Architectural
DRAFTING & DESIGN

Architectural
DRAFTING & DESIGN

Second
Edition

Alan Jefferis
David A. Madsen

The authors are architectural designers and instructors in Drafting
Technology, Authorized Autodesk Training Center, Clackamas Community
College, Oregon City, Oregon.

Delmar Publishers Inc.®

NOTICE TO THE READER

Cover photos courtesy of Piercy & Barclay Designers. Cover design by Mary Beth Vought.

DELMAR STAFF

Senior Administrative Editor: Michael McDermott
Developmental Editor: Mary Ormsbee
Project Supervisor: Marlene McHugh Pratt
Production Coordinator: Bruce Sherwin
Design Supervisor: Susan C. Mathews

For information, address Delmar Publishers Inc.
3 Columbia Circle Drive, Box 15-015
Albany, New York 12212

Printed in the United States of America
Published simultaneously in Canada
by Nelson Canada,
a division of The Thomson Corporation

10 9 8 7 6

Library of Congress Cataloging-in-Publication Data
Jefferis, Alan.
   Architectural drafting and design/Alan Jefferis, David A.
Madsen.— 2nd ed.
      p. cm.
   ISBN 0-8273-3674-8
   1. Architectural drawing. 2. Architectural design. I. Madsen,
David A. II. Title.
NA2700.J44, 1991
720'.28'4—dc20
                                                            90-37061
                                                            CIP

Contents

Preface

ARCHITECTURAL DRAFTING AND DESIGN is a practical, comprehensive textbook that is easy to use and understand. The content may be used as presented, by following a logical sequence of learning activities for residential and light commercial architectural drafting, or the chapters may be rearranged to accommodate alternate formats for traditional or individualized instruction. This text is the only reference needed by students of architectural drafting.

APPROACH

Practical

Architectural Drafting and Design provides a practical approach to architectural drafting as it relates to current common practices. The emphasis on standardization is an excellent and necessary foundation of drafting training as well as implementing a common approach to drafting nationwide. After students become professional drafters, this text will serve as a valuable desk reference.

Realistic

Chapters contain realistic examples, illustrations, step-by-step layout techniques, drafting problems, and related tests. The examples demonstrate recommended drafting presentation with actual architectural drawings used for reinforcement. The correlated text explains drafting techniques, and provides useful information for skill development. Step-by-step layout methods provide a logical approach to beginning and finishing complete sets of working drawings.

Practical Approach to Problem Solving

The professional architectural drafter's responsibility is to convert architects', engineers', and designers' sketches and ideas into formal drawings. The text explains how to prepare formal drawings from design sketches by providing the learner with the basic guidelines for drafting layout, and minimum design and code requirements in a knowledge-building format; one concept is learned before the next is introduced. The concepts and skills learned from one chapter to the next allow students to prepare complete sets of working drawings in residential and light commercial drafting. Problem assignments are presented in order of difficulty, and in a manner that provides students with a wide variety of architectural drafting experiences.

The problems are presented as preliminary designs or design sketches in a manner that is consistent with actual architectural office practices. It is not enough for students to duplicate drawings from given assignments; they must be able to think through the process of drawing development with a foundation of how drawing and construction components are implemented. The goals and objectives of each problem assignment are consistent with recommended evaluation criteria based on the progression of learning activities. The drafting problems and tests recommend that work be done using drafting skills on actual drafting materials with either professional manual or computer drafting equipment. A problem solution or test answer should be accurate and demonstrate proper drafting technique.

FEATURES OF THE TEXT

Applications

Special emphasis has been placed on providing realistic drafting problems. Problems are presented as design sketches or preliminary drawings in a manner that is consistent with industry practices. The problems have been supplied by architectural designers. Each problem solution is based on the step-by-step layout procedures provided in the chapter discussions.

Problems are given in order of complexity so that students may be exposed to a variety of drafting experiences. Problems require students to go through the same thought and decision-making processes that a professional drafter faces daily, including scale and paper size selection, view layout, dimension placement, section placement, and many other activities. Problems may be solved using manual or computer drafting, as determined by individual course guidelines. Chapter tests provide a complete coverage of each chapter and may be used for student evaluation or as study questions.

Illustrations

Drawings and photos are used liberally throughout this text to amplify the concepts presented. Two-color treatment enhances the learning value. Abundant step-by-step illustrations take students through the drafting process and clarify the detailed stages. This new edition also incorporates many CADD-drawn illustrations.

Computer-Aided Design Drafting (CADD)

CADD is presented as a valuable tool that is treated no differently from manual drafting tools. The complete discussion of computer graphics introduces the workstation, environment, terminology, drafting techniques, and sample drawings. While individual course guidelines may elect to solve architectural drafting problems using either computer or manual drafting equipment, the concepts remain the same; the only difference is the method of presentation.

Systems Drafting

Systems drafting techniques that are commonly used in the architectural drafting industry, such as overlay, repetitive elements, and drawing restoration, are covered early in the text content so that individual procedures may be implemented as appropriate to course guidelines.

Codes and Construction Techniques

National building codes UBC, SBC, and BOCA are introduced and compared throughout the text as they relate to specific instructions and applications. Construction techniques differ throughout the country. This text clearly acknowledges the difference in construction methods, and introduces the student to the format used to make complete sets of working drawings for each method of construction. Students may learn to prepare drawings for each construction method or, more commonly, for the specific construction techniques that are used in their locality. The problem assignments are designed to provide drawings that involve a variety of construction alternatives.

FEATURES OF THE NEW EDITION

Expanded CADD Coverage

We feel that our CADD coverage is the most comprehensive available in a major architectural drafting and design text. We have devoted a full chapter to CADD in architectural drafting, with coverage on the CADD environment in the architectural office, CADD methods and techniques, and professional CADD applications, such as layering and drawing management.

In addition to the strong chapter coverage on CADD, we have placed CADD applications in chapters where their specific use pertains to the content. These applications discuss and display real-world examples of how CADD is used in the architectural drafting and design community.

Revised Basic Skills Coverage

This coverage presents a thorough and focused discussion of the skills, techniques, and equipment most germane to architectural drafting.

Expanded Commercial Coverage

This coverage lets students and teachers explore the use of CADD for commercial and multifamily projects and for drawing structural details. In addition, a *new chapter* on structural drafting discusses such topics as order of precedence, detail coordination, and occupancy, with problems focusing on roof drainage plans, truss details, exterior elevations, project coordination, and more.

Revised Step-by-Step Illustrations

These are an important learning tool in this text. Many of these step by steps have been completely redrawn for refined clarity. We feel that students will find these new drawings much easier to interpret. Previous steps are printed in gray, with the new step added in black; all new steps are called out in blue.

Code Updates

The Council of American Building Officials (CABO) issued a revised code in April of 1990. The new provisions of this national code have been integrated wherever applicable.

ORGANIZING YOUR COURSE

Architectural drafting is the primary emphasis of many technical drafting curricula, whereas other programs offer only an exploratory course in this field. This text is appropriate for either application, in that its content reflects the common elements in an architectural drafting curriculum.

Prerequisites

An interest in architectural drafting, plus basic arithmetic, written communication, and reading skills are the only prerequisites required. Basic drafting skills and layout techniques are presented as appropriate. Students with an interest in architectural drafting who begin using this text will end with the knowledge and skills required to prepare complete sets of working drawings for residential and light commercial architectural drafting.

Fundamental Through Advanced Coverage

This text may be used in the architectural drafting curriculum that covers the basics of residential architecture in a one-, two-, or three-semester sequence. In this application, students use the chapters directly associated with the preparation of a complete set of working drawings for a residence, where the emphasis is on the use of fundamental skills and techniques. The balance of the text may remain as a reference for future study or as a valuable desk reference.

The text may also be used in the comprehensive architectural drafting program where a four- to six-semester sequence of residential and light commercial architectural drafting and design is required. In this application, students may expand on the primary objective of preparing a complete set of working drawings for the design of residential and light commercial projects with the coverage of any one or all of the following areas: systems drafting, energy-efficient construction techniques, solar and site orientation design applications, heating and cooling thermal performance calculations, structural load calculations, presentation drawings.

Section Length

Chapters are presented in individual learning segments that begin with elementary concepts and build until each chapter provides complete coverage of every topic. Instructors may choose to present lectures in short, 15-minute discussions or divide each chapter into 40- to 50-minute lectures.

Drafting Equipment and Materials

Identification and use of manual and computer-aided drafting equipment is given. Students will require an inventory of equipment available for use as listed in the chapters. Professional drafting materials are explained, and it is recommended that students prepare problem solutions using actual drafting materials.

SUPPLEMENTS

Instructor's Guide

The instructor's guide for the main text contains learning objectives, test and problem solutions, and supplementary text materials.

Workbooks and CADD Disks

We have developed a series of workbooks and CADD workdisks to correlate with *Architectural Drafting and Design*. They are available in the following formats:

Workbook I—Basic Drafting. This workbook is correlated with the main text and contains "survival information" related to the topics covered. The plentiful problem assignments take the beginning architectural drafting student from the basics of line and lettering techniques to drawing a complete set of residential plans. Problems may be done manually or on CADD.

Workbook II—Residential Drafting and Design. This workbook provides the student with a series of complete residential plans presented as architectural design problems. The plans range from simple to complex and give the student an opportunity to vary the design elements of the home. Survival information is again correlated with the main text to provide additional instruction. Problems may be done on CADD or manually.

Workbook III—Light Commercial Drafting and Design. This workbook is for the advanced student and provides a variety of complete light commercial drafting and design projects. The types of projects include multifamily residential, tilt-up concrete, steel, and heavy timber construction. Survival information is correlated with the commercial chapters of the main text. This information leads the student into the comprehensive drafting and design projects.

Student CADD Workdisk Package. A package of four CADD workdisks for each workbook (twelve disks in all) is available. Each set of disks is designed to allow the student to prepare a complete set of working drawings on the CADD system. Students are given parts of the architectural layout for each element of the set of drawings. The student is asked to use AutoCAD to complete the plans as specified in the detailed instructions.

Instructor's CADD Solution Disks. Instructors will receive three disks with a complete set of solutions to the architectural drawing problems on the student workdisks. Instructors may also use these complete sets of working drawings as instructional aids.

House Plans

House plans are a full set of residential drawings representing the houses featured in the main text's step-by-step illustrations.

ACKNOWLEDGMENTS

We would like to thank and acknowledge the many professionals who reviewed the manuscript to help us publish our architectural drafting text. A special acknowledgment is due the following instructors who reviewed the chapters in detail:

Andrew Staudt
Bemidji High School

John List
Etiwanda High School

Joseph Yamello
Greater Lowell Regional Vo-Tech

Mike Hudson
Bastrop Vo-Tech

Pierre Couture
Milford Sr. High School

Wayne Stiffler
Western Reserve High School

Joseph Cutrone
Island Drafting & Technical Institute

John Rainone, Jr.
Hall Institute

Darrell Horn
Knox County AVEC

Eldon Divine
The School of the Ozarks

Larry Tindle
St. Louis Tech

Bruce Downing
New England Institute of Technology

Bruce Bainbridge
Clinton Community College

Tom Peterson
Des Moines Area Community College

Dr. Dale Visger
Walla Walla College

Charles Case
ITT Technical Institute

Michael Jordan
Dalton College

Jim Leslie
Central Piedmont Community College

Ian Thomson
National Business Institute

The quality of this text is also enhanced by the support and contributions from architects, designers, engineers, and vendors. The list of contributors is extensive and acknowledgment is given at each illustration; however, the following individuals and companies gave an extraordinary amount of support:

Dan Kovac
Piercy & Barclay Designers, Inc.

Alan Mascord
Alan Mascord Design Associates, Inc.

Charles Talcott
Home Planners, Inc.

Ken Smith
Structureform Masters, Inc.

Bob Ringland
Southland Corporation

James Bihr
International Conference of
  Building Officials

Robert E. DeWeese
Mutoh America, Inc.

Duane Snyder
Cascade Architectural
  and Engineering Supply

Vincent A. Trippy
Kathleen McCarthy
Vincent Donofrio, Jr.
Joan Fleming
KOH-I-NOOR Rapidograph, Inc.

Cynthia Ann Murphy
Danier Partner
Computervision Corporation

Walter Stein
Home Building Plan Service, Inc.

Steve Webb
Lennox Industries Inc.

Renee Randall
CALCOMP

Howard Kaufman
John Doleva
Chartpak

Walter Underwood III
Oregon Blueprint Company

Jim Mackay
Berol Corporation

Pat Bowlin
American Plywood Association

Richard Branham
National Concrete Masonry Association

E. Henry Fitzgibbon, AIA
Soderstrom Architects

Approximately 180 illustrations are reproduced from *Mechnical Drafting*, by Madsen, Shumaker, and Stewart, Delmar Publishers, Inc. Special thanks to the students who provided step-by-step drawings: Cheryl Day, Andy Baethke, Ken Prouty.

TO THE STUDENT

Architectural Drafting and Design is designed for you, the student. The development and format of the presentation have been tested in actual conventional and individualized classroom instruction. The information presented is based on architectural standards, drafting room practice, and trends in the drafting industry. This text is the only architectural drafting reference that you will need. Use the text as a learning tool while in school, and take it along as a desk reference when you enter the profession. The amount of written text is complete, but kept to a minimum. Examples and illustrations are used extensively. Drafting is a graphic language, and most drafting students learn best by observation of examples. Here are a few helpful hints.

1. *Read the text.* The text content is intentionally designed for easy reading. Sure, it doesn't read the same as an exciting short story, but it does give the facts in as few, easy-to-understand words as possible. Don't pass up the reading, because the content will help you to understand the drawings clearly.

2. *Look carefully at the examples.* The figure examples are presented in a manner that is consistent with drafting standards. Look at the examples carefully in an attempt to understand the intent of specific applications. If you are able to understand why something is done a certain way, it will be easier for you to apply those concepts to the drawing problems and, later, to the job. Drafting is a precise technology based on rules and guidelines. The goal of a drafter is to prepare drawings that are easy to interpret. There will always be situations when rules must be altered to handle a unique situation. Then you will have to rely on judgment based on your knowledge of accepted standards. Drafting is often like a puzzle; there may be more than one way to solve a problem.

3. *Use the text as a reference.* Few drafters know everything about drafting standards, techniques, and concepts, so always be ready to use the reference if you need to verify how a specific application is handled. Become familiar with the definitions and use of technical terms. It would be difficult to memorize everything noted in this text but, after considerable use of the concepts, architectural drafting applications should become second nature.

4. *Learn each concept and skill before you continue to the next.* The text is presented in a logical learning sequence. Each chapter is designed for learning development, and chapters are sequenced so that drafting knowledge grows from one chapter to the next. Problem assignments are presented in the same learning sequence as the chapter content, and also reflect progressive levels of difficulty.

5. *Practice.* Development of good manual and computer drafting skills depends to a large extent on practice. Some individuals have an inherent talent for manual drafting, and some people are

readily compatible with computers. If you fit into either group, great! If you don't, then practice is all you may need. Practice manual drafting skills to help improve the quality of your drafting presentation, and practice communicating and working with a computer. A good knowledge of drafting practice is not enough if the manual skills are not satisfactory. When the computer is used, however, most manual skills are not needed.

6. *Use sketches or preliminary drawings.* When drawing manually or with a computer, the proper use of a sketch or preliminary drawing can save a lot of time in the long run. Prepare a layout sketch or preliminary layout for each problem. This will give you a chance to organize thoughts about drawing scale, view selection, dimension and note placement, and paper size. After you become a drafting veteran, you may be able to design a sheet layout in your head, but, until then, you will be sorry if you don't use sketches.

7. *Use professional equipment and materials.* For the best possible learning results and skill development, use the professional drafting equipment, supplies, and materials that are recommended.

Alan Jefferis
David A. Madsen

CM-1430

FRONT ELEVATION

Section One

Introduction to Architectural Drafting

Chapter 1
Professional Architectural Careers, Office Practice, and Opportunities

AS YOU begin working with this text, you are opening the door to many exciting careers. Each career in turn has many different opportunities within it. Whether your interest lies in theoretical problem solving, artistic creations, or working with your hands creating something practical, a course in residential architecture will help prepare you to satisfy that interest. This statement is no late night television advertisement but one of reality. An architectural drafting class can lead to a career as a drafter, designer, architect, or engineer.

Of course, you will not be able to step into these fields by simply reading this book and taking one class but once you have mastered the information and skills presented in this text, you will be prepared for each of these fields as well as many others. You may be anxious to get to drawing and creating, but slow down and first become familiar with some of the possibilities that exist for you as you progress through this class.

DRAFTER

If you will take a moment to thumb through the pages of this book you will see many drawings that are drawn in a step-by-step manner. The goal of these illustrations is to help you understand the basic tasks that a drafter is required to perform. A drafter is the person who draws the drawings and details for another person's creations. It is the drafter's responsibility to use the proper line and lettering quality and to lay out properly the required drawings necessary to complete a project. Such a task requires a great attention to detail as the drafter redraws the supervisor's sketches. Because the drafter could possibly be working for several architects or engineers within an office, the drafter must also be able to get along well with others.

The Beginning Drafter

As a beginning or junior drafter, your job will generally consist of making corrections to drawings that have been drawn by others. There may not be a lot of mental stimulation to making changes but it is a very necessary job. It is also a good introduction to the procedures and quality standards within an office.

As your line and lettering quality improve, your responsibilities will be expanded. Typically your supervisor will give you a sketch and expect you to

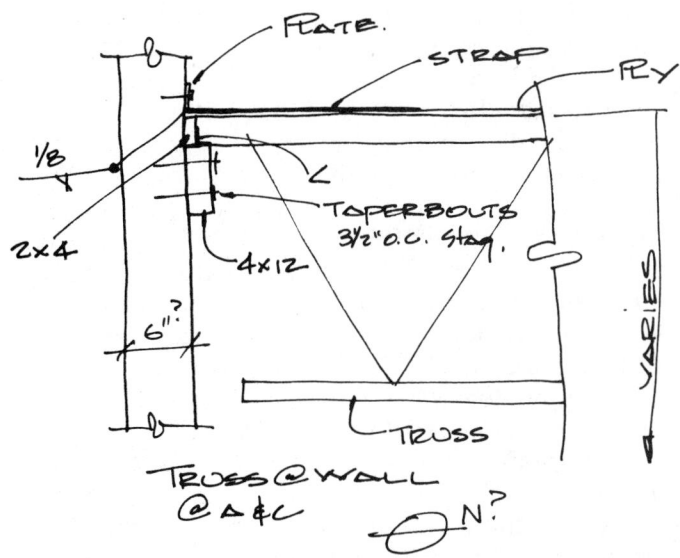

Figure 1–1 A sketch is usually given to a junior drafter to follow for a first drawing. The drafter can find information for completing the drawing by examining similar jobs in the office.

draw the required drawing. Figure 1–1 shows an engineer's sketch. Figure 1–2 shows the drawing created by a drafter. As you gain an understanding of the drawings that you are making and gain confidence in your ability, the sketches that you are given generally will become more simplified. Eventually your supervisor may just refer you to a similar drawing and expect you to be able to make the necessary adjustments to fit it to the new application.

The decisions involved in making drawings without sketches require the drafter to have a good understanding of what is being drawn. This understanding does not come just from a textbook. To advance as a drafter, you will need to spend time at construction sites observing buildings being constructed. An even better way to gain an understanding of what you are drafting is to spend time working at a construction site. Understanding what a craftsman must do as a result of what you have drawn is necessary if you are to advance as a drafter.

Depending on the size of the office where you work, you may also spend a lot of your time as a beginning drafter running prints, making deliveries, obtaining permits, and other such office chores. Don't get the idea that a drafter only does the menial chores around an office. You do need to be prepared, as you go to your first drafting job, to do things other than drafting. Many entry-level drafters expect that they will go to their first job and start designing great works for humanity. As an entry-level drafter it will not be so.

The Experienced Drafter

Although your supervisor may prepare the basic design for a project, experienced drafters are expected to make construction design decisions. These might include determining structural sizes, connection methods for intersecting beams, drawing renderings, making job visitations and supervising beginning drafters. The types of drawings that you will be

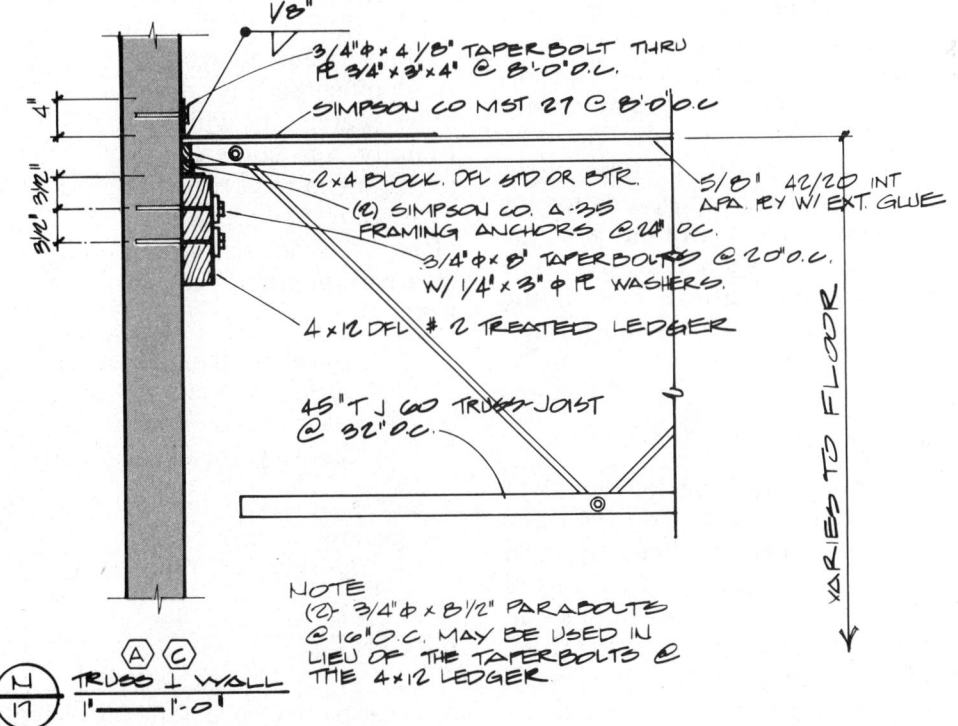

Figure 1–2 A detail drawn by a drafter using the sketch shown in Figure 1–1.

working on will also be affected as you gain experience. Instead of drawing plot plans, cabinet elevations, roof plans, or revising existing details, an experienced drafter will be working on the floor and foundation plans, elevations, and sections. Probably your supervisor will still make the initial design drawings, but will pass these drawings on to you as soon as a client approves the preliminary drawings.

In addition to drafting, you will most likely work with the many city and state building departments that govern your work. This will require you to do research in the many codes that govern the building industry. Not only will you be required to do research with building codes, but you will also need to become familiar with vendor catalogs. The most common of these catalogs is the Sweet's Catalog. Sweet's, as it is known, is a series of books that contain product information on a wide variety of building products. Information within these catalogs is listed by manufacturer, trade name, and type of product. In addition to these catalogs, a drafter will often be required to research design data in such books as *Architectural Graphics* or *Time Saver Standards*. Each contains a wide variety of information needed for design drafting.

Employment Opportunities

As a drafter, you may find employment in firms of all sizes. Designers, architects, and engineers all require entry-level and advanced drafters to help produce their drawings. Many drafters are employed by suppliers of architectural equipment. This work might include drawing construction details for a steel fabricator, making layout drawings for a cabinet shop, or designing ductwork for a heating and air-conditioning installer. Many manufacturing companies hire drafters with an architectural background to help draw and sometimes sell a product. Drafters might be called upon to draw installation diagrams for instruction booklets or sales catalogs. Drafters are also employed by many government agencies. These jobs range from working in planning, utility, or building departments, survey crews, or other related municipal jobs.

Educational Requirements

In order to get your first drafting job you will need a solid education, good line and lettering quality, and the ability to *sell* yourself to an employer. Good linework and lettering will come as a result of practice. The education required for a drafter can range from one or more years in a high school drafting program, a diploma from a one-year accredited technical school, a degree from a two-year college program, all the way to a masters degree in architecture.

Helpful areas of study for an entry-level drafter would include math, writing, and drawing. As a drafter, the math required will range from simple addition to calculus. Although the drafter may spend most of the day adding dimensions expressed in feet and inches, a knowledge of geometry will be helpful for solving many building problems. Writing skills will also be very helpful. As a drafter, you often will be required to complete the paperwork that accompanies any set of plans such as permits, requests for variances, written specifications, or environmental impact reports. In addition to standard drafting classes, classes in photography, art, surveying, and construction could be helpful to the drafter.

Many drafters are quite satisfied with the field of architectural drafting and remain in this position throughout their career. Others use drafting as a steppingstone to other fields.

DESIGNER

The meaning of the term designer varies from state to state. In some areas, anyone who can spell designer can be a designer. Many states restrict the use of the term designer by requiring anyone using the term to have had formal training and to have passed a competency test.

A designer's responsibilities are very similar to that of an experienced drafter and are usually based on both education and experience. A designer is usually the coordinator of a team of drafters. The designer may work under the direct supervision of an architect or engineer or both and supervise the work schedule of the drafting team.

In addition to working in a traditional architectural office setting, designers often have their own office practice in which they design residential, multifamily, and some types of light commercial buildings. State laws vary on the types and sizes of buildings a designer may work on without requiring the stamp of an architect or engineer. Students wishing more information about this career can obtain information from:

The American Institute of
Building Design (AIBD)
1412 Nineteenth Street
Sacramento, CA 95814

Students can also contact The American Institute of Design and Drafting, the U.S. Department of Labor, or the U.S. Office of Education.

ARCHITECT

An architect performs the tasks of many professionals including designer, artist, project manager, and construction supervisor. Few architects work full time in residential design. Although many architects design some homes, most devote their time to commercial construction projects such as schools, offices, hospitals, etc. An architect is responsible for the design of a structure and for the way the building relates to the environment. The architect will often serve as a coordinator on a project to ensure that all aspects of the structure blend together to form a pleasing relationship. This coordinating includes working with the client, the contractors, and a multitude of engineering firms that may be working on the project.

Use of the term architect is legally restricted to use by individuals who have been licensed by the state where they will have their practice. Obtaining a license requires passing several written tests. There are two routes a person can take to prepare for these tests. A drafter or designer can prepare to take the licensing test through practical work experience. Although standards vary for each state, five to seven years of experience under the direct supervision of a licensed architect or engineer usually is required. An alternative to this method is to obtain a bachelor degree from an accredited college and three years of professional experience with a licensed architect or engineer.

Education

High school and two-year college students can prepare for a degree program by taking classes in fine arts, math, science and social science. Many two-year drafting programs offer drafting classes that can be used for credit in four- or five-year architectural programs. A student planning to transfer to a four-year program should verify with the new college which classes can be transferred.

Fine arts classes such as drawing, sketching, design, and art along with architectural history will provide a helpful background for the humanities classes that will be required in a four-year degree program. Such classes will help the future architect develop an understanding of the cultural significance of structures and help transform ideas into reality. Math and science, including algebra, geometry, trigonometry, and physics, will provide a stable base for the advanced structural classes that will be required. Sociology, psychology, studies of group behavior, cultural anthropology and classes dealing with human environments will help develop an understanding of the people that will use the structure. Because architectural students will need to read, write, and think clearly about abstract concepts, preparation should also include literature and philosophy courses.

In addition to formal study, students should discuss with local architects the opportunities and pos-sible disadvantages that may await them in pursuing the study and practice of architecture.

Areas of Study

The study of architecture is not limited to the design of buildings. Although the architectural curriculum typically is highly structured for the first two years of study, students begin to specialize in an area of interest during the third year of the program.

Students in a bachelor program may choose courses leading to a degree in several different areas of architecture such as urban planning, landscape architecture and interior architecture. Urban design is the study of the relationship among the components within a city. Rather than designing specific buildings, the professional urban planner helps guide the growth of entire cities. Interior architects work specifically with the interior of a structure to ensure that all aspects of the building will be functional. Landscape architects specialize in relating the exterior of a structure to the environment. Students wishing further information on training or other related topics can contact:

American Institute of Architects
1735 New York Avenue, NW
Washington, D.C. 20006

American Society of Landscape Architects
1750 Old Meadow Road
McLean, VA 22101

American Institute of Landscape Architects
501 E. San Juan Avenue
Phoenix, AZ 85012

Association of Collegiate Schools of
Architecture
1735 New York Avenue, NW
Washington, D.C. 20006

ENGINEER

Engineers are typically among the most sought-after graduates by the construction and business world. Similar to the requirements for becoming an architect, a license is required to function as an engineer. The license can be applied for after several years of practical experience, or after obtaining a bachelor degree and three years of practical experience.

Education

Students entering an engineering program must have a very strong background in science and math. An architect may do the initial design work for a

Figure 1-3 Drawings are often prepared by an architectural illustrator to help convey design concepts. *Drawing by Huxley, Courtesy Structureform Masters, Inc.*

structure, but an engineer usually assumes the responsibility for determining that it will safely resist the forces of nature. Training for this responsibility dictates that the student will spend a tremendous amount of time in math classes and science labs. Students are normally required to complete classes including advanced calculus, differential equations, vector analysis and numerical calculus. While taking these background classes, the student will also be taking classes dealing with specific areas of the analysis and design of structures.

Areas of Study

Civil, electrical, and mechanical engineering are the areas that are related to the construction industry.

Civil engineers plan, design, and manage the construction and operation of public and private facilities including buildings, power plants, dams, highways and transportation systems, and water and wastewater treatment systems. There are many areas of study in electrical engineering. The field of electrical power engineering would provide the background for supplying and controlling the power within a structure. A degree in mechanical engineering would open career paths in energy conservation and utilization. For further information on the field of engineering you may contact:

American Society of Civil Engineers
345 E. 47th Street
New York, NY 10017

RELATED FIELDS

So far we've only covered the opportunities that are similar because of their drawing, design and creative nature. In addition to these careers, there are many related careers that require an understanding of drafting principles to be successful. Some of these include illustrator, model maker, specification writer, estimator, inspector, and construction related trades.

Illustrator

Many drafters, designers and architects have the basic skills to draw architectural renderings. Very few though have the expertise to make this type of drawing rapidly. Most illustrators have a background in art. By combining their artistic talent with a basic understanding of architectural principles, the illustrator is able to produce drawings that realistically show a proposed structure. Figure 1-3 shows a drawing that was prepared by an architectural illustrator. Section 10 will provide an introduction to presentation drawings.

Figure 1-4 Models such as this one of the KOIN Center of Portland, Oregon, are often used in public displays to convey design ideas. *Courtesy KOIN Center, Olympia & York Properties (Oregon), Inc.*

Model Maker

In addition to presentation drawings, many architectural offices use models of a building or project to help convey design concepts. Models such as the one shown in Figure 1-4 are often used as a public display to help gain support for large projects. Model makers need basic drafting skills to help interpret the plans required to build the actual project. Model makers may be employed within a large architectural firm, or for a company that only makes models for architects.

Specification Writer

Specifications are written instructions for methods, materials, and quality of construction. Figure 1-5 shows an example of written specifications. Written specifications will be introduced in Section 11. Although no special training is required, a specification writer must have a very thorough understanding of the construction process and have a good ability to read plans. Generally, a writer will have had classes in technical writing at the two-year college level.

Inspector

Building departments require that plans and the construction process be inspected to ensure that the required codes for public safety have been met. A plan examiner must be licensed by the state to certify

8 Architectural Drafting and Design

GENERAL NOTES

1. ALL CONSTRUCTION SHALL COMPLY WITH THE GOVERNING BUILDING CODES AND REGULATIONS.

2. THE CONTRACTOR SHALL VERIFY ALL DIMENSIONS AND CONDITIONS AT THE JOB SITE BEFORE COMMENCEMENT OF WORK AND SHALL REPORT ANY DISCREPANCIES OR OMISSIONS TO STRUCTUREFORM IN WRITING.

3. DETAILS OF CONSTRUCTION NOT SPECIFICALLY SHOWN SHALL BE CONSTRUCTED IN ACCORDANCE WITH DETAILS SHOWN FOR SIMILAR CONDITIONS AND MATERIALS.

4. EACH SUBCONTRACTOR IS CONSIDERED AN EXPERT IN HIS RESPECTIVE FIELD AND SHALL PRIOR TO THE SUBMISSION OF BID OR PERFORMANCE OF WORK NOTIFY THE GENERAL CONTRACTOR OR OWNER OF ANY WORK CALLED OUT ON THE DRAWINGS IN HIS TRADE THAT CANNOT BE FULLY GUARANTEED.

5. THE CONTRACTOR SHALL COORDINATE ALL MECHANICAL AND ELECTRICAL EQUIPMENT AS TO WEIGHTS AND EXACT LOCATIONS WITH STRUCTURAL SUPPORTS. IN THE EVENT THAT THE PURCHASED EQUIPMENT DEVIATES IN WEIGHT AND LOCATION FROM THOSE INDICATED ON THE PLANS, STRUCTUREFORM MUST BE NOTIFIED, AND APPROVAL OBTAINED PRIOR TO INSTALLATION.

6. THIS STRUCTURE IS DESIGNED AS A STABLE UNIT AFTER ALL COMPONENTS ARE IN PLACE. THE CONTRACTOR SHALL BE RESPONSIBLE TO PROVIDE TEMPORARY BRACING AS REQUIRED TO INSURE THE VERTICAL AND LATERAL STABILITY OF THE ENTIRE STRUCTURE OR ANY PORTION THEREOF DURING CONSTRUCTION.

7. WHERE SPECIAL INSPECTION IS REQUIRED ON THE PLANS, IT SHALL BE PERFORMED BY A REGISTERED DEPUTY INSPECTOR, APPROVED BY THE GOVERNING JURISDICTION. COPIES OF THE INSPECTION REPORTS SHALL BE SUBMITTED TO THE BUILDING DEPARTMENT AND STRUCTUREFORM. (OWNER SHALL EMPLOY SPECIAL INSPECTOR)

8. TRADE NAMES AND MANUFACTURERS REFERRED TO ARE FOR QUALITY STANDARDS ONLY. SUBSTITUTIONS WILL BE PERMITTED AS APPROVED BY STRUCTUREFORM.

9. STRUCTUREFORM IS TO BE NOTIFIED IN WRITING WHEN CONSTRUCTION AT THE SITE BEGINS.

10. WHENEVER REQUIRED, SHOP DRAWINGS APPROVED BY THE CONTRACTOR SHALL BE SUBMITTED TO STRUCTUREFORM FOR REVIEW.

11. ANY QUESTIONS RELATED TO INTERPRETATION OR INTENT OF THESE DRAWINGS SHALL BE REFERRED TO STRUCTUREFORM.

FOUNDATION NOTES

1. ALL EARTHWORK AND GRADING SHALL BE ACCOMPLISHED IN ACCORDANCE WITH THE RECOMMENDATIONS OF THE FOUNDATION INVESTIGATION BY _____

2. A COMPACTION REPORT MUST BE SUBMITTED TO AND APPROVED BY THE BUILDING INSPECTION DEPARTMENT PRIOR TO PLACEMENT OF ANY FOUNDATION CONCRETE ON FILL.

3. ALL UTILITY TRENCHES SHALL BE COMPACTED TO A MINIMUM OF 90% RELATIVE DENSITY.

4. ALL FINISH GRADES AROUND BUILDING SHALL BE SLOPED TO DRAIN SURFACE WATER AWAY.

REINFORCING STEEL

1. ALL REINFORCING STEEL TO BE NEW DEFORMED INTERMEDIATE GRADE CONFORMING TO A.S.T.M. A-615-68, GRADE 40, UNLESS NOTED OTHERWISE.

2. USE LOW HYDROGEN ELECTRODES, GRADE E-7018, FOR WELDING REINFORCING BARS. SPECIAL INSPECTION IS REQUIRED FOR ALL FIELD WELDING.

3. ALL REINFORCING SHALL BE SECURELY TIED AND BRACED IN PLACE PRIOR TO PLACING CONCRETE OR GROUTING MASONRY.

4. PROVIDE THE FOLLOWING MINIMUM PROTECTIVE COVERING OF CONCRETE :

BELOW GRADE (FORMED)   3" CLR.
BELOW GRADE (UNFORMED)   3" CLR.
PRECAST WALL PANELS   3/4" CLR.
CAST-IN-PLACE WALLS   1 1/2" CLR.

5. LAP BARS A MINIMUM OF 40 DIAMETERS IN MASONRY AND 30 DIAMETERS IN CONCRETE.

CONCRETE

1. ALL CONCRETE SHALL HAVE AN ULTIMATE COMPRESSIVE STRENGTH OF AT LEAST 2,000 PSI IN 28 DAYS OR AS SPECIFIED.

2. CONCRETE WITH SPECIFIED DESIGN COMPRESSIVE STRESS GREATER THAN 2,000 PSI IN 28 DAYS SHALL BE PLACED UNDER CONTINUOUS INSPECTION.

3. DRYPACK SHALL BE COMPOSED OF ONE PART PORTLAND CEMENT TO NOT MORE THAN THREE PARTS SAND.

4. PORTLAND CEMENT SHALL CONFORM TO A.S.T.M. C150-72, TYPE I OR II.

5. CONCRETE FLATWORK TO BE 3 1/2" MINIMUM THICKNESS WITH EXPANSION JOINTS AT STREET SIDEWALKS, INTERSECTING CONCRETE CHANGE IN CONCRETE WIDTH, AND AT FORTY FOOT INTERVALS ON STRAIGHT RUNS. PROVIDE SCORE LINES AT APPROXIMATELY TEN FOOT INTERVALS.

6. ANCHOR BOLTS, DOWELS, INSERTS, ETC. SHALL BE SECURELY TIED IN PLACE PRIOR TO PLACING CONCRETE.

MASONRY

1. MASONRY UNITS SHALL BE GRADE 'N' UNITS CONFORMING TO A.S.T.M. C90-70 AND TO THE REQUIREMENTS OF THE QUALITY CONTROL STANDARDS OF THE MASONRY INSTITUTE OF AMERICA.

2. DOWELS IN FOOTINGS FOR MASONRY WALLS SHALL BE THE SAME SIZE AND SPACING AS MASONRY WALL REINFORCING.

3. ALL CELLS CONTAINING REINFORCING STEEL OR ANCHORS SHALL BE FILLED SOLID WITH GROUT. ALL HORIZONTAL STEEL SHALL BE PLACED IN DEEP CUT BOND BEAM UNITS. ALL GROUT SHALL BE CONSOLIDATED AT TIME OF POURING BY PUDDLING OR VIBRATING AND THEN RECONSOLIDATED BY AGAIN PUDDLING LATER, BEFORE PLASTICITY IS LOST. RETAINING WALLS AND WALLS BELOW GRADE SHALL BE GROUTED SOLID TO A POINT 6" ABOVE GRADE.

4. MORTAR SHALL BE TYPE 'S', WITH A MINIMUM COMPRESSIVE STRENGTH OF 1,800 PSI AT 28 DAYS. PROPORTIONS BY VOLUME : 1 PART OF PORTLAND CEMENT, 1 1/4 PART MINIMUM TO 1 1/2 PART MAXIMUM HYDRATED LIME NOT LESS THAN 2 1/4 AND NOT MORE THAN 3 TIMES THE SUM OF THE VOLUME OF THE CEMENT AND LIME USED.

5. GROUT SHALL ATTAIN A MINIMUM COMPRESSIVE STRENGTH OF 2,000 PSI AT 28 DAYS. PROPORTIONS BY VOLUME : 1 PART PORTLAND CEMENT TO WHICH MAY BE ADDED NOT MORE THAN 1/10 PART HYDRATED LIME OR LIME PUTTY AND 2 TO 3 PARTS SAND, AND NOT MORE THAN 2 PARTS GRAVEL.

6. EXPOSED MORTAR JOINTS TO BE CONCAVE AND OTHER JOINTS TO BE FINISHED FLUSH UNLESS SHOWN OTHERWISE.

LUMBER

1. ALL METAL HANGERS AND FRAMING CONNECTORS SHALL BE "STRONG-TIE" BY SIMPSON COMPANY.

2. ALL FRAMING LUMBER, UNLESS NOTED OTHERWISE, SHALL BE STAMPED D.F./LARCH.

BEAMS, HEADERS, AND POSTS   #1
(4" LARGER IN WIDTH)

JOISTS AND RAFTERS   #2

STUDS   STANDARD AND BETTER

MAXIMUM MOISTURE CONTENT OF WOOD MEMBERS TO BE 19%.

3. ALL STRUCTURAL PLYWOOD SHALL BE C-D APA INTERIOR GRADE WITH EXTERIOR GLUE AND CONFORM TO PRODUCT STANDARD PS-1 (LATEST EDITION), UNLESS NOTED OTHERWISE.

4. GLU-LAMINATED BEAMS TO BE DFL COMBINATION 24F, FB: 2400 PSI, FV: 165 PSI & FC: 450 PSI, UNLESS OTHERWISE NOTED. CONTINUE BOTTOM TENSION LAMINATIONS OVER BEARING POINT.

5. ALL WOOD BEARING ON CONCRETE OR MASONRY FOUNDATIONS SHALL BE PRESSURE-TREATED DFL #2. ALL OTHER PLATES SHALL BE DFL #2.

6. IT SHALL BE THE RESPONSIBILITY OF THE GENERAL CONTRACTOR TO PROVIDE THE DEPARTMENT OF BUILDING INSPECTION WITH "A.I.T.C. CERTIFICATE OF CONFORMANCE" FOR GLU-LAMINATED WOOD MEMBERS PRIOR TO THEIR INSTALLATION.

7. PLACE DOUBLE JOISTS UNDER ALL PARALLEL PARTITIONS UNLESS DIRECTLY SUPPORTED BELOW. PLACE 2" DFL SOLID BLOCKING BETWEEN ALL JOISTS AND RAFTERS AT SUPPORTS AND UNDER ALL PARTITIONS.

8. PROVIDE 2"x DFL SOLID BLOCKING OR 1"x3" CROSS BRIDGING OR METAL CROSS BRIDGING AS FOLLOWS :

   A. AT ROOF JOISTS OVER 8" IN DEPTH AND SPACE AT 10'-0" O.C. MAXIMUM OR AT MIDSPAN.

   B. AT FLOOR JOISTS OVER 10" IN DEPTH AND OVER 8'-0" SPAN SPACE AT 8'-0" O.C. MAXIMUM OR AT MIDSPAN.

9. WHERE STUD PARTITIONS JOIN MASONRY WALLS, THE END STUD SHALL BE ANCHORED WITH 1/2"φ ANCHOR BOLTS, 12" FROM THE TOP AND BOTTOM AND AT 48" O.C. ALONG STUD.

10. POWER ACTUATED SILL PINS SHALL BE "RAMSET" #3340 WITH 3/8"φ HEAD AND 0.218"φ SHANK (ICBO #1147), UNLESS NOTED OTHERWISE.

11. BOLTS IN WOOD SHALL BE NOT LESS THAN 7-DIA. FROM THE END AND 4-DIA. FROM THE EDGE UNLESS OTHERWISE NOTED.

12. BOLT HOLES IN WOOD SHALL BE 1/16" LARGER THAN THE BOLT DIAMETER. THE THREADED PORTION OF THE BOLT SHALL NOT BEAR ON WOOD.

13. NAILING SCHEDULE : (USE COMMON WIRE OR BOX-NAILS)

JOIST TO SILL OR GIRDER, TOE NAIL	3-8d
BRIDGING TO JOIST, TOE NAIL EA. END	2-8d
1"x6" SUBFLOOR OR LESS TO EA. JOIST, FACE NAIL	2-8d
WIDER THAN 1"x6" SUBFLOOR TO EA. JOIST, FACE NAIL	3-8d
2" PLANK TO JOIST OR GIRDER, BLIND & FACE NAIL	2-16d
SOLE PLATE TO JOIST OR BLOCKING, FACE NAIL	16d AT 16" O.C.
TOP PLATE TO STUD, END NAIL	2-16d
STUD TO SOLE PLATE, TOE NAIL	4-8d
DOUBLED STUDS, FACE NAIL	16d AT 24" O.C.
DOUBLED TOP PLATES, FACE NAIL	16d AT 16" O.C.
TOP PLATES, LAPS & INTERSECTIONS, FACE NAIL	2-16d
CONTIN. HEADER, TWO PIECE	16d AT 16" O.C. EA. EDGE
CEILING JOISTS TO PLATE, TOE NAIL	3-8d
CONTIN. HEADER TO STUD, TOE NAIL	4-8d
CEILING JOISTS, LAPS OVER PARTITIONS, FACE NAIL	3-16d
CEILING JOISTS TO PARALLEL RAFTERS, FACE NAIL	3-16d
RAFTER TO PLATE, TOE NAIL	3-8d
1" BRACE TO EA. STUD & PLATE, FACE NAIL	2-8d
1"x8" SHEATHING OR LESS TO EA. BEARING, FACE NAIL	2-8d
WIDER THAN 1"x8" SHEATHING TO EA. BEARING, FACE NAIL	2-8d
BUILT-UP CORNER STUDS	16d AT 24" O.C.
BUILT-UP GIRDER AND BEAM	20d AT 32" O.C. AT TOP & BOTTOM & STAGGERED 2 20d AT ENDS AND AT EACH SPLICE

STRUCTURAL STEEL

1. STRUCTURAL STEEL SHALL COMPLY WITH THE FOLLOWING A.S.T.M. DESIGNATIONS :

STEEL TUBES	A500, GRADE B (FY: 46KSI)
ROLLED SHAPES &	A36
MISC. METAL	
UNFINISHED BOLTS	A307

2. PROVIDE FULL BEARING ON UNTHREADED PORTION OF SHANK FOR BOLTS AT ALL STEEL MEMBER CONNECTIONS.

3. ALL WELDING SHALL BE DONE BY CERTIFIED WELDERS USING THE SHIELDED ARC METHOD AND E-70XX LOW HYDROGEN ELECTRODES. FIELD WELDING SHALL HAVE CONTINUOUS SPECIAL INSPECTION. (OWNER SHALL EMPLOY SPECIAL INSPECTOR)

4. MATERIAL AND WORKMANSHIP SHALL COMPLY WITH A.I.S.C. SPECIFICATIONS FOR THE DESIGN, FABRICATION AND ERECTION OF STRUCTURAL STEEL FOR BUILDINGS. WELDING SHOPS MUST BE APPROVED BY A RECOGNIZED TESTING LABORATORY OR WELDING MUST HAVE CONTINUOUS SPECIAL INSPECTION. A RECOGNIZED TESTING LAB IS ONE SUPERVISED BY A STATE REGISTERED ENGINEER.

DRAWN BY: KS
REVISIONS:
DATE: 3-14-83
JOB No: 83-1-3A
(C 1983)

structureform STAFF
444-8182
353 E. PARK AVE., SUITE 4.
EL CAJON, CA.
92020

10 of 18

Figure 1-5 Drafters are often required to print specifications that explain the criteria for construction quality. *Courtesy Structureform Masters, Inc.*

minimum understanding of the construction process. In most states, there are different levels of examiners. An experienced drafter or designer may be able to qualify as a low-level or residential-plan inspector. Generally, a degree in engineering or architecture is required to advance to an upper-level position.

The construction that results from the plans must also be inspected. Depending on the size of the building department, the plan examiner may also serve as the building inspector. In large building departments, one group inspects plans and another inspects construction. To be a construction inspector requires an exceptionally good understanding of codes limitations, print reading, and construction methods. Each of these skills has its roots in a beginning drafting class.

Jobs in Construction

Many drafters are employed directly by construction companies. The benefits of this type of position have already been discussed. These drafters typically not only do drafting, but also work part time in the field. Many drafters give up their jobs for one of the high paying positions in the construction industry. The ease of interpreting plans as a result of a background in drafting would be of great benefit to any construction worker.

PROFESSIONAL ARCHITECTURAL CAREERS, OFFICE PRACTICE, AND OPPORTUNITIES TEST

DIRECTIONS

Answer the questions with short complete statements or drawings as needed on an 8½ × 11 drawing sheet as follows:

1. Use ⅛ in. guidelines for all lettering.
2. Letter your name, Professional Architectural Careers, Office Practice, and Opportunities Test, and the date at the top of the sheet.
3. Letter the question number and provide the answer. You do not need to write out the question.
4. Do all lettering with vertical-style letters. If the answer requires line work, use proper drafting tools and technique. Answers may be prepared on a word processor if appropriate with course guidelines.

QUESTIONS

1. List five types of work that a junior drafter might be expected to perform.

2. What three skills are usually required of a junior drafter for advancement?
3. What types of drawings should a junior drafter expect to be drawing?
4. Describe what the junior drafter might be given to assist in making drawings.
5. List three types of work a drafter might be expected to perform.
6. List four sources of written information that a drafter will need to be able to use.
7. What types of drawings might a designer be working on?
8. Why would a student in an architectural degree program need to take classes in logic, art, psychology and philosophy?
9. Why are engineering students required to have such a good understanding of math and science?
10. List and briefly describe some different careers in which drafting would be helpful.

Chapter 2
Architectural Drafting Equipment

DRAFTING TOOLS and equipment are available from a number of vendors that sell professional drafting supplies. For accuracy and long life, always purchase high-quality equipment. Local vendors can be found by looking in the yellow pages of your telephone book under headings such as: Drafting Room Equipment & Supplies, Blueprinting, Architects' Supplies, Engineering Equipment & Supplies, or Artists' Materials & Supplies.

DRAFTING EQUIPMENT KITS

Drafting supplies and equipment can be purchased in a kit or items can be bought individually. Many vendors have produced drafting kits which are often available at college bookstores for economical prices. Whether equipment is purchased in a kit or by the individual tool, the items that are normally needed include the following:

- One mechanical lead holder with 4H, 2H, H, and F grade leads. This pencil and lead assortment allows for individual flexibility of line and lettering control, or use in sketching.
- One 0.3 mm automatic drafting pencil with 4H, 2H, and H leads.
- One 0.5 mm automatic drafting pencil with 4H, 2H, H, and F leads.
- One 0.7 mm automatic drafting pencil with 2H, H, and F leads.
- One 0.9 mm automatic drafting pencil with H, F, and HB leads. The automatic drafting pencils allow for constant line and lettering widths without sharpening. The 0.7 and 0.9 mm pencils with soft (H, F, or HB) leads are good for sketching. Drafters may elect to purchase two or more pencils and use a different grade of lead in each. Doing so will reduce the need to change leads constantly. Some drafters use a light-blue, non-reproducible lead for layout work.
- Lead sharpener.
- 6-in. bow compass.
- Dividers.
- Eraser. Select an eraser that is recommended for drafting with pencil on paper.

- Erasing shield.
- 3/10-in. 30°–60° triangle.
- 3/10-in. 45° triangle.
- Irregular curve.
- Adjustable triangle.
- Scales:
  1. Triangular architect's scale.
  2. Triangular civil engineer's scale.
- Drafting tape.
- Architectural floor plan template, ¼″ = 1′–0″ (for residential plans).
- Circle template (small holes).
- Lettering guide.
- Sandpaper sharpening pad.
- Dusting brush.

Not all of the items listed here are used in every school or workplace. Additional equipment and supplies may be needed depending upon the specific application, for example:

- Technical pen set.
- Drafting ink.
- Lettering template.
- Assorted architectural drafting templates.

DRAFTING FURNITURE

Tables

There is a large variety of drafting tables available ranging from economical models to complete professional work stations, Figure 2–1. Drafting tables are generally sized by the dimensions of their tops. Standard table-top sizes range from 24 × 36 in. to 42 × 84 in.

The features to look for in a good-quality, professional table include:

- One-hand tilt control.
- One-hand or foot height control.
- The ability to position the board vertically.

Figure 2–1 Drafting work station. *Courtesy Mayline Company, Inc.*

- An electrical outlet.
- A drawer for tools and/or drawings.

Some manufacturers ship tables with tops that are ready to draw on. Others ship tables with tops of steel or basswood that need to be covered. Basswood can be a drawing surface; however, most offices commonly cover drafting-table tops with smooth, specially designed surfaces. The material, usually vinyl, provides the proper density for effective use under normal drafting conditions. After compass or divider points have pierced the surface, the small holes close and so provide a smooth surface for continued use. Drafting tape is commonly used to adhere drawings to the table top, although some drafting tables have magnetized tops and use magnetic strips to attach drawings.

Chairs

Better drafting chairs have the following characteristics:

- Padded or contoured seat design.
- Height adjustment.
- Foot rest.
- Fabric that allows air to circulate.
- Sturdy construction.

DRAFTING PENCILS, LEADS, AND SHARPENERS

Mechanical Pencils

The term *mechanical pencil* is applied to a pencil which requires a piece of lead to be manually inserted and by some physical action such as twist, push, or pull, the lead is mechanically, or semiautomatically, advanced to the tip. A common lead holder, shown in Figure 2–2, is a mechanical pencil that many drafters favor. Pressing the thumb button on the end of this model opens the chuck (clamping jaws) and releases the lead. For proper use, the lead should extend about ¼-in. beyond the end of the chuck. Mechanical pencils vary in price. Some are made of plastic while others are made of metal. Get one that is comfortable and well made. Some inexpensive lead holders wear out quickly, and often the

Figure 2–2 Mechanical pencil also known as a lead holder. *Courtesy Koh-I-Noor Rapidograph, Inc.*

chuck at the tip fails to hold the lead tightly during use.

Leads are bought separately although one lead usually comes with the holder. You will need to purchase other leads so that you can correctly make a variety of lines and letters. Leads are graded by hardness and designated by a number and letter, or one or two letters. The designation is usually found along or on one end of the lead. Always sharpen the end opposite the designation.

Automatic Pencils

The term *automatic pencil* refers to a pencil with a lead chamber that, at the push of a button or tab, will advance the lead from the chamber to the writing tip. Automatic pencils are designed to hold leads of one width that do not need to be sharpened. These pencils are available in several different lead thickness sizes. Figure 2–3 shows a popular automatic pencil. Many drafting technicians will have several automatic or mechanical pencils. Each pencil will have a different grade of lead hardness and be used for lettering or a specific type of line or technique.

Wooden Pencils

Wooden pencils are not often used by professional drafters because they are time consuming to sharpen, waste much lead when sharpened, and become uncomfortable to use as the pencils become short. Wooden pencils will produce results equal to the other two kinds of drafting pencils. With wooden pencils you will need a knife or a special drafting pencil sharpener and a sanding block to keep the point sharp. All wooden pencils have the lead hardness marked only on one end, so be careful not to sharpen that end otherwise you will not know the hardness of that pencil.

Lead Grades

The leads that you select for your line work depend upon the amount of pressure you apply and other technique factors. You should experiment until you identify the leads that give you the best line quality. Leads commonly used for thick lines range from 2H to F, while leads for thin lines range from 4H to H, depending upon individual preference. Con-

Figure 2–3 Automatic pencil. *Courtesy Pentel of America, Ltd.*

9H 8H 7H 6H 5H 4H	3H 2H H F HB B	2B 3B 4B 5B 6B 7B
HARD	MEDIUM	SOFT
4H AND 6H ARE COMMONLY USED FOR CONSTRUCTION LINES.	H AND 2H ARE COMMON LEAD GRADES USED FOR LINE WORK. H AND F WOULD BE FOR LETTERING AND SKETCHING.	THESE GRADES ARE FOR ART WORK. THEY ARE TOO SOFT TO KEEP A SHARP POINT AND THEY SMUDGE EASILY.

Figure 2–4 The range of lead grades.

struction lines for layout and guidelines are very lightly drawn with a 6H or 4H lead. Figure 2–4 shows the different lead grades. Generally, softer leads are used for sketching than those used for making formal lines. Good sketching leads are H, F, or HB.

Polyester and Special Leads

Polyester leads, also known as plastic leads, are for drawing on *polyester drafting film*, often called by its trade name, *Mylar*®. Plastic leads come in grades equivalent to F, 2H, 4H, and 5H and are usually labelled with an "S," as in 2S. Some companies make a combination lead for use on both vellum and polyester film. See Chapter 3 for information about the techniques and use of polyester leads.

Colored leads have special uses. Red or yellow lead is commonly used to make corrections. Red or yellow lines appear black on a print. Blue lead can be used on the original drawing for information that is not to show on a print such as for notes, lines, and outlines of areas to be corrected. Blue lines do not appear on the print when the original is run through a Diazo machine. Some drafters use light-blue lead for all layout work and guidelines because it will not reproduce.

Basic Pencil Motions

Keep your pencil straight from side to side and tilted about 60° with the direction of travel. Try not to tilt the lead under or away from the straightedge. Rotate a lead holder or wooden pencil between your fingers as you draw a line so that the tip stays uniformly conical. Automatic pencils do not require such rotation, although some drafters feel more comfortable rotating any pencil. Provide enough pressure to make a line dark and crisp. Take care not to make it too thick. Figure 2–5 shows some basic pencil motions.

Sanding Block

One of the simplest devices used to put a point on a pencil is a piece of sandpaper. Several strips of

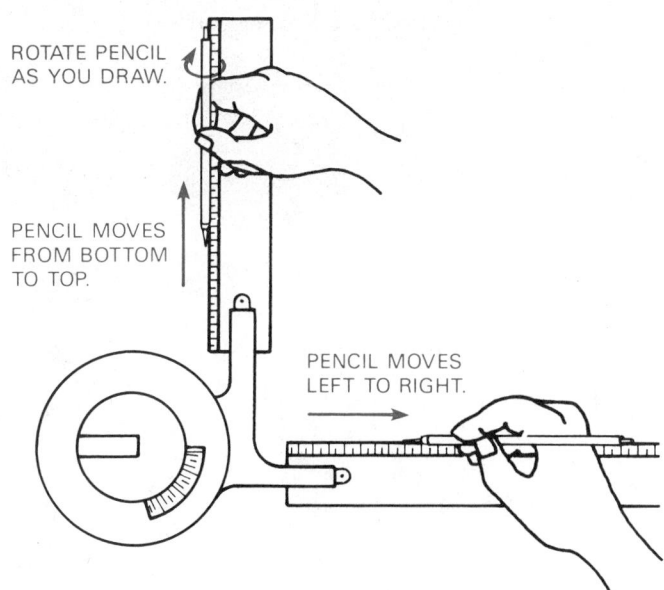

Figure 2-5 Basic pencil motions.

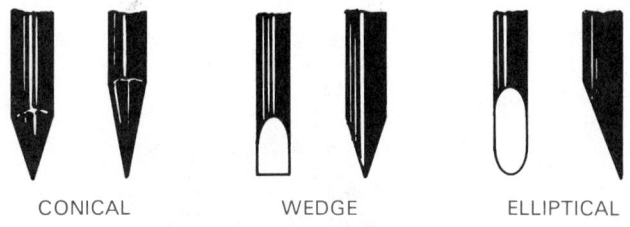

CONICAL   WEDGE   ELLIPTICAL

Figure 2-6 Types of drafting points.

sandpaper stapled to a wooden paddle is called a sanding block. Plastic lead will fill up sandpaper rapidly so several sheets will be needed as compared to graphite lead. To avoid smudging your drawing, use the sanding block away from your drawing table and dispose of the graphite carefully. The sanding block is a good instrument to use to obtain a wedge or elliptical point. With a sanding block you can also make a conical point, although other sharpeners are better for that purpose. Figure 2-6 shows three common drafting points.

To obtain an elliptical point, stroke the lead in a back-and-forth motion on the sandpaper on one side only at about a 30° angle. The elliptical point is usually used in a compass, but some drafters like to use it for all straight lines on a drawing.

Caution: Do not rotate your pencil when drawing a line with an elliptical point.

To obtain a wedge point, use the same action as making the elliptical point except turn your pencil 180° and sharpen the opposite side as well. The wedge point may also be made using a side-to-side motion. This point is preferred by some drafters for drawing straight lines only. Usually the lead tip is held at a slight angle when drawing a line and only the corner is used. When this edge becomes dull, turn it 180° and use the other corner.

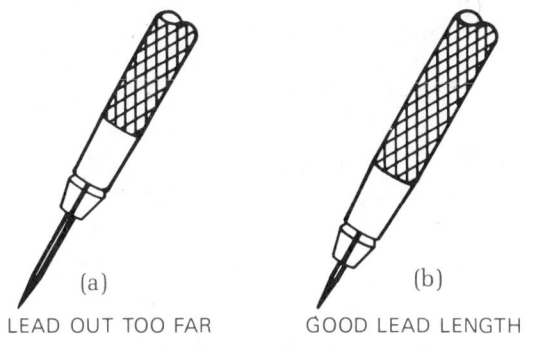

(a) LEAD OUT TOO FAR   (b) GOOD LEAD LENGTH

Figure 2-7 Lead length.

Caution: Do not rotate your pencil when drawing a line with the wedge point.

Normally, other kinds of pencil sharpeners are used to make a conical point but sandpaper can also be used. Just keep rotating your lead as you draw it back-and-forth across the sandpaper. When drawing a line, you will need to rotate your pencil in order to keep the conical point sharp. This point is preferred by most drafting technicians because you can letter and draw straight and curved lines with the same point.

When you have sharpened the tip of plastic lead, push the lead back in the holder as far as practical because plastic lead is weaker than graphite and will break easier. Pushing the lead back is a good practice with graphite lead also. Figure 2-7(a) shows the lead extended too far, while 2-7(b) shows a good length for convenient use.

Pocket Pointer

A portable sharpener for mechanical pencils is the pocket pointer shown in Figure 2-8. This pointer

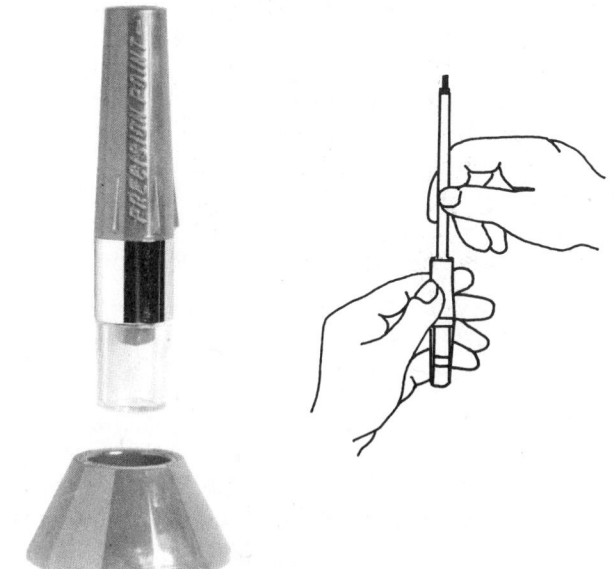

Figure 2-8 Pocket pointer. *Courtesy Koh-I-Noor Rapidograph, Inc.*

contains blades that sharpen lead to a conical point. To sharpen a point, you either hold the pencil still with one hand and rotate the sharpener with the other hand, or vice versa. The cutting blades on this sharpener will wear out with use and must be replaced periodically. The pocket pointer will work with either graphite or plastic lead.

Sandpaper Desk-top Pointer

Another common sharpener used to obtain a conical point with mechanical holders uses a sandpaper disk. See Figure 2–9. This sharpener works well with graphite, but not so well with polyester lead. To sharpen a point you hold the pencil and use it as a handle while you rotate the top of the pointer in a circular motion. The lead rubs on the sandpaper disk to make the point.

These pointers are heavy enough to sit on the table top, but take care not to turn the sharpener over as it will spill graphite. The sanding disk must be replaced often and the unit should be cleaned periodically away from the drawing board.

Pencil Point Cleaners

Point cleaners are available with most sharpeners. Press the sharpened pencil point into the point cleaner to remove graphite particles. This practice helps keep your drawing free of smudges.

Cutting-wheel Pointer

The best type of conical-point sharpener for mechanical pencil holders is a mechanical lead pointer with a tool-steel cutting wheel as seen in Figure 2–10. This unit must be clamped to the drawing board. Use the slots provided in the top to expose the right length of lead to get a sharp or slightly dull point. The slightly dull point is used for lettering. This sharpener will sharpen graphite or polyester leads equally well. The cutting wheel lasts a long time and the unit is easy to clean by washing it in a sink. An occasional drop of light machine oil on the shaft will keep the cutting wheel working properly.

Electric Lead Pointer

The electric lead pointer is an excellent device for quick pencil sharpening. Most units have gages for proper lead extension and will sharpen points to a perfect taper in about half a second. Their heavy-duty motors are quiet and maintenance free. Usually this machine has a storage area for lead holders. Lead pointer attachments are also available that will turn an electric eraser into a pencil pointer.

Figure 2–9 Sandpaper desk-top pointer. *Courtesy Charvoz-Carsen Corporation.*

TO GET A SHARP OR DULL POINT, USE SLOTS PROVIDED FOR LENGTH OF LEAD ADJUSTMENT IN TOP.

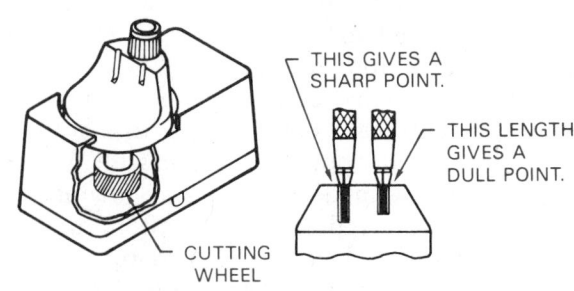

THIS GIVES A SHARP POINT.

THIS LENGTH GIVES A DULL POINT.

CUTTING WHEEL

Figure 2–10 Cutting-wheel lead pointer. *Courtesy Berol USA RapiDesign.*

Advice Regarding Pencil Points

The conical point, shown in Figure 2–6, is most commonly used but is not the only one that is favored by drafters. Some drafters claim that the wedge point will produce a better fine line with the advantage of having two corners of the edge to use. Still others claim that lead is manufactured so it is harder on the outside edge. The elliptical point, shown in Figure 2–6 takes advantage of this feature. The elliptical point is, of course, excellent for compass work. Students must experiment with different lead points and grades of lead in mechanical pencils to determine their best individual results. A comparison should also be made between the mechanical and automatic pencils to determine best results.

TECHNICAL PENS AND ACCESSORIES

Technical Pens

Also known as technical fountain pens, technical pens have improved over the past few years in quality and ability to produce excellent inked lines. These pens function on a capillary action where a needle acts as a valve to allow ink to flow from a storage cylinder through a small tube which is designed to meter the ink so that a specific line width is created. A technical pen is shown in Figure 2–11. Technical pens may be purchased individually or in sets. The different tip sizes used to make various line widths range from a narrow number 6 × 0 (.005 in./0.13 mm) to a wide number 7 (.079 in./2 mm). Figure 2–12 shows a comparison of some of the different line widths available with technical pens.

Technical pens are available in different price ranges as determined by the kind of material used to make the point. Each kind of point has a recommended use. Stainless steel points are made for use on vellum and tracing paper. These points will wear out very rapidly when used on polyester film. Tungsten carbide points are recommended for polyester film and can be used on vellum. Jewel points provide the longest life and can be used on vellum or Mylar with the best results. They also provide the smoothest ink flow on polyester film.

In addition to having the advantage of a constant line width, technical pens have a reservoir that allows the drafter to make inked lines for a long period of time before ink must be added. Technical pens may be used with templates to make circles, arcs, and symbols. Compass adapters to hold technical pens are also available for use as seen in Figure 2–13. Technical pen tips are designed to fit into scribers for use with lettering guides. This concept is discussed further in Chapter 4.

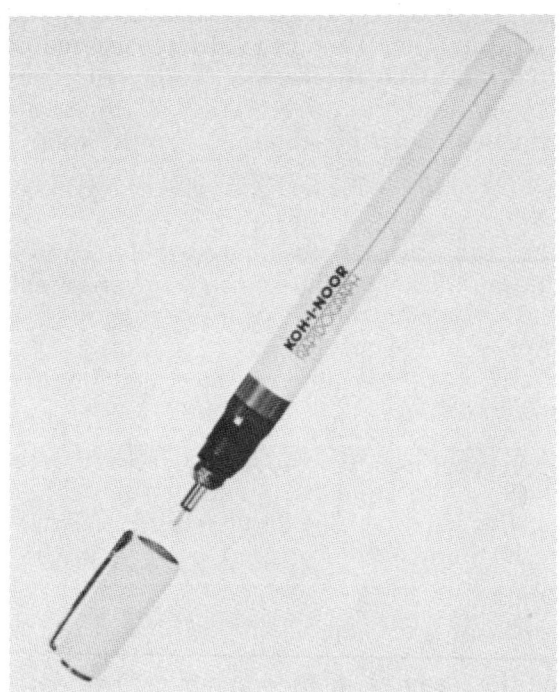

Figure 2–11 Technical pen. *Courtesy Koh-I-Noor Rapidograph, Inc.*

6x0	4x0	3x0	00	0	1	2	2½	3	3½	4	6	7
.13	.18	.25	.30	.35	.50	.60	.70	.80	1.00	1.20	1.40	2.00
005 in	007 in	010 in	012 in	014 in	020 in	024 in	028 in	031 in	039 in	047 in	055 in	079 in
13mm	18mm	25mm	30mm	35mm	50mm	60mm	70mm	80mm	100mm	120mm	140mm	200mm

Figure 2–12 Technical pen line widths. *Courtesy Koh-I-Noor Rapidograph, Inc.*

Figure 2–13 Technical pen compass adapter. *Courtesy J.S. Staedtler, Inc.*

Most pen manufacturers have designed pen holders or caps that help keep pen points moist and ready for use. When pens are used daily, cleaning may be necessary only periodically. Some symptoms to look for when pens need cleaning include the following:

- Ink constantly creates a drop at the pen tip.
- Ink tends to flow out around the tip holder.
- The point plunger does not activate properly. If you do not hear and feel the plunger when you shake the pen, then it is probably clogged with thick or dried ink.
- When drawing a line, ink does not flow freely.
- Ink flow starts with difficulty.

The ink level in the reservoir should be kept between one-quarter to three-quarters full. If the cylinder is too full, the ink may not flow well; if too little ink is present, then the pen may skip when in use.

Pen Cleaning

Read the cleaning instructions that come with the brand of pen that you purchase. Some pens require disassembly for cleaning while others should not be taken apart. Some manufacturers strongly suggest that pen tips remain assembled. The main parts of a technical pen include the cap, nib, pen body, ink

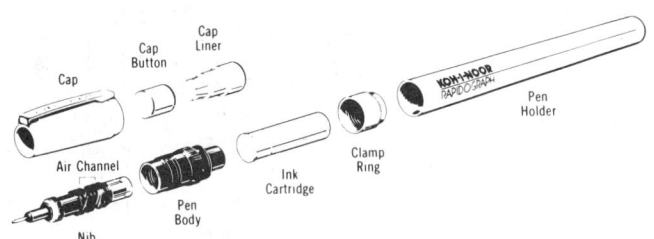

Figure 2–14 The parts of a technical pen. *Courtesy Koh-I-Noor Rapidograph, Inc.*

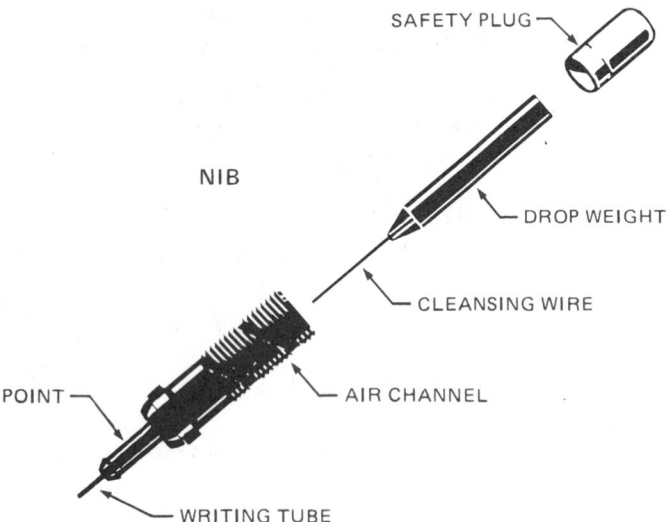

Figure 2–15 Parts of a technical pen nib. *Courtesy Koh-I-Noor Rapidograph, Inc.*

cartridge (or reservoir), and pen holder as seen in Figure 2–14. The nib contains a cleansing wire with drop weight and a safety plug, shown in Figure 2–15. Most manufacturers recommend that the nib remain assembled during cleaning as the cleansing wire is easily damaged. To fill the technical pen, unscrew the cap, holder, and clamp ring from the pen body. Remove the cartridge and fill it with ink to within ¼ of the top. Slowly replace the cartridge and assemble the parts. Pens should be cleaned before each filling or before being stored for a long period of time. Clean the technical pen nib, cartridge, and body separately in lukewarm water or special cleaning solution.

Ultrasonic pen cleaners are available to clean points. Pens are placed in a tank where millions of energized microscopic bubbles, generated by ultrasonic action, carry cleaning solution into the smallest openings of the drawing point to scrub the tube inside and out.

Syringe pressure pen cleaners and point starters are also available for cleaning pens. These cleaners use pressure and suction for the cleaning action. These units are provided with a connector for use as a pen starter. Specially formulated pen cleaner should be used for best results in either the ultrasonic or syringe units. Pen cleaner can also be used to soak pen points for cleaning by hand.

Ink

Drafting inks should be opaque or have a matte or semiflat black finish that will not reflect light. The ink should reproduce without hot spots or line variation. Drafting ink should have excellent adhesion properties for use on paper or film. Certain inks are recommended for use on film in order to avoid peeling, chipping, or cracking. Inks recommended for use in technical pens also have nonclogging characteristics. This property is especially important for use in high-speed computer-graphics plotters.

When selecting an ink, be sure to purchase one that will do the job that you want done. First, determine how the ink will be applied, that is, from a technical pen, computer plotter, air brush, fountain pen, calligraphy pen, or with a brush. Second, determine the surface the ink will be used on, such as paper (vellum or bond), polyester film (Mylar), or acetate. Third, determine if your use requires the ink to be opaque, fast drying, waterproof, or erasable.

ERASERS AND ACCESSORIES

The common shapes of erasers are rectangular and stick. You will find that the stick eraser works best in small areas. There are three basic types of erasers:

pencil, pen, and plastic. The plastic eraser is used for plastic lead or ink on polyester film. These erasers are identified by their white or translucent color. Select an eraser that is recommended for the particular material used.

Kinds of Erasers

Gray Ink-eraser. The gray ink-eraser contains a large quantity of pumice (an abrasive material) and is very firm to the touch. This eraser is designed to remove ink from paper but must be used with care or it will quickly wear a hole in the drawing.

Red Pencil Eraser. The red eraser is the most firm of all the pencil erasers and contains the greatest amount of pumice. It should be used with care to prevent tearing the paper.

White Pencil Eraser. The white pencil eraser is used for removing pencil marks from paper. It contains a small amount of pumice but can be used as a general-purpose pencil eraser.

Pink Pencil Eraser. A pink pencil eraser contains less pumice than the white pencil eraser. It can be used to erase pencil marks from most kinds of office paper without doing any damage to the surface.

Soft-green or Soft-pink Pencil Eraser. Both the soft-green and soft-pink erasers contain no pumice and are designed for use on even the most delicate types of paper without doing damage to the surface. The color difference is maintained only to satisfy long-established individual preferences.

Kneaded Eraser. Kneaded erasers are soft, stretchable, and nonabrasive. They can be formed into any size you need. Kneaded erasers are used for erasing pencil and charcoal; they are also used for shading. In addition, kneaded erasers are handy for removing graphite from the tip of a freshly sharpened pencil and smudges from a drawing and for cleaning a drawing surface.

Vinyl Eraser. The vinyl or plastic eraser contains no abrasive material. This eraser is used on drafting film to erase plastic lead or ink. When used with ink, apply very light pressure and take the utmost care because the friction developed by the speed of erasure can easily damage the drafting film surface and prevent the adhesion of ink when redrawing over the erased area. Moistening the eraser during use will help to reduce any damage to the drawing surface.

India Ink Erasing Machine Refill. The India ink refill eraser is for removing India ink from vellum or film. It contains a solvent that dissolves the binding agents in the ink and the vinyl, then removes the ink. This eraser does not work well with pencil lead.

Erasing Tips

When erasing, the idea is to remove an unwanted line or letter. You do not want to remove the surface of the paper or Mylar®. Erase only hard enough to remove the unwanted line. However, you must bear down hard enough to eliminate the line completely. If all the line does not disappear, ghosting will result. A ghost is a line that should have been eliminated but still shows on a print. Lines that have been drawn so hard as to make a groove in the drawing sheet can cause a ghost too. To remove ink from vellum, use a pink or green eraser, or an electric eraser. Work the area slowly. Do not apply too much pressure or erase in one spot too long or you will go through the paper. On polyester film, use a vinyl eraser and/or a moist cotton swab. The inked line will usually come off easily, but use caution. If you destroy the mat surface of either a vellum or Mylar® sheet, you will not be able to redraw over the erased area, especially not over smooth Mylar®.

Electric Erasers

Professional drafters use electric erasers. Those with cords that plug in are best, but cordless, rechargeable units are also available. When working with an electric eraser, you do not need to use very much pressure because the eraser operates at high speed. The purpose of the electric eraser is to remove unwanted lines quickly. Use caution, these erasers can also remove paper quickly! Eraser refills for electric units are available in pink, green, white, red, gray, yellow, and vinyl. Figure 2–16 shows an electric eraser and its optional lead pointer attachment.

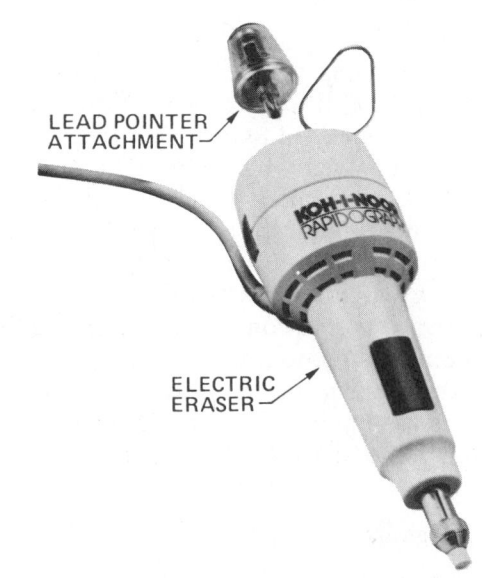

Figure 2–16 Electric eraser with optional lead pointer attachment. *Courtesy Koh-I-Noor Rapidograph, Inc.*

Figure 2-17 Erasing shield. *Courtesy Koh-I-Noor Rapidograph, Inc.*

Erasing Shield

Erasing shields are thin metal or plastic sheets with a number of differently shaped holes in them. They are used to erase small, unwanted lines or areas. For example, if you have a corner overrun, place one of the slots of the erasing shield over the area to be removed while covering the good area. Erase the overrun through the slot as shown in Figure 2-17.

Use a sketch for all preliminary layout work so as to help avoid the need to use erasers when you are working on the final drawing. Plan ahead. In addition, keep your hands and equipment clean to avoid unnecessary smudges. Drafting is a clean and neat profession. But because no one is perfect there are a variety of professional drafting erasers available.

Eradicating Fluid

Eradicating fluid is primarily used with ink on film or for removal of lines from sepia (brown) prints. Sepia prints are often used to make corrections rather than correcting the original drawing. The eradicating fluid is most often applied with a brush or cotton swab. If in doubt about its application, follow the manufacturer's instructions; however, application is usually done by lightly moistening the area to be corrected. Then the solution is wiped with a tissue, with care being taken to remove all residue. This process is continued until all residue is gone. Eradicating fluid is especially effective for removing aged ink lines and for erasure of large areas.

Cleaning Agents

Special eraser particles are available in a shaker-top can or a pad. Both types are used to sprinkle the eraser particles on a drawing to help reduce smudging

Figure 2-18 Dusting brush. *Courtesy of Koh-I-Noor Rapidograph, Inc.*

and to keep the drawing and your equipment clean. The particles also help float triangles, straightedges, and other drafting equipment to reduce line smudging. Cleaning powders are designed to prepare the drafting surface prior to working on it. Dry cleaning pads are fabric covered and contain fine, graded art gum that sifts through the fabric weave when the pad is tapped on the drawing surface. Use this material sparingly since too much of it can cause your lines to become fuzzy. Cleaning powders are not recommended for use on ink drawings, nor on polyester film.

Dusting Brush

Use a dusting brush to remove eraser particles from your drawing. Doing so will help reduce the possibility of smudges. Avoid using your hand to brush away eraser particles because the hand tends to cause smudges which reduces drawing neatness. A clean, dry cloth works better than your hand for removing eraser particles, but a brush is preferred. Figure 2-18 shows a typical dusting brush.

DRAFTING INSTRUMENTS

Kinds of Compasses

Compasses are used to draw circles and arcs. However, using a compass can be time consuming. Use a template, whenever possible, to make circles or arcs more quickly. A compass is especially useful for large circles.

There are several basic types of compasses:

1. A friction-head compass is not as accurate or stable as other types. This compass is not one that is usually chosen by professional drafters.
2. A drop-bow compass is mostly used for drawing small circles. The center rod contains the needle point and remains stationary while the pencil, or pen, leg revolves around it. See Figure 2-19.
3. The circuit-scribing instrument is a modified drop-bow compass used to cut terminal pads or prepare printed circuit layouts on scribe-coat film.

4. The center-wheel bow compass is most commonly used by professional drafters. This compass operates on the screwjack principle by turning the large knurled center wheel. The bow compass, shown in Figure 2–20, is used for most drawings. This is the type of compass commonly used by professionals.

5. A beam compass is a bar with an adjustable needle and a pencil or pen attachment for swinging large arcs or circles as shown in Figure 2–21. Also available is a beam that is adaptable to the bow compass. Such an adapter works only on bow compasses that have a removable break point, not on the fixed point models.

Compass Use

Keep both the compass needle point and lead point sharp. The points are removable for easy replacement. The better compass needle points have a shoulder on them. The shoulder helps keep the point from penetrating the paper more than necessary. Compare the needle points in Figure 2–22.

The compass lead should, in most cases, be one grade softer than the lead you use for straight lines because less pressure is used on a compass than a pencil. Keep the compass lead sharp. An elliptical point is commonly used with the bevel side inserted away from the needle leg. Keep the lead and the point equal in length. Figure 2–23 shows properly aligned and sharpened points on a compass.

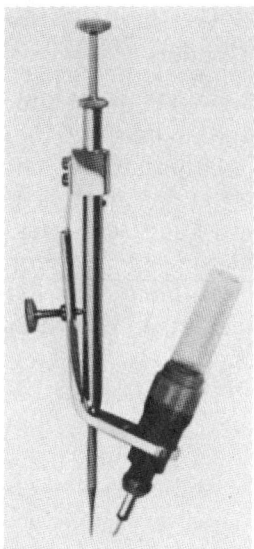

Figure 2–19 Drop-bow compass technical pen and pencil models. *Courtesy J.S. Staedtler, Inc.*

Figure 2–21 Beam compass. *Courtesy Teledyne Post.*

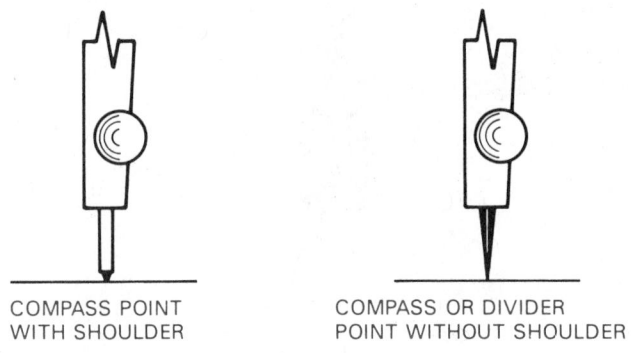

COMPASS POINT WITH SHOULDER

COMPASS OR DIVIDER POINT WITHOUT SHOULDER

Figure 2–22 Compass points.

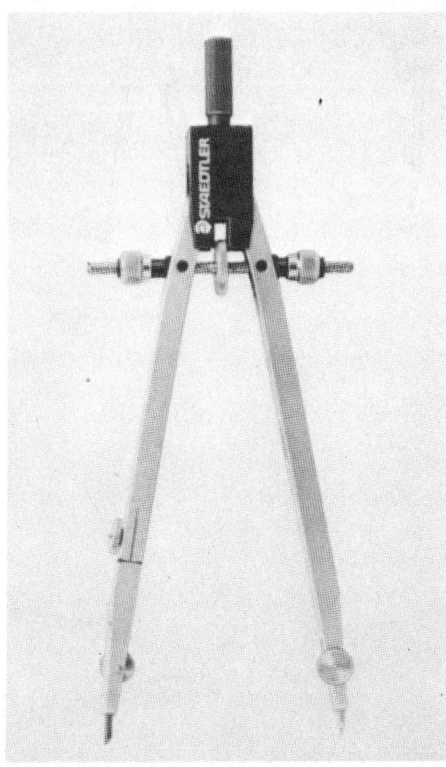

Figure 2–20 Bow compass. *Courtesy J.S. Staedtler, Inc.*

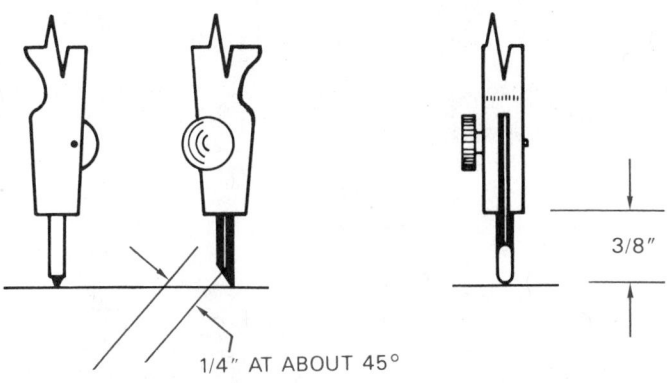

3/8"

1/4" AT ABOUT 45°

Figure 2–23 Properly sharpened and aligned elliptical compass point.

Use a sandpaper block to sharpen the elliptical point. Be careful to keep the graphite residue away from your drawing and off your hands. Remove excess graphite from the point with a tissue or cloth after sharpening. Sharpen the lead often to keep it sharp.

Some drafters prefer to use a conical point in their compass. This is the same point used in a lead holder. If you want to try this point, sharpen a piece of lead in your lead holder, then transfer it to your compass.

If you are drawing a number of circles from the same center, you will find that the compass point will cause an ugly hole in your drawing sheet. Reduce the chance of making such a hole by placing a couple of pieces of drafting tape at the center point for protection. There are small plastic circles available for just this purpose. Place one at the center point, then pierce the plastic with your compass.

Dividers

Dividers are used to transfer dimensions or to divide a distance into a number of equal parts. Figure 2-24 shows a dividers.

Note: Do not try to use dividers as a compass!

Some drafters prefer to use a bow dividers because the center wheel provides the ability to make fine adjustments easily. Also, the setting remains more stable than with standard friction dividers.

A good dividers should not be too loose or tight. It should be easily adjustable with one hand. In fact, you should control dividers with one hand as you lay out equal increments or transfer dimensions from one feature to another. Figure 2-25 shows how the dividers should be handled when used.

Proportional Dividers

Proportional dividers are used to reduce or enlarge an object without the need of mathematical calculations or scale manipulations. The center point of the dividers is set at the correct point for the proportion you want. Then you measure the original size line with one side of the proportional dividers and the other side automatically determines the new reduced or enlarged size. Figure 2-26 shows a proportional dividers.

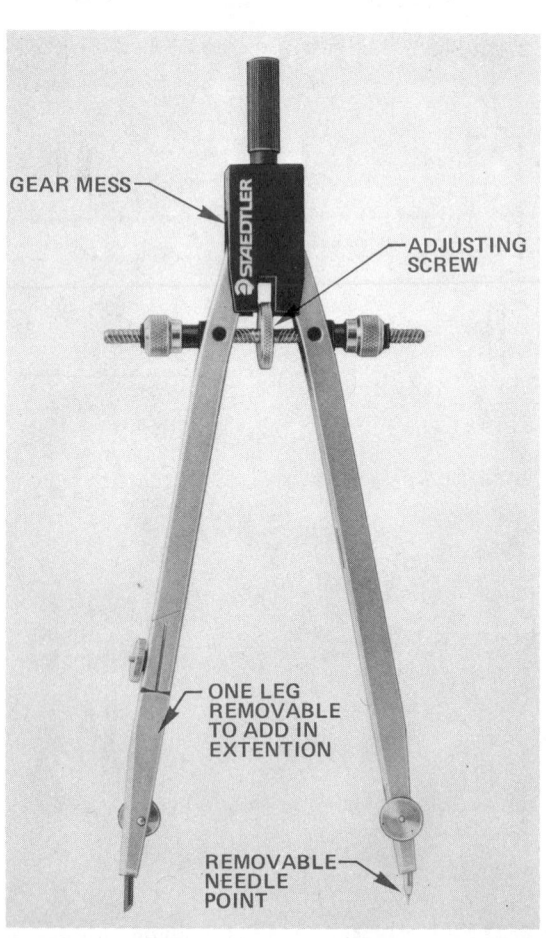

Figure 2-24 Dividers and its parts. *Courtesy Teledyne Post.*

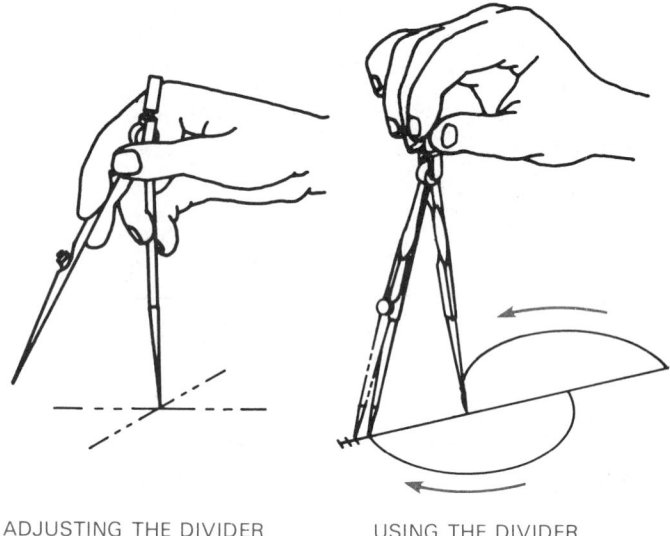

ADJUSTING THE DIVIDER   USING THE DIVIDER

Figure 2-25 Using dividers.

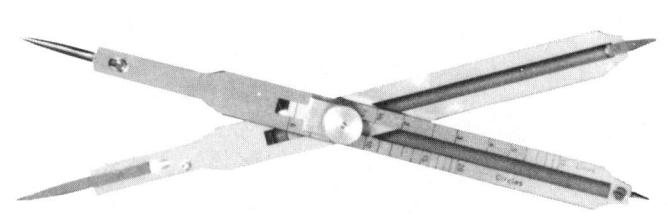

Figure 2-26 Proportional dividers. *Courtesy Teledyne Post.*

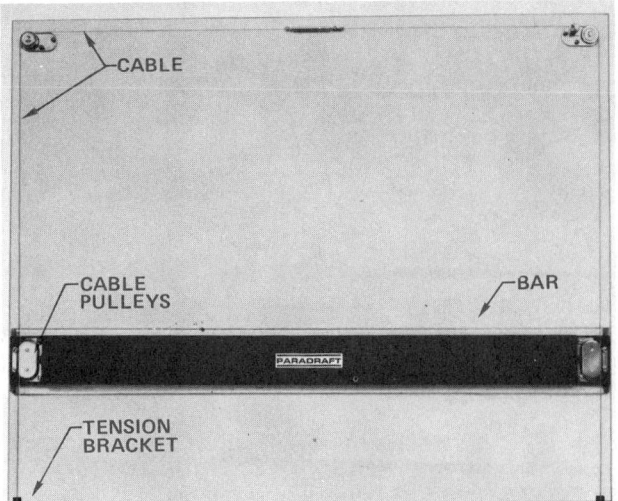

Figure 2-27 Parallel bar. *Courtesy Charvoz-Carsen Corporation.*

Parallel Bar

The parallel bar slides up and down the drafting board on cables that are attached to pulleys mounted at the top and bottom corners of the table. See Figure 2-27. The function of the parallel bar is to allow you to draw horizontal lines. Vertical lines and angles are made with triangles in conjunction with the parallel bar as shown in Figure 2-28. Angled lines are made with either standard or adjustable triangles.

The parallel bar is commonly found in architectural drafting offices because architectural drawings are frequently very large. Architects and architectural drafters often need to draw straight lines the full length of their boards and the parallel bar is ideal for such lines. Drafting machines take up a great amount of table space and are not as convenient for drawing long, straight lines. The parallel bar may be used with the board in an inclined position. Triangles and the parallel bar must be held securely when used in any position. Professional units have a brake that may be used to lock the parallel bar in place during use.

Figure 2-28 Drawing vertical lines with the parallel bar and triangle. *Courtesy Cascade Architectural and Engineering Supply.*

Triangles

There are two standard triangles. One has angles of 30°-60°-90° and is known as the 30°-60° triangle. The other has angles of 45°-45°-90° and is known as the 45° triangle.

Some drafting technicians prefer to use triangles in place of a vertical drafting machine scale. The machine protractor or the triangle can be used to make angled lines. Drafters that use parallel bars (or T-squares) rather than drafting machines also use triangles to make vertical and angled lines.

Triangles may also be used as a straightedge to connect points for drawing lines without the aid of a parallel bar or machine scale. Triangles are used individually or in combination to draw angled lines in 15° increments. See Figure 2-29. Also available are adjustable triangles with built-in protractors that are used to make angles of any degree up to a 45° angle. See Figure 2-30.

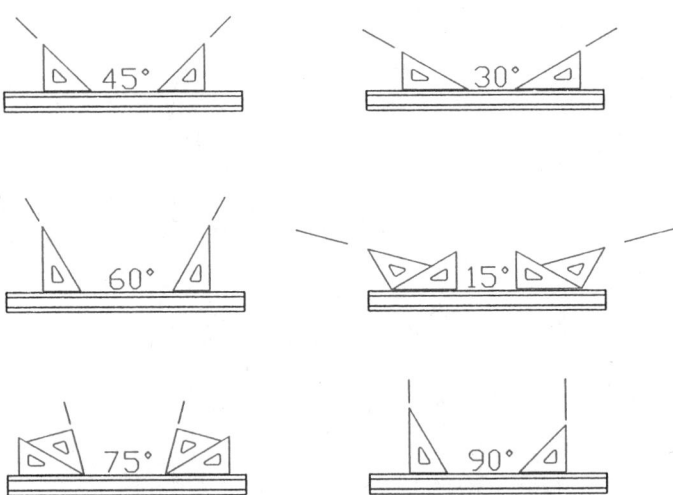

Figure 2-29 Angles that may be made with the 30°-60° and 45° traingles individually or in combination.

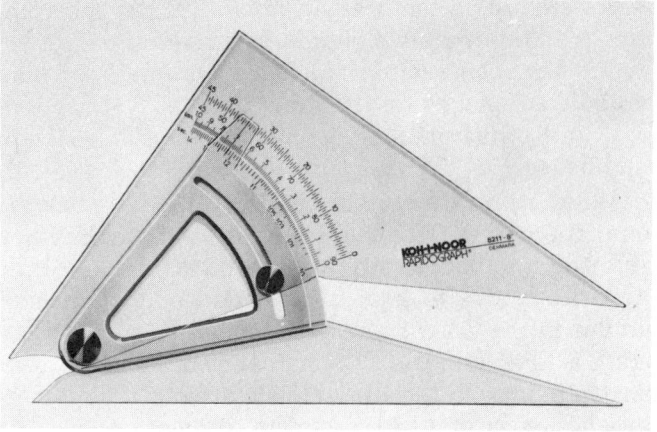

Figure 2-30 Adjustable triangle. *Courtesy Koh-I-Noor Rapidograph, Inc.*

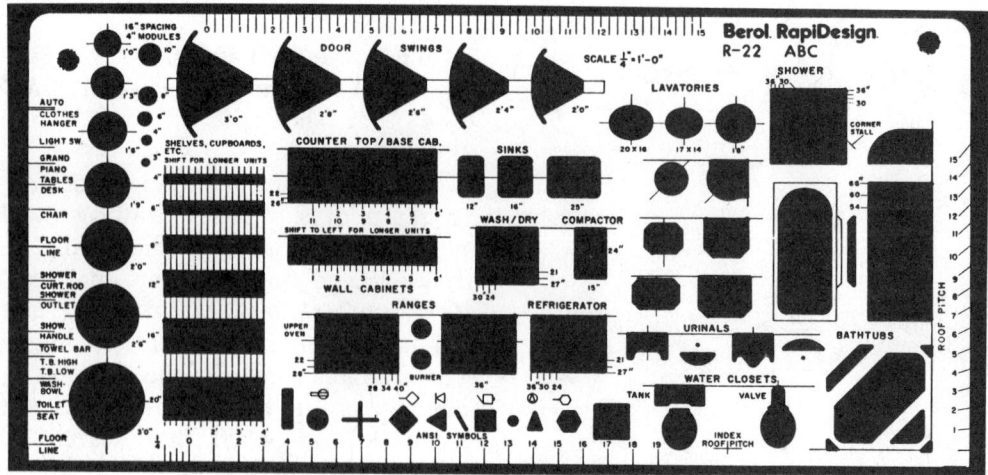

Figure 2–31 Architectural floor plan symbol template. *Courtesy Berol USA Rapi-Design.*

Architectural Templates

Templates are plastic sheets that have standard symbols cut through them for tracing. There are as many standard architectural templates as there are architectural symbols to draw. Templates may be scaled to match a particular application, such as floor plan symbols, or they may be unscaled for use on drawings that do not require a scale.

One of the most common architectural templates used is the residential floor plan template as shown in Figure 2–31. This template is typically available at a scale of $\frac{1}{4}'' = 1'-0''$ which coincides with the scale usually used for residential floor plans. Features that are often found on a floor plan template include circles, door swings, sinks, bathroom fixtures, kitchen appliances, and electrical symbols. Other floor plan templates are available for both residential and commercial applications. Additional architectural templates will be introduced in chapters where their specific applications are discussed.

Template Use. Always use a template when you can. Templates save time, are very accurate, and help standardize features on drawings. For most applications the template should be used only after the layout has been established. For example, floor plan symbols are placed on the drawing after walls, openings, and other main floor plan features have been established.

When using a template, carefully align the desired template feature with the layout lines of the drawing. Hold the template firmly in position while you draw the feature. Try to keep your pencil or pen perpendicular to the drawing surface for best results. When using a template and a technical pen, keep the pen perpendicular to the drawing sheet. Some templates have risers built in to keep the template above the drawing sheet. Without this feature there is a risk of ink running under a template that is flat against

the drawing. If your template does not have risers, purchase and add template lifters, use a few layers of tape placed on the underside of the template (although tape does not always work well), or place a second template with a large circle under the template you are using. See Figure 2–32.

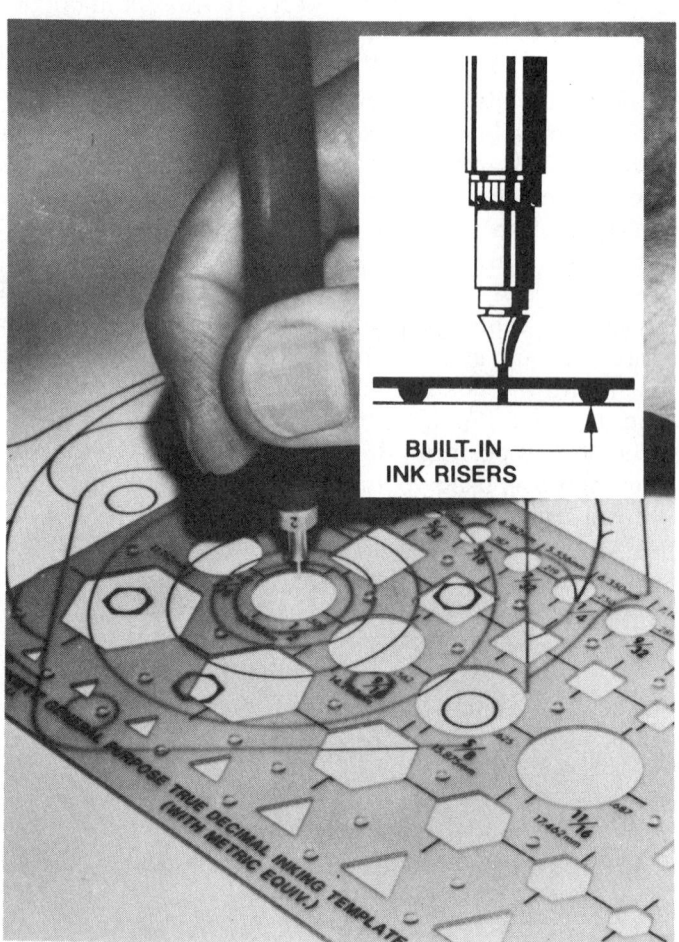

BUILT-IN INK RISERS

Figure 2–32 A template with built-in risers. *Courtesy Chartpak.*

Irregular Curves

Irregular curves are commonly called French curves. These curves have no constant radii. A selection of irregular curves is shown in Figure 2–33. Also available are ship's curves which become progressively larger and, like French curves, have no constant radii. They are used for layout and development of ships' hulls. Flexible curves are made of plastic and have a flexible core. See Figure 2–34. They may be used to draw almost any curve desired by bending and shaping.

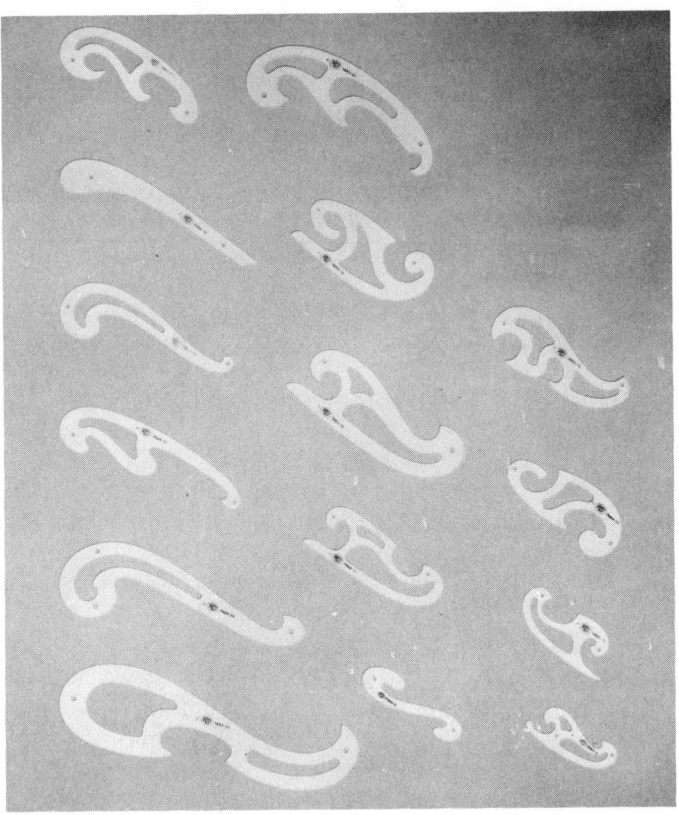

Figure 2–33 Irregular or French curves. *Courtesy Teledyne Post.*

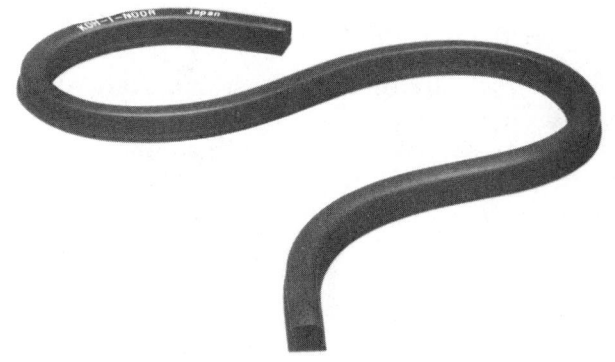

Figure 2–34 Flexible curve. *Courtesy Koh-I-Noor Rapidograph, Inc.*

Irregular curves are used for a variety of applications in architectural drafting. Some drafters use the curves to draw floor plan electrical runs or leader lines that connect notes to features on the drawing.

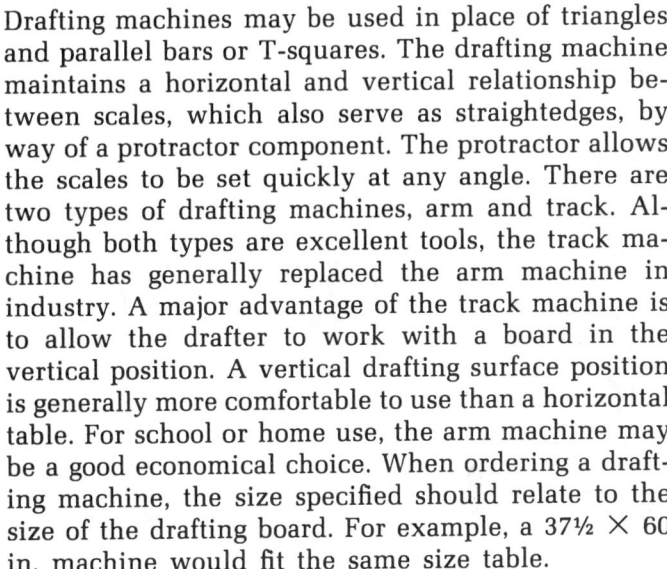

DRAFTING MACHINES

Drafting machines may be used in place of triangles and parallel bars or T-squares. The drafting machine maintains a horizontal and vertical relationship between scales, which also serve as straightedges, by way of a protractor component. The protractor allows the scales to be set quickly at any angle. There are two types of drafting machines, arm and track. Although both types are excellent tools, the track machine has generally replaced the arm machine in industry. A major advantage of the track machine is to allow the drafter to work with a board in the vertical position. A vertical drafting surface position is generally more comfortable to use than a horizontal table. For school or home use, the arm machine may be a good economical choice. When ordering a drafting machine, the size specified should relate to the size of the drafting board. For example, a 37½ × 60 in. machine would fit the same size table.

Drafting Machine Care

The drafting machine is a piece of precision-manufactured equipment that requires reasonable care in its use. There are locks that are used to stop the movement of the vertical and horizontal tracks of the track drafting machine. Be sure these locks are free before attempting to move the tracks. The drafting machine head automatically locks every 15°. The convenient thumb release must be pressed before you can move the head from these positions. There is a small lever that is used to lock the drafting machine head at angles other than the 15° increments. Always unlock this lever before moving the machine head; the drafting machine should work smoothly. These mechanisms are explained in detail in the following discussion. If at any time something does not work smoothly, see if any of the items described are in the locked position. Never force the equipment. Improper use and failure to keep the equipment clean may result in breakage or poor performance.

Arm Drafting Machine

The arm drafting machine is compact and less expensive than a track machine. The arm machine clamps to a table and through an elbow-like arrangement of supports allows the drafter to position the protractor head and scales anywhere on the board.

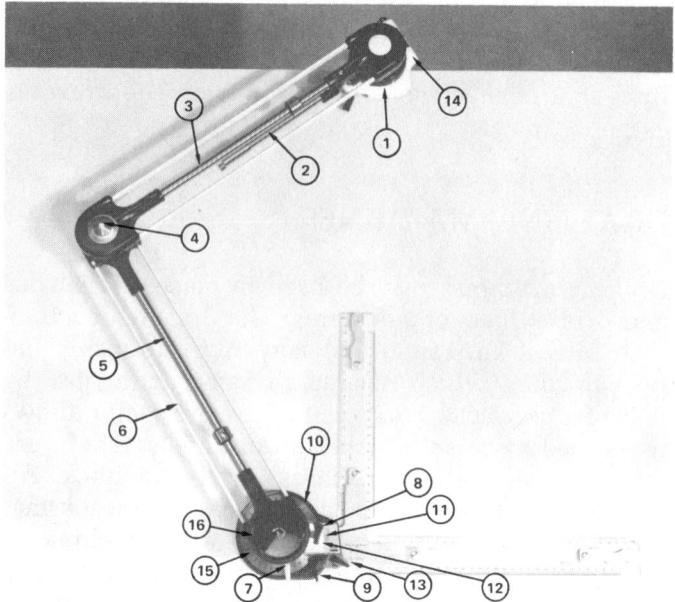

Figure 2–35 Arm drafting machine and its parts. *Courtesy Mutoh America, Inc.*

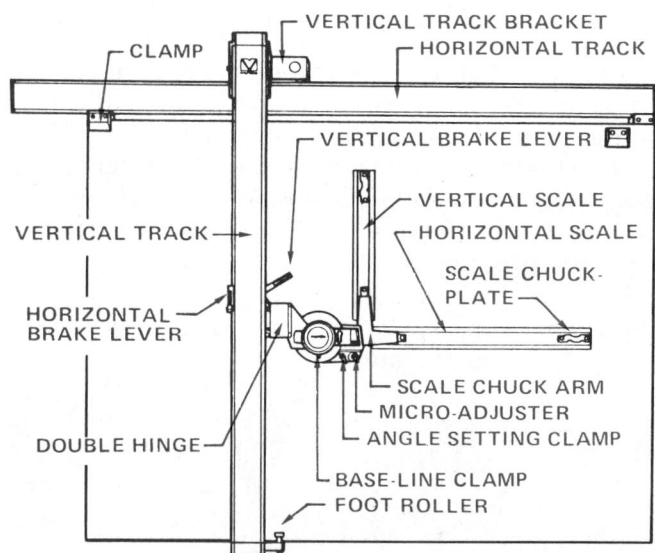

Figure 2–36 Track drafting machine and its parts. *Courtesy Mutoh America, Inc.*

The components of an arm drafting machine, shown in Figure 2–35, are as follows in numbered order:

1. Single screw board clamp with quick leveling nut that makes it easy to shift the machine along the board edge and to compensate for board warp.
2. Cartridge stabilizer balances the machine on boards inclined to 25°.
3. Single tension bar permits band adjustment.
4. Adjustable disk brake hand-tightens to increase machine stability on boards inclined to 35°.
5. Stainless steel tension bars and bands assure dependability and accuracy.
6. Semirigid band covers permit an instant check on band tension.
7. 360° base-line setting with positive lock baseline clamp. Allows for a fast alignment of the scale to any reference line on a drawing.
8. Dual action index control. Press the control for automatic 15° settings; press and lift to release the index for free rotation to any angle.
9. Vernier clamp locks the protractor at any angle.
10. Protractor scale. Engine divided to 1° to 180° in both directions.
11. Vernier scale. Engine divided to 5′ (minutes).
12. Magnifier to magnify readings.
13. Microadjuster assures fine scale alignment to the base line.
14. Swing-free hinge permits the machine to be raised to a rest position vertical to the board.

15. Protractor cover protects against dust and grime.
16. Cushion-grip protractor head for easy grip and comfort.

Track Drafting Machines

A track drafting machine has a traversing arm that moves left and right across the table and a head unit that moves up and down the traversing arm. There is a locking device for both the head and the traversing arm. The shape and placement of the controls of a track machine vary with the manufacturer although most brands have the same operating features and procedures. Figure 2–36 shows the component parts of a track drafting machine.

As with the arm machines, track drafting machines have a vernier head that allows the user to measure angles accurately to 5′ (minutes).

Digital Display Drafting Machine

Some track drafting machines are available with a digital display of angles and X-Y coordinates along with a memory function. These machines are more expensive than other track drafters; however, some companies have found them to have a speed and accuracy advantage over the old-style machines.

Controls and Machine Head Operation

The drafting machine head contains the controls for horizontal, vertical, and angular movement. Although each brand of machine contains similar fea-

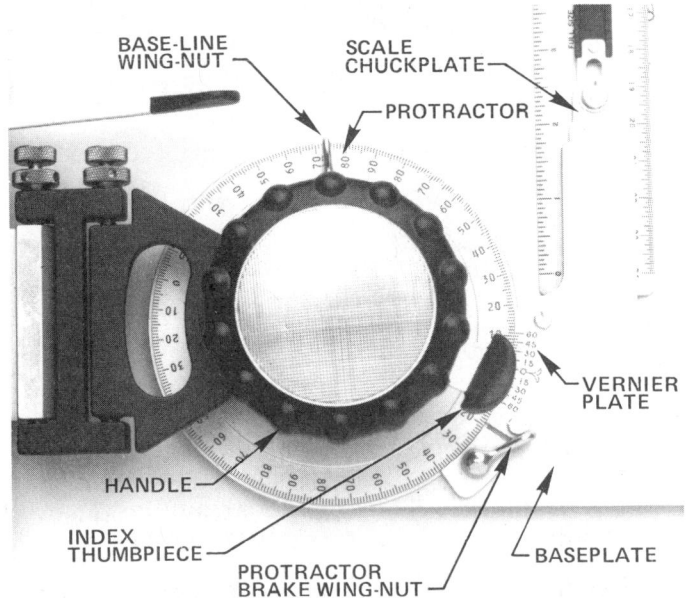

Figure 2–37 Drafting machine head controls and parts. *Courtesy Vemco.*

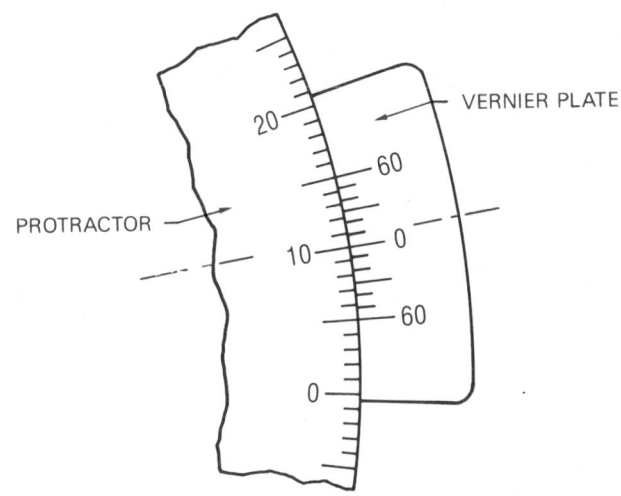

Figure 2–38 Vernier plate and protractor showing a reading of 10°.

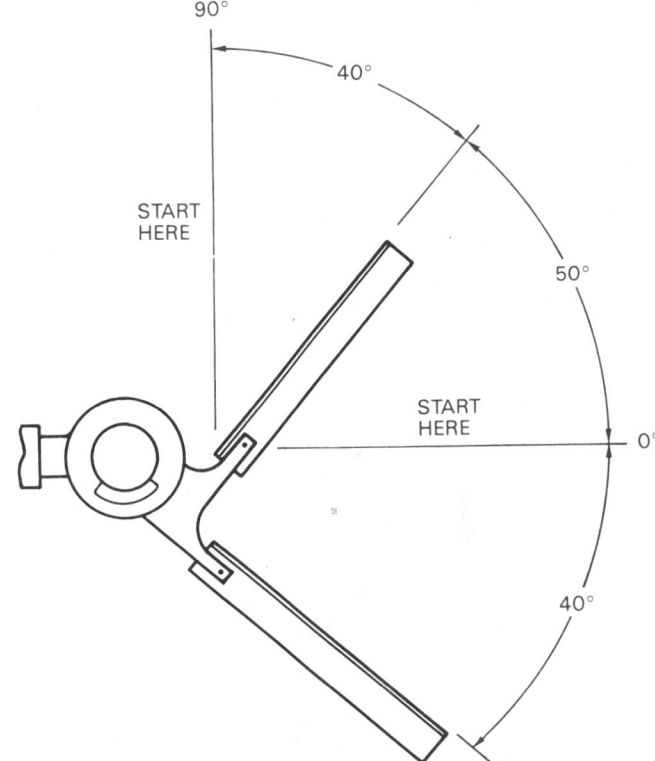

Figure 2–39 Angle measurement.

tures, controls may be found in different places on different brands. See Figure 2–37. Most machines have the following controls:

1. Base-line adjustment. This will release the scales so they can move independently from the protractor.
2. Index control. This permits automatic stops every 15°. It can also be pushed in and locked to enable you to adjust the machine to any angle.
3. Indexing clamp. The indexing clamp will lock the protractor at intermediate angles (those other than 15° increments) so you can draw a line accurately without the protractor moving.

To operate the drafting machine protractor head, place your hand on the handle and using your thumb, depress the index thumb-piece. Doing so will allow the head to rotate. Each increment marked on the protractor is one degree with a label every 10 degrees. See Figure 2–38. As the vernier plate (the small scale numbered from 0 to 60) moves past the protractor, the zero on the vernier will align with the angle that you wish to read. For example, Figure 2–38 shows a reading of 10°. As you rotate the handle, notice that the head will automatically lock every 15°. To move the protractor past the 15° increment, you must again depress the index thumb-piece. Figure 2–37 shows the index thumb-piece.

Having rotated the protractor head 40° clockwise, the machine will be in the position shown in Figure 2–39. The vernier plate at the protractor will read 40° which means that both the horizontal and vertical scale will have moved 40° from their original position at 0° and 90° respectively. The horizontal scale will

read directly from the protractor starting from 0°. The vertical scale reading begins from the 90° position. The key to measuring angles is to determine if the angle is to be measured from the horizontal or vertical starting point. See the examples in Figure 2–40.

Measuring full degree increments is easy since you simply match the zero mark on the vernier plate with a full degree mark on the protractor. See the reading of 12° in Figure 2–41. The vernier scale will allow you to measure angles as accurately as 5′ (min-

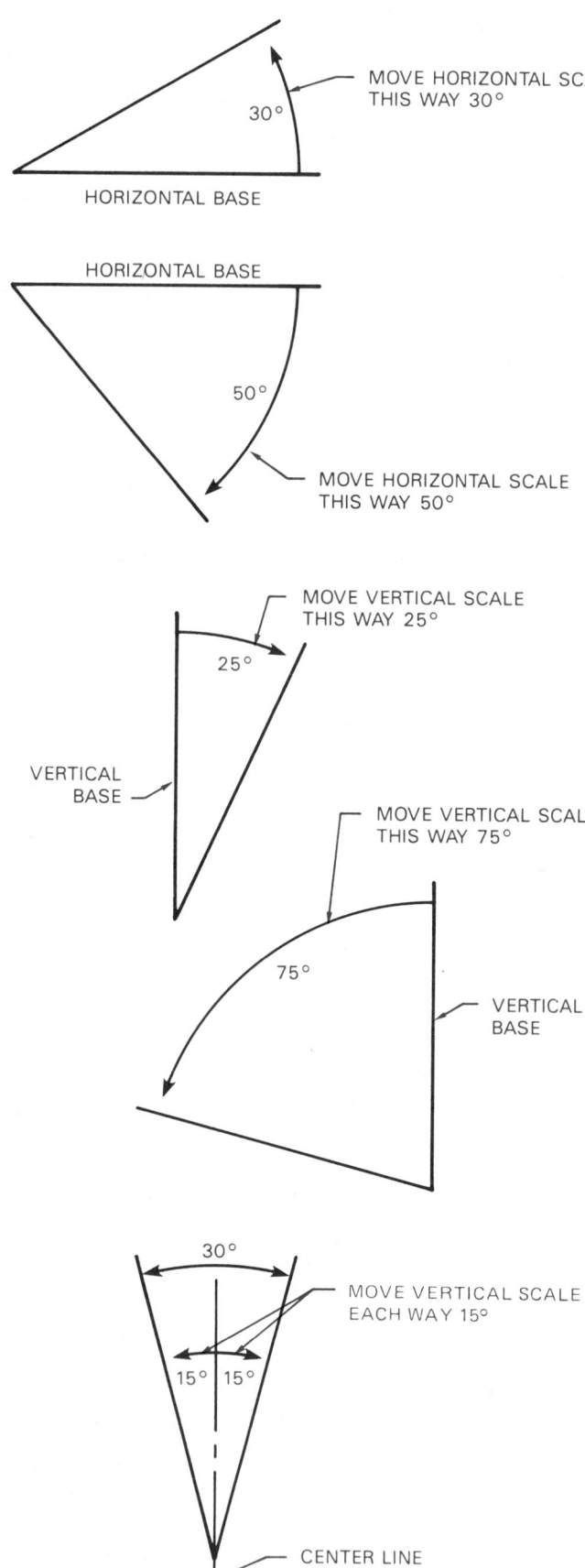

Figure 2-40 Angle measurements from either a horizontal or vertical reference line.

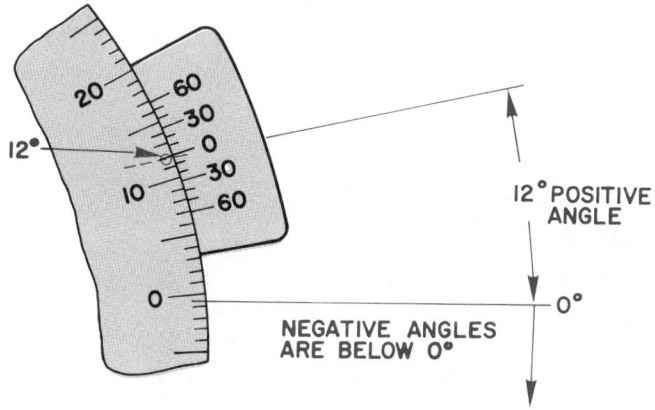

Figure 2-41 Measuring full degrees.

utes). Remember, 1 degree equals 60 minutes ($1° = 60'$) and 1 minute equals 60 seconds ($1' = 60''$).

Reading and Setting Angles with the Vernier. To read an angle other than a full degree we will assume the vernier scale is set at a *positive angle* as shown in Figure 2-42. Positive angles read upward and negative angles read downward from zero. Each mark on the vernier scale represents 5'. First see that the angle to be read is between 7° and 8°. Then find the 5' mark on the *upper* half of the vernier (the direction in which the scale has been turned) that is most closely aligned with a full degree on the protractor. In this example, it is the 40' mark. Add the minutes to the degree just past. The correct reading, then, is 7°40'. The procedure for reading *negative* angles is the same, except to read the minute marks on the *lower* half of the vernier. The example shown in Figure 2-43 reads 4°25'.

Suppose you wished to set the angle 7°40' as shown in Figure 2-42. First release the protractor brake and disengage the indexing mechanism with the thumb control. Rotate the protractor arm counterclockwise until the zero of the vernier is at 7°. Then slowly continue the rotation until the 40' mark on the upper half of the vernier aligns with the nearest degree mark on the protractor. Lock the pro-

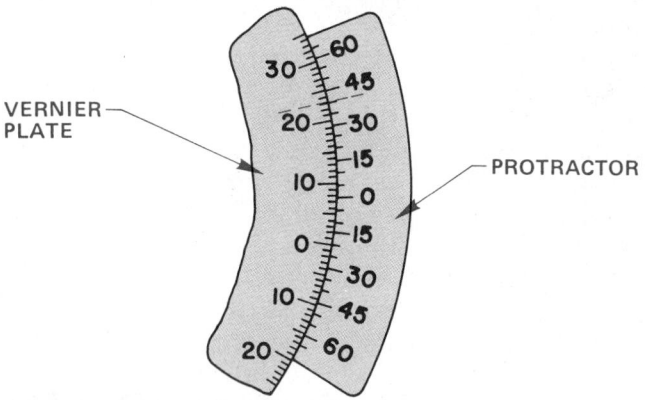

Figure 2-42 Reading positive angles with the vernier.

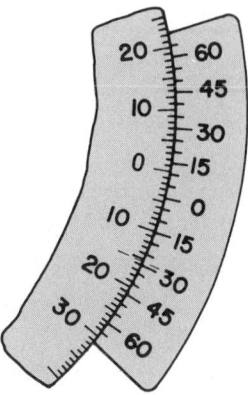

Figure 2–43 Reading negative angles with the vernier.

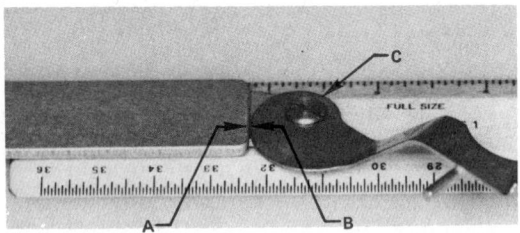

Figure 2–44 Scale removal. *Courtesy Vemco.*

tractor brake and draw the line. The procedure for setting negative angles is essentially the same except for turning the protractor head in a clockwise direction. For example, to set the reading of Figure 2–43, rotate the protractor arm clockwise until the zero aligns with the 4° mark, then slowly continue the rotation until the 25′ mark on the lower half of the vernier aligns with the nearest degree mark on the protractor.

Machine Set-up

To insert a scale in the baseplate chuck, place the scale flat on the board and align the scale chuckplate with the baseplate chuck on the protractor head. Firmly press but do not drive the scale chuckplate into the baseplate chuck. To remove a scale, use the scale wrench as shown in Figure 2–44. With the pin side of the wrench pointing down, slip the wrench over screw C and turn clockwise, thus pressing curved section B strongly against section A of the baseplate chuck. Removing a scale by hand without the aid of a key could result in damage to the scale and/or machine.

Scale Alignment. Before drawing with any drafting machine, the scales should be checked for alignment and, if needed, be adjusted at right angles to each other. For best results with a track drafting machine, the scales should also be aligned with respect to the horizontal track. Both operations can be accomplished through the following procedure:

Step 1.   Tighten the flat-head screw nearest the end of the scale on each scale chuckplate. Insert the scales in the baseplate chuck and press them firmly into place. Release the inner scale-chuckplate lock-screw on the horizontal scale. Set the scale near the center of its angular range of adjustment, and tighten the lock-screw. See Figure 2–45. Be careful not to overtighten any screw.

Step 2.   Draw a reference line parallel to the horizontal track by:

a. Locking the vertical brake and releasing the horizontal brake.
b. Placing a pencil point at zero on the horizontal scale and moving both the pencil and protractor head together laterally along the board. See Figure 2–46. *Caution:* Merely drawing the pencil along the scale will not assure the line being parallel to the horizontal track.

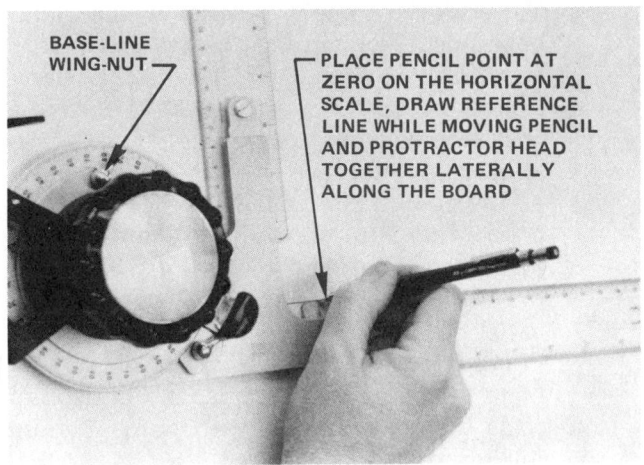

Figure 2–46 Step 2: Draw the horizontal reference line.

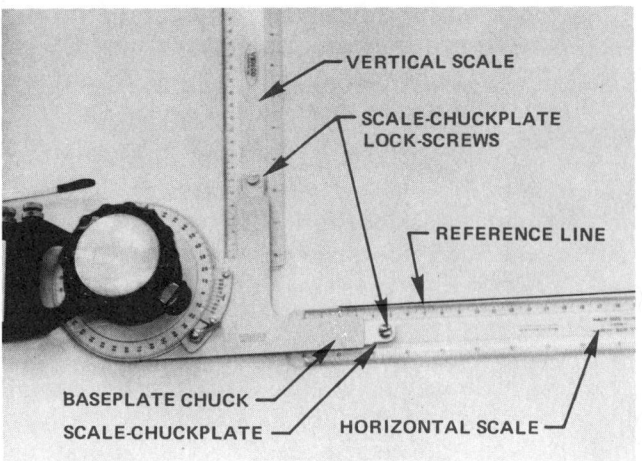

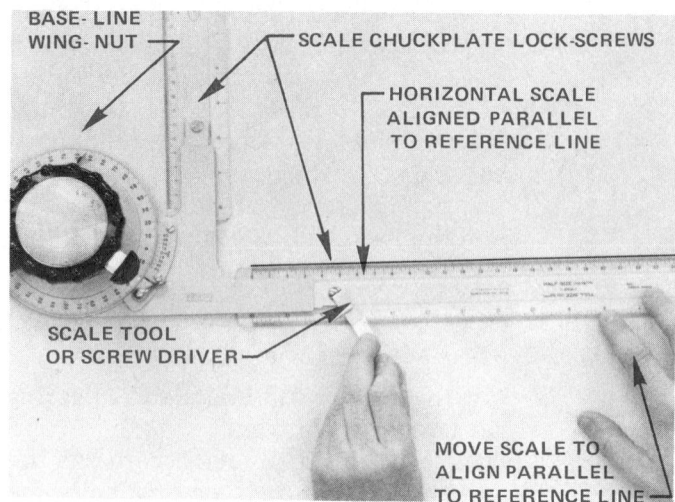

Figure 2–47 Steps 3 and 4: Align the horizontal scale with the reference line.

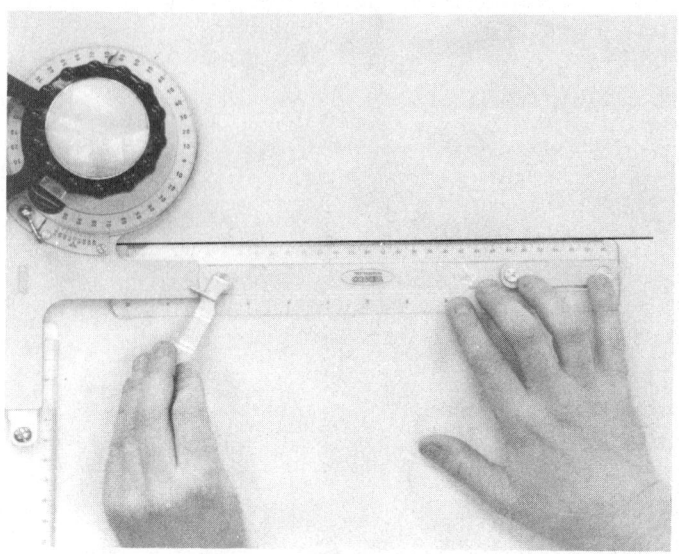

Figure 2–48 Step 5: Rotate the drafting machine head 90° and align the vertical scale with the reference line.

Step 3.   Release the lock nut on the micrometer base-line screw and turn this screw until the scale is brought parallel to the reference line. See Figure 2–47. Tighten the lock nut firmly. Some machines have a base-line wing-nut. If yours does, release the base-line wing-nut and bring the scale parallel to the reference line. Tighten the base-line wing-nut. For those machines that have a base-line zero on the protractor (usually found to the left of the handle), first loosen the base-line wing-nut and align the arrow to 0°. Then lock the base-line wing-nut. Finally, loosen the horizontal scale-chuckplate lock-screw and adjust the horizontal scale to the reference line, then retighten the screw.

Step 4.   Remove the horizontal scale, turn it 180° and replace it. Loosen the scale-chuckplate lock-screw, adjust the scale parallel to the reference line, and tighten the lock-screw. Now the horizontal scale is properly aligned when inserted from either end.

Step 5.   Move the head 90° clockwise and adjust both ends of the vertical scale in the same manner as the horizontal scale and along the same reference line drawn in step 2 b. See Figure 2–48.

After the horizontal scale has been properly adjusted, the vertical scale may be aligned 90° to the horizontal scale by placing the 90° angle of a 30°–60° or 45° triangle between the two scales. Be sure the drafting machine scales fit tightly against the triangle before tightening the screws.

By following this procedure, you have established a reference line setting that is parallel to the hori-

zontal track and have adjusted the scales so that they are parallel to the track and perpendicular to each other. For satisfactory results when drawing, the screws on the scales must be tight and the scale chuckplates pressed firmly into the chucks. Use good judgment when tightening any mechanism as too much force can cause components to break or wear out rapidly.

The alignment procedure of steps 1 and 2 should be checked periodically, even daily. Doing so may seem like a lot of work and trouble, but once you have gone through the procedure several times it will become routine. By checking and adjusting the scale alignment often, you will be sure that your drawings are accurate. One of a drafter's great frustrations is to prepare a layout and then discover that the machine is not properly aligned.

SCALES

Scale Shapes

There are four basic scale shapes as shown in Figure 2–49. The two-bevel scales are also available with chuck plates for use with standard arm or track drafting machines. These machine scales have typical calibrations, and some have no scale reading for use as a straightedge alone. Drafting machine scales are

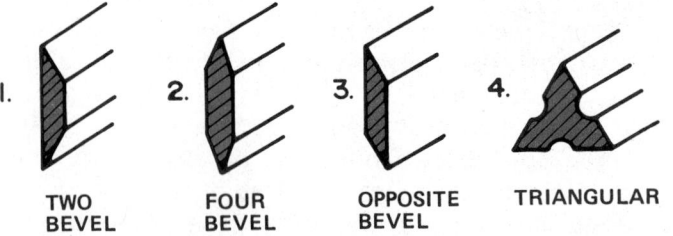

Figure 2–49 Scale shapes.

purchased by designating the length needed, 12, 18, or 24 in., and the scale calibration such as metric, engineer's full scale in 10ths and half scale in 20ths, or architect's scale ¼″ = 1′–0″ and ½″ = 1′–0″. Of course, many other scales are available.

Scale Notation

The scale of a drawing is usually noted in the title block or below the view of an object that differs in scale from that given in the title block. Drawings are scaled so that the object represented can be illustrated clearly on standard sizes of paper. It would be difficult, for example, to draw a shopping mall or even a house full size; thus a scale that reduces the size of such large objects must be used.

The scale selected, then, depends upon:

- The actual size of the structure.
- The amount of detail to be shown.
- The paper size selected.
- The amount of dimensions and notes required on the part.
- Common practice that regulates certain scales.

The following scales and their notation are frequently used on architectural drawings:

1/8″ = 1′–0″	3/8″ = 1′–0″	1 1/2″ = 1′–0″
3/32″ = 1′–0″	1/2″ = 1′–0″	3″ = 1′–0″
3/16″ = 1′–0″	3/4″ = 1′–0″	12″ = 1′–0″
1/4″ = 1′–0″	1″ = 1′–0″	

Some scales used in civil drafting are noted as follows:

1″ = 10′	1″ = 50′	1″ = 300′
1″ = 20′	1″ = 60′	1″ = 400′
1″ = 30′	1″ = 100′	1″ = 500′
1″ = 40′	1″ = 200′	1″ = 600′

Metric Scale

According to the American National Standards Institute (ANSI): The commonly used SI (International System of Units) linear unit used on drawings is the millimeter. On drawings where all dimensions are either in inches or millimeters, individual identification of units is not required. However, the drawing shall contain a note stating: UNLESS OTHERWISE SPECIFIED, ALL DIMENSIONS ARE IN INCHES (or MILLIMETERS, as applicable). Where some millimeters are shown on an inch-dimensioned drawing, the millimeter value should be followed by the symbol, mm. Where some inches are shown on a millimeter-dimensioned drawing, the inch value should be followed by the abbreviation, IN.

Metric symbols are as follows:

millimeter = mm

centimeter = cm
decimeter = dm
meter = m
dekameter = dam
hectometer = hm
kilometer = km

Some metric-to-metric equivalents are the following:

10 millimeters = 1 centimeter
10 centimeters = 1 decimeter
10 decimeters = 1 meter
10 meters = 1 dekameter
10 dekameters = 1 kilometer

Some metric-to-U.S. customary equivalents are the following:

1 millimeter = .03937 inch
1 centimeter = .3937 inch
1 meter = 39.37 inches
1 kilometer = .6214 mile

Some U.S. customary-to-metric equivalents are the following:

1 mile = 1.6093 kilometers = 1609.3 meters
1 yard = 914.4 millimeters = .9144 meter
1 foot = 304.8 millimeters = .3048 meter
1 inch = 25.4 millimeters = .0254 meter

To convert inches to millimeters, multiply inches by 25.4 mm.

One advantage of metric scales is that any scale is a multiple of 10; therefore, any reductions or enlargements are easily performed. In most cases, no mathematical calculations should be required when using a metric scale. Whenever possible, select a direct reading scale. If no direct reading scale is available, you may use multiples of other scales. To avoid the possibility of error, avoid multiplying or dividing metric scales by anything but multiples of ten. See "Using Metric" in Chapter 16.

Architect's Scale

The triangular architect's scale contains 11 different scales. On ten of them each inch represents a foot and is subdivided into multiples of 12 parts to represent inches and fractions of an inch. The eleventh scale is the full scale with a 16 in the margin. The 16 denotes that each inch is divided into 16 parts and each part is equal to 1/16th of an inch. Figure 2–50 shows an example of the full architect's scale while Figure 2–51 shows the fraction calibrations.

Look at the architect's scale examples in Figure 2–52. Note the form in which scales are expressed on a drawing. The scale is expressed as an equation

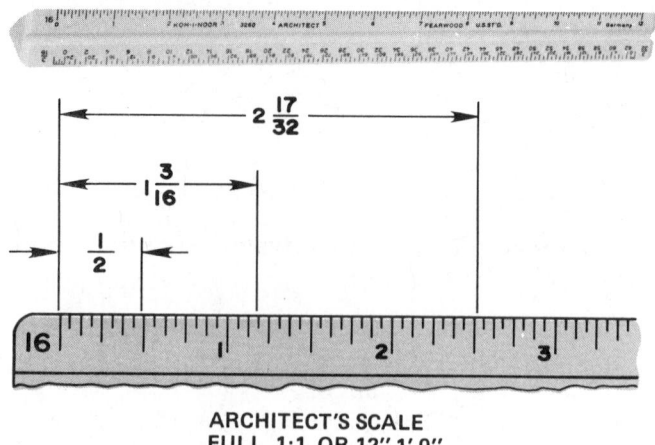

ARCHITECT'S SCALE
FULL, 1:1, OR 12″ 1′ 0″

Figure 2–50 Full (1:1), or 12″ = 1′–0″, architect's scale. *Photo courtesy Koh-I-Noor Rapidograph, Inc.*

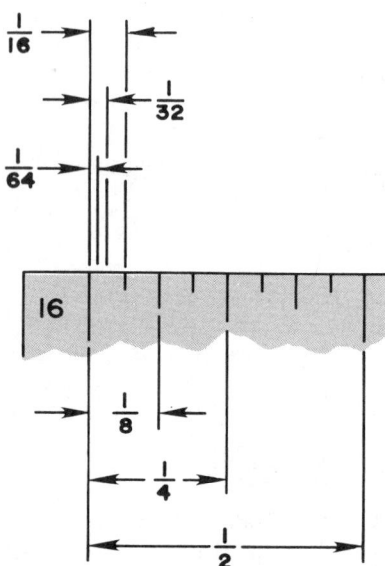

Figure 2–51 Enlarged view of architect's (16) scale.

of the drawing size in inches or fractions of an inch to one foot. For example: 3″ = 1′–0″, ½″ = 1′–0″, or ¼″ = 1′–0″. The architect's scale commonly has scales running in both directions along an edge. Be careful when reading a scale from left to right so as to not confuse its calibrations with the scale that reads from right to left.

When selecting scales for preparing a set of architectural drawings, there are several factors that must be considered. Some parts of a set of drawings are traditionally drawn at a certain scale. For example, the floor plans for most residential structures are drawn at ¼″ = 1′–0″. Although some applications may require a larger or smaller scale, commercial buildings are often drawn at ⅛″ = 1′–0″ when they are too large to draw at the same scale as a residence. Exterior elevations are commonly drawn at ¼″ = 1′–0″, although some architects prefer to draw the front or most important elevation at ¼″ = 1′–0″ and the balance of the elevations at ⅛″ = 1′–0″. Construction details and cross sections may be drawn at larger scales to help clarify specific features. Some cross sections can be drawn at ¼″ = 1′–0″ with clarity, but complex cross sections require a scale of ⅜″ = 1′–0″ or ½″ = 1′–0″ to be clear. Construction details may be drawn at any scale between ½″ = 1′–0″ and 3″ = 1′–0″, depending upon the amount of information presented.

Civil Engineer's Scale

The architectural drafter may need to use the civil engineer's scale to draw plot plans, maps, subdivision plats, or read existing land documents. Most land related plans such as construction site plot plans are drawn using the civil engineer's scale although some are drawn with an architect's scale. Common architect's scales used are ⅛″ = 1′–0″, 3/32″ = 1′–0″, or 1/16″ = 1′–0″. The triangular civil engineer's scale

contains six scales, one on each of its sides. The civil engineer's scales are calibrated in multiples of ten. The scale margin denotes the scale represented on a particular edge. The following table shows some of the many scale options available when using the civil engineer's scale. Keep in mind that any multiple of ten is available with this scale.

CIVIL ENGINEER'S SCALE				
Divisions	Ratio	Scales Used With This Division		
10	1:1	1″=1″	1″=1′	1″=10′	1″=100′
20	1:2	1″=2″	1″=2′	1″=20′	1″=200′
30	1:3	1″=3″	1″=3′	1″=30′	1″=300′
40	1:4	1″=4″	1″=4′	1″=40′	1″=400′
50	1:5	1″=5″	1″=5′	1″=50′	1″=500′
60	1:6	1″=6″	1″=6′	1″=60′	1″=600′

The 10 scale is used in civil drafting for scales of 1″ = 10′ or 1″ = 100′ and so on. See Figure 2–53. The 20 scale is used for scales of 1″ = 2′, 1″ = 20′, 1″ = 200′ as shown in Figure 2–54.

The remaining scales on the civil engineer's scale may be used in a similar fashion. The 50 scale is popular in civil drafting for drawing plats of subdivisions.

PROTRACTORS

When a drafting machine is not used or when combining triangles does not provide enough flexibility for drawing angles, a protractor is the instrument to use. Protractors can be used to measure angles to within ½° or even closer if you have a good eye.

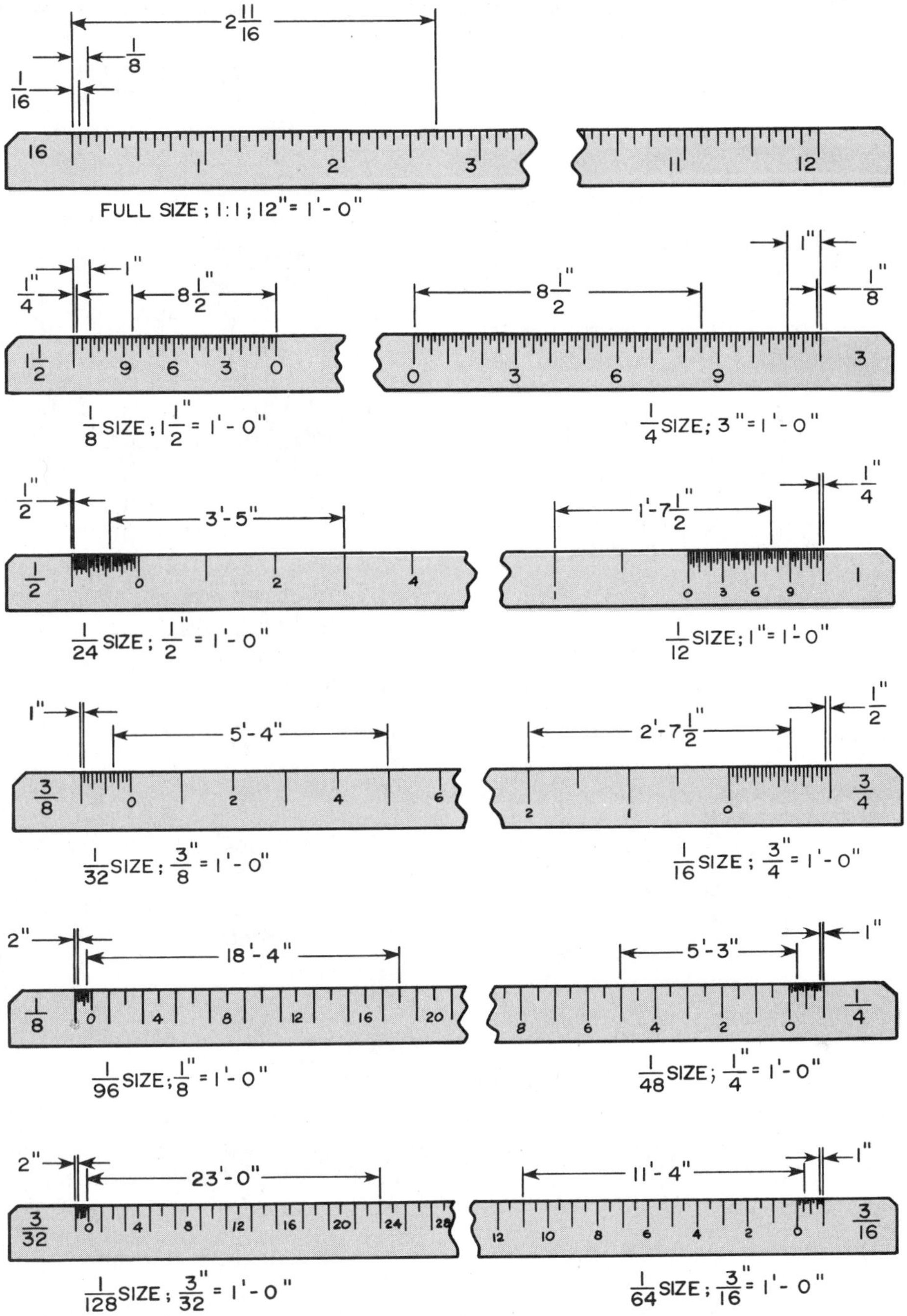

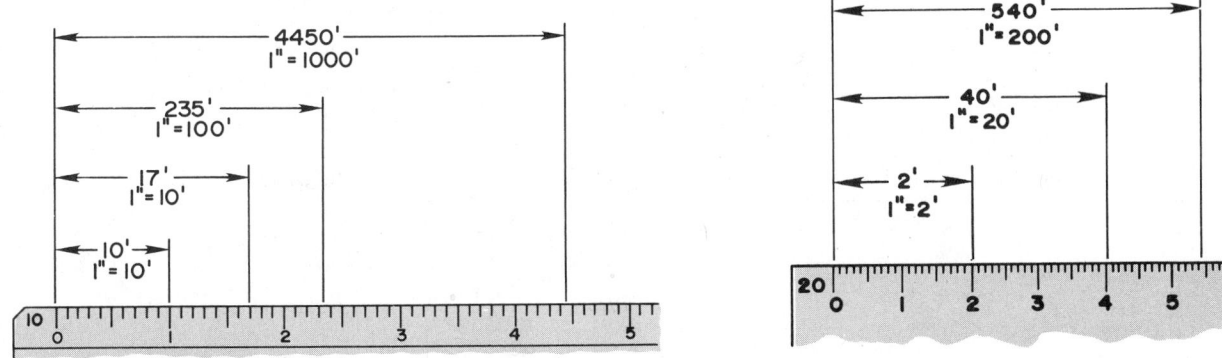

Figure 2-52 Architect's scales.

Figure 2-53 Civil engineer's scale, units of 10.

Figure 2-54 Civil engineer's scale, units of 20.

EQUIPMENT TEST

DIRECTIONS

Answer the questions with short complete statements or drawings as needed on 8½ × 11 in. lined paper as follows:

1. Letter your name, Equipment Test, and the date at the top of the sheet.
2. Letter the question number and provide the answer. You do not need to write out the question.
3. Prepare your answers with upper-case letters to the best of your ability. Proper architectural lettering techniques will be discussed in Chapter 4. Answers may be prepared on a word processor if appropriate with course guidelines.

PART 1: QUESTIONS

1. Describe a mechanical drafting pencil.
2. Describe an automatic drafting pencil.
3. List three lead sizes available for automatic pencils.
4. Identify how graphite leads are labeled.
5. Name the type of technical pen tip that will normally provide longer life.
6. What precautions should be taken when disassembling a technical pen?
7. List three characteristics recommended for technical pen inks.
8. Describe one advantage and disadvantage of using an electric eraser.
9. Name the type of compass most commonly used by professional drafters.
10. Why should templates be used whenever possible?
11. Why should a compass point with a shoulder be used when possible?
12. Identify two lead points that are commonly used in compasses.
13. What is the advantage of placing drafting tape or plastic at the center of a circle before using a compass?
14. A good dividers should not be too loose or too tight. Why?
15. List two uses for dividers.
16. At what number of degree increments will most drafting machine heads automatically lock?
17. How many minutes are there in one degree; seconds in one minute?
18. Why should drafting machine scales be checked for alignment daily?
19. In combination, the 30°–60° and 45° triangles may be used to make what range of angles?
20. Show how the following scales are noted on an architectural drawing: ⅛ in., ¼ in., ½ in., ¾ in., 1½ in., and 3 in.
21. Identify a civil engineer's scale that is commonly used for subdivision plats.
22. What scale is usually used for drawing residential floor plans?
23. List three factors that influence the selection of a scale for a drawing.

PART 2: SCALE USE

Determine the length of the following lines using both an architect's and civil engineer's scale. The scales to use when measuring are given above each line. The architect's scale is first; the civil engineer's scale is second; and the metric scale is third.

24. a. Scale: ⅛″ = 1′–0″   b. 1″ = 10′–0″   c. 1:1 (metric)

25. a. Scale: ¼″ = 1′–0″   b. 1″ = 20′–0″   c. 1:2 (metric)

26. a. Scale: ⅜″ = 1′–0″   b. 1″ = 30′–0″   c. 1:5 (metric)

27. a. Scale: ½″ = 1′–0″   b. 1″ = 40′–0″   c. 1:25 (metric)

28. a. Scale: ¾″ = 1′–0″   b. 1″ = 50′–0″   c. 1:35 (metric)

29. a. Scale: 1″ = 1′–0″   b. 1″ = 60′–0″   c. 1:35 (metric)

30. a. Scale: 1½″ = 1′–0″   b. 1″ = 100′   c. 1:75 (metric)

31. a. Scale: 3″ = 1′–0″   b. 1″ = 200′   c. 1:75 (metric)

Chapter 3
Drafting Media and Reproduction Methods

THIS CHAPTER will cover the types of media that are used for the drafting and the reproduction of architectural drawings. Drawings are generally prepared on precut drafting sheets with printed graphic designs for company borders and title blocks. Drawing reproductions or copies are made for use in the construction process so that the original drawings will not be damaged. Alternate material options and reproduction methods will be discussed as they relate to common practices.

PAPERS AND FILMS

Selection of Drafting Media

There are several factors that should influence the purchase and use of drafting media. The consid-erations include durability, smoothness, erasability, dimensional stability, transparency, and cost.

Durability is a factor that should be considered if the original drawing wil have a great deal of use. Originals may tear or wrinkle and the images become difficult to see if the drawings are used often.

Smoothness relates to how the medium will accept line work and lettering. The material should be easy to draw on so that the image is dark and sharp without a great deal of effort on the part of the drafter.

Erasability is important because errors will need to be corrected and changes will frequently be made. When images are erased, ghosting should be kept to a minimum. *Ghosting* is the residue that remains when lines are difficult to remove. These unsightly ghost images will be reproduced in a print. Materials that have good erasability are easy to clean up.

Dimensional stability is the quality of the media to not alter size due to the effects of atmospheric conditions such as heat and cold. Some materials are more dimensionally stable than others.

Transparency is one of the most important char-acteristics of drawing media. The diazo reproduction method requires light to pass through the material. The final goal of a drawing is good reproduction, so the more transparent the material the better the reproduction, assuming that the image drawn is professional quality.

Cost is a factor that may also influence the se-lection of drafting media. When the absolute best reproduction, durability, dimensional stability, smoothness, and erasability are important, then there may be few cost alternatives. If drawings are to have normal use and reproduction quality, then the cost of the drafting media may be kept to a minimum. The following discussion on available materials will help you evaluate cost differences.

Vellum

Vellum is drafting paper that is specially designed to accept pencil or ink. Lead on vellum is probably the most common combination used for manual drafting. There are many vendors that manufacture quality vellum for drafting purposes. Each claims to have specific qualities that should be considered in the selection of paper. Vellum is the least expensive material having good smoothness and transparency. Use vellum originals with care. Drawings made on vellum that require a great deal of use could deteriorate, as vellum is not as durable a material as others. Also, some brands have better erasable qualities than others. Affected by humidity and other atmospheric conditions, vellum generally is not as dimensionally stable as other materials.

Polyester Film

Polyester film, also known by its trade name, Mylar®, is a plastic material that offers excellent dimensional stability, erasability, transparency, and durability. Drawing on Mylar® is best accomplished using ink or special polyester leads. Do not use regular graphite leads as they will smear easily. Drawing techniques that drafters use with polyester leads are similar to graphite leads except that polyester leads are softer and feel like a crayon when used.

Mylar® is available with a single or double mat surface. Mat is surface texture. The double mat film has texture on both sides so that drawing can be done on either side if necessary. Single mat film is the most common in use and has a slick surface on one side. When using Mylar® you must be very careful not to damage the mat by erasing. Erase at right angles to the direction of your lines and do not use too much pressure. Doing so will help minimize damage to the mat surface. Once the mat is destroyed and removed, the surface will not accept ink or pencil. Also, be cautious about getting moisture on the Mylar® surface. Moisture from your hands can cause your pen to skip across the material.

Normal handling of drawing film is bound to soil it. Inked lines applied over soiled areas do not adhere well and in time will chip off or flake. It is always good practice to keep the film clean. Soiled areas can be cleaned effectively with special film cleaner.

Mylar® is much more expensive than vellum; however, it should be considered where excellent reproductions, durability, dimensional stability, and erasability are required of original drawings.

Reproductions

The one thing most designers, engineers, architects, and drafters have in common is that their finished drawings are made with the intent of being reproduced. The goal of every professional is to produce drawings of the highest quality that will give the best possible prints when they are reproduced.

Reproduction is the most important factor that influences the selection of media for drafting. The primary combination that will achieve the best reproduction is the blackest, most opaque lines or images on the most transparent base or material. Each of the materials mentioned will make good prints if the drawing is well done. If the only concern is the quality of the reproduction, then ink on Mylar® is the best choice. Some products have better characteristics than others. Some individuals prefer certain products. It is up to the individual or company to determine the combination that will work best for their needs and budget. The question of reproduction is especially important when sepias must be made. (Sepias are second or third generation originals. See Sepias in this chapter.)

Look at Figure 3–1 and you will see a magnified view of graphite on vellum, plastic lead on Mylar®, and ink on Mylar®. Judge for yourself which material and application will provide the best reproduction. As you can see from Figure 3–1, the best reproduction is achieved with a crisp, opaque image on transparent material. If your original drawing is not good quality, it will not get better on the print.

SHEET SIZES, TITLE BLOCKS, AND BORDERS

All professional drawings have title blocks. Standards have been developed for the information put into the title block and on the sheet adjacent to the border so that the drawing will be easier to read and file than drawings that do not follow a standard format.

Sheet Sizes

Drafting materials are available in standard sizes which are determined by manufacturer's specifications. Paper and Mylar® may be purchased in either cut sheets or in rolls. Architectural drafting offices generally use cut sheet sizes of 18 × 24 in., 24 × 36 in., 28 × 42 in., 30 × 42 in., 30 × 48 in., or 36 × 48 in. Roll sizes vary in width from 18 to 48 in.

GOOD   BETTER   BEST

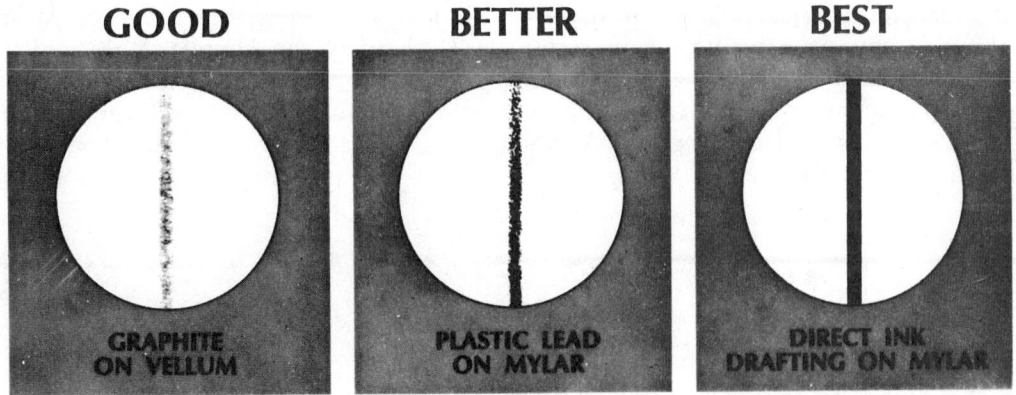

GRAPHITE ON VELLUM   PLASTIC LEAD ON MYLAR   DIRECT INK DRAFTING ON MYLAR

Figure 3–1 A comparison of graphite on vellum, plastic lead on Mylar®, and ink on Mylar®. *Courtesy Koh-I-Noor Rapidograph, Inc.*

Zoning

Some companies use a system of numbers along the top and bottom margins, and letters along the left and right margins called zoning. Zoning allows the drawing to be read similar to a road map. For example, the reader can refer to the location of a specific item as D-4, which means that the item can be found on or near the intersection of D across and 4 up or down. Zoning may be found on some architectural drawings although it is more commonly used in mechanical drafting.

Architectural Drafting Title Blocks

Title blocks and borders are normally preprinted on drawing paper or Mylar® to help reduce drafting time and cost. Some companies use an adhesive title block so that one standard title block can be attached to any size drawing sheet. These title blocks may also be a cost saving practice as preprinted borders and title blocks are a little more expensive. Most architectural drafting firms, however, use one basic sheet size with preprinted borders and title blocks.

Drawing sheet borders are thick lines that go around the entire sheet. Top, bottom, and right-side border lines are usually between ⅜ and ½ in. away from the paper edge while the left border may be between ¾ and 1½ in. away. This extra-wide left margin allows for binding drawing sheets. Some companies do not use any border lines and drafters are requested to keep drawing information a given distance away from the sheet edge.

Preprinted architectural drawing title blocks are generally placed along the right side of the sheet although some companies do place them across the bottom of the sheet. Each company will use a slightly different title block design, but the same general information is found in almost all blocks:

1. Drawing number. This may be a specific job or file number for the drawing.

2. Company name, address, and phone number.
3. Project or client. This is an identification of the project by company or client name, project title, or location.
4. Drawing name. This is where the title of the drawing may be placed. For example, MAIN FLOOR PLAN, or ELEVATIONS. Most companies leave this information off the title block and place it on the face of the sheet below the drawing.
5. Scale. Some company title blocks provide a location for the drafter to fill in the general scale of the drawing. Any view or detail on the sheet that differs from the general scale must have the scale of that view identified below the view title and both placed directly below the view. Most companies leave the scale out of the title block and place it on the sheet directly below the title of each individual plan, view, or detail.
6. Drawing or sheet identification. Each sheet will be numbered in relation to the entire set of drawings. For example, if the complete set of drawings has eight sheets then each consecutive sheet will be numbered: 1 of 8, 2 of 8, 3 of 8, and so on to 8 of 8.
7. Date. The date noted is the one on which the drawing or project is completed.
8. Drawn by. This is where the drafter, designer, or architect that prepared this drawing places his or her initials or name.
9. Checked by. This is the identification of the individual that approves the drawing for release.
10. Architect or designer. Most title blocks provide for the identification of the individual that designed the structure.
11. Revisions. Many companies provide a revision column where drawing changes are identified and recorded. After a set of drawings is released for construction, there may be some

need for drawing changes. When this is necessary there is usually a written request for change that comes from the contractor, owner, or architect. The change is then implemented on the drawings that are affected. Where changes are made on the face of the drawing, a circle with a revision number will accompany the change. This revision number will be keyed to a place in the drawing title block where the revision number, revision date, initials of the individual making the change, and an optional brief description of the revision

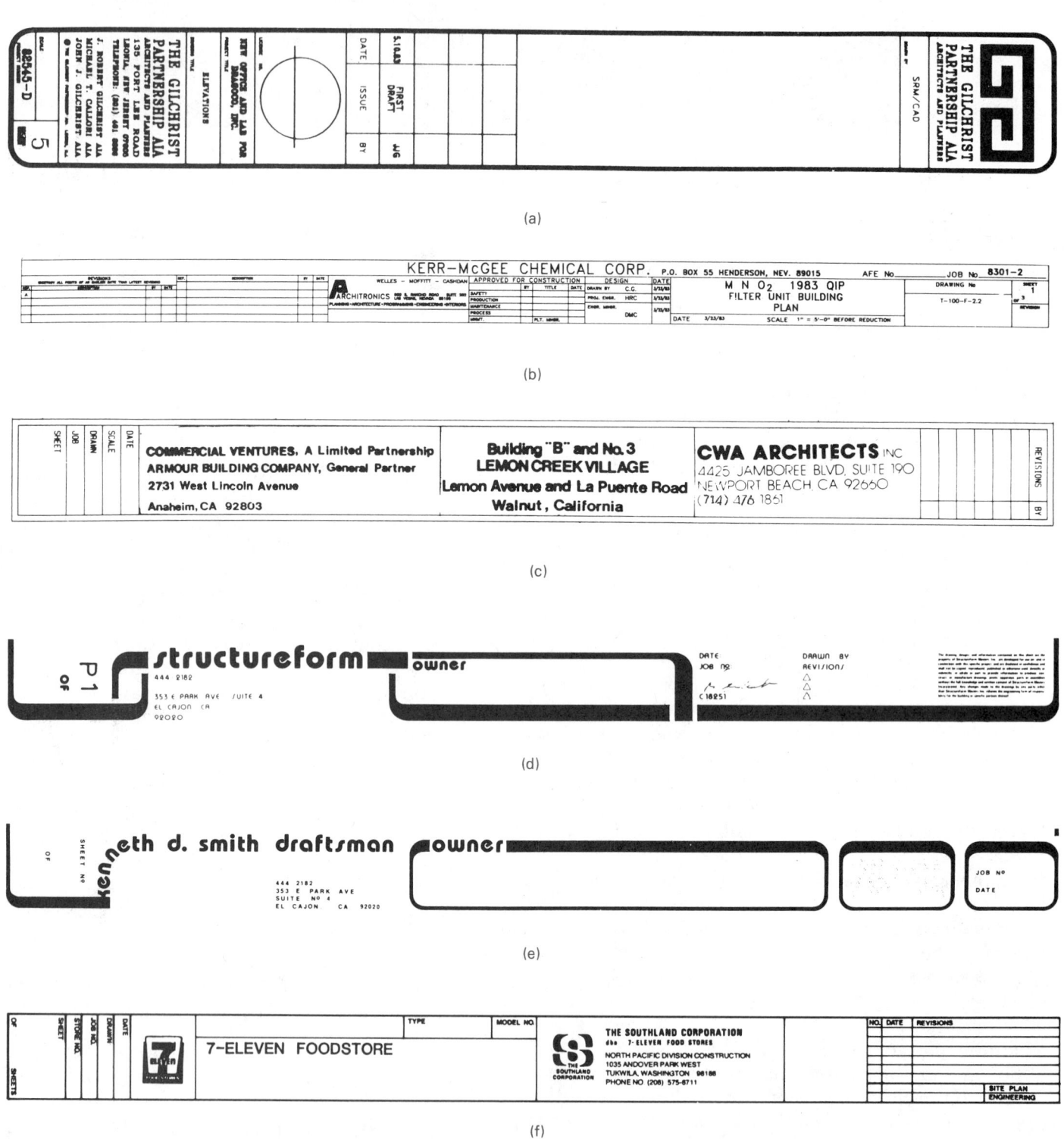

Figure 3–2 Sample title blocks. (a) and (b) *Courtesy Summagraphics Corporation;* (c) *courtesy T & W Systems Inc.; (d) courtesy Structureform; (e) courtesy Ken Smith Drafting; (f) courtesy Southland Corporation.*

are located. For further record of the change, the person making the change may also fill out a form that is called a change notice. This change notice will contain complete information about the revision for future reference.

Figure 3–2(a)–(f) shows several different architectural title blocks. Notice the similarities and differences among title blocks. The location of specific items may differ slightly and some companies require more detailed information than others, but, in general, the title block format is the same.

DIAZO REPRODUCTION

The Diazo Printer

Diazo prints, also known as ozalid dry prints, or blue-line prints, are made with a printing process that uses an ultraviolet light that passes through a translucent original drawing to expose a chemically coated paper or print material underneath. The light, of course, does not go through the dense, black lines on the original drawing. Thus the chemical coating on the paper beneath the lines is not exposed. The print material is then exposed to ammonia vapor which will activate the remaining chemical coating to produce blue, black, or brown lines on a white or clear background. The print that results is a diazo, or blue-line print, not a blueprint. The term *blueprint* is now a generic term that is used to refer to diazo prints even though they are not true blueprints.

Diazo is a direct print process and the print remains relatively dry. There are other processes available that require a moist development. Blueprinting, for example, is an older method of making prints which uses a light to expose sensitized paper placed under an original drawing. The prints are developed in a water wash which turns the background dark blue. The lines from the original are not fixed by the light and wash out leaving the white paper to show. So a true blueprint has a dark blue background with white lines.

The diazo process is less expensive and less time consuming than most other reproductive methods. The diazo printer is designed to make quality prints from all types of translucent paper, film, or cloth originals. Diazo prints may be made on coated roll-stock or cut sheets. The operation of all diazo printers is similar, but be sure to read the instruction manual or check with someone familiar with a particular machine if you are using a machine that is new to you. A diazo printing machine is shown in Figure 3–3.

Figure 3–3 Diazo printer. *Courtesy Ozalid Corporation.*

Diazo Printer Speed. All machines have an on/off switch. Many machines have a forward and reverse control and all machines have a speed selector. Some machines have a HI/LO speed control which allows you to select a speed range, while the actual speed control provides a fine adjustment of speed within the high or low range.

The operating speed of the machine will be determined by the speed of the diazo material and by the transparency of the original. For example, Mylar® may be run faster than vellum. The speed of the diazo material also influences the quality of the print. Diazo materials that are classified as slow will produce a higher-quality print than fast material. Some materials, such as fast-speed blue-line print paper, require a high- or fast-speed setting. Other materials, such as some sepias, require a low- or slow-speed setting. You will become familiar with the proper speed to use as you gain experience with a particular machine.

Testing the Printer. Before you run a print using a complete sheet, run a test strip to determine the quality of the print you will get. Cut a sheet of diazo material into strips, then use a strip to obtain the proper speed setting. This will save a great deal of money because diazo material is expensive. You know you have the proper speed setting when the lines and letters are dark blue and the background is almost all white. Once you are satisfied with the quality of the test strip, you are ready to run a full sheet to make a print.

Making a Diazo Print

To make a diazo print, place the diazo material on the feedboard, coated (yellow) side up. Position the original drawing, image side up, on top of the

Figure 3–4 Feeding the original drawing and diazo material into the machine. *Courtesy Ozalid Corporation.*

diazo material, making sure to align the leading edges. See Figure 3–4.

Using fingertip pressure from both hands, push the original and diazo material into the machine. The light will pass through the original and expose the sensitized diazo material except where images (lines and lettering) exist on the original. When the exposed diazo material and the original drawing emerge from the printer section, remove the original and carefully feed the diazo material into the developer section, as shown in Figure 3–5.

In the developer section the sensitized material that remains on the diazo paper will activate with ammonia vapor and blue lines will form. Thus, the term diazo is also known as blue-line print. Some diazo materials, however, make black or brown lines. Special materials are also available to make other

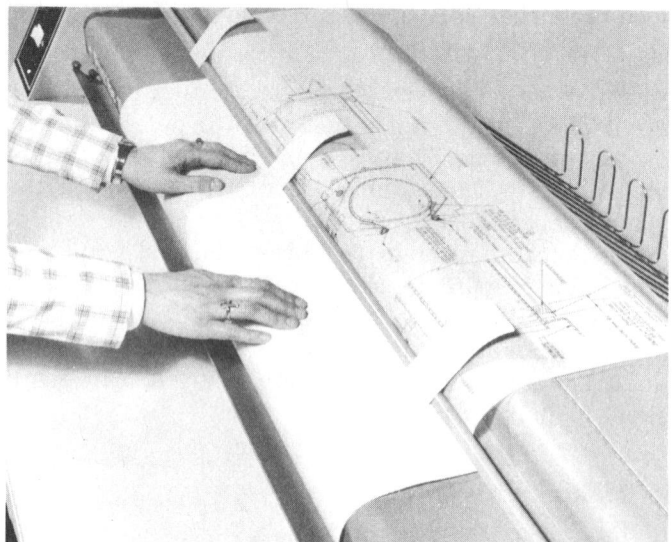

Figure 3–5 Feeding the exposed, sensitized diazo material into the developer section. *Courtesy Ozalid Corporation.*

colored lines, or to make transfer sheets and transparencies. Many machines will automatically shut off after a one to two minute inactive period. Other machines must be turned off manually.

Improving Print Quality

Examination of the processed print will serve as a basis for any speed adjustments necessary. See Figure 3–6 as you consider the following reasons for poor quality prints and the steps needed to correct them:

- Weak lines and no background indicate that the speed is too slow. The printing lamps are burning off the image. The printing speed should be increased.
- Dark lines and dark background indicate that the printing speed is too fast. Light from the printing lamps is not fully penetrating the original. The printing speed should be reduced.
- A processed print with strong lines and slight background color indicates the ideal speed/sensitivity combination.

Print quality is a matter of personal preference. However, experience has shown that a print with a slight background color is an indication that the print contains all the data appearing on the original.

Storage of Diazo Materials

Diazo materials are light sensitive so they should always be kept in a dark place until ready for use. Long periods of exposure to room light will cause the diazo chemicals to deteriorate and reduce the quality of your print. If you notice brown or blue edges around the unexposed diazo material, it is getting old. Always keep it tightly stored in the shipping package and in a dark place such as a drawer. Some people prefer to keep all diazo material in a small, dark refrigerator. Doing so will preserve the chemical for a long time.

Sepias

Sepias are diazo materials that are used to make secondary originals. A secondary, or second-generation, original is actually a print of an original drawing that can be used as an original. Changes can be made on the secondary original while the original drawing remains intact. The diazo process is performed with material called sepia. Sepia prints will normally form dark brown lines on a clear (translucent) background; therefore, they are sometimes called brownlines. In addition to being used as an original to make alterations to a drawing without changing the original,

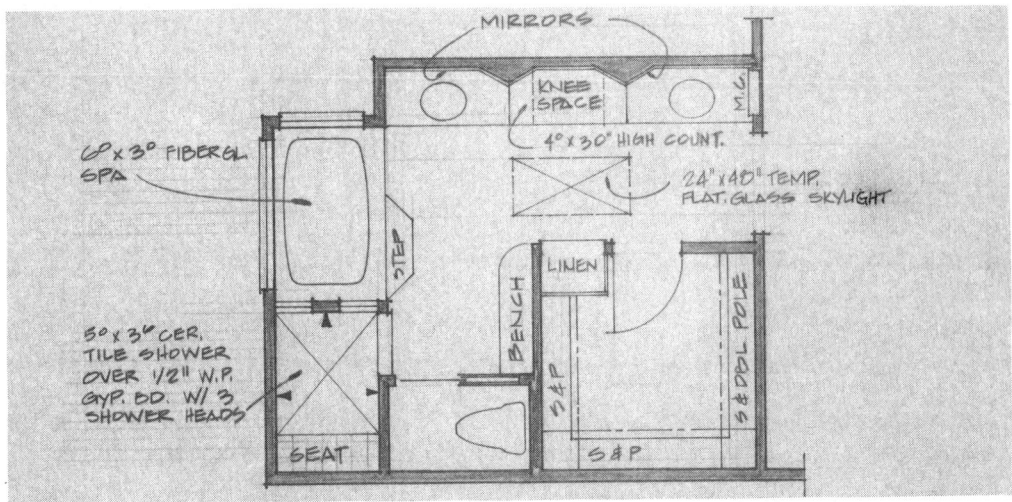

TOO DARK

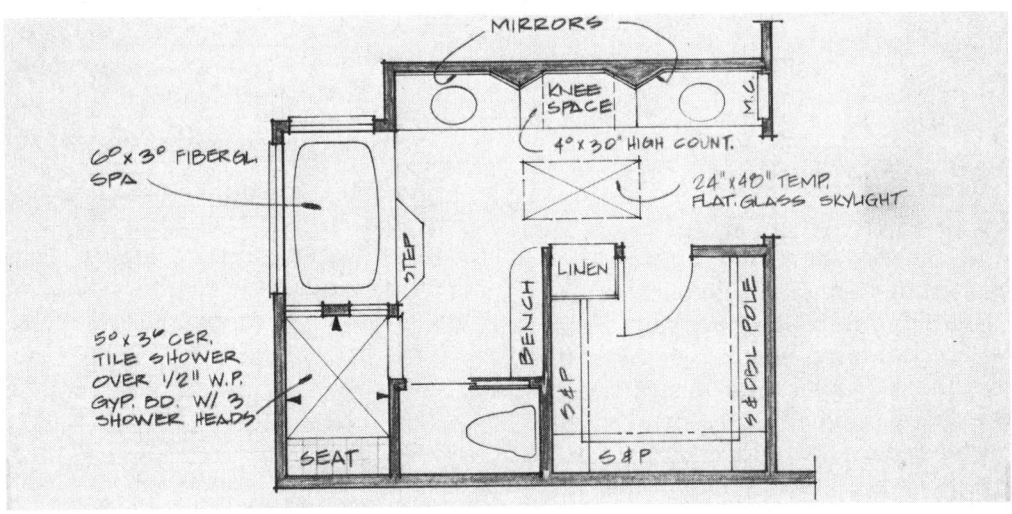

JUST RIGHT

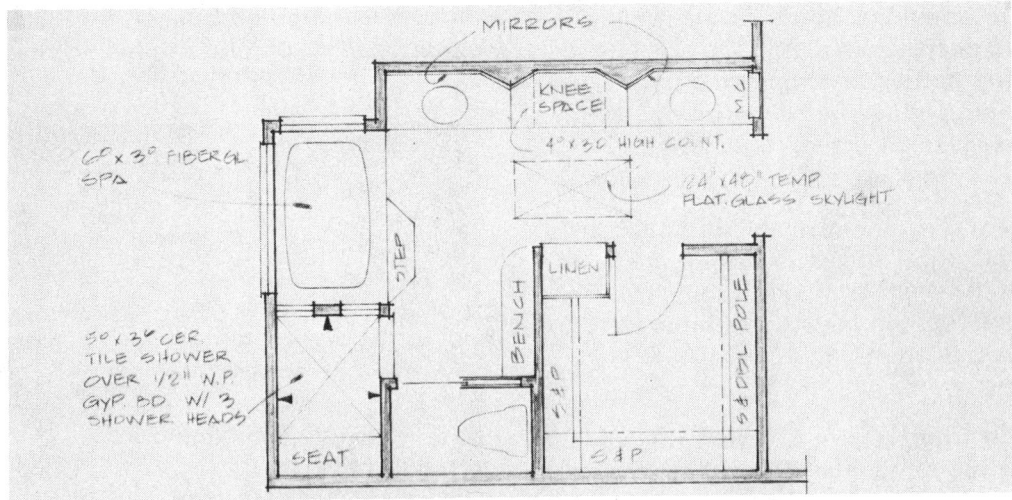

TOO LIGHT

Figure 3-6 A comparison of diazo prints that are too dark, just right, and too light.

sepias are also used when originals are required at more than one company location.

Sepias are normally made with the original face down on the sensitized sepia material. The balance of the print process is the same as just described except that the sepia should be fed into the developer coated-side down. Doing so will allow the coating on the sepia material to come into direct exposure with the ammonia in the development chamber. Experiment both ways and observe the quality of your reproduction. Standard diazo copies may reproduce better with the coated-side down; it depends on your machine and materials.

Sepias are made in reverse (reverse sepias) so that corrections or changes can be made on the mat side (face side) and erasures can be made on the sensitized side. Sepia materials are available in paper or polyester. The resulting paper sepia is similar to vellum and the polyester sepia is Mylar®. Drawing changes can be made on sepia paper with pencil or ink, and on sepia Mylar® with polyester lead or ink.

DIAZO SAFETY PRECAUTIONS

Ammonia

Ammonia has a strong, unmistakable odor. It may be detected, at times, while operating your diazo printer. The levels encountered would be extremely low and harmless. Diazo printers are designed and built to provide safe operation from ammonia exposure. Some machines have ammonia filters while others require outside exhaust fans. When print quality begins to deteriorate and it has been determined that the print paper is in good condition, then the ammonia may be old. Ammonia bottles should be changed periodically as determined by the quality of prints. When the ammonia bottle is changed it is generally time to change the filter also.

When handling bottles of ammonia or when replacing a bottle supplying a diazo printer, the following precautions are required.

Eye Protection. Extreme care should be taken to avoid direct contact of ammonia with your eyes. Always wear safety goggles, or equivalent eye protection, when handling ammonia containers directly or handling ammonia supply systems.

Ammonia and Filter Contact. Avoid the contact of ammonia and the ammonia filter with your skin or clothing. Ammonia and ammonia residue on the filter can cause uncomfortable irritation and burns when in direct contact with your skin.

Ammonia Fumes Inhalation. The disagreeable odor of ammonia is usually sufficient to prevent breathing harmful concentrations of ammonia vapors. Avoid prolonged periods of inhalation close to open containers of ammonia or where strong, pungent odors are present. The care, handling and storage of ammonia containers should be in accordance with the suppliers' instructions and all applicable regulations.

First Aid. If ammonia is spilled on your skin, promptly wash with plenty of water, and remove your clothing if necessary, to flush affected areas adequately. If your eyes are affected, irrigate with water as quickly as possible for at least 15 minutes, and, if necessary, consult a physician.

Anyone overcome by ammonia fumes should be removed to fresh air at once. Apply artificial respiration, preferably with the aid of oxygen if breathing is labored or has stopped. Obtain medical attention at once in event of eye contact, burns to the nose or throat, or if the person is unconscious.

Ultraviolet Light Exposure

Under the prescribed operating instructions there is no exposure to the ultraviolet rays emitted from the illuminated printing lamps. However, to avoid possible eye damage, no one should attempt to look directly at the illuminated lamps under any circumstances.

PHOTOCOPY REPRODUCTION

The Xerox brand 2080 printer shown in Figure 3–7 makes prints up to 24 in. wide, and up to 25 ft long from originals up to 36 in. wide by 25 ft long. Prints can be made on bond paper, vellum, polyester film, colored paper, or other translucent materials. The

Figure 3–7 Xerox brand 2080 photocopy printer. *Courtesy Oregon Blueprint Company.*

reproduction capabilities also include instant print sizes ranging from 45 to 141 percent of the original size. Larger or smaller sizes are possible by enlarging or reducing in two or more steps, that is by making a second print from a print.

Almost any large original can be converted into a smaller sized reproducible print and then the secondary original used to generate diazo or photocopy prints for distribution, inclusion in manuals, or for more convenient handling. Also, a random collection of mixed-scale drawings can be enlarged or reduced and converted to one standard scale and format. Reproduction clarity is so good that halftone illustrations (photographs) and solid or fine line work has excellent resolution and density.

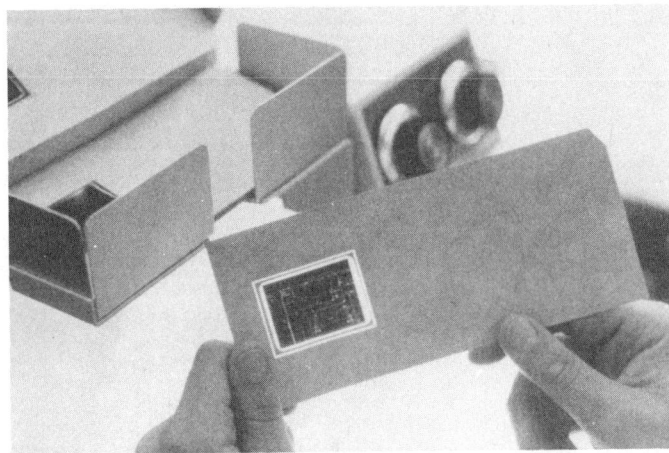

Figure 3–8 Aperture card with microfilm. *Courtesy 3M Company.*

MICROFILM

In many companies original drawings are filed in drawers by drawing number. When a drawing is needed the drafter will find the original, remove it, and make a copy. This process works well although, depending upon the size of the company or the number of drawings generated, drawing storage often becomes a problem. Sometimes an entire room is needed for drawing storage cabinets. Another problem occurs when originals are used over and over. They often become worn and damaged, and old vellum becomes yellowed and brittle. Also, in case of a fire or other kind of destruction, originals may be lost and endless hours of drafting will vanish. For these and other reasons many companies are using microfilm for the storage and reproduction of original drawings. Microfilm is used by industry for the photographic reproduction of original drawings into a film-negative format. Cameras used for microfilming are usually one of three sizes: 16, 35 or 70 mm. Microfilming processor cameras are now available that prepare film ready for use in about 20 seconds.

Aperture Card

The microfilm is generally prepared as one frame, or drawing, attached to an aperture card or as many frames in succession on a roll of film. The aperture card shown in Figure 3–8 becomes the engineering document and replaces the original drawing. A 35 mm film negative is mounted in an aperture card, which is a standard computer card. Some companies file and retrieve these cards manually, while other companies punch the cards for computerized filing and retrieval. The aperture card, or data card as it is often called, is convenient to use. All drawings are converted to one size, regardless of the original dimensions. All engineering documents are filed together, instead of having originals ranging in size from 8½ × 11 in. to 34 × 44 in. Then for easy retrieval each card is numbered with a sequential engineering drawing and/or project number.

When a drawing is prepared on microfilm, generally two negatives are made. One negative is placed in an active file and the other is placed in safe storage in case the first is damaged or if an alternate is needed to make drawing changes and revisions. In many cases the original drawings are either stored out of the way or destroyed.

Microfilm Enlarger Reader-printer

Microfilm from aperture cards or rolls can be displayed on a screen for review, or enlarged and reproduced as a copy on plain bond paper, vellum or offset paper-plates. Most microfilm printer readers can enlarge and reproduce prints ranging in size from A to C. Prints are then available for disbursement to construction, sales, or other department personnel. See Figure 3–9.

Computerized Microfilm Filing and Retrieval

The next step in the automation of drawing filing systems is the computerized filing and retrievel of microfilm aperture cards. The implementation of this kind of system remains very expensive. Large companies and independent microfilming agencies are able to take advantage of this technology. Small companies can send their architectural documents to local microfilm companies known as job shops where microfilm can be prepared and stored. Companies that are able to use computerized microfilm systems can have a completed drawing from the architect microfilmed, stored in a computer, and available on-line in the construction office within a few minutes.

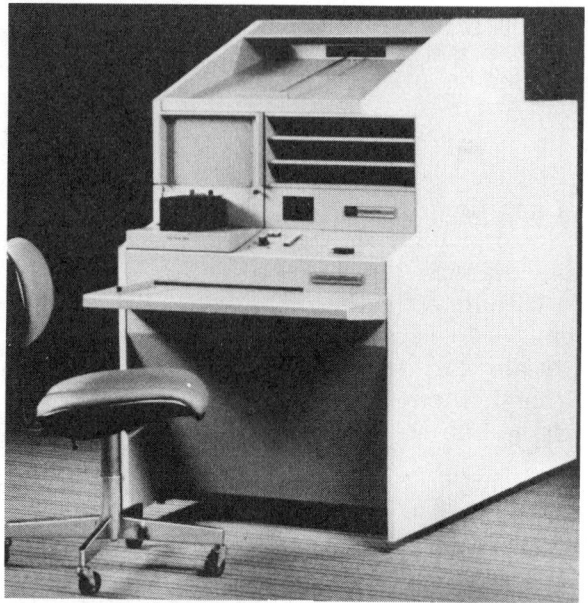

Figure 3-9 Microfilm from aperture cards or rolls to prints or secondary originals. *Courtesy 3M Company.*

DRAFTING MEDIA AND REPRODUCTION METHODS TEST

DIRECTIONS

Answer the questions with short complete statements or drawings as needed on 8½ × 11 vellum as follows:

1. Place a piece of lined paper under your drawing sheet, or draw very light lines on the sheet to help keep your answers in straight lines. The use of guidelines for freehand lettering will be discussed in Chapter 4.
2. Letter your name, Drafting Media and Reproduction Methods Test, and the date at the top of the sheet.
3. Letter the question number and provide the answer. You do not need to write out the question.
4. Prepare answers with upper-case letters to the best of your ability. Proper architectural lettering techniques will be discussed in Chapter 4. Answers may be prepared on a word processor if appropriate with course guidelines.

QUESTIONS

1. List five factors that influence the purchase and use of drafting materials.
2. Why is media transparency so important when reproducing copies using the diazo process?
3. Describe vellum.
4. Describe polyester film.
5. What is another name for polyester film?
6. Define mat and describe the difference between single and double mat.
7. Which of the following combinations would yield the best reproduction: graphite on vellum, plastic lead on Mylar®, or ink on Mylar®?
8. What are the primary elements that will give the best reproduction?
9. Identify three standard sheet sizes that may commonly be used by architectural offices.
10. Describe zoning.
11. List six elements that normally may be found in a standard architectural title block.
12. Identify two different locations where the scale may be located on an architectural drawing.
13. What is another name for the diazo print?
14. Is a diazo the same as a blueprint? Explain.
15. Describe how the diazo process functions.
16. How does the speed of the diazo printer affect the resulting print?
17. Describe how to run a test strip, and the importance of this test.
18. What should a good quality diazo print look like?
19. Describe the characteristics of slightly exposed or old diazo materials.
20. Define sepias and their use.
21. Why are sepias generally made in reverse (reverse sepia)?
22. Discuss the safety precautions involving the handling of ammonia.
23. Describe the recommended first aid for the following ammonia accidents: ammonia spilled on the skin, ammonia in the eyes, inhaling excess ammonia vapor.
24. List four advantages of the photocopy reproduction method over the diazo process.
25. Define the microfilm process.
26. What is the big advantage of microfilm?
27. What are the two common microfilm formats, and which microfilm format is the most popular, and why?

Chapter 4
Lines and Lettering

DRAFTING IS a universal graphic language that uses lines, symbols, and notes to describe a structure to be built. Lines and lettering on a drawing must be of a quality that will reproduce clearly. Properly drawn lines are dark, crisp, sharp, and of a uniform thickness. There should be no variation in darkness, only a variation in thickness known as line contrast. Certain lines may be drawn thick so that they stand out clearly from other information on the drawing. Other lines are drawn thin. Thin lines are not necessarily less important than thick lines, but they may be subordinate for identification purposes. In mechanical drafting recommended line thicknesses are much more defined than in architectural drafting.

Architectural drafting line standards have traditionally been more flexible and the creativity of the individual drafter or company may influence line and lettering applications. This is not to say that each drafter can do anything that he or she desires when preparing an architectural drawing. This chapter will present some general guidelines, styles, and techniques that are recommended for architectural drafters.

TYPES OF LINES

Construction Lines and Guidelines

Construction lines are used for laying out a drawing. Construction lines are drawn very lightly so that they will not reproduce and will not be mistaken for any other lines on the drawing. Construction lines are drawn with a very little amount of pressure using a 4H to 6H pencil, and if drawn properly will not need to be erased. Use construction lines for all preliminary work.

Guidelines are like construction lines and will not reproduce when properly drawn. Guidelines are drawn to guide your lettering. For example, if lettering on a drawing is ⅛ in. high, then the lightly drawn guidelines will be placed ⅛ in. apart. A rule of thumb for construction and guideline darkness is when the paper is placed at arm's length the lines should be difficult to see.

Some drafters prefer to use a light-blue lead rather than a graphite lead for all construction and guidelines. Light-blue lead will not reproduce and is usually cleaner than graphite.

Outlines

In mechanical drafting the outline lines, or object lines as they are commonly called, are a specific thickness so that they stand out from other lines as they form the outline of views. In architectural drafting this concept is not quite so specific. Outline lines are used to define the outline and characteristic features of architectural plan components, but the method of presentation may differ slightly from one office to another. The following techniques may be alternatives for outline line presentation:

1. One popular technique is to enhance certain drawing features so that they clearly stand out from outer items on the drawing. For example, the outline of floor plan walls and partitions, or beams in a cross section may be drawn thicker than other lines so that they are more apparent than the outer lines on the drawing. These thicker lines may be drawn with a rounded conical point in an H or F lead mechanical pencil or a 0.9 mm automatic pencil. See Figure 4–1. This technique may also use

light shading to further accentuate the walls of a floor plan. Dark shading would not be used as it would nullify the thicker outline lines.

2. Another technique is for all lines of the drawing to be the same thickness. This method does not differentiate one type of line from another, except that construction lines are always very lightly drawn. The idea of this technique is to make all lines medium thick to save drafting time. The drafter will use a lead that works best for the individual although a slightly rounded conical point 2H or H lead in a mechanical pencil, or 0.5 mm automatic pencil, is popular. See Figure 4–2(a). This technique may use dark shading to accentuate features such as walls in floor plans as shown in Figure 4–2(b). Remember, the idea is to get all lines dark and crisp. If the lines are fuzzy, they will not reproduce well.

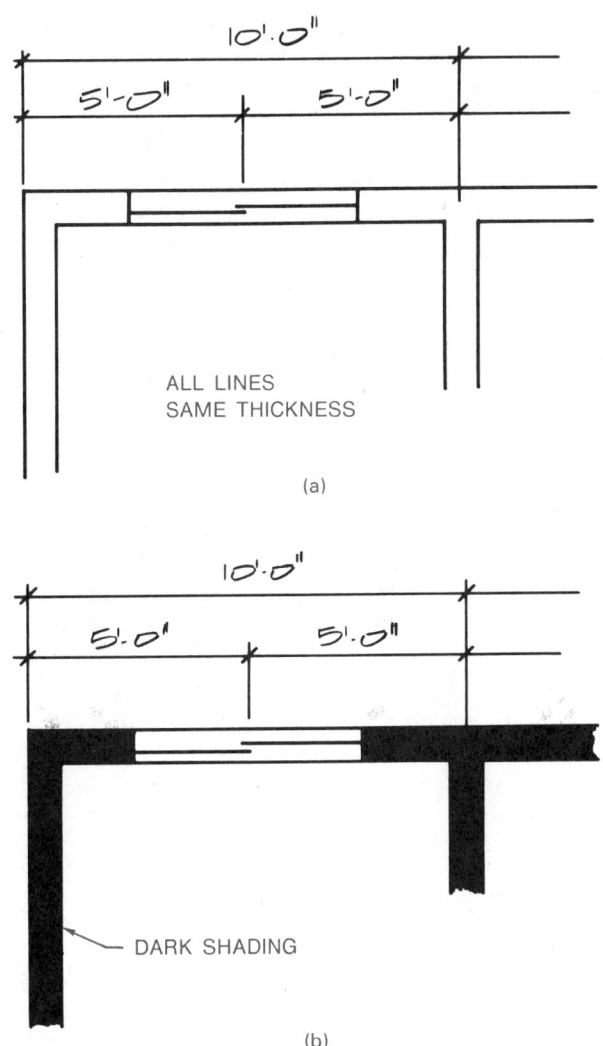

(a)

(b)

Figure 4–2 (a) All lines the same thickness; (b) accent with shading.

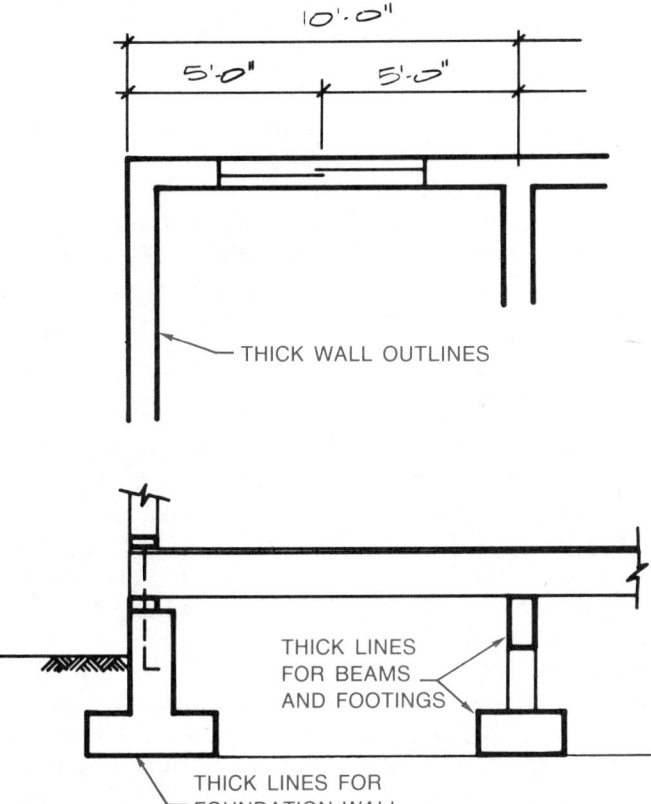

Figure 4–1 Thick outlines.

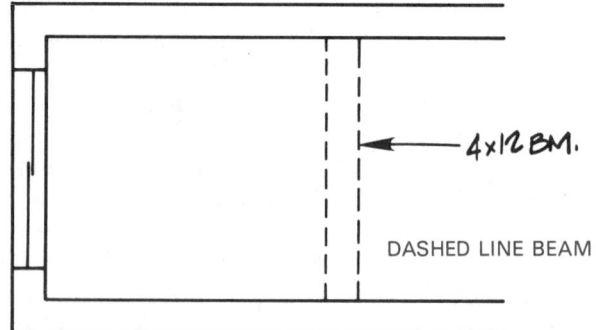

Figure 4–3 Dashed line beam.

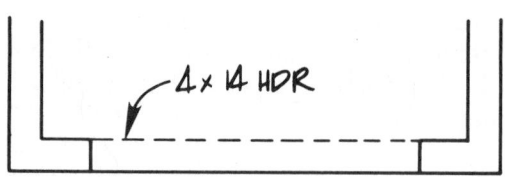

Figure 4–4 Dashed line header.

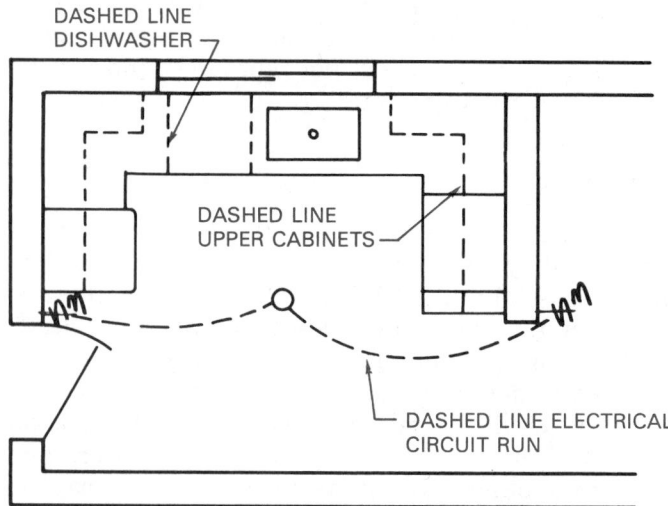

Figure 4–5 Dashed lines used for upper kitchen cabinets, dishwasher, and electrical circuit run.

Dashed Lines

In mechanical drafting dashed lines are called hidden lines. In architectural drafting dashed lines may also be considered as hidden lines since they are used to denote drawing features that are not visible in relationship to the view or plan. These dashed features may also be subordinate to the main emphasis of the drawing. Dashed lines vary slightly from one office to the next. These lines are thin and generally drawn about ⅛ to ⅜ in. in length with a space of 1/16 to ⅛ in. between each dash. The dashes should be kept uniform in length on the drawing, for example, all ¼ in. with approximately equal spaces. Dashed lines are thin, and the spacing should be by eye, never measured. Drawing dashed lines takes practice to do well. Recommended leads are a slightly rounded mechanical pencil or a 0.5 mm automatic pencil of 2H or H hardness. Examples of dashed line representations include beams, Figure 4–3; headers, Figure 4–4; upper kitchen cabinets, under counter appliances (dishwasher) or electrical circuit runs, Figure 4–5. These concepts will be discussed further in later chapters.

Extension and Dimension Lines

Extension lines show the extent of a dimension, and dimension lines show the length of the dimension and terminate at the related extension lines with slashes, arrowheads, or dots. The dimension numeral in feet and inches is placed above and near the center of the solid dimension line. Figure 4–6 shows several dimension and extension line examples. Further dis-

cussion and examples will be provided as needed in later chapters. Extension lines are generally thin, dark, crisp lines that may be drawn with a sharp 2H, 3H, or 4H lead in a mechanical pencil or an 0.5 mm automatic pencil.

Leader Lines

Leader lines are also thin, sharp, crisp lines. These lines are used to connect notes to related features on a drawing. Leader lines may be drawn freehand or with an irregular curve. Do them freehand if you can do a good job but if they are not smooth, then use an irregular curve. The leader should start from the vertical center at the beginning or end of a note and be terminated with an arrowhead at the feature. Some companies prefer that leaders be straight line segments that begin with a short shoulder and angle to the intended feature. Figure 4–7 shows several examples.

Break Lines

The two types of break lines are the long break line and the short break line. The type of break line that is normally associated with architectural drafting is the long break line. The break symbol is generally drawn freehand. Break lines are used to terminate features on a drawing when the extent of the feature has been clearly defined. Figure 4–8(a) shows several examples. The short break line may be found on some architectural drawings. This line, as shown in Figure 4–8(a) is an irregular line drawn freehand and may be used for a short area. Keep in mind that it is not as common as the long break line. Breaks in cylindrical objects such as steel bars and pipes are shown in Figure 4–8(b).

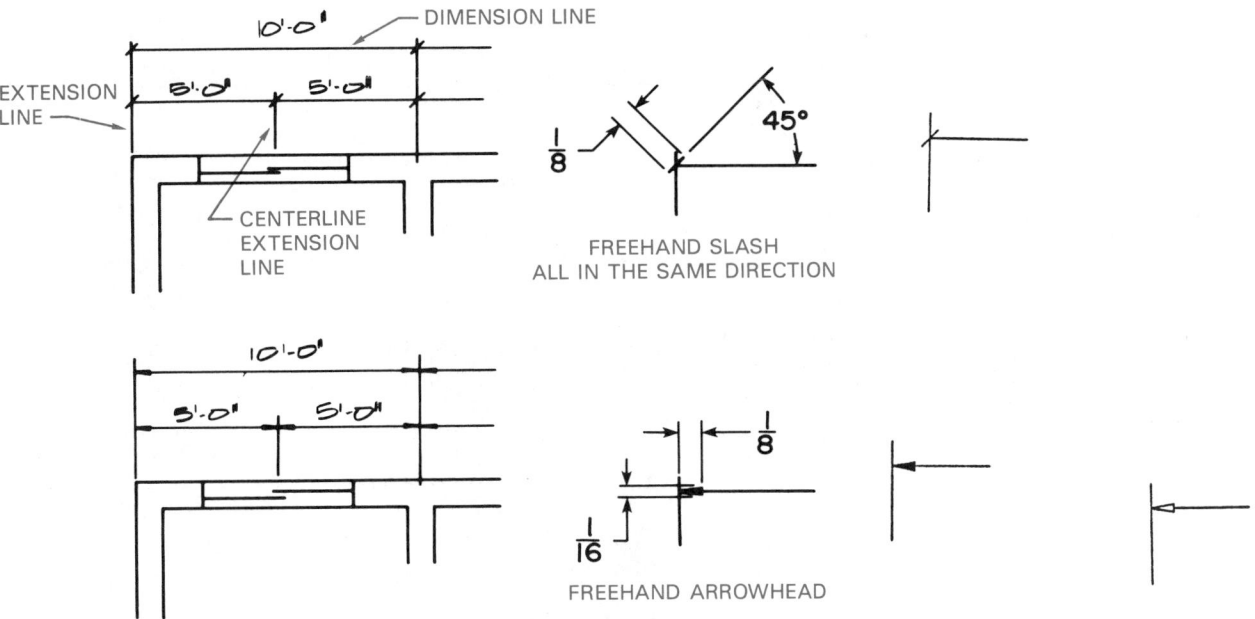

Figure 4-6 Dimension and extension lines.

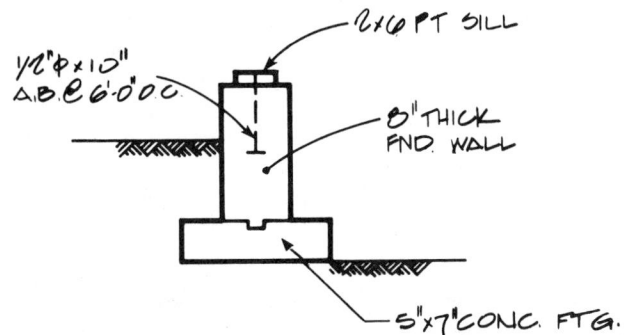

Figure 4-7 Sample leader lines.

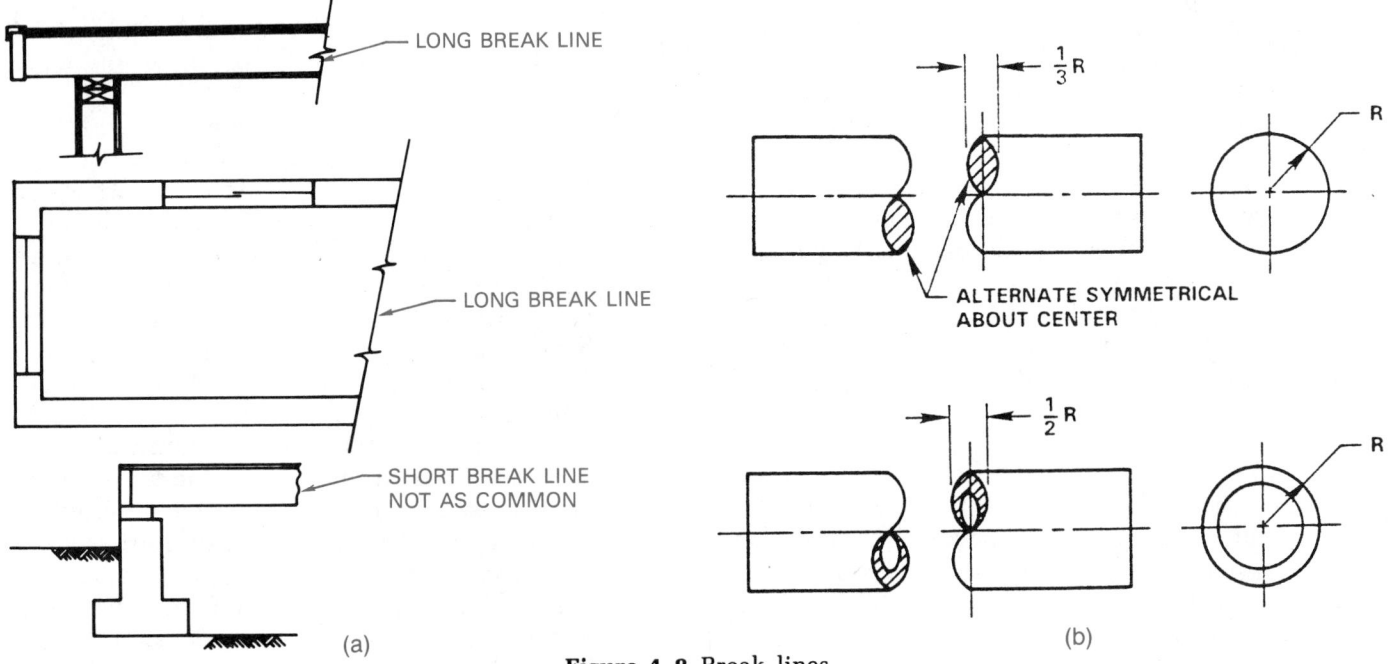

Figure 4-8 Break lines.

LINE TECHNIQUES

When working on vellum or Mylar® using pencil, polyester lead, or ink, use these basic techniques to help make the completion of the drawing easier:

1. Prepare a sketch to help organize your thoughts before beginning the formal drawing.
2. Do all layout work using construction lines. If you make an error, it will be easy to correct.
3. Begin the formal drawing by making all horizontal lines from the top of the sheet to the bottom. Try to avoid going back over lines that have been drawn any more than necessary.
4. If right handed, draw all vertical lines from left to right. If left handed, draw vertical lines from right to left.
5. Place all symbols on the drawing. Try to work from one side of the sheet to the other.
6. Do all lettering last. Place a clean piece of paper under your hand when lettering to avoid smudging lines or perspiring on the drawing.
7. Most important, keep your hands and equipment clean.

Pencil Line Methods on Vellum

To see if your lines are dark and crisp enough, turn your drawing over and hold it up to the light or put it on a light table. The lines should have a dark, consistent density. Problems to look for are lines that you can see through, or that have rough or fuzzy edges. The following hints may help to make a proper line:

1. Be sure that the mechanical lead is sharp and slightly rounded. A dull lead is a prime cause of fuzzy lines.
2. Use a lead of the proper hardness. A lead that is too hard will not make a dark line without a lot of extra work. A lead that is too soft will get dull too fast and cause fuzzy lines.
3. Draw with the pencil tilted about 45° in the direction of travel and perpendicular with the scale.
4. Rotate a mechanical pencil between your fingers as you draw a line. This will help keep the conical point uniformly sharp longer and will help avoid flat spots that cause fuzzy lines. If you are using an automatic pencil it is not as important to rotate it, although some drafters feel that rotation does help. See Figure 4–9.
5. Use enough pressure on the pencil. The amount of pressure depends on the individual. You may need to experiment with different lead hardnesses and pressures to find the right combination. Too much pressure can engrave the

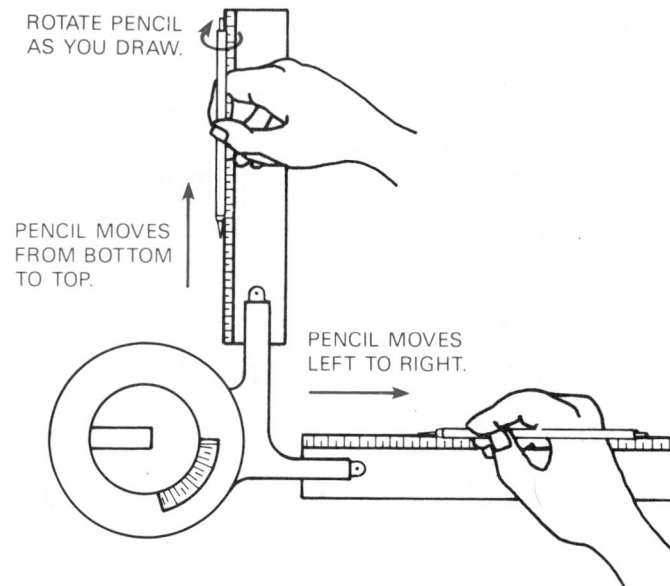

Figure 4–9 Basic pencil motions.

paper or break the point while not enough pressure may make fuzzy lines.
6. Some drafters may need to go over lines more than once to make them dark. Try to avoid doing so as it will slow you down and can cause an unwanted double line.

Polyester Lead Methods on Mylar®

Some companies use polyester lead on Mylar® to help improve line and lettering quality without using ink. Polyester lead is faster to use than ink and, in general, will produce a better print than graphite on vellum. After working with graphite on vellum the use of polyester lead will take some practice. Using polyester lead is similar to drawing with a crayon. Here are some basic techniques that will be helpful:

1. Always draw on the mat side of the Mylar®.
2. Draw with a slightly greater angle than that used for drawing graphite lines. Sharp angles may penetrate the mat surface and lesser angles may reduce line quality. Maintain the proper angle throughout the line. There is a tendency to increase the angle at the end of a line which may cause gouging of the mat.
3. Draw a single line in one direction. Retracing a line in both directions deposits a double line which will smear and damage the mat.
4. Draft with a light touch. Drafting films require up to 40 percent less pressure than other media. Smearing and embossing can be reduced with less pressure.
5. Draw with a slightly rounded point when using a mechanical lead holder, or use an automatic lead holder.

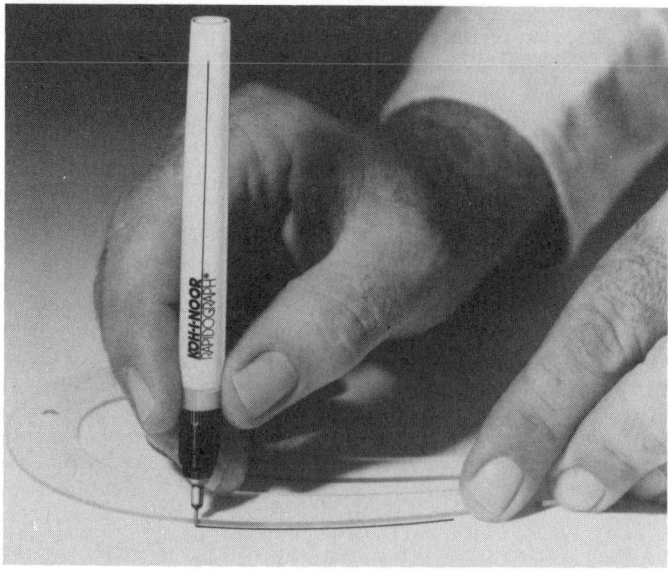

Figure 4–10 Inking with the technical pen. *Courtesy Koh-I-Noor Rapidograph, Inc.*

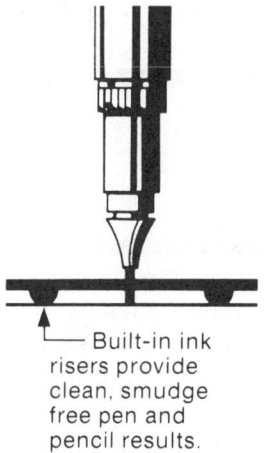

└─ Built-in ink risers provide clean, smudge free pen and pencil results.

Figure 4–11 Templates with built-in risers. *Courtesy Chartpak.*

6. As you move the pencil, rotate it. This will help keep lines uniform in width and reduce point wear.
7. Erase with a vinyl eraser. If an electric eraser is used, be very careful not to destroy the mat surface.

Inking Methods on Vellum or Mylar®

When inking on either vellum or Mylar®, be sure to ink on the textured surface. On Mylar® the textured surface is the mat side. On vellum the inking surface either has a water mark, printed label, or title block and border. Inking can be easy if you remember that ink is wet until it turns a dull color. If the ink is shiny, do not move your equipment over it. Follow the same recommended procedures as previously discussed. The following are some helpful hints to make inking easier.

1. When using technical pens, hold the pen perpendicular to the vellum or Mylar®. Move the pen at a constant speed that is not too fast. Do not slow at the end of a line since this may cause widening of the line or a drop of ink to form at the end of a line. Do not apply any pressure to the pen. Allow the pen to flow easily over the vellum or Mylar®. See Figure 4–10.
2. Care should be taken to provide a space between the instrument edge and the ink so that it does not flow under the instrument and smear. Drafting machine scales have long been manufactured with edge relief for inking. Now templates, triangles, and other equipment are

being made with ink risers built in. See Figure 4–11. Other ways to keep instruments away from inked lines include the use of adhesive template lifters as seen in Figure 4–12, or template risers which are long plastic strips that fit on the template edges as shown in Figure 4–13. If these devices are not available, then it is possible to place a second template with a larger opening under the template being used.
3. Periodically check pens for leaks around the tip or a drop of ink at the end of the tip. Have a piece of tissue paper or cloth available to help keep the tip free of ink drops.
4. Keep technical pens clean and the reservoir between ¼ and ¾ full.

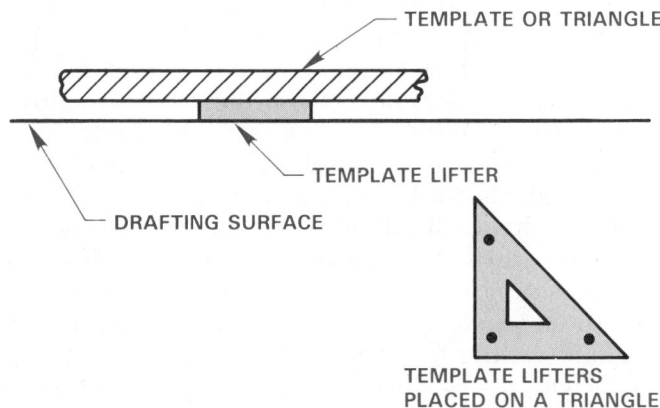

TEMPLATE OR TRIANGLE

TEMPLATE LIFTER

DRAFTING SURFACE

TEMPLATE LIFTERS PLACED ON A TRIANGLE

Figure 4–12 Template lifters for inking.

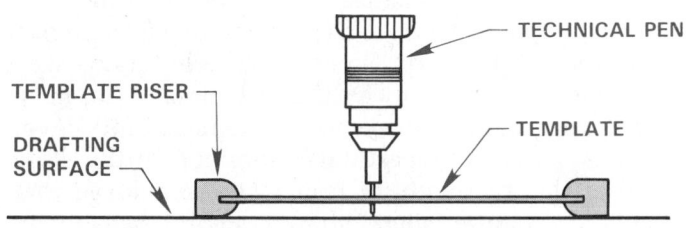

TECHNICAL PEN

TEMPLATE RISER

DRAFTING SURFACE

TEMPLATE

Figure 4–13 Template risers for inking.

5. Drafters often shake technical fountain pens to get the ink started but do not shake the pen over your drawing.

LETTERING

Information on drawings that cannot be represented graphically by lines may be presented by lettered dimensions, notes, and titles. It is extremely important that these lettered items be exact, reliable, and entirely legible in order for the user to have confidence in them and never have any hesitation as to their meaning. This is especially important when using reproduction techniques that require a drawing to be reduced in size such as with a photocopy or microfilm, or when secondary originals are made. Secondary originals are copies that may be used as originals to make changes and other copies. The quality of each generation of the secondary original is reduced, thus requiring the highest quality from the original drawing. Poor lettering will ruin an otherwise good drawing.

Single-stroke Gothic Lettering

The standard lettering that has been used for generations by mechanical drafters is vertical single-stroke Gothic letters. The term single stroke comes from the fact that each letter is made up of single straight or curved line elements that make them easy to draw and clear to read. There are uppercase and lowercase Gothic letters although the industry has traditionally used uppercase lettering. Figure 4–14 shows the recommended strokes that are used to form the uppercase Gothic letters. Architectural designers and drafters do not use the same structured single-stroke Gothic lettering used by mechanical drafters. However, the architectural style is derived from the single-stroke concept. Architectural drafting is more individualized and some people may say that it is more artistic than mechanical drafting. This may or may not be true but architectural drafting is less structured. Architectural lettering styles range from standard Gothic forms to more avant-garde characters. Figure 4–15 shows a typical representation of architectural lettering. As a beginning drafter you would do well to be conservative. Too much emphasis on flair may cause unnatural lettering. One important point for lettering technique is to make letter forms consistent. Do not make a letter one way one time and another way the next time. Also, keep letters vertical and always use guidelines. Entry-level drafters should pay particular attention to the style used at the architectural firm where employed and match it. A professional drafter should be able to letter rapidly with clarity and neatness. As you study

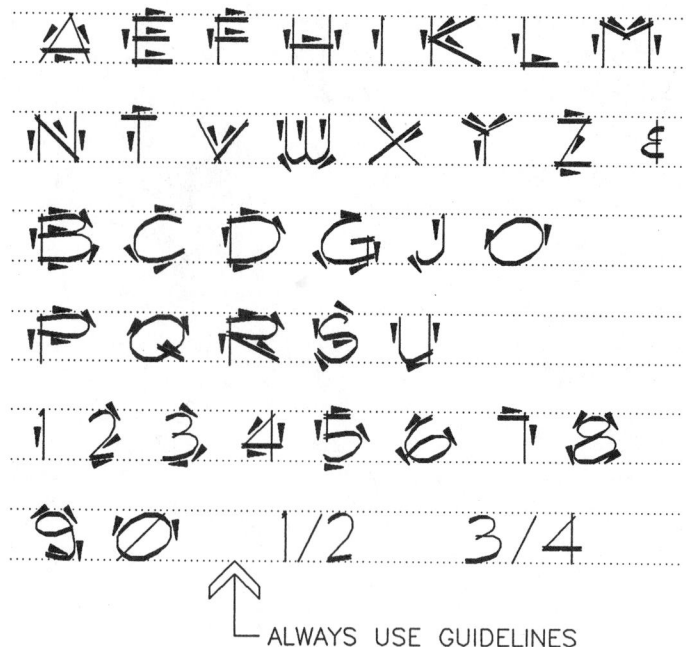

Figure 4–14 Vertical straight element letters, curved element letters, and numerals and fractions.

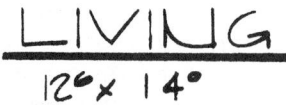

Figure 4–15 Architectural lettering.

this textbook, notice the variety of lettering styles on the drawings.

Lettering Size

Minimum lettering height should be ⅛ in. Some companies use 3/32 in. high lettering. All dimension numerals, notes, and other lettered information should be the same height except for titles, drawing numbers, and other captions. Titles and subtitles, for example, may be 3/16 or ¼ in. high. Verify the specific requirements with your instructor or employer.

Lettering Legibility

Lettering should be dark, crisp, and sharp for the best reproducibility. The composition of letters in words and the space between words in sentences should be such that the individual letters are uniformly spaced with approximately equal background areas. To achieve such spacing usually requires that letters such as I, N, or S be spaced slightly farther apart than L, A, or W. A minimum recommended space between letters is approximately 1/16 in. The space between words in a note or title should be about the same as the height of the letters. When a note is made up of more than one sentence, the space between sentences should be at least twice the height of the letters.

When lettering notes, sentences, or dimensions that require more than one line, the space between the lines should be a minimum of one-half the height of letters. Some companies prefer more space between lines of lettering, but usually never more than equal to the height of the lettering. Notes should be lettered horizontally on the sheet or, in some cases where space dictates, notes may be lettered vertically so that they read from the right side of the sheet. For some applications, some companies may prefer that lettering be done using a lettering template or guide.

Computer graphics is here to stay and ultimately there will be little, if any, need for freehand lettering. Architectural drafters, however, will probably attempt to keep their skill and artistic talent for at least one generation after the change to computer aided drafting has taken place. There is no doubt that computer generated lettering is fast, easily done, and legible.

Professional Lettering Hints

Vertical freehand lettering is the standard for architectural drafting. The ability to quickly make good quality lettering is important. A common comment among employers hiring entry-level drafters is about their ability (or lack of it) to do quality lettering and line work. The following suggestions may help establish good lettering skills:

1. Always use guidelines, which are lightly drawn horizontal or vertical lines spaced equal to the height of the letters. Guidelines should be so light that they will not reproduce.

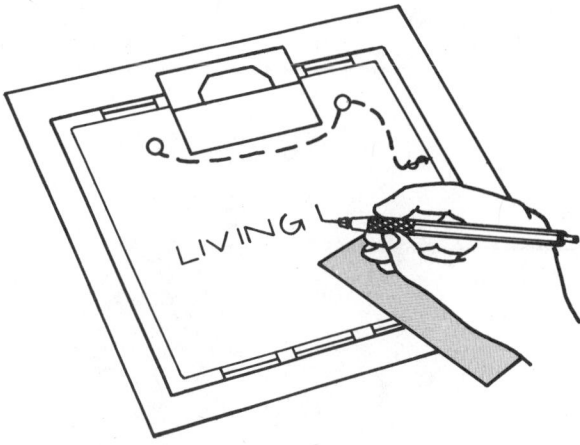

Figure 4–16 Place a clean sheet of blank paper under your hand when lettering.

2. If using a mechanical pencil, experiment with a 2H, H, or F lead and a slightly rounded point for best control.
3. If using an automatic pencil, try one that is 0.5 mm wide with H, F, or HB lead. These pencils are usually easy to control for effective lettering and they do not require sharpening.
4. Protect the drawing by resting your hand on a clean protective sheet placed over the drawing. This will help prevent smearing and smudging as shown in Figure 4–16.
5. Lettering composition is spacing letters so that the background areas look the same. This is done by eye and there is no substitute for experience. In general, space vertical line letters farther apart than angled or curved line letters.
6. If your letters are wiggly or if you are nervous, try using a straight edge for vertical strokes or try making each letter rapidly. This tends to eliminate wiggly letters. Another option, if the problem continues, is to try using a softer lead and be sure that the lead does not extend too far out of the pencil tip.
7. Make sure your hand and arm are comfortable on the board. Do not letter with your arm going over a parallel rule or other equipment.

MAKING GUIDELINES

Guidelines, as previously discussed, are lines very lightly drawn and equal to the height of the letters in distance apart. Some drafters prefer the use of a light-blue lead so that guidelines will not reproduce. A rule of thumb is that guidelines should be drawn so lightly that when the drawing is held at arm's length the lines should be very difficult or impossible to see.

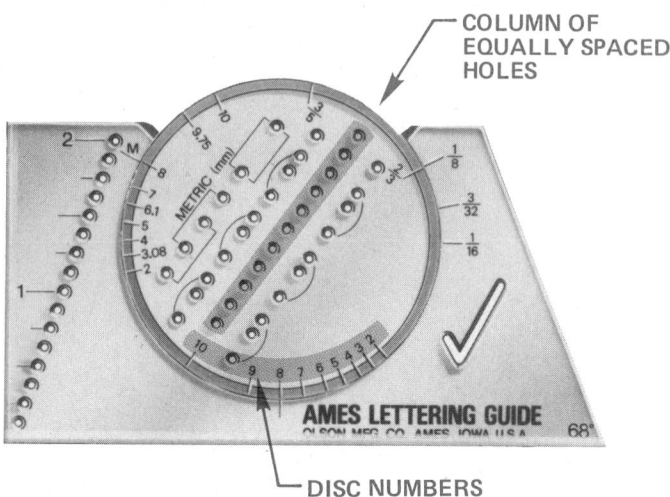

Figure 4-17 Ames Lettering Guide. *Courtesy Olson Manufacturing Co.*

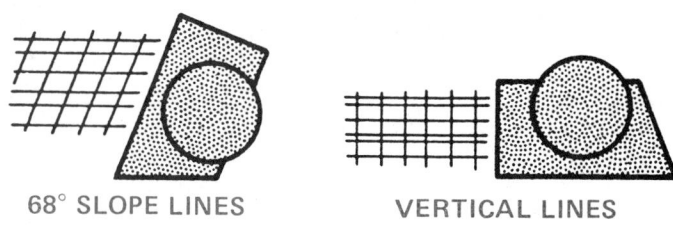

Figure 4-18 Inclined or vertical guidelines. *Courtesy Olson Manufacturing Co.*

Ames Lettering Guide

Probably the most commonly used device for making guidelines is the versatile Ames Lettering Guide. With your Ames Lettering Guide it is possible to draw guidelines and sloped lines for lettering from 1/16 to 2 in. in height. Disk numbers from 10 to 2 denote the height of letters in thirty-seconds of an inch. If ¼ in. high letters are required, simply rotate the disk so that the 8 (8/32″ = ¼″) is at the index mark on the bottom of the frame. See Figure 4-17.

Use a sharpened 4H or harder drawing pencil and place the guide, readable side up, against the top of the straightedge. Place the pencil in the top hole. Keep the pencil perpendicular to the paper and slightly inclined in the direction of travel. With the pencil in the top hole, slide the guide to the right, lightly drawing a line. Keep the base of the guide in contact with the straightedge until the end of the line has been reached. To make the remaining guidelines, move the pencil down hole by hole, and alternately slide the guide to the left and then to the right. You now have one set of three guidelines ¼ in. high. To draw two more sets, repeat the procedure using the remaining holes in this column.

If no middle guideline is desired, or for ⅛ in. lettering, use the same 8 setting. If 3/32 or 1/16 in. heights are desired with no middle guideline, use the 6 or 4 setting respectively at the bottom of the disk or use the index mark on the disk (near the ⅔ fraction) and set the disk at the desired mark on the frame.

Cross Sectioning. To make parallel lines for such purposes as brick, tile, or concrete block section lines, set the index mark on the disk (near the ⅔ fraction) at the desired mark on the frame (⅛, 3/32 or 1/16). Set your straightedge parallel to the desired lines and draw lines alternately to the right and left.

Slanted or Vertical Lines. Slanted or vertical guidelines can be drawn easily to help keep the letters vertical for mechanical drafting or slanted for structural drafting. Look at Figure 4-18. Always remember to draw sloped lines lightly and use only enough to maintain slope uniformity.

Metric Guidelines. The numbers and set of six holes to the left of the disk relate to metric heights for guidelines. This column of six holes offers the drafter the option of spacing guidelines equally (right brackets) or at half space (left brackets). The 3.08, 6.1 and 9.75 mm calibrations are for standard letter heights used in United States drawings. By setting 3.08 opposite the left frame index M, the guideline spacing will be .12 in. Similarly, setting 6.1 and 9.75 opposite M will give .24 and .38 in. high guidelines respectively. Other metric heights are calibrated on the disk for use if desired.

Other Lettering Aids and Guidelines

Guideline lettering aids for equidistant spacing of lines have parallel slots ranging in width from 1/16 to ¼ in. These lettering guideline aids are not as complex as the Ames Lettering Guide, but they are also not as versatile nor as flexible for drawing guidelines. See Figure 4-19 for an example of a parallel-slot lettering aid.

Another method of making guidelines used by a few drafters is to place ⅛ in. grid paper under the drawing. The grid paper lines show through the drawing sheet and guidelines need not be drawn.

Figure 4-19 Lettering aid. *Courtesy Berol USA RapiDesign.*

Points to Remember

1. Always use two guidelines.
2. Make all letters and numbers on the drawing at least ⅛ in. high, none smaller. All letters should be the same height. Be consistent.
3. Make all lettering dark. You may have to press hard on your pencil to get dark letters.
4. Practice lettering no more than 15 minutes per day otherwise your hand will cramp and any further practice will be of little value. Attempt to gain speed and neatness as you practice.

OTHER LETTERING STYLES

Slanted Lettering

Some companies prefer slanted lettering. The general slant of these letters is 68°. Structural drafting is one field where slanted lettering may be commonly found. Figure 4–20 shows slanted uppercase letters.

LETTERING GUIDE TEMPLATES

Although professional drafters are excellent at lettering, each individual's lettering is slightly different. Some companies prefer that drafting technicians use lettering guides so that uniformity is maintained. Standard lettering guide templates are available with vertical Gothic letters and numerals ranging in let-

$$A\ B\ C\ D\ E\ F\ G\ H\ I\ J\ K\ L\ M$$
$$N\ O\ P\ Q\ R\ S\ T\ U\ V\ W\ X\ Y\ Z$$
$$1\ 2\ 3\ 4\ 5\ 6\ 7\ 8\ 9\ 0$$

Figure 4–20 Uppercase inclined letters and numbers.

tering height from 3/32 to ⅜ in. See Figure 4–21(a) and 4–21(b). Lettering guides are also available in many other lettering styles, including slanted Gothic, block, Futura, Old English, and Microfont letters in either uppercase or lowercase.

MECHANICAL LETTERING EQUIPMENT

Mechanical lettering equipment is available in kits with templates for letters and numerals in a wide range of sizes. See Figure 4–22. A complete lettering equipment kit includes a scriber plus templates, tracing pins and lettering pens. Figure 4–23 shows the component parts of a lettering equipment set.

Templates

Most templates have a convenient scale on the bottom edge for quick centering and letter spacing. Also, the distance between the bottom of the letters and the bottom of each template is uniform so templates can be exchanged without changing the position of the straightedge.

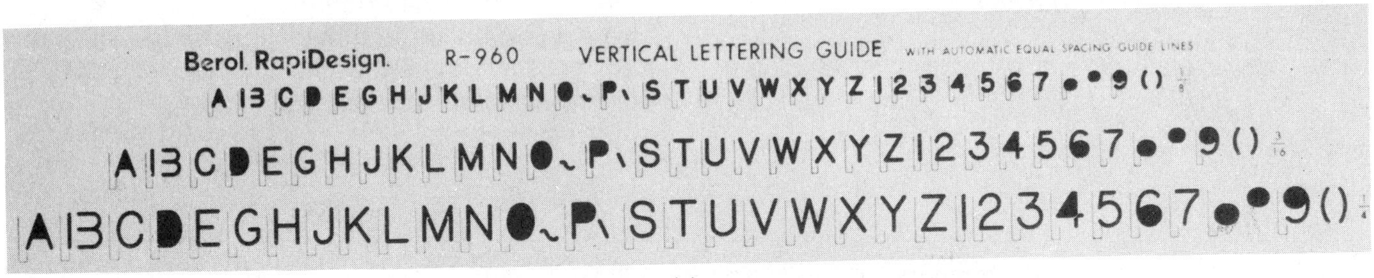

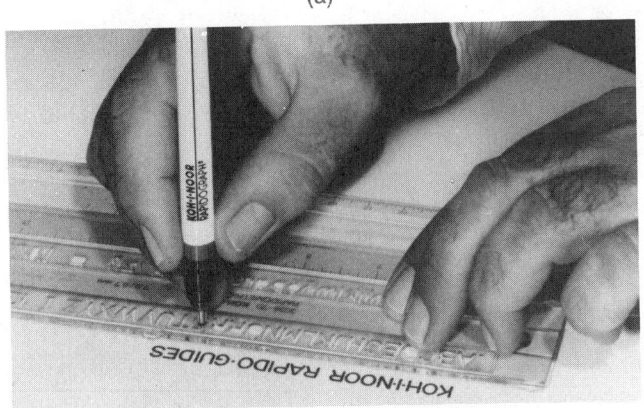

(a)

(b)

Figure 4–21 (a) Lettering guide template; (b) lettering guide template in use.
(a) *Courtesy Berol USA RapiDesign;* (b) *courtesy Koh-I-Noor Rapidograph, Inc.*

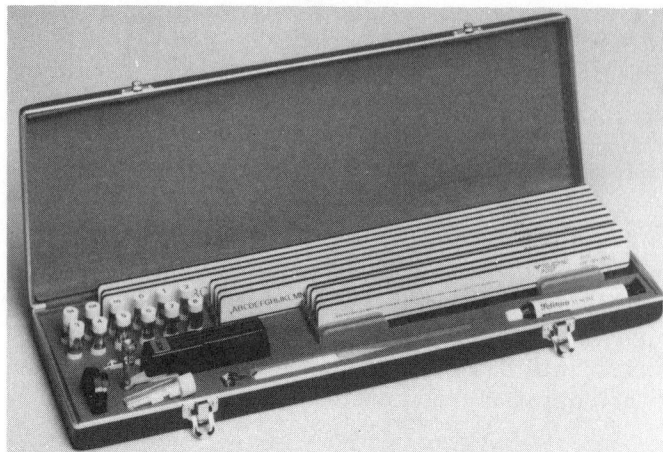

Figure 4–22 Mechanical lettering equipment kit. *Courtesy Teledyne Post.*

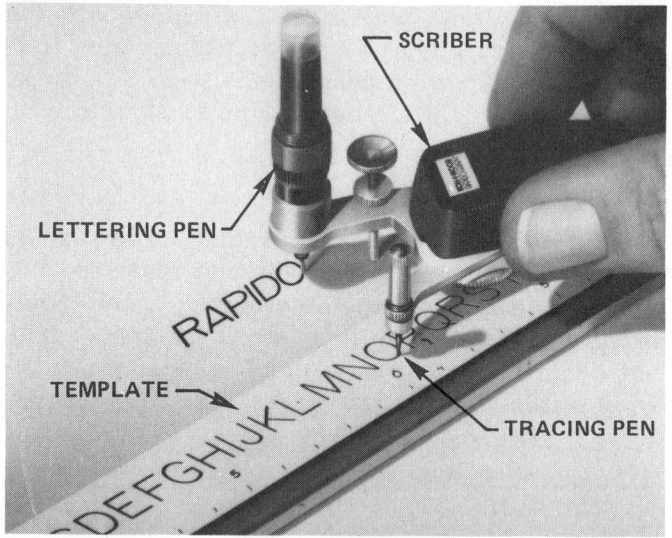

Figure 4–23 Components of a lettering equipment set. *Courtesy Koh-I-Noor Rapidograph, Inc.*

Scriber

The scriber is used with templates up to 500 CL and with pens from number 04 to 8. The scriber is adjustable from vertical to 22° forward slanted letters by opening and closing the scriber arm. It is not necessary to move the templates or change position when adjusting to different slants.

Lettering Pens

The lettering pen consists of two basic parts: the inkwell and the cleaning pin. The cleaning pin is inserted through the top of the pen and ensures a smooth ink flow. Pens numbered 04 to 1 also have a special clip which is used to hold the fragile cleaning pin in place. The scriber will hold either the standard lettering pen or the technical fountain pen.

Many drafters prefer technical pens for use in mechanical lettering equipment since they contain a large reservoir of ink for continued use. Standard lettering pens are convenient for use when only a limited amount of lettering will be done and the pens are easy to clean and put away. Lettering kits are available with either standard lettering pens or technical fountain pens.

Important Points to Remember

- Always lay the template along a straightedge.
- Insert the pen into the scriber until its shoulder is perfectly seated, then tighten the side screw.
- Use the proper tracing pin.
- Rest the scriber on the scriber stand when not in use.
- Clean pens after use.
- Practice.

MACHINE LETTERING

Lettering machines are available that produce a variety of fonts, styles, and letter sizes to prepare drawing titles, labels, or special headings. These types of lettering features are especially useful for making display letters, cover sheets, or drawing titles. Most machines use a typewriter keyboard for quick preparation of lettering. A personal computer may also interface with the lettering machine to increase speed and provide additional flexibility. Lettering machines prepare strips of lettering on clear adhesive-backed tape for placement on drawing originals. The tape is also available in a variety of colors for special displays and presentation drawings.

TRANSFER LETTERING

A large variety of transfer lettering fonts, styles, and sizes are available on sheets. These transfer letters may be used in any combination to prepare drawing titles, labels, or special headings. They may be used to improve the quality of a presentation drawing, or for titles on all drawings. Some vendors have over 300 lettering fonts and sizes available for use.

Transfer letters may be purchased as vinyl sheets where individual letters are removed from a sheet and placed on the drawing in the desired location. Transfer letters are also available on sheets where letters are placed on the drawing by rubbing with a burnishing tool as shown in Figure 4–24. Rub-on letters, as they are often called, offer a high quality lettering that is excellent for drawing titles and special displays.

1. POSITION THE LETTER.

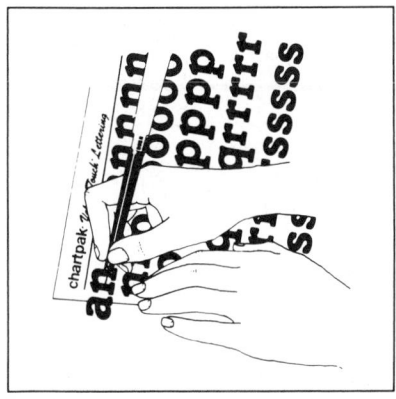

2. RUB OVER THE LETTER WITH A BURNISHER. BE SURE TO COVER ALL AREAS AND FINE LINES.

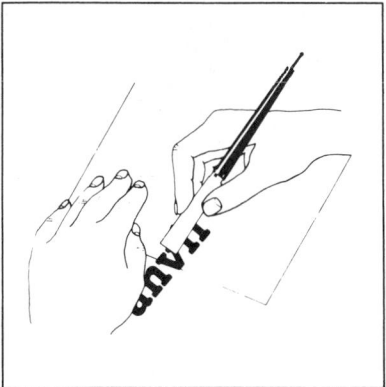

3. REMOVE THE SHEET BY CAREFULLY LIFTING IT FROM THE CORNER. FOR MAXIMUM ADHESION, PLACE THE BACKING SHEET OVER LETTER AND RUB AGAIN WITH THE BURNISHER.

Figure 4–24 Using rub-on letters. *Courtesy Chartpak.*

Special drawing transfers are also manufactured that can be used on presentation drawings. For example, a wide assortment of home furnishings or plant and office products may be purchased for use in preparing layout drawings. Other special items that are available are scales, call-outs, trees, landscaping items, people representations, and transportation figures.

Drawing aids in the form of transfer tapes may be used to prepare borders, line drawings, or special symbols.

Some vendors prepare custom transfer templates for architectural customers. Such transfer templates may be used as standard drawing details.

LINES AND LETTERING TEST

DIRECTIONS

Answer the questions with short complete statements or drawings as needed on 8½ × 11 vellum as follows:

1. Use ⅛ in. guidelines for all lettering.
2. Letter your name, Lines and Lettering Test, and the date at the top of the sheet.
3. Letter the question number and provide the answer. You do not need to write out the question.
4. Do all lettering with vertical, single-stroke architectural letters. If the answer requires line work, use proper drafting tools and technique. Answers may be prepared on a word processor if appropriate with course guidelines.

QUESTIONS

1. Is there any recommended variation in line darkness or are all properly drawn lines the same darkness?
2. What are construction lines used for, and how should they be drawn?
3. Discuss line uniformity and line contrast.
4. Define guidelines.
5. What is the recommended thickness of outlines?
6. Identify two items that dashed lines represent on a drawing.
7. Describe a situation where an extension line is the centerline of a feature.
8. Extension lines are thin lines that are used for what purpose?
9. Where should extension lines begin in relationship to the object and end in relationship to the last dimension line?
10. Describe leaders.
11. Describe and show an example of three methods used to terminate dimension lines at extension lines.
12. How does architectural line work differ from mechanical drafting line work?
13. What is the advantage of drawing certain outlines thicker than other lines on the drawing?

14. If all lines on a drawing are the same thickness, how can walls and partitions, for example, be represented so that they stand out clearly on a floor plan?
15. Discuss the proper recommended technique of using a mechanical pencil with graphite lead on vellum.
16. How will the line technique differ when using a mechanical pencil as compared to using an automatic pencil?
17. Describe the proper technique to use when drawing lines with a technical pen.
18. How does architectural lettering compare to vertical single-stroke freehand Gothic lettering?
19. What are the minimum recommended lettering heights?
20. How should the letters within words be spaced?
21. What is the recommended space between words in a note?
22. What is the recommended horizontal space between lines?
23. When should guidelines be used for lettering on a drawing?
24. Why are guidelines necessary for freehand lettering?
25. Describe the recommended leads and points used in mechanical and automatic pencils for freehand lettering.
26. Identify a method to use to help avoid smudging the drawing when lettering.
27. When lettering fractions, what is the recommended relationship of the fraction division line?
28. List two manual methods that can be used to make guidelines rapidly.
29. Why should the mechanical lettering template be placed along a straightedge when lettering?
30. Identify an advantage for using lettering guides.
31. Describe a use for lettering machines.
32. Describe four uses for transfer materials.

LINES AND LETTERING PROBLEMS

DIRECTIONS

1. Read all instructions carefully before you begin.
2. Use an 8½ × 11 vellum or bond paper drawing sheet for each drawing or lettering exercise.
3. Use the architect's scale of ¼″ = 1″-0″ for each drawing.
4. Draw the floor plan described in Problem 4–1 twice. On the first drawing, use thick lines for the walls and thin lines for extension, dimension, and symbol lines. On the second drawing, make all lines the same thickness. Each drawing will represent a line thickness technique discussed in this chapter.
5. Use guidelines for all lettering. Using architectural lettering, letter the title, FLOOR PLAN, centered below the drawing in ¼ in. high letters. In ⅛ in. high letters and centered below the title, letter the following, SCALE: ¼″ = 1′-0″. Letter your name and all other notes and dimensions using ⅛ in. high architectural lettering.
6. Lightly lay out the drawing using construction lines. When you are satisfied with the layout, darken all lines.
7. For the lettering exercise, use ⅛ in. guidelines with ⅛ in. space between the lines.
8. Leave a ¾ in. margin around the lettering exercise sheet.
9. Make a diazo print or photocopy of your original drawings or lettering exercise sheet as specified by your instructor.
10. Submit your copies and originals for grade evaluation.

Problem 4–1 Lines and lettering. Given the following information, draw the garage floor plan:

1. Overall dimensions are 24′-0″ × 24′-0″. Dimensions are measured to the outside of walls.
2. Make all walls 4″ thick.
3. Center a 16′-0″ wide garage door in the front wall.
4. Using dashed lines, draw a 4 × 12 header over the garage door and label it, 4 × 12 HEADER.
5. Label the garage floor as 4″ CONC OVER 4″ GRAVEL FILL.

Problem 4–2 Lettering practice. Using architectural lettering, letter the following statement as instructed:

YOUR NAME
MOST ARCHITECTURAL DRAWINGS THAT ARE NOT MADE WITH CAD EQUIPMENT ARE LETTERED USING VERTICAL FREEHAND LETTERING. THE QUALITY OF THE FREEHAND LETTERING GREATLY AF-

FECTS THE APPEARANCE OF THE ENTIRE DRAWING. MANY ARCHITECTURAL DRAFTERS LETTER WITH PENCIL ON VELLUM OR POLYESTER LEAD ON MYLAR®. LETTERING IS COMMONLY DONE WITH A SOFT, SLIGHTLY ROUNDED LEAD IN A MECHANICAL PENCIL OR A .5-MILLIMETER LEAD IN AN AUTOMATIC PENCIL. LETTERS ARE MADE BETWEEN VERY LIGHTLY DRAWN GUIDELINES. GUIDELINES ARE PARALLEL AND SPACED AT A DISTANCE EQUAL TO THE HEIGHT OF THE LETTERS. GUIDELINES ARE REQUIRED TO HELP KEEP ALL LETTERS THE SAME UNIFORM HEIGHT. THE SPACE BETWEEN LINES OF LETTERING MAY BE BETWEEN ½ TO EQUAL THE HEIGHT OF THE LETTERS. ALWAYS USE GUIDELINES. WHEN LETTERING FREEHAND, LEARN TO RELAX SO THAT THE STROKES FOR EACH LETTER FLOW SMOOTHLY. WHEN YOUR HAND BECOMES TIRED, REST FOR A WHILE BEFORE BEGINNING AGAIN.

Chapter 5
Sketching and Orthographic Projection

graph paper to help establish the coordinates for drawing components. Some drafters use sketches to help record the stages of progress when designing until a final design is ready for implementation into formal drawings. A sketch can be a useful form of illustration in technical reports. Sketching is also used in job shops where one-of-a-kind products are made. In the job shop, the sketch is often used as a formal production drawing. When the drafter's assignment is to prepare working drawings for existing parts or products, the best method to gather shape and size descriptions about the project is to make a sketch. The sketch can be used to quickly lay out dimensions of features for later transfer to a formal drawing.

SKETCHING IS freehand drawing, that is, drawing without the aid of drafting equipment. Sketching is convenient since all that is needed is paper, pencil and an eraser. There are a number of advantages and uses for freehand sketching. Sketching is fast visual communication. The ability to make an accurate sketch quickly can often be an asset when communicating with people at work or at home. Especially when technical concepts are the topic of discussion, a sketch may be the best form of communication. Most drafting technicians will prepare a preliminary sketch to help organize thoughts and minimize errors on the final drawing. The computer graphics technician will usually prepare a sketch on

TOOLS AND MATERIALS

Sketching equipment is not very elaborate. As mentioned, all you need is a pencil, eraser, and paper. The pencil should have a soft lead; a common number 2 pencil will work fine. A mechanical pencil with an F or HB lead is also good, as is an automatic 7 or 9 mm pencil with F or HB lead. The pencil lead should not be sharp. A dull, slightly rounded pencil point is best. Different thickness of line, if needed, can be drawn by changing the amount of pressure that you apply to the pencil. The quality of the paper is not too critical either. A good sketching paper is newsprint, although most any kind will work. Actually, paper with a surface that is not too smooth is best. Many architectural designs have been created on a napkin around a lunch table. Sketching paper should not be taped down to the table so there is no need for tape. The best sketches are made when you are able to move the paper to the most comfortable drawing position. Some people make horizontal lines better than vertical lines. If this is your situation, then move the paper so that vertical lines become horizontal. Such movement of the paper may not always be possible, so it does not hurt to keep practicing all forms of lines for best results.

◣ STRAIGHT LINES

Lines should be sketched lightly in short connected segments as shown in Figure 5-1. If you sketch one long stroke in one continuous movement, your arm tends to make the line curved rather than straight, as shown in Figure 5-2. Also, if you make a dark line, you may have to erase it if you make an error, whereas if you draw a light line, often there will be no need to erase.

Following is the procedure used to sketch a horizontal straight line with the dot-to-dot method:

Step 1.   Mark the starting and ending positions, as in Figure 5-3. The letters A and B are only for instruction. All you need are the points.

Step 2.   Without actually touching the paper with the pencil point, make a few trial motions between the marked points to adjust the eye and hand to the anticipated line.

Step 3.   Sketch very light lines between the points by stroking in short light strokes, 2 to 3 in. long. By using a blank stare, keep one eye directed towards the end point while keeping the other eye directed on the pencil point. With each stroke, an attempt should be made to correct the most obvious defects of the preceding stroke so that the finished light lines will be relatively straight. Look at Figure 5-4.

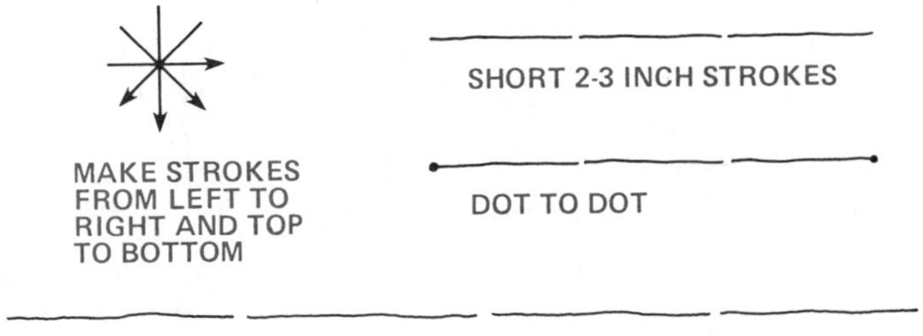

Figure 5-2 Long hand movement tends to cause the line to curve.

A ·   · B

Figure 5-3 Step 1: Dot-to-dot.

Figure 5-4 Step 3: Short light strokes.

Figure 5-5 Step 4: Darken to finish the line.

Step 4.   Darken the finished line with a dark, distinct, uniform line directly on top of the light line. Usually the darkness can be obtained by pressing hard on the pencil. See Figure 5-5.

Start with light lines so that corrections can be made without erasing. Do not tape down your paper so you can turn it to different angles for easier sketching.

Exercise 5-1. For practice, take a few pieces of newsprint or tablet paper and sketch a series of horizontal lines on one sheet, vertical lines on another, and diagonal lines on a third. Keep the lines as parallel as possible and use your preferred grade of soft lead.

CIRCULAR LINES

Figure 5-6 shows the parts of a circle. There are three sketching techniques to use when making a circle: the box method, trammel method, and hand-compass method.

Box Method

Step 1.   Sketch a box as square as possible with the sides of the box equal to the diameter

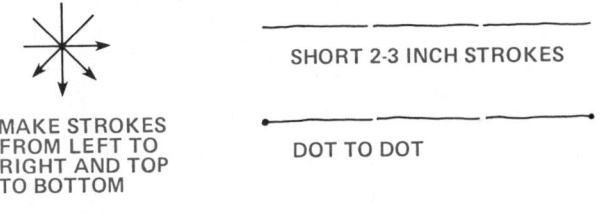

Figure 5-1 Sketching short line segments.

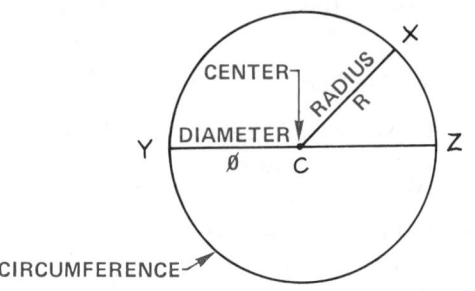

Figure 5-6 Parts of a circle.

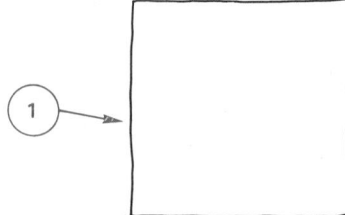

Figure 5–7 Step 1: Box method.

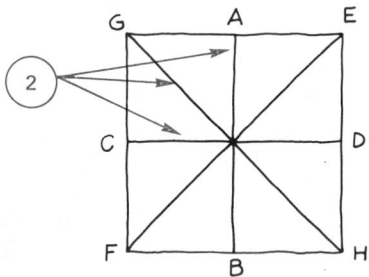

Figure 5–8 Step 2: Box method.

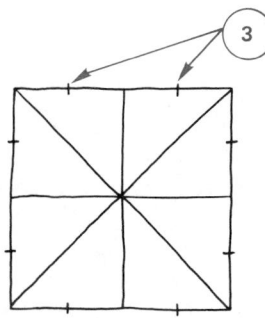

Figure 5–9 Step 3: Box method.

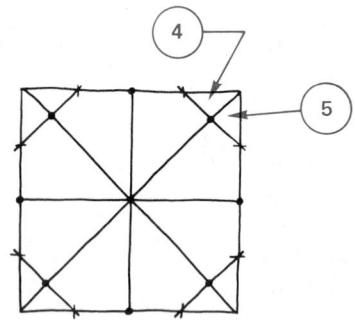

Figure 5–10 Steps 4 and 5: Box method.

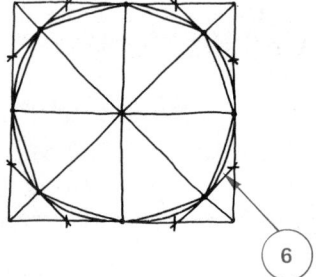

Figure 5–11 Step 6: Box method.

of the circle or arc. Use very light construction lines, as in Figure 5–7.

Step 2. Sketch the diagonal, vertical and horizontal elements, A–B, C–D, E–F, and G–H, as in Figure 5–8. The intersections of the horizontal and vertical lines with the sides of the box give you four points on the circle.

Step 3. To get four other points on the circle, first divide each of the eight line segments in half. See Figure 5–9.

Step 4. Connect each point with a light straight line as shown in Figure 5–10.

Step 5. Where the lines intersect the diagonal, another point on the circle has been located. See Figure 5–10.

Step 6. Connect the dots with a smooth, circular line lightly drawn. See Figure 5–11.

Step 7. When satisfied with results after correcting any misalignment, darken the desired portion of the circle or arc, as in Figure 5–12.

Trammel Method

Step 1. Make a trammel. If you wanted to sketch a 6 in. diameter circle, you would tear a strip of paper approximately 1 in. wide and longer than the radius, 3 in. On the strip of paper mark an approximate 3 in. radius with tick marks such as A and B in Figure 5–13.

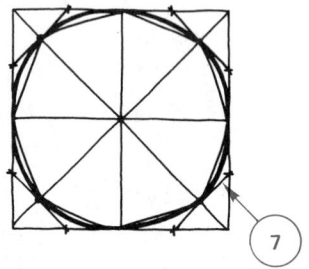

Figure 5–12 Step 7: Box method.

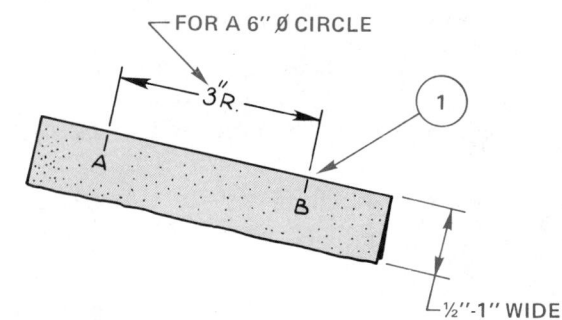

Figure 5–13 Step 1: Trammel method.

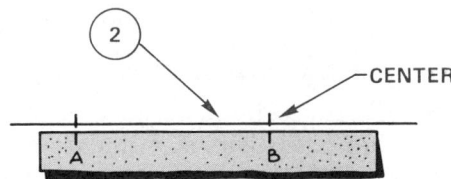

Figure 5–14 Step 2: Trammel method.

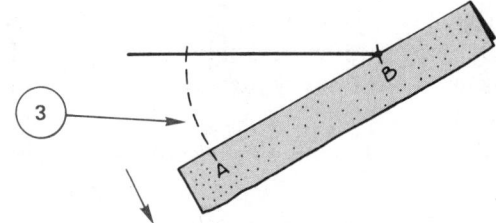

Figure 5–15 Step 3: Trammel method.

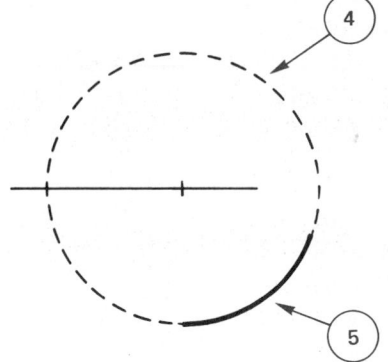

Figure 5–16 Step 4: Trammel method.

Step 2. Sketch a straight line representing the circle diameter at the place where the circle is to be located. On the sketched line, locate with a dot the center of the circle to be sketched. Use the marks on the trammel to mark the other end of the radius line as shown in Figure 5–14. With the trammel next to the sketched line, be sure point B on the trammel is aligned with the center of the circle you are about to sketch.

Step 3. Pivot the trammel at point B, making tick marks at point A as you go, as shown in Figure 5–15, until you have a complete circle as shown in Figure 5–16.

Step 4. Lightly sketch the circumference over the tick marks to complete the circle, then darken it in, as shown in Figure 5–16.

Hand Compass Method

The hand compass method is a quick and fairly accurate method of sketching circles, although it is a method that takes some practice.

Step 1. Be sure that your paper is free to rotate completely around 360°. Remove anything from the table that might stop such a rotation.

Step 2. To use your hand and a pencil as a compass, place the pencil in your hand between your thumb and the upper part of your index finger so that your index finger becomes the *compass point* and the pencil becomes the *compass lead*. The other end of the pencil will rest in your palm as shown in Figure 5–17.

Step 3. Determine the circle radius by adjusting the distance between your index finger and the pencil point. Now, with the desired approximate radius established, place your index finger on the paper at the proposed center of the circle.

Step 4. With your desired radius established, keep your hand and pencil point in one place while you rotate the paper with your other hand. Try to keep the radius steady as you rotate the paper. Look at Figure 5–18.

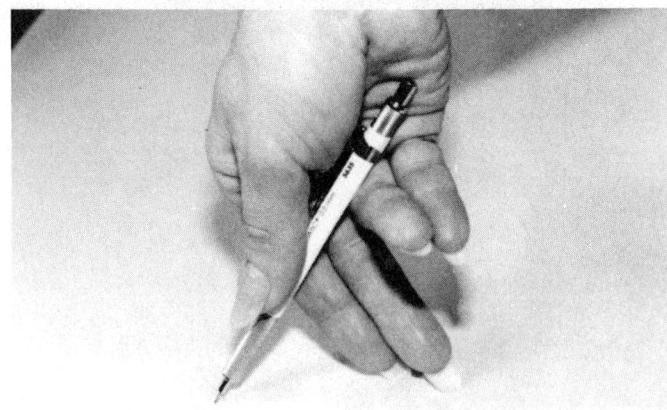

Figure 5–17 Step 2: Hand compass method.

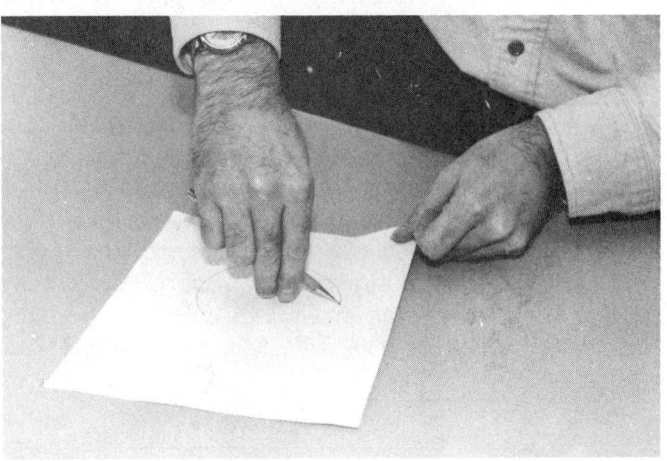

Figure 5–18 Step 4: Hand compass method.

Figure 5–19 Step 5: Hand compass method.

Step 5. You can perform step 4 very lightly and then go back and darken the circle or, if you have had a lot of practice, you may be able to draw a dark circle as you go. See Figure 5–19.

Another method generally used to sketch large circles is to tie a string between a pencil and a pin. The distance between the pencil and pin will be the radius of the circle. Use this method when a large circle is to be sketched since the other methods may not work as well.

◀ MEASUREMENT LINES AND PROPORTIONS

When sketching objects, all the lines which make up the object are related to each other by size and direction. In order for a sketch to communicate accurately and completely, it must be drawn in the same proportion as the object. The actual size of the sketch depends upon the paper size and how large you want the sketch to be. The sketch should be large enough to be clear, but the proportions of the features are more important than the size of the sketch.

Look at the lines in Figure 5–20. How long is line #1? How long is line #2? Answer these questions without measuring either line, but instead relate each line to the other. For example, line 1 could be stated as being half as long as line 2, or line 2 called twice as long as line 1. Now you know how long each line is in relationship to the other (proportion), but we do not know how long either line is in relationship to a measured scale. No scale is used for sketching,

LINE 1 _____

LINE 2 _____

Figure 5–20 Measurement lines.

so this is not a concern. So, whatever line you decide to sketch first will determine the scale of the drawing. This first line sketched is called the *measurement line.* You will relate all the other lines in your sketch to that first line. This is one of the secrets in making a sketch look like the object being sketched.

The second thing you must know about the relationship of the two lines in the above example is their direction and position to each other. For example, do they touch each other, are they parallel, perpendicular, or at some angle to each other? When you look at a line ask yourself the following questions:

(For this example use the two lines given in Figure 5–21.)

1. How long is the second line?
   a. same length as the first line?
   b. shorter than the first line? How much shorter?
   c. longer than the first line? How much longer?
2. In what direction and position is the second line related to the first line?

A typical answer to these questions about the lines in Figure 5–21 would be as follows:

1. The second line is about three times as long as the first line.
2. Line two touches the lower end of line one with about a 90° angle between them.

Carrying this concept a step further, a third line can relate to the first line or the second line and so forth. Again, the first line drawn (measurement line) sets the scale for the whole sketch.

This idea of relationship can also apply to spaces. In Figure 5–22, the location of a table in a room can be determined by space proportions.

A typical verbal location for the table in this floor plan might be as follows: The table is located about one-half the table width from the top of the floor plan or about two table widths from the bottom, and about one table width from the right side or about three table widths from the left side of the floor plan.

Figure 5–21 Measurement line.

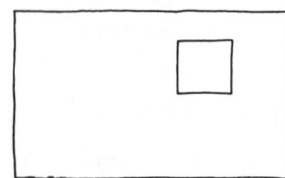

Figure 5–22 Space proportions.

Block Technique

Any illustration of an object can be surrounded overall with a rectangle as shown in Figure 5–23. Before starting a sketch, see the object to be sketched inside a rectangle in your mind's eye. Then use the measurement-line technique with the rectangle, or block, to help you determine the shape and proportions of your sketch.

Procedures in Sketching

Step 1. When starting to sketch an object, try to visualize the object surrounded with a rectangle overall. Sketch this rectangle first with very light lines. Sketch it in the proper proportion with the measurement-line technique, as shown in Figure 5–24.

Step 2. Cut sections out or away using proper proportions as measured by eye. Use light lines as shown in Figure 5–25.

Step 3. Finish the sketch by darkening the desired outlines for the finished sketch. See Figure 5–26.

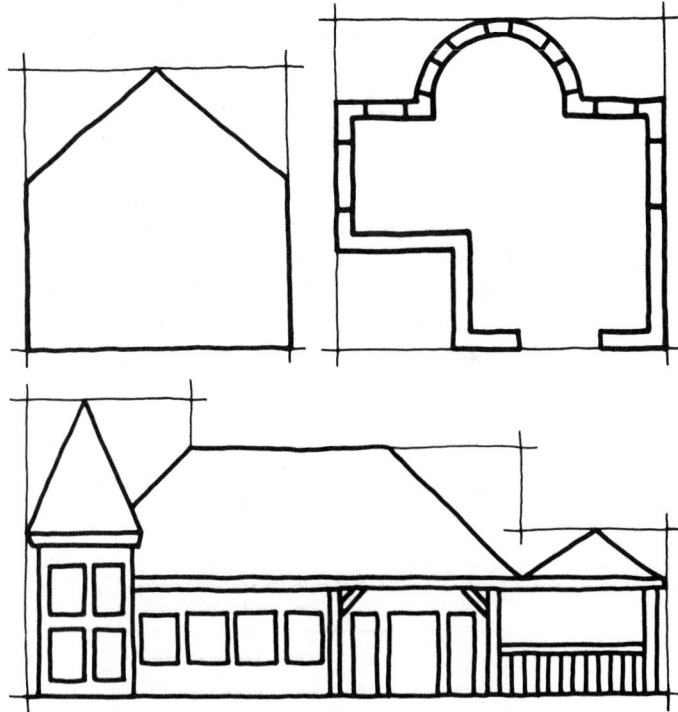

Figure 5–23 Block technique.

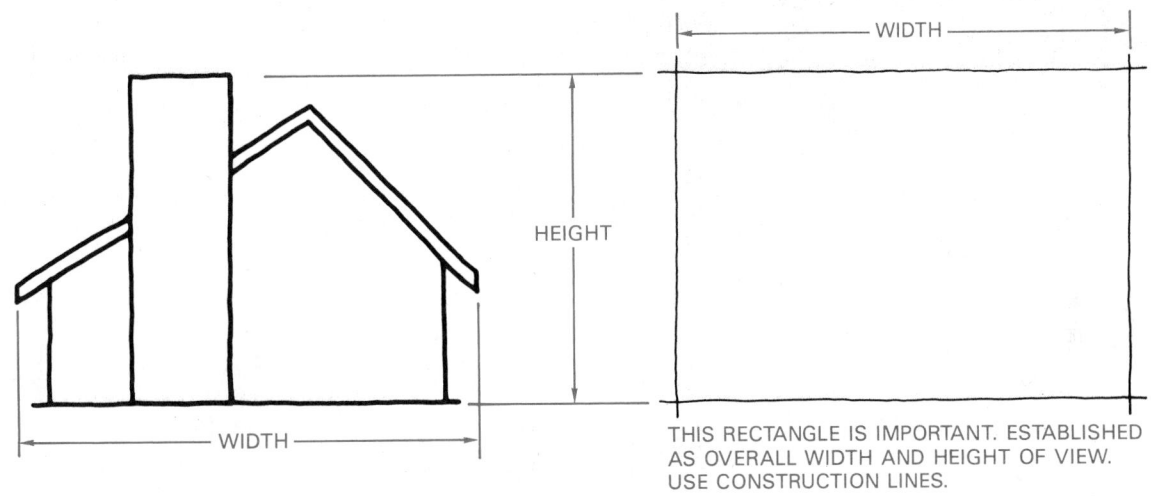

THIS RECTANGLE IS IMPORTANT. ESTABLISHED AS OVERALL WIDTH AND HEIGHT OF VIEW. USE CONSTRUCTION LINES.

Figure 5–24 Step 1: Block technique.

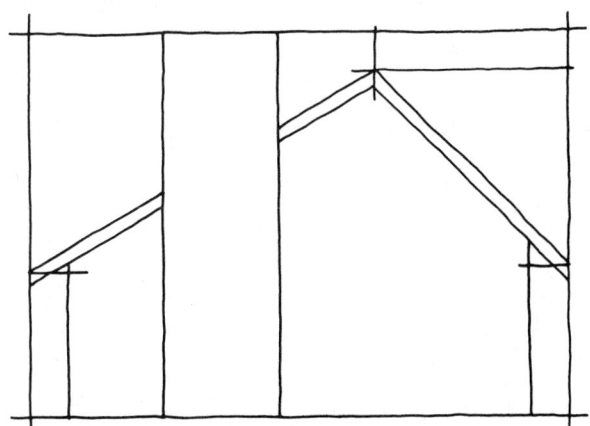

Figure 5–25 Step 2: Block technique.

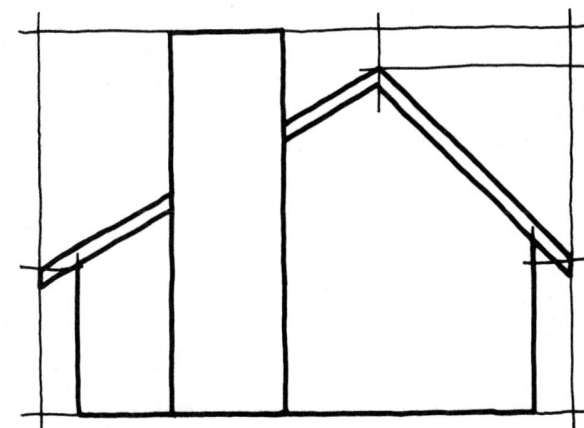

Figure 5–26 Step 3: Block technique.

Irregular Shapes

By using a frame of reference or an extension of the block method, irregular shapes can be sketched easily to their correct proportions. Follow these steps to sketch the freeform swimming pool shown in Figure 5–27.

Step 1.   Place the object in a lightly constructed box. See Figure 5–28.

Step 2.   Next, draw several random or equally spaced horizontal, vertical or diagonal lines that will cross or touch features of the object such as corners, edges, etc. Many drafters prefer the evenly spaced grid method shown in Figure 5–29(a). Figure 5–29(b) shows the random line format. If you are sketching an object already drawn, just draw your reference lines on top of the object lines to establish a frame of reference. If you are sketching an object directly, you will have to visualize these reference lines on the object you sketch.

Step 3.   On your sketch, correctly locate a proportioned box similar to the one established on the original drawing or object, as shown in Figure 5–30.

Step 4.   Using the drawn box as a frame of reference, include the grid or random lines in correct proportion, as seen in Figure 5–31(a) or 5–31(b).

Step 5.   Then, using the grid, sketch the small irregular arcs and lines that match the lines of the original, as in Figure 5–32(a) or 5–32(b).

Step 6.   Darken the outline for a complete proportioned sketch, as shown in Figure 5–33.

Figure 5–27 Freeform swimming pool.

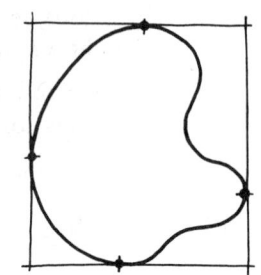

Figure 5–28 Imaginary box.

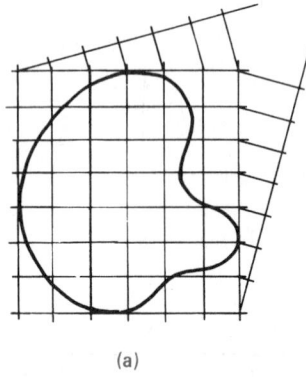

(a)   (b)

Figure 5–29 (a) Evenly spaced grid; (b) random grid.

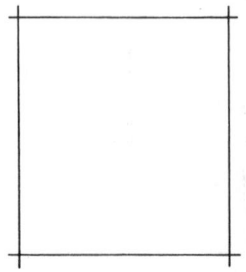

Figure 5–30 Proportioned box.

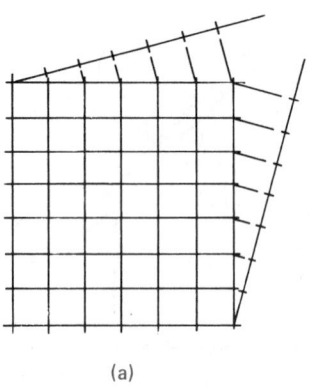 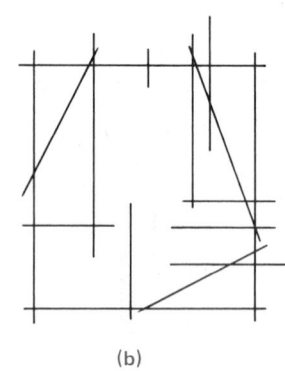

(a)   (b)

Figure 5–31 (a) Regular grid; (b) random grid.

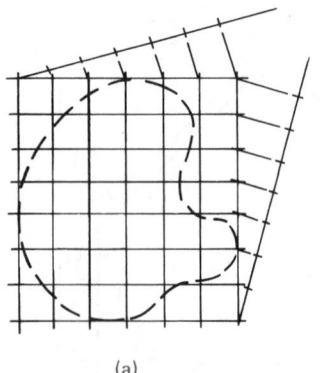 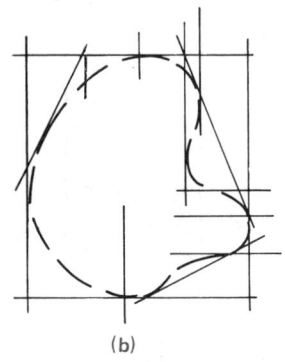

(a)   (b)

Figure 5–32 (a) Sketching the shape using a regular grid; (b) sketching the shape using a random grid.

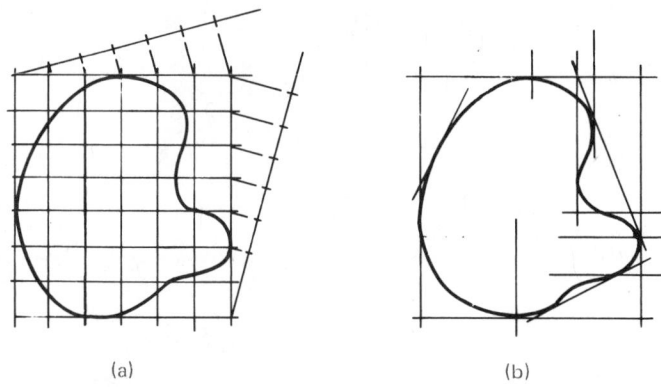

(a)   (b)

Figure 5–33 Completely darken the object.

MULTIVIEW SKETCHES

Multiviews, or multiview projection, is also known as orthographic projection. In architectural drafting such drawings are referred to as elevation views. Elevation views are two-dimensional views of an object (a house, for example) that are established by a line of sight that is perpendicular (90°) to the surface of the object. When making multiview sketches, a systematic order should be followed. Learning to make these multiview sketches will help you later

as you begin to prepare elevation drawings as discussed in Chapter 25.

Multiview Alignment

To keep your drawing in a standard form, sketch the front view in the lower left portion of the paper, the top view directly above the front view, and the right-side view to the right side of the front view. See Figure 5–34. The views needed may differ depending upon the object.

Multiview Sketching Technique

Steps in sketching:

Step 1.   Sketch and align the proportional rectangles for the front, top and right side of the object given in Figure 5–35. Sketch a 45° line to help transfer width dimensions. The 45° line is established by projecting the width from the top view across and the width from the right-side view up until the lines intersect as shown in Figure 5–36.

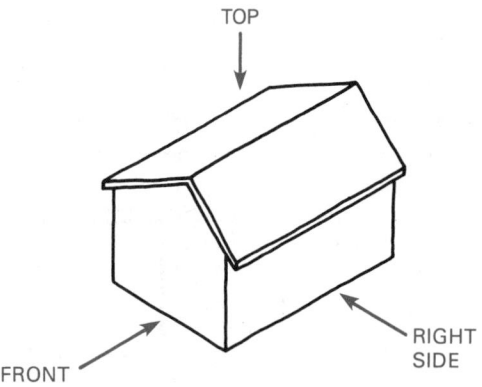

Figure 5–35 Pictorial view.

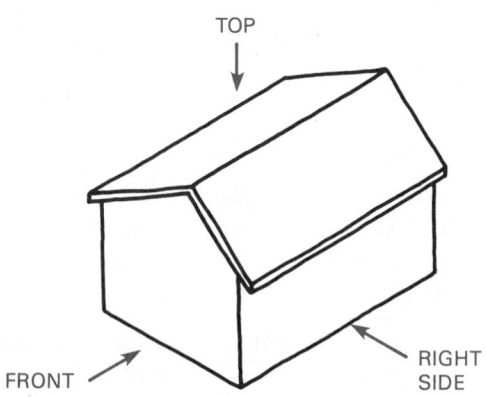

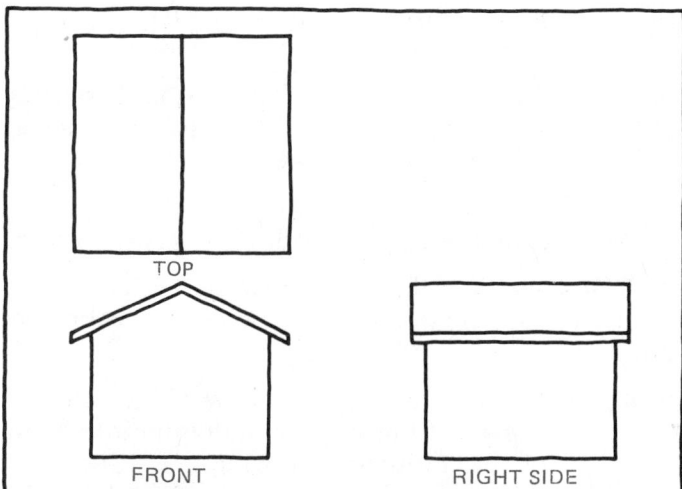

Figure 5–34 Multiviews.

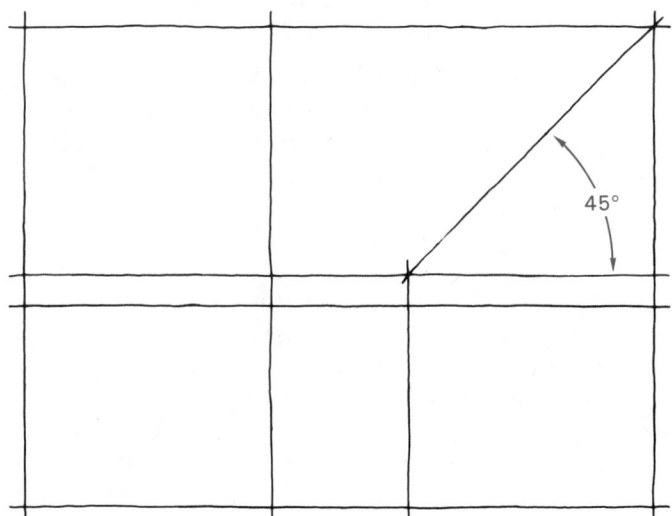

Figure 5–36 Step 1: Block out views and establish a 45° line.

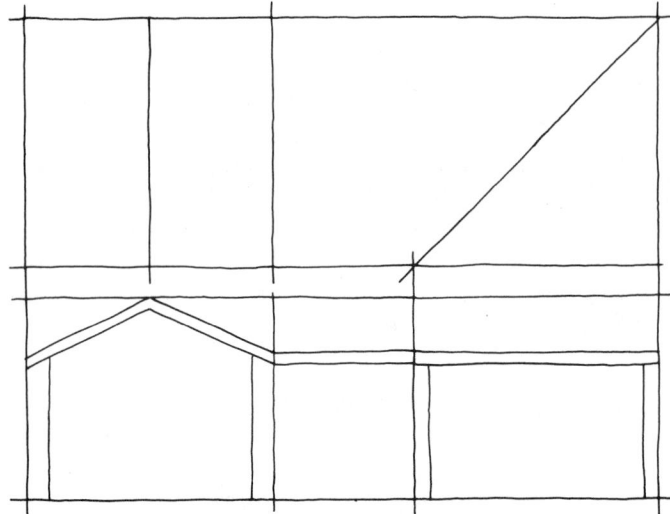

Figure 5-37 Step 2: Block out shapes.

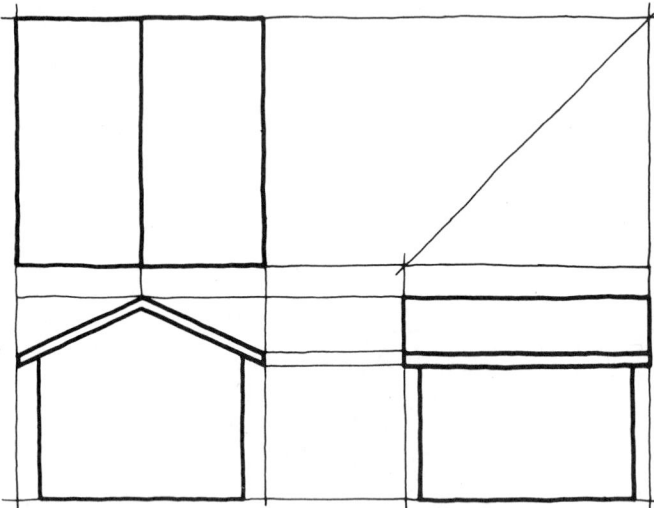

Figure 5-38 Step 3: Darken all object lines.

Step 2.   Complete the shapes within the blocks as shown in Figure 5-37.

Step 3.   Darken the lines of the object as in Figure 5-38. Remember, keep the views aligned for ease of sketching and understanding.

ISOMETRIC SKETCHES

Isometric sketches provide a three-dimensional pictorial representation of an object such as the shape of a building. Isometric sketches are easy to draw and make a fairly realistic exhibit of the object. Isometric sketches tend to represent the objects as they appear to the eye. Isometric sketches help in the visualization of an object because three sides of the object are sketched in a single three-dimensional view.

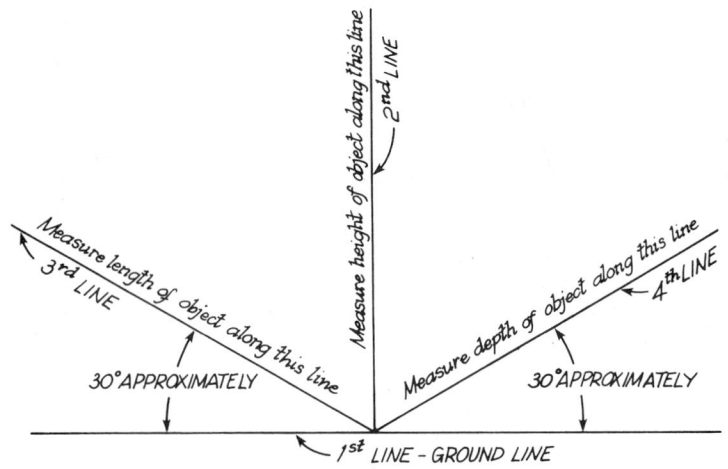

Figure 5-39 Isometric axes.

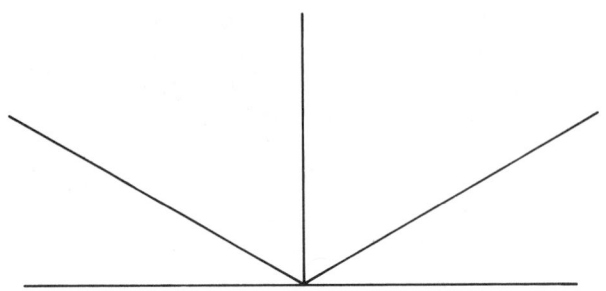

Figure 5-40 Step 3: Isometric axis.

Establishing Isometric Axes

To establish isometric axes, you need four beginning lines: a horizontal reference line, two 30° angular lines, and one vertical line. Draw them as very light construction lines. Look at Figure 5-39.

Step 1.   Sketch a horizontal reference line (consider this the ground-level line).

Step 2.   Sketch a vertical line perpendicular to the ground line somewhere near its center. The vertical line will be used to measure height.

Step 3.   Sketch two 30° angular lines each starting at the intersection of the first two lines as shown in Figure 5-40.

Making an Isometric Sketch

The steps in making an isometric sketch from a multiview drawing or when viewing the real object are as follow:

Step 1.   Select an appropriate view of the object to use as a front view or study the front view of the multiview drawing.

Step 2.   Determine the best position in which to show the object.

Begin your sketch by setting up the isometric axes as just described. See Figure 5–40.

By using the measurement-line technique, draw a rectangular box to correct proportion which could surround the object to be drawn. Use the object shown in Figure 5–41

for this explanation. Imagine the rectangular box in your mind, as in Figure 5–42. Begin to sketch the box by marking off the width at any convenient length (measurement line), as in Figure 5–43. Next estimate and mark the length and height as related to the measurement line. A typical verbal description could be, the length is about one and one-fourth as long as the width. The height is about one and one-half as long as the width. See Figure 5–44. Sketch the three dimensional box by using lines parallel to the original axis lines. See Figure 5–45. Sketching the box is the most critical part of the construction. It must be

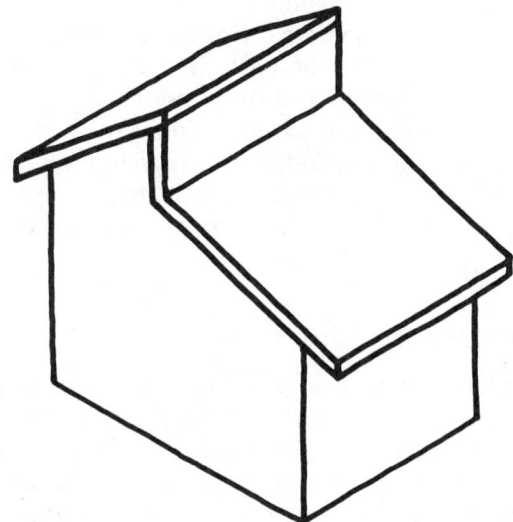

Figure 5–41 Given structure.

Figure 5–42 Step 4: Imagine a box around the structure.

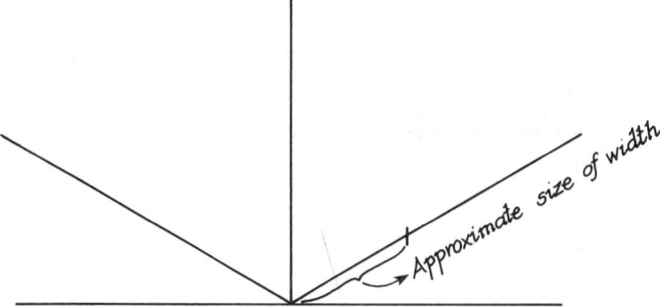

Figure 5–43 Step 4: Lay out the width.

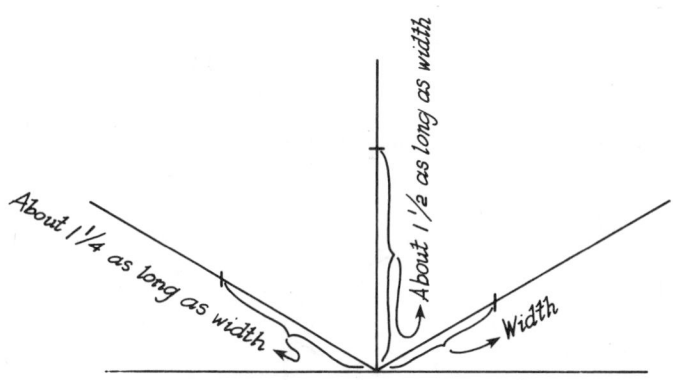

Figure 5–44 Step 4: Lay out the length and height.

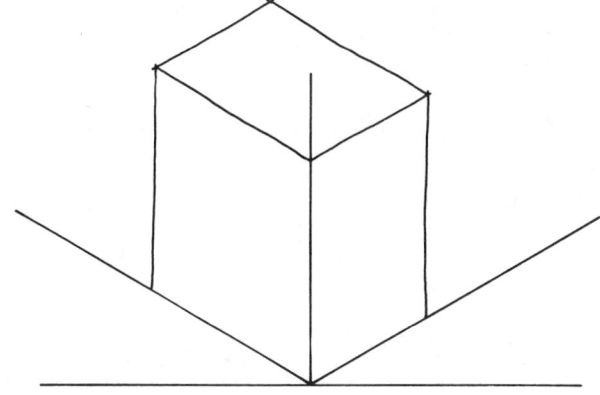

Figure 5–45 Step 4: Sketch the three-dimensional box.

done correctly; otherwise your sketch will be out of proportion. All lines drawn in the same direction must be parallel.

Step 5.   Lightly sketch the features which will define the details of the object. By estimating distances on the rectangular box, the features of the object are easier to sketch in correct proportion than trying to draw them without the box. See Figure 5–46.

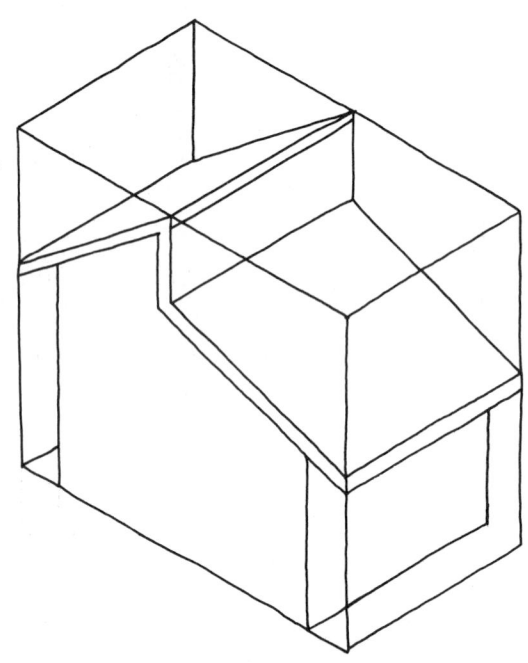

Figure 5–46 Step 5: Sketch features.

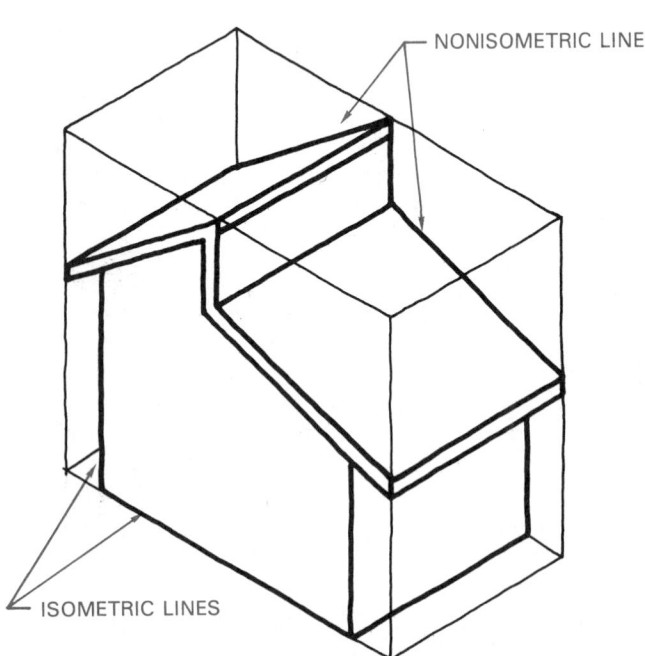

— NONISOMETRIC LINES

ISOMETRIC LINES

Figure 5–47 Step 6: Darken the outlines.

Step 6.   To finish the sketch, darken all the object lines (outlines), as in Figure 5–47. For clarity, do not show any hidden object lines.

Nonisometric Lines

Isometric lines are lines which are on or parallel to the three original axes lines. All other lines are nonisometric lines. Isometric lines can be measured true length. Nonisometric lines appear either longer or shorter than they actually are. See Figure 5–47.

You can measure and draw nonisometric lines by connecting their end points. You can find the end points of the nonisometric lines by measuring along isometric lines. To locate where nonisometric lines should be placed, you have to relate to an isometric line.

Sketching Isometric Circles

Circles and arcs appear as ellipses in isometric views. To sketch isometric circles and arcs correctly, you need to know the relationship between circles and the faces, or planes, of an isometric cube. Depending on which face the circle is to appear, isometric circles look like one of the ellipses shown in Figure 5–48. The angle the ellipse (isometric circle) slants is determined by the surface on which the circle is to be sketched. See Figure 5–48.

Four-Center Method. The four-center method of sketching an isometric ellipse is simple to perform, but care must be taken to form the ellipse arcs properly so the ellipse does not look distorted.

Step 1.   Draw an isometric cube similar to Figure 5–49.

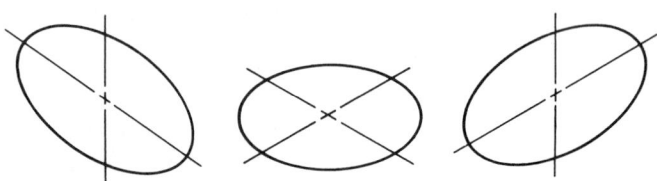

Figure 5–48 Isometric circles.

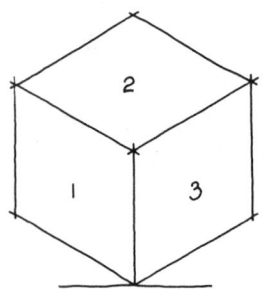

Figure 5–49 Step 1: Isometric cube.

Step 2.   On each surface of the box draw line segments that connect the 120° corners to the centers of the opposite sides. See Figure 5–50.

Step 3.   With points 1 and 2 as the centers, sketch arcs that will begin and end at the centers of the opposite sides on each isometric surface. See Figure 5–51.

Step 4.   On each isometric surface, with points 3 and 4 as the centers, complete the isometric ellipses by sketching arcs that will meet the arcs sketched in step 3. See Figure 5–52.

The four-center method is fast, but care should be taken to keep the isometric ellipses from looking like the examples in Figure 5–53.

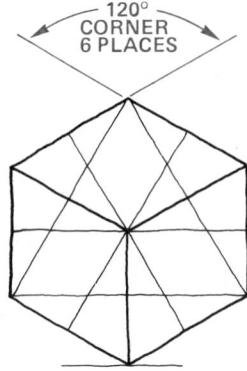

Figure 5–50 Step 2: Four-center isometric ellipse construction.

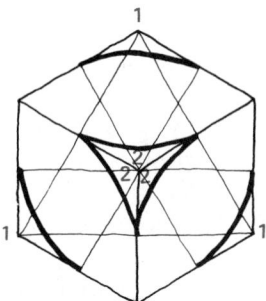

Figure 5–51 Step 3: Sketch arcs from points 1 and 2.

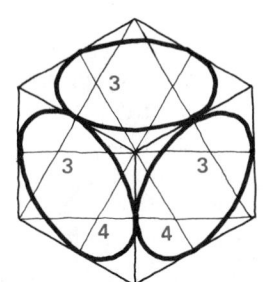

Figure 5–52 Step 4: Sketch arcs from points 3 and 4.

Figure 5–53 Poorly sketched isometric ellipses.

Sketching Isometric Arcs

Sketching isometric arcs is similar to sketching isometric circles. First, block out the overall configuration of the object, then establish the centers of the arcs. Finally, sketch the arc shapes. Remember that isometric arcs, just as isometric circles, must lie in the proper plane and have the correct shape.

ORTHOGRAPHIC PROJECTION

Orthographic projection is any projection of features of an object onto an imaginary plane called a plane of projection. The projection of the features of the object is made by lines of sight that are perpendicular to the plane of projection. When a surface of the object is parallel to the plane of projection, the surface will appear in its true size and shape on that plane. In Figure 5–54, the plane of projection is parallel to the surface of the object. The line of sight (projection from the object) from the object is perpendicular to

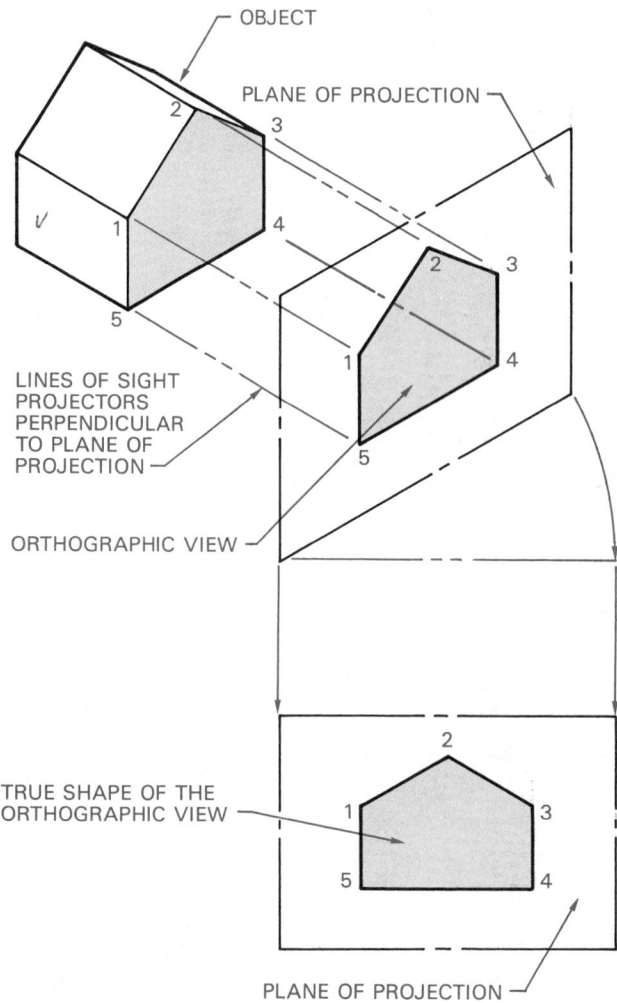

Figure 5–54 Orthographic projection to form orthographic view.

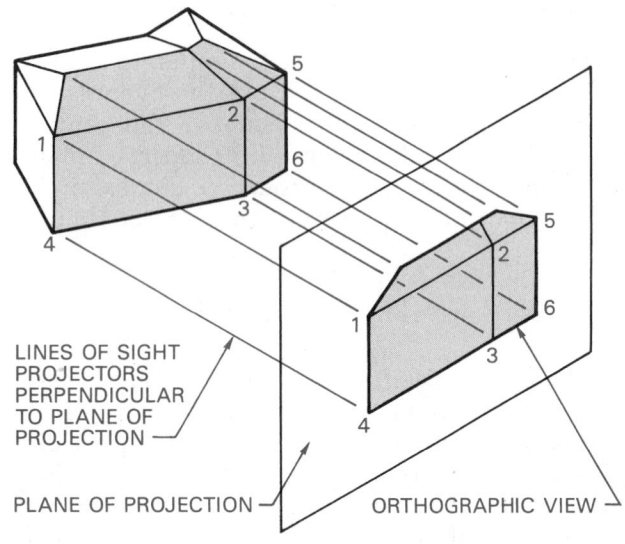

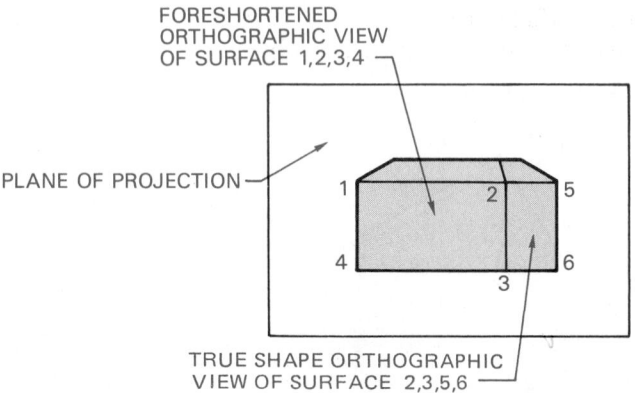

Figure 5–55 Projection of a foreshortened orthographic surface.

the plane of projection. Notice also that the object appears three dimensional (width, depth, and height) while the view on the plane of projection is two dimensional (width and height). In situations where the plane of projection is not parallel to the surface of the object, the resulting orthographic view is foreshortened, or shorter than the true length. See Figure 5–55.

MULTIVIEW PROJECTION

Multiview projection establishes two or more views of an object as projected upon two or more planes of projection by using orthographic projection techniques. The result of multiview projection is a multiview drawing. Multiview drawings represent the shape of an object using two or more views. Consideration should be given to the choice and number of views so, when possible, the surfaces of the object are shown in their true size and shape.

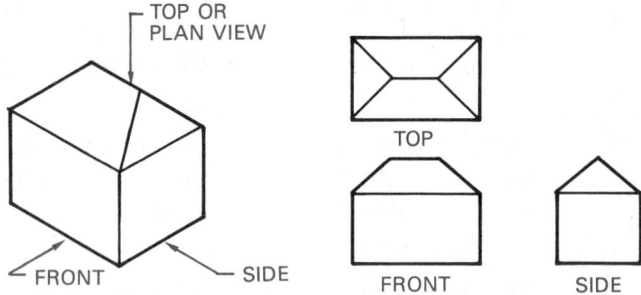

Figure 5–56 Comparison of a pictorial and multiview.

Elevations are Multiviews

It is often easier for an individual to visualize a three-dimensional drawing of a structure than it is to visualize a two-dimensional drawing. In architectural drafting, however, it is more common to prepare construction drawings that show two-dimensional exterior views of a structure that provide representations of exterior materials. These drawings are referred to as elevations. The method used to draw elevations is known as multiview projection. A more detailed discussion of elevation drawing is found in Chapters 24 and 25. Figure 5–56 shows an object represented by a three-dimensional drawing, called a pictorial drawing, and three two-dimensional views, or multiviews, also known as orthographic projection. This method of drafting will represent the shape description of the object.

Glass Box

If we place the object in Figure 5–56 in a glass box so that the sides of the box are parallel to the major surfaces of the object, we can project the surfaces of the object onto the sides of the glass box and create multiviews, Figure 5–57. Imagine the sides of the glass box are the planes of projection previously described. Look at Figure 5–58. If we look at all sides of the glass box, we will see six views: front, top, right side, left side, bottom and rear. Now let's unfold the glass box as if the corners were hinged about the front view (except the rear view which is attached to the left-side view) as demonstrated in Figure 5–59. These hinge lines are commonly called fold lines.

Completely unfold the glass box onto a flat surface and you have the six views of an object represented in multiview. Figure 5–60 shows the glass box unfolded. Notice also that the views are labeled, front, top, right side, left side, rear, and bottom. It is in this arrangement that the views will always be found when using multiviews. Analyze Figure 5–60 in detail so you see the features that are common between views. Knowing how to identify the features of an object that are common between views will aid you later in the visualization of elevations.

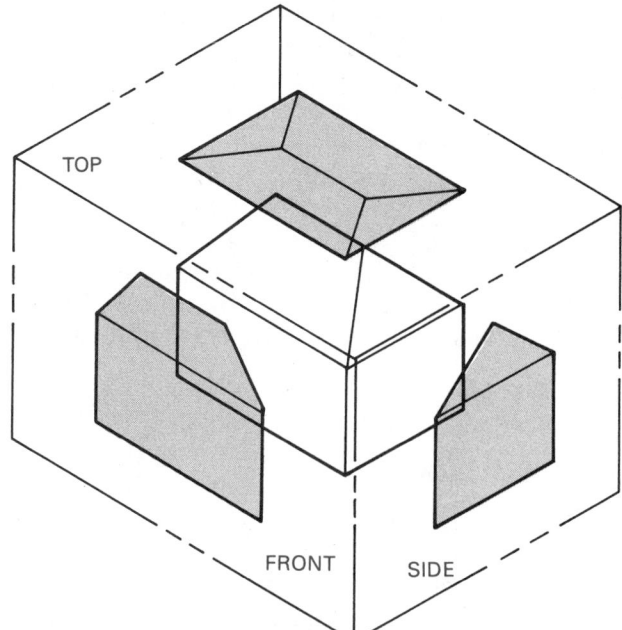

Figure 5-57 Glass box.

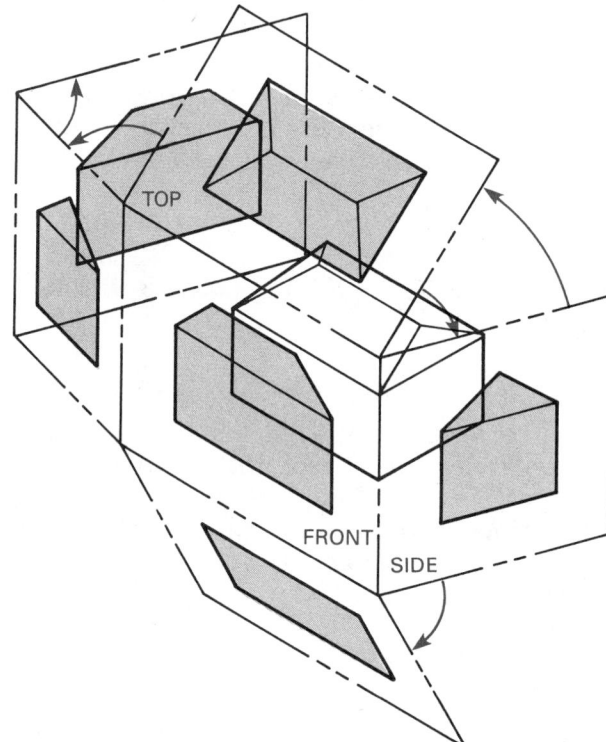

Figure 5-58 Unfolding the glass box at hinge lines, also called fold lines.

Notice how the views are aligned. The top view is directly above and the bottom view is directly below the front view. The left side is directly to the left while the right side is directly to the right of the front view. This alignment allows the drafter to project features directly from one view to the next to help establish each view.

Now, look closely at the relationship between the front, top, and right-side views. A similar relationship exists using the left-side view. Figure 5–61 shows a 45° projection line established by projecting the fold, or reference line (hinge), between the front and side view up and the fold line between the front and top view over. All of the features established on the top view can be projected to the 45° line and then down onto the side view. This is possible because the depth dimension is seen in both the top and side views. The reverse is also true. Features from the side view may be projected to the 45° line and then over to the top view.

The transfer of features achieved in Figure 5–61 using the 45° line can also be accomplished by using

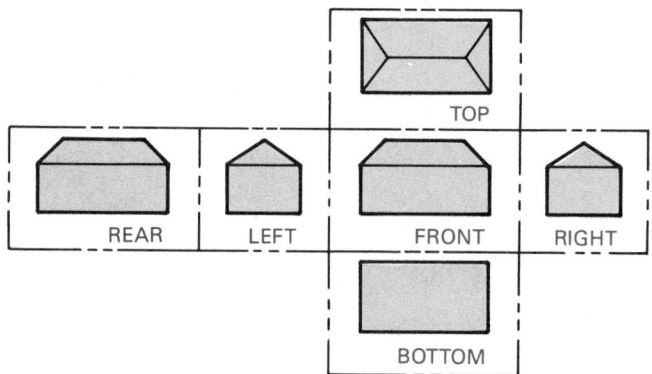

Figure 5-59 Glass box unfolded.

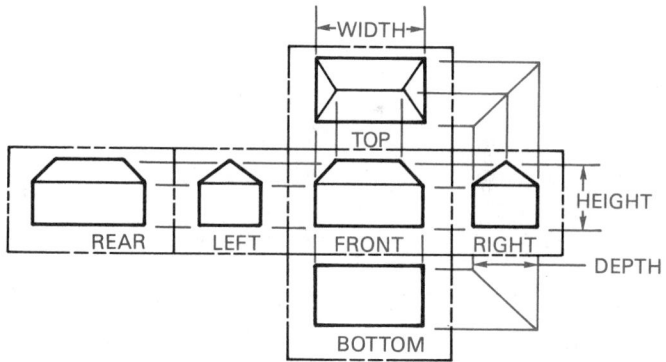

Figure 5-60 View alignment.

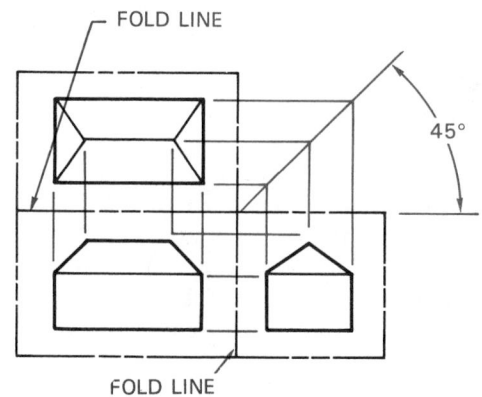

Figure 5-61 Establishing a 45° projection line.

72   Architectural Drafting and Design

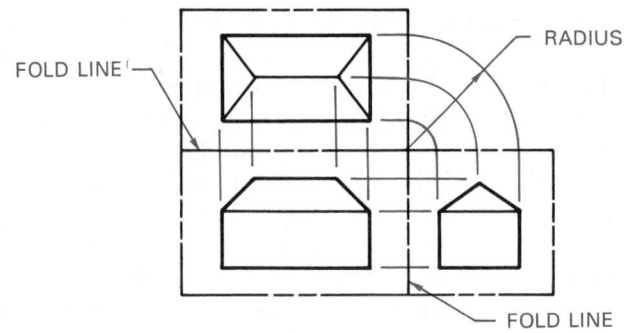

Figure 5-62 Projection with a compass.

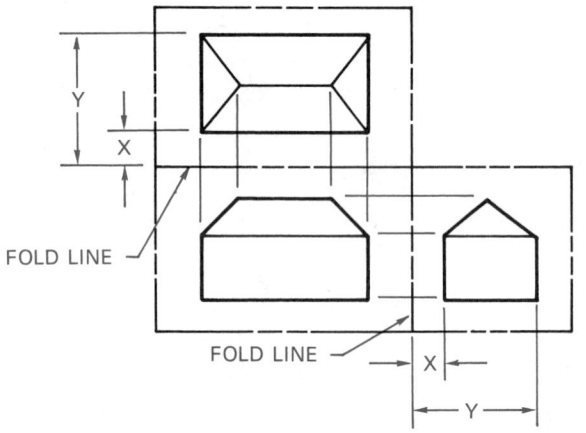

Figure 5-63 Using dividers to transfer view projections.

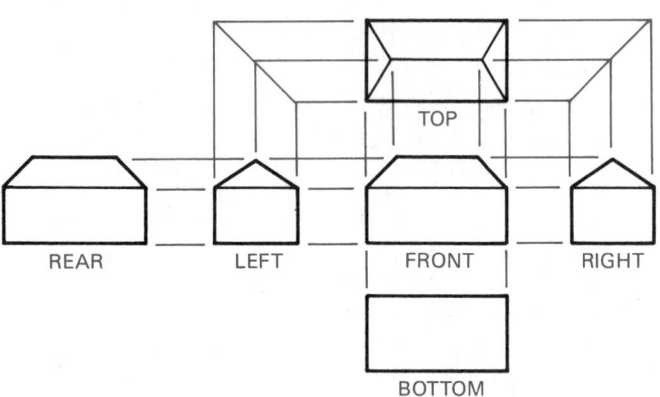

Figure 5-64 Multiview orientation.

a compass with one leg at the intersection of the horizontal and vertical fold lines. The compass will establish the common relationship between the top and side views as shown in Figure 5-62.

Another method that is commonly used to transfer the size of features from one view to the next is the use of dividers to transfer distances from the fold line at the top view to the fold line at the side view.

The relationship between the fold lines and the two views is the same as shown in Figure 5-63.

The front view is usually the most important view since it is the one from which the other views are established. There is always one dimension common between adjacent views. For example, the width is common between the front and top views and the height between the front and side views. This knowledge will allow you to relate information from one view to another. Take one more look at the relationship between the six views as shown in Figure 5-64.

View Selection

There are six primary views that you may select to completely describe a structure. In architectural drafting the front, left side, right side, and rear views are used as elevations to describe the exterior appearance of a structure completely. Elevation drawings are discussed in more detail in Chapters 24 and 25. The top view is called the roof plan view. This view shows the roof of the structure and provides construction information and dimensions. Roof plans are discussed in more detail in Chapters 33 and 34. The bottom view is often used in mechanical drafting but never used in architectural drafting.

PROJECTION OF FEATURES FROM AN INCLINED PLANE

Rectangular Features on an Inclined Plane

When a rectangular feature such as a skylight projects out of a sloped roof, the intersection of the skylight with the roof appears as a line when the roof also appears as a line. This intersection location may then be projected onto adjacent views as shown in Figure 5-65.

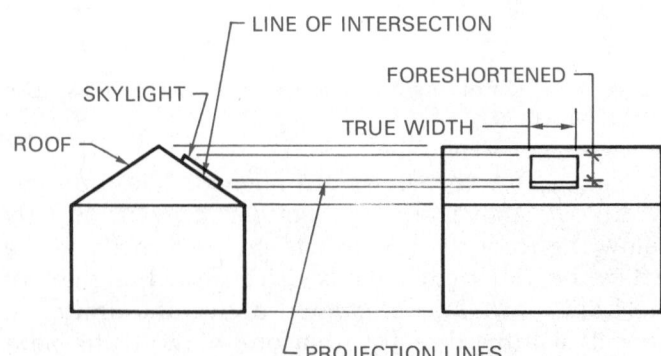

Figure 5-65 Rectangular features on an inclined plane.

Circles on an Inclined Plane

When the line of sight in a view is perpendicular to a circle, such as a round window, the window appears round as shown in Figure 5–66. When a circle is projected onto an inclined surface, such as a round skylight projected onto a sloped roof, the view of the inclined circle is elliptical. See Figure 5–67.

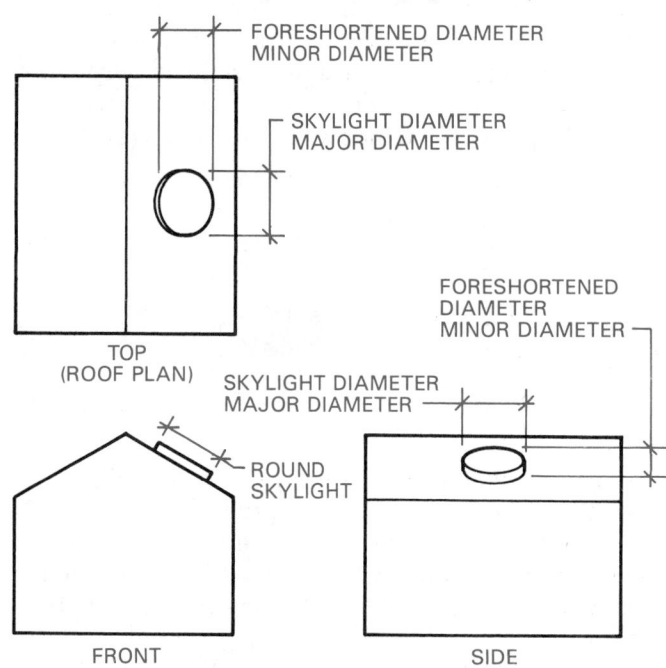

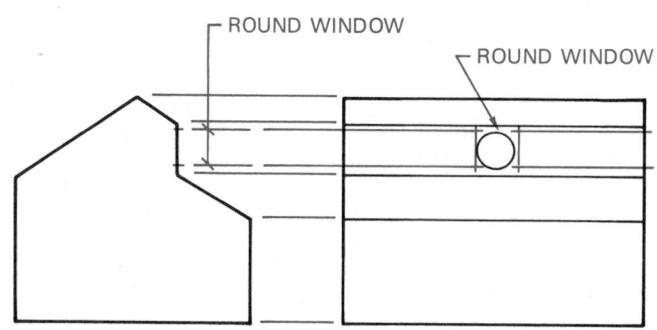

Figure 5–66 Round window is a circle when the line of sight is perpendicular.

Figure 5–67 Circle projected onto an inclined surface appears as an ellipse.

SKETCHING AND ORTHOGRAPHIC PROJECTION TEST

DIRECTIONS

Answer the questions with short, complete statements or drawings as needed on 8½ × 11 vellum as follows:

1. Use ⅛ in. wide guidelines for all lettering.
2. Letter your name, Sketching and Orthographic Projection Test, and the date at the top of the sheet.
3. Letter the question number and provide the answer. You do not need to write out the question.
4. Do all lettering with vertical, single-stroke architectural letters. If the answer requires line work, use proper sketching techniques. Answers may be prepared on a word processor if appropriate with course guidelines.
5. Your grade will be based on correct answers and quality of line technique.

QUESTIONS

1. Define sketching.
2. How are sketches useful as related to computer graphics?
3. Describe the proper sketching tools.
4. Should the paper be taped to the drafting board or table when sketching? Why?
5. What kind of problem can occur if a long straight line is drawn without moving the hand?
6. What type of paper should be used for sketching?
7. Name the two methods that can be used to sketch irregular shapes.
8. Define an isometric sketch.
9. What is the difference between an isometric line and a nonisometric line?
10. What do the use of proportions have to do with sketching techniques?
11. Define orthographic projection.
12. What is the relationship between the orthographic plane of projection and the projection lines from the object or structure?
13. When is a surface foreshortened in an orthographic view?
14. How many principal multiviews of an object are possible?
15. Give at least two reasons why the multiviews of an object are aligned in a specific format.
16. In architectural drafting, what are the exterior front, right side, left side, and rear views also called?

17. If a round window appears as a line in the front view and the line of sight is perpendicular to the window in the side view, what shape is the window in the side view?

18. If a round skylight is positioned on a 5/12 roof slope and appears as a line in the front view, what shape will the skylight be in the side view?

SKETCHING AND ORTHOGRAPHIC PROJECTION PROBLEMS

DIRECTIONS

Use proper sketching materials and techniques to solve the following sketching problems, on 8½″ × 11″ bond paper or newsprint. Use very lightly sketched construction lines for all layout work. Darken the lines of the object but do not erase the layout lines.

Problem 5–1 Sketch the front view of your home or any local single family residence using the block technique. Use the measurement line method to approximate proper proportions.

Problem 5–2 Use the box method to sketch a circle with an approximate 4 in. diameter. Sketch the same circle using the trammel and hand compass methods.

Problem 5–3 Find an object with irregular shapes, such as a French (irregular) curve, and sketch a two dimensional view using either the regular or random grid method. Sketch the object to correct proportions without measuring.

Problem 5–4 Use the same structure you used for Problem 5–1, or a different structure, to prepare an isometric sketch.

Problem 5–5 Use the same structure you used for Problem 5–4 to sketch a front and right-side view.

Problem 5–6 Use a scale of ¼″ = 1′-0″ to draw a 38° acute angle with one side horizontal and both sides 8′-6″ long.

Chapter 6
Systems Drafting

SYSTEMS DRAFTING is a general term that is frequently used to identify a group of drafting techniques and processes that are designed to save drafting time, improve productivity, and improve drawing control. Systems drafting is not necessarily computer aided drafting although CAD may be used as a tool for most systems drafting procedures. Systems drafting includes such techniques as paste-up drafting, scissors drafting, opaquing, restoration, photodrafting, overlay drafting, or the use of duplicated repetitive elements.

There are a number of advantages to using systems drafting techniques. The biggest advantage is saving time. Estimates on time savings have been reported from 30 to 90 percent depending upon the technique used and the task performed. These short cut methods do not reduce drawing quality; on the contrary, drawing quality is generally improved. The concept of systems drafting techniques is to reduce the need to redraw repetitious features and thus release drafting time for creative work. Systems drafting methods often use ink on Mylar® although pencil on vellum is used for some applications. Photographic techniques are commonly used to increase the flexibility of systems drafting. Even companies that do not have photographic capabilities can call on independent specialists to handle the task or use some of the many photographic materials that are available that do not require special facilities. There are even certain systems drafting methods that can be performed using the diazo or photocopy reproduction processes. Special diazo materials are available, including sepias, that make many applications possible at a substantial cost reduction over photographic methods.

PASTE-UP DRAFTING

Paste-up drafting is a time saving process that may be used when an existing drawing is to be changed, added to, or substantially rearranged. The idea with any systems drafting technique is to use drawings or views that already exist so that valuable drafting time may be used to make original documents. The procedure for paste-up drafting is as follows:

Step 1. An existing drawing is photographed and a clear film reproduction is made. See Figure 6–1.

Step 2. The desired elements are cut from the clear film reproduction and then taped onto a new drawing sheet in the place desired. Transparent tape is used. See Figure 6–2.

Step 3. This new drawing sheet with the elements taped down is then photographed. The end result is a new smooth drawing on Mylar® where all tape marks and other unwanted elements have been eliminated. See Figure 6–3.

Step 4. The photo Mylar® is now the new drawing and is ready for drawing additional information such as more views, details, dimensions, or notes, if any.

The result is a new drawing without spending very much drafting time. With the use of photo materials that may be processed in normally lighted working conditions and with common diazo reproduction machines, the need for elaborate darkrooms and photo processing equipment is not necessary. Check with vendors such as Kodak and Fuji for specific details and instructions.

SCISSORS DRAFTING

Scissors drafting allows you to avoid redrawing any portion of a drawing that already exists. This technique may be used when a portion of an existing drawing is to be removed, when an existing drawing requires reformatting, or when parts of one or more existing drawings are to be combined into a new drawing with or without additional drawing changes.

One example of scissors drafting would be when a company has changed the general format of its drawing sheets by using a new title block and border line design. The company would like to update all its existing drawings by changing them to the new sheet format. The process is easy using scissors drafting as follows:

Step 1. Tape the new format drawing sheet onto a thick paperboard sheet mounted on the drafting table.

Step 2. Tape the existing drawing sheet in the desired location over the new sheet.

Step 3. Use a sharp knife or single-edge razor blade

to cut through both the existing drawing and the new format drawing sheet at the same time. Try to cut rectangular areas using a straightedge rather than cut freehand or on a curve. See Figure 6–4.

Step 4. Remove the unwanted border from the existing drawing and remove the blank area cut from the new sheet. This will leave a *window* in the new sheet that the cut portion of the existing drawing will fit exactly. See Figure 6–5.

Step 5. With a few pieces of drafting tape, carefully tape the existing drawing into the window of the new sheet. Only a few pieces of tape placed in several spots around the cut are necessary to hold the existing drawing in the window temporarily. See Figure 6–6.

Step 6. Remove from the drawing board the new format sheet with the taped-in existing drawing and turn over this composite piece (old element and new format) on the drawing table.

Step 7. On the back side of the sheet, use transparent tape to carefully tape the seam between the new format and the existing drawing. Do not allow the tape to overlap at corners.

Step 8. After taping the seams, turn the composite face up. Remove the pieces of drafting tape from the front.

Step 9. Complete the new drawing title block and add additional notes, dimensions, or details if needed. See Figure 6–7.

Step 10. The new drawing is ready to print. If using diazo reproduction, run the machine at a speed that will burn out any tape shadow without burning out wanted information.

The same scissors drafting methods can be used to reformat parts from different existing drawings using the originals or sepias if the originals must remain intact. Some companies use scissors drafting in a manner that is similar to paste-up drafting where copies of the desired drawing components are cut out and pasted or taped together to form a new drawing layout. This new layout is then photographed and a composite on Mylar® is ready for additional drafting or other use. A combination of scissors and paste-up drafting and the photocopying process can be used to create a new drawing by merging information and views from existing drawings as shown in Figure 6–8.

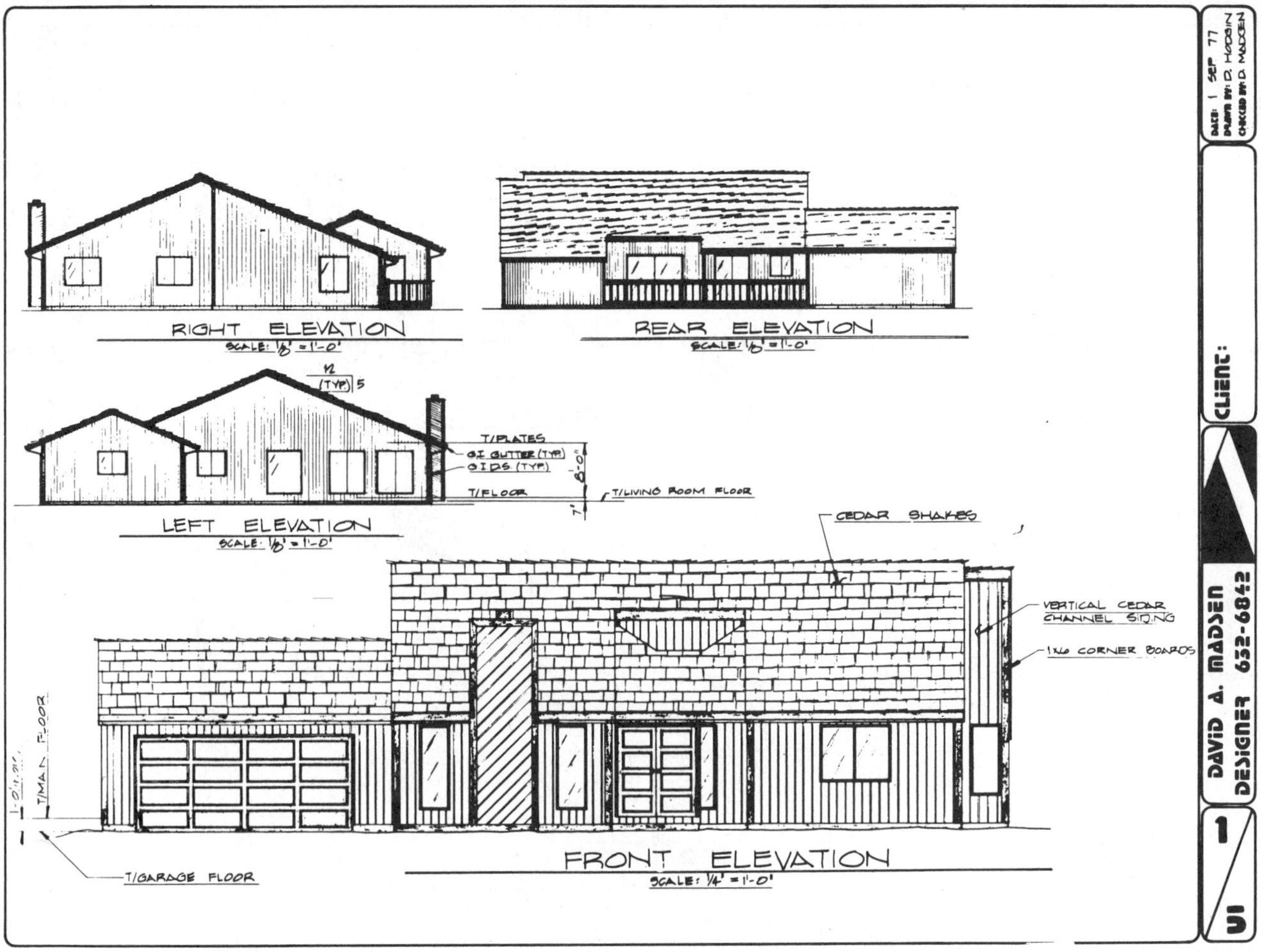

Figure 6–1 Paste-up; clear film reproduction of an existing drawing.

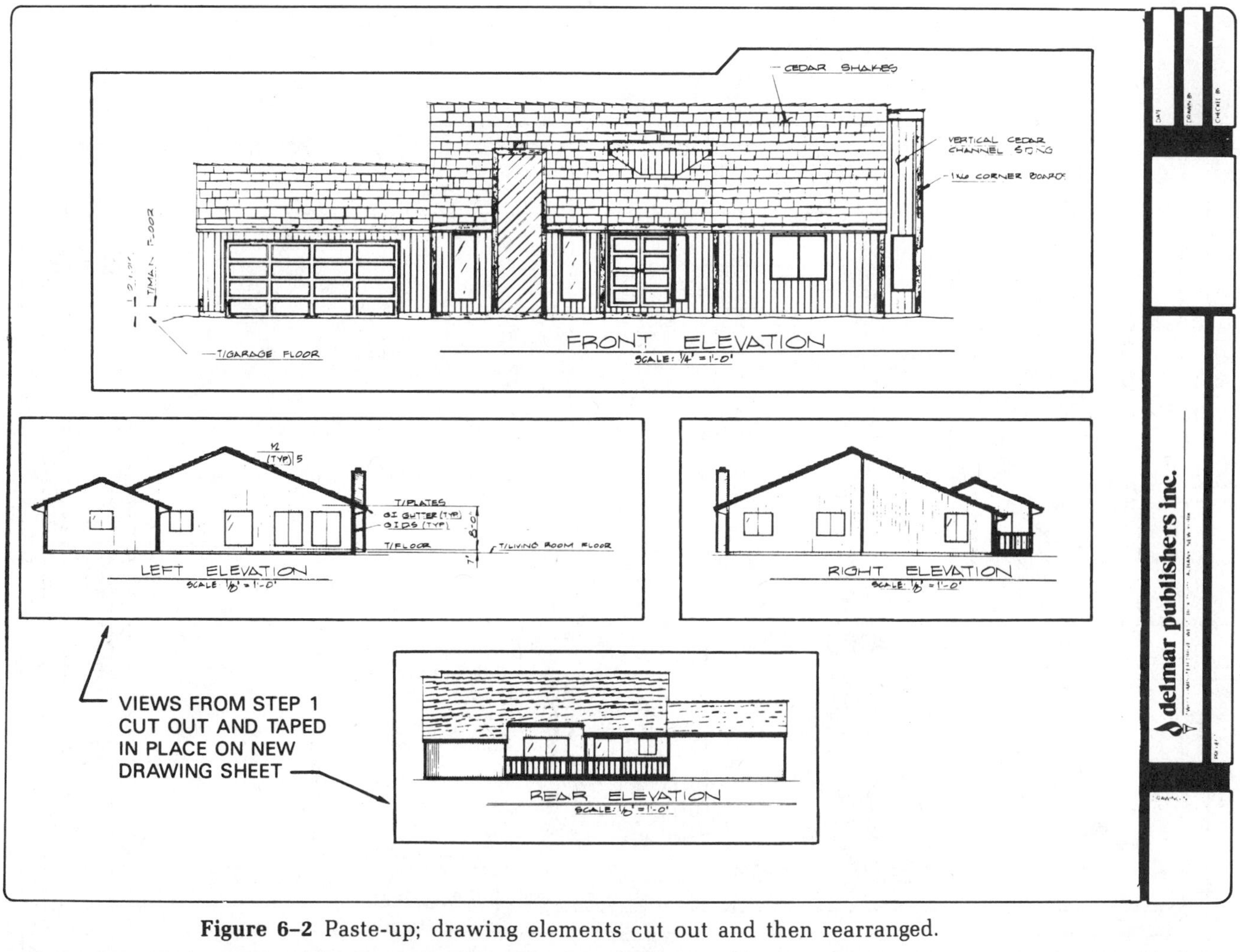

VIEWS FROM STEP 1
CUT OUT AND TAPED
IN PLACE ON NEW
DRAWING SHEET

Figure 6–2 Paste-up; drawing elements cut out and then rearranged.

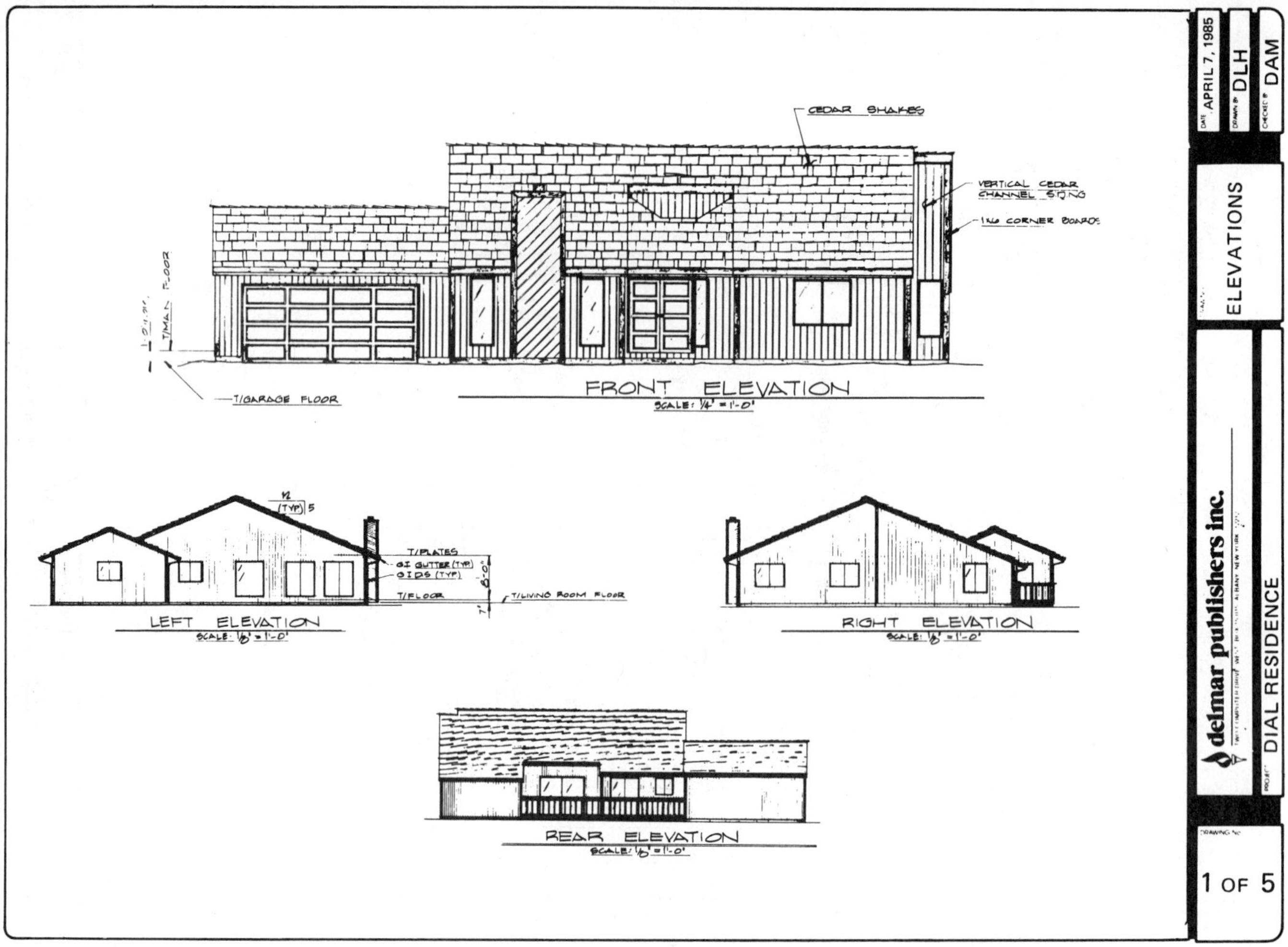

Figure 6–3 Paste-up; new sheet format photographed on Mylar® and ready for use.

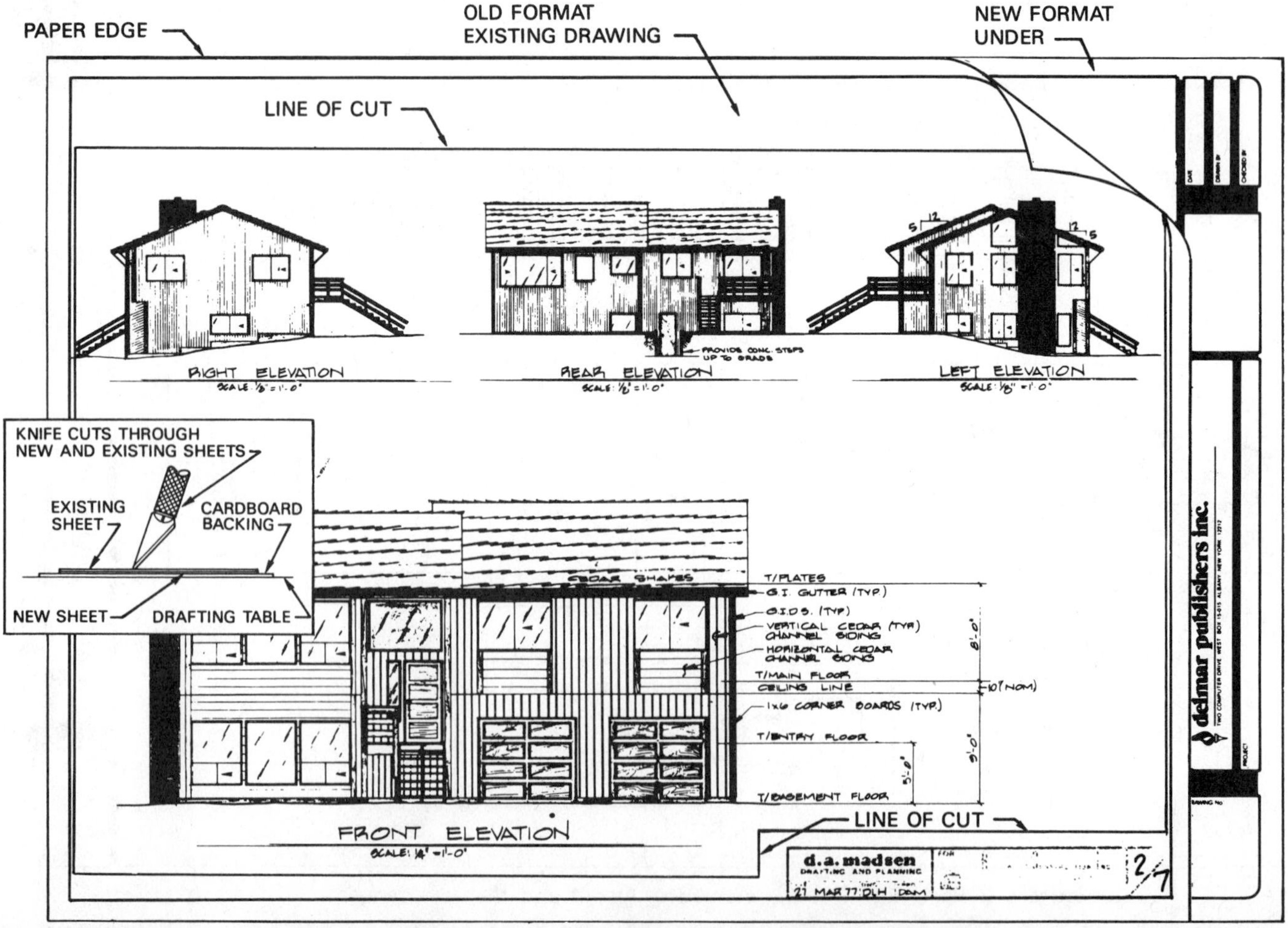

Figure 6–4 Scissors drafting; cutting out blocks of a drawing.

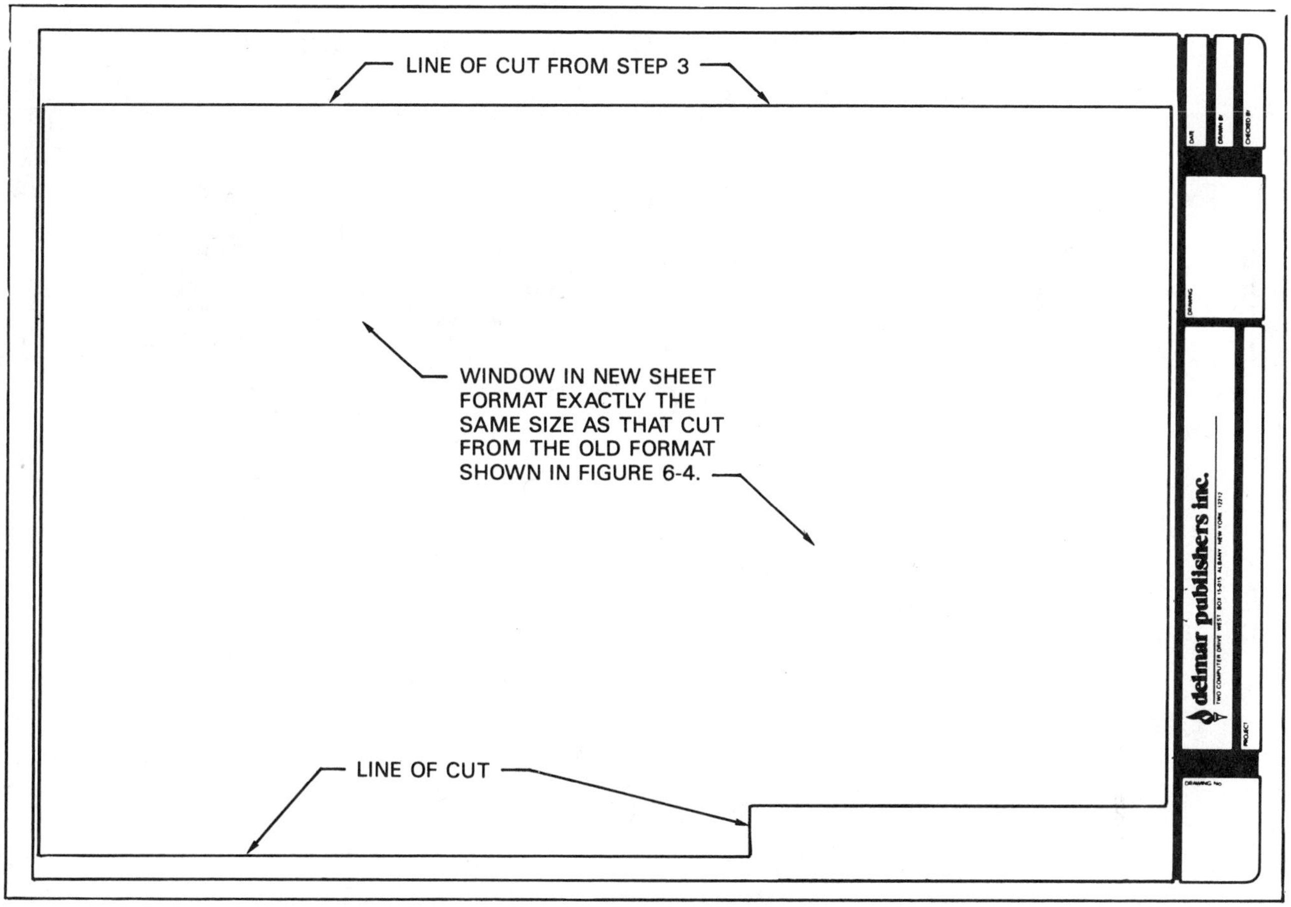

Figure 6–5 Scissors drafting; window cut in the new sheet.

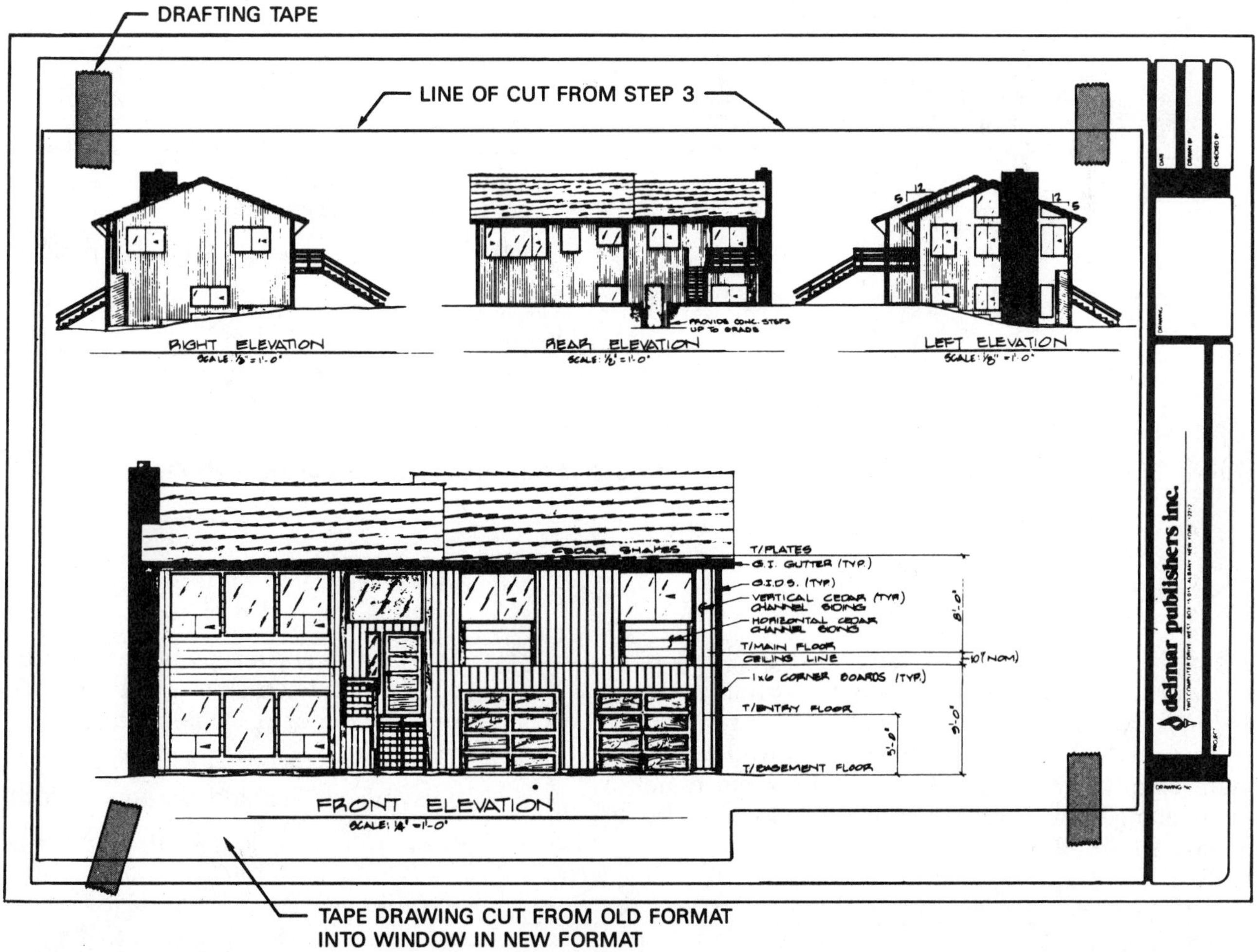

Figure 6–6 Temporarily tape the existing drawing that had been cut in the window of the new sheet.

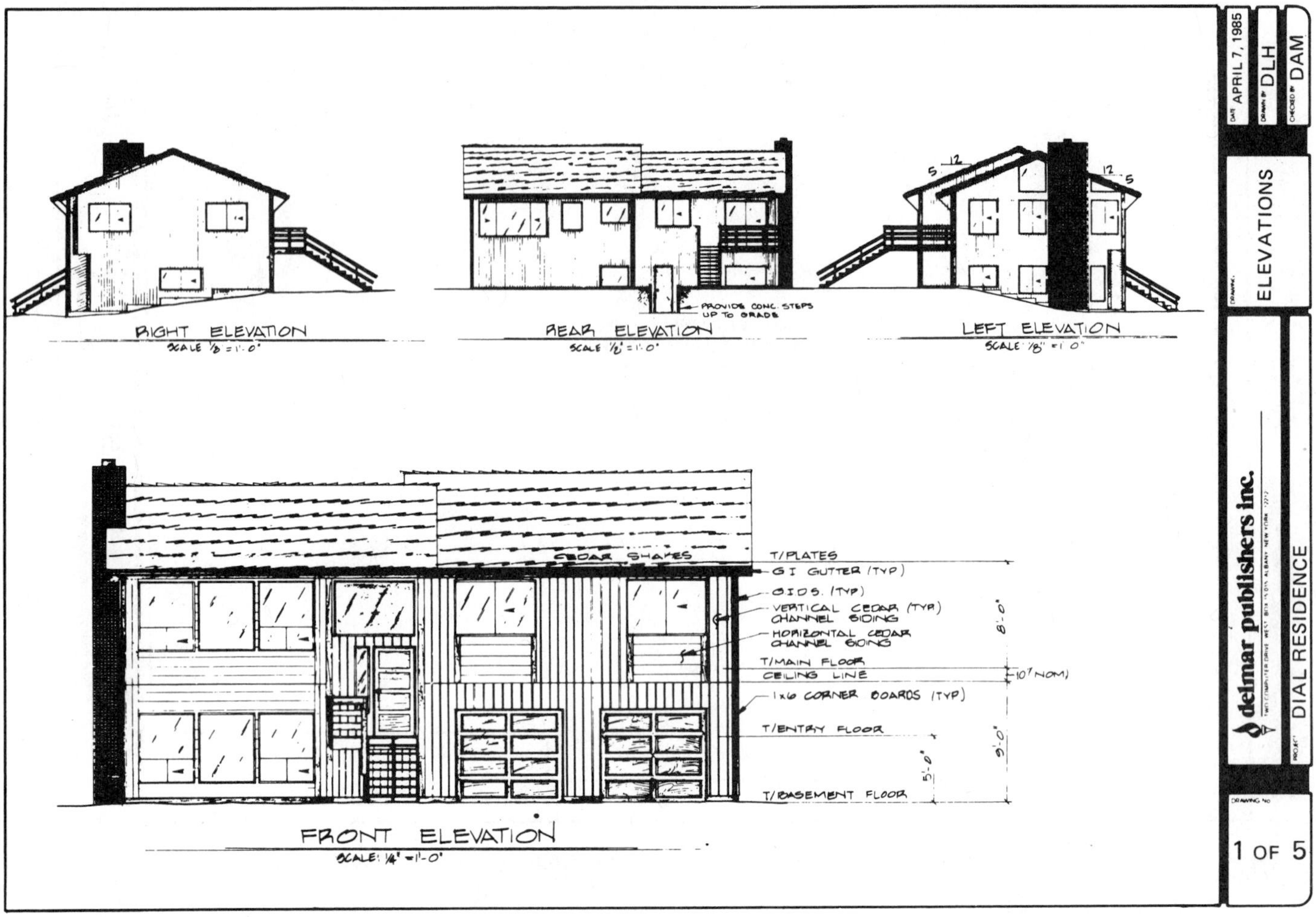

Figure 6-7 Complete new drawing.

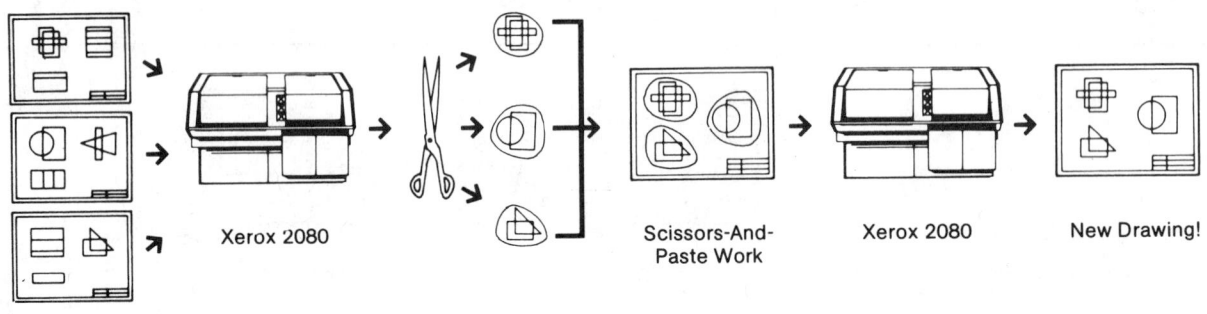

Existing Drawings

Figure 6-8 Create a new drawing by merging information and views from existing drawings. *Courtesy Xerox Corporation.*

MASKING

Masking is a systems drafting technique that may be used when only a relatively small portion of an existing drawing must be removed. This may occur, for example, when a floor plan or elevation will remain essentially the same except for some minor design changes or alternatives. The following procedure works well with sepia reproduction materials:

Step 1.   Make a reverse Mylar® sepia copy of the existing original drawing.

Step 2.   On the new sepia copy use eradicating fluid on the emulsion side of the sepia sheet to remove the area to be changed.

Step 3.   Turn the Mylar® sheet over and on the drawing surface add the new information.

Step 4.   Now you have a new drawing ready for

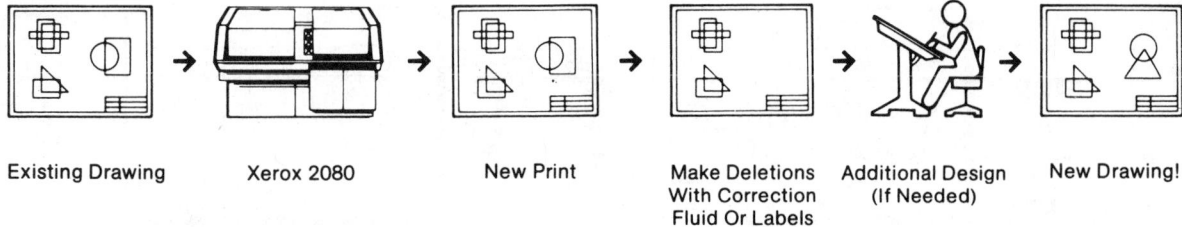

Figure 6–9 Making drawing deletions by masking unwanted information with correction fluid. *Courtesy Xerox Corporation.*

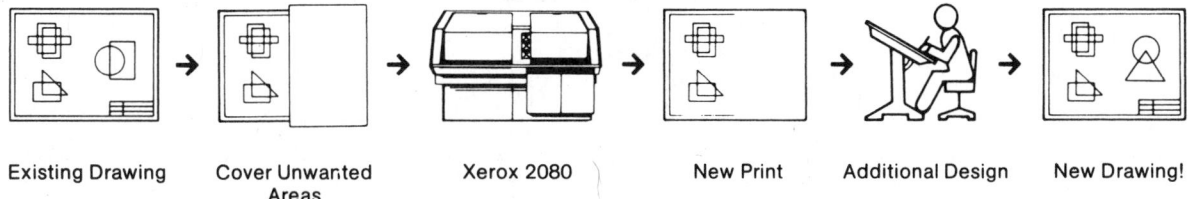

Figure 6–10 Deleting large areas using paper masking techniques. *Courtesy Xerox Corporation.*

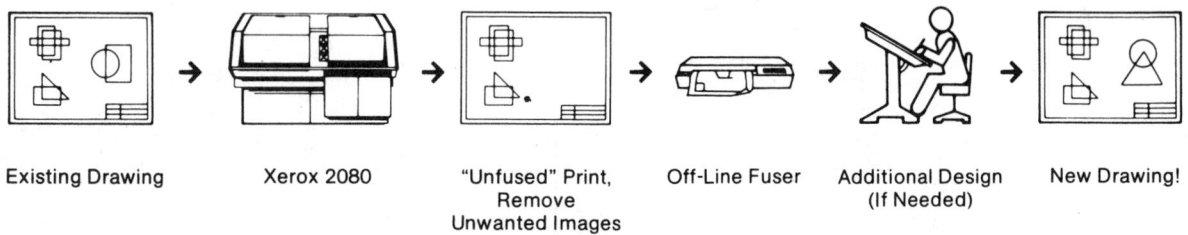

Figure 6–11 Removal of unwanted information from an unfused photocopy print. *Courtesy Xerox Corporation.*

use. This same technique may be used in conjunction with the photocopy process as shown in Figure 6–9.

Drawing changes can also be made using the photocopy process by covering unwanted information on the original with opaque paper. The resulting secondary original can then be used to add revised information as shown in Figure 6–10.

Another method is to use the photocopy process to generate a print with an unfused image on material designed for this purpose and then wipe away unwanted areas. The remaining image will then be fused to the paper with a fuser, which is a special piece of equipment. After the fusing process is complete, additional information may be added to the drawing and it is ready for service. See Figure 6–11.

Traditionally, masking is done photographically by making a photo negative of an original drawing. The unwanted information is covered over using opaque photo correcting fluid. After the unwanted area is removed, a photo positive is made on Mylar®.

The new drawing information, if any, can be added to the Mylar® and the new drawing is ready for use.

SEPIA BURN-OUT

Sepia burn-out is a technique that can be performed using the diazo machine and regular diazo products. The idea here is to copy part of an existing drawing onto a new drawing sheet to which you can add a new view or other details.

Step 1. Make a diazo copy of the existing drawing on heavy-weight diazo paper. Align the print carefully with the original. See Figure 6–12.

Step 2. Cut out the unwanted area or areas from the diazo print with a scissors or knife as shown in Figure 6–13.

Step 3. Carefully align the diazo copy with the unwanted information removed over a fresh

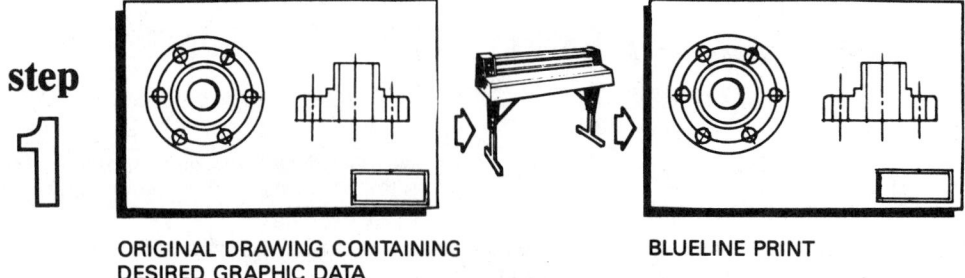

ORIGINAL DRAWING CONTAINING
DESIRED GRAPHIC DATA

BLUELINE PRINT

Figure 6–12 Step 1: Sepia burn-out. *Courtesy Blu-Ray, Inc.*

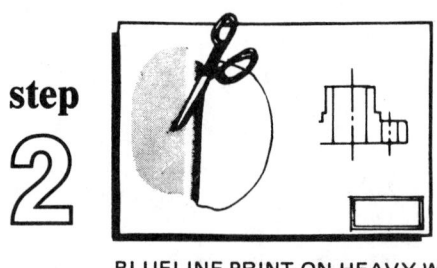

BLUELINE PRINT ON HEAVY-WEIGHT
DIAZO PAPER USED AS MASK

Figure 6–13 Step 2: Sepia burn-out. *Courtesy Blu-Ray, Inc.*

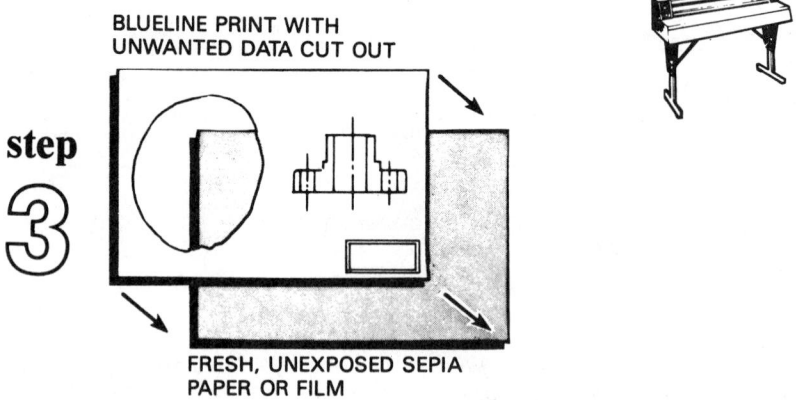

BLUELINE PRINT WITH
UNWANTED DATA CUT OUT

FRESH, UNEXPOSED SEPIA
PAPER OR FILM

Figure 6–14 Step 3: Sepia burn-out. *Courtesy Blu-Ray, Inc.*

piece of sepia paper or Mylar®. See Figure 6–14.

Step 4. Run the two sheets from Step 3 through the light chamber of the diazo machine. Remember, only the light chamber. The idea here is to remove the sepia emulsion from the cutaway area while saving the emulsion on the balance of the drawing sheet. See Figure 6–15

Step 5. Take the sepia material from Step 4 and place the existing drawing over it so that the unwanted information is located in the area that was burned away in Step 4. With both sheets carefully aligned, expose and develop in the diazo machine just as if you were making a sepia copy. See Figure 6–16.

Step 6. The resulting sepia will have the desired information present and the unwanted material removed. Now, the sepia is ready to have other drawing information added as seen in Figure 6–17.

PHOTODRAFTING

In some situations a photograph can be used as a drawing. Photodrawings are a combination of a photograph together with line work and lettering on a drawing. Photodrafting is used in mechanical drafting to prepare an assembly drawing of a product from a prototype or in electronic drafting to label the component parts of a circuit board. Photodrafting may also be used in architectural drafting to display the

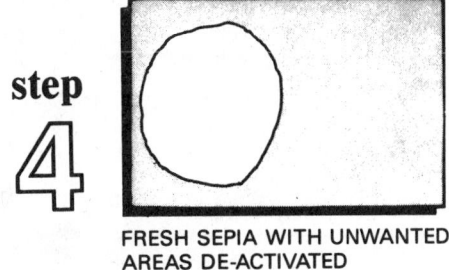

FRESH SEPIA WITH UNWANTED
AREAS DE-ACTIVATED

Figure 6–15 Step 4: Sepia burn-out. *Courtesy Blu-Ray, Inc.*

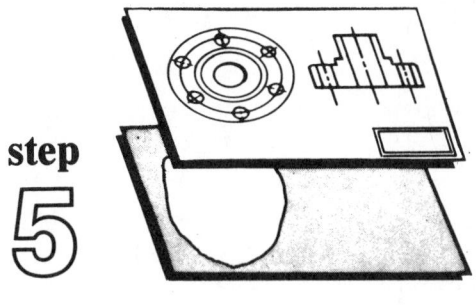

COPY ORIGINAL DRAWING
ONTO PREPARED SEPIA

Figure 6–16 Step 5: Sepia burn-out. *Courtesy Blu-Ray, Inc.*

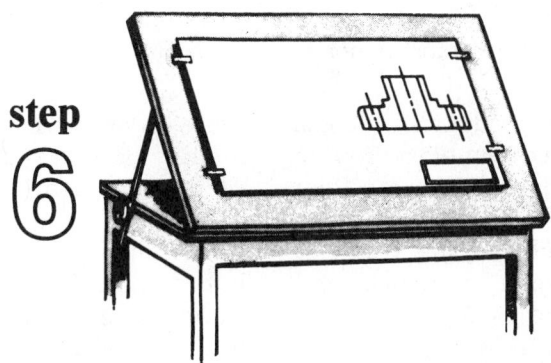

Figure 6–17 Step 6: Sepia burn-out. *Courtesy Blu-Ray, Inc.*

elevations of an existing structure rather than drawing the views.

One method of photodrafting uses only photographic reproduction as follows:

Step 1.   Take a photograph of the desired structure.

Step 2.   Have the photo reproduced photographically onto a sheet of drafting Mylar® using a halftone or dot pattern.

Step 3.   Add additional information to complete the drawing.

A second method of photodrafting combines photographic and sepia reproduction as follows:

Step 1.   Have a halftone positive made of the desired photograph.

Step 2.   Using the halftone photo and a sheet of single mat Mylar® sepia, make a reverse sepia of the photo.

Step 3.   Using the sepia as an original drawing surface, add all of the necessary information to the photo on the mat side of the sepia. The completed drawing is then ready for use.

Catalog illustrations for vendors' products are frequently prepared using photodrafting. In this appli-

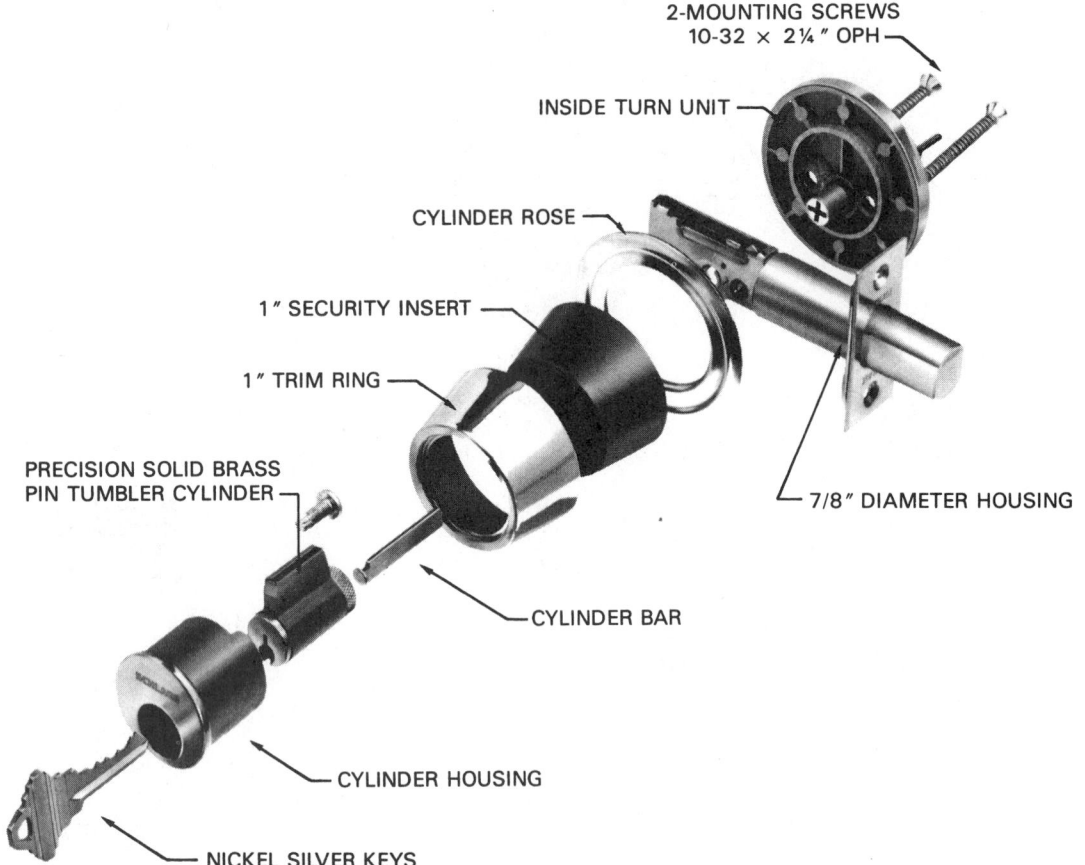

2-MOUNTING SCREWS
10-32 × 2¼″ OPH

INSIDE TURN UNIT

CYLINDER ROSE

1″ SECURITY INSERT

1″ TRIM RING

PRECISION SOLID BRASS
PIN TUMBLER CYLINDER

7/8″ DIAMETER HOUSING

CYLINDER BAR

CYLINDER HOUSING

NICKEL SILVER KEYS

Figure 6–18 Photodrafting for vendor's catalog display. *Photo courtesy Schlage Lock Company.*

cation a photograph is taken of a product and labels are added. Another option is to disassemble a product and take photos of each part. These photos are then arranged in order of assembly while a photo is made of the display. Labels are added and the result is used in a promotion catalog, repair manual, or installation instructions. See Figure 6–18.

OVERLAY DRAFTING

Overlay drafting, or pin-registered drafting as it is often called, is a process of making drawings in layers, each perfectly aligned with the other. Each layer will contain its own independent information and all of the overlays may be reproduced as one composite drawing. Overlay drafting is frequently used in commercial architectural drafting although this technique is also used in residential architecture.

In overlay drafting there are two main types of drawings: base sheets and overlay sheets. The base sheet contains general information that is common to the entire project. For example, a base sheet might show the main exterior structure with the permanent bearing walls and partitions. Each overlay sheet will contain independent information related to the base sheet, but the base sheet information will not be

redrawn each time. There may be a separate overlay for the electrical, mechanical, HVAC (Heating, Ventilating and Air Conditioning), and plumbing plan. There may be over a hundred overlays for a large commercial structure. Time is saved since the base information does not have to be redrawn each time. The basic components of overlay drafting are shown in Figure 6–19. The pin bar is a manufactured plastic

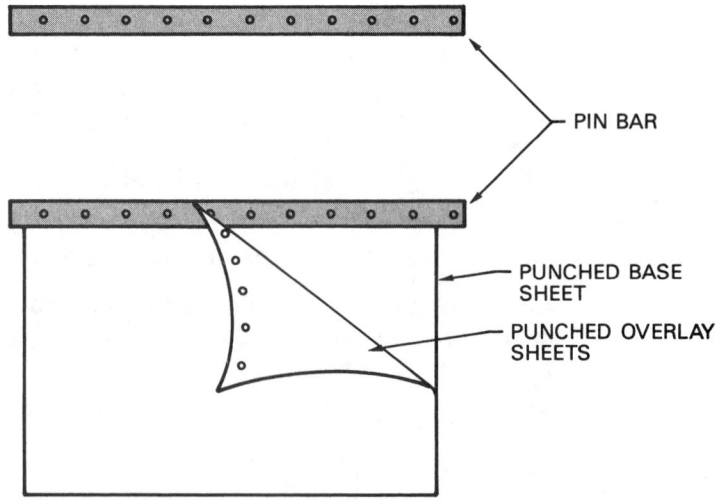

PIN BAR

PUNCHED BASE SHEET

PUNCHED OVERLAY SHEETS

Figure 6–19 Overlay drafting components.

or metal bar with precisely positioned pins that extend up from its surface. This pin bar is fastened with tape to the drafting table and in careful alignment with the drafting machine or parallel bar. The base and overlay sheets are generally prepunched (some companies punch their own) so that each sheet will register perfectly over the pin bar. Polyester drafting film, at least 3 mils (.003 in.) thick, is usually used for base and overlay sheets because of its durability, dimensional stability, and reproduction quality when used in conjunction with ink or polyester lead.

The overlay drafting process is described as follows:

Step 1. When using the overlay technique the base sheet drawing is prepared on prepunched polyester film. The information on this drawing will be unchanging from one overlay to the next. See Figure 6–20.

Step 2. After the base sheet drawing is complete, then diazo copies of the base sheet are made on prepunched clear polyester diazo reproduction material. These sheets, called slicks, are used as secondary base sheets. A slick will be given to each drafter or subcontractor for use as the base sheet in preparation of the specific overlays.

Step 3. The individual drafter or engineer will place a clean overlay sheet over the slick and add information by drawing on the overlay. Figure 6–21 shows interior partitions with related dimensions and specifications that have been drawn on an overlay that covers the floor plan base. The overlay is shown highlighted in color over the base, or slick, shown in black. The process continues with the foundation drawing shown in Figure 6–22. The slick is shown in black under the foundation with related dimensions and specifications. Figure 6–23 shows the roof framing plan over the slick. Some companies have several different departments so that one overlay may be prepared by the mechanical group, another by the plumbing department, and so on. Even small companies that do all engineering and drafting in one place by one or a few people can benefit from this technique. In some cases a slick may be sent to a subcontractor in another state for preparation of related overlays.

Step 4. The base sheet and the completed overlay sheets can be registered together with registration clips and a composite diazo or

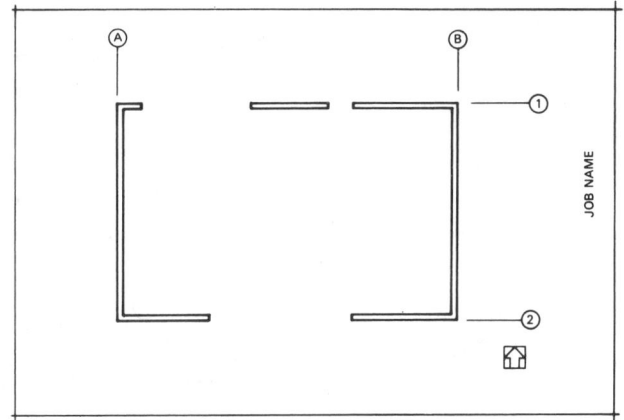

1 BASE SHEET

Figure 6–20 Step 1: Base sheet drawing. *Courtesy Structureform.*

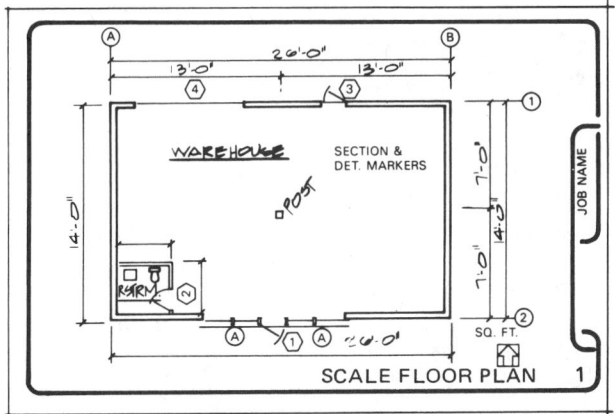

2 FLOOR PLAN OVERLAY

Figure 6–21 Step 3: Overlay of interior partitions. *Courtesy Structureform.*

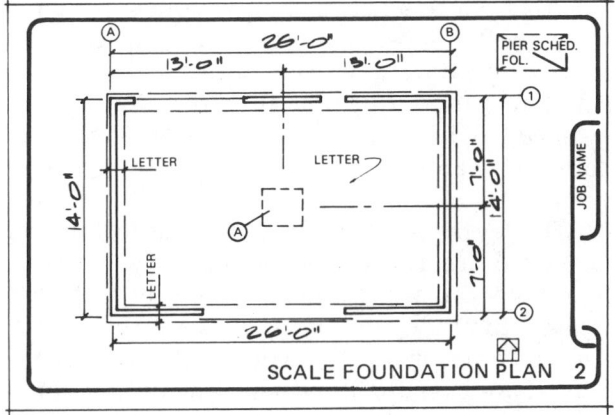

3 FOUNDATION PLAN OVERLAY

Figure 6–22 Foundation overlay. *Courtesy Structureform.*

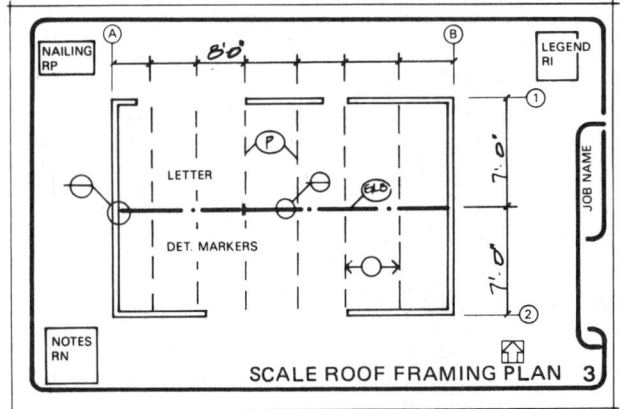

4 ROOF FRAMING PLAN OVERLAY

Figure 6–23 Roof framing plan overlay. *Courtesy Structureform.*

photocopy made that integrates the components of all or any specific combination of sheets. The total process can be seen in Figure 6–24 through 6–27.

The advantages of overlay drafting include the following:

1. Time saving which directly relates to cost saving.
2. It is easy to make interior designs using a separate overlay for each floor.
3. Subcontractor work will be easy and fast. With each working on his or her own base and overlays, the information required by one subcontractor will not get mixed up with another and quality control is improved. Each subcontractor can be working simultaneously with the others thus speeding progress on the complete set of drawings.
4. Composite prints may be made by combining the base sheet and any combination of overlays.

Overlay drafting and Computer Aided Design and Drafting (CADD) can be used together to achieve even more productivity. The CADD system is used to generate a base sheet and then overlay sheets are developed that are registered to the base. Some CADD systems software is designed to make drawings in layers.

CADD layers must perform two basic functions: they must differentiate independent information and differentiate pen weights for plotting. In addition to the layer identification system established by the CADD software, many companies set up other layer systems based on their own project needs. For example, layers may be identified with a layer identification system where the elements are divided into three groups: the major group, minor group, and basic group. The major group contains the *type* of drawing, such as Floor Plan. The minor group identifies the *element* on the drawing, such as Electrical, and the basic group labels the *type* of information, such as Lines or Text. An example of this method of layer identification is FL1 ELEC L, which means first-floor plan, electrical plan, and lines. A typical layout of the three groups follows:

MAJOR GROUP	MINOR GROUP	BASIC GROUP
BSMT	HVAC	LINE
FL1	ELEC	TXT
FL2	PLUMB	DIM
GAR	WALLS	INSERT
SITE	DOORS	HATCH
SCHED	WINDOWS	
NOTES	APPL	
FDN		
ELEV		
ROOF		
REFLECT		

Layer identification may also contain a number identifying the pen width used to produce the plot. For example, 1 = .025 pen width, 2 = .035 pen width, 3 = .050 pen width, and 4 = .070 pen width.

The following are the layers grouped by drawing type developed by E. Henry Fitzgibbon AIA, Soderstrom Architects PC.

LAYERS GROUPED BY DRAWING TYPE	
Site Plans	Buildings
	Roads
	Curbs, Walks, Site-stairs, Parking-stripes
	Trees, Cars
	Demolition
	Fences
	Property-Line, Project-Boundary, Scope-of-Work
	Utilities, Power

Floor Plans	Walls, Light-Walls, Overhead, Floor-patterns
	Columns
	Stairs
	Doors, Windows, Cabinets, Decking
	Appliances, Equipment, Plumbing
	Wall-pocket, Specialties
	Demolition
	Partitions
Building Elevations	Walls, Light-Walls, Reveal, Punch
	Doors, Windows, Roofing, Siding
	Flashing
	Footings
	Grade-Line
Building Sections	Walls, Light-Walls, Punch
	Joist, Trusses, Beams
	Insulation, Wall-Pocket
	Footings
	Earth-Gravel
	Light, Medium, Heavy
Details	Light, Medium, Heavy, Punch
Reflected Ceiling Plans	Walls
	Ceiling-Grid
	Lighting
Structural Framing Plans	Foundation, Footing
	Columns, Joist, Beams, Hangers
	Rafters, Roof-plan
	Walls-below
Interior Floor Plans	Walls, Partitions
	Stairs
	Furniture, Accessories
	Equipment
	Wall-Pocket
Interior Elevations	Walls, Light-walls
	Doors, Windows
	Fixtures, Plumbing
	Cabinets, Dashed-Cabinets
	Toilet-Partitions
	Floor-base
Annotation Used with All Drawing Types:	Light-text, Dark-Text, Room-Text, Grid-Text, Attribute-Text, Mark-Text, Titleblock-Text
	Grid
	Dimensions
	Pochet
	Architectural-Symbols
	Titleblock
	Key-plan
Layers Used as Tools:	Trace, Non-print, Baseplan

REPETITIVE ELEMENTS

On many drawings there are certain details, symbols, or even labels that are used over and over again. To redraw these elements every time they are needed is very time consuming and time would be saved if a standard stencil could be used instead. This concept is similar in some respects to drawing symbols with a template. Computer aided drafting is especially useful for the rapid duplication of repetitive features or drawing elements.

There are vendors of transfer materials that have standard transfers available, and they will also prepare custom transfers to be used for repetitive elements. These transfers are generally produced on an adhesive-backed Mylar® sheet. The element needed is peeled off its backing sheet and added to the drawing in the desired location. These elements may be used with or without additional labels, notes, or dimensions.

Repetitive elements may also be prepared by an architectural office as follows:

Step 1. Draw the desired repetitive element on Mylar® using ink. Pay particular attention to line darkness and detail. See Figure 6–28.

Step 2. Use a photocopy machine or a photographic process to duplicate as many of the original elements as will fit on a standard size sheet. An 8½″ × 11″ sheet is preferred. The copies should be as black as possible. If the photocopies are not dark enough, you may need to touch them up with ink.

Step 3. Cut the elements out of the individual sheets from Step 2 and tape them together in a neat and orderly pattern on one sheet. See Figure 6–29.

Step 4. Use the photocopy machine or a photographic process again to make a Mylar® copy of the composite sheet from Step 3.

Step 5. Using the Mylar® sheet from Step 4, make diazo copies or photocopies of the elements on adhesive-backed Mylar® sheets. Cut each element from the adhesive sheet as needed. Place an element on a drawing in any desired location. Additional information may now be added.

When drafting with CADD, standardized symbols or details should be drawn only once. One advantage of a CADD system is the productivity gained when standard and repetitive elements are brought into the drawing automatically. An operator simply calls up a specific "block" from the computer and places it wherever needed in the drawing. The term block refers to a standard symbol or drawing that is stored in the computer for use in any drawing at any time. Standard blocks may be completely labeled and dimensioned, or specific information can be added to customize the detail after a block has been inserted. With most CADD systems you can also "stretch" or "trim" block features.

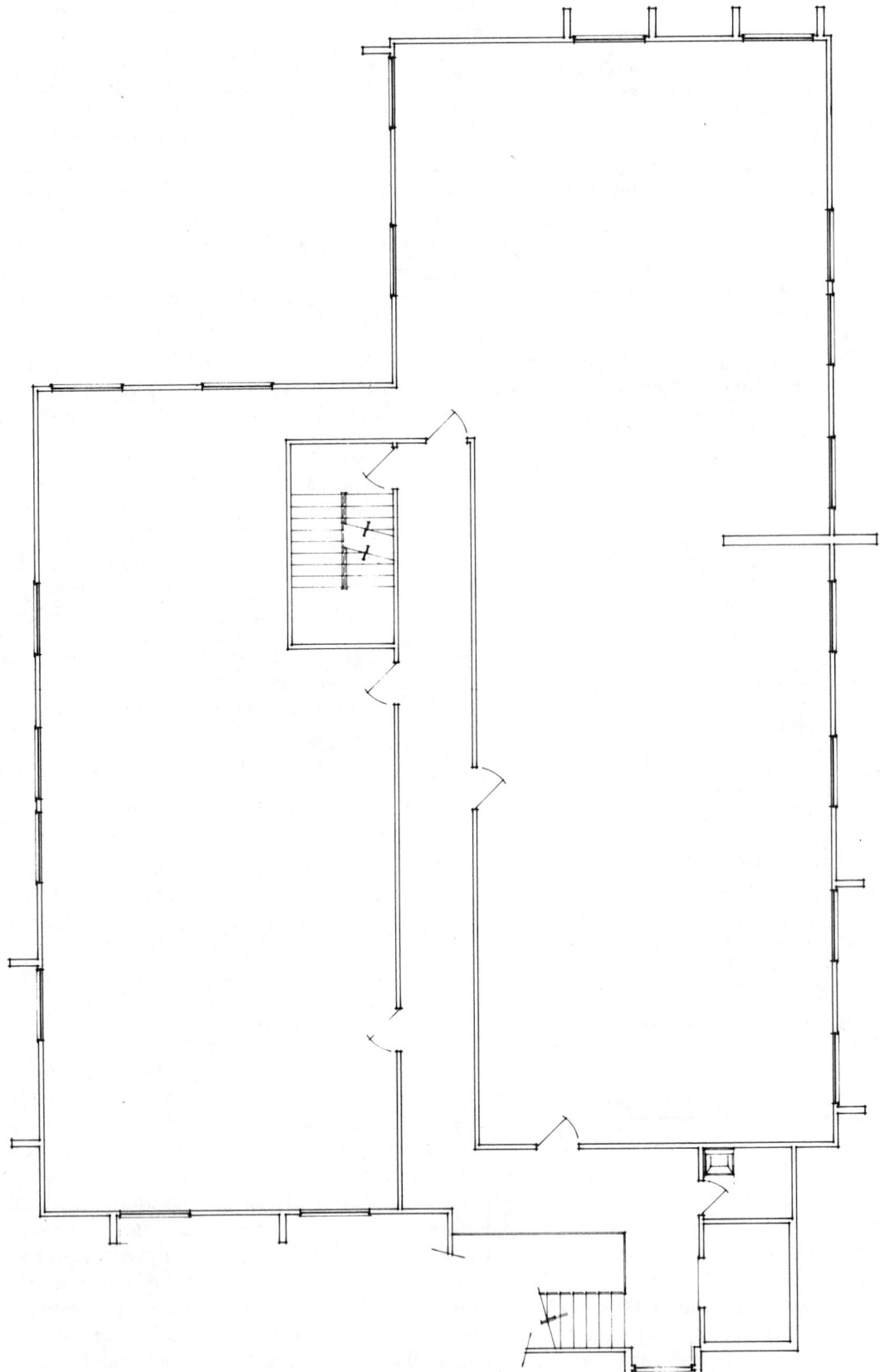

Figure 6-24 Exterior and support structure base sheet is unchanged throughout the project. *Courtesy Structureform.*

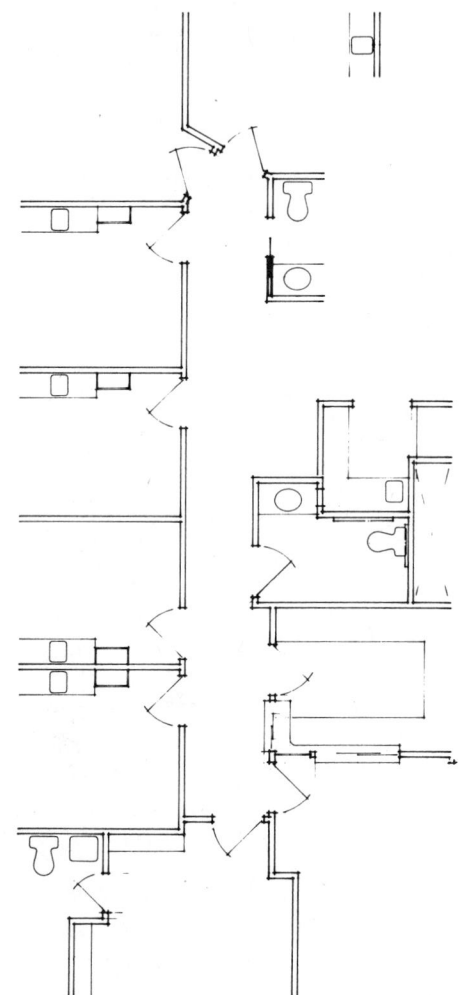

Figure 6-25 Interior design of nonbearing partitions may be changed as desired using overlays. *Courtesy Structureform.*

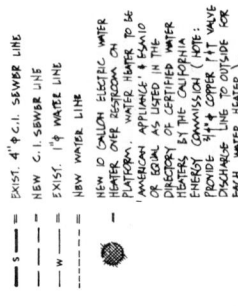

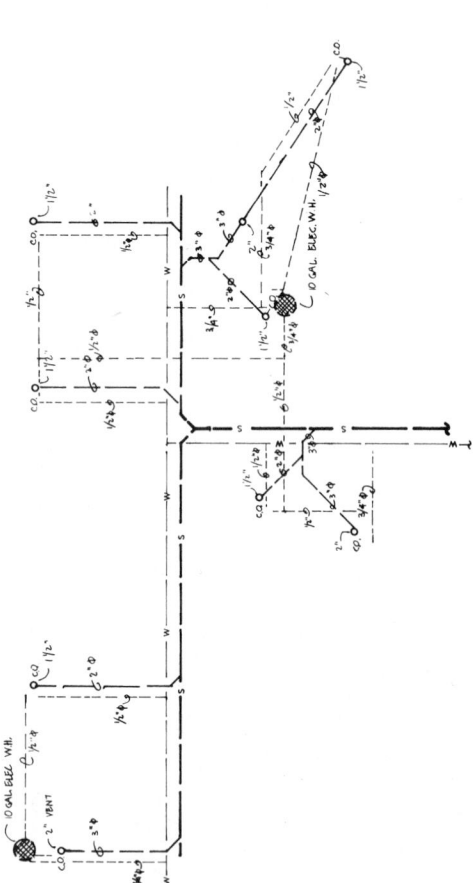

PLUMBING

Figure 6-26 Plumbing overlay. *Courtesy Structureform.*

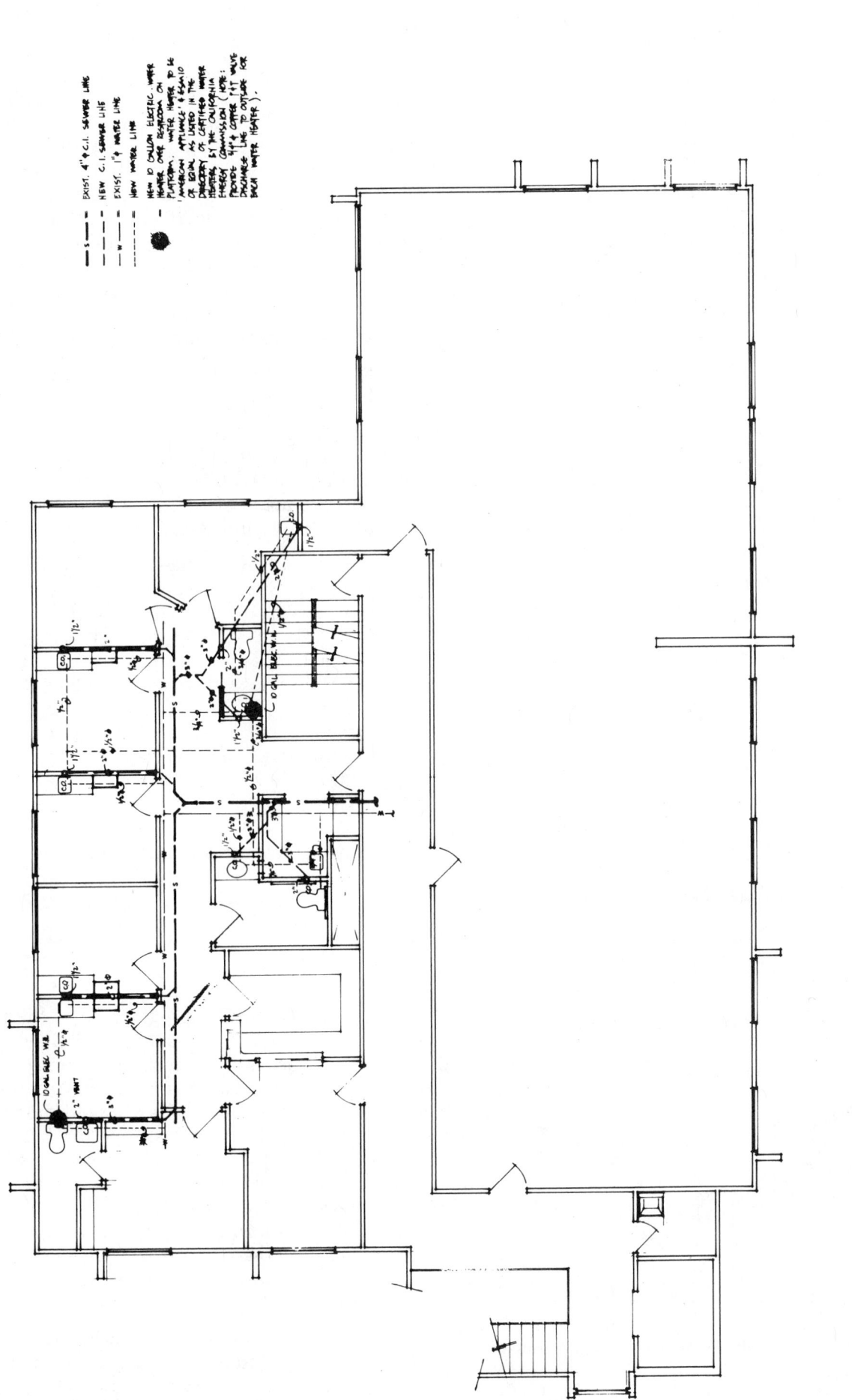

PLUMBING

Figure 6-27 Composite of base sheet and overlays. *Courtesy Structureform.*

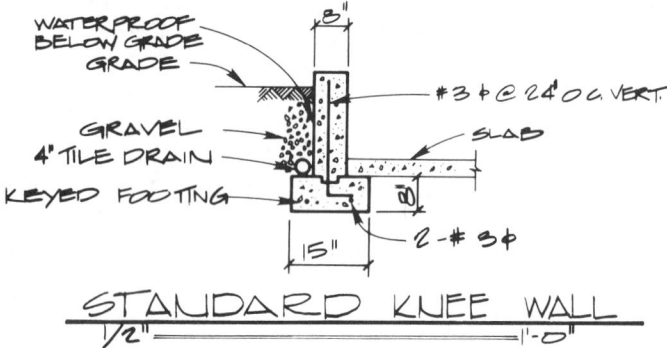

Figure 6–28 Draw a single element with ink on Mylar®.

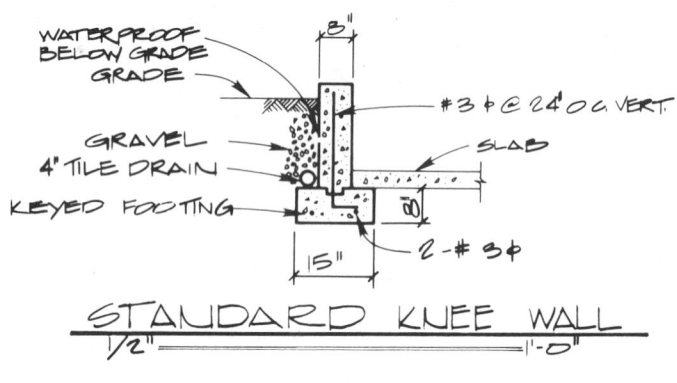

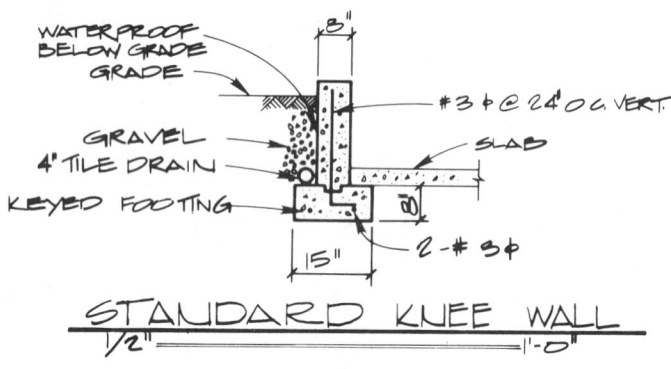

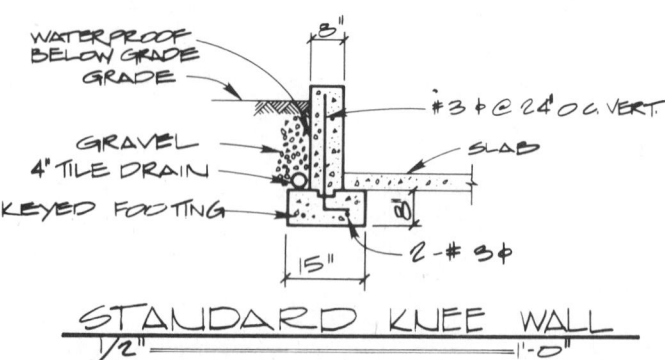

Figure 6–29 Copies of the single element from step 1 combined in a group.

SCREENED IMAGES

Also known as phantom or subdued images, screened image drawings may be used to show a subordinate drawing subdued in the background while specific information is highlighted. An advantage of this technique is that the screened information is present if needed for reference while the emphasized main drawing is very dark and clear. This method may be used, for example, for showing a specific utility highlighted on a plat of land that has been screened. This same technique could be used in overlay drafting where the base sheet is subdued and the overlays are dark. Screened images may be made as follows:

Step 1.   Make an original base sheet of the area to be screened.

Step 2.   Use the photocopy process to add an overlay of white dots that make up the screen. See Figure 6–30. Or have a halftone photo positive made of the drawing on polyester film. See Figure 6–31.

Step 3.   Use the screened image as a base sheet for the preparation of pin registered overlay sheets. The overlay sheets will be drawn with ink on Mylar® for dark images. An alternative is to draw directly on the screened image sheet made in Step 2. This method will allow one drawing with a screened image under a highlighted image to be drawn. See Figure 6–32. A variation of this alternative method is to make a reverse sepia of the Mylar® sheet from Step 2. Then use the reverse sepia to make a drawing of the desired highlighted features.

RESTORATION

Restoration, also known as reprographics, is the process of bringing old, worn, or damaged drawings back to life without the necessity of costly redrawing. With CADD now in use, some companies are going through the process of updating and redrawing old drawings with the computer. This is not always the best restoration process because the CADD system is usually used for helping architects, designers, and drafters create new projects. The CADD tool is more valuable on new projects. Also, in most cases it is less costly to renovate old drawings than it is to recreate them using CADD. Companies may get involved in drawing restoration for several reasons:

1. If a company is converting all drawing files to microfilm it is often necessary to recondition

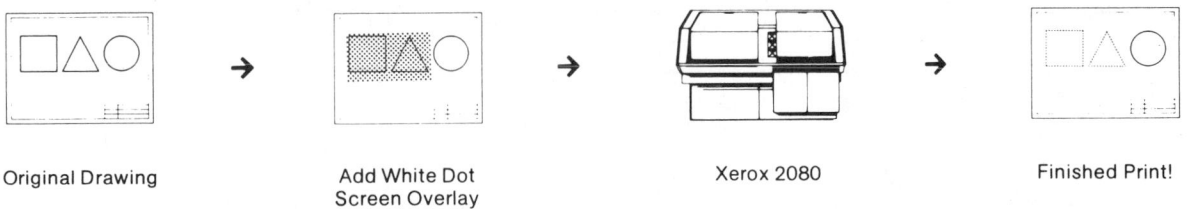

Original Drawing   Add White Dot   Xerox 2080   Finished Print!
                          Screen Overlay

Figure 6–30 Create a screened base sheet by overlaying the original drawing with a dot screen. *Courtesy Xerox Corporation.*

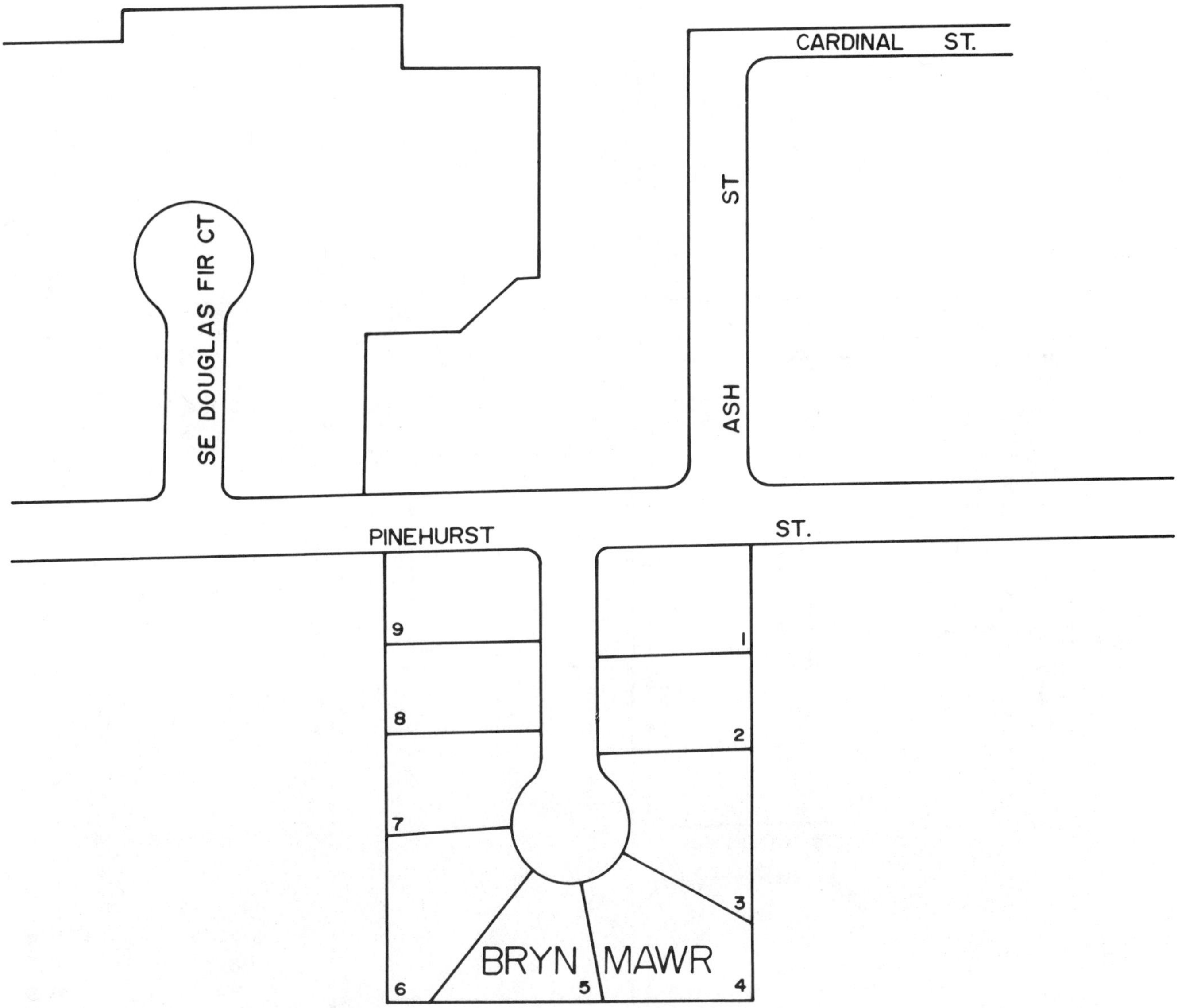

CARDINAL ST.

ST

ASH

SE DOUGLAS FIR CT

PINEHURST   ST.

9   I

8   2

7

          3

BRYN MAWR

6   5   4

Figure 6–31 Halftone photo positive of base sheet drawing on film.

old drawings before they are ready to meet microfilming standards.

2. When old drawings continue to be used on a regular basis it is necessary to restore them so the construction prints are clear.

3. In some cases, drawings are legal documents and their clarity must be maintained for ac-

curacy such as for surveys and plats (map of a subdivision of land).

Restoration may be accomplished in a few different ways. Some companies do their own restoration using diazo, photocopy, or photo reproduction equipment, while other companies send old drawings

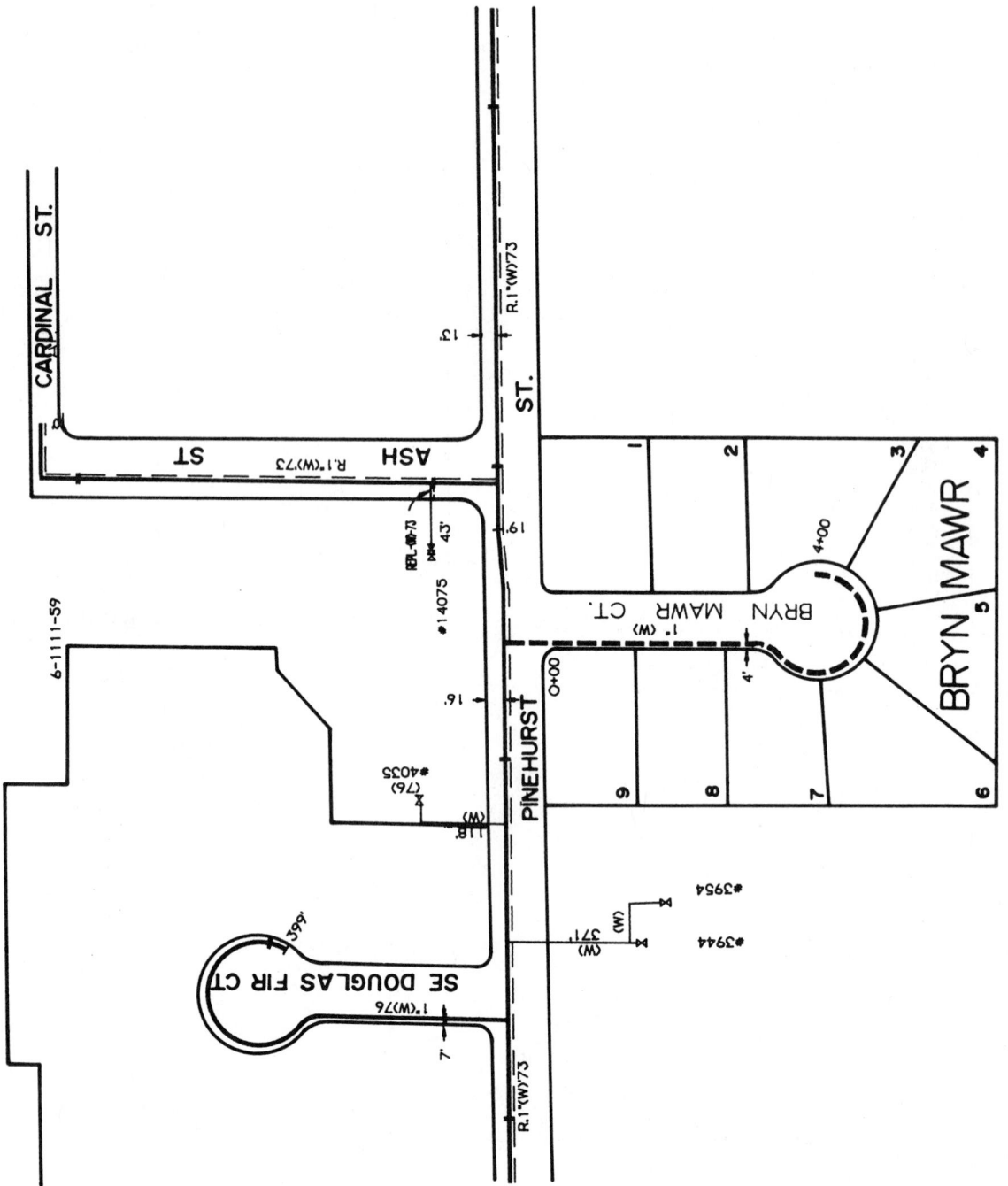

Figure 6-32 Composite of screened-image base sheet and black image on overlay sheet. *CADD drawing layout courtesy Northwest Natural Gas Company.*

to independent reprographics businesses for restoration. The best solution to restoration is through the use of photographic methods; however, a fine job of restoration can be accomplished using the diazo or photocopy machines and special materials.

Preliminary Restoration

There are a number of tasks that can be performed on an old drawing before it ever gets to the camera, diazo, or photocopy machine:

Step 1. The first task in preparation for restoration is an inspection and cleaning of the drawing. A lot of surface damage can be reduced by cleaning. First, erase smears and smudges with a soft eraser. Second, clean the back of the drawing with an eraser and cleaning pad that is recommended for the type of original material. A cleaning pad full of art gum powder works well on vellum. Brush off all eraser particles.

Step 2. After years of use, drawings get torn and creased. These tears and creases can be repaired. Bring the edges of a tear back to their original positions, then apply a piece of transparent tape. Creases can be partly or totally removed with an iron. Place the area to be pressed between two pieces of soft paper and then using a warm iron or photo drying press carefully apply dry heat and pressure to the area.

Step 3. Evaluate lines that you know will not reproduce well. Using the same medium (pencil or ink) that was used on the original, carefully go over the lines that need improvement.

Old drawings often become stained or discolored. In many cases this problem can be reduced during the reproduction process. Any discoloration problems that remain can be eliminated with a mask during the balance of the restoration process.

Diazo Process

Most companies have a diazo machine. It is best if the diazo machine is in top working order with good lights. Do the following after preliminary preparation is complete:

Step 1. Use the old cleaned original to make a clear sepia-film copy. Machine speed is critical so the background is burned out while keeping the lines and lettering clear. There is a fine line between good and adequate success here.

Step 2. Take a close look at the original in comparison to the new sepia film. Use eradicating fluid that is recommended for the material to remove carefully all unwanted areas such as shadows, crease and tear lines, and other flaws.

Step 3. The completed clear sepia from Step 2 is now ready to copy. If additional drafting work is to be done on the restored secondary original, then a reverse Mylar® sepia should be made. Any additional drafting can be done in ink or polyester lead.

Photocopy Process

The photocopy process will actually improve line and lettering quality and remove some background discoloration. A photocopy duplicator with a nonfusing feature along with an off-line fuser can be used to restore old drawings.

Step 1. Make an unfused Mylar® print of the old drawing to be restored.

Step 2. Using an eradicator, remove all unwanted background smudges, smears, unwanted lines, and tear marks.

Step 3. Run the repaired drawing through the off-line fuser.

Step 4. Do any additional touch-up work, drawing changes, or drawing additions and the new drawing is ready for use. See Figure 6–33.

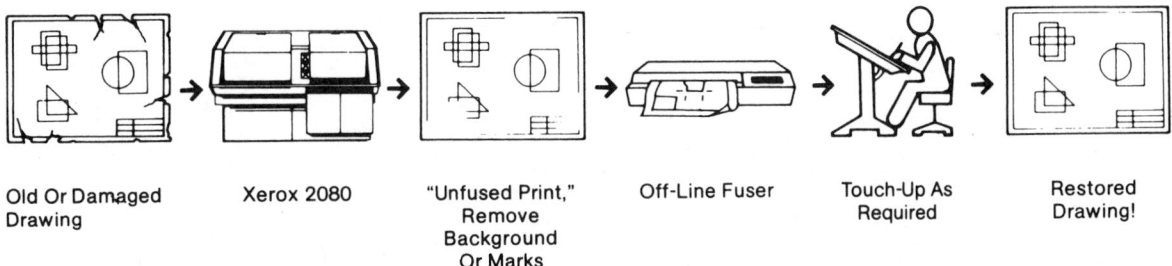

Old Or Damaged Drawing   Xerox 2080   "Unfused Print," Remove Background Or Marks   Off-Line Fuser   Touch-Up As Required   Restored Drawing!

Figure 6–33 Use a photocopy machine nonfusing feature and special lens aperture setting to make old drawings look new. *Courtesy Xerox Corporation.*

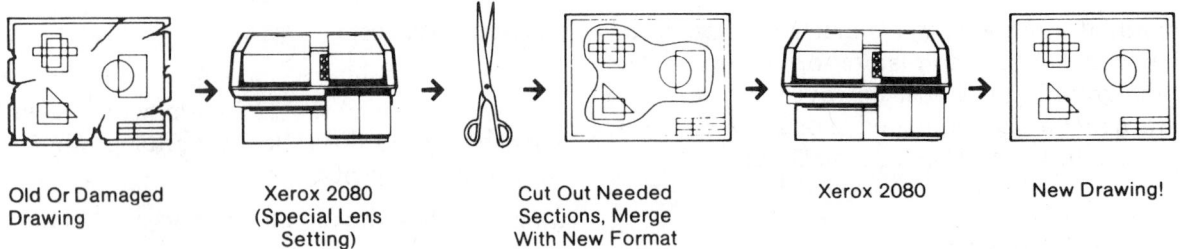

Figure 6–34 Use scissors-and-paste drafting to restore drawings. *Courtesy Xerox Corporation.*

The photocopy process can also be used without an off-line fuser with the aid of scissors-and-paste drafting techniques.

Step 1. Use a photocopy machine with a special lens setting recommended for this application and make a copy of the old drawing.

Step 2. Cut out the needed parts of the drawing while cutting away unwanted deteriorated areas. Remove the entire title block and border line.

Step 3. Attach the cut portions from Step 2 to a new drawing sheet. Carefully align the elements and tape them down.

Step 4. Make a photocopy of this paste-up on Mylar® or vellum. The new drawing is ready for additional drafting or production. See Figure 6–34.

Photographic Process

Photographic restoration of old drawings will help improve deteriorated line and lettering quality and remove a great deal of the background blemishes. Some companies have camera reproduction capabilities while others may send old drawings to a reprographic business for restoration. The photographic process is as follows:

Step 1. Make a negative of the old drawing. Many labs make a reduced-scale negative be-cause it has less surface area to work with and increases line density.

Step 2. Use photo opaquing fluid on the negative to opaque stains, tear lines, and other flaws. Also, use a scribe (special tool for removing the black film surface) to improve the quality of faded or unclear lines.

Step 3. Make a positive second original on Mylar® from the film negative. If the negative was reduced, bring the positive back to the original scale.

There is little doubt that systems drafting can save time and money while improving drawing control and clarity. A number of systems drafting techniques are used in industry today, and the implementation of these methods depends upon the type of equipment available and the desired end result. Most companies can do most systems drafting procedures with standard drafting reproduction equipment and specific materials designed for the intended purpose. The best solution to any reprographics problem is to first find out what materials are available from vendors that can be used to accomplish the desired task. Some vendors have training workshops developed to assist companies or individuals in reprographic techniques. Vendors that supply materials and equipment for drawing restoration will usually be glad to send a representative to discuss specific reprographic needs. Look in the telephone book under reproduction equipment and supplies or reprographics.

SYSTEMS DRAFTING TEST

DIRECTIONS

Answer the questions with short complete statements or drawings as needed on 8½ × 11 vellum as follows:

1. Use ⅛ in. guidelines for all lettering.
2. Letter your name, Systems Drafting Test, and the date at the top of the sheet.
3. Letter the question number and provide the answer. You do not need to write out the question.
4. Do all lettering with vertical uppercase architectural letters. If the answer requires line work, use proper drafting tools and technique. Answers may be prepared on a word processor if appropriate with course guidelines.
5. Your grade will be based on correct answers and quality of line technique.

QUESTIONS

1. Define systems drafting.
2. Identify three advantages that are associated with systems drafting techniques.
3. Describe the paste-up drafting technique.
4. Discuss how scissors drafting can be a time-saving technique.
5. How are paste-up drafting techniques different from scissors drafting techniques?
6. When can masking be used effectively as a systems drafting technique?
7. How is the sepia burn-out method similar to masking?
8. Give an example of how photodrafting can be used as an architectural drafting technique.
9. What is another name for overlay drafting?
10. List four possible overlays that may be prepared for a typical architectural project.
11. Name the two main types of drawings used in overlay drafting.
12. What is the pin bar used for?
13. Why is Mylar® the best material to use in overlay drafting?
14. Describe slicks.
15. Describe how overlay drafting and CADD may be compatible.
16. Discuss an example of how repetitive elements can be used in architectural drafting.
17. Why is CADD so successful in the preparation of repetitive elements?
18. What is another name for screened images?
19. Describe the intended result of using the screened image technique.
20. What is another name for drawing restoration?
21. What is the main advantage of using restoration techniques on an old, worn-out drawing?
22. Why is restoration used in many situations rather than redrawing with CADD?
23. Describe the preliminary restoration steps.
24. How is drawing restoration possible using the diazo process?
25. Why is it not always necessary to have expensive photographic equipment and facilities to perform many systems drafting techniques?

Chapter 7
Computer-aided Design and Drafting in Architecture

IN CHAPTER 2 you learned about the traditional manual drafting workstation with modern conveniences such as an adjustable drafting table, and a drafting machine or parallel bar. Also available to enhance your speed and accuracy are automatic pencils, electric erasers, and templates of all kinds. As a professional drafting technician, or even as you become a designer or architect, you will continue to see the traditional equipment. However, drafting is changing. The concepts and theories are the same, but the tools are changing. Recently a panel of experts acknowledged that traditional manual drafting, in general, will convert to computer-aided design and drafting (CADD) within the next few years. This is not to say that the traditional manual drafting workstation that you are familiar with will not be around. It will stay with us. However, computer graphics is now available in most drafting schools and either is being used or soon will be used in many architectural firms. Companies that do not have computer graphics may have computers to do other tasks such as the storage and retrieval of information.

MICROCOMPUTERS

Initially in industry the large main frame computer was standard equipment for CADD technology. A company would provide a special air conditioned room to house a half-million dollar computer. Several workstations were supported by this computer for creating the first computer-aided architectural designs.

The movement in CADD is toward microcomputers. These are desk-top models that will perform a multitude of tasks at a comparatively low installation cost and may be purchased from a variety of vendors. A complete workstation can be purchased for an amount between $8,000 and $15,000 depending upon its capabilities. Some of the lower-cost units are much slower than the more expensive models. The availability of software, or programs, to operate microcomputers has increased greatly. Inexpensive

Figure 7–1 Microcomputer graphics workstation. *Courtesy Applicon.*

software is available that will perform all types of drafting tasks. The capabilities of microcomputers are improving as memory storage is expanded. Microcomputers are in virtually every business and industry. Placed on individual desk tops, they can also be connected to interact between stations. Figure 7–1 shows an example of a typical microcomputer workstation.

PRODUCTIVITY

There is agreement among CADD users that a drafter's productivity is increased with computer graphics over traditional manual drafting methods. While estimates range from a three-times productivity increase to a twenty-times increase, the reality is that any increase in productivity depends upon the task, the system, and how quickly employees learn to use CADD. For many duties, CADD easily can multiply productivity several times. For other tasks, it may be determined that manual drafting is the appropriate method of performance. It is especially true that the computer will perform redundant and time-consuming tasks much faster and more accurately than can be done by manual techniques. A great advantage of CADD is that the time needed by the designer and drafter for creativity has increased while their time spent on the actual preparation of drawings has been reduced. Some of the business tasks related to architectural design and drafting, such as construction cost analysis, specifications writing, computations, materials inventory, time scheduling, and information storage can be done better and faster on a computer.

With some units, a designer can look at several design alternatives at one time. The drafter can draw in layers where one layer may be the plan perimeter, the next layer fixtures, the next electrical, and another layer dimensions and notes. It is even common for each layer to appear in a different color for easy comparison. Productivity is also related directly to the amount of time a company has had CADD on line (in working order) coupled with employee acceptance and experience. Most companies can expect more productivity after the users become more comfortable with the capabilities of the equipment.

DESIGNING

Architectural designers will continue to make sketches even as the computer waits for input. The old methods of making circles to determine preliminary room arrangement will continue to be with us. Designers will still form small renderings in an effort to establish design ideas. The computer can help in the design process, but individual creativity may often take place before the computer is turned on.

There are a number of design functions that the CADD system can perform in a manner that will often exceed many expectations. Plan components, such as room arrangements, can be stored in a design file which will allow the designer to call upon a series of these components for rearrangements in a new design. Another factor that aids design is that a given plan can be quickly reduced or enlarged in size while all components maintain their proper proportion. A particular room can be changed while the balance of the design remains the same. The design capabilities of drawing layers allows the architect to prepare a preliminary layout on one layer while changing and rearranging components on another layer.

Not only can creativity be enhanced with CADD, but also the repetitive aspects of design can be handled more effectively. For example, when designing an apartment or condominium complex an initial unit can be designed and then any number of the same units can be attached to one another in any manner very quickly. Alternate designs can also be made. Some units can be expanded or reduced in size or bedroom and bath alternatives can quickly be implemented.

ERGONOMICS

Ergonomics is the study of a worker's relationship to physical and psychological environments. As drafting technicians begin to make a transition from traditional drafting methods to computer graphics, there is mounting concern about the effect of this new working environment on the individual. Some studies have shown that workers should not work continuously at a computer workstation for more than about four hours. In reality, this is impossible as most companies do not want to give full pay for half a day's work. The various problems that are addressed by computer manufacturers should also be considered when purchasing a system.

Keyboard design in old mechanical typewriters was based on the importance of position. Keys were placed so they would not jam when used. Keyboard design can now be rearranged as electronics eliminates the old problem of jamming. Keys are arranged to help facilitate easier use. Also, a good keyboard will have key tops that are dished to help reduce finger slippage. For some people, keyboards should either be adjustable or separate from the computer to provide more flexibility. Also, when keys are depressed a slight sound should be heard to give assurance that the key has made contact.

The cathode-ray tube (CRT) screen, or monitor, is one of the biggest concerns. The operator should be able to see images clearly without glare. One primary problem has been eye strain and headache with extended use. Many manufacturers have green monitor screens which tend to be easier to view than black and white. Also, if the position of the monitor is adjustable, the operator can tilt or turn the screen to help reduce glare from overhead or adjacent lighting. Some users have found that a small amount of background light is helpful.

The chair should be designed for easy adjustments to allow each operator to have optimum comfort. The chair should be comfortably padded. The user's back should be straight, feet should be flat on the floor, and the elbow to hand movement should be horizontal when working the keyboard or digitizer. The digitizer should be in close proximity to the monitor so that movement is not strained and equipment use is flexible. The operator should not have to move a great deal to look directly over the cursor to activate commands.

The plotter creates some noise and is best located in a separate room adjacent to the workstation. Some companies put the plotter in a central location with small office workstations around the plotter. Others prefer to have plotters near the individual workstations that may be surrounded by acoustical partition walls or partial walls.

The working environment may be different from traditional drafting rooms in that air conditioning and ventilation should be designed to accommodate the computers and equipment. Carpets should be antistatic. Noise should be kept to a minimum. If smoking is permitted, the room should have special ventilation. Smoke or other contaminants can affect computer graphics equipment.

Drafters who are required to do tedious, repetitive tasks on the computer could develop symptoms of fatigue often known as job burn-out. Consideration should be given to allowing computer graphics employees to do a variety of jobs. Rotating jobs from CADD to traditional drafting work every few weeks should provide enough variety to prevent boredom.

THE COMPUTER GRAPHICS WORKSTATION

The computer graphics workstation is different from the traditional station because the tools have changed. For example, the new table is flat and contains a computer, digitizer, and plotter on or adjacent to the workstation.

The Computer

There are two basic computer aided workstations. Some companies may have a large centrally located computer that is generally in a special room of its own. This main frame computer, as it is called, can serve several independent workstations. With the other layout, each workstation will contain its own computer. Whichever way the company selects to use computer graphics, the result is the same and the computer is the core of the CADD workstation. Figure 7–2 shows a computer graphics workstation. The monitor is similar to a TV screen, and resting below or attached to it is the keyboard. The monitor displays alphanumeric (characters and numbers) in-

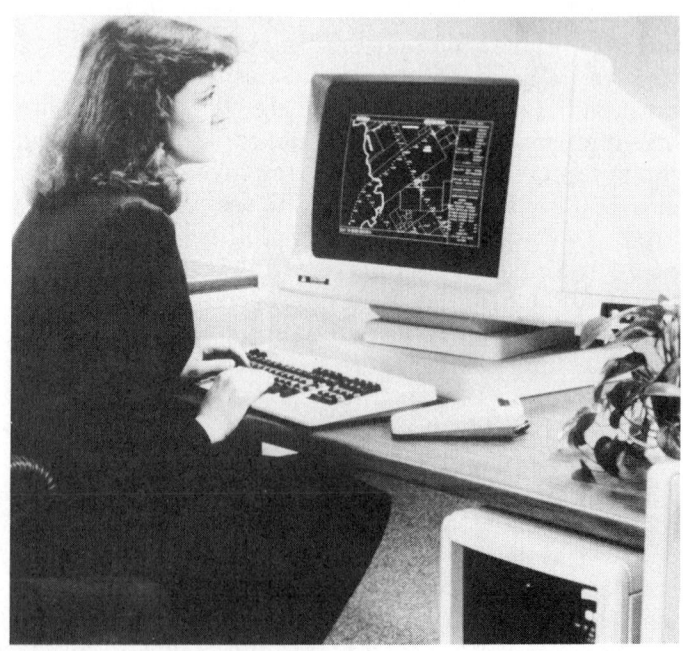

Figure 7–2 Computer graphics workstation. *Courtesy Calcomp.*

formation from input given at the keyboard. Input is any data or information that the operator puts into the computer. The monitor also displays graphics (lines, symbols, or pictures) as input from the keyboard or digitizer.

The Digitizer

The digitizer is an electronically sensitized drafting board. The digitizer may be adjacent to the monitor or built into the unit. Digitizers may be equipped with a pen-like instrument called a stylus, or a hand-held device called a cursor that contains a cross-hair lens and command buttons. Input will be displayed on the monitor from the keyboard in the form of alphanumeric information or as graphics by providing the coordinates of the ends of a line or other geometric shape. The digitizer, however, can allow the operator to perform the graphics tasks more rapidly and with greater ease. Provided with a list of symbols, lines, or words known as a menu, the operator can instantly input information on the monitor. The reason that the related group of commands is called a menu is because each symbol or element can be ordered for immediate display with a touch of the stylus or cursor. Figure 7–3 shows a digitizer used to establish coordinate points for drawing lines.

Another method used to input graphics is to place a sketch over the digitizer surface or to work from a sketch or series of commands adjacent to the digitizer. Here the stylus or cursor is used to establish coordinate points or geometric shapes by a touch on the active surface of the digitizer. The position of the command is transmitted from the electronic sensing device inside the digitizer to the monitor. For example, press the stylus at the beginning and end

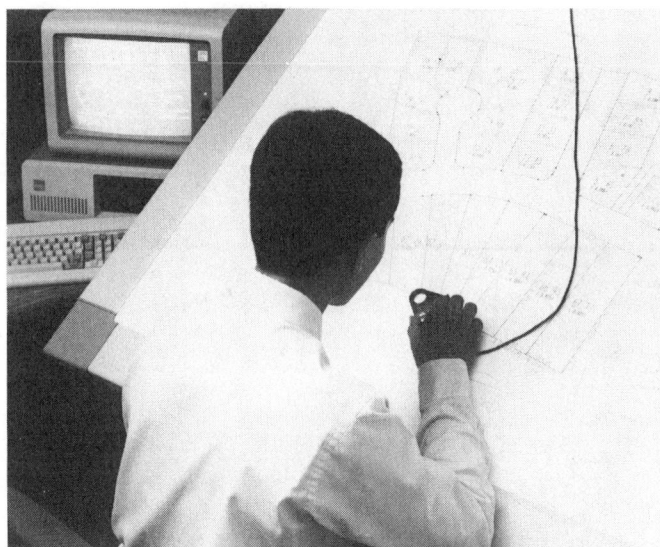

Figure 7–3 Digitizer used to establish coordinate points for drawing lines. *Courtesy Calcomp.*

points of a line and the coordinates of the line ends are transmitted to the computer, and a line is shown as output. Output is any information the computer has to show or tell the operator. A computer graphics operator can digitize an entire drawing in this manner.

The Plotter and Printers

Once a drawing has been put into the computer and a desired monitor image has been established, then an actual drawing is needed. The plotter is the mechanism that makes the drawing. There are two basic types of pen plotters: flatbed, Figure 7–4, and

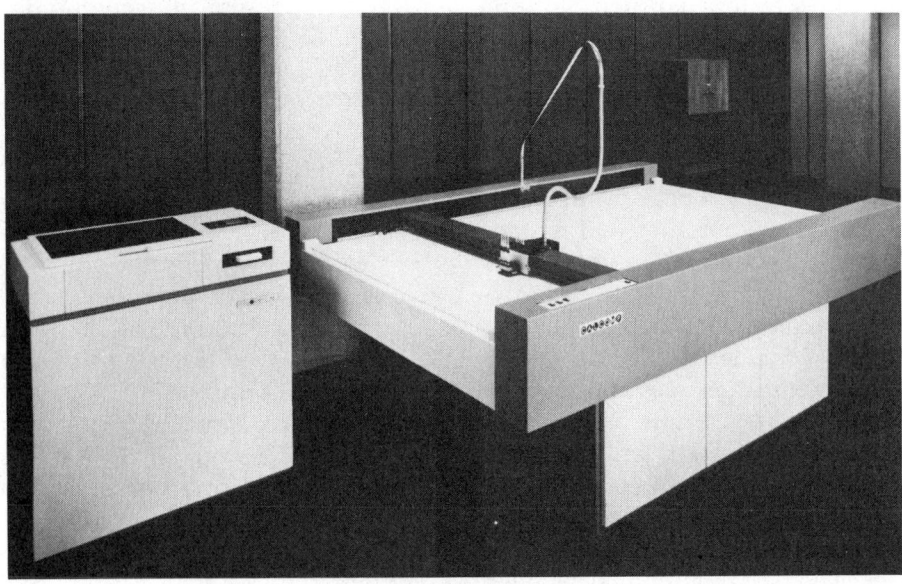

Figure 7–4 Flatbed plotter. *Courtesy Calcomp.*

Figure 7–5 Drum plotter. *Courtesy Hewlett-Packard Company.*

drum, Figure 7–5. Pen plotters use liquid ink or felt- or roller-tip pens to reproduce the computer image on plotter bond paper, vellum, or polyester film. The liquid-ink pens, similiar in construction to technical fountain pens, produce the highest quality drawings. Liquid ink pens are available in disposable and re-fillable models. Also available, but at greater cost, are the electrostatic plotters used where a large volume of plots must be made. Electrostatic plotters produce plots faster and more quietly than pen plotters. The electrostatic process uses a line of closely spaced electrically charged wire nibs to produce dots on coated paper. Pressure or heat is then used to permanently attach ink to the charged dots. These plotters are about ten times faster than pen plotters.

There are two basic types of printers that generate printed copy: impact and nonimpact printers. Impact printers operate by striking a ribbon to transfer ink from the ribbon to the paper. Two well known members of this family are the daisy-wheel printer and the dot-matrix printer. The daisy-wheel printer produces characters similiar to a typewriter and is considered to be a letter-quality printer. The dot-matrix printers create images composed of tiny dots. Usually, a dot-matrix printer that can strike 24 dots at one time (a 24-pin printer) is considered to be a letter-quality printer. Many companies use dot-matrix printers to run economical check prints. Nonimpact printers are thermal, electrostatic, ink-jet, and laser printers. The thermal printer uses tiny heat elements to burn dot-matrix characters into treated paper. The ink-jet sprays droplets of ink onto the paper to produce dot-matrix images. The best quality image comes from the laser printer. A laser draws lines on a revolving plate that is charged with a high voltage. The laser light causes the plate to discharge. An ink toner then adheres to the laser-drawn images. The ink is then bonded to the paper by pressure or heat.

COMPUTER GRAPHICS TERMINOLOGY

CADD: Computer-Aided Design and Drafting

Hardware: The workstation components such as the computer, digitizer, keyboard, and plotter.

Software: The programs or instructions that run the computer.

Input: Information given from the operator to the computer.

Output: Information given from the computer to the operator.

Program: The system that runs the computer and a set of instructions.

Commands: Operator-supplied information that results in a task performed by the computer.

Menu: A group of commands that are related in some way and allow the operator to order items needed to make a drawing.

Soft Copy: The image on the CRT screen or monitor

Hard Copy: A drawing produced on paper or film.

Bit: Smallest amount of information a computer can read, either 0 or 1.

Byte: Eight bits that make up letters or numbers.

Storage: The disk or tape is the storage device for information.

Memory: There are two kinds of memory.

   RAM: Random Access Memory. In the computer, a program goes from the disk to the RAM, which is made of computer chips. Information is held in the RAM until stored on the disk or power is removed.

   ROM: Read Only Memory. A computer chip with fixed data that is not lost when power is removed.

Default Value: One or more values that are established by the program. Alternates must be selected or default values take precedence. For example, the default value for character height may be .125 in. The computer will always output .125 in. lettering unless the size is changed by the operator.

Disk Drive: Used to write data to, and read data from, a Floppy Disk.

Display: Information placed on the monitor or screen.

Edit: To change an existing or new drawing.

Floppy Disk: A thin disk coated with magnetic material used to store data.

Joystick: A control similar to that used on video games that, when shifted, moves a cross-hair target on the screen. Used for digitizing information. Another type on some units is two thumbwheels which, when moved, control the X and Y axis of the cross hairs on the screen.

Load: To move a program from storage to the computer.

Relocate: A command that allows the operator to change the origin of a drawing or portion of a drawing.

Digitizer Tablet: The digitizer tablet is similar to the drafting table. It is an input device that converts graphic data (points) into X-Y coordinates for computer to use. The tablet usually is equipped with an electronic cursor (sometimes called a puck) or a stylus.

CADD EMPLOYMENT OPPORTUNITIES

Job openings for drafters will continue to fluctuate in response to the health of the economy, but the position of drafter will be around for years to come. The job title is changing though. Most often, a CADD drafter is termed a CADD operator. But *operator* can mean almost anyone who uses a CADD system. Hence, we may begin to see the use of CADD drafter, CADD designer, or CADD design-drafter.

As a drafter gains experience, he or she may move into a design position or that of *technician*, depending on the company, the nature of the work, and the job titles the company chooses to use. Drafters have always had the opportunity to advance into engineering, sales, estimating, contracting, managerial positions, and even company ownership. (See Figure 7–6.) The introduction of computers has opened other avenues of advancement for the CADD drafter. After gaining experience with a specific system, a drafter may move into programming and customizing company software (computer programs) and symbol libraries (files of regularly used symbols). This could even lead to positions of systems analyst, computer sales, CADD training, or CADD instructor in public and private schools. (See Figure 7–7.)

The present need for CADD operators is great. Most companies that purchase a new CADD system train their existing employees to operate it. Also, they may hire drafters with CADD experience to help implement the new system. The demand for experienced CADD operators and students with CADD training will continue to be high for several years as industry adjusts to accommodate the new tools.

EDUCATIONAL PREPARATION FOR CADD

Computer literacy is a term heard often, and everyone has a different opinion regarding its meaning. How

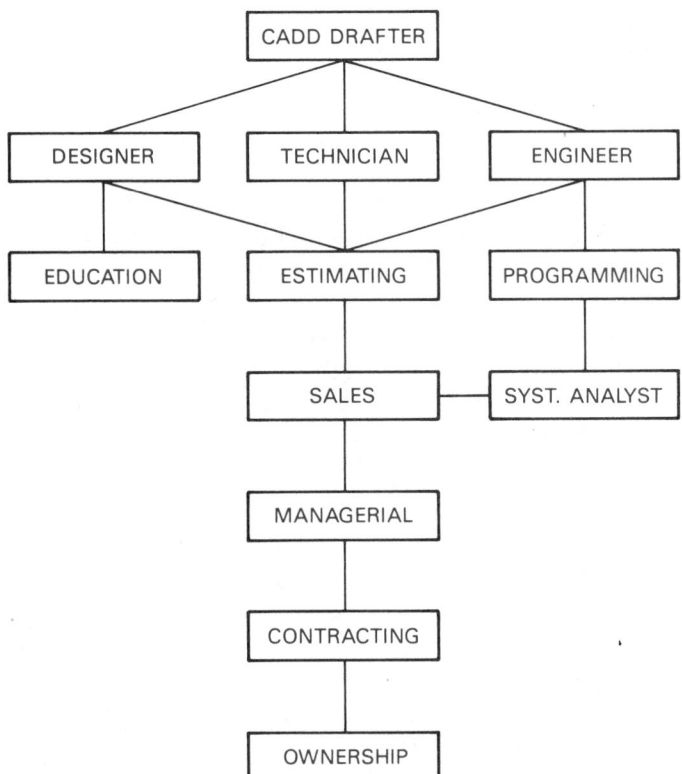

Figure 7–6 This chart shows the many different positions to which a CADD drafter can advance.

Figure 7–7 Drafters with CADD experience can become instructors in public schools or vendors of CADD systems. *Courtesy Houston Instruments Incorporated.*

much do we need to know about computers to be literate? How much does a drafting or engineering student need to know about the operation of a computer-aided drafting system in order to become a good CADD operator? Are skills learned on one CADD system transferable to another? Will the skills change in a few years? Such questions continue to arise and probably will be debated for years.

In the meantime, you, the drafting student, need to keep a few things in mind. The position of drafter is not being eliminated; only the tools have changed. The best CADD operators are those people trained in the time-proven techniques and concepts of creating a nice looking drawing. Every CADD operator needs a strong drafting and design education spiced liberally with mathematics, problem solving and analytical skills. Employers are looking for people with a solid, basic education, which means possessing the ability to read, write, and spell correctly, think logically, communicate effectively, deal with people rationally, and accept responsibility.

A knowledge of computer programming and programming language is not necessary to become a CADD operator. What is most important is to gain some familiarity with the basic operations of a computer and the other pieces of equipment at a CADD workstation. After all, almost everyone learns how to drive a car without learning to be a mechanic. Most companies who hire entry-level drafters do not expect them to have been trained on their specific system. There is always a period of training so the new employee can learn company standards and how to apply them to the CADD system. Once you learn the basics of operating a computer, you can operate any of them with a minimum amount of training. The greatest time is spent learning how to run computer software.

Unfortunately, many experts and computer programmers have generated a cloud of mystery about computers, programming, the operation of computers, and the understanding of the entire field. The instruction manuals accompanying equipment and programs have often reinforced this mystery by being written in a jargon-filled language that only other experts and programmers could understand. Today, however, the better programs are accompanied by well-written manuals that first-time users can understand.

CADD Training in School

The pressure is high for educators to develop computer-aided drafting classes and purchase CADD systems. This is not always possible or feasible. Even if your school drafting department does not have CADD, it should not deter you from studying the technology. Attending demonstrations, cooperative

work exchanges, conventions, conferences, workshops and seminars where CADD equipment is found and taking field trips to industrial sites that use CADD equipment can develop and strengthen one's knowledge of computer-aided drafting. Remember, what is important is not whether your school has a computer drafting system, but whether you study computer-aided drafting.

The purpose of this textbook is not to instruct the reader in the workings of any one specific brand of computer-aided drafting system. Such instruction is covered in detail in the operating manuals of each system. The references in this text to CADD equipment, skills, techniques, and concepts used in the industry are intended to be general. All of the assignments in this book can be done manually or on any CADD system your school may have. From this book you will learn the techniques of drafting, while the specifics of operating your CADD system will be learned from the manufacturer's instruction manual and hands-on experience.

THE LANGUAGE OF THE COMPUTER

Probably one of the most difficult aspects of communicating with computers is just that: communicating. Computers were taught to communicate by people who developed computer programming languages, and unfortunately those languages instruct computers to use words and terms unfamiliar to most people. Anyone interested in computers has been forced to learn to communicate with them on their level. But we are beginning to see a reversal and computers are beginning to communicate with people on the human level. Until such communication becomes universal, some of us will learn programming languages and the rest of us will learn the vocabulary and jargon that enable humans and computers to get along. You won't be studying programming in this text, but we will take a brief look at the words and languages used to communicate with computers.

Vocabulary and Jargon

Any subject requires a knowledge of certain terms. Most jobs or hobbies involve the use of specific items or concepts which have names and meanings. The more involved we get in our pursuits the more knowledge we acquire about the equipment, techniques, and concepts used in that pursuit. We are often unknowingly learning a specialized vocabulary, and to speak to anyone about an aspect of our interest demands the use of specific words.

The world of computers is full of jargon, which is the specialized, technical vocabulary associated with a subject. All of the words and acronyms have a meaning, but often plain English does a better job of explaining what we mean, especially to a person not skilled in the field. An acronym, by the way, is a word that is formed from the initial letters of a name, such as BASIC (Beginner's All-purpose Symbolic Instruction Code). As you become familiar with CADD you will learn many terms, some useful and others seldom used but impressive sounding. Try to sift through the vocabulary and retain those words that you need. Using vocabulary correctly is an asset for any skilled person, but tossing jargon around indiscriminately may only serve to confuse and irritate those unfamiliar with the field.

Computer Languages

Computers receive immediate instructions from information that the user provides. This immediate instruction activates a block of detailed instructions inside the computer program. The program is written in one of several different programming languages, a few of which are listed here.

BASIC (Beginner's All-purpose Symbolic Instruction Code. BASIC is a programming language that is easy to learn and easy to use. BASIC has a relatively small number of commands and statement formats, and is in wide use on many computers. There are many versions of BASIC developed to operate on specific brands of computers. BASIC is not a structured programming language and can be difficult to interpret if the program was not logically designed. BASIC was developed at Dartmouth College in the mid 1960s.

FORTRAN (Formula Translator or Translation). FORTRAN is a high-level programming language that is used for scientific, mathematical, and engineering applications. It was developed by the IBM Company in 1954 and is widely used for CADD programs.

Pascal. Pascal is another high-level language and was developed in the early 1970s. It is noted for its structured design and simplicity. It was named after Blaise Pascal, the 17th century French mathematician who developed the first desk calculator.

C. C is a high-level structured programming language designed for use on microcomputers. It was developed by Bell Laboratories.

The operator of a CADD system does not need to know computer programming techniques. In fact the operator does not need to know anything about programming to create drawings with a CADD system, just as a person who drives a car doesn't have to be an automobile mechanic. But a CADD drafter's potential is greatly increased if he or she possesses some knowledge of programming. Drafters with pro-

gramming ability may be able to customize the software to accommodate company standards and requirements. Drafters with such skills may even be able to move into positions of programmer, systems analyst, or troubleshooter for the system.

As a drafting student you will find it in your best interest to take computer programming courses while in school. Start with a course in BASIC, and if it seems to be something you'd like to continue, move on to FORTRAN and Pascal. The avenues of job advancement will be enhanced with programming abilities.

Commands and Prompts

Computers follow instructions well, but not blindly. They often ask questions in response to instructions issued to them. Instructions and questions are two important forms of computer communication to which you are exposed as soon as you turn on the machine. When you wish to get a program running in a computer you must first load the program into the computer. Type the word LOAD, and you have issued a command to the computer. A command is a specific instruction, which, when entered by the user, causes a certain action to occur, such as loading the program, or getting an error message. You may then type RUN, which commands the computer to run the program. Some systems execute the load and run procedure automatically.

Once the program is up and running (known as having been booted) the user will issue many commands in the drawing process. For instance, you may tell the computer to draw a polygon. The computer will gladly do this, but it needs additional information to perform the task. The computer may prompt you, that is, ask you a question such as, "How many sides?" You must respond with a number. What would happen if you typed a letter by mistake? You would then get an error message, or prompt on the screen, such as "incorrect response," or "please enter a number." The prompts vary from one program to the next. Some programs are claimed to be *user friendly* and others are noticeably *user hostile.* Such terms refer to the ability of the computer to relate in human terms, and so reflect the ability of the programmer to think in such a manner.

The command and prompt form of communication will become familiar to you after just a few minutes of working at the computer. This form of communication is displayed on the video screen for your reference. Some displays begin at the top of the screen and move (scroll) down, while others begin at the bottom and scroll up. As you continue to work with the computer you will eventually encounter audible prompts called beeps. These often indicate an error on the part of the operator but can also be an acknowledgement. Responding to an audible output is not critical to operating a CADD system; therefore, hearing is not a criterion for becoming an operator. Most systems use more than one tone to indicate different things, which you will quickly learn.

INPUT AT THE KEYBOARD

The layout of computer keyboards varies greatly. One keyboard is shown in Figure 7–8. The standard QWERTY typewriter keys are arranged the same, but beyond that, anything goes, and the additional keys can be found anywhere. Consider the following descriptions of some of the most common keys found on a CADD system keyboard.

Return Key

The name of this key varies, but it is most commonly labeled RETURN, ENTER, END or END LINE, and is usually located at the right side of the keyboard. It is similar to the carriage return key on a typewriter. The computer responds to a line of data entry after this key is pressed.

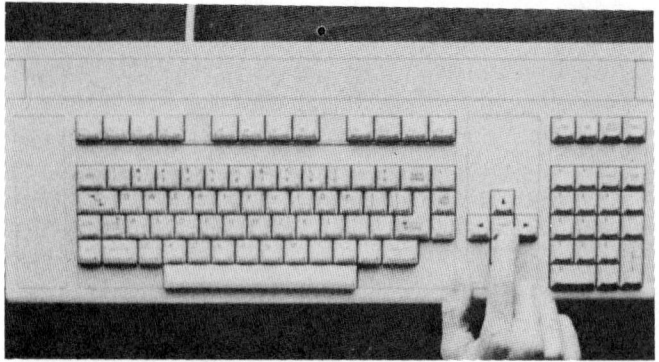

Figure 7–8 Typical alphanumeric computer keyboard. *Courtesy Sharp and Texas Instruments Incorporated.*

Escape Key

This key allows you to escape from the current command or activity that you're engaged in.

Cursor Keys

The function of these keys is to move the screen cursor. They are arranged in a group and appear as four arrows pointing in the four compass directions. They are often called arrow keys. Some keyboards may only have two cursor keys for left and right cursor movement.

Home Key

This key is used in conjunction with the cursor keys. It moves the cursor to either the top left corner of the screen or to the beginning of the line. It can be found in the center of the cluster of cursor keys or at the upper left of the keyboard.

Backspace Key

If you make a mistake in typing, press this key and you can delete what you just typed. This key can also serve to move the screen cursor back along the line just typed.

Control Key

This key is similar to a typewriter shift key because it is usually pressed along with another key (or keys) to initiate a function or command within the program. The control key is used extensively in word processing but its operation is often replaced with function keys in CADD systems.

Function Keys

These are additional keys located just about anywhere on the keyboard. (See Figure 7–8.) A popular location is along the top of the keyboard. The number and grouping pattern varies by manufacturer. They are used by the program to activate specific functions or commands. Their use may change in the program, or from one program to the next, and hence the need for function key masks or overlays. The overlay is usually a plastic template with written labels that fits around the keys. Some computers and programs display the labels of the function keys at the bottom of the screen, which eliminates the need for key overlays.

Calculator Keypad

This cluster of keys is usually referred to as the keypad and contains the numbers 0 through 9, a decimal point and arithmetic function symbols.

Remember that standards exist only as a common ground from which to deviate, and the layout of terminal keyboards is no exception. Become intimately familiar with the keyboard you will be working with, and you will be rewarded with less wasted time searching for keys and smoother-running sessions at the computer overall.

DRAWING LINES WITH CADD

Creating good drawings with a CADD system hinges on just a few things. One of the most important is your ability to learn and remember. Another is your hand-to-eye coordination between the digitizing surface and the screen. A third is your ability to un-

derstand and visualize coordinate systems as they apply to shapes on different planes and at a variety of rotation angles. The fourth is your typing ability, although this varies between CADD systems.

In this section we will describe in general the concepts, techniques, and commands used when working with any computer drafting system. A familiarity with the basics of CADD allows you to grasp the particulars of any system.

Cartesian Coordinate System

Absolute Coordinates. The Cartesian coordinate system is a rectangular coordinate system that locates a point by its distances from intersecting, perpendicular planes. The word Cartesian comes from Cartesius, the Latinized form of Descartes, a seventeenth century French mathematician and scientist. Drawings done with a computer are based on the Cartesian (rectangular) coordinate system, so it is imperative that you develop a thorough understanding of it.

The two-dimensional rectangular coordinate system is illustrated in Figure 7–9. The point of intersection of the dark vertical and horizontal lines (planes) is called the *origin*. The origin has a value of zero. Values along the horizontal line increase as you move to the right. This is called the *X axis*. The *Y axis* is the vertical line and values increase as you move upward from the origin. The values just mentioned are positive. Note in Figure 7–9 that each axis can also have negative values. Negative X values are to the left of the vertical axis, and negative Y values are below the horizontal axis. Study this figure carefully before continuing.

The best way to understand the rectangular coordinate system is to work with a piece of ten lines

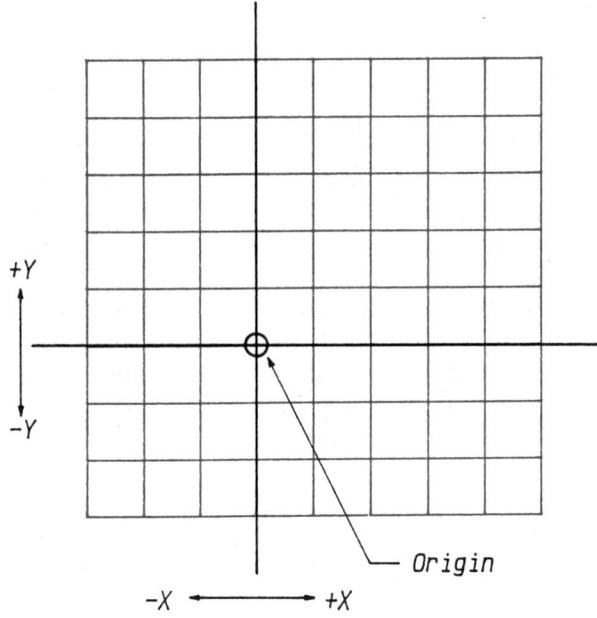

Figure 7–9 Two-dimensional Cartesian (rectangular) coordinate system.

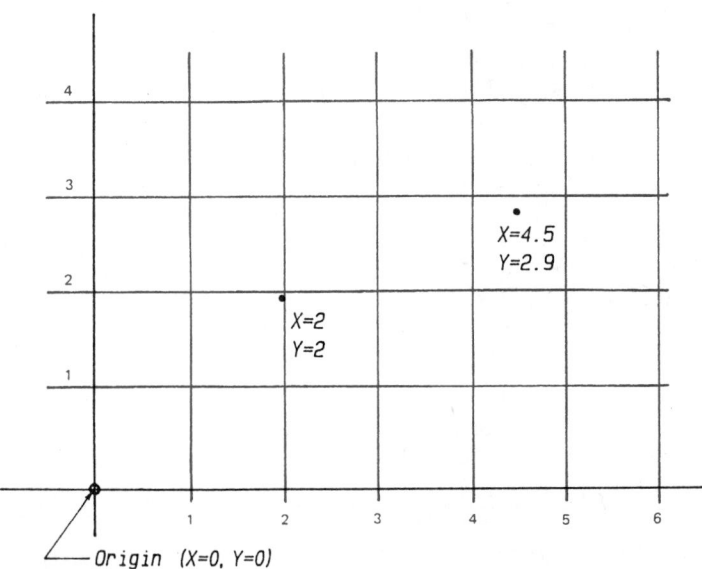

Figure 7–10 Points located on a rectangular coordinate grid.

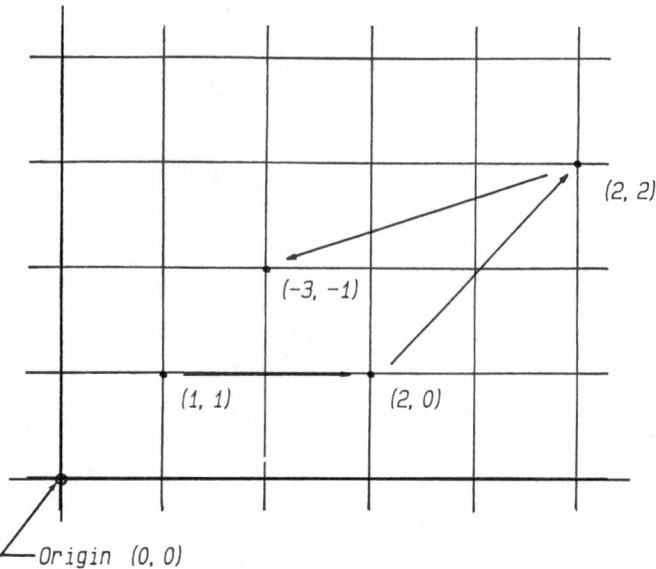

Figure 7–11 Points located using incremental (absolute) coordinates.

to the inch graph paper. Locate the intersection of any two heavy perpendicular grid lines on your graph paper. Mark this point as the origin. Both X and Y have values of zero at the origin. At each inch mark on the horizontal line to the right of the origin, write the values 1, 2, 3, 4, etc. Do the same for the inch lines above the origin along the vertical axis line. (See Figure 7–10.) Now locate the point of X=2, Y=2. First count two inches to the right on the X axis, then count two inches straight up on the Y axis. This point has the value of X=2, Y=2. Only one point in this coordinate system can have that value.

Not all points will have even inch values. Locate the point X=4.5, Y=2.9 on your grid paper. This point is located directly from the origin and not from any other point. Coordinate values are always written with the X value given first. Therefore, this point could be written 4.5, 2.9 and you would know what it means. Count the grid squares along the X and Y axes to find this point, or use a scale and measure. Remember that every point must have at least two coordinate values. A point of just 4.5 could be any location 4.5 in. from the vertical line. Well, how did you do locating this point? Are you ready to draw an object?

Incremental Coordinates. The Cartesian coordinate system uses absolute coordinates. That means that each point is referenced to the origin of the coordinate system and not the values of the points around it. The origin is fixed and does not move. Objects can also be drawn using a moving origin. In this method, each point becomes the origin and the next point is located in relation to the previous point. This method is called *incremental*, or *delta*, coordinates by some CADD systems. If each point becomes the origin for the next point, then numbers to the left and below the origin are negative. See Figure 7–11 for an example of this method.

The incremental coordinate method may be useful when using the dimensions of each line to lay out a part. It is important that you keep in mind the positive and negative aspects of this method, because each point becomes the origin of a coordinate system. For example, moving to the left of a point gives the next point a negative X value. The object in Figure 7–12 shows the relationship of points on an object constructed with incremental coordinates.

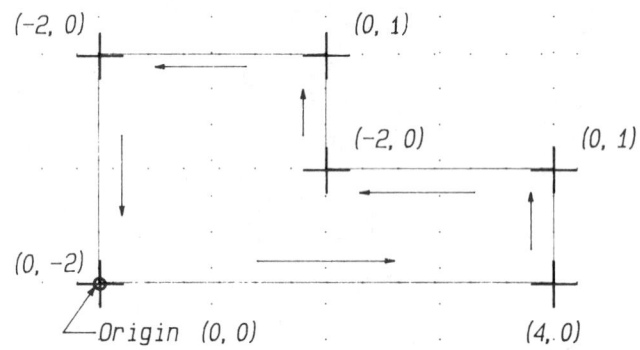

Figure 7–12 Object drawn using incremental (absolute) co-ordinates.

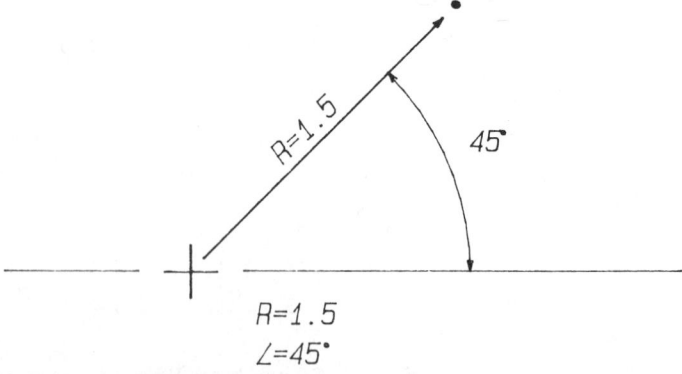

Figure 7–13 Locating a point using polar coordinates.

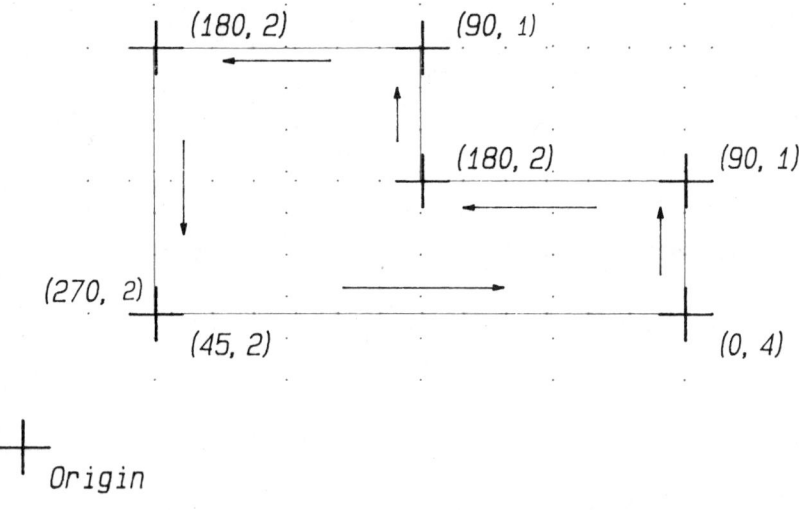

Figure 7-14 Object drawn using polar coordinates.

Polar Coordinates. Not all points can be located properly with a rectangular coordinate system. For example, a point may be at a 45° angle from horizontal at a radius distance of 1.5 in. from a reference point. Such a location defines a point by *polar* coordinates. Note in Figure 7-13 that the horizontal line has a value of 0°. Angles are measured in a counterclockwise direction from horizontal. The radius distance is measured from a specified reference, or center, point.

Polar coordinates are incremental and can be used to create a drawing if all the angles of the part are known. Figure 7-14 is the same object drawn in Figure 7-12, but the values given are polar coordinates. The first number at each corner of the object is the angle from the previous point (origin), and the second number is the radius from the origin. Study this object until you are familiar with the concept of polar coordinates.

DRAWING GEOMETRIC SHAPES WITH CADD

The process used for drawing geometric shapes involves three steps:

1. Select the command.
2. Locate the feature.
3. Input the parameters; that is, draw the feature.

Shapes

Circle. A circle, for example, may be drawn several different ways. After selecting the CIRCLE command, the information that you have about the circle

will determine the method by which you draw it. The methods are shown in Figure 7-15 (a) through (d). The first method (a) requires that two points, the center (1) and a point on the circle (2), be digitized before the circle can be drawn. The second, example (b), requires that two opposite points (1 and 2) on the circumference (the diameter) be digitized. The third, example (c), requires that three points be digitized on the circumference. The final method (d) requires that the center point be digitized and the radius be entered as a number selected from the keypad on the menu tablet, or typed from the keyboard.

Ellipse. Ellipses are quick and easy to draw on a CADD system. Most programs have a command such as ELLIPSE. In this command you are asked for the major and minor diameters and the computer automatically draws an ellipse with the information.

Arc. Arcs are constructed in the same manner as circles. But arcs are only portions of circles and therefore the two end points of the arc must be digitized. The methods of constructing an arc are shown in Figure 7-16 (a) through (d). The fourth method (d) has two variations, each requiring numerical input. The first variation requires point number 1 (beginning point) to be digitized, as well as point number 2, a location on the arc. Then a numerical value for the radius and length of the arc must be entered from the menu keypad or from the keyboard. The second variation requires the same two points, but instead of entering the radius, the center point location of the arc is entered at the keypad.

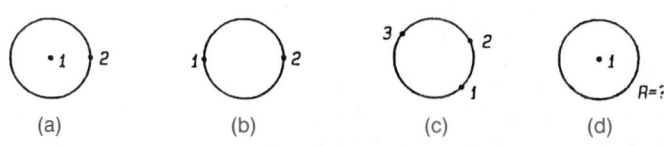

Figure 7-15 Four ways to digitize a circle.

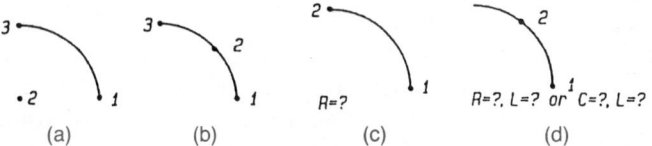

Figure 7-16 Four ways to digitize an arc.

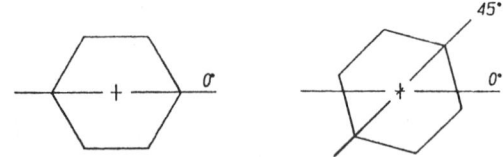

Figure 7–17 Polygon starting angles.

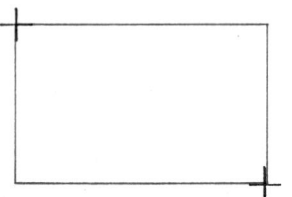

Figure 7–18 Rectangle construction using opposite corners.

Tangencies. Tangencies are easy to draw with the computer. Most CADD programs have a command or option such as TANGENT which allows you to pick a circle or arc and automatically draw a line or another circle or arc tangent to the selected object.

Polygon. A polygon can be drawn using the same methods as the circle command, but some additional information is needed. Since polygons have corners, or vertices, the computer needs to know where the first vertex should be located. A prompt asking for the location will appear on the screen and the answer should be in degrees. Figure 7–17 shows two examples of polygons that have been given different starting angles. The final bit of information the computer needs is the number of sides. After this number is entered from the menu or keyboard, the polygon is drawn.

Rectangle. A rectangle is one of the easiest shapes to draw. Only two points are needed. The first is one corner of the rectangle which may be any of the four corners. Once you digitize this corner, the direction location of the second point has already been determined. The second point is the corner of the rectangle opposite the first corner that was digitized. The computer then connects these two points with the straight lines needed to form the rectangle. Figure 7–18 illustrates this process. Of course rectangles and boxes can be drawn using the LINE command, but it takes longer.

LETTERING WITH CADD

Lettering with a CADD system is one of the easiest tasks associated with computer drafting. It is just a matter of deciding on the style or font of lettering to use, and then locating the text where it is needed.

The CADD drafter often rejoices when the time comes to place text and notes on the drawing because

no freehand lettering is involved. The computer will place text of a consistent shape and size on a drawing in any number of styles, or fonts. The FONT or TEXT command is one of several that can be found in a section of the menu labeled text, or text attributes. The drafter is also able to specify the height, width, and slant angle of characters (letters and numbers). Most systems maintain a certain size of text called the *default* size that will be used if the operator does not specify one. The term default refers to any value that is maintained by the computer for a command or function that has variable parameters. The default text height may be ⅛ in., but the user can change it if need be.

Lettering Styles

Many CADD systems possess a variety of lettering styles, or fonts. The drafter can select the style to use simply by pressing a menu-pad command or symbol, or by typing a command at the keyboard. Figure 7–19(a) shows some of the styles and sizes of characters that can be used in CADD. The size and style of characters used is dictated by the nature of the drawing. Some CADD lettering font styles include symbols such as the mapping symbols shown in Figure 7–19(b).

ABCDEFGHIJKLMNOPQRSTUVWXYZ
1234567890

ABCDEFGHIJKLMNOPQRSTUVWXYZ
1234567890

ABCDEFGHIJKLMNOPQRSTUVW
XYZ   1234567890

ABCDEFGHIJKLMNOPQRSTUVW
XYZ   1234567890

(a)

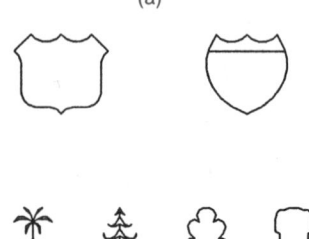

(b)

Figure 7–19 (a) Some character styles and sizes that can be used with CADD; (b) mapping symbols.

Figure 7–20 Some points on text that can be used for location purposes.

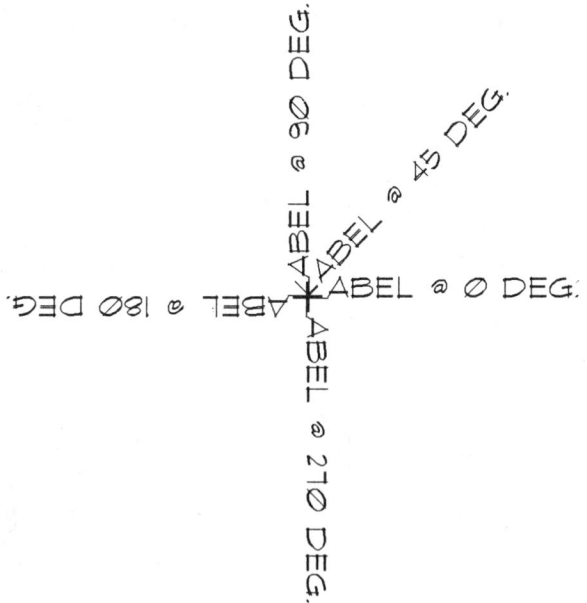

Figure 7–21 Label relationships.

Locating Text

The process of locating text has not changed. The drafter still needs to decide where to locate dimensions, notes, parts lists, and the like, but with CADD the process of placing notes is just a bit more technical. Most CADD systems provide for keyboard entry of location and size coordinates, thus allowing the drafter to accurately locate the text. But using the keyboard to input text location coordinates is a tedious process. Often key strokes are combined with digitizer stylus commands to generate text.

How is text located? By pointing to one of several places on the lettering. Figure 7–20 shows an example of several points on the text that can be used for location purposes. Not all CADD systems use all the points shown, but most systems have a command known as *text* that is used for placing written information on the drawing. Some systems may allow the operator to locate text between two points. The computer calculates the size of each letter to enable the text to fit in the desired space.

The first decision regarding text is to determine its height, width, and slant angle. Most CADD systems maintain a default text size that is used by the computer if the operator forgets or decides not to change it. The angle of rotation, direction, or text path is also determined by the drafter. The text path is the angle from horizontal that the text will lie on. An example of text path is shown in Figure 7–21. Text located on a horizontal line has a direction of 0°, and text that reads from the bottom up vertically has a direction of 90°.

CADD Dimension and Extension Lines

Extension lines are drawn by digitizing the beginning of the extension line with a small space between the structure and the line. The end of the line should extend about .125 in. past the last dimension line. The sketch will help determine the distance from the object to the last dimension line. See Figure 7–22. Dimension lines are often drawn by establishing the beginning of the line, then the command specifying the direction of the line. For

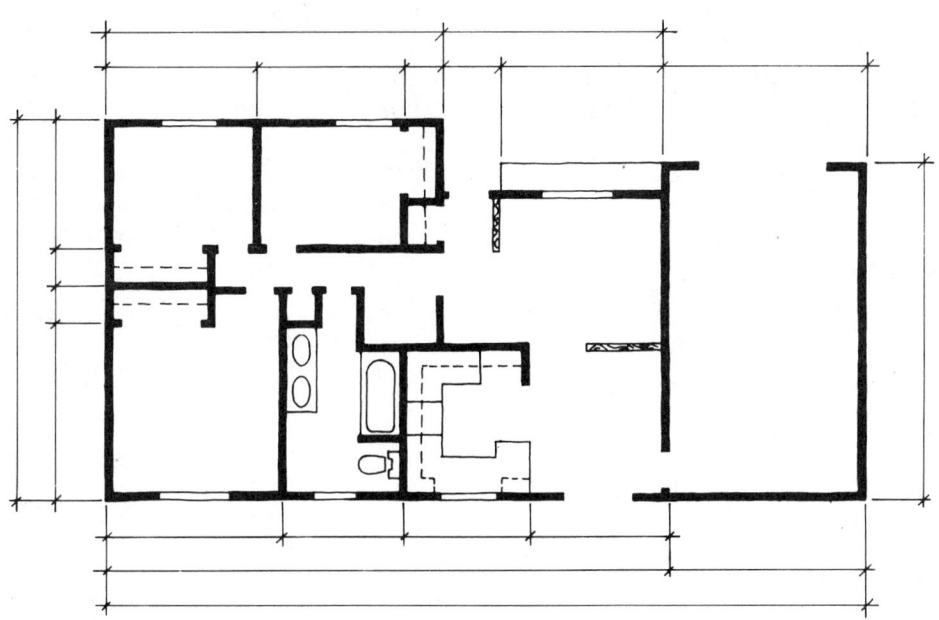

Figure 7–22 Use a layout sketch before starting the CADD drawing.

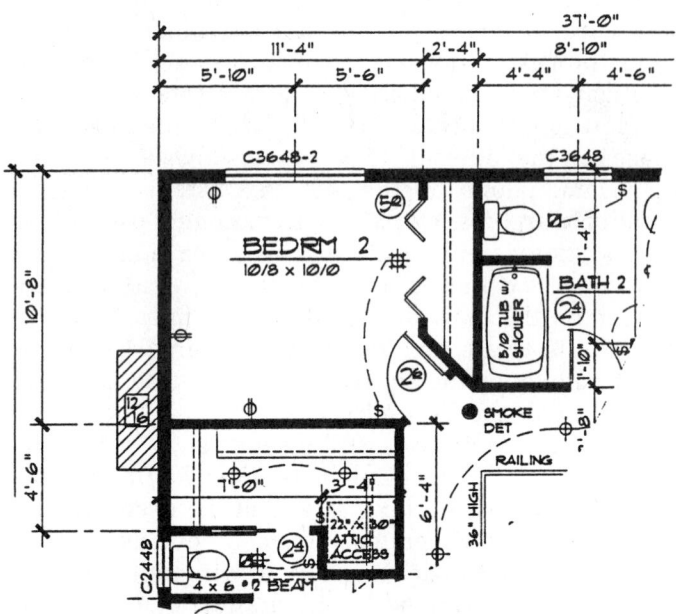

Figure 7–23 Dimension and extension lines. *Courtesy Piercy & Barclay Designers, Inc.*

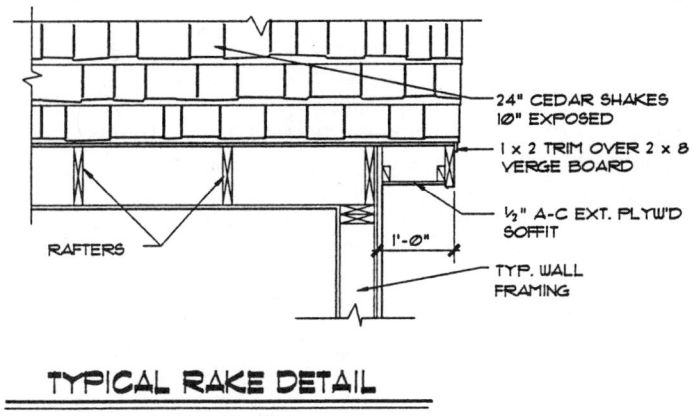

Figure 7–24 Leaders. *Courtesy Piercy & Barclay Designers, Inc.*

example, zero degrees is horizontal and to the right from the beginning point, and 90° is vertical from the beginning point. The next command would be the length of the dimension from the beginning extension line to the ending extension line. This information should be input as feet and inches. The dimension line will be drawn, capped on the ends with arrowheads or slashes, and the dimension numeral added at the center and above the dimension line or in a space provided in a break of the dimension line, as seen in Figure 7–23.

Leaders

Digitize leader lines by establishing the start of the leader and then the shoulder of the leader if a leader is to be straight with a shoulder. Point to the end of the leader if the leader is an arc. The procedure used depends upon the program. The leader will end with an arrowhead or point. See Figure 7–24.

CADD Drawing Symbols

Menus of related architectural symbols should be created. Each menu contains several boxes and one symbol is assigned to each box. Symbols are created by drawing once the feature that is to be the symbol. After it is drawn, the symbol is named and stored in the computer for future use. A group of related symbols are combined under a common menu name such as floor plan symbols. A company may want to create menus for electrical, plumbing, HVAC, foundation, cabinet or elevation symbols. Figure 7–25 shows a typical architectural menu.

Symbols are drawn on plans by placing the cursor or stylus on the menu box that contains the symbol desired. For example, if an exterior door is to be drawn, the door location would be digitized and the direction of rotation is specified. The drafter touches the cursor or stylus to the exterior door symbol on the menu. The symbol then appears on the monitor in the desired location. Each symbol has an established insertion point. The insertion point helps the drafter place the symbol on the drawing. Figure 7–26 shows the insertion point of several common architectural symbols. This same procedure is used to draw windows, plumbing fixtures, or any other architectural symbol required on a drawing. Figure 7–27 shows an architectural drawing with its many symbols created using computer graphics.

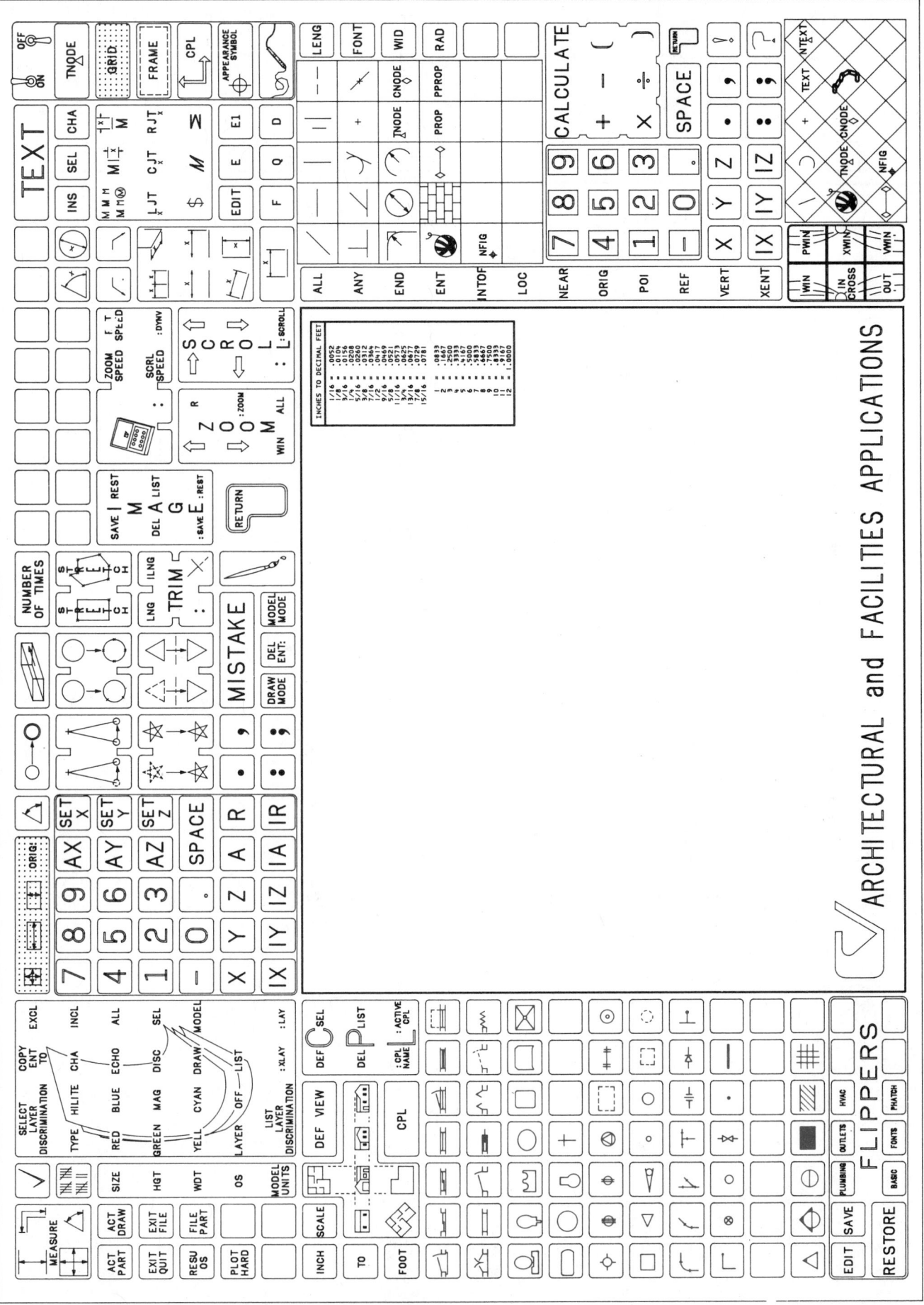

Figure 7-25 An architectural menu. *Courtesy Computervision.*

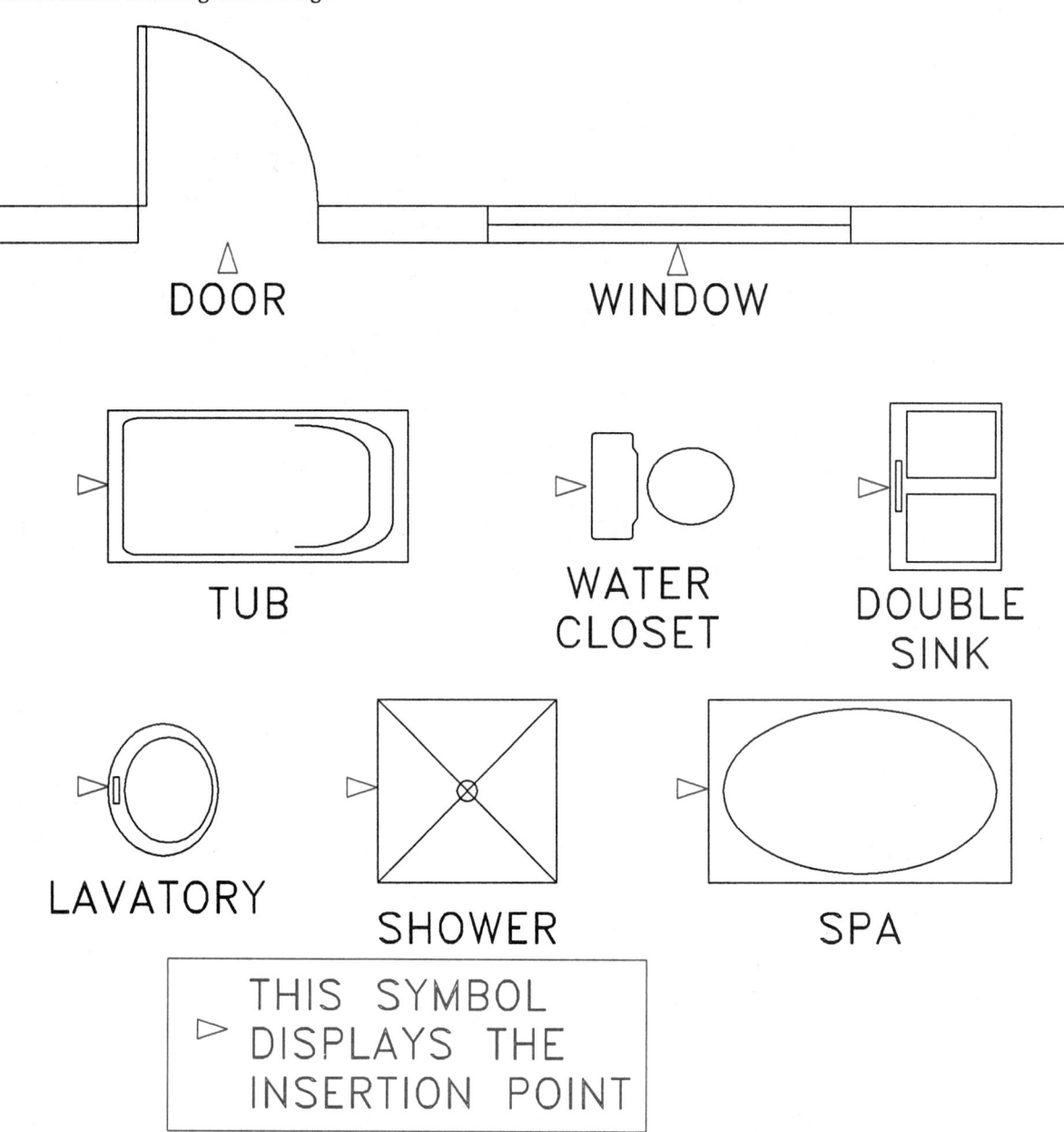

DOOR

WINDOW

TUB

WATER
CLOSET

DOUBLE
SINK

LAVATORY

SHOWER

SPA

THIS SYMBOL
▷ DISPLAYS THE
INSERTION POINT

Figure 7–26 Insertion points for several architectural symbols.

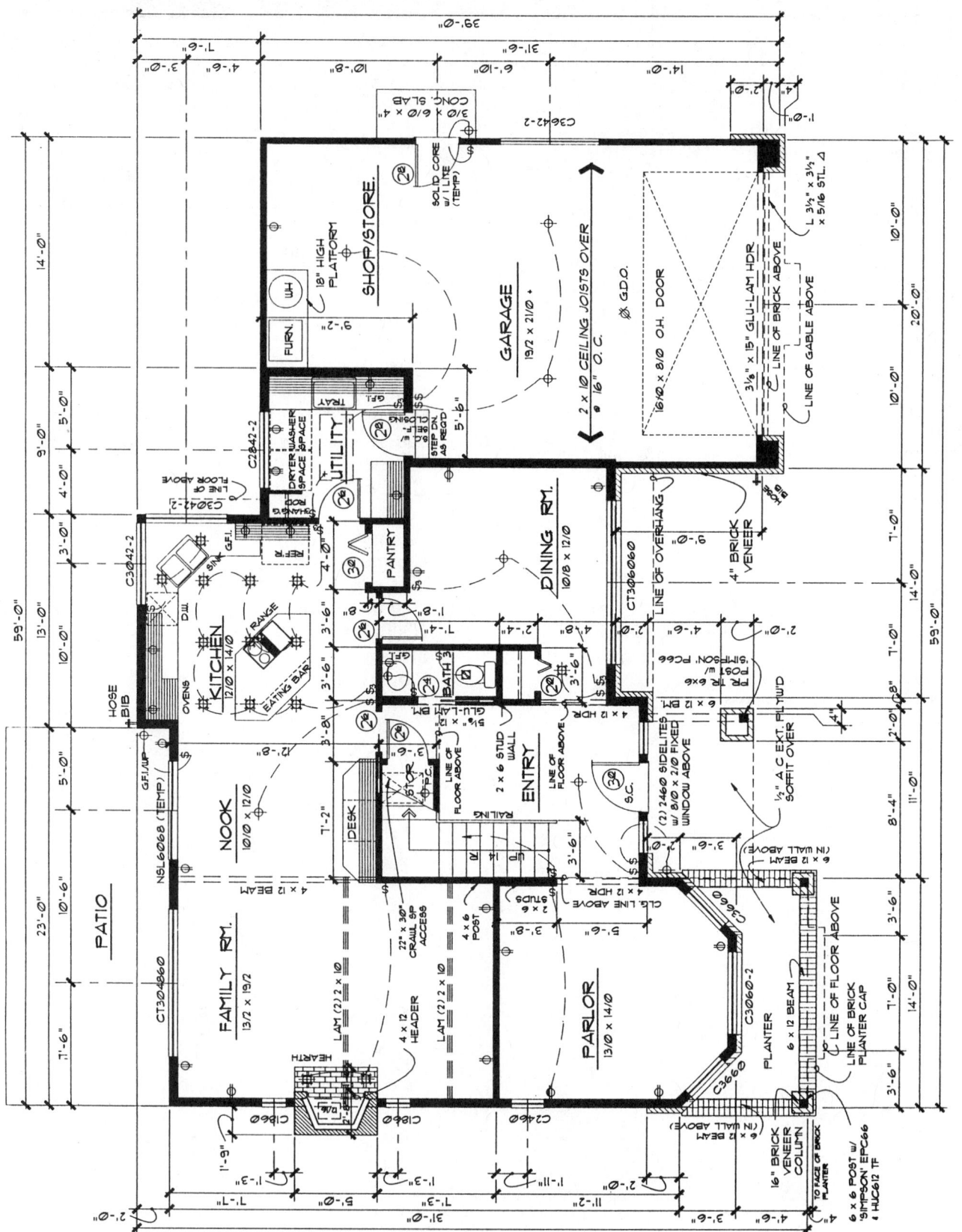

Figure 7-27 Computer-generated drawing of a floor plan with its many symbols. *Courtesy Piercy & Barclay Designers, Inc.*

COMPUTER-AIDED DESIGN AND DRAFTING IN ARCHITECTURE TEST

DIRECTIONS

Answer the questions with short, complete statements or drawings as needed on 8½ × 11 vellum as follows:

1. Use a CADD workstation or word processor to prepare the answers to the test questions. If these workstations are not available or appropriate with your course guidelines then prepare the answers using ⅛ in. high architectural lettering. Use guidelines if freehand lettering is used.
2. Place your name, Computer Aided Design and Drafting in Architecture Test, and the date at the top of the sheet.
3. Letter the question number and provide the proper answer. You do not need to write out the question.

QUESTIONS

1. What does the abbreviation CADD denote?
2. Define microcomputer in general terms.
3. Identify three factors that influence an increase in productivity with CADD.
4. Identify five nondrafting related tasks that may be performed by a computer.
5. Describe how drawing layers can be prepared on a computer graphics system.
6. Describe three ways architectural design functions are improved with a CADD system.
7. Define ergonomics.
8. Describe three factors that are potential disadvantages of CADD.
9. Describe the following computer graphics workstation components:
   a. Computer
   b. CRT
   c. Digitizer
   d. Plotter
10. Define the following computer graphics terminology:
    a. Hardware
    b. Software
    c. Program
    d. Commands
    e. Soft copy
    f. Default value
    g. Disk drive
    h. Storage
    i. Floppy disk
    j. Menu

first floor plan

CM-1430

Section Two
Residential Design

Chapter 8

Building Codes and Interior Design

BUILDING CODES have a great impact on the design and construction of a structure. As a drafter, you will be required to work frequently with codes. If you have been dreaming of a career in architecture in which you thought you could just sit down and let your creative powers flow, building codes may put a damper on your dream. Building codes place restraints on the visions of designers and architects but they are intended to protect the public by establishing minimum standards of safety for buildings. These guidelines come in the form of structural, mechanical, plumbing, electrical, fire, and security codes.

Building codes are designed to provide for public safety. As a drafter, you will hear lots of complaints about *the codes*, and you will probably have some of your own. Reading building codes and comparing cross-referenced material that you may not fully understand can be very frustrating. Don't let your frustration with the codes cause you to ignore the structures that have settled unevenly because of an inadequate foundation, roofs that have been ripped off by high winds, walls that have rotted from termite damage, or homes that have slid down steep hills from inadequate support. Building codes are intended to help spare the consumer from such problems and many others. They may seem confusing at times, but building codes not only protect the buyer of a house, they also help the designer by providing minimum guidelines so that someone's dreamhouse will remain standing after a storm.

Each city, county, or state has the authority to write its own building codes to protect its population. Some areas have chosen to have no building codes. Some areas have codes, but only on a voluntary compliance basis. Other areas have building codes but exempt residential construction. This wide variety of attitudes has produced over 2,000 different codes in the United States. Trying to design a structure can be quite challenging when faced with so many possibilities.

NATIONAL CODES

Most states have adopted one of three national codes. The *Uniform Building Code* (UBC) has predominantly been adopted throughout the western and southwestern states. The *Basic National Building Code* (BNBC) has been adopted in many areas of the midwest and northeast. This code is often referred to as BOCA which is an acronym for Building Officials and Code Administrators who publish this code. Several states in the southeast have adopted the *Standard Building Code* (SBC). It is important to remember that there are many variations to these three building codes. For example, your state may have adopted the UBC. Your county may have also adopted the UBC but with their own standards to override some areas of the code. Different cities within your county may each have their own codes. This is why the architectural drafter must carefully research and determine which governing body has jurisdiction over the construction site before drawings are begun.

To supplement the three national codes, the Council of American Building Officials have developed CABO, One- and Two-Family Dwelling Code. CABO combines parts of each major code to form one code. Areas that were once covered by a national code have adopted CABO for a single-family residence, while keeping another code for multifamily or commercial structures. In addition to these national codes, the Department of Housing and Urban Development (HUD) and the Federal Housing Authority (FHA) each publish their own guidelines for minimum property standards for residential construction.

CODES AND DESIGN

Building codes have their major influence on construction methods rather than on design. Code influences on construction methods will be discussed in Sections 3, 4, 5 and 7 of this text. There are several areas that drafters and designers need to be familiar with in order to meet minimum design standards. Some of the major areas of the residential codes that you should be familiar with include exit facilities, room dimensions, and light, ventilation, and sanitation requirements.

The UBC, BOCA, and SBC divide structures into different categories or occupancies. Houses are a Group R occupancy. This occupancy includes hotels, apartments, convents, single family dwellings, and lodging houses. The R occupancy is further divided into three categories. A single family dwelling and apartments with less than ten inhabitants are defined as R–3. This designation allows the least restrictive type of construction and fire rating group. Keep in mind that this is only an introduction to building codes. As a drafter and designer you will need to become familiar with and constantly use the building code which governs your area. Chapter 50 will give you a more detailed look at the codes. Because of the similarities of the national codes, all references in this text will be to the UBC unless otherwise noted.

Exit Facilities

The major subjects to be considered in this area of the code include doors, emergency egress (exits), and stairs.

Doors. Each house, or dwelling unit as they are referred to in the codes, must have a minimum of one door that is at least 3 ft wide and 6 ft 8 in. tall. This is very rarely a problem in the design stage. If you have ever moved in or out of a house, you know the benefits of wide doors. A problem that arises in door design and placement is that a door cannot swing over a step that is more than 7½ in. (8½" CABO) below the level of the door. This often becomes a design problem when trying to place a door near a stairway. Figure 8–1 shows some common door and landing problems and their solutions.

Emergency Egress Openings. Egress is used in most building codes to specify areas of access or exits. It is typically used in reference to doors, windows, and hallways. Windows are a major consideration when designing exits. All sleeping areas below the fourth floor must have at least one openable door

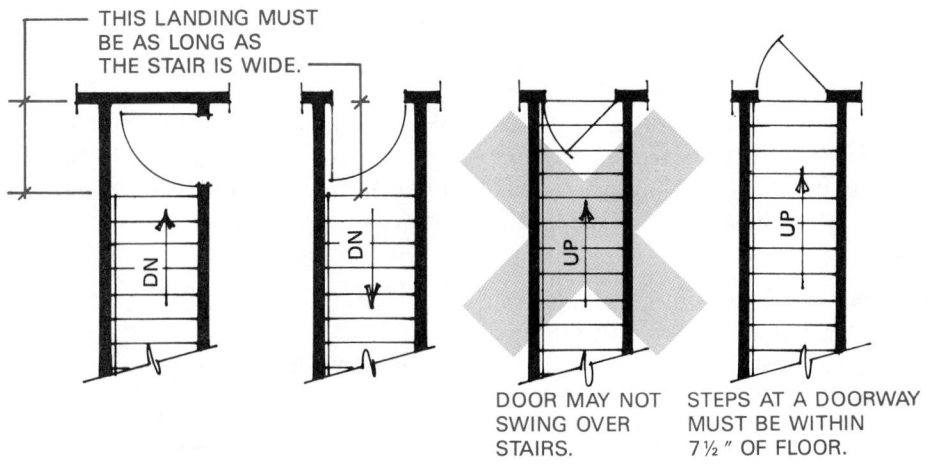

Figure 8–1 Placement of doors near stairs.

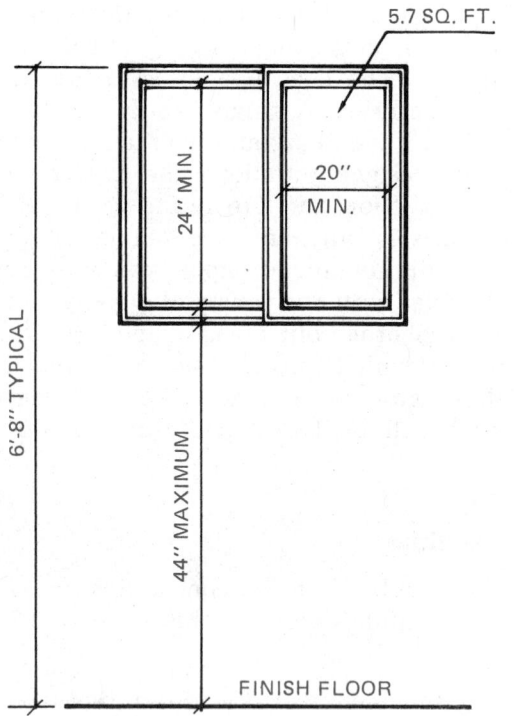

Figure 8–2 Minimum window size for emergency egress of bedrooms below the fourth floor.

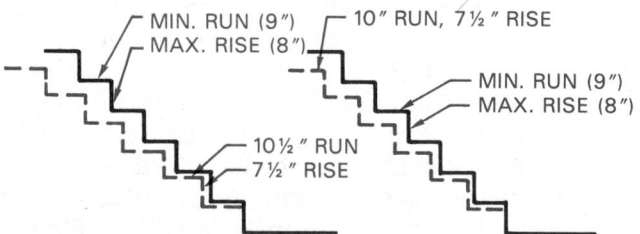

	UBC	CABO	BOCA	SBC
WIDTH (min.)	30″	36″	36″	36″
RISE (max.)	8″	8¼″	8¼″	7¾″*
TREAD (min.)	9″	9″	9″	10″

* Treads and risers must be proportioned so that the sum of two risers and a tread (exclusive of tread nosing) must not be less than 24″ and not more than 25″.

Figure 8–3 A comparison of basic design values for stairs according to major building codes.

Figure 8–4 Stair layouts comparing minimum run and maximum rise with common design alternatives.

or window that has a minimum area of 5.7 sq ft. This area must be 20 in. minimum in width and be within 44 in. of the floor. This door or window provides occupants in each sleeping area with a method of escape in case of a fire. See Figure 8–2.

Smoke Detectors. Closely related to emergency egress is the use of smoke detectors. Smoke detectors are warning devices that provide an opportunity for safe exit through early detection of fire and smoke. CABO requires one smoke detector on every floor near sleeping areas and on each additional floor OVER stairs. The smoke detector must be located either within 12 in. of the ceiling or mounted on the ceiling. It must be connected to the electrical wiring. For a one-story residence, the smoke detector must be located at the start of every hall that serves a bedroom. For a multi-level residence, a detector is required on every level with a bedroom and must be located over the stairs leading to that level. Smoke detectors should not be placed in kitchens or near fireplaces because of the strong possibility of false alarms from small amounts of smoke.

Halls. Hallways must be a minimum of 36 in. wide. This is very rarely a design consideration because hallways are often laid out to be 42 in. wide or wider to create an open feeling and to enhance accessibility from room to room.

Stairs. Stairs often can dictate the layout of an entire structure. Because of their importance in the design process, stairs must be considered early in the design stage. For a complete description of stair construction see Chapter 31. Code requirements for stair design vary greatly as seen in Figure 8–3. By following any of the minimum standards, stairs that are extremely steep, very narrow, and have very little room for foot placement would result. Good design practice would provide stairs with a width of between 36 and 42 in. for ease of movement. A common tread width is between 10 and 10½ in. with a rise of about 7½ in. Figure 8–4 shows the difference between the minimum stair layout and some common alternatives.

Spiral stairs are often thought to be the perfect stair by many clients having a residence designed. The UBC places restrictions on this type of stair. When a spiral stair is the only stair serving an upper floor area, problems are created in getting furniture from one floor to another. Building codes place limitations on the size of floor area spiral stairs may serve. Spiral stairs may not be used as an exit when the area exceeds 400 sq ft.

Headroom over stairs must also be considered as the residence is being designed. Stairs are required to have 6'-8″ minimum headroom by CABO. This headroom can have a great effect on wall placement on the upper floor over the stairwell. Figure 8–5 shows some alternatives in wall placement around stairs.

Room Dimensions

Room dimension requirements affect the size and ceiling height of rooms. Every dwelling unit is required to have at least one room that has a minimum of 150 sq ft. Other habitable rooms are required to

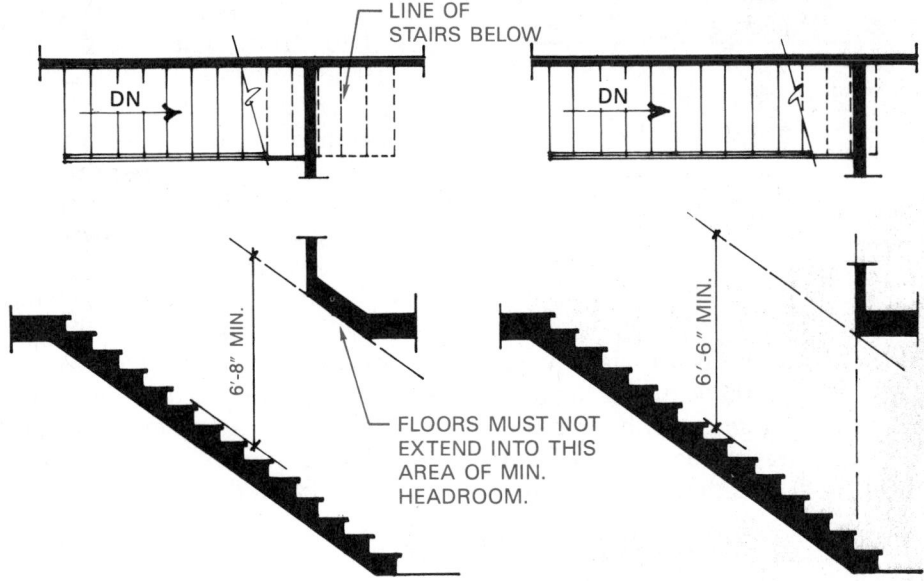

Figure 8–5 Wall placement over stairs.

have 70 sq ft. These code requirements rarely affect home design. One major code requirement affecting room size governs the space allowed for a toilet. A toilet is typically referred to as a water closet in most codes. A space 30 in. wide must be provided for water closets. This can often affect the layout of a bathroom.

Ceiling height requirements have much more effect on the design of a residence. Habitable rooms must have a ceiling height of 7'-6" minimum, but supporting beams are sometimes allowed to extend into this area. Bathrooms, kitchens, and hallways must have 7 ft high ceilings. This lowered ceiling can often be used for lighting or for heating ducts. In rooms that have a sloping ceiling, the minimum ceiling must be maintained in at least half of the room. The balance of the room height may slope to 5 ft minimum. Any part of a room that has less than 5 ft high ceilings may not be included as habitable square footage. See Figure 8–6.

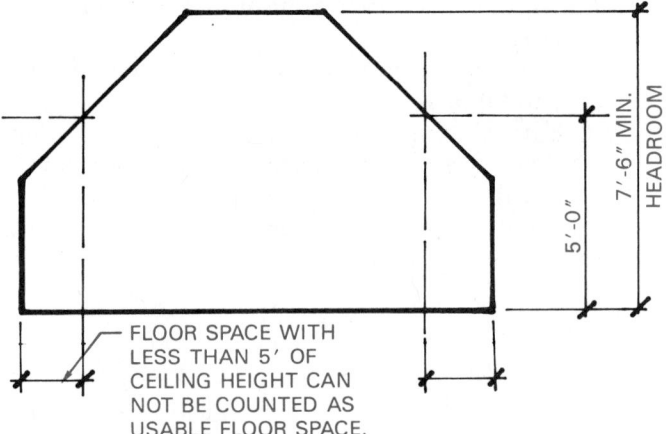

Figure 8–6 Minimum ceiling heights for habitable rooms.

The requirements described are just some of the minimum standards established for residential construction that affect interior design. Of greater effect to the design process are the client's request and guidelines for room arrangement and size.

Light, Ventilation, and Sanitation Requirements

The light and ventilation requirements of building codes have a major effect on window size and placement. The sanitation requirements are so minimal that they will rarely affect the design process. Each house is required to have a bathroom that has a water closet, lavatory, and either a shower or a tub. Each house is also required to have a kitchen with a sink. Each sink, lavatory, and tub or shower must also have hot and cold water.

The codes covering light and ventilation will have a broad impact on the design of the house. Many preliminary designs often show entire walls of glass to take advantage of beautiful surroundings. At the other extreme, some houses have very little glass and thus no view but very little heat loss. Building codes will affect both types of designs.

All habitable rooms must have natural light provided by windows. Habitable rooms would include living, dining, and family rooms, bedrooms and dens. Nonhabitable rooms would include workshops, and storage and utility rooms. Kitchens are habitable rooms but are not required to meet the light and ventilation requirements.

Figure 8–7 shows a comparison of building code requirements for windows. A bedroom that is 9 × 10 ft. would be required to have a window with a glass area of 7.2 sq ft to meet BOCA, CABO, and SBC standards, and 9 sq ft to meet the minimum

	UBC	CABO	BOCA	SBC
LIGHT	10% 10 sq ft min.	8%	8%	8%
VENTILATION	5% 5 sq ft min.	4%	4%	4%

Figure 8–7 Light and ventilation requirements according to major building codes.

standards of UBC. Maximum limits of glass vary between 17 and 22 percent of the exterior heated wall area of the entire house. Homes can have more glass, but typically it is required to be triple glazed to help cut down heat loss. Another limit to the amount of glass area would be in locations that are subject to strong winds or earthquakes. Because of the lateral movement created by winds and earthquakes, window and wall areas must be carefully proportioned to provide lateral stability.

Windows are also required to provide natural ventilation in habitable rooms as shown in Figure 8–7. An exception to this requirement is to provide mechanical ventilation for all rooms except sleeping areas. Bathrooms and laundry rooms must be provided with an openable window or a fan that can provide five air changes per hour. These fans must be vented to outside air. For lighting and ventilation requirements, rooms may be considered adjoining when half of the wall dividing the two rooms is open and unobstructed.

BUILDING CODES AND INTERIOR DESIGN TEST

DIRECTIONS

Answer the questions with short complete statements or drawings as needed on an 8½ × 11 drawing sheet as follows:

1. Use ⅛ in. guidelines for all lettering.
2. Letter your name, Building Codes and Interior Design Test, and the date at the top of the sheet.
3. Letter the question number and provide the answer. You do not need to write out the question.
4. Do all lettering with vertical uppercase architectural letters. If the answer requires linework, use proper drafting tools and technique. Answers may be prepared on a word processor if appropriate with course guidelines.
5. Your grade will be based on correct answers and quality of line technique.
6. Answers should be based on the UBC unless otherwise noted.

QUESTIONS

1. What is the minimum required size for an entry door?
2. Give the maximum rise for stair treads for:
   a. UBC
   b. SBC
   c. BOCA
   d. CABO
3. According to UBC, all habitable rooms must have what percent of floor area in glass for natural light?
4. What is the required width for hallways?
5. List the minimum width for residential stairs according to the CABO.
6. What is the minimum ceiling height for a kitchen?
7. What is the maximum height that bedroom windows can be above the finish floor?
8. Toilets must have a space how many inches wide?
9. What are the maximum areas of glass that are allowed without special provisions?
10. List three sanitation requirements for a residence.
11. What are the area limitations of spiral stairs?
12. For a bedroom that is 10′ × 12′, what area is required to provide the minimum ventilation requirements?
13. List the minimum square footage required for habitable rooms.
14. For a sloping ceiling, what is the lowest height that is allowed for usable floor area according to SBC?
15. What is the minimum size opening for an emergency egress?

Chapter 9
Room Relationships and Sizes

AS A junior drafter, you will not usually be involved in the design process. An understanding of basic design relationships and sizes will be helpful, however, so that you may advance in your architectural career. Architecture probably has more amateur *experts* than any other field. Wide exposure to houses causes many people to feel that they can design their own house. Because they know what they like, many people attempt to draw their own plans only to have them rejected by building departments. Or worse yet is the person who has drawn and built his or her own home only to sell it because it does not meet the family's needs. Designing houses can be done by most anyone. Designing a home to meet a variety of family needs takes more knowledge.

This chapter will introduce the major areas of interior design that need to be considered when designing a home including information that goes beyond the scope of just designing a residence. You will become familiar with room relationships and sizing that affect the livability of the living, sleeping,

and service areas of a home. Not all families will need each of these areas, and in some houses they may be combined. As you read this chapter, you will be exposed to several different floor plans. Each is a residence designed for a specific family and a specific site. Faults can be found in each of these homes. But, at this point, avoid spending too much time in finding fault with each house, and concentrate on studying how the three areas of the homes relate to one another.

LIVING AREA

The living area can be considered the living, dining, and family rooms, den and nook. These are the rooms or areas of a house where family and friends will spend most of their leisure time.

Living Room

Depending on the size of the house, the living room may be either a formal or informal area. In a home without a family room or basement, the living room must serve as an entertainment area and also as a place where the family can relax. A room of about 13' × 18' will serve adequately for most furniture arrangements. This area can be made to seem larger if the living room is attached to the dining

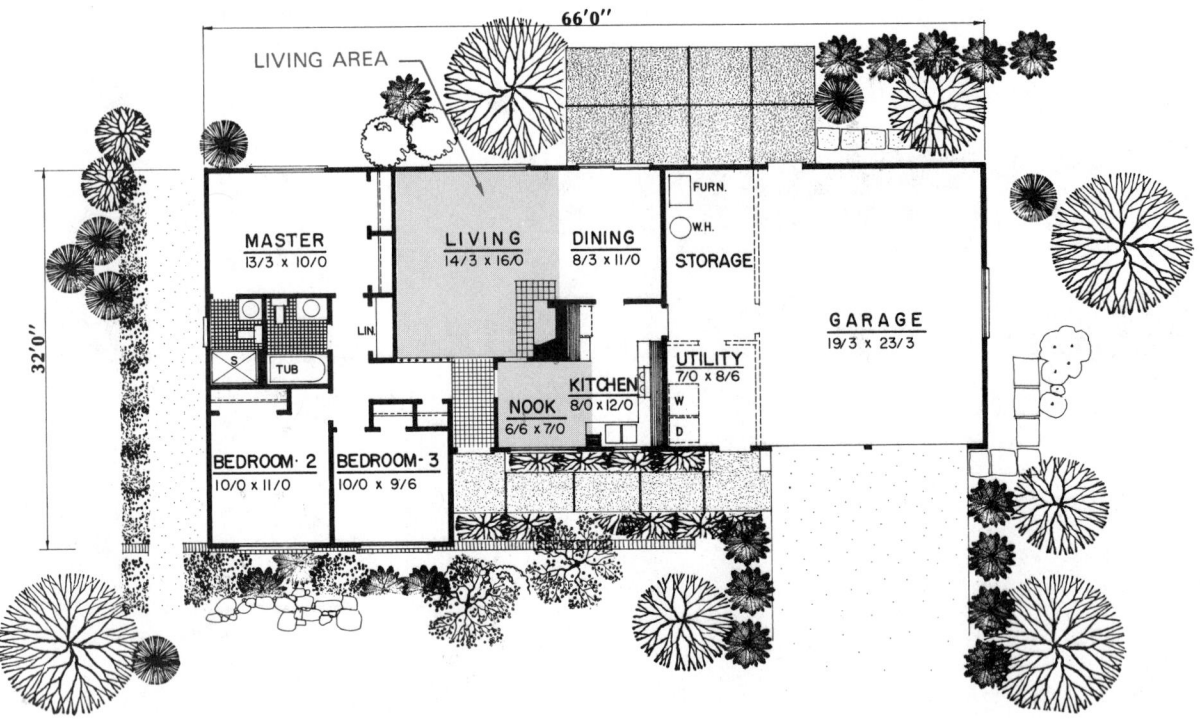

Figure 9–1 The living area of a small home. Although the room sizes are small, they appear larger because they are open to each other. *Courtesy Piercy & Barclay Designers, Inc.*

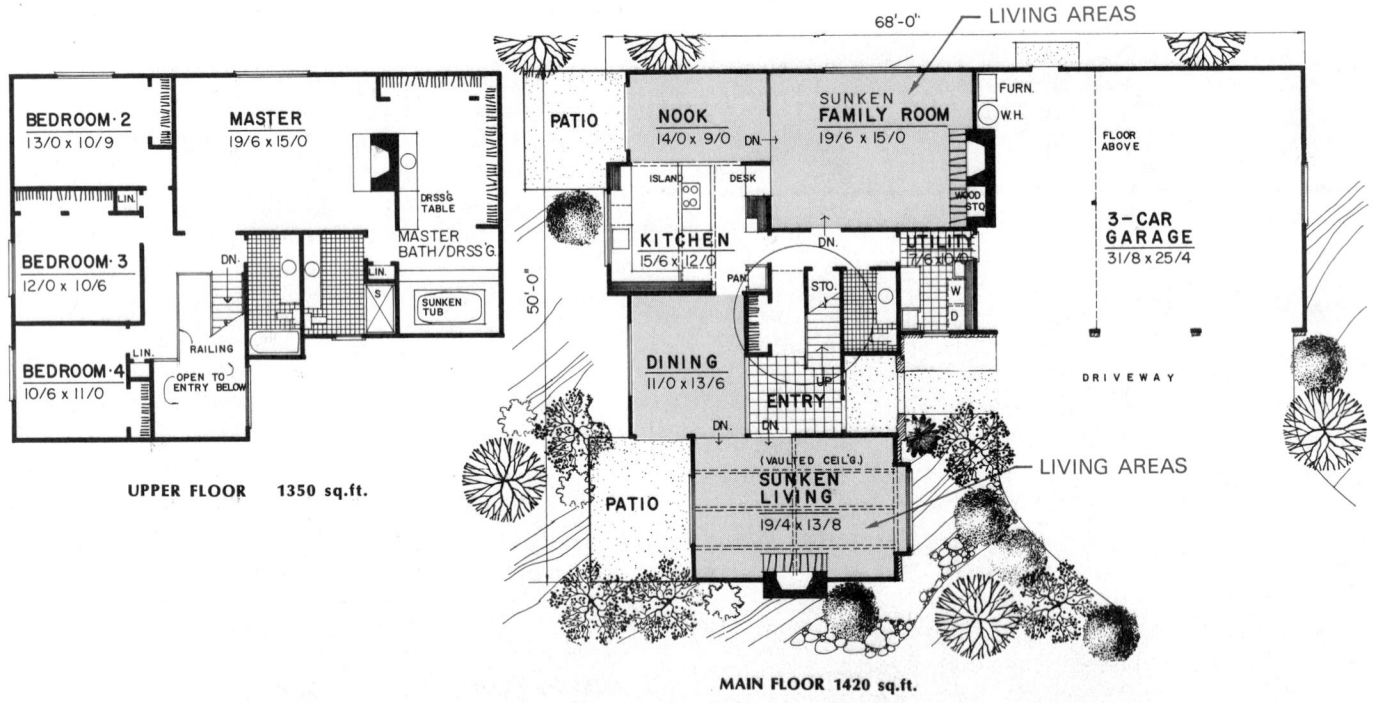

Figure 9–2 Living areas of a large home. Each room is separated from the others for privacy but easily accessible for entertaining. *Courtesy Piercy & Barclay Designers, Inc.*

area as shown in Figure 9–1. In larger residences, the living room is often set apart from other living areas to give it a more formal effect. It becomes a room where guests are entertained and a room for

quiet conversation apart from the noisier activities of other rooms of the living area. See Figure 9–2.

The living room is usually placed near the entry so that guests may enter the living room without having to pass through the rest of the house. When placed on the west side of the house, the room will have natural light in the evening when the room is most commonly used.

Family Room

A family room is probably the most used area in the house. A multipurpose area, it is used for such activities as watching television, informal entertaining, sorting laundry, playing pool, or eating. With such a wide variety of possible uses, planning the family room can be quite difficult. The noise from the family room needs to be separated from the living room. The family room needs to be near the kitchen since it is often used as an eating area.

Sizes can vary greatly depending on the design criteria for the residence. When designed for a specific family, the size of the family room can be planned to meet their needs. When the room is being designed for a house where the owners are unknown, the room must be of sufficient size to meet a variety of needs. An area of about 13′ × 16′ should be the minimum size considered for a family room. This would be a small room but it would provide sufficient area for most activities. If a wood stove is in the family room, the room should be large enough to allow for the heat from the stove. Often in an enclosed room where air does not circulate well, the area around a stove or fireplace is too warm to sit comfortably.

Dining Room

Dining areas, depending on the size and atmosphere of the residence, can be treated in several ways. The dining area is often part of, or adjoining, the living area as was seen in Figure 9–1. For a more formal eating environment the dining area will be near but separate from the living area. The two areas are usually adjoining so that guests may go easily from one area to the other without passing through other areas of the house.

Casual dining rooms can be as small as 9′ × 11′ if the area is open to another area. A formal dining room should be about 11′ × 14′. This will allow room for a hutch or china cabinet as well as the table and chairs. It will also allow for chair placement and room to walk around the table.

Nook

When space and finances will allow, a nook or breakfast area is often included in the design. This area is typically where the family will eat most of its meals or snacks. The dining room then becomes an area for formal eating only. Both the dining room

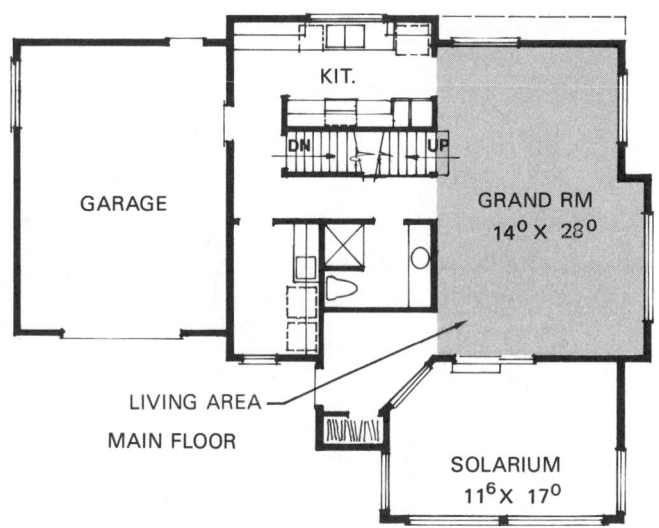

Figure 9–3 The great room is one large room which serves as the living, dining, and family rooms. *Courtesy Jeff's Residential Designs.*

and the nook need to be near the kitchen. If possible, the nook should also be near the family room.

Figure 9–3 shows another alternative for the living, dining, and family rooms. Where space is at a premium, these areas are often placed together in one room called a grand room.

SLEEPING AREA

Quite simply, the sleeping area consists of the bedrooms. These rooms should be placed away from the noise of the living and service areas and out of the normal traffic patterns. Bedrooms are generally located with access from a hallway for privacy from living areas and to be near bathrooms. Care must be taken to keep the bathroom plumbing away from bedroom walls. One way to accomplish this is to place a closet between the bedroom and the bath. If plumbing must be placed in a bedroom wall, use a 2 × 6 stud wall with insulation to help control noise. See Section 3 for other methods.

Bedrooms

Bedrooms will function best on the southeast side of the house. This location will place morning sunlight in the rooms. When a two-level layout is used, bedrooms are often placed on the upper level away from the living areas. Not only does this arrangement provide a quiet sleeping area, but bedrooms can often be heated by the natural convection of heat rising from the living area. Another option is placing the bedrooms in a daylight basement as shown in Figure

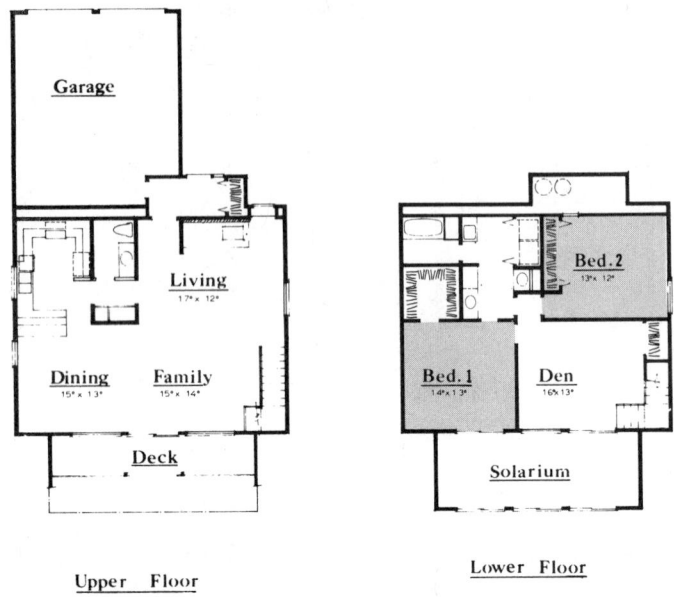

Upper Floor   Lower Floor

Figure 9-4 Bedrooms in a daylight basement. This plan is a variation of the plan in Figure 9-3, with the levels reversed. *Courtesy Jeff's Residential Designs.*

9-4. Care must be taken in basement bedrooms to provide direct exits to the outside as specified in the previous chapter. An advantage of a bedroom in a daylight basement is the cool sleeping environment that the basement provides.

Size needs vary greatly with bedrooms. Spare or children's bedrooms are often as small as 9′ × 10′. This might be adequate for a sleeping area but not if the room is also to be used as a study or play area. Ideally each bedroom should have enough space so that older children or teenagers have an area to

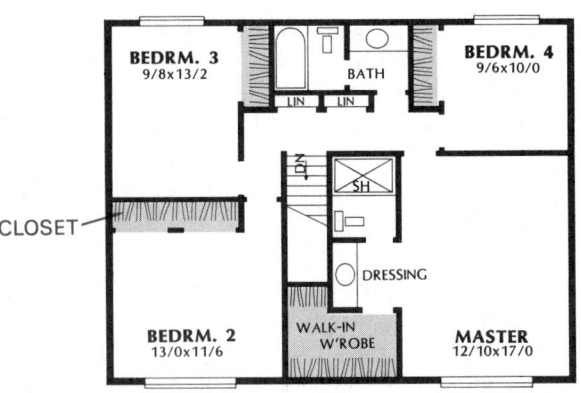

Figure 9-6 Closets can be used as a noise buffer between rooms. *Courtesy Piercy & Barclay Designers, Inc.*

play or study away from the rest of the family. This requires a space of about 12′ × 14′ plus closet areas. The master bedroom should be at least 12′ × 14′ plus closet areas. An area of 13′ × 16′ will make a spacious bedroom suite. Try to arrange bedrooms so that at least two walls can be used for bed placement. This is especially important in the master bedroom to allow for periodic furniture movement.

Closets

Each bedroom should have its own closet with a minimum length of 4′. If the closet must be small, a double-pole system can be used to double the storage space as seen in Figure 9-5. Closets can often be used as a noise buffer between rooms as shown in Figure 9-6. Master bedrooms often will have a walk-in closet. It should be a minimum of 6′ × 6′

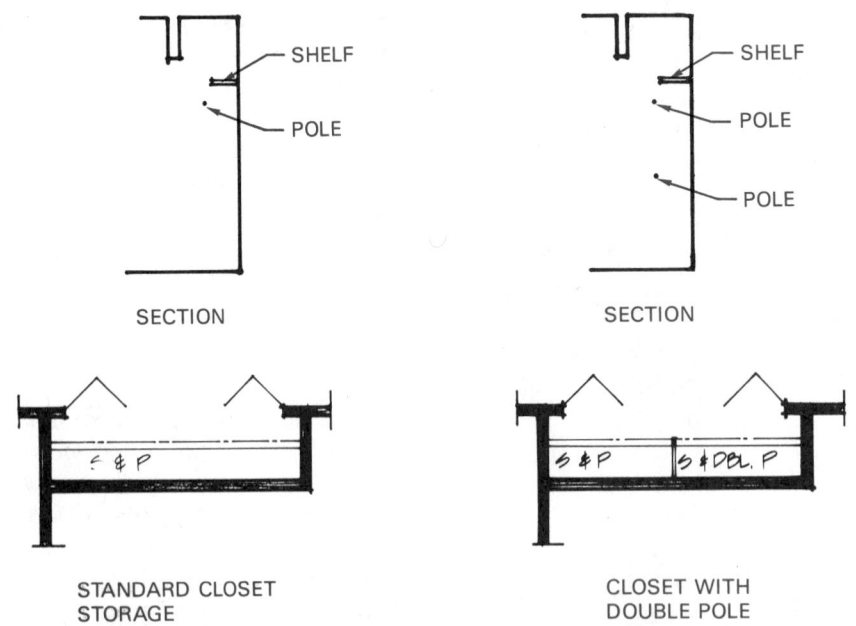

Figure 9-5 Wardrobe storage can be increased by the addition of a second pole. Some single-pole storage should be provided for long garments.

to provide adequate space for clothes storage. A closet of 6′ × 8′ provides much better access to all clothes. Space must also be provided near the bedrooms for linen storage. A space 2 ft wide and 18 in. deep would be minimal but try to provide a closet that is 4 ft long and 24 in. deep. Refer to FHA (Federal Housing Administration) minimum property standards for further information.

SERVICE AREA

Bath, kitchen, and utility rooms and the garage are each considered a part of the service area. Notice that three of the four areas have plumbing in them. Because of the plumbing and the services that each provides, an attempt should be made to keep the service areas together. Another consideration in placing the service area is noise. Each of these four areas tends to have noises that will interrupt activities of the living and sleeping areas.

Bathrooms

Bathrooms are often placed so that access is gained from a short hallway in order to provide privacy from living areas. A house with only one bathroom must have it located for easy access from both the living and sleeping areas. Access to the bathroom should not require having to pass through the living or sleeping areas. See Figure 9–7.

When a residence has two or more baths, they are often placed back-to-back to help reduce plumbing costs similar to the baths shown in Figure 9–8. This allows one bathroom to serve both the living and children's sleeping areas and the other to serve only the master bedroom. A second bathroom is a

SECOND FLOOR PLAN
985 SQUARE FEET

Figure 9–8 Bathrooms are often placed back-to-back to reduce plumbing costs. *Courtesy Home Building Plan Service.*

desirable feature and will help the resale of the home. Figure 9–9 shows a common alternative for bathroom layouts with a half-bath downstairs, and two full bathrooms upstairs. This allows guests convenient access to a bathroom from the living areas, and still provides full facilities for the bedrooms. A half-bath contains a lavatory and water closet.

Kitchens

A kitchen is used through most of a family's waking hours. It needs to be located close to the dining areas so that serving meals does not require extra steps. The kitchen and eating areas in Figure 9–10 provide a formal dining area with a separate area for family dining.

The kitchen should also be near the family room. This will allow those preparing meals to still be part of family activities. When possible, avoid placing the kitchen in the southwest corner of the home. This location will receive the greatest amount of natural sunlight and could easily cause the kitchen to overheat. With the kitchen creating its own heat, try to place it in a cooler area of the house unless venting and shading precautions are taken. One advantage of a western placement is the natural sunlight available in the late evening.

When designing a house for families with young children, a kitchen with a view of indoor and outdoor play areas is a valuable asset. This will allow for the supervision of playtimes and control of traffic in and out of the house.

The kitchen is often closely related to the utility area. Because these are the two major workstations in the home, a kitchen close to the utility room can save valuable time and energy as the daily house

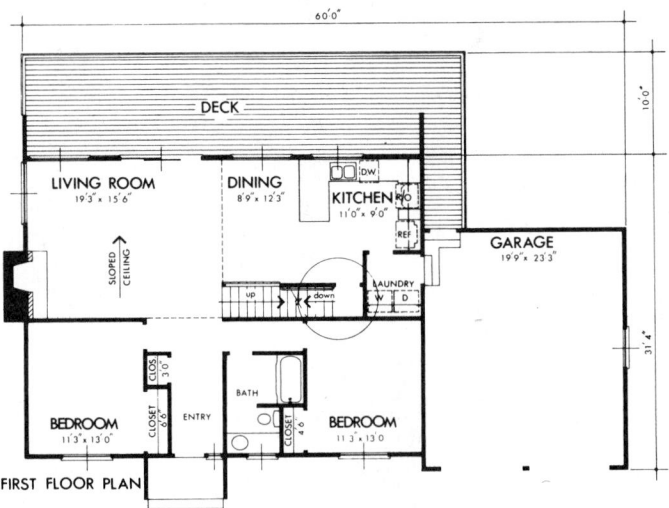

Figure 9–7 Bathroom access should not require having to pass through the living or sleeping areas. *Courtesy Home Building Plan Service.*

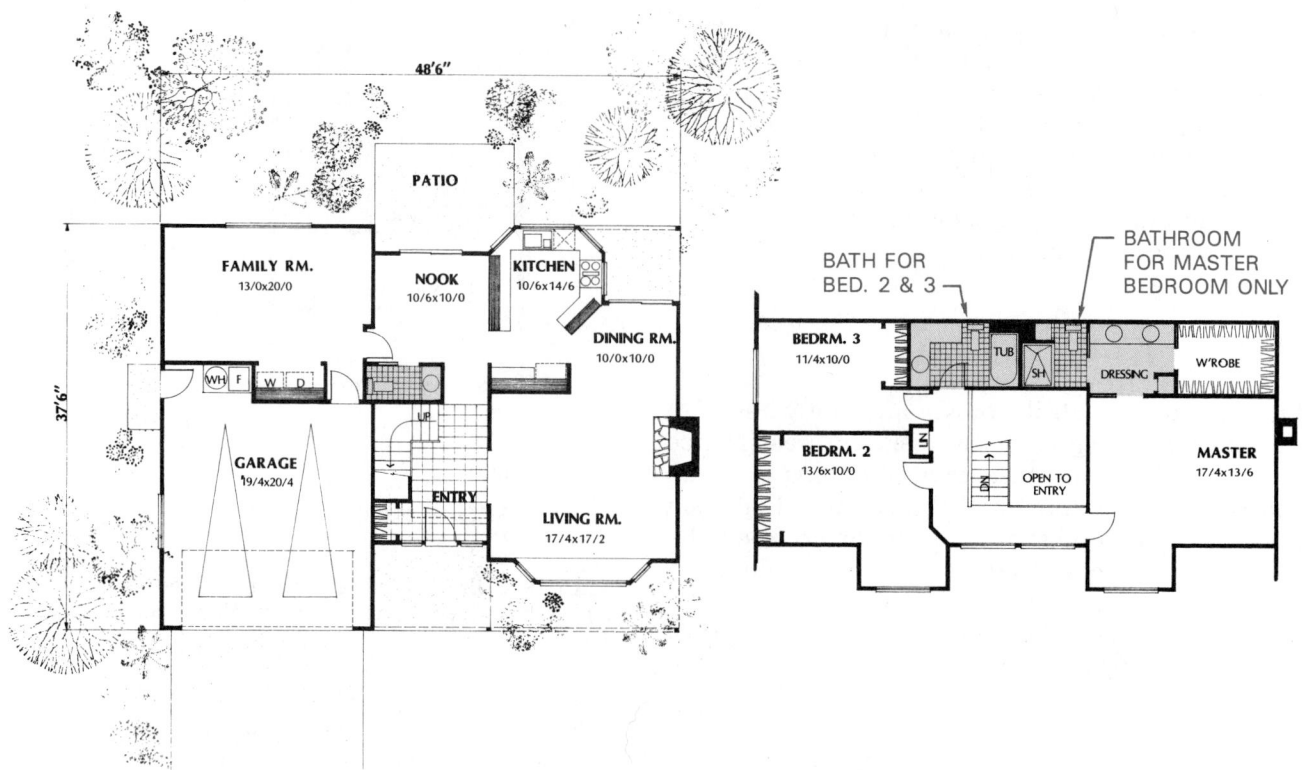

Figure 9-9 A half-bath downstairs with two full bathrooms upstairs. The lower bathroom can easily serve all the rooms on the lower floor. The upper bathrooms can be reached from the bedrooms or may be used by guests from the lower floor. *Courtesy Piercy & Barclay Designers, Inc.*

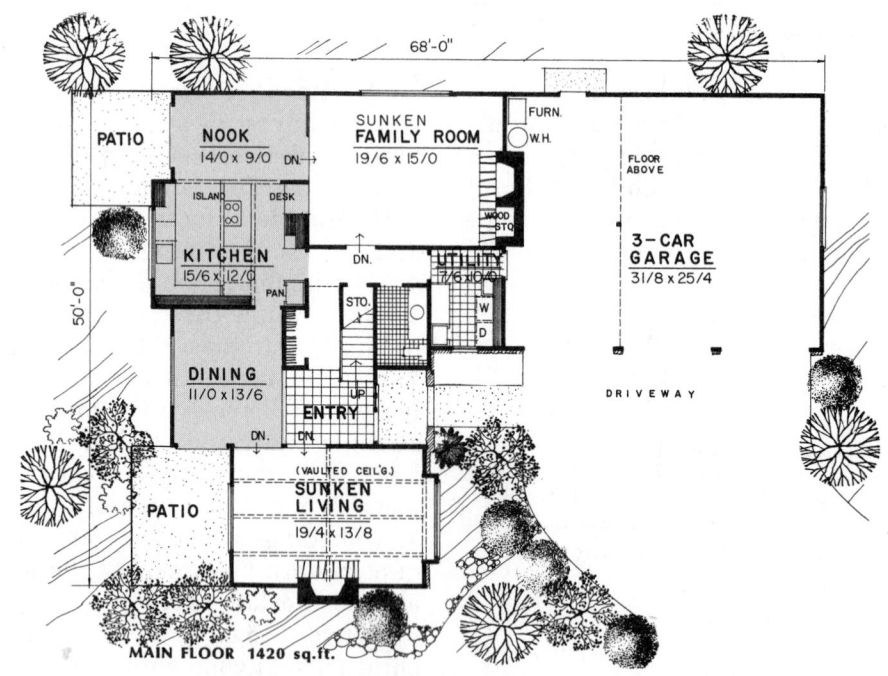

Figure 9-10 The kitchen and eating areas need to be closely related. This kitchen provides for casual eating in the nook and formal eating in the dining room. *Courtesy Piercy & Barclay Designers, Inc.*

chores are done. Also helpful in kitchen planning is to place the kitchen near the garage or carport. This location will allow groceries to be unloaded easily.

Not only must the kitchen location be given much thought, but the space within the kitchen also demands great consideration. Perhaps the greatest challenge facing the designer is to create a workable layout in a small kitchen. Layout within the kitchen includes the relationship of the appliances to the work areas. In addition, the relationship of the kitchen to other rooms also needs to be considered. If care is not taken in the design process the kitchen can become a hallway. The kitchen needs to be in a central location but traffic must flow around the kitchen, not through it. Figure 9–11(a), 9–11(b), and 9–11(c) shows the traffic pattern in three different kitchens. The kitchen in Figure 9–11(a) has no through traffic to disrupt the work areas. The kitchen in Figure 9–11(b) has traffic that goes through the kitchen but not through its major working areas. The kitchen in Figure 9–11(c) has a traffic pattern that would be disruptive to food preparation.

In addition to the traffic patterns from the kitchen to other rooms, consideration must be given to the traffic pattern within the kitchen. Figure 9–12 shows several different kitchen layouts and their traffic patterns. The traffic pattern, or work triangle as it is known, shows the relationship of the sink, refrigerator, and the stove.

The kitchen sink is often placed under a window. This allows for supervision of outdoor activities and provides a source of light at this workstation. If the residence is being designed for an area where freezing is a problem, the plumbing wall can be framed with

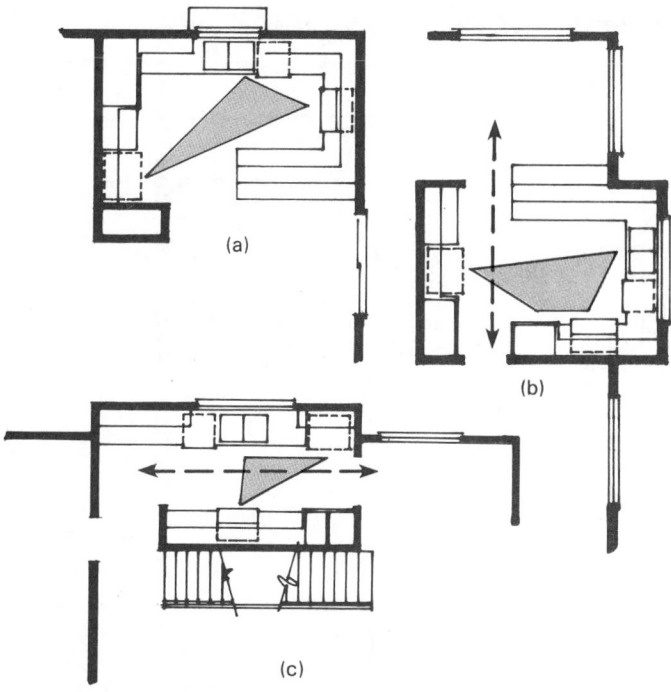

Figure 9–11 The traffic flow through the kitchen can often disrupt work. (a) This kitchen has no through traffic; (b) this kitchen has cross traffic but not through the work area; (c) this kitchen has disruptive traffic going through the work area.

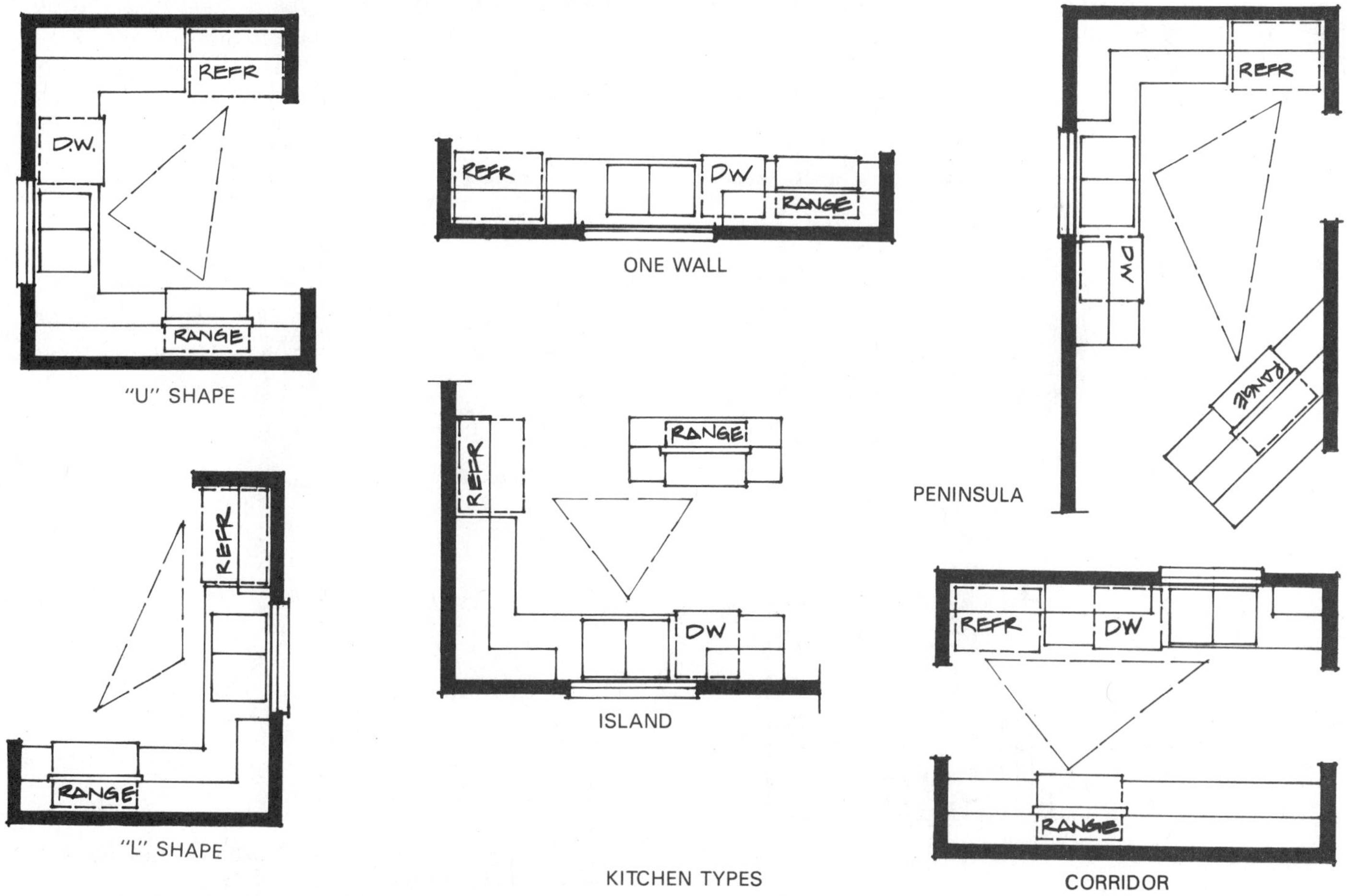

"U" SHAPE

"L" SHAPE

ONE WALL

ISLAND

KITCHEN TYPES

PENINSULA

CORRIDOR

Figure 9–12 Kitchen layout. The arrangement of the cabinets will affect the location of the appliances and the work triangle formed between them.

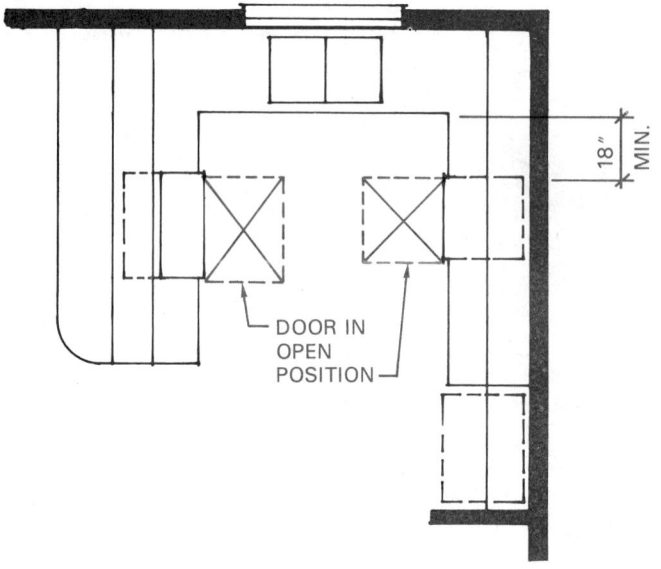

18″ MIN.

DOOR IN
OPEN
POSITION

Figure 9–13 Placement of the stove and dishwasher can often hamper access to other areas of the kitchen.

thicker studs to allow for more insulation around the water lines. Try to avoid placing the sink and dishwasher on different counters even if just around the counter from each other. Such a layout often leads to accidents in the kitchen from water dripping onto the floor. The open door of the dishwasher also hampers access to other areas of the kitchen as shown in Figure 9–13.

The refrigerator is usually placed at the end of a counter within five or six feet of the sink and stove. The refrigerator needs to have a counter space of about 18″ beside it for temporary food storage as the refrigerator is loaded and unloaded.

The stove should be placed so that the person using it will not be standing in the path of traffic flowing through the kitchen. This will help eliminate the chance of hot utensils being knocked from the stove. Stoves should be placed so that there is approximately 18″ of counter space between the stove and the end of the counter to prevent burns to people passing by. Stoves should not be placed within 18″ of an interior cabinet corner. This precaution will allow the oven door to be open and still allow access to the interior cabinet.

When a cooktop and an oven are used, try to place them within three or four steps of each other. Be careful not to place the stove next to a refrigerator, trash compactor, or a storage area for produce and breads.

In addition to the major appliances of the kitchen, care must also be given to other details such as breadboards, counter workspaces, and specialized storage areas. The breadboard should be placed near the sink and the stove but not in a corner. Ideally a minimum of 5′ of counter space can be placed between each appliance to allow for food preparation. Specialized storage often needs to be considered to meet clients' needs. These needs will be covered as cabinets are explained in Section 8.

Figure 9–14 The island counter can be a serving, eating, or preparation area.

A kitchen with an island is often desired. These are useful in gaining extra counter workspace as well as an area for placing the stove near the sink and refrigerator. Islands are often used as an eating area as well as a workspace. Figure 9–14 shows several island options. Try to keep a minimum of 4′ between the island and other counters to allow for traffic around the island.

Utility Rooms

Utility rooms are often placed by either the bedrooms or kitchen area. There are advantages to both locations. Placing the utility room near the bath and sleeping area places the washer and dryer near the primary source of the laundry. Care must be taken to insulate the sleeping area from the noise of the washer and dryer.

Placing the utilities near the kitchen allows for a much better traffic flow between the two major work areas of the home. With the utility room near the kitchen, space can often be provided in the utility room for additional kitchen storage. If bedrooms are on the upper floor, a laundry chute to the utility room can be a very nice convenience. The utility room often has a door leading to the exterior. This allows the utility room to function as a mudroom. A mudroom is a combination of a utility room and a bathroom. Entry can be made from the outside directly into the mudroom where dirty clothes can be removed. This allows for cleanup near the service entry and helps keep the rest of the house clean. Figure 9–15 shows this type of utility layout. Another common use for a utility room is to provide an area for sewing and ironing as seen in Figure 9–16.

Garage or Carport

Believe it or not, some people actually park their car in the garage. For those who don't, the garage often becomes a storage area, a second family room, or a place for the water heater and furnace. A double-car garage should be a minimum of 20 feet wide and 22 feet deep. Additional space should also be included for a workbench. A garage of 22′ × 24′ feet would provide space for parking, storage and room to walk around. The garage location is dictated by the site. If possible try to place the garage so that it can act as a windbreak for the rest of the home.

In areas where cars do not need to be protected from the weather, a carport can provide an inexpensive alternative to a garage. Provide lockable storage space on one side of the carport if possible. This can usually be provided between the supports at the exterior end.

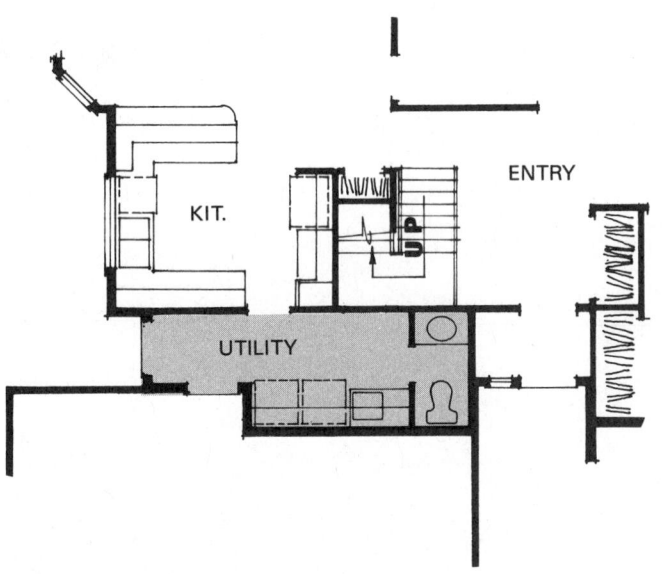

Figure 9–15 The utility room may serve as a service entry where dirty clothes can be removed as the home is entered.

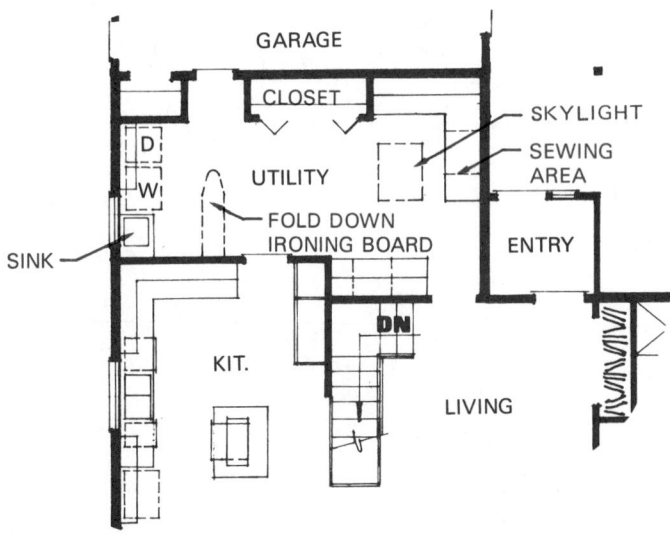

Figure 9–16 This utility room provides a spacious layout for home-care chores.

ROOM RELATIONSHIPS AND SIZES TEST

DIRECTIONS

Answer the questions with short complete statements or drawings as needed on an 8½ × 11 drawing sheet as follows:

1. Use ⅛ in. guidelines for all lettering.
2. Letter your name, Room Relationships and Sizes Test, and the date at the top of the sheet.
3. Letter the question number and provide the answer. You do not need to write out the question.
4. Do all lettering with vertical uppercase architectural letters. If the answer requires line work, use proper drafting tools and technique. Answers may be prepared on a word processor if appropriate with course guidelines.
5. Your grade will be based on correct answers and quality of line technique.

QUESTIONS

1. What are the three main areas of a home?
2. How much closet area should be provided for each bedroom?
3. What rooms should the kitchen be near? Why?
4. What are the functions of a utility room?
5. Give the standard size for a two-car garage.
6. List five functions of a family room.
7. What are the advantages of bedrooms placed on an upper floor?
8. What are the advantages of bedrooms placed on a lower floor?
9. List four design criteria to consider when planning the dining room.
10. What are the service areas of the home?

Chapter 10
Exterior Design Factors

THE DESIGN of a house does not stop once the room arrangements have been determined. The exterior of the residence must also be considered. Often a client will have a certain style in mind that will dictate the layout of the floor plan. In this chapter, ideas will be presented to help you better understand the design process. To properly design a structure, consideration must be given to the site, the floor plan style and shape, and exterior styles.

SITE CONSIDERATIONS

Several site factors will affect the design of a house. Among the most important to consider are the neighborhood, and access to the lot. For a complete description of each item see Section 9.

Neighborhood

In the initial planning of a residence, the neighborhood in which it will be built must be considered. It is extremely poor judgment to design a $200,000 residence in a neighborhood of $80,000 houses. This is not to say the occupants will not be able to coexist with their neighbors, but the house will have poor resale value because of the lower value of the houses in the rest of the neighborhood. The style of the houses in the neighborhood should also be considered. Not that all houses should look alike, but some unity of design can help keep the value of all the property in the neighborhood high.

Review Boards

In order to help keep the values of the neighborhood uniform, many areas have architectural control committees. These are review boards made up of citizens within an area that determine what may or may not be built. Although once found only in the most exclusive neighborhoods, review boards are now common in undeveloped subdivisions, recreational areas, and retirement areas. These boards often set standards for minimum square footage, height limitations, and the type and color of siding and roofing materials. The homeowner is usually required to submit preliminary designs to the review board showing floor plans and exterior elevations.

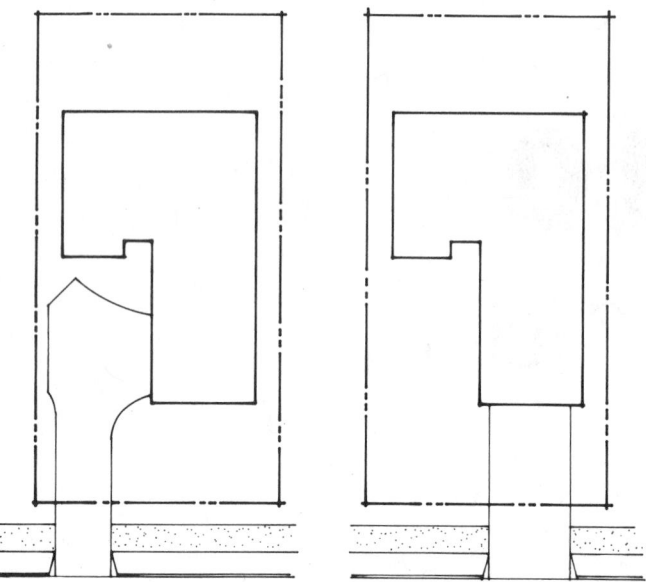

Figure 10–1 Access to an inner lot is limited by the street and garage location.

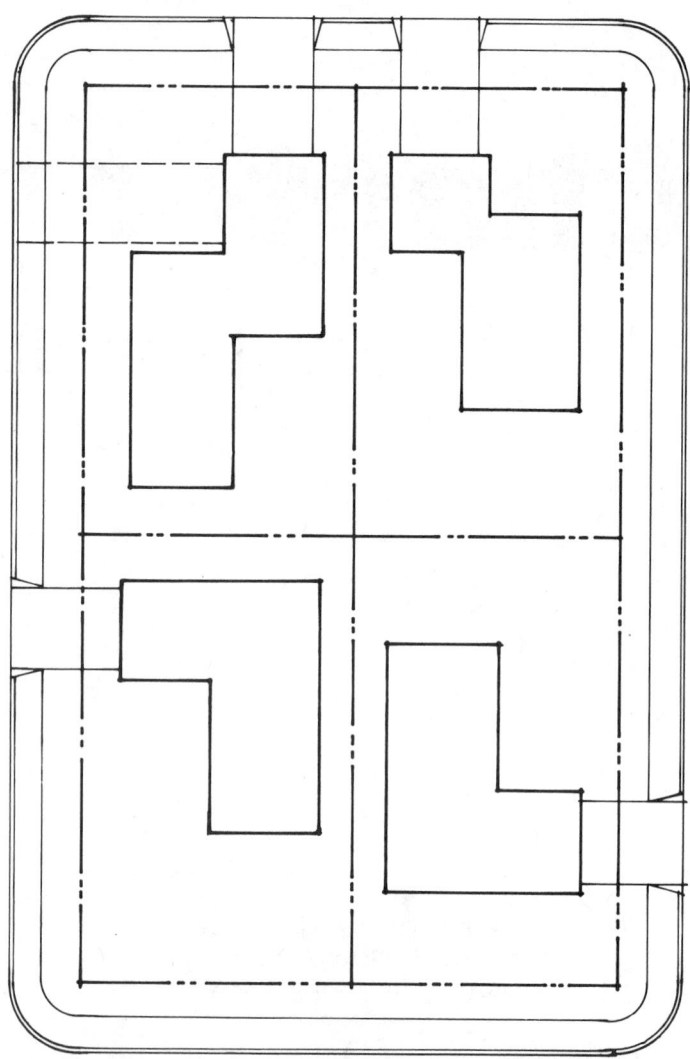

Figure 10–2 A corner lot offers several options for the shape and location of a residence.

Access

Site access can have a major effect on the design of the house. The narrower the lot, the more the access will affect the location of the entry and the garage. Figure 10–1 shows typical access and garage locations for a narrow lot with access from one side. Usually only a straight driveway is used on interior lots because of space restrictions. When a plan is being developed for a corner lot, there is much more flexibility in the garage and house placement. Figure 10–2 shows some possible design alternatives for corner lots. When a residence is being planned for a rural site, weather and terrain can affect the access to the home site. Studying the weather patterns at the job site will help reveal areas of the lot that may be inaccessible during parts of the year due to poor water drainage or drifted snow. The shape of the land will determine where the access to the house can be placed.

 FLOOR PLAN STYLES

Many clients will come to a designer with very specific ideas about the kind and number of levels they desire in a house. Some clients want homes with only one level so that no stairs will be required. For other clients, the levels in the house are best determined by the topography of the lot. Common floor plan layouts include single, split-level, daylight basement, two story, dormer, tri-level, and multilevel.

Single-level

The single-level house has become one of the most common styles built. This style has become a standard of many builders because it can be built with minimal expense. A one-level layout provides stair-free access to all rooms which makes it attractive to people with limited mobility. It is also preferred by many homeowners because it is easy to maintain and can be used with a variety of exterior styles. See Figure 10–3.

Split-level

The split-level, seen in Figure 10–4, is an attempt to combine the features of a one- and a two-story residence. This style is best suited to sloping sites which allow one area of the house to be two stories and one area to be one story. Many clients like the

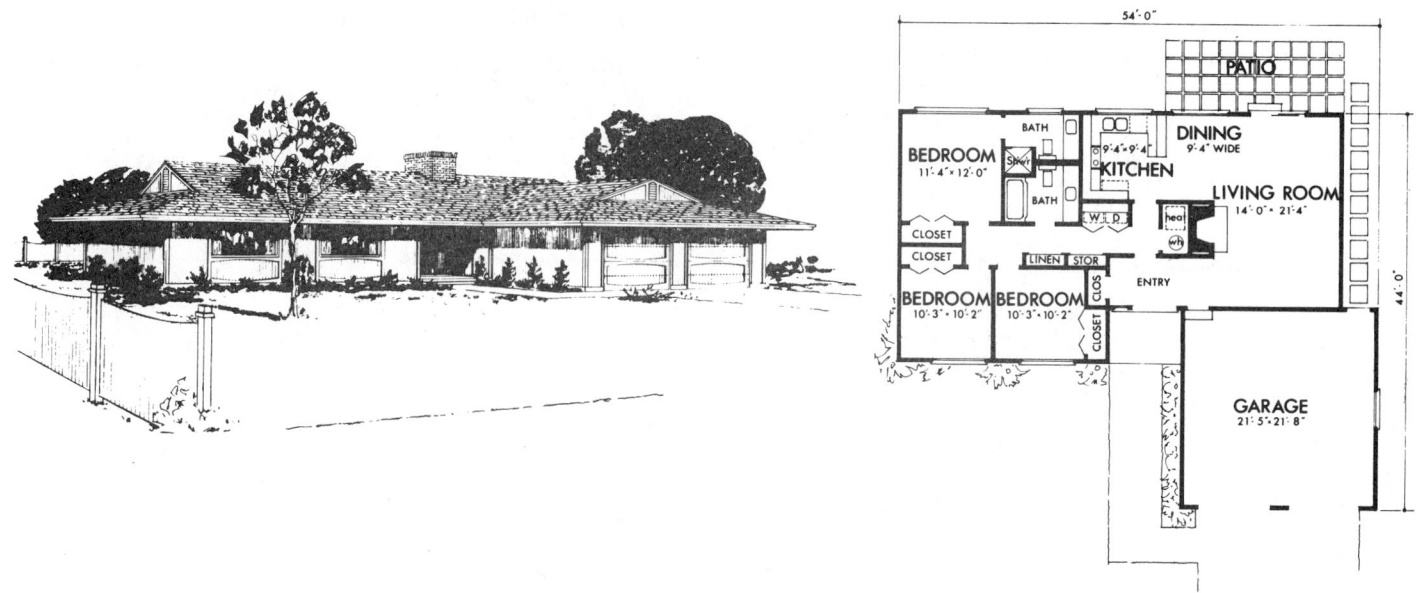

Figure 10–3 The single-level plan has become one of the most popular floor plan styles because of the lack of stairs and ease of maintenance. *Courtesy Home Building Plan Service.*

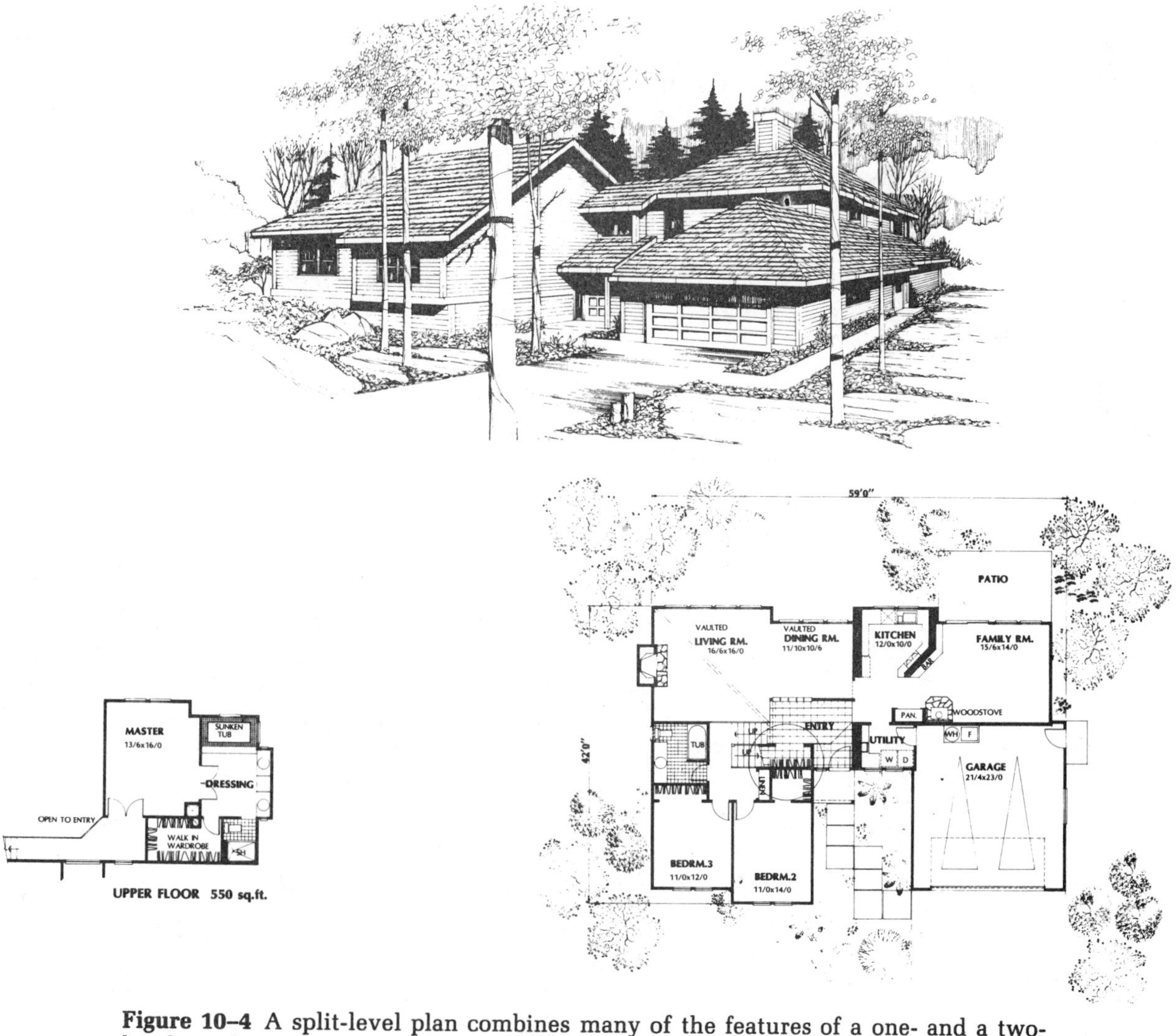

Figure 10–4 A split-level plan combines many of the features of a one- and a two-level residence. *Courtesy Piercy & Barclay Designers, Inc.*

reduced number of steps from one level to another that is found in the split-level design. The cost of construction for a split-level plan is usually greater than the cost of a single-level structure of the same size because of the increased foundation cost that the sloping lot will require.

Daylight Basement

Although called a daylight basement, this style of house could be either a one-story house over a basement or garage, or two complete living levels. This style of house is well suited for a sloping lot. From the high side of the lot, the house will appear to be a one-level structure. From the low side of the lot, both levels of the structure can be seen. See Figure 10–5.

Two-Story

The two-story house of Figure 10–6 provides many options for families that don't mind stairs. Living and sleeping areas can be easily separated, and a minimum of land will be used for the building site. On a sloping lot, depending on the access, the living area can be on either the upper or lower level. The most popular feature of a two-level layout is its ability to provide the maximum building area at a lower cost per square foot than other styles of houses. This savings results from less material being used on the foundation, exterior walls, and the roof of a two-story structure compared to other styles of houses.

Dormer

The dormer style provides for two levels with the upper level usually about half of the square footage of the lower floor. This floor plan is best suited to an exterior style which incorporates a steep roof. See Figure 10–7. The dormer level is formed in what would have been the attic area. The dormer has many of the same economic features of a two-story home.

Tri-Level

The tri-level plan of Figure 10–8 has three living areas connected by two sets of stairs. This type of house is best suited to contemporary styles of exterior design. It provides its owners with the benefits of two-story living, but can create the feeling of much more interior space with ceiling levels flowing from one level to the next.

Multilevel

With this style of layout, the possibilities for floor levels are endless. Site topography will dictate this style as much as the owners' living habits. Figure 10–9 shows a multilevel layout. The cost for this type of home exceeds all other styles because of the problems of excavation, foundation construction, and roof intersections.

SHANES OF FLOOR PLANS

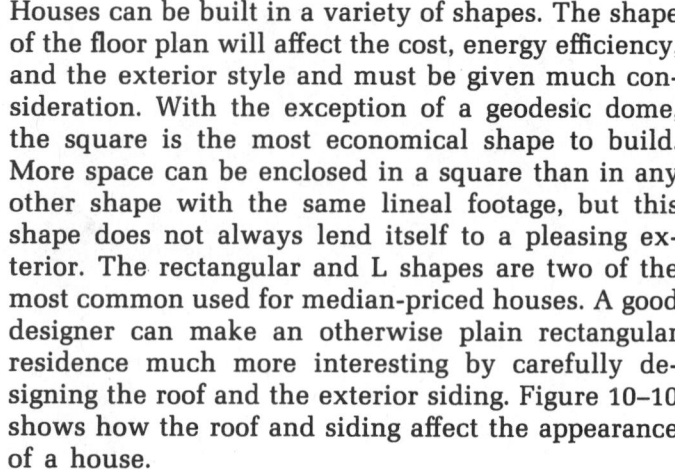

Houses can be built in a variety of shapes. The shape of the floor plan will affect the cost, energy efficiency, and the exterior style and must be given much consideration. With the exception of a geodesic dome, the square is the most economical shape to build. More space can be enclosed in a square than in any other shape with the same lineal footage, but this shape does not always lend itself to a pleasing exterior. The rectangular and L shapes are two of the most common used for median-priced houses. A good designer can make an otherwise plain rectangular residence much more interesting by carefully designing the roof and the exterior siding. Figure 10–10 shows how the roof and siding affect the appearance of a house.

The more the shape of the structure varies from a rectangle, the higher the cost of construction. A free-flowing shape is well suited to a sloping lot as seen in Figure 10–11. A varied shape will also allow a house to be entwined in the trees so that it blends better with the site.

EXTERIOR STYLES

A client often has a specific exterior style in mind for a house. The exterior design also must be considered as the floor plan style and shape are being developed. For example, the designer should not be using the rambling layout of a ranch style plan if the owner wants a colonial facade. It is the designer's ability to blend the style of the facade with the floor plan shape and layout that will determine the acceptance of the project by the client.

Exterior style is often based on the styles of houses from the past. Some early colonists lived in lean-to shelters called wigwams. These shelters were formed with poles and covered with twigs woven together and then covered with mud or clay. Log cabins were introduced by Swedish settlers in Delaware and soon were used throughout the colonies by the poorer

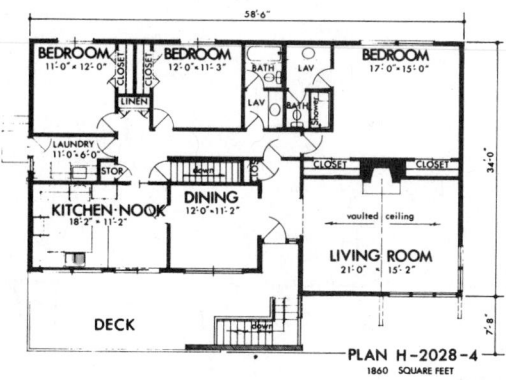

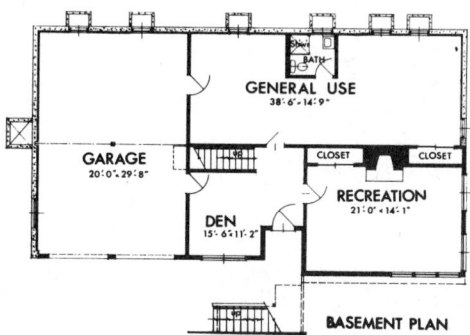

Figure 10–5 A daylight basement floor plan style offers many of the features of a two-level home in one plan. *Courtesy Home Building Plan Service.*

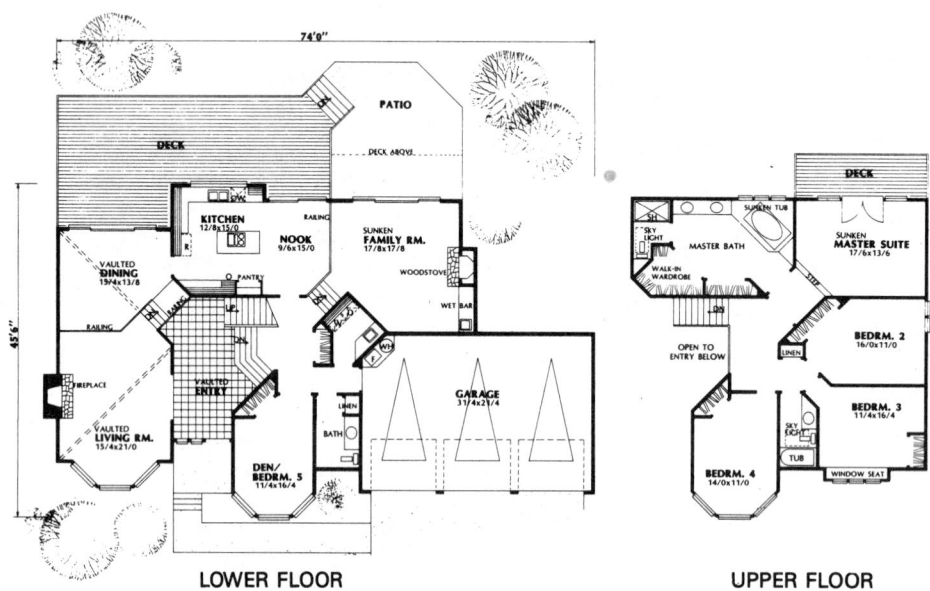

LOWER FLOOR UPPER FLOOR

Figure 10-6 The two-level home style offers good separation between the living and sleeping areas to those families that don't mind stairs. *Courtesy Piercy & Barclay Designers, Inc.*

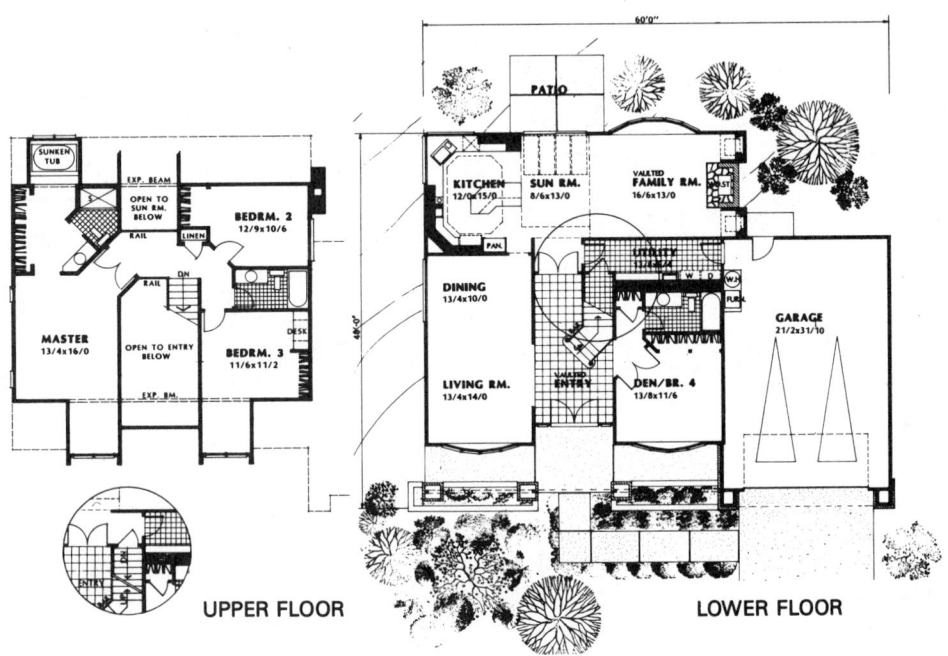

UPPER FLOOR   LOWER FLOOR

Figure 10–7 A dormer style of home with the upper level placed in what would have been the attic area. *Courtesy Piercy & Barclay Designers, Inc.*

MAIN FLOOR LOWER FLOOR

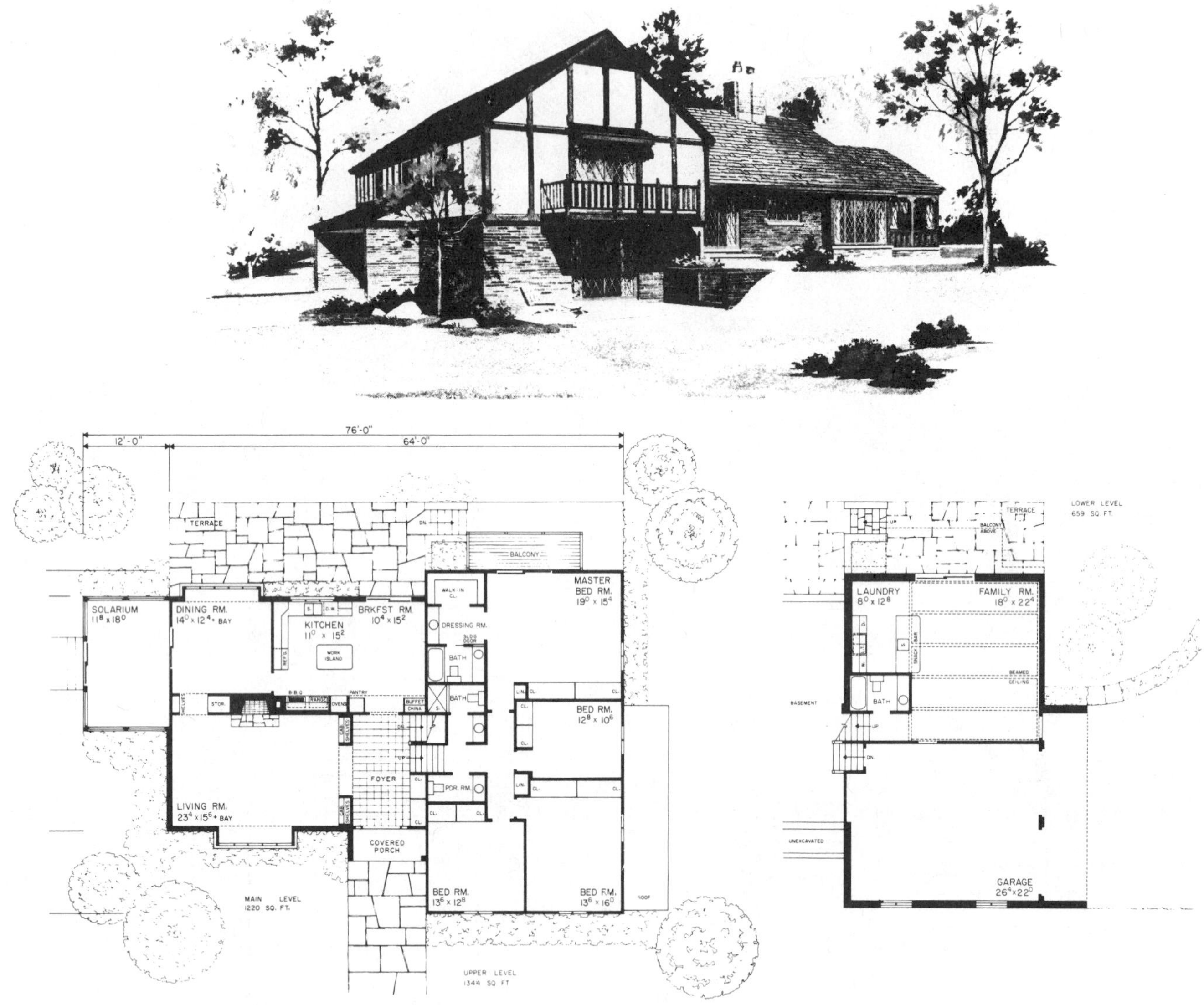

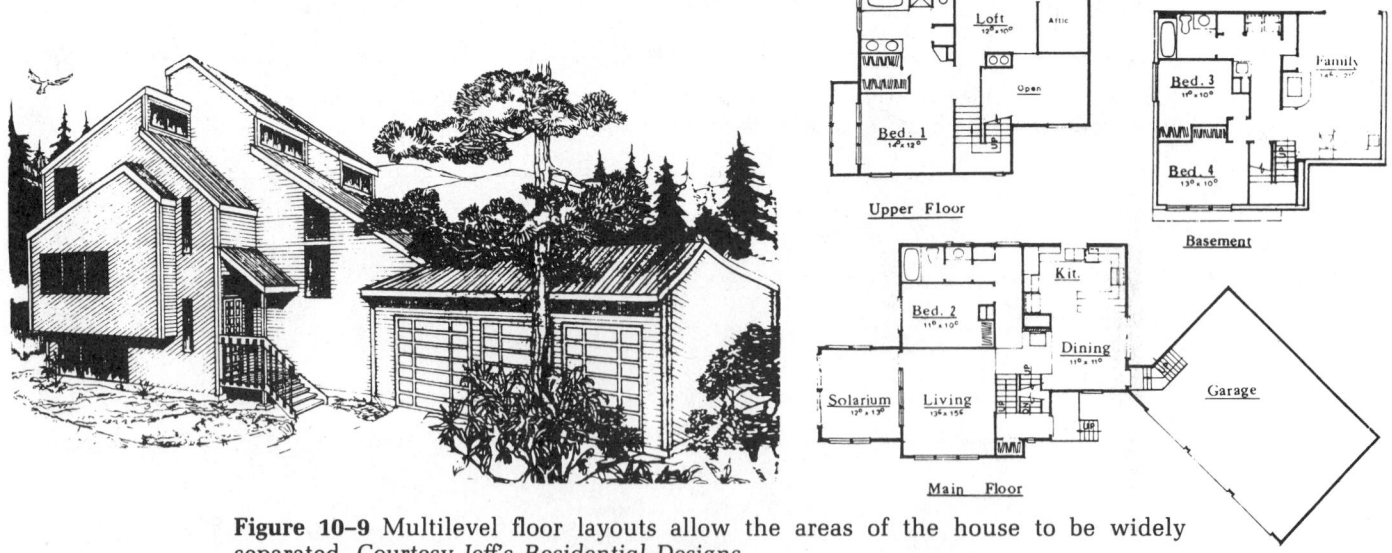

Figure 10–8 A tri-level home with the living areas on three different levels. *Courtesy Home Planners, Inc.*

Figure 10–9 Multilevel floor layouts allow the areas of the house to be widely separated. *Courtesy Jeff's Residential Designs.*

Figure 10-10 The exterior shape of the home need not be exotic to create interest. This home uses the basic cube with many different breaks to achieve its distinctive appeal. Design by Pulliam & Mathews, Los Angeles. *Courtesy Red Cedar Shingle and Handsplit Shake Bureau.*

Figure 10-11 This multileveled, varied-shaped residence was designed by architects Confer & Nance to blend with the sloping site. *Courtesy Red Cedar Shingle and Handsplit Shake Bureau.*

settlers. Many companies now sell plans and precut kits for assembling log houses. Figure 10-12 shows an example of a modern log residence. Many of the colonial houses were similar in style to the houses that had been left behind in Europe. Construction methods and materials were varied because of the weather and building materials available.

Colonial influence can still be seen in houses that are built to resemble the Georgian, saltbox, garrison, Cape Cod, and southern colonial styles of houses. Other house styles from the colonial period include influences of the English, Dutch, French, and Spanish.

Figure 10-12 A popular style for rural settings is the traditional log residence. No longer just a log cabin, plans and kits are available for building log houses. *Courtesy Wilderness Log Homes.*

Georgian

The Georgian style of design is a good example of a basic style that was modified throughout the colonies to meet the needs of available material and weather. This style receives its name for the kings of England who were in power as this style flourished. The Georgian style follows the classical principles of design used by the ancient Greeks. The principles of form and symmetry can be seen throughout the structure but are most evident in the front elevation. The front entry is centered on the wall, and equally spaced windows are placed on each side. The front entry is usually covered with a columned porch and the doorway trimmed with carved wood detailing. When constructed in the South much of the facade is built of brick. In the northern states, wood siding is the major covering. Other common exterior materials include stucco or stone. An example of Georgian styling can be seen in the plan in Figure 10-13.

Figure 10-13 The Georgian style of architecture uses the classic form and symmetry of the ancient Greeks. *Courtesy Home Planners, Inc.*

Figure 10–14 The saltbox reflects the symmetry of Georgian architecture, but is usually constructed of wood. The front of the house has two levels, while the back half of the house has only one. The two areas are connected by a steep roof. *Courtesy Home Planners, Inc.*

Figure 10–15 The garrison style maintained the symmetry of window and door placement of other styles, but the upper level extends past the lower level and is supported by carved timbers. *Courtesy Home Planners, Inc.*

Figure 10–16 The Cape Cod style reflects the symmetry and balance of other styles but adds dormers and shutters. *Courtesy Home Planners, Inc.*

Figure 10–17 A southern colonial, or colonial plantation, style of architecture maintains classic symmetry in a typically brick structure, with a large entry porch to protect windows from the summer sun. *Courtesy Home Building Plan Service.*

Saltbox

One of the most common modifications of the Georgian style is the saltbox. The saltbox maintained the symmetry of the Georgian style, but omitted much of the detailing. A saltbox is typically a two-story structure at the front, but tapers to one story at the rear. Window areas are usually protected with shutters to provide protection from winter winds. Figure 10–14 shows features of saltbox styling in a residence.

Garrison

The garrison style combines the styling of the saltbox and Georgian houses with the construction methods of log buildings. The garrison was originally modeled after the lookout structures of early forts. The upper level extends past the lower level, and on the fort made the walls harder to scale. Originally, heavy timbers were used to support the overhang and were usually carved. Figure 10–15 shows the features of the garrison-style residence.

Cape Cod

Cape Cod styling is typically one level with a steep roof. Windows are symmetrically placed around the door and have shutters. An example of Cape Cod styling can be seen in Figure 10–16.

Southern Colonial

The southern colonial homes are similar to the Georgian style with their symmetrical features. The southern colonial style usually has a flat, covered porch which extends the length of the house to protect the windows from the summer sun. Figure 10–17 shows an example of southern colonial styling.

English

English style houses are fashioned after houses that were built in England prior to the early 1800s. These houses feature an unsymmetrical layout and walls that are usually constructed of stone, brick, or heavy timber and plaster. Window glass is typically diamond shaped rather than the more traditional rectangle. Figure 10–18 shows common features of English Tudor styling.

Figure 10-18 An English Tudor, or English half-timber, remains a popular style with its combination of brick or stone, plaster, and timbers. *Courtesy Piercy & Barclay Designers, Inc.*

Dutch

The Dutch colonial style has many of the same features of houses already described. The major difference is in the roof shape. A Dutch colonial style features a gambrel roof which in many areas is also known as a barn roof. This roof is made of two levels. The lower level is usually very steep, and serves as the walls for the second floor of the structure. The upper area of the roof is the more traditional gable roof. An example of Dutch colonial styling can be seen in Figure 10-19. The gambrel roof will be described in Section 7.

French

French colonial styling is also a matter of roof design. Similar to the gambrel with its steep lower roof, French colonial styling uses a hip or mansard roof to hide the upper floor area. A mansard roof is basically an angled wall and will be discussed in Section 7. Figure 10-20 shows an example of French colonial styling.

Spanish

Spanish colonial buildings were constructed of adobe or plaster and were usually one story. Arches and tiled roofs are two of the most common features of Spanish, or mission-style, architecture. Timbers are often used to frame a flat or very low-pitched roof. Windows with grilles or spindles and balconies with wrought iron railings are also common features. Figure 10-21 shows an example of Spanish style architecture.

Farmhouse

The farmhouse style of residence makes use of two-story construction and is usually surrounded by a covered porch. The trim and detail work that is common on many other styles of architecture is rarely found on this style of home. Figure 10-22 shows an example of farmhouse style.

Figure 10-19 Dutch colonial styling features the use of a gambrel roof to cover the upper level. *Courtesy Home Planners, Inc.*

Figure 10-20 French colonial styling blends many features of other styles with its steep-pitched, hip, or mansard roof. *Courtesy Home Planners, Inc.*

Figure 10-21 Spanish or mission styling is reflected in the use of low-sloping tile roofs, arches, and window grilles. *Courtesy Home Planners, Inc.*

Figure 10-22 Farmhouse styling with its simple lines and wraparound porch remains popular in many areas of the country. *Courtesy Home Building Plan Service.*

Figure 10–23 Ranch-style houses feature a rambling floor layout, with low-sloped roofs. *Courtesy Piercy & Barclay Designers, Inc.*

Figure 10–24 Victorian structures are often very ornate with angular shapes, arched windows, and towers. *Courtesy Home Building Plan Service.*

Ranch

The ranch style of construction comes from the Southwest. This style is usually defined by a one-story, rambling layout which is made possible because of the mild climate and plentiful land on which such houses are built. The roof shape is typically low pitched with a large overhang to block the summer sun. The major exterior material is usually stucco or adobe. Figure 10–23 shows the ranch style.

Victorian

The Victorian and Queen Anne styles of house from the late 1800s are also still being copied in many parts of the country. These styles of house feature irregular-shaped floor plans and very ornate detailing throughout the residence. Victorian houses often include many other styles of architecture including partial mansard roofs, arched windows, and towers. Exterior materials include a combination of wood and brick. Wrought iron is often used. Figure 10–24 shows an example of the Victorian style.

Contemporary

It is important to remember that a client may like the exterior look of one of the traditional styles, but very rarely would the traditional floor plan of one of those houses be desired. Quite often the floor plans of the older style of house produced very small rooms with very poor traffic flow. A designer must take the best characteristics of a particular style of house and work them into a plan that will best suit the needs of the owner.

Contemporary, or modern, does not denote any special style of house. Some houses are now being designed to meet a wide variety of needs, and others reflect the particular lifestyle of the owner. Figures 10–25 through 10–29 show a few of the wide variety of contemporary houses.

Figure 10–25 A contemporary Chalet-style residence with its steep roof to shed snow and open floor plan make this style popular in many mountain areas. *Courtesy Piercy & Barclay Designers, Inc.*

Figure 10–26 Contemporary houses often are designed with very simple lines that are offset to create interest. *Courtesy Home Building Plan Service.*

Figure 10–27 Because of increased land cost, many home owners share property lines to reduce property and construction cost. This duplex further reduces cost by using passive solar heating. *Courtesy Jeff's Residential Designs.*

Figure 10–28 Many American families are forsaking the single-family residence for townhouses, apartments, or condominiums. Design by McCool, McDonald & Associates. *Courtesy Shakertown Corp.*

Figure 10–29 Subterranean living has become a popular method to provide energy-efficient construction. *Courtesy Weather Shield Mfg., Inc.*

EXTERIOR DESIGN FACTORS TEST

DIRECTIONS

Answer the questions with short complete statements or drawings as needed on an 8½ × 11 drawing sheet as follows:

1. Use ⅛ in. guidelines for all lettering.
2. Letter your name, Exterior Design Factors Test, and the date at the top of the sheet.
3. Letter the question number and provide the answer. You do not need to write out the question.

4. Do all lettering with vertical uppercase architectural letters. If the answer requires line work, use proper drafting tools and technique. Answers may be prepared on a word processor if appropriate with course guidelines.
5. Your grade will be based on correct answers and quality of line technique.

QUESTIONS

1. Explain how the neighborhood can influence the type of house that will be built.
2. Sketch three alternatives for access to a house on a corner lot.
3. Sketch a simple two-bedroom house in two of the following shapes: L, U, T, or V.
4. List four functions of a review board.
5. Describe four floor plan styles and explain the benefits of each.
6. What factors make a two-story house more economical to build than a single-story house of similar size?
7. What house shape is the most economical to build?
8. Photograph or sketch examples of the following historical styles found in your community:
   a. Dutch colonial
   b. Garrison
   c. Saltbox
   d. Victorian
9. List the major features of the following styles of house.
   a. Ranch
   b. Tudor
   c. Cape Cod
   d. Spanish
10. Photograph or sketch three contemporary houses that have no apparent historic style.
11. What period of architecture influenced the Georgian style?
12. Sketch a Dutch colonial house.
13. Sketch or photograph a house in your community built with a traditional influence, and explain which styles this house has copied.
14. What are some of the drawbacks of having a traditional house style?

Chapter 11
Site Orientation

SITE ORIENTATION is the placement of a structure on the property with certain environmental and physical factors taken into consideration. Site orientation is one of the preliminary factors that an architect or designer takes into consideration when beginning the design process. The specific needs of the occupants such as individual habits, perceptions, aesthetic values and so on are important and need to be considered. The designer or architect has the responsibility of putting together the predetermined values of the owner and other factors that influence the location of the structure when designing the home or business. In some cases site orientation is predetermined. For example, in a residential subdivision where all of the lots are 50' × 100', the street frontage clearly dictates the front of the house. The property line setback requirements do not allow much flexibility. In such a case, site planning has a minimal amount of influence on the design. This chapter will present concepts that may influence site orientation, including terrain, view, solar, wind, and sound.

TERRAIN ORIENTATION

The terrain is the characteristic of the land upon which the proposed structure will be placed. Terrain will affect the type of structure to be built. A level construction site is a natural location for a single-level or two-story home. Some landscape techniques on a level site may allow for some alternatives.

For example, the excavation material plus extra top soil could be used to construct an earth berm, which is a mound or built-up area. The advantage of the berm is to help reduce the height appearance of a second story or to add earth insulation to part of the structure. See Figure 11–1.

Sloped sites are a natural location for multilevel or daylight basement homes. A single-level home is a poor choice on a sloped site due to the extra construction cost in excavation or building up the foundation. See Figure 11–2. Figure 11–3 shows how the terrain can be an important influence on housing types.

Subterranean construction is gaining popularity due to some economical advantages in energy consumption. The terrain of the site is an important factor to consider in the implementation of these designs. See Figure 11–4.

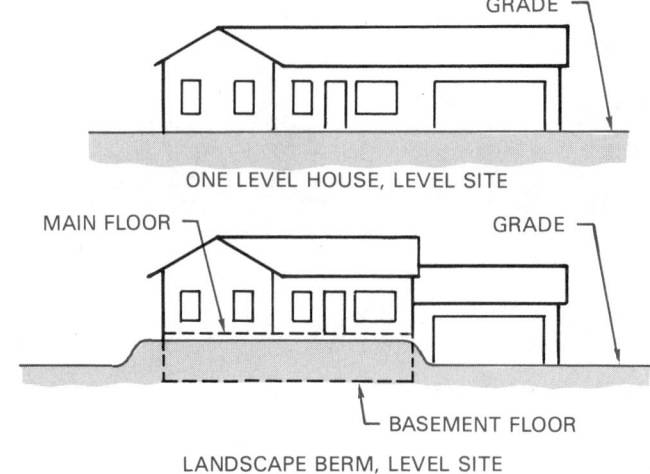

GRADE

ONE LEVEL HOUSE, LEVEL SITE

MAIN FLOOR

GRADE

BASEMENT FLOOR

LANDSCAPE BERM, LEVEL SITE

Figure 11–1 Level site.

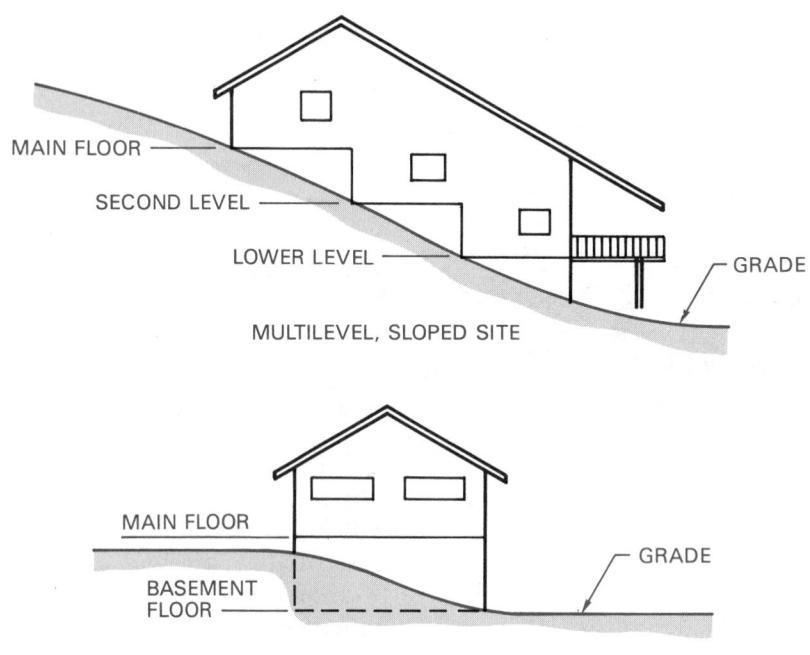

MAIN FLOOR

SECOND LEVEL

LOWER LEVEL

GRADE

MULTILEVEL, SLOPED SITE

MAIN FLOOR

BASEMENT FLOOR

GRADE

DAYLIGHT BASEMENT, SLOPED SITE

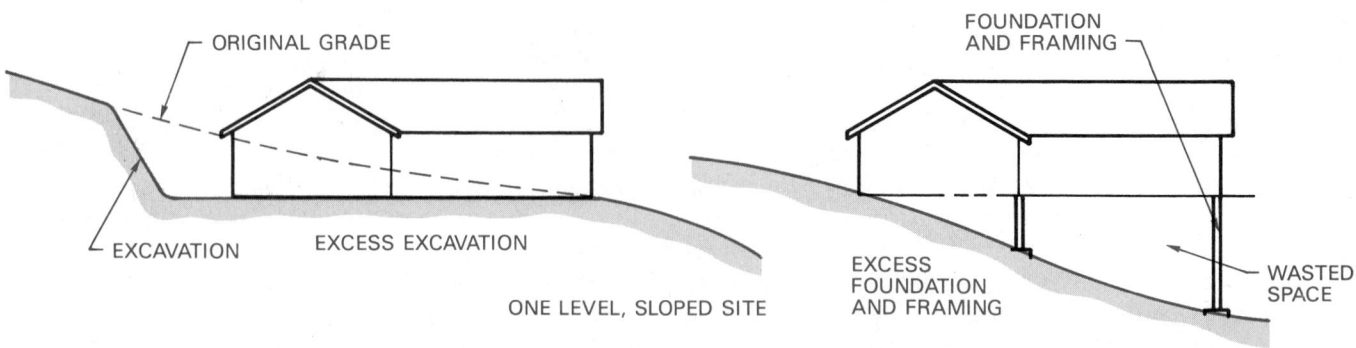

ORIGINAL GRADE

FOUNDATION AND FRAMING

EXCAVATION

EXCESS EXCAVATION

ONE LEVEL, SLOPED SITE

EXCESS FOUNDATION AND FRAMING

WASTED SPACE

Figure 11–2 Sloped sites.

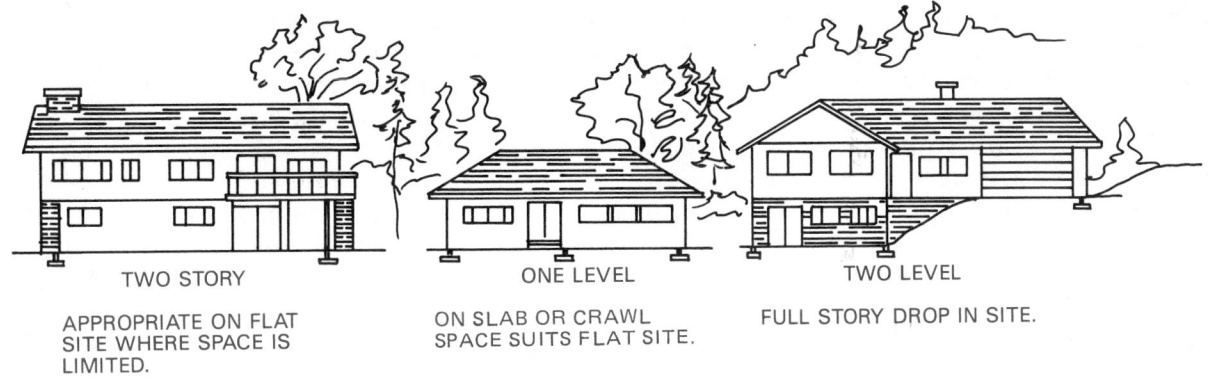

TWO STORY — APPROPRIATE ON FLAT SITE WHERE SPACE IS LIMITED.

ONE LEVEL — ON SLAB OR CRAWL SPACE SUITS FLAT SITE.

TWO LEVEL — FULL STORY DROP IN SITE.

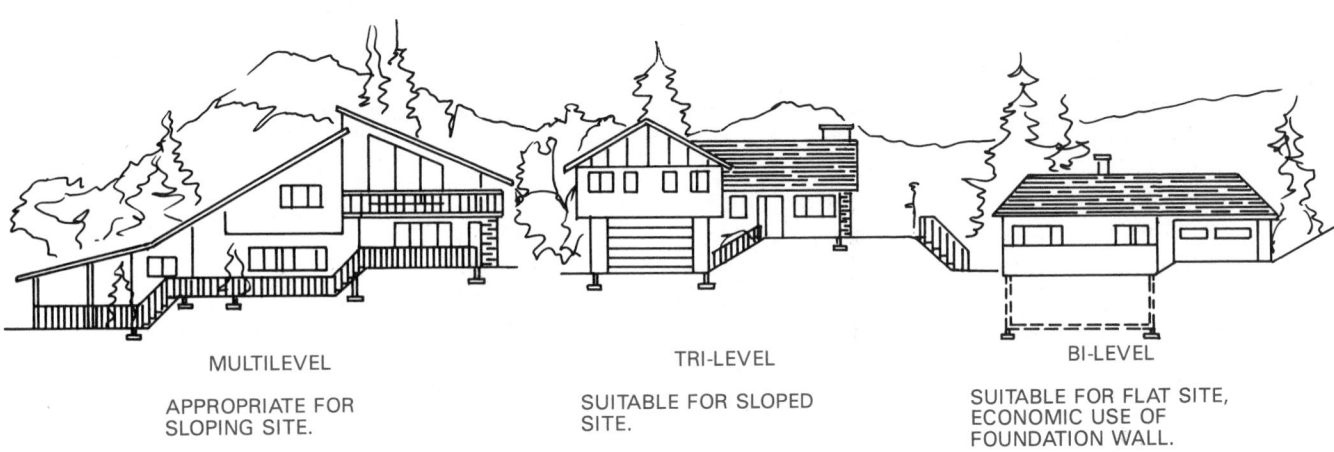

MULTILEVEL — APPROPRIATE FOR SLOPING SITE.

TRI-LEVEL — SUITABLE FOR SLOPED SITE.

BI-LEVEL — SUITABLE FOR FLAT SITE, ECONOMIC USE OF FOUNDATION WALL.

Figure 11-3 Terrain determines housing types.

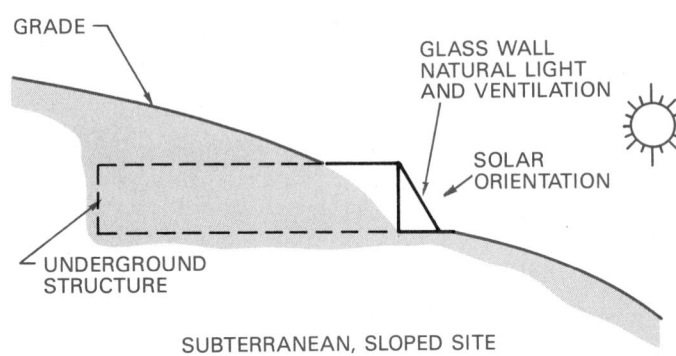

SUBTERRANEAN, SLOPED SITE

Figure 11-4 Subterranean construction site.

VIEW ORIENTATION

In many situations future home owners will purchase a building site even before they begin the home design. In a large number of these cases the people are buying a view. The view may be of mountains, city lights, a lake, the ocean, or even a golf course. These view sites are usually more expensive than comparable sites without a view. The architect's obligation to the client in this situation is to provide a home design that will optimize the view. Actually the best situation is to provide an environment that allows the occupants to feel as though they are part of the view. Figure 11-5 shows a dramatic example of a view as part of the total environment.

View orientation may conflict with the advantages of other orientation factors such as solar or wind. When a client pays a substantial amount to purchase a view site, such a trade-off may be necessary. When

Figure 11-5 View orientation. *Courtesy Peachtree.*

the view dictates that a large glass surface face a wind-exposed nonsolar orientation, some energy saving alternatives should be considered. Provide as much solar-related glass as possible. Use small window surfaces in other areas to help minimize heat loss. Use triple-glazed windows in the exposed view surface as well as in the balance of the structure if economically possible. Insulate to stop air leakage.

SOLAR ORIENTATION

The sun is an important factor in home orientation. Real estate advertisements in the local newspaper often will read, "Solar orientation, perfect southern exposure." These types of sites allow for excellent exposure to the sun. There should not be obstacles such as tall buildings, evergreen trees, or hills that have the potential to block the sun. Generally a site located on the south slope may have these characteristics.

When a site has southern exposure that will allow solar orientation, a little basic astronomy can contribute to proper placement of the structure. Figure 11-6 shows how a southern orientation in relationship to the sun's path will provide the maximum solar exposure.

Establishing South

A perfect solar site will allow the structure to have unobstructed southern exposure. When a site has this potential then true south should be determined. This determination should be established in the preliminary planning stages. Other factors that contribute to orientation, such as view, also may be taken into consideration at this time. If view orientation requires that a structure be turned slightly away from south, it is possible that the solar potential will not be significantly reduced.

True south is determined by a line from the north to the south poles. When a compass is used to establish north-south, the compass points to magnetic north. Magnetic north is not the same as true north. The difference between true north and magnetic north is known as the magnetic declination. Figure 11-7 shows the compass relationship between true north-south and magnetic north. The magnetic declination differs throughout the country. Figure 11-8 shows a map of the United States with lines that represent the magnetic declination at different locations.

A magnetic declination of 18° east, which occurs in northern California, means that the compass needle

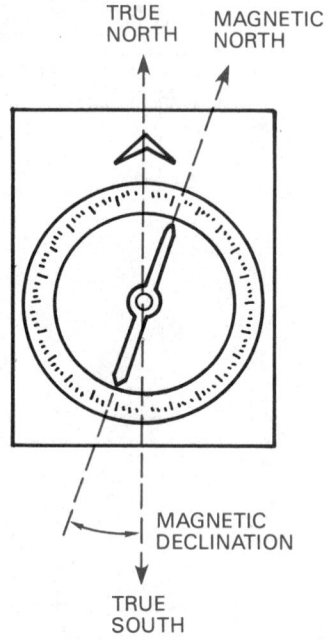

Figure 11-7 Magnetic declination.

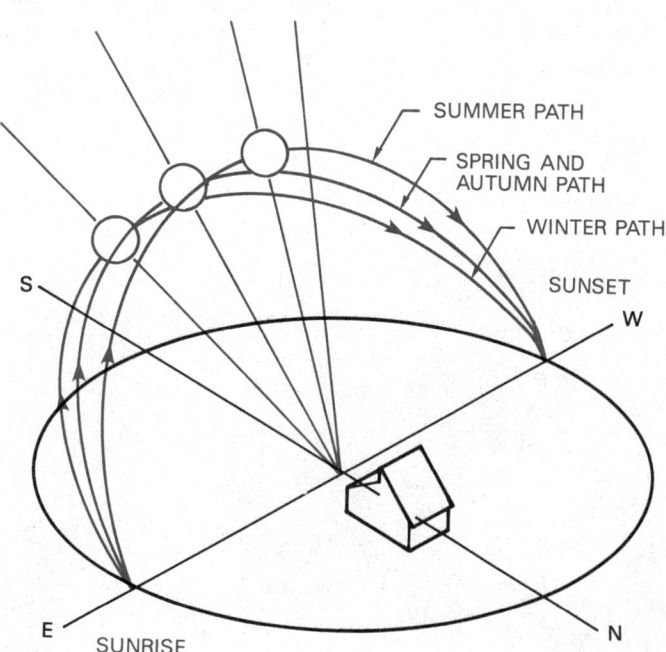

Figure 11-6 Southern exposure.

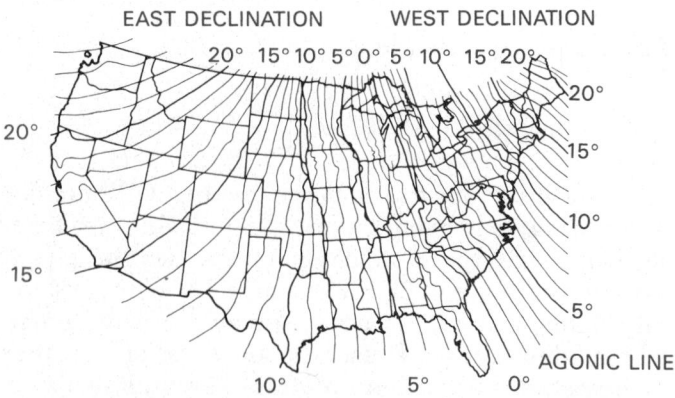

Figure 11-8 United States magnetic declination grid.

Figure 11-9 Viewing through the Solar Site Selector. *Courtesy Lewis and Associates.*

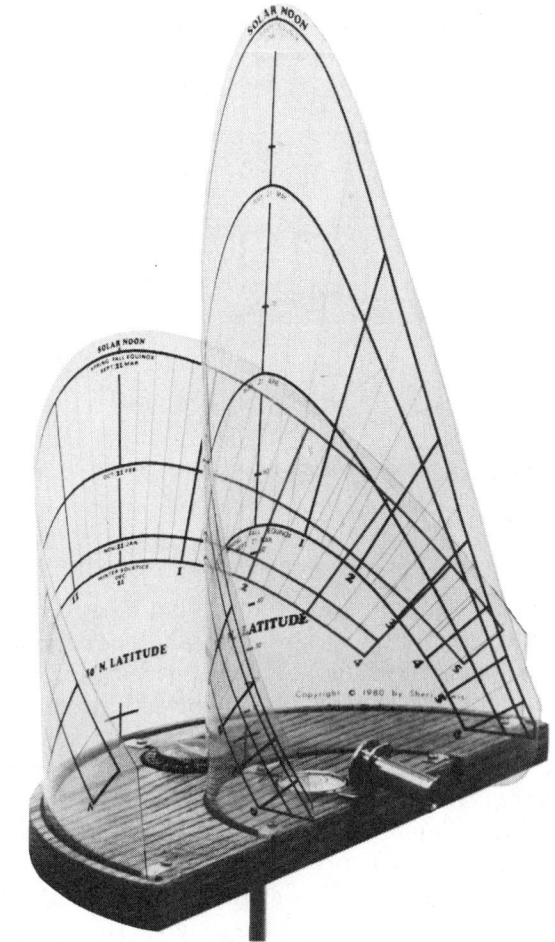

Figure 11-10 Solar Site Selector. *Courtesy Lewis and Associates.*

will point 18° to the east of true north, or 18° to the west of true south. So, in this location, as you face toward magnetic south, true south will be 18° to the left.

Solar Site Planning Tools

The Solar Site Selector is an instrument that calculates solar access and demonstrates shading patterns for any given site or surface throughout the year. Solar access refers to the availability of direct sunlight to a structure or construction site. Solar access is calculated by using silkscreened grids that function as solar windows when viewed through the 180° eyepiece as seen in Figure 11-9. The sunpaths, hour lines, and insolation (sun's rays) segments are superimposed on the site being studied and instantly show shading patterns that make possible a simple visual calculation of hours of solar access. The instrument also enables a quick computation of the percent of occlusion and percent of incident solar radiation (insolation) for that site. The instrument fits on a handle or photographic tripod and is oriented with a built-in compensating compass and bubble level.

Take the Solar Site Selector to the site or building you wish to study for solar access, siting, and orientation. Accurate readings can be made for the entire year at any time of day, in clear or cloudy weather. Figure 11-10 shows an example of the Solar Site Selector.

Monthly solar availability may be determined by using the monthly sunpath diagram. Seasonal diagrams, as shown in Figure 11-11, allow a quick estimation of the percent of available solar energy during specific seasons and for specific heating purposes. Seasonal diagrams are available for determining annual solar hot water heating, passive solar space heating, active solar space heating, and solar swimming pool heating requirements.

Figure 11-11 Solar Pathfinder. *Courtesy Solar Pathways, Inc.*

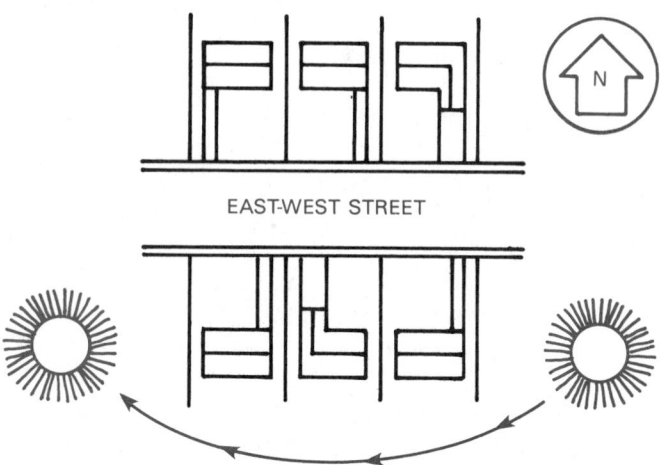

Figure 11–12 East–west street orientation.

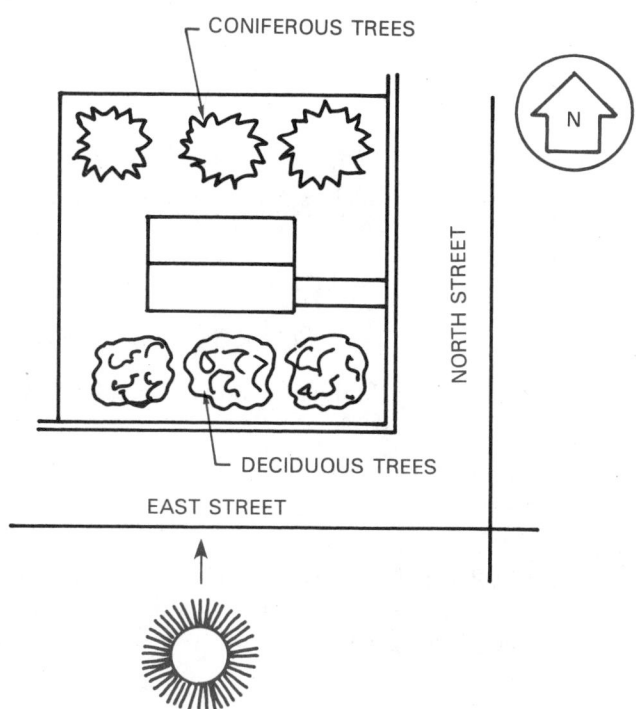

Figure 11–13 Solar orientation with trees.

Solar Site Location

A solar site in a rural or suburban location where there may be plenty of space to take advantage of a southern solar exposure allows the designer a great deal of flexibility. Some other factors, however, may be considered when selecting an urban solar site. Select a site where zoning restrictions have maximum height requirements. This will prevent future neighborhood development from blocking the sun from an otherwise good solar orientation. Avoid a site where large coniferous trees hinder the full potential of the sun exposure. Sites that have streets running east-west and 50′ × 100′ lots provide fairly limited orientation potential. Adjacent homes can easily block the sun unless southern exposure is possible. Figure 11–12 shows how the east-west street orientation can provide the maximum solar potential. If you love the trees but also want solar orientation, then consider a site where the home could be situated so that southern exposure can be achieved with coniferous trees to the north and deciduous trees on the south side. The coniferous trees can effectively block the wind exposure without interfering with the solar orientation. The deciduous trees provide shade relief from the hot summer sun. In the winter when these trees have lost their leaves, the winter sun exposure is not substantially reduced. Figure 11–13 shows a potential solar site with trees. For more information on solar designing refer to Chapter 12.

WIND ORIENTATION

The term *prevailing winds* refers to the direction from which the wind most frequently blows in a given area of the country. For example, if the prevailing winds are said to be southwesterly that means that the winds in the area most generally flow from the southwest. There are some locations that may have southwesterly prevailing winds, but then during certain times of the year there may be severe winds that blow from the northeast. The factors that influence these particular conditions may be mountains, large bodies of water, valleys, canyons, or river basins. The prevailing winds in the United States are from west to east although some local areas have wind patterns that differ from this.

Wind conditions should be taken into consideration in the orientation of a home or business. There is, in many cases, a conflict between the different aspects of site orientation. For example, the best solar orientation may be in conflict with the best wind orientation. The best view may be out over the ocean, but the winter winds may also come from that direction.

One of the factors used to evaluate orientation may outweigh another. Personal judgment may be the final ruling factor. A good combination may be achieved if careful planning is used to take all of the environmental factors into consideration.

Site Location

Evaluate the direction of the prevailing winds in an area by calling the local weather bureau or by a discussion with local residents. Select an area where winter winds are at a minimum or where there is protection from these winds. Within a 25 mile radius of a given area there may be certain locations where wind is more of a problem than in others. A hill, mountain, or forest can protect the building site from

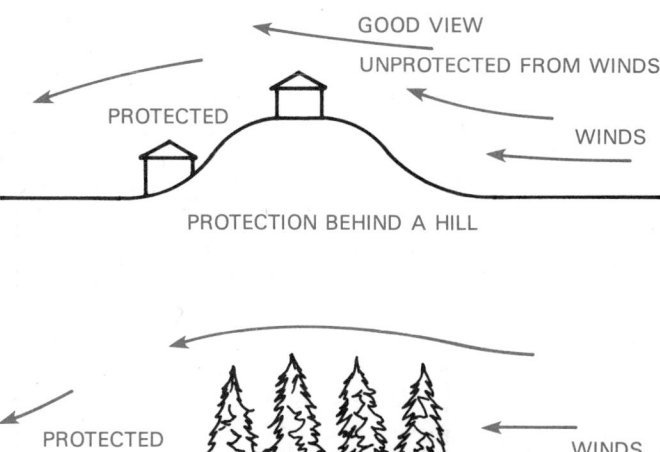

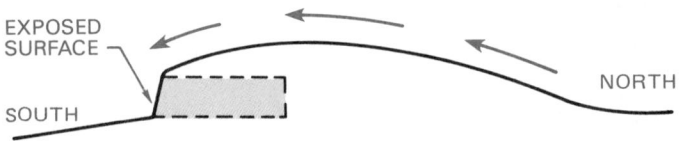

Figure 11-14 Locations protected from wind.

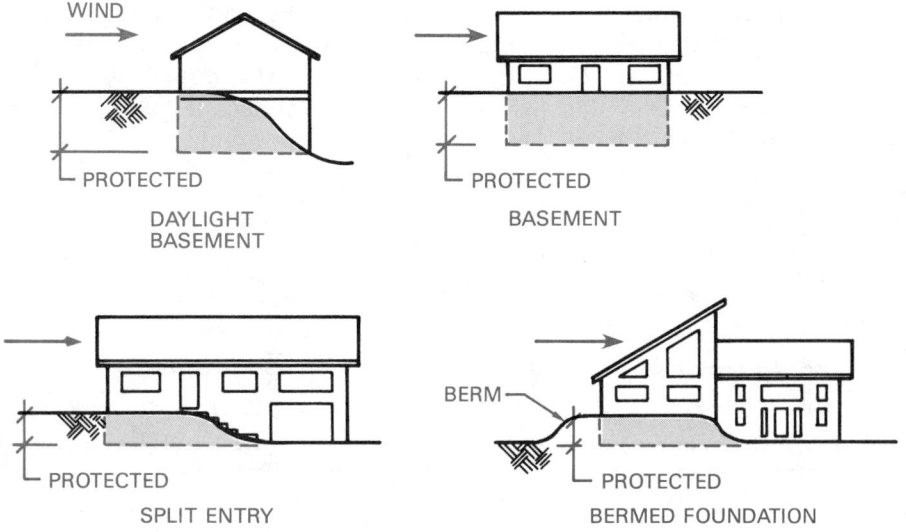

Figure 11-15 Subterranean wind protection.

general wind conditions. Figure 11–14 shows some examples of site locations that may be protected from prevailing winds.

It may be very difficult to completely avoid the negative effects of winds in a given location. When a site has been selected and wind continues to be a concern, there are other factors such as construction or landscaping techniques that can contribute to a satisfactory environment. A subterranean structure may totally reduce the effects of wind. These un-

derground homes, when placed with the below-grade portion against the wind, can create a substantial wind control as seen in Figure 11–15.

When subterranean housing is not considered a design alternative, then some other techniques can be used. Building the structure partly into the ground with a basement or using berming may be a successful alternative. Proper foundation drainage is a factor to consider when these methods are used. Figure 11–16 shows how wind protection can be achieved with proper use of the earth. Landscaping can also add an effective break between the cold winter wind and the home site. Coniferous trees or other evergreen landscaping materials can provide an excellent windbreak. These trees should be planted in staggered rows. Two rows is a suggested minimum while three rows may be better. Some hedge plants could be planted in one row to provide wind protection. Figure 11–17 shows how landscaping can protect the structure from cold wind.

Room and construction design can also influence wind protection. Place rooms that do not require a great deal of glass for view or solar use on the north side or the side toward which severe winter winds are a problem. A garage, even though unheated, is an insulator and can provide an excellent break between the cold winter winds and the living areas of the home. Bedrooms with fairly small windows may be placed to provide a barrier between the wind and the balance of the home. A common method of exterior construction design that helps deflect wind is a long sloping roof. A flat two-story surface causes a great deal of wind resistance. A better alternative is achieved when a long sloping roof is used to reduce wind resistance resulting in more energy efficient construction. Figure 11–18 shows how roof construction can effectively deflect prevailing winds.

Figure 11-16 Wind protection using earth.

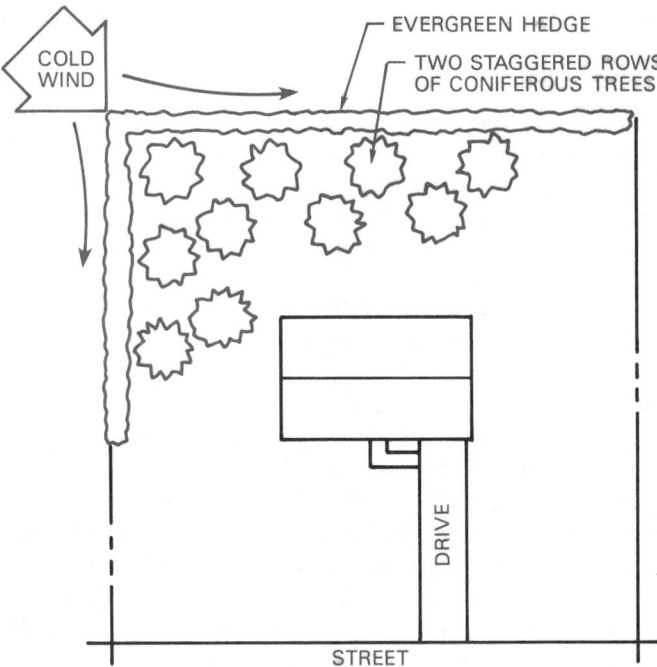

Figure 11–17 Wind protection with landscaping.

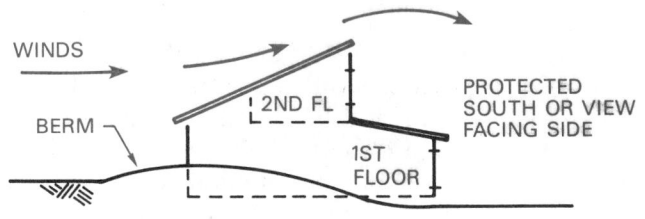

Figure 11–18 Roof slope wind protection.

Summer Cooling Winds

Summer winds may be mild and help provide for a more comfortable living environment. Comfort can be achieved through design considerations for natural ventilation and through landscape design. Effective natural ventilation can be achieved when a structure has openings in opposite walls that allow for cross ventilation. In a two- or multiple-story structure, the openings can be effectively tied into the stair wells to provide for continuous ventilation. Figure 11–19

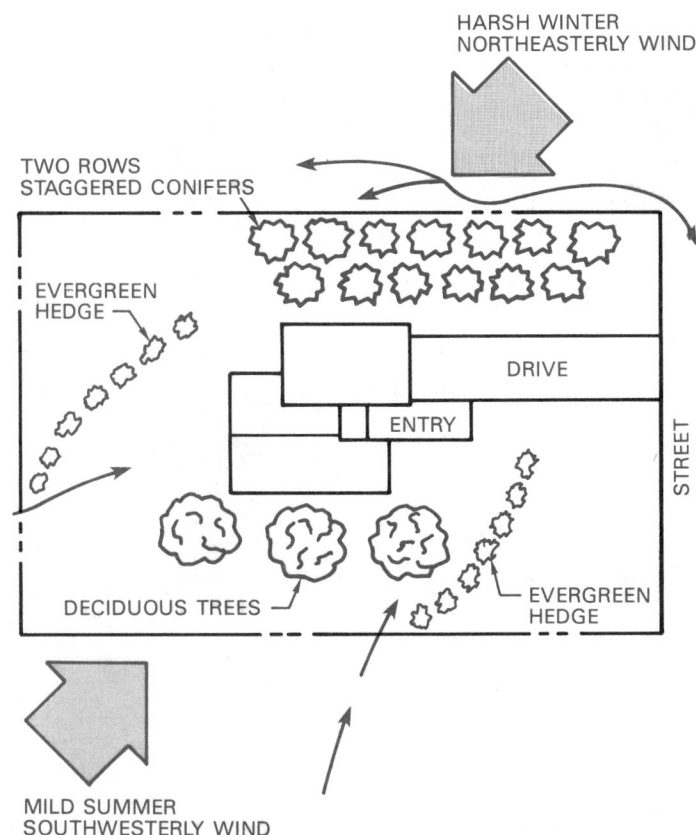

Figure 11–20 Landscaping for wind control.

shows an example of how good natural ventilation can be achieved.

Landscaping can also help provide summer cooling. The discussion of wind protection showed how coniferous trees can protect against cold winter winds. These evergreen trees can also be used in conjunction with deciduous trees to help funnel summer winds into the home site and help provide natural summer cooling. Fences or other buildings can also help create a wind funnel. Deciduous trees serve a triple purpose. In the summer they provide needed shade and act as a filter to cool heated wind. In the winter they loose their leaves thus allowing the sun's rays to help warm the house. Figure 11–20 shows how an effective landscape plan can be used to provide a total environment.

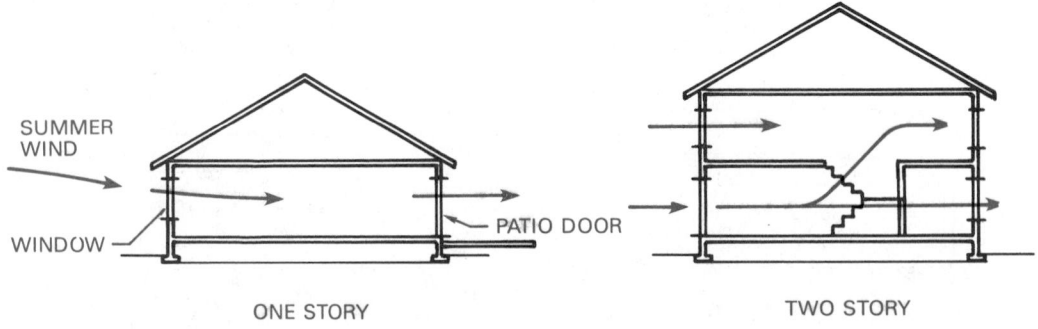

Figure 11–19 Natural ventilation.

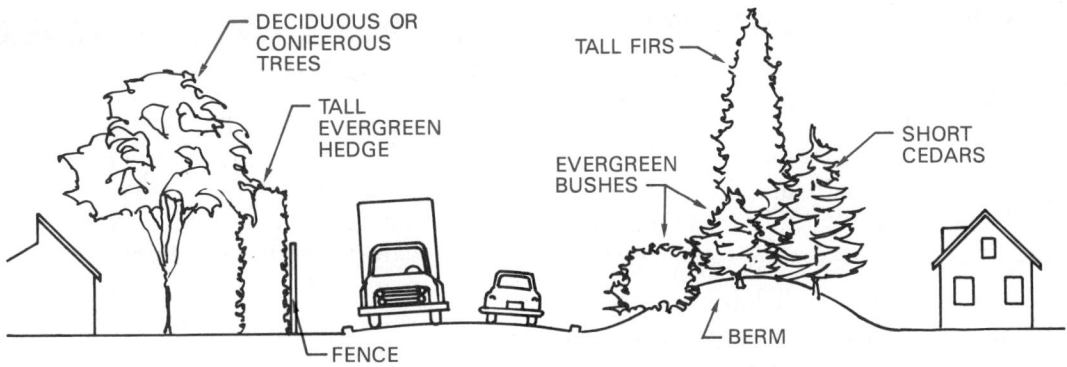

Figure 11-21 Sound insulation landscaping.

SOUND ORIENTATION

If your construction site is located in the country near the great outdoors, then sound orientation may not be a concern. The sounds that you will contend with are singing birds, croaking frogs, chirping crickets, and a few road noises. It is very difficult to eliminate road sounds from most locations. A site that is within a mile of a major freeway may be plagued by the droning sounds of excessive road noise. A building site that is level with or slightly below a road may have less noise than a site that is above and overlooking the sound source.

There are a few landscaping designs that can contribute to a quieter living environment. Berms, trees, hedges, and fences can all be helpful. Some landscape materials deflect sounds while others may absorb sounds. The density of the sound barrier has an influence on sound reduction although even a single hedge can reduce a sound problem to a certain extent. A mixture of materials can most effectively reduce sound. Keep in mind that while deciduous trees and plants help reduce noise problems during the summer, they are a poor sound insulation in the winter. See Figure 11-21.

As previously shown, trees can effectively provide a barrier to wind and they may also provide sound insulation. The greater the width of the plantings for sound insulation, the better the control. Trees planted in staggered rows provide the best design. Figure 11-22 shows the plan view of a site with sound barrier plants. Notice, also, in Figure 11-22 that the garage is placed between the living areas of the home

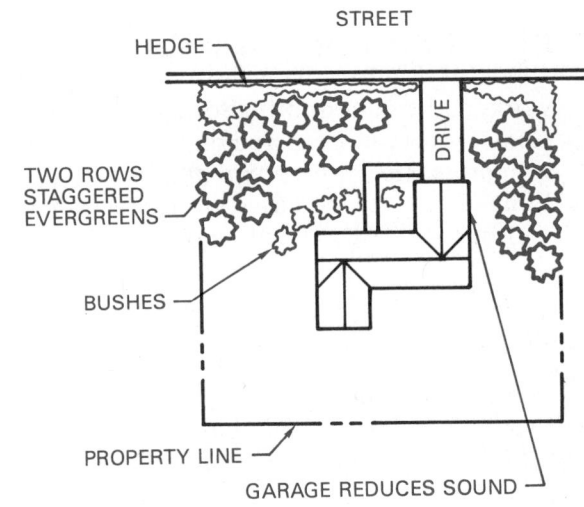

Figure 11-22 Sound reduction: home and landscape plan.

and the street to help reduce sound problems substantially.

There are a number of factors that influence site orientation. Solar orientation may be important to one builder while another homeowner may have view orientation as the main priority. A perfect construction site will have elements of each site orientation design feature. When a perfect site is not available then it is a challenge for the designer or architect to orient the structure to take the best advantage of each potential design feature. As you have seen, it is possible to achieve some elements of good orientation with excavation and landscaping techniques. Always take advantage of the natural conditions whenever possible.

SITE ORIENTATION TEST

DIRECTIONS

Answer the questions with short complete statements or drawings as needed on an 8½ × 11 drawing sheet as follows:

1. Use ⅛ in. guidelines for all lettering.
2. Letter your name, Site Orientation Test, and the date at the top of the sheet.
3. Letter the question number and provide the answer. You do not need to write out the question.
4. Do all lettering with vertical uppercase architectural letters. If the answer requires line work, use proper drafting tools and technique. Answers may be prepared on a word processor if appropriate with course guidelines.
5. Your grade will be based on correct answers and quality of line technique.

QUESTIONS

1. Define site orientation.
2. Describe in short complete statements five factors that influence site orientation.
3. Define magnetic declination.
4. What is the magnetic declination of the area where you live?
5. Name and describe two types of obstacles that can block the sun in an otherwise good solar site.
6. Describe how trees can be an asset in solar orientation.
7. What are prevailing winds?
8. Name two features that can protect the structure from wind.
9. Show in a sketch how landscaping can be used for winter wind protection and summer cooling.
10. Show in a sketch how landscaping can be an effective sound control.
11. List at least two factors that must be considered in subterranean construction.
12. List at least two disadvantages of a two-story house on a narrow treeless lot.
13. List at least five advantages of considering site orientation in the planning of a home.
14. Name at least one solar site planning tool.

Chapter 12
Solar Energy Designs

SOLAR ENERGY

SUNLIGHT BECOMES solar energy when it is transferred to a medium that has the capacity or ability to provide useful heat. This useful solar energy may be regulated in order to heat water or the inside of a building, or create power to run electrical utilities. Most areas of the earth receive about 60 percent direct sunlight each year while in very clear areas up to 80 percent of the annual sunlight is available for use as solar energy. When the sun's rays reach the earth, air and the things on the earth become heated. Certain dense materials such as concrete can absorb more heat than less dense materials such as wood. During the day the dense materials absorb and store solar energy. Then at night with the source of energy gone, the stored energy is released in the form of heat. Some substances, such as glass, absorb thermal radiation while transmitting light. This concept, in part, is what makes solar heating possible. Solar radiation enters a structure through a glass panel and warms the surfaces of the interior areas. The glass keeps the heat inside by absorbing the radiation.

Two basic residential and commercial uses for solar energy are heating spaces and hot water. Other uses are industrial and include drying materials such as lumber, masonry, or crops. Solar energy has also been used for nearly a century with desalinization plants to provide fresh water from either mineral or salt water.

The types of solar space heating systems available are either passive, active, or a combination of the two. Passive, or architectural, systems use no mechanical devices to retain, store, and radiate solar heat. Active, or mechanical, systems do use mechanical devices to absorb, store, and use solar heat.

SOLAR DESIGN

The potential reduction of fossil fuel energy consumption can make solar heat an economical alternative. There are a number of factors that contribute to the effective use of solar energy. Among them are building a structure with energy efficient construction techniques and fully insulating the building to reduce heat loss and air infiltration. These concepts are covered in detail in Chapter 13.

An auxiliary heating system is often used as a backup or supplemental system in conjunction with solar heat. The amount of heat needed from the auxiliary system depends upon the effectiveness of the solar system. Both the primary and supplemental systems should be professionally engineered for optimum efficiency and comfort.

A southern exposure, when available, provides the best site orientation for solar construction. A perfect solar site will allow the structure to have an unobstructed southern exposure.

Room placement is another factor to consider when taking advantage of solar heat. Living areas, such as the living and family rooms, should be on the south side of the house while inactive rooms, such as bedrooms, laundries, and baths, should be located on the north side of the structure where a cooler environment is desirable. If possible the garage should be placed on the north, northeast, or northwest side of the home. A garage can act as an effective barrier for insulating the living areas from cold exterior elements.

Another energy efficient element of the design is an air-lock entry, known as a vestibule. This is an entry that provides a hall or chamber between an exterior and interior door to the building. The vestibule should be designed so that neither interior nor exterior door should be open at the same time. See Figure 12–1. The distance between doors should be at least 7' to help force the occupants to close one door before they reach the other. The main idea behind a vestibule entry is to provide a chamber that is always closed to the living area by a door. When the exterior door is opened, the air lock loses heat, but the heat loss is confined to the small space of the vestibule and the warm air of the living area is not exposed to loss.

Figure 12–1 also shows this plan to be a solar design with living areas and a solarium, or sun room, at the southern exposure where extensive glass allows the rooms to be warmed by solar heat. The inactive rooms including the bedrooms, baths, laundry, pantry, and garage shelter the living area from the northern exposure. The use of masonry walls also allow the house to be built into a slope on its northern side or for berms to be used as shelter from the elements.

LIVING WITH SOLAR ENERGY SYSTEMS

The use of solar energy and energy efficient construction requires a commitment to energy conservation. Each individual must evaluate cost against potential savings and become aware of the responsibility of living with energy conservation.

Solar systems that provide some heat from the sun and require little or no involvement from the occupant to assist the process can be designed. Such a minimal energy-saving design is worth the effort in most cases. Active solar space heating systems are available that can provide a substantial amount of needed heat energy. These systems are automatic and also do not generally require involvement from the homeowner although he or she should be aware of operation procedures and maintenance schedules. On the other hand, some passive solar heating systems require much participation by the occupant. For example, a mechanical shade that must be maneuvered by the homeowner can be used to block the summer sun's rays from entering southern exposure windows. During the winter months when the sun is heating the living area, the heat should be retained as long as possible. In the morning the homeowner will need to open shutters or drapes to allow sunlight to enter and heat the rooms. In the early evening before the heat begins to radiate out of the house, the occupant should close the shutters or drapes to keep the heat within.

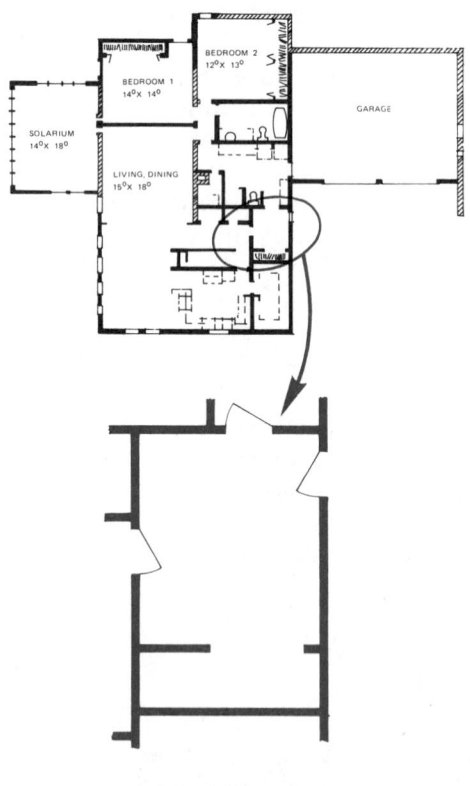

AIR LOCK ENTRY

Figure 12–1 Solar design. *Courtesy Residential Designs.*

CODES AND SOLAR RIGHTS

Building permits are generally required for the installation of active solar systems or the construction of passive solar systems. Some installations also require plumbing and electrical permits. Verify the exact requirements for solar installations with local building officials. During the initial planning process, always check the local zoning ordinances to determine the feasibility of the installation. For example, many areas have dwelling height restrictions. If the planned solar system encroaches upon this zoning rule, then a different approach or a variance to the restriction should be considered.

The individual's rights to solar access are not always guaranteed. A solar home may be built in an area that has excellent solar orientation and then a few years later, a tall structure may be built across the street that blocks the sun. The neighbor's trees may even grow tall and reduce solar access. Determine the possibility of such a problem arising before construction begins. Some local zoning ordinances, laws, or even deed restrictions do protect the individual's *right to light*. In the past, laws generally provided the right to receive light from above the property, but not from across neighboring land. This situation is changing in many areas of the country.

ROOF OVERHANG

Since the sun's angle changes from season to season, lower on the horizon in the winter and higher in the summer, the addition of overhang can shield a major glass area from the heat of the summer sun and also allow the lower winter sun to help warm the home. Figure 12–2 shows an example of how a properly designed overhang can aid in the effective use of the sun's heat.

An overhang that will provide about 100 percent of shading at noon on the longest day of the year can be calculated with a formula that divides the window height by a factor determined in relationship to the latitude of the construction:

$$\text{Overhang} = \frac{\text{Windowsill Height}}{F}$$

NORTH LATITUDE	F
28°	8.4
32°	5.2
36°	3.8
40°	3.0
44°	2.4
48°	2.0
52°	1.7
56°	1.4

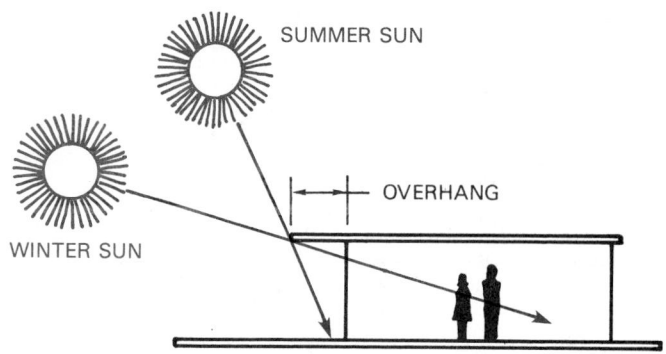

Figure 12–2 Effective overhang.

Calculate the recommended southern overhang for a location at 36° latitude and provide for a 6'–8" window height.

$$\text{Overhang (OH)} = \frac{6'-8'' \ (\text{Window Height})}{3.8 \ (\text{F at 36° latitude})}$$

$$\text{OH} = \frac{6.6}{3.8} = 1.8 = \text{Approx. } 1'-10''$$

The overhang recommendation would be greater for a more northerly latitude. For example a 48° latitude calculation with 6'–8" window height would be:

$$\text{OH} = \frac{6'-8''}{2.0} = 3'-4''$$

Figure 12–3 shows the effects of the summer and winter sun on the 3'–4" overhang calculation for the 48° latitude. The valuable heat from the winter sun is allowed to enter the home while the summer heat is excluded.

Overhang protection can be constructed in ways other than a continuation of the roof structure. An awning, porch cover, or trellis may be built to serve the same function. There is a great deal of flexibility in architectural design that will provide the same function. Alternate methods of shading from summer heat and exposing the window areas to winter sun

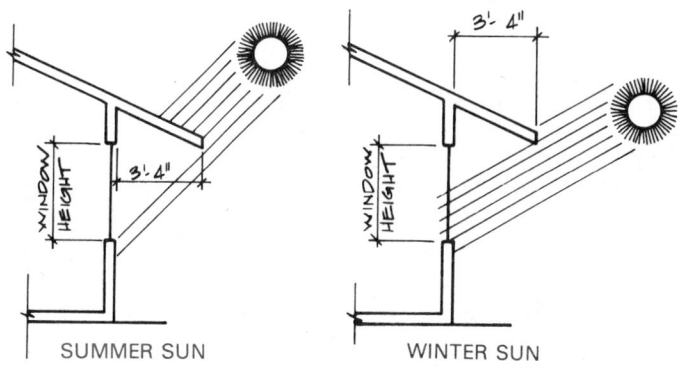

Figure 12–3 Effective overhang on summer and winter sun.

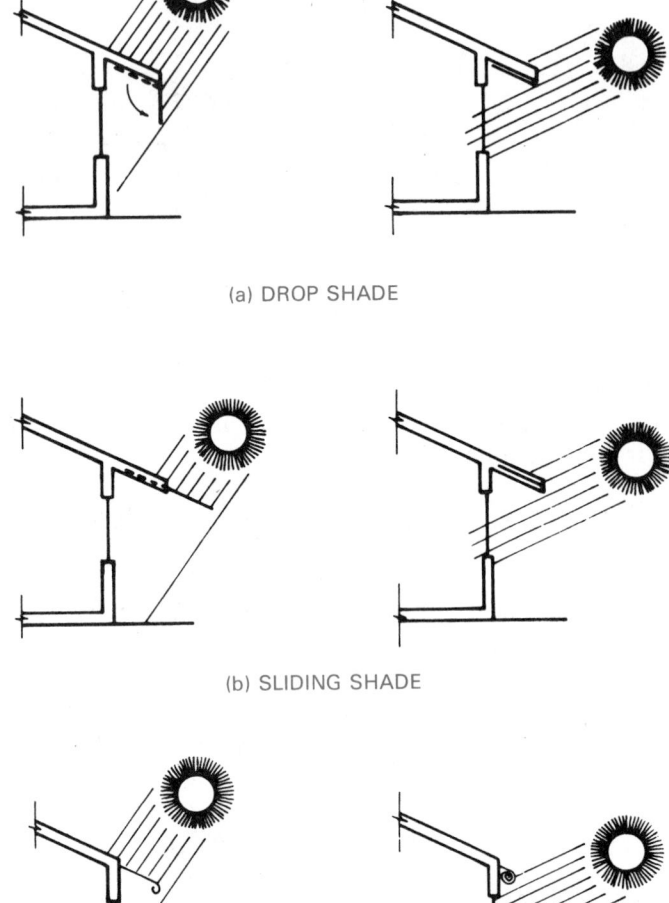

(a) DROP SHADE

(b) SLIDING SHADE

(c) AWNING SHADE

Figure 12-4 Optional shading devices.

can be achieved with mechanical devices. These movable devices require that the occupant be aware of the need for shade or heat at different times of the year. Figure 12-4(a), 12-4(b), and 12-4(c) shows a display of some shading options.

PASSIVE SOLAR SYSTEMS

In passive solar architecture, the structure is designed so the sun will directly warm the interior. A passive solar system allows the sun to enter the structure and be absorbed into a structural mass. The stored heat then warms the living space. Shutters or drapes are used to control the amount of sun entering the home, and vents help provide temperature control. In passive solar construction, the structure is the system. The amount of material needed to store heat

depends on the amount of sun, the desired temperature within the structure, and the heat storage ability of the material used. Materials such as water, steel, concrete, or masonry have good heat capacity while wood does not. There are several passive solar architectural methods that have been used individually and together including south facing glass, thermal storage walls, water storage, roof ponds, solariums, and envelope construction.

South-facing Glass

Direct solar gain is a direct gain in heat created by the sun. This direct gain is readily created in a structure through south-facing windows. Large window areas facing south can provide up to 60 percent of a structure's heating needs when the windows are insulated at night with tight-fitting shutters or insulated curtains. When the window insulation is not used at night, the heat gain during the day will quickly be lost. The sun's energy must heat a dense material in order to be retained. Floors and walls are often covered or made of materials other than traditional wood and plasterboard. Floors constructed of or covered with tile, brick, or concrete, and special walls made of concrete or masonry, or containing water tubes can provide heat storage for direct gain applications. Figure 12-5 shows a typical direct-gain south-facing glass application.

Clerestory windows can be used to provide light and direct solar gain to a second floor living area and increase the total solar heating capacity of a house. Figure 12-6 shows a design using clerestory windows. These clerestory units can also be used to help ventilate a structure during the summer months when the need for cooling may be greater than heating. Look at Figure 12-7.

Skylights can be used effectively for direct solar gain. When skylights are placed on a south-sloping

Figure 12-5 South-facing glass provides direct gain. *Courtesy Residential Designs.*

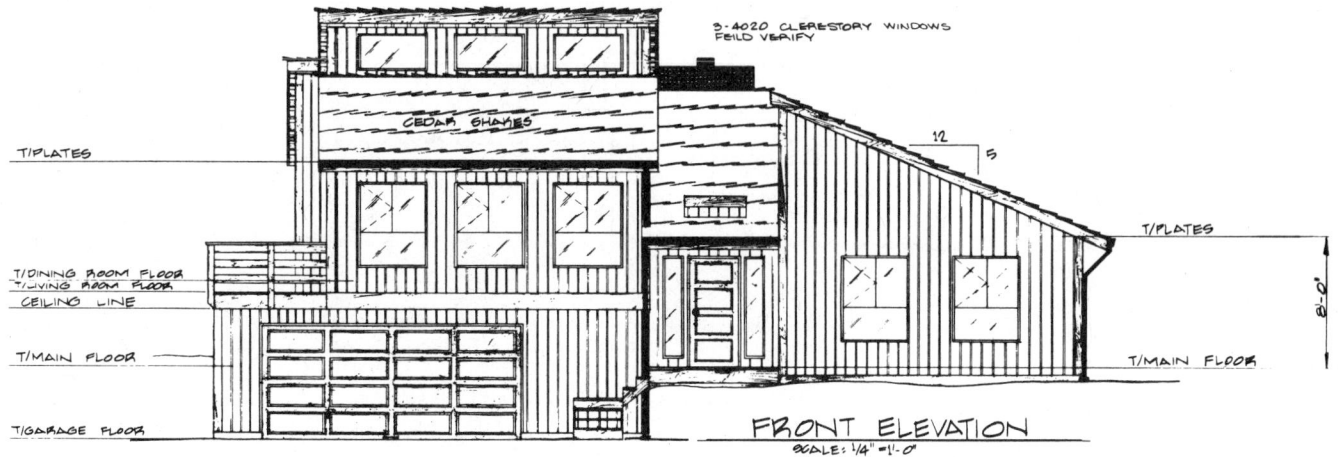

3-4020 CLERESTORY WINDOWS
FEILD VERIFY

CEDAR SHAKES

T/PLATES

T/DINING ROOM FLOOR
T/LIVING ROOM FLOOR
CEILING LINE

T/MAIN FLOOR

T/GARAGE FLOOR

12
5

T/PLATES

8'-0"

T/MAIN FLOOR

FRONT ELEVATION
SCALE: 1/4" = 1'-0"

Figure 12-6 Clerestory windows. *Courtesy Madsen Designs.*

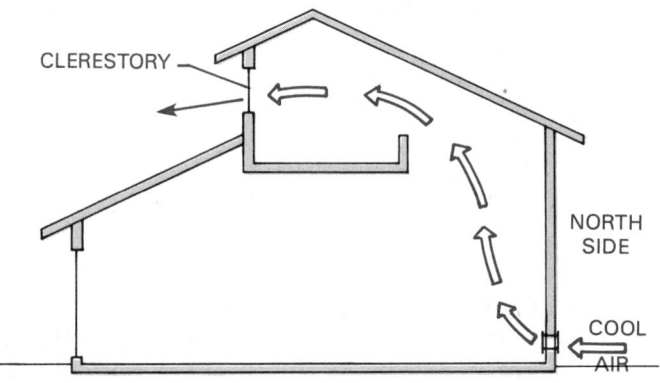

CLERESTORY

NORTH
SIDE

COOL
AIR

Figure 12-7 Clerestory circulation.

roof, they provide needed direct gain during the winter. In the summer, these units can cause the area to overheat unless additional care is taken to provide for ventilation or a shade cover. Some manufacturers have skylights that open which may provide sufficient ventilation. Figure 12–8 shows an application of openable skylights.

Thermal Storage Walls

Thermal storage walls can be constructed of any good heat-absorbing material such as concrete, masonry, or water-filled cylinders. The storage wall can be built inside and adjacent to a large southern exposed window or group of windows. The wall receives and stores energy during the day and releases the heat slowly at night.

The Trombe wall, designed by French scientist Dr. Felix Trombe, is a commonly used thermal storage wall. The Trombe wall is a massive dark-painted masonry or concrete wall situated a few inches inside and adjacent to south-facing glass. The sun heats the air between the wall and the glass. The heated air rises and enters the room through vents at the top

Figure 12-8 Skylights. *Courtesy VELUX-AMERICA, INC.*

of the wall. At the same time, cool air from the floor level of adjacent rooms is pulled in through vents at the bottom of the wall. The vents in the Trombe wall must be closable to avoid losing the warm air from within the structure through the windows at night. The heat absorbed in the wall during the day radiates back into the room during night hours. The Trombe wall will also act to cool the structure during the summer. This happens when warm air rises between the wall and glass and is vented to the outside. The air currents thus created work to pull cooler air from an open north-side window or vent. Figure 12–9 shows an example of the thermal storage wall.

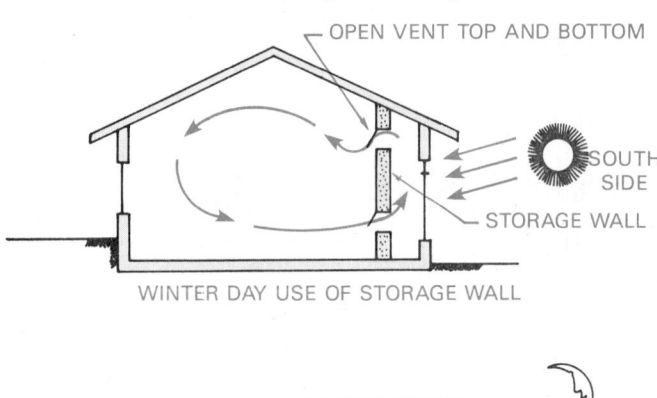

OPEN VENT TOP AND BOTTOM

SOUTH SIDE

STORAGE WALL

WINTER DAY USE OF STORAGE WALL

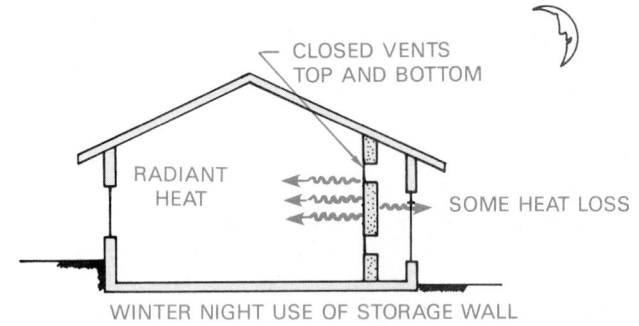

CLOSED VENTS TOP AND BOTTOM

RADIANT HEAT

SOME HEAT LOSS

WINTER NIGHT USE OF STORAGE WALL

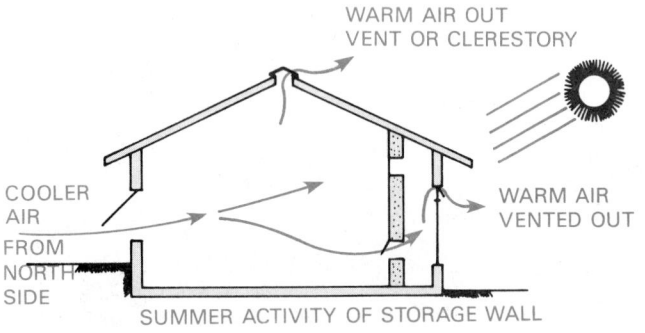

WARM AIR OUT VENT OR CLERESTORY

COOLER AIR FROM NORTH SIDE

WARM AIR VENTED OUT

SUMMER ACTIVITY OF STORAGE WALL

Figure 12-9 Thermal storage wall.

Some passive solar structures use water as the storage mass where large vertical water-filled tubes or drums painted dark to absorb heat are installed as the Trombe wall. The water functions excellently as a medium to store heat during the day and release heat at night.

Roof Ponds

Roof ponds are used occasionally in residential architecture, although they are more commonly used in commercial construction. A roof pond is usually constructed of containers filled with antifreeze and water on a flat roof. The water is heated during the winter days and then at night the structure is covered with insulation which allows the absorbed heat to radiate into the living space. This process functions in reverse during the summer. The water-filled units are covered with insulation during the day and uncovered at night to allow any stored heat to escape. In order to assist in the radiation of heat at night,

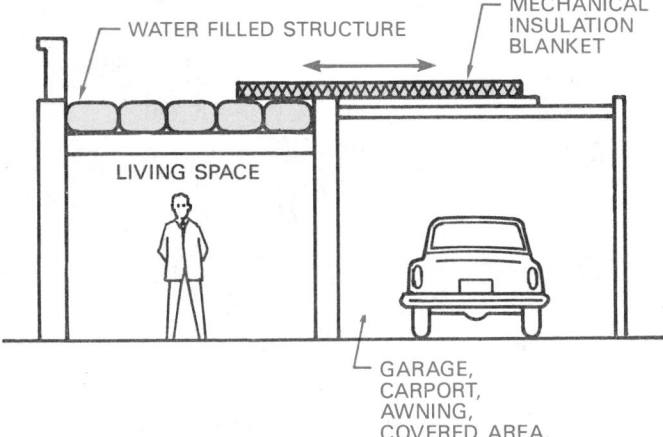

WATER FILLED STRUCTURE

MECHANICAL INSULATION BLANKET

LIVING SPACE

GARAGE, CARPORT, AWNING, COVERED AREA.

Figure 12-10 Roof ponds.

the structure should be constructed of a good thermal conducting material such as steel. Figure 12-10 shows an example of the roof pond system.

Solariums

A solarium, sometimes called a sun room or solar greenhouse, is designed to be built on the south side of a house adjacent to the living area. Solariums are a nice part of the living area when designed into a new home, and are one of the most common passive solar additions to existing structures. The additional advantage of the solarium is the greenhouse effect. These rooms allow plants to grow well all year around.

The theory behind the solarium is to absorb a great amount of solar energy and transmit it to the balance of the structure. A thermal mass as previously described may also be used in conjunction with the solarium. Heat from the solarium can be circulated throughout the entire house by natural convection or through a forced-air system. The circulation of hot air during the winter and cool air during the summer in the solar greenhouse functions similar to a Trombe wall.

The solarium can overheat during long, hot summer days. This potential problem can be reduced by mechanical ventilators. The addition of a mechanical humidifier may also be recommended. Exterior shading devices are often advantageous where a cover can be rolled down over the greenhouse glass area. The use of landscaping with southern deciduous trees as discussed in Chapter 11 is a suggested alternative. Figure 12-11 shows how the solarium operates to provide solar heat and circulate summer cooling.

Solar greenhouses are a popular design feature of some restaurants. The feeling of outside dining is a desirable alternative to traditional dining rooms. See Figure 12-12. It is not at all uncommon for a passive solar design to use several of the concepts previously

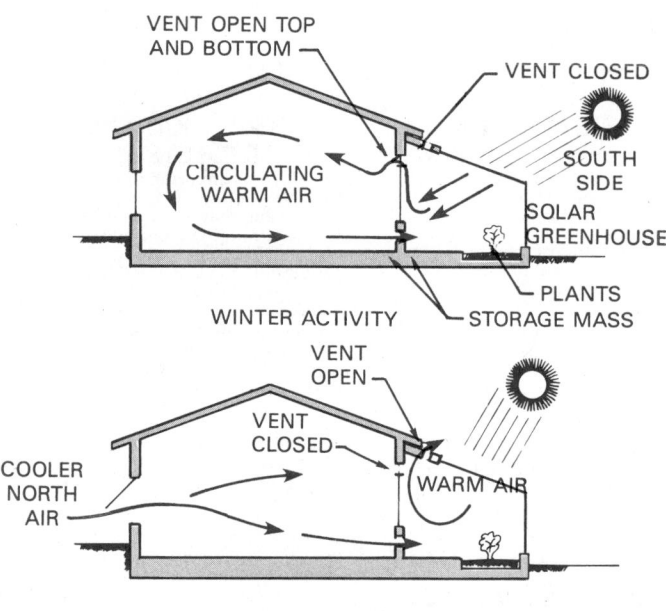

Figure 12–11 Solarium construction.

Figure 12–12 Solar greenhouse. *Courtesy Janco Greenhouses, J.A. Nearing Co., Inc.*

discussed in one structure. Figure 12–13 shows examples of how passive solar elements can be used in one home.

Envelope Design

The envelope design is based on the idea of constructing an envelope or continuous cavity around the perimeter of the structure. A solarium is built on the south side with insulating double-pane glass to act as a solar collector. During the winter when solar energy is required to heat the structure the warm air that is created in the solarium rises and the convection currents cause the heated air to flow

around the structure through the envelope cavity. Look at Figure 12–14.

Notice that the envelope crawl space floor is a storage mass. The rock will store heat during the day and release the energy slowly at night. This functions in reverse during the summer to help cool the cavity and the structure. The greenhouse floor acts as a vent with floor decking spaced to allow air currents to pass through and provide the continuous current. The heated air in the envelope cavity will help keep the living space at a constant temperature. The properly designed envelope structure can completely eliminate the need for a backup heating system. Some envelope dwellings use a wood- or coal-burning appliance for backup heat while others use small forced-air systems.

The summer heat is often a concern in solar design although an envelope can effectively cool when the sun is high in the sky. Deciduous shade trees are an added advantage for summer cooling when planted on the south side. The function of the cooling process is a reverse of the heating operation. The clerestory windows are opened and heated air is allowed to escape as it rises. Another design feature that assists in cooling is the underground pipe or tube that is constructed in connection with the cool crawl space. The underground temperature remains about 55° F and when open to outside air ventilation, a convection current is again created. This time the flow of air is cool and flows under the cool crawl space and around the envelope. This same system can be used in conjunction with the solar greenhouse. Figure 12–15 shows how the envelope design can cool during the summer.

Insulation is an important factor in the envelope design with both the outer shell and the inner shell being insulated. Generally R-19 insulation is adequate on the outer shell while R-11 insulation on the inner shell is common. Insulative values in excess of these amounts generally do not add greater efficiency to the structure. Foundation walls at the crawl space perimeter and floor should be adequately insulated.

The passive envelope system is an effective method of reducing energy consumption and creating an excellent living environment. Standard construction techniques are generally used although the cost of two walls and roof structures is a factor. Another problem is the framing and installation of windows and openings in the double walls of the envelope. Research local and national building codes when considering the envelope design. Factors that should be discussed include fire safety. Codes often require that specific safety precautions be taken to mechanically damper the cavity in case of fire. The same air currents that carry the air around the envelope will also allow flames to engulf the structure quickly.

LARGE, SOUTH FACING WINDOWS

The most widely applied form of passive solar heating requires large areas of south-facing windows to provide direct heat gain. The amount of window area needed will depend upon the amount of heating required and the amount of sunshine available. As a rule of thumb, about one square foot of south-facing window area would be provided for every three to five square feet of floor space. Draperies or shades are used to prevent unnecessary heat loss.

OVERHANGING ROOFS

A distinguishing feature of any passive solar home is the use of overhanging roofs. The principal is simple: The high sun angle during the summer, if not blocked by overhangs, would adversely boost interior temperatures. But during the winter, with a lower sun angle, sunlight can stream unimpeded through the windows, warming the house. The length of the overhang is dependent on the latitude, which for our region is typically fifty percent of the window height.

VENTILATION

Proper ventilation is essential in a passive solar home...as it is in a conventional structure. Air movement during summer months can contribute significantly to natural cooling. Through adequate ventilation design, the need for artificial cooling can be reduced.

INSULATION AND WEATHER STRIPPING

It is important to ensure that the dwelling is properly insulated and that heat loss is kept to a minimum. There would be little value in using solar features to capture the sun's energy if the heat gained is lost due to inadequate insulation. Floor, wall and ceiling insulation as well as weatherstripping, caulking, storm doors and windows are essential to maximize the effectiveness of passive solar. Pacific Power can help you determine if you have enough insulation.

ORIENTATION

Proper orientation in relation to the sun and clear access to the sun's rays are particularly important. The essence of passive solar is direct access to the sun.

EARTH BERM

LEAFING TREES

Trees, besides being pleasant to look at, play a key role in passive solar design. Deciduous trees permit natural shading during the hot summer months but lose their leaves in winter, allowing sunshine to enter and warm the home.

TROMBE WALL

A special kind of heat storage wall is the Trombe wall. This method utilizes direct heat gain through south-facing windows coupled with a large storage wall positioned relatively close to the windows (see illustration). The wall mass absorbs heat during the day, then radiates the stored heat back into the living space at night. *The distinguishing feature of the Trombe wall is the use of dampers to control airflow direction.* Through the use of airflow controls, a reverse circulation is prevented. Sufficient space should be left between the wall and window for opening and closing drapes and window cleaning.

HEAT STORAGE

The key to passive solar home heating is storage of daytime heat for controlled release later when the temperature drops. Collected solar heat can be stored in concrete walls, slate floors, rock beds under the floor or in special storage walls designed as a feature of the building's interior.

The best material for heat storage is water, which is approximately five times as effective as masonry.

Some modern passive designs have incorporated water tanks discretely into storage walls. Or, if masonry is used, a rule of thumb is that 150 lbs. is recommended for every square foot of south-facing window area.

Figure 12–13 Passive solar elements. *Courtesy Pacific Power and Light Company.*

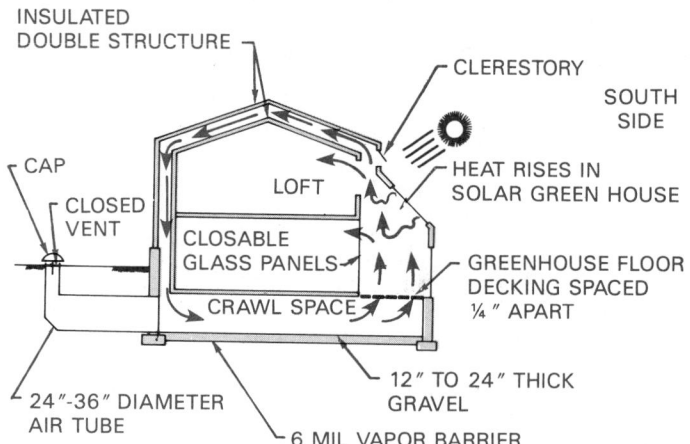

Figure 12–14 Winter envelope activity.

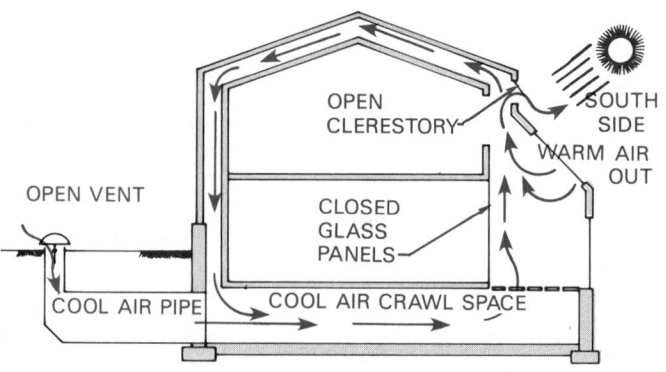

Figure 12–15 Summer envelope activity.

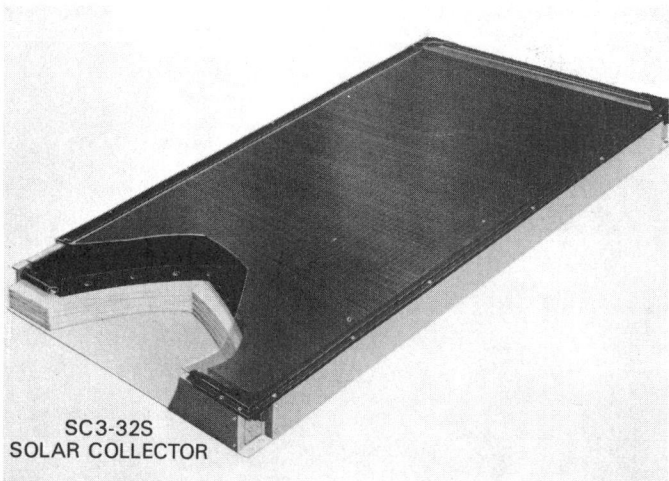

Figure 12–16 Solar collector. *Courtesy Lennox Industries, Inc.*

If proper precautions are not taken, a fire in the home can turn the envelope into a giant wooden flue, and the inside of the house will ultimately become the firebox and proliferate the flames into an all-fuel fireplace. National Codes, in general, specify fire blocking at the floor and ceiling plates, and require the home designer to submit alternatives for the envelope design. Most alternatives include the addition of smoke activated dampers in the cavity at the floor and ceiling lines plus lining the air chamber with drywall. The liner may improve the efficiency of the structure but add tremendously to the cost. Some envelope designs have proven better at cooling in the summer than heating in the winter which may be a plus. However, the popularity of the envelope design is declining due to the added cost compared to other systems. The potential energy cost savings may not be much better than that achieved with excellent energy efficient construction.

ACTIVE SOLAR SYSTEMS

Active solar systems for space heating use collectors to gather heat from the sun which is transferred to a fluid. Fans, pumps, valves, and thermostats move the heated fluid from the collectors to an area of heat storage. The heat collected and stored is then distributed to the structure. Heat in the system is transported to the living space by insulated ducts which are similar to the duct work used in a conventional forced-air heating system. The active solar heating system generally requires a back-up heating system that is capable of handling the entire heating needs of the building. Some back-up systems are forced-air systems that use the same ducts as the solar system. The back-up system may be heated by electricity, natural gas, or oil. Some people rely on wood- or coal-burning appliances for supplemental heat. Active solar systems are commonly adapted to existing homes or businesses that normally use a forced-air heating system.

Collectors

As the name implies, solar collectors catch sunlight and convert this light to heat. Well designed solar collectors are nearly 100 percent efficient. Figure 12–16 shows an example of a solar collector.

The number of solar collectors needed to provide heat to a given structure depends upon the size of the structure and volume of heat needed. These are the same kinds of determinations made when sizing a conventional heating system. Collectors are commonly placed in rows on a roof or on the ground adjacent to the structure as shown in Figure 12–17. The best placement requires an unobstructed southern exposure. The angle of the solar collectors should be in proper relationship to the angle of the sun during winter months when the demand for heat is greatest. Verify the collector angle that is best suited for the specific location. Some collectors are designed to be positioned at 60° from horizontal so that winter sun hits at about 90° to the collector. While this is the ideal situation, a slight change from this angle

Typical Applications

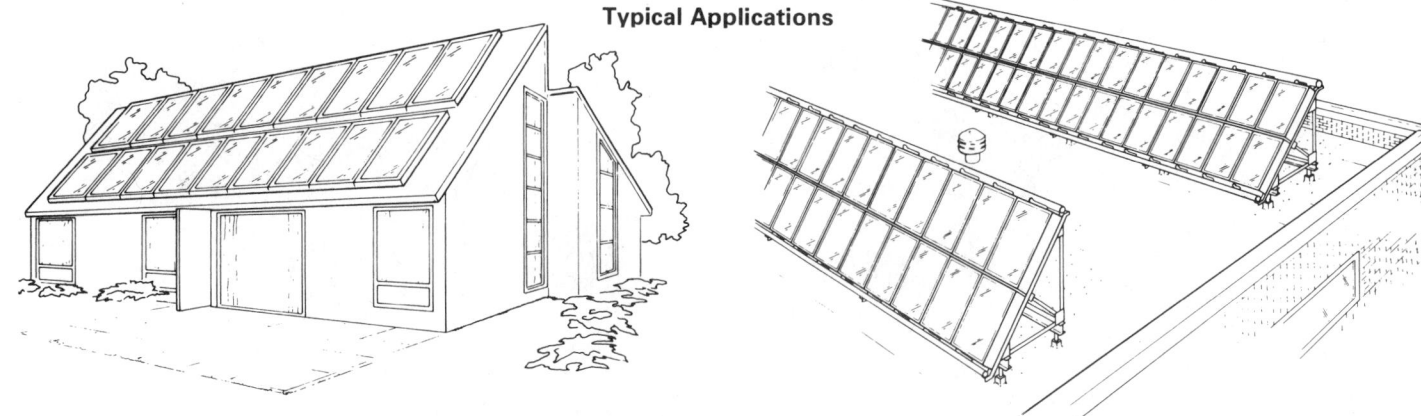

Figure 12–17 Typical application of solar hot-water collectors. *Courtesy Lennox Industries, Inc.*

of up to 15° may not alter the efficiency very much. Other collectors are designed to obtain solar heat by direct and reflected sunlight. Reflecting, or focusing, lenses help concentrate the light on the collector surface. Figure 12–18 shows an example of solar collector tilt.

Solar collectors for space heating are designed to be positioned for optimum effect during winter months. Solar hot water collectors may be positioned at an angle that would produce an average solar gain throughout the year. For example, if space heat collectors are placed at 60° to take advantage of the low winter sun angle, then hot water collectors may be placed at a more average angle of 45° for heat absorption throughout the year. Space heat needs are more demanding in the winter while hot water is required all year around.

Storage

During periods of sunlight the active solar collectors transfer the heat energy to a storage area and then to the living space. After the demand for heat is met, the storage facilities allow the heat to be contained for use when solar activity is reduced such as at night or during cloud cover.

The kind of storage facilities used depends upon the type of collector system used. There are water, rock, or chemical storage systems. Water storage is excellent since water has a high capacity for storing heat. Water in a storage tank is used to absorb heat from a collector. When the demand for heat exceeds the collector's output, the hot water from the storage tank is pumped into a radiator, or through a water-to-air heat exchanger for dispersement to the forced-air system. Domestic hot water may be provided by a water-to-water heat exchanger in the storage tank.

Rock storage is often used when air is the fluid used by the collectors rather than water. The heated air flows over a rock storage bed. The rock absorbs some heat from the air while the balance is distributed to the living space. When the solar gain is minimal, then cooler air passes over the rock storage where it absorbs heat and is distributed by fans to the living space. Domestic hot water may also be provided by an air-to-water heat exchanger situated in the rock storage or in the hot air duct leading from the collector.

Chemical storage systems are gaining popularity. Chemicals used in collectors and in storage facilities absorb large amounts of heat at low temperatures. Many of these systems claim to absorb heat on cloudy

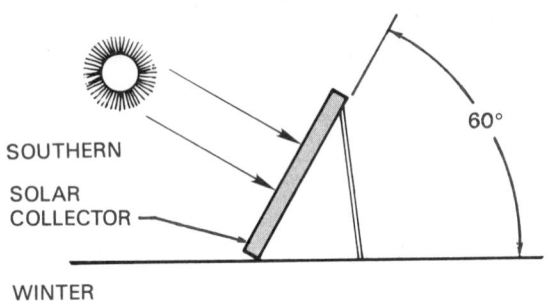

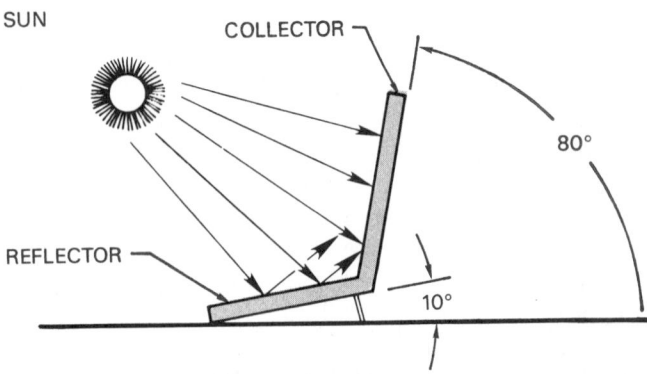

Figure 12–18 Solar collector tilt.

days or even when the collectors are snow covered. Chemicals with very low freezing temperatures can actually absorb heat during winter months when the outside temperature is low.

Freon-charged Solar Collectors

Freon-charged solar collectors operate on a sealed system principle that is much like a refrigerator but with no compressor. The sun's energy will boil and compress the semiazeotrope fluids (any mixture which has a semiconstant boiling point at a specific concentration) into a vapor at 80° F just as water would turn to steam at 212° F. The heated vapor will rise to a heat exchanger above the solar collector plate through which the storage fluid is circulated. Energy is transferred from the vapor to circulating water which condenses the vapor back to a liquid state. The liquid returns to the bottom of the solar collecting plate completing the cycle. Figure 12–19 shows a space heating or cooling diagram. Figure 12–20

shows a typical roof-level installation. Ground level installations are also commonly used.

Solar Architectural Cement Products

Solar collectors may be built into the patio, driveway, tennis court, pool deck, or tile roof.

Solar architectural cement products make the most versatile solar collector on the market. It can be used as a driveway, sidewalk, patio, pool deck, roofing material, or the side surface of a building wall or fence. The finished surface can resemble cobblestone, brick, or roof tiles. Pigments are added to the specially formulated material which give it a lasting color that is pleasing to the eye. These solar products are completely different from all other solar collectors in that they add to the aesthetic value of the property. These products are manufactured from a specially formulated mixture which is strong and dense, allowing it to be very conductive and waterproof. Solar architectural cement products absorb and collect heat from

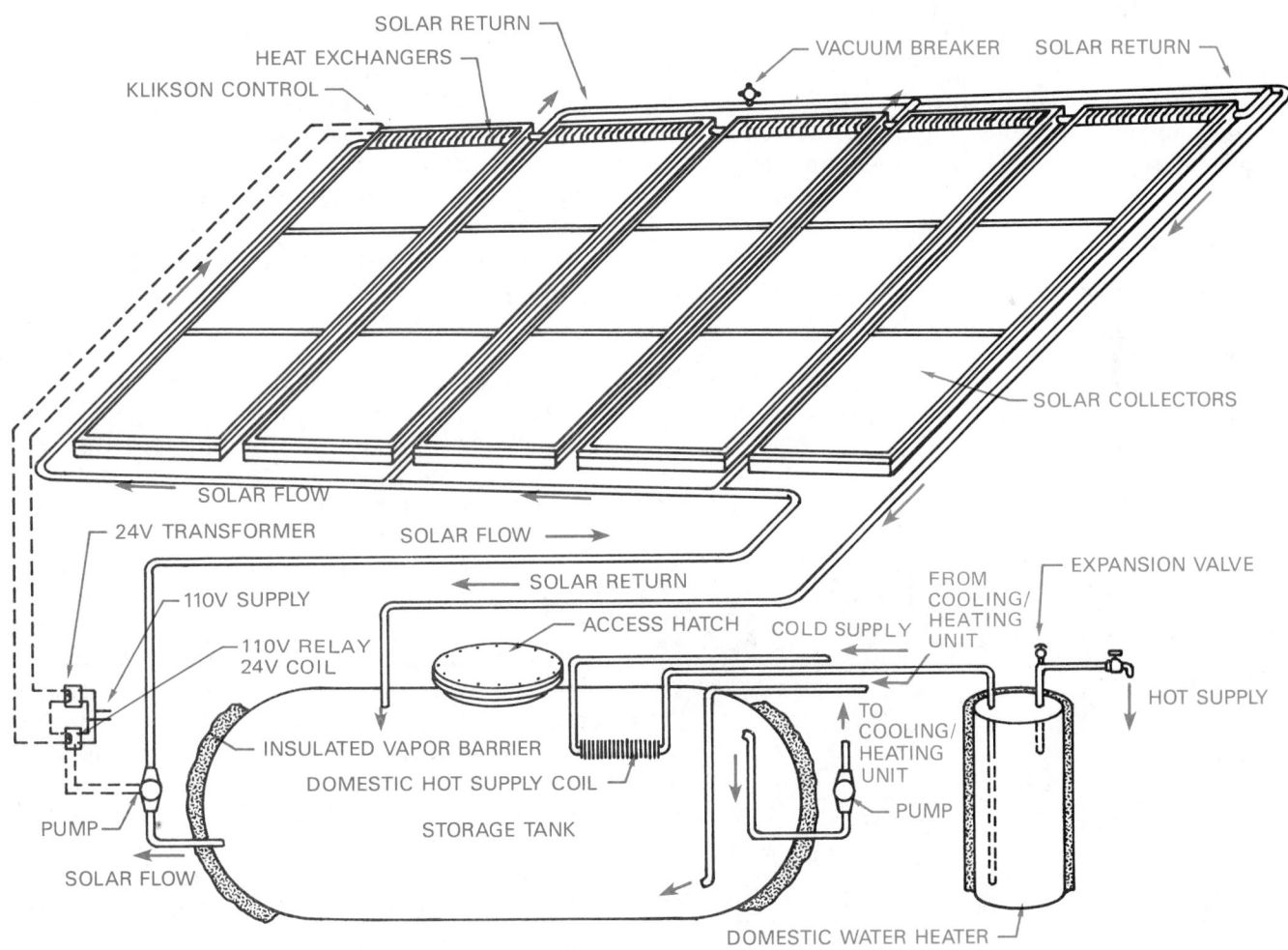

Figure 12–19 Space heating or cooling solar bank. *Courtesy Solar Oriented Environmental Systems, Inc.*

Figure 12–20 Typical roof level solar collector installation. *Courtesy Lennox Industries, Inc.*

the sun and outside air, and transfer the heat into water, glycol, or other heat transferring fluid passing through imbedded tubes. Figure 12–21 shows examples of solar architectural cement in use.

Geothermal Systems

Geothermal heating and cooling equipment is designed to use the constant, moderate temperature of the ground to provide space heating and cooling, or domestic hot water, by placing a heat exchanger in the ground, or in wells, lakes, rivers, or streams.

A geothermal system operates by pumping ground water from a supply well and then circulating it through a heat exchanger where either heat or cold

is transferred by freon. The water, which has undergone only a temperature change, is then returned through a discharge well back to the strata as shown in Figure 12–22. Lakes, rivers, ponds, streams, and swimming pools may be alternate sources of water. Rather than pumping the water up to the heat exchanger, a geothermal freon exchanger can be inserted into a lake, river, or other natural body of water to extract heat or cold as desired as shown in Figure 12–23.

Another alternative is to insert a geothermal freon exchanger directly into a well where the natural convection of the ground water temperature, assisted by the normal flow of underground water in the strata, is used to transfer the hot or cold temperature that is required. Sometimes the thermal transfer must be assisted by forcing the freon to circulate through tubes within the well by a low horsepower pump. See Figure 12–24.

A geothermal system may assist a solar system that uses water as a heat storage and transfer medium. After the water heated by solar collectors has given up enough heat to reduce its temperature to below 100° F, this water becomes the source for operating the geothermal system. See Figure 12–25.

When an adequate supply of water is not available, the ground, which always maintains a constant temperature below the frost line, can be used to extract either heat or cold. The thermal extraction is done through the use of a closed-loop system consisting of polybutylene tubing filled with a glycol solution and circulated through the geothermal sys-

Figure 12–21 Solar architectural concrete installation.

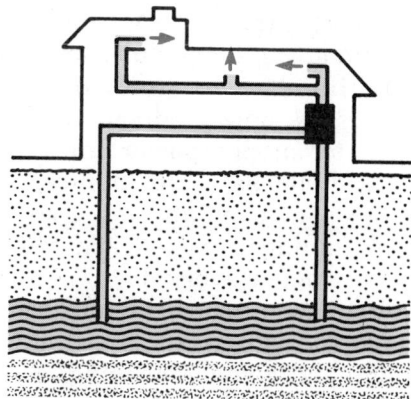

Figure 12–22 Ground water system. *Courtesy Solar Oriented Environmental Systems, Inc.*

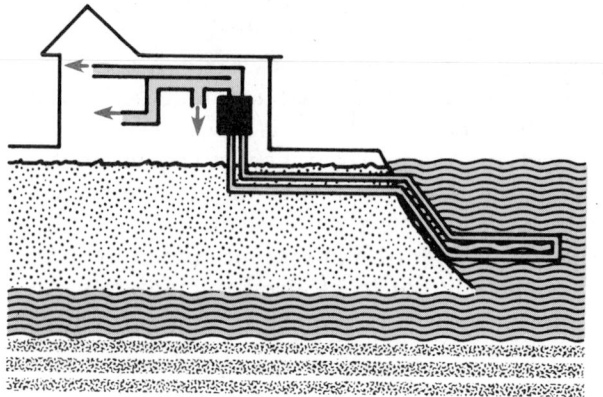

Figure 12–23 Geothermal freon exchanger in a lake. *Courtesy Solar Oriented Environmental Systems, Inc.*

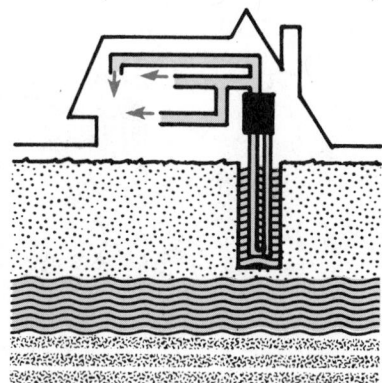

Figure 12–24 Geothermal freon exchanger in a well. *Courtesy Solar Oriented Environmental Systems, Inc.*

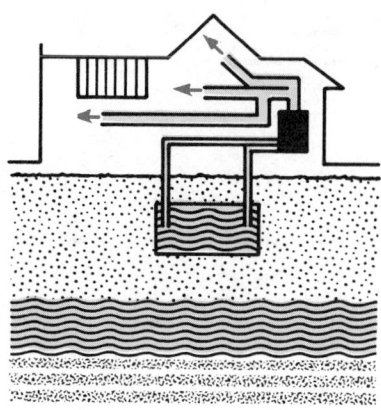

Figure 12–25 Solar assisted system. *Courtesy Solar Oriented Environmental Systems, Inc.*

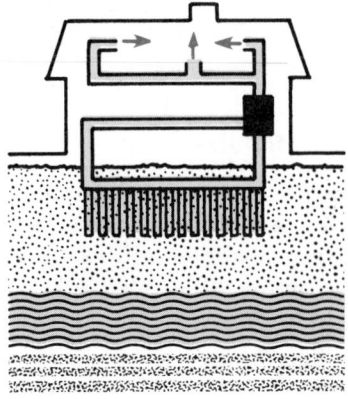

Figure 12–26 Ground loop system. *Courtesy Solar Oriented Environmental Systems, Inc.*

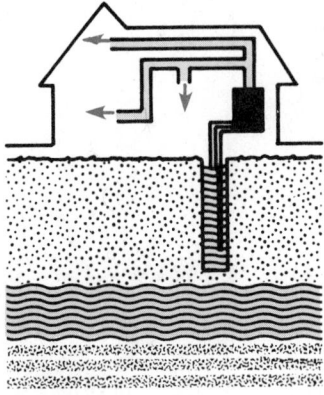

Figure 12–27 Vertical dry system. *Courtesy Solar Oriented Environmental Systems, Inc.*

tem. One alternative system is shown in Figure 12–26. Another method is to use a vertical dry-hole well which is sealed to enable it to function as a closed-loop system as shown in Figure 12–27.

The geothermal system is mechanically similar to a conventional heat pump, except that it uses available water to cool the refrigerant or to extract heat as opposed to using 90° F air for cooling, or 20 to 40° F air for heating. Water can store great amounts of geothermal energy due to its high specific heat (the amount of energy required to raise the temperature of any substance 1° F). The specific heat of air is only 0.018 so it can absorb and release only 1/50 of the energy that water can. Fifty times more air by weight must pass through a heat pump to produce as much heat as the same amount of water.

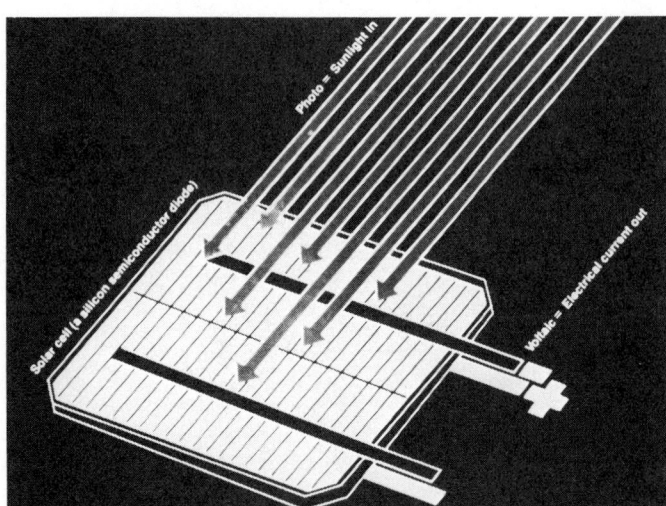

Figure 12-28 Photovoltaic cell. *Courtesy Arco Solar, Inc.*

Photovoltaics Modules

Solar electricity from photovoltaic cells was once considered to be an exotic technology appropriate only for powering space satellites or an occasional terrestrial experiment. Solar electricity is a practical means of producing energy for everyday use.

Photovoltaic technology has been developed and refined, and photovoltaic modules are now powering thousands of installations worldwide. Solar photovoltaic systems are now producing millions of watts of electricity to supply power for remote cabins, homes, railroad signals, water pumps, telecommunications stations and even utilities. Uses for this technology are continuing to expand, and new installations are being constructed every day.

Photovoltaic cells turn light into electricity. The word photovoltaic is derived from the Greek *photo*, meaning *light*, and *voltaic*, meaning to *produce electricity by chemical action*. Figure 12-28 shows that photons strike the surface of a silicon wafer, which is a semiconductor diode, to stimulate the release of mobile electric charges that can be guided into a circuit to become a useful electric current.

Photovoltaic modules produce direct current (DC) electricity. This type of power is useful for many applications and for charging storage batteries. When alternating current (AC) is required, DC can be changed to AC by an inverter. Some photovoltaic systems are designed to use immediately the energy produced as is often the case in water-pumping installations. When the energy produced by solar electric systems is not to be used immediately, or when an energy reserve is required for use when sunlight

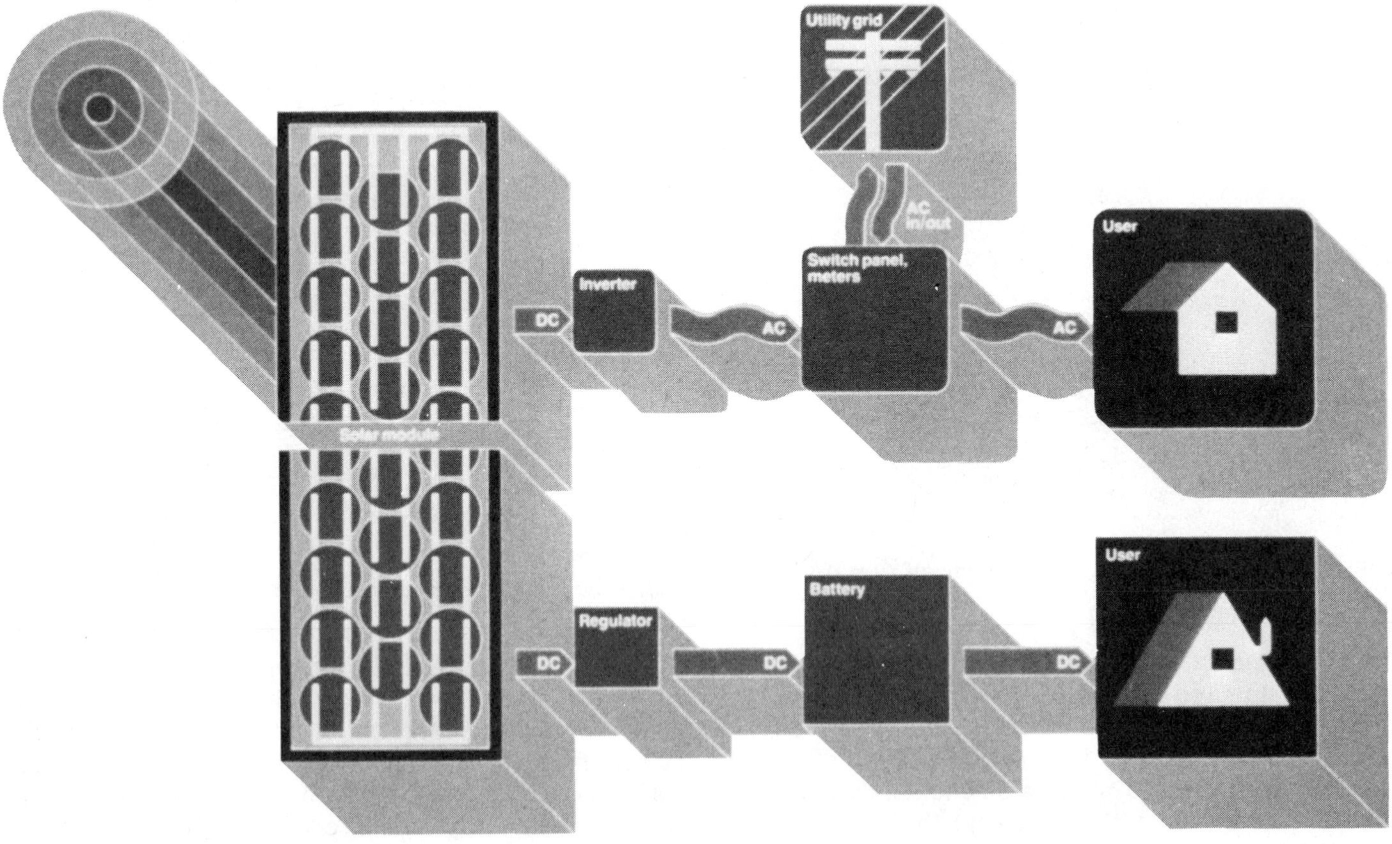

Figure 12-29 Function of the photovoltaic solar system. *Courtesy Arco Solar, Inc.*

is not available, the energy must be stored. The most common storage devices used are batteries.

Although both DC and AC systems can stand alone, AC systems can also be connected to a utility grid. During times of peak power usage, the system can draw on the grid for extra electricity if needed. At other times, such a system may actually return extra power to the grid. In most areas of the country the utility (grid) is required to purchase excess power. Figure 12–29 shows the function of a typical solar system.

Correct site selection is vitally important. The solar modules should be situated where they will receive maximum exposure to direct sunlight for the longest period of time every day. Other considerations are distance from the load (appliance), shade from trees or buildings, which changes with the seasons, and accessibility. Figure 12–30 is a photovoltaic solar installation on a remote home.

The future looks bright for solar technologies. The costs and efficiencies of high technology systems are improving. As homeowners watch their heating and cooling costs rise and become more concerned about shortages of oil and gas, solar heating becomes an attractive alternative. When preparing a preliminary design, solar alternatives should be considered. A qualified solar engineer should evaluate the site and recommend solar design alternatives. Additional assistance is usually available from state or national

Figure 12–30 Photovoltaic solar installation. *Courtesy Arco Solar, Inc.*

Departments of Energy. Verify the availability of tax credits or other incentives to help make solar energy systems more feasible. Always evaluate the cost of the system, including any tax incentives, against the estimated payback period, which is the amount of time it should take to save enough on energy usage to pay for the system.

SOLAR ENERGY DESIGNS TEST

DIRECTIONS

Answer the questions with short complete statements or drawings as needed on an 8½ × 11 drawing sheet as follows:

1. Use ⅛ in. guidelines for all lettering.
2. Letter your name, Solar Energy Designs Test, and the date at the top of the sheet.
3. Letter the question number and provide the answer. You do not need to write out the question.
4. Do all lettering with vertical uppercase architectural letters. If the answer requires line work, use proper drafting tools and techniques. Answers may be prepared on a word processor if appropriate with course guidelines.
5. Your grade will be based on correct answers and quality of line technique.

QUESTIONS

1. What are the two basic residential and commercial uses for solar heat?
2. Describe passive and active solar heating.
3. List and describe three factors that influence a good solar design.
4. Discuss the concept of right to light.
5. Define and show a sketch of how each of the following solar systems function:
   a. south-facing glass
   b. clerestory windows
   c. thermal storage wall
   d. roof ponds
   e. solarium
   f. envelope design
6. Define solar collector.
7. Describe a freon-charged solar collector.
8. What are solar architectural cement products and how do they function?
9. Describe three applications of geothermal heating and cooling systems.
10. Define the function of photovoltaic cells.

Chapter 13
Energy-Efficient Design

ENERGY-CONSCIOUS individuals have been experimenting with energy-efficient construction for decades. Their goal has been to reduce home heating and cooling costs. In recent years there have been several formal studies done around the country which have been sponsored by various private and governmental agencies with a commitment to conservation as a result of rising energy costs. The experimental programs have had the following goals:

- Create a better living environment.
- Meet consumer demand for more economical living.
- Evaluate realistic material and construction alternatives that may be used to alter building codes in the future.

Today's home buyers are as concerned about energy-efficient design as they are about large, expansive floor plans and conveniences such as brick fireplaces. Many purchasers have long-term energy saving as their first priority when selecting a new home. Home buyers expect energy-efficient design and construction to be a part of the total home package and, in fact, such design and construction can be achieved without a great deal of additional cost. For example, consumers know that some fireplaces can be a source of heat loss. They are willing to spend the few additional dollars to get an efficient fireplace, one that is constructed with an outside source of combustible air and a built-in heat exchanger. In addition, they look for construction that uses double- or triple-pane windows and air infiltration barriers. Air infiltration barriers are important because when air infiltration is reduced, the amount of unconditioned air that must be heated or cooled to the desired temperature is also reduced. Such construction increases comfort while reducing energy costs.

A survey of 1,400 home buyers made by the Owens-Corning Fiberglas Corporation found that 80 percent considered low energy consumption to be more important than home size, lot size, or luxury features. In fact, low energy cost was their first consideration in looking for a new home. Figure 13–1 is a bar graph that shows the results of the survey. The consumer logic is good. Fuel costs undoubtedly will continue to rise, thus energy cost savings will continue to increase.

Home builders around the country have realized

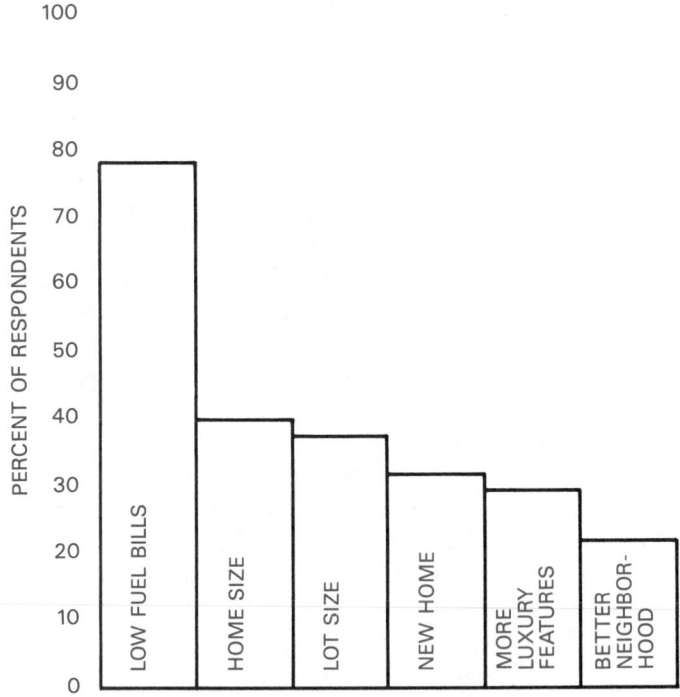

Figure 13-1 What home buyers are looking for. *Courtesy Owens-Corning Fiberglas Corporation.*

the advantages of energy-efficient construction for both consumers and themselves. An energy-efficient home is easier to sell and will sell sooner than ordinary construction. This is especially true during a time when a consumer's ratio of income to purchasing power makes it difficult for a potential home buyer to qualify for a loan. The person applying for a mortgage loan on an energy-efficient home will qualify sooner than for ordinary construction because the estimated energy savings will reduce the purchaser's monthly expenses. The money saved on energy will thus be available for mortgage payments. This concept can be seen in the operation of the Federal Home Loan Mortgage Corporation, or Freddie Mac, as it is called. Freddie Mac is a secondary mortgage lender, which is a place where banks and mortgage companies can sell portfolios, or blocks, of loans they have made for individual mortgages. The money obtained from Freddie Mac allows the lenders to make more housing loans. Freddie Mac has made a commitment to energy efficiency which is acknowledged by the local lenders. Freddie Mac realizes that a borrower's ability to make monthly payments is enhanced when a home is energy efficient and the borrower is required to devote less of his or her income to utility expenses. As a result, Freddie Mac allows banks and other lenders to be more flexible in evaluating the debt-to-income ratio on loans secured by energy-efficient homes. There are several nationwide programs that are recognized to assist

lenders in identifying energy efficiency. These programs include the following:

- National Association of Home Builders (NAHB) thermal performance guidelines
- Virginia and Maryland Homebuilders E-7 Program
- Owens-Corning Fiberglas Corporation Energy Performance Design System (EPDS)
- Massachusetts Home Energy Rating System
- (VEPCO), Energy Saver Home Program
- Western Resources Center, Residential Energy Evaluation Program
- Tennessee Valley Authority Energy Saver Home Program
- Bonneville Power Administration and Oregon Department of Energy, The Oregon Home

EXPERIMENTAL ENERGY-EFFICIENT PROJECTS

There have been several experimental projects in the United States and Canada that have used different methods to evaluate the results of energy-efficient construction. Elements of the programs differ from passive vs. active solar systems or heat pumps vs. zoned heat. The common criteria among these programs are limiting air infiltration and providing large amounts of insulation. Notice as you look at the illustrations of the homes involved in the test cases that there is nothing different in appearance between energy-efficient and conventional homes. The energy-efficient design elements are generally internal and may be used in any style of architecture. The test cases also clearly show that there are many different techniques that may be used to implement energy-efficient design. The methods used may vary with personal preference and budget until such time that local and national building codes are changed to include specific methods in all homes.

Energy-efficient Residence (EER)

Two homes of the same size were built on adjacent lots in Mt. Airy, Maryland, about 40 miles north of Washington, D.C. The U.S. Department of Housing and Urban Development sponsored the design and construction of an energy-efficient residence (EER), and a conventional comparison home (CCH) was sponsored by the National Association of Home Builders. The objective of the research was to demonstrate and measure residential energy conservation potential by comparing two homes of the same size. One house was conventionally designed and built while the other was designed to be energy efficient using available products and techniques. Both houses were built on lots that sloped sharply downward toward the south so that the basement of each home was completely below grade on the north and above grade on the south. Thus both houses had good solar orientation, and the basements of each were approximately one half below grade. Each house had 1196 sq ft on the basement and main floor. Figure 13–2(a) and (b) show the floor plan of each home.

The following table shows how the two homes differed in design and construction:

CONVENTIONAL (CCH)	ENERGY (EER)
Design	
South-facing windows	Unconditioned vestibule and storage room buffers
East glass shaded by carport	Air lock entrance
West windows 1.5 percent of floor area	7'-6" ceiling height
	Closable family room
	Fireplace with glass doors and heat exchanger
	Increased number of south-facing windows
	Roof overhang designed to shade completely south windows in summer
	North windows area reduced and east-west windows omitted
Insulation	
R-11 in walls	R-19 in walls
R-19 in ceilings	R-38 in ceilings
R-8 in basement walls	R-19 in basement walls
	R-5 sheathing
	R-19 perimeter band joist
	Continuous 6 mil vapor barrier in walls and ceiling

After a year of testing in which the families of equal size were asked to keep the thermostats at the same levels, the performance of the EER home was substantially better than the CCH home. The EER home required 71 percent less energy to heat and 31 percent less energy to cool. The comfort level was higher in the EER home because of the high insulation levels which reduced the differences in interior room temperature.

Arkansas Home

The Arkansas Power and Light Company monitored the energy requirements of eighteen homes. Nine homes were built to energy-efficient specifications and nine others were standard code construction. The following table compares the differences between the energy-efficient homes and the standard homes.

The Arkansas home also used advanced framing techniques that helped reduce the amount of wood used and increased the insulation installed. For ex-

STANDARD	ENERGY EFFICIENT
Insulation	
R-3.5 slab perimeter	R-10 slab perimeter
R-11 walls	R-19 walls
R-19 ceilings	R-38 ceiling
	Vapor barrier in walls, ceilings, and floors
	Air leaks caulked and insulated

ample, 2 × 6 studs, 24" on center were used with a single top plate. The trusses were placed directly over and connected to each exterior stud with truss-to-stud connectors.

The study results determined that the Arkansas energy-efficient homes used 80 percent less energy for heating and 60 percent less energy for cooling. The builders involved in the program also reported that the construction costs were about the same due to the special framing and smaller sized HVAC equipment in the energy-efficient homes.

The Energy Showcase Program

The energy showcase program conducted in Saskatchewan, Canada, tested the energy efficiency of thirteen homes. The climate in this area provided a grueling test for energy-efficient construction. The energy features in these homes included two-wall construction for R-40 wall insulation and advanced truss construction to allow for R-60 to R-80 ceiling insulation. Quadruple-paned windows were used. Careful installation reduced air infiltration to near zero. Some homes received ventilation and heat storage systems to help save heat from solar gain. Air-to-air heat exchangers were used to provide ventilation at a minimal loss of heat to the outside air. See Chapter 19 for a discussion of air-to-air heat exchangers.

The results of the testing conducted in this cold climate control program were very impressive. One of the 1,800 sq ft homes cost only $146 (Canadian) to heat in one entire year. That was a total of only 6,477 kilowatt hours of electricity consumed.

The Oregon Home

Beginning in 1984, the Oregon Department of Energy and Bonneville Power Administration jointly sponsored the construction of 700 energy conservation homes in Oregon, Washington, Montana, and Idaho. There were 200 individually constructed energy conservation homes and 30 matched pairs of homes built in Oregon. The criterion for evaluation was established as the Model Conservation Standards (MCS). Each home was scientifically monitored for

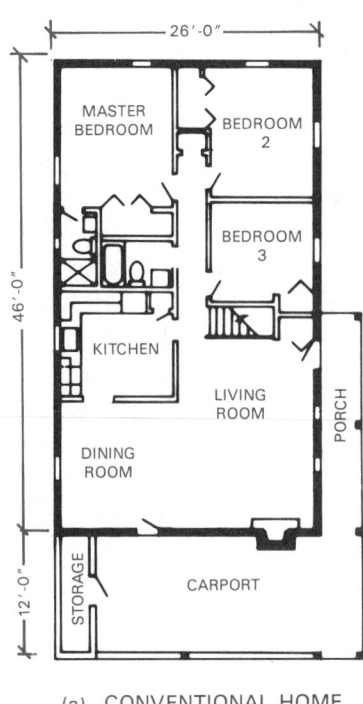

(a) CONVENTIONAL HOME

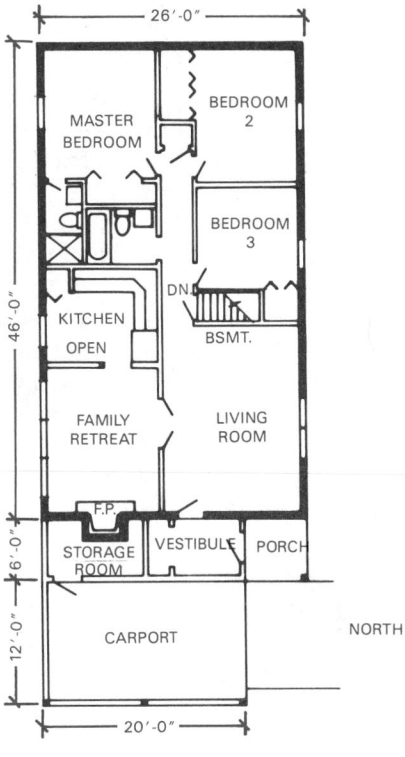

(b) EER HOME

Figure 13–2 (a) Conventional residence compared to (b) an energy-efficient residence. *Courtesy Owens-Corning Fiberglas Corporation.*

one complete year. The data would determine specifically how much energy was consumed in space heating, water heating, operating appliances and lighting. The monitoring would also evaluate indoor air quality to determine if building a too-tightly insulated home can result in poor air quality. Other tests would determine levels of formaldehyde and radon. The sponsors of this program predicted that the energy-efficient homes will use only about one third of the heating energy used by homes built to standard building codes.

Builders involved in the construction of these homes were required to select one of four different methods for meeting the model conservation standards:

• Prescriptive requirements approach
• Point system approach
• Energy budget approach
• Component approach

Prescriptive Requirements and Point System Options. One of these two methods of energy-efficient

construction were selected most often by builders. The rationale for this MCS is that specific requirements for insulation levels, vapor barriers, and glass areas are prescribed. As long as these prescriptions are met, no calculations have to be done. The point system specifically allows for easy modifications of the prescriptive approach. The method assigns positive points to components that exceed the prescriptive requirements and negative points to features that reduce energy savings. After the points are determined for all of the building features, there must be a balance between positive and negative points.

Energy Budget Option. The energy budget approach establishes an energy budget for the building in BTU/sq ft/yr, or kwh/sq ft/yr. A calculation is done to determine if the building meets the budget. This is a flexible method but requires some knowledge of energy analysis. This approach was selected for situations involving passive solar design or unusual construction methods.

Component Approach. The component approach option allowed for lowering the insulation in one component while increasing the insulation in another. The overall U-value of the building must not increase. This method allowed for flexibility in the design and construction of a building. The advantage was for builders using a computer spreadsheet program and related heat loss calculations.

Comparison of Matched Pair of Houses. Further program requirements were that homes must contain at least 1,200 sq ft, be totally electric, and may not use a heat pump in any home under 2,000 sq ft. A very important part of the total study was the construction in Oregon of thirty matched pairs of homes. Each house of the matched pair had to be the same design and close to one another. The difference in the two houses of each pair was that one was built to current code and practice while the other was MCS construction. The results of energy calculations for the MCS home compared to the current practice home as determined in these Oregon climatic zones are shown in Figure 13–3. The following specifications represent the difference between the current code and MCS using the prescriptive path approach for a typical matched pair of houses built in Oregon City, Oregon.

The cost analysis of the Oregon City matched pair of houses indicated that the total cost difference between the current practice home and the MCS home was only $2,000 more for the MCS home. This amount helps conclude that it does not cost very much more to build a more energy-efficient home. Figure 13–4 provides a complete sample set of plans that were used by the Oregon Department of Energy as a builder's guide.

CURRENT	MCS
Walls R-11 Ceiling R-30 Floors R-19 Under slab perimeter R-7 Vapor barrier, none	Walls R-19 Ceiling R-38 Floors R-30 Under slab perimeter R-16 Vapor barrier, 6 mil plastic sheet continuous wrap floor, walls, ceiling
Electric forced-air furnace	Zoned heat Air-to-air heat exchanger required
Two-pane insulated windows Solid-core wood exterior doors plus weatherstripping Ground, 6 mil visqueen to footing	Triple-pane insulated windows Steel, insulated exterior doors plus weatherstripping Ground, 6 mil plastic sheet up foundation wall to sill; caulk and seal all sills, plates, penetrations; special wiring and plumbing to avoid installation in exterior walls; humidifiers, and timed exhaust fans with self-closing dampers; special framing including insulated headers, 2 × 6 exterior studs 24″ o.c., insulated corners, cantilevered truss for full plate line insulation.

ENERGY-EFFICIENT CONSTRUCTION TECHNIQUES

In the several controlled situations where energy-efficient construction techniques were implemented to determine if there would be a significant reduction in energy consumption, the results clearly show that there is energy savings. There are a number of techniques that can be used that do not cost much more than standard construction to implement. To the other extreme, there are some energy conservation construction techniques that are complex and involve labor and material intensive installations. With an unlimited budget and where a commitment to careful craftsmanship and expenditure of time is a possibility, it is possible to provide nearly perfect energy efficiency. Some of the energy-efficient construction designs preclude the necessity for first-time users to research the advantages and disadvantages of specific construction techniques. For the present, a compromise between current and experimental methods will be used by most energy-conscious builders.

Local and national building codes are in the process of implementing energy concepts. Be sure to communicate with local building officials regarding acceptable practice before completing an energy-efficient design.

The Owens-Corning Fiberglas Corporation has an energy performance design program called the thermal crafted home. Their system provides builders

CURRENT USE VS MODEL STANDARD USE

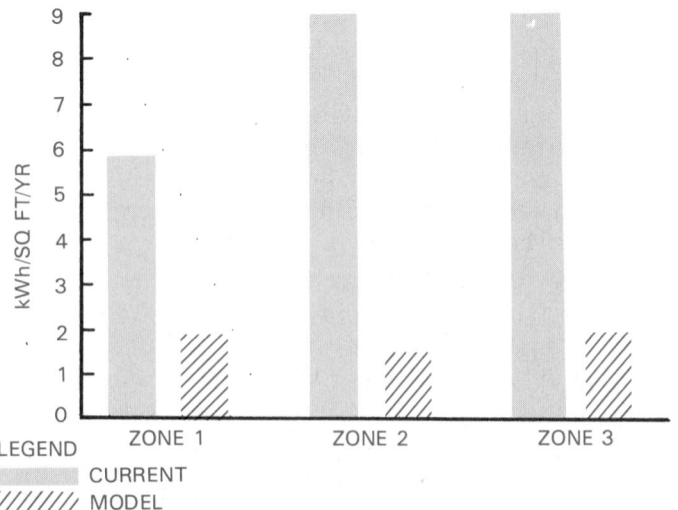

Figure 13–3 Current use compared to model standard use. *Oregon State University and Oregon Department of Energy.*

with a computer analysis of building plans to evaluate potential energy efficiency.

A CHECKLIST FOR ENERGY-EFFICIENT DESIGN

1. Site
   - ____ Avoid windy locations
   - ____ Advantageous solar orientation
   - ____ Landscape to block cold winds and provide for cool shading
   - ____ Effective use of the terrain
2. Room Layout and Design
   - ____ Place living spaces on south side: living, family, dining, kitchen
   - ____ Place passive rooms on north side: bedrooms, baths, laundries, stairs, utilities, halls, garage
   - ____ Provide air lock entries
3. Construction Methods
   - ____ Roof construction to maximize eave insulation
   - ____ Wall construction to reduce wood and increase insulation
   - ____ Floor construction to maximize insulation
   - ____ Foundation construction to decrease air leakage and increase insulation
4. Windows
   - ____ Orient major windows toward south
   - ____ Minimize north-facing windows
   - ____ Keep west-facing windows small
   - ____ Place windows to allow passive cooling
   - ____ Use windows designed for energy efficiency; well weather-stripped, lightly sealed when closed, casements, double hung, awnings
   - ____ Triple pane
5. Doors
   - ____ Energy efficient steel insulated
   - ____ Well weather-stripped
6. Insulation
   - ____ Emphasize craftsmanship
   - ____ Extra insulation in walls, ceiling, and floors
   - ____ Install insulation carefully to avoid blank and compressed areas
   - ____ Keep recessed fixtures, appliances, plumbing, and electrical wiring out of exterior walls
7. Ventilation
   - ____ Vent attics and ceilings adequately
8. Air Infiltration
   - ____ Emphasize craftsmanship at all phases
   - ____ Install continuous interior vapor barrier
   - ____ Caulk and seal joints
   - ____ Use air-to-air heat exchanger
   - ____ Place vent fans on humidistats
9. Heating Systems
   - ____ Properly size heating system
   - ____ Insulate well any required duct work
   - ____ Provide programmable controls
   - ____ Place heat-producing equipment and appliances inside house rather than in the garage
10. Water Heating
    - ____ Set temperature at 120° F
    - ____ Use self-heating dishwasher
    - ____ Insulate tank and pipes
    - ____ Use low-flow shower heads

COMMON ENERGY-EFFICIENT DESIGN SPECIFICATIONS

Although construction methods and materials may vary, these specifications are typically added to the general specifications. See Chapter 43 for a complete discussion of construction specifications.

Framing

1. Frame all exterior walls with 2 × 6 studs at 24 in. Trusses to be aligned with studs.
2. Set sole plates on 1 × 6 fiberglass batt or on silicone caulking.
3. Unless noted on the framing plan, use 4 in. wide header in 6 in. wide exterior walls and back w/ 2 in. rigid insulation behind header. Use 2× nailer at the bottom of the header for sheetrock and sheathing nailing.

Caulking and Insulation

NOTE: CAULKING AND INSULATION ARE THE SINGLE MOST IMPORTANT INGREDIENTS IN THE ENERGY EFFICIENCY OF THIS HOME. DO NOT SUBSTITUTE OR TAKE SHORTCUTS TO THIS IMPORTANT FEATURE.

All insulation to be installed after plumbing and wiring is installed.

1. Insulate all exterior walls around heated areas with 6 in. fiberglass batts, R-19 minimum. Insulate exterior walls prior to installation of tub or shower units.
2. Insulate all flat ceilings with two layers of 6 in. batts, R-38 minimum. Lower layer to have foil face on heated side. Insulate vaulted ceilings with 10 in. batts, R-30 minimum with paper face toward the heated side.
3. Insulate all wood floor areas with 6 in. batts, R-19 minimum between floor joist.

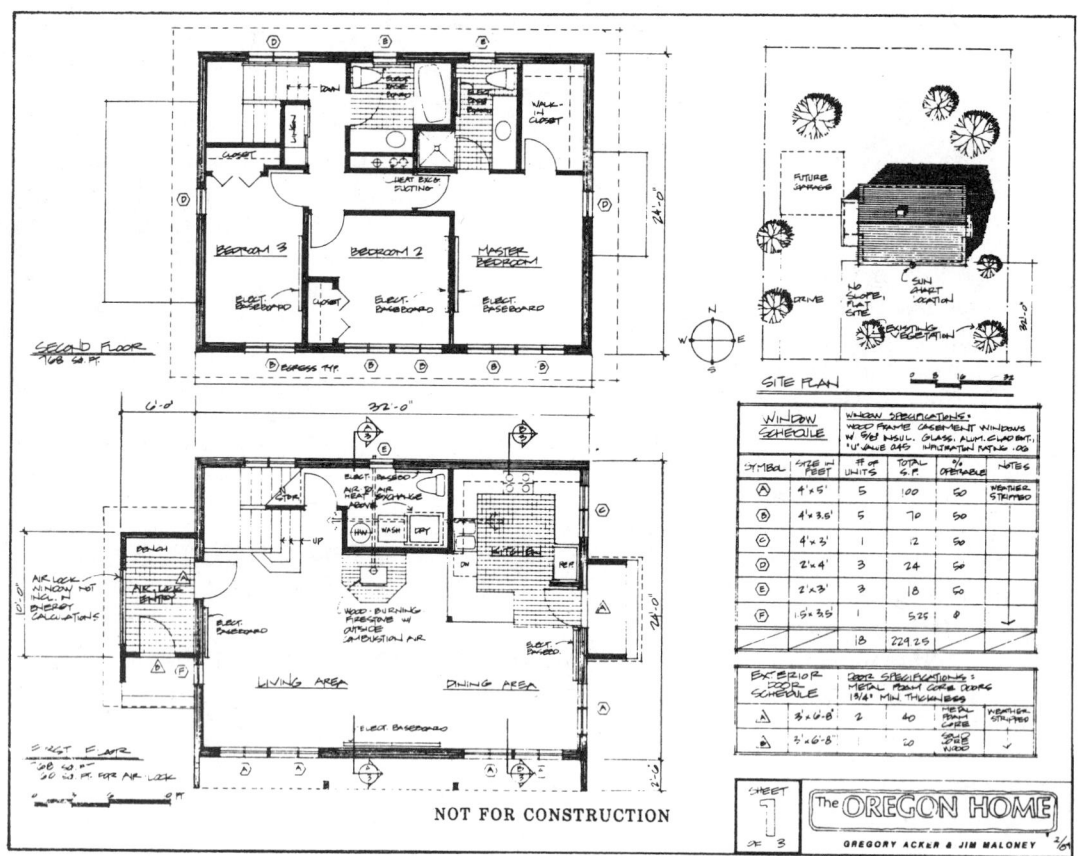

NOT FOR CONSTRUCTION

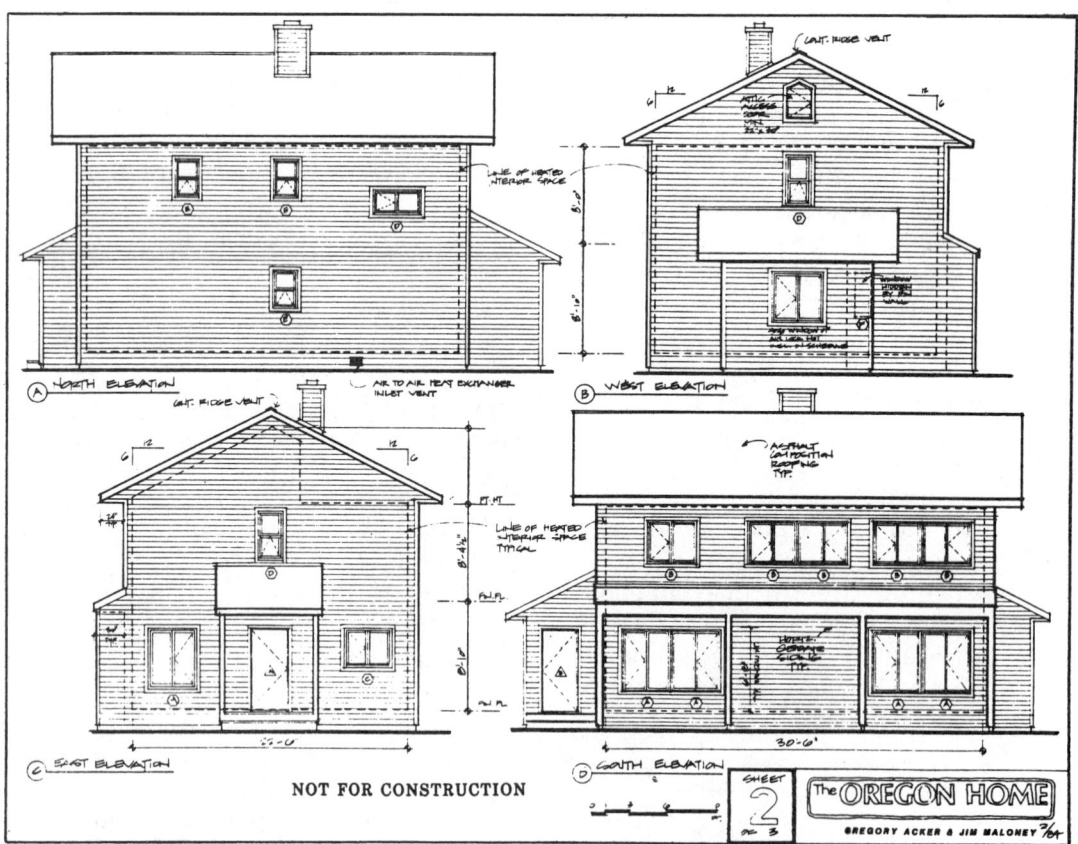

NOT FOR CONSTRUCTION

Figure 13-4 Complete set of energy design plans. *Courtesy Oregon State University and Oregon Department of Energy.*

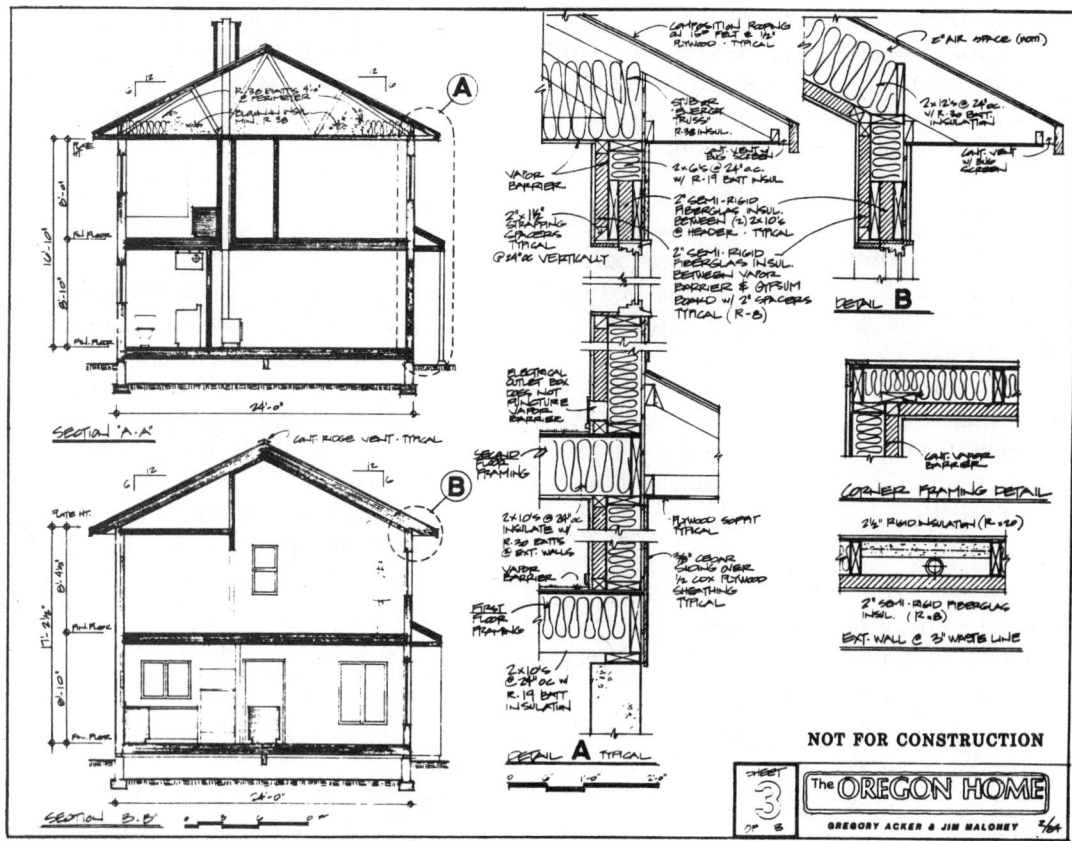

Figure 13–4 Continued.

4. Cover all exterior walls on the exterior side with TYVEK vapor barrier and omit 15# felt. Lap all joints 6 in. minimum and tape all joints.

5. Caulk the following openings with expanded foam or backer rods; polyurethane, elastomeric copolymer, and siliconized acrylic latex caulks may also be used where appropriate:

> Any space between window and door frames and the wall framing.
>
> Between all exterior wall sole plates and the structural floor.
>
> On top of rim joist prior to plywood floor sheathing being applied.
>
> From wall sheathing or siding to top plate.
>
> Around openings for ducts, plumbing, electricity, telephone, and gas lines in walls, ceilings, and floors. All voids around piping running through framing or sheathing are to be packed with gasketing or oakum to provide an airtight barrier.
>
> On perimeter of house. To all sheetrock walls, apply a continuous bead of caulk at the top of the sheetrock to the top plate; apply another continuous bead at the base of the sheetrock to the sill.

6. Seal the sheathing at all corners, joints, doors, windows, and foundation sills with silicone caulking.

7. Weatherstrip the attic and crawl access doors. Insulate attic side of access door to R-38

Electrical and Mechanical

1. All electrical runs in exterior walls are to be in the bottom 6 in. of the studs.

2. Recessed lights in exterior ceilings are to be insulative cover rated.

3. Electrical outlet plate gaskets shall be installed on receptacles, switches, and other electrical boxes in exterior walls.

4. Provide a separate circuit for microwave oven. Verify location with owner.

5. Provide thermostatically controlled exhaust fans in attic with manual override.

6. Heating to be by electric forced-air heating. Provide cold air returns as high as possible in each room with vaulted ceilings.

7. All fans vented outside. All fan ducts to have automatic dampers and be rated 3.0 sones or less with a capacity of 50—100 cfm. Provide a timer switch for all bathroom fans.

8. The hot water tank is to be insulated to R-12 or better.

9. Insulate all hot water pipe runs to R-4 minimum.

10. Provide 6 sq ft of vent from outside for combustion air for fireplace. Connect directly to firebox. Combustion air intake ducts should be wrapped with 1 in. blanket insulation. Provide a fully closeable combustion air inlet.

Concrete and Foundation

1. Provide an 18 in. minimum crawl area below floor joist and 12 in. minimum below beams. Cover crawl space with .006 (6 mil) black vapor barrier.
2. Provide 24″ × 6″ screened vents at 10 ft O.C. (1 sq. ft. for each 150 sq ft of under-floor area).
3. Provide .006 (6 mil) black visqueen lap joints 12 in. minimum and extend up stem wall and staple to mudsill.

Doors

1. Exterior doors from heated rooms must have a thermal U value of less than 0.54. Wood doors to comply with ANSI/NWMA IS-2-80 standards. Metal doors to comply with ISDSI standard 104.
2. Sliding glass doors to have a thermal U value of less than 0.65.

Window and Skylight

1. All skylights to be designed to support a 40 psf live load. Skylights must have a thermal value of less than 0.65.
2. All windows to have a thermal U value of less than 0.65.
3. All skywalls to have low-E glass by Duralite or equal.
4. Provide an alternate bid for all low-E glass.
5. Provide an alternate bid for all glass to have thermal break.

ENERGY-EFFICIENT DESIGN TEST

DIRECTIONS

Answer the questions with short complete statements or drawings as needed on an 8½ × 11 drawing sheet as follows:

1. Use ⅛ in. guidelines for all lettering.
2. Letter your name, Energy-Efficient Design Test, and the date at the top of the sheet.
3. Letter the question number and provide the answer. You do not need to write out the question.
4. Do all lettering with vertical uppercase architectural letters. If the answer requires line work, use proper drafting tools and technique. Answers may be prepared on a word processor if appropriate with course guidelines.
5. Your grade will be based on correct answers and quality of line technique.

QUESTIONS

1. Describe four factors that are common among the experimental energy-efficient construction programs discussed.
2. List three reasons why energy-efficient construction techniques are becoming important.
3. Describe two factors that may be disadvantages of energy-efficient construction.
4. How, in general, will future building codes be expected to change with the implications of energy-efficient construction?
5. What is the primary goal of energy-efficient design and construction?
6. Why might it be easier to qualify for a mortgage to purchase an energy-efficient home as opposed to a nonenergy-efficient home?
7. List the two main common criteria between experimental energy-efficient design and construction cases.
8. Why is it possible to use energy-efficient design in any architectural style?
9. Why is it possible to implement some energy-efficient design in every new home?
10. List two site factors that contribute to energy-efficient design.
11. List two room layout factors that contribute to energy-efficient design.
12. List two window placement factors that contribute to energy-efficient design.
13. List two factors that influence a reduction in air infiltration into a structure.
14. List two factors that affect heating systems in energy-efficient designs.

Chapter 14
Design Sequence

DESIGNING A home for a client can be an exciting but difficult process. Very rarely can an architect sit down and dash off a design that meets the needs of the client perfectly. The time required to design a home can range from a few days to several months. It's important for you to understand the design process and the role the drafter plays in it. This requires an understanding of basic design principles, financial considerations, and common procedures of design. In Chapter 1 the differences between architects, designers, and drafters were explained. Throughout this section the terms architect and designer can be thought of as synonymous.

As you begin your drafting career, you need to remember that very rarely will you be asked to design something. Typically the designing and much of the drafting will already be done before the project is given to the junior drafter. As experience and confidence are gained, the junior drafter will enter the design process at earlier stages.

DESIGN BASICS

Good design is a very abstract concept. What appeals to one person may be repulsive to another. Following certain basic design guidelines can help achieve a pleasing design regardless of the floor plan shape and layout, or the looks of the facade of the building. These guidelines include rhythm, balance, proportion, and unity.

Rhythm

Rhythm in music usually can be determined by most people. The beat of a drum gives a repetitive element that sets the foot tapping. In design, a repetitive element provides rhythm. A consistent pattern of shapes, sizes, or material can create a house that is pleasing to the eye as well as providing a sense of ease for the inhabitants. Figure 14–1 shows elements of rhythm in a structure.

Balance

Balance is the relationship between the various areas of the structure as they relate to an imaginary centerline. Balance may be either formal or informal. Formal balance is symmetrical so that one side of the structure matches the opposite side in size. The residence in Figure 14–2 is an example of formal balance. Both sides of the home are of similar mass.

Figure 14–1 Rhythm in design. The repetition of wood and glass patterns helps create a pleasing appearance for this structure by Herbert Nadel, A.I.A., and partners. *Photo by Wes Thompson. Courtesy California Redwood Association.*

With informal balance, or a nonsymmetrical shape, balance can be achieved by placing shapes of different size in various positions around the imaginary centerline. This type of balance can be seen in Figure 14–3.

Proportion

Proportion is related to both size and balance. It can be thought of in terms of size, as in Figure 14–4, where one exterior area is compared to another. Proportion can also be thought of in terms of how the residence relates to its environment. Proportions must also be considered inside the house. A house with a large living and family area needs to have the rest of the structure in proportion to these areas.

Figure 14–2 Formal balance can be seen in the shape of this home as each side is balanced to reflect the size and shape of the other. *Courtesy Home Planners, Inc.*

Figure 14–3 Informal balance is used on this office building in Boulder, Colorado. Although the structure has more mass on the right side than on the left, the building has a very pleasing effect. Designed by John J. Williams, Jr., of Knudson and Williams Architects. *Photo by T.S. Gordon. Courtesy California Redwood Association.*

Figure 14–4 Proportion can be seen in the pleasing shapes of this home as each area relates to the other areas of the structure. Designed by Dickerson Homes. *Courtesy Shakertown Corp.*

Figure 14–5 Unity is the blending of varied shapes and sizes into a pleasing appearance as shown by this office structure in Santa Rosa, California, by Lawrence Simons and Associates, A.I.A. *Courtesy Shakertown Corp.*

The length, width and height of each individual room should also be in proportion to one another to create a pleasing appearance. A room 10 ft wide and 25 ft long is an example of a room that has poor proportions. A more pleasing relationship for room dimensions is found in the proportions of 2 units of width to 3 units of length. Another common proportion is 3 units wide by 5 units long. In large rooms the height must also be considered. A 24′ × 34′ family room is too large to have an 8′ high flat ceiling. This standard-height ceiling would be out of proportion to the room size. A 10′ high or a vaulted ceiling would be much more in keeping with the size of the room.

Unity

Unity relates to rhythm, balance, and proportion. Unity ties a structure together with a common design or decorating pattern. Similar features that relate to each other can give a sense of well-being. You should avoid adding features to a building that appear to be just there or tacked on. See Figure 14–5.

As an architectural drafter, you should be looking for these basic elements in residences that you see. Walk through houses at every opportunity to see how other designers have used these basics of design. Many magazines are available that feature interior and exterior home designs. Study the photos for pleasing relationships and develop a scrapbook of styles and layouts that are pleasing to you. This will provide valuable resource material as you advance in your drafting career and become a designer or architect.

FINANCIAL CONSIDERATIONS

Both designers and drafters need to be concerned with costs. Money will influence decisions made by the drafter about framing methods and other structural considerations. Often the advanced drafter must decide between methods that require more materials with less labor or those that require less materials but more labor. These are decisions of which the owner may never be aware, but they can make the difference in the house being affordable or not.

The designer will make the major financial decisions that will affect the cost and size of the project. The designer will need to determine the client's budget at the beginning of the design process and work to keep the project within these limits.

Through past experience and contact with builders, the designer should be able to make an accurate estimate of the finished cost of a house. This estimate is often made on a square footage basis in the initial stages of design. For instance, in some areas a modest residence can be built for approximately $40 per sq ft. In other areas this same house may cost approximately $70 per sq ft. A client wishing to build a 2,500 sq ft house could expect to pay between $100,000 and $175,000, depending on where the home will be built. Keep in mind that these are estimates. A square footage price tells very little about the home. In the design stage, square footage estimates help set parameters for the design. The final cost of the project is determined once the house is completely drawn and a list of materials is determined. With a list of materials, contractors are then able to make accurate decisions about cost.

The source of the finances can also affect the design process of the project. Certain lending institutions may require some drawings that the local building department may not. Federal Housing Administration (FHA) and Veterans Administration (VA) loans often require extra forms, drawings, and specifications that need to be taken into account in the initial design stages.

THE CLIENT

Most houses are not designed for one specific family. In order to help keep costs down, houses are often built in subdivisions and designed to appeal to a wide variety of people. Often one basic plan can be built with several different options, thus saving the contractor the cost of paying for several different complete plans. See Figure 14–6. Some families may make minor changes to an existing plan. These modified *stock plans* allow the prospective home buyer a chance to have a personalized design at a cost far below that of custom-drawn plans. See Figure 14–7. If finances allow, or if a stock plan cannot be found to meet their needs, a family can have a plan custom designed. It does not matter if the residence is designed for mass appeal or for a specific family; the design and drafting procedure is similar. Previous chapters have dealt with the design process in general terms; now it will be examined in relation to a specific family.

THE DESIGN PROCESS

The design of a residence can be divided into several stages. These generally include initial contact, preliminary design studies, presentation drawings, initial working drawings, final design considerations, completion of working drawings, permit procedures, and job supervision.

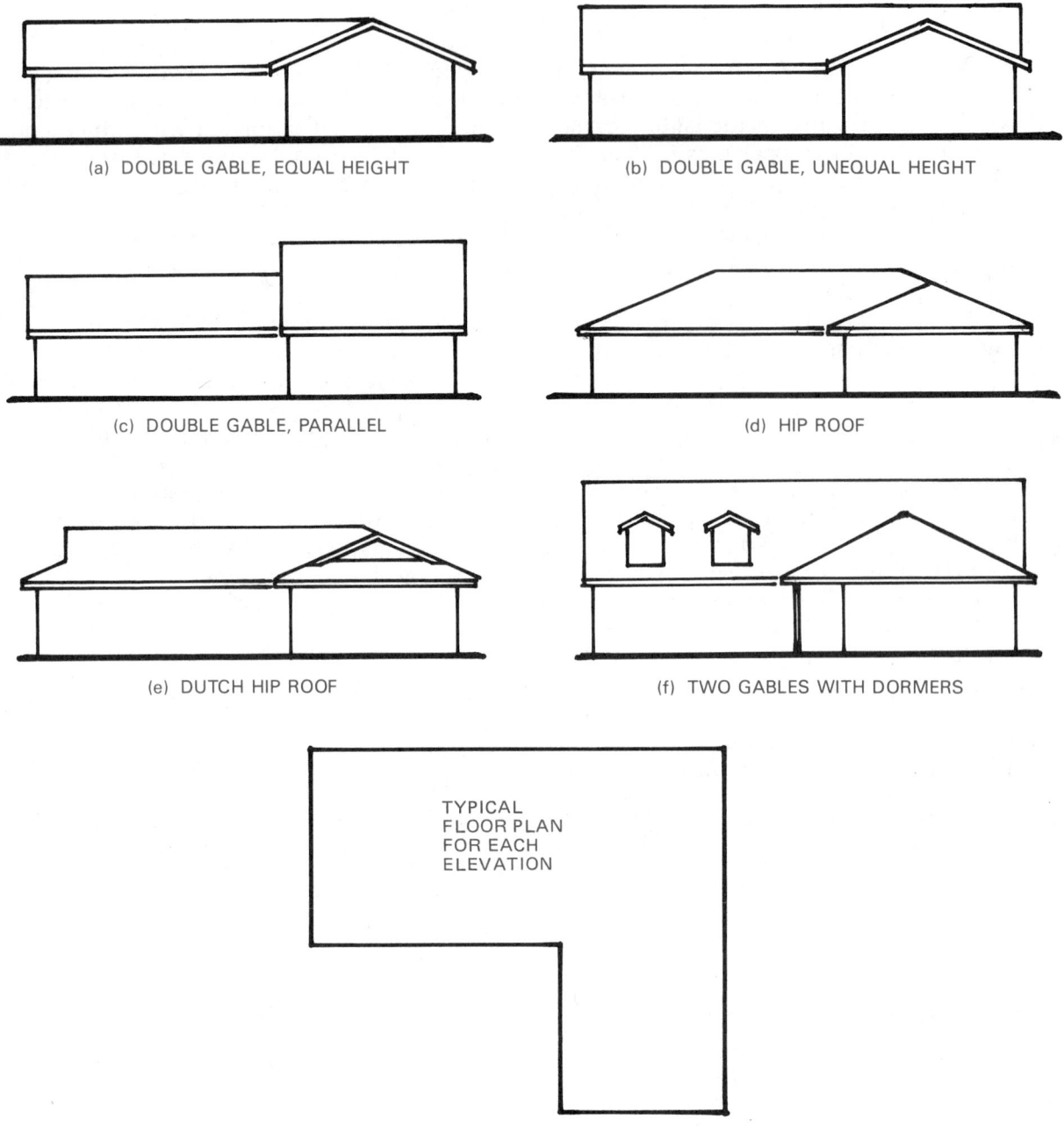

(a) DOUBLE GABLE, EQUAL HEIGHT

(b) DOUBLE GABLE, UNEQUAL HEIGHT

(c) DOUBLE GABLE, PARALLEL

(d) HIP ROOF

(e) DUTCH HIP ROOF

(f) TWO GABLES WITH DORMERS

TYPICAL FLOOR PLAN FOR EACH ELEVATION

Figure 14–6 Often a plan can be drawn with several different options.

Initial Contact

Whether designed for a contractor or a specific owner, the initial contact will set the standard for the rest of the design process. The initial contact can be divided into the stages of shopping and selection.

A client who approaches an architect or designer is often *just shopping*. This is the stage where the client is trying to obtain background information on the designer or architect. Design fees, schedules, and the compatibility of personalities are but a few of the basic questions to be answered. This stage may take place by telephone conversation or a personal visit.

The questions asked are important to both the architect and the client. The client needs to pick a designer that can work within budget and time limitations. The designer needs to screen a client. An architect's client frequently becomes anxious to have a new home once he or she has decided to build and so claim to need plans "yesterday," that is, on a very short schedule. The designer needs to determine if the client's needs fit within his or her office schedule.

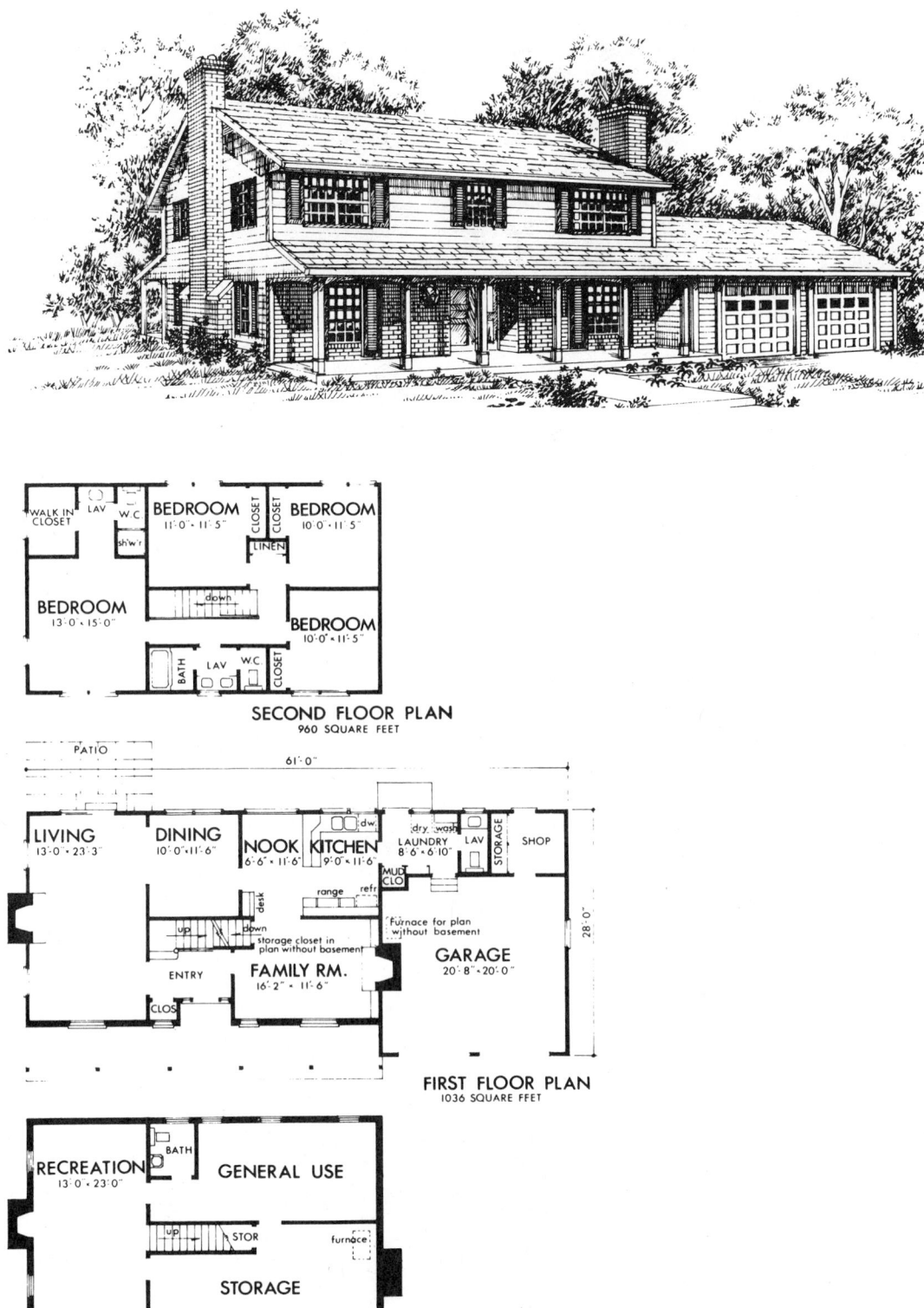

Figure 14–7 An example of a stock design. A plan with wide appeal can often be used by many families, thus eliminating the expense of a custom-designed home. *Courtesy Home Building Plan Service.*

Once the client has chosen someone to draw the plans, the preliminary design work can begin. This selection process usually begins with the signing of a contract to set guidelines to identify which services will and will not be provided, and when payment will be provided. This is also the time when the

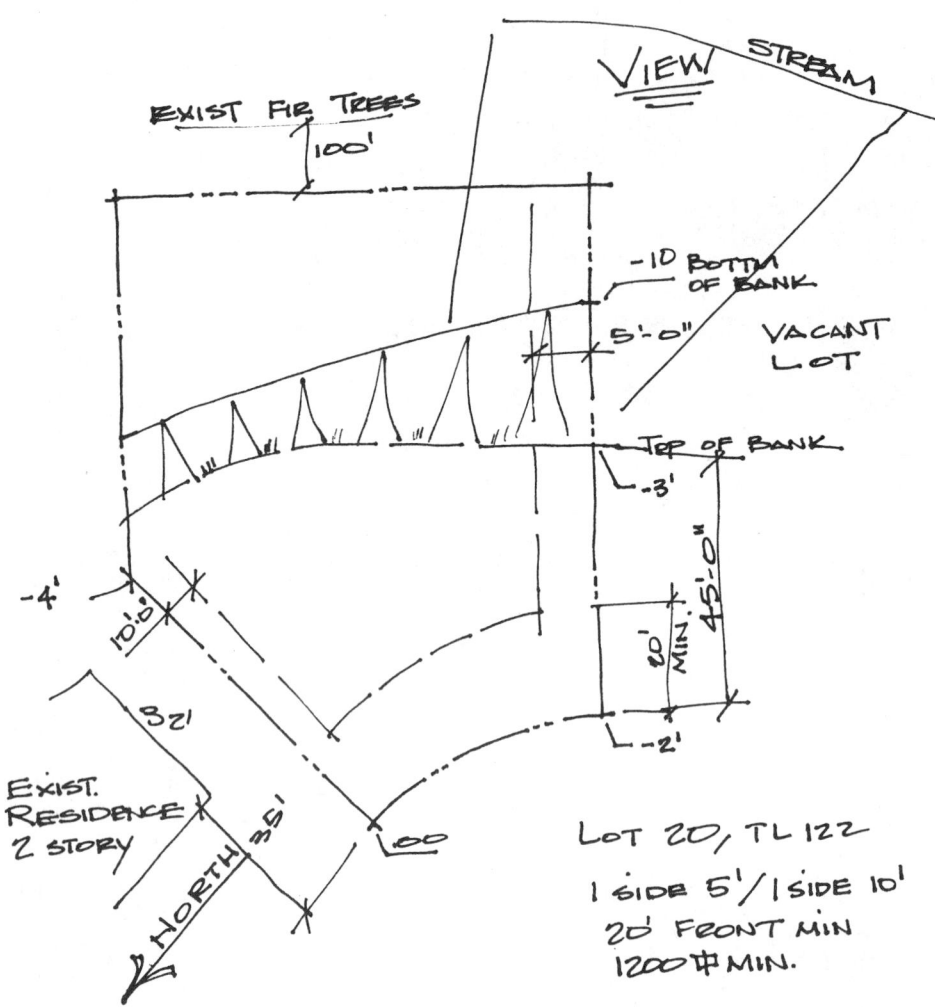

Figure 14-8 A sketch of a plot plan showing the results of the lot visitation.

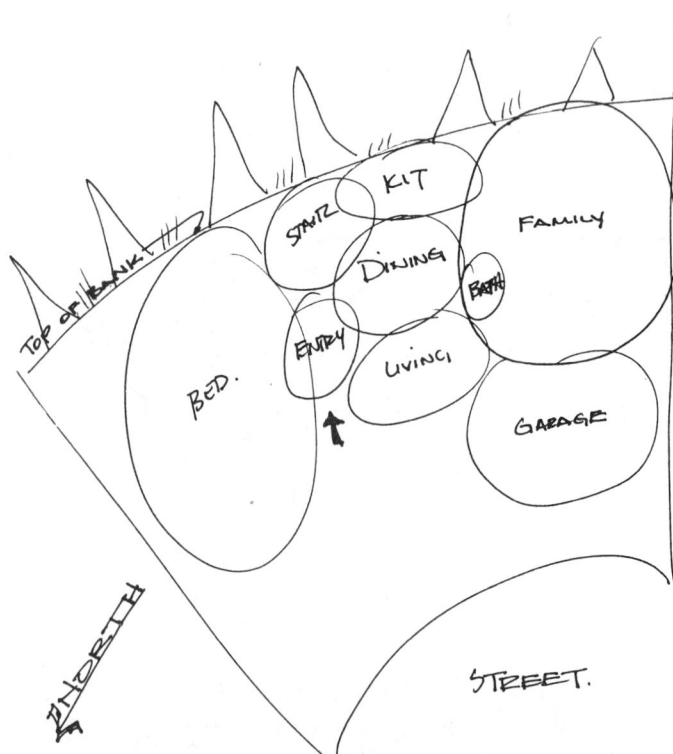

Figure 14-9 Bubble designs are the first drawings in the design process. These drawings are used to explore room relationships.

initial criteria for the project will be determined. Generally, the client will have a basic size and a list of specifics in mind. Sometimes the owner will even have a sketch. In addition to these general guidelines, the owners often have a file full of pictures of items that they would like in their house. During this initial phase of design it is important to become familiar with the life-style of the client as well as the site where the house will be built.

Preliminary Designs

With a thorough understanding of the client's lifestyle, design criteria, and financial limits, the preliminary studies can begin. These include research with the building and zoning departments that govern the site, investigation of the site, and discussions with any board of review that may be required.

Figure 14–8 shows a preliminary plot plan with the initial design criteria included. Once this initial research has been done, preliminary design studies can be started. The preliminary drawings usually take two stages: bubble drawings and ⅛" = 1'-0" scale sketches.

Bubble drawings are freehand sketches used to help determine room locations and relationships. See Figure 14–9. It is during this stage of the preliminary design that consideration is given to the site and solar efficiency of the home.

Once a satisfactory layout has been sketched these shapes are transformed into scaled sketches. Usually several sets of sketches are developed to explore different design possibilities. It is in this stage of design that consideration is given to building code regulations and room relationships and sizes. After the options to the design are explored, the designer

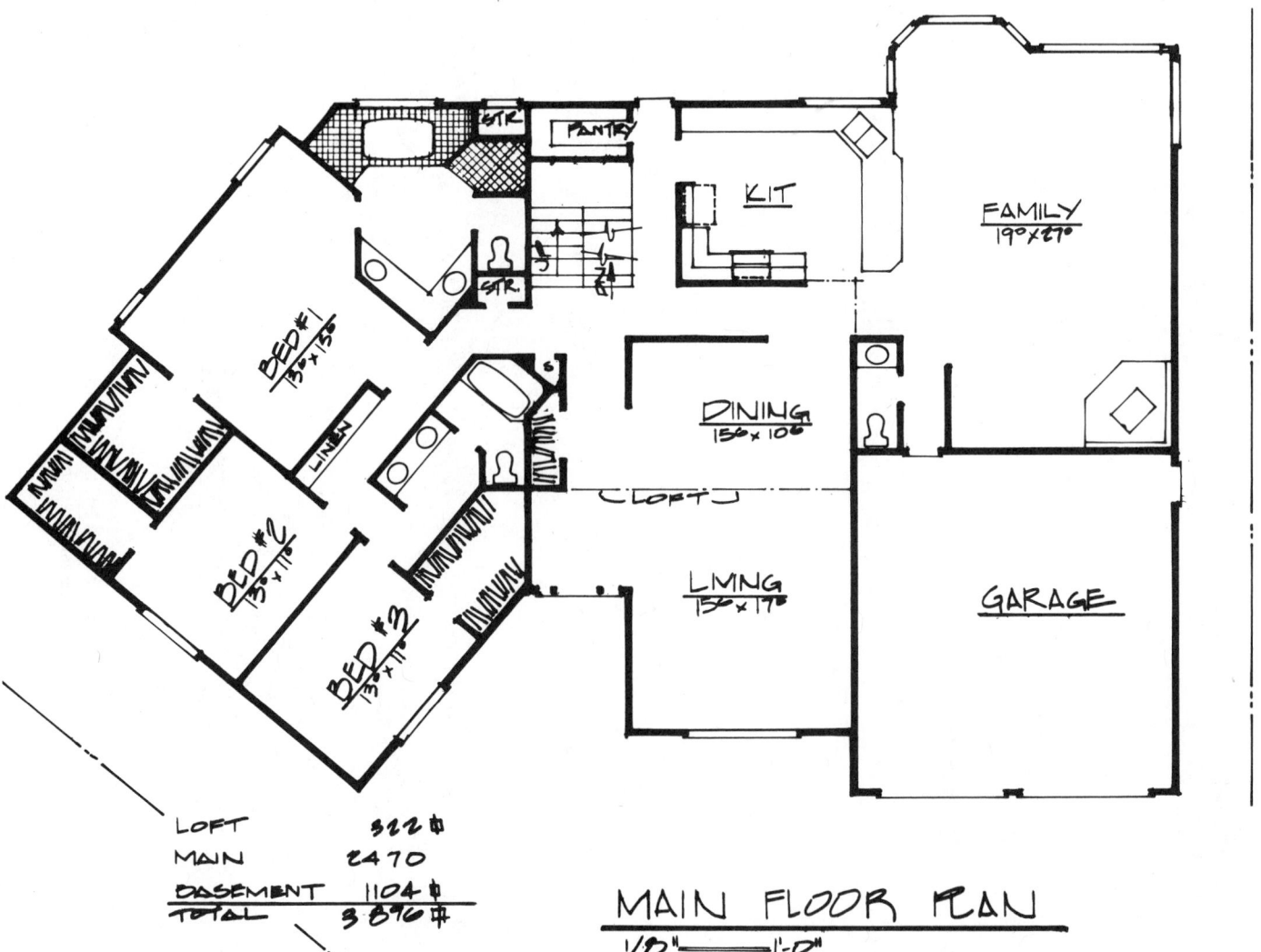

Figure 14–10 Preliminary drawings. The initial bubble drawings are transformed into scaled preliminary drawings to determine basic room sizes and relationships and exterior styling of the home.

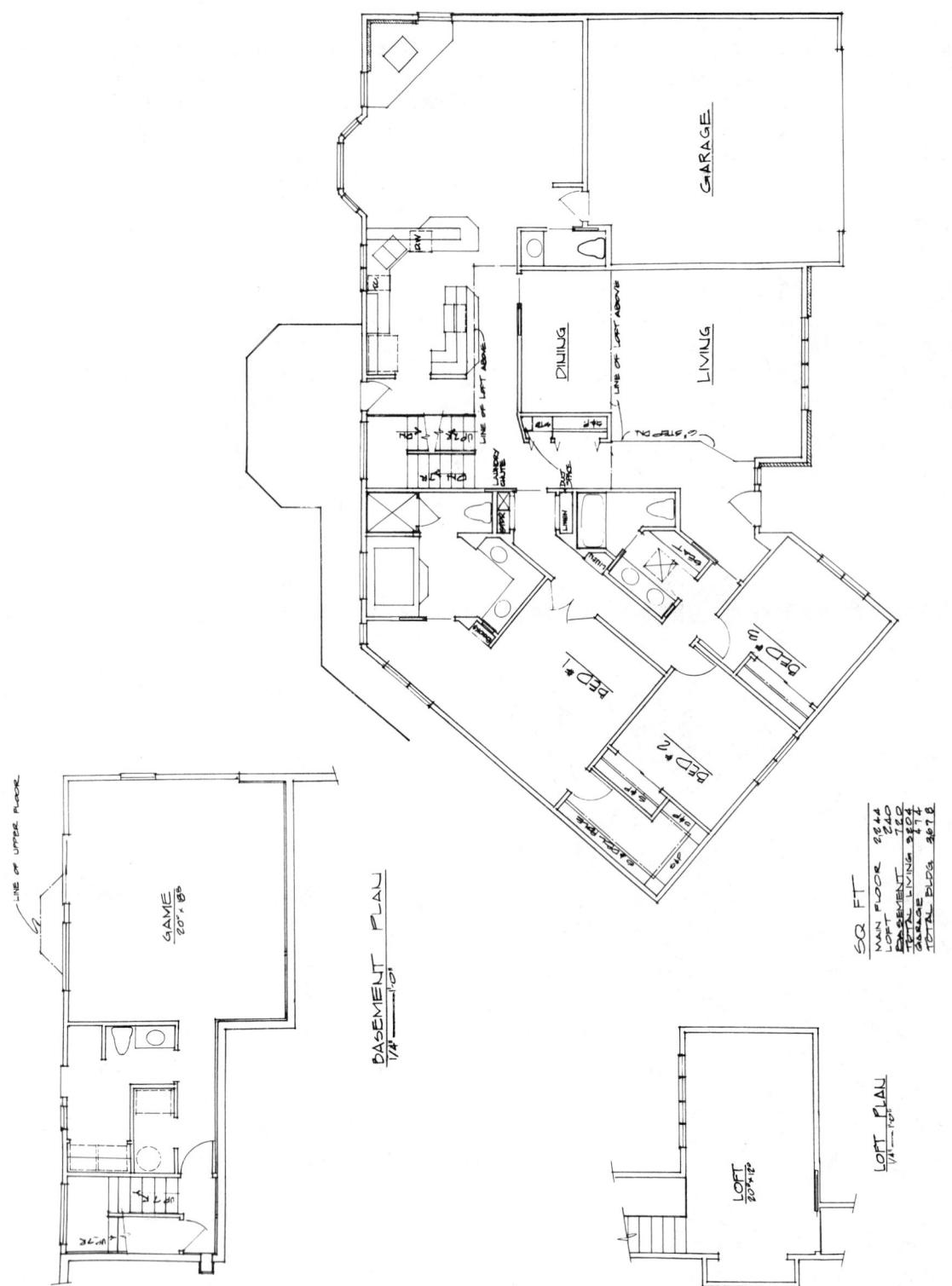

Figure 14-11 The preliminary floor plan is redrawn at a larger scale and final details are considered before the working drawings are started.

selects a plan to prepare for the clients. This could be the point where a drafter first becomes involved in the design process. Depending on the schedule of the designer, a skilled drafter might prepare the refined preliminary drawings. These would include floor plans and an elevation. It is at this time that the floor plan and the style of the exterior are coordinated. These drawings are then presented to the client. See Figure 14–10. Changes and revisions are made at this time. Once the plans are approved by the client, the preliminary drawings are ready to be converted to design drawings.

Presentation Drawings

A drafter will usually convert the ⅛″ = 1′–0″ drawings to ¼″ = 1′–0″ drawings. The floor plan and each elevation and a typical section are laid out but not drawn in great detail. These drawings are still regarded as preliminary. Chapter 40 gives a complete description of the types of drawings that are done at this stage. Although the smaller scale drawings have been approved, changes still occur. Consideration is usually given to furniture placement and room usage, and changes might include minor size adjustments, or adding or moving windows. Once approved, these drawings will become the core of the working drawings. See Figures 14–11 through 14–13.

Room Planning. As the design is transformed to ¼″ = 1′–0″ scale, room usage must be considered. Typically the designer will have talked with the owners about how each room will be used and what types of furniture will be included. Occasionally, placement of a family heirloom will dictate the entire layout. When this is the case, the owner should specify the size requirements for a particular piece of furniture.

When placing furniture outlines to determine the amount of space in a room, the drafter can use transfer silhouette shapes known as rub-ons, templates, or freehand sketching methods. Rub-ons provide a fast method of representing furniture, but they can also prove to be expensive. Furniture can be drawn with a template or sketched quickly if the drafter will take time to practice sketching the outlines of common furniture pieces. Figure 14–14 shows examples of the outlines of common pieces of furniture using both rub-on and hand-drawn methods. Figure 14–15 shows typical sizes for common pieces of furniture. Figure 14–16 shows a preliminary floor plan with the furniture added.

Initial Working Drawings

With the preliminary drawings approved, a drafter can begin to lay out the working drawings. The procedure will vary with each office but generally each of the drawings required for the project will be started. These would include the foundation, plot, roof, electrical, cabinet, and framing plans. At this stage the drafter must rely on past experience for drawing the size of beams and other structural members. Beams and other structural material will be located, but exact sizes are not usually determined until the entire project has been laid out.

Final Design Considerations

Once the drafter has the drawings laid out, the designer will generally meet with the client one last time. This conference is used to get final information on flooring, electrical needs, cabinets, and other finish materials. This conference will result in a set of marked drawings that the drafter will use to complete the working drawings.

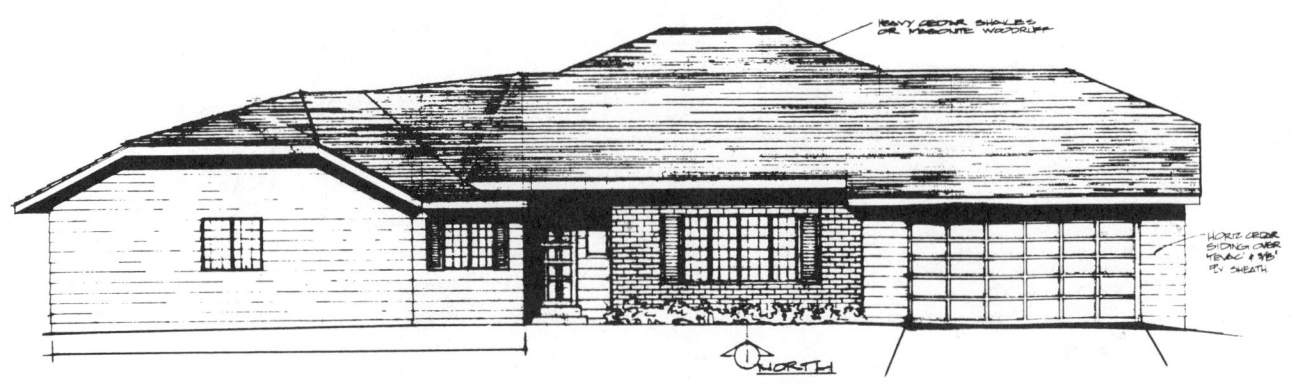

Figure 14–12 The preliminary elevations are redrawn at a larger scale so that the exterior details may be planned before the working drawings are started.

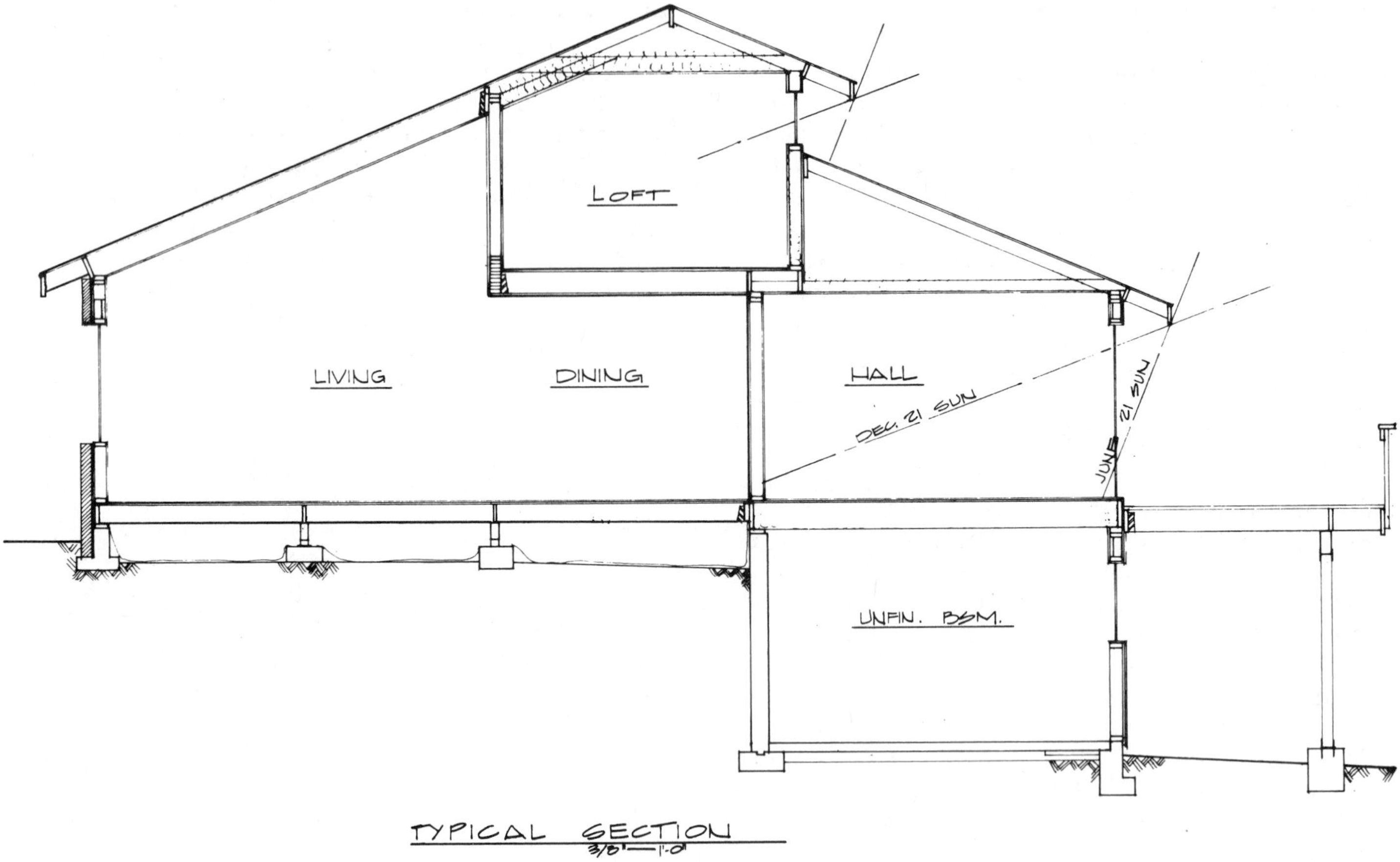

LOFT

LIVING

DINING

HALL

DEC. 21 SUN

JUNE 21 SUN

UNFIN. BSM.

TYPICAL SECTION
3/8" = 1'-0"

Figure 14-13 A section showing typical construction is often drawn for the client during the preliminary design stage. When final approval is given to the design, this will become one of the working drawings.

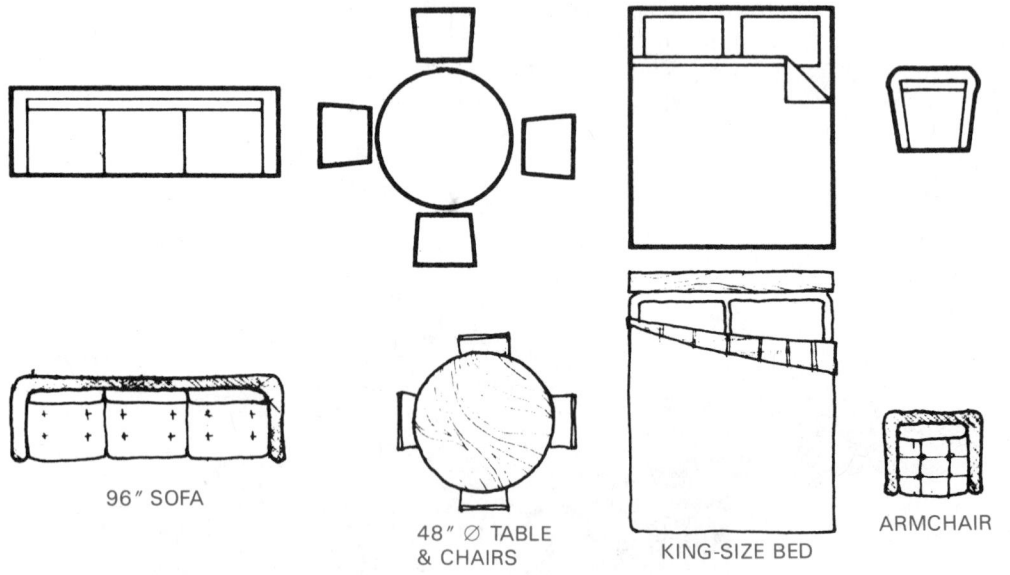

96" SOFA

48" Ø TABLE
& CHAIRS

KING-SIZE BED

ARMCHAIR

Figure 14-14 Furniture can be drawn with rub-ons (above) or freehand (below) to help determine how rooms will be used.

COMMON FURNITURE SIZES

Living Room and Family Room

Sofas	34 × 76	End	18 × 18	Arm	18 × 21
	34 × 90	Tables	18 × 24	Chairs	18 × 24
	34 × 96		18 × 30		22 × 24
	34 × 102		18 × 36		28 × 32
			24 × 24		32 × 34
Sectional	26 × 30		26 × 26		
Pieces	26 × 53		24 hex	Recliners	30 × 29
	26 × 62		26 hex		to 66
				Piano	24 × 56
Love	32 × 50	Coffee	18 × 36		
Seats	30 × 66	Tables	20 × 52	Grand	
			20 × 60	Piano	58 × 75
			20 × 75		

Dining Room

Oval Tables	54 × 76	Hutch	18 × 36 × 72
Round Tables	30	Chairs	16 × 18
	32		18 × 20
	36		
	42	Tea Cart	16 × 24
	48		18 × 33
Rectangular	30 × 34		
Tables	36 × 44 to 108		
	42 × 48 to 108		

Bedroom

Beds:		Dressers	18 × 30 to 82
Cribs	20 × 50		
	30 × 54	Desks	24 × 30
			24 × 36
Twin	44 × 80		24 × 42
			32 × 42
Double	54 × 75		32 × 48
			32 × 60
Queen	65 × 80		
		Night	12 × 15
King	72 × 84	Stands	15 × 15 to 21

Figure 14–15 Common furniture sizes. Because of the wide variation in sizes, a drafter will typically need to verify exact sizes with the owner.

Completion of Working Drawings

The drawings are now ready to be completed. The complexity of the residence will determine which drawings are required. Most building departments require a plot plan, floor plan, foundation plan, elevations and one cross section as the minimum drawings to get a building permit. On a complicated plan, a wall framing plan, roof framing plan, grading plan, and construction details may be required. Depending on the lending institution, interior elevations, cabinet drawings, and finish specifications may be required. Figures 14–17 through 14–21 show a complete set of working drawings.

The skills of the drafter will determine his or her participation in preparing the working drawings. As an entry-level drafter, you will often be given the job of making corrections on existing drawings or drawing plot plans, cabinets, or other drawings. Although you will not receive a title change or a promotion, as you gain skill you will be given more drawing responsibility. With increased ability, you will start to share in the design responsibilities.

If the drafter is working in an office that has a CAD system, many of the preliminary drawings can be used for the working drawings. With the use of layers, information such as furniture layout can be turned off to eliminate clutter from the working drawings. Other layers containing electrical information or plumbing dimensions can be added to the preliminary drawing. The specific computer application for each will be covered in Section 3.

As you progress through this text, you will be exposed to each type of working drawing. It is important to understand that a drafter would rarely draw one complete drawing and then go on to another drawing. Because the drawings in a set of plans are so interrelated, often one drawing is started, and then another drawing is started so that relationships between the two can be studied before the first drawing is completed. For instance, floor plans may be laid out, and then a section may be drawn to work out the relationships between floors or any headroom problems.

When the plans are completely drawn, they must be checked. Dimensions must be checked carefully and cross referenced from one floor plan to another and to the foundation plan. Bearing points from beams must be followed from the roof down through the foundation system. Perhaps one of the hardest jobs for a new drafter is coordinating the drawings. As changes are made throughout the design process, the drafter must be sure that those changes are reflected on all affected drawings. When the drafter has completed checking the plans, the drafting supervisor will again review the plans before they leave the office.

Permit Procedure

When the plans are complete, the owner will ask several contractors to estimate the cost of construction. Once a contractor is selected to build the house, a construction permit is obtained. Although the drafter is sometimes responsible for obtaining the permits, this is usually done by the owner or contractor. The process for obtaining a permit varies depending on the local building department and the complexity of the drawings. Permit reviews generally take from two to three weeks. Once the review is complete either a permit is issued or the drafter is required to make changes to the plans.

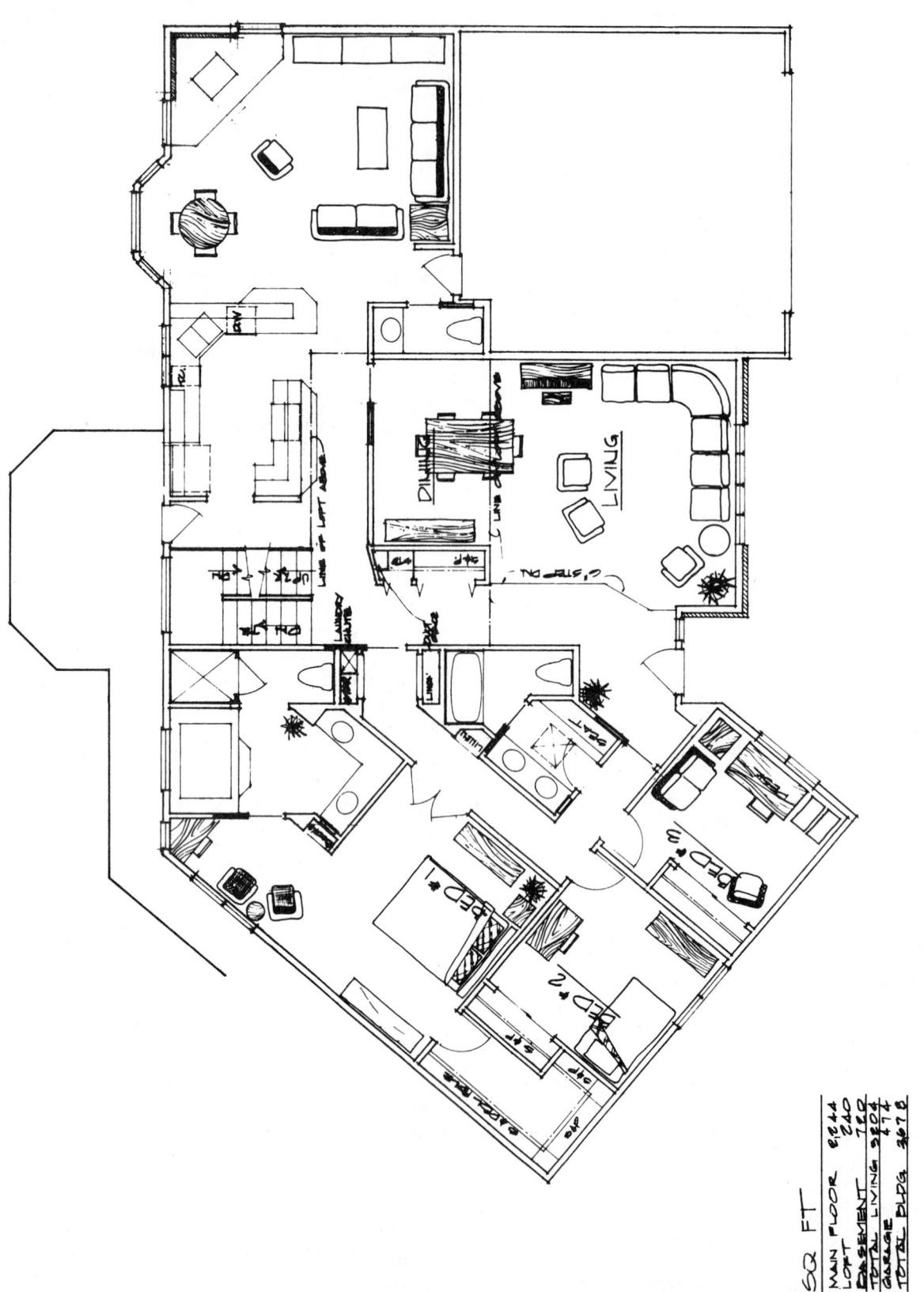

Figure 14-16 Floor plan with furniture placement.

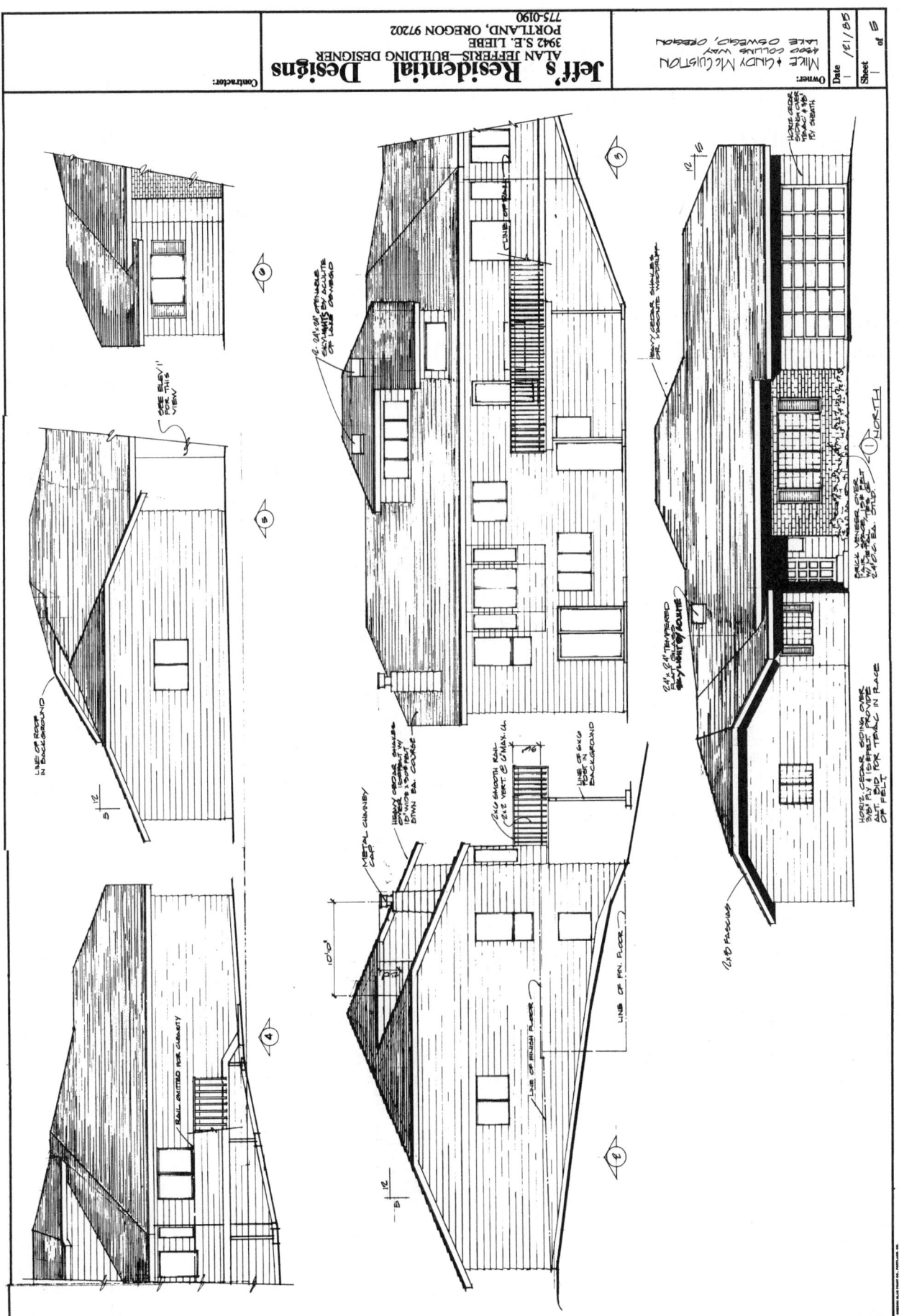

Figure 14-17 Complete callouts for all exterior materials are added to the elevations that were drawn during the preliminary design stage. The rear and side elevations are drawn with the addition of courtyard elevations.

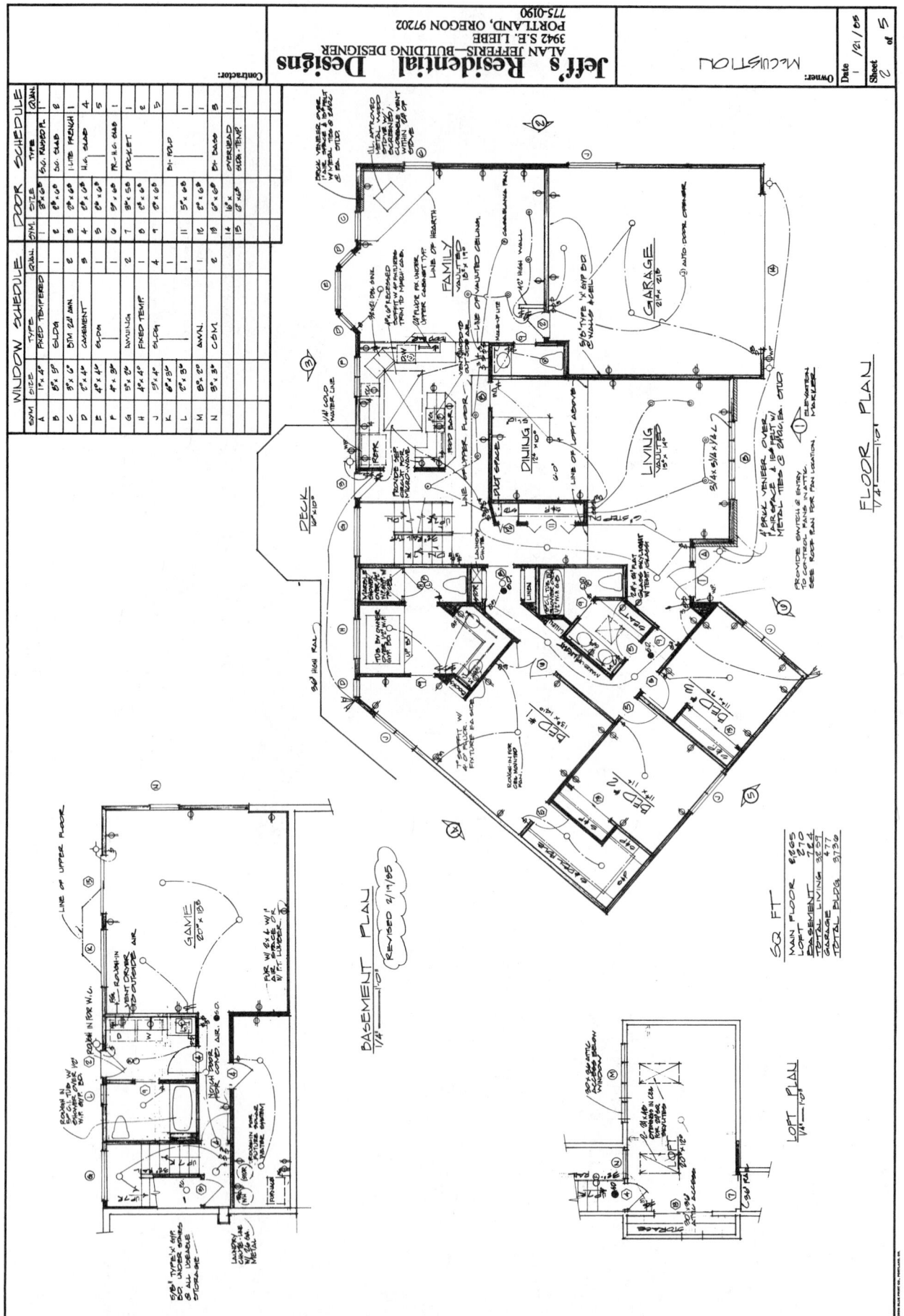

Figure 14-18 Architectural and electrical information has been added to the floor plan used in the preliminary stage. There are several changes that have been made to the floor plans in the final design stages. These changes are drawn by the junior drafter.

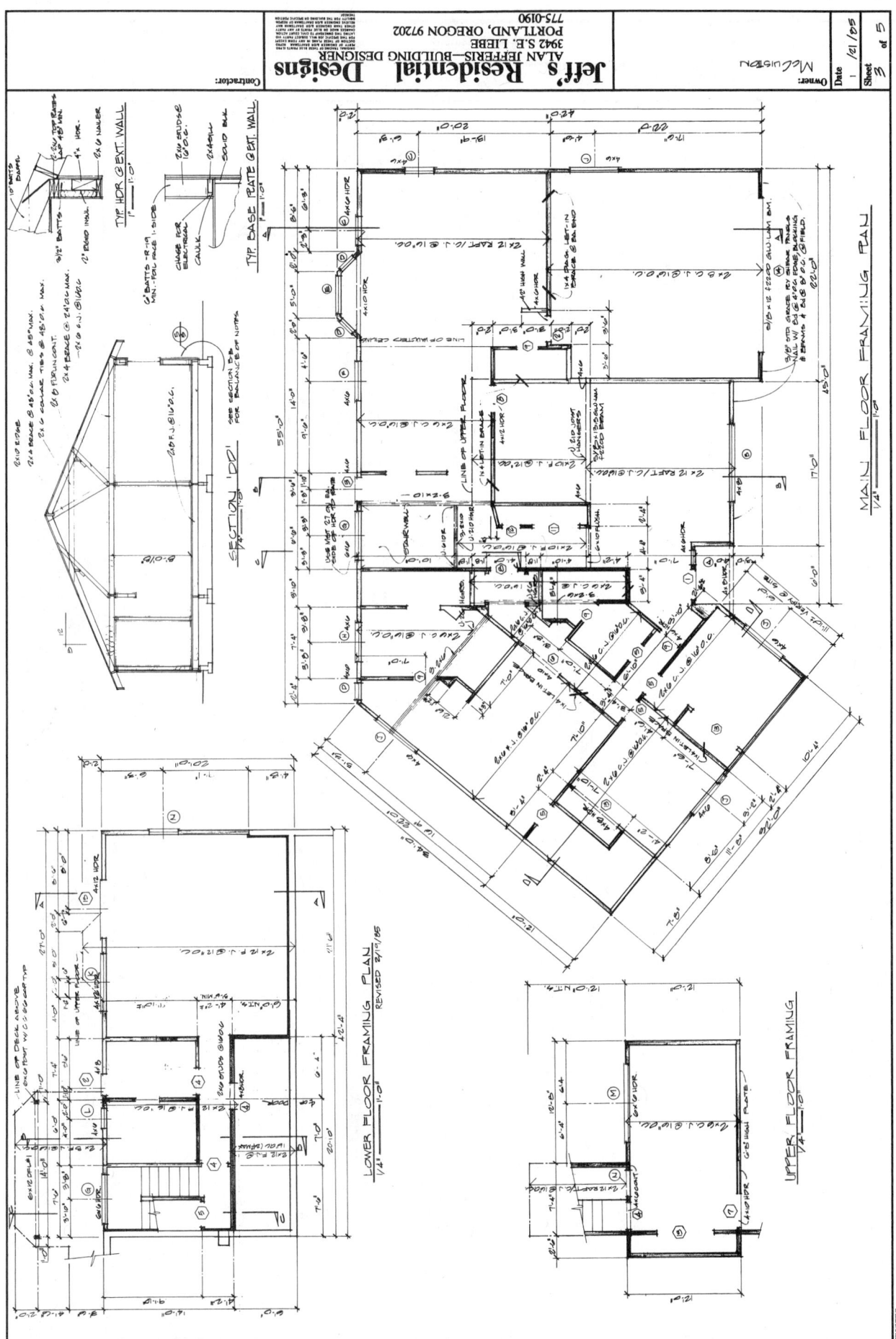

Figure 14-19 Dimensions and structural information are often placed on a separate floor plan so it does not become too crowded. A drafter is required to have a good understanding of construction methods before drawing the framing plans.

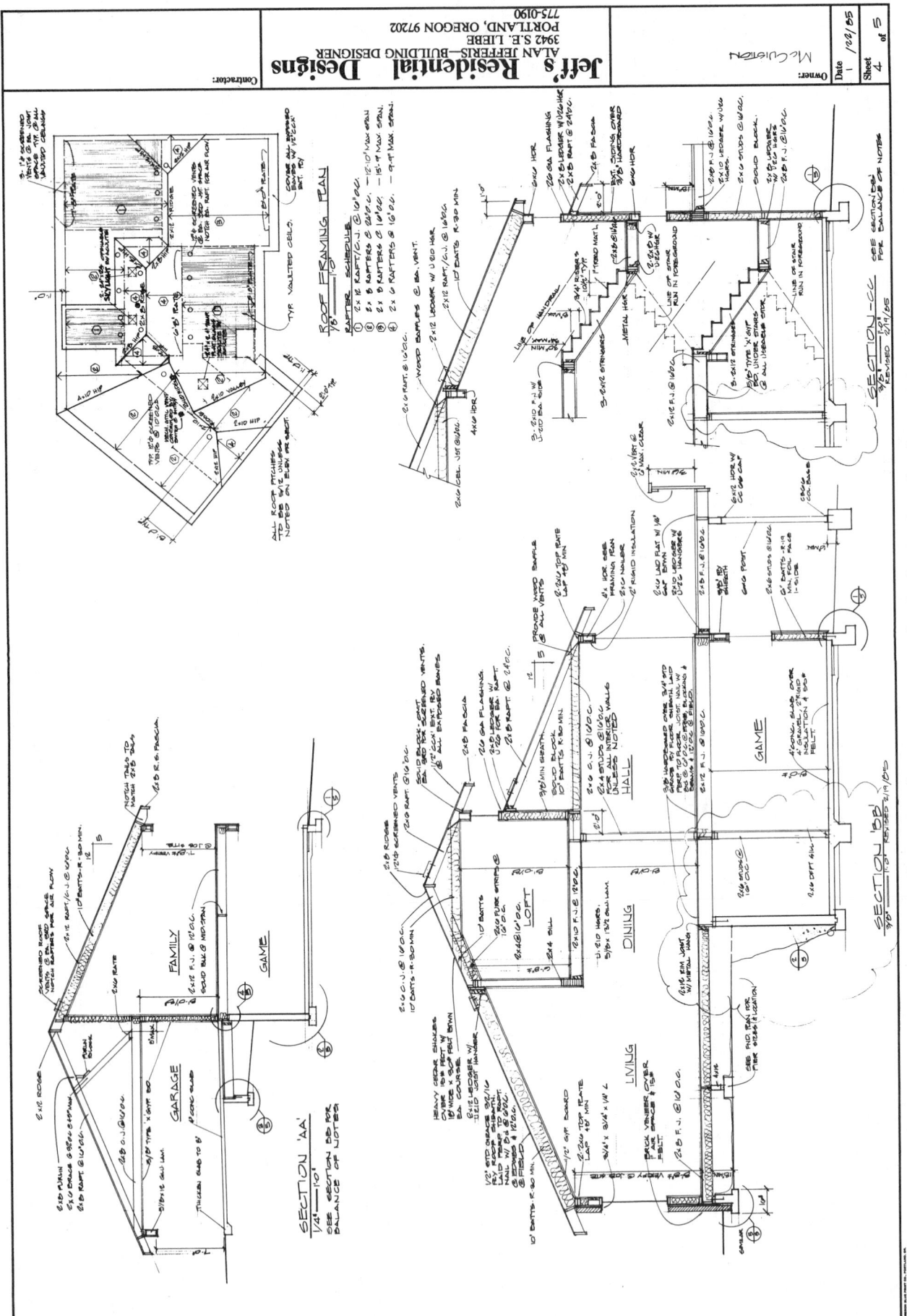

Figure 14–20 The original section is completely lettered and other sections are drawn to show framing details throughout the home. Notice that areas of this drawing have been revised. Because the revisions occurred during the construction process, each one was circled so it would be noticed.

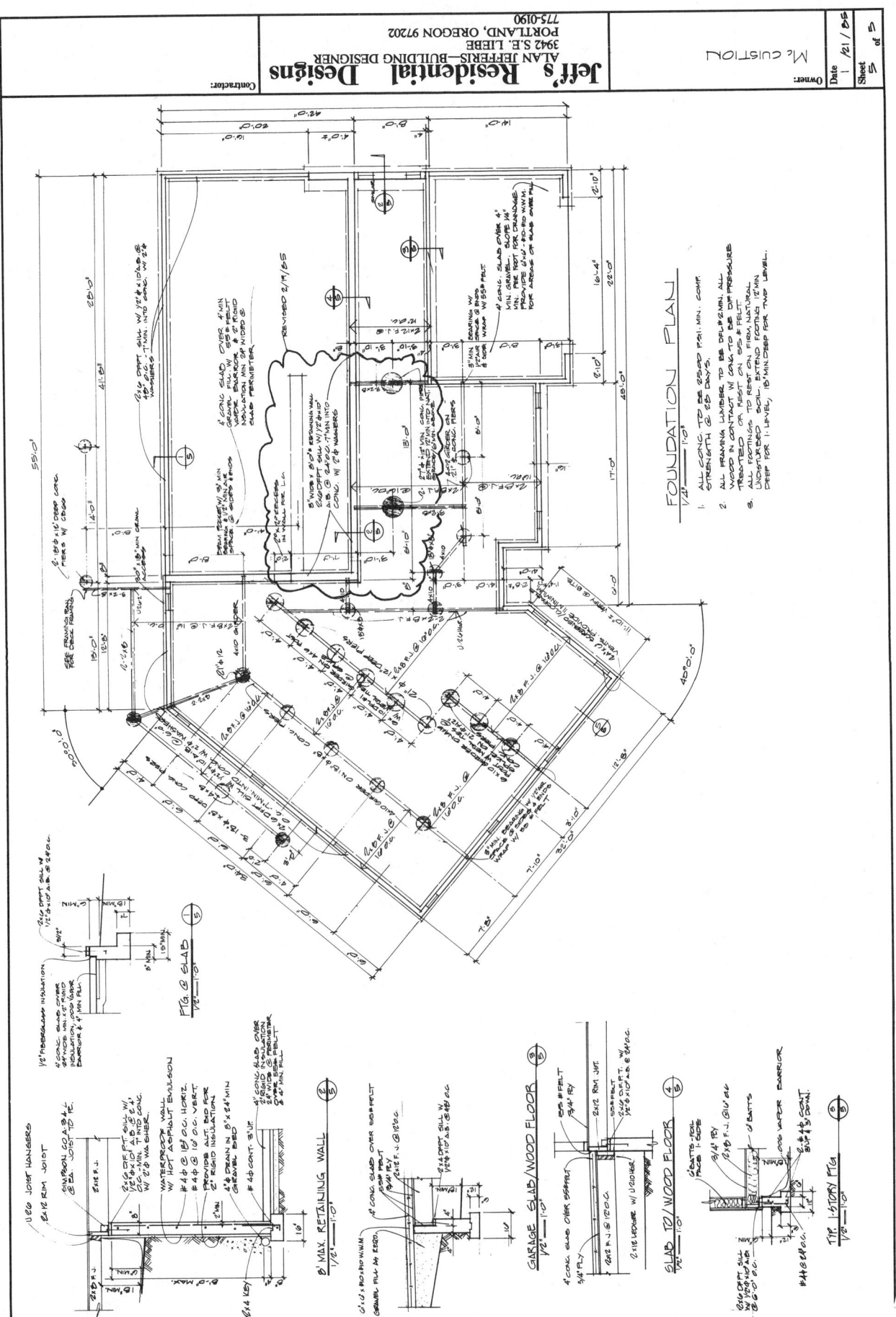

Figure 14-21 The foundation plan is drawn to describe the concrete and lower floor system. The same change that was shown on the section is also reflected.

Job Supervision

In residential construction, job supervision is rarely done when working for a designer, but it is quite often provided when an architect has drawn the plans. Occasionally a problem at the job site will require the designer or drafter to go to the site to help find a solution. In light commercial or structural drafting, the architect is often required by the contract to make visits to the job site to insure that the materials specified on the plans are being properly installed. The architect basically serves as a liaison between the contractor and the owner.

DESIGN SEQUENCE TEST

DIRECTIONS

Answer the questions with short complete statements or drawings as needed on an 8½ × 11 drawing sheet as follows:

1. Use ⅛ in. guidelines for all lettering.
2. Letter your name, Design Sequence Test, and the date at the top of the sheet.
3. Letter the question number and provide the answer. You do not need to write out the question.
4. Do all lettering with vertical uppercase architectural letters. If the answer requires line work, use proper drafting tools and technique. Answers may be prepared on a word processor if appropriate with course guidelines.
5. Your grade will be based on correct answers and quality of line technique.

QUESTIONS

1. List and describe the steps of the design process.
2. What are the functions of the drafter in the design process?
3. Define and sketch examples of rhythm, balance, and unity.
4. What is the purpose of a bubble drawing?
5. What drawings are usually part of the first scaled sketches of the design process?
6. Why do you think furniture placement should be considered in the preliminary design process?
7. What would be the minimum drawings required to get a building permit?
8. List five additional drawings that may be required for a complete set of house plans in addition to the five basic drawings.
9. List three methods of drawing furniture on the floor plan.
10. Following the principles of this section, sketch a bubble sketch for a home with the following specifications:

   a. 75′ × 120′ lot with a street on the north side of the lot.
   b. A gently sloping hill to the south.
   c. South property line is 75′ long.
   d. 40′ oak trees along the south property line.
   e. 3 bedrooms, 2½ baths, living, dining, with separate eating area off kitchen.
   f. Exterior style as per your choice.

   Explain why you designed the house that you did.

Section Three
Floor Plans

Chapter 15
Floor-Plan Symbols

THE FLOOR plans for a proposed home provide the future homeowner with the opportunity to evaluate the design in terms of livability and suitability for the needs of the family. In addition, the floor plans quickly communicate the overall construction requirements to the builder. Symbols are used on floor plans to describe items that are associated with living in the home such as doors, windows, cabinets, and plumbing fixtures. Other symbols that are more closely related to the construction of the home may include such items as electrical circuits and material sizes and spacing. One of the most important concerns of the drafter is to combine carefully all of the symbols, notes, and dimensions on the floor plan so that the plan remains easy to read and as uncluttered as possible.

Floor plans that are easy to read are also easy to build since there is less of a possibility of construction errors than with unorganized, cluttered plans. Figure 15–1 shows a typical complete floor plan.

Figure 15–2 shows that floor plans are the representation of an imaginary horizontal cut made approximately 4 ft above the floor line. Residential floor plans are generally drawn at a scale of ¼″ = 1′–0″.

Architectural templates are available with a wide variety of floor-plan symbols at the proper scale. Figure 15–3 shows a typical floor plan template.

In addition to knowing the proper symbols to use, architects, designers, and architectural drafters should be familiar with standard products that the symbols represent. Products used in the structures they design such as plumbing fixtures, appliances, windows, and doors are usually available from local vendors. Occasionally some special items must be ordered from a factory far enough in advance to ensure delivery to the job site at the time needed. By becoming familiar with the standard products, you will become familiar with their cost also. Knowing costs will allow you to know if the product you are considering using will be affordable within the owner's budget.

One of the best sources of standard product information is Sweet's Catalogs. Sweet's publishes several sets of catalogs in different categories, and the set you would use depends on the kind of building you are designing. For residential designs, you would most likely use Sweet's *Home Building and Remodeling* catalog. Sweet's, as it is known, is a set of books containing building products manufacturers' catalogs arranged by category. For example, catalogs of several window manufacturers are found together arranged alphabetically by manufacturer's name. The catalog information will provide you with the specifications for the product, and often includes installation drawings which will aid you when drawing your floor plans.

WALL SYMBOLS

Exterior Walls

Exterior wood-frame walls are generally drawn 6 in. thick at a ¼″ = 1′–0″ scale, as seen in Figure 15–4. Six in. exterior walls are common when 2 × 4 studs

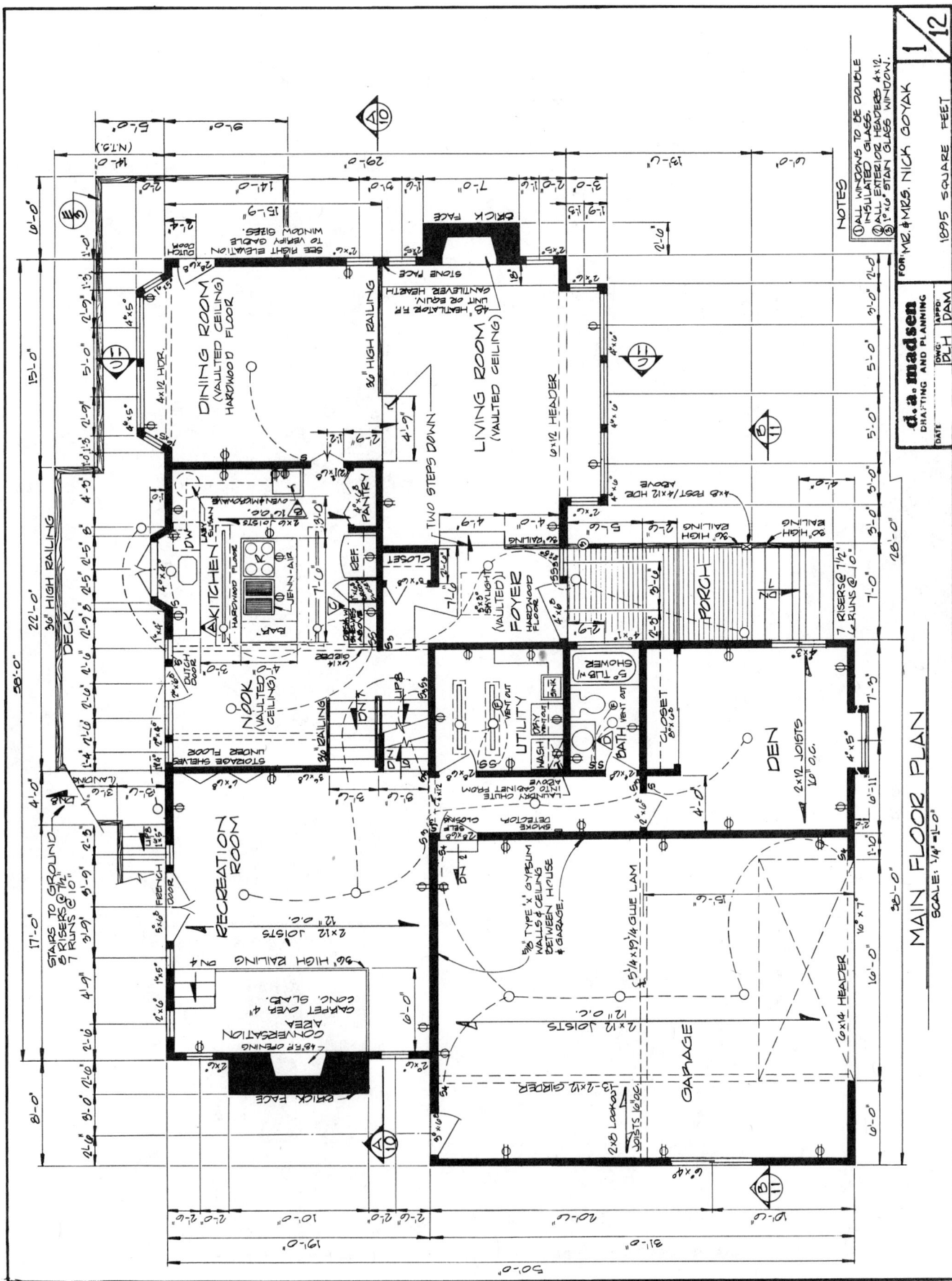

Figure 15-1 Complete floor plan. *Courtesy Madsen Designs.*

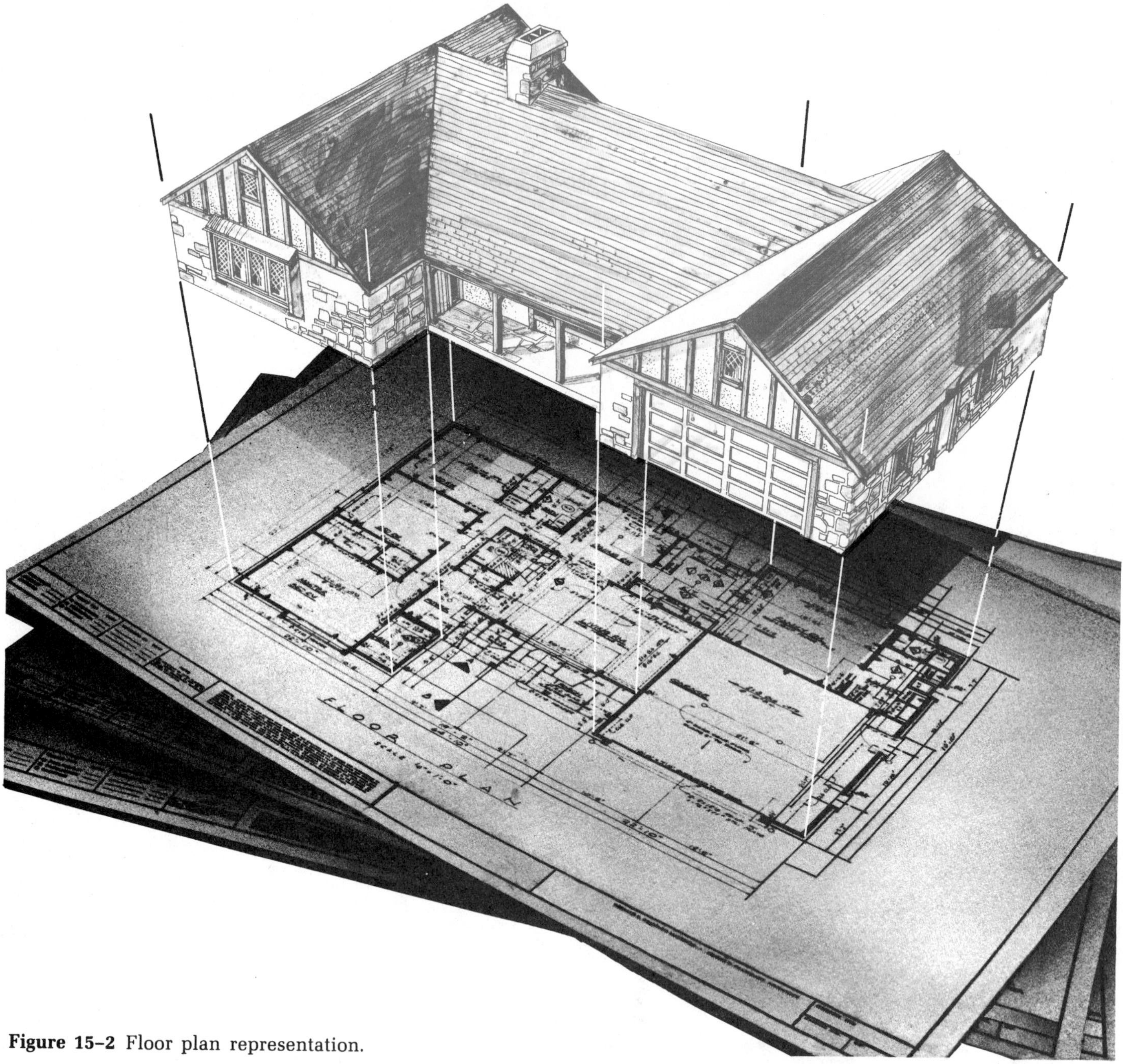

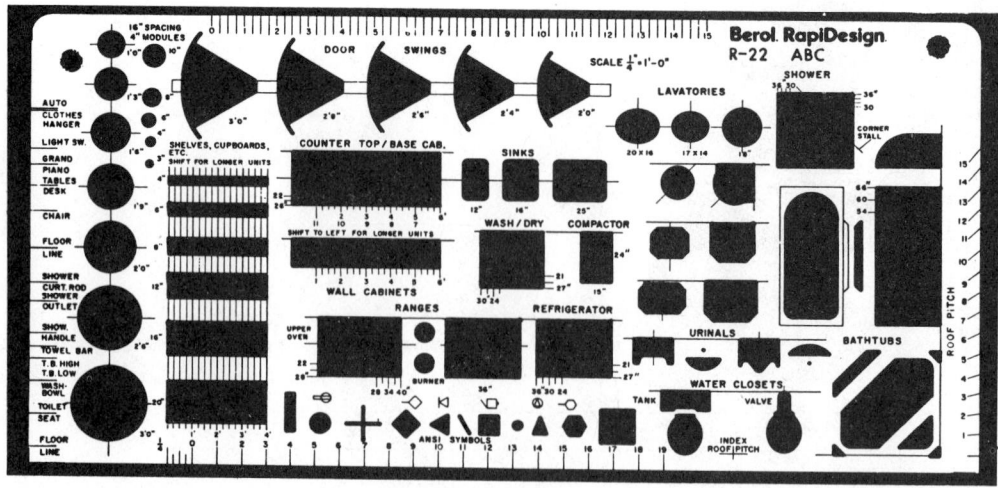

Figure 15–2 Floor plan representation.

Figure 15–3 Architectural floor plan template. *Courtesy Berol USA RapiDesign.*

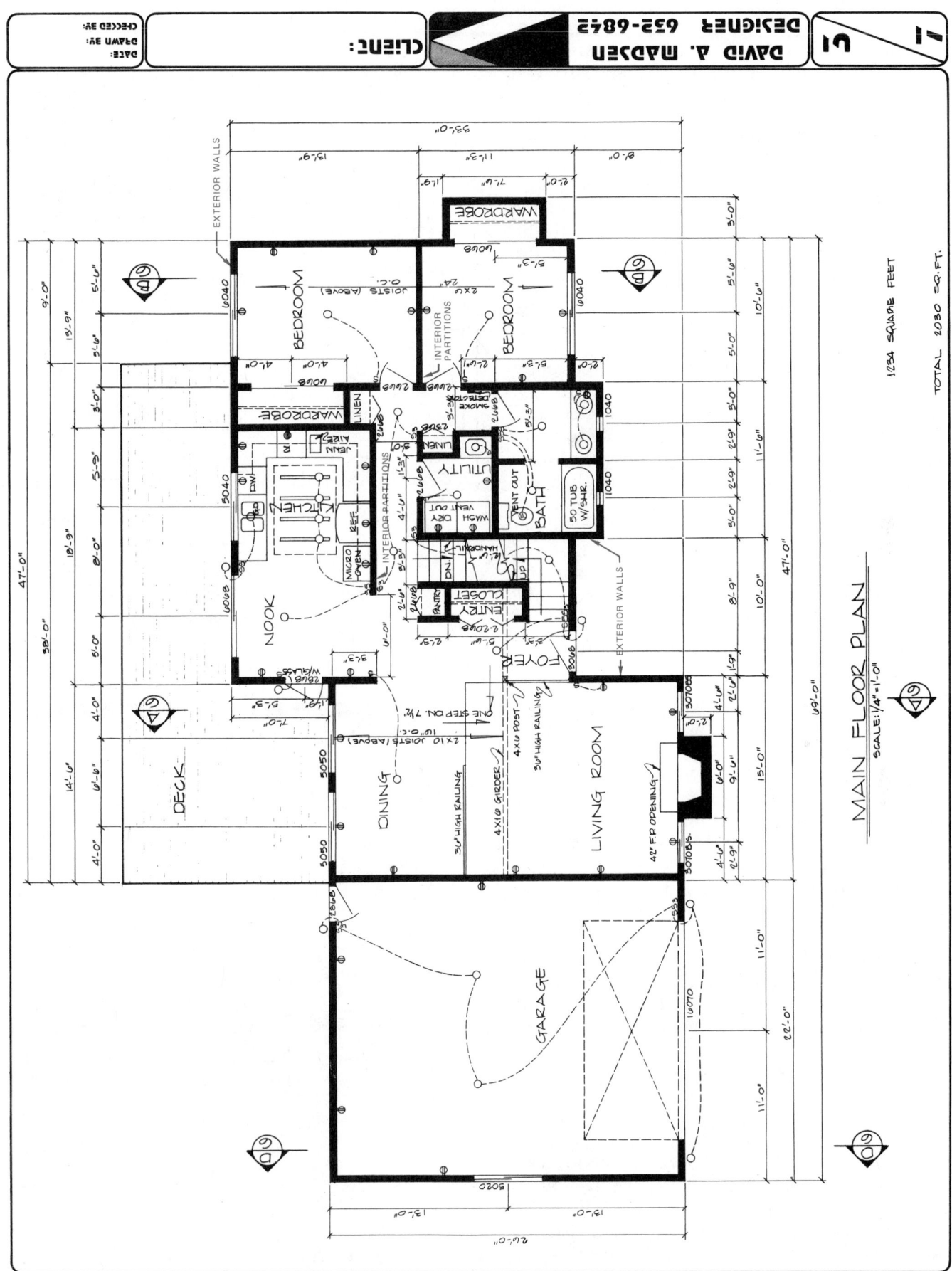

Figure 15–4 Typical floor plan. *Courtesy Madsen Designs.*

are used. The 6 in. is approximately equal to the thickness of wall studs plus interior and exterior construction materials. When 2 × 6 studs are used, the exterior walls may be drawn thicker. The wall thickness depends on the type of construction. If the exterior walls are to be concrete or masonry construction with wood framing to finish the inside surface, then they will be drawn substantially thicker as shown in Figure 15–5. Exterior frame walls with masonry veneer construction applied to the outside surface are drawn an additional 4 in. thick with the masonry veneer represented as 4 in. thick over the 6 in. wood frame walls as seen in Figure 15–6.

Interior Partitions

Interior walls, known as partitions, are frequently drawn 5 in. thick when 2 × 4 studs are used with drywall applied to each side. Walls with 2 × 6 studs are generally used where additional plumbing is required within the wall cavity. This additional plumbing may occur behind a toilet to accommodate the soil pipe. Occasionally masonry veneer is used on interior walls and is drawn in a manner similar to the exterior application shown in Figure 15–6. In many architectural offices wood-frame exterior and interior walls are drawn the same thickness to save time. The result is a wall representation that clearly communicates the intent.

Wall Shading

There are several methods used to shade walls which is done so that the walls will stand out clearly from the balance of the drawing. Wall shading should be the last drafting task performed. Wall shading should be done on the back of the drawing although some drafters shade on the front, a practice that could cause the drawing to become smudged easily. When shading is done on the back of the sheet, blank paper should be placed on the drawing table to avoid transferring lines from the drawing image to the drafting table. Some drafters shade walls very dark for accent while others shade the walls lightly for a more subtle effect as shown in Figure 15–7. Wall shading should be done with a rounded, soft (F or HB) pencil lead. The shading technique is known as poché. Other wall shading techniques include closely spaced thin lines, wood grain effect, or the use of colored pencils.

Office practice that requires light wall shading may also use thick wall lines to help accent the walls and partitions so that they stand out from other floor-plan features. Thick wall lines may be achieved with a slightly rounded H or F lead in a mechanical pencil or an H or F lead in a 7 mm automatic pencil. Figure 15–8 shows how walls and partitions appear when

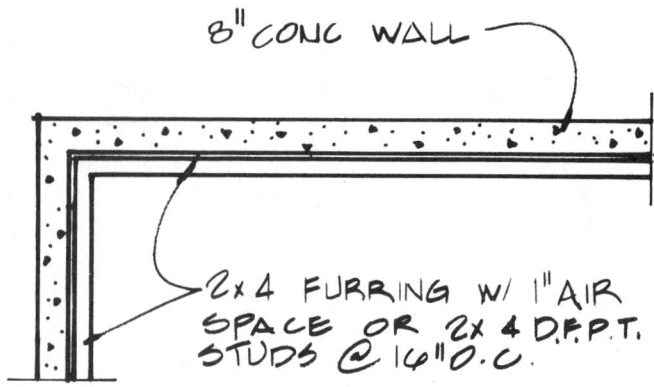

Figure 15–5 Concrete exterior wall.

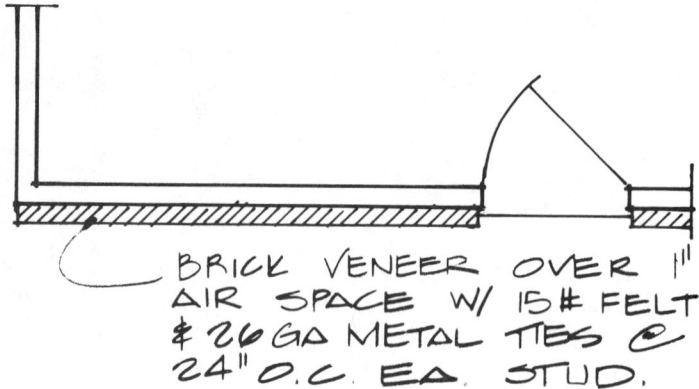

Figure 15–6 Exterior masonry veneer.

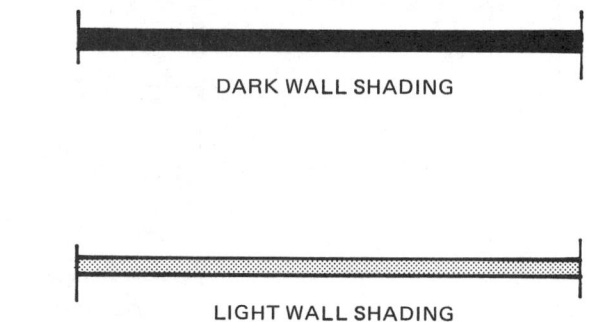

Figure 15–7 Wall shading.

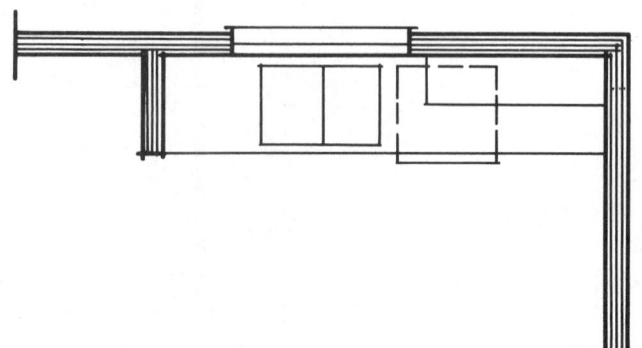

Figure 15–8 Thick lines used on walls and partitions.

outlined with thick lines. This method is not used when dark wall shading is used since the darker shading results in walls and partitions that clearly stand out from other floor-plan features. Some architectural drafters prefer to draw walls and partitions unshaded with a thick outline.

Partial Walls

Partial walls are used as room dividers in situations where an open environment is desired, as guard rails at balconies, or adjacent to a flight of

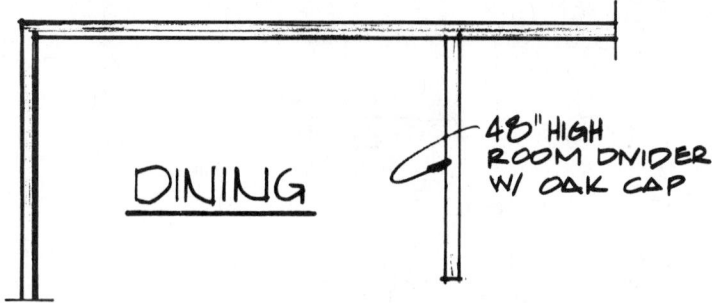

Figure 15–9 Partial wall used as a partition wall or room divider.

stairs. Partial walls require a minimum height above the floor of 36 in. and are often capped with wood or may have decorative spindles that connect to the ceiling. Partial walls are differentiated from other walls by wood grain or very light shading and should be defined with a note that specifies the height as shown in Figure 15–9.

Guardrails

Guardrails are used for safety at balconies, lofts, stairs, and decks over 30 in. above the next lower level. Residential guardrails should be noted on floor plans as being at least 36 in. above the floor and may include a note specifying that intermediate rails should not have more than a 6 in. open space. The minimum space will help ensure that small children will not fall through. Decorative guardrails are also used as room dividers especially at a sunken area or to create an open effect between two rooms. Guardrails are commonly made of wood or wrought iron. Creatively designed guardrails add a great deal to the aesthetics of the interior design. Figure 15–10 shows guardrail designs and how they are drawn on a floor plan.

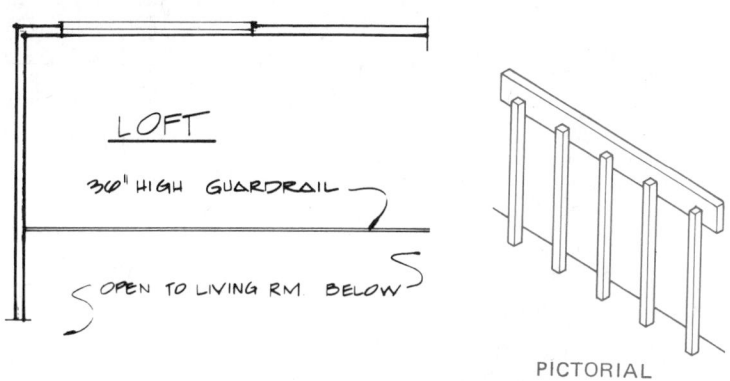

GUARDRAIL AT LOFT OR BALCONY

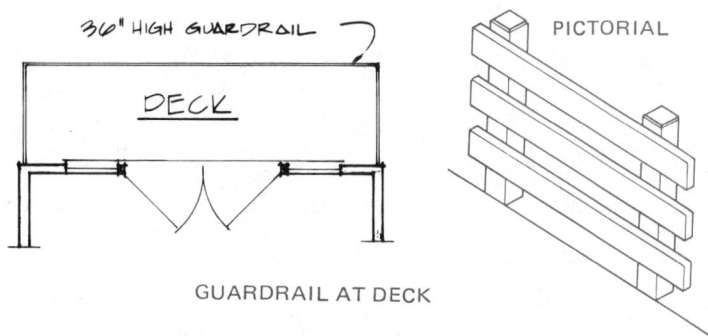

GUARDRAIL AT DECK

Figure 15–10 Guardrails.

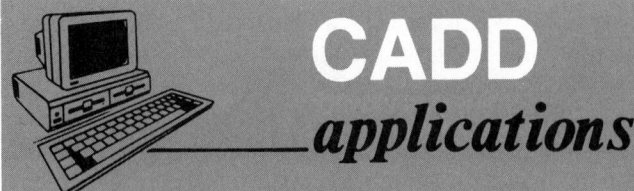

CADD *applications*

CADD FLOOR PLAN SYMBOLS

A variety of architectural CADD software packages are available that provide complete floor plan symbol library templates. The architectural template shown in Figure 1 is a tablet menu-driven package that has extensive architectural applications including window and door symbols, tags, structural, plumbing,

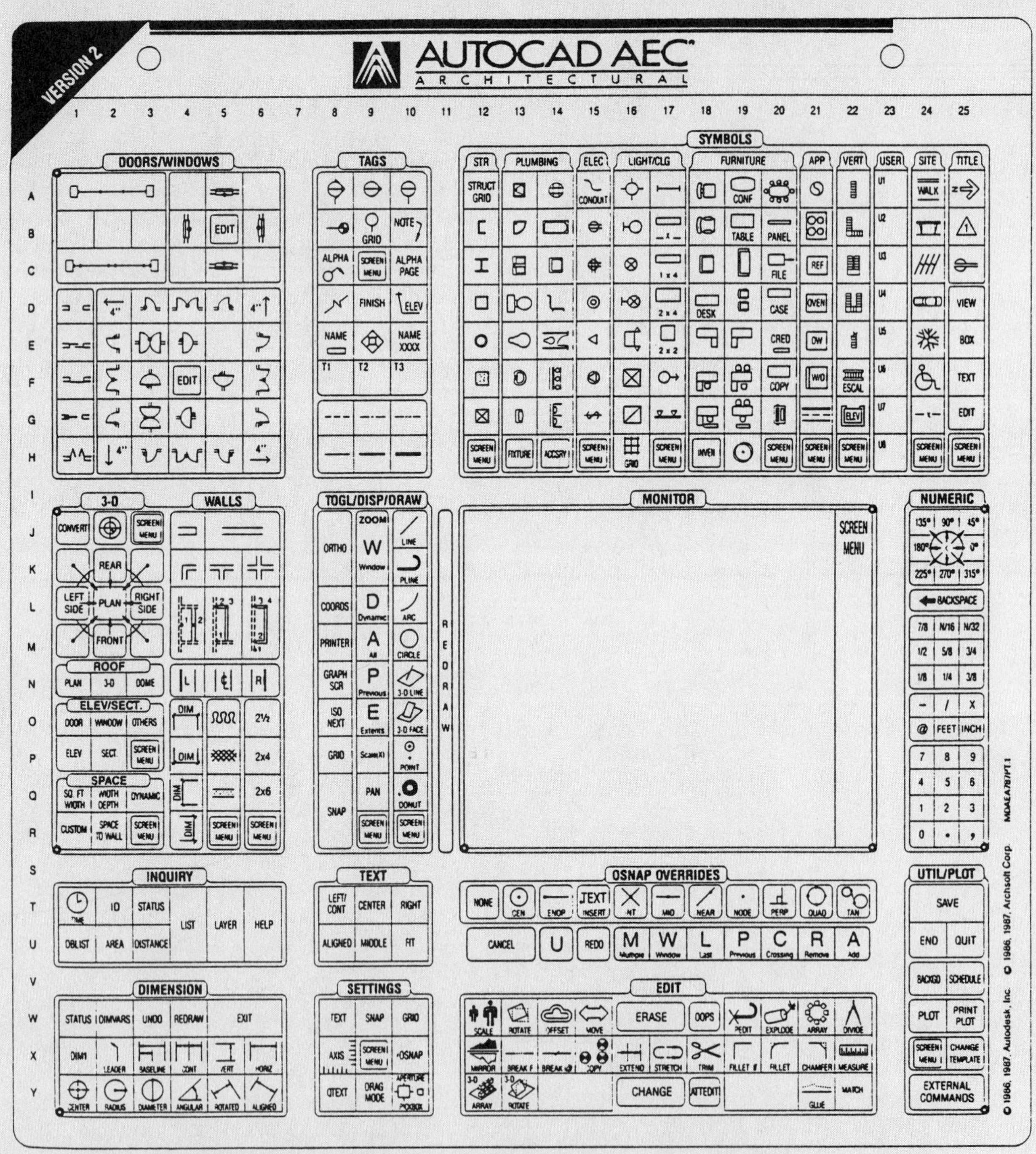

Figure 1 This tablet menu-driven package has extensive architectural details. *Courtesy Autodesk, Inc.*

Figure 2 Multiple sink arrangement.

Figure 3 The stairs were automatically drawn.

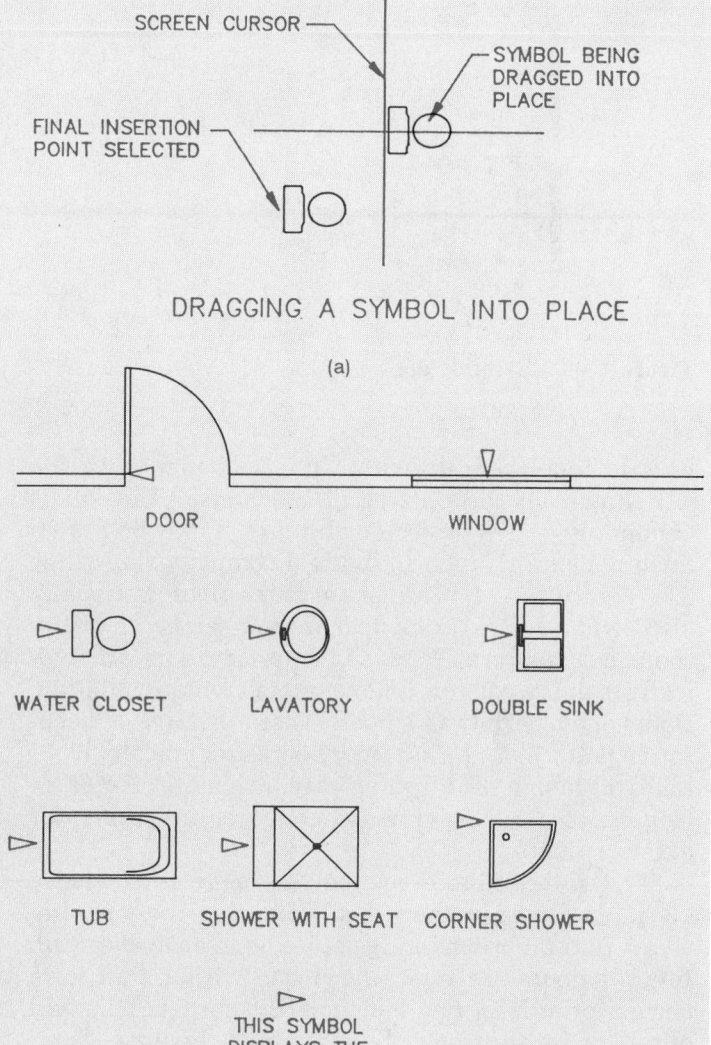

Figure 4 (a) Dragging symbol into place; (b) insertion points for common symbols.

electrical, furniture, appliance, stairs, and site-plan symbols. Also available are titles, drawing and editing functions, and complete dimensioning capabilities. The CADD commands provide (1) residential and commercial symbols for single insertion and (2) commercial symbols for multiple insertion. The multiple-insertion symbols are based on parametric design where you provide specifications for several variables and the CADD system automatically draws the units. For example, if you design a restroom for a hotel, all you do is select vanity sinks for multiple insertion, and you are given several sink types to choose from. You continue by specifying the sink size, the number of units, and the distance between walls. You also specify the cabinet width, height, and the backsplash dimensions. Figure 2 shows the multiple sink arrangement previously described.

Drawing stairs is also easy with the CADD system. All you have to do is pick the start point of the stairs, specify the number of steps to the landing, give the stair width and direction, give the total rise, and the program automatically calculates the rise of each step. The program asks you to provide handrails with or without ballisters, and provides you with several options of handrail ends. After you have provided all the required information, the stair is automatically drawn, as shown in Figure 3.

In most cases, the symbol you select is "dragged" onto the screen by the screen cursor at the symbol-insertion point. The term drag defines the CADD command that allows you to move the symbol to a desired location where it is fixed in place on the drawing. If you decide at a later time that you do not like the selected position, you can use commands such as MOVE and ROTATE to reposition the symbol; you might also use ERASE to get rid of it all together. Figure 4 shows a symbol being dragged into position and displays the insertion point of several common symbols. The insertion point refers to a convenient point on the symbol that is used when placing the symbol on the drawing.

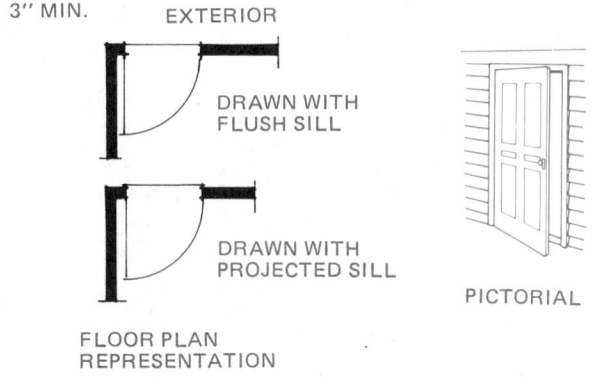

3″ MIN.

EXTERIOR

DRAWN WITH
FLUSH SILL

DRAWN WITH
PROJECTED SILL

FLOOR PLAN
REPRESENTATION

PICTORIAL

Figure 15–11 Exterior door.

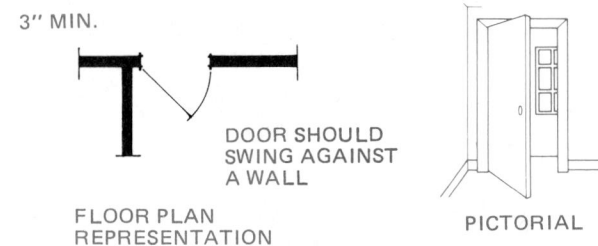

3″ MIN.

DOOR SHOULD
SWING AGAINST
A WALL

FLOOR PLAN
REPRESENTATION

PICTORIAL

Figure 15–12 Interior door.

DOOR SYMBOLS

Exterior doors are drawn on the floor plan with the sill shown on the outside of the house. The sill is commonly drawn projected although it may be drawn flush depending upon individual company standards. See Figure 15–11. The main entry door is usually 3′–0″ wide. An exterior door from a garage or utility room is usually 2′–8″ wide. Exterior doors are typically solid wood or hollow metal with insulation. Doors may be either smooth, slab, or have a decorative pattern on the surface. Doors are typically 6′–8″ high, although 8′–0″ doors are available. Refer to Chapter 8 for a review of code requirements for exterior doors.

The interior door symbol, as shown in Figure 15–12, is drawn without a sill. Interior doors should swing into the room being entered and against a wall. Interior doors are typically placed within 3 in. of a corner, or at least two feet from the corner. This will allow for furniture placement behind the door. Common interior door sizes are:

2′–8″ utility rooms
2′–8″—2′–6″ bedrooms, dens, family, and dining rooms
2′–6″—2′–4″ bathrooms
2′–4″—2′–0″ closets

The larger size door would normally be used on more expensive homes with wider halls; smaller size doors are usually used on homes where space is at a premium. Interior doors are usually slabs but may be the raised-panel type or have glass panels.

Pocket doors are commonly used when space for a door swing is limited as in a small room. Look at Figure 15–13. Pocket doors should not be placed where the pocket will be in an exterior wall or where there is interference with plumbing or electrical wiring. The size of pocket doors should follow the same guidelines as interior swinging doors. Pocket doors are more expensive to purchase and install than standard interior doors because the pocket door frame must be built while the house is being framed. The additional cost is often worth the results, however.

FLOOR PLAN
REPRESENTATION

PICTORIAL

Figure 15–13 Pocket door.

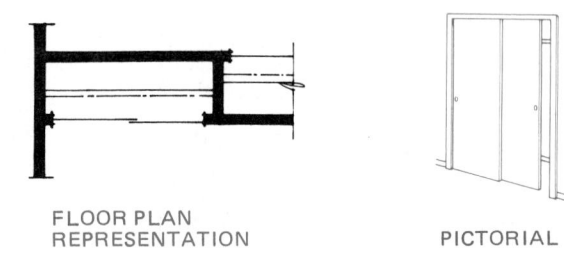

FLOOR PLAN
REPRESENTATION

PICTORIAL

Figure 15–14 Bipass door.

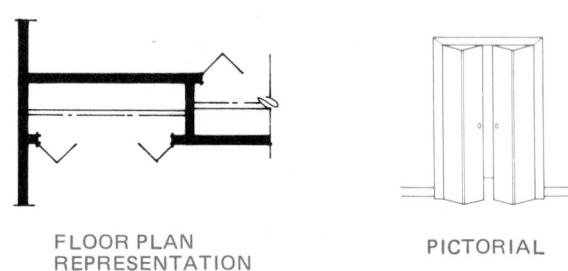

FLOOR PLAN
REPRESENTATION

PICTORIAL

Figure 15–15 Bifold door.

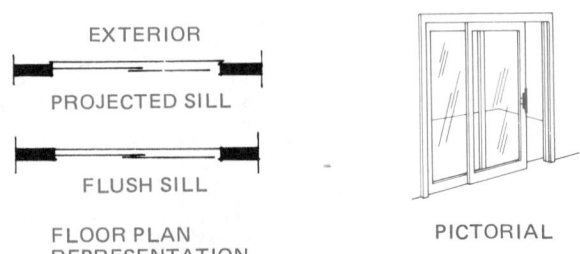

EXTERIOR

PROJECTED SILL

FLUSH SILL

FLOOR PLAN
REPRESENTATION

PICTORIAL

Figure 15–16 Glass sliding door.

A common economical wardrobe door is the bipass door as shown in Figure 15–14. Bipass doors normally range in size from 4'-0" through 12'-0" wide in one-foot intervals. Pairs of doors are usually adequate for widths up to about eight feet. Three panels are usually provided for doors between eight and ten feet wide, and four panels are normal for doors wider than ten feet. Bifold wardrobe or closet doors are used when complete access to the closet is required. Sometimes bifold doors are used on a utility closet that houses a washer and dryer or other utilities. See Figure 15–15. Bifold wardrobe doors often range in size from 4'-0" through 9'-0" wide, in six-inch intervals.

Double-entry doors are common where a large formal foyer design requires a more elaborate entry than can be achieved by one door. The floor-plan symbol for double-entry and French doors is the same; therefore, the door schedule should clearly identify the type of doors to be installed.

Glass sliding doors are made with wood or metal frames and tempered glass for safety. Figure 15–16 shows the floor-plan symbol for both a flush and projected exterior sill representation. These doors are used to provide glass areas and are excellent for access to a patio or deck. Glass sliding doors typically range in size from 5'-0" through 12'-0" wide at one foot intervals. 6'-0" wide is the most common size.

French doors are used in place of glass sliding doors when a more traditional door design is required. Glass sliding doors are associated with contemporary design and do not take up as much floor space as French doors. French doors may be purchased with wood mullions and muntins (the upright and bar partitions respectively) between the glass panes or with one large glass pane and a removable grill for easy cleaning. See Figure 15–17. French doors range in size from 2'-4" through 3'-6" wide in two inch increments. Doors may be used individually, in pairs, or in groups of threes or fours. The three- and four-panel doors typically have one or more fixed panels which should be specified.

Double-acting doors are often used between a kitchen and eating area so that the doors will swing in either direction for easy passage. Double-acting doors may also create a classic western design when used to enter the home bar or party room. See Figure 15–18. Common size for pairs of doors range from 2'-6" through 4'-0" wide in two inch increments.

Dutch doors are used when it is desirable to have a door that may be half open and half closed. The top portion may be opened and used as a pass through. Look at Figure 15–19. Dutch doors range in size from 2'-6" through 3'-6" wide in two inch increments.

Accordion doors may be used at closets or wardrobes, or they are often used as room dividers where an openable partition is needed. Figure 15–20 shows

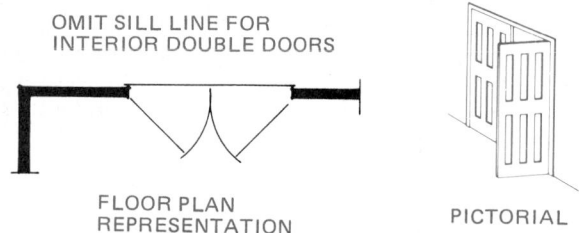

Figure 15–17 Double-entry or French doors.

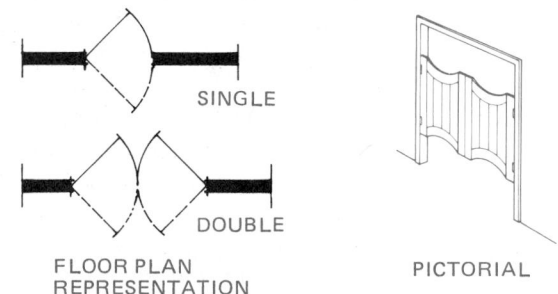

Figure 15–18 Double-acting doors.

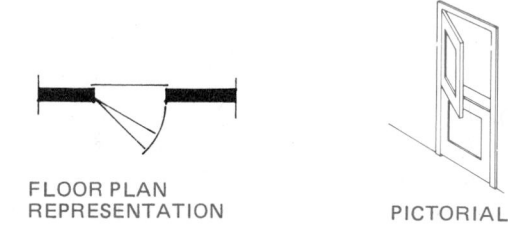

Figure 15–19 Dutch doors.

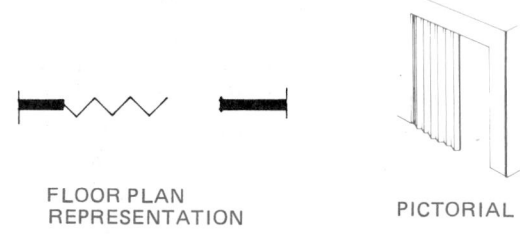

Figure 15–20 Accordion door.

the accordion door floor-plan symbol. Accordion doors range in size from 4'-0" through 12'-0" in one foot increments.

The floor-plan symbol for an overhead garage door is shown in Figure 15–21. The dashed lines denote the size and extent of the garage door when open. The extent of the garage door is typically only shown when the door will interfere with something on the ceiling.

Garage doors range in size from 8'-0" through 16'-0" wide. An 8'-0" door is common for a single car width. A door 9'-0" is common for a single door and will accommodate a pick-up truck with a camper or trailer. A door 16'-0" is common for a double car door. Door heights are typically 7'-0" high, although 8'-0" or 10'-0" high doors are common for campers or recreational vehicles.

WINDOW SYMBOLS

Window symbols are drawn with a sill on the outside and inside. The sliding window, as shown in Figure 15–22, is a popular 50 percent openable window. Notice that windows may be drawn with exterior sills projected or flush, and the glass pane may be drawn with single or double lines. The method used should be consistent throughout the plan and should be determined by the preference of the specific architectural office. Many offices draw all windows with a projected sill and one line to represent the glass; they then specify the type of window in the window schedule. This allows the drafter to draw all windows on the floor plan even though the owner or contractor has not yet determined the window style.

Windows typically come in sizes that range from 2'-0" through 12'-0" wide at intervals of about six inches. Typically, windows with an aluminum frame offer greater size variations than wood frames.

The location of the window in the house and the way the window opens will have an effect on the size. A window between 6'-0" to 12'-0" wide is common for a living, dining, or family room. To take advantage of any possible view while sitting, windows in these rooms are normally between 4'-0" to 5'-0" deep.

Windows in bedrooms are typically between 3'-0" to 6'-0" wide. The depth often ranges from 3'-6" to 4'-0". The type of window used in the bedroom is important because of emergency egress requirements of most codes. See chapter 8 for a review.

Kitchen windows are often between 3'-0" to 5'-0" wide and between 3'-0" to 3'-6" deep. Wide windows are nice to have in a kitchen for the added light they provide, but some of the upper cabinets may be eliminated. If the tops of windows are at the normal 6'-8" height, windows deeper than 3'-6" will interfere with the counter tops.

Bathroom windows often range between 2'-0" and 3'-0" wide with an equal depth. A longer window with less depth is often specified if the window is to be located in a shower area. Most bathroom windows have obscure glass.

Casement windows may be 100 percent openable and are best used where extreme weather conditions require a tight seal when the window is closed although these windows are in common use everywhere. See Figure 15–23. Casement windows may be more expensive than sliding units.

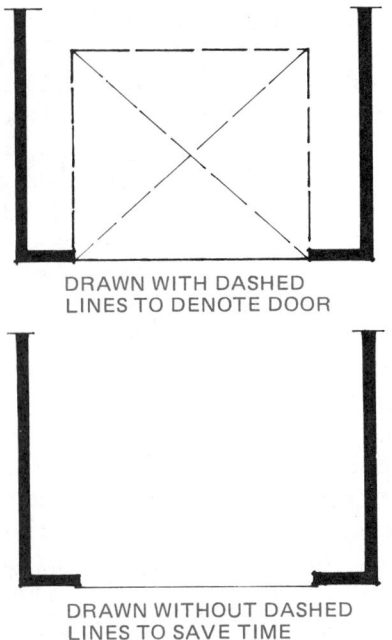

DRAWN WITH DASHED LINES TO DENOTE DOOR

DRAWN WITHOUT DASHED LINES TO SAVE TIME

Figure 15–21 Overhead garage door.

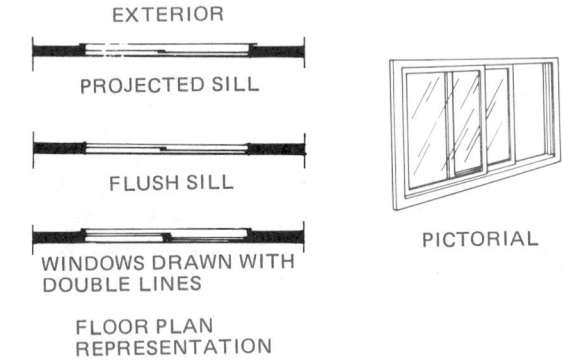

EXTERIOR

PROJECTED SILL

FLUSH SILL

WINDOWS DRAWN WITH DOUBLE LINES

FLOOR PLAN REPRESENTATION

PICTORIAL

Figure 15–22 Horizontal sliding window.

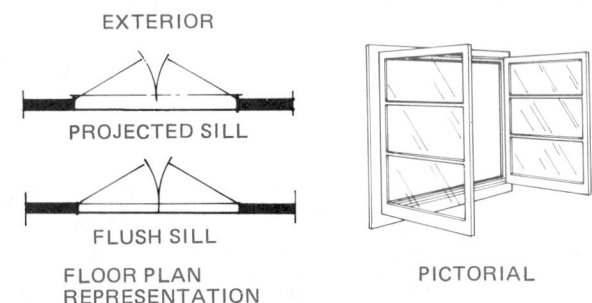

EXTERIOR

PROJECTED SILL

FLUSH SILL

FLOOR PLAN REPRESENTATION

PICTORIAL

Figure 15–23 Casement window.

The traditional double-hung window has a bottom panel that slides upward as shown in Figure 15–24. Double-hung wood-frame windows are designed for energy efficiency and are commonly used in traditional as opposed to contemporary architectural designs. Double-hung windows are typically deeper than they are wide. Single windows usually range in width from 1'-6" through 4'-0". It is very common to have double-hung windows grouped together in pairs of two or more.

Awning windows often are used in basements or below a fixed window to provide ventilation. Another common use places awning windows between two different roof levels; this provides additional ventilation in vaulted rooms. These windows would then be opened with a long pole connected to the opening device. These windows are hinged at the top and swing outward as shown in Figure 15–25. Hopper windows are drawn in the same manner; however, they hinge at the bottom and swing inward. Jalousie windows are used when a louvered effect is desired as seen in Figure 15–26.

Fixed windows are popular when a large unobstructed area of glass is required to take advantage of a view or to allow for solar heat gain. Figure 15–27 shows the floor plan symbol of a fixed window.

Bay windows are often used when a traditional style is desired. Figure 15–28 shows the representation of a bay. Usually the sides are drawn at 45 or 30 degrees. The depth of the bay is usually between 18″ and 24″. The total width of a bay is limited by the size of the center window which is typically either a fixed panel, double-hung, or casement window. Bays can be either premanufactured or built at the job site.

A garden window, as shown in Figure 15–29, is a popular style for utility rooms or kitchens. Garden windows usually project between 12″–18″ from the residence. Depending on the manufacturer, either the side or top panels will open.

Skylights

When additional daylight is desirable in a room or for natural light to enter an interior room, consider using a skylight. Skylights are available fixed or openable. They are made of plastic in a dome shape or

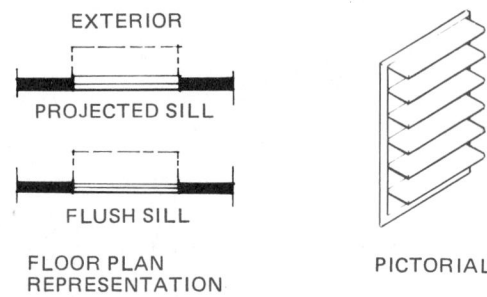

Figure 15–26 Jalousie window.

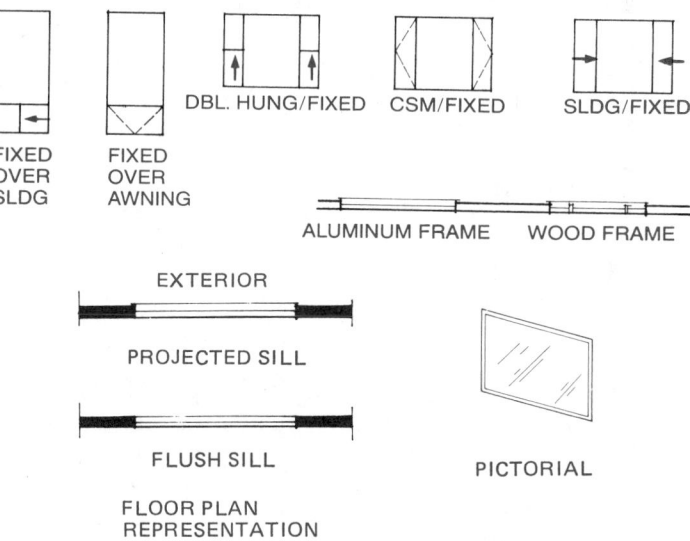

Figure 15–27 Fixed window.

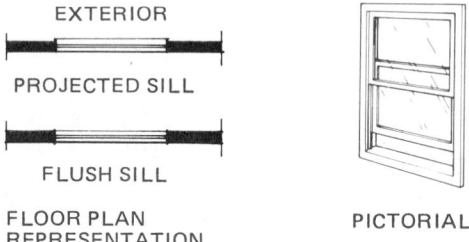

Figure 15–24 Double-hung window.

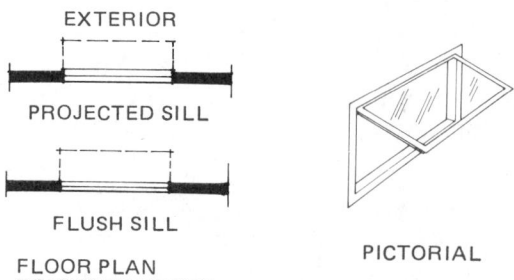

Figure 15–25 Awning window.

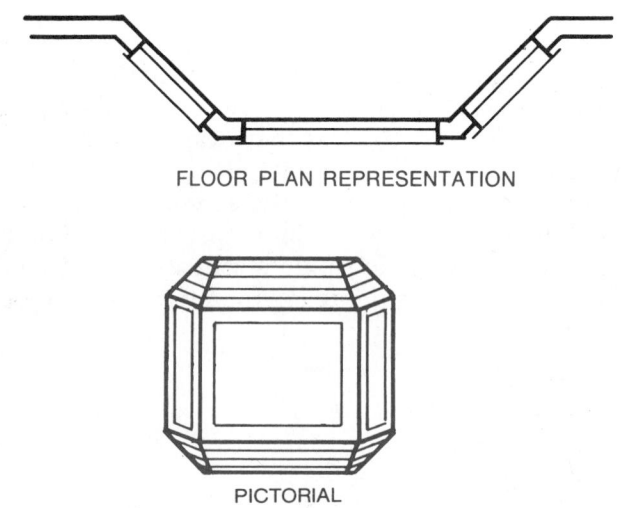

Figure 15–28 Bay window.

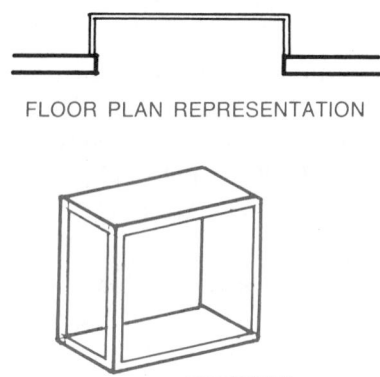

FLOOR PLAN REPRESENTATION

PICTORIAL

Figure 15–29 Garden window.

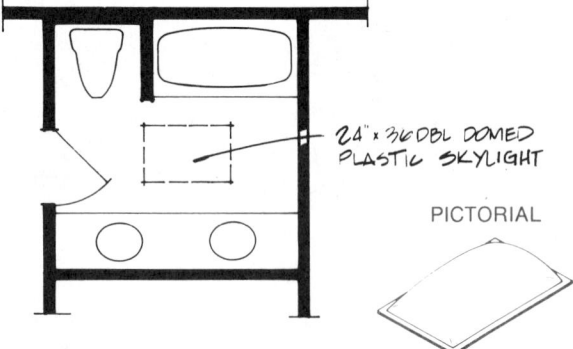

24" x 36 DBL DOMED PLASTIC SKYLIGHT

PICTORIAL

Figure 15–30 Skylight representation.

flat tempered glass. Tempered double-pane insulated skylights are energy efficient, do not cause any distortion of view, and generally are not more expensive than plastic skylights. Figure 15–30 shows how a skylight is represented in the floor plan.

◣ SCHEDULES

Numbered symbols used on the floor plan key specific items to charts known as schedules. Schedules are used to describe items such as doors, windows, appliances, materials, fixtures, hardware, and finishes. See Figure 15–31. Schedules help keep drawings clear of unnecessary notes since the details of the item are off the drawing and on another sheet. There are many different ways to set up a schedule, but it may include any or all of the following information about the product:

- vendor's name
- product name
- model number
- quantity
- size
- rough opening size
- color

WINDOW SCHEDULE

SYM	SIZE	MODEL	ROUGH OPEN	QUAN.
A	1° x 5°	JOB BUILT	VERIFY	2
B	8° x 5°	W 4 N 5 CSM.	8'-0³⁄₄ x 5'-0⅛	1
C	4° x 5°	W 2 N 5 CSM.	4'-0³⁄₄ x 5'-0⅛	2
D	4° x 3⁶	W 2 N 3 CSM	4'-0³⁄₄ x 3'-6½	2
E	3⁶ x 3⁶	2 N 3 CSM	3'-6½ x 3'-6½	2
F	6° x 4°	G 64 SLDG.	6'-0½ x 4'-0½	1
G	5° x 3⁶	G 536 SLDG.	5'-0½ x 3'-6½	4
H	4° x 3⁶	G 436 SLDG.	4'-0½ x 3'-6½	1
J	4° x 2°	A 41 AWN.	4'-0½ x 2'-0⅛	3

(a)

DOOR SCHEDULE

SYM.	SIZE	TYPE	QUAN
1	3° x 6⁸	S.C. R.P. METAL INSULATED	1
2	3° x 6⁸	S.C. FLUSH METAL INSULATED	2
3	2⁸ x 6⁸	S.C. SELF CLOSING	2
4	2⁸ x 6⁸	HOLLOW CORE	5
5	2⁶ x 6⁸	HOLLOW CORE	5
6	2⁶ x 6⁸	POCKET SLDG.	2

(b)

Figure 15–31 Window and door schedule.

During the early stages of plan development the drafter or designer will refer to manufacturers' catalogs for products to be used in the design and so begin to establish the schedule data.

Schedule Key

When doors and windows are described in a schedule, they must be keyed from the drawing to the schedule. The key may be to label doors with a number and windows with a letter. You can enclose the letters or numbers in different geometric figures such as the following:

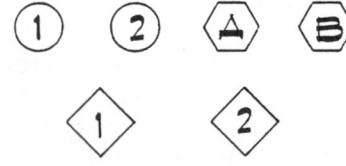

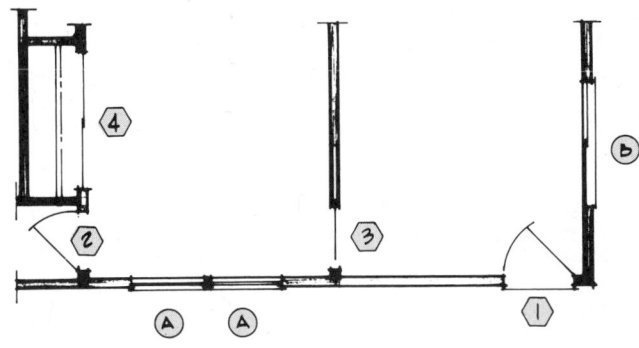

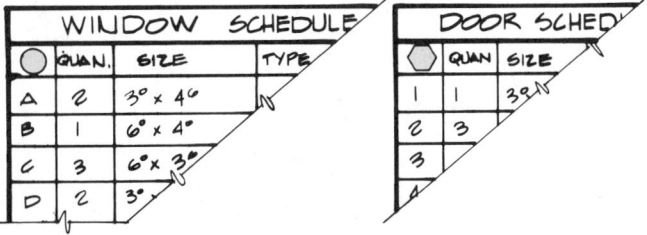

Figure 15–32 Method of keying windows and doors from the floor plan to the schedules.

See also Figure 15–32. As an alternative method, you may consider using a divided circle for the key. You would place the letter D for door or W for window above the dividing line and the number of the door or window, using consecutive numbers, below the line as shown:

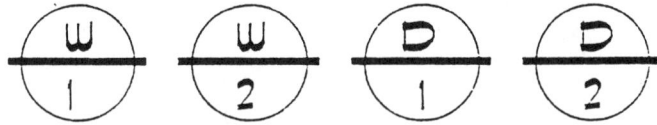

The exact method of representation depends upon individual company standards.

Schedules are also used to identify finish materials used in different areas of the structure. Figure 15–33 shows a typical interior finish schedule.

Door and window sizes also may be placed on the floor plan next to their symbols. This method, as shown in Figure 15–34, is used by some drafting technicians to save time. While this method is easy to do, it may not be used when specific data must be identified. The sizes are the numbers adjacent to the windows and doors in Figure 15–34. Notice that the first two numbers indicate the width. For example, 30 means 3′-0″. The second two numbers indicate the height; 68 means 6′-8″. A 6040 window means 6′-0″ wide by 4′-0″ high, and a 2868 door means 2′-8″ wide by 6′-8″ high. Standard door height is 6′-8″. Some drafters use the same system in a slightly different manner by presenting the sizes as 2⁸ × 6⁸ meaning 2′-8″ wide by 6′-8″ high or with actual dimensions given such as 2′-8″ × 6′-8″. This

INTERIOR FINISH SCHEDULE

| ROOM | FLOOR | | | | | WALLS | | | | CEIL. | | |
	VINYL	CARPET	TILE	HARDWOOD	CONCRETE	PAINT	PAPER	TEXTURE	SPRAY	SMOOTH	BROCADE	PAINT
ENTRY					●							
FOYER			●			●			●		●	●
KITCHEN			●					●			●	●
DINING				●		●			●		●	●
FAMILY		●				●			●		●	●
LIVING		●				●		●			●	●
MASTER BED.		●				●			●		●	●
MASTER BATH.			●					●		●		●
BATH #2			●			●			●		●	●
BED. #2		●				●			●		●	●
BED. #3		●				●			●		●	●
UTILITY	●					●			●		●	●

Figure 15–33 Finish schedule.

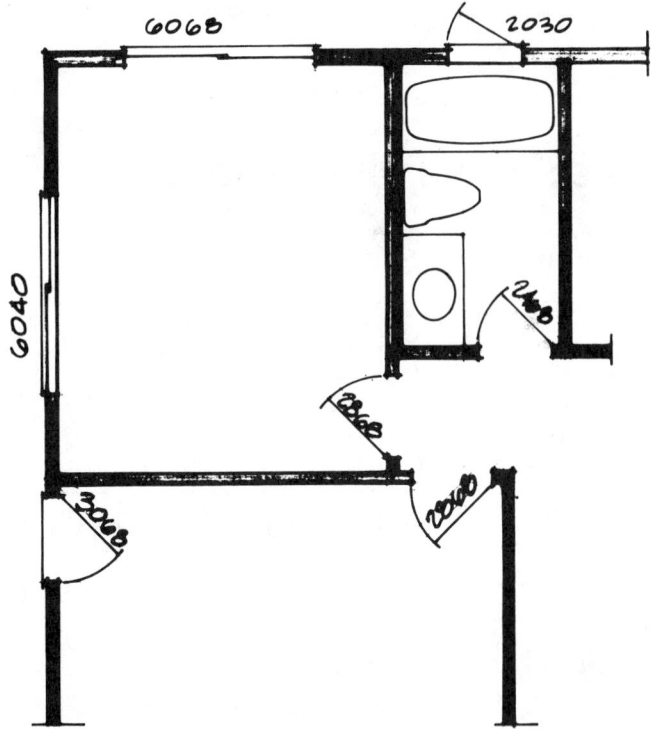

Figure 15–34 Simplified method of labeling doors and windows.

simplified method of identification is better suited for development housing in which doors, windows, and other items are not specified on the plans as to a given manufacturer. These details will be included in a description of materials or specification sheet

Doors with Beveled, Leaded Glass

Widths: 3'0"—single; 6'0"—double.
Heights: 6'8", 6'10", 7'0".

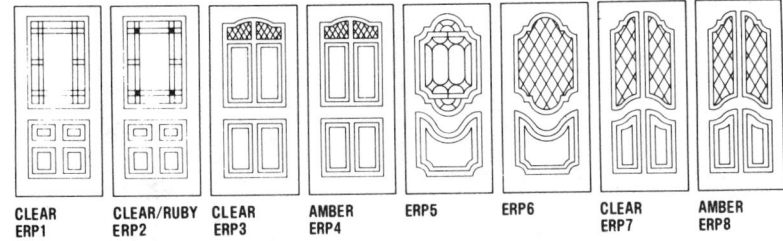

Embossed Doors

Widths: 2'8", 2'10", 3'0"—single; 5'4", 5'8", 6'0"—double.
Heights: 6'6", 6'8", 6'10",7'0".
NA: Certain styles not available in sizes as marked.

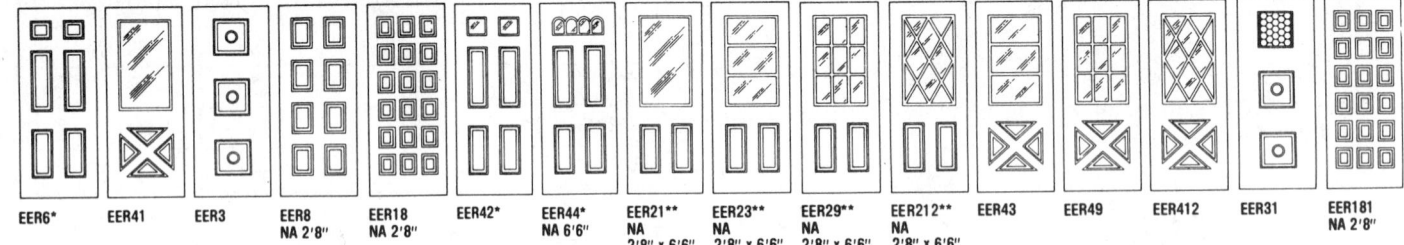

*Deadlocks on 2'8" 6-panel Embossed Doors must have a 2⅜" backset.
**Deadlocks on 2'8" 6-panel Embossed Doors with half-glass lites must have
a 2⅜" backset and a 2" rose.

Flush Doors with Raised Trim

Widths: 2'6", 2'8", 2'10", 3'0", 3'6"—single;
        5'0", 5'4", 5'8", 6'0"—double.
Heights: 6'6", 6'8", 6'10", 7'0".

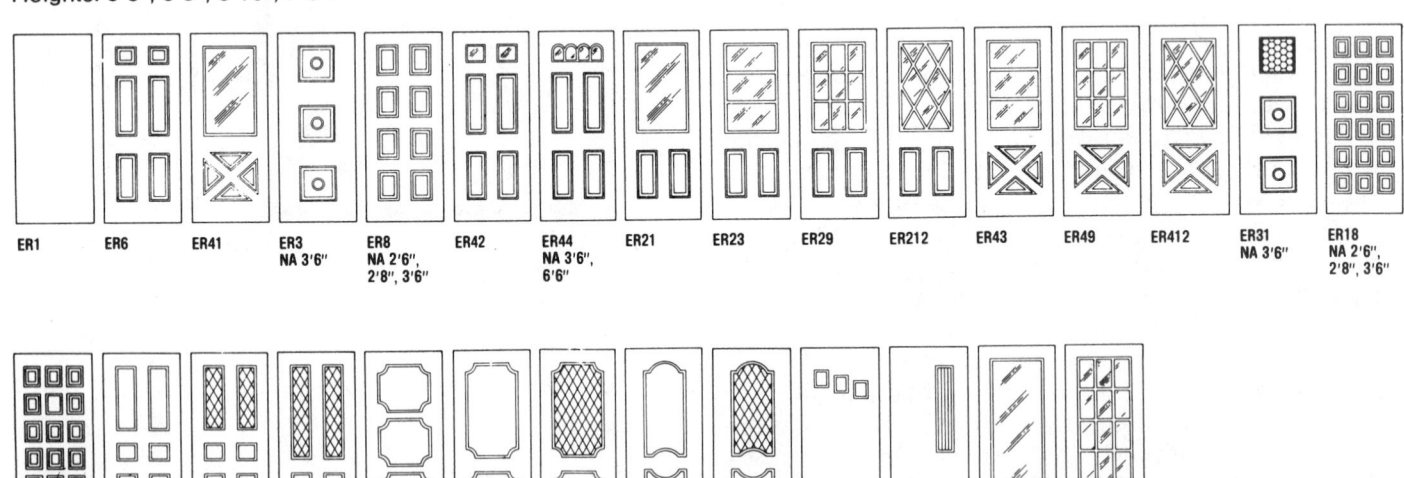

Figure 15–35 Door catalog page. *Courtesy Ceco Corporation.*

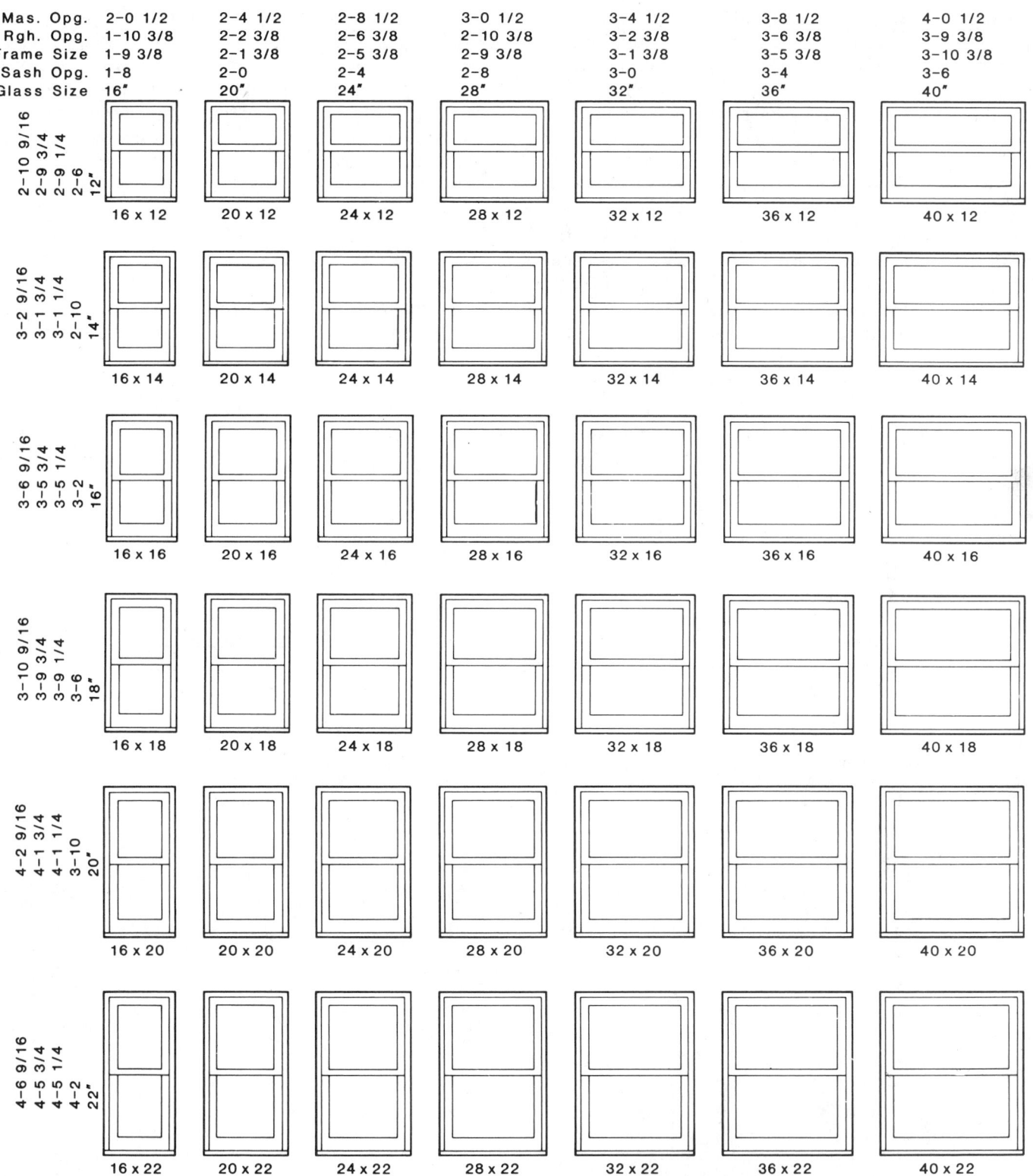

Mas. Opg.	2-0 1/2	2-4 1/2	2-8 1/2	3-0 1/2	3-4 1/2	3-8 1/2	4-0 1/2
Rgh. Opg.	1-10 3/8	2-2 3/8	2-6 3/8	2-10 3/8	3-2 3/8	3-6 3/8	3-9 3/8
Frame Size	1-9 3/8	2-1 3/8	2-5 3/8	2-9 3/8	3-1 3/8	3-5 3/8	3-10 3/8
Sash Opg.	1-8	2-0	2-4	2-8	3-0	3-4	3-6
Glass Size	16"	20"	24"	28"	32"	36"	40"

Figure 15–36 Window catalog page. *Courtesy Marvin Windows.*

for each individual house. The principal reason for using this system is to reduce drafting time by omitting schedules. The building contractor may be required to submit alternate specifications to the client so that actual items may be clarified.

When preparing a set of residential plans, you should give specific details about doors and windows regarding standard size, material, type of finish, energy efficiency and style. This information is available through vendors' specifications. As an architectural drafter you should obtain copies of vendors' specifications from manufacturers that have products available in your local area. Figure 15–35 shows a typical page from a door catalog that shows styles

and available sizes. Figure 15–36 is a page from a window catalog that describes the sizes of a particular product. Notice that specific information is given for the rough opening (framing size), finish size, and amount of glass. Vendors' catalogs also provide construction details and actual specifications for each product as shown in Figure 15–37.

CABINETS, FIXTURES, AND APPLIANCES

Cabinets are found in kitchens, baths, dressing areas, utility rooms, bars and work shops. Specialized cab-

2x4 Frame Construction,
1/2" Drywall, 1/2" Sheathing,
Single Glazing with an optional
Alpine Combination Storm & Screen.

2x4 Frame Construction,
1/2" Drywall, 1/2" Sheathing,
Insulated Glass, Brick Veneer

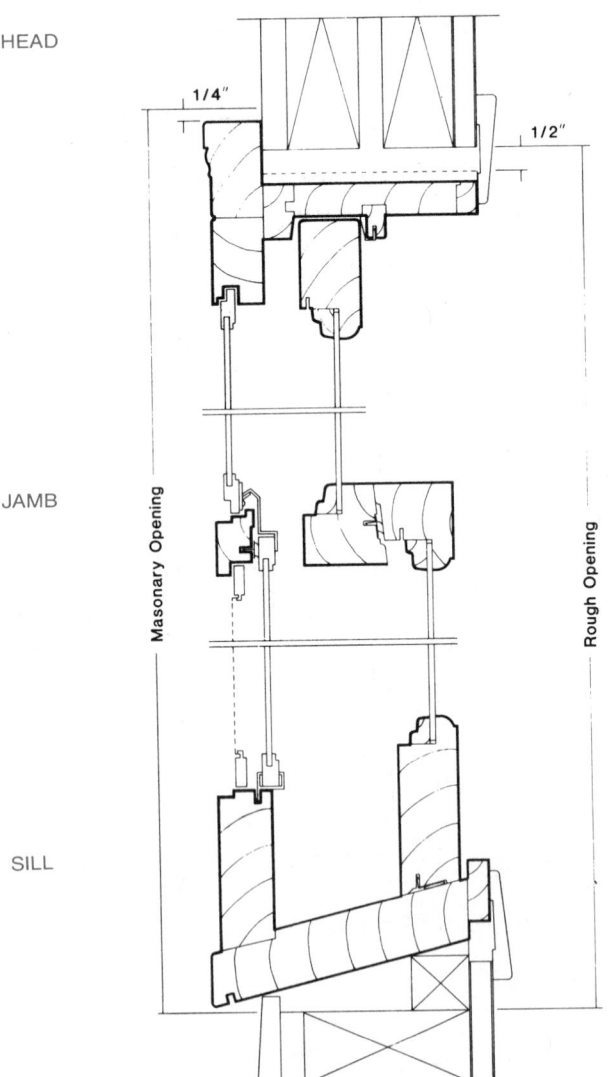
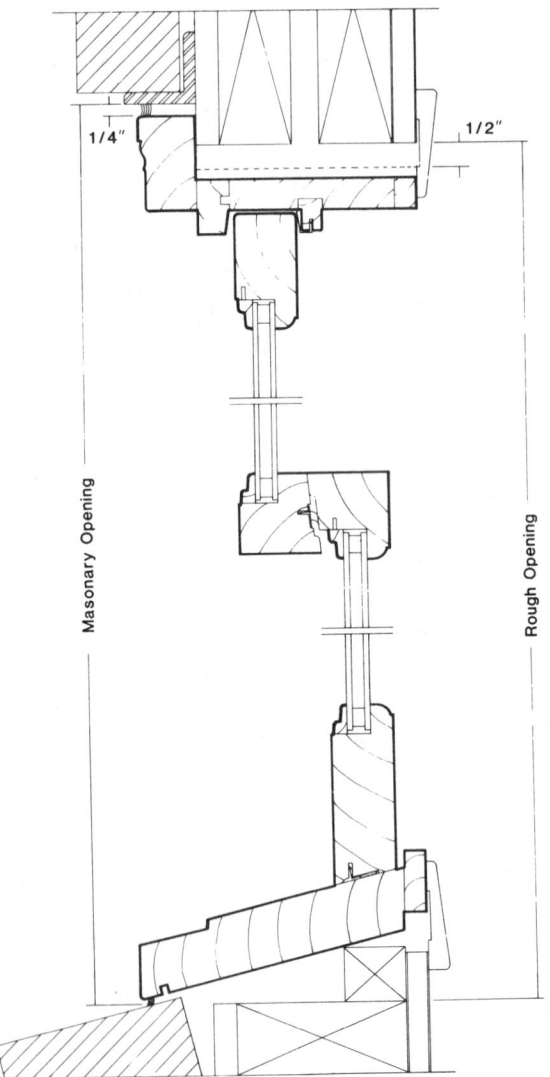

Figure 15–37 Vendor catalog details. *Courtesy Marvin Windows.*

inets such as desks or built-in dressers may be found in bedrooms. In general, the cabinets that are drawn on the floor plans are built-in units.

Kitchens

In conjunction with cabinets, you will locate fixtures such as sinks, butcher block cutting board counter tops, and lighting, and appliances such as the range, refrigerator, dishwasher, trash compactor, and garbage disposal. Figure 15–38 shows the floor plan view of the kitchen cabinets, fixtures, and appliances. Some drafters prefer to show upper cabinets as in Figure 15–39.

The range should have a hood with a light and fan. You should note how the fan will vent. Some

ranges do not require a hood because they vent through the floor or wall. Vent direction should be specified on the plan. Some homes may have a range top with a built-in oven or an oven and microwave unit. There are many options. The size of the range and refrigerator may vary between 30 and 48 in. wide. Decide on the size you want from a vendor's catalog. Label the garbage disposal with a note or with the abbreviation G.D. Houses with septic tanks should not have garbage disposals.

Pantries are popular and may be drawn as shown in Figure 15–40. A pantry may also be designed to be part broom closet and part shelves for storage. Figure 15–41 shows typical floor plan representation and cabinet sizes for a kitchen layout.

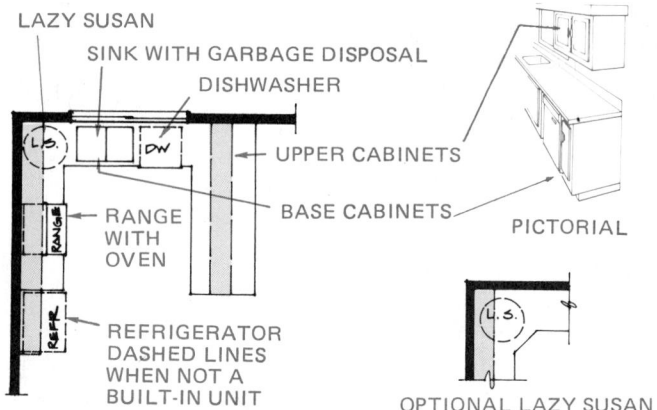

Figure 15–38 Kitchen cabinets, fixtures, and appliances.

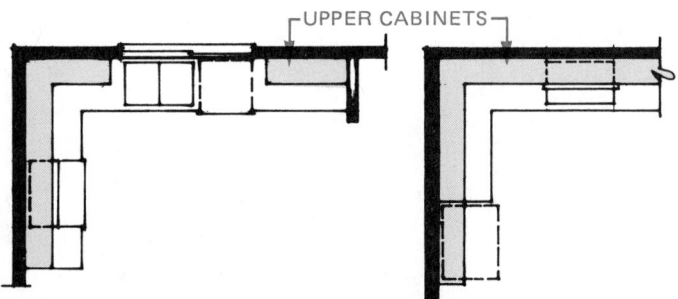

Figure 15–39 Alternate upper cabinet floor plan symbols.

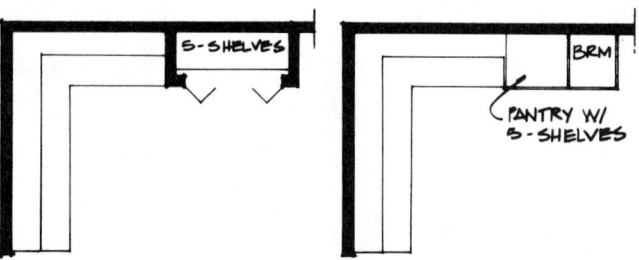

Figure 15–40 Kitchen pantry.

Bathrooms

Bathroom cabinets and fixtures are shown in several typical floor plan layouts in Figure 15–42. The vanity may be any length depending upon the space you have. The shower may be smaller or larger than the one shown depending upon the vendor. Verify the size for a prefabricated shower unit before you draw one. Showers that are built on the job may be any size or design. They are usually lined with tile, marble, or other materials. The common size of tubs is 30″ × 60″, but larger and smaller ones are available. Sinks can be round, oval or other shapes.

Figure 15–43 shows a variety of products that are available for use when something special is required in a bathroom design. Verify the availability of products and vendors' specifications as you design and draw the floor plan. Figure 15–44 shows the floor-plan representation of a 60″ × 72″ raised bathtub in a solarium. Often, due to cost considerations, the space available for bathrooms is minimal. Figure 15–45 shows some minimum sizes to consider.

Utility Rooms

The symbols for the clothes washer, dryer, and laundry tray are shown in Figure 15–46. The clothes washer and dryer symbols may be drawn with dashed lines if these items are not part of the construction contract. Laundry utilities may be placed in a closet when only minimum space is available as shown in Figure 15–47. Ironing boards may be built into the laundry room wall or attached to the wall surface as shown in Figure 15–48. Provide a note to the electrician if power is required to the unit or provide an adjacent outlet.

The furnace and hot water heater are sometimes placed together in a location central to the house. They may be placed in a closet as shown in Figure 15–49. These utilities may also be placed in a separate room, the basement, or the garage.

Wardrobes and closets are utilitarian in nature as they are used for clothes and storage. Bedroom closets should be labeled WARDROBE. Other closets may be labeled ENTRY CLOSET, LINEN CLOSET, BROOM

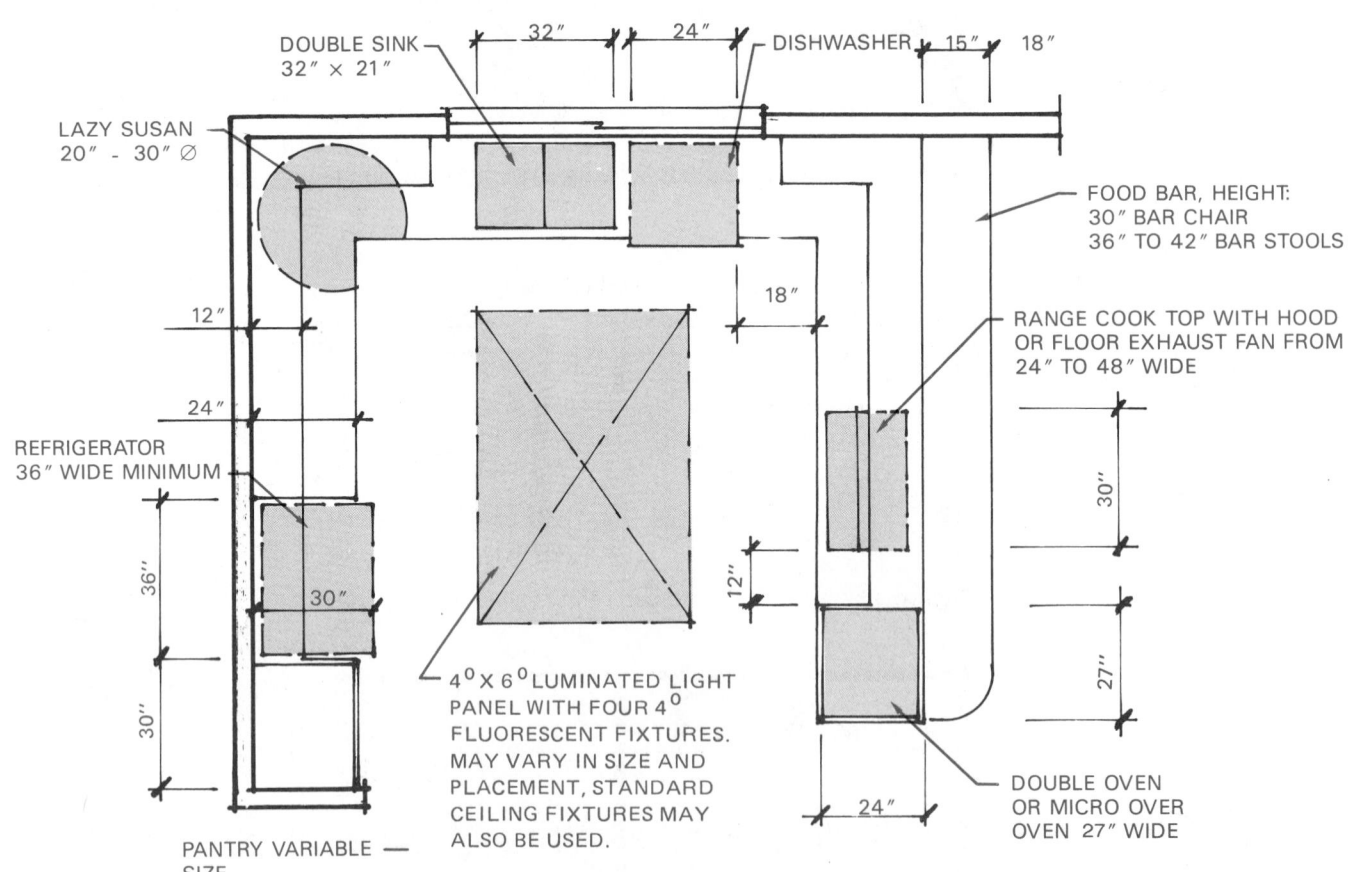

Figure 15–41 Standard kitchen cabinet, fixture, and appliance sizes.

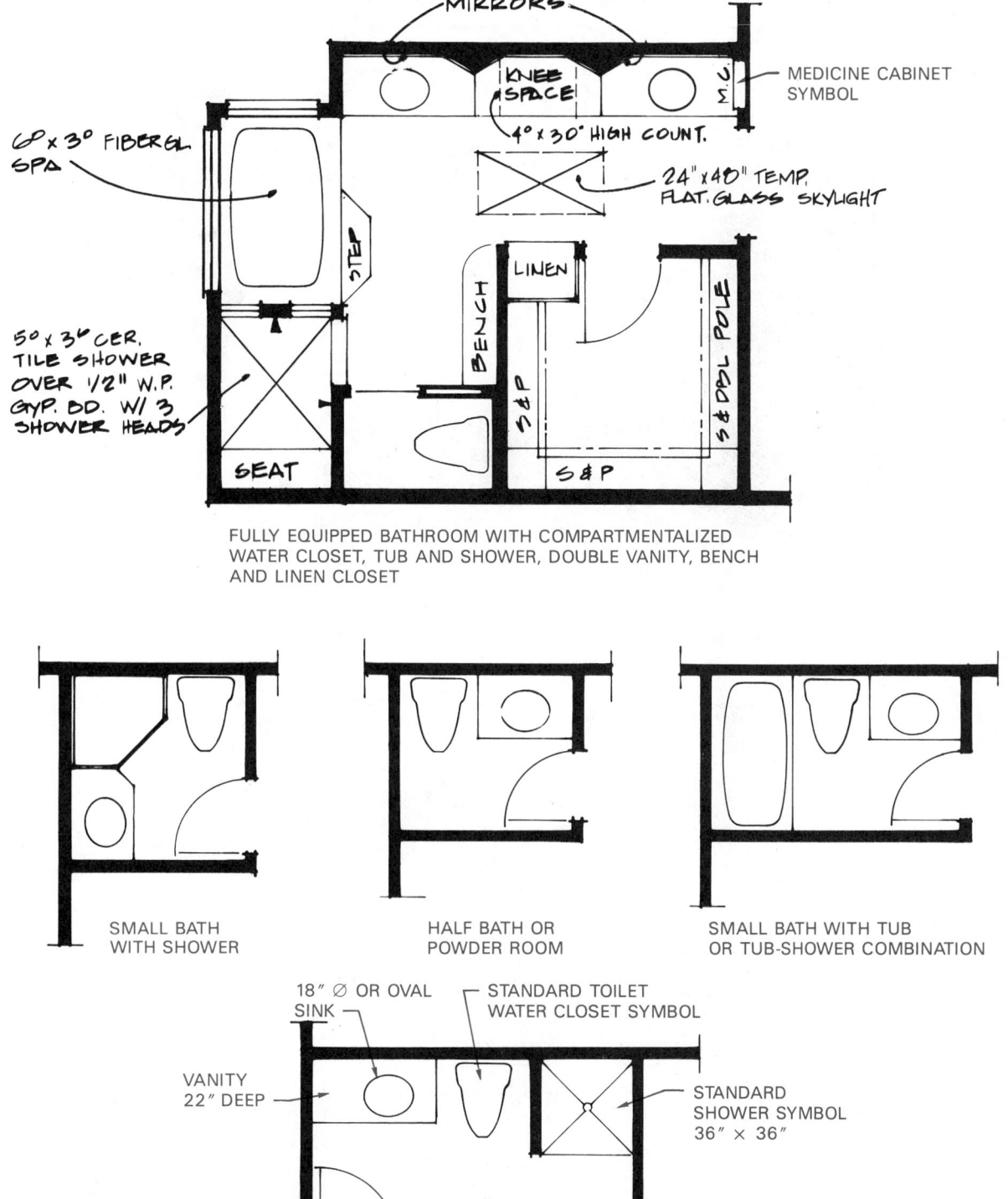

MIRRORS

MEDICINE CABINET SYMBOL

KNEE SPACE

4°x30° HIGH COUNT.

6°x3° FIBERGL. SPA

24"x48" TEMP. FLAT GLASS SKYLIGHT

LINEN

5°x3° CER. TILE SHOWER OVER 1/2" W.P. GYP. BD. W/ 3 SHOWER HEADS

BENCH

S & DBL POLE

S & P

S & P

STEP

SEAT

FULLY EQUIPPED BATHROOM WITH COMPARTMENTALIZED WATER CLOSET, TUB AND SHOWER, DOUBLE VANITY, BENCH AND LINEN CLOSET

SMALL BATH WITH SHOWER

HALF BATH OR POWDER ROOM

SMALL BATH WITH TUB OR TUB-SHOWER COMBINATION

18" ∅ OR OVAL SINK

STANDARD TOILET WATER CLOSET SYMBOL

VANITY 22" DEEP

STANDARD SHOWER SYMBOL 36" × 36"

STANDARD TUB SYMBOL 5'-0" x 2'-8"

TYPICAL BATHROOM

Figure 15–42 Layout of bathroom cabinet and fixture floor plan symbols.

Figure 15–43 Unique bathroom products. *Courtesy Jacuzzi Whirlpool Bath.*

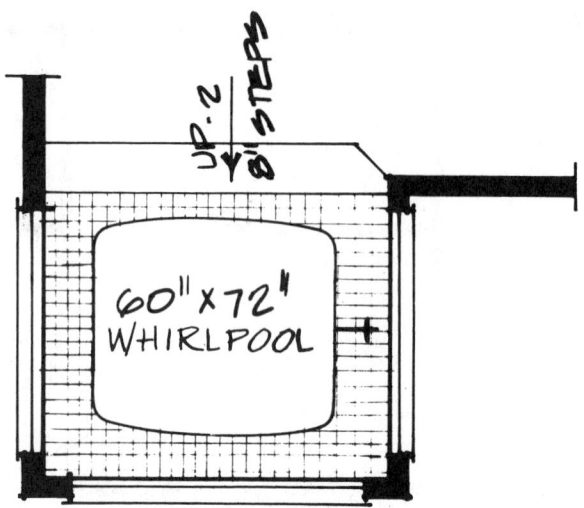

Figure 15–44 Raised bathtub and solarium.

CLOSET, etc. Wardrobe or guest closets should be provided with a shelf and pole. The shelf and pole may be drawn with a thin line to represent the shelf and a centerline to show the pole as shown in Figure 15–50. Some drafters use two dashed lines to symbolize the shelf and pole.

When a laundry room is below the bedroom area, provide a chute from a convenient area near the bedrooms through the ceiling and into a cabinet directly in the utility room. The cabinet should be above or adjacent to the clothes washer. Figure 15–51 shows a laundry chute noted in the floor plan.

FLOOR-PLAN MATERIALS

Finish Materials

Finish materials used in construction may be identified on the floor plan with notes, characteristic symbols, or key symbols that relate to a finish schedule. The key symbol is also placed on the finish schedule next to the identification of the type of finish needed at the given location on the floor plan. Finish schedules may also be set up on a room-by-room basis. When flooring finish is identified, the

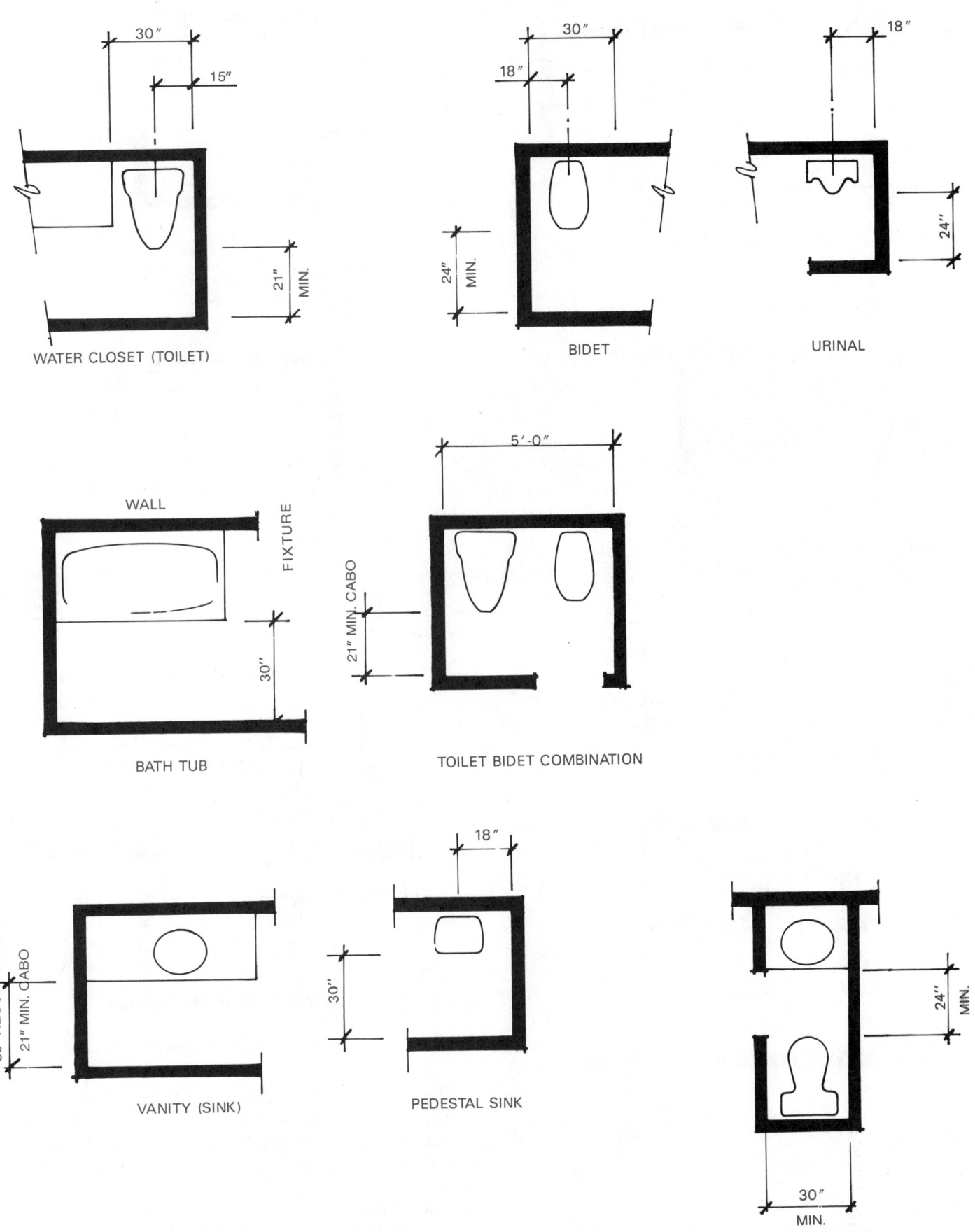

Figure 15–45 Minimum bath spaces.

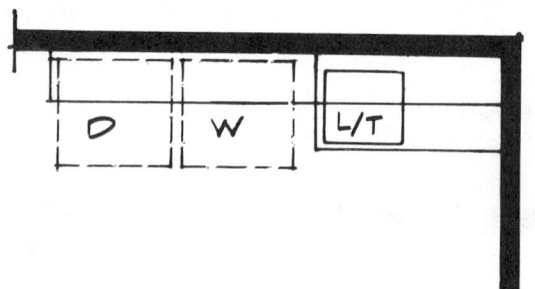

Figure 15–46 Washer, dryer, and laundry tray.

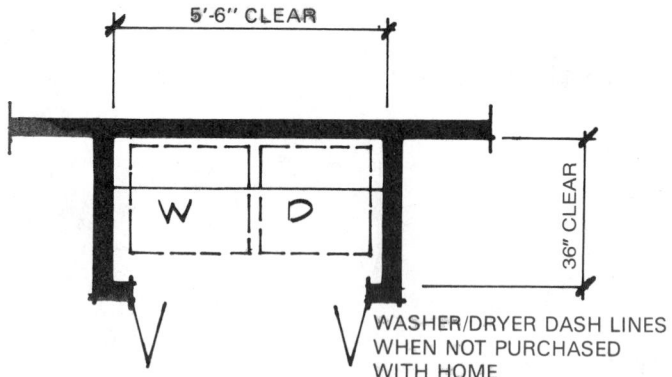

Figure 15–47 Minimum washer and dryer space.

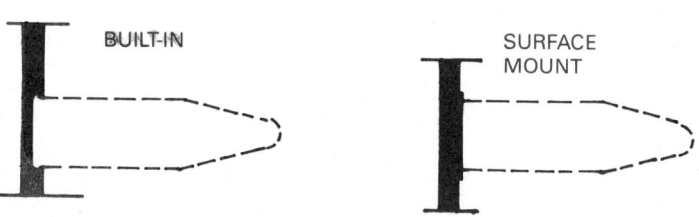

Figure 15–48 Ironing boards.

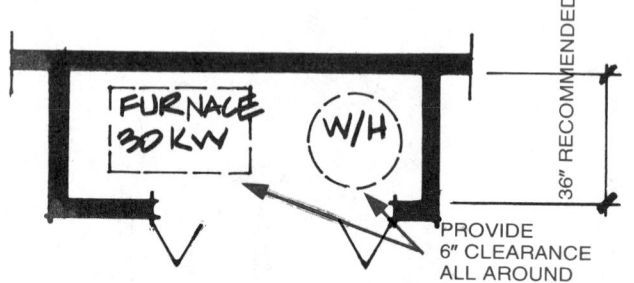

Figure 15–49 Furnace and water heater.

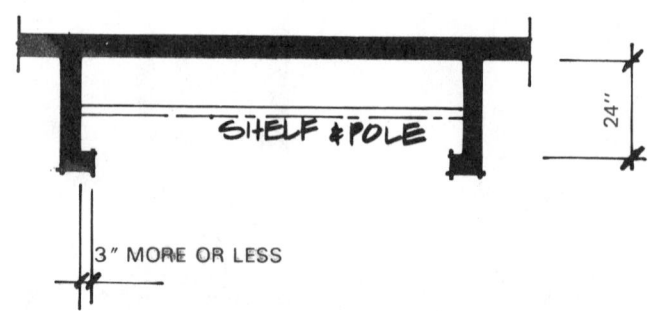

Figure 15–50 Standard wardrobe closet.

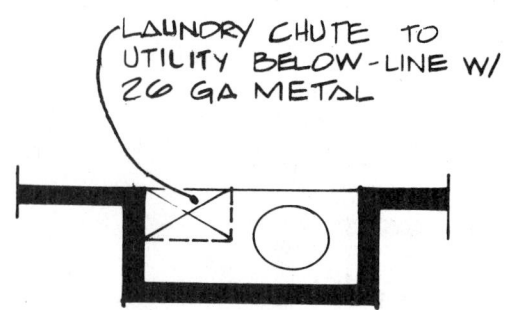

Figure 15–51 Laundry chute.

Figure 15–52 Room labels with floor finish material noted.

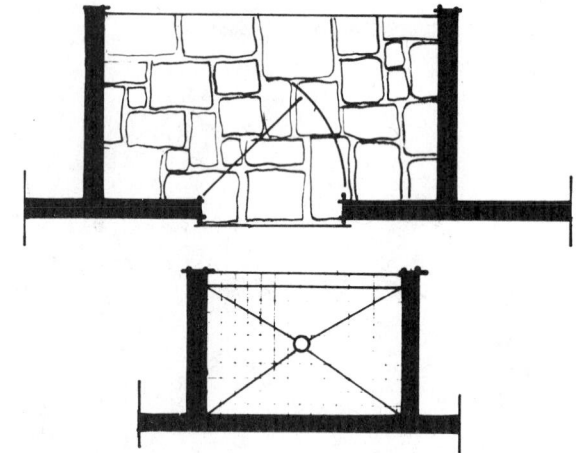

Figure 15–53 Finish material symbols.

easiest method is to label the material directly under room designation as shown in Figure 15–52. Other methods include using representative material symbols and a note to describe the finish materials as shown in Figure 15–53.

Drafting technicians with an artistic flair may draw floor-plan material symbols freehand. Other drafters may use adhesive material symbols that are available in sheet form. You use this product by

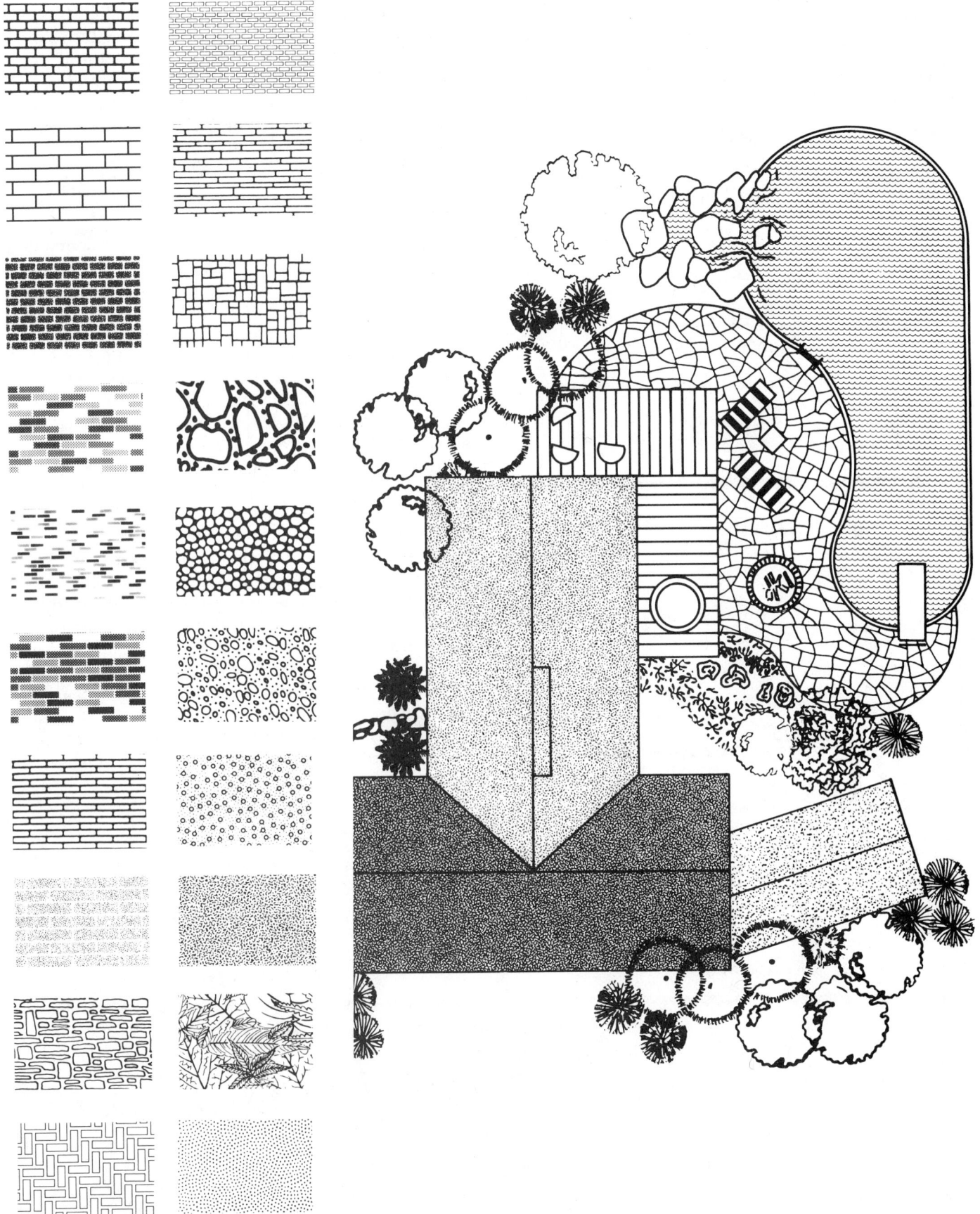

Figure 15-54 Adhesive patterns for finish materials. *Courtesy Chartpak.*

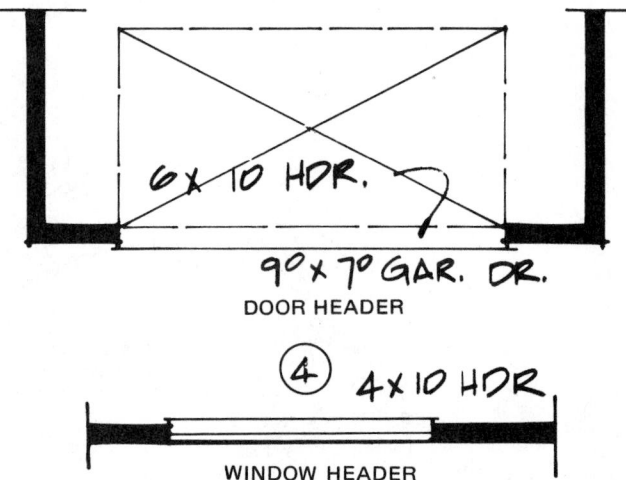

Figure 15–55 Header representations and notes.

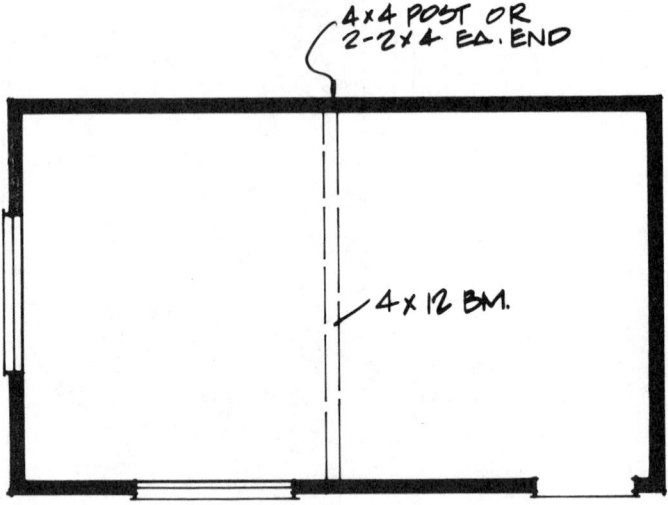

Figure 15–56 Beam and post representation and note.

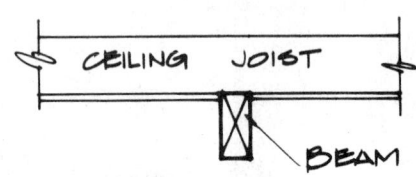

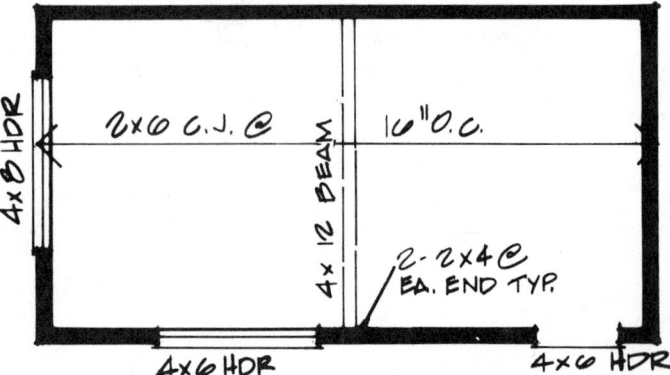

Figure 15–57 Identification of joists and joists over beam.

removing a section of the sheet that is slightly larger than the area to be covered. Then, with a sharp knife, cut away the extra material. Be careful to cut only the symbol material and not your drawing original. Remove the symbol material from areas where the pattern is not needed then firmly press the pattern onto the desired area. Figure 15–54 shows some patterns that are available.

Structural Materials

Structural materials are identified on floor plans with notes and symbols. The symbolic representation of a specific header size over a garage door opening is a dashed line as are all overhead fixtures. See Figure 15–55. Other specific header sizes may be shown as a note over a window as in Figure 15–55.

Ceiling beams, when shown on a floor plan, are generally shown with dashed lines and labeled as shown in Figure 15–56. Construction members, such as beams, joists, rafters, or headers that are labeled on the floor plan are considered to be at the ceiling level unless otherwise specified.

Ceiling joists, trusses, or roof joists for a vaulted ceiling are identified in the floor plan with an arrow that shows the direction and extent of the span. Ceilings are generally considered to be flat unless specified as vaulted, which denotes a sloping ceiling. The size and spacing of the members are noted along the arrow, as shown in Figure 15–57. Notice in the section at the beam in Figure 15–57 that the ceiling joists go over the beam which leaves the beam exposed. The exposed beam may be made of quality material for a natural appearance or it may be wrapped with sheetrock or other material for a finished appearance.

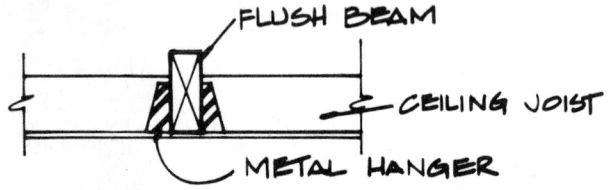

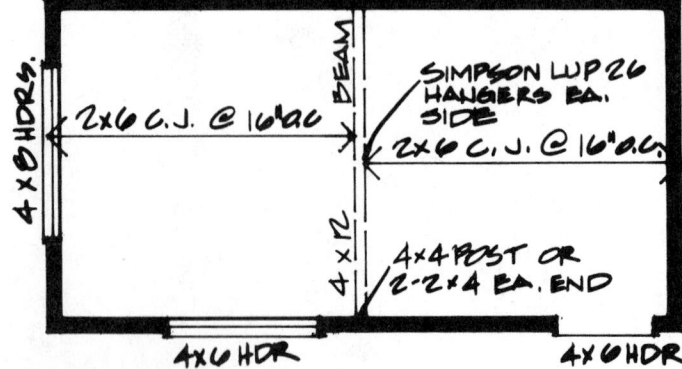

Figure 15–58 Joist hangers used at beam for a flush ceiling.

When it is not desirable to have a beam exposed in the room the joists should intersect flush with the bottom of the beam. To accomplish such an intersection, steel joist hangers are often used as labeled in Figure 15–58. When the joists span the shortest distance across a room from one bearing wall to another and no beam is needed for central support, then you have a situation similar to Figure 15–59.

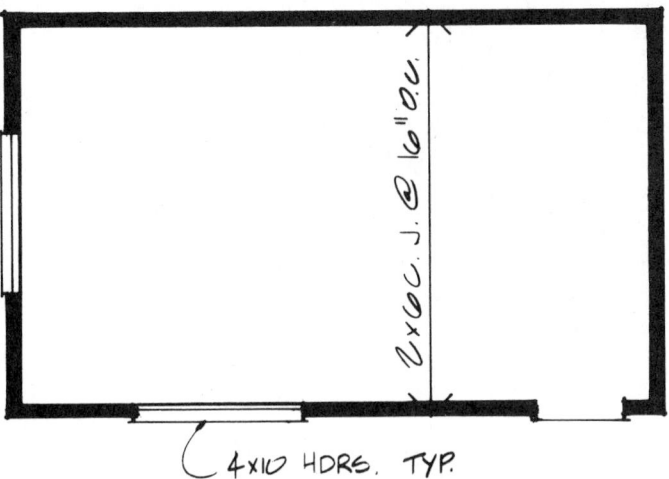

Figure 15–59 Noting ceiling joists, roof joists, or trusses at shortest span.

There are a number of structural connectors that can be used in residential construction to connect joists to walls. The best thing to do is obtain a vendor's catalog from a company that manufactures structural connectors and become familiar with the many construction methods that are shown as examples in the catalog.

All construction members that relate directly to the floor plan but are not clearly identified in cross sections or details must be drawn and labeled on the floor plan. There is a great deal of information that must be included and it is often difficult to include all the necessary data without crowding the drawing. If you are in doubt whether or not an item is clearly identified, then be sure to add it to your drawing. It is better to be too clear than to omit some important information.

STAIRS

Stair Planning

The design of a multistory home is often made complex by the need to plan stairs. Figure 15–60 shows several common flights of stairs. Stairs should be conveniently located for easy access. Properly

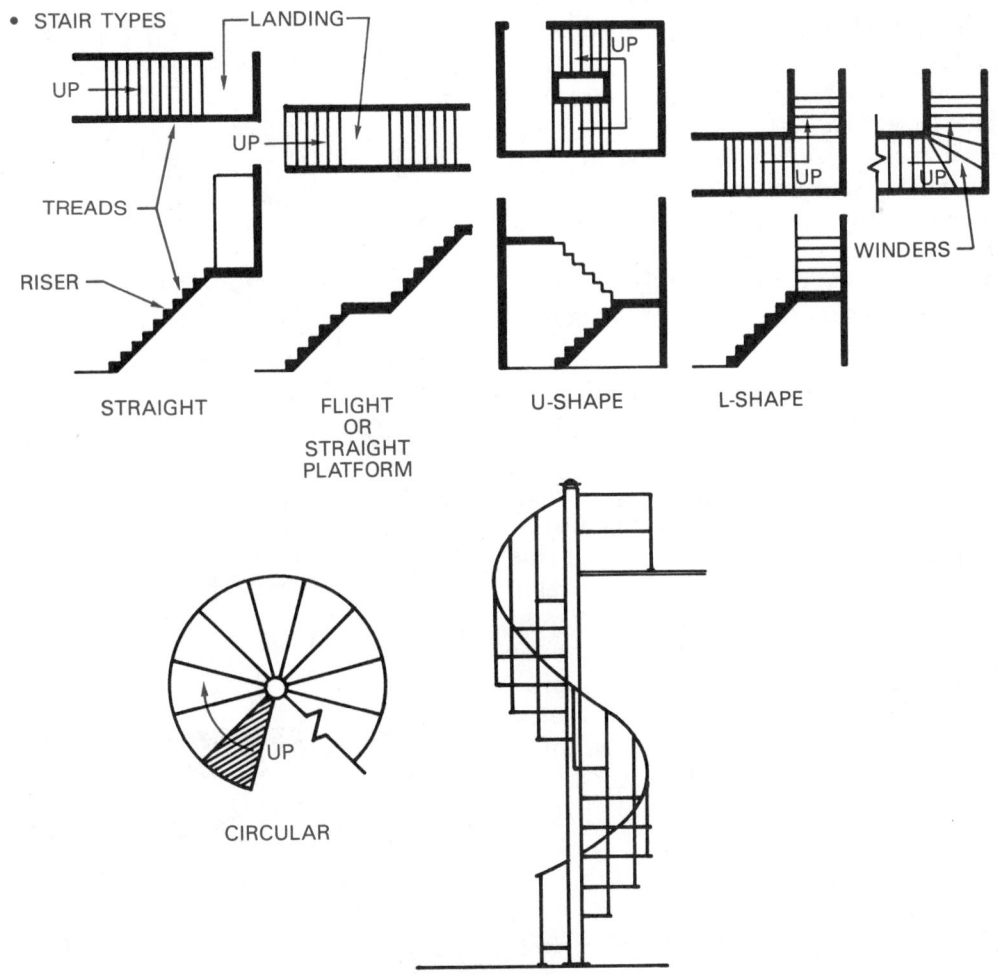

Figure 15–60 Stair types.

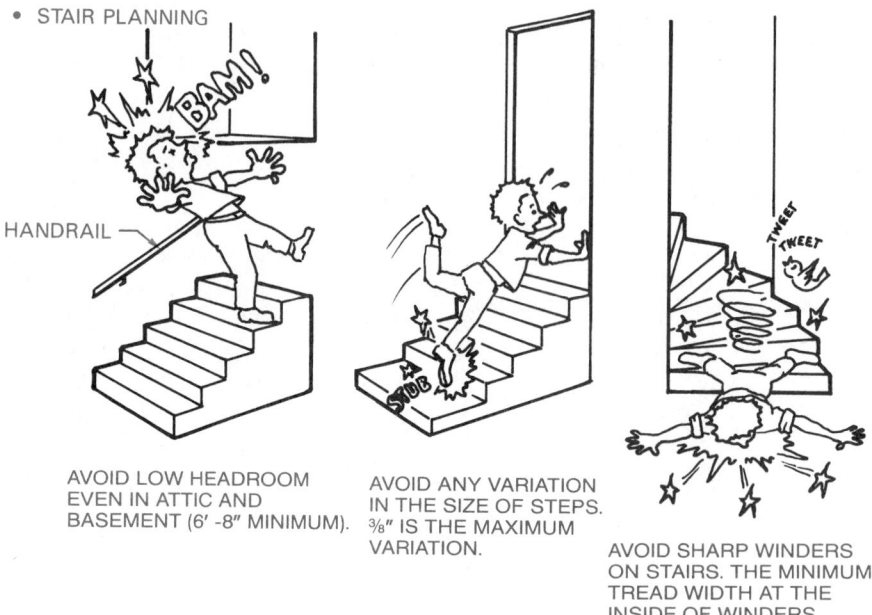

Figure 15–61 Stair design considerations.

designed stairs have several important characteristics based on CABO requirements:

- Minimum stair width is 30 in. but 36 to 48 in. is preferred.
- Stair tread length should be 10 to 12 in. with 9 in. minimum.
- Individual risers may range between 7 and 8¼" in. in height. Risers should not vary more than ⅜ in. A comfortable riser height is 7¼ in.
- Landings at the top and bottom of stairs should be at least equal in size to the width of the stairs.
- A clear height of 6'–8" is the minimum amount of headroom required for the length of the stairs. A height of 7 ft is preferred.

See Figure 15–61. These characteristics along with stair calculation and construction are discussed in detail in Chapter 31.

Handrails are placed at a blank wall along a flight of stairs to be used for support while going up or down. Handrails should run the whole length of the stairs even though the stairs are enclosed between two walls. Stairs with over three risers require handrails. Guardrails are placed where there is no protective wall. They serve the dual purpose of protecting people from falling off the edge of the stairs and providing a rail for support. Stair wells, or stair openings in the floor, should be enclosed with strong railings extending 6 in. past the edge of the first step. See Figure 15–62.

Stairs on Floor Plans

Stairs are shown on floor plans by the width of the tread, the direction and number of risers, and

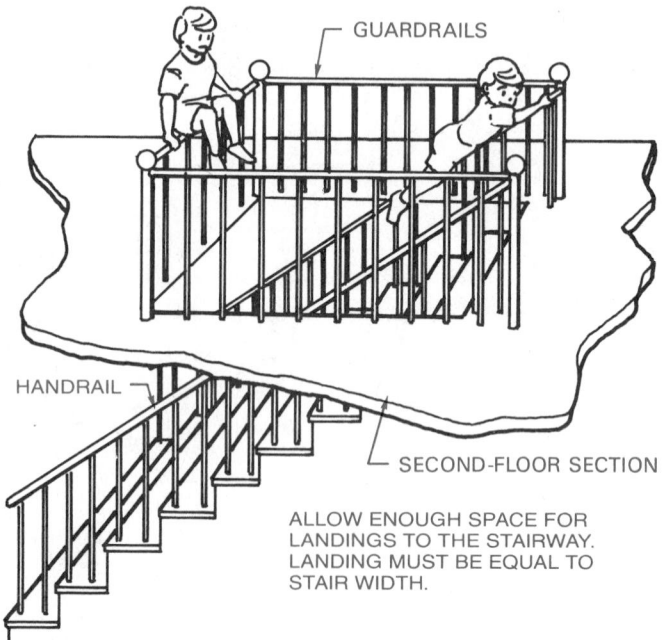

Figure 15–62 Stair design considerations.

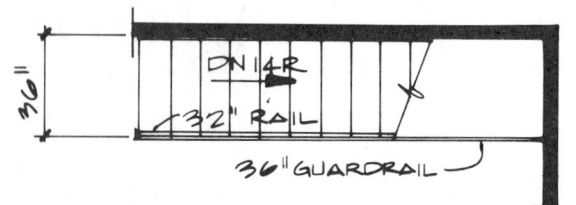

Figure 15–63 Stairs with a wall on one side and a guardrail on the other.

Figure 15–64 Stairs with guardrails all around.

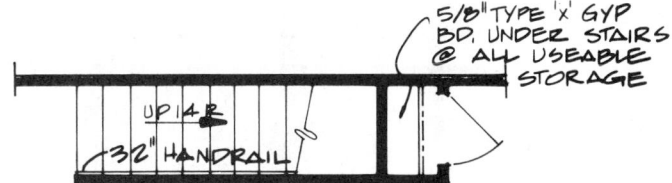

Figure 15–65 Stairs between two walls.

the lengths of handrails or guardrails. Abbreviations used are DN for down, UP for up, and R for risers. A note of 14R would mean there are 14 risers in the flight of stairs.

Stair layout depends upon the amount of space available. There is always one less run than rise. Run is the individual tread and rise is each individual riser. Consider the average set of stairs to have 14 risers. To figure the length of stairs, multiply the length of a tread by the number of runs. For example, stairs with 14 risers have 13 runs. If each individual run is 10 in. then $10'' \times 13 = 130''$ or $10'-10''$. Keep in mind that landings take up more space and they should be as long as the stairs are wide. If a 36 in. wide stairway should have a landing, the landing should measure $36'' \times 36''$.

Figure 15–63 shows a common straight stair layout with a wall on one side and a guardrail on the other. Figure 15–64 shows a flight of stairs with guardrails all around at the top level and a handrail running down the stairs. Figure 15–65 shows stairs between two walls. Notice also that the stairs are drawn broken with a long break line at approximately mid-height. Figure 15–66 shows parallel stairs with one flight going up and the other down. This situation is common when access from the main floor to both the second floor and basement is designed for the same area.

Stairs with winders and spiral stairs may be used to conserve space. Winders are used to turn a corner instead of a landing. They must not be any smaller than 6 in. at the smallest dimension. Spiral stairs should be at least 30 in. wide from the center post to the outside and the center post should have a 6 in. minimum diameter. Spiral stairs and custom winding stairs may be manufactured in several designs. Figure 15–67 shows the plan view of winder and spiral stairs.

A sunken living room or family room is a popular design feature. When a room is either sunken or raised, there will be one or more steps into the room. The steps are noted with an arrow as shown in Figure 15–68. The few steps up or down do not require a handrail unless there are over three risers, but provide a handrail next to the steps when there are four or more. The guardrail shown in Figure 15–68 is for decoration only.

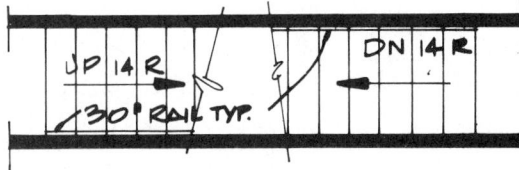

Figure 15–66 Stairs up and down in the same area.

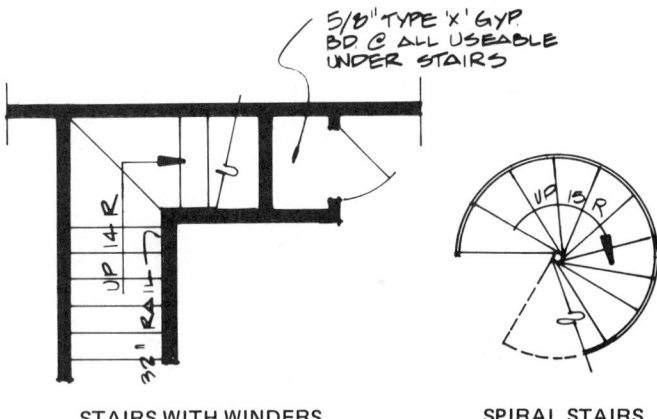

STAIRS WITH WINDERS   SPIRAL STAIRS

Figure 15–67 Winder and spiral stairs.

FIREPLACES

Floor Plan

The dimensions shown on the fireplace floor plan symbol in Figure 15–69 are minimums. Figure 15–70 shows several typical fireplace floor plan representations. Common fireplace opening sizes in inches are shown in the following table:

OPENING WIDTH	OPENING HEIGHT	UNIT DEPTH
36	24	22
40	27	22
48	30	25
60	33	25

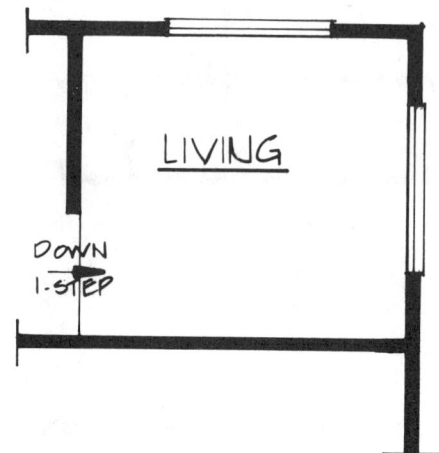

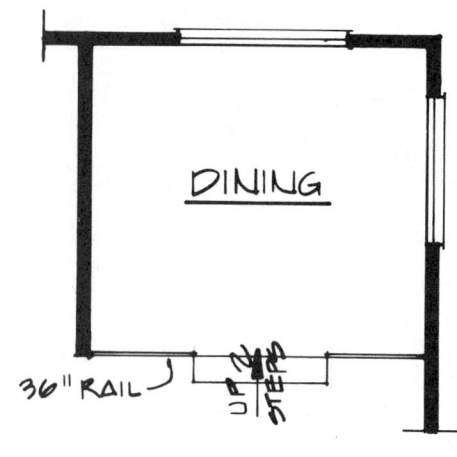

Figure 15–68 Sunken or raised rooms.

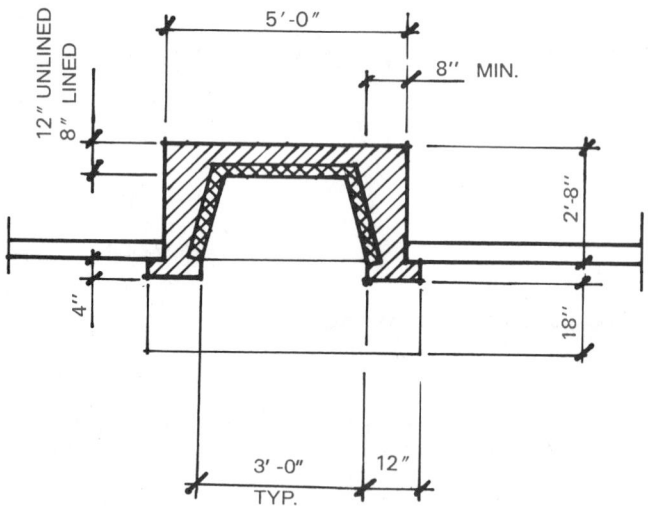

Figure 15–69 Single masonry minimum fireplace dimensions not generally shown on the plan.

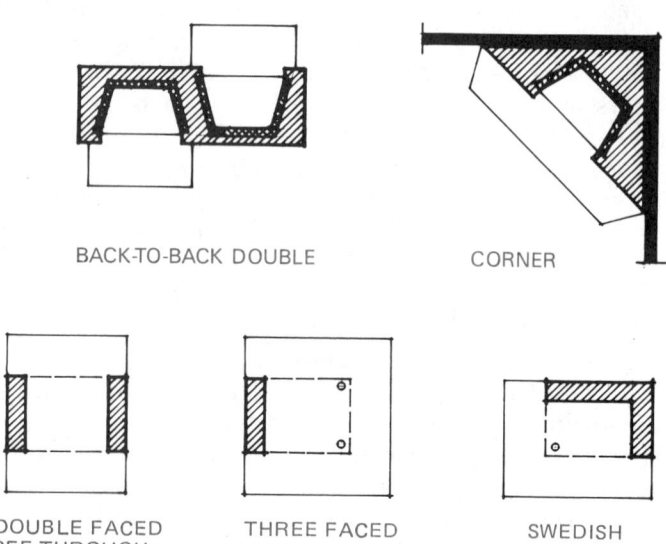

BACK-TO-BACK DOUBLE   CORNER

DOUBLE FACED
SEE THROUGH   THREE FACED   SWEDISH

Figure 15–70 Floor plan representations of typical masonry fireplace.

Steel Fireplaces

Fireplace fireboxes made of steel are available from various manufacturers. The fireplace you draw on the floor plan will look the same whether the firebox is prefabricated of steel or constructed of masonry materials. See Figure 15–71. These prefabricated fireplaces are popular because of their increased efficiency. Some units add to their efficiency with fans that are used to circulate air around the firebox and into the room. Some contractors tie the heat source of the firebox into the central heating system, but confirm the acceptability of such a practice with local building codes.

There are also insulated fireplace units made of steel that can be used with wood-framed chimneys. These units are often referred to as zero-clearance units. Zero clearance means that the insulated metal fireplace unit and flue can be placed directly adjacent to a wood-frame structure. Verify building codes and vendor's specifications before calling for its use. The popularity of these fireplaces has increased due to their low construction cost as compared to masonry fireplace and chimney construction. See Figure 15–72. Figure 15–73 shows some common sizes of fireplace units that are available.

Wood Storage

Fireplace wood may be stored near the fireplace. A special room or an area in a garage adjacent to the fireplace may be ideal. A wood compartment built into the masonry next to a fireplace opening may also be provided for storing a small amount of wood. The floor-plan representation of such a wood storage box is shown in Figure 15–74.

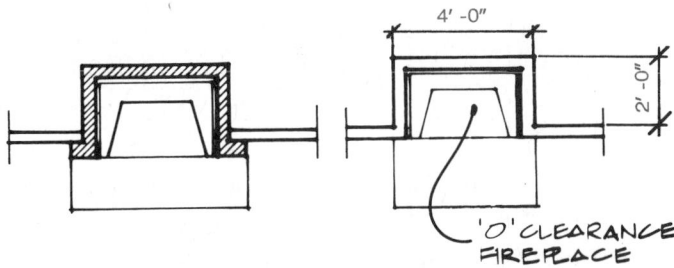

Figure 15–71 Manufactured firebox framed in masonry.

Figure 15–72 Manufactured firebox in wood frame.

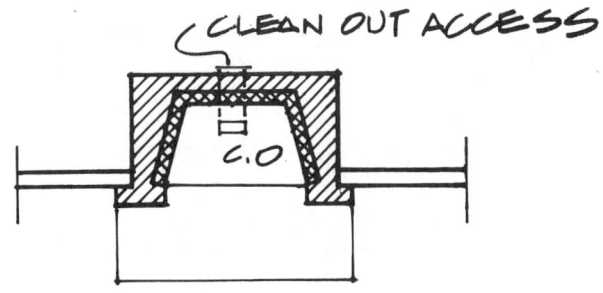

Figure 15–75 Fireplace cleanout.

DIMENSION A OPENING SIZE IN INCHES
28
32
36
40
48
60

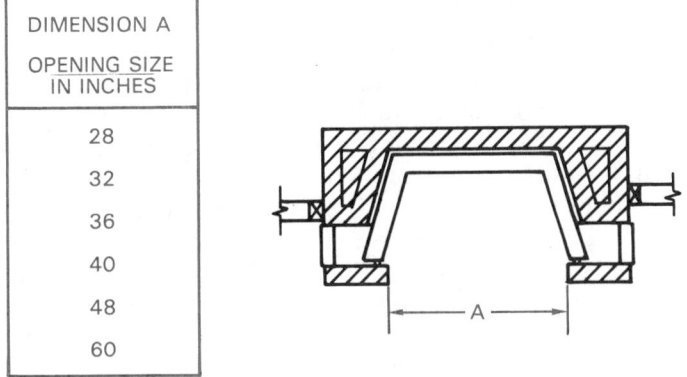

Figure 15–73 Prefabricated fireplace opening sizes. Courtesy Heatilator, Inc.

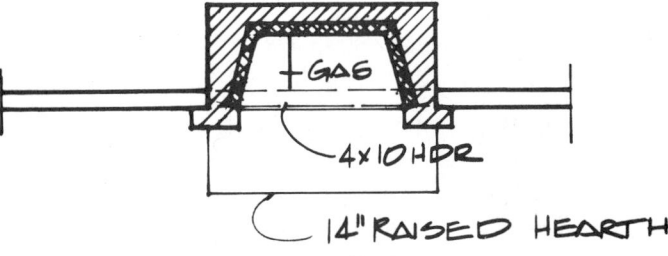

Figure 15–76 Gas supply to fireplace.

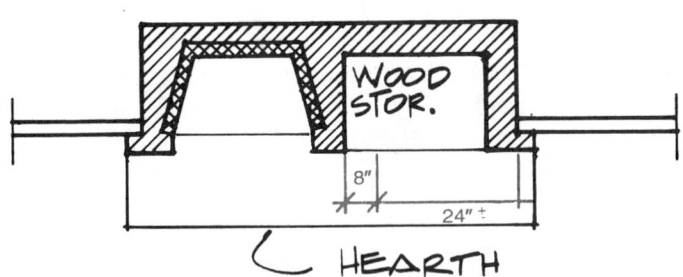

Figure 15–74 Wood storage.

Fireplace Cleanout

When you can provide easy access to the base of the fireplace, provide a cleanout (CO). The cleanout is a small door in the floor of the fireplace firebox that allows ashes to be dumped into a hollow cavity built into the fireplace below the floor. Access to the fireplace cavity to remove the stored ashes is provided from the basement or outside the house. Figure 15–75 shows a fireplace cleanout noted in the plan view.

Combustion Air

Building codes require that combustion air be provided to the fireplace. Combustion air is outside air supplied in sufficient quantity for fuel combustion. The air is supplied through a screened duct that is built by masons from the outside into the fireplace combustion chamber. By providing outside air, this venting device will prevent the fireplace from using the heated air from the room thus maintaining indoor oxygen levels and keeping heated air from going up the chimney. A note should be placed on the floor plan next to the fireplace that states the following: PROVIDE OUTSIDE COMBUSTION AIR TO WITHIN 24″, or PROVIDE SCREENED CLOSABLE VENT TO OUTSIDE AIR WITHIN 24″ OF FIREBOX.

Gas-burning Fireplace

Natural gas may be provided to the fireplace either for starting the wood fire or for fuel to provide flames on artificial logs. The gas supply should be noted on the floor plan as shown in Figure 15–76.

Built-in Masonry Barbecue

When a home has a fireplace in a room next to the dining room, nook, or kitchen, the masonry structure may also incorporate a built-in barbecue. The floor-plan representation for a barbecue is shown in Figure 15–77. A built-in barbecue may be purchased as a prefabricated unit that is set into the masonry structure that surrounds the fireplace. There may be a gas or electricity supply to the barbecue as a source of heat for cooking. As an alternative, the barbecue unit may be built into the exterior structure of a fireplace for outdoor cooking. The barbecue may also be installed separately from a fireplace although there is some cost savings when the cooking unit is combined with the fireplace structure.

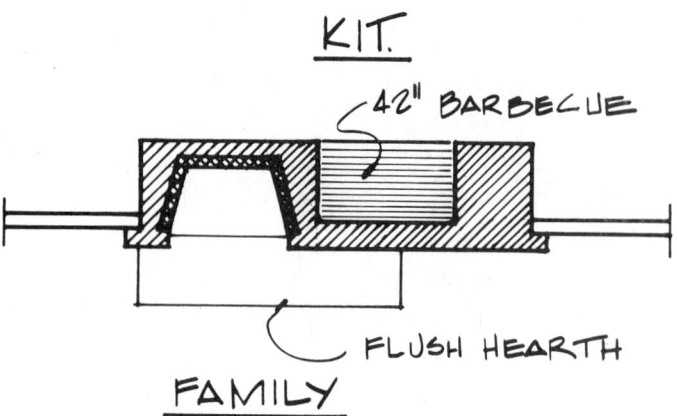

Figure 15–77 Barbecue in fireplace.

SOLID FUEL-BURNING APPLIANCES

Solid fuel-burning appliances are such items as air-tight stoves, free-standing fireplaces, fireplace stoves, room heaters, zero-clearance fireplaces, antique and homemade stoves, and fireplace inserts for existing masonry fireplaces. This discussion shows the floor plan representation and minimum distance requirements for the typical installations of some approved appliances.

Appliances that comply with nationally recognized safety standards may be noted on the floor plan with a note such as:

ICBO APPROVED WOOD STOVE AND INSTALLATION REQUIRED (ICBO = International Conference of Building Officials)

VERIFY ACTUAL INSTALLATION REQUIREMENTS WITH VENDORS' SPECIFICATIONS AND LOCAL FIRE MARSHAL OR BUILDING CODE GUIDELINES.

General Rules (Verify with Local Fire Marshal or Building Code Guidelines)

Floor Protection. Combustible floors must be protected. Floor protection material shall be noncombustible, with no cracks or holes, and strong enough not to crack, tear or puncture with normal use. Materials commonly used are brick, stone, tile or metal.

Wall Protection. Wall protection is critical whenever solid fuel-burning units are designed into a structure. Direct application of noncombustible materials will not provide adequate protection. When solid fuel-burning appliances are installed at recommended distances to combustible walls, a one-inch air space is necessary between the wall and floor to the noncombustible material, plus a bottom opening for air intake and a top opening for air exhaust to provide positive air change behind the structure. This helps reduce superheated air adjacent to combustible material, Figure 15–78. Noncombustible materials include brick, stone or tile over cement asbestos board. Minimum distances to walls should be verified in regard to vendors' specifications and local requirements.

Combustion Air. Combustion air is generally required as a screened closable vent installed within 24″ of the solid fuel-burning appliance.

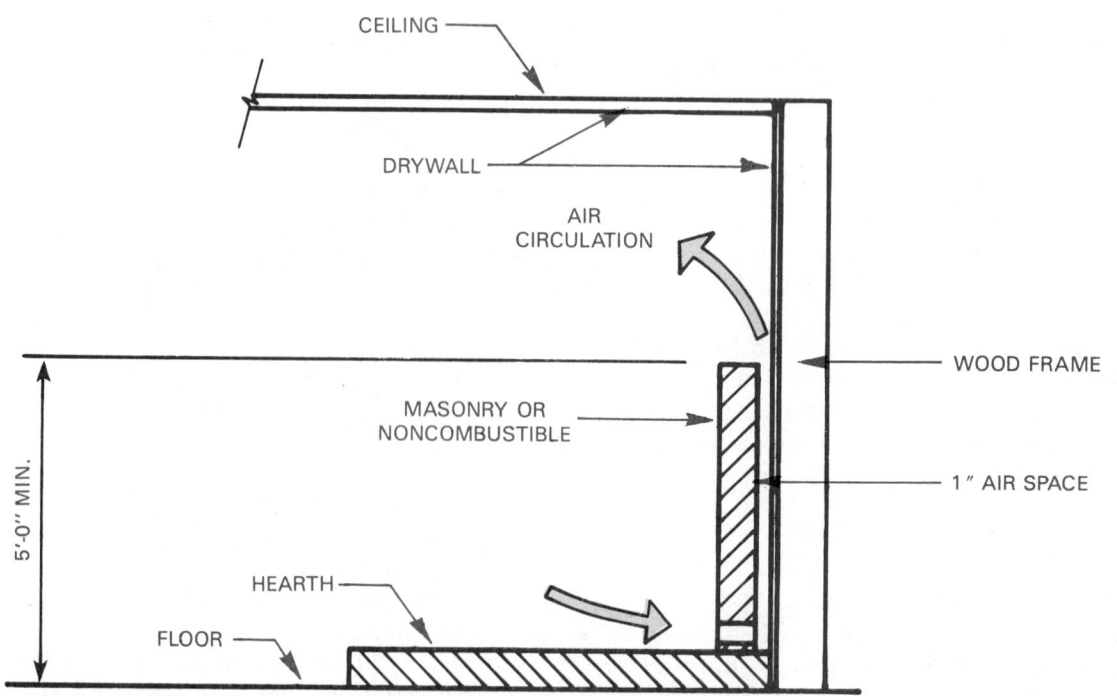

Figure 15–78 Air circulation around wall protection.

Air Pollution. Some local areas have initiated guidelines that help control air pollution from solid fuel-burning appliances. The installation of a catalytic converter or other devices may be required. Check with local regulations.

Figure 15–79 shows floor plan representations of common wood stove installations.

A current trend in housing is to construct a masonry alcove within which a solid fuel unit is installed. The floor plan layout for a typical masonry alcove is shown in Figure 15–80.

ROOM TITLES

Rooms are labeled with a name on the floor plan. Generally the lettering is larger than that used for other notes and dimensions. Room titles may be lettered using 3/16 or ¼ in. high letters as shown in Figure 15–81. Occasionally the interior dimensions of the room are lettered under the title as shown in Figure 15–82.

OTHER FLOOR-PLAN SYMBOLS

Hose Bibb

A hose bibb is an outdoor water faucet to which a garden hose may be attached. Hose bibbs should be placed at locations convenient for watering lawns or gardens and for washing a car. The floor-plan symbol for a hose bibb is shown in Figure 15–83.

Concrete Slab

Concrete slabs used for patio walks, garages, or driveways may be noted on the floor plan. A typical example would be 4″ THICK CONCRETE WALK. Concrete slabs used for the floor of a garage should slope toward the front. The slope is to allow water to drain. The amount of slope is ⅛ in./ft minimum. A garage slab is noted in Figure 15–84. Calling for a slight slope on patios and driveway aprons is also common.

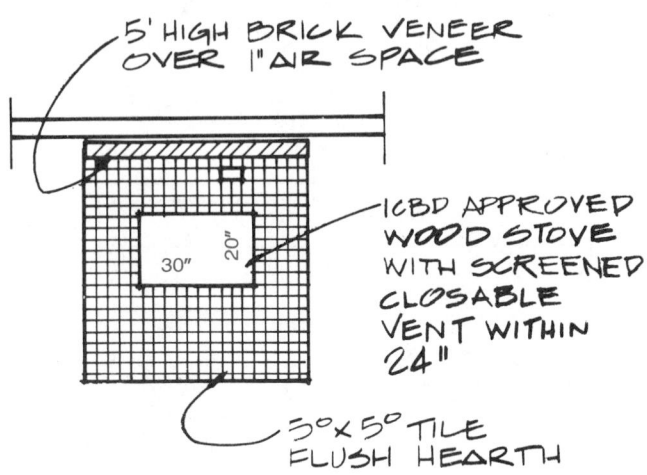

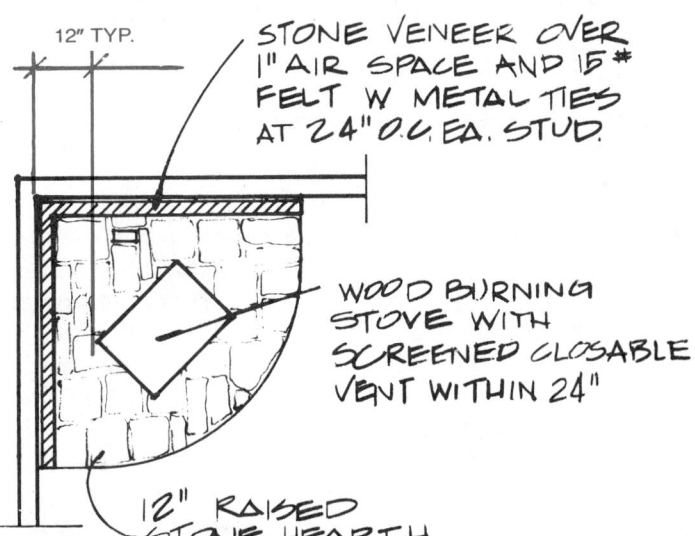

Figure 15–79 Wood stove installation.

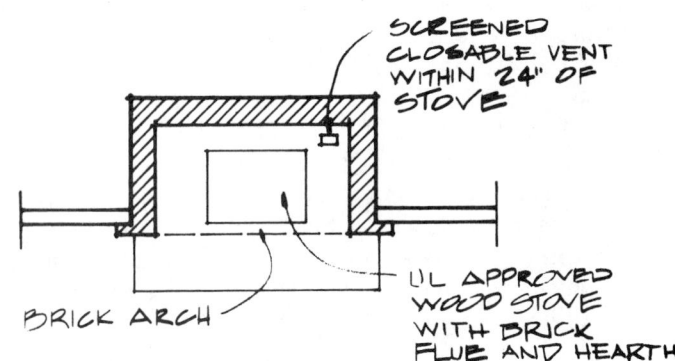

Figure 15–80 Masonry alcove for solid-fuel-burning stove.

LIVING　　BED.#1　　KIT.

Figure 15–81 Room titles.

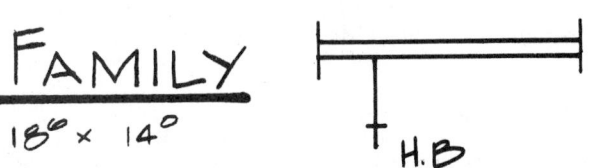

Figure 15–82 Room titles with room sizes noted.

Figure 15–83 Hose bibb symbol.

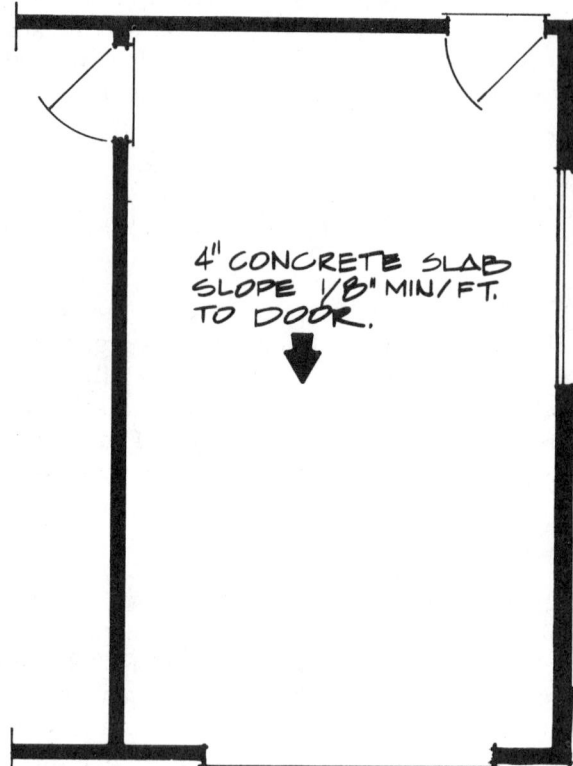

Figure 15–84 Garage slab note.

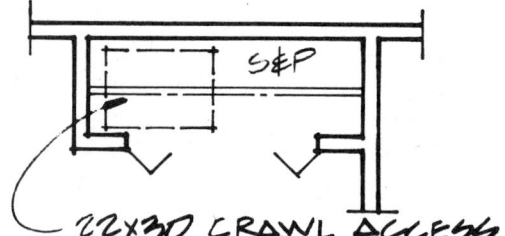

Figure 15–85 Crawl space access note.

Figure 15–86 Shower symbol showing floor drain.

Attic and Crawl Space Access

Access is necessary to attics and crawl spaces. The crawl access may be placed in any convenient location such as a closet or hallway. The minimum size of the attic access must be 22″ × 30″ as shown in Figure 15–85. The crawl access should be 22″ × 30″ if located in the floor. The attic access may include a fold-down ladder if the attic is to be used for storage. A minimum of 30″ must be provided above the attic access. Crawl space access may be shown on the foundation plan when it is constructed through the foundation wall. When in the foundation wall, the access can be 24″ × 18″.

Floor Drains

A floor drain is shown on the floor-plan symbol for a shower seen in Figure 15–86. Floor drains should be used in any location where water could accumulate on the floor such as the laundry room, bathroom, or garage. The easiest application of a floor drain is in a concrete slab floor although drains may be designed in any type of floor construction. Figure 15–87 shows a floor drain in a utility room.

Cross-section Symbol

The location on the floor plan where a cross section is taken is identified with symbols known as cutting-plane lines. These symbols place an imagi-

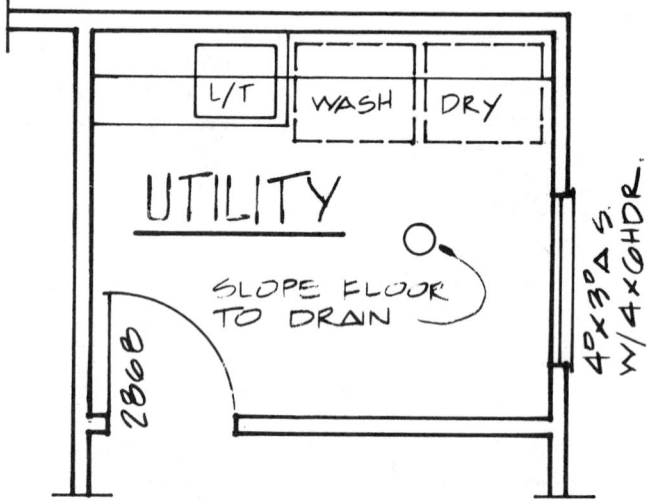

Figure 15–87 Floor drain symbol (symbol may also be square).

nary cutting plane through the house at a particular location. The cross-section view that relates to the cutting-plane line is usually found on another sheet although both views may be on the same sheet if there is room. The arrows of the cutting plane are drawn ¼″ × 3/32″ and labeled with a letter. The same letter is used to identify the cross-section view. Figure 15–88 shows a cross-section symbol (cutting-plane line). There are a number of methods used in industry to label sections. The example in Figure 15–88 is a simple version. Other methods of identifying cutting-planes and cross sections are more

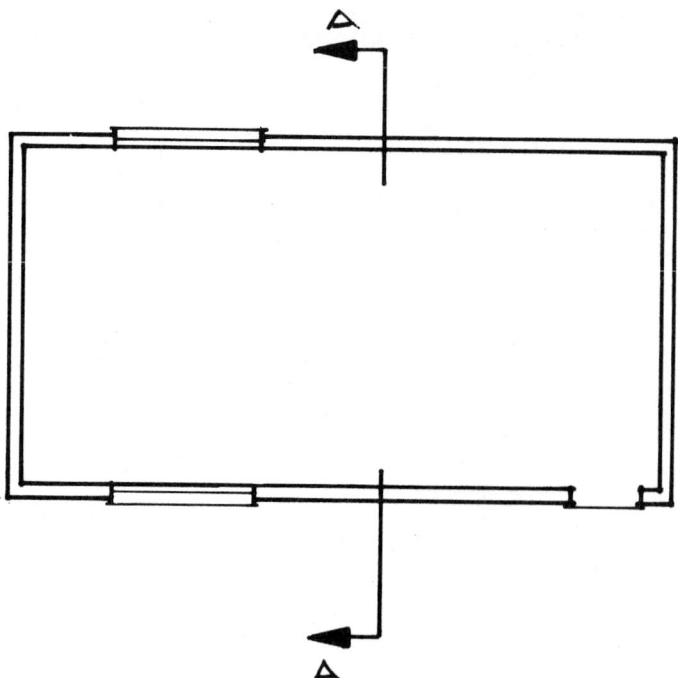

Figure 15-88 Simplified cutting-plane line symbol.

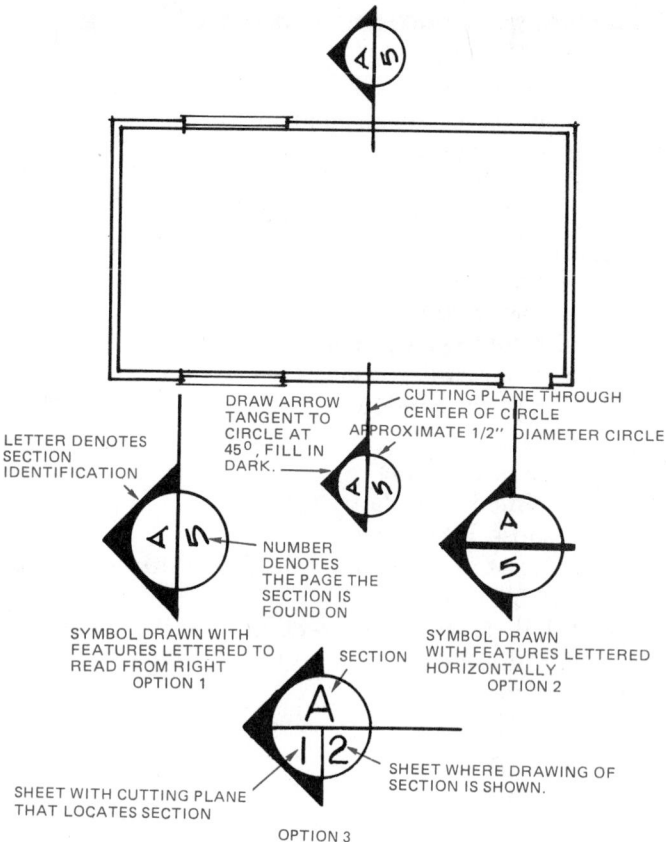

Figure 15-89 Cutting-plane symbols.

elaborate. Figure 15-89 shows three optional methods that are commonly used. The identification usually includes a letter designating the section and a number designating the drawing sheet where the letter is to be found. The identification letters and numbers may be drawn to read from the right side or bottom of the sheet. The method used depends upon company practice.

Floor plans are a key element in a complete set of architectural drawings. Clients are interested in floor plans so they can see how their future home

or business will be laid out. As you have seen in this chapter, there are a large variety of symbols and drawing techniques that go into preparing a floor plan. The challenge to the architectural drafter is to be sure to include all the necessary symbols and notes needed for construction and yet make the plan easy to read.

FLOOR-PLAN SYMBOLS TEST

DIRECTIONS

Answer the questions with short complete statements or drawings as needed on an 8½ × 11 drawing sheet as follows:

1. Use ⅛ in. guidelines for all lettering.
2. Letter your name, Floor-Plan Symbol Test, and the date at the top of the sheet.
3. Letter the question number and provide the answer. You do not need to write out the question.
4. Do all lettering with vertical uppercase architectural letters. If the answer requires line work, use proper drafting tools and technique.

Answers may be prepared on a word processor if appropriate with course guidelines.
5. Your grade will be based on correct answers and quality of line technique.

QUESTIONS

1. Exterior walls for a wood-frame residence are usually drawn how thick?
2. Interior walls are commonly drawn how thick?
3. How does the floor-plan symbol for an interior door differ from the symbol for an exterior door?

4. What are the recommended spaces required for the following?
   a. wardrobe closet depth
   b. water closet compartment
   c. stair width
   d. fireplace hearth depth
5. Describe an advantage of using schedules for windows and doors.
6. Sketch the following floor-plan symbols:
   a. pocket door
   b. bifold closet door
   c. casement window
   d. sliding window
   e. skylight
   f. ceiling beam
   g. single run stairs, up
   h. hose bibb
7. Letter the note that would properly denote a 48" high wall.
8. What is the required minimum height of guardrails?
9. Provide the appropriate note used to identify a guardrail at a balcony overlooking the living room.
10. What door would you recommend for use when space for a door swing is not available?
11. Name the window that you would recommend when a 100 percent openable unit is required.
12. What does the note 6040 next to a window on the floor plan denote?
13. Show how 2 × 8, 16" on-center ceiling joists would be properly labeled on the floor plan.
14. What is the minimum crawl space or attic access required?
15. What is the abbreviation for garbage disposal?
16. When should the clothes washer and dryer be shown with dashed lines on the floor plan?
17. Identify in short complete statements four factors to consider in stair planning.
18. Show the note used to identify the steps at a two-step sunken living room.
19. What is the amount of slope for a concrete garage floor and why should it have a slope?

Chapter 16
Floor-Plan Dimensions

ALIGNED DIMENSIONS

THE DIMENSIONING system most commonly used in architectural drafting is known as aligned dimensioning. With this system dimensions are placed in line with the dimensions lines and read from the bottom or right side of the sheet. Dimension numerals are centered on and placed above the solid dimension lines. Figure 16–1 shows a floor plan that has been dimensioned using the aligned dimensioning system.

FLOOR-PLAN DIMENSIONS

Basic Dimensioning Concepts

You should place dimensions so that the drawing does not appear crowded. Doing so is often difficult because of the great number of dimensions that must be placed on an architectural drawing. When placing dimensions, space dimension lines a minimum of ⅜ in. from the object and from each other. If there is room, ½ in. is preferred. Some drafters use 1 in. or more if space is available. Other drafting technicians place the first dimension line 1 in. away from the plan and space additional dimensions equally at ½ or ¾ in. apart. The minimum recommended spacing

of dimensions is shown in Figure 16–2. Regardless of distance chosen, be consistent so that dimension lines are evenly spaced.

Extension and dimension lines are drawn thin and dark. They are drawn in this manner so they do not distract from the overall appearance and balance of the drawing. Dimension lines terminate at extension lines with dots, arrowheads, or slash marks that are each drawn in the same direction. See Figure 16–3.

Dimension numerals are drawn ⅛ in. high with the aid of guidelines. The dimension units used are feet and inches for all lengths over 12 in. Inches and fractions are used for units less than 12 in. Foot units are followed by the symbol (′) and inch units are shown with the symbol (″). Some drawing dimensions may not use the foot and inch symbols if company standards are to omit them.

Exterior Dimensions

The overall dimensions on frame construction are understood to be given to the outside of the stud frame of the exterior walls. The reason for locating dimensions on the outside of the stud frame is that the frame is established first and windows, doors, and partitions are usually put in place before sheathing and other wall covering material is applied. The first line of dimensions on the plan is the smallest distance from the exterior wall to the center of windows, doors, and partition walls. The second line of dimensions generally gives the distance from the outside walls to partition centers. The third line of dimensions is usually the overall distance between two exterior walls. See Figure 16–4. This method of applying dimensions eliminates the need for workers

235

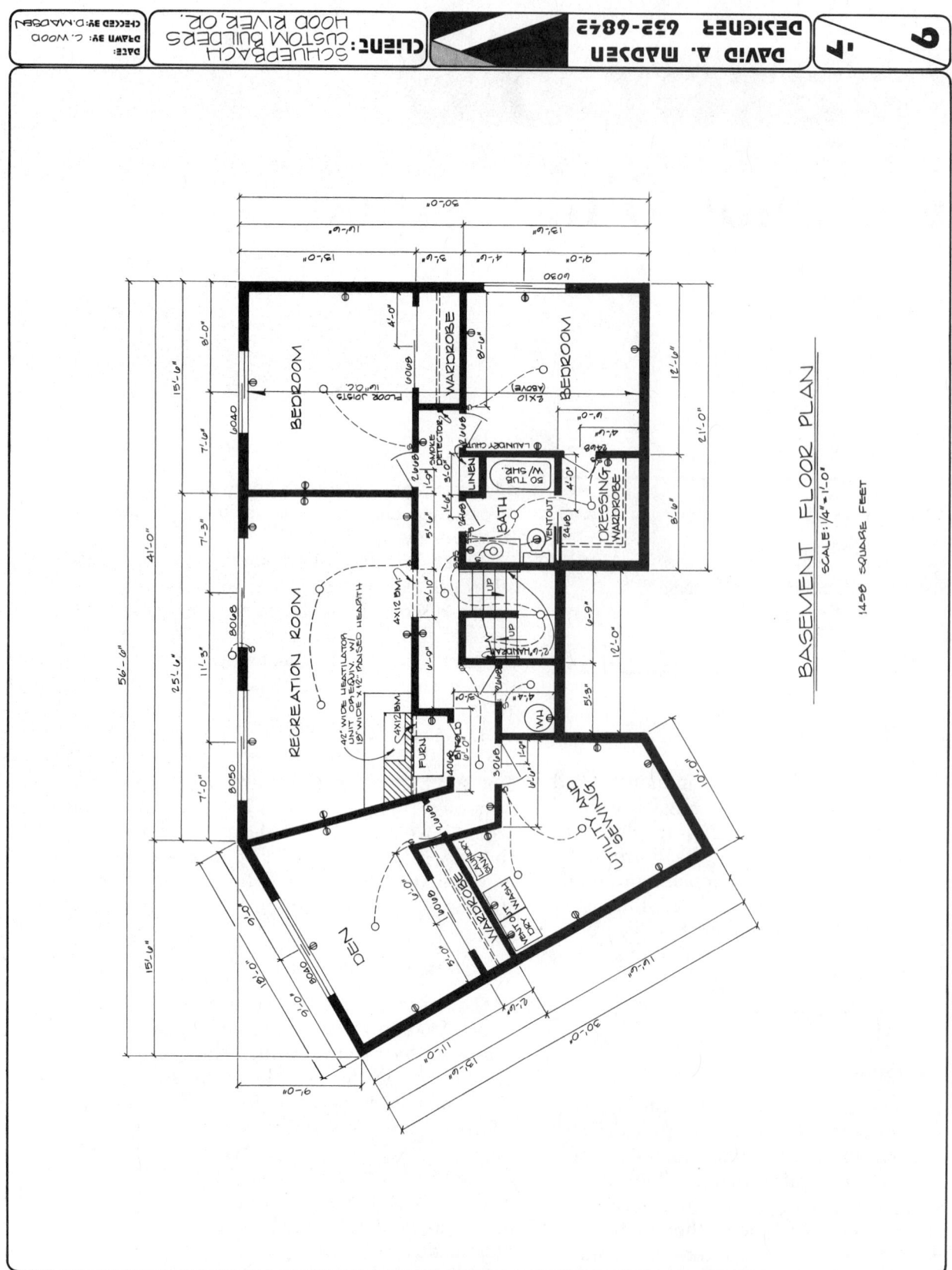

Figure 16–1 Aligned dimensions on a floor plan. *Courtesy Madsen Designs.*

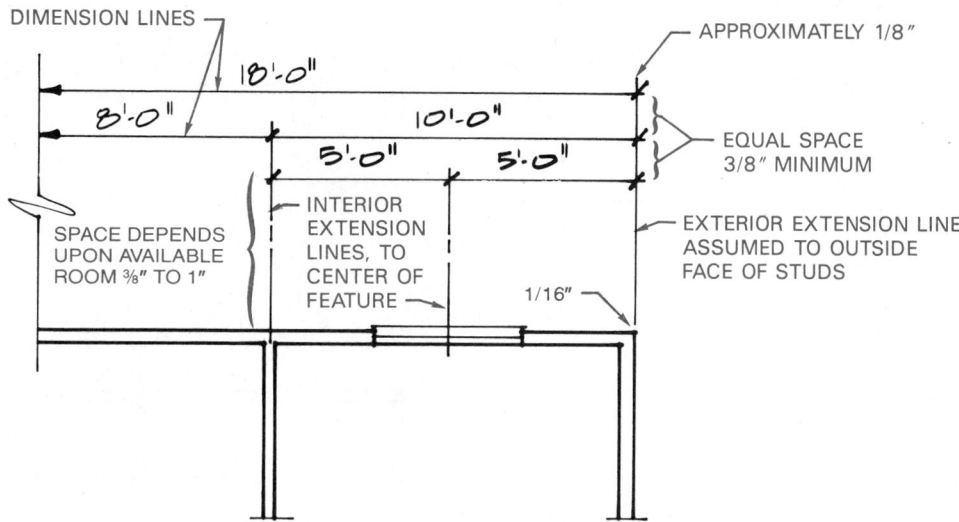

Figure 16–2 Dimension line spacing.

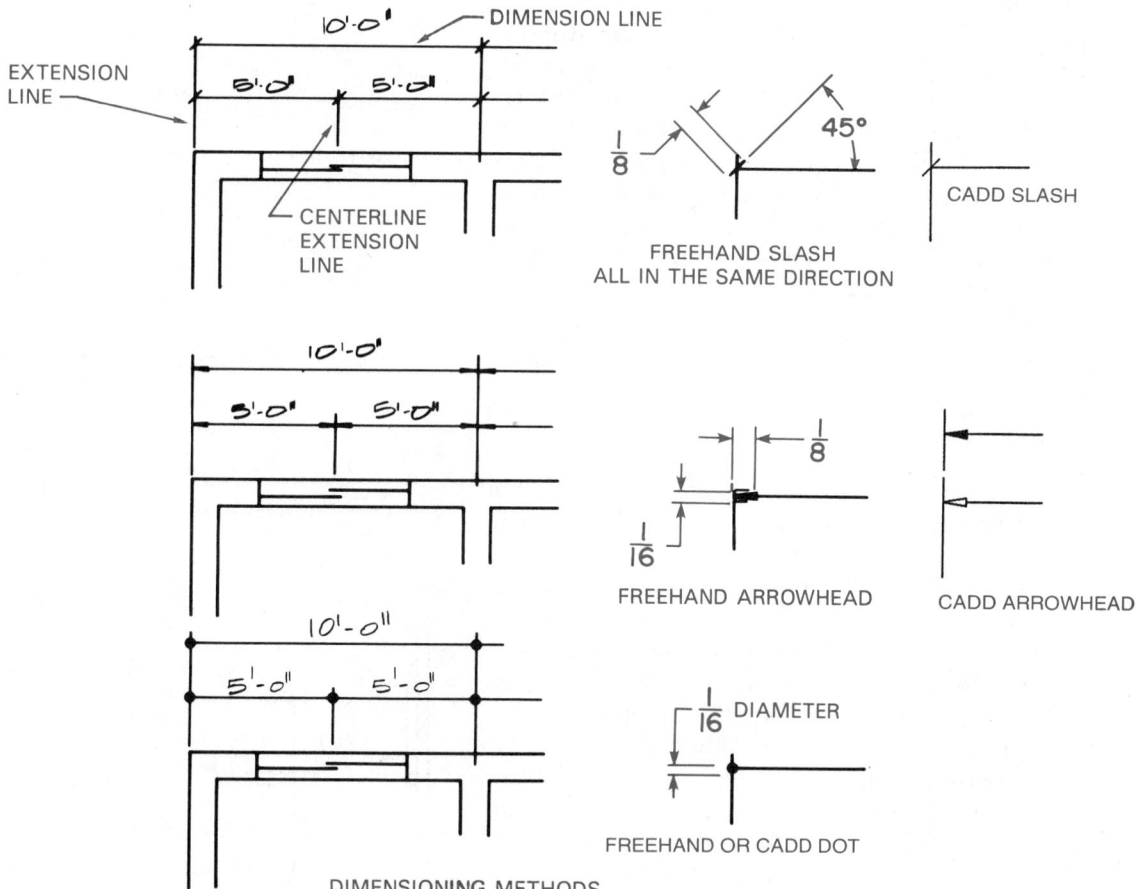

DIMENSIONING METHODS

Figure 16–3 Terminating dimension lines.

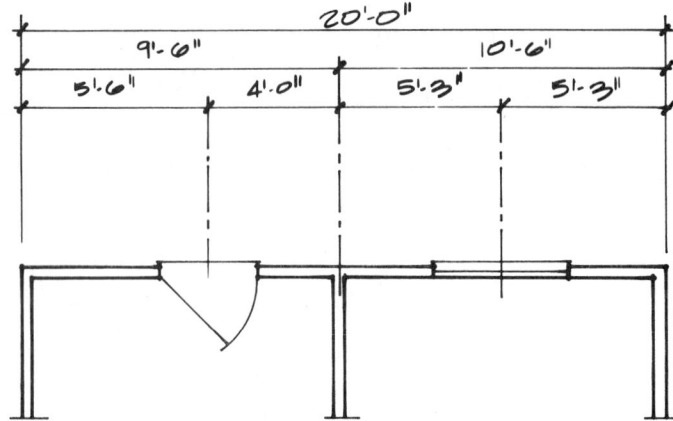

Figure 16-4 Exterior dimensions.

to add dimensions at the job site and reduces the possibility of making an error.

Interior Dimensions

Interior dimensions will locate all interior partitions and features in relationship to exterior walls. Figure 16-5 shows some common interior dimensions. Notice how they relate to the outside walls. Notice also that wall shading is omitted so that dimension lines that cross walls or measure to the centerline of partitions can be seen easily. When dimensioning interior features, ask yourself if you have provided workers with enough dimensions to build the house. The contractor should not have to guess where a wall or feature should be located. Nor should workers ever have to use a scale to try to locate items on a plan.

Standard Features

Some interior features that are considered to be standard sizes may not require dimensions. Figure 16-6 shows a situation where the drafter elected not to dimension the depth of the pantry since it is directly adjacent to a refrigerator which has an assumed depth of 30 in. Notice that the refrigerator width is given because there are many different widths available. The base cabinet is not dimensioned as they are typically 24 in. deep. When there is any doubt, it is better to apply a dimension. The refrigerator and other appliances may be drawn with dashed lines or marked with the abbreviation NIC (not in contract) if the unit will not be supplied according to the contract for the home being constructed. Follow the practice of the architect's office in which you work.

Other situations where dimensions may be assumed are when a door is centered between two

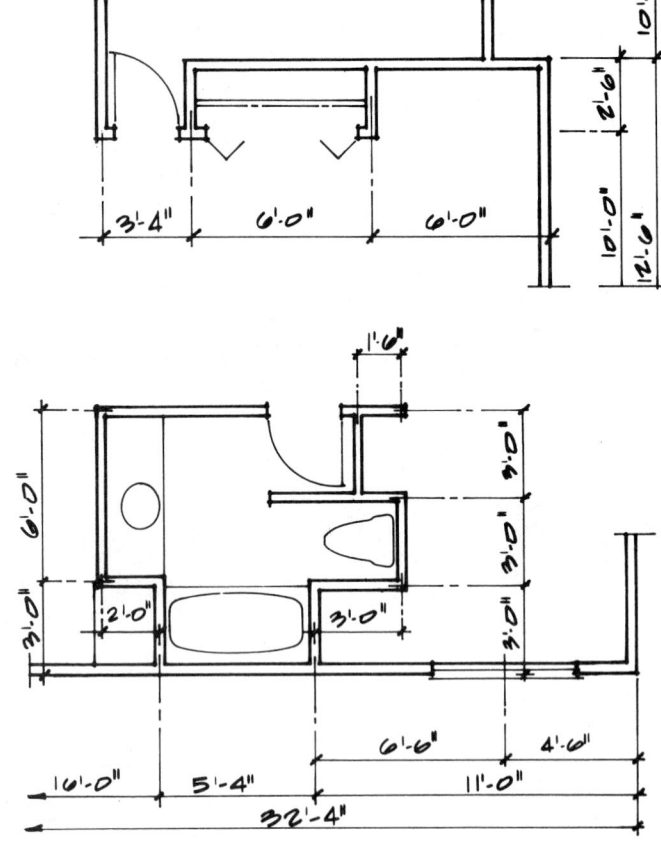

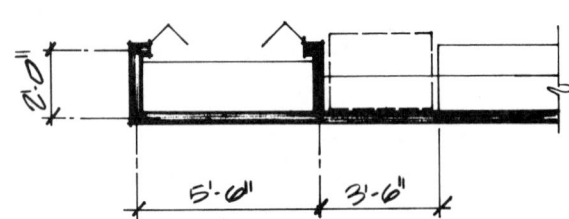

Figure 16-5 Interior dimensions.

Figure 16-6 Assumed dimensions.

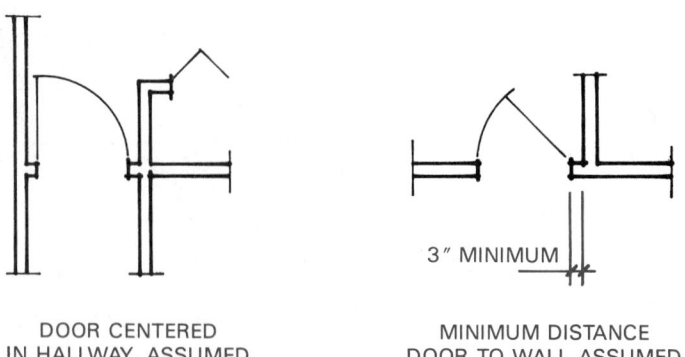

DOOR CENTERED
IN HALLWAY, ASSUMED

3″ MINIMUM

MINIMUM DISTANCE
DOOR TO WALL ASSUMED

Figure 16-7 Assumed location of features without dimensions given.

walls as at the end of a hallway, or when a door enters a room and the minimum distance from the wall to the door is assumed. See the examples in Figure 16–7. Some dimensions may be provided in the form of a note for standard features as seen in Figure 16–8. The walls around a shower need not be dimensioned when the note, 36″ square shower, defines the inside dimensions. The shower must be located, however.

One of the best ways to learn how experienced drafters lay out dimensions is to study and evaluate existing plans.

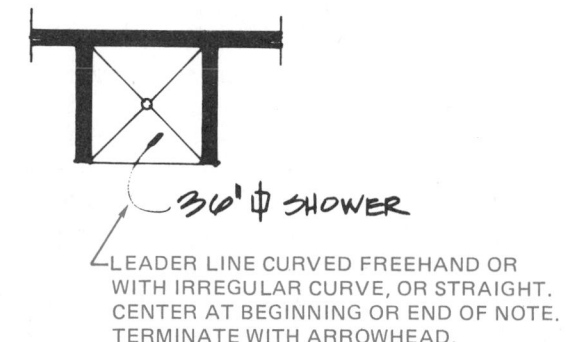

Figure 16–8 Standard features dimensioned with a specific note.

PLACING ARCHITECTURAL DIMENSIONS WITH CADD

Most CADD architectural dimensions automatically terminate with tick marks, which are popular in architectural drafting. Many architectural drafters prefer to use the tick mark for all dimensions and then change to another format, such as an arrow option, for all leader-line terminators. Figure 1 shows an example of each type of dimension-line terminator.

Architectural dimensions are commonly placed using the continuous, or point-to-point, dimensioning method. Most architectural CADD programs allow this to happen automatically. When you pick the DIMENSION command, the computer prompts you to select either vertical, horizontal, or aligned dimensioning. Aligned dimensions are placed in alignment with an angled wall or feature. After you make this selection you are asked for the first extension-line location. All you have to do is pick the origin of the first extension line. The program automatically places the traditional small gap between the building and the beginning of the extension line. Next you are asked to pick the second extension line location followed by the dimension line location. Now the computer automatically draws the extension lines, dimension line, tick marks, and places the dimension text. After the first dimension is placed, the computer asks you to pick the next extension line location. The second dimension is automatically placed, and this procedure continues until all dimensions are drawn as shown in Figure 2. The CADD drawing is extremely accurate. If you draw the walls or other features where they are supposed to be, then the dimensions are perfect every time.

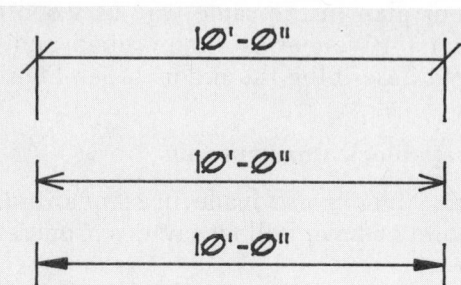

Figure 1 Examples of dimension line terminators.

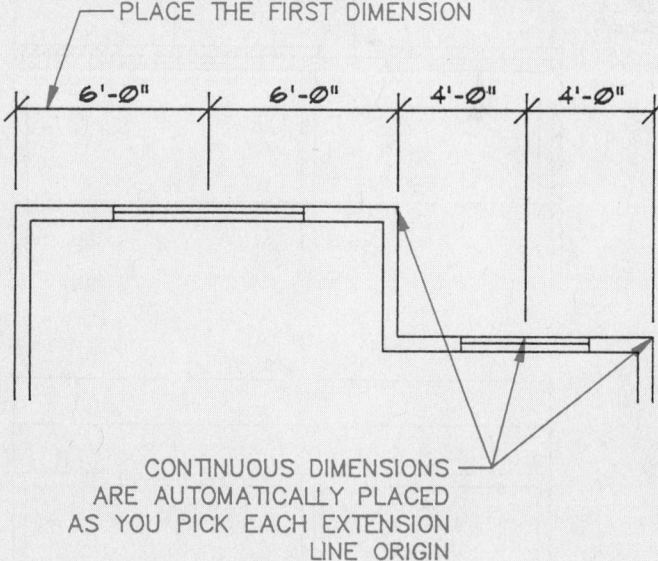

Figure 2 CADD drawing with completed dimensions.

Notes, specifications, and titles are easily drawn with CADD. All you have to do is select the TEXT command, pick the desired location for the text, and type the desired information. Some examples of CADD notes are shown in Figure 16–12.

DIMENSIONING FLOOR-PLAN FEATURES

Masonry Veneer

The dimensioning discussion thus far has provided examples of floor-plan dimensioning for wood-framed construction. Other methods of residential construction include masonry veneer, concrete block, and solid concrete. Masonry veneer construction is the application of thin masonry, such as stone or brick, to the exterior of a wood-framed structure. This kind of construction provides a long-lasting, attractive exterior. Masonry veneer may also be applied to interior frame partitions where the appearance of stone or brick is desired. Brick or stone may cover an entire wall that contains a fireplace, for example. Occasionally either material may be applied to the lower half of a wall and another material extend to the ceiling for a contrasting decorative effect. Masonry veneer construction is dimensioned on the floor plan in the same way as wood framing except that the veneer is dimensioned and labeled with a note describing the product. See Figure 16–9.

Concrete-block Construction

Concrete blocks are made in standard sizes and may be solid or have hollow cavities. Concrete block

may be used to construct exterior or interior walls of residential or commercial structures. Some concrete blocks have a textured or sculptured surface to provide a pleasant exterior appearance. Most concrete-block construction must be covered such as by masonry veneer for a finished look. Some structures use concrete block for the exterior bearing walls and wood-framed construction for interior partitions.

Dimensioning concrete-block construction is different from wood-framed construction in that each wall, partition, and window and door opening is dimensioned to the edge of the feature as shown in Figure 16–10. While this method is most common, some drafters do prefer to dimension the concrete-block structure in the same way as wood-framed construction. To do so they must add specific information in notes or section views about wall thicknesses and openings.

Solid Concrete Construction

Solid concrete construction is used in residential and commercial structures. In residences it is mostly limited to basements and subterranean homes. Concrete is poured into forms that mold the mixture to the shape desired. When the concrete cures (hardens) the forms are removed and the structure is complete.

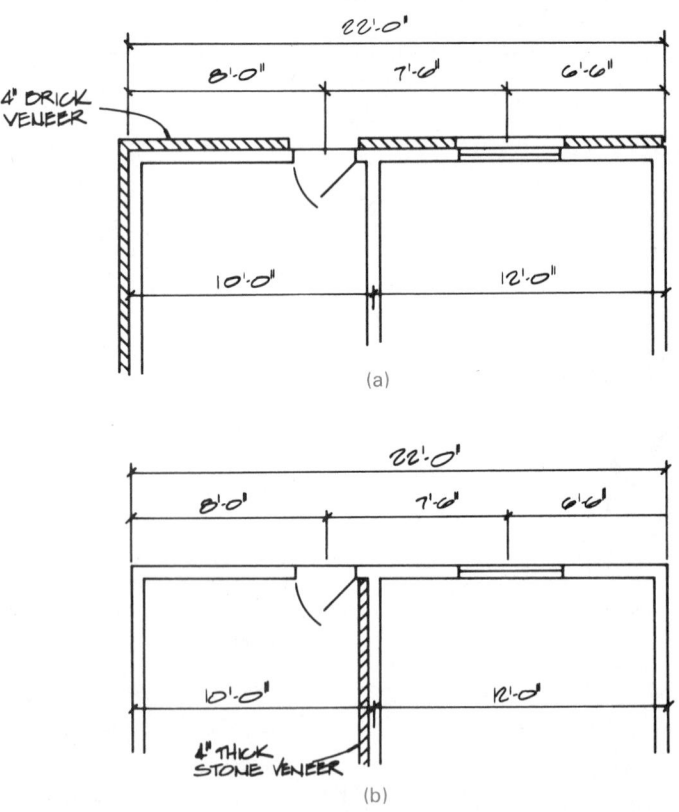

Figure 16–9 Dimensioning (a) brick; (b) stone veneer construction.

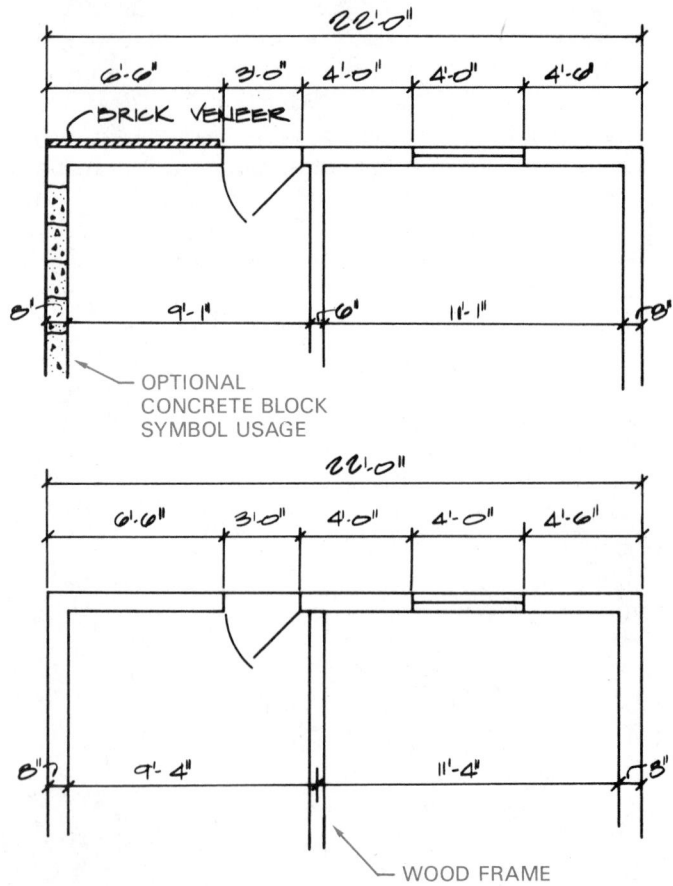

Figure 16–10 Dimensioning concrete-block construction.

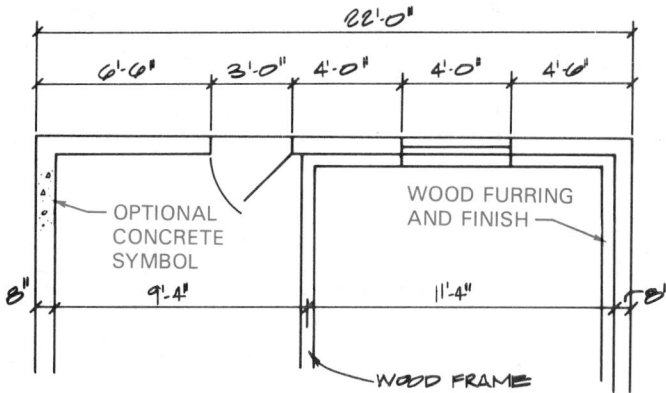

Figure 16–11 Dimensioning solid concrete construction.

Masonry veneer may be placed on either side of concrete walls for appearance. Wood framing and typical interior finish materials may also be added to the inside of concrete walls. The wood framing attached to the concrete walls is in the form of furring which is usually nailed in place with special nails. Standard interior finish materials such as drywall or paneling may be added to the furring. Solid concrete construction is typically dimensioned the same as concrete-block construction. See Figure 16–11.

More information about covering masonry and concrete construction in a residence will be found in Chapters 26 through 28.

NOTES AND SPECIFICATIONS

Notes on plans are either specific or general. Specific notes relate to specific features within the floor plan such as the header size over a window opening. The specific note is often connected to the feature with a leader line. Specific notes are also called local notes since they identify isolated features. Common information that should be specified in the form of local notes.

1. Window schedule. Place all windows in a schedule. Group by type (sldg, fixed, awning, etc.) from largest to smallest. Window size and type can also be placed directly on the floor plan.
2. Door schedule. Place all doors in schedule. Group by type (solid core, slab, sldg, bifold, etc.) from largest to smallest. Door size and type can be placed directly on the floor plan.
3. Place room names in the center of all habitable rooms (¼″ lettering) with the interior size below (⅛″ lettering).
4. Label appliances such as furnace, water heater, dishwasher, compactor, stove, and refrigerator. Items that can be distinguished by shape such as toilets and sinks do not need to be identified.

5. Label all tubs, showers, or spas giving size, type and material.
6. Label fireplace or woodstove. Specify vent within 24″, hearth, U.L. approved materials, and wood box.
7. Label stairs giving direction of travel, number of risers, and rail height.
8. Label all closets with shelves, S&P (shelf and pole), linen, broom, or pantry.
9. Specify attic and crawl access openings.
10. Designate 1-hour firewall between garage and residence with "⅝" type 'x' gypsum board from floor to ceiling.
11. On multilevel structures, call out 'line of upper floor,' balcony above, line of lower floor, or other projections of one level beyond another.

General notes apply to the drawing overall rather than to specific items. General notes are commonly lettered in the *field* of the drawing. The field is any area that surrounds the principal views. A common location for general notes is the lower right corner of the sheet. Notes should not be placed closer than ½ in. from the drawing border. Some typical general notes are seen in Figure 16–12.

Some specific notes that are too complex or take up too much space may be lettered with the general notes and keyed to the floor plan with a short identification such as with the phrase: see NOTE #1 or

COMMON FRAMING NOTES:

1. ALL FRAMING LUMBER TO BE D.F. L. #2 OR BETTER.
2. ALL EXTERIOR WALLS @ HEATED LIVING AREAS TO BE 2 x 6 @ 24" O.C.
3. ALL EXTERIOR HEADERS TO BE 2 2x12 UNLESS NOTED, W/ 2" RIGID INSULATION BACKING UNLESS NOTED.
4. ALL SHEAR PANELS TO BE ⅜ STD. GRADE 32/16 PLY W/ 8d @ 4" O.C.@ EDGE, HDRS, & BLOCKING AND 8d @ 8" O.C. @ FIELD UNLESS NOTED.
5. PROVIDE ⅝" TYPE 'X' GYP. BD. UNDER STAIRS @ ALL USEABLE STORAGE.
6. PROVIDE ½" W.P.GYP. BD. AROUND ALL TUBS, SHOWERS & SPAS.
7. VENT DRYER AND ALL FANS TO OUTSIDE AIR THRU VENT W/ DAMPER
8. ALL METAL CONNECTORS TO BE BY SIMPSON CO. OR EQUAL.
9. INSULATE W.H. TO R-11 AND PLACE ON 18" HIGH PLATFORM (GARAGE LOCATIONS ONLY)
10. BRICK VENEER TO BE OVER 1" AIR SPACE W/ 15# FELT AND METAL TIES @ 24" O.C. @ EA. STUD.
11. ALL TRUSSES TO BE @ 24" O.C. (DIRECTLY OVER STUDS). SUBMIT TRUSS CALCS. TO BUILDING DEPT. PRIOR TO ERECTION.
12. ALL BEDROOM WINDOWS TO BE WITHIN 44" OF FIN. FLOOR.
13. ALL DOORS TO BE 6'8" HIGH UNLESS NOTED. GARAGE DOOR TO BE 7'-0" HIGH
14. ENTRY DOOR TO BE RAISED PANEL, METAL INSULATED.
15. ALL WINDOWS AND GLASS DOORS TO BE THERMAL PANE W/ BRONZE ANODIZED FRAMES
16. ALL GLASS WITHIN 18" OF DOORS TO BE TEMPERED.
17. ALL SKYLITES TO BE _" x _" DBL DOMED PLASTIC SKYLITES BY VELOX OR EQUAL.
(OR)
ALL SKYLITES TO BE _" x _"TEMPERED FLAT GLASS BY VELOX OR EQUAL.

Figure 16–12 Some typical general notes.

SEE NOTE 1, or with a number within a symbol such as ①.

Written specifications are separate notes that specifically identify the quality, quantity or type of materials and fixtures that are used in the entire project. Specifications for construction are prepared in a format different from drawing sheets. Specifications may be printed in a format that categorizes each phase of the construction and indicates the precise methods and materials to be used. Architects and designers may publish specifications for a house so that the client will know exactly what the home will contain, even including the color and type of paint. This information will also set a standard that will allow contractors to prepare construction estimates on an equal basis.

Lending institutions require material specifications to be submitted with plans when builders apply for financing. Generally each lender has a form to be used that will supply the description of all construction materials and methods along with a cost analysis of the structure. More information about specifications will be found in Chapters 43 and 44.

◢ USING METRIC

The unit of measure commonly used is the millimeter (mm). It is based on the International System of Units (SI). Canada is one country that uses metric dimensioning.

When materials are purchased from the United States, it is often necessary to make a *hard conversion* to metric units. This means that the typical inch units are converted directly to metric. For example, a 2 × 4 that is plained to 1½ in. × 3½ in. converts to 38 × 89 mm. When making the conversion from the imperial inch to millimeters, use the formula 25.4 × inch = millimeters.

The preferred method of metric dimensioning is called a *soft conversion*. This means that the lumber is milled directly to metric units. The 2 × 4 lumber would be 40 × 90 mm using the soft conversion. This method is much more convenient to use when drawing plans and measuring in construction. When plywood thickness is measured in metric units, ⅝ in. thick equals 17 mm, and ¾ in. thick equals 20

mm. The length and width of plywood also changes from 48 × 96 in. to 1,200 × 2,400 mm. Modules for architectural design and construction in the United States are typically 12 in. or 16 in. In countries using metric measurement, the dimensioning module is 100 mm. For example, construction members may be spaced 24 in. on center (oc) in the United States, while the spacing in Canada would be 600 mm oc. Or the spacing between studs at 16 in. oc in the United States would be 400 mm oc in Canada. These metric modules allow the 1,200 × 2,400 mm plywood to fit exactly on center with the construction members. Interior dimensions are also designed in 100-mm increments. For example, the kitchen base cabinet would measure 600 mm deep.

Expressing Metric Units on a Drawing

When placing metric dimensions on a drawing, all dimensions within dimension lines are in millimeters, and the millimeter symbol (mm) is omitted. When more than one dimension is quoted, the millimeter symbol (mm) is placed only after the last dimension. For example, the size of a plywood sheet would read 1,200 × 2,400 mm, or the size and length of a wood stud would read 38 × 89 × 600 mm. The millimeter symbol is omitted in the notes associated with a drawing, except when referring to a single dimension such as the thickness of material or the spacing of members. For example, a note might read 90 × 1,200 BEAM, while the reference to material thickness of 12 mm Gypsum or the spacing of joists of 400 mm oc.

Metric Scales

In Chapter 2 metric scales were introduced with respect to the use of the metric scale as a drafting tool. When drawings are produced in metric, the floor plans, elevations, and foundation plans are generally drawn at a scale of 1:50 rather than the ¼″ = 1′-0″ scale used in the imperial system. Larger scale drawings, such as construction details, are often drawn at a scale of 1:5. Small-scale drawings, such as plot plans, may be drawn at a scale of 1:500. Figure 16–13 shows a floor plan completely drawn using metric dimensioning. The preferred method of soft conversion is used, and the metric scale is 1:50.

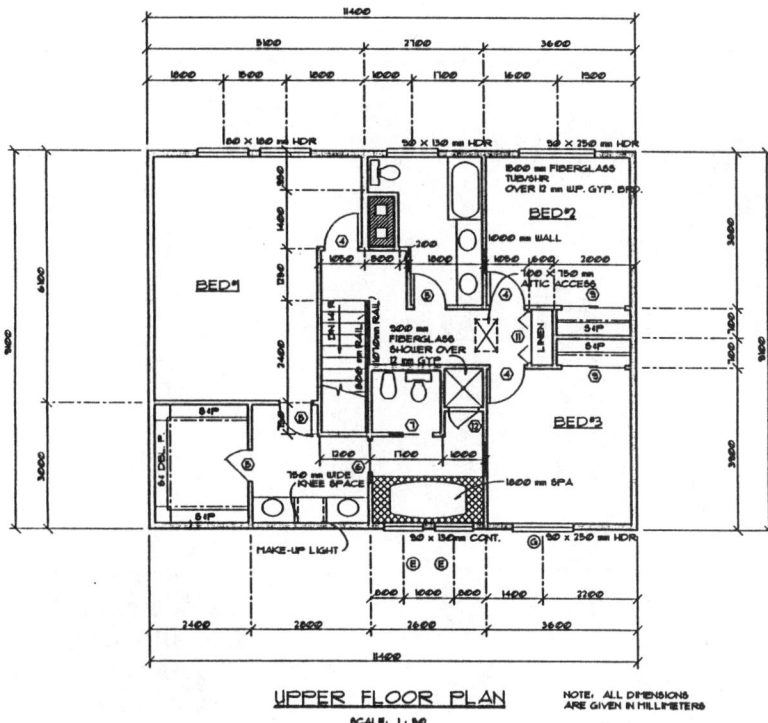

Figure 16–13 Floor plan drawn using metric dimensioning.

FLOOR-PLAN DIMENSIONS TEST

DIRECTIONS

Answer the questions with short complete statements or drawings as needed on an 8½ × 11 drawing sheet as follows:

1. Use ⅛ in. guidelines for all lettering.
2. Letter your name, Floor-Plan Dimensions Test, and the date at the top of the sheet.
3. Letter the question number and provide the answer. You do not need to write out the question.
4. Do all lettering with vertical uppercase architectural letters. If the answer requires line work, use proper drafting tools and technique. Answers may be prepared on a word processor if appropriate with course guidelines.
5. Your grade will be based on correct answers and quality of line technique.

QUESTIONS

1. Define aligned dimensioning.
2. Why should dimension lines be spaced evenly and to avoid crowding?
3. Should extension and dimension lines be drawn thick or thin?
4. Show an example of how dimension numerals that are less than one foot are lettered.
5. Show an example of how dimension numerals that are greater than one foot are lettered.
6. Are the overall dimensions on frame construction given to the outside of the stud frame at exterior walls?
7. When three lines of dimensions are used, describe the dimensional information provided in each line.
8. Describe and give an example of a specific note.
9. What is another name for a specific note?
10. Describe and give an example of a general note.
11. Show an example of dimensioning a wood-framed structure on a floor plan. Show at least one interior partition, one exterior door, and one window.
12. Show an example of how masonry veneer is dimensioned on a floor plan when used with wood-framed construction.
13. Show an example of a floor plan constructed with concrete block. Show at least one wood-frame interior partition, one exterior door, and one window.
14. Show an example of a floor plan constructed with solid concrete exterior walls. Show at least one interior wood-frame partition, one wall with interior wood furring, one exterior door, and one window.

Chapter 17
Electrical Plans

ELECTRICAL CIRCUIT DESIGN

THE DESIGN of the electrical circuits in a home is important because of the number of electrical appliances that make modern living enjoyable. Discuss with the client any anticipated needs for electric energy in the home. Such a discussion would include the intended use of each of the rooms and the potential placement of furniture in them. Try to design the electrical circuits so that there will be enough outlets and switches at convenient locations. National Electrical Code requirements dictate the size of some circuits and the placement of certain outlets and switches within the home.

In addition to convenience and code requirements, you will have to consider cost. A client may want outlets 4 ft apart in each room, but the construction budget may not allow such an extravagant luxury. Try to establish budget guidelines and then work closely with the client to achieve desired results. While switches, convenience outlets, and electrical wire and boxes may not seem to cost very much individually, their installation in great quantity could be costly. In addition, attractive and useful light fixtures required in most rooms can also be very expensive.

Some common items to consider when designing electrical circuits based on convenience and national and local codes include the following:

- Duplex convenience outlets (wall plugs) should be a maximum of 12 ft apart. Closer spacing is desirable although economy is a factor.
- Duplex outlets should be no more than 6 ft from a corner, and there should be a duplex outlet in any wall over 36 in. long.
- Consider furniture layout, if possible, so that duplex outlets do not become inaccessible behind large pieces.
- Place a duplex outlet next to or behind a desk or table where light is needed, or near a probable reading area.
- Place a duplex outlet near a fireplace.
- Place a duplex outlet in a hallway.
- Duplex outlets should be placed close together in kitchens, and should be installed where fixed and portable appliances will be located for use. Some designs include an outlet in a pantry for use with portable appliances. Kitchen, bathroom, laundry, and outdoor circuits are required to be protected by ground-fault circuit-interrupters (GFI or GFCI). The function of the GFI is to trip a circuit breaker when there is any unbalance in the current in the circuit. This protection is required for any electric fixture within 5 ft. of water. Fixtures and appliances produce a potential hazard for electrocution.
- Each bath sink or makeup table should have a duplex outlet.
- Each enclosed bath or laundry (utility) room should have an exhaust fan. Those rooms with openable windows do not require fans, although they are desirable.
- A lighting outlet is necessary outside all entries and exterior doors.
- A waterproof duplex outlet should be placed at a convenient exterior location, such as a patio.
- Ceiling lights are common in children's bedrooms for easy illumination. Master bedrooms

may have a switched duplex outlet for a bedside lamp.

- The kitchen may have a light over the sink, although in a very well-lighted kitchen this may be an extra light.
- Bathroom lights are commonly placed above the mirror at the vanity, and located in any area that requires additional light. In a large bath, a recessed light should be placed in a shower or above a tub.
- Place switches in a manner that will provide the easiest control of the lights.
- Locate lights in large closets or any alcove or pantry that requires light.
- Light stairways well.
- Place lights and outlets in garages or shops in relationship to their use. For example, a welder or shop equipment will require 220-volt outlets.
- Place exterior lights properly to illuminate walks, drives, patios, decks, and other high-use areas.

ENERGY CONSERVATION

Energy efficiency is a very important consideration in today's home design and construction market. There are a number of steps that can easily help contribute to energy savings for the home owner at little additional cost. Some of these items will have to be explained by specific or general notes or included in construction specifications while other methods must be defined with detail drawings. Energy-efficient considerations related to the electrical design include the following:

- Keep electrical outlets and recessed appliances or panels to a minimum at exterior walls. Any

units recessed into an exterior wall will eliminate or severely compress the insulation and reduce its insulating value.

- Fans or other exhaust systems exhausting air from the building should be provided with back draft or automatic dampers to limit air leakage.
- Timed switches or humidistats should be installed on exhaust fans to control unnecessary operation.
- Electrical wiring is often located in exterior walls at a level convenient for electricians to run wires. This practice causes insulation to become compacted, and a loss of insulating value results. Wires should be run along the bottom of the studs at the bottom plate. This is easily accomplished during framing by cutting a V groove in the stud bottoms while the studs are piled at the site after delivery. Figure 17–1 shows a comparison of standard and energy saving installation methods.
- Select energy efficient appliances such as a self-heating dishwasher or a high insulation water heater. Evaluate the vendor's energy statement before purchase.
- Use energy saving fluorescent lighting fixtures where practical such as in the kitchen, laundry, utility, garage, or shop.
- Fully insulate above and around recessed lighting fixtures. Verify code and vendor specifications for this practice.
- Carefully caulk and seal around all light and convenience outlets. Also, caulk and seal where electrical wires penetrate the top and bottom plates. Figure 17–2 shows some methods that could be used to increase energy efficiency, although some of these techniques may not be cost effective.

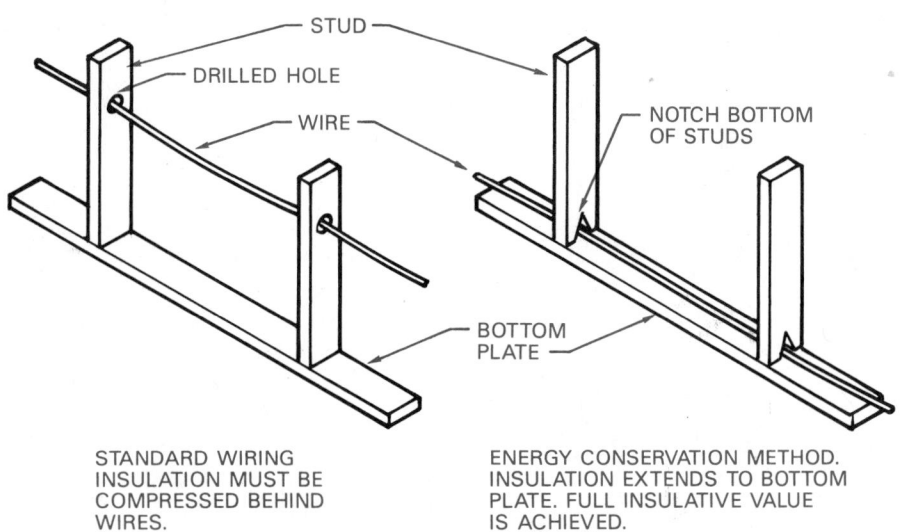

STANDARD WIRING INSULATION MUST BE COMPRESSED BEHIND WIRES.

ENERGY CONSERVATION METHOD. INSULATION EXTENDS TO BOTTOM PLATE. FULL INSULATIVE VALUE IS ACHIEVED.

Figure 17–1 Wiring technique for energy conservation.

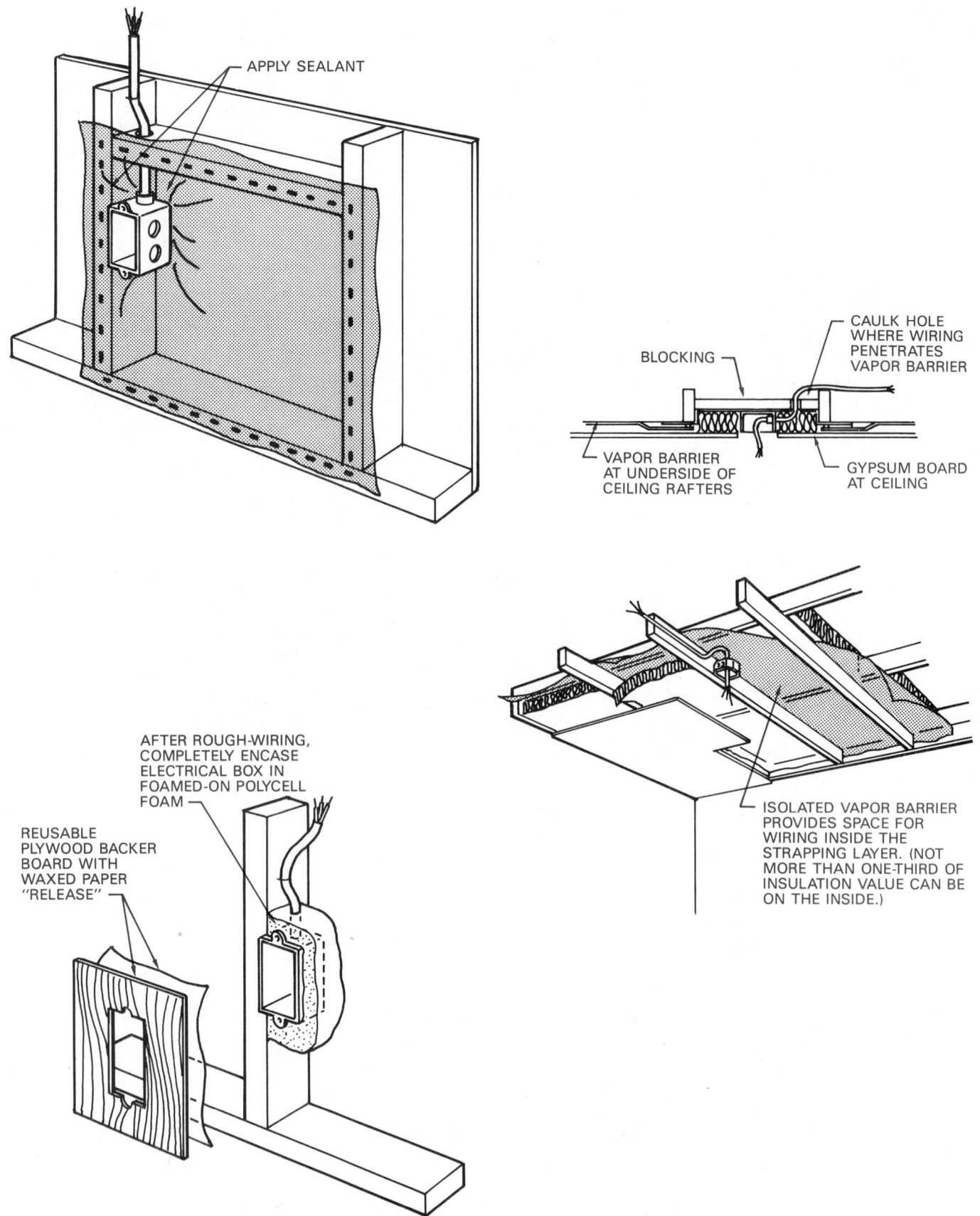

APPLY SEALANT

BLOCKING

CAULK HOLE
WHERE WIRING
PENETRATES
VAPOR BARRIER

VAPOR BARRIER
AT UNDERSIDE OF
CEILING RAFTERS

GYPSUM BOARD
AT CEILING

ISOLATED VAPOR BARRIER
PROVIDES SPACE FOR
WIRING INSIDE THE
STRAPPING LAYER. (NOT
MORE THAN ONE-THIRD OF
INSULATION VALUE CAN BE
ON THE INSIDE.)

AFTER ROUGH-WIRING,
COMPLETELY ENCASE
ELECTRICAL BOX IN
FOAMED-ON POLYCELL
FOAM

REUSABLE
PLYWOOD BACKER
BOARD WITH
WAXED PAPER
"RELEASE"

Figure 17-2 Energy conservation techniques.

CADD
applications

DRAWING ELECTRICAL SYMBOLS WITH CADD

In most cases, electrical symbols are drawn on a separate CADD layer. The floor plan serves as the base sheet. So, by turning the electrical layer ON you have a composite drawing with the floor plan, electrical symbols, and electrical layout. You also have the flexibility to turn the electrical layer OFF when you want to display the floor plan without electrical. Many companies provide two separate drawings for commercial projects—the floor plan completely dimensioned and the floor plan with only the walls and electrical layout. All you have to do is turn ON or OFF specific layers as needed to display what you want. Most architectural CADD programs are tablet menu driven with a symbols library for electrical applications, as shown in Figure 1. A drafter simply selects the desired symbol from the tablet menu and then drags the symbol into position on the drawing. Parametric design plays an important role in applications such as ceiling lighting grids. You specify the room width, length, and grid size; the computer then automatically draws the entire ceiling grid. Figure 2 shows a complete floor plan with electrical symbols.

Figure 1 CADD symbols library for electrical applications. *Courtesy Autodesk, Inc.*

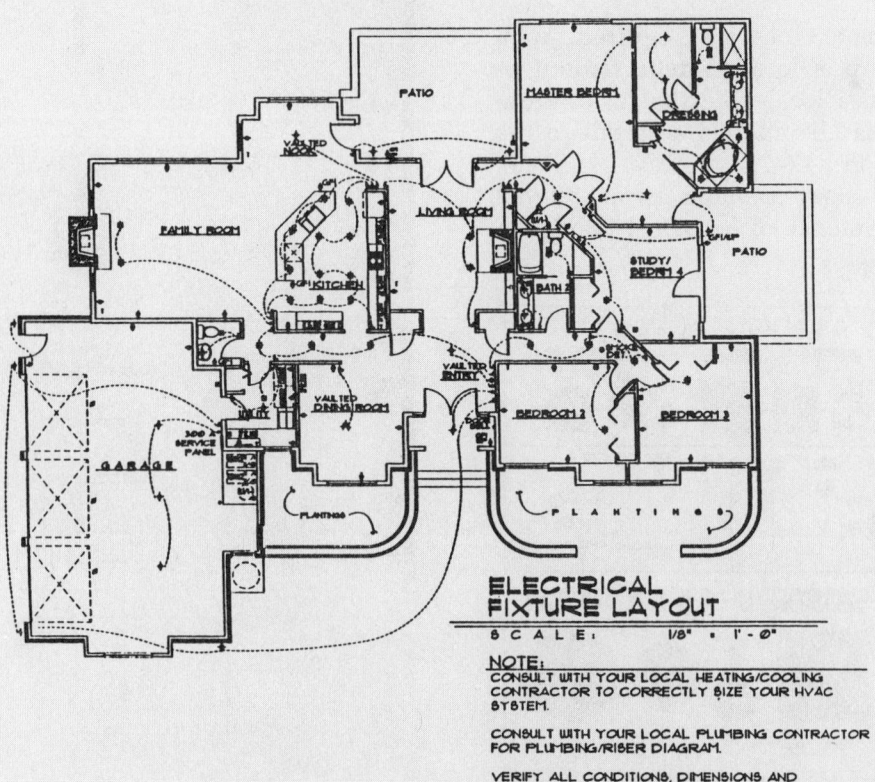

Figure 2 Complete floor plan with electrical symbols. *Courtesy Piercy & Barclay Designers, Inc.*

ELECTRICAL SYMBOLS

Electrical symbols are used to show the lighting arrangement desired in the home. This includes all switches, fixtures and outlets. Lighting fixture templates are available with a variety of fixture shapes for drafting convenience as shown in Figure 17–3. Switch symbols are generally lettered freehand.

All electrical symbols should be drawn with ⅛ in. diameter circles as seen in Figure 17–4. The electrical layout should be subordinate to the plan and not clutter or distract from the other information. All lettering for switches and other notes should be ⅛ or 3/32 in. high depending upon space requirements and office practice.

Switch symbols are generally drawn perpendicular to the wall and are placed to read from the right side or bottom of the sheet. Look at Figure 17–5. Also, notice that the switch relay should intersect the symbol at right angles to the wall or the relay may begin adjacent to the symbol. Verify the preference of your instructor or employer and do not mix methods.

Figure 17–6 shows several typical electrical installations with switches to light outlets. The switch leg or electrical circuit line may be drawn with an irregular (French) curve or may be drawn freehand. Individuals using freehand electrical relay lines should have a very good command of freehand drawing. If there is any doubt about line quality, use an irregular curve.

When special characteristics are required, such as a specific size fixture, a location requirement or any other specification, a local note that briefly describes the situation may be applied adjacent to the outlet as shown in Figure 17–7.

Figure 17–8 shows some common errors related to the placement and practice of electrical floor plan layout.

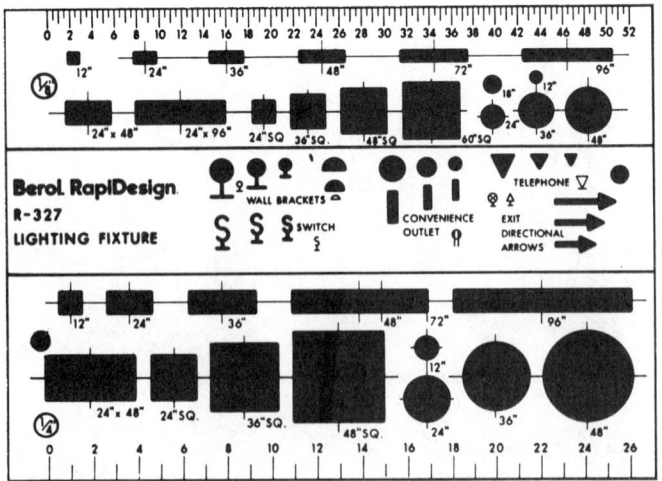

Figure 17–3 Lighting fixture template. *Courtesy Berol USA RapiDesign.*

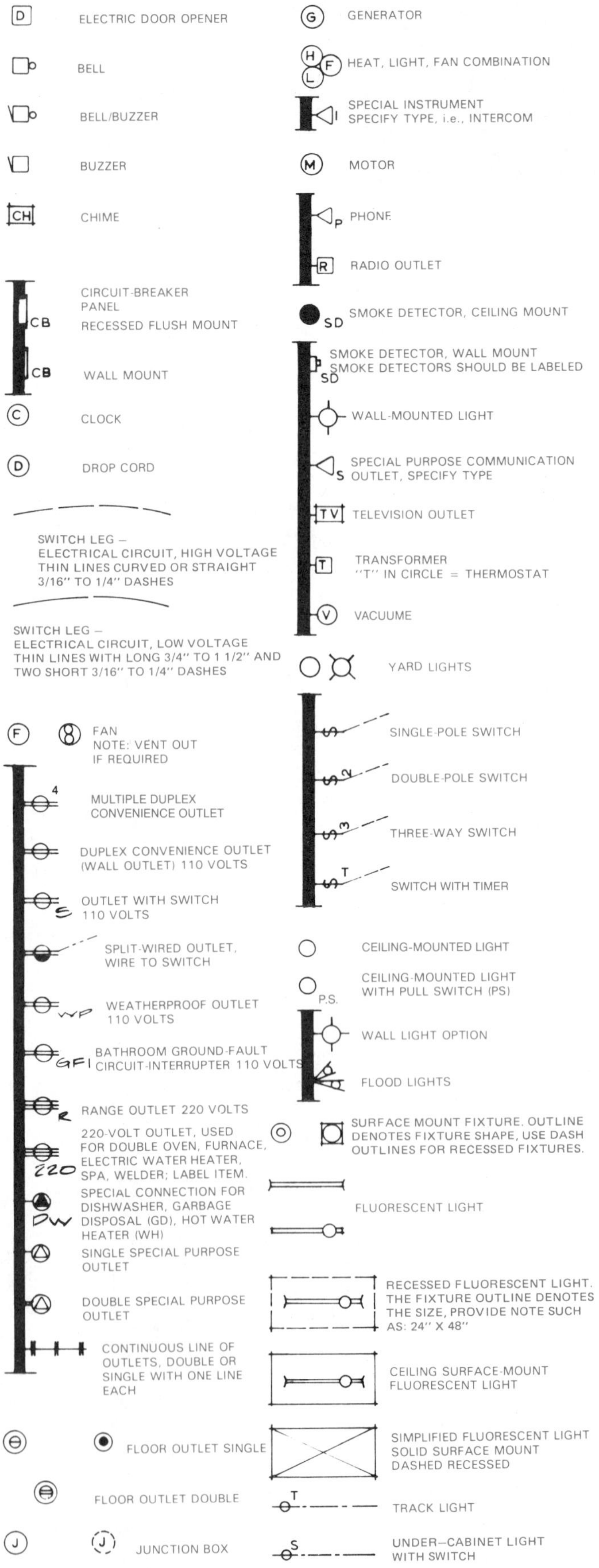

Figure 17–4 Common electrical symbols.

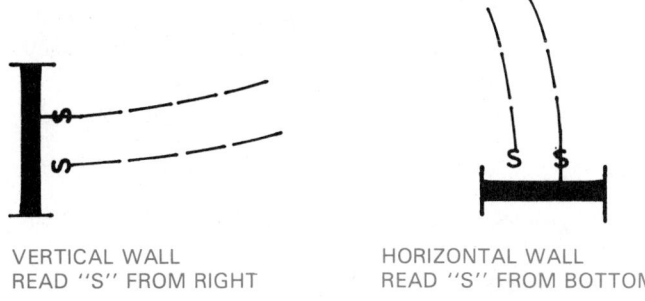

VERTICAL WALL
READ "S" FROM RIGHT

HORIZONTAL WALL
READ "S" FROM BOTTOM

Figure 17-5 Switch symbol placement.

Figure 17-9 shows some examples of maximum spacing recommended for installation of wall outlets.

Figure 17-10 shows some examples of typical electrical layouts. Figure 17-11 shows a bath layout. Figure 17-12 shows a typical kitchen electrical layout.

ELECTRICAL WIRING SPECIFICATIONS

The following specifications describing the installation of the service entrance and meter base for a residence has been adapted from information furnished by Home Building Plan Service.

Service Entrance and Meter Base Installation

Before proceeding with the installation of the service entrance and meter base, the following questions must be resolved:

- What is the service capacity to be installed?
- Where is the service entrance to be located?
- Where will the meter base be located?
- Where will the distribution panelboard be located?

1. For capacity of service, the average single-family residence should be equipped with a 200-amp service entrance. If heating, cooking, water heating, and similar heavy loads are supplied by energy sources other than electricity, then the service entrance conductors may be sized for 100 amps provided local codes are not violated. Some local codes require a minimum capacity of 200 amps for each single dwelling. Local inspection authorities and the power company serving the area can be of assistance if difficulty is encountered in sizing the service entrance.

2. The service entrance location depends upon whether the power company serves the houses in the area from an overhead or underground distribution system. The underground service entrance, shown in Figure 17-13, is the most

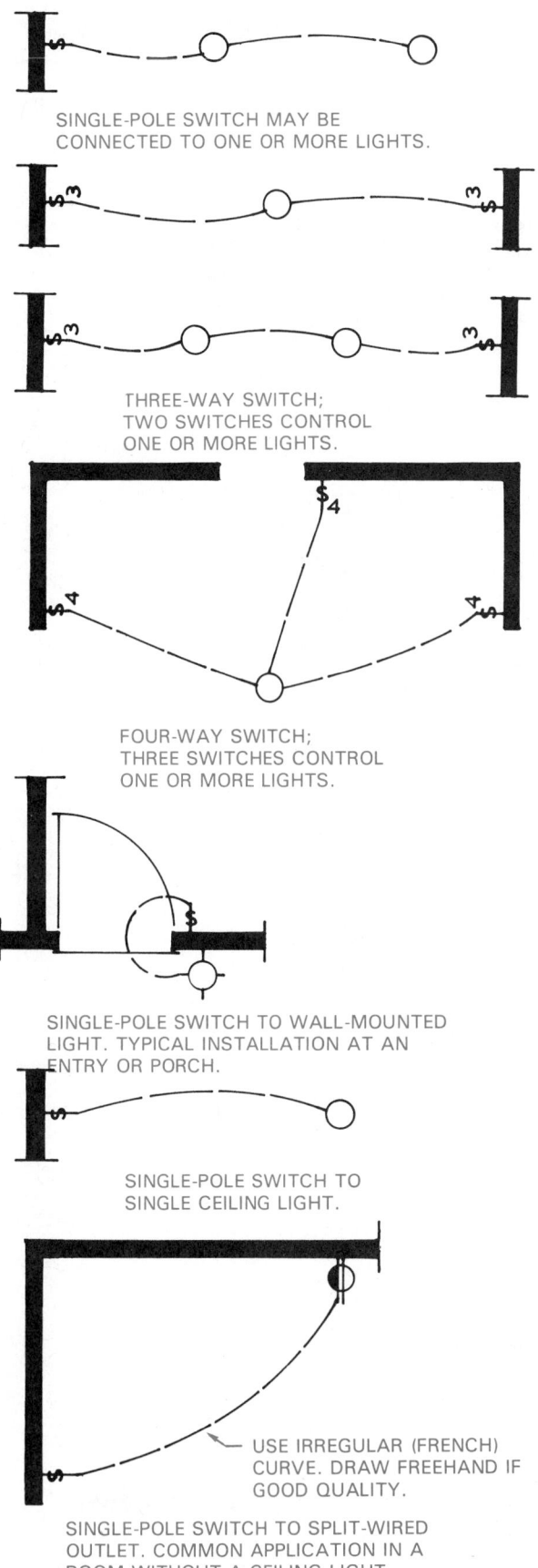

SINGLE-POLE SWITCH MAY BE CONNECTED TO ONE OR MORE LIGHTS.

THREE-WAY SWITCH; TWO SWITCHES CONTROL ONE OR MORE LIGHTS.

FOUR-WAY SWITCH; THREE SWITCHES CONTROL ONE OR MORE LIGHTS.

SINGLE-POLE SWITCH TO WALL-MOUNTED LIGHT. TYPICAL INSTALLATION AT AN ENTRY OR PORCH.

SINGLE-POLE SWITCH TO SINGLE CEILING LIGHT.

USE IRREGULAR (FRENCH) CURVE. DRAW FREEHAND IF GOOD QUALITY.

SINGLE-POLE SWITCH TO SPLIT-WIRED OUTLET. COMMON APPLICATION IN A ROOM WITHOUT A CEILING LIGHT. ALLOWS SWITCHING A TABLE LAMP.

Figure 17-6 Typical electrical installations.

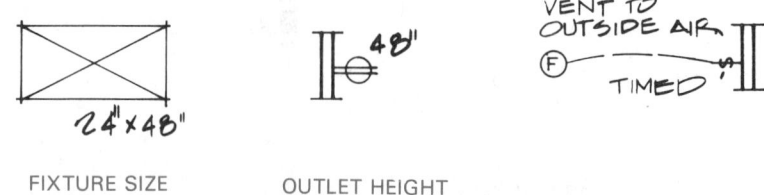

24" x 48"
48"
VENT TO
OUTSIDE AIR
TIMED
FIXTURE SIZE
OUTLET HEIGHT

Figure 17–7 Special notes for electrical fixtures.

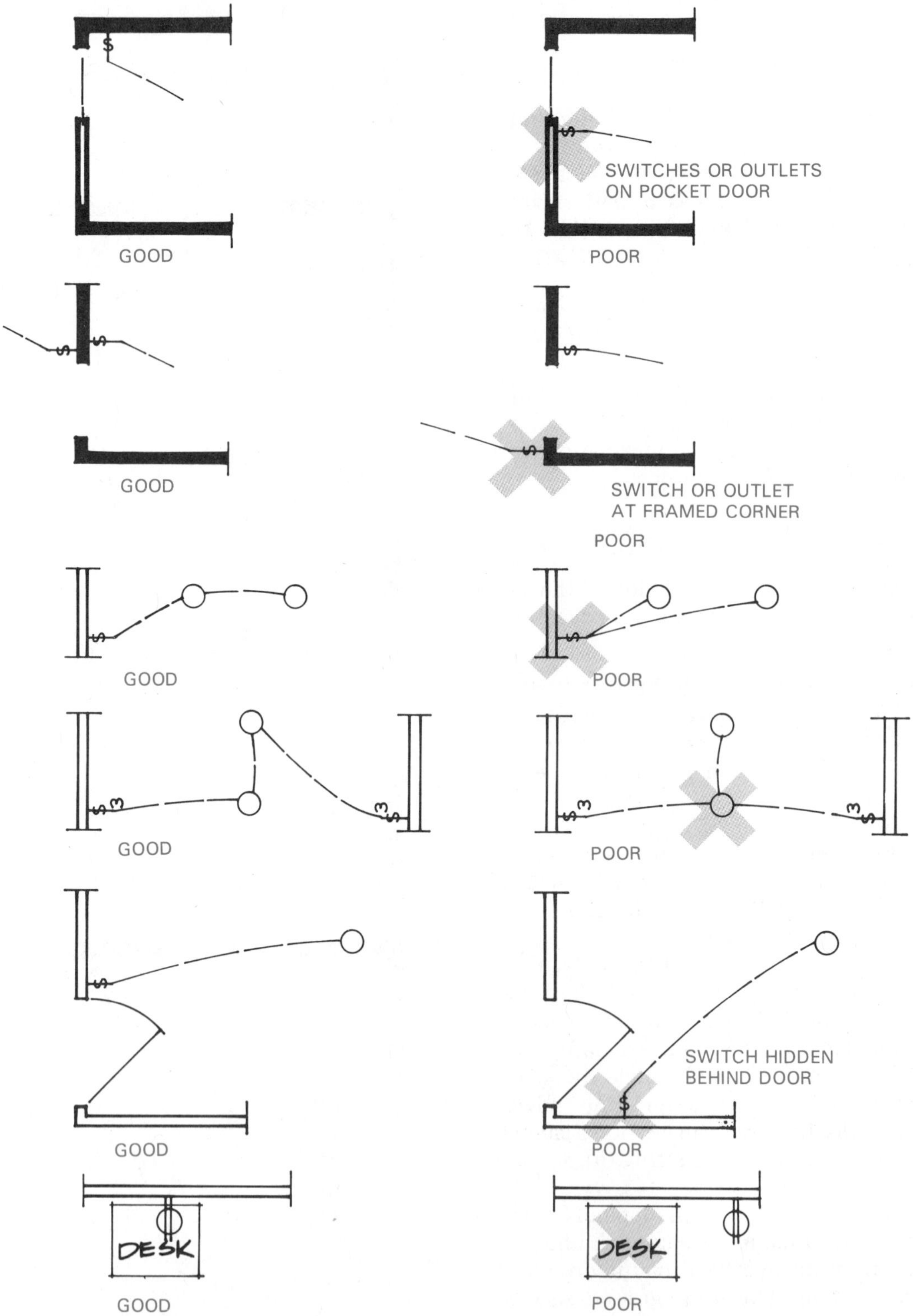
GOOD
POOR
SWITCHES OR OUTLETS
ON POCKET DOOR
GOOD
SWITCH OR OUTLET
AT FRAMED CORNER
POOR
GOOD
POOR
GOOD
POOR
GOOD
SWITCH HIDDEN
BEHIND DOOR
POOR
DESK
GOOD
DESK
POOR

Figure 17–8 Electrical layout techniques.

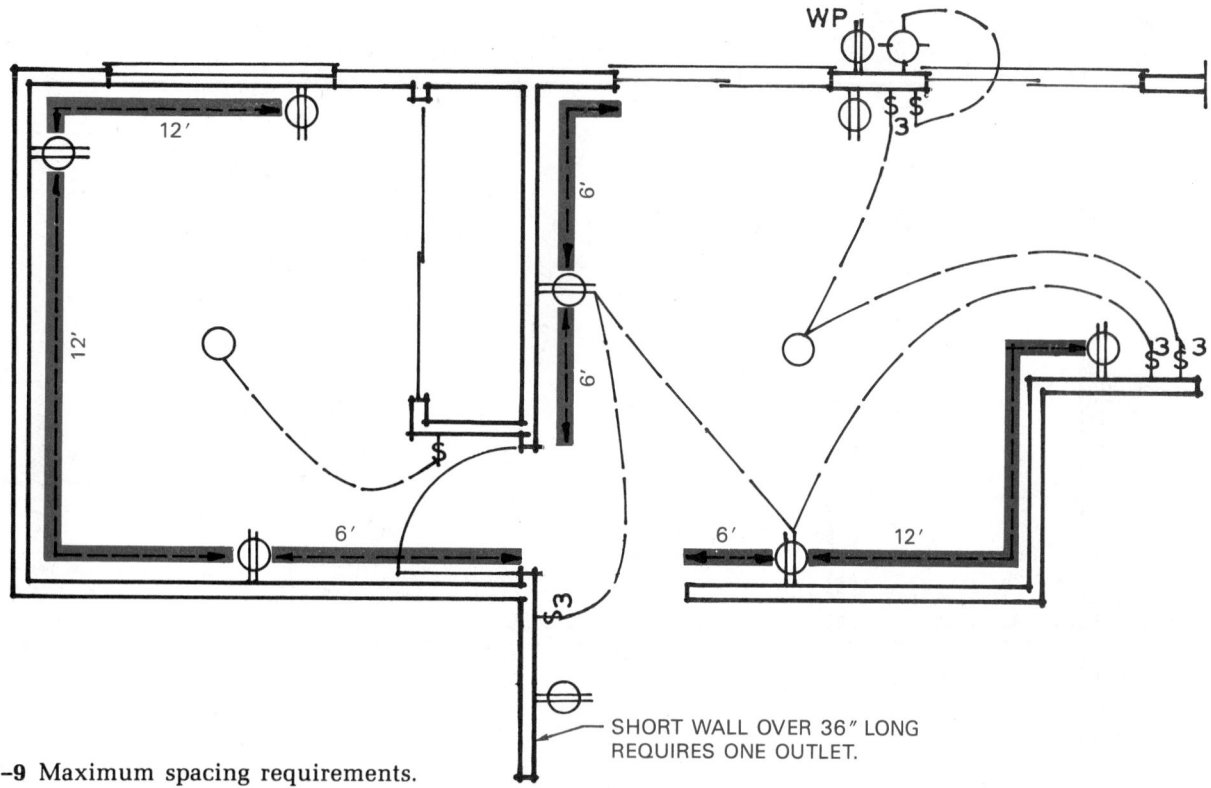

Figure 17-9 Maximum spacing requirements.

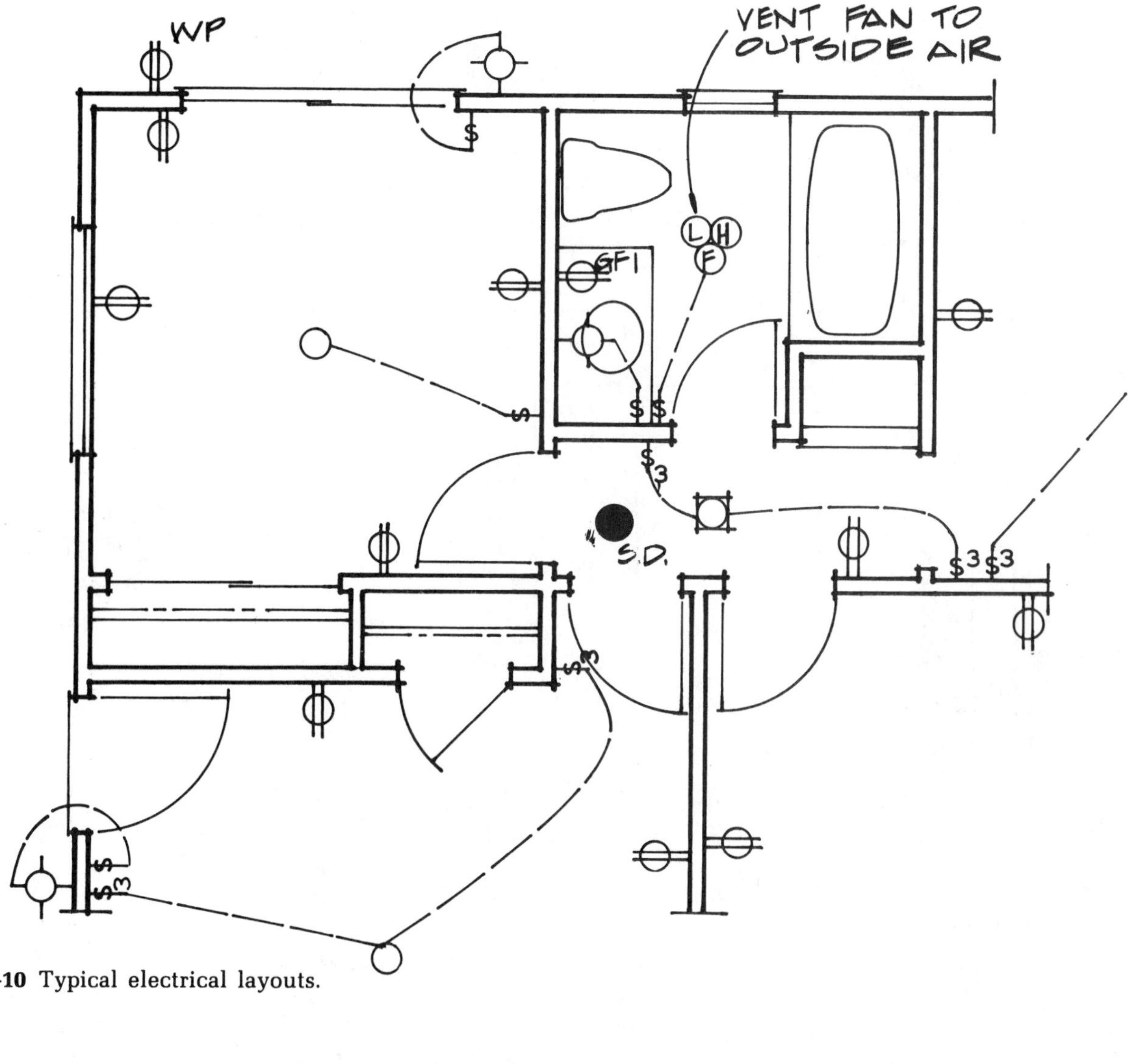

SHORT WALL OVER 36″ LONG
REQUIRES ONE OUTLET.

Figure 17-10 Typical electrical layouts.

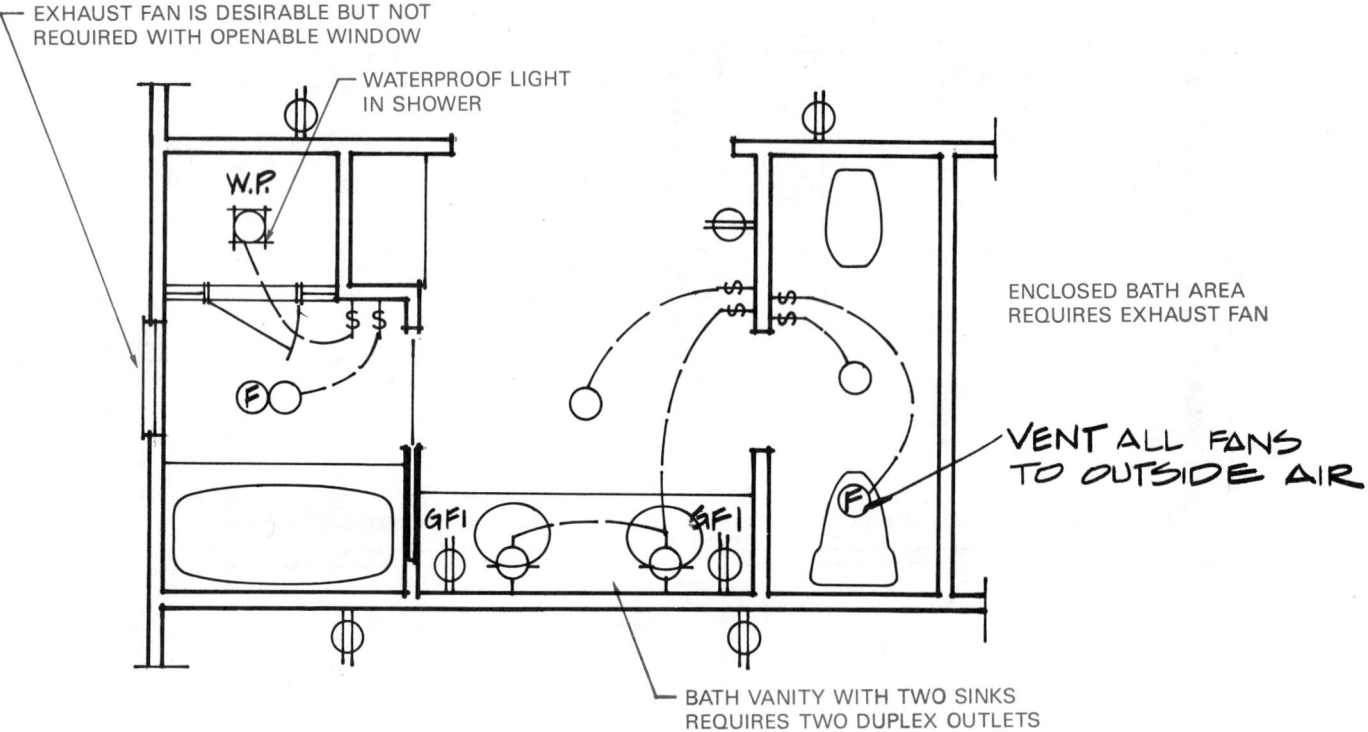

Figure 17–11 Bath electrical layout.

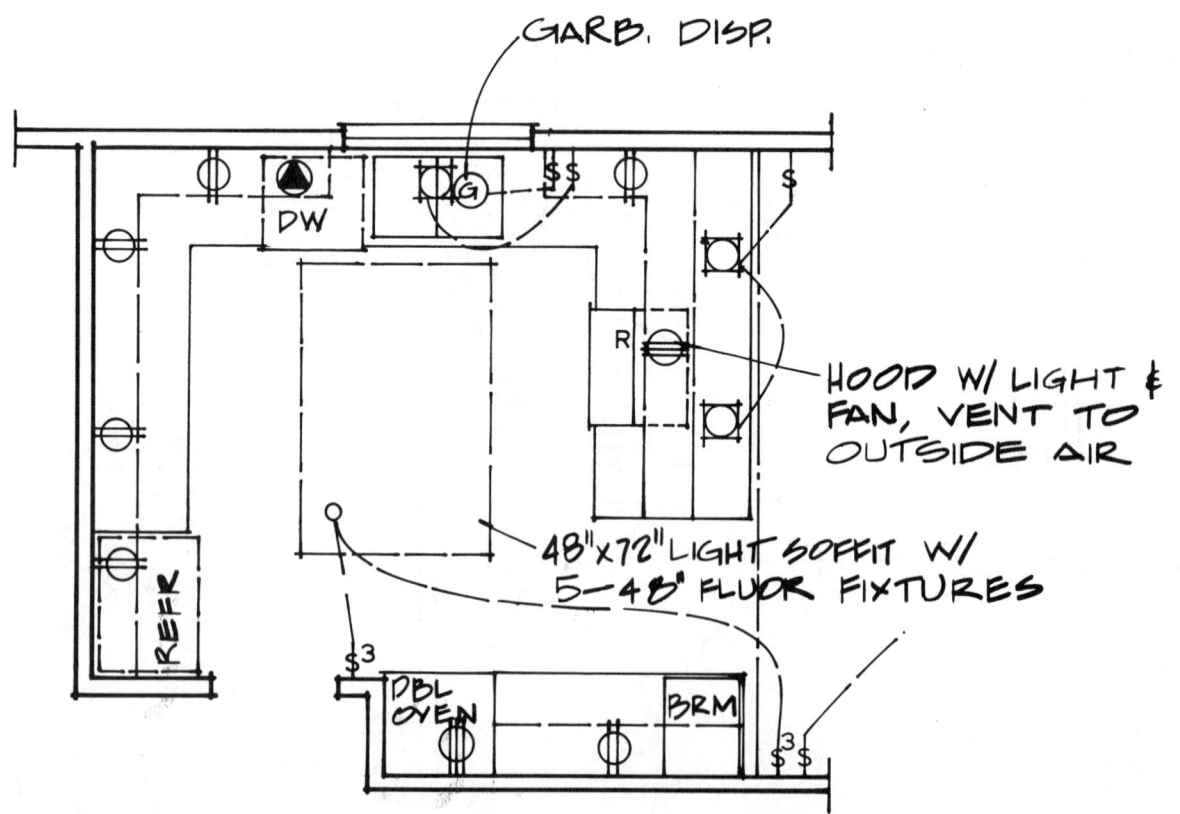

Figure 17–12 Kitchen electrical layout.

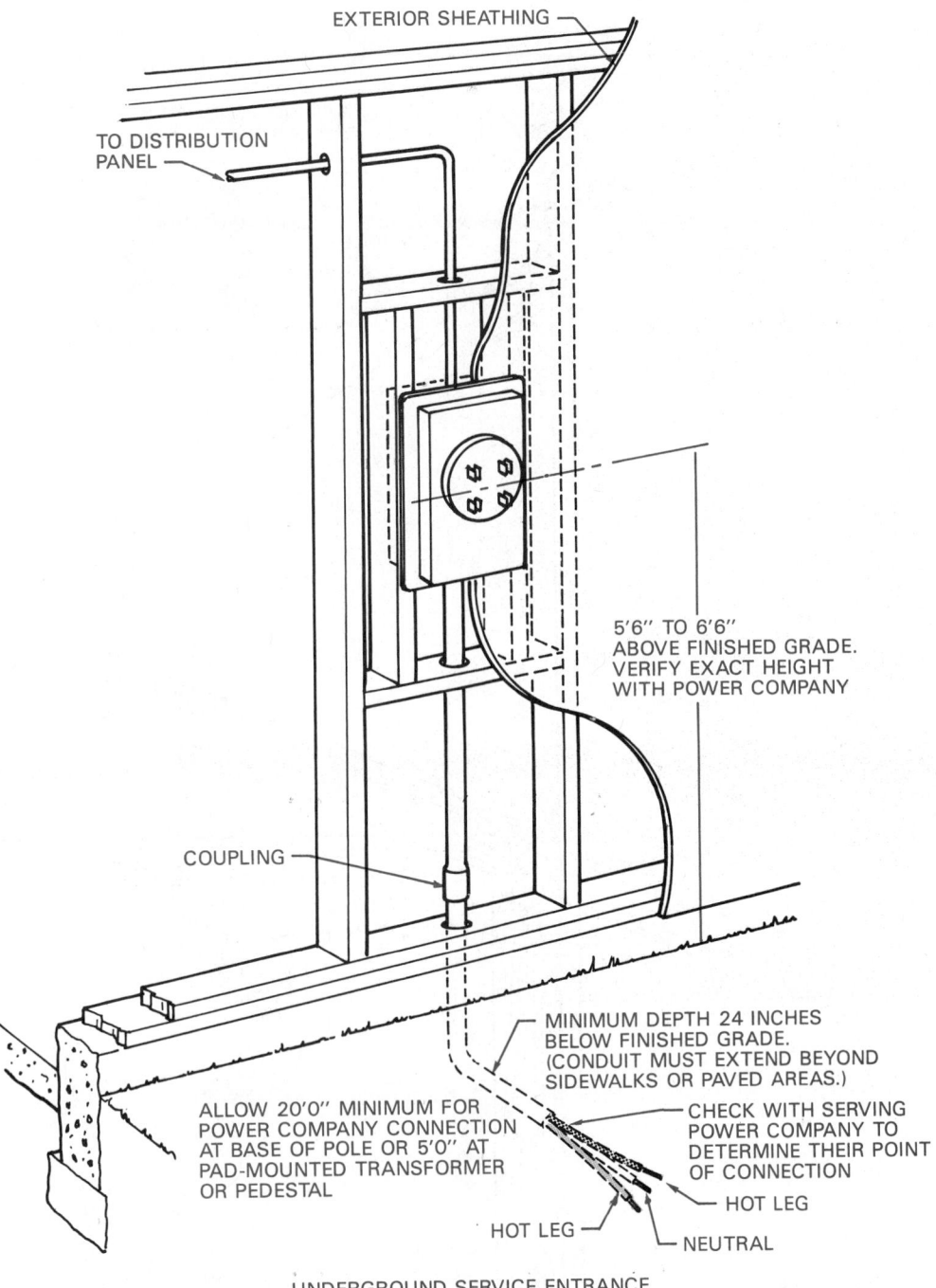

EXTERIOR SHEATHING

TO DISTRIBUTION PANEL

5'6" TO 6'6" ABOVE FINISHED GRADE. VERIFY EXACT HEIGHT WITH POWER COMPANY

COUPLING

MINIMUM DEPTH 24 INCHES BELOW FINISHED GRADE. (CONDUIT MUST EXTEND BEYOND SIDEWALKS OR PAVED AREAS.)

ALLOW 20'0" MINIMUM FOR POWER COMPANY CONNECTION AT BASE OF POLE OR 5'0" AT PAD-MOUNTED TRANSFORMER OR PEDESTAL

CHECK WITH SERVING POWER COMPANY TO DETERMINE THEIR POINT OF CONNECTION

HOT LEG

HOT LEG

NEUTRAL

UNDERGROUND SERVICE ENTRANCE
OUTSIDE VIEW OF METER BASE

Figure 17–13 Underground service entrance. *Courtesy Home Building Plan Service.*

desirable from both an aesthetic and reliability standpoint. However, if the power company services the area from an overhead pole line, an underground service entrance may be impractical, prohibitively expensive, or even impossible. Overhead service installations are shown in Figures 17–14 and 17–15.

3. The meter base must always be mounted so that the meter socket is on the exterior of the house and preferably on the side wall of a garage. The meter base should not be installed

on the front of the house for aesthetic reasons. If the house does not have a garage, the meter base should be located on an exterior side wall as near to the distribution panel as practical.

4. The preferred location for the distribution panel is on an inside garage wall and close to the heaviest electrical loads, such as a range, clothes dryer, electric furnace, etc. The panel should be mounted flush unless the location does not permit this. If the house does not have a garage, the panel should be located in a readily ac-

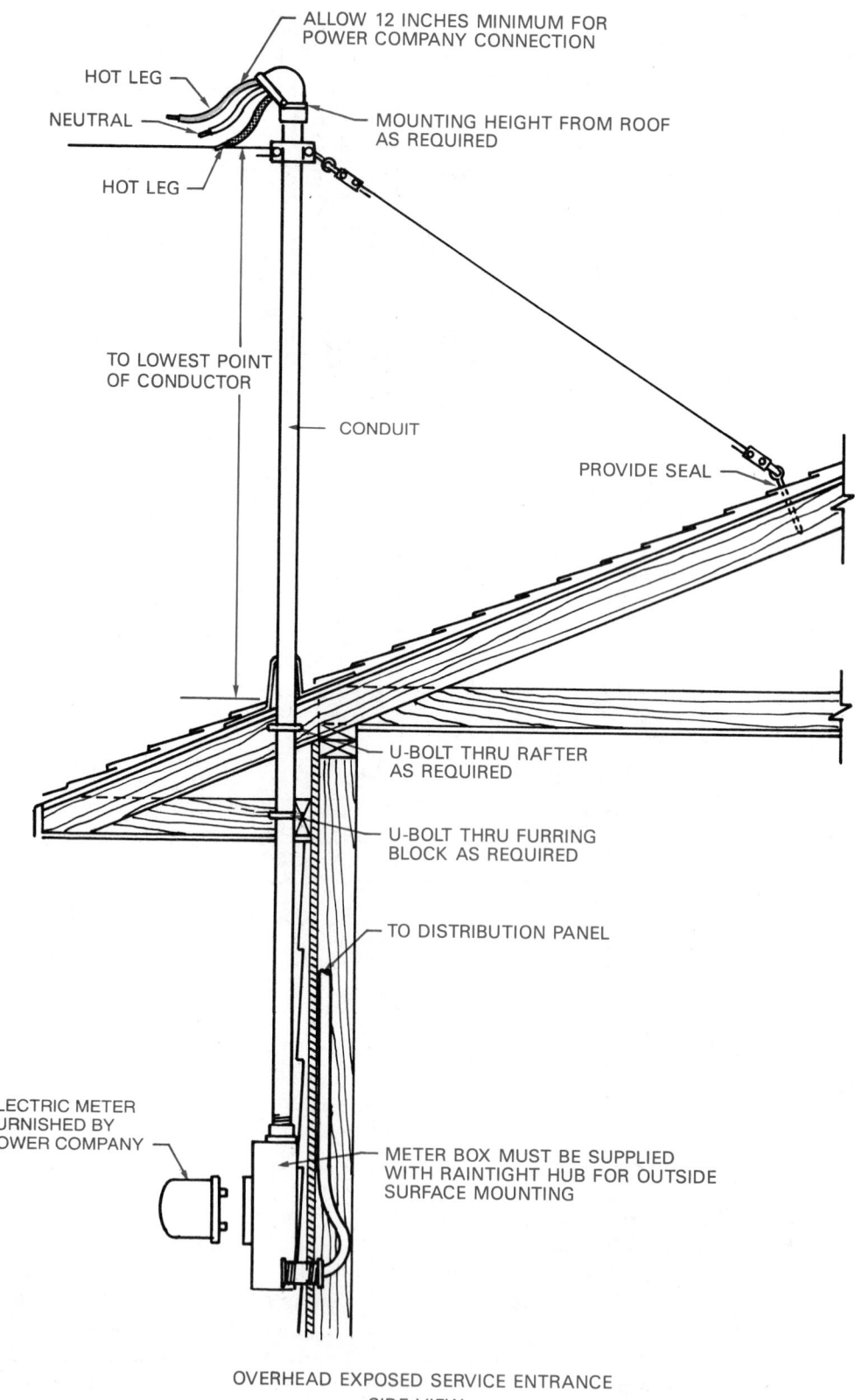

ALLOW 12 INCHES MINIMUM FOR
POWER COMPANY CONNECTION

HOT LEG

NEUTRAL

MOUNTING HEIGHT FROM ROOF
AS REQUIRED

HOT LEG

TO LOWEST POINT
OF CONDUCTOR

CONDUIT

PROVIDE SEAL

U-BOLT THRU RAFTER
AS REQUIRED

U-BOLT THRU FURRING
BLOCK AS REQUIRED

TO DISTRIBUTION PANEL

ELECTRIC METER
FURNISHED BY
POWER COMPANY

METER BOX MUST BE SUPPLIED
WITH RAINTIGHT HUB FOR OUTSIDE
SURFACE MOUNTING

OVERHEAD EXPOSED SERVICE ENTRANCE
SIDE VIEW

Figure 17–14 Overhead exposed service entrance. *Courtesy Home Building Plan Service.*

cessible area such as a utility room, kitchen wall, etc.

5. Select the appropriate service entrance detail or combination thereof from the foregoing examples after the required data is known.

6. In some localities the electrical power billing structure requires two meters. For example, lighting and general use energy may be billed at a rate different from energy used for space and water heating. In such a situation, provide two meter bases and two distribution panels to suit requirements.

7. For an overhead service entrance, dimension "A" shall be 8'–0" if the roof slope is less than 4 in. in 12 in. If the slope is greater, then 3'–0" for dimension "A" is permissible. If dimension "B" is 4'–0" or less, dimension "A" can be 1'–6" regardless of roof slope. See Figure 17–14.

8. Dimension "C" is the service conductor clearance to ground. The required distance for dimension "C" is 10'–0" when above finish grade, sidewalks, or any area that the service conductors can be reached. If the service conductors extend over a driveway or parking area, dimension "C" shall be not less than 12'–0". See Figure 17–14.

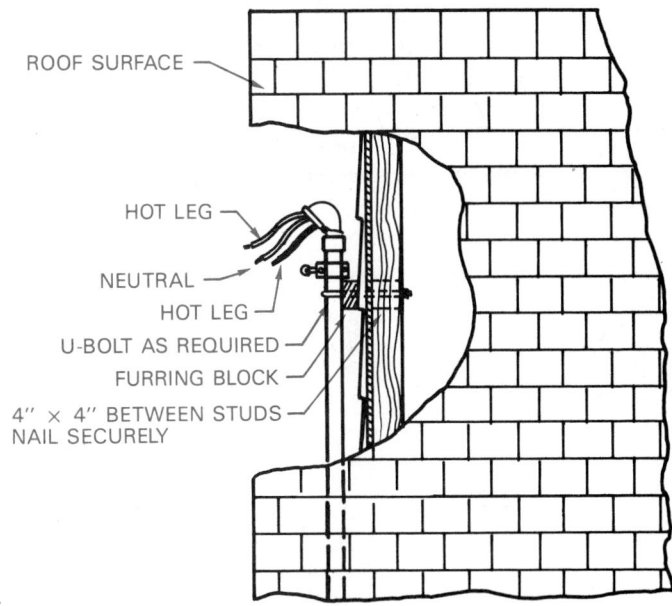

ROOF SURFACE
HOT LEG
NEUTRAL
HOT LEG
U-BOLT AS REQUIRED
FURRING BLOCK
4" × 4" BETWEEN STUDS NAIL SECURELY

Figure 17–15 Overhead exposed service entrance, typical cable mounting. *Courtesy Home Building Plan Service.*

ELECTRICAL PLANS TEST

DIRECTIONS

Answer the questions with short complete statements or drawings as needed on an 8½ × 11 drawing sheet as follows:

1. Use ⅛ in. guidelines for all lettering.
2. Letter your name, Electrical Plans Test, and the date at the top of the sheet.
3. Letter the question number and provide the answer. You do not need to write out the question.
4. Do all lettering with vertical uppercase architectural letters. If the answer requires line work, use proper drafting tools and technique. Answers may be prepared on a word processor if appropriate with course guidelines.
5. Your grade will be based on correct answers and quality of line technique.

QUESTIONS

1. Duplex convenience outlets should be a maximum of how many feet apart?
2. Duplex convenience outlets should be no more than how many feet from a corner?
3. Describe at least four energy efficient considerations related to electrical design.
4. Draw the proper floor-plan symbol for:

   a. Duplex convenience outlet
   b. Range outlet
   c. Recessed circuit breaker panel
   d. Phone
   e. Light
   f. Wall-mounted light
   g. Single-pole switch
   h. Simplified fluorescent light fixture
   i. Fan

5. Draw a typical floor-plan representation of the following:

   a. Three-way switch controlling three ceiling-mounted lighting fixtures.
   b. Four-way switch to one ceiling-mounted lighting fixture.
   c. Single-pole switch to wall-mounted light fixture.
   d. Single-pole switch to split-wired duplex convenience outlet.
   e. Typical small bathroom layout with tub, water closet, one sink vanity, one wall-mounted light over sink with single-pole

switch at door, GFCI duplex convenience outlet next to sink, ceiling-mounted light-fan-heat unit with timed switch at door, proper vent note for fan.

f. Typical kitchen layout with double light above sink, dishwasher, range with oven below and proper vent note, refrigerator, centered ceiling-recessed fluorescent light-ing fixture, adequate GFI duplex convenience outlets, and garbage disposal.

6. Why is it poor practice to place a switch behind a door swing?

7. What is a GFI duplex convenience outlet?

8. The average single-family residence should be equipped with how many amps of electrical service?

Chapter 18
Plumbing Plans

ENERGY CONSERVATION
PLUMBING SCHEDULES
PLUMBING DRAWINGS
WATER SYSTEMS
DRAINAGE AND VENT SYSTEMS
ISOMETRIC PLUMBING DRAWINGS
SOLAR HOT WATER
SEWAGE DISPOSAL
TEST

THERE ARE two classifications of piping: industrial and residential. Industrial piping is used to carry liquids and gases used in the manufacture of products. Steel pipe with welded or threaded connections and fittings is used in heavy construction.

Residential piping is called plumbing and carries fresh water, gas, or liquid and solid waste. The pipe used in plumbing may be made of copper, plastic, galvanized steel, or cast iron. Copper pipes have soldered joints and fittings, and are used for carrying hot or cold water. Plastic pipes have glued joints and fittings, and are used for vents and for carrying fresh water or solid waste. Very little galvanized steel pipe is used except where conditions require such installation. Steel pipe has threaded joints and fittings and is used to carry natural gas. Cast iron pipe is commonly used to carry solid and liquid waste as the sewer pipe that connects the structure with the local or regional sewer system.

Residential plans may not require a complete plumbing plan. The need for a complete plumbing plan should be verified with the local building code. In most cases, the plumbing requirements can be clearly provided on the floor plan in the form of symbols for fixtures and notes for specific applications or conditions. The plumbing fixtures are drawn in their proper locations on the floor plans at a scale of ¼″ = 1′-0″. Templates with a large variety of floor plan plumbing symbols are available as shown in Figure 18–1.

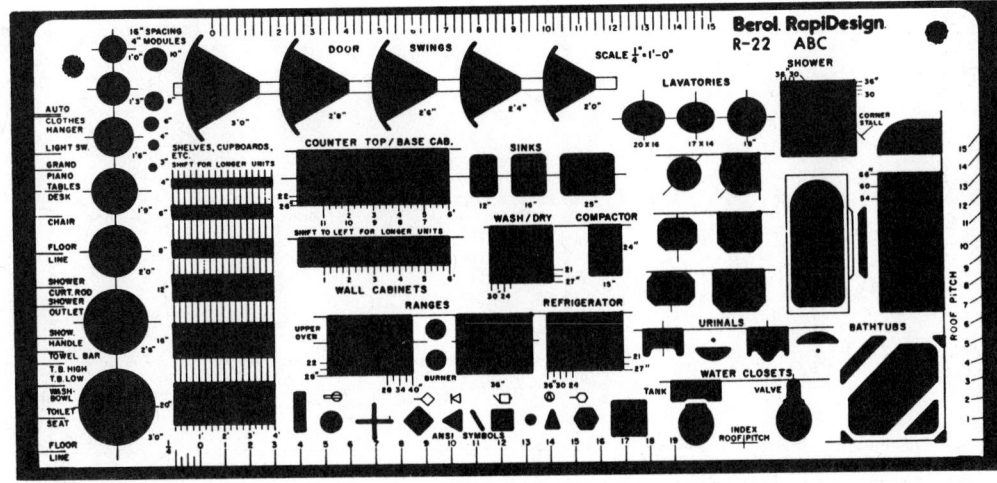

Figure 18–1 Architectural floor plan template. *Courtesy Berol USA RapiDesign.*

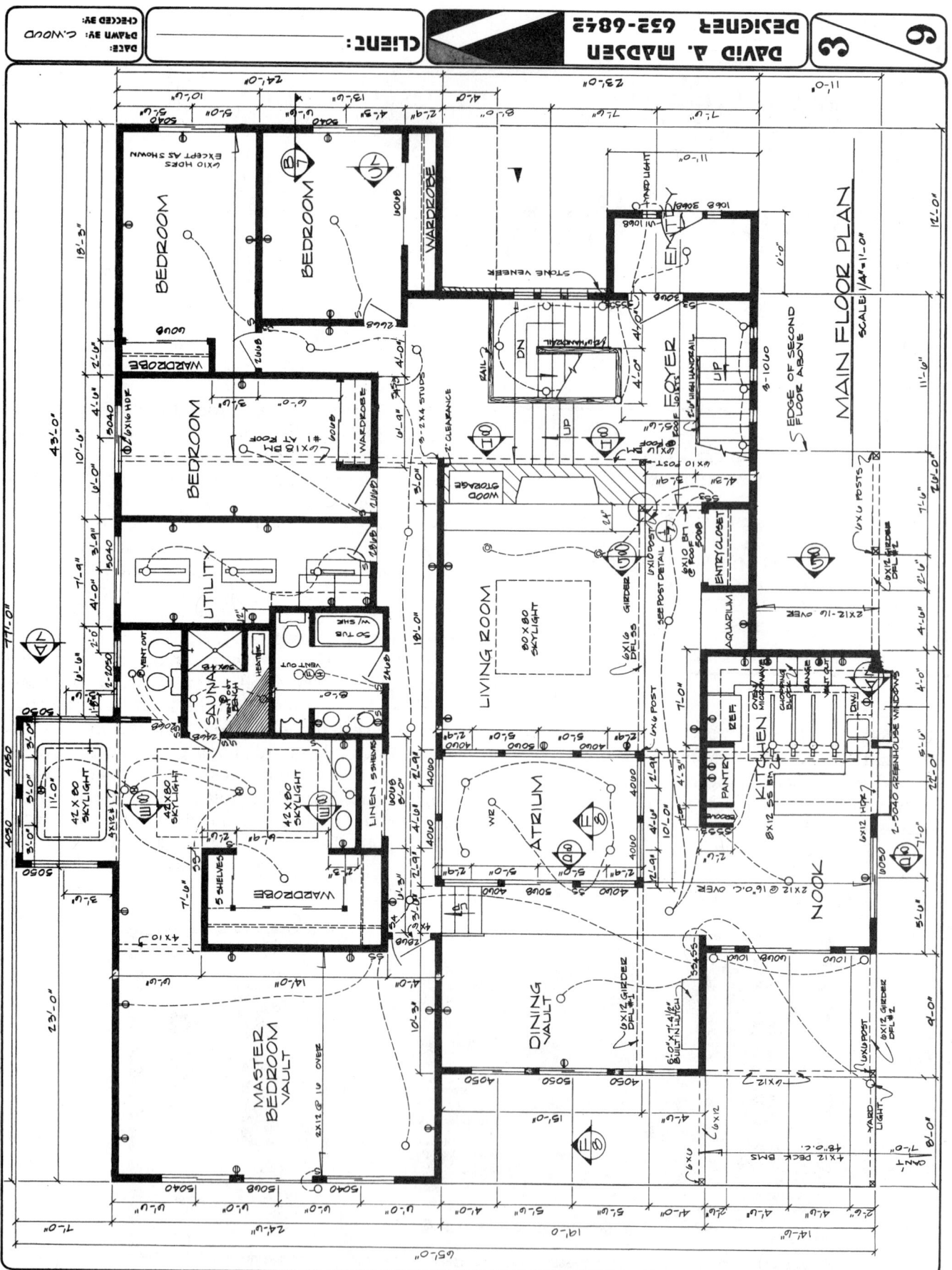

Figure 18-2 A complete residential floor plan. Courtesy Madsen Designs.

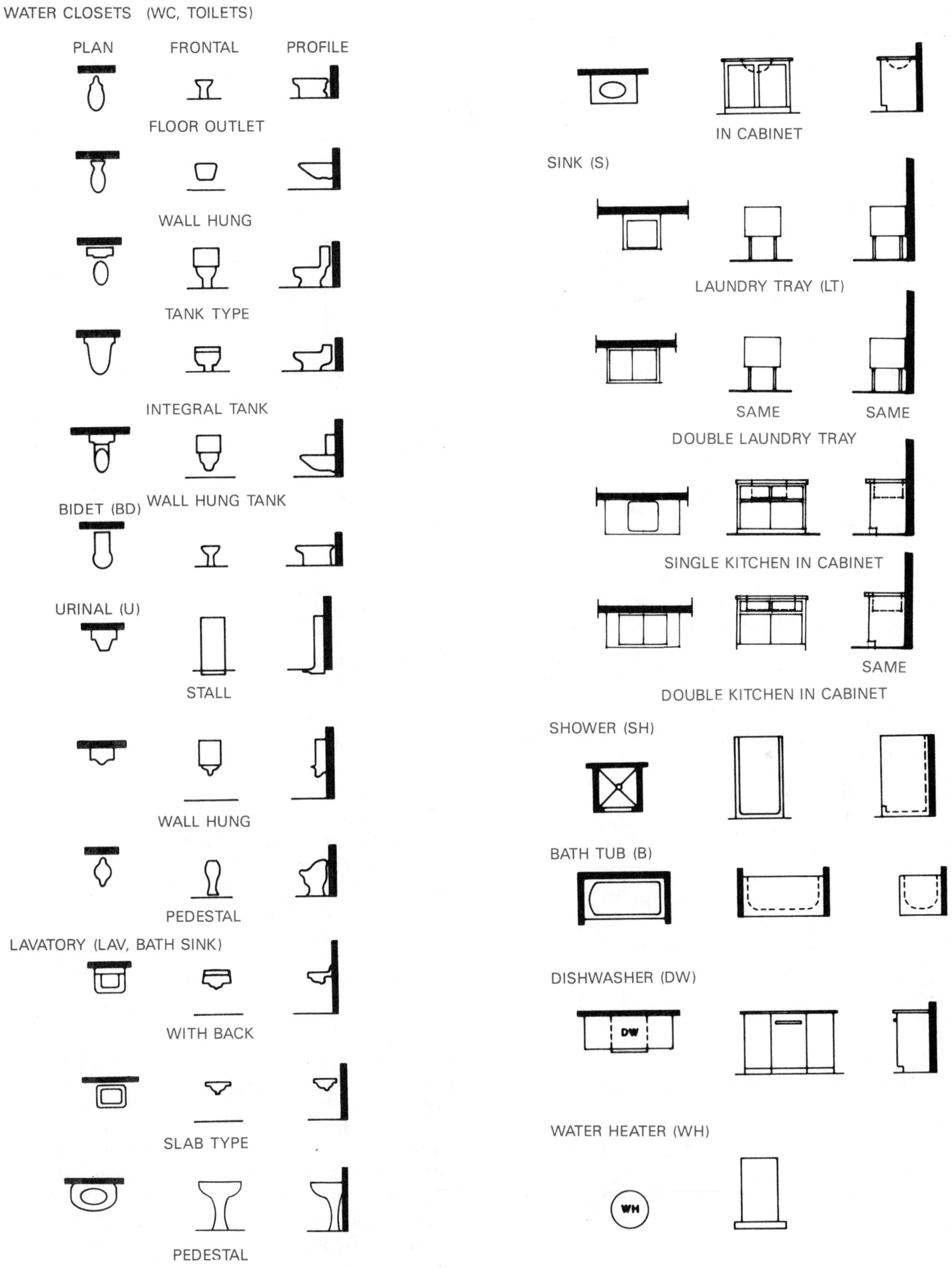

WATER CLOSETS (WC, TOILETS)

PLAN   FRONTAL   PROFILE

FLOOR OUTLET

WALL HUNG

TANK TYPE

INTEGRAL TANK

WALL HUNG TANK   BIDET (BD)

URINAL (U)

STALL

WALL HUNG

PEDESTAL

LAVATORY (LAV, BATH SINK)

WITH BACK

SLAB TYPE

PEDESTAL

IN CABINET

SINK (S)

LAUNDRY TRAY (LT)

SAME   SAME

DOUBLE LAUNDRY TRAY

SINGLE KITCHEN IN CABINET

SAME

DOUBLE KITCHEN IN CABINET

SHOWER (SH)

BATH TUB (B)

DISHWASHER (DW)

DW

WATER HEATER (WH)

WH

Figure 18–3 Plumbing fixture symbols.

Other plumbing items to be added to the floor plan include floor drains, vent pipes, and sewer or water connections. Floor drains are shown in their approximate location and are identified with a note identifying size, type, and slope to drain. Vent pipes are shown in the wall where they are to be located and labeled by size. Sewer and water service lines are located in relationship to the position in which these utilities enter the home. The service lines are commonly found on the plot plan. In the situation described here, where a very detailed plumbing layout is not provided, the plumbing contractor will be required to install quality plumbing in a manner that will meet local code requirements and also be economical. Figure 18–2 shows a complete floor plan including plumbing symbols. Figure 18–3 shows plumbing fixture symbols in plan, frontal, and profile view.

ENERGY CONSERVATION

Energy conservation methods of construction can be applied to the plumbing installation. If these types of methods are used, they can be applied to the drawing in the form of specific or general notes on detailed drawings or in construction specifications. Some energy conservation methods include:

- Insulating all exposed hot-water pipes. Cold-water pipes should be insulated in climates where freezing is a problem.
- Running water pipes in insulated spaces where possible.
- Keeping water pipes out of exterior walls where practical.
- Placing thermosiphon traps in hot-water pipes to reduce heat loss from excess hot water in the pipes.
- Locating the hot-water heater in a heated space and insulating it well.
- Selecting low-flow shower heads.
- Putting flow restrictors in faucets.
- Completely caulking plumbing pipes where they pass through the plates. See Figure 18–4.

PLUMBING SCHEDULES

Plumbing schedules are similar to door, window, and finish schedules. Schedules provide specific information regarding plumbing equipment, fixtures, and supplies. The information is condensed in a chart so that the floor plan will not be unnecessarily crowded with information. Figure 18–5 shows a typical plumbing fixture schedule.

Other schedules may include specific information regarding floor drains, water heaters, pumps, boilers,

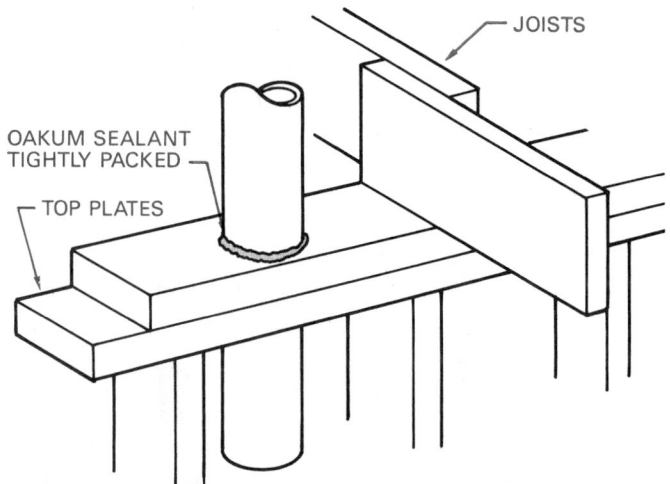

Figure 18–4 Sealing around plumbing pipes.

or radiators. These schedules generally key specific items to the floor plan with complete information describing size, manufacturer, type, and other specifications as appropriate.

Description of Plumbing Fixtures and Materials

Mortgage lenders may require a complete description of materials for the structure. Part of the description often includes a plumbing section in which certain plumbing specifications are described as shown in Figure 18–6.

PLUMBING DRAWINGS

Plumbing drawings usually are not drawn on the same sheet as the complete floor plan. The only plumbing items shown on the floor plans are fixtures as previously shown. The drafting technician or designer will prepare an accurate outline of the floor plan showing all walls, partitions, doors, windows, plumbing fixtures, and utilities. This outline can be used as a preliminary drawing for client approval and can also be used to prepare a sepia or photocopy secondary original. This secondary original will allow the drafter to save the original drawing for the complete floor plan. The secondary original will save drafting time so that the drafter will not have to prepare another outline for the plumbing drawing.

Plumbing drawings may be prepared by a drafting technician in an architectural office or in conjunction with a plumbing contractor. In some situations, when necessary, plumbing contractors will work up their own rough sketches or field drawings. Plumbing drawings are made up of lines and symbols that show how liquids, gases, or solids are transported to various locations in the structure. Plumbing lines and features are drawn thicker than wall lines so that they are clearly distinguishable. Symbols identify types of pipes, fittings, valves, and other components of the system. Sizes and specifications are provided in local or general notes. Figure 18–7 shows some typical plumbing symbols. Certain abbreviations are commonly used in plumbing drawings as shown in Figure 18–8.

WATER SYSTEMS

Water supply to a structure begins at a water meter for public systems or from a water storage tank for private well systems. The water supply to the home or business, known as the main line, is generally 1 in. plastic pipe. This size may vary in relationship

PLUMBING FIXTURE SCHEDULE

LOCATION	ITEM	MANUFACTURER	REMARKS
MASTER BATH	36" F.G. SHR. COLOR BIDET C.I. SR. COLOR LAV. COLOR W. C.	HYTEC K-4868 K-2904 K-3402-PBR	M2620 BRASS K1940 BRASS M4625 BRASS PLAS. SEAT
BATH #2	KEG STYLE TUB C.I. COLOR PED. LAV. COLOR W.C.	KOHLER KOHLER K3402-PBR	M2850 BRASS M4625 BRASS PLAS. SEAT
BATH #3	URINAL F.G. SHOWER C.I. LAVS.	K-4980 HYTEC K2904	M2620 BRASS M4625 BRASS
KITCHEN	C.I. 3 HOLE SINK	K5960	M7531 BRASS
WATER HTR.	82 GAL. ELEC.	MORFIO	P & T VALVE
UTILITY	F.G. LAUN. TRAY	24 X21	D2121 BRASS

Figure 18–5 Plumbing fixture schedule.

PLUMBING:

Fixture	Number	Location	Make	Mfr's Fixture Identification No.	Size	Color
Sink						
Lavatory						
Water closet						
Bathtub						
Shower over tub △						
Stall shower △						
Laundry trays						

△□ Curtain rod   △□ Door   □ Shower pan: material _____

Water supply: □ public; □ community system; □ individual (private) system. ★

<u>Sewage disposal</u>: □ public; □ community system; □ individual (private) system. ★

★*Show and describe individual system in complete detail in separate drawings and specifications according to requirements.*

House drain (inside): □ cast iron; □ tile; □ other _____   House sewer (outside): □ cast iron; □ tile; □ other _____

Water piping: □ galvanized steel; □ copper tubing; □ other _____   Sill cocks, number _____

Domestic water heater: type _____ ; make and model _____ ; heating capacity _____

_____ gph 100° rise.   Storage tank: material _____ ; capacity _____ gallons.

Gas service: □ utility company; □ liq. pet. gas; □ other _____   Gas piping: □ cooking; □ house heating.

Footing drains connected to: □ storm sewer; □ sanitary sewer; □ dry well.   Sump pump; make and model _____

_____ ; capacity _____ ; discharges into _____

Figure 18–6 Plumbing description of materials.

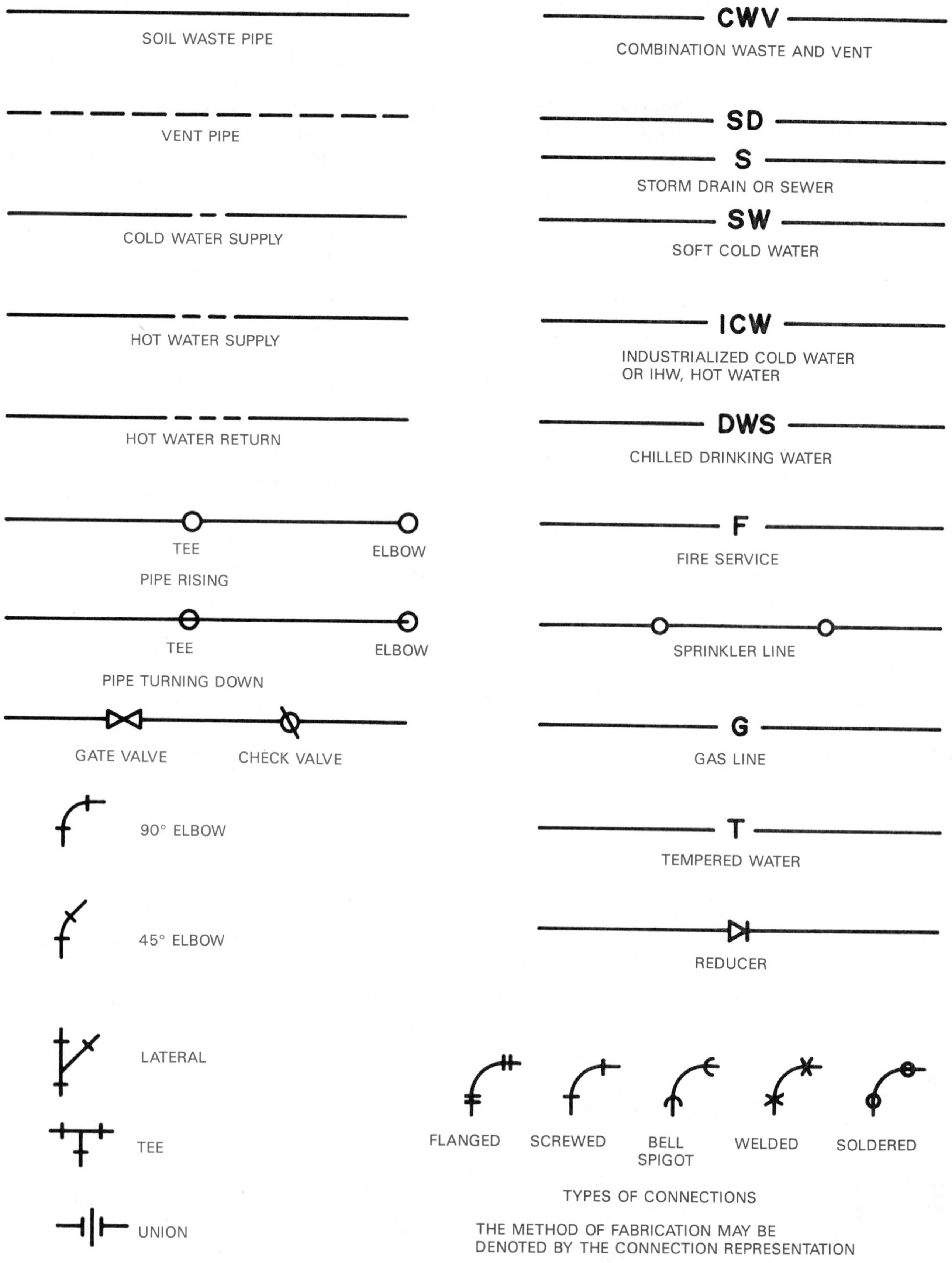

SOIL WASTE PIPE

VENT PIPE

COLD WATER SUPPLY

HOT WATER SUPPLY

HOT WATER RETURN

TEE   ELBOW

PIPE RISING

TEE   ELBOW

PIPE TURNING DOWN

GATE VALVE   CHECK VALVE

90° ELBOW

45° ELBOW

LATERAL

TEE

UNION

CWV

COMBINATION WASTE AND VENT

SD

S

STORM DRAIN OR SEWER

SW

SOFT COLD WATER

ICW

INDUSTRIALIZED COLD WATER
OR IHW, HOT WATER

DWS

CHILLED DRINKING WATER

F

FIRE SERVICE

SPRINKLER LINE

G

GAS LINE

T

TEMPERED WATER

REDUCER

FLANGED   SCREWED   BELL   WELDED   SOLDERED
SPIGOT

TYPES OF CONNECTIONS

THE METHOD OF FABRICATION MAY BE
DENOTED BY THE CONNECTION REPRESENTATION

Figure 18-7 Typical plumbing symbols.

CURRENT		MCS	
CW	Cold-Water Supply	WC	Water Closet (Toilet)
HW	Hot-Water Supply	LAV	Lavatory (Bath Sink)
HWR	Hot-Water Return	B	Bathtub
HB	Hose Bibb	S	Sink
CO	Clean Out	U	Urinal
DS	Downspout	SH	Shower
RD	Rain Drain	DF	Drinking Fountain
FD	Floor Drain	WH	Water Heater
SD	Shower Drain	DW	Dishwasher
CB	Catch Basin	BD	Bidet
MH	Manhole	GD	Garbage Disposal
VTR	Vent Thru Roof		

Figure 18-8 Typical plumbing abbreviations.

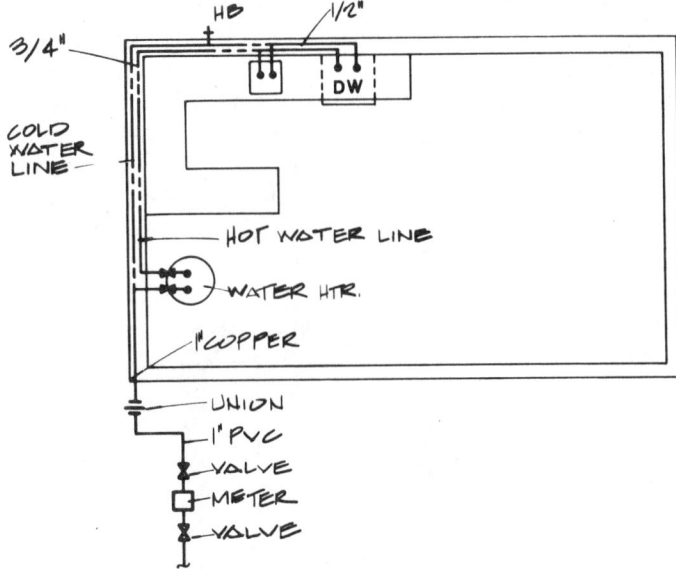

Figure 18-9 Water supply system.

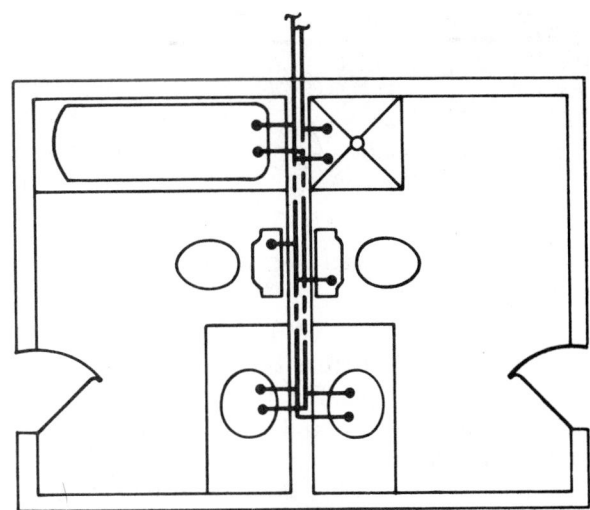

Figure 18-10 Common plumbing wall with back-to-back baths.

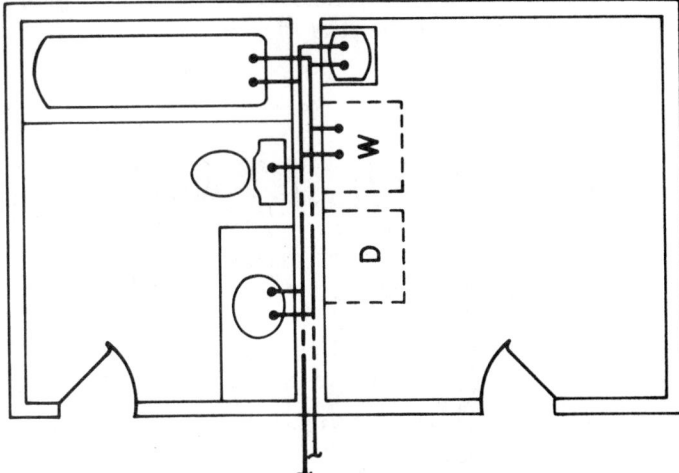

Figure 18-11 Common plumbing wall with a bath in back of a laundry.

Figure 18-12 Hot-water temperature.

to the service needed. The plastic main line joins a copper line within a few feet of the structure. The balance of the water system piping is usually copper pipe although plastic pipe is increasing in popularity for cold-water applications. The 1 in. main supply often changes to ¾ in. pipe where a junction is made to distribute water to various specific locations. From the ¾ in. distribution lines, ½ in. pipe usually supplies water to specific fixtures, for example, the kitchen sink. Figure 18-9 shows a typical installation from the water meter of a house with distribution to a kitchen. The water meter location and main line representation are generally shown on the plot plan. Verify local codes regarding the use of plastic pipe.

There is some advantage to placing plumbing fixtures adjacent or back-to-back when possible. This practice will save materials and labor costs. Also, when designing a two-story structure, placing plumbing fixtures one above the other aids in an economical installation. If the functional design of the floor plan clearly does not allow for such economy measures,

then good judgment should be used in the placement of plumbing fixtures so that the installation of the plumbing is physically possible. Figure 18-10 shows a back-to-back bath situation. If the design allows, another common installation may be a bath and laundry room next to each other to provide a common plumbing wall. See Figure 18-11. If a specific water temperature is required, that specification can be applied to the hot water line as shown in Figure 18-12.

CADD
applications

DRAWING PLUMBING SYMBOLS WITH CADD

In residential architecture, the plumbing drawings usually amount to placing floor-plan symbols such as sinks, water closets, and tubs. In commercial architecture applications, a separate plumbing drawing shows the complete plumbing layout with symbols and pipes on a separate CADD layer. The floor plan serves as the base sheet. So, by turning the plumbing layer ON you have a composite drawing with the floor plan, plumbing symbols, and plumbing layout shown. You also have the flexibility to turn the plumbing layer OFF when you want to display the floor plan without plumbing. Many companies show two separate drawings on commercial projects—the (1) floor plan completely dimensioned and (2) the floor plan walls and plumbing layout. This is easy to do, because all you have to do is turn ON or OFF specific layers as needed to display what you want. Most architectural CADD programs are tablet menu driven with a symbols library for plumbing applications, as shown in Figure 1. A drafter simply selects

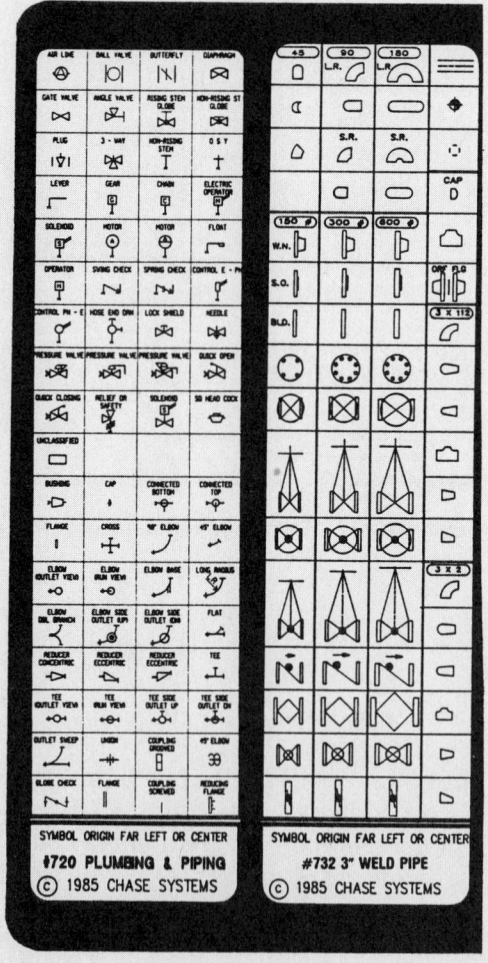

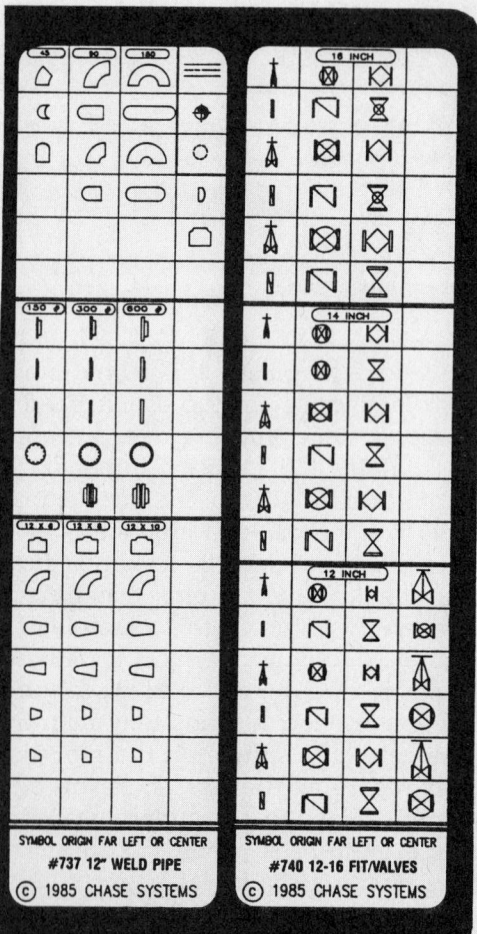

(a)

Figure 1 CADD symbols library for plumbing applications. *Courtesy Chase Systems.*

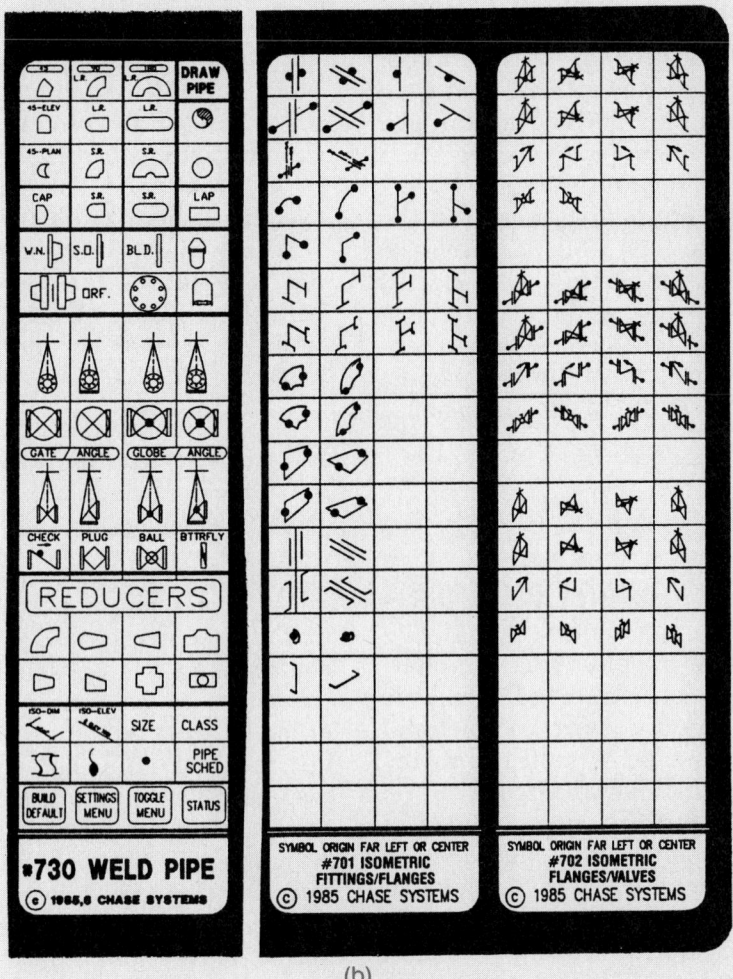

(b)

Figure 1 Continued.

the desired symbol from the tablet menu and then drags the symbol into position on the drawing. Parametric design plays an important role in applications such as multiple water closet stalls in a commercial building rest room. You specify the distance between walls or the width of each stall, the number of stalls, the stall length, and the door-swing direction; the computer then automatically draws the entire series of rest room stalls as shown in Figure 2.

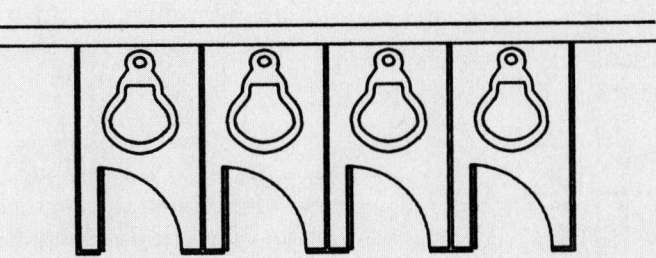

Figure 2 A series of stalls drawn using CADD.

DRAINAGE AND VENT SYSTEMS

The drainage system provides for the distribution of solid and liquid waste to the sewer line. The vent system allows for a continuous flow of air through the system so that gases and odors may dissipate and bacteria will not have an opportunity to develop. These pipes throughout the house are generally made of PVC plastic, although the pipe from the house to the concrete sewer pipe is commonly 3 or 4 in. cast iron. Drainage and vent systems, as with water systems, are drawn with thick lines using symbols, abbreviations, and notes. Figure 18–13 shows a sample drainage vent system. Figure 18–14 shows a house plumbing plan.

 ISOMETRIC PLUMBING DRAWINGS

Isometric drawings may be used to provide a three-dimensional representation of a plumbing layout. Figure 18–15 shows an isometric plumbing template. Especially for a two-story structure, an isometric drawing provides an easy-to-understand pictorial drawing. Figure 18–16 shows an isometric drawing of the system shown in plan view in Figure 18–13. Figure 18–17 shows a detailed isometric drawing of a typical drain, waste, and vent system. Figure 18–18 shows a single-line isometric drawing of the detailed isometric drawing shown in Figure 18–17. Figure 18–19 shows a detailed isometric drawing of a hot- and cold-water supply system. Figure 18–20 shows a single-line isometric drawing of that same system.

SOLAR HOT WATER

Solar hot-water collectors are available for new or existing residential, commercial, or industrial instal-

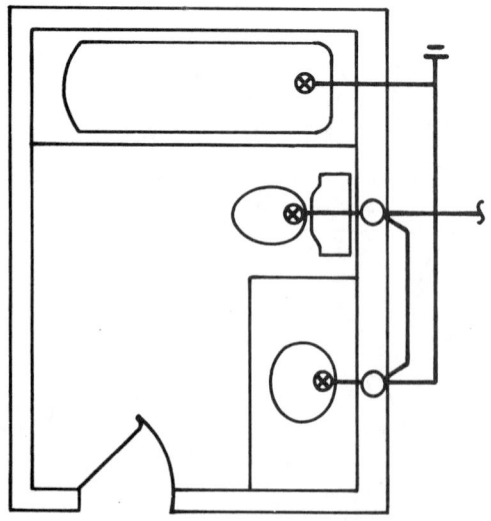

Figure 18–13 Drainage and vent drawing.

lations. Solar collectors may be located on a roof, wall, or on the ground. Figure 18–21 shows a typical application of solar collectors. Solar systems vary in efficiency. The number of collectors needed to provide heat to a structure depends upon the size of the structure and the volume of heat needed.

The flat-plate collector is the heart of a solar system. Its main parts are the transparent glass cover, absorber plate, flow tubes, and insulated enclosure. See Chapter 12 for a complete discussion of solar collectors. Figure 18–22 displays a typical piping and wiring drawing for a complete solar hot-water heating system.

SEWAGE DISPOSAL

Public Sewers

Public sewers are available in and near most cities and towns. The public sewers are generally located under the street or an easement adjacent to the construction site. In some situations the sewer line may have to be extended to accommodate the addition of another home or business in a newly developed area. The cost of this extension may be the responsibility of the developer. Usually the public sewer line is under the street so that the new construction will have a line from the structure to the sewer. The cost of this construction usually includes installation expenses, street repair, sewer tap, and permit fees. Figure 18–23 shows an illustration of a sewer connection and the plan view usually found on the plot plan.

Private Sewage Disposal, a Septic System

The septic system consists of a storage tank and an absorption field and operates as follows. Solid and liquid waste enters the septic tank where it is stored and begins decomposition into sludge. Liquid material, or effluent, flows from the tank outlet and is dispersed into a soil-absorption field, or drain field (also known as leach lines). When the solid waste has effectively decomposed, it also dissipates into the soil absorption field. The owner should use a recommended chemical to work as a catalyst for complete decomposition of solid waste. Septic tanks may become overloaded in a period of up to ten years and may require pumping.

The characteristics of the soil must be verified for suitability for a septic system by a soil feasibility test, also known as a percolation test. This test, performed by a soil scientist or someone from the local government, will determine if the soil will accommodate a septic system. The test should also identify certain specifications that should be followed for system installation. The Federal Veterans Administra-

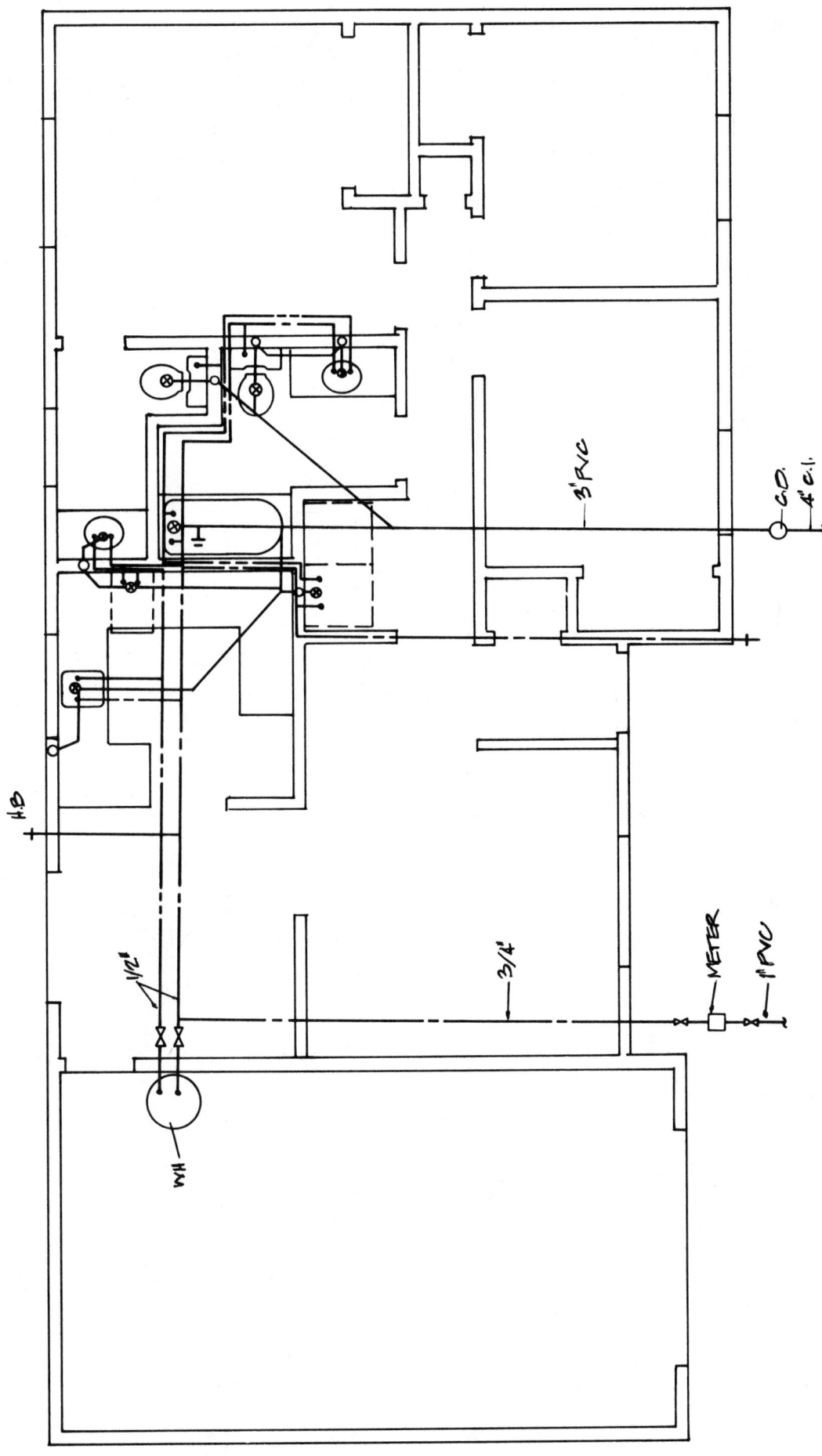

Figure 18-14 House plumbing plan.

tion (VA) and the Federal Housing Administration (FHA) require a minimum of 240 ft of field line or more if the soil feasibility test shows it necessary. Verify these dimensions with local building officials. When the soil characteristics will not allow a conventional system, there may be some alternatives such as a sand filter system, which filters the effluent through a specially designed sand filter before it enters the soil absorption field. Check with your local code officials before calling for such a system. Figure 18–24 shows a typical serial septic system. The serial system allows for one drain field line to fill before the next line is used. The drain field lines must be level and must follow the contour of the land perpendicular to the slope. The drain field should be at least 100 ft from a water well but verify the distance with local codes. There is usually no minimum distance to a public water supply.

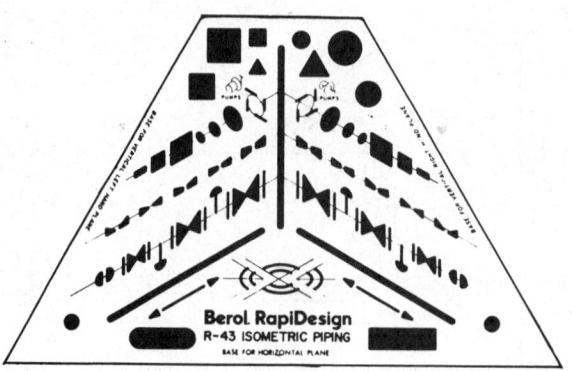

Figure 18–15 Isometric piping template. *Courtesy Berol USA RapiDesign.*

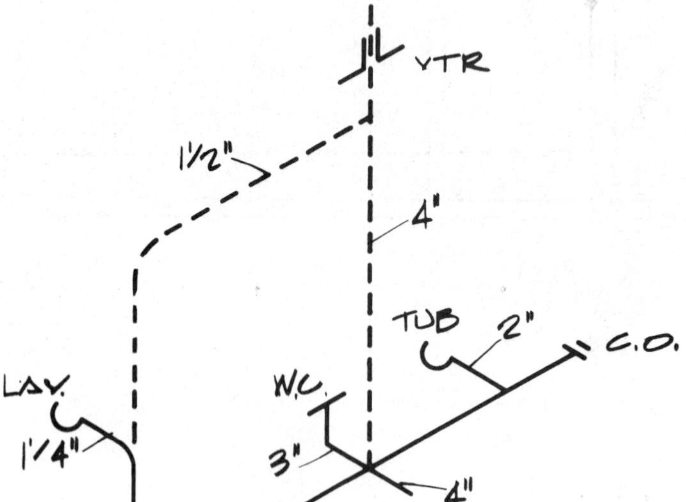

Figure 18–16 Single-line isometric layout of drainage and vent drawing.

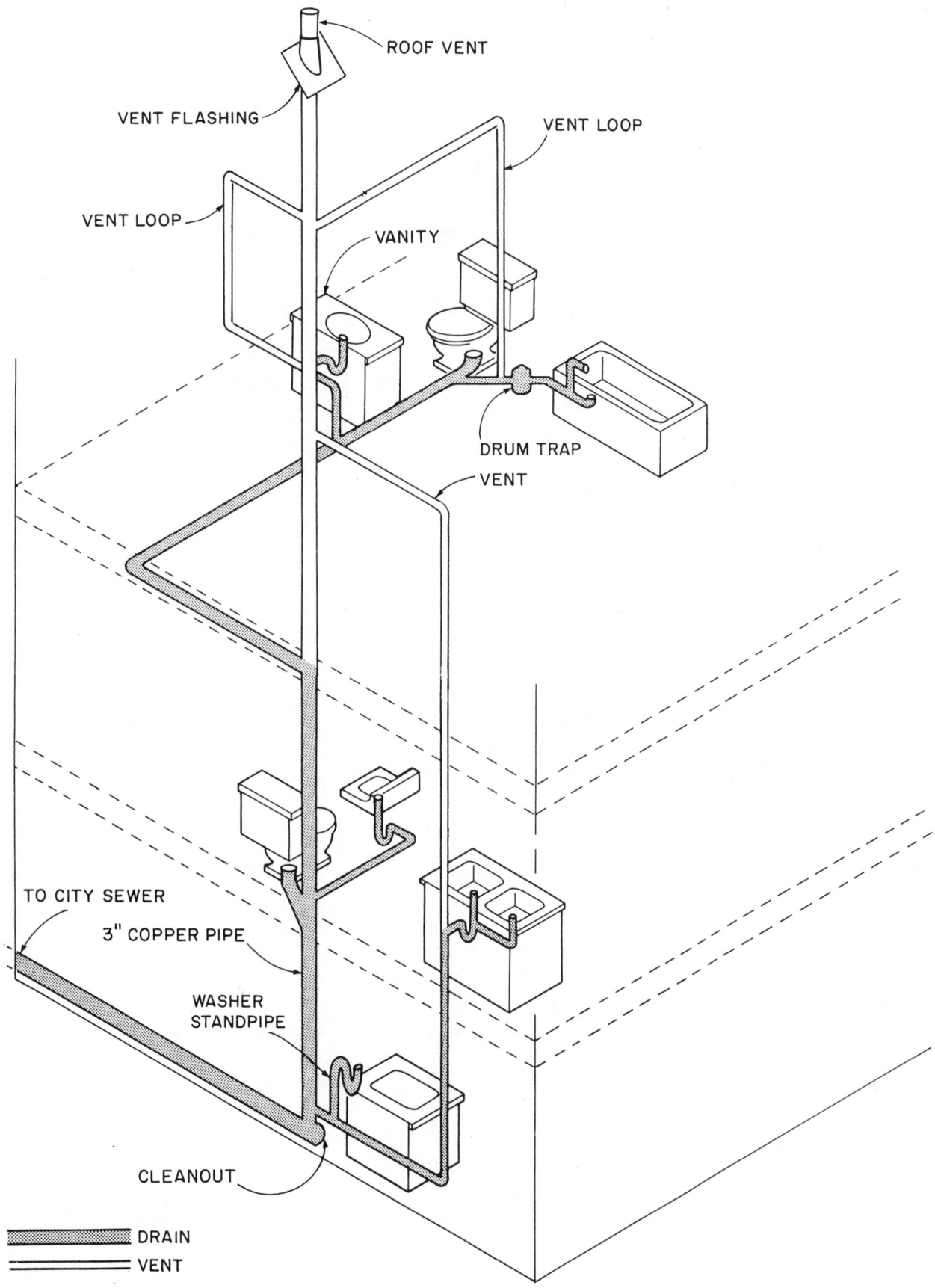

Figure 18–17 Detailed isometric drawing of drain, waste, and vent system. *From Huth*, Understanding Construction Drawings, *Delmar Publishers Inc.*

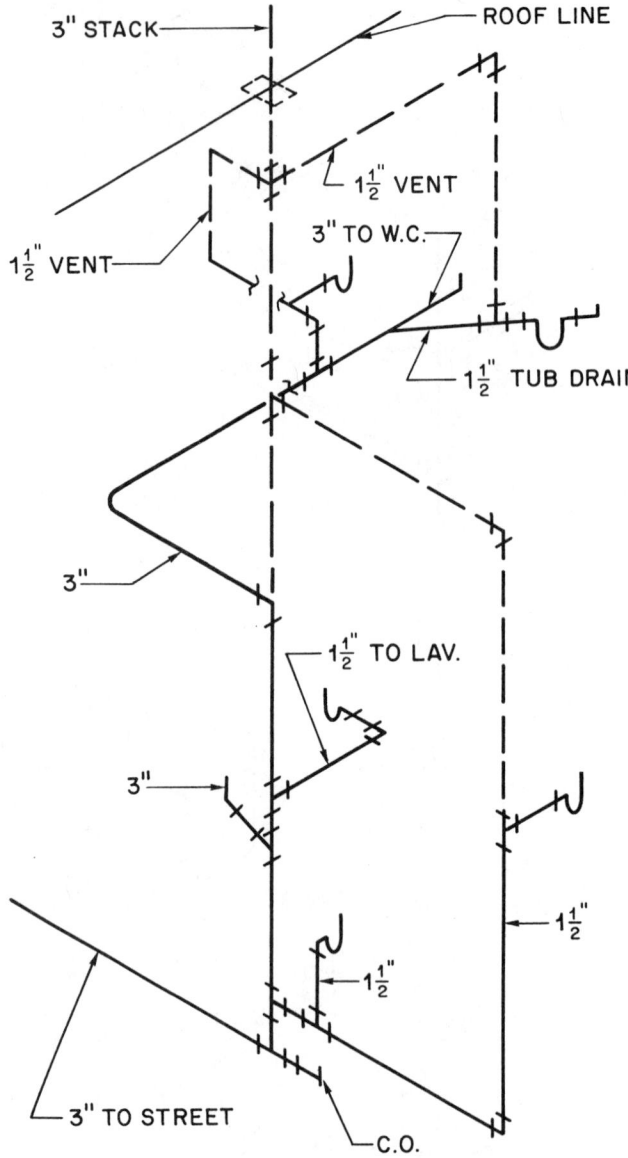

Figure 18-18 Single-line isometric view of drain, waste, and vent system. *From Huth,* Understanding Construction Design, *Delmar Publishers Inc.*

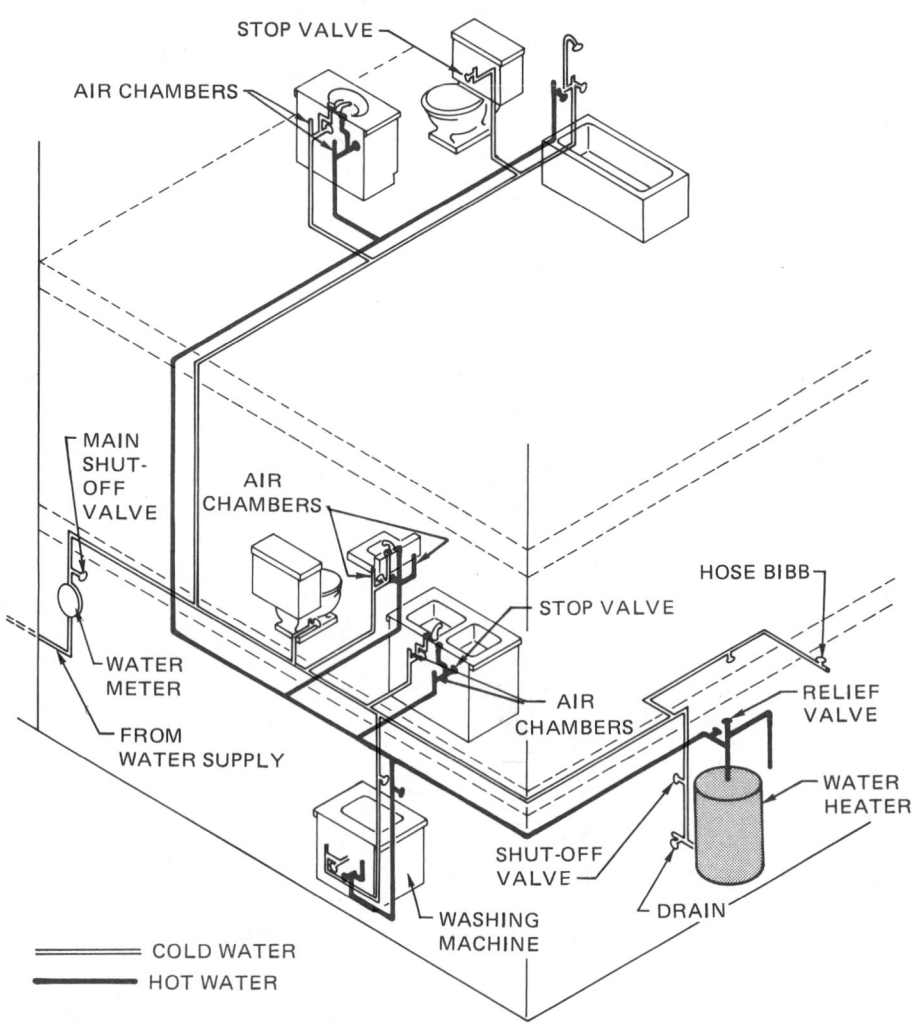

Figure 18–19
Detailed isometric
drawing of hot- and
cold-water system.

STOP VALVE

AIR CHAMBERS

MAIN SHUT-OFF VALVE

AIR CHAMBERS

WATER METER

FROM WATER SUPPLY

STOP VALVE

HOSE BIBB

AIR CHAMBERS

RELIEF VALVE

WATER HEATER

SHUT-OFF VALVE

DRAIN

WASHING MACHINE

COLD WATER

HOT WATER

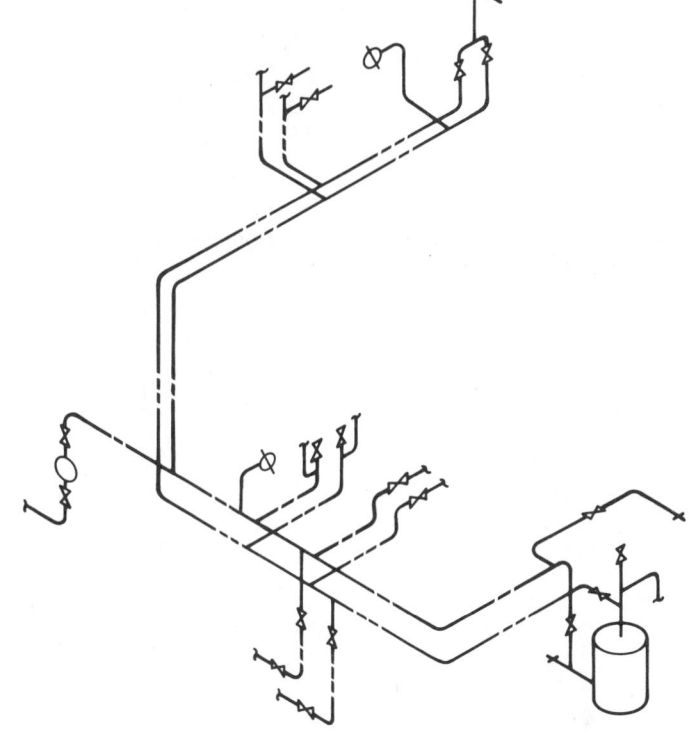

Figure 18–20 Single-line
isometric drawing of hot-
and cold-water system.

Typical Applications

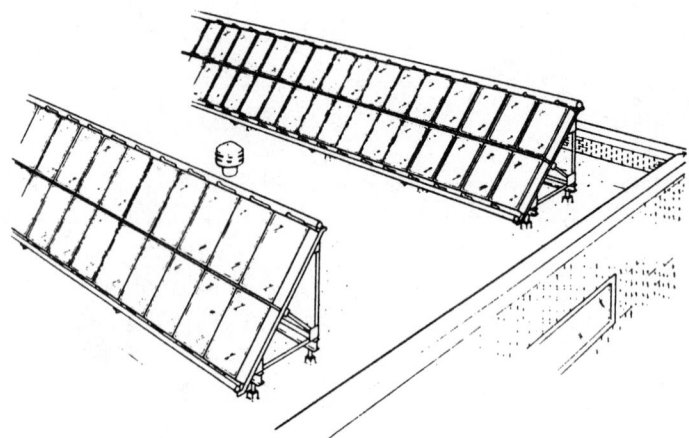

Figure 18–21 Typical application of solar hot-water collectors. *Courtesy Lennox Industries, Inc.*

TWO-TANK SYSTEM
TYPICAL PIPING AND WIRING

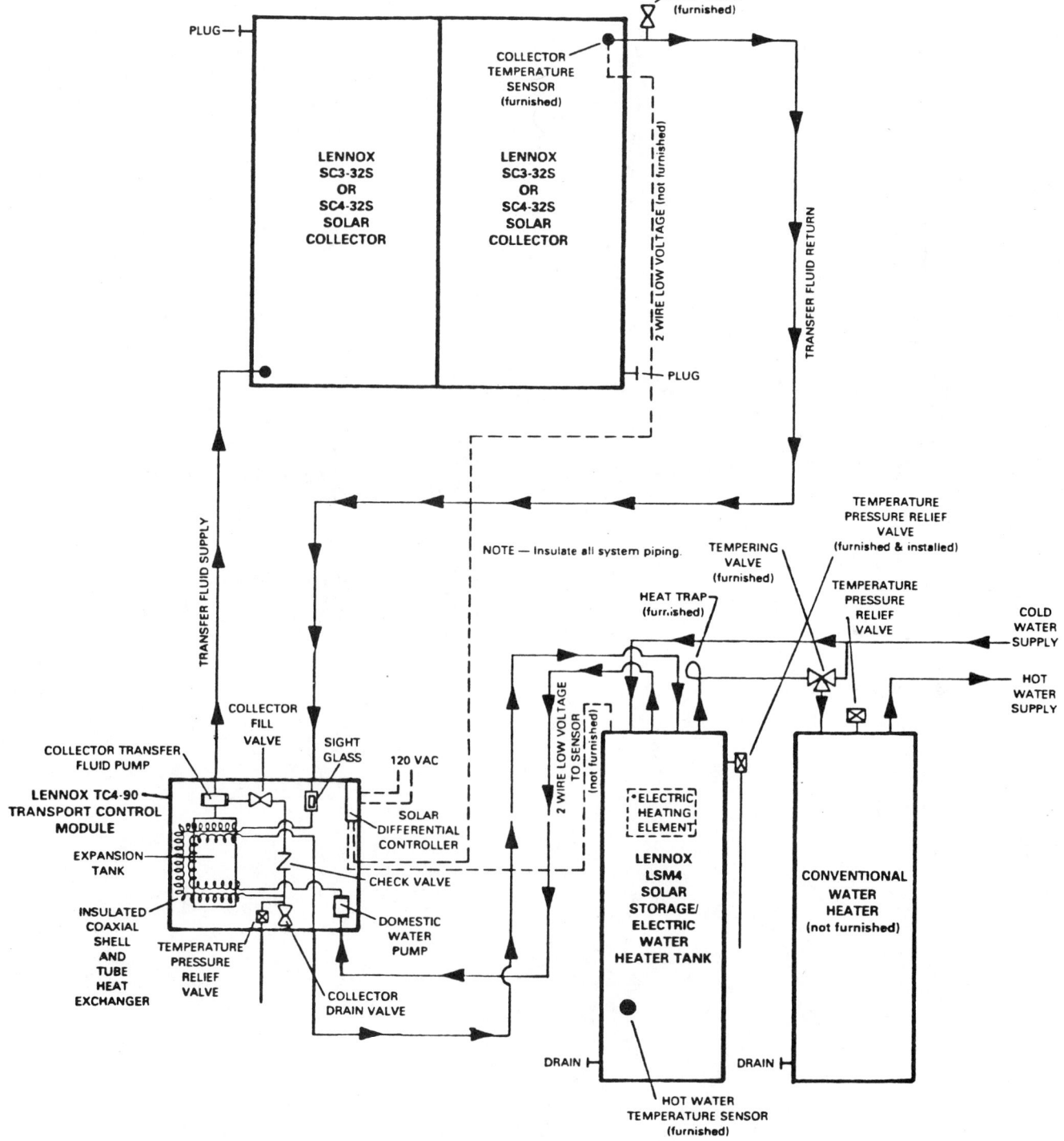

Figure 18–22 Piping and wiring diagram for two-tank solar hot-water system. *Courtesy Lennox Industries, Inc.*

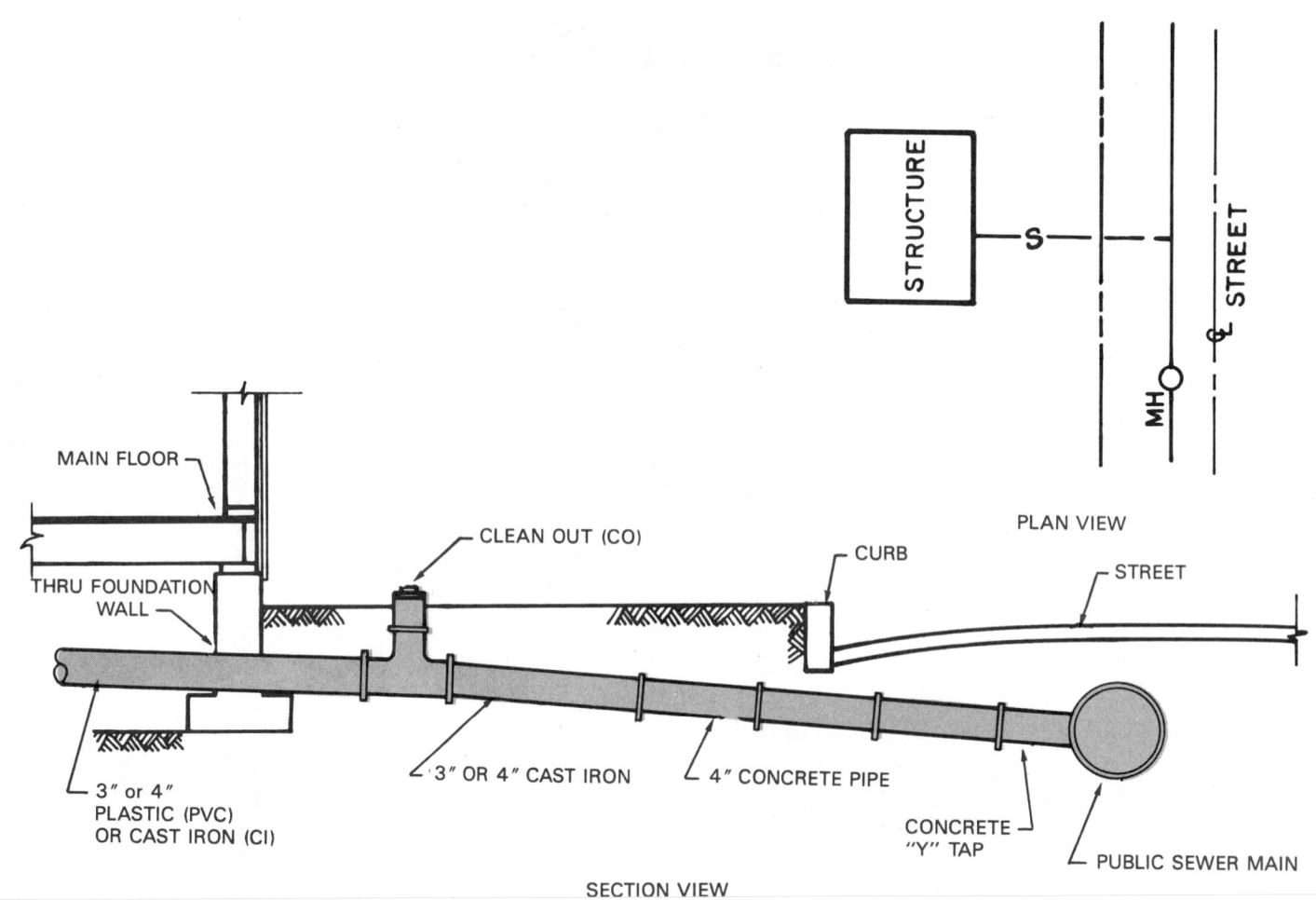

MAIN FLOOR

CLEAN OUT (CO)

CURB

STREET

PLAN VIEW

STRUCTURE

S

℄ STREET

MH

THRU FOUNDATION WALL

3″ or 4″ PLASTIC (PVC) OR CAST IRON (CI)

3″ OR 4″ CAST IRON

4″ CONCRETE PIPE

CONCRETE "Y" TAP

PUBLIC SEWER MAIN

SECTION VIEW

Figure 18–23 Public sewer system.

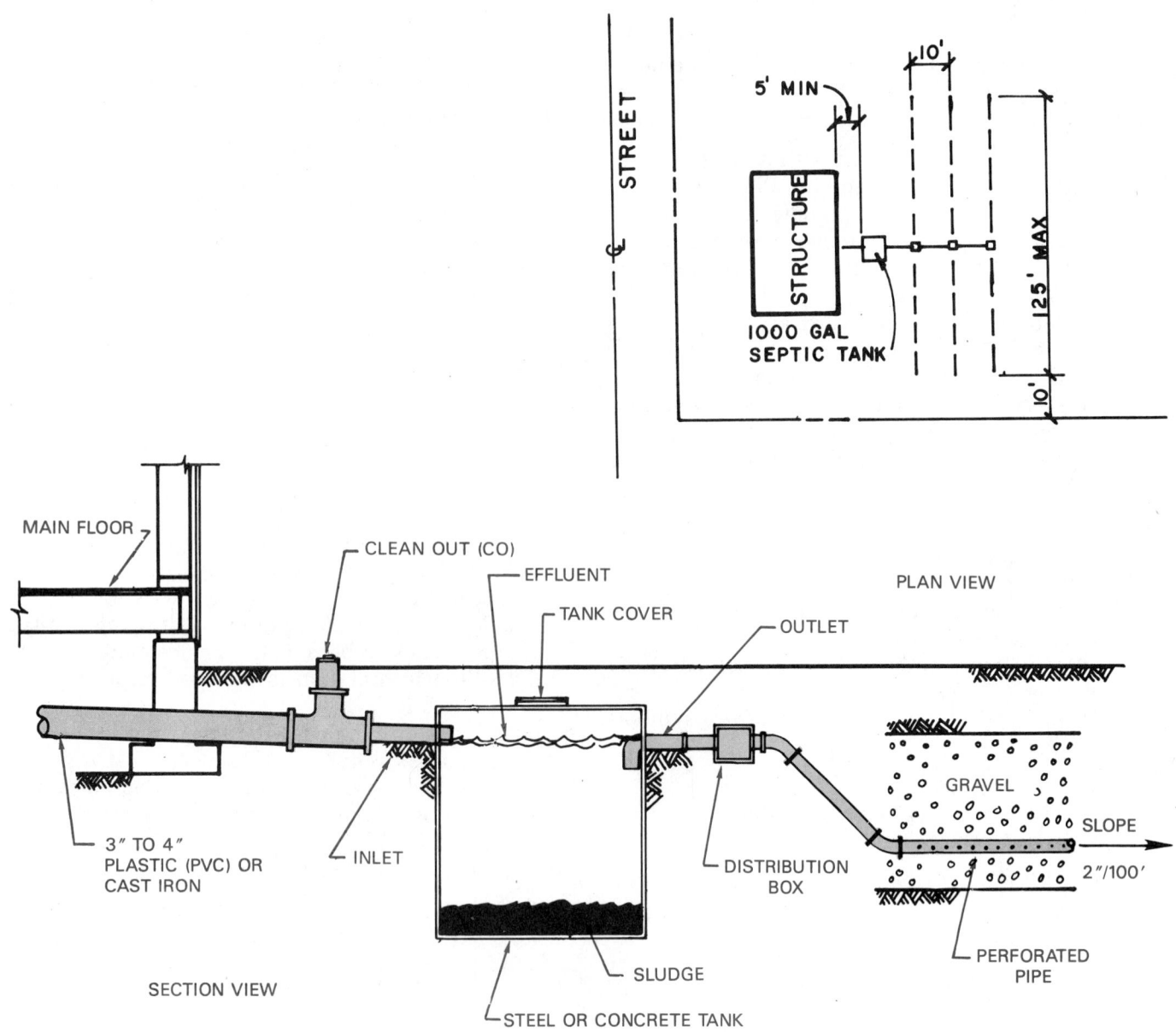

STREET

5' MIN

10'

125' MAX

10'

STRUCTURE

1000 GAL
SEPTIC TANK

PLAN VIEW

MAIN FLOOR

CLEAN OUT (CO)

EFFLUENT

TANK COVER

OUTLET

3" TO 4"
PLASTIC (PVC) OR
CAST IRON

INLET

DISTRIBUTION
BOX

GRAVEL

SLOPE
2"/100'

PERFORATED
PIPE

SLUDGE

SECTION VIEW

STEEL OR CONCRETE TANK

Figure 18–24 Septic sewer system.

PLUMBING PLANS TEST

DIRECTIONS

Answer the questions with short complete statements or drawings as needed on an 8½ × 11 drawing sheet as follows:

1. Use ⅛ in. guidelines for all lettering.
2. Letter your name, Plumbing Plans Test, and the date at the top of the sheet.
3. Letter the question number and provide the answer. You do not need to write out the question.
4. Do all lettering with vertical uppercase architectural letters. If the answer requires line work, use proper drafting tools and technique. Answers may be prepared on a word processor if appropriate with course guidelines.
5. Your grade will be based on correct answers and quality of line technique.

QUESTIONS

1. Floor plan plumbing symbols are generally drawn at what scale?
2. Identify four methods that can contribute to energy efficient plumbing.
3. Draw the following plumbing fixture symbols in plan view:

   a. Water closet
   b. 5'–0" long × 2'–6" wide bathtub
   c. Shower 3'–0" × 3'–0"
   d. Urinal
   e. Lavatory cabinet with oval sink
   f. Laundry tray

4. Draw the following plumbing piping symbols:

   a. Hot-water supply
   b. Cold-water supply
   c. Soil waste pipe
   d. Gate valve
   e. 90° elbow
   f. Tee

5. Define the following plumbing abbreviations:

   a. CO
   b. FD
   c. VTR
   d. WC
   e. WH
   f. SH

6. Make a single-line isometric drawing of a typical kitchen sink piping diagram.
7. Make a single-line isometric drawing of a typical drain, waste, and vent system.
8. Make a floor-plan plumbing drawing of a typical back-to-back bath arrangement.
9. What information is required on a plumbing schedule?
10. Are plumbing drawings required by all contractors? Why?
11. List at least one advantage and one disadvantage of solar hot-water systems.
12. Briefly explain how the public sewer and private septic systems differ.

Chapter 19
Heating, Ventilating, and Air Conditioning

◄ CENTRAL FORCED-AIR SYSTEMS

ONE OF the most common systems for heating and air conditioning circulates the air from the living spaces through or around heating or cooling devices. A fan forces the air into sheet metal or plastic pipes called ducts and the ducts connect to openings called diffusers, or air supply registers. Warm air (WA) or cold air (CA) passes through the ducts and registers to enter the rooms and either heats or cools them as needed.

Air then flows from the room through another opening into the return duct, or return air register (RA). The return duct directs the air from the rooms over the heating or cooling device. If warm air is required, the return air is either passed over the surface of a combustion chamber (the part of a furnace where fuel is burned) or a heating coil. If cool air is required, the return air passes over the surface

of a cooling coil. Finally, the conditioned air is picked up again by the fan and the air cycle is repeated. Figure 19–1(a) and 19–1(b) shows the air cycle in a forced-air system.

Heating Cycle

If the air cycle just described is used for heating, the heat is generated in a furnace. Furnaces for residential heating produce heat by burning fuel oil or natural gas, or from electric heating coils. If the heat comes from burning fuel oil or natural gas, the combustion (burning) takes place inside a combustion chamber. The air to be heated does not enter the combustion chamber but absorbs heat from the outer surface of the chamber. The gases given off by combustion are vented through a chimney. In an electric furnace, the air to be heated is passed directly over the heating coils. This type of furnace does not require a chimney.

Cooling Cycle

If the air from the room is to be cooled, it is passed over a cooling coil. The most common type of residential cooling system is based on two principles:

1. As liquid changes to vapor, it absorbs large amounts of heat.
2. The boiling point of a liquid can be changed by changing the pressure applied to the liquid. This is the same as saying that the temperature of a liquid can be raised by increasing its pressure and lowered by reducing its pressure.

Common refrigerants can boil (change to a vapor) at very low temperatures; some as low as 21° F below zero.

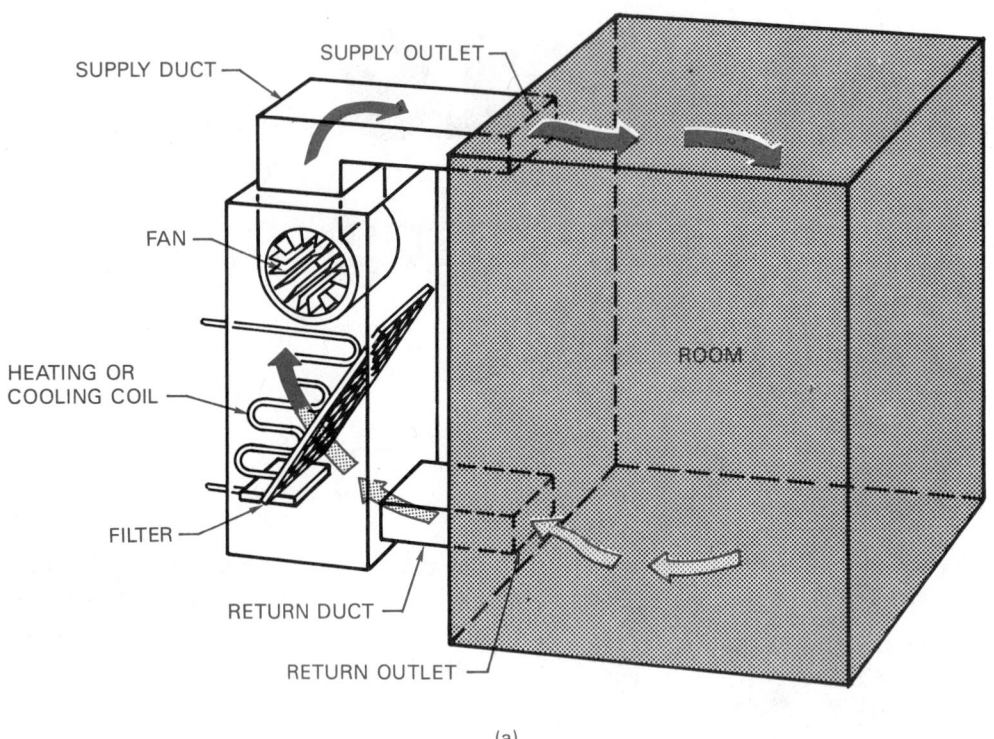

(a)

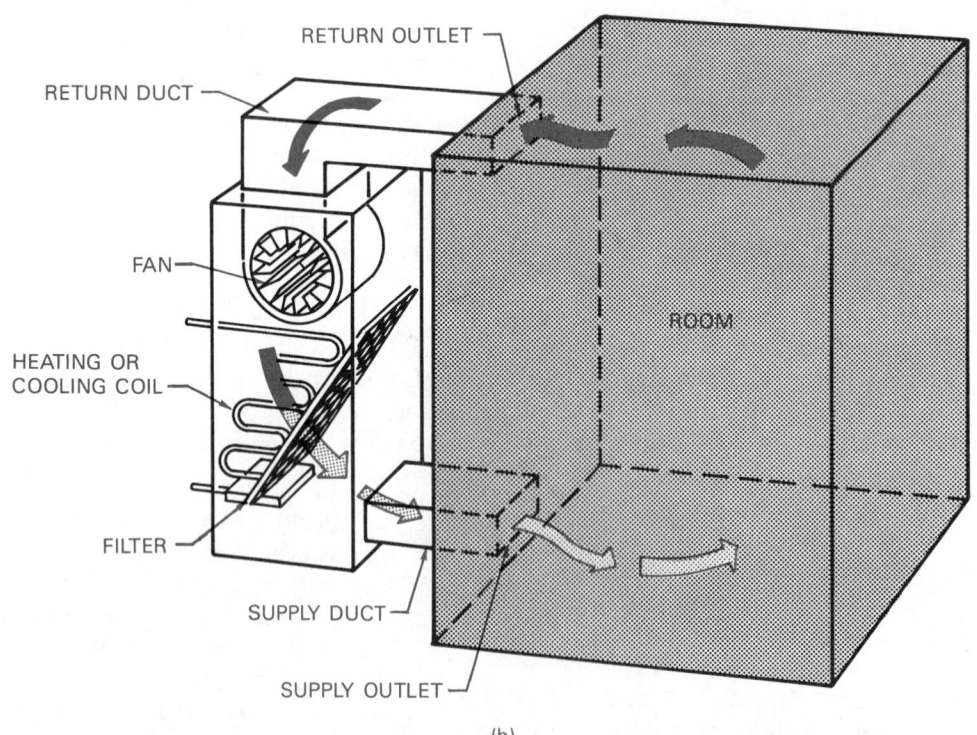

(b)

Figure 19–1 (a) Down-draft forced-air system heated air cycle. *From Huth,* Understanding Construction Drawings, *Delmar Publishers Inc.,* (b) up-draft forced-air system heated air cycle.

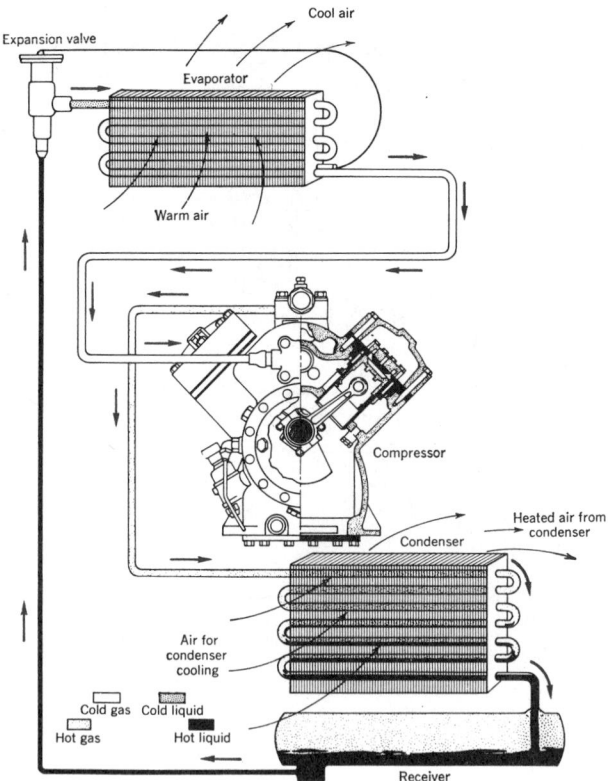

Figure 19–2 Schematic diagram of cooling cycle. *From Lang, Principles of Air Conditioning, 3rd ed., Delmar Publishers Inc.*

The principal parts of a refrigeration system are the cooling coil (evaporator), compressor, the condenser, and the expansion valve. Figure 19–2 shows a diagram of the cooling cycle. The cooling cycle operates as follows. Warm air from the ducts is passed over the evaporator. As the cold liquid refrigerant moves through the evaporator coil it picks up heat from the warm air. As the liquid picks up heat, it changes to a vapor. The heated refrigerant vapor is then drawn into the compressor where it is put under high pressure. This causes the temperature of the vapor to rise even more.

Next, the high-temperature, high-pressure vapor passes to the condenser where the heat is removed. This is done by blowing air over the coils of the condenser. As the condenser removes heat the vapor changes to a liquid. It is still under high pressure, however. From the condenser, the refrigerant flows to the expansion valve. As the liquid refrigerant passes through the valve, the pressure is reduced which lowers the temperature of the liquid still further so that it is ready to pick up more heat.

The cold low-pressure liquid then moves to the evaporator. The pressure in the evaporator is low enough to allow the refrigerant to boil again and absorb more heat from the air passing over the coil of the evaporator.

Forced-air Heating Plans

Complete plans for the heating system may be needed when applying for a building permit or a mortgage depending upon the requirements of the local building jurisdiction or the lending agency. If a complete heating layout is required, it can be prepared by either the architectural drafter or heating contractor.

When forced-air electric, gas, or oil heating systems are used, the warm-air outlets and return air locations may be shown as in Figure 19–3. Notice that the registers are normally placed in front of a window so that warm air will be circulated next to the coldest part of the room. As the warm air rises, a circulation action is created as the air goes through the complete heating cycle. Cold-air returns are often placed in the ceiling or floor of a central location.

A complete forced-air heating plan will show the size, location and number of Btu dispersed to the rooms from the warm-air supplies. Btu stands for British thermal unit which is a measure of heat. The location and size of the cold-air return and the location, type and output of the furnace is also shown.

The warm-air registers are sized in inches, for example, 4 × 12. The size of the duct is also given, as shown in Figure 19–4. The note 20/24 denotes a 20″ × 24″ register while a number 8 next to a duct denotes an 8″ diameter duct. This same system may be used as a central cooling system when cool air is forced from an air conditioner through the ducts and into the rooms. WA denotes warm air, and RA is return air. CFM is cubic feet per minute, the rate of air flow.

HOT-WATER SYSTEMS

In a hot-water system, the water is heated in an oil- or gas-fired boiler and then circulated through pipes to radiators or convectors in the rooms. The boiler is supplied with water from the fresh water supply for the house. The water is circulated around the combustion chamber where it absorbs heat.

In one kind of system, one pipe leaves the boiler and runs through the rooms of the building and back to the boiler. In this one-pipe system the heated water leaves the supply, is circulated through the outlet, and is returned to the same pipe, as shown in Figure 19–5. In a two-pipe system, two pipes run throughout the building. One pipe supplies heated water to all of the outlets. The other is a return pipe which carries the water back to the boiler for reheating, as seen in Figure 19–6.

Hot-water systems use a pump, called a circulator, to move the water through the system. The water is kept at a temperature between 150°–180° F in the

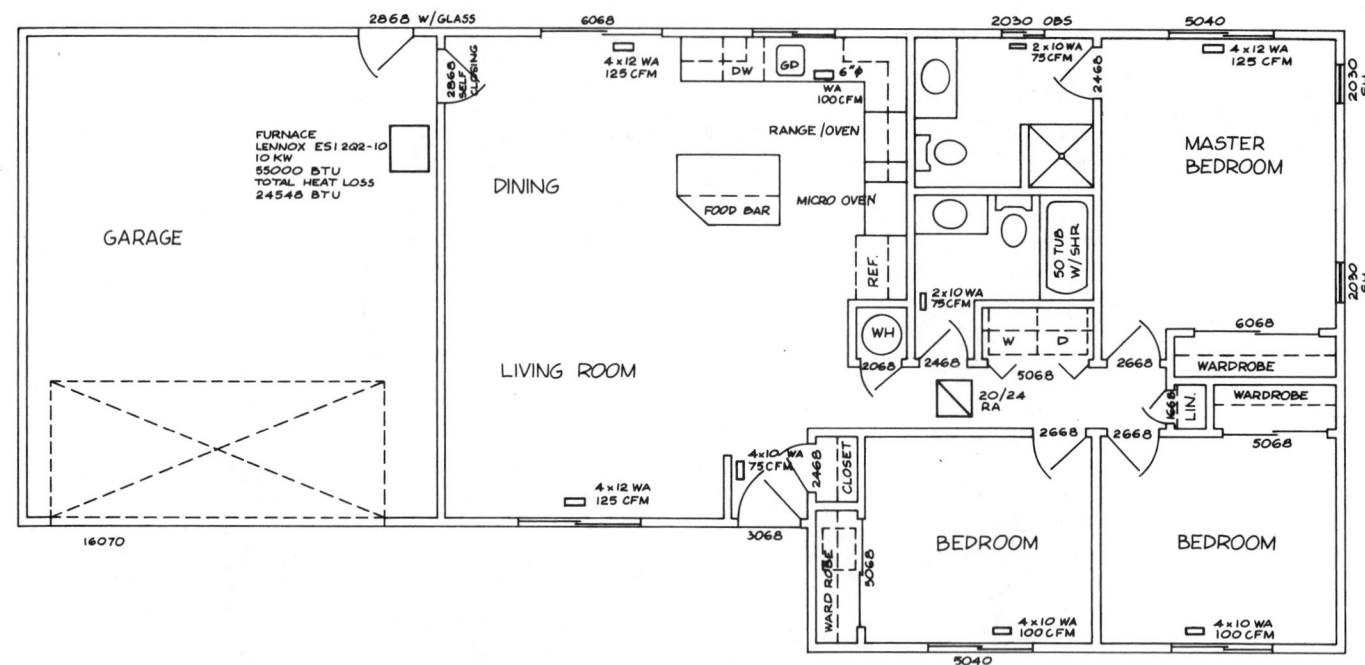

Figure 19–3 Simplified forced-air plan.

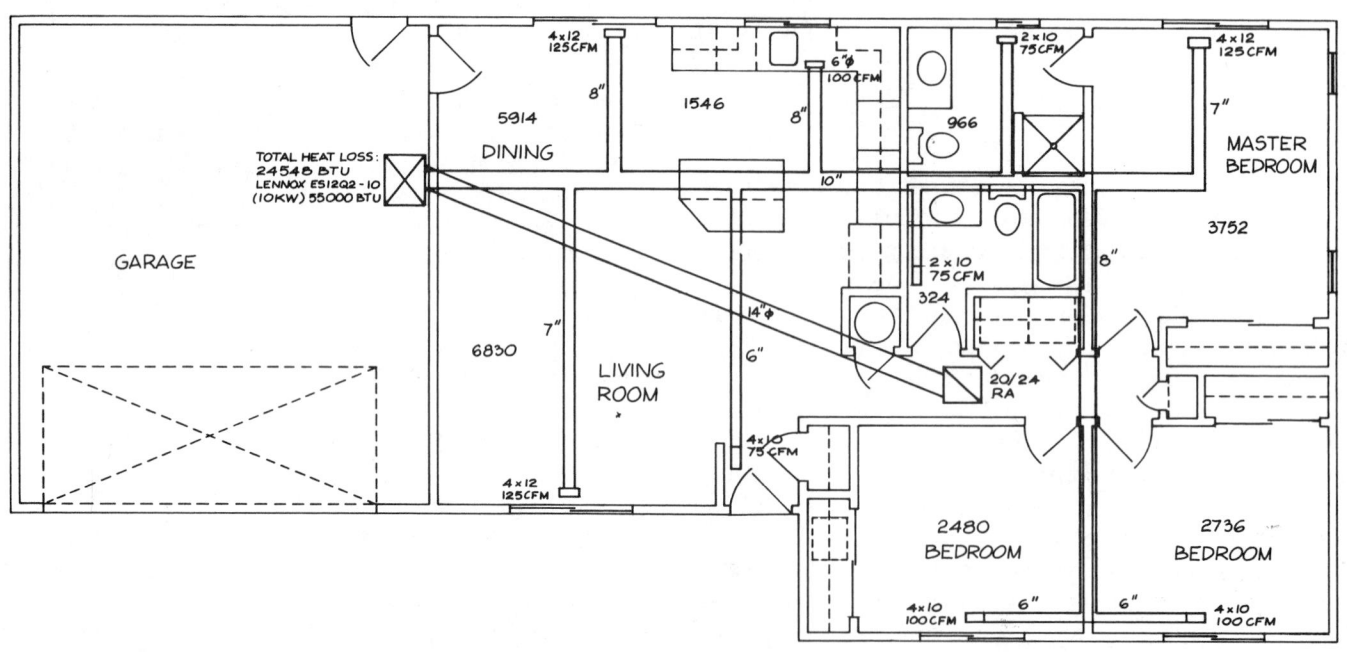

Figure 19–4 Detailed forced-air plan.

boiler. When heat is needed, the thermostat starts the circulator which supplies hot water to the convectors in the rooms.

HVAC SYMBOLS

There are over a hundred heating, ventilating and air conditioning (HVAC) symbols that may be used in residential and commercial heating plans. Only a few of the symbols are typically used in residential HVAC drawings. Figure 19–7 shows some common HVAC symbols. Figure 19–8 shows a sheet metal conduit template and a heating and air conditioning template. These templates are time-saving devices that are used to help improve the quality of drafting for HVAC systems.

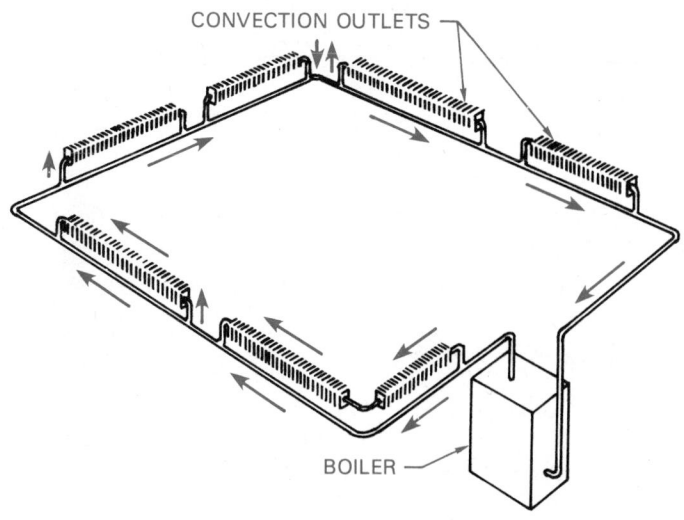

Figure 19-5 One-pipe hot-water system. *From Huth, Understanding Construction Drawings, Delmar Publishers Inc.*

Figure 19-6 Two-pipe hot-water system. *From Huth, Understanding Construction Drawings, Delmar Publishers Inc.*

CADD
applications

HVAC PICTORIALS

CADD applications often make pictorial representations much easier to implement, especially when the HVAC program allows direct conversion from the plan view to the pictorial. The CADD pictorials, known as graphic models, may be used to view the HVAC system from any angle or orientation. Some CADD programs automatically analyze the layout for obstacles where an error in design may result in a duct that does not have a clear path. One of the biggest advantages of a CADD system occurs when changes are made to the HVAC plan. These changes are simultaneously corrected on all drawings, schedules, and lists of materials. Figure 1 shows a CADD-generated perspective of HVAC duct routing.

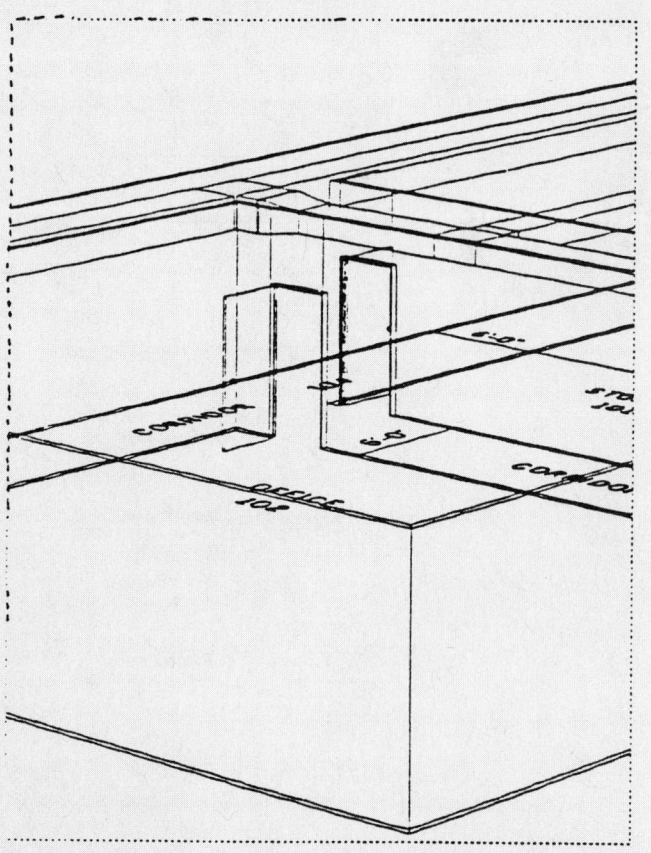

Figure 1 CADD-generated perspective of HVAC duct routing.

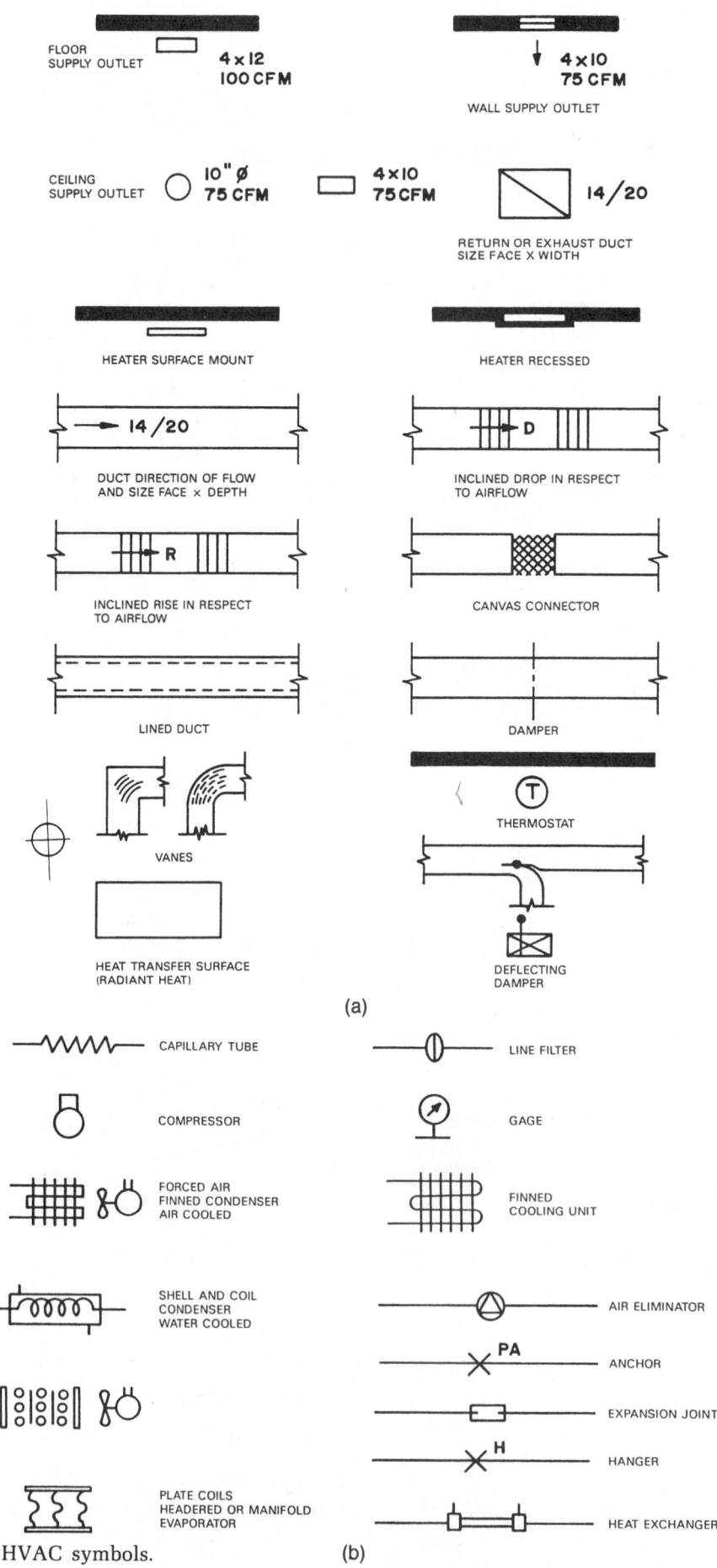

Figure 19-7 Common HVAC symbols.

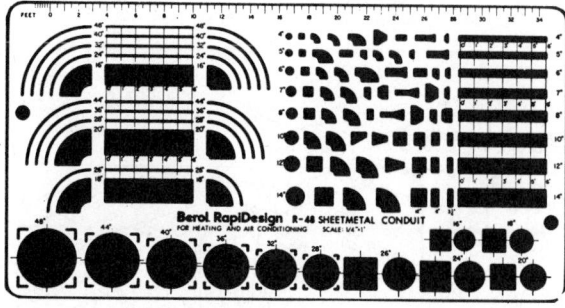

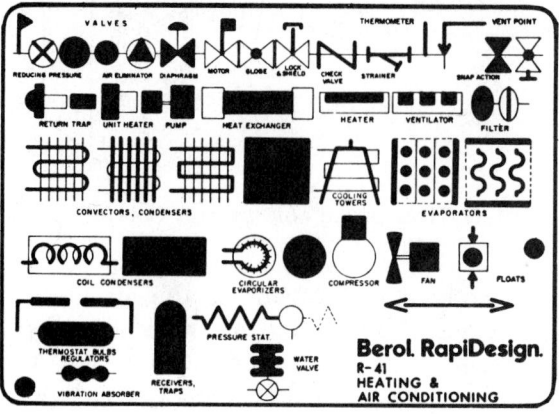

Figure 19-8 HVAC templates. *Courtesy Berol USA Rapi-Design.*

HEAT PUMP SYSTEMS

The heat pump is a forced-air central heating and cooling system. It operates using a compressor and a circulating refrigerant system. Heat is extracted from the outside air and pumped inside the structure. The heat pump supplies up to three times as much heat per year for the same amount of electrical consumption as a standard electric forced-air heating system. In comparison, this can result in a 30 to 50 percent annual energy savings. In the summer the cycle is reversed and the unit operates as an air conditioner. In this mode, the heat is extracted from the inside air and pumped outside. On the cooling cycle the heat pump also acts as a dehumidifier. Figure 19-9 shows a graphic example of how a heat pump works.

ZONE CONTROL SYSTEMS

A zoned heating system requires one heater and one thermostat per room. No ductwork is required, and only the heaters in occupied rooms need be turned on.

One of the major differences between a zonal and a central system is flexibility. A zonal heating system allows the home occupant to determine how many rooms are heated, how much energy is used, and how much money is spent on heat. A zonal system allows the home to be heated to the family's needs while a central system requires using all the heat produced. If the air flow is restricted, the efficiency of the central system is reduced. There is also a 10 to 15 percent heat loss through ductwork in central systems.

Regardless of the square footage in a house, its occupants normally use less than 40 percent of the entire area on a regular basis. A zoned system is very adaptable to heating the 40 percent of the home that is occupied using automatic controls that will allow for night setback, day setback and nonheated areas. The homeowner can save as much as 60 percent on energy costs through controlled heating systems. Figure 19-10 shows a graphic example comparing central and zoned heating. Residential heat pumps vary in size from two to five tons. Some vendors carry two-stage heat pumps that alternate between three and five tons, for example. During minimal demand the more efficient three-ton phase is used, while the five-ton phase is operable during peak demand. Each ton of rating removes approximately 12,000 Btu per hour (Btuh) of heat.

Residential or commercial structures that, either due to size or design, cannot be uniformly heated or

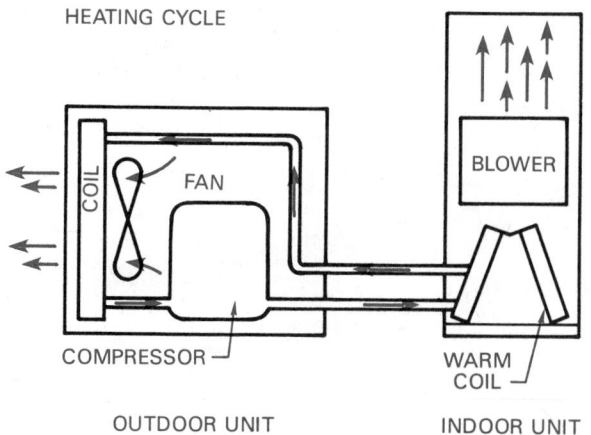

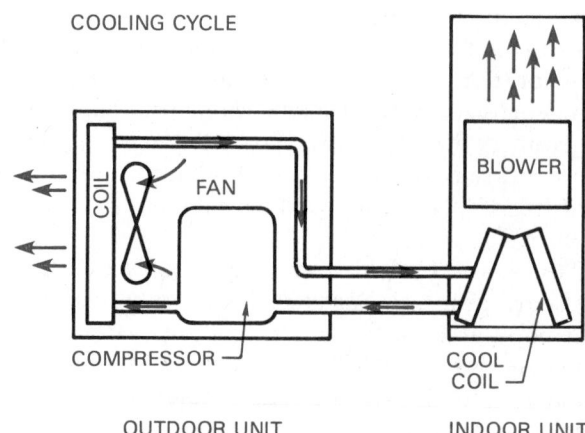

Figure 19-9 Heat pump heating and cooling cycle. *Courtesy Lennox Industries, Inc.*

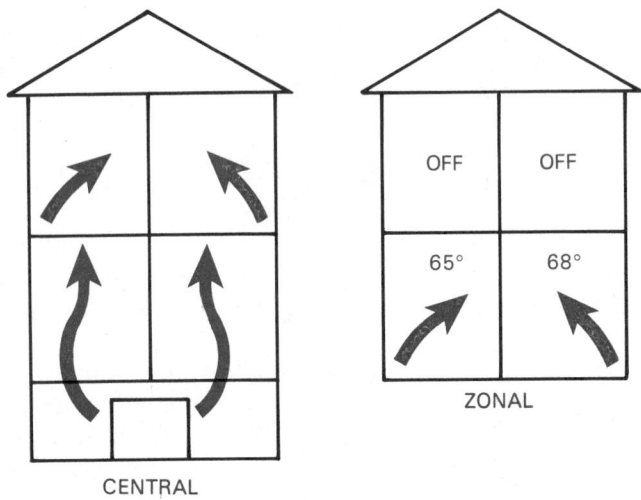

Figure 19-10 Comparison of central and zoned heating. *Courtesy Cadet Mfg. Co.*

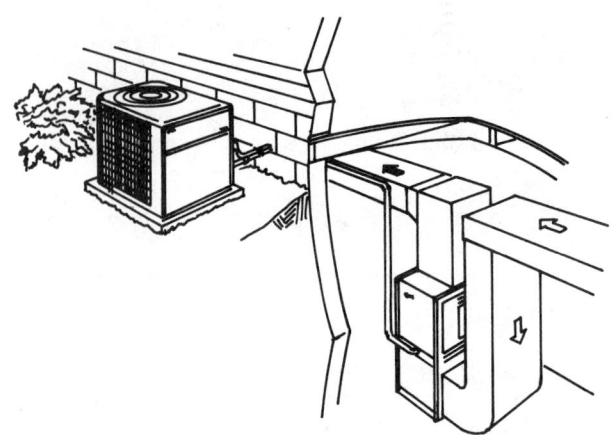

Figure 19-11 Heat pump compressor. *Courtesy Lennox Industries, Inc.*

cooled from one compressor may require a split system with two or more compressors. The advantage to such an arrangement may be that two smaller units can more effectively control the needs of two zones within the structure.

Other features such as an air cleaner, humidifier, or air freshener can be added to the system. In general, the initial cost of the heat pump will be over twice as much as a conventional forced-air electric heat system. However, the advantages and long range energy savings make it a significant option for heating. Keep in mind that if cooling is a requirement the cost difference is less. The total heat pump system uses an outside compressor, an inside blower to circulate air, a back-up heating coil, and complete duct system. Heat pump systems move a large volume of air; therefore, the return air and supply ducts must be adequately sized. Figure 19–11 shows the relationship between the compressor and the balance of the system. The compressor should be placed in a location where some noise will not cause a problem. The compressor should be placed on a concrete slab about 36″ × 48″ × 6″ in size in a location that will allow adequate service access. Do not connect the slab to the structure to avoid transmitting vibration. Show or note the concrete slab on the foundation plan. Verify vendor's specifications. In some areas of the country heat pumps may not be as efficient as in other areas because of annual low or high temperatures. Verify the product efficiency with local vendors.

There are typically two types of zone heaters: baseboard and fan. Baseboard heaters have been the most popular type for zoned heating systems for the past several decades. They are used in many different climates and under various operating conditions. There are no ducts, motors, or fans required. Baseboard units have an electric heating element which

causes a convection current as the air around the unit is heated. The heated air rises into the room and is replaced by cooler air that falls to the floor. Baseboard heaters should be placed on exterior walls under or adjacent to windows or other openings. These units do project a few inches into the room at floor level. Some homeowners do not care for this obstruction in comparison to the floor duct vent of a central system or the recessed wall-mounted fan heater. Furniture arrangements should be a factor in locating any heating element. Figure 19–12 shows a typical baseboard heater.

Fan heaters are generally mounted in a wall recess. A resistance heater is used to generate the heat, and a fan circulates the heat into the room. These units should be placed to circulate the warmed air in each room adequately. Avoid placing the heaters on exterior walls as the recessed unit will reduce or eliminate the insulation in that area. Figure 19–13 shows a fan heater.

Heat pumps may require a split system in very large homes. Split systems are also possible using zonal heat in part of the home and central heat in the balance of the structure. An alternative is to install a heat pump for the areas used most often and zoned heaters for the remainder of the house. This is also an option for additions to homes that

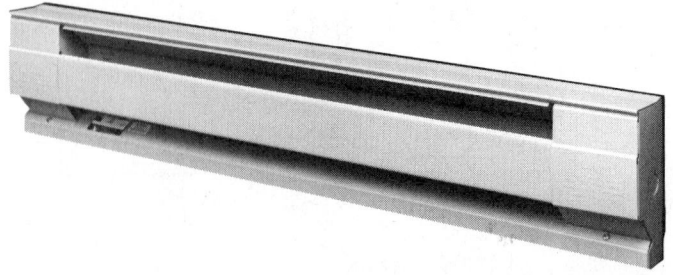

Figure 19-12 Baseboard heater. *Courtesy Cadet Mfg., Co.*

Figure 19–13 Recessed wall-mounted fan heater. *Courtesy Cadet Mfg., Co.*

have a central system. Zoned heat can be used effectively in an addition so that the central system is not overloaded or required to be replaced.

RADIANT HEAT

Radiant heating and cooling systems provide a comfortable environment by means of controlling surface temperatures and minimizing excessive air motion within the space. Warm ceiling panels are effective for winter heating because they warm the floor surfaces and glass surfaces by direct transfer of radiant energy. The surface temperature of well-constructed and properly insulated floors will be 2° F to 3° F above the ambient air temperature, and the inside surface temperature of glass will be increased significantly. As a result of these heated surfaces, downdrafts are minimized to the point where no discomfort is felt.

Radiant heat systems generate operating cost savings of 20 to 50 percent annually compared to conventional convective systems. This savings is accomplished through lower thermostat settings. Savings are also due to the superior, cost-effective design inherent in radiant heating products.

It is generally accepted that 3 to 4 percent of the energy cost is saved for each degree the thermostat is lowered. Users of surface mounted radiant panels take advantage of this fact in two ways. First, they are able to achieve comfort at a lower ambient air temperature, normally 60° F to 64° F as compared with convection heating air temperatures of 68° F to 72° F. Second, they are able to practice comfortable day and night temperature setback of about 58° F in areas used frequently, 55° F in areas used occasionally, and 50° F in those areas seldom used.

Radiant heat may be achieved with oil- or gas-heated hot water piping in the floor or ceiling, to electric coils, wiring, or elements either in or above the ceiling gypsum board, and transferred to metal

radiator panels generally mounted by means of a bracket about an inch below the ceiling surface. A relatively recent evolution of the 25-year-old radiant panel concept is manufactured by Solid State Heating Corporation. This product offers installation versatility and greater economy than other radiant systems or convection heating systems. It is a lightweight, quick response, totally zone-controlled panel system which may be mounted directly to the ceiling surface, on joists, or placed in a suspended ceiling grid. The radiant solid-state heating panels are available in a full range of sizes and voltages which are ideal for both remodeling and new construction applications as primary or auxiliary heating.

Zone radiant heating panels are an alternative when space is limited or the location of built-in zone heaters may be a factor. Figure 19–14 shows an example of radiant heating panels.

THERMOSTATS

The thermostat is an automatic mechanism for controlling the amount of heating or cooling given by a

Figure 19–14 Radiant heat panel installation. *Courtesy Solid State Heating, Corp.*

central or zonal heating or cooling system. The thermostat floor-plan symbol is shown in Figure 19–15.

The location of the thermostat is an important consideration to the proper functioning of the system. For zoned heating or cooling units thermostats may be placed in each room or a central thermostat panel that controls each room may be placed in a convenient location. For central heating and cooling systems there may be one or more thermostats depending upon the layout of the system or the number of units required to service the structure. For example, a very large home or office building may have a split system that divides the structure into two or more zones. Each individual zone will have its own thermostat.

Several factors contribute to the effective placement of the thermostat for a central system. A good common location is near the center of the structure and close to a return air duct for a central forced-air system. The air entering the return air duct is usually temperate, thus causing little variation in temperature on the thermostat. A key to successful thermostat placement is to find a stable location where an average temperature reading can be achieved. There should be no drafts that would adversely affect temperature settings. The thermostat should not be placed in a location where sunlight or a heat register would cause an unreliable reading. The same rationale suggests that a thermostat not be placed close to an exterior door where temperatures can change quickly. Thermostats should be placed on inside partitions rather than on outside walls where a false temperature reading could also be obtained. Avoid placing the thermostat near stairs or a similar traffic area where significant bouncing or shaking could cause the mechanism to alter the actual reading.

Energy consumption can be reduced by controlling thermostats in individual rooms. Central panels are available which make it easy to lower or raise temperatures in any room where each panel switch controls one remote thermostat. See Figure 19–16.

Programmable microcomputer thermostats are also available which effectively help reduce the cost of heating or cooling. Some units automatically switch from heat to cool while minimizing temperature deviation from the setting under varying load conditions. These computers can be used to alter heating and cooling temperature settings automatically for different days of the week or different months of the year. Figure 19–17 shows an example of a microcomputer thermostat.

HEAT RECOVERY AND VENTILATION

Sources of Pollutants

Air pollution in a structure is the principal reason for installing a heat recovery and ventilation system. There are a number of sources that contribute to an unhealthy environment within a home or business:

- Moisture in the form of relative humidity can cause structural damage as well as health problems such as respiratory problems. The source of relative humidity is the atmosphere, steam from cooking and showers, and individuals who can produce up to 1 gal. of water vapor per day.
- Incomplete combustion from gas-fired appliances or wood-burning stoves and fireplaces can

Figure 19–15   Thermostat floor-plan symbol.

Figure 19–16   Central panel thermostat. *Courtesy Eaton Corporation.*

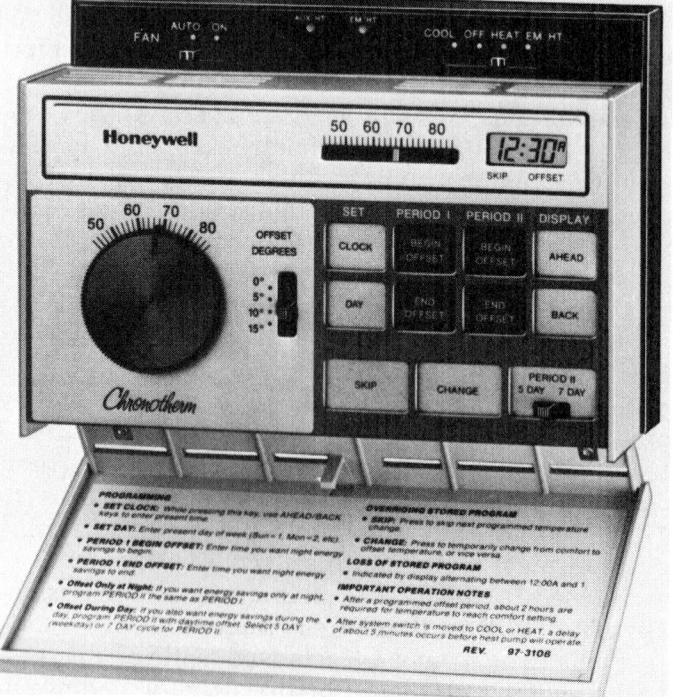

Figure 19–17   Microcomputer thermostat. *Courtesy Honeywell.*

generate a variety of pollutants including carbon monoxide, aldehydes, and soot.

- Humans and pets can transmit bacterial and viral diseases through the air.
- Tobacco smoke contributes chemical compounds to the air which can affect both smokers and nonsmokers alike.
- Formaldehyde, when present, is considered a factor in the cause of eye irritation, certain diseases, and respiratory problems. Formaldehyde is found in carpets, furniture, and the glue used in construction materials such as plywood and particle board as well as some insulation products.
- Radon is a naturally occurring radioactive gas that breaks down into compounds that are carcinogenic (cancer causing) when large quantities are inhaled over a long period of time. Radon may be more apparent in a structure that contains a large amount of concrete or in certain areas of the country. Radon can be monitored scientifically at a nominal cost, and barriers can be built that will help reduce concern about radon contamination.
- Household products such as those available in aerosol spray cans and craft materials such as glues and paints can contribute a number of toxic pollutants.

Air-to-air Heat Exchangers

Government energy agencies, architects, designers, and contractors around the country have been evaluating construction methods that are designed to reduce energy consumption. Some of the tests have produced super insulated, vapor barrier lined, airtight structures. The result has been a dramatic reduction in heating and cooling costs; however, the air quality in these houses has been significantly reduced and

may even be harmful to health. In essence, the structure does not breathe and the stale air and pollutants have no place to go. A recent technology has emerged from this dilemma in the form of an air-to-air heat exchanger. In the past the air in a structure was exchanged due to leakage through walls, floors, ceilings, and around openings. Although this random leakage was no insurance that the building was properly ventilated, it did ensure a certain amount of heat loss. Now, with the concern of energy conservation, it is clear the internal air quality of a home or business cannot be left to chance.

An air-to-air heat exchanger is a heat recovery and ventilation device that pulls polluted, stale warm air from the living space and transfers the heat in that air to fresh, cold air being pulled into the house. Heat exchangers do not produce heat, they only exchange heat from one air stream to another. The heat transfer takes place in the core of the heat exchanger which is designed to avoid mixing the two air streams to ensure that indoor pollutants are expelled. Moisture in the stale air condenses in the core and is drained from the unit. Figure 19–18 shows the function and basic components of an air-to-air heat exchanger.

The recommended minimum effective air change rate is 0.5 air changes per hour (ach). Codes in some areas of the country have established a rate of 0.7 ach. The American Society of Heating, Refrigeration, and Air Conditioning Engineers, Inc. (ASHRAE) recommends ventilation levels based on the amount of air entering a room. The recommended amount of air entering most rooms is 10 cubic ft per minute (cfm). The rate for kitchens is 100 cfm and bathrooms is 50 cfm. Mechanical exhaust devices vented to outside air should be added to kitchens and baths to maintain the recommended air exchange rate.

The minimum heat exchanger capacity needed for a structure can easily be determined. Assume a

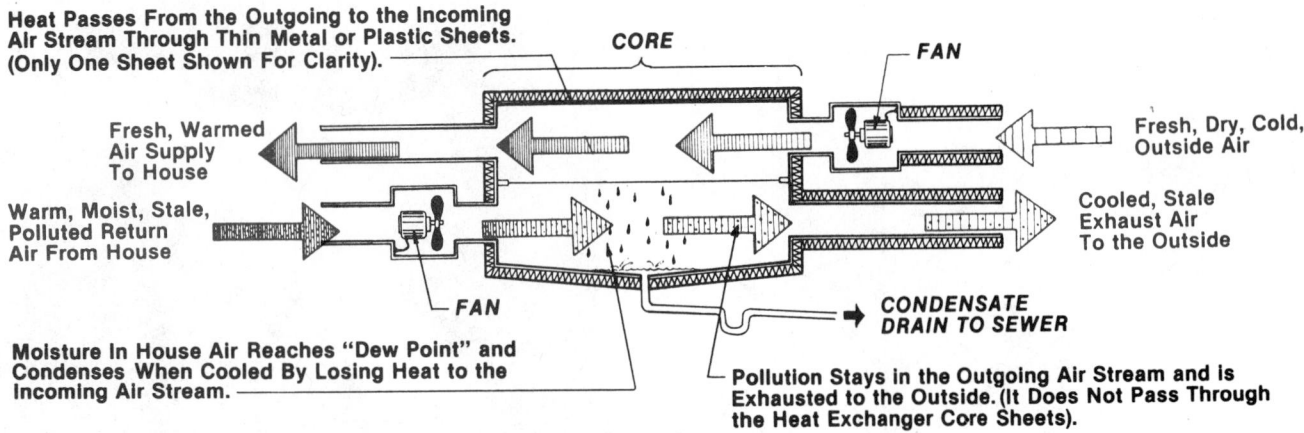

Figure 19–18 Components and function of air-to-air heat exchanger. *Courtesy U.S. Department of Energy.*

0.5 ach rate in a 1,500 sq ft single level, energy efficient house and follow these steps:

1. Determine the total floor area in sq ft. Use the outside dimensions of the living area only.

$$30' \times 50' = 1,500 \text{ sq ft}$$

2. Determine the total volume within the house in cubic ft by multiplying the total floor area by the ceiling height.

$$1,500 \text{ sq ft} \times 8' = 12,000 \text{ cu ft}$$

3. Determine the minimum exchanger capacity in cfm by first finding the capacity in cubic feet per hour (cfh). Multiply the house volume by the ventilation rate required from the exchanger.

$$12,000 \text{ cu ft} \times 0.5 \text{ ach} = 6,000 \text{ cfh}$$

4. Convert the cfh rate to cfm by dividing the cfh rate by 60 min.

$$6,000 \text{ cfh} \div 60 \text{ min} = 100 \text{ cfm}$$

There is a percentage of capacity loss due to mechanical resistance that should be considered by the system designer.

Most homeowners do not have the knowledge of potential air pollution and how internal air may be adequately controlled by ventilation. Therefore the architect of an energy efficient home must plan the proper ventilation. Figure 19–19 shows the duct work required for an air-to-air heat exchanger. The ducts, intake, and exhaust for such a system should be located on the advice of a ventilation consultant or a knowledgeable HVAC contractor.

CENTRAL VACUUM SYSTEMS

There are a number of advantages that central vacuum systems have over portable vacuum cleaners.

1. Some systems cost no more than a major appliance
2. Increased resale value of home
3. Removes dirt too heavy for most portable units
4. Exhausts dirt and dust out of the house or office
5. No motor unit or electric cords
6. No noise
7. Saves cleaning time
8. Vacuum pressure may be varied

A well-designed system will require only a few inlets to cover the entire home or business, including exterior use. The hose plugs into a wall outlet and the vacuum is ready for use as shown in Figure 19–20. The hose is generally lightweight and without a portable unit to carry, it is often easier to vacuum in hard-to-reach places. The central canister empties easily as shown in Figure 19–21 to remove the dust and debris from the house or business. The floor plan symbol for vacuum cleaner outlets is shown in Figure 19–22. The central unit may be shown in the garage or storage area as a circle that is labeled Central Vacuum System.

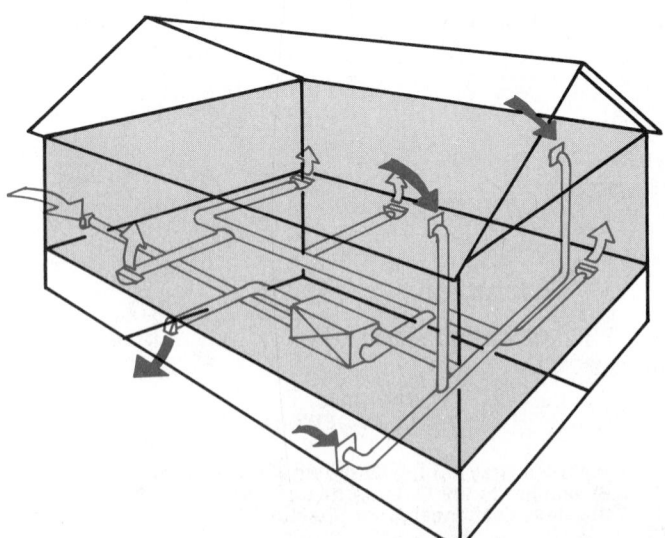

Figure 19–19 Ducted air-to-air heat exchanger system. *Courtesy U.S. Department of Energy.*

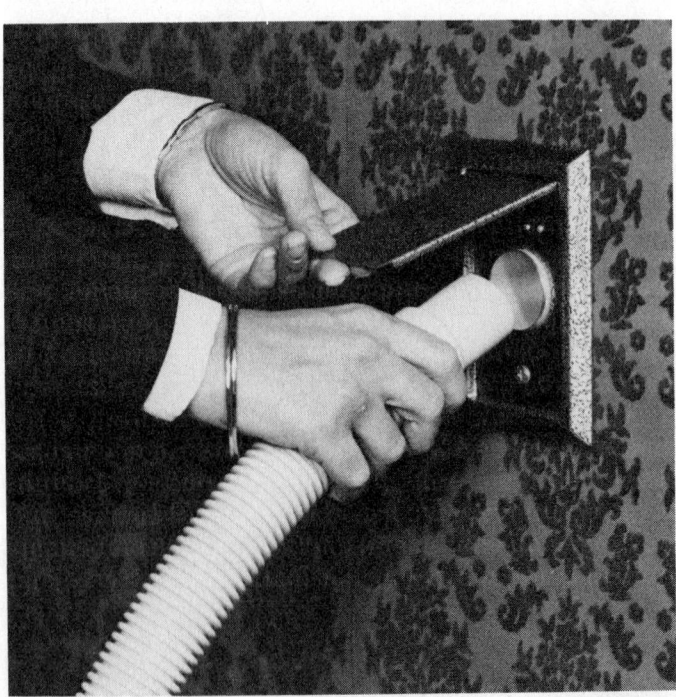

Figure 19–20 Vacuum wall outlet. *Courtesy Vacu-maid, Inc.*

Figure 19–21 Central vacuum canister. *Courtesy Vacu-maid, Inc.*

Figure 19–22 Vacuum outlet floor plan symbol.

THERMAL CALCULATIONS FOR HEATING/COOLING

Development of Heat Loss Estimation Methodology

The basic methodology used to estimate residential heat loss today has been in use since the early 1900s. Historically, its primary use was to calculate the design heat load of houses in order to estimate the size of gas and oil heating systems required. Because home designers, homebuilders, and heating system installers did not want to receive complaints from cold homeowners, they commonly designed the heating system for worst case weather conditions with a bias toward overestimating the design heat load to insure the furnace would never be too small. Consequently, many gas and oil furnaces were over-sized.

As early as 1915 an engineer for a gas utility began modifying the design heat load with a degree-day method to estimate annual energy consumption. Oil companies also began using this method to predict when to refill their customers' tanks. Data from this period, for houses with little or no insulation, indicated that the proportionality between annual heating energy requirements and average outside temperature began at 65° F in residential buildings. This was the beginning of the 65° F base for degree days. Studies made by the American Gas Association up to 1932 and by the National District Heating Association in 1932 also indicated a 65° F base was appropriate for houses of that period.

Experience in the 1950s and early 1960s with electrically heated homes indicated the traditional degree day procedure was overestimating annual heating loads. This was due primarily to tighter, better insulated houses with balance temperatures below 65° F, and to more appliances. These later studies led to use of the modified degree day procedure incorporating a modifying factor, C. This C factor compensates for such things as higher insulation levels and more heat-producing appliances in the house. The high insulation levels found in homes built to current codes, and those that have been retrofitted with insulation, cause even lower balance temperatures than those of houses built in the 1950s and 1960s. This history has been adapted from *Standard Heat Loss Methodology of July, 1983,* Bonneville Power Administration.

Terminology

Outdoor Temperature. Outdoor temperatures are related to average winter and summer temperatures for a local area. If the outdoor winter design temperature is 20°, this means that the temperature during the winter will be 20° or higher 97½ percent of the time. If the outdoor summer design temperature in an area is 100° this means that the temperature during the summer will be 100° or less 97½ percent of the time. Figures for each area of the country have been established by the American Society of Heating, Refrigerating, and Air Conditioning Engineers. Verify the outdoor temperature with your local building department or heating contractor.

Indoor Temperature. The indoor design temperature is generally 60 to 70° F.

Temperature Difference. The temperature difference is the indoor temperature less the outdoor temperature.

Heat Transfer Multiplier. The heat transfer multiplier is the amount of heat that flows through 1 sq ft of the building surface. The product depends upon the type of surface and whether it is applied to heating or cooling.

Infiltration. Infiltration is the inward flow of air through a porous wall or crack. In a loosely constructed home infiltration substantially increases heat loss. Infiltration around windows and doors is calculated in cubic feet per minute (cfm) per linear foot of crack. Window infiltration greater than 0.5 cfm per linear foot of crack is excessive.

Mechanical Ventilation. Amount of heat lost through mechanical ventilators such as range hood fans, or bathroom exhaust fans.

Duct Loss. Heat loss through duct work in an unheated space has an effect upon total heat loss. Insulating those ducts helps increase efficiency.

R Factor. Resistance to heat flow is the R factor. The more resistance to heat flow the higher the R value. For example, 3½″ of mineral wool insulation has a value of R-11 while 6″ of the same insulation has a value of R-19. R is equal to the reciprocal of the U factor, $1 / U = R$.

U Factor. The U factor is the coefficient of heat transfer expressed to Btuh sq ft/°F of surface area.

Btu, British thermal unit. A unit of measure determined by the amount of heat required to raise one pound of water one degree Fahrenheit. Heat loss is calculated in Btus per hour (Btuh).

Sensible Load Calculations. Load calculations associated with temperature change that occurs when a structure loses or gains heat.

Compass Point. When referring to cooling calculations it is important to evaluate the amount of glass in each wall as related to compass orientation. This is due to the differences effected by solar gain.

Internal Heat Gain. Internal heat gain is associated with factors such as heat transmitted from appliances, lights, other equipment, and occupants.

Latent Load. Latent (invisible) loads are the effects of moisture entering the structure from the outside by humidity infiltration or from the inside produced by people and plants, and daily activities such as cooking, showers, and laundry.

Outdoor Wet Bulb. A wet-bulb thermometer is one in which the bulb is kept moistened and is used to determine humidity level when compared to a dry-bulb thermometer. Outdoor wet bulb relates to the use of a wet-bulb thermometer outside.

Indoor Wet Bulb. The indoor wet bulb relates to the use of the wet-bulb thermometer inside.

Grains. The amount of moisture in the air (grains of moisture in one cubic foot). Air at different temperatures and humidities holds different amounts of moisture. The effects of this moisture content in the southern and midwestern states becomes more of a factor than in other parts of the country.

Figure 19–23 is a completed Residential Heating Data Sheet. The two-page data sheet is divided into several categories with calculations resulting in total heat loss for the structure shown in Figure 19–24. The large numbers by each category refer to the following steps used in completing the form. Notice that the calculations are rounded off to the nearest whole unit.

Steps in Filling Out the Residential Heating Data Sheet

Refer to Figure 19–23.

1. Outdoor Temperature. Use the recommended outdoor design temperature for your area. The area selected for this problem is Dallas, Texas, with an outdoor design temperature of 22° F which has been rounded off to 20° F to make calculations simple to understand. The proper calculations would interpolate the tables for a 22° F outdoor design temperature.
2. Indoor Temperature: 70° F.
3. Temperature Difference:

$$70° - 20° = 50° \text{ F.}$$

4. Movable Glass Windows: Select double glass; find area of each window (frame length × width) then combine for total: 114 sq ft.
5. Btuh Heat Loss: Using 50° design temperature difference find 46 approximate heat transfer multiplier:

$$46 \times 114 = 5244 \text{ Btuh.}$$

6. Sliding Glass Doors: Select double glass; find total area of 34 sq ft.
7. Btuh Heat Loss:

$$34 \times 48 = 1632 \text{ Btuh.}$$

8. Doors: Weatherstripped solid wood; 2 doors at 39 sq ft.
9. Btuh Heat Loss:

$$39 \times 30 = 1170 \text{ Btuh.}$$

10. Walls: Excluding garage; perimeter in running feet 132 × ceiling height 8 feet = Gross wall area 1056 sq ft. Subtract window and door areas − 187 sq ft = net wall area 869 sq ft.
11. Frame wall: No masonry wall above or below grade. When there is masonry wall subtract the square footage of masonry wall from total wall for the net frame wall. Fill in net amount on approximate insulation value; 869 sq ft frame wall, R-13 (given).
12. Btuh Heat Loss:

$$869 \times 3.5 = 3042 \text{ Btuh.}$$

13–14. No masonry above grade in this structure.
15–16. No masonry below grade in this structure.
17. Heat loss subtotal: Add together items 5, 7, 9, and 12; 11,088 Btuh. Transfer the amount to the top of page 2 of the form.
18. Ceilings: R-30 insulation (given), same square footage as floor plan 976 sq ft (given).
19. Btuh heat loss:

$$976 \times 1.6 = 1562 \text{ Btuh.}$$

RESIDENTIAL HEATING DATA SHEET

JOB NAME:	DATE
ADDRESS:	

1 OUTDOOR TEMP: 20°   **2** INDOOR TEMP: 70°   **3** TEMP. DIFFERENCE: 50°

4

MOVABLE GLASS WINDOWS	SQUARE FEET	DESIGN TEMPERATURE DIFFERENCE														BTUH HEAT LOSS
		30	35	40	45	(50)	55	60	65	70	75	80	85	90	95	
		HEAT TRANSFER MULTIPLIER														
SINGLE GLASS		39	45	52	58	65	71	78	84	90	97	103	110	116	123	
SINGLE GLASS W/STORM		21	25	28	31	35	38	42	45	49	52	56	59	63	66	
DOUBLE GLASS	114	28	32	37	41	(46)	50	55	60	64	69	73	78	82	87	5244
DOUBLE GLASS W/STORM		16	19	21	24	27	29	32	35	37	40	42	45	48	50	

5

6

SLIDING GLASS DOORS	SQUARE FEET	DESIGN TEMPERATURE DIFFERENCE														BTUH HEAT LOSS
		30	35	40	45	(50)	55	60	65	70	75	80	85	90	95	
		HEAT TRANSFER MULTIPLIER														
SINGLE GLASS		42	48	55	62	69	76	83	90	97	104	110	117	124	131	
SINGLE GLASS W/STORM		22	26	29	33	37	40	44	48	51	55	59	62	66	70	
DOUBLE GLASS	34	29	34	39	43	(48)	53	58	63	67	72	77	82	87	91	1632

7

8

DOORS	SQUARE FEET	DESIGN TEMPERATURE DIFFERENCE														BTUH HEAT LOSS
		30	35	40	45	(50)	55	60	65	70	75	80	85	90	95	
		HEAT TRANSFER MULTIPLIER														
SOLID WOOD		31	36	41	46	51	56	62	67	72	77	82	87	92	97	
SOLID WOOD**	39	18	21	24	27	(30)	33	36	39	42	45	47	50	53	56	1170
METAL URETHANE		23	27	30	34	38	42	45	49	53	57	60	64	68	72	
METAL URETHANE**		13	16	18	20	22	25	27	29	31	33	36	38	40	42	
**Weatherstripped or Storm																

9

10 WALLS

RUNNING FEET	132
CEILING HEIGHT	X 8
GROSS WALL	= 1056
WINDOWS & DOOR AREAS	− 187
NET WALL AREA	869

11

FRAME WALL	SQUARE FEET	DESIGN TEMPERATURE DIFFERENCE														BTUH HEAT LOSS
		30	35	40	45	(50)	55	60	65	70	75	80	85	90	95	
		HEAT TRANSFER MULTIPLIER														
NO INSULATION		8	10	11	12	14	15	17	18	19	21	22	23	25	26	
R-11, 3" INSULATION		2.7	3.1	3.6	4.0	4.5	4.9	5.4	5.8	6.3	6.7	7.2	7.6	8.1	8.5	
R-13, 3-1/2" INSULATION	869	2.1	2.4	2.8	3.2	(3.5)	3.8	4.2	4.6	4.9	5.3	5.6	5.9	6.3	6.6	3042
R-13 + 1" POLYSTYRENE		1.8	2.1	2.4	2.7	3.0	3.3	3.6	3.9	4.2	4.5	4.8	5.1	5.4	5.7	
R-19 + 1/2" POLYSTYRENE		1.6	1.9	2.2	2.5	2.8	3.0	3.3	3.6	3.8	4.1	4.4	4.7	4.9	5.2	

12

13

MASONRY WALL ABOVE GRADE	SQUARE FEET	DESIGN TEMPERATURE DIFFERENCE														BTUH HEAT LOSS
		30	35	40	45	50	55	60	65	70	75	80	85	90	95	
		HEAT TRANSFER MULTIPLIER														
NO INSULATION		16	18	21	23	26	28	31	33	36	38	41	44	46	49	
R-5, 1" INSULATION		4.3	5.0	5.8	6.5	7.2	7.9	8.6	9.4	10.1	10.8	11.5	12.2	13.0	13.7	
R-11, 3" INSULATION		2.3	2.7	3.1	3.5	3.8	4.2	4.6	5.0	5.4	5.8	6.2	6.5	6.9	7.3	
R-19, 6" INSULATION		1.4	1.7	1.9	2.2	2.4	2.6	2.9	3.1	3.4	3.6	3.8	4.1	4.3	4.6	

14

15

MASONRY WALL BELOW GRADE	SQUARE FEET	DESIGN TEMPERATURE DIFFERENCE														BTUH HEAT LOSS
		30	35	40	45	50	55	60	65	70	75	80	85	90	95	
		HEAT TRANSFER MULTIPLIER														
NO INSULATION		4.4	5.1	5.9	6.6	7.3	8.1	8.8	9.6	10.3	11.0	11.8	12.5	13.2	14.0	
R-5, 1" INSULATION		2.6	3.0	3.5	3.9	4.3	4.8	5.2	5.7	6.1	6.5	7.0	7.4	7.8	8.3	
R-11, 3" INSULATION		1.8	2.1	2.4	2.7	3.0	3.3	3.6	3.9	4.2	4.5	4.8	5.1	5.4	5.7	
R-19, 6" INSULATION		1.2	1.4	1.6	1.8	2.0	2.2	2.4	2.6	2.8	3.0	3.2	3.4	3.6	3.8	

16

HEAT LOSS SUBTOTAL	11088

17

Figure 19–23 Completed residential heating data sheet form. *Courtesy Lennox Industries, Inc.*

Heat Loss Subtotal from Page 1 → 11088 **17**

18 / **19**

CEILING	SQUARE FEET	30	35	40	45	50	55	60	65	70	75	80	85	90	95	BTUH HEAT LOSS
		DESIGN TEMPERATURE DIFFERENCE / HEAT TRANSFER MULTIPLIER														
NO INSULATION		18	21	24	27	30	33	36	39	42	45	48	51	54	57	
R-11, 3" INSULATION		2.6	3.1	3.5	4.0	4.4	4.8	5.3	5.7	6.2	6.6	7.0	7.5	7.9	8.4	
R-19, 6" INSULATION		1.6	1.9	2.1	2.4	2.6	2.9	3.2	3.4	3.7	4.0	4.2	4.5	4.8	5.0	
R-30, 10" INSULATION	976	1.0	1.2	1.3	1.5	1.6	1.8	2.0	2.1	2.3	2.5	2.6	2.8	3.0	3.1	1562
R-38, 12" INSULATION		0.8	0.9	1.0	1.2	1.3	1.4	1.6	1.7	1.8	2.0	2.1	2.2	2.3	2.5	

20 / **21**

FLOOR OVER AN UNCONDITIONED SPACE	SQUARE FEET	30	35	40	45	50	55	60	65	70	75	80	85	90	95	BTUH HEAT LOSS
		DESIGN TEMPERATURE DIFFERENCE / HEAT TRANSFER MULTIPLIER														
NO INSULATION		10	11	13	14	16	17	19	21	22	24	25	27	28	30	
R-11, 3" INSULATION		2.4	2.8	3.2	3.6	4.0	4.4	4.8	5.2	5.6	6.0	6.4	6.8	7.2	7.6	
R-19, 6" INSULATION	976	1.6	1.8	2.1	2.3	2.6	2.9	3.1	3.4	3.6	3.9	4.2	4.4	4.7	4.9	2538
R-30, 10" INSULATION		1.1	1.3	1.5	1.7	1.8	2.0	2.2	2.4	2.6	2.8	3.0	3.1	3.3	3.5	

22 / **23**

BASEMENT FLOOR	SQUARE FEET	30	35	40	45	50	55	60	65	70	75	80	85	90	95	BTUH HEAT LOSS
		DESIGN TEMPERATURE DIFFERENCE / HEAT TRANSFER MULTIPLIER														
BASEMENT FLOOR		0.8	1.0	1.1	1.3	1.4	1.5	1.7	1.8	2.0	2.1	2.2	2.4	2.5	2.7	

24 / **25**

CONCRETE SLAB WITHOUT PERIMETER SYSTEM	LINEAR FOOT	30	35	40	45	50	55	60	65	70	75	80	85	90	95	BTUH HEAT LOSS
		DESIGN TEMPERATURE DIFFERENCE / HEAT TRANSFER MULTIPLIER														
NO EDGE INSULATION		25	29	33	37	41	45	49	53	57	61	65	69	73	77	
1" EDGE INSULATION		13	15	17	19	21	23	25	27	29	31	33	35	37	39	
2" INSULATION		6.3	7.4	8.4	9.4	10.5	11.5	12.6	13.6	14.7	15.8	16.8	17.8	18.9	20.0	

26 / **27**

CONCRETE SLAB WITH PERIMETER SYSTEM	LINEAR FOOT	30	35	40	45	50	55	60	65	70	75	80	85	90	95	BTUH HEAT LOSS
		DESIGN TEMPERATURE DIFFERENCE / HEAT TRANSFER MULTIPLIER														
NO EDGE INSULATION		57	67	76	86	95	105	114	124	133	143	152	162	171	181	
1" EDGE INSULATION		34	40	46	52	57	63	69	74	80	86	91	97	103	109	
2" EDGE INSULATION		28	33	37	42	47	51	56	61	65	70	75	79	84	89	

An additional infiltration load is calculated **only if** the home is loosely constructed or when window infiltration is greater than .5 CFM per linear foot of crack.

28 INFILTRATION/ VENTILATION

976 FLOOR SQ. FT. x 8 CEILING HEIGHT = 7808 CUBIC FT

0.40 x 7808 CUBIC FT ÷ 60 = 52 CFM

MECHANICAL VENTILATION CFM = FRESH AIR INTAKE

29

	CFM	30	35	40	45	50	55	60	65	70	75	80	85	90	95	BTUH HEAT LOSS
		DESIGN TEMPERATURE DIFFERENCE / HEAT TRANSFER MULTIPLIER														
INFILTRATION	52	33	39	44	50	55	61	66	72	77	83	88	94	99	105	2860
MECHANICAL VENTILATION	52	33	39	44	50	55	61	66	72	77	83	88	94	99	105	2860

HEAT LOSS SUBTOTAL → 20908 **30**

DUCT LOSS	BTUH HEAT LOSS
R-4, 1" Flexible Blanket Insulation: ADD 15% (.15)	3138
R-7, 2" Flexible Blanket Insulation: ADD 10% (.10)	

31 / **31**

TOTAL HEAT LOSS → 24046 **32**

NOTE: All Heat Transfer Multipliers from ACCA Manual "J" Sixth Edition.

HL-841-L7   002344

Litho U.S.A.

Figure 19–23 Continued.

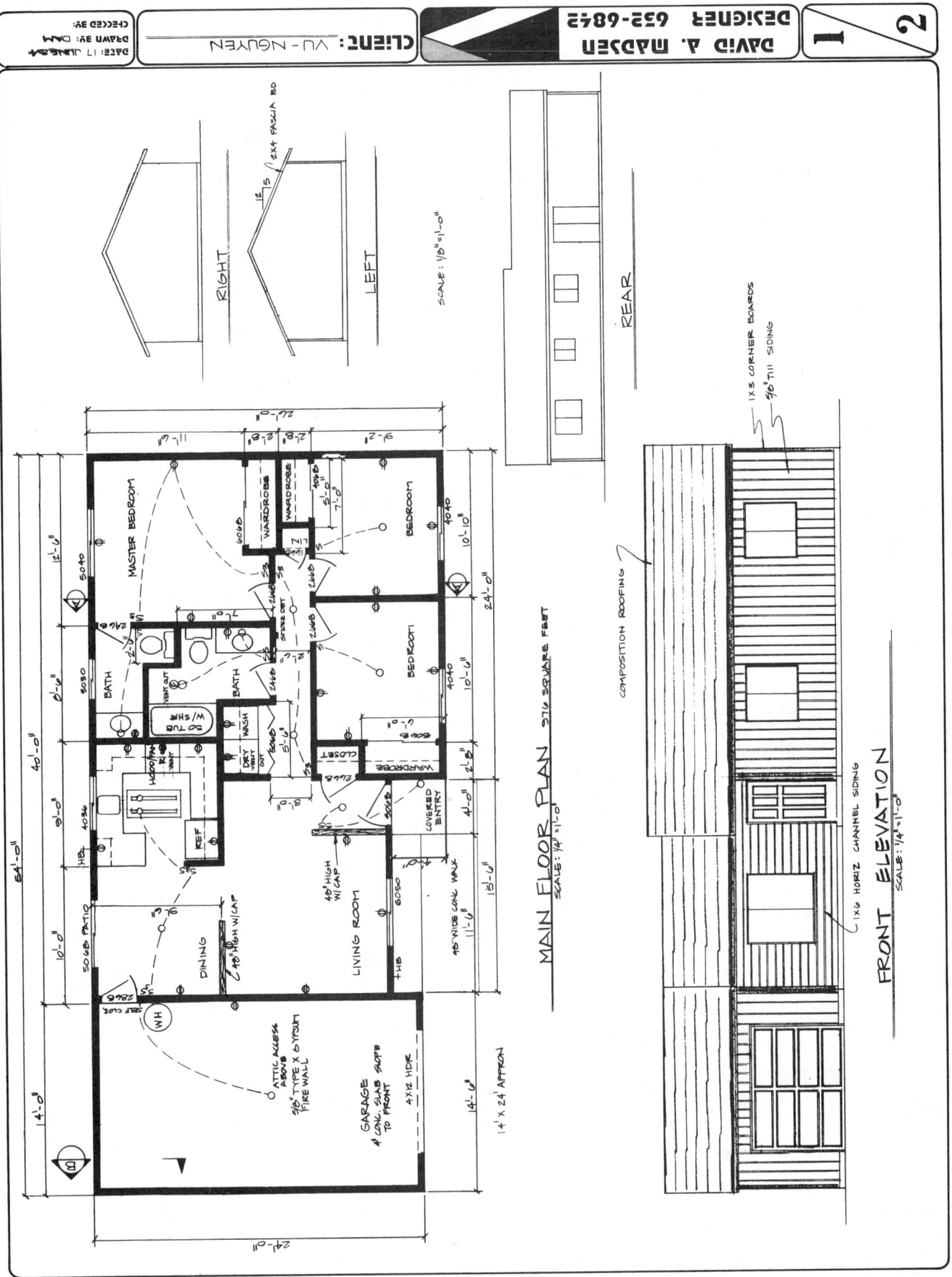

Figure 19-24 Sample floor plan for heat loss and heat gain calculations. *Courtesy Madsen Designs.*

20. Floor over an unconditioned space: R-19 insulation (given), 97 sq ft.
21. Btuh heat loss:

$$976 \times 2.6 = 2538 \text{ Btuh.}$$

22–23. Basement floor: Does not apply to this house.
24–25. Concrete slab without perimeter system: Does not apply to this house.
26–27. Concrete slab with perimeter system: Does not apply to this house.
28. Infiltration 976 sq ft floor $\times$ 8 feet ceiling height = 7808 cu ft.

$$0.40 \times 7808 \text{ cu ft} \div 60 = 52 \text{ cfm.}$$

Infiltration = mechanical ventilation cfm = Fresh air intake.
29. Btuh heat loss:

$$52 \times 55 = 2860 \text{ Btuh.}$$

30. Heat loss subtotal. Add together items 17, 19, 21, and 29; 20,908 Btuh.
31. Duct loss: R-4 insulation (given); Add 15 percent to item 30;

$$.15 \times 20,923 = 3138.$$

When no ducts are used exclude this item.
32. Total heat loss: Add together items 30 and 31; 24,046 Btuh.

Figure 19–25 is a completed residential cooling data sheet. The two-page data sheet is divided into several categories with calculations resulting in total sensible and latent heat gain for the same structure, shown in Figure 19–24, used for heat loss calculations. The large numbers by each category refer to the following steps used in completing the form.

Steps in Filling Out the Residential Cooling Data Sheet

Refer to Figure 19–25.

1. Outdoor temperature: 100° F.
2. Indoor temperature: 70° F.
3. Temperature difference. 100° − 70° = 30° F.
4–13. Glass no shade, double glazed.
4. North glass: Including sliding glass door; 81 sq ft.
5. Btuh heat gain:

$$81 \times 28 = 2268 \text{ Btuh.}$$

6–7. NE and NW glass: None, house faces N, E, W, S.
8–9. East and West glass: None in this plan.
10–11. SE and SW glass: None, house faces N, E, W, S.
12. South glass: 67 sq ft.

13. Btuh heat loss:

$$67 \times 43 = 2881 \text{ Btuh.}$$

14–23. Applies to glass with inside shade. This house is sized without the consideration of inside shade. If items 14–23 are used then omit items 4–13.
24. Doors: Solid wood weatherstripped, 2 doors; 39 sq ft.
25. Btuh heat gain:

$$39 \times 9.6 = 374 \text{ Btuh.}$$

26. Walls (excluding garage walls):

$$132 \text{ ft} \times 8 \text{ ft} = 1056 \text{ sq ft} - 187 \text{ sq ft} = 869 \text{ sq ft net wall area.}$$

27. Frame wall: 869 sq ft.
28. Btuh heat gain:

$$869 \times 2.5 = 2173 \text{ Btuh.}$$

29–30. Masonry wall above grade: None in this house.
31. Sensible heat gain subtotal. Add together items 5, 13, 25, 28. 7696 Btuh heat gain. Transfer the amount to the top of page 2 of the form.
32. Ceiling: R-30 insulation; 976 sq ft.
33. Btuh heat gain:

$$976 \times 1.7 = 1659 \text{ Btuh.}$$

34. Floor over unconditioned space: R-19 insulation; 976 sq ft.
35. Btuh heat gain:

$$976 \times 1.2 = 1171 \text{ Btuh.}$$

36. Infiltration/ventilation:

$$976 \text{ sq ft} \times 8 \text{ ft} = 7808 \text{ cu ft}$$
$$0.40 \times 7808 \text{ cu ft} \div 60 = 52 \text{ cfm.}$$

37. Btuh heat gain:

$$52 \times 32 = 1664 \text{ Btuh.}$$

38. Internal heat gain: Number of people (assume 4 for this house) 4 $\times$ 300 Btuh per person = 1200 Btuh. Kitchen allowance given 1200 Btuh.
39. Sensible heat gain subtotal: Add together items 31, 33, 35, 37, and 38; 15,054 Btuh.
40. Duct gain:

$$15,054 \times .15 = 2258 \text{ Btuh.}$$

41. Total sensible heat gain: Add together items 39 and 40; 17,312 Btuh.
42–45. Latent load calculations.
42. Determine the local relative humidity conditions, either wet, medium, medium dry, or dry. Our selected location is medium, which is 35 grains.
43. Latent load infiltration:

RESIDENTIAL COOLING DATA SHEET

JOB NAME:	DATE
ADDRESS:	

①OUTDOOR TEMP: 100°	②INDOOR TEMP: 70°	③TEMP DIFFERENCE: 30°

SENSIBLE LOAD CALCULATIONS

GLASS NO SHADE		SINGLE						DOUBLE						TRIPLE						BTUH HEAT GAIN
		DESIGN TEMPERATURE DIFFERENCE																		
COMPASS POINT	GLASS AREA SQ. FEET	10	15	20	25	30	35	10	15	20	25	30	35	10	15	20	25	30	35	
		HEAT TRANSFER MULTIPLIER																		
④N	81	25	29	33	37	41	45	20	22	24	26	28	30	15	16	18	19	20	21	2268 ⑤
⑥NE & NW		55	60	65	70	75	80	50	52	54	56	58	60	37	38	40	41	42	44	⑦
⑧E & W		80	85	90	95	100	105	70	72	74	76	78	80	55	56	58	59	60	62	⑨
⑩SE & SW		70	74	78	82	86	90	60	62	64	66	68	70	47	49	51	52	53	54	⑪
⑫S	67	40	44	48	52	56	60	35	37	39	41	43	45	26	27	29	31	32	33	2881 ⑬

GLASS INSIDE SHADE		SINGLE						DOUBLE						TRIPLE						BTUH HEAT GAIN
		DESIGN TEMPERATURE DIFFERENCE																		
COMPASS POINT	GLASS AREA SQ. FEET	10	15	20	25	30	35	10	15	20	25	30	35	10	15	20	25	30	35	
		HEAT TRANSFER MULTIPLIER																		
⑭N		15	19	23	27	31	35	15	17	19	21	23	25	10	12	14	16	17	19	⑮
⑯NE & NW		35	39	43	47	51	55	30	32	34	36	38	40	22	24	26	28	30	31	⑰
⑱E & W		50	54	58	62	66	70	45	47	49	51	53	55	35	36	38	40	42	44	⑲
⑳SE & SW		40	44	48	52	56	60	35	37	39	41	43	45	29	30	32	34	36	38	㉑
㉒S		25	29	33	37	41	45	20	22	24	26	28	30	16	18	20	22	24	26	㉓

DOORS	SQUARE FEET	DESIGN TEMPERATURE DIFFERENCE						BTUH HEAT GAIN
		10	15	20	25	30	35	
		HEAT TRANSFER MULTIPLIER						
SOLID WOOD		6.3	8.6	10.9	13.2	14.4	15.5	
㉔SOLID WOOD **	39	4.2	5.7	7.3	8.8	9.6	10.4	374 ㉕
METAL URETHANE		2.6	3.5	4.5	5.4	5.9	6.4	
METAL URETHANE **		2.2	3.0	3.8	4.6	5.0	5.4	
** Weatherstripped or Storm								

㉖ WALLS	RUNNING FEET 132 CEILING HEIGHT X 8 GROSS WALL = 1056 WINDOWS & DOOR AREAS − 187 NET WALL AREA [869]

FRAME WALL	SQUARE FEET	DESIGN TEMPERATURE DIFFERENCE						BTUH HEAT GAIN
		10	15	20	25	30	35	
		HEAT TRANSFER MULTIPLIER						
NO INSULATION		3.7	5.0	6.4	7.8	8.5	9.1	
R-11, 3" INSULATION		1.2	1.7	2.1	2.6	2.8	3.0	
㉗R-13, 3-1/2" INSULATION	869	1.1	1.5	1.9	2.3	2.5	2.7	2173 ㉘
R-13 + 1" POLYSTYRENE		0.8	1.1	1.4	1.7	1.8	2.0	
R-19 + 1/2" POLYSTYRENE		0.7	1.0	1.3	1.6	1.7	1.8	

㉙MASONRY WALL ABOVE GRADE	SQUARE FEET	DESIGN TEMPERATURE DIFFERENCE						BTUH HEAT GAIN ㉚
		10	15	20	25	30	35	
		HEAT TRANSFER MULTIPLIER						
NO INSULATION		3.2	5.8	8.3	10.9	12.2	13.4	
R-5, 1" INSULATION		0.9	1.6	2.3	3.1	3.5	3.8	
R-11, 3" INSULATION		0.5	0.9	1.3	1.6	1.8	2.0	
R-19, 6" INSULATION		0.3	0.5	0.8	1.0	1.2	1.3	

SENSIBLE HEAT GAIN SUBTOTAL	7696 ㉛

Figure 19–25 Completed residential cooling data sheet form. *Courtesy Lennox Industries, Inc.*

| | | Sensible Heat Gain Subtotal from Page 1 | | 7696 | | **31** |

CEILING	SQUARE FEET	DESIGN TEMPERATURE DIFFERENCE						BTUH HEAT GAIN
		10	15	20	25	30	35	
		HEAT TRANSFER MULTIPLIER						
No Insulation		14.9	17.0	19.2	21.4	22.5	23.6	
R-11, 3" Insulation		2.8	3.2	3.7	4.1	4.3	4.5	
R-19, 6" Insulation		1.8	2.1	2.3	2.6	2.8	2.9	
R-30, 10" Insulation	976	1.1	1.3	1.5	1.6	(1.7)	1.8	1659
R-38, 12" Insulation		0.9	1.0	1.1	1.3	1.3	1.4	

32   **33**

FLOOR OVER UNCONDITIONED SPACE	SQUARE FEET	DESIGN TEMPERATURE DIFFERENCE						BTUH HEAT GAIN
		10	15	20	25	30	35	
		HEAT TRANSFER MULTIPLIER						
No Insulation		1.9	3.9	5.8	7.7	8.7	9.6	
CARPET FLOOR-NO INSULATION		1.3	2.5	3.8	5.1	5.7	6.3	
R-11, 3" INSULATION		0.4	0.8	1.3	1.7	1.9	2.1	
R-19, 6" INSULATION	976	0.3	0.5	0.8	1.1	(1.2)	1.3	1171
R-30 10" INSULATION		0.2	0.4	0.6	0.7	0.8	0.9	

34   **35**

36 INFILTRATION/ VENTILATION

976 FLOOR SQ. FT. x __8__ CEILING HEIGHT = 7808 CUBIC FT

0.40 x 7808 CUBIC FT ÷ 60 = __52__ CFM

MECHANICAL VENTILATION CFM – FRESH AIR INTAKE

	CFM	DESIGN TEMPERATURE DIFFERENCE						BTUH HEAT GAIN
		10	15	20	25	30	35	
		HEAT TRANSFER MULTIPLIER						
INFILTRATION	52	11.0	16.5	22.0	27.0	(32.0)	38.0	1664
MECHANICAL VENTILATION	52	11.0	16.5	22.0	27.0	(32.0)	38.0	1664

37

INTERNAL HEAT GAIN	BTUH HEAT GAIN
Number of People __4__ x 300	1200
Kitchen Allowance	1,200

38   **38**

SENSIBLE HEAT GAIN SUBTOTAL	15054

39

DUCT GAIN	BTUH HEAT GAIN
R-4, 1" Flexible Blanket Insulation: ADD 15% (.15)	2258
R-7, 2" Flexible Blanket Insulation: ADD 10% (.10)	

40   **40**

TOTAL SENSIBLE HEAT GAIN	17312

41

LATENT LOAD CALCULATIONS

Conditions	Outdoor Wet Bulb	Indoor Wet Bulb	Grains
Wet	80	62.5	50
Medium	75	62.5	(35)
Medium Dry	70	62.5	20
Dry	65	62.5	0

42

Based on 75°F Indoor Dry Bulb at 50% RH.

LATENT LOAD-INFILTRATION	
0.68 x __35__ Grains x __52__ Infiltration CFM	1238

43   **43**

LATENT LOAD-VENTILATION	
0.68 x __35__ Grains x __52__ Ventilation CFM	1238

44   **44**

LATENT LOAD-PEOPLE	
Number of People __4__ x 230	920

45   **45**

TOTAL LATENT HEAT GAIN	3396

46

TOTAL SENSIBLE AND LATENT HEAT GAIN	20716

47

NOTE: All Heat Transfer Multipliers from ACCA Manual "J" Sixth Edition and for a medium outdoor daily temperature range.

241 17 002345

Litho U.S.A.

Figure 19–25 Continued.

0.68 × 35 grains × 52 cfm (from item 36) = 1238 Btuh.

44. Latent load ventilation:

   0.68 × 35 grains × 52 cfm = 1238 Btuh.

45. Latent load people:

   4 people × 230 Btuh = 920 Btuh.

46. Total latent heat gain: Add together items 43, 44, and 45; 3396 Btuh.

47. Total sensible and latent heat gain: Add together items 41 and 46; 20,708 Btuh.

HVAC DRAWINGS

Drawings for the HVAC system show the size and location of all equipment, duct work, and components with accurate symbols, specifications, notes, and schedules that form the basis of contract requirements for construction. Specifications are documents that accompany the drawings and contain all pertinent written information related to the HVAC system.

HVAC drawings for residential structures may or may not be necessary depending upon the requirements of the local building jurisdiction or the lending agency. Drawings may be prepared by the architect, architectural drafter, or the heating contractor when a complete HVAC layout is necessary. Figure 19–26 shows a heating plan for a residential structure.

For commercial structures the HVAC plan may be prepared by an HVAC engineer as a consultant for the architect. The consulting engineer will be responsible for the HVAC design and installation. The engineer will determine the placement of all equipment and the location of all duct runs and components. He or she will also determine all of the specifications for unit and duct size based on calculations of structure volume, exterior surface areas and construction materials, rate of air flow, and pressure. The engineer may prepare single-line sketches or submit data and calculations to a design drafter who will prepare design sketches or final drawings. Drafters without design experience will work from engineering or design sketches to prepare formal drawings. A single-line engineer's sketch is shown in Figure 19–27. The next step in the HVAC design is for the drafter to convert the rough sketch into a preliminary drawing. This preliminary drawing will go back to the engineer and architect for verification and corrections or changes. The final step in the design process is for the drafter to implement the design changes on the preliminary drawing to establish the final HVAC drawing. The final HVAC drawing is shown in Figure 19–28.

When the drafter converts an engineering sketch to a formal drawing, the easiest to read format should be used. For example:

1. Draw duct runs using thick (.7 or .9 mm) line widths.
2. Label duct sizes within the duct when appropriate, or use a note with a leader to the duct in other situations.
3. Duct sizes may be noted as 22 × 12 or 22/12, where the first number, 22, denotes the duct width and the second numeral, 12, indicates the duct depth.
4. Place notes on the drawing to avoid crowding. Aligned techniques may be used where horizontal notes read from the bottom of the sheet

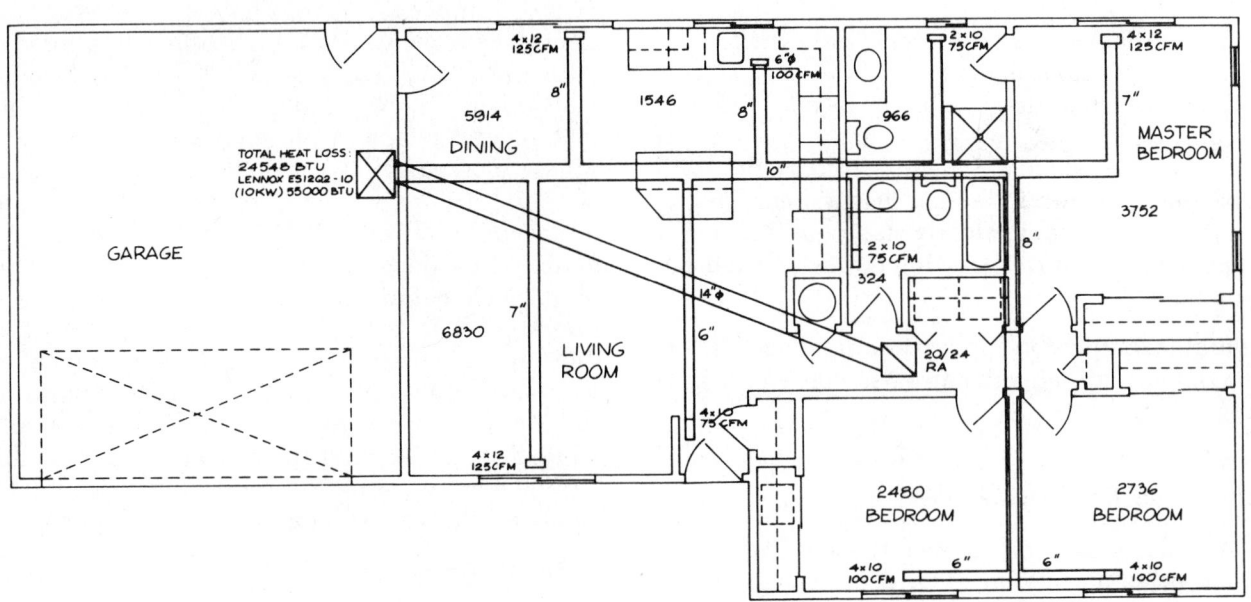

Figure 19–26 Heating plan for a residential structure.

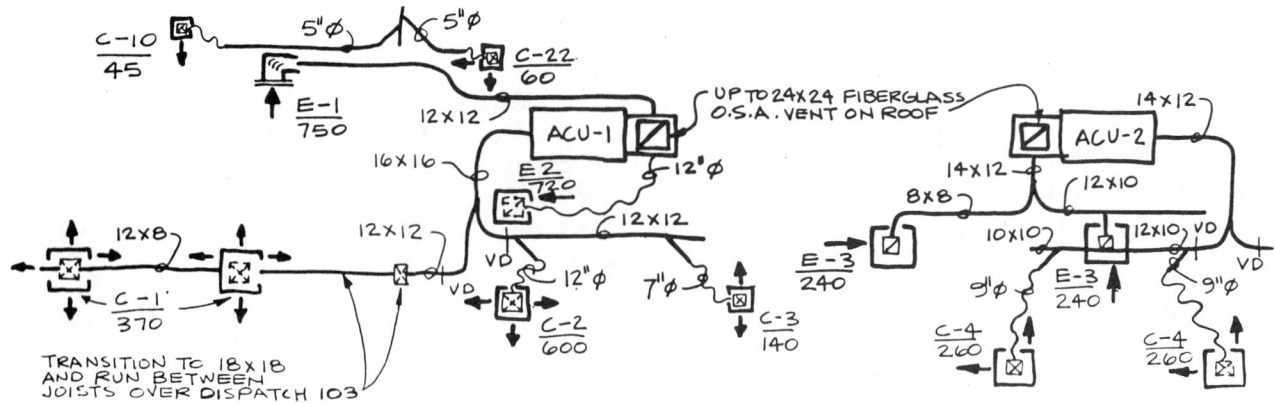

Figure 19–27 A single-line HVAC plan engineer's sketch.

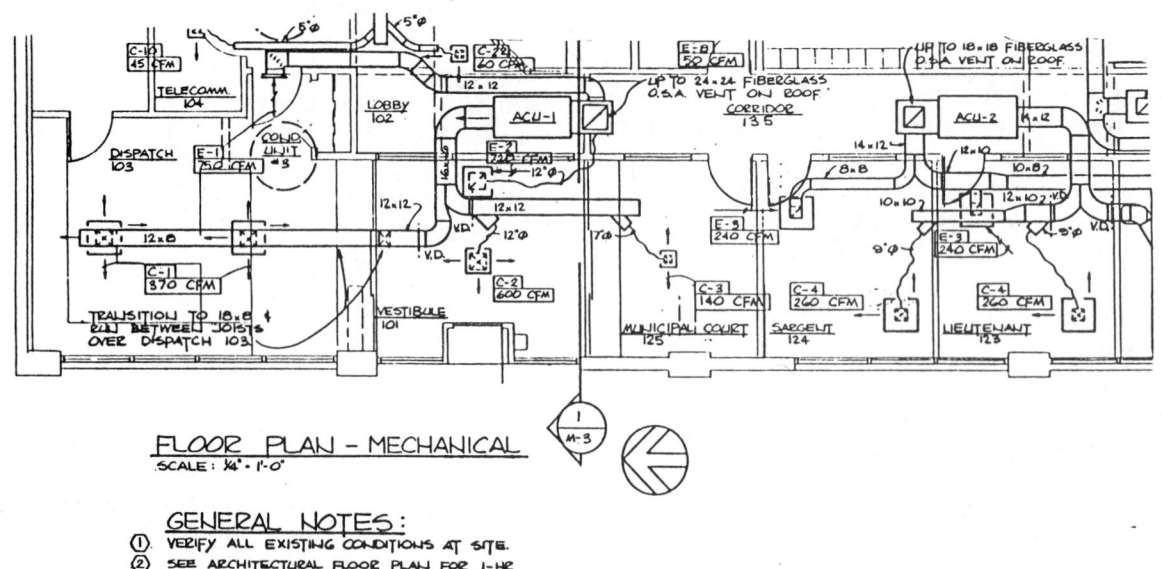

Figure 19–28 HVAC plan for the engineer's sketch shown in Figure 19–27. *Courtesy W. Alan Gold Consulting Mechanical Engineer and Robert Evenson Associates AIA Architects.*

and vertical notes read from the right side of the sheet. Make notes clear and concise.

5. Refer to schedules to obtain specific drawing information that may not otherwise be available on the sketch. Schedule information will be found in the following discussion.

6. Label equipment to clearly stand out from other information on the drawing either blocked out or bold.

Several examples of duct system elements are shown comparing the engineering sketch and formal drawing in Figure 19–29.

Single- and Double-line HVAC Plans

HVAC plans are drawn over the outline of the floor plan or as an overlay. The floor plan layout is drawn first using thin lines as a base sheet for the HVAC layout and other overlays. The HVAC plan is then drawn using thick lines and notes for contrast with the floor plan. The HVAC plan will show the placement of equipment and duct work. The size (in inches) and shape (with symbols, $\emptyset$ = round, $\square$ = square or rectangular) of duct work and system component labeling is placed on the drawing or keyed to schedules. Drawings may be either single line or double line, depending on the needs of the client or how much detail must be shown. Single-line drawings are easier and faster to draw. In many situations they are adequate to provide the equipment placement and duct routing as shown in Figure 19–30. Double-line drawings take up more space and are more time consuming than single line, but they are often necessary when complex systems require more detail as shown in Figure 19–28.

Detail Drawings

Detail drawings are used to clarify specific features of the HVAC plan. Single- and double-line

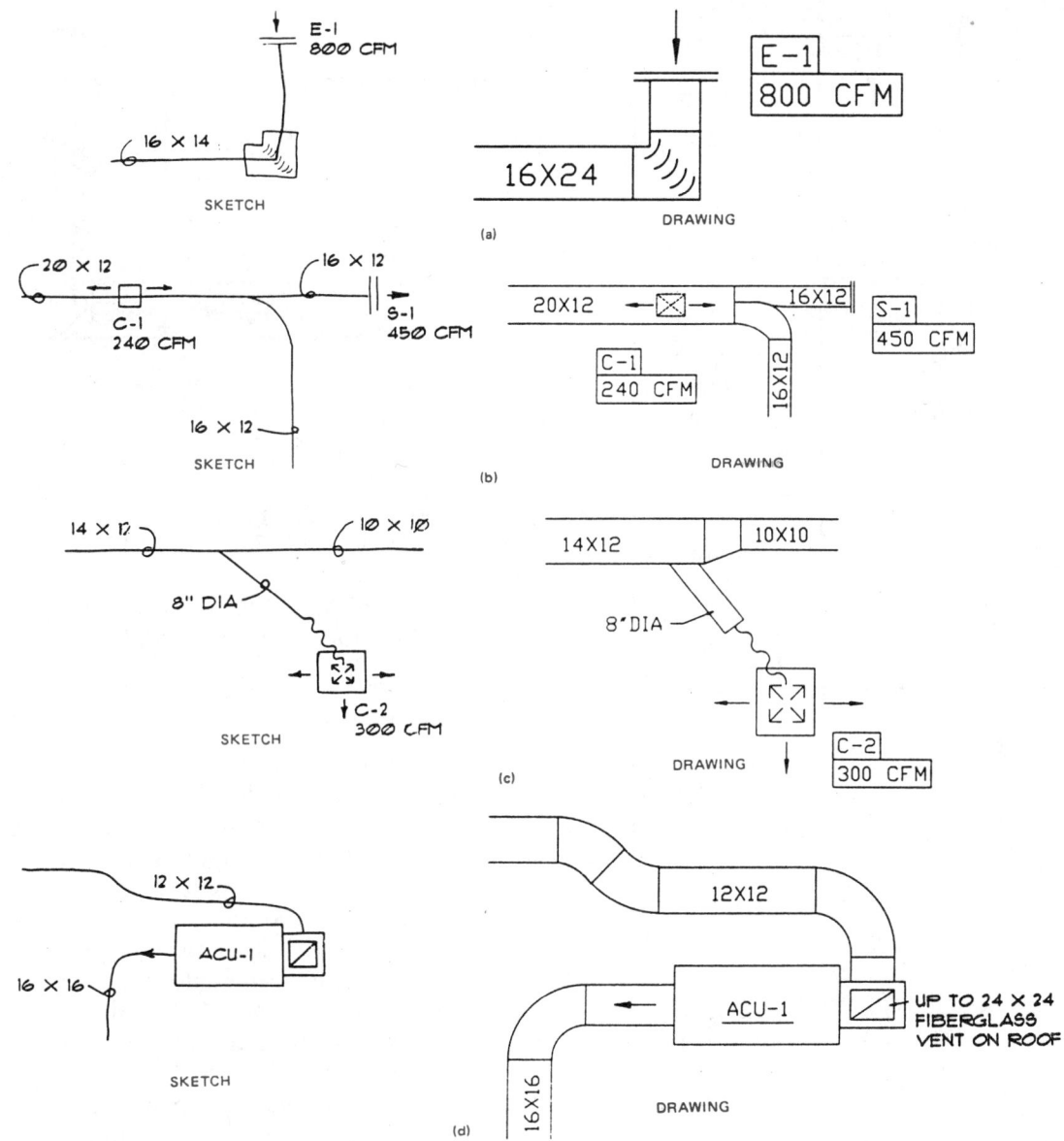

Figure 19-29 Examples showing engineering sketches converted to formal HVAC plan drawings.

drawings are intended to establish the general arrangement of the system; they do not always provide enough information to fabricate specific components. When further clarification of features is required, detail drawings are made. A detail drawing is an enlarged view(s) of equipment, equipment installations, duct components, or any feature that is not defined on the plan. Detail drawings may be scaled or unscaled and provide adequate views and dimensions for sheet metal shops to prepare fabrication patterns as shown in Figure 19-31.

Section Drawings

Sections or sectional views are used to show and describe the interior portions of an object or structure that would otherwise be difficult to visualize. Section drawings may be used to provide a clear representation of construction details or a profile of the HVAC plan as taken through one or more locations in the building. There are two basic types of section drawings used in HVAC. One method is used to show the construction of the HVAC system in relationship to the structure. In this case the building is sectioned and the duct system is shown unsectioned. This drawing provides a profile of the HVAC system. There may be one or more sections taken through the structure, depending on the complexity of the project. The building structure may be drawn using thin lines as shown in Figure 19-32. Figure 19-32 is a section through the HVAC plan shown in Figure 19-28. The other sectioning method is used to show detail of

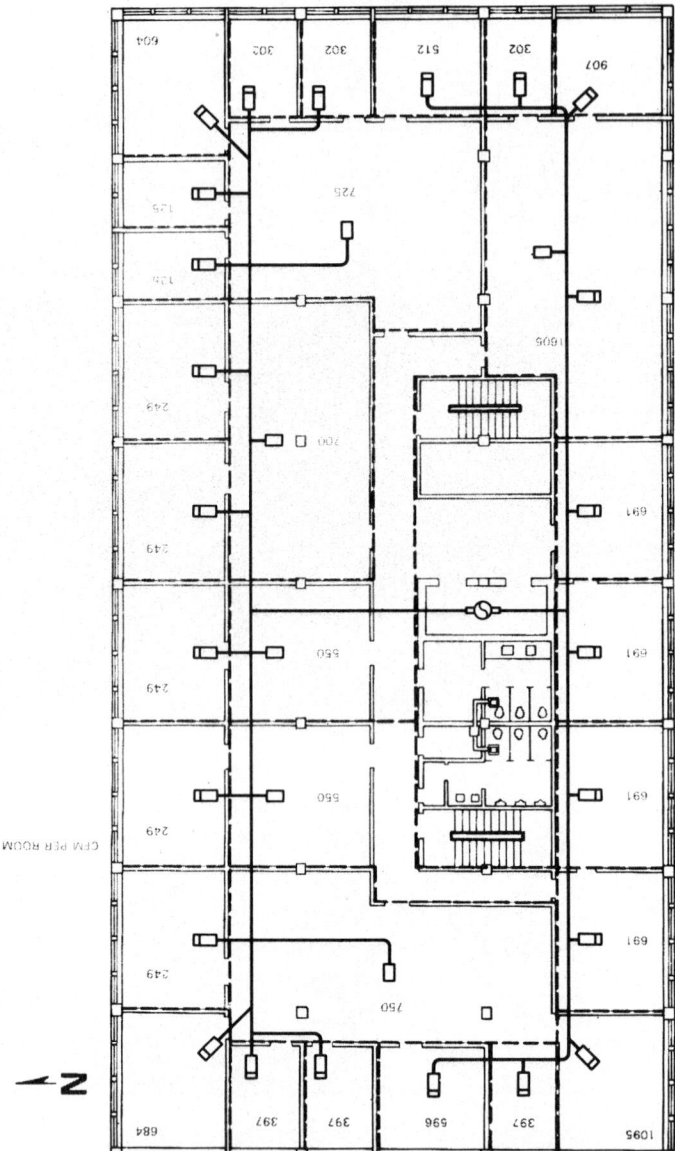

Figure 19-30 Single-line ducted system showing a layout of the proposed trunk and runout ductwork. *Courtesy The Trane Company, LaCrosse, WI.*

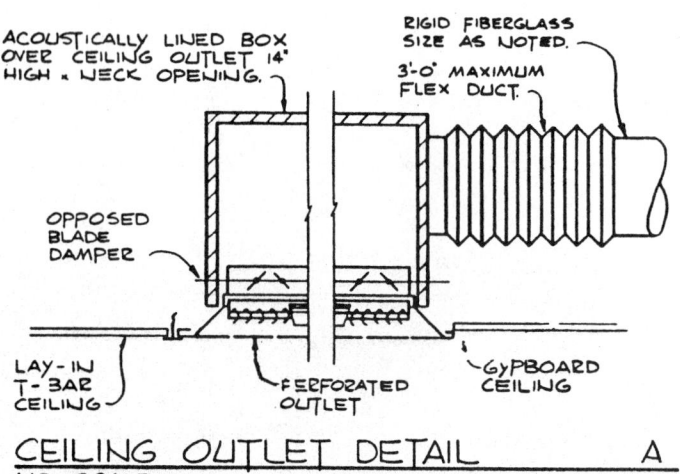

CEILING OUTLET DETAIL   A
NO SCALE   M-3

Figure 19-31 Detail drawings. *Courtesy W. Alan Gold Consulting Mechanical Engineer and Robert Evenson Associates AIA Architects.*

equipment, or to show how parts of an assembly fit together. (See Figure 19-33.)

Schedules

Numbered symbols that are used on the HVAC plan to key specific items to charts are known as schedules. These schedules are used to describe items such as ceiling outlets, supply and exhaust grills, hardware, and equipment. Schedules are charts of materials or products that include size, description, quantity used, capacity, location, vendor's specification, and any other information needed to construct or finish the system. Schedules aid the drawing by keeping it clear of unnecessary notes. They are generally placed in any convenient area of the drawing field or on a separate sheet. Items on the plan may be keyed to schedules by using a letter and number combination such as C-1 for CEILING OUTLET NO. 1, E-1 for EXHAUST GRILL NO. 1, or ACU-1 for

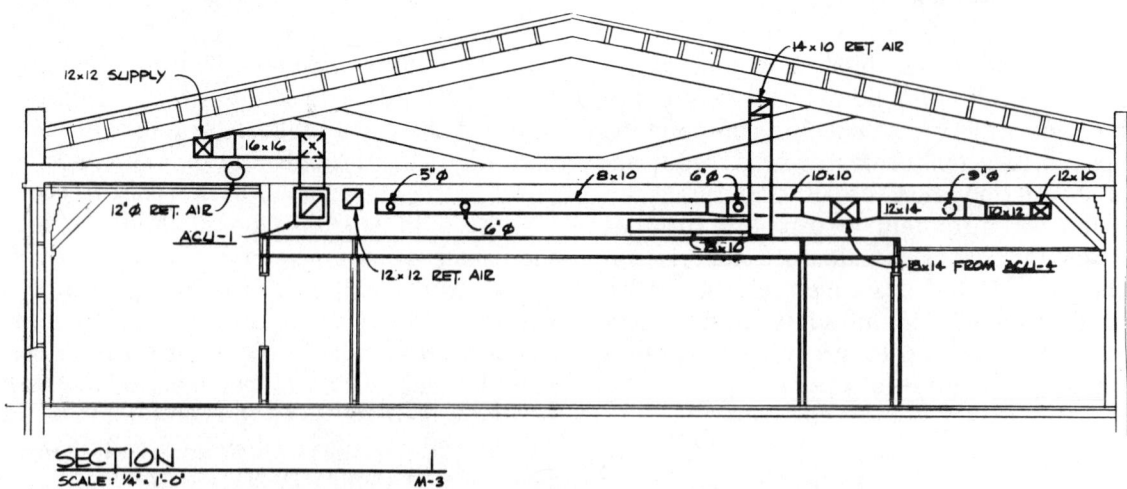

SECTION
SCALE: ¼" = 1'-0"   M-3

Figure 19-32 Section drawing. *Courtesy W. Alan Gold Consulting Mechanical Engineer and Robert Evenson Associates AIA Architects.*

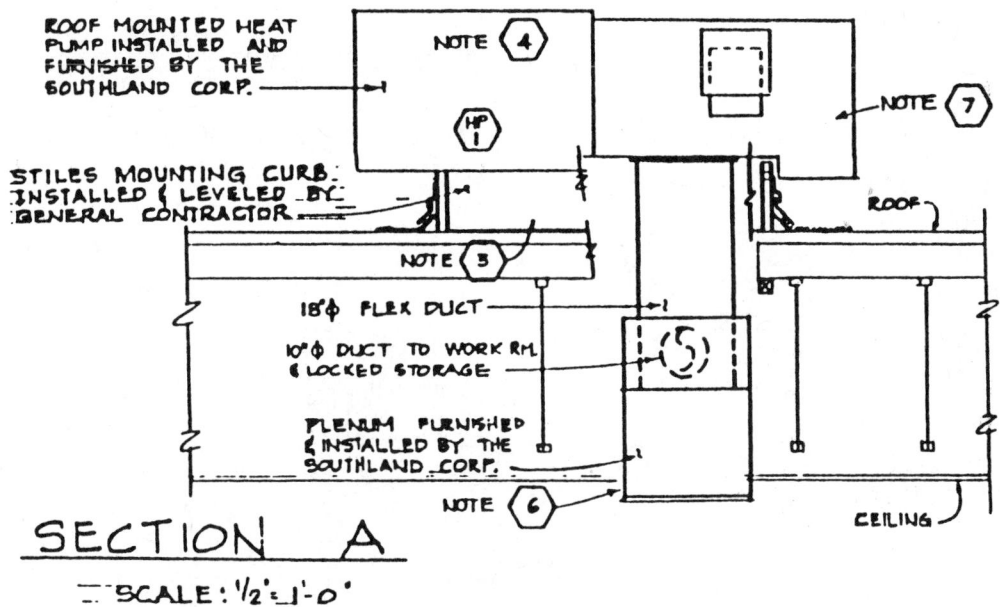

SECTION   A

SCALE: 1/2" = 1'-0"

Figure 19-33 Detailed section showing HVAC equipment installation. *Courtesy The Southland Corporation.*

EXHAUST GRILL SCHEDULE

SYMBOL	SIZE	CFM	LOCATION	FIRE DPR.	KEY OP. OPP BLD	KEY OP. EXTR	NO. DPR.	TYPE	REMARKS
				DAMPER TYPE					
E–1	24x12	750	HIGH WALL					4	
E–2	18x18	720	CEILING					2	
E–3	10x10	240	CEILING					1	24x24 PANEL
E–4	10x10	350	CEILING					1	
E–5	12x12	280	CEILING					1	
E–6	10x10	500	CEILING					1	
E–7	6x6	350						2	
E–8	12x6	50						3	
E–9	12x6	200						3	
E–10	12x8	150						3	
E–11	10x10	290						3	
E–12	9x4	160						1	24x24 PANEL
E–13	9x4	75	HIGH WALL					4	

TYPE 1: KRUGER 1190 SERIES STEEL PERFORATED FRAME 23 FOR LAY-IN TILE

TYPE 2: KRUGER 1190 SERIES STEEL PERFORATED FRAME 22 FOR SURFACE MOUNT

TYPE 3: KRUGER EGC-5: 1/2"x1/2"x1/2" ALUMINUM GRID.

TYPE 4: KRUGER S80H: 35° HORIZ. BLADES 3/4"O.C.

Figure 19-34 Exhaust grill schedule.

EQUIPMENT UNIT NO. 1. The exhaust grill schedule keyed to the HVAC plan in Figure 19–27 may be set up as a chart as shown in Figure 19–34.

Pictorial Drawings

Pictorial drawings may be isometric or oblique as shown in Figure 19–35. Pictorial drawings are usually not drawn to scale. They are used in HVAC for a number of applications, such as assisting in visualization of the duct system, and when the plan and sectional views are not adequate to show difficult duct routing. Manually drawn pictorials are time consuming and generally not used unless necessary.

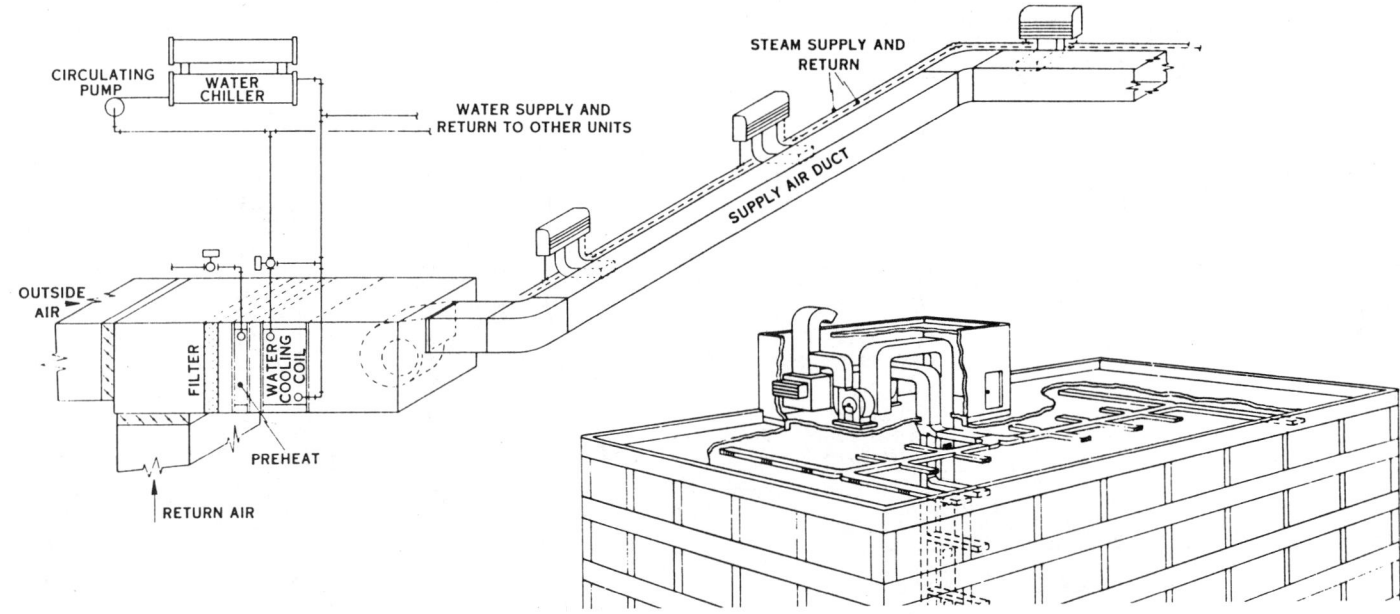

Figure 19–35 Pictorial drawings. *Courtesy The Trane Company, LaCrosse, WI.*

CADD
applications

CADD USES IN THE HVAC INDUSTRY

HVAC CADD software is available that allows you to place duct fittings and then automatically sizes ducts in accordance with common mechanical equipment supplier's specifications. The floor plan is commonly used as a reference layer, and the HVAC plan is a separate layer. Then, the CADD drafter follows these simple steps:

Step 1.   The drawing begins with the preliminary layout drawn as the duct centerlines as shown in Figure 1.

Step 2.   Select supply and return registers from a template menu symbols library, and add the symbols to the end of the centerlines where appropriate as shown in Figure 2.

Step 3.   The program then automatically identifies and records the lengths of individual duct runs, and tags each run. Fittings are located and identified by the type of intersection as shown in Figure 3. While all of this drawing information is added to the layout, the computer automatically gathers design

information into a file for duct-sizing based on a specific mechanical manufacturer's specifications that you select.

Step 4.   After the fitting location and sizes are determined, the program transforms each fitting into accurate double-line symbols exactly to the ANSI Y32.2.4 standard, as shown in Figure 4.

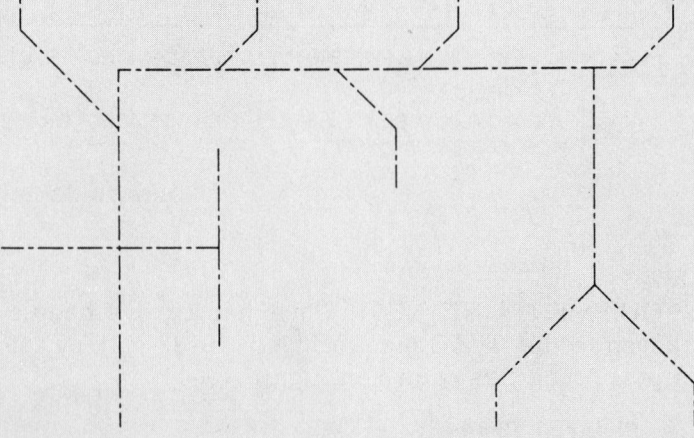

Figure 1 CADD-generated perspective of HVAC duct routing. *Courtesy Computervision Corporation.*

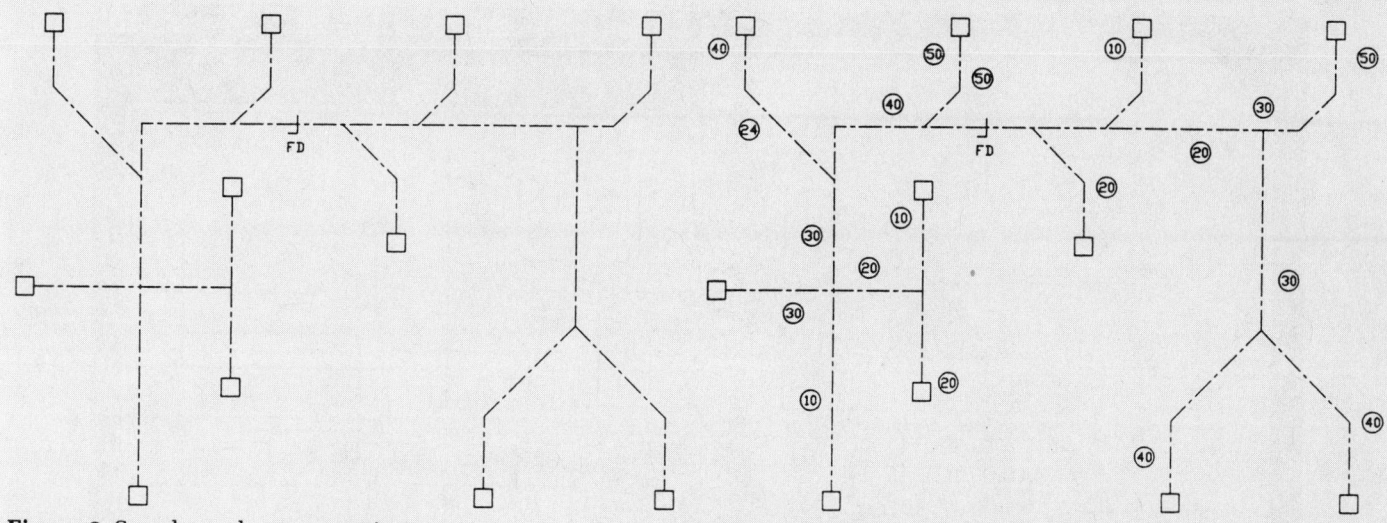

Figure 2 Supply and return registers.

Figure 3 Fittings located and identified.

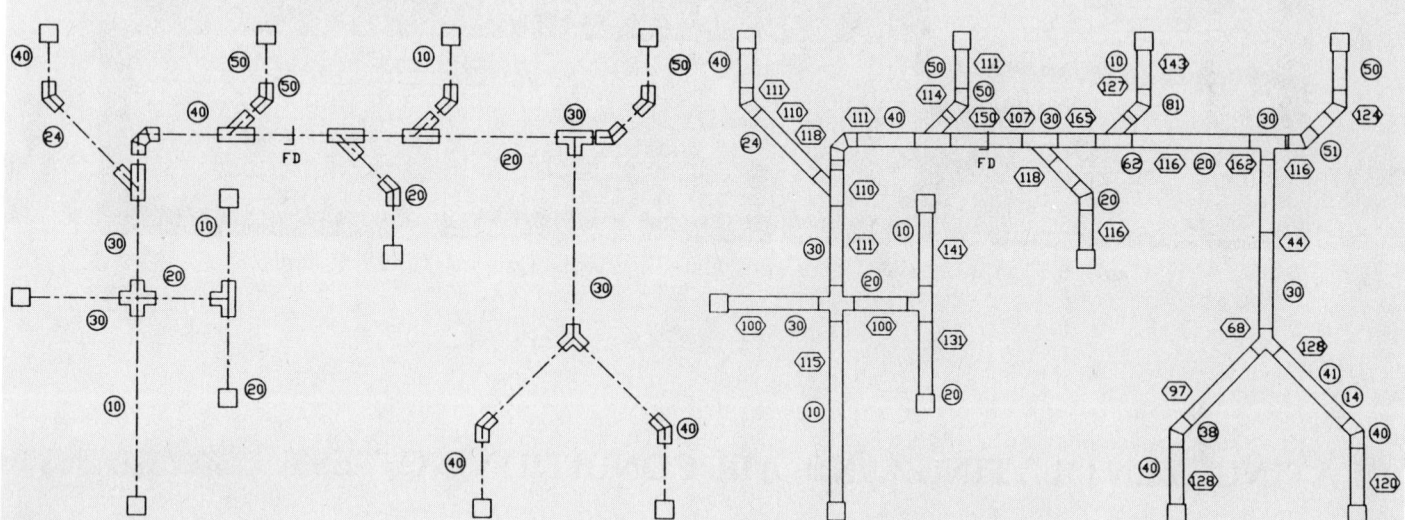

Figure 4 Fitting symbols.

Figure 5 Complete HVAC layout.

Step 5. When the fittings are in place, the program calculates and draws the connecting ducts and adds couplings automatically at the maximum duct lengths. If a transition is needed in a duct run, the program recommends the location; all you have to do is pick a transition fitting from the menu library. See Figure 5 for the complete HVAC layout.

The increase in productivity over manual methods is excellent. Plus, the program automatically records information, while you draw, to generate a complete bill of materials. The systems that offer you the greatest flexibility and productivity are designed as a parametric package. This program type allows you to set the design parameters that you want. Then, the computer automatically draws and details according to these settings. As you draw, information is placed with each fitting including type-of-fitting, CFM, and gauge. A complete HVAC plan and related schedules are shown in Figure 6.

CADD HVAC packages provide a variety of tablet menu overlays that assist in the rapid selection of symbols. Some of these tablet menu overlays are shown in Figure 7.

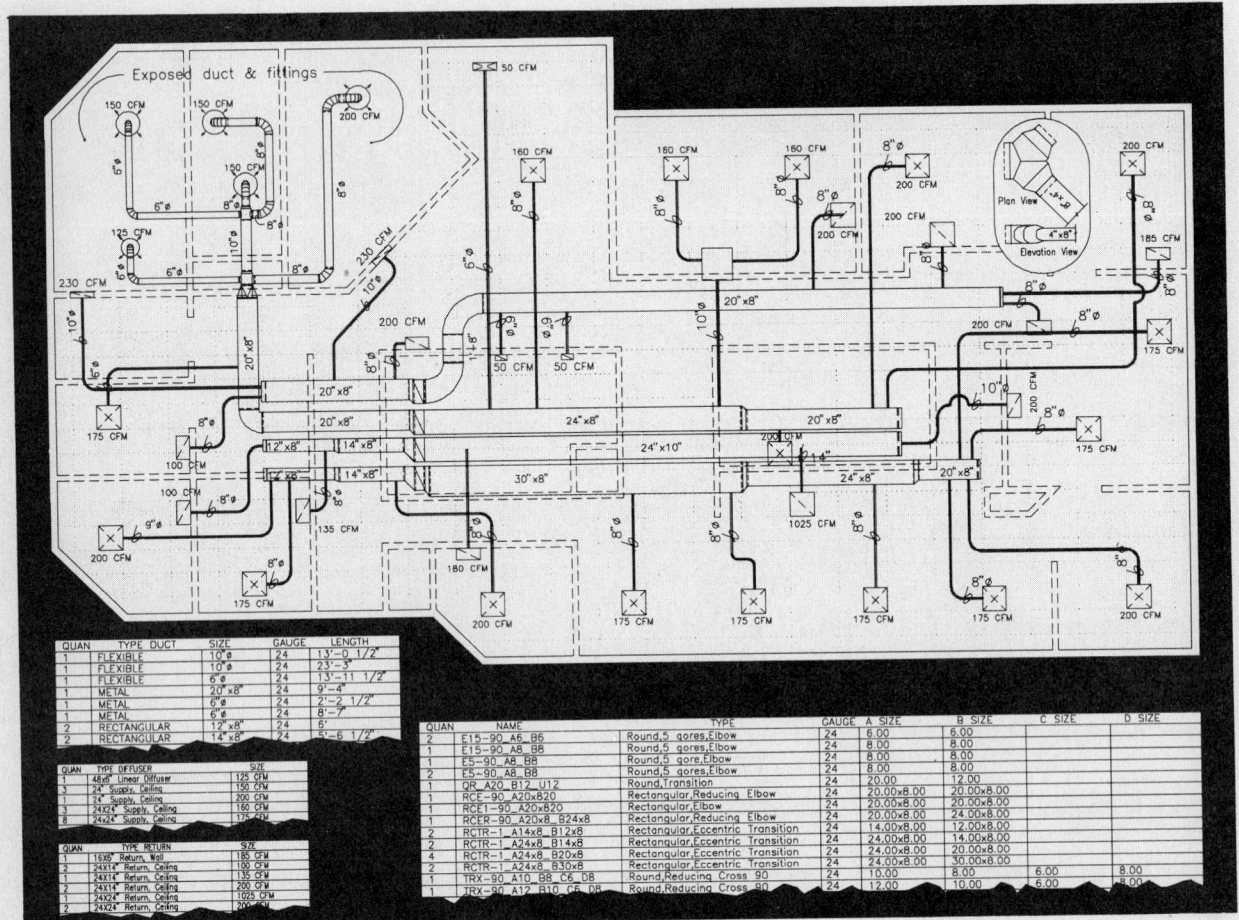

Figure 6 Complete HVAC plan and related symbols. *Courtesy Chase Systems.*

HEATING, VENTILATING, AND AIR CONDITIONING TEST

DIRECTIONS

Answer the questions with short complete statements or drawings as needed on an 8½ × 11 drawing sheet as follows:

1. Use ⅛ in. guidelines for all lettering.
2. Letter your name, HVAC Test, and the date at the top of the sheet.
3. Letter the question number and provide the answer. You do not need to write out the question.
4. Do all lettering with vertical uppercase architectural letters. If the answer requires line work, use proper drafting tools and technique. Answers may be prepared on a word processor if appropriate with course guidelines.
5. Your grade will be based on correct answers and quality of line technique.

QUESTIONS

1. Describe the following heating and cooling systems:
   a. central forced air
   b. hot water
   c. heat pump
   d. zoned heating
2. Describe a type of zoned heating called radiant heat.
3. List two advantages and two disadvantages of zonal heat over central forced-air heating.
4. A heat pump may supply up to how many times as much heat per year for the same amount of electrical consumption as a standard electric forced-air system?
5. Discuss four factors that influence the placement of a thermostat.

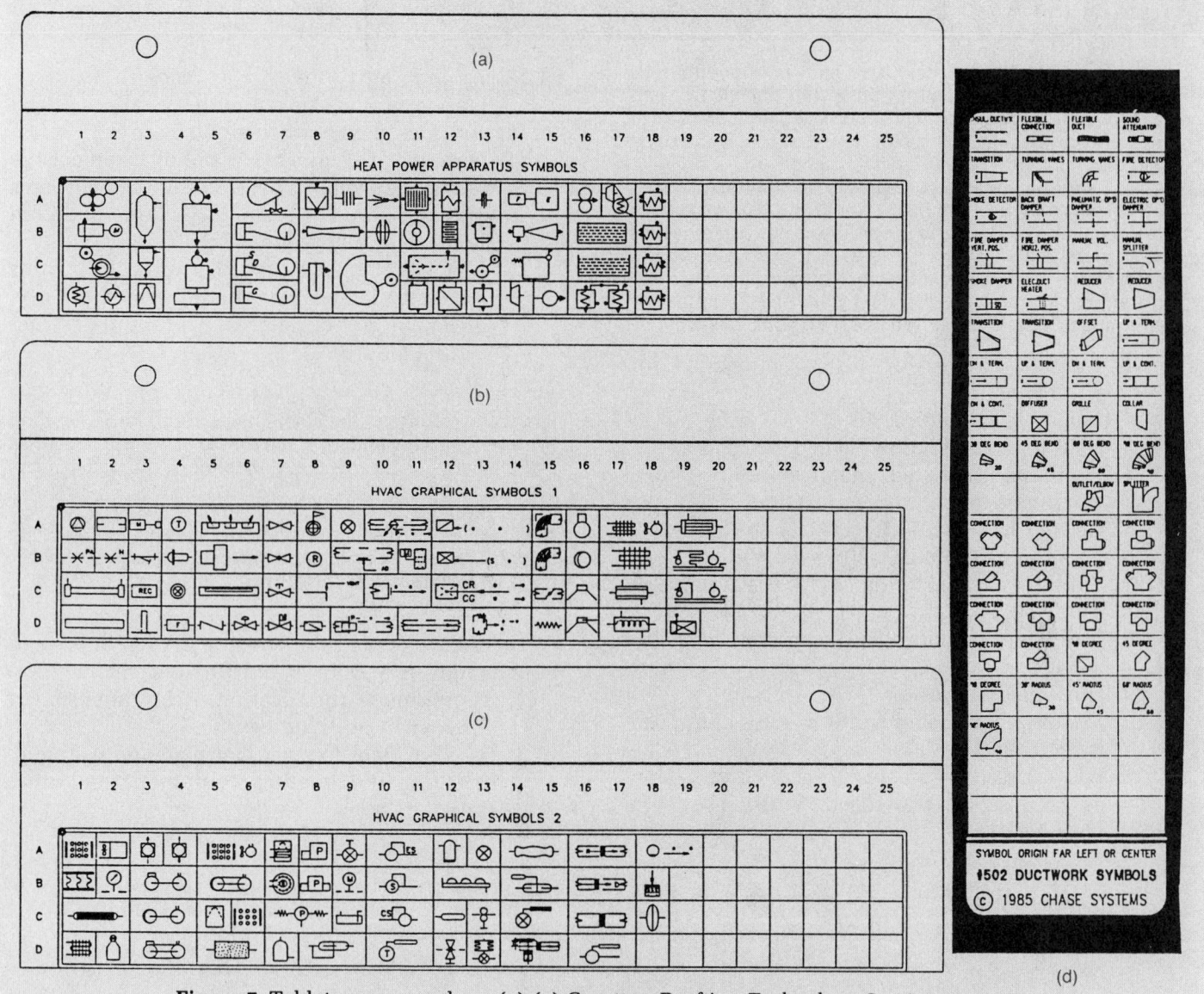

Figure 7 Tablet menu overlays. (a)–(c) *Courtesy Drafting Technology Services, Inc., Bartlesville, OK;* (d) *courtesy Chase Systems.*

6. Describe five sources that can contribute to an unhealthy living environment.
7. Discuss the function of an air-to-air heat exchanger.
8. List five advantages of a central vacuum system.
9. Define the following terms related to thermal performance calculations:

   a. Outdoor temperature
   b. Indoor temperature
   c. Temperature difference
   d. Infiltration
   e. Mechanical ventilation
   f. Duct loss
   g. R factor
   h. U factor
   i. Btu
   j. Compass point
   k. Internal heat gain
   l. Latent load
   m. Grains

HVAC PROBLEMS

Problem 19–1. Prepare heat loss and gain calculations for one of the floor plans found at the end of Chapter 20, Floor Plan Problems. You may use the floor plan of your choice or your instructor will assign a floor plan. Use the residential heating data sheets and the residential cooling data sheets (found in the Instructor's Guide) provided by your instructor, or prepare your own data sheets by copying the proper headings from Figures 19–23 and 19–25. Complete the data sheets according to the method used in this chapter to solve for the total winter heat loss and summer heat gain. Use the following criteria unless otherwise specified by your instructor:

1. Outdoor temperature as recommended for your area.
2. Indoor temperature: 70° F.
3. Double glass windows and glass doors.
4. Urethane insulated metal exterior doors, weatherstripped.
5. Ceiling height: 8'-0".
6. Ceiling insulation: R-30.
7. Frame wall insulation: R-19 + ½" polystyrene.
8. Insulation in floors over unconditioned space: R-19.
9. Duct insulation: R-4.
10. Masonry above and below grade as required in plan used.
11. Basement floor or concrete slab construction as required in plan used. Verify use with your instructor.
12. Assume entry foyer door faces south to establish window orientation.
13. Assume glass with inside shade.
14. Number of occupants is optional. Select the family size you desire or count the bedrooms and add one. For example, a three-bedroom home plus one equals four people.
15. Use latent load conditions typical for your local area. Select wet, medium, medium dry, or dry as appropriate. Consult your instructor.

Problem 19–2. Calculate the minimum heat exchanger capacity for one of the floor plans found in Floor Plan Problems at the end of Chapter 20. Use the formulas established earlier in the Air-to-air Heat Exchangers section of this chapter.

Problem 19–3. Given: Residential heating engineering sketch of main floor plan and basement. Do the following on appropriately sized vellum (2 B size sheets or 1 C size is recommended):

1. Make a formal double-line HVAC floor plan layout at a ¼ in. = 1 ft 0 in. scale.
2. Approximate the location of undimensioned items such as windows.
3. Use thin lines for the floor plan and use thick lines for the heating equipment and duct runs.

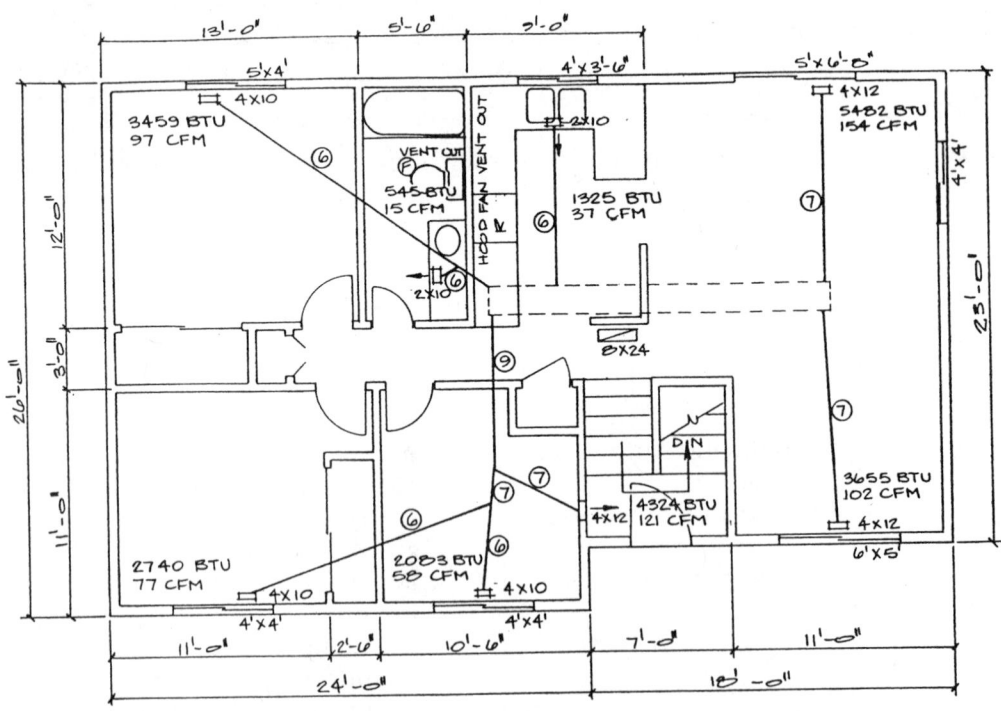

TOTAL HEAT LOSS 23,885 BTU
675 CFM

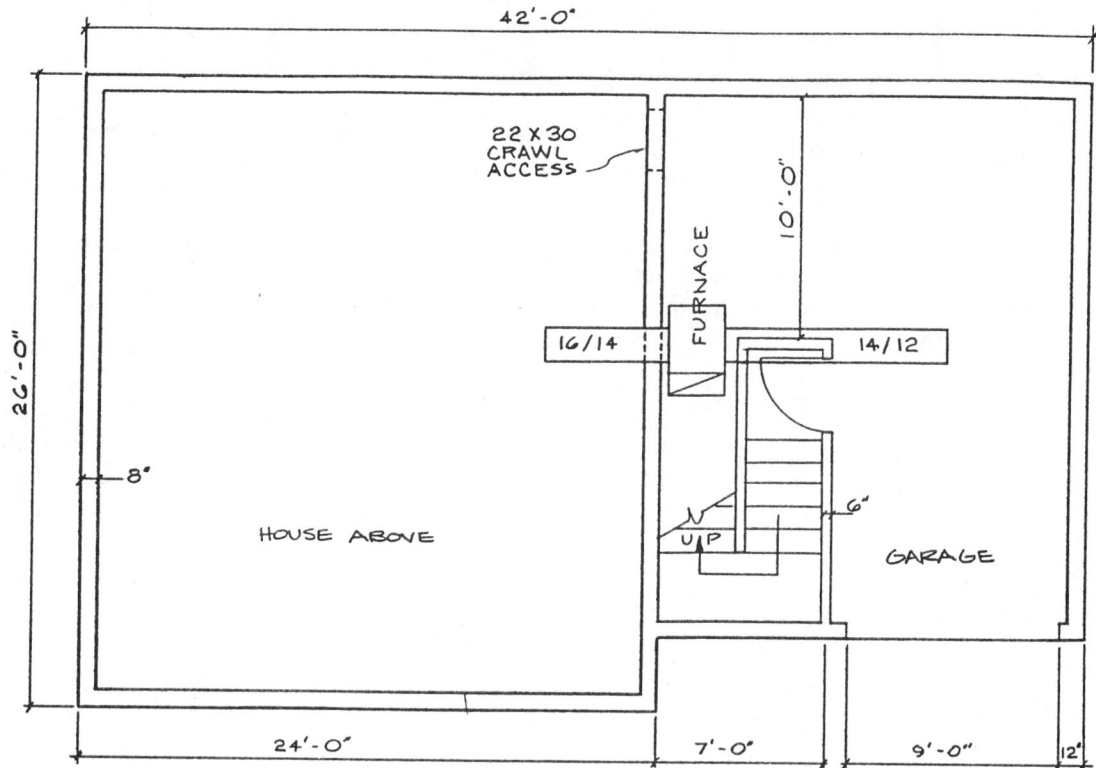

BASEMENT FURNANCE HEATING PLAN

Problem 19–4. Given: Residential air-to-air heat exchanger ducting engineering sketch of basement floor plan. Do the following on appropriately sized vellum (one B or C size sheet is recommended):

1. Make a formal single-line air-to-air heat exchanger floor plan layout at a ¼ in. = 1 ft 0

in. scale.

2. Approximate the location of undimensioned items such as doors.

3. Use thin lines for the floor plan and use thick lines for the air-to-air heat exchanger equipment and duct runs.

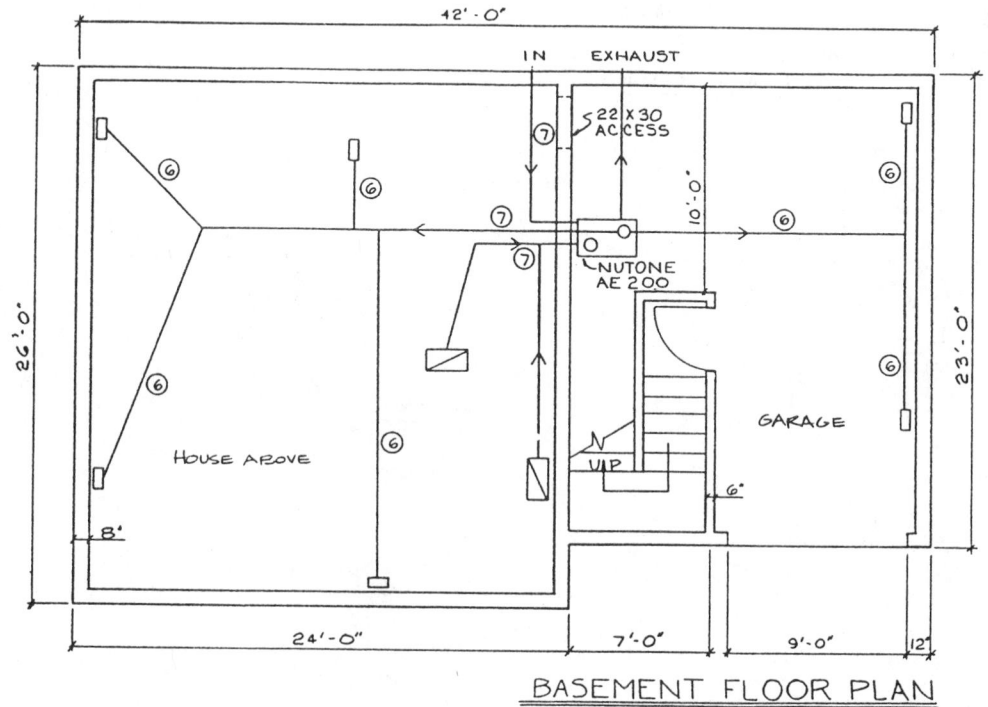

BASEMENT FLOOR PLAN
AIR-TO-AIR HEAT EXCHANGER PLAN

Problem 19–5. Given the following:

1. HVAC floor plan engineering layout at approximately 1/16 in. = 1 ft 0 in. The engineer's layout is rough, so round off dimensions to the nearest convenient units. For example, if the dimension you scale reads 24 ft 3 in. round off to 24 ft 0 in. The floor plan will not require dimensioning; therefore, the representation is more important than the specific dimensions.
2. Related schedules.
3. Engineer's sketch for exhaust hood.

Do the following on appropriately sized vellum (C or D size is recommended; all required items will fit on one sheet with careful planning):

1. Make a formal double-line HVAC floor plan layout at a ¼ in. = 1 ft 0 in. scale. (NOTE: You measured the given engineer's sketch at 1/16 in. = 1 ft 0 in.) Now convert the established dimensions to a formal drawing at ¼ in. = 1 ft 0 in. Approximate the location of the HVAC duct runs and equipment in proportion to the presentation on the sketch.
2. Prepare correlated schedules in the space available. Set up the schedules in a manner similar to the examples below.
3. Make a detail drawing of the exhaust hood either scaled or unscaled. Make the detail large enough to clearly show the features. Refer to the detail drawings below for examples.

SCHEDULES

CEILING OUTLET SCHEDULE

SYMBOL	SIZE	CFM	DAMPER TYPE	PANEL SIZE
C-10	9 × 9	230	Key Operated	12 × 12
C-11	8 × 8	185	Key Operated	12 × 12
C-12	6 × 6	40	Key Operated	12 × 12
C-13	6 × 6	45	Key Operated	12 × 12
C-14	6 × 18	300	Fire Damper	24 × 24

SUPPLY GRILL SCHEDULE

SYMBOL	SIZE	CFM	LOCATION	DAMPER TYPE
S-1	20 × 8	450	High Wall	Key Operation
S-2	20 × 8	450	High Wall	External Operation

EXHAUST GRILL SCHEDULE

SYMBOL	SIZE	CFM	LOCATION	DAMPER TYPE
E-5	18 × 24	1000	Low Wall	No Damper

ROOF EXHAUST FAN SCHEDULE

SYMBOL	AREA SERVED	CFM	FAN SPECIFICATIONS
REF-1	Solvent Tank	900	1/4 HP, 12 in. Non-spark Wheel, 1050 Max. Outlet Velocity

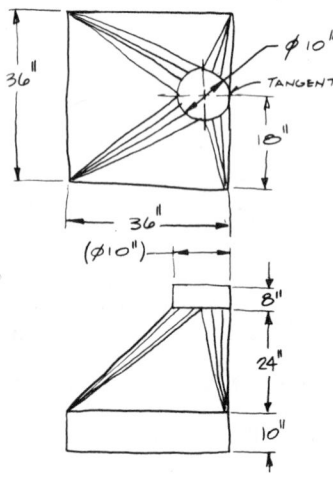

EXHAUST HOOD DETAIL

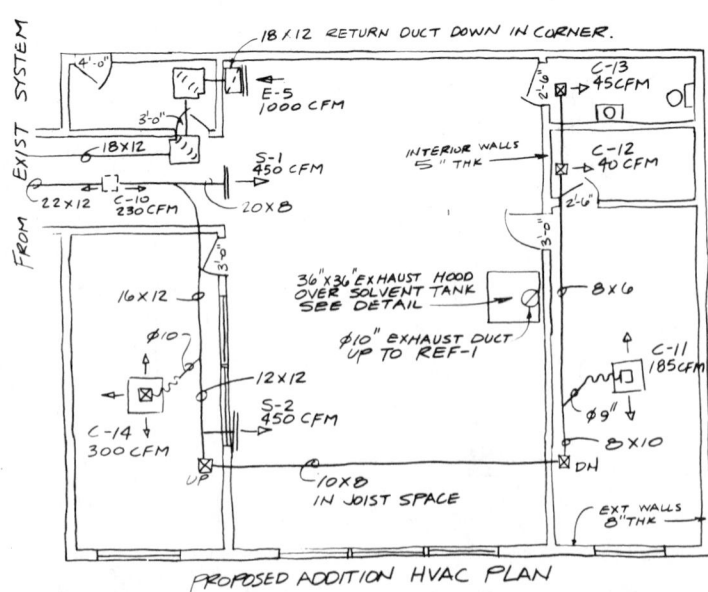

PROPOSED ADDITION HVAC PLAN

Chapter 20
Floor-Plan Layout

RESIDENTIAL PLANS are commonly drawn on 17″ × 22″, 18″ × 24″, 22″ × 34″, or 24″ × 36″ drawing sheets. This discussion will explain floor-plan layout techniques using 17″ × 22″ vellum. The layout methods may be used with any sheet size. A complete floor plan is shown in Figure 20–1. The step-by-step method used to draw this floor plan will provide you with a method for laying out any floor plan. As you progress through the step-by-step discussion of the floor-plan layout, refer back to previous chapters to review specific floor-plan symbols and dimensioning techniques. Keep in mind that these layout techniques represent a suggested typical method used to establish a complete floor plan. You may alter these layout steps to suit your individual preference as your skills develop and knowledge increases.

LAYING OUT A FLOOR PLAN

Before you begin the floor-plan layout be sure that your hands and equipment are clean, tape your drawing sheet down very tightly, and align and square the scales of your drafting machine if you use one.

Step 1. Determine the working area of the paper to be used. This is the distance between borders. In Figure 20–2, the 17″ × 22″ vellum has a 16″ vertical and 19½″ horizontal distance.

Step 2. Determine the drawing area which is approximately the area that the floor plan

plus dimensions will require when completely drawn. Residential floor plans are drawn to a scale of ¼″ = 1′–0″ while most commercial floor plans are drawn to a scale of ⅛″ = 1′–0″ due to the size of the structure. The house to be drawn is 60 ft long and 36 ft wide. At a scale of ¼″ = 1′–0″ the house will be drawn 15 in. by 9 in. (60′ ÷ 4 = 15″ by 36′ ÷ 4 = 9″). This size does not take into consideration any area needed for dimensions. However, it appears that in this case there is adequate space for dimensions because the house size is substantially less than the working area. When you consider the need for at least 2 in. on each side of the house for dimensions but this added length or width does not fit within the working area, you have a problem that can only be solved by one of the following choices:

- Select a larger size drawing sheet. When the paper size is increased for one sheet, this size is generally used for the entire set of drawings.
- Crowd the dimensions. This can only be done to the point where you begin to sacrifice clarity. Be careful.
- Reduce the floor-plan scale. This is not normally done, as floor plans are usually drawn at ¼″ to 1′–0″, except for some commercial applications where ⅛″ = 1′–0″ or 3/16″ = 1′–0″ may be used.

Step 3. Center the drawing within the working area using these calculations:

$$
\begin{array}{r}
\text{Working area length} = 19.5″ \\
\underline{\text{Drawing area length} = -15.0″} \\
4.5″
\end{array}
$$

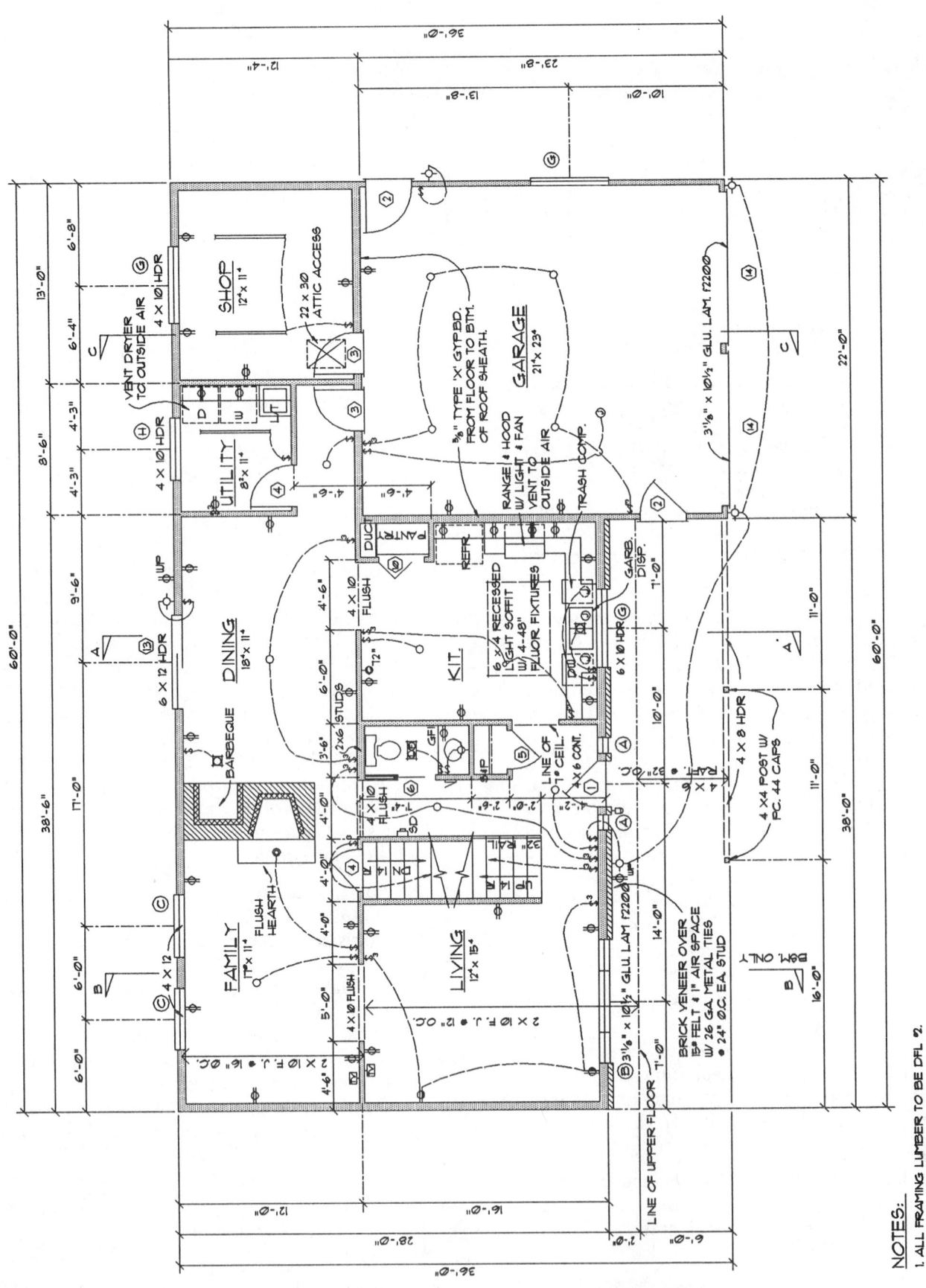

MAIN FLOOR PLAN

SCALE : ¼" = 1'-0"

Figure 20–1 The complete floor plan.

NOTES:
1. ALL FRAMING LUMBER TO BE DFL 2.
2. ALL EXT. STUDS TO BE 2x6 @16" O.C.
   • HEATED AREAS.
3. ALL METAL CONNECTORS TO BE SIMPSON
   CO. OR EQUAL.
4. VENT ALL FANS TO OUTSIDE AIR

TITLE BLOCK

CHECKED BY

DRAWN BY

DATE

PROJECT

DRAWING

DRAWING No.

delmar publishers inc.

TWO COMPUTER DRIVE WEST BOX 15-015 ALBANY NEW YORK 12212

19 1/2"

16"

BORDER LINE

Figure 20-2 Working area.

$$4.5'' \div 2 = 2.25''$$

2.25″ = Space on each side of floor plan.

Working area height =   16″

Drawing area height = − 9″

               7″

$$7'' \div 2 = 3.5''$$

3.5″ = Space above and below floor plan.

Figure 20–3 shows the drawing area centered within the working area. Use construction lines drawn very lightly with a 6H or 4H lead to outline the drawing area. This method of centering a drawing is important for beginning drafting technicians. It can be quite frustrating to start a drawing and find that there is not adequate room to complete it. More experienced drafting technicians may not use this process to this extent, although they will make some quick calculations to determine where the drawing should be located. In actual practice, the drawing does not have to be perfectly centered, but a well-balanced drawing is important. Several factors contribute to a well-balanced drawing:

- Actual size of the required drawing
- Scale of the drawing
- Amount of detail
- Size of drawing sheet
- Amount of dimensions needed
- Amount of general and local notes required

Step 4.   Lay out all exterior walls 6 in. thick within the drawing area using construction lines. Construction lines are very lightly drawn with a 6H or 4H lead and easy to erase if you make an error. If properly drawn, however, construction lines need not be erased. Properly drawn construction lines are too light to reproduce using a diazo print although they may show as very light lines on a photocopy reproduction. Some technicians use a light-blue pencil lead for preliminary layout work because the light-blue will not reproduce. Use your ¼″ = 1′-0″ architect's scale. Look at Figure 20–4.

Step 5.   Lay out all interior walls 4″ thick within the floor plan using construction lines. See Figure 20–4.

Step 6.   Block out all doors and windows in their proper locations using construction lines as shown in Figure 20–5. Be sure that doors and windows are centered within the desired areas.

Step 7.   Using construction lines, draw all cabinets. Base kitchen cabinets are 24 in., upper cabinets 12 in., and bath vanities 22 in. wide as shown in Figure 20–6.

Step 8.   Draw all appliances and utilities using construction lines. Draw the refrigerator 36″ × 30″, range 30 in. wide, dishwasher 24 in. wide, furnace 24″ × 30″, water heater 24 in. in diameter, and the washer and dryer 30″ × 30″ each. See Figure 20–6.

Step 9.   Draw all plumbing fixtures, sinks, and toilets as seen in Figure 20–6.

Step 10.   Use construction lines to draw a 5 ft wide, single-face fireplace with a 36 in. wide opening and an 18″ × 5′ hearth. Include a 30″ × 18″ barbecue. Add 4 in. brick veneer to the front wall as shown in Figure 20–6.

Step 11.   Lightly draw the stairs representation providing several 12 in. wide treads to a long break line with necessary handrails or guardrails. See Figure 20–6.

Step 12.   Check your accuracy and then darken all the construction lines that you have drawn. Add all door and window floor-plan symbols. Draw lines and symbols from top to bottom and from left to right if you are right handed or from right to left if left handed. Try to avoid passing your hands and equipment over darkened lines to help minimize smudging. Darken walls with a slightly rounded H or F lead, or a 0.7 or 0.9 mm pencil with H lead. For inked drawings or computer generated drawings use a 0.7 mm technical pen. All cabinets, appliances, fixtures, and other items are drawn with a sharp 2H or H lead or a 0.5 mm pencil. These are only suggestions, and each drafter will select leads that work best for him or her judging from practice and experience. Look at Figure 20–7. At this point, the floor plan is ready to use as a preliminary drawing for client approval.

Step 13.   Lay out all exterior dimension lines using construction lines. Place an overall dimension line on all sides of the residence. The second row of dimensions should go from exterior face to exterior face of major jogs. A third line should be used to go from exterior face of exterior walls to the center of interior walls. There is a common exception: Dimension to the exterior face of the walls between the garage and the residence because of the change in foundation materials. A fourth line should be used to go from each wall to the center of each

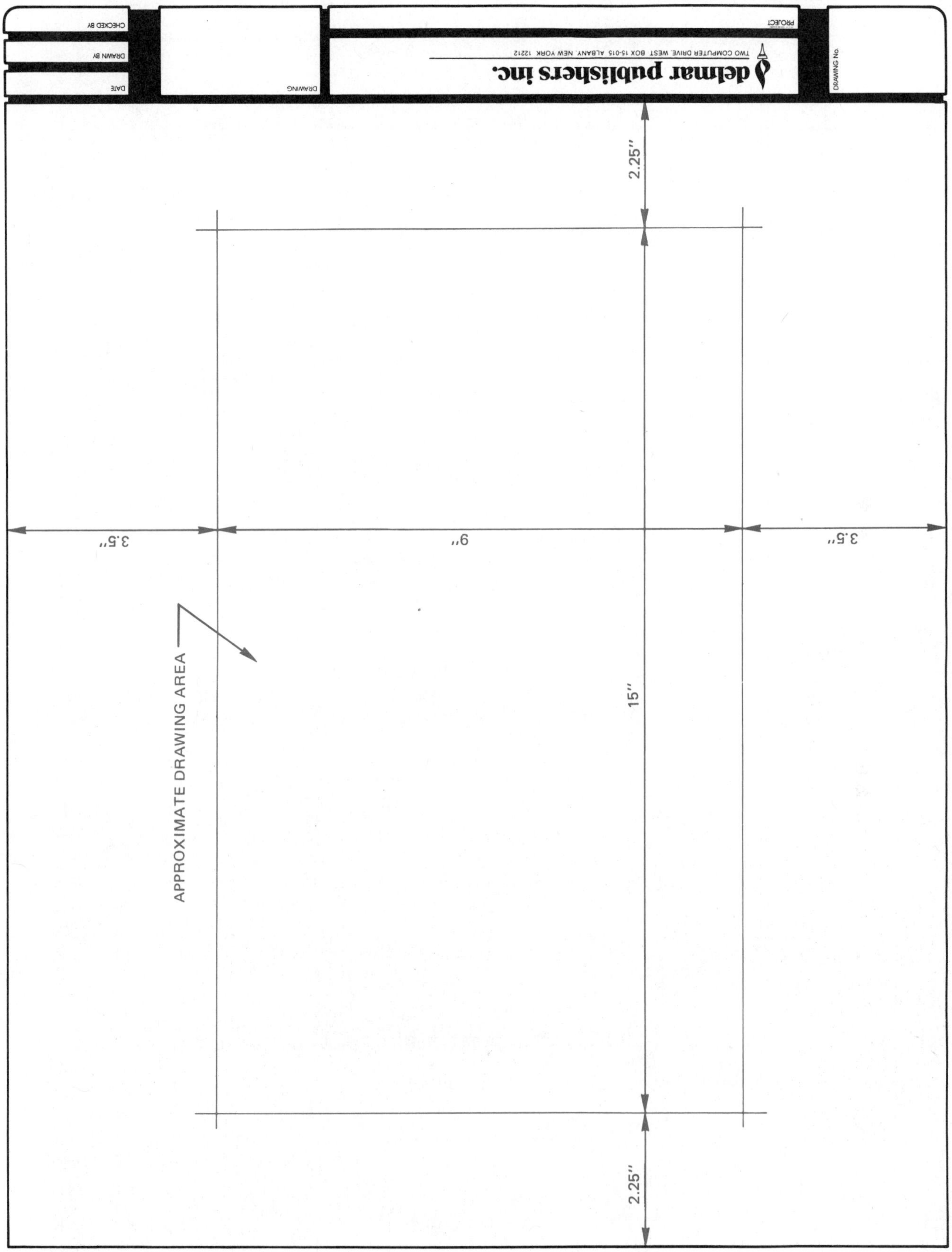

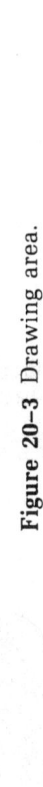

CHECKED BY

DRAWN BY

DATE

DRAWING

PROJECT

DRAWING No.

delmar publishers inc.
TWO COMPUTER DRIVE WEST, BOX 15-015, ALBANY, NEW YORK 12212

2.25″

3.5″

9″

3.5″

15″

2.25″

APPROXIMATE DRAWING AREA

Figure 20-3 Drawing area.

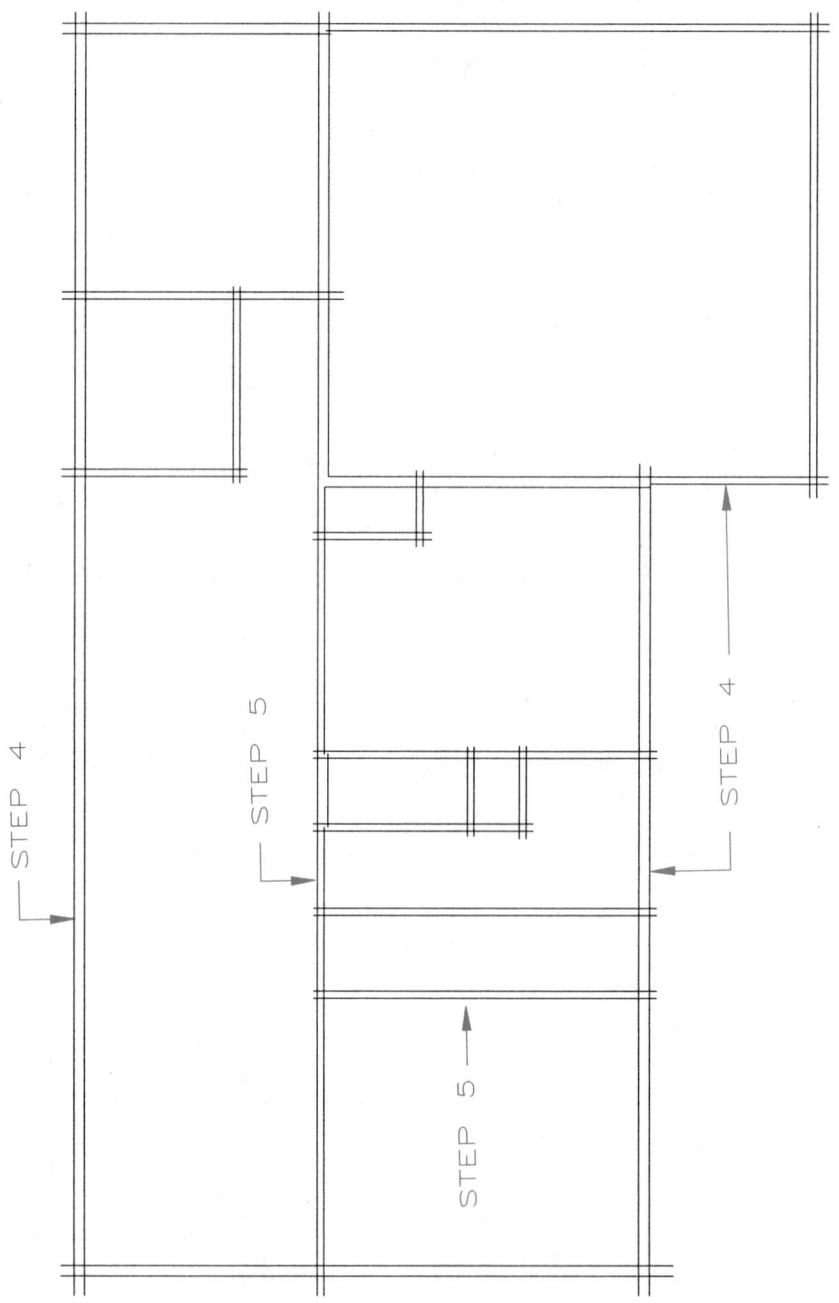

Figure 20–4 Steps 4 and 5: Lay out exterior walls and interior partitions with construction lines.

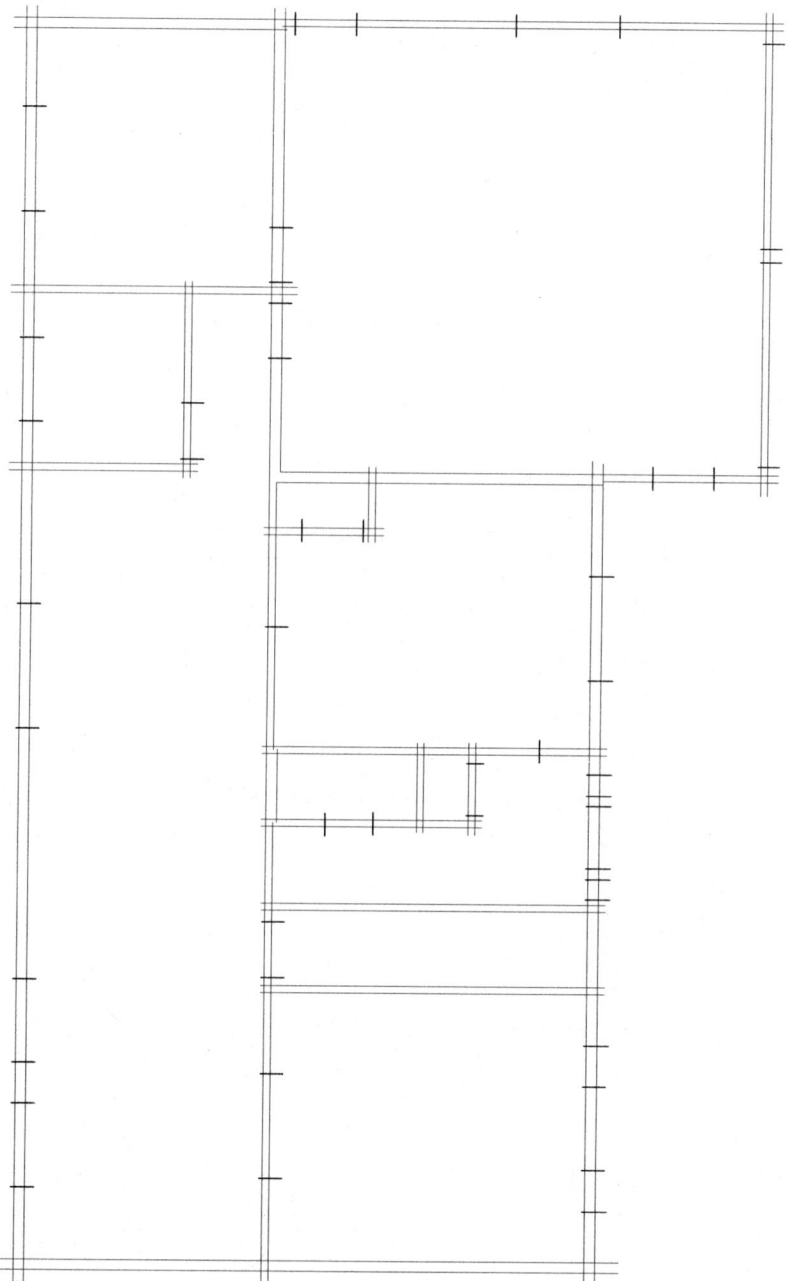

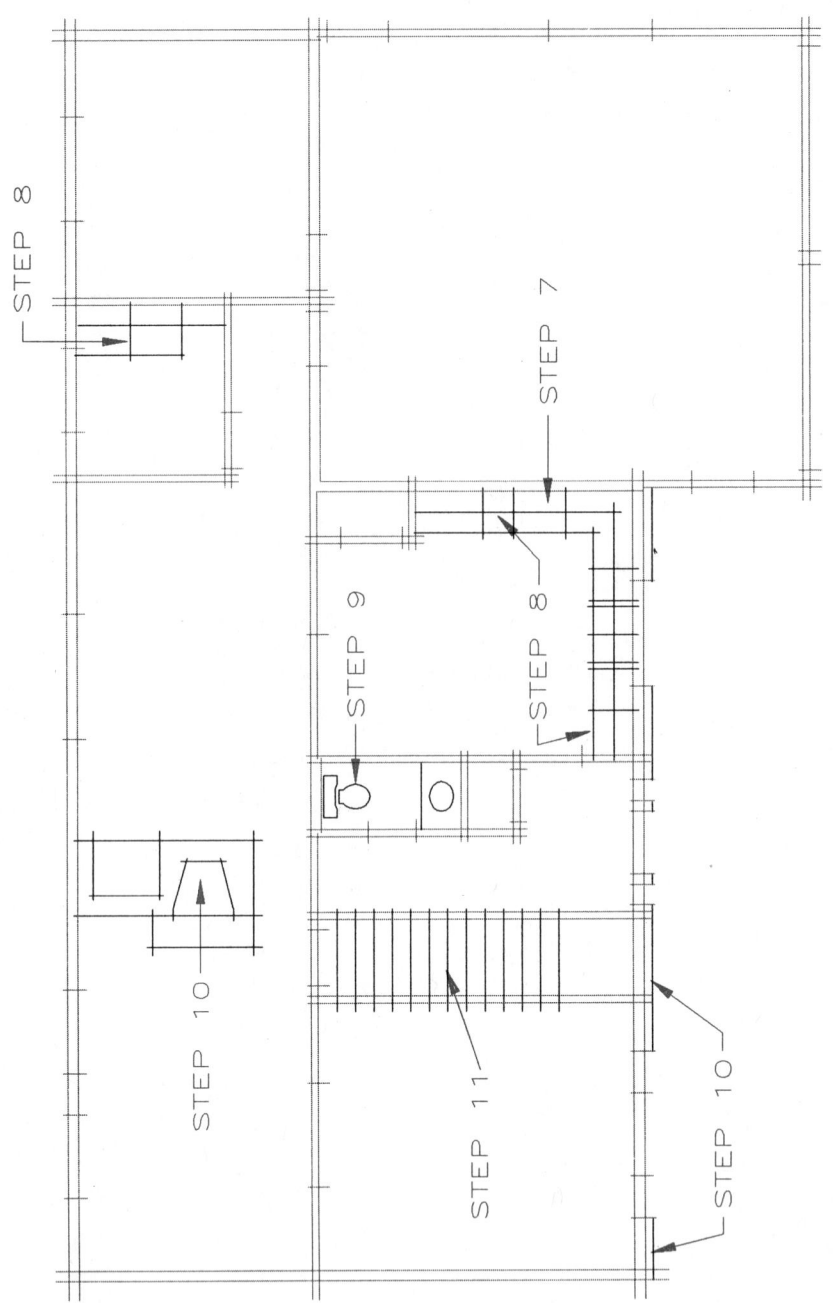

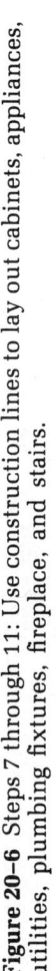

Figure 20–6 Steps 7 through 11: Use construction lines to lay out cabinets, appliances, utilities, plumbing fixtures, fireplace, and stairs.

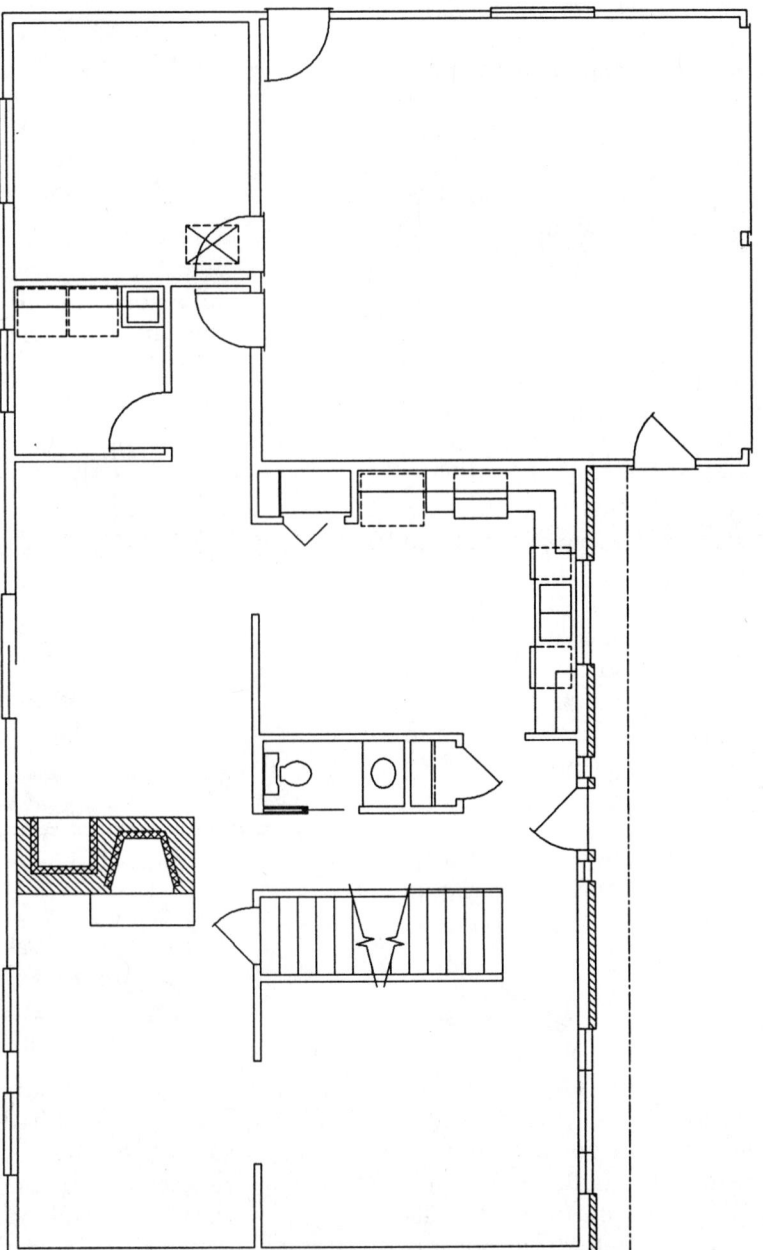

Figure 20–7 Step 12: Darken all items previously drawn; add door and window symbols.

door and window. There is also a common exception: Do not locate the doors in the garage on the floor plan. These will be dimensioned on the floor plan. See Chapter 16 for a complete review of common dimensioning practices. Do not place dimensions numerals on at this time. Add symbols for door and window schedules. See Figure 20-8.

Step 14. Lay out all interior dimensions as needed. Locate interior dimensions from the exterior dimensions. Do not place dimension numerals at this time. See Figure 20-8. Darken all extension and dimension lines using a sharp 2H or H lead or a 0.5 mm pencil. Use a 0.5 mm technical pen for inked lines. *Some drafters prefer to darken dimension and extension lines as they are drawn.*

Step 15. Letter all switch locations and light fixture locations. Use a ⅛ in. diameter circle for light fixtures. If electrical symbols are too large, they distract from the total drawing. Draw electrical circuits or switch legs from switches to fixtures using an irregular curve and a sharp 2H or H pencil lead. Keep your pencil sharp for all electrical symbols. Other methods may be used to draw relay lines such as drawing them freehand if approved by your instructor. Figure 20-9 shows the switches, lights, and relay lines added to the floor plan.

Step 16. Add all outlets to the floor plan. Verify maximum spacing of outlets and proper symbols from Chapter 17. Look at Figure 20-9.

Step 17. Letter all dimension numerals centered above each dimension line. Dimension numerals should read from the bottom on horizontal dimension lines and from the right side of the sheet on vertical dimension lines. Prepare very light, ⅛ in. high guidelines within 1/16 in. from the dimension lines for all numerals. Do not letter without guidelines. Place a clean piece of paper under your hand as you letter to help avoid smudging. Use a slightly rounded soft (H or F) lead in a mechanical pencil, or an H or F lead in a 0.5 mm pencil for lettering. For ink work, use a 0.5 mm technical pen. Add arrowheads rather than slashes if preferred by your instructor. Provide window and door sizes. See Figure 20-10.

Step 18. Add all beam, header, joist, and rafter symbols and specifications. Use ⅛ or 3/32 in. guidelines for all lettering and add cross section indicators as shown in Figure 20-10.

Step 19. Draw ⅛ or 3/32 in. guidelines and add all other local notes such as those for a cantilever second floor or concrete slabs. Add notes for specific appliances such as dishwasher (DW), water heater (WH), furnace, garbage disposal (GD), hood with fan over range, oven, and microwave if any. All exhaust fans must be noted to vent to outside air, and fireplace specifications must be added. Look at Figure 20-11.

Step 20. Label all rooms using 3/16 in. high guidelines for lettering. The interior room dimensions may be placed under the room designation if required by your instructor. Use ⅛ in. guidelines for room sizes if included as in the following example:

LIVING ROOM
12'-6" X 14'-0"

Letter the title and scale of the drawing directly below and centered upon the floor plan. Use ¼ in. high guidelines for the title. Underline the title and letter the scale using ⅛ in. guidelines. For example:

MAIN FLOOR PLAN
SCALE: 1/4"=1'-0"

The scale may be omitted if it is located in the title block. Add all other general notes as required in the project or as specified by your instructor. Letter all title block information. Look at Figure 20-11.

Step 21. Add all material symbols such as tile or stone, if any. Shade all walls and handrails as required by your instructor. Wood grain representation may be used on handrails, guardrails and partial walls. Exterior and interior walls may be shaded on the back of the drawing using a rounded soft F or HB lead. Shade on the back of the sheet to avoid smudging lines on the front. Turn the drawing over onto a blank sheet of scratch paper and carefully shade all walls. Do not shade without scratch paper between the drawing and table because lines from the drawing may transfer to the table. Figure 20-12 shows the completed floor plan.

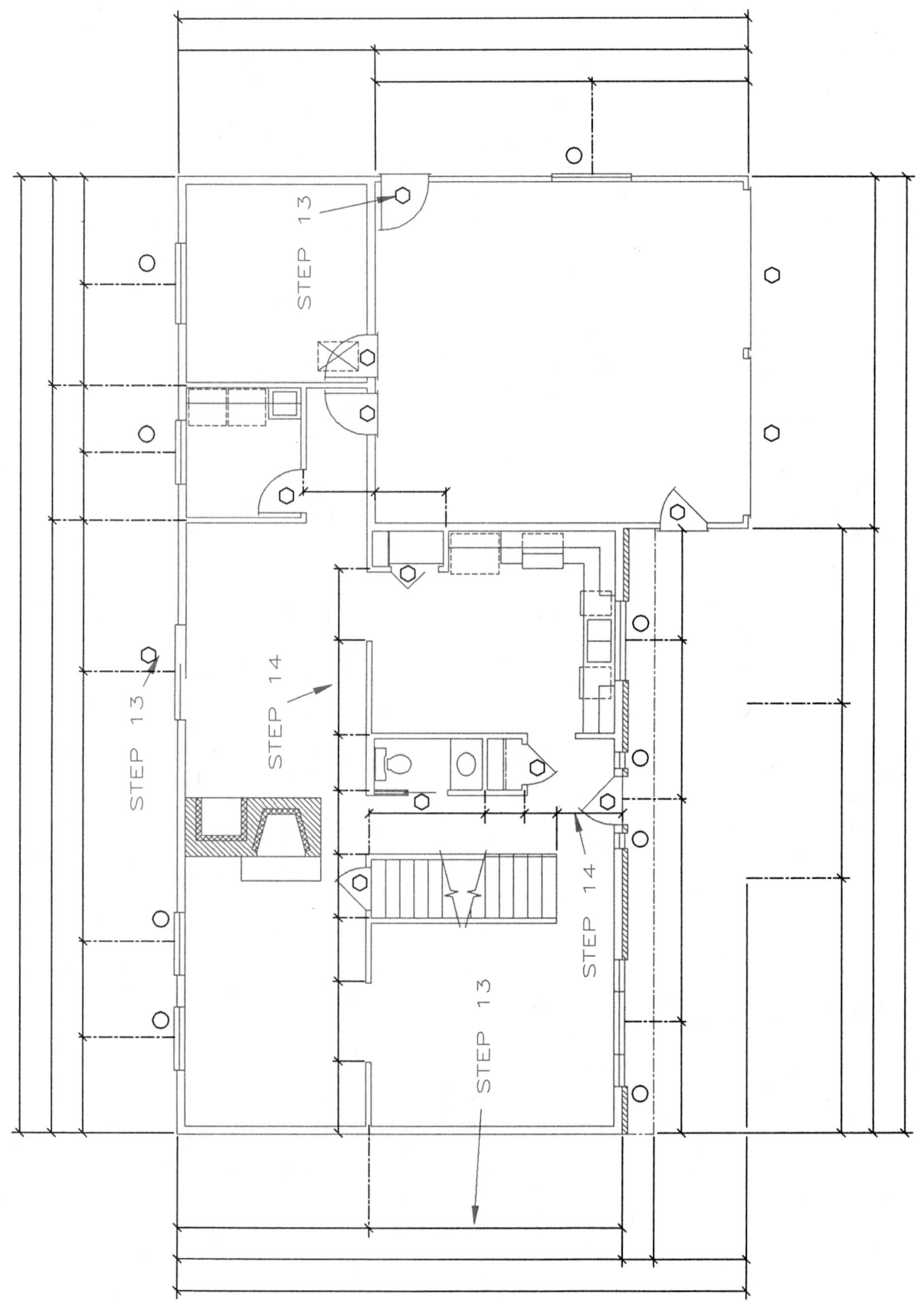

STEP 13

STEP 14

STEP 13

STEP 14

STEP 13

STEP 13

Figure 20–8 Steps 13 and 14: Lay out exterior and interior dimensions, and door and window schedule symbols.

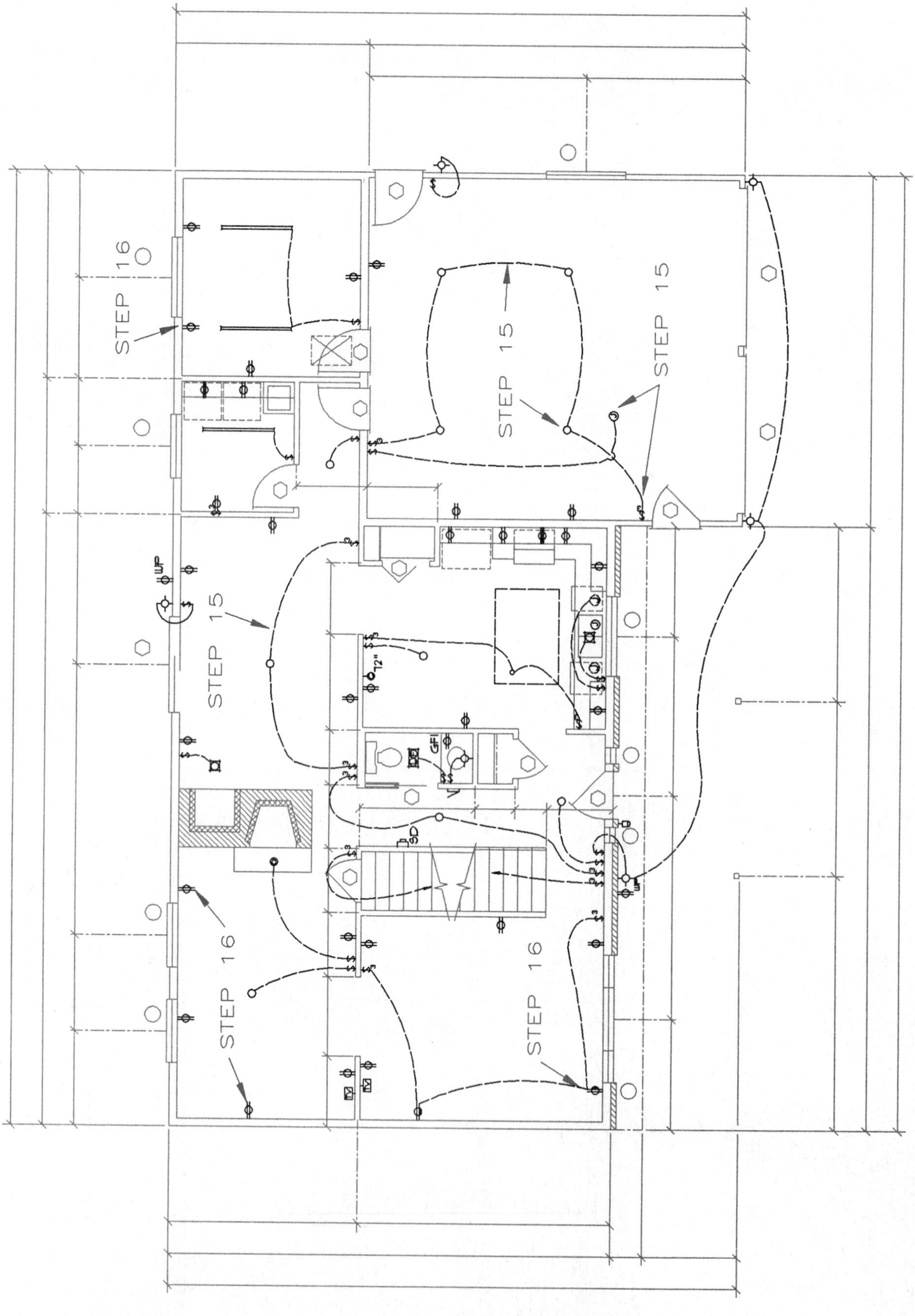

Figure 20-9 Steps 15 and 16: Lay out the electrical system.

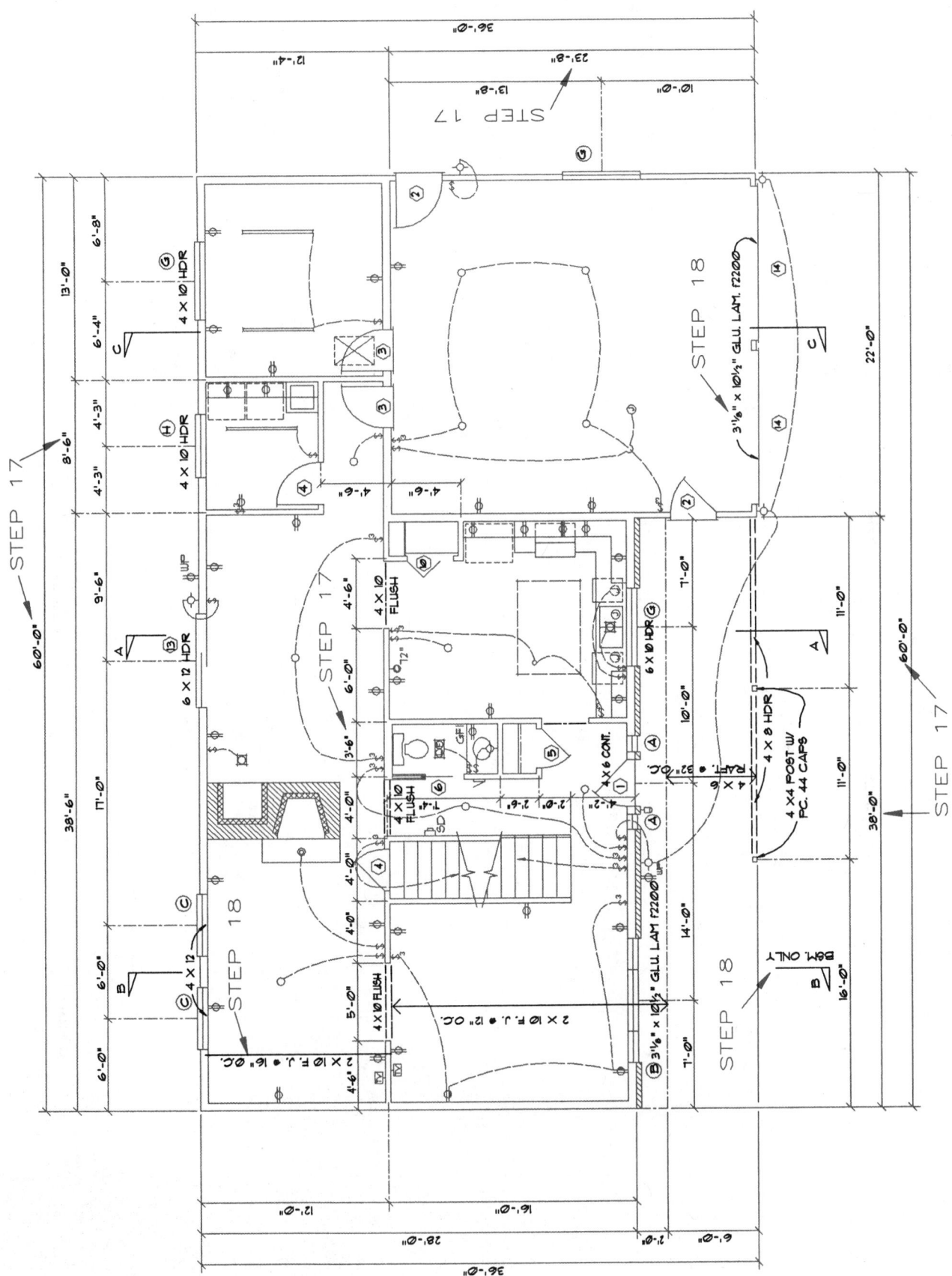

Figure 20–10 Steps 17 and 18: Lay out all dimension numerals, window and door sizes, and construction members including headers, beams, joists, and trusses.

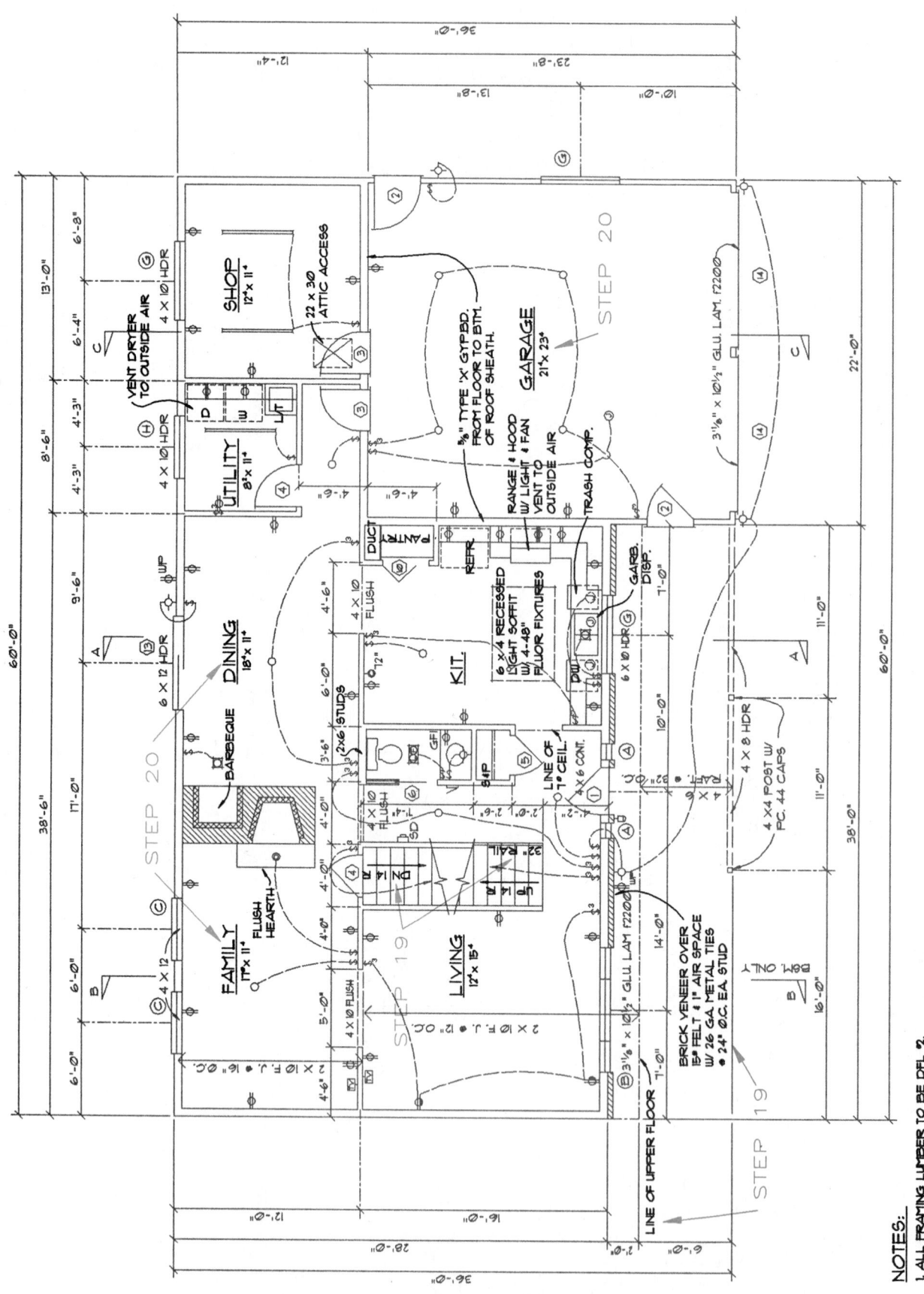

MAIN FLOOR PLAN

SCALE : ¼" = 1'-0"

Figure 20–11 Steps 19 and 20: Lay out all specific and general notes.

NOTES:

1. ALL FRAMING LUMBER TO BE DFL #2.
2. ALL EXT. STUDS TO BE 2x6 @16" O.C.
   ● HEATED AREAS.
3. ALL METAL CONNECTORS TO BE SIMPSON
   CO. OR EQUAL
4. VENT ALL FANS TO OUTSIDE AIR

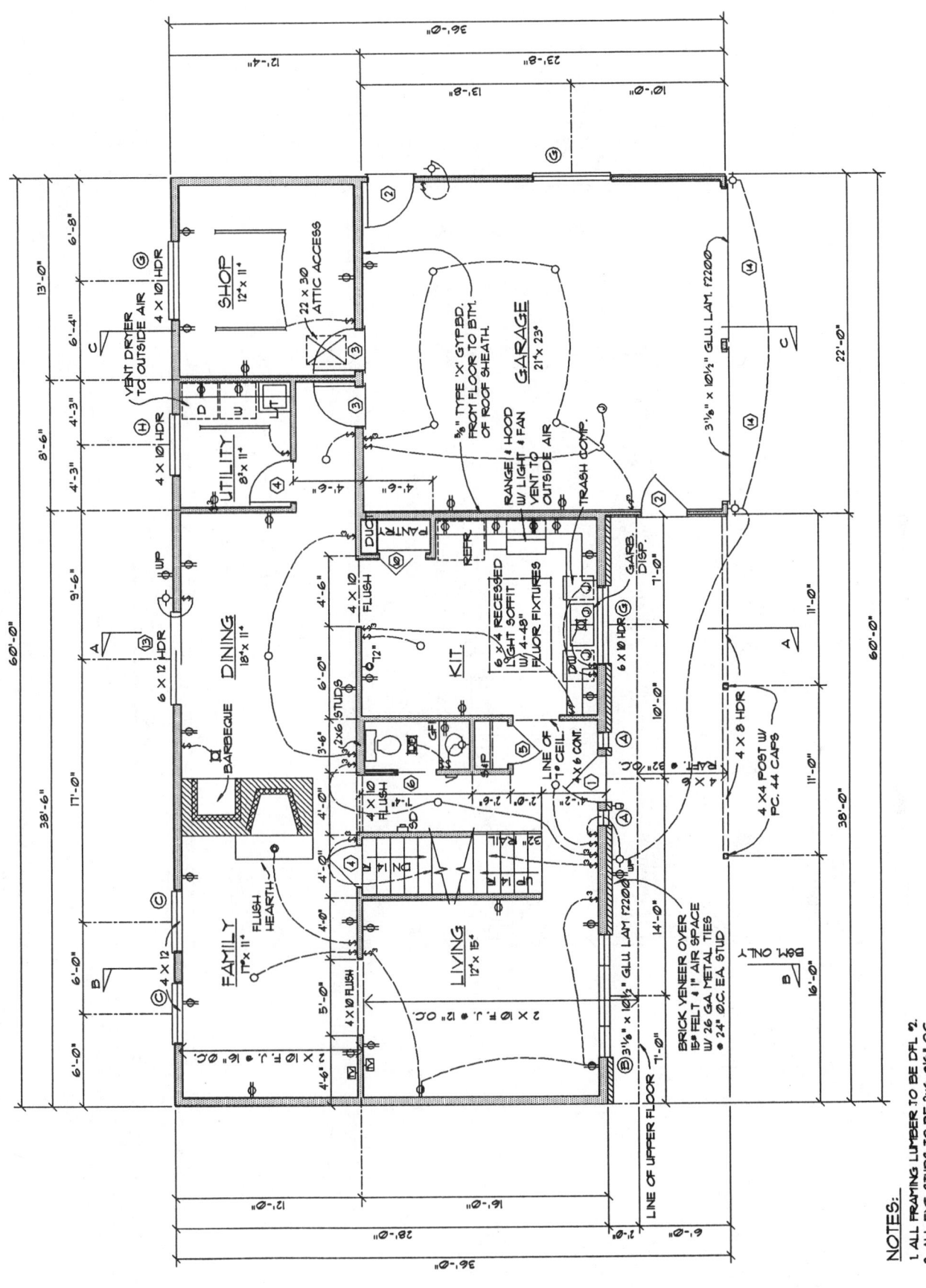

MAIN FLOOR PLAN
SCALE : ¼" = 1'-0"

Figure 20-12 Step 21: Complete the floor plan by adding finish materials, shading the walls and partitions, and filling in the title block information.

NOTES:
1. ALL FRAMING LUMBER TO BE DFL #2.
2. ALL EXT. STUDS TO BE 2x6 @16" O.C.
   ● HEATED AREAS.
3. ALL METAL CONNECTORS TO BE SIMPSON CO. OR EQUAL.
4. VENT ALL FANS TO OUTSIDE AIR

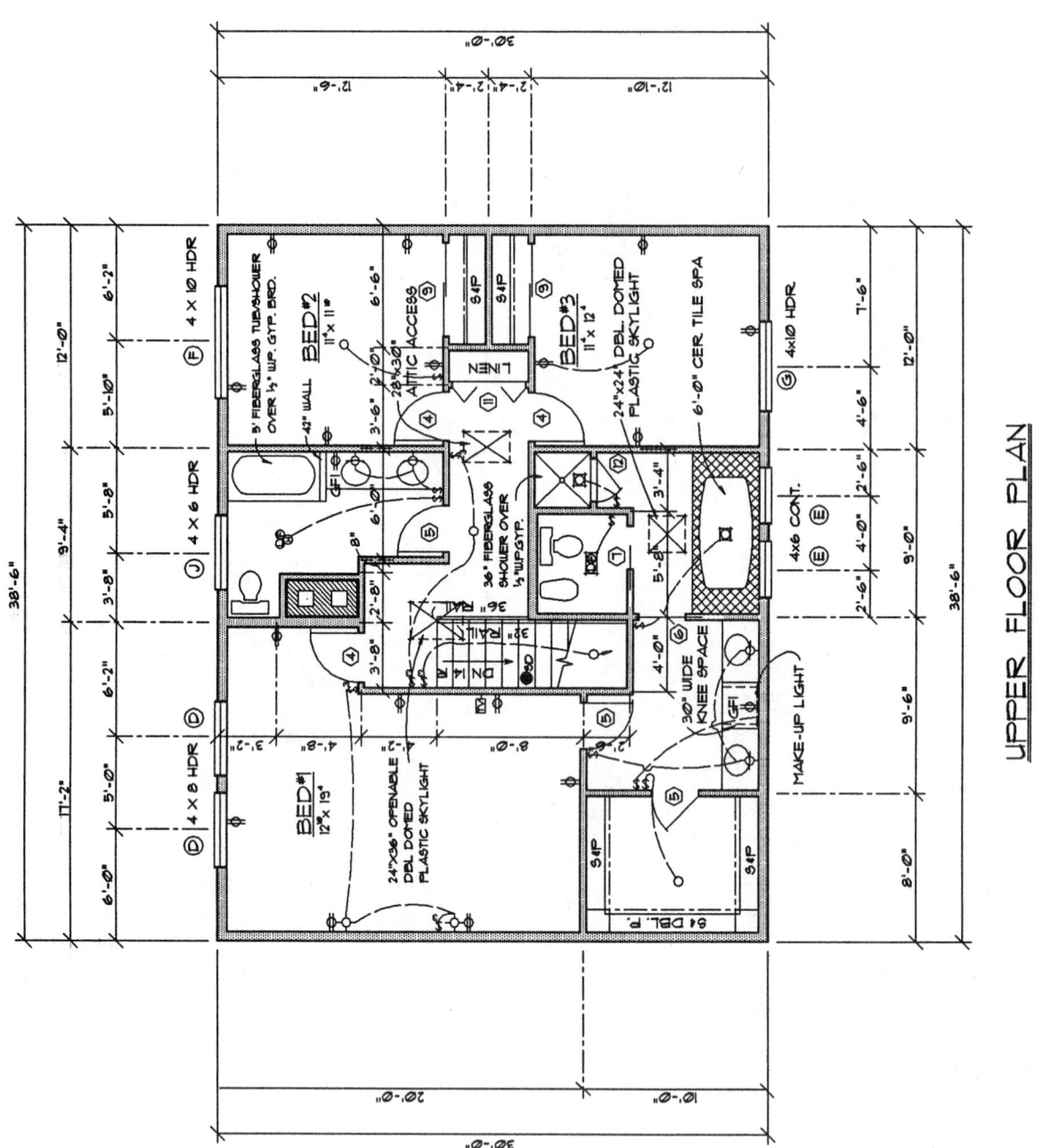

Figure 20-13 Complete second floor plan with window and door schedules.

WINDOW SCHEDULE				
SYM.	SIZE	MODEL	ROUGH OPEN	QUAN
A	$1^{0} \times 5^{0}$	JOB-BUILT		2
B	$8^{0} \times 5^{0}$	W4N5 CSM	8'-2¾"x5'-5⅞"	1
C	$4^{0} \times 5^{0}$	W2N5 CSM	4'-2¼"x5'-5⅞"	2
D	$4^{0} \times 3^{6}$	W2N3 CSM	4'-2¼"x3'-5½"	2
E	$3^{6} \times 3^{6}$	2N3 CSM	3'-5¼"x3'-5½"	2
F	$6^{0} \times 4^{0}$	G64 SLDG	6'-0½"x4'-0½"	1
G	$5^{0} \times 3^{6}$	G536 SLDG	5'-0½"x3'-6½"	4
H	$4^{0} \times 3^{6}$	G436 SLDG	4'-0½"x3'-6½"	1
J	$4^{0} \times 2^{0}$	A41 AWN	4-0½"x2'-0⅝"	3
K	$4^{0} \times 2^{0}$	G42 SLDG	4'-0½"x2'-0½"	3

DOOR SCHEDULE			
SYM.	SIZE	TYPE	QUAN
1	$3^{0} \times 6^{8}$	S.C. R.P. METAL INSULATED	1
2	$3^{0} \times 6^{8}$	S.C.-FLUSH-METAL INSUL	2
3	$2^{8} \times 6^{8}$	S.C-SELF CLOSING	2
4	$2^{8} \times 6^{8}$	H.C.	5
5	$2^{6} \times 6^{8}$	H.C.	5
6	$2^{6} \times 6^{8}$	POCKET	2
7	$2^{4} \times 6^{8}$	POCKET	1
8	FR $2^{6} \times 6^{8}$	H.C.	1
9	$5^{0} \times 6^{8}$	BI-PASS	2
10	$3^{0} \times 6^{8}$	BI-FOLD	1
11	$4^{0} \times 6^{8}$	BI-FOLD	1
12	$2^{0} \times 6^{0}$	SHATTER PROOF	1
13	$6^{0} \times 6^{8}$	WOOD FRAME-TEMP. SLDG. GL.	1
14	$9^{0} \times 7^{0}$	OVERHEAD GARAGE	2

WALL AREAS *	2275 SQ. FT.
WINDOWS	250 SQ. FT.
SKYLITES	10 SQ. FT.
DOORS	77 SQ. FT.
TOTAL OPENINGS	337 SQ. FT.
% OPENINGS	15%

*BASEMENT EXCLUDED.

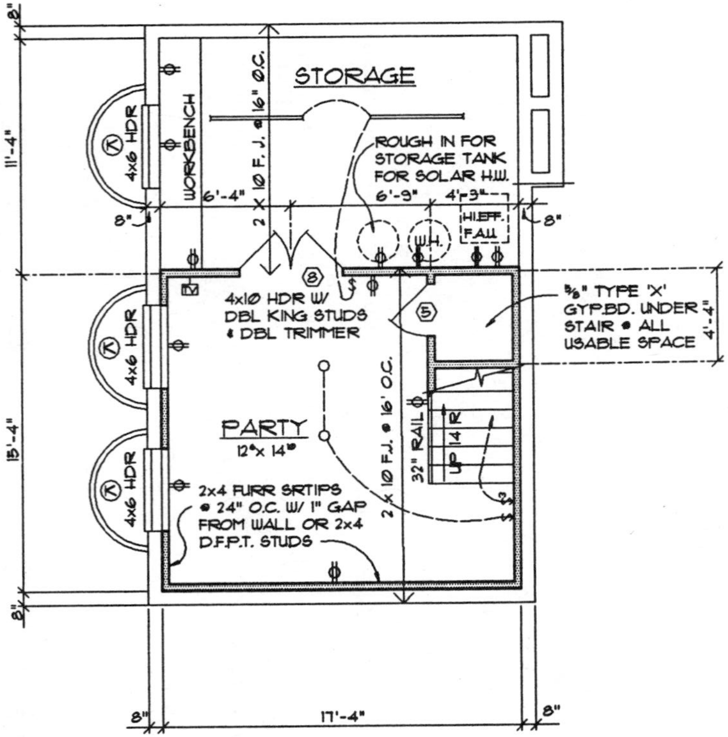

LOWER FLOOR PLAN

SCALE : ¼" = 1'-0"

Figure 20–14 Basement plan layout.

SECOND-FLOOR PLAN LAYOUT

The second-floor plan must be scaled so that it will fit over the main-floor plan. The exterior walls (unless cantilevered or supported beyond the main floor), the continued interior bearing partitions, and stairs must line up directly with the main floor. Be sure to check the scale of the print for accuracy as prints may expand or contract slightly. An easy way to do this is to run a print of the main-floor plan and tape it to your table. Place your new drawing sheet for the second-floor plan over the print and adjust the new sheet so that the drawing area for the second floor is over the first-floor outline. On the second sheet take into consideration adequate area for dimensions, notes, and possible schedules. If the second-floor plan is smaller than the main-floor plan there may be additional space on the sheet for door and window schedules. These schedules should be near the floor plans when practical.

Tape the second drawing sheet to the board after adjusting it to the desired position. Lay out the second-floor plan using Steps 1 through 21 previously described. Figure 20–13 shows a complete second-floor plan with door and window schedules provided.

BASEMENT-PLAN LAYOUT

When a home has a basement, the basement-plan layout is accomplished in the same way as described in the second-floor-plan layout. When a basement plan is very simple or possibly when left unfinished, it may be drawn in conjunction with the foundation plan. Use good judgment since you do not want to create a plan that will result in confusion to the contractors. Figure 20–14 shows a partial basement represented in the floor plan. A full basement would be under the entire main floor.

USING CADD TO DRAW FLOOR PLANS

Procedures for laying out floor plans with CADD are similar to manual drafting. However, the drafter does not need to lay out the walls and interior partitions with construction lines. The floor plan begins with walls and interior partitions drawn in place. If an error is made, it is easy to erase from the screen and redraw. After the walls are drawn you may begin placing the symbols for doors, windows, plumbing fixtures, cabinets, and appliances. The drawing at this stage should look like Figure 20–7. The next step is to place dimensions on the drawing. Dimensions are easily placed with CADD, and each dimension is accurate. As you draw individual dimensions, the computer gives you the exact dimension numeral so you can instantly see if the drawing is correct or if it requires alteration. With most Architectural CADD systems the drawing elements are placed on individual layers. This allows you to control the display of these items. For example, if you want the floor plan shown without dimensions, turn off the dimension layer. Refer to Chapter 6 for a discussion of drawing with CADD layers.

Some residential architects choose to display the electrical layout on the floor plan while others create the electrical layout on background drawings—a subset of the information contained in the floor plan. For example, the only information shown on the electrical background drawing is the electrical layout. This drawing is sent to the electrical contractor for biding and construction purposes. Sending the electrical layout without unnecessary detail often reduces biding errors and construction errors and simplifies the biding process. With CADD, the drafter has the flexibility to display the floor plan with or without the background drawings. A composite drawing exists when the layer and background drawings are displayed together. A composite CADD floor plan drawing is shown in Figure 1.

In commercial applications, the background drawings become an even more important feature of the CADD capabilities. Background drawings are created for areas such as plumbing, mechanical (heating, ventilating, and air conditioning), structural, and interior design. These concepts are discussed in Chapter 49.

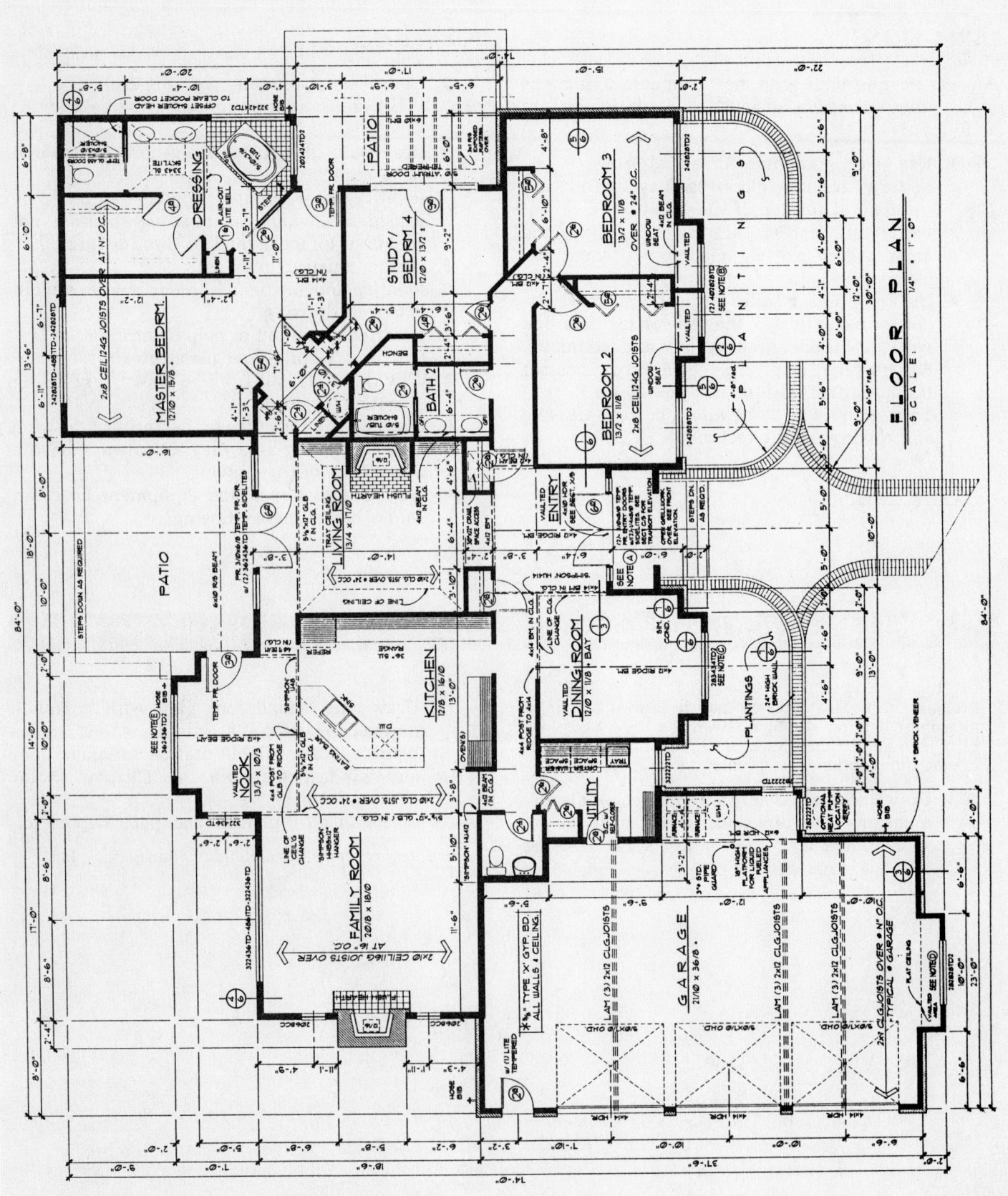

Figure 1 Composite CADD floor plan. *Courtesy Piercy & Barclay Designers, Inc.*

FLOOR-PLAN LAYOUT TEST

DIRECTIONS

Answer the questions with short complete statements or drawings as needed on an 8½ × 11 drawing sheet as follows:

1. Use ⅛ in. guidelines for all lettering.
2. Letter your name, Floor-Plan Layout Test, and the date at the top of the sheet.
3. Letter the question number and provide the answer. You do not need to write out the question.
4. Do all lettering with vertical uppercase architectural letters. If the answer requires line work, use proper drafting tools and technique. Answers may be prepared on a word processor if appropriate with course guidelines.
5. Your grade will be based on correct answers and quality of line technique.

QUESTIONS

1. Describe the drawing working area.
2. What are the dimensions of a C-size drawing sheet?
3. Residential floor plans are generally drawn at what scale?
4. Identify two alternative actions that could be considered when the drawing space is not adequate to accommodate the drawing.
5. Define construction lines.
6. Identify four factors that contribute to a well-balanced drawing.
7. Describe a method to help determine the layout for a second-floor plan quickly.
8. Why should layout work be drawn very lightly or with blue lead?
9. Discuss why formulas for centering a drawing in the working area may not always be the way to lay out a drawing.
10. Why should hands and equipment be clean before beginning a drawing?

FLOOR-PLAN LAYOUT PROBLEMS

Problem 20–1. This problem may be drawn manually or using computer graphics. Given the Cape Cod floor plan with approximate interior dimensions, do the following unless otherwise specified by your instructor:

1. Draw the main-floor plan with complete dimensions and notes using the scale ¼″ = 1′–0″. Use a 17″ × 22″ or 18″ × 24″ drawing sheet. This is sheet 2 of 5.

2. Draw the second-floor plan with complete dimensions using the scale ¼″ = 1′–0″. In the blank space available draw a complete door and window schedule. See Chapter 15 for size guidelines.
3. Establish all dimensions as per Chapter 16.

Illustration courtesy Home Building Plan Service, Inc.

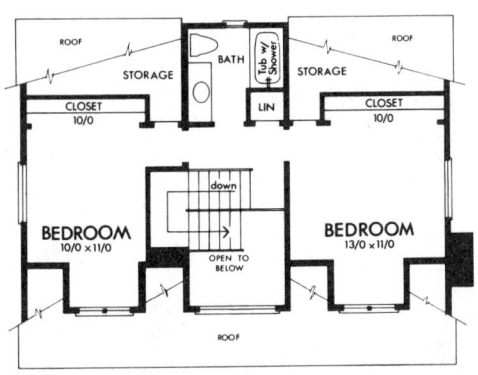

SECOND FLOOR PLAN
456 SQUARE FEET

ROOF   ROOF

STORAGE   BATH   STORAGE

CLOSET
10/0   LIN   CLOSET
10/0

down

BEDROOM
10/0 x 11/0   BEDROOM
13/0 x 11/0

OPEN TO
BELOW

ROOF

72'-0"

22'-0"   12'-0"   38'-0"

GARAGE
21/0 x 21/0

22'-0"

32'-0"

DW   REF   WH   Sh'r

KITCHEN
10/0 x 11/0   BATH   CLOSET
7/6   BEDROOM
11/0 x 11/6

R/O   W
D   heat

up   GUEST   LIVING ROOM
13/0 x 15/0

FIRST FLOOR PLAN
1008 SQUARE FEET
484 SQUARE FEET – GARAGE

OPEN TO
ABOVE

DINING
12/0 x 16/0   ENTRY

Problem 20–2. This problem may be drawn manually or using computer graphics. Given the cabin floor plan with approximate interior dimensions, do the following unless otherwise specified by your instructor:

1. Draw the main-floor plan with complete dimensions and notes using the scale ¼″ = 1′-0″. Use a 17″ × 22″ or 18″ × 24″ drawing sheet. This is sheet 2 of 3.

2. Draw a complete door and window schedule.

3. Determine all beam and joist sizes based on your area.

Illustration courtesy Home Building Plan Service, Inc.

SECOND FLOOR PLAN
256 SQUARE FEET

FIRST FLOOR PLAN
648 SQUARE FEET

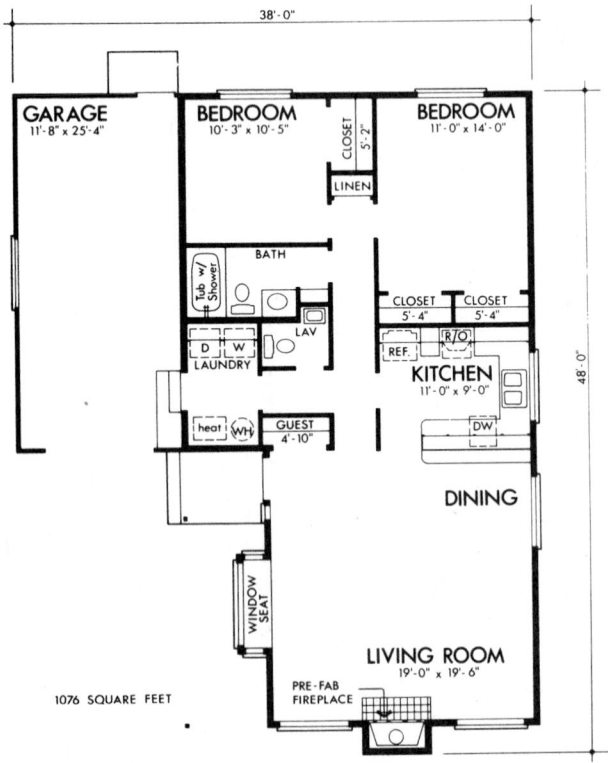

1076 SQUARE FEET

Problem 20–3. This problem may be drawn manually or using computer graphics. Given the ranch floor plan with approximate interior dimensions, do the following unless otherwise specified by your instructor:

1. Draw the main-floor plan with complete dimensions and notes using the scale ¼″ = 1′-0″.

2. In the blank space available draw a complete door and window schedule.

3. Determine all beam and joist sizes based on your area.

Illustration courtesy Home Building Plan Service, Inc.

FRONT VIEW

Problem 20–4. This problem may be drawn manually or using computer graphics. Given the Spanish floor plan with approximate interior dimensions, do the following unless otherwise specified by your instructor:

1. Draw the main-floor plan with complete dimensions and notes using the scale ¼″ = 1′–0″.
2. In the blank space available draw a complete door and window schedule.

3. Determine all joist and beam sizes based on your area loads.
4. If the weather patterns of your area require it, design a pitch roof with clay tiles. Verify design with your instructor prior to completion of drawings.

Illustration courtesy Home Building Plan Service, Inc.

Problem 20-5. This problem may be drawn manually or using computer graphics. Given the early American floor plan with approximate interior dimensions, do the following unless otherwise specified by your instructor:

1. Draw the main-floor plan with complete dimensions using the scale ¼″ = 1′-0″.
2. Draw the second-floor plan with complete dimensions and notes using the scale ¼″ = 1′-0″. In the blank space available draw a complete door and window schedule.

3. Design and draw the basement-floor plan with complete dimensions using the scale ¼″ = 1′-0″. Design the basement so it may be used for one bedroom, a recreation room, and a bathroom. There will be a bearing wall directly under the main floor plan wall between the dining room and kitchen, entry and lav.

Illustration courtesy Home Building Plan Service, Inc.

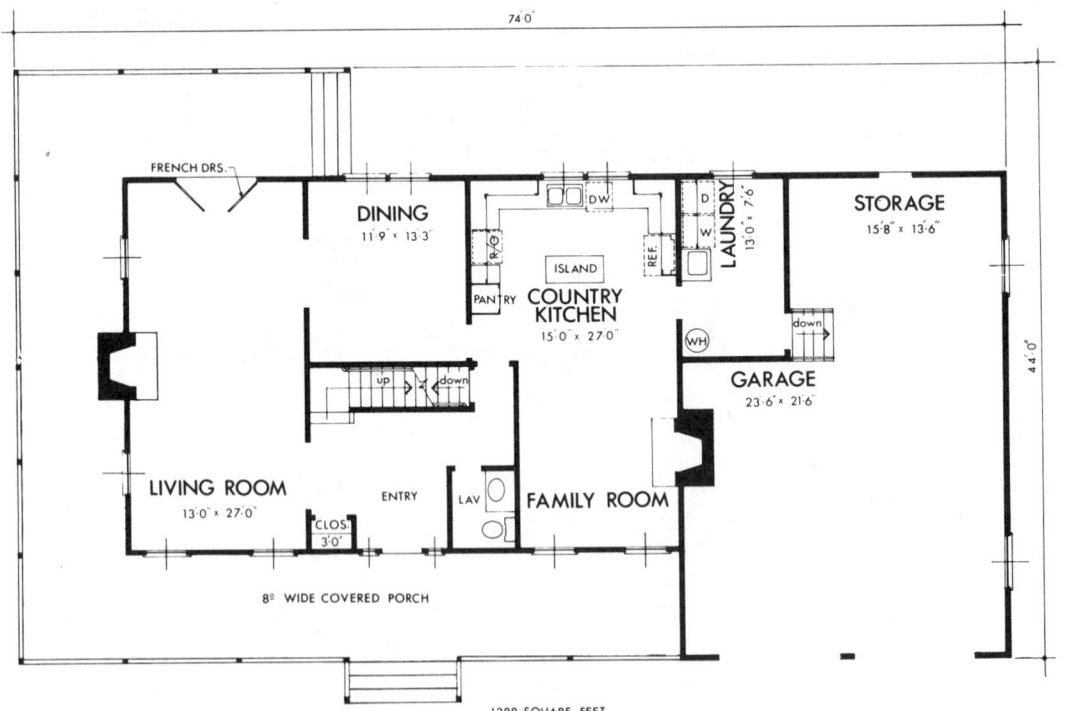

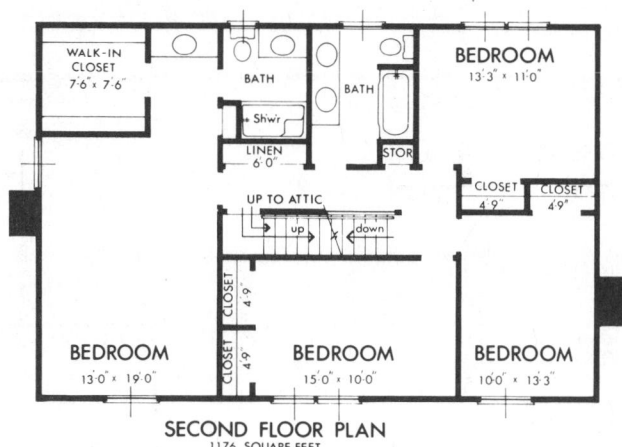

SECOND FLOOR PLAN
1176 SQUARE FEET

Problem 20–6. This problem may be drawn manually or using computer graphics. Given the side-to-rear sloped-lot (contemporary) floor plan with approximate interior dimensions, do the following unless otherwise specified by your instructor:

1. Draw the main-floor plan with complete dimensions using the scale ¼″ = 1′-0″.
2. Draw the second-floor plan with complete dimensions and notes using the scale ¼″ = 1′-0″. In the blank space available draw a complete door and window schedule. This is sheet 3 of 7.
3. Draw the basement-floor plan with complete dimensions using the scale ¼″ = 1′-0″. This is sheet 4 of 7.
4. Design all joist and beams based on the codes for your area.

Illustration courtesy Home Building Plan Service, Inc.

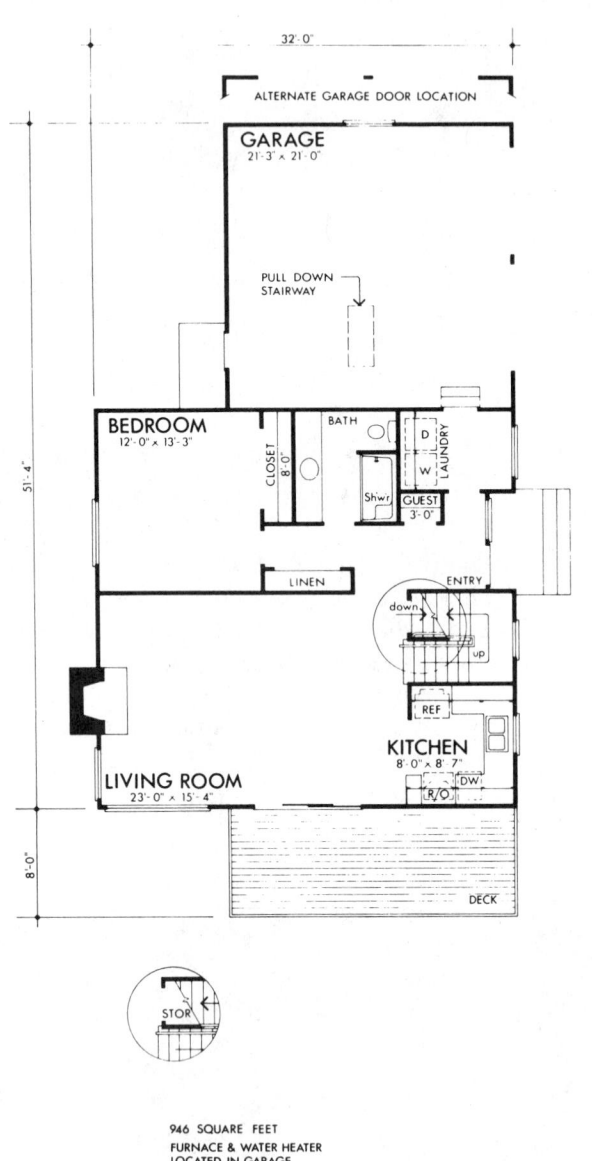

32'-0"

ALTERNATE GARAGE DOOR LOCATION

GARAGE
21'-3" × 21'-0"

PULL DOWN
STAIRWAY

BEDROOM
12'-0" × 13'-3"

CLOSET
8'-0"

BATH

D
W
LAUNDRY

GUEST
3'-0"

Shwr

51'-4"

LINEN

ENTRY

down

up

REF

KITCHEN
8'-0" × 8'-7"

DW

R/O

LIVING ROOM
23'-0" × 15'-4"

8'-0"

DECK

STOR

946 SQUARE FEET
FURNACE & WATER HEATER
LOCATED IN GARAGE

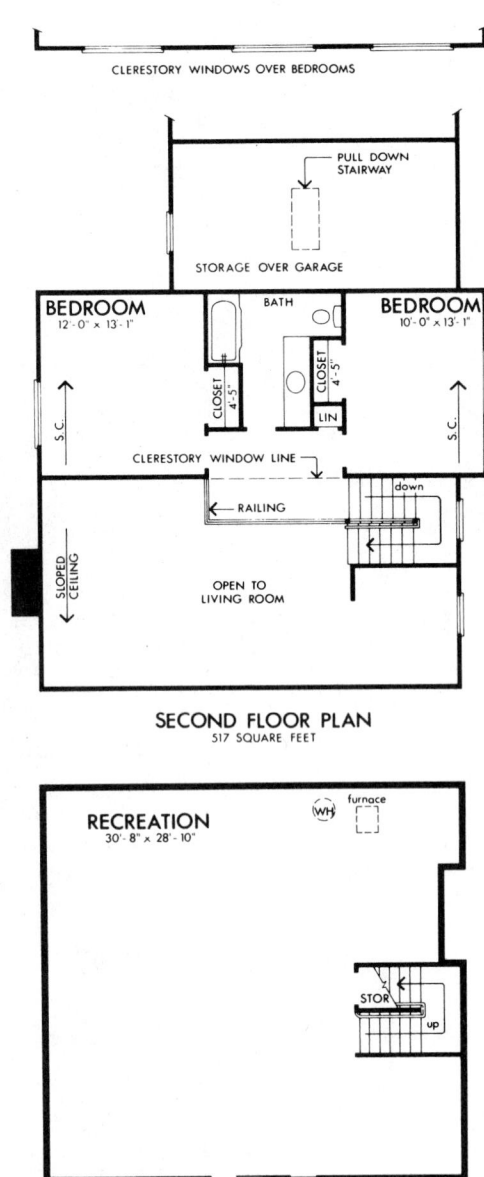

CLERESTORY WINDOWS OVER BEDROOMS

PULL DOWN
STAIRWAY

STORAGE OVER GARAGE

BEDROOM
12'-0" × 13'-1"

BATH

BEDROOM
10'-0" × 13'-1"

CLOSET
4'-5"

CLOSET
4'-5"

LIN

S.C.

S.C.

CLERESTORY WINDOW LINE

RAILING

down

SLOPED
CEILING

OPEN TO
LIVING ROOM

SECOND FLOOR PLAN
517 SQUARE FEET

RECREATION
30'-8" × 28'-10"

WH

furnace

STOR

up

BASEMENT PLAN
814 SQUARE FEET

Problem 20–7. This problem may be drawn manually or using computer graphics. Given the ranch duplex floor plan with approximate interior dimensions, do the following unless otherwise specified by your instructor:

1. Draw the main-floor plan with complete dimensions and notes using the scale ¼″ = 1′–0″. In the blank space available, draw a complete door and window schedule.
2. Design all joist and beams based on the codes for your area.

Illustration courtesy Home Building Plan Service, Inc.

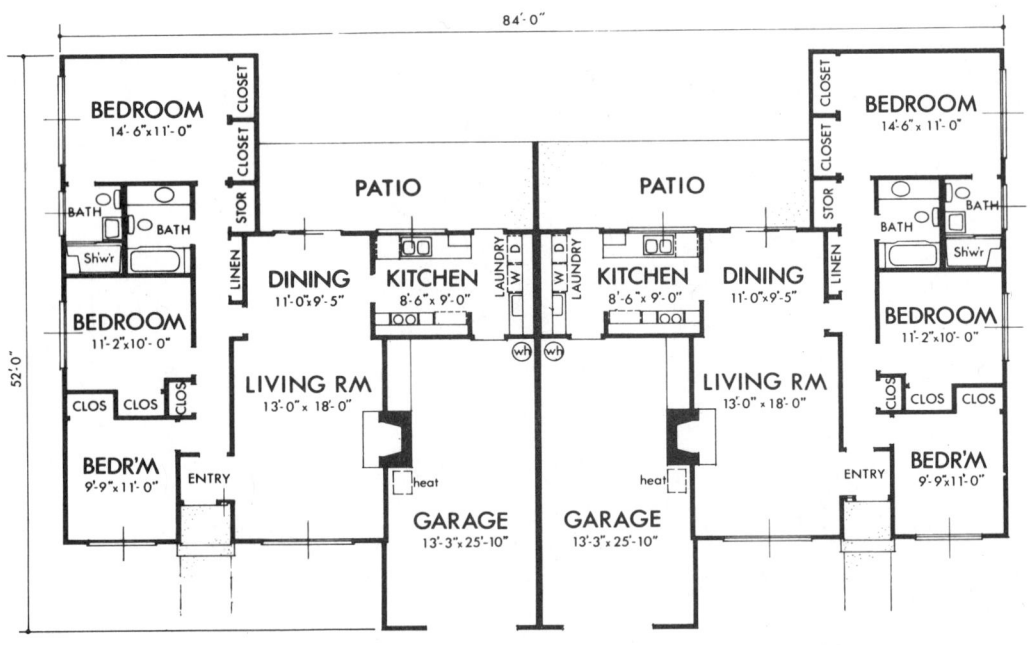

2 THREE-BEDROOM UNITS
2386 SQUARE FEET

FOUNDATION PLAN

CM-1430

Section Four
Foundation Plans

Chapter 21
Foundation Systems

ALL STRUCTURES are required to have a foundation. The foundation provides a base to distribute the weight of the structure onto the soil. The weight, or loads, must be evenly distributed over enough soil to prevent them from compressing it.

In addition to resisting the loads from gravity, the foundation must resist floods, winds, and earthquakes. Where flooding is a problem, the foundation system must be designed for the possibility that much of the supporting soil may be washed away. The foundation must also be designed to resist any debris that may be carried by flood waters.

The forces of wind on a structure can cause severe problems for a foundation. The walls of a structure act as a large sail. If the structure is not properly anchored to the foundation, the walls can be ripped away by the wind. Not only does wind try to push a structure sideways but upward as well. Because the structure is securely bonded together at each intersection, wind pressure will build under the roof overhangs and inside the structure and cause an upward tendency. Proper foundation design will resist this upward movement.

Depending on the risk for seismic damage, special design considerations may be required of a foundation. Although earthquakes cause both vertical and horizontal movement, it is the horizontal movement that causes the most damage to structures. The foundation system must be designed so that it can move with the ground yet keep its basic shape. Steel reinforcing and welded wire mesh are often required to help resist or minimize damage due to the movement of the earth.

SOIL CONSIDERATIONS

In addition to the forces of nature, the nature of the soil supporting the foundation must also be considered. The texture of the soil and the tendency of the soil to freeze will influence the design of the foundation system.

Soil Texture

The texture of the soil will affect its ability to resist the loads of the foundation. Before the foundation can be designed for a structure, the bearing capacity of the soil must be known. The soil bearing capacity is a design value specifying the amount of weight a square foot of soil can support. In residential construction, the type of soil can often be determined from the local building department. In commercial construction, a soils engineer is usually required to study the various types of soil that are at the job site and make recommendations for foundation design. The soil bearing values must be determined before a suitable material for the foundation can be selected. In addition to the texture, the tendency of freezing must also be considered.

Freezing

Don't confuse ground freezing with blizzards. Even in the warmer southern states ground freezing can be a problem. Figure 21–1 shows the average frost penetration depths for the United States. A foundation should be built to a depth where the ground is not subject to freezing. Soil expands as it freezes and then contracts as it thaws. A foundation must rest on stable soil so that the foundation does not

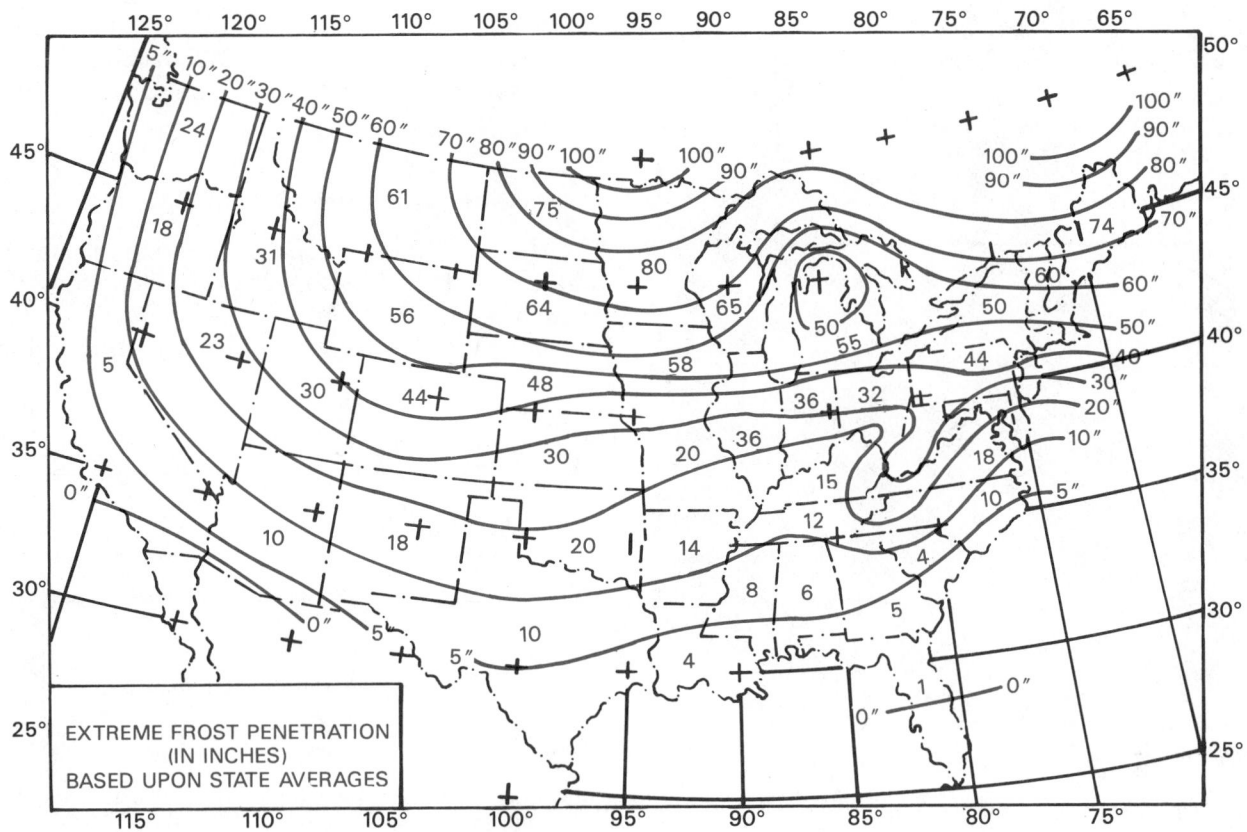

Figure 21–1 Average frost depth in the United States. The depth of freezing can greatly affect the type of foundation used for a structure.

crack. The drafter will have to verify the required depth of foundations with the local building department. Once the soil bearing capacity and the depth of freezing are known the type of foundation system to be used can be determined.

TYPES OF FOUNDATIONS

The foundation is usually constructed of pilings, continuous footings or grade beams.

Pilings

A piling is a type of foundation system that uses a column to support the loads of the structure. Beams are placed below each bearing wall and a piling is used to support each end of the beam. This type of foundation system is typically used for hillside or beach residential construction where erosion might be a problem. Figure 21–2 shows an example of how a piling foundation system might be used. When the upper levels of soil are soft or shifting, the piling is placed through these layers to firm soil layers below. Steel, pressure-treated wood, and concrete columns are typically used for pilings. Piling foundations are also used when conventional trenching equipment

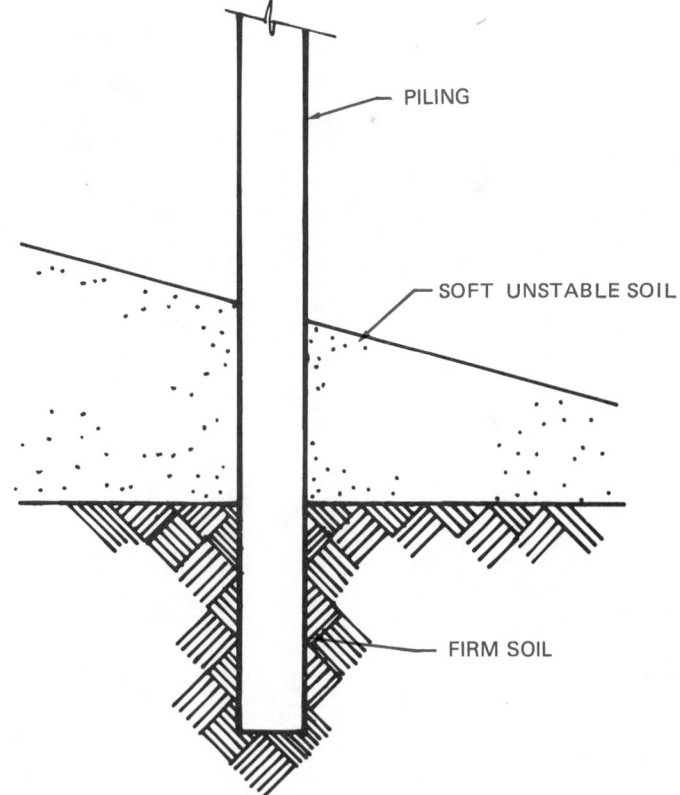

Figure 21–2 Pilings are used when upper soil levels are unstable. The piling is sunk until firm, undisturbed soil is found.

Figure 21-3 A piling foundation is often used when the job site is too steep for traditional foundation methods. *Courtesy American Plywood Association.*

cannot be used safely. Figure 21-3 shows a home that has a piling foundation. When pilings are drawn on a foundation plan, they are usually drawn as shown in Figure 21-4.

Continuous or Spread Foundations

The most typical type of foundation used in residential and light commercial construction is a continuous or spread foundation. This type of foundation consists of a footing and wall. A footing is the base

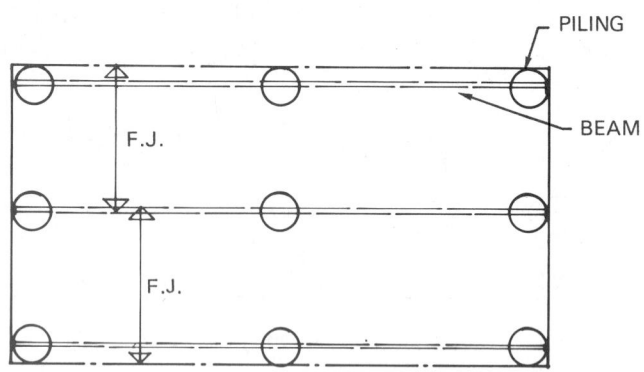

Figure 21-4 Pilings are usually drawn with solid lines on a foundation plan.

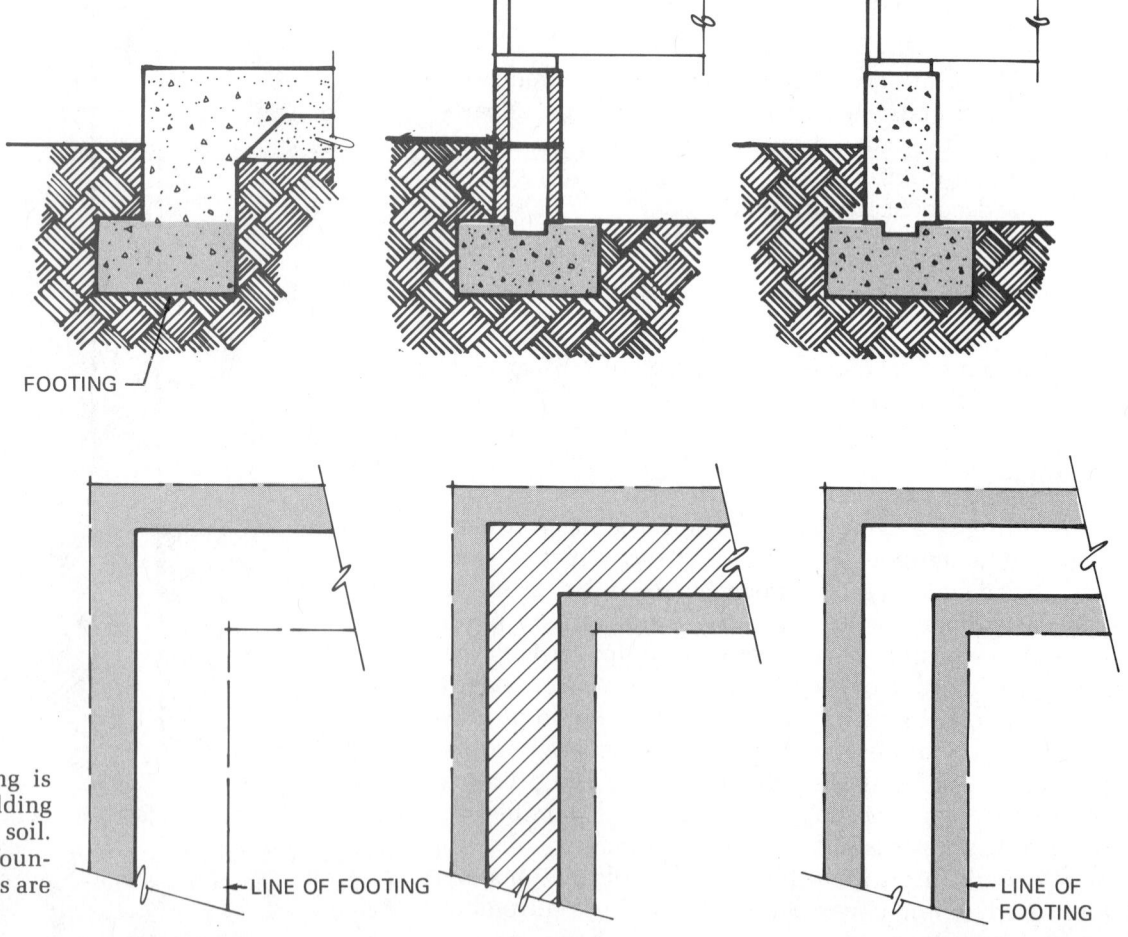

Figure 21-5 The footing is used to disperse building loads evenly into the soil. When drawn on the foundation plan, hidden lines are used.

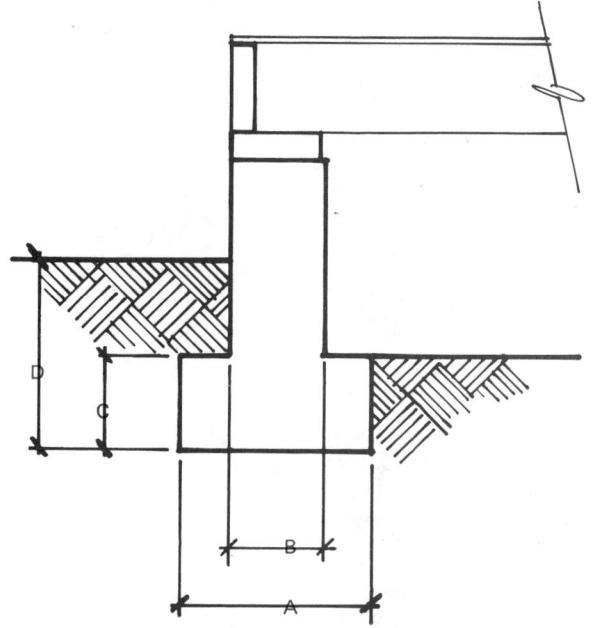

UNIFORM BUILDING CODE FOOTING REQUIREMENTS				
Building Height	Footing Width (A)	Wall Width (B)	Footing Height (C)	Depth into Undisturbed Grade (D)
1 Story	12″	6″	6″	12″
2 Story	15″	8″	7″	18″
3 Story	18″	10″	8″	24″

Figure 21–6 Footing design according to the Uniform Building Code and the Basic National Building Code. Verify exact depth with your local building department.

of the foundation system and is used to displace the building loads over the soil. Figure 21–5 shows a typical footing and how it is usually drawn on foundation plans. Footings are typically made of poured concrete and placed so that they extend below the freezing level. Figure 21–6 shows common footing sizes and depths as required by building codes. The strength of the concrete must also be specified, based on the location of the concrete in the structure and its chance of freezing. Figure 21–7 lists typical values.

When footings are placed over areas of soft soil or fill material, reinforcement steel is often placed in the footing. Concrete is extremely durable when it supports a load and is compressed, but is very weak when in tension. Figure 21–8 shows a footing in both compression and tension. Steel is placed in the footing to help resist the forces of tension.

The material used to construct the foundation wall and the area in which the building is to be located will affect how the wall and footing are tied together. If the wall and footing are made at different times, a keyway is placed in the footing. The keyway is formed by placing a 2 × 4 in the top of the concrete footing while the concrete is still wet. Once the

TYPE OR LOCATION OF CONCRETE	MINIMUM COMPREHENSIVE STRENGTH WEATHER POTENTIAL		
	NEGLIGIBLE	MODERATE	SEVERE
Basement walls and foundations not exposed to weather	2,500	2,500	2,500
Basement slabs and interior slabs on grade, except garage floor slabs	2,500	2,500	2,500
Basement walls, foundation walls, exterior walls, and other vertical concrete work exposed to weather	2,500	3,000	3,000
Porches, concrete slabs and steps exposed to the weather, and garage floor slabs	2,500	3,000	3,500

Figure 21–7 The compressive strength of concrete based on CABO.

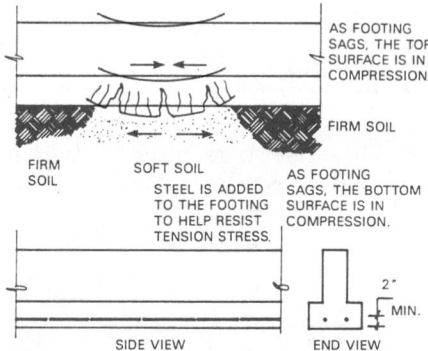

Figure 21–8 Steel is often placed in the footing to help resist tension.

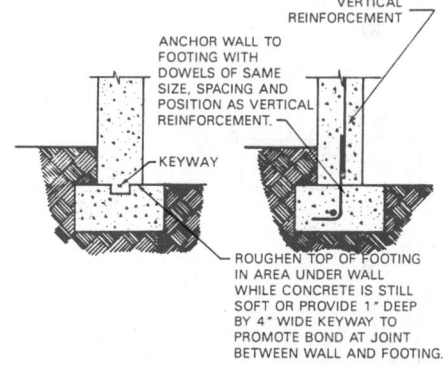

Figure 21–9 The footing can be bonded to the foundation wall with a key or with steel. *Courtesy National Concrete Masonry Association.*

concrete has set, the 2 × 4 is removed leaving a keyway in the concrete. When the concrete for the wall is poured, it will form a key by filling in the keyway. If a stronger bond is desired, steel is often used to tie the footing to the foundation wall. Both methods of bonding the foundation wall to the footing can be seen in Figure 21–9. Footing steel is not drawn on the foundation plan but is usually specified in a general note and shown in footing detail similar to that shown in Figure 21-10.

Fireplace Footings

The fireplace will need to be supported on a footing. Building codes usually require the footing to be a minimum of 12 in. deep. The footing is required to extend 6 in. past the face of the fireplace on each side. Figure 21-11 shows how fireplace footings are shown on the foundation plan.

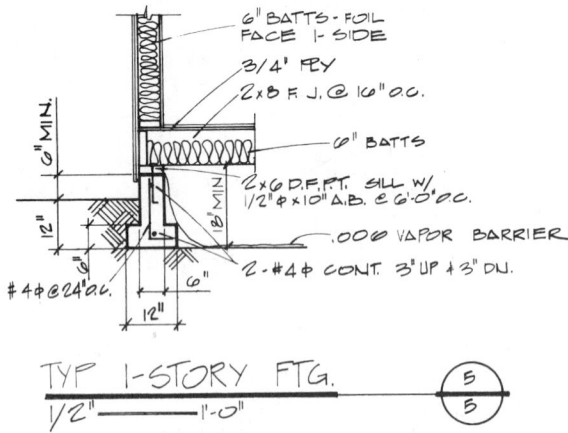

Figure 21-10 When steel is required in the foundation, it is usually specified in a general note or in a detail.

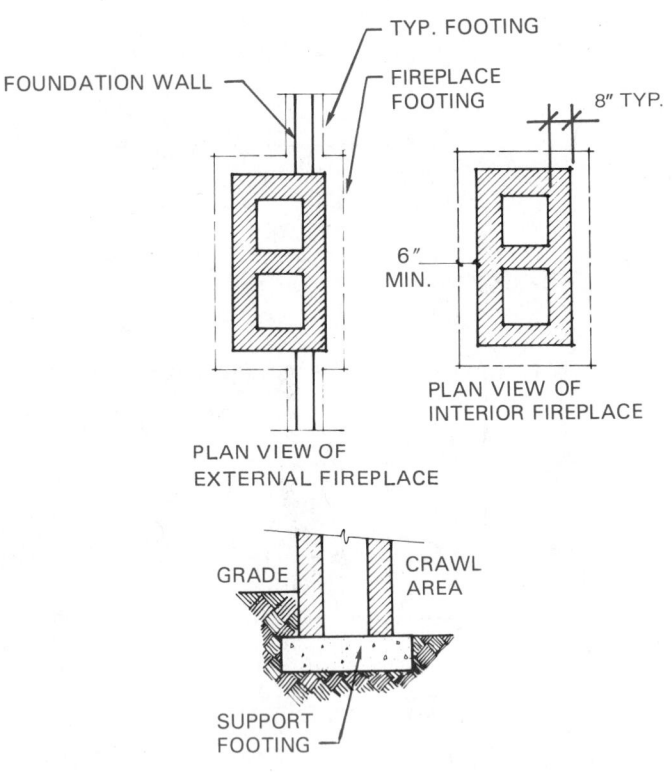

Figure 21-11 A masonry fireplace is required to have a 12-in. deep footing that extends 6 in. past the face of the fireplace.

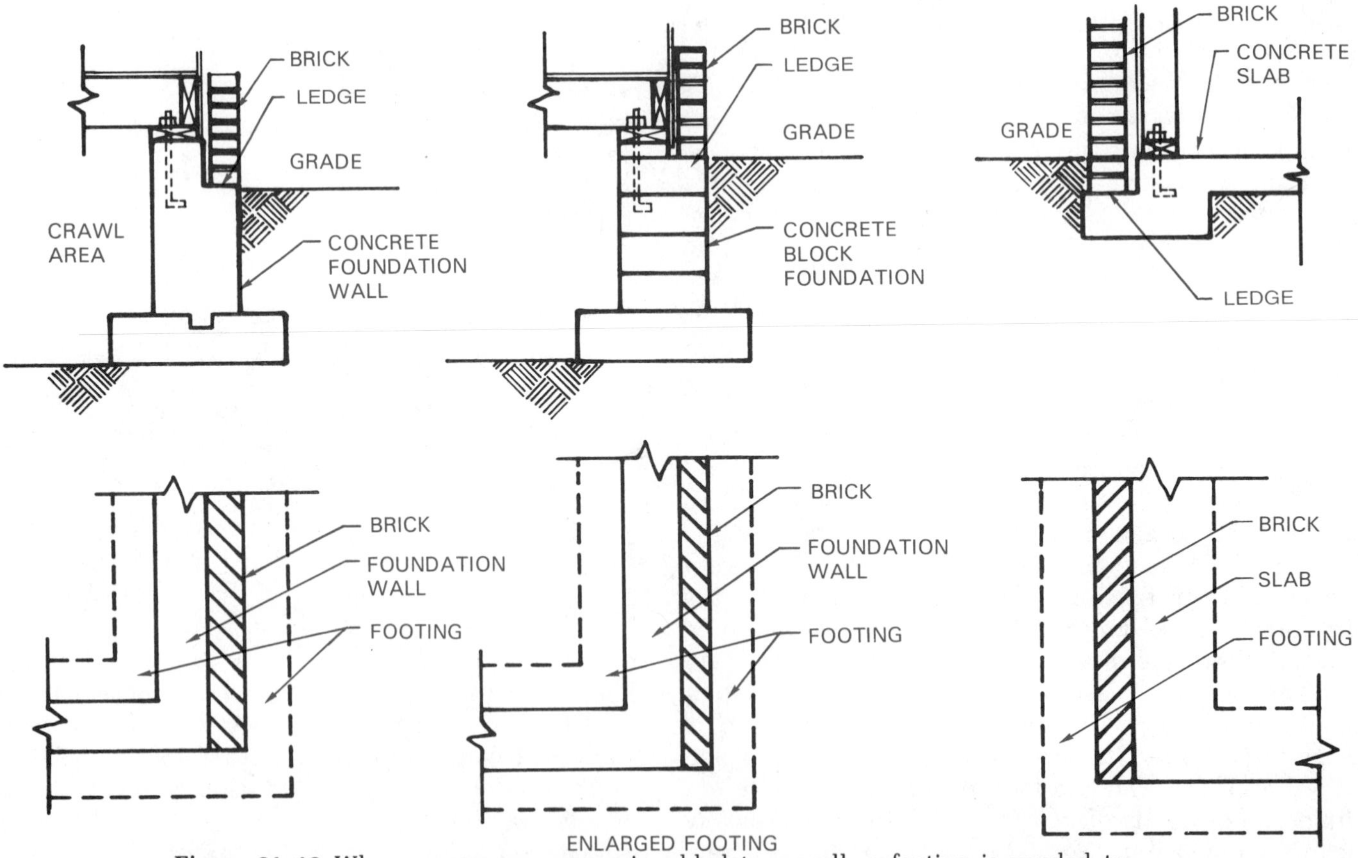

Figure 21-12 When a masonry veneer is added to a wall, a footing is needed to provide support.

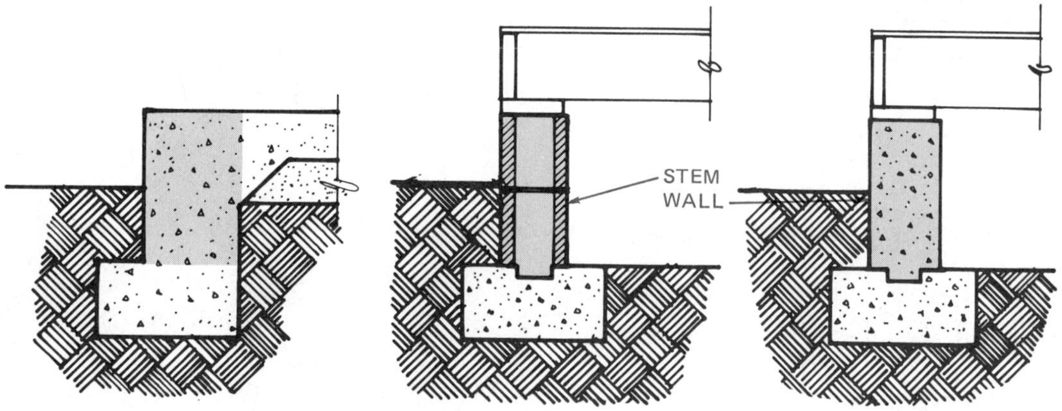

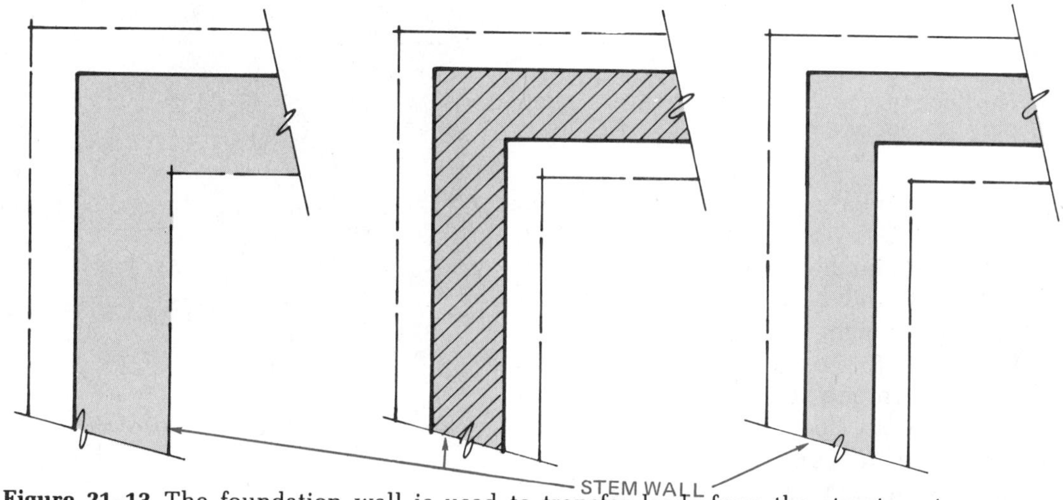

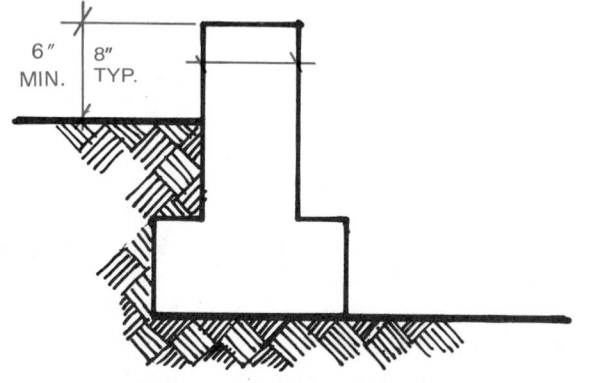

Figure 21–13 The foundation wall is used to transfer loads from the structure to the footing. The wall also serves to keep soil away from the wood structure.

WIDTH		
Story	Concrete	Unit Masonry
1	6″	6″
2	8″	8″
3	10″	10″

Figure 21–14 Foundation wall thickness based on the Uniform Building Code.

Veneer Footings

If masonry veneer is used, the footing must be wide enough to provide adequate support for the veneer. Depending on the type of veneer material to be used, the footing is typically widened by 4 to 6 in. Figure 21–12 shows common methods of providing footing support for veneer.

Foundation Wall

The foundation wall is the vertical wall which extends from the top of the footing up to the first floor level of the structure as shown in Figure 21–13. The foundation wall is usually centered on the footing to help equally disperse the loads being supported. The height of the wall will extend either 6 or 8 in. above the ground, depending on which building code you are following. This height reflects the minimum distance that is required between wood-framing members and the grade. The required width of the wall varies depending on the code used. Figure 21–14 shows common wall dimensions.

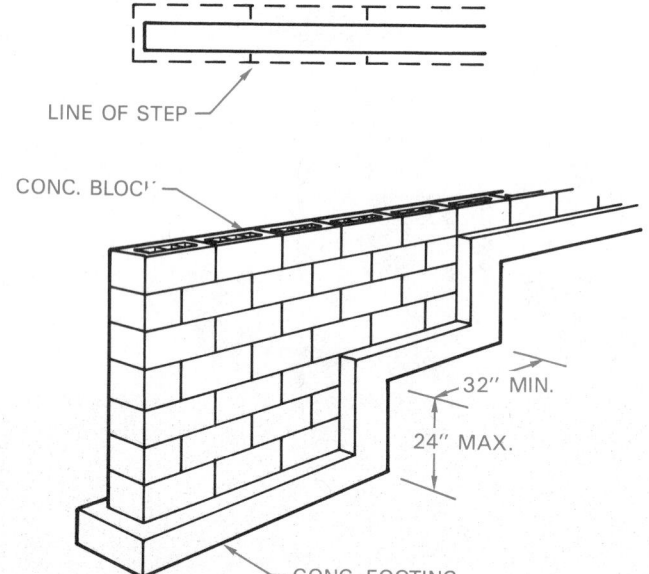

Figure 21–15 The footing and foundation wall are often stepped on sloping lots to save material.

The top of the foundation wall must be level. When the building lot is not level, the foundation wall is often stepped. This helps reduce the material needed to build the foundation wall. As the ground slopes downward, the height of the wall is increased as shown in Figure 21–15. Foundation walls may not step more than 24 in. in one step, and wood framing between the wall and any floor being supported may not be less than 14 in. in height.

Although brick and stone are occasionally used, the foundation wall is usually made from either poured concrete or from concrete blocks. Steel anchor bolts are placed in the top of the wall to secure the wood mudsill to the concrete. If concrete blocks are used, the cell in which the bolt is placed must be filled with grout. Figure 21–16 shows anchor bolts and lists minimum requirements of building codes. The mudsill is required to be pressure treated or be made of some other water-resistant wood so that it will not absorb moisture from the concrete. A 2 in. round washer is placed over the bolt projecting through the mudsill before the nut is installed to increase the holding power of the bolts.

The mudsill must also be protected from termites in many parts of the country. Among the most common methods of protection are the use of metal caps between the mudsill and the wall, chemical treatment of the soil around the foundation, and chemically treated wood near the ground. Figure 21–17 shows a metal termite shield in place.

If the house is to have a wood flooring system, some method of securing support beams to the foundation must be provided. Typically a cavity or beam pocket is built into the foundation wall. The cavity provides both a method of supporting the beam and

BUILDING CODE REQUIREMENTS FOR ANCHOR BOLTS		
	UBC/CABO	BOCA
Min. size	½ ∅	½ ∅
Depth into concrete	7″	8″
Depth into masonry	15″	15″
Max. spacing	6′-0″	8′-0″

Figure 21–16 Anchor bolts are set in concrete to hold down the wood framing members.

helps tie the floor and foundation system together. A 3-in. minimum amount of bearing surface must be provided for the beam. A ½ in. air space is provided around the beam in the pocket for air circulation. Figure 21–18 shows common methods of beam support at the foundation wall. Air must also be allowed to circulate under the floor system. To provide ventilation under the floor, vents must be set into the foundation wall. Figure 21–19 shows how foundation vents are located in the foundation wall. If an access opening is not provided in the floor, an opening will need to be provided in the foundation wall for access to the crawl space under the floor. Figure 21–20 shows how the crawl space access can be shown on the foundation plan.

If the foundation is for an energy efficient structure, insulation is often added to the wall. Two-inch

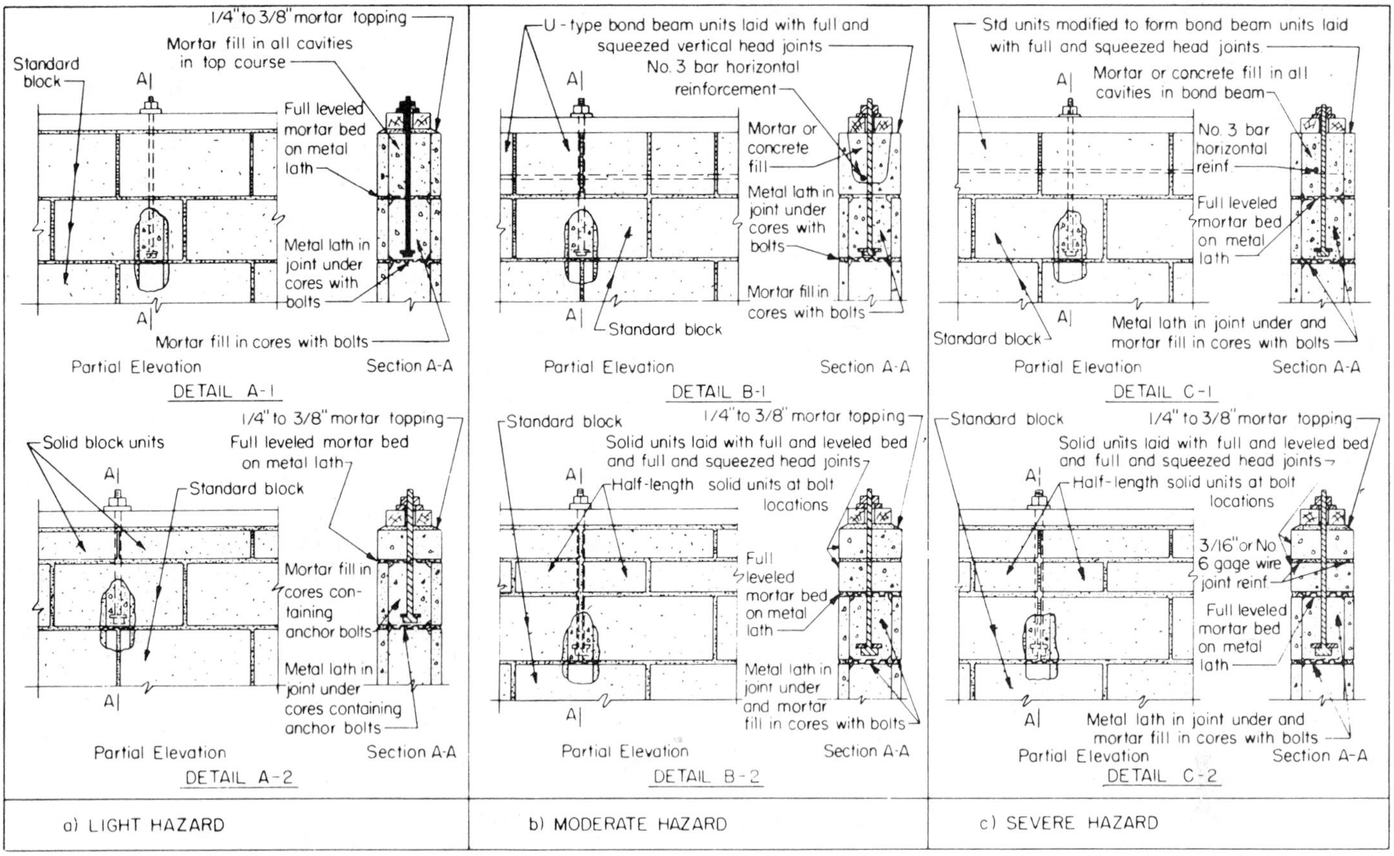

a) LIGHT HAZARD

DETAIL A-1

1/4" to 3/8" mortar topping

Mortar fill in all cavities in top course

Standard block

Full leveled mortar bed on metal lath

Metal lath in joint under cores with bolts

Mortar fill in cores with bolts

Partial Elevation   Section A-A

DETAIL A-2

Solid block units

Standard block

1/4" to 3/8" mortar topping

Full leveled mortar bed on metal lath

Mortar fill in cores containing anchor bolts

Metal lath in joint under cores containing anchor bolts

Partial Elevation   Section A-A

b) MODERATE HAZARD

DETAIL B-1

U-type bond beam units laid with full and squeezed vertical head joints

No. 3 bar horizontal reinforcement

Mortar or concrete fill

Metal lath in joint under cores with bolts

Mortar fill in cores with bolts

Standard block

Partial Elevation   Section A-A

DETAIL B-2

Standard block

1/4" to 3/8" mortar topping

Solid units laid with full and leveled bed and full and squeezed head joints

Half-length solid units at bolt locations

Full leveled mortar bed on metal lath

Metal lath in joint under and mortar fill in cores with bolts

Partial Elevation   Section A-A

c) SEVERE HAZARD

DETAIL C-1

Std units modified to form bond beam units laid with full and squeezed head joints

Mortar or concrete fill in all cavities in bond beam

No. 3 bar horizontal reinf

Full leveled mortar bed on metal lath

Standard block

Metal lath in joint under and mortar fill in cores with bolts

Partial Elevation   Section A-A

DETAIL C-2

Standard block

1/4" to 3/8" mortar topping

Solid units laid with full and leveled bed and full and squeezed head joints

Half-length solid units at bolt locations

3/16" or No 6 gage wire joint reinf

Full leveled mortar bed on metal lath

Metal lath in joint under and mortar fill in cores with bolts

Partial Elevation   Section A-A

Figure 21-17 Recommended methods of capping concrete masonry foundations supporting wood frame construction in termite-infested areas. *Courtesy National Concrete Masonry Association.*

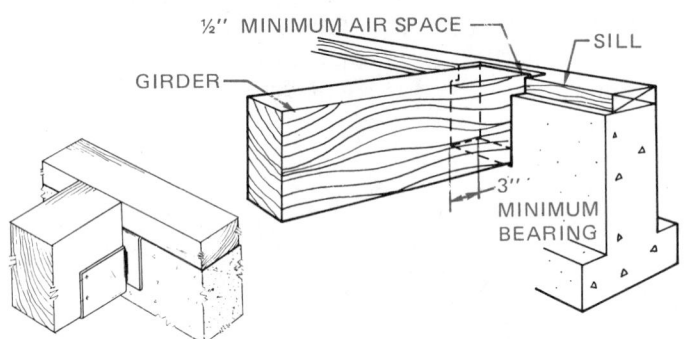

1/2" MINIMUM AIR SPACE

GIRDER

SILL

3" MINIMUM BEARING

Figure 21-18 A beam seat, or pocket, can either be recessed into the foundation wall or the beam may be supported by metal connectors. *Connectors courtesy Simpson Strong-Tie Company, Inc.*

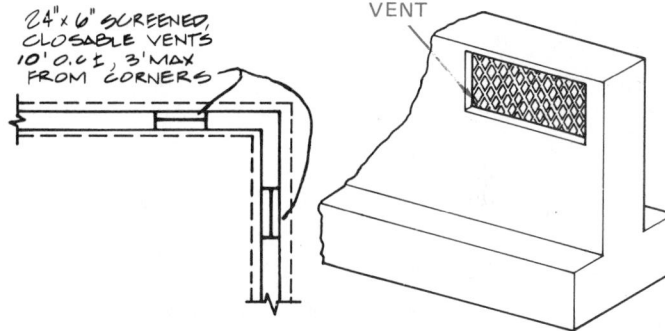

24"x6" SCREENED, CLOSABLE VENTS 10'0.c±, 3' MAX FROM CORNERS

VENT

Figure 21-19 Foundation vents must be placed in the foundation wall to provide 1 sq ft ventilation for each 150 sq ft of crawl space. Vents must be placed within 3 ft of a corner.

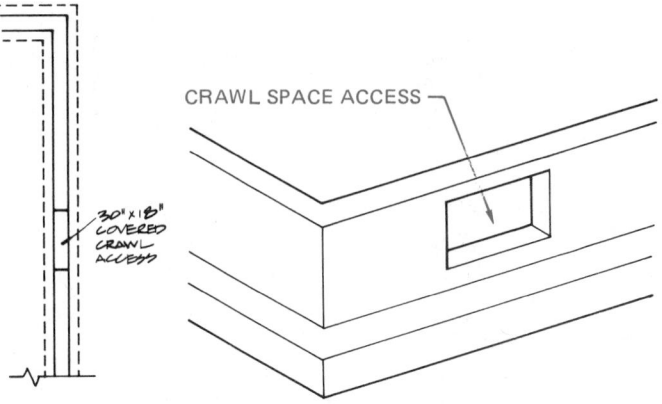

30"x 18" COVERED CRAWL ACCESS

CRAWL SPACE ACCESS

BUILDING CODE REQUIREMENTS		
UBC	CABO	SBC
18" × 30"	18" × 24"	18" × 24"

Figure 21-20 Minimum foundation access required if a crawl space is provided below the floor system.

rigid insulation is used to protect the wall from cold weather. This can be placed on either side of the wall. If the insulation is placed on the exterior side of the wall, the wall will retain heat from the building. This placement does cause problems in protecting the insulation from damage. Insulation placed on the interior side of the wall does not need protection, but a continuous layer may be hard to obtain. Figure

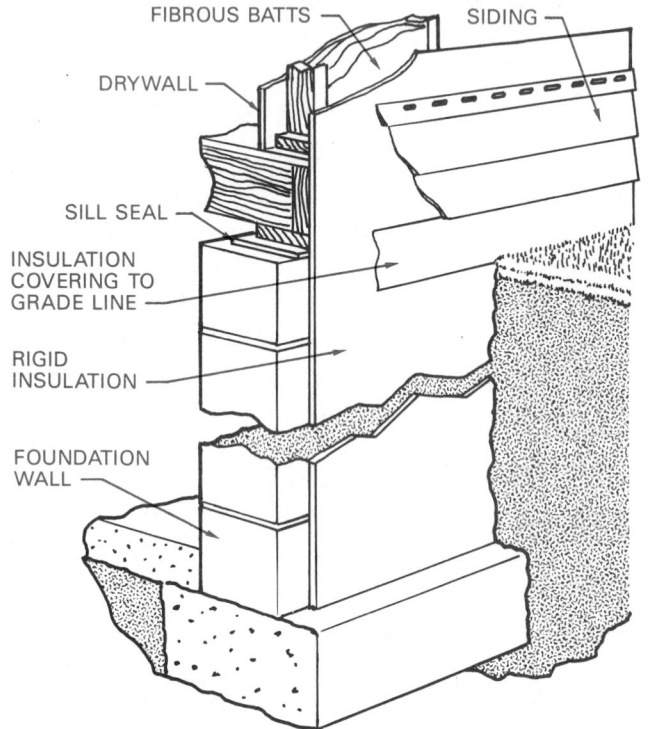

FIBROUS BATTS
SIDING
DRYWALL
SILL SEAL
INSULATION
COVERING TO
GRADE LINE
RIGID
INSULATION
FOUNDATION
WALL

Figure 21–21 Insulation is often placed on the foundation wall to help cut heat loss.

21–21 shows exterior insulation placement.

In addition to supporting the loads of the structure, the foundation walls also must resist the lateral pressure of the soil pressing against the wall. When the wall is over 24 in. in height, vertical steel is usually added to the wall to help reduce tension in the wall. Horizontal steel is also added to foundation walls in some seismic zones to help strengthen the wall.

Retaining Walls

Retaining or basement walls are primarily made of concrete blocks or poured concrete. The material used will depend on labor trends in your area. The material used will affect the height of the wall. If concrete blocks are used, the wall is typically 12 blocks high from the top of the footing. If poured concrete is used, the wall will normally be 8 ft high from the top of the footing. This will allow 4 × 8 sheets of plywood to be used as forms for the sides of the wall.

Regardless of which material is used, basement walls serve the same functions as the shorter foundation walls. Because of the added height, the lateral forces acting on the side of these walls are magnified. As seen in Figure 21–22, this lateral soil pressure tends to bend the wall inward, thus placing the soil side of the wall in compression and the interior face of the wall in tension. To resist this tensile stress, steel reinforcing may be required by the building department. The seismic zone will affect the size and placement of the steel. Figures 21–23 and 21–24 show common patterns of steel placement.

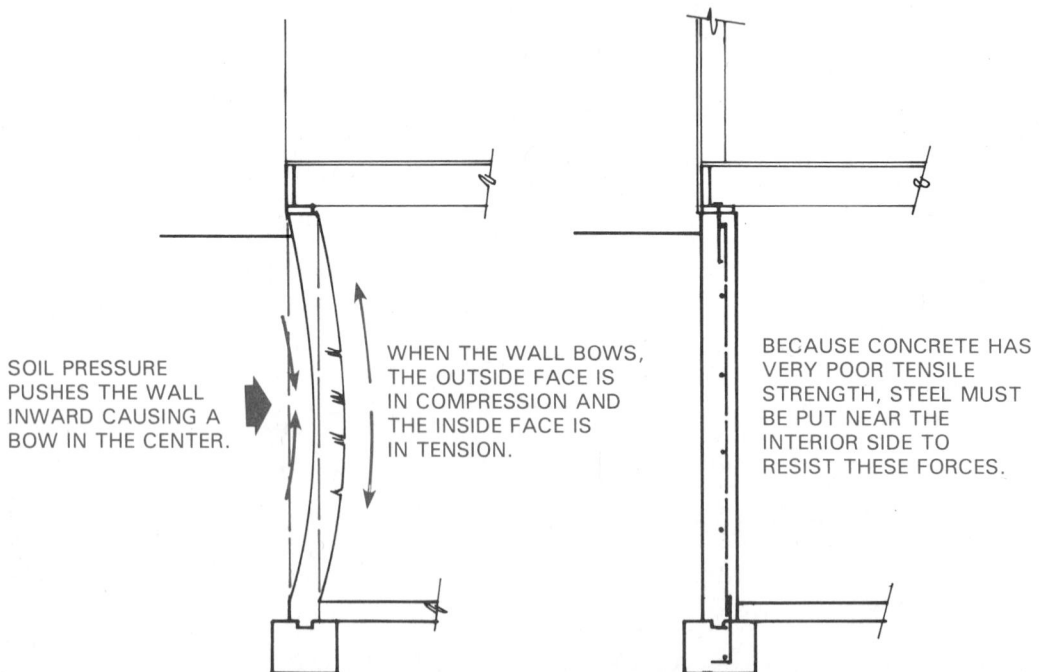

SOIL PRESSURE PUSHES THE WALL INWARD CAUSING A BOW IN THE CENTER.

WHEN THE WALL BOWS, THE OUTSIDE FACE IS IN COMPRESSION AND THE INSIDE FACE IS IN TENSION.

BECAUSE CONCRETE HAS VERY POOR TENSILE STRENGTH, STEEL MUST BE PUT NEAR THE INTERIOR SIDE TO RESIST THESE FORCES.

Figure 21–22 Stresses acting on a beam retaining wall. The wall serves as a beam spanning between each floor, and the soil is the supported load.

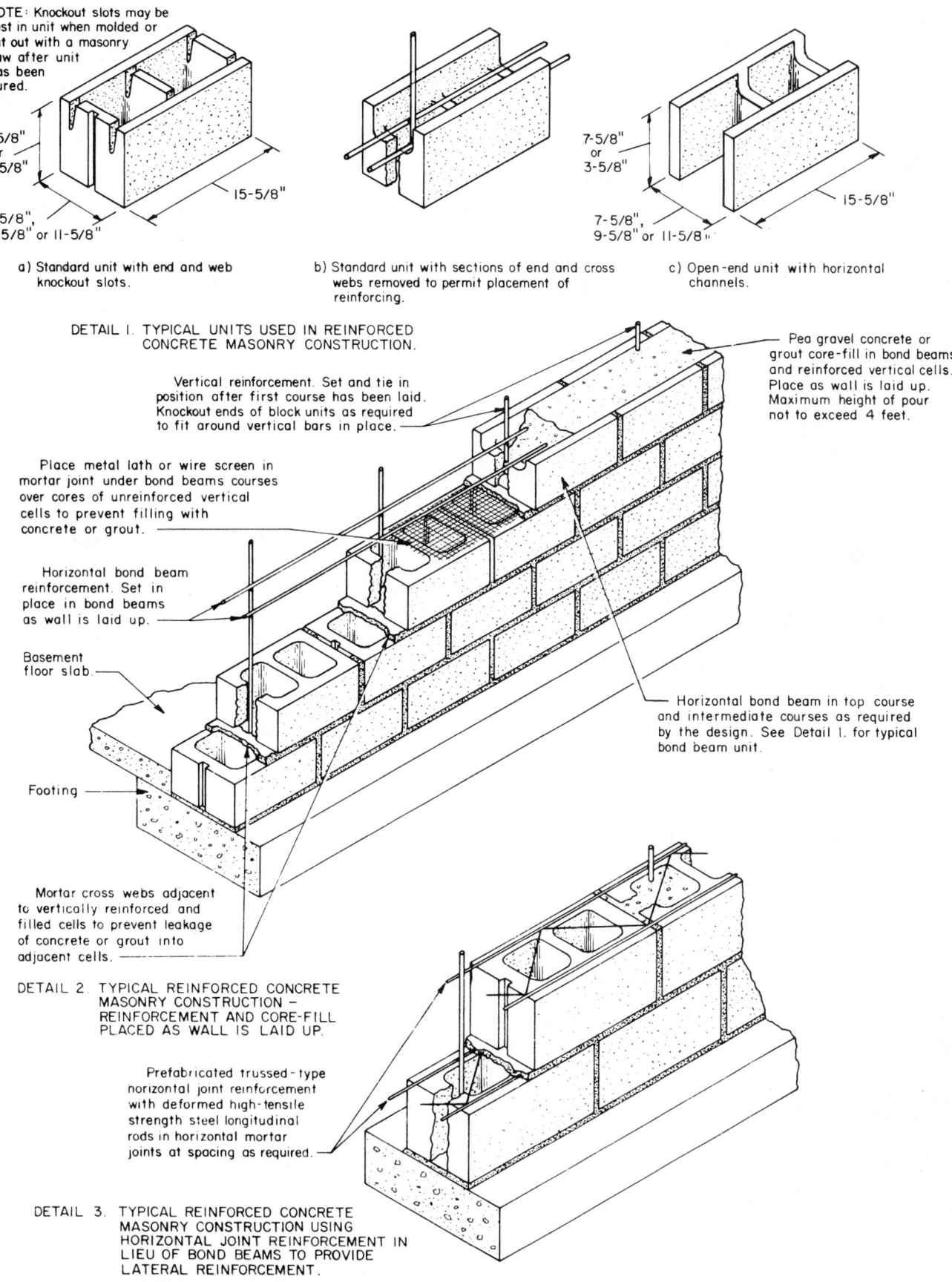

NOTE: Knockout slots may be cast in unit when molded or cut out with a masonry saw after unit has been cured.

7-5/8" or 3-5/8"

7-5/8", 9-5/8" or 11-5/8"

15-5/8"

a) Standard unit with end and web knockout slots.

b) Standard unit with sections of end and cross webs removed to permit placement of reinforcing.

c) Open-end unit with horizontal channels.

7-5/8" or 3-5/8"

7-5/8", 9-5/8" or 11-5/8"

15-5/8"

DETAIL I. TYPICAL UNITS USED IN REINFORCED CONCRETE MASONRY CONSTRUCTION.

Vertical reinforcement. Set and tie in position after first course has been laid. Knockout ends of block units as required to fit around vertical bars in place.

Place metal lath or wire screen in mortar joint under bond beams courses over cores of unreinforced vertical cells to prevent filling with concrete or grout.

Horizontal bond beam reinforcement. Set in place in bond beams as wall is laid up.

Basement floor slab.

Footing

Pea gravel concrete or grout core-fill in bond beams and reinforced vertical cells. Place as wall is laid up. Maximum height of pour not to exceed 4 feet.

Horizontal bond beam in top course and intermediate courses as required by the design. See Detail I. for typical bond beam unit.

Mortar cross webs adjacent to vertically reinforced and filled cells to prevent leakage of concrete or grout into adjacent cells.

DETAIL 2. TYPICAL REINFORCED CONCRETE MASONRY CONSTRUCTION - REINFORCEMENT AND CORE-FILL PLACED AS WALL IS LAID UP.

Prefabricated trussed-type horizontal joint reinforcement with deformed high-tensile strength steel longitudinal rods in horizontal mortar joints at spacing as required.

DETAIL 3. TYPICAL REINFORCED CONCRETE MASONRY CONSTRUCTION USING HORIZONTAL JOINT REINFORCEMENT IN LIEU OF BOND BEAMS TO PROVIDE LATERAL REINFORCEMENT.

Figure 21-23 Suggested construction details for reinforced concrete masonry foundation walls. *Courtesy National Concrete Masonry Association.*

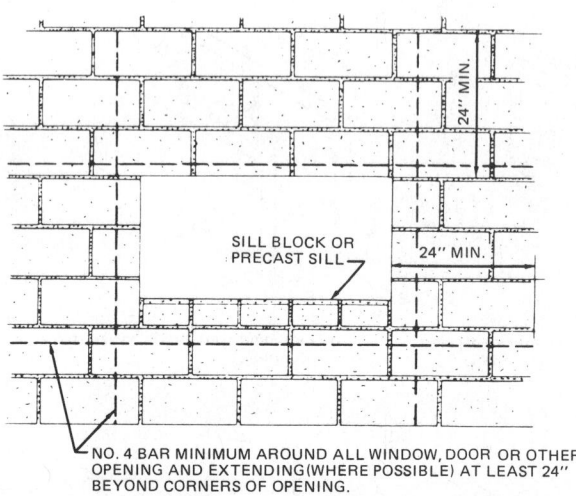

RECOMMENDED REINFORCEMENT AROUND OPENINGS

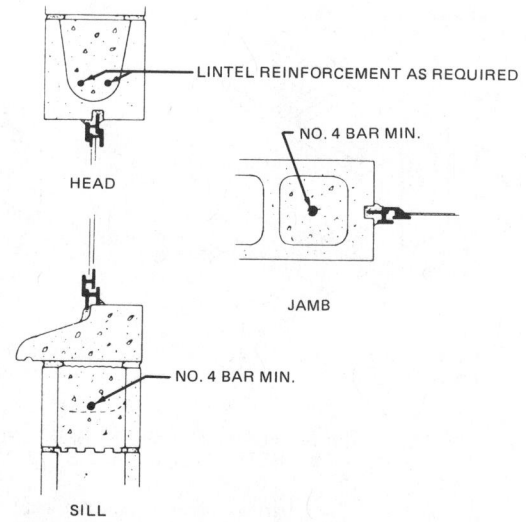

TYPICAL STEEL BASEMENT WINDOW DETAILS

Figure 21–24 Typical reinforcing and window detail at opening in reinforced concrete masonry basement walls. *Courtesy National Concrete Masonry Association.*

The footing for a retaining wall is usually 16 in. wide and either 8 or 12 in. deep. The depth will depend on the weight to be supported. Steel is typically extended from the footing into the wall. At the top of the wall anchor bolts are placed in the wall in the same method as with a foundation wall. Anchor bolts for retaining walls are typically placed much closer together than for shorter walls. It is very important that the wall and the floor system be securely tied together. The floor system is used to help strengthen the wall and resist the soil pressure. Where seismic danger is great, metal angles are added to the anchor bolts to make the tie between the wall and the floor joist extremely rigid. Figure 21–25 shows common wall-to-floor connections for a retaining wall.

If a wall will be submitted to severe lateral pressure, a pilaster may be added to the wall. A pilaster is a thickened area of wall and is used to reduce the lateral pressure against the wall by reducing the length of the wall. A pilaster is also used to transfer vertical loads down to the footing. Pilasters can be built in several different ways as seen in Figure 21–26.

To reduce soil pressure next to the footing, a drain is installed. The drain is set at the base of the footing to collect and divert water from the face of the wall. Figure 21–27 shows how the drain is typically placed. Generally the area above the drain is filled with gravel so that subsurface water will percolate easily down to the drain and away from the wall. By reducing the water content of the soil, the lateral pressure on the wall is reduced. The drain is not drawn on the foundation plan but must be specified in a note.

No matter what the soil condition, the basement wall should be waterproofed to help reduce moisture from passing through the wall into the living area. Figure 21–28 lists common methods of waterproofing a basement wall. Adding windows to the basement can help cut down the moisture content of the basement. This will sometimes require adding a window well to prevent the ground from being pushed in front of the window. Figure 21–29 shows how a window well, or areaway as it is sometimes called, can be drawn on the foundation plan.

Similar to a foundation wall, the basement wall also needs to be protected from termites. Figure 21–30 shows common ways that wood can be protected. When drawing the foundation plan, the metal shield will not be drawn, but it should be called out in a note.

Restraining Walls

As seen in Figure 21–31 when a structure is built on a sloping site the masonry wall may not need to be full height. Although less soil is retained than with a full height wall, more problems are encountered. Figure 21–32 shows the tendencies for bending for this type of wall. Because the wall is not supported at the top by the floor, the soil pressure must be resisted through the footing. This requires a larger footing than for a full-height wall. If the wall and footing connection is rigid enough to keep the wall in position, the soil pressure will tend to try to overturn the whole foundation. The extra footing width is to resist the tendency to overturn. Figure

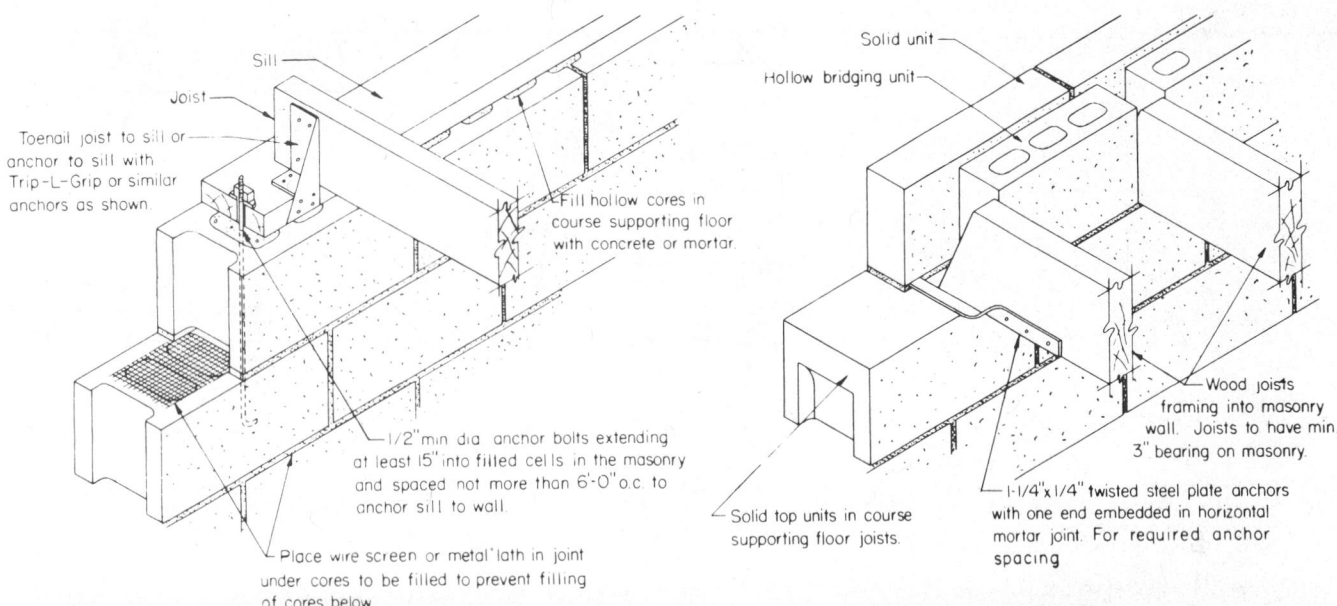

Toenail joist to sill or anchor to sill with Trip-L-Grip or similar anchors as shown.

Sill

Joist

Fill hollow cores in course supporting floor with concrete or mortar.

1/2" min. dia. anchor bolts extending at least 15" into filled cells in the masonry and spaced not more than 6'-0" o.c. to anchor sill to wall.

Place wire screen or metal lath in joint under cores to be filled to prevent filling of cores below.

ANCHORAGE OF WOOD JOISTS TO FOUNDATION IN WOOD FRAME CONSTRUCTION.

Solid unit

Hollow bridging unit

Wood joists framing into masonry wall. Joists to have min. 3" bearing on masonry.

1-1/4"x1/4" twisted steel plate anchors with one end embedded in horizontal mortar joint. For required anchor spacing.

Solid top units in course supporting floor joists.

ANCHORAGE OF WOOD JOISTS TO FOUNDATION IN MASONRY CONSTRUCTION

SUGGESTED METHODS OF ANCHORING WOOD JOISTS
BEARING ON CONCRETE MASONRY FOUNDATION WALLS.

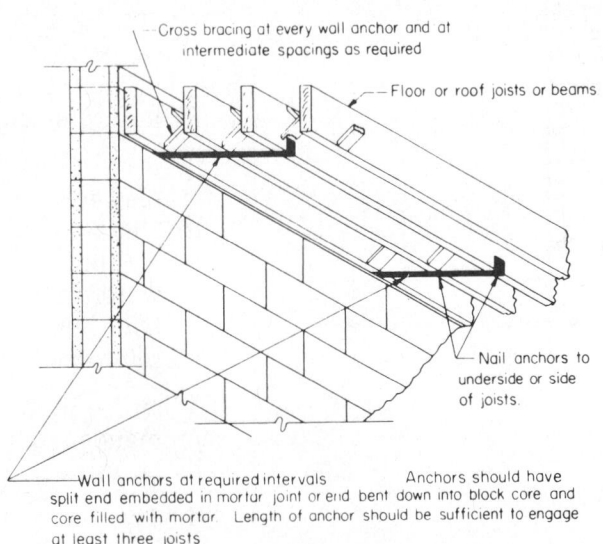

Cross bracing at every wall anchor and at intermediate spacings as required

Floor or roof joists or beams

Nail anchors to underside or side of joists.

Wall anchors at required intervals split end embedded in mortar joint or end bent down into block core and core filled with mortar. Length of anchor should be sufficient to engage at least three joists.

Anchors should have end bent down into block core and core filled with mortar.

TYPICAL DETAIL FOR ANCHORAGE OF CONCRETE
MASONRY WALLS TO PARALLEL WOOD JOISTS OR BEAMS.

Figure 21–25 Metal angles and straps are typically used on basement walls to ensure a rigid connection between the floor and wall. *Courtesy National Concrete Masonry Association.*

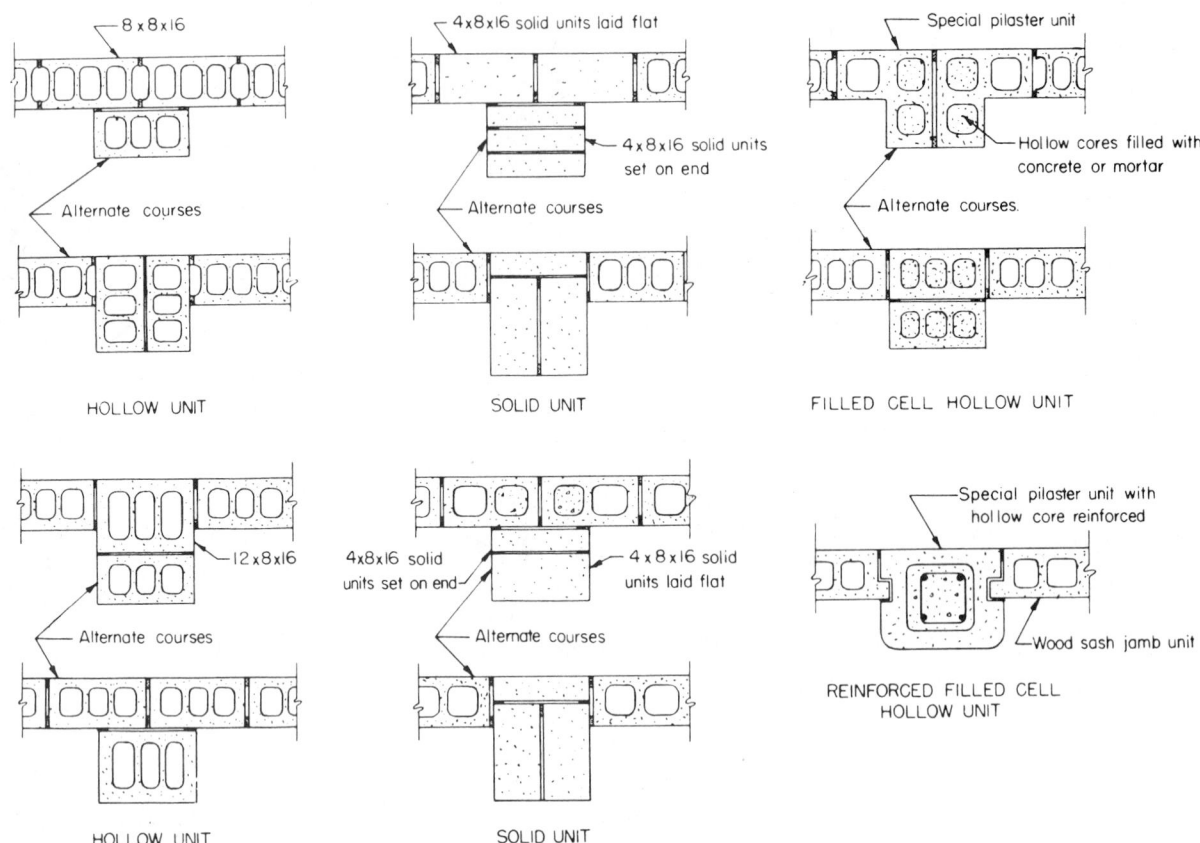

Figure 21–26 Typical concrete masonry pilaster designs. *Courtesy National Concrete Masonry Association.*

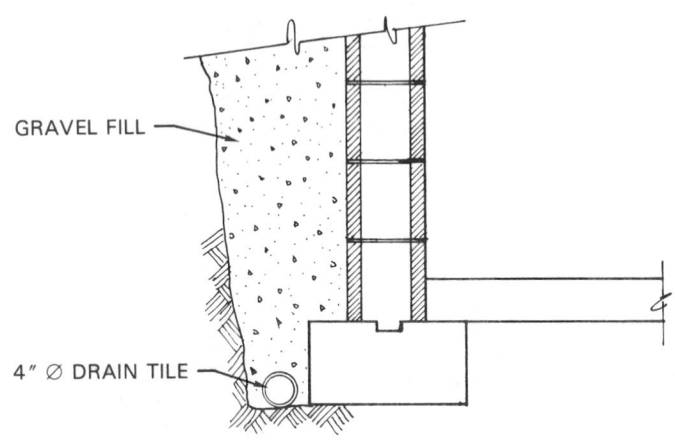

Figure 21–27 A drain is placed in a gravel bed to help disperse water away from the wall area.

When built in well-drained soils, it is recommended that the exterior face of the basement walls be protected with either:

1. Two ¼-in. thick coats of portland cement plaster.
2. One ¼-in. thick coat of portland cement plaster plus two brush coats of bituminous waterproofing.
3. One heavy troweled-on coat of cold, fiber-reinforced asphaltic mastic.

When built in wet, poorly drained soils, it is recommended that the exterior face of basement walls be protected with either:

1. Two ¼-in. thick coats of portland cement plaster plus two brush coats of bituminous waterproofing.
2. One ¼-in. thick coat of portland cement plaster, plus one heavy troweled-on coat of cold, fiber-reinforced asphaltic mastic.

Figure 21–28 Common methods of waterproofing basement walls. *Courtesy National Concrete Masonry Association.*

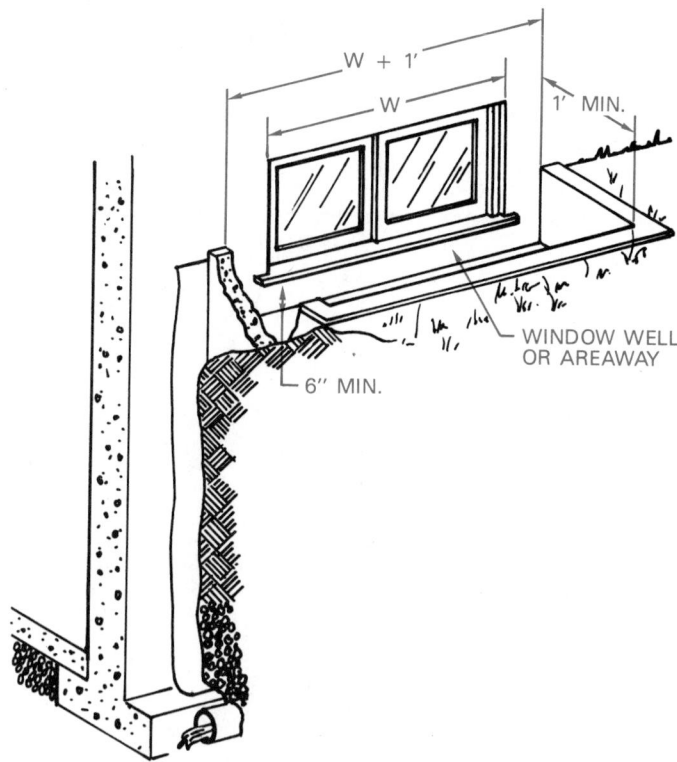

Figure 21-29 When a window is placed in a basement wall, a window well may be required to keep soil away from the window.

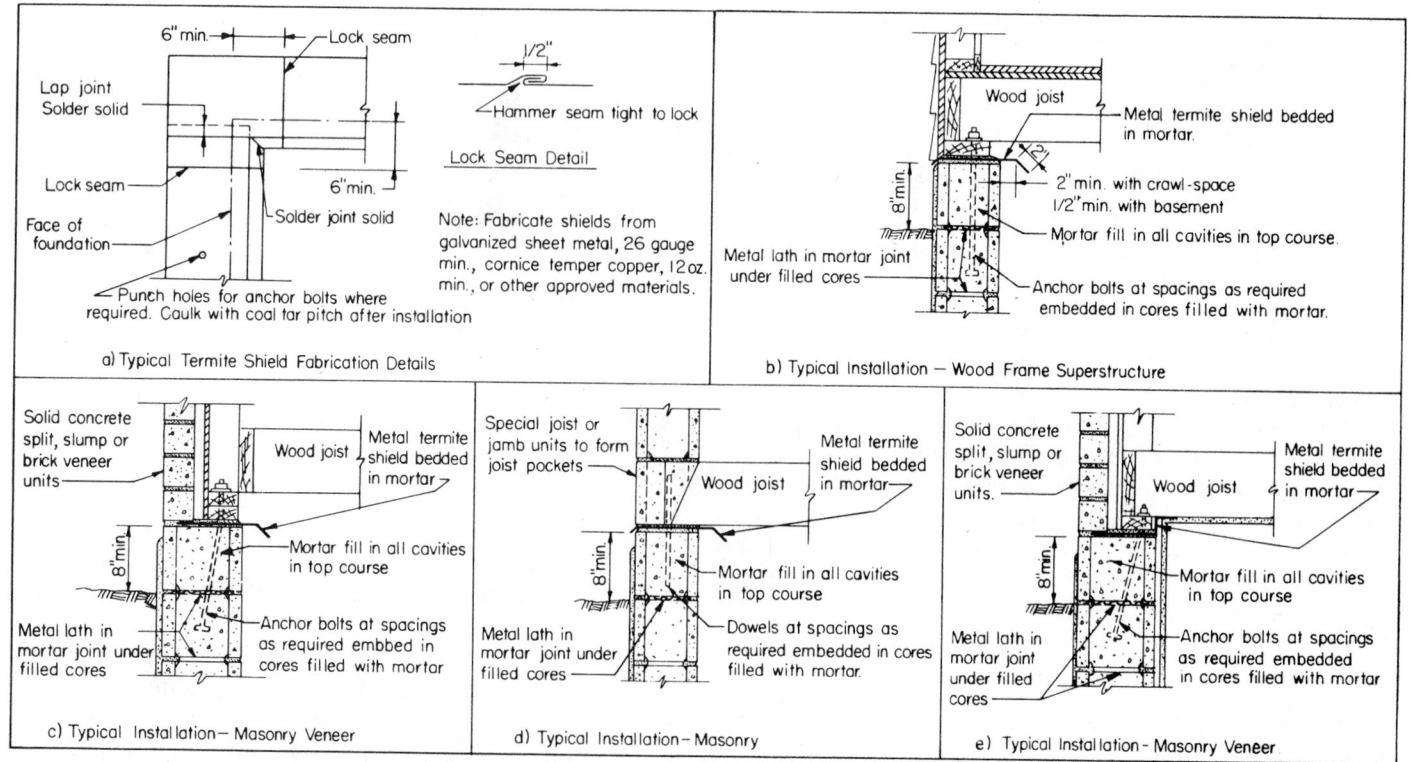

Figure 21-30 Termite shield details for retaining walls. *Courtesy National Concrete Masonry Association.*

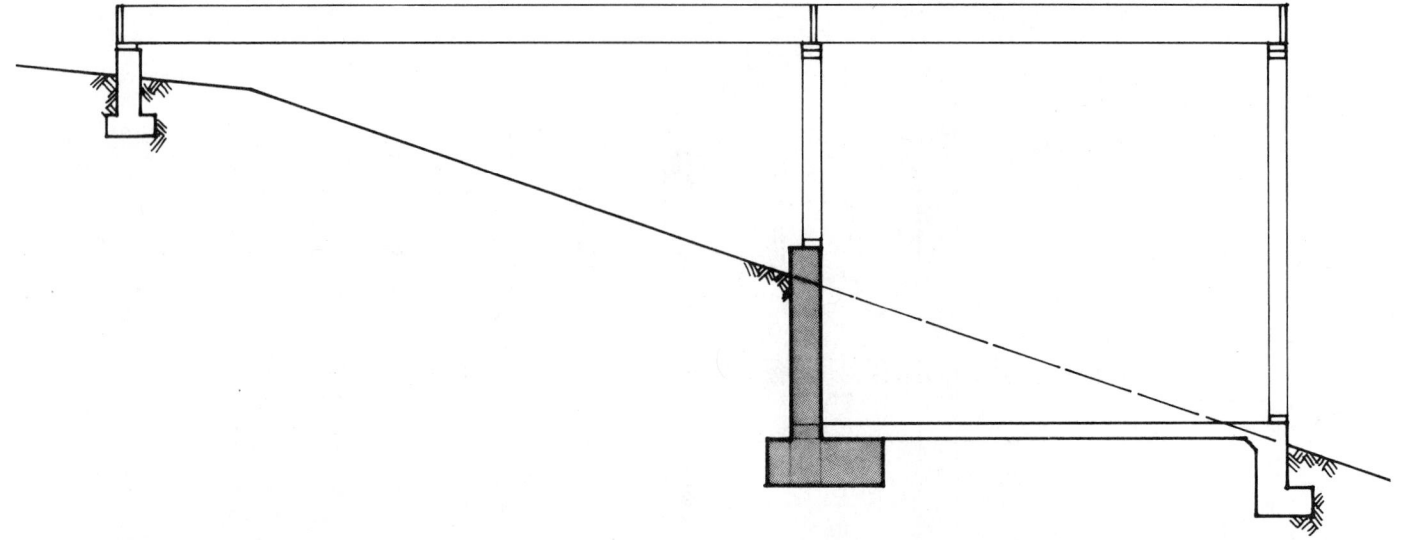

Figure 21–31 An 8-ft. high retaining wall is usually not required on sloping lots. A partial restraining wall with wood-framed walls above it is often used.

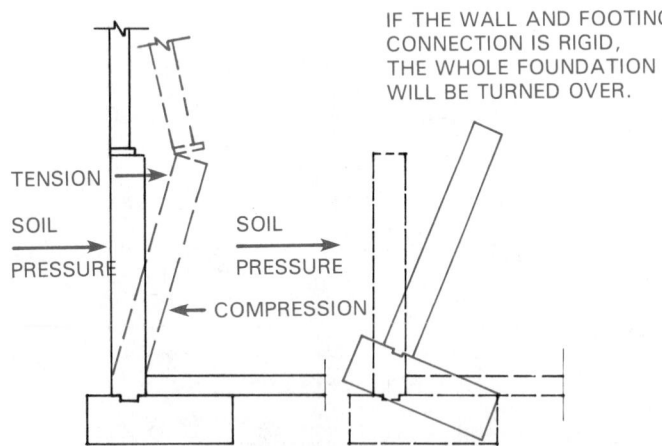

IF THE WALL AND FOOTING CONNECTION IS RIGID, THE WHOLE FOUNDATION WILL BE TURNED OVER.

TENSION

SOIL PRESSURE

SOIL PRESSURE

COMPRESSION

Figure 21–32 When a wall is not held in place at the top, soil pressure will tend to move the wall inward. The intersection of the wood and concrete walls is called a hinge point because of the tendency to move.

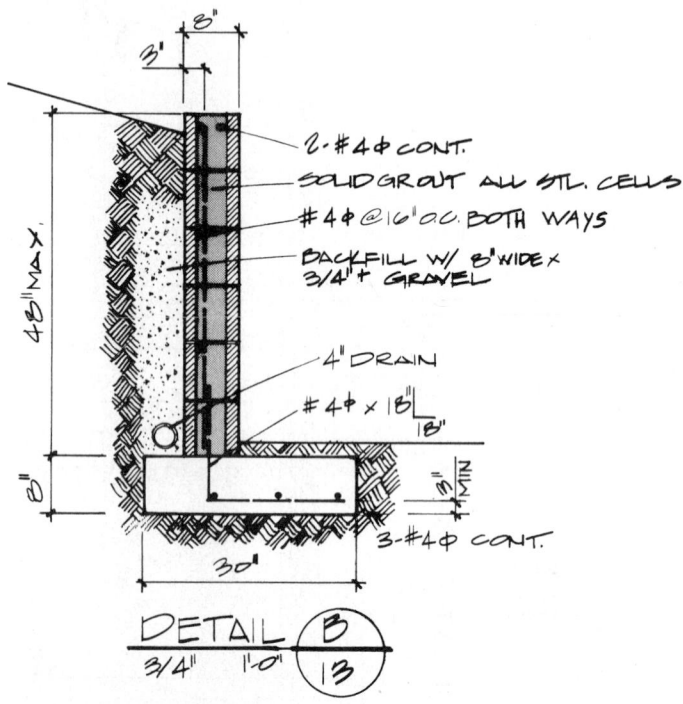

Figure 21–33 A detail of a partial wall.

21–33 shows an example of a detail that a drafter might be required to draw and how the wall would be represented on the foundation plan. Depending on the slope of the ground being supported, a key may be required as seen in Figure 21–34. A keyway on the top of the footing has been discussed. This key is added to the bottom of the footing to help keep it from sliding as a result of soil pressure against the wall. Generally the key is not shown on the foundation plan but is shown in a detail of the wall.

Interior Supports

Foundation walls and footings are typically part of the foundation system that supports the exterior shape of the structure. Interior loads are generally supported on spot footings, or piers. Pier depth is generally required to match that of the footings. The placement of piers will be determined by the type of floor system to be used and will be discussed in Chapter 22. The size of the pier will depend on the load being supported and will be explained in Chapter 47. Piers are usually drawn on the foundation plan with dotted lines as shown in Figure 21–35.

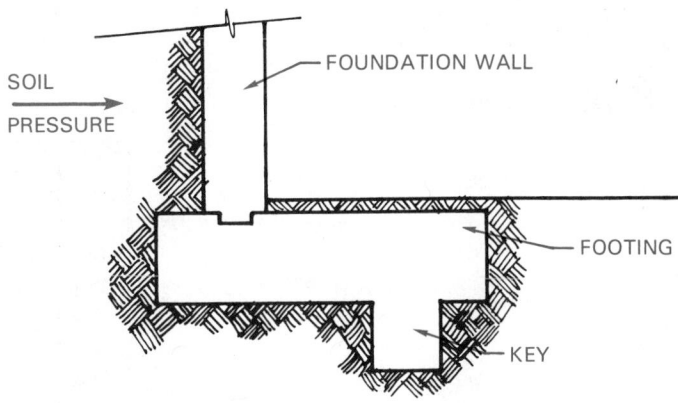

Figure 21–34 When soil pressure is too great for the wall to withstand, a key may be added to the bottom of the footing. The key provides added surface area to help resist sliding.

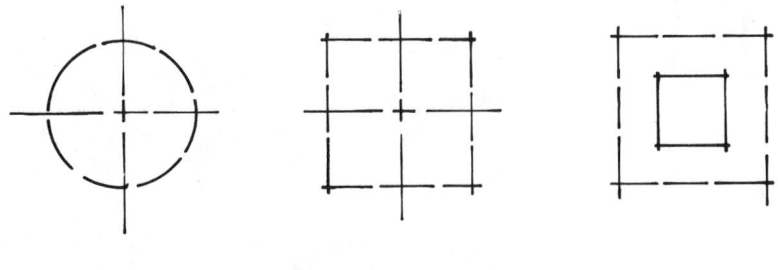

PLAN VIEW OF PIERS

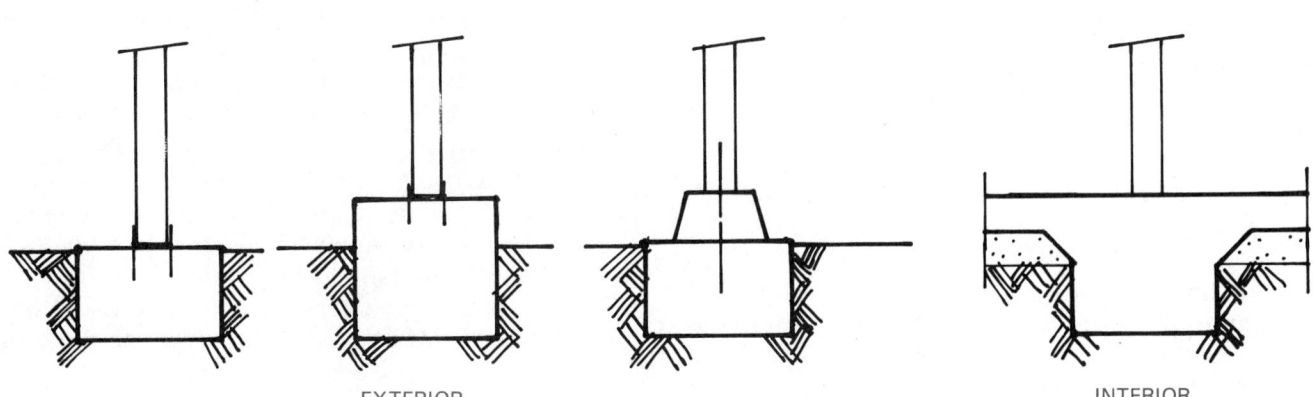

EXTERIOR

INTERIOR

PIERS IN SIDE ELEVATION

Figure 21–35 Concrete piers are used to support interior loads. Most building codes require wood to be at least 6 in. above the grade, which means that piers must also extend 6 in. above the grade.

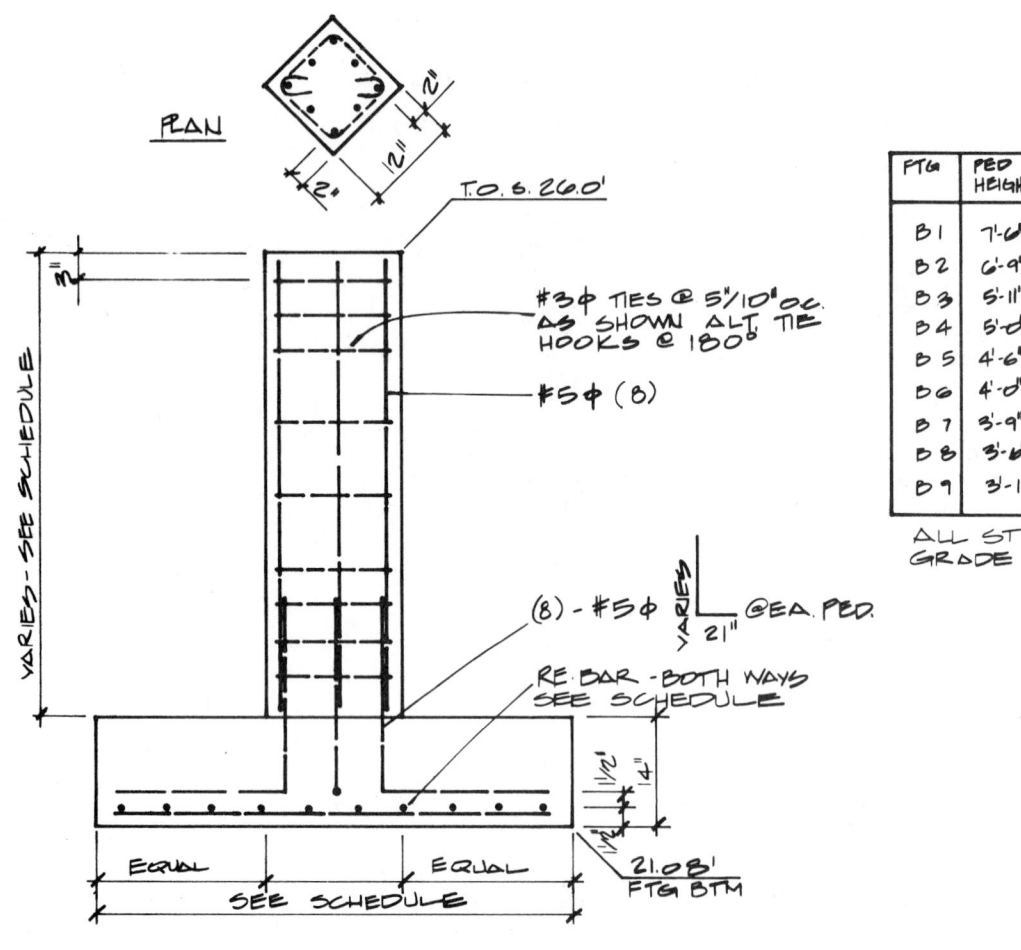

FTG	PED HEIGHT	SIZE	REINFORCING STEEL
B1	7'-6"	7'-0"	#6 φ @ 10' O.C.
B2	6'-9"	6'-6"	#6 φ @ 12' O.C.
B3	5'-11"	6'-6"	#6 φ @ 12' O.C.
B4	5'-0"	7'-0"	#6 φ @ 10' O.C.
B5	4'-6"	6'-0"	#5 φ @ 15' O.C.
B6	4'-0"	7'-0"	#6 φ @ 10' O.C.
B7	3'-9"	6'-6"	#6 φ @ 12' O.C.
B8	3'-6"	6'-6"	#6 φ @ 12' O.C.
B9	3'-1"	6'-0"	#5 φ @ 15' O.C.

ALL STEEL TO BE ASTM GRADE 60, UNLESS NOTED

Figure 21–36 Pedestals are often used if upper soil levels are unstable.

Pedestals

A pedestal is a column built on top of a footing. Pedestals are often built on piers to protect wooden posts from water in flood zones. Pedestals are also used when a structure is built on loose-fill material. The footing is placed on firm soil and the pedestal extends through the loose-fill material to a point above grade. Figure 21–36 shows examples of each type of pier and how they are drawn on foundation plans.

Metal Connectors

Metal connectors are often used at the foundation level. Three of the most commonly used metal connectors are shown in Figure 21–37. Each is accompanied by a table of standard dimensions. The drafter is often required to determine the proper size connector and to specify it on the foundation plan. How the connector is used will determine how it is specified. Figure 21–38 shows how these connectors might be specified on the foundation plan.

DIMENSIONING FOUNDATION COMPONENTS

Throughout this chapter we have seen the typical components of a foundation system and how they are drawn on the foundation plan. The manner in which they are dimensioned is equally important to the construction crew. The line quality for the dimension and leader lines is the same as was used on the floor plan. Jogs in the foundation wall are dimensioned using the same methods used on the floor plan. A different method is used to dimension the interior walls, however. Foundation walls are dimensioned from face-to-face rather than from face-to-center as on the floor plan. Footings widths are also usually dimensioned. Each type of dimension can be seen in Figure 21–39.

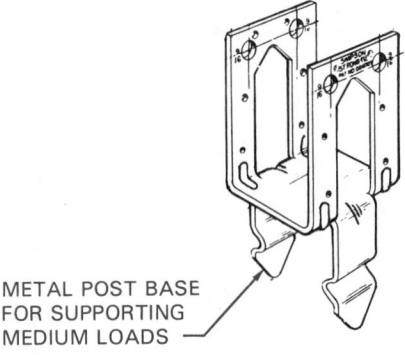

METAL POST BASE
FOR SUPPORTING
MEDIUM LOADS

Model No.	DIMENSIONS		I.C.B.O. LOADS (12-16d NAILS)		U.B.C. Calc. (2)-½" Dia.
	W	L	Vert. Up	Lateral	Vert. Up
PB44	3⁹/₁₆"	3⅜"	1320	1320	—
PB46	5½"	3⅜"	1320	1320	—
PB66	5½"	5⅜"	1610	1610	3225
PB44R	4"	3⅜"	1540	1540	—
PB46R	6"	3⅜"	1320	1320	3225
PB66R	6"	5⅜"	1610	1610	3225

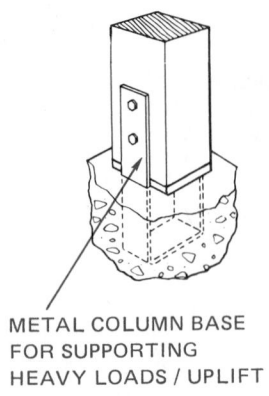

METAL COLUMN BASE
FOR SUPPORTING
HEAVY LOADS / UPLIFT

Model No.	W	L	Material / Stirrups	Bolts	Uplift Design Loads
CB44	3⁹/₁₆"	3⅝"	³/₁₆"x2"	(2) ⅝"	5030
CB46	3⁹/₁₆"	5½"	³/₁₆"x2"	(2) ⅝"	5030
CB48	3⁹/₁₆"	7½"	³/₁₆"x2"	(2) ⅝"	5030
CB5	5¼"	Specify	³/₁₆"x3"	(2) ⅝"	5030
CB66	5½"	5½"	³/₁₆"x3"	(2) ⅝"	5030
CB68	5½"	7½"	³/₁₆"x3"	(2) ⅝"	5030
CB610	5½"	9½"	³/₁₆"x3"	(2) ⅝"	5030
CB612	5½"	11½"	³/₁₆"x3"	(2) ⅝"	5030
CB7	6⅞"	Specify	¼"x3"	(2) ¾"	7230
CB88	7½"	7½"	¼"x3"	(2) ¾"	7230
CB810	7½"	9½"	¼"x3"	(2) ¾"	7230
CB812	7½"	11½"	¼"x3"	(2) ¾"	7230
CB9	8⅞"	Specify	¼"x3"	(2) ¾"	7230
CB1010	9½"	9½"	¼"x3"	(2) ¾"	7230
CB1012	9½"	11½"	¼"x3"	(2) ¾"	7230
CB1212	11½"	11½"	¼"x3"	(2) ¾"	7230

Model No.	Dimensions					Bolt Attachment			Average Test Ultimate	Design Load Value[5,6,7] When Installed On Stud Thickness Of					Maximum Allowable Short Term Loading	Minimum Weld
	GA.	H¹	W	D	SO²	CL³	Concrete		Stud		1½"	2"	2½"	3"	3½"		
							DIA.	Min.⁴ Embedment									
HD2	7	5³/₄"	2½"	2⅝"	2½"	1³/₈"	⅝"	9"	(2)-⅝"MB	13,200	2065	2520	2520	2520	2520	3360	³/₁₆"×2"
HD5	7	6⁵/₁₆"	2⅞"	3½"	3⅛"	2⅛"	¾"	11"	(2)-¾"MB	19,000	2485	2365	3610	3610	3610	4810	³/₁₆"×8"
HD6	¼"	12½"	2⅞"	3³/₁₆"	3"	1⁷/₈"	1"	14"	(3)-¾"MB	18,600	3730	4895	5410	5410	5410	6080	¼"×2½"
HD7	¼"	11¹¹/₁₆"	3½"	4"	2⁷/₈"	2⅛"	1"	14"	(3)-⅞"MB	28,600	4355	5775	6500	6500	6500	8665	¼"×9½"
HD7	¼"	11¹¹/₁₆"	3½"	4"	2⁷/₈"	2⅛"	1⅛"	15"	(3)-⅞"MB	28,600	4355	5775	7195	7500	7500	9530	¼"×9½"
HD9	¼"	16½"	3½"	4¼"	3³/₈"	2⅛"	1⅛"	27"	(3)-1"MB	—	—	—	—	—	11,210	14,940	¼"×9½" Bottom, ³/₈" ea. face
HD12	¼"	20½"	3½"	4¼"	3³/₈"	2⅛"	1⅛"	32"	(4)-1"MB	48,000	—	—	—	—	14,945	16,000	¼"×9½" Bottom, ³/₈" ea. face
HD15	¼"	24½"	3½"	4¼"	3³/₈"	2⅛"	1¼"	38"	(5)-1"MB	55,300	—	—	—	—	18,336	18,330	¼"×9½" Bottom, ³/₈" ea. face
HD2N	12	7⁷/₈"	2¼"	2"	1½"	1⅛"	⅝"	9"	(2)-⅝"MB	8,800	2070	2520	2520	2520	2520	2520	⅛"×1" (¼" face, ¾" top) ea. side
HD5N	10	9³/₈"	2⅝"	2¼"	2³/₁₆"	1¼"	¾"	11"	(2)-¾"MB	11,600	2485	3265	3610	3610	3610	3610	⅛"×1" (³/₈" face, ⅝" top) ea. side
HD7N	7	12"	3³/₈"	2⁷/₈"	2⁷/₈"	1⁹/₁₆"	1"	14"	(2)-1"MB	20,300	3305	4410	5510	6490	6500	6500	³/₁₆"×1⅛" (½" face, ⅝" top) ea. side

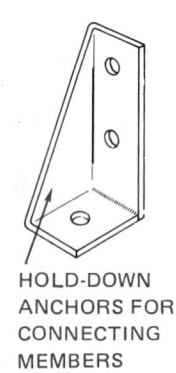

HOLD-DOWN
ANCHORS FOR
CONNECTING
MEMBERS

Figure 21–37 Three of the most common types of metal connectors used on the foundation system. Drafters are often required to use vendor information when drawing foundation plans. *Courtesy Simpson Strong-Tie Company, Inc.*

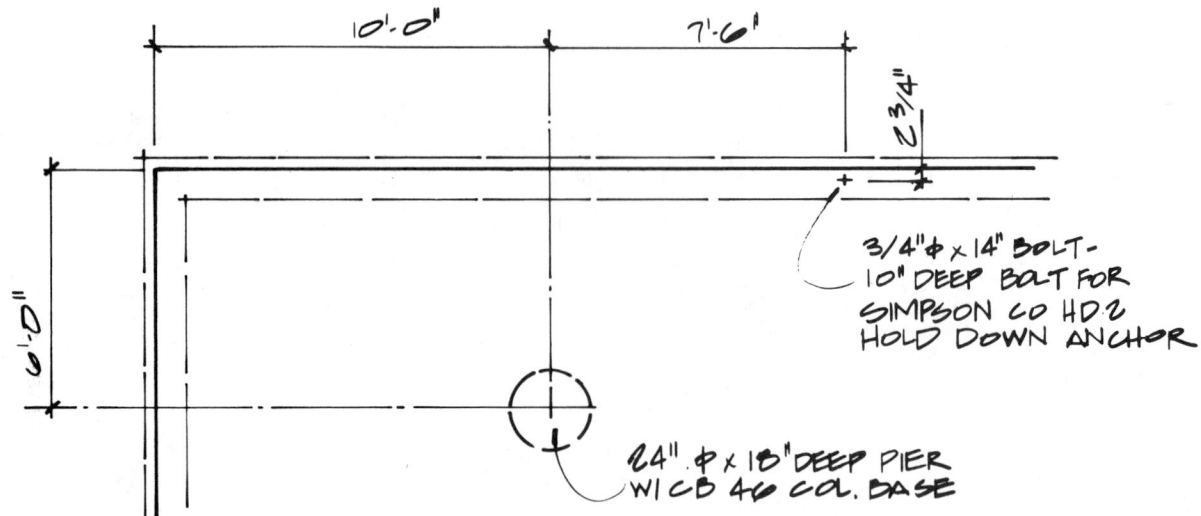

10'-0"   7'-6"   2 3/4"

6'-0"

3/4"⌀ x 14" BOLT-
10" DEEP BOLT FOR
SIMPSON CO HD2
HOLD DOWN ANCHOR

24" ⌀ x 18" DEEP PIER
W/ CB 46 COL. BASE

Figure 21-38 Metal connector locations must be specified on the foundation plan. When centered in a pier, the dimension for the pier will locate the connector. When the connector is in a foundation wall, the connector must be located with dimensions.

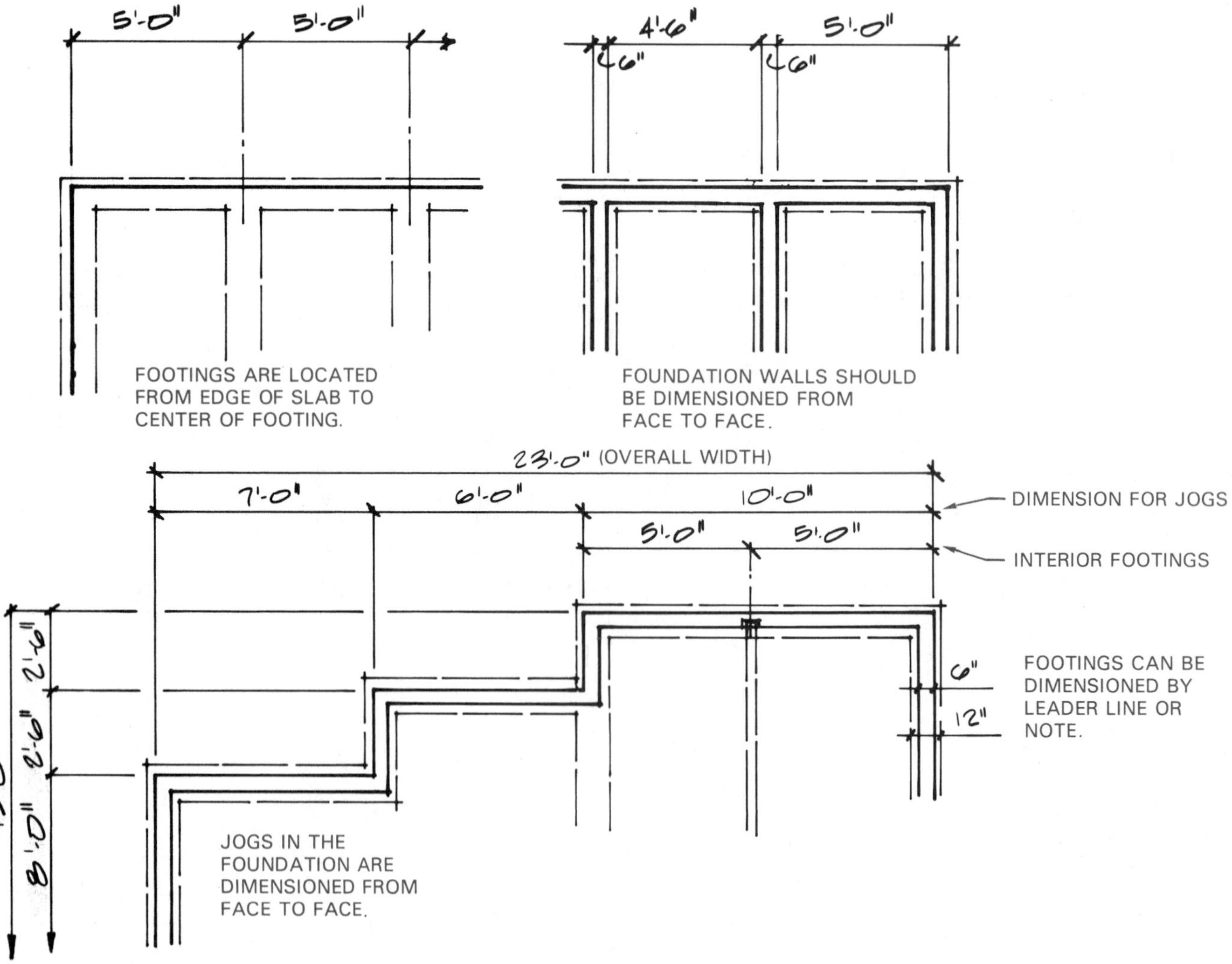

5'-0"   5'-0"

FOOTINGS ARE LOCATED
FROM EDGE OF SLAB TO
CENTER OF FOOTING.

4'-6"   5'-0"
6"   6"

FOUNDATION WALLS SHOULD
BE DIMENSIONED FROM
FACE TO FACE.

23'-0" (OVERALL WIDTH)

7'-0"   6'-0"   10'-0"   ———— DIMENSION FOR JOGS

5'-0"   5'-0"   ———— INTERIOR FOOTINGS

13'-0"   8'-0"   2'-0"   2'-0"

6"

12"

FOOTINGS CAN BE
DIMENSIONED BY
LEADER LINE OR
NOTE.

JOGS IN THE
FOUNDATION ARE
DIMENSIONED FROM
FACE TO FACE.

Figure 21-39 Dimensioning techniques for foundation plans.

FOUNDATION SYSTEMS TEST ▮▮▮▮▮▮▮▮▮▮

DIRECTIONS

Answer the questions with short complete statements or drawings as needed on an 8½ × 11 drawing sheet as follows:

1. Use ⅛ in. guidelines for all lettering.
2. Letter your name, Foundation Systems Test, and the date at the top of the sheet.
3. Letter the question number and provide the answer. You do not need to write out the question.
4. Do all lettering with vertical uppercase architectural letters. If the answer requires line work, use proper drafting tools and technique. Answers may be prepared on a word processor if appropriate with course guidelines.
5. Your grade will be based on correct answers and quality of line technique.

QUESTIONS

1. What are the major parts of the foundation system?
2. What methods are used to determine the size of footings?
3. List five forces that a foundation must withstand.
4. How can the soil texture influence a foundation?
5. List the major types of material used to build foundation walls.
6. Why is steel placed in footings?
7. Describe when a stepped footing might be used.
8. What size footing should be used with a basement wall?
9. What influences the size of piers?
10. Describe the difference between a retaining and a restraining wall.

Chapter 22
Floor Systems and Foundation Support

THE FOUNDATION plan not only shows the concrete footings and walls, but also the members that are used to form the floor. Two common types of floor systems are typically used in residential construction. These include floor systems with a crawl space or cellar below the floor system, and a floor system built at grade level. Each has its own components and information that must be put on a foundation plan.

ON GRADE FOUNDATIONS

A concrete slab is often used for the floor system of either residential or commercial structures. A concrete slab provides a firm floor system with little or no maintenance and generally requires less material and labor than conventional wood floor systems. The floor slab is usually poured as an extension of the foundation wall and footing as shown in Figure 22–1. Other common methods of pouring the foundation and floor system are shown in Figure 22–2.

A 3½ in. concrete slab is the minimum thickness allowed by major building codes for residential floor slabs. Commercial slabs are often 5 or 6 in. thick depending on the floor loads to be supported. The slab is only used as a floor surface and is not used to support the weight of the walls or roof. If load-bearing walls must be supported, the floor slab must be thickened as shown in Figure 22–3. If a load is concentrated in a small area, a pier may be placed under the slab to help disperse the weight as seen in Figure 22–4. Depending on the size of the slab, joints may be placed in the slab. Joints are used so the construction crew can pour several small slabs

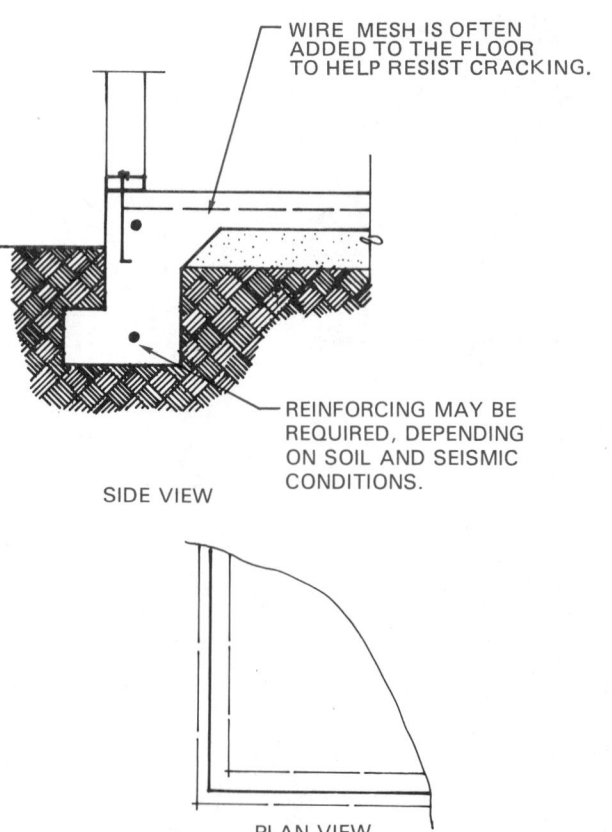

SIDE VIEW

WIRE MESH IS OFTEN ADDED TO THE FLOOR TO HELP RESIST CRACKING.

REINFORCING MAY BE REQUIRED, DEPENDING ON SOIL AND SEISMIC CONDITIONS.

PLAN VIEW

Figure 22–1 The foundation and floor systems can often be constructed in one pour, which saves time and money.

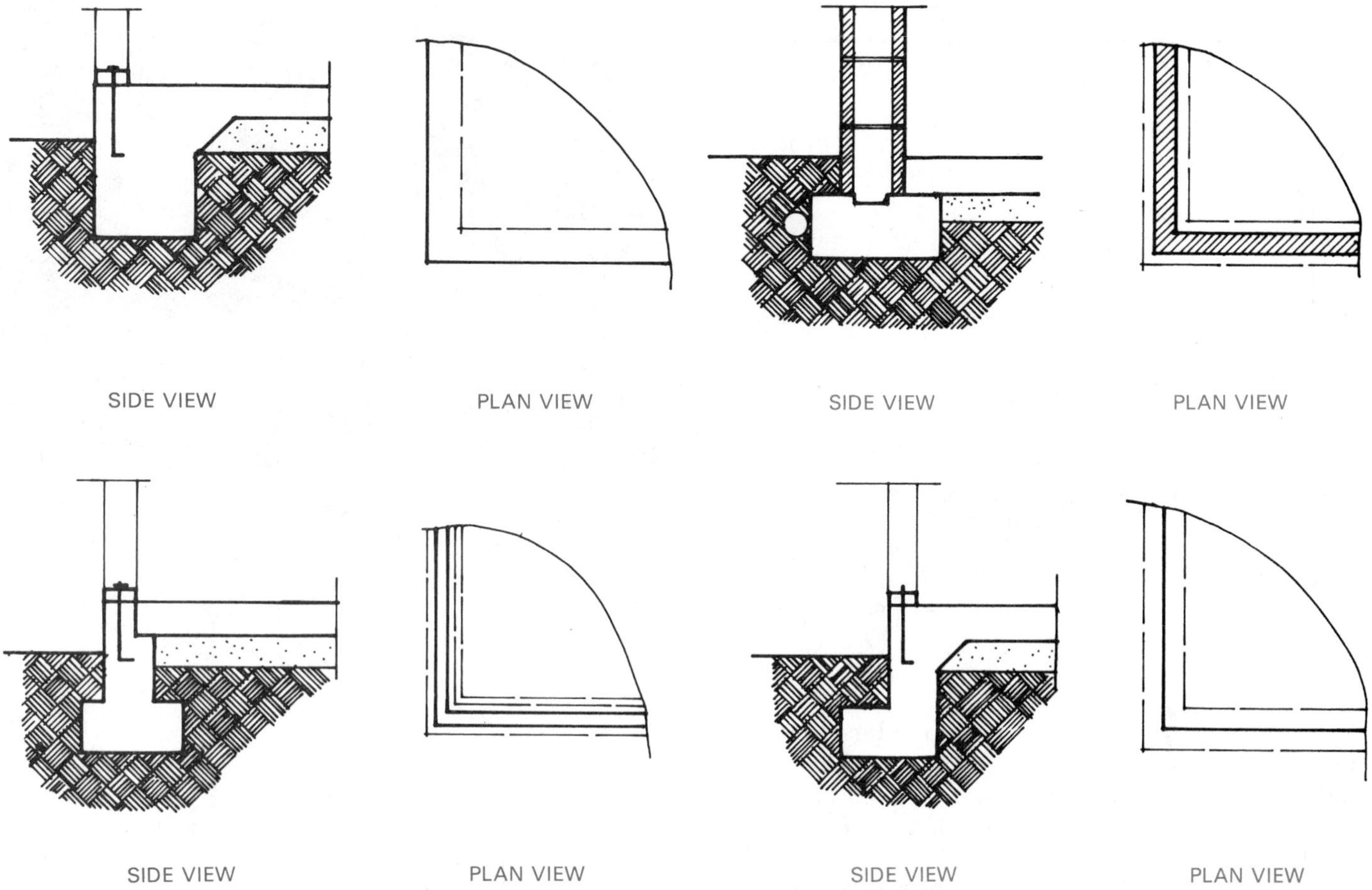

SIDE VIEW	PLAN VIEW	SIDE VIEW	PLAN VIEW

SIDE VIEW	PLAN VIEW	SIDE VIEW	PLAN VIEW

Figure 22–2 Common foundation and slab intersections.

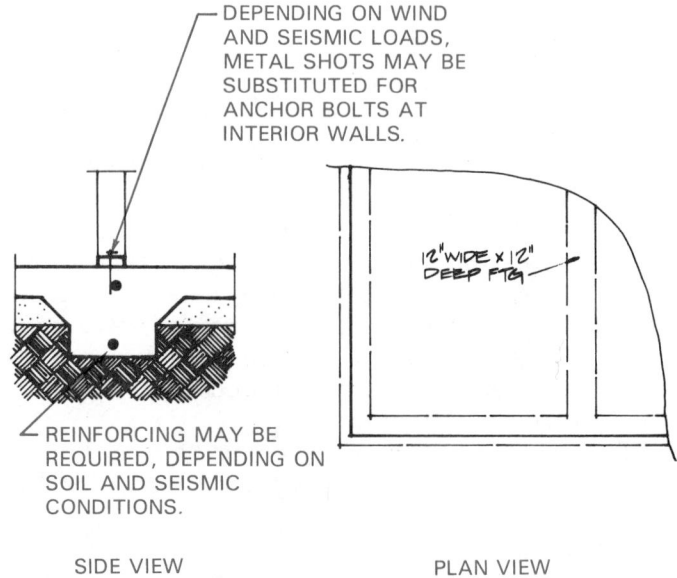

DEPENDING ON WIND AND SEISMIC LOADS, METAL SHOTS MAY BE SUBSTITUTED FOR ANCHOR BOLTS AT INTERIOR WALLS.

12" WIDE × 12" DEEP FTG

REINFORCING MAY BE REQUIRED, DEPENDING ON SOIL AND SEISMIC CONDITIONS.

SIDE VIEW   PLAN VIEW

Figure 22–3 Footing and floor intersections at an interior load-bearing wall.

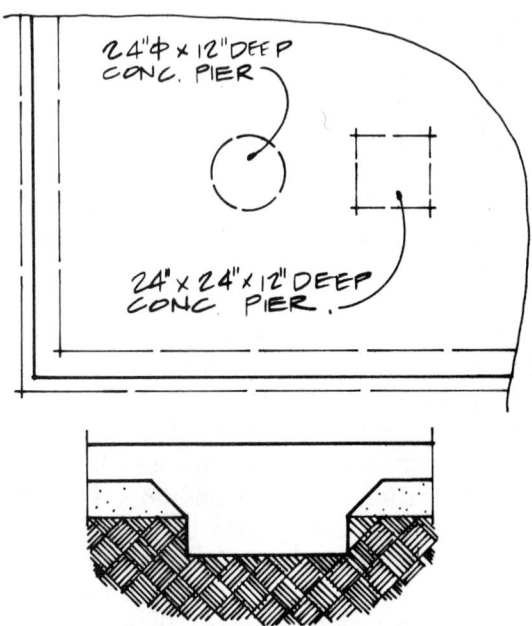

24"Φ × 12" DEEP CONC. PIER

24" × 24" × 12" DEEP CONC. PIER.

Figure 22–4 A concrete pier can be poured under loads concentrated in small areas. Piers are typically round or rectangular with the size of the pier determined by the load to be supported.

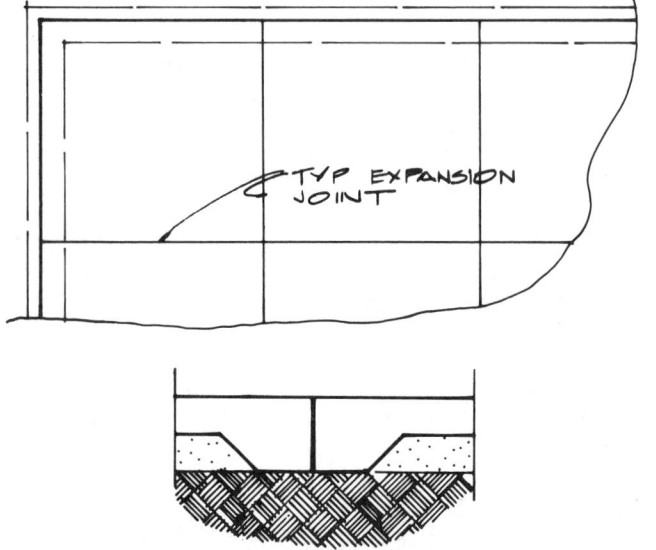

Figure 22–5 Control joints are often placed in large slabs to resist cracking and to allow the construction crew manageable areas to pour.

Figure 22–6 Welded wire mesh is often placed in concrete slabs to help reduce cracking.

instead of one large one and to help reduce the spread of cracks throughout the slab. By using control or expansion joints, any cracks that develop in one area will not spread to other areas of the slab. Control joints can be seen in Figure 22–5.

The slab may be placed either above, below or at grade level. Residential slabs are rarely placed above grade because of the expense of filling the area between the slab and the natural grade level. Slabs below grade are most commonly used in basements. When used at grade, the slab is usually placed just above grade level. Most building codes require the top of the slab to be eight inches above the finish grade to keep structural wood away from the ground moisture.

No matter where the slab is placed, it must be placed on a 4-in.-minimum base of compacted sand or gravel fill. The area for which the building is designed will dictate the type of fill material that is typically used. The fill material provides a level base for the concrete slab and helps eliminate cracking in the slab caused by settling of the ground under the slab. The fill material is not shown on the foundation plan but is specified with a note.

When the slab is placed on more than 4 in. of uncompacted fill, mesh should be placed in the slab to help resist cracking. Typically a steel mesh of number 10 wire in 6 in. grids is used for residential floor slabs. Figure 22–6 shows an example of the mesh used in concrete slabs. In commercial buildings, steel reinforcing bars may also be used to resist floor cracking. Generally the mesh or steel is not shown on the foundation plan but is specified by note.

In most areas, the slab is required to be placed over 6 mil polyethylene sheet plastic to protect the

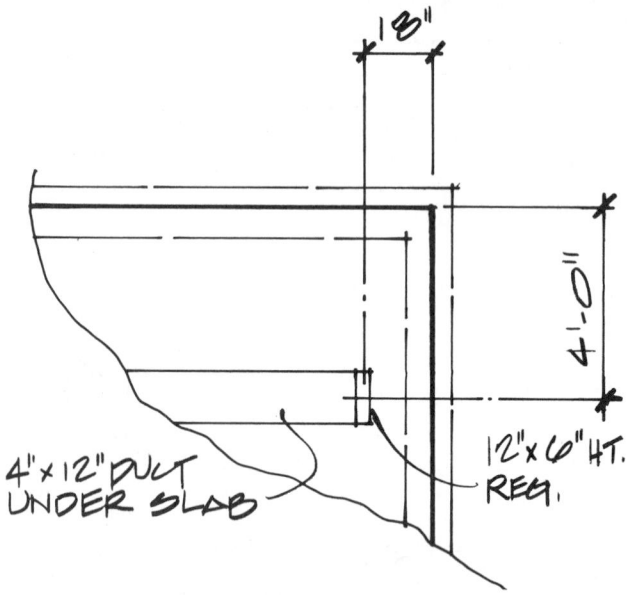

Figure 22–7 HVAC ducts and registers that are to be located in the floor must be located on the foundation plan.

floor from ground moisture. This vapor barrier is not drawn but specified with a general note on the foundation plan. Depending on the risk of freezing, a layer of rigid insulation may be placed under the slab at the perimeter to help reduce heat loss from the floor into the ground.

Plumbing and heating ducts must be placed under the slab before the concrete is poured. On residential plans plumbing is usually not shown on the foundation plan. Generally the skills of the plumbing contractor are relied on for the placement of required utilities. If heating ducts are to be run under the slab, they are usually drawn on the foundation plan as shown in Figure 22–7. Drawings for commercial construction usually include both a plumbing and mechanical plan.

Some codes require the slab to be placed over 6 ml. vapor barrier over 2″ of sand and 4″ of gravel.

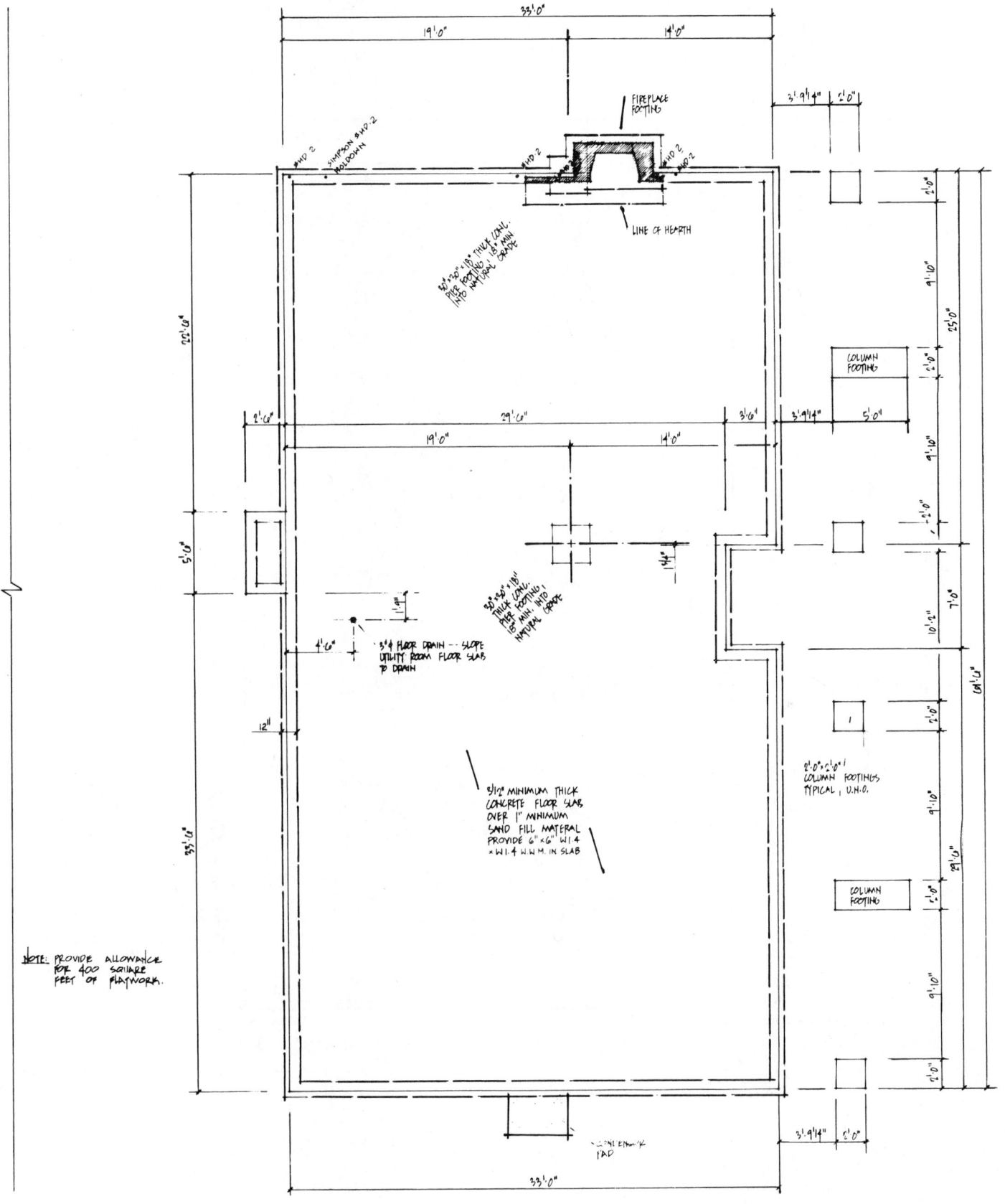

Figure 22–8 A foundation plan for a residence with a concrete slab. *Courtesy Ken Smith Drafting.*

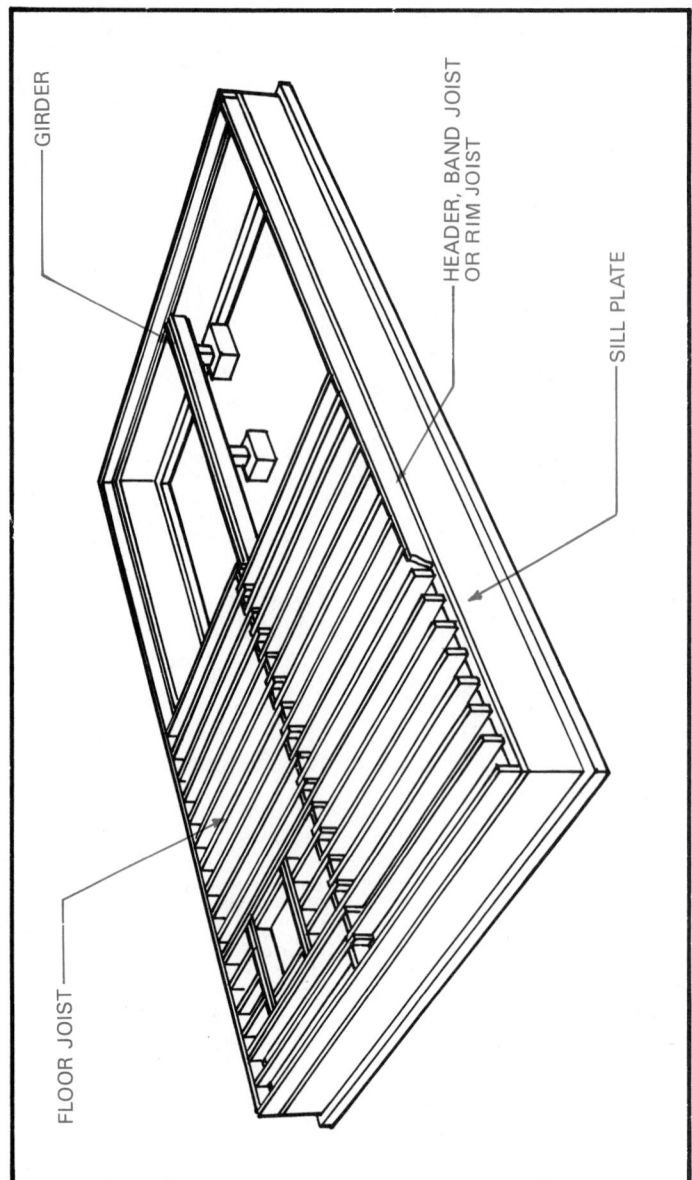

Figure 22-9 A joist floor system uses individual framing members placed at 12, 16, or 24 in. O.C. to support the subfloor.

Common Components Shown on a Slab Foundation

Refer to Figure 22–8. Dimensions are needed for each of the following items to provide location information.

- Outline of slab
- Interior footing locations
- Changes in floor level
- Floor drains
- Exterior footing locations
- Ducts for mechanical
- Metal anchors
- Patio slabs

Common Components Specified by Note Only

See Figure 22–8.

- Slab thickness and fill material
- Wire mesh
- Mudsill size
- Vapor barriers
- Pier sizes
- Assumed soil strength
- Reinforcing steel
- Anchor bolt size and spacing
- Insulation
- Slab slopes
- Concrete strength

CRAWL SPACE FLOOR SYSTEMS

The crawl space is the area formed between the floor system and the ground. Building codes require a minimum of 18 in. from the bottom of the floor to the ground and 12 in. from the bottom of beams to the ground. Two common methods of providing a crawl space below the floor are the conventional method using floor joists and the post-and-beam system. An introduction to each system is needed to complete the foundation. Both floor systems will be discussed in detail in relationship to the entire structure in Section 6.

Joist Floor Framing

The most common method of framing a wood floor is with wood members called floor joists. Floor joists are used to span between the foundation walls. The floor joists are usually placed at 16 in. on center, but the spacing of joists may change depending on the span and the load to be supported. Section 12 will provide a complete explanation of joist spans and sizing.

Figure 22–9 shows a floor system framed with joists or stick framing methods. To construct this

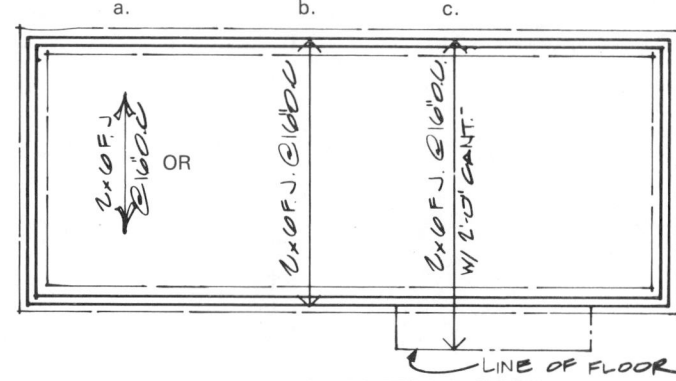

a. AN ARROW REPRESENTS THE DIRECTION OF SPAN AND SPACING.

b. AN ARROW IS DRAWN FROM BEARING POINT TO BEARING POINT.

c. WHEN FLOOR JOISTS EXTEND PAST THE FOUNDATION WALL, THE LENGTH SHOULD BE SHOWN.

Figure 22–10 Common methods of representing floor joists in plan view.

type of floor, a pressure-treated sill is bolted to the top of the foundation wall with the anchor bolts that were placed when the foundation was formed. The floor joists can then be nailed to the sill. With the floor joists in place, plywood floor sheathing is installed to provide a base for the finish floor. Figure 22–10 shows common methods of drawing floor joists on the foundation plan.

When the distance between the foundation walls is too great for the floor joists to span, a girder is used to support the joists. A girder is a horizontal load-bearing member that spans between two or more supports at the foundation level. Depending on the load to be supported and the area you are in, either a wood or steel member may be used for the girder and for the support post. The girder is usually supported in a beam pocket where it intersects the foundation wall. A concrete pier is put under the post to resist settling. Figure 22–11 shows methods of drawing the girders, posts, piers, and beam pocket on the foundation plan.

Common Components Shown with a Joist Floor System

See Figure 22–12. Unless indicated with an (*), all components require dimensions to provide location information.

- Foundation wall
- Door opening in foundation wall
- Fireplace
- Floor joist
- Girders (bearing walls & floor support)
- Girder pockets
- Crawl access*

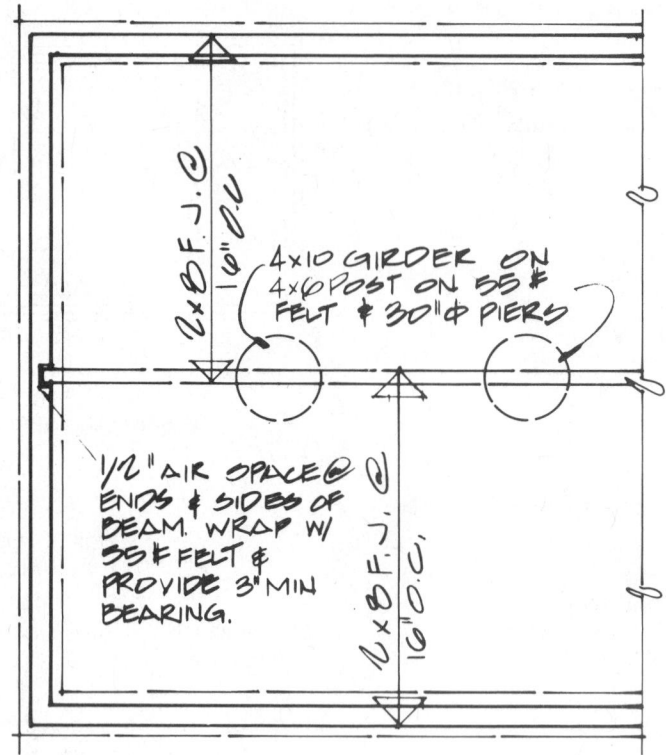

2×8 F.J. @ 16" O.C.

4×10 GIRDER ON
4×6 POST ON 55#
FELT & 30"Φ PIERS

1/2" AIR SPACE @
ENDS & SIDES OF
BEAM. WRAP W/
55# FELT &
PROVIDE 3" MIN
BEARING.

2×8 F.J. @ 16" O.C.

Figure 22-11 Common methods of foundation components in plan view.

- Exterior footings
- Metal anchors
- Fireplace footings
- Outline of cantilevers
- Interior piers
- Changes in floor levels
- Vents for crawl space*

Common Components Specified by Note Only

See Figure 22-12.

- Floor joist size and spacing
- Anchor bolt size and spacing
- Insulation
- Crawl height
- Assumed soil strength
- Subfloor material
- Girder size
- Mudsill size
- Vapor barrier
- Concrete strength
- Wood type and grade

Post-and-beam Floor Systems

A post-and-beam floor system is built using a standard foundation system. Rather than having floor joists span between the foundation walls, a series of beams are used to support the subfloor as shown in Figure 22-13. Once the mudsill is bolted to the foundation wall the beams are placed so that the top of each beam is flush with the top of the mudsill. The beams are usually placed at 48 in. on center but the spacing can vary depending on the size of the floor decking to be used. Generally 2-in.-thick material is used to span between the beams to form the subfloor.

The beams are supported by wooden posts as they span between the foundation walls. Posts are usually placed about 8 ft on center but spacing varies depending on the load to be supported. Each post is supported by a concrete pier. Beams, posts, and piers can be drawn on the foundation plan as shown in Figure 22-14.

Common Components Shown for a Post-and-beam System

See Figure 22-15. Unless indicated with an (*), all components require dimensions to provide location information.

- Foundation wall
- Openings in wall for doors
- Fireplace
- Girders (Beams)
- Girder pockets
- Crawl access*
- Exterior footings
- Metal anchors
- Fireplace footings
- Piers
- Changes in floor levels
- Vents for crawl space*

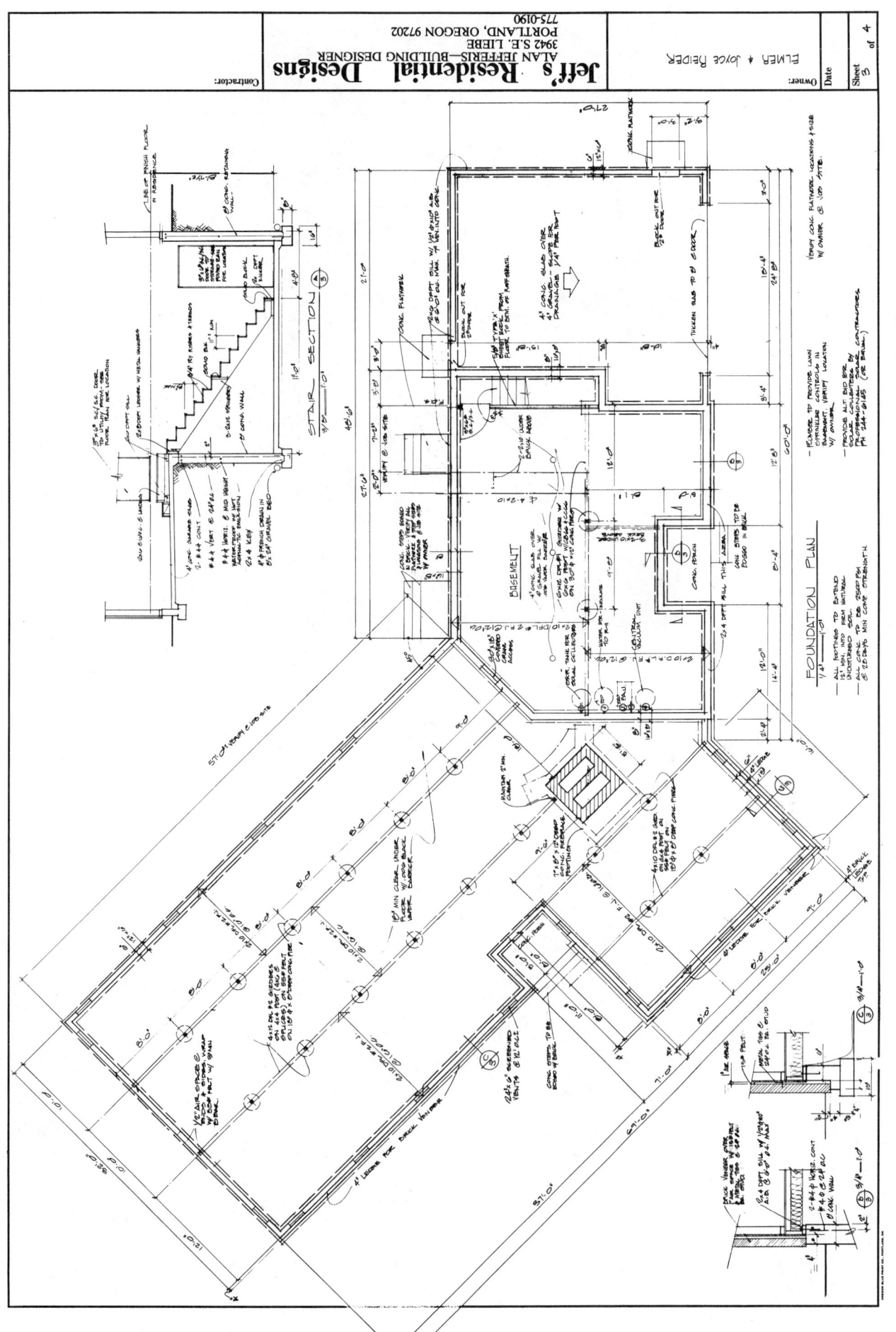

Figure 22-12 A foundation plan for a residence with floor joist. Courtesy of Jeff's Residential Designs.

Figure 22–13 A post-and-beam floor system on a traditional foundation system. Beams are usually placed at 48 in. O.C., with supports placed at approximately 8′–0″ O.C.

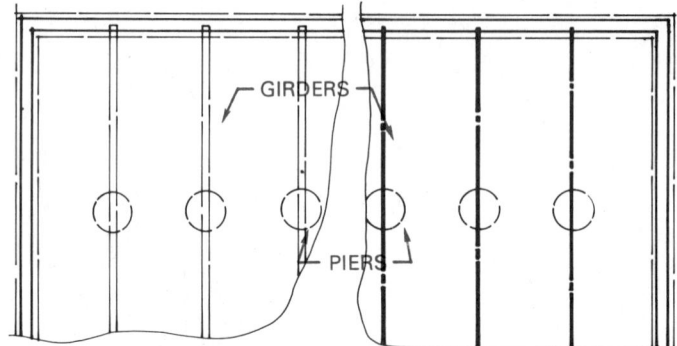

Figure 22–14 Common methods of drawing post-and-beam components in plan view.

Common Components Specified by Note Only

See Figure 22–15.

- Anchor bolt spacing
- Mudsill size
- Insulation
- Minimum crawl height
- Subfloor material
- Girder size
- Vapor barrier
- Concrete strength
- Wood type and grade
- Assumed soil strength

Combined Floor Methods

Floor and foundation methods may be combined depending on the building site. This is typically done on partially sloping lots when part of a structure may be constructed with a slab and part of the structure with a joist floor system as seen in Figure 22–16.

One component typically used when floor systems are combined is a ledger. A ledger is used to provide support for floor joist and subfloor when they intersect the concrete. Unless felt is placed between the concrete and the ledger, the ledger must be pressure-treated lumber. The ledger can be shown on the foundation plan as shown in Figure 22–17.

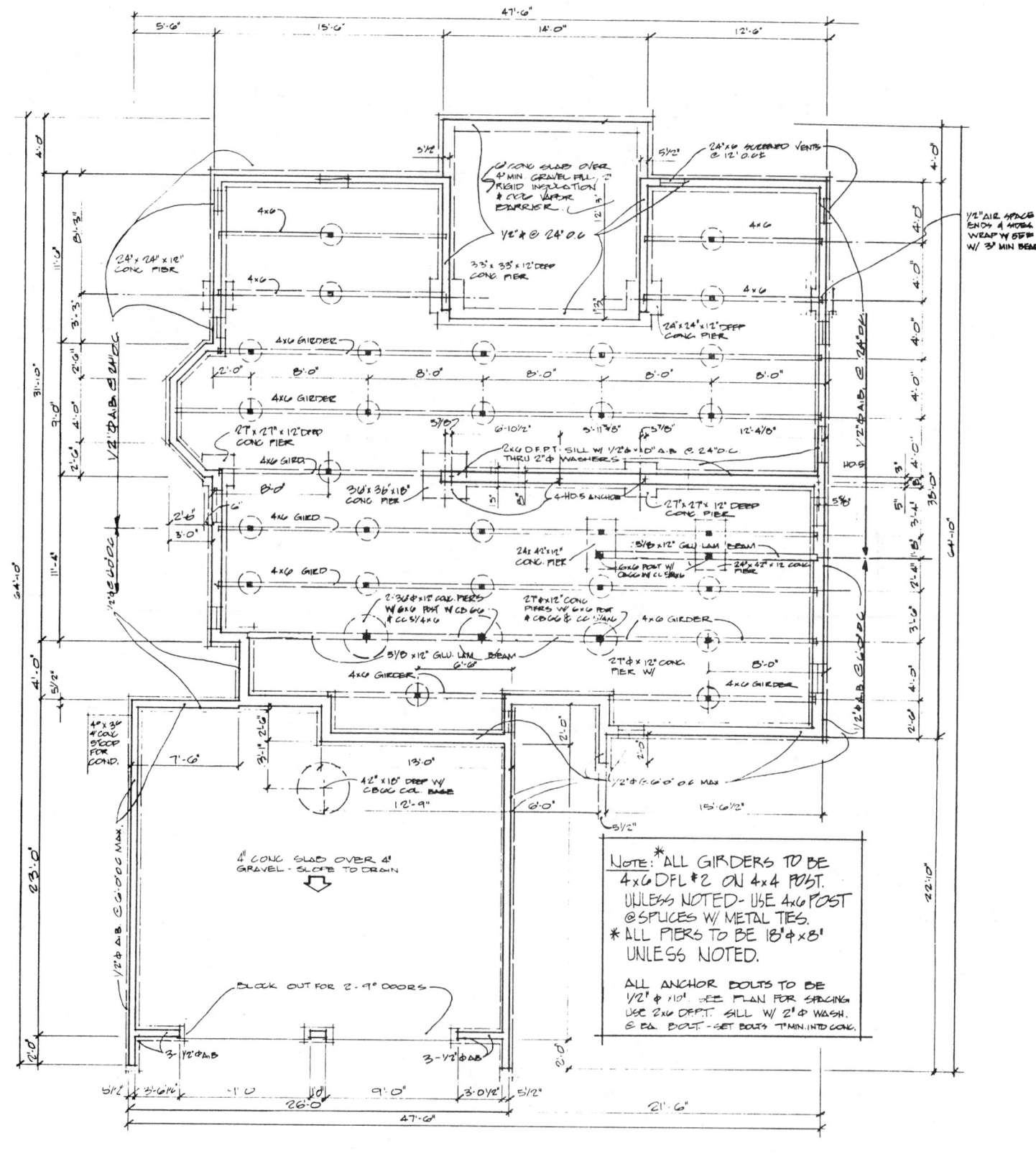

FOUNDATION PLAN

1/4" = 1'-0"

ALL CONC TO BE 2500 PSI @ 28 DAYS MIN. COMP. STRENGTH.
ALL FOOTINGS TO REST ON FIRM, NATURAL UNDISTURBED SOIL.
CRAWL SPACE TO HAVE 18" MIN CLEAR - BTM OF FLOOR TO GRADE - COVER W/ .006 BLACK VAPOR BARRIER

Figure 22–15 A foundation plan for a residence with a post-and-beam floor system.

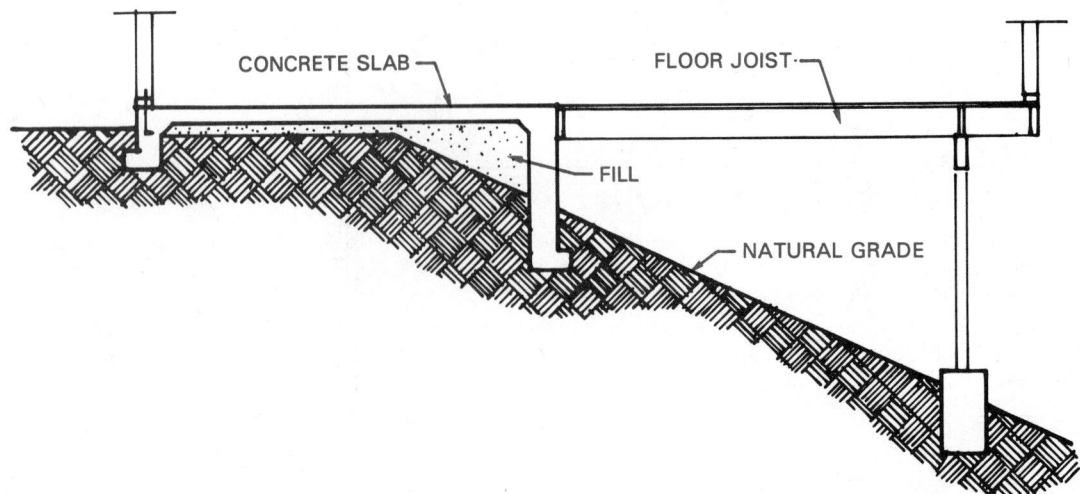

Figure 22–16 Concrete slab and floor joist systems are often combined on sloping sites to help minimize fill material.

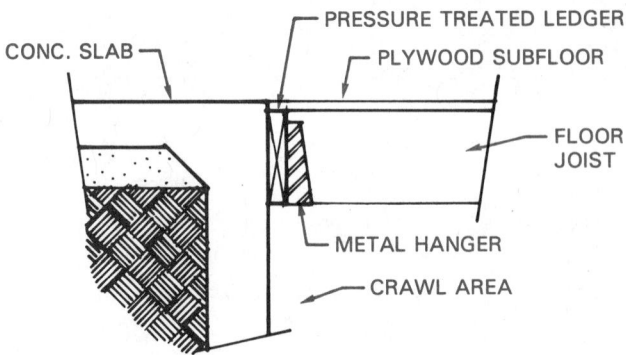

Figure 22–17 A ledger is used to provide anchorage to floor joists where they intersect the concrete slab. Metal joist hangers are used to join the joists to the ledger.

FLOOR SYSTEMS AND FOUNDATION SUPPORT TEST

DIRECTIONS

Answer the questions with short complete statements or drawings as needed on an 8½ × 11 drawing sheet as follows:

1. Use ⅛ in. guidelines for all lettering.
2. Letter your name, Floor Systems and Foundation Support Test, and the date at the top of the sheet.
3. Letter the question number and provide the answer. You do not need to write out the question.
4. Do all lettering with vertical uppercase architectural letters. If the answer requires line work, use proper drafting tools and technique. Answers may be prepared on a word processor if appropriate with course guidelines.
5. Your grade will be based on correct answers and quality of line technique.

QUESTIONS

1. Why is a concrete slab called an on grade floor system?
2. What is the minimum thickness for a residential slab?
3. Why are control joints placed in slabs?
4. What is the minimum amount of fill placed under a slab?
5. What thickness of vapor barrier is to be placed under a slab?
6. What is the minimum height required in the crawl area?
7. What is the purpose of a girder?
8. How are floor joists attached to the foundation wall?
9. How are girders supported at the foundation wall?
10. What is a common spacing for beams in a post-and-beam floor?

Chapter 23
Foundation-Plan Layout

THE FOUNDATION plan is typically drawn at the same scale as the floor plan that it will support. Although the floor plan can be traced to obtain overall sizes, this practice can lead to major errors in the foundation plan. If you trace a floor plan that is slightly out of scale, you will reproduce the same errors in the foundation plan. A better method is to draw the foundation plan using the dimensions that are found on a print of the floor plan. If the foundation cannot be drawn using the dimensions on the floor plan, your floor plan may be missing dimensions or contain errors. Great care needs to be taken with the foundation plan. If the foundation plan is not accurate, changes may be required that affect the entire structure.

This chapter includes guidelines for several types of foundation plans which include joist construction, concrete slab, basement slab and joist, post and beam, and a piling foundation. Each is based on the floor plan that was used for examples in Section 3. Before attempting to draw a foundation plan, study the completed plan that precedes each example so you will know what the finished drawing should look like.

The foundation plan can be drawn by dividing the work into the six stages of foundation layout, drawing foundation members, drawing floor framing members, dimensioning, lettering, and evaluation. As you progress through the drawing, you will use several types of line quality. For layout steps, construction lines in nonreproducible blue or with a 6H lead will be best. When drawing finished quality lines, use the following:

A 5 mm lead, #0 pen, or sharp 3H lead for thin lines

A 7 mm lead, #2 pen, or sharp H lead for bold lines

A 9 mm lead, #3 pen, or H lead and draw two parallel lines very close for very bold lines

FOUNDATION PLAN WITH JOIST CONSTRUCTION

The following steps can be used to draw a foundation plan showing continuous footings and floor joists. When complete, your drawing should resemble Figure 23–1. Use construction lines for steps 1 through 9. Each step can be seen in Figure 23–2.

Step 1. Using the dimensions on your floor plan, lay out the exterior face of the foundation wall.

Step 2. Determine the foundation wall thickness and lay out the interior face of the foundation wall. See Figure 21–6 for a review of foundation footing and wall dimensions.

Step 3. Block out doors in the garage area. Typically the door size plus 4 in. is provided as the foundation is formed. This extra space allows for door framing.

Step 4. Block out a 30-in.-wide minimum crawl access.

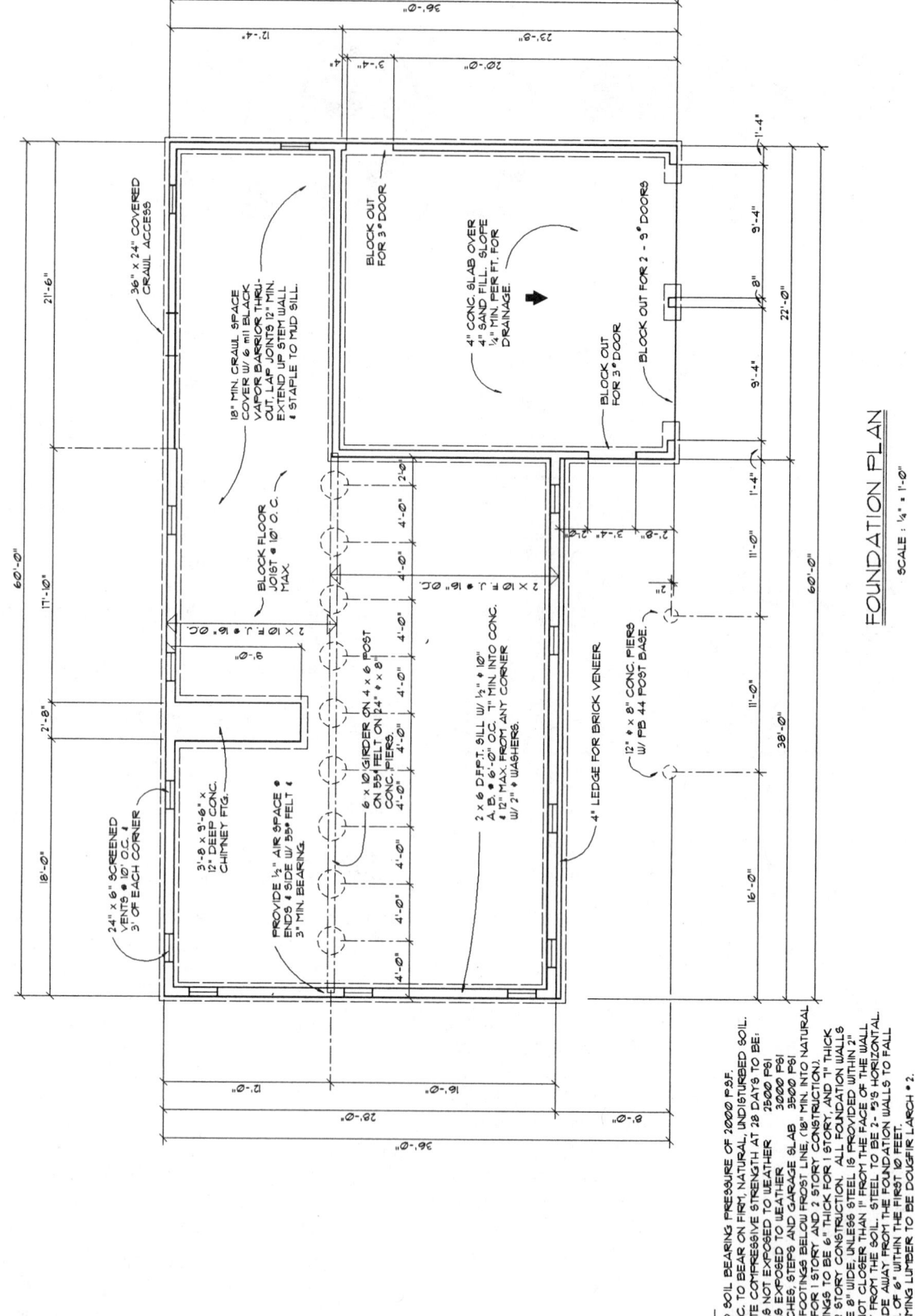

Figure 23-1 A foundation plan using joist construction.

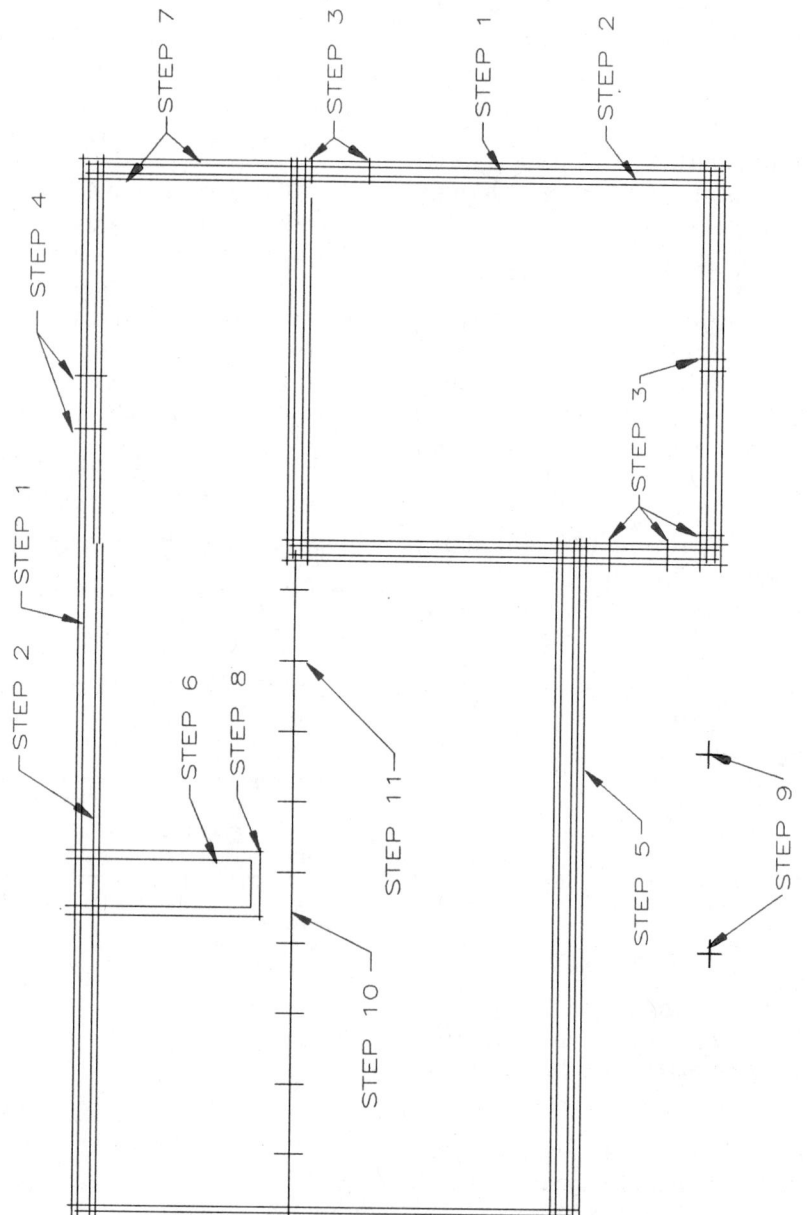

Figure 23-2 Initial layout of a foundation plan with joist construction.

Step 5. Lay out a support ledge if masonry veneer is to be used.

Step 6. Lay out the size of the fireplace using the measurements on the floor plan.

Step 7. Lay out the footing width around the perimeter. See Figure 21–6.

Step 8. Lay out the footing under the fireplace so that it extends a minimum of 6 in. past the face of the fireplace.

Step 9. Lay out any exterior piers required for porches or deck support.

Step 10. Lay out girder locations to support floor joists and load-bearing walls and changes in floor elevation.

Step 11. Locate the center of all support piers.

Step 12. Darken all items drawn in steps 1 through 9. Use bold lines to represent the materials drawn in steps 1 through 6. Use thin dashed lines for steps 7 through 9. When finished with this step, your drawing should resemble Figure 23–3.

See Figure 23–4 for steps 13 through 18. The items to be drawn in these steps are not drawn with construction lines. Because of their simplicity these items can be drawn using finished lines and need not be traced.

Step 13. Using thin dashed lines, draw the girders with the proper thickness.

Step 14. Draw arrows to represent the floor joist direction.

Step 15. Draw the piers to support the girders using thin lines.

Step 16. Draw beam pockets with thin lines.

Step 17. Draw 24-in. length vents in the walls surrounding the crawl space. Use bold lines to represent the edges and thin lines to represent the vent.

Step 18. Crosshatch the masonry chimney using thin lines if concrete blocks are used.

You now have all of the information drawn that is required to represent the floor and foundation systems. Follow steps 19 through 24 to dimension these items. Use thin lines for all extension and dimension lines. When complete, your drawing should resemble Figure 23–5.

Step 19. Draw extension and dimension lines to locate the overall size on each side of the foundation.

Step 20. Draw extension and dimension lines to locate the jogs in the foundation wall.

Step 21. Draw extension and dimension lines to locate door openings in the foundation wall.

Step 22. Draw extension and dimension lines to locate the fireplace.

Step 23. Draw extension and dimension lines to locate all girders and piers. Place extension lines on the outside of the foundation if possible.

Step 24. Draw extension and dimension lines to locate all metal connectors.

All materials have now been drawn and located. The final drawing procedure is to place dimensions and specify the material to be used. This is done with general and local notes in a method similar to that which was used on the floor plan. Figure 23–6 shows how the notes might appear on the foundation plan. Use the following steps as a guideline to completing the foundation plan.

Step 25. Compute all dimensions and place them in their appropriate locations.

Step 26. Neatly letter all required general notes.

Step 27. Neatly letter all required local notes.

Step 28. Place a title and scale under the drawing.

Step 29. Use a print of your plan to evaluate your drawing using the following checklist.

FOUNDATION-PLAN CHECKLIST	
CORRECT SYMBOL & LOCATION	**CORRECT STRUCTURAL MATERIALS**
Walls	Proper footing sizes
Footings	Proper wall size
Crawl access	Proper beam placement
Vents	Proper beam size
Doors	Proper joist size and direction
Girders	Proper pier locations and sizes
Joist	
Piers	
REQUIRED LOCAL NOTES	
Joist size and spacing	Veneer ledges
Beam sizes	Door blockouts
Beam pockets	Fireplace footing size
Metal connectors	Vent size and spacing
Anchor bolts and mudsill	
Garage slab thickness	
Fill and slope direction	
REQUIRED GENERAL NOTES	**REQUIRED DIMENSIONS**
Soil bearing information	Overall
Concrete strength	Jogs
Crawl space covering	Openings
Framing lumber grade and species	Girder locations
	Pier locations
	Metal connectors

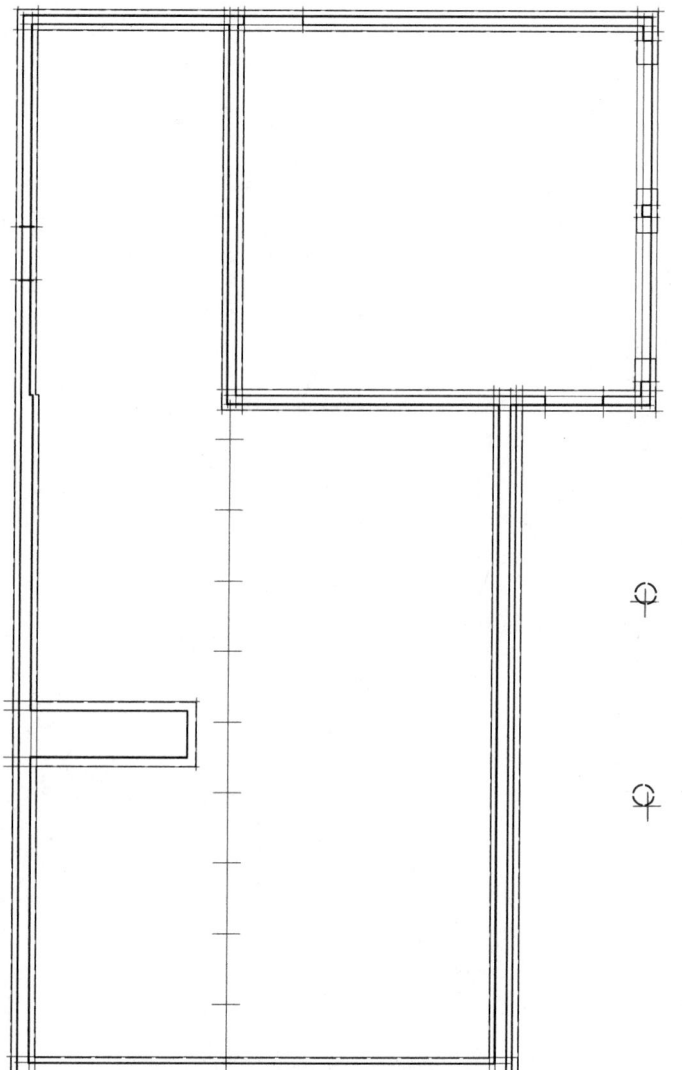

Figure 23-3 Darken all items drawn in steps 1 through 11.

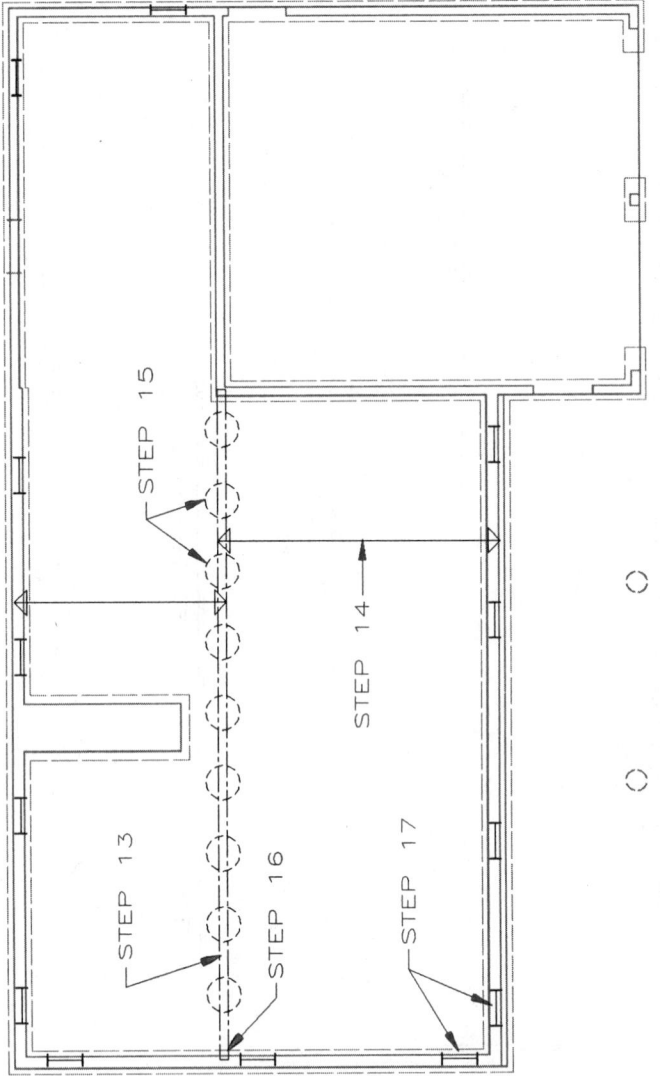

Figure 23–4 Draw floor members with finished quality lines.

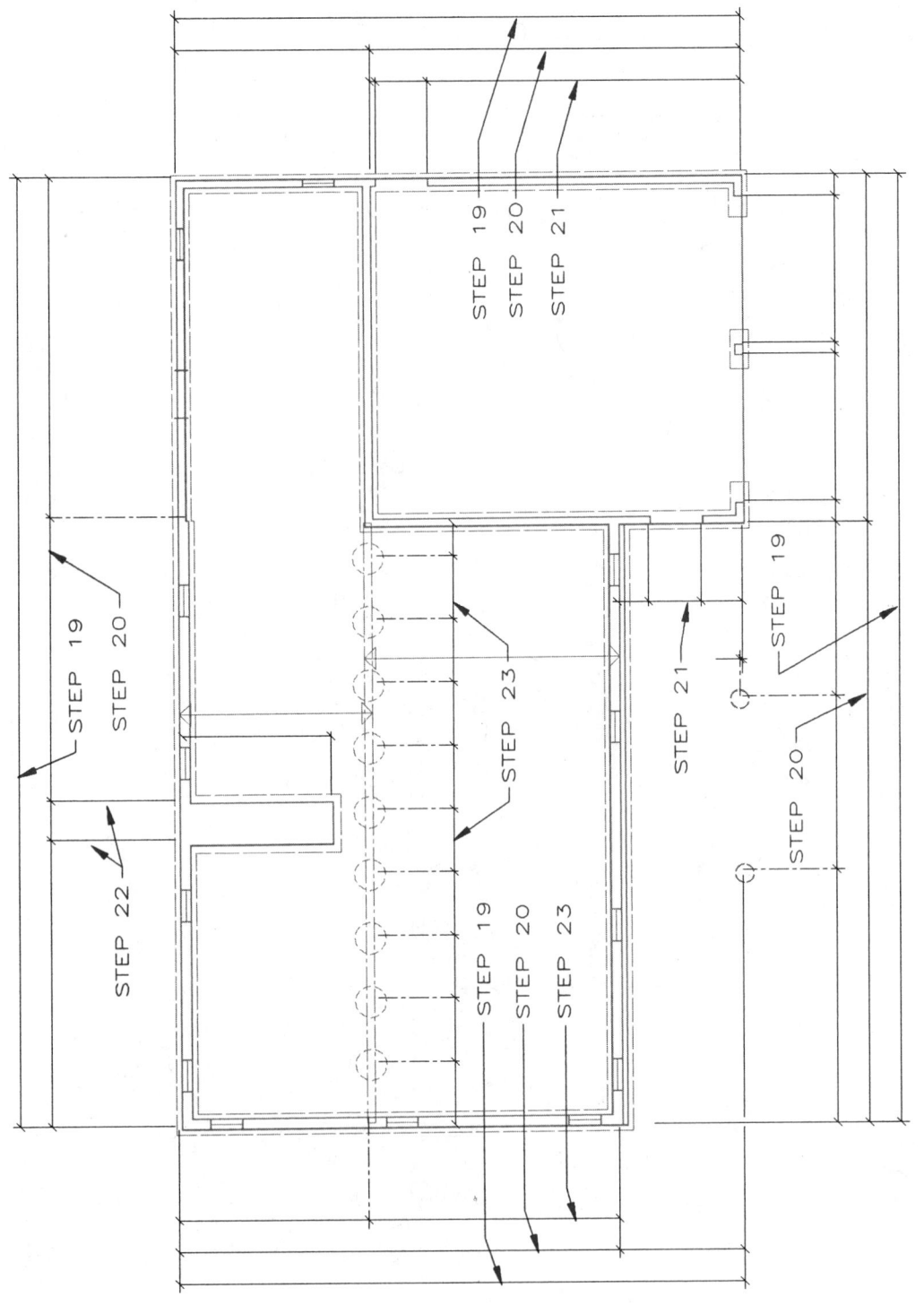

Figure 23-5 Prepared for dimensions.

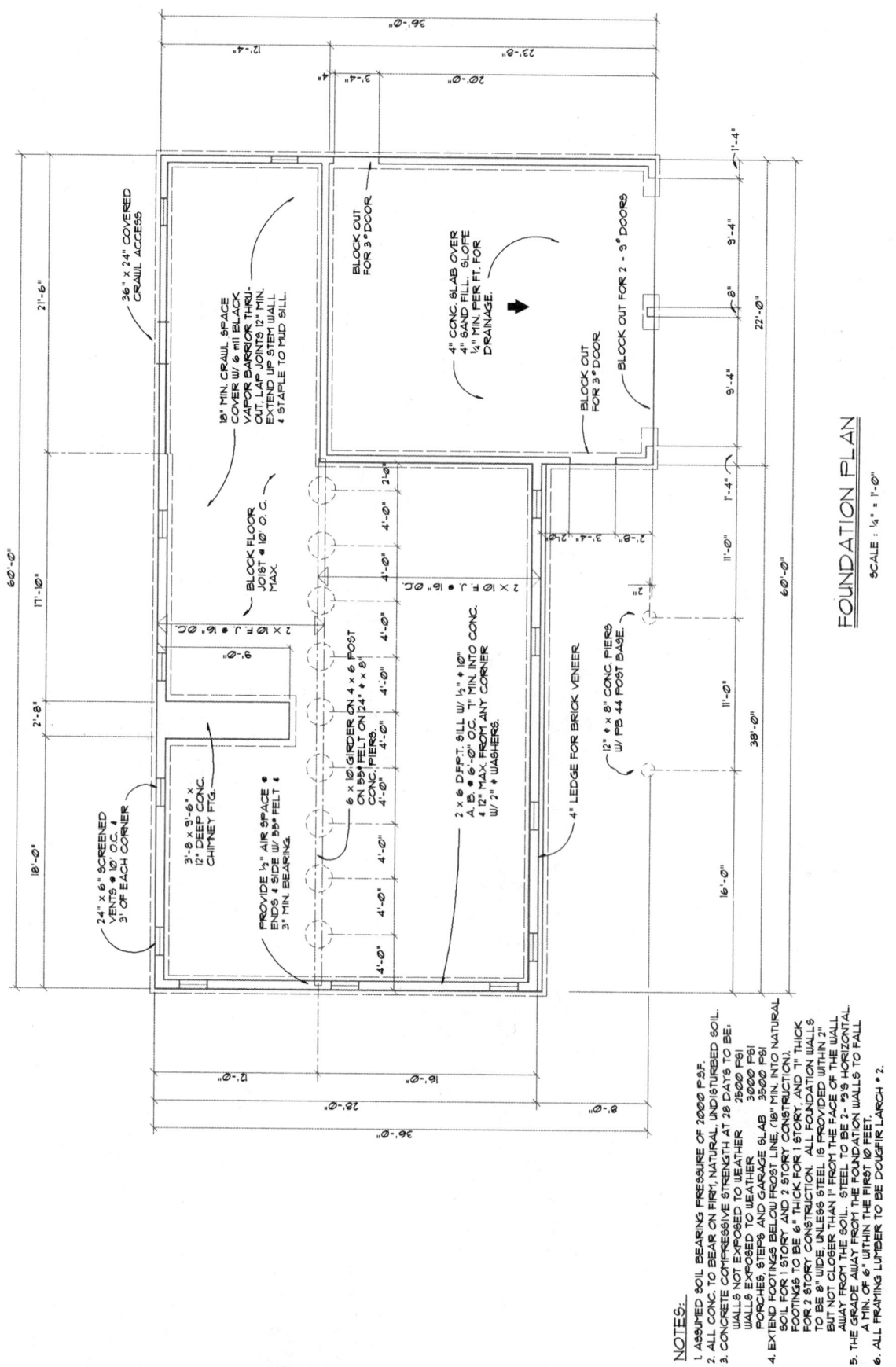

FOUNDATION PLAN

SCALE : 1/4" = 1'-0"

NOTES:

1. ASSUMED SOIL BEARING PRESSURE OF 2000 P.S.F.
2. ALL CONC. TO BEAR ON FIRM, NATURAL, UNDISTURBED SOIL.
3. CONCRETE COMPRESSIVE STRENGTH AT 28 DAYS TO BE:
   WALLS NOT EXPOSED TO WEATHER   2500 PSI
   WALLS EXPOSED TO WEATHER   3000 PSI
   PORCHES, STEPS AND GARAGE SLAB   3500 PSI
4. EXTEND FOOTINGS BELOW FROST LINE, 18" MIN. INTO NATURAL
   SOIL FOR 1 STORY AND 2 STORY CONSTRUCTION).
   FOOTINGS TO BE 6" THICK FOR 1 STORY, AND 7" THICK
   FOR 2 STORY CONSTRUCTION. ALL FOUNDATION WALLS
   TO BE 8" WIDE, UNLESS STEEL IS PROVIDED WITHIN 2"
   BUT NOT CLOSER THAN 1" FROM THE FACE OF THE WALL
   AWAY FROM THE SOIL. STEEL TO BE 2 - #5'S HORIZONTAL
5. THE GRADE AWAY FROM THE FOUNDATION WALLS TO FALL
   A MIN. OF 6" WITHIN THE FIRST 10 FEET.
6. ALL FRAMING LUMBER TO BE DOUGFIR LARCH #2.

Figure 23-6 Dimensions and notes added.

CONCRETE SLAB FOUNDATION LAYOUT

A concrete slab is drawn using a method similar to the foundation plan with joist construction. When the concrete slab foundation is complete, it should resemble the plan shown in Figure 23-7. Use construction lines for steps 1 through 9. Each step can be seen in Figure 23-8.

Step 1. Using the dimensions on your floor plan, lay out the exterior edge of the slab. The edge of the slab should match the exterior side of the exterior walls on the floor plan.

Step 2. Draw the interior side of the stem wall around the slab at the garage area. See Figure 21-6 for a review of foundation dimensions.

Step 3. Block out doors in the stem walls. Allow for the door size plus 4 in.

Step 4. Lay out a support ledge if brick veneer is to be used.

Step 5. Lay out the exterior footing width. See Figure 21-6 for a review of foundation sizes.

Step 6. Lay out the size of the fireplace based on measurements from the floor plan.

Step 7. Lay out the fireplace footing so that it extends 6 in. minimum beyond the face of the fireplace.

Step 8. Lay out interior footings.

Step 9. Lay out any exterior piers that might be required for decks or porches.

Step 10. Darken all items that were drawn in steps 1 through 9. Use bold lines to draw steps 1 through 4 with finished line quality. Use thin dashed lines to draw steps 4, 7, 8, and 9 with finished line quality. Your drawing should now resemble the drawing in Figure 23-9.

See Figure 23-10 for steps 11 through 14. Because the following items are simple, they can be drawn without the use of construction lines. These items may or may not be required depending on your plan.

Step 11. Draw changes in the floor levels.

Step 12. Draw metal connectors.

Step 13. Draw floor drains.

Step 14. Draw heating registers.

You now have all of the information drawn that is required to represent the floor and foundation systems. Follow steps 15 through 20 to place the required dimensions on the drawing. Use thin lines for all extension and dimension lines. Your drawing should resemble Figure 23-11 when complete.

Step 15. Draw extension and dimension lines to locate the overall size on each side of the foundation.

Step 16. Draw the extension and dimension lines to locate jogs in the foundation walls.

Step 17. Draw the extension and dimension lines to locate door openings in the stem wall.

Step 18. Draw the leader and dimension lines to locate interior footings.

Step 19. Draw the leader and dimension lines to locate the fireplace.

Step 20. Draw the leader and dimension lines to locate heating and plumbing materials.

The final drawing procedure is to place dimensions and specify the materials that are to be used. Figure 23-12 is an example of the notes that are required on the foundation. Use the following steps to complete the foundation plan.

Step 21. Compute and neatly letter all dimensions in the appropriate location.

Step 22. Neatly letter all required general notes.

Step 23. Neatly letter all required local notes.

Step 24. Place a title and scale under drawing.

Step 25. Using a print of your plan, evaluate your drawing using the following checklist.

SLAB FOUNDATION-PLAN CHECKLIST	
CORRECT SYMBOL & LOCATION	CORRECT STRUCTURAL MATERIALS
Outline of slabs	Proper footing size
Walls	Proper footing location
Footings and piers	Proper pier size
Doors	Proper pier location
Ductwork	
Plumbing	
Floor slopes	
REQUIRED LOCAL NOTES	REQUIRED GENERAL NOTES
Concrete slab thickness, fill, and reinforcement	Soil bearing pressure
Veneer ledges	Concrete strength
Door blockouts	Anchor bolt size & spacing
Fireplace footings	Vapor barriers
Pier sizes	Slab insulation
Footing sizes	Reinforcement
Floor drains	
Heating registers	

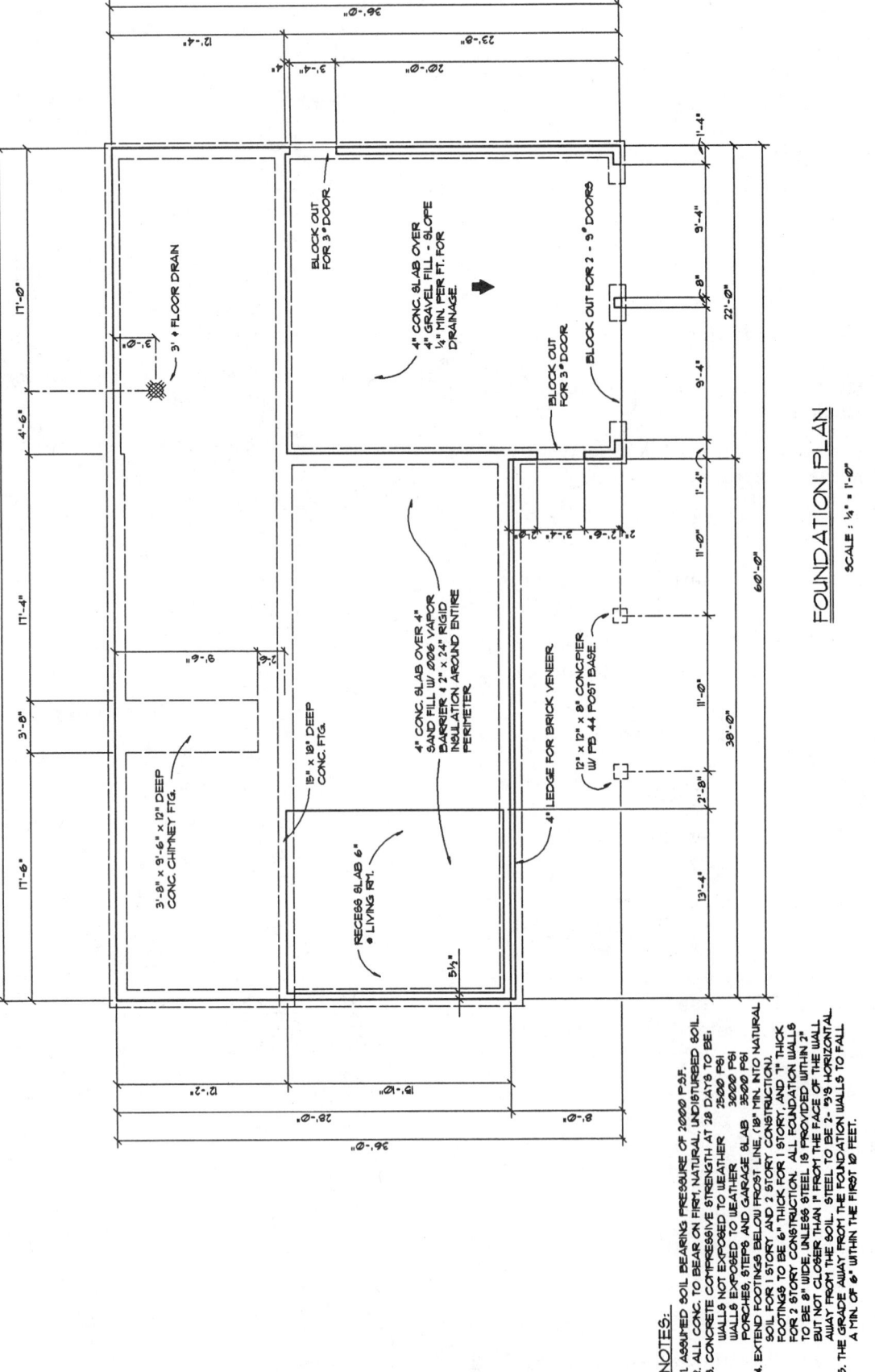

Figure 23-7 A completed foundation plan for a concrete slab floor system.

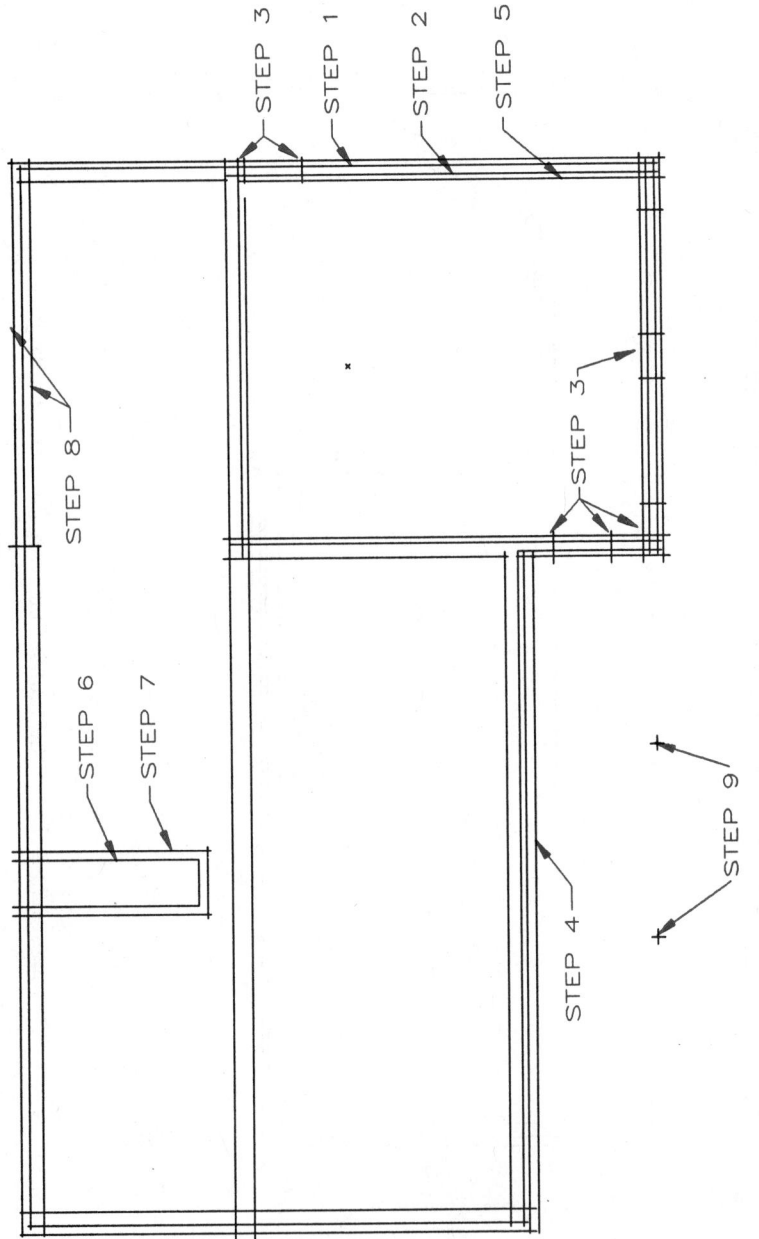

Figure 23-8 Layout of the foundation and slab floor.

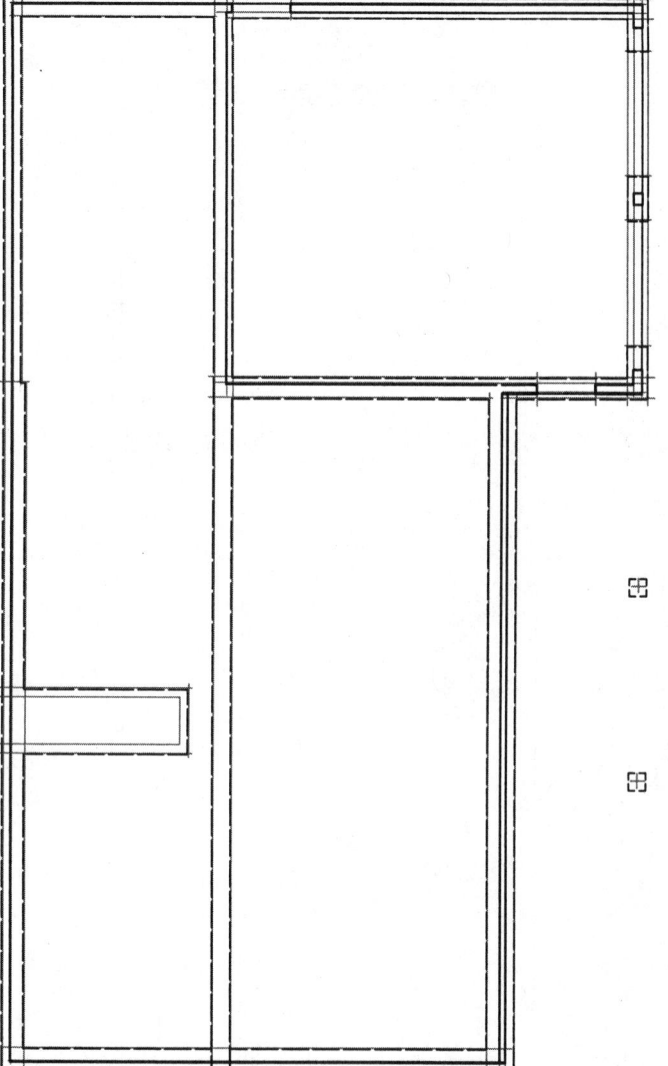

Figure 23-9 Draw the foundation with finished quality lines.

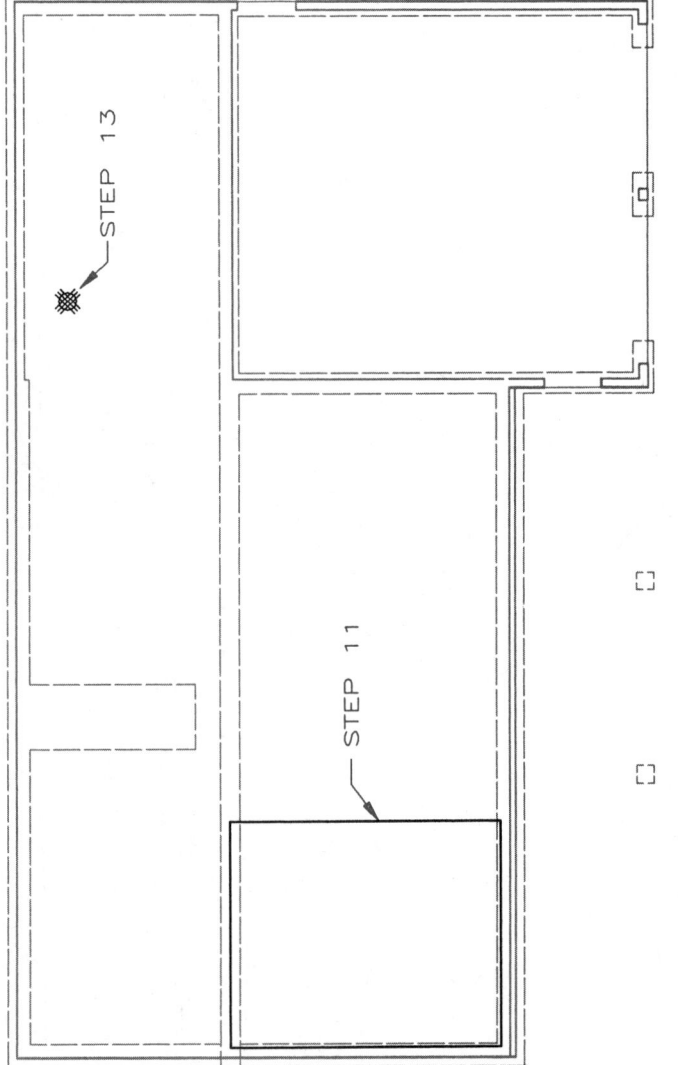

Figure 23–10 Representing items in the floor.

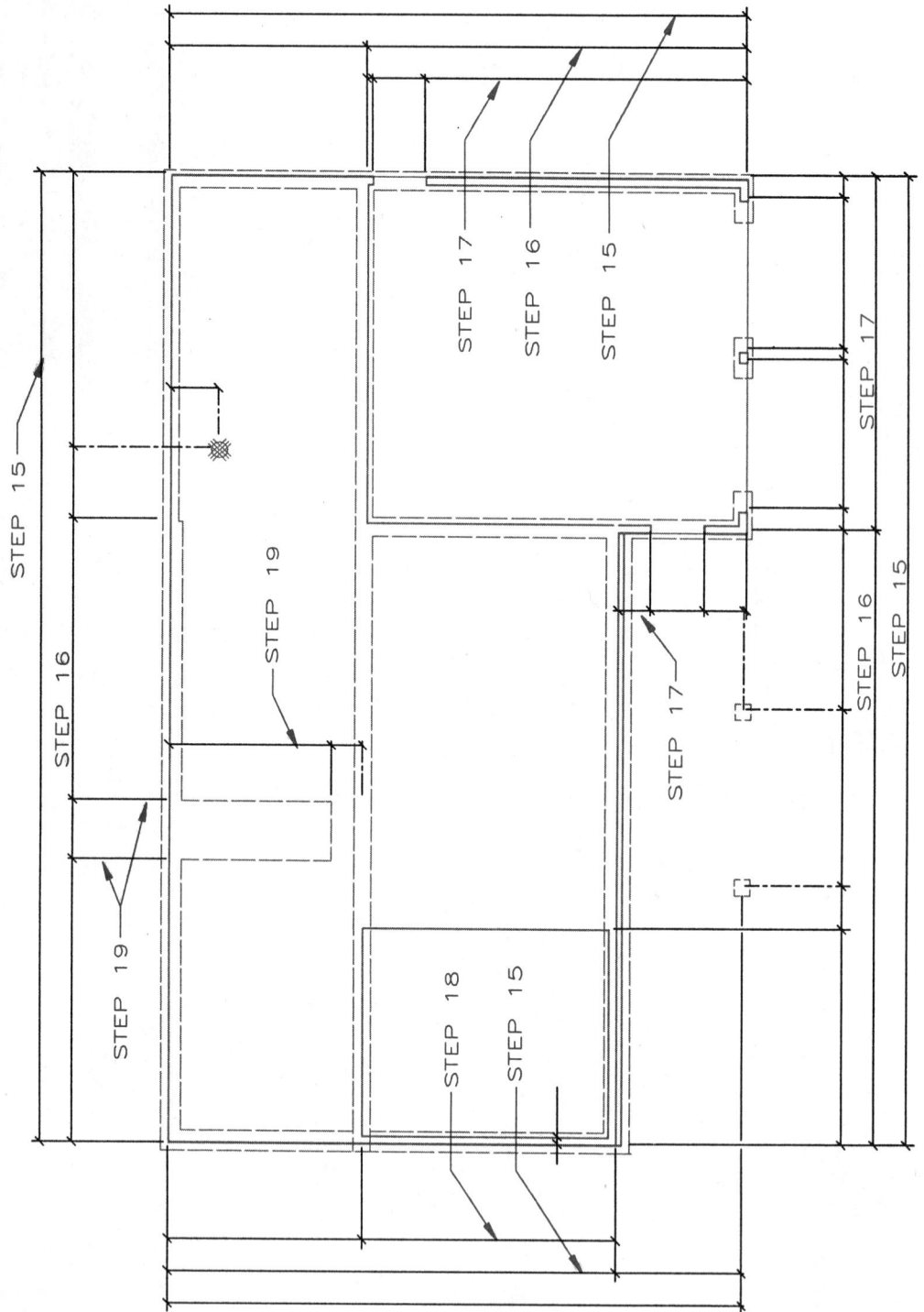

STEP 15

STEP 17

STEP 16

STEP 15

STEP 17

STEP 15

STEP 19

STEP 16

STEP 15

STEP 16

STEP 19

STEP 17

STEP 19

STEP 18

STEP 15

Figure 23-11 Prepared to place dimensions.

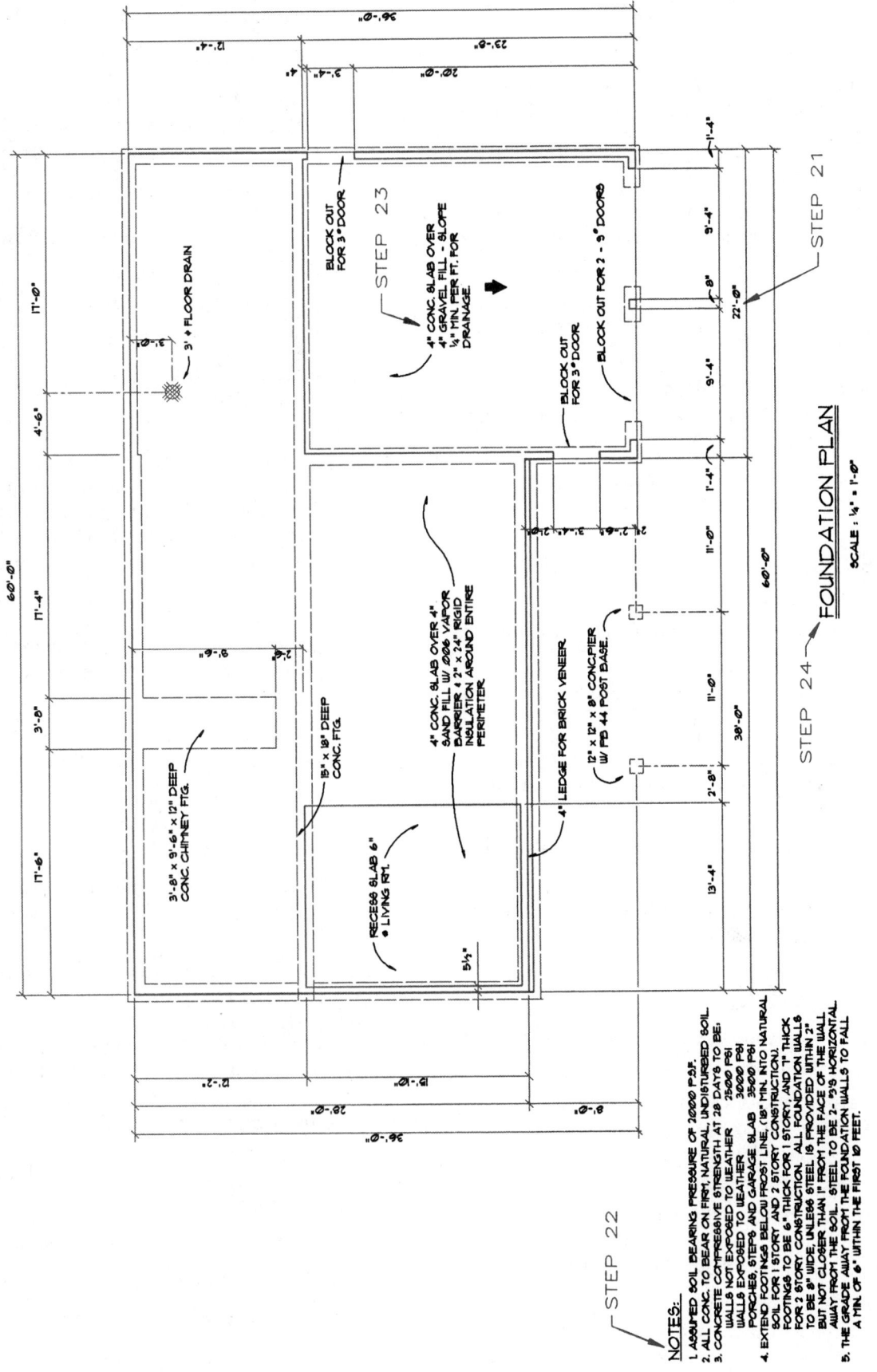

STEP 23

4" CONC. SLAB OVER
4" GRAVEL FILL - SLOPE
¼" MIN. PER FT. FOR
DRAINAGE

BLOCK OUT
FOR 3" DOOR

BLOCK OUT
FOR 3" DOOR

BLOCK OUT FOR 2 - 5" DOORS

STEP 21

3' ∅ FLOOR DRAIN

15" x 18" DEEP
CONC. FTG.

3'-8" x 9'-6" x 12" DEEP
CONC. CHIMNEY FTG.

4" CONC. SLAB OVER 4"
SAND FILL W/ .006 VAPOR
BARRIER 4' 2" x 24" RIGID
INSULATION AROUND ENTIRE
PERIMETER

RECESS SLAB 6"
@ LIVING RM.

4" LEDGE FOR BRICK VENEER

12" x 12" x 8' CONC.PIER
W/ PB 44 POST BASE.

STEP 24

FOUNDATION PLAN
SCALE : ¼" = 1'-0"

STEP 22

NOTES:
1. ASSUMED SOIL BEARING PRESSURE OF 2000 P.S.F.
2. ALL CONC. TO BEAR ON FIRM, NATURAL, UNDISTURBED SOIL.
3. CONCRETE COMPRESSIVE STRENGTH AT 28 DAYS TO BE:
   WALLS NOT EXPOSED TO WEATHER   2500 PSI
   WALLS EXPOSED TO WEATHER   3000 PSI
   PORCHES, STEPS AND GARAGE SLAB   3500 PSI
4. EXTEND FOOTINGS BELOW FROST LINE, (18" MIN. INTO NATURAL
   SOIL FOR 1 STORY AND 2 STORY CONSTRUCTION).
   FOOTINGS TO BE 6" THICK FOR 1 STORY, AND 7" THICK
   FOR 2 STORY CONSTRUCTION. ALL FOUNDATION WALLS
   TO BE 8" WIDE, UNLESS STEEL IS PROVIDED WITHIN 2"
   BUT NOT CLOSER THAN 1" FROM THE FACE OF THE WALL
5. THE GRADE AWAY FROM THE SOIL STEEL TO BE 2 - 5"8 HORIZONTAL
   AWAY FROM THE FOUNDATION WALLS TO FALL
   A MIN. OF 6" WITHIN THE FIRST 10 FEET.

Figure 23-12 Placing the dimensions and notes.

COMBINATION SLAB AND CRAWL SPACE PLANS

A structure may require a combined slab and floor joist system. The foundation plan will have similarities to both a foundation with joist and a slab foundation system. Figure 23–13 is an example of a foundation plan with a basement slab and a crawl space with joist construction. The following steps can be used to draw the foundation plan. Use construction lines for steps 1 through 12. Each step can be seen in Figure 23–14.

Step 1.   Using the dimensions on your floor plan, lay out the exterior face of the foundation walls.

Step 2.   Determine the wall thickness and lay out the interior face of the foundation walls. See Figure 21–6 for foundation dimensions.

Step 3.   Block out door and window openings in the foundation walls. Allow for actual size plus 4 in.

Step 4.   Block out a 30-in.-wide minimum crawl access.

Step 5.   Lay out a support ledge if masonry veneer is to be used.

Step 6.   Lay out the size of the fireplace based on the size drawn on the floor plan.

Step 7.   Lay out the footing under the fireplace so that it extends a minimum of 6 in. past the face of the fireplace.

Step 8.   Lay out the footing width under all foundation walls.

Step 9.   Lay out the footing width under all interior load-bearing walls.

Step 10.   Lay out any exterior piers required for porches and deck support.

Step 11.   Lay out girder locations to support floor and load-bearing walls.

Step 12.   Locate the center of all interior support piers.

Step 13.   Darken all items drawn in steps 1 through 12. Use bold lines for steps 1 through 6. Use thin dashed lines for items 7 through 10 and step 12. When complete, your drawing should resemble Figure 23–15.

See Figure 23–16 for steps 14 through 21. These items have not been drawn with construction lines. Each can be drawn using finished quality lines and need not be traced.

Step 14.   Draw the girders using dashed lines.

Step 15.   Draw piers with thin dashed lines.

Step 16.   Draw beam pockets with thin lines.

Step 17.   Draw 24-in.-long vents in the crawl area only. Draw the edge of the vents with bold lines, and the vents with thin lines.

Step 18.   Draw windows with thin lines.

Step 19.   Draw window wells using thin lines.

Step 20.   If concrete blocks are used for the foundation walls, crosshatch the wall with thin lines at a 45° angle.

Step 21.   Crosshatch the chimney with thin lines at a 45° angle.

You now have all of the information drawn that is needed to represent the floor and foundation systems. Follow steps 22 through 25 to dimension these items. Use thin lines for all extension and dimension lines. When complete, your drawing should resemble Figure 23–17.

Step 22.   Draw extension and dimension lines to locate the overall size on each side of the foundation.

Step 23.   Draw extension and dimension lines to locate jogs in the foundation walls.

Step 24.   Draw extension and dimension lines to locate all openings in the foundation walls except for vents.

Step 25.   Draw extension lines to locate all girders and piers.

All materials have now been drawn and located. The final drawing procedure is to place dimensions and specify the materials that were used. Materials may be specified with general and local notes. Figure 23–18 is an example of the notes that can be found on the foundation plan. Use the following steps as guidelines to complete the foundation plan.

Step 26.   Compute all dimensions and place them in the appropriate location.

Step 27.   Neatly letter all required general notes.

Step 28.   Neatly letter all required local notes.

Step 29.   Place a title and scale under the drawing.

Step 30.   Using a print of your plan, evaluate your drawing using the following checklist.

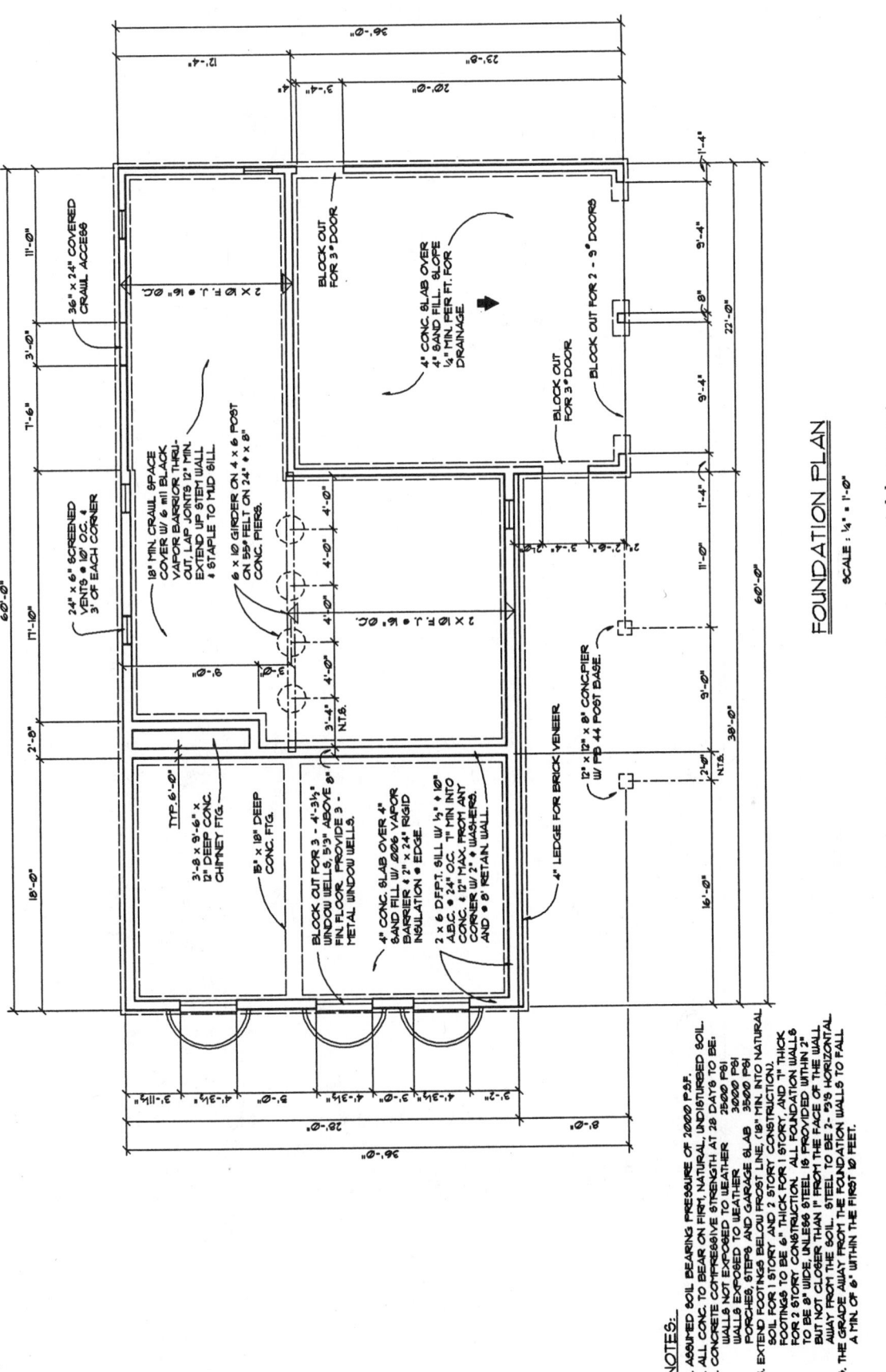

Figure 23-13 A complete foundation plan for a partial basement.

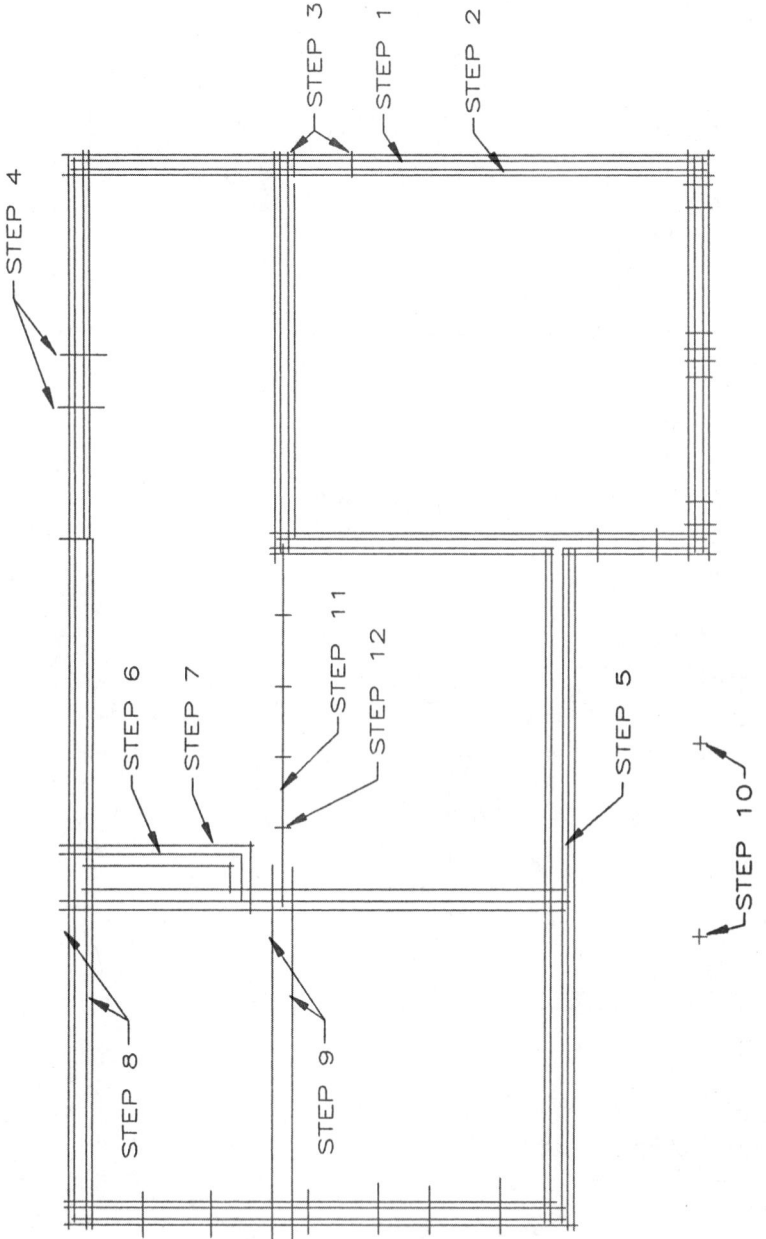

Figure 23-14 Layout of the partial basement plan.

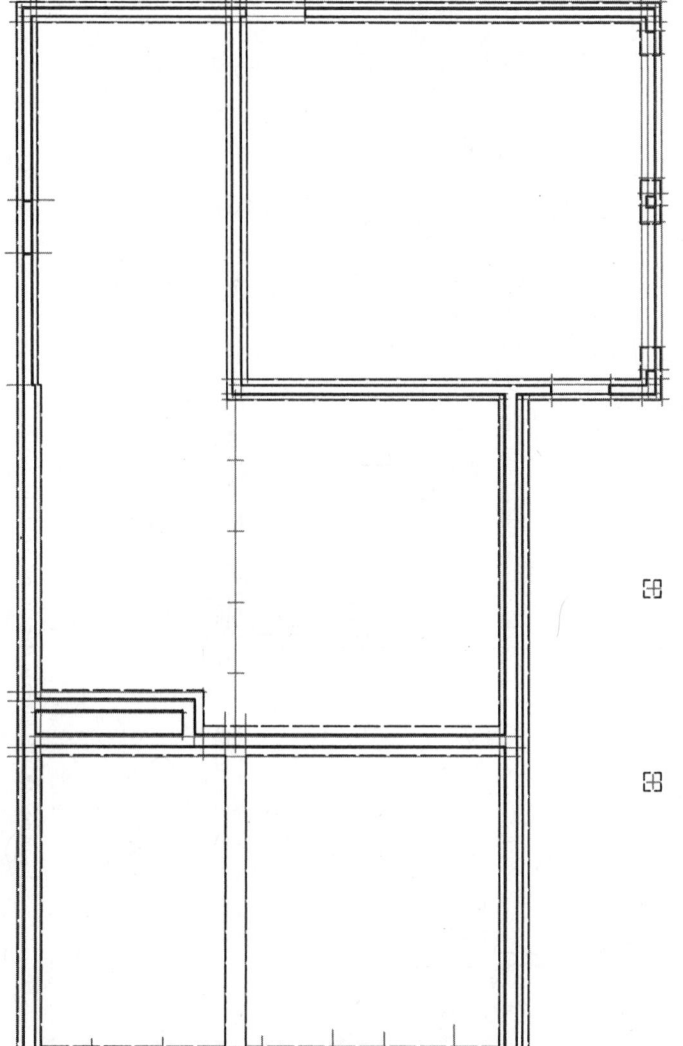

Figure 23-15 Draw the foundation plan with finished quality lines.

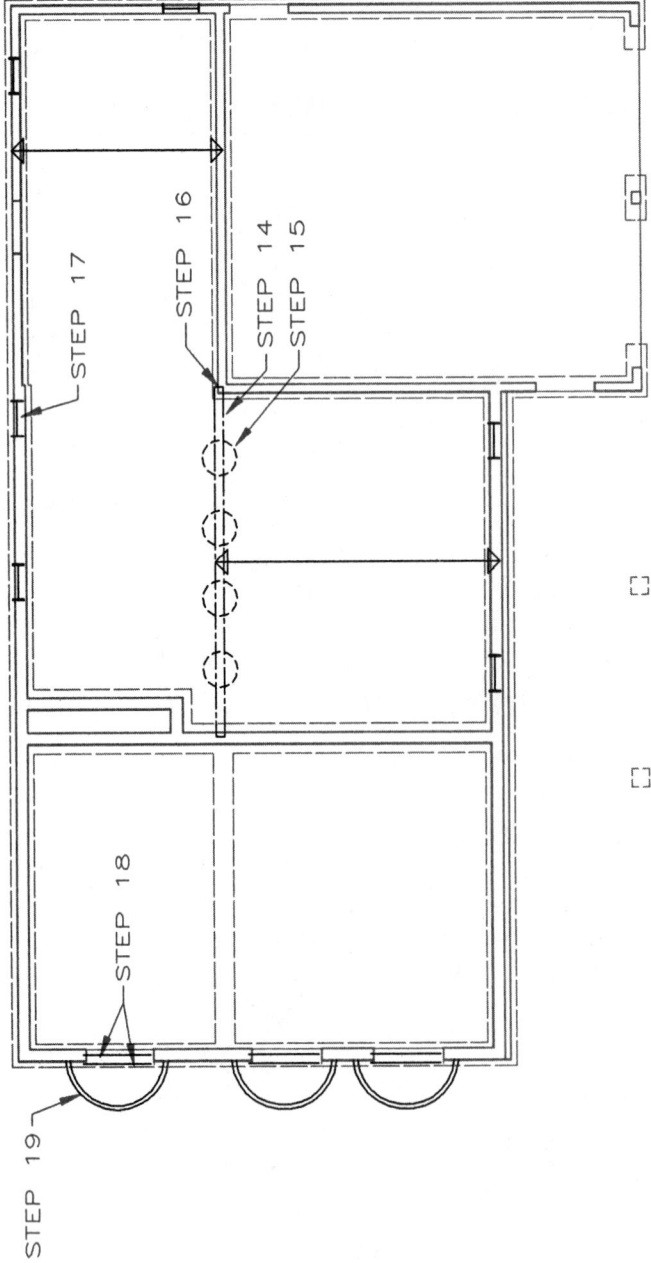

Figure 23-16 Draw floor materials with finished quality lines.

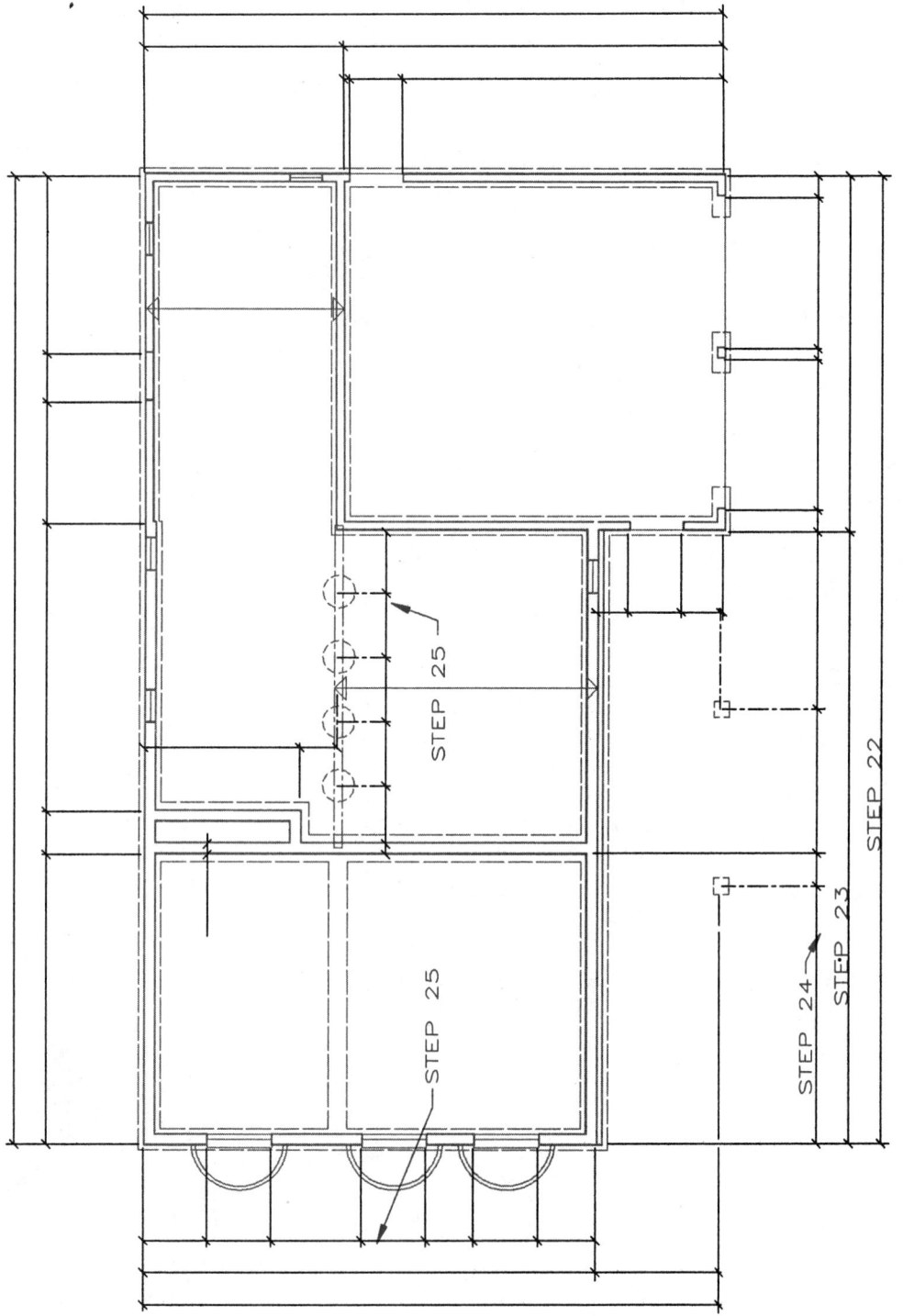

Figure 23-17 Determine materials to be dimensioned.

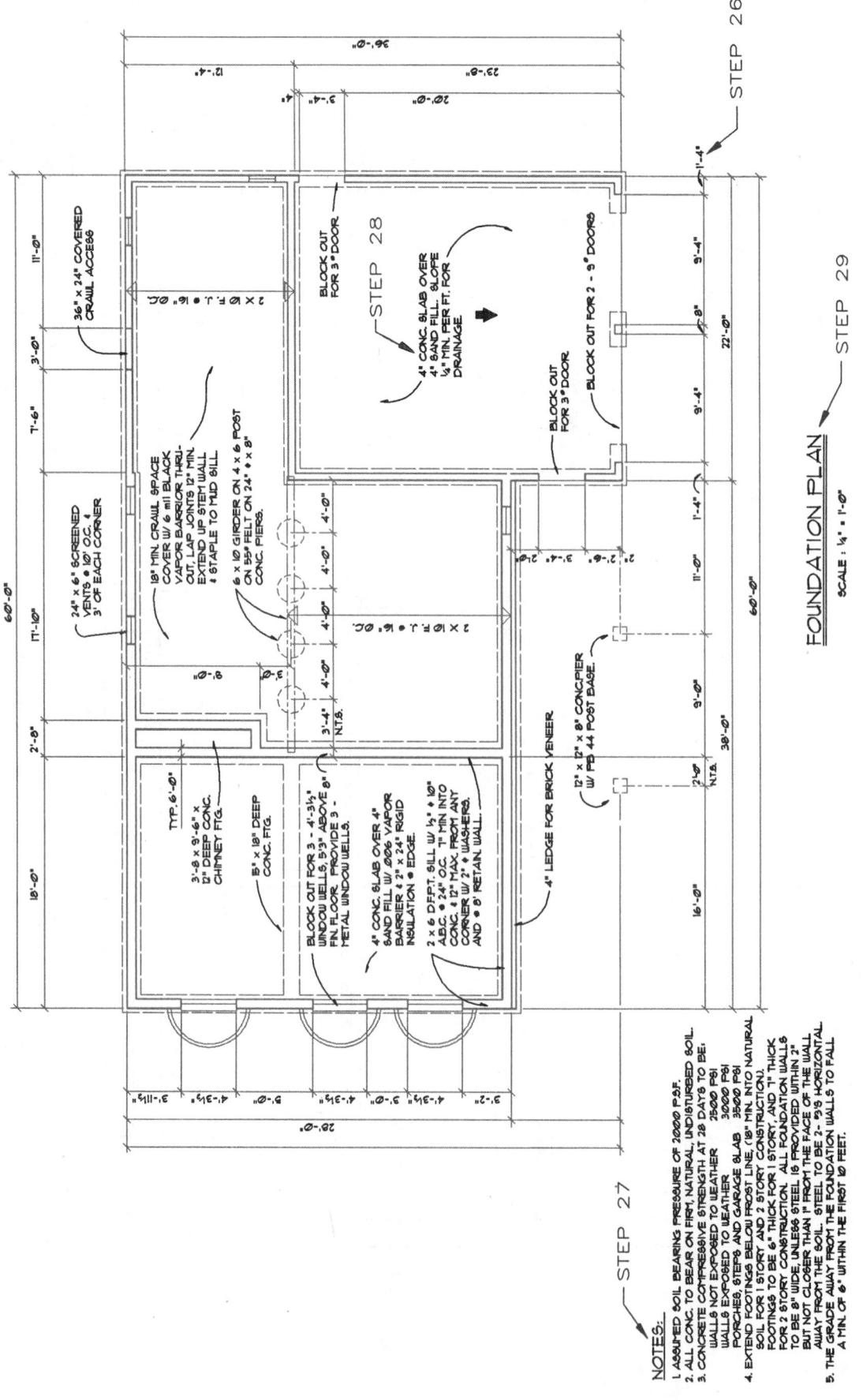

Figure 23-18 Specify size and location of all materials with notes and dimensions.

CHECKLIST FOR PARTIAL SLAB AND FLOOR JOIST FOUNDATION	
CORRECT SYMBOL & LOCATION	**CORRECT STRUCTURAL MATERIALS**
Walls	Footing size
Footings	Wall size
Crawl access	Beam placement
Vents	Beam size
Doors	Joist size
Girders and joist	Pier location
Piers	Beam location
Slabs	Pier sizes
REQUIRED LOCAL NOTES	**REQUIRED GENERAL NOTES**
Joist size and spacing	Soil bearing value
Beam size	Concrete strength
Beam pockets	Crawl space covering
Metal connectors	Framing lumber grade and species
Anchor bolts	Slab insulation
Mudsill	
Slab thickness	
Fill	
Slope direction of slab	

STANDARD FOUNDATION WITH POST-AND-BEAM FLOOR SYSTEM

When your drawing is complete, it should resemble the plan in Figure 23–19. Use construction lines for drawing steps 1 through 12. Each step can be seen in Figure 23–20.

Step 1.   Using the dimensions on your floor plan, lay out the exterior edge of the foundation wall.

Step 2.   Determine the foundation wall thickness and lay out the interior face of the foundation wall. See Figure 21–6 for a review of foundation footing and wall dimensions.

Step 3.   Block out doors in the garage area. Typically the door size plus 4 in. is provided as the foundation is formed.

Step 4.   Block out for a 30-in.-wide minimum crawl access.

Step 5.   Lay out the support ledge if masonry veneer is to be used.

Step 6.   Lay out the size of the fireplace using measurements from the floor plan.

Step 7.   Lay out the footing under the foundation walls.

Step 8.   Lay out the footing under the fireplace, providing 6 in. minimum around the perimeter.

Step 9.   Lay out any exterior piers required to support porches and decks.

Step 10.   Lay out the center of each load-bearing wall.

Step 11.   Lay out all girders.

Step 12.   Lay out the center for the piers to support the girders.

See Figure 23–21 for step 13.

Step 13.   Darken all items in steps 1 through 12. Use bold lines to represent the material in steps 1 through 6. Use thin dashed lines to represent the material in steps 7 through 9, and 12.

Step 14.   Use thin dashed lines or a very bold dashed line to represent the girders. When finished with this step your drawing should resemble the drawing in Figure 23–22.

See Figure 23–23 for steps 15 through 18. The items to be drawn in these steps have not been drawn with construction lines. Because of their simplicity you can draw these items with finished lines.

Step 15.   Draw beam pockets with thin lines.

Step 16.   Draw 24-in.-long vents in the walls surrounding the crawl space. Use bold lines to represent the ends and a thin line to represent the vent.

Step 17.   If the walls are formed using concrete blocks, crosshatch the walls with thin lines at a 45° angle.

Step 18.   Crosshatch the chimney using thin lines on a 45° angle.

You now have all of the information drawn to represent the floor and foundation systems. Follow steps 19 through 25 to dimension these items. Use thin lines for extension and dimension lines. When complete, your foundation plan should resemble Figure 23–24.

Step 19.   Draw extension and dimension lines to locate the overall size of the foundation.

Step 20.   Draw extension and dimension lines to locate the jogs in the foundation walls.

Step 21.   Draw extension and dimension lines to locate all openings in the foundation walls except for vents.

Step 22.   Draw extension and dimension lines to locate the fireplace.

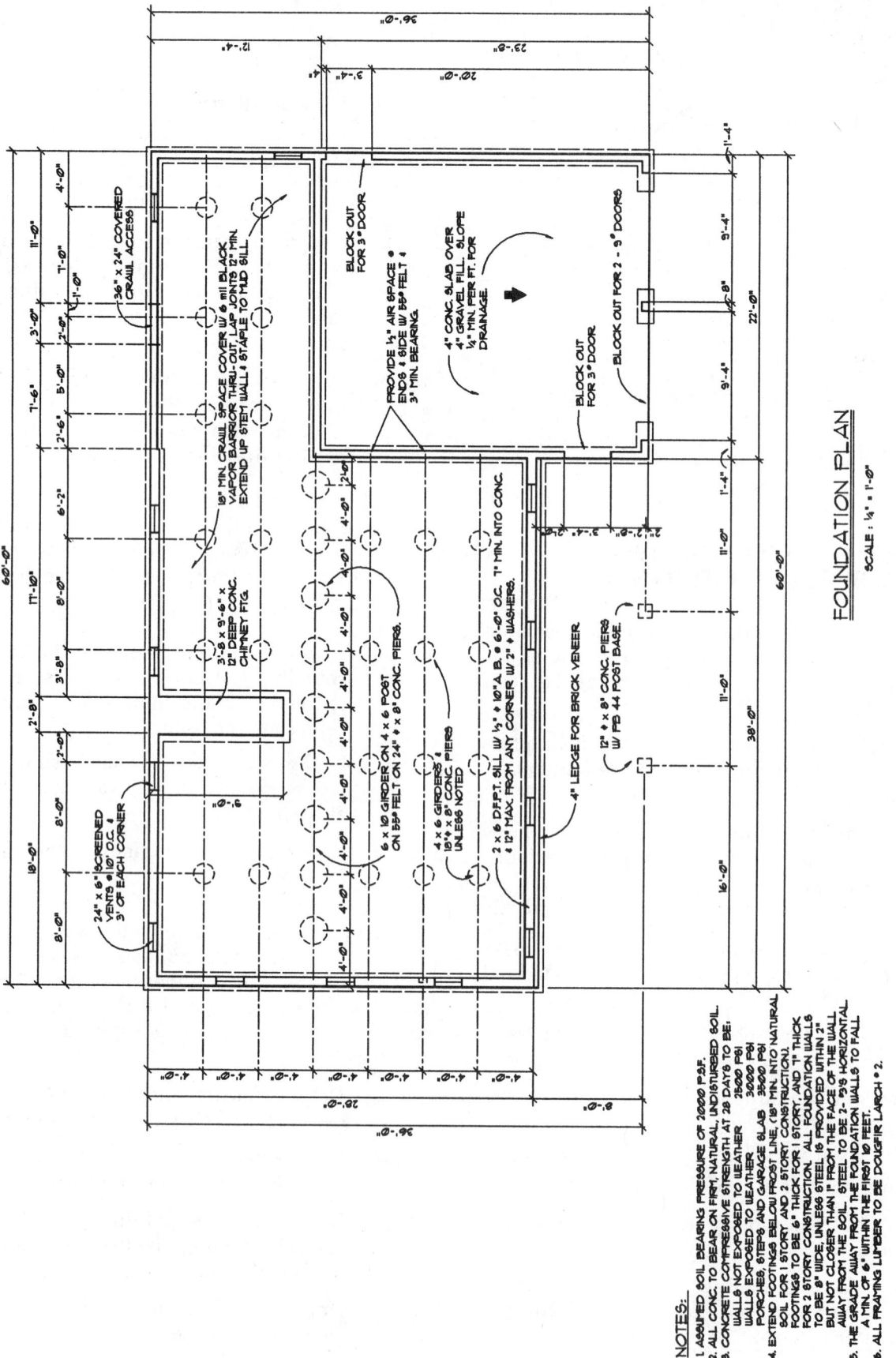

FOUNDATION PLAN

SCALE : ¼" = 1'-0"

Figure 23-19 A completed post-and-beam foundation plan.

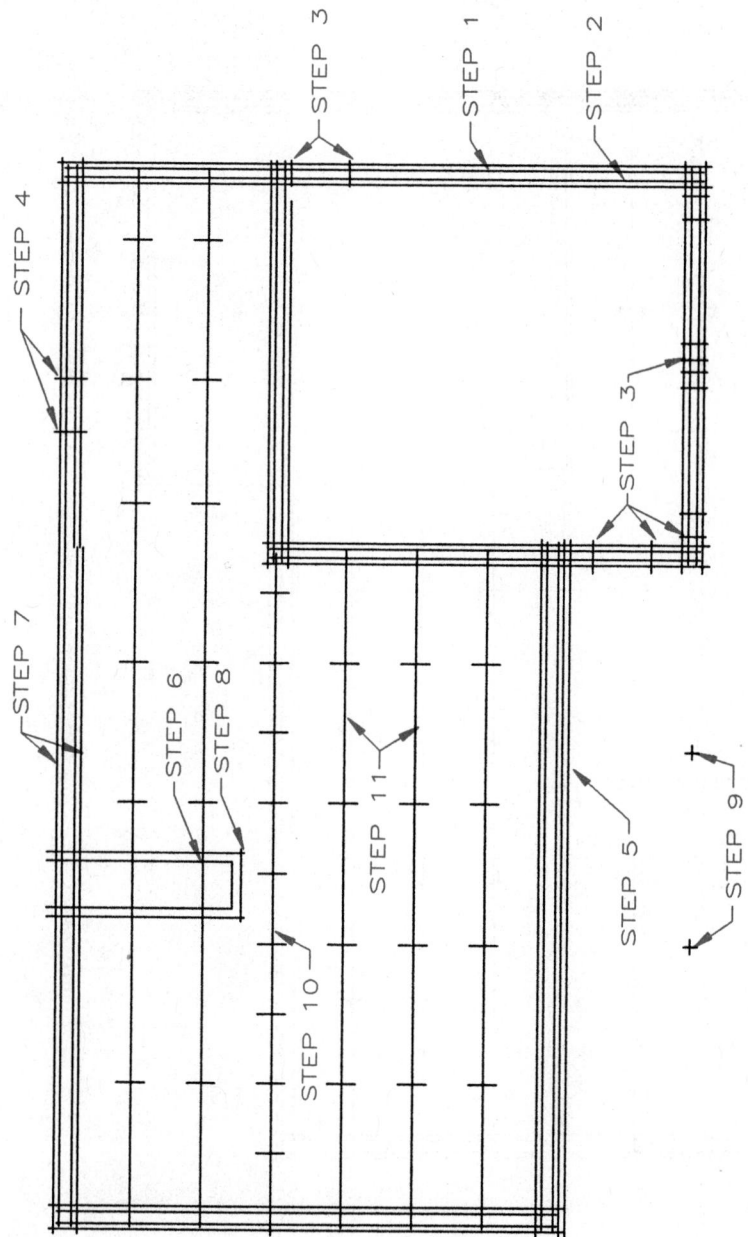

Figure 23–20 Layout of the post-and-beam foundation plan.

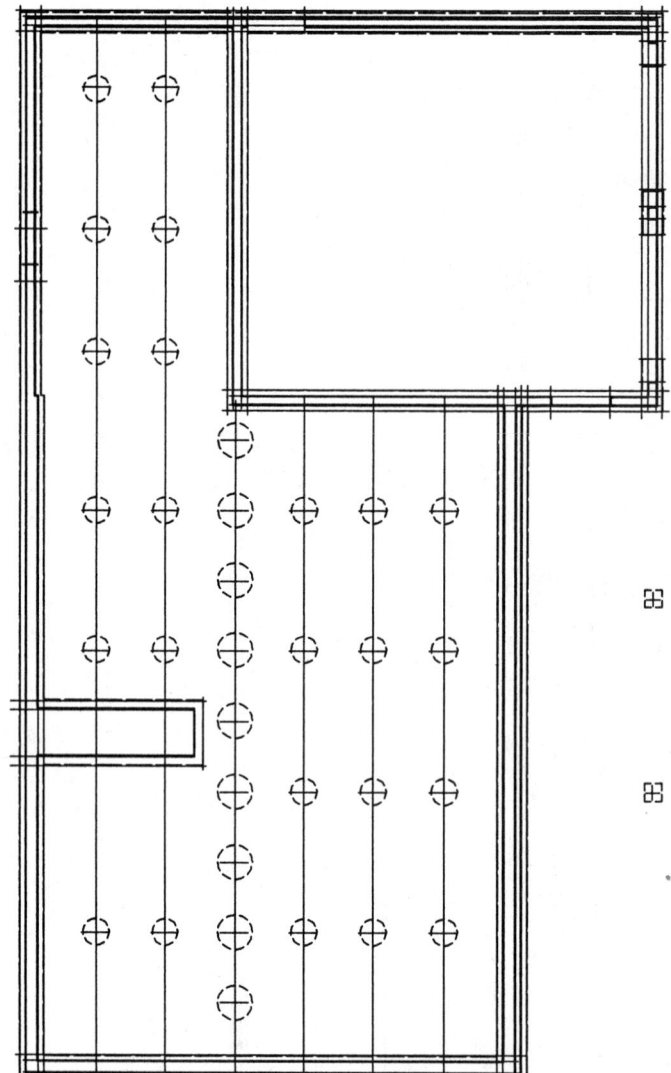

Figure 23-21 Drawing concrete members with finished quality lines.

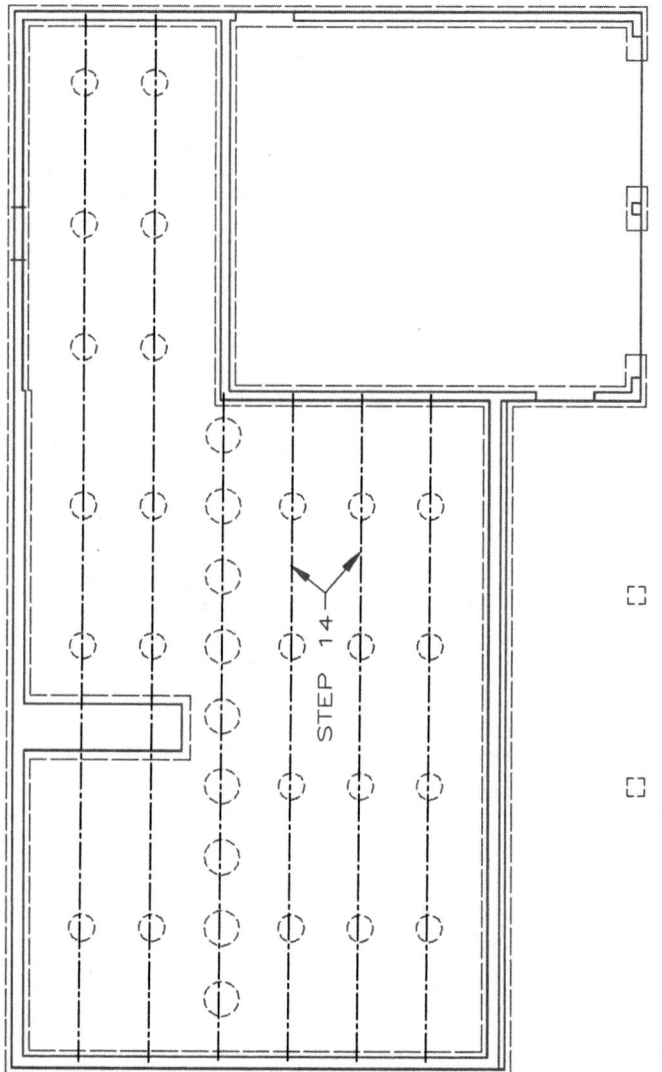

Figure 23-22 Drawing girders with finished quality lines.

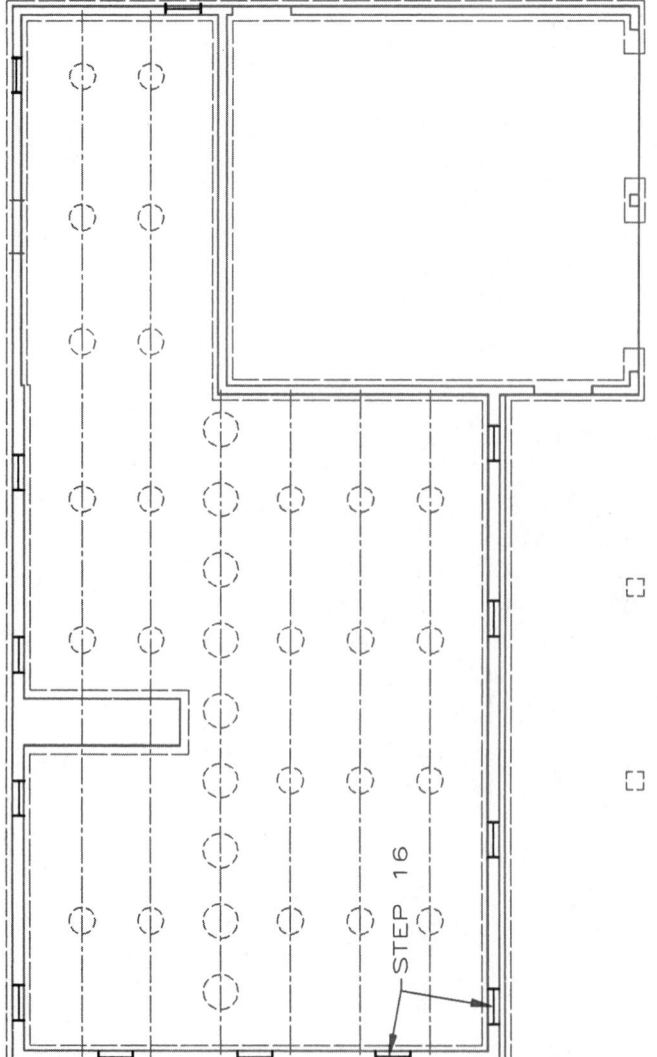

Figure 23-23 Drawing supplemental material with finished quality lines.

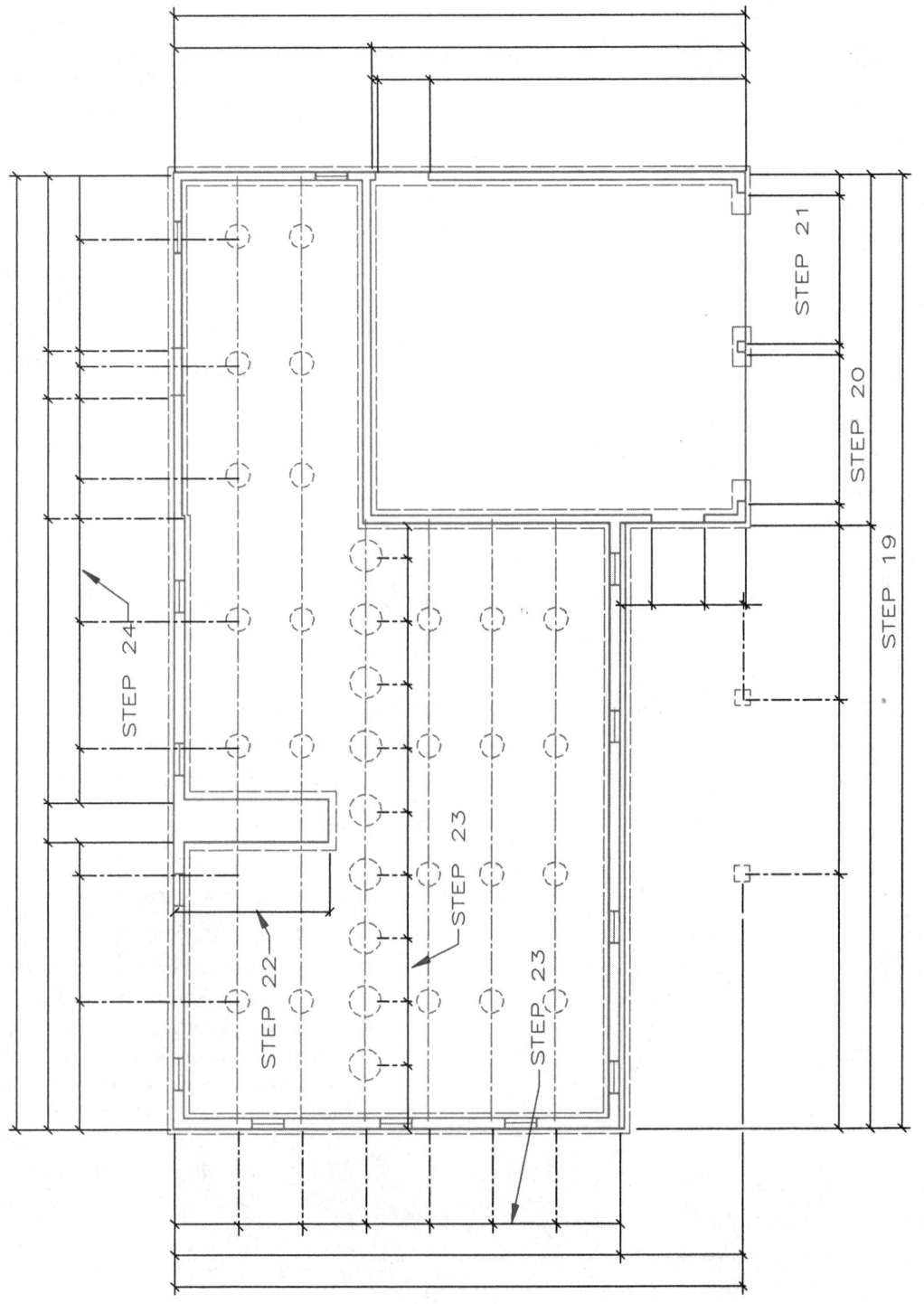

Figure 23-24 Prepared for dimensions.

Step 23. Draw extension and dimension lines to locate all girders.

Step 24. Draw extension and dimension lines to locate all piers.

Step 25. Draw extension and dimension lines to locate all metal connectors.

All materials have now been drawn to represent the floor and foundation systems. The final drafting procedure is to place dimensions and specify the material to be used. This is done by the use of general and local notes in a similar method that was used on the floor plan. Figure 23–25 shows how notes can be placed on the foundation plan. Complete the foundation plan using the following steps.

Step 26. Compute and neatly letter dimensions in the appropriate place.

Step 27. Neatly letter all required general notes.

Step 28. Place a title and scale below the drawing.

Step 29. Using a print of your plan, evaluate your drawing using the following checklist.

POST-AND-BEAM CHECKLIST	
CORRECT SYMBOL & LOCATION	**CORRECT STRUCTURAL MATERIALS**
Walls	Proper footing sizes
Footings	Proper wall size
Crawl access	Proper beam placement
Vents	Proper pier placement
Doors	Veneer ledges
Girders and piers	
Line of slabs	
Fireplace	
REQUIRED LOCAL NOTES	**REQUIRED GENERAL NOTES**
Beam size	Soil bearing values
Beam pockets	Concrete values
Metal connectors	Crawl space covering
Anchor bolts and mudsills	Crawl space insulation
Garage slab thickness, fill, slope direction	Framing lumber grade and species
Fireplace note	
Vent size and spacing	
Veneer ledges	
Door blockouts	
REQUIRED DIMENSIONS	
Overall	Girder locations
Jogs	Pier locations
Wall openings	Metal locations
	Fireplace location

PILING FOUNDATION AND JOIST FLOOR SYSTEM

When your drawing is complete, it should resemble the plan in Figure 23–26. Use construction lines for drawing steps 1 through 13. Each step can be seen in Figure 23–27.

Step 1. Outline the shape of the entire structure using the measurements from your floor plan.

Step 2. Lay out the shape of the slab.

Step 3. Lay out the foundation wall. See Figure 21–6.

Step 4. Block out doors in the garage area. Typically the door size plus 4 in. is provided as the foundation is formed.

Step 5. Lay out the support ledge if masonry veneer is to be used.

Step 6. If a masonry fireplace is to be used, lay out the size of the fireplace.

Step 7. Lay out the footing under the foundation walls.

Step 8. Lay out the footing under the fireplace.

Step 9. Lay out any piers or footings for interior walls or posts.

Step 10. Lay out the centerline of girders under load-bearing walls.

Step 11. Locate the center of pilings.

Step 12. Lay out the girder and pilings for any decks or porches.

Step 13. Lay out the centerline for any piers for decks and porches.

Step 14. Darken all items drawn with construction lines in steps 1 through 13. Use bold long-short-long dashed lines for step 1. Use bold lines for steps 2, 3, 4, 5, and 6. Use thin dashed lines to represent the material of steps 7, 8, 9, 11, 12, and 13. Use thin lines to represent the girders of steps 10 and 12. When this step is complete, your drawing should resemble Figure 23–28.

See Figure 23–29 for steps 15 through 19. These items have not been drawn using construction lines. Because of their simplicity, each may be drawn with finished quality lines and need not be traced.

Step 15. With a bold long-short-long dashed line draw the ledger.

Step 16. Draw arrows to represent joist span and direction with thin lines.

Step 17. Crosshatch the masonry for the chimney with thin lines at a 45° angle.

Step 18. Indicate crossbracing between wood or steel pilings.

Step 19. Place detail markers to indicate details to be drawn.

You now have all of the needed items drawn to represent the floor and foundation systems. Use steps 20 through 28 to locate these items. Use thin lines for the extension and dimension lines. When complete, your drawing should resemble Figure 23–30.

Step 20. Draw extension and dimension lines to locate the perimeter of the structure on each side.

Step 21. Draw extension and dimension lines to locate the limits of the slab.

Step 22. Draw extension and dimension lines to locate jogs in the slab and foundation walls.

Step 23. Draw extenion and dimension lines to locate openings in the foundation walls.

Step 24. Draw extension and dimension lines to locate the fireplace.

Step 25. Draw extension and dimension lines to locate the girders.

Step 28. Draw extension and dimension lines to locate all pilings.

Step 27. Draw extension and dimension lines to locate all piers.

Step 28. Draw extension and dimension lines to locate all metal connectors.

All materials have now been drawn and located. The final drawing procedure is to place dimensions and specify the material to be used. This is done with the use of general and local notes. Figure 23–31 shows notes that are typically required. Use the following steps as a guideline to complete the foundation.

Step 29. Compute all dimensions and place them in the appropriate location.

Step 30. Neatly letter all required general notes.

Step 31. Neatly letter all required local notes.

Step 32. Place a title and scale below the drawing.

Step 33. Using a print of your plan, evaluate your drawing using the following checklist.

PILING FOUNDATION AND JOIST FLOOR SYSTEM CHECKLIST

CORRECT SYMBOL & LOCATION	CORRECT STRUCTURAL MATERIALS
Walls	Proper footing size
Footings	Proper wall size
Structure perimeter	Proper wall and footing location
Slab perimeter	
Girders	Proper pier or piling location
Pilings or piers	Proper girder location
Metal connectors	Proper girder size
Openings in walls	Proper joist size
Fireplace	Proper joist direction

REQUIRED GENERAL NOTES	REQUIRED LOCAL NOTES
Soil bearing pressure	Joist size and spacing
Concrete strength	Beam size
Crossbracing between wood and steel pilings or posts	Post sizes
	Metal connectors
	Pier or piling size
Framing lumber grade and species	Anchor bolt and mudsill size
	Veneer ledges
	Door blockouts in stemwall
	Fireplace footing size

REQUIRED DIMENSIONS

Overall
Jogs
Pilings or piers
Continuous footing centers
Girders
Metal connectors

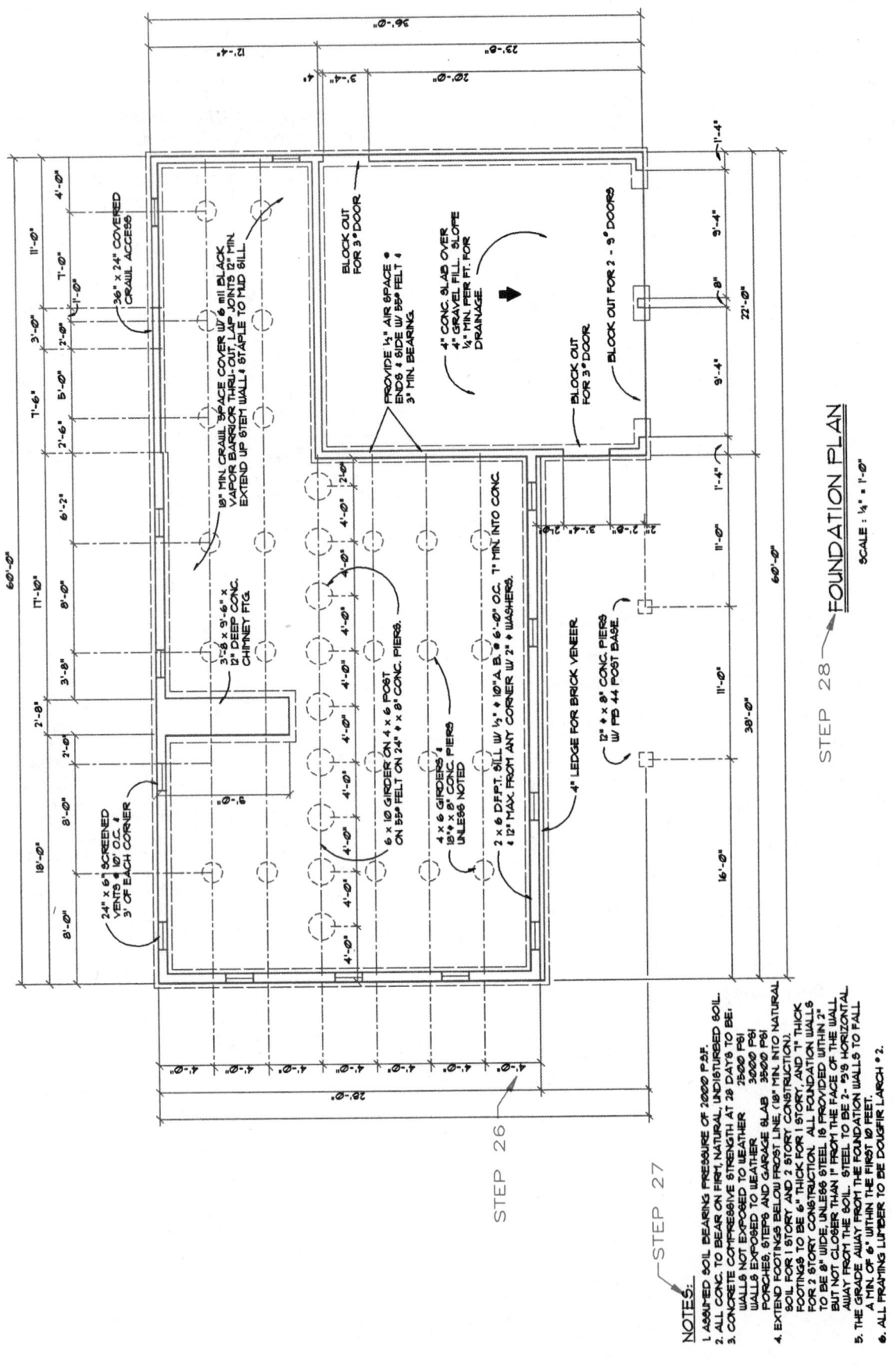

Figure 23-25 Placing dimensions and notes.

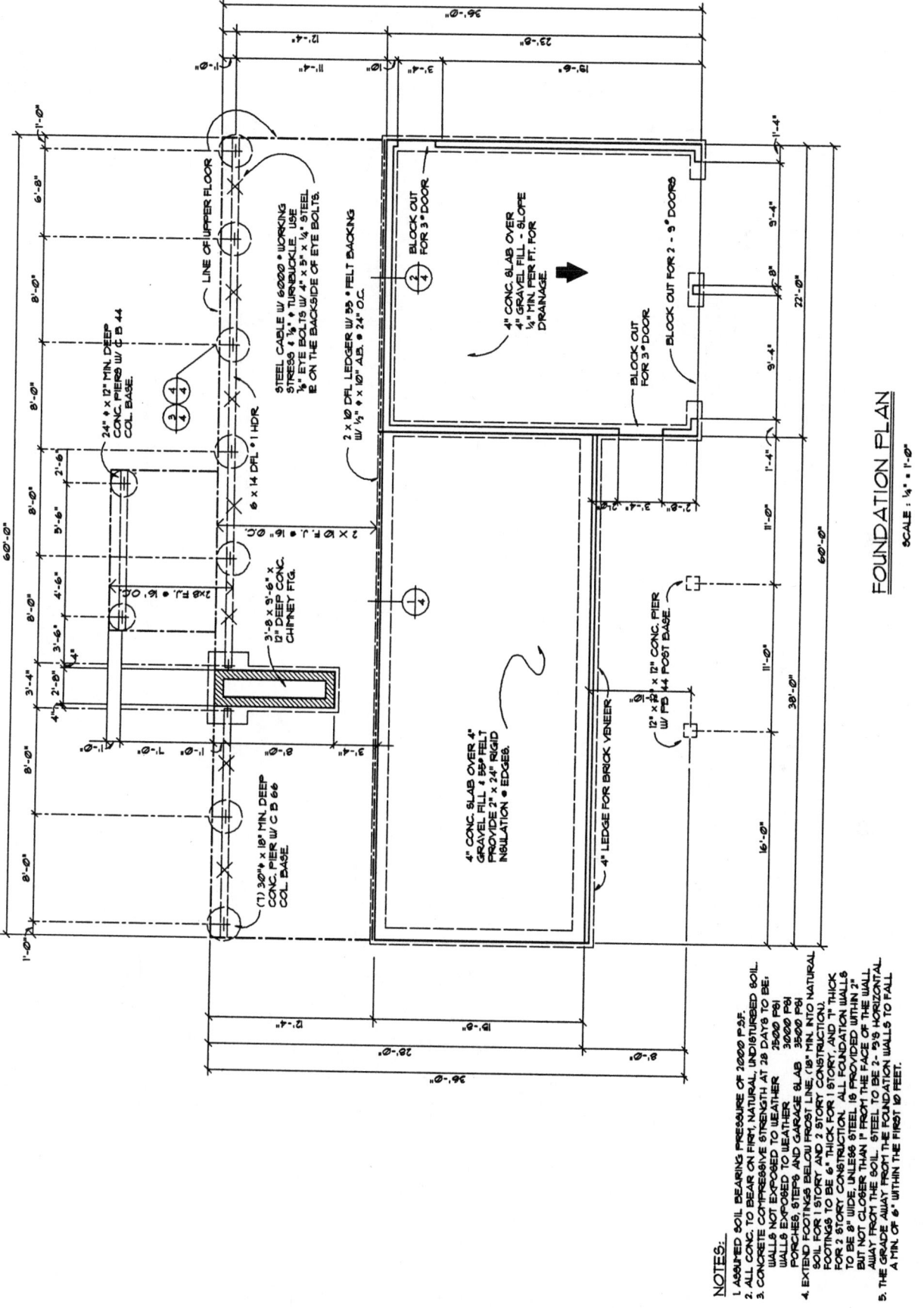

Figure 23–26 A completed foundation plan using pilings.

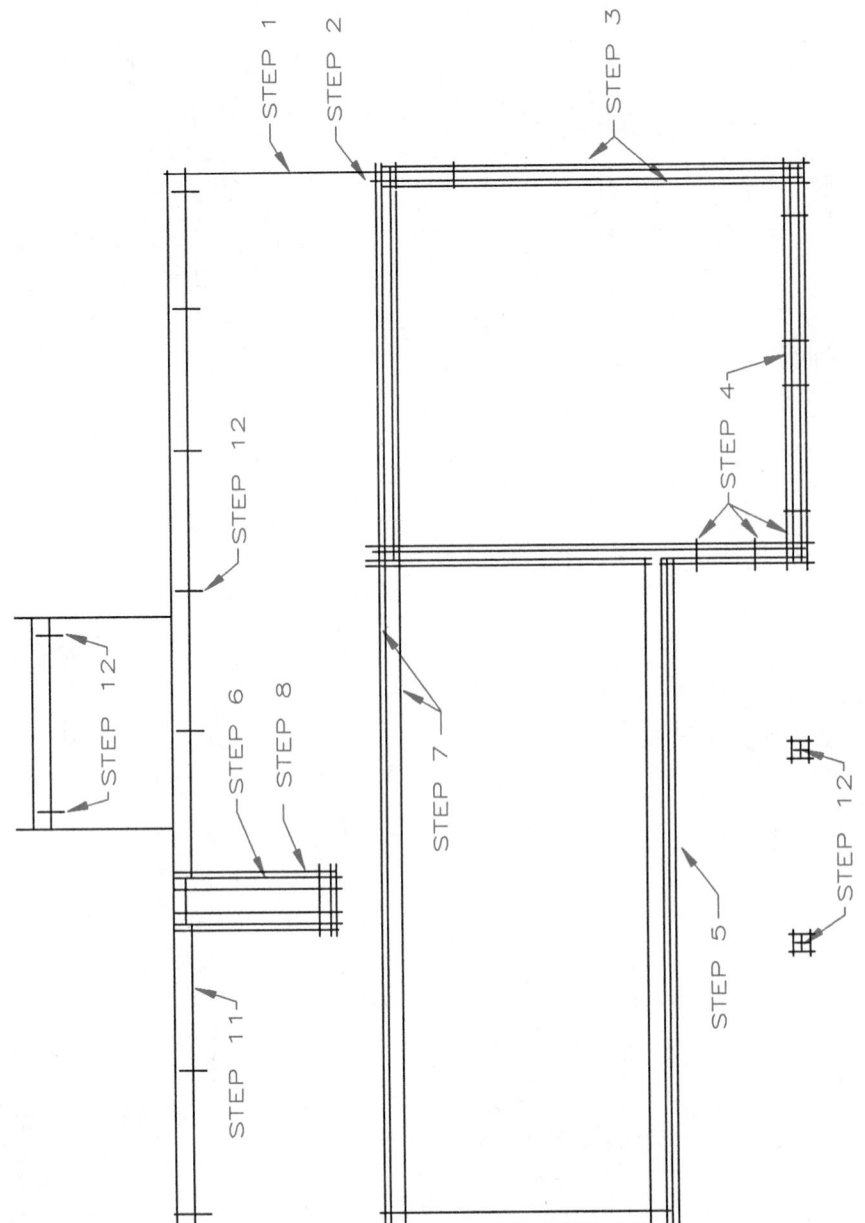

Figure 23–27 Layout of a piling foundation. Steps 9 and 10 are not required on this plan.

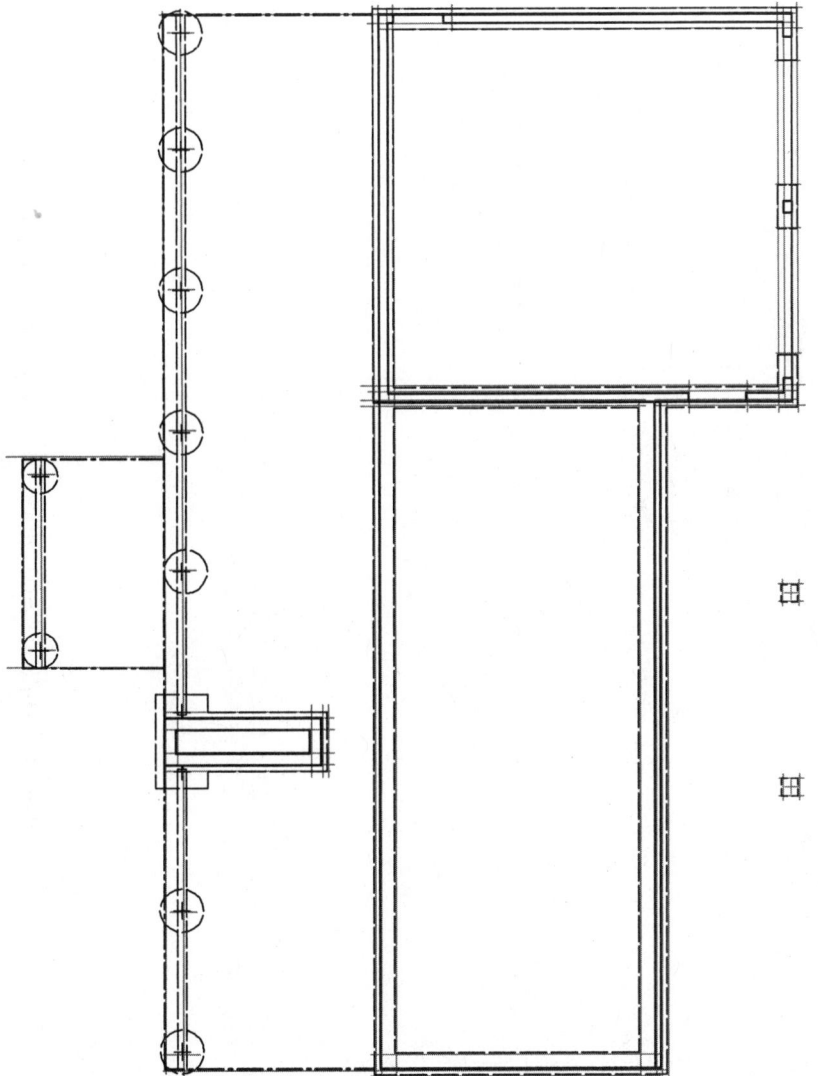

Figure 23–28 Drawing the foundation plan with finished quality lines.

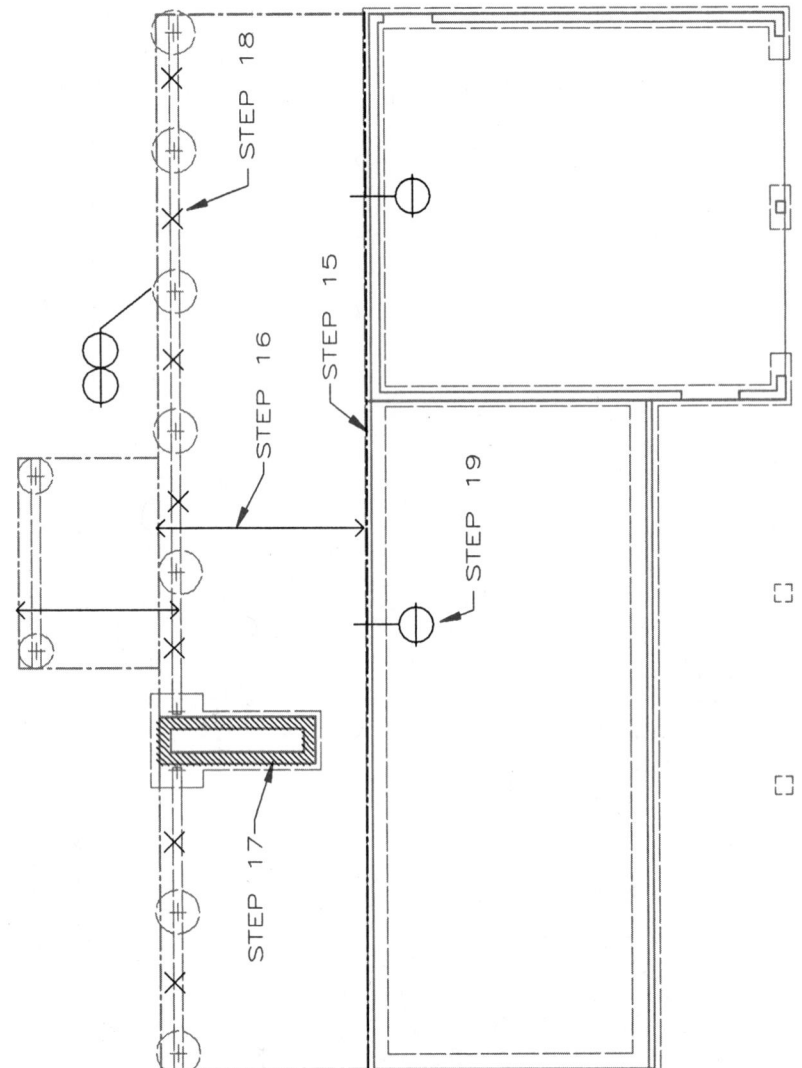

Figure 23–29 Drawing supplemental information with finished quality lines.

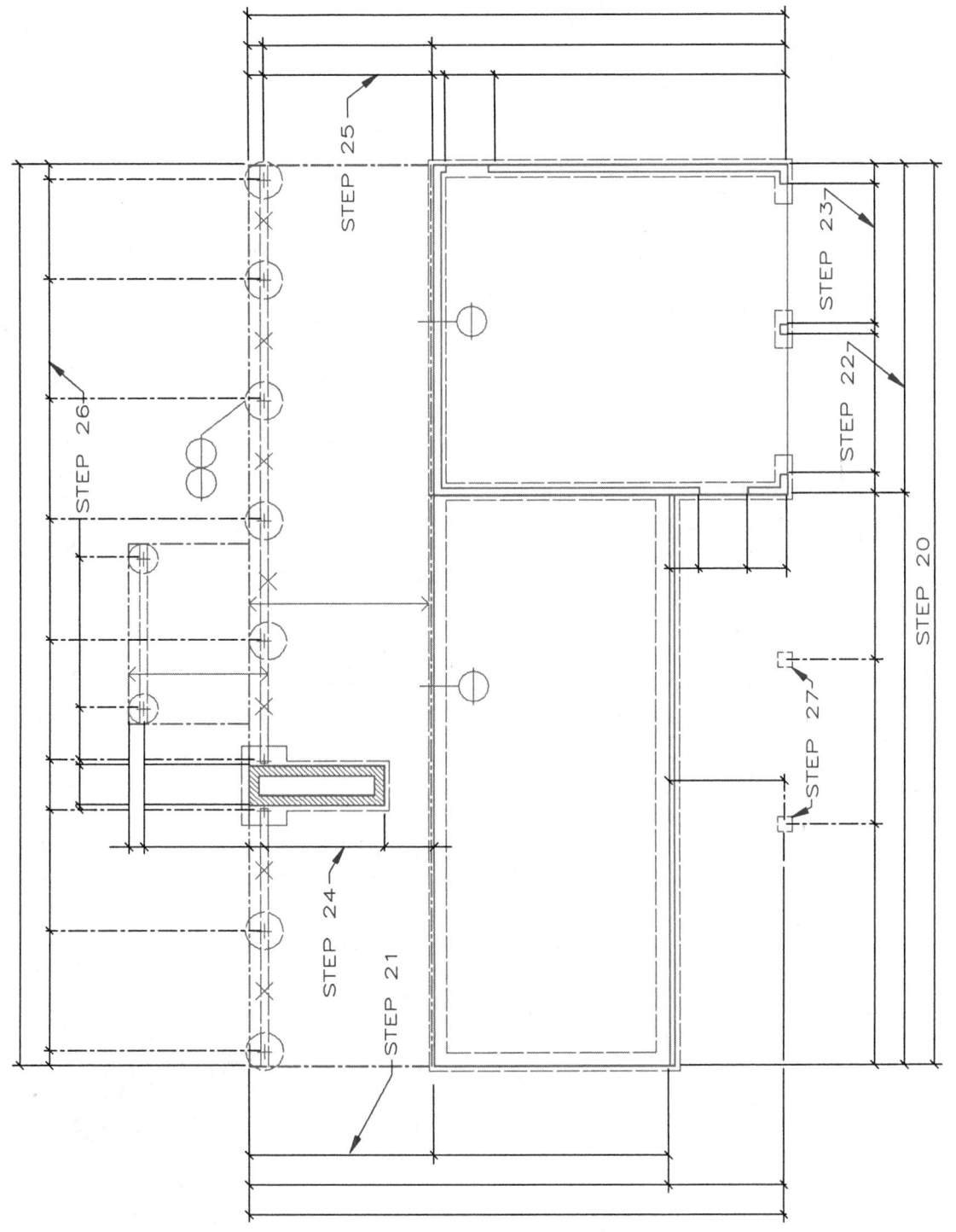

Figure 23-30 Placing extension and dimension lines.

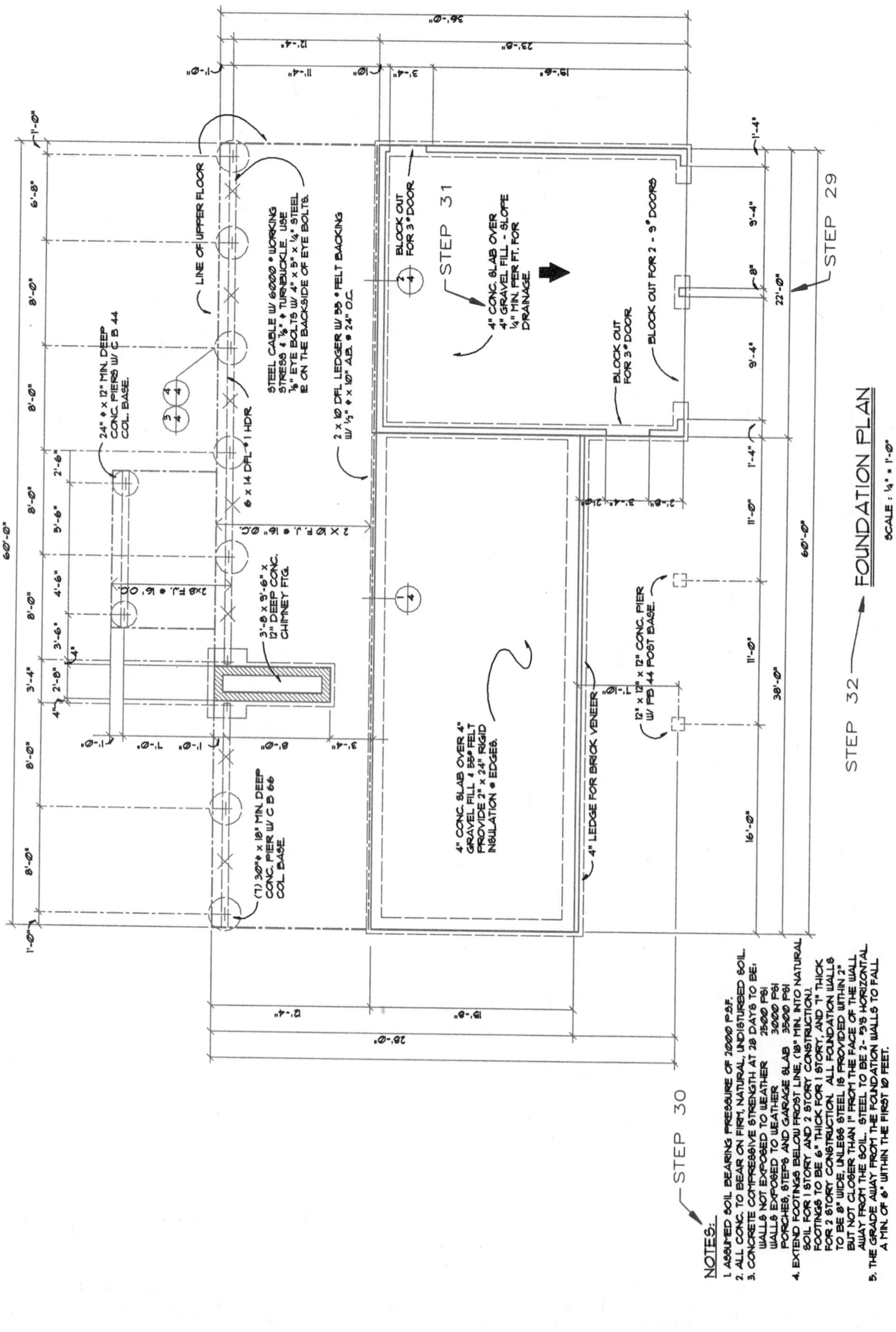

Figure 23-31 Completion of the foundation plan.

LINE OF UPPER FLOOR

24" Ø x 12" MIN. DEEP CONC. PIERS W/ C B 44 COL. BASE.

STEEL CABLE W/ 6000 # WORKING STRESS & ⅜" Ø TURNBUCKLE. USE ¼" EYE BOLTS W/ 4" x 5" x ¼" STEEL ℗ ON THE BACKSIDE OF EYE BOLTS.

2 x 10 DFL LEDGER W/ 55 # FELT BACKING W/ ½" Ø x 10" AB. @ 24" O.C.

6 x 14 DFL #1 HDR

2 x 10 F.J. @ 16" O.C.

3'-6 x 9'-6" x 12" DEEP CONC. CHIMNEY FTG.

(1) 30" Ø x 18" MIN. DEEP CONC. PIER W/ C B 66 COL. BASE.

BLOCK OUT FOR 3' DOOR

4" CONC. SLAB OVER 4" GRAVEL FILL - SLOPE ¼" MIN. PER FT. FOR DRAINAGE.

STEP 31

BLOCK OUT FOR 3' DOOR

BLOCK OUT FOR 2 - 9' DOORS

4" CONC. SLAB OVER 4" GRAVEL FILL & 55# FELT PROVIDE 2" x 24" RIGID INSULATION @ EDGES.

4" LEDGE FOR BRICK VENEER

12" x 12" CONC. PIER W/ PB 44 POST BASE

STEP 32 → FOUNDATION PLAN

SCALE : ¼" = 1'-0"

STEP 29

STEP 30

NOTES:

1. ASSUMED SOIL BEARING PRESSURE OF 2000 P.S.F.
2. ALL CONC. TO BEAR ON FIRM, NATURAL, UNDISTURBED SOIL.
3. CONCRETE COMPRESSIVE STRENGTH AT 28 DAYS TO BE:
   WALLS NOT EXPOSED TO WEATHER   2500 PSI
   WALLS EXPOSED TO WEATHER   3000 PSI
   PORCHES, STEPS AND GARAGE SLAB   3500 PSI
4. EXTEND FOOTINGS BELOW FROST LINE, (18" MIN. INTO NATURAL SOIL. FOR 1 STORY AND 2 STORY CONSTRUCTION). FOOTINGS TO BE 6" THICK FOR 1 STORY, AND 1" THICK FOR 2 STORY CONSTRUCTION. ALL FOUNDATION WALLS TO BE 8" WIDE. UNLESS STEEL IS PROVIDED WITHIN 2" BUT NOT CLOSER THAN 1" FROM THE FACE OF THE WALL
5. THE GRADE AWAY FROM THE SOIL. STEEL TO BE 2 - 5% HORIZONTAL AWAY FROM THE FOUNDATION WALLS TO FALL A MIN. OF 6" WITHIN THE FIRST 10 FEET.

CADD
applications

USING CADD TO DRAW FOUNDATION PLANS

Early in this chapter you learned that it is possible to trace from the floor plan to create a foundation plan using manual drafting. However, it was explained that this practice is dangerous because errors or scale inaccuracies are transferred to the foundation plan. While this is true with manual drafting practices, CADD applications are different. Floor plans drawn using CADD will be accurate if the information you give the computer is accurate. You do not have the same kind of accuracy problems, such as misreading a scale, as you have with manual drafting. For this reason, the CADD floor plan may be used as an accurate basis for drawing the foundation plan. Display the floor plan on a layer and then begin the foundation drawing directly over the

floor plan on another layer. With this procedure, you can lay out the foundation exactly. All foundation walls, bearing footings, and support beams will be in their correct locations. When you are finished drawing the foundation plan, turn OFF or FREEZE the floor plan layer to have a ready-to-plot foundation plan. A complete CADD foundation is shown in Figure 1.

The process of drawing the foundation with CADD increases productivity enough for many architectural drafters to add floor-framing plans to the complete set of working drawings. For many residential applications, framing plans are not needed, but the addition of these plans increases construction accuracy and reduces the number of contractor-to-architect questions. These added drawing features can be included with little or no added time when compared to manual drafting.

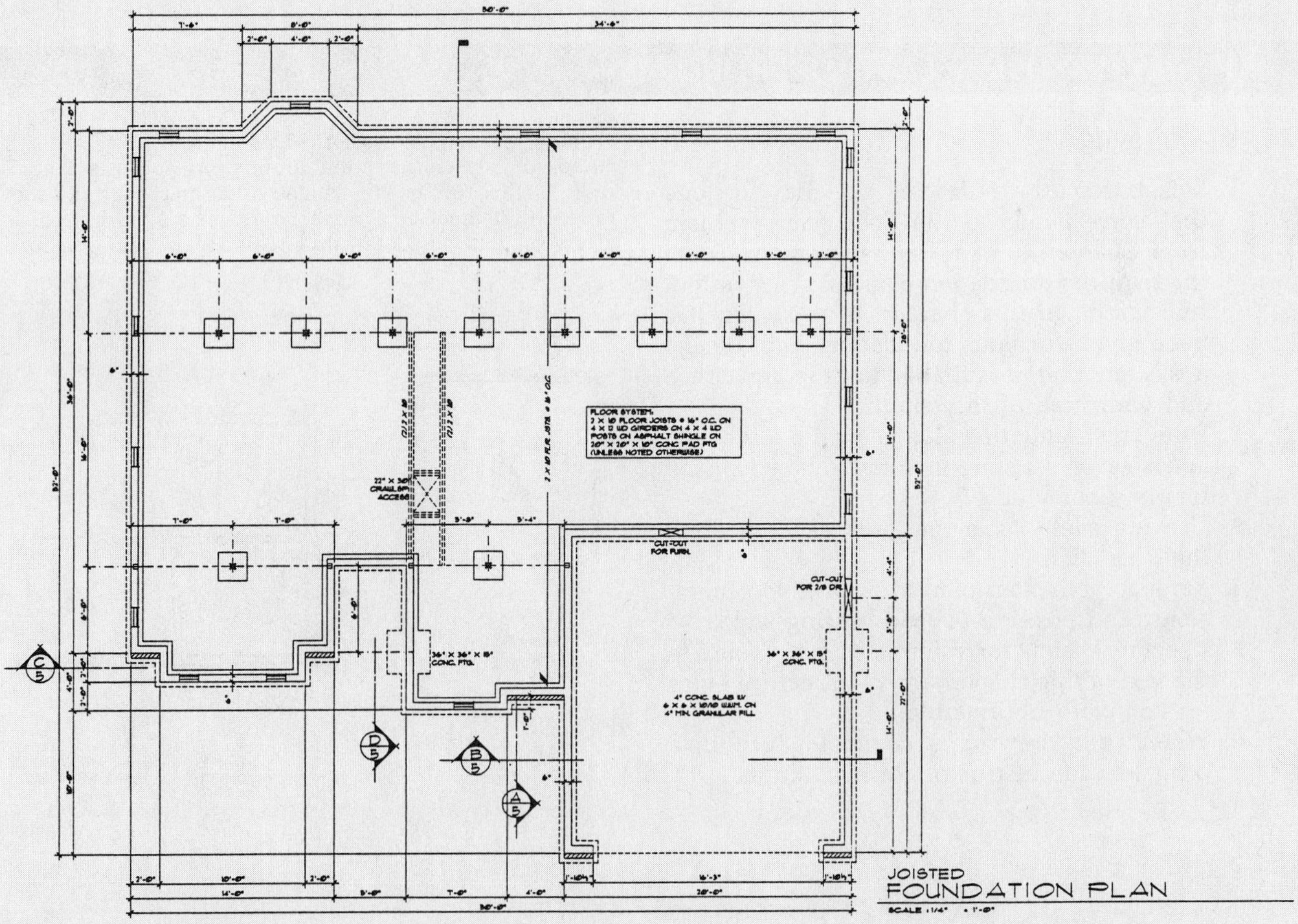

JOISTED
FOUNDATION PLAN
SCALE : 1/4" = 1'-0"

Figure 1 A complete CADD foundation plan. *Courtesy Alan Mascord Design Associates.*

FOUNDATION-PLAN LAYOUT TEST

DIRECTIONS

Answer the questions with short complete statements or drawings as needed on an 8½ × 11 drawing sheet as follows:

1. Use ⅛ in. guidelines for all lettering.
2. Letter your name, Foundation-Plan Layout Test, and the date at the top of the sheet.
3. Letter the question number and provide the answer. You do not need to write out the question.
4. Do all lettering with vertical uppercase architectural letters. If the answer requires line work, use proper drafting tools and techniques. Answers may be prepared on a word processor if appropriate with course guidelines.
5. Your grade will be based on correct answers and quality of your line and lettering technique.

QUESTIONS

1. At what scale will the foundation be drawn?
2. List five items that must be shown on a foundation plan for a concrete slab.
3. What general categories of information must be dimensioned on a slab foundation?
4. Show how floor joists are represented on a foundation plan.
5. How large an opening should be provided in the stem wall for an 8'–0" wide garage door?
6. How much space should be provided for a 3 ft entry door in a post-and-beam foundation? Explain your answer.
7. How are the footings represented on a foundation plan?
8. Show two methods of representing girders.
9. What type of line quality is typically used to represent beam pockets?
10. What are the disadvantages of tracing a print of the floor plan to lay out a foundation plan?

FOUNDATION-PLAN LAYOUT PROBLEMS

DIRECTIONS

1. Select from the following sketches the one that corresponds to the floor plan problem from Chapter 20 that you have drawn. Draw the required foundation plan using the guidelines given in this chapter. If no sketch has been given for your foundation plan, design a system that is suitable for the residence and your area of the country.
2. Draw the foundation plan using the same type and size of drawing material that you used for the floor plan.
3. Use the same scale that was used to draw the floor plan.
4. Refer to your floor plan to determine dimensions, and position of load-bearing walls.
5. Use the sketch for reference only. Refer to the text of this chapter and class lecture notes for complete information.
6. When your drawing is complete, turn in a print to your instructor for evaluation.

Problem 23–1. CAPE COD. This floor plan requires a standard joist construction foundation and has a stick roof. A stick roof is constructed of ceiling joists and roof rafters that meet at a ridge board. The kind of roof is given so you can determine which partitions are load bearing.

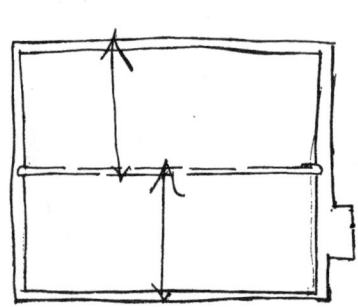

Problem 23-2. CABIN. This floor plan requires a piling foundation and has a stick roof. A stick roof is constructed of ceiling joists and roof rafters that meet at a ridge board. The kind of roof is given so you can determine which partitions are load bearing. Note the alternate foundation layout.

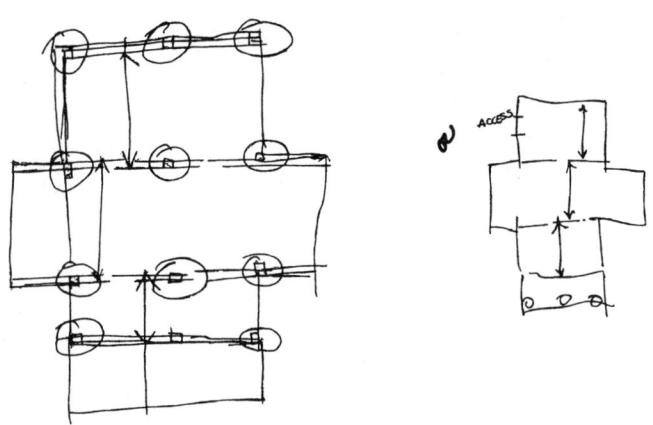

Problem 23-3. RANCH. This floor plan requires a post-and-beam foundation and has a truss roof. A truss roof requires no interior bearing walls. The kind of roof is given so you can determine which partitions are load bearing.

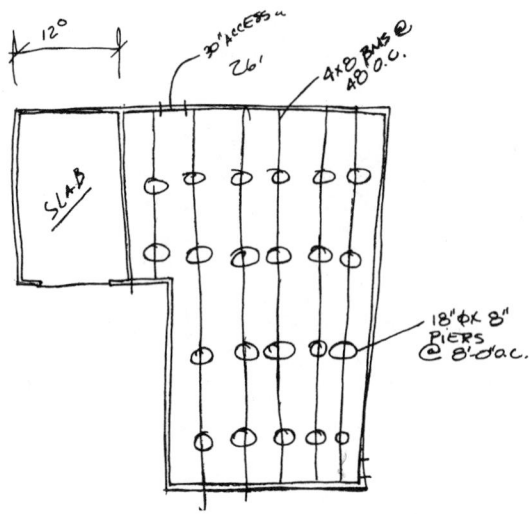

Problem 23-4. SPANISH. This floor plan requires a concrete slab foundation and has a stick roof. A stick roof is constructed of ceiling joists and roof rafters that meet at a ridge board. The kind of roof is given so you can determine which partitions are load bearing.

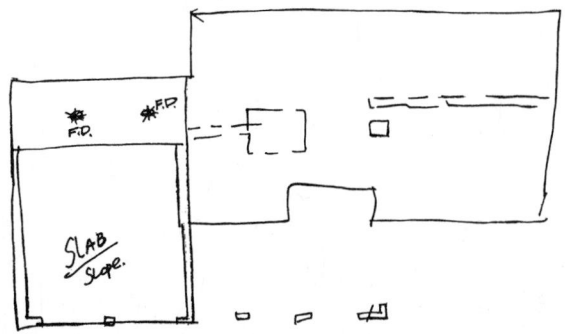

Problem 23-5. EARLY AMERICAN. This floor plan will be drawn with a basement foundation system. The roof and floors will be framed using conventional framing methods. Provide support at the foundation level for all bearing walls. Determine the size of all footings and piers using the information in this section and Chapters 46, 47, and 48.

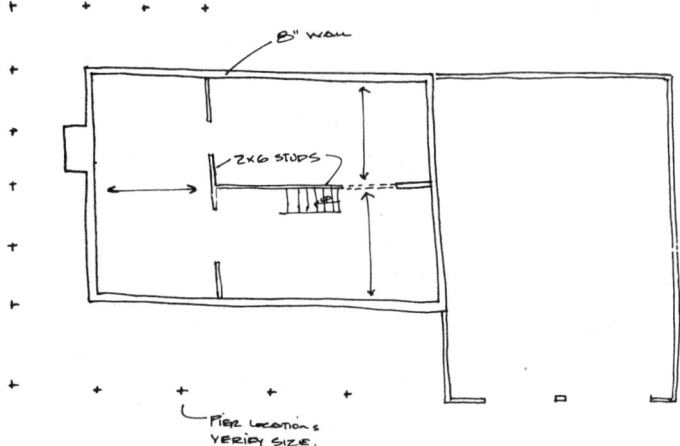

Problem 23-6. CONTEMPORARY. This floor plan will be drawn with a daylight basement. The roof and floors will be framed using conventional framing methods. Provide support at the foundation level for all bearing walls. Determine the size of all footings and piers using the information in this section and Chapters 46, 47, and 48. Determine the size of windows and doors, and type of basement materials, based on common practices in your area or according to lectures by your instructor.

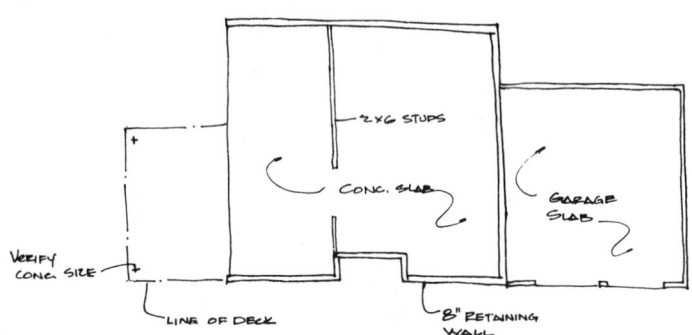

Problem 23-7. DUPLEX. Without the use of a designer's sketch, design a suitable foundation for this structure using the information presented in this section and Chapters 46, 47, and 48. Determine the type of roof framing system to be used, and design an appropriate foundation system. Sketch the foundation plan showing all required footings and piers and have it approved by your instructor prior to starting your drawing.

FRONT ELEVATION

LEFT-SIDE ELEVATION

CM-1430

Section Five
Elevations

Chapter 24
Introduction to Elevations

ELEVATIONS ARE an essential part of the design and drafting process. The elevations are a group of drawings which show the exterior of a building. An elevation is an orthographic drawing that shows one side of a building. Elevations are projected as shown in Figure 24–1. Elevations are drawn to show exterior shapes and finishes as well as the vertical relationships of the building levels. By using the elevations, sections, and floor plans the exterior shape of a building can be determined.

REQUIRED ELEVATIONS

Typically, four elevations will be required to show the features of a building. On a simple building, only three elevations will be needed as seen in Figure 24–2. When drawing a building with an irregular shape, parts of the house may be hidden. An elevation of each different surface should be drawn as shown in Figure 24–3. If a building has walls that are not at 90° to each other, a true orthographic drawing could be very confusing. In the orthographic projection, part of the elevation will be distorted as can be seen in Figure 24–4. Elevations of this type of

building are usually expanded so that a separate elevation of each different face is drawn similar to Figure 24–5.

TYPES OF ELEVATIONS

Elevations can be drawn as either presentation drawings or working drawings. Presentation drawings were introduced in Chapter 14 and will be covered in depth in Chapter 40. These are drawings that are a part of the initial design process and may range from sketches to very detailed drawings intended to help the owner and lending institution understand the basic design concepts. See Figure 24–6.

Working elevations are part of the working drawings and are drawn to provide information for the building team. This would include information on roofing, siding, openings, chimneys, land shape, and sometimes even the depth of footings as shown in Figure 24–7. When used with the floor plans, the elevations provide the information for the contractor to determine surface areas. Once surface areas are known, exact quantities of material can be determined. The elevations are also necessary when making heat loss calculations as described in Chapter 19. The elevations are used to determine the surface area of walls and wall openings for the required heat loss formulas.

ELEVATION SCALES

Elevations are typically drawn at the same scale as the floor plan. For most plans, this means a scale of

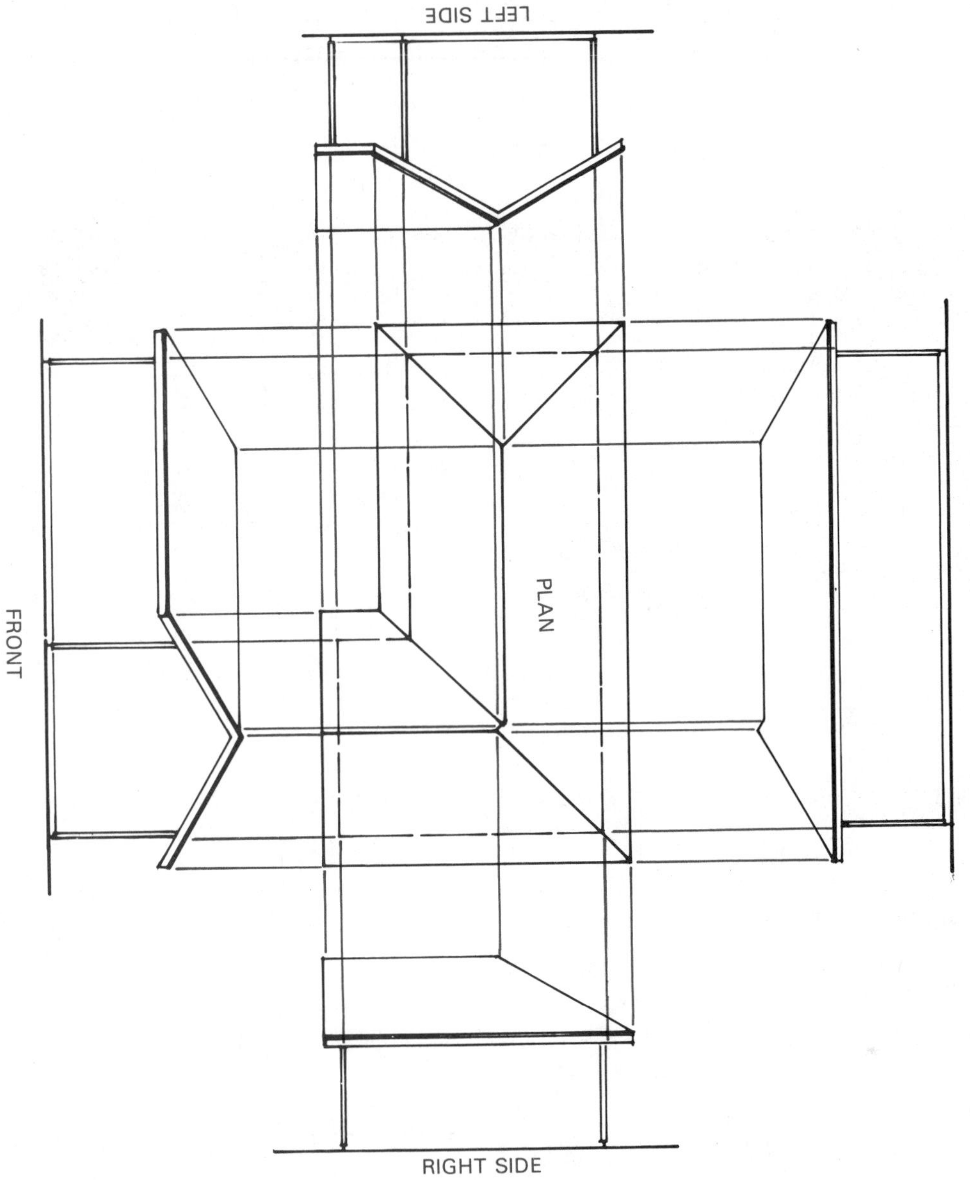

LEFT SIDE

FRONT

PLAN

REAR

RIGHT SIDE

Figure 24–1 Elevations are orthographic projections showing each side of a structure.

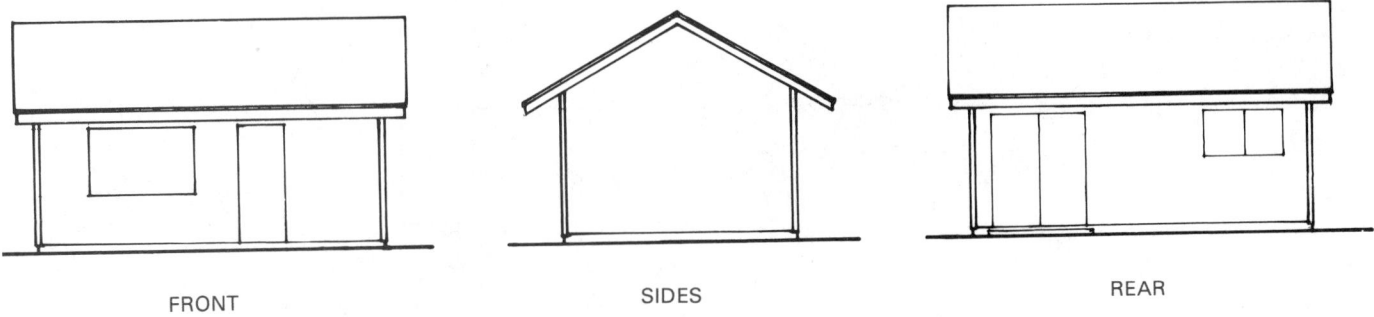

FRONT

SIDES

REAR

Figure 24–2 Elevations are used to show the exterior shape and material of a building. On a simple structure, only three views are required.

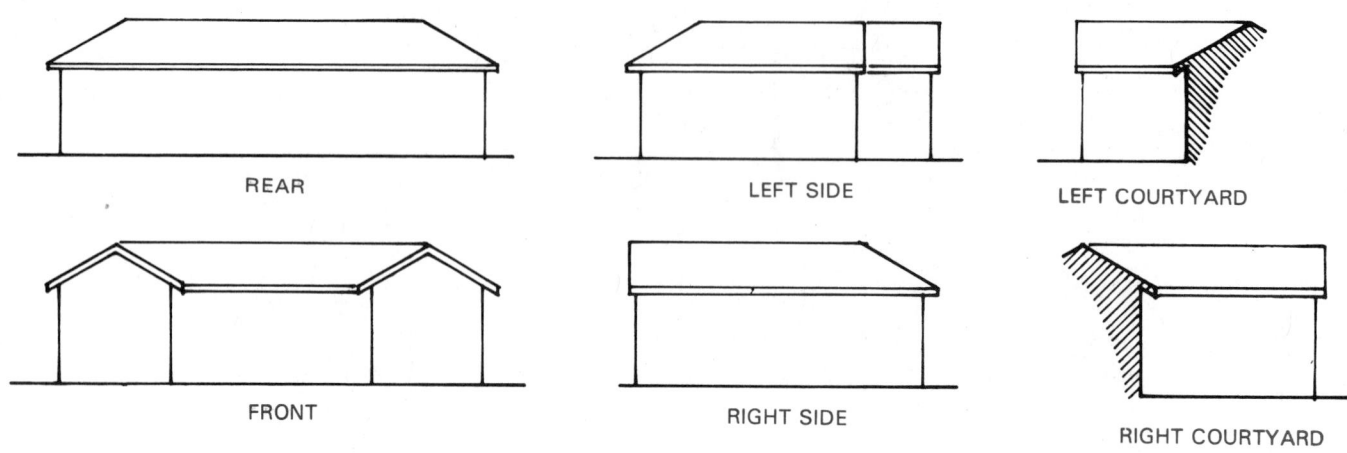

REAR   LEFT SIDE   LEFT COURTYARD

FRONT   RIGHT SIDE   RIGHT COURTYARD

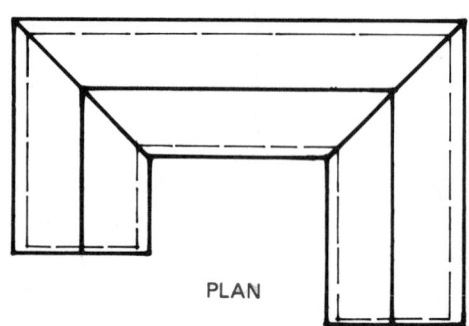

PLAN

Figure 24–3 Plans of irregular shapes often require an elevation of each surface.

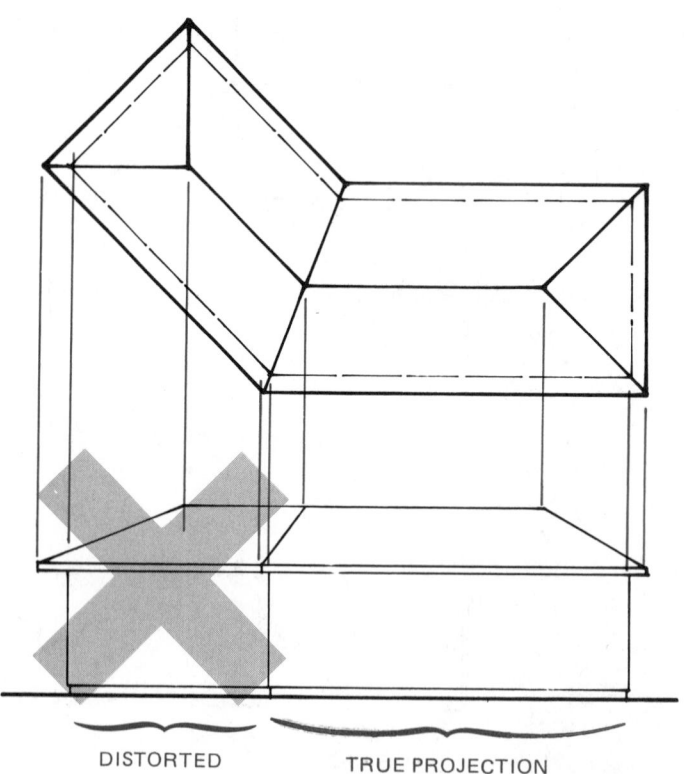

DISTORTED   TRUE PROJECTION

Figure 24–4 Using true orthographic projection methods with a plan of irregular shapes will result in a distortion of part of the view.

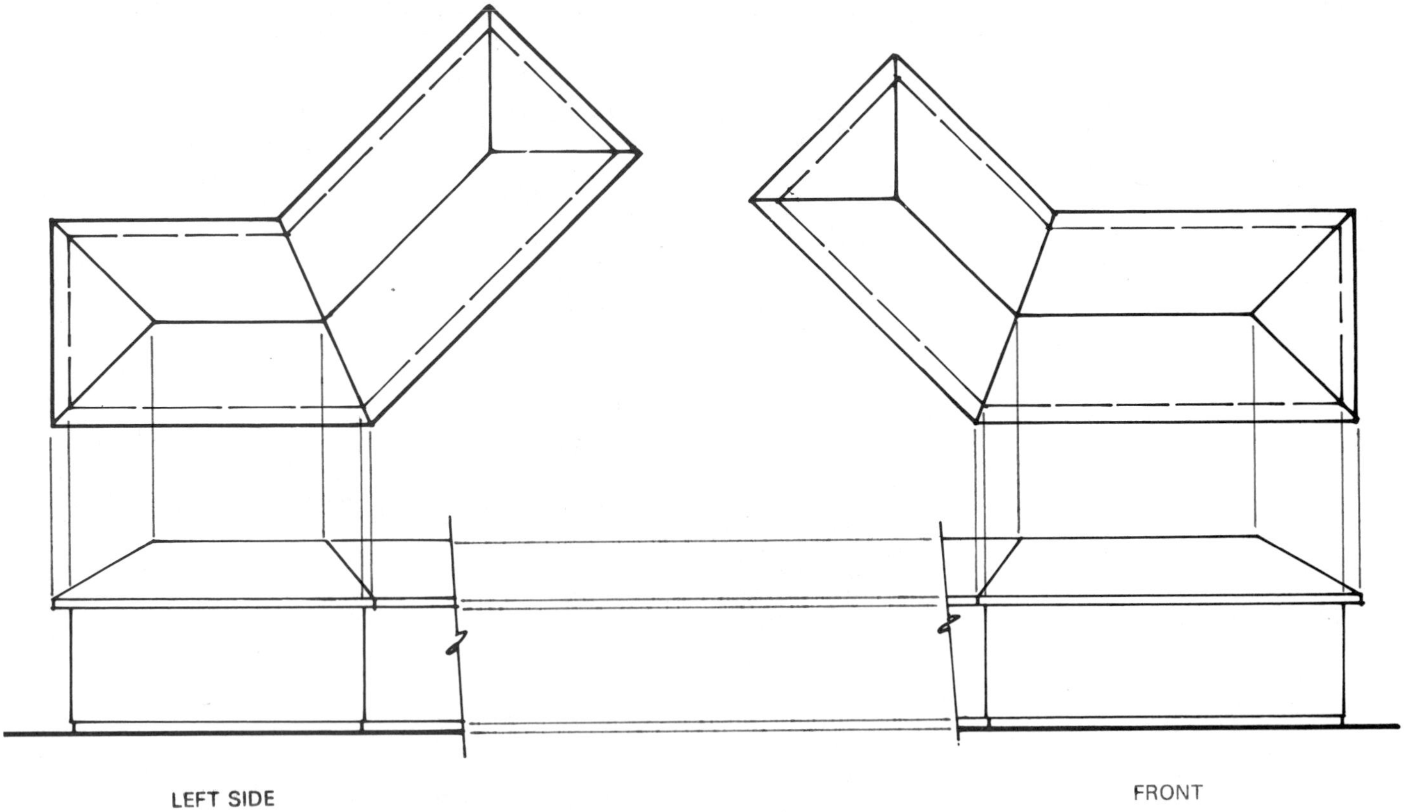

LEFT SIDE   FRONT

Figure 24-5 When drawing elevations with walls that are not at right angles to each other, expanded elevations should be drawn.

"STUCCATO"
PANEL SIDING
(FRONT ELEV. ONLY)
1 x 6 R/S CEDAR
CORNER TRIM

FRONT ELEVATION

SCALE : 1/4" = 1' - 0"

Figure 24-6 Presentation elevations are highly detailed drawings used to present the structure. *Courtesy Piercy & Barclay, Inc.*

¼″ = 1′–0″ will be used. This allows for the elevations to be projected directly from the floor plans. Some floor plans for multifamily and commercial projects may be laid out at a scale of 1/16″ equals 1 ft or even as small as 1/32 in. equals 1 ft. When a scale of ⅛ in. or less is used, generally very little detail is placed on the drawing as seen in Figure 24–8. Depending on the complexity of the project or the amount of space on a page the front elevation may be drawn at ¼ in. scale and the balance of the elevations drawn at a smaller scale.

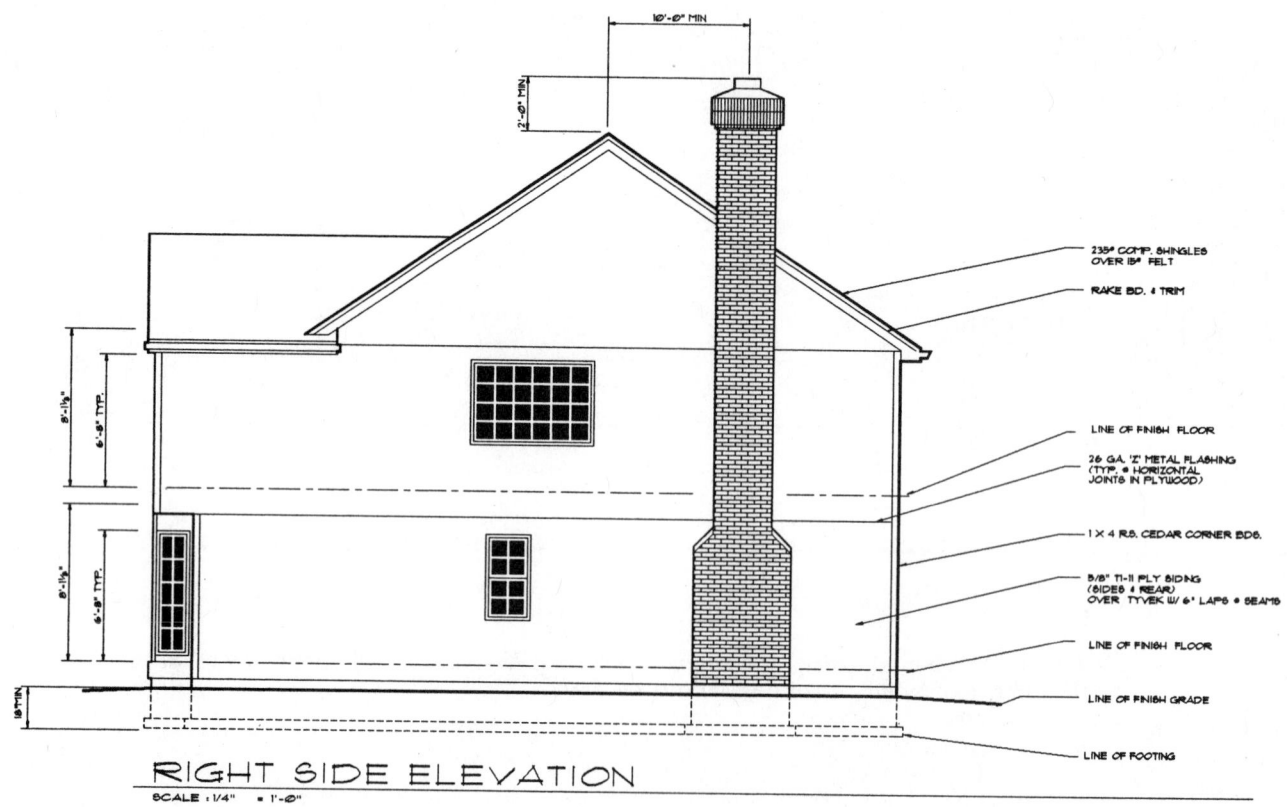

Figure 24–7 Working elevations are the drawings for the construction crew and show less detail than a presentation drawing. *Courtesy Alan Mascord Design Associates.*

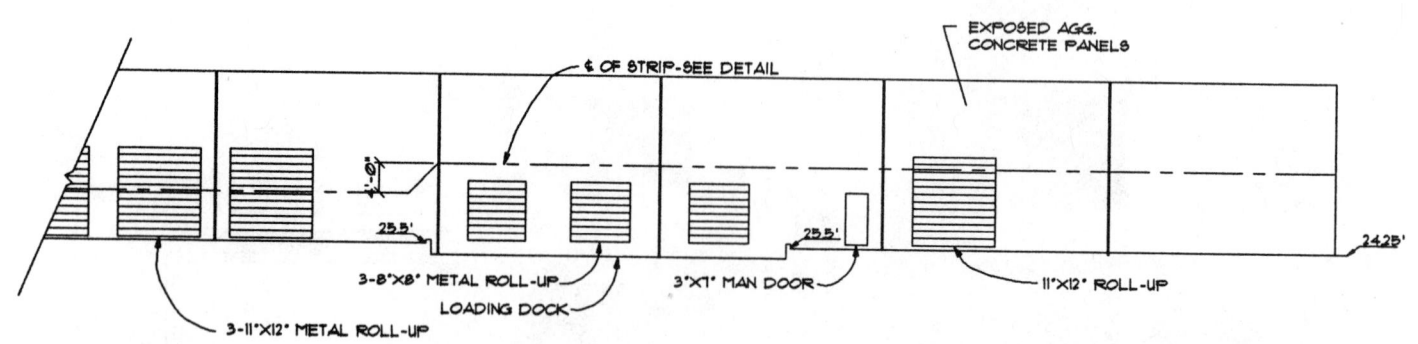

Figure 24–8 Elevations of large structures are typically drawn at a small scale such as 1/16″ = 1′–0″ with very little detail shown.

CADD
applications

CADD ELEVATION SYMBOLS

Drawing exterior and interior elevation features with CADD is easy. Most architectural CADD programs have a variety of elevation symbols representing doors, windows, and materials. For example, when selecting symbols, pick a DOOR or WINDOW symbol from a tablet menu library—a screen menu will display your options. You then pick doors such as entrance, flush, or French. You can also add trim and door knobs. When you pick WINDOW from the tablet menu library, you get options such as sliders, casement, double hung, awning, and fixed. Figure 1 shows door and window tablet menu overlays. You can customize your window symbols with divided lites, arrows, reflection marks, solid black glass, or hinge marks. Figure 2 shows a variety of CADD elevation door and window symbols.

After you manually draw an elevation with fine-detail materials such as brick, stone or shake roofing, you should have an opportunity to see how these items are drawn using CADD. All you do is pick the symbol, define the boundaries of the material, and the computer automatically draws the material within those boundaries. Bricks, stone, or roofing material symbols come out perfectly every time, as shown in Figure 3.

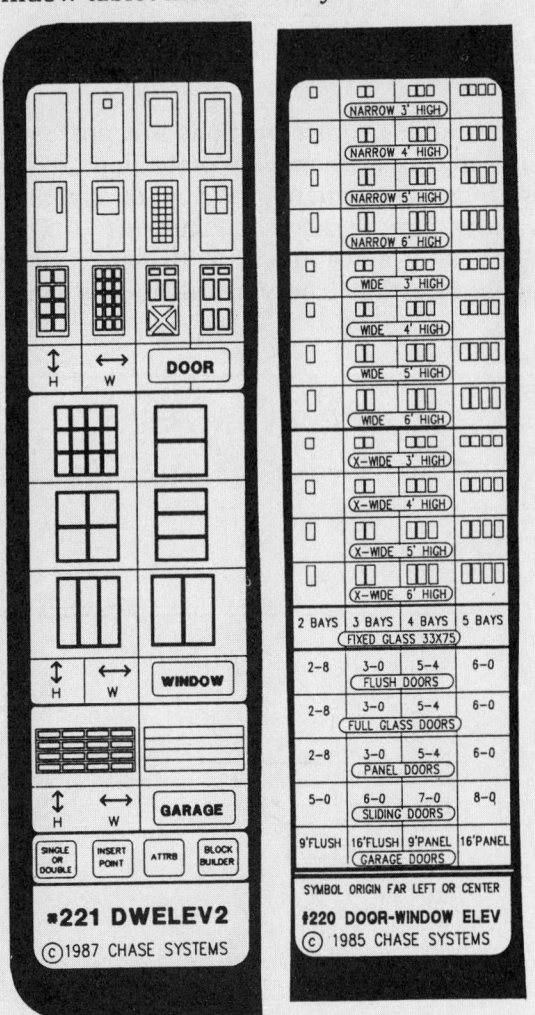

Figure 1 Door and window tablet menu overlays. *Courtesy Chase Systems.*

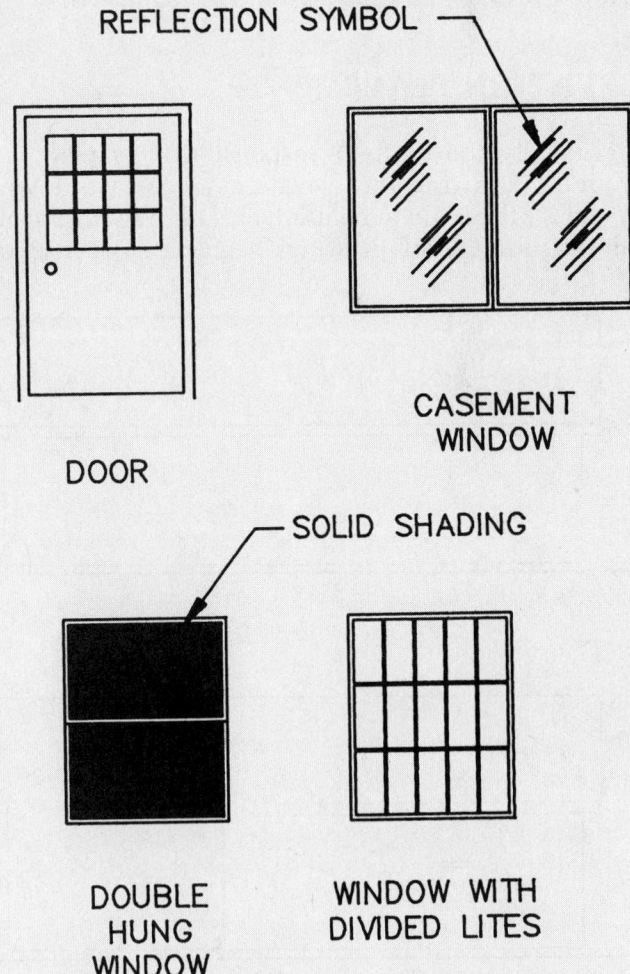

Figure 2 CADD elevation door and window symbols.

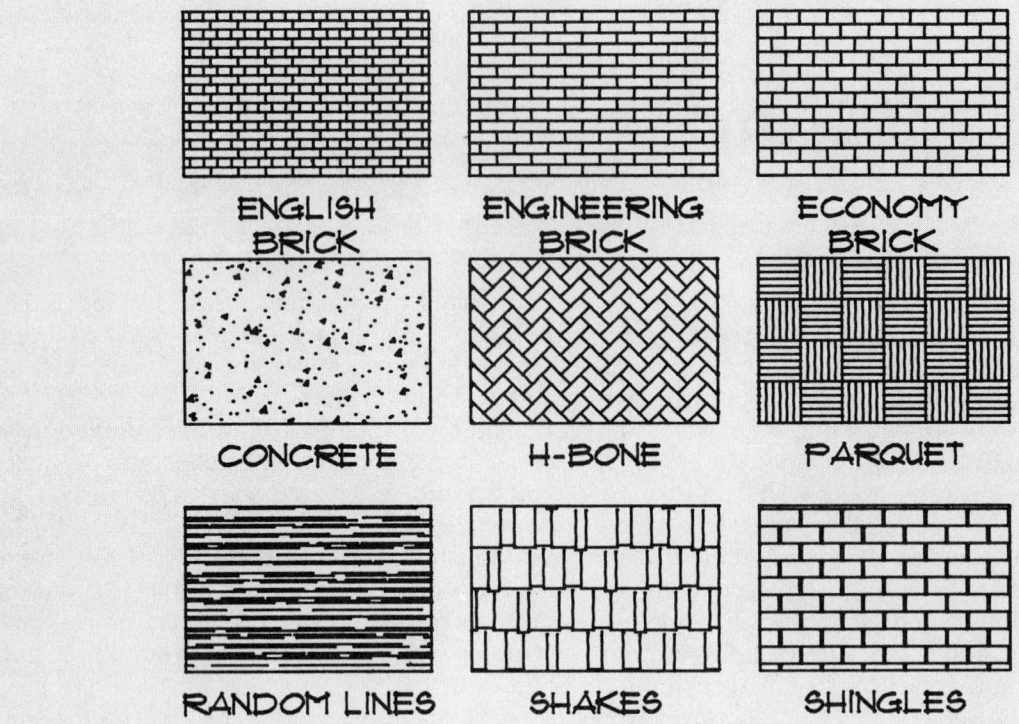

Figure 3 CADD representations of building materials.

ELEVATION PLACEMENT

It is usually the drafter's responsibility to plan the layout for drawing the elevations. The layout will depend on the scale to be used, size of drawing sheet, and the number of drawings required. Because of size limitations, the elevations are not usually laid out in the true orthographic projection of Front, Side, Rear, Side. A common method of layout for four elevations can be seen in Figure 24–9. This layout places a side elevation by both the front and rear elevations so that true vertical heights may be pro-

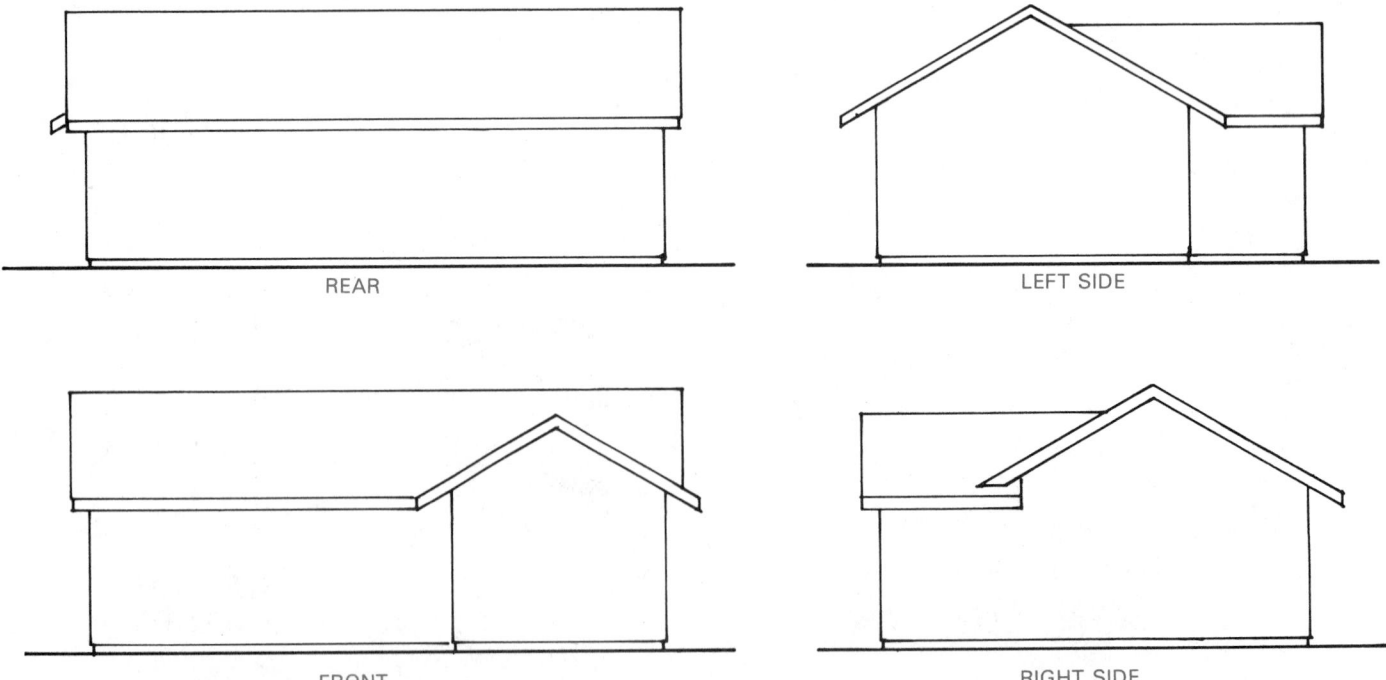

Figure 24–9 A common method of elevation layout is to place a side elevation beside both the front and the rear elevation. This allows for heights to be directly transferred from one view to the other.

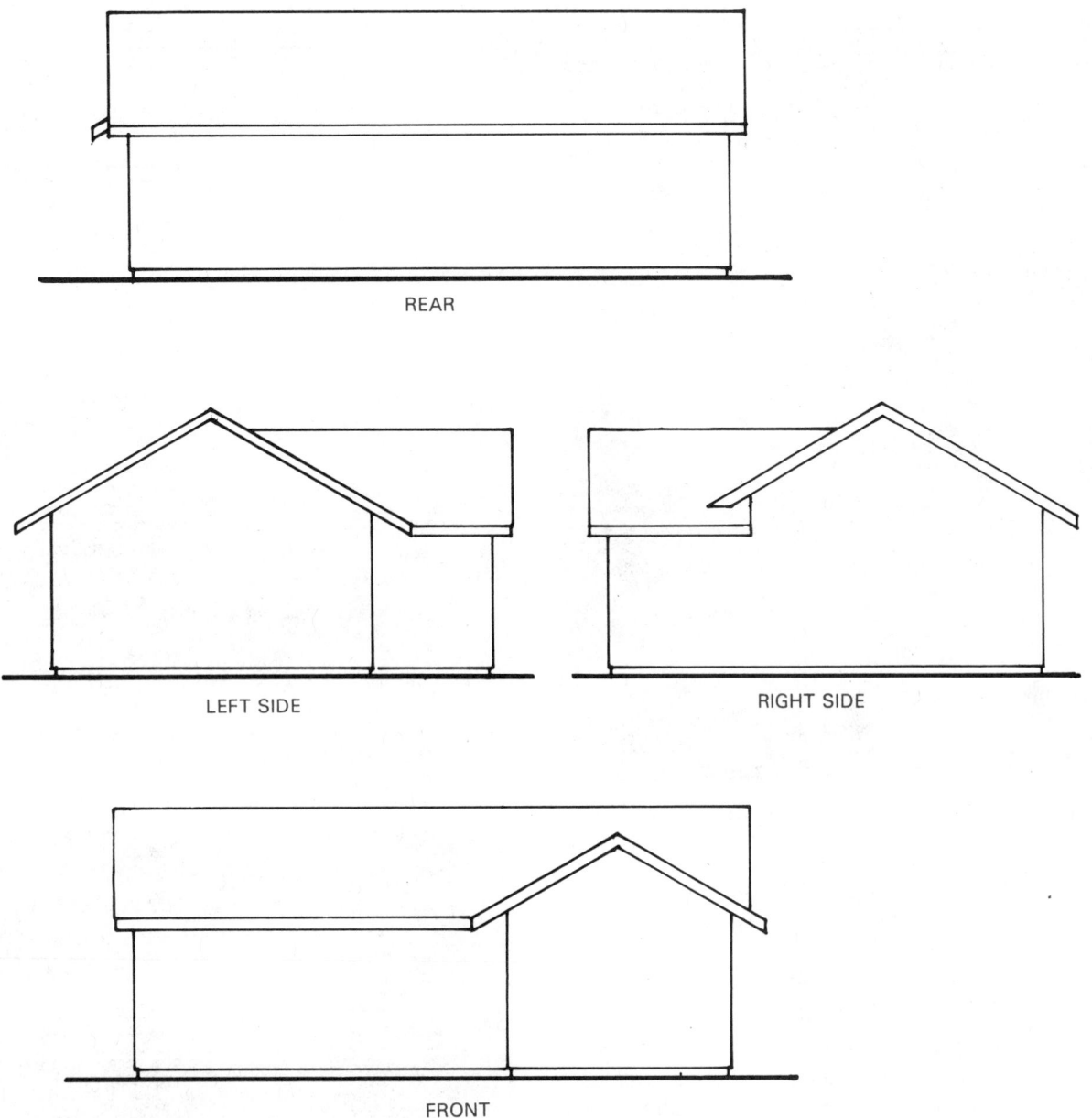

Figure 24–10 An alternative elevation arrangement is to place the two shortest elevations side by side.

jected from one view to another. If the drawing paper is not long enough for this placement, the layout of Figure 24–10 may be used. This arrangement often is used when the elevations are placed next to the floor plan to conserve space. A drawback to this layout is that the heights established on the side elevations cannot be quickly transferred. A print of one elevation will have to be taped next to the location of the next elevation so that heights can be transferred.

SURFACE MATERIALS IN ELEVATION

The materials that are used to protect the building from the weather need to be shown on the elevations.

This information will be considered in the categories of roofing, wall coverings, doors, and windows.

Roofing Materials

There are several common materials that are used to protect the roof. Among the most frequently used are asphalt shingles, wood shakes and shingles, clay and concrete tiles, metal sheets, and built-up roofing materials. It is important that the architectural drafter have an idea of what each material looks like so that it can be drawn in a realistic style. It is also important to remember that the purpose of the elevations is for the framing crew. The framer's job will not be made easier by seeing every shingle drawn or other techniques that are used on presentation drawings

Figure 24–11 A common alternative to the uniform size and texture of 235# composition shingles are 300# shingles. The random pattern is typified in this photo of "Architect 80." *Courtesy Genstar Roofing Products Company.*

and renderings. The elevations need to have materials represented clearly and quickly.

Asphalt Shingles. Asphalt shingles come in many colors and patterns. Figure 24–11 shows a roof covered with the random pattern of 300# asphalt shingles. Asphalt shingles are typically drawn using the method seen in Figure 24–12.

Wood Shakes and Shingles. Figure 24–13 shows a roof protected with wood shakes. Other materials such as Masonite are used to simulate wood shakes and can be seen in Figure 24–14. Shakes and Masonite create a jagged surface at the ridge and the edge. These types of materials are often represented as shown in Figure 24–15.

Tile. Concrete, clay, or a lightweight simulated tile material present a very rugged surface at the ridge and edge as well as many shadows throughout the roof. Figure 24–16 shows flat tile. This type of tile is usually drawn in a manner similar to the drawing in Figure 24–17. Figure 24–18 shows a roof with Spanish tile. This type of tile is often drawn as shown in Figure 24–19. Rub-on films are available for some types of tile roofs. Figure 24–20 shows an

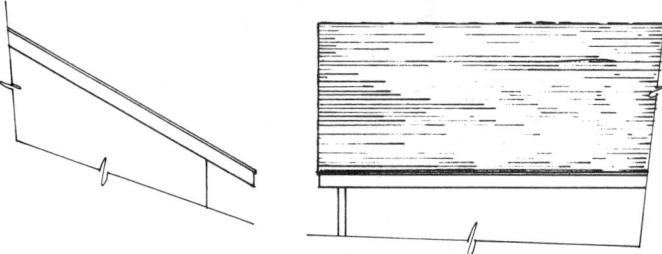

Figure 24–12 Drawing asphalt shingles.

Figure 24–13 Wood shakes and shingles have much more texture than asphalt shingles.

Figure 24–14 Shingles are made to resemble wood shakes. These shingles are Masonite. *Courtesy Masonite Corporation.*

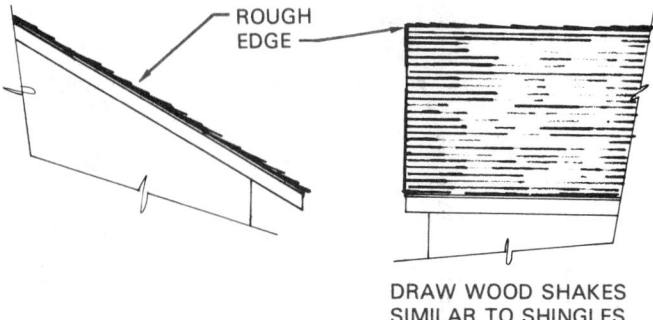

ROUGH EDGE

DRAW WOOD SHAKES SIMILAR TO SHINGLES

Figure 24–15 Drawing wood shakes and shingles.

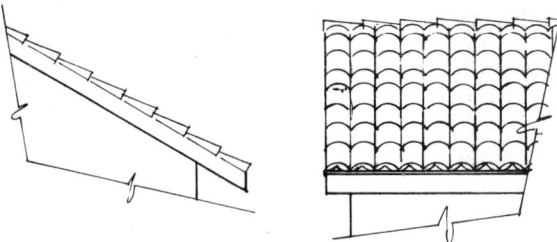

Figure 24–19 Drawing curved tiles.

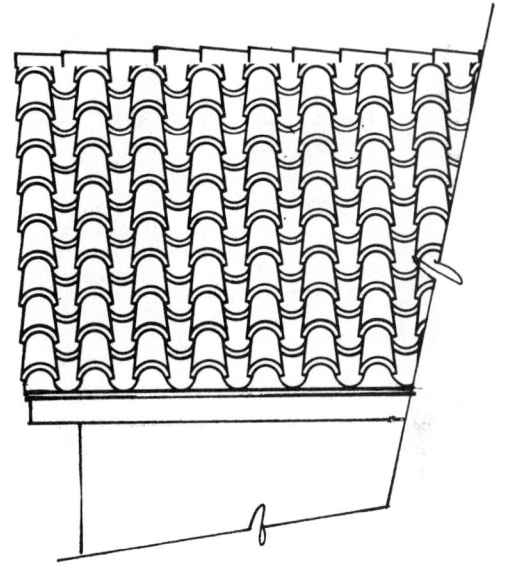

Figure 24–20 Tiles may be drawn in elevation by using rub-on film. *Courtesy Chartpak.*

Figure 24–16 Flat tiles are a very common roofing material in many parts of the country.

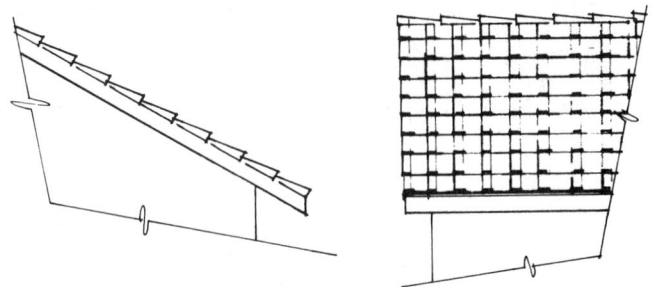

Figure 24–17 Flat tiles are drawn using methods similar to drawing shakes.

Figure 24–21 Built-up roofing with a gravel cover is common in many areas where there is mild weather all year long.

Figure 24–18 Curved, or Spanish, tiles are a very traditional roofing material in many areas of the country.

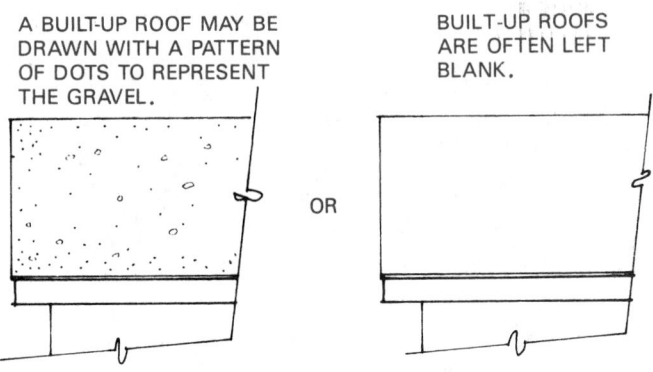

A BUILT-UP ROOF MAY BE DRAWN WITH A PATTERN OF DOTS TO REPRESENT THE GRAVEL.

BUILT-UP ROOFS ARE OFTEN LEFT BLANK.

OR

Figure 24–22 Drawing built-up roofs.

elevation where the drafter used a rub-on film to represent the tile rather than drawing each tile.

Metal. Metal shingles and panels are common on many types of roofs. Metal shingles would usually be drawn in a manner similar to asphalt shingles. Metal panels come in many styles.

Built-up Roofs. Built-up roofing, or hot tar roofs, are used on very low pitched roofs. Because of the low pitch and the lack of surface texture, built-up roofs are usually outlined and left blank. Occasionally a built-up roof will be covered with 2- or 3-in.-

(a)

(b)

Figure 24–23 (a) Domed and (b) flat glass skylights are a common feature of many roofs. (a) *Courtesy Duralite;* (b) *courtesy VELUX-AMERICA, INC.*

diameter rock as seen in Figure 24–21. The drawing technique for this roof can be seen in Figure 24–22.

Skylights. Skylights may be made of either flat glass or domed plastic. Although they come in a variety of shapes and styles, skylights usually resemble those shown in Figure 24–23. Depending on the pitch of the roof, skylights may or may not be drawn. On very low-pitched roofs a skylight may be unrecognizable. On roofs over 3/12 pitch the shape of the skylight can usually be drawn without creating confusion. Unless the roof is very steep, a rectangular skylight will appear almost square. The flatter the roof, the more distortion there will be in the size of the skylight. Figure 24–24 shows common methods of drawing both flat glass and domed skylights.

Wall Coverings

Exterior wall coverings are usually made of wood, wood substitutes, masonry, metal, plaster or stucco. Each has its own distinctive look in elevation.

Wood. Wood siding can either be installed in large sheets or in individual pieces. Plywood sheets are a popular wood siding because of the low cost and ease of installation. Individual pieces of wood provide an attractive finish but usually cost more than plywood. This higher cost results from differences in material and the labor to install each individual piece.

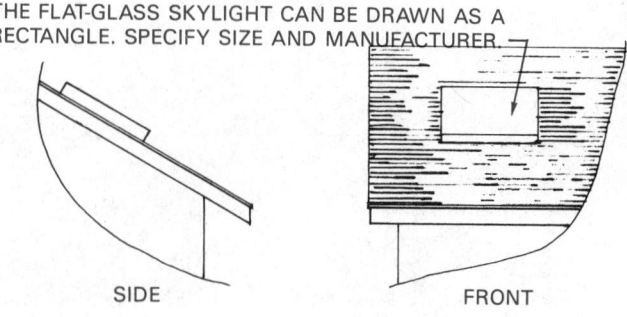

A DOUBLE-DOMED SKYLIGHT SHOULD HAVE A SLIGHTLY CURVED SURFACE TO REFLECT THE CURVED PLASTIC. SPECIFY SIZE AND MANUFACTURER.

SIDE   FRONT

DOUBLE-DOMED SKYLIGHT

THE FLAT-GLASS SKYLIGHT CAN BE DRAWN AS A RECTANGLE. SPECIFY SIZE AND MANUFACTURER.

SIDE   FRONT

FLAT-GLASS SKYLIGHT

Figure 24–24 Common methods of drawing skylights.

Figure 24–25 Plywood T–1–11 is a common siding. *Courtesy American Plywood Association.*

Figure 24–26 Batt-on-board siding. *Courtesy Weather Shield Mfg., Inc.*

Plywood siding can have many textures, finishes, and patterns. Textures and finishes are not shown on the elevations but may be specified in a general note. Patterns in the plywood are usually shown. The most common patterns in plywood are T-1-11 shown in Figure 24–25, reverse board and batten shown in Figure 24–26, and plain or rough-cut ply in Figure 24–27. Figure 24–28 shows methods for drawing each type of siding.

Lumber siding comes in several types and is laid in many patterns. Among the most common lumber for sidings are cedar, redwood, pine, fir, spruce, and hemlock. Common styles of lumber siding are tongue and groove, bevel, and channel siding. Each kind can be seen in Figures 24–29 through 24–31. Each of

Figure 24–27 Plywood siding can be seen on this home designed by the Santa Rosa, CA, architectural firm of Roland/Miller/Associate. *Courtesy American Plywood Association.*

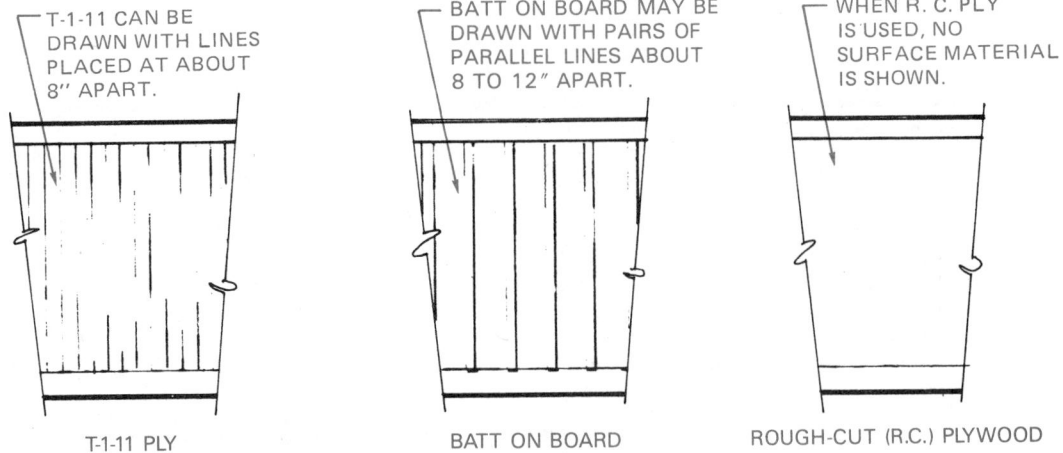

Figure 24–28 Drawing plywood siding in elevation.

Figure 24–29 Tongue and groove siding. *Courtesy Western Wood Products Association.*

Figure 24–30 Bevel siding can be seen on this residence in Idyllwild, CA, designed by Outback Design & Construction. *Courtesy California Redwood Association.*

Figure 24–31 Channel siding.

these materials can be installed in a vertical, horizontal, or diagonal position. The material and type of siding must be specified in a general note on the elevations. The pattern in which the siding is to be installed must be shown on the elevations in a manner similar to Figure 24–32. The type of siding and the position in which it is laid will affect how the siding appears at a corner. Figure 24–33 shows two common methods of corner treatment.

Wood shingles can either be installed individually or in panels. Shingles are often drawn as shown in Figure 24–34.

Wood Substitutes. Hardboard, aluminum, and vinyl siding can be produced to resemble lumber siding. Figure 24–35 shows a home finished with hardboard siding. Hardboard siding is generally installed in large sheets similar to plywood but often has more detail than plywood or lumber siding. It is typically drawn using methods similar to those used for drawing

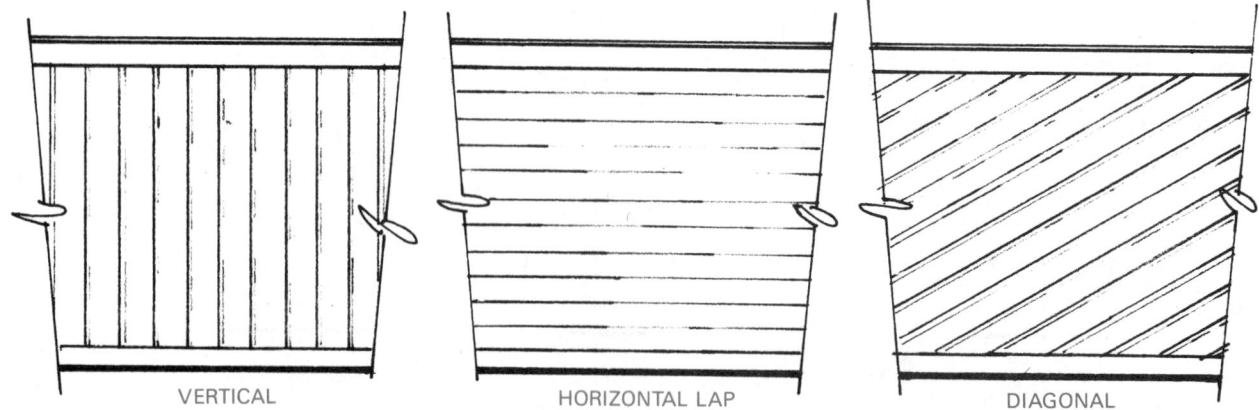

VERTICAL   HORIZONTAL LAP   DIAGONAL

Figure 24–32 The type of siding and the position in which it is to be installed must be shown on the elevations.

Figure 24–33
Common methods of corner treatment to be shown on elevations.

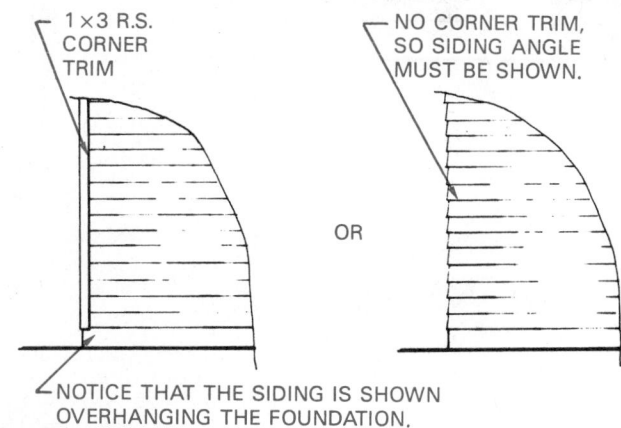

1 × 3 R.S. CORNER TRIM

NO CORNER TRIM, SO SIDING ANGLE MUST BE SHOWN.

OR

NOTICE THAT THE SIDING IS SHOWN OVERHANGING THE FOUNDATION.

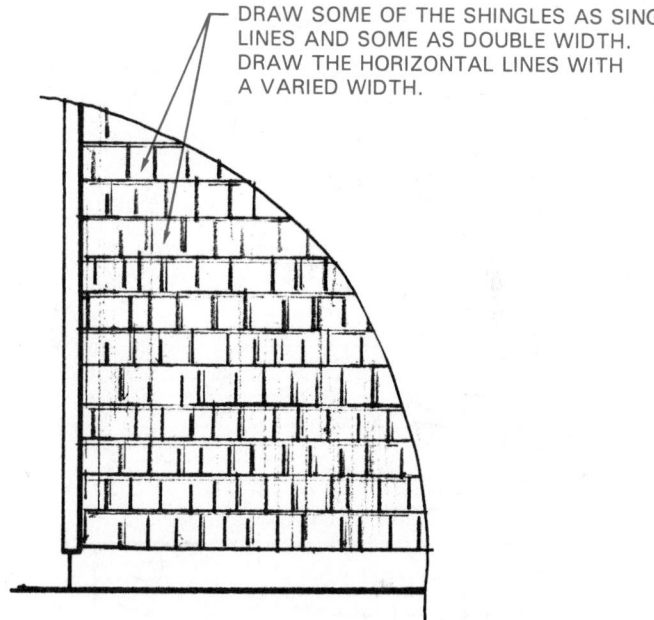

DRAW SOME OF THE SHINGLES AS SINGLE LINES AND SOME AS DOUBLE WIDTH. DRAW THE HORIZONTAL LINES WITH A VARIED WIDTH.

Figure 24–34 Drawing shingles. Notice the contrast in line weights to create shadows and texture.

Figure 24–35 Hardboard siding. *Courtesy Georgia-Pacific Corporation.*

Figure 24–36 Aluminum and vinyl sidings resemble wood siding. *Courtesy Vinyl Improvement Products Company.*

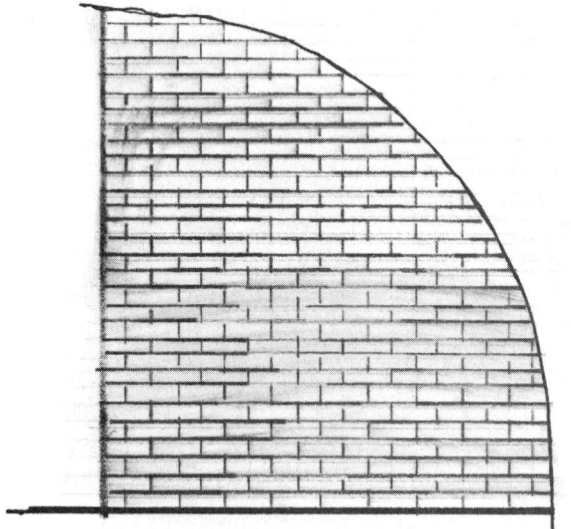

Figure 24–37 Drawing brick in elevation.

Figure 24–38 Drawing brick with a quill pen and ink wash.

lumber sidings. Aluminum and vinyl sidings also resemble lumber siding in appearance as shown in Figure 24–36. Aluminum and vinyl sidings are drawn similar to their lumber counterpart.

Masonry. Masonry finishes may be made of brick, concrete block or stone.

Figure 24–39 Rub-on brick patterns. *Courtesy Chartpak.*

Figure 24–40 Methods of representing concrete blocks in elevation.

Bricks come in a variety of sizes, patterns, and textures. When drawing elevations the drafter must represent the pattern of the bricks on the drawing and the material and texture in the written specifications. Methods for drawing bricks are shown in Figure 24–37 and 24–38. Although bricks are not usually drawn exactly to scale, the proportions of the brick must be maintained. Figure 24–39 shows common patterns available for rub-on bricks.

A drafter will often be required to show size, pattern, and texture on the elevation when drawing concrete blocks. Figure 24–40 shows methods of representing some of the various concrete blocks.

Stone or rock finishes also come in a wide variety of sizes and shapes, and are laid in a variety of patterns as shown in Figure 24–41. Stone or rock may be either natural or artificial. Both will appear the same when drawn in elevation. When representing stone and rock surfaces in elevation, the drafter must be careful to represent the irregular shape as shown in Figure 24–42.

Metal. Although primarily a roofing material, metal can be used as an attractive wall covering. Drawing metal in elevation uses a method similar to drawing lumber siding.

Figure 24–41 Stone is used in a variety of shapes and patterns. *Courtesy Stucco Stone Products, Inc., Napa, CA.*

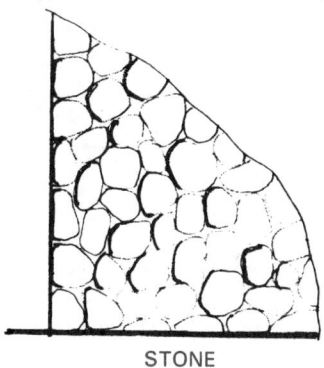
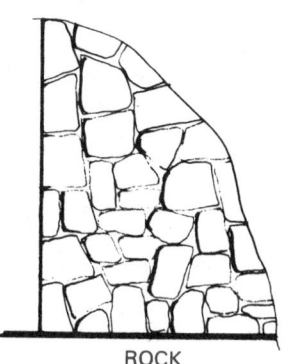

STONE   ROCK

Figure 24–42 Drawing stone and rock surfaces in elevation.

Plaster or Stucco. Although primarily used in areas with little rainfall, plaster or stucco can be found throughout the country. Figure 24–43 shows an example of a common stucco pattern. No matter what the pattern, stucco is typically drawn as shown in Figure 24–44.

Doors

Many styles of doors were shown in Chapter 15. On the elevations, doors are drawn to resemble the type of door specified in the door schedule. The drafter should be careful not to try to reproduce an exact likeness of a door. This is especially true on entry doors and garage doors. Typically these doors have a decorative pattern on them. It is important to show this pattern, but don't spend time trying to

Figure 24–43 Stucco is used in many patterns and textures. *Courtesy Ken Smith Drafting.*

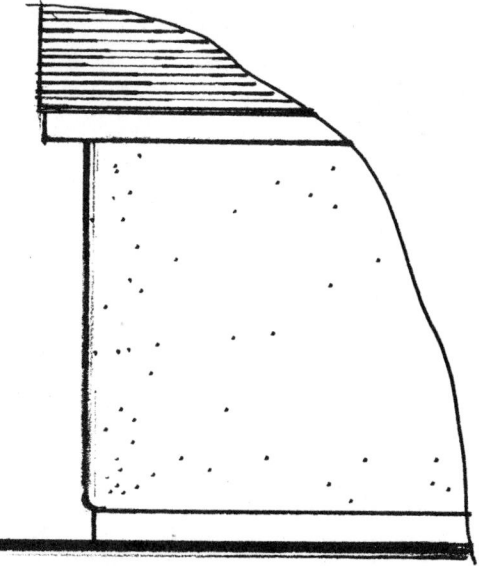

Figure 24–44 Drawing stucco or plaster in elevation.

reproduce the exact pattern. Since the door is manufactured, the drafter is wasting time on details that add nothing to the plan. Figure 24–45 shows the layout of a raised-panel door and Figure 24–46 shows how other common types of doors can be drawn.

Windows

The same precautions about drawing needless details for doors should be taken when drawing windows. Care must be given to the frame material when drawing windows. Wooden frames are wider than metal frames. When the elevations are started in the preliminary stages of design, the drafter may not know what type of frames will be used. In this case,

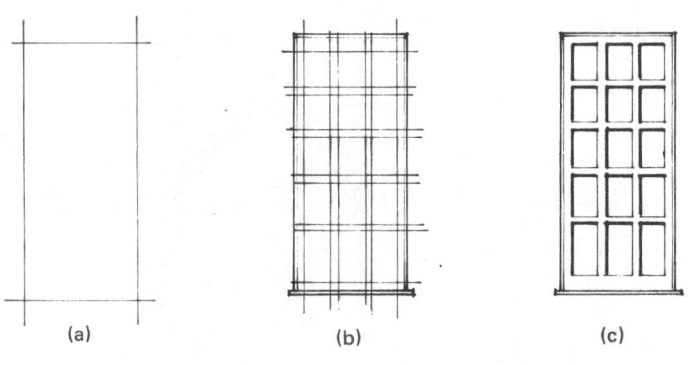

(a)   (b)   (c)

Figure 24–45 Layout steps for drawing a raised-panel door.

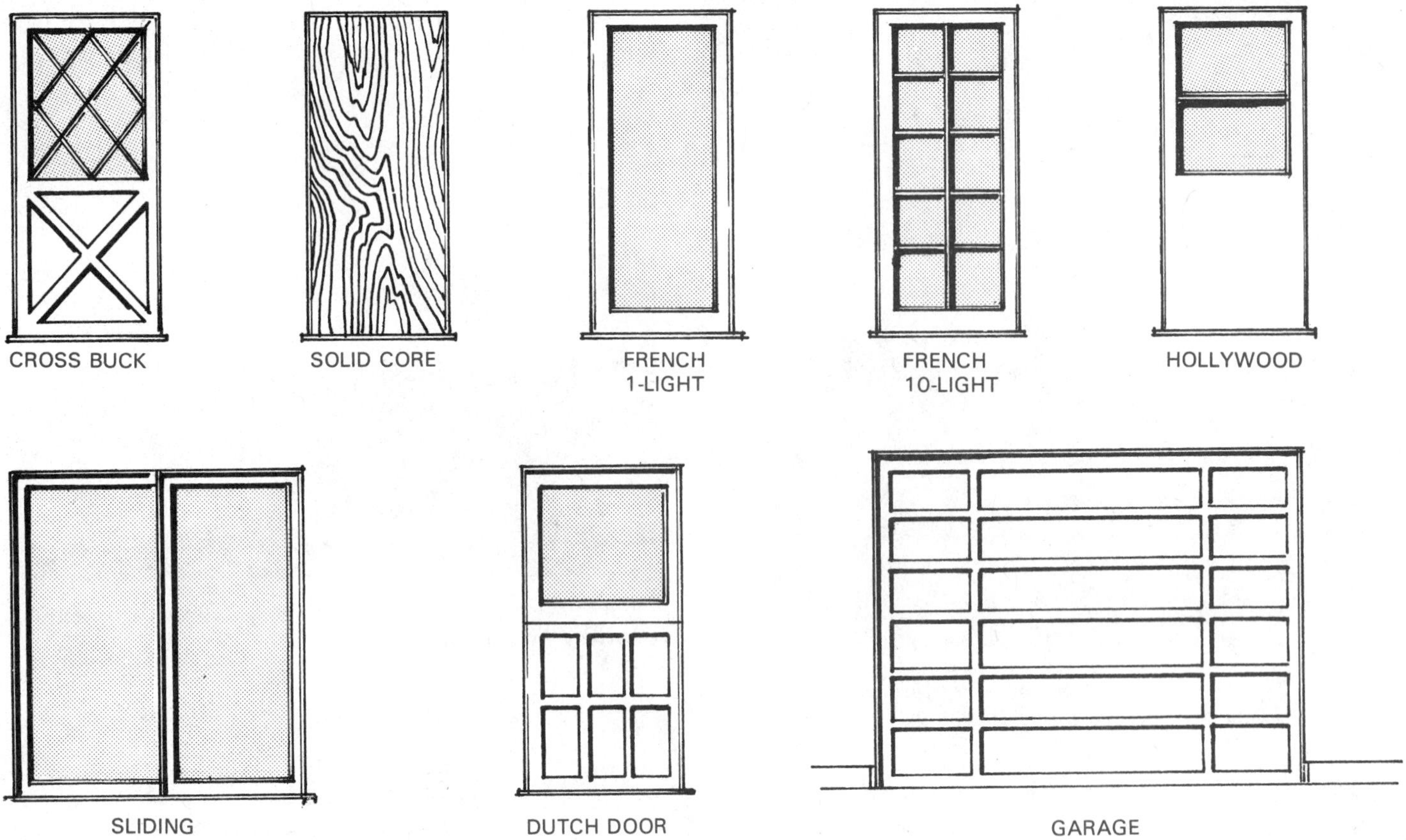

CROSS BUCK   SOLID CORE   FRENCH 1-LIGHT   FRENCH 10-LIGHT   HOLLYWOOD

SLIDING   DUTCH DOOR   GARAGE

Figure 24–46 Common doors represented in elevations.

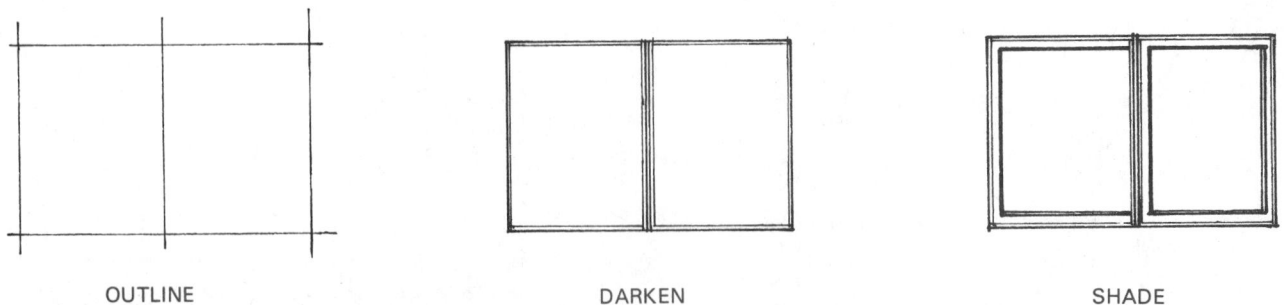

OUTLINE   DARKEN   SHADE

Figure 24–47 Layout steps for a sliding window.

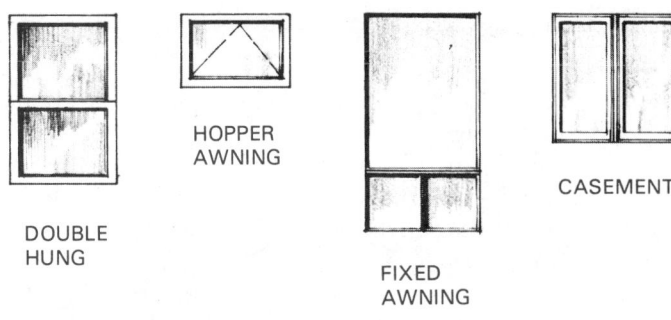

DOUBLE
HUNG

HOPPER
AWNING

FIXED
AWNING

CASEMENT

Figure 24–48 Representing common window shapes on elevations.

Figure 24–49 Common types of railings.

the drafter should draw the windows in the most typical usage for the area. Figure 24–47 shows the layout steps for an aluminum sliding window. Figure 24–48 shows how other common types of windows can be drawn.

Rails

Rails can be either solid to match the wall material or open. Open rails are typically made of wood or wrought iron. Although spacing varies vertical rails are usually required to be no more than 6 in. clear. Rails are often drawn as shown in Figure 24–49. Although it is not necessary to measure the location of each vertical, care must be taken to space the rails evenly.

Shutters

Shutters are sometimes used as part of the exterior design and must be shown on the elevations. Figure 24–50 shows a typical shutter and how it could be drawn. Although the spacing should be uniform, the drafter should try to lay out the shutter by eye rather than measuring each louver.

Eave Vents

Drawing eave vents is similar to drawing shutters. Figure 24–51 shows common methods of drawing eave vents.

Chimney

Several different methods can be used to represent a chimney. Figure 24–52 shows examples of wood and masonry chimneys.

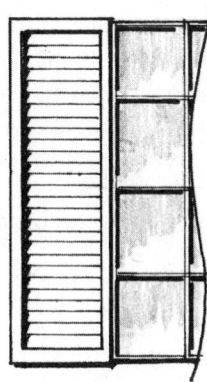

Figure 24–50 Representing shutters in elevation.

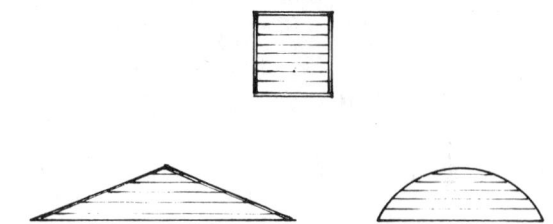

Figure 24–51 Common methods of representing attic vents on elevations.

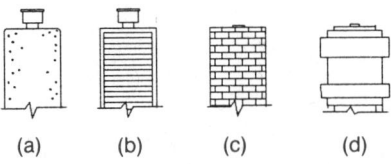

(a)   (b)   (c)   (d)

Figure 24–52 Common methods of drawing chimneys: (a) stucco chase with metal cap; (b) horizontal wood siding with metal cap; (c) common brick; (d) decorative masonry.

INTRODUCTION TO ELEVATIONS TEST

DIRECTIONS

Answer the questions with short complete statements or drawings as needed on an 8½ × 11 drawing sheet as follows:

1. Use ⅛ in. guidelines for all lettering.
2. Letter your name, Introduction to Elevations Test, and the date at the top of the sheet.
3. Letter the question number and provide the answer. You do not need to write out the question.
4. Do all lettering with vertical uppercase architectural letters. If the answer requires line work, use proper drafting tools and technique. Answers may be prepared on a word processor if appropriate with course guidelines.
5. Your grade will be based on correct answers and quality of line technique.

QUESTIONS

1. Under what circumstances could a drafter be required to draw only three elevations?
2. When would more than four elevations be required?
3. What are the goals of an elevation?
4. What is the most common scale for drawing elevations?
5. Would an elevation drawn at a scale of 1/16″ = 1′-0″ require the same methods to draw finishing materials as an elevation drawn at a larger scale?
6. Describe two methods of transferring the heights of one elevation to another.
7. Describe two different methods of showing concrete tile roofs.
8. What are the two major types of wood siding?
9. When drawing a home with plywood siding, how should the texture of the wood be expressed?
10. Sketch the most typically used pattern for brick work.
11. What problems is the drafter likely to encounter when drawing stone?
12. Sketch the way wood shingles would look when looking at the gable end of a roof.
13. Give the major consideration when drawing doors in elevation.
14. What are the two most common materials used for rails?
15. When drawing stucco, how should the pattern be expressed?

Chapter 25
Elevation Layout and Drawing Techniques

FOR DRAFTERS and students alike, drawing elevations is one of the most enjoyable projects in architecture. As a student, though, you should keep in mind that a beginning drafter very rarely gets to draw the main elevations. The architect or designer usually draws the main elevations in the preliminary stage of design and then a drafter gets to finish the elevations. As a beginner you may be introduced to elevations at your first job by making corrections resulting from design changes. Not a lot of creativity is involved in corrections, but it is a start. As you display your ability you'll most likely be involved in earlier stages of the drawing process. Elevations are drawn in the three steps of layout, drawing, and lettering. Usually you will be given the preliminary design elevation or the designer's sketch to use as a guide.

LAYOUT

Before you draw any lines on the paper, review the information of the last chapter. The size of drawing sheet you'll be using will affect the scale, placement and layout of the elevations. Because C-sized paper is so commonly used, these instructions will assume the drawing is to be made on that size sheet. Usually two elevations cannot be placed side-by-side on C-sized material. Thus you will not be able to use a side elevation for projecting heights onto the front or rear elevations. The following instructions will be given for drawing the front elevation at a scale of $\frac{1}{4}'' = 1'-0''$ and the rear and both side elevations at a scale of $\frac{1}{8}'' = 1'-0''$. Using two scales will require more steps than when all of the elevations are drawn at one scale.

The layout process can be divided into the stages of overall shape, roof layout, and opening layout. Use construction lines for each stage.

Overall-shape Layout

Step 1.   With a clean sheet of drawing paper in place, tape down a print of the floor plans to use as a guide for all horizontal measurements. Each horizontal measurement can be projected as shown in Figure 25–1.

Step 2.   See Figure 25–2 for steps 2 through 8. Lay out a baseline to represent the finish grade.

Step 3.   Project lines down from the floor plan to represent the edges of the house.

Step 4.   Establish the finish floor line. See Figure 25–3 for help in determining minimum measurements.

Step 5.   Measure up 8'–0" from the finished floor line and draw a line to represent the ceiling level. Although the actual measurement may be slightly more or less than 8'–0", this difference will cause no problems.

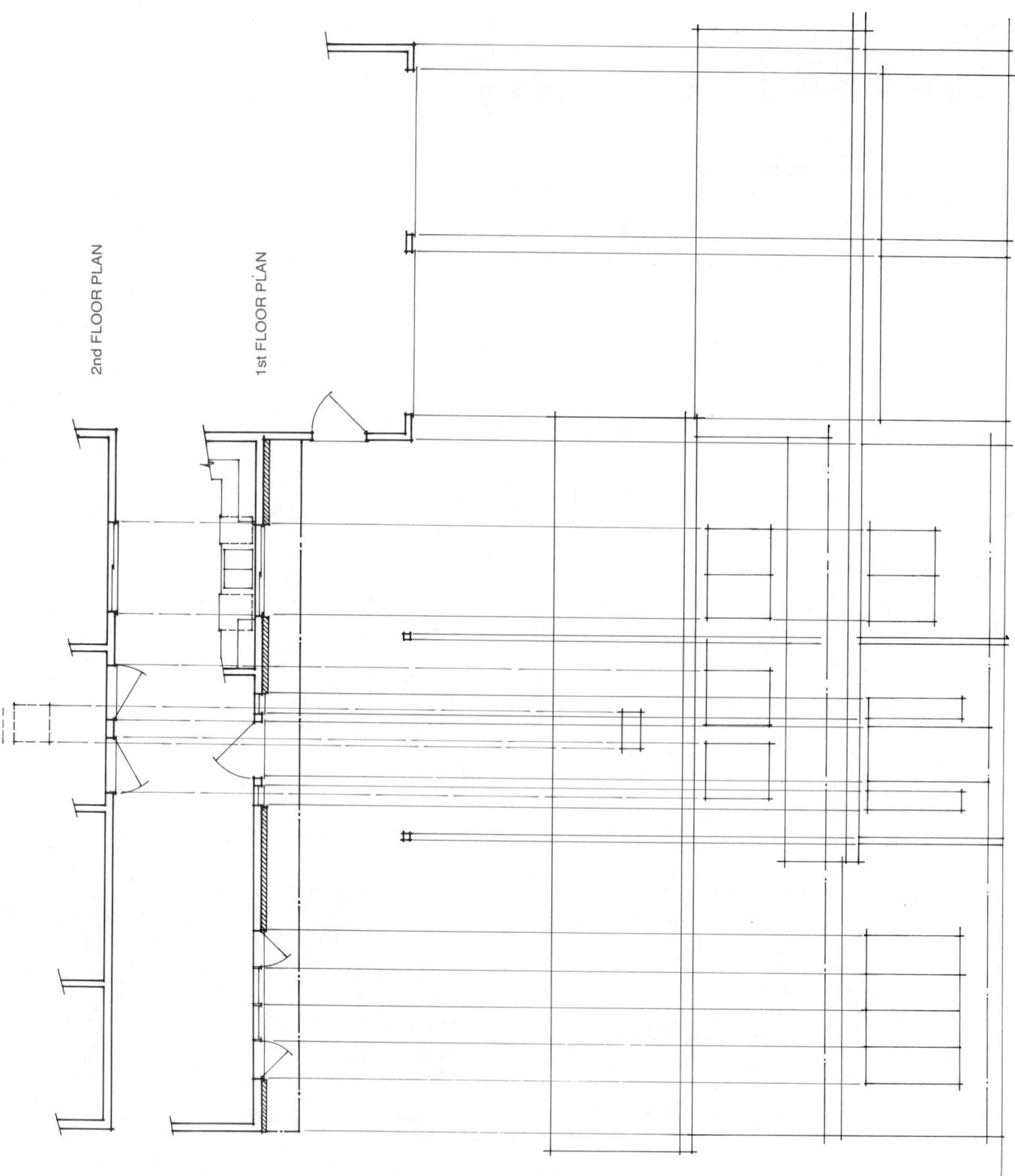

2nd FLOOR PLAN

1st FLOOR PLAN

Figure 25-1 The layout of an elevation. With a print of the floor plans taped above the area where the elevations will be drawn, horizontal distances can be projected down to the elevation.

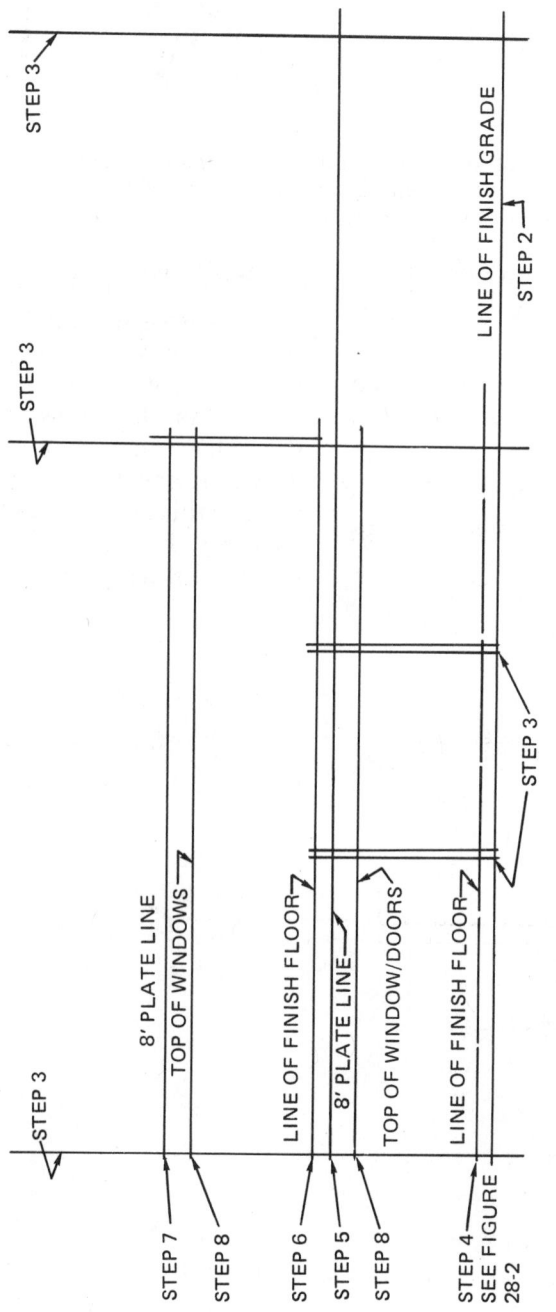

Figure 25–2 Layout of the overall shape of the front elevation.

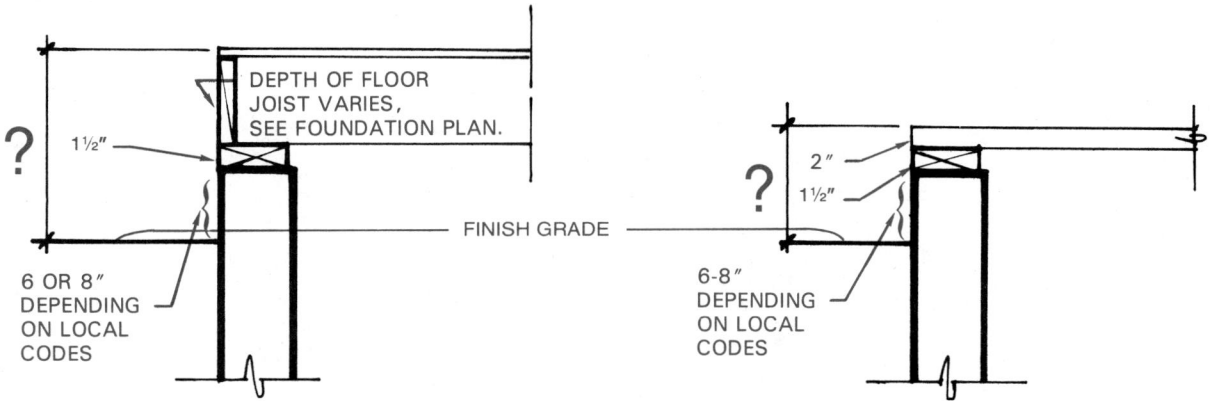

Figure 25–3 The height of the finish floor above grade will be determined by the type of the floor framing system. Exact framing sizes are often rounded up to the nearest inch when drawing elevations.

Step 6. Measure up the depth of the floor joist to establish the finished floor level of the second floor.

Step 7. Measure up 8'–0" from the second finished floor line and draw a line to represent the upper ceiling level.

Step 8. Measure up from each finished floor line 6'–8" and draw a line to represent the tops of the windows and doors.

Roof Layout

Because a side elevation is not being drawn beside the front elevation there is no easy way to determine the true roof height. If the sections have been drawn before the elevations, the height from the ceiling to the ridge could be measured on one of the section drawings and then transferred to the elevations. Although this might save time, it also might duplicate an error. If the roof was incorrectly drawn on the section drawing, the error will be repeated if di-

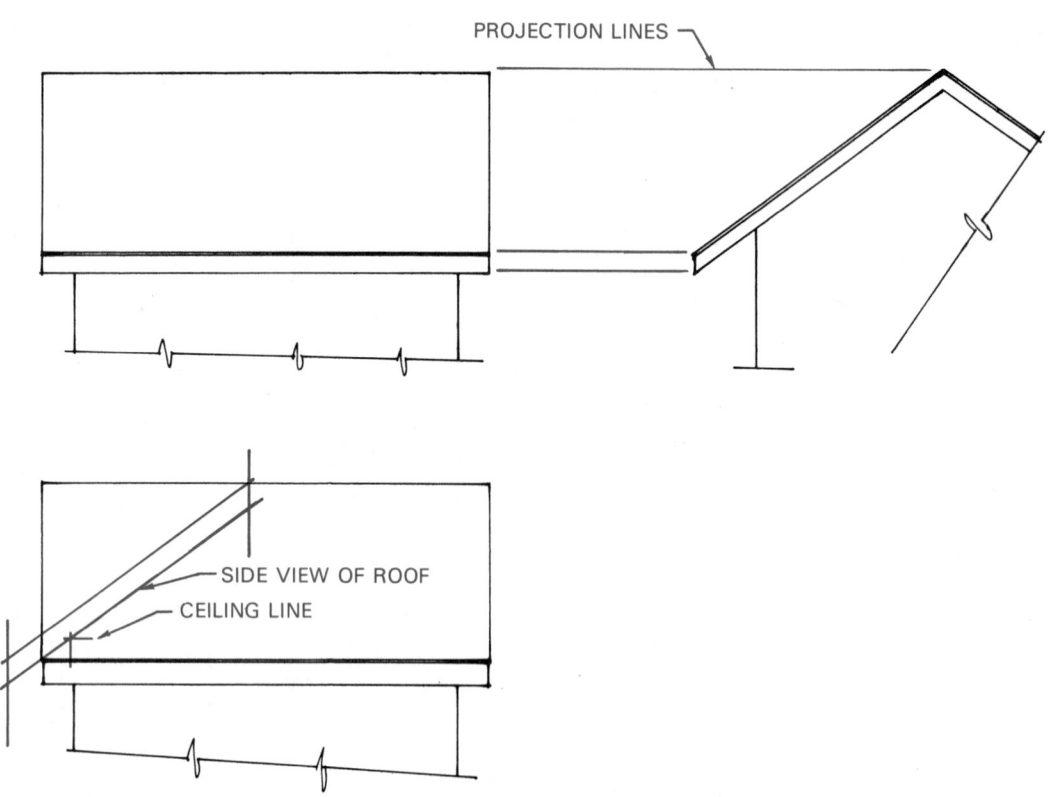

Figure 25–4 Roof height layout. When elevations are drawn side by side, heights can be projected with construction lines. When only one elevation is drawn, a side elevation will need to be drawn in the middle of what will become the front elevation.

mensions are simply transferred from section to elevation.

The best procedure to determine the height of the roof in the front view is to lay out a side view lightly. This can be done in the middle of what will become the front view. An example of this can be seen in Figure 25–4. On this home, three different roofs must be drawn. These include the roof over the two-story area, garage, and porch. It would be best to lay out the porch roof last since it is a projection of the garage roof. The upper or garage roof can be drawn by following steps 9 through 19 in Figure 25–5.

Step 9.   Lay out a line 1'–0" from the end of each wall to represent the edge of the roof.

Step 10.   Lay out a line 2'–0" from one of the end walls to represent the overhang projection.

Step 11.   Lay out a line to represent the ridge. This should be halfway between each wall if the slope of each side of the roof is equal.

Step 12.   Determine the roof slope. For this home draw the roof at a 5/12 pitch. A 5/12 slope equals 22½ degrees. See Section 7 for a complete explanation of pitches.

Step 13.   At the intersection of the wall and ceiling lines (lines drawn in steps 3 and 7), draw a line at the desired angle to represent the roof. This line will represent the bottom of the truss or rafter.

Step 14.   Measure up 6 in. and draw a line parallel to the line just drawn which will represent the top of the rafter. On the elevations, it is not important that the exact depth of the rafters be represented.

Step 15.   Establish the top of the roof. The true height of the roof can be measured where the line from step 14 intersects the line from step 11.

Step 16.   Establish the bottom of the eave. This can be determined from the intersection of the line from step 10 with the lines of steps 13 and 14.

Step 17.   Lay out the upper roof using the same procedure of drawing a partial side elevation and projecting exact heights.

The porch roof will be an extension of the garage roof, so much of the layout work will have been done. Only the left end and the upper limits of the roof must be determined. Because the ends of the upper and garage roof extend 12 in., this distance will be maintained. The upper edge of the roof will be formed by the intersection of the roof and the wall for the upper floor. This height can be determined by following steps 18 and 19.

Step 18.   Place a line on the slope lines (the lines from steps 13 and 14) to represent the distance from the garage wall to the front wall on the upper floor plan.

Step 19.   At the intersection of the lines from steps 14 and 18, project a line to represent the top of the roof.

You now have the basic shape of the walls and roof blocked out. The only items to be drawn now are the door and window openings.

Layout of Openings

See Figure 25–6 for steps 20 through 23.

Step 20.   Lay out the width of all doors, windows, and skylights by projecting their location from the floor plan.

Step 21.   Lay out the bottom of the windows and doors. The doors should extend to the line representing the finished floor. Determine the depth of the windows from the window schedule and draw a line to represent the correct depth.

Step 22.   Determine the height of the skylights. This must be done by measuring the true size of the skylights on the line from step 14, and then projecting this height to the proper location.

Step 23.   Draw the shape of the garage doors. Remember that the height of these doors is measured from the line representing the ground and not from the finished floor level.

You now have the front elevation blocked out. The same steps can be used to draw the right and left side and rear elevations. The reduced scale of these elevations will really test your visual skills. The major difference in laying out these elevations is that the widths of walls, windows, and doors cannot be projected from the floor plan. To lay out these items you will need to rely on the dimensions of the floor plan. Although slower than the projection method, drawing at a reduced scale is a great way to check the accuracy of your dimensions. Remember, if the dimensions are not accurate when drawing the elevations, they will not be accurate as the framers are trying to lay out the home.

Start by drawing either side elevation. The side elevation can be drawn by following the procedure for the layout of the front elevation. Figure 25–7 shows a completed side elevation. Once this is drawn, use the heights of the side elevation to establish the heights for the other side and the rear elevation as shown in Figure 25–8.

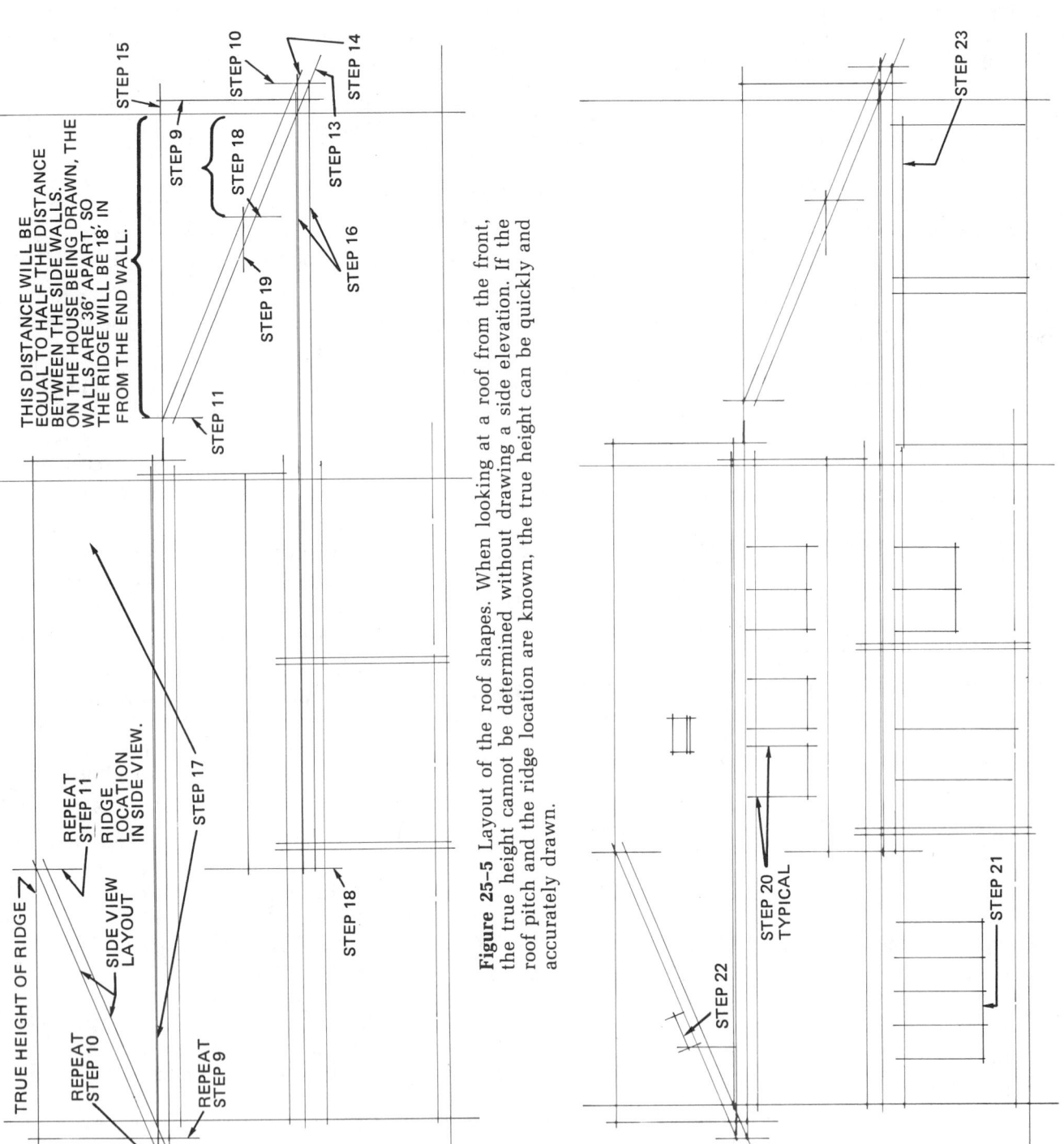

Figure 25–5 Layout of the roof shapes. When looking at a roof from the front, the true height cannot be determined without drawing a side elevation. If the roof pitch and the ridge location are known, the true height can be quickly and accurately drawn.

Figure 25–6 Layout of the doors, windows, and skylights. The widths can be projected down from the floor plan. Vertical heights for windows came from the window schedule.

THIS DISTANCE WILL BE
EQUAL TO HALF THE DISTANCE
BETWEEN THE SIDE WALLS.
ON THE HOUSE BEING DRAWN, THE
WALLS ARE 36' APART, SO
THE RIDGE WILL BE 18' IN
FROM THE END WALL.

STEP 15
STEP 10
STEP 14
STEP 9
STEP 18
STEP 13
STEP 16
STEP 19
STEP 11
STEP 17
STEP 18

TRUE HEIGHT OF RIDGE
REPEAT STEP 11
RIDGE LOCATION IN SIDE VIEW.
SIDE VIEW LAYOUT
REPEAT STEP 10
REPEAT STEP 9

STEP 23
STEP 20 TYPICAL
STEP 21
STEP 22

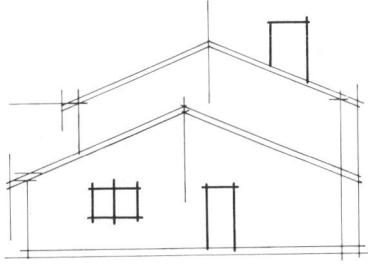

Figure 25-7 The layout of a side elevation is similar to the layout of the front elevation.

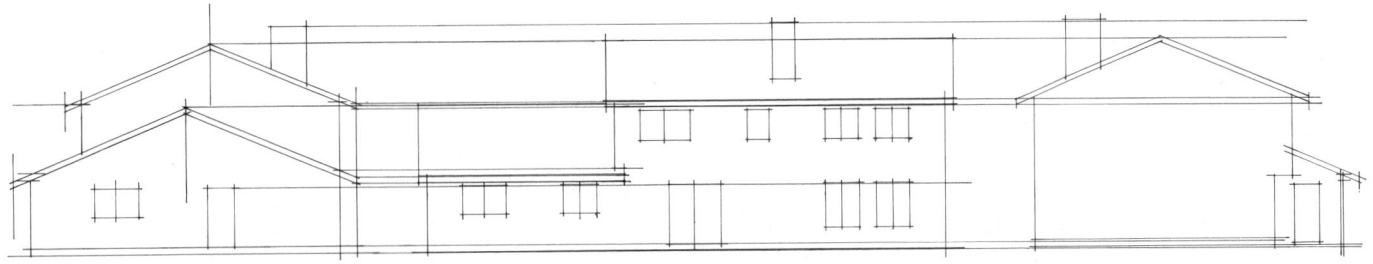

Figure 25-8 With a side elevation drawn, heights for the rear and other side can be projected quickly.

Figure 25-9 Drawing the front elevation using finished quality lines.

DRAWING FINISHED QUALITY LINES

With all of the elevations drawn with construction lines, they must now be completed with finished quality lines. An H and 2H lead will provide good contrast for many of the materials. The use of ink and graphite will also produce a very nice effect. Methods for drawing items required in elevations were discussed in Chapter 24. This line quality cannot be overstressed. By using varied line widths and density, a more realistic elevation can be created.

A helpful procedure for completing the elevations is to begin to darken the lines at the top of the page first and work down the page to the bottom. Because you will be using a soft lead it will tend to smear easily. If the lower elevations are drawn first, cover them with a sheet of paper when they are complete to prevent smearing.

Another helpful procedure for completing the elevations is to start at the top of one elevation and work toward the ground level. Also start by drawing surfaces that are in the foreground and work toward the background of the elevation. This procedure will help cut down on erasing background items for items that are in the foreground. Figure 25–9 shows a completed front elevation. It can be drawn by following steps 24 through 28.

Step 24.   Draw the outline of all roofs.

Step 25.   Draw the roofing material.

Step 26.   Draw all windows and doors.

Step 27.   Draw all corner trim and posts.

Step 28.   Draw the siding.

At this point your front elevation is completely drawn. The same procedures can be used to finish the rear and side elevations. These elevations are shown in Figure 25–10. Notice that only a small portion of the siding has been shown in these elevations. It is common practice to have the front elevation highly detailed and have the other elevations show just the minimum information for the construction crew.

LETTERING

With the elevations completely drawn, the material must now be specified. If the elevations are all on one page, a material only needs to be specified on one elevation. Use Figures 25–9 and 25–10 as guides for placing notes. The notes needed include the following:

1. Siding. Generally the kind of siding, its thickness and the backing material must be specified.
2. Corner and decorative trims.
3. Chimney height (2 ft minimum above any roof within 10 ft).
4. Flatwork which would include any decks or concrete patios.
5. Posts and headers.
6. Fascias and barge rafters.

7. Roof material.
8. Roof pitch.
9. Dimensions. The use of dimensions on elevations varies greatly from office to office. Some companies place no dimensions on elevations using the sections to show all vertical heights. Other companies show the finished floor lines on the elevations and dimension floor to ceiling levels. Unless your instructor tells you otherwise, no dimensions will be placed on the elevations.

DRAWING IRREGULAR SHAPES

Not all plans that will be drawn have walls constructed at 90° to each other. When the house has an irregular shape, a floor plan and a roof plan will be required to draw the elevations. The process is similar to the process just described but will require more patience in projecting all of the roof and wall intersections. The projection of an irregularly shaped home can be seen in Figure 25–11. See Section 7 for an explanation of how the roof plan is drawn. Once the roof plan has been determined, it can be drawn on a print of the floor plan and the intersections of the roof can be projected to the elevation.

PROJECTING GRADES

The term grade is often used to describe the shape of the ground level. Projecting ground levels is required on elevations when a structure is being constructed on a hillside. Figure 25–12 shows the layout of a hillside residence. To complete this elevation a plot, floor, and roof plan were used to project locations. Usually the grading plan and the floor plan are drawn at different scales. The easiest method of projecting the ground level onto the elevation is to measure the distance on the plot plan from one contour line to the next. This distance can then be marked on the floor plan and projected onto the elevation.

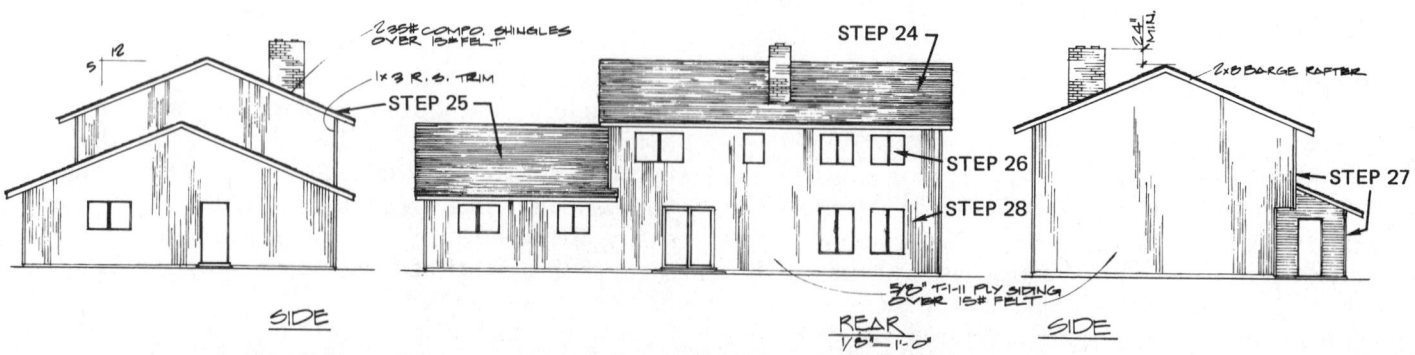

Figure 25–10 Drawing small-scale elevations does not require drawing all of the finishing materials. The same procedures used on the front elevation can be used on the side and rear elevations.

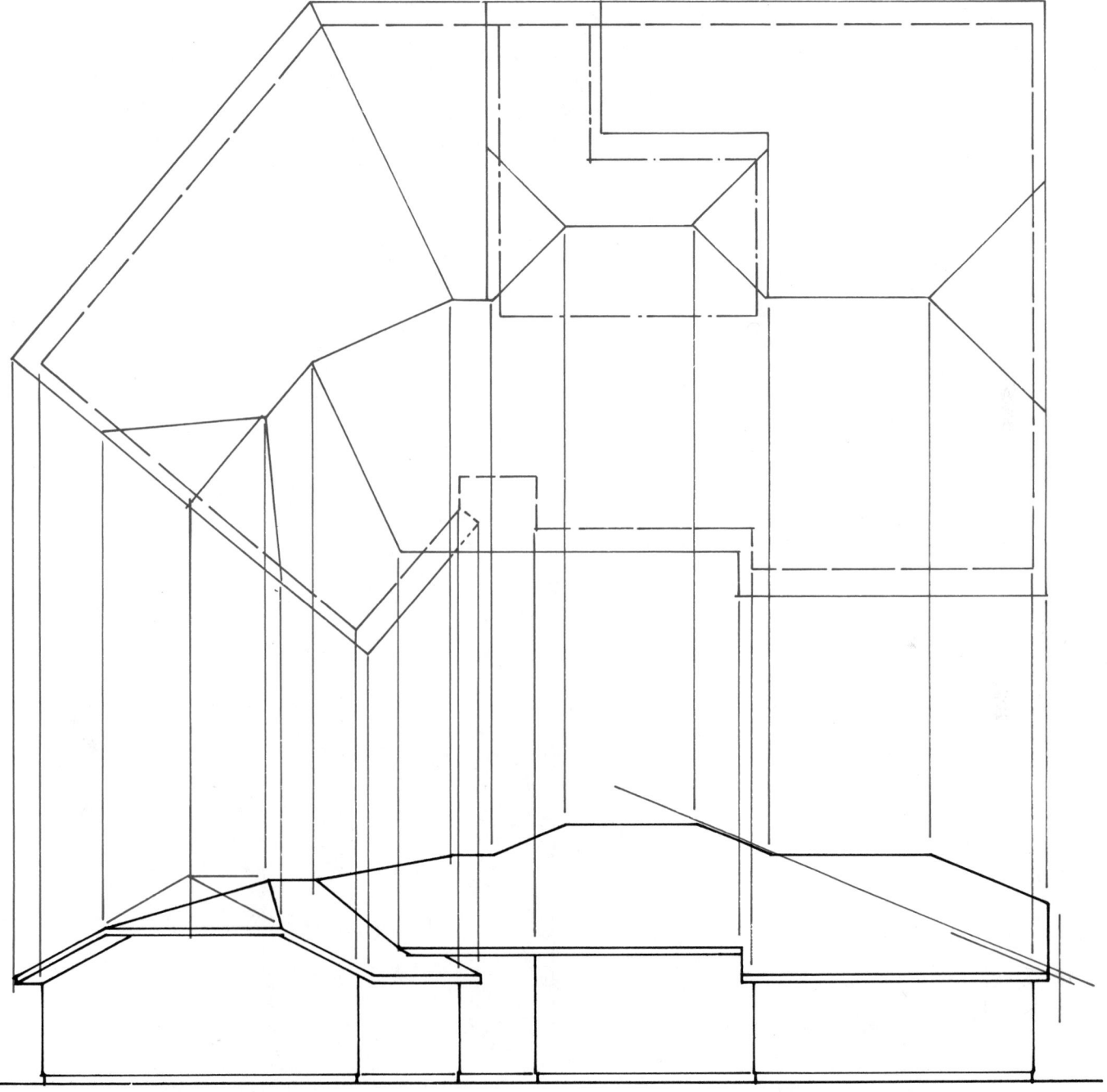

Figure 25–11 When drawing the elevations of a structure with an irregular shape, great care must be taken in the projection methods. This elevation was drawn by drawing the outline of the roof on a print of the floor plan and then projecting the needed intersections down to the drawing area. Notice on the right side of the elevation a line at the required angle has been drawn to represent the proper roof angle for establishing the true heights.

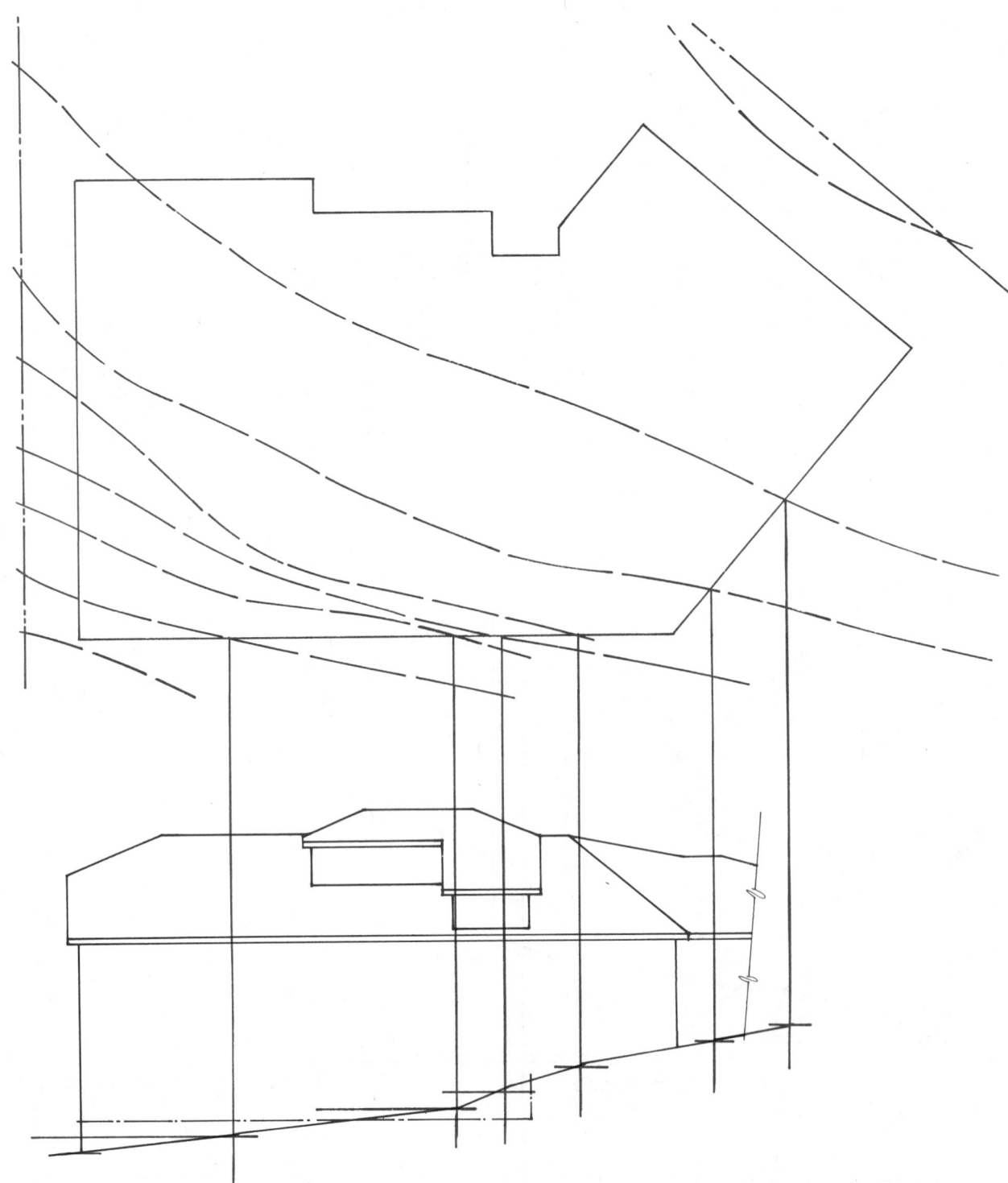

Figure 25–12 Projecting grades is similar to the method used to project roof lines. This elevation was drawn by using the information on the roof, floor, and grading plans. Only the projection lines for the grades are shown for clarity.

CADD
applications

DRAWING ELEVATIONS WITH CADD

Drawing exterior elevations with CADD is similar to techniques used to draw elevations manually. With manual drafting, you project lines from the floor plan to create lines for the elevation drawing. This was shown in Figure 25–1. With CADD, you do the same thing using a computer screen as a drawing table. After you draw the floor plan, you make it a BLOCK— a custom symbol or drawing that can be transferred between drawings and displayed at any time. Once a floor plan is made into a block, you can display it on the screen to create the elevation drawing. The computer is the drawing tool; you follow the same steps you use to draw an elevation manually. It is best to have the projection lines on a separate layer because they are eliminated as soon as the projection line layer is turned off. Also, ERASE the floor plan, so only the preliminary elevation drawing remains.

If the roof of the building is complex, you can create the roof elevation in the same manner by projecting from the roof plan into the elevation drawing, as shown in Figure 25–11.

Now you have a preliminary elevation with all the outlines of the building shown. All you have to do to complete the elevation is add the detailed door, window, and material symbols, and add dimensions and notes as necessary. A complete CADD elevation using the methods described is shown in Figure 1.

FRONT ELEVATION
SCALE   1/4" • 1'-0"

Figure 1 A complete CADD elevation. *Courtesy of Piercy & Barclay Designers, Inc.*

ELEVATION LAYOUT AND DRAWING TECHNIQUES TEST

DIRECTIONS

Answer the questions with short complete statements or drawings as needed on an 8½ × 11 drawing sheet as follows:

1. Use ⅛ in. guidelines for all lettering.
2. Letter your name, Elevation Layout and Drawing Test, and the date at the top of the sheet.
3. Letter the question number and provide the answer. You do not need to write out the question.
4. Do all lettering with vertical uppercase architectural letters. If the answer requires line work, use proper drafting tools and techniques. Answers may be prepared on a word processor if appropriate with course guidelines.
5. Your grade will be based on correct answers and quality of your line and lettering technique.

QUESTIONS

1. Who typically draws the main elevations of a structure? Explain.
2. List three methods of projecting heights from one elevation to another.
3. What scales are typically used to draw elevations?
4. What is the best method of determining the height of a roof when it is being viewed in a manner that does not show the pitch?
5. What lines should be drawn first when using finished line quality?
6. What drawings are required to project grades onto an elevation? Briefly explain the process.
7. What drawings are required to draw a structure with an irregular shape?
8. Sketch the method of showing the chimney height, and provide the minimum dimensions that must be shown.
9. What dimensions are typically shown on elevations?
10. What angle is used to represent a 4/12 pitch?

ELEVATION LAYOUT AND DRAWING TECHNIQUES PROBLEMS

DIRECTIONS

1. Select from the following sketches the one that corresponds to your floor-plan problem from Chapter 20 and draw the required elevations.
2. Draw the required elevations using the same type and size of drawing material that you used to draw your floor plan.
3. See each sketch to determine the scale and method of layout to be used. If no sketch has been given for the elevations of your plan, design the structure using materials suitable for your area.
4. Refer to your floor plan to determine all sizes and locations. If you find material that cannot be located using your floor plan, make additions to your floor plan as required.
5. Use the sketch as a reference only. Refer to the text of this chapter and notes from class lectures to complete the drawings.
6. When your drawing is complete, turn in a print for evaluation to your instructor.

Problem 25-1. CAPE COD.

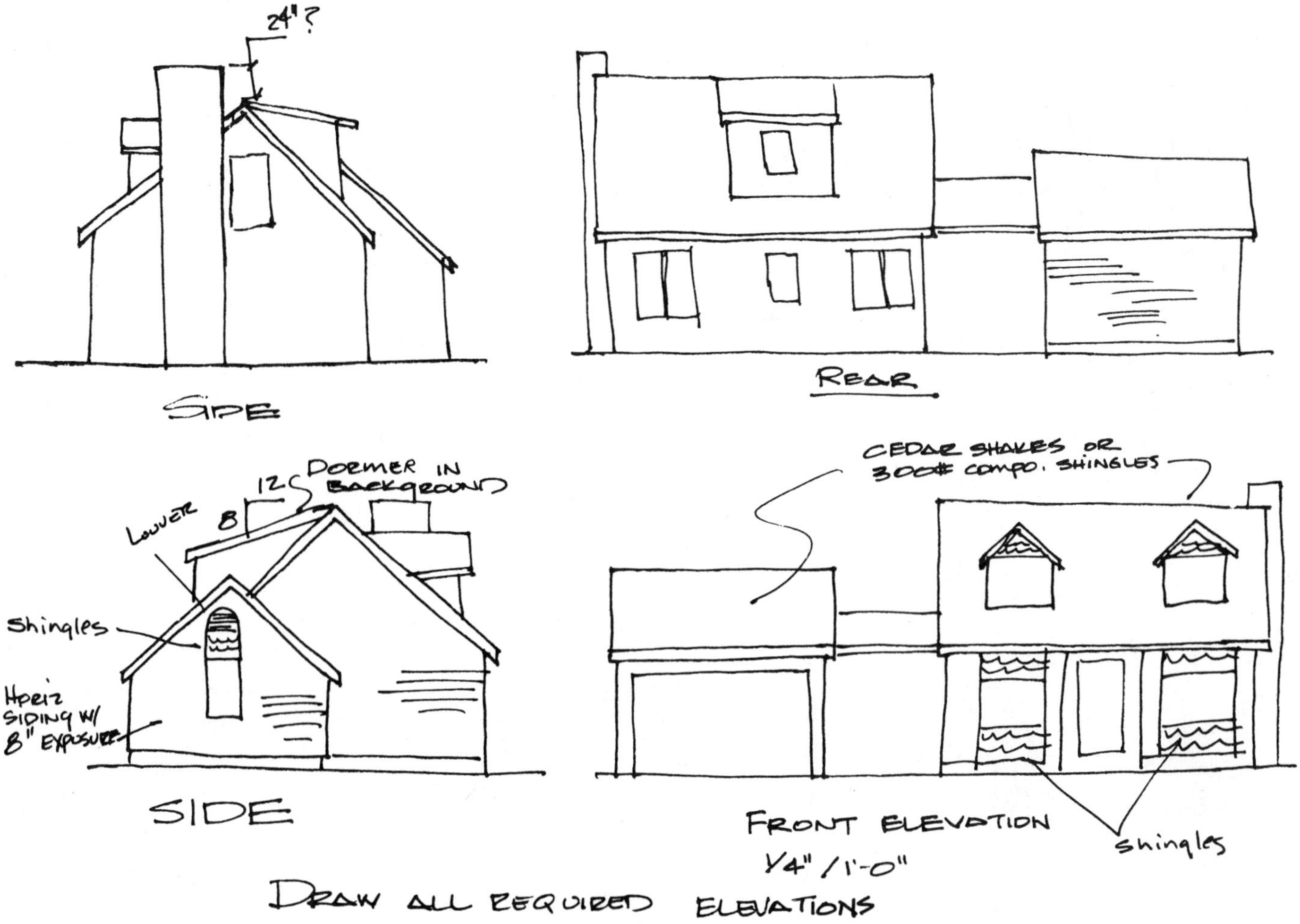

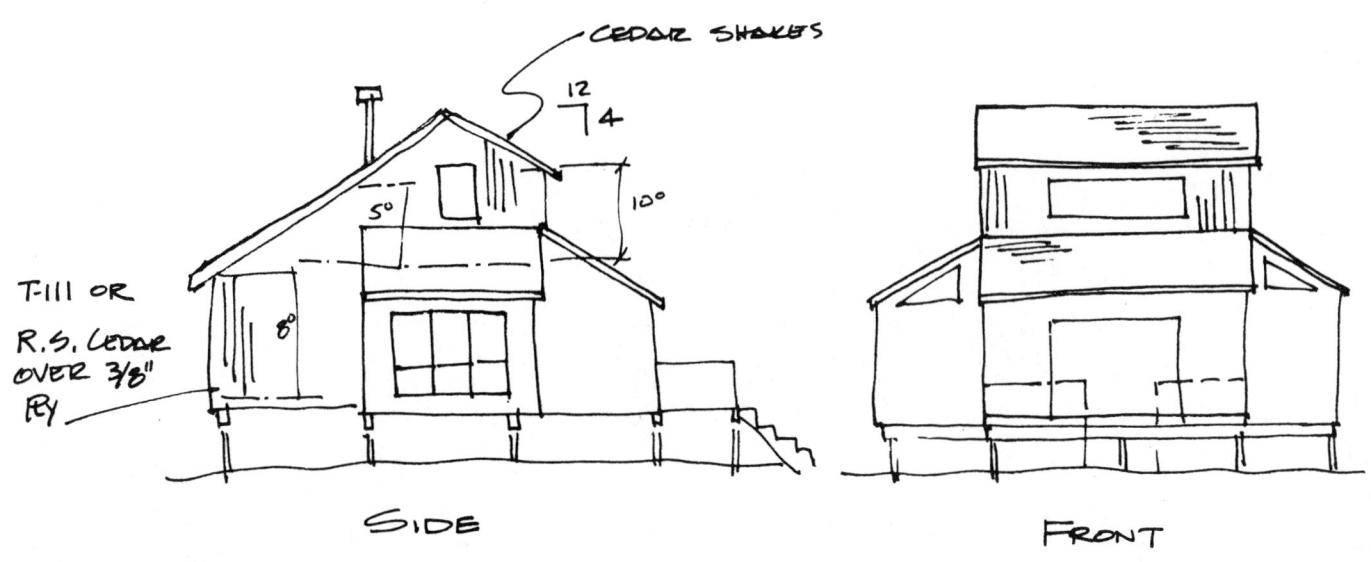

24"?

SIDE

REAR

DORMER IN
BACKGROUND
12
Louver   8
Shingles
Horiz
Siding w/
8" Exposure

SIDE

CEDAR SHAKES OR
300# COMPO. SHINGLES

FRONT ELEVATION
¼" / 1'-0"
Shingles

DRAW ALL REQUIRED ELEVATIONS

Problem 25-2. CABIN.

CEDAR SHAKES
12
7 4
5°
10°
8°

T-111 OR
R.S. CEDAR
OVER ⅜"
PLY

SIDE

FRONT

Problem 25-3. RANCH.

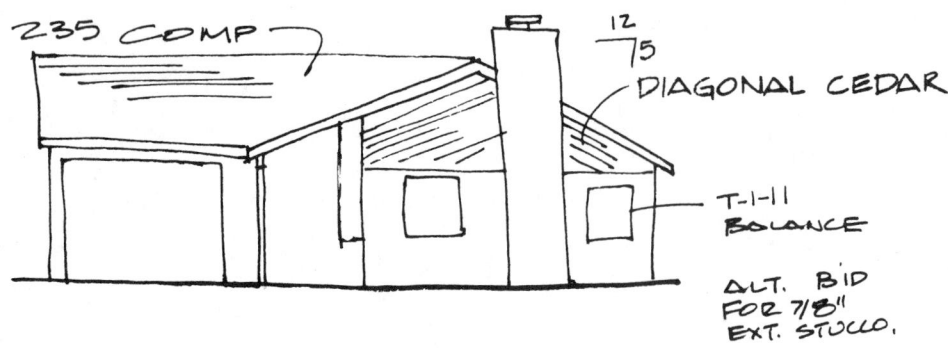

235 COMP

12
/5

DIAGONAL CEDAR

T-1-11
BALANCE

ALT. BID
FOR 7/8"
EXT. STUCCO.

Problem 25-4. SPANISH.

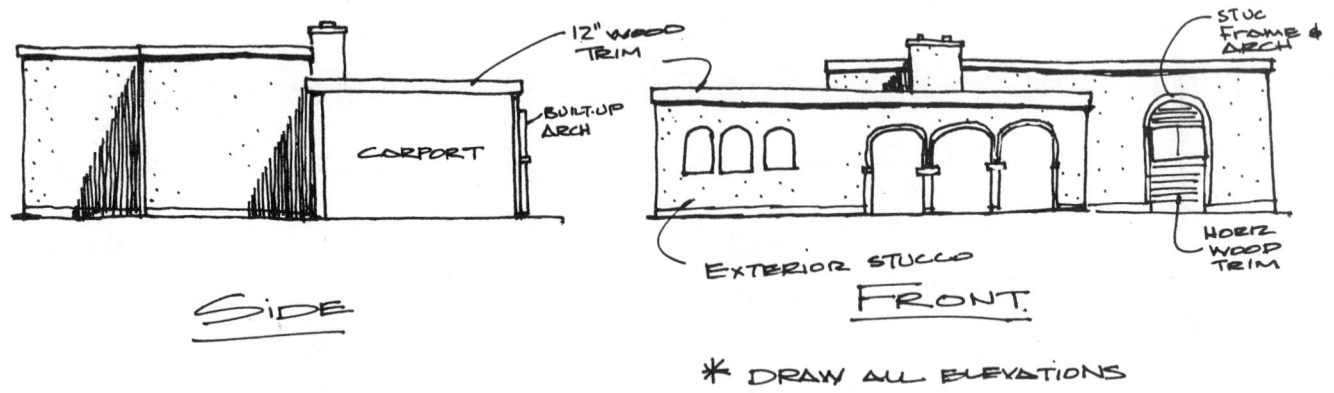

12" WOOD TRIM

BUILT-UP ARCH

CORPORT

Side

STUC FRAME & ARCH

HORIZ WOOD TRIM

EXTERIOR STUCCO

FRONT

* DRAW ALL ELEVATIONS

Problem 25-5. EARLY AMERICAN.

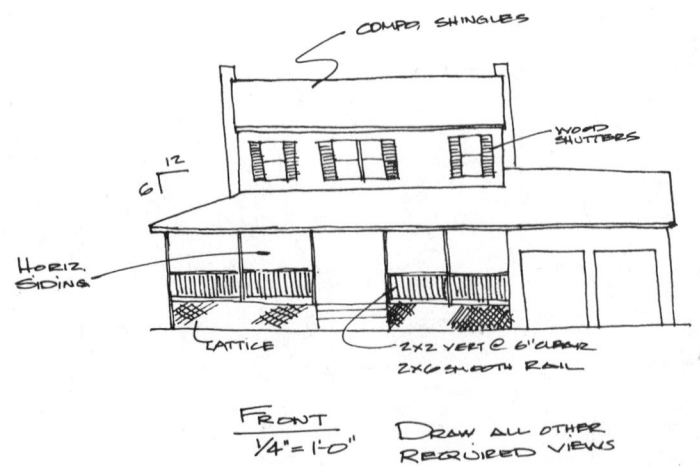

COMPO, SHINGLES

WOOD SHUTTERS

12
6/

HORIZ. SIDING

LATTICE

2x2 VERT @ 6" CLEAR
2x6 SMOOTH RAIL

FRONT
1/4" = 1'-0"

DRAW ALL OTHER REQUIRED VIEWS

Problem 25-6. CONTEMPORARY.

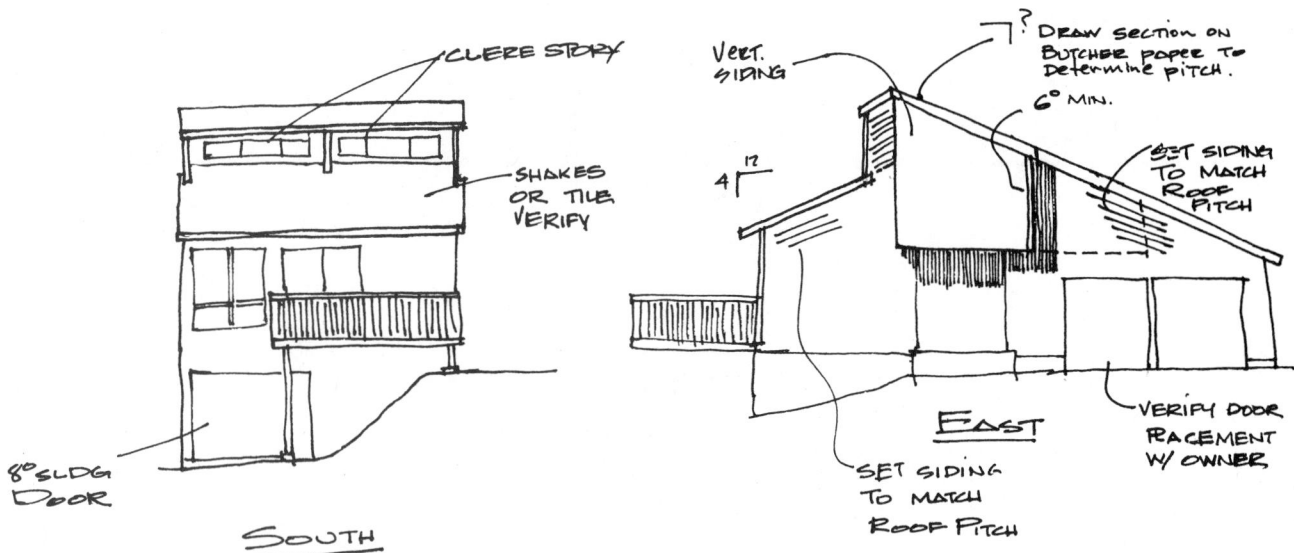

SOUTH

Problem 25-7. DUPLEX. Design this structure using suitable roof pitch and materials for your area. Sketch an elevation for each surface that will need to be drawn and have it approved by your instructor prior to starting your drawing.

TYPICAL WALL SECTION

CM-1430

Section Six
Sections

Chapter 26
Framing Methods

MORE SO than any other drawing to be done by the drafter, drawing sections requires a thorough understanding of the materials and the process of construction. A drafter can successfully complete the floor and foundation plans with minimal understanding of the structural processes that are involved. To draw the sections and show how the building is to be constructed requires the drafter to have an understanding of basic construction principles.

In Chapter 21 you were introduced to different types of foundation systems. There are also different types of framing systems that the drafter must understand. Wood, masonry, and concrete are the most common materials used in the construction of residential and small office buildings. With each material there are several different framing methods that can be used to assemble the components. Wood is the most widely used material for the framing of houses and apartments. The most common framing systems used with wood include balloon, platform, and post-and-beam. There have also been several variations of platform framing in recent years to provide for better energy efficiency.

BALLOON FRAMING

Although balloon framing is not widely used, a knowledge of this system will prove helpful if an old building is being remodeled. With the balloon or Eastern framing method, the exterior studs run from the top of the foundation to the top of the highest level as seen in Figure 26–1. This is one of the benefits of the system. Wood has a tendency to shrink as the moisture content decreases and will shrink more in width than it will in length. Because the wall members are continuous from foundation to the roof, fewer horizontal members are used resulting in less shrinkage. Since brick veneer or stucco is often applied to the exterior face of the wall, the minimal shrinkage of the balloon system helps to keep the exterior finish from cracking.

Because of the long pieces of lumber needed, a two-story structure was the maximum that could be built easily using balloon framing. Floor framing at the midlevel was supported by a ledger set into the studs. Structural members were usually spaced at 12, 16, or 24 in. on center. Figure 26–2 shows typical construction methods used in the balloon framing system.

Although the length of the wood gave the building stability, it also caused the demise of the system. The major flaw with balloon framing is fire danger. A fire starting in the lower level could quickly race through the cavities formed in the wall or floor systems of the building. Blocking or smoke-activated dampers are now required by many building codes at all levels to resist the spread of fire. See Figures 26–3(a) and 26–3(b).

PLATFORM FRAMING

Platform or Western platform framing is the most common framing system now in use. The system gets its name from the platform created by each floor as the building is being framed. The framing crew is able to use the floor as a platform to assemble the

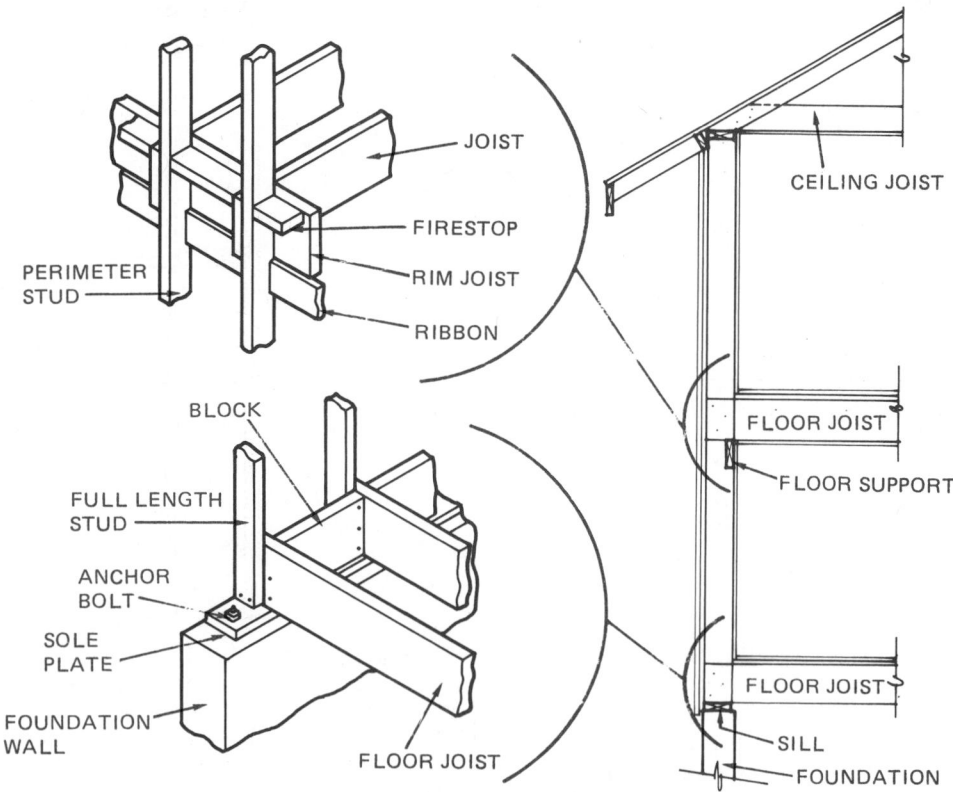

Figure 26-1 Balloon framing wall members extend from the foundation to the roof level in one continuous piece.

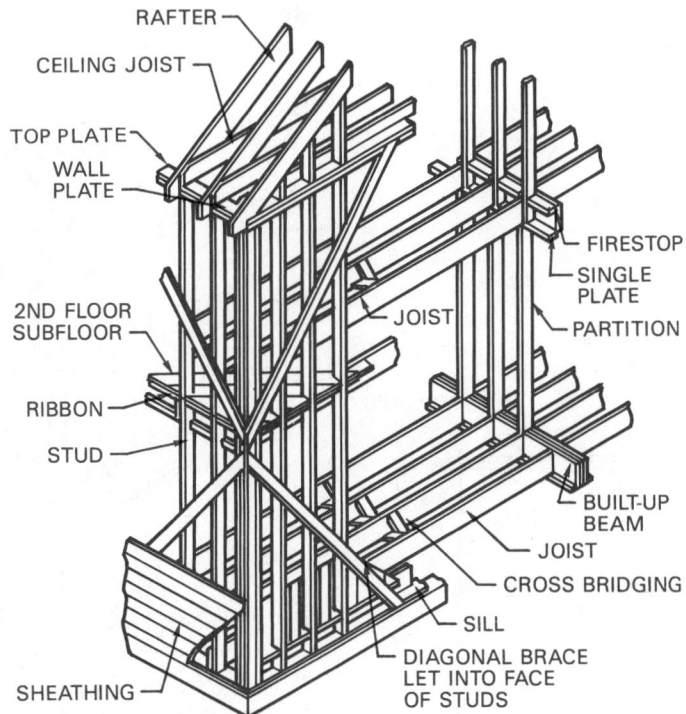

Figure 26-2 Structural members of the balloon framing system are typically spaced at 12, 16, or 24 in. O.C. Exterior walls are erected first, and then the upper floor is hung from the walls.

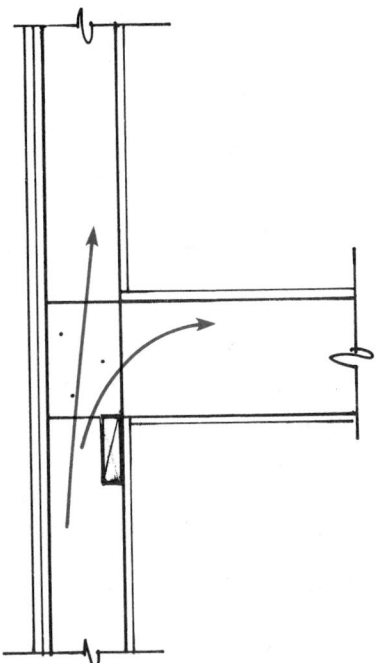

Figure 26–3(a) The risk of fire spreading with balloon framing is very great because flames can race through the floor and wall systems.

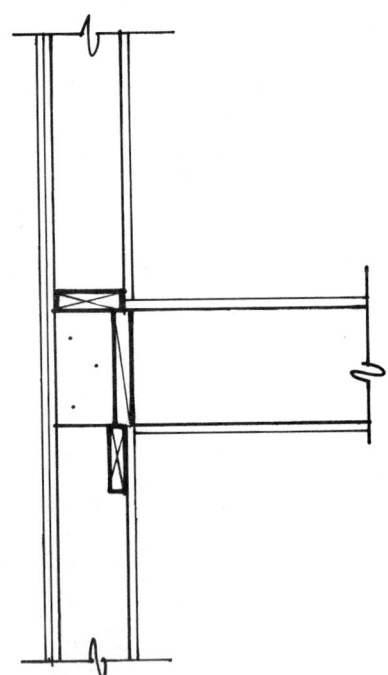

Figure 26–3(b) Blocking, or fire blocking, is required by building codes to be added to the intersection of each floor and wall to resist the spread of fire and smoke through the floor and wall systems of a structure.

walls for that level. Platform framing grew out of the need for the fireblocks in the balloon framing system. The fireblocks that had been put in individually between the studs in balloon framing became continuous members placed over the studs to form a solid bearing surface for the floor or roof system. See Figure 26–4.

Building with the Platform System

Once the foundation is in place, the framing crew will set the girders and the floor members. The major components of platform construction can be seen in

Figure 26–5. Floor joists ranging in size from 2 × 6 through 2 × 14 can be used depending on the distance they are required to span. Plywood of either ½, ⅝, or ¾ in. thickness can be used for the subfloor which covers the floor joists. The plywood usually has a tongue-and-groove (T&G) pattern in the edge to help minimize floor squeaking. Occasionally T&G

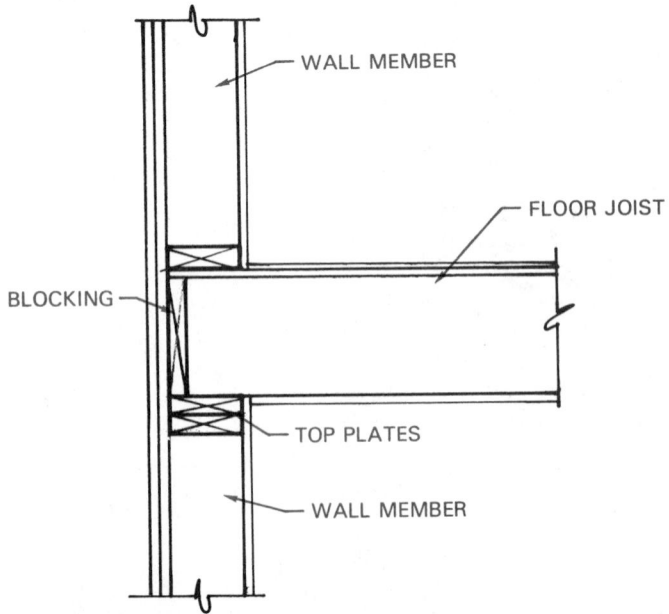

Figure 26–4 The fireblocks of the balloon system gave way to continuous supports at each floor and ceiling level.

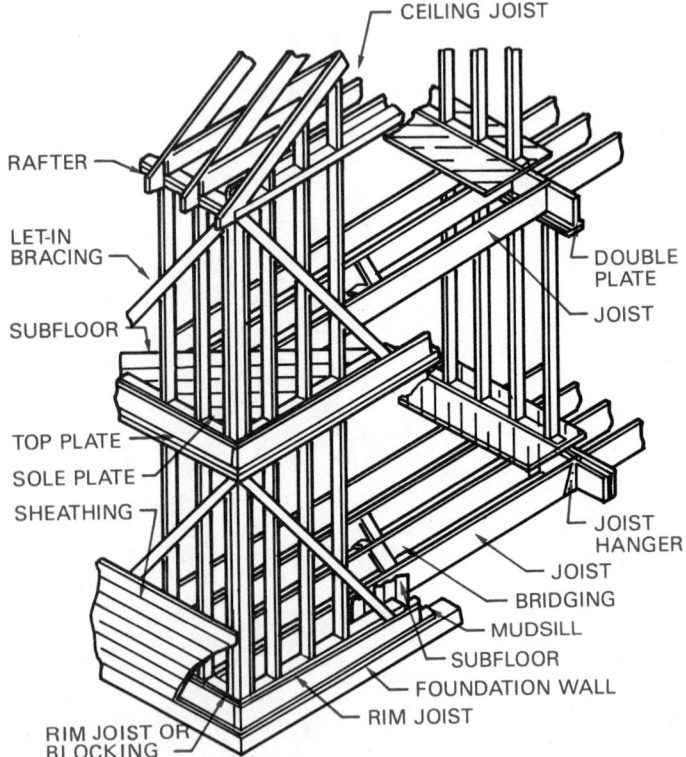

Figure 26–5 Structural members of the platform framing system.

lumber 1 × 4 or 1 × 6 will be laid diagonal to the floor joists to form the floor system, but plywood is primarily used because of the speed with which it can be installed.

Figure 26–6 Using western platform construction methods, the floor provides a flat surface to form walls (background) and to lift them into place. *Courtesy American Plywood Association.*

Figure 26–7 An apartment building under construction using western platform construction methods. *Courtesy Southern Forest Products Association.*

With the floor in place, the walls are constructed using the floor as a clean, flat, layout surface. Walls are typically built flat on the floor using a bottom plate, studs, and two top plates. With the walls squared, sheathing can be nailed to the exterior face of the wall, and then the wall tilted up into place as shown in Figure 26–6. When all of the bearing walls are in place the next level can be started. Similar to the balloon system, studs are typically placed at 12, 16, or 24 in. O.C. Figure 26–7 shows a building constructed with platform framing methods.

POST-AND-BEAM FRAMING

Post-and-beam construction places framing members at greater distances apart than platform methods. Figure 26–8 shows a comparison of platform and post-and-beam construction. In residential construction, posts and beams are usually spaced at 48 in. on

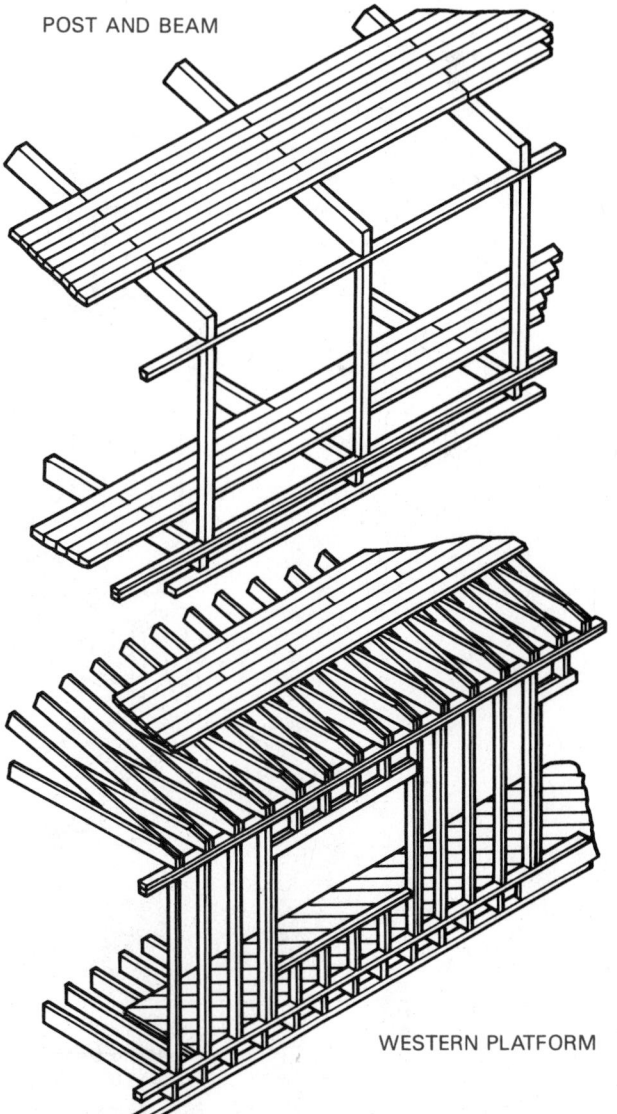

Figure 26–8 Structural members of platform construction are usually placed at 12, 16, or 24 in. on center. Post-and-beam members are usually placed at 48 in. O.C.

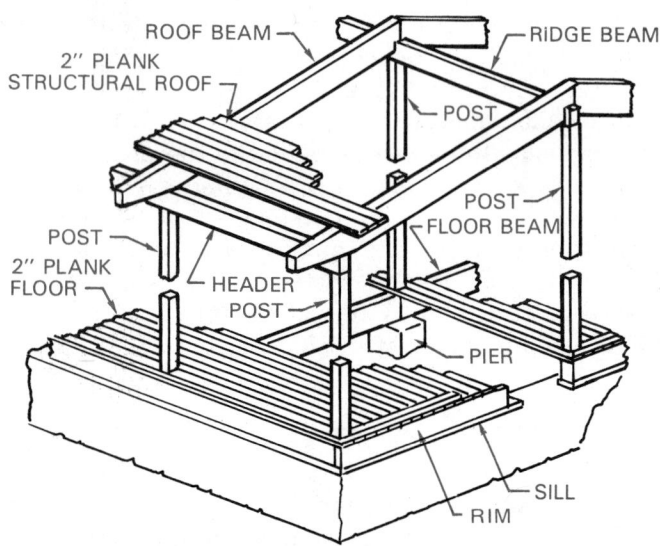

Figure 26–9 Structural members of a post-and-beam framing system. In residential construction, supporting members are usually placed at 48 in. on center. In commercial uses, spacing may be 20 ft or greater.

center. In light commercial applications, supports may be placed at even greater intervals. Although the system uses less lumber than other methods, the members required are larger. Sizes vary depending on the span, but beams of 4 or 6 in. wide are typically used. The subflooring and roofing over the beams is commonly 2 × 6, 2 × 8, or 1⅛ in. T&G plywood. Figure 26–9 shows typical construction members of post-and-beam construction.

Post-and-beam construction can offer great savings in both the lumber and nonstructural materials. This savings results from careful planning of the locations of the posts, and doors and windows that will be located between them. Savings also result by having the building conform to the modular dimensions of the material being used.

Although an entire home can be framed with this method, many contractors will use the post-and-beam system for supporting (1) the lower floor (when no basement is required) and (2) roof systems, then use conventional framing methods for the walls and up-

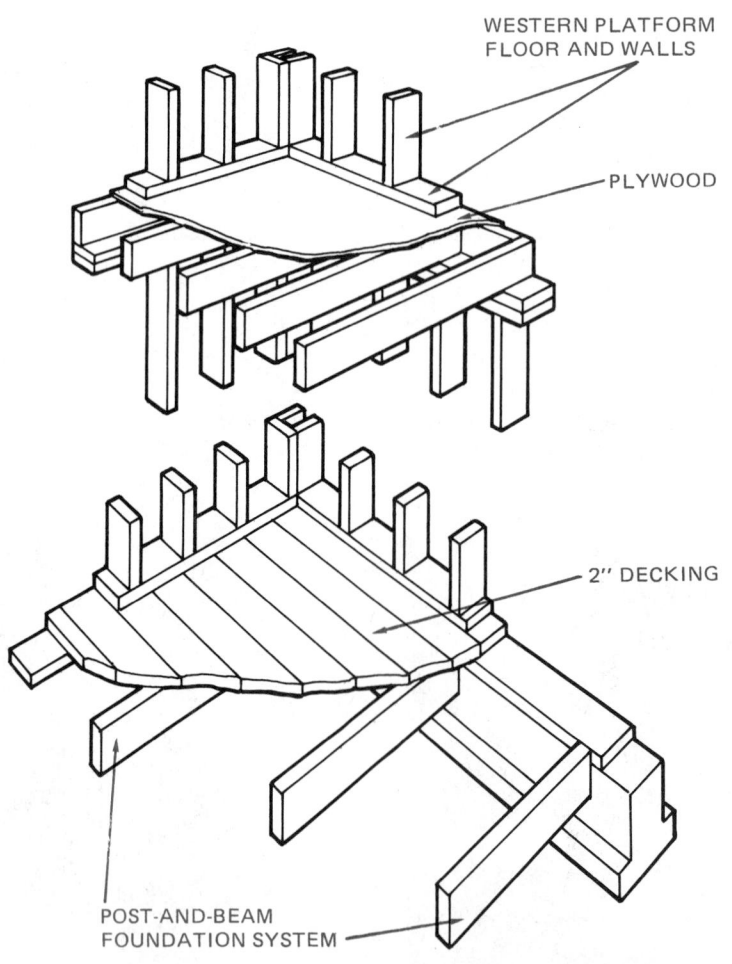

Figure 26–10 Post-and-beam construction is often mixed with platform construction.

Figure 26–11 A post-and-beam floor system being constructed. *Courtesy American Plywood Association.*

per levels as seen in Figure 26–10. Figure 26–11 shows plywood decking being installed on the beams of a post-and-beam floor system.

BRICK AND STONE CONSTRUCTION

A common method of using brick and stone in residential construction is as a veneer. Veneer is a nonload-bearing material. Using brick as a veneer over wood frame construction offers the charm and warmth of brick, with a lower construction cost than structural brick. Brick veneer can be used with any of the common methods of frame construction. Figure 26–12 shows a typical method of attaching brick veneer to wood-framed walls.

ENERGY-EFFICIENT CONSTRUCTION

No matter what system of construction is used, energy efficiency can be a part of the construction process. Some of the following construction techniques may seem like excessive protection and depending on the area of the country where you live some of the methods would be inappropriate. The

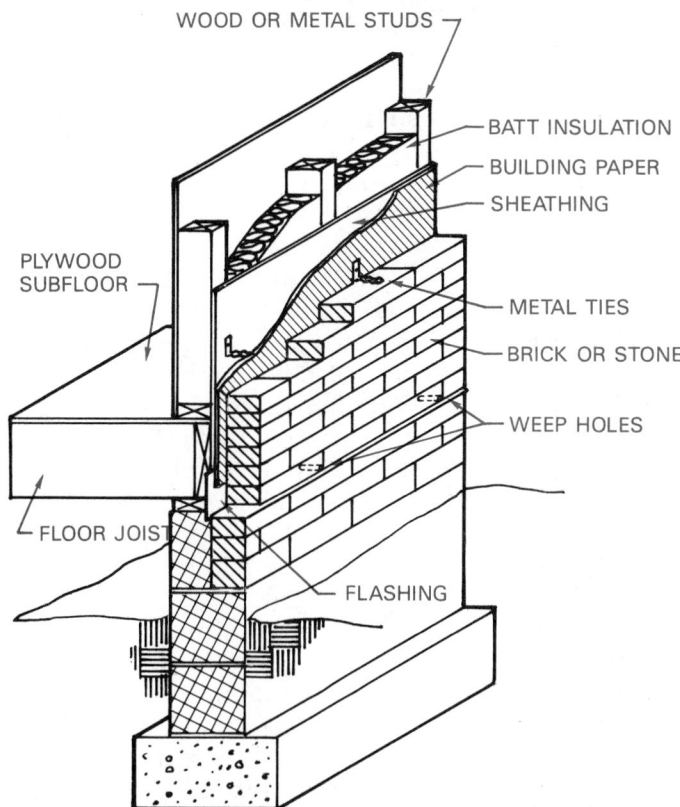

WOOD OR METAL STUDS

BATT INSULATION
BUILDING PAPER
SHEATHING

PLYWOOD SUBFLOOR

METAL TIES
BRICK OR STONE

WEEP HOLES

FLOOR JOIST

FLASHING

Figure 26–12 Brick is typically used as a nonload-bearing veneer attached to wood or concrete construction with metal ties.

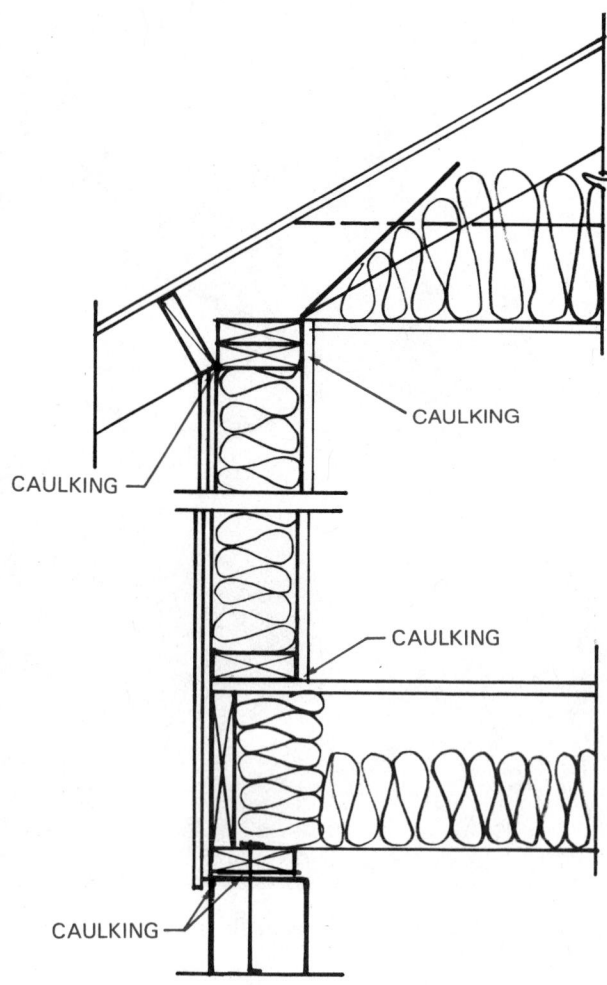

CAULKING

CAULKING

CAULKING

CAULKING

Figure 26–13 Caulking is often added to help eliminate drafts.

examples given are simply examples of various methods that have been used and found effective for special conditions. During your drafting career you'll find clients with varied interest in energy conservation. For many, standard construction methods will be just fine. Other clients may have determined to never spend another extra dime for heating fuel. For those clients much research will be required to help determine the most cost effective method of reducing heat loss and air infiltration in your area. The goal of energy-efficient construction is to decrease the dependency on the heating system. This is best done by the use of caulking, vapor barriers, and insulation.

Caulking

Caulking normally consists of filling small seams in the siding or the trim to reduce air drafts. In energy-efficient construction, caulking is added during construction at all seams or intersections of floors and walls to further reduce the chance of air infiltration. Figure 26–13 shows typical areas where caulking can be added. These beads of caulk will keep air from leaking between joints in construction materials. It may seem like extra work for a small

effect, but caulking is well worth the effort. Caulking involves minimal expense for material and labor.

Vapor Barriers

For an energy-efficient system, air tightness is critical. The ability to eliminate air infiltration through small cracks is imperative if heat loss is to be minimized. Vapor barriers are a very effective method of decreasing heat loss. Most building codes require 6 mil thick plastic to be placed over the earth in the crawl space, and foil to be placed on the interior surfaces of the wall and ceiling insulation. Many energy efficient construction methods use these precautions and add a continuous vapor barrier to the walls. This added vapor barrier is designed to keep exterior moisture from the walls and insulation.

Under normal conditions, wall and ceiling insulation with a foil face on the interior side will allow small amounts of air to leak in at each seam. To eliminate this leakage, a continuous vapor barrier can be installed. To be effective, the vapor barrier must be lapped and sealed to keep air from penetrating through the seams in the plastic. A common element in each of the following illustrations is the

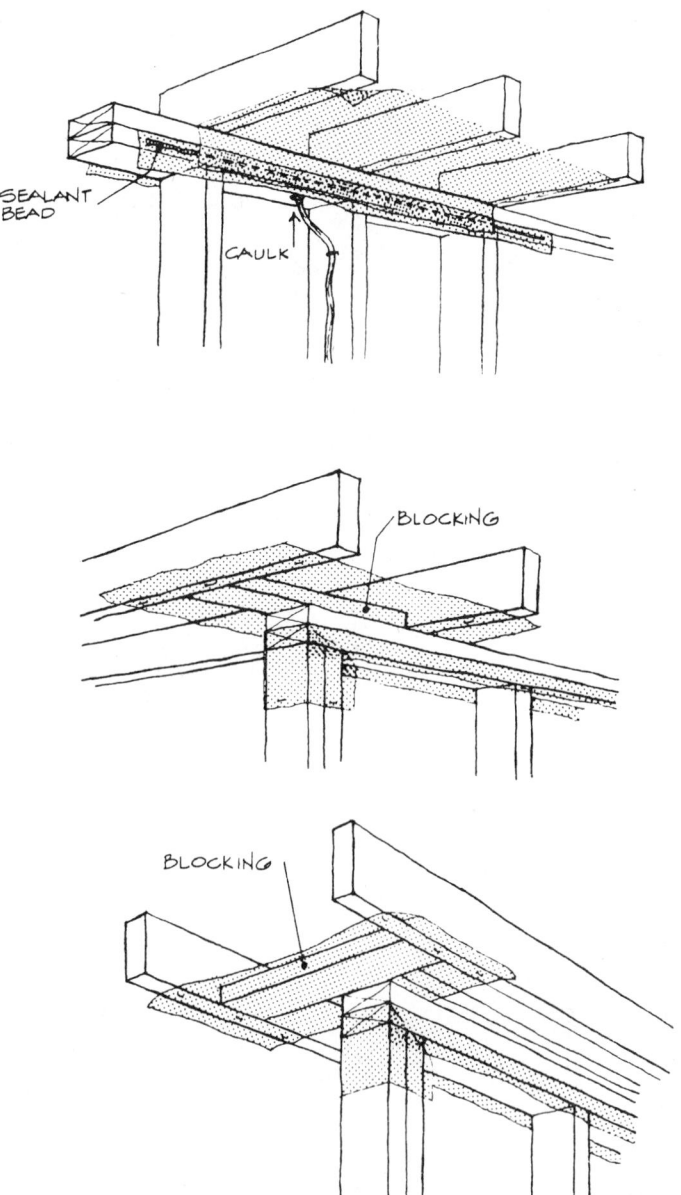

Figure 26-14 Ceiling application of vapor barriers. *Courtesy Oregon Department of Energy.*

care taken to seal the laps in the vapor barrier.

The vapor barrier can be installed in the ceiling, walls, and floor system for effective air control. Figure 26-14 shows three different applications of the vapor barrier in the ceiling. Each is designed to help prevent small amounts of heated air from escaping to the attic. Figure 26-15 shows methods of controlling air infiltration at an exterior wall and interior partition. Figure 26-16 shows several ways to lap the vapor barrier at a floor. All the effort required to keep the vapor barrier intact at the seams must be continued wherever an opening in the wall or ceiling is required.

The cost of materials for a vapor barrier will be low compared to the overall cost of the project. The expense of the vapor barrier will come in the labor to install and to maintain its seal. Great care is required by the entire construction crew to maintain the barrier. This extra care by plumbers, electricians, sheetrockers, and other craftsmen to maintain the barrier after it is installed could greatly add to the labor cost of the home.

Insulation

Many energy-efficient construction methods depend on added insulation to help reduce air infiltration and heat loss. Some of these systems require not only adding more insulation to the structure, but also require adding more framing material to contain the insulation.

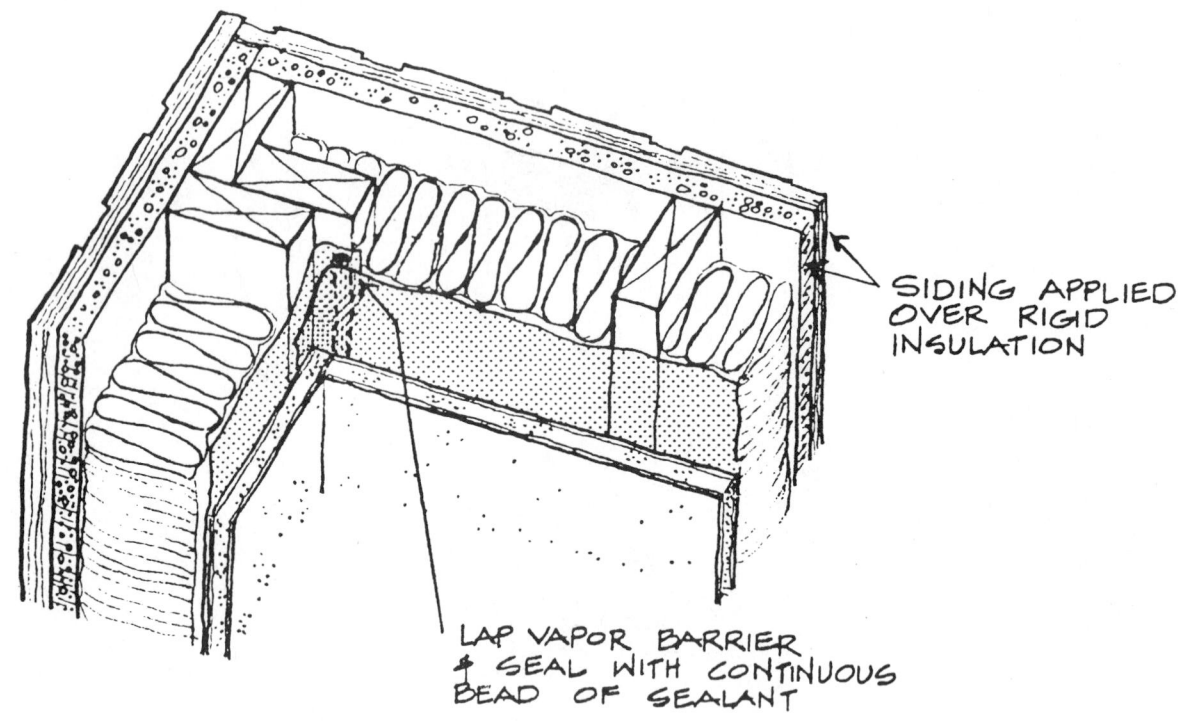

SIDING APPLIED OVER RIGID INSULATION

LAP VAPOR BARRIER & SEAL WITH CONTINUOUS BEAD OF SEALANT

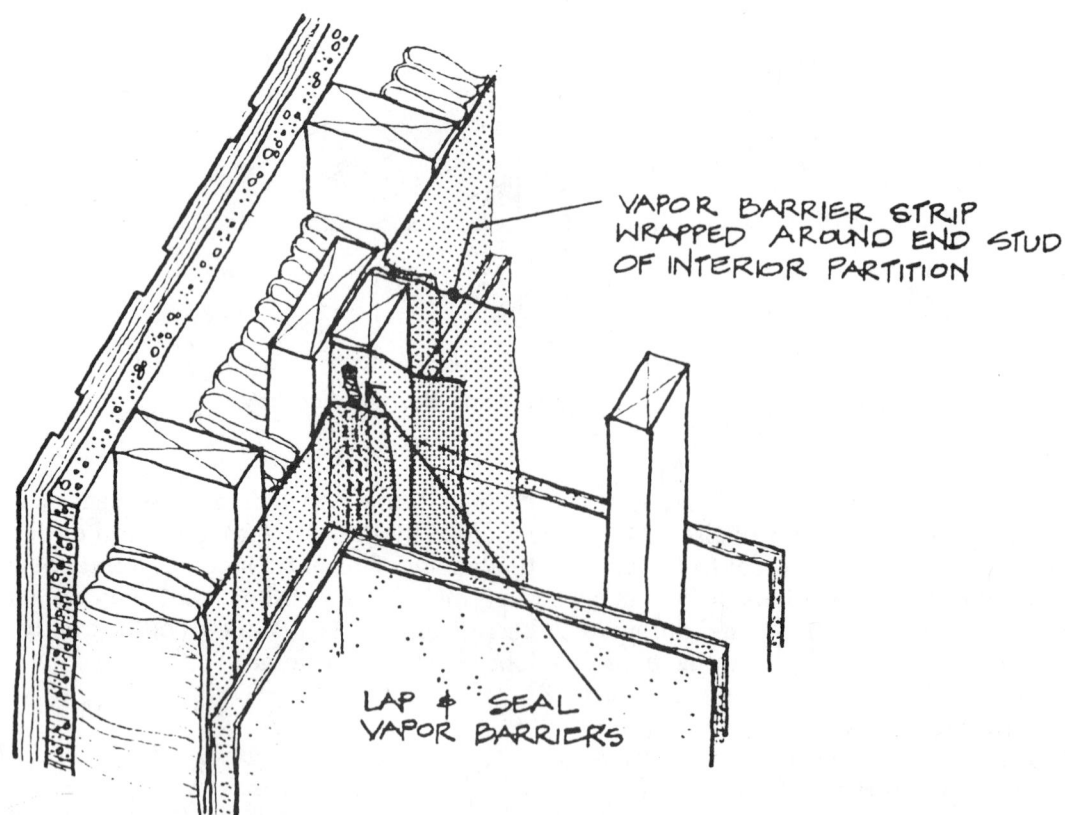

VAPOR BARRIER STRIP WRAPPED AROUND END STUD OF INTERIOR PARTITION

LAP & SEAL VAPOR BARRIERS

Figure 26–15 The vapor barrier at an exterior wall and partition. *Courtesy Oregon Department of Energy.*

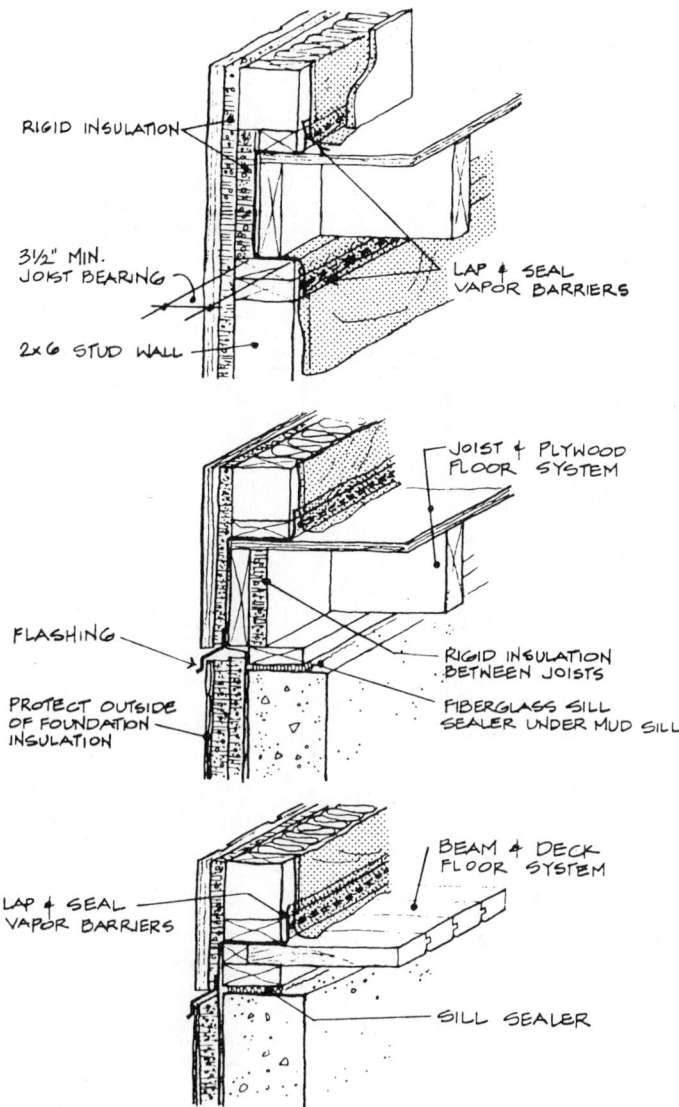

RIGID INSULATION

3½" MIN.
JOIST BEARING

2x6 STUD WALL

LAP & SEAL
VAPOR BARRIERS

JOIST & PLYWOOD
FLOOR SYSTEM

FLASHING

PROTECT OUTSIDE
OF FOUNDATION
INSULATION

RIGID INSULATION
BETWEEN JOISTS

FIBERGLASS SILL
SEALER UNDER MUD SILL

LAP & SEAL
VAPOR BARRIERS

BEAM & DECK
FLOOR SYSTEM

SILL SEALER

Figure 26–16 Typical methods of lapping the vapor barrier at the floor level. *Courtesy Oregon Department of Energy.*

Building codes require a minimum of R-19 insulation in sloped ceilings and R-30 insulation in flat ceilings to help retain heat. In energy-efficient homes, the R value of the ceiling insulation may range from R-38 to R-80. A ceiling of 16 in. of cellulose fibers is often used in energy-efficient structures to provide an R value of 60.

Building codes require a minimum of R-11 insulation in the walls of a residence. A common practice in many areas has been to use 2 × 6 studs so that 6 in. batt insulation with a value of R-19 can be used. This allows for added insulation in the walls as well as the addition of insulation behind the header as shown in Figure 26–17.

Some codes regulate the insulation based on the efficiency of the heating system and the amount of openings. For instance, a house with an 80% efficient furnace could have the following minimum insulation R values:

Ceiling R–30
Walls R–11
Floor R–19

Wall openings, such as windows, doors, and skylights, cannot exceed 17% of the total heated wall area without increasing other energy-conservation methods.

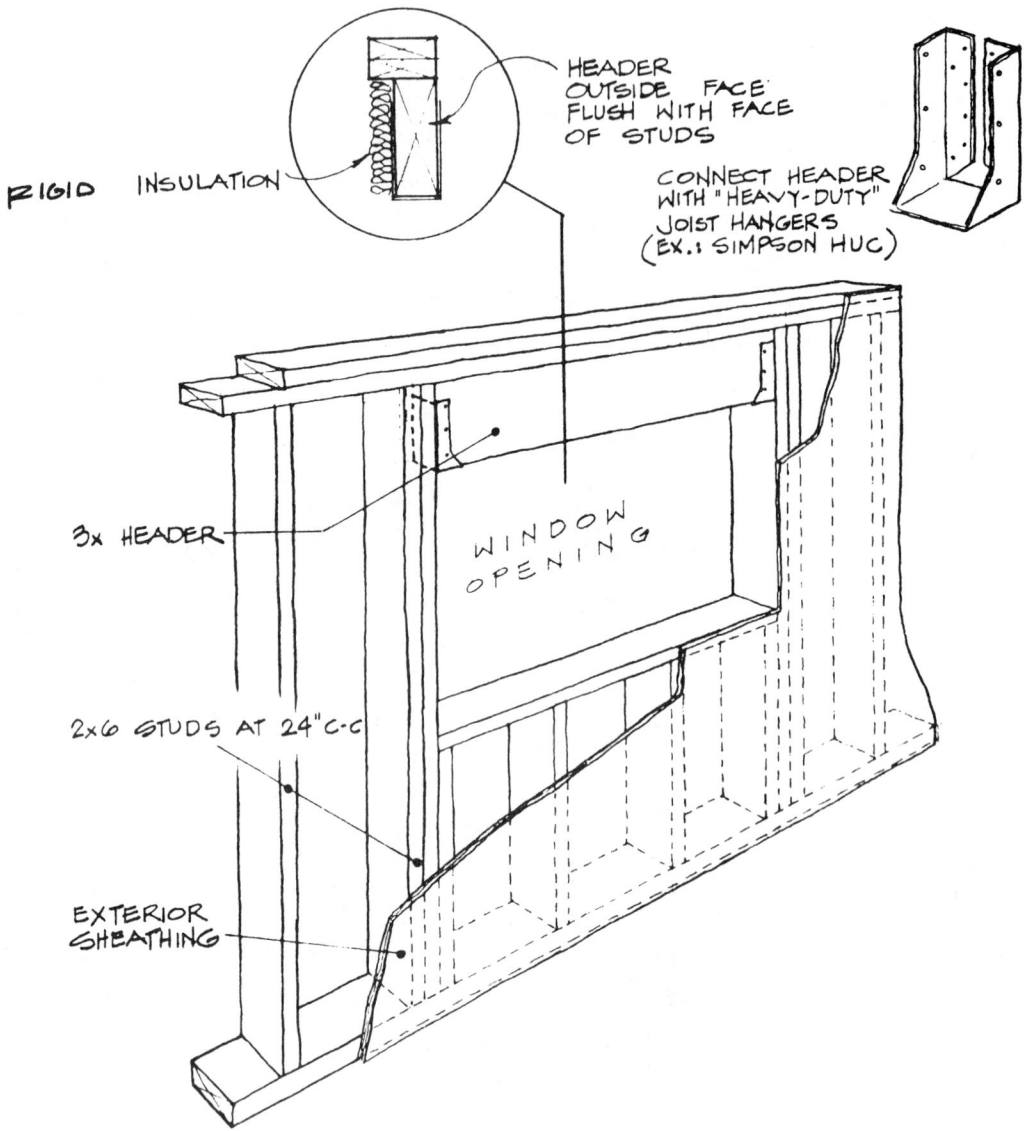

Figure 26–17 Walls formed of 2 × 6 studs allow for the use of 6 in. insulation batts. More important, space is provided for 2 in. rigid insulation behind the header. *Courtesy Oregon Department of Energy.*

FRAMING METHODS TEST

DIRECTIONS

Answer the questions with short complete statements or drawings as needed on an 8½ × 11 drawing sheet as follows:

1. Use ⅛ in. guidelines for all lettering.
2. Letter your name, Framing Methods Test, and the date at the top of the sheet.
3. Letter the question number and provide the answer. You do not need to write out the question.

4. Do all lettering with vertical uppercase architectural letters. If the answer requires line work, use proper drafting tools and technique. Answers may be prepared on a word processor if appropriate with course guidelines.
5. Your grade will be based on correct answers and quality of line technique.

QUESTIONS

1. List and explain two advantages of platform framing.
2. Sketch the platform construction methods for a one-level house.
3. Why is balloon framing not commonly used today?
4. What are two goals of an energy efficient construction system?
5. Sketch a section showing a post-and-beam foundation system.
6. How is brick typically used in residential construction?
7. What factor dictates the reinforcing in masonry walls?
8. Why would a post-and-beam construction roof be used with platform construction walls?
9. List three general materials for energy efficient construction.
10. What is the typical spacing of posts and beams in residential construction?
11. Name two items that can be used at the floor levels of balloon framing to reduce the spread of fire.
12. What is the thickness of common floor framing materials for platform construction?
13. What is the common thickness for roof sheathing for beam construction?
14. What are two materials typically used to reinforce concrete block construction?
15. What is caulking and where is it typically used?
16. What is the thickness for a vapor barrier in a crawl space?
17. List the typical R value for the following uses:
    a. flat ceilings
    b. vaulted ceilings
    c. energy efficient ceiling
    d. walls

Chapter 27
Structural Components

AS WITH every phase of drafting, section drawing includes its own terminology. The terms referred to in this chapter are basic for structural components of sections. The terms will cover floors, walls, and roofs.

FLOOR CONSTRUCTION

Two common methods of framing the floor system are conventional joist and post and beam. In some areas of the country it is common to use post-and-beam framing for the lower floor when a basement is not used and conventional framing for the upper floor. The architect will choose the floor system or systems to be used. The size of the framing crew and the shape of the ground at the job site are the two main factors in the choice of framing methods. As a drafter, you will need to understand both types of floor systems.

Conventional Floor Framing

Conventional, or stick, framing involves the use of 2-in.-wide members placed one at a time in a repetitive manner. Basic terms of the system include mudsill, floor joist, girder, and rim joist. Each can be seen in Figure 27–1 and throughout this chapter.

The mudsill, sill, or base plate, is the first of the structural lumber used in framing the home. The mudsill is the plate which rests on the masonry foundation and provides a base for all framing. Because of the moisture content of concrete and soil, the mudsill is required to be pressure treated or made of foundation-grade redwood or cedar. Mudsills are set along the entire perimeter of the foundation and attached to the foundation with anchor bolts. The size of the mudsill is typically 2 × 6.

With the mudsills in place the girders can be set to support the floor joists. A girder is another name for a beam. The girder is used to support the floor joists as they span across the foundation. Floor joists are usually set on top of the girder, as shown in Figure 27–2, but they also may be hung from the girder with joist hangers.

Posts are used to support the girders. Steel columns may be used in place of a wooden post depending on the load to be transferred to the foundation. Because a wooden post will draw moisture out of the concrete foundation it must rest on 55 pound felt. Sometimes an asphalt roofing shingle is used between the post and the girder.

Once the framing crew has set the support system, the floor joists can be set in place. Floor joists are the structural members used to support the subfloor, or rough floor. Floor joists usually span between the foundation and a girder, but as shown in Figure 27–3, a joist may extend past its support. This extension is known as a cantilever. Floor joists can range in size from 2 × 6 through 2 × 14 and may be spaced at 12, 16, or 24 in. on center depending on the load, span, and size of joist to be used. See Chapter 46 for a complete explanation of sizing joists. Floor joists

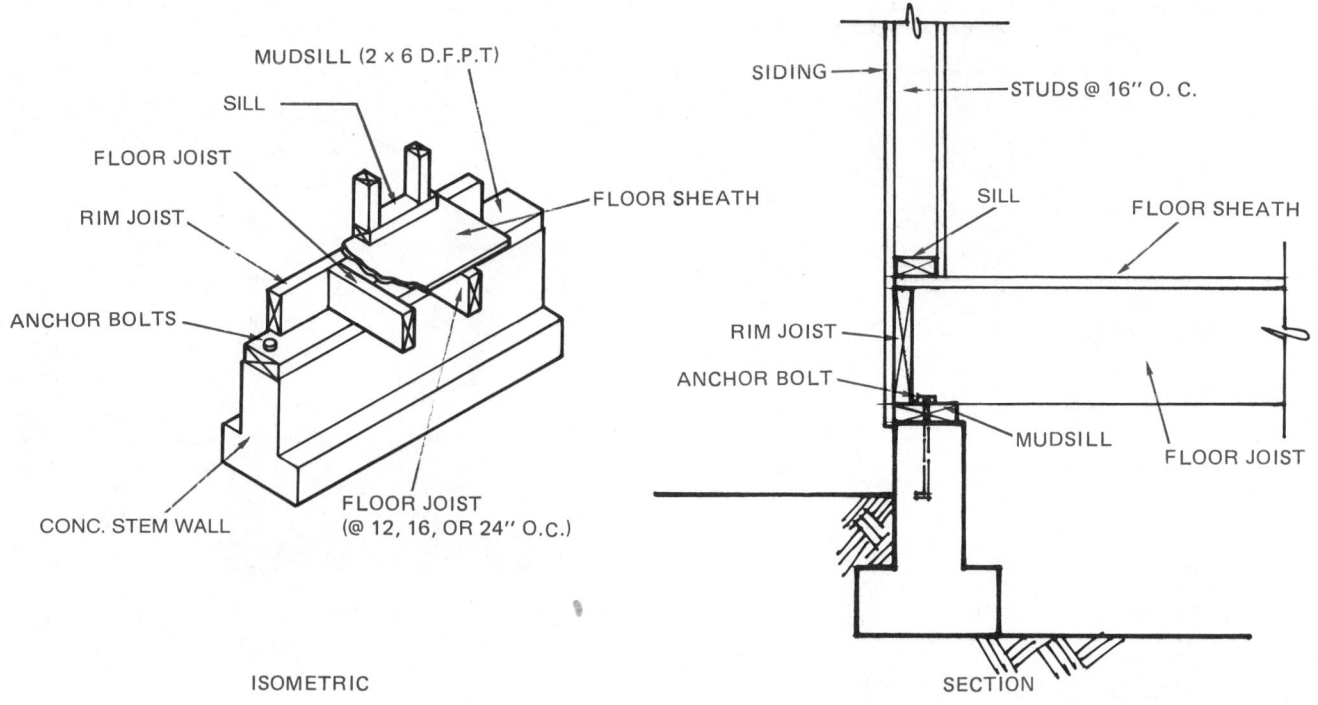

Figure 27–1 Conventional, or stick, floor framing at the concrete perimeter wall.

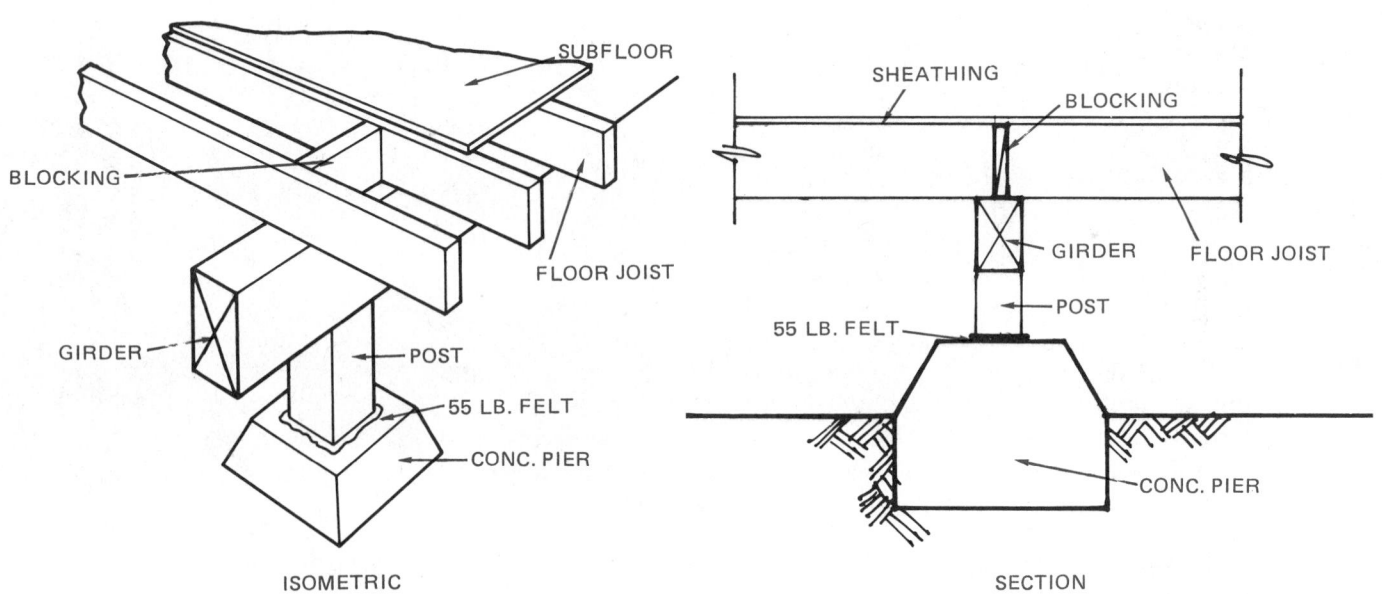

Figure 27–2 Floor joists supported by a girder.

can also be made from plywood. These joists, called truss joists, allow the members to be lighter and longer than conventional floor joists. See Figure 27–4. Trusses can also be used for floor support when a large area needs to be spanned. Figure 27–5 shows the use of trusses for a floor system.

A rim, or band joist (or header, as it is sometimes called) is usually aligned with the outer face of the foundation and mudsill. Some framing crews will set a rim joist around the entire perimeter and then end-nail the floor joists. An alternative to the rim joist is to use solid blocking at the sill between each floor joist. See Figure 27–6.

Blocking in the floor system is used to keep floor joists from rolling over on their sides. One use of blocking is at the center of the joist span as shown in Figure 27–2. Spans longer than 10 ft must be blocked at the center to help transfer lateral forces

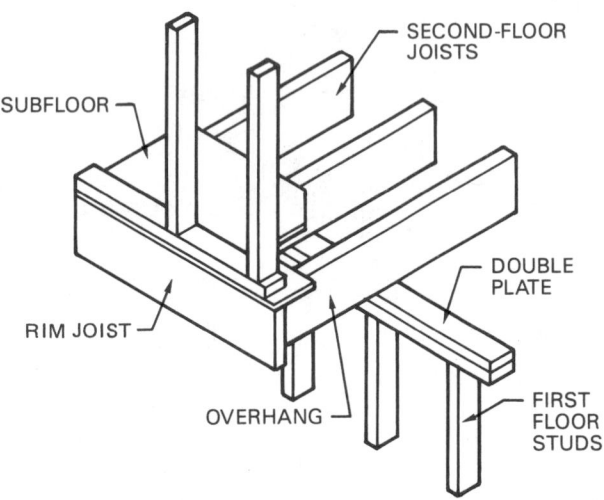

FRAMING A SECOND-FLOOR OVERHANG

Figure 27–3 A floor joist or beam that extends past its supporting member is cantilevered.

Figure 27–4 Plywood truss joists are often used for a lightweight, uniform floor system. *Courtesy Trus Joist Corporation.*

from one joist to another and then to the foundation system. Another use of blocking is at the end of the floor joists at their bearing point. See Figure 27–6. These blocks help keep the entire floor system rigid. Blocking is also used to reduce the spread of fire and smoke through the floor system.

Floor sheathing is installed over the floor joists to form the subfloor. The sheathing provides a surface for the base plate of the wall to rest on. Until the mid 1940s, 1 × 4s or 1 × 6s laid perpendicularly or diagonally to the floor joists were used for floor sheathing. Plywood is now the most common floor sheathing. Depending on the spacing of the joist, ½, ⅝, or ¾ in. plywood is used for sheathing because of its labor-saving advantages. Plywood is usually laid so that the face grain on each surface is perpendicular to the floor joist. This provides a rigid floor system without having to block the edges of the plywood.

ment. The underlayment is not installed until the walls, windows, and roof are in place making the house weathertight. The underlayment provides a smooth surface on which to install the finished flooring. Underlayment is usually ⅜ or ½ in. hardboard. The hardboard underlayment may be omitted if the holes in the plywood are filled.

Post-and-Beam Construction

Terms to be familiar with when working with post-and-beam floor systems include girder, post, decking, and finished floor. Notice there are no floor joists with this system. See Figure 27–7 for the location of post-and-beam components.

A mudsill is installed with post-and-beam construction just as with platform construction. Once set, the girders are also placed. With post-and-beam

Figure 27–5 Trusses can be used in place of floor joists. *Courtesy American Plywood Association.*

construction the girder is supporting the floor decking instead of floor joists. Girders are usually 4 × 6 beams spaced at 48 in. O.C., but the size and distance may vary depending on the loads to be supported. Similar to conventional methods, posts are used to support the girders. Typically a 4 × 4 is the minimum size used for a post, with a 4 × 6 post used to support joints in the girders. With the support system in place, the floor system can be installed.

Decking is the material laid over the girders to form the subfloor. Typically decking is 2 × 6 or 2 × 8

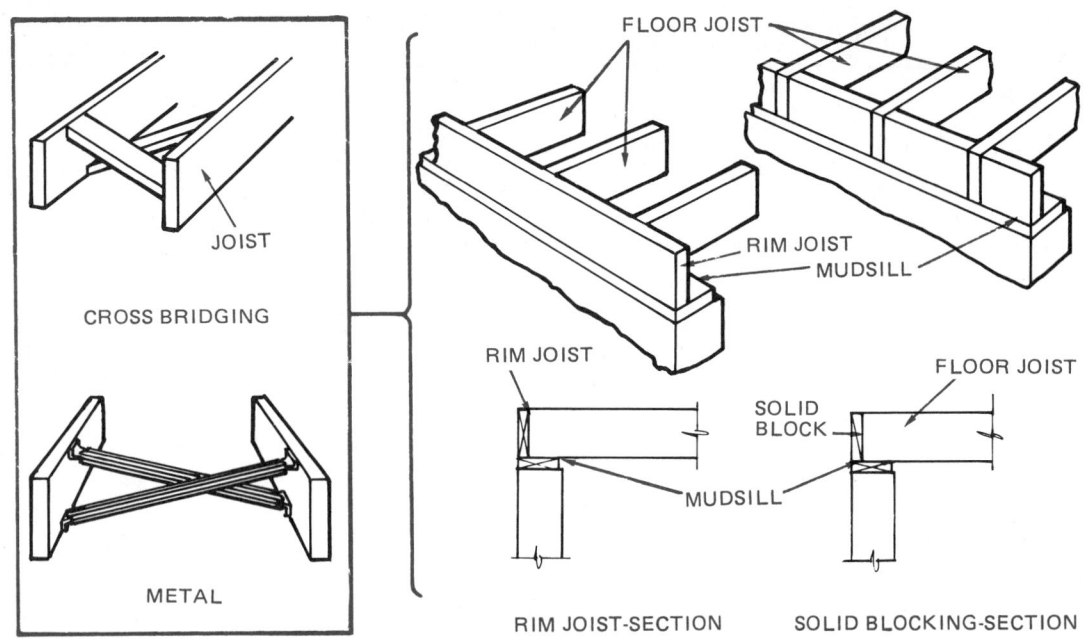

Figure 27–6 Floor joist blocking at the center and end of the span. At midspan, solid or cross blocking may be used. At the ends of the floor joists, solid blocking or a continuous rim joist may be used to provide stability.

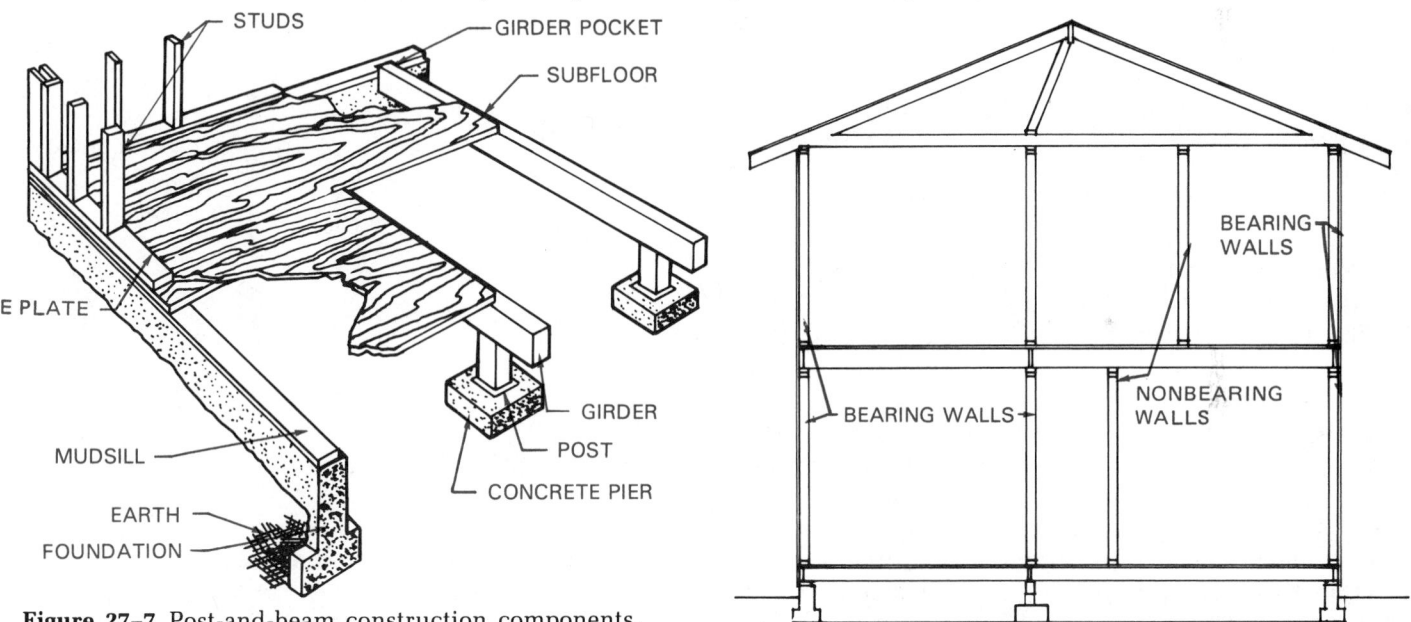

Figure 27–7 Post-and-beam construction components.

Figure 27–8 Bearing and nonbearing walls. A bearing wall supports its own weight and the weight of floor and roof members. A nonbearing wall only supports its own weight. Most building codes allow ceiling weight to be supported on a wall and still be considered a nonbearing wall.

tongue and groove (T&G) boards or 1⅛ in. T&G plywood. The decking is usually finished in similar fashion to conventional decking with a hardboard overlay.

FRAMED WALL CONSTRUCTION

As a drafter you will be concerned with two types of walls, bearing and nonbearing. A bearing wall not only supports itself but also the weight of the roof or other floors constructed above it. A bearing wall requires some type of support under it at the foundation or lower floor level in the form of a girder or another bearing wall. Nonbearing walls are sometimes called partitions. A nonbearing wall serves no structural purpose. It is a partition used to divide rooms and could be removed without causing damage to the building. Bearing and nonbearing walls can be seen in Figure 27–8. In post-and-beam construction, any exterior walls placed between posts are nonbearing walls.

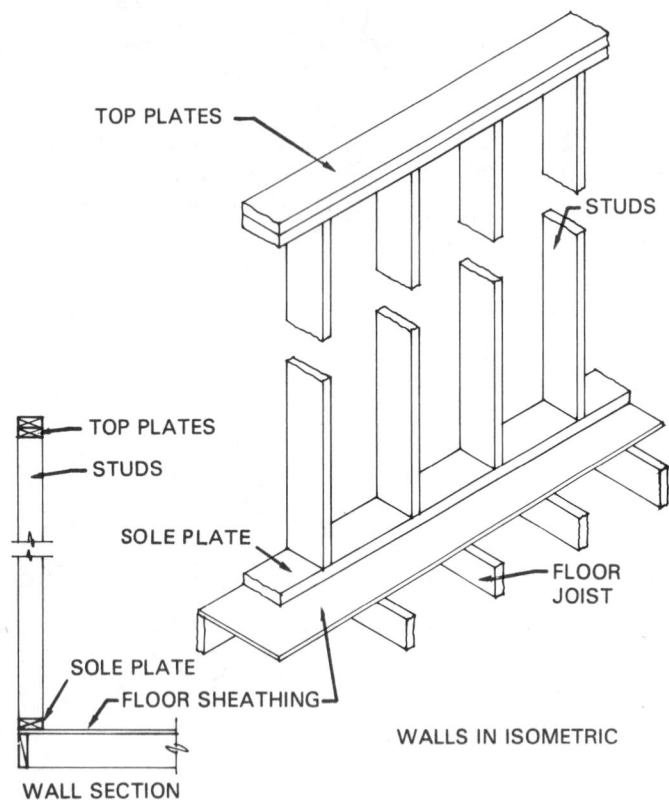

TOP PLATES

STUDS

TOP PLATES

STUDS

SOLE PLATE

FLOOR JOIST

SOLE PLATE

FLOOR SHEATHING

WALL SECTION

WALLS IN ISOMETRIC

Figure 27–9 Standard wall construction uses a double top plate on the top of the wall, a sole plate at the bottom of the wall, and studs.

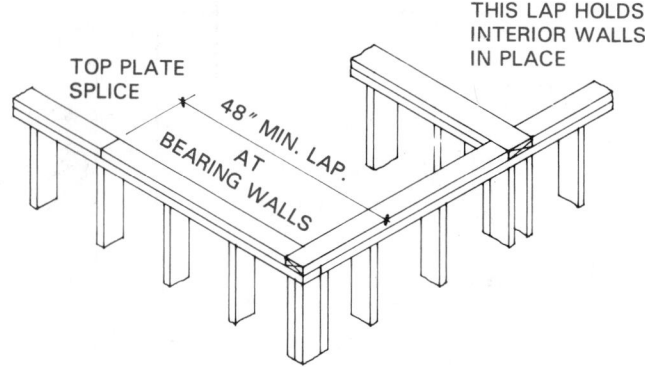

TOP PLATE SPLICE

48" MIN. LAP. AT BEARING WALLS

THIS LAP HOLDS INTERIOR WALLS IN PLACE

Figure 27–10 Top plate laps are required to be 48 in. minimum in bearing walls or held together with steel straps.

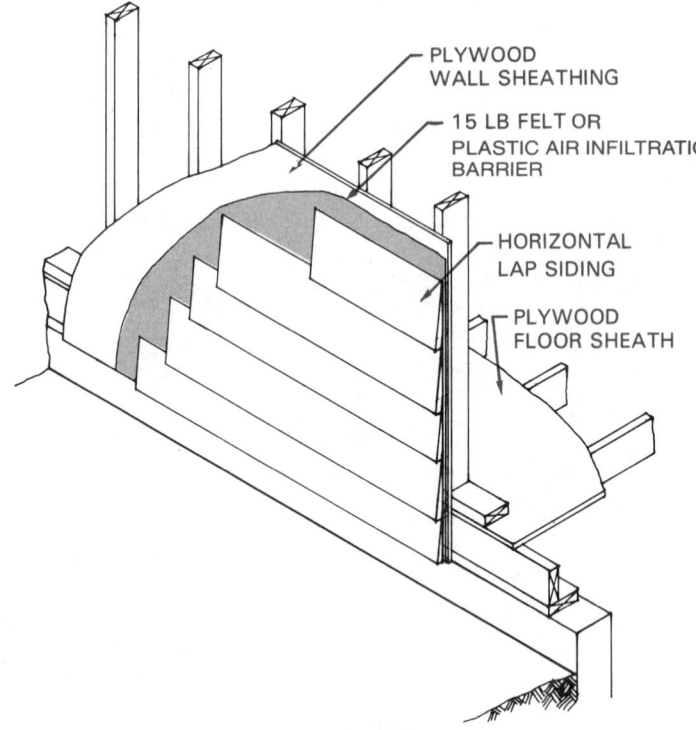

PLYWOOD WALL SHEATHING

15 LB FELT OR PLASTIC AIR INFILTRATIO BARRIER

HORIZONTAL LAP SIDING

PLYWOOD FLOOR SHEATH

Figure 27–11 The use of sheathing on walls varies throughout the country. In some areas siding is applied over the sheathing to provide double wall construction.

Bearing and nonbearing walls are both constructed with similar materials using a sole plate, studs, and a top plate. Each can be seen in Figure 27–9. The sole, or bottom, plate is used to help disperse the loads from the wall studs to the floor system. The sole plate also holds the studs in position as the wall is being tilted into place. Studs are the vertical framing members used to transfer loads from the top of the wall to the floor system. Typically studs are spaced at 16 in. O.C. and provide a nailing surface for the wall sheathing on the exterior side and the sheetrock on the interior side. The top plate is located on top of the studs and is used to hold the wall together. See Figure 27–10. Two top plates are required on bearing walls, and each must lap the other a minimum of 48 in. This lap distance provides a continuous member on top of the wall to keep the studs from separating. An alternative to the double top plate is to use one plate with a steel strap at each joint in the plate. The top plate also provides a bearing surface for the floor joists from an upper level or for the roof members.

Plywood sheathing is primarily used as an insulator against the weather and also as a backing for the exterior siding as shown in Figure 27–11. Sheathing may be considered optional depending on your area of the country. When sheathing is used on exterior walls, it provides what is called double-wall construction. Single-wall construction is when wall sheathing is not used. With single-wall construction, the siding is attached over building paper to the studs as in Figure 27–12. The cost of the home and its location will have a great influence on whether wall sheathing is to be used. In areas where wood is plentiful, ⅜ in. plywood is used on exterior walls as an underlayment. Many builders prefer to use ½ in. plywood for a better nailing surface for the siding.

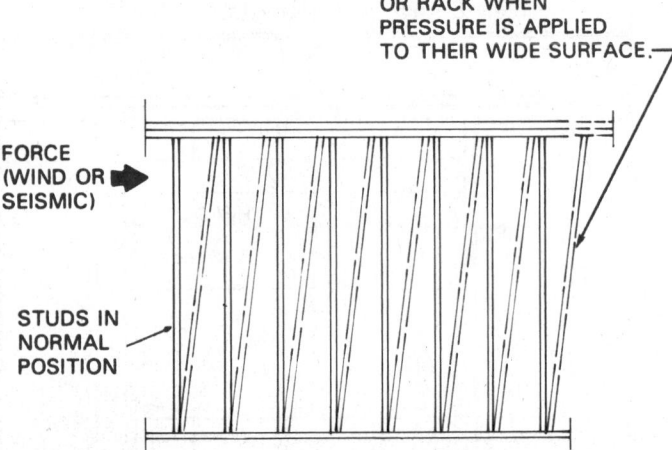

Figure 27-12 With single-wall construction, siding is applied directly over the building paper and studs. *Courtesy American Plywood Association.*

Figure 27-13 Wall racking occurs when wind or seismic forces push the studs out of their normal position. Plywood panels can be used to resist these forces and keep the studs perpendicular to the floor. These plywood panels are called shear panels.

By using ½ in. plywood as sheathing, the builders need only order one thickness of plywood for the entire home.

In areas where wood is neither inexpensive nor plentiful, plywood is used for its ability to resist the tendency of a wall to twist or rack. Racking can be caused from wind or seismic forces. Plywood used to resist these forces is called a shear panel. See Figure 27-13 for an example of racking and how plywood can be used to resist this motion.

In areas where plywood is not required for shear panels or for climatic reasons, the studs can be kept from racking by using let-in braces. Figure 27-14 shows how a brace can be used to stiffen the studs. A notch is cut into the studs and a 1 × 4 is laid flat in this notch at a 45° angle to the studs.

Prior to the mid-1960s, blocking was common in walls to help provide stiffness. Blocking for structural or fire reasons is now no longer required unless a wall exceeds 10 ft in height. Blocking is often installed for a nailing surface for mounting cabinets and plumbing fixtures. Blocking is sometimes used to provide extra strength in some seismic zones.

In addition to the wall components mentioned, there are several other terms that the drafter needs to be aware of. These are terms that are used to

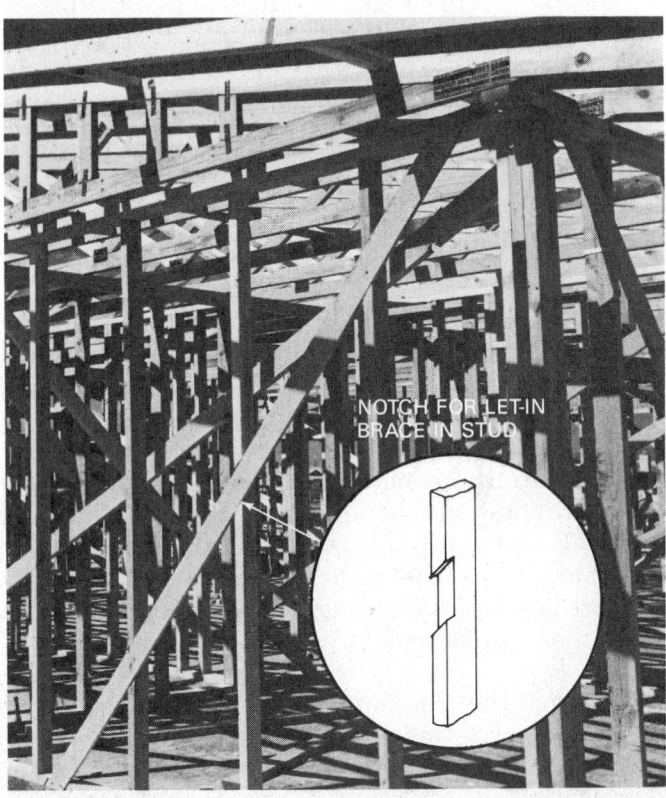

Figure 27-14 Let-in braces can sometimes be used instead of shear panels to resist wall racking. *Courtesy Gang-Nail Systems, Inc.*

describe the parts used to frame around an opening in a wall. These include headers, subsill, trimmers, king studs, and jack studs. Each can be seen in Figure 27-15.

A header in a wall is used over an opening such as a door or window. When an opening is made in

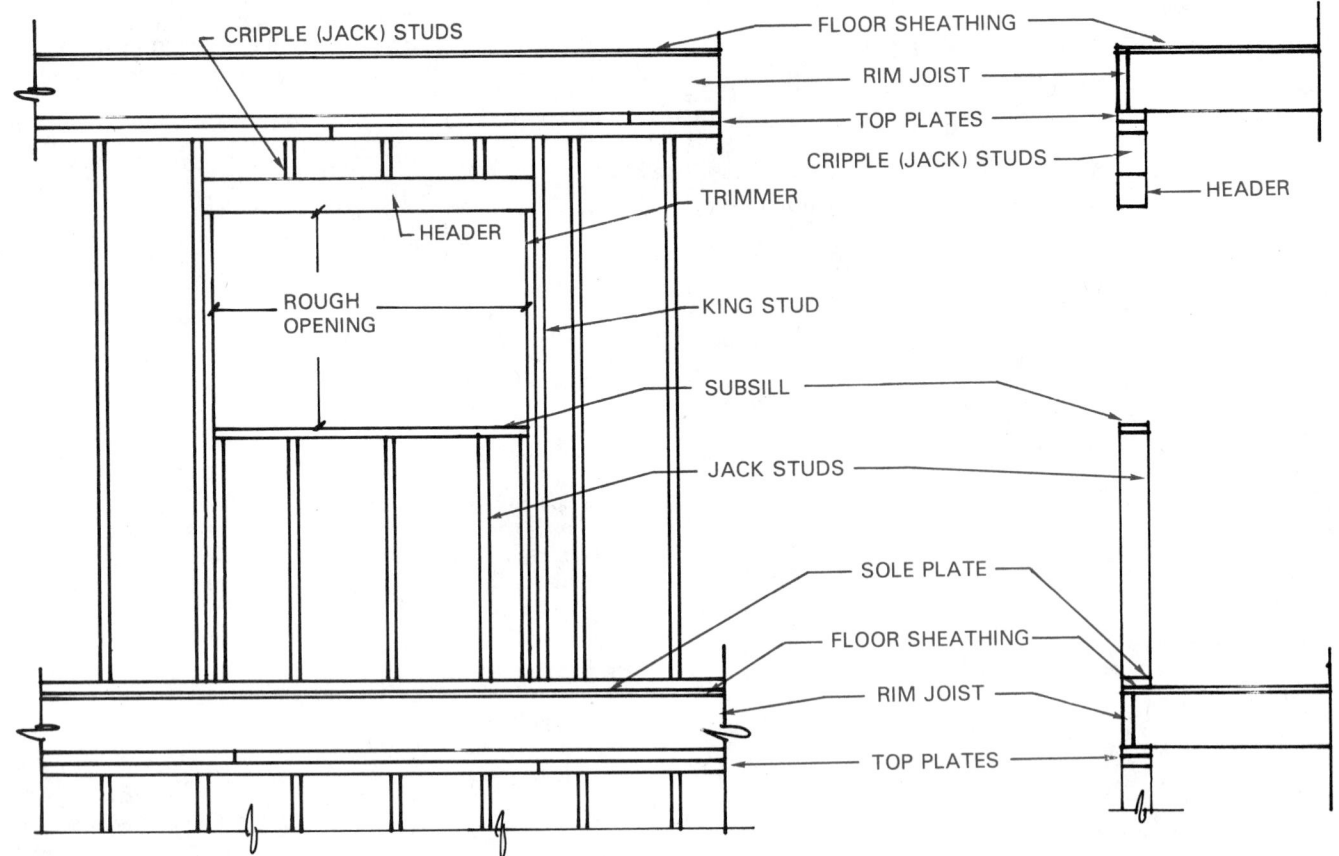

Figure 27-15 Construction components at an opening.

a wall, one or more studs must be omitted. A header is used to support the weight that the missing studs would have carried. The header is supported on each side by a trimmer. Depending on the weight the header is supporting, double trimmers may be required. The trimmers also provide a nailing surface for the window and the interior and exterior finishing materials. A king stud is placed beside each trimmer and extends from the sill to the top plates. It provides support for the trimmers so that the weight imposed from the header can only go downward and not sideways.

Between the trimmers is a subsill located on the bottom side of a window opening. It provides a nailing surface for the interior and exterior finishing materials. Jack studs, or cripples, are studs that are not full height. They are placed between the sill and the sole plate and between a header and the top plates.

MASONRY WALL CONSTRUCTION

Concrete block and brick construction offer many advantages for construction. A structure made of masonry will be practically maintenance free and can last for centuries. Although concrete blocks are used to form the exterior walls of some houses, the primary use of blocks is for residential foundations and commercial structures. Construction methods with concrete blocks can be reviewed in Chapter 21.

The most common method of using brick is as a veneer on a wood-framed structure as seen in Figure 27-16. Using brick as veneer allows the amount of brick used to be cut in half resulting in a large financial saving while still providing an attractive exterior appearance. Great care must be taken with brick veneer to protect the wood frame from moisture and to keep the brick from pulling away from the wood. To protect the wood from moisture a vapor barrier of 55# felt or 6 mil plastic is installed in a 1 in. minimum air space between the brick and the wood frame. The brick is normally attached to the wall with galvanized metal straps at 24 in. on center at each stud.

Masonry Patterns

One of the most popular features of brick is the wide variety of positions and patterns in which it can be placed. These patterns are achieved by placing the brick in various positions to each other. The position in which the brick is placed may alter what the brick is called. Figure 27-17 shows the names of common brick positions.

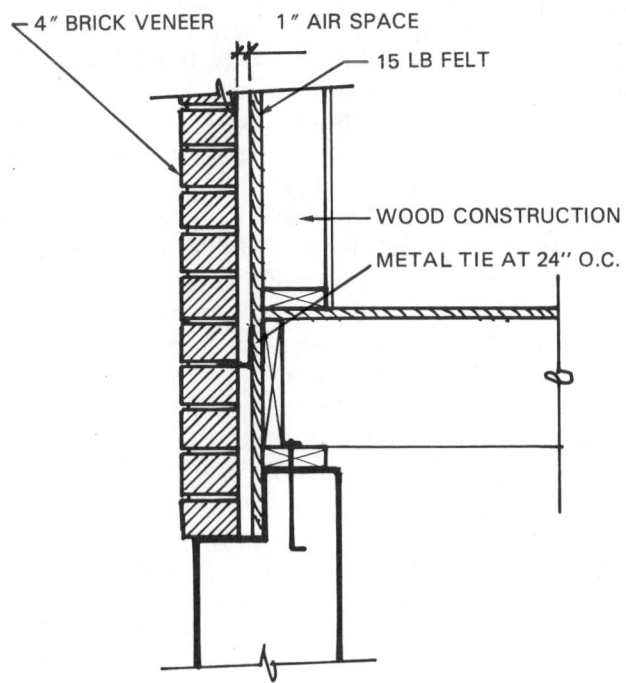

Figure 27-16 A brick veneer wall is the most common use of brick in residential construction.

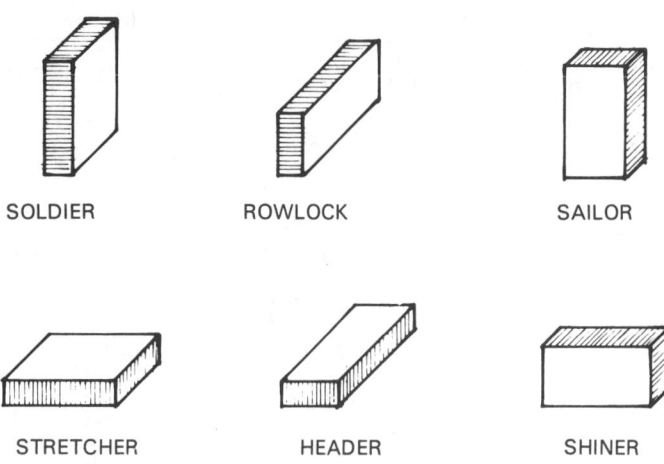

Figure 27-17 The position in which a brick is placed alters the name of the unit.

Bricks can be placed in various positions to form a variety of bonds and patterns. A bond is the connecting of two wythes to form stability within the wall. The pattern is the arrangement of the bricks within one wythe. The Flemish and English bonds in Figure 27-18 are the most common methods of bonding two wythes or vertical section of a wall that is one brick thick. The Flemish bond consists of alternating headers and stretchers in every course. A course of brick is one row in height. An English bond consists of alternating courses of headers and stretchers. The headers span between wythes to keep the wall from separating.

There are many patterns that can be used when laying brick and Figure 27-19 shows some of the most common. The pattern used depends on the desired effect and the economy associated with constructing the wall.

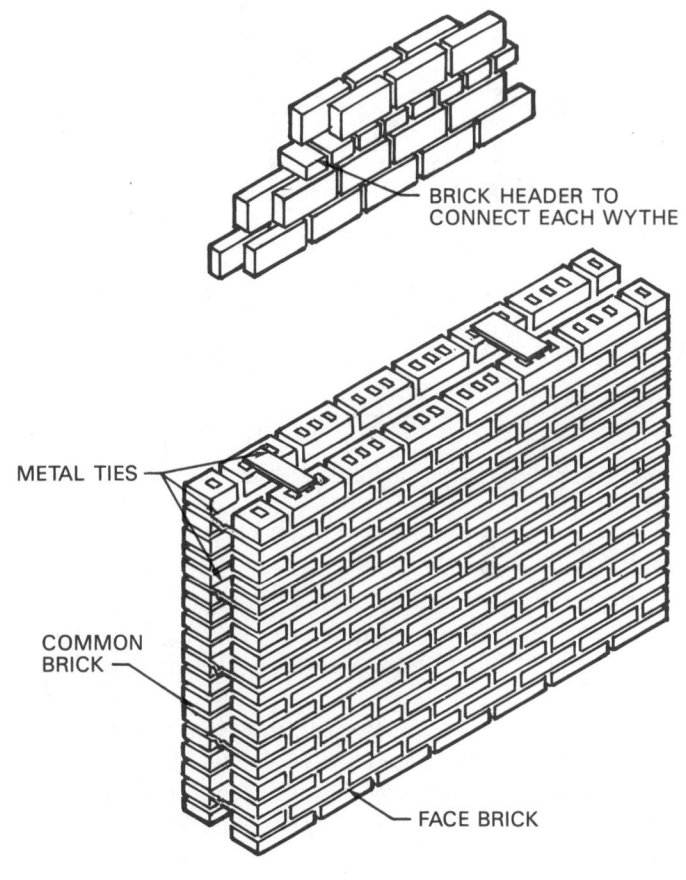

ROOF CONSTRUCTION

Roof framing includes both conventional and truss framing methods. Each has its own special terminology but there are many terms that apply to both systems. These common terms will be described first, followed by the terms for conventional and truss framing methods.

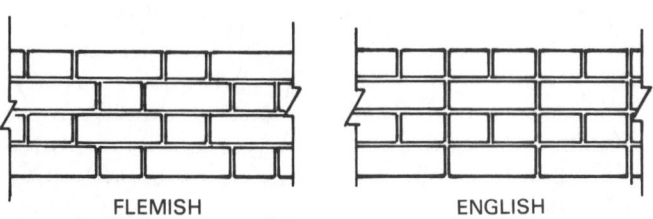

Figure 27-18 Brick walls can be strengthened by metal ties or bricks connecting each wythe. The most common types of brick bonds are the Flemish and English bonds.

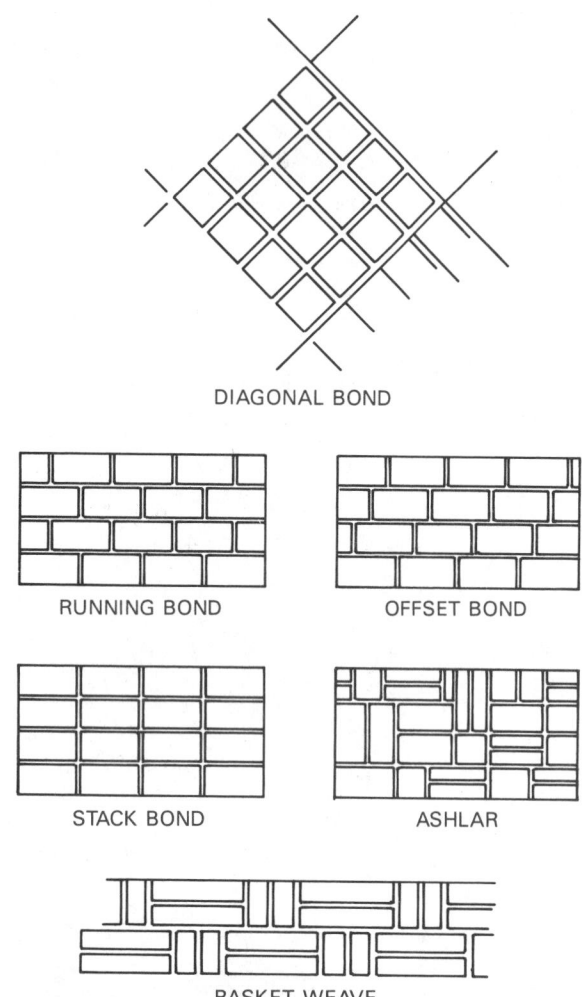

DIAGONAL BOND

RUNNING BOND   OFFSET BOND

STACK BOND   ASHLAR

BASKET WEAVE

Figure 27–19 Common patterns for brickwork.

Basic Roof Terms

Roof terms common to conventional and trussed roofs include eave, cornice, eave blocking, fascia, ridge, sheathing, finishing roofing, flashing and roof pitch dimensions.

The eave is the portion of the roof that extends beyond the walls. The cornice is the covering that is applied to the eaves. Common methods for constructing the cornice can be seen in Figure 27–20. Eave, or bird, blocking is a spacer block placed between the rafters or truss tails at the eave. This block keeps the spacing of the rafters or trusses uniform and keeps small animals from entering the attic. It also provides a cap to the exterior siding as seen in Figure 27–21.

A fascia is a trim board placed at the end of the rafters or truss tails and usually perpendicular to the building wall. It hides the truss or rafter tails from sight and also provides a surface where the gutters may be mounted. See Figure 27–21. The fascia is typically 2 in. deeper than the rafters or truss tails. At the opposite end of the rafter from the fascia is

the ridge. The ridge is the highest point of a roof and formed by the intersection of the rafters or the top chords of a truss. See Figure 27–22.

Roof sheathing is similar to wall and floor sheathing in that it is used to cover the structural members. Roof sheathing may be either solid or skip. The area of the country and the finished roofing to be used will determine which type of sheathing is used. For solid sheathing, ½ in. thick CDX plywood is generally used. CDX is the specification given by the American Plywood Association to designate standard grade plywood. It provides an economical, strong covering for the framing as well as an even base for installing the finished roofing.

Skip sheathing is generally used with either tile or shakes. Typically 1 × 4s are laid perpendicular to the rafters with a 4 in. space between each piece of sheathing. A water-resistant sheathing must be used when the eaves are exposed to weather. This usually consists of plywood rated CCX or 1 in. T&G decking. CCX is the specification for exterior use plywood. It is designated for exterior use because of the glue and the type of veneers used to make the panel.

The finished roofing is the weather protection system. Typically roofing might include built-up roofing, asphalt shingles, fiberglass shingles, cedar, tile, or metal panels. For a complete discussion of roofing materials see Chapters 24 and 33. Flashing is generally 20 to 26 gage metal used at wall and roof intersections to keep water out. See Figure 27–23.

Pitch, span and overhang are dimensions that are needed to define the angle, or steepness, of the roof. Each can be seen in Figure 27–24. Pitch is used to describe the slope of the roof. Pitch is the ratio between the horizontal run and the vertical rise of the roof. The run is the horizontal measurement from the outside edge of the wall to the centerline of the ridge. The rise is the vertical distance from the top of the wall to the highest point of the rafter being measured. See Chapter 33 for a complete discussion of roof pitch. The span is the measurement between the outside edges of the supporting walls. The overhang is the horizontal measurement between the exterior face of the wall and the end of the rafter tail.

Conventionally Framed Roof Terms

Conventional, or stick, framing methods involve the use of wood members placed in repetitive fashion. Stick framing involves the use of such members as a ridge board, rafter, and ceiling joists. See Figure 27–25 for their location and relationship to each other.

The ridge board is the horizontal member at the ridge which runs perpendicular to the rafters. The ridge board is centered between the exterior walls

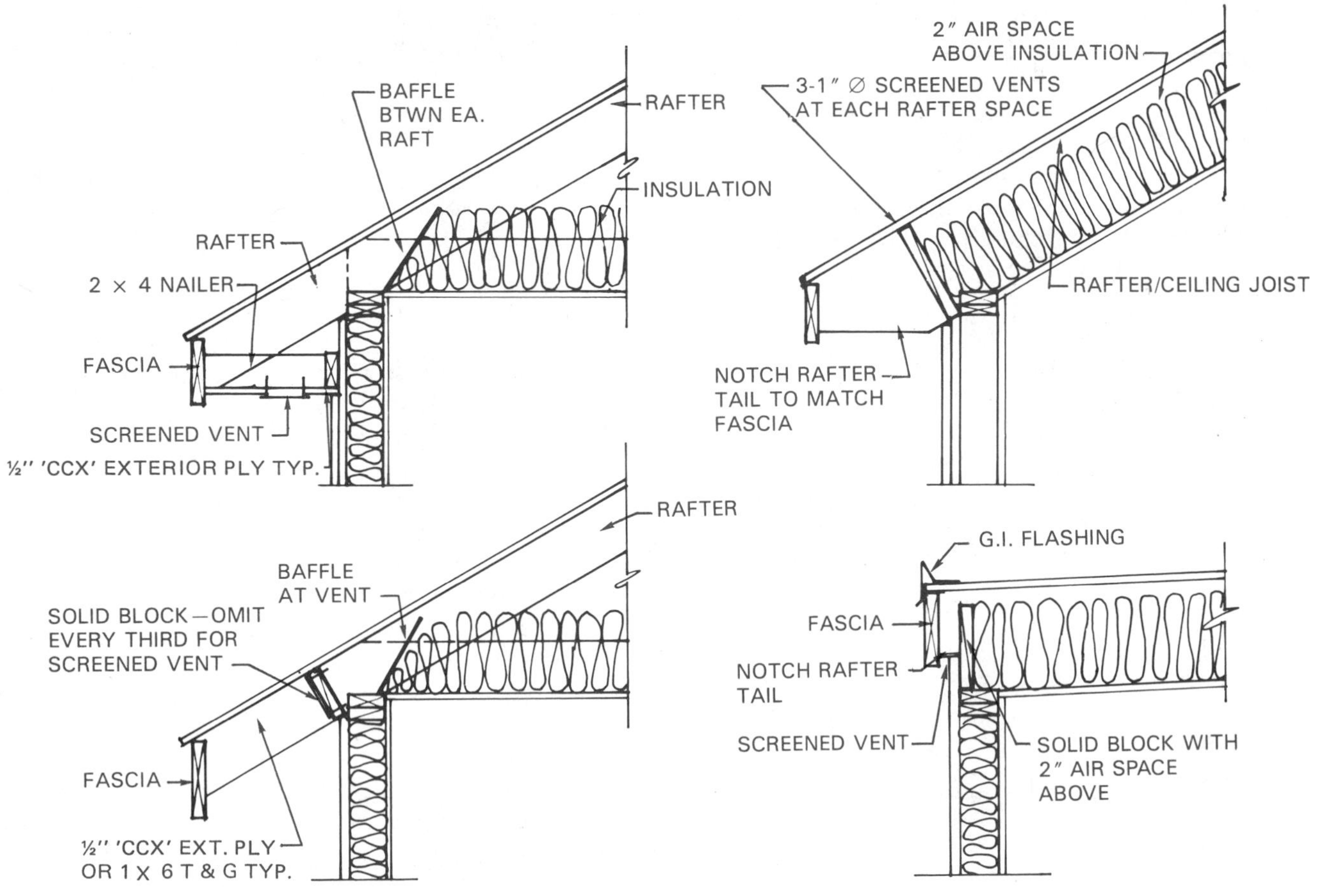

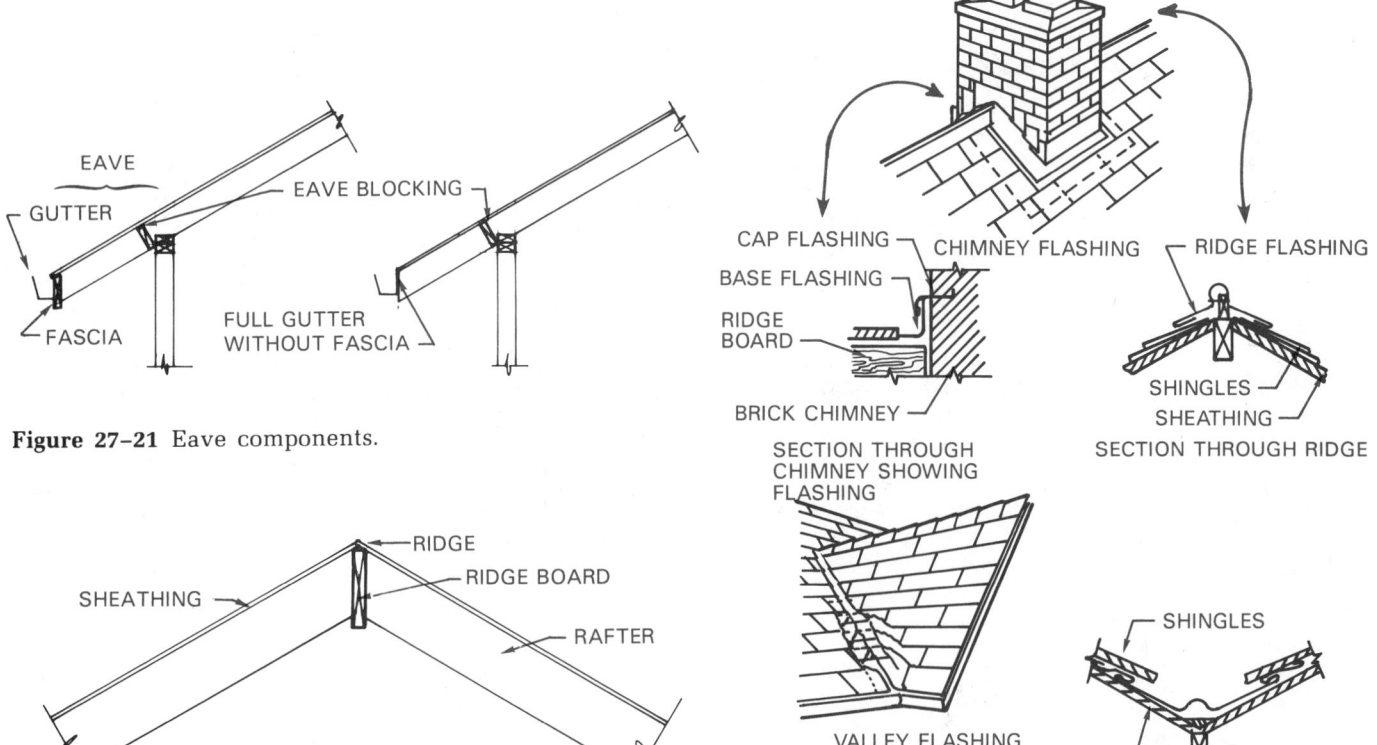

BAFFLE BTWN EA. RAFT

RAFTER

INSULATION

RAFTER

2 × 4 NAILER

FASCIA

SCREENED VENT

½'' 'CCX' EXTERIOR PLY TYP.

2" AIR SPACE ABOVE INSULATION

3-1" Ø SCREENED VENTS AT EACH RAFTER SPACE

RAFTER/CEILING JOIST

NOTCH RAFTER TAIL TO MATCH FASCIA

SOLID BLOCK—OMIT EVERY THIRD FOR SCREENED VENT

BAFFLE AT VENT

RAFTER

FASCIA

½'' 'CCX' EXT. PLY OR 1 × 6 T & G TYP.

G.I. FLASHING

FASCIA

NOTCH RAFTER TAIL

SCREENED VENT

SOLID BLOCK WITH 2" AIR SPACE ABOVE

Figure 27-20 Typical methods for constructing a cornice.

EAVE

GUTTER

EAVE BLOCKING

FASCIA

FULL GUTTER WITHOUT FASCIA

Figure 27-21 Eave components.

SHEATHING

RIDGE

RIDGE BOARD

RAFTER

Figure 27-22 Ridge construction.

CAP FLASHING

BASE FLASHING

RIDGE BOARD

BRICK CHIMNEY

CHIMNEY FLASHING

SECTION THROUGH CHIMNEY SHOWING FLASHING

RIDGE FLASHING

SHINGLES

SHEATHING

SECTION THROUGH RIDGE

VALLEY FLASHING

SHINGLES

SHEATHING

Figure 27-23 Roof flashing is typically used at intersections such as hips and valleys, and ridges.

when the pitch on each side is equal. The ridge board resists the downward thrust resulting from gravity trying to force the rafters into a V shape between the walls. The ridge board does not support the rafters but is used to align the rafters so that their forces are pushing against each other.

Rafters are the sloping members used to support the roof sheathing and finished roofing. Rafters are typically spaced at 12, 16, or 24 in. O.C. There are various kinds of rafters including common, hip, valley and jack rafters. Each can be seen in Figure 27–25.

A common rafter is used to span and support the roof loads from the ridge to the top plate. Common rafters run perpendicular to both the ridge and the wall supporting them. The upper end rests squarely against the ridge board and the lower end receives a bird's mouth notch and rests on the top plate of the wall. A bird's mouth is a notch cut in a rafter at the point where the rafter intersects a beam or bearing wall. This notch increases the contact area of the rafter by placing more rafter surface against the top of the wall as shown in Figure 27–26.

Hip rafters are used when adjacent slopes of the roof meet to form an inclined ridge. The hip rafter extends diagonally across the common rafters and provides support to the upper end of the rafters. The hip is inclined at the same pitch as the rafters. A valley rafter is similar to a hip rafter. It is inclined at the same pitch as the common rafters that it supports. Valley rafters get their name because they are located where adjacent roof slopes meet to form a valley. Jack rafters span from a wall to a hip or valley rafter. They are similar to a common rafter but span a shorter distance. Typically, a section will only show common rafters, with hip, valley and jack rafters reserved for a very complex section.

Before moving on to other roof terms it is important to understand the function of the rafters in relation to the other framing members. As can be seen in Figure 27–27, rafters tend to settle because of the weight of the roof and because of gravity. As the rafters settle, they push supporting walls outward. These two actions, downward and outward, require special members to resist these forces. These members include ceiling joists, ridge bracing, collar ties, purlins, and purlin blocks and braces. Each can be seen in Figure 27–28.

Ceiling joists span between the top plates of bearing walls to resist the outward force placed on the walls from the rafters. The ceiling joists also support the finished ceiling. Collar ties are also used to help resist the outward thrust of the rafters. They are

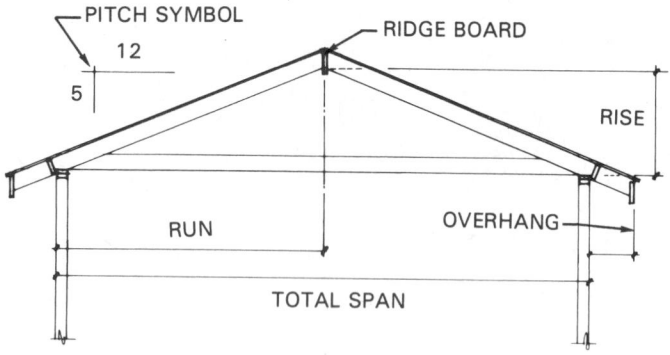

Figure 27–24 Roof dimensions needed for construction.

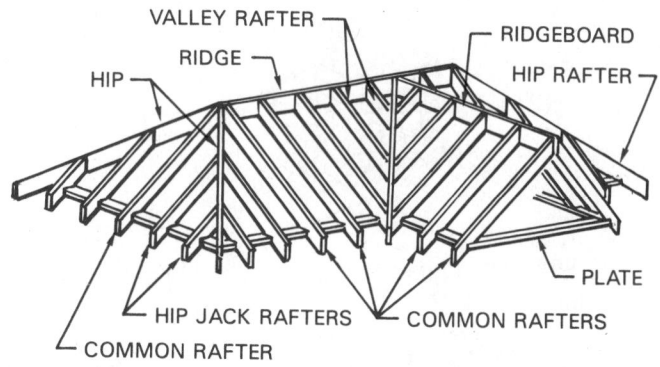

Figure 27–25 Roof members in conventional construction.

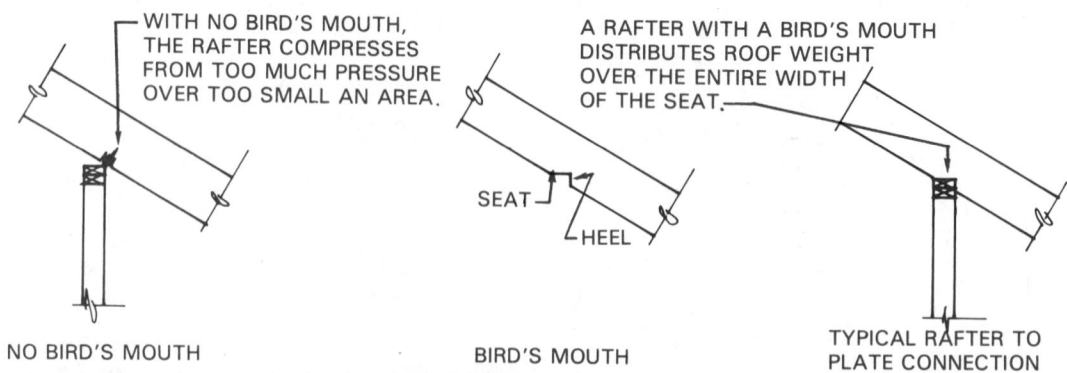

Figure 27–26 A bird's mouth is a notch cut into the rafter to increase the bearing surface.

usually the same cross section size as the ceiling joists and placed in the upper third of the roof.

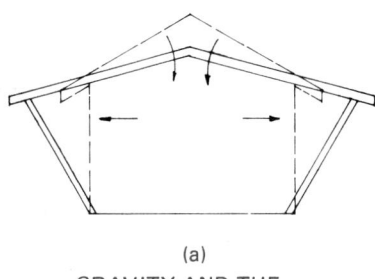

(a)

GRAVITY AND THE WEIGHT OF ROOFING MATERIALS TEND TO TRY TO FORCE THE RAFTERS DOWNWARD AND OUTWARD.

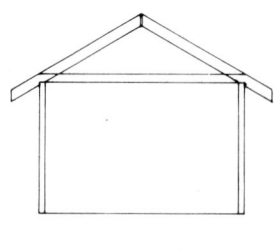

(b)

A CEILING JOIST IS USED TO RESIST THE OUTWARD FORCES FROM THE RAFTERS.

Figure 27–27 Roof actions and reactions.

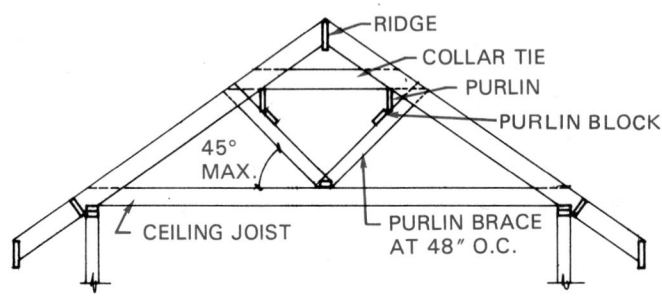

RIDGE
COLLAR TIE
PURLIN
PURLIN BLOCK
45° MAX.
CEILING JOIST
PURLIN BRACE AT 48″ O.C.

Figure 27–28 Common roof supports.

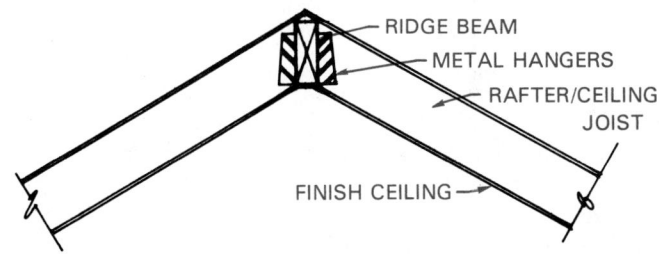

RIDGE BEAM
METAL HANGERS
RAFTER/CEILING JOIST
FINISH CEILING

Figure 27–29 A flush ridge beam.

Ridge braces are used to support the downward action of the ridge board. The brace is usually a 2 × 4 spaced at 48 in. O.C. maximum. The brace must be set at 45° maximum to the ceiling joist. A purlin is a brace used to provide support for the rafters as they span between the ridge and the wall. The purlin is usually the same cross section size as the rafter and is placed below the rafter to reduce the span. As the rafter span is reduced, the size of the rafter can be reduced. See Chapter 46 for a further explanation of rafter sizes. A purlin brace is used to support the purlins. They are typically 2 × 4s spaced at 48 in. O.C. along the purlin and transfer weight from the purlin to a supporting wall. The brace is supported by an interior wall, or a 2 × 4 lying across the ceiling joist. They can be installed at no more than 45° from vertical. A scrap block of wood is used to keep the purlin from sliding down the brace. When there is no wall to support the ridge brace, a strong back is added. A *strong back* is a beam placed over the ceiling joist to support the ceiling and roof loads.

If a vaulted ceiling is desired, the drafter will need to be familiar with two additional terms. These are rafter/ceiling joist and ridge beam. Both can be seen in Figure 27–29. A rafter/ceiling joist, or rafter joist, is a combination of rafter and ceiling joist. The rafter/ceiling joist is used to support both the roof loads and the finished ceiling. Typically a 2 × 12 rafter/ceiling joist is used. This allows room for 10 in. of insulation and 2 in. of air space above the insulation.

A ridge beam is used to support the upper end of the rafter/ceiling joist. Since there are no horizontal ceiling joists, metal joist hangers must be used to keep the rafters from separating from the ridge beam.

The final terms that you will need to be familiar with to draw a stick roof are header and trimmer. Both are terms that are used in wall construction, and they have a similar function when used as roof members. See Figure 27–30. A header at the roof level consists of two members nailed together to support rafters around an opening such as for a skylight or chimney. Trimmers are two rafters nailed together to support the roofing on the inclined edge of an opening.

Truss Roof Construction Terms

Truss construction is generally considered non-conventional construction. A truss is a component used to span large distances without intermediate supports. Trusses can be either prefabricated or job built. Prefabricated trusses are commonly used in residential construction. Assembled at the truss company and shipped to the job site, the truss roof can quickly be set in place. A roof that might take two

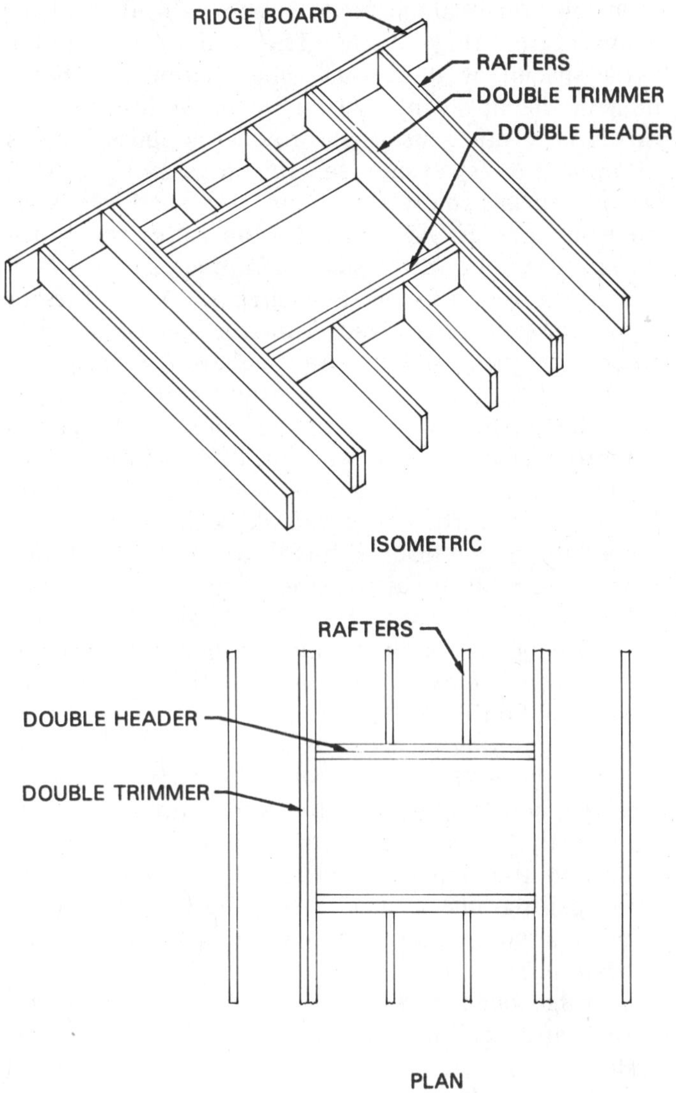

RIDGE BOARD
RAFTERS
DOUBLE TRIMMER
DOUBLE HEADER

ISOMETRIC

RAFTERS
DOUBLE HEADER
DOUBLE TRIMMER

PLAN

Figure 27–30 Typical construction at roof openings.

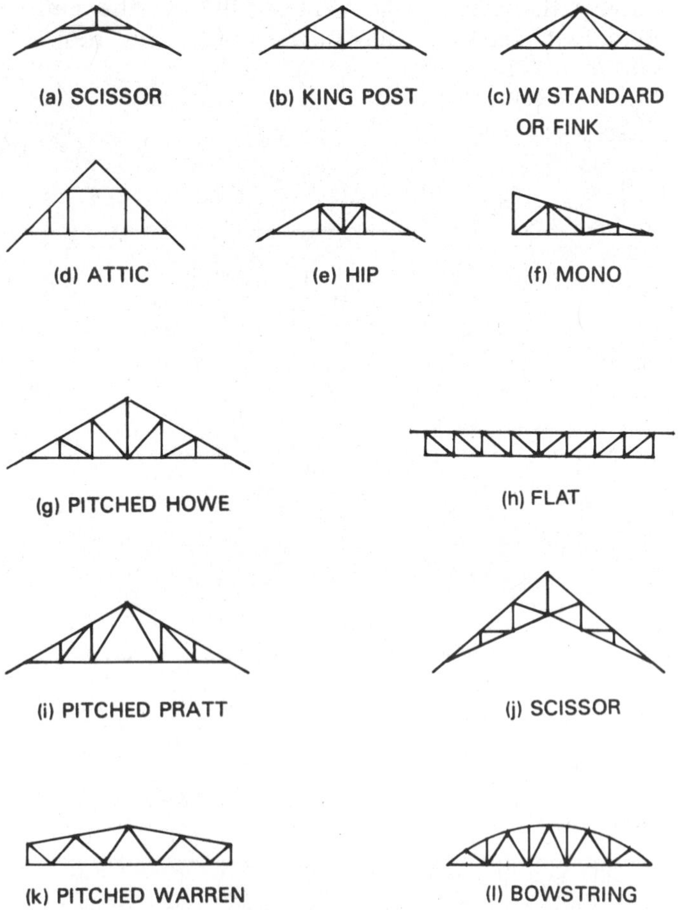

(a) SCISSOR   (b) KING POST   (c) W STANDARD OR FINK

(d) ATTIC   (e) HIP   (f) MONO

(g) PITCHED HOWE   (h) FLAT

(i) PITCHED PRATT   (j) SCISSOR

(k) PITCHED WARREN   (l) BOWSTRING

Figure 27–31 Types of trusses. Types (a) through (f) are typically used in residential construction. Types (g) through (l) are common in commercial construction.

or three days for a crew to frame can be set in place in two or three hours using trusses. In addition, the size of the material used in trusses is smaller than with conventional frames. Typically, truss members need only be 2 × 4s set at 24 in. on center.

Job-built trusses are similar to prefabricated trusses except the framing crew builds the trusses on site. Job-built trusses are laid out on the floor and then lifted into place. Although this method is only slightly faster than conventional framing, it has the advantage of using smaller members to build the trusses.

There are several shapes and types of trusses that are available for residential use. See Figure 27–31. The W, or Fink, truss is the most common. This shape, which places some members in tension and others in compression, is the reason smaller wood sizes can be used when building trusses. See Figure 27–32.

As a drafter you will not be required to design or size the truss members. This will be done by an

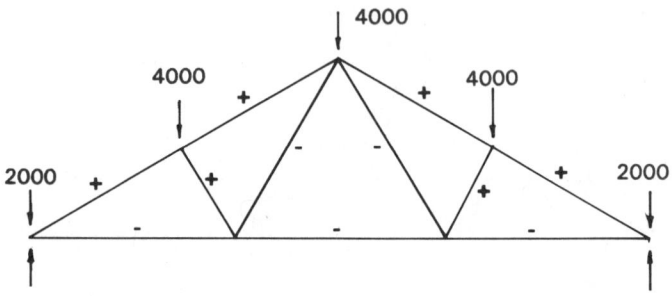

Figure 27–32 Trusses are designed so that the weight to be supported is spread to the outer walls. This is done by placing some members in tension and some in compression. A member in compression is indicated by a plus sign (+) and one in tension is represented by a minus sign (−).

engineer or will be supplied with the trusses by the manufacturer. A drafter's job is to draw the basic shape of the truss in cross section. A knowledge of truss terms will be helpful in doing this. Terms that will be helpful are top chord, bottom chord, web, ridge block and truss clips. Each can be seen in Figure 27–33.

The top chord serves a function similar to a common rafter in stick frame construction. It is the inclined member used to support the sheathing and finished roof material. The bottom chord serves a function similar to a ceiling joist in stick framing. It is the horizontal member which both resists the outward forces of the top chord and supports the finished ceiling.

In stick construction a continuous ridge board is used. Since a truss is a self-contained unit, no ridge

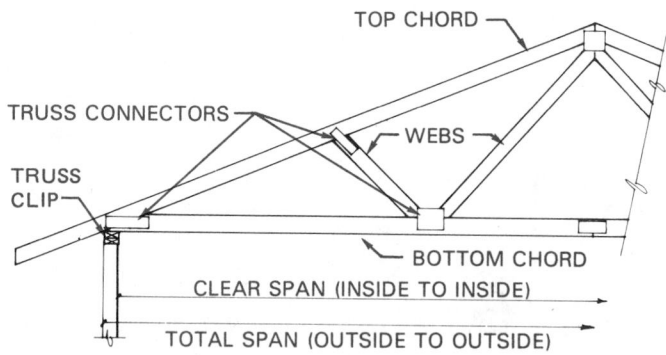

Figure 27-33 Truss construction members.

board is required. Instead, a block is often placed between each truss to help the framing crew maintain uniform spacing and provide a nailing surface for the plywood at the ridge. Figure 27-34 shows truss connections typically shown on sections.

Truss clips hold the truss down on the wall. The truss clip, or hurricane tie, resists the tendency to lift the truss and roof off the wall from wind pushing upward on the eave. It is important that the drafter specify these clips on the cross section to assure proper truss attachment to the top plate. This clip transfers the force of any wind uplift acting on the trusses down through the walls and into the foundation. See Figure 27-35.

Metal Hangers

Metal hangers are used on floor, ceiling, and roof members. These hangers are typically used to keep structural members from separating. Figure 27-36 shows several common types of connectors that are used in light construction. These connectors keep beams from lifting off posts, keep posts from lifting off foundations, or hold one beam or joist to another.

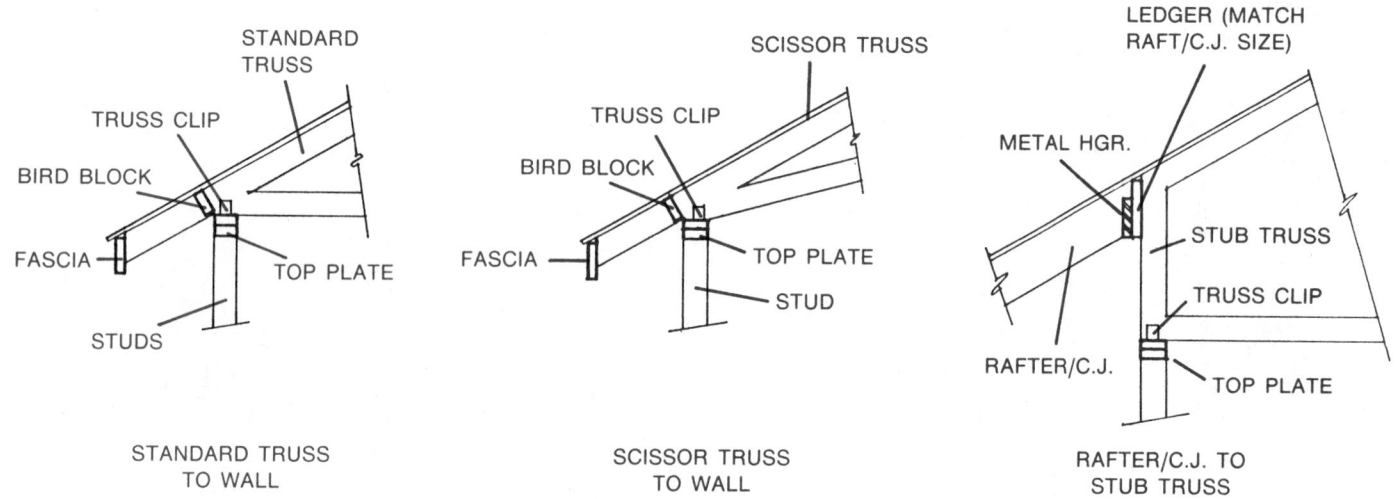

Figure 27-34 Common truss connections normally shown in the sections. Notice that the top chord aligns with the outer face of the top plate. When detailing a scissor truss, the bottom chord is typically drawn a minimum of 2 pitches less than the top chord.

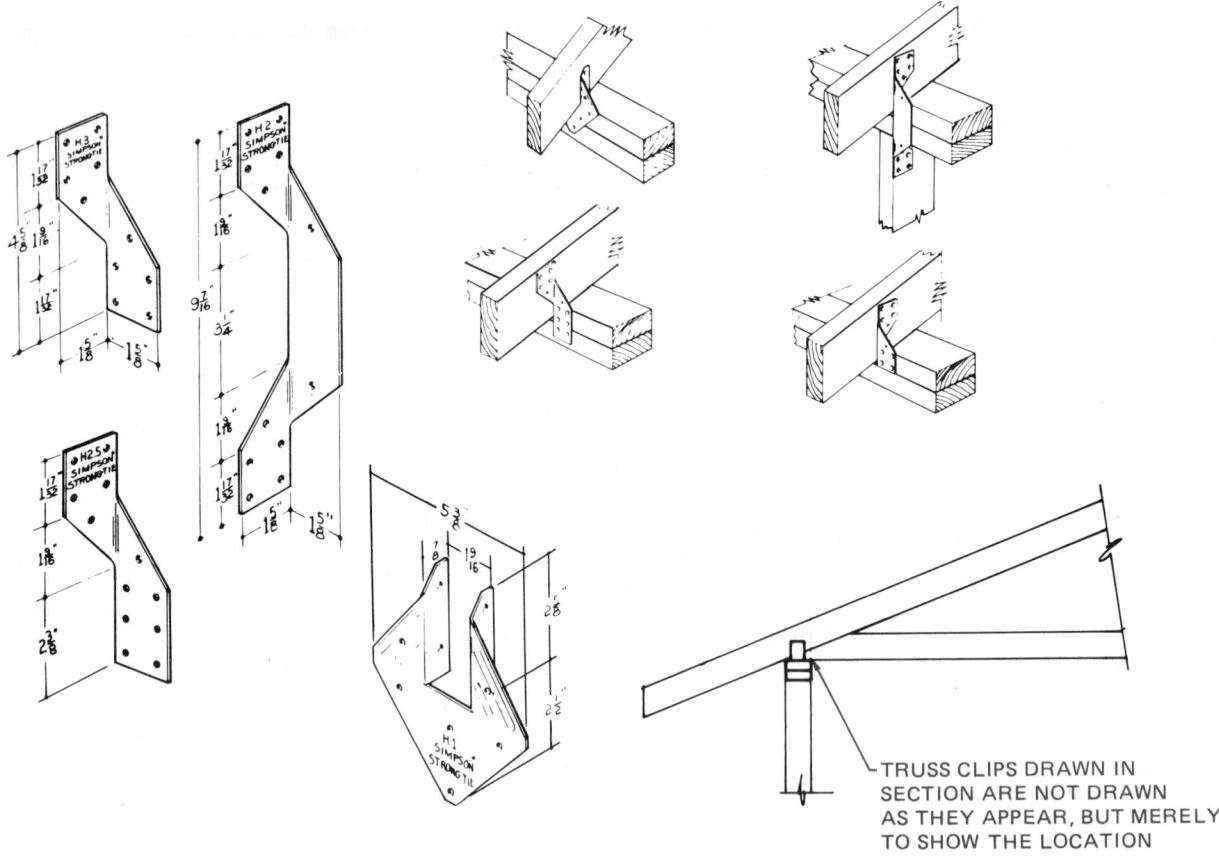

TRUSS CLIPS DRAWN IN
SECTION ARE NOT DRAWN
AS THEY APPEAR, BUT MERELY
TO SHOW THE LOCATION

Figure 27–35 Truss clips hold the truss to the wall to resist upward forces. *Courtesy Simpson Strong-Tie Company, Inc.*

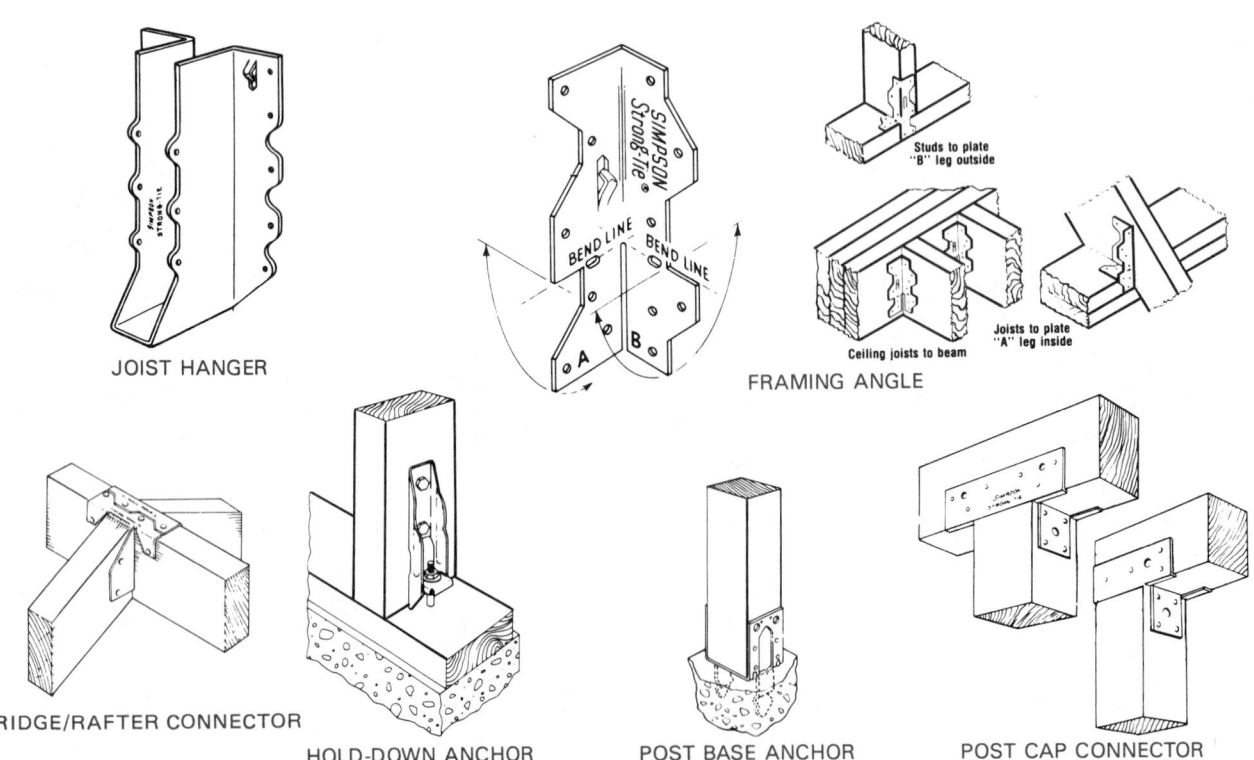

JOIST HANGER

FRAMING ANGLE

Studs to plate "B" leg outside

Ceiling joists to beam

Joists to plate "A" leg inside

RIDGE/RAFTER CONNECTOR

HOLD-DOWN ANCHOR

POST BASE ANCHOR

POST CAP CONNECTOR

Figure 27–36 Common metal framing connectors for residential framing. *Courtesy Simpson Strong-Tie Company, Inc.*

STRUCTURAL COMPONENTS TEST

DIRECTIONS

Answer the questions with short complete statements or drawings as needed on an 8½ × 11 drawing sheet as follows:

1. Use ⅛ in. guidelines for all lettering.
2. Letter your name, Structural Components Test, and the date at the top of the sheet.
3. Letter the question number and provide the answer. You do not need to write out the question.
4. Do all lettering with vertical uppercase architectural letters. If the answer requires line work, use proper drafting tools and technique. Answers may be prepared on a word processor if appropriate with course guidelines.
5. Your grade will be based on correct answers and quality of line technique.

QUESTIONS

1. List two different types of floor framing methods and explain the differences. Provide sketches to help illustrate your answer.
2. What is the difference between a girder, header, and beam?
3. List the differences between a rim joist and solid blocking at the sill.
4. Explain the difference between a bearing and nonbearing wall.
5. What are let-in braces and wall sheathing used for?
6. A let-in brace must be at what maximum angle?
7. What is the minimum lap for top plates in a bearing wall?
8. How is a foundation post protected from the moisture in the concrete support?
9. Blocking is required in walls over how many feet high?
10. Sketch, label, and define the members supporting the loads around a window.
11. What purpose does the bird's mouth of a rafter serve?
12. What do the numbers 4/12 mean when placed on a roof pitch symbol?
13. Explain the difference between ridge, ridge blocking, and ridge board.
14. What is the most common spacing for rafters?
15. Sketch, list, and define five types of rafters.
16. List two functions of a ceiling joist.
17. Define the four typical parts of a truss.
18. What is the function of the top plate of a wall?
19. Define the term mudsill.
20. What function does a purlin serve?

Chapter 28
Sectioning Basics

SECTIONS ARE drawn to show the vertical relationships of the structural materials called for on the floor, framing, and foundation plans. The sections show the methods of construction for the framing crew. Before drawing sections it is important to understand the different types of sections, their common scales, and the relationship of the cutting plane to the section.

TYPES OF SECTIONS

Three types of sections may be drawn for a set of plans. These include full sections, partial sections, and details.

For a simple home, only one section might be required to explain fully the types of construction to be used. A full section is a section that cuts through the entire building. A full section can be seen in Figure 28–1. On a more complex home, a full section showing typical framing techniques and a partial section may be required. The partial section can be used to show atypical construction methods such as variations of the roof or foundation. Figure 28–2 shows a partial section. On a complex set of plans, several full and partial sections may be required. Depending on the complexity of the project, details or enlargements of a section may also be required. An area of the section where several items intersect or where many small items are required are examples of when a detail might be required.

Some offices have stock details. These are details of items such as footings that typically remain the same. By using a stock footing detail, the drafter is saved the time of having to relabel all of this information each time this part is drawn in section. See Figure 28–3.

By combining the information on the framing plans and the sections, the contractor should be able to make accurate estimates of the amount of material required and the cost of completing the project. To help make the sections easier to read, sections have become somewhat standardized in several areas. These include the areas of scales and alignment.

SCALE

Sections are typically drawn at a scale of $\frac{3}{8}'' = 1'-0''$. Scales of $\frac{1}{8}$ or $\frac{1}{4}$ in. may be used for supplemental sections requiring little detail. A scale of $\frac{3}{4}'' = 1'-0''$ or larger may be required to draw some construction details. Several factors influence the choice of scale to use when drawing sections:

1. Size of the drawing sheet to be used.
2. Size of the project to be drawn.
3. Purpose of the section.
4. Placement of the section.

Factors 1 and 2 need little discussion. The floor plan determines the size of the project. Once the sheet size is selected for the floor plan, that size should be used throughout the entire project. The placement of the section as it relates to other drawings should have only a minor influence on the scale. It may be practical to put a partial section in a blank corner of a drawing, but don't let space dictate the scale.

The most important influence should be the use of the section. If the section is merely to show the

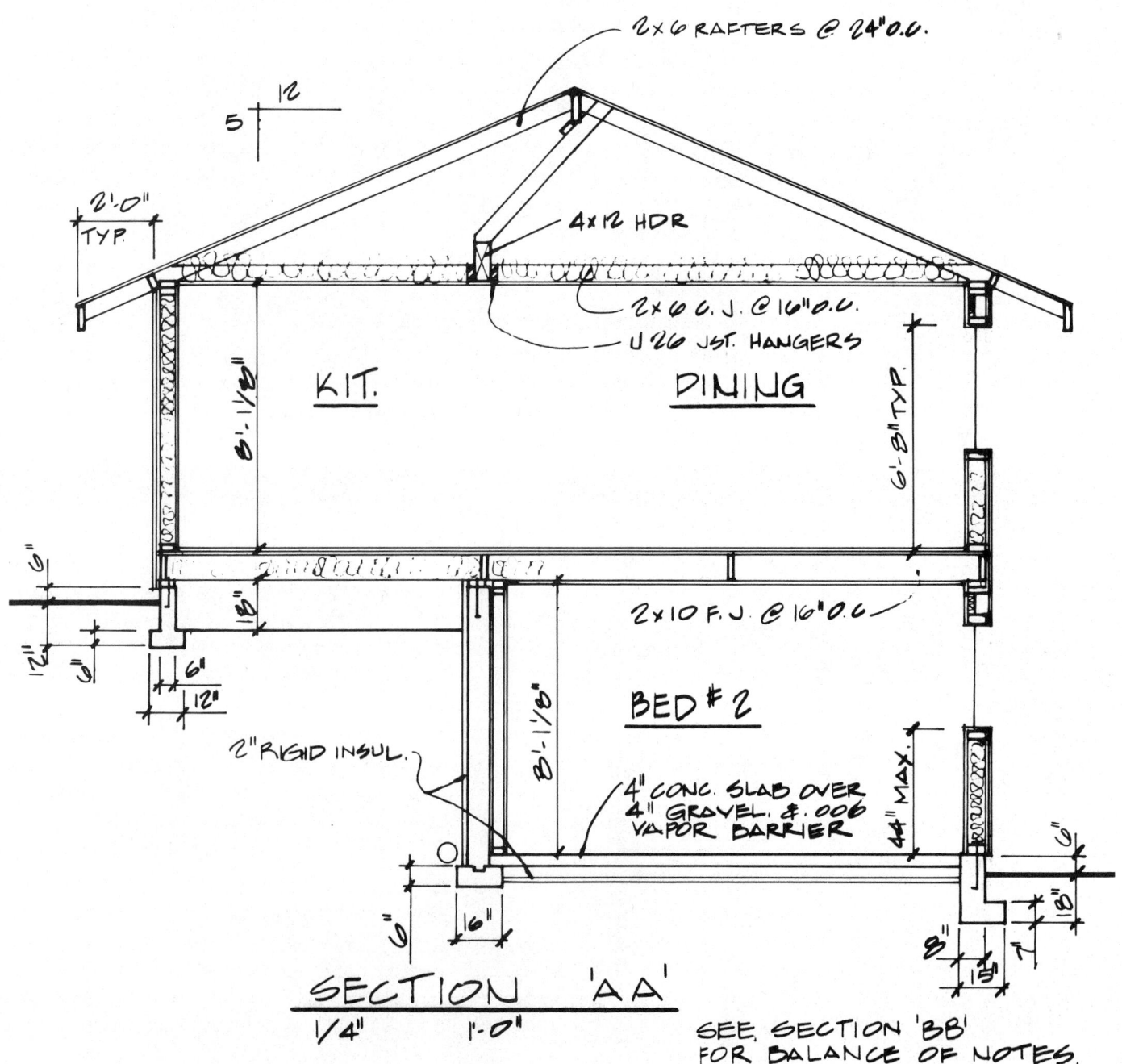

Figure 28–1 A full cross section showing the layout of the structural members. *Courtesy Jeff's Residential Designs.*

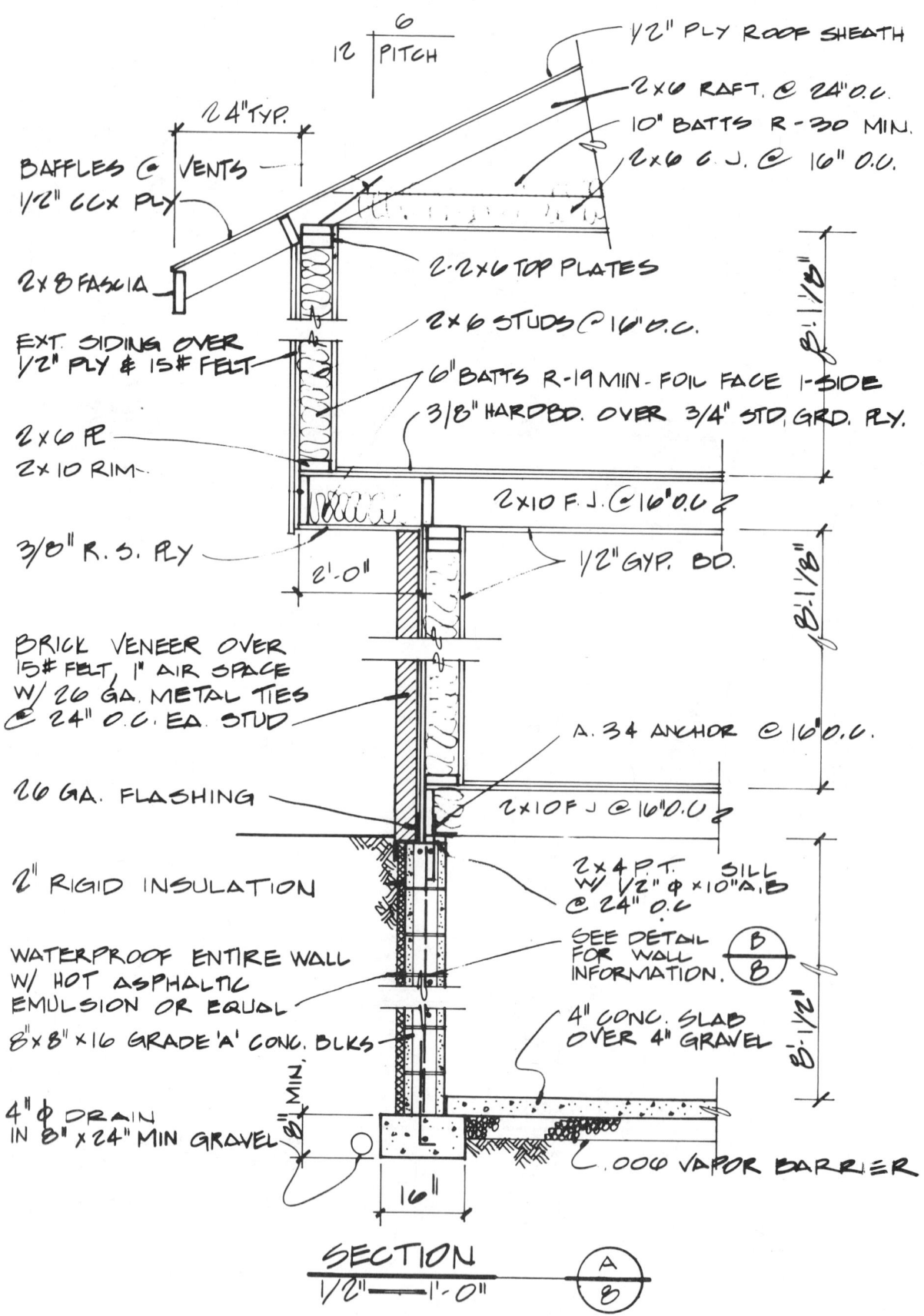

12 $\frac{6}{\text{PITCH}}$

1/2" PLY ROOF SHEATH

2×6 RAFT. @ 24" O.C.

10" BATTS R-30 MIN.

2×6 C.J. @ 16" O.C.

24" TYP.

BAFFLES @ VENTS
1/2" CCX PLY

2×8 FASCIA

2·2×6 TOP PLATES

2×6 STUDS @ 16" O.C.

EXT. SIDING OVER
1/2" PLY & 15# FELT

6" BATTS R-19 MIN.- FOIL FACE 1-SIDE
3/8" HARDBD. OVER 3/4" STD. GRD. PLY.

2×6 PL.
2×10 RIM.

2×10 F.J. @ 16" O.C.

1/2" GYP. BD.

3/8" R.S. PLY

2'-0"

BRICK VENEER OVER
15# FELT, 1" AIR SPACE
W/ 26 GA. METAL TIES
@ 24" O.C. EA. STUD

A. 34 ANCHOR @ 16" O.C.

26 GA. FLASHING

2×10 F.J @ 16" O.C.

2" RIGID INSULATION

2×4 P.T. SILL
W/ 1/2" φ ×10" A.B.
@ 24" O.C

SEE DETAIL
FOR WALL
INFORMATION. (B/B)

WATERPROOF ENTIRE WALL
W/ HOT ASPHALTIC
EMULSION OR EQUAL

4" CONC. SLAB
OVER 4" GRAVEL

8"×8"×16 GRADE 'A' CONC. BLKS.

4" φ DRAIN
IN 8"×24" MIN GRAVEL

8" MIN.

16"

.006 VAPOR BARRIER

8'-1 1/8"

8'-1 1/8"

8'-1 1/2"

SECTION
1/2" ——— 1'-0"   (A/8)

Figure 28-2 A partial cross section may be used to supplement the full section by showing atypical construction methods.

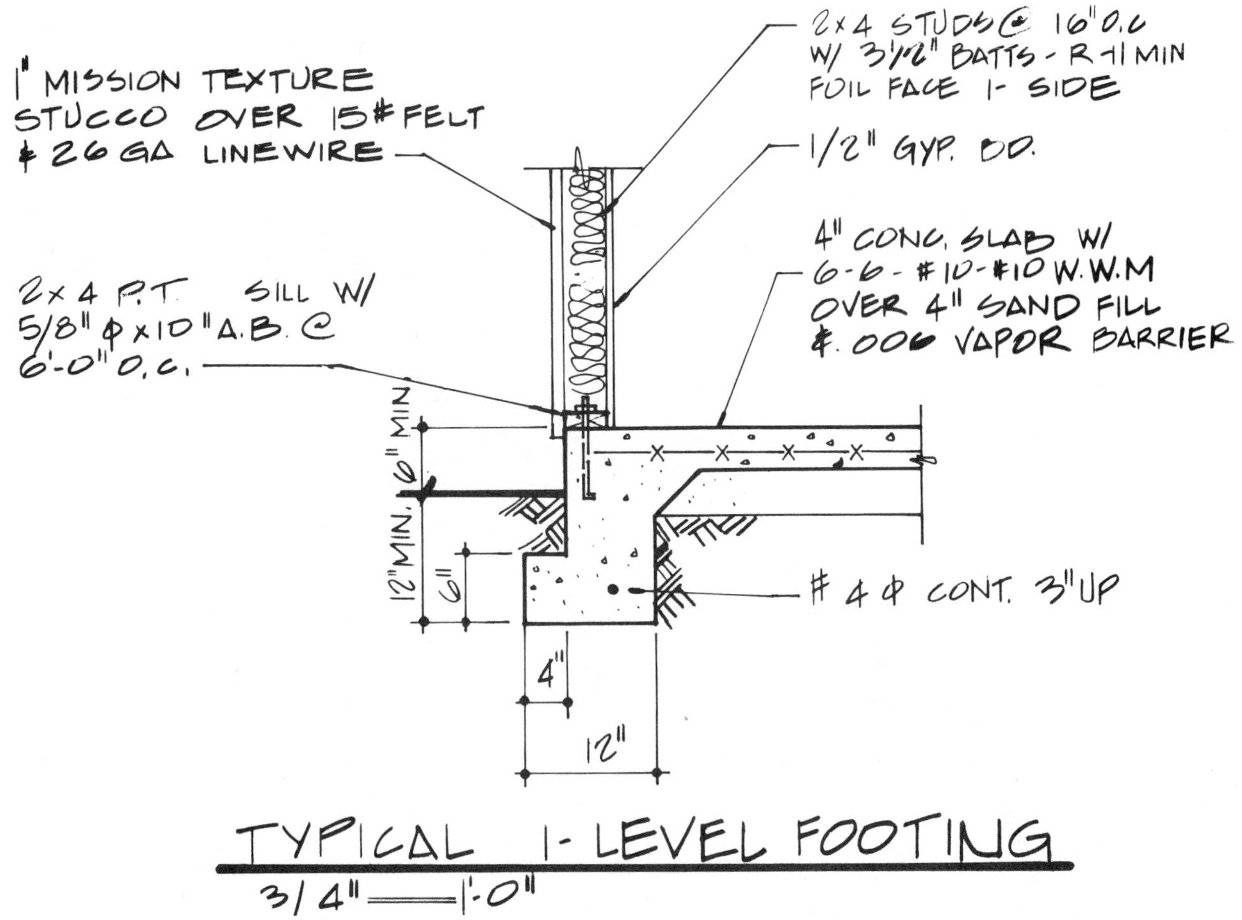

1" MISSION TEXTURE
STUCCO OVER 15# FELT
& 26 GA LINEWIRE

2×4 STUDS @ 16" O.C
W/ 3½" BATTS - R-11 MIN
FOIL FACE 1-SIDE

1/2" GYP. BD.

2×4 P.T SILL W/
5/8" Φ ×10" A.B. @
6'-0" O.C.

4" CONC. SLAB W/
6-6-#10-#10 W.W.M
OVER 4" SAND FILL
& .006 VAPOR BARRIER

12" MIN. 6" MIN

6"

4 Φ CONT. 3" UP

4"

12"

TYPICAL 1-LEVEL FOOTING
3/4" ═══ 1'-0"

Figure 28–3 Details are an enlargement of an area from a section.

shape of the project, a scale of ⅛″ = 1'-0″ would be fine. This type of section is rarely required in residential drawings but is often used when drawing apartments or office buildings. See Figure 28–4 for an example of a shape section.

The primary section is typically drawn at a scale of ⅜″ = 1'-0″. This scale provides two benefits, one to the print reader and one to the drafter. The main advantage of using this scale is the ease of distinguishing each structural member. At a smaller scale separate members such as the finished flooring and the rough flooring are difficult to draw and read. Without good clarity problems could arise at the job site. At ⅜ in. scale, the drafter will have a bigger drawing on which to place the notes and dimensions.

The scale of ½″ = 1'-0″ is not widely used in most offices. Using this scale does offer great clarity, but sections are so large that a great deal of paper

is required to complete the project. Often, if more than one section must be drawn, the primary section is drawn at ⅜″ = 1'-0″, and the other sections are drawn at ¼″ = 1'-0″. By combining drawings at these two scales, typical information can be placed on the ⅜ in. section, and the ¼ in. sections are used to show variations with little detail.

SECTION ALIGNMENT

In drawing sections, as with other parts of the plans, the drawing is read from the bottom or right side of the page. The cutting plane on the floor plan shows which way the section is being viewed. The arrows of the cutting plane should be pointing to the top or left side of the paper depending on the area of the building being sectioned. See Figure 28–5.

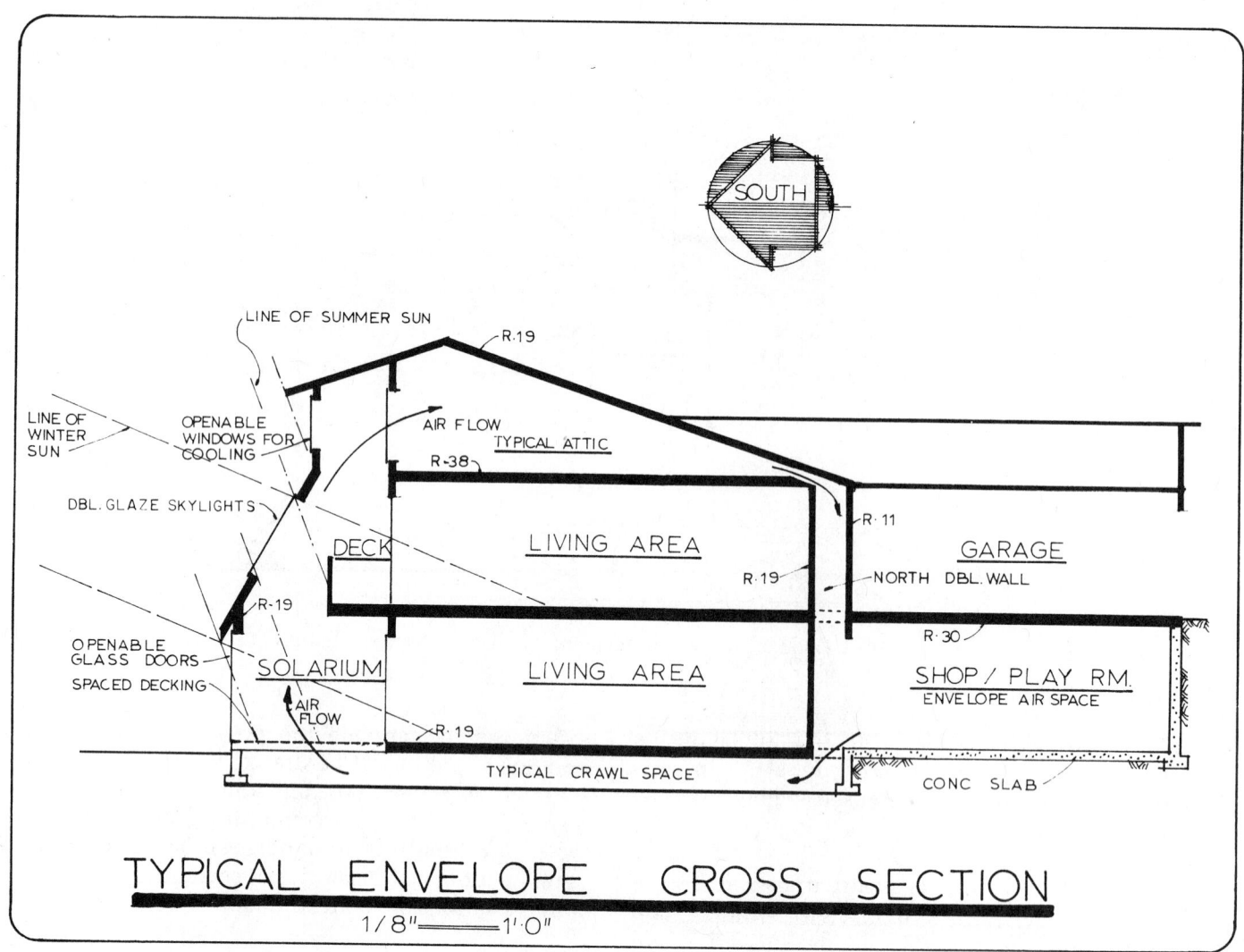

Figure 28–4 A shape section showing the outline of living areas with no structural information. *Courtesy Jeff's Residential Designs.*

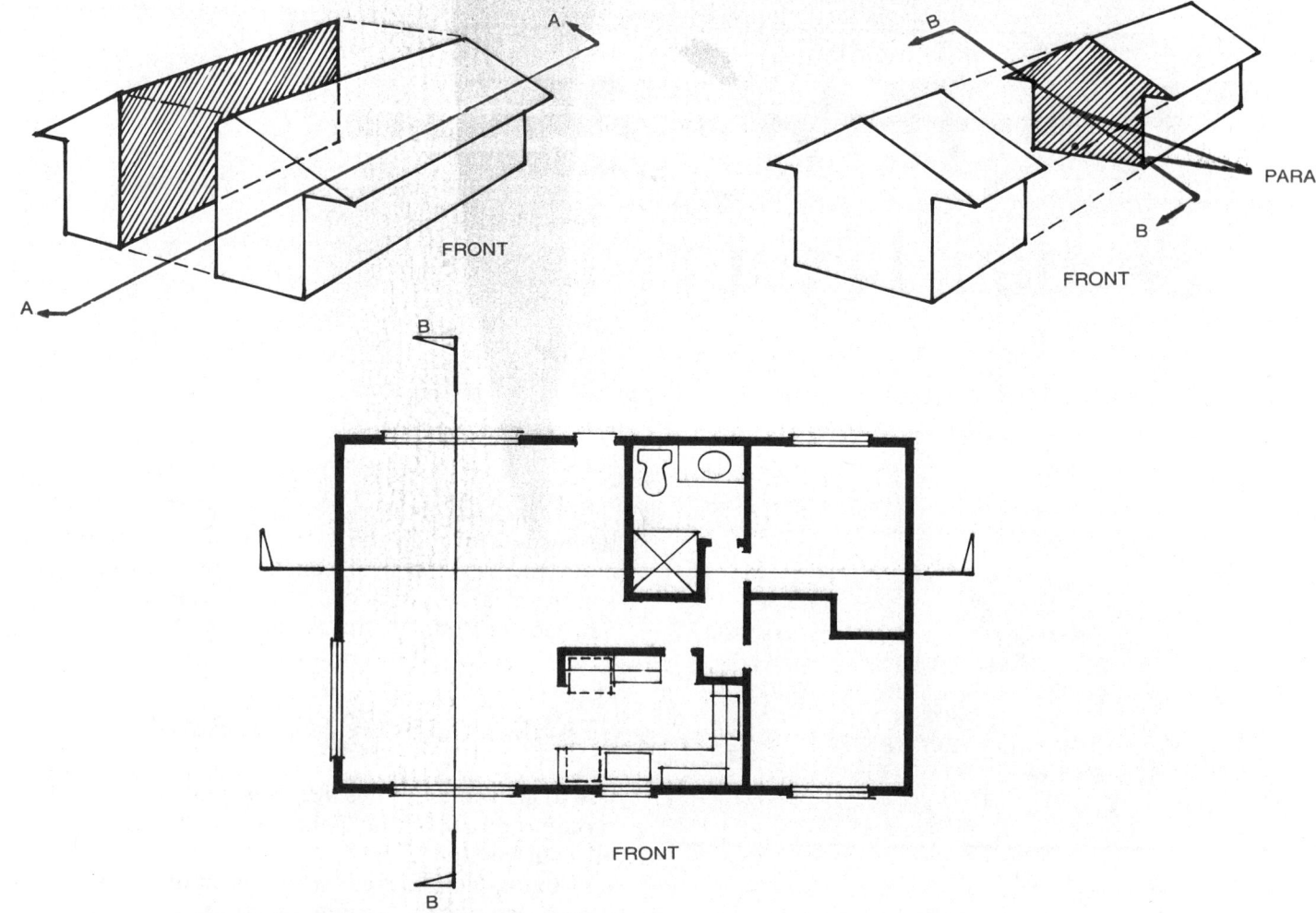

Figure 28–5 Cutting planes on the floor plan show the direction the section is to be viewed. Always try to keep the cutting plane arrows pointing to the left or to the top of the page.

SECTIONING BASICS TEST

DIRECTIONS

Answer the questions with short complete statements or drawings as needed on an 8½ × 11 drawing sheet as follows:

1. Use ⅛ in. guidelines for all lettering.
2. Letter your name, Sectioning Basics Test, and the date at the top of the sheet.
3. Letter the question number and provide the answer. You do not need to write out the question.
4. Do all lettering with vertical uppercase architectural letters. Answers may be prepared on a word processor if appropriate with course guidelines.
5. Your grade will be based on correct answers and quality of line technique.

QUESTIONS

1. What is a full section?
2. When could a partial section be used?
3. What is a stock detail and when would it be used?
4. From which drawings does a drafter get the needed information to draw a section?
5. Name the most common scale for drawing full sections.
6. What factors do you think would influence the scale of a detail?
7. What is a cutting plane and how does it relate to a section?
8. In which directions should the arrows on a cutting plane be pointing?
9. What type of section might be drawn at a scale of ⅛″ = 1′–0″?
10. What factors influence the choice of scale for the section?

Chapter 29
Section Layout

DRAWING SECTIONS will be accomplished in seven major stages. By following the step-by-step procedure for each stage, sections can be easily drawn and understood. Read through each stage and carefully compare the step-by-step instructions with the corresponding illustrations.

STAGE 1: EVALUATE NEEDS

Using a print of the floor and foundation plans, evaluate the major types of construction needed on the project. The differences in the construction required include the following:

- The right side of the plan is one story and the left side is two story.
- The rear at right is a stick floor and the front is a concrete slab.
- The left side of the roof is vaulted and stick while the right side is truss.

To provide the needed information to the framing crew a minimum of two full sections is required. One will cut through the family room and kitchen and show the stick floor, walls, the upper floor cantilever, and the truss roof. A full section will also be needed through the garage area to show the concrete and wooden floor construction. Partial sections should also be provided to show the stairs and the vaulted roof over bedroom number 1.

STAGE 2: LAY OUT THE SECTION

Use construction lines for this entire stage. Use a nonreproducible blue pencil or a 6H lead to draw all construction lines.

Having determined which sections need to be drawn, lay out the primary section at ⅜″ = 1′–0″. To determine sizes and locations of structural members, refer to the floor and foundation plans. The entire layout process can be seen in Figure 29–1. For the layout of a post-and-beam, slab, or basement foundation, see Chapter 30. See Figure 29–2 for steps 1 through 5.

Stick Floor Layout

Step 1.   Lay out the width of the building.

Step 2.   Establish a baseline about 2 in. above the border.

Before laying out steps 3 through 8, it may be necessary to review the basics of foundation design in Section 4. All sizes given in the following steps are based on the minimum standards of the Uniform Building Code (unless otherwise noted) and should be compared with local standards.

Step 3.   Measure the footing thickness. Measure up from the baseline the required thickness for a footing. Minimum footing depths are 6 in. for one-story, 7 in. for two-story, and 8 in. for three-story construction.

482

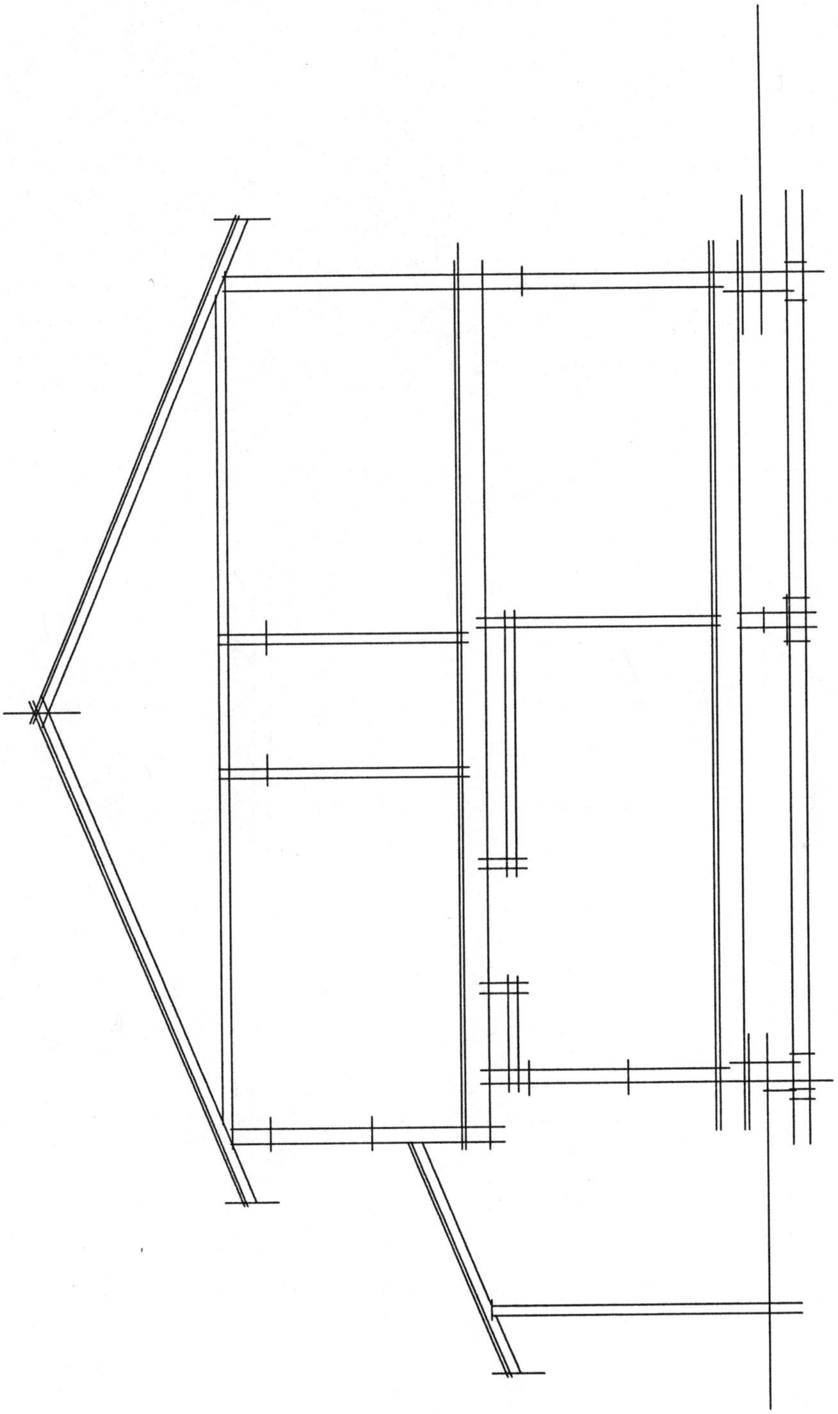

Figure 29-1 A layout of a cross section with all work done with construction lines.

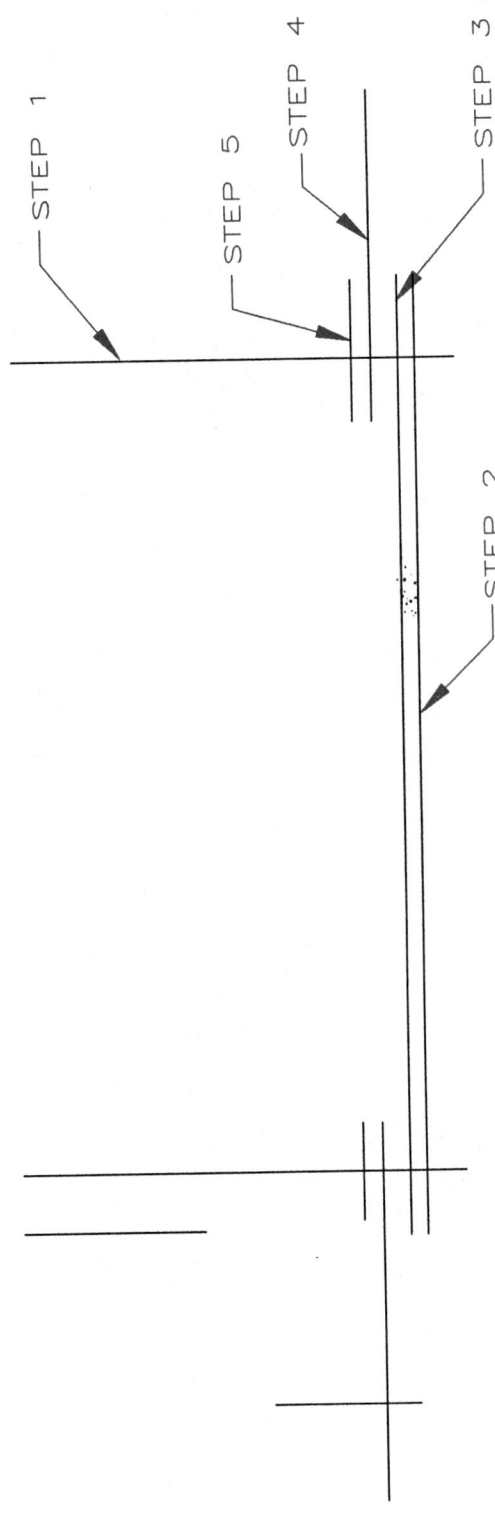

STEP 1

STEP 5

STEP 4

STEP 3

STEP 2

Figure 29-2 Initial steps of the section layout.

Step 4. Locate the finished grade. Footings must extend into the natural grade a minimum of 12 in. for one-story, 18 in. for two-story, and 24 in. for three-story construction. In addition to these guidelines, footings must also extend below the frost line. See Section 4 for a review of frost conditions.

Step 5. Locate the top of the stem wall. All wood is required to be: UBC (6″ min.), CABO, BOCA, and SBC (8″ min.) above finished grade.

See Figure 29–3 for steps 6 through 15.

Step 6. Block out the width of the stem wall. Stem walls are required to be 6 in. for one-story, 8 in. for two-story, and 10 in. for three-story construction.

Step 7. Block out 4 in. wide by 8 in. high ledge for brick veneer.

Step 8. Block out the required width for footings. Center the footing below the stem walls. Footings are required to be 12 in. for one-story, 15 in. for two-story, and 18 in. for three-story construction.

Step 9. Add 4 in. in width to the footing to support the brick ledge.

Step 10. Locate the depth for the 2 × 6 mudsill. The top of the mudsill also becomes the bottom of the floor joists.

Step 11. Locate the depth of the floor joists.

Step 12. Lay out the plywood subfloor. Draw a line as close to the floor joist as possible to represent the plywood while still leaving a gap between the plywood and the joist.

Step 13. Lay out the girder.

Step 14. Lay out the post.

Step 15. Lay out the concrete piers centered under the post.

Wall Layout

With the foundation and floor system lightly drawn, proceed now to lay out the walls for the main level using construction lines. See Figure 29–4 for the layout of steps 16 through 22.

Step 16. Locate the top of the top plates. Measure up 8′-0″ above the floor and draw a line to represent the top of the top plate. In a one-level house, this would also represent the bottom of the ceiling.

Step 17. Locate the interior side of the exterior walls.

Step 18. Locate the interior walls.

After locating the interior walls, make sure that any interior bearing walls line up over a girder. If they do not line up, there is a mistake. The mistake could either be in your measurements, math calculations, or a conflict between the dimensions of the floor and foundation plans.

Step 19. Lay out the tops of doors and windows. Headers for doors and windows are typically set at 6′-10″ above the floor. Measure up from the plywood to locate the bottom of the header. The top will be drawn later.

Step 20. Lay out the subsills. To establish the subsill location you must know the window size. This can be found on either the floor plan or on the window schedule. Measure down the required distance from the bottom of the header to establish the subsill location.

Step 21. Lay out the 7′-0″ ceilings for soffits in areas such as kitchens, baths, or hallways.

Step 22. Lay out the patio post width and height.

Lay out the upper floor area following the same steps that were used for the lower level. See Figure 29–5 for steps 23 through 29.

Step 23. Lay out exterior walls. Remember the 2′-0″ cantilever of the upper floor past the lower level walls.

Step 24. Locate the depth of the floor joists.

Step 25. Draw the plywood subfloor.

Step 26. Lay out the ceiling 8′-0″ above the floor.

Step 27. Lay out the interior side of exterior walls.

Step 28. Lay out the interior walls.

Step 29. Lay out the windows.

Truss Roof Layout

Steps 30 through 37 can be seen in Figure 29–6. For the layout of other types of roofs, see Chapter 30.

Step 30. Locate the ridge.

Step 31. Locate the overhang on each side (see the elevations).

Step 32. Lay out the bottom side of the top chord. Starting at the intersection of the outer wall and the ceiling line draw a line at a 5/12 pitch. Do this for both sides. The lines should intersect at the ridge. A 5/12 pitch means that you measure up 5 units and over 12 units. A 5/12 pitch may also be drawn with a protractor or a drafting machine since it equals 22½°.

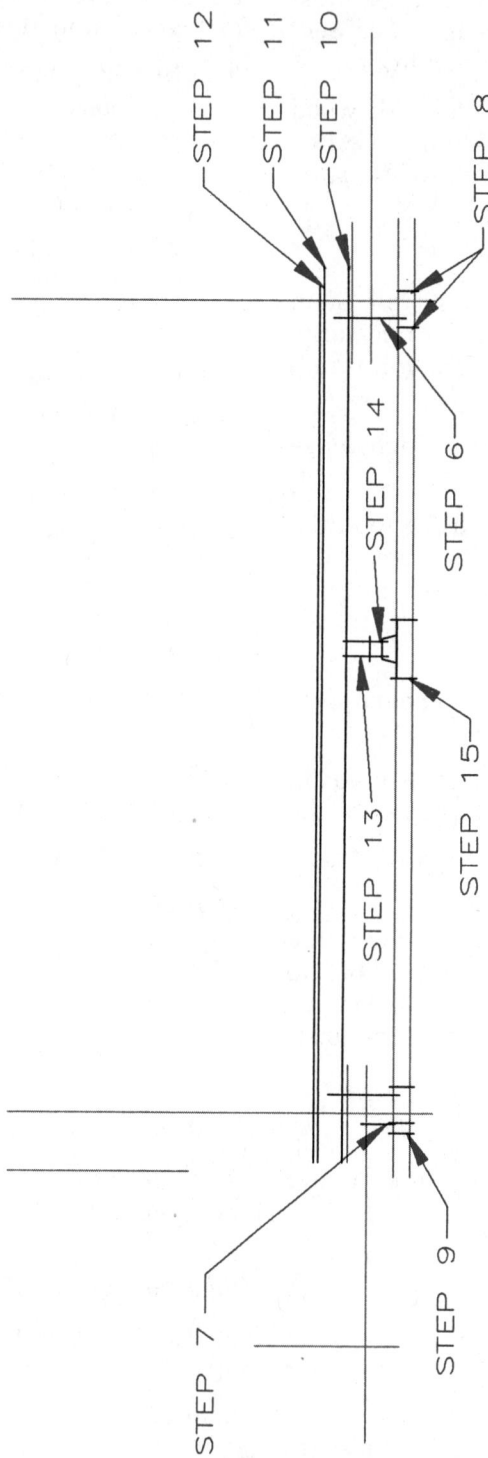

Figure 29-3 Layout of a stick floor system.

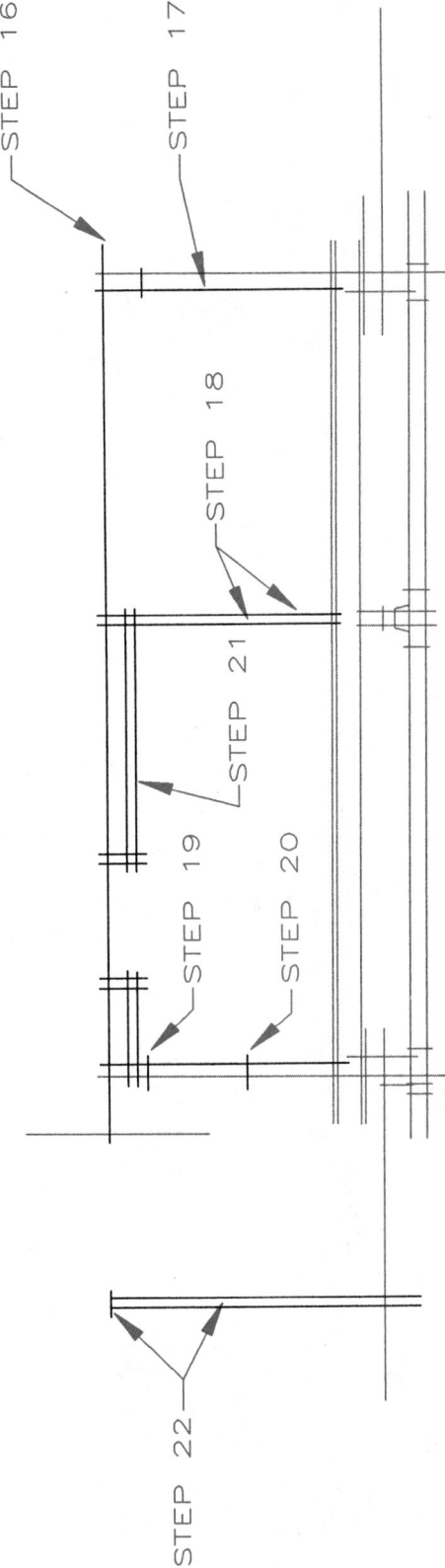

Figure 29–4 Layout of the ceiling level.

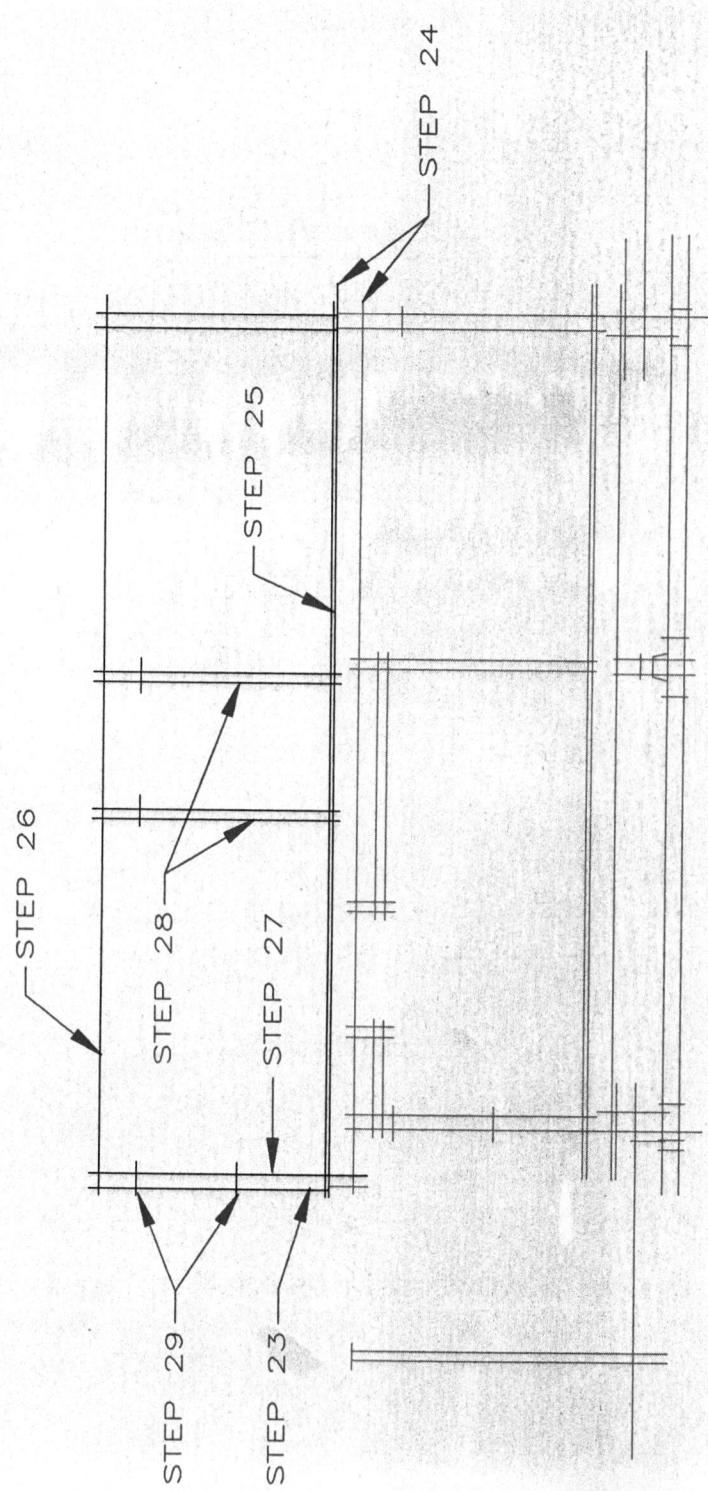

Figure 29-5 Layout of the upper floor level.

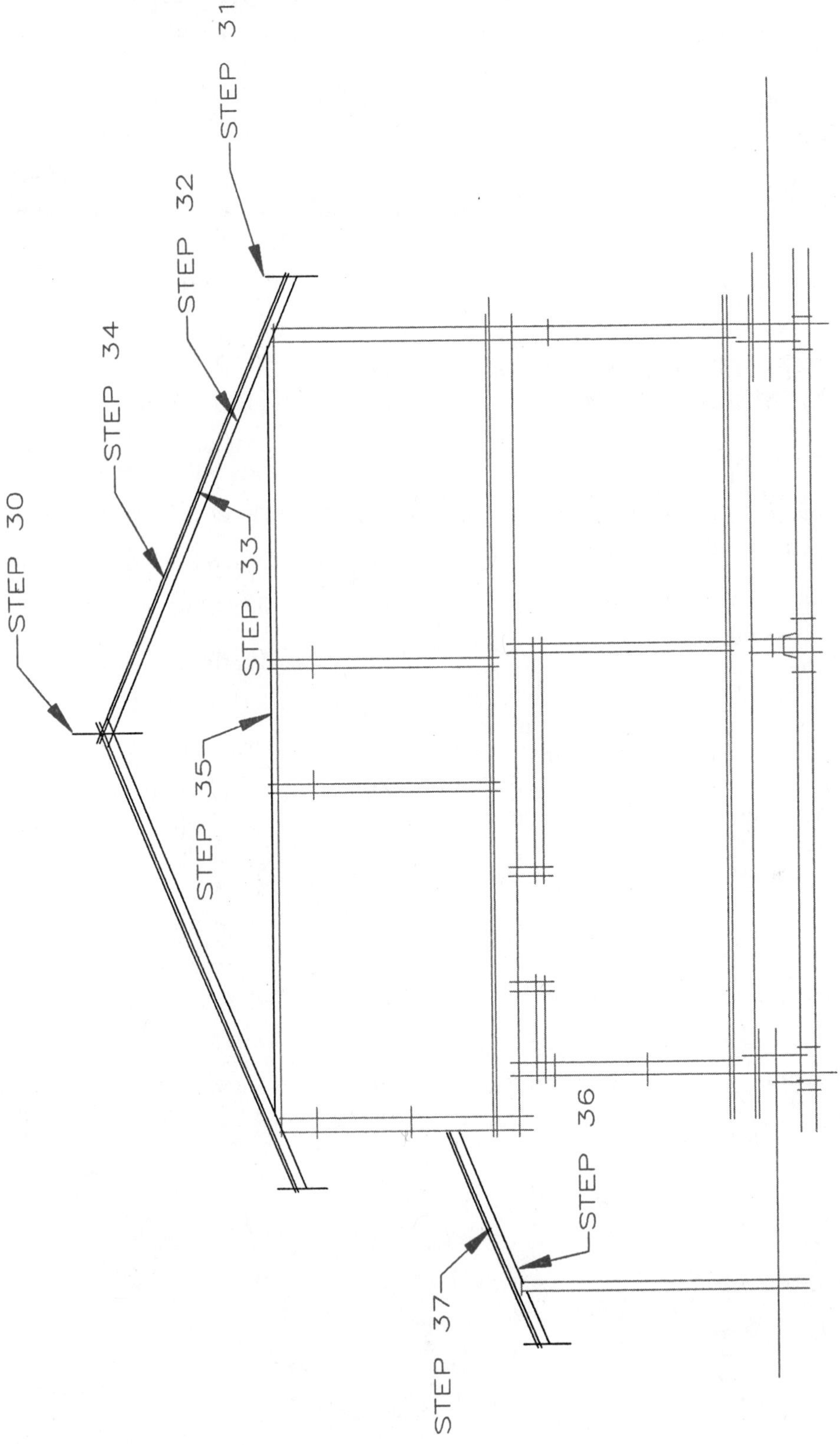

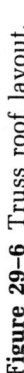

STEP 31

STEP 32

STEP 34

STEP 30

STEP 33

STEP 35

STEP 36

STEP 37

Figure 29-6 Truss roof layout.

Step 33. Lay out the top side of the top chord. Assume chords to be 4 in. deep.

Step 34. Lay out the plywood roof sheathing.

Step 35. Lay out the top side of the bottom chord.

Step 36. Lay out the patio roof. Starting at the intersection of the inner wall and the ceiling, draw a line at a 5/12 pitch to represent the rafter.

Step 37. Lay out the 1 in. tongue and groove roof sheathing.

The entire section has now been outlined.

◢ STAGE 3: FINISHED QUALITY LINES— STRUCTURAL MEMBERS ONLY

When drawing with finished quality lines, start at the roof and work down. This will help you keep the drawing clean. The steps used will be divided into truss roof, walls, upper floor, walls, lower floor, and foundation.

Continuous members shown in section are traditionally drawn with a diagonal cross (X) placed in the member. Blocking is drawn with one diagonal line (/) through the member. This method of representing sectioned members is time consuming to draw and may be difficult to read on small scale sections. Rather than drawing symbols, the members can be drawn much easier with different line qualities as shown in Figure 29–7.

Three types of lines are used to draw structural material for the sections:

Thin. Use a 5 mm lead, a #0 pen or a sharp 3H lead.

Bold. Use a 9 mm lead, a #2 pen or an H lead with a wedge tip.

Very bold. Use a 9 mm lead and draw two parallel lines with no white space between them, or a #4 pen or an unpointed H lead.

As you read through these steps you will be asked to draw items that have not been laid out. These are items that can be drawn by eye and need not be traced. Just be careful to keep 2 in. members a uniform size so that they do not become 4 in. members. When finished, your drawing should look like Figure 29–8.

Roof

To gain speed, draw all parallel lines on one side of the roof before drawing the opposite side. Roof steps 1 through 7 are shown in Figure 29–9.

Step 1. Use thin lines to draw the plywood sheathing.

Step 2. Draw the top chord with thin lines.

Step 3. Draw the eave blocking with bold lines.

Step 4. Repeat steps 1 through 3 on the opposite side of the roof.

Step 5. Draw the fascias with bold lines.

Step 6. Draw the bottom chord with thin lines.

Step 7. Draw the ridge blocking with a bold line.

Upper Walls and Floor

See Figure 29–10 for steps 8 through 18.

Step 8. Draw all double top plates with bold lines.

Step 9. Draw walls with thin lines.

Step 10. Draw all headers with bold lines.

Step 11. Draw all subsills with bold lines.

Step 12. Draw all bottom plates with bold lines.

Step 13. Draw exterior sheathing with thin lines.

Step 14. Draw the porch rafters and decking with thin lines.

Step 15. Draw fascia, block, header, and ledger for the porch roof with bold lines.

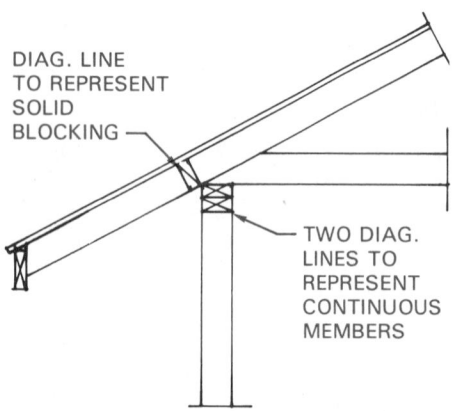
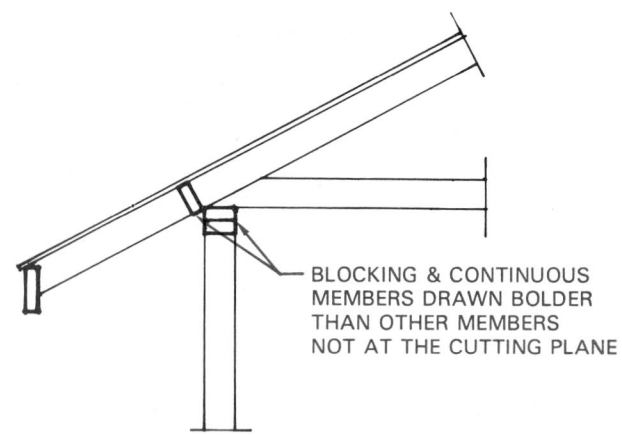

DIAG. LINE TO REPRESENT SOLID BLOCKING

TWO DIAG. LINES TO REPRESENT CONTINUOUS MEMBERS

BLOCKING & CONTINUOUS MEMBERS DRAWN BOLDER THAN OTHER MEMBERS NOT AT THE CUTTING PLANE

Figure 29–7 Finished quality lines for structural members.

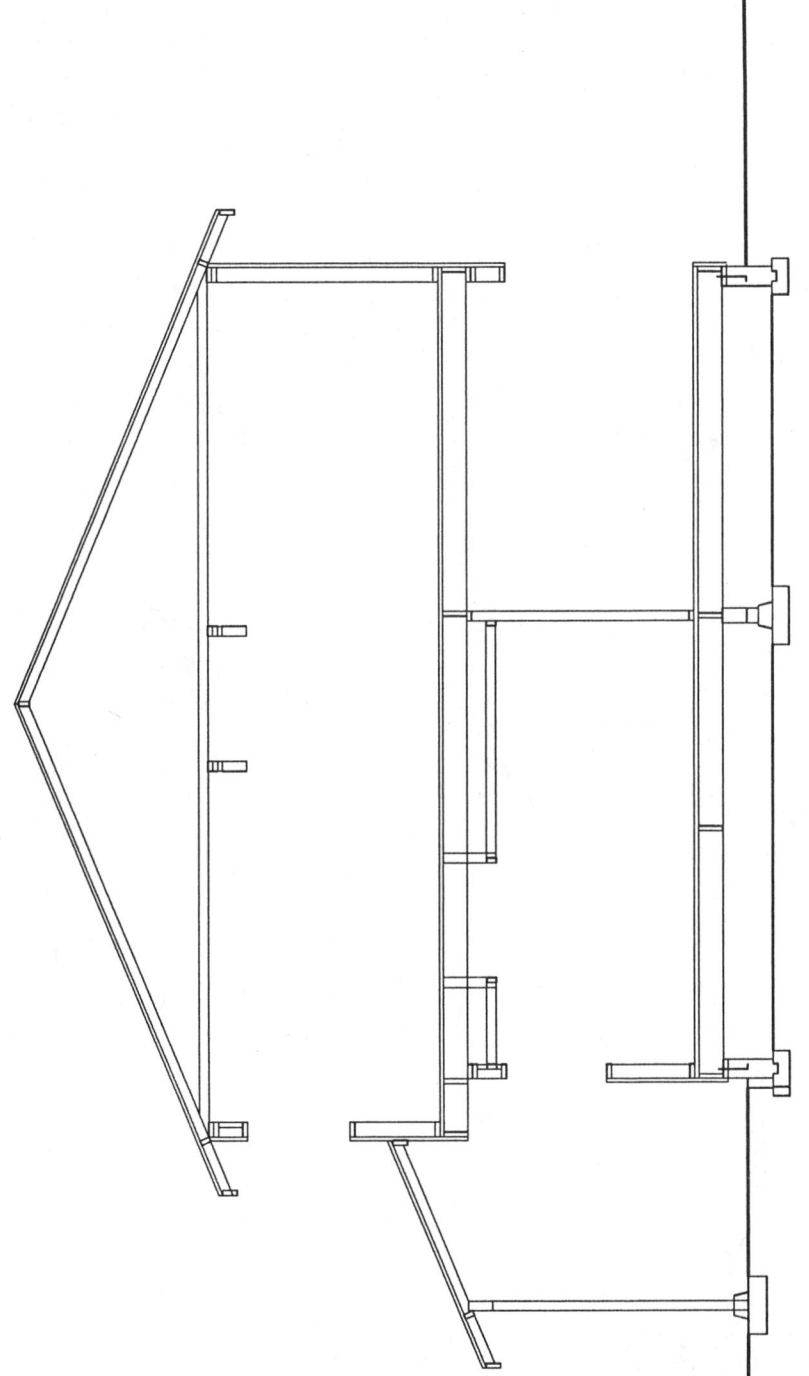

Figure 29-8 Cross section 'AA' with all structural members drawn with finished quality lines.

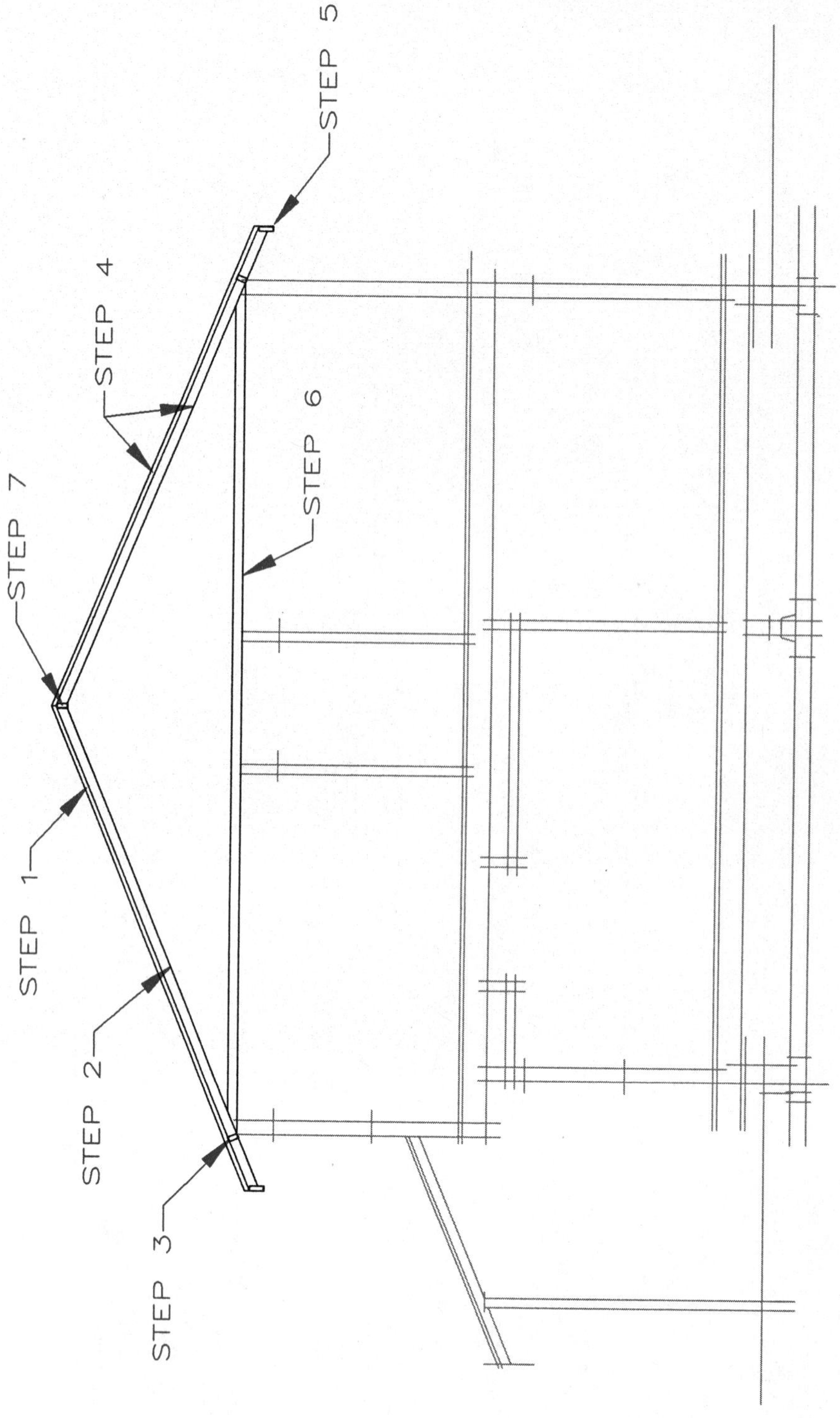

STEP 5

STEP 4

STEP 7

STEP 6

STEP 1

STEP 2

STEP 3

Figure 29-9 Truss roof construction drawn with finished quality lines.

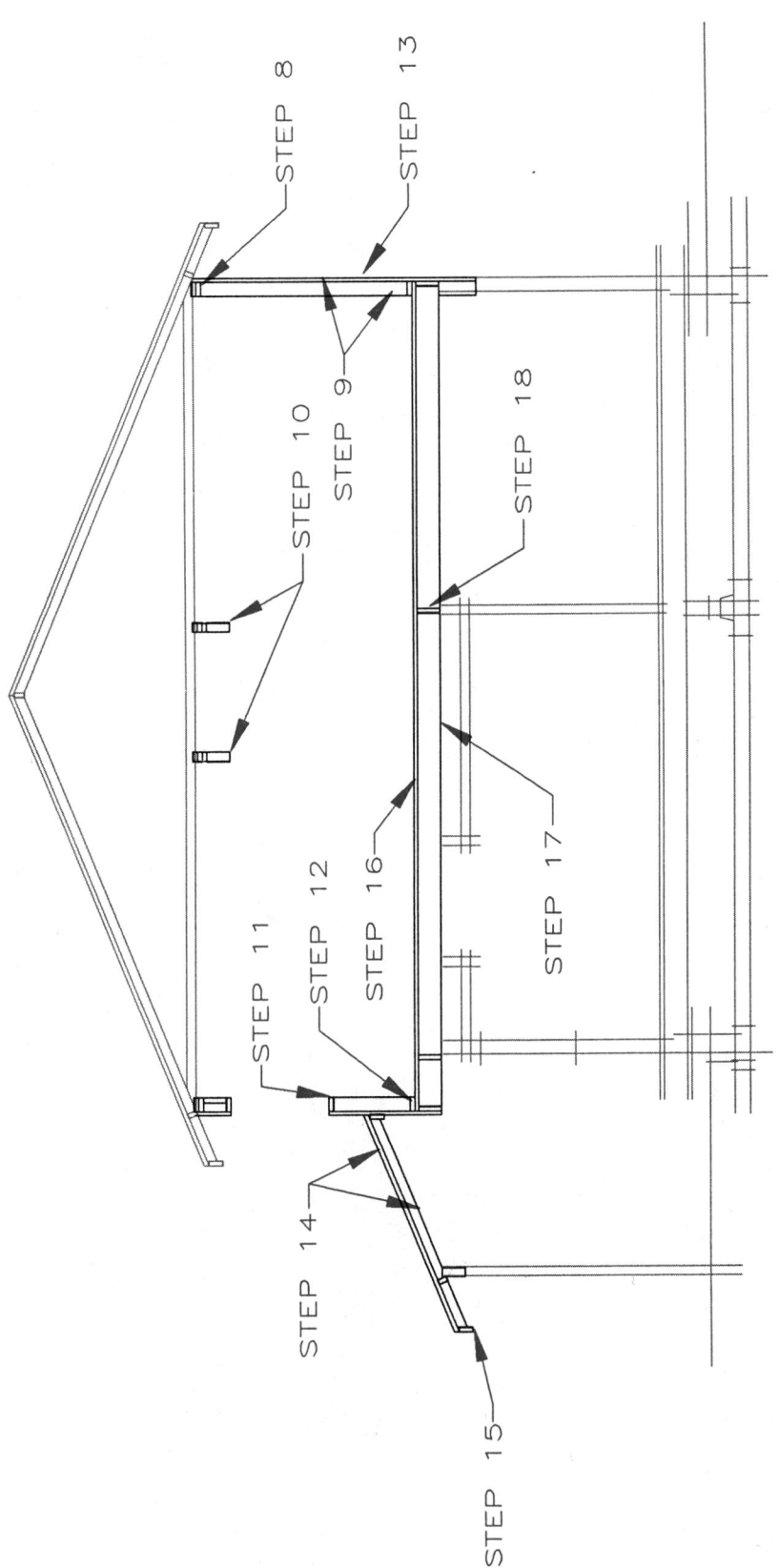

Figure 29-10 Upper floor structural members drawn with finished quality lines.

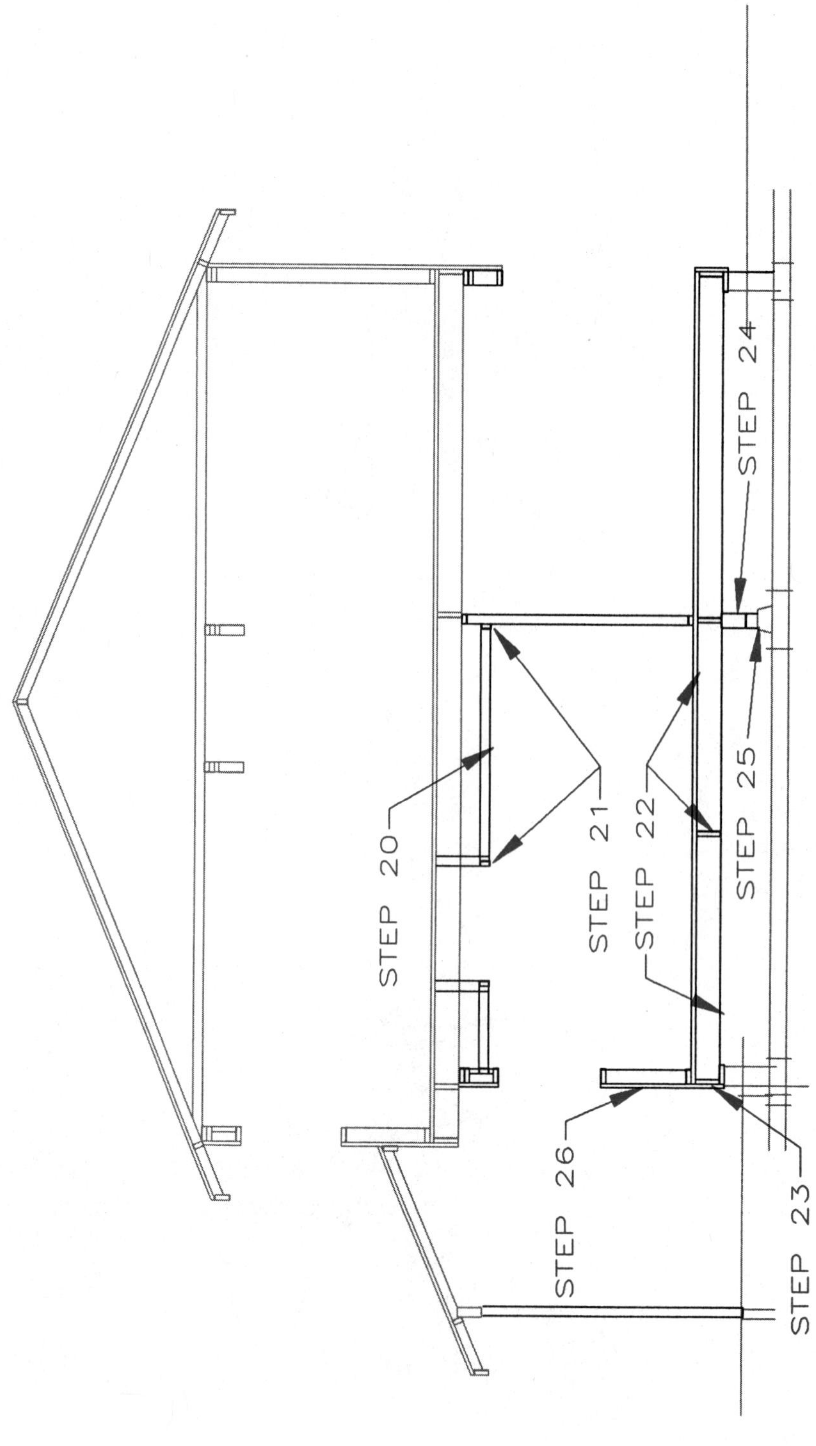

STEP 20

STEP 21

STEP 22

STEP 24

STEP 25

STEP 26

STEP 23

Figure 29–11 Structural members of the main floor level drawn with finished quality lines.

Step 16. Draw plywood subfloor with thin lines.

Step 17. Draw floor joists with thin lines.

Step 18. Draw floor blocks with bold lines.

Lower Level Walls and Floor

See Figure 29–11 for steps 19 through 26.

Step 19. Repeat steps 8 through 13.

Step 20. Draw furred ceiling with thin lines.

Step 21. Draw all blocks and ledgers for ceiling with bold lines.

Step 22. Repeat steps 16 through 18.

Step 23. Draw mudsills with bold lines.

Step 24. Draw girders with bold lines.

Step 25. Draw post with thin lines.

Step 26. Draw all exterior wall sheathing with thin lines.

Foundation

See Figure 29–12 for steps 27 through 30.

Step 27. Draw stem walls and footings with very bold lines. Note that Figure 29–12 shows two kinds of footings. Have your instructor explain which is the most common in your area. Make sure you use the same kind on each side.

Step 28. Draw the piers with very bold lines.

Step 29. Draw anchor bolts with bold lines.

Step 30. Use a very bold line to draw the finished grade.

All structural material is now drawn.

STAGE 4: DRAWING FINISHING MATERIALS

The material drawn in stage 3 forms the frame of the building. The material drawn in this stage seals the exterior from the weather and finishes the interior. Start at the roof and work down to the foundation to keep the drawing clean. Use thin lines for this entire stage unless otherwise noted. See Figure 29–13 for steps 1 through 14.

Roof

Step 1. Draw hurricane ties (approximately 3 in. square).

Step 2. Draw baffles with a bold line.

Step 3. Draw the finished ceiling.

Step 4. Draw insulation in the ceiling approximately 10 in. deep.

Step 5. Draw ridge vents.

Step 6. Draw gutters.

Walls

Step 7. Draw the exterior siding.

Step 8. Draw all windows.

Step 9. Draw all interior finishes and insulation.

Step 10. Draw and crosshatch the brick veneer.

Floors and Crawl Spaces

Step 11. Draw the hardboard underlayment. Note that the plywood subfloor extends under all walls but the hardboard underlayment does not go under any walls.

Step 12. Draw floor insulation.

Step 13. Draw the vapor barrier freehand, leaving a small space between the ground and the barrier.

Step 14. Draw the metal connectors and flashing for the porch.

STAGE 5: DIMENSIONING

Now that the section is drawn, all structural members must be dimensioned so that the framing crew knows their vertical location. Figure 29–14 shows the needed dimensions. All leader lines should be thin, similar to those used on the floor and foundation plans. All lettering should be aligned.

Step 1. Floor to ceiling. Place a dimension line from the top of the floor sheathing to the bottom of the floor or ceiling joist.

Step 2. Determine the floor-to-floor dimensions. The walls were drawn 8′–0″ high, but this is not their true height. The true height is the sum of the thickness of two top plates, the studs and the base plate. The plates

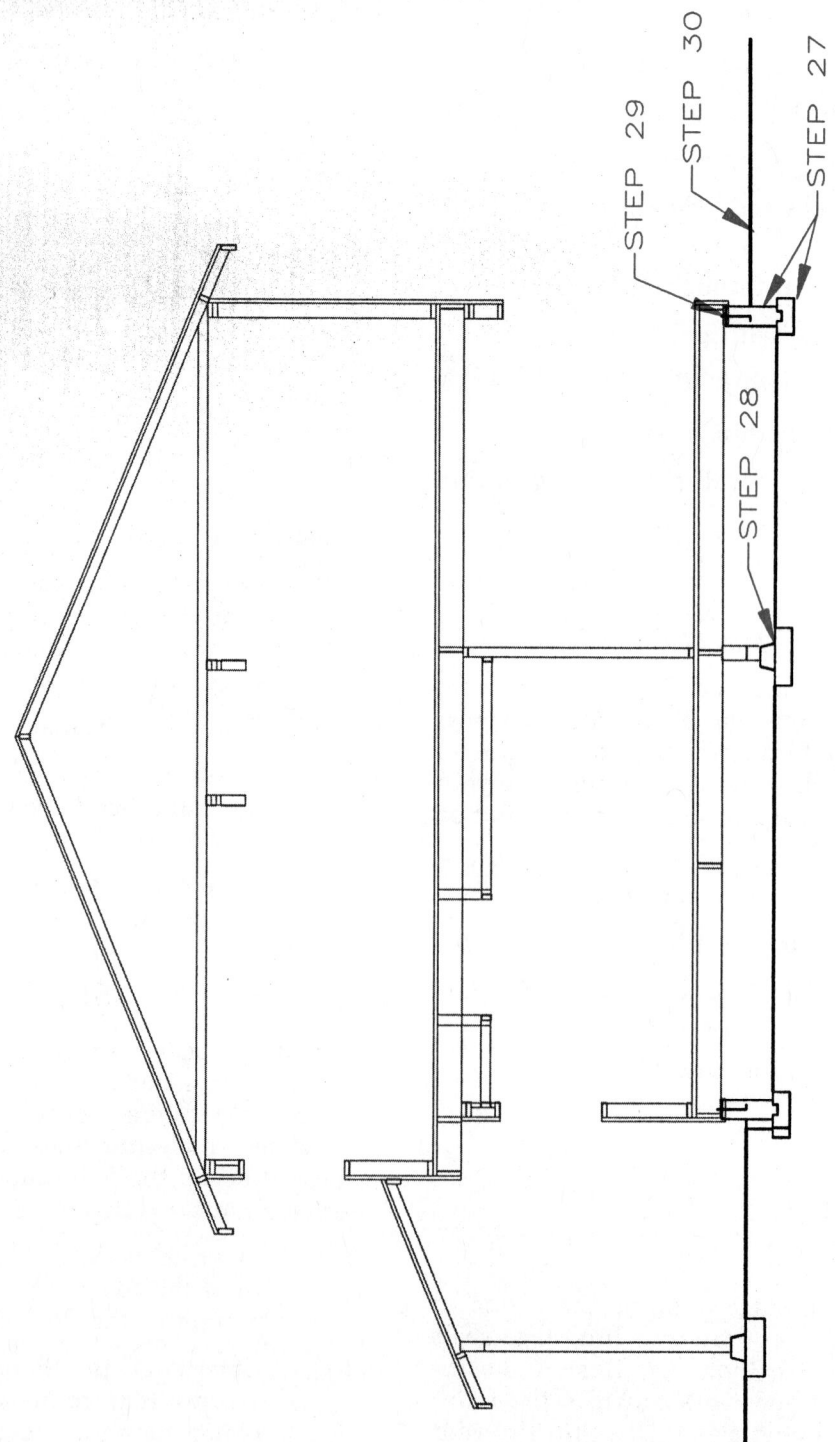

Figure 29-12 Structural members of the foundation level drawn with finished quality lines.

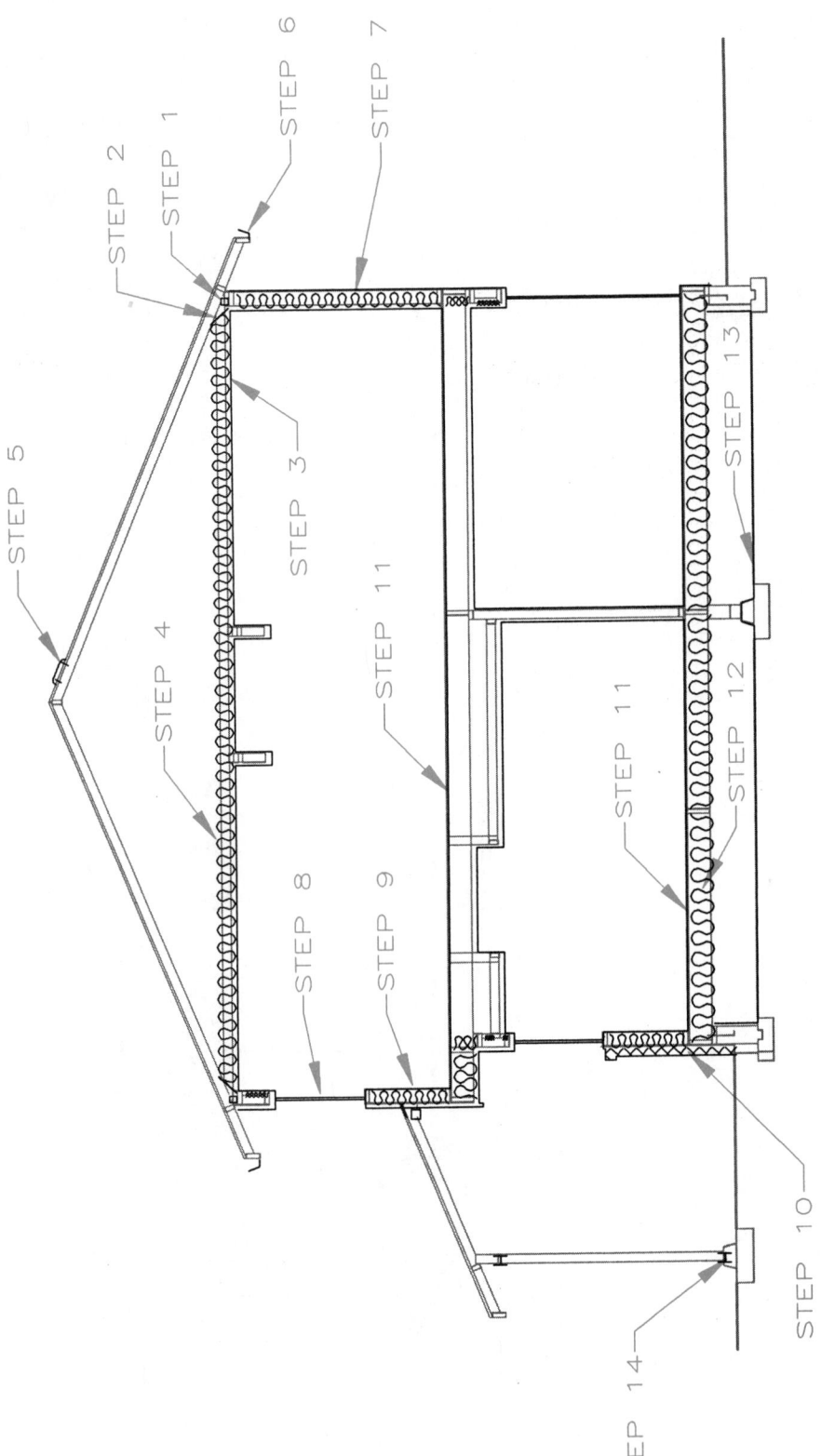

Figure 29-13 Cross section "AA" with all of the finishing materials for the roof, walls, floors, and foundations.

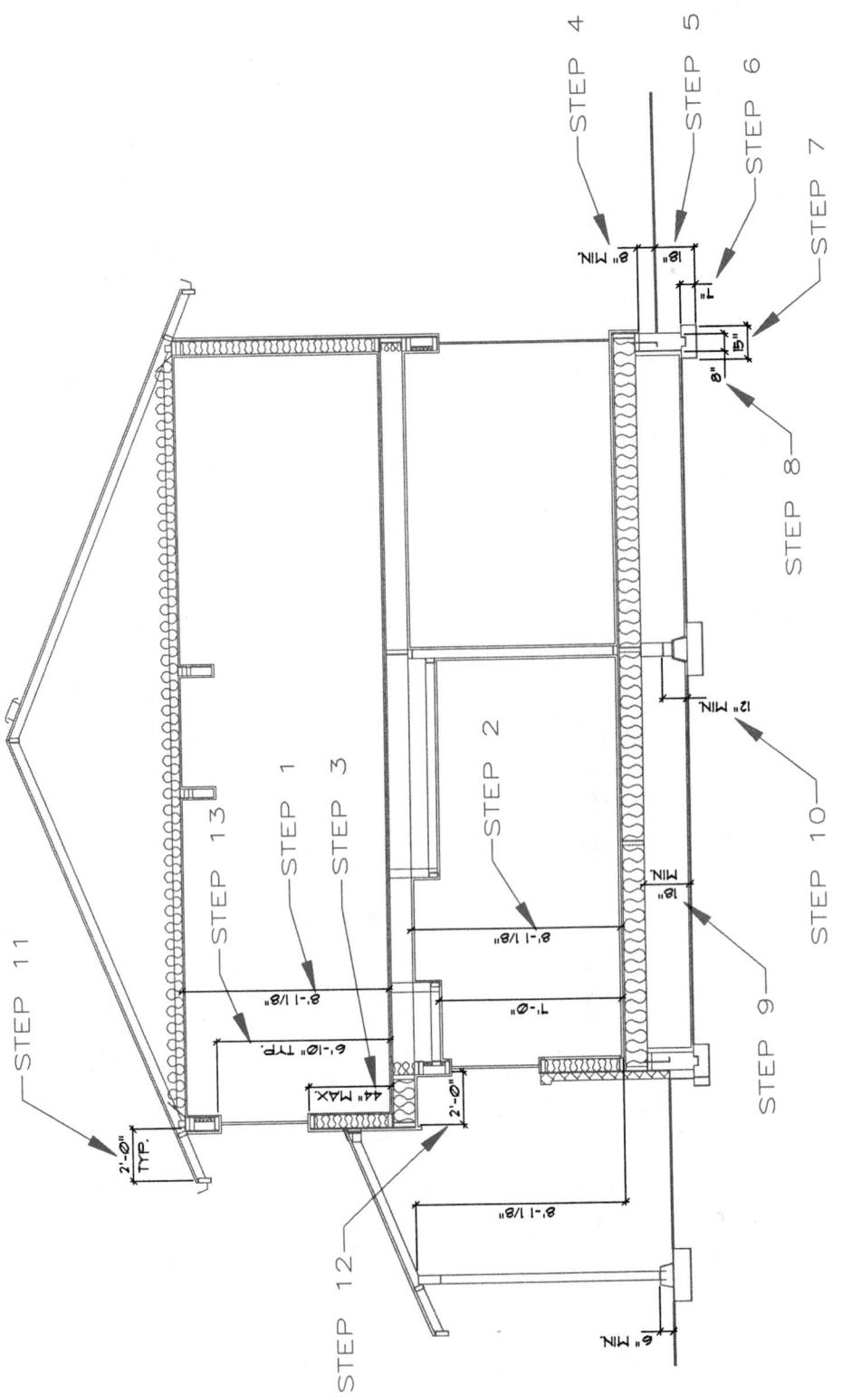

Figure 29–14 Cross section 'AA' with all of the required dimensions.

Long Stud (in.)		Short Stud (in.)
3	2 TOP PLATES	3
92 5/8	STUD HEIGHT	88 5/8
+ 1 1/2	BASE PLATE	+ 1 1/2
97 1/8	TOTAL HEIGHT	93 1/8
8'-1 1/8"	DIMENSION TO APPEAR ON SECTION	7'-9 1/8"

Figure 29–15 Determining floor to ceiling dimensions. Add the depth of the top plates, base plate, and the height of the studs. Notice that the heights for two common stud lengths are given.

are made from 2 in. material, which is actually 1½ in. thick. The studs are either milled in 88⅝ or 92⅝ in. lengths. Check with your instructor to see which size you should use. See Figure 29–15 to determine the true height of the walls.

Place the required leader and dimension lines to locate the following dimensions:

Step 3. Floor to bottom of bedroom windows (44 in. maximum).

Step 4. Finished grade to top of stem wall.

Step 5. Depth of footing into grade.

Step 6. Height of footing.

Step 7. Width of footing.

Step 8. Width of stem wall.

Step 9. Crawl space depth.

Step 10. Bottom of girders to grade.

Step 11. Eave overhangs.

Step 12. Cantilevers.

Step 13. Header heights from rough floor.

Step 14. Height of brick veneer if necessary.

Step 15. Lean back and relax! You're almost done.

STAGE 6: LETTERING NOTES

Everything that has been drawn and located must be explained. Place guidelines around the perimeter of the drawing and align the required notes on the guidelines as seen in Figure 29–16. Doing so will help make your drawing neat and easy to read. Not all of the following notes will need to go on every section you draw. Typically, the primary section will be fully notated and then other sections will have

only construction notes. You will notice as you go through the list of general notes that some are marked (*). These marked items have several options. Review Chapter 27 to help you decide which option to use. Ask your instructor for help in determining which grade of material to use.

One other important concept to remember is that the following list is just a guideline. You, the drafter, will need to evaluate each section prior to placing the required notes. In an office setting your supervisor might give you a print with all of the notes that need to be placed on the original. As you gain confidence you will probably be referred to a similar drawing for help in deciding which notes are needed. Eventually you will be able to draw and notate a section without any guidelines. The general notes that may appear on sections are as follows:

Roof

*1. RIDGE BLOCK, or 2 × __ RIDGE BOARD (Fill in the blank.)

2. SCREENED RIDGE VENTS @ 10' O.C. ±.

*3. ½" STD GRADE 32/16 PLY ROOF SHEATH. LAID PERP. TO TRUSSES. NAIL W/ 8d @ 6" O.C. @ EDGE AND 8d @ 12" O.C. FIELD.
   or
   1 × 4 SKIP SHEATHING W/ 3½" SPACING.

*4. 235# (or 300#) COMPO. ROOF SHINGLES OVER 15# FELT.
   or
   MED. CEDAR SHAKES OVER 15# FELT W/ 30# × 18" WIDE FELT BETWEEN EACH COURSE W/ 10½" EXPOSURE.
   or
   CONC. ROOF TILES BY (give manufacturer's name, and color and weight of tiles). INSTALL AS PER MANUF. SPECS.

5. STD. ROOF TRUSSES @ 24" O.C. SEE DRAW. BY MANUF.
   or
   2 × __ RAFT. @ __" O.C.
   2 × __ C.J. @ __" O.C. (Fill in the blanks with sizes.)

*6. 10" BATTS, R-30 PAPER FACE @ HEATED SIDE.
   or
   10" BLOWN-IN INSULATION R-30 MIN.

7. BAFFLES AT EAVE VENTS.

8. SOLID BLOCK—OMIT EA. 3rd FOR SCREENED VENTS.

9. TRUSS CLIPS @ EA. TAIL TO PLATE.

10. __ × __ FASCIA W/ GUTTER (Fill in the blanks with sizes.)

11. ½" 'CCX' EXT. PLY @ ALL EXPOSED EAVES.
    or
    1 × 4 T&G DECKING @ ALL EXPOSED EAVES.

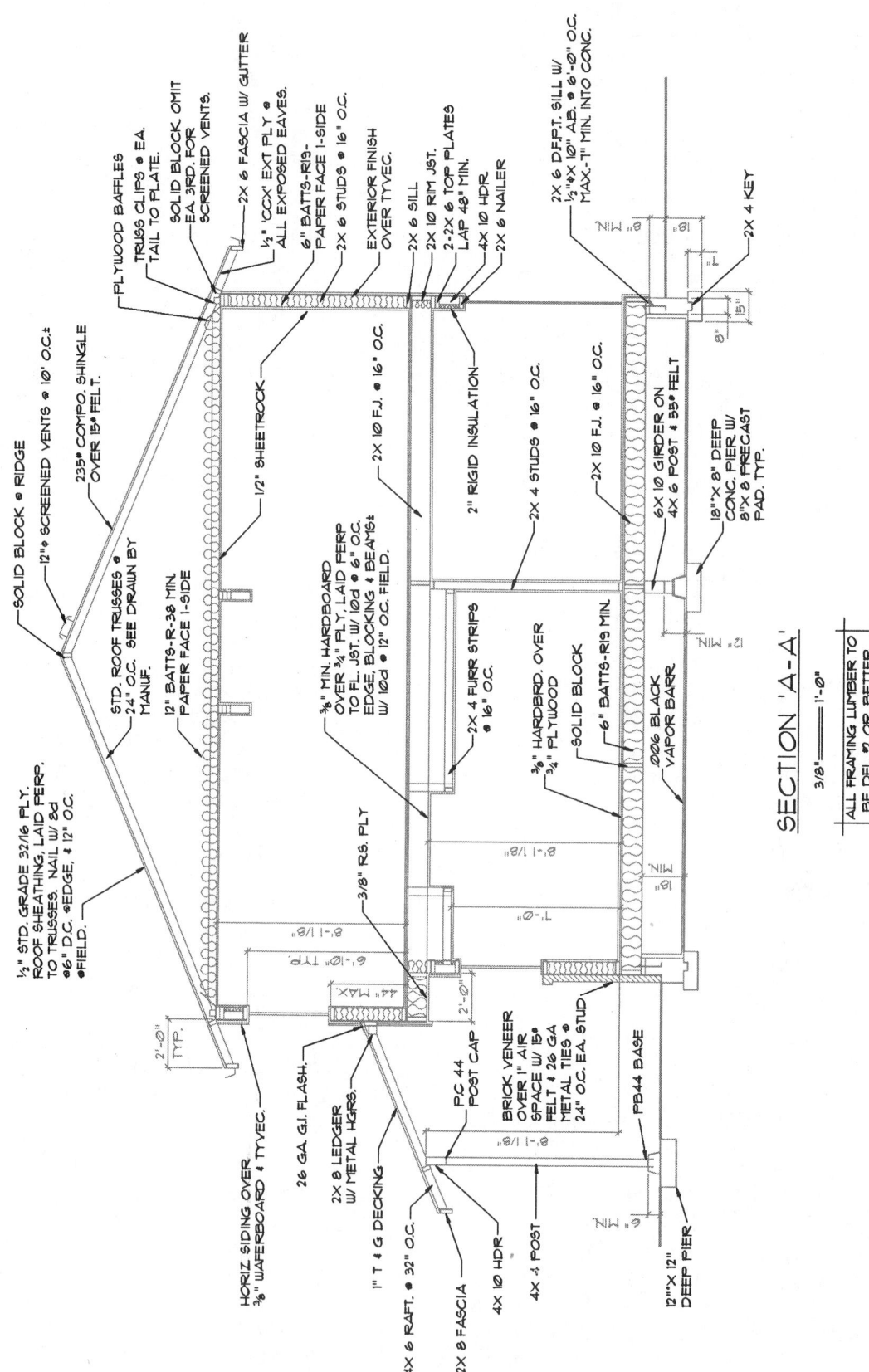

Figure 29-16 Cross section "AA" completed with all structural and finishing material drawn, dimensioned, and lettered.

Walls

*1. 2—2 × __ TOP PLATES, LAP 48″ MIN. (Fill in the blank.)
*2. 2 × __ STUDS @ __″ O.C. (Fill in the blanks.)
*3. 2 × __ SILL (Fill in the blank.)
*4. EXT. SIDING OVER ⅜″ PLY. & TYVEK.
*5. 3½ FIBERGLASS BATTS, R-11 MIN.—PAPER FACE ONE SIDE.

or

6″ FIBERGLASS BATTS, R-19, PAPER FACE ONE SIDE.
*6. __ × __ HEADER (Fill in the blanks.)
7. LINE OF INTERIOR FINISH.
8. SOLID BLOCK AT MID HEIGHT FOR ALL WALLS OVER 10′.
9. ⅝″ TYPE 'X' GYP. BD. FROM FLOOR TO BOTTOM OF ROOF SHEATH.

or

⅝″ TYPE 'X' GYP. BD. WALLS AND CEIL.
10. BRICK VENEER OVER 1″ AIR SPACE & 15# FELT W/ METAL TIES @ 24″ O.C. EA. STUD.

Floors and Foundation

1. ⅜″ MIN. HARDBOARD UNDERLAYMENT.
*2. ¾″ 42/16 PLY. FLOOR SHEATH. LAID PERP. TO FLOOR JOISTS. NAIL W/ 10d @ 6″ O.C. EDGE, BLOCKING, & BEAMS. USE 10d @ 12″ O.C. @ FIELD.
3. SOLID BLOCK @ 10′ O.C. MAX.
4. 6″ BATTS—R-19 MIN.
*5. __ × __ GIRDERS (Fill in the blanks. See foundation plan to verify size.)
*6. 4 × 4 POST, 4 × 6 @ SPLICES, W/ METAL TIES ON 55# FELT ON __ × __ DEEP CONC. PIERS. (Fill in the blanks.)
7. .006 BLACK VAPOR BARRIER or 55# ROLLED ROOFING.
*8. 2 × __ P.T. SILL W/ ½″ ∅ A.B. @ 6′-0″ O.C. MAX.—7″ MIN. INTO CONC. W/ 2″ ∅ WASHERS (Fill in the blank.)
9. Give the section a title such as SECTION 'AA'.
10. Give the drawing a scale such as ⅜″ = 1′-0″.
11. List general notes near the title or near the title block.
*ALL FRAMING LUMBER TO BE D.F.L. #2 OR BETTER
(Instead of D.F.L. you may need to substitute a different type of wood.)
SEE SECTIONS 'BB' & 'CC' FOR BALANCE OF NOTES.

Give your eyes and fingers a well-deserved rest. You now have 99 percent of the section complete.

STAGE 7: EVALUATE YOUR WORK

Don't assume because you did the work and it took a long time that the drawing is complete. Run a print and evaluate your work for accuracy and quality. Don't just compare it to someone else's drawing. Use the checklist and make sure your section matches the material and location that you have specified on the floor and foundation plans. Your best chance of finding your own mistakes is to get away from your drawing for an hour or two before checking it. Use the following checklist to evaluate your drawing before giving it to your instructor.

Roof

1. Line quality: uniform thickness/weight.
2. Drawn at correct pitch.
3. Truss, overhang, blocking, fascia, plywood, insulation, pitch callout, truss ties.
4. Notes.

Walls

1. Line quality: uniform thickness/weight.
2. Uniform size of studs and plates.
3. Insulation.
4. Siding.
5. Proper relationship to floor/finished floor.
6. Proper notes.

Floors

1. Floor sheathing and finished floor thickness.
2. Floor joist size.
3. Girders, post, piers, insulation.
4. Vapor barrier, pressure-treated plate/anchor bolts.
5. Finished grade.

Dimensions

1. Grade to top of footing and grade to bottom of footing.
2. Width of footing and width of wall.
3. Crawl space depth and beam depth.
4. Floor to floor.
5. Floor to header and floor to bedroom subsill.
6. Cantilevers.
7. Overhangs.
8. Veneers.

Line Quality

1. Line contrast, structural and finished quality lines.
2. Line uniformity. Uniform weight/size of like members.
3. Clarity/crispness of lines.

Lettering

1. Lettering proper size and location.
2. Proper notes and callouts.

Coordination

1. Structural members of section match floor and/or foundation plans.

CADD
applications

DRAWING SECTIONS AND DETAILS WITH CADD

The steps for drawing sections presented in this chapter are used for both manual and computer-aided drafting. However, using the computer has some advantages: standard sections and details can be brought into the drawing from a menu library; placing notes on the section is easy with CADD. Also, some architectural CADD packages automatically draw a pre-

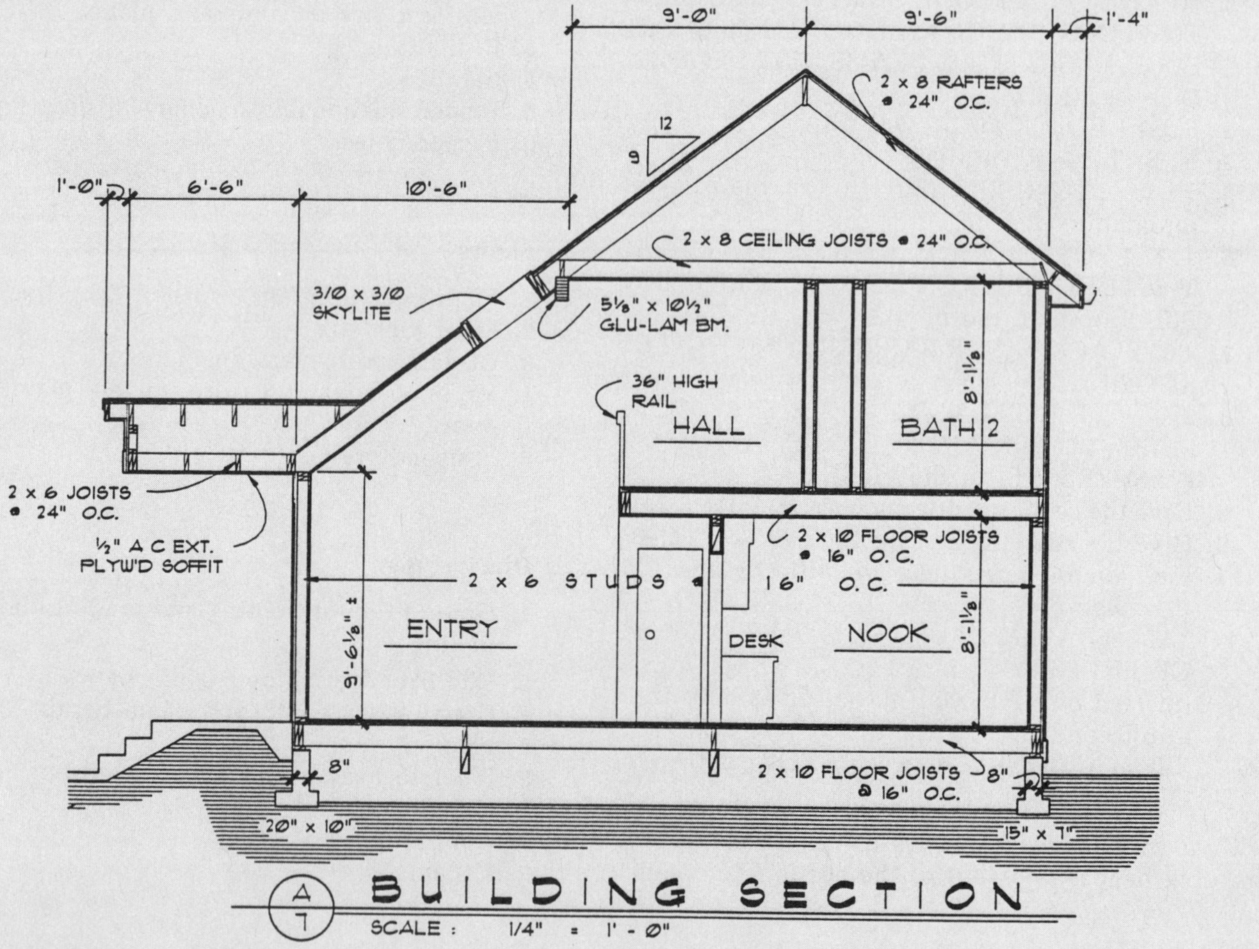

Figure 1 CADD section drawing.

liminary section from information you provide in relationship to the floor plan. This type of parametric design requires that an imaginary cutting plane line be placed through the floor plan in the desired section location. This is followed by computer prompts requesting information such as roof pitch and structural floor thicknesses. In programs of this type, the floor plan walls are drawn with heights established, so these dimensions automatically convert to wall height information in the sectional view. The result is called a preliminary section; it is an outline of the sectional view similar to Figure 29–6. All you do to complete the section is add material symbols, dimensions, and notes. A complete CADD section drawing is shown in Figure 1.

Some architectural CADD packages have template library menu overlays that contain typical section elements such as details, materials, and tags. A sample menu library is shown in Figure 2. After architects have used the CADD system awhile, they begin to save all typical or standard construction details as BLOCKS. These BLOCKS are commonly placed in a library manual for easy reference and can be called up and displayed at any time in any drawing. The standard details should be clearly labeled with an identification code for easy reference. Each CADD user should have a copy of the library reference manual, and every time a new detail is drawn, the reference manual should be updated with a drawing of the detail and the reference code. A typical CADD detail drawing is shown in Figure 3.

Many of the major window and door manufacturers, such as Pella and Anderson, have CADD software programs available that integrate with major CADD software packages. These handy additions are useful in providing floor plan layouts, complete specifications, and standard construction details, as shown in Figure 4.

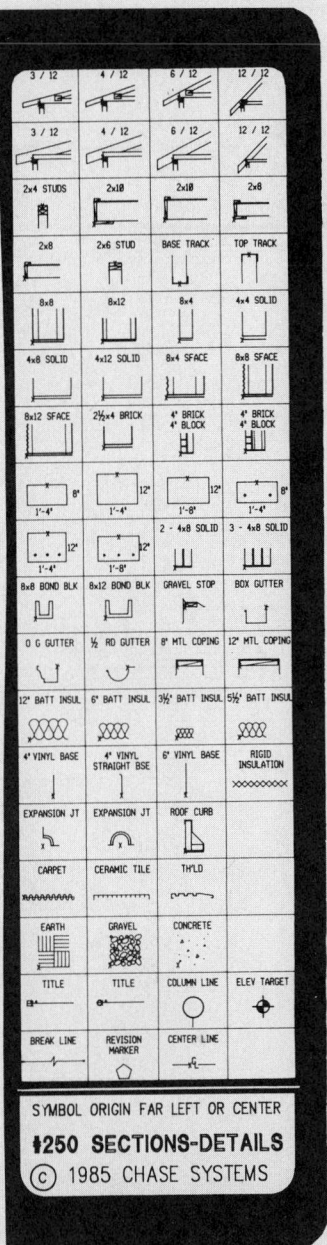

Figure 2 CADD template library menu.

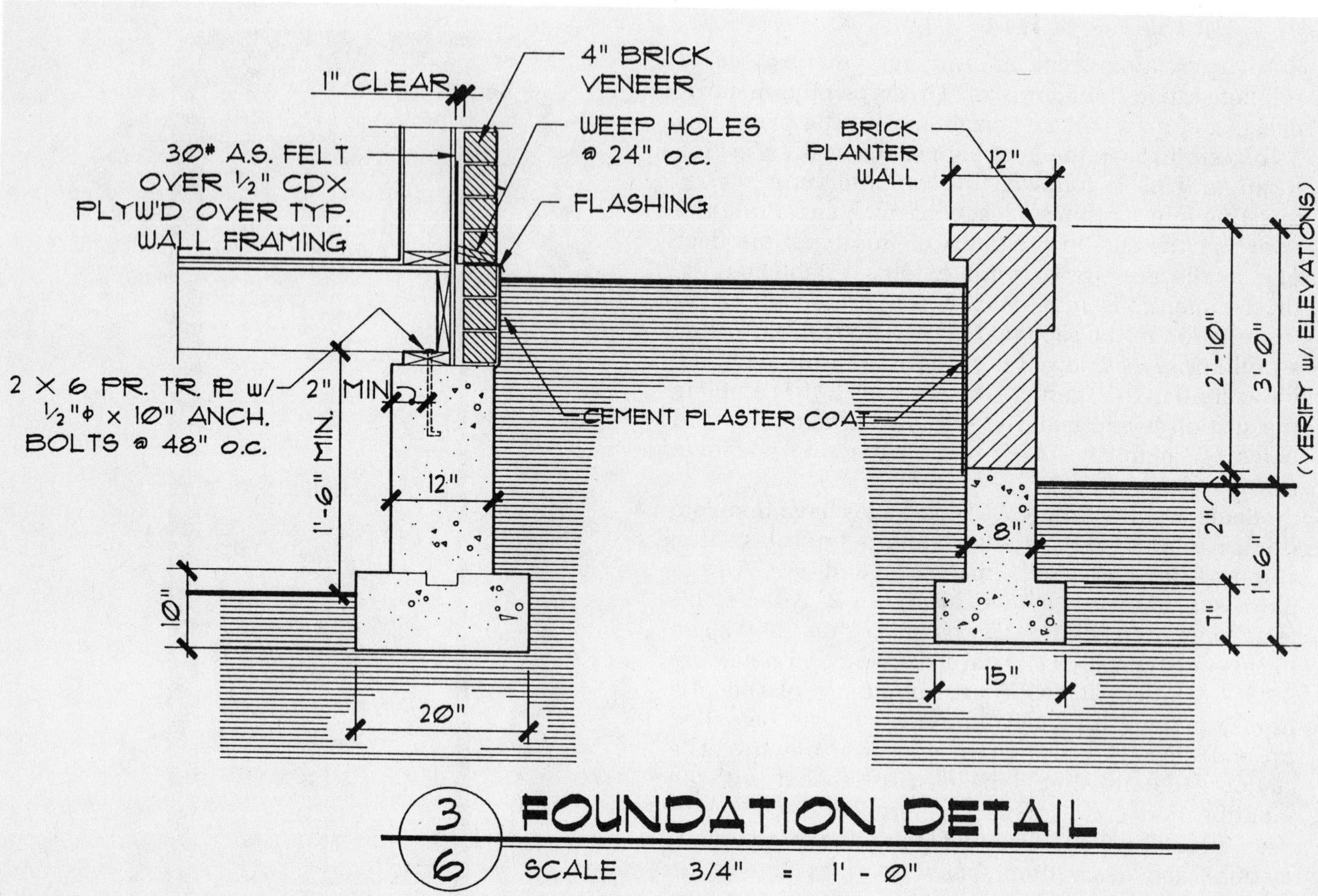

1" CLEAR

4" BRICK VENEER

WEEP HOLES @ 24" o.c.

BRICK PLANTER WALL

30# A.S. FELT OVER ½" CDX PLYW'D OVER TYP. WALL FRAMING

FLASHING

12"

2 X 6 PR. TR. P w/ ½"φ x 10" ANCH. BOLTS @ 48" o.c.

2" MIN.

1'-6" MIN.

12"

CEMENT PLASTER COAT

8"

(VERIFY w/ ELEVATIONS)

2'-10"

3'-0"

2"

1'-6"

7"

10"

20"

15"

③/⑥ FOUNDATION DETAIL

SCALE   3/4" = 1'-0"

Figure 3 CADD detail drawing.

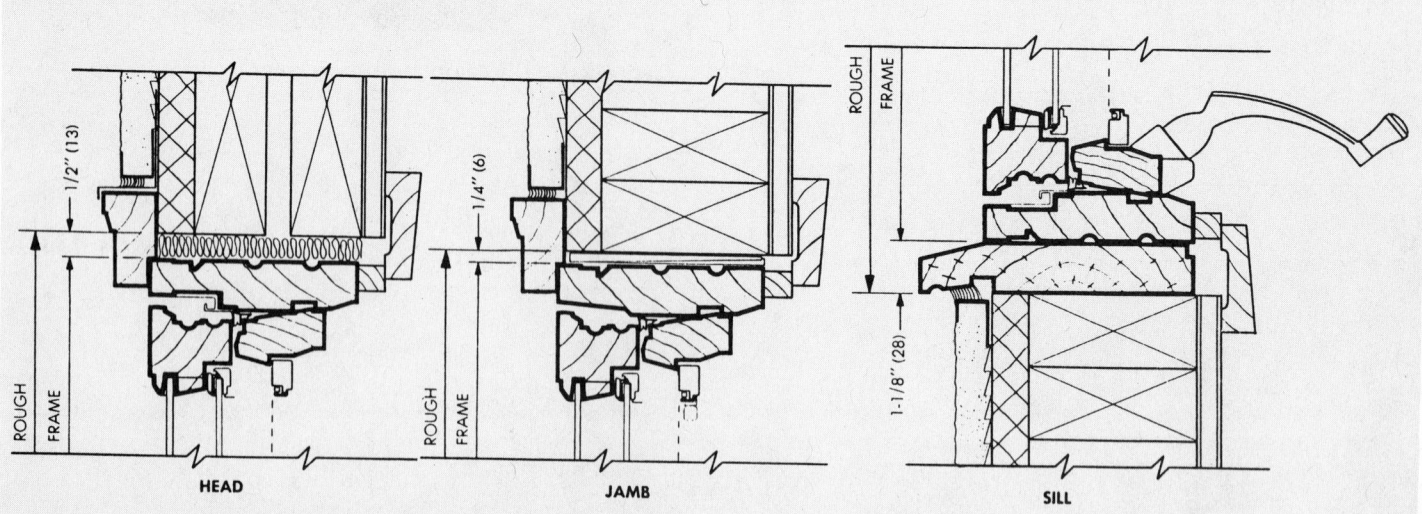

HEAD

½" (13)

ROUGH FRAME

JAMB

¼" (6)

ROUGH FRAME

SILL

ROUGH FRAME

1-1/8" (28)

Figure 4 Use for manufacturer-supplied CADD program.

SECTION LAYOUT TEST

DIRECTIONS

Answer the questions with short complete statements or drawings as needed on an 8½ × 11 drawing sheet as follows:

1. Use ⅛ in. guidelines for all lettering.
2. Letter your name, Section Layout Test, and the date at the top of the sheet.
3. Letter the question number and provide the answer. You do not need to write out the question.
4. Do all lettering with vertical uppercase architectural letters. If the answer requires line work, use proper drafting tools and technique. Answers may be prepared on a word processor if appropriate with course guidelines.
5. Your grade will be based on correct answers and quality of line technique.

QUESTIONS

1. Define the following terms.

   a. Rafter
   b. Truss
   c. Ceiling joist
   d. Collar tie
   e. Jack stud
   f. Rim joist
   g. Chord
   h. Sheathing

2. On a blank sheet of paper sketch a section view of a conventionally framed roof showing all interior supports.
3. Give the typical sizes for the following materials.

   a. Mudsill
   b. Stud height
   c. Roof sheathing
   d. Wall sheathing
   e. Floor decking
   f. Underlayment

4. List three common scales for drawing sections and tell when they are best used.
5. List the seven stages of drawing a section.
6. List two different types of drawings for which stock drawings are typically used.

Chapter 30
Alternate Layout Techniques

POST-AND-BEAM FOUNDATIONS
CONCRETE SLAB FOUNDATIONS
BASEMENT WITH CONCRETE SLAB
CONVENTIONAL (STICK) ROOF FRAMING
VAULTED CEILINGS
GARAGE/RESIDENCE SECTION
TEST

CHAPTER 29 presented the basic methods for drawing a section with a crawl space, floor joists and truss roof. Those methods will not meet the needs of all drafters because of the job site, the contractor's personal preference for framing, or the area of the country in which the house is to be built. This chapter will provide you with other common construction methods to meet a variety of needs. Unless noted, all sizes given in the following steps are based on the minimum standards of the Uniform Building Code and should be compared with local standards.

▶ POST-AND-BEAM FOUNDATIONS

Section 4 presented an introduction to post-and-beam construction. This chapter will only describe post-and-beam construction as it applies to the foundation and lower floor.

Layout

Use construction lines for steps 1 through 14. See Figure 30–1 for steps 1 through 10.

Step 1. Lay out the width of the building.

Step 2. Lay out a baseline for the bottom of the footings.

Step 3. Lay out the footing thickness of 6 in. for one-story, 7 in. for two-story, or 8 in. for three-story construction.

Step 4. Lay out the finished grade. Footings must extend 12 in. into natural grade for a one-story, 18 in. into natural grade for a two-story, or 24 in. into natural grade for a three-story building.

Step 5. Locate the top of the stem wall 8 in. minimum above the finished grade.

Step 6. Block out the width of the stem wall using 6 in. for a one-story, 8 in. for a two-story, or 10 in. for a three-story building.

Step 7. Block out the width of the footings, centered under the stem wall. Footings are required to be 12 in. for one-story, 15 in. for two-story, or 18 in. for three-story construction.

Step 8. Block out a 4″ × 8″ ledge for the brick veneer.

Step 9. Add 4 in. width to the footing to support the brick ledge.

Step 10. Locate the 2 × 6 mudsill.

See Figure 30–2 for steps 11 through 13.

Step 11. Lay out the depth of the 2 in. floor decking.

Step 12. Lay out the girders and the support posts.

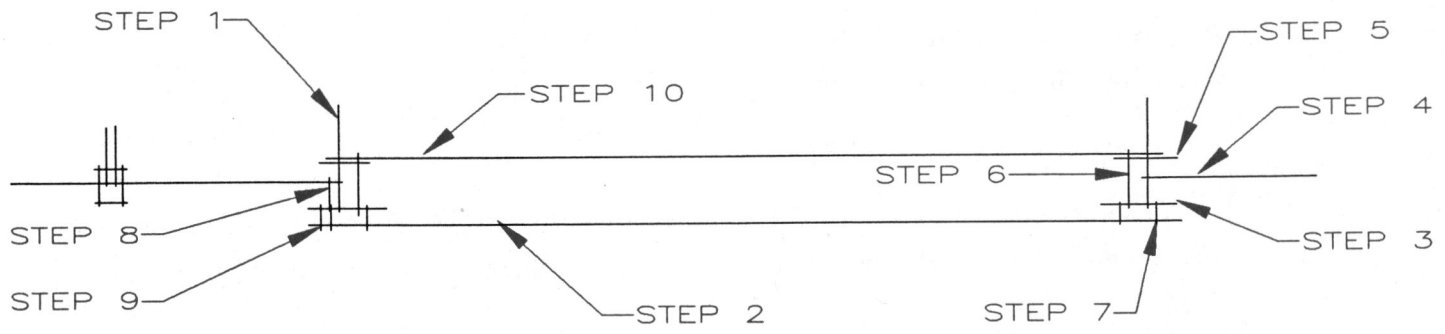

Figure 30–1 Layout for the post-and-beam foundation system using construction lines.

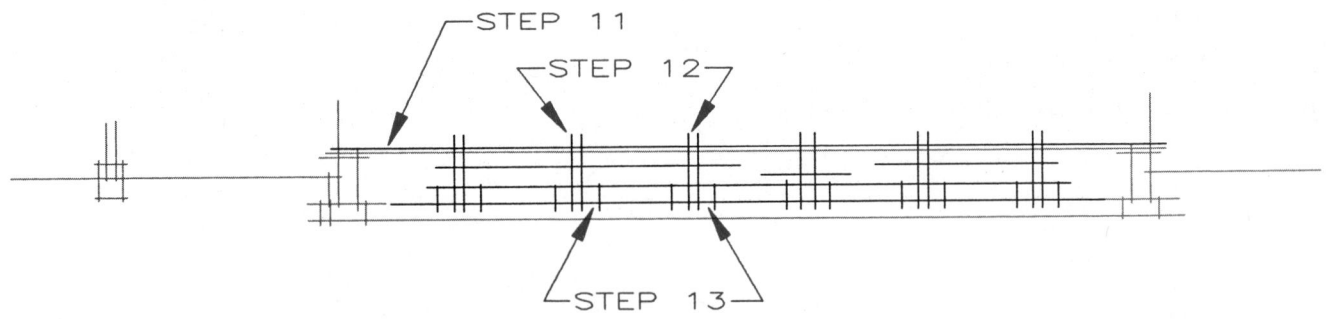

Figure 30–2 Layout of the interior supports for a post-and-beam foundation.

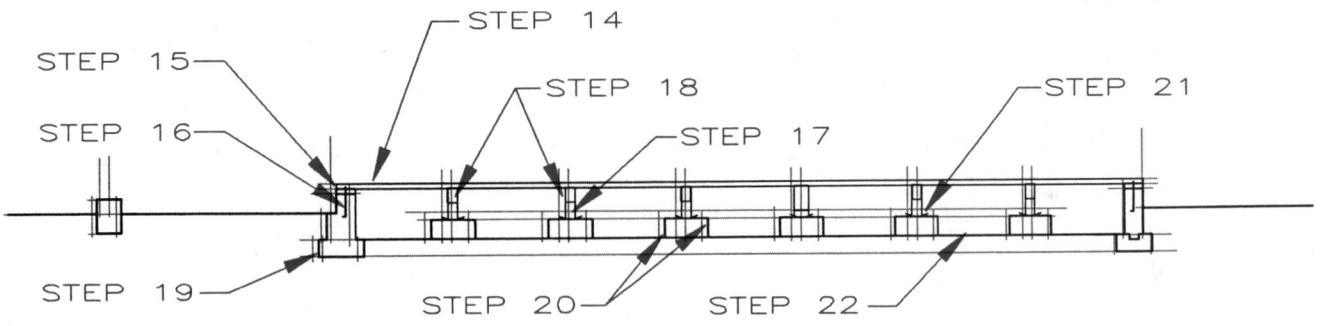

Figure 30–3 Finished quality lines on the structural members of a post-and-beam foundation system.

Step 13. Lay out the concrete support piers centered under the posts. Lay out the width first for each pier and then draw one continuous guideline to represent the top of all piers.

Finished Quality Lines—Structural Material

For drawing structural members with finished quality lines, use line quality as described in Chapter 29 unless otherwise noted. See Figure 30–3 for steps 14 through 22. You will notice that some items will be drawn that have not been laid out. These are items that are simple enough that they can be drawn by estimation.

Step 14. With thin lines, draw the tongue and groove (T&G) decking. Do not show the actual T&G pattern. This is only done when details are shown at a larger scale such as $\frac{3}{4}'' = 1'-0''$.

Step 15. Draw the mudsills using bold lines.

Step 16. Draw anchor bolts with bold lines.

Step 17. Draw all posts with thin lines.

Step 18. Draw all girders with bold lines.

Step 19. Draw the stem walls and footings with very bold lines. Figure 30–3 shows two methods for drawing the footings. Have your instructor explain which method is the most common in your area. Make sure you draw the same system on each side of the section.

Step 20. Draw piers with very bold lines.

Step 21. Draw the post pads freehand with bold lines.

Step 22. Draw the finished grade with very bold lines.

Finished Quality Lines—Finishing Material

The materials in this section will be used to seal the exterior walls from the weather and to finish the interior. Use thin lines for each step, unless otherwise noted. See Figure 30–4 for steps 23 through 25.

Step 23. Draw the hardboard subfloor from wall to wall.

Step 24. Draw the insulation.

Step 25. Draw the vapor barrier freehand.

Dimensioning

See Figure 30–5 for steps 26 through 32. Place the needed leader and dimension lines to locate the following dimensions:

Step 26. Finished grade to the top of the stem wall.

Step 27. Depth of the footing into grade.

Step 28. Height of the footing.

Step 29. Width of the footing.

Step 30. Width of the stem wall.

Step 31. Crawl space depth (18 in. minimum).

Step 32. Bottom of girders to grade (12 in. minimum).

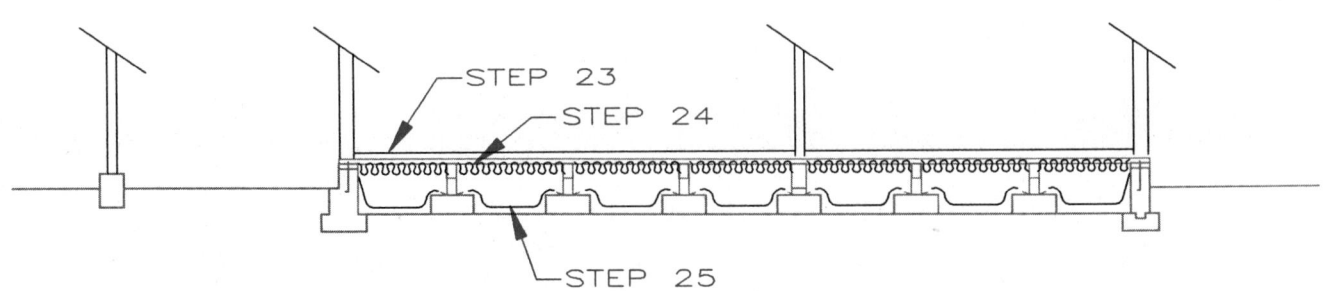

Figure 30–4 Finishing materials for a post-and-beam foundation system.

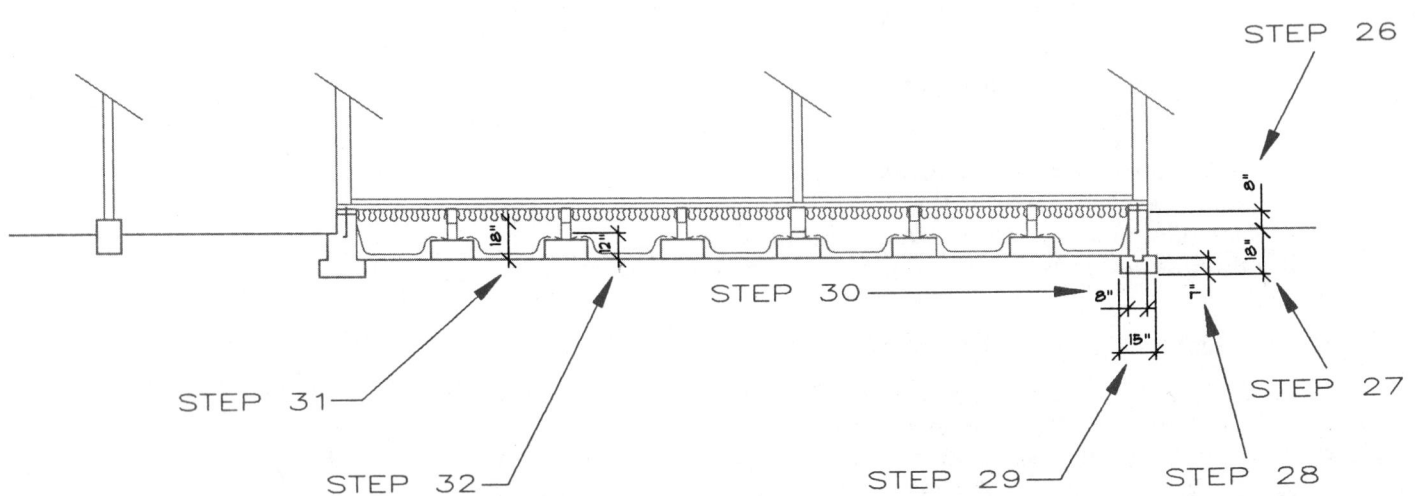

Figure 30–5 Required dimensions for a post-and-beam foundation system.

Notes

Step 33. Letter the floor and foundation notes as shown in Figure 30–6. Typical notes should include the following:

a. ⅜″ HARDBOARD OVERLAY
b. 2 × 6 T&G DECKING
c. 6″ BATTS, R-19 MIN.
d. __ × __ GIRDERS
e. 4 × 4 POST ON 55# FELT
f. __″ DIA × __″ DEEP CONC. PIERS
g. .006 BLACK VAPOR BARRIER or 55# ROLLED ROOFING
h. 2 × 6 P.T. SILL W/ ½″ DIA × 10″ A.B. @ 6′-0″ O.C. MAX.—7″ MIN. INTO CONC. THRU 2″ DIA WASHERS.

Step 34. Complete the section as per Chapter 29.

CONCRETE SLAB FOUNDATIONS

Structural Layout

Use light construction lines for steps 1 through 11. See Figure 30–7.

Step 1. Lay out the width of the building.

Step 2. Lay out a baseline for the bottom of the footings.

Step 3. Lay out the footing thickness using 6 in. for a one-story, 7 in. for a two-story, or 8 in. for a three-story building.

Step 4. Lay out the finish grade. Footings must extend 12 in. minimum into natural grade for a one-story, 18 in. minimum into nat-

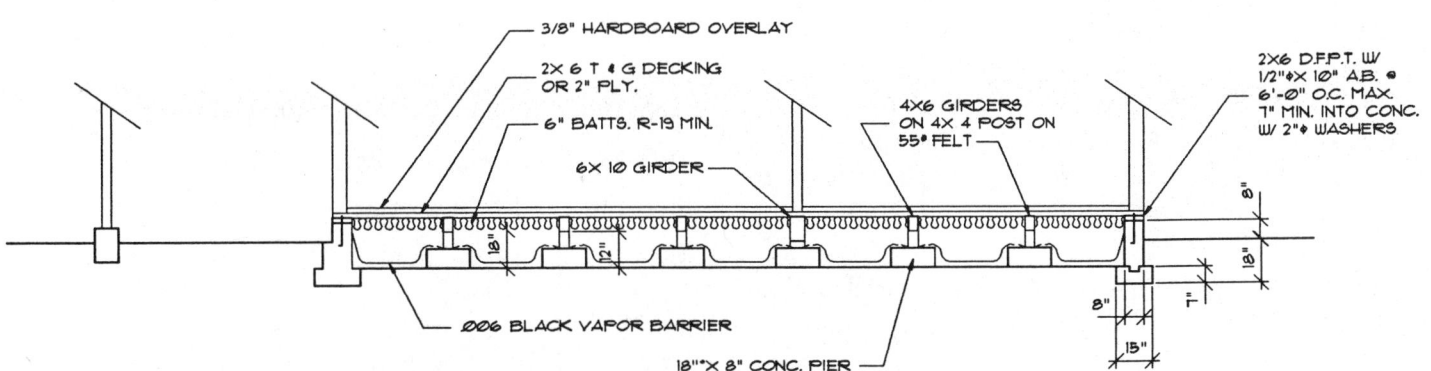

Figure 30–6 Typical notes for a post-and-beam foundation system.

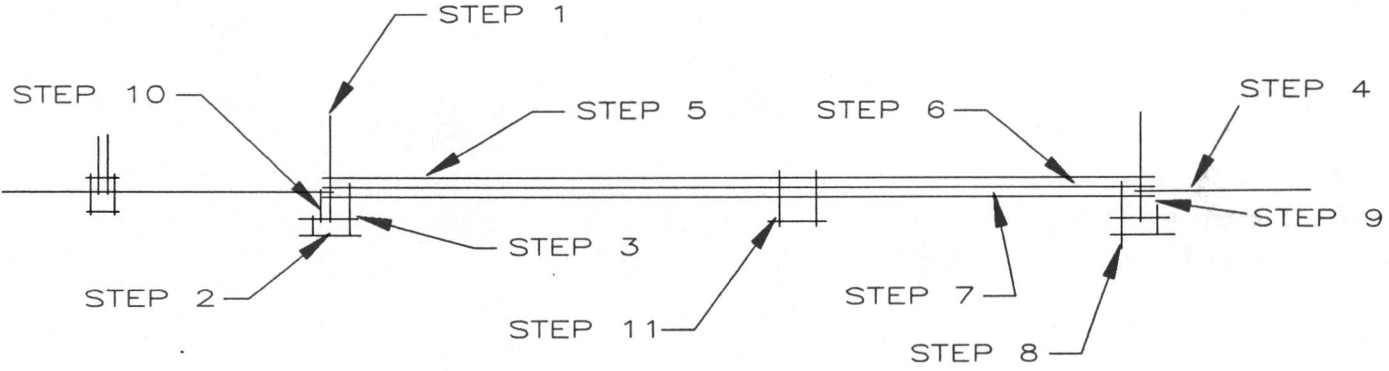

Figure 30–7 Layout methods for a concrete slab foundation.

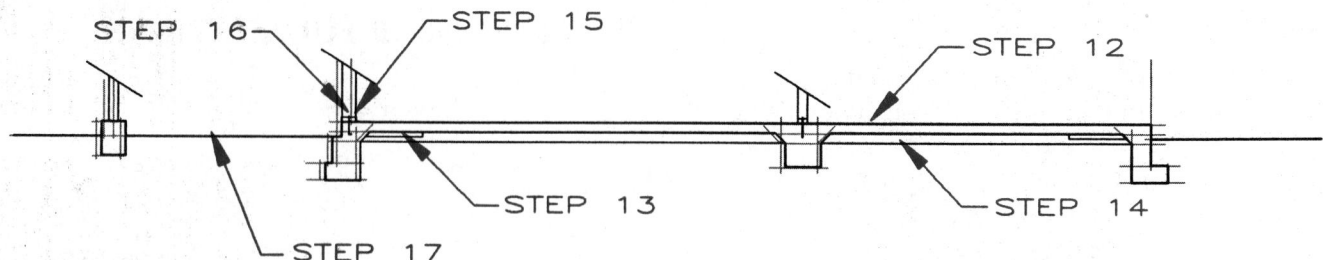

Figure 30–8 Finished quality lines for concrete slab structural materials.

ural grade for a two-story, or 24 in. minimum into natural grade for a three-story structure.

Step 5.   Locate the top of the slab. Building codes typically require all wood to be 6 in. minimum above the finish grade.

Step 6.   Lay out the bottom of the 4 in. slab.

Step 7.   Lay out 4 in. of fill material under the slab.

Step 8.   Lay out the width of the stem wall. Minimum widths are 6 in. for a one-story, 8 in. for a two-story, and 10 in. for a three-story building.

Step 9.   Lay out the width of the footings. Footings must be 12 in. for a one-story, 15 in. for a two-story, and 18 in. for a three-story structure.

Step 10. Lay out the 4″ × 8″ ledge for brick veneer.

Step 11. Block out the interior footings for load-bearing walls.

Finished Quality Lines

See Figure 30–8 for steps 12 through 17.

Step 12. Draw the outline of the concrete using very bold lines.

Step 13. Draw the 24″ × 2″ insulation with thin lines.

Step 14. Draw the 4 in. fill material with a thin line.

Step 15. Draw the mudsills with bold lines.

Step 16. Draw the anchor bolts (7 in. deep into the concrete) with bold lines.

Step 17. Draw the finished grade with a very bold

Dimensions

See Figure 30–9 for steps 18 through 22. Place the required extension and dimension lines to locate the following dimensions:

Step 18. Finished grade to top of slab (6 in. minimum).

Step 19. Finished grade to bottom of footing.

Step 20. Height of footing.

Step 21. Width of footing.

Step 22. Width of stem wall.

Notes

Step 23. Letter the foundation notes as shown in Figure 30–10. Typical notes should include:

a. 2 × 6 P.T. SILL W/ ½″ DIA × 10″ A.B. @ 6′-0″ O.C. MAX.—7″ MIN. INTO CONC. W/ 2″ DIA WASHERS.

b. 4″ CONC. SLAB OVER 4″ GRAVEL, 6 MIL VAPOR BARRIER, AND 2″ SAND FILL.

or

4″ CONC. SLAB OVER 4″ GRAVEL FILL OVER 55# FELT.

c. 2″ × 24″ RIGID INSULATION.

Step 24. Complete the section as per Chapter 29.

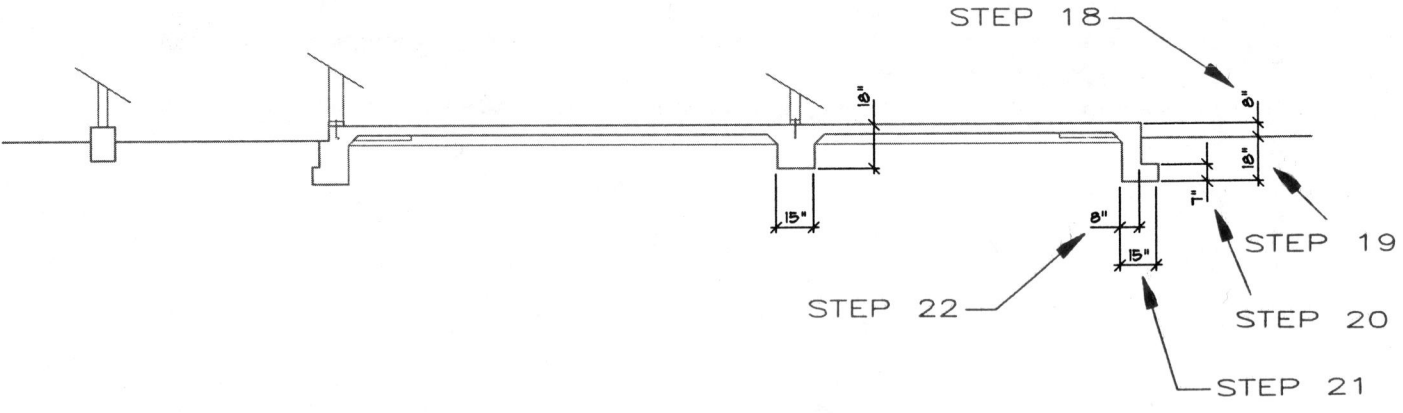

STEP 18

STEP 19

STEP 22

STEP 20

STEP 21

Figure 30–9 Required dimensions for a concrete slab foundation system.

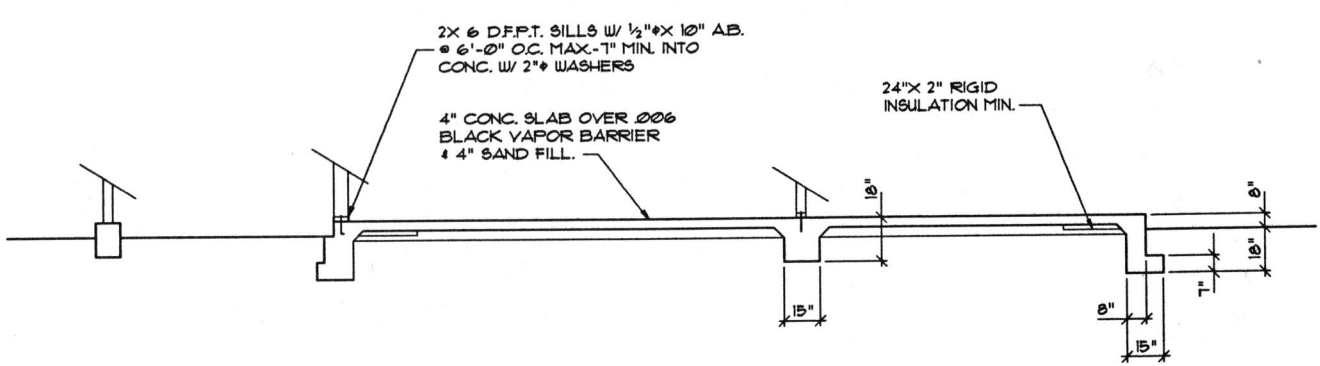

2X 6 D.F.P.T. SILLS W/ ½"⌀X 10" A.B.
@ 6'-0" O.C. MAX.-7" MIN. INTO
CONC. W/ 2"⌀ WASHERS

4" CONC. SLAB OVER .006
BLACK VAPOR BARRIER
& 4" SAND FILL.

24"X 2" RIGID
INSULATION MIN.

Figure 30–10 Typical notes for a concrete slab foundation system.

◢ BASEMENT WITH CONCRETE SLAB

For the basement layout use light construction lines. Depending on the seismic zone for which you are drawing, an engineer's drawing may be required for this kind of foundation. If so, you will need to follow engineer's design standards similar to those shown in Figure 30–11. Understanding engineer's design standards, or calculations (calcs), can be very frustrating. Calcs are generally divided into the areas of the item to be designed, the formulas to determine the size, and the solution.

The drafter does not need to understand the formulas that are used, but he or she must be able to convert the solution into a drawing. The solution in Figure 30–11 is the notes that are listed under the heading USE. For an entry-level drafter, the engineer will usually provide a sketch similar to the drawing in Figure 30–12 to explain the calculations. By using

8' HIGH BEAM TYPE BLOCK RETAINING WALL

StructureForm Masters Inc.

KEN SMITH—PRESIDENT
353 E. PARK AVE. SUITE 4 EL CAJON CALIF. 92020

DESIGN TYPE. - 8' BEAM TYPE BLOCK RETAINING WALL

$$M = (0.1283)(960)(8) = 985'\#$$

TRY #5 ϕ @ 16"O.C. VERT. PLACED 2" FROM
INSIDE FACE OF 8" BLOCK.

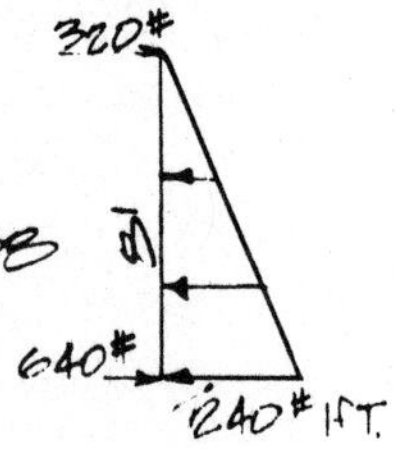

$$np = \frac{(43)(0.31)}{(16)(5.62)} = 0.148, \quad J = .861 \quad 2/KJ = .558$$

$$f_m = \frac{(1.33)(12)(985)(558)}{(16)(5.62)^2} = 174.5 \text{ PSI}$$

$$f_s = \frac{(12)(1.33)985}{(0.31)(.861)(5.62)} = 10,500 \text{ PSI} \qquad U = (11.0)\left(\frac{16}{1.963}\right) = 88.5 \text{ PSI}$$

$$V = \frac{(1.33)(640)}{(16)(.861)(5.62)} = 11.0 \text{ PSI} \qquad ht = \frac{96}{8} = 12$$

$$f_a = (135)(.94) = 127 \text{ P.S.I.}$$

ALLOW FOR ROOF, 2ND FLOOR & IST. FL. LOADING OF WALL FOR f_a

$$f_a = \frac{(40)(40) + (8)(32) + (2)(8)(16) + (4)(137) + (8)(63) + (8)(63) + (12)(3)}{(7.62)(12)}$$

$$f_a = 29.6 \text{ P.S.I.}$$

MIN. HORZ STEEL = (.0.007)(8)(96) = 0.54 in², $\quad \dfrac{174.5}{225} + \dfrac{29.4}{127} = \boxed{1.00}$ (OK)

USE:
— #5ϕ VERT @ 16"O.C. - PLACED 2" FROM FACE OF BLOCK AWAY FROM DIRT.
— USE 8" GRADE 'A' CONC. BLOCK - SOLID GROUT ALL STEEL CELLS.
— INTERMEDIATE GRADE DEFORMED BARS LAP 40 DIA. @ SPLICES.
— DBL. ALL VERT. STEEL BESIDE OPENINGS, & WALL ENDS & MATCH
  ALL DOWEL STEEL OUT OF FTGS. FOR SIZE & POSITION.
— USE 2-#4 UNDER & OVER ALL OPENINGS (UNLESS NOTED OTHERWISE)
  & EXTEND 24" BEYOND OPENINGS. PLACE 1½"- 2" UP FROM BTM.
  OF LINTEL IN INVERTED BOND BEAM BLOCK OR EQUAL & GROUT
  LINTEL CELLS SOLID
— USE 4-#4ϕ CONT. @ TOP OF WALL IN 8"x16" BLOCK BOND BM.
  & 2 #4ϕ CONT. IN BOND BLOCK @ MID-HEIGHT (4' MAX)
— GROUT AS PER SECTION 2403 (R) & MORTAR AS PER TABLE 24-A
  TYPE 'S'- 1982 UBC. W/ CENTERING BRACKET @ TOP & BTM.
— PROVIDE CLEANOUT HOLES @ BTM. OF STL. CELLS WHERE WALLS
  ARE GROUTED IN MORE THAN 4' LIFTS.
— AT TOP OF WALL, USE 4"x3' ¼"x 3" LONG (OR EQUAL) L W/
  ¾"x10" A.B THRU 3" LEG & PLATE INTO WALL & ¾" BOLT
  THRU 4" LEG & JOIST (OR BLOCK, WHERE ⊥ TO WALL W/
  2"ϕ WASH. AGAINST WOOD. WHERE JOIST ∥ WALL, BLOCK
  OUT 4' @ 32"O.C. & USE 10d @ 4"O.C. FOR SUB FLOOR.
— WATER PROOF ENTIRE WALL & USE 4"ϕ DRAIN TILE & GRAVEL
  @ BTM. OF WALL.
— DO NOT BACK FILL UNTIL FLOOR IS IN PLACE.

Figure 30–11 A drafter is often required to work from engineer's calculations when drawing retaining walls. Calculations usually show the math formulas to solve a problem and the written solution to the problem. It is the written solution to the problem that the drafter must make into a drawing. *Courtesy Ken Smith, Structureform Masters Inc.*

the written calculations and the sketch, a drafter can make a drawing similar to Figure 30–18.

The basement can be drawn by following steps 1 through 13. See Figure 30–13.

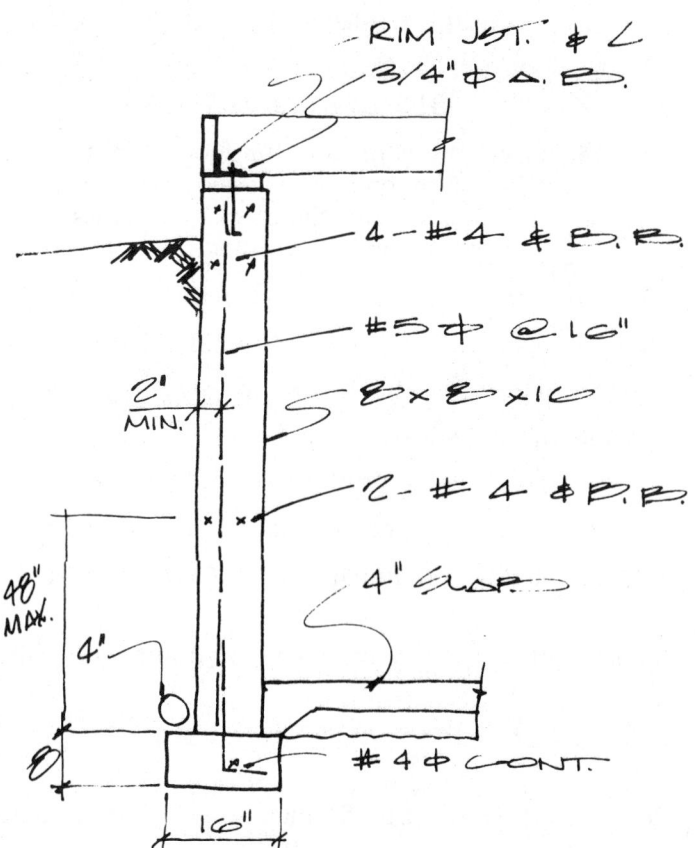

Step 1. Lay out the width of the building.

Step 2. Lay out a baseline for the bottom of the footings.

Step 3. Measure up from the baseline for the footings. Footings thickness is typically 8 in. deep for a one-story building and 12 in. deep for two or more stories.

Step 4. Lay out the 4 in. concrete slab.

Step 5. Lay out the wooden floor. The height of the basement will vary from 7'-0" to 8'-0" depending on its intended use.

Step 6. Lay out the 2 in. mudsill.

Step 7. Lay out the finished grade 8 in. minimum below the mudsill.

Step 8. Block out the width of the retaining wall. Walls are usually made from 8 in. thick material, but they can be made from 6 in. thick material if the support steel is increased.

Step 9. Block out the width of the footing. Footings for this type of wall are usually 16 in. wide, centered under the retaining wall.

Step 10. Lay out the 4 in. ledge and add 4 in. to the footing to support the brick veneer. An alternative to the ledge method is to form the wall 4 in. out from the face of the exterior wall to support the brick. See Figure 30–14.

Step 11. Draw a line to show the 4 in. fill material under the slab.

Figure 30–12 A sketch is often given to the drafter to help explain the written calculations. Many of the written calculations appear on the sketch but are not written in proper form.

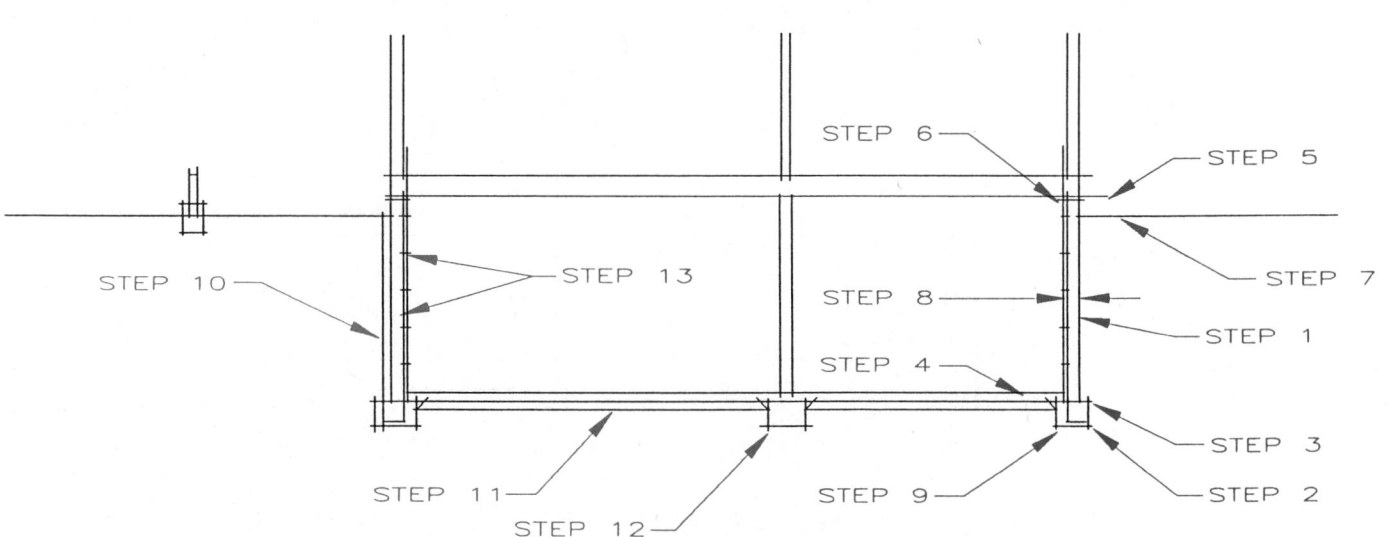

Figure 30–13 Retaining wall layout.

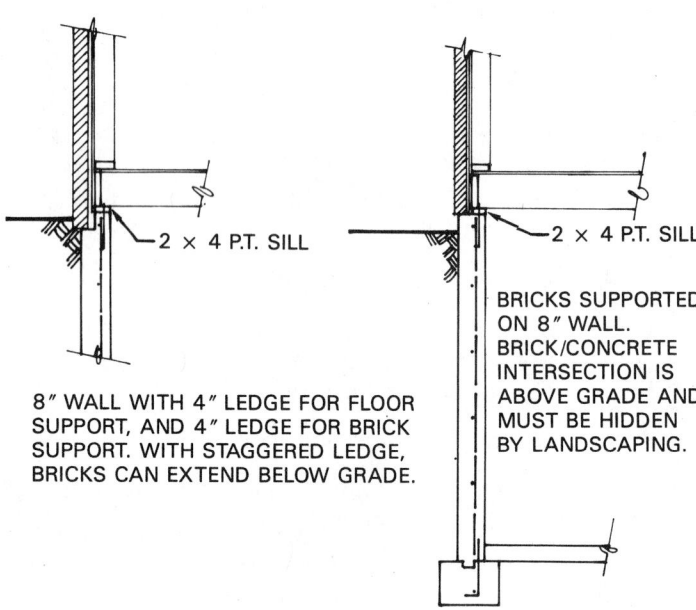

Figure 30-14 Common methods used for supporting brick veneer.

2 × 4 P.T. SILL

8" WALL WITH 4" LEDGE FOR FLOOR SUPPORT, AND 4" LEDGE FOR BRICK SUPPORT. WITH STAGGERED LEDGE, BRICKS CAN EXTEND BELOW GRADE.

2 × 4 P.T. SILL

BRICKS SUPPORTED ON 8" WALL. BRICK/CONCRETE INTERSECTION IS ABOVE GRADE AND MUST BE HIDDEN BY LANDSCAPING.

Step 12. Lay out the interior footings for bearing walls.

Step 13. Lay out the steel reinforcing for the wall. This will vary greatly depending on the seismic area you are in and how the wall is to be loaded. One typical placement pattern puts the vertical steel 2 in. from the inside face, and the horizontal steel 18 in. O.C. starting at the footing.

Finished Quality Lines—Structural Material Only

See Figure 30-15 for steps 14 through 21.

Step 14. Draw the plywood flooring with thin lines.

Step 15. Draw the floor joists with thin lines. Draw the floor joists with bold lines when they are perpendicular to the wall.

Step 16. Draw the mudsills and anchor bolts with bold lines.

Step 17. Draw the blocks with bold lines.

Step 18. Draw the walls and the footings with bold lines. If concrete blocks are used, draw the division lines of the blocks and crosshatch the blocks with thin lines.

Step 19. Draw the concrete slab with bold lines.

Step 20. Draw the wall steel with bold dashed lines.

Step 21. Complete the section as per Chapter 29.

Finishing Materials

See Figure 30-16 for steps 22 through 28.

Step 22. Draw the floor insulation with thin lines.

Step 23. Draw the finished grade with very bold lines.

Step 24. Draw the 4 in. diameter drain with thin lines.

Step 25. Draw the 8" × 24" gravel bed at the base of the wall.

Step 26. Draw the 4 in. fill materials with thin lines.

Step 27. Draw the brick veneer and the crosshatching with thin lines.

Step 28. Draw the welded wire mesh with thin dashed lines.

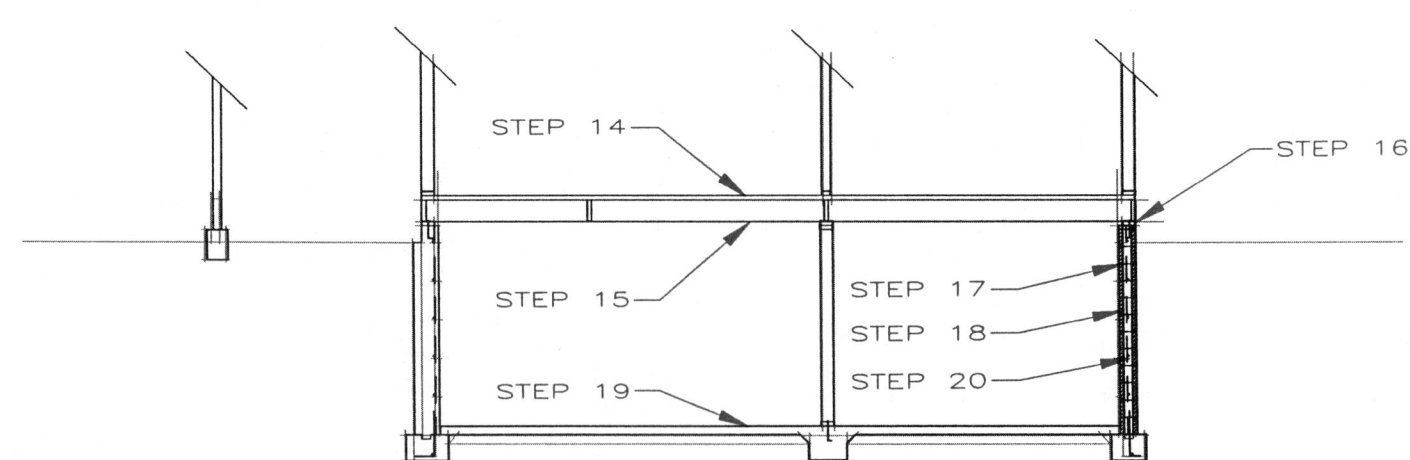

STEP 14

STEP 16

STEP 15

STEP 17

STEP 18

STEP 20

STEP 19

Figure 30-15 Finished quality lines of the structural material for a basement foundation system. The left wall is drawn showing a poured concrete wall. The right wall is drawn showing 8 × 8 × 16 concrete blocks. Generally the two wall systems are not used together.

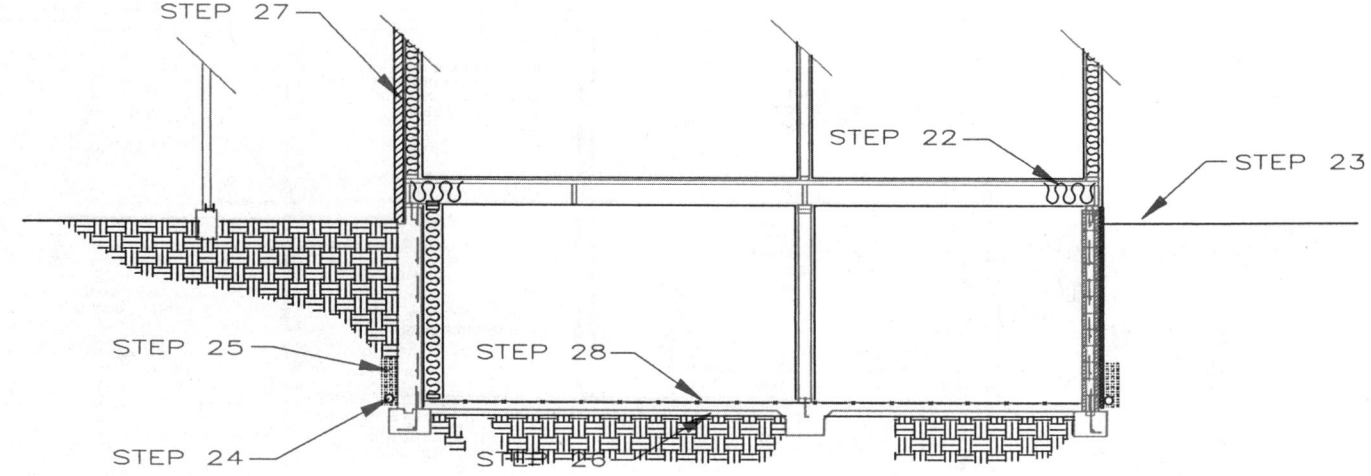

Figure 30–16 Finishing materials for a basement foundation system.

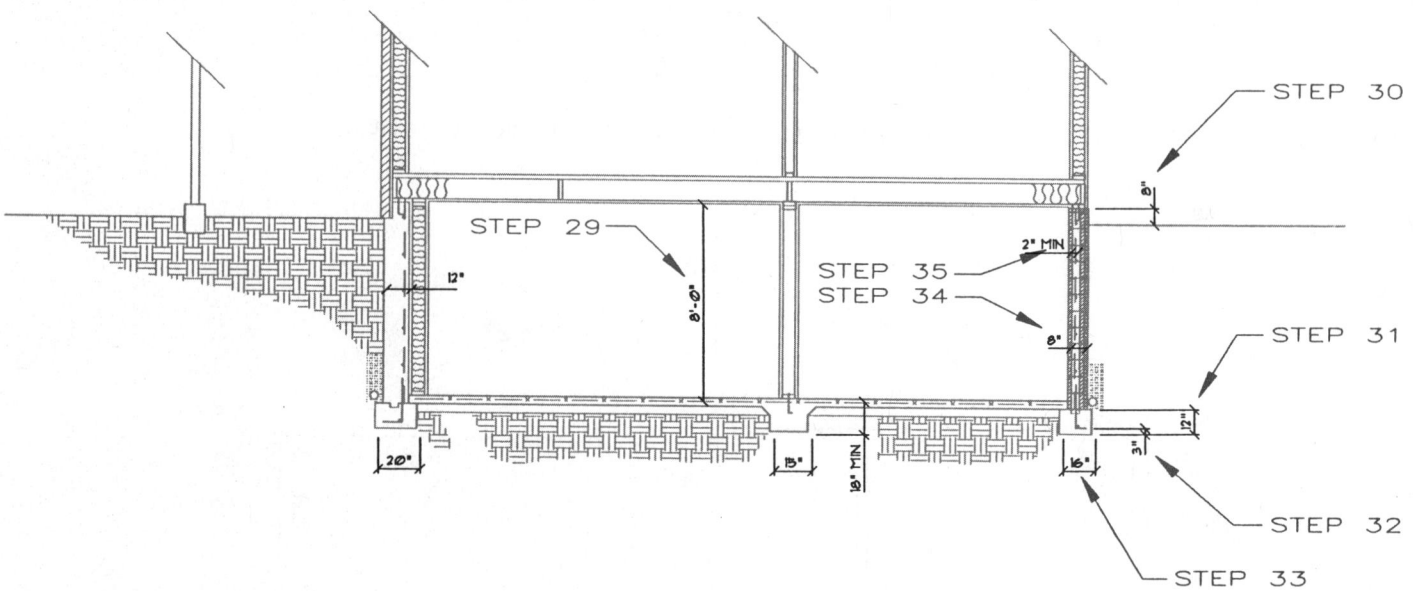

Figure 30–17 Required dimensions for a basement foundation system.

Dimensions

See Figure 30–17 for steps 29 through 35. Place the needed leader and dimensions lines to locate the following dimensions:

Step 29. Floor to ceiling.

Step 30. Top of wall to finished grade.

Step 31. Height of footing.

Step 32. Footing steel to bottom of footing.

Step 33. Footing width.

Step 34. Wall width.

Step 35. Edge of wall to vertical steel.

Notes

Step 36. Letter the section notes as shown in Figure 30–18. Remember that these notes are only guidelines and may vary slightly because of local standards. Typical notes should include the following:

a. 2 × __ FLOOR JOIST @ __″ O.C.

b. SOLID BLOCK @ 48″ O.C.—48″ OUT FROM WALL WHERE JOISTS ARE PARALLEL TO WALL.

c. 2 × __ RIM JOIST W/ A-34 ANCHORS BY SIMPSON CO. OR EQUAL.

d. 2 × 6 P.T. SILL W/ ½″ DIA × 10″ A.B. @ 24″ O.C. W/ 2″ DIA WASHERS.

e. 8″ CONC. WALL W/ #4 @ 18″ O.C. EA. WAY.
8 × 8 × 16 GRADE 'A' CONC. BLOCKS W/ #4 @ 16″ O.C. EA. WAY—SOLID GROUT ALL STEEL CELLS.

f. WATERPROOF THIS WALL W/ HOT ASPHALTIC EMULSION.

g. 4″ DIA DRAIN IN 8 × 24 MIN. GRAVEL BED.

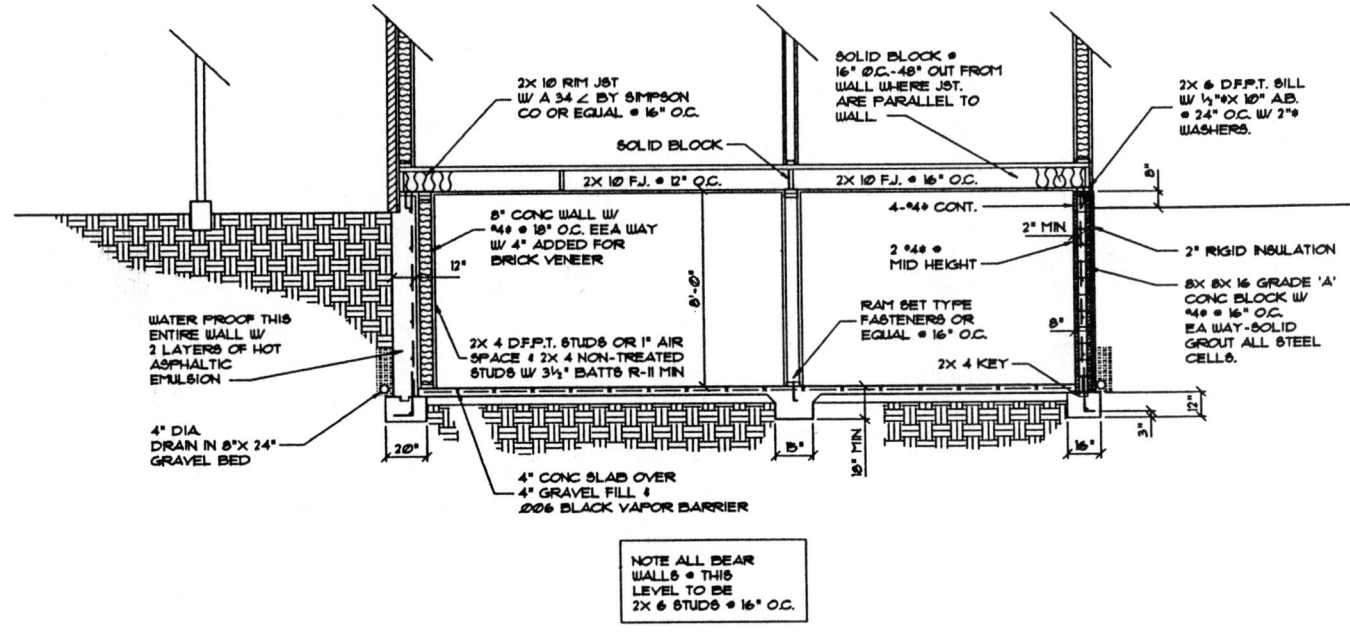

Figure 30-18 Typical notes for a basement foundation system.

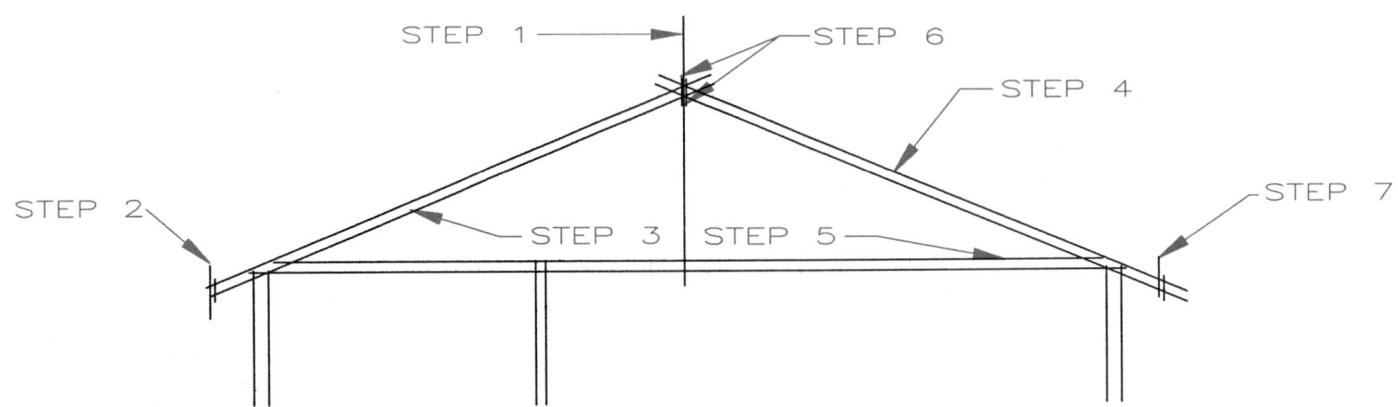

Figure 30-19 Layout of a conventionally framed roof.

h. 2 × 4 KEY.

i. 4″ CONC. SLAB OVER 4″ GRAVEL FILL AND 55# ROLLED ROOFING.

or

4″ CONC. SLAB OVER 4″ SAND FILL AND 6 MIL VAPOR BARRIER, AND 2″ SAND FILL.

Note: Wire mesh is often placed in the concrete slab to help control cracking. This mesh is typically called out on the sections and foundation plan as 6″ × 6″—#10 × #10 W.W.M.

◤ CONVENTIONAL (STICK) ROOF FRAMING

The two types of conventional roof framing presented are flat and vaulted ceilings. You will notice many similar features between the two styles.

Flat Ceiling

Use light construction lines to lay out the drawing. See Figure 30-19 for steps 1 through 7.

Step 1.   Place a vertical line to represent the ridge.

Step 2.   Locate each overhang.

Step 3.   Lay out the bottom side of the rafter. Starting at the intersection of the ceiling and the interior side of the exterior wall, draw a line at a 5/12 pitch. Do this for both sides of the roof. Both lines should meet at the ridge line.

Step 4.   Lay out the top side of the rafters.

Step 5.   Lay out the top side of the ceiling joist.

Step 6.   Lay out the ridge board.

Step 7.   Lay out the fascias.

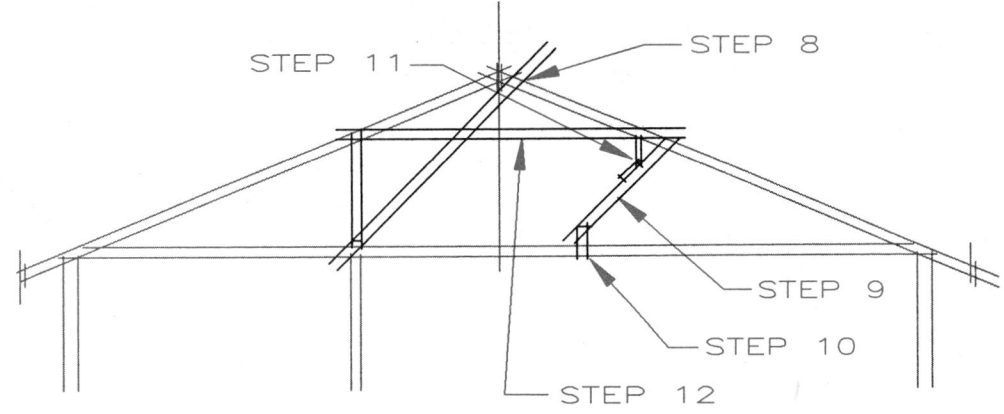

Figure 30–20 Layout of interior supports for a conventionally framed roof.

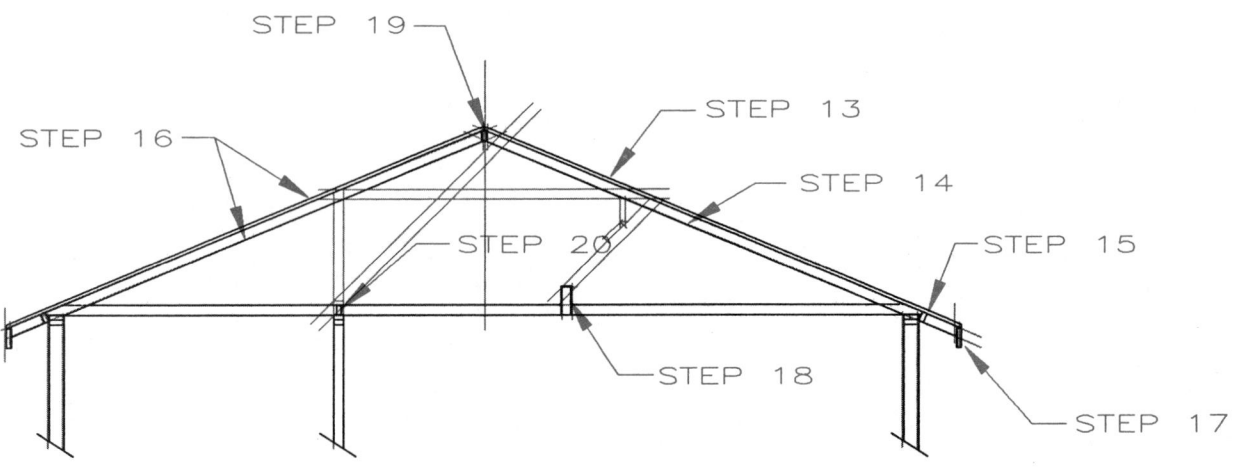

Figure 30–21 Finished quality lines of structural materials for a conventionally framed roof.

Lay Out the Interior Supports

See Figure 30–20 for steps 8 through 12.

Step 8.   Lay out the ridge brace and support.

Step 9.   Lay out the purlin braces and supports.

Step 10. Lay out the strong backs.

Step 11. Lay out the purlins.

Step 12. Lay out the collar ties.

Finished Quality Lines—Structural Members Only

See Figure 30–21 for steps 13 through 20.

Step 13. Draw the plywood sheathing with thin lines.

Step 14. Draw the rafters with thin lines.

Step 15. Draw the eave blocking with bold lines.

Step 16. Repeat steps 13 through 15 for the opposite side of the roof.

Step 17. Draw the fascias with bold lines.

Step 18. Draw the strong backs with bold lines.

Step 19. Draw the ridge board with bold lines.

Step 20. Draw blocking with bold lines.

Interior Support Finished Quality Lines

See Figure 30–22 for steps 21 through 24.

Step 21. Draw all plates with bold lines.

Step 22. Draw all braces with thin lines.

Step 23. Draw all purlins with bold lines.

Step 24. Draw the collar tie with thin lines.

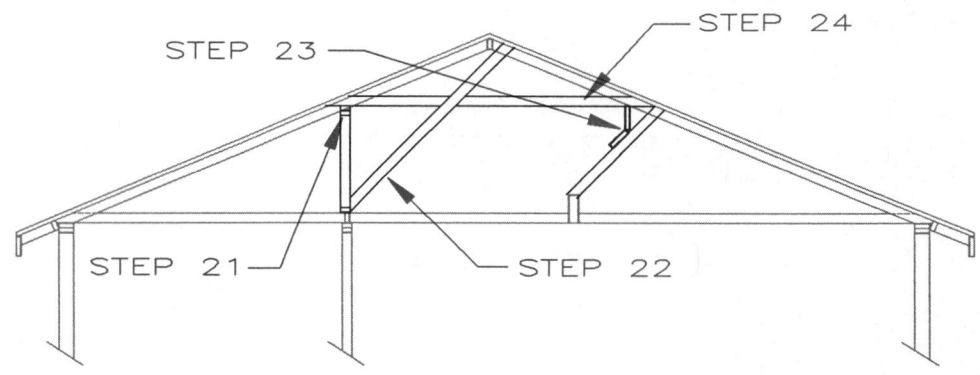

Figure 30–22 Finished quality lines of interior supports.

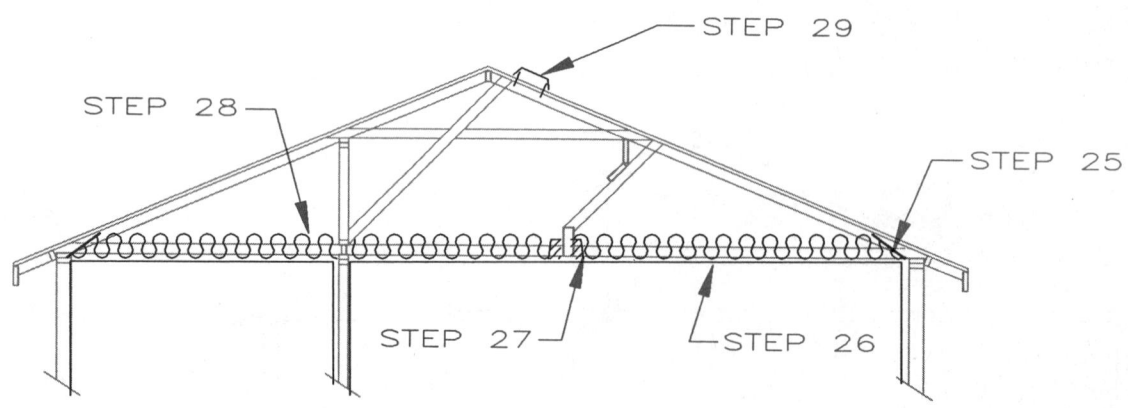

Figure 30–23 Finishing materials for a conventionally framed roof.

Dimensions

There are usually no dimensions required for the roof framing.

Finishing Materials

See Figure 30–23 for steps 25 through 29.

Step 25.   Draw baffles with bold lines.

Step 26.   Draw the finished ceiling with thin lines.

Step 27.   Draw joist hangers with thin lines.

Step 28.   Draw the 10 in. thick insulation.

Step 29.   Draw the ridge vents.

Notes

See Chapter 29 for a complete listing of notes that apply to the roof. In addition to those notes, see

Figure 30–24 for the notes needed to describe the interior supports. Roof notes should include the following:

a. 2 × __ RIDGE BOARD.
b. 2 × __ RAFTERS @ __" O.C.
c. 2 × __ COLLAR TIE @ 48" O.C. MAX.
d. 2 × __ PURLIN.
e. 2 × 4 BRACE @ 48" O.C. MAX.

VAULTED CEILINGS

If the entire roof level is to have vaulted ceilings, the process of laying it out is very similar to the procedure for laying out a stick roof with flat ceilings. Usually though, part of the roof has 2 × 6 rafters with flat ceilings and a vaulted ceiling using 2 × 12 rafter/ceiling joists. In order to make the two roofs align on the outside, the plate must be lowered in

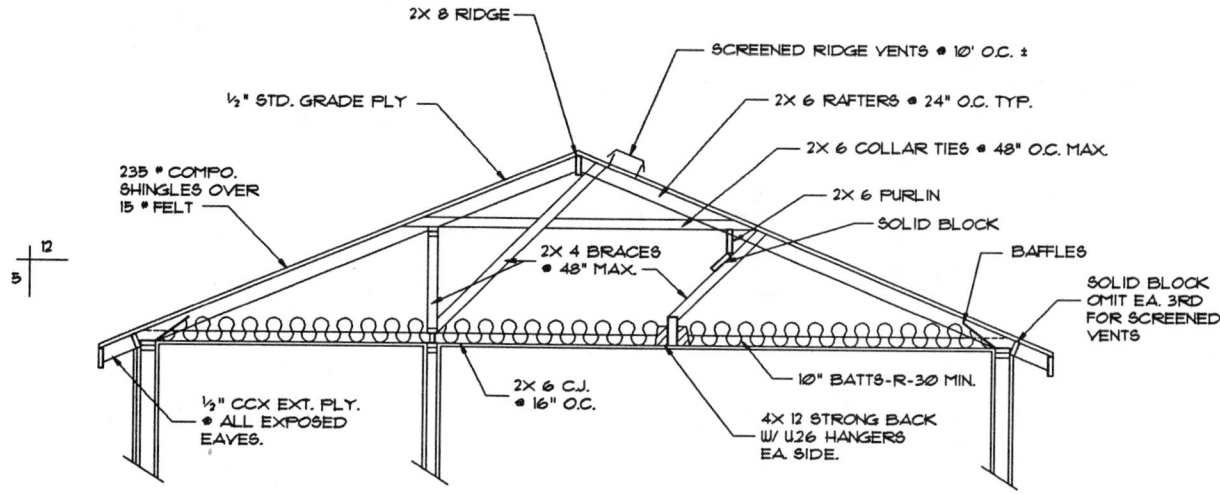

Figure 30–24 Typical notes for a conventionally framed roof.

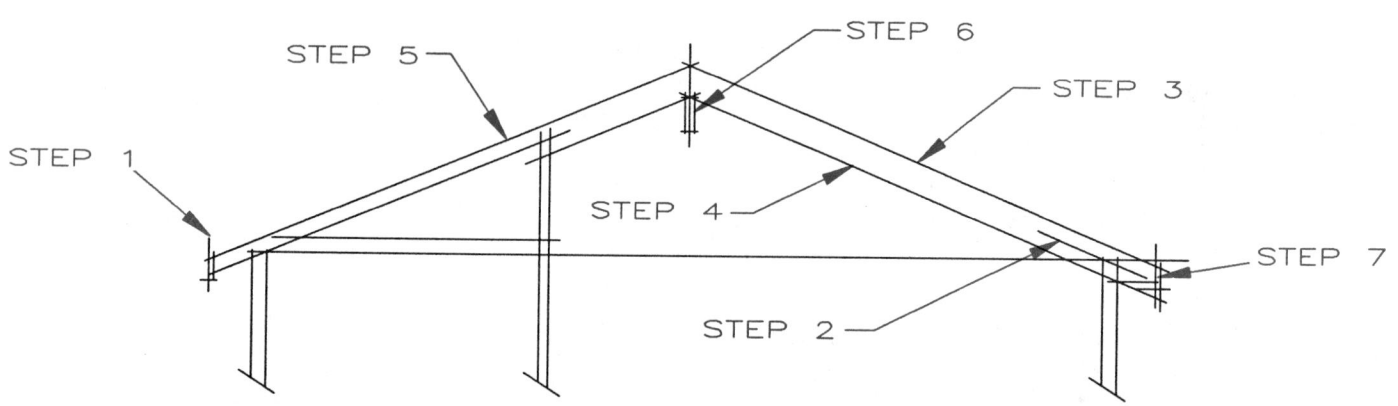

Figure 30–25 Layout of a vaulted ceiling.

the area having the vaulted ceilings. See Figure 30–25 for steps 1 through 7 of laying out the vaulted ceiling. Use construction lines for all steps.

Step 1.   Lay out the overhangs.

Step 2.   Lay out the bottom side of the 2 × 6 rafter.

Step 3.   Lay out the top side of the 2 × 6 rafter. For this example, this size rafter is used throughout the balance of the house, not the 2 × 12 rafter/ceiling joist.

Step 4.   Measure down from the top side of the rafter drawn in step 3 to establish the bottom of the 2 × 12 rafter/ceiling joist. Notice that the 2 × 12 extends below the top plate of the wall.

Step 5.   Repeat steps 2 through 4 for the opposite side of the roof.

Step 6.   Lay out the ridge beam. See Figure 30–26 for two common methods of placing the ridge beam.

Step 7.   Lay out the fascias and the rafter tail cut for the 2 × 12 rafter/ceiling joists.

Finished Quality Lines—Structural Members Only

See Figure 30–27 for steps 8 through 12.

Step 8.   Draw the plywood sheathing with thin lines.

Step 9.   Draw the rafter/ceiling joist with thin lines.

Step 10.   Draw all blocks, plates, and fascias with bold lines.

Step 11.   Draw the ridge beam with bold lines.

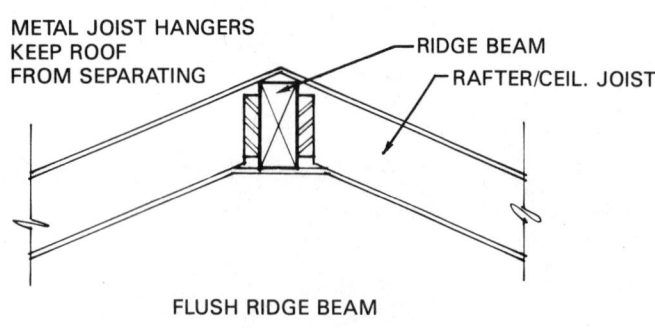

METAL JOIST HANGERS
KEEP ROOF
FROM SEPARATING

RIDGE BEAM

RAFTER/CEIL. JOIST

FLUSH RIDGE BEAM

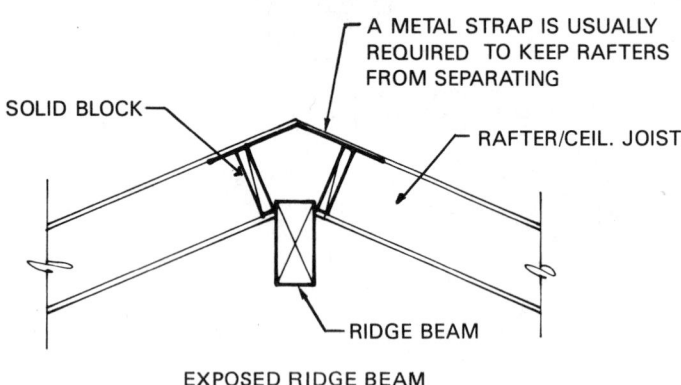

A METAL STRAP IS USUALLY
REQUIRED TO KEEP RAFTERS
FROM SEPARATING

SOLID BLOCK

RAFTER/CEIL. JOIST

RIDGE BEAM

EXPOSED RIDGE BEAM

Figure 30–26 The ridge beam placement can be either flush or exposed.

Step 12. Repeat steps 8 through 10 for the opposite side of the roof.

Finishing Materials

See Figure 30–28 for steps 13 through 17.

Step 13. Draw the baffles with bold lines.

Step 14. Draw the insulation with thin lines.

Step 15. Draw the ceiling interior finish with thin lines.

Step 16. Draw the ridge vents and notches with thin lines.

Step 17. Draw the metal hangers and crosshatch with thin lines. Depending on the ridge beam option that you drew, joist hangers may not be required.

Dimensions

No dimensions are needed to describe the roof. You will need to give the floor-to-plate dimension. List this dimension as 7'-6" ± VERIFY AT JOB SITE.

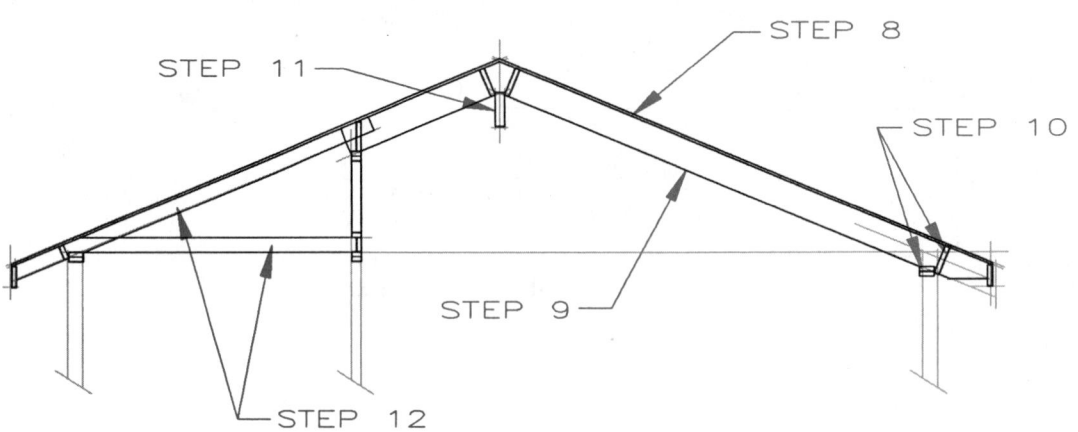

STEP 11   STEP 8

STEP 10

STEP 9

STEP 12

Figure 30–27 Finished quality lines of structural materials for a vaulted roof.

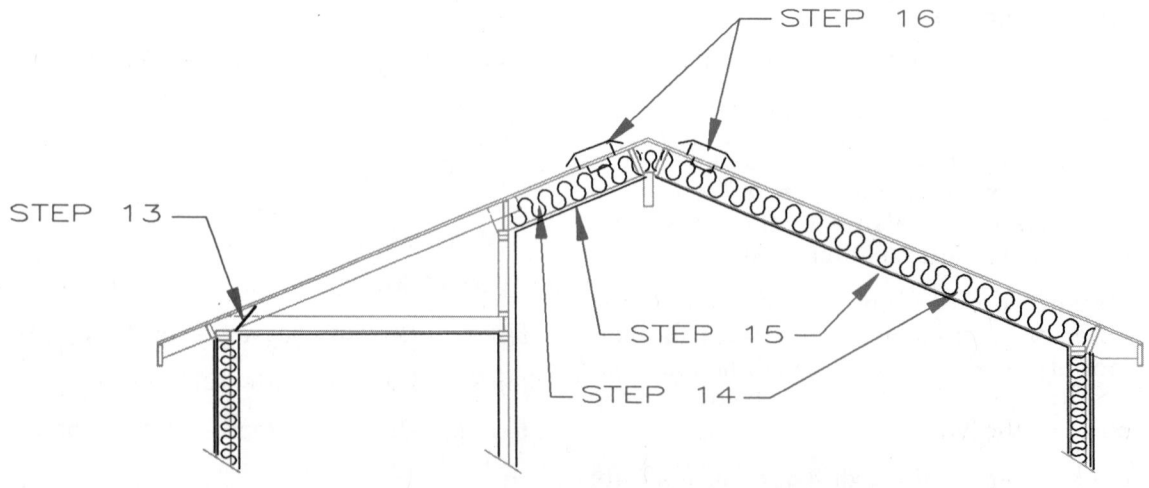

STEP 16

STEP 13

STEP 15

STEP 14

Figure 30–28 Finishing materials for a vaulted roof.

By telling the framer to verify the height at the job site you are alerting the framer to a problem. This is a problem that can be solved much easier at the job site than at the drafting table.

Notes

See Chapter 29 for a complete listing of notes that apply to the roof. In addition to those notes, see Figure 30–29 for the notes needed to describe the roof completely. The notes should include the following:

a. __ × __ RIDGE BEAM.
b. 2 × __ RAFT./C.J. @ __" O.C.
c. U-210 JST. HGR. BY SIMPSON CO. OR EQUAL.
d. SCREENED RIDGE VENTS @ EA. 3RD. SPACE. NOTCH RAFT. FOR AIR FLOW.
e. SOLID BLOCK W/ 3-1" DIA SCREENED VENTS @ EA. SPACE.
f. NOTCH RAFTER TAILS AS REQD.
g. LINE OF INTERIOR FINISH.
h. 10" BATTS—R-30 MIN.

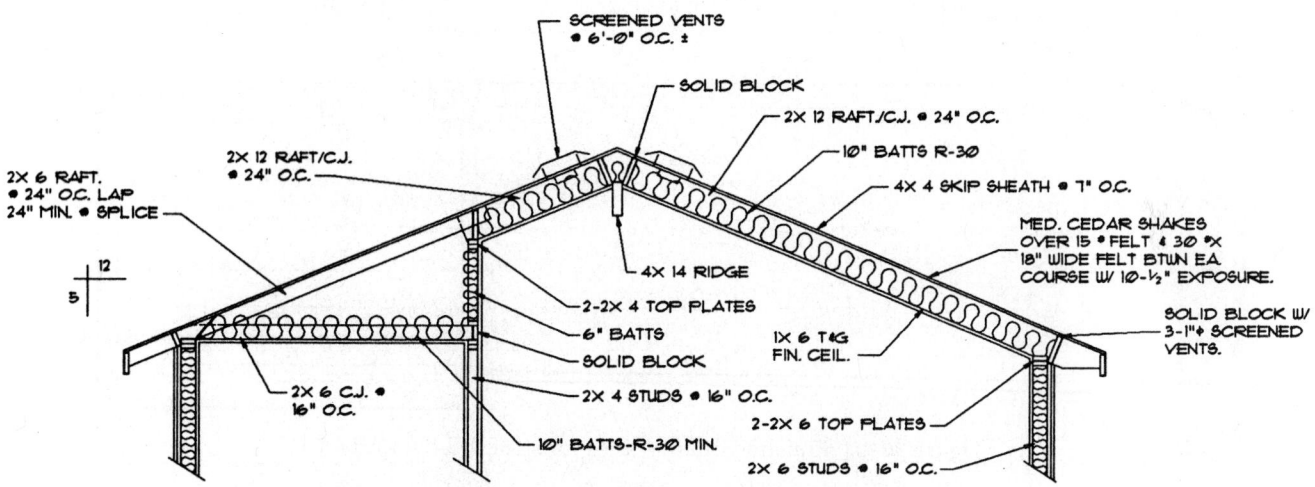

Figure 30–29 Notes for a vaulted ceiling.

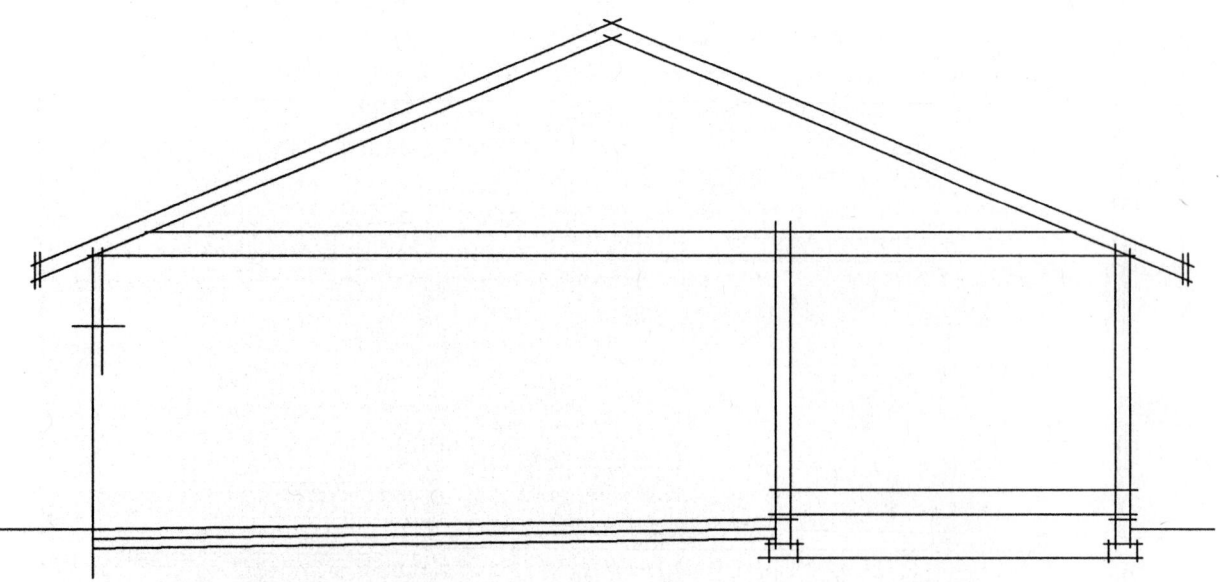

Figure 30–30 Layout of a section drawn through the garage and living area.

GARAGE/RESIDENCE SECTION

Drawing this section is similar to drawing the sections just described since it is a combination of several types of sections. The steps needed to draw this section can be seen in Figures 30–30 through 30–34.

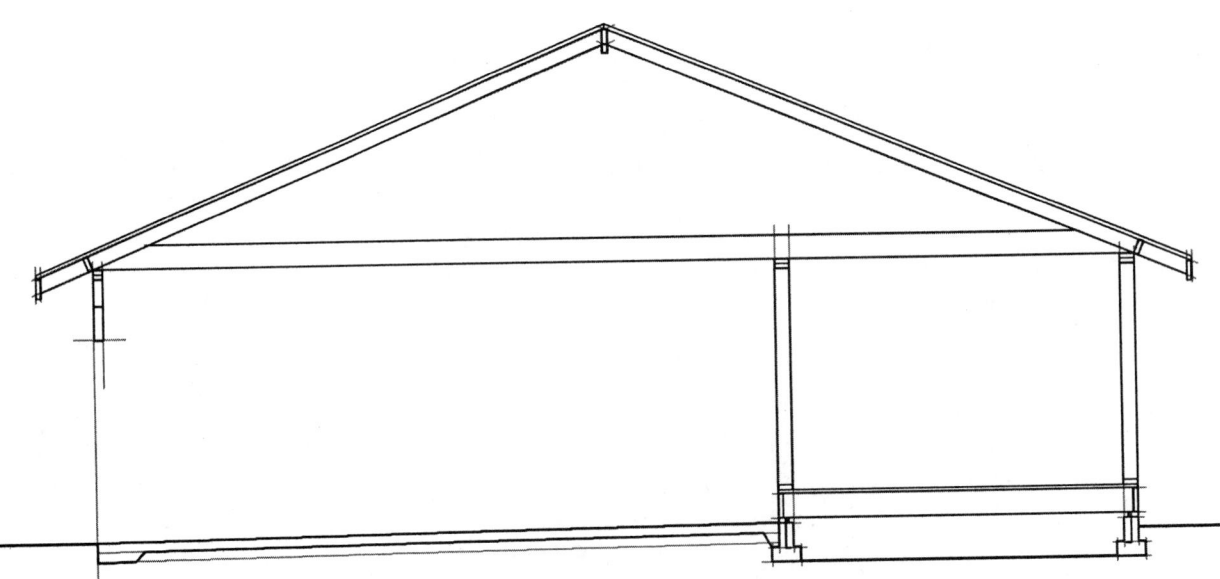

Figure 30–31 Finished quality lines for structural materials.

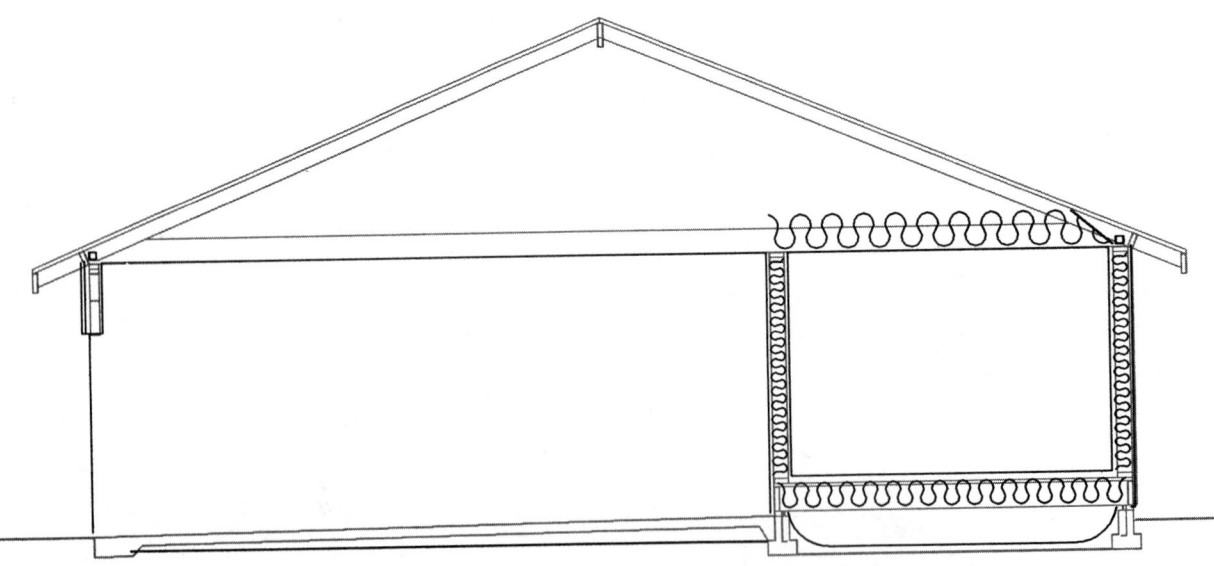

Figure 30–32 Finishing materials.

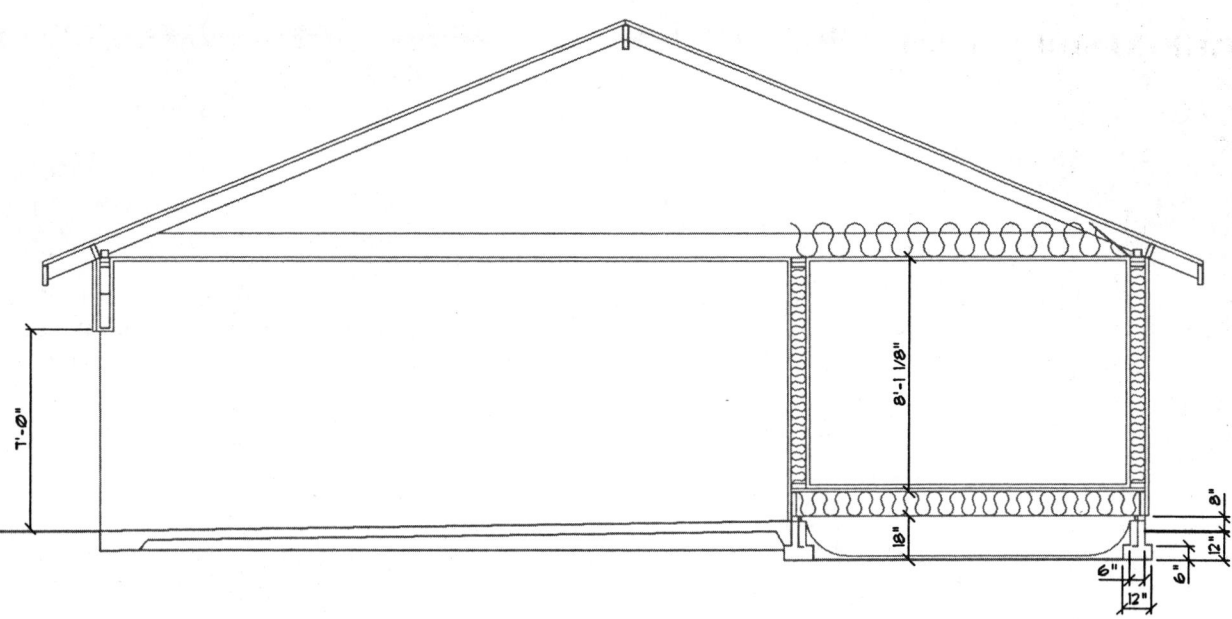

Figure 30–33 Typical dimensions.

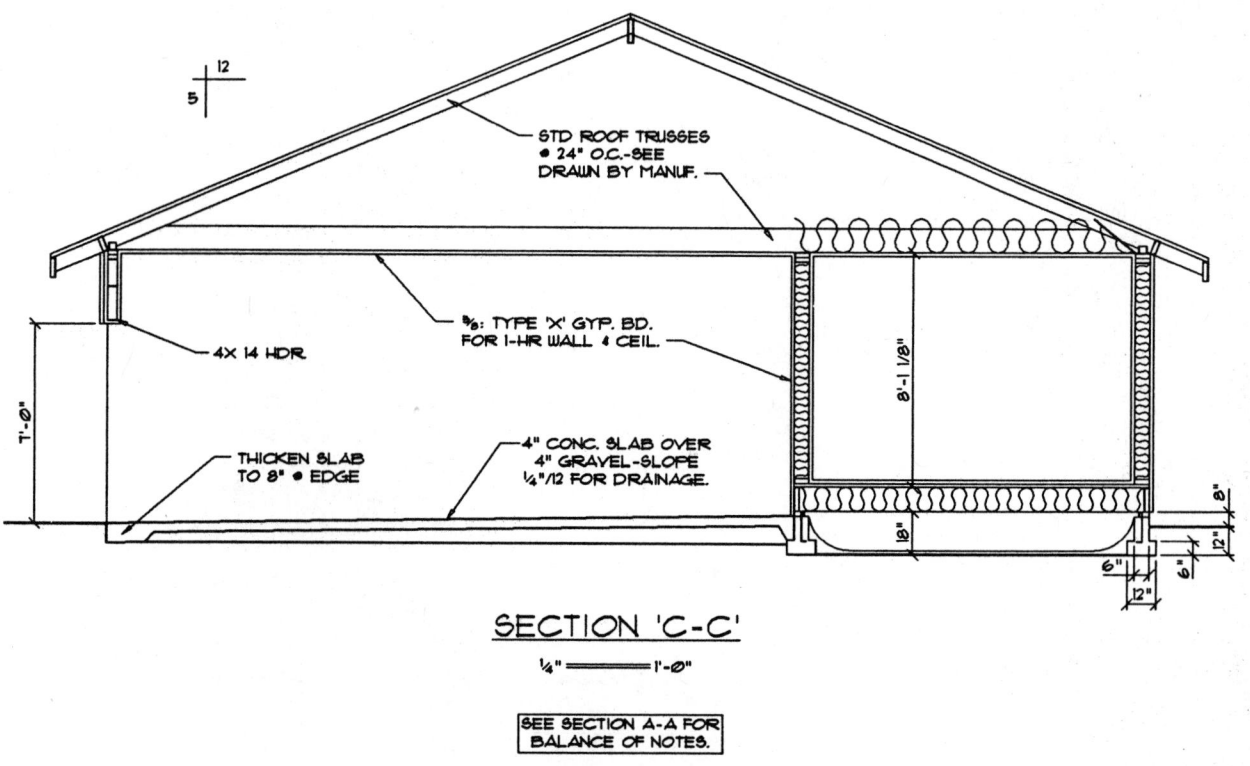

STD ROOF TRUSSES
@ 24" O.C.-SEE
DRAWN BY MANUF.

⅝: TYPE 'X' GYP. BD.
FOR I-HR WALL & CEIL.

4X 14 HDR

THICKEN SLAB
TO 8" @ EDGE

4" CONC. SLAB OVER
4" GRAVEL-SLOPE
¼"/12 FOR DRAINAGE.

SECTION 'C-C'

¼" ══════ 1'-∅"

SEE SECTION A-A FOR
BALANCE OF NOTES.

Figure 30–34 A completed section through the garage and living area.

ALTERNATE LAYOUT TECHNIQUES TEST

DIRECTIONS

Use an 8½ × 11 drawing sheet and identify each numbered part on the section drawing shown on pp. 524 and 525 with its complete name. Observe the following:

1. Use ⅛ in. guidelines for all lettering.
2. Letter your name, Alternate Layout Techniques Test, and the date at the top of the sheet.

3. Letter the part number and provide the name of that part.
4. Do all lettering with vertical uppercase architectural letters. Answers may be prepared on a word processor if appropriate with course guidelines.
5. Your grade will be based on correct answers and quality of lettering technique.

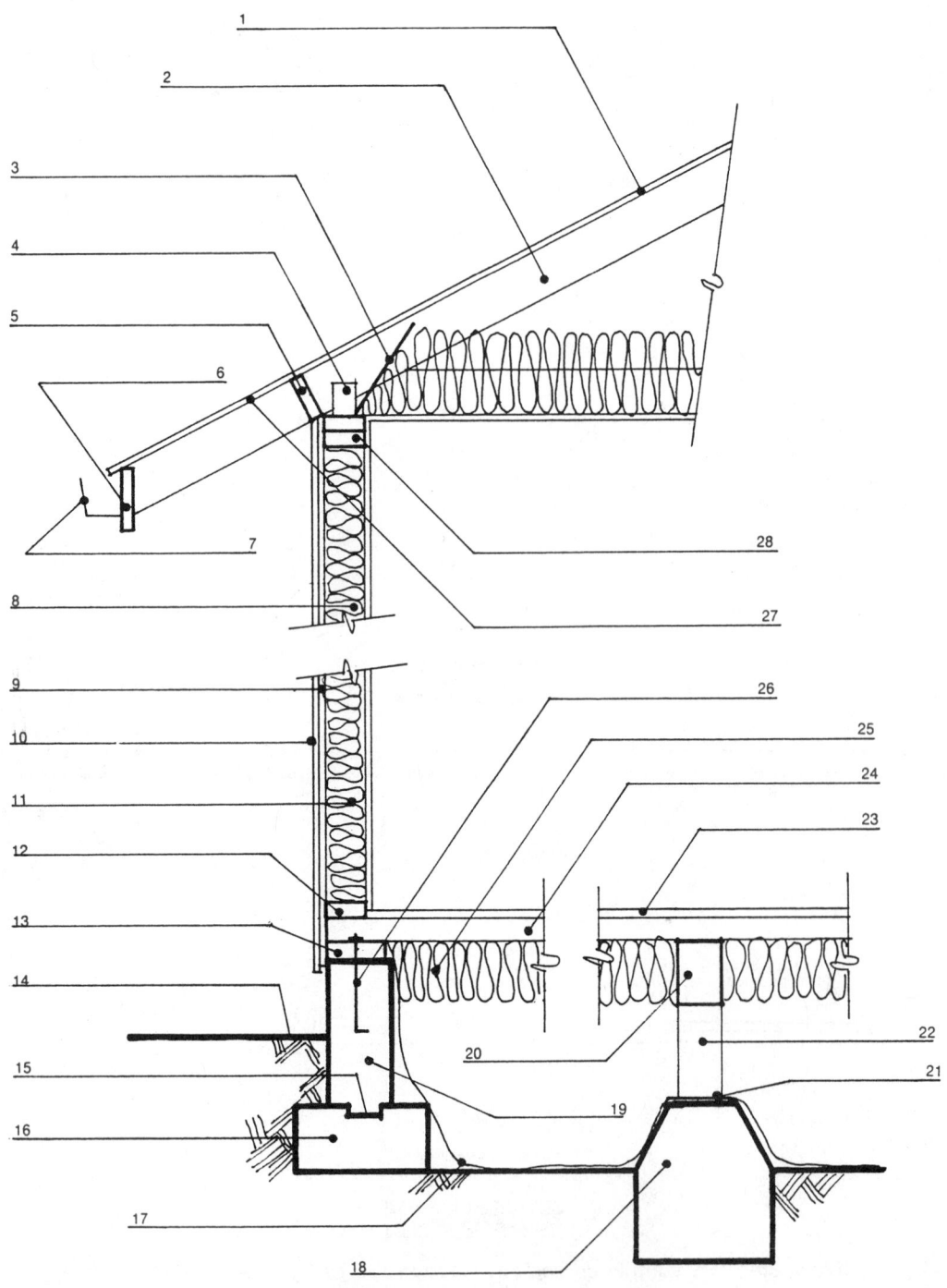

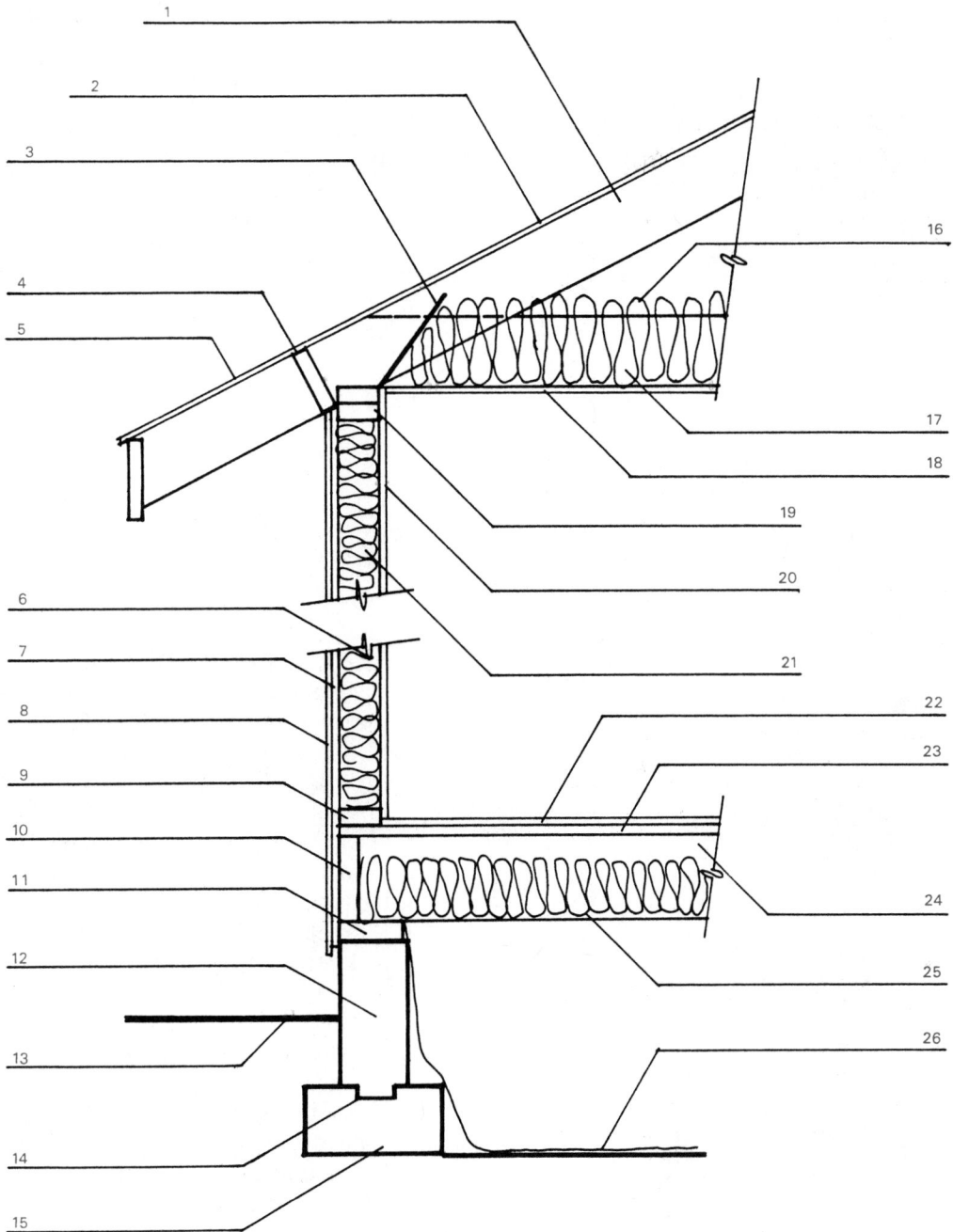

QUESTIONS

1. Sketch and dimension an exterior footing for a concrete slab supporting two floors.
2. What thickness of floor decking is typically used for floors using the post-and-beam method?
3. What type of line quality is used to represent the mudsill?
4. How are stem walls represented on the finished drawing?
5. What is the thickness of the vapor barrier used under a crawl space?
6. The top of the concrete slab must be ___" above the finished grade.
7. Basement walls are typically ___" wide.
8. What determines the amount of structural steel placed in a retaining wall?
9. Describe a common blocking pattern that is typically used to support the top of a concrete retaining wall.
10. Sketch and label the framing for a stick framed roof showing rafters, ceiling joists, ridge, purlins, purlin blocks, and braces.
11. On a separate sheet of paper, list each part shown on the accompanying drawings.

Chapter 31
Stair Construction and Layout

STAIRS WERE introduced with floor plans in Section 3. Minimal information was provided in that section so that you could draw stairs on floor plans. This chapter will show you how to draw stairs in section. Step-by-step instructions will be given for the layout and drawing of straight run, open, and U-shaped stair layouts.

STAIR TERMINOLOGY

There are several basic terms you will need to be familiar with when working with stairs. Each can be seen in Figure 31–1.

- *Run.* The run is the horizontal distance from end to end of the stairs.
- *Rise.* The rise is the vertical distance from top to bottom of the stairs.
- *Tread.* The tread is the horizontal step of the stairs. It is usually made from 1 in. material on enclosed stairs and 2 in. material for open stairs. Tread width is the measurement from the face of the riser to the nosing. The nosing is the portion of the tread that extends past the riser.

- *Riser.* The riser is the vertical backing between the treads. It is usually made from 1 in. material for enclosed stairs and is not used on open stairs.
- *Stringer.* The stringer, or stair jack, is the support for the treads. A 2 × 12 notched stringer is typically used for enclosed stairs. For an open stair a 4 × 14 is common, but sizes vary greatly. Figure 31–2 shows the stringers, risers, and treads.
- *Kick Block.* The kick block, or kicker, is used to keep the bottom of the stringer from sliding on the floor when downward pressure is applied to the stringer.
- *Headroom.* Headroom is the vertical distance measured from the tread nosing to a wall or floor above the stairs. Building codes will specify a minimum size.
- *Handrail.* The handrail is the railing that you slide your hand along as you walk down the stairs.
- *Guardrail.* The guardrail is the railing placed around an opening for the stairs.

Type X gypsum (GYP.) board ⅝ in. thick is required by the U.B.C. for enclosing all usable storage space under the stairs. This is a gypsum board that has a 1 hr fire rating. Figure 31–3 shows common stair dimensions from three codes.

DETERMINING RISE AND RUN

Building codes dictate the maximum rise of the stairs. To determine the actual rise, the total height from floor to floor must be known. Review Chapter 29,

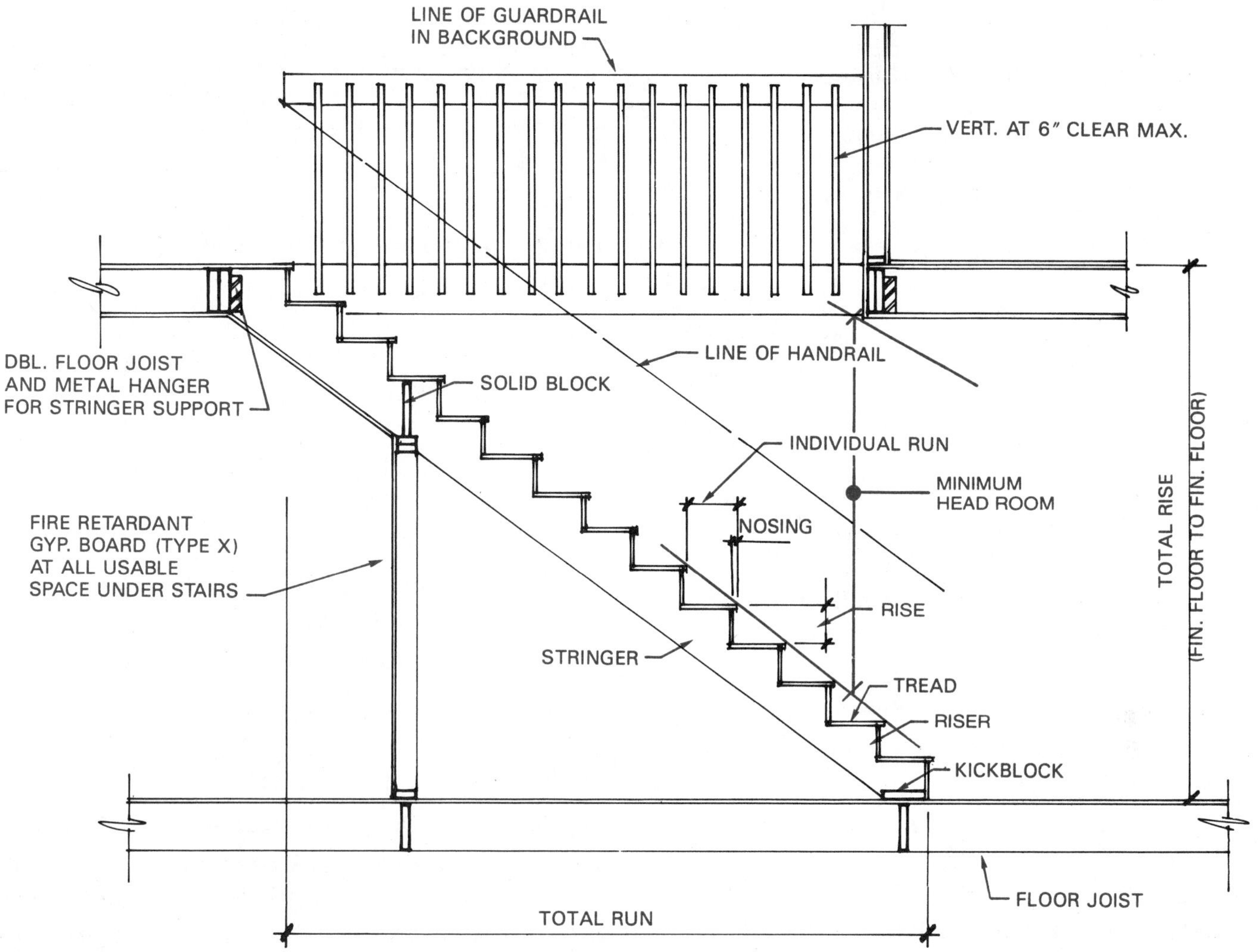

LINE OF GUARDRAIL IN BACKGROUND

VERT. AT 6″ CLEAR MAX.

LINE OF HANDRAIL

DBL. FLOOR JOIST AND METAL HANGER FOR STRINGER SUPPORT

SOLID BLOCK

INDIVIDUAL RUN

MINIMUM HEAD ROOM

FIRE RETARDANT GYP. BOARD (TYPE X) AT ALL USABLE SPACE UNDER STAIRS

NOSING

RISE

TOTAL RISE (FIN. FLOOR TO FIN. FLOOR)

STRINGER

TREAD

RISER

KICKBLOCK

FLOOR JOIST

TOTAL RUN

Figure 31–1 Common stair terms.

Figure 31–2 Multilevel stairs with the upper level stringers in place, ready for the treads and risers. The lower-level stairs are complete. *Courtesy Southern Forest Products Association.*

TYPE	UBC	CABO/BOCA*	SBC
Straight Treads			
Rise	8″ max.	8¼″ max.	7¾″ max.
Run	9″ min.	9″ min.	**9″ min. excluding nosing 10″ min. including nosing
Headroom	6′–6″ min.	6′–6″ min. 6′–8″ min. CABO	6′–6″ min.
Tread Width	30″ min.	36″ min.	36″ min.
Handrail	30″ min. 34″ max.	30″ min.	30″ min. 34″ max.
Guardrail	36″ min.	36″ min.	36″ min.
Winders			
Tread Depth	9″ @ 12″ 6″ min.	9″ @ 12″ 6″ min.	9″ @ 12″ 6″ min.
Spiral			
Tread Depth	7½″ @ 12″	7½″ @ 12″	7½″ @ 12″
Rise	9½″ max.	9½″ max.	9½″ max.
Radius	26″ min.	26″ min.	26″ min.

* CABO/BOCA requirements are the same except as noted.
** Treads and risers of required stairs shall be proportioned so that the sum of two risers and one tread, excluding nosing, is not less than 24 in. or more than 25 in.

Figure 31–3 Basic stair dimensions according to the four national building codes.

| Step 1. | Determine the total rise in inches. |
| | 3/4   plywood |

Step 1.   Determine the total rise in inches.
              3/4   plywood
              9 1/4   floor joist
              3   top plates
              92 5/8   studs
              1 1/2   bottom plate
          107.125 in. total rise

Step 2.   Find the number of risers required. Divide rise by 8 (8 in. is the maximum rise of UBC).

$$8 \overline{)107.125} = 13.4$$

Since you cannot have .4 risers, the number will be rounded up to 14 risers.

Step 3.   Find the number of treads required. Number of treads equals Rise − Run. 14 − 1 = 13 treads required.

Step 4.   Multiply the length of each tread by the number of treads to find the total run.

Figure 31–4 Determining the rise and run needed for a flight of stairs.

Figure 29–15, for the floor-to-ceiling calculation. By adding the floor-to-ceiling height, the depth of the floor joist, and the depth of the floor covering, the total rise can be found. The total rise can then be divided by the maximum allowable rise to determine the number of steps required as shown in Figure 31–4.

Once the required rise is determined, this information should be stored in your memory for future reference. Of the residential stairs you will lay out in your career as a drafter, probably 99 percent will have the same rise. So with a standard 8'-0" ceiling, you will always need 14 risers.

Once the rise is known, the required number of treads can be found easily since there will always be one less tread than the number of risers. Thus, a typical stair for a house with 8'-0" ceilings will have 14 risers and 13 treads. If each tread is 10½ in. wide, the total run can be found by multiplying 10½ in. (the width) by 13 (the number of treads required). Armed with this basic information, you are now ready to lay out the stairs. The layout for a straight stairway will be described first.

◤ STRAIGHT STAIR LAYOUT

The straight-run stair is by far the most common type of stair that will need to be drawn. It is a stair that goes from one floor to another in one straight run. An example of a straight-run stair can be seen in Figure 31–5. See Figure 31–6 for steps 1 through 4.

Step 1.   Lay out walls that may be near the stairs.

Step 2.   Lay out each floor level.

Step 3.   Lay out one end of the stairs. If no dimensions are available on the floor plans, scale your drawing.

Step 4.   Figure and lay out the total run of the stairs.

Step 5.   Lay out the required risers. See Figure 31–7.

Step 6.   Lay out the required treads. See Figure 31–7.

Step 7.   Lay out the stringer, and outline the treads and risers as shown in Figure 31–8.

Drawing the Stairs with Finished Quality Lines

Use a thin line to draw the stairs unless otherwise noted. See Figure 31–9 for steps 8 through 11.

Step 8.   Draw the treads and risers.

Step 9.   Draw the bottom side of the stringer.

Step 10.   Draw the upper stringer support or support wall where the stringer intersects the floor.

Step 11.   Draw metal hangers and crosshatch them if there is no support wall.

See Figure 31–10 for steps 12 through 17.

Step 12.   Draw the kick block with bold lines.

Step 13.   Draw any intermediate support walls.

Step 14.   Draw solid blocking with bold lines.

Step 15.   Draw the ⅝ in. type X gypsum board.

Step 16.   Draw any floors or walls which are over the stairs.

Step 17.   Draw the handrail with thin dashed lines.

Dimensions and Notes

See Figure 31–11 for steps 18 through 24. Place the required leader and dimension lines to locate the following needed dimensions:

Step 18.   Total rise

Step 19.   Total run

Step 20.   Rise

Step 21.   Run

Step 22.   Headroom

Step 24.   Handrail

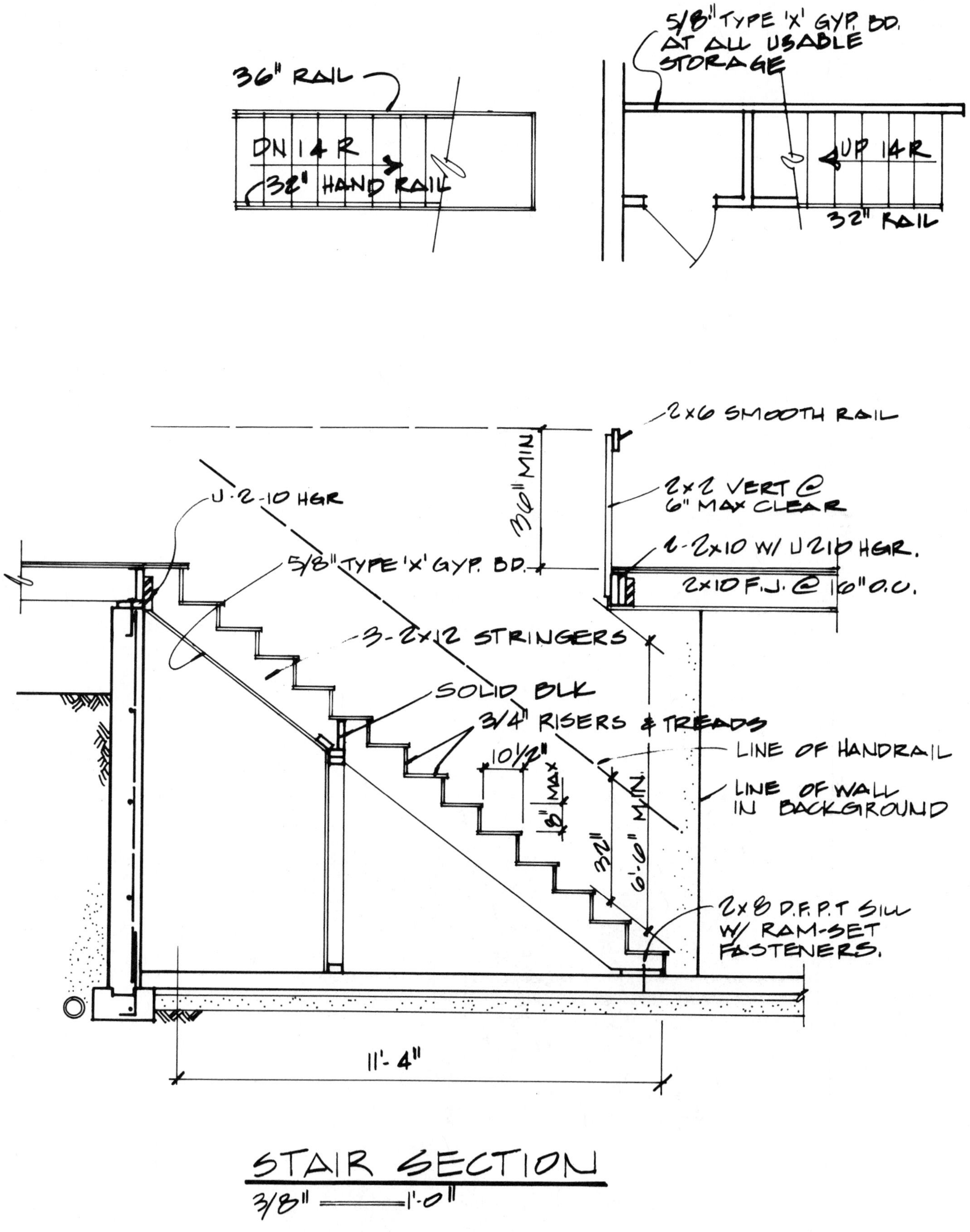

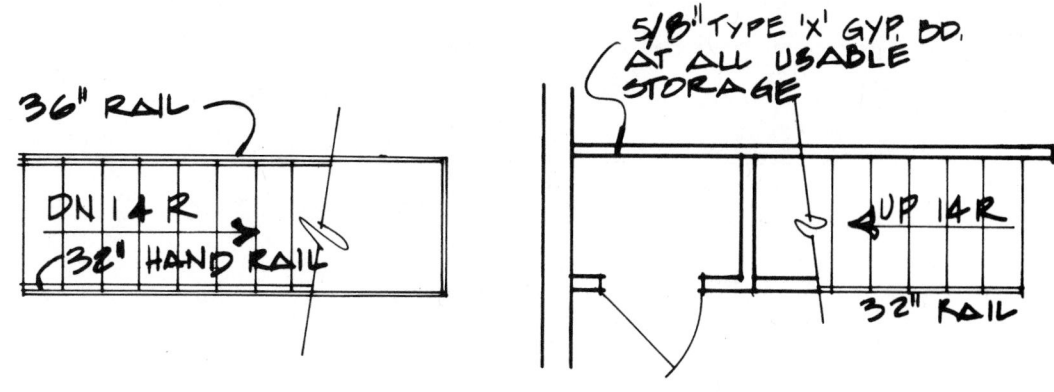

36" RAIL

DN 14 R
32" HAND RAIL

5/8" TYPE 'X' GYP. BD.
AT ALL USABLE
STORAGE

UP 14 R

32" RAIL

2x6 SMOOTH RAIL

U-2-10 HGR

5/8" TYPE 'X' GYP. BD.

3-2x12 STRINGERS

SOLID BLK
3/4" RISERS & TREADS

10½"

8" MAX

32"

30" MIN

2x2 VERT @
6" MAX CLEAR

1-2x10 W/ U2I0 HGR.

2x10 F.J. @ 16" O.C.

LINE OF HANDRAIL

LINE OF WALL
IN BACKGROUND

6'-0" MIN.

2x8 D.F.P.T SILL
W/ RAM-SET
FASTENERS.

11'-4"

STAIR SECTION
3/8" ——— 1'-0"

Figure 31–5 Straight-run enclosed stairs.

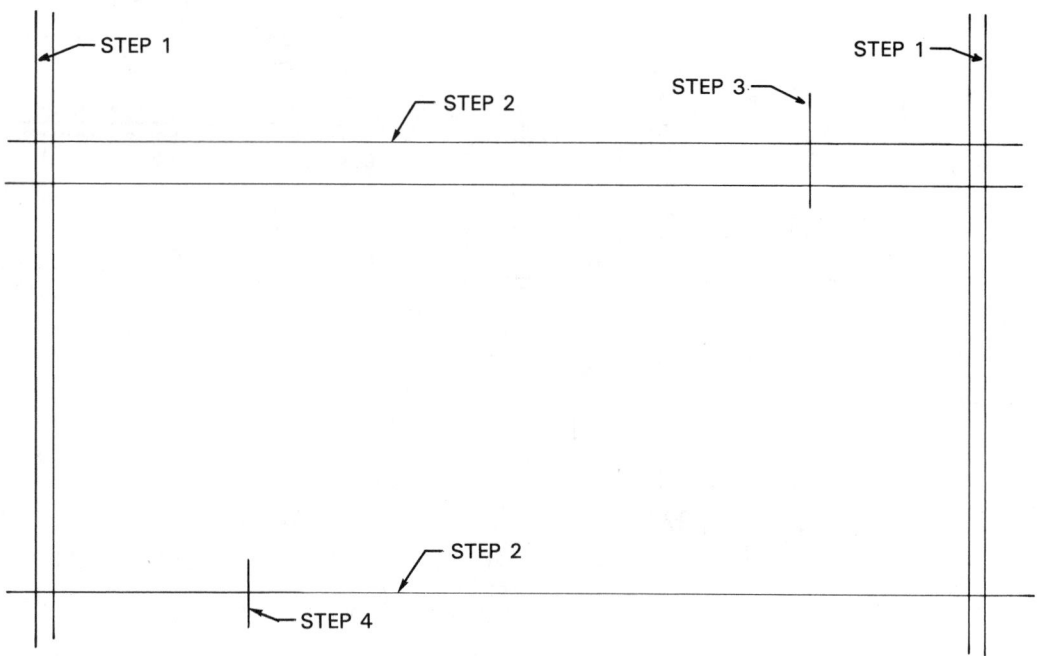

Figure 31–6 Lay out walls, floor, and each end of the stairs.

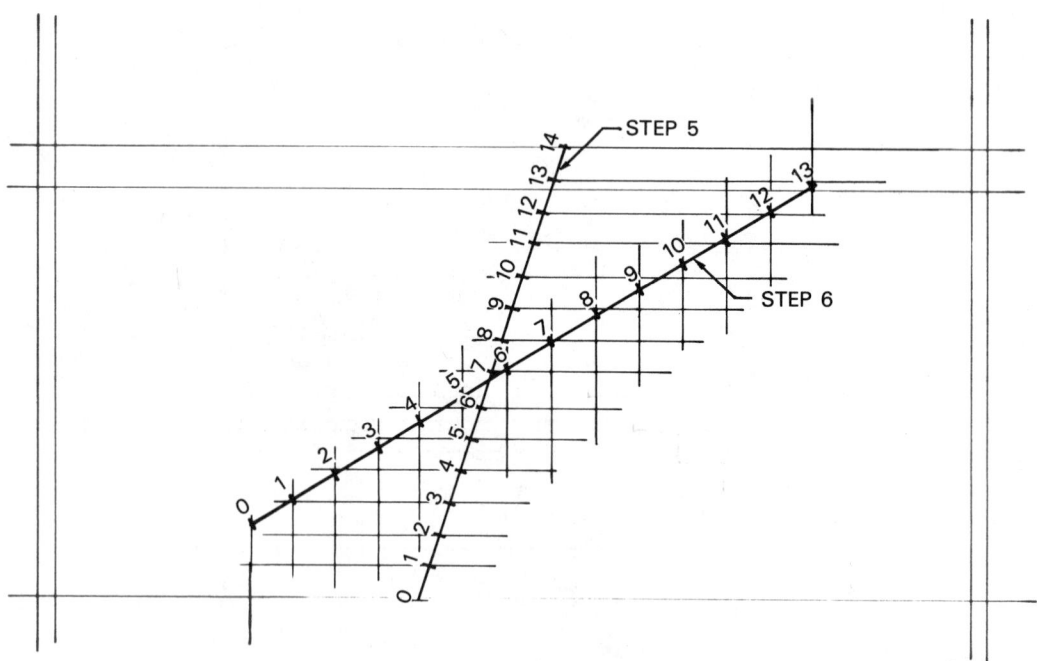

Figure 31–7 Layout of the risers and treads.

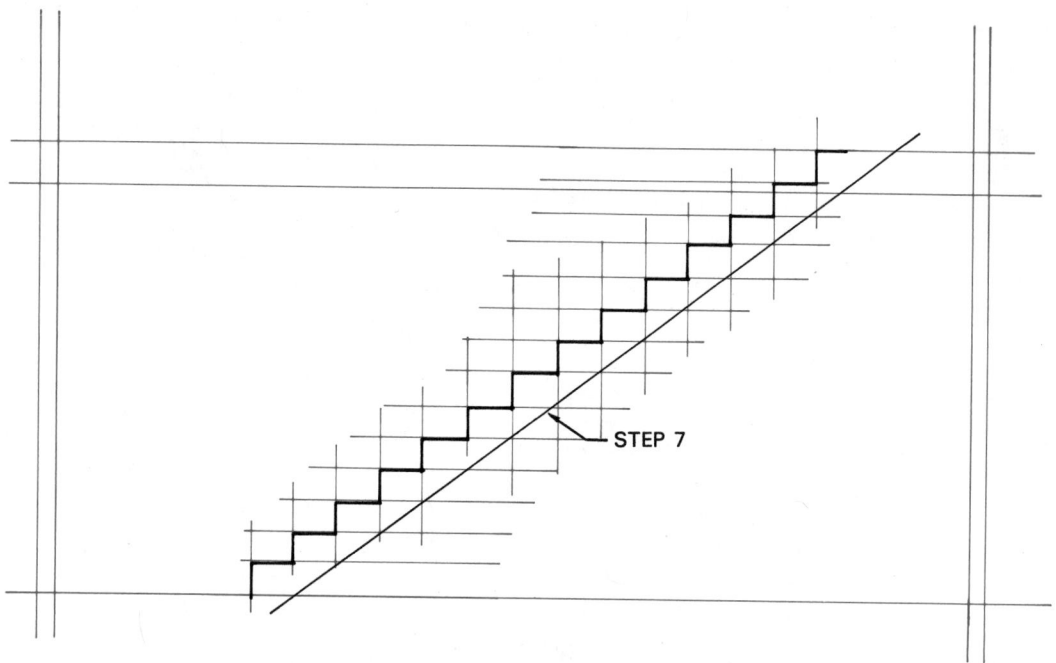

Figure 31-8 Outline the treads, stringer, and risers.

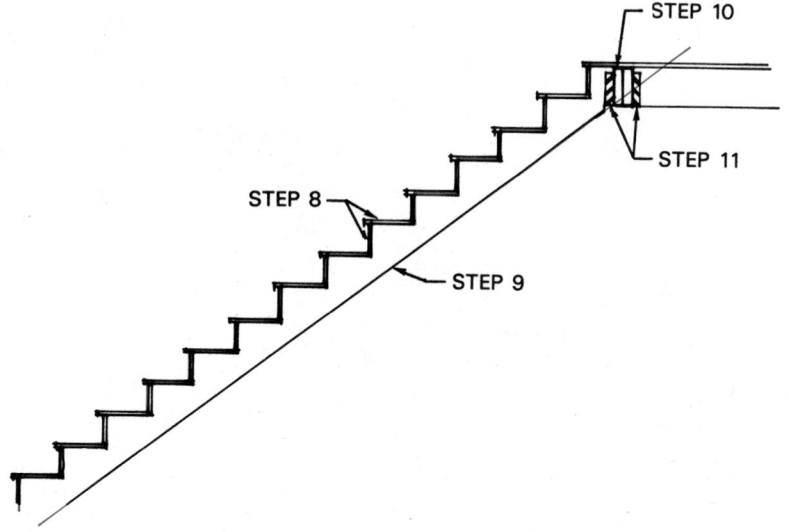

Figure 31-9 Finished quality lines for treads, risers, and the stringer.

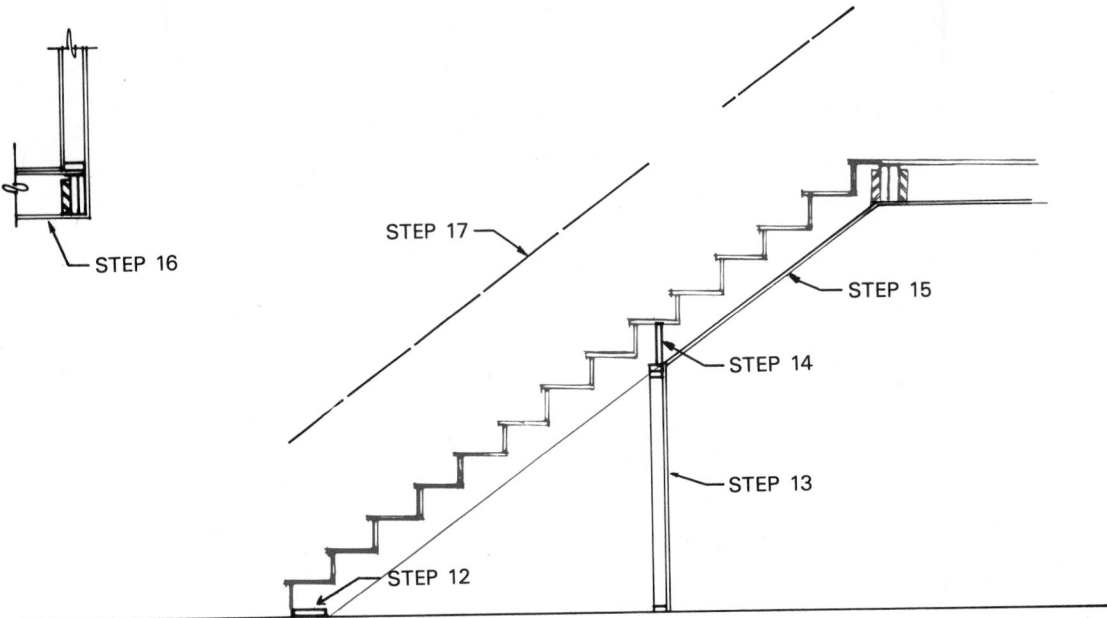

Figure 31–10 Finishing materials.

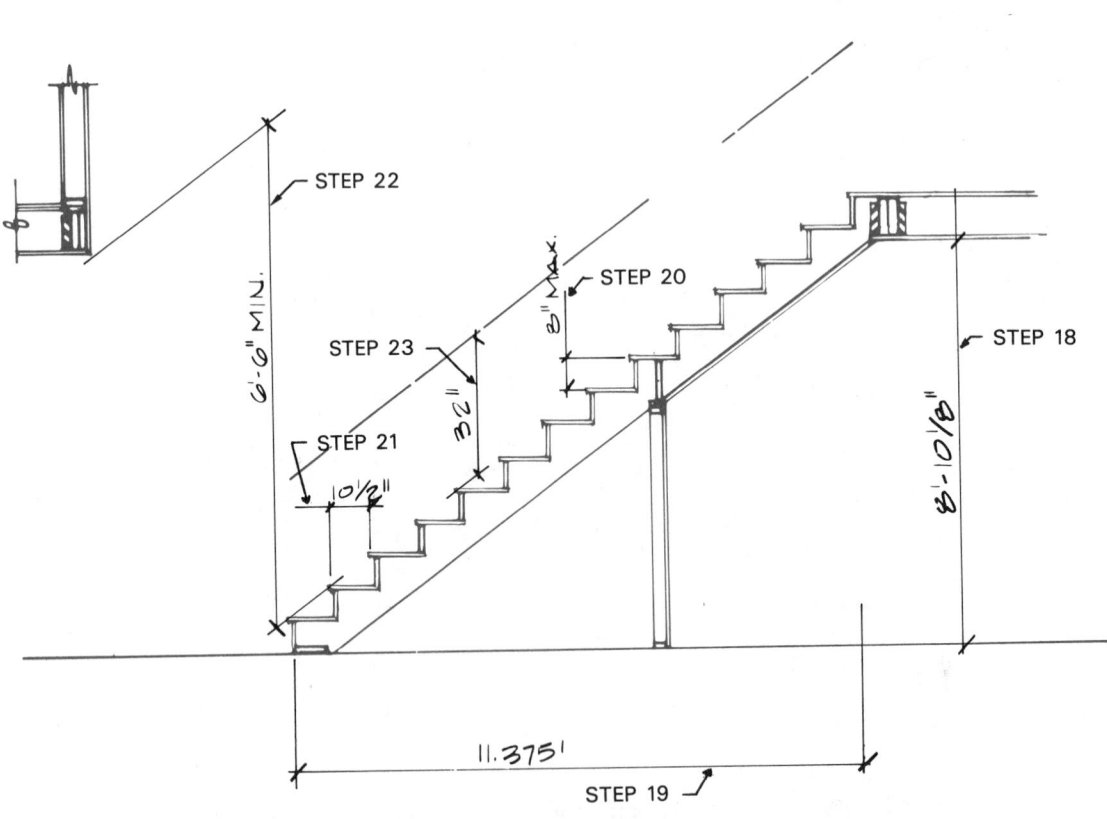

Figure 31–11 Stair dimensions.

CADD *applications*

DRAWING STAIRS WITH CADD

Drawing stairs is easy with a parametric CADD system. All you have to do is pick the starting point of the stairs, specify the number of steps required, give the stair width and direction, and give the total rise; the program then automatically calculates the rise of each step. The program asks you to provide handrails with or without ballisters and provides you with several options of handrail ends. After you have given the required information, the stair is automatically drawn. A sample of the common stair floor plan representations is shown in Figure 1.

There are also CADD stair detailing systems that reduce detailing from hours to minutes. The CADD program uses your specifications for type of stair construction, total rise, and total run. It then automatically calculates the individual rise and run. You specify the tread, riser type, thickness, stringer dimensions, and railing specifications. After all design variables are input, the computer automatically draws, completely dimensions and labels the stair section. Figure 2 shows stair detail drawn by CADD.

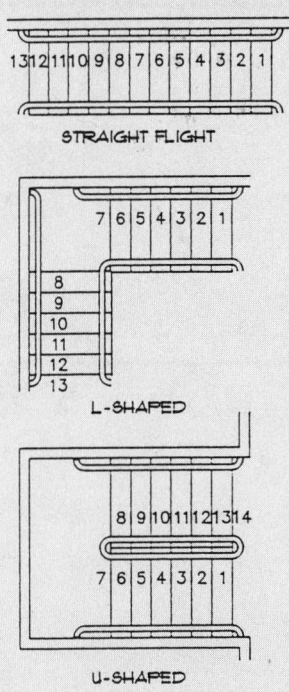

Figure 1 CADD floor plan representations.

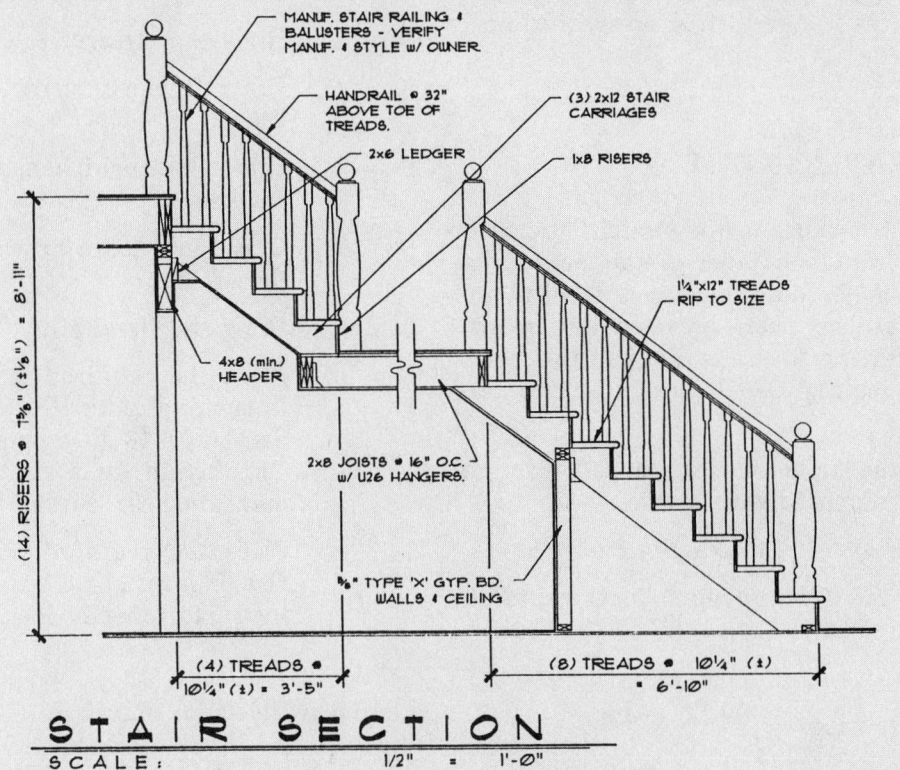

Figure 2 Stair detail drawn by CADD.

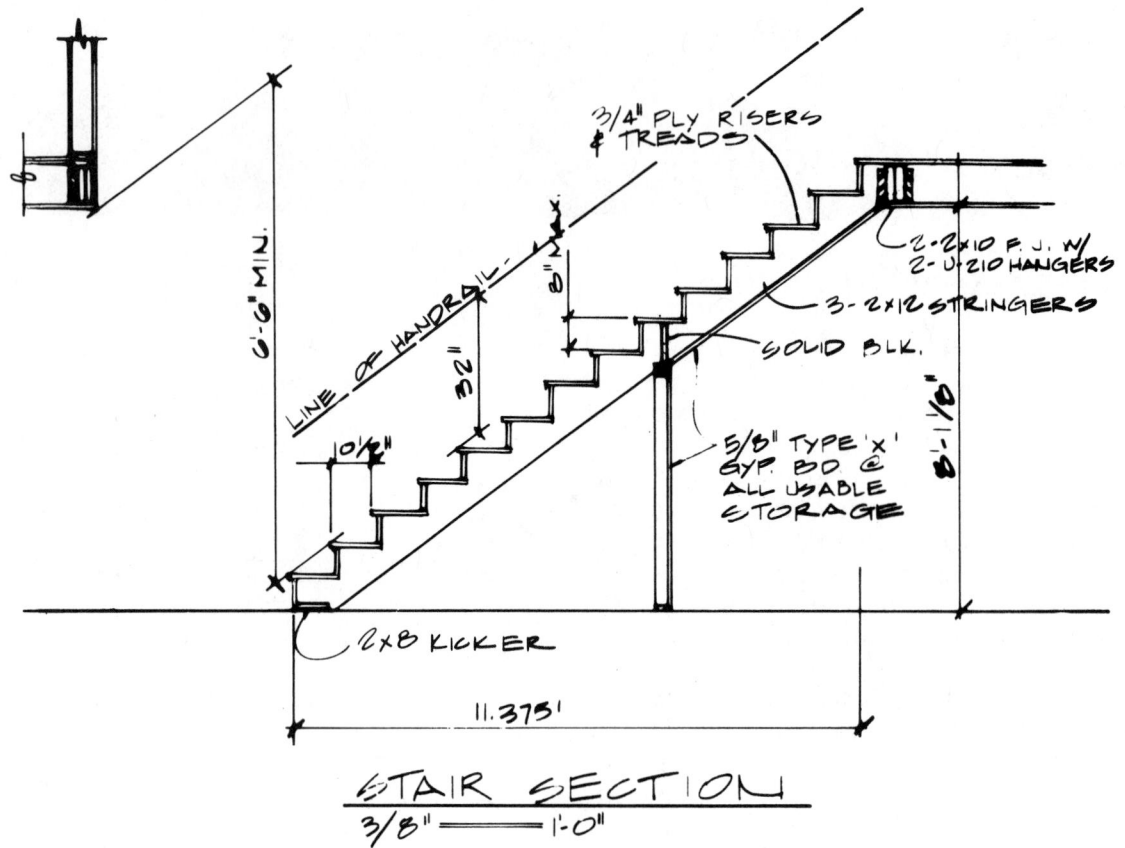

Figure 31–12 Stair notes.

See Figure 31–12 for typical notes that are placed on stair sections. Have your instructor specify local variations.

 OPEN STAIRWAY LAYOUT

An open stairway is similar to the straight enclosed stairway. It goes from one level to the next in a straight run. The major difference is that with the open stair, there are no risers between the treads. This allows for viewing from one floor to the next, creating an open feeling. See Figure 31–13 for an open stairway.

Step 1.   Lay out the stairs following steps 1 through 4 of the enclosed stair layout.

Step 2.   Lay out the 3 × 12 treads. See Figure 31–14.

Step 3.   Lay out the 14 in. deep stringer centered on the treads.

Finished Quality Lines

Use thin lines for each step unless otherwise noted. See Figure 31–15 for steps 4 through 9.

Step 4.   Draw the treads with a bold line.

Step 5.   Draw the stringer.

Step 6.   Draw the upper stringer supports with bold lines.

Step 7.   Draw the metal hangers for the floor and stringer.

Step 8.   Draw any floors or walls which are near the stairs.

Step 9.   Draw the handrail.

Step 10.   Place the required leader and dimension lines to provide the needed dimensions. See steps 18 through 24 of the enclosed stair layout for a guide to the needed dimensions. See Figure 31–16.

Step 11.   Place the required notes on the section. Use Figure 31–16 as a guide. Have your instructor specify local variations.

U-SHAPED STAIRS

The U-shaped stair is often used in residential design. Rather than going up a whole flight of steps in a

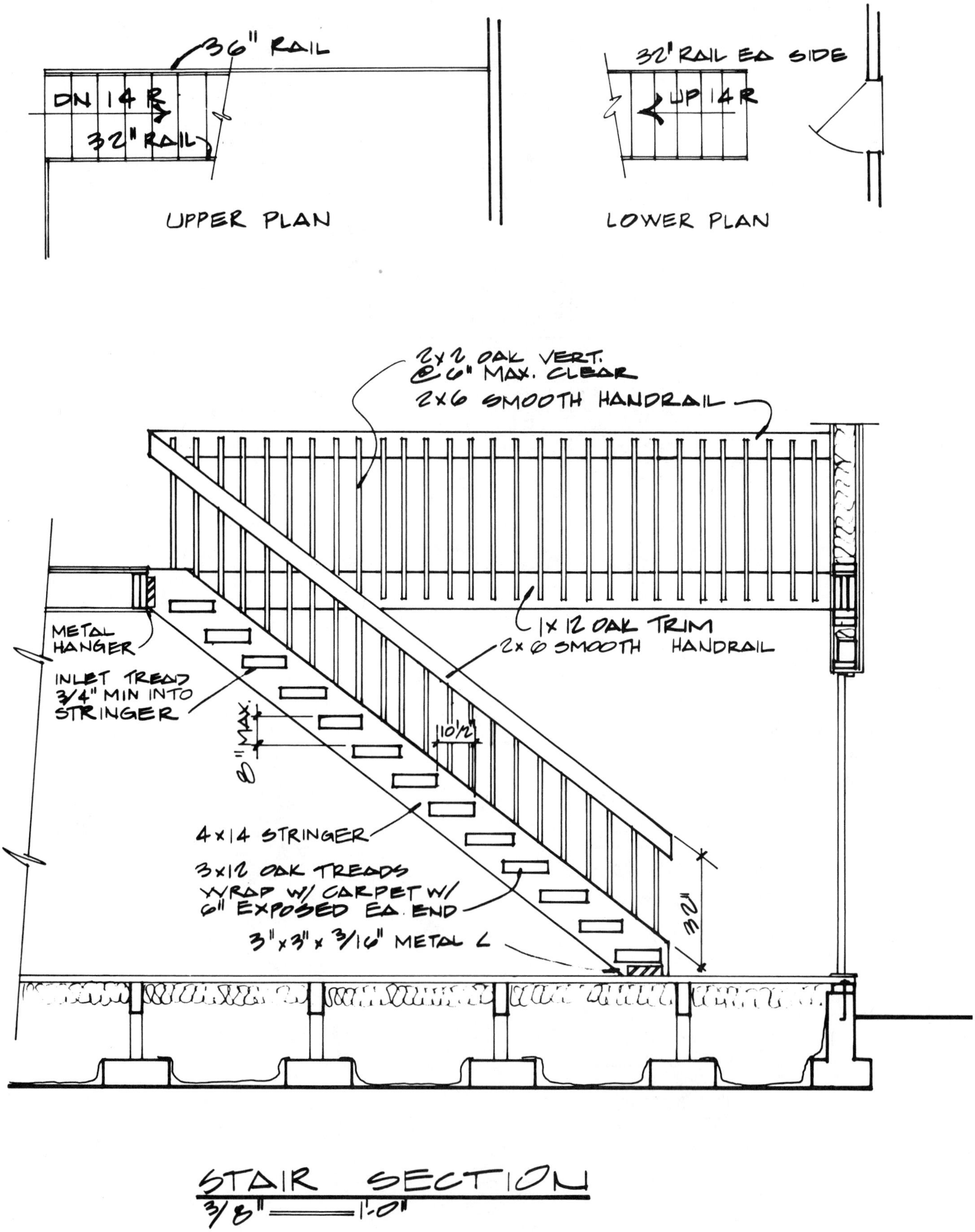

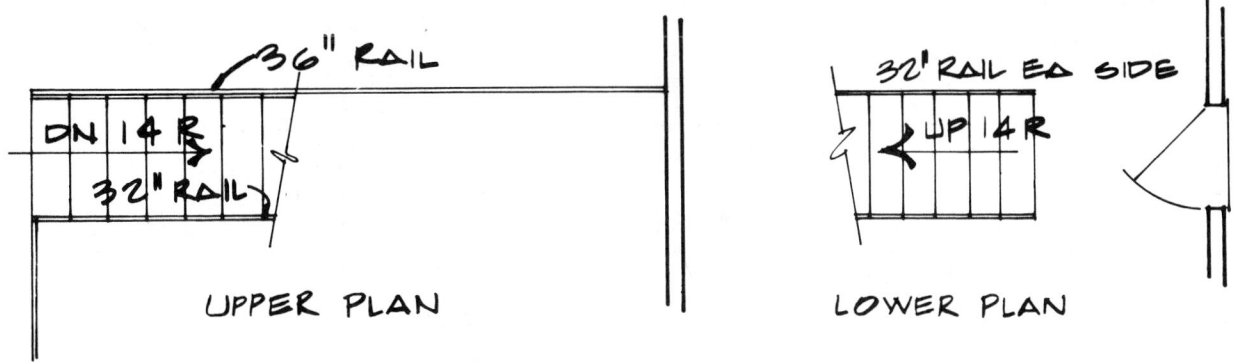

36" RAIL
DN 14 R
32" RAIL
UPPER PLAN
32' RAIL EA SIDE
UP 14 R
LOWER PLAN
2x2 OAK VERT.
@ 6" MAX. CLEAR
2x6 SMOOTH HANDRAIL
METAL HANGER
1x12 OAK TRIM
2x6 SMOOTH HANDRAIL
INLET TREAD 3/4" MIN INTO STRINGER
8" MAX.
10 1/2"
4x14 STRINGER
3x12 OAK TREADS WRAP W/ CARPET W/ 6" EXPOSED EA. END
3"x3"x 3/16" METAL L
32"
STAIR SECTION
3/8" = 1'-0"

Figure 31–13 Open tread stairs.

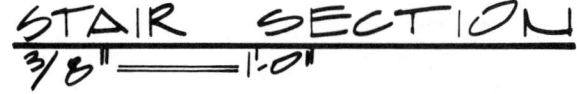

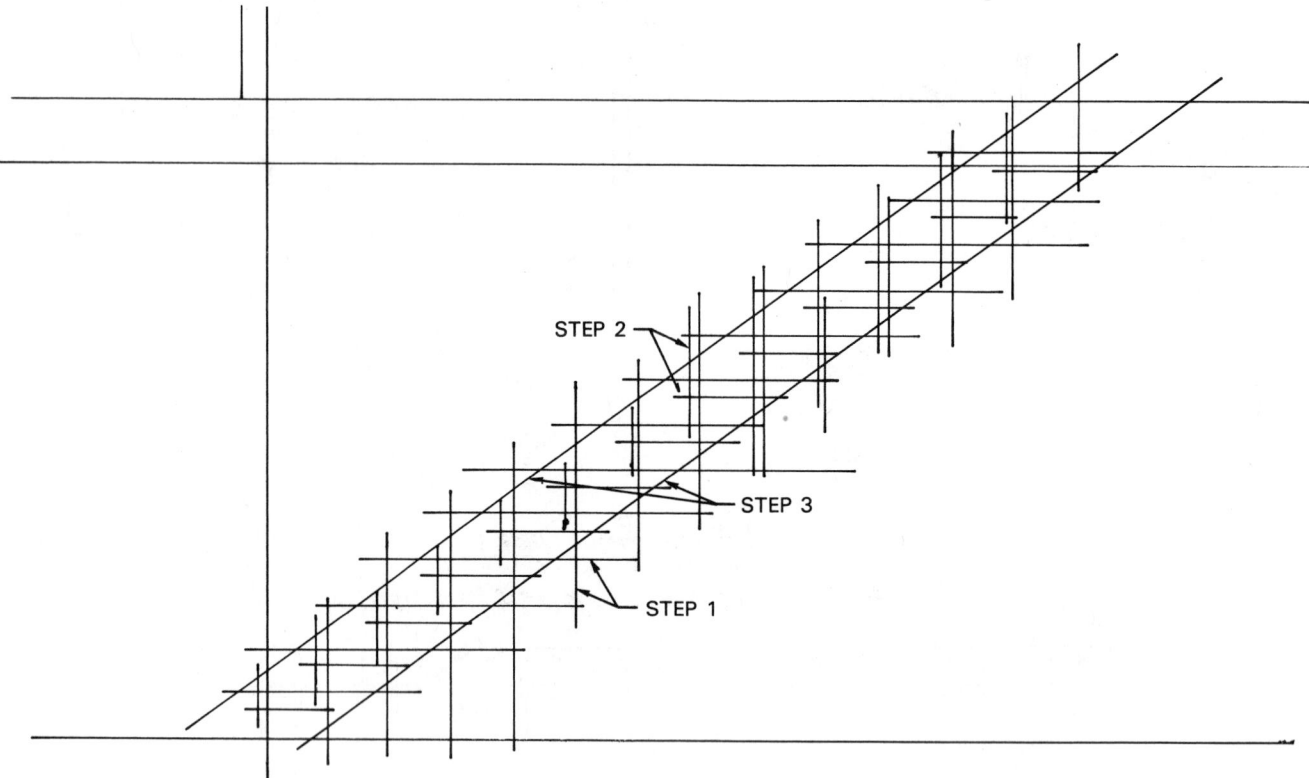

STEP 2

STEP 3

STEP 1

Figure 31–14 Lay out the open tread stairs.

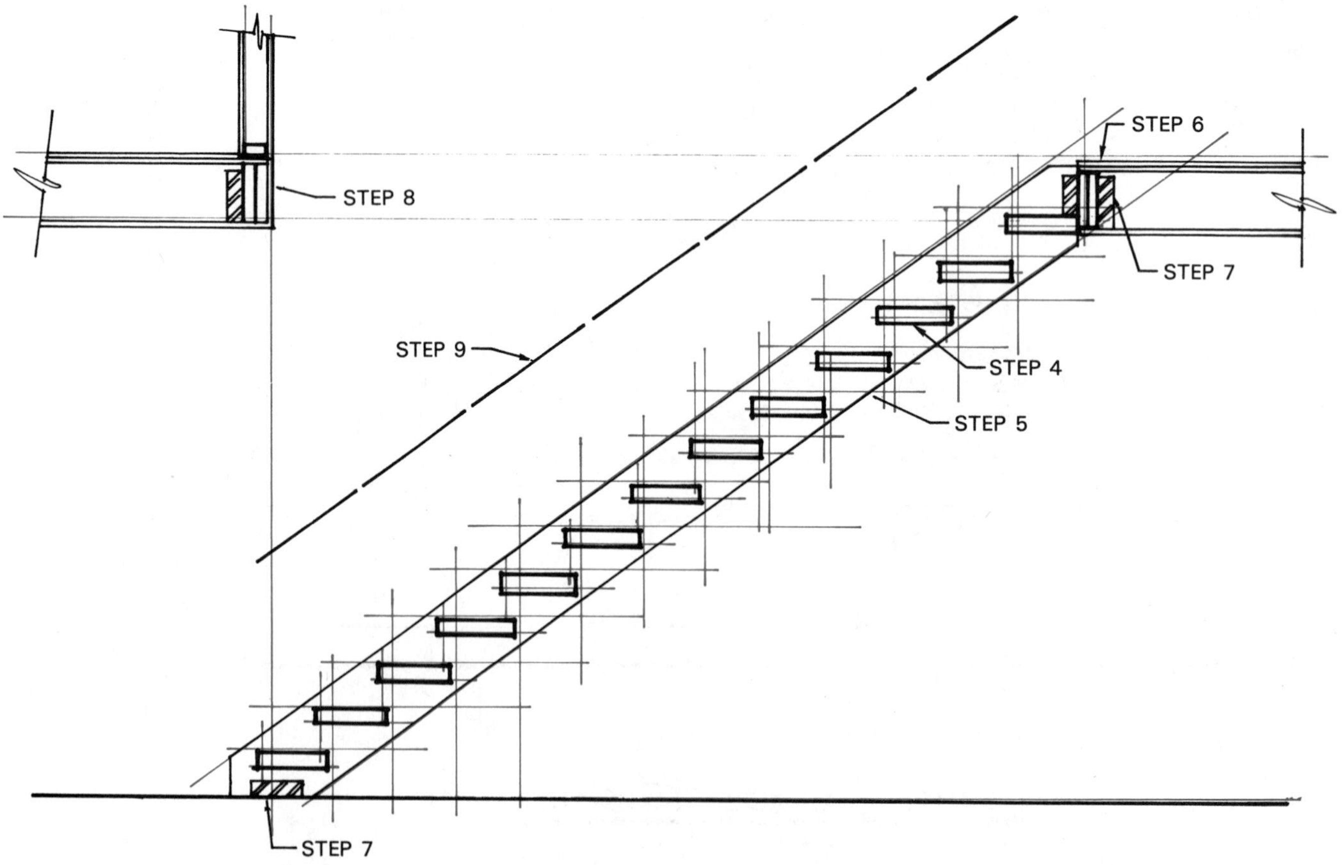

STEP 8

STEP 6

STEP 7

STEP 9

STEP 4

STEP 5

STEP 7

Figure 31–15 Finished quality lines for structural material on open stairs.

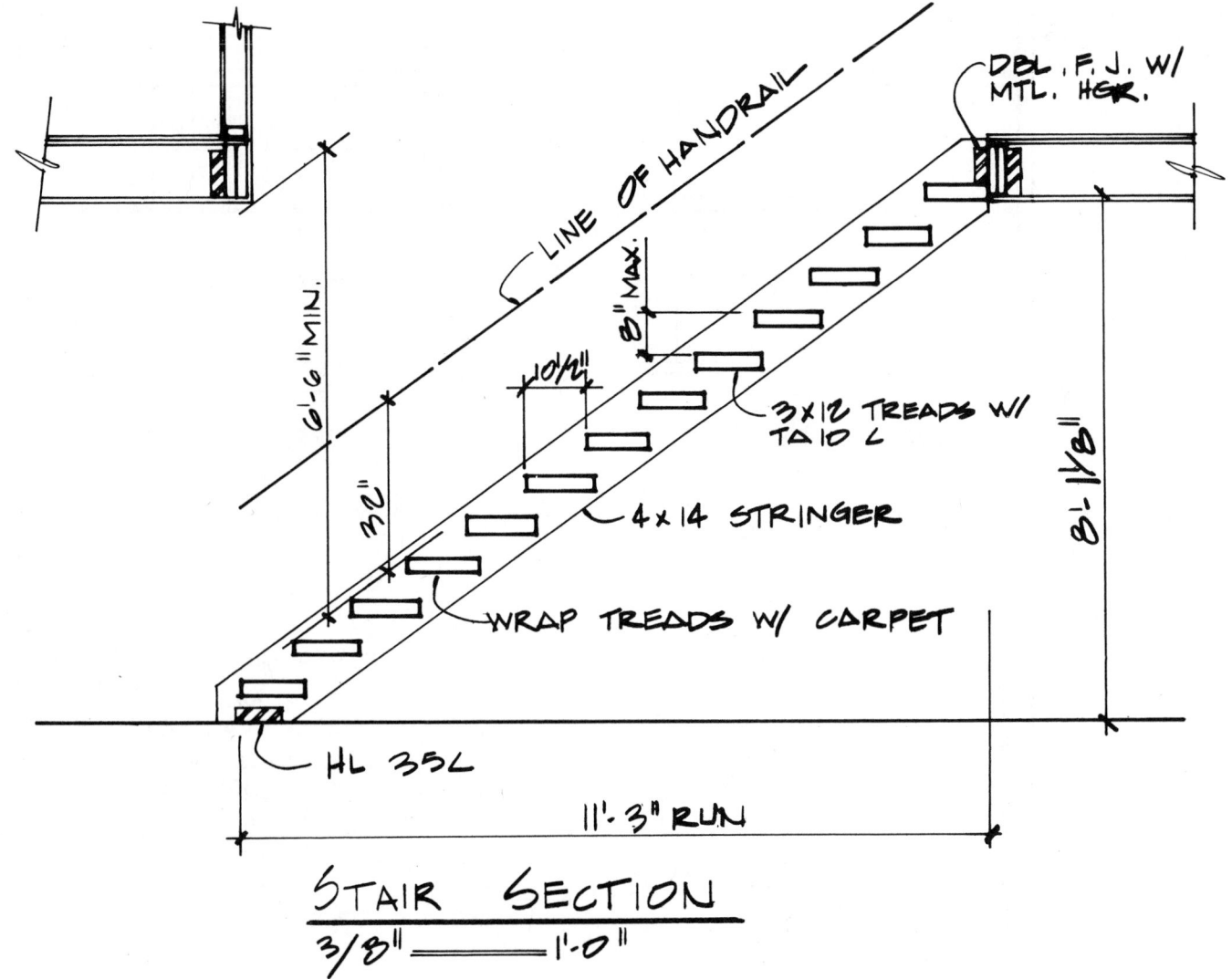

Figure 31–16 The completed open stair with dimensions and notes added.

straight run, this stair layout introduces a landing. The landing is usually located at the midpoint of the run but it can be offset depending on the amount of room allowed for stairs on the floor plan. Figure 31–17 shows what a U-shaped stair looks like on the floor plan and in section.

The stairs may be either open or enclosed depending on the location. The layout of the stair is similar to the layout of the straight-run stair. It requires a little more planning in the layout stage because of the landing. Lay out the distance from the start of the stairs to the landing, based on the floor-plan measurements. Then proceed using a method similar to that used to draw the straight-run stair. See Figure 31–18 for help in laying out the section.

EXTERIOR STAIRS

It is quite common to need to draw sections of exterior stairs on multilevel homes. Figure 31–19 shows two different types of exterior stairs. Although there are many variations, these two options are common. Both can be laid out by following the procedure for the straight-run stairs. There are some major differences in the finishing materials. Notice there is no riser on the wood stairs, and the tread is thicker than the tread of an interior step. Usually the same material that is used on the deck is used for tread material. In many parts of the country a nonskid material should also be called for to cover the treads.

The concrete stair can also be laid out by following the straight-run stairs. Once the risers and run have been marked off, the riser can be drawn. Notice that the riser is drawn on a slight angle. It can be drawn at about 10° and not labeled. This is something the flatwork crew will determine at the job site, depending on their forms.

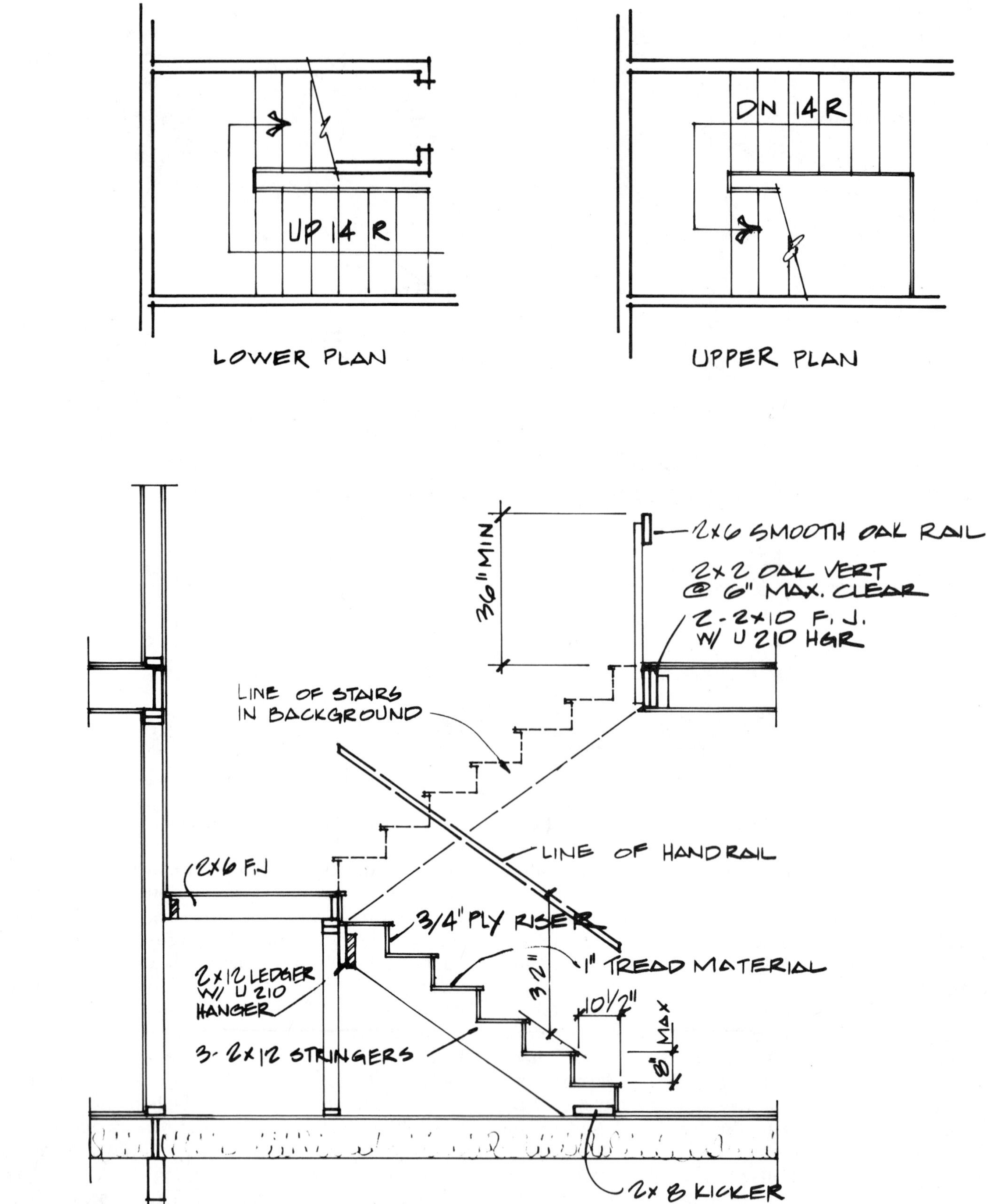

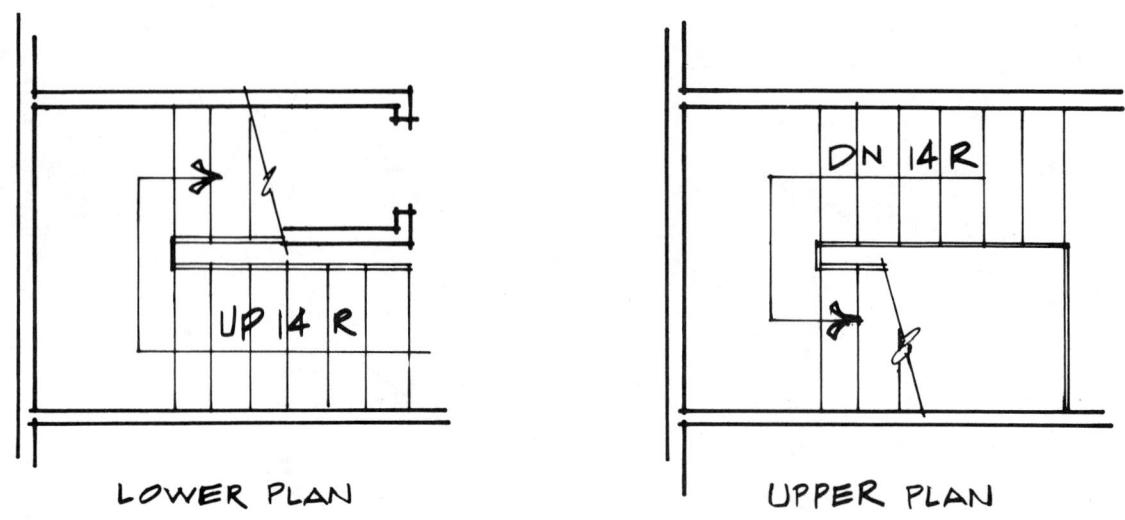

UP 14 R
LOWER PLAN
DN 14 R
UPPER PLAN
2x6 SMOOTH OAK RAIL
2x2 OAK VERT
@ 6" MAX. CLEAR
2-2x10 F.J.
W/ U 210 HGR
36" MIN
LINE OF STAIRS
IN BACKGROUND
LINE OF HANDRAIL
2x6 F.J
3/4" PLY RISER
1" TREAD MATERIAL
2x12 LEDGER
W/ U 210
HANGER
32"
10 1/2"
8" MAX
3-2x12 STRINGERS
2x 8 KICKER

Figure 31–17 The U-shaped stair.

Figure 31–18 The layout of U-shaped stair runs.

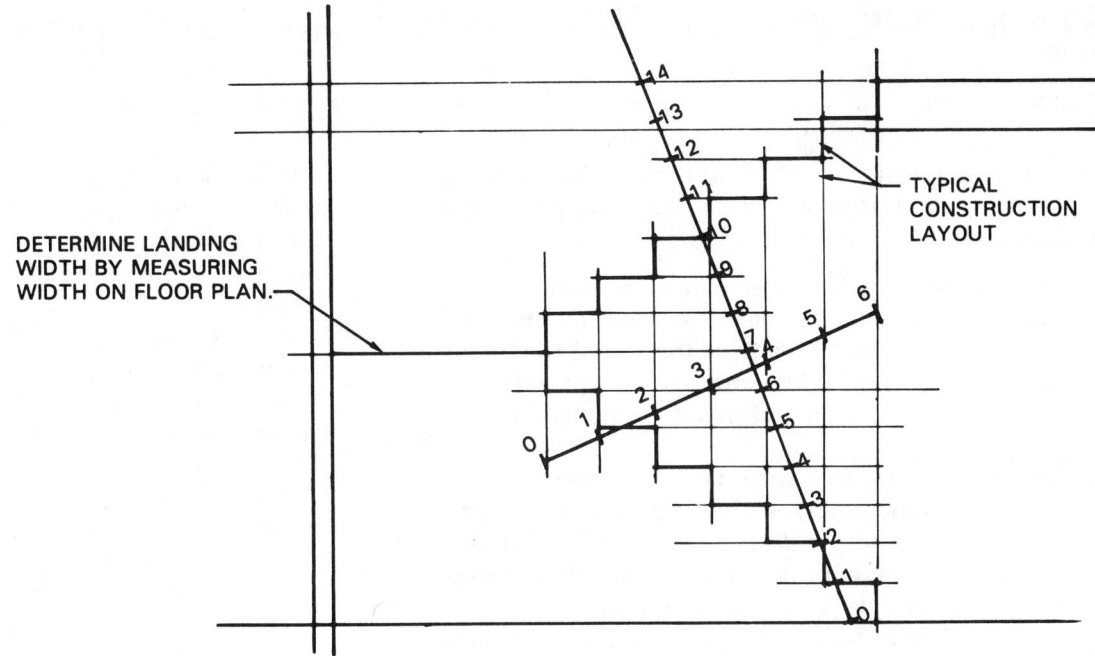

DETERMINE LANDING WIDTH BY MEASURING WIDTH ON FLOOR PLAN.

TYPICAL CONSTRUCTION LAYOUT

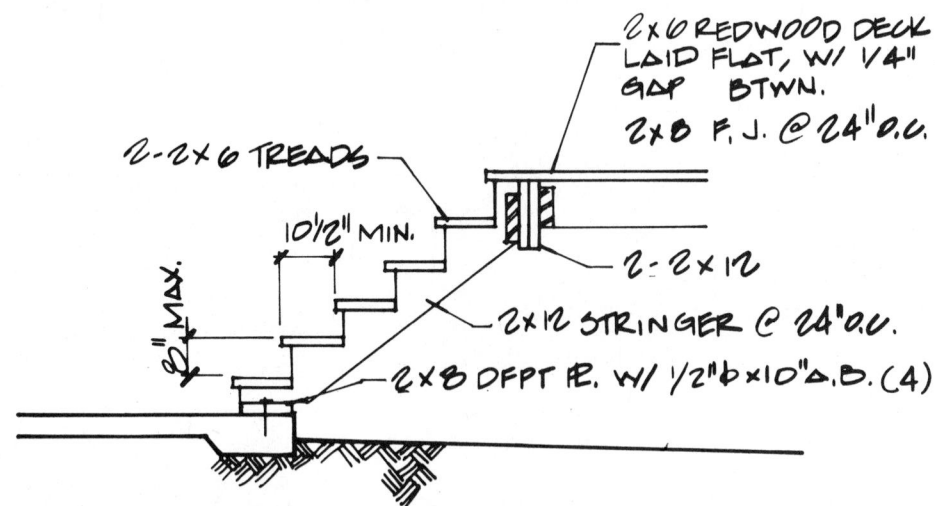

2 x 6 REDWOOD DECK LAID FLAT, W/ 1/4" GAP BTWN.

2 x 8 F. J. @ 24" O.C.

2 - 2 x 6 TREADS

10 1/2" MIN.

6" MAX.

2 - 2 x 12

2 x 12 STRINGER @ 24" O.C.

2 x 8 DFPT FR. W/ 1/2" b x 10" A.B. (4)

EXTERIOR DECK STAIRS
3/8" ——— 1'-0"

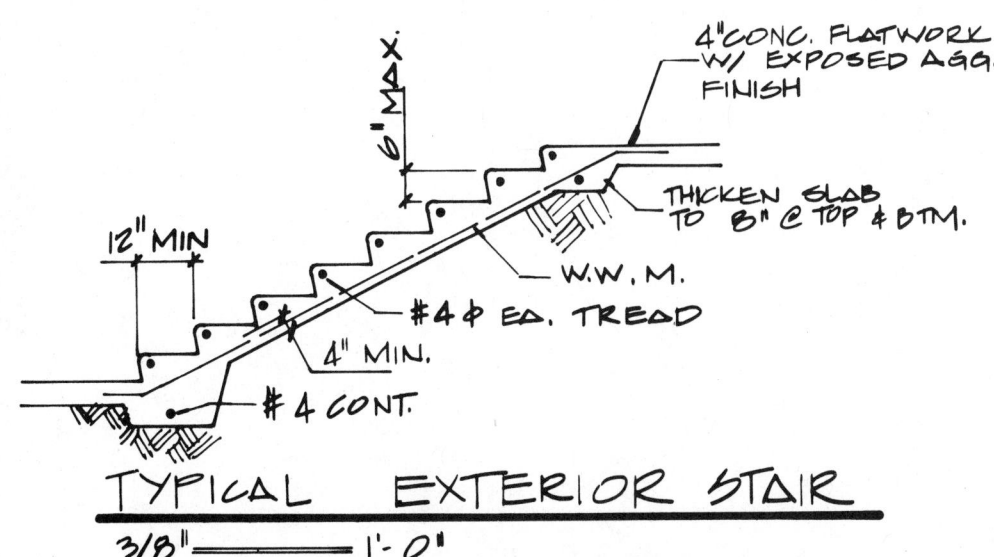

4" CONC. FLATWORK W/ EXPOSED AGG. FINISH

6" MAX.

THICKEN SLAB TO 8" @ TOP & BTM.

W.W.M.

12" MIN

#4 Φ EA. TREAD

4" MIN.

#4 CONT.

TYPICAL EXTERIOR STAIR
3/8" ——— 1'-0"

Figure 31–19 Common types of exterior stairs.

STAIR CONSTRUCTION AND LAYOUT TEST ▬▬▬▬

DIRECTIONS

Answer the questions with short complete statements or drawings as needed on an 8½ × 11 drawing sheet as follows:

1. Use ⅛ in. guidelines for all lettering.
2. Letter your name, Stair Construction and Layout Test, and the date at the top of the sheet.
3. Letter the question number and provide the answer. You do not need to write out the question.
4. Do all lettering with vertical uppercase architectural letters. If the answer requires line work, use proper drafting tools and technique. Answers may be prepared on a word processor if appropriate with course guidelines.
5. Your grade will be based on correct answers and quality of line technique.

QUESTIONS

1. What is a tread?
2. What is the minimum headroom required for a residential stair?
3. What is the maximum individual rise of a step?
4. What member is used to support the stairs?
5. What spacing is required between the verticals of a railing?
6. Describe the difference between a handrail and a guardrail.
7. How many risers are required if the height between floors is 10 ft?
8. Sketch three common stair types.
9. If a run of 10 in. is to be used, what will be the total run when the distance between floors is 9 ft?
10. What is a common size for treads on an open-tread layout?

Chapter 32
Fireplace Construction and Layout

THOUGHT WAS given to the type and location of the fireplace when the floor plan was drawn. As the sections are being drawn, consideration must be given to the construction of the fireplace and chimney. The most common construction materials for a fireplace and chimney are masonry or metal. The metal, or zero clearance fireplace, is manufactured and does not require a section to explain its construction. As an architectural drafter, you should be familiar with the components of a masonry fireplace and chimney so that you can draw them.

FIREPLACE TERMS

Figure 32–1 shows the parts of a fireplace and chimney. Each of these parts should be understood to help you draw a fireplace section.

Fireplace Parts

- *Hearth.* The hearth is the floor of the fireplace and consists of an inner and outer hearth. The inner hearth is the floor of the firebox. The hearth is made of fire-resistant brick and holds the burning fuel. An ash dump is usually located in the inner hearth. The outer hearth may be made of any incombustible material. The material is usually selected to blend with other interior design features and may include brick, tile, marble, or stone. The outer hearth protects the combustible floor around the fireplace. Figure 32–2 shows the minimum sizes for the outer hearth.
- *Ash Dump.* The ash dump is an opening in the hearth that the ashes can be dumped into. The ash dump normally is covered with a small metal plate which can be removed to provide access to the ash pit.
- *Ash Pit.* The ash pit is the space below the fireplace where the ashes can be stored.
- *Fireplace Opening.* The fireplace opening is the area between the side and top faces of the fireplace. The size of the fireplace opening should be given much consideration since it is important for the appearance and operation of the fireplace. If the opening is too small, the fireplace will not produce a sufficient amount of heat. If the opening is too large, the fire could make a room too hot. The Masonry Institute of America suggests that the opening be approximately 1/30 of the room area for small rooms, and 1/65 of the room area for large rooms. Figure 32–3 shows suggested fireplace opening sizes compared to room size. The ideal dimensions for a single-face fireplace have been determined to be 36 in. wide and 26 in. high. These dimensions may be varied slightly to meet the size of the brick or to fit other special dimensions of the room.
- *Firebox.* The firebox is where the combustion of the fuel occurs. The side should be slanted slightly to radiate heat into the room. The rear

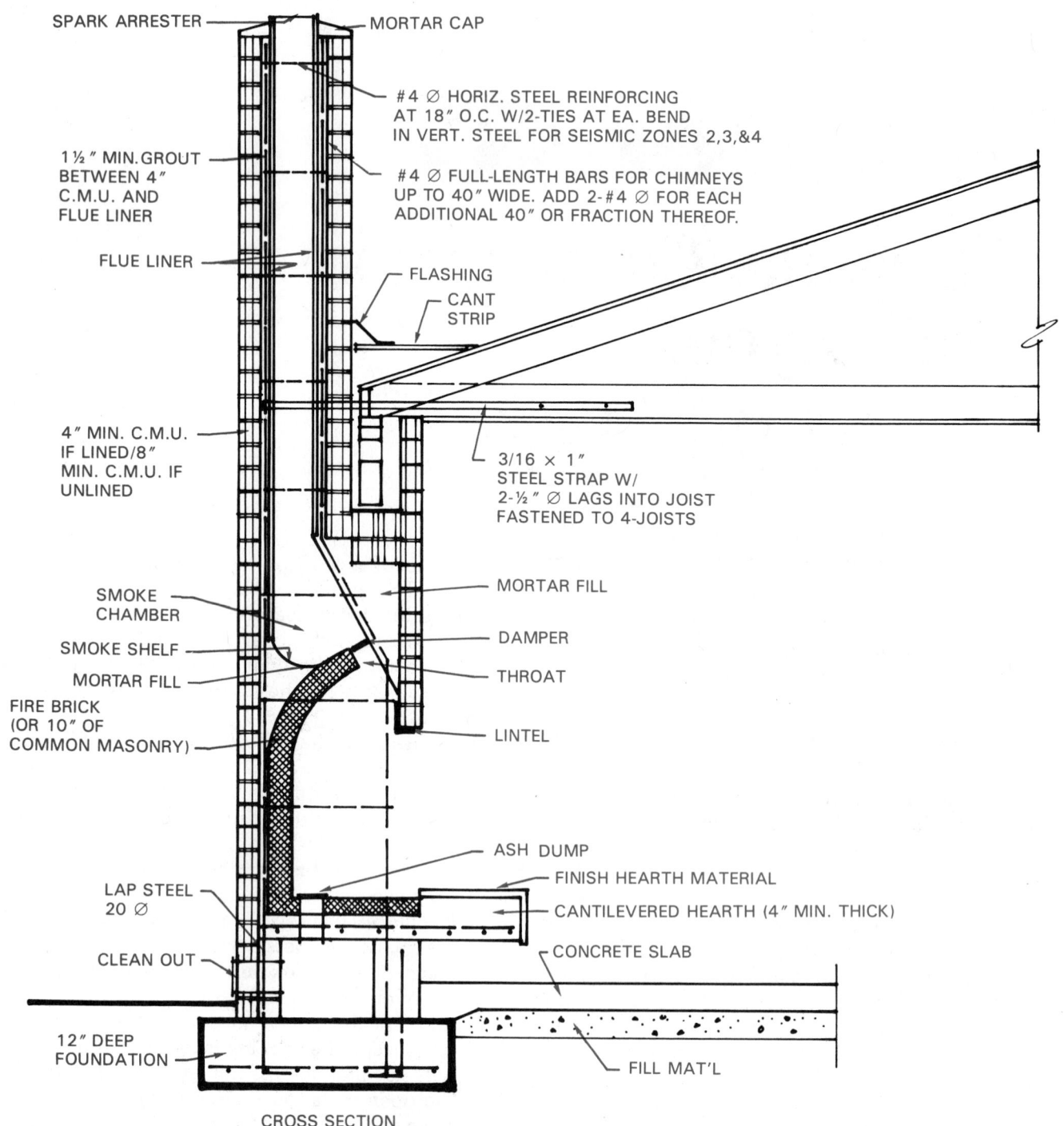

SPARK ARRESTER — MORTAR CAP

#4 ⌀ HORIZ. STEEL REINFORCING
AT 18″ O.C. W/2-TIES AT EA. BEND
IN VERT. STEEL FOR SEISMIC ZONES 2,3,&4

#4 ⌀ FULL-LENGTH BARS FOR CHIMNEYS
UP TO 40″ WIDE. ADD 2-#4 ⌀ FOR EACH
ADDITIONAL 40″ OR FRACTION THEREOF.

1½″ MIN.GROUT
BETWEEN 4″
C.M.U. AND
FLUE LINER

FLUE LINER

FLASHING

CANT
STRIP

4″ MIN. C.M.U.
IF LINED/8″
MIN. C.M.U. IF
UNLINED

3/16 × 1″
STEEL STRAP W/
2-½″ ⌀ LAGS INTO JOIST
FASTENED TO 4-JOISTS

SMOKE
CHAMBER

MORTAR FILL

SMOKE SHELF

DAMPER

MORTAR FILL

THROAT

FIRE BRICK
(OR 10″ OF
COMMON MASONRY)

LINTEL

ASH DUMP

FINISH HEARTH MATERIAL

LAP STEEL
20 ⌀

CANTILEVERED HEARTH (4″ MIN. THICK)

CONCRETE SLAB

CLEAN OUT

12″ DEEP
FOUNDATION

FILL MAT'L

CROSS SECTION

Figure 32–1 Parts of a fireplace and chimney.

wall should be curved to provide an upward draft into the upper part of the fireplace and chimney. The firebox is usually constructed of fire-resistant brick set in fire-resistant mortar. Figure 32–2 shows minimum wall thickness for the firebox.

The firebox depth should be proportional to the size of the fireplace opening. By providing a proper depth, smoke will not discolor the front face (breast) of the fireplace. With an opening of 36″ × 26″, a depth of 20″ should be provided

for a single-face fireplace. Figure 32–4 lists recommended fireplace opening-to-depth proportions.

- *Lintel.* The lintel is a steel angle above the fireplace opening that supports the fireplace face.
- *Throat.* The throat of a fireplace is the opening at the top of the firebox which opens into the chimney. The throat should be able to be closed when the fireplace is not in use. This is done by installing a damper.

GENERAL CODE REQUIREMENTS

ITEM	Letter	Uniform Building Code ✱ 1979 & 1982 Edition	FHA & VA	Local or Special Requirements
Hearth Slab Thickness	A	4"	4"	
Hearth Slab Width (Each side of opening)	B	8" Fireplace opg. <6 sq. ft. 12" Fireplace opg. ≥6 sq. ft.	8"	
Hearth Slab Length (Front of opening)	C	16" Firepl. opg. <6 sq. ft. 20" Firepl. opg. ≥6 sq. ft.	16"	
Hearth Slab Reinforcing	D	Reinforced to carry its own weight and all imposed loads.	Required if cantilevered in connection with raised wood floor construction.	
Thickness of Wall of Firebox	E	10" common brick or 8" where a fireback lining is used. Jts. in fireback ¼" max.	8" including minimum 2" fireback lining—12" when no lining is provided.	
Distance from Top of Opening to Throat	F	6"	6" min.; 8" recommended.	
Smoke Chamber Edge of Shelf	G		½" offset.	
Rear Wall—Thickness		6"	6" plus paraging may be omitted if wall thickness is 8" or more of solid masonry. Form damper is required.	
Front & Side wall—Thickness		8"		
Chimney Vertical Reinforcing	**H	Four #4 full length bars for chimney up to 40" wide. Add two #4 bars for each additional 40" or fraction of width or each additional flue.	Four #4 bars full length, no splice unless welded.	
Horizontal Reinforcing	J	¼" ties at 18" and two ties at each bend in vertical steel.	¼" bars at 24"	
Bond Beams	K	No specified requirements. L.A. City requirements are good practice	Two ¼" bars at top bond beam 4" high. Two ¼" bars at anchorage bond beam 5" high.	
Fireplace Lintel	L	Incombustible material	2½" x 3" x 3/16" angle with 3" end bearing	
Walls with Flue Lining	M	Brick with grout around lining. 4" min. from flue lining to outside face of chimney.	Brick with grout around lining. 4" min. from outside flue lining to outside face of chimney.	
Walls with Unlined Flue	N	8" Solid masonry	8" Solid masonry	
Distance Between Adjacent Flues	O	4" including flue liner	4" wythe for brick	
Effective Flue Area (Based on Area of Fireplace Opening)	P	Round lining—1/12 or 50 sq. in. min. Rectangular lining 1/10 or 64 sq. in. min. Unlined or lined with firebrick—1/8 or 100 sq. in. min.	1/10 for chimneys over 15' high and over 1/8 for chimneys less than 15' high	
Clearances Wood Frame Combustible Material Above Roof	R	1" when outside of wall or ½" gypsum board 1" when entirely within structure 6" min. to fireplace opening. 12" from opening when material projecting more than 1/8 for ea. 1" 2' at 10'	¾" from subfloor or floor or roof sheathing. 2" from framing members 3½" to edge of fireplace 12" from opening when projecting more than 1½" 2' at 10'	
Anchorage Strap Number Embedment into chimney Fasten to Bolts	S	3/16" x 1" 2 12" hooked around outer bar w/6"ext. 4 Joists Two ½" Dia.	1/4" x 1" 2 18" hooked around outer bar 3 joists Two ½" Dia.	
Footing Thickness Width	T	12" min. 6" each side of fireplace wall	8" min. for 1 story chimney 12" min. for 2 story chimney 6" each side of fireplace wall.	
Outside Air Intake	U	Optional	Required	6 sq. in. minimum area (California Energy Commission Requirement)
Glass Screen Door		Optional	Required but shall not interfere with energy conservation improving devices	Required but shall not interfere with energy conservation improving devices

*Applies to Los Angeles County and Los Angeles City requirements.

**H EXCEPTION. Chimneys constructed of hollow masonry units may have vertical reinforcing bars spliced to footing dowels, provided that the splice is inspected prior to grouting of the wall.

Figure 32–2 General code requirements for fireplace and chimney construction. The letters in the second column will be helpful in locating a specific item in Figures 32–6 through 32–9. *Reprinted from Residential Fireplace and Chimney Construction Details and Specifications, with permission from the Masonry Institute of America, Los Angeles, CA.*

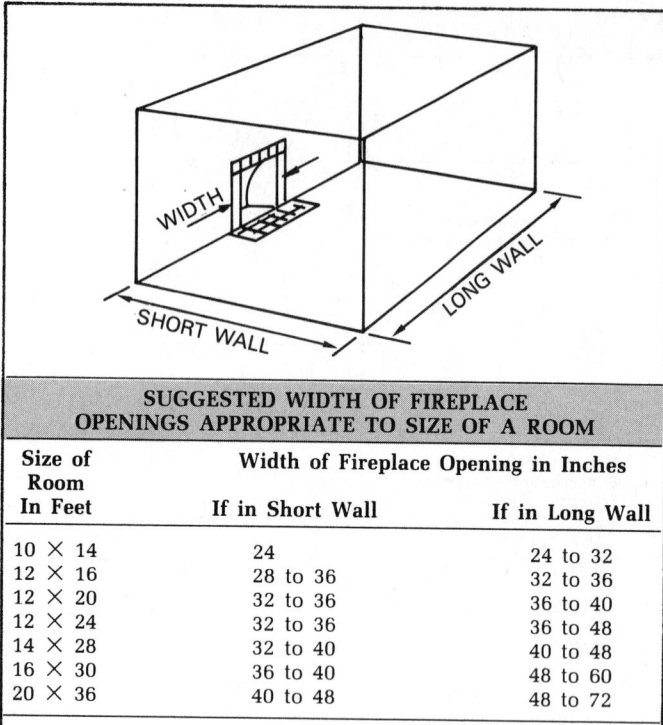

		SUGGESTED WIDTH OF FIREPLACE OPENINGS APPROPRIATE TO SIZE OF A ROOM	

Size of Room In Feet	Width of Fireplace Opening in Inches	
	If in Short Wall	If in Long Wall
10 × 14	24	24 to 32
12 × 16	28 to 36	32 to 36
12 × 20	32 to 36	36 to 40
12 × 24	32 to 36	36 to 48
14 × 28	32 to 40	40 to 48
16 × 30	36 to 40	48 to 60
20 × 36	40 to 48	48 to 72

Figure 32–3 The size of the fireplace should be proportioned to the size of the room. This will give both a pleasing appearance and a fireplace that will not overheat the room. *Reprinted from* Residential Fireplace and Chimney Construction Details and Specifications, *with permission from the Masonry Institute of America, Los Angeles, CA.*

Fireplace Type	Width of Opening w, inches	Height of Opening h, inches	Depth of Opening d, inches
Single Face			
	28	24	20
	30	24	20
	30	26	20
	36	26	20
	36	28	22
	40	28	22
	48	32	25
Two faces adjacent "L" or corner type	34	27	23
	39	27	23
	46	27	23
	52	30	27
Two face ▲ Opposite Look thru	32	21	30
	35	21	30
	42	21	30
	48	21	34
Three face ▲ 2 long, 1 short 3 way opening	39	21	30
	46	21	30
	52	21	34
Three face ▲ 1 long, 2 short 3 way opening	43	27	23
	50	27	23
	56	30	27

▲ NOTE: Fireplaces open on more than front and one end are NOT recommended.

Figure 32–4 Fireplace opening-to-depth proportion guide. *Reprinted from* Residential Fireplace and Chimney Construction Details and Specifications, *with permission from the Masonry Institute of America, Los Angeles, CA.*

chimney will be determined by the type of flue construction. Figure 32–2 shows the minimum wall thickness for chimneys.

Chimney Parts

- *Flue.* The flue is the opening inside the chimney that allows the smoke and combustion gases to pass from the firebox away from the structure. A flue may be constructed of normal masonry products or may be covered with a flue liner. The size of the flue must be proportional to the size of the firebox opening and the number of open faces of the fireplace. A flue that is too small will not allow the fire to burn well and will cause smoke to exit through the front of the firebox. A flue that is too large for the firebox will cause too great a draft through the house as the fire draws its combustion air. Flue sizes are generally required to equal either ⅛ or 1/10 of the fireplace opening. Figure 32–5 shows recommended areas for residential fireplaces.
- *Chimney Liners.* A chimney liner is usually built of fire clay or terra cotta. The liner is built into the chimney to provide a smooth surface to the

- *Damper.* The damper extends the full width of the throat and is used to prevent heat from escaping up the chimney when the fireplace is not in use. When fuel is being burned in the firebox, the damper can be opened to allow smoke from the firebox into the smoke chamber of the chimney.
- *Smoke Chamber.* The smoke chamber acts as a funnel between the firebox and the chimney. The shape of the smoke chamber should be symmetrical so that the chimney draft pulls evenly and creates an even fire in the firebox. The smoke chamber should be centered under the flue in the chimney and directly above the firebox.
- *Smoke Shelf.* The smoke shelf is located at the bottom of the smoke chamber behind the damper. The smoke shelf prevents down drafts from the chimney from entering the firebox.
- *Chimney.* The chimney is the upper extension of the fireplace and is built to carry off the smoke from the fire. The main components of the chimney are the flue, lining, anchors, cap, and spark arrester. The wall thickness of the

Type of Fireplace	Width of Opening w in.	Height of Opening h in.	Depth of Opening d in.	Area of Fireplace opening for flue determination sq. in.	Flue Size Required at 1/10 Area of fireplace opening	Flue Size Required at 1/8 Area of fireplace opening (FHA Requirement)*
	28	24	20	672	8½ x 13	8½ x 17
	30	24	20	720	8½ x 17	13" round
	30	26	20	780	8½ x 17	10 x 18
	36	26	20	936	10 x 18	13 x 17
	36	28	22	1008	10 x 18	10 x 21
	40	28	22	1120	10 x 18	10 x 21
	48	32	25	1536	13 x 21	17 x 21
	60	32	25	1920	17 x 21	21 x 21
	34	27	23	1107	10 x 18	10 x 21
	39	27	23	1223	10 x 21	13 x 21
	46	27	23	1388	10 x 21	13 x 21
	52	30	27	1884	13 x 21	17 x 21
	64	30	27	2085	17 x 21	21 x 21
	32	21	30	1344	13 x 17 or 10 x 21	17 x 17 or 13 x 21
	35	21	30	1470	17 x 17 or 13 x 21	17 x 21
	42	21	30	1764	17 x 21	17 x 21
	48	21	34	2016	17 x 21	21 x 21
	39	21	30	1638	13 x 21 or 17 x 17	17 x 21
	46	21	30	1932	17 x 21	21 x 21
	52	21	34	2184	17 x 21	21 x 21
	43	27	23	1782	13 x 21 or 17 x 17	17 x 21
	50	27	23	1971	17 x 21	17 x 21
	56	30	27	2490	21 x 21	21 x 21 or 2 — 10 x 21 ▲
	68	30	27	2850	13 x 21 & ▲ 10 x 21	2 — 13 x 21 or 2 — 17 x 17 or ▲ 10 x 18 & 17 x 21

* FHA Requirement if chimney is less than 15' high. Use 1/10 ratio if chimney is 15' or more in height.

▲ Rather than using 2 flue liners in chimney, many times the flue is left unlined with 8" masonry walls. Unlined flues must have a minimum area of 1/8 fireplace opening.

Figure 32–5 Recommended flue areas for residential fireplaces. *Reprinted from* Residential Fireplace and Chimney Construction Details and Specifications, *with permission from the Masonry Institute of America, Los Angeles, CA.*

flue wall and to reduce the width of the chimney wall. The smooth surface of the liner will help to reduce the build-up of soot which could cause a chimney fire.

- *Chimney Anchors.* The anchors are steel straps that connect the fireplace to the framing members at each floor and ceiling level. Steel straps approximately 3/16" × 1" are embedded into the grout of the chimney or wrapped around the reinforcing steel and then bolted to the framing members.
- *Chimney Reinforcement.* A minimum of four ½ in. diameter (#4) vertical reinforcing bars should be used in the chimney extending from the foundation up to the top of the chimney. Typically these vertical bars are supported at 18 in. intervals with ¼ in. horizontal rebars known as ties. Usually ties are also installed when the

vertical steel is bent for a change in chimney width.

- *Chimney Cap.* The chimney cap is the sloping surface on the top of the chimney. The slope prevents rain from collecting on the top of the chimney. The flue normally projects 2 to 3 in. above the cap so that water will not run down the flue.
- *Chimney Hood.* The chimney hood is a covering which may be placed over the flue for protection from the elements. The hood can be made of either masonry or metal. The masonry cap is built so that openings allow for the prevailing wind to blow through the hood and create a draft in the flue. The metal hood can usually be rotated by wind pressure to keep the opening of the hood downwind and thus prevent rain or snow from entering the flue.

- *Spark Arrester.* The spark arrester is a screen placed at the top of the flue to prevent combustibles from leaving the flue.

DRAWING THE FIREPLACE SECTION

The fireplace section can be a valuable part of the working drawings. Although a fireplace drawing is required by most building departments when a home has a masonry fireplace and chimney, a drafter may not be required to draw a fireplace section. Because of the similarities of fireplace design, a fireplace drawing is often kept on file as a stock detail at many offices. When a house is being drawn that has a fireplace, the drafter needs only to get the stock detail from a file, make the needed copies, and attach them to the prints of the plans.

In some areas, rather than the drafter providing the drawing, a standard fireplace drawing by the Masons Association may be attached to the plans as shown in Figure 32–6. Not all building departments will accept these drawings so check with your building department before you submit plans for a permit.

Fireplace Guidelines

If you are required to draw a fireplace section, use the drawings by the Masonry Institute of America as a guide. Fireplace drawings are also included in some codes such as *Dwelling Construction Under the Uniform Building Code* and would be helpful for the beginning drafter to use as a guide.

A print of the floor plans will be needed to help determine wall locations and the size of the fireplace. As the drawing for the fireplace is started, use construction lines. See Figure 32–7 for steps 1 through 4.

Layout of the Fireplace

Step 1. Lay out the width of the fireplace (20 in. for the firebox and 8 in. for the rear wall).

Step 2. Lay out all walls, floors, and ceilings that are near the fireplace. Be sure to maintain the required minimum distance from the masonry to the wood as determined by the code in your area.

Step 3. Lay out the foundation for the fireplace. The footing is typically 6 in. wider on each side than the fireplace and 12 in. deep.

Step 4. Lay out the hearth in front of the fireplace. The hearth will vary in thickness depending on the type of finishing material used. If the fireplace is being drawn for a house with a wood floor, the hearth will require

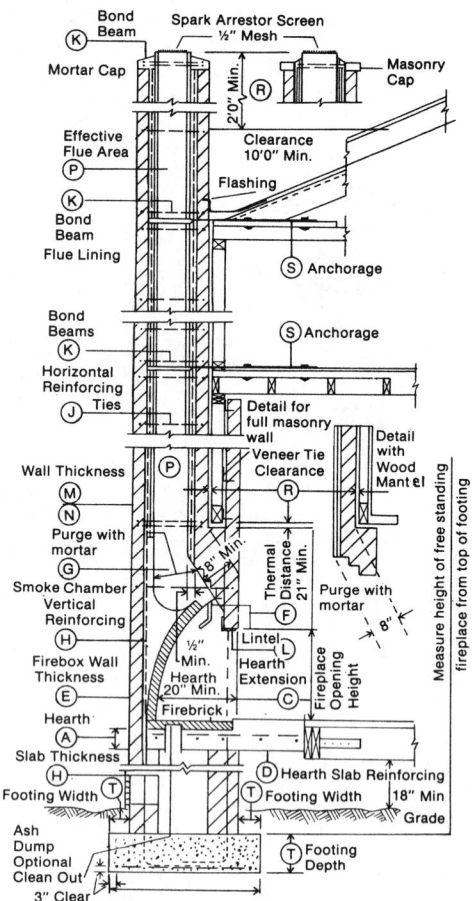

BRICK FIREBOX AND CHIMNEY— SECTIONAL SIDE VIEW ON WOOD FLOOR

Figure 32–6 A brick fireplace and chimney with a wood-framed floor. The circled letters refer to item references listed in Figure 32–2. *Reprinted from Residential Fireplace and Chimney Construction Details and Specifications,* with permission from the Masonry Institute of America, Los Angeles, CA.

a 4 in. minimum concrete slab projecting from the fireplace base to support the finished hearth.

See Figure 32–8 for steps 5 through 8.

Step 5. Lay out the firebox. Assume that a 36″ × 26″ × 20″ firebox will be used. See Figure 32–9 for guidelines for laying out the firebox.

Step 6. Determine the size of flue required. A 36″ × 26″ opening has an area of 936 sq in. By examining Figure 32–10, you can see that a flue with an area of 91 sq in. is required. The flue walls can be constructed using either 8 in. of masonry, or 4 in. of masonry and a clay flue liner. If a liner is used, a 13 in. round liner would be the minimum size required.

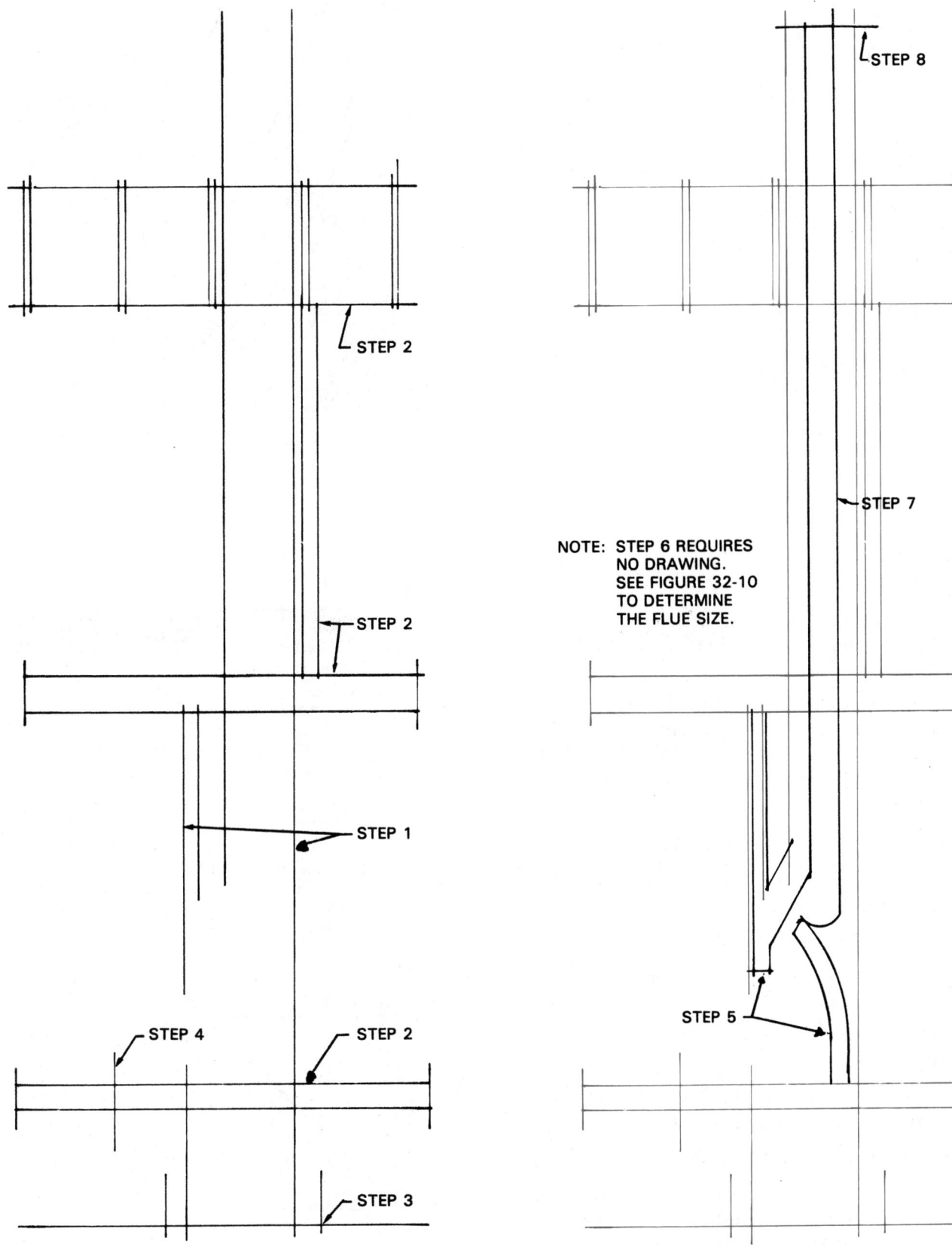

NOTE: STEP 6 REQUIRES
NO DRAWING.
SEE FIGURE 32-10
TO DETERMINE
THE FLUE SIZE.

Figure 32–7 Fireplace layout using construction lines.

Figure 32–8 Layout of the firebox and flue using construction lines.

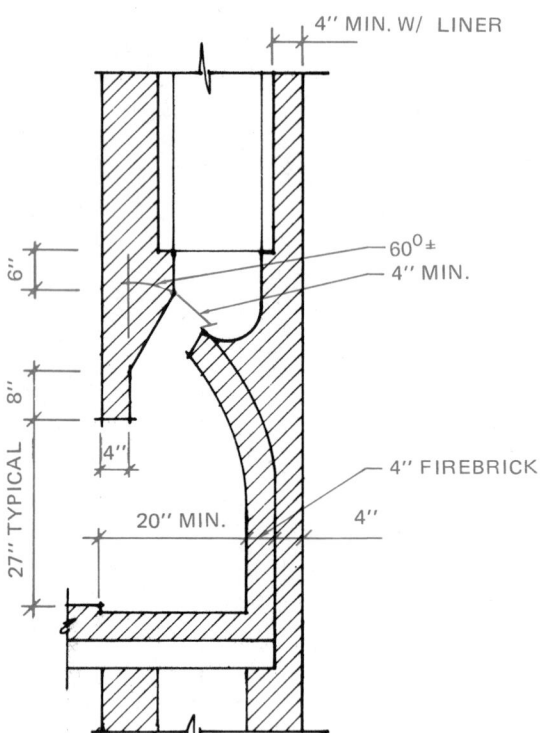

Figure 32-9 Firebox layout.

Step 7. Lay out the flue with a liner. Draw the interior face of the liner. The thickness will be shown later.

Step 8. Determine the height of the chimney. Most building codes require the chimney to project 24 in. minimum above any construction within 10 ft of the chimney. See Figure 32–11.

Drawing With Finished Quality Lines

Step 9. Use bold lines to outline all framing materials as shown in Figure 32–12.

See Figure 32–13 for steps 10 through 12.

Step 10. Use bold lines to outline the masonry, flue liner, and hearth.

Step 11. Use thin lines at a 45° angle to crosshatch the masonry.

Step 12. Crosshatch the firebrick with lines at a 45° angle so that a grid is created.

See Figure 32–14 for steps 13 through 15.

Step 13. Draw all reinforcing steel with bold lines. Verify with local building codes to determine what steel will be required.

Step 14. Draw the lintel with a very bold line.

Step 15. Draw the damper with a very bold line.

See Figure 32–15 for steps 16 and 17.

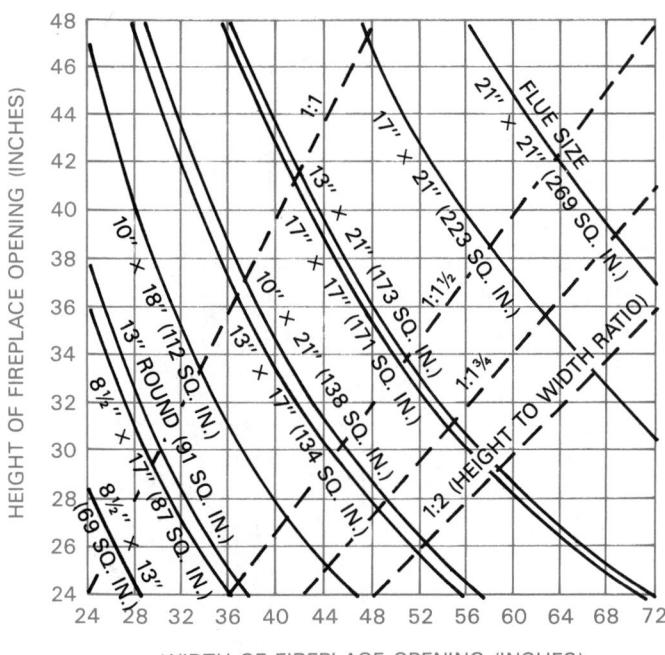

WIDTH OF FIREPLACE OPENING (INCHES)

GRAPH TO DETERMINE THE PROPER FLUE SIZE FOR A SINGLE-FACE FIREPLACE. BY MATCHING THE WIDTH AND HEIGHT OF THE FIREPLACE OPENING, THE MINIMUM FLUE SIZE CAN BE DETERMINED. ONCE THE MINIMUM FLUE SIZE HAS BEEN DETERMINED, THE CHIMNEY SIZE CAN BE DETERMINED.

Nominal Dimension of Flue Lining	Actual Outside Dimensions of Flue Lining	Effective Flue Area	Max. Area of Fireplace Opening	Minimum Outside Dimension of Chimney
8½" Round	8½" Round	39 sq. in.	390 sq. in.	17" x 17"
8½" x 13" oval	8½" x 12¾"	69 sq. in.	690 sq. in.	17" x 21"
8½" x 17" oval	8½" x 16¾"	87 sq. in.	870 sq. in.	17" x 25"
13" Round	12¾" Round	91 sq. in.	1092 sq. in.	21" x 21"
10" x 18" oval	10" x 17¾"	112 sq. in.	1120 sq. in.	19" x 26"
10" x 21" oval	10" x 21"	138 sq. in.	1380 sq. in.	19" x 30"
13" x 17" oval	12¾" x 16¾"	134 sq. in.	1340 sq. in.	21" x 25"
13" x 21" oval	12¾" x 21"	173 sq. in.	1730 sq. in.	21" x 30"
17" x 17" oval	16¾" x 16¾"	171 sq. in.	1710 sq. in.	25" x 25"
17" x 21" oval	16¾" x 21"	223 sq. in.	2230 sq. in.	25" x 30"
21" x 21" oval	21" x 21"	269 sq. in.	2690 sq. in.	30" x 30"

Figure 32-10 Flue and chimney sizes based on the area of the fireplace opening. *Reprinted from Residential Fireplace and Chimney Construction Details and Specifications, with permission from the Masonry Institute of America, Los Angeles, CA.*

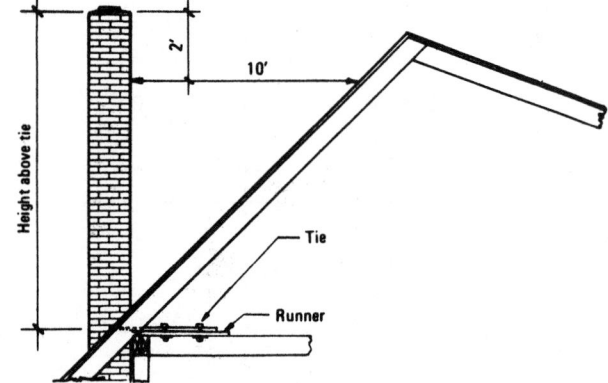

Figure 32-11 The chimney is required to extend 2 ft. above any part of the structure that is within 10 ft. *Reprinted from Residential Fireplace and Chimney Construction Details and Specifications, with permission from the Masonry Institute of America, Los Angeles, CA.*

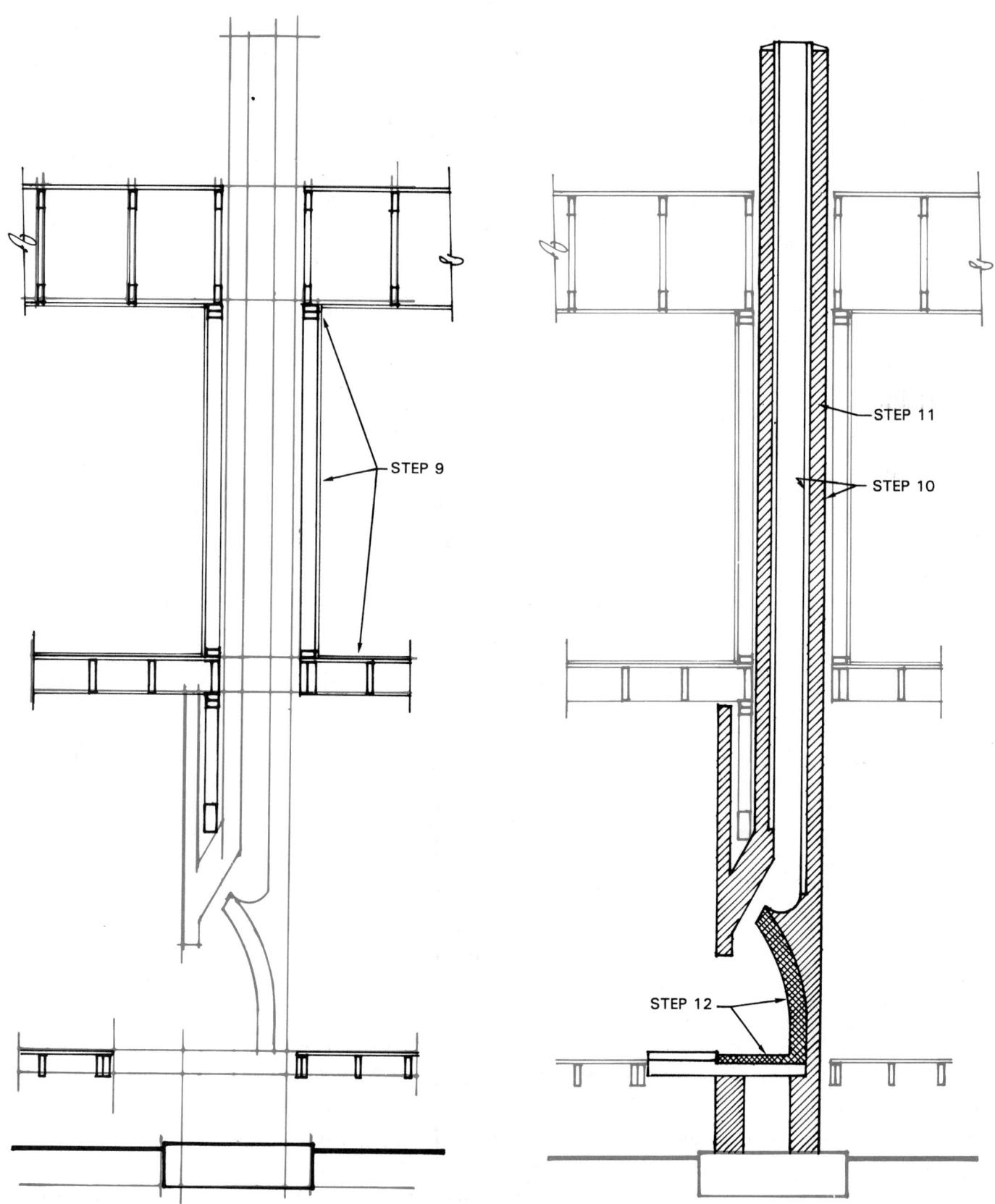

STEP 9

STEP 11

STEP 10

STEP 12

Figure 32–12 Draw all framing members with finished quality lines.

Figure 32–13 Darken all masonry.

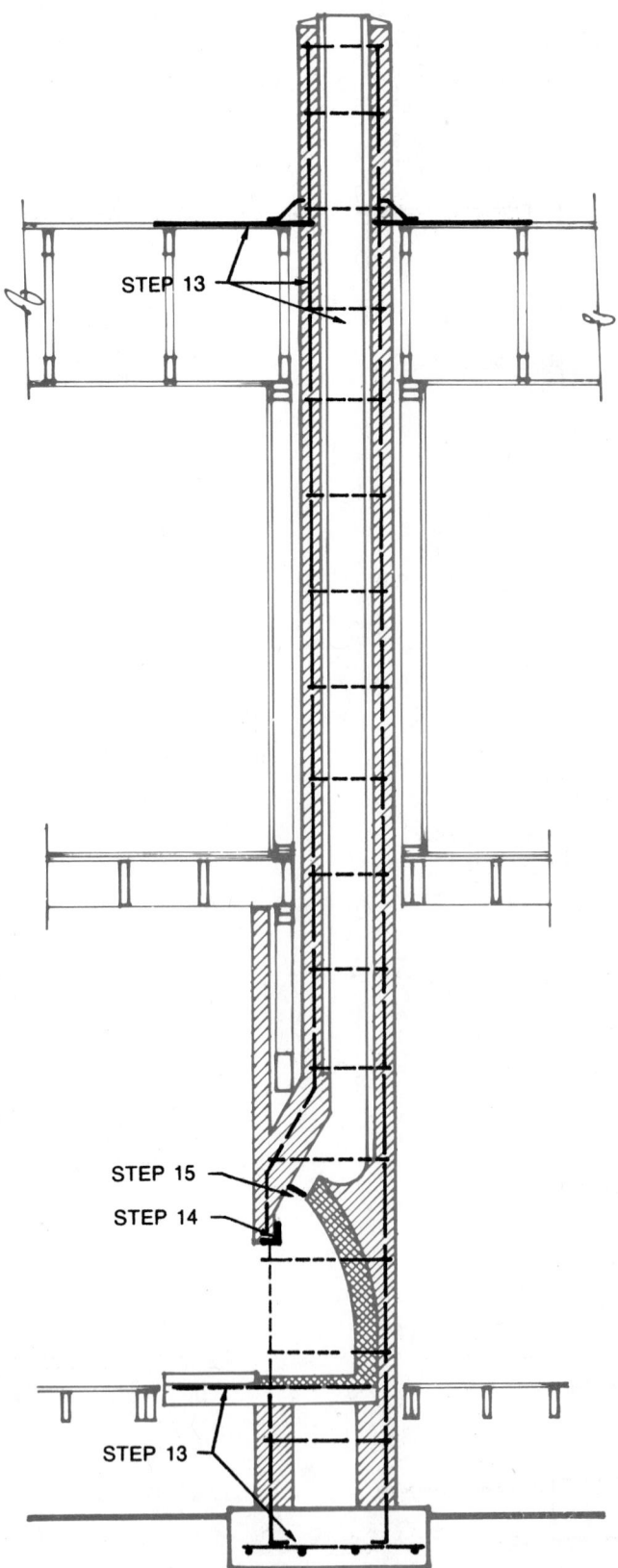

STEP 13

STEP 15

STEP 14

STEP 13

Figure 32–14 Draw all reinforcing steel.

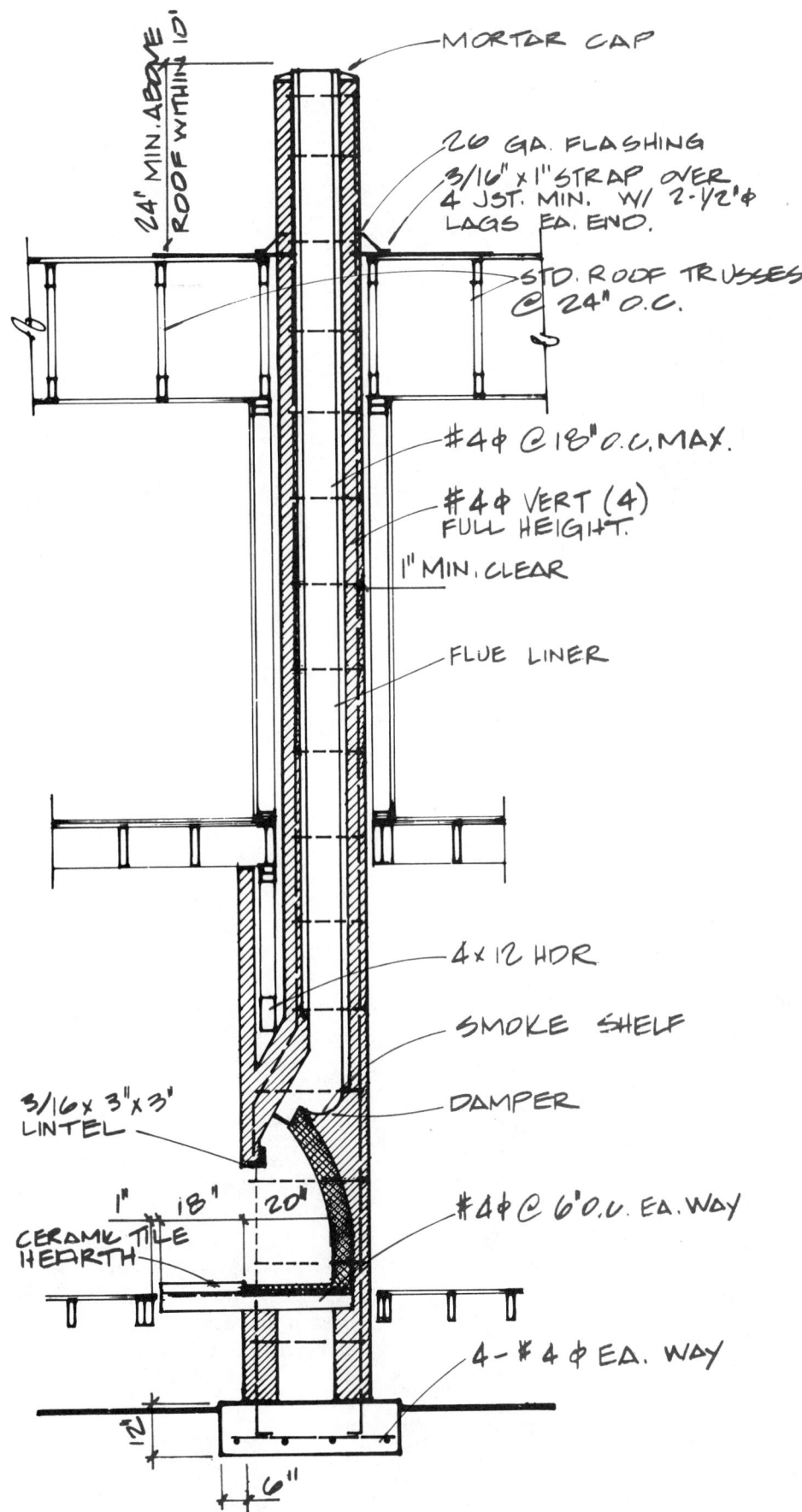

MORTAR CAP

24" MIN. ABOVE ROOF WITHIN 10'

26 GA. FLASHING
3/16" X 1" STRAP OVER
4 JST. MIN. W/ 2-1/2"∅
LAGS EA. END.

STD. ROOF TRUSSES
@ 24" O.C.

#4∅ @ 18" O.C. MAX.

#4∅ VERT (4)
FULL HEIGHT.

1" MIN. CLEAR

FLUE LINER

4 X 12 HDR

SMOKE SHELF

DAMPER

3/16 X 3" X 3"
LINTEL

1" 18" 20"

CERAMIC TILE
HEARTH

#4∅ @ 6" O.C. EA. WAY

4 - #4∅ EA. WAY

12"

6"

Figure 32–15 Place the notes and dimensions.

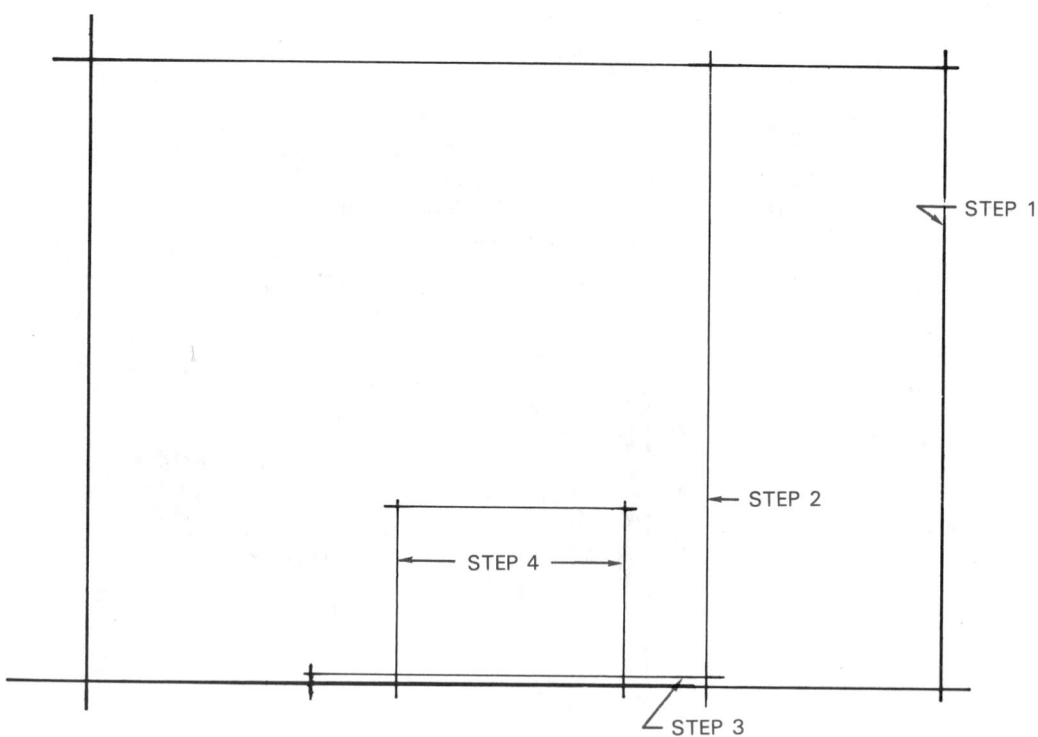

Figure 32-16 Fireplace elevation layout.

Step 16. Dimension the drawing. Items that must be dimensioned include the following:

   a. Height above roof
   b. Width of hearth
   c. Width and height of firebox
   d. Width and depth of footings
   e. Wood to masonry clearance

Step 17. Place notes on the drawing using Figure 32-15 as a guide. Remember that notes will vary depending on the code that you follow and depending on the structural material that has been specified on the floor and foundation plans.

 **FIREPLACE ELEVATIONS**

The fireplace elevation is the drawing of the fireplace as viewed from inside the home. Fireplace elevations typically show the size of the firebox and the material that will be used to decorate the face of the fireplace. Fireplace elevations can be drawn by using the following steps. See Figure 32-16 for steps 1 through 4.

Elevation Layout

Step 1. Lay out the size of the wall that will contain the fireplace.

Step 2. Lay out the width of the chimney.

Step 3. Lay out the height and width of the hearth if a raised hearth is to be used.

Step 4. Lay out the fireplace opening.

Finished Quality Lines

Usually the designer will provide the drafter with a rough sketch similar to Figure 32-17 to describe the finishing materials on the face of the fireplace. By using this sketch and the methods described in Chapter 24, the fireplace elevation can be drawn. See Figure 32-18. Once the finishing materials have been drawn, the elevation can be lettered and dimensioned as seen in Figure 32-19. Notes will need to be placed on the drawing to describe all materials. Dimensions will be required to describe:

   1. Room height
   2. Hearth height
   3. Fireplace opening height and width
   4. Mantel height

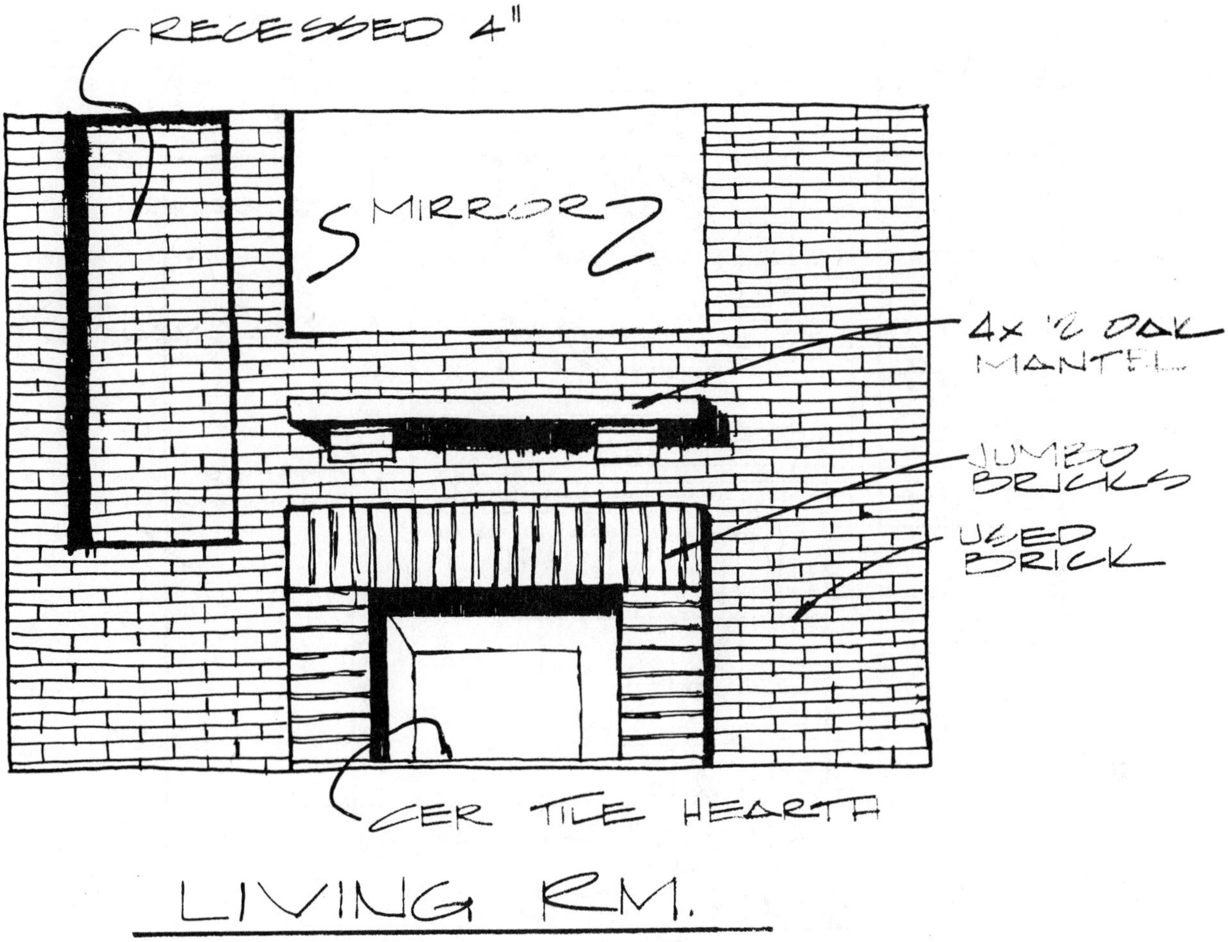

RECESSED 4"

MIRROR

4x '2 OAK MANTEL

JUMBO BRICKS

USED BRICK

CER TILE HEARTH

LIVING RM.

Figure 32–17 The drafter can often use the designer's preliminary sketch as a guide when drawing the finishing materials for a fireplace elevation.

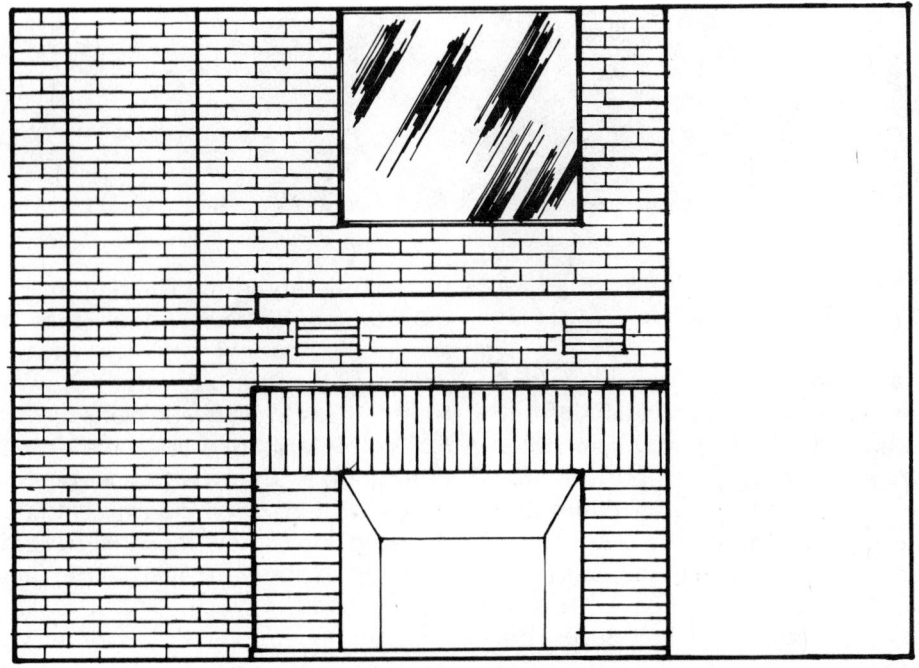

Figure 32–18 Drawing the finished elevation.

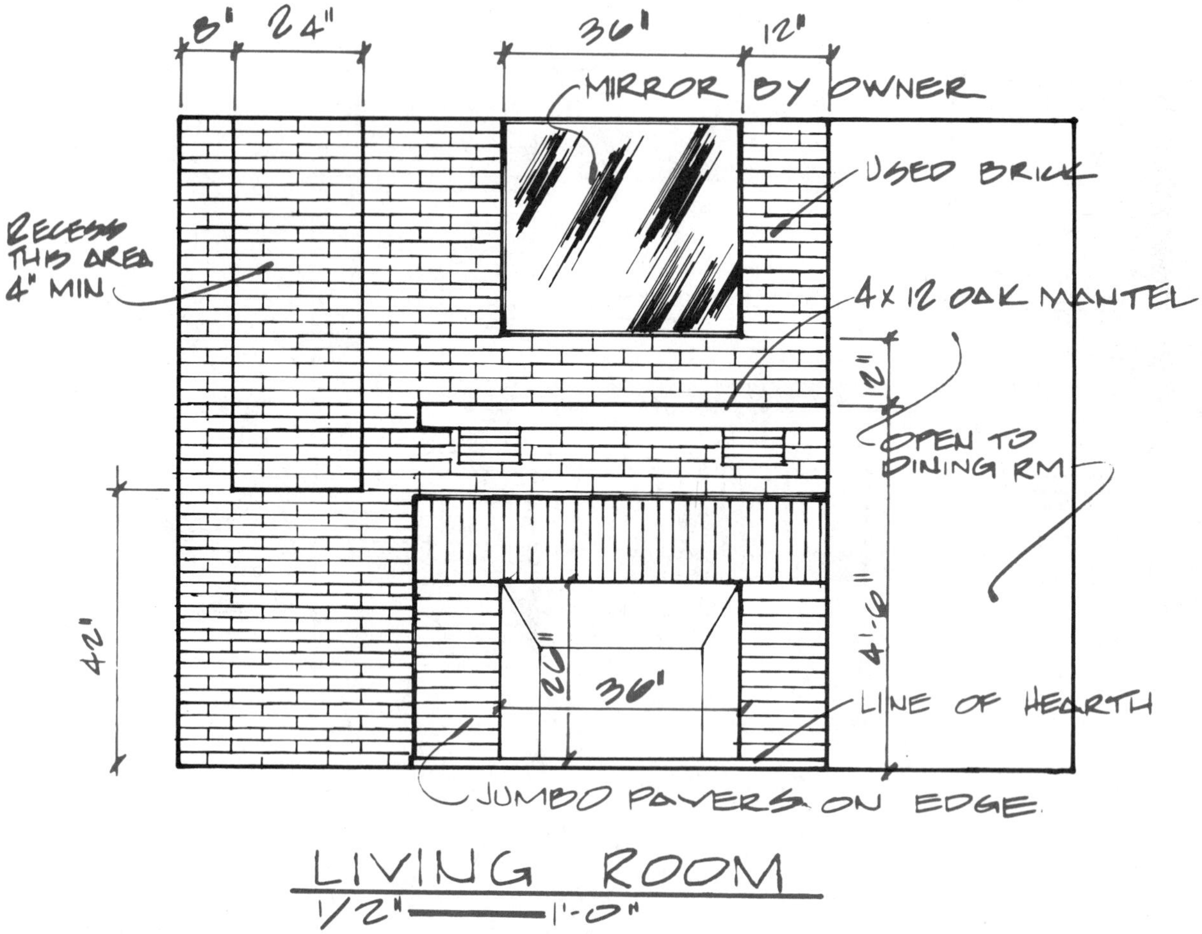

RECESS
THIS AREA
4" MIN

MIRROR BY OWNER

USED BRICK

4 X 12 OAK MANTEL

OPEN TO
DINING RM

LINE OF HEARTH

JUMBO PAVERS ON EDGE.

8" 24" 36" 12"

42" 36" 4'-0"

LIVING ROOM
1/2" = 1'-0"

Figure 32–19 Lettering and dimensions for a fireplace elevation.

CADD
applications

DRAWING FIREPLACE SECTIONS AND ELEVATIONS WITH CADD

A drafter uses standard fireplace sections whenever possible. Standard fireplace sections are available from the Masons Association and in the abridged code book *Dwelling Construction Under the Uniform Building Code*. This is also true when doing computer aided drafting. In many cases the architectural firm draws a number of standard fireplace sections and details. These typical sections are then saved in the CADD symbols library and called up when necessary to insert on a drawing. The standard sections may be completely dimensioned and noted, or the dimensions and specific notes may be added after the section is brought into the drawing. With manual drafting, the drafter either draws the section each time or uses Mylar® stick-ons as discussed in Chapter 6. The Mylar® stick-ons save drawing time, but they often look as though they were stuck onto the drawing. With CADD, standard sections are added to the drawing, and they look as if they are part of the drawing. A standard CADD fireplace section is shown in Figure 1.

Drawing fireplace elevations with CADD is easy because a fireplace elevation is normally either a

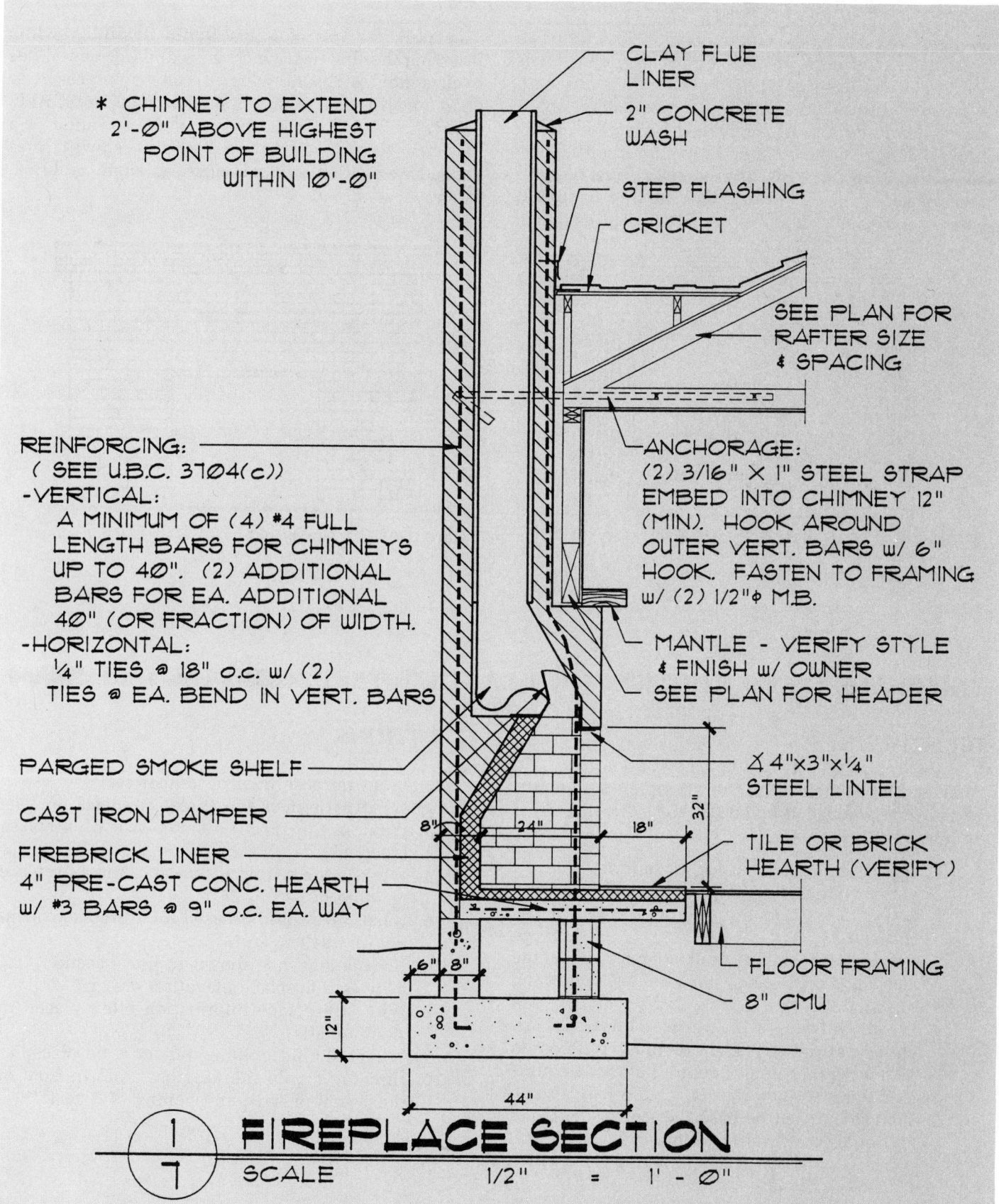

* CHIMNEY TO EXTEND 2'-Ø" ABOVE HIGHEST POINT OF BUILDING WITHIN 10'-Ø"

CLAY FLUE LINER

2" CONCRETE WASH

STEP FLASHING

CRICKET

SEE PLAN FOR RAFTER SIZE & SPACING

REINFORCING:
(SEE U.B.C. 3704(c))
-VERTICAL:
   A MINIMUM OF (4) #4 FULL LENGTH BARS FOR CHIMNEYS UP TO 40". (2) ADDITIONAL BARS FOR EA. ADDITIONAL 40" (OR FRACTION) OF WIDTH.
-HORIZONTAL:
   ¼" TIES @ 18" o.c. w/ (2) TIES @ EA. BEND IN VERT. BARS

ANCHORAGE:
(2) 3/16" X 1" STEEL STRAP EMBED INTO CHIMNEY 12" (MIN). HOOK AROUND OUTER VERT. BARS w/ 6" HOOK. FASTEN TO FRAMING w/ (2) 1/2"φ M.B.

MANTLE - VERIFY STYLE & FINISH w/ OWNER
SEE PLAN FOR HEADER

PARGED SMOKE SHELF

CAST IRON DAMPER

FIREBRICK LINER

4" PRE-CAST CONC. HEARTH w/ #3 BARS @ 9" o.c. EA. WAY

∠ 4"x3"x¼" STEEL LINTEL

TILE OR BRICK HEARTH (VERIFY)

FLOOR FRAMING

8" CMU

8"   24"   18"   32"

6"   8"

12"

44"

① / ⑦ **FIREPLACE SECTION**
SCALE   1/2"   =   1' - Ø"

Figure 1 CADD fireplace section.

fireplace box and a surrounding mantel, or a fireplace box and a masonry wall. In either case the job is simple. If you are drawing fireplace elevations with a surrounding mantel, draw a few standard applications and add one of them to the drawing at any time. Figure 2 shows a standard mantel in a fireplace elevation. With most CADD programs, these symbols are dragged onto the drawing where the computer gives you a chance to scale the display up or down.

This provides you with maximum flexibility while inserting the drawing. Once the standard mantel has been added to the drawing, it can be increased or decreased in size with commands such as SCALE, TRIM, or STRETCH. If the fireplace elevation is a masonry wall, all you do is define the area with lines and add elevation symbols such as stone or brick, as shown in Figure 3.

Figure 2 CADD mantel.

Figure 3 CADD representation of a fireplace masonry wall.

FIREPLACE CONSTRUCTION AND LAYOUT TEST

DIRECTIONS

Answer the questions with short complete statements or drawings as needed on an 8½ × 11 drawing sheet as follows:

1. Use ⅛ in. guidelines for all lettering.
2. Letter your name, Fireplace Construction and Layout Test, and the date at the top of the sheet.
3. Letter the question number and provide the answer. You do not need to write out the question.
4. Do all lettering with vertical uppercase architectural letters. Answers may be prepared on a word processor if appropriate with course guidelines.
5. Your grade will be based on correct answers and quality of line technique.

QUESTIONS

1. What purpose does a damper serve?
2. What parts does the throat connect?
3. What is the most common size of fireplace opening?
4. What is the required flue area for a fireplace opening of 44″ × 26″?
5. What flues could be used for a fireplace opening of 1,340 sq in.?
6. How is masonry shown in cross section?
7. Why is a fireplace elevation drawn?
8. Why is fireplace information often placed in stock details?
9. Where should chimney anchors be placed?
10. How far should the hearth extend in front of the fireplace with an opening of 7 sq ft?

FIREPLACE CONSTRUCTION AND LAYOUT PROBLEMS

Problem 32–1. Cape Cod. Using a print of your floor and foundation plans, evaluate the construction methods used and determine which sections and partial sections need to be drawn. Lay out a freehand sketch of the sections you will need showing all wall locations, floor supports, and roof construction. Include sections show-ing stair and masonry fireplace construction if required. Use a C-size drawing sheet to lay out and draw all needed sections. Choose a scale based on the reading material in this section and use the examples given in each chapter to help you complete your drawings.

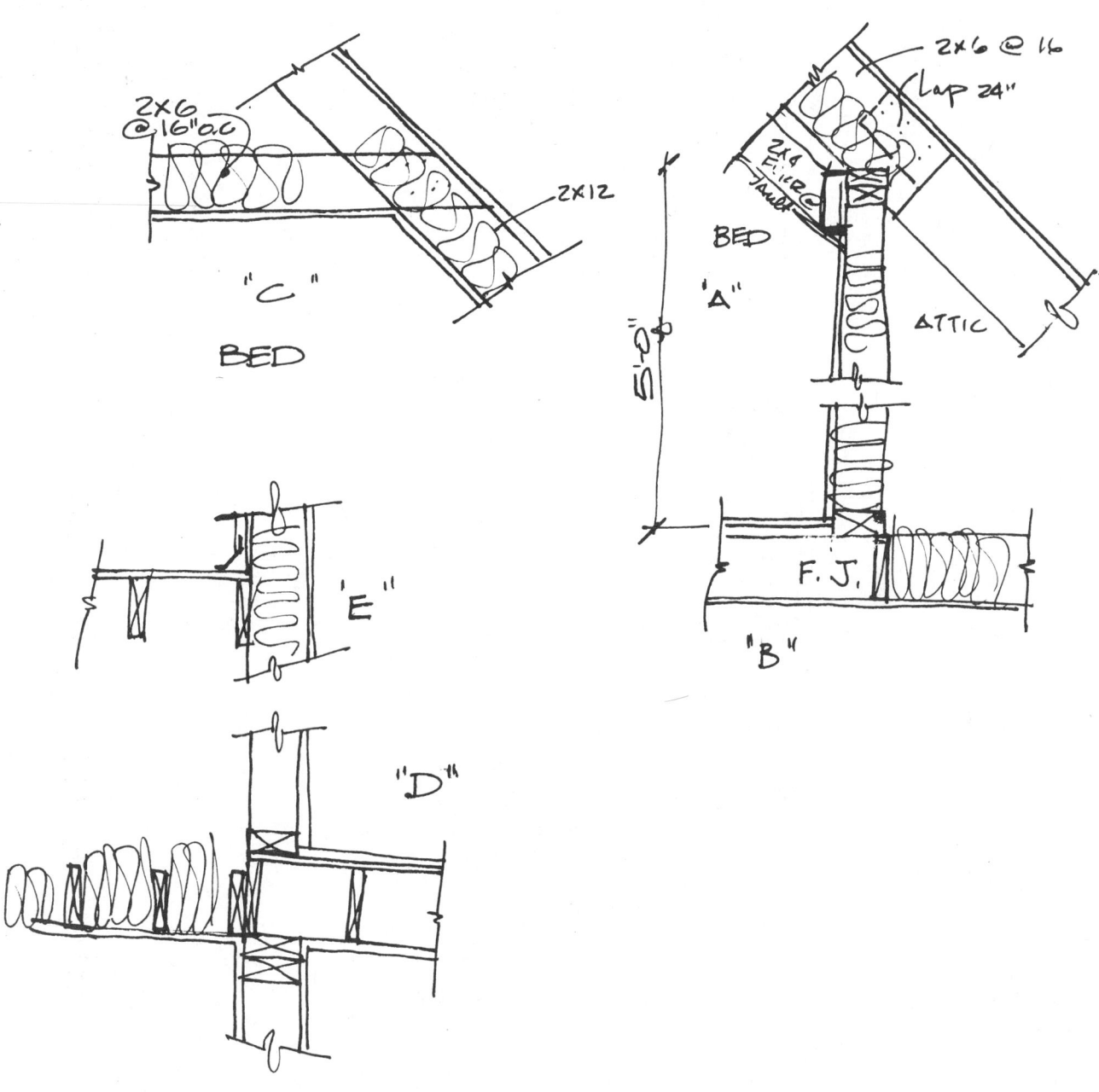

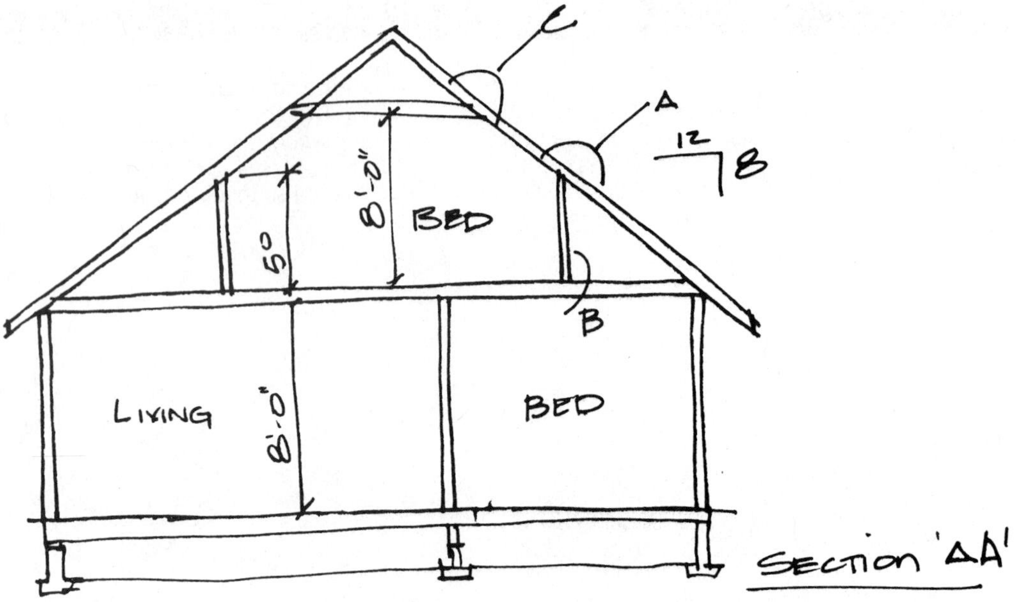

C

A

12 ⌐ 8

8'-0"

5°

BED

B

LIVING

8'-0"

BED

SECTION 'AA'

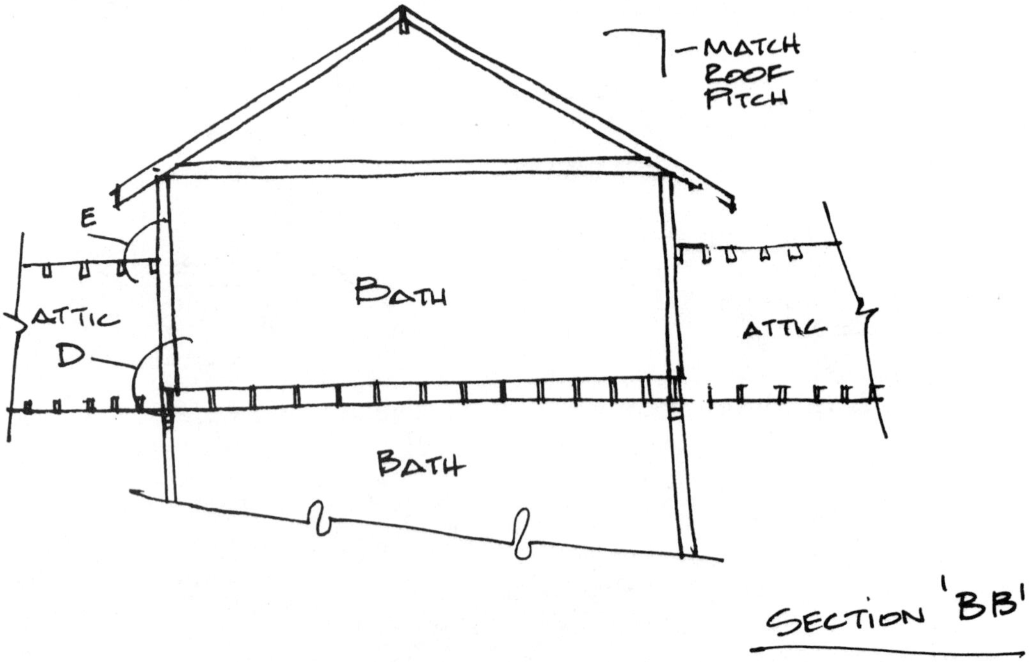

⌐MATCH ROOF PITCH

E

ATTIC

D

BATH

ATTIC

BATH

SECTION 'BB'

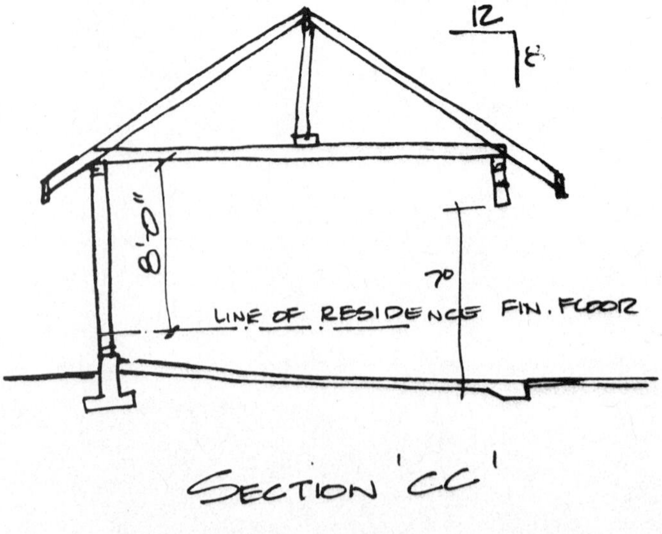

12 ⌐ 8

8'-0"

7°

LINE OF RESIDENCE FIN. FLOOR

SECTION 'CC'

Problem 32-2. Cabin. Using a print of your floor and foundation plans, evaluate the construction methods used and determine which sections and partial sections need to be drawn. Lay out a freehand sketch of the sections you will need showing all wall locations, floor supports, and roof construction. Include sections showing cantilevers, and stair construction. Use a C-size drawing sheet to lay out and draw all needed sections. Choose a scale based on the reading material in this section and use the examples given in each chapter to help you complete your drawings. Assume:

2 × 12 rafters @ 16″ O.C. w/10″ batts.
2 × 10 floor joists at 16″ O.C. at the upper floor level.
2 × 6 exterior studs at 16″ O.C.

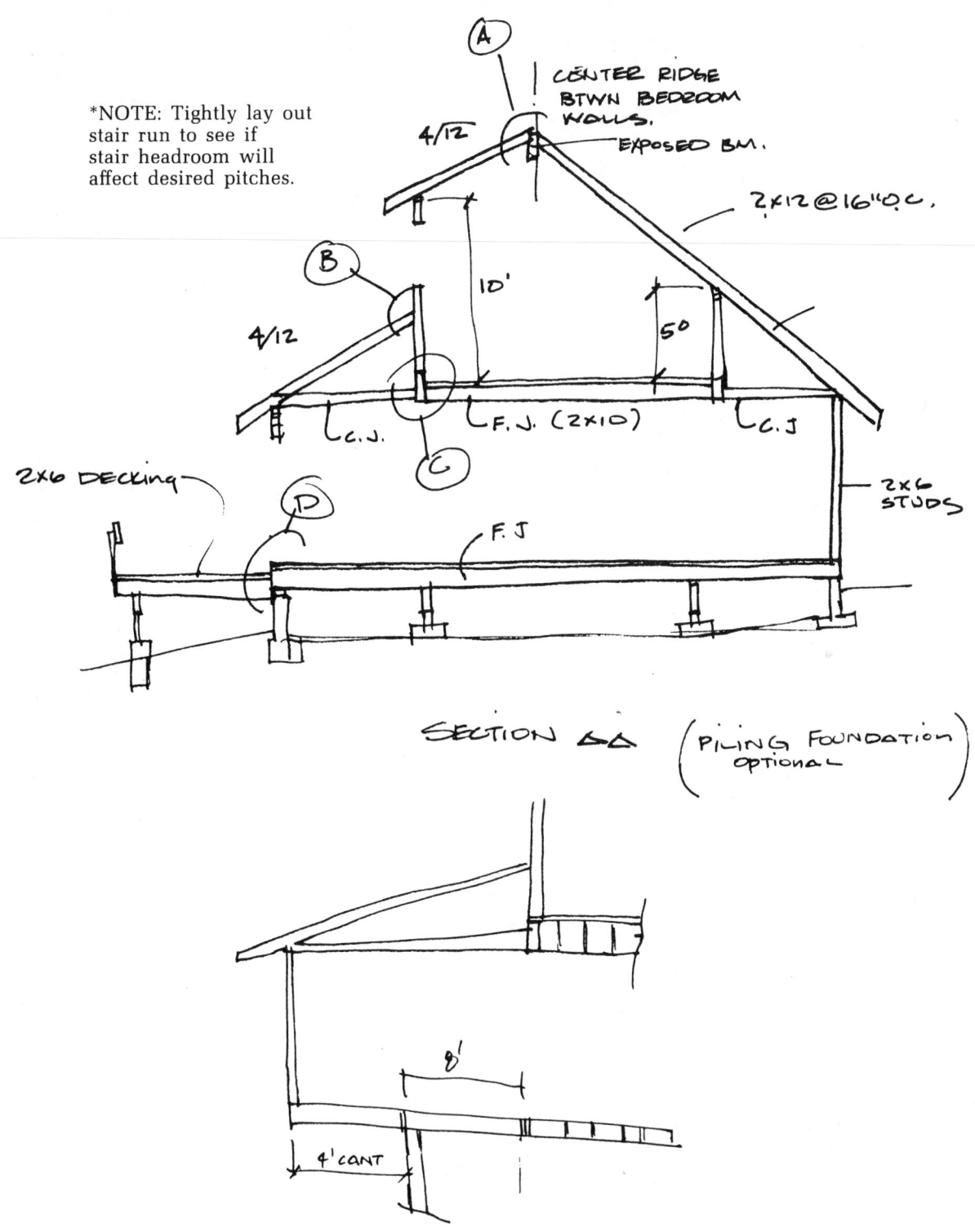

*NOTE: Tightly lay out stair run to see if stair headroom will affect desired pitches.

A
CENTER RIDGE BTWN BEDROOM WALLS.
4/12
EXPOSED BM.
2×12 @ 16″ O.C.
B
10'
4/12
50
2×6 DECKING
C.J.   F.J. (2×10)   C.J
C
2×6 STUDS
D
F.J

SECTION AA   (PILING FOUNDATION OPTIONAL)

8'
4' CANT

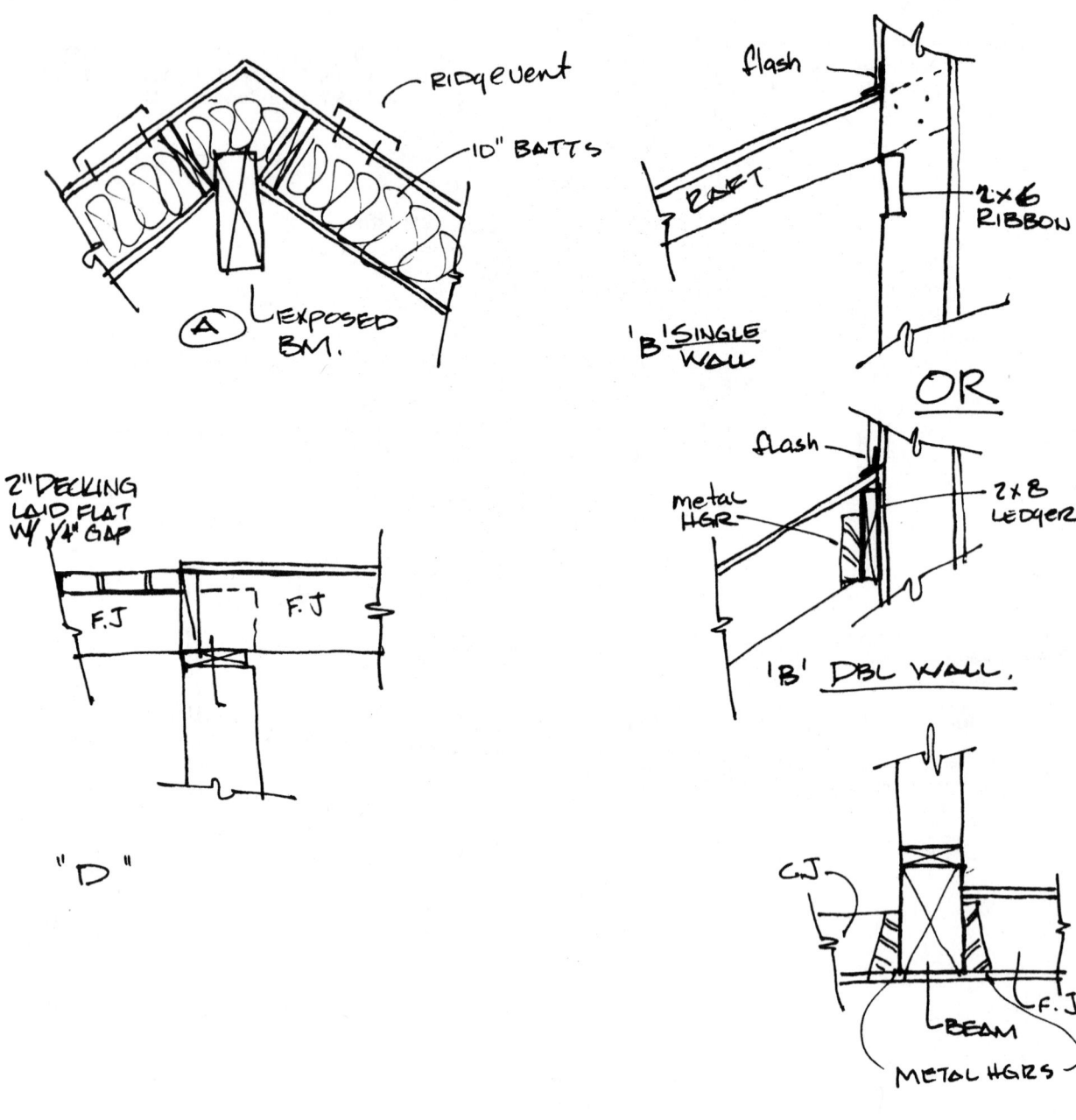

RIDGE VENT

10" BATTS

(A) EXPOSED BM.

flash

RAFT

2×6 RIBBON

'B' SINGLE WALL

OR

flash

metal HGR

2×8 LEDGER

'B' DBL WALL.

2" DECKING LAID FLAT W/ 1/4" GAP

F.J

F.J

"D"

C.J

BEAM

F.J

METAL HGRS

'C'

Problem 32–3. Ranch. Using a print of your floor and foundation plans, evaluate the construction methods used and determine which sections and partial sections need to be drawn. Lay out a freehand sketch of the sections you will need showing all wall locations, floor supports, and roof construction. Use a C-size drawing sheet to lay out and draw all needed sections. Choose a scale based on the reading material in this section and use the examples given in each chapter to help you complete your drawings. Ask your instructor what type of floor system to use. Assume:

Truss roof @ 24″ O.C.
Scissor trusses over living room. Interior pitch @ 3/12.

Use 2 × 6 rafters in areas where trusses cannot be used. Determine spacing.

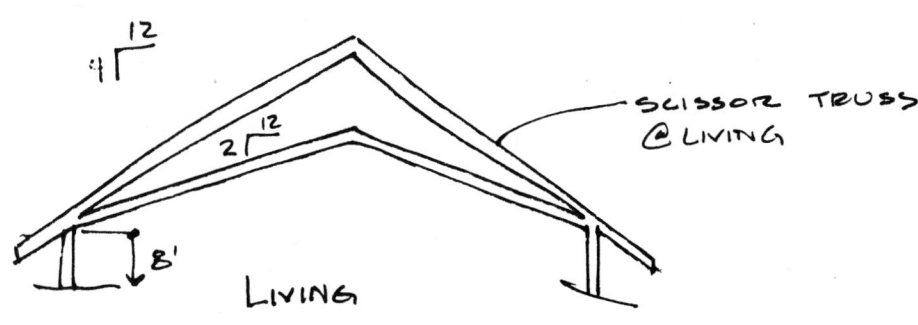

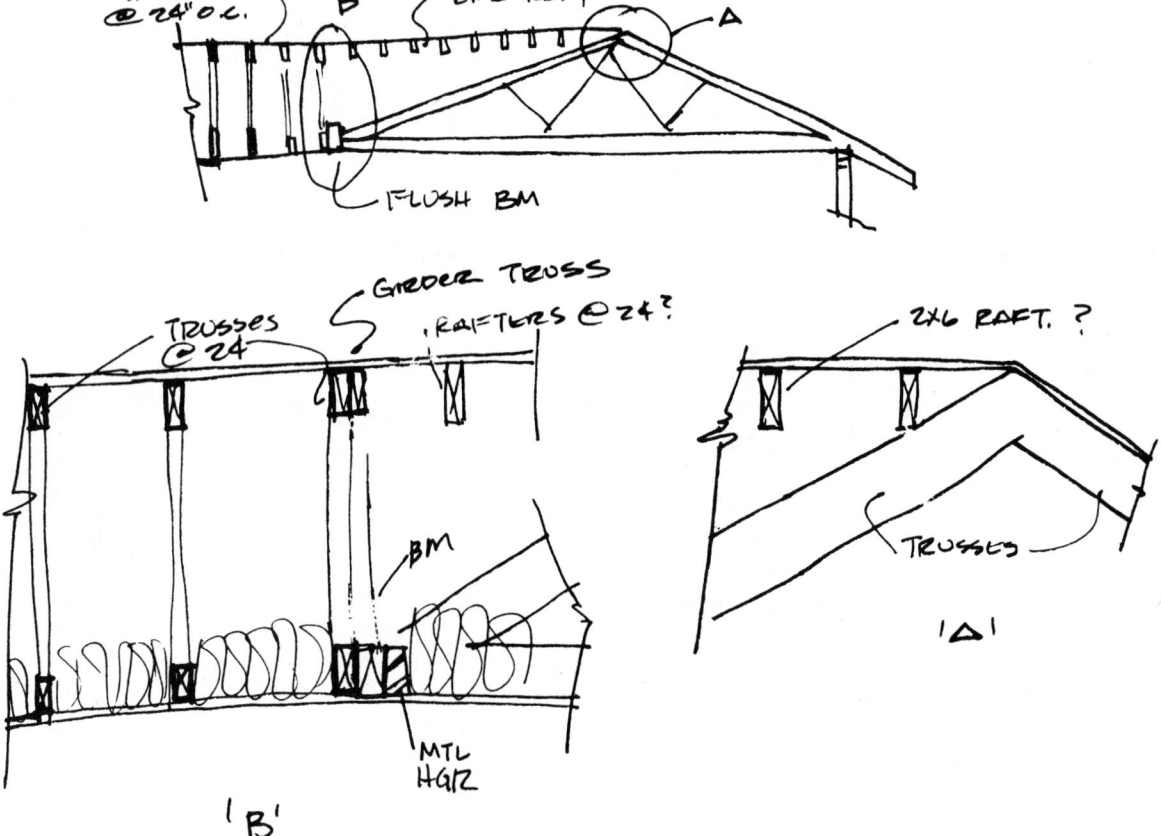

Problem 32-4. Spanish. Using a print of your floor and foundation plans, evaluate the construction methods used and determine which sections and partial sections need to be drawn. Lay out a freehand sketch of the sections you will need showing all wall locations, floor supports, and roof construction. Include a section showing masonry fireplace construction, if required. Use a C-size drawing sheet to lay out and draw all needed sections. Choose a scale based on the reading material in this section and use the examples given in each chapter to help you complete your drawings. Ask your instructor what type of floor system to use. Assume:

Rafter/C.J. @ 16″ O.C.
¼″ per 12″ min. roof pitch.

Use 2 × 6 rafters in areas where trusses can't be used. Determine spacing.

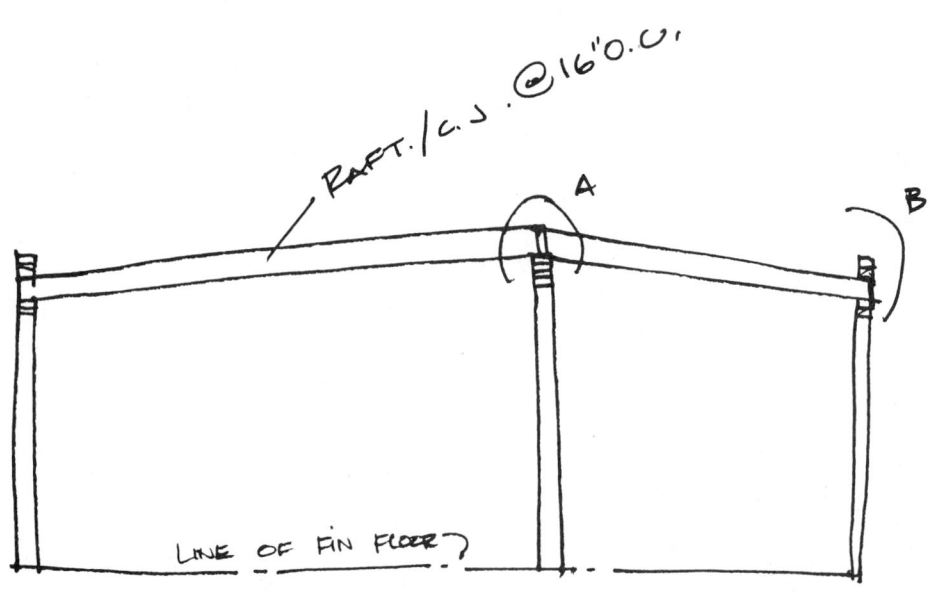

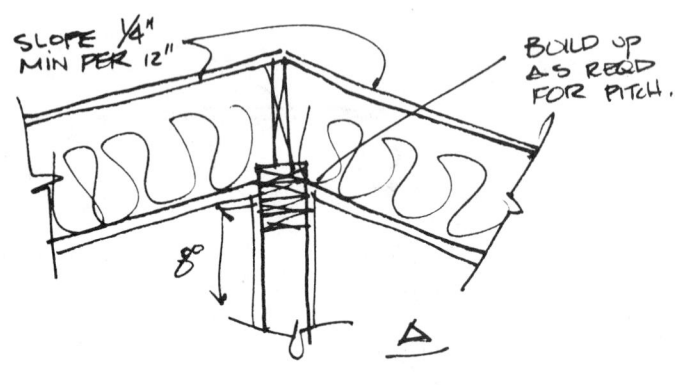

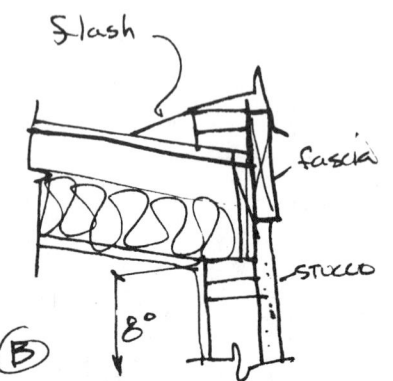

Problem 32–5. Early American. Using a print of your floor and foundation plans, evaluate the construction methods used and determine which sections and partial sections need to be drawn. Lay out a freehand sketch of the sections you will need showing all wall locations, floor supports, and roof construction. Include sections showing stair and masonry fireplace construction if required. Use a C-size drawing sheet to lay out and draw all needed sections. Choose a scale based on the reading material in this section and use the examples given in each chapter to help you complete your drawings. Assume:

Rafter/C.J. @ 16″ O.C. over master bedroom.
Rafters @ 24″ O.C. except at vaulted ceilings.
Determine proper sizes for floor joists.

Unless your instructor tells you otherwise, use concrete blocks for the basement walls.

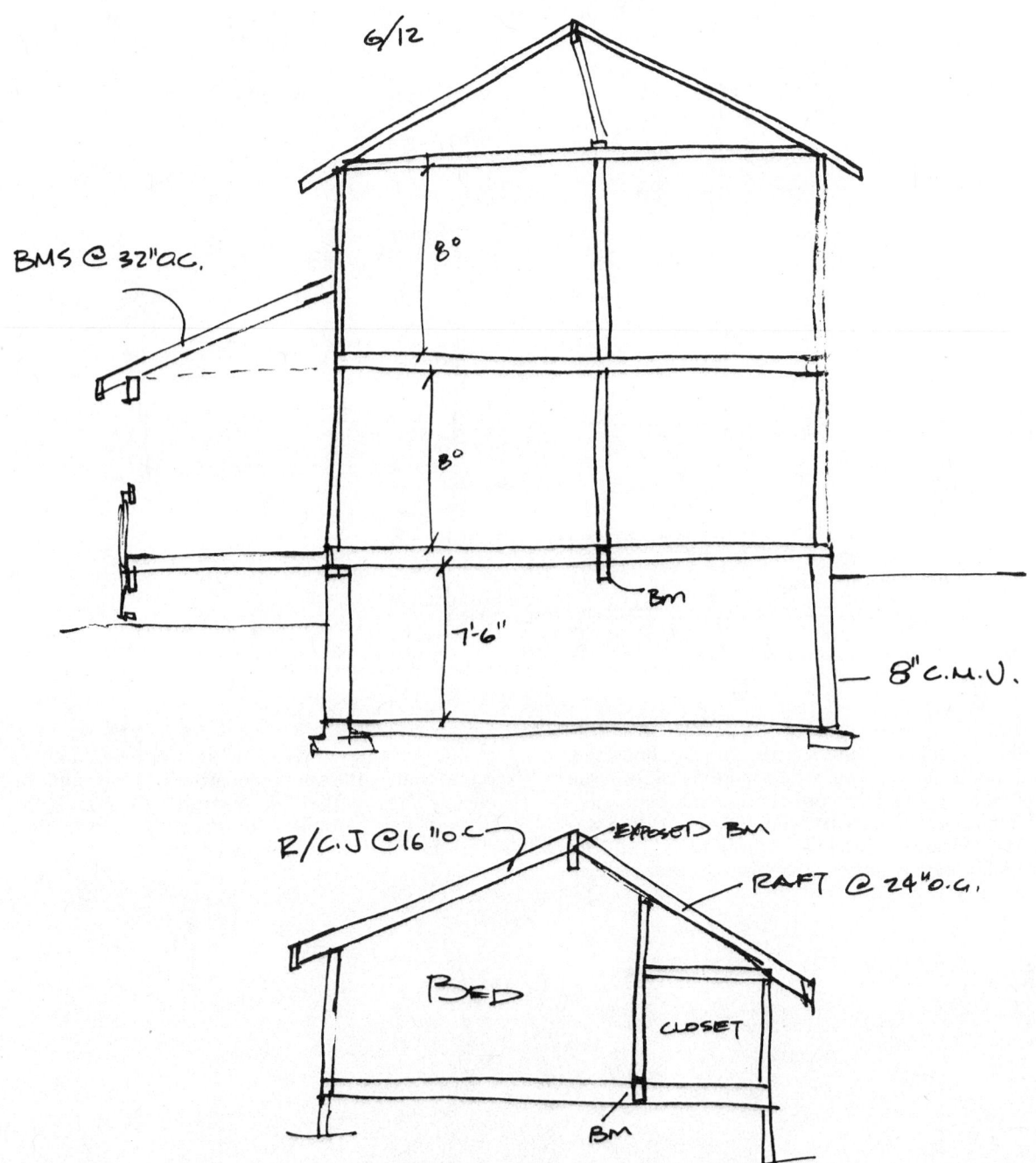

Problem 32–6. Contemporary. Using a print of your floor and foundation plans, evaluate the construction methods used and determine which sections and partial sections need to be drawn. Lay out a freehand sketch of the sections you will need showing all wall locations, floor supports, and roof construction. Include sections showing stair and masonry fireplace construction. Use a C-size drawing sheet to lay out and draw all needed sections. Choose a scale based on the reading material in this section and use the examples given in each chapter to help you complete your drawings. Determine proper sizes for all framing members.

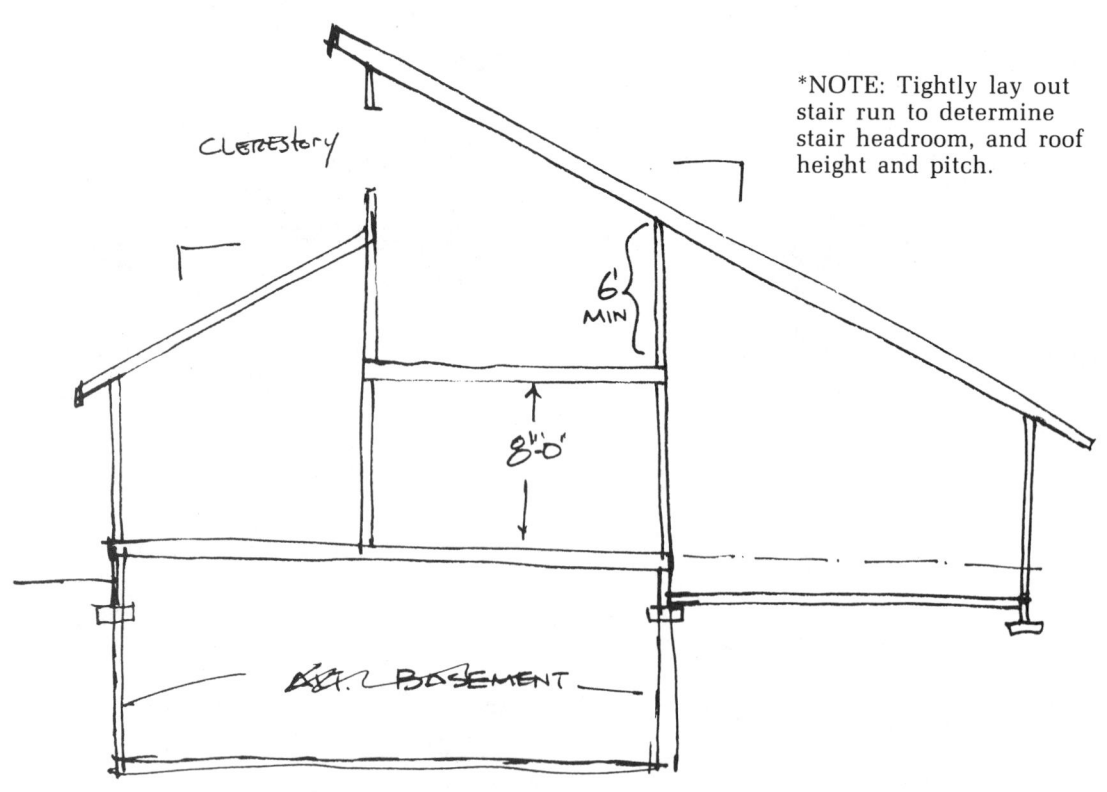

*NOTE: Tightly lay out stair run to determine stair headroom, and roof height and pitch.

Problem 32–7. Duplex. Using a print of your floor and foundation plans, determine what sections should be drawn. Use energy-efficient construction methods suitable for your area. Check with your local building department to determine if special treatment is required for the wall between the two units. Use D-size vellum to lay out and complete all required sections. Choose a scale that will allow construction information to be clearly shown. Use the examples given in each chapter to help you complete the drawings. Determine proper sizes for all framing members.

Section Seven
Roof Plans

Chapter 33
Roof Plan Components

Figure 33-1 The shape of the roof can play an important role in the design of the structure as seen in this home by architect Robert Roloson. *Photo courtesy Red Cedar Shingle & Handsplit Shake Bureau.*

Figure 33-2 In addition to aesthetic considerations, the roof is often used to resist wind and seismic forces when walls of the structure contain large amounts of glass as seen in this home by architect Claude Miquelle. *Photo courtesy Red Cedar Shingle & Handsplit Shake Bureau.*

THE DESIGN of the roof must be considered long before the roof plan is drawn. The architect or designer will typically design the basic shape of the roof as the floor plan and elevations are drawn in the preliminary design stage. This does not mean that the designer plans the entire structural system for the roof during the initial stages, but the general shape and type of roofing material to be used will be planned. By examining the structure in Figure 33-1, you can easily see how much impact the roof design has on the structure. Often the roof can present a larger visible surface area than the walls. In addition to aesthetic considerations, the roof can also be used to provide rigidity in a structure when wall areas are filled with glass as seen in Figure 33-2. To insure that the roof will meet the designer's criteria, a roof plan is usually drawn by the drafter to provide construction information. In order to draw the roof plan, a drafter should understand types of roof plans, various pitches, common roof shapes, and common roof materials.

TYPES OF ROOF PLANS

The plan that is drawn of the roof area may be either a roof plan or a roof framing plan. For some types of roofs a roof drainage plan may also be drawn.

Roof Plans

A roof plan is used to show the shape of the roof and the size and direction of its major construction materials. Other materials such as the roofing material, vents and their location, and the type of underlayment are also typically specified on the roof plan and can be seen in Figure 33–3. Roof plans are typically drawn at a scale smaller than the scale used for the floor plan. A scale of ⅛″ = 1′-0″ or 1/16″ = 1′-0″ is commonly used when drawing a roof plan. When drawing residential projects, the roof framing will usually be shown on a roof plan. The project may even be simple enough that the structural in-

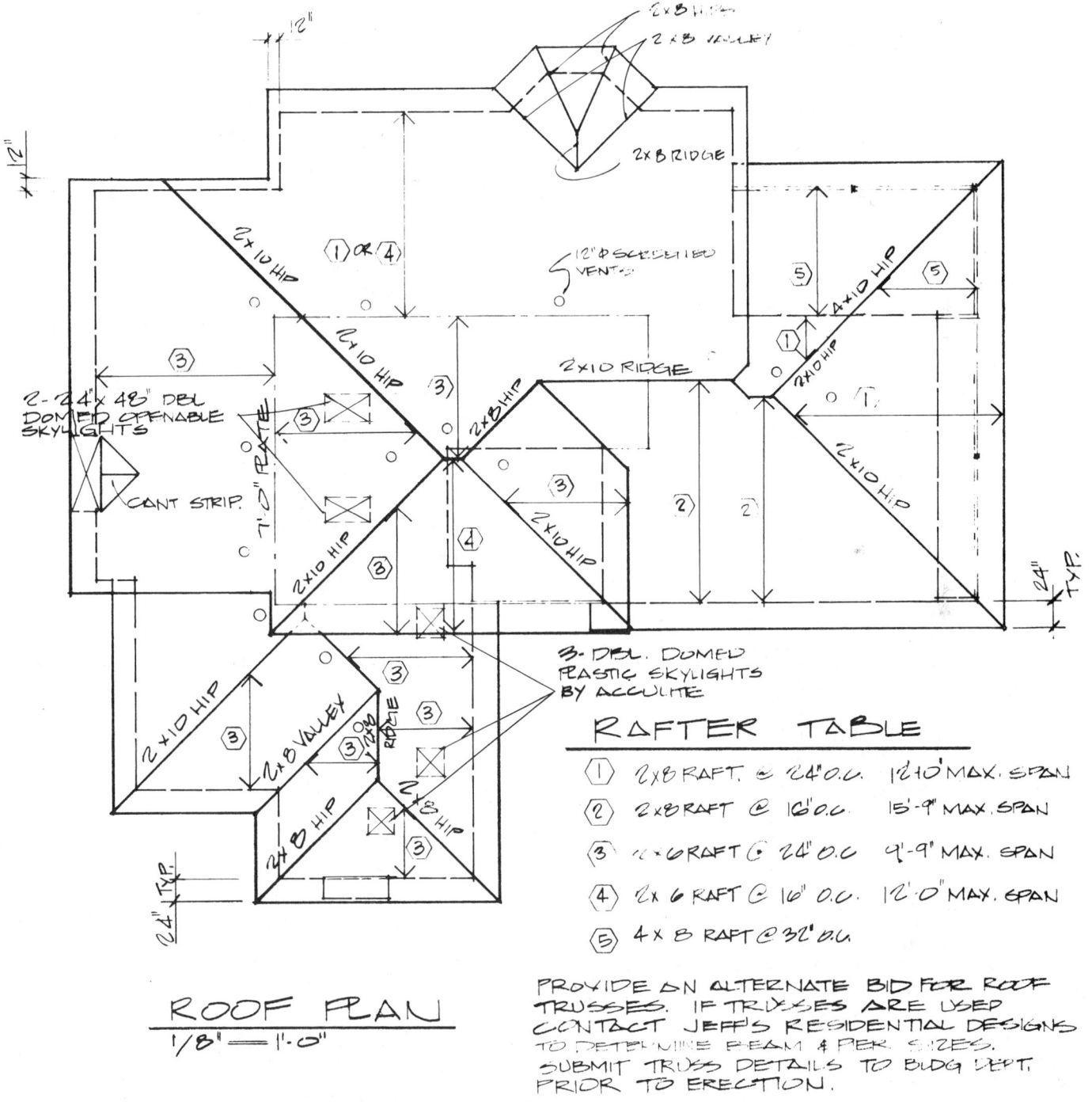

Figure 33–3 A roof plan is drawn to show the shape of the roof and the size and direction of framing members. *Courtesy Jeff's Residential Designs.*

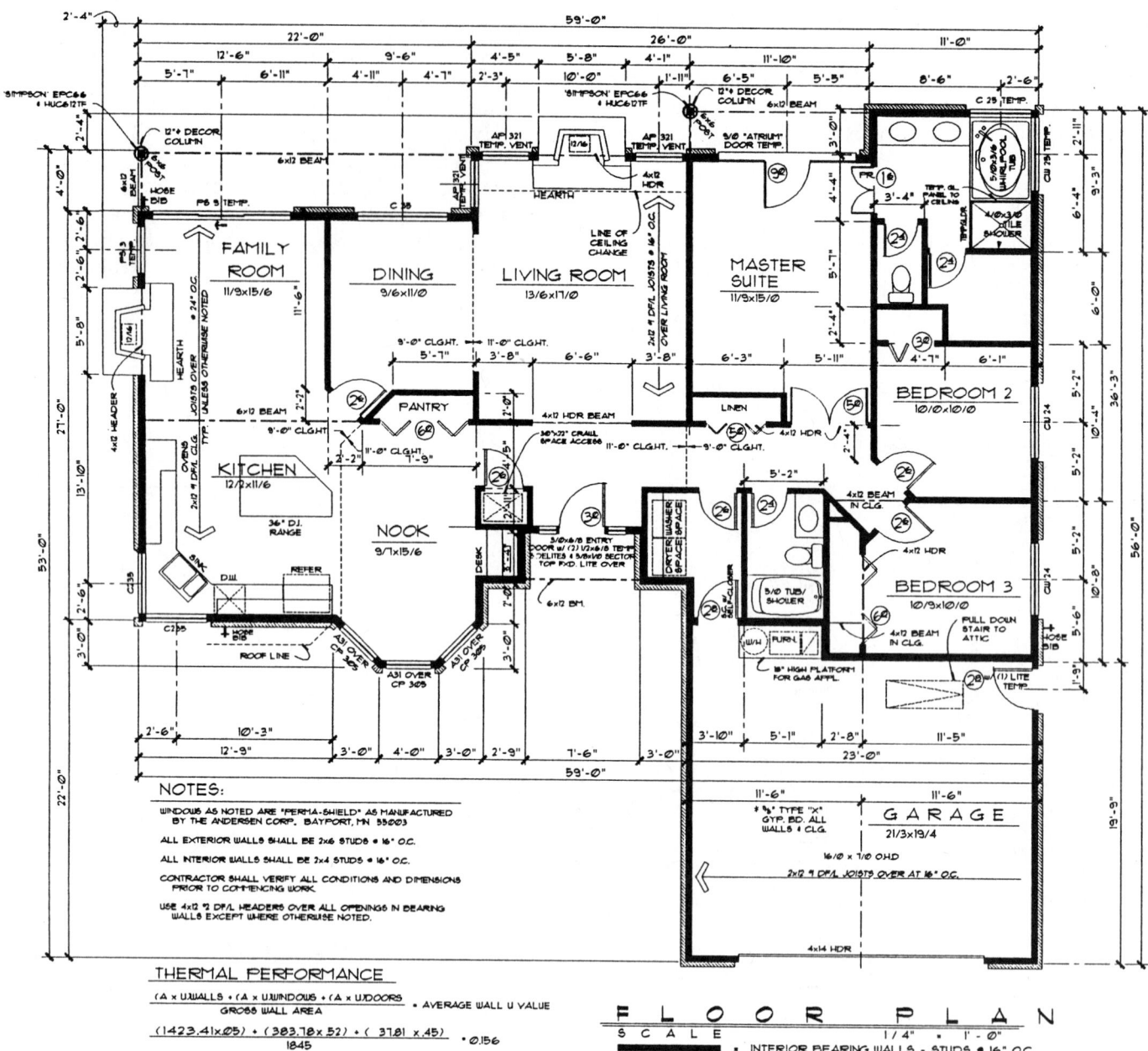

Figure 33-4 On simple roof shapes, the structural material can often be shown on the floor plan. *Courtesy Wally Greiner A.I.B.D. Sunridge Designs.*

formation can be placed on the floor plan, and other related information can be shown on the sections. Projects framed with trusses often do not require a roof plan. See Figure 33-4 for a floor plan that contains roof framing information.

Roof Framing Plans

Roof framing plans are usually required on complicated residential roof shapes and with most com-

mercial projects. A roof framing plan shows the size and direction of every construction member that is required to frame the roof. Figure 33-5 shows an example of a roof framing plan. Don't skim over the word *every*. A residential roof framing plan typically shows each member required to frame the roof. On a commercial project with repetitive members, only a portion of the roof is usually drawn as shown in Figure 33-6. On a complicated structure, a roof framing plan is drawn to locate the framing members,

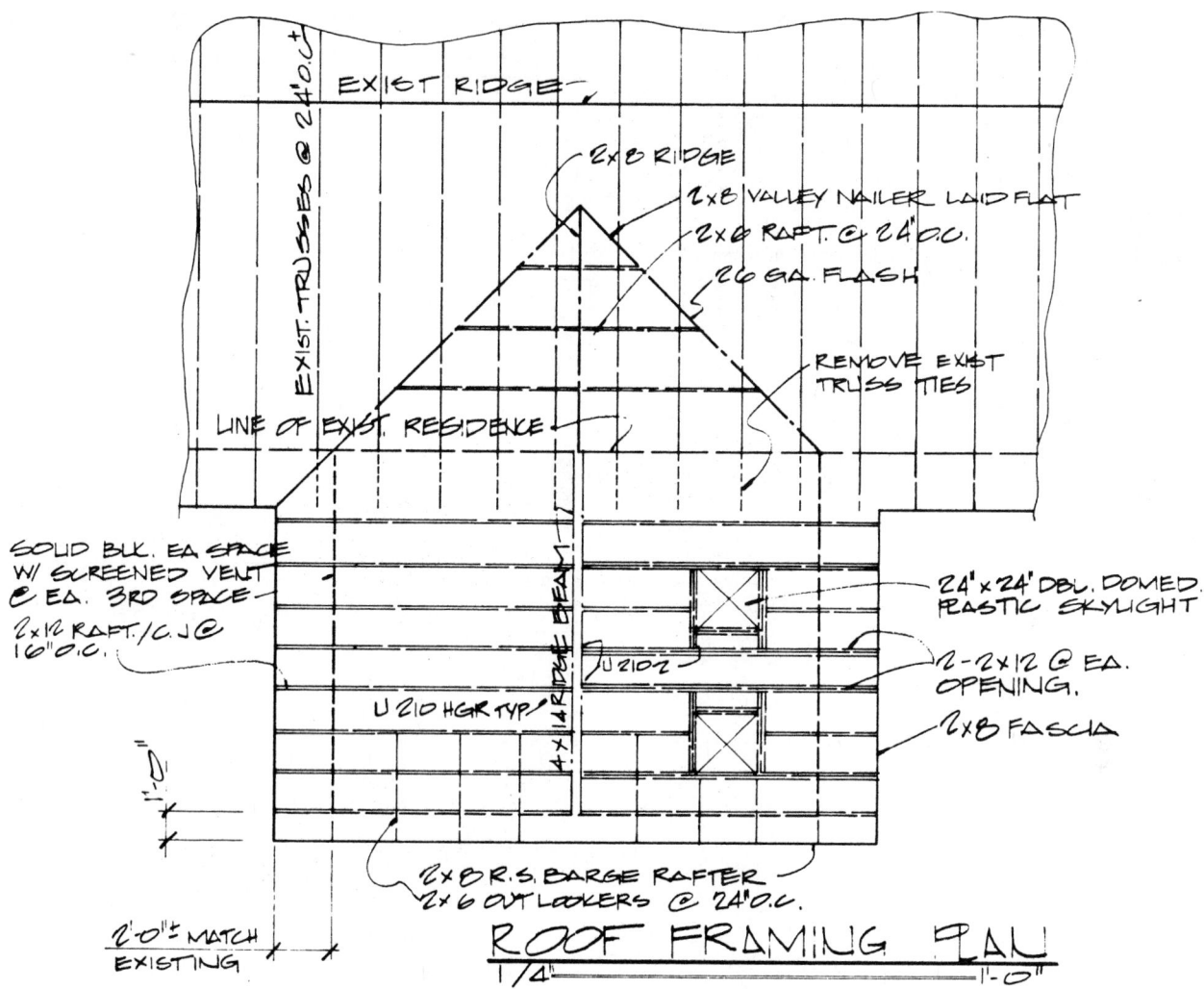

EXIST RIDGE

EXIST. TRUSSES @ 24'0.C.

2x8 RIDGE

2x8 VALLEY NAILER LAID FLAT
2x6 RAFT. @ 24" O.C.
26 GA. FLASH

REMOVE EXIST
TRUSS TIES

LINE OF EXIST. RESIDENCE

SOLID BLK. EA SPACE
W/ SCREENED VENT
@ EA. 3RD SPACE
2x12 RAFT./C.J @
16" O.C.

4 x 14 RIDGE BEAM

U 210 Z

U 210 HGR TYP.

24"x 24" DBL. DOMED.
PLASTIC SKYLIGHT

2-2x12 @ EA.
OPENING.

2x8 FASCIA

2x8 R.S. BARGE RAFTER
2x6 OUTLOOKERS @ 24'0.C.

ROOF FRAMING PLAN
1/4" = 1'-0"

2'-0"± MATCH
EXISTING

Figure 33–5 A roof framing plan may be drawn for complicated roofs to show the size and location of every structural member. *Courtesy Jeff's Residential Designs.*

and a roof plan is drawn to locate drains, vents, and other nonstructural materials. The framing plan is usually drawn at the same scale as the floor plan.

Roof Drainage Plans

A roof drainage plan is a plan showing how water will be diverted over and away from the roof system. Figure 33–7 shows an example of a roof drainage plan. The roof drainage plan will typically show ridges or valleys in the roof, roof drains, and downspouts. On a residence or small commercial project this information can be placed on the roof plan. On large commercial jobs, a separate plan is usually required to show this material. Because of its simplicity, the plan is usually drawn at a scale much smaller than the floor plan. Scales of 1/16" = 1'-0" or 1/32" = 1'-0" are commonly used. On both the

roof and the framing plan, the pitch, the type of roof, and kind of roofing material will need to be considered by the drafter in order to complete the plan.

ROOF PITCHES

Roof pitch, or slope, is a description of the angle of the roof that compares the horizontal run to the vertical rise. The slope is shown when the elevations and sections are drawn and were shown in Chapters 25 and 29. The intersections that result from various roof pitches must be shown on the roof plan. In order to correctly plot the intersection between two roof surfaces, the drafter must understand how various roof pitches are drawn. Figure 33–8 shows how the pitch can be visualized. The drafter can plot the roof shape using this method for any pitch. Adjustable

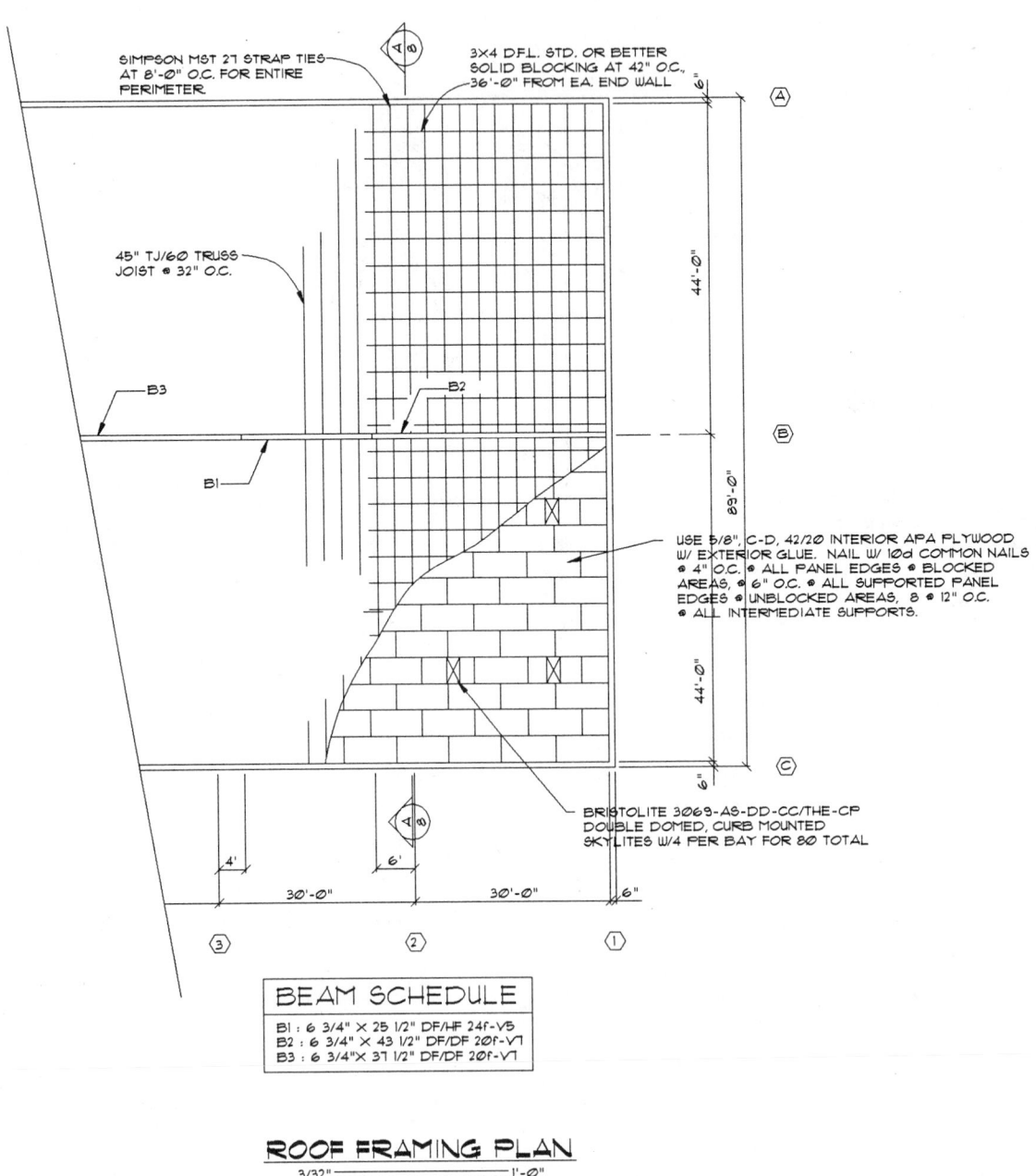

Figure 33–6 On projects with repetitive elements, only a portion of the roof will usually be drawn.

triangles for plotting roof angles are available and save the time of having to measure the rise and run of a roof. The roof can also be drawn if the drafter knows the proper angle that a certain pitch represents. Knowing that a 4/12 roof equals 18½° allows the drafter to plot the correct angle without having to plot the layout or use special equipment. Figure 33–9 shows angles for common roof pitches.

When drawing a roof plan for a structure with equal roof pitches, the intersection, or ridge, will be formed halfway between the two walls supporting the rafters as shown in Figure 33–10. When the roof pitches are unequal, the drafter must plot the proper pitches and determine the location of the intersection. This same method of plotting pitches must be used when supporting walls for the rafters are at different heights, or when the roof is constructed with multiple shapes as seen in Figure 33–11. The pitch also can determine the size of the rafter to be used. When a rafter is at an angle of 30° or less from vertical, the roof member can actually be considered as a wall member rather than a rafter. See Figure 33–12.

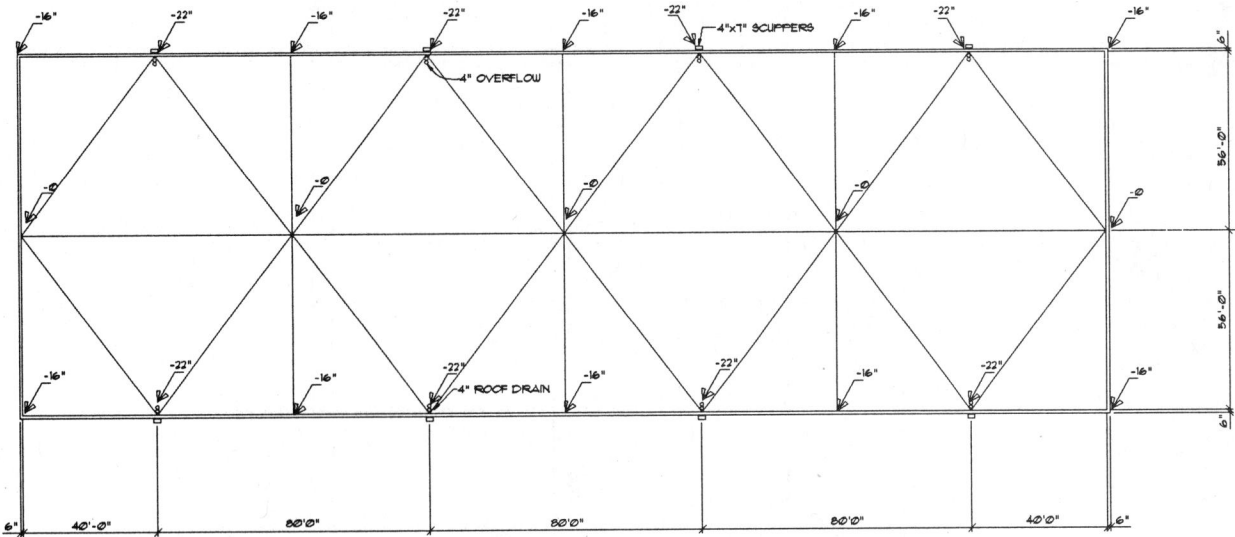

ROOF DRAINAGE PLAN
1/16" ═══════ 1'-0"

GENERAL NOTES:

1. ROOF AND OVERFLOW DRAINS TO BE GENERAL PURPOSE
   W/ NON-FERROUS DOMES AND 4" DIA. OUTLETS.

2. OVERFLOW DRAINS TO BE SET W/ INLET 2" ABOVE DRAIN INLETS
   SHELL BE CONNECTED TO DRAIN LINES INDEPENDENT OF
   ROOF LINES.

3. SCUPPERS TO BE 4" H, X 7" W W/ 4" RECTANGULAR CORRUGATED
   DOWNSPOUTS. PROVIDE A 6" X 9" CONDUCTOR HEAD AT THE TOP
   OF THE DOWN SPOUTS.

Figure 33-7 The roof drainage plan is often used to show the shape of the roof and drainage system.

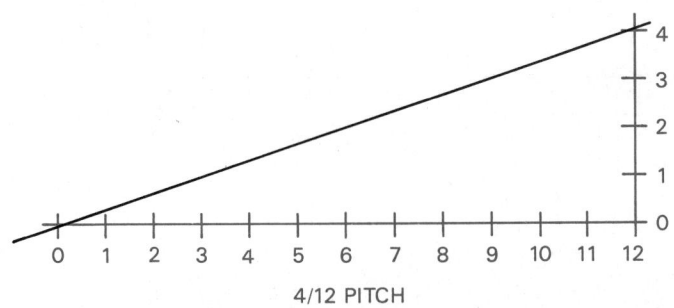

4/12 PITCH

Figure 33-8 When plotting a roof slope, the angle is expressed as a comparison of equal units. Units may be inches, feet, meters, etc., as long as the horizontal and vertical units are of equal length.

COMMON ANGLES FOR DRAWING ROOF PITCHES	
Roof Pitch	**Angle**
1/12	4°–30'
2/12	9°–30'
3/12	14°–0'
4/12	18°–30'
5/12	22°–30'
6/12	26°–30'
7/12	30°–0'
8/12	33°–45'
9/12	37°–0'
10/12	40°–0'
11/12	42°–30'
12/12	45°–0'

Figure 33-9 Common roof pitches and angles. Angles shown are approximate, and are to be used for drawing purposes only.

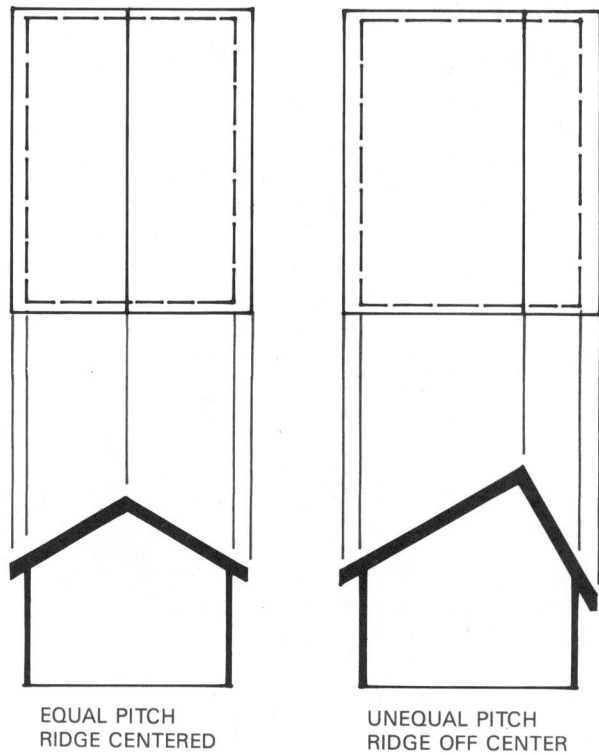

EQUAL PITCH
RIDGE CENTERED

UNEQUAL PITCH
RIDGE OFF CENTER

Figure 33–10 Roof pitches will affect the intersection of each surface.

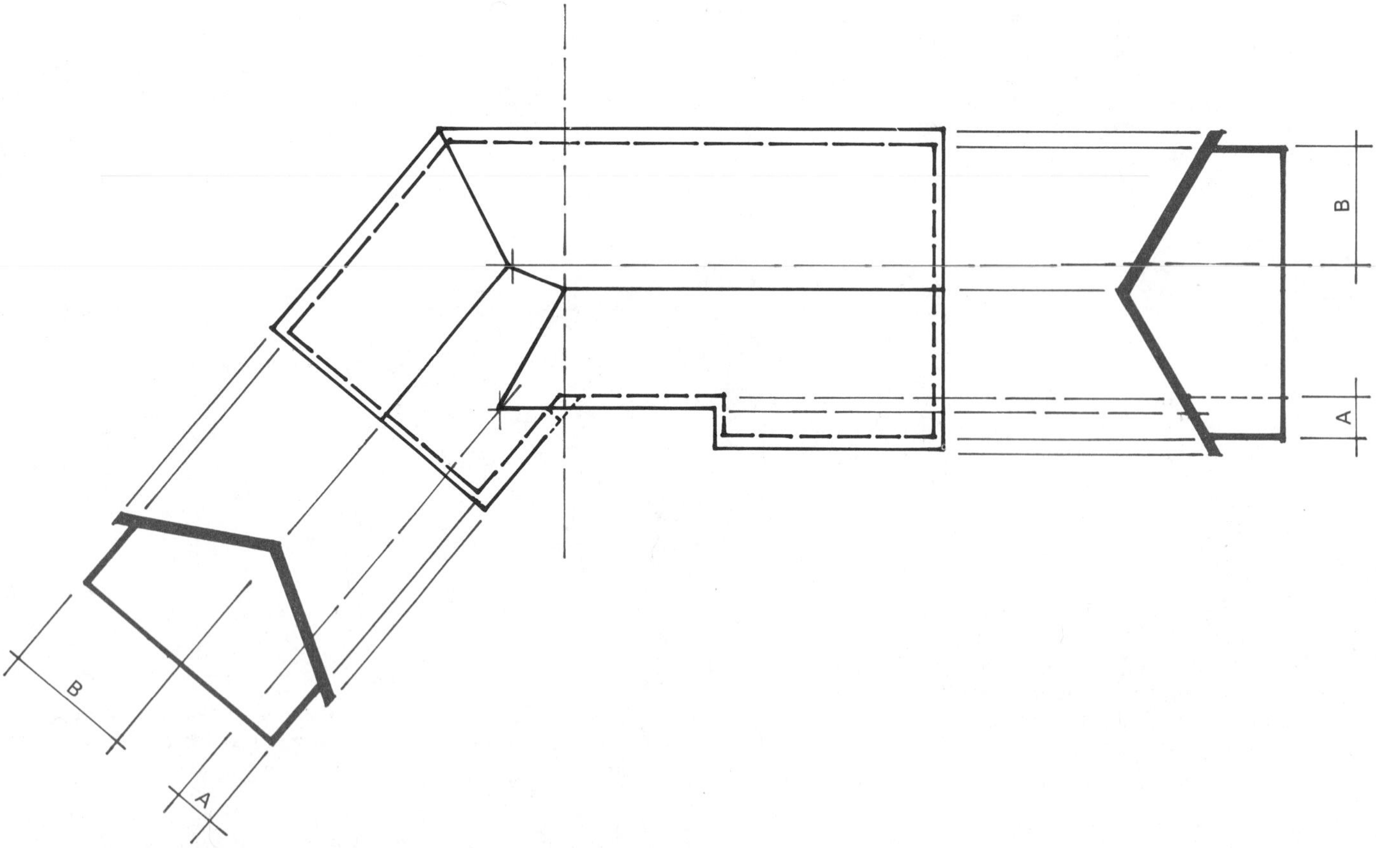

Figure 33–11 When roofs have multiple shapes, the intersection can be difficult to draw. A section often needs to be drawn near the roof plan to project distances from one roof surface to another.

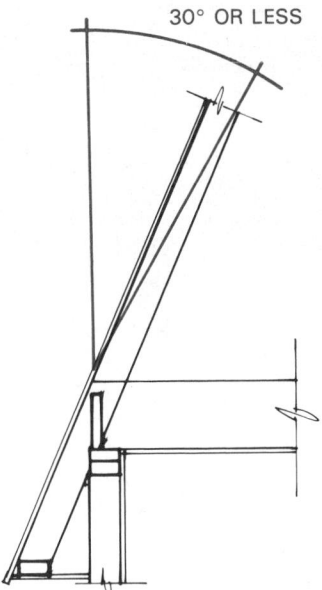

Figure 33-12 The roof pitch can often affect the size of the framing members. When a rafter is within 30° of vertical, it may be sized as a wall member rather than a roof member.

ROOF SHAPES

By changing the roof pitch the shape of the roof may be changed. Common roof shapes include flat, shed, gable, A-frame, gambrel, hip, Dutch hip, and mansard. Each can be seen in Figure 33-13. See Chapter 27 for a review of roof framing terms.

Flat Roofs

The flat roof is a very common style of roof in areas with little rain or snow. In addition to being used in residential construction, the flat roof is typically used on commercial structures to provide a platform for heating and other mechanical equipment. The flat roof is economical to construct because ceiling joists are eliminated and rafters are used to support both the roof and ceiling loads. Figure 33-14 shows the common materials used to frame a flat roof. Figure 33-15 shows how a flat roof could be represented on the roof plan.

Often the flat roof has a slight pitch in the rafters. A pitch of 1/8 in. per ft is often used to help prevent water from ponding on the roof. As water flows to the edge, a metal diverter is usually placed at the eave to prevent dripping at walkways. A flat roof will often have a parapet, or false wall, surrounding the perimeter of the roof. Figure 33-16 provides an example of a parapet wall. This wall can be used for decoration or for protection of mechanical equipment. When used it must be shown on the roof plan.

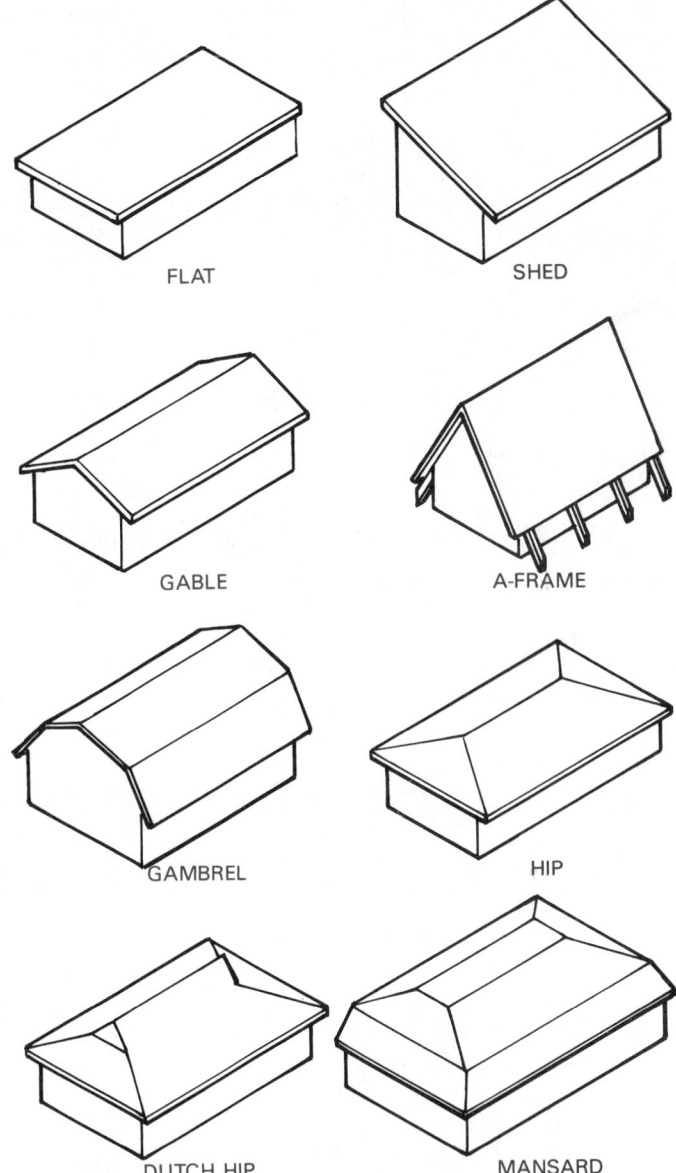

Figure 33-13 Common roof shapes for residential architecture.

Shed Roofs

The shed roof gets its name from its original use, but should not be thought of as a roof for storage buildings. See Figure 33-17. The shed roof offers the same simplicity and economical construction methods of a flat roof, but does not have the drainage problems associated with a flat roof. Figure 33-18 shows the construction methods of shed roofs. The shed roof may be constructed at any pitch. The roofing material and the desired aesthetic considerations are the only limiting factors of the pitch. When drawn in plan view, the shed roof will resemble the flat roof, as seen in Figure 33-19.

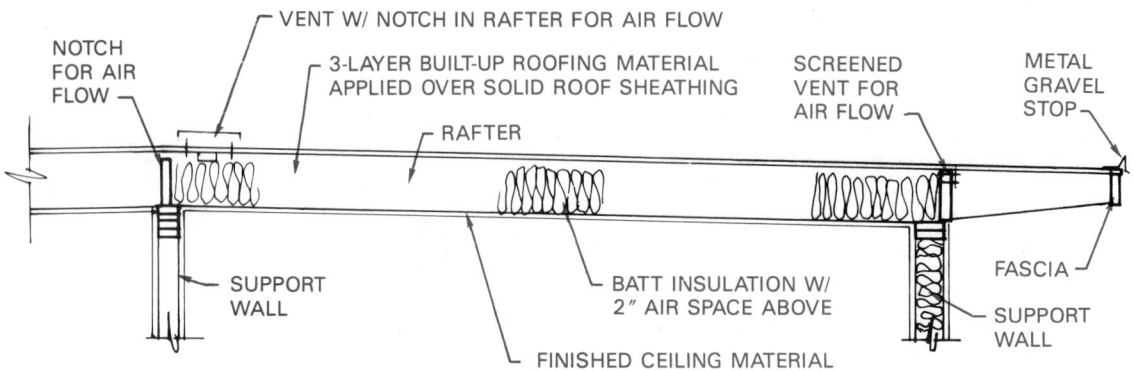

Figure 33–14 Common construction components of a flat roof.

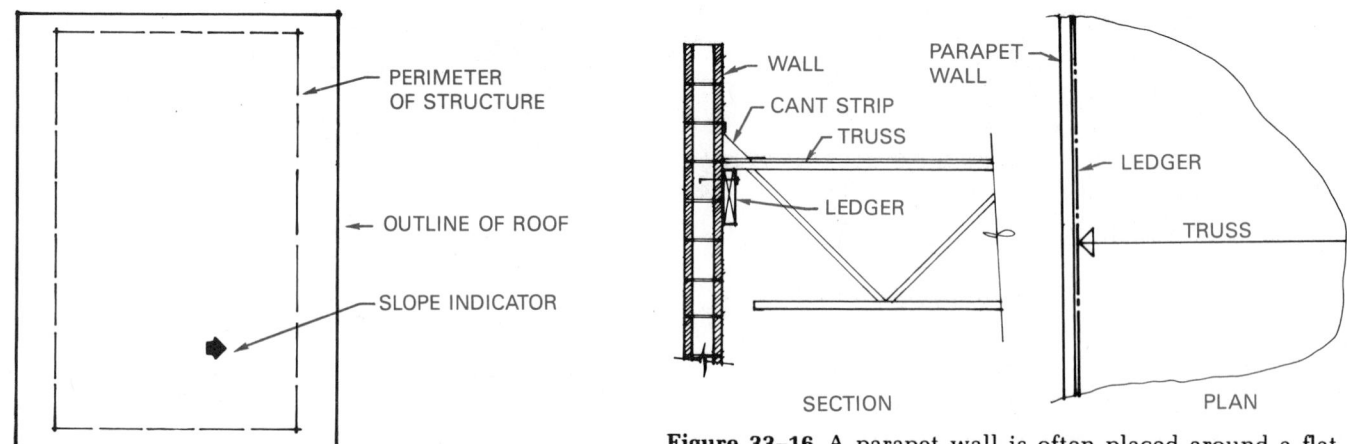

Figure 33–15 A flat roof in plan view.

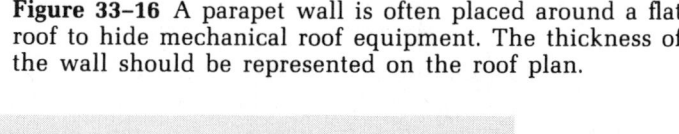

Figure 33–16 A parapet wall is often placed around a flat roof to hide mechanical roof equipment. The thickness of the wall should be represented on the roof plan.

Figure 33–17 A shed roof is a simple, economical, and attractive roof alternative. *Courtesy American Plywood Association.*

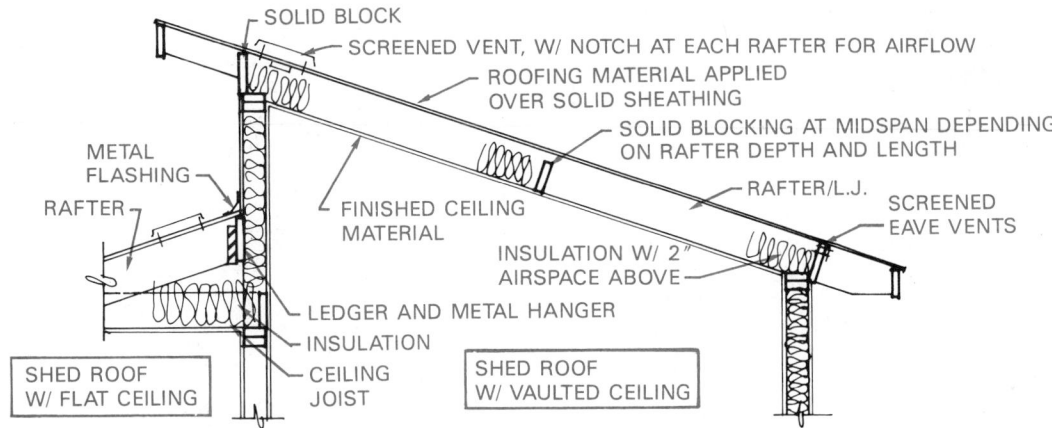

Figure 33-18 Common construction components of shed roofs.

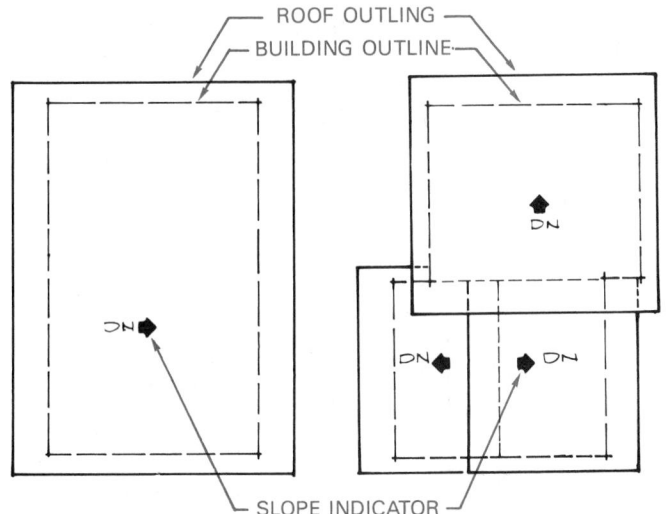

Figure 33-19 Shed roof shapes in plan view.

Gable Roofs

A gable roof is one of the most common types of roof used in residential construction. A gable roof uses two shed roofs that meet to form a ridge between the support walls. Figure 33-20 shows the construction of a gable roof system. The gable can be con-

structed at any pitch with the choice of pitch limited only by the roofing material and the effect desired. A gable roof is often used on designs seeking to maintain a traditional appearance with formal balance. Figure 33-21 shows how a gable roof is typically represented in plan view. Many plans use two or more gables at 90° angles to each other. The intersections of gable surfaces are called either hips or valleys. Typically the valley and hip are specified on the roof plan.

To give a gable roof a less traditional appearance, the gable ends of the roof are often extended beyond their normal limits as shown in Figure 33-22. These extensions are supported on beams or rafters typically called lookout rafters, or outlookers. These extending members must be specified on the roof plan.

A-frame Roofs

An A-frame is a method of framing walls as well as a system of framing roofs. An A-frame structure uses rafters to form its supporting walls as shown in Figure 33-23. The structure gets its name from the letter A that is formed by the roof and floor systems. The roof plan for an A-frame is very similar to the

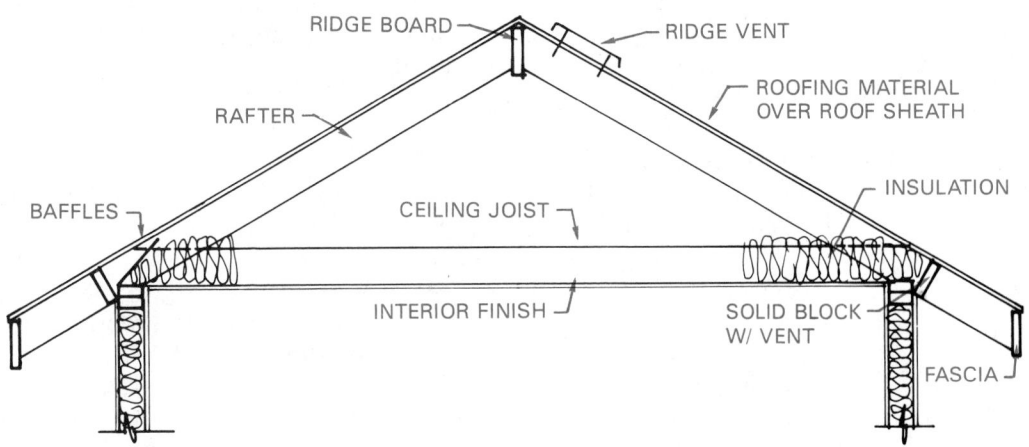

Figure 33-20 Common construction components of a gable roof.

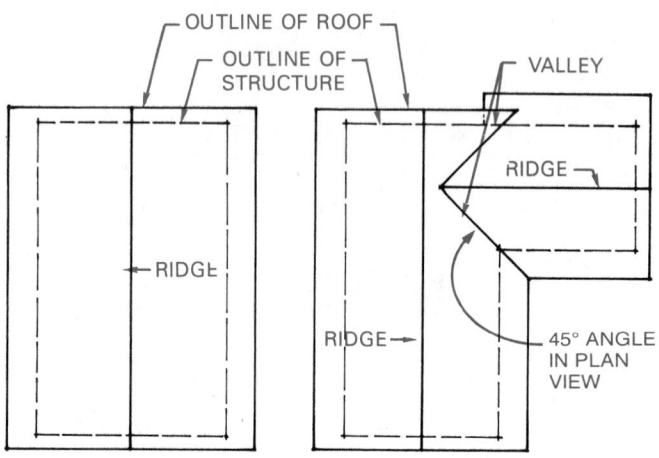

Figure 33–21 A gable roof represented in plan view.

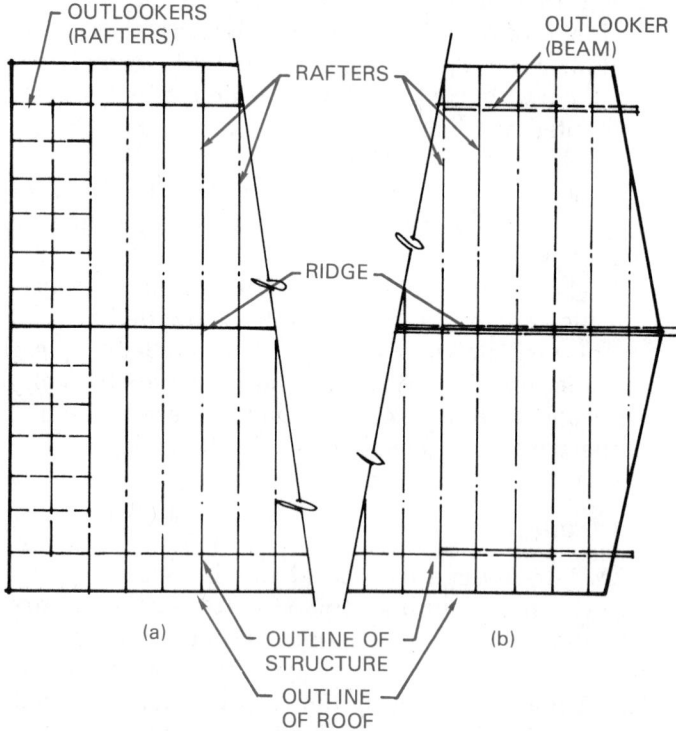

Figure 33–22 Support for the gable end. Illustration (a) shows a common method of supporting the roof at the gable end. When the roof extends more than about 36 in. past the structure, beams are usually cantilevered to support the roof weight as shown in illustration (b).

plan for a gable roof. However, the materials and rafter sizes are usually quite different. Figure 33–24 shows how an A-frame can be represented on the roof plan.

Gambrel Roofs

A gambrel roof can be seen in Figure 33–25. The gambrel roof is a very traditional roof shape that dates back to the colonial period. Figure 33–26 shows the construction methods of a gambrel roof. Typically

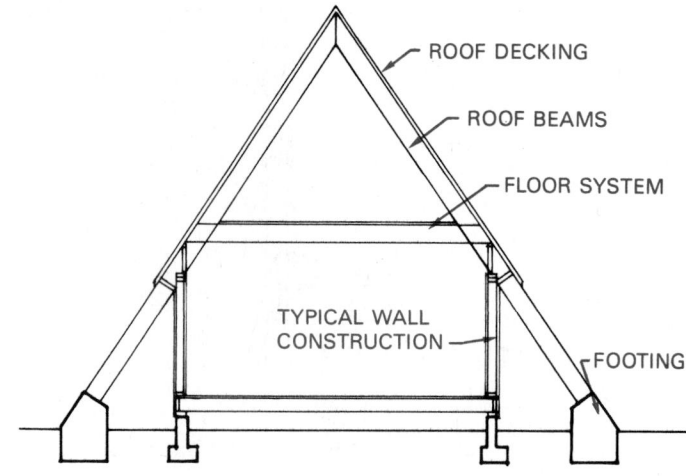

Figure 33–23 Common components of A-frame construction.

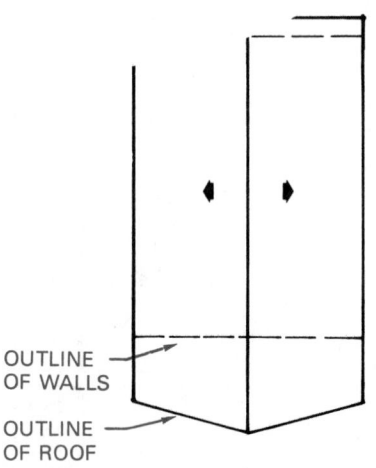

Figure 33–24 Representing an A-frame in plan view.

used on two-level structures, the upper level is covered with a steep roof surface which connects into a roof system with a slighter pitch. By covering the upper level with roofing material rather than siding, the height of the structure will appear shorter than it is. This roof system can also be used to reduce the cost of siding materials with less expensive roofing materials. Figure 33–27 shows a plan view of a gambrel roof.

Hip Roofs

The hip roof of Figure 33–28 is a traditional roof shape. This shape can be used to help eliminate some of the roof mass and create a structure with a smaller appearance as seen in Figure 33–29. A hip roof has many similarities to a gable roof but instead of having two surfaces the hip roof has four. The intersection between each surface is called a hip. If built on a square structure, the hips will come together to form a point. If built on a rectangular structure, the hips will form two points with a ridge spanning between

Figure 33–25 The gambrel roof is often used to enhance the traditional appearance of a residence. This plan was designed by architect Russell Swinton Oatman, R.A., Princeton, MA. *Photo courtesy Cabot's Stains.*

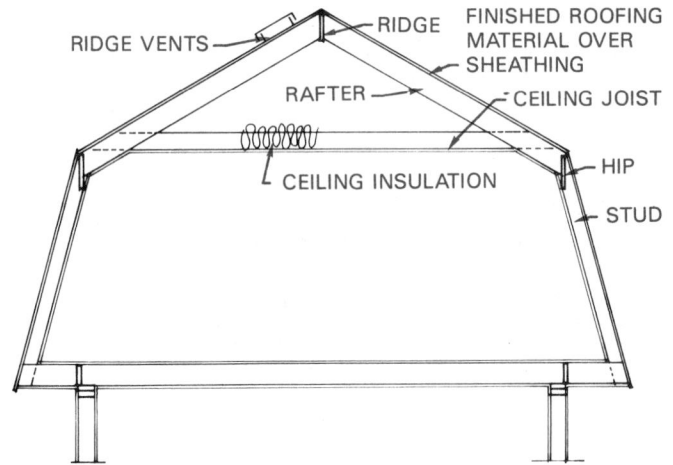

Figure 33–26 Common construction components of a gambrel roof.

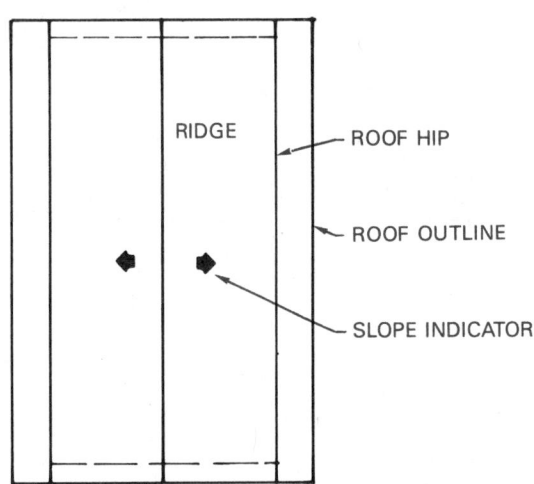

Figure 33–27 Representing a gambrel roof in plan view.

Figure 33–28 A hip roof is often used to decrease the amount of roof that is visible. *Photo courtesy Masonite Corporation.*

Figure 33-29 The hip roof can help hide the mass of a structure by reducing the amount of visible surface area.

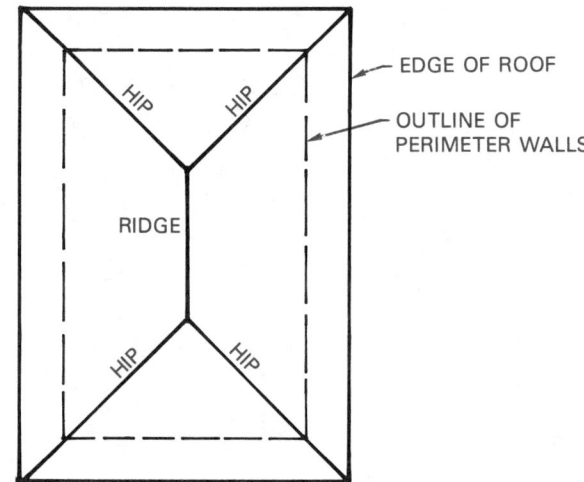

Figure 33-30 A hip roof in plan view.

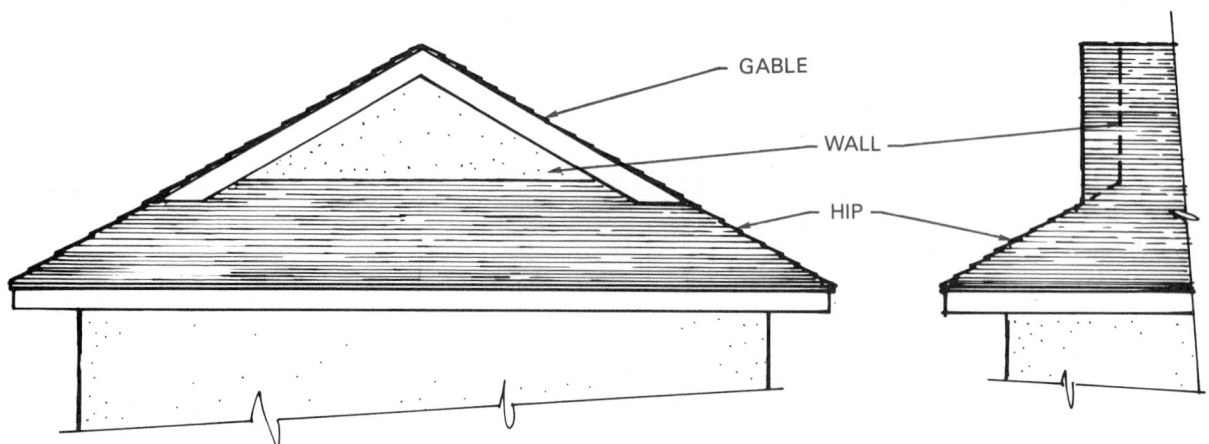

Figure 33-31 A wall is formed between the hip and gable roof.

them. When hips are placed over an L- or T-shaped structure, an interior intersection will be formed that is called a valley. The valley of a hip roof is the same as the valley for a gable roof. Hip roofs can be seen in plan view as shown in Figure 33-30.

Dutch Hip Roofs

The Dutch hip roof is a combination of a hip and a gable roof. The center section of the roof is framed in a method similar to a gable roof. The ends of the roof are framed with a partial hip that blends into the gable. A small wall is formed between the hip and the gable roofs as seen in Figure 33-31. On the roof plan, the shape, distance, and wall location must be shown similar to the plan in Figure 33-32.

Mansard Roofs

The mansard roof is similar to a gambrel roof but has the angled lower roof on all four sides rather than just two. The mansard roof is often used as a

parapet wall to hide mechanical equipment on the roof or can be used to help hide the height of the upper level of a structure. Examples of each can be seen in Figure 33-33. Mansard roofs can be constructed in many different ways. Figure 33-34 shows two common methods of constructing a mansard roof. The roof plan for a mansard roof will resemble the plans shown in Figure 33-35.

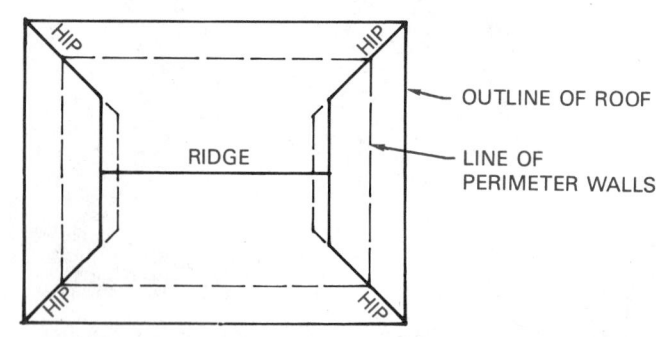

Figure 33-32 Representing a Dutch hip roof in plan view.

Figure 33–33 Mansard roofs are often used to hide equipment on the roof or to help disguise the height of the structure. *Landow and Landow, AIA, Architects, Smithtown, NY; photo courtesy Follansbee Steel Corporation.*

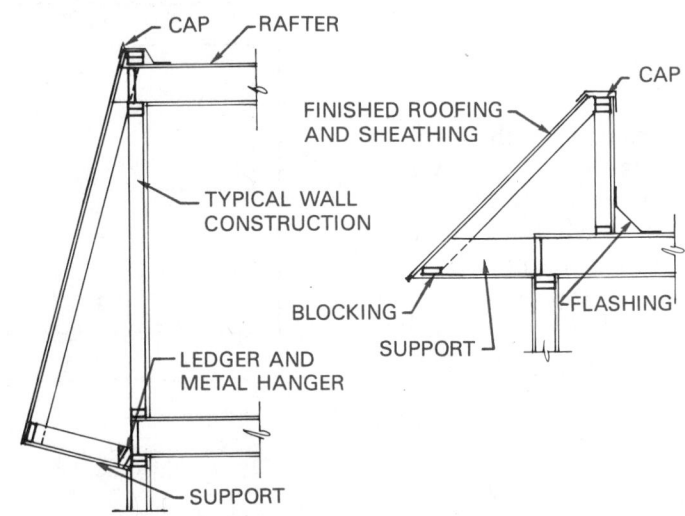

Figure 33–34 Common methods of constructing a mansard roof.

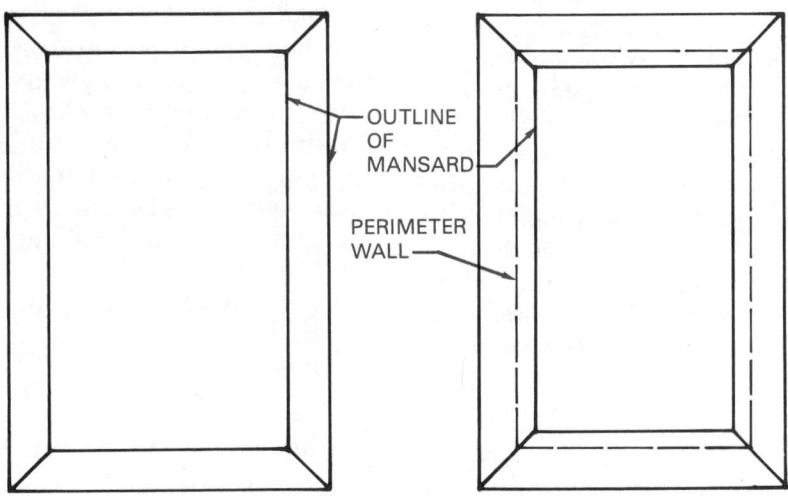

Figure 33–35 The mansard in plan view.

Figure 33–36 Dormers are often added to help enhance the traditional appearance. *Photo courtesy Genstar Roofing Products Company.*

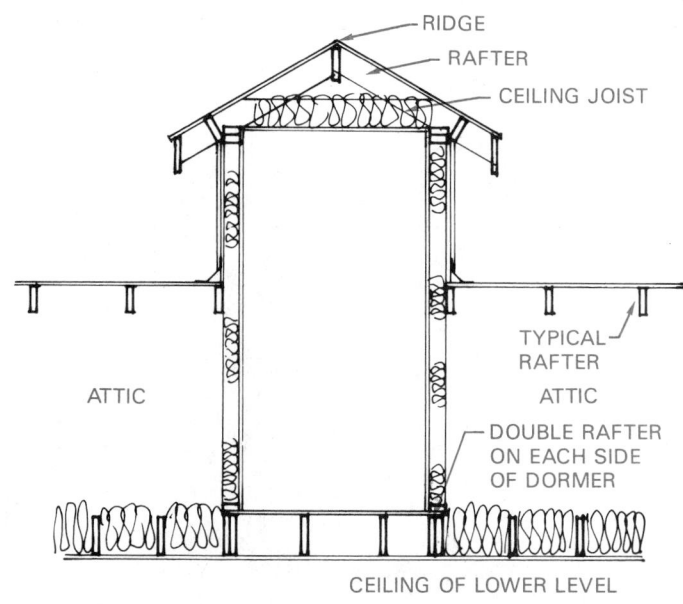

Figure 33–37 Typical components of dormer construction.

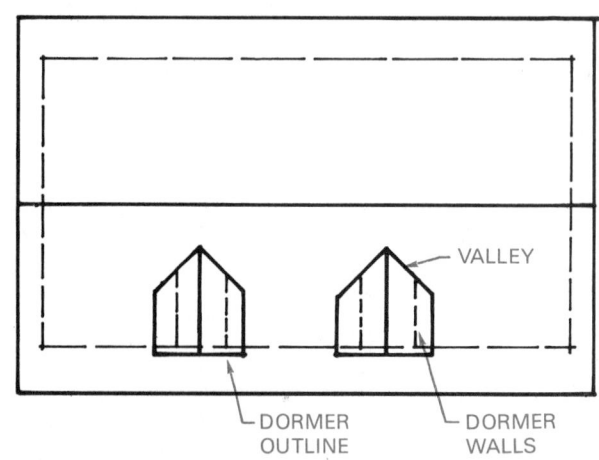

Figure 33–38 Dormers in plan view.

Dormers

A dormer is an opening framed in the roof to allow for window placement. Figure 33–36 shows an example of dormers that have been added to provide light and ventilation to rooms in what would have been attic space. Dormers are most frequently used on traditional style roofs such as the gable or hip. Figure 33–37 shows one of the many ways that dormers can be constructed. Dormers are usually shown on the roof plan as seen in Figure 33–38.

ROOFING MATERIALS

The material to be used on the roof is dependent on the pitch, exterior style, weather, and cost of the structure. Common roofing materials include built-up roofing, composition and wood shingles, clay and cement tiles, and metal panels. When ordering or specifying these materials, the term square is often used. A square is used to describe an area of roofing that covers 100 sq ft. The drafter will need to be aware of the weight per square and the required pitch as the plan is being drawn. The weight of the roofing material will affect the size of the framing members all the way down to the foundation level. The material will also affect the required pitch and the appearance that results from the selected pitch.

Built-up Roofing

Built-up roofing of felt and asphalt is typically used on flat or low-sloped roofs below a 3/12 pitch. When the roof has a low pitch, water will either pond or drain very slowly. To prevent water from leaking into a structure, built-up roofing is used because of its lack of seams. On a residence a built-up roof may consist of three alternate layers of felt and hot asphalt placed over solid roof decking. The decking is usually plywood. In commercial uses, a four- or five-layer roof is used to provide added durability. Gravel is often used as a finishing layer to help cover the felt. On roofs with a pitch over 2/12, course rocks 2 or 3 in. in diameter are used for protecting the roof and for appearance. When built-up roofs are to be specified on the roof plan, the note should include the number of layers, the material to be used, and the size of the finishing material.

Shingles

Asphalt, asbestos-cement, fiberglass, and wood are the most typical types of shingles used as roofing materials. Most building codes and manufacturers require a minimum roof pitch of 4/12 with an underlayment of one layer of 15 lb felt. Asphalt and fiberglass shingles can be laid on roofs as low as 2/12 if two layers of 15 lb felt are laid under the shingles and if the shingles are sealed. Asbestos-cement and wood shingles must usually be installed on roofs having a pitch of at least 3/12. Asphalt, asbestos-cement and fiberglass are similar in appearance and application. Each comes in many different patterns and colors.

Composition and fiberglass shingles typically weigh 235 lb per square. Shingles resembling wood shingles are also available. These shingles weigh approximately 300 lbs per square. Asbestos-cement shingles weigh approximately 560 lb per square depending on the manufacturer and the pattern of shingles used. When shingles are specified on the roof plan, the note should include the manufacturer, the material, the weight, the color, and the underlayment.

Wood is also used for shakes and shingles. Wood shakes are thicker than shingles and are also more irregular in their texture. Wood shakes and shingles are generally installed on roofs with a minimum pitch of 4/12 using a base layer of 15 lb felt. An additional layer of 15 lb by 18-in.-wide felt is also placed between each course or layer of shingles. Wood shakes and shingles can be installed over solid or spaced sheathing. The weather, material availability, and labor practices will affect the type of underlayment used. In colder climates solid sheathing is typically used because of its added insulation value. Also, plywood can be installed much faster than individual strips of sheathing. Spaced sheathing does allow for better expansion and contraction in the roof due to humidity in the attic.

Depending on the area of the country, shakes and shingles are usually made of cedar, redwood, or cypress. They are also produced in various lengths. When shakes or shingles are specified on the roof plan, the note should usually include the thickness, the material, the exposure, the underlayment, and the type of sheathing.

Metal is sometimes used for roof shingles. Metal shingles provide a durable, fire-resistant roofing material but they are generally not used in residential construction because of their high cost. Metal shingles are usually installed using the same precautions applied to asphalt shingles. Metal shingles are typically specified on the roof plan in a note listing the manufacturer, the type of shingle, and the underlayment.

Clay and Cement Tiles

Clay or concrete tiles provide an extremely durable roof covering. Roof tiles are manufactured in both curved or flat shapes. Curved tiles are often called Spanish tiles and come in a variety of curved shapes and colors. The flat, or barr, tiles are also produced in many different colors and shapes. The drafter should carefully study vendor catalogs prior to specifying tiles on the roof plan to assure that the tile that the designer or architect intended is being used.

Tiles are typically installed on roofs having a roof pitch of 4/12 or greater. Interlocking roof tiles may be placed on roofs as low as a 3/12 pitch if a 15 lb minimum underlayment is used. Tiles can be placed over either spaced or solid sheathing. If solid sheathing is used, wood strips are generally added on top of the sheathing to support the tiles.

When tile is to be used, the drafter must take special precautions with the design of the structure. Tile roofs weigh between 850 and 1000 lb per square. These weights will require rafters, headers, and other supporting members to be larger than normally required for other types of roofing material. Tiles are generally specified on the roof plan in a note which lists the manufacturer, style, color, weight, fastening method, and underlayment.

Metal Panels

Metal roofing panels often provide savings because of the speed and ease of installation. Panels are typically produced in either 22 or 24 gage metal in widths of either 18 or 24 in. The length of the panel can be specified to meet the needs of the roof in lengths up to 40 ft. Metal roofs are manufactured in many colors and patterns and can be used to blend with almost any material. When specifying metal roofing on the roof plan, the note should include the manufacturer, the pattern, the material, the underlayment, and the trim and flashing.

ROOF VENTILATION AND ACCESS

As the roof plan is drawn, the drafter must determine the size of the attic space. The attic is the space formed between the ceiling joists and the rafters. The U.B.C., S.B.C. and B.O.C.A. each require that the attic space be provided with vents that are covered with ¼ in. screen mesh. These vents must have an area equal to 1/150 of the attic area. This area can be reduced to 1/300 of the attic area if a vapor barrier is provided on the heated side of the attic floor and half of the required vents are placed in the upper half of the roof area.

The method used to provide the required vents varies throughout the country. Vents may be placed in the gabled end walls near the ridge. This allows the roof surface to remain vent free. In other areas, a continuous vent is placed in the eaves or a vent may be placed in each third rafter space. The drafter will need to specify the proper area of vents that are required and the area in which they are to be placed.

The drafter must also specify how to get into the attic space. The actual opening into the attic is usually shown on the floor plan, but its location must be considered while drawing the roof plan. The size of the access opening will vary depending on the code that you are using. The U.B.C. requires an opening that is 22″ × 30″ with 30 in. minimum of headroom. The S.B.C. requires an access opening of 22″ × 36″ with 24 in. minimum of headroom. While planning the roof shape, the drafter must find a suitable location for the attic access that meets both code and aesthetic requirements. The access should be placed where it can be easily reached but should not be placed where it will visually dominate a space. Avoid placing the access in areas with high moisture content, such as bathrooms, or in bedrooms that will be used by young children. Hallways usually provide an area to place the access that is both easily accessible but not in a focal point of the structure.

ROOF PLAN COMPONENTS TEST

DIRECTIONS

Answer the questions with short complete statements or drawings as needed on an 8½ × 11 drawing sheet as follows:

1. Use ⅛ in. guidelines for all lettering.
2. Letter your name, Roof Plan Components Test, and the date at the top of the sheet.
3. Letter the question number and provide the answer. You do not need to write out the question.
4. Do all lettering with vertical uppercase architectural letters. If the answer requires line work, use proper drafting tools and technique. Answers may be prepared on a word processor if appropriate with course guidelines.
5. Your grade will be based on correct answers and quality of line technique.

QUESTIONS

1. List and describe three different types of roof plans.
2. When describing roof pitch, what do the numbers 4/12 represent?
3. What angle represents a 6/12 pitch?
4. Is a surface built at a 28° angle from vertical a wall or a roof?
5. What are two advantages of using a flat roof?
6. What is the major disadvantage of using a flat roof?
7. List three traditional roof shapes.
8. Sketch and define the difference between a hip and a Dutch hip roof.
9. What are two uses for a mansard roof?
10. List two common weights for asphalt or fiberglass shingles.
11. What are two common shapes of clay roof tiles?
12. What advantage do metal roofing panels have over other roofing materials?
13. According to the S.B.C., what is the minimum headroom required at the attic access?
14. What is the minimum size of an attic access opening according to the U.B.C.?
15. What type of roof is both a roof system and a framing system?

Chapter 34
Roof Plan and Roof Framing Plan Layout

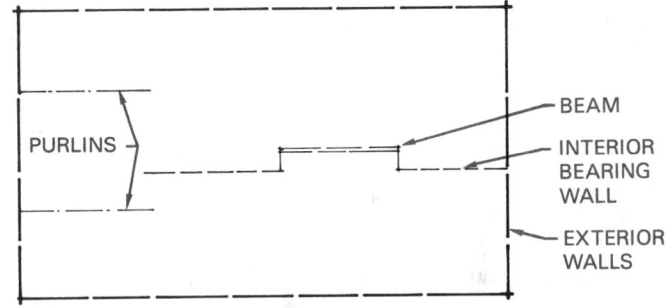

Figure 34-1 Drawing roof supports.

LINES AND SYMBOLS

SEVERAL DIFFERENT types of lines and symbols are required when drawing the roof or framing plan. These include lines used to represent the roof supports, roof shapes, structural materials, nonstructural materials, dimensions, and written specifications.

Supports

Exterior walls, interior bearing walls, purlins, beams, and outlookers are the supports for the roof structure. Each must be shown on the roof plan. Exterior walls are generally shown with bold dashed lines. The length of the dashes will vary depending on the size of the roof to be drawn. Interior bearing walls are often drawn using thin dashed lines similar to those used to represent the exterior walls. Purlins

are often drawn with thin dashed lines in a long-short-long pattern. Beams and outlookers are usually drawn with two thin parallel lines. Figure 34-1 shows these methods for drawing each type of roof support.

Roof Shape

The overhang of the roof which forms the outline is usually drawn with bold solid lines. The size of the overhang will vary depending on the pitch of the roof and the amount of shade desired. As seen in Figure 34-2, the steeper the roof pitch, the smaller the overhang that is required to shade an area. If you are drawing a home for a southern location, an overhang large enough to protect glazing from direct sunlight is usually desirable. In northern areas, the overhang is usually restricted to maximize the amount of sunlight received during winter months. Figure

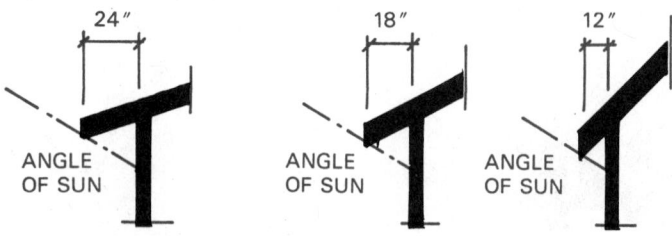

Figure 34–2 The steeper the roof pitch, the more shadow will be cast. Typically the overhang is decreased as the pitch is increased.

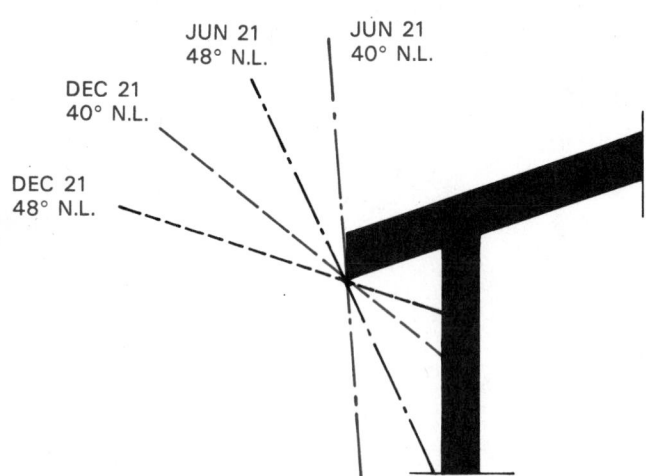

Figure 34–3 The overhang will block different amounts of sunlight at different times of the year. Notice the difference in the sun's angles at 40° and 48° north latitudes.

34–3 compares the effect of an overhang at different times of the year.

Changes in the shape of the roof such as ridges, hips, Dutch hips and valleys are also drawn with solid lines. Each can be seen in Figure 34–4. These changes in shape can be drawn easily when the pitches are of equal angle. Because the ridge is centered between the two bearing walls, it can be located by measuring the distance between the two supporting walls and dividing that distance in half. A faster method of locating the ridge is to draw two 45° angles as shown in Figure 34–5. The ridge extends through the intersection of the two angles. This same procedure is used when locating hips. When formed between two equally spaced, equally angled roofs, hips will form a 45° intersection.

A Dutch hip is drawn by first lightly drawing a hip as shown in Figure 34–6. Once the hip is drawn, determine the location of the gable wall. The wall is usually located over a rafter. If the rafters are spaced at 24 in. on center, the wall is typically located 48 or 72 in. from the exterior wall. With the wall located, the overhang can be drawn in a similar manner to a gable roof. The overhang line will intersect the hip lines to form the outline of the Dutch hip.

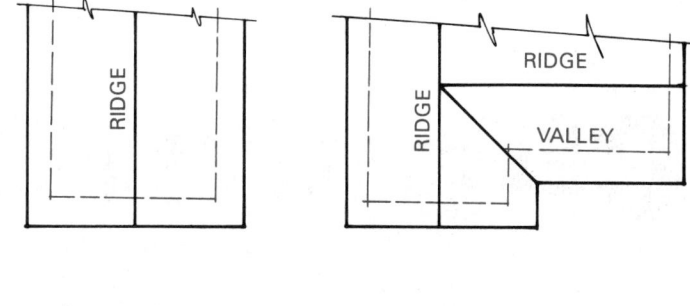

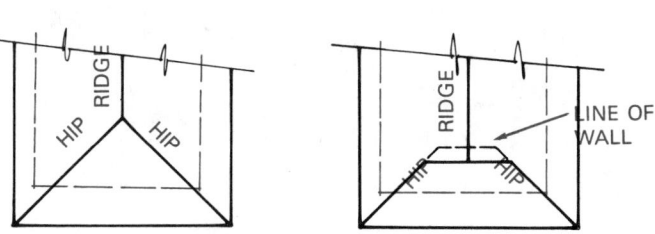

Figure 34–4 Changes in roof shape are shown with solid lines.

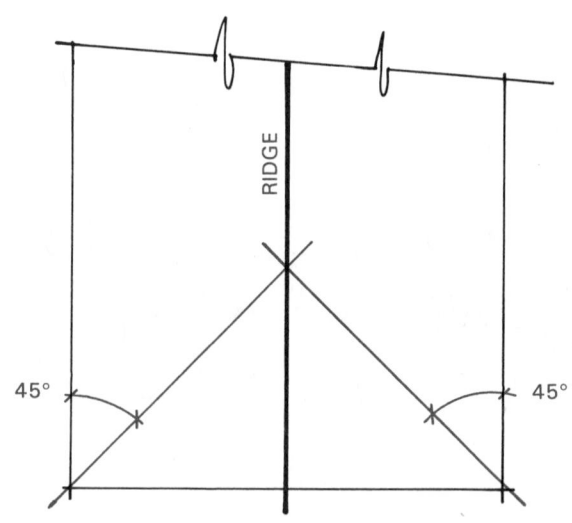

Figure 34–5 The ridge between two equal roof surfaces can be plotted by drawing two 45° angles. The ridge extends through the intersection.

When two perpendicular roofs intersect each other as shown in Figure 34–7, a valley will be formed at 45° to the walls. The drafter must consider both the distance between supporting walls and the pitch to determine how the intersection is represented on the plan. Notice in Figure 34–8 that the shape of the roof changes dramatically as the width between the walls is changed. Remember that when the pitches are equal, the wider the distances between the walls, the higher the roof will be.

When the walls are equally spaced, but not perpendicular, the hip, valley, and ridge intersection will occur along a line as shown in Figure 34–9. With unequal distances between the supporting walls, the hips, valleys, and ridge can be drawn as shown in Figure 34–10. Such a drawing is often a difficult

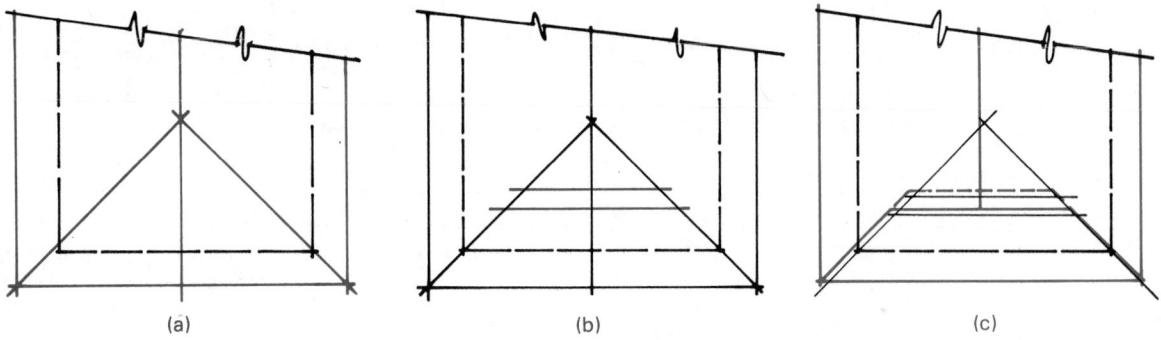

Figure 34-6 Layout of a Dutch hip roof: (a) Establish the ridge and hip locations; (b) locate the gable end wall; (c) use bold lines to complete the roof.

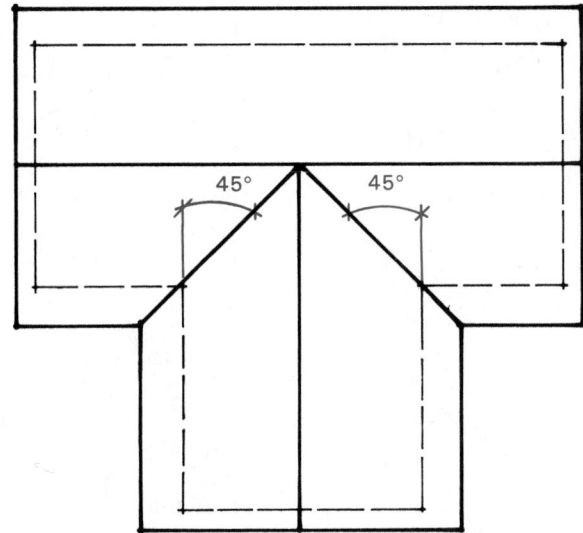

Figure 34-7 When two perpendicular roofs intersect, a valley is formed at 45° to the ridge.

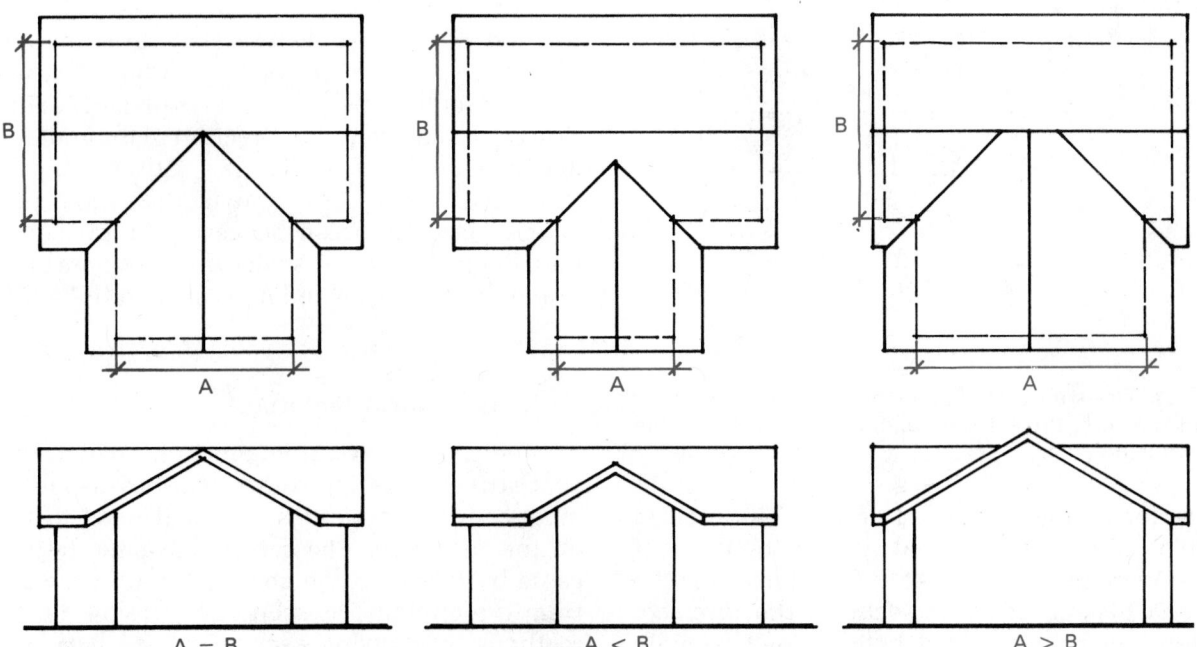

Figure 34-8 Although the basic shape remains the same, the roof plan and elevations change as the distance between walls varies.

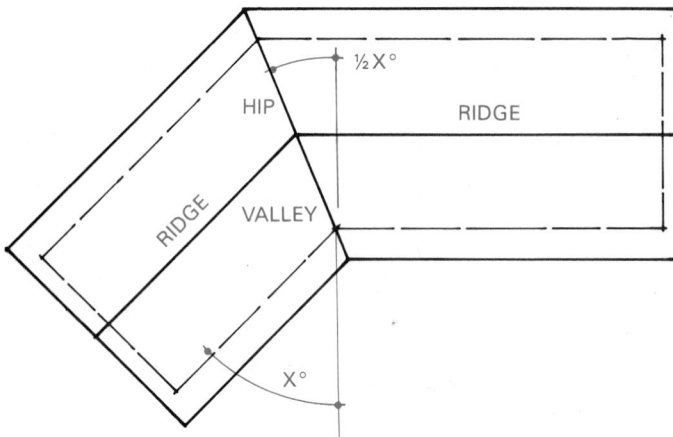

Figure 34-9 When walls are equally spaced, but not perpendicular, the roof surfaces will occur along a line as shown.

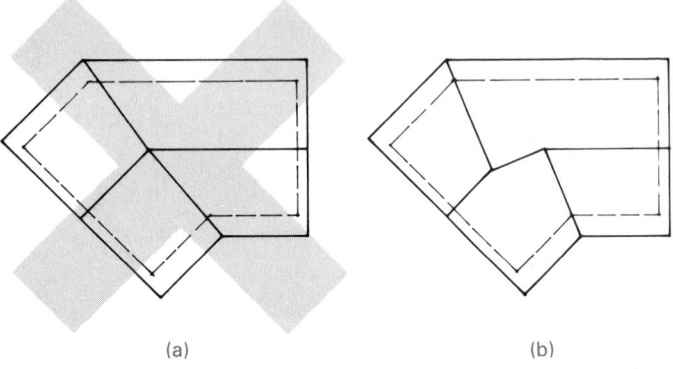

(a)   (b)

Figure 34-10 When walls are unequally spaced, a drafter may be tempted to draw the roof as shown at (a). The actual intersection can be seen at (b).

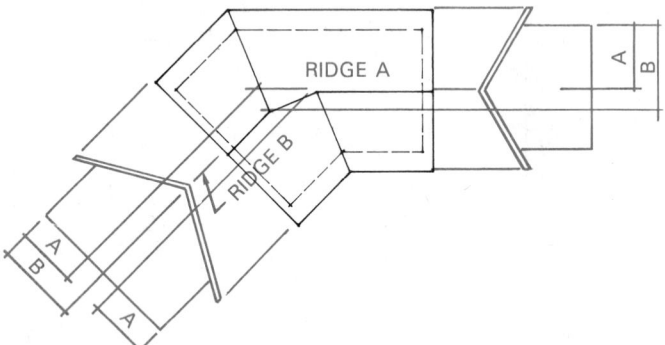

Figure 34-11 The true roof shape can be seen by drawing sections of the roof. Project the heights represented on the sections onto the roof.

procedure for an inexperienced drafter. The process is simplified if you draw partial sections by the roof plan as shown in Figure 34-11. By comparing the heights and distances in the sections, the intersections often can be visualized better. Don't hesitate to draw partial sections like these as you plot complicated roof shapes.

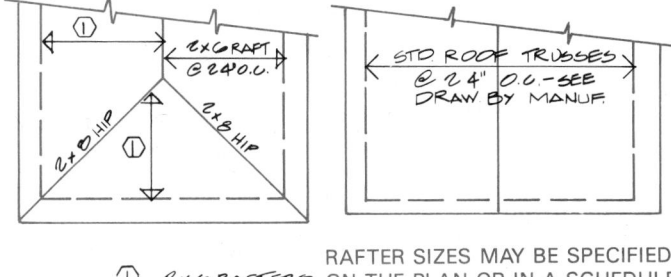

RAFTER SIZES MAY BE SPECIFIED ON THE PLAN OR IN A SCHEDULE

Figure 34-12 Rafters or trusses are typically represented on the roof plan by a thin line showing the proper direction and span.

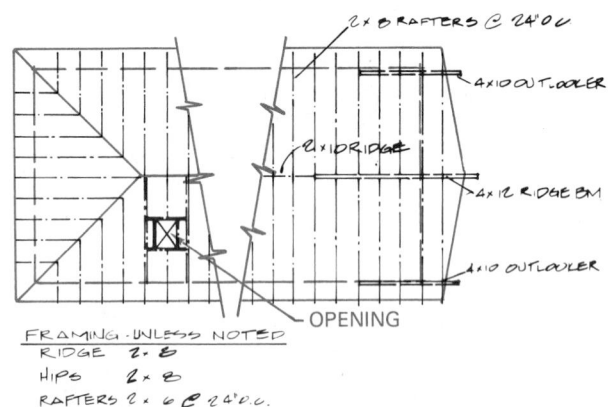

Figure 34-13 When drawing a roof framing plan, each rafter is drawn. When an opening is required, the rafters on each side of the opening are doubled.

Structural Material

The type of plan to be drawn will affect the method used to show the structural material. If a roof plan is to be drawn, the rafters or trusses can be represented as shown in Figure 34-12. A thin line is used to represent the direction of the roof members, and a note specifies the size and spacing. If a roof framing plan is to be drawn, thin lines in a long-short-long pattern can be used to represent the rafters. Beams and other structural members are usually drawn with thin dashed lines as seen in Figure 34-13.

Nonstructural Materials

Vents, chimneys, skylights, solar panels, diverters, cant strips, slope indicators, and downspouts are the most common materials that will need to be shown on the roof plan. The cant strip or saddle is a small gable built behind the chimney to divert water away from the chimney as seen in Figure 34-14. Common methods of showing each of the nonstructural materials listed can be seen in Figure 34-15. These materials are not shown on a roof framing plan.

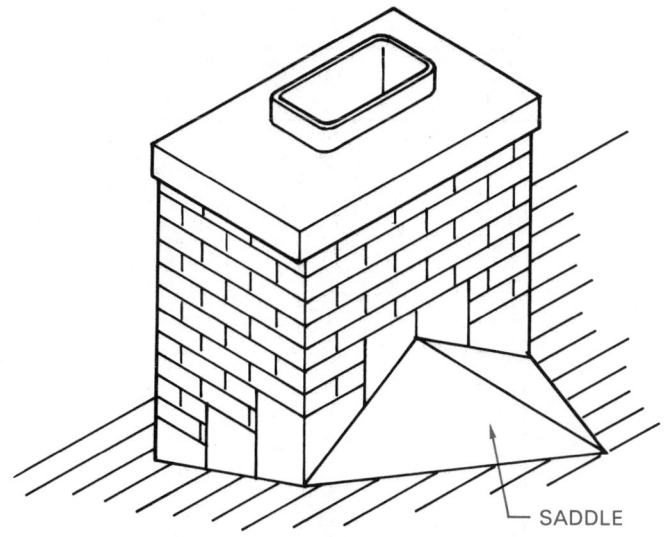

Figure 34–14 A saddle or cant strip is used to divert water around the chimney.

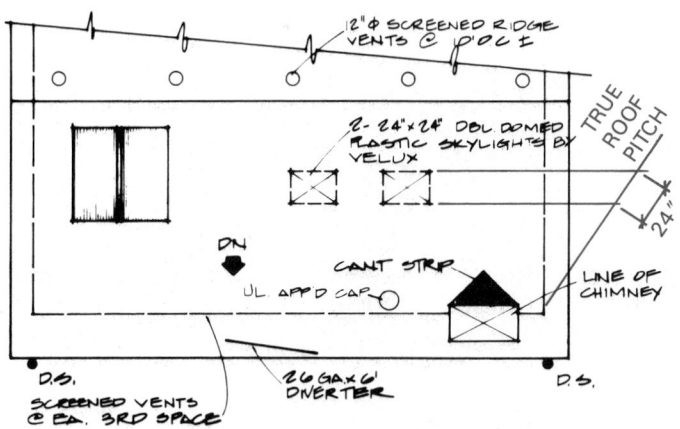

Figure 34–15 Nonstructural materials shown on the roof plan.

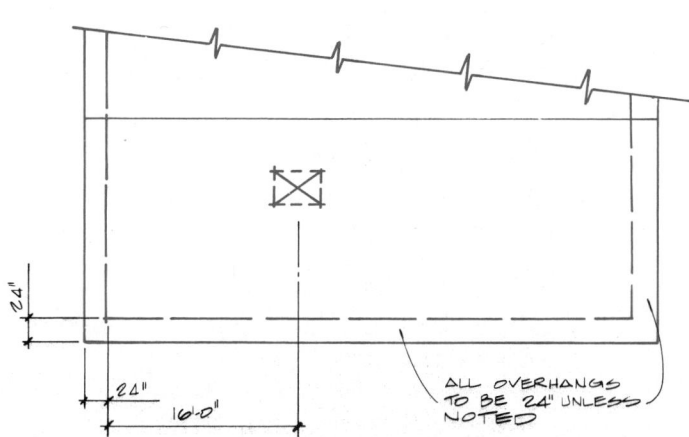

Figure 34–16 Dimensions may be placed by using leader and extension lines or in a note.

Dimensions

The roof plan and framing plan require very few dimensions. Typically only the overhangs and openings will be dimensioned. These may even be specified in note form rather than with dimensions. Figure 34–16 shows how dimensions are placed on roof and framing plans. When drawing framing plans for commercial projects, beam locations are often dimensioned to help in estimating the materials required.

Notes

As with the other drawings, notes on the roof or framing plans can be divided into general and local notes. General notes might include the following:

- Vent Notes
- Sheathing information
- Roof covering
- Eave sheathing
- Pitch
- Rafter size and spacing if uniform

Material that should be specified in local notes includes the following:

- Skylight type, size, and material
- Metal anchors
- Chimney caps
- Solar panel type and size
- Framing materials
- Cant strips
- Metal diverters

In addition to these notes, the drafter should also place a title and scale on the drawing.

DRAWING THE ROOF PLAN

The following instructions are for the roof plan to accompany the residence that has been used in each of the preceding layout chapters. The plan will be drawn using a gable roof. Use construction lines for steps 1 through 7. Each step can be seen in Figure 34–17.

Step 1.   Using the dimensions of the floor plan, draw the perimeter walls.

Step 2.   If the roof is to be framed using stick framing methods, draw interior bearing walls. These walls can be omitted with truss framing since only the outer walls are normally bearing walls. Because our example is of a trussed frame roof, no interior walls are shown.

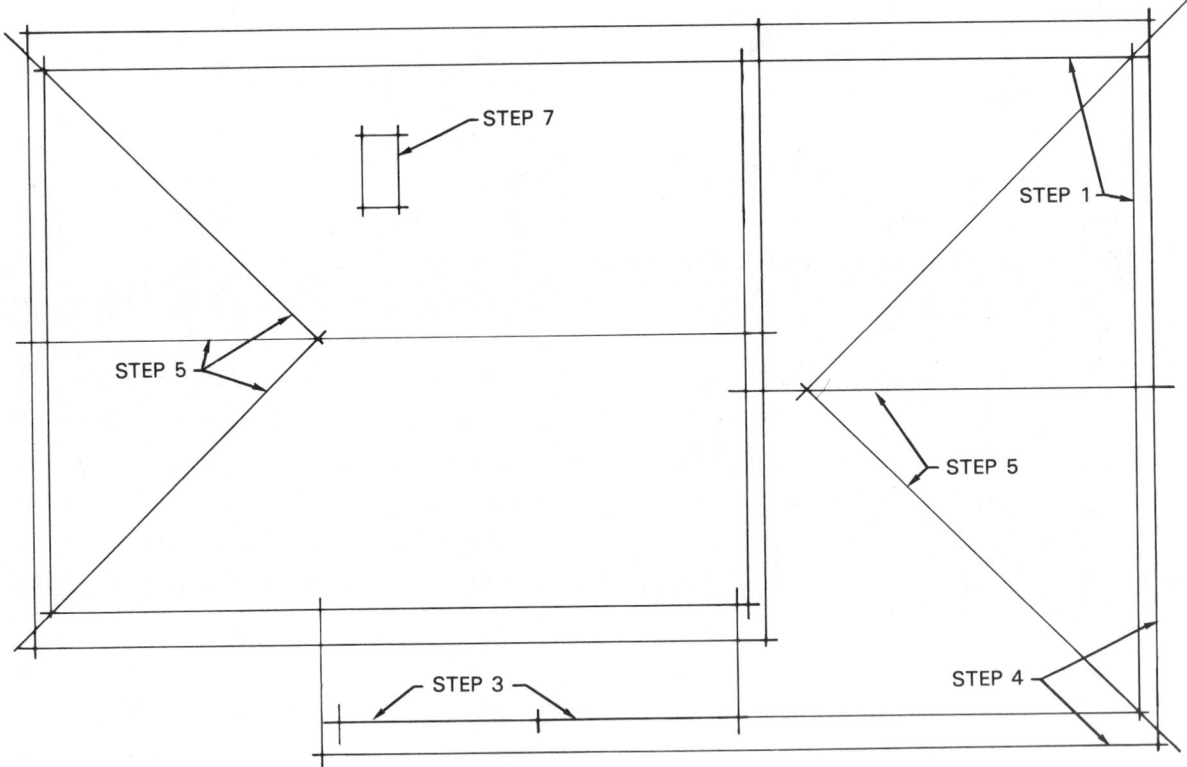

Figure 34–17 The layout of the roof plan should be done with construction lines. Interior walls (step 2) do not need to be drawn when using trusses.

Step 3. Using the dimensions from the floor or foundation plan, locate any posts and headers that are required for covered porches.

Step 4. Draw the limits of the overhangs. Unless your instructor provides different instructions, use 1'–0" overhangs for the gable end walls and 2'–0" overhangs for the eaves.

Step 5. Locate and draw the ridge or ridges.

Step 6. Locate and draw all hips and valleys required by design. On this particular project, no hips or valleys are required.

Step 7. Using measurements from the upper floor plan, locate the chimney.

Step 8. Using line quality described in this chapter, draw the materials of steps 1 through 7. Draw the outline of the upper roof and then work down to lower levels. Your drawing should now resemble Figure 34–18.

Use the line quality described in this chapter to draw steps 9 through 14. Each step can be seen in Figure 34–19.

Step 9. Draw any skylights that are specified on the floor plans.

Step 10. Calculate the area of the attic and determine the required number of vents. Assume that 12 in. round vents will be used.

Draw the required vents on a surface of the roof that will make the vents least visible.

Step 11. Draw the cant strip by the chimney if a masonry chimney or wood chase was used. A *wood chase* is the vertical enclosure for a metal chimney.

Step 12. Draw solar panels.

Step 13. Draw the arrows to represent all structural materials.

Step 14. Draw the downspouts.

Step 15. Add dimensions for the overhangs and skylights. Your drawing should now resemble the roof plan in Figure 34–20.

Step 16. Label all materials using local and general notes. Your drawing should now resemble Figure 34–21.

Step 17. Evaluate your drawing for quality and completeness. Remember to include proper symbols for walls, overhangs, ridge, hips, valleys, purlins and beams, fireplace, cant strip, vents, skylights and solar panels. Remember also proper dimensions for overhangs, openings, and solar panels. Add local and general notes, a title and scale.

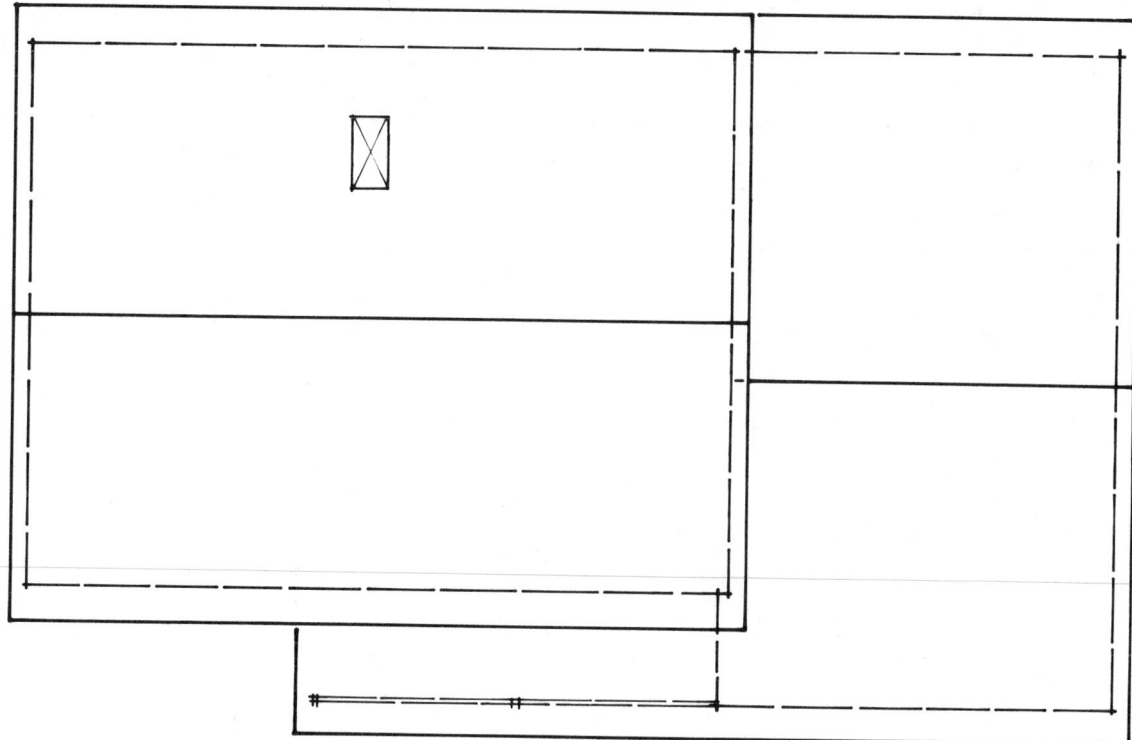

Figure 34–18 Drawing the roof plan using finished quality lines.

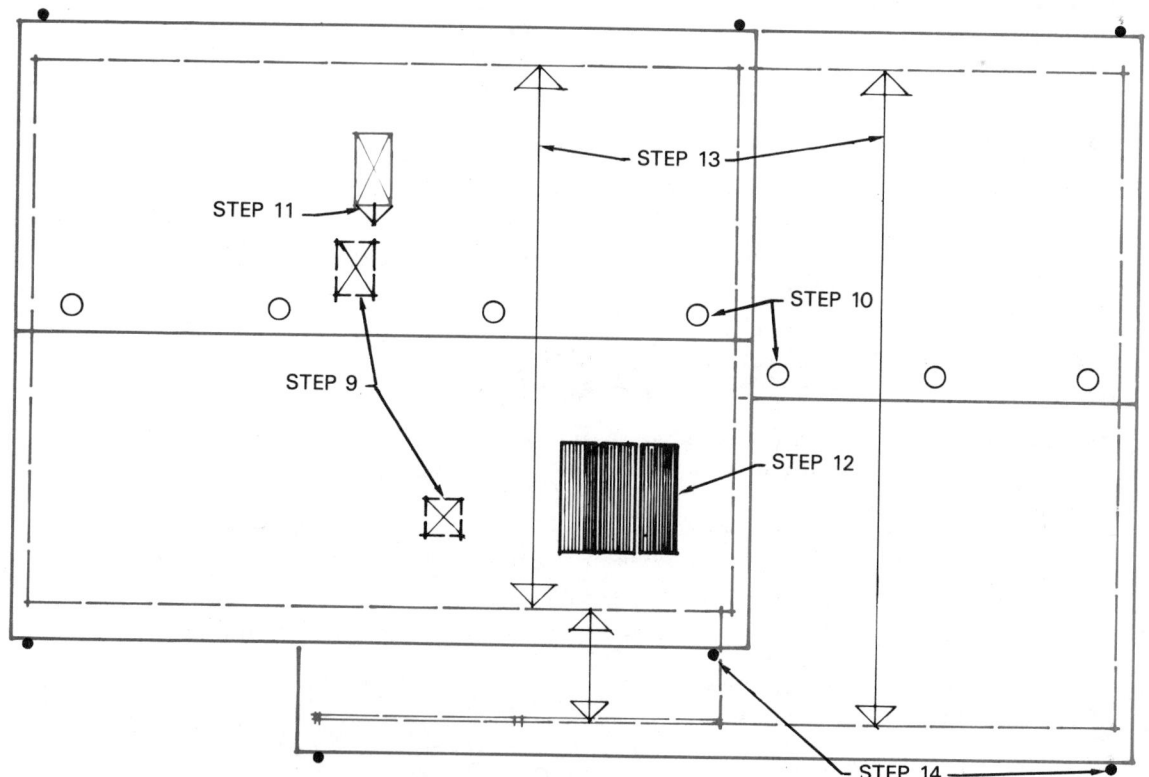

Figure 34–19 Drawing the nonstructural material.

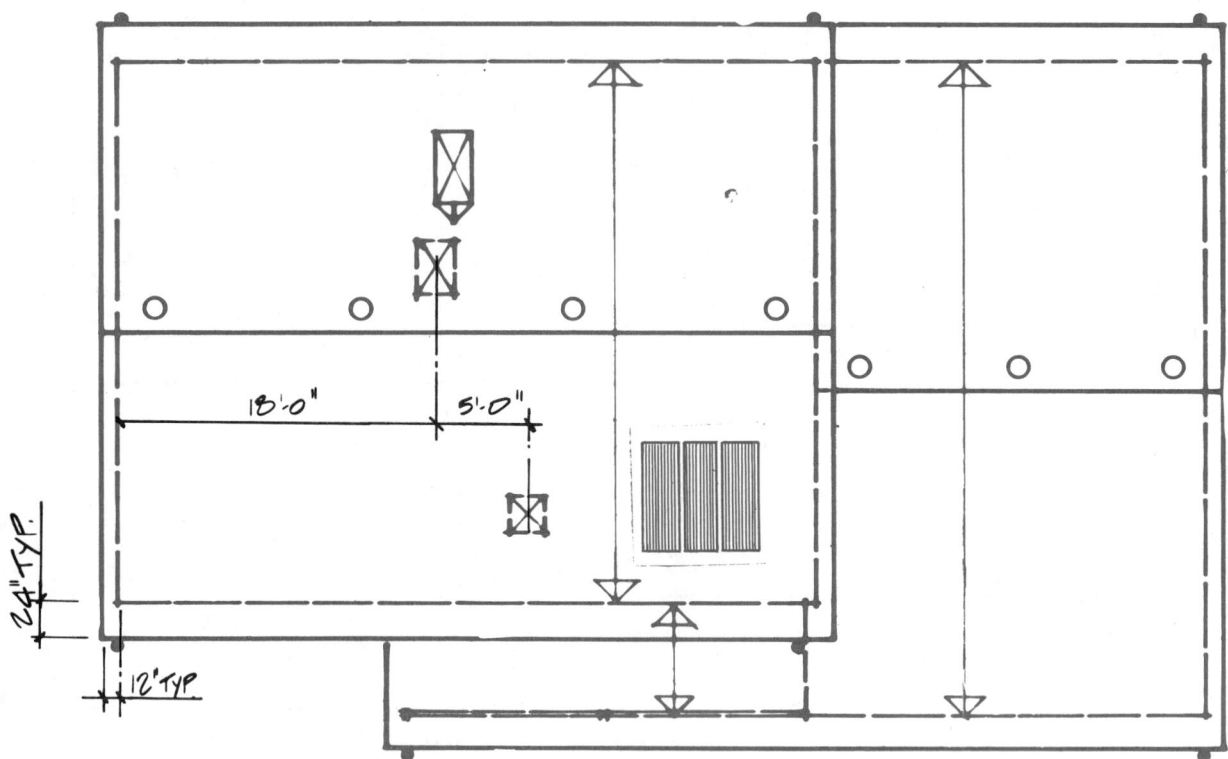

Figure 34-20 The overhangs and all openings should be dimensioned.

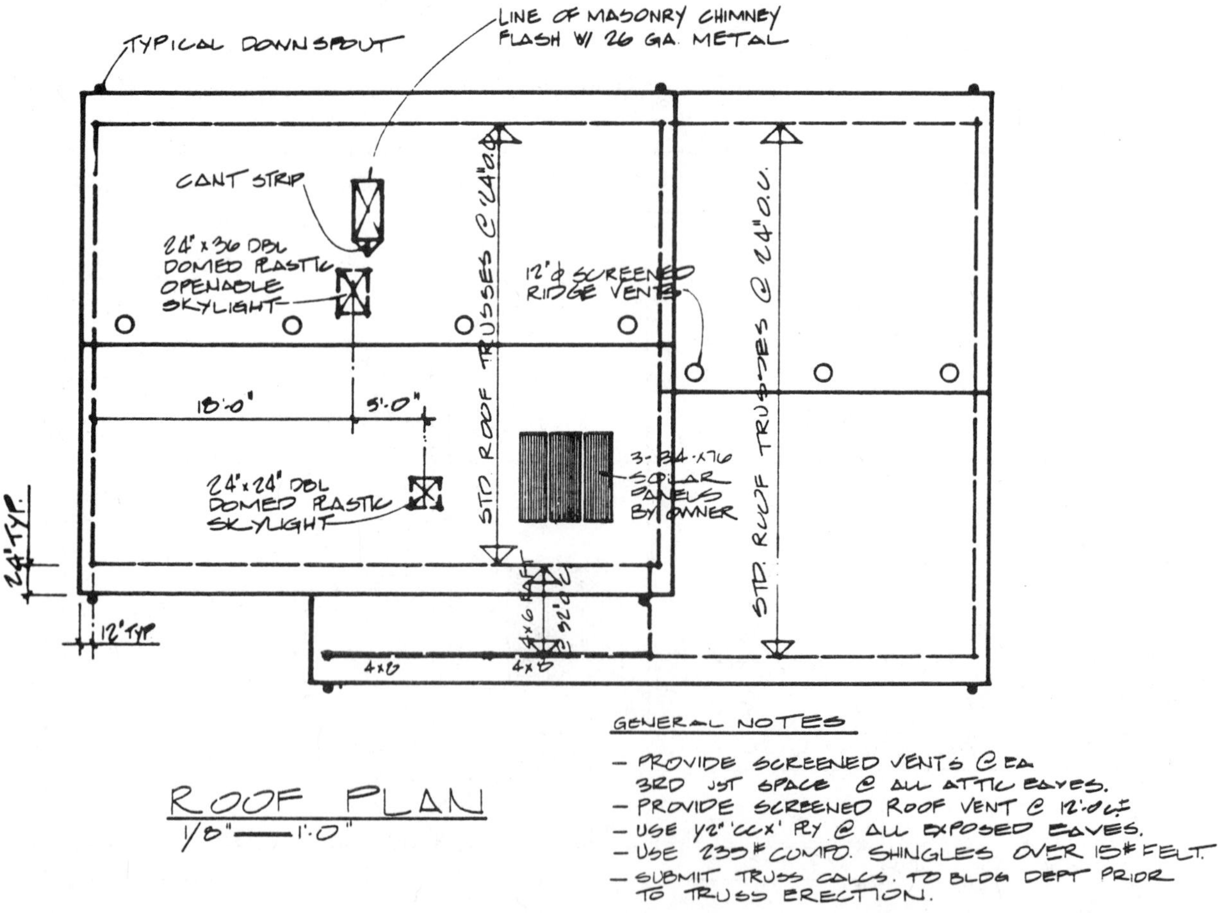

TYPICAL DOWNSPOUT

LINE OF MASONRY CHIMNEY
FLASH W/ 26 GA. METAL

CANT STRIP

24" x 36 DBL
DOMED PLASTIC
OPENABLE
SKYLIGHT

12" ⌀ SCREENED
RIDGE VENTS

STD. ROOF TRUSSES @ 24 o.c.

STD. RUOF TRUSSES @ 24" o.c.

24" x 24" DBL
DOMED PLASTIC
SKYLIGHT

3-24 x 76
SOLAR
PANELS
BY OWNER

4 x 6 RAFT.

2 x 6 @ 24"

4 x 6

4 x 6

GENERAL NOTES

– PROVIDE SCREENED VENTS @ EA
  3RD JST SPACE @ ALL ATTIC EAVES.
– PROVIDE SCREENED ROOF VENT @ 12'-0"±
– USE ½" CCX PLY @ ALL EXPOSED EAVES.
– USE 235# COMPO. SHINGLES OVER 15# FELT.
– SUBMIT TRUSS CALCS. TO BLDG DEPT PRIOR
  TO TRUSS ERECTION.

ROOF PLAN
1/8" — 1'-0"

Figure 34-21 A completed roof plan should show local and general notes.

DRAWING THE ROOF FRAMING PLAN

In the preceding steps instructions were given for drawing a roof plan. The following instructions are for a roof framing plan to accompany the same residence. Keep in mind that on an actual set of working drawings both plans would not be required. This plan will be drawn using a gable roof with stick construction methods. The ceiling over the master bedroom will be vaulted. Use construction lines for steps 1 through 10. Each step can be seen in Figure 34–22.

Step 1.   Using the dimensions of the floor plans, draw the perimeter walls.

Step 2.   Using the dimensions on the floor plans, draw the interior wall locations.

Step 3.   Using the dimensions on the floor and foundation plans, locate any posts and headers that are required for the covered porches.

Step 4.   Determine all rafter sizes. At this point, you would use the procedures described in Chapter 46 to determine the size and spacing of the rafters. For this project the following sizes will be required:

Over garage: 2 × 6 rafters @ 24″ O.C.
Over porch: 4 × 8 beams @ 48″ O.C. exposed.
Over bedroom 1: 2 × 12 raft/c.j. @ 16″ O.C.
Ridge beam at bedroom 1: 4 × 14 exposed.
Purlins at upper floor: 2 × 6.
Purlins at garage: 2 × 8.

Step 5.   Based on rafter size, locate and draw needed purlins.

Step 6.   Draw the limits of the overhangs. Unless your instructor provides different information, use 1′-0″ overhangs for the gable end walls and 2′-0″ overhangs for the eaves.

Step 7.   Locate and draw the ridge.

Step 8.   Locate and draw all hips and valleys required by the design. On this particular drawing there are no hips or valleys required.

Step 9.   Draw the chimney based on the measurements of the upper floor.

Step 10.   Draw any skylights that are specified on the floor plan.

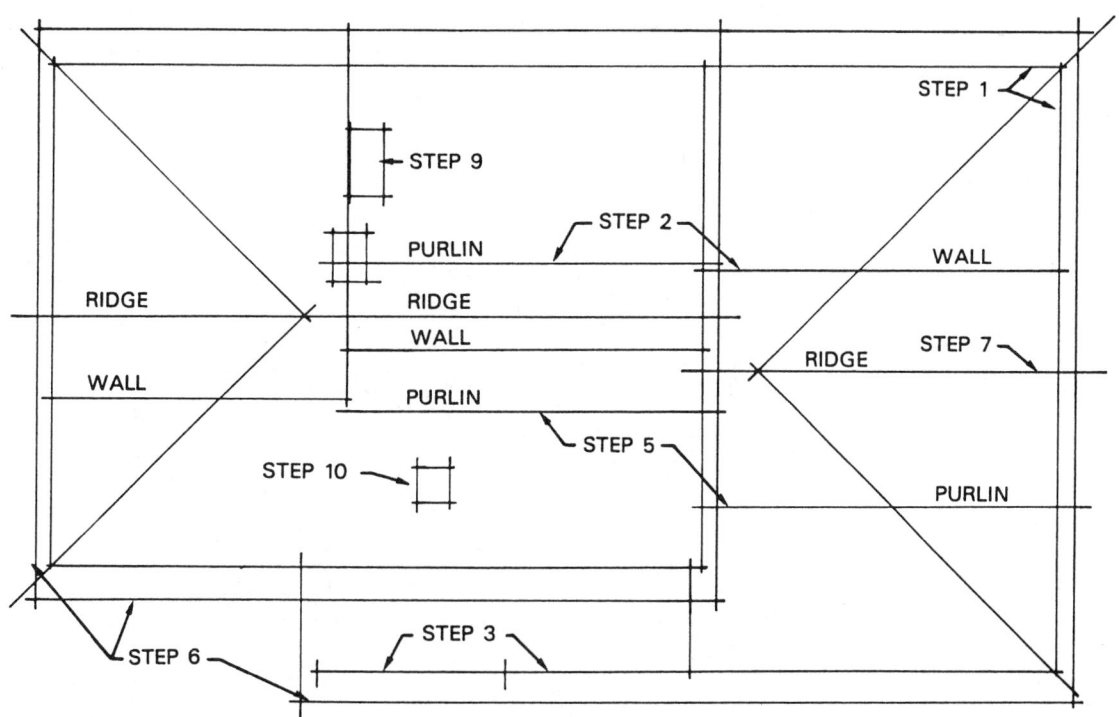

Figure 34–22 Using construction lines, draw the roof framing plan similar to the roof plan of Figure 34–17.

Use line quality as described earlier in this chapter for the following steps.

Step 11.   Draw the material blocked out in steps 1 through 8. Your drawing should now resemble Figure 34–23.

Step 12.   Draw the framing around openings. Your drawing should now resemble Figure 34–24.

Step 13.   Draw all rafters starting with the largest and working to the smallest. If all rafters are the same size, start in an area with the least amount of openings. Your drawing should now resemble Figure 34–25.

See Figure 34–26 for steps 14 and 15.

Step 14.   Add dimensions to locate all overhangs and openings in the roof.

Step 15.   Label all materials using local and general notes.

Step 16.   Evaluate your drawing for quality and completeness. Look for proper symbols for walls, overhangs, ridges, hips, valleys, purlins, beams, fireplace, and skylights; proper dimensions for overhangs, beams, and openings in the roof; plus local and general notes, a title and scale.

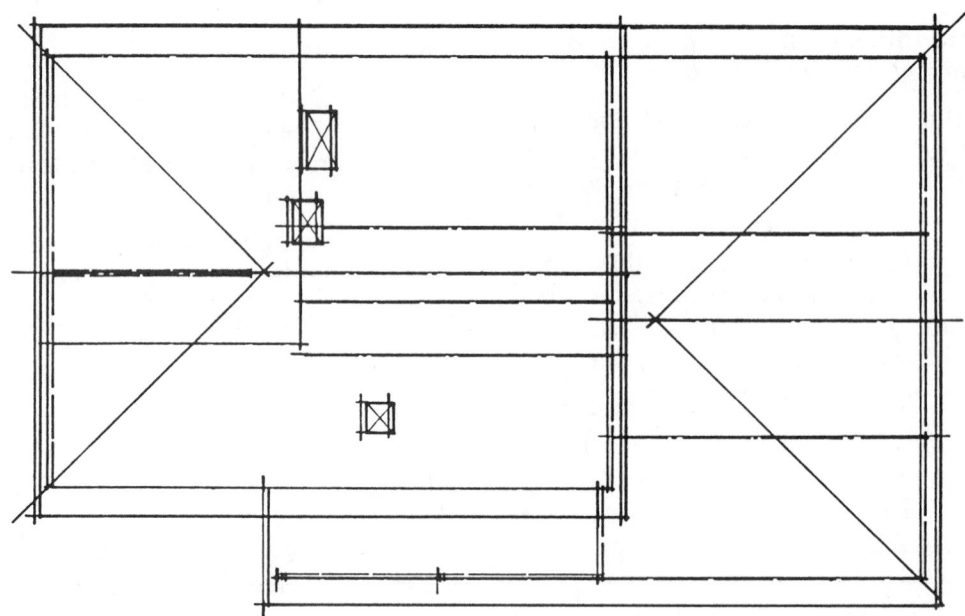

Figure 34–23 The outline of the roof and structural supports drawn with finished quality lines.

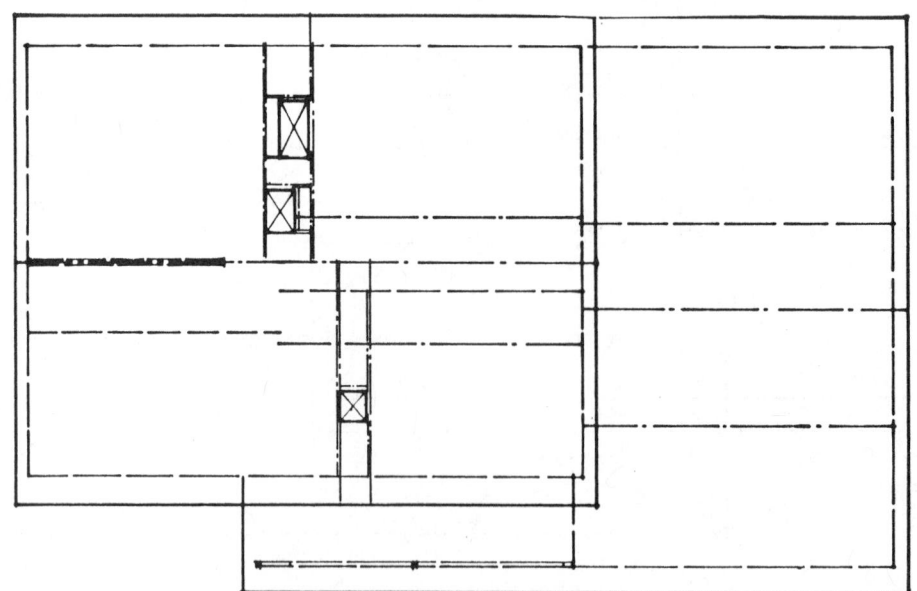

Figure 34–24 Draw any special framing required to support openings.

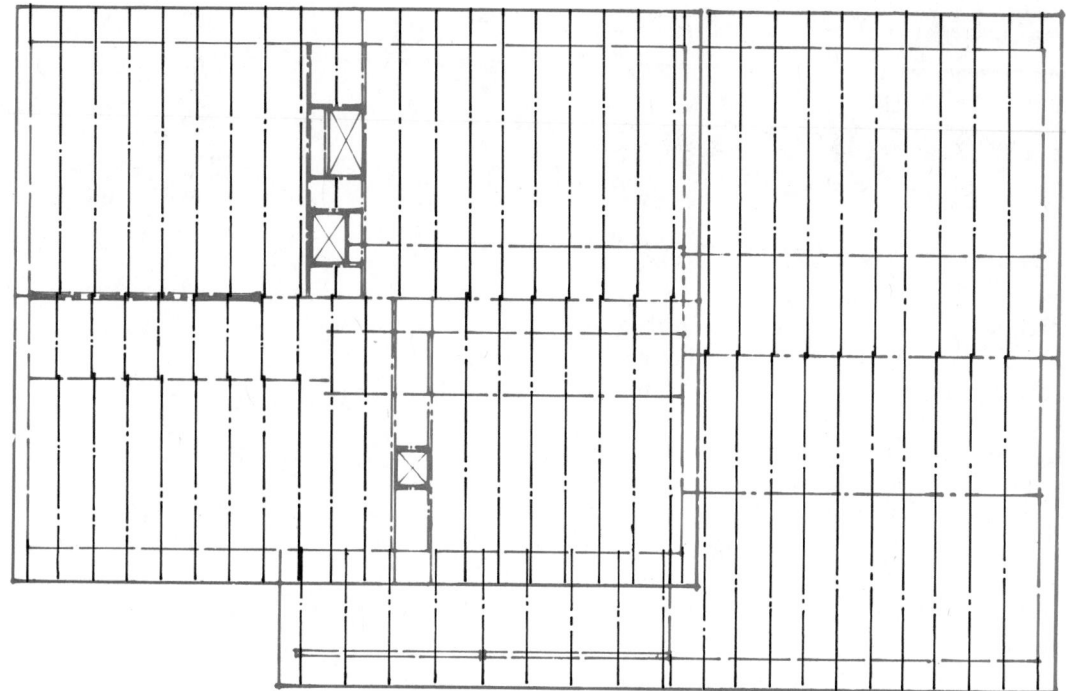

Figure 34–25 Each rafter is shown on a roof framing plan.

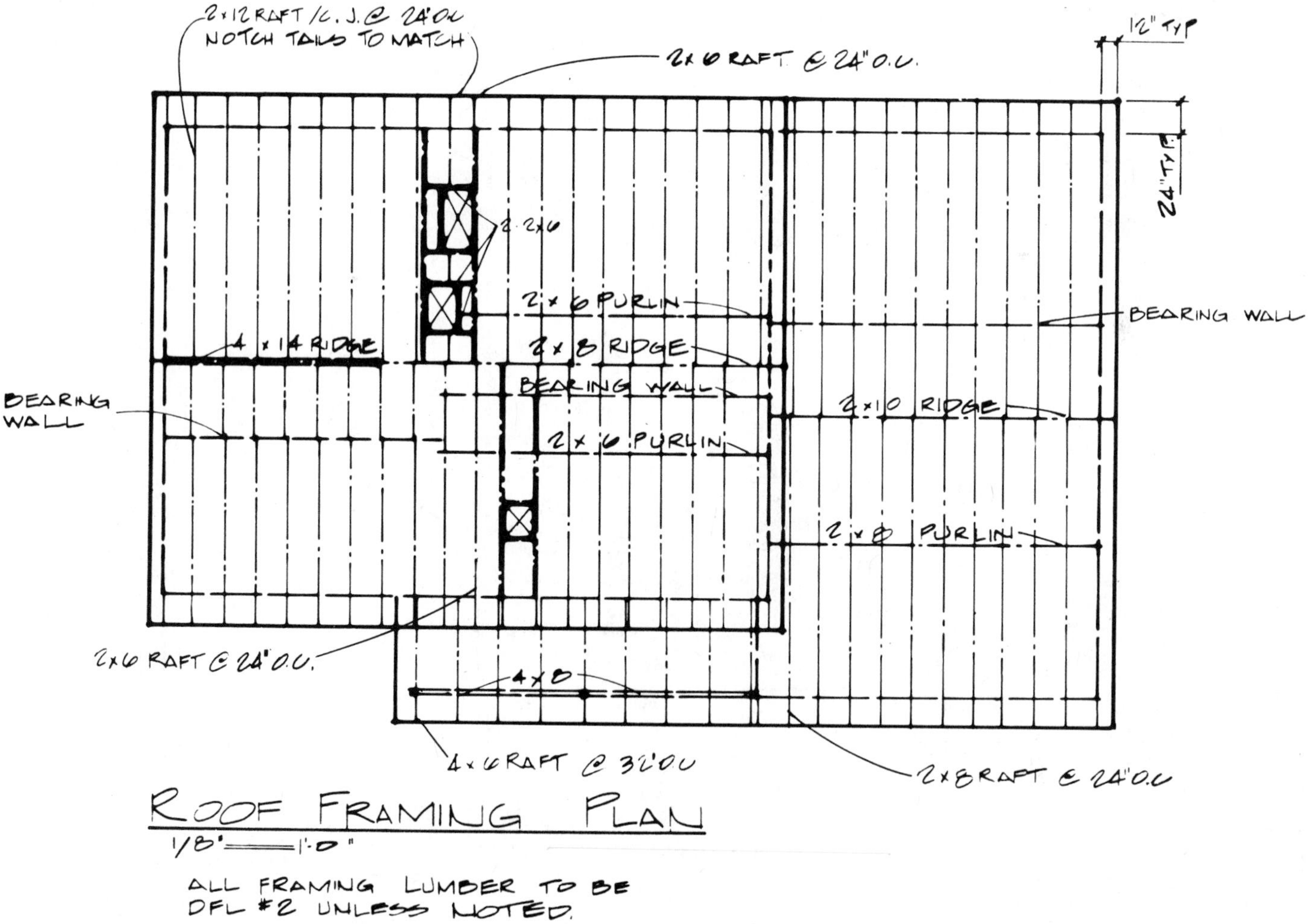

2×12 RAFT/C. J. @ 24'OC
NOTCH TAILS TO MATCH

2×6 RAFT @ 24"O.C.

12" TYP

24" TYP

2-2×6

2×6 PURLIN

2×8 RIDGE

BEARING WALL

BEARING WALL

4×14 RIDGE

BEARING WALL

2×10 RIDGE

BEARING WALL

2×6 PURLIN

2×8 PURLIN

2×6 RAFT @ 24'O.U.

4×8

4×6 RAFT @ 32'O.U.

2×8 RAFT @ 24'O.U.

ROOF FRAMING PLAN
1/8" = 1'-0"

ALL FRAMING LUMBER TO BE
DFL #2 UNLESS NOTED.

Figure 34–26 A completed roof framing plan showing dimensions and notes.

DRAWING ROOF PLANS WITH CADD

Some architectural CADD programs can automatically generate a basic roof plan from the floor plan. They use the floor plan as a base layer. The drafter then provides the roof overhang, specifies span by picking the building width on the floor plan, and identifies hip and valley lines. The computer then draws a roof plan similar to the examples shown in Figure 1. After the roof plan is drawn, the drafter adds dimensions and notes to complete the drawing. CADD makes drawing roof plans so easy that many architects and designers use CADD to draw roof framing plans; they show roof construction in greater detail than a roof plan. Figure 2 shows a comparison between a CADD-drawn roof plan and a roof framing plan.

When the roof plan gets complicated, some ar-

Figure 1 CADD roof plan.

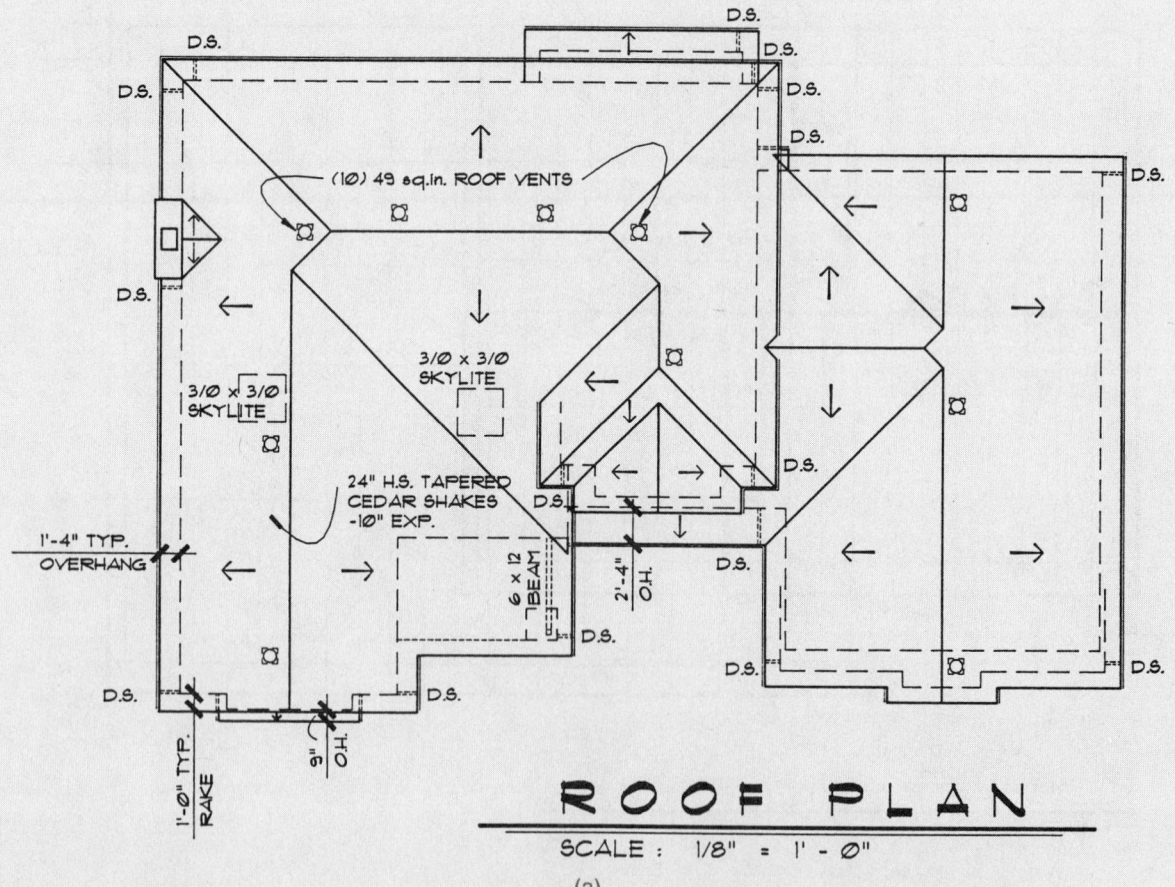

(a)

Figure 2 CADD-drawn plans showing (a) roof plan and (b) roof framing plan.

chitects prefer to draw in three dimensions (3-D). The 3-D drawing allows you to see the roof slopes more clearly than a plan view. You also have the flexibility to rotate a 3-D view to any position, so

you can determine lines of intersection between complex roof pitches. After the roof is completely drawn in the 3-D format, you can automatically establish the plan view.

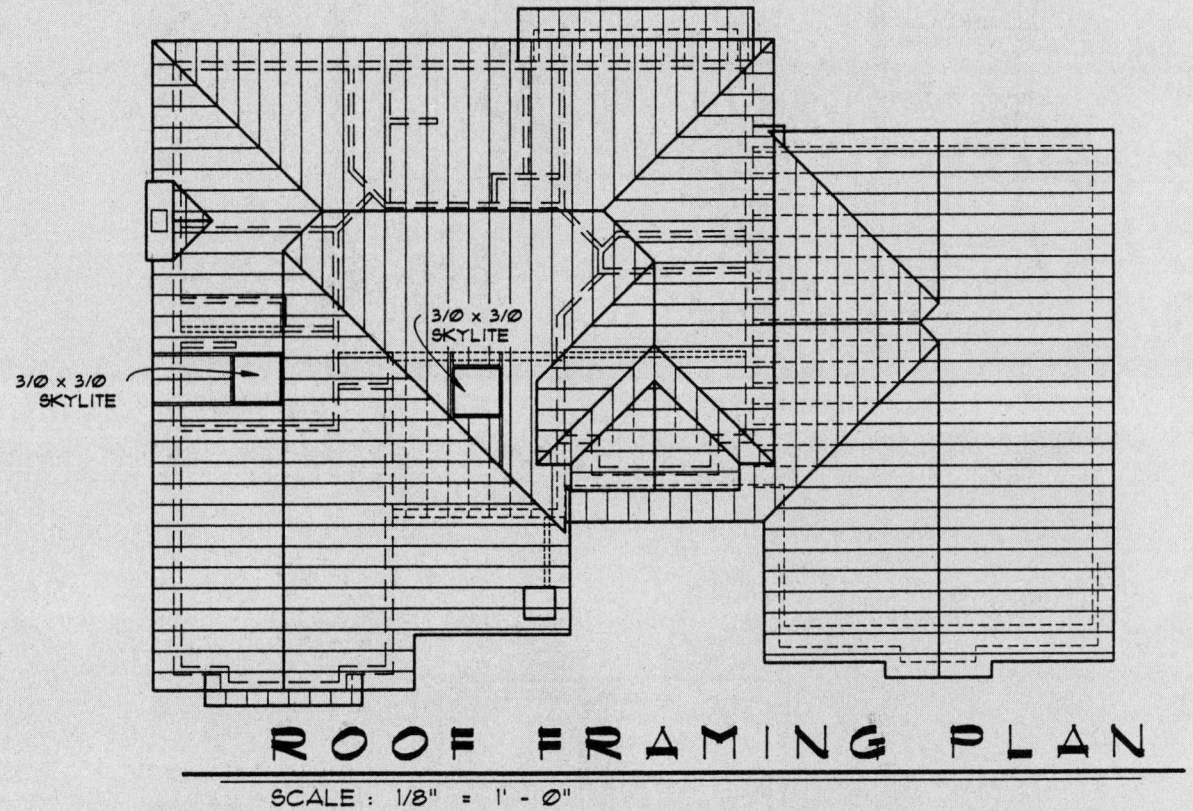

3/0 x 3/0
SKYLITE

3/0 x 3/0
SKYLITE

ROOF FRAMING PLAN

SCALE : 1/8" = 1' - 0"

NOTES :
1.   ALL RAFTERS TO BE 2 x 8 *2 & BTR. DF/L @ 24" O.C.
2.   ALL HIP AND RIDGE BOARDS TO BE 2 x 10 *2 DF/L.
3.   DOUBLE FRAMING AT ALL ROOF PENETRATIONS.

(b)

Figure 2 Continued.

ROOF PLAN AND ROOF FRAMING PLAN LAYOUT PROBLEMS

DIRECTIONS

1. Using a print of your floor plan and elevation drawn for problems from Chapters 20, 23, and 25, draw a roof or roof framing plan for your house. If no sketch has been given for the plan you have drawn, design a roof system appropriate for your area that will support local wind or snow loads. Draw the type of plan that the

construction method dictates. Use a scale suitable for the complexity of the plan.

2. Place the plan on the same sheet as the elevations if possible. If a new sheet is required, place the drawing so that other drawings can be put on the same sheet.

3. When you have completed your drawing, turn in a diazo copy to your instructor for evaluation.

Problem 34–1. CAPE COD.

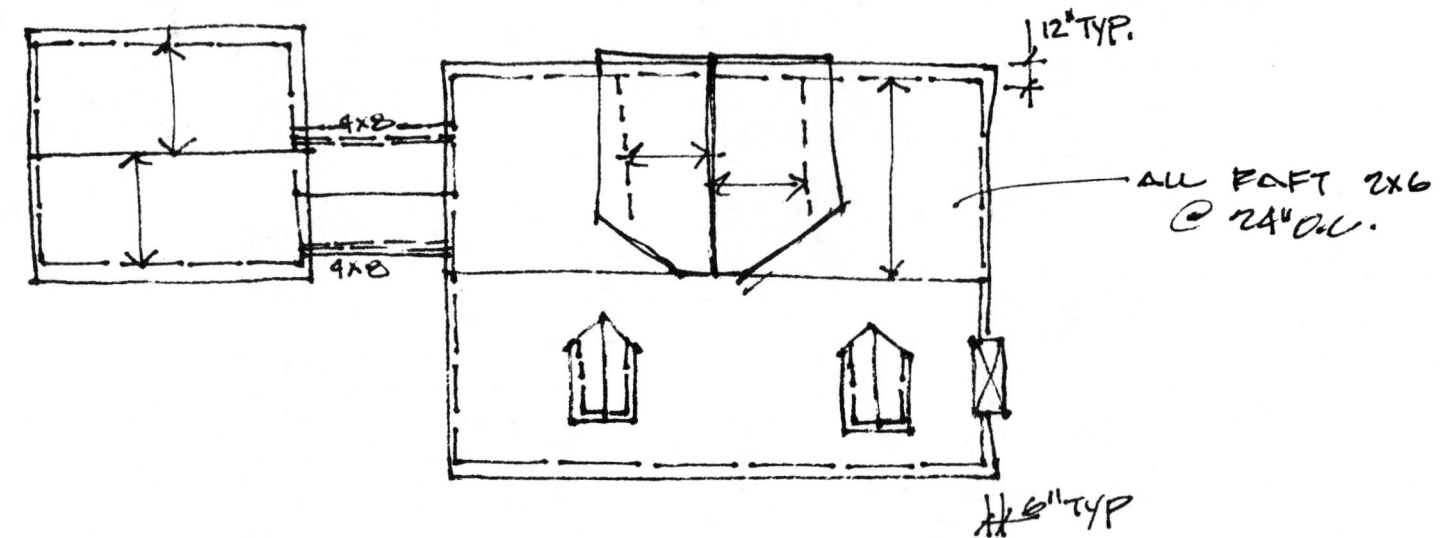

All RAFT 2×6 @ 24" O.C.

12" TYP.

4×8

4×8

6" TYP

Problem 34–2. CABIN.

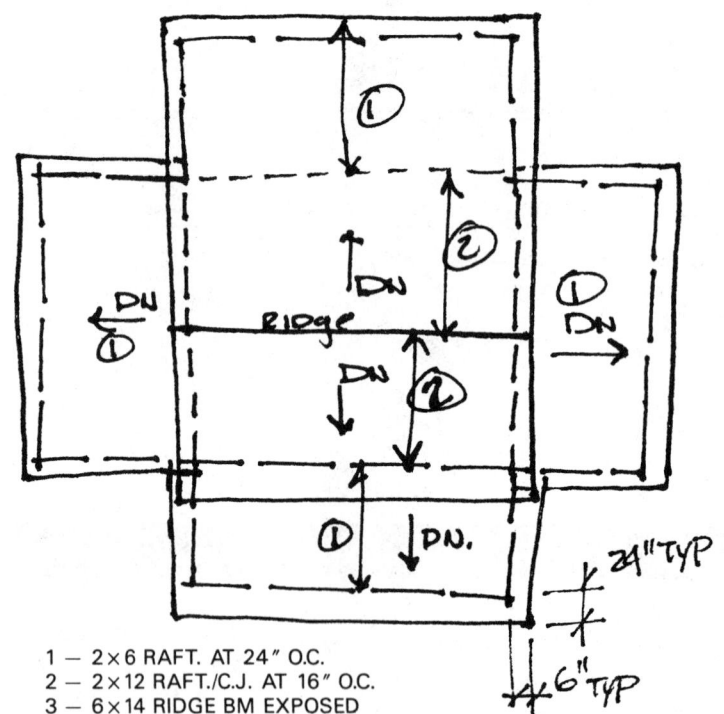

RIDGE

DN

DN

DN

DN

DN

DN.

24" TYP

6" TYP

1 — 2×6 RAFT. AT 24" O.C.
2 — 2×12 RAFT./C.J. AT 16" O.C.
3 — 6×14 RIDGE BM EXPOSED

Problem 34–3. RANCH.

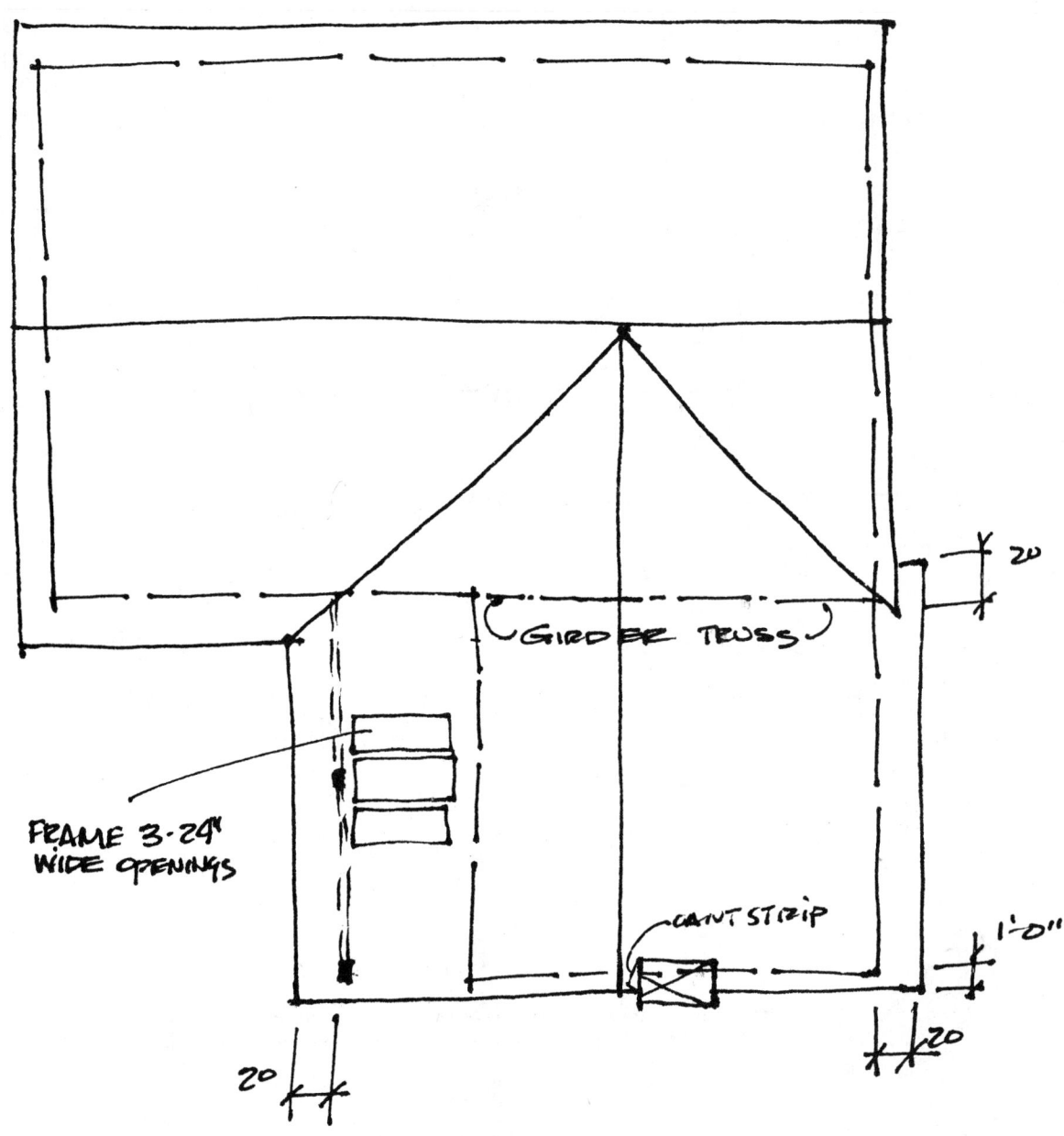

FRAME 3·24"
WIDE OPENINGS

GIRDER TRUSS

CANT STRIP

20

1'-0"

20

20

Problem 34–4. SPANISH.

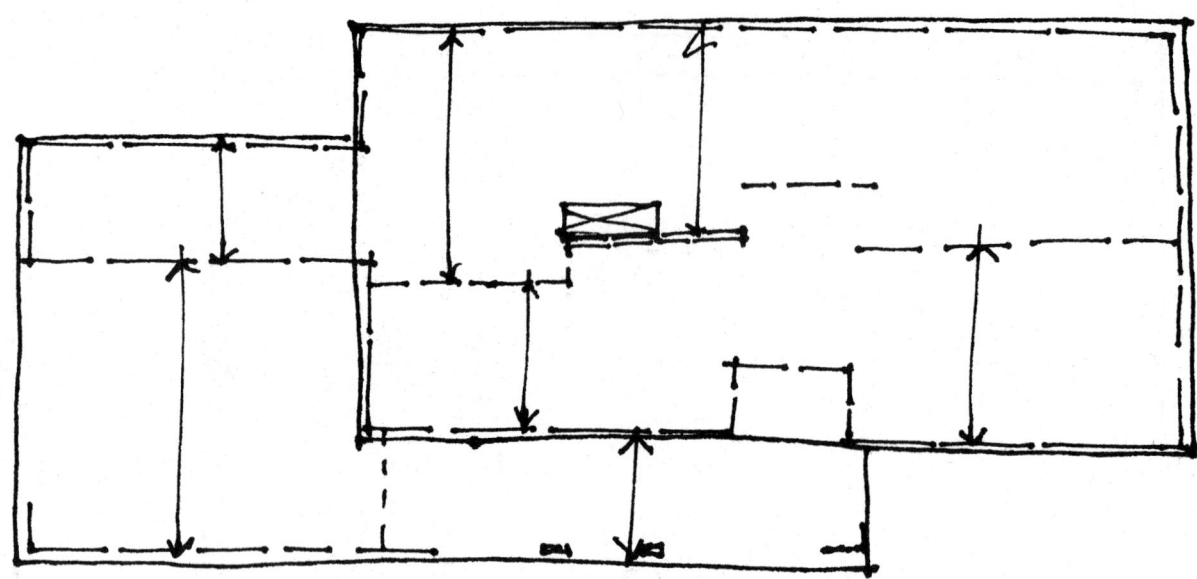

USE 4 × 8 @ 32″ O.C. EXPOSED
@ PORCH

ALL RAFT/C.J. TO BE 2 × 12
@ 16″ O.C.

2″ OVERHANG TYPICAL

Problem 34–5. EARLY AMERICAN.

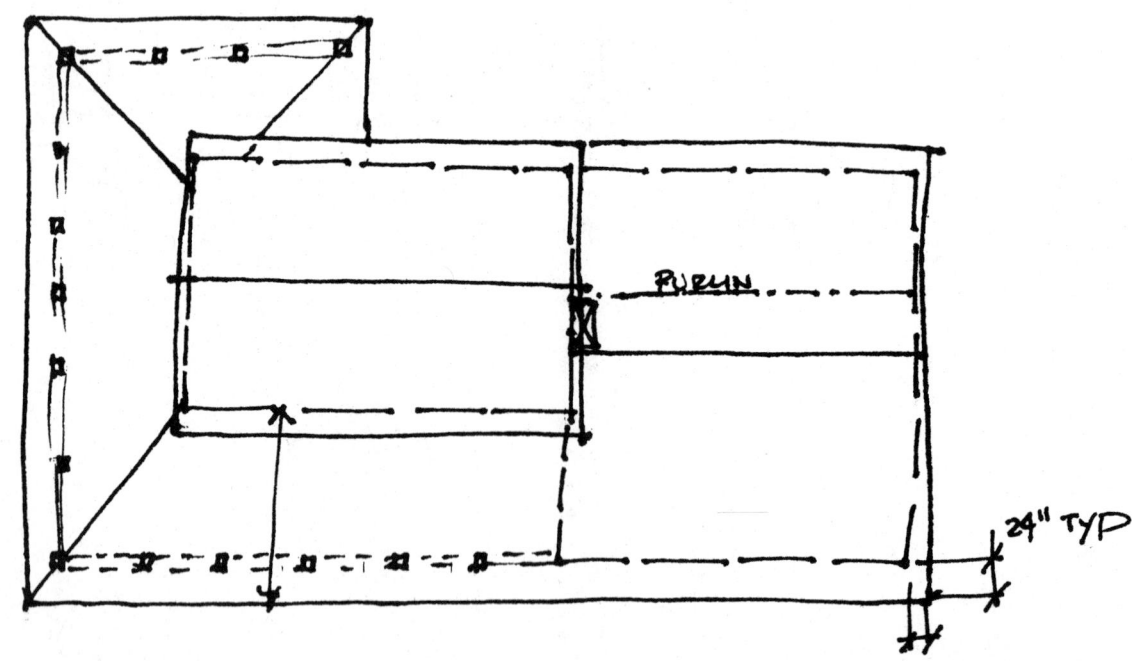

PURLIN

24″ TYP

DETERMINE ALL RAFTER SIZES

Problem 34-6. CONTEMPORARY.

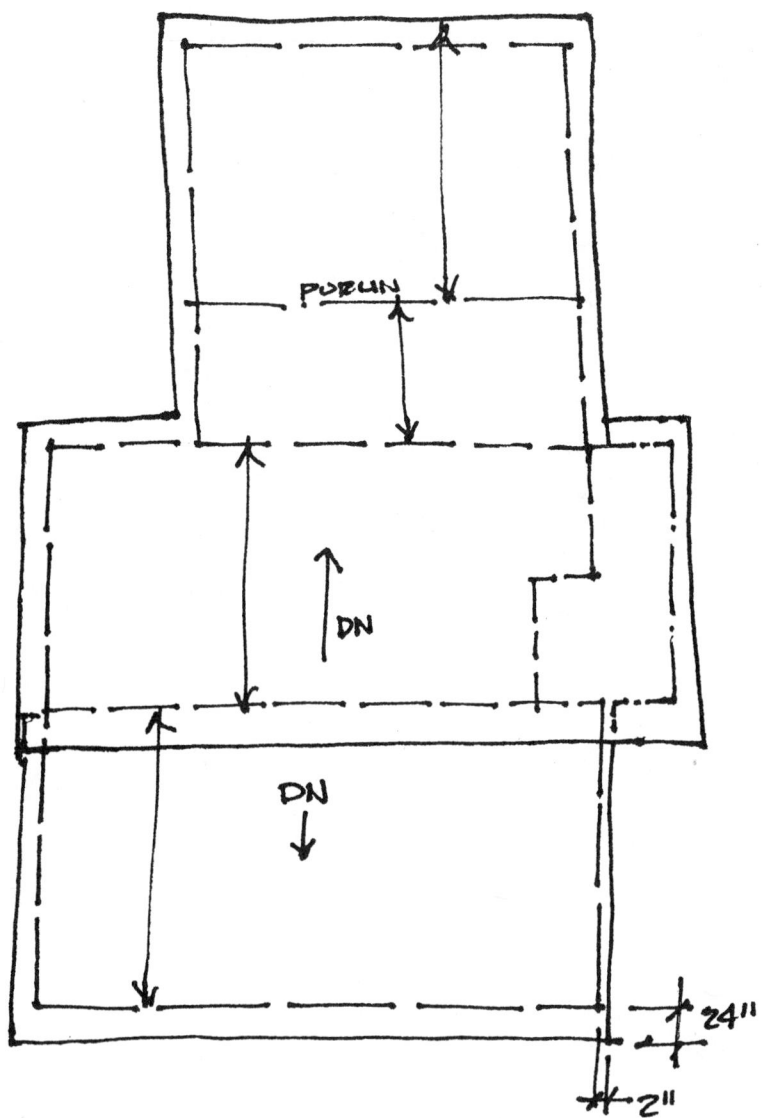

PURLIN

DN

DN

24"

2"

DETERMINE ALL RAFTER SIZES

Problem 34-7. DUPLEX. Without the use of a sketch, design a roof plan for this structure. Sketch the layout you will use and have it approved by your instructor prior to starting your drawing.

CM-1430

Section Eight
Cabinets

Chapter 35
Millwork and Cabinets

CABINET CONSTRUCTION is an element of the final details of a structure known as millwork. Millwork is any item that is considered finish trim or finish woodwork. Architects, designers, and drafters do not always draw complete details of millwork items. The practice of drawing millwork representations depends upon the specific requirements of the project. For example, the custom plans for a residential or commercial structure may show very detailed and specific drawings of the finish woodwork in the form of plan views, elevations, construction details, and written specifications. Plans of a house that is one of many to be built with a group of houses may only show floor plan views of cabinetry. The reason for this is that the building contractor may want the flexibility of being able to use available millwork without strict requirements placed on selection. Other factors that determine the extent of millwork drawings on a set of plans are the requirements of specific lenders and local code jurisdictions. In most situations when a set of plans is ready for construction, it must be submitted to a lender for loan approval and to code officials for a building permit. The lender approval is not necessary if the structure is to be built with cash, which does not happen very often. The approval of local building officials is always necessary in areas where building permits are required. Before a set of plans can be completed, verify the requirements of the client, the lender, and the local building officials.

TYPES OF MILLWORK

Millwork may be designed for appearance or for function. When designed for appearance, ornate and decorative millwork may be created with a group of shaped wooden forms placed together to capture a style of architecture. Molded millwork may be reproduced in as many styles as the designer can imagine. There are also vendors that manufacture a wide variety of prefabricated millwork moldings that are available at less cost than custom designs. See Figure 35–1. Millwork that is used for function may be very plain in appearance. This type of millwork is also less expensive than standard sculptured forms. In some situations wood millwork may be replaced with plastic or ceramic products. For example, in a public restroom or in a home laundry room a plastic strip may be used around the wall at the floor to protect the wall. This material will stand up to abuse better than wood. In some cases drafters will be involved

Figure 35–1 Prefabricated millwork. *Courtesy Cumberland Woodcraft Co., Inc., Carlisle, PA.*

in drawing details for specific millwork applications. There are as many possible details as there are design ideas. The following discussion will provide a general example of the items to help define the terms.

Baseboards

Baseboards are placed at the intersection of walls and floors and are generally used to protect the wall from damage as shown in Figure 35–2. Baseboards

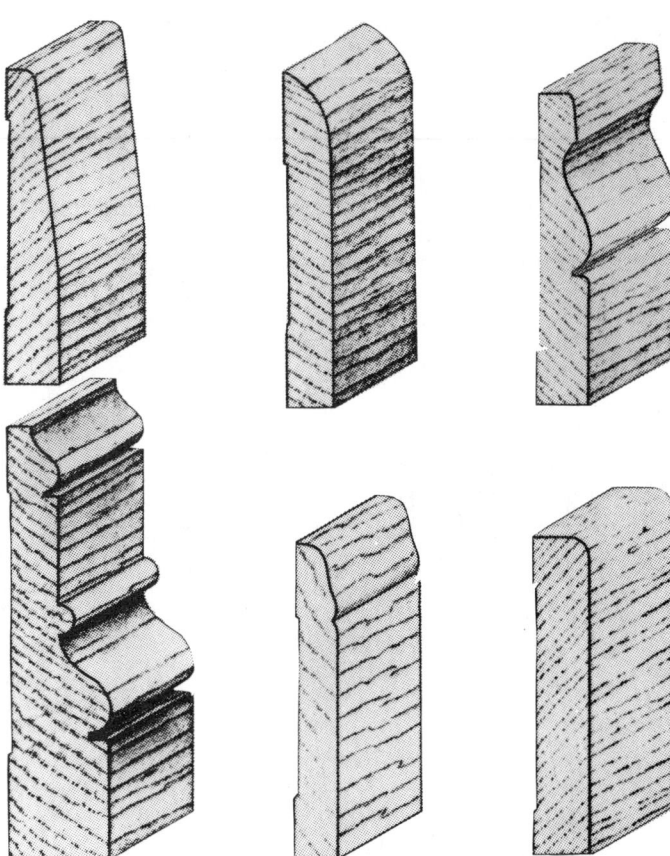

Figure 35–3 Standard baseboards. *Courtesy Hillsdale Pozzi Co.*

can be as ornate or as plain as the specific design or location dictates. In some designs, baseboards are the same shape as other millwork members, such as trim around doors and windows. Figure 35–3 shows some standard molded baseboards.

Wainscots

A wainscot is any wall finish where the material on the bottom portion of the wall is different from the upper portion. The lower portion is called the wainscot, and the material used is called wainscoting. Wainscots may be used on the interior or exterior of the structure. As previously discussed, exterior wainscoting is often brick veneer. Interior wainscoting may be any material that is used to divide walls into two visual sections. For example, wood paneling, plaster texture, ceramic tile, wallpaper, or masonry may be used as wainscoting. Figure 35–4 shows the detail of wood wainscot with plywood panels. The plywood panel may have an oak or other hardwood outer veneer to match the surrounding hardwood material. This is a less expensive method of constructing an attractive wood wainscot than with the hardwood panels shown in Figure 35–5.

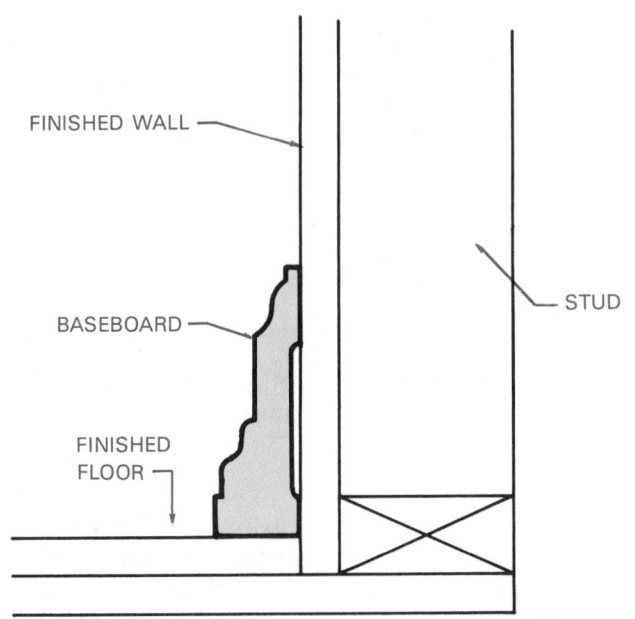

FINISHED WALL

STUD

BASEBOARD

FINISHED FLOOR

Figure 35–2 Baseboard.

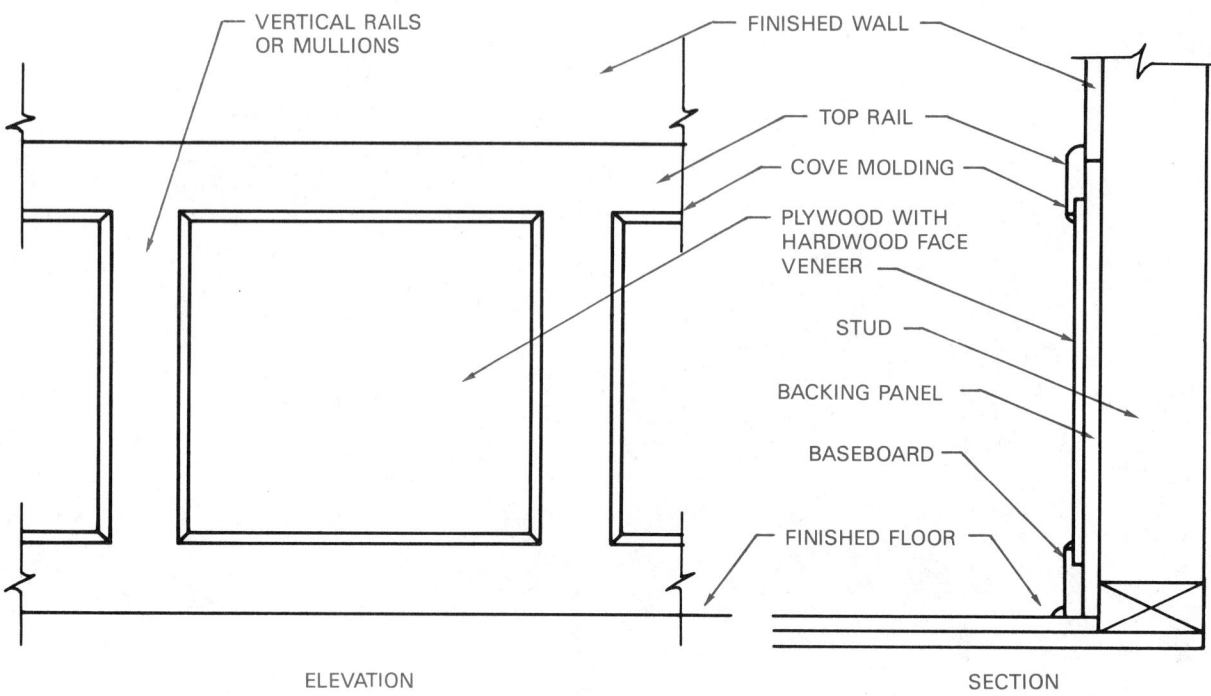

Figure 35-4 Plywood panel wood wainscot.

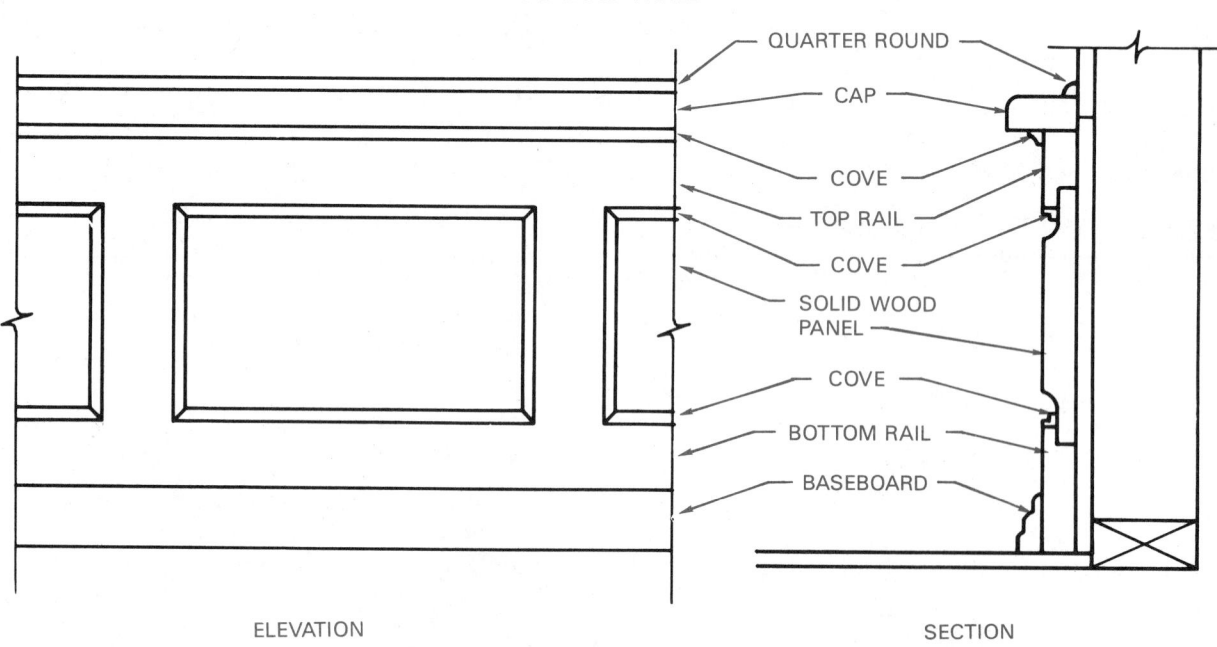

Figure 35-5 Solid wood-panel wainscot.

Chair Rail

The chair rail has traditionally been placed horizontally on the wall at a height where chair backs would otherwise damage the wall. See Figure 35-6. Chair rails, when used, are usually found in the dining room, den, office, or in other areas where chairs are frequently moved against a wall. Chair rails may be used in conjunction with wainscoting. In some applications the chair rail is an excellent division between two different materials or wall textures. Figure 35-7 shows sample chair rail moldings.

Cornice

The cornice is decorative trim placed in the corner where the wall meets the ceiling. A cornice may be a single shaped wood member called cove or crown molding as seen in Figure 35-8, or the cornice may be a more elaborate structure made up of several

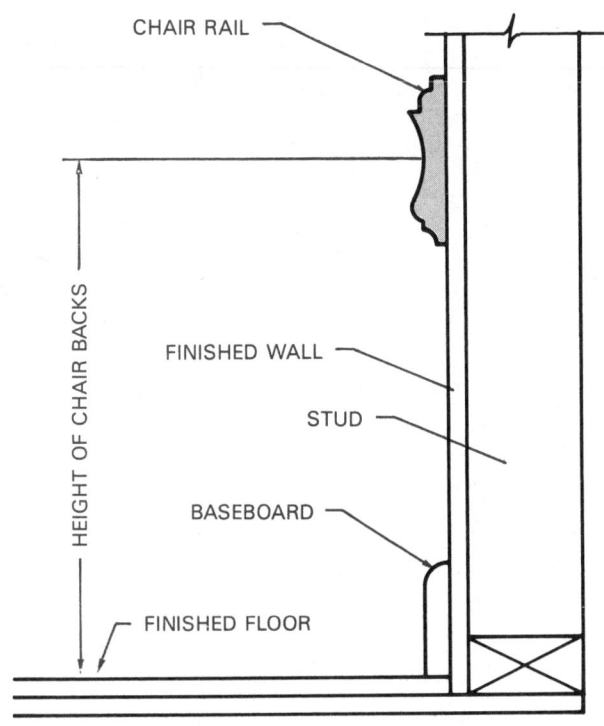

Figure 35-6 Chair rail.

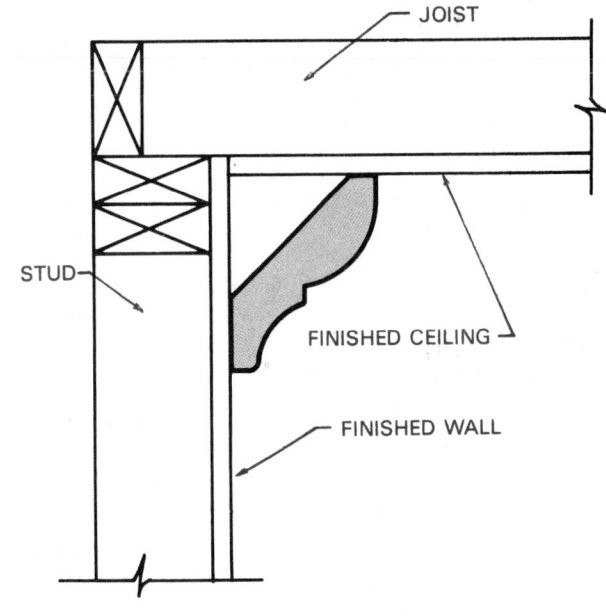

Figure 35-8 Individual piece cornice.

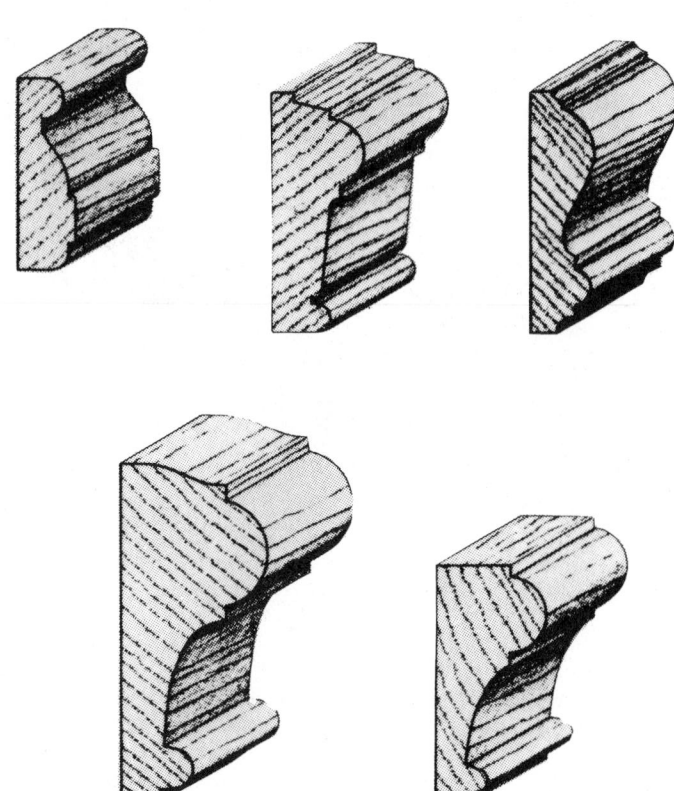

Figure 35-7 Standard chair rails. *Courtesy Hillsdale Pozzi Co.*

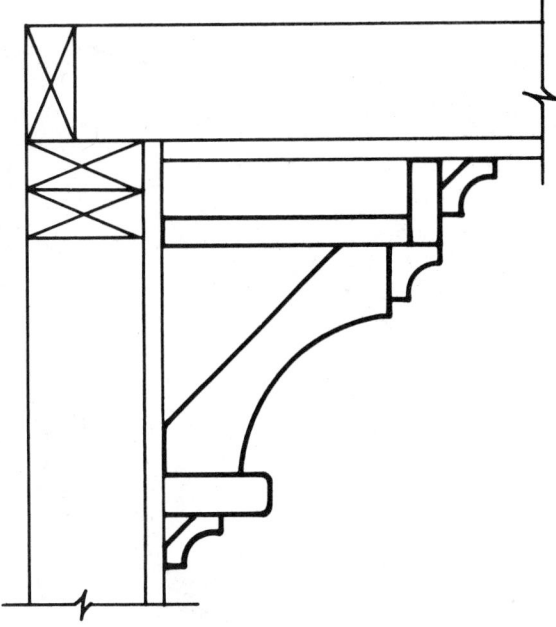

Figure 35-9 Multipiece cornice.

individual wood members as shown in Figure 35-9. Cornice boards are not commonly used, as they traditionally fit into specific types of architectural styles such as English Tudor, Victorian, or colonial. Figure 35-10 shows some standard cornice moldings. In most construction, where contemporary architecture or cost saving is important, wall to ceiling corners are left square.

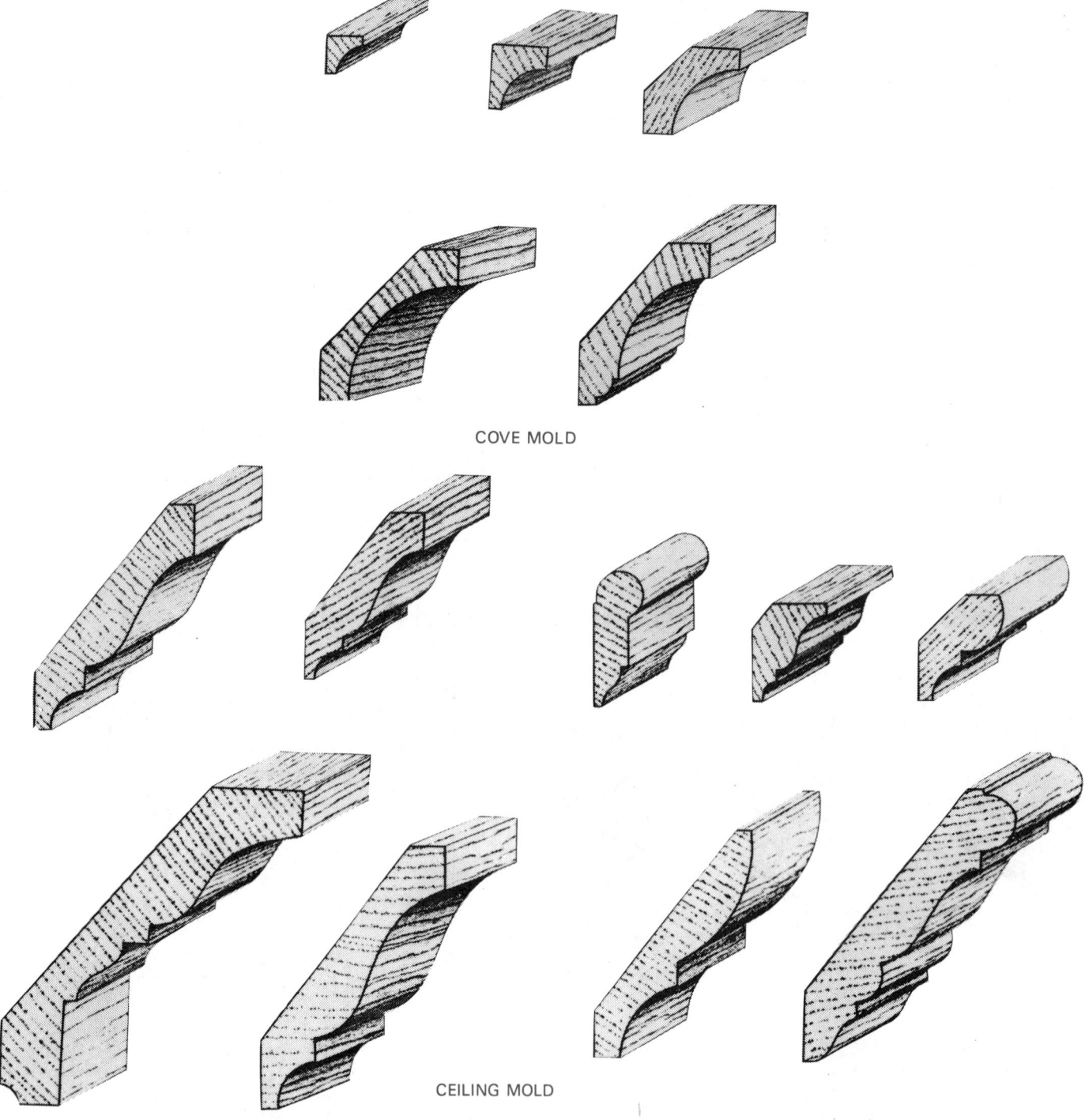

COVE MOLD

CEILING MOLD

Figure 35–10 Standard cornice (cove and ceiling) moldings. *Courtesy Hillsdale Pozzi Co.*

Casings

Casings are the members that are used to trim around windows and doors. Casings are attached to the window or door jamb (frame) and to the adjacent wall as shown in Figure 35–11. Casings may be decorative to match other moldings or plain to serve the functional purpose of covering the space between the door or window jamb and the wall. Figure 35–12 shows a variety of standard casings.

Mantels

The mantel is an ornamental shelf or structure that is built above a fireplace opening as seen in Figure 35–13. Mantel designs vary with individual

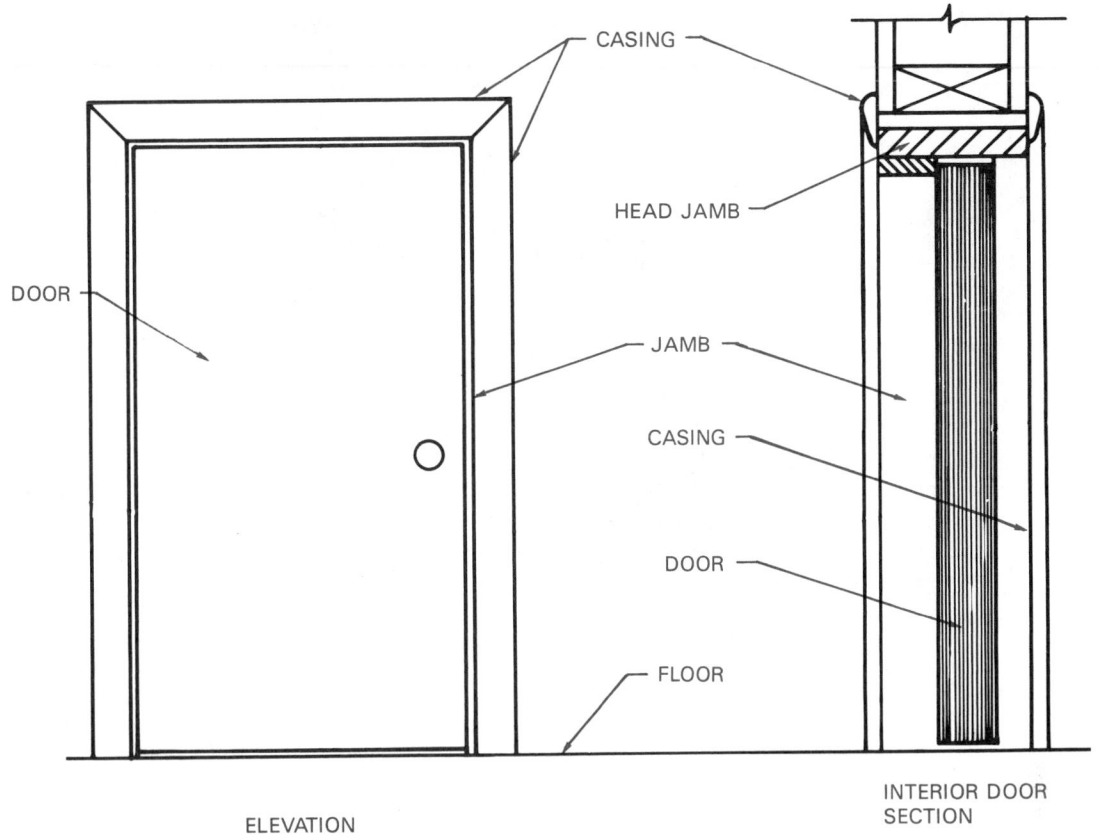

Figure 35-11 Casings.

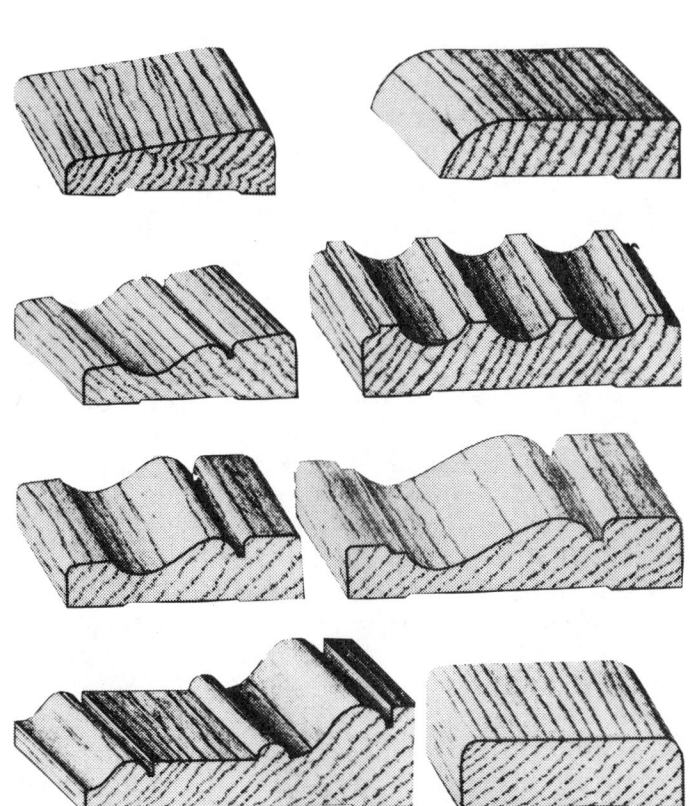

Figure 35-12 Standard casings. *Courtesy Hillsdale Pozzi Co.*

Figure 35-13 Mantel. *Photo by Bruce Davies, courtesy Park Place Wood Products, Inc.*

preference. Mantels may be made of masonry as part of the fireplace structure, or ornate decorative wood moldings, or even a rough-sawn length of lumber bolted to the fireplace face. Figure 35-14 shows a traditional mantel application.

Book Shelves

Book and display shelves may have simple construction with metal brackets and metal or wood shelving, or they may be built detailed as fine fur-

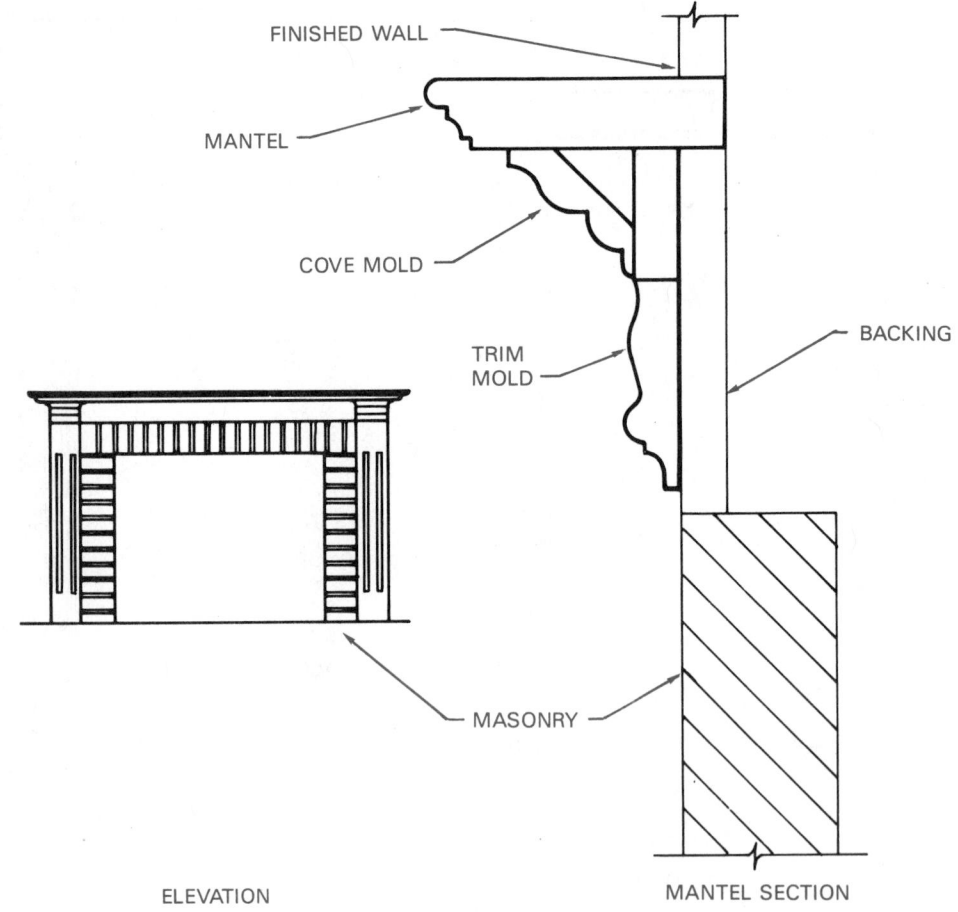

FINISHED WALL

MANTEL

COVE MOLD

TRIM
MOLD

BACKING

MASONRY

ELEVATION

MANTEL SECTION

Figure 35–14 Traditional mantel.

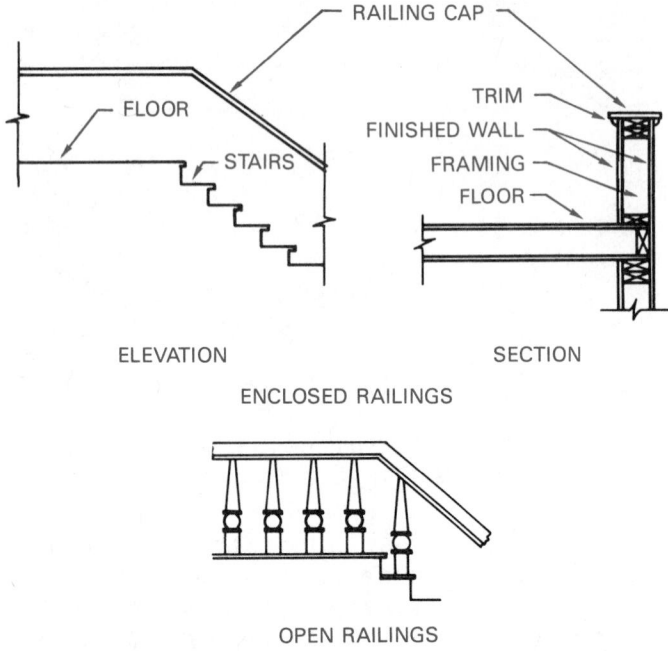

RAILING CAP

FLOOR

STAIRS

TRIM
FINISHED WALL
FRAMING
FLOOR

ELEVATION

SECTION

ENCLOSED RAILINGS

OPEN RAILINGS

Figure 35–15 Railings.

niture. Book shelves are commonly found in such rooms as the den, library, office, or living room. Shelves that are designed to display items other than books are also found in almost any room of the house.

A common application is placing shelves on each side of a fireplace. Shelves are also used for functional purposes in storage rooms, linen closets, laundry rooms, and any other location where additional storage is needed.

Railings

Railings are used for safety at stairs, landings, decks, and open balconies where people could fall. Rails are recommended at any rise that measures 24 in. or is three or more stair risers. Verify the size with local codes. Railings may also be used as decorative room dividers or for special accents. Railings may be built enclosed or open and constructed of wood or metal. Enclosed rails are often the least expensive to build because they require less detailed labor than open rails. A decorative wood cap is typically used to trim the top of enclosed railings. See Figure 35–15. Open railings can be one of the most attractive elements of interior design. Open railings may be as detailed as the designer's or craftsperson's imagination. Detailed open railings built of exotic hardwoods can be one of the most expensive items in the structure. Figure 35–16 shows some standard railing components.

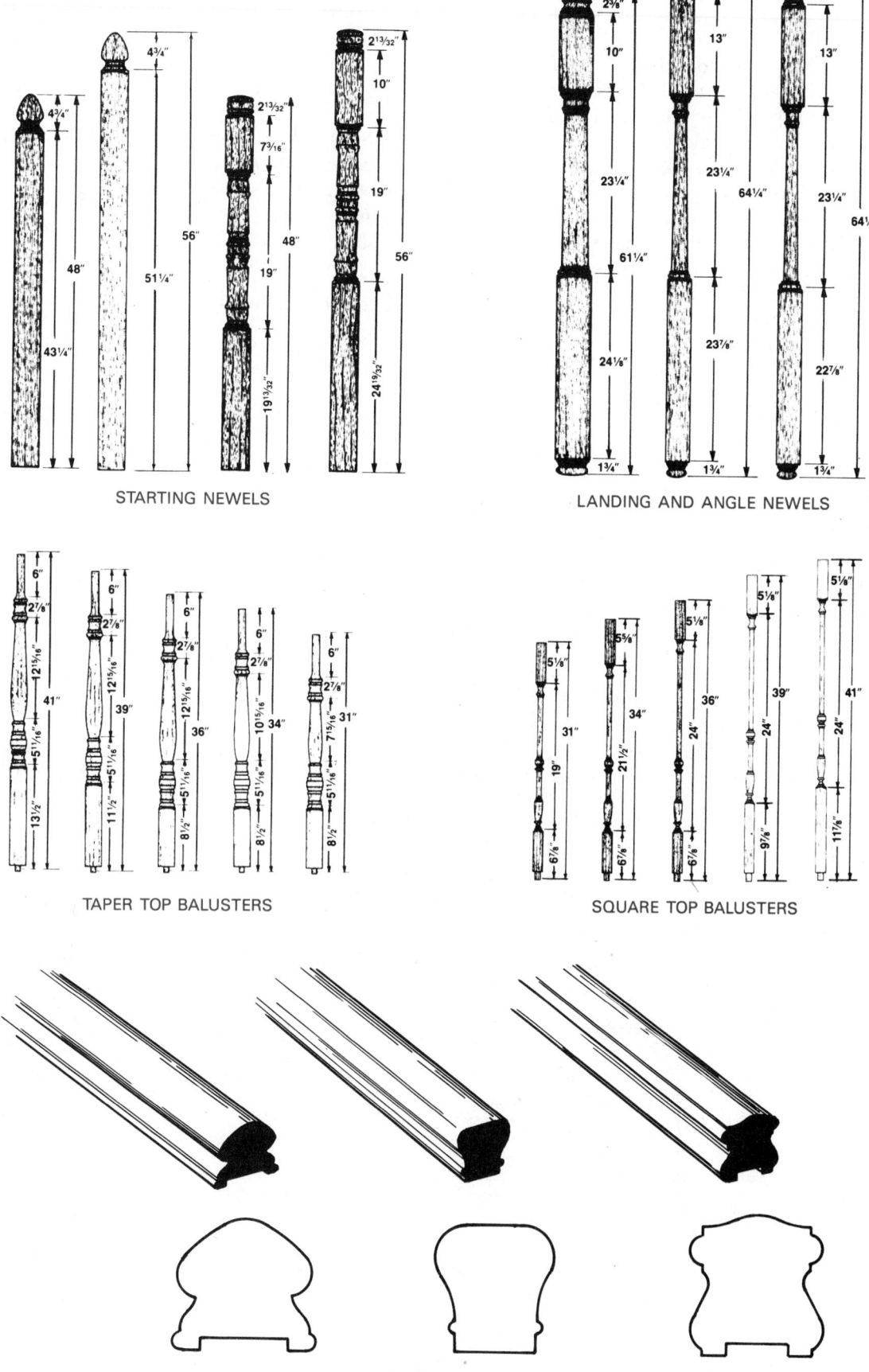

STARTING NEWELS

LANDING AND ANGLE NEWELS

TAPER TOP BALUSTERS

SQUARE TOP BALUSTERS

HAND RAILS

Figure 35–16 Examples of standard railing components. *Courtesy Hillsdale Pozzi Co.*

CABINETS

One of the most important items for buyers of a new home is the cabinets. The quality of cabinetry can vary greatly. Cabinet designs may reflect individual tastes and a variety of styles are available for selection. Cabinets are used for storage and as furniture. The most obvious locations for cabinets are the kitchen and bath. The design and arrangement of kitchen cabinets has been the object of numerous studies. Over the years design ideas have resulted not only in attractive but also functional kitchens. Kitchen cabinets have two basic elements: the base cabinet and the upper cabinet. See Figure 35–17. Drawers, shelves, cutting boards, pantries, and appliance locations must be carefully considered. Bathroom cabinets are called vanities, linen cabinets, and medicine cabinets. See Figure 35–18. Other cabinetry may be found throughout a house such as in utility or laundry rooms for storage. For example, a storage cabinet above a washer and dryer is common.

Cabinet Types

There are as many cabinet styles and designs as the individual can imagine. However, there are only two general types of cabinets based upon their method of construction. These are modular, or prefabricated cabinets, and custom cabinets.

Modular Cabinets

The term modular refers to prefabricated cabinets because they are constructed in specific sizes called modules. The best use of modular cabinets is when a group of modules can be placed side by side in a

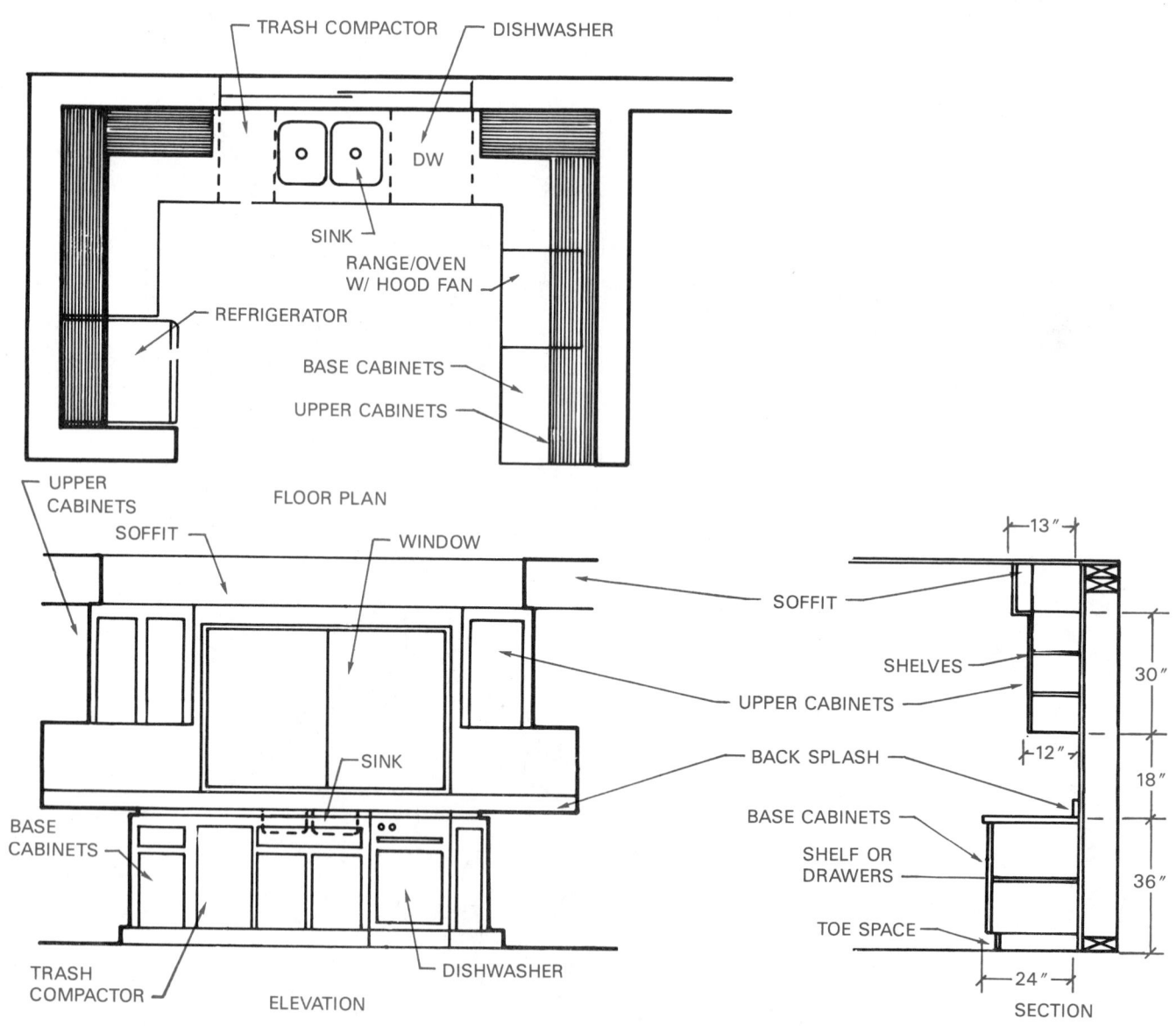

Figure 35–17 Kitchen cabinet components.

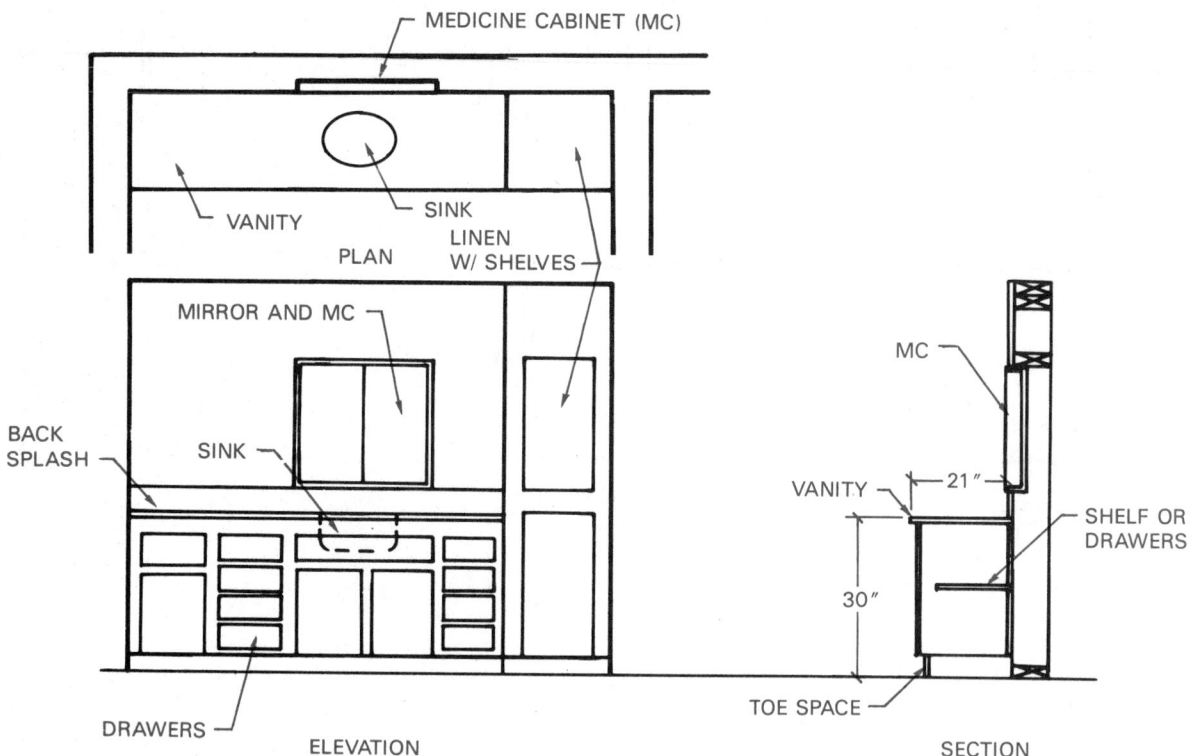

Figure 35–18 Bath cabinet components.

given space. If a little more space is available, then pieces of wood, called filler, are spliced between modules. Many brands of modular cabinets are available that are well crafted and very attractive. Most modular cabinet vendors offer different door styles, wood species, or finish colors on their cabinets. Modular cabinets are sized in relationship to standard or typical applications although many modular cabinet manufacturers can make cabinet components that will fit nearly every design situation. See Figure 35–19.

The modular cabinet layout begins with standard manufactured cabinet components which include wall, or upper, cabinets, base cabinets, vanity cabinets, tall cabinets, and accessories. When modular cabinets are used, the architect or designer will incorporate the individual units into the floor plan based upon the manufacturer's sizes and specifications. The actual floor plan will look the same as any of the cabinet representations presented in Chapter 15.

Custom Cabinets

The word *custom* denotes made to order. Some modular cabinet manufacturers advertise that their cabinets are made to order. The big difference between custom cabinets and modular cabinets is that

custom cabinets are generally fabricated locally in a shop to the specifications of an architect or designer, and after construction they are delivered to the job site and installed in large sections. The modular cabinets are often manufactured nationally and delivered in modules.

One of the advantages of custom cabinets is that their design is limited only by the imagination of the architect and the cabinet shop. Custom cabinets may be built for any situation such as for any height, space, type of exotic hardwood, type of hardware, geometric shape, or other design critera. Anything that is available in standard modular cabinets is also available in custom cabinets. Some custom cabinet shops use manufactured doors because they are attractive and may be less expensive than building from the beginning. Custom cabinet builders are not limited to these given styles. Many shops can build any unique design. In some cases it could take a little longer to get delivery of custom cabinets than modulars although this should be verified with local shops and compared to the availability of modular units. In most cases, if cabinets are ordered as soon as framing is completed, the cabinets should be delivered on time.

Custom cabinet shops will estimate a price based on the architectural drawings. The actual cabinets will be constructed from measurements taken at the job site after the building has been framed.

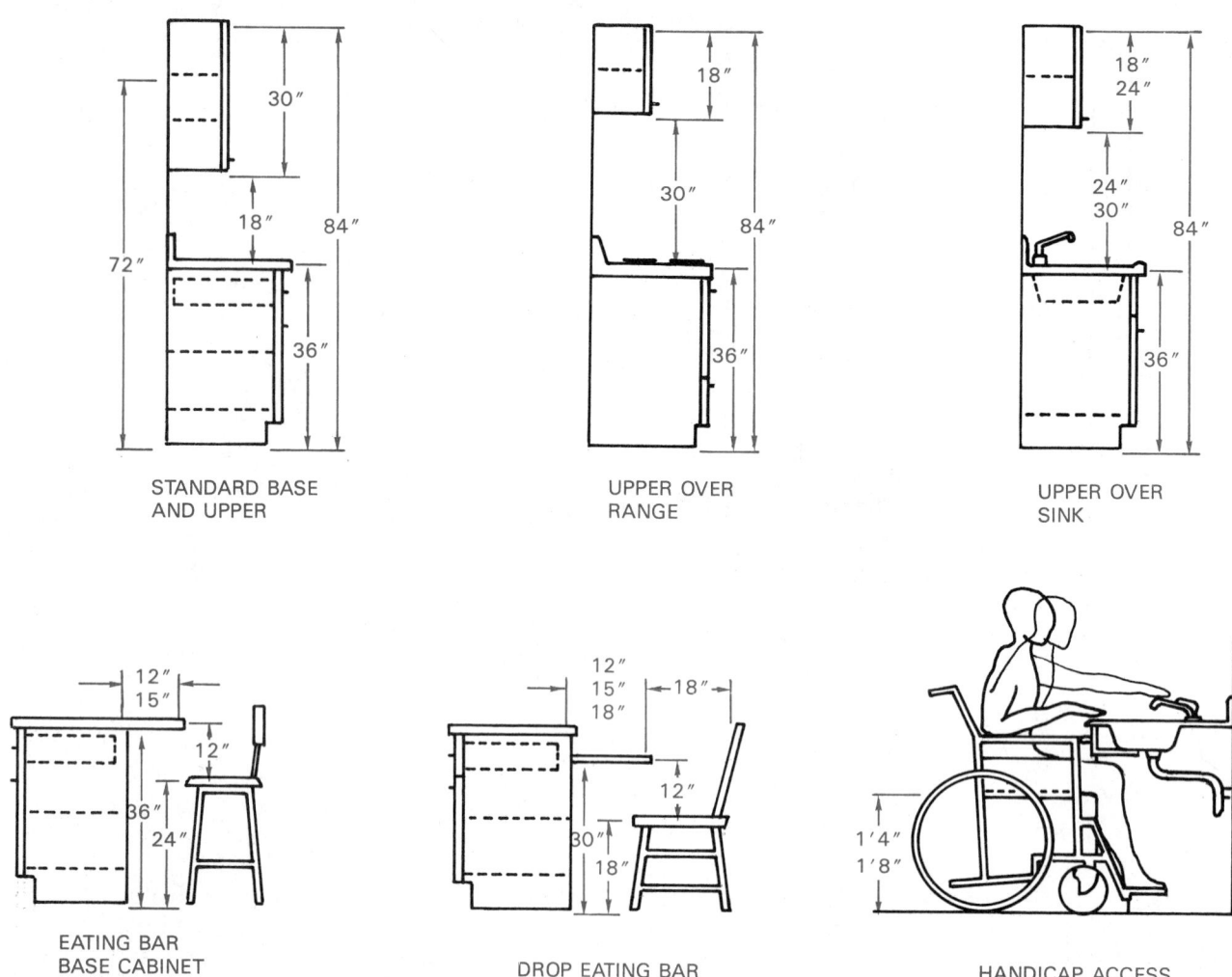

Figure 35–19 Standard cabinet dimensions.

Cabinet Options

Some of the cabinet design alternatives that are available from either custom or modular cabinet manufacturers include the following:

- Door styles, materials, and finishes.
- Self-closing hinges.
- A variety of drawer slides, rollers, and hardware.
- Glass cabinet fronts for a more traditional appearance.
- Wooden range hoods.
- Specially designed pantries, appliance hutches, and a lazy Susan or other corner cabinet design for efficient storage.
- Bath, linen storage, and kitchen specialties.

MILLWORK AND CABINETS TEST

DIRECTIONS

Answer the questions with short complete statements or drawings as needed on an 8½ × 11 drawing sheet as follows:

1. Use ⅛ in. guidelines for all lettering.
2. Letter your name, Millwork and Cabinets Test, and the date at the top of the sheet.
3. Letter the question number and provide the answer. You do not need to write out the question.
4. Do all lettering with vertical uppercase architectural letters. If the answer requires line work, use proper drafting tools and technique. Answers may be prepared on a word processor if appropriate with course guidelines.
5. Your grade will be based on correct answers and quality of line technique.

QUESTIONS

1. Define millwork.
2. Give an example of when plastic or ceramic products may be used rather than wood millwork.
3. What are baseboards used for?
4. Describe wainscots.
5. Define cornice.
6. When is the application of cornice millwork appropriate?
7. Where are casings used?
8. Where are mantels used?
9. Give an example of where book shelves may be used effectively as millwork in the interior design of a structure.
10. Give two examples of where railings may be used.
11. Describe modular cabinets.
12. Describe custom cabinets.
13. What is another name for modular cabinets?
14. What is the big difference between modular and custom cabinets?
15. How is it possible to compare cabinetry and millwork to fine furniture?

Chapter 36
Cabinet Elevations and Layout

CABINET FLOOR plan layouts and symbols were discussed in Chapter 15. Cabinet elevations or exterior views are developed directly from the floor plan drawings. The purpose of the elevations is to show how the exterior of the cabinets will look when completed and to give general dimensions, notes, and specifications. Cabinet elevations may be as detailed as the architect or designer feels is necessary. The factors that may influence the decision of how cabinet elevations should be represented are the following:

1. The decision of whether or not cabinet elevations are required as discussed in Chapter 35.
2. The cost of the structure. Cabinet elevations for a $75,000 house may be drawn with less detail than the elevations for a $275,000 house.
3. The requirements of the client may dictate the amount of detail that is represented in the cabinet elevations. Some individuals may want a very clear drawing of the cabinetry and other millwork to be sure that the finish work meets their specifications.
4. The amount of design input that is obtained from the cabinet builder or vendor may have some influence on the formal cabinet drawings. Some architects or designers may not prepare cabinet elevations but instead request the cabinet supplier to draw them. In this situation the cabinet supplier will prepare cabinet drawings that are then attached to the complete set of drawings.
5. The office practice of the architect will determine, in most cases, the amount of detail that is used on cabinet drawings. Some designers and architects take a great deal of pride in their drafting product and so put a little extra effort into the quality and appearance of the drawings. Figures 36–1(a) and 36–1(b) show two examples of cabinet elevations. In Figure 36–1(a), the cabinet elevations are very clear and well done without any detail or artwork that is not specifically necessary to construct the cabinets. In Figure 36–1(b), the cabinet elevations are more artistically drawn. Neither set of cabinet drawings is necessarily more functional than the other.

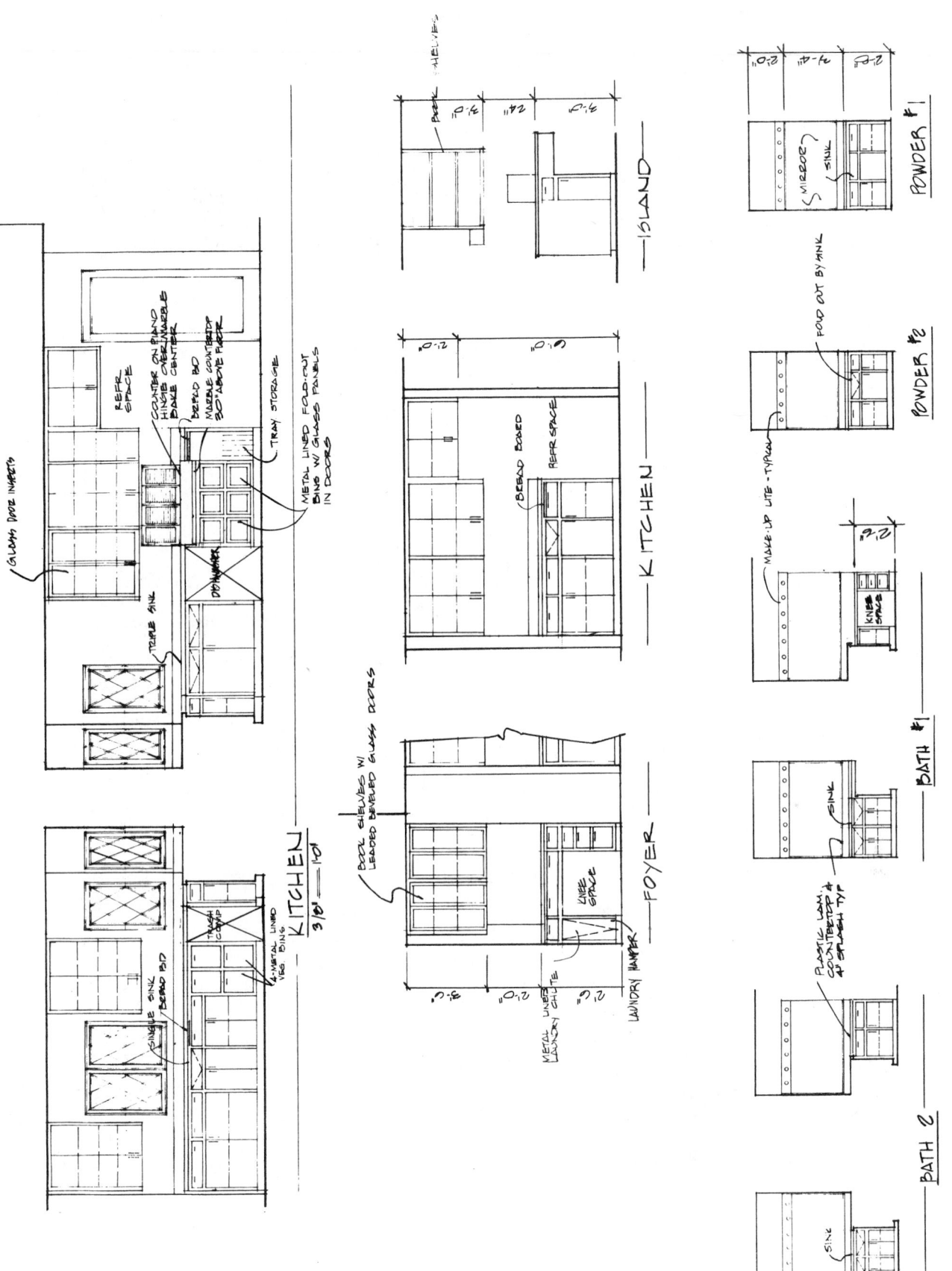

Figure 36-1(a) Simplified cabinet elevations. *Courtesy Jeff's Residential Designs.*

E ⟶ BATH ELEVATION
SCALE: 1/4"=1'-0"

D ⟶ BATH ELEVATION
SCALE: 1/4"=1'-0"

A ⟶ KITCHEN ELEVATION
SCALE: 1/4"=1'-0"

B ⟶ KITCHEN ELEVATION
SCALE: 1/4"=1'-0"

F ⟶ MASTER BATH ELEVATION
SCALE: 1/4"=1'-0"

C ⟶ KITCHEN ELEVATION
SCALE: 1/4"=1'-0"

Figure 36-1(b) Detailed cabinet elevations. *Courtesy Madsen Designs.*

Figure 36-2 Simplified floor plan and elevation cabinet location symbol.

KEYING CABINET ELEVATIONS TO FLOOR PLANS

There are several methods that may be used to key the cabinet elevations to the floor plan. In Figure 36–1(a), the designer keyed the cabinet elevations to the floor plans with such room titles as KITCHEN CABINET ELEVATIONS or BATH AND UTILITY ELEVATIONS. In Figure 36–1(b), the designer used an arrow with a letter inside, similar to the one shown in Figure 36–2, to correlate the elevation to the floor plan. For example, in Figure 36–3 the E and F arrows pointing to the vanities are keyed to letters E and F that appear below the vanity elevations.

Given the commercial drawing shown in Figure 36–4, notice that the floor plan has identification numbers within a combined circle and arrow. The symbols, similar to that shown in Figure 36–5, are pointing to various areas that correlate to the same symbols labeled below the related elevations. A similar method may be used to relate cabinet construction details to the elevations. The detail identification symbol as shown in Figure 36–6 is used to correlate a detail to the location from which it originated on the elevation. With some plans, small areas such as the women's rest room and men's rest room have interior elevations without specific orientation to the floor plan. The reason for this is that the relationship of floor plan to elevations is relatively obvious.

There may be various degrees of detailed representation needed for millwork depending upon its complexity and the design specifications. The sheet from a set of architectural working drawings shown in Figure 36–7 is an example of how millwork drawings can provide very clear and precise construction techniques.

CABINET LAYOUT

Cabinet layout is possible after the floor plan drawings are complete. The floor plan cabinet drawings are used to establish the cabinet elevation lengths. Cabinet elevations may be projected directly from the floor plan or dimensions may be transferred from the floor plan to the elevations with a scale or dividers.

Kitchen Cabinet Layout

The cabinet elevations are drawn as though you were standing in the room looking directly at the cabinets. Cabinet elevations are two dimensional. Height and length are shown in an external view and depth is shown where cabinets are cut with a cutting plane that is the line of sight. See Figure 36–8. For the kitchen shown in Figure 36–8 there will be two elevations: one looking at the sink and dishwasher cabinet group, the other viewing the range, refrigerator, and adjacent cabinets.

Given the floor-plan drawing shown in Figure 36–8 draw the cabinet elevations using the following methods:

Step 1. Make a copy of the cabinet floor-plan area and tape the copy to the drafting table above the area where the elevations are to be drawn. Transfer length dimensions from the floor plan onto the blank drafting surface in the location where the desired elevation is to be drawn using construction lines as shown in Figure 36–9. Some drafters prefer to transfer dimensions from the floor-plan drawings with a scale or dividers. As you gain layout experience, you will probably prefer to transfer dimensions. Notice that when the elevations are transferred directly from the floor plan, the scale will be the same as the floor plan, ¼″ = 1′–0″. Cabinet elevations may be drawn at ¼″ = 1′–0″, but keep a sharp pencil at this scale. Other scales are also used such as ⅜″ = 1′–0″ or ½″ = 1′–0″ when additional clarity is needed to show small detail. When the cabinet elevation scale is different from the floor-plan scale, the dimensions may not be projected. In this case the dimensions will be established from the floor plan

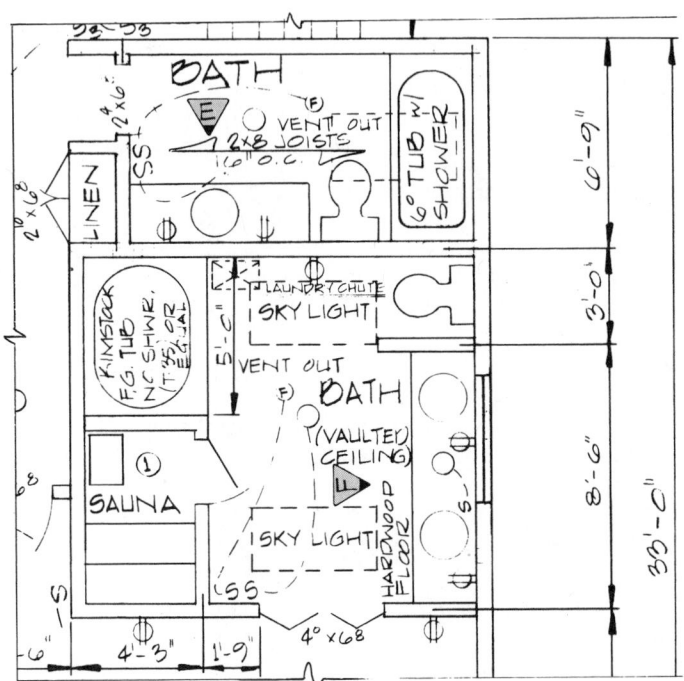

Figure 36–3 Using the floor plan and elevation cabinet location symbol. *Courtesy Madsen Designs.*

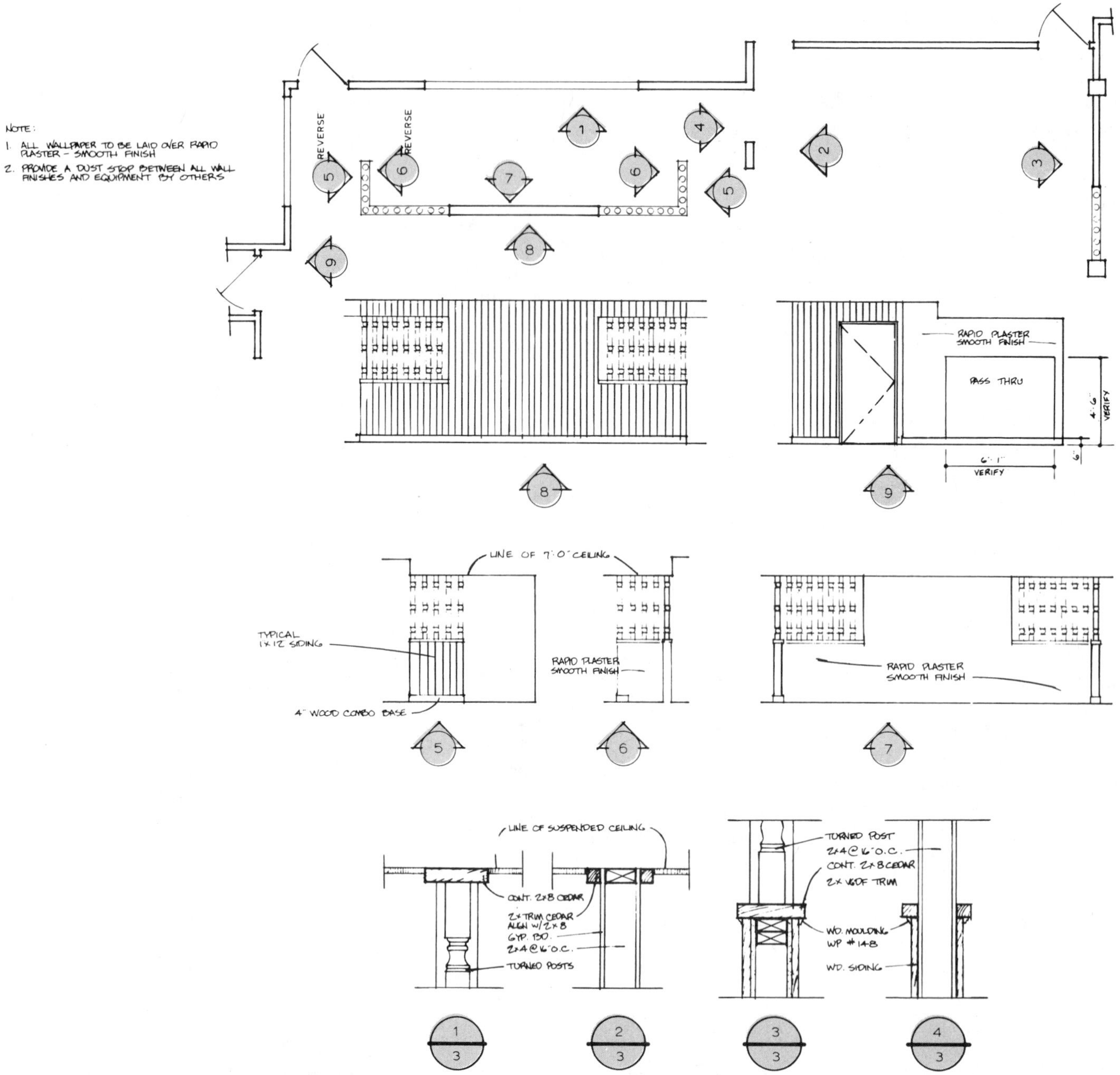

NOTE:
1. ALL WALLPAPER TO BE LAID OVER RAPID PLASTER - SMOOTH FINISH
2. PROVIDE A DUST STOP BETWEEN ALL WALL FINISHES AND EQUIPMENT BY OTHERS
REVERSE
REVERSE
RAPID PLASTER SMOOTH FINISH
PASS THRU
VERIFY
VERIFY
LINE OF 7'-0" CEILING
TYPICAL 1×12 SIDING
4" WOOD COMBO BASE
RAPID PLASTER SMOOTH FINISH
RAPID PLASTER SMOOTH FINISH
LINE OF SUSPENDED CEILING
CONT. 2×8 CEDAR
GYP. BD.
TURNED POSTS
TURNED POST
CONT. 2×8 CEDAR
WD. SIDING

Figure 36–4 Commercial floor plan with cabinet identification and location symbols. *Courtesy Ken Smith Structureform Masters, Inc.*

5
ELEVATION IDENTIFICATION NUMBER

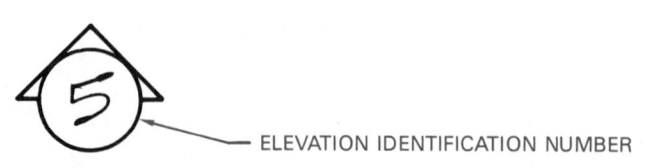

Figure 36–5 Floor plan and elevation cabinet identification and location symbol.

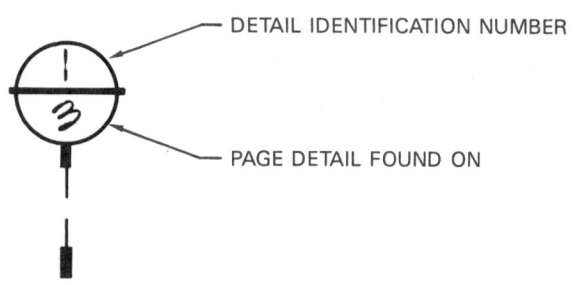

DETAIL IDENTIFICATION NUMBER
1
3
PAGE DETAIL FOUND ON

Figure 36–6 Detail identification symbol.

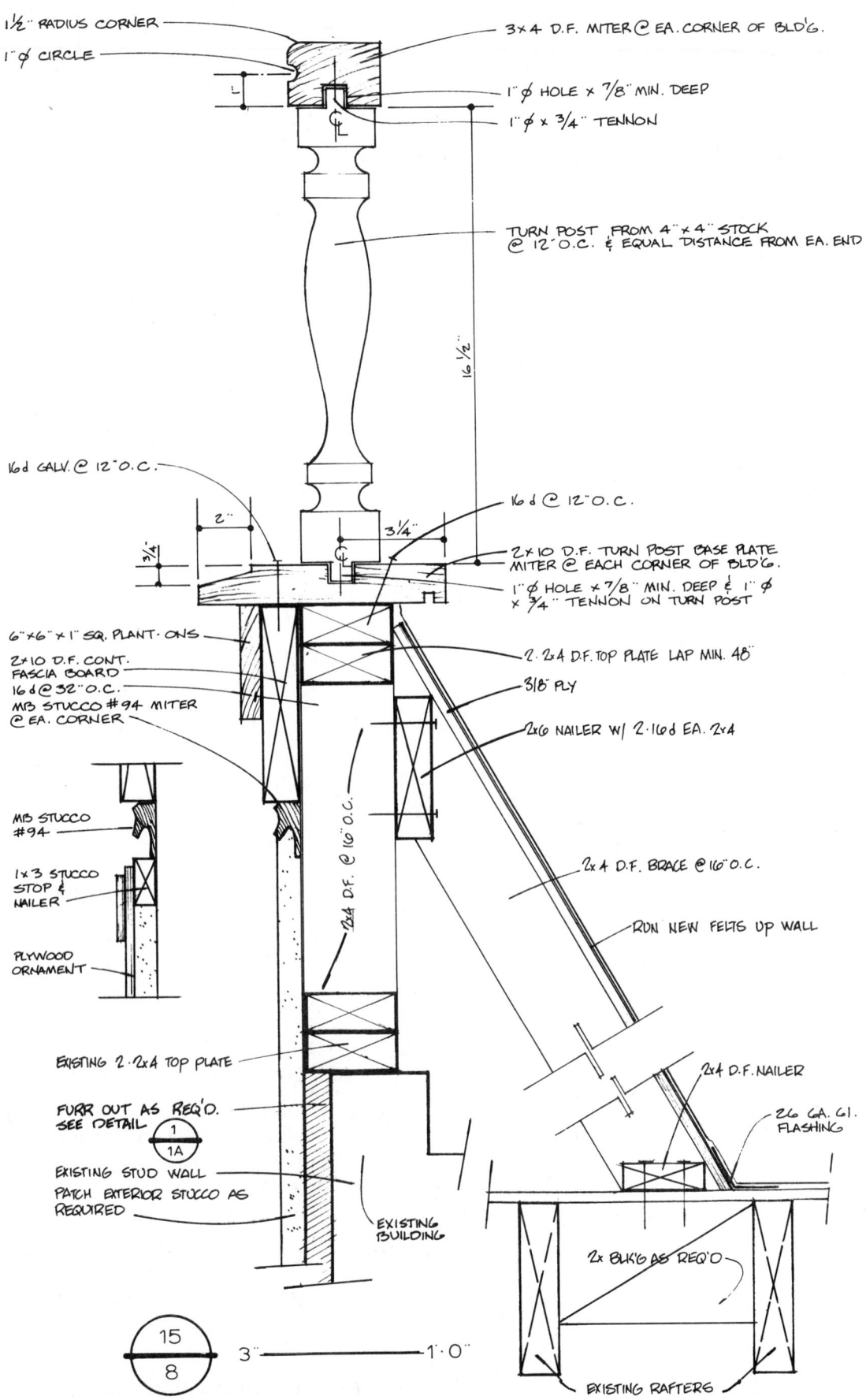

1½" RADIUS CORNER

1" ∅ CIRCLE

3×4 D.F. MITER @ EA. CORNER OF BLD'G.

1" ∅ HOLE × ⅞" MIN. DEEP

1" ∅ × ¾" TENNON

TURN POST FROM 4" × 4" STOCK @ 12" O.C. & EQUAL DISTANCE FROM EA. END

16d GALV. @ 12" O.C.

16d @ 12" O.C.

2"

3¼"

¾"

2×10 D.F. TURN POST BASE PLATE MITER @ EACH CORNER OF BLD'G.

1" ∅ HOLE × ⅞" MIN. DEEP & 1" ∅ × ¾" TENNON ON TURN POST

6"×6" × 1" SQ. PLANT. ONS

2×10 D.F. CONT. FASCIA BOARD

16d @ 32" O.C.

MB STUCCO #94 MITER @ EA. CORNER

2 · 2×4 D.F. TOP PLATE LAP MIN. 48"

3/8" PLY

2×6 NAILER W/ 2·16d EA. 2×4

MB STUCCO #94

1×3 STUCCO STOP & NAILER

PLYWOOD ORNAMENT

2×4 D.F. @ 16" O.C.

2×4 D.F. BRACE @ 16" O.C.

RUN NEW FELTS UP WALL

EXISTING 2·2×4 TOP PLATE

FURR OUT AS REQ'D. SEE DETAIL

1
1A

EXISTING STUD WALL PATCH EXTERIOR STUCCO AS REQUIRED

EXISTING BUILDING

2×4 D.F. NAILER

26 GA. G.I. FLASHING

2× BLK'G AS REQ'D

EXISTING RAFTERS

15
8

3 ———— 1'·0"

Figure 36–7 Millwork and cabinet construction details. *Courtesy Ken Smith Structureform Masters, Inc.*

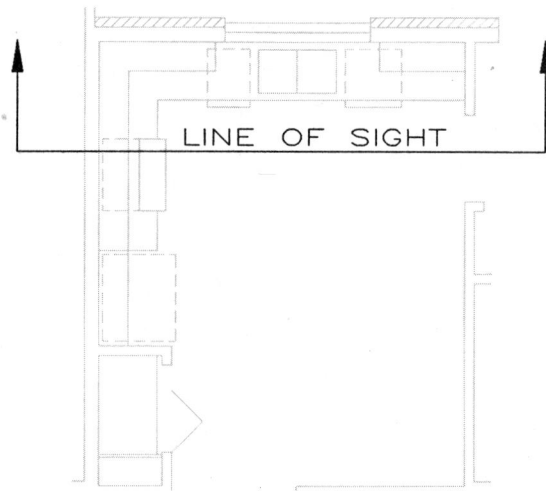

Figure 36–8 Establishing the line of sight for cabinet elevations.

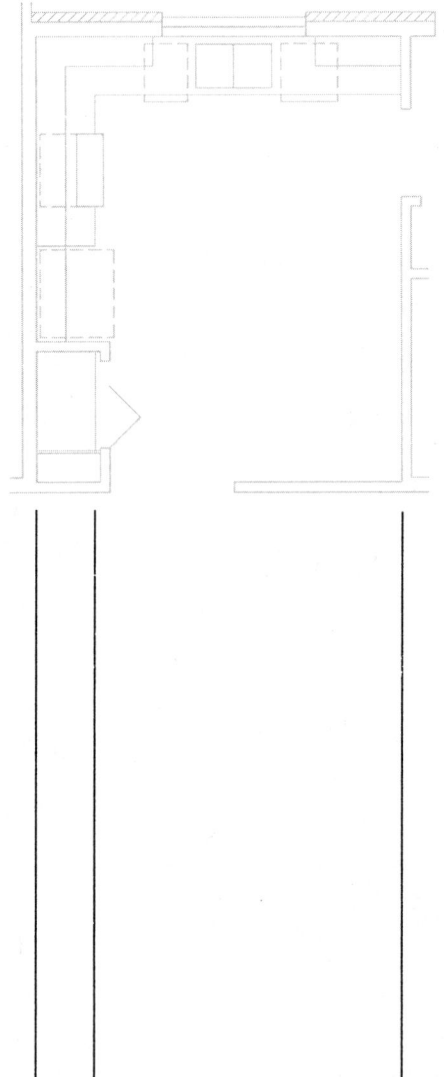

Figure 36–9 Step 1: Transfer length dimensions from the floor plan to the cabinet elevation using construction lines.

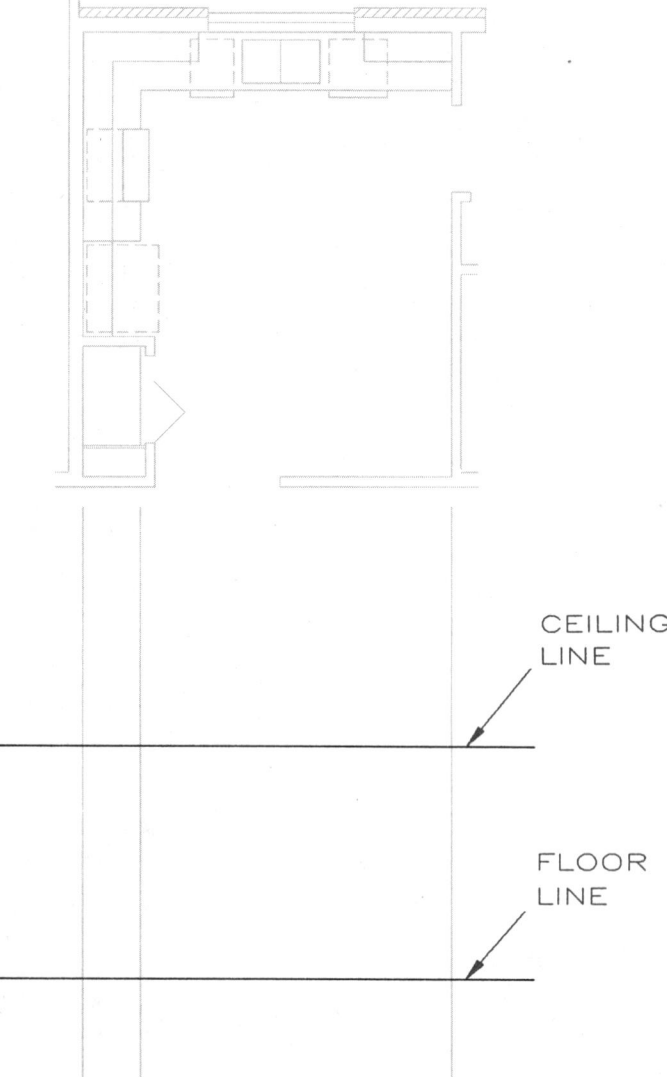

CEILING
LINE

FLOOR
LINE

Figure 36–10 Step 2: Establish the floor and ceiling lines using construction lines.

and a scale change will be implemented before transfer to the elevation drawing.

Step 2.   Establish the room height from floor to ceiling. If the floor to ceiling height is 8 ft, then draw two lines 8 ft apart with construction lines using the ¼″ = 1′–0″ scale. See Figure 36–10.

Step 3.   Establish the portion of the cabinetry where the line of sight cuts through base and upper cabinets, and soffits. Use construction lines to lightly draw in these areas as shown in Figure 36–11.

Step 4.   Use construction lines to draw cabinet elevation features such as doors, drawers, and appliances. See Figure 36–12. Also, draw

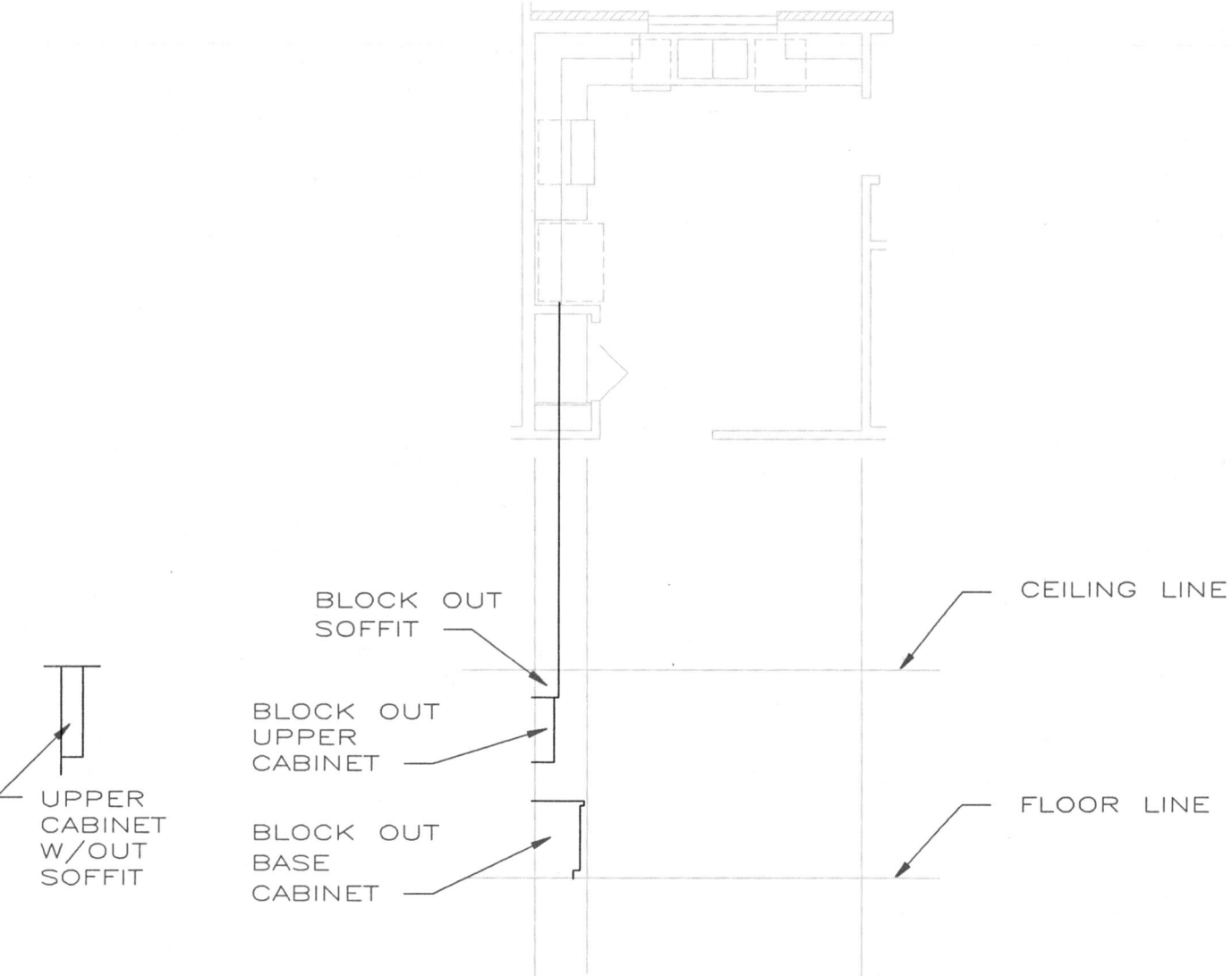

Figure 36–11 Step 3: Establish base cabinets, upper cabinets, and soffits using construction lines.

background features such as back splash, windows, and doors if any. Notice the rectangular shape that is drawn to the left of the dishwasher and below the countertop where the sink would be. This is called a false front that is designed to look like a drawer. An actual drawer cannot be placed here as it would run into the sink. A false drawer front is used to establish the appearance of a line of drawers just below the base cabinet top and before doors are used. Some designs use cabinet doors from the toe kick to the base cabinet top although this method is not as common.

Step 5. Darken all cabinet lines. Some drafters use the technique of drawing the outline of the ends of the cabinets and surrounding areas with a thick line. Draw dashed lines that denote hidden features such as sinks, and shelves as seen in Figure 36–13.

Step 6. Add dimensions and notes. See Figure 36–13.

Follow the same process for the remaining cabinet elevations. See Figure 36–14. The same procedure may be used to draw bath vanity elevations as shown in Figure 36–15 or other special cabinet or millwork elevations and details.

Figure 36–12 Step 4:
Use construction
lines to establish
cabinet elevation
features.

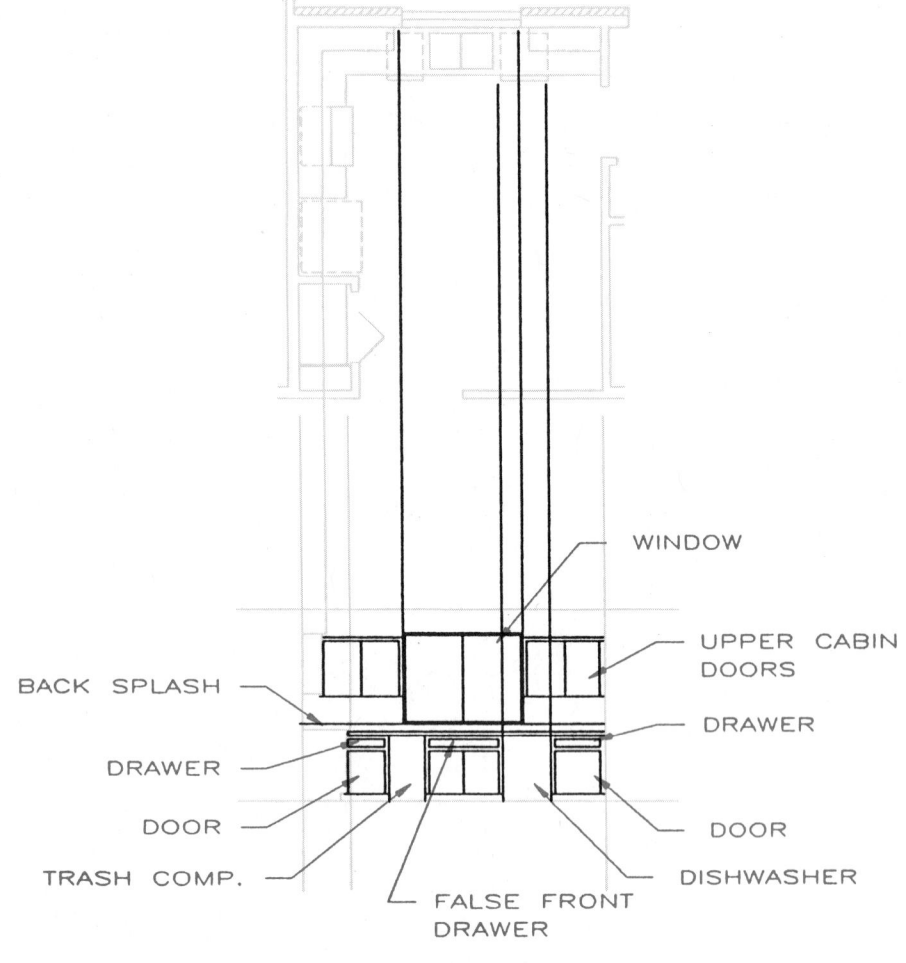

BACK SPLASH

WINDOW

UPPER CABIN
DOORS

DRAWER

DRAWER

DOOR

DOOR

TRASH COMP.

DISHWASHER

FALSE FRONT
DRAWER

Figure 36–13 Steps 5 and 6:
Darken all cabinet lines and
add dimensions and notes.

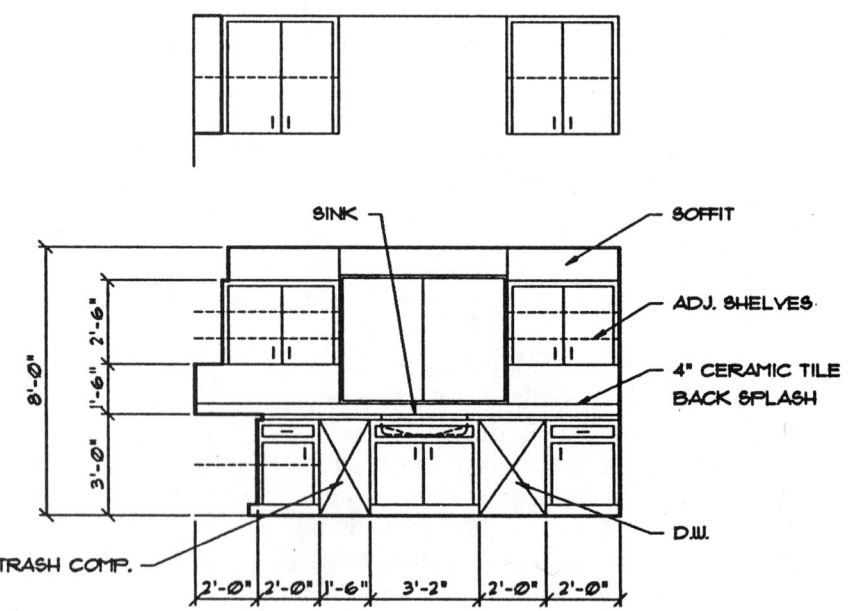

SINK

SOFFIT

ADJ. SHELVES

4" CERAMIC TILE
BACK SPLASH

D.W.

TRASH COMP.

2'-0" 2'-0" 1'-6" 3'-2" 2'-0" 2'-0"

8'-0"   2'-6"   1'-6"   3'-0"

KITCHEN CABINET ELEV.

SCALE: ¼"=1'-0"

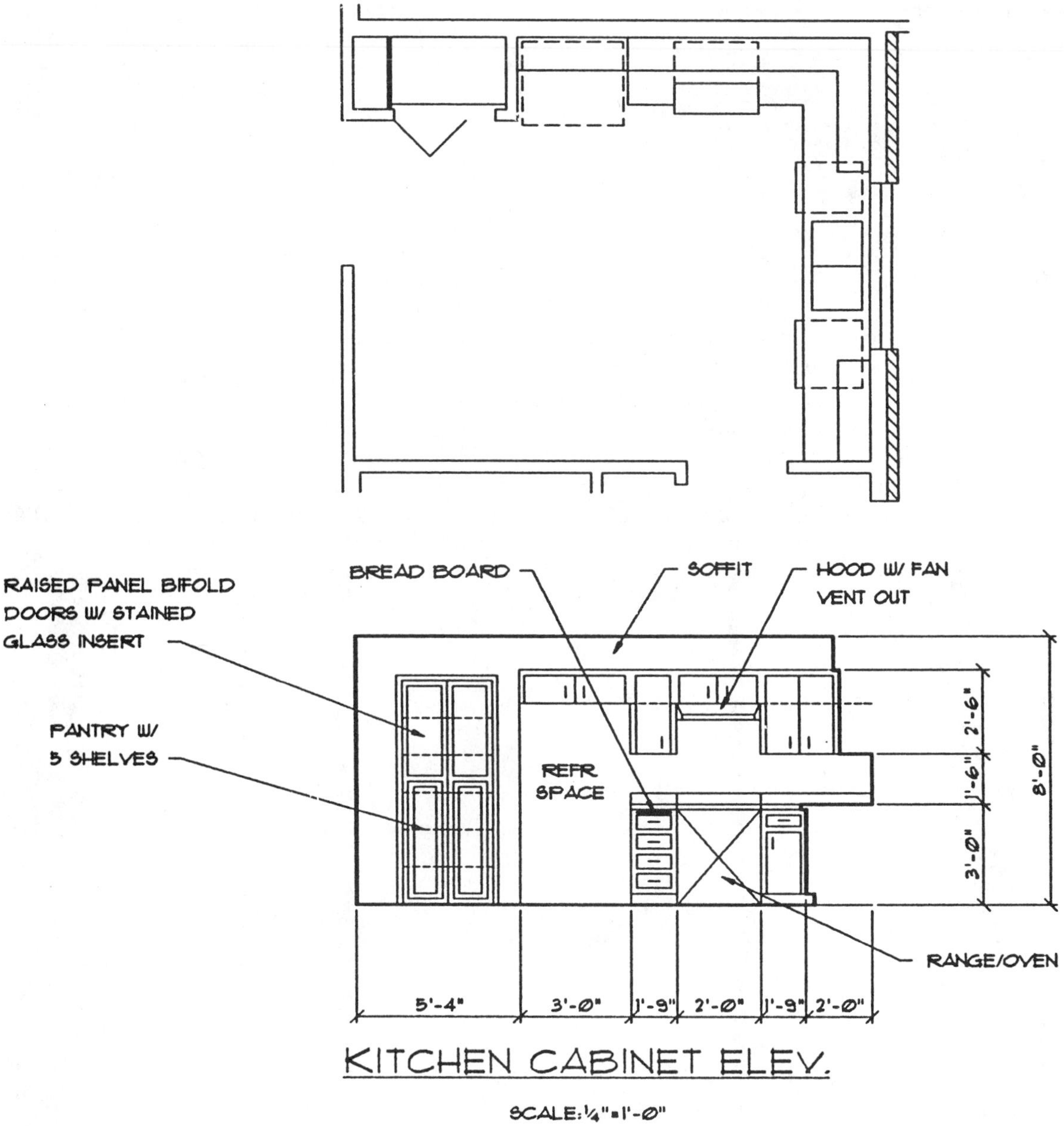

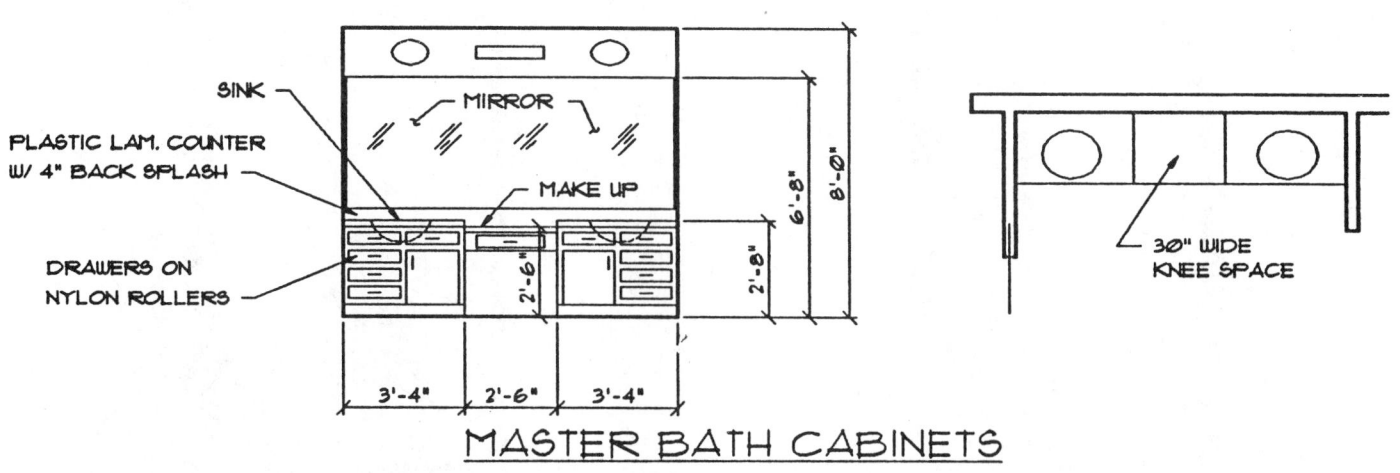

RAISED PANEL BIFOLD
DOORS W/ STAINED
GLASS INSERT

BREAD BOARD

SOFFIT

HOOD W/ FAN
VENT OUT

PANTRY W/
5 SHELVES

REFR
SPACE

2'-6"

1'-6"

8'-0"

3'-0"

RANGE/OVEN

5'-4"   3'-0"   1'-9" 2'-0" 1'-9" 2'-0"

KITCHEN CABINET ELEV.

SCALE: 1/4" = 1'-0"

Figure 36–14 Follow steps 1 through 6 to draw the other cabinet elevations.

SINK

MIRROR

PLASTIC LAM. COUNTER
W/ 4" BACK SPLASH

MAKE UP

8'-0"

6'-8"

2'-6"

2'-8"

DRAWERS ON
NYLON ROLLERS

3'-4"   2'-6"   3'-4"

30" WIDE
KNEE SPACE

MASTER BATH CABINETS

SCALE: 1/4" = 1'-0"

Figure 36–15 Use cabinet layout steps 1 through 6 to draw all bath cabinet elevations.

CADD
applications

DRAWING MILLWORK AND CABINET ELEVATIONS WITH CADD

CADD makes it easy to draw millwork details and sections with the use of tablet menu symbol libraries that contain millwork profiles as shown in Figure 1.

CADD tablet menu commands for cabinet floor plan layouts place base and upper cabinets on the drawing, then add symbols for appliances and kitchen or bath features. Draw cabinet elevations with CADD by selecting cabinet module symbols from a template menu library, then organize them on the drawing. These cabinet modules are combinations of (1) a cabinet door and drawer or (2) banks of drawers for the base units and door modules for the upper units. There are also typical cabinet profiles that display the section of a cabinet through the end view. For bath cabinet elevations, there are modules with base units and mirror or medicine cabinets. Figure 2 shows a CADD tablet menu library used to draw cabinet elevations. A complete set of CADD cabinet elevation drawings is shown in Figure 3.

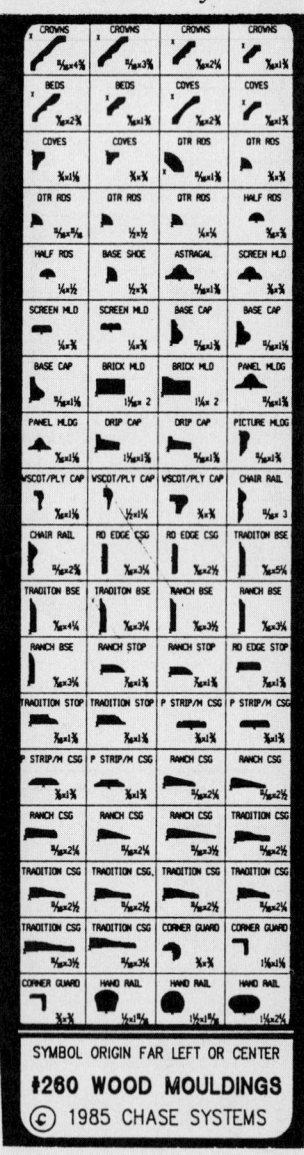

Figure 1 CADD tablet menu symbol library for millwork profiles.

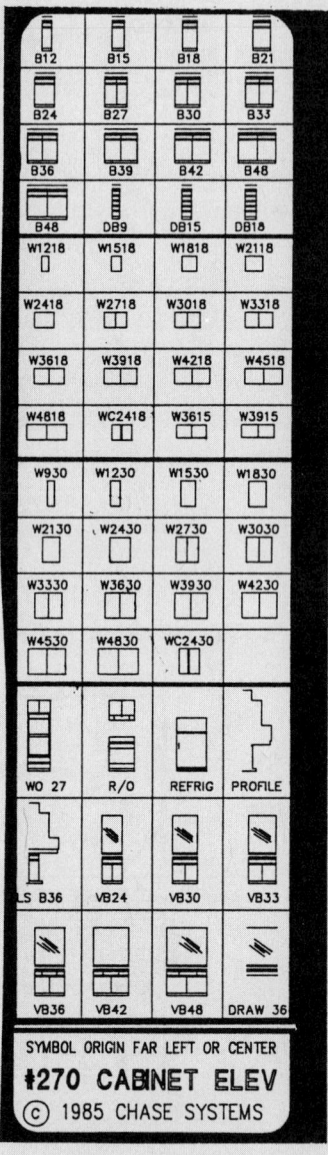

Figure 2 CADD tablet menu library for cabinet elevations.

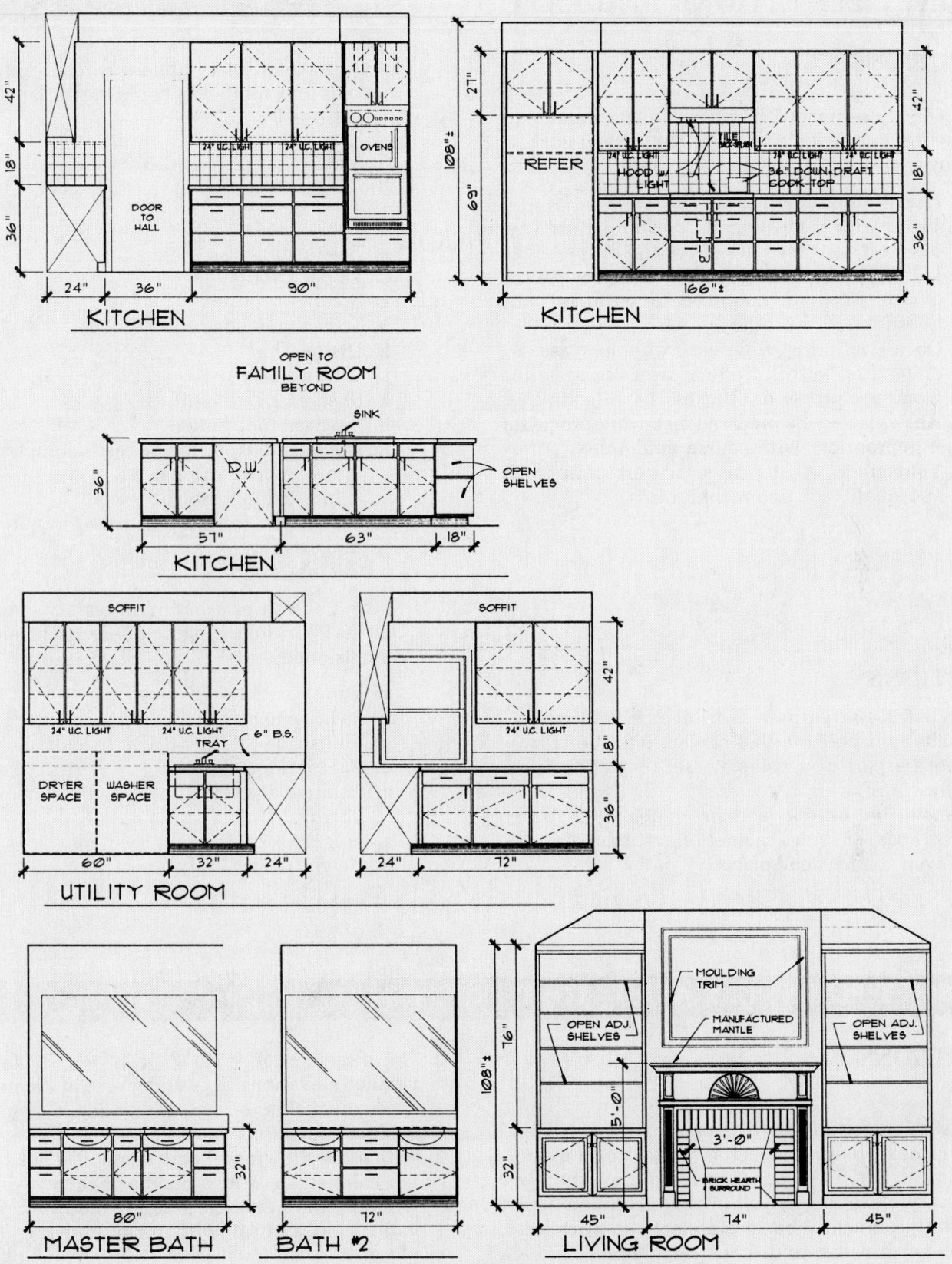

CABINET ELEVATIONS

S C A L E   3/8" = 1' - 0"

Figure 3 CADD cabinet elevations.

CABINET ELEVATIONS AND LAYOUT TEST

DIRECTIONS

Answer the questions with short complete statements or drawings as needed on an 8½ × 11 drawing sheet as follows:

1. Use ⅛ in. guidelines for all lettering.
2. Letter your name, Cabinet Elevations and Layout Test, and the date at the top of the sheet.
3. Letter the question number and provide the answer. You do not need to write out the question.
4. Do all lettering with vertical uppercase architectural letters. If the answer requires line work, use proper drafting tools and technique. Answers may be prepared on a word processor if appropriate with course guidelines.
5. Your grade will be based on correct answers and quality of line technique.

QUESTIONS

1. What is the purpose of cabinet elevations?
2. Why is it possible that cabinet elevations may not be part of a complete set of architectural drawings?
3. Show by sketch and/or explanation three methods of how cabinet elevations may be keyed to the floor plans.

4. Make a sketch of a kitchen cabinet elevation that has the following components labeled or dimensioned:
   a. Drawers
   b. False front
   c. Toe space
   d. Back splash
   e. Base cabinet
   f. Upper cabinet
   g. Soffit
   h. Range and hood
   i. Dishwasher
   j. Cutting board
   k. Shelves
   l. Base cabinet height
   m. Dimension from top of base cabinet to bottom of upper cabinet
   n. Upper cabinet height
   o. Dimension from top of range to bottom of range hood
   p. Cabinet doors

5. Make a sketch of a bathroom vanity elevation that has the following components labeled or dimensioned:
   a. Vanity cabinet
   b. Back splash
   c. Toe space
   d. Cabinet doors
   e. Cabinet drawers
   f. Mirror
   g. Medicine cabinet
   h. Height of vanity cabinet

CABINET ELEVATIONS AND LAYOUT PROBLEM

DIRECTIONS

1. Using as a guide the floor plan of the problem you have been drawing as a project or a floor plan assigned by your instructor, draw the necessary elevations for all kitchen, bath, and specialty cabinets. The specific location of cabinet doors, drawers, and other features is flexible. Verify your cabinet designs with the contents of this chapter and your instructor's guidelines. The placement of appliances and fixtures is predetermined by the floor-plan drawing unless otherwise specified by your instructor.

2. Use a scale of ¼″ = 1′-0″ or ⅜″ = 1′-0″ for the cabinet elevations depending on the amount of space available on your drawing sheet. The cabinet elevations may be placed on a sheet with other drawings if convenient. Do not crowd the cabinet elevations on the sheet you select. If there is not enough area for the cabinet elevations on a sheet with other drawings, then place them on a separate sheet. Avoid placing cabinet elevations on a sheet with exterior elevations or the main floor plan.

3. These elevations may be prepared using computer graphics if appropriate with course guidelines.

CM-1430

Section Nine
Plot Plans

Chapter 37
Legal Descriptions

METES AND BOUNDS SYSTEM
RECTANGULAR SYSTEM
LOT AND BLOCK SYSTEM

VIRTUALLY EVERY piece of property in the United States is described for legal purposes. Legal descriptions of properties are filed in local jurisdictions, generally the county or parish courthouse. Legal descriptions are public record and may be reviewed at any time. This section deals with plot plan characteristics and requirements. A plot is an area of land generally one lot or construction site in size. The term plot is synonymous with lot. A plat is a map of part of a city or township showing some specific area such as a subdivision made up of several individual plots or lots. There are usually many plots in a plat. Some dictionary definitions, however, do not differentiate between plot and plat.

There are three basic types of legal descriptions: metes and bounds, rectangular system, and lot and block.

METES AND BOUNDS SYSTEM

Metes, or measurements, and bounds, or boundaries, may be used to identify the perimeters of any prop-

erty. The metes are measured in feet, yards, rods (rd), or surveyor's chains (ch). There are 3 feet in 1 yard, 5.5 yards or 16.5 feet in one rod, and 66 feet in one surveyor's chain. The boundaries may be a street, fence, creek, or river. Boundaries are also established as bearings. Bearings are directions with reference to one of the quadrants of the compass. There are 360° in a circle or compass and each quadrant has 90°. Degrees are divided into minutes and seconds. There are 60 minutes (60') in 1 degree

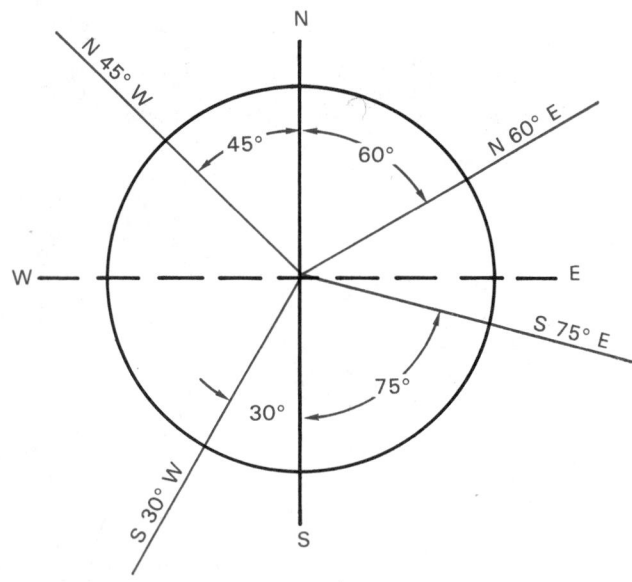

Figure 37–1 Bearings.

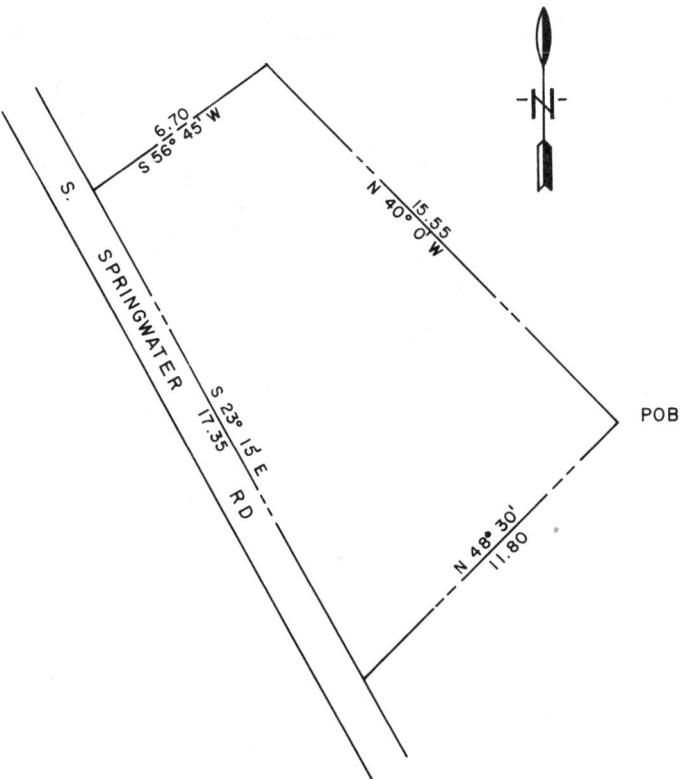

Beginning at a point 20 chains north 40° 0′ west from the southeast corner of the Asa Stone Donation Land Claim No. 49, thence north 40° 0′ west 15.55 chains to a pipe, thence south 56° 45′ west 6.70 chains to center of road, thence south 23° 15′ east 17.35 chains, thence north 48° 30′ east 11.80 chains to place of beginning.

Figure 37-2 Metes and bounds plot plan and legal description for the plot.

and there are 60 seconds (60″) in 1 minute. Bearings are measured clockwise or counterclockwise from either north or south. For example, a reading 45° from north toward west would be labeled N 45° W. See Figure 37-1. If a bearing reading required great accuracy, fractions of a degree would be used. For example, S 30° 20′ 10″ E, would read from south 30 degrees 20 minutes 10 seconds toward east.

The metes and bounds land survey begins with a monument known as the point-of-beginning. This point is a fixed location and in times past has been a pile of rocks, a large tree or an iron rod driven into the ground. Figure 37-2 shows an example of a plot plan that is laid out using metes and bounds and the legal description for the plot.

RECTANGULAR SYSTEM

The states in an area of the United States starting with the western boundary of Ohio, and including some southeastern states, to the Pacific Ocean, were described as public land states. Within this area the

United States Bureau of Land Management devised a system for describing land known as the rectangular system.

Parallels of latitude and meridians of longitude were used to establish areas known as great land surveys. The point of beginning of each great land survey is where two basic reference lines cross. The lines of latitude, or parallels, are termed the base lines and the lines of longitude, or meridians, are called principal meridians. There are 31 sets of these lines in the continental United States with three in Alaska. At the beginning the principal meridians were numbered, and the numbering system ended with the sixth principal meridian passing through Nebraska, Kansas and Oklahoma. The remaining principal meridians were given local names. The meridian through one of the last great land surveys near the west coast is named the Willamette Meridian because of its location in the Willamette Valley of Oregon. The principal meridians and base lines of the great land surveys are shown in Figure 37-3.

Townships

The great land surveys were, in turn, broken down into smaller surveys known as townships and sections. The base lines and meridians were divided into blocks called townships. Each township measures 6 miles square. The townships are numbered by tiers running east-west. The tier numbering system is established either north or south of a principal base line. For example, the fourth tier south of the base line is labeled, Township Number 4 South, or abbreviated T. 4 S. Townships are also numbered according to vertical meridians, known as ranges. Ranges are established either east or west of a principal meridian. The third range east of the principal meridian is called Range Number 3 East, or abbreviated R. 3 E. Now, if we combine T. 4 S. and R. 3 E. we have located a township or a piece of land 6 mi by 6 mi or a total of 36 sq mi. Figure 37-4 shows the township just described.

Sections

To further define the land within a 6 mi square township, the area was divided into units 1 mi square. These 1 mi by 1 mi areas are called sections. Sections in a township are numbered from 1 to 36. Section 1 always begins in the upper right corner and consecutive numbers are arranged as shown in Figure 37-5. The legal descriptions of land can be carried one stage further. For example, Section 10 in the township given would be described as Sec. 10, T. 4 S., R. 3 E. This is an area of land 1 mi square. Sections are divided into acres. One acre equals 43,560 sq ft and 1 section of land contains 640 acres.

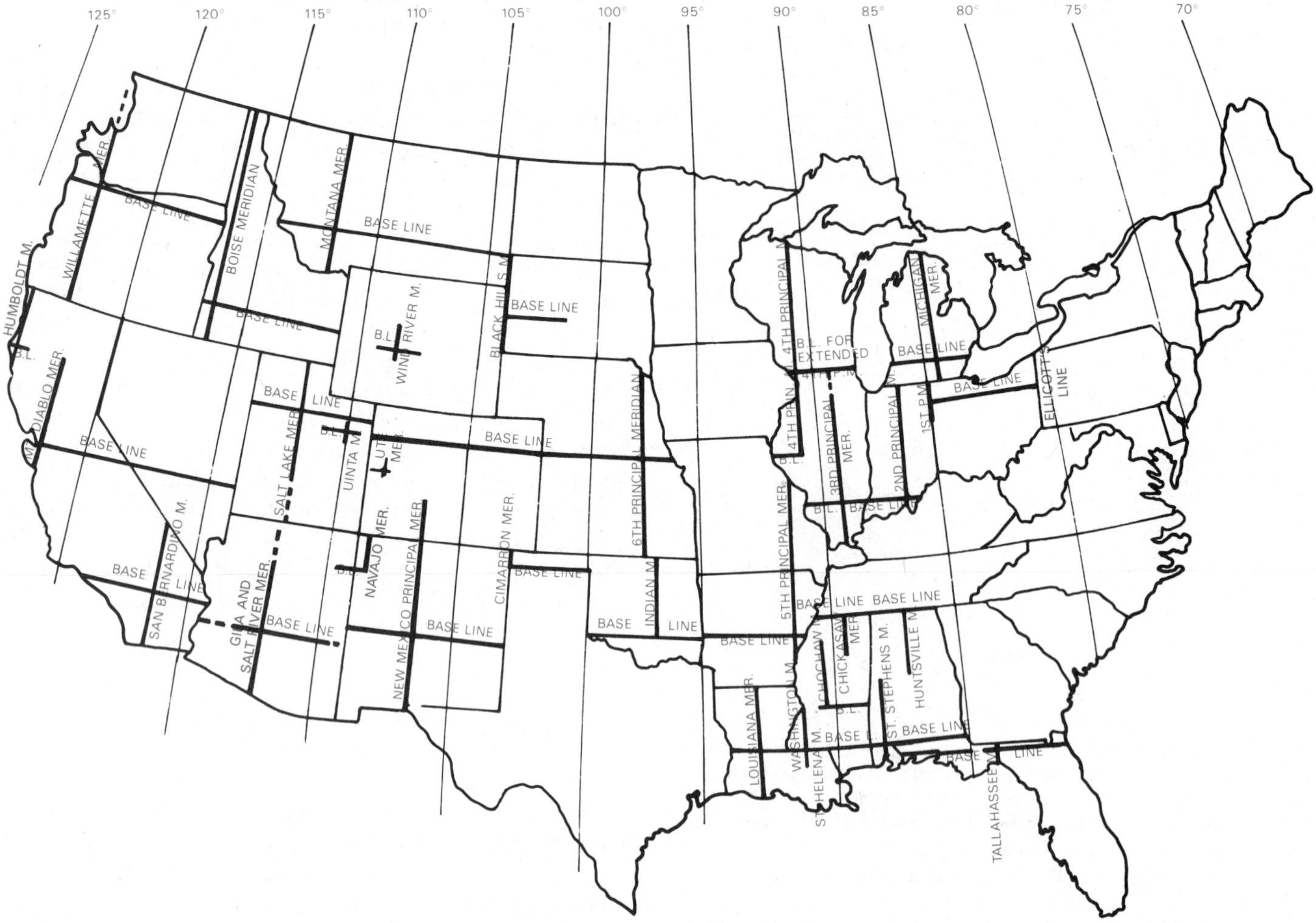

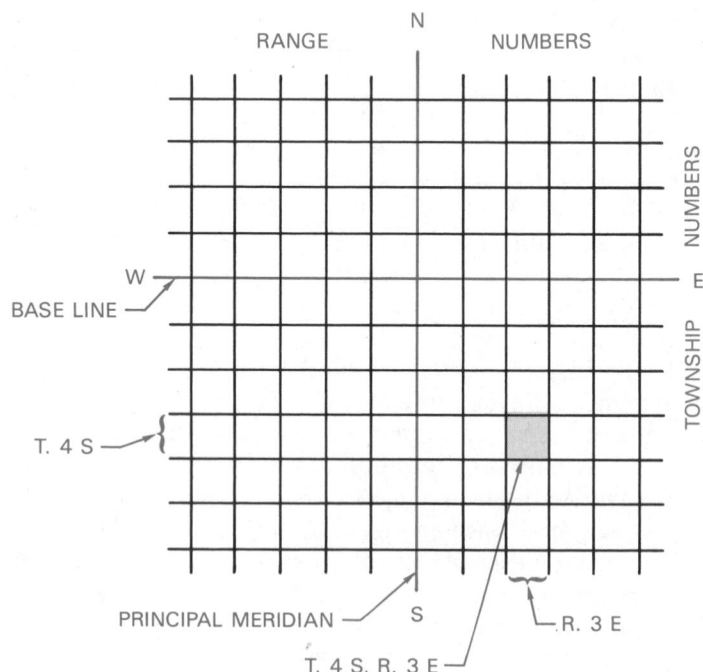

Figure 37–3 The principal meridians and base lines of the great land survey (not including Alaska).

Figure 37–4 Townships.

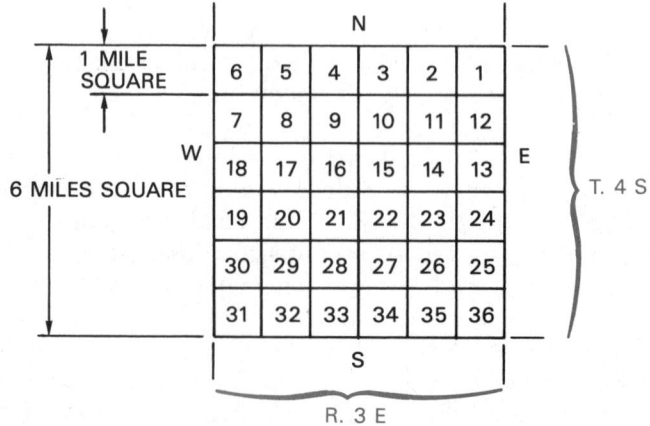

Figure 37–5 Sections.

In addition to dividing sections into acres, sections are also divided into quarters as shown in Figure 37–6. The northeast one-quarter of Section 10 is a 160-acre piece of land described as NE ¼, Sec. 10, T. 4 S., R. 3 E. When this section is keyed to a specific meridian, then it can only be one specific 160-acre area. The section can be broken further by dividing each quarter into quarters as shown in Fig-

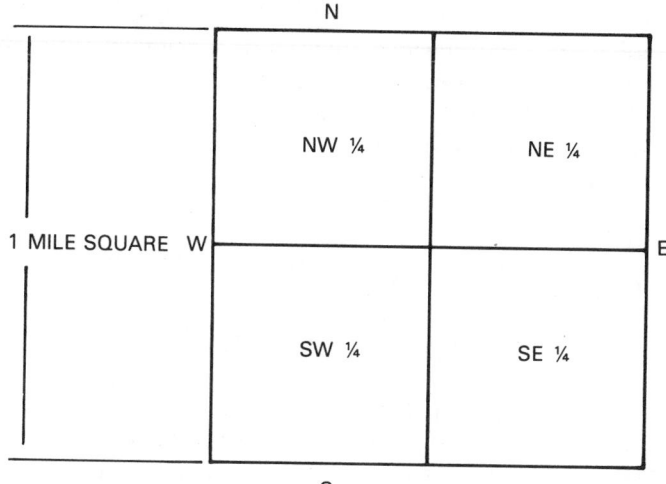

Figure 37-6 Section quarters.

ure 37-7. If the SW ¼ of the NE ¼ of Section 10 were the desired property, then we would have 40 acres known as SW ¼, NE ¼, Sec. 10, T. 4 S., R. 3 E. The complete rectangular system legal description of a 2.5 acre piece of land in Section 10 would read: SW ¼, SE ¼, SE ¼, SE ¼ Sec. 10, T. 4 N., R. 8 W. of the San Bernardino Meridian, in the County of Los Angeles, State of California. See Figure 37-8.

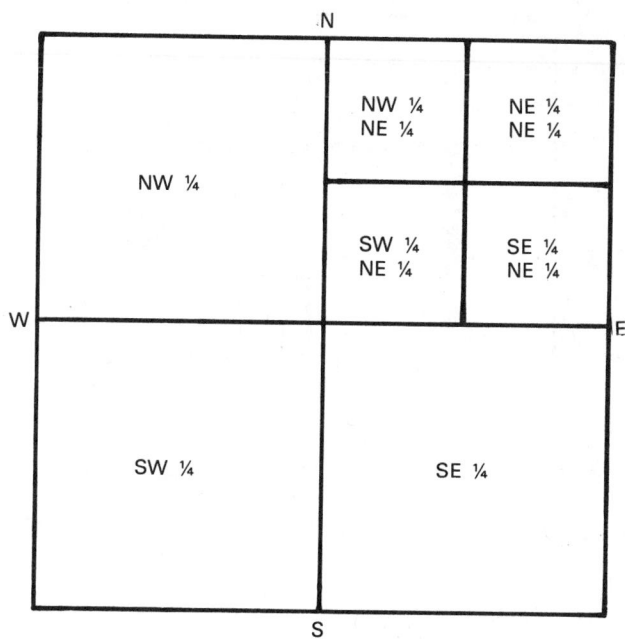

Figure 37-7 Dividing a quarter section.

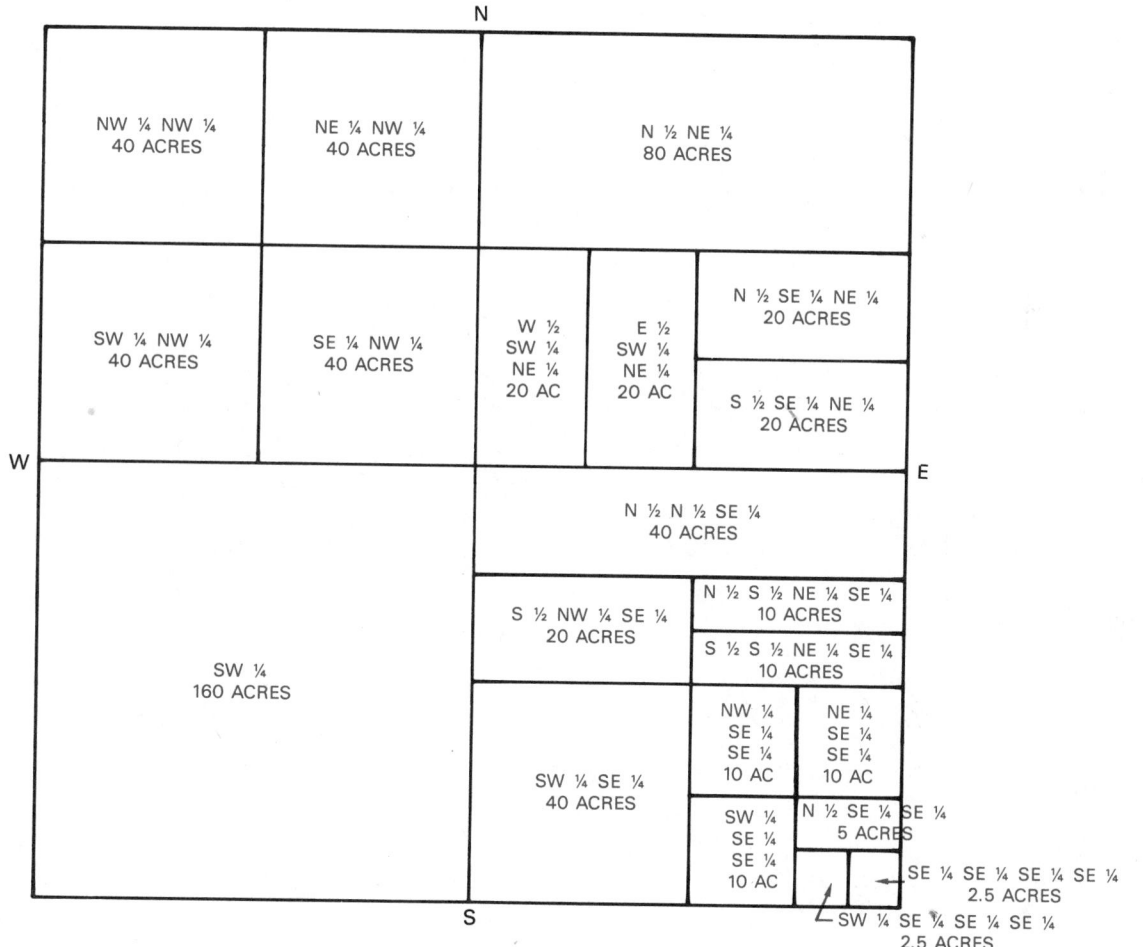

Figure 37-8 Sample divisions of a section.

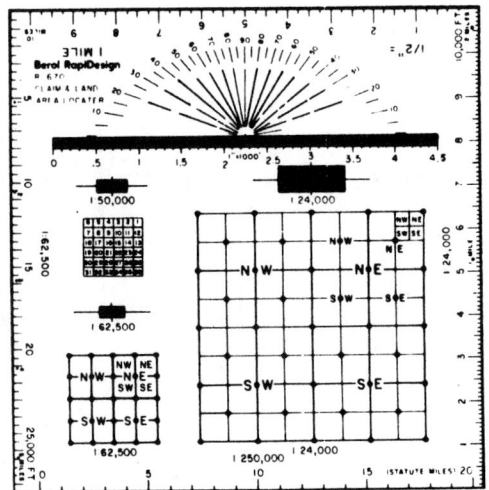

Figure 37-9 Claim and land area locater. *Courtesy Berol USA RapiDesign.*

The rectangular system of land survey may be used to describe very small properties by continuing to divide the section of a township. Oftentimes the township section legal description may be used to describe the location of the point of beginning of a metes and bounds legal description especially when the surveyed land is an irregular plot within the rectangular system. A handy template that is used as a convenient claim and land area locater is shown in Figure 37-9.

LOT AND BLOCK SYSTEM

The lot and block legal description system can be derived from either the metes and bounds or the rectangular systems. Generally when a portion of land is subdivided into individual building sites the subdivision must be established as a legal plot and recorded as such in the local county records. The subdivision is given a name and broken into blocks of lots. A subdivision may have several blocks each divided into a series of lots. Each lot may be 50' × 100', for example, depending upon the zoning requirements of the specific area. Figure 37-10 shows an example of a typical lot and block system.

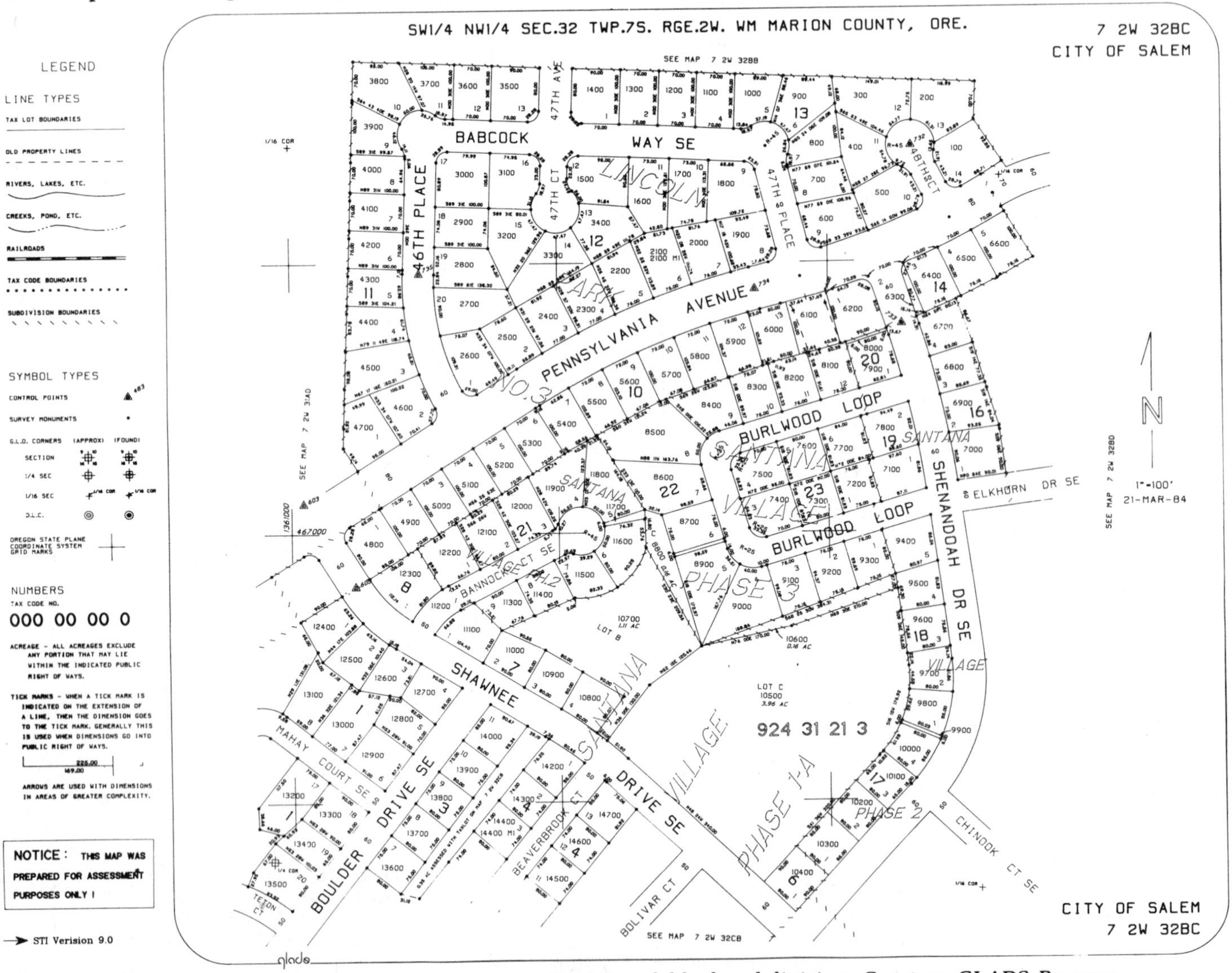

Figure 37-10 A computer-generated plat of a lot and block subdivision. *Courtesy GLADS Program.*

Chapter 38
Plat and Plot Plan Requirements

A PLOT plan, also known as a lot plan, is a map of a piece of land that may be used for any number of purposes. Plot plans may show a proposed construction site for a specific property. Plots may show topography with contour lines or the numerical value of land elevations may be given at certain locations. Plot plans are also used to show how a construction site will be excavated and are then known as a grading plan. While plot plans can be drawn to serve any number of required functions they all have some similar characteristics which include showing the following:

- A legal description of the property based on a survey
- Property line bearings and directions
- North direction
- Roads and easements
- Utilities
- Elevations
- Map scale

Plats are maps that are used to show an area of a town or township. They show several or many lots and may be used by a builder to show a proposed subdivision of land.

TOPOGRAPHY

Topography is a physical description of land surface showing its variation in elevation, known as relief, and locating other features. Surface relief can be shown with graphic symbols that use shading methods to accentuate the character of land or the differences in elevations can be shown with contour lines. Plot plans that require surface relief identification generally use contour lines. These lines connect points of equal elevation and help show the general lay of the land.

A good way to visualize the meaning of contour lines is to look at a lake or ocean shore line. When the water is high during the winter or at high tide, a high-water line establishes a contour at that level. As the water recedes during the summer or at low tide, a new lower level line is obtained. This new line represents another contour. The high-water line goes all around the lake at one level and the low-water line goes all around the lake at another level.

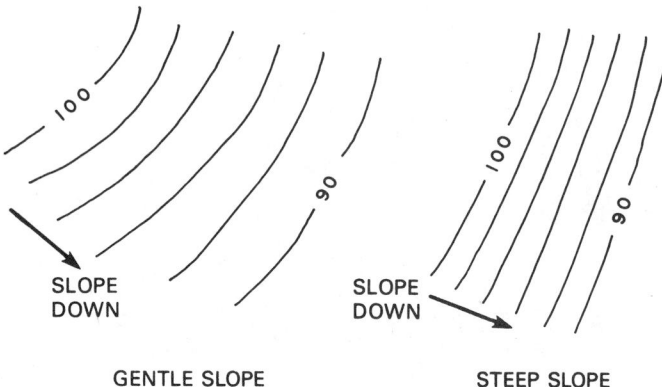

Figure 38-1 Contour lines showing both gentle and steep slopes.

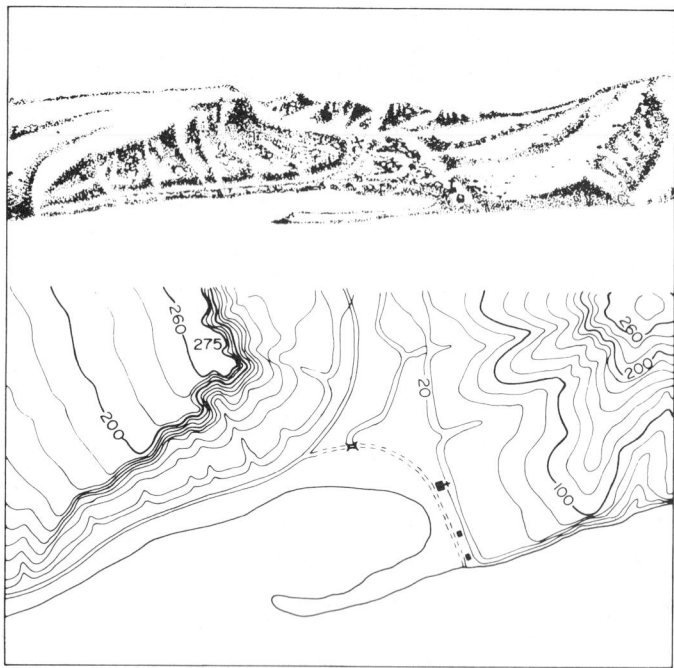

Figure 38-2 Land relief pictorial and contour lines. *Courtesy U.S. Department of the Interior, Geological Survey.*

These two lines represent contours, or lines of equal elevation. The vertical distance between contour lines is known as contour interval. When the contour lines are far apart, the contour interval shows relatively flat or gently sloping land. When the contour lines are close together, then the contour interval shows a land that is much steeper. Drawn contour lines are broken periodically and the numerical value of the contour elevation above sea level is inserted. Figure 38-1 shows sample contour lines. Figure 38-2 shows a graphic example of land relief in pictorial form and contour lines of the same area.

Plot plans do not always require contour lines showing topography. Verify the requirements with the local building codes. In most instances the only contour-related information required is property corner elevations, street elevation at a driveway, and the elevation of the finished floor levels of the structure. Additionally, slope may be defined and labeled with an arrow.

PLOT PLANS

Plot plan requirements vary from one local jurisdiction to the next although there are elements of plot plans that are similar around the country. Guidelines for plot plans can be obtained from the local building official or building permit department. Some agencies, for example, require that the plot plan be drawn on specific size paper such as 8½″ × 14″. Typical plot plan items include the following:

- Plot plan scale.
- Legal description of the property.
- Property line bearings and dimensions.
- North direction.
- Existing and proposed roads.
- Driveways, patios, walks, and parking areas.
- Existing and proposed structures.
- Public or private water supply.
- Public or private sewage disposal.
- Location of utilities.
- Rain and footing drains, and storm sewers or drainage.
- Topography including contour lines or land elevations at lot corners, street centerline, driveways, and floor elevations.
- Setbacks, front, rear, and sides.
- Specific items on adjacent properties may be required.
- Existing and proposed trees may be required.

Figure 38-3 shows a plot plan layout that is used as an example at a local building department. Figure 38-4 shows a basic plot plan for a proposed residential addition.

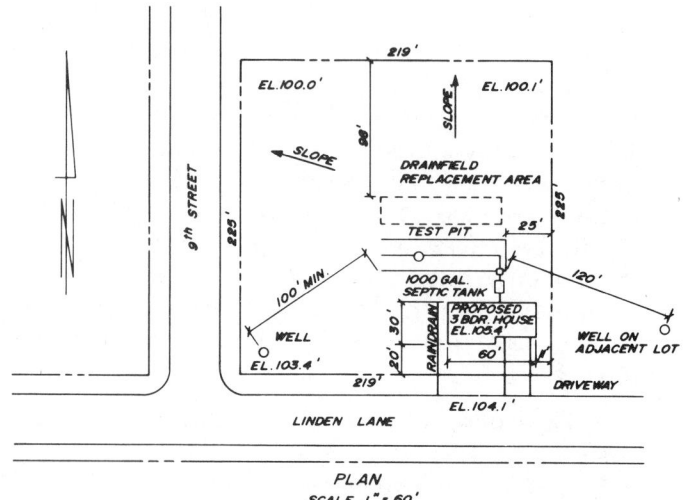

Figure 38-3 Recommended typical plot plan layout.

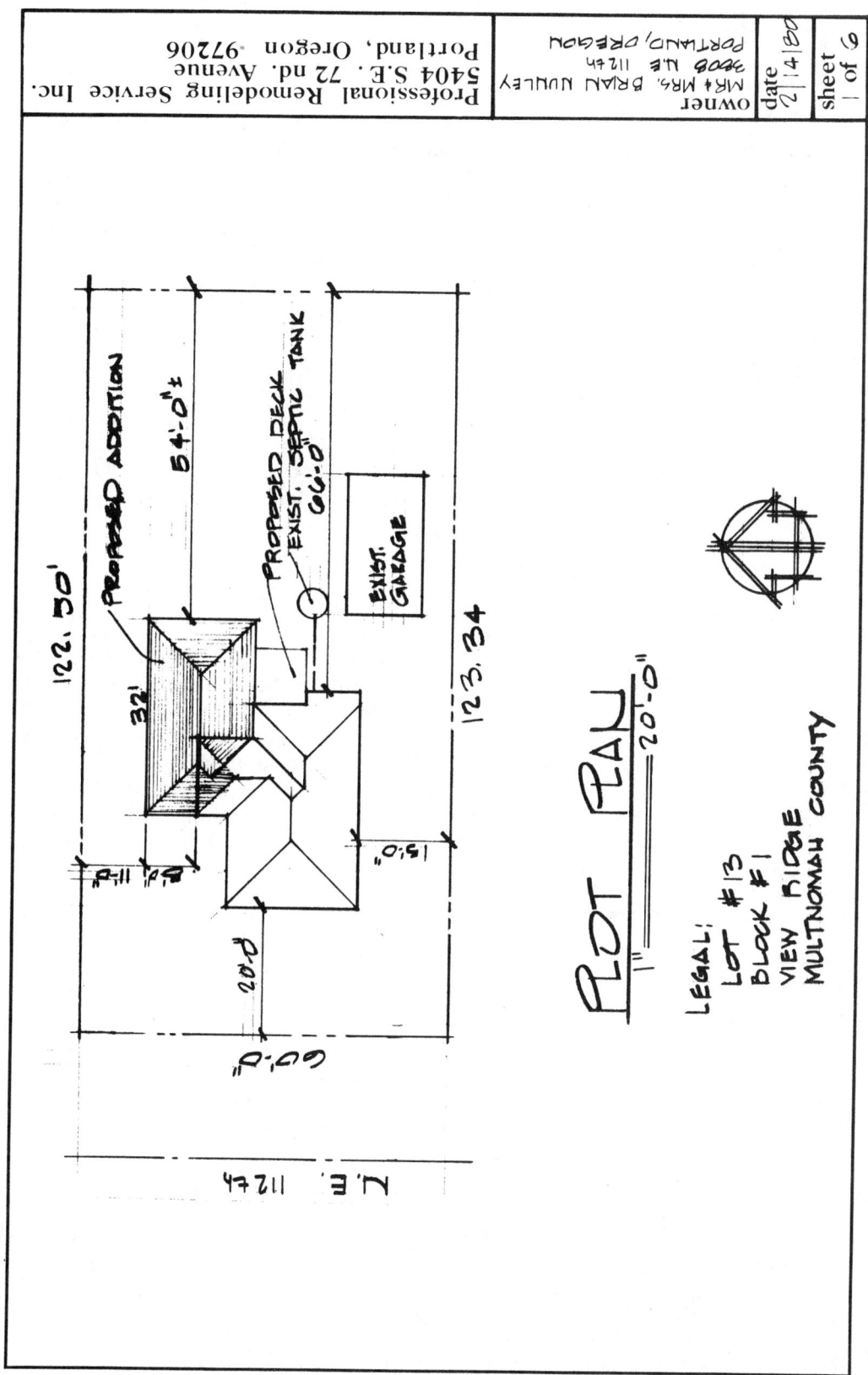

Professional Remodeling Service Inc.
5404 S.E. 72 nd. Avenue
Portland, Oregon 97206

owner
MR & MRS, BRIAN NULLEY
3808 N.E. 112th
PORTLAND, OREGON
date 2/14/80
sheet 1 of 6

PLOT PLAN
1" = 20'-0"

LEGAL:
LOT #13
BLOCK #1
VIEW RIDGE
MULTNOMAH COUNTY

PROPOSED ADDITION
54'-0"±
122.50'
32'
PROPOSED DECK
EXIST. SEPTIC TANK
66'-0"
EXIST. GARAGE
123.34
8'-11"
15'-0"
20'-0"
60'-0"
N.E. 112th

Figure 38-4 Sample plot plan. *Courtesy Jeff's Residential Designs.*

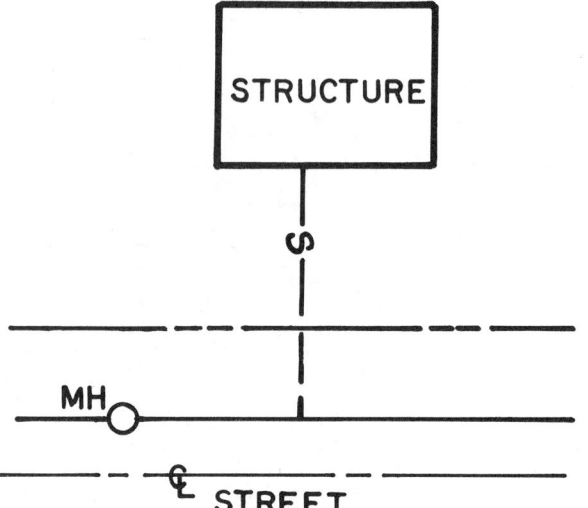

Figure 38–5 Plot plan showing a public sewer connection.

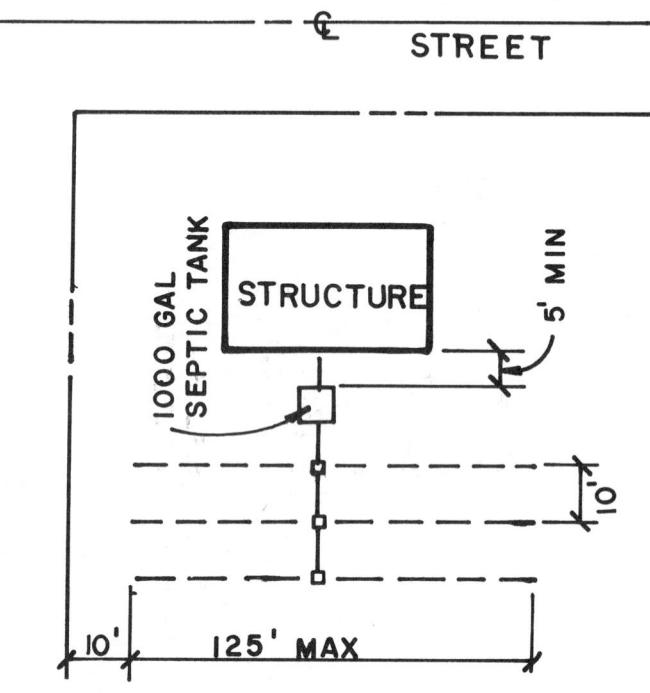

Figure 38–6 Plot plan showing a private septic sewage system.

The method of sewage disposal is generally an important item shown on a plot plan drawing. There are a number of alternative methods of sewage disposal including public sewers and private systems. Chapter 18 gives more details of sewage disposal methods. The plot plan representation of a public sewer connection is shown in Figure 38–5. A private septic sewage disposal system is shown in a plot plan example in Figure 38–6.

GRADING PLAN

Grading plans are plots of construction sites that generally show existing and proposed topography. The outline of the structure may be shown with elevations at each building corner and the elevation given for each floor level. Figure 38–7 shows a detailed grading plan for a residential construction site. Notice that the legend identifies symbols for existing and finished contour lines. This particular grading plan provides retaining walls and graded slopes to accommodate a fairly level construction site from the front of the structure to the extent of the rear yard. The finished slope represents an embankment that establishes the relationship of the proposed contour to the existing contour. This particular grading plan also shows a proposed irrigation and landscaping layout. Grading plan requirements may differ from one location to the next. Some grading plans may also show a cross section through the site at specified intervals or locations to evaluate the contour more fully.

SITE ANALYSIS PLAN

In areas where zoning and building permit applications require a design review, a site analysis plan may be required. The site analysis should provide the basis for the proper design relationship of the proposed development to the site and to adjacent properties. The degree of detail of the site analysis is generally appropriate to the scale of the proposed project. A site analysis plan, as shown in Figure 38–8, often includes the following:

- A vicinity map showing the location of the property in relationship to adjacent properties, roads, and utilities.
- Site features such as existing structures and plants on the property and adjacent property.
- The scale.
- North direction.
- Property boundaries.
- Slope shown by contour lines, cross sections, or both.
- Plan legend.
- Traffic patterns.
- Solar site information if solar application is intended.
- Pedestrian patterns.

SUBDIVISION PLANS

Local requirements for subdivisions should be confirmed as there are a variety of procedures depending upon local guidelines and zoning rules.

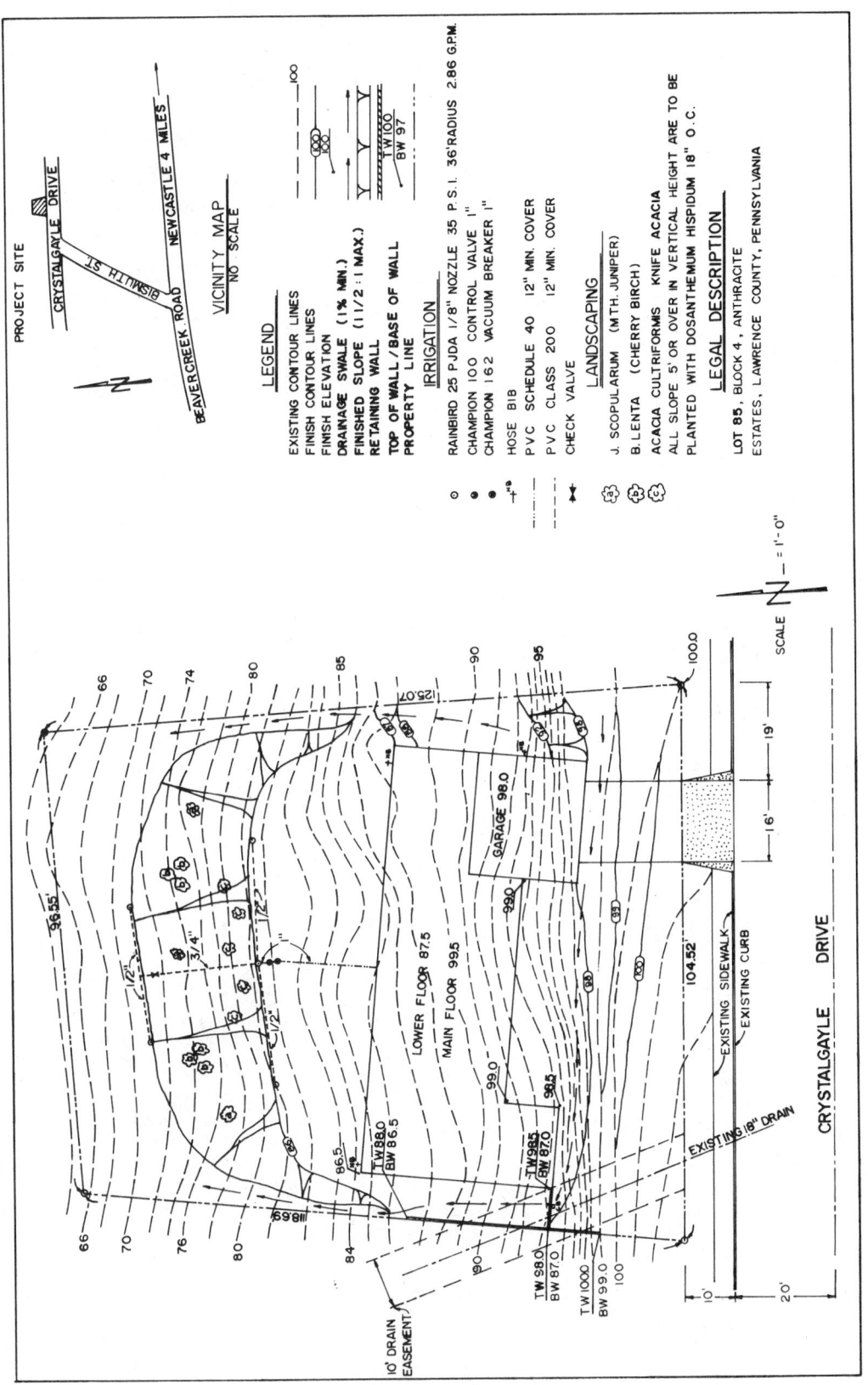

Figure 38-7 Grading plan.

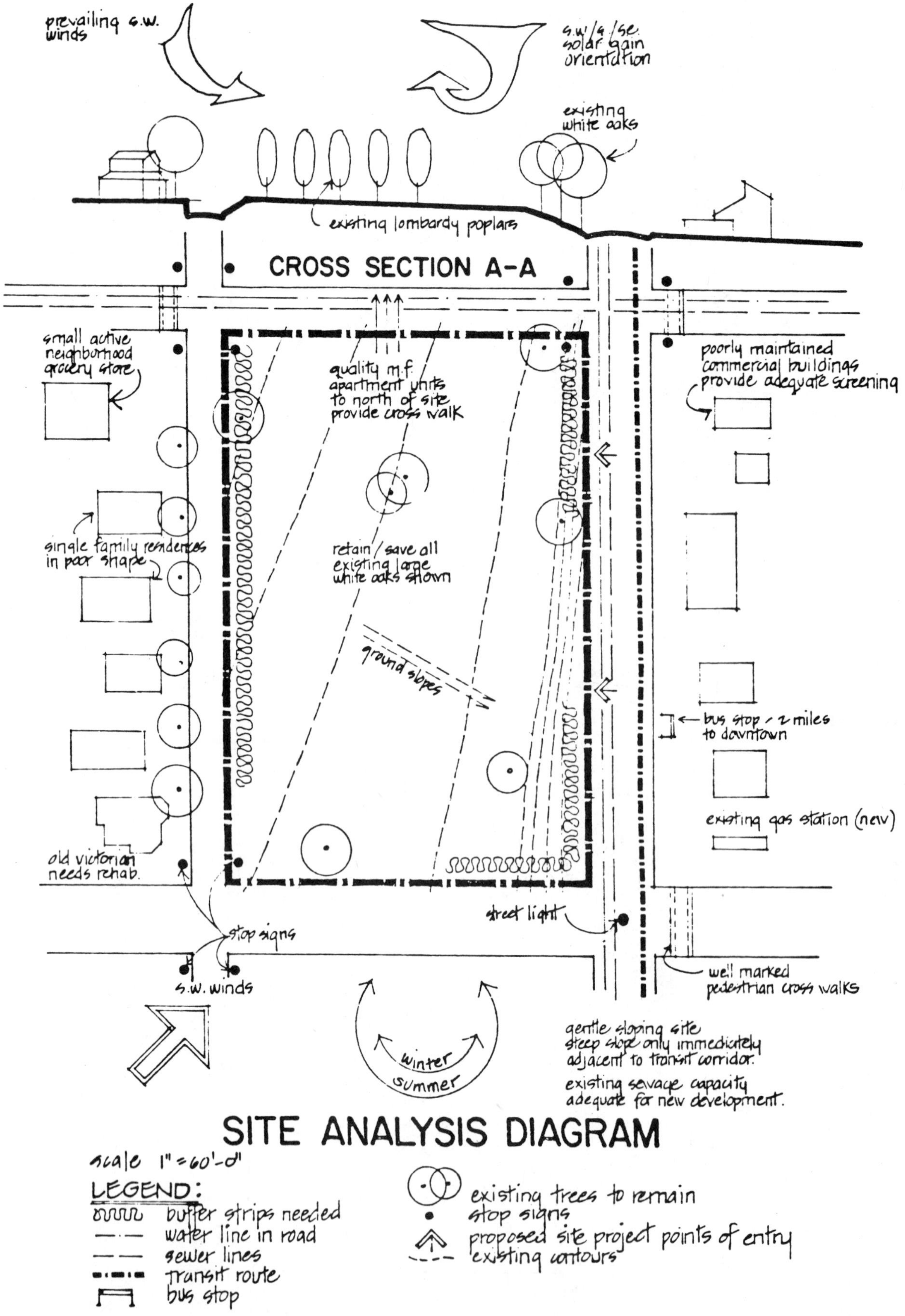

prevailing s.w. winds

s.w./s./se. solar gain orientation

existing white oaks

existing lombardy poplars

CROSS SECTION A-A

small active neighborhood grocery store

poorly maintained commercial buildings provide adequate screening

quality m.f. apartment units to north of site provide cross walk

single family residences in poor shape

retain/save all existing large white oaks shown

ground slopes

bus stop - 2 miles to downtown

existing gas station (new)

old victorian needs rehab.

street light

well marked pedestrian cross walks

stop signs

s.w. winds

winter summer

gentle sloping site steep slope only immediately adjacent to transit corridor.

existing sewage capacity adequate for new development.

SITE ANALYSIS DIAGRAM

scale 1" = 60'-0"

LEGEND:
- ᴗᴗᴗᴗ buffer strips needed
- ——— water line in road
- – – – sewer lines
- –·–·– transit route
- ⊓ bus stop

- existing trees to remain
- • stop signs
- proposed site project points of entry
- – – – existing contours

Figure 38–8 Site analysis plan. *Courtesy Planning Department, Clackamas County, OR.*

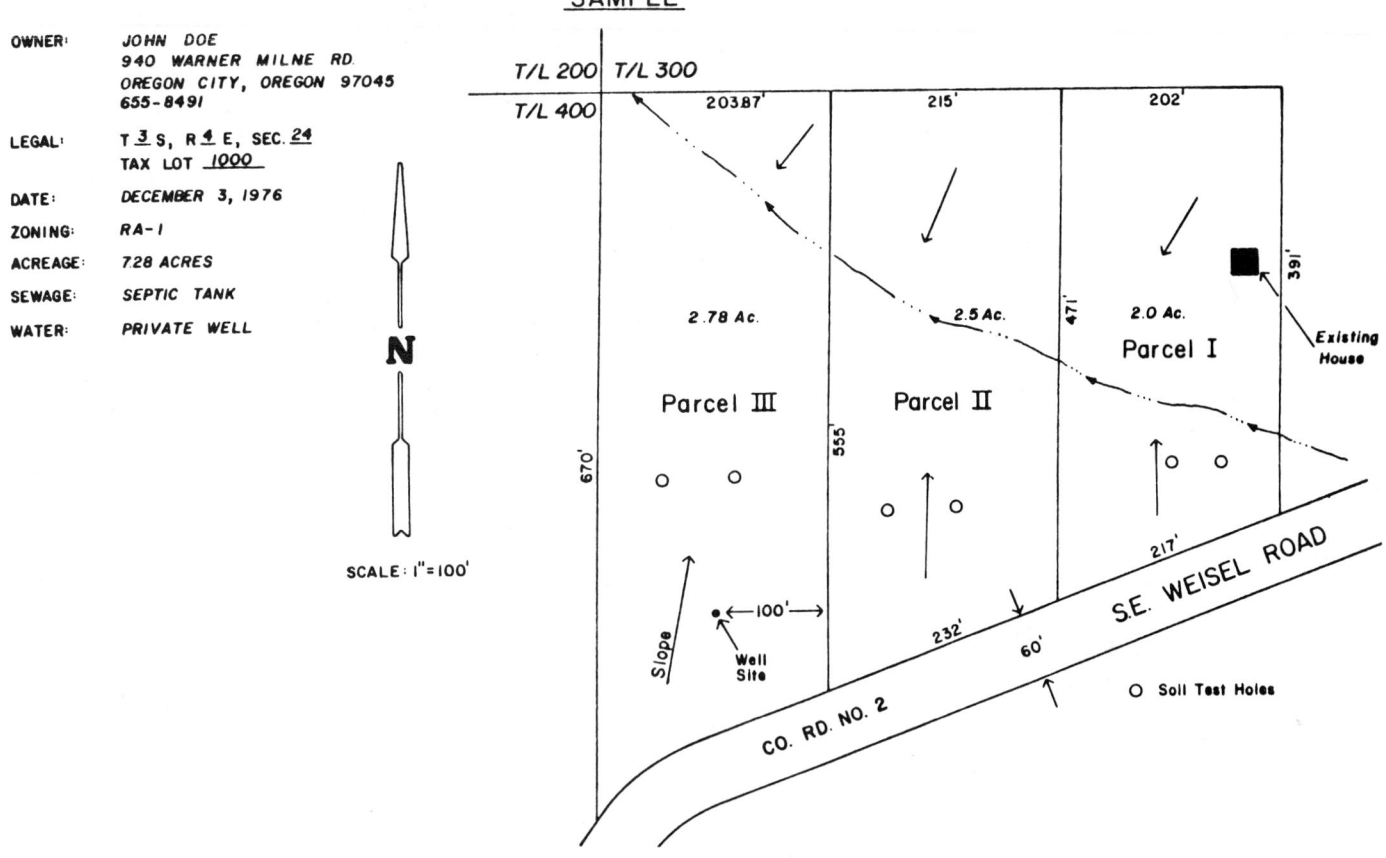

Figure 38–9 Subdivision with three proposed lots. *Courtesy Planning Department, Clackamas County, OR.*

Some areas have guidelines for small subdivisions that differ from large subdivisions such as dividing a property into three or fewer parcels. The plat required for a minor subdivision may include the following:

1. Legal description.
2. Name, address, and telephone number of applicant.
3. Parcel layout with dimensions.
4. Direction of north.
5. All existing roads and road widths.
6. Number identification of parcels such as Parcel 1, Parcel 2.
7. Location of well or proposed well, or name of water district.
8. Type of sewage disposal, that is, septic tank or public sanitary sewers. Name of sewer district.
9. Zoning designation.
10. Size of parcel(s) in square feet or acres.
11. Slope of ground. (Arrows pointing down slope.)
12. Setbacks of all existing buildings, septic tanks, and drainfields from new property lines.
13. All utility and drainage easements.

14. Any natural drainage channels. Indicate direction of flow and whether drainage is seasonal or year-round.
15. Map scale.
16. Date.
17. Building permit application number, if any.

Figure 38–9 shows a typical subdivision of land with three proposed parcels.

A major subdivision may require plats that are more detailed than a minor subdivision. Some of the items that may be included on the plat or in separate cover are the following:

1. The name, address and phone number of the property owner, applicant, and engineer or surveyor.
2. Source of water.
3. Method of sewage disposal.
4. Existing zoning.
5. Proposed utilities.
6. Calculations justifying the proposed density.
7. Name of the major partitions or subdivision.
8. Date the drawing was made.
9. Legal description.

10. North arrow.
11. Vicinity sketch showing location of the subdivision.
12. Identification of each lot or parcel and block by number.
13. Gross acreage of property being subdivided or partitioned.
14. Dimensions and acreage of each lot or parcel.
15. Streets abutting the plat including name, direction of drainage, and approximate grade.
16. Streets proposed including names, approximate grades, and radius of curves.
17. Legal access to subdivision or partition other than public road.
18. Contour lines at two-foot interval for slopes of 10 percent or less, five foot interval if exceeding a 10 percent slope.
19. Drainage channels, including width, depth, and direction of flow.
20. Existing and proposed easements locations.
21. Location of all existing structures, driveways, and pedestrian walkways.
22. All areas to be offered for public dedication.
23. Contiguous property under the same ownership, if any.
24. Boundaries of restricted areas, if any.
25. Significant vegetative areas such as major wooded areas or specimen trees.

Figure 38–10 shows an example of a major subdivision plat.

PLANNED UNIT DEVELOPMENT

A creative and flexible approach to land development is a planned unit development. Planned unit developments may include such uses as residential areas, recreational areas, open spaces, schools, libraries, churches or convenient shopping facilities. Developers involved in these projects must pay particular attention to the impact on local existing developments. Generally the plats for these developments must include all of the same information shown on a subdivision plat, plus:

1. A detailed vicinity map as shown in Figure 38–11.
2. Land use summary.

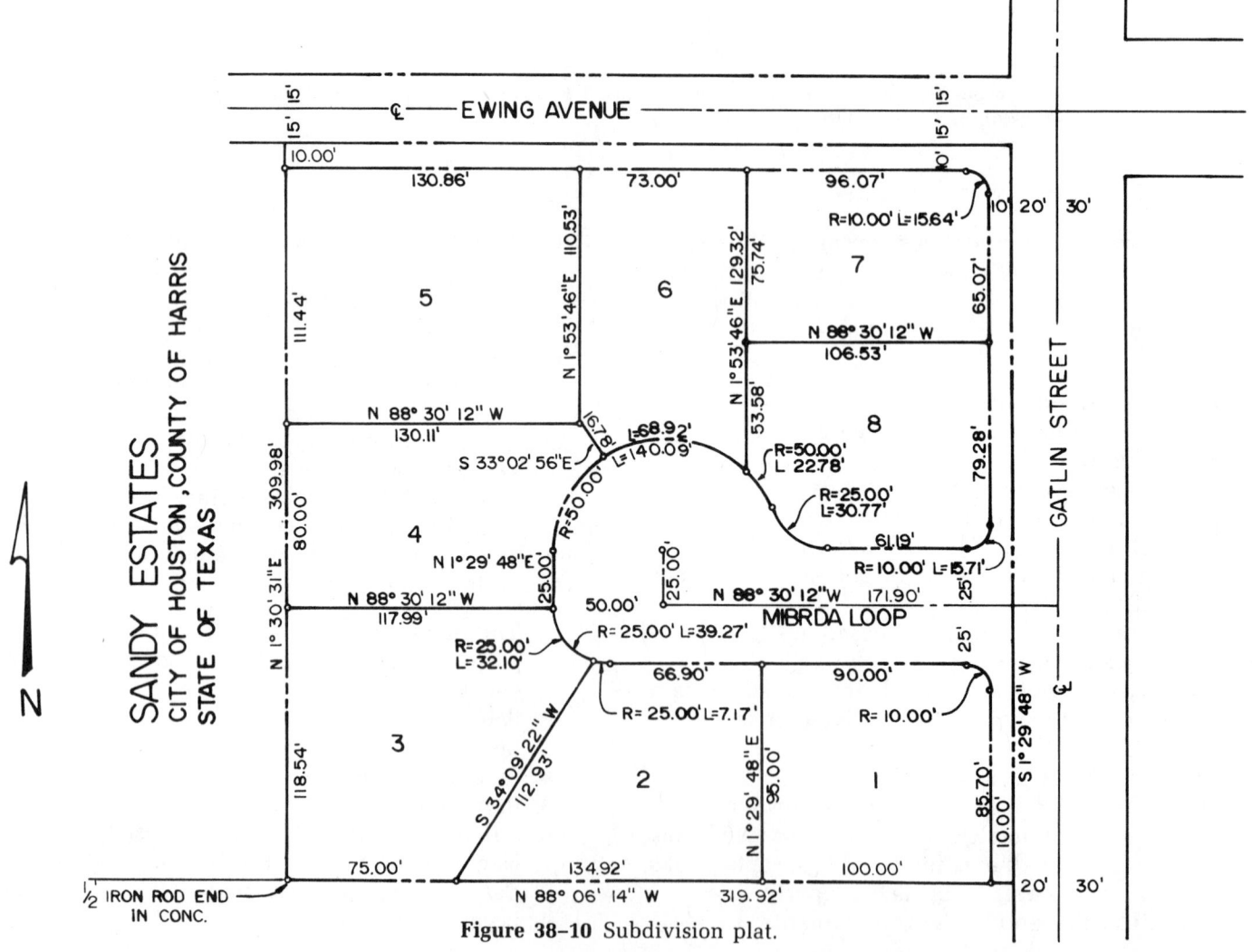

Figure 38–10 Subdivision plat.

3. Symbol legend.

4. Special spaces such as recreational and open spaces, or other unique characteristics.

Figure 38–12 shows a typical planned unit development plan. These plans, as in any proposed plat plan, may require changes before the final drawings are approved for development.

There are several specific applications for a plot or plat plan. The applied purpose of each will be different, although the characteristics of each type of plot plan may be similar. Local districts will have guidelines for the type of plot plan required. Be sure to evaluate local guidelines before preparing a plot plan for a specific purpose. Prepare the plot plan in strict accordance with the requirements in order to receive acceptance.

A variety of plot plan-related templates are available that can help make the preparation of these plans a little easier. See Figure 38–13.

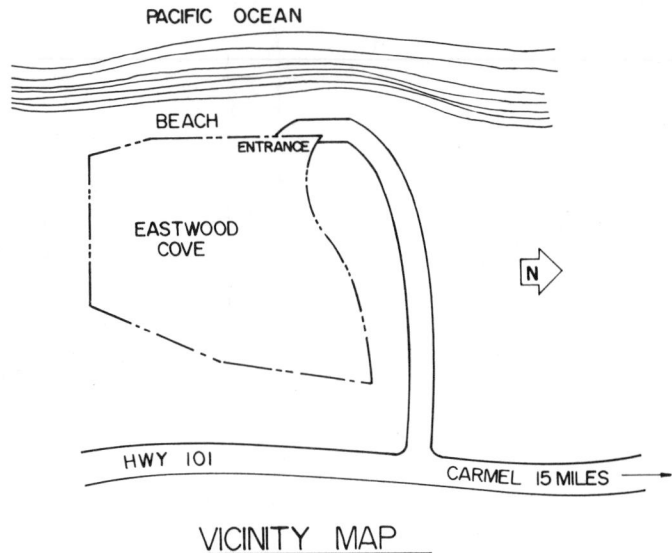

Figure 38–11 Vicinity map.

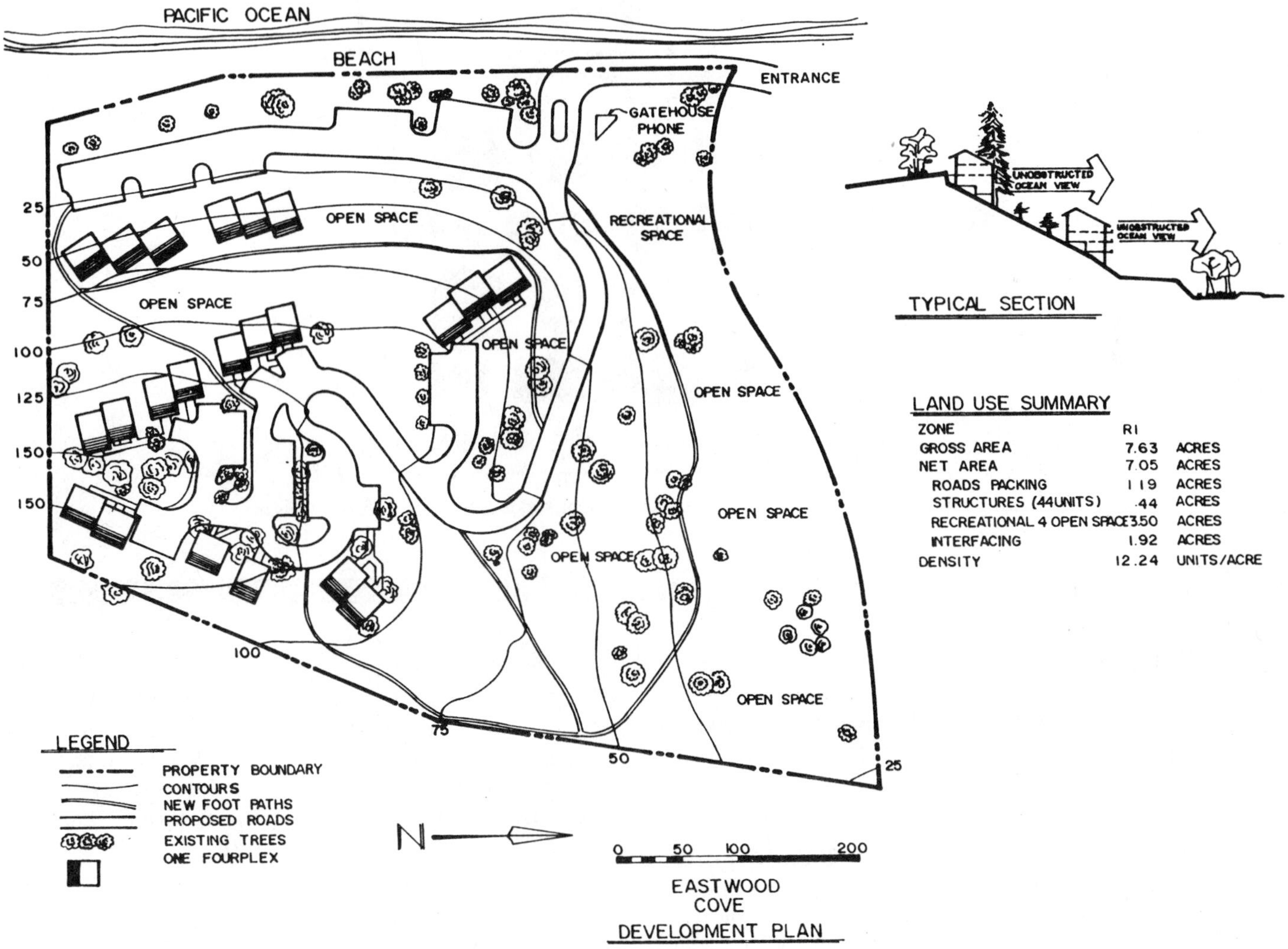

Figure 38–12 Planned unit development plan.

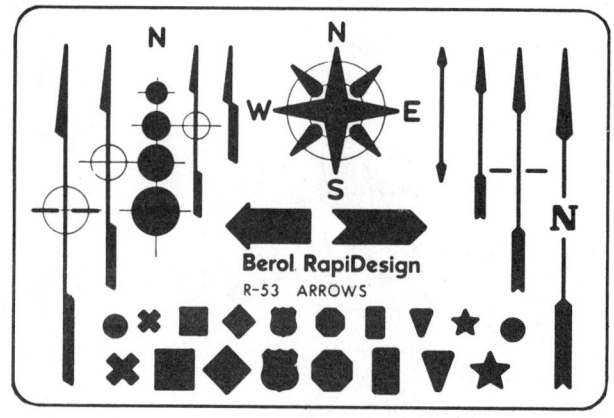

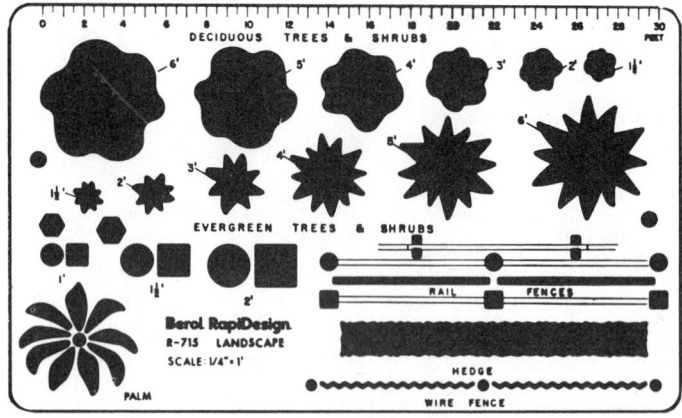

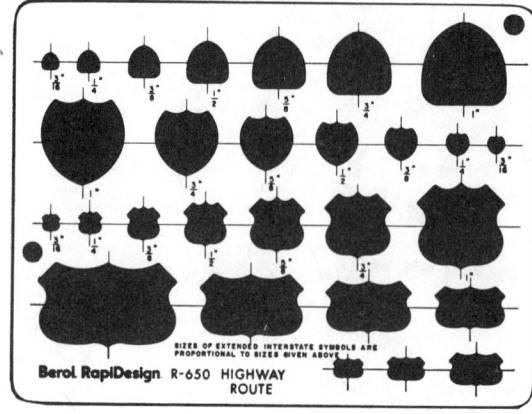

Figure 38–13 Plot plan-related templates. *Courtesy Berol USA RapiDesign.*

PLAT AND PLOT PLAN REQUIREMENTS TEST

DIRECTIONS

Answer the questions with short complete statements or drawings as needed on an 8½ × 11 drawing sheet as follows:

1. Use ⅛ in. guidelines for all lettering.
2. Letter your name, Plat and Plot Plan Requirements Test, and the date at the top of the sheet.
3. Letter the question number and provide the answer. You do not need to write out the question.
4. Do all lettering with vertical uppercase architectural letters. If the answer requires line work, use proper drafting tools and technique. Answers may be prepared on a word processor if appropriate with course guidelines.
5. Your grade will be based on correct answers and quality of line technique.

QUESTIONS

1. Define the following terms:
   a. Plot plan
   b. Topography
   c. Contour lines
   d. Contour intervals
2. Describe in short complete statements five different types of plot plans.
3. How does a plat differ from a plot?
4. List six characteristics that are similar on plot plans.
5. What is a vicinity map?
6. Describe the purpose of a grading plan.
7. What specific information is provided on a site analysis plan?
8. Describe the difference between a minor and major subdivision.
9. Describe the purpose of a planned unit development.
10. Why should verification of local requirements be made before beginning a site development plan for any function?

Chapter 39
Plot Plan Layout

INTRODUCTION

PLOT PLANS may be drawn on media (bond paper, vellum, Mylar® or computer plot paper) ranging in size from 8½″ × 11″ up to 24″ × 36″ depending upon the purpose of the plan and the guidelines of the local government agency requiring the plot plan. Many local jurisdictions recommend that plot plans be drawn on an 8½″ × 14″ size sheet.

Before you begin the plot plan layout there is some important information that you will need. This information can often be obtained from the legal documents for the property, the surveyor's map, the local assessor's office, or the local zoning department. Figure 39–1 is a plat from a surveyor's map that can be used as a guide to prepare the plot plan. The scale of the surveyor's plat may vary, although in this case it is 1″ = 200′. The plot plan to be drawn may have a scale ranging from 1″ = 10′ to 1″ = 200′. The factors that influence the scale include the following:

- Sheet size
- Plat size
- Amount of information required
- Amount of detail required

Additional information that should be determined before the plat can be completed usually includes the following:

- Legal description
- North direction
- All existing roads, utilities, water, sewage disposal, drainage, and slope of land
- Zoning information including front, rear, and side yard setbacks
- Size of proposed structures
- Elevations at property corners, driveway at street, or contour elevations

STEPS IN PLOT PLAN LAYOUT

Follow these steps to draw a plot plan.

Step 1. Select the paper size. In this case the size is 8½″ × 11″. Evaluate the plot to be drawn. Lot 2 of Sandy Estates shown in Figure 39–1 will be used. Determine the scale to use by considering how the longest dimension (134.92 ft) fits on the sheet. Always try to leave at least a ½ in. margin around the sheet.

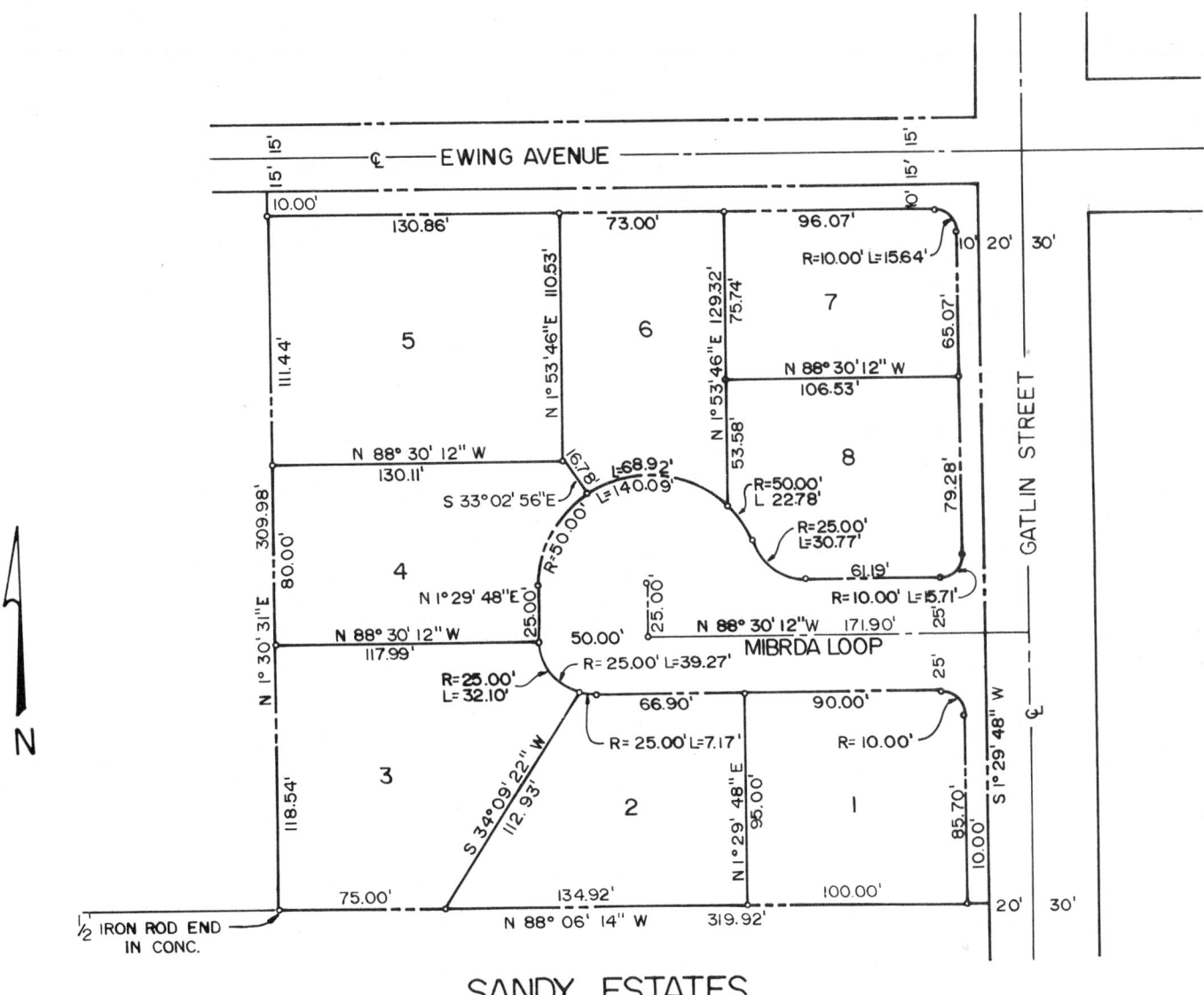

SANDY ESTATES
CITY OF HOUSTON, COUNTY OF HARRIS
STATE OF TEXAS

Figure 39-1 Plat from surveyor's map.

Step 2. Use the given plat as an example to lay out the proposed plot plan. If a plat is not available, then the plot plan can be laid out from the legal description by establishing the boundaries using the bearings and dimensions in feet. Lay out the entire plot plan using construction lines. If errors are made, the construction lines are very easy to erase. See Figure 39-2.

Step 3. Lay out the proposed structure using construction lines. The proposed structure in this example is 54 ft long and 26 ft wide. The front setback is 25 ft and the east side is 20 ft. Lay out all roads, driveways, walks, and utilities. Look at Figure 39-3.

Step 4. Darken all property lines, structures, roads, driveways, walks, and utilities as shown in Figure 39-4. Some drafters use a thick line or shading for the structure.

Step 5. Add dimensions and contour lines (if any) or elevations. Add all labels including the road name, property dimensions and bearings (if used), utility names, walks, and driveways as shown in Figure 39-5.

Step 6. Complete the plot plan by adding the north indicator, the legal description, title, scale, client's name, and other title block information. Figure 39-6 shows a complete plot plan.

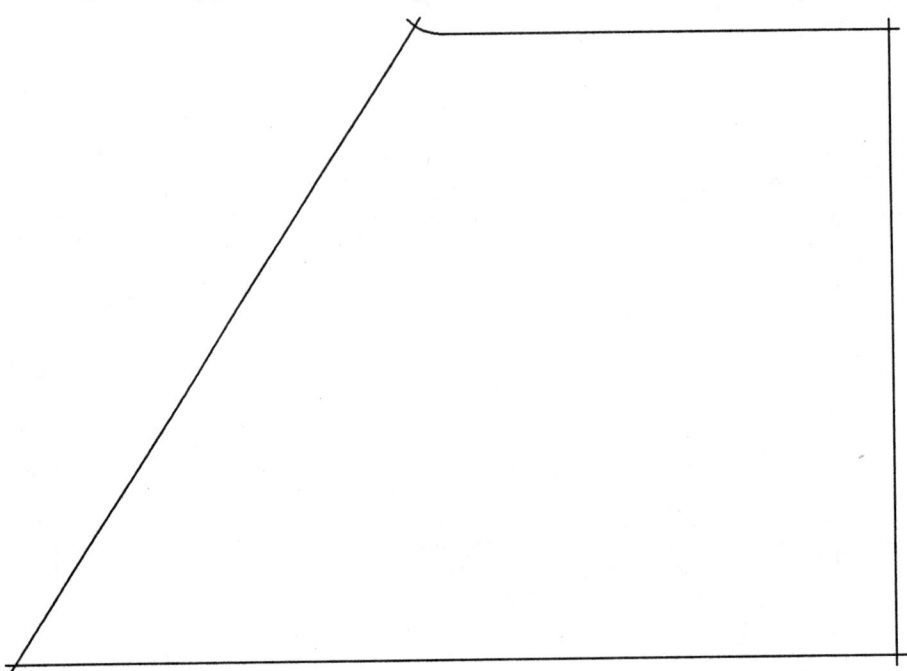

Figure 39-2 Step 2: Lay out the plot plan with construction lines.

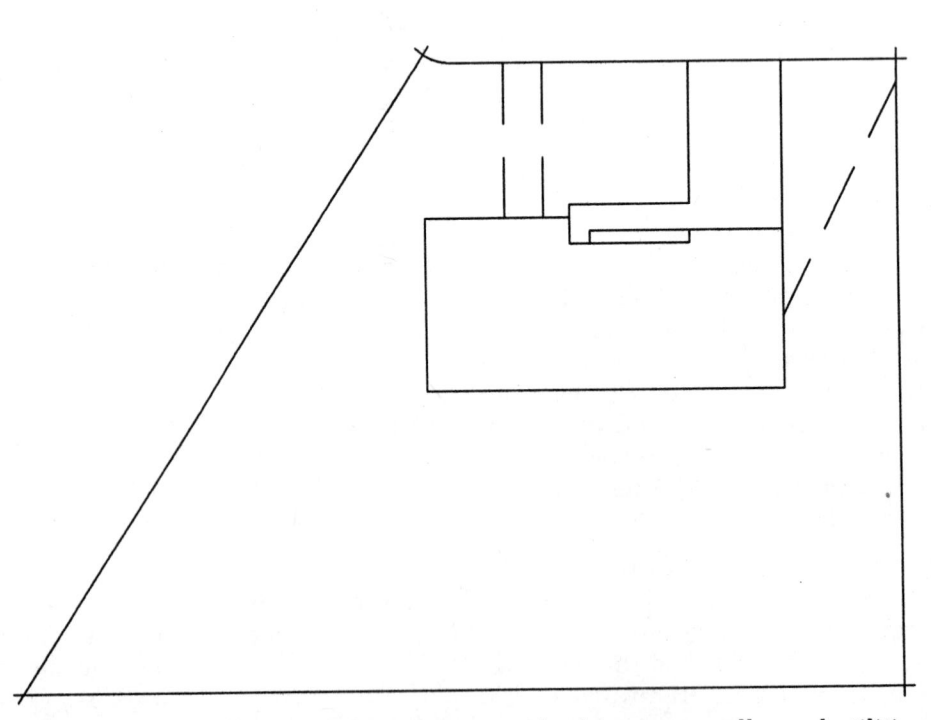

Figure 39-3 Step 3: Lay out the structures, roads, driveways, walks, and utilities.

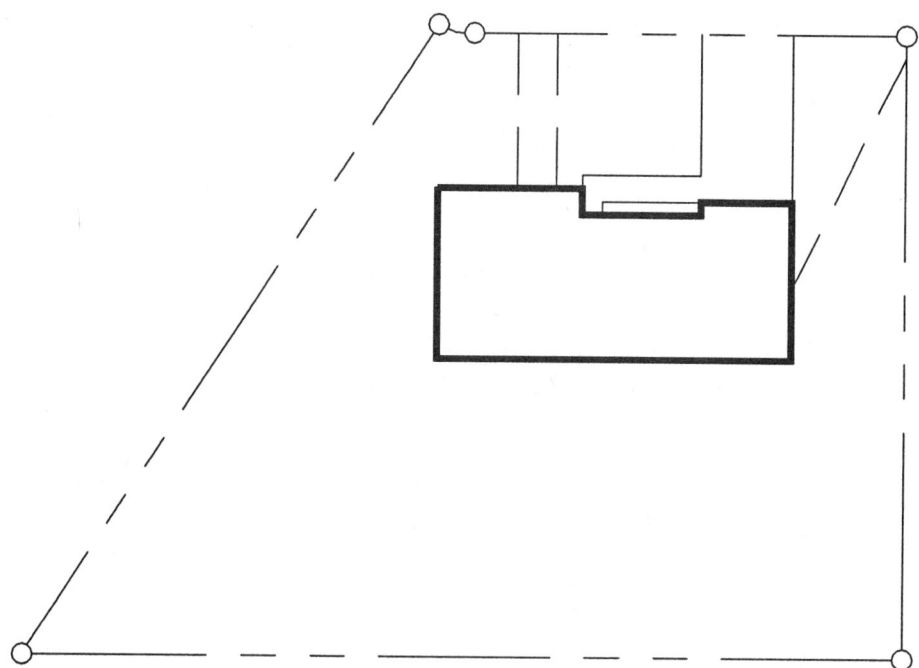

Figure 39–4 Step 4: Darken boundary lines, structures, roads, driveways, walks, and utilities.

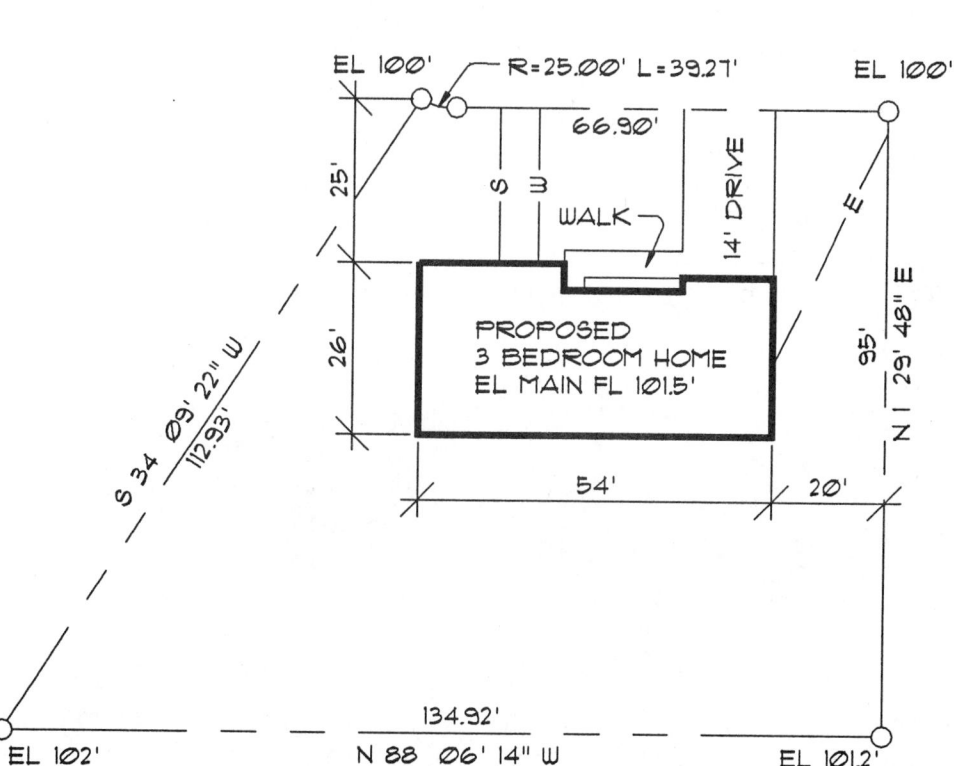

Figure 39–5 Step 5: Add dimensions and elevations; then label all roads, driveways, walks, and utilities.

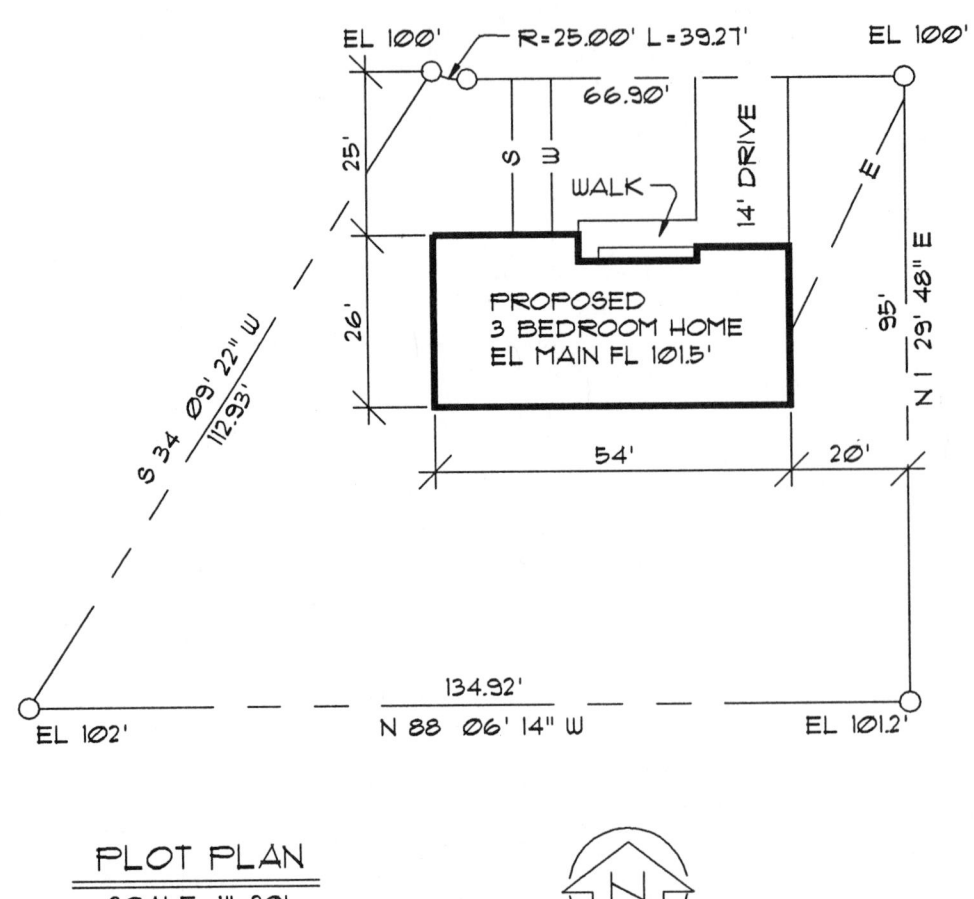

PLOT PLAN
SCALE: 1"=20'

LEGAL:
LOT 2 SANDY ESTATES
CITY OF HOUSTON,
COUNTY OF HARRIS,
STATE OF TEXAS

Figure 39-6 Step 6: Complete the plot plan. Add title, scale, north arrow, legal description, and other necessary information, such as owner's name if required.

CADD
applications

USING CADD TO DRAW PLOT PLANS.

There are CADD software packages that may easily be customized to assist in drawing plot plans. Also available are complete CADD mapping packages that allow you to draw topographic maps, cut and fill layouts, grading plans, and land profiles. It all depends on the nature of your business and how much power you need in the CADD mapping program. One of the benefits of CADD over manual drafting is accuracy. For example, you can draw a property boundary line by giving the length and bearing. The

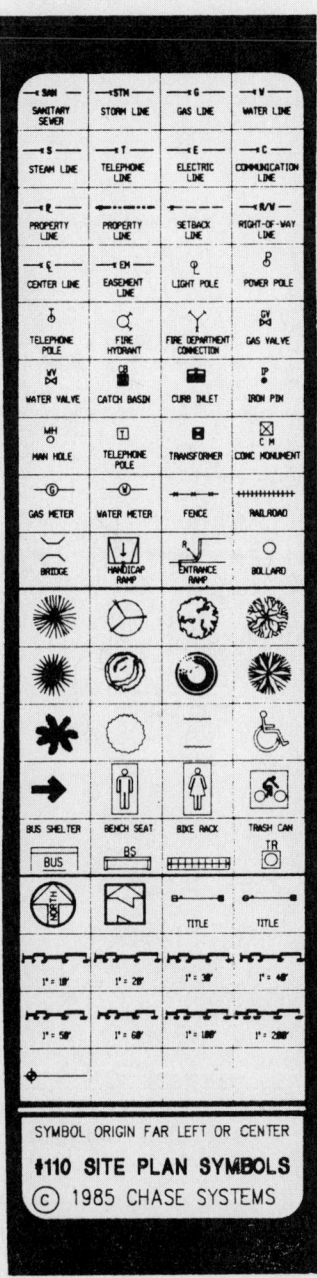

Figure 1 CADD tablet menu overlay showing plot plan symbols.

computer automatically draws the line, then it labels the length and bearing. Continue by entering information from surveyor's notes to draw the entire property boundary in just a few minutes. Such features increase the speed and accuracy of drawing plot plans, but there are tablet menu overlays available that provide powerful plot plan capabilities, including standard symbols, scales, titles, North arrows, and landscaping features, as shown in Figure 1. A residential grading plan, drawn using CADD mapping software, is shown in Figure 2.

The needs of the commercial site plan are a little different from the residential requirements. The commercial CADD site plan package should use the same features as the residential application but, additionally, have the ability to design street and parking lot layouts. A CADD template overlay with this capability is shown in Figure 3. The commercial CADD drafter uses features from both symbol libraries, including utility symbols, street, curb and gutter designs, landscaping, parking lot layouts, titles, and scales. A commercial site plan is shown in Figure 4.

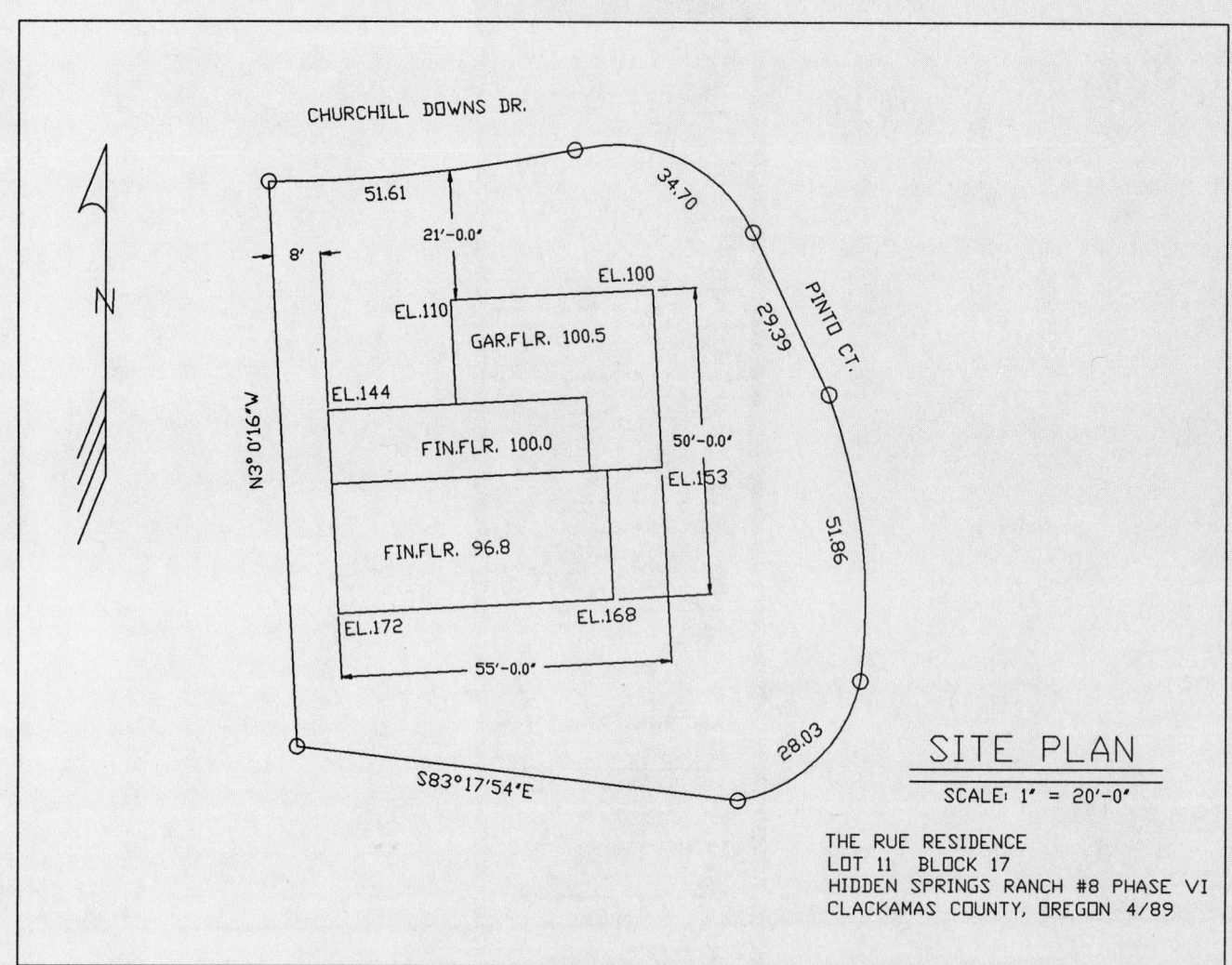

Figure 2 CADD-drawn site plan. *Courtesy Henry Fitzgibbon.*

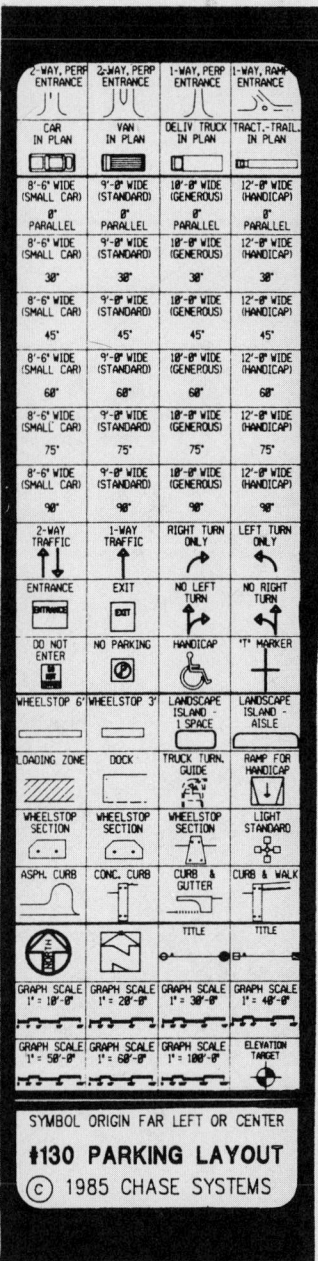

Figure 3 CADD tablet menu overlay for commercial site planning.

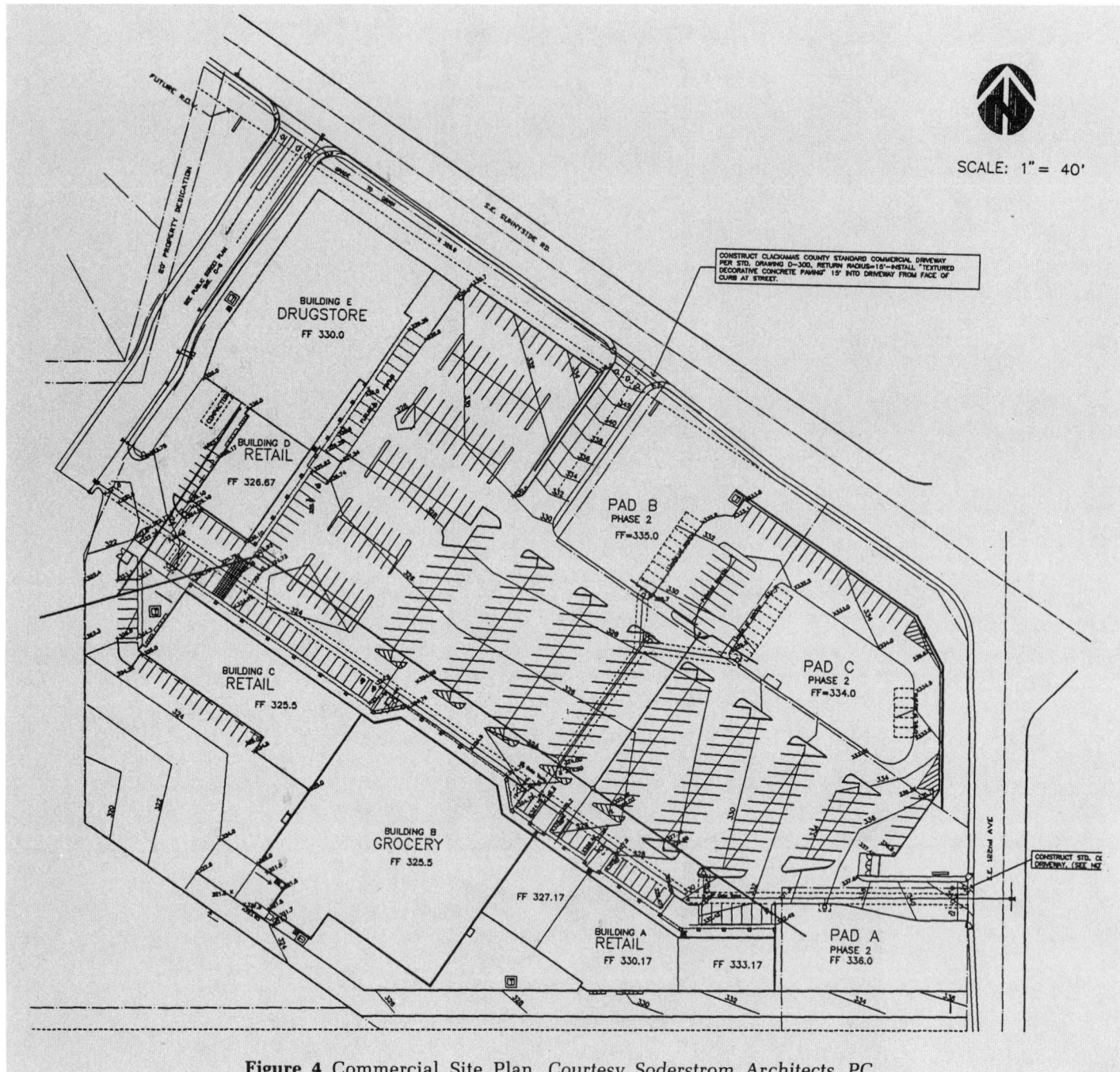

SCALE: 1" = 40'

Figure 4 Commercial Site Plan. *Courtesy Soderstrom Architects, PC.*

PLOT PLAN LAYOUT TEST

DIRECTIONS

Answer the questions with short complete statements or drawings as needed on an 8½ × 11 drawing sheet as follows:

1. Use ⅛ in. guidelines for all lettering.
2. Letter your name, Plot Plan Layout Test, and the date at the top of the sheet.
3. Letter the question number and provide the answer. You do not need to write out the question.
4. Do all lettering with vertical uppercase architectural letters. If the answer requires line work, use proper drafting tools and technique. Answers may be prepared on a word processor if appropriate with course guidelines.
5. Your grade will be based on correct answers and quality of line technique.

QUESTIONS

1. What influences the size of the drawing sheet recommended for plot plans?
2. What four factors influence scale selection when drawing a plot plan?
3. List five elements of information that should be determined before starting a plot plan drawing.
4. Why are construction lines helpful in plot plan layout?
5. Information used to prepare a plot plan may come from one or more of several available sources; list four possible sources.

PLOT PLAN LAYOUT PROBLEM

DIRECTIONS

Select, or have your instructor assign, one of the three different plot plan sketches that follow. Additional selections may be used if pertinent to individual curriculum goals. The problems may be done using computer graphics if appropriate with course guidelines.

Problem 39–1. Using the structure from the architectural problem or problems that you have drawn as a complete set of plans, draw a complete plot plan with appropriate elements as described in the plot plan chapters.

1. Use an 8½ × 14 drawing sheet.
2. Select an appropriate scale.
3. The minimum front setback is 25'-0".
4. The minimum rear yard setback is 25'-0".
5. The minimum side yard setback is 7'-0".

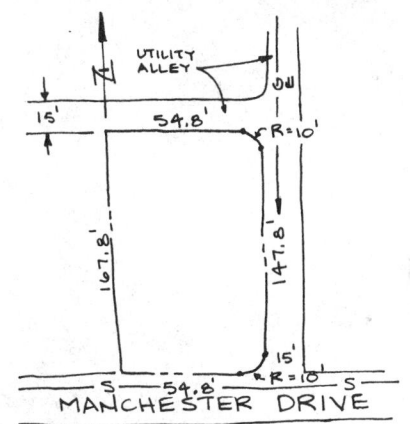

LOT 17, BLOCK 3, PLAT OF GARTHWICK, YOUR CITY, COUNTY, STATE

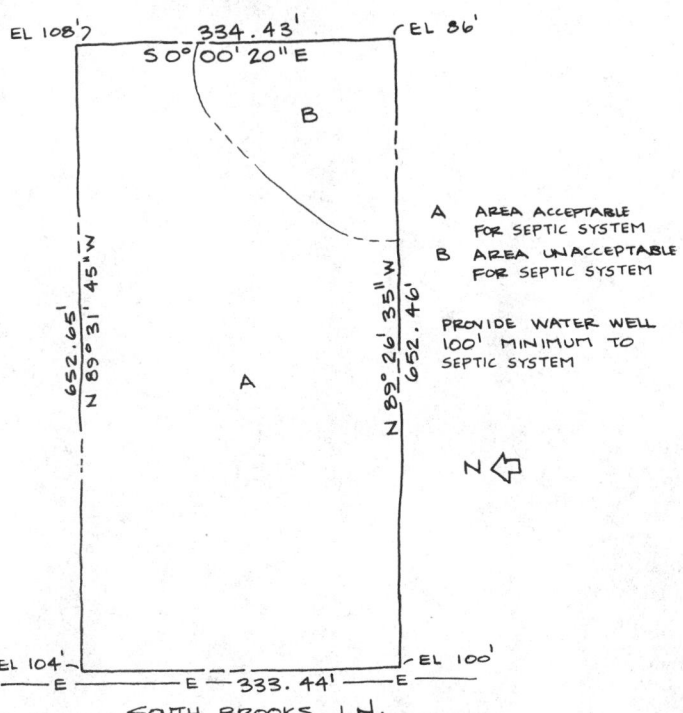

TAX LOT 2300, LOT 12 CLARKES ESTATES SECTION 17, T.4S., R.3E., SALT LAKE MERIDIAN, TOOELE COUNTY, UTAH

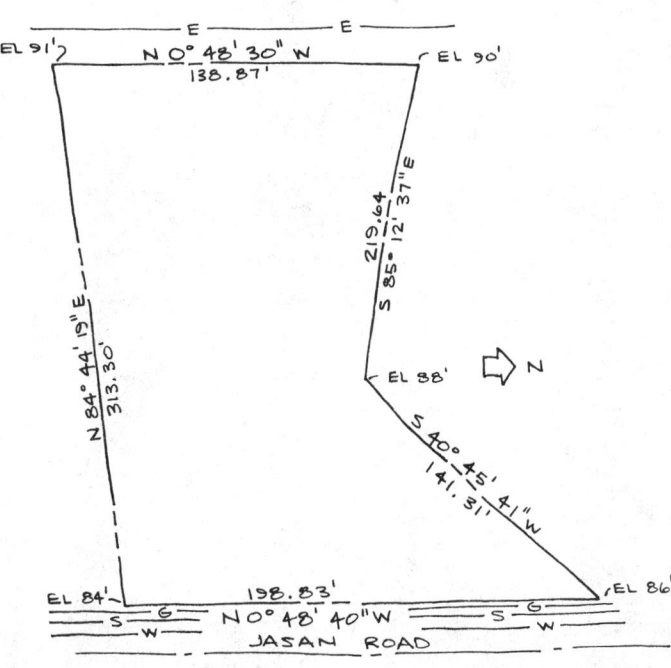

LOT 7, BLOCK 2, KYLEE ESTATES SECTION 12, T.12N., R.14E., LOUISIANA MERIDIAN, RAPIDES PARISH, LOUISIANA.

FRONT ELEVATION

CM-1430

Section Ten

Architectural Rendering

Chapter 40
Presentation Drawings

THE TERM presentation drawings was first introduced during the discussion of the design sequence in Chapter 14. As the residence was being designed, the floor plan and a rendering were drawn to help the owners understand the designer's ideas. Presentation drawings are the drawings that are used to convey basic design concepts from the design team to the owner or other interested persons. Presentation drawings are a very important part of public hearings and design reviews as a structure is studied by government and private agencies to determine its impact on the community. In residential architecture, presentation drawings are frequently used to help advertise existing stock plans.

Your artistic ability, the type of drawing to be done, and the needs of the client will affect how the presentation drawing will be done and who will produce the drawings. Some offices may have an architectural illustrator do all presentation drawings. As discussed in Chapter 1, an illustrator combines the skills of an artist with the techniques of drafting. Other offices allow design drafters to make the presentation drawings. A drafter may be able to match the quality of an illustrator, but not the speed. Many of the presentation drawings that are contained throughout this book would take an illustrator only a few hours to draw. As a drafter you should be familiar with each type of presentation drawing but realize that they are typically done by design drafters, architects, or illustrators.

TYPES OF PRESENTATION DRAWINGS

The same type of drawings that are required for the working drawings can also be used to help present the design ideas. Because the owner, user, or general public may not be able to fully understand the working drawings, each can be drawn as a presentation drawing to present basic information. The most common types of presentation drawings are renderings, elevations, floor plans, plot plans, and sections.

Renderings

Renderings are the best type of presentation drawing for showing the shape or style of a structure. The term rendering can be used to describe an artistic process applied to a drawing. Each of the presentation drawings can be rendered using one of the artistic styles soon to be discussed. Rendering can also be

Figure 40–1 The most common type of presentation drawing is a rendering, or perspective, drawing. The rendering presents an image of how the structure will look when complete. *Courtesy Paul Franks.*

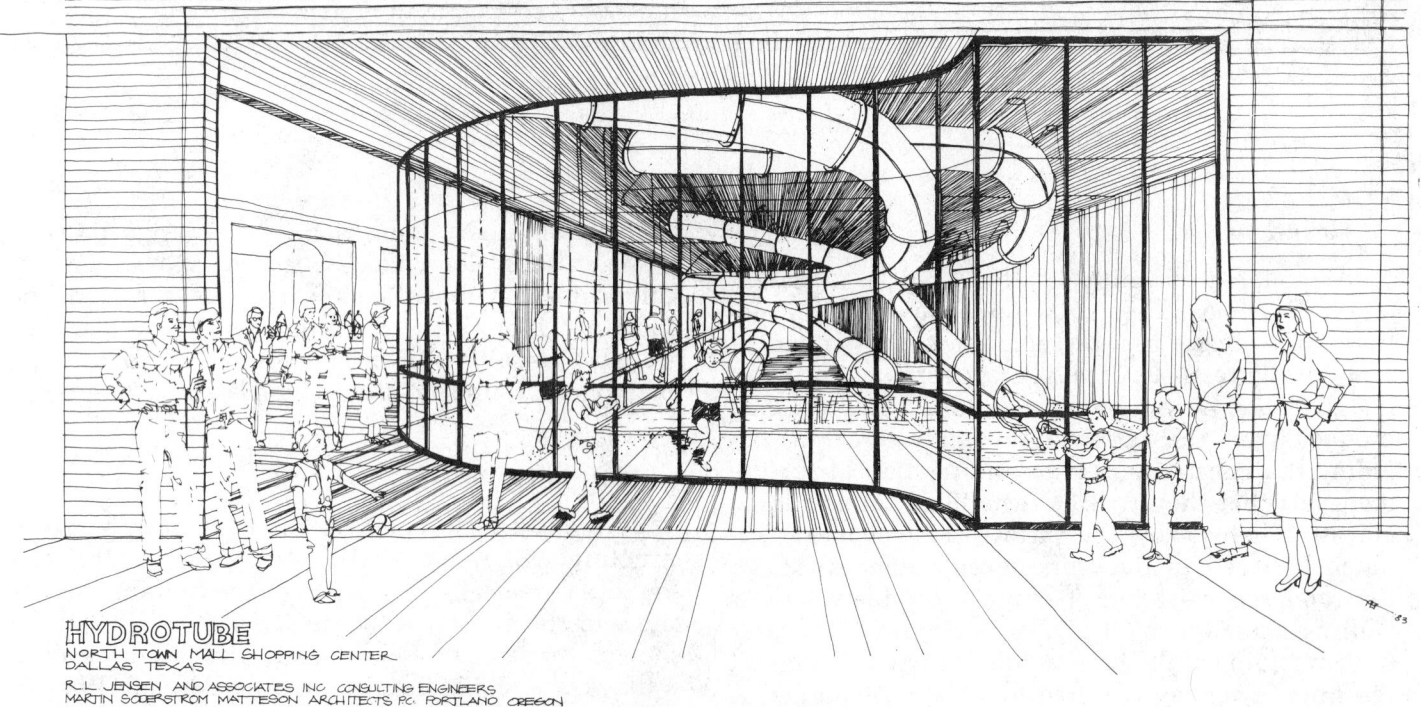

HYDROTUBE
NORTH TOWN MALL SHOPPING CENTER
DALLAS TEXAS
R.L. JENSEN AND ASSOCIATES INC. CONSULTING ENGINEERS
MARTIN SODERSTROM MATTESON ARCHITECTS PC. PORTLAND OREGON

Figure 40–2 Renderings are often helpful for showing the relationships of interior spaces. *Courtesy Paul Franks, and Martin Soderstrom, Matteson Architects.*

used to refer to a drawing created using the perspective layout method which will be presented in Chapter 41. Although rendering is the artistic process used on a perspective drawing, the term is also often applied to the drawings.

Figure 40–1 shows an example of a rendering. A rendering is used to present the structure as it will appear in its natural setting. A rendering can also be very useful for showing the interior shape and layout of a room as seen in Figure 40–2. Interior renderings are usually drawn using a one-point perspective method.

Figure 40–3 A presentation elevation helps show the shape of the structure without requiring the amount of time that is required to draw a rendering. *Courtesy Jeff's Residential Designs.*

Elevations

A rendered elevation is often used as a presentation drawing to help show the shape of the structure. An example of a presentation elevation can be seen in Figure 40–3. This type of presentation drawing gives the viewer an accurate idea of the finished product while the working drawing is aimed at providing the construction crew information about the materials that they will be installing. The rendered elevation helps show the various changes in surface much better than the working elevation. Although the rendered elevation does not show the depth as well as a rendering, it allows the viewer a clearer understanding of the project without having to invest the time or money required to draw a rendering. A rendered elevation will usually include all of the material shown on a working elevation with the addition of shades and plants. Depending on the artistic level of the drafter, people and automobiles are often shown also.

Floor Plans

Floor plans are often used as presentation drawings to convey the layout of interior space. Similar to the preliminary floor plan in the design process, a presentation floor plan is used to show room relationships, openings such as windows and doors, and basic room sizes. Furniture and traffic patterns are also usually shown. Figure 40–4 provides an example of a presentation floor plan.

Plot Plans

A rendered plot plan is used to show how the structure will relate to the job site and to the surrounding area. The placement of the building on the site and the north arrow are the major items to be shown. As seen in Figure 40–5, streets, driveways, walkways, and plantings are usually shown. Although most of these items are shown on the working plot plan, the presentation plot plan presents this material in a more artistic fashion than shown on the plot plan in the set of working drawings.

Sections

Sections are often drawn as part of the presentation drawings to show the vertical relationships within the structure. As seen in Figure 40–6, a section

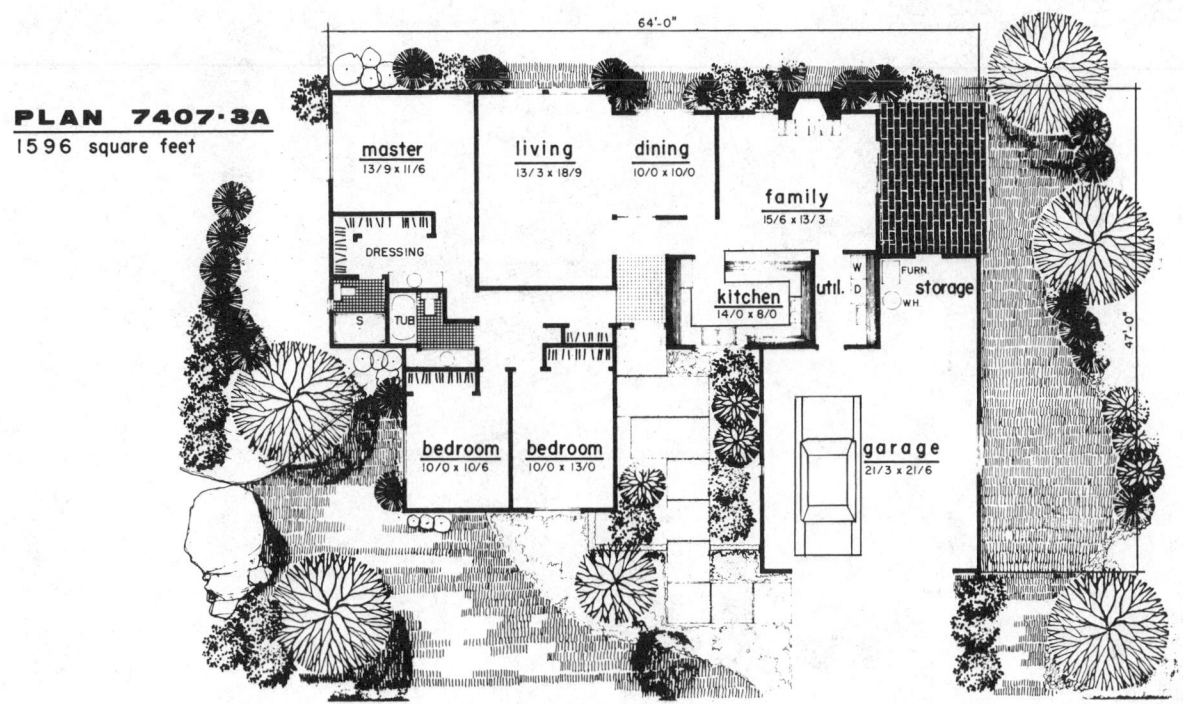

PLAN 7407·3A
1596 square feet

master
13/9 x 11/6

living
13/3 x 18/9

dining
10/0 x 10/0

family
15/6 x 13/3

DRESSING

kitchen
14/0 x 8/0

util.

storage

FURN

W
D

WH

S

TUB

bedroom
10/0 x 10/6

bedroom
10/0 x 13/0

garage
21/3 x 21/6

64'-0"

47'-0"

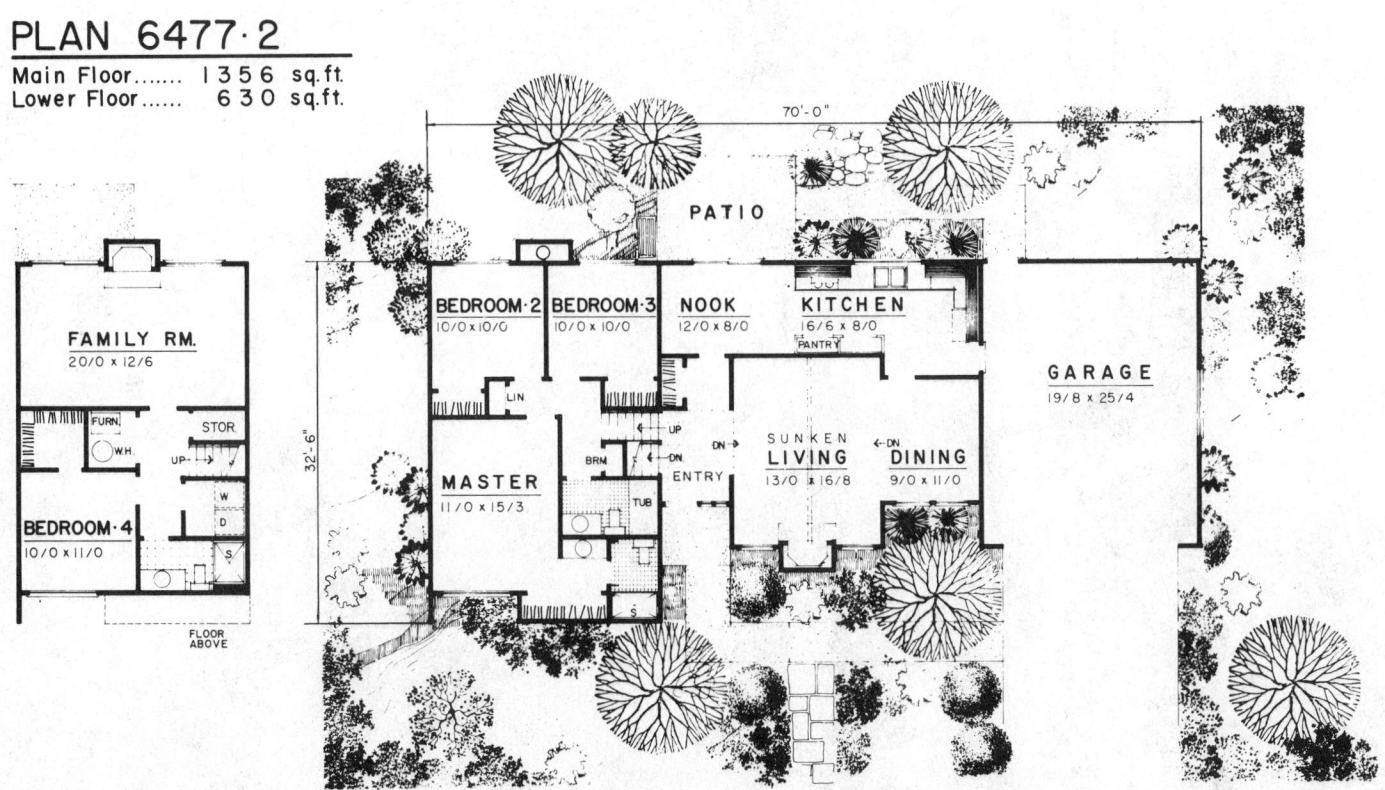

PLAN 6477·2

Main Floor....... 1356 sq.ft.
Lower Floor...... 630 sq.ft.

FAMILY RM.
20/0 x 12/6

FURN.

W.H.

STOR.

UP

W
D

S

BEDROOM·4
10/0 x 11/0

FLOOR
ABOVE

PATIO

BEDROOM·2
10/0 x 10/0

BEDROOM·3
10/0 x 10/0

NOOK
12/0 x 8/0

KITCHEN
16/6 x 8/0

PANTRY

GARAGE
19/8 x 25/4

LIN

UP

DN

DN

MASTER
11/0 x 15/3

BRM

DN

ENTRY

SUNKEN
LIVING
13/0 x 16/8

DINING
9/0 x 11/0

TUB

S

70'-0"

32'-6"

Figure 40-4 A floor plan is often part of the presentation drawings and is used to show room relationships. *Courtesy Piercy & Barclay Designers, Inc.*

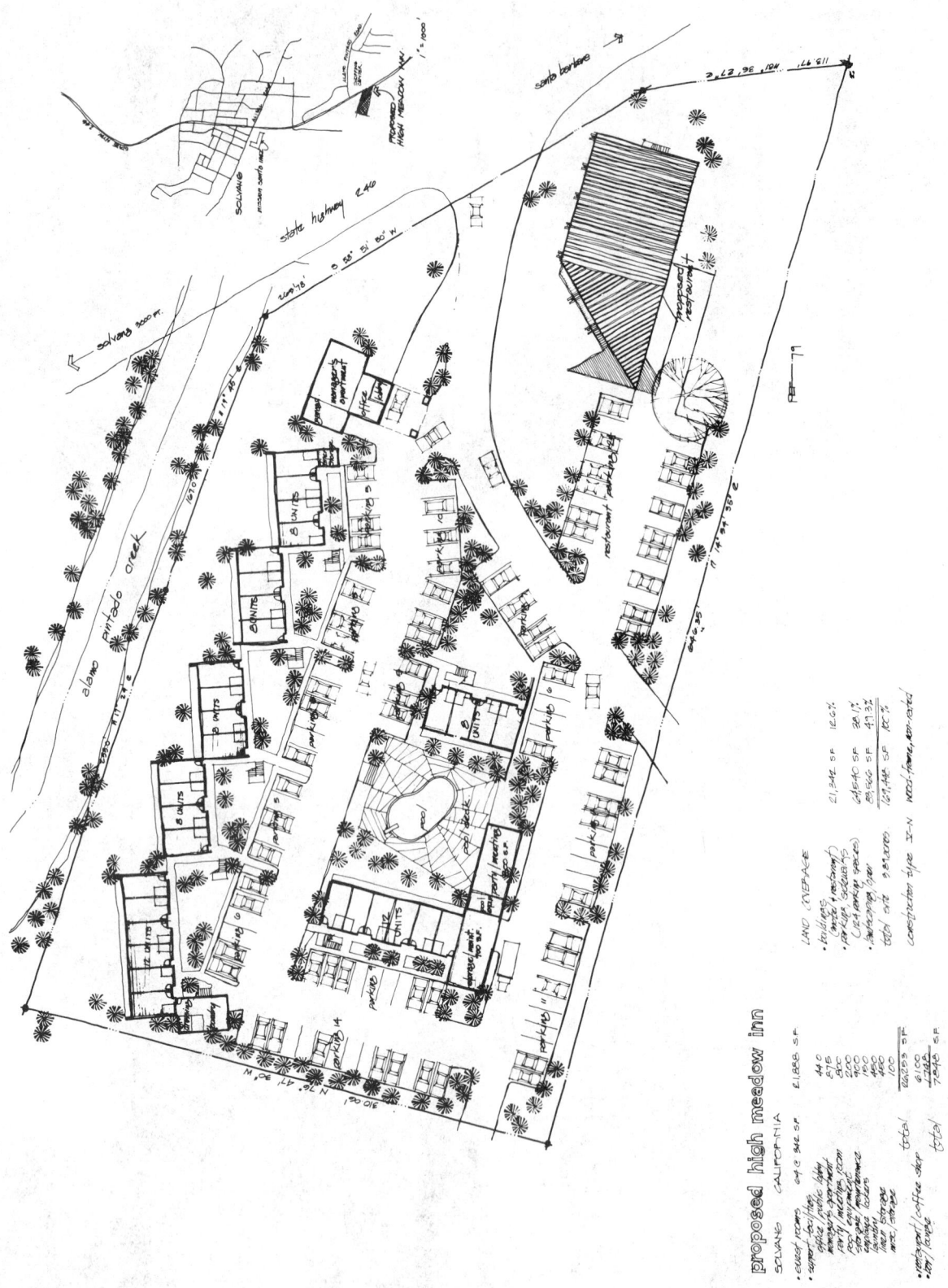

Figure 40-5 A rendered plot plan is used to show how structures relate to the job site. *Courtesy Paul Franks.*

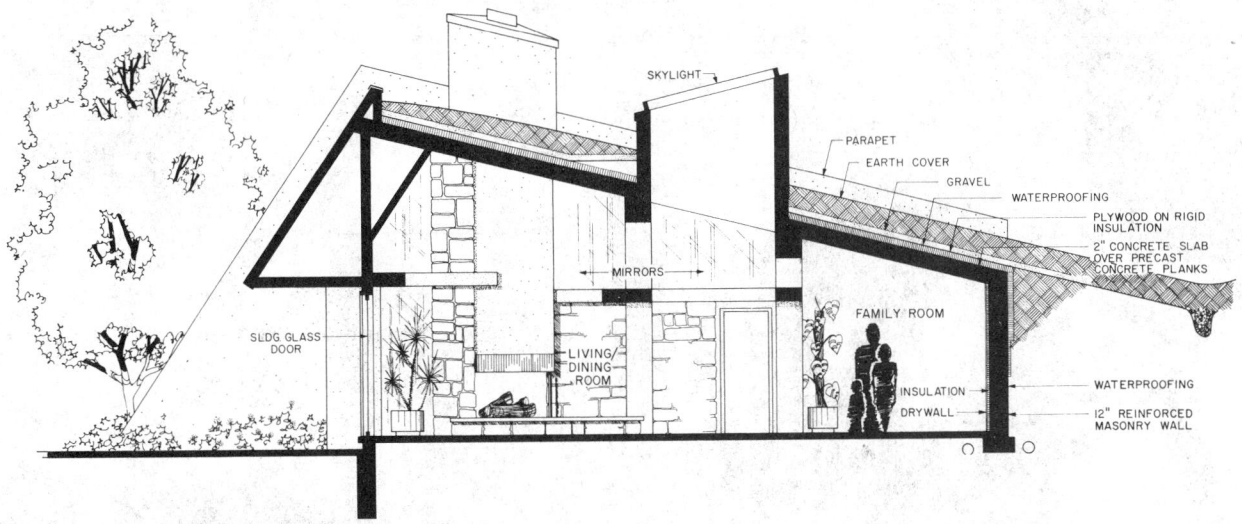

Figure 40-6 Presentation sections are used to show vertical relationships. *Courtesy Home Planners, Inc.*

can be used to show the changes of floor or ceiling levels, vertical relationships, and sun angles. Working sections show these same items with emphasis on structural materials. The presentation sections may show some structural material, but the emphasis is on spacial relationships.

METHODS OF PRESENTATION

No matter the type of drawing to be made, each can be drawn on any one of several different media. The drawings are made using different materials and line techniques.

Common Media

Common media for presentation drawings include sketch paper, vellum, Mylar®, and illustration board. Sketch paper is often used for the initial layout stages of presentation drawings, and some drawings are even done in their finished state on sketch paper. Most drawing materials will adhere to sketch paper; but because of its thinness, it does not provide good durability. Drafting vellum can be a very durable drawing medium but will wrinkle when used with some materials. Vellum is best used with graphite or ink. Graphite can produce a great variety of line qualities on vellum. Ink reproduces well on vellum but can be very unforgiving if a mistake is made.

Mylar® is often used in presentation drawings because of the ease of correcting errors. A 4 mil, clear polyester film will provide both durability and a quality surface for making photographic reproductions. Ink is the most common element used on Mylar® but some types of watercolors and polyester leads can also be used.

Illustration board is extremely durable and provides a suitable surface for all types of drawing materials. When the materials are to be photographed, a white board is usually used. Beige, gray, and light blue board also can give a pleasing appearance for presentation drawings. Because of the difficulty of correcting mistakes, illustration board is not usually used by beginners. Until experience is gained, presentation drawings can be drawn on vellum and then mounted on illustration board.

When drawing on illustration board, the drafter must plan the arrangement of the entire layout carefully prior to placing the first lines. Drawings are usually drawn on sketch paper first and then transferred to the illustration board. To transfer a drawing onto the board, lightly shade the back side of the sketch with a soft graphite lead. The graphite on the back of the lines will act as carbon paper when the original lines are traced to transfer them onto illustration board. Excess graphite can also be transferred. To avoid smearing, graphite should be placed only over each line to be transferred and not over the entire backside of the drawing. Graphite paper can also be used to transfer the drawing onto the illustration board.

A pleasing effect can be achieved by combining media. A rendering can be drawn using overlay principles and combining vellum or Mylar®, and illustration board. For example, the structure may be drawn on illustration board and the landscaping drawn in color on Mylar®. Because of the air space between the Mylar® and the illustration board, an illusion of depth is created.

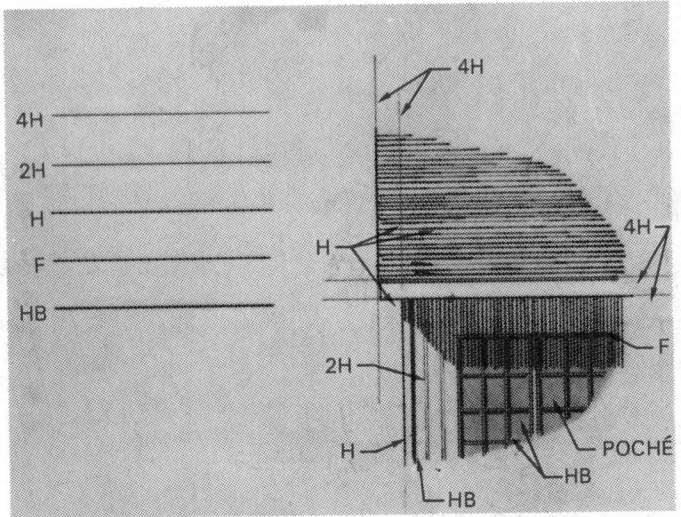

Figure 40–7 Types of graphite lines that are typically used on renderings.

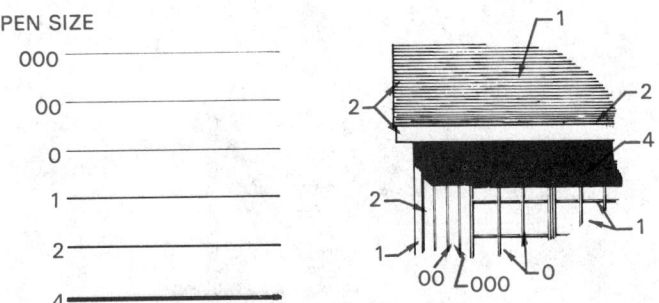

Figure 40–8 Common pen point sizes used for presentation work. The size of the drawing and the amount of detail to be shown will affect the size of point to be used.

Drawing Materials

Common materials used to draw presentation drawings include graphite, ink, colored pencil, felt tip pens, and watercolor.

Because of the ease of correcting errors, graphite is a good material for the beginning drafter to experiment with. Lead softer than that used for working drawings is typically used for renderings. Using softer lead allows for more contrast in the line work and thus creates a better sense of realism. Common leads that are used for presentation work include 4H or 5H for layout work and 2H, H, F, HB, and 4B for drawing object lines. The actual choice of lead will vary depending on the object to be drawn and the surface of the media being drawn upon. Figure 40–7 shows the different qualities that can be achieved with graphite on vellum.

Because of its reproductive qualities, ink is commonly used for presentation drawings. Ink lines have a uniform density which can be easily reproduced photographically. However, ink lines are hard to remove when a mistake occurs. Careful planning is required when working with ink to assure that the drawing is properly laid out prior to inking. Planning is also required to determine the order in which the lines will be drawn. With proper planning you can draw in one area while the ink dries in another area of the drawing.

The complexity of the drawing will affect the size of the pen points to be used. Three points generally will be required to help create a sense of depth and realism. The particular technique to be used will dictate which pen points will be used. Common points used for presentation work include numbers 0, 1, and 2. Many drafters and illustrators also add the use of 000, 00, and number 4 points to get a greater

Figure 40–9 Renderings can be drawn with opaque water color. These drawings can be reproduced easily in color or black and white. *Courtesy Home Building Plan Service, Inc.*

variation in line contrast. Figure 40–8 shows examples of various line weights available for ink work.

Color is often added to a presentation drawing by the use of colored pencils, markers, or pastels. The skill of the drafter and the use of the drawing will affect where the color is to be placed. Color is usually added to the original drawing when the illustration is to be reproduced. When the drawing is to be displayed, color is often placed on the print rather than to an original drawing. Best results are achieved when color is used to highlight a drawing rather than coloring every item in the drawing. The use of watercolors is common among professional illustrators because of the lifelike presentations that can be achieved. See Figure 40–9.

Line Techniques

Two techniques commonly used for drawing lines in presentation drawing are mechanical and freehand methods. Each uses the same methods for layout, but each varies in the method of achieving finished line quality. Figure 40–10 shows an example of a rendering drawn mechanically using a straightedge to produce lines. If a more casual effect is desired, initial layout lines can be traced without using tools. Figure 40–11 shows an example of a freehand rendering.

In addition to line methods, many styles of lettering are also used on presentation drawings. Lettering may be placed with mechanical methods such as with a lettering guide or rub-ons. Many illustrations are lettered with freehand lettering similar to Figure 40–12.

Figure 40–10 Renderings drawn with tools to provide straight lines. *Courtesy Piercy & Barclay Designers, Inc.*

RENDERING PROCEDURE FOR DRAWINGS

Because of the number of steps required to make a perspective drawing, one- and two-point perspectives will be covered in the following chapters. Other drawings can be rendered as follows.

Figure 40–11 Presentation drawings are often drawn using freehand methods. *Courtesy Paul Franks.*

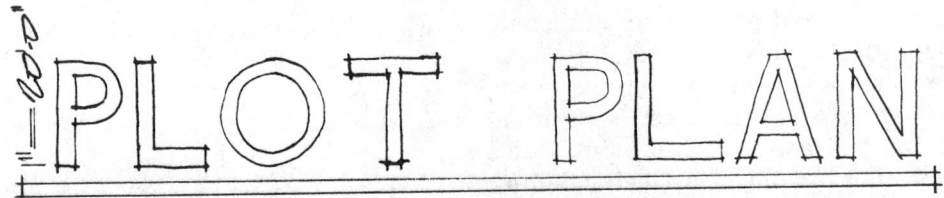

Figure 40-12 Lettering can either be drawn by using mechanical methods, such as a LeRoy Lettering Guide, rub-ons, or with freehand techniques.

Elevations

Presentation elevations can be drawn by following the initial layout steps described in Chapter 25. The elevations are usually drawn at the same scale as the floor plan. Once the elevation is drawn with construction lines, the drafter should plan the elements to be included in the presentation. For our example, this will be limited to plants and shading. Care must be taken to ensure that the surroundings in the drawing do not overshadow the main structure.

Plants. Your artistic ability will determine how plants are to be drawn. Rub-on plants are great time savers, but they should not be your only means of representing plants. Because of the expense and limited selection of rub-on plants, you should learn to draw trees and shrubs.

The method of drawing plantings should match the method used to draw the structure. If the elevation is to be drawn as a freehand sketch, or with watercolors, the plants should be drawn with a similar method. No matter the method, plants are typically kept very simple. The area of the country where the structure will be built will determine the types of plants that are shown on the elevation. Figure 40-13 shows common types of trees that can be placed on the elevations. Be sure to use plants that are typically seen in your area.

Start the presentation elevations using the same methods used on the working drawings. Sketch the area where the plants will be placed as seen in Figure 40-14. Plants that will be in the foreground should be drawn prior to drawing the structure with finished quality lines. Figure 40-15 shows the foreground planting in place. Once the foreground trees have

been drawn, the material on the elevations can be drawn by following the same steps that were used for the working drawings. The elevation should now resemble the drawing in Figure 40-16.

Shading. Shadows are often used on presentation drawings to show surface changes and help create a sense of realism. Before shadows can be drawn, a light source must be established. A light source should be selected that will give the best presentation. The source of light will be influenced by the shape of the building. This can be seen in Figure 40-17. Even though the sun may strike the structure as shown on the left, so little of the structure is left unshaded that it is hard to determine the appearance of the building. By moving the light source to the other side of the drawing, as seen at the right, more of the features of the building surface are identified.

Once the light source has been selected, the amount of shadow to be seen should be determined. Figure 40-18 shows the effect of moving the light source away from the horizon. The drafter should determine where shadows will be created and the amount of shade that will be created. This can be done by projecting a line from the light source across the surface to be shaded as seen in Figure 40-19. If you are not happy with the amount of shade, raise or lower the light source. Once the first shadow is projected, the proportions of the other shadows must be maintained. Be sure and use a very light line as you are lining out the location of shadows.

Shade can be drawn using several different methods. Figure 40-20 shows common methods of using graphite or ink. Determine the method of shading you will be using and then lay out the area where the shadows will be placed. The final drawing pro-

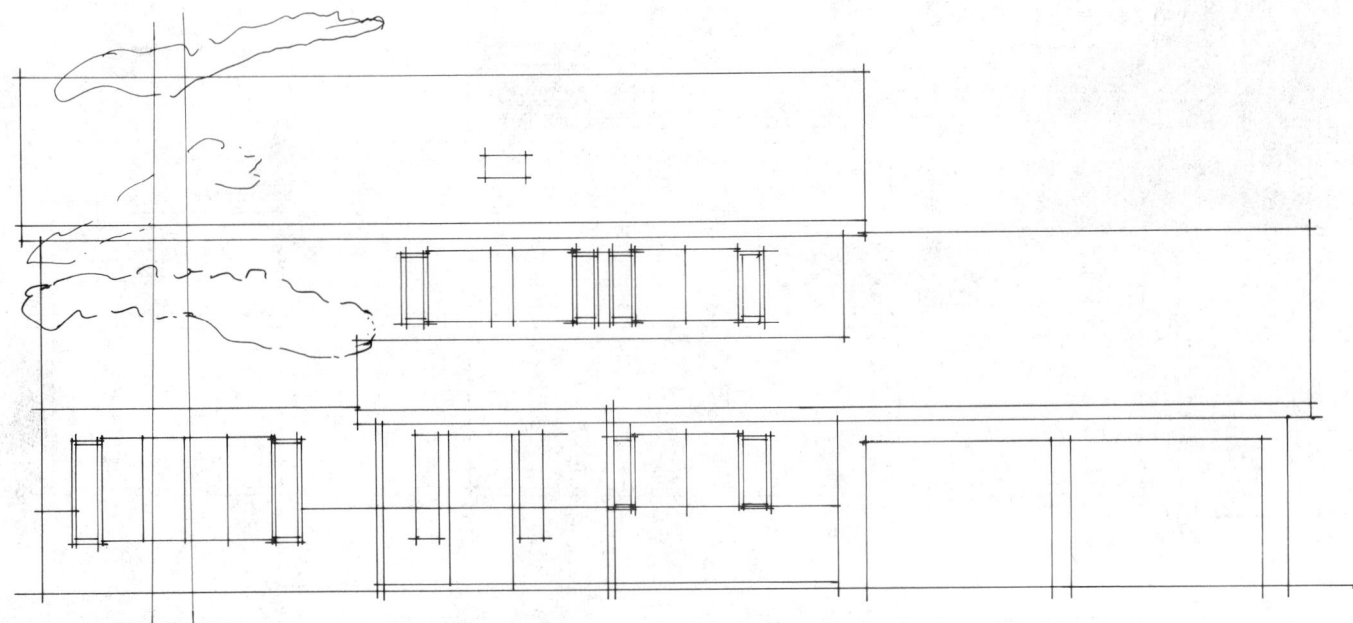

Figure 40–13 Common types of trees typically placed on presentation elevations. Trees should be simple and not distract from the structure. *Courtesy Home Building Plan Service, Inc.; Home Planners, Inc.; and Piercy & Barclay Designers, Inc.*

Figure 40–14 With the elevation drawn with construction lines, trees in the foreground should be drawn. Be sure to draw trees that grow in the vicinity of where the structure will be built.

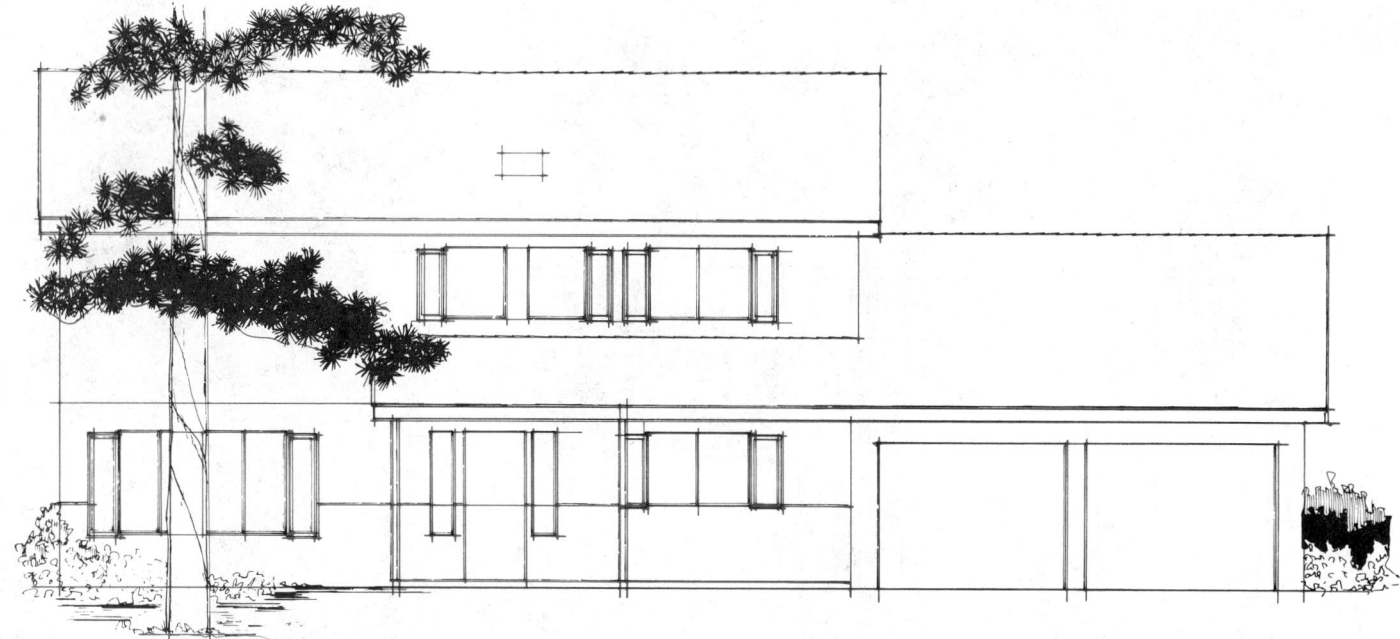

Figure 40–15 Plantings that will be in the foreground should be drawn before drawing the elevation.

Figure 40–16 The presentation elevation can be completed using similar steps to those used to draw the working elevations of Chapter 25.

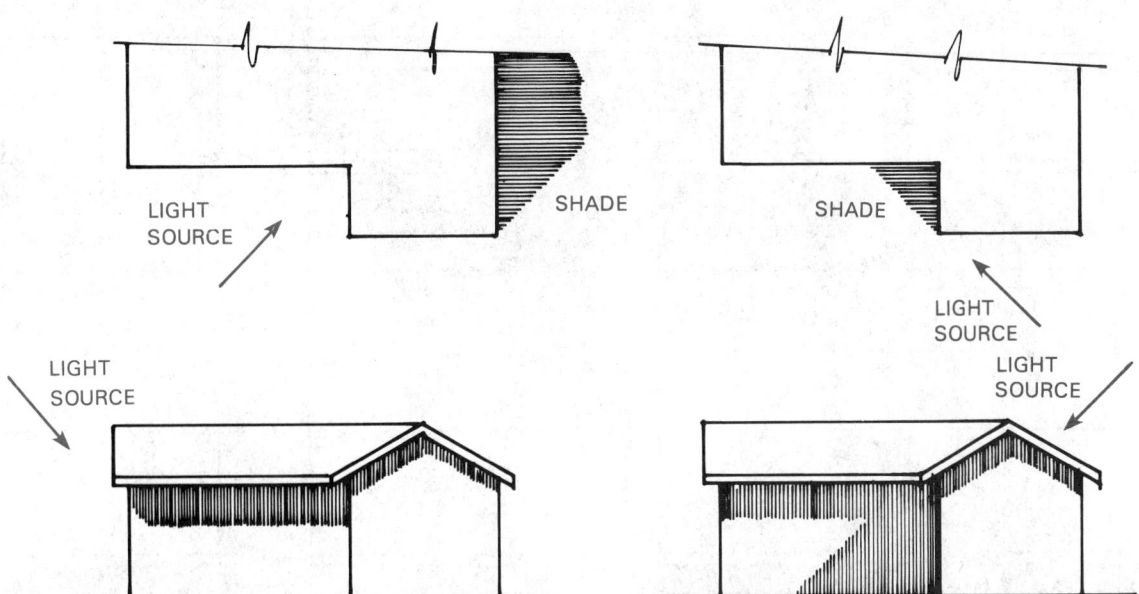

Figure 40–17 The shape of the structure will influence the selection of the light source. Select a source that will accent depth but will not dominate a surface.

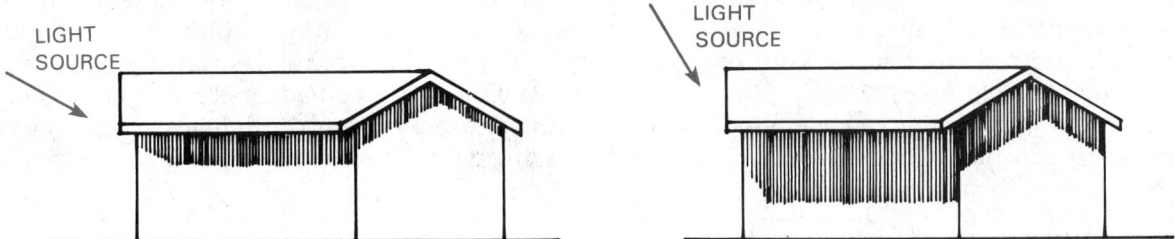

Figure 40–18 As the light source is moved above the horizon line, the depth of the shadow will be increased.

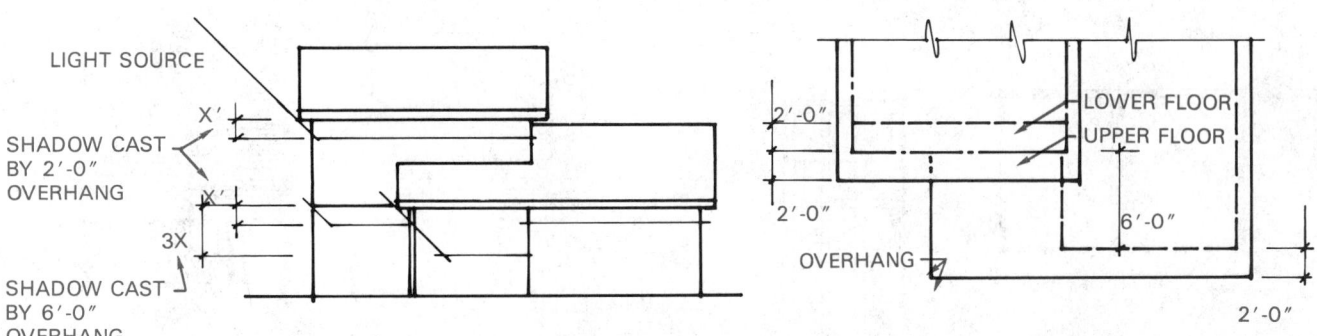

Figure 40–19 Shadows are placed by determining a light source. The depth of the shadow can be determined by the illustrator. Select a depth that does not cover important information. Once the first shadow has been drawn, keep other shadows in proportion. Keep shadow outlines very light.

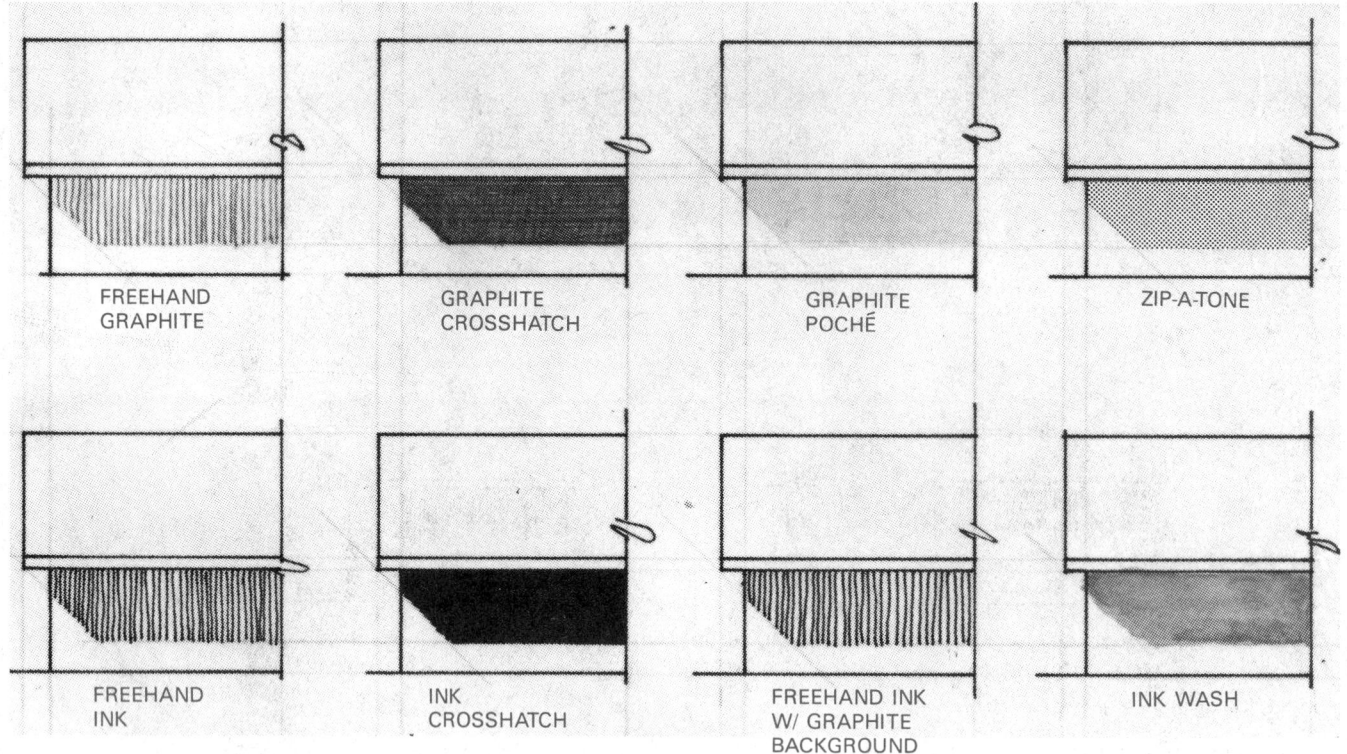

Figure 40–20 Shading can be drawn using several methods.

cedure is to draw the small shadows created by changes in surface material. Figure 40–21 shows common areas that should receive shading. Your drawing should now resemble Figure 40–22.

With all material now drawn and rendered, basic materials should be specified. Complete specifications

do not need to be given for the products to be used but general specifications should be included. For example, on the working elevations in Chapter 25, the roofing was specified as 235 lb composition shingles over ½ in. ply and 15 lb felt. On the presentation drawing only the basic material of 235 lb composition

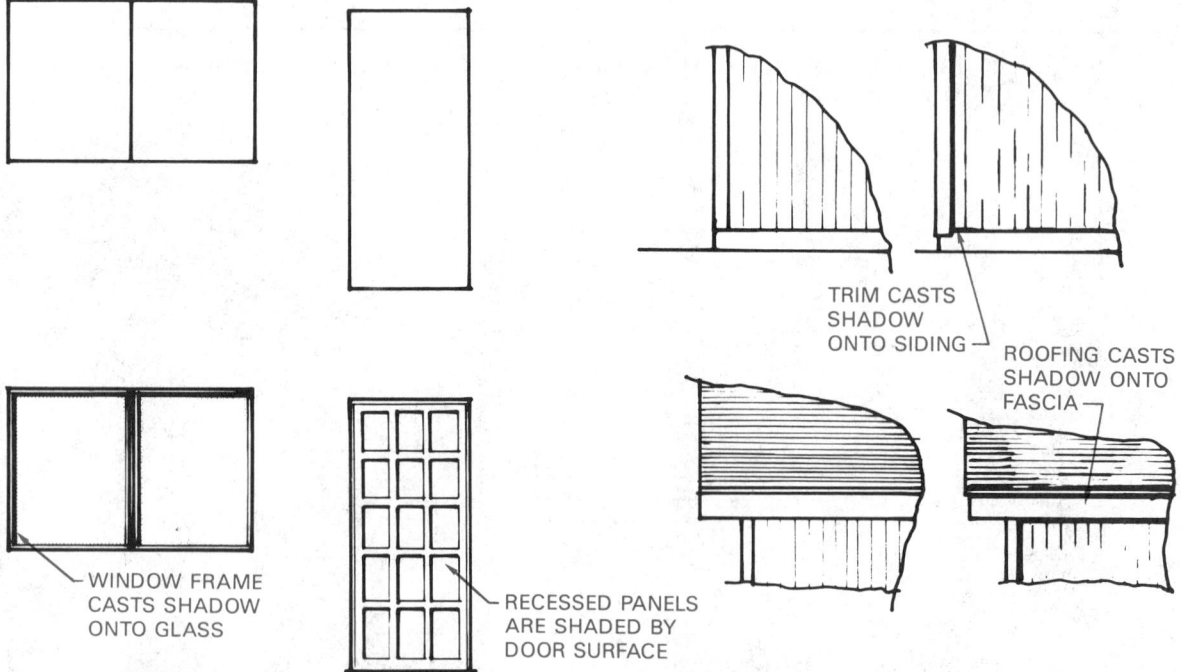

Figure 40–21 Shading can affect the realism of a drawing. Shadows will be cast at each surface change.

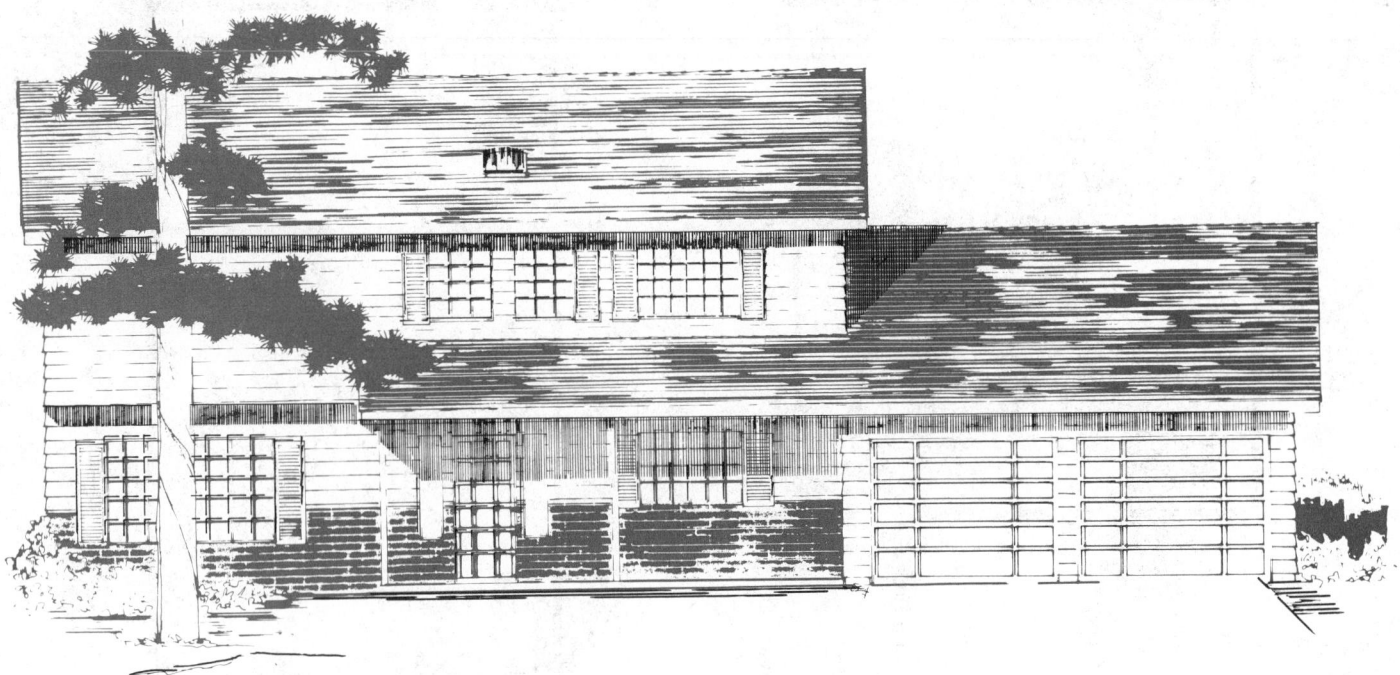

Figure 40–22 The presentation elevation with shadows applied. Shadows were drawn with ink on a graphite background.

shingles needs to be specified. Figure 40–23 shows examples of notes that are often placed on the elevations.

Floor Plan

The use of the presentation floor plan will determine the scale at which it will be drawn. If the plan is to be mounted and displayed, the layout space will determine the scale to be used. When the plan will be reproduced, plans are typically drawn at a scale of either ¼″ = 1′–0″ or ⅛″ = 1′–0″ and then photographically reduced. The presentation floor plan can be drawn using many of the same steps that were described in Chapter 20. Figure 40–24 shows

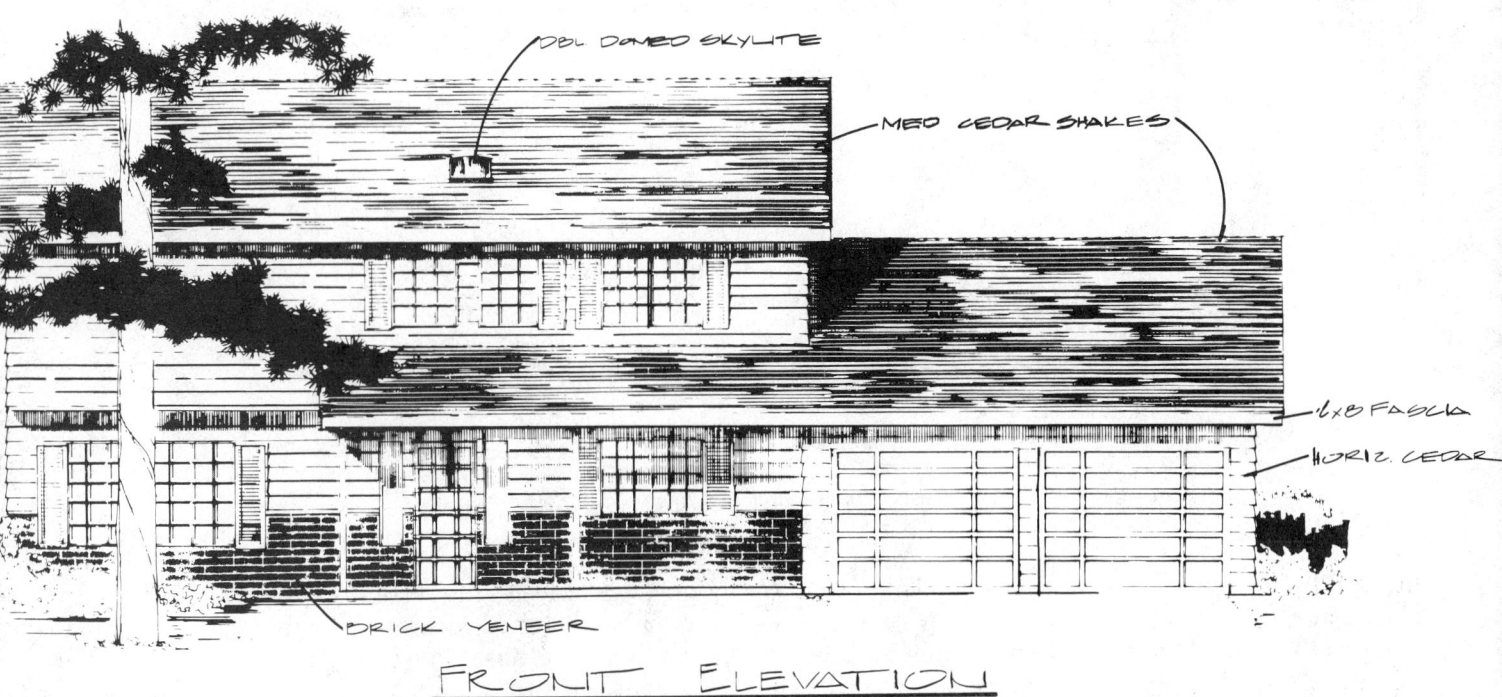

FRONT ELEVATION
1/4″ ——— 1′-0″

Figure 40–23 Notes are added to the presentation elevation to explain major surface materials but are not as specific as the notes on the working elevation.

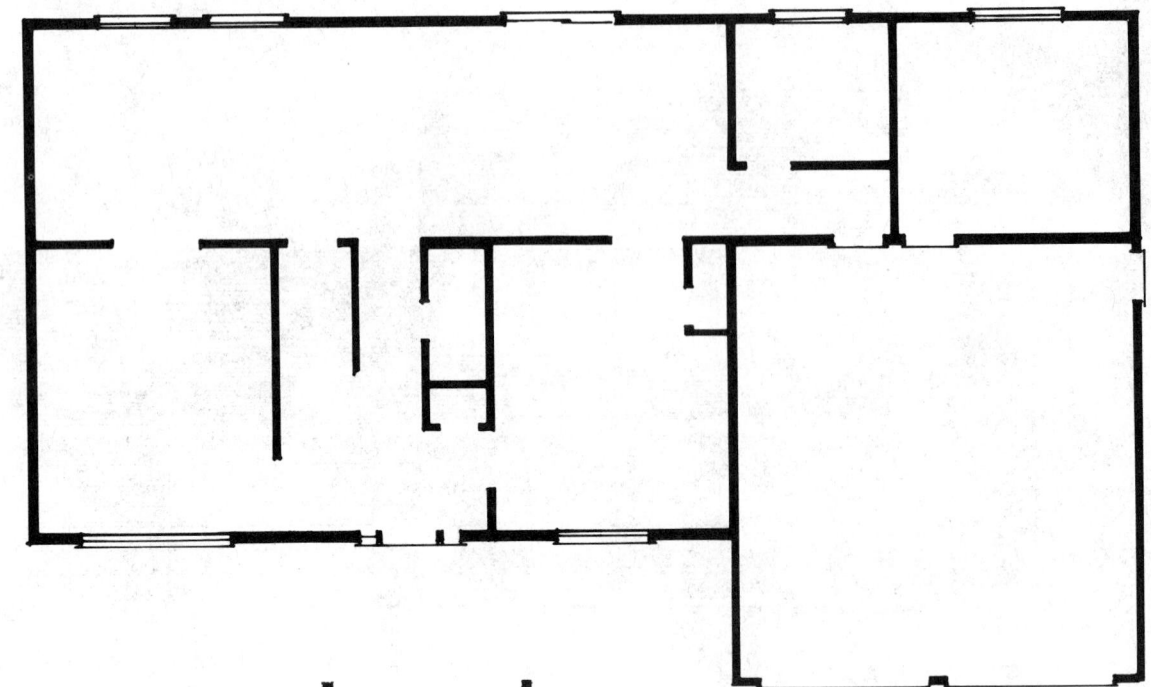

Figure 40–24 The presentation floor plan is drawn using layout procedures similar to those for the working floor plan in Chapter 20.

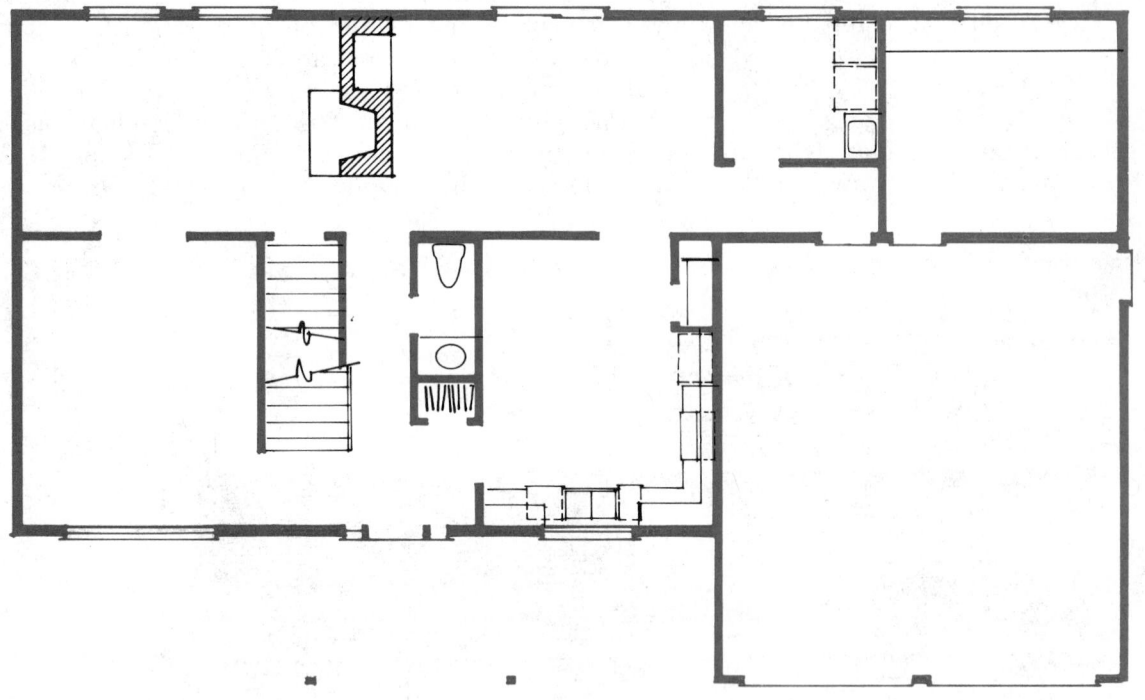

Figure 40–25 With the walls, doors, and windows drawn, the cabinets, stairs, and other interior features can be added.

the wall layout for floor plan for the house presented in Chapter 20.

Once the walls are drawn, the symbols for plumbing and electrical appliances can be drawn. Closets and storage areas are usually represented on the floor plan. These symbols can be seen in Figure 40–25. Furniture is often shown on the floor plan to help show possible living arrangements. Furniture can either be sketched, drawn with templates, or put in place with rub-ons. Figure 40–26 shows the floor plan with the furniture added.

When brick, stone, or tile is used for a floor covering, it is often shown on the floor plan. A directional arrow may be shown on a floor plan to

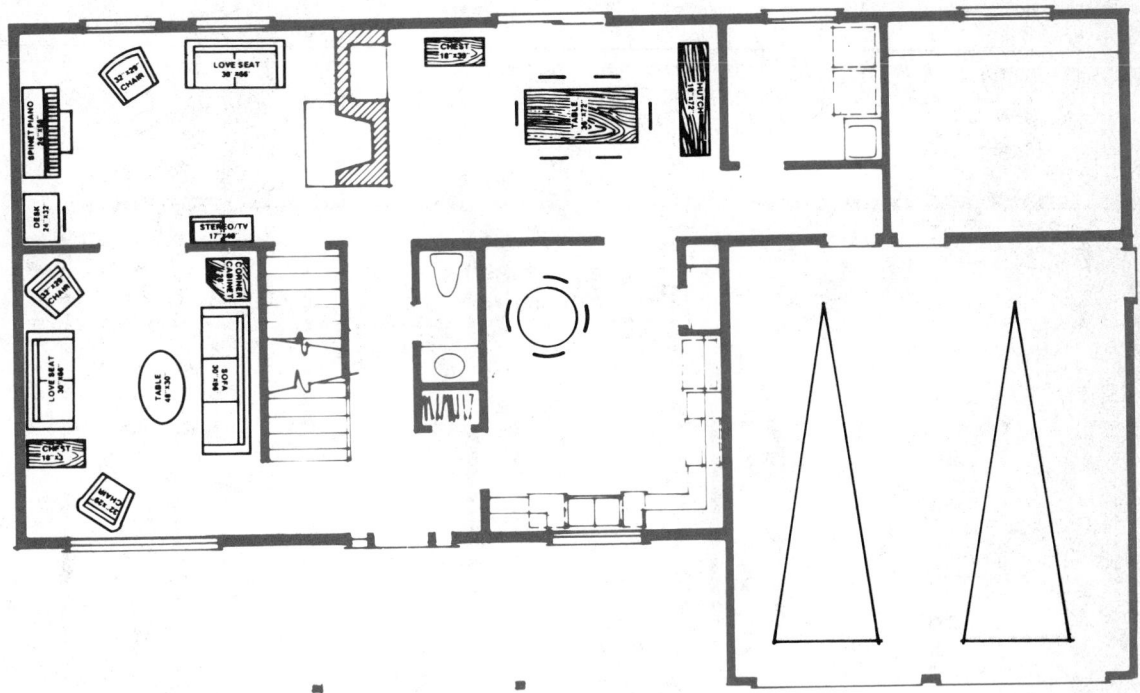

Figure 40–26 Furniture is often shown on the floor plan to help visualize how interior space can be used.

help orient the viewer to the position of the sun or to surrounding landmarks. The symbols for brick and tile floor covering have been added to the floor plan of Figure 40–27.

Written specifications on the floor plan are usually limited to room types and sizes, appliances, and general titles. Figure 40–28 shows the completed presentation floor plan for the plan that was presented in Chapter 20.

Plot Plan

The plot plan can be drawn by following many of the steps of Chapter 39. Once the lot and structure have been outlined, walks, driveways, decks, and pools should be drawn. Figure 40–29 shows the plot plan in the initial layout stage. The lot lines are drawn in the same manner as the lines on the work-

ing plot plan. Once the structure is located, plantings and walkways are usually indicated on the plan as shown in Figure 40–30. As with the other types of presentation drawings, basic sizes are specified on the plot plan as shown on Figure 40–31.

Sections

Section presentation drawings are made by using the same methods described in Chapters 29 and 30. Sections are usually drawn at a scale similar to the presentation floor plan. The initial section layout for the house of Chapter 20 can be seen in Figure 40–32. Lines of sun angles at various times of the year and lines of sight are typically indicated on the section. Room names and ceiling heights are also specified on the section. Methods of presenting this type of information can be seen in Figure 40–33.

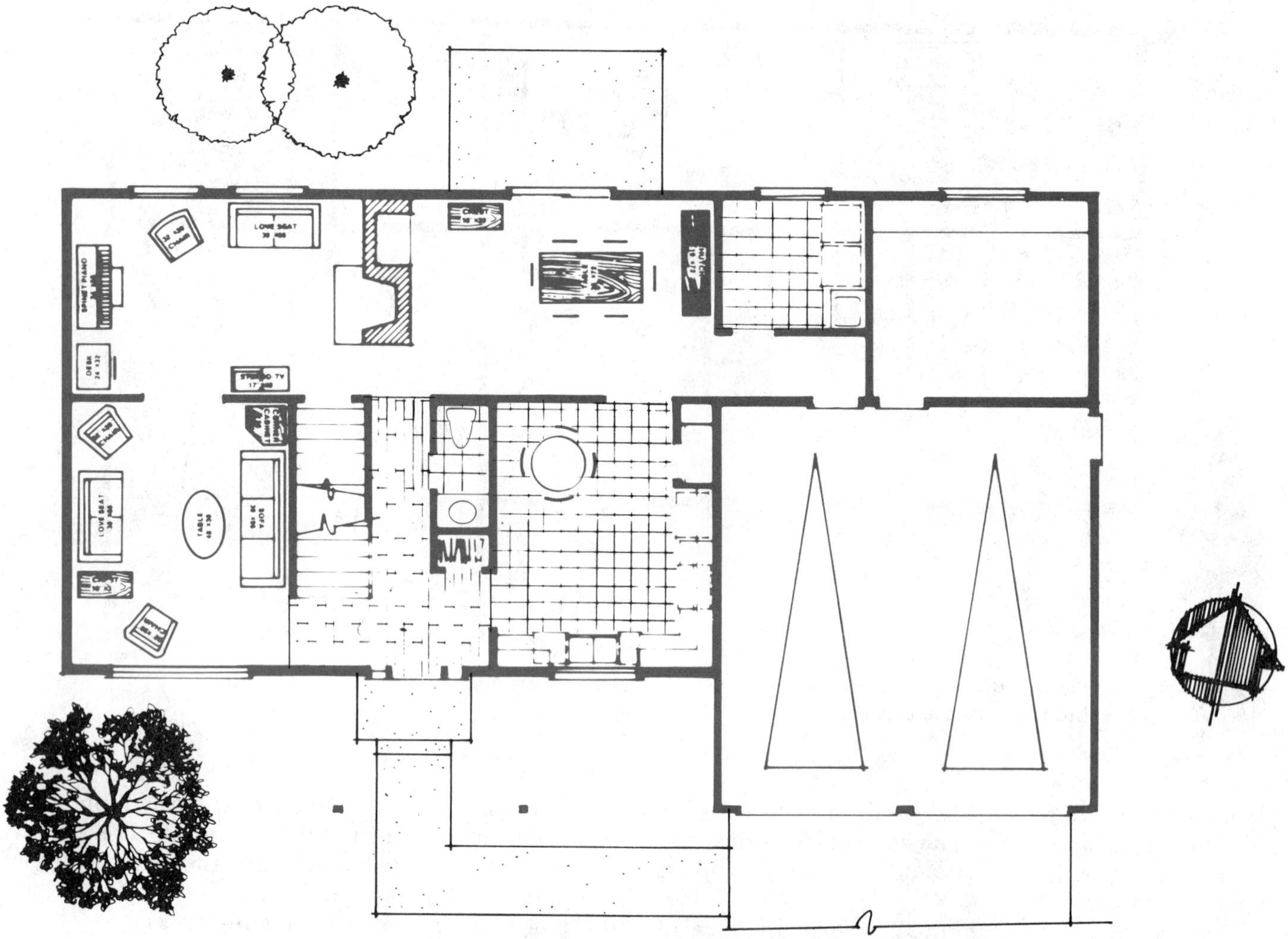

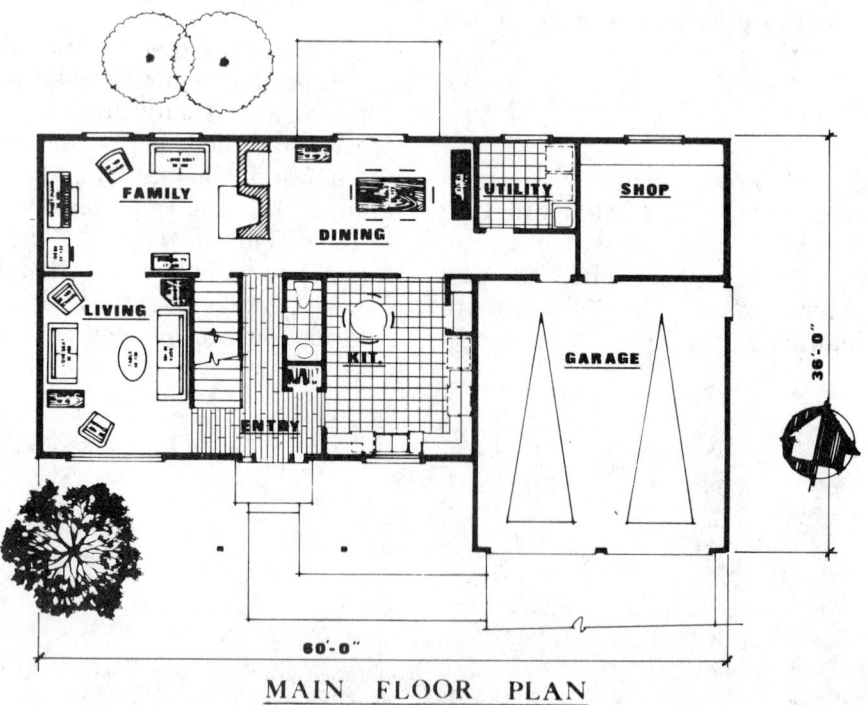

Figure 40–27 Floor materials are drawn to help clarify the design.

MAIN   FLOOR   PLAN

Figure 40–28 The completed floor plan is a useful tool for presenting the arrangement of interior space.

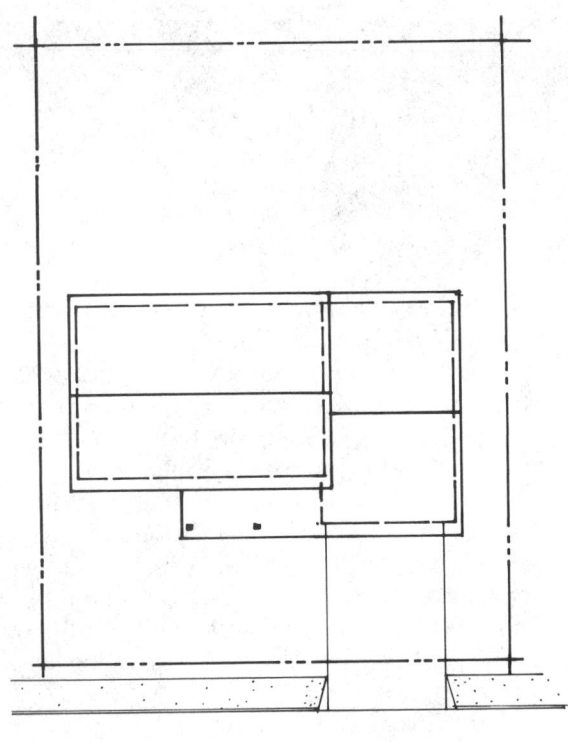

Figure 40–29 The presentation plot plan is drawn using procedures similar to those that were used in Chapter 39 with the working plot plan.

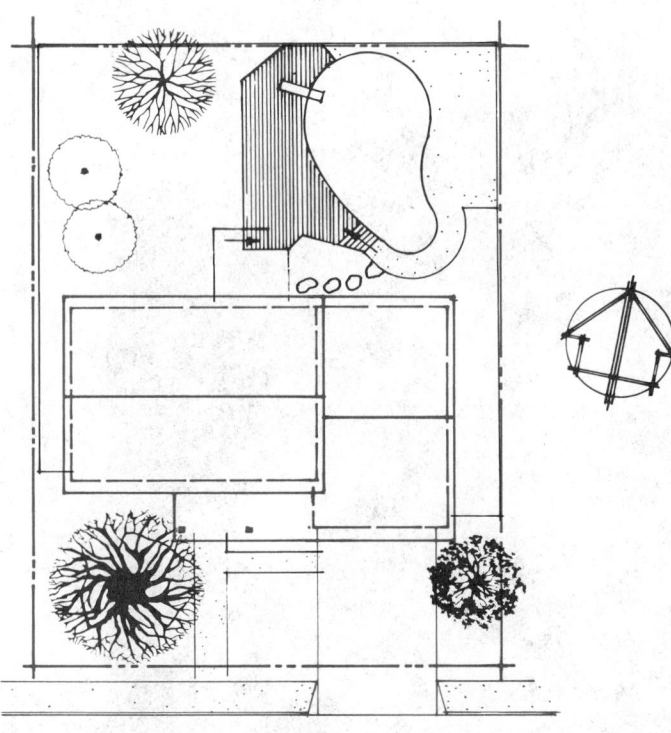

Figure 40–30 Landscaping, decks, and pools should be shown on the presentation plot plan to show how the structure will blend with its surroundings.

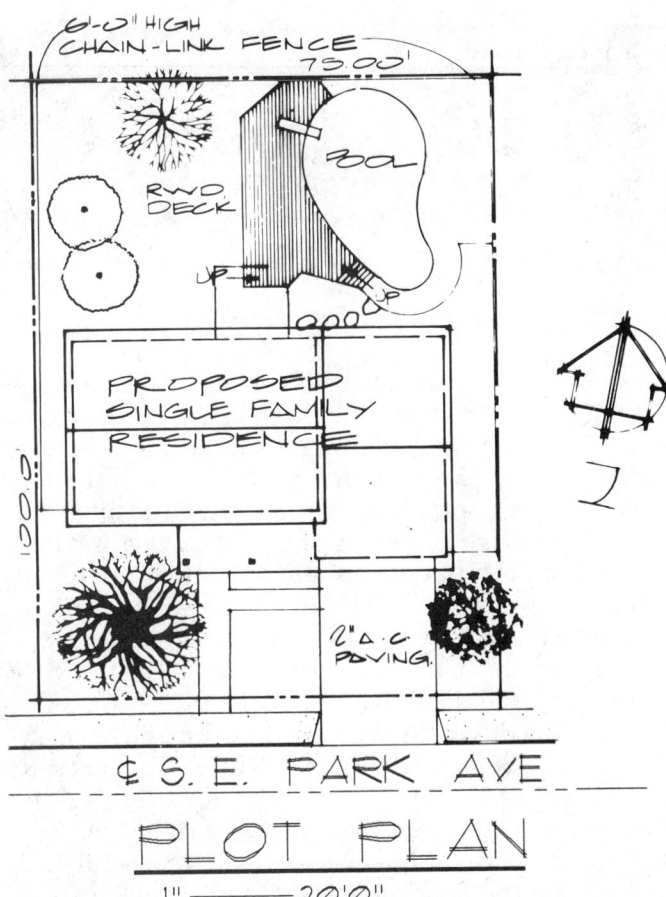

Figure 40–31 Major items should be specified on the plot plan to help the viewer better understand the project.

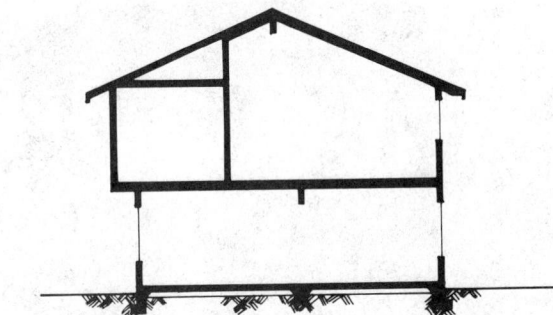

Figure 40–32 The initial layout of the section can be drawn using procedures similar to those that were used for the layout of the working section in Chapters 29 and 30.

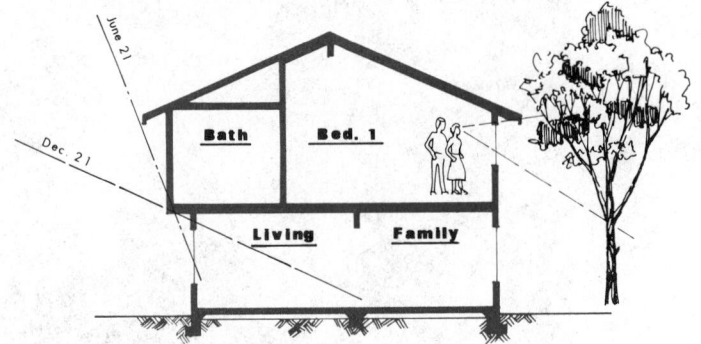

Figure 40–33 The presentation section is often used to show sun angles and views. Label rooms so that the viewer will understand which areas are being shown.

CADD
applications

USING CADD TO MAKE PRESENTATION DRAWINGS

When CADD is used to draw elevations (Chapters 24 and 25) the material representations look so realistic that they may also be used as presentation drawings. Most architectural drafters even add such things as trees and cars to the drawings, because with CADD these items can be placed on the drawing in seconds. You simply pick a symbol from the tablet menu library, and add it to the elevation in the desired location. This process is so easy that elevation drawings often contain such presentation features as landscaping and shading.

Preparing three dimensional (3-D) drawings is easy with CADD. Some of the powerful CADD packages, such as AutoCAD's AEC Architectural, allow you to automatically generate a 3-D drawing from the floor plan layout. Wall and header heights are established as you draw the floor plan. When it is complete, you can view the drawing in 3-D from any selected point

in space. You can change the viewpoint until you find the view that displays the building best. Many architectural firms have renderers on staff who prepare artistic presentation drawings. These people are needed to provide customers with a realistic presentation of a completed building. Some architects have found that a combination of 3-D CADD presentation of the building and the artistic addition of landscaping features create beautiful presentation drawings in a shorter period of time. The 3-D presentation of a multifamily housing project with the building drawn with CADD and the landscaping drawn by an artist is shown in Figure 1.

There are also CADD rendering programs available that let you turn 3-D line drawings into realistically shaded pictures. AutoSHADE by Autodesk is one such program. You can create a drawing that looks like a photographer's image by adjusting camera and lighting locations. You can produce both color and black-and-white drawings with this process.

Figure 1 CADD 3-D representation.

PRESENTATION DRAWINGS TEST

DIRECTIONS

Answer the questions with short complete statements or drawings as needed on an 8½ × 11 drawing sheet as follows:

1. Use ⅛ in. guidelines for all lettering.
2. Letter your name, Presentation Drawings Test, and the date at the top of the sheet.
3. Letter the question number and provide the answer. You do not need to write out the question.
4. Do all lettering with vertical uppercase architectural letters. Answers may be prepared on a word processor if appropriate with course guidelines.
5. Your grade will be based on correct answers and quality of line technique.

QUESTIONS

1. What is the use of presentation drawings?
2. What is the major difference between the information provided on a presentation drawing and a working drawing?
3. What are some of the factors that might influence the selection of the person who will draw the presentation drawings?
4. List and describe the major information found on each type of presentation plan.
5. What type of drawing is best used to show the shape and style of a structure?
6. List four different media that are often used for presentation drawings.
7. Which drawing material is most often used for presentation drawings?
8. What common methods are used to add color to a drawing?
9. At what scale are sections usually drawn?
10. What scale is typically used when a floor plan will be reproduced photographically?

Chapter 41
Perspective Drawing Techniques

ALL OF the drawings that you have done so far have been orthographic projections which have allowed the size and shape of a structure to be accurately presented in a drawing. Orthographic projection is a great method for conveying information, but is quite unlike what the eye would see when viewing the project. To develop a drawing similar to what is seen when looking at the project requires the use of perspective drawing methods. Perspective drawing methods present structures very much as they appear in their natural setting. Figure 41–1 presents two elevations for a residence. This same residence can be seen in a perspective drawing in Figure 41–2, and in a photograph in Figure 41–3. As you can see, the perspective drawing resembles the photo much more than does the working drawing.

 TYPES OF PERSPECTIVE DRAWINGS

Three methods are used to draw perspective drawings. They are the three-, two-, and one-point methods. The three-point method is primarily used to draw very tall multilevel structures as seen in Figure 41–4. This method will not be covered in this text.

Figure 41–2 is an example of a two-point perspective. Notice that all horizontal lines merge into the horizon. This method of perspective drawing is the most typical one used on presentation drawings. With this method at least two surfaces of the structure will be seen. Two-point perspective is generally used to present the exterior views of a structure, but the technique can also be used to present interior shapes as seen in Figure 41–5.

The one-point perspective method is used primarily for presenting interior space layouts. Figure 41–6 shows an example of an interior space drawn using the one-point perspective method. Notice that all lines merge into one central point. The one-point method can also be used to present exterior views such as courtyards.

PERSPECTIVE TERMS

In the drawing of perspective views, six terms will be used frequently. These terms are the ground line, station point, horizon line, vanishing points, picture plane, and the true-height line. The relationship of these lines, points, and planes can be seen in Figure 41–7.

The Ground Line (G.L.)

The ground line represents the horizontal surface at the base of the perspective drawing. It is this surface that gives the viewer a base from which to judge heights. The drafter uses the ground line as a base when making vertical measurements.

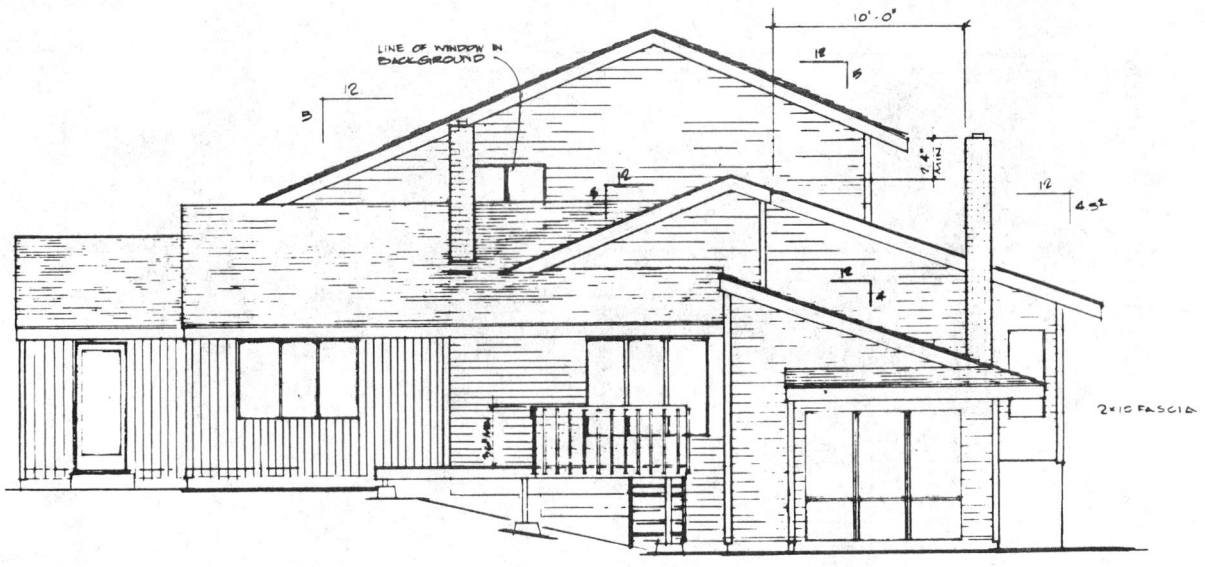

WEST ELEVATION

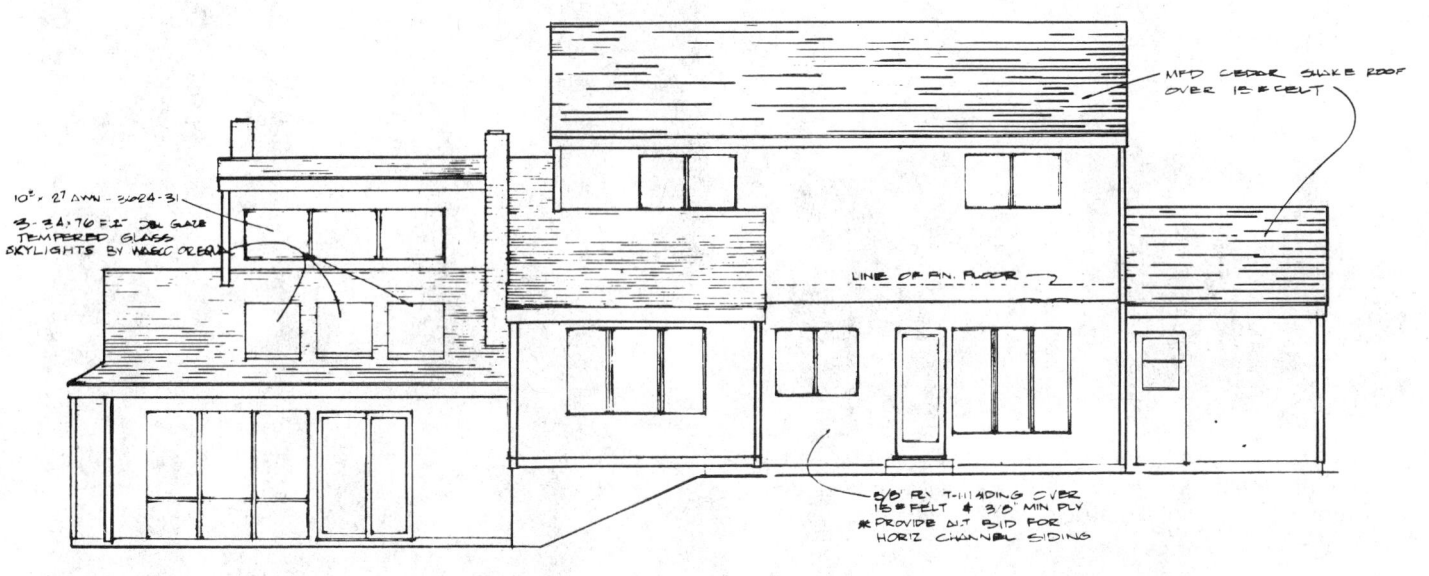

SOUTH ELEVATION

Figure 41–1 Orthographic drawings are used to present information regarding the construction of a structure. Many people outside the construction field have a difficult time interpreting those drawings. *Courtesy Jeff's Residential Designs.*

Figure 41–2 A two-point perspective is a drawing method that closely resembles a photograph. *Courtesy Jeff's Residential Designs.*

Figure 41–3 Many people who are unable to interpret orthographic drawings are able to visualize a project when they see a photograph. *Courtesy Jeff's Residential Designs.*

Figure 41–4 A three-point perspective drawing method is used to present tall structures. *Courtesy Olympia & York Properties, Inc.*

Figure 41–5 Although the two-point perspective is primarily used to present the exterior of a structure, it can also be used to present large interior areas. *Courtesy Paul Franks.*

Figure 41–6 The one-point perspective method is used to present interior views of a structure. Notice that all horizontal lines appear to converge at one point. *Courtesy Paul Franks.*

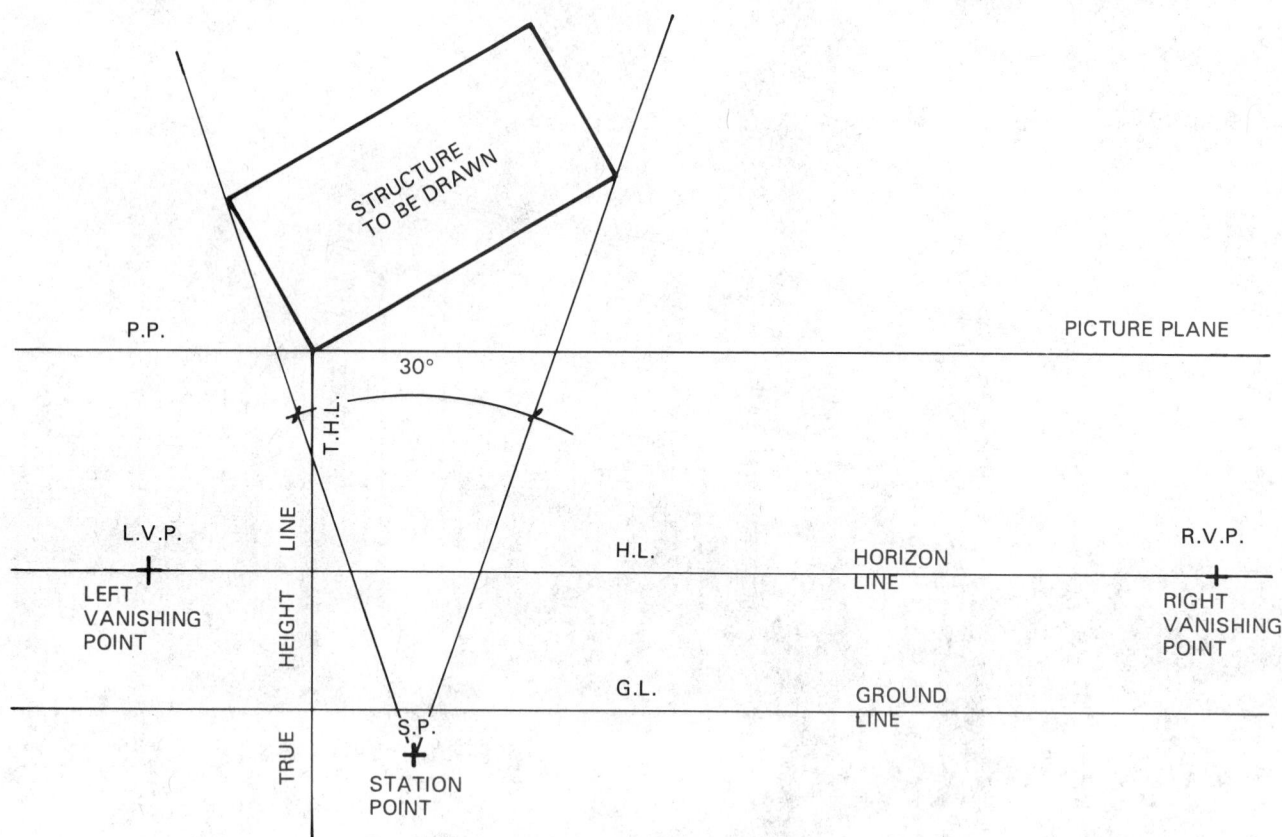

TWO-POINT PERSPECTIVE

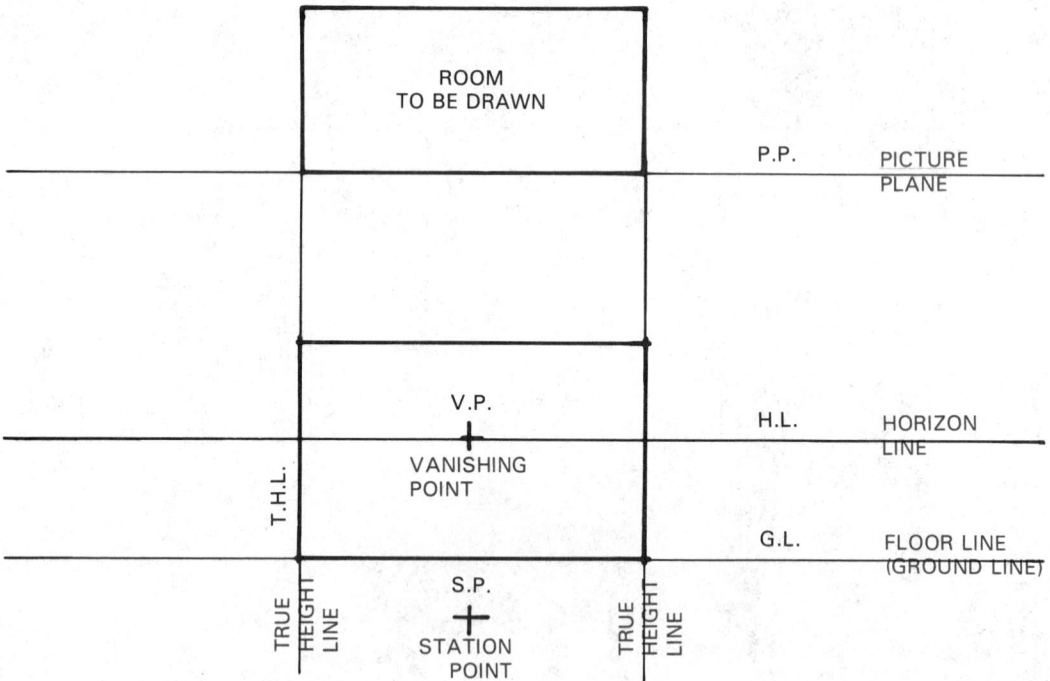

ONE-POINT PERSPECTIVE

Figure 41–7 When drawing perspectives, six terms will be used repeatedly. These include the ground line, station point, horizon line, vanishing points, picture plane, and the true-height line.

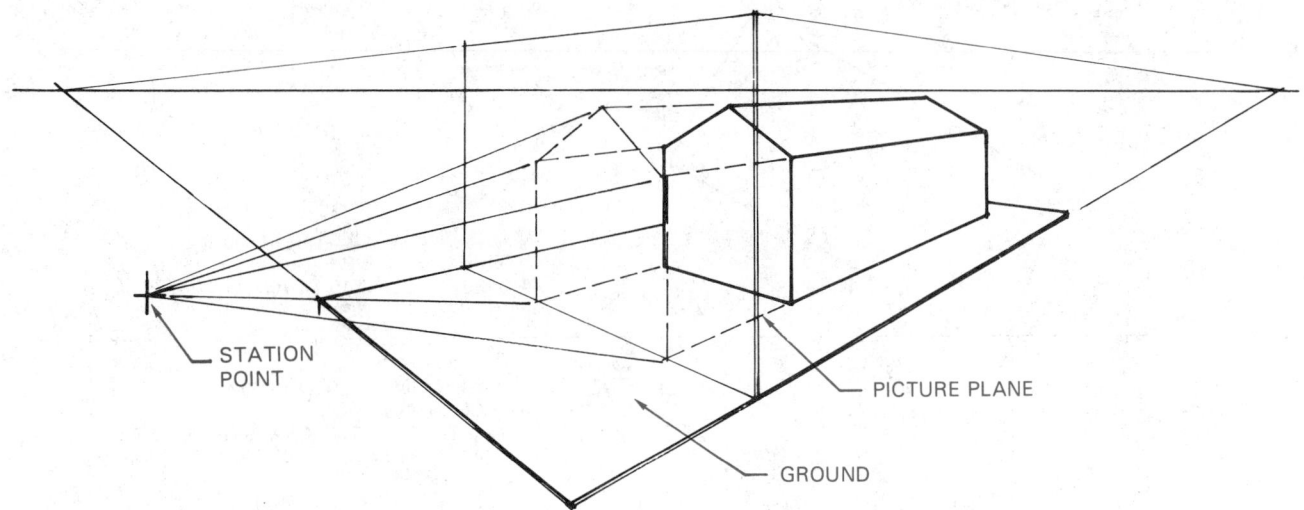

Figure 41-8 The station point represents the location of the viewer. All points on the floor plan will converge at the station point (S.P.).

The Station Point (S.P.)

The station point represents the position of the observer's eye. Figure 41-8 shows the theoretical positioning of the station point. The station point will be used in a manner similar to a vanishing point. Since the S.P. represents the location of the observer, all measurements of width will converge at the station point.

Figure 41-9 shows the method used to find the horizontal location of a surface. A straight line is projected from each corner of the surface in the plan view to the S.P. From the intersection of each line with the picture plane, another line is projected at 90° to the picture plane down to the area where the perspective will be drawn. When a surface extends past the P.P., a line is projected from the S.P. to the surface and then up to the P.P. as shown in Figure 41-10.

The location of the station point will affect the total size of the finished drawing. Figure 41-11 shows the effect of moving the station point in relationship to the picture plane. As the distance between the S.P. and the P.P is decreased, the width of the drawing will be decreased. Likewise as the distance is increased between the S.P. and the P.P., the perspective will become larger.

The station point can also affect the view of each surface to be presented in the perspective drawing. The station point can be placed anywhere on the drawing but is usually placed so that the structure will fit within a cone that is 30° wide. This can be seen in Figure 41-7. As the S.P. is moved in a horizontal direction, the width of each surface to be projected will be affected. Figure 41-12 shows the effect of moving the S.P.

The Horizon Line (H.L.)

The horizon line is drawn parallel to the ground line and represents the intersection of ground and sky. As the distance between the horizon line and ground line is varied, the view of the structure will be greatly affected. Figure 41-13 shows the differences that can be created as the horizon line is varied. The H.L. is usually placed at an eye level of between 5 to 6 ft. It can be placed anywhere on the drawing, depending on the view desired. When placed above the highest point in the elevation, the viewer will be able to look down on the structure. Moving the H.L. above eye level can be very helpful if a roof with an intricate shape needs to be displayed. The H.L. can also be placed below the normal line of vision. This placement will allow the viewer to see items that are normally hidden by eave overhangs. Avoid placing the horizon line at the top or bottom of the object to be drawn.

Vanishing Points (V.P.)

When drawing one- or two-point perspectives, the vanishing point or points will always be on the horizon line. As the structure is drawn, all horizontal lines will converge at the horizon line as seen in Figure 41-14. On a one-point perspective the vanishing point may be placed anywhere on the horizon line. Figure 41-15 shows the effect of changing the location of the vanishing point.

The vanishing points will be on the horizon line in a two-point perspective, but their location will be determined by the location of the station point and the angle of the floor plan to the picture plane. Figure

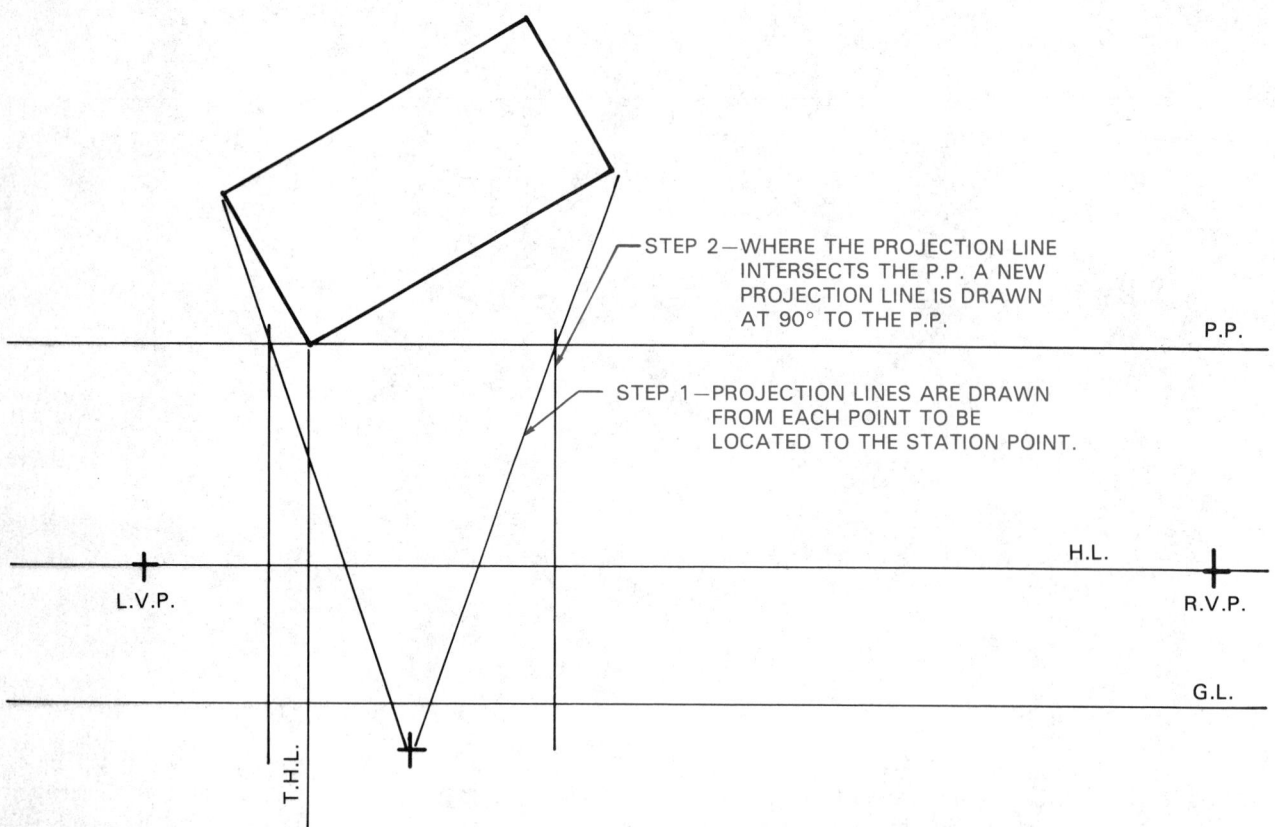

STEP 2—WHERE THE PROJECTION LINE
INTERSECTS THE P.P. A NEW
PROJECTION LINE IS DRAWN
AT 90° TO THE P.P.

STEP 1—PROJECTION LINES ARE DRAWN
FROM EACH POINT TO BE
LOCATED TO THE STATION POINT.

P.P.

H.L.

L.V.P.

R.V.P.

G.L.

T.H.L.

PROJECTING WIDTHS IN TWO-POINT PERSPECTIVE

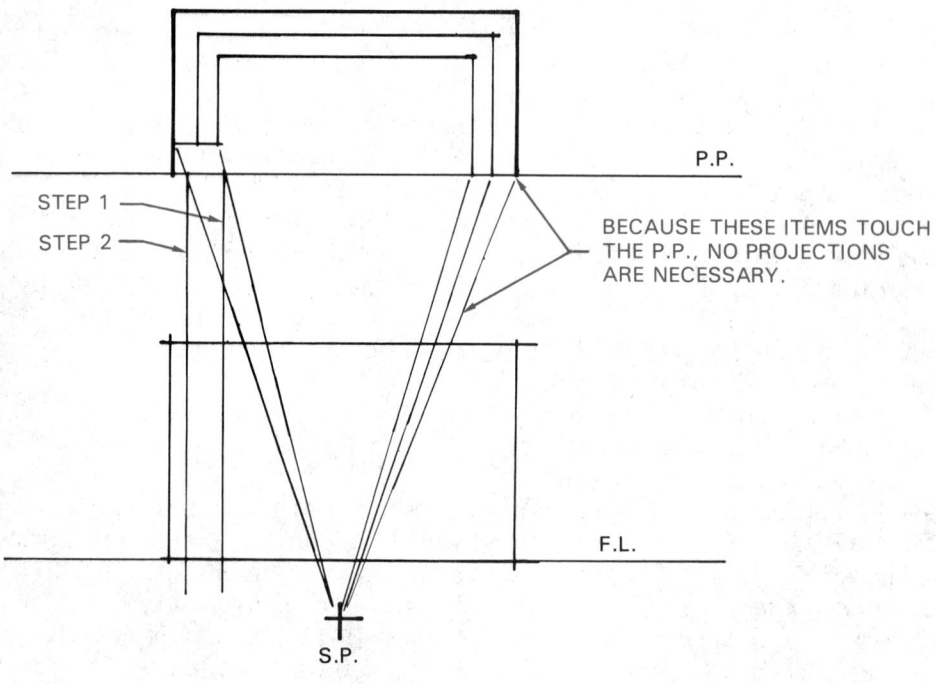

P.P.

STEP 1

STEP 2

BECAUSE THESE ITEMS TOUCH
THE P.P., NO PROJECTIONS
ARE NECESSARY.

F.L.

S.P.

PROJECTING WIDTHS IN ONE-POINT PERSPECTIVE

Figure 41–9 The station point is used to project the width of the object to be drawn.

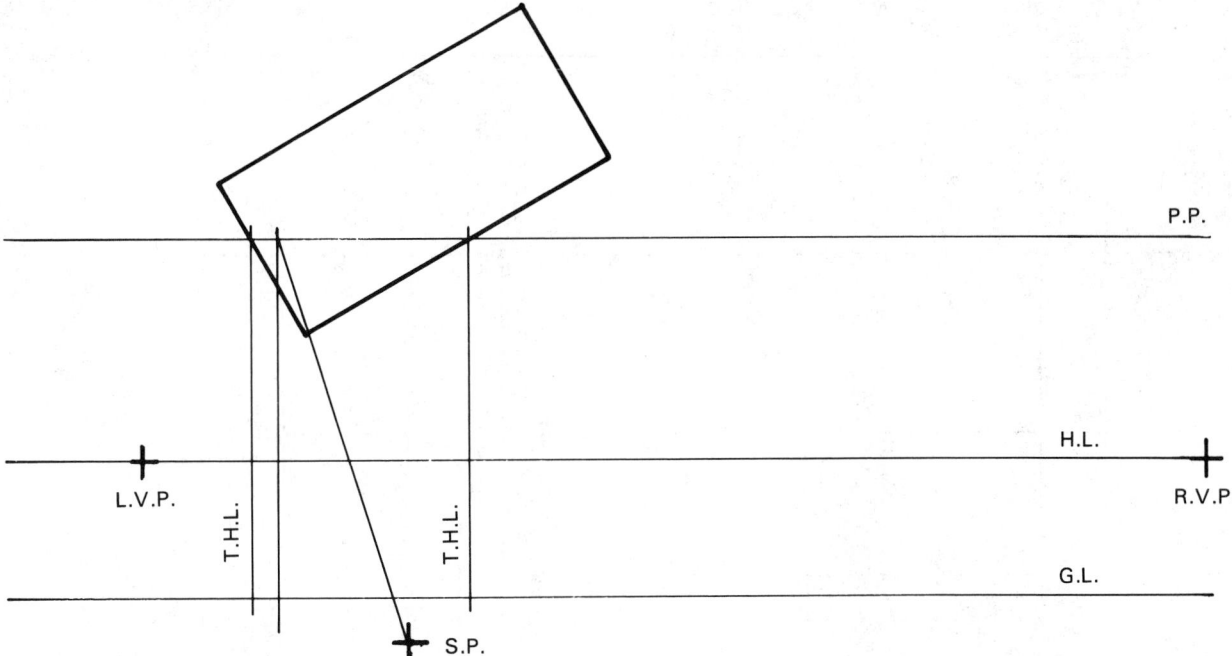

Figure 41–10 When a structure extends past the picture plane, a line is projected from the station point through the point up to the picture plane. From this point on the picture plane, a line, perpendicular to the picture plane, is projected to the drawing area.

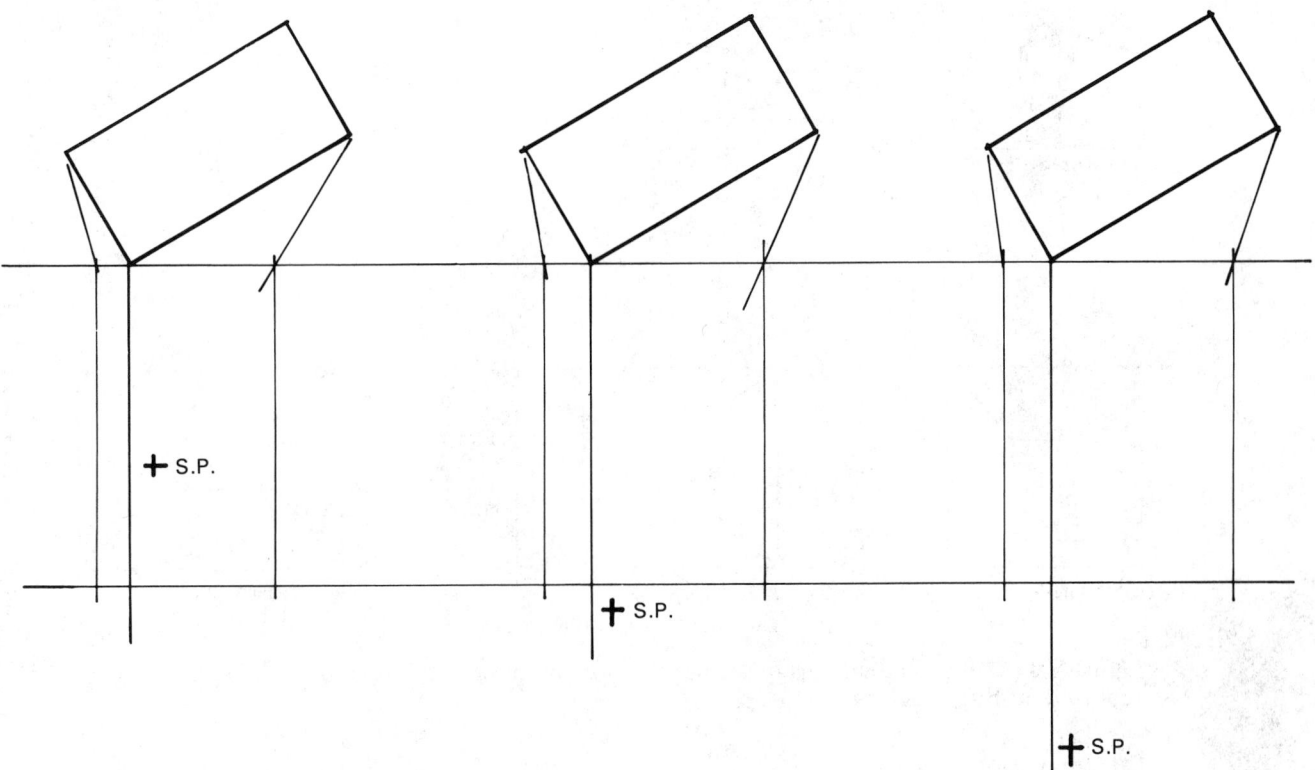

Figure 41–11 As the distance between the picture plane and the station point is increased, the width of the drawing is also increased.

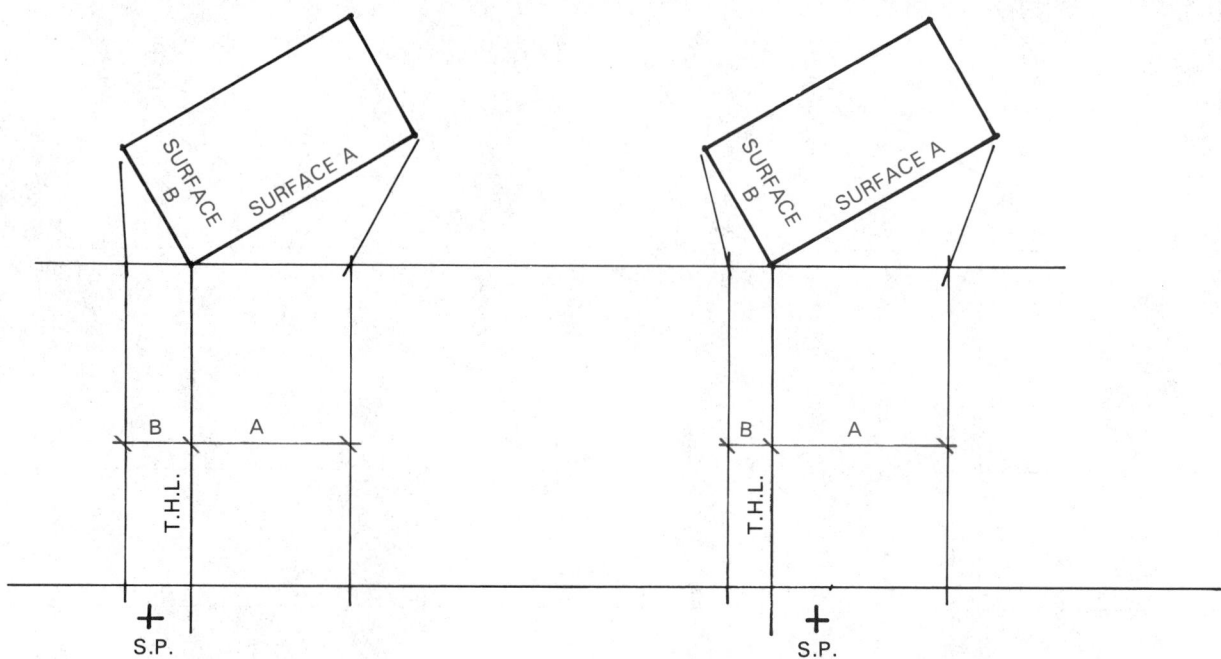

Figure 41–12 As the station point is shifted to the left or right of the true-height line, the width of each surface is affected.

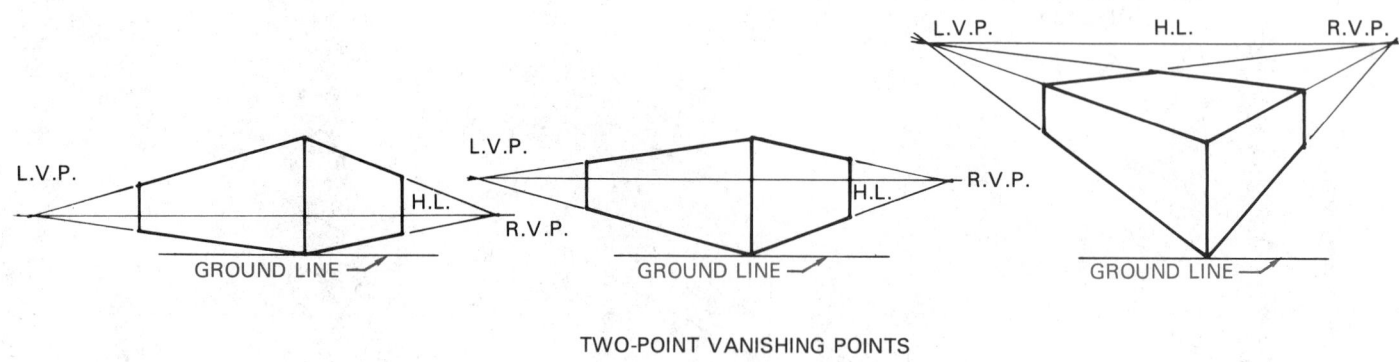

TWO-POINT VANISHING POINTS

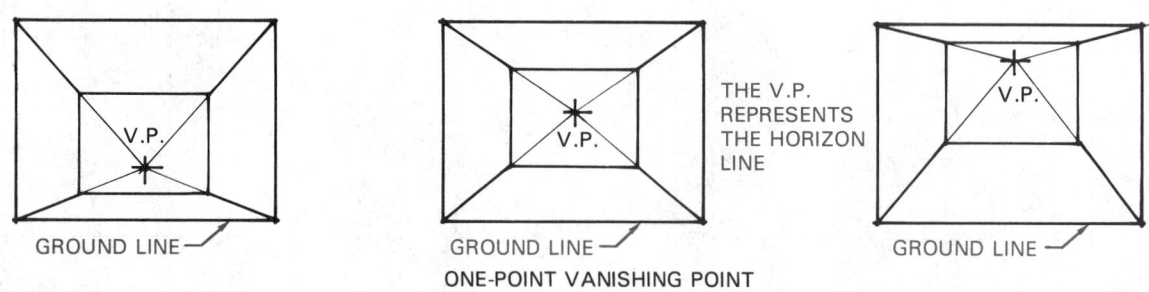

ONE-POINT VANISHING POINT

Figure 41–13 Changing the distance from the horizon line to the ground line affects the view of the structure.

41–16 shows how the vanishing points are established. With the floor plan and S.P. established, lines parallel to the floor plan can be projected from the S.P. These lines are extended from the S.P. until they intersect the P.P. A line at 90° to the P.P. is extended from this intersection down to the horizon line. The point where this line intersects the horizon line forms the vanishing point. Be sure that you project the line from the S.P. all the way to the P.P. A common mistake in the layout is to project the angle directly onto the horizon line. This will result in a perspective that is greatly reduced in size.

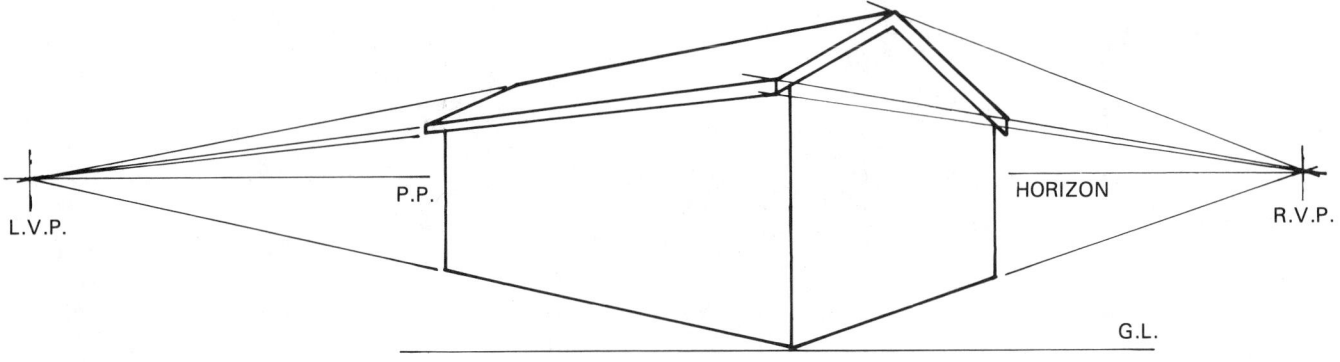

Figure 41–14 In a two-point perspective, all horizontal lines will converge at the vanishing points.

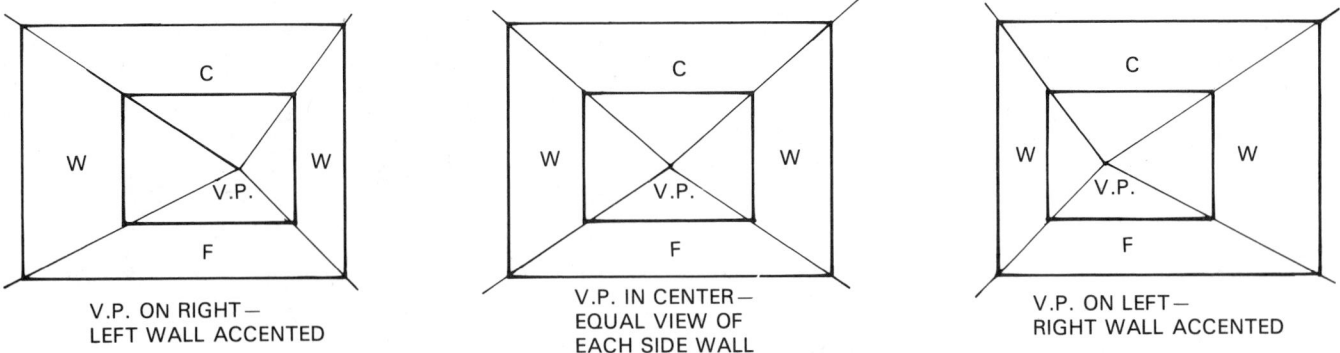

Figure 41–15 In a one-point perspective, the vanishing point may be placed anywhere. As the vanishing point (V.P.) is shifted from side to side, the shape of the walls is changed. The station point (S.P.) should always be kept below the V.P.

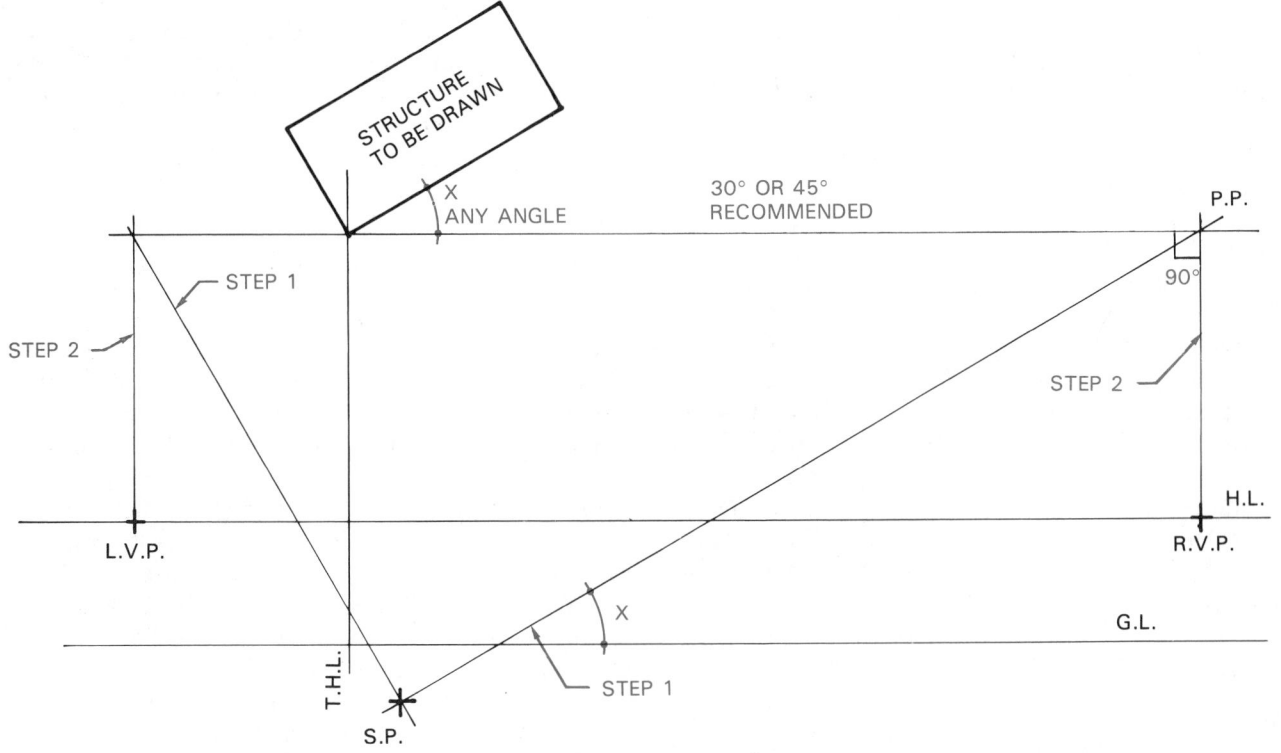

Figure 41–16 The vanishing points on a two-point perspective can be located with two easy steps. Start by projecting lines parallel to the structure from the station point (S.P.) to the picture plane (P.P.). Where these lines intersect the P.P., project a second line down to the horizon line at a 90° angle. Each vanishing point (V.P.) is located where the second projection line intersects the horizon line.

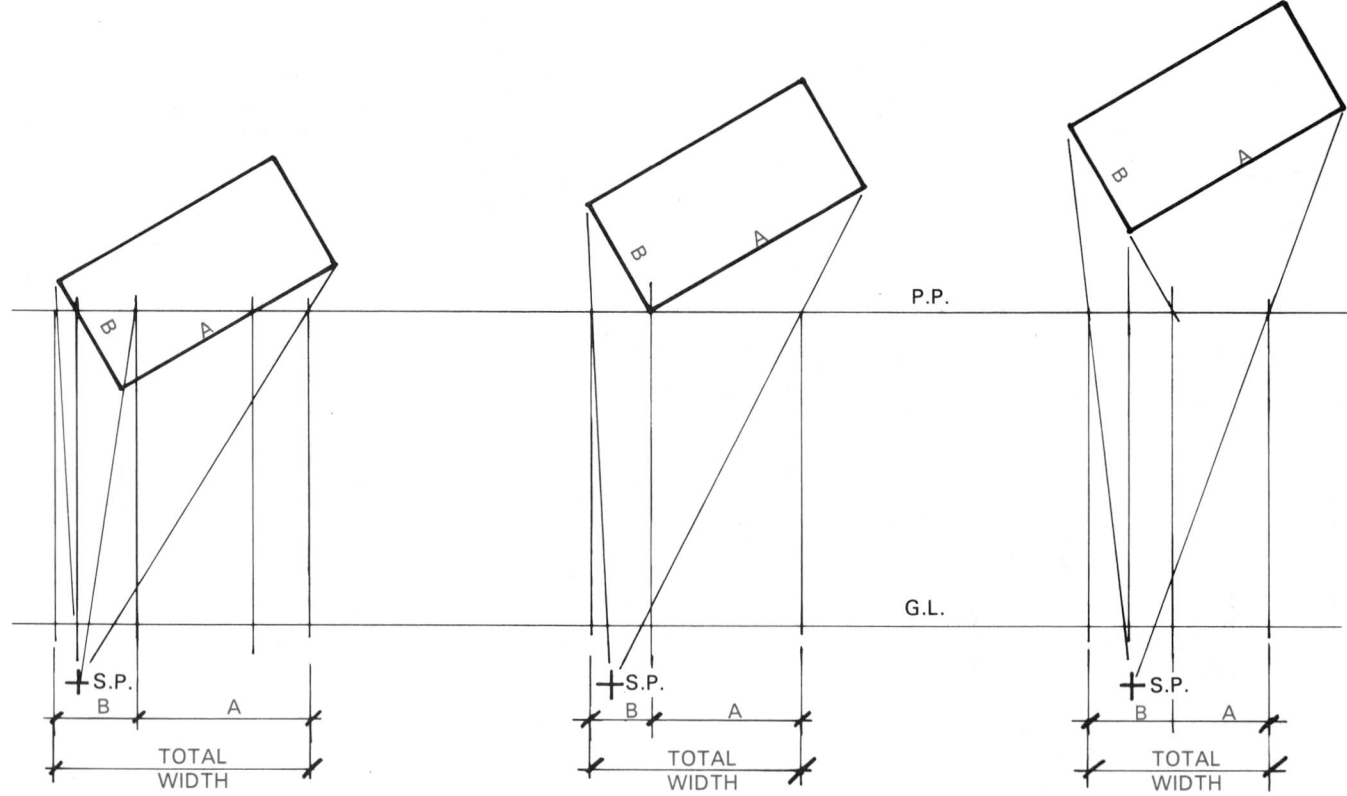

Figure 41–17 Areas of the structure that extend past the picture plane will appear enlarged. When the structure is behind the picture plane (P.P.), its size will be reduced.

Picture Plane (P.P.)

The picture plane represents the plane that the view of the object is projected onto. Figure 41–8 shows how the theory of the picture plane affects a perspective drawing. The picture plane is represented by a horizontal line when drawing perspectives. It is a reference line on which the floor plan of the structure to be drawn is placed. Any point of the structure that is on the picture plane will be drawn in its true size in the perspective drawing. Parts of the structure that are above the picture plane will appear smaller in the perspective drawing, and parts of the structure that lie below the picture plane line will become larger. The relationship of the structure to the picture plane can be seen in Figure 41–17.

The relationship of the floor plan to the picture plane not only controls the height of the structure but also the amount of surface area that will be exposed. As a surface of the floor plan is rotated away from the picture plane its length will be shortened in the perspective drawing. Figure 41–18 shows the effect of rotating the floor plan away from the picture plane.

The structure to be drawn can be placed at any angle to the picture plane. Using an angle of 45°, 30°, or 15° will be helpful in some of the projecting steps

if you use a drafting machine. The key factor in choosing the angle should be the effect desired of the presentation drawing. If one side of the structure is very attractive and the other side to be shown is plain, choose an angle that will shorten the plain side.

True-height Line (T.H.L.)

In the discussion of the picture plane you learned that where the object to be drawn touches the picture plane is the only place where true height can be determined. Often in a two-point perspective only one corner of the structure touches the picture plane line. The line projected from that point is called the true-height line. All other surfaces must have their height projected to this line and then projected to the vanishing point. To save the drafter time, an elevation is used to project the height of the structure to the true-height line. This method can be seen in Figure 41–19.

Projecting true heights tends to be the most difficult aspect of drawing the perspective drawing for the beginning illustrator. ALL heights can be projected from the elevation to the T.H.L. Once projected to the T.H.L., the height must be taken to the vanishing point as shown in Figure 41–20. If the height

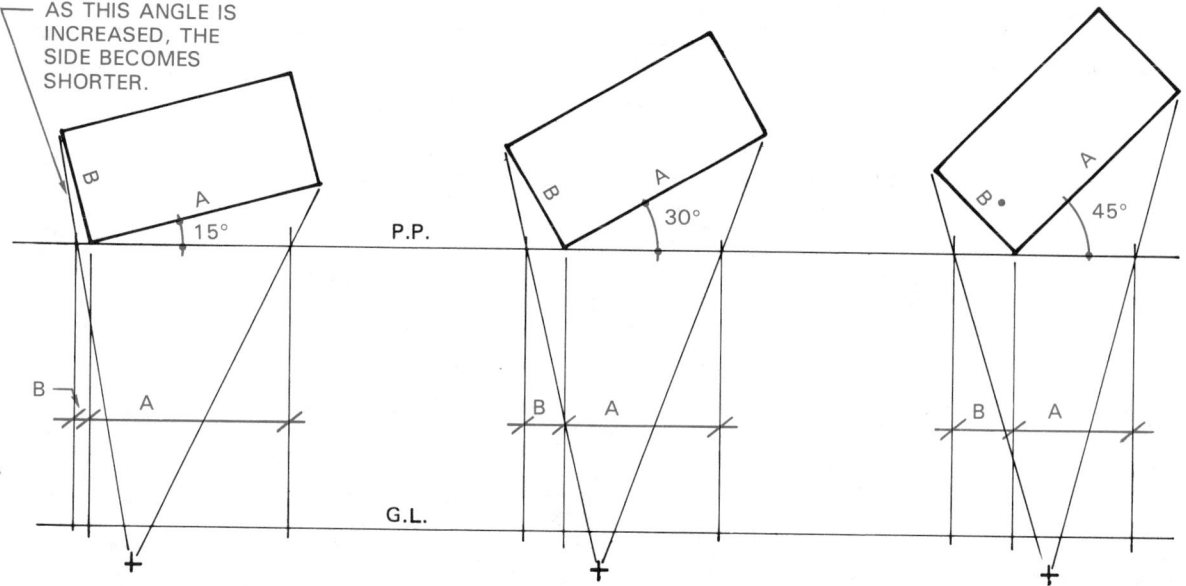

Figure 41–18 As a surface is rotated away from the picture plane (P.P.), it will become foreshortened in the perspective view.

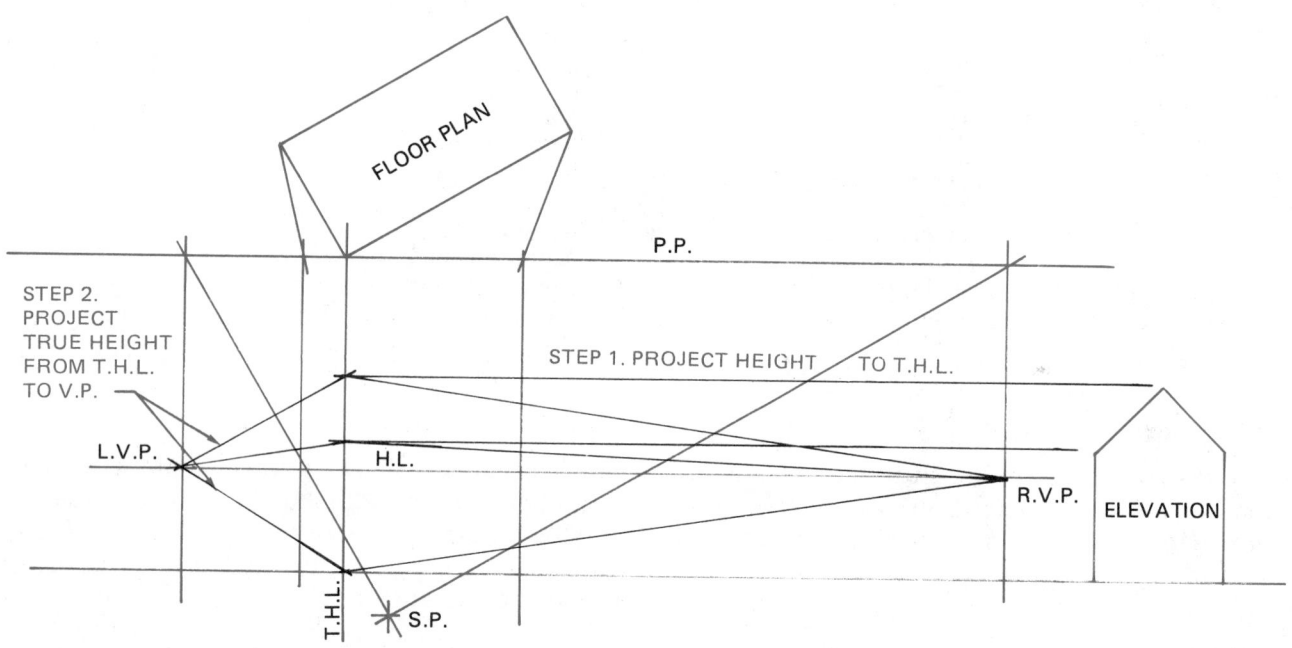

Figure 41–19 Heights from an elevation are projected to the true-height line (T.H.L.) and then to the vanishing point (V.P.).

is for a surface that is not on the picture plane, an additional step is required as seen in Figure 41–21. This procedure requires the height to be projected to the T.H.L., back towards the V.P., and then back to the true location.

Combining the Effects

It takes plenty of experience to help get over the initial confusion caused by the relationship of these points, lines, and planes. On your initial drawings,

keep one corner of the floor plan on the P.P. Experiment with changing the drawing size once you feel comfortable with the process of projecting heights. A typical layout for your first few drawings would be to keep the plan view at either a 30° or 45° angle to the picture plane. Using an angle of less than 30° will usually place one of the vanishing points off your layout area. On your first few drawings keep the distance from the S.P. to the P.P. about twice the height of the object to be drawn. It should also be kept near the true-height line to help avoid dis-

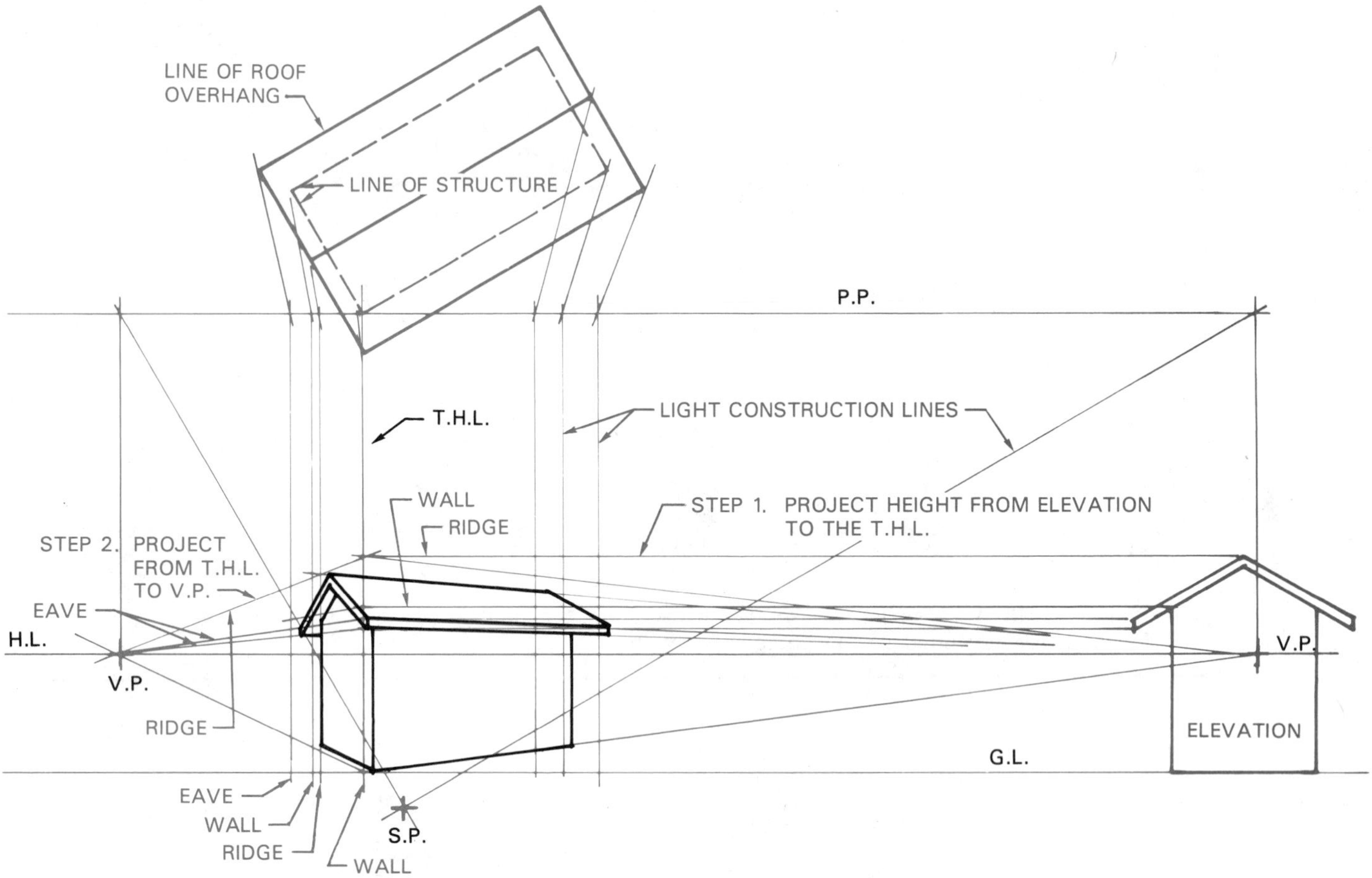

Figure 41–20 All heights are initially projected to the true-height line (T.H.L.) and from the T.H.L. to a vanishing point (V.P.). The actual height is established where the height projection line intersects the location line from the plan view.

tortion of a surface. As you begin to feel confidence with the perspective method, start by changing one variable, then another, and then change others as needed.

 TWO-POINT PERSPECTIVE DRAWING METHOD

There are numerous ways to draw two-point perspectives. Each has its own advantages and disadvantages. As you continue with your architectural training, you will be exposed to many other methods. Don't be afraid to experiment with a method. Keep in mind that this chapter is intended to be only an introduction to perspective methods.

To begin your drawing you will need a print of your floor plan and an elevation. Run a print of your drawings. *Never work with the original drawings when making layouts.* You will find it helpful to draw the outline of the roof on the print of the floor plan. You will also need a sheet of paper about 4 ft long and 2 ft high on which to do the initial layout work. Butcher paper or the back of a sheet of blueprint paper will provide a durable surface for drawing. The use of colored pencils can also help you keep track of various lines. Some students like to draw all roof lines in one color, all wall lines in a second color, and all window and door lines in a third color. The residence that was drawn in Chapter 20 will be drawn for our example.

Setup of Basic Elements

See Figure 41–22 for steps 1 through 10.

Step 1.   Draw a line at the top of your paper to represent the P.P.

Step 2.   Tape a print of your floor plan on the paper so that a corner of the building touches the P.P. For this example a 30° angle between the long side of the floor plan and

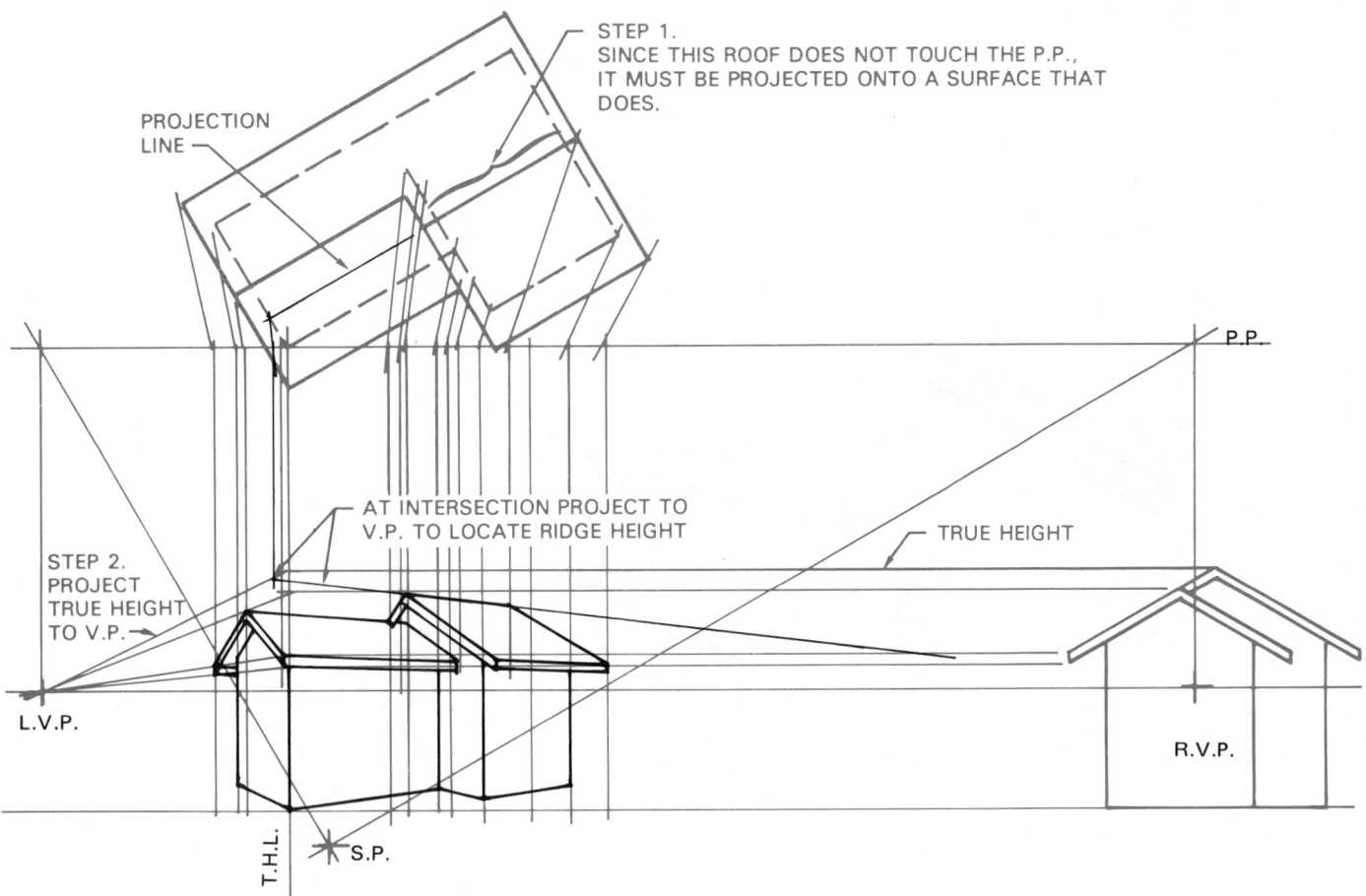

STEP 1.
SINCE THIS ROOF DOES NOT TOUCH THE P.P.,
IT MUST BE PROJECTED ONTO A SURFACE THAT
DOES.

PROJECTION
LINE

P.P.

AT INTERSECTION PROJECT TO
V.P. TO LOCATE RIDGE HEIGHT

TRUE HEIGHT

STEP 2.
PROJECT
TRUE HEIGHT
TO V.P.

L.V.P.

R.V.P.

T.H.L.

S.P.

Figure 41–21 When a surface does not touch the picture plane, it must be projected to a surface that does and then to the station point.

the P.P. was used, but the plan may be placed at any angle.

Step 3. Draw the line of any cantilevers for the upper floor.

Step 4. Draw the outline of the roof on the floor plan.

Step 5. Establish a ground line. The distance from the G.L. to the P.P. should be greater than the height of the structure to be drawn to avoid overlapping layout lines.

Step 6. Tape a print of the elevation to the side of the drawing area with the ground of the elevation touching the G.L.

Step 7. Establish the true-height line by projecting the intersection of the floor plan and the P.P. down at 90° from the P.P.

Step 8. Establish the station point. Keep the S.P. within an inch of the T.H.L., and a distance

of about twice the height of the object to be drawn.

Step 9. Establish the horizon line at about 6 scale ft above the ground.

Step 10. Establish the vanishing points. Start at the S.P. and project lines parallel to the floor plan up to the P.P. From the point where these lines intersect the P.P., project a line down at 90° to the H.L. The V.P.s are established where this line intersects the H.L.

You are now ready to project individual points from the floor plan down to the area where the perspective drawing will be drawn. Start by determining the maximum size of the house.

Step 11. Project lines from each corner of the roof down to the S.P. Even though the lines converge on the S.P., stop the lines just after they pass the P.P. See Figure 41–23.

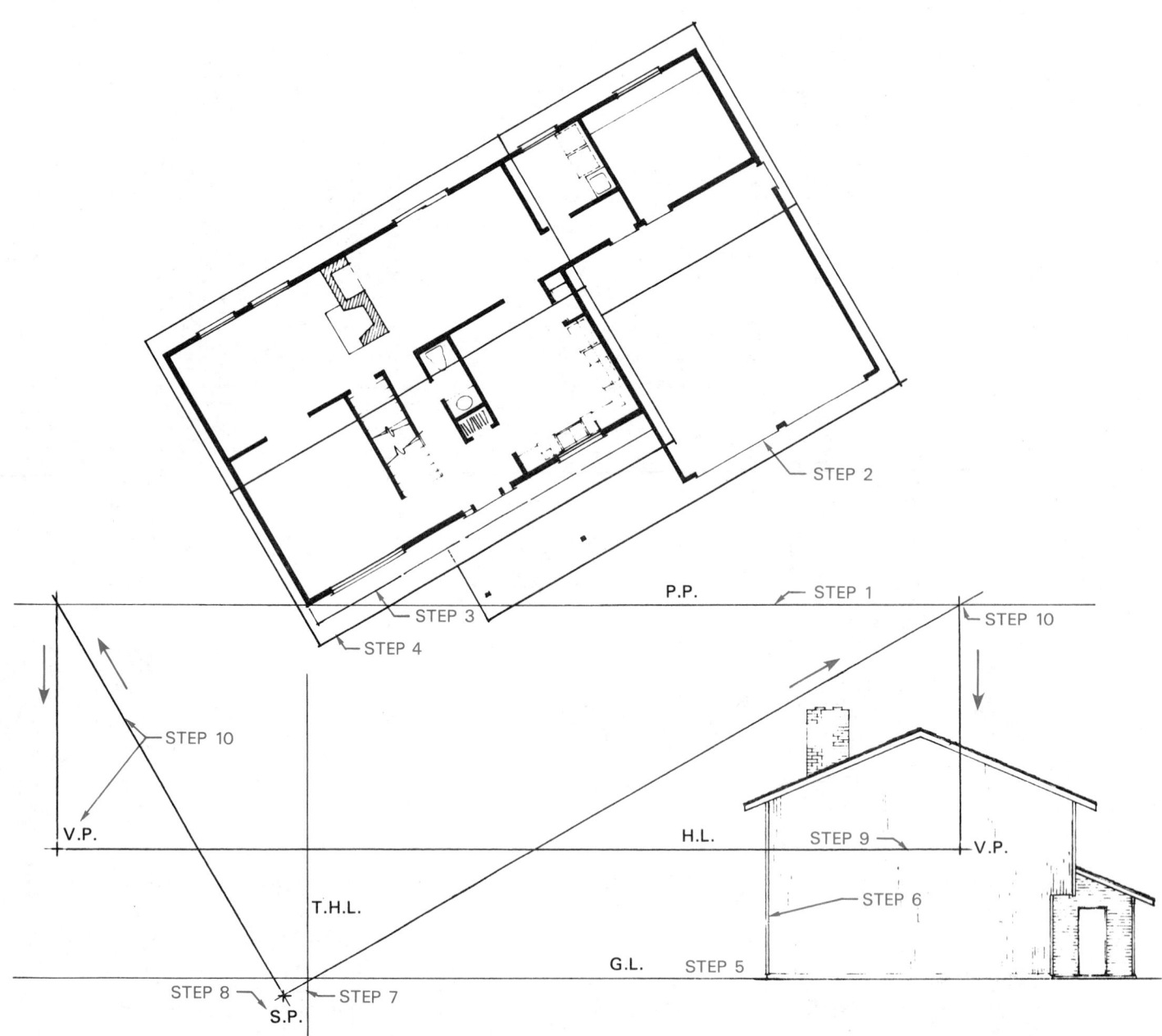

Figure 41–22 Initial layout for a two-point perspective. Establish the picture plane (P.P.), horizon line (H.L.), ground line (G.L.), true-height line (T.H.L.), station point (S.P.), and the vanishing points (V.P.s).

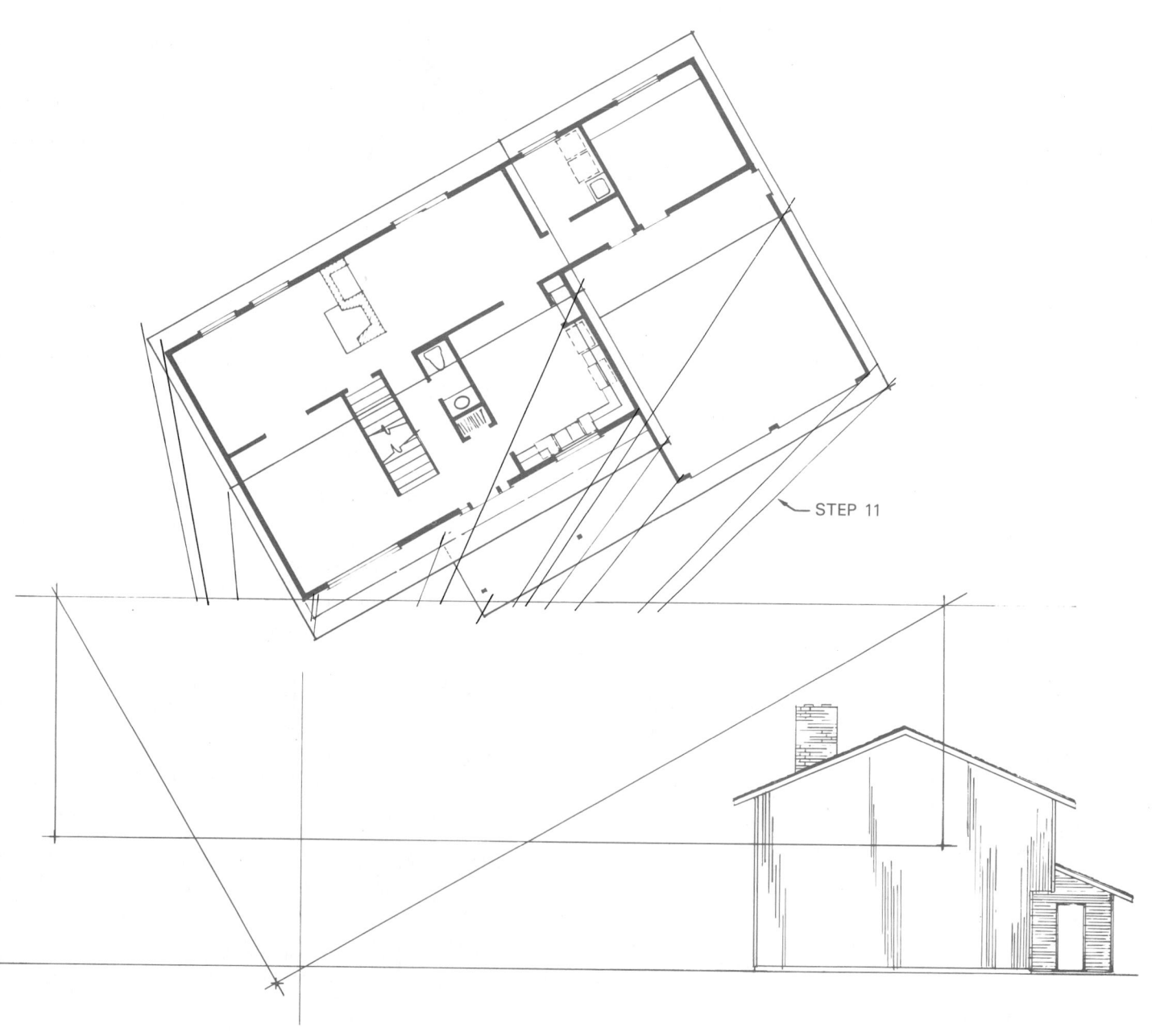

STEP 11

Figure 41-23 Layout of the roof shape. Project corner locations from the plan to the station point (S.P.).

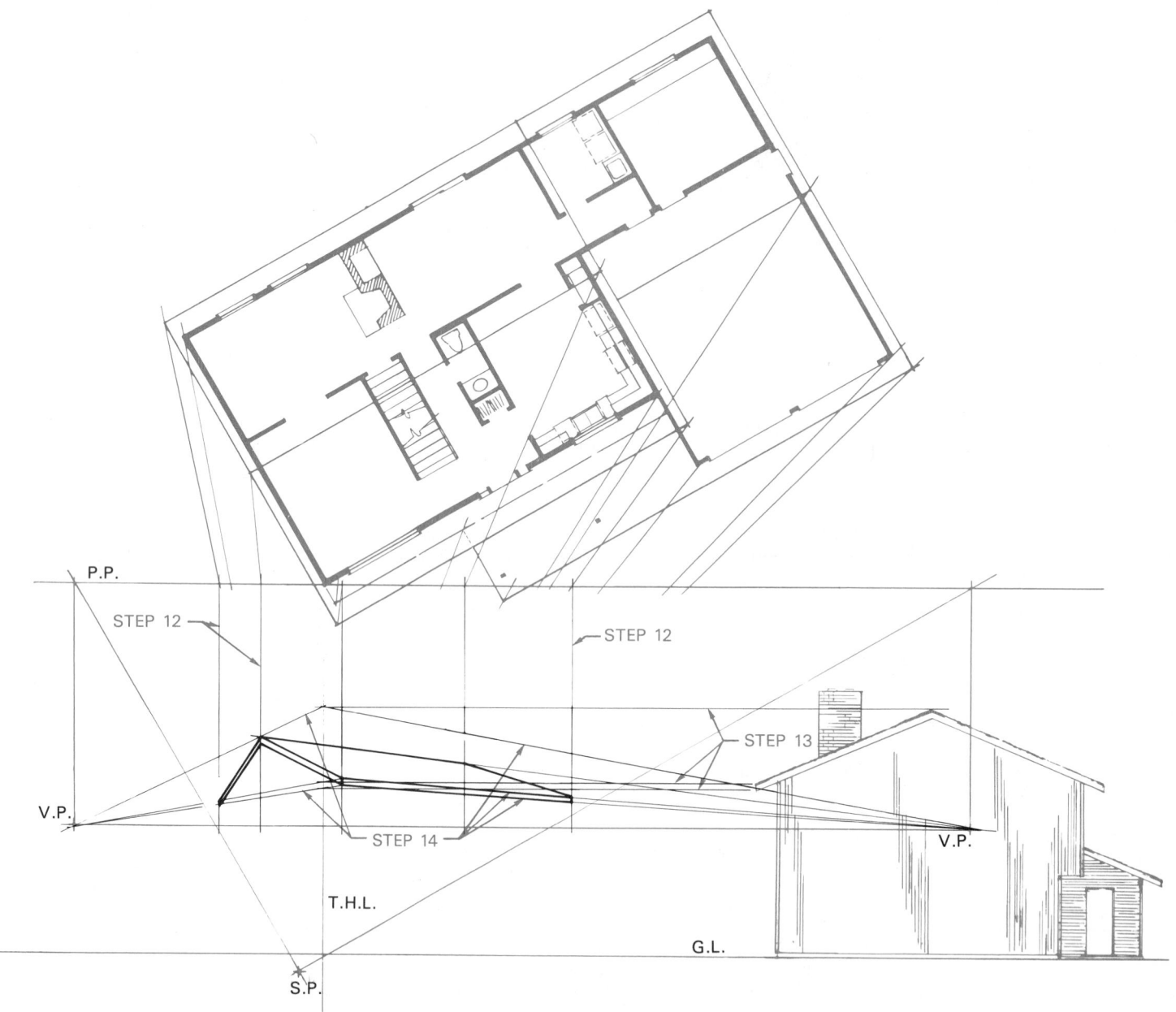

Figure 41–24 The roof shape can be drawn by projecting the width and height lines. The roof plan must be drawn on the floor plan before it can be projected to the drawing area.

See Figure 41–24 for steps 12 through 14.

Step 12. Project a line down from the P.P. to the drawing area to represent each corner of the roof.

Step 13. Project the height for the roof onto the T.H.L.

Step 14. Project the heights of the roof on the T.H.L. back to each V.P. As width and height lines

intersect, you can begin to lay out the basic roof shape.

Step 15. Continue to project height and width lines for each roof surface. Work from front to back and top to bottom. When all roof surfaces are projected, your drawing will resemble Figure 41–25.

You now have the roof shape blocked out plus a multitude of lines that may have you getting tense.

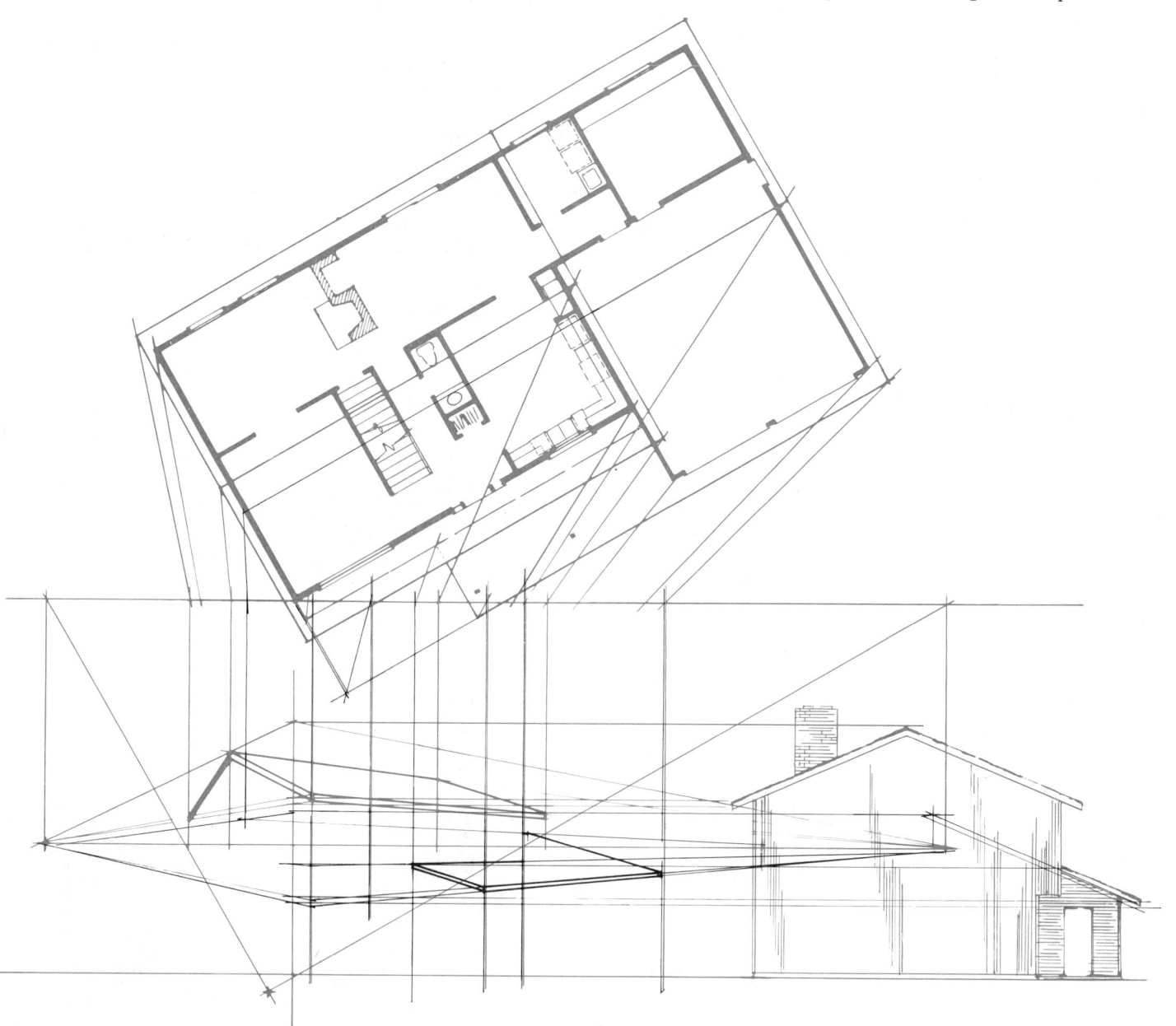

Figure 41-25 Lay out the upper roof by projecting heights from the elevation to the true-height line (T.H.L.) and then back to the vanishing points (V.P.s). Corresponding points from the picture plane (P.P.) are projected down to the drawing area.

Don't panic; there are more lines to come. To help you keep track of them, use colored pencils for the walls' projection lines. See Figure 41–26 for steps 16 and 17.

Step 16. Project a line from the corner of each wall to the S.P., stopping at the P.P.

Step 17. Project a line from the P.P. to the drawing area to represent each wall.

Step 18. Using a different color than was used for roof and wall projections, plot the outline for all windows and doors. Project the height from the elevations and the locations from the floor plan.

Your drawing should now resemble Figure 41–27, and is now ready to be transformed into a rendered presentation drawing. The steps for completing this process will be discussed in the following chapter.

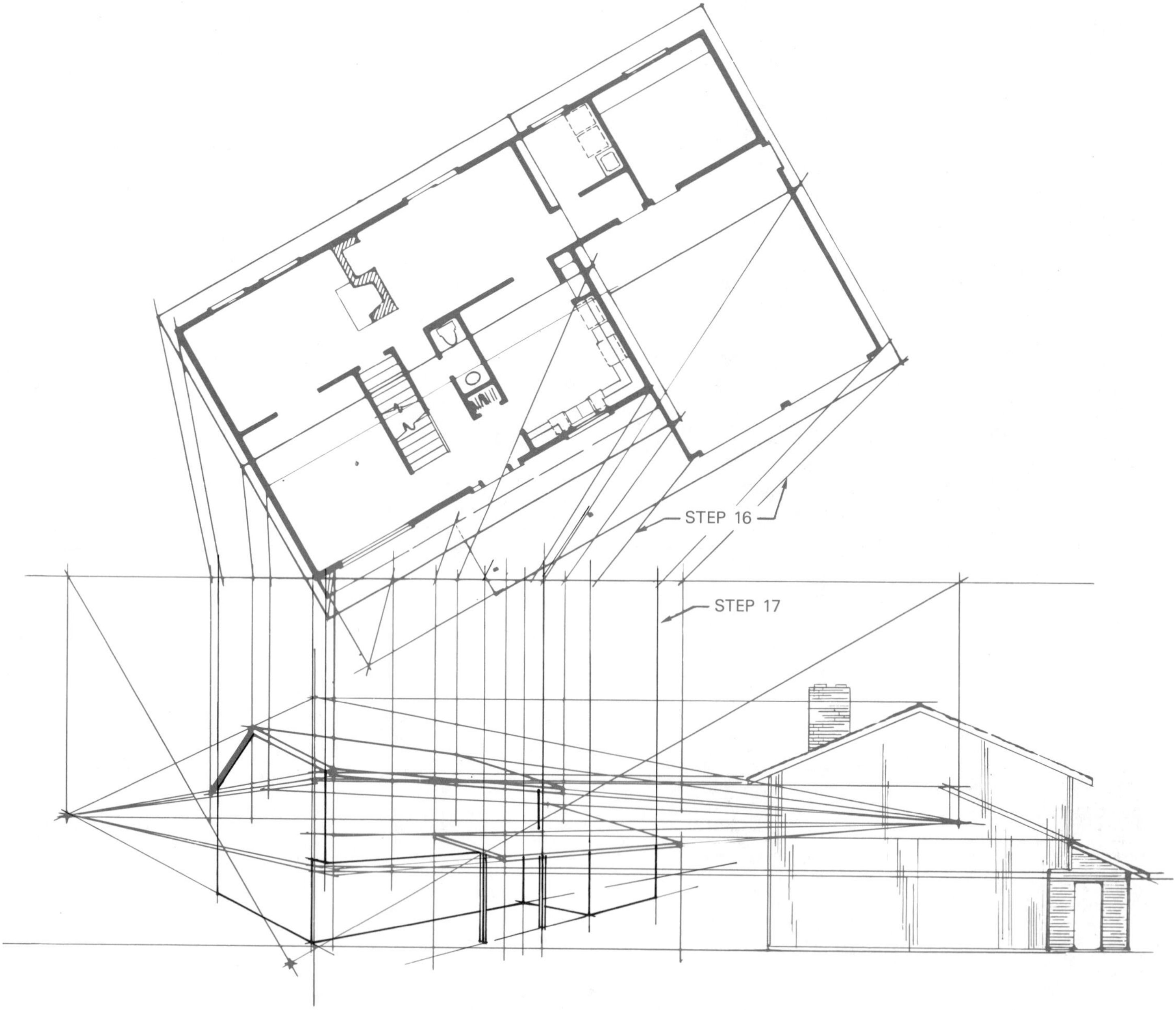

STEP 16

STEP 17

Figure 41–26 The shape of the two-point perspective can be finished by connecting the height and width lines. Work from top to bottom and from front to back.

 ## ONE-POINT PERSPECTIVE DRAWING METHOD

Much of the process for drawing the one-point perspective is similar to drawing the two-point perspective. Differences in procedure will be explained in a step-by-step process. To begin your drawing you will need a sheet of butcher paper and a print of your floor plan. Depending on the complexity of the area to be drawn, you may need to draw an elevation. If you are working on a simple interior, you may be able to mark the heights on the T.H.L. rather than drawing an elevation. Depending on the size of the area you will be drawing, the floor plan may need

to be enlarged. Often your drawing will seem very small if you start with a ¼″ = 1′-0″ floor plan. Because kitchens are such a common item to be drawn in presentation drawings, the kitchen from the residence in Chapter 20 will be drawn for our example. See Figure 41–28 for steps 1 through 7.

Step 1. Establish the picture plane.

Step 2. Tape a print of the floor plan to the P.P. Remember to redraw the floor plan at a larger scale.

Step 3. Locate the S.P. using the same consideration as with the two-point method.

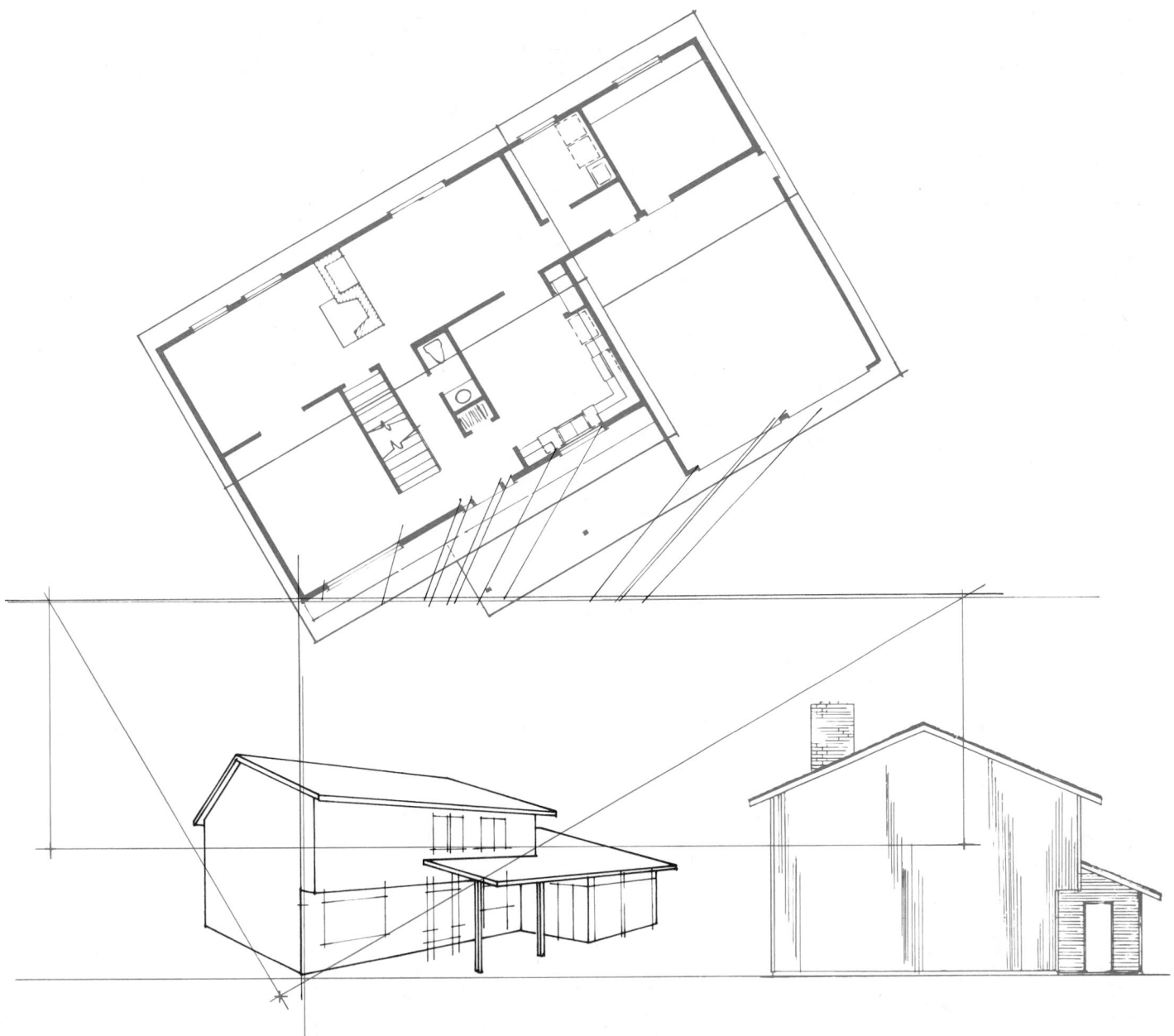

Figure 41–27 The perspective drawing is now complete. Proceed to Chapter 42 for an explanation on how to render the drawing with finished quality lines.

Step 4. Establish the ground line. In a one-point perspective this line represents the floor.

Step 5. Measure up from the ground line and establish the ceiling line. Notice that both lines will be parallel. All lines that are parallel to the P.P. will remain parallel in the drawing.

Step 6. Establish the width of the drawing by projecting the points where the walls intersect the P.P. down to the drawing area.

Step 7. Establish a vanishing point. The V.P. can go at any height but should be kept above the S.P.

See Figure 41–29 for steps 8 through 10.

Step 8. Project lines from each of the room corners to the V.P. to begin establishing the side walls, floor, and ceiling.

Step 9. Project lines from each room corner of the plan to the S.P. Extend the lines to just past the P.P. to avoid construction lines in the area where the perspective will be drawn.

Step 10. Lay out the floor, walls, and ceiling. These can be determined where the wall line intersects the lines that were projected from the floor and ceiling to the V.P.

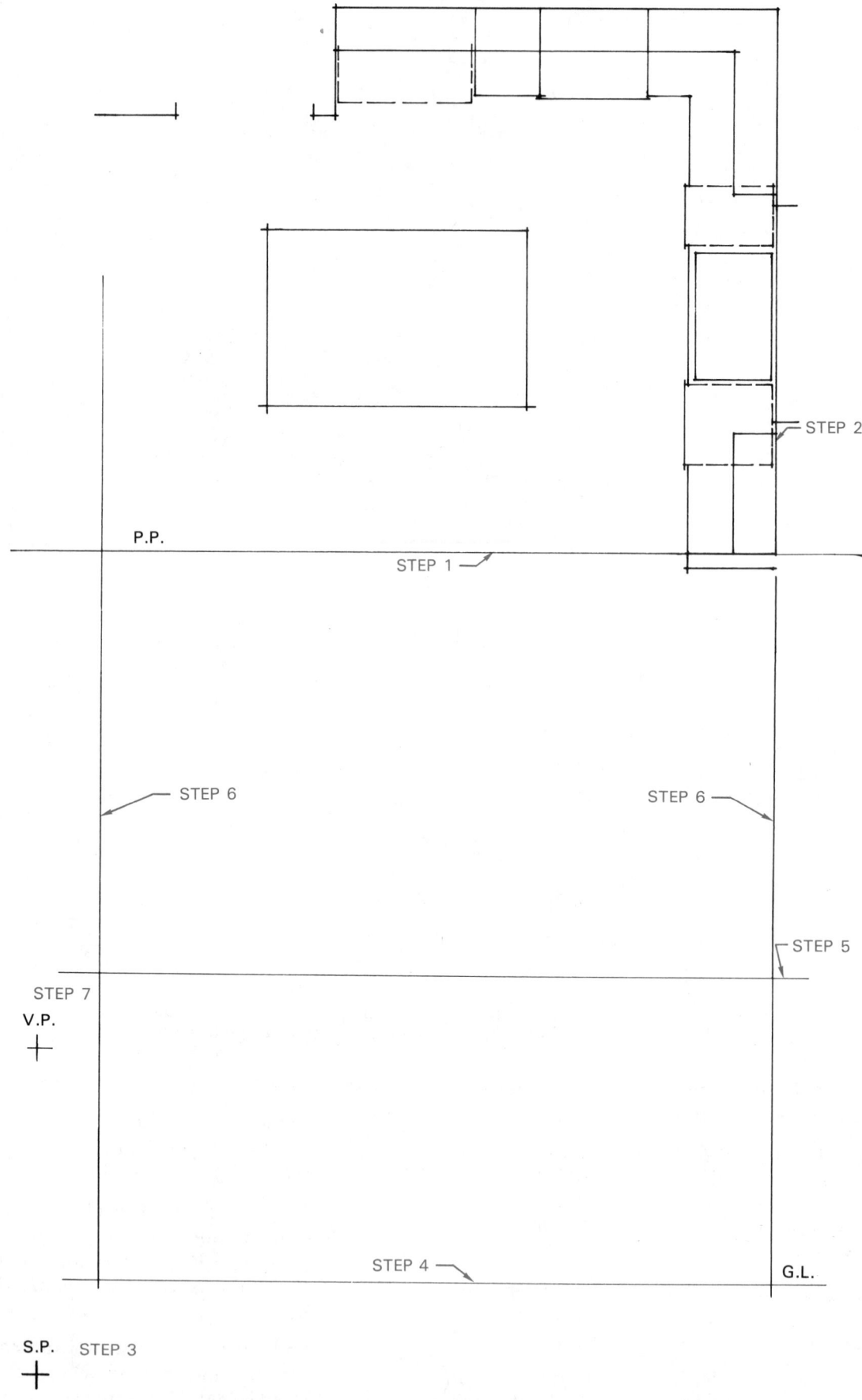

P.P.

STEP 1

STEP 2

STEP 6   STEP 6

STEP 5

STEP 7
V.P.

STEP 4   G.L.

S.P.   STEP 3

Figure 41–28 The initial layout for a one-point perspective. Start by taping a print of the floor plan to the picture plane.

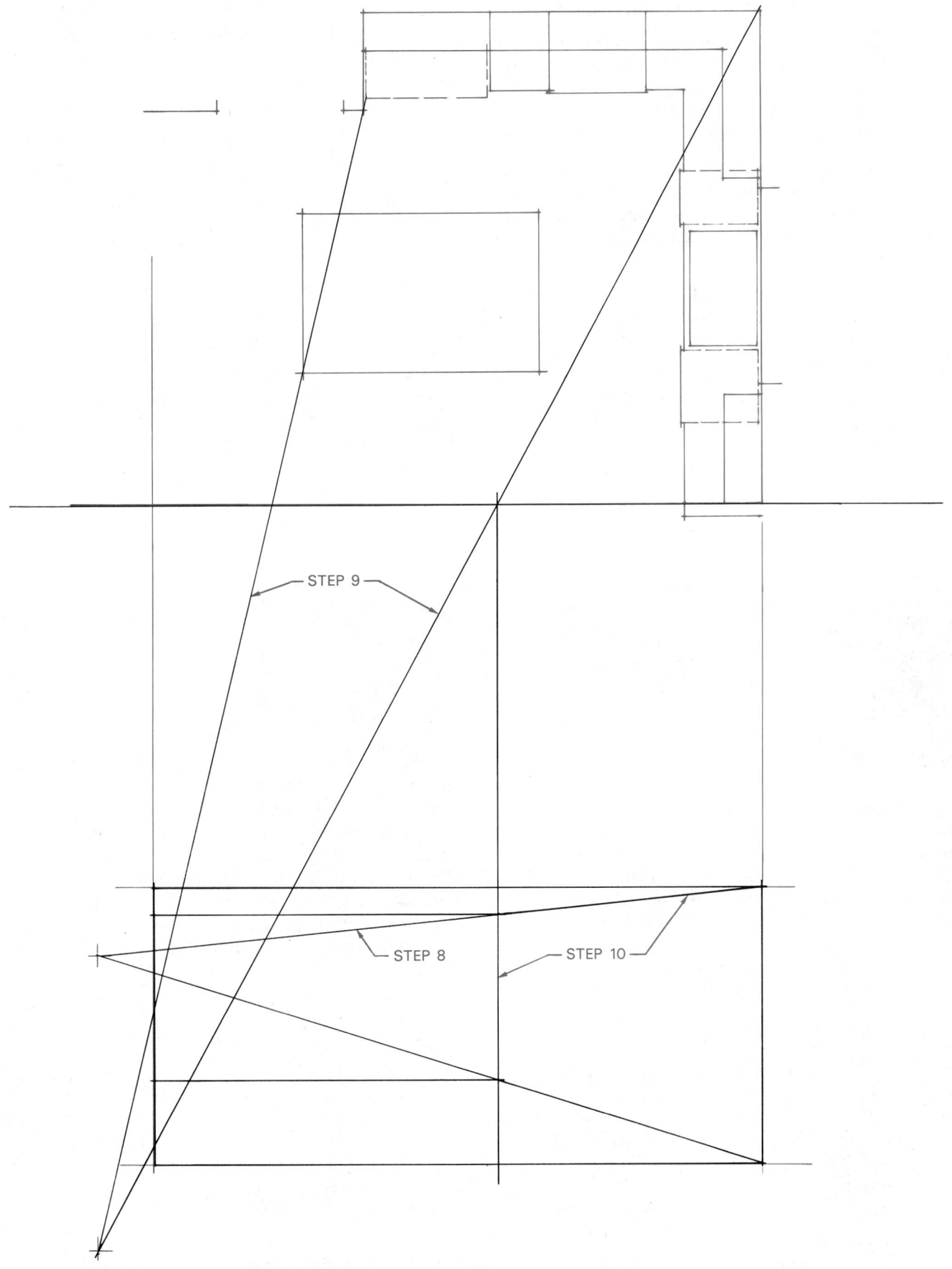

Figure 41-29 Establishing the walls, floor, and ceiling.

See Figure 41–30 for steps 11 through 14.

Step 11.   Measure the height of the cabinets on the cabinet elevations of Chapter 36, and project these heights on either of the T.H.L. In a one-point perspective, each side of the drawing is a T.H.L.

Step 12.   Lay out the shape of the base cabinet. This can be done by projecting the width from the floor plan and measuring the height on the T.H.L. Project the height back to the V.P.

Step 13.   Lay out the cabinet on the back wall by projecting the intersection point on the floor plan down onto the perspective.

Step 14.   Lay out the upper cabinet following the same procedure used to lay out the base cabinet.

See Figure 41–31 for steps 15 through 17. Similar to the two-point perspective, your drawing is probably starting to get cluttered with projection lines. Don't hesitate to use multiple colors for projection lines.

Step 15.   Lay out the widths for all cabinets and appliances by projecting their widths to the S.P. and then down to the drawing. To determine heights, mark the true height on the T.H.L. and then project the height back to the V.P.

Step 16.   Block out any windows.

Step 17.   Block out soffits, skylights, or other items in the ceiling.

You now have the basic materials drawn for the one-point perspective. Your drawing should resemble the drawing in Figure 41–32. Chapter 42 will introduce you to the basics of rendering the perspective drawing.

CADD applications

USING CADD TO MAKE PERSPECTIVES

Preparing perspective drawings is easy with CADD. Some of the powerful CADD packages allow you to automatically generate a perspective drawing from the floor plan layout. Wall and header heights are established while you draw the floor plan. When the floor plan is complete you can view the drawing in perspective from any selected point in space. You can change the view point until you find the perspective view that displays the building best. When you move the view point, the CADD system automatically adjusts the picture plane, station point, and vanishing points, but the ground plane always remains the same. Interior perspectives may be drawn in the same manner, or you can create the drawing directly in 3-D. Some systems have a split screen that allows you to draw in plan view on one part of the screen while generating a 3-D view on the other. The perspective of a multifamily housing project drawn using CADD is shown in Figure 1.

Figure 1 CADD perspective drawing of a multifamily housing project. *Courtesy Soderstrom Architects PC.*

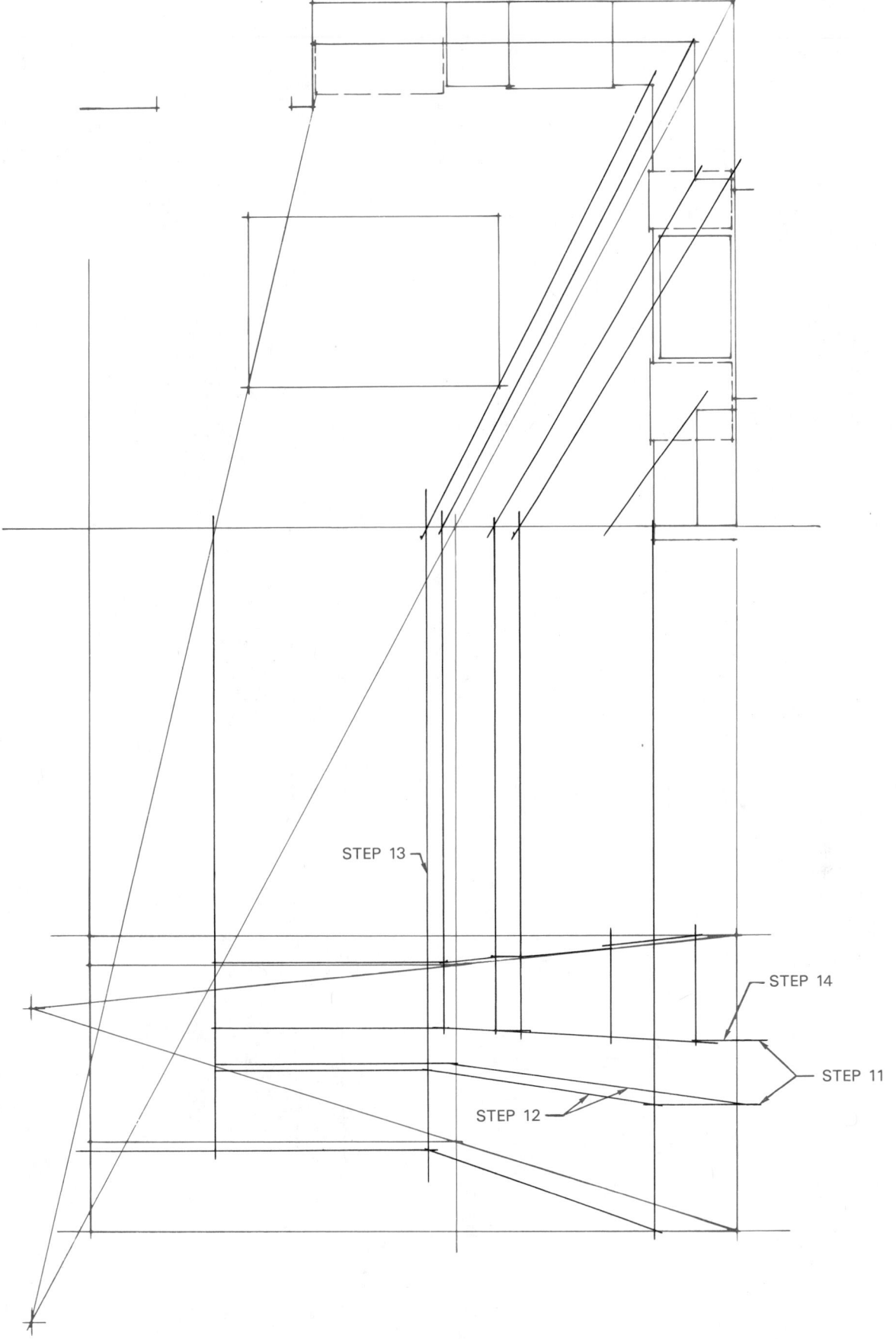

STEP 13

STEP 14

STEP 11

STEP 12

Figure 41–30 Lay out the basic cabinet shapes by projecting each location from the floor plan.

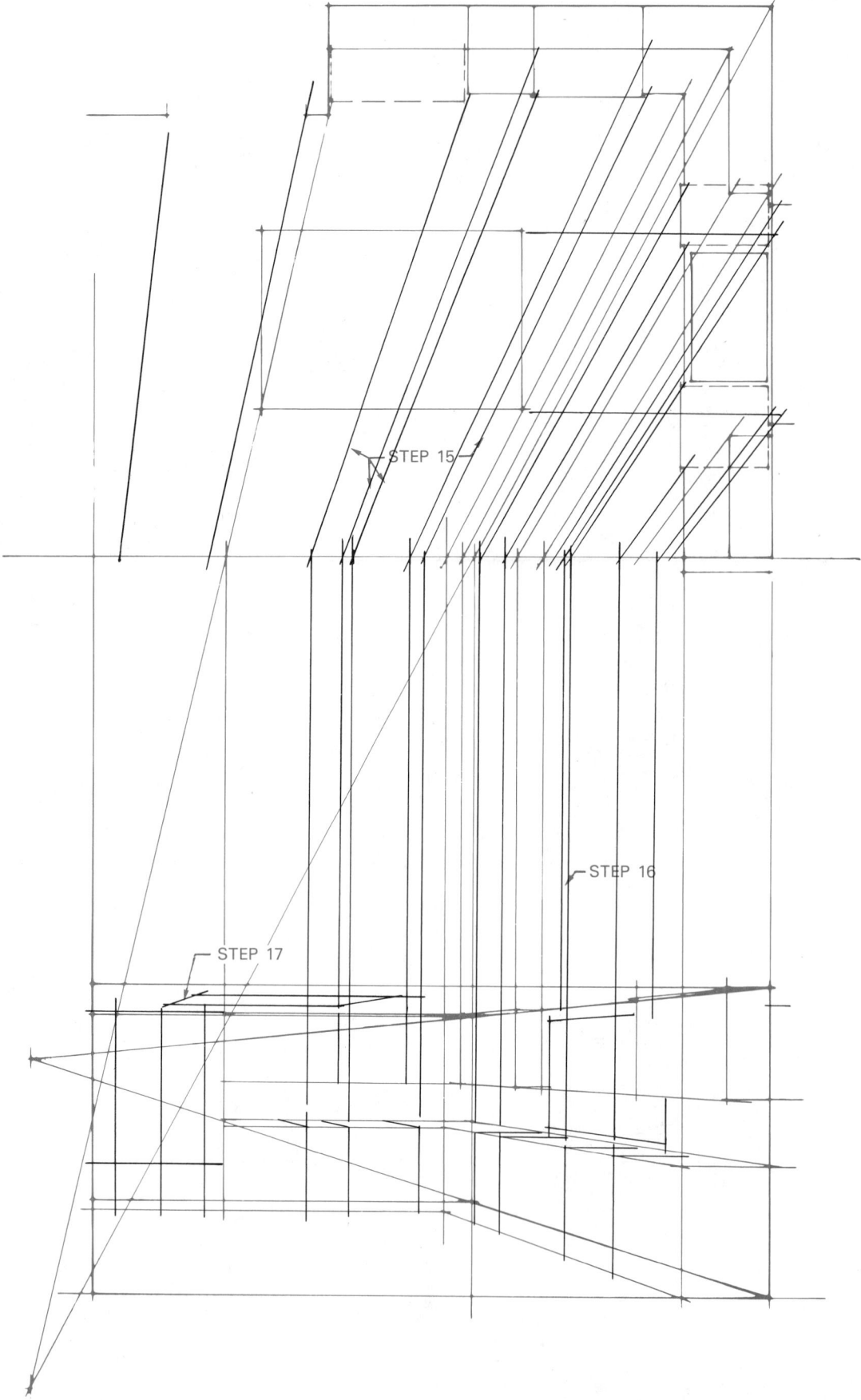

Figure 41–31 Block out individual cabinets. Use drawings of the cabinet elevations to establish each location.

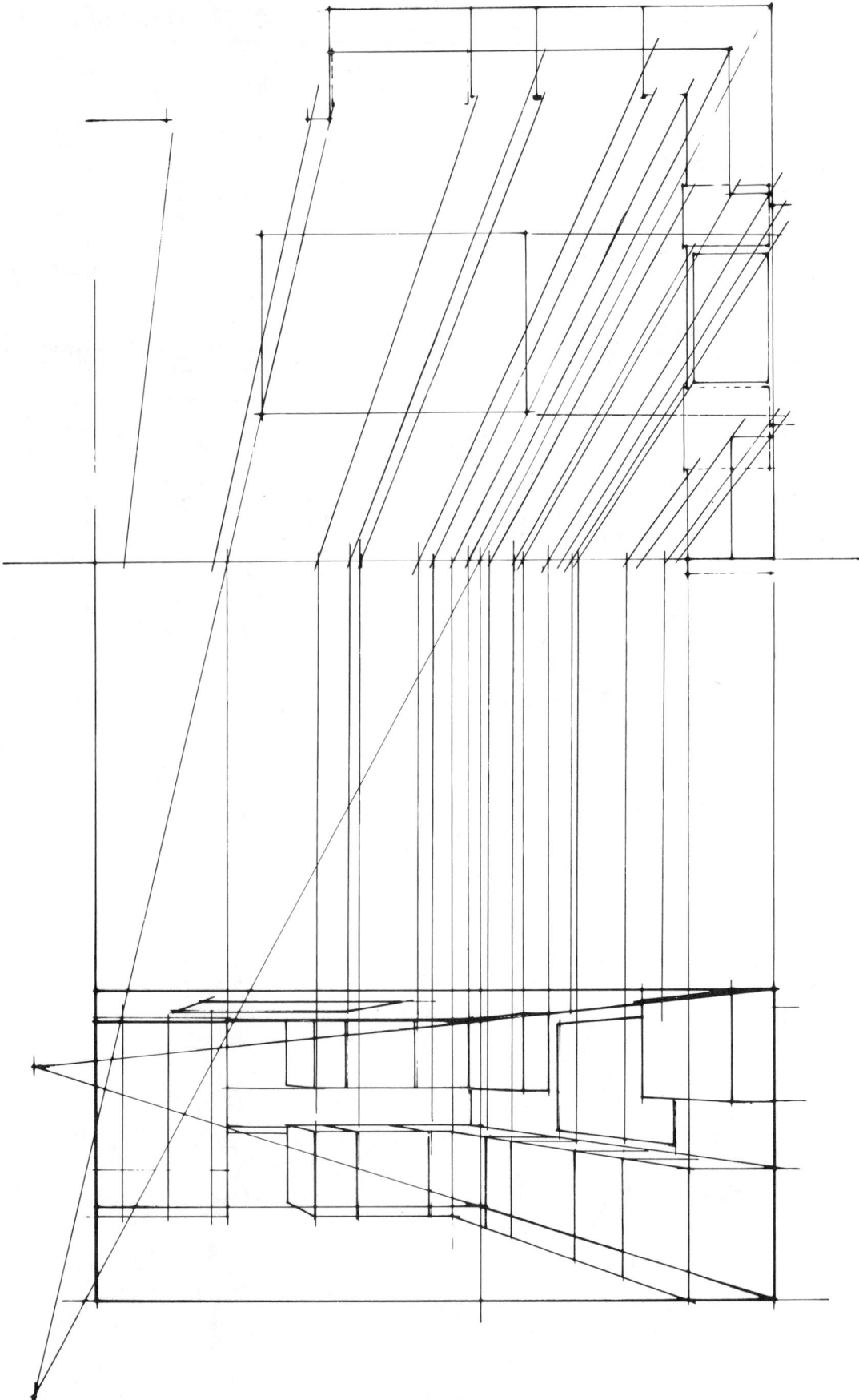

Figure 41–32 The completed one-point perspective ready to be rendered. See Chapter 42 for an explanation of how to render the drawing with finished quality lines.

PERSPECTIVE DRAWING TECHNIQUES TEST

DIRECTIONS

Answer the questions with short complete statements or drawings as needed on an 8½ × 11 drawing sheet as follows:

1. Use ⅛ in. guidelines for all lettering.
2. Letter your name, Perspective Drawing Techniques Test, and the date at the top of the sheet.
3. Letter the question number and provide the answer. You do not need to write out the question.
4. Do all lettering with vertical uppercase architectural letters. If the answer requires line work, use proper drafting tools and technique. Answers may be prepared on a word processor if appropriate with course guidelines.
5. Your grade will be based on correct answers and quality of line technique.

QUESTIONS

1. What are the major types of perspective drawings?
2. On a two-point perspective, where will all horizontal lines meet?
3. Explain the effect of moving the station point.
4. What are the most common uses for a one-point perspective?
5. Sketch the method of locating the vanishing points for a two-point perspective and describe each step that is used.
6. How does the placement of the floor plan affect the layout of a perspective?
7. Where is the actual height of the structure shown in the perspective?
8. How are three-point perspectives typically used?
9. What drawings are required to draw a two-point perspective?
10. What represents the horizontal surface at the base of the perspective?

PERSPECTIVE DRAWING TECHNIQUES PROBLEMS

DIRECTIONS

Lay out the following problems on butcher paper. When complete, trace the object onto vellum using either ink or graphite.

Problem 41–1.

1. Draw the following object as a perspective drawing. Enlarge 3×.
2. Place the G.L. 7 in. away from the P.P.
3. Set the H.L. 5½ in. above the G.L.
4. Set the S.P. ⅜ in. below the G.L. and ¼ in. to the left of the T.H.L.
5. Set point 2 on the P.P. with line 1–2 at a 30° angle to the P.P.
6. Lay out the perspective drawing. Leave all construction lines.
7. Darken all object lines using graphite.
8. Repeat steps 1 through 7 using an H.L. that is 3 in. above the G.L.
9. Repeat steps 1 through 7 using a S.P. that is ⅜ in. below the ground and ¼ in. to the right of the T.H.L.

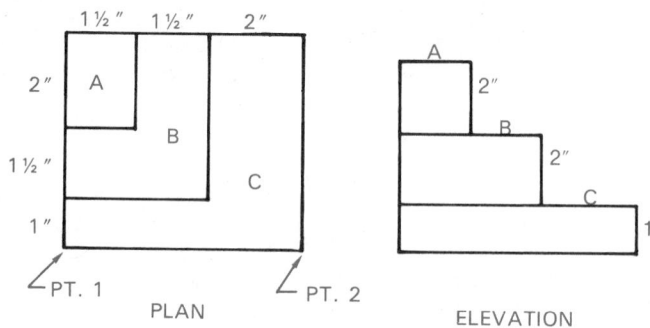

PLAN   ELEVATION

Problem 41–2.

1. Make a perspective drawing of the following object.
2. Place the plan at a 45° angle to the P.P.
3. Select your own V.P. and S.P.

4. Leave all construction lines. Darken all object lines.
5. Draw the object a second time at 15° to the P.P.

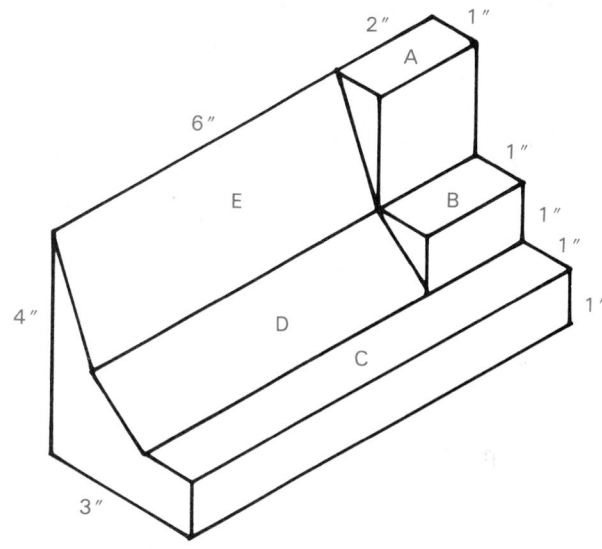

Problem 41–3.

1. Draw a perspective drawing of the following object.
2. Select a horizon line that will not accent the height.
3. Select an angle for the floor plan placement that will equally accent each surface.
4. Set point 1 on the P.P.
5. Trace this drawing onto a sheet of vellum using ink.

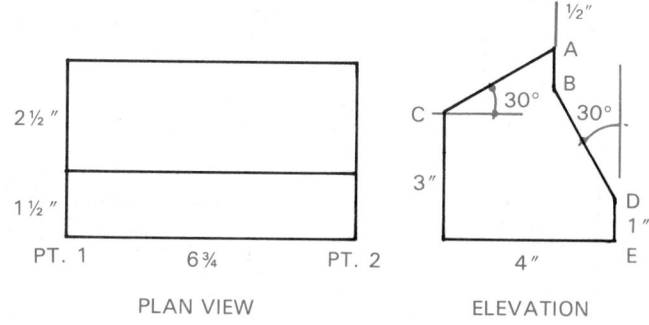

PLAN VIEW   ELEVATION

Problem 41–4.

1. Make two perspective drawings of the following object.
2. Set point 1 on the P.P.
3. Draw perspective A with the H.L. above the ridge.
4. Draw perspective B with the H.L. below the eave.
5. Use the same S.P. for each drawing.
6. Trace your drawings onto a sheet of vellum using ink.

Problem 41–5.

1. Draw a one-point perspective of the following object at a scale of ½″ = 1′–0″.
2. Draw a floor plan on the P.P.
3. Set the G.L. 8 in. below the P.P.
4. Set the V.P. in the center of the drawing at a point above B.
5. Set the S.P. 4 in. directly below the V.P.
6. Darken all object lines using graphite. Leave all construction lines.

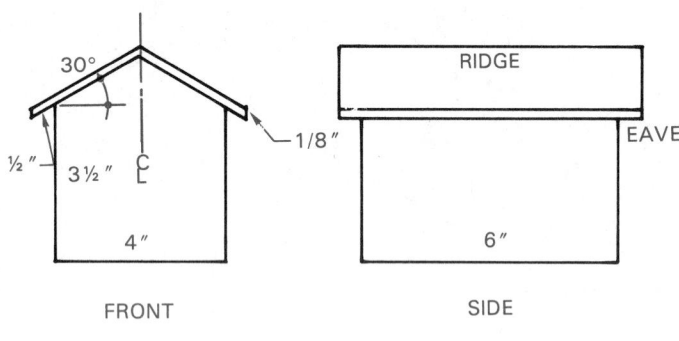

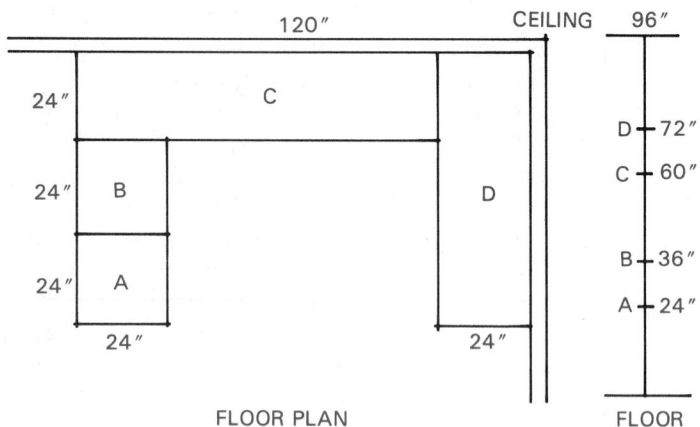

Problem 41–6.

1. Draw a one-point perspective of the following object at a scale of ½″ = 1′–0″.
2. Draw the floor plan on the P.P.
3. Establish your own G.L. and S.P.
4. Set the V.P. in the left third of the drawing, at a point above D.
5. Darken all object lines using graphite. Leave all construction lines.
6. Redraw this object using steps 1 through 3. Set the V.P. at any point above the G.L. in the right third of the drawing. Darken all object lines using graphite. Leave all construction lines.

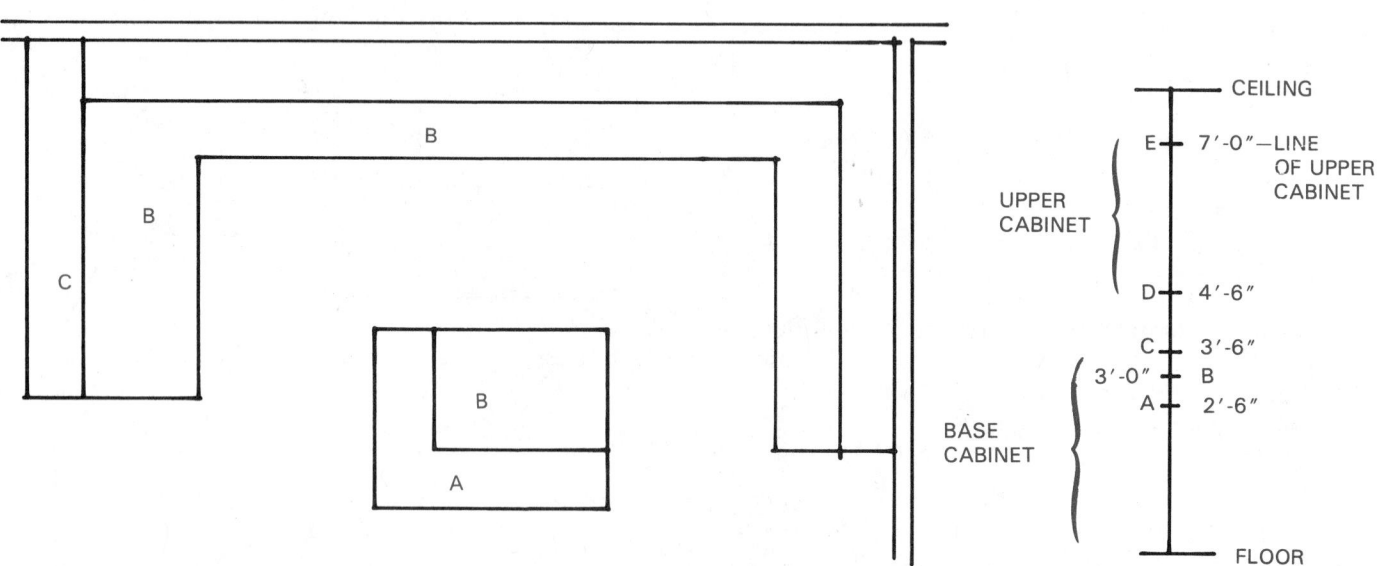

Problem 41-7. Using a print of your floor plan and elevation draw a two-point perspective of the residence that you have drawn for your project. Select a view that will not accent one surface greatly over the other. Leave all lines as construction lines. This drawing will be used in the next chapter for your rendering project.

Problem 41-8. Using a print of your floor plan and cabinet elevations draw a one-point perspective of one of the rooms. Do all work on butcher paper. Leave all lines as construction lines. This drawing will be used in the next chapter for your rendering project.

Chapter 42
Rendering Methods for Perspective Drawings

FIGURE 41-27 shows an example of a perspective drawing. It presents a better view of the structure than an orthographic drawing, but it still does not appear very realistic. In order to transform the perspective drawing into a realistic presentation of the structure, the drawing must be rendered. You have already been exposed to the process of rendering other types of presentation drawings. Similar materials and media are used when rendering perspective drawings. A rendered perspective drawing will typically show depth, shading, reflections, texture, and entourage, or surroundings.

More than any other type of presentation drawing, a rendered perspective can be a very intimidating project for the beginning student. On other forms of

presentation drawings you will be able to use standard drafting tools to form the lines. When rendering perspective drawings, you will need to rely on your artistic ability. Don't panic if you feel you will never be able to draw a rendering. The techniques needed require lots of practice, but they can be mastered. Start by developing a scrapbook of renderings done by professional illustrators in various materials. Also collect photos of people, trees, and cars. Until you gain confidence in your artistic ability, you can use one of the photos or renderings from your scrapbook as a guide or, if necessary, you could even trace it.

Your renderings will also be enhanced if you will take the time to notice and sketch the things around you. Pay special attention to trees and shadows that are cast by and onto buildings. You will notice that, depending on the location and intensity of sunlight, surfaces will take on different appearances. Try and reproduce these effects in your sketches.

PRESENTING DEPTH

Figure 42-1 provides an example of how depth and surface texture can be shown. The perspective drawing itself shows the illusion of depth by presenting three surface areas in one view. On a two-point perspective, the feeling of depth is often shown at such areas as windows, doors, fascias, surface intersections, and trim boards. The feeling of depth can

Figure 42–1 A rendered perspective drawing can show depth and texture, creating a realistic look to the drawing. *Courtesy Home Building Plan Service.*

be created by using off-setting lines and by using different line weights. Figure 42–2 shows examples of how depth can be created.

The same guidelines for showing depth should be used on the one-point perspective. Cabinet doors, drawers, and appliances typically project past the face of a cabinet and should be shown on the perspective drawing. Figure 42–3 shows an example of how depth can be shown on a one-point perspective.

SHADE AND SHADOWS

Shade and shadows provide an excellent method of presenting depth. Shadows will be cast anytime a surface blocks light from striking another surface.

Figure 42–3 Depth can be seen in this one-point rendering. *Courtesy Shakertown Corp.*

Figure 42–4 shows an example of the effect of shadows on a structure. No matter if you are an architect or a drafter, you should have a basic understanding of how shadows are cast, and how they are drawn on a perspective drawing.

The principles for projecting shadows in perspective are similar to the methods used in orthographic

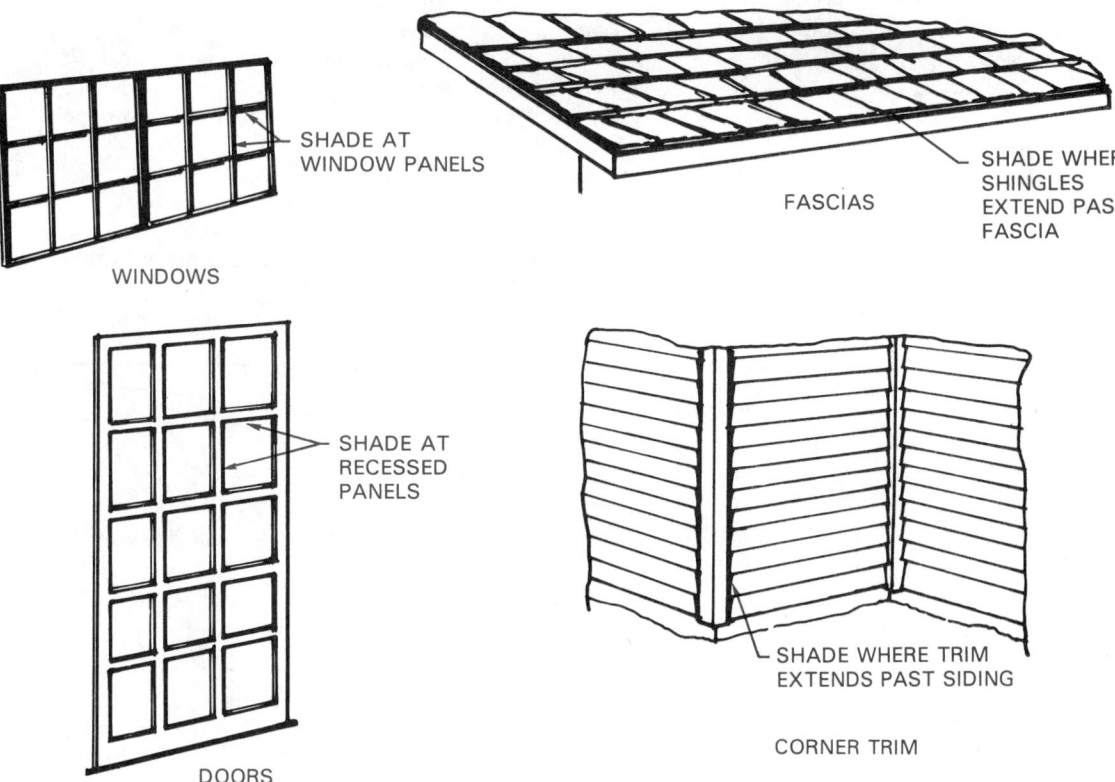

Figure 42–2 Depth can be shown at surface changes by using thicker lines to represent shadows.

Figure 42–4 Shades and shadows are used to show depth. *Courtesy Piercy & Barclay Designers, Inc.*

drawings. Before any shadows can be projected, a light source must be established using the same guidelines that were used for presentation elevations. Keep the light source in a position so that major features of the structure will not be hidden.

Shadows are usually projected at an angle of 30°, 45°, or 50°. The use of these angles will save time in projecting because of the ease of using one standard triangle or drafting machine setting. Figure 42–5 shows the effects of changing the angle of the light source.

Two principles will affect the layout of shade and shadows if the light source is drawn parallel to the picture plane.

1. A vertical wall or surface will cast a shadow on the adjacent ground or horizontal surface in the direction in which the light rays are traveling.
2. The shadow on a plane, caused by a line parallel to the plane, will form a shadow line parallel to the line. Both will converge at the same vanishing point.

Both principles can be seen in Figure 42–6. The vertical lines cast their shadows according to the first rule, and the horizontal lines cast a shadow according to the second rule. These same two principles can be applied as the shadows are cast onto other parts of the structure as seen in Figure 42–7. When a structure has an overhang, the same principles can be applied to project the shaded areas.

You will often be required to project the height of a horizontal surface onto an inclined surface. This can be done by following the procedure shown in Figure 42–8. A similar problem is created when trying to project the shadow of an inclined surface onto a flat surface. Figure 42–9 shows how the shadow created by a roof can be projected onto the ground.

One of the problems of casting shadows parallel to the picture plane is that this method requires one

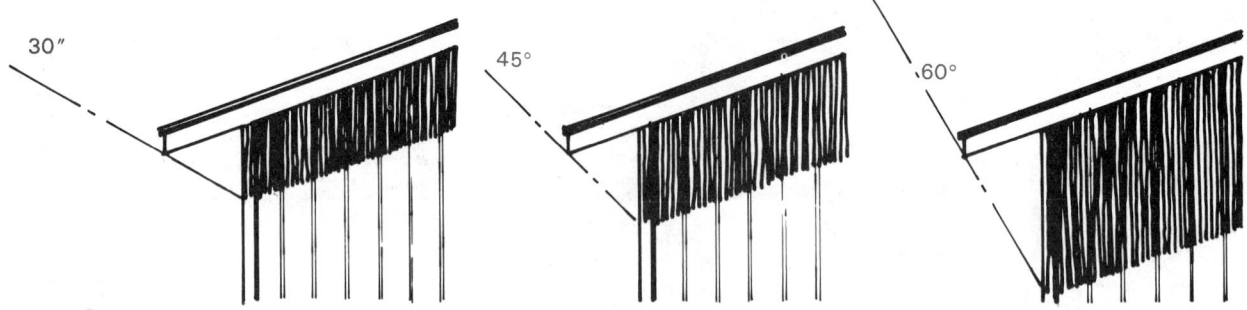

Figure 42–5 As the angle of light becomes steeper, the length of shadow becomes longer.

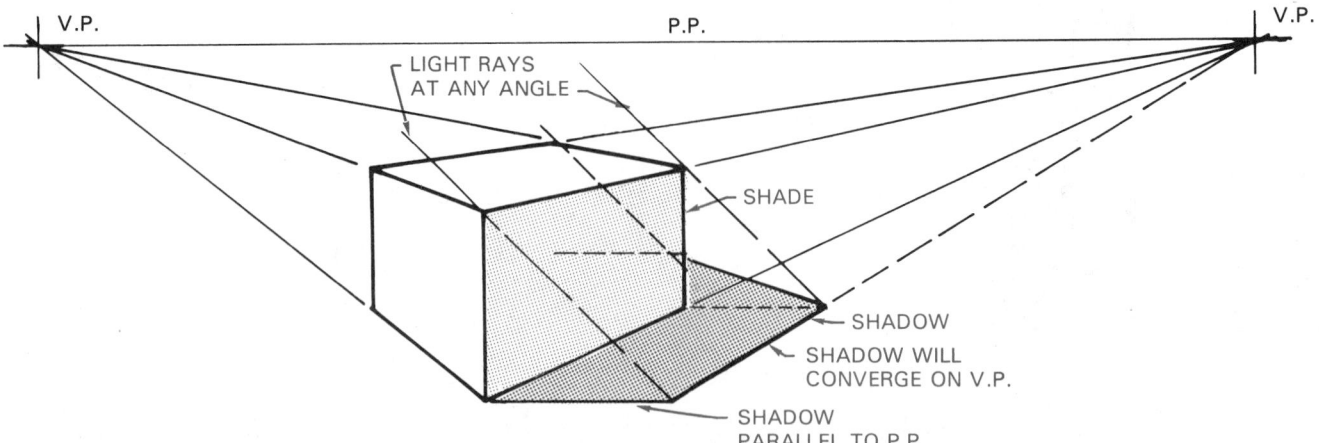

Figure 42–6 A vertical surface will cast a shadow on a horizontal surface in the direction that the light rays are traveling. The shadow that is created will be parallel to the surface that created it and will converge at the same vanishing point.

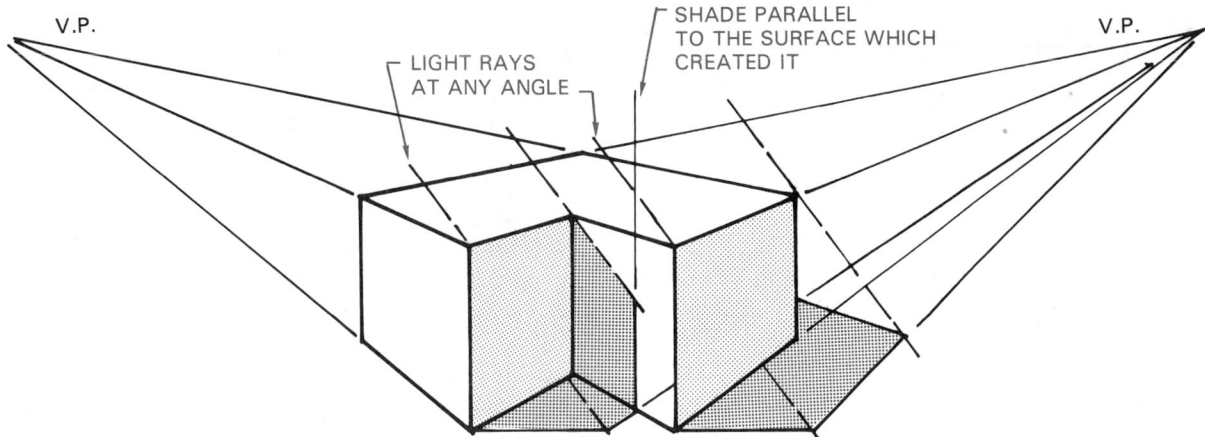

Figure 42–7 Shadows cast onto a vertical wall are projected using the same methods used to project shadows onto the ground.

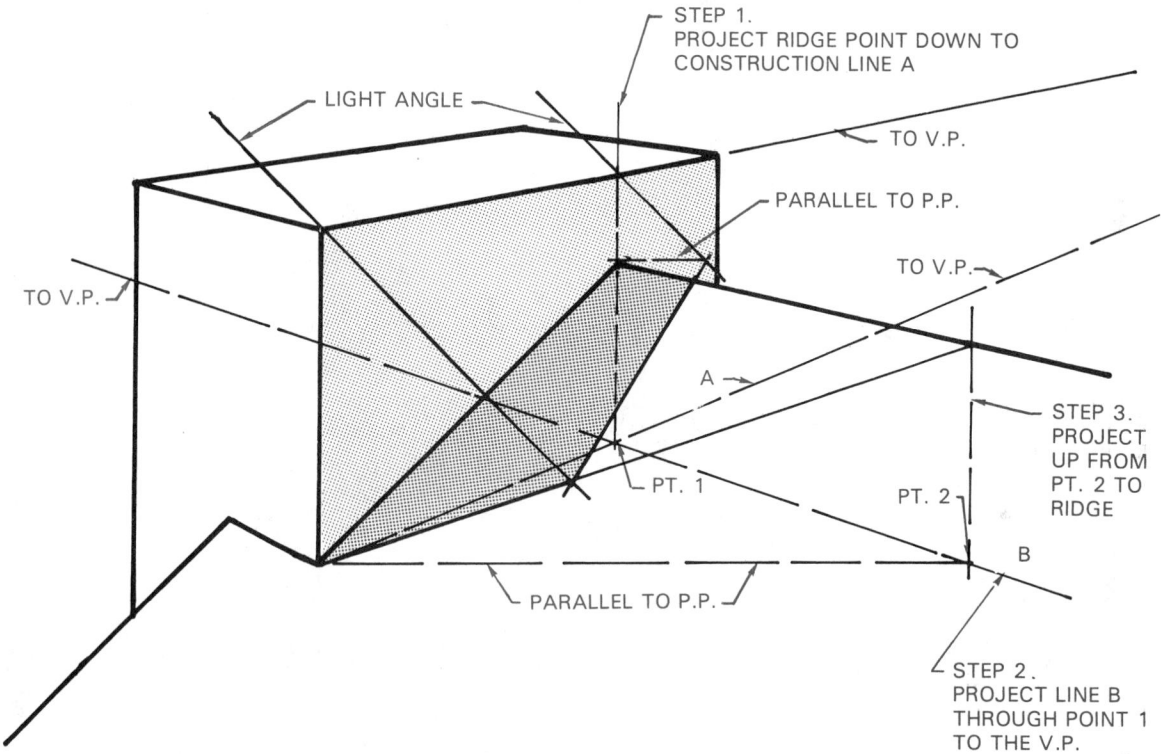

Figure 42–8 A method of projecting shadows onto an angled surface.

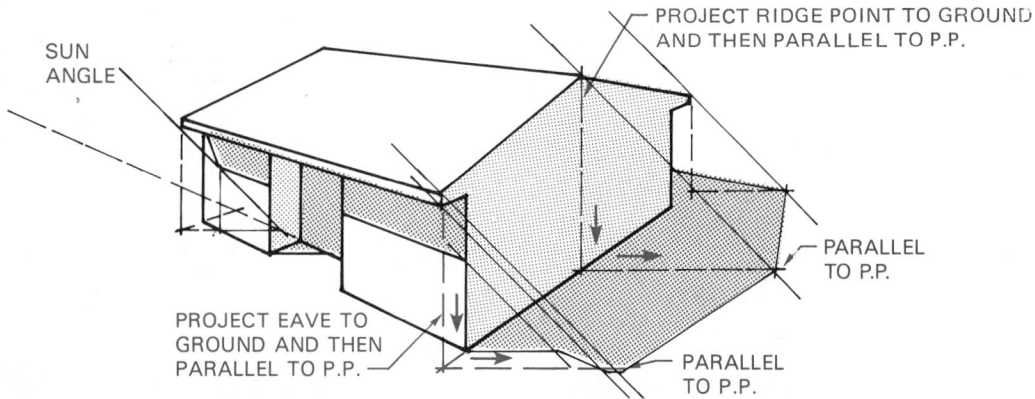

Figure 42–9 Projecting shadows from an inclined roof onto a horizontal surface.

Figure 42–10 The sun is often placed behind the viewer's back so that shadows will be cast while each surface remains in the sunlight. *Courtesy Piercy & Barclay Designers, Inc.*

of the two wall surfaces to be in the shade. Material can still be seen when it is in the shade, but it will not be as prominent as the same material in direct sunlight. Shading film, ink wash, and graphite shading are the most common methods of showing shaded areas. These same materials are used to show shadows, but they must be applied using a denser pattern. Methods similar to those for drawing shadows can be used on perspective drawings that were used on the rendered elevation.

If you would like to have both surfaces of a structure in direct sunlight, the light source will need to be moved so that it is no longer parallel to the picture plane. Figure 42–10 shows a rendering drawn

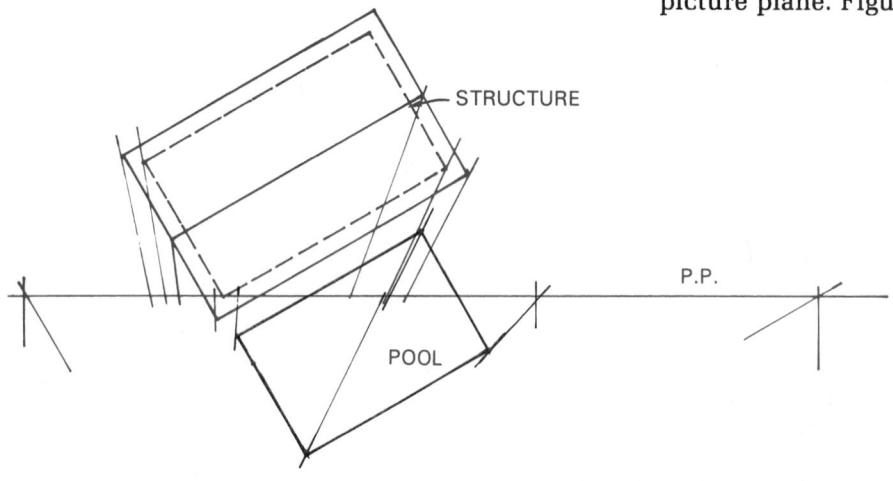

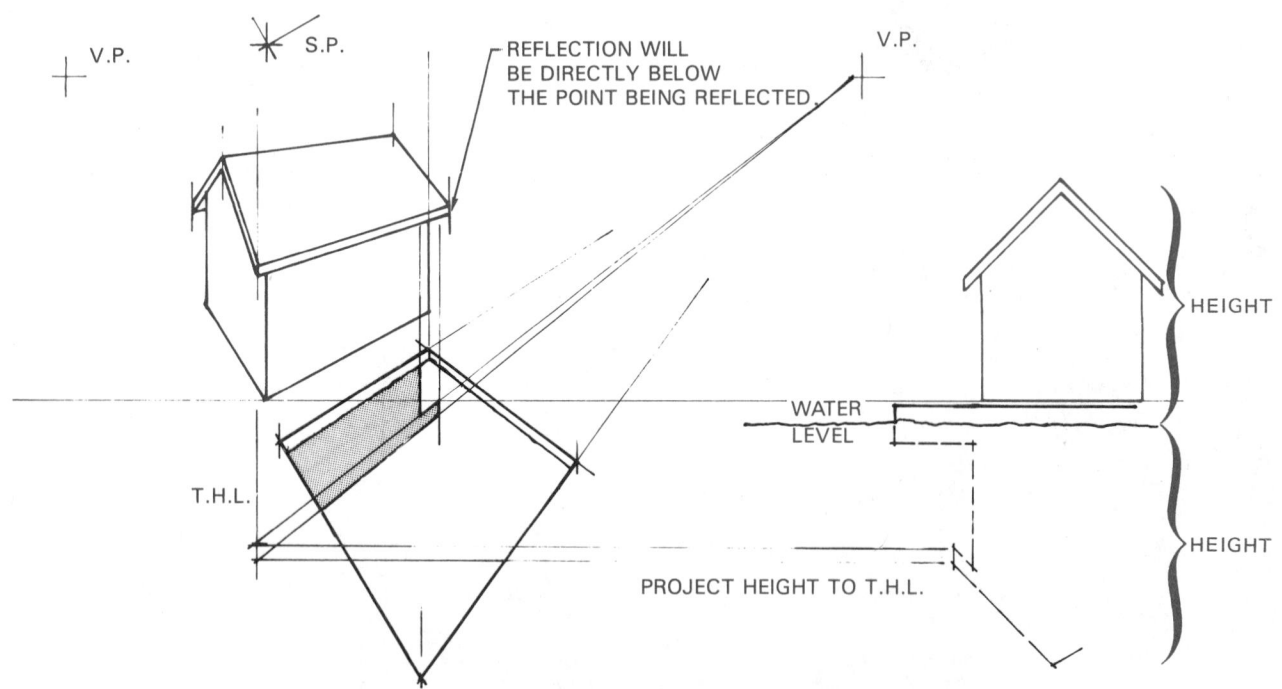

Figure 42–11 Projecting reflections on water. The reflected image will fall directly below the point to be projected. The depth of the reflection will be equal to the distance that the point is above the reflecting surface.

with the light source behind the viewer so that both sides are in sunlight.

REFLECTIONS

Reflections in perspective drawings are typically caused by either water or glass. When casting a reflection caused by water, the point to be projected will fall directly below that point and the depth of the reflection will be equal to the distance that the point is above the water's surface. Figure 42–11 shows how these two principles can be used to project a reflection. Figure 42–12 shows another method for rendering water.

Large areas of glass in a perspective drawing can often appear very dull unless rendered. Figure 42–13 shows common methods of rendering glass. Glass is often rendered solid black with small areas of white

Figure 42–12 Reflections on water. *Courtesy Home Planners, Inc.*

Figure 42–13 Glass can be rendered using several techniques. *Courtesy Home Building Plan Service.*

to indicate reflections. Glass can also be left unrendered and all material in the background can be shown. A third alternative is to use an ink wash. A wash is a combination of water and ink applied with a small paintbrush that gives a gray tone rather than the solid black color of ink. Small areas of reflection are often left white or shaded with a soft graphite.

TEXTURE

An important part of the rendered perspective is to show the texture of the materials used to build the structure. Most materials can be drawn on the perspective drawing in styles similar to those used to draw an elevation. Although the material will appear similar, the actual lines used to represent the material should be different on a perspective drawing.

Roofing Materials

Shingles, tiles, and metal panels are the major types of materials that will be rendered on the roof. Horizontal construction lines that represent each course of shingles or tiles are usually drawn using tools and then traced using freehand techniques as shown in Figure 42–14. Bar tiles are represented using

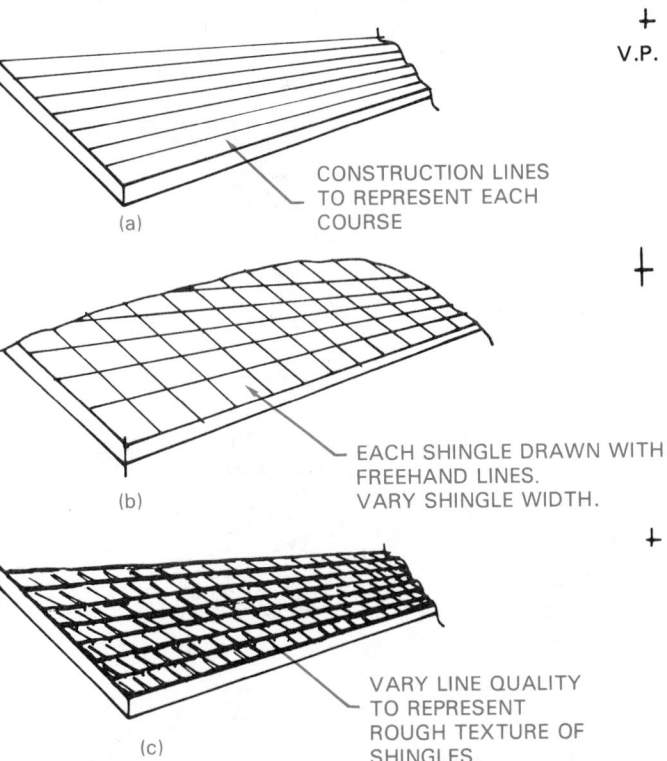

Figure 42–14 Drawing shingles. Shingles can be drawn by lightly drawing lines to the vanishing point (V.P.) to represent each course. Lines can then be drawn to represent each shingle. With each shingle drawn, the original horizontal lines should then be redrawn freehand to represent the rough texture of shingles.

V.P.

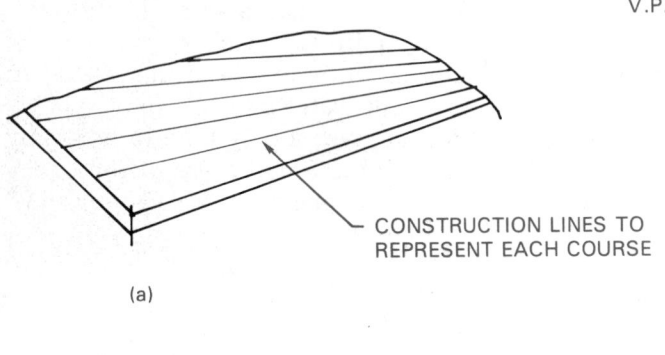

CONSTRUCTION LINES TO
REPRESENT EACH COURSE

(a)

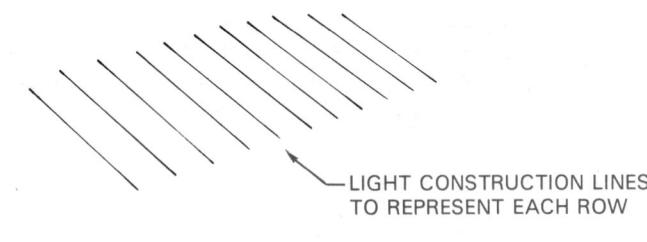

LIGHT CONSTRUCTION LINES
TO REPRESENT EACH ROW

(b)

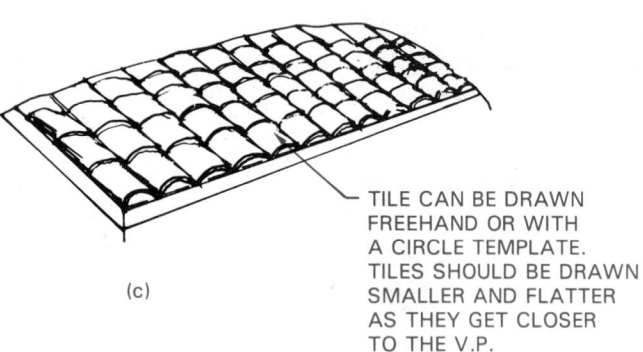

TILE CAN BE DRAWN
FREEHAND OR WITH
A CIRCLE TEMPLATE.
TILES SHOULD BE DRAWN
SMALLER AND FLATTER
AS THEY GET CLOSER
TO THE V.P.

(c)

Figure 42–15 Drawing curved tiles is similar to the layout procedure used when drawing shingles. Tiles should be drawn smaller as they get closer to the vanishing point (V.P.).

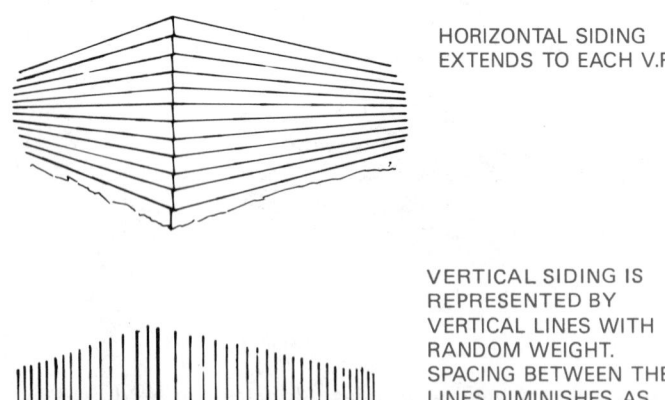

HORIZONTAL SIDING
EXTENDS TO EACH V.P.

VERTICAL SIDING IS
REPRESENTED BY
VERTICAL LINES WITH
RANDOM WEIGHT.
SPACING BETWEEN THE
LINES DIMINISHES AS
THE LINES GET CLOSER
TO THE V.P.

Figure 42–16 Drawing horizontal or vertical siding.

methods similar to shingles. Curved tiles can be drawn as shown in Figure 42–15.

Siding or Paneling

Siding will be drawn using either horizontal or vertical lines. If horizontal siding is used, the lines representing the siding will merge at the vanishing points. When horizontal lap siding intersects another surface, a sawtooth shade pattern will result.

Vertical siding can be drawn using the same methods used on the rendered elevation. On some types of siding, both thickness and texture must be drawn. Figure 42–16 shows common methods of drawing siding. Paneling is usually drawn using a combination of vertical straightedge and freehand lines to represent the wood grain.

ENTOURAGE

Entourage, the term for the surroundings of a building, consists of ground cover, trees, people, and cars. The entourage helps to create an attractive, realistic drawing. In addition it helps define the scale of the drawing. The illustrator must be very careful that the entourage is not allowed to compete with the structure. The surroundings should accent rather than draw attention away from the building. Figure 42–17 shows an example of entourage that blends well with the structure. Notice that rocks, plants, and trees help present the residence as it might appear, but do not draw attention away from the actual structure.

Plants

Plants can be drawn either by hand or applied as rub-ons. A wide variety of rub-on trees and plants are available for use on perspectives. If rub-ons are to be used, they should be placed on the drawing after the line work has been completed. This will help keep the plants from being peeled off the illustration as you draw. Care must be taken to outline the shape of the plant so that the lines of the structure are not placed where the plants will go. If a diazo copy will be made, entourage can be placed on the

Figure 42–17 Entourage should be used to help present the structure in a lifelike setting. *Courtesy Piercy & Barclay Designers, Inc.*

Figure 42–18 Ground cover will often show individual plants. *Courtesy Home Building Plan Service.*

back of the drawing. If the drawing will be photographically reproduced, the rub-ons must be placed on the front side of the drawing material.

Although rub-on plants may be convenient, every drafter should know how to draw entourage. Freehand entourage can best be drawn by spending time observing and sketching various kinds of trees and plants. The method used to draw the entourage should be consistent with the method used to draw the structure. A wide variety of plants can be seen by studying the rendered perspective drawings presented throughout this text. Practice drawing trees and plants that typically grow in your area until you

gain confidence in your work. Keep trees in proportion to the structure. Heights for plants can be projected using methods similar to those used for the structure.

Another common element that should be included when drawing plantings is a method of drawing a ground cover such as grass. Broad strokes of a soft lead are often used to represent grass and the shape of the ground as shown in Figure 42–18. Ground cover provides a method to fill in the white space around a structure without distracting the viewer from it.

People

Many illustrators include people as part of their entourage. If properly drawn, people can help set the scale of the structure and give depth to the drawing. The heights of the people in your drawing should be projected from the vanishing point to the area where they will be placed, so that they will be consistent with the height of the structure. Figure 42–19 shows how people can be drawn in a rendering. As you study the people shown in the renderings throughout this text, you will notice that some of the figures have been outlined, while others have been finely detailed.

Figure 42–19 People are often placed within a drawing to give the viewer a sense of belonging. *Courtesy Paul Franks and Gary M. Larsen, Architects.*

Figure 42–20 Furniture helps show how a space can be used. *Courtesy Paul Franks.*

The method used to draw people should be consistent with the scale of the drawing, and their location should not detract from the main focus of the drawing. Depending on your artistic ability, you may want to collect from magazines and clothes catalogs illustrations of people of various sizes posed in different positions. Such pictures could then be traced onto your rendering.

Furniture

For an interior rendering, furniture and people together help to provide a reference for scale. Furniture should be kept simple and consistent with the line quality of the drawing. Figure 42–20 shows how the use of furniture, people, and interior plants can help draw the viewer into the drawing to create a sense of realism rather than showing just a drawing of a room.

Cars

Cars can be a very attractive addition to the rendering, but can easily overshadow the structure. Be careful not to detail the car so completely that the viewer is thinking about the car rather than the structure. Care must be taken in the placement of the car so that it blends with the surroundings. Drawing people near cars helps tie the scale of the entourage.

Content

You've been exposed to many of the elements that are typically placed in renderings, but you still must consider which elements should be used on

your rendering and where these elements should be placed. The entourage should be consistent with the purpose of the drawing and not obscure the structure. Three guidelines will be helpful in planning your drawing to maintain a proper relation between the structure and the entourage.

1. Use only entourage that is necessary to show the location, scale, and usage of the structure.
2. Draw the entourage with only enough detail to illustrate the desired material.
3. Never obscure structural elements with entourage.

PLANNING THE DRAWING

Successful rendering of a drawing will give the illusion of depth, proportion, and reality. By contrasting areas and surfaces of light and dark, the structure can be emphasized making it the most important part of the drawing. Before rendering a presentation drawing, the illustrator should do several sketches to determine the effectiveness of a layout. Consideration should be given to the placement of the building, people, landscaping, and contrasting values that will be created by the layout. Figure 42–21 is an example of a rendering that has made good use of contrast to help present the structure. Entourage has been used to create black and white surfaces against which the structure can be contrasted.

In Chapter 14 you were introduced to the idea of formal and informal balance. The type of drawing that you are rendering should affect the type of balance that is used in your presentation. Don't try to present a formal business in an informal manner. When making presentation drawings of residential projects, an informal method of balance will typically be most appropriate. Figure 42–22 shows an example of a presentation drawing using formal balance. Notice that the entourage is used as a frame to present the structure. Figure 42–23 shows an example of informal balance with mass of the structure and the entourage offsetting each other.

Figure 42–21 Entourage should be used to accent the structure. *Courtesy Home Building Plan Service.*

Figure 42–22 Formal balance in presentation can be seen in the location of trees used to frame the residence. *Courtesy Home Building Plan Service.*

Figure 42–23 Informal balance can be seen in this drawing as the trees are used to offset the mass of the structure. *Courtesy Home Building Plan Service.*

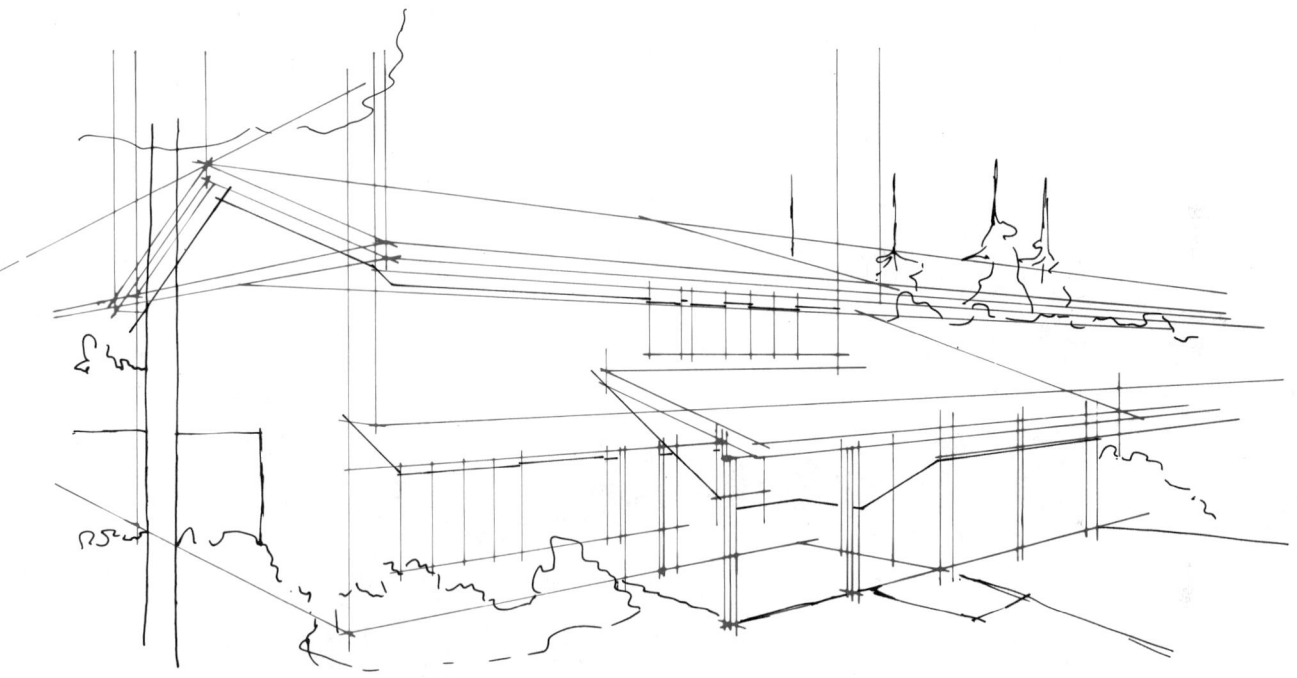

Figure 42–24 With the perspective drawn using construction lines, entourage should be sketched in.

TWO-POINT PERSPECTIVE RENDERING

See Figure 42–24 for steps 1 through 3.

Step 1. Tape your perspective layout to your drawing surface. If you are using graphite and vellum, cover your layout with a thin sheet of sketch paper. This will keep the layout from being traced onto the back of your vellum as you trace the layout.

Step 2. Lay out areas in the foreground where entourage will be placed.

Step 3. Lay out areas that will be shaded.

See Figure 42–25 for steps 4 through 6.

Step 4. Draw trees that will be placed in the foreground.

Step 5. Draw people and cars that will be placed on the drawing. On residential renderings, people and cars are not usually drawn.

Step 6. Draw entourage to help tie the structure to the ground.

Step 7. Render the structure by first drawing material in the foreground and then work into the background. See Figure 42–26.

See Figure 42–27 for steps 8 through 10.

Step 8. Draw major areas of shades and shadows.

Figure 42–25 Draw the foreground entourage prior to drawing the structure. Background and ground cover can also be added.

Figure 42–26 The structure can be rendered once the foreground entourage is drawn. Work from the top to bottom, and from front to back.

Step 9.   Highlight areas in materials that will cast shadows.

Step 10. Letter the job title or owner's name in an appropriate place.

ONE-POINT PERSPECTIVE RENDERING

The one-point perspective can be drawn by following the same procedure that was used for a two-point perspective. The entourage that will be shown for

Figure 42-27 Highlights are added to surface changes.

Figure 42-28 The perspective shown in Figure 41-32 is rendered to show depth and texture.

an interior view will be different from an exterior illustration; however, the interior rendering must be drawn in the same sequence as an exterior view. That is, draw the foreground entourage before drawing the cabinets or furniture in the background. See Figure 42-28.

RENDERING METHODS FOR PERSPECTIVE DRAWINGS TEST

DIRECTIONS

Answer the questions with short complete statements or drawings as needed on an 8½ × 11 drawing sheet as follows:

1. Use ⅛ in. guidelines for all lettering.
2. Letter your name, Rendering Methods for Perspective Drawings Test, and the date at the top of the sheet.
3. Letter the question number and provide the answer. You do not need to write out the question.
4. Do all lettering with vertical uppercase architectural letters. Answers may be prepared on a word processor if appropriate with course guidelines.
5. Your grade will be based on correct answers and quality of line technique.

QUESTIONS

1. What two principles affect the layout of shade and shadows?
2. Sketch an example of how shakes would appear in a rendering.
3. List three steps that could help improve a drafter's rendering technique.
4. At what angles are shadows usually projected? Explain.
5. If you would like to have both surfaces in a two-point perspective in direct sunlight, where would you place the light source?
6. What is entourage?
7. List three guidelines for planning entourage.
8. Sketch four examples of how glass can be rendered.
9. Sketch examples of how depth can be shown at a window.
10. Describe the elements to be considered in planning a rendering.

RENDERING METHODS FOR PERSPECTIVE DRAWINGS PROBLEMS

Problem 42–1. Using your two-point perspective drawing from Problem 41–7, render the residence using either graphite or ink. Draw entourage by hand; do not use rub-ons. Use the examples found in this text as guidelines for drawing your entourage.

Problem 42–2. Using your one-point perspective drawing from Problem 41–8, render the interior illustration using either graphite or ink. Draw entourage freehand; do not use rub-ons. Use the examples found in this text as guidelines for drawing your entourage.

COMMON FRAMING NOTES:

1. ALL FRAMING LUMBER TO BE D.F. L. #2 OR BETTER.
2. ALL EXTERIOR WALLS @ HEATED LIVING AREAS TO BE 2 x 6 @ 24" O.C.
3. ALL EXTERIOR HEADERS TO BE 2 2x12 UNLESS NOTED, W/ 2" RIGID INSULATION BACKING UNLESS NOTED.
4. ALL SHEAR PANELS TO BE ½ STD. GRADE 32/16 PLY. W/ 8d @ 4" o.c.@ EDGE, HDRS., & BLOCKING AND 8d @ 8" o.c. @ FIELD UNLESS NOTED.
5. PROVIDE 1" TYPE "X" GYP. BD. UNDER STAIRS @ ALL USEABLE STORAGE.
6. PROVIDE ½" W.P.GYP. BD. AROUND ALL TUBS, SHOWERS & SPAS.
7. VENT DRYER AND ALL FANS TO OUTSIDE AIR THRU VENT W/ DAMPER.
8. ALL METAL CONNECTORS TO BE BY SIMPSON CO. OR EQUAL.
9. INSULATE W.H. TO R-11 AND PLACE ON 18" HIGH PLATFORM (GARAGE LOCATIONS ONLY)
10. BRICK VENEER TO BE OVER 1" AIR SPACE W/ 15# FELT AND METAL TIES @ 24" o.c. @ EA. STUD.
11. ALL TRUSSES TO BE @ 24" o.c. (DIRECTLY OVER STUDS). SUBMIT TRUSS CALCS. TO BUILDING DEPT. PRIOR TO ERECTION.
12. ALL BEDROOM WINDOWS TO BE WITHIN 44" OF FIN. FLOOR.
13. ALL DOORS TO BE 6'8" HIGH UNLESS NOTED. GARAGE DOOR TO BE 7'-0" HIGH.
14. ENTRY DOOR TO BE RAISED PANEL, METAL INSULATED.
15. ALL WINDOWS AND GLASS DOORS TO BE THERMAL PANE W/ BRONZE ANODIZED FRAMES
16. ALL GLASS WITHIN 18" OF DOORS TO BE TEMPERED.
17. ALL SKYLITES TO BE ___" x ___" DBL DOMED PLASTIC SKYLITES BY VELOX OR EQUAL.
    (OR)
    ALL SKYLITES TO BE ___" x ___"TEMPERED FLAT GLASS BY VELOX OR EQUAL.

CM-1430

Section Eleven

General Construction Specifications

Chapter 43
General Construction Specifications

CONSTRUCTION SPECIFICATIONS

BUILDING PLANS, including all of the elements that make up a complete set of residential or commercial drawings, contain most general and some specific information about the construction of the structure. However, it is very difficult to provide all of the required information on a set of plans. Schedules, as discussed in detail in Section 3, provide a certain amount of subordinate information. Information that cannot be clearly or completely provided on the drawing or in schedules are provided in construction specifications. Specifications are an integral part of any set of plans. Specifications may not be required when applying for a building permit for a simple residential structure, but they are generally needed for loan approval when financing is required. Most lenders have their own format for residential con- struction specifications, although these forms are gen- erally similar. The Federal Housing Administration (FHA) or the Federal Home Loan Mortgage Corpo- ration (FHLMC) has a specification format entitled, Description of Materials. This specifications form is used widely in a revised or identical manner by most residential construction lenders. The same form is used by Farm Home Administration (FmHA) and by the Veterans Administration (VA). Figure 43–1 shows a completed FHA Description of Materials form for a typical structure. The set of plans, construction specifications, and building contract together become the legal documents for the construction project. These documents should be prepared very carefully in co- operation with the architect, client, and contractor. Any deviation from these documents should be ap- proved by all three parties. When brand names are used, a clause specifying, "or equivalent," may be added. This means that another brand of equivalent value to the one specified may be substituted with the construction supervisor's approval.

TYPICAL MINIMUM CONSTRUCTION SPECIFICATIONS

Minimum construction specifications as established by local building officials vary from one location to the next and their contents are dependent upon spe- cific local requirements, climate, codes used, and the

FHA Form 2005
VA Form 26-1852
Form FmHA 424-2
Rev. 4/77

□ Proposed Construction

□ Under Construction

U. S. DEPARTMENT OF HOUSING AND URBAN DEVELOPMENT
FEDERAL HOUSING ADMINISTRA۱ION
For accurate register of carbon copies, form
may be separated along above fold. Staple
completed sheets together in original order.

DESCRIPTION OF MATERIALS No. _____

(To be inserted by FHA, VA or FmHA)

Form Approved
OMB No. 63-R0055

Property address _____ LAKE HOUSE _____   City _____   State _____

Mortgagor or Sponsor _____   _____
(Name)   (Address)

Contractor or Builder _____   _____
(Name)   (Address)

INSTRUCTIONS

1. For additional information on how this form is to be submitted, number of copies, etc., see the instructions applicable to the FHA Application for Mortgage Insurance, VA Request for Determination of Reasonable Value, or FmHA Property Information and Appraisal Report, as the case may be.
2. Describe all materials and equipment to be used, whether or not shown on the drawings, by marking an X in each appropriate check-box and entering the information called for in each space. If space is inadequate, enter "See misc." and describe under item 27 or on an attached sheet. THE USE OF PAINT CONTAINING MORE THAN THE PERCENTAGE OF LEAD BY WEIGHT PERMITTED BY LAW IS PROHIBITED.
3. Work not specifically described or shown will not be considered unless

required, then the minimum acceptable will be assumed. Work exceeding minimum requirements cannot be considered unless specifically described.
4. Include no alternates, "or equal" phrases, or contradictory items. (Consideration of a request for acceptance of substitute materials or equipment is not thereby precluded.)
5. Include signatures required at the end of this form.
6. The construction shall be completed in compliance with the related drawings and specifications, as amended during processing. The specifications include this Description of Materials and the applicable Minimum Property Standards.

1. EXCAVATION:
Bearing soil, type ___ SANDY LOAM ___

2. FOUNDATIONS:
Footings: concrete mix _____; strength psi _2500 @ 28 D._ Reinforcing _2 - #4_
Foundation wall: material ___CONCRETE BLOCK___   Reinforcing _HORIZONTAL @ 24"_
Interior foundation wall: material _CONCRETE BLOCK_   Party foundation wall _____
Columns: material and sizes _TS3 1/2 X 3 1/2 X .250_   Piers: material and reinforcing _____
Girders: material and sizes _SEE DRAWINGS_   Sills: material _2 X 10/CELOTEX SILL SEAL_
Basement entrance areaway _____   Window areaways _____
Waterproofing _2 COATS ASPHALT BELOW GRADE_   Footing drains _____
Termite protection _____
Basementless space: ground cover _____; insulation _R-7.2 FOAM BD_; foundation vents_____
Special foundations _____
Additional information: _3/8"φ X 12" ANCHOR BOLTS @ 3'-0"_

3. CHIMNEYS:
Material _TRIPLE-WALL STEEL_   Prefabricated *(make and size)* _MAJESTIC 9"_
Flue lining: material _STAINLESS STEEL_   Heater flue size _____   Fireplace flue size _____
Vents *(material and size)*: gas or oil heater _____; water heater _____
Additional information: _INSTALLED IN ACCORDANCE W/MAJESTIC INSTRUCTIONS_

4. FIREPLACES:
Type: ☒ solid fuel; □ gas-burning; □ circulator *(make and size)* _MAJESTIC #M28_   Ash dump and clean-out _____
Fireplace: facing _FACE BRICK_; lining _____; hearth _FACE BRICK_; mantel _____
Additional information: _____

5. EXTERIOR WALLS:
Wood frame: wood grade, and species _HEM-FIR #2_   ☒ Corner bracing. Building paper or felt _3/4"CDX PLY. WD._
Sheathing _R-5.4 FOAM BD._; thickness _3/4"_; width ___; □ solid; □ spaced ___" o. c.; □ diagonal; ___
Siding _PLYWOOD_; grade _EXT._; type _T1-11_; size _1/2"_; exposure ___"; fastening _AL. NAILS_
Shingles ___; grade ___; type ___; size ___; exposure ___"; fastening ___
Stucco ___; thickness ___"; Lath ___; weight ___ lb.
Masonry veneer ___   Sills ___   Lintels ___   Base flashing ___
Masonry: □ solid □ faced □ stuccoed; total-wall thickness ___"; facing thickness ___"; facing material ___
Backup material ___; thickness ___"; bonding ___
Door sills _OAK_   Window sills ___   Lintels ___   Base flashing ___
Interior surfaces: dampproofing, ___ coats of ___; furring _1 X 3 @ 16" O.C._
Additional information: _____
Exterior painting: material _STAIN_; number of coats _1_
Gable wall construction: ☒ same as main walls; □ other construction _____

6. FLOOR FRAMING:
Joists: wood, grade, and species _DOUG. FIR. #2_; other ___; bridging ___; anchors ___
Concrete slab: ☒ basement floor; □ first floor; ☒ ground supported; □ self-supporting; mix _2500 PSI @ 28 DAYS_; thickness _4_";
reinforcing _6 X 6 - 10/10 WWM_; insulation ___; membrane _4-MIL POLYETHELENE_
Fill under slab: material _R.O.B. GRAVEL_; thickness _6_". Additional information: _R-14.6 FOAM BD._
INSULATION UNDER HEAT SINK

7. SUBFLOORING: *(Describe underflooring for special floors under item 21.)*
Material: grade and species _CD GRADE PLYWOOD_; size _1/2"_; type ___
Laid: □ first floor; □ second floor; □ attic ___ sq. ft.; □ diagonal; □ right angles. Additional information: _ALL FRAMED_
FLOOR NOT DESCRIBED UNDER ITEM 21 TO HAVE 3/8" PLY. WD. UNDERLAY AT RIGHT ANGLES.

8. FINISH FLOORING: *(Wood only. Describe other finish flooring under item 21.)*

LOCATION	ROOMS	GRADE	SPECIES	THICKNESS	WIDTH	BLDG. PAPER	FINISH
First floor	LOFT	SELECT	R. OAK	25/32	2 1/2	YES	FILL & 2 COATS POLYURETHANE
Second floor							
Attic floor		___ sq. ft.					
Additional information:							

FHA Form 2005
VA Form 26-1852
Form FmHA 424-2

DESCRIPTION OF MATERIALS

Figure 43-1 Completed FHA Description of Materials for a structure. From *Huth, Understanding Construction Drawings, Delmar Publishers Inc.*

9. PARTITION FRAMING:
Studs: wood, grade, and species ___HEM-FIR #2___ size and spacing ___2 X 4 @ 16" O.C.___ Other _____
Additional information: _____

10. CEILING FRAMING:
Joists: wood, grade, and species ___HEM-FIR #2___ Other _____ Bridging _____
Additional information: _____

11. ROOF FRAMING:
Rafters: wood, grade, and species ___HEM-FIR #2___ Roof trusses (see detail): grade and species _____
Additional information: _____

12. ROOFING:
Sheathing: wood, grade, and species ___1/2" CDX PLY. WD.___ ; ☐ solid; ☐ spaced ___" o.c.
Roofing ___COMP. SHINGLES___ ; grade ___#235___ ; size _____ ; type _____
Underlay ___ASPHALT SATURATED FELT___ ; weight or thickness ___#15___ ; size _____ ; fastening _____
Built-up roofing _____ ; number of plies _____ ; surfacing material _____
Flashing: material ___ALUMINUM___ ; gage or weight ___28 GA.___ ; ☐ gravel stops; ☐ snow guards
Additional information: ___ALUMINUM DRIP EDGE___

13. GUTTERS AND DOWNSPOUTS:
Gutters: material _____ ; gage or weight _____ ; size _____ ; shape _____
Downspouts: material _____ ; gage or weight _____ ; size _____ ; shape _____ ; number _____
Downspouts connected to: ☐ Storm sewer; ☐ sanitary sewer; ☐ dry-well. ☐ Splash blocks: material and size _____
Additional information: _____

14. LATH AND PLASTER
Lath ☐ walls, ☐ ceilings: material _____ ; weight or thickness _____ Plaster: coats ____ ; finish _____
Dry-wall ☒ walls, ☒ ceilings: material ___GYPSUM___ ; thickness ___1/2"___ ; finish ___PAINTED___ ,
Joint treatment ___TAPE & COMPOUND WITH METAL CORNER BEADS___

15. DECORATING: *(Paint, wallpaper, etc.)*

Rooms	Wall Finish Material and Application	Ceiling Finish Material and Application
Kitchen	LOW LUSTER ENAMEL - - 2 COATS	ALL CEILINGS - - ONE COAT
Bath	VINYL WALLCOVERING	FLAT LATEX/ONE COAT
Other	FLAT LATEX - - 2 COATS	STIPPLED LATEX

Additional information: _____

16. INTERIOR DOORS AND TRIM:
Doors: type _____ ; material ___WOOD DOORS BIRCH OR PINE___ ; thickness _____
Door trim: type ___RANCH___ ; material ___PINE___ Base: type ___RANCH___ ; material ___PINE___ ; size ___3 1/2"___
Finish: doors ___SEMIGLOSS LATEX ENAMEL - 2 CTS.___ ; trim ___SEMIGLOSS LATEX ENAMEL - - 2 COATS___
Other trim (item, type and location) ___BEAM CASINGS - - PINE W/2 COATS SEMIGLOSS; RAILING & LADDER - - WOOD___
Additional information: ___PARTS, SANDED & 2 COATS POLYURETHANE - - METAL PARTS, 2 COATS RUST-RESISTANT SEMIGLOSS ENAMEL.___

17. WINDOWS:
Windows: type ___SLIDING___ ; make ___CAPITOL___ ; material ___THERM-BRK. AL.___ ; sash thickness _____
Glass: grade ___INSULATING___ ; ☐ sash weights; ☐ balances, type _____ ; head flashing ___INTEGRAL FLANGE___
Trim: type ___GYP. BD. RETURN___ ; material _____ Paint ___AS WALL___ ; number coats _____
Weatherstripping: type ___FACTORY INSTALLED___ ; material _____ Storm sash, number _____
Screens: ☒ full; ☐ half; type _____ ; number _____ ; screen cloth material ___ALUMINUM___
Basement windows: type _____ ; material _____ ; screens, number _____ ; Storm sash, number _____
Special windows ___SKYLIGHT - - SKYVUE #DV 2852___
Additional information: ___WOOD DRIP CAPS___

18. ENTRANCES AND EXTERIOR DETAIL:
Main entrance door: material ___HOLLOW CORE STEEL___ ; width ___3'-0"___ ; thickness ___1 3/4___". Frame: material ___WOOD___ , thickness ___".
Other entrance doors: material ___SAME___ ; width _____". thickness _____". Frame: material _____ ; thickness _____"
Head flashing _____ Weatherstripping: type ___MAGNETIC___ saddles ___OAK___
Screen doors: thickness ___" ; number _____ ; screen cloth material _____ Storm doors: thickness ___" ; number _____
Combination storm and screen doors: thickness ___" ; number ____ ; screen cloth material _____
Shutters: ☐ hinged; ☐ fixed. Railings _____ , Attic louvers _____
Exterior millwork: grade and species ___#1 PINE___ Paint ___STAIN___ ; number coats ___1___
Additional information: ___ALL DECK LUMBER TO BE TREATED W/COPPER-BASE PRESERVATIVE___

19. CABINETS AND INTERIOR DETAIL:
Kitchen cabinets, wall units: material ___SCHEIRCH, GARDEN GROVE___ ; lineal feet of shelves _____ ; shelf width _____
  Base units: material ___GARDEN GROVE___ ; counter top ___PLASTIC LAMINATE___ ; edging _____
  Back and end splash ___MOLDED___ Finish of cabinets ___FACTORY FINISHED___ ; number coats _____
Medicine cabinets: make ___MIAMI-CAREY___ ; model ___UP-CRP3418/DWN-CRP-306-AL___
Other cabinets and built-in furniture ___BENCH IN L.R. - - AC PLYWOOD, SANDED, 1 COAT FIRZITE___
Additional information: ___2 COATS SEMIGLOSS ENAMEL___

20. STAIRS:

Stair	Treads		Risers		Strings		Handrail		Balusters	
	Material	Thickness	Material	Thickness	Material	Size	Material	Size	Material	Size
Basement	OAK	5/4	PINE	1" NOM.	PINE	5/4				
Main	OAK	5/4	PINE	1" NOM.	PINE	5/4	OAK	5/4" X 3"	STEEL	1"
Attic										

Disappearing: make and model number _____
Additional information: _____

Figure 43–1 Continued.

2

21. SPECIAL FLOORS AND WAINSCOT: *(Describe Carpet as listed in Certified Products Directory)*

	LOCATION	MATERIAL, COLOR, BORDER, SIZES, GAGE, ETC.	THRESHOLD MATERIAL	WALL BASE MATERIAL	UNDERFLOOR MATERIAL
FLOORS	Kitchen	QUARRY TILE (N.I.C.)	OAK	PINE	1" CONC.
	Bath	UNGLAZED CERAMIC TILE	MARBLE	TILE	1" CONC.
	L.R. & D.R.	QUARRY TILE (N.I.C.)		PINE	CONC.

	LOCATION	MATERIAL, COLOR, BORDER, CAP. SIZES, GAGE, ETC.	HEIGHT	HEIGHT OVER TUB	HEIGHT IN SHOWERS (FROM FLOOR)
WAINSCOT	Bath	CERAMIC TILE	4'-0"	4'-0" FROM TUB	TO CLG.

Bathroom accessories: ☒ Recessed; material ___CHINA___; number ___5___; ☒ Attached; material ___CHINA___; number ___7___
Additional information: _____

22. PLUMBING:

FIXTURE	NUMBER	LOCATION	MAKE	MFR'S FIXTURE IDENTIFICATION NO.	SIZE	COLOR
Sink	1	KITCHEN	MOEN	S3322-4		S.S.
Lavatory	3		UNIVERSAL-RUNDLE	163330	PER DWGS.	BY OWNER
Water closet	3		UNIVERSAL-RUNDLE	4055-15		BY OWNER
Bathtub	1		UNIVERSAL-RUNDLE	118-2	5'-0"	BY OWNER
Shower over tub △	1		MOEN			CROME
Stall shower △	1		KINKEAD INDUSTRIES	MARBLEMOLD	3'-0" X 3'-0"	
Laundry trays						

△☒ Curtain rod   △☒ Door   ☐ Shower pan: material ___SYNTHETIC HARD RUBBER___
Water supply: ☐ public; ☐ community system; ☒ individual (private) system. ★
Sewage disposal: ☐ public; ☐ community system; ☐ individual (private) system. ★
★ *Show and describe individual system in complete detail in separate drawings and specifications according to requirements.*
House drain (inside): ☐ cast iron; ☐ tile; ☒ other ___PVC___   House sewer (outside): ☐ cast iron; ☐ tile; ☒ other ___PVC___
Water piping: ☐ galvanized steel; ☒ copper tubing; ☐ other _____   Sill cocks, number ___2___
Domestic water heater: type ___ELECTRIC___; make and model ___STATE-CENSIBLE___; heating capacity _____
_____ gph. 100° rise. Storage tank: material ___GLASS___; capacity ___40___ gallons.
Gas service: ☐ utility company; ☐ liq. pet. gas; ☐ other _____   Gas piping: ☐ cooking; ☐ house heating.
Footing drains connected to: ☐ storm sewer; ☐ sanitary sewer; ☐ dry well. Sump pump; make and model _____
_____; capacity _____; discharges into _____

23. HEATING:
☐ Hot water. ☐ Steam. ☐ Vapor. ☐ One-pipe system. ☐ Two-pipe system.
  ☐ Radiators. ☐ Convectors. ☐ Baseboard radiation. Make and model _____
  Radiant panel: ☐ floor; ☐ wall; ☐ ceiling. Panel coil: material _____
  ☐ Circulator. ☐ Return pump. Make and model _____; capacity _____ gpm.
  Boiler: make and model _____ Output _____ Btuh.; net rating _____ Btuh.
Additional information: _____
Warm air: ☐ Gravity. ☐ Forced. Type of system _____
  Duct material: supply _____; return _____ Insulation _____, thickness _____ ☐ Outside air intake.
  Furnace: make and model _____ Input _____ Btuh.; output _____ Btuh.
  Additional information: _____
☐ Space heater; ☐ floor furnace; ☐ wall heater. Input _____ Btuh.; output _____ Btuh.; number units _____
  Make, model _____ Additional information: _____
Controls: make and types _____
Additional information: _____
Fuel: ☐ Coal; ☐ oil; ☐ gas; ☐ liq. pet. gas; ☐ electric; ☐ other _____; storage capacity _____
  Additional information: _____
Firing equipment furnished separately: ☐ Gas burner, conversion type. ☐ Stoker: hopper feed ☐; bin feed ☐
  Oil burner: ☐ pressure atomizing; ☐ vaporizing _____
  Make and model _____ Control _____
  Additional information: _____
Electric heating system: type ___BASEBOARD RESISTANCE___ Input _____ watts; @ _____ volts; output _____ Btuh.
  Additional information: ___SEE SCHEDULE___
Ventilating equipment: attic fan, make and model _____; capacity _____ cfm.
  kitchen exhaust fan, make and model ___GENERAL ELECTRIC #JV330___
Other heating, ventilating, or cooling equipment _____

24. ELECTRIC WIRING:
Service: ☐ overhead; ☒ underground. Panel: ☐ fuse box; ☒ circuit-breaker; make ___SQUARE D___ AMP's ___200___ No. circuits ___40___
Wiring: ☐ conduit; ☐ armored cable; ☒ nonmetallic cable; ☐ knob and tube; ☐ other _____
Special outlets: ☒ range; ☒ water heater; ☐ other ___CLOTHES DRYER___
☐ Doorbell. ☒ Chimes. Push-button locations ___KITCHEN ENTRANCE___ Additional information: ___ONE TELEPHONE___
___JACK IN EACH LIVING SPACE TO BE COMPATIBLE W/LOCAL TELEPHONE UTILITY___

25. LIGHTING FIXTURES:
Total number of fixtures ___22___ Total allowance for fixtures, typical installation, $ ___$450___
Nontypical installation _____
Additional information: _____

DESCRIPTION OF MATERIALS

26. INSULATION:

Location	Thickness	Material, Type, and Method of Installation	Vapor Barrier
Roof	9"	R-30 FIBERGLASS	4 MIL POLYETHYLENE
Ceiling			
Wall	6"	R-19 FIBERGLASS	4 MIL POLYETHYLENE
Floor			
MASONARY WALLS - - 1", R-7.2 FOAM BD BETWEEN FURRING			

27. MISCELLANEOUS: *(Describe any main dwelling materials, equipment, or construction items not shown elsewhere; or use to provide additional information where the space provided was inadequate. Always reference by item number to correspond to numbering used on this form.)*

2. HEATSINK – 12" R.Q.B. GRAVEL MINIMUM OVER UNEXCAVATED EARTH. BLOCK UNDER CONCRETE AT HEAT SINK TO BE LAID FLAT W/3/8" JOINTS & NO MORTAR.

19. VANITIES - - SCHEIRICH GARDEN GROVE

HARDWARE: *(make, material, and finish.)* KWIK-SET: ENTRANCES - - BRONZE
BATHS - - CHROME
OTHERS - - BRASS

SPECIAL EQUIPMENT: *(State material or make, model and quantity. Include only equipment and appliances which are acceptable by local law, custom and applicable FHA standards. Do not include items which, by established custom, are supplied by occupant and removed when he vacates premises or chattles prohibited by law from becoming realty.)*

APPLIANCES NOT INCLUDED ABOVE - - NOT IN CONTRACT

PORCHES:
DECKS ACCORDING TO DRAWINGS - - ALL LUMBER TO BE CCA TREATED OR EQUAL. FASTENERS TO BE GALVANIZED STEEL.

TERRACES:

GARAGES:
ACCORDING TO PLAN, NO INSULATION, OVERHEAD DOOR - - WOOD FRAME W/HARDBOARD PANELS, ONE SECTION GLAZED.

WALKS AND DRIVEWAYS:
Driveway: width SEE DWG ; base material GRADE ; thickness ____"; surfacing material CLEAN GRAVEL ; thickness 6 "
Front walk: width 3'-0" ; material STONE ; thickness 4 ". Service walk: width ____ ; material ____ ; thickness ____ "
Steps: material ____ ; treads ____"; risers ____". Cheek walls ____

OTHER ONSITE IMPROVEMENTS:
(Specify all exterior onsite improvements not described elsewhere, including items such as unusual grading, drainage structures, retaining walls, fence, railings, and accessory structures.)

LANDSCAPING, PLANTING, AND FINISH GRADING:
Topsoil 2 " thick: ☒ front yard; ☒ side yards; ☒ rear yard to PROPERTY LINE feet behind main building.
Lawns *(seeded, sodded, or sprigged)*: ☒ front yard SEED ; ☒ side yards SEED ; ☒ rear yard SEED
Planting: ☐ as specified and shown on drawings; ☐ as follows:
____ Shade trees, deciduous, ____" caliper. ____ Evergreen trees. ____' to ____', B & B.
____ Low flowering trees, deciduous, ____' to ____' ____ Evergreen shrubs. ____' to ____', B & B.
____ High-growing shrubs, deciduous, ____' to ____' ____ Vines, 2-year ____
____ Medium-growing shrubs, deciduous, ____' to ____'
____ Low-growing shrubs, deciduous, ____' to ____'

Identification.—This exhibit shall be identified by the signature of the builder, or sponsor, and/or the proposed mortgagor if the latter is known at the time of application.

Date ____ Signature ____

Signature ____

FHA Form 2005
VA Form 26–1852
Form FmHA 424–2

4

Figure 43–1 Continued.

extent of coverage. Verify the local requirements for a construction project as they may differ from those given here. The following are some general classifications of construction specifications.

Room Dimensions

- Minimum room size is to be 70 sq ft.
- Ceiling height minimum is to be 7'–6" in 50 percent of area except 7'–0" may be used for bathrooms and hallways.

Light and Ventilation

- Minimum window area is to be 1/10 floor area with not less than 10 sq ft for habitable rooms and 3 sq ft for bathrooms and laundry rooms. Not less than one-half of this required window area is to be openable. Every sleeping room is required to have a window or door for emergency exit. Windows with an openable area of not less than 5 sq ft with no dimension less than 22 in. meet this requirement, and the sill height is to be not more than 44 in. above the floor.
- Glass subject to human impact is to be tempered glass.
- Glass doors in shower and tub enclosures are to be tempered glass or fracture-resistant plastic.
- Attic ventilation is to be a minimum of 1/300 of the attic area, one-half in the soffit and one-half in the upper area.
- Bathroom and kitchen fans and dryer are to vent directly outside.

Foundation

- Concrete mix is to have a minimum ultimate compressive strength of 2000 psi at 28 days and shall be composed of 1 part cement, 3 parts sand, 4 parts of 1 in. maximum size rock, and not more than 7½ gallons of water per sack of cement.
- Foundation mud sills, plates, and sleepers are to be pressure treated or of foundation-grade redwood. All footing sills shall have full bearing on the footing wall or slab and shall be bolted to the foundation with ½" × 10" bolts embedded at least 7 in. into the concrete or reinforced masonry, or 15 in. into unreinforced grouted masonry. Bolts shall be spaced not to exceed 6 ft on center with bolts not over 12 in. from cut end of sills.
- Crawl space shall be ventilated by an approved mechanical means or by openings with a net area not less than 1½ sq ft for each 25 linear ft of exterior wall. Openings shall be covered with not less than ¼ in. or more than ½ in. of corrosion-resistant wire mesh. If the crawl space is to be heated, closeable covers for vent openings shall be provided. Water drainage and 6 mil black ground cover shall be provided in the crawl space.
- Access to crawl space is to be a minimum of 18" × 24".
- Basement foundation walls with a height of 8 ft or less supporting a well-drained porous fill of 7 ft or less, with soil pressure not more than 30 lb per sq ft equivalent fluid pressure, and with the bottom of the wall supported from inward movement by structural floor systems may be of plain concrete with an 8 in. minimum thickness and minimum ultimate compressive strength of 2500 psi at 28 days. Basement walls supporting backfill and not meeting these criteria shall be designed in accordance with accepted engineering practices.
- Concrete forms for footings shall conform to the shape, lines, and dimensions of the members as called for on the plans and shall be substantial and sufficiently tight to prevent leakage of mortar and slumping out of concrete in the ground contact area.

Framing

- Lumber. All joists, rafters, beams, and posts 2 to 4 in. thick shall be No. 2 Grade Douglas fir-larch or better. All posts and beams 5 in. and thicker shall be No. 1 Grade Douglas fir-larch or better.
- Beams (untreated) bearing in concrete or masonry wall pockets shall have air space on sides and ends. Beams are to have not less than 4 in. of bearing on masonry or concrete.
- Wall Bracing. Every exterior wood stud wall and main cross partition shall be braced at each end and at least every 25 ft of length with 1 × 4 diagonal let-in braces or equivalent.
- Joists are to have not less than 1½ in. of bearing on wood or metal nor less than 3 in. on masonry.
- Joists under bearing partitions are to be doubled.
- Floor joists are to have solid blocking at each support and at the ends except when the end is nailed to a rim joist or adjoining studs. Joists 2 × 14 or larger are to have bridging at maximum intervals of 8 ft.
- Two in. clearance is required between combustible material and the walls of an interior fireplace or chimney. One in. clearance is required when the chimney is on an outside wall. (½ in. moisture-resistant gypsum board may be used in lieu of the 1 in. clearance requirement).

- Rafter purlin braces are to be not less than 45° to the horizontal.
- Rafters, when not parallel to ceiling joists, are to have ties that are 1 × 4 minimum spaced not more than 4 ft on center.
- Provide a double top plate with a minimum 48 in. lap splice.
- Metal truss tie-downs are to be required for manufactured trusses.
- Plant manufactured trusses (if used) shall be of an approved design with an engineered drawing.
- Fire blocking shall be provided for walls over 10'–0" in height, also for horizontal shafts 10'–0" on center, and for any concealed draft opening.
- Garage walls and ceiling adjacent to or under dwelling require one-hour fire-resistant construction on the garage side. A self-closing door between the garage and dwelling is to be a minimum 1⅜ in. solid core construction.
- Ceramic tile, or approved material, is to be used in a water-splash area.
- Building paper, or other approved material, is to be used under siding.
- Framing in the water-splash area is to be protected by waterproof paper, waterproof gypsum, or other approved substitute.
- Post-and-beam connections. A positive connection shall be provided between beam, post, and footing to ensure against uplift and lateral displacement. Untreated posts shall be separated from concrete or masonry by a rust-resistant metal plate or impervious membrane and be at least 6 in. from any earth.

Stairways

- Maximum rise is to be 8 in., minimum run 9 in., minimum head room to be 6'–6", and minimum width to be 30 in.
- Winding and curved stairways are to have a minimum inside tread width of 6 in.
- Enclosed usable space under stairway is to be protected by one-hour fire-resistant construction (⅝ in. type X gypsum board).
- Handrails are to be from 30 to 34 in. above tread nosing and intermediate rails are to be such that no object 5 in. in diameter can pass through.
- Generally, for commercial or public structures, all unenclosed floor and roof openings, balconies, decks, and porches more than 30 in. above grade shall be protected by a guardrail not less than 42 in. in height with intermediate rails or dividers such that no object 9 in. in diameter can pass through. Generally, guardrails for residential occupancies may be not less than 36 in. in height. Specific applications are subject to local or national building codes.

Roof

- Composition shingles on roof slopes between 4 to 12 and 7 to 12 shall have an underlayment of not less than 15 lb felt. For slopes from 2 to 12 to less than 4 to 12, Building Department approval of roofing manufacturers' low-slope instructions is required.
- Shake roofs require solid roof sheathing (in lieu of solid sheathing, spaced sheathing may be used but shall not be less than 1 × 4 with not more than 3 in. clearance between) with an underlayment of not less than 15 lb felt with an interlace of not less than 30 lb felt. For slopes less than 4 to 12, special approval is required.
- Attic scuttle is to have a minimum of 22 by 30 in. of headroom above.

Chimney and Fireplace

- Reinforcing. Masonry constructed chimneys extending more than 7 ft above the last anchorage point (example: roof line) must have not less than four number 4 steel reinforcing bars placed vertically for the full height of the chimney with horizontal ties not less than ¼ in. diameter spaced at not over 18 in. intervals. If the width of the chimney exceeds 40 in., two additional number 4 vertical bars shall be provided for each additional flue or for each additional 40 in. in width or fraction thereof.
- Anchorage. All masonry chimneys over 18 ft high shall be anchored at each floor and/or ceiling line more than 6 ft above grade, except when constructed completely within the exterior walls of the building.

Thermal Insulation and Heating

- Thermal designs employing the R factor must meet minimum R factors as follows:

  a. Ceiling or roof: R–30
  b. Walls: R–11, vapor barrier required. Minimum one permeability rating.
  c. Floors over unheated crawl space or basements: R–19 including reflective foil.
  d. Foundation walls: R–4.5 to ½ ft below exterior finished grade line.
  e. Slab-on-Grade: R–4.5 around perimeter a minimum of 18 in. horizontally or vertically.

- Thermal glazing. Heated portions of buildings located in the 5,000 or less degree-day zone do not require thermal glazing on that portion of the glazing that is less than 20 percent of the total area of exterior walls including doors and windows. Heated portions of buildings located in zones over 5,000 degree days shall be provided with special thermal glazing in all exterior wall areas.

- Duct insulation. Supply and return air ducts used for heating and/or cooling located in unheated attics, garages, crawl spaces, or other unheated spaces other than between floors or interior walls shall be insulated with an R–3.5 minimum.
- Heating. Every dwelling unit and guest room shall be provided with heating facilities capable of maintaining a room temperature of 70° F at a point 3 ft above the floor.

Fire Warning System

- Every dwelling shall be provided with approved detectors of products of combustion mounted on the ceiling or a wall within 12 in. of the ceiling at a point centrally located in the corridor or area giving access to and not over 12 ft from rooms used for sleeping. Where sleeping rooms are on an upper level, the detector shall be placed at the high area of the ceiling near the top of the stairway.

SPECIFICATIONS FOR COMMERCIAL CONSTRUCTION

Specifications for commercial construction projects are often more complex and comprehensive than the documents for residential construction. Commercial project specifications may provide very detailed instructions for each phase of construction. Specifications may establish time schedules for the completion of the project. Also, in certain situations, the specifications will include inspections that are in conjunction with or in addition to required local jurisdiction inspections.

Construction specifications often follow the guidelines of the individual architect or engineering firm although a common format has been established by the Construction Specification Institute (CSI). The CSI format is made up of 17 major divisions. Within each major division are several subsections. The major categories are numbered in order beginning at Division 0 through Division 16. The subdivisions of each general category are numbered with five-digit numbers. For example, one of the division 15 subsections is numbered 15050. When specific divisions or subdivisions are not required as elements of the project, they are excluded. The numbering system continues as normal with these unnecessary elements left out. Figure 43–2 shows the categorical breakdown of the CSI system.

The CSI format is an effective system for indexing large project specifications. Much of the CSI format cannot be effectively used in some light commercial or residential construction. When comprehensive specifications are required for residential construction, an abridged format of the CSI system may be used. This short form may include the major divisions and exclude the subdivisions. Figure 43–3 provides a set of written specifications for the same structure described in the FHA Description of Materials; notice the similarities and differences.

DIVISION 0 - BIDDING AND CONTRACT REQUIREMENTS

00010	PRE-BID INFORMATION
00100	INSTRUCTIONS TO BIDDERS
00200	INFORMATION AVAILABLE TO BIDDERS
00300	BID/TENDER FORMS
00400	SUPPLEMENTS TO BID/TENDER FORMS
00500	AGREEMENT FORMS
00600	BONDS AND CERTIFICATES
00700	GENERAL CONDITIONS OF THE CONTRACT
00800	SUPPLEMENTARY CONDITIONS
00950	DRAWINGS INDEX
00900	ADDENDA AND MODIFICATIONS

SPECIFICATIONS—DIVISIONS 1-16

DIVISION 1 - GENERAL REQUIREMENTS

01010	SUMMARY OF WORK
01020	ALLOWANCES
01030	SPECIAL PROJECT PROCEDURES
01040	COORDINATION
01050	FIELD ENGINEERING
01060	REGULATORY REQUIREMENTS
01070	ABBREVIATIONS AND SYMBOLS
01080	IDENTIFICATION SYSTEMS
01100	ALTERNATES/ALTERNATIVES
01150	MEASUREMENT AND PAYMENT
01200	PROJECT MEETINGS
01300	SUBMITTALS
01400	QUALITY CONTROL
01500	CONSTRUCTION FACILITIES AND TEMPORARY CONTROLS
01600	MATERIAL AND EQUIPMENT
01650	STARTING OF SYSTEMS
01660	TESTING, ADJUSTING, AND BALANCING OF SYSTEMS
01700	CONTRACT CLOSEOUT
01800	MAINTENANCE MATERIALS

DIVISION 2 - SITE WORK

02010	SUBSURFACE INVESTIGATION
02050	DEMOLITION
02100	SITE PREPARATION
02150	UNDERPINNING
02200	EARTHWORK
02300	TUNNELLING
02350	PILES, CAISSONS AND COFFERDAMS
02400	DRAINAGE
02440	SITE IMPROVEMENTS
02480	LANDSCAPING
02500	PAVING AND SURFACING
02580	BRIDGES
02590	PONDS AND RESERVOIRS
02600	PIPED UTILITY MATERIALS AND METHODS
02700	PIPED UTILITIES
02800	POWER AND COMMUNICATION UTILITIES
02850	RAILROAD WORK
02880	MARINE WORK

DIVISION 3 - CONCRETE

03010	CONCRETE MATERIALS
03050	CONCRETING PROCEDURES
03100	CONCRETE FORMWORK
03150	FORMS
03180	FORM TIES AND ACCESSORIES
03200	CONCRETE REINFORCEMENT
03250	CONCRETE ACCESSORIES
03300	CAST-IN-PLACE CONCRETE
03350	SPECIAL CONCRETE FINISHES
03360	SPECIALLY PLACED CONCRETE
03370	CONCRETE CURING
03400	PRECAST CONCRETE
03500	CEMENTITIOUS DECKS
03600	GROUT
03700	CONCRETE RESTORATION AND CLEANING

Figure 43-2
CSI format for specifications. Reproduced from MASTERFORMAT, 1983 edition, courtesy Construction Specifications Institute.

DIVISION 4 - MASONRY

04050	MASONRY PROCEDURES
04100	MORTAR
04150	MASONRY ACCESSORIES
04200	UNIT MASONRY
04400	STONE
04500	MASONRY RESTORATION AND CLEANING
04550	REFRACTORIES
04600	CORROSION RESISTANT MASONRY

DIVISION 5 - METALS

05010	METAL MATERIALS AND METHODS
05050	METAL FASTENING
05100	STRUCTURAL METAL FRAMING
05200	METAL JOISTS
05300	METAL DECKING
05400	COLD-FORMED METAL FRAMING
05500	METAL FABRICATIONS
05700	ORNAMENTAL METAL
05800	EXPANSION CONTROL
05900	METAL FINISHES

DIVISION 6 - WOOD AND PLASTICS

06050	FASTENERS AND SUPPORTS
06100	ROUGH CARPENTRY
06130	HEAVY TIMBER CONSTRUCTION
06150	WOOD-METAL SYSTEMS
06170	PREFABRICATED STRUCTURAL WOOD
06200	FINISH CARPENTRY
06300	WOOD TREATMENT
06400	ARCHITECTURAL WOODWORK
06500	PREFABRICATED STRUCTURAL PLASTICS
06600	PLASTIC FABRICATIONS

DIVISION 7 - THERMAL AND MOISTURE PROTECTION

07100	WATERPROOFING
07150	DAMPPROOFING
07200	INSULATION
07250	FIREPROOFING
07300	SHINGLES AND ROOFING TILES
07400	PREFORMED ROOFING AND SIDING
07500	MEMBRANE ROOFING
07570	TRAFFIC TOPPING
07600	FLASHING AND SHEET METAL
07800	ROOF ACCESSORIES
07900	SEALANTS

DIVISION 8 - DOORS AND WINDOWS

08100	METAL DOORS AND FRAMES
08200	WOOD AND PLASTIC DOORS
08250	DOOR OPENING ASSEMBLIES
08300	SPECIAL DOORS
08400	ENTRANCES AND STOREFRONTS
08500	METAL WINDOWS
08600	WOOD AND PLASTIC WINDOWS
08650	SPECIAL WINDOWS
08700	HARDWARE
08800	GLAZING
08900	GLAZED CURTAIN WALLS

DIVISION 9 - FINISHES

09100	METAL SUPPORT SYSTEMS
09200	LATH AND PLASTER
09230	AGGREGATE COATINGS
09250	GYPSUM WALLBOARD
09300	TILE
09400	TERRAZZO
09500	ACOUSTICAL TREATMENT
09550	WOOD FLOORING
09600	STONE AND BRICK FLOORING
09650	RESILIENT FLOORING
09680	CARPETING
09700	SPECIAL FLOORING
09760	FLOOR TREATMENT
09800	SPECIAL COATINGS
09900	PAINTING
09950	WALL COVERING

DIVISION 10 - SPECIALITIES

10100	CHALKBOARDS AND TACKBOARDS
10150	COMPARTMENTS AND CUBICLES
10200	LOUVERS AND VENTS
10240	GRILLES AND SCREENS
10250	SERVICE WALL SYSTEMS
10260	WALL AND CORNER GUARDS
10270	ACCESS FLOORING
10280	SPECIALTY MODULES
10290	PEST CONTROL
10300	FIREPLACES AND STOVES
10340	PREFABRICATED STEEPLES, SPIRES, AND CUPOLAS
10350	FLAGPOLES
10400	IDENTIFYING DEVICES
10450	PEDESTRIAN CONTROL DEVICES
10500	LOCKERS
10520	FIRE EXTINGUISHERS, CABINETS, AND ACCESSORIES
10530	PROTECTIVE COVERS
10550	POSTAL SPECIALTIES
10600	PARTITIONS
10650	SCALES
10670	STORAGE SHELVING
10700	EXTERIOR SUN CONTROL DEVICES
10750	TELEPHONE ENCLOSURES
10800	TOILET AND BATH ACCESSORIES
10900	WARDROBE SPECIALTIES

DIVISION 11 - EQUIPMENT

11010	MAINTENANCE EQUIPMENT
11020	SECURITY AND VAULT EQUIPMENT
11030	CHECKROOM EQUIPMENT
11040	ECCLESIASTICAL EQUIPMENT
11050	LIBRARY EQUIPMENT
11060	THEATER AND STAGE EQUIPMENT
11070	MUSICAL EQUIPMENT
11080	REGISTRATION EQUIPMENT
11100	MERCANTILE EQUIPMENT
11110	COMMERCIAL LAUNDRY AND DRY CLEANING EQUIPMENT
11120	VENDING EQUIPMENT
11130	AUDIO-VISUAL EQUIPMENT
11140	SERVICE STATION EQUIPMENT
11150	PARKING EQUIPMENT
11160	LOADING DOCK EQUIPMENT
11170	WASTE HANDLING EQUIPMENT
11190	DETENTION EQUIPMENT
11200	WATER SUPPLY AND TREATMENT EQUIPMENT
11300	FLUID WASTE DISPOSAL AND TREATMENT EQUIPMENT
11400	FOOD SERVICE EQUIPMENT
11450	RESIDENTIAL EQUIPMENT
11460	UNIT KITCHENS
11470	DARKROOM EQUIPMENT
11480	ATHLETIC, RECREATIONAL, AND THERAPEUTIC EQUIPMENT
11500	INDUSTRIAL AND PROCESS EQUIPMENT
11600	LABORATORY EQUIPMENT
11650	PLANETARIUM AND OBSERVATORY EQUIPMENT
11700	MEDICAL EQUIPMENT
11780	MORTUARY EQUIPMENT
11800	TELECOMMUNICATION EQUIPMENT
11850	NAVIGATION EQUIPMENT

DIVISION 12 - FURNISHINGS

12100	ARTWORK
12300	MANUFACTURED CABINETS AND CASEWORK
12500	WINDOW TREATMENT
12550	FABRICS
12600	FURNITURE AND ACCESSORIES
12670	RUGS AND MATS
12700	MULTIPLE SEATING
12800	INTERIOR PLANTS AND PLANTINGS

DIVISION 13 - SPECIAL CONSTRUCTION

13010	AIR SUPPORTED STRUCTURES
13020	INTEGRATED ASSEMBLIES
13030	AUDIOMETRIC ROOMS
13040	CLEAN ROOMS
13050	HYPERBARIC ROOMS
13060	INSULATED ROOMS
13070	INTEGRATED CEILINGS
13080	SOUND, VIBRATION, AND SEISMIC CONTROL
13090	RADIATION PROTECTION
13100	NUCLEAR REACTORS
13110	OBSERVATORIES
13120	PRE-ENGINEERED STRUCTURES
13130	SPECIAL PURPOSE ROOMS AND BUILDINGS
13140	VAULTS
13150	POOLS
13160	ICE RINKS
13170	KENNELS AND ANIMAL SHELTERS
13200	SEISMOGRAPHIC INSTRUMENTATION
13210	STRESS RECORDING INSTRUMENTATION
13220	SOLAR AND WIND INSTRUMENTATION
13410	LIQUID AND GAS STORAGE TANKS
13510	RESTORATION OF UNDERGROUND PIPELINES
13520	FILTER UNDERDRAINS AND MEDIA
13530	DIGESTION TANK COVERS AND APPURTENANCES
13540	OXYGENATION SYSTEMS
13550	THERMAL SLUDGE CONDITIONING SYSTEMS
13560	SITE CONSTRUCTED INCINERATORS
13600	UTILITY CONTROL SYSTEMS
13700	INDUSTRIAL AND PROCESS CONTROL SYSTEMS
13800	OIL AND GAS REFINING INSTALLATIONS AND CONTROL SYSTEMS
13900	TRANSPORTATION INSTRUMENTATION
13940	BUILDING AUTOMATION SYSTEMS
13970	FIRE SUPPRESSION AND SUPERVISORY SYSTEMS
13980	SOLAR ENERGY SYSTEMS
13990	WIND ENERGY SYSTEMS

DIVISION 14 - CONVEYING SYSTEMS

14100	DUMBWAITERS
14200	ELEVATORS
14300	HOISTS AND CRANES
14400	LIFTS
14500	MATERIAL HANDLING SYSTEMS
14600	TURNTABLES
14700	MOVING STAIRS AND WALKS
14800	POWERED SCAFFOLDING
14900	TRANSPORTATION SYSTEMS

DIVISION 15 - MECHANICAL

15050	BASIC MATERIALS AND METHODS
15200	NOISE, VIBRATION, AND SEISMIC CONTROL
15250	INSULATION
15300	SPECIAL PIPING SYSTEMS
15400	PLUMBING SYSTEMS
15450	PLUMBING FIXTURES AND TRIM
15500	FIRE PROTECTION
15600	POWER OR HEAT GENERATION
15650	REFRIGERATION
15700	LIQUID HEAT TRANSFER
15800	AIR DISTRIBUTION
15900	CONTROLS AND INSTRUMENTATION

DIVISION 16 - ELECTRICAL

16050	BASIC MATERIALS AND METHODS
16200	POWER GENERATION
16300	POWER TRANSMISSION
16400	SERVICE AND DISTRIBUTION
16500	LIGHTING
16600	SPECIAL SYSTEMS
16700	COMMUNICATIONS
16850	HEATING AND COOLING
16900	CONTROLS AND INSTRUMENTATION

Figure 43–2
Continued.

SPECIFICATIONS FOR LAKE HOUSE
CONTENTS

GENERAL CONDITIONS

GENERAL REQUIREMENTS	01000
SITE WORK	02000
CONCRETE	03000
MASONRY	04000
STRUCTURAL STEEL	05000
WOOD & PLASTICS	06000
THERMAL & MOISTURE PROTECTION	07000
DOORS & WINDOWS	08000
FINISHES	09000
FIREPLACE	10000
EQUIPMENT	11000
MECHANICAL	15000
ELECTRICAL	16000

(Divisions 12000, 13000, and 14000 are not used.)

GENERAL CONDITIONS

The General Conditions of the Contract For Construction, AIA Document A107, whether or not bound herein, are hereby incorporated into and made a part of this contract and these specifications.

01000 GENERAL REQUIREMENTS

A. ARCHITECT'S SUPERVISION
The architect will have continual supervisory responsibility for this job.

B. TEMPORARY CONVENIENCES
The general contractor shall provide suitable temporary conveniences for the use of all workers on this job. Facilities shall be within a weathertight, painted enclosure complying with legal requirements. The general contractor shall maintain all temporary toilet facilities in a sanitary condition.

C. PUMPING
The general contractor shall keep the excavation and the basement free from water at all times and shall provide, maintain, and operate at his own expense such pumping equipment as shall be necessary.

D. PROTECTION
The general contractor shall protect all existing driveways, parking areas, sidewalks, curbs, and existing paved areas on, or adjacent to, the owner's property.

E. GRADES, LINES, LEVELS, AND SURVEYS
The owner shall establish the lot lines.
The general contractor shall:
1. Establish and maintain bench marks.
2. Verify all grades, lines, levels, and dimensions as shown on the drawings, and report any errors or inconsistencies before commencing to work.
3. Lay out the building accurately under the supervision of the architect.

F. FINAL CLEANING
In addition to the general room cleaning, the general contractor shall do the following special cleaning upon completion of the work:
1. Wash and polish all glass and cabinets.
2. Clean and polish all hardware.
3. Remove all marks, stains, fingerprints, and other soil or dirt from walls, woodwork, and floors.

G. GUARANTEES
The general contractor shall guarantee all work performed under the contract against faulty materials or workmanship. The guarantee shall be in writing with duplicate copies delivered to the architect. In case of work performed by subcontractors where guarantees are required, the general contractor shall secure written guarantees from those subcontractors. Copies of these guarantees shall be delivered to the architect upon completion of the work. Guarantees shall be signed by both the subcontractor and the general contractor.

H. FOREMAN
The general contractor shall have a responsible foreman at the building site from the start to the completion of construction. The foreman shall be on duty during all working hours.

I. FIRE INSURANCE
The owner shall effect and maintain builder's risk completed-value insurance on this job.

02000 SITE WORK

WORK INCLUDED
This work shall include, but shall not be limited by the following:
A. Cleaning site.
B. Excavating, backfilling, grading, and related items.
C. Removal of excess earth.
D. Protection of existing trees to remain on the site.

All excavation and backfill required for heating, plumbing, and electrical work will be done by the respective contractors and are not included under site work.

It is the contractor's responsibility to field inspect existing conditions to determine the scope of work.

02100 CLEARING

A. Clean the area within the limits of the building of all trees, shrubs, or other obstructions as necessary.
B. Within the limits of grading work as shown on the drawings, remove such trees, shrubs, or other obstructions as are indicated on the drawings to be removed, without injury to trunks, interfering branches, and roots of trees to remain. Do cutting and trimming only as directed. Box and protect all trees and shrubs in the construction area to remain; maintain boxing until finished grading is completed.

Figure 43-3
Specifications for the lake house. *From Huth, Understanding Construction Drawings, Delmar Publishers Inc.*

C. Remove all debris from the site; do not use it for fill.

02200 EXCAVATION

A. Carefully remove all sod and soil throughout the area of the building and where finish grade levels are changed. Pile on site where directed. This soil is to be used later for finished grading.

B. Do all excavation required for footings, piers, walls, trenches, areas, pits, and foundations. Remove all materials encountered in obtaining indicated lines and grades required.

Beds for all foundations and footings must have solid, level, and undisturbed bed bottoms. No backfill will be allowed and all footings shall rest on unexcavated earth.

C. The contractor shall notify the architect when the excavation is complete so that he may inspect all soil before the concrete is placed.

D. Excavate to elevations and dimensions indicated, leaving sufficient space to permit erection of walls, waterproofing, masonry, and the inspection of foundations. Protect the bottom of the excavation from frost.

02260 BACKFILL

A. All outside walls shall be backfilled to within 6 inches of the finished grade with clean fill. Backfill shall be thoroughly compacted.

B. Unless otherwise directed by the architect, no backfill shall be placed until after the first floor framing is in place. No backfill shall be placed until all walls have developed such strength to resist thrust due to filling operations.

02270 GRADING

A. Do all excavating, filling, and rough grading to bring entire area outside of the building to levels shown on the drawings.

B. Where existing trees are to remain, if the new grade is lower than the natural grade under the trees, a sloping mound shall be left under the base of the tree extending out as far as the branches; if the grade is higher, a well shall be constructed around the base of the tree to provide the roots with air and moisture.

C. After rough grading has been completed and approved, spread topsoil evenly to the previously stripped area. Prepare the topsoil to receive grass seed by removing stone, debris, and unsuitable materials. Hand rake to remove water pockets and irregularities. Seeding will be done by the owner.

D. Furnish and place run of bank gravel as approved under all floor slabs.

03000 CONCRETE

WORK INCLUDED
Provide all materials, labor, equipment, and services necessary to furnish, deliver, and install all work of this Section, as shown on the drawings, as specified herein, and/or as required by job conditions including but not limited to the following:

A. Concrete for all footings and piers
B. Concrete for all slabs on ground
C. Concrete for slab at heat sink
D. Furnishing and installation of all required anchors.
E. Supplying fabrication and placement of all reinforcing bars and mesh and wire reinforcement for concrete where shown, called for, or required with proper supporting devices.
F. Erection of all wood forms required for the concrete work and removal upon completion of the work.
G. The finishing of all concrete work as hereinafter specified.
H. Porous fill below slabs on ground.

03010 MATERIAL

A. *Fine Aggregate*
Fine aggregates for concrete shall consist of natural sand having clean, hard, sharp, uncoated grains free from injurious amounts of dust, lumps, soft or flaky particles, shale, alkali, organic matter, loam or other deleterious substances.

B. *Coarse Aggregate (Stone)*
Coarse aggregates shall consist of crushed stone or gravel having clean, hard, strong, durable, uncoated particles, free from injurious amounts of soft, friable, thin, elongated or laminated pieces, alkali, organic or other deleterious matter.

C. *Water*
All water used in connection with concrete work shall be clean and free from deleterious materials or shall be the water used for drinking daily.

D. *Portland Cement*
Portland cement shall be an approved domestic brand complying with Standard Specifications for Portland Cement, ASTM Designation C-150, Type 1. Only one brand of cement shall be used throughout the course of the work.

E. All concrete is to be machine mixed in an approved mixer with a water metering device. Concrete is to reach a compressive strength of 2500 psi after 28 days.

F. *Reinforcement*
All reinforcing, unless otherwise shown or specified, shall conform to ASTM A-615, Grade 60. Wire mesh reinforcing shall have a minimum ultimate tensile strength of 70,000 psi, and shall conform to ASTM Specifications A-185, latest edition.

03320 INSPECTION & PLACING

A. All reinforcing shall be free of rust, scale, oil, or other coatings that tend to reduce the bond to concrete. All reinforcing is to be tied with 18-gauge wire at intersections and shall be securely held in position during the pouring of concrete.

B. The architect will inspect all footing beds, forms, and reinforcing just prior to placing concrete for footings and slabs.

Figure 43–3
Continued.

C. All concrete shall be placed upon clean surfaces, and properly compacted fill, free from standing water. The concrete shall be compacted and worked into corners and around reinforcing.

D. All concrete to be true and level as indicated on drawings to within ± 1/4 inch in 10 feet.

03330 FINISHING

A. Slabs in occupied spaces shall be troweled smooth and free of trowel marks.

B. Slabs in unoccupied spaces will have wood float finish.

04000 MASONRY

WORK INCLUDED
This work shall include but shall not be limited by the following:

A. Brickwork
B. Concrete blockwork
C. Mortar for brick and blockwork

04010 MATERIALS

A. Delivery and storage:

All materials shall be delivered, stored, and handled so as to prevent the inclusion of foreign materials and the damage of the materials by water or breakage.

Packaged materials shall be delivered and stored in the original packages until they are ready for use.

B. Materials showing evidence of water or other damage shall be rejected.

C. Brick shall be chosen by the owner from approved samples. Brick shall be carefully protected during transportation and shall be unloaded by hand and carefully piled; dumping is not permitted.

D. Concrete block shall be load bearing, hollow, concrete masonry units and shall conform to the standard specifications of ASTM C-145-71.

E. Mortar used for laying brick and concrete block shall consist of one (1) part masonry cement to three (3) parts sand. The mortar ingredients shall comply with the following requirements:

1. Masonry cement: ASTM C-91 T Type 2.
2. Aggregates: ASTM C-144.
3. Water: Clean, fresh, free from acid, alkali, sewage, or organic material.

F. Reinforcing: reinforcing material for masonry walls shall be prefabricated welded steel.

04220 INSTALLATION

A. All work shall be laid true to dimensions, plumb, square, and in bond, and properly anchored. All courses shall be level and joints shall be of uniform width; no joints shall exceed the size specified.

B. Joints shall be finished as follows:

C. All brick shall be laid on full mortar bed with a shoved joint. All joints shall be completely filled with mortar. All horizontal and vertical joints shall be raked 3/8 of an inch deep.

D. All mortar joints for concrete block masonry shall have full mortar coverage on vertical and horizontal face shells.

E. Vertical joints shall be shoved tight. Full mortar bedding shall have ruled joints.

F. Horizontal reinforcement shall be placed in every third bed joint of block work. Reinforcement shall be placed in the first and second bed joints above and below all openings.

G. Concealed work shall have joints cut flush.

H. Fill voids in top course with masonry and set anchor bolts as shown on construction drawings.

I. Protection: cover the wall each night and when the work is discontinued due to weather.

04240 CLEANING AND POINTING

1. Point up all the voids and open joints with mortar. Remove all of the excess mortar and dirty spots from the entire surface.

2. Upon completion, all brickwork shall be thoroughly cleaned with clean water and stiff fiber brushes and then rinsed with clear water. The use of acids or wire brushes is not permitted.

05000 STRUCTURAL STEEL

WORK INCLUDED
This work shall include but shall not be limited by the following:

A. Structural tube columns.
B. Welded flanges and plates.
C. Structural steel rafters and beams.
D. Stanchions at railings: this contractor shall supply fabricated stanchions to be installed by others.
E. Grouting base plates.

05010 MATERIALS

A. All structural steel to conform to ASTM A-36.
B. Welding electrodes to conform to American Welding Society A5.1, E70 series.

05100 FABRICATION & ERECTION

A. Drilling or punching of holes in columns, beams, and rafters shall not be permitted unless approved.

B. Welds shall be by qualified operators and shall achieve complete penetration without voids, cracks, or porosity.

C. Concealed structural steel shall have one coat of approved rust-resistant primer.

06000 WOOD & PLASTICS

WORK INCLUDED
All lumber, plywood, rough hardware, trim, paneling, and finish carpentry joinery and millwork required or implied by drawings and/or specifications. Cabinets and countertops are not included in this section.

06010 MATERIAL

A. Grade or trademark is required on each piece of lumber; only official marks of association under whose rules it is graded will be accepted.

Figure 43-3
Continued.

B. Plywood shall conform to U.S. Product Standards PS-66 and shall be branded or stamped with type and grade.

C. Moisture content shall not exceed 19% for framing lumber, 12% for plywood, 8% for finish millwork.

D. Work that is to be finished or painted shall be free from defects or blemishes on surfaces exposed to view that will show after the finish coat of paint or stain is applied. Defective materials not up to specifications for quality and grade for its intended use, or otherwise not in proper conditions, shall be rejected.

E. Rough lumber shall be dressed four (4) sides, air-dried, well-seasoned, sound, and free from splits, cracks, shakes and wanes, loose or unsound knots, and decay and excessive warp. Species and grades shall be those listed:

Douglas fir or hem-fir for rough carpentry

—Each piece marked as to grade and free from defect

—No. 1 light framing with not more than 25% No. 2 framing allowed for all lumber 2x6 or larger

—No. 2 construction grade for studs

Treated lumber: Southern yellow pine, CCA treated per AWPA standards

Finish lumber and millwork: clear white pine or ponderosa pine

F. All nails, spikes, screws, bolts, joist hangers, and timber connectors as indicated, noted or detailed on drawings, and as required to produce a safe, substantial and workmanlike job in all respects

G. Laminated plastic to be Micarta, Formica, or Textolite in decorator colors as selected by the owner

06100 ROUGH CARPENTRY

A. Install all rough wood framing, nailers, edge members, curbs, blocking, grounds, rough sills, backing, furring, and the like as indicated, detailed, noted, or required to properly support, back up, and complete the work this section and of any or all trades under these contracts.

—Securely attach and anchor to adjacent construction as detailed or as approved if detail is not provided.

—Shim to line if so required to provide a uniform base for any other work.

B. Provide double studs adjacent to and headers of size indicated over all openings.

C. Double joists under parallel partitions.

06200 FINISH CARPENTRY

A. Provide all rabbets, splines, ploughs, and other cuts as detailed or required for neat, tight, solid fitting and joining.

B. Finish millwork where indicated to have a clear finish shall be dressed and sanded, free from machine and tool marks, abrasions, raised grain and other defects on surfaces exposed to view. Construction and workmanship of millwork items shall conform to or exceed, the requirements of AWI and good shop practice.

C. Joints shall be tight and so formed as to conceal shrinkage.

D. Interior millwork, running finish, and trim shall be in as long lengths as practicable, shall be spliced

only where necessary, and only when approved by the Architect. All such splices shall be beveled and jointed where solid fastenings can be made.

07000 THERMAL & MOISTURE PROTECTION

WORK INCLUDED
A. Dampproofing basement walls
B. Vapor barriers
C. Thermal insulation
D. Roofing
E. Flashing
F. Caulking and sealants

07010 MATERIALS

A. Dampproofing on basement walls to be Sonneborn Building Products, Semi-mastic Hydrocide 600 or approved equal
B. Vapor barriers under concrete slabs to be 4 mil thick polyethylene
C. Vapor barriers on insulated walls and roofs to be 4 mil thick polyethylene
D. Insulation exposed to earth shall be Dow Styrofoam SM, R-5.4 per inch.
E. All rigid board insulation not exposed to earth shall be Owens/Corning, High-R Sheathing, R-7.2 per inch.
F. Batt insulation shall be Owens/Corning Fiberglass, unfaced, or approved equal.
  —3 1/2" thickness, R-11
  —6" thickness, R-19
  —9" thickness, R-30
G. Roofing underlayment, #15 asphalt-saturated felt
H. Composition roofing, Johns Mannville 12"x36" asphalt shingles, 235 lb per square
I. Metal flashing, 28 gauge aluminum
J. Caulking to be acrylic polymer conforming to F.F. TT-S-00230

07150 DAMPPROOFING

A. Apply two coats of asphalt dampproofing over all masonry wall surfaces to receive earth backfill.
B. Apply polyethylene vapor barrier over gravel fill at all concrete slabs.
C. Vapor barrier sheets to be lapped 6" minimum.
D. Apply polyethylene vapor to the heated side of insulated frame walls and roofs.

07200 THERMAL INSULATION

A. Pack all voids and cavities in exterior walls and roof. Avoid compressing batt insulation.
B. Cut and fit insulation and vapor barriers as necessary for snug fit.
C. Allow minimum air space of 1/2" between insulation and roof sheathing.
D. Rigid insulation is to be nailed and glued with Dow Mastic number 11, according to manufacturer's instructions.

07300 ROOFING

A. Apply asphalt-saturated felt underlayment with 6" lap to all roof surfaces.
B. Install roof shingles according to manufacturer's printed instructions.
C. Roof shingles to be applied with zinc-coated, barbed roofing nails, 4 nails per shingle.

Figure 43–3
Continued.

07600 FLASHING

A. Apply factory-painted aluminum drip edge at all roof edges.
B. Chimney to be flashed at roof with Majestic number 9-6-12 galvanized flashing.
C. Flash all pipes at roof with neoprene flashing of the proper size.
D. Flash at all intersections of roofs and vertical surfaces and as otherwise shown on construction drawings.
E. Flashing to be nailed at 3″ intervals with aluminum roofing nails.

07900 CAULKING

Caulk all windows, doors, and other openings.

08000 DOORS & WINDOWS

WORK INCLUDED

All doors, door frames, windows, skylights, trim for each, and all hardware not included elsewhere.

08010 PRODUCTS

A. Hollow metal doors to be manufactured by Pease, or approved equal. Skin to be 16 gauge steel with phenolic honeycomb core.
B. Wood doors by Iroquois Millwork or approved equal. Birch plywood skin with phenolic impregnated Kraft core.
C. All door frames to be of clear pine in standard patterns as shown on the construction drawings. Side lites to be Iroquois, Weather Guard SL with 5/8″ insulating glass.
D. Windows to be Capitol, Series E-700 aluminum frame, thermal break with factory-applied enamel finish. Windows to include aluminum screens by the same manufacturer.
E. Skylight to be Skyvue, number DV2852.
F. Door trim to be standard WM patterns milled from clear pine.
G. Contractor shall allow $500 for locksets, latches, bi-fold hardware, hinges, weatherstripping, medicine cabinets, closet rods, and shower curtain rods.

08100 DOORS

A. Frames to be plumb and square with accurately fitted joints. Set exposed nails with a nail set.
B. Accurately align doors with frames and adjust hardware as necessary for smooth operation.
C. Install molding as shown on construction drawings with accurately mitered corners.

08500 WINDOWS & SKYLIGHTS

A. Install all windows true and plumb, and according to the manufacturer's recommendations to produce a weathertight installation.
B. Install all hardware and accessories, and check all moving sections for smooth operation.

08900 HARDWARE

A. Install all door and window hardware according to the manufacturer's recommendations and check for smooth operation.
B. Install a closet rod in each closet. Closet rod to be secured through wall finish to blocking installed with rough carpentry.
C. Install shower curtain rods over tub and shower stall. Shower curtain rods to be secured through wall finish to blocking installed with rough carpentry.
D. Install a medicine cabinet (by owner) over each lavatory.

09000 FINISHES

WORK INCLUDED

A. Gypsum wallboard
B. Ceramic tile in baths and toilet rooms
C. Quarry tile floors
D. Painting and varnishing

09250 WALLBOARD

MATERIAL

A. All wallboard material to be the product of one manufacturer; U.S. Gypsum, Flintkote, or approved equal. Drywall in bath, toilet rooms, and tub room to be moisture resistant.

INSTALLATION

A. Gypsum wallboard shall be installed with joints centered over framing or furring.
B. Fasten gypsum wallboard with power-driven drywall screws or ring-shank drywall nails located not over 12 inches O.C. at all edges and in the field.
C. Outside corners are to be protected with metal corner bead.
D. Finish all joints with a minimum of three coats of joint compound and standard gypsum board reinforcing tape in accordance with the manufacturer's printed instructions.
E. Dimples at screwheads or nailheads shall receive three coats of compound.

09300 TILE

MATERIAL

A. Wall tile to be American-Olean Tile Company standard grade bright glazed in color selected. Bathroom accessories to be same manufacturer and color.
B. Floor tile in bath, toilet, and tub rooms to be American-Olean unglazed 1″ x 1″ ceramic mosaic tile in color selected.
C. Quarry tile to be installed in this specification will be 6″ x 6″ shale-and-clay tile provided by owner.
D. Marble thresholds at all doors adjacent to mosaic tile floors shall be Vermont Marble 7/8″ x 3 1/2″.

INSTALLATION

A. Lay out ceramic tile on walls and floors so that no tiles of less than one-half size occur.
B. Cut and fit tile around toilets, tubs, and other abutting devices.
C. Install all floor tile by thin-set method in accordance with TCA recommendations.
D. Install wall tile in mastic cement conforming to the recommendations of the tile manufacturer.
E. Grout all tile work to completely fill joints.
F. Clean all tile surfaces to present a workmanlike job.
G. Install 12 bathroom accessories as follows:
   • 2 soap dishes
   • 3 toilet paper holders
   • 7 towel bars

Figure 43–3
Continued.

09900 PAINTING

MATERIAL

A. Exterior stain: one coat Minwax exterior stain or approved equal, in color by owner
B. Interior walls — flat: two coats Martin Senour, Bright Life alkyd flat or approved equal, in colors by owner
C. Interior walls — semigloss: two coats Martin Senour, Bright Life alkyd semigloss or approved equal, in colors by owner
D. Interior painted woodwork: two coats Martin Senour, Bright Life alkyd semigloss, or approved equal, in colors by owner
E. Metal: two coats DeRusto rust-resistant enamel or approved equal, in colors by owner
F. Polyurethane: two coats United Gilsonite Laboratories, ZAR gloss
G. Primers: all primer to be that recommended by manufacturer of top coat.

APPLICATION

A. Repair all minor defects by patching, puttying, or filling as normally performed by painting contractors.
B. Prime uncoated wood surfaces with tinted primer and touch up previously painted surfaces.
C. Sand all surfaces smooth before each coat of paint to produce a smooth and uniform job at completion.
D. Protect all adjacent surfaces and other work incorporated into project against damage or defacement.
E. Coat all surfaces according to the following painting schedule and as indicated on the drawings. All colors are to be selected by the owner.

EXTERIOR WALLS & TRIM	Stain
METAL RAILINGS	Rust-resistant enamel
PLAYROOM	Walls: Flat / Ceiling: Flat
ALL BATHS	Walls: Semigloss / Ceilings: Semigloss
HALLS & CLOSETS	Walls: Flat / Ceilings: Flat
LIVING ROOM	Walls: Flat / Ceiling: Flat
DINING ROOM	Walls: Flat / Ceiling: Flat
KITCHEN	Walls: Semigloss / Ceiling: Semigloss
BEDROOMS	Walls: Flat / Ceilings: Flat
LOFT	All except floor and ladder: Flat
LOFT FLOOR & LADDER	Polyurethane
INTERIOR DOORS	Polyurethane
INTERIOR STAIRS	Polyurethane
UNSCHEDULED INTERIOR TRIM	Semigloss

10000 FIREPLACE

WORK INCLUDED

Provide and install fireplace, chimney, and accessories as indicated on the construction drawings. Related masonry is not included in this section.

10310 EQUIPMENT

A. Majestic Company fireplace number M28.
B. Majestic Company chimney with 8-inch flue.
C. All chimney accessories required to conform with printed instructions of Majestic Company.

10320 INSTALLATION

Fireplace and chimney are to be installed according to printed instructions of Majestic Company and as indicated on the construction drawings. All equipment is to be installed level and plumb and finished to provide a workmanlike appearance.

11000 EQUIPMENT

WORK INCLUDED

A. Provide and install kitchen cabinets and countertop.
B. Provide and install vanity cabinets. This section does not include lavatories or related plumbing.
C. Provide necessary cutouts for installation of kitchen sink, by plumbing contractor; cooktop, by owner; grill, by owner; oven, by owner.

11910 MATERIAL

A. Cabinets and vanities shall be H.J. Scheirich Company, Garden Grove style.
B. Countertops shall be Formica brand or approved equal with molded backsplash in color by owner.

11920 INSTALLATION

A. Cabinets shall be installed level and true with no less than four screws per base unit and present a workmanlike appearance.
B. Countertop shall be installed with concealed screws at 18-inch intervals front and back.
C. Exposed ends of countertop shall be veneered with matching plastic laminate.
D. Cutouts for other equipment shall be neatly trimmed to proper dimensions according to the equipment manufacturer.

15000 MECHANICAL

This division includes heating, ventilating, air conditioning, and plumbing. It is omitted here because these topics have not been covered earlier in the textbook.

16000 ELECTRICAL

This division covers all aspects of electrical work. It is omitted here because these topics have not been covered earlier in the textbook.

Figure 43–3
Continued.

GENERAL CONSTRUCTION SPECIFICATIONS TEST ▬▬▬

DIRECTIONS

Answer the questions with short complete statements or drawings as needed on an 8½ × 11 drawing sheet as follows:

1. Use ⅛ in. guidelines for all lettering.
2. Letter your name, General Construction Specifications Test, and the date at the top of the sheet.
3. Letter the question number and provide the answer. You do not need to write out the question.
4. Do all lettering with vertical uppercase architectural letters. If the answer requires line work, use proper drafting tools and technique. Answers may be prepared on a word processor if appropriate with course guidelines.
5. Your grade will be based on correct answers and quality of line technique.

QUESTIONS

1. Give a general definition of construction specifications.
2. Identify the basic differences between residential and commercial specifications.
3. List four factors that influence the specific requirements of minimum construction specifications established by local building officials.
4. Using general terms, list the typical minimum construction requirements for the following categories:

   a. Room dimensions
   b. Light and ventilation
   c. Foundation
   d. Framing
   e. Stairways
   f. Roof
   g. Chimney and fireplace
   h. Thermal insulation and heating
   i. Fire warning system

   A partial example would be as follows:
   4. d. Framing
        1. lumber grades
        2. beams bearing area
5. Describe the format established by the Construction Specifications Institute (CSI) for construction specifications.

GENERAL CONSTRUCTION SPECIFICATIONS PROBLEM ▬

DIRECTIONS

Obtain a blank copy of the FHA Description of Materials form from your instructor or local FHA office. Using your set of architectural plans for the residence you have been drawing as a continuing problem, complete the FHA form. If you have more than one set of plans, select only one set or have your instructor select the set of plans to use.

Chapter 44
Construction Supervision Procedures

LOAN APPLICATIONS **INDIVIDUAL APPRAISAL REQUIREMENTS** **MASTER APPRAISAL REQUIREMENTS** **CHANGE ORDERS** **BUILDING PERMITS** **CONTRACTS** **COMPLETION NOTICE** **BIDS** **CONSTRUCTION INSPECTIONS** **TEST**

THE DESIGNER or architect may often be involved with several phases of preparation before construction of the project begins. The level of commitment may go beyond the preparation of plans to the complete supervision of the entire construction project. There are several items that any client may need before construction starts depending upon the complexity or unique requirements of the project. Architects are often involved with post-drafting work including zone changes when necessary, specification preparation, building permit applications, bonding requirements, client financial statement, lender approval, and building contractor estimates and bid procurement.

LOAN APPLICATIONS

Loan applications vary depending upon the requirements of the lender. Most applications for construction financing contain a variety of similar information. The FHA-proposed construction appraisal requirements are, in part, as follows:

1. Plot plan (three copies per lot).
2. Prints (three copies per plan). Prints should include the following:

   Four elevations including front, rear, right side, and left side.
   Floor plan.
   Foundation plan.
   Wall section.
   Roof plan.
   Cross sections of exterior walls, stairs, etc.
   Cabinet detail including a cross section.
   Fireplace detail (manufacturer's detail if fireplace is prefabricated).
   Truss detail (include name and address of supplier).
   Heating plan. If forced air, show size and location of ducts and registers plus cubic feet per minute (CFM) at register.
   Location of wall units with watts and CFM at register.
3. Specifications (one copy per blueprint). Areas

commonly missed on specifications are the following:

List all appliances with make and model number.

List smoke detector with make and model number, and "Direct Wire".

If landscaped, supply a typical detail for each plan type.

List plumbing fixtures with make, model number, size, and color.

List carpet by brand, style, and directory number.

List carpet pad by brand, style, thickness, and directory number.

Include name and address of manufacturer of trusses.

Include name of manufacturer of fireplace and model number if applicable.

4. Public Utility District (PUD) heat loss calculation (one per specification sheet). A room-by-room Btu heat loss count showing the total Btu heat loss for the dwelling as well as the total output of the heating system.

5. Proposed sale price.

6. Copy of earnest money agreement in blank or completed if a presale.

7. If a presale, the buyer must sign the specification sheet as well as the builder.

INDIVIDUAL APPRAISAL REQUIREMENTS

The subdivision should be FHA approved or a letter must accompany the submission with the following information:

1. Total number of lots in the subdivision.
2. Evidence of acceptance of streets and utilities by local authorities for continued maintenance.
3. One copy of the recorded plat and covenants.

MASTER APPRAISAL REQUIREMENTS

A minimum of five lots for each plan type is required for a master. The subdivision must be FHA or VA approved and contain the following information:

1. Location map and a copy of the recorded plat and covenants.
2. A letter from the builder that includes the following information:

a. The number of lots in the area owned by the builder and the number of lots proposed to be built upon.

b. The number of homes presently under construction and the number completed and unsold.

If the builder has not worked with the FHA previously, an equal employment opportunity certificate and an affirmative fair housing marketing plan must be submitted for either a master or individual appraisal request.

CHANGE ORDERS

Any physical change in the plans or specifications should be submitted to the FHA on FHA Form 2577. It should be noted whether the described change will be an increase or decrease in value and by what dollar amount. It must be signed by the lender, the builder, and, if sold, the purchaser, who must also sign prior to submission to the FHA.

Most lending institutions' applications are not as comprehensive as the FHA while others may require additional information. The best practice is to always research the lender to identify the needed information. A well-prepared set of documents and drawings usually stands a better chance of funding.

BUILDING PERMITS

The responsibility of completing the building permit application may fall to the architect or designer. The architect should contact the local building official to determine the process to be followed. Generally, the building permit application is a basic form that identifies the major characteristics of the structure to be built, the legal description and location of the property, and information about the applicant. The application is usually accompanied by two sets of plans and up to five sets of plot plans. The fee for a building permit usually depends upon the estimated cost of construction. The local building official will determine the amount based upon a standard schedule at a given cost per square foot. The fees are often divided into two parts: a plan-check fee paid upon application and a building-permit fee paid when the permit is received. There are other permits and fees that may or may not be paid at this time. In some cases the mechanical, sewer, plumbing, electrical, and water permits are obtained by the general or subcontractors. Water and sewer permits may be expensive depending upon the local assessments for these utilities.

CONTRACTS

Building contracts may be very complex documents for large commercial construction or short forms for residential projects. The main concern in the preparation of the contract is that all parties understand what will be specifically done, in what period of time and for what reimbursement. The contract becomes an agreement between the client, general contractor, and architect. Figure 44–1 shows an example of a typical building contract.

It is customary to specify the date by which the project is to be completed. On some large projects, dates for completion of the various stages of construction are specified. Usually, the contractor receives a percentage of the contract price for the completion of each stage of construction. Payments are typically made three or four times during construction. Another method is for the contractor to receive partial payment for the work done each month. Verify the method used with the lending agency.

The owner is usually responsible for having the property surveyed. The architect may be responsible for administering the contract. The contractor is responsible for the construction and security of the site during the construction period.

Certain kinds of insurance are required during construction. The contractor is required to have liability insurance. This protects the contractor against being sued for accidents occurring on the site. The owner is required to have property insurance including fire, theft, and vandalism. Workman's compensation is another form of insurance that provides income for contractors' employees if they are injured at work.

The contract describes conditions under which the contract may be ended. Contracts may be terminated if one party fails to comply with the contract, when one of the parties is disabled or dies, and for several other reasons.

There are two kinds of contracts in use for most construction. One is the fixed-sum and the other is the cost-plus contract. Each of these offers certain advantages and disadvantages.

Fixed-sum (sometimes called lump-sum) contracts are used most often. With a fixed-sum contract, the contractor agrees to complete the project for a certain amount of money. The greatest advantage of this kind of contract is that the owner knows in advance exactly what the cost will be. However, the contractor does not know what hidden problems may be encountered and so the contractor's price must be high enough to cover unforeseen circumstances such as excessive rock in the excavation or sudden increases in the cost of materials.

A cost-plus contract is one in which the contractor agrees to complete the work for the actual cost, plus a percentage for overhead and profit. The advantage of this type of contract is that the contractor does not have to allow for unforeseen problems, so the final price is apt to be less. A cost-plus contract is also useful when changes are to be made during the course of construction. The main disadvantage of this kind of contract is that the owner does not know exactly what the cost will be until the project is completed.

COMPLETION NOTICE

The completion notice is a document that should be posted in a conspicuous place on or adjacent to the structure. This legal document notifies all parties involved in the project that work has been substantially completed. There may be a very small part of work or cleanup to be done but the project, for all practical purposes, is complete. The completion notice must be recorded in the local jurisdiction. Completion notices serve several functions. Subcontractors and suppliers have a certain given period of time to file a claim or lien against the contractor or client to obtain reimbursement for labor or materials that have not been paid for. Lending institutions often hold a percentage of funds for a given period of time after the completion notice has been posted. It is important for the contractor to have this document posted so that the balance of payment can be obtained. The completion notice is often posted in conjunction with a final inspection that includes the local building officials and the client. Some lenders require that all building inspection reports be submitted before payment is given and may also require a private inspection by an agent of the lender. Figure 44–2 shows a sample completion notice.

BIDS

Construction bids are often obtained by the architect for the client. The purpose is to obtain the best price for the best work. Some projects require that work be given to the lowest bidder, while other projects do not necessarily go to the lowest bid. In some situations, especially in the private sector, other factors are considered such as an evaluation of the builder's history based upon quality, ability to meet schedules, cooperation with all parties, financial stability, and license, bond, and insurance.

FORM No. 144—BUILDING CONTRACT (Fixed Price—No Service Charge).

TN

THIS AGREEMENT, Made the ....day of ...., 19..........., by and between ...., hereinafter called the Contractor, and ...., hereinafter called the Owner, WITNESSETH:

The parties hereto, each in consideration of the promises of the other, agree as follows:

ARTICLE I: The contractor shall and will perform all the work for the

as shown on the drawings and described in the specifications therefor prepared by ....

....;

said drawings, specifications and this contract hereinafter, for brevity, are called "contract documents"; they are identified by the signatures of the parties hereto and hereby are made a part hereof. All said work is to be done under the direction of ....

....who, for brevity hereinafter is designated as "supervisor." (Publisher's note: If the owner himself is to supervise said work, simply insert the word "owner" in the blank space immediately preceding.) The supervisor's decision as to the true construction and meaning of the drawings and specifications shall be final and binding upon both parties. All of said drawings and specifications including those hereinafter mentioned have been and will be prepared by the owner at his expense and are to remain his property; said drawings and specifications are loaned to the contractor for the purposes of this contract and at the completion of the work are to be returned to the owner; none of said contract documents shall be used by, submitted or shown to third parties without owner's written consent.

ARTICLE II: The contractor shall commence work within .... days from the date hereof and substantially complete the same on or before ...., 19......... . At all times the supervisor shall have access to said work for the purpose of inspecting the same and the progress thereof. Should completion be delayed by reason of the fault of the owner or of any other contractor employed by him or by fire, casualty, strikes, delays in obtaining materials or other reasons beyond the contractor's control, then the completion date shall be extended for a period equivalent to the time lost for such reasons. Should the parties be unable to agree as to the period of such extension, the question shall be referred to arbitration as hereunder provided. However, the contractor shall take special precautions to protect his work during freezing weather and shall be fully responsible for the effect of such weather upon said work.

ARTICLE III: Subject to the provisions for adjustment set forth in ARTICLE V hereof, the owner shall pay to the contractor for the performance of this contract, in current funds, the sum of $................................, payable at the following times:

NOTE—This form not suitable for use as a retail installment contract where a finance charge is being made.

Figure 44–1 Standard building contract. *Courtesy Stevens-Ness Law Publishing Co.*

Sales tax, if any, shall be paid by the owner in addition to the fixed price mentioned above. Should any progress payments be provided for above, the same shall not include or be based upon any salary, allowance or compensation to the contractor, if an individual, or any officer of the contractor, if a corporation, nor shall it include any of the contractor's overhead or general expenses of any kind; before any such progress payment is made, the contractor shall deliver to the supervisor receipts, vouchers or other evidence satisfactory to the supervisor showing contractor's payment for materials, labor and other items for which the contractor seeks payment, including payments to subcontractors, if any. After three days' written notice to the contractor, bills for labor or materials not paid by the contractor when due, may be paid by the owner and deducted from any payment due or to become due to the contractor. After similar notice, liens, if any are filed, including attorney's fees and costs claimed therein, may be paid, settled or compromised by the owner and amounts paid therefor shall likewise be deducted. However, the contractor shall have the right to contest any such bills, claims or liens.

Final payment shall be made within .... days after the completion of said work as certified in writing by the supervisor; however, before the latter shall so certify, the contractor shall submit evidence satisfactory to the supervisor that all payrolls, material bills and other indebtedness connected with the work have been fully paid, including those incurred by each and all of contractor's subcontractors. Provided always, that no payment made to the contractor pursuant to the terms hereof shall be construed as an acceptance of any work or materials not in accordance with the contract documents.

ARTICLE IV: In his performance of said work, contractor shall obtain at his own expense all necessary permits and comply with all applicable laws, ordinances, building codes and regulations of any public authority and be responsible for any infraction or violation thereof and any expense or damages resulting from any such infraction or violation. If the parties are unable to agree upon the dollar amount of contractor's responsibility under this paragraph, the matter shall be referred to arbitration as hereinafter provided. Any work claimed by the supervisor to be defective shall be uncovered by the contractor so that a complete inspection may be made; the contractor further agrees promptly (1) to remove from the job site all materials, whether or not incorporated in the work, condemned by any public authority, (2) to take down and remove all portions of the work likewise condemned or deemed by the supervisor as failing in any way to conform to any of said contract documents and (3) to replace all faulty work and materials.

ARTICLE V: No eliminations or alterations shall be made in the work except upon written order of the supervisor. Should any such eliminations or alterations require new plans or specifications, the owner shall supply the same at his expense. Should any of said eliminations or alterations require an adjustment of the agreed price (upward or downward) such adjustment shall be evidenced by the written agreement of the parties. Should they not be able so to agree, the work shall go on nevertheless under the order mentioned above and the determination of the proper adjustment shall be referred to arbitration as hereinafter provided.

ARTICLE VI: The owner reserves the right to let other contracts in connection with the improvement of which the work herein undertaken by the contractor is a part. In such event, due written notice of such other contracts shall be given promptly to the contractor and the latter shall afford said other contractors a reasonable opportunity for the storage of their materials and the execution of their contracts and shall properly coordinate his work within theirs. In this connection, should the contractor suffer loss by reason of any delay brought about by said other contractors, the owner agrees to reimburse the contractor for such loss; on the other hand, the contractor agrees that if he shall delay the work of said other contractors so as to cause loss for which the owner shall become liable, then he shall reimburse the owner for any such loss. If the parties are unable to agree as to the amounts so to be reimbursed, all questions relative thereto shall be submitted to arbitration as hereinafter provided.

ARTICLE VII: The contractor may subcontract any part of said work but not the whole thereof. Within seven days after entering into any such subcontract, the contractor shall notify the supervisor in writing of the names of said subcontractors and the work to be undertaken by each of them. In this connection, the contractor shall be fully responsible to the owner for the acts and omissions of any of said subcontractors or of persons either directly or indirectly employed by them. Nothing contained herein shall create any contractual relation between any such subcontractor and the owner.

ARTICLE VIII: At no time shall the contractor or any of his subcontractors employ on the work any unfit person or anyone not skilled in the work assigned to him. Any employee adjudged by the supervisor to be incompetent or unfit immediately shall be discharged and shall not again be employed upon the work. Should the contractor at any time be adjudged a bankrupt or should a receiver be appointed for his affairs or should he neglect to supply sufficient properly skilled workmen or supply materials of the proper quality or fail in any respect to prosecute the work with promptness and diligence (except because of matters for which an extension of the completion date is above provided for) or comply with said contract documents or any thereof, then in any of such events, after seven days' written notice to the contractor, the owner may, if the contractor is still in default, terminate the contractor's right to continue said work and may take exclusive possession of the premises and of all materials, tools and appliances thereon and finish the work by whatever method he may deem expedient. In such case the contractor shall not be entitled to receive any further payment until the work is finished. If the unpaid balance of the contract price shall exceed the expense of finishing the work, including compensation to the owner for additional managerial and administrative expenses, such excess shall be paid to the contractor; however, if such expense shall exceed such unpaid balance, the contractor shall pay the difference to the owner. If the parties are unable to agree upon the amounts so to be paid, the question shall be submitted to arbitration as hereinafter provided.

ARTICLE IX: All materials incorporated in any structure in connection with said work by the contractor shall, as soon as incorporated, become the property of the owner. At all times the owner, at his expense shall effect and maintain fire insurance, with extended coverage, upon the entire structure on which the work under this contract is to be done, in an amount equal to the full insurable value thereof; said insurance shall cover materials on the work site intended by the contractor to be incorporated into said structure but not yet incorporated as well as contractor's temporary buildings incident to the said work. The insured in such policy or policies shall include the owner, the contractor and such other persons as either of them may designate. Loss, if any, shall be made payable to said insured as their respective interests may appear. Certificates showing the existence of such insurance shall be delivered to the contractor if he so requests. The owner shall have power, in his sole discretion to adjust and settle any loss with the insurer which he may deem reasonable. If loss should occur and the parties hereto are unable to agree as to the division of the proceeds thereof, the question as to the amount as to which each insured shall be entitled shall be referred to arbitration as hereinafter provided.

ARTICLE X: At all times the contractor shall take all necessary precautions for the safety of persons on the work by whomsoever employed; he shall comply with all workers' compensation and similar legislation and further shall maintain at his expense public liability insurance against claims for damages because of bodily injury, including death and property damage, which may arise during his operations and those of all subcontractors under him. The insured in all such liability policies shall be the parties hereto and any others which they, or either of them, shall designate. The said insurance shall be written for not less than $........................... for injuries, including death, to any one person in any one accident; not less than $........................... for bodily injury, including death, to more than one person in any one accident, and $........................... property damage. The contractor shall deliver to the owner within ten days after the date hereof, one or more certificates from a responsible insurance company or companies satisfactory to the owner, showing the existence of such insurance. No such insurance shall be cancelled without ten days' prior written notice to the owner.

ARTICLE XI: All disputes, claims or questions subject to arbitration under this contract shall be submitted to three arbitrators, one to be designated by the owner, one by the contractor and the two thus selected to choose the third arbitrator; each party hereto shall have the right to appear before said arbitrators either in person, by attorney or other representative and to present witnesses or evidence, if desired; the decision of the majority of said arbitrators shall be final, binding and conclusive upon all parties hereto; the parties further agree that the decision of the arbitrators shall be a condition precedent to any right of legal action which either party hereto may have against the other. The work herein contracted for shall not be delayed during any arbitration proceedings except by mutual written agreement of the parties. The expense of such arbitration shall be shared equally by the parties hereto.

Figure 44–1 Continued.

ARTICLE XII: The contractor shall keep the premises (especially that part thereof under the floors thereof) free from accumulation of waste materials or rubbish and at the completion of the work shall remove all of his tools, scaffoldings and supplies and leave the premises broom-clean, or its equivalent.

ARTICLE XIII: If the owner should require a completion bond from the contractor, the premium therefor shall be added to the contract price and paid by the owner on delivery of said bond to him.

ARTICLE XIV: If the contractor employs a foreman or superintendent on said work, all directions and instructions given to the latter shall be as binding as if given to the contractor.

ARTICLE XV: The contractor agrees at all times to keep said work and the real estate on which the same is to be constructed free and clear of all construction and materialmen's liens, including liens on behalf of any subcontractor or person claiming under any such subcontractor and to defend and save the owner harmless therefrom.

ARTICLE XVI: In all respects the contractor shall be deemed to be an independent contractor.

ARTICLE XVII: In the event of any suit or action arising out of this contract, the losing party therein agrees to pay to the prevailing party therein the latter's costs and reasonable attorney's fees to be fixed by the trial court and in the event of an appeal, the prevailing party's costs and reasonable attorney's fees in the appellate court to be fixed by the appellate court.

ARTICLE XVIII: Any notice given by one party hereto to the other shall be sufficient if in writing, contained in a sealed envelope with postage thereon fully prepaid and deposited in the U. S. Registered Mails; any such notice conclusively shall be deemed received by the addressee thereof on the day of such deposit. If such notice is intended for the owner, the envelope containing the same shall be addressed to the owner at the following address: ....
....,

and if intended for the contractor, if addressed to ....
....

ARTICLE XIX: In construing this contract and where the context so requires, the singular shall be deemed to include the plural, the masculine shall include the feminine and the neuter and all grammatical changes shall be made and implied so that this contract shall apply equally to individuals and to corporations; further, the word "work" shall mean and include the entire job undertaken to be performed by the contractor as described in the contract documents, and each thereof, together with all services, labor and materials necessary to be used and furnished to complete the same, except for the preparation of the said plans and specifications and further except the compensation of the said supervisor.

ARTICLE XX: The parties hereto further agree

IN WITNESS WHEREOF, the parties have hereunto set their hands in duplicate.

....
CONTRACTOR   OWNER

....

Figure 44–1 Continued.

FORM No. 748
STEVENS-NESS LAW PUBLISHING CO., PORTLAND, OR. 97204
1976

COMPLETION NOTICE

Notice hereby is given that the building or structure on the following described premises, to-wit (insert legal description including street address, if known):

has been completed.

All persons claiming a lien upon the same under Oregon's Construction Lien Law hereby are notified to file a claim of lien as required by ORS 87.035.

Dated ...., 19........

....
Owner or Mortgagee

By ....

P. O. Address ....

....

STATE OF OREGON   )
)ss.
County of ....)

I, ..., being first duly sworn, depose and say:

That on my behalf or as agent for ....

....

I did on the .... day of .... , 19........, duly post a notice of which the above is a true copy, in a conspicuous place upon the land or upon the improvement situated thereon described in said notice, to-wit: by posting, nailing, tacking, pasting, fastening or ....(indicate which) such notice at the front entrance on the building or improvement constructed, altered or repaired on the above described land. (If no building, state in what manner posted.)

....

....

....

....

Subscribed and sworn to before me this.............

day of ...., 19.........

....
Notary Public for Oregon.

My commission expires:

(SEAL)

Record with recording officer within 5 days after posting —ORS 87.045 (3).

STATE OF OREGON   )
) ss.
County of ....)

I certify that the within instrument was filed in my office on the .... day of ...., 19........, at............ o'clock .....M., and recorded in book .... on page .... or as file/reel number .... of the Construction Lien Book of said County.

Witness my hand and seal of County affixed.

....
Recording Officer.

By ....
Deputy.

Figure 44–2 Completion notice. *Courtesy Stevens-Ness Law Publishing Co.*

The bid becomes part of the legal documents for completion of the project. The legal documents may include plans, specifications, contracts, and bids. The following items are part of a total analysis of costs for residential building construction. The architect and client should clearly know what the bid includes.

1. Plans
2. Permits, fees, specifications
3. Roads and road clearing
4. Excavation
5. Water connection (well and pump)
6. Sewer connection (septic)
7. Foundation, waterproofing
8. Framing including materials, trusses, and labor
9. Fireplace including masonry
10. Plumbing, both rough and finished
11. Wiring, both rough and finished
12. Windows
13. Roofing including sheetmetal and vents
14. Insulation
15. Drywall or plaster
16. Siding
17. Gutters, downspouts, sheet metal and rain drains
18. Concrete flatwork and gravel
19. Heating
20. Garage and exterior doors
21. Painting and decorating
22. Trim and finish interior doors including material and labor
23. Underlayment
24. Carpeting including the amount of carpet and padding, and the cost of labor
25. Vinyl floor covering amount and cost of labor
26. Formica
27. Fixtures and hardware
28. Cabinets
29. Appliances
30. Intercom/stereo system
31. Vacuum system
32. Burglar alarm
33. Weatherstripping and venting
34. Final grading, cleanup, and landscaping
35. Supervision, overhead, and profit
36. Subtotal of land costs
37. Financing costs

CONSTRUCTION INSPECTIONS

When the architect or designer is responsible for the supervision of the construction project, then it will be necessary to work closely with the building contractor to obtain the proper inspections at the necessary times. There are two types of inspections that most frequently occur. The regularly scheduled code inspections that are required during specific phases of construction. These inspections help ensure that the construction methods and materials meet local and national code requirements. The general intent of these inspections is to protect the safety of the occupants and the public. Another type of inspection is often conducted by the lender during certain phases of construction. The purpose of these inspections is to ensure that the materials and methods described in the plans and specifications are being used. The lender has a valuable interest here. If the materials and methods are inferior or not of the standard expected, then the value of the structure may not be what the lender had considered when a preliminary appraisal was made. Another reason for these inspections, and probably the reason that the builder likes best, is the dispersement inspection. These inspections may be requested at various times, such as monthly, or they may be related to a specific dispersement schedule of four times during construction, for example. The intended result of these inspections is the release of funds for payment of work completed.

When the architect or designer supervises the total construction, then he or she must work closely with the contractor to ensure that the project is completed in a timely manner. When a building project remains idle, the overhead costs, such as construction interest, begin to add up quickly. A contractor that bids a job high but builds quickly may be able to save money in the final analysis. Some overhead costs go on daily even when work has stopped or slowed. The supervisor should also have a good knowledge of scheduling so that inspections can be obtained at the proper time. If an inspection is requested when not ready, the building official may charge a fee for excess time spent. Always try to develop a good rapport with building officials so that each encounter goes as smoothly as possible.

CONSTRUCTION SUPERVISION PROCEDURES TEST

DIRECTIONS

Answer the questions with short complete statements or drawings as needed on an 8½ × 11 drawing sheet as follows:

1. Use ⅛ in. guidelines for all lettering.
2. Letter your name, Construction Supervision Procedures Test, and the date at the top of the sheet.
3. Letter the question number and provide the answer. You do not need to write out the question.
4. Do all lettering with vertical uppercase architectural letters. If the answer requires line work, use proper drafting tools and technique. Answers may be prepared on a word processor if appropriate with course guidelines.
5. Your grade will be based on correct answers and quality of line technique.

QUESTIONS

1. Define and list the elements of the following construction-related documents:

   a. loan applications
   b. contracts
   c. building permits
   d. completion notice
   e. bids
   f. change orders

2. Outline and briefly discuss the required building construction inspections.

Section Twelve

Design Criteria for Joists and Beams

Chapter 45
Design Criteria for Structural Loading

AS A beginning drafter you need not be concerned about how the structure to be drawn is supported. To advance in the field of architecture, however, requires a very thorough understanding of how the weight of the materials used for construction will be supported. This will require a knowledge of loads and determining how they are dispersed throughout a structure.

 TYPES OF LOADS

As a drafter you will need to be concerned with several types of loads acting upon a building. These include dead, live, and dynamic loads. Because of the complexity of determining these loads exactly, building codes have tables of conventional safe loads which can be used to help determine the amount of weight or stress acting on any given member.

Dead Loads

Dead loads consist of the weight of the structure including walls, floors, and roofs plus any permanently fixed loads such as fixed service equipment. The symbol DL is often used to represent the values for dead loads. Common dead loads can be seen in Figure 45–1.

Live Loads

Live loads are loads which are superimposed on the building through its use. These loads include such things as people and furniture, and weather-related items such as ice, snow, and water (rain). The most commonly encountered live loads include floor, moving, roof, and snow loads. Live loads are represented by the symbol LL.

Floor Live Loads. Buildings are designed for a specific use or occupancy. Depending on the occupancy, the floor live load will vary greatly. Figure 45–2 shows common minimum design live loads. Notice that the LL for residential floors is 40 lb per sq ft (psf).

Moving Live Loads. In residential and light construction, moving loads typically occur only in garage areas due to the weight of a car or truck. When the weight is being supported by a slab over soil, these loads do not usually cause concern. When moving weights are being supported by wood, the designer

748

WEIGHTS OF BUILDING MATERIALS			
MATERIAL	PSF	MATERIAL	PSF
CEILINGS		**ROOFING**	
Acoustical tile	1.0	Asbestos, corrugated 1/4″	3.0
Channel suspended system	1.0	15 lb felt	.85
1/2″ gypsum board	2.2	3 ply and gravel	5.5
5/8″ gypsum board	2.8	4 ply and gravel	6.0
		5 ply and gravel	6.5
DECKING		Shingles	
2″	4.4	Asphalt	2.0
		Asbestos cement	4.0
FLOOR FINISHES		Book tile 2″	12.0
Asphalt tile	2.0	Book tile 3″	20.0
Brick pavers	10.0	Cement tile	16.0
Ceramic tile 3/4″	10.0	Clay tile	14.0
Concrete (lightweight per in.)	10.0	Fiberglass	0.5
Concrete (reinforced per in.)	12.0	Ludowici	10.0
Hardwood 1″	4.0	Roman	12.0
Linoleum	2.0	Slate 1/4″	10.0
Marble	30.0	Spanish	19.0
Subfloor per in. of depth	3.0	Wood	3.0
Quarry tile 3/8″	5.0		
Terrazzo 1″	13.0	**WALLS**	
Vinyl asbestos tile	1.3	4″ glass block	18.0

Wood floor joists:

	12″O.C.	16″O.C.
2 × 6	6.0	5.0
2 × 8	6.0	6.0
2 × 10	7.0	6.0
2 × 12	8.0	7.0

MATERIAL	PSF
Glass 1/4″ plate	3.3
Window (glass, frame, sash)	8.0
Glazed tile	18.0
Gypsum board 1/2″	2.2
Gypsum board 5/8″	2.8
Marble	15.0
Masonry 4″ thick unless noted	
Brick	38.0
Concrete block	
4″ hollow	30.0
6″ hollow	42.0
8″ hollow	55.0
Hollow clay tile	18.0
Hollow gypsum tile	13.0
Limestone	55.0
Terra-cotta tile	25.0
Stone	55.0
Plaster 1″	8.0
Plaster 1″ w/ wood lath	10.0
Porcelain enamel. steel	3.0
Stucco 7/8″	10.0

MATERIAL	PSF
INSULATION	
Rigid 1″	1.5
Fiberboard 1″	2.0
Foamboard per in.	0.2
Poured in place	2.0
4″ batts	1.7
6″ batts	2.5
10″ batts	4.5
PLYWOOD SHEATHING	
3/8″	1.1
1/2″	1.5
5/8″	1.8
3/4″	2.2
1″	3.0
1 1/8″	3.3

For more exact weights, see manufacturers' specifications.

Figure 45–1 Standard weights of common building materials.

needs to take special care in the design. Consult with the local building department to determine what design weight should be used for moving loads.

Roof Live Loads. Roof live loads vary from 20 to 40 psf depending on the pitch and the use of the roof. Some roofs also are used for sundecks and are designed in a manner similar to floors. Other roofs are so steep that they may be designed like a wall. Many building departments use 30 psf as a safe live load for roofs. Consult the building department in your area for roof live load values.

Snow Loads. Snow loads may or may not be a problem in the area for which you are designing. You may be designing in an area where snow is something you dream about, not design for. If you are designing in an area where winter is something you shovel, it is also something you must allow for in your design. Because snow loads vary so greatly, the designer should consult the local building department to determine what amount of snow load should be considered. In addition to climatic variables, the elevation, wind frequency, duration of snowfall, and the exposure of the roof all influence the amount of live load design.

Dynamic Loads

Dynamic loads are the loads imposed on a structure from a sudden gust of wind or from an earthquake.

Minimum Uniformly Distributed Live Load Table

Basic Building Code - 1978 Edition, as administered by Building Officials & Code Administration International, Inc. (BOCA)

Standard Building Code - Revised to 1978 Editions, as administered by Southern Building Code Congress International, Inc. (SBC)

Uniform Building Code - 1979 Edition, as administered by International Conference of Building Officials (UBC)

Occupancy or Use	BOCA	SBC	UBC
Apartments (see residential)			
Armories & drill rooms	150	150	150
Assembly halls & places of assembly:			
Fixed seats	60	50	50
Movable seats	100	100	100
Platforms	100	100	125
Balcony (exterior)	100	60	—
One- & two-family residences	70	40	60
Bowling alleys, poolrooms & similar recreational areas	75	75	—
Cornices	75	—	60
Corridors	100	100	100
Dance halls & ballrooms	100	100	—
Dining rooms & restaurants	100	100	—
Dwellings (see residential)	—	—	—
Fire escapes:	100	100	100
On multi-or single family residential buildings	40	40	—
Garages, general storage and/or repair	—	—	100
Private passenger car storage	50	50	50
Gymnasiums, main floor & balconies	100	100	—
Hospitals:			
Operating rooms	60	60	40
Private rooms	40	40	40
Wards	40	40	40
Corridors above first floor	80	80	—
Hotels (see residential)	—	—	—
Libraries:			
Reading rooms	60	60	60
Stack rooms	150	125	125
Corridors above first floor	80	80	—
Manufacturing:			
Light	125	100	75
Heavy	250	150	125
Marquees	75	75	60
Office buildings:			
Offices	50	50	50
Lobbies	100	100	100
Corridors above first floor	80	80*	100

Occupancy or Use	BOCA	SBC	UBC
Penal institutions:			
Cell blocks	40	40	—
Corridors	100	100	—
Printing plants:			
Press rooms	—	—	150
Composing & linotype rooms	—	—	100
Residential:			
Multi-family, private apartments	40	40	40
Public rooms	100	100	—
Corridors	80	80	—
Dwellings:			
First floor	40	—	40
Second floor & habitable attics	30	30	40
Sleeping rooms	30	30	30
Uninhabitable attics	20	30	40
All other rooms	—	40	40
Hotels:			
Guest rooms	40	40	40
Public rooms	100	100	100
Corridors serving public rooms	100	100	100
Corridors	80	80	100
Reviewing stands & bleachers	100	100	100
Schools:			
Classrooms	40	40	40
Corridors	80	80	100
Stairs & exitways	100	100	100
Storage warehouses:			
Light	125	125	125
Heavy	250	250	250
Stores:			
Retail:			
First floor rooms	100	75	75
Upper floors	75	75	75
Wholesale	125	100	100
Theaters:			
Aisles, corridors & lobbies	100	100	—
Orchestra floors	60	50	—
Balconies	60	50	—
Stage floors	150	150	125

These live loads were obtained from the editions of the "model" codes as indicated above. The designer is cautioned to ascertain load requirements for his immediate area or governing building code.

Figure 45–2 Minimum uniform design loads. *Reprinted from the* Wood Truss Handbook, *courtesy Gang-Nail Systems, Inc.*

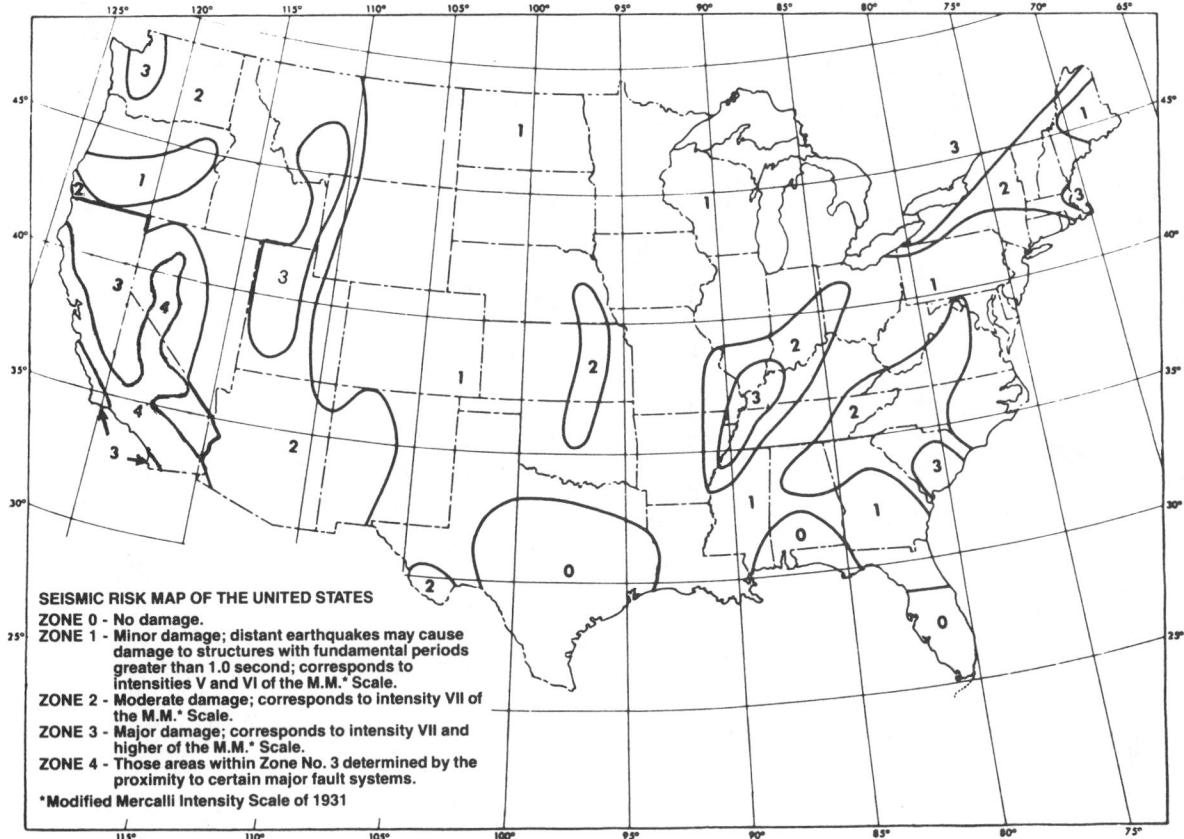

Figure 45–3 Seismic zone maps can be used to help determine the potential risk of damage from earthquakes. *Reproduced from the* Uniform Building Code, *1985 edition. Courtesy The International Conference of Building Officials.*

Wind Loads. The problem of designing for wind is similar to that encountered when designing for snow. Because such wide variations are encountered, the designer must rely on the local building department to provide information on wind speeds.

Seismic Loads. Seismic loads result from earthquakes. Figure 45–3 shows a seismic map of the United States and the risk of each area to damage from earthquakes. The UBC, BOCA, and CABO all specify specific requirements for seismic design.

LOAD DESIGN

Now that you know the source of loads, some information about structural layout is needed. Once the floor plan and elevations have been designed, the designer can start the process of determining how the structure will resist the loads that will be imposed on it. To determine the sizes of material required, it is always best to start at the roof and work down to the foundation. By calculating from the top down the loads will be accumulating and when you work down to the foundation, you will have the total loads needed to size the footings. Use a print of the floor plans, the foundation plan and the sections to help

you visualize the building as you size the various members.

If you consider the examples from past chapters, you will notice that all of the structural information was given to you. How to draw various parts of structures was explained but not why the structural members were of a certain size. That was because as a beginning drafter you are not expected to be designing the structural components. In most offices the structural design of even the simplest buildings is done by a designer or an engineer. The information of this chapter is a brief introduction into the size of structural members. The design of even simple beams can be very complex.

LOAD DISTRIBUTION

Figure 45–4 shows the bearing walls on the various levels of a typical building. This building has a bearing wall that is located approximately halfway between the exterior walls. For this type of building, one-half of the total building loads will be on the central bearing wall, and one-quarter of the total building loads will be on each exterior wall. Examine this building one floor at a time and see why.

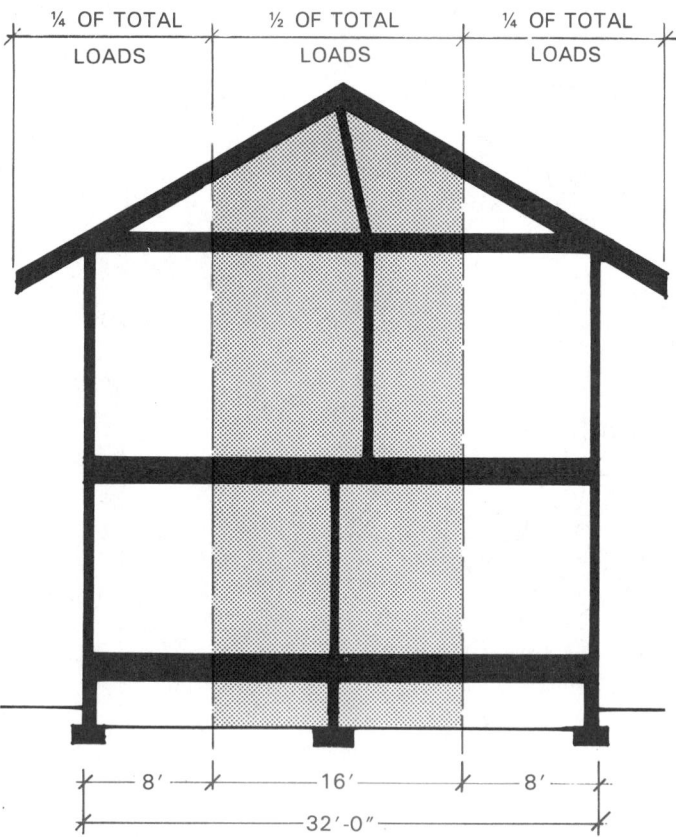

MEMBER	DL	LL	TOTAL
Floor	10	40	50
Decks	10	60	70
Ceiling	5	10	15
Roofs			
235 lb Comp.	8	30	38
Cedar Shakes	7	30	37
Tile	25	30	55
Built-up	8	30	38

Figure 45–6 Typical loads for residential construction. See Appendix B for CABO revisions.

the ceiling and the other floor levels the loading is the same. One-half of each joist is supported at the center wall and half at the outer wall.

Now let's add some numbers and see what it all means. As a starting point we will work on a house that has no snow, no wind problems, and no danger of earthquakes. Figure 45–6 shows a simplified loading chart for residential construction. Using these loads, the weights being supported can be determined. To determine the total weight that a wall supports is a matter of determining the area being supported and multiplying by the weight.

Figure 45–4 Bearing walls and load distribution of a typical home.

The Upper Floor

At the upper floor level, the roof and ceiling loads are being supported. In a building 32′ × 15′, as shown in Figure 45–5, each rafter is spanning 16 ft. Of course the rafter is longer than 16 ft, but remember that the span is a horizontal measurement. If the loads are uniformly distributed throughout the roof, half of the weight of the roof will be supported at each end of the rafter. At the ridge, half of the total roof weight is being supported. At each exterior wall one-quarter of the total roof load is being supported. At

Roof

The area being supported is 15 ft long by 8 ft wide. This is an area of 120 sq ft. The roof load equals the sum of the live and dead loads. Assume a live load of 30 psf. For the dead load we will assume the roof is built with asphalt shingles, ½ in. ply, and 2 × 8 rafters for a dead load of approximately 8.5 psf. For simplicity 8.5 can be rounded up to 10 psf for the dead load. By adding the dead and live loads you can determine that the total roof load is 40 psf. The total roof weight the wall is supporting is 4800 pounds (120 × 40 lb = 4800 lb).

Because the center area in our example is twice as big, the weight will also be twice as big. But just to be sure, check the total weight on the center wall. You should be using 15 × 16 × 40 lb for your calculations. The wall is 15 ft long and holds 8 ft of rafters on each side of the wall for a total of 16 ft. Using a LL of 40 lb, the wall is supporting 9600 pounds.

Ceiling

The procedure for calculating a ceiling is the same as for a roof, but the loads are different. A typical loading pattern for a ceiling is 15 lb. At the outer walls the formula would be 15 × 8 × 15 lb, or 1800 pounds. The center wall would be holding 15 × 16 × 40 lb or 3600 pounds.

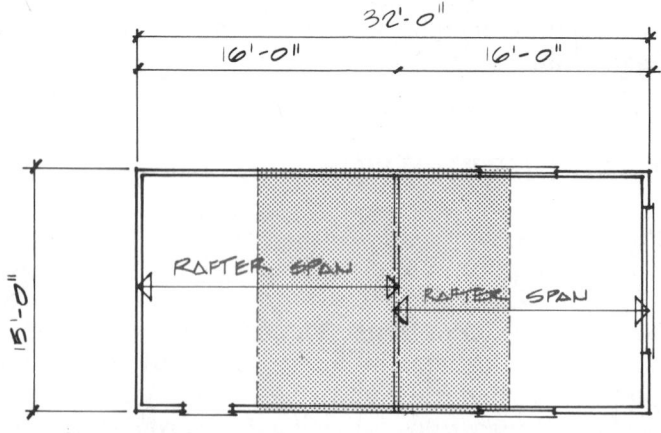

Figure 45–5 Load distribution on a simple beam.

The Lower Floor

Finding the weight of a floor is the same as finding the weight of a ceiling, but the loads are much greater. The LL for residential floors is usually 40 lb and the DL is 10 lb for a total of 50 lb per sq ft.

Walls

The only other weight left to be determined is the weight of the walls. Generally, walls will average about 10 lb per sq ft. Determine the height of the wall and multiply by the length of the wall to find its area. Multiply the area by the weight per square foot and you will have the total wall weight. Figure 45–7 shows the total weight that will be supported by the footings.

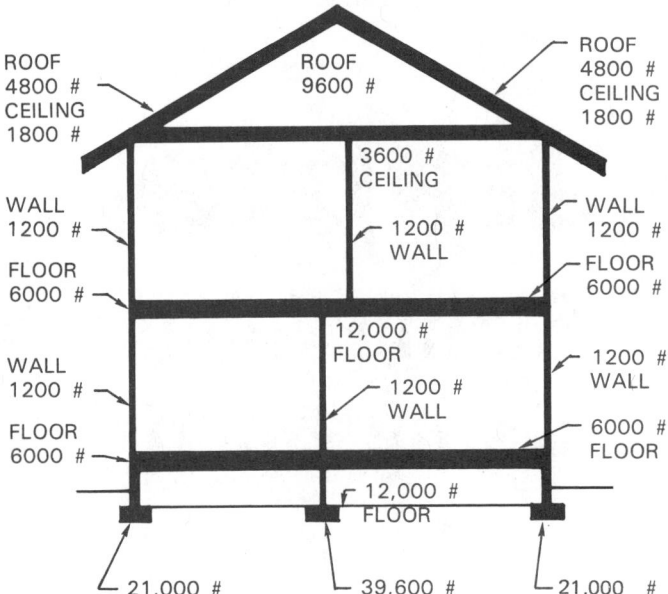

Figure 45–7 Total loads supported by footings. Using the assumed loads multiplied by 15 (the length of the building) produces the total loads.

DESIGN CRITERIA FOR STRUCTURAL LOADING TEST

DIRECTIONS

Answer the questions with short complete statements or drawings as needed on an 8½ × 11 drawing sheet as follows:

1. Use ⅛ in. guidelines for all lettering.
2. Letter your name, Design Criteria and Structural Loading Test, and the date at the top of the sheet.
3. Letter the question number and provide the answer. You do not need to write out the question.
4. Use the illustrations in this chapter to answer the questions. Draw loading sketches as required and show all work.
5. Do all lettering with vertical uppercase architectural letters. For questions 7, 8, and 9 provide loading sketches and show all work. Answers may be prepared on a word processor if appropriate with course guidelines.
6. Your grade will be based on correct answers and quality of line technique.

QUESTIONS

1. What are the two major categories of loads that affect buildings?

2. What is the safe design live load for a residential floor?
3. What is the safe design total load for a residential floor?
4. What factors cause snow loads to vary so widely within the same area?
5. On a uniformly loaded joist, how will the weight be distributed?
6. What load will a floor 15 ft wide by 25 ft long generate?
7. If the floor in problem 6 had a girder to support it 7'–6" in from the edge (centered), how much weight will the girder be supporting?
8. A building is 20 ft wide with a tile roof supported by trusses. The roof shape is a gable and the building is 30 ft long. What amount of roof weight are the walls supporting? What amount of weight is a footing at the bottom of the wall supporting?
9. A one-story home with a post-and-beam floor needs a foundation design. Girders will be placed at 4 ft O.C. with support every 8 ft. What weight will the girders be supporting? What weight will the stem wall at the end of the girder be supporting?
10. Why is it important to be able to solve problems like these?

Chapter 46
Sizing Joists and Rafters Using Span Tables

LOADING REACTIONS OF WOOD MEMBERS
DETERMINING WOOD CHARACTERISTICS
DETERMINING SIZE AND SPAN
TEST

ON THE house that was used as an example of drafting methods in Chapter 20, all structural members were given. A drafter will often need to determine the size of the framing members. Standard framing practice is to place structural members at 12, 16, or 24 in. on center. Because of this practice, standard tables have been developed for the sizing of repetitive members. These tables can be found in most code books. In addition to building codes, many building departments publish their own standards for repetitive framing members. In order to use these tables you must understand a few basic facts including typical loading reactions of framing members and the structural capabilities of various species and grades of wood.

LOADING REACTIONS OF WOOD MEMBERS

For every action there is an equal and opposite reaction. This is a law of physics that affects every

structure ever built. There are two actions, or stresses, that must be understood before beam reactions can be considered. These are fiber bending stress and modulus of elasticity. There are many other stresses that act on a structural member, but they do not need to be understood to use standard loading tables. You do not need to know how these stresses are generated, only that they exist, to determine the size of a framing member using standard loading tables. Each term will be covered in greater depth in the next chapter.

Fiber Bending Stress

Fiber bending stresses are represented on span tables by the symbol F_b. The figures that are listed on span tables are the safe allowable fiber bending stresses for a specific load over a specific span. The designer must compare the calculated values of F_b that must be supported, with the F_b values listed for the species and grade of lumber used to support the load.

Modulus of Elasticity

The modulus of elasticity deals with the stiffness of a structural member. Represented by the symbol E, the modulus of elasticity, or deflection, is concerned with how much a structural member sags.

DETERMINING WOOD CHARACTERISTICS

Before a span table can be used, the values for F_b and E must be determined. Before these can be determined, you must be familiar with the species and grade of wood being used for framing in your area. Some of the most common types of lumber in use for framing are Douglas fir—larch (DFL #2), southern pine (SP #2), spruce—pine—fir (SPF #2), hemlock—fir (Hem—Fir #2) and hemlock (Hem #2). Notice that

each species is followed by #2. This number refers to the grade value of the species. Usually only #1 or #2 grade lumber is used as structural lumber.

Once the type of framing lumber is known, the safe working values can be determined. Figure 46–1 shows the safe working stresses for joists and rafters. Notice that all values are given in terms of F_b and E. A useful procedure for using such a table would be as follows:

1. Determine the type of wood to be used. For example, DFL #2.

SPECIES AND GRADE	SIZE	ALLOWABLE UNIT STRESS IN BENDING F_b			MODULUS OF ELASTICITY E 1 x 10⁶ psi
		FLOOR OR CEILING MEMBERS	ROOF MEMBERS[1] SNOW LOADING	NO SNOW LOADING	
DOUGLAS FIR—LARCH					
DOUGLAS FIR—LARCH (NORTH)					
Construction	2x4	1200	1380	1500	1.5
Standard		675	780	840	1.5
Utility		325	370	410	1.5
Studs		925	1060	1160	1.5
No. 1 & Appearance	2x5 and wider	1750	2010	2190	1.8
Dense No. 2		1700	1960	2120	1.7
No. 2		1450	1670	1810	1.7
No. 3		850	980	1060	1.5
DOUGLAS FIR SOUTH					
Construction	2x4	1150	1320	1440	1.1
Standard		650	750	810	1.1
Utility		300	340	380	1.1
Studs		875	1010	1090	1.1
No. 1 & Appearance	2x5 and wider	1650	1900	2060	1.4
No. 2		1350	1550	1690	1.3
No. 3		800	920	1000	1.1
EASTERN HEMLOCK—TAMARACK					
EASTERN HEMLOCK (NORTH)					
WESTERN HEMLOCK (NORTH)⁵					
Construction	2x4	1050	1210	1310	1.0(1.3)
Standard		575	660	720	1.0(1.3)
Utility		275	320	340	1.0(1.3)
Studs		800	920	1000	1.0(1.3)
No. 1 & Appearance	2x5 and wider	1500	1720	1880	1.3(1.6)
No. 2		1200	1380	1500	1.1(1.4)
No. 3		725	830	910	1.0(1.3)
HEM—FIR					
HEM—FIR (NORTH)					
MOUNTAIN HEMLOCK—HEM—FIR⁶					
Construction	2x4	925	1060	1160	1.2(1.0)
Standard		525	600	660	1.2(1.0)
Utility		250	290	310	1.2(1.0)
Studs		700	800	880	1.2(1.0)
No. 1 & Appearance	2x5 and wider	1350	1550	1690	1.5(1.3)
No. 2		1100	1260	1380	1.4(1.1)
No. 3		650	750	810	1.2(1.0)
LODGEPOLE PINE					
Construction	2x4	875	1010	1090	1.0
Standard		500	580	620	1.0
Utility		225	260	280	1.0
Studs		675	780	840	1.0
No. 1 & Appearance	2x5 and wider	1300	1500	1620	1.3
No. 2		1050	1210	1310	1.2
No. 3		625	720	780	1.0

SPECIES AND GRADE	SIZE	ALLOWABLE UNIT STRESS IN BENDING F_b			MODULUS OF ELASTICITY E 1 x 10⁶ psi
		FLOOR OR CEILING MEMBERS	ROOF MEMBERS[1] SNOW LOADING	NO SNOW LOADING	
MOUNTAIN HEMLOCK					
Construction	2x4	1000	1150	1250	1.0
Standard		575	660	720	1.0
Utility		275	315	340	1.0
Studs		775	890	970	1.0
No. 1 & Appearance	2x5 and wider	1450	1670	1815	1.3
No. 2		1200	1380	1500	1.1
No. 3		700	850	875	1.0
NORTHERN PINE					
Construction	2x4	950	1090	1190	1.1
Standard		525	600	660	1.1
Utility		250	290	310	1.1
Studs		725	830	910	1.1
No. 1 & Appearance	2x5 and wider	1400	1610	1750	1.4
No. 2		1100	1260	1380	1.3
No. 3		650	750	810	1.1
SOUTHERN PINE (Surfaced dry)					
Construction	2x4	1150	1320	1440	1.4
Standard		675	775	840	1.4
Utility		300	345	375	1.4
Studs		900	1035	1125	1.4
No. 1	2x5 and wider	1700	1955	2125	1.7
No. 1 Dense		2000	2300	2500	1.8
No. 2		1400	1610	1750	1.6
No. 2 Dense		1650	1900	2060	1.6
No. 3		800	920	1000	1.4
No. 3 Dense		925	1060	1155	1.5
SPRUCE—PINE—FIR					
Construction	2x4	850	980	1060	1.2
Standard		475	550	590	1.2
Utility		225	260	280	1.2
Stud		650	750	810	1.2
No. 1 & Appearance	2x5 and wider	1200	1380	1500	1.5
No. 2		1000	1150	1250	1.3
No. 3		575	660	720	1.2
WESTERN CEDARS					
WESTERN CEDARS (NORTH)					
Construction	2x4	875	1010	1090	.9
Standard		500	580	620	.9
Utility		225	260	280	.9
Studs		675	780	840	.9
No. 1 & Appearance	2x5 and wider	1300	1500	1620	1.1
No. 2		1050	1210	1310	1.0
No. 3		625	720	780	.9

TABLE NO. 25-A-1—WORKING STRESSES FOR JOISTS AND RAFTERS— VISUAL GRADING

These F_b values are for use where repetitive members are spaced not more than 24 inches. For wider spacing, the F_b values should be reduced 13 percent.

Values are for surfaced dry or surfaced green lumber, except for southern pine as indicated. Values apply at 19 percent maximum moisture content in use.

[1] Values for the allowable unit stress in bending F_b for roof members have been increased 15 percent for snow loading and 25 percent for no snow loading in accordance with U.B.C. Section 2504 (c).

[2] Values for modulus of elasticity shown in ( ) apply to balsam fir.

[3] Values for modulus of elasticity shown in ( ) apply to northern aspen.

[4] Values for modulus of elasticity shown in ( ) apply to coast species.

[5] Values for modulus of elasticity shown in ( ) apply only to western hemlock (north).

[6] Values for modulus of elasticity shown in ( ) apply to mountain hemlock-hem-fir.

[7] Values for modulus of elasticity shown in ( ) apply to white woods (mixed species).

Figure 46–1 Working stress values for common framing woods. See Appendix B for CABO revisions. *Reproduced from the Dwelling Construction Under the Uniform Building Code, 1985 edition. Courtesy The International Conference of Building Officials.*

2. Determine the use. Rafter for example. This typically means that you will be using the 2 × 5 and wider values.

3. If working on a rafter, determine snow or no snow.

4. Select the needed values. For DFL #2 the values are F_b floor = 1450, rafter (no snow) = 1810, rafter (snow) = 1670, E = 1.7.

These are the safe unit working values for the lumber. Given the proper formula, the designer can determine the amount of loads that will be placed on the lumber. If the loading values exceed the safe working values, the lumber fails and part of the structure could collapse.

DETERMINING SIZE AND SPAN

Once the safe working values of the framing lumber are known, the size and span can be determined. Each code provides allowable span tables for floor joists, ceiling joists and rafters. Determine how the wood is to be used and proceed to the proper table.

Sizing Floor Joists

A few simple headings must be located at the top of the table before any spans can be identified. See

Figure 46–2 to become familiar with the basics of the span table. Some of the key things to be gleaned from this part of the table are the following:

- *The Title.* Most codes include about ten different span charts and it is extremely easy to use the wrong table. Double-check the title to see that you have the right table.

- *The Loads.* Within some categories of tables, the values for the table are determined by the loads assumed to be supported. In Figure 46–2, the table is based on an assumed LL value of 40 lb per sq ft. The values in this table will work fine for a residence, but will not work for an office. Because an office has different live loads than a residence, a different table must be used.

- *Listed Values.* Once you determine that you have the right table, determine which values are actually being given. The span is always governed by F_b or E. Notice in Figure 46–2 that this table gives spans that are governed by E. To use this table, the safe E working stress must be known. This value was given as 1.7 for DFL #2 in Figure 46–1.

- *Size and Spacing of Lumber.* The left side of most span tables is usually reserved for the size and spacing of the framing lumber. In Figure 46–2 you will notice that each size of structural

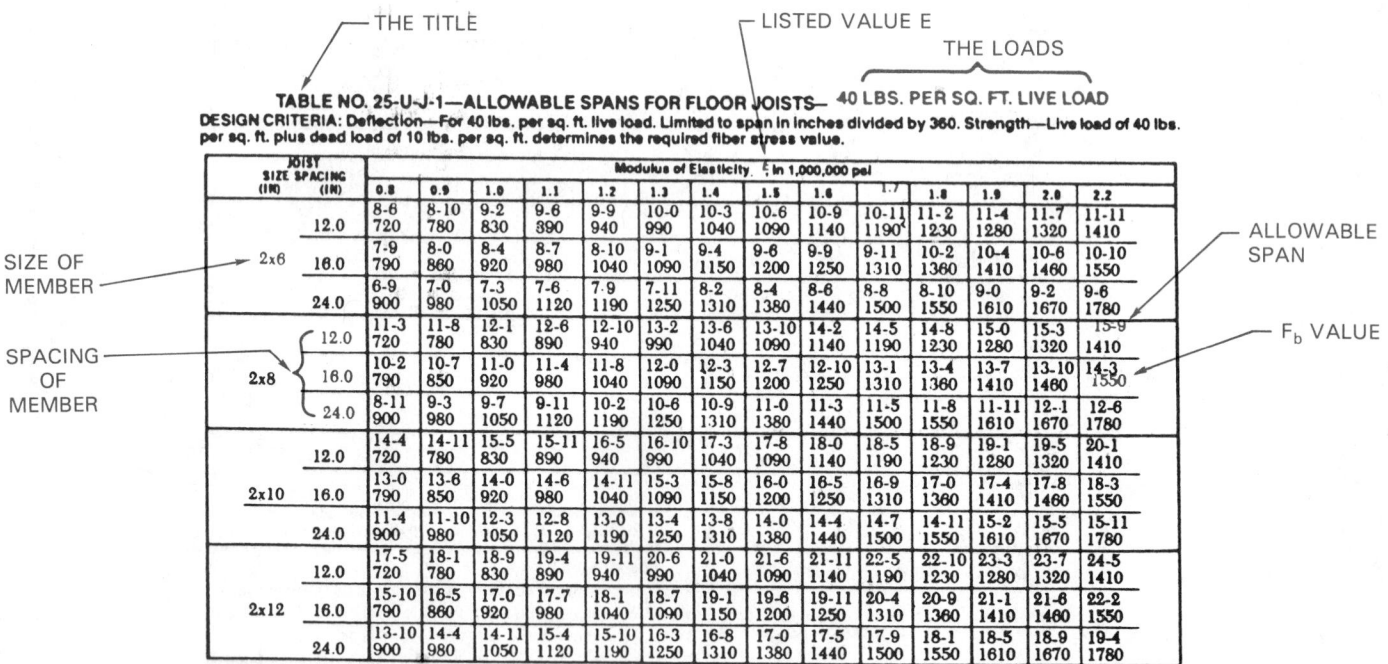

TABLE NO. 25-U-J-1—ALLOWABLE SPANS FOR FLOOR JOISTS— 40 LBS. PER SQ. FT. LIVE LOAD

DESIGN CRITERIA: Deflection—For 40 lbs. per sq. ft. live load. Limited to span in inches divided by 360. Strength—Live load of 40 lbs. per sq. ft. plus dead load of 10 lbs. per sq. ft. determines the required fiber stress value.

JOIST SIZE (IN)	SPACING (IN)	Modulus of Elasticity, E in 1,000,000 psi														
		0.8	0.9	1.0	1.1	1.2	1.3	1.4	1.5	1.6	1.7	1.8	1.9	2.0	2.2
2x6	12.0	8-6 720	8-10 780	9-2 830	9-6 890	9-9 940	10-0 990	10-3 1040	10-6 1090	10-9 1140	10-11 1190	11-2 1230	11-4 1280	11-7 1320	11-11 1410
	16.0	7-9 790	8-0 860	8-4 920	8-7 980	8-10 1040	9-1 1090	9-4 1150	9-6 1200	9-9 1250	9-11 1310	10-2 1360	10-4 1410	10-6 1460	10-10 1550
	24.0	6-9 900	7-0 980	7-3 1050	7-6 1120	7-9 1190	7-11 1250	8-2 1310	8-4 1380	8-6 1440	8-8 1500	8-10 1550	9-0 1610	9-2 1670	9-6 1780
2x8	12.0	11-3 720	11-8 780	12-1 830	12-6 890	12-10 940	13-2 990	13-6 1040	13-10 1090	14-2 1140	14-5 1190	14-8 1230	15-0 1280	15-3 1320	15-9 1410
	16.0	10-2 790	10-7 850	11-0 920	11-4 980	11-8 1040	12-0 1090	12-3 1150	12-7 1200	12-10 1250	13-1 1310	13-4 1360	13-7 1410	13-10 1460	14-3 1550
	24.0	8-11 900	9-3 980	9-7 1050	9-11 1120	10-2 1190	10-6 1250	10-9 1310	11-0 1380	11-3 1440	11-5 1500	11-8 1550	11-11 1610	12-1 1670	12-6 1780
2x10	12.0	14-4 720	14-11 780	15-5 830	15-11 890	16-5 940	16-10 990	17-3 1040	17-8 1090	18-0 1140	18-5 1190	18-9 1230	19-1 1280	19-5 1320	20-1 1410
	16.0	13-0 790	13-6 850	14-0 920	14-6 980	14-11 1040	15-3 1090	15-8 1150	16-0 1200	16-5 1250	16-9 1310	17-0 1360	17-4 1410	17-8 1460	18-3 1550
	24.0	11-4 900	11-10 980	12-3 1050	12-8 1120	13-0 1190	13-4 1250	13-8 1310	14-0 1380	14-4 1440	14-7 1500	14-11 1550	15-2 1610	15-5 1670	15-11 1780
2x12	12.0	17-5 720	18-1 780	18-9 830	19-4 890	19-11 940	20-6 990	21-0 1040	21-6 1090	21-11 1140	22-5 1190	22-10 1230	23-3 1280	23-7 1320	24-5 1410
	16.0	15-10 790	16-5 860	17-0 920	17-7 980	18-1 1040	18-7 1090	19-1 1150	19-6 1200	19-11 1250	20-4 1310	20-9 1360	21-1 1410	21-6 1460	22-2 1550
	24.0	13-10 900	14-4 980	14-11 1050	15-4 1120	15-10 1190	16-3 1250	16-8 1310	17-0 1380	17-5 1440	17-9 1500	18-1 1550	18-5 1610	18-9 1670	19-4 1780

NOTES:

(1) The required extreme fiber stress in bending (F_b) in pounds per square inch is shown below each span.

(2) Use single or repetitive member bending stress values (F_b) and modulus of elasticity values (E) from Tables Nos. 25-A-1 and 25-A-2 of the Uniform Building Code.

(3) For more comprehensive tables covering a broader range of bending stress values (F_b) and modulus of elasticity values (E), other spacing of members and other conditions of loading, see U.B.C. Standard No. 25-21.

(4) The spans in these tables are intended for use in covered structures or where moisture content in use does not exceed 19 percent.

Figure 46–2 Information typically found on a span table. *Reproduced from the* Dwelling Construction Under the Uniform Building Code, *1985 edition. Courtesy The International Conference of Building Officials.*

member has a value for the spacings of 12, 16, or 24 in. on center.

Using the Span Tables

To use Figure 46–2, find the column that represents proper E value for the lumber used in your area. For our example, Douglas fir #2 for a floor will be used which means that the 1.7 column will contain all the span information we need. The first listing in this column is 10–11 over the number 1190. The 10–11 represents a maximum allowable span of 10′–11″. The 1190 is the F_b value that 40 lb per sq ft would place on this member. Because 1190 is less than the safe working stress of 1450, the member is safe to use. By following the table over to the left side you will see that these values correspond to a 2 × 6 at 12 in. O.C.

Using Figure 46–3, determine the distance a 2 × 10 DFL #2 floor joist will span at 16 in. O.C. Use the 1.7 E column. Work down the left side until you come to 2 × 10. Now work to the right in the 16 in. spacing row. The 1.7 E column and the 16 in. spacing row will intersect at 16–9 over 1310. The span for a 2 × 10 at 16 in. O.C. is 16′–9″ with a fiber bending value of 1310. Because the safe limit is 1450, the 2 × 10 is safe to use. As you use the floor joist tables, start with the 16 in. spacing. Floor joists are most commonly laid out at 16 in. O.C.

Sizing Ceiling Joists

To determine the size of a ceiling joist, use the same procedure that was used to size a floor joist using the proper table. Because they are both horizontal members, they will have similar loading patterns. A table for sizing ceiling joists can be seen in Figure 46–4. It is very similar to the floor joist span table of Figure 46–3, and the two can be confused easily when you are in a hurry. The major difference between the two tables are the loads. Remember, for floors the live load was 40 lb. For ceiling joists the load is only 10 lb. Using table 46–4, determine the smallest size ceiling joist that will span 16 ft at 16 in. O.C. By using the 1.7 column, you will find that a 2 × 6 at 16 in. O.C. will span 18′–1″ with an F_b of 1290. The safe limit, remember, is 1450.

Sizing Rafters

There are many different tables that can be used for selecting rafter spans depending on the use, roof pitch, and the roofing material. The rafter tables are used when the structure has an attic, and rafter/ceiling joist tables are used for vaulted ceilings. Figure 46–5 shows examples of several different types of tables which can be used for rafters. In addition to being separated by use, rafter tables are also divided into categories by pitch. Low slope roofs are

TABLE NO. 25-U-J-1—ALLOWABLE SPANS FOR FLOOR JOISTS—40 LBS. PER SQ. FT. LIVE LOAD

DESIGN CRITERIA: Deflection—For 40 lbs. per sq. ft. live load. Limited to span in inches divided by 360. Strength—Live load of 40 lbs. per sq. ft. plus dead load of 10 lbs. per sq. ft. determines the required fiber stress value.

JOIST SIZE (IN)	SPACING (IN)	Modulus of Elasticity, E, in 1,000,000 psi													
		0.8	0.9	1.0	1.1	1.2	1.3	1.4	1.5	1.6	1.7	1.8	1.9	2.0	2.2
2x6	12.0	8-6 / 720	8-10 / 780	9-2 / 830	9-6 / 890	9-9 / 940	10-0 / 990	10-3 / 1040	10-6 / 1090	10-9 / 1140	10-11 / 1190	11-2 / 1230	11-4 / 1280	11-7 / 1320	11-11 / 1410
	16.0	7-9 / 790	8-0 / 860	8-4 / 920	8-7 / 980	8-10 / 1040	9-1 / 1090	9-4 / 1150	9-6 / 1200	9-9 / 1250	9-11 / 1310	10-2 / 1360	10-4 / 1410	10-6 / 1460	10-10 / 1550
	24.0	6-9 / 900	7-0 / 980	7-3 / 1050	7-6 / 1120	7-9 / 1190	7-11 / 1250	8-2 / 1310	8-4 / 1380	8-6 / 1440	8-8 / 1500	8-10 / 1550	9-0 / 1610	9-2 / 1670	9-6 / 1780
2x8	12.0	11-3 / 720	11-8 / 780	12-1 / 830	12-6 / 890	12-10 / 940	13-2 / 990	13-6 / 1040	13-10 / 1090	14-2 / 1140	14-5 / 1190	14-8 / 1230	15-0 / 1280	15-3 / 1320	15-9 / 1410
	16.0	10-2 / 790	10-7 / 850	11-0 / 920	11-4 / 980	11-8 / 1040	12-0 / 1090	12-3 / 1150	12-7 / 1200	12-10 / 1250	13-1 / 1310	13-4 / 1360	13-7 / 1410	13-10 / 1460	14-3 / 1550
	24.0	8-11 / 900	9-3 / 980	9-7 / 1050	9-11 / 1120	10-2 / 1190	10-6 / 1250	10-9 / 1310	11-0 / 1380	11-3 / 1440	11-5 / 1500	11-8 / 1550	11-11 / 1610	12-1 / 1670	12-6 / 1780
2x10	12.0	14-4 / 720	14-11 / 780	15-5 / 830	15-11 / 890	16-5 / 940	16-10 / 990	17-3 / 1040	17-8 / 1090	18-0 / 1140	18-5 / 1190	18-9 / 1230	19-1 / 1280	19-5 / 1320	20-1 / 1410
	16.0	13-0 / 790	13-6 / 850	14-0 / 920	14-6 / 980	14-11 / 1040	15-3 / 1090	15-8 / 1150	16-0 / 1200	16-5 / 1250	16-9 / 1310	17-0 / 1360	17-4 / 1410	17-8 / 1460	18-3 / 1550
	24.0	11-4 / 900	11-10 / 980	12-3 / 1050	12-8 / 1120	13-0 / 1190	13-4 / 1250	13-8 / 1310	14-0 / 1380	14-4 / 1440	14-7 / 1500	14-11 / 1550	15-2 / 1610	15-5 / 1670	15-11 / 1780
2x12	12.0	17-5 / 720	18-1 / 780	18-9 / 830	19-4 / 890	19-11 / 940	20-6 / 990	21-0 / 1040	21-6 / 1090	21-11 / 1140	22-5 / 1190	22-10 / 1230	23-3 / 1280	23-7 / 1320	24-5 / 1410
	16.0	15-10 / 790	16-5 / 860	17-0 / 920	17-7 / 980	18-1 / 1040	18-7 / 1090	19-1 / 1150	19-6 / 1200	19-11 / 1250	20-4 / 1310	20-9 / 1360	21-1 / 1410	21-6 / 1460	22-2 / 1550
	24.0	13-10 / 900	14-4 / 980	14-11 / 1050	15-4 / 1120	15-10 / 1190	16-3 / 1250	16-8 / 1310	17-0 / 1380	17-5 / 1440	17-9 / 1500	18-1 / 1550	18-5 / 1610	18-9 / 1670	19-4 / 1780

NOTES:
(1) The required extreme fiber stress in bending (F_b) in pounds per square inch is shown below each span.
(2) Use single or repetitive member bending stress values (F_b) and modulus of elasticity values (E) from Tables Nos. 25-A-1 and 25-A-2 of the Uniform Building Code.
(3) For more comprehensive tables covering a broader range of bending stress values (F_b) and modulus of elasticity values (E), other spacing of members and other conditions of loading, see U.B.C. Standard No. 25-21.
(4) The spans in these tables are intended for use in covered structures or where moisture content in use does not exceed 19 percent.

Figure 46–3 Once the safe value for E is known, a specific size and spacing for a floor joist can be determined. *Reproduced from the Dwelling Construction Under the Uniform Building Code, 1985 edition. Courtesy The International Conference of Building Officials.*

TABLE NO. 25-U-J-6—ALLOWABLE SPANS FOR CEILING JOISTS—10 LBS. PER SQ. FT. LIVE LOAD
(Drywall Ceiling)

DESIGN CRITERIA: Deflection—For 10 lbs. per sq. ft. live load. Limited to span in inches divided by 240. Strength—Live load of 10 lbs. per sq. ft. plus dead load of 5 lbs. per sq. ft. determines the required fiber stress value.

JOIST SIZE (IN)	SPACING (IN)	Modulus of Elasticity, E, in 1,000,000 psi													
		0.8	0.9	1.0	1.1	1.2	1.3	1.4	1.5	1.6	1.7	1.8	1.9	2.0	2.2
2x4	12.0	9-10	10-3	10-7	10-11	11-3	11-7	11-10	12-2	12-5	12.8	12-11	13-2	13-4	13-9
		710	770	830	880	930	980	1030	1080	1130	1180	1220	1270	1310	1400
	16.0	8-11	9-4	9-8	9-11	10-3	10-6	10-9	11-0	11-3	11-6	11-9	11-11	12-2	12-6
		780	850	910	970	1030	1080	1140	1190	1240	1290	1340	1390	1440	1540
	24.0	7-10	8-1	8-5	8-8	8-11	9-2	9-5	9-8	9-10	10-0	10-3	10-5	10-7	10-11
		900	970	1040	1110	1170	1240	1300	1360	1420	1480	1540	1600	1650	1760
2x6	12.0	15-6	16-1	16-8	17-2	17-8	18-2	18-8	19-1	19-6	19-11	20-3	20-8	21-0	21-8
		710	770	830	880	930	980	1030	1080	1130	1180	1220	1270	1310	1400
	16.0	14-1	14-7	15-2	15-7	16-1	16-6	16-11	17-4	17-8	18-1	18-5	18-9	19-1	19-8
		780	850	910	970	1030	1080	1140	1190	1240	1290	1340	1390	1440	1540
	24.0	12-3	12-9	13-3	13-8	14-1	14-5	14-9	15-2	15-6	15-9	16-1	16-4	16-8	17-2
		900	970	1040	1110	1170	1240	1300	1360	1420	1480	1540	1600	1650	1760
2x8	12.0	20-5	21-2	21-11	22-8	23-4	24-0	24-7	25-2	25-8	26-2	26-9	27-2	27-8	28-7
		710	770	830	880	930	980	1030	1080	1130	1180	1220	1270	1310	1400
	16.0	18-6	19-3	19-11	20-7	21-2	21-9	22-4	22-10	23-4	23-10	24-3	24-8	25-2	25-11
		780	850	910	970	1030	1080	1140	1190	1240	1290	1340	1390	1440	1540
	24.0	16-2	16-10	17-5	18-0	18-6	19-0	19-6	19-11	20-5	20-10	21-2	21-7	21-11	22-8
		900	970	1040	1110	1170	1240	1300	1360	1420	1480	1540	1600	1650	1760
2x10	12.0	26-0	27-1	28-0	28-11	29-9	30-7	31-4	32-1	32-9	33-5	34-1	34-8	35-4	36-5
		710	770	830	880	930	980	1030	1080	1130	1180	1220	1270	1310	1400
	16.0	23-8	24-7	25-5	26-3	27-1	27-9	28-6	29-2	29-9	30-5	31-0	31-6	32-1	33-1
		780	850	910	970	1030	1080	1140	1190	1240	1290	1340	1390	1440	1540
	24.0	20-8	21-6	22-3	22-11	23-8	24-3	24-10	25-5	26-0	26-6	27-1	27-6	28-0	28-11
		900	970	1040	1110	1170	1240	1300	1360	1420	1480	1540	1600	1650	1760

NOTES:

(1) The required extreme fiber stress in bending (F_b) in pounds per square inch is shown below each span.

(2) Use single or repetitive member bending stress values (F_b) and modulus of elasticity values (E) from Tables Nos. 25-A-1 and 25-A-2 of the Uniform Building Code.

(3) For more comprehensive tables covering a broader range of bending stress values (F_b) and modulus of elasticity values (E), other spacing of members and other conditions of loading, see U.B.C. Standard No. 25-21.

(4) The spans in these tables are intended for use in covered structures or where moisture content in use does not exceed 19 percent.

Figure 46–4 The span table for determining ceiling joist spans is similar to the table used to size floor joists. *Reproduced from the Dwelling Construction Under the Uniform Building Code, 1985 edition. Courtesy The International Conference of Building Officials.*

those with a pitch of less than 3/12, and high slope roofs are those steeper than 3/12.

Another distinguishing feature of the rafter tables is the finished roof material. The tables are divided into light and heavy roofs. A tile roof would be an example of a heavy roof. Composition shingles, shakes, or metal panels are examples of light roofing materials.

The biggest difference you will find in the rafter tables from the other tables described is the way the information is presented. Rafter values are given in terms of F_b rather than E. Go back to the Working Stresses for Joist and Rafters in Figure 46–1 and determine the F_b for the type of wood to be used. For Douglas fir #2, this will be 1670 for snow loading, and 1810 for no snow. Figure 46–6 shows one of the most common rafter tables from the Uniform Building Code. Figure 46–7 and 46–8 are also frequently used in many types of construction. Before trying to determine spans, remember to study the top part of the table. Determine the weights, pitch, and type of member the table was designed for.

One new problem is presented in the use of the rafters tables. The safe working value for DFL #2 is 1810. If you check Figure 46–6 carefully, you will notice that there is no column headed 1810. The closest you can come to the desired value is 1800. Don't panic; use the closest value to the safe working stress of the lumber you are working with, without exceeding it.

Another key element to sizing rafters is that they are usually placed at 24 in. O.C. rather than the 16 in. centers of floor and ceiling joists. As you enter the tables, use the 24 in. spacing as a starting point. Now give the tables a try. Determine the size of rafter needed to span 14'-0" in an area where it never snows, on a house with a 5/12 pitch and composition shingles. By using the rafter table in Figure 46–6, you will find a 2 × 4 will span 7'-1" at 24 in. O.C., a 2 × 6 will span 11'-1" at 24 in. O.C., and a 2 × 8 will span 14'-7". The 2 × 8 is the right choice.

TABLE NO. 25-U-R-1—ALLOWABLE SPANS FOR LOW- OR HIGH-SLOPE RAFTERS
20 LBS. PER SQ. FT. LIVE LOAD (Supporting Drywall Ceiling)

DESIGN CRITERIA: Strength—15 lbs. per sq. ft. dead load plus 20 lbs. per sq. ft. live load determines required fiber stress. Deflection—For 20 lbs. per sq. ft. live load. Limited to span in inches divided by 240. RAFTERS: Spans are measured along the horizontal projection and loads are considered as applied on the horizontal projection.

RAFTER SIZE (IN)	SPACING (IN)	Allowable Extreme Fiber Stress in Bending F_b (psi)														
		500	600	700	800	900	1000	1100	1200	1300	1400	1500	1600	1700	1800	1900
	12.0	8-6 / 0.26	9-4 / 0.35	10-0 / 0.44	10-9 / 0.54	11-5 / 0.64	12-0 / 0.75	12-7 / 0.86	13-2 / 0.98	13-8 / 1.11	14-2 / 1.24	14-8 / 1.37	15-2 / 1.51	15-8 / 1.66	16-1 / 1.81	16-7 / 1.96

TABLE NO. 25-U-R-2—ALLOWABLE SPANS FOR LOW- OR HIGH-SLOPE RAFTERS
30 LBS. PER SQ. FT. LIVE LOAD (Supporting Drywall Ceiling)

DESIGN CRITERIA: Strength—15 lbs. per sq. ft. dead load plus 30 lbs. per sq. ft. live load determines required fiber stress. Deflection—For 30 lbs. per sq. ft. live load. Limited to span in inches divided by 240. RAFTERS: Spans are measured along the horizontal projection and loads are considered as applied on the horizontal projection.

RAFTER SIZE (IN)	SPACING (IN)	Allowable Extreme Fiber Stress in Bending F_b (psi)														
		500	600	700	800	900	1000	1100	1200	1300	1400	1500	1600	1700	1800	1900
	12.0	7-6 / 0.27	8-2 / 0.36	8-10 / 0.45	9-6 / 0.55	10-0 / 0.66	10-7 / 0.77	11-1 / 0.89	11-7 / 1.01	12-1 / 1.14	12-6 / 1.28	13-0 / 1.41	13-5 / 1.56	13-10 / 1.71	14-2 / 1.86	14-7 / 2.02

TABLE NO. 25-U-R-7—ALLOWABLE SPANS FOR LOW-SLOPE RAFTERS, SLOPE 3 IN 12 OR LESS
20 LBS. PER SQ. FT. LIVE LOAD (No Ceiling Load)

DESIGN CRITERIA: Strength—10 lbs. per sq. ft. dead load plus 20 lbs. per sq. ft. live load determines required fiber stress. Deflection—For 20 lbs. per sq. ft. live load. Limited to span in inches divided by 240. RAFTERS: Spans are measured along the horizontal projection and loads are considered as applied on the horizontal projection.

RAFTER SIZE (IN)	SPACING (IN)	Allowable Extreme Fiber Stress in Bending F_b (psi)														
		500	600	700	800	900	1000	1100	1200	1300	1400	1500	1600	1700	1800	1900
	12.0	9-2 / 0.33	10-0 / 0.44	10-10 / 0.55	11-7 / 0.67	12-4 / 0.80	13-0 / 0.94	13-7 / 1.09	14-2 / 1.24	14-9 / 1.40	15-4 / 1.56	15-11 / 1.73	16-5 / 1.91	16-11 / 2.09	17-5 / 2.28	17-10 / 2.47

TABLE NO. 25-U-R-8—ALLOWABLE SPANS FOR LOW-SLOPE RAFTERS, SLOPE 3 IN 12 OR LESS
30 LBS. PER SQ. FT. LIVE LOAD (No Ceiling Load)

DESIGN CRITERIA: Strength—10 lbs. per sq. ft. dead load plus 30 lbs. per sq. ft. live load determines required fiber stress. Deflection—For 30 lbs. per sq. ft. live load. Limited to span in inches divided by 240. RAFTERS: Spans are measured along the horizontal projection and loads are considered as applied on the horizontal projection.

RAFTER SIZE (IN)	SPACING (IN)	Allowable Extreme Fiber Stress in Bending F_b (psi)														
		500	600	700	800	900	1000	1100	1200	1300	1400	1500	1600	1700	1800	1900
	12.0	7-11 / 0.32	8-8 / 0.43	9-5 / 0.54	10-0 / 0.66	10-8 / 0.78	11-3 / 0.92	11-9 / 1.06	12-4 / 1.21	12-10 / 1.36	13-3 / 1.52	13-9 / 1.69	14-2 / 1.86	14-8 / 2.04	15-1 / 2.22	15-6 / 2.41

TABLE NO. 25-U-R-10—ALLOWABLE SPANS FOR HIGH-SLOPE RAFTERS, SLOPE OVER 3 IN 12
20 LBS. PER SQ. FT. LIVE LOAD (Heavy Roof Covering)

DESIGN CRITERIA: Strength—15 lbs. per sq. ft. dead load plus 20 lbs. per sq. ft. live load determines required fiber stress. Deflection—For 20 lbs. per sq. ft. live load. Limited to span in inches divided by 180. RAFTERS: Spans are measured along the horizontal projection and loads are considered as applied on the horizontal projection.

RAFTER SIZE (IN)	SPACING (IN)	Allowable Extreme Fiber Stress in Bending F_b (psi)														
		500	600	700	800	900	1000	1100	1200	1300	1400	1500	1600	1700	1800	1900
	12.0	5-5 / 0.20	5-11 / 0.26	6-5 / 0.33	6-10 / 0.40	7-3 / 0.48	7-8 / 0.56	8-0 / 0.65	8-4 / 0.74	8-8 / 0.83	9-0 / 0.93	9-4 / 1.03	9-8 / 1.14	9-11 / 1.24	10-3 / 1.36	10-6 / 1.47

TABLE NO. 25-U-R-11—ALLOWABLE SPANS FOR HIGH-SLOPE RAFTERS, SLOPE OVER 3 IN 12
30 LBS. PER SQ. FT. LIVE LOAD (Heavy Roof Covering)

DESIGN CRITERIA: Strength—15 lbs. per sq. ft. dead load plus 30 lbs. per sq. ft. live load determines required fiber stress. Deflection—For 30 lbs. per sq. ft. live load. Limited to span in inches divided by 180. RAFTERS: Spans are measured along the horizontal projection and loads are considered as applied on the horizontal projection.

RAFTER SIZE (IN)	SPACING (IN)	Allowable Extreme Fiber Stress in Bending F_b (psi)														
		500	600	700	800	900	1000	1100	1200	1300	1400	1500	1600	1700	1800	1900
	12.0	4-9 / 0.20	5-3 / 0.27	5-8 / 0.34	6-0 / 0.41	6-5 / 0.49	6-9 / 0.58	7-1 / 0.67	7-5 / 0.76	7-8 / 0.86	8-0 / 0.96	8-3 / 1.06	8-6 / 1.17	8-9 / 1.28	9-0 / 1.39	9-3 / 1.51

TABLE NO. 25-U-R-13—ALLOWABLE SPANS FOR HIGH-SLOPE RAFTERS, SLOPE OVER 3 IN 12
20 LBS. PER SQ. FT. LIVE LOAD (Light Roof Covering)

DESIGN CRITERIA: Strength—7 lbs. per sq. ft. dead load plus 20 lbs. per sq. ft. live load determines required fiber stress. Deflection—For 20 lbs. per sq. ft. live load. Limited to span in inches divided by 180. RAFTERS: Spans are measured along the horizontal projection and loads are considered as applied on the horizontal projection.

RAFTER SIZE (IN)	SPACING (IN)	Allowable Extreme Fiber Stress in Bending F_b (psi)														
		500	600	700	800	900	1000	1100	1200	1300	1400	1500	1600	1700	1800	1900
	12.0	6-2 / 0.29	6-9 / 0.38	7-3 / 0.49	7-9 / 0.59	8-3 / 0.71	8-8 / 0.83	9-1 / 0.96	9-6 / 1.09	9-11 / 1.23	10-3 / 1.37	10-8 / 1.52	11-0 / 1.68	11-4 / 1.84	11-8 / 2.00	12-0 / 2.17

TABLE NO. 25-U-R-14—ALLOWABLE SPANS FOR HIGH-SLOPE RAFTERS, SLOPE OVER 3 IN 12
30 LBS. PER SQ. FT. LIVE LOAD (Light Roof Covering)

DESIGN CRITERIA: Strength—7 lbs. per sq. ft. dead load plus 30 lbs. per sq. ft. live load determines required fiber stress. Deflection—For 30 lbs. per sq. ft. live load. Limited to span in inches divided by 180. RAFTERS: Spans are measured along the horizontal projection and loads are considered as applied on the horizontal projection.

RAFTER SIZE (IN)	SPACING (IN)	Allowable Extreme Fiber Stress in Bending F_b (psi)														
		500	600	700	800	900	1000	1100	1200	1300	1400	1500	1600	1700	1800	1900
	12.0	5-3 / 0.27	5-9 / 0.36	6-3 / 0.45	6-8 / 0.55	7-1 / 0.66	7-5 / 0.77	7-9 / 0.89	8-2 / 1.02	8-6 / 1.15	8-9 / 1.28	9-1 / 1.42	9-5 / 1.57	9-8 / 1.72	10-0 / 1.87	10-3 / 2.03

Figure 46–5 There is a wide variety of rafter span tables that can be used depending on the type of roof framing system, roofing material, and roof pitch. See Appendix B for CABO schedules. *Reproduced from the Dwelling Construction Under the Uniform Building Code, 1985 edition. Courtesy The International Conference of Building Officials.*

TABLE NO. 25-U-R-14—ALLOWABLE SPANS FOR HIGH-SLOPE RAFTERS, SLOPE OVER 3 IN 12
30 LBS. PER SQ. FT. LIVE LOAD (Light Roof Covering)

DESIGN CRITERIA: Strength—7 lbs. per sq. ft. dead load plus 30 lbs. per sq. ft. live load determines required fiber stress. Deflection—For 30 lbs. per sq. ft. live load. Limited to span in inches divided by 180. RAFTERS: Spans are measured along the horizontal projection and loads are considered as applied on the horizontal projection.

RAFTER SIZE (IN)	SPACING (IN)	Allowable Extreme Fiber Stress in Bending F_b (psi). 500	600	700	800	900	1000	1100	1200	1300	1400	1500	1600	1700	1800	1900
2x4	12.0	5-3 / 0.27	5-9 / 0.36	6-3 / 0.45	6-8 / 0.55	7-1 / 0.66	7-5 / 0.77	7-9 / 0.89	8-2 / 1.02	8-6 / 1.15	8-9 / 1.28	9-1 / 1.42	9-5 / 1.57	9-8 / 1.72	10-0 / 1.87	10-3 / 2.03
	16.0	4-7 / 0.24	5-0 / 0.31	5-5 / 0.39	5-9 / 0.48	6-1 / 0.57	6-5 / 0.67	6-9 / 0.77	7-1 / 0.88	7-4 / 0.99	7-7 / 1.11	7-11 / 1.23	8-2 / 1.36	8-5 / 1.49	8-8 / 1.62	8-10 / 1.76
	24.0	3-9 / 0.19	4-1 / 0.25	4-5 / 0.32	4-8 / 0.39	5-0 / 0.47	5-3 / 0.55	5-6 / 0.63	5-9 / 0.72	6-0 / 0.81	6-3 / 0.91	6-5 / 1.01	6-8 / 1.11	6-10 / 1.21	7-1 / 1.32	7-3 / 1.43
2x6	12.0	8-3 / 0.27	9-1 / 0.36	9-9 / 0.45	10-5 / 0.55	11-1 / 0.66	11-8 / 0.77	12-3 / 0.89	12-9 / 1.02	13-4 / 1.15	13-10 / 1.28	14-4 / 1.42	14-9 / 1.57	15-3 / 1.72	15-8 / 1.87	16-1 / 2.03
	16.0	7-2 / 0.24	7-10 / 0.31	8-5 / 0.39	9-1 / 0.48	9-7 / 0.57	10-1 / 0.67	10-7 / 0.77	11-1 / 0.88	11-6 / 0.99	12-0 / 1.11	12-5 / 1.23	12-9 / 1.36	13-2 / 1.49	13-7 / 1.62	13-11 / 1.76
	24.0	5-10 / 0.19	6-5 / 0.25	6-11 / 0.32	7-5 / 0.39	7-10 / 0.47	8-3 / 0.55	8-8 / 0.63	9-1 / 0.72	9-5 / 0.81	9-9 / 0.91	10-1 / 1.01	10-5 / 1.11	10-9 / 1.21	11-1 / 1.32	11-5 / 1.43
2x8	12.0	10-11 / 0.27	11-11 / 0.36	12-10 / 0.45	13-9 / 0.55	14-7 / 0.66	15-5 / 0.77	16-2 / 0.89	16-10 / 1.02	17-7 / 1.15	18-2 / 1.28	18-10 / 1.42	19-6 / 1.57	20-1 / 1.72	20-8 / 1.87	21-3 / 2.03
	16.0	9-5 / 0.24	10-4 / 0.31	11-2 / 0.39	11-11 / 0.48	12-8 / 0.57	13-4 / 0.67	14-0 / 0.77	14-7 / 0.88	15-2 / 0.99	15-9 / 1.11	16-4 / 1.23	16-10 / 1.36	17-4 / 1.49	17-11 / 1.62	18-4 / 1.76
	24.0	7-8 / 0.19	8-5 / 0.25	9-1 / 0.32	9-9 / 0.39	10-4 / 0.47	10-11 / 0.55	11-5 / 0.63	11-11 / 0.72	12-5 / 0.81	12-10 / 0.91	13-4 / 1.01	13-9 / 1.11	14-2 / 1.21	14-7 / 1.32	15-0 / 1.43
2x10	12.0	13-11 / 0.27	15-2 / 0.36	16-5 / 0.45	17-7 / 0.55	18-7 / 0.66	19-8 / 0.77	20-7 / 0.89	21-6 / 1.02	22-5 / 1.15	23-3 / 1.28	24-1 / 1.42	24-10 / 1.57	25-7 / 1.72	26-4 / 1.87	27-1 / 2.03
	16.0	12-0 / 0.26	13-2 / 0.34	14-3 / 0.43	15-2 / 0.53	16-2 / 0.63	17-0 / 0.74	17-10 / 0.85	18-7 / 0.97	19-5 / 1.09	20-1 / 1.22	20-10 / 1.35	21-6 / 1.49	22-2 / 1.63	22-10 / 1.78	23-5 / 1.93
	24.0	9-10 / 0.19	10-9 / 0.25	11-7 / 0.32	12-5 / 0.39	13-2 / 0.47	13-11 / 0.55	14-7 / 0.63	15-2 / 0.72	15-10 / 0.81	16-5 / 0.91	17-0 / 1.01	17-7 / 1.11	18-1 / 1.21	18-7 / 1.32	19-2 / 1.43

NOTES:
(1) The required modulus of elasticity (*E*) in 1,000,000 pounds per square inch is shown below each span.
(2) Use single or repetitive member bending stress values (F_b) and modulus of elasticity values (*E*) from Tables Nos. 25-A-1 and 25-A-2 of the Uniform Building Code. For duration of load stress increases, see Section 2504 (c) 4 of the Uniform Building Code.
(3) For more comprehensive tables covering a broader range of bending stress values (F_b) and modulus of elasticity values (*E*), other spacing of members and other conditions of loading, see U.B.C. Standard No. 25-21.
(4) The spans in these tables are intended for use in covered structures or where moisture content in use does not exceed 19 percent.

Figure 46–6 A rafter span table is used in a method similar to that for a floor joist table. Notice that the values for this table are given in terms of F_b rather than E. *Reproduced from the Dwelling Construction Under the Uniform Building Code, 1985 edition. Courtesy The International Conference of Building Officials.*

TABLE NO. 25-U-R-8—ALLOWABLE SPANS FOR LOW-SLOPE, RAFTERS SLOPE 3 IN 12 OR LESS
30 LBS. PER SQ. FT. LIVE LOAD (No Ceiling Load)

DESIGN CRITERIA: Strength—10 lbs. per sq. ft. dead load plus 30 lbs. per sq. ft. live load determines required fiber stress. Deflection—For 30 lbs. per sq. ft. live load. Limited to span in inches divided by 240. RAFTERS: Spans are measured along the horizontal projection and loads are considered as applied on the horizontal projection.

RAFTER SIZE (IN)	SPACING (IN)	Allowable Extreme Fiber Stress in Bending F_b (psi) 500	600	700	800	900	1000	1100	1200	1300	1400	1500	1600	1700	1800	1900
2x6	12.0	7-11 / 0.32	8-8 / 0.43	9-5 / 0.54	10-0 / 0.66	10-8 / 0.78	11-3 / 0.92	11-9 / 1.06	12-4 / 1.21	12-10 / 1.36	13-3 / 1.52	13-9 / 1.69	14-2 / 1.86	14-8 / 2.04	15-1 / 2.22	15-6 / 2.41
	16.0	6-11 / 0.28	7-6 / 0.37	8-2 / 0.47	8-8 / 0.57	9-3 / 0.68	9-9 / 0.80	10-2 / 0.92	10-8 / 1.05	11-1 / 1.18	11-6 / 1.32	11-11 / 1.46	12-4 / 1.61	12-8 / 1.76	13-1 / 1.92	13-5 / 2.08
	24.0	5-7 / 0.23	6-2 / 0.30	6-8 / 0.38	7-1 / 0.46	7-6 / 0.55	7-11 / 0.65	8-4 / 0.75	8-8 / 0.85	9-1 / 0.96	9-5 / 1.08	9-9 / 1.19	10-0 / 1.31	10-4 / 1.44	10-8 / 1.57	10-11 / 1.70
2x8	12.0	10-6 / 0.32	11-6 / 0.43	12-5 / 0.54	13-3 / 0.66	14-0 / 0.78	14-10 / 0.92	15-6 / 1.06	16-3 / 1.21	16-10 / 1.36	17-6 / 1.52	18-2 / 1.69	18-9 / 1.86	19-4 / 2.04	19-10 / 2.22	20-5 / 2.41
	16.0	9-1 / 0.28	9-11 / 0.37	10-9 / 0.47	11-6 / 0.57	12-2 / 0.68	12-10 / 0.80	13-5 / 0.92	14-0 / 1.05	14-7 / 1.18	15-2 / 1.32	15-8 / 1.46	16-3 / 1.61	16-9 / 1.76	17-2 / 1.92	17-8 / 2.08
	24.0	7-5 / 0.23	8-1 / 0.30	8-9 / 0.38	9-4 / 0.46	9-11 / 0.55	10-6 / 0.65	11-0 / 0.75	11-6 / 0.85	11-11 / 0.96	12-5 / 1.08	12-10 / 1.19	13-3 / 1.31	13-8 / 1.44	14-0 / 1.57	14-5 / 1.70
2x10	12.0	13-4 / 0.32	14-8 / 0.43	15-10 / 0.54	16-11 / 0.66	17-11 / 0.78	18-11 / 0.92	19-10 / 1.06	20-8 / 1.21	21-6 / 1.36	22-4 / 1.52	23-2 / 1.69	23-11 / 1.86	24-7 / 2.04	25-4 / 2.22	26-0 / 2.41
	16.0	11-7 / 0.28	12-8 / 0.37	13-8 / 0.47	14-8 / 0.57	15-6 / 0.68	16-4 / 0.80	17-2 / 0.92	17-11 / 1.05	18-8 / 1.18	19-4 / 1.32	20-0 / 1.46	20-8 / 1.61	21-4 / 1.76	21-11 / 1.92	22-6 / 2.08
	24.0	9-5 / 0.23	10-4 / 0.30	11-2 / 0.38	11-11 / 0.46	12-8 / 0.55	13-4 / 0.65	14-0 / 0.75	14-8 / 0.85	15-3 / 0.96	15-10 / 1.08	16-4 / 1.19	16-11 / 1.31	17-5 / 1.44	17-11 / 1.57	18-5 / 1.70
2x12	12.0	16-3 / 0.32	17-9 / 0.43	19-3 / 0.54	20-6 / 0.66	21-9 / 0.78	23-0 / 0.92	24-1 / 1.06	25-2 / 1.21	26-2 / 1.36	27-2 / 1.52	28-2 / 1.69	29-1 / 1.86	29-11 / 2.04	30-10 / 2.22	31-8 / 2.41
	16.0	14-1 / 0.28	15-5 / 0.37	16-8 / 0.47	17-9 / 0.57	18-10 / 0.68	19-11 / 0.80	20-10 / 0.92	21-9 / 1.05	22-8 / 1.18	23-6 / 1.32	24-4 / 1.46	25-2 / 1.61	25-11 / 1.76	26-8 / 1.92	27-5 / 2.08
	24.0	11-6 / 0.23	12-7 / 0.30	13-7 / 0.38	14-6 / 0.46	15-5 / 0.55	16-3 / 0.65	17-0 / 0.75	17-9 / 0.85	18-6 / 0.96	19-3 / 1.08	19-11 / 1.19	20-6 / 1.31	21-2 / 1.44	21-9 / 1.57	22-5 / 1.70

NOTES: (1) The required modulus of elasticity (*E*) in 1,000,000 pounds per square inch is shown below each span.
(2) Use single or repetitive member bending stress values (F_b) and modulus of elasticity values (*E*) from Tables Nos. 25-A-1 and 25-A-2. For duration of load stress increases, see Section 2504 (c) 4.
(3) For more comprehensive tables covering a broader range of bending stress values (F_b) and modulus of elasticity values (*E*), other spacing of members and other conditions of loading, see U.B.C. Standard No. 25-21.
(4) The spans in these tables are intended for use in covered structures or where moisture content in use does not exceed 19 percent.

Figure 46–7 Rafter spans for low-sloped roofs that are typically used with built-up roofing. *Reproduced from the Dwelling Construction Under the Uniform Building Code, 1982 edition. Courtesy The International Conference of Building Officials.*

TABLE NO. 25-U-R-2—ALLOWABLE SPANS FOR LOW- OR HIGH-SLOPE RAFTERS
30 LBS. PER SQ. FT. LIVE LOAD (Supporting Drywall Ceiling)
DESIGN CRITERIA: Strength—15 lbs. per sq. ft. dead load plus 30 lbs. per sq. ft. live load determines required fiber stress.
Deflection—For 30 lbs. per sq. ft. live load. Limited to span in inches divided by 240. **RAFTERS:** Spans are measured along the horizontal projection and loads are considered as applied on the horizontal projection.

RAFTER SIZE (IN)	SPACING (IN)	Allowable Extreme Fiber Stress in Bending F_b (psi).														
		500	600	700	800	900	1000	1100	1200	1300	1400	1500	1600	1700	1800	1900
2x6	12.0	7-6 / 0.27	8-2 / 0.36	8-10 / 0.45	9-6 / 0.55	10-0 / 0.66	10-7 / 0.77	11-1 / 0.89	11-7 / 1.01	12-1 / 1.14	12-6 / 1.28	13-0 / 1.41	13-5 / 1.56	13-10 / 1.71	14-2 / 1.86	14-7 / 2.02
	16.0	6-6 / 0.24	7-1 / 0.31	7-8 / 0.39	8-2 / 0.48	8-8 / 0.57	9-2 / 0.67	9-7 / 0.77	10-0 / 0.88	10-5 / 0.99	10-10 / 1.10	11-3 / 1.22	11-7 / 1.35	11-11 / 1.48	12-4 / 1.61	12-8 / 1.75
	24.0	5-4 / 0.19	5-10 / 0.25	6-3 / 0.32	6-8 / 0.39	7-1 / 0.46	7-6 / 0.54	7-10 / 0.63	8-2 / 0.72	8-6 / 0.81	8-10 / 0.90	9-2 / 1.00	9-6 / 1.10	9-9 / 1.21	10-0 / 1.31	10-4 / 1.43
2x8	12.0	9-10 / 0.27	10-10 / 0.36	11-8 / 0.45	12-6 / 0.55	13-3 / 0.66	13-11 / 0.77	14-8 / 0.89	15-3 / 1.01	15-11 / 1.14	16-6 / 1.28	17-1 / 1.41	17-8 / 1.56	18-2 / 1.71	18-9 / 1.86	19-3 / 2.02
	16.0	8-7 / 0.24	9-4 / 0.31	10-1 / 0.39	10-10 / 0.48	11-6 / 0.57	12-1 / 0.67	12-8 / 0.77	13-3 / 0.88	13-9 / 0.99	14-4 / 1.10	14-10 / 1.22	15-3 / 1.35	15-9 / 1.48	16-3 / 1.61	16-8 / 1.75
	24.0	7-0 / 0.19	7-8 / 0.25	8-3 / 0.32	8-10 / 0.39	9-4 / 0.46	9-10 / 0.54	10-4 / 0.63	10-10 / 0.72	11-3 / 0.81	11-8 / 0.90	12-1 / 1.00	12-6 / 1.10	12-10 / 1.21	13-3 / 1.31	13-7 / 1.43
2x10	12.0	12-7 / 0.27	13-9 / 0.36	14-11 / 0.45	15-11 / 0.55	16-11 / 0.66	17-10 / 0.77	18-8 / 0.89	19-6 / 1.01	20-4 / 1.14	21-1 / 1.28	21-10 / 1.41	22-6 / 1.56	23-3 / 1.71	23-11 / 1.86	24-6 / 2.02
	16.0	10-11 / 0.24	11-11 / 0.31	12-11 / 0.39	13-9 / 0.48	14-8 / 0.57	15-5 / 0.67	16-2 / 0.77	16-11 / 0.88	17-7 / 0.99	18-3 / 1.10	18-11 / 1.22	19-6 / 1.35	20-1 / 1.48	20-8 / 1.61	21-3 / 1.75
	24.0	8-11 / 0.19	9-9 / 0.25	10-6 / 0.32	11-3 / 0.39	11-11 / 0.46	12-7 / 0.54	13-2 / 0.63	13-9 / 0.72	14-4 / 0.81	14-11 / 0.90	15-5 / 1.00	15-11 / 1.10	16-5 / 1.21	16-11 / 1.31	17-4 / 1.43
2x12	12.0	15-4 / 0.27	16-9 / 0.36	18-1 / 0.45	19-4 / 0.55	20-6 / 0.66	21-8 / 0.77	22-8 / 0.89	23-9 / 1.01	24-8 / 1.14	25-7 / 1.28	26-6 / 1.41	27-5 / 1.56	28-3 / 1.71	29-1 / 1.86	29-10 / 2.02
	16.0	13-3 / 0.24	14-6 / 0.31	15-8 / 0.39	16-9 / 0.48	17-9 / 0.57	18-9 / 0.67	19-8 / 0.77	20-6 / 0.88	21-5 / 0.99	22-2 / 1.10	23-0 / 1.22	23-9 / 1.35	24-5 / 1.48	25-2 / 1.61	25-10 / 1.75
	24.0	10-10 / 0.19	11-10 / 0.25	12-10 / 0.32	13-8 / 0.39	14-6 / 0.46	15-4 / 0.54	16-1 / 0.63	16-9 / 0.72	17-5 / 0.81	18-1 / 0.90	18-9 / 1.00	19-4 / 1.10	20-0 / 1.21	20-6 / 1.31	21-1 / 1.43

NOTES: (1) The required modulus of elasticity (*E*) in 1,000,000 pounds per square inch is shown below each span.

(2) Use single or repetitive member bending stress values (*F$_b$*) and modulus of elasticity values (*E*) from Tables Nos. 25-A-1 and 25-A-2. For duration of load stress increases, see Section 2504 (c) 4.

(3) For more comprehensive tables covering a broader range of bending stress values (*F$_b$*) and modulus of elasticity values (*E*), other spacing of members and other conditions of loading, see U.B.C. Standard No. 25-21.

(4) The spans in these tables are intended for use in covered structures or where moisture content in use does not exceed 19 percent.

Figure 46–8 Rafter spans for rafter/ceiling joist of any pitch to allow for a vaulted ceiling. *Reproduced from the* Dwelling Construction Under the Uniform Building Code, *1982 edition. Courtesy The International Conference of Building Officials.*

SIZING JOISTS AND RAFTERS USING SPAN TABLES TEST

DIRECTIONS

Answer the questions with short complete statements or drawings as needed on an 8½ × 11 drawing sheet as follows:

1. Use ⅛ in. guidelines for all lettering.
2. Letter your name, Sizing Joists and Rafters Using Span Tables Test, and the date at the top of the sheet.
3. Letter the question number and provide the answer. You do not need to write out the question.
4. Use the tables in this chapter to answer the questions as appropriate.
5. Do all lettering with vertical uppercase architectural letters. Answers may be prepared on a word processor if appropriate with course guidelines.
6. Your grade will be based on correct answers.

QUESTIONS

1. List four common types of lumber used for framing throughout the country.
2. How is fiber bending stress represented in engineering formulas?
3. What does the term modulus of elasticity mean?
4. How is modulus of elasticity represented in engineering formulas?
5. Give the safe working stresses in fiber bending and modulus of elasticity for the following types of lumber. Assume all are grade #2 floor joist.
   a. Douglas Fir—Larch
   b. Hem—Fir.
   c. Southern pine
   d. SPF
6. Using SPF #2, determine the size of floor joist that will be required to span 15'-0" if spaced at 16 in. O.C.
7. You are considering the use of 2 × 8 Hem—Fir #2 floor joists to span 14'-0". Will they work?
8. Using 2 × 6 SP #2 at 16 in. O.C. for ceiling joists, determine their maximum safe span.
9. A friend of yours wants to add a family room to a home in San Diego. It will have a vaulted ceiling covered with cedar shakes to match the existing roof. Your friend has written to you for some advice. If DFL #2 lumber is to be used, what size members will be needed to span 16 ft if the members are at 16 in. O.C.? What if they are at 24 in. O.C.?

Chapter 47
Determining Simple Beams with Uniform Loads

AS YOU advance in your architectural skills, the need to determine the size of structural members will occur frequently. There are several skills that you will need to develop in order to determine easily the size of structural members. These skills include the ability to distinguish loading patterns on the member, recognize standard engineering symbols used in beam formulas, recognize common causes of beam failure, and select beams to resist these tendencies.

LOADING AND SUPPORT PATTERNS OF BEAMS

There are two common ways to load and support a beam. Loads can be uniformly distributed over the entire span of the beam or can be concentrated in one small area of a beam. In Chapter 45, uniformly distributed loads were discussed. Those were loads which came from a floor, roof, or wall and were evenly dispersed over the supporting member. A concentrated load is one that comes about as a result of a large load acting on only one area of a beam. Examples are a support post from an upper floor resting on a beam on a lower floor, the weight of a car being transferred through a wheel onto a floor system, or an air conditioning unit resting on the roof members.

A simple introduction about the support of beams is needed before proceeding. Usually a beam is supported at each end. Common alternatives are to support a beam at the center of the span in addition to the ends or to provide support at one end and near the other end. The type of beam that extends past the support is called a cantilevered beam. Examples of each type of load and support system can be seen in Figure 47–1. Only simple beams with uniform loads will be considered in this chapter.

DESIGN LOADS AND STRESSES

Design loads have been discussed in past chapters. See Figure 45–6 for a simplified list of design live (LL) and dead (DL) loads.

The allowable unit stresses for lumber have also been discussed in past chapters. Figure 47–2 shows a simplified stress table for common types of con-

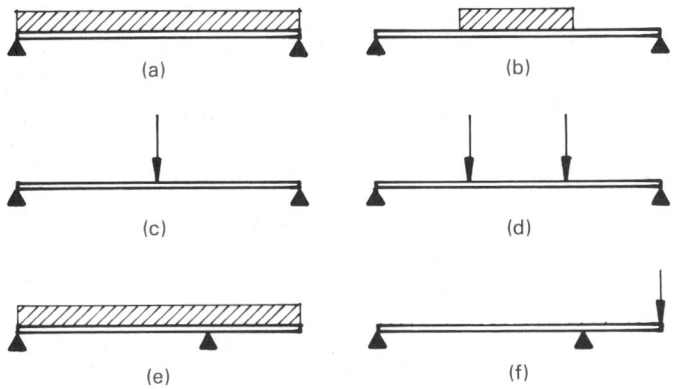

Figure 47–1 Common loading patterns on a beam include the following: (a) simple beam with a uniformly distributed load; (b) simple beam with a partially distributed load at the center; (c) simple beam with a concentrated load at the center; (d) simple beam with two equal concentrated loads placed symmetrically; (e) cantilevered beam with a uniform load; (f) cantilevered beam with a concentrated load at the free end.

struction lumber. Stresses for beams are shown in a manner similar to stresses for joists. The beam stress table includes the now-familiar column of values for fiber bending stress (F_b) and modulus of elasticity (E) plus a column for horizontal shear (F_v) as well as several other values. The other values will not be discussed at this time, but you will need to understand horizontal shear.

Horizontal shear is the tendency of a beam to split parallel to the grain of the wood as the beam transfers its loads to its supports. Figure 47–3 shows examples of beam failures that would result from the different stresses.

NOTATIONS FOR FORMULAS

Standard symbols have been adopted by engineering and architectural communities to simplify the design of beams. Figure 47–4 gives a partial list of these notations. As a beginning designer, it is not important that you understand why the formulas work, but it is important that you know the notations to be used in the formulas.

METHODS OF BEAM DESIGN

Four methods of beam design will be introduced. These include a span computer, a computer program, wood design books, and, of course, the old-fashioned way of pencil, paper, and a few formulas.

A span computer is very similar to a slide rule. Figure 47–5 shows an illustration of a span computer made by the Western Wood Products Association. Beam sizes are determined by lining up values of the lumber to be used with a distance to be spanned.

DESIGN STRESS VALUES FOR COMMON WOOD BEAMS			
Member	Fiber bending stress F_b	Horizontal shear F_v	Modulus of elasticity E
Douglas fir	1300	85	1.6
Eastern hemlock	1150	80	1.2
Western hemlock	1150	85	1.4
Hemlock-fir	1050	70	1.3
Southern pine	1200	85	1.5
Spruce-pine-fir	900	65	1.3

Figure 47–2 Simplified listing of values of common types of lumber used for beams. *From Table 25 A–1 of the* Uniform Building Code, *1985 edition. Courtesy The International Conference of Building Officials.*

BEAM IN HORIZONTAL SHEAR

BEAM IN EQUILIBRIUM

BEAM IN BENDING STRESS

Figure 47–3 Types of beam failure.

BEAM FORMULA NOTATIONS		
b	=	breadth of beam in inches
d	=	depth of beam in inches
D	=	deflection due to load
E	=	modulus of elasticity
F_b	=	allowable unit stress in extreme fiber bending
F_v	=	unit stress in horizontal shear
I	=	moment of inertia of the section
l	=	span of beam in inches
L	=	span of beam in feet
M	=	bending or resisting moment
P	=	total concentrated load in pounds
S	=	section modulus
V	=	end reaction of beam
W	=	total uniformly distributed load in pounds
w	=	load per linear foot of beam in pounds

Figure 47–4 Common notations used in beam formulas.

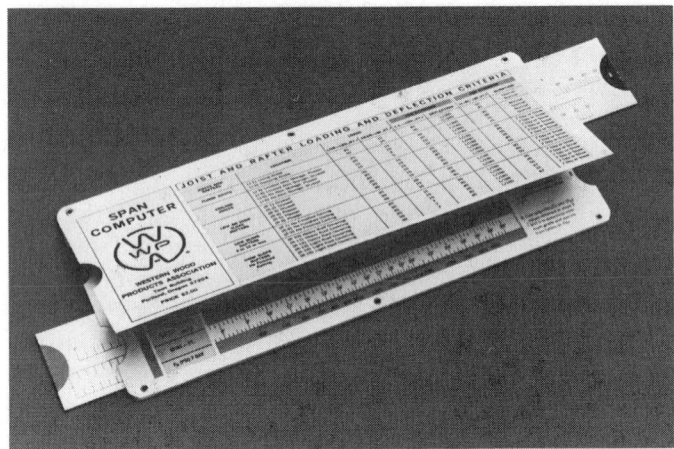

Figure 47–5 A span computer used to determine joist and beam sizes. *Courtesy Western Wood Products Association.*

Computer programs are now available for many personal and business computers that will size beams. These programs will typically ask for loading information and then proceed to determine the span size within seconds. Using a computer program to solve beam spans is extremely easy, but you do have to be able to answer questions that require an understanding of the basics of beam design and loading.

Another practical method of sizing beams is through the use of books published by various wood associations. Two of the most common span books used in architectural offices are *Wood Structural Design Data* from the National Forest Products Association and the *Western Woods Use Book* from the Western Wood Products Association. These books contain design information of wood members, standard formulas, and design tables that provide beam loads for a specific span. Figure 47–6 shows a partial eight-foot span table. By following the instructions provided with the table, information on size, span, and loading patterns can be determined.

The final method of beam design is to use standard formulas to determine how the beam will be stressed.

Figure 47–7 shows the formulas and the loading, shear, and moment diagrams for a simple beam. These are diagrams that can be drawn by the designer to determine where the maximum stress will occur. With a simple beam and a uniformly distributed load, the diagrams typically are not drawn because the results remain constant.

SIZING WOOD BEAMS

Wood beams can easily be determined by following these steps:

1. Determine the area to be supported by the beam.
2. Determine the weight supported by one linear foot of beam.
3. Determine the reactions.
4. Determine the pier sizes.
5. Determine the bending moment.
6. Determine the horizontal shear.
7. Determine the deflection.

Determining the Area to be Supported

To determine the size of a beam, the weight the beam is to support must be known. To find the weight, find the area the beam is to support and multiply by the total loads. Figure 47–8 shows a sample floor plan with a beam of undetermined size. The beam is supporting an area 10'–0" long (the span) multiplied by 10'–0" wide (half of each floor joist supported). With an LL of 40 lb and a DL of 10 lb, this beam is holding a total of 5000 lb which represents the total weight supported by the beam. In beam formulas, the total weight is represented by the letter W. Refer to Figure 47–4.

Determining Linear Weight

In some formulas only the weight per linear foot of beam is desired. This is represented by the letter w. In Figure 47–9, it can be seen that w is the product of the area to be supported, multiplied by the weight per sq ft. It can also be found by dividing the total weight (W) by the length of the beam. In our example, if the span (represented by L) is 10 ft, w = 5000/10 or 500 lb.

Determining Reactions

Even before the size of the beam is known, the supports for the beam can be determined. These supports for the beam are represented by the letter, R, for reactions. The letter V is also sometimes used in place of the letter R. On a simple beam, half of the weight it is supporting will be dispersed to each

WOOD BEAMS—SAFE LOAD TABLES

Symbols used in the tables are as follows:

F_b = Allowable unit stress in extreme fiber in bending, psi.

W = Total uniformly distributed load, pounds

w = Load per linear foot of beam, pounds

F_v = Horizontal shear stress, psi, induced by load W

E = Modulus of elasticity, 1000 psi, induced by load W for $l/360$ limit

Beam sizes are expressed as nominal sizes, inches, but calculations are based on net dimensions of S4S sizes.

SIZE OF BEAM		F_b									
		900	1000	1100	1200	1300	1400	1500	1600	1800	2000
8'- 0" SPAN CONT'D											
2 x 14	W	3291	3657	4023	4389	4754	5120	5486	5852	6583	7315
	w	411	457	502	548	594	640	685	731	822	914
	F_v	124	138	151	165	179	193	207	220	248	276
	E	489	543	597	652	706	760	815	869	978	1086
6 x 8	W	3867	4296	4726	5156	5585	6015	6445	6875	7734	8593
	w	483	537	590	644	698	751	805	859	966	1074
	F_v	70	78	85	93	101	109	117	125	140	156
	E	864	960	1055	1152	1247	1343	1439	1535	1727	1919
4 x 10	W	3743	4159	4575	4991	5407	5823	6238	6654	7486	8318
	w	467	519	571	623	675	727	779	831	935	1039
	F_v	86	96	105	115	125	134	144	154	173	192
	E	700	778	856	934	1011	1089	1167	1245	1401	1556
3 x 12	W	3955	4394	4833	5273	5712	6152	6591	7031	7910	8789
	w	494	549	604	659	714	769	823	878	988	1098
	F_v	105	117	128	140	152	164	175	187	210	234
	E	576	640	704	768	832	896	959	1024	1151	1279
8 x 8	W	5273	5859	6445	7031	7617	8203	8789	9375	10546	11718
	w	659	732	805	878	952	1025	1098	1171	1318	1464
	F_v	70	78	85	93	101	109	117	125	140	156
	E	864	960	1055	1151	1247	1343	1439	1535	1727	1919
3 x 14	W	5486	6095	6705	7315	7924	8534	9143	9753	10972	12191
	w	685	761	838	914	990	1066	1142	1219	1371	1523
	F_v	124	138	151	165	179	193	207	220	248	276
	E	489	543	597	652	706	760	815	869	978	1086
4 x 12	W	5537	6152	6767	7382	7998	8613	9228	9843	11074	12304
	w	692	769	845	922	999	1076	1153	1230	1384	1538
	F_v	105	117	128	140	152	164	175	187	210	234
	E	576	640	703	768	832	896	960	1023	1151	1279
6 x 10	W	6204	6894	7583	8272	8962	9651	10341	11030	12409	13788
	w	775	861	947	1034	1120	1206	1292	1378	1551	1723
	F_v	89	98	108	118	128	138	148	158	178	197
	E	682	757	833	909	985	1061	1136	1212	1364	1515
3 x 16	W	7267	8075	8882	9690	10497	11305	12112	12920	14535	16150
	w	908	1009	1110	1211	1312	1413	1514	1615	1816	2018
	F_v	142	158	174	190	206	222	238	254	285	317
	E	424	472	519	566	613	660	708	755	849	944
4 x 14	W	7973	8859	9745	10631	11517	12403	13289	14175	15946	17718
	w	996	1107	1218	1328	1439	1550	1661	1771	1993	2214
	F_v	126	140	154	168	182	196	210	225	253	281
	E	480	533	586	640	693	746	800	853	960	1066

Figure 47–6 A partial listing of a typical span table. Once W, w, F_b, E, and F_v are known, spans can be determined for a simple beam. See Appendix A for complete listing. *From Wood Structural Design Data. Courtesy National Forest Products Association.*

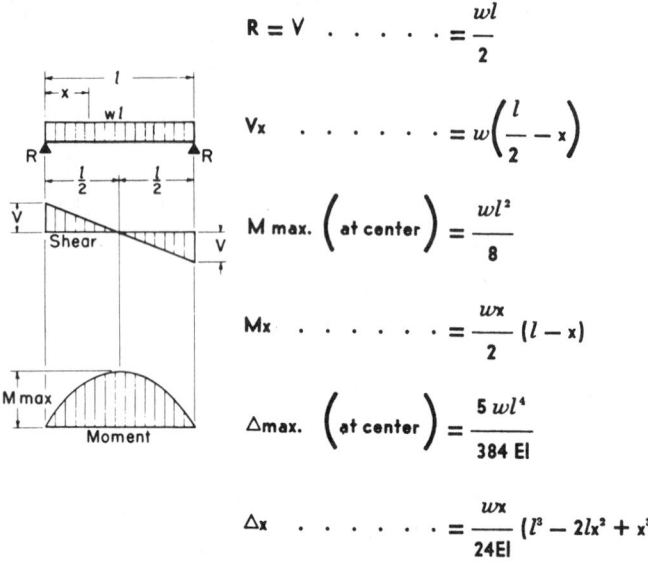

$$R = V \ldots \ldots = \frac{wl}{2}$$

$$V_x \ldots \ldots = w\left(\frac{l}{2} - x\right)$$

$$M \text{ max.} \left(\text{at center}\right) = \frac{wl^2}{8}$$

$$M_x \ldots \ldots = \frac{wx}{2}(l - x)$$

$$\Delta \text{max.} \left(\text{at center}\right) = \frac{5\,wl^4}{384\,EI}$$

$$\Delta_x \ldots \ldots = \frac{wx}{24EI}(l^3 - 2lx^2 + x^3)$$

Figure 47–7 Loading, shear, and moment diagrams for a simple beam with uniform loads showing where stress will affect a beam and the formulas for computing these stresses. *From Wood Structural Design Data. Courtesy National Forest Products Association.*

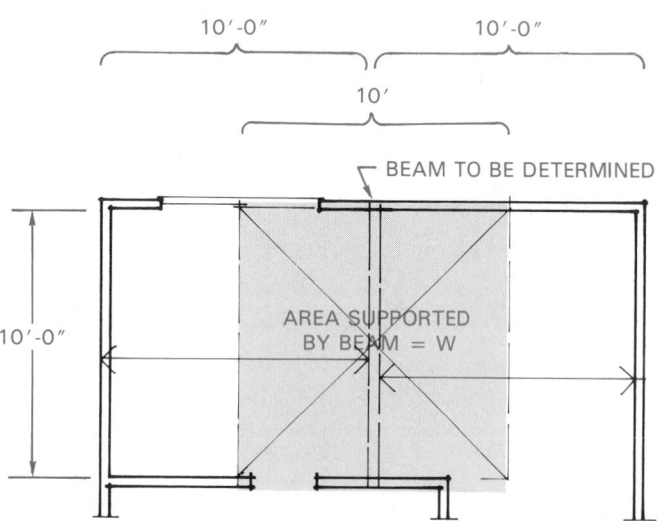

Figure 47–8 A floor plan with a beam to be determined. This beam is supporting an area of 100 sq ft, with an assumed weight of 50 lb per sq ft, W = 5000 lb.

end. In our example, W = 5000 lb and so R = 2500 lb. See Figure 47–10. At this point W, w, and R have been determined (W = 5000 lb, w = 500 lb, and R = 2500 lb.)

Determining Pier Sizes

We found that each support post is holding 2500 lb. Of course, something must support the bottom of the post or it will settle. Usually a concrete pier is used to support the loads at the foundation level. To determine the size of the pier, the working stress of the concrete and the bearing value of the soil must be taken into account.

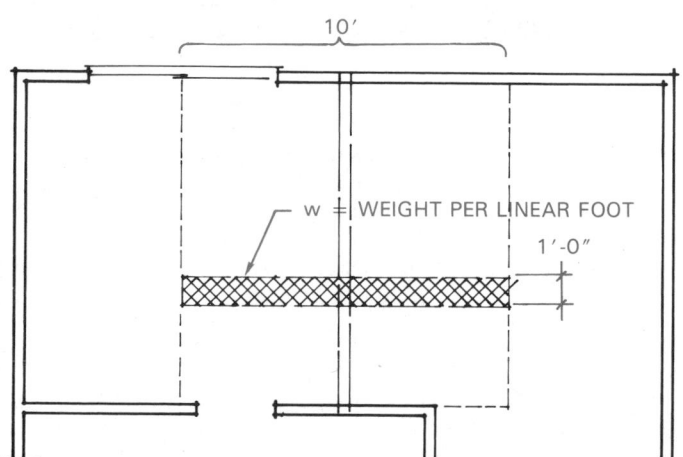

Figure 47–9 Determining linear weights. An area of 10 sq ft, with an assumed weight of 50 lb per sq ft, w = 500 lb.

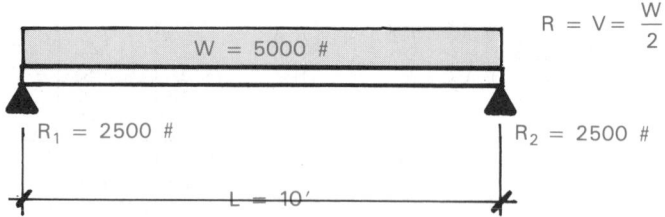

Figure 47–10 Determining beam reactions is a matter of sizing the supports for the beam.

Usually concrete with a working stress of between 2000 to 2500 lb is used in residential construction. The working stress of concrete specifies how much weight in pounds can be supported by each square inch (psi) of concrete surface. If each square inch of concrete can support 2500 lb, only 1 sq in. of concrete would be required to support a load of 2500 pounds. Don't stop now though, because something must support the concrete.

The safe bearing values of soil vary greatly. See Figure 47–11 for safe soil-loading values. Although there are some areas where only 1000 pounds per square foot (psf), are used, most building departments use 2000 psf for the assumed safe working value of soil.

Don't skim over these numbers. The concrete is listed in pounds per square inch. Soil is listed in pounds per square foot. A pier supporting 2500 lb must be divided by 2000 lb (the soil-bearing value) to find the area of the pier needed. This will result in an area of 1.25 sq ft of concrete needed to support the load. See Figure 47–12 to determine the size of pier needed to obtain the proper soil support area.

Determining the Bending Moment

A moment is the tendency of a force to cause rotation about a certain point. In figuring a simple beam, W is the force and R is the point around which the force rotates. To determine the bending moment

TABLE NO. 29-B—ALLOWABLE FOUNDATION AND LATERAL PRESSURE

CLASS OF MATERIALS[2]	ALLOWABLE FOUNDATION PRESSURE LBS. SQ. FT.[3]	LATERAL BEARING LBS./SQ. FT./ FT. OF DEPTH BELOW NATURAL GRADE[4]	LATERAL SLIDING[1]	
			COEF- FICIENT[5]	RESISTANCE LBS./SQ. FT.[6]
1. Massive Crystalline Bedrock	4000	1200	.79	
2. Sedimentary and Foliated Rock	2000	400	.35	
3. Sandy Gravel and/or Gravel (GW and GP)	2000	200	.35	
4. Sand, Silty Sand, Clayey Sand, Silty Gravel and Clayey Gravel (SW, SP, SM, SC, GM and GC)	1500	150	.25	
5. Clay, Sandy Clay, Silty Clay and Clayey Silt (CL, ML, MH and CH)	1000[7]	100		130

[1]Lateral bearing and lateral sliding resistance may be combined.
[2]For soil classifications OL, OH and PT (i.e., organic clays and peat), a foundation investigation shall be required.
[3]All values of allowable foundation pressure are for footings having a minimum width of 12

Figure 47-11 Safe soil-bearing values. *Reproduced from the Uniform Building Code, 1985 edition. Courtesy The International Conference of Building Officials.*

PIER AREAS AND SIZES	
ROUND PIERS	**SQUARE PIERS**
15" DIA. = 1.23 SQ FT	15" SQ = 1.56 SQ FT
18" DIA. = 1.77 SQ FT	18" SQ = 2.25 SQ FT
21" DIA. = 2.40 SQ FT	21" SQ = 3.06 SQ FT
24" DIA. = 3.14 SQ FT	24" SQ = 4.00 SQ FT
27" DIA. = 3.97 SQ FT	27" SQ = 5.06 SQ FT
30" DIA. = 4.90 SQ FT	30" SQ = 6.25 SQ FT
36" DIA. = 7.07 SQ FT	36" SQ = 9.00 SQ FT
42" DIA. = 9.60 SQ FT	42" SQ = 12.25 SQ FT

Figure 47-12 Common pier areas and sizes. By dividing the load to be supported by the soil-bearing pressure, the area of the concrete pier can be determined. Areas are shown for common pier sizes.

is to calculate the size of the beam needed to resist the tendency for W to rotate around R.

To determine the size of the beam required to resist the force (W), use the following formula:

$$M = \frac{(w)(l)}{8}$$

Once the moment is known, it can be divided by the F_b of the wood to determine the size of beam required to resist the load. This whole process can be simplified by using the formula:

$$S = \frac{(3)(w)(L^2)}{(2)(F_b)}$$

Use the values for Douglas fir from Figure 47-2, and apply this formula to the beam span from Figure 47-8.

$$S = \frac{(3)(500)(100)}{(2)(1300)} = \frac{150,000}{2600} = 57.69$$

What you have just found is the minimum section modulus required to support a load of 5000 pounds. Look at the table that is Figure 47-13 to determine the size of lumber needed for the beam. A beam must be selected that has an S value larger than the S value found. By examining the S column of the table, you will find that a 4 × 12 has an S of 73.8 and 6 × 10 has an S value of 82.7. Each of these sizes of beams is suitable to resist the forces of bending moment.

Determining Horizontal Shear Values

Failure by horizontal shear is the tendency of the beam's fibers to slide past each other in a direction

PROPERTIES OF STRUCTURAL LUMBER						
NOMINAL SIZE	(b)(d)	(2)(b)(d)	S	A	I	(384)(E)(I) *
2 × 6	1.5 × 5.5	16.5	7.6	8.25	20.8	12,780
2 × 8	1.5 × 7.25	21.75	13.1	10.875	47.6	29,245
2 × 10	1.5 × 9.25	27.75	21.4	13.875	98.9	60,764
2 × 12	1.5 × 11.25	33.75	31.6	16.875	177.9	109,302
2 × 14	1.5 × 13.25	39.75	43.9	19.875	290.8	178,668
4 × 6	3.5 × 5.5	38.5	17.6	19.25	48.5	29,798
4 × 8	3.5 × 7.25	50.75	30.7	25.375	111.0	68,198
4 × 10	3.5 × 9.25	64.75	49.9	32.375	230.8	141,804
4 × 12	3.5 × 11.25	78.75	73.8	39.375	415.3	255,160
4 × 14	3.5 × 13.5	94.5	106.3	47.250	717.6	440,893
6 × 8	5.5 × 7.5	82.5	51.6	41.25	193.4	118,825
6 × 10	5.5 × 9.5	104.5	82.7	52.25	393.0	241,459
6 × 12	5.5 × 11.5	126.5	121.2	63.25	697.1	428,298
6 × 14	5.5 × 13.5	148.5	167.1	74.25	1127.7	692,859

* 384 × E × I values are listed in units per million, with E value assumed to be 1.6 for DFL.

Figure 47-13 Structural properties of wood beams. The (2)(b)(d) and the (384)(E)(I) columns are parts of formulas that are always needed. These two columns are set up for Douglas fir. If a different type of wood is to be used, you must use different values for these columns.

parallel to the grain of the wood. Wood used to span short distances and support heavy loads tends to fail by horizontal shear. Frequently, a beam large enough to support bending stresses may not be large enough to resist the forces of horizontal shear.

To compute the size of a beam required to resist the forces of horizontal shear, use the following formula:

$$F_v = \frac{(3)(V)}{(2)(b)(d)}$$

For a simple beam, $V = R$. To determine b and d, use the actual size of the beam determined for bending. For this example, use the 4 × 12 value. The actual size of a 4 × 12 is 3.5 × 11.25 in. Figure 47–13 shows the product of (2bd) to be 78.75. These values can be inserted into the formula to find the shear on the beam.

$$F_v = \frac{(3)(V)}{(2)(b)(d)} = \frac{3 \times 2500}{78.75} = \frac{7500}{78.75} = 95.238$$

This answer is meaningless unless you know the safe shear value in horizontal shear for the type of wood in question. The safe limit for lumber in horizontal shear can be determined from the table in Figure 47–2. The value for DFL is 85. If the product of the formula is larger than the safe working stress, the beam fails. In the example above, 95.238 exceeds the limit for Douglas fir. At this point, the designer must select a larger beam and the formula must be reworked. The figures on the top of the formula will remain the same because these values are the result of the load, which has not changed. Insert the values for a 4 × 14 beam. Now the formula should read:

$$F_v = \frac{7500}{94.5} = 79.37$$

Since this new value is less than 85, the beam works.

A 4 × 12 was found to have adequate stiffness to resist the load but not enough size to prevent horizontal shear from occurring. Either a 4 × 14 or a 6 × 10 beam will be needed. Even though the 6 × 10 has not been proven by the formula, you should be able to tell that it will work. The value in the (2bd) column of Figure 47–13 for a 6 × 10 beam is 104.5, which is larger than the value for the 4 × 14 beam. When the 104.5 value is inserted into the formula, it will produce a smaller F_v value and so the 6 × 10 is a safer beam.

Another way to determine F_v is to multiply V times 1.5 and then divide by the F_v value for the lumber being used.

$$F_v = \frac{3V}{85} = \# > \text{ than (2bd) value for selected bm}$$

$$F_v = \frac{3 \times 2500}{85} = 88.23 = 4 \times 14 \text{ or } 6 \times 10$$

This will produce a minimum area required to resist the stress in horizontal shear. You have now determined W, w, R, V, S, and F_v. The last value to be determined is the stress for modulus of elasticity.

Determining Deflection

Modulus of elasticity is the deflection, or sag, in a beam. Deflection affects the area around the beam more than it affects the beam itself. In other words, the beam may not fail, but it might sag enough to crack the ceiling material supported by the beam. Deflection limits are determined by building codes and are expressed as a fraction of an inch in relation to the span of the beam in inches. Limits set by the Uniform Building Code are: for floors and ceilings, 1/360; roofs under 3/12 pitch, 1/240; and roofs over 3/12 pitch, 1/180.

To determine deflection limits, the maximum allowable limit must first be known. Use the formula:

$$D_{max.} = \frac{L \times 12}{360}$$

This formula requires the span in feet (L) to be multiplied by 12 (12 inches per foot) and then divided by 360 (the safe limit for floors and ceilings).

In the example used in this chapter, L equals 10 ft. The maximum safe limit would be:

$$D_{max.} = \frac{L \times 12}{360} = \frac{10 \times 12}{360} = D = \frac{120}{360} = 0.33 \text{ in.}$$

The maximum amount the beam is allowed to sag is 0.33 in. Now you need to determine how much the beam will actually sag under the load it is supporting.

The values for E and I need to be determined before the deflection can be determined. These values can be found in Figure 47–13. You will also need to know l^3 and W, but these values are not available in tables. W has been determined. For our example:

$$l = 10 \times 12 = 120 \text{ in.}$$
$$l^3 = (l)(l)(l) = (120)(120)(120) = 1{,}728{,}000$$

Because the E value was reduced from 1,600,000 to 1.6, we will change the l^3 value from 1,728,000 to 1.728. Each of these numbers is much easier to use when calculating.

To determine how much a beam will sag, use the following formula:

$$D = \frac{5(W)(l^3)}{(384)(E)(I)} \text{ or } D = 22.5 \frac{(W)(l^3)}{(E)(I)}$$

The values determined thus far are W = 5000, w = 500, R = V = 2500, L = 10, l = 120, l³ = 1.728 and I = 393 (see Figure 47–13, column I). Find also the value of (384)(E)(I) for a 6 × 10 beam from the table in Figure 47–13 (241,459). Now insert the values into the formula.

$$D = \frac{5(W)(L^3)}{384(E)(I)} = \frac{5 \times 5000 \times 1.728}{241,459} = \frac{43,200}{241,459} = 0.178 \text{ in.}$$

Because 0.178 in. is less than the maximum allowable deflection of 0.33 in., a 6 × 10 beam can be used to support the loads.

REVIEW

In what may have seemed like an endless string of formulas, tables, and values, you have determined the loads and stresses on a 10-ft-long beam. Seven basic steps were required as follows:

1. Determine the values for W, w, L, l, l³ and R.
   W = area to be supported × weight (LL + DL)
   w = W/L
   L = span in feet
   l = span in inches
   l³ = (l)(l)(l)
   R = V = W/2
2. Determine S. $S = \frac{(3)(w)(L^2)}{(2)(F_b)}$
   A usable S value answer is smaller than the S value in the table.
3. Determine F_v.
   $F_v = \frac{(3)(V)}{(2)(b)(d)} = 85$ or $\frac{(3)(V)}{85} = (2)(b)(d)$
   A usable F_v value answer is smaller than the F_v value in the table.
4. Determine maximum value for D. D = l/360
5. Determine D. $D = \frac{(5)(W)(l^3)}{(384)(E)(I)}$
6. Determine post supports. R = W/2
7. Determine piers size. R/soil bearing pressure

Figure 47–14 shows a floor plan with a ridge beam that needs to be determined. The beam will be SPF with no snow loads. Using the seven steps, determine the size of the beam.

Step 1. Determine the values.
   W = 10 × 12 × 40 = 4800 lb
   w = W/L = 4800/12 = 400 lb
   R = V = 2400
   L = 12′
   L² = 144
   l = 12′ × 12″ = 144
   l³ = 2.986
   F_b = 900
   F_v = 65 max.
   E = 1.3 max.

Step 2. Determine the section modulus.
$$S = \frac{(3)(w)(L^2)}{(2)(F_b)} = \frac{3 \times 400 \times 144}{2 \times 900} = \frac{172,800}{1800} = 96$$

Use a 4 × 14 or a 6 × 12 to determine F_v.

Step 3. Determine horizontal shear. The value from the table is 65.

$$4 \times 14 \ F_v = \frac{(3)(V)}{(2)(b)(d)} = \frac{3 \times 2400}{2 \times 3.5 \times 13.5} =$$

$$\frac{7200}{94.5} = 76.19 > 65$$

Since the computed value is larger than the table value, the 4 × 14 beam is inadequate. Try a 6 × 12.

$$6 \times 12 \ F_v = \frac{7200}{126.5} = 56.92$$

Finally, this beam works. Now solve for D.

Step 4. Determine D_{max}. $D_{max} = \frac{l}{180} = \frac{144}{180} = 0.8''$

Step 5. Determine D.

$$D = \frac{(5)(W)(l^3)}{(384)(E)(I)} = \frac{5 \times 4800 \times 2.986}{384 \times 1.3 \times 697} = \frac{71,664}{347,942}$$

D = 0.20

Step 6. Determine reactions. R = W/2 = 2400

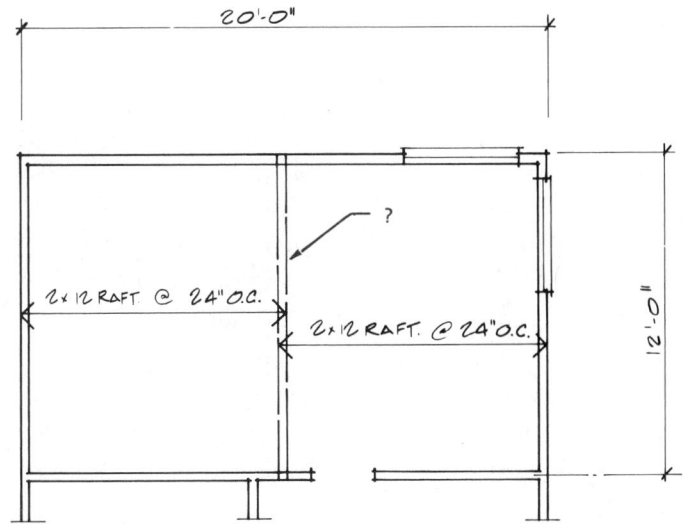

Figure 47–14 Sample floor plan with a beam of undetermined size.

Step 7. Determine piers. R/soil value (assume 2000 lb)

$$\frac{2400}{2000} = 1.2 \text{ sq ft}$$

According to the table (Figure 47–12) use either a 15 in. diameter or 15 in. square pier.

SPAN TABLES

You have already been introduced to span tables. Now that you have labored sizing a beam by solving for S, F_v, and E, you can better understand why span tables should be used whenever possible. The CABO code now includes charts for sizing very simple beams for one- or two-story residences. The National Forest Products Association offers tables that are easy to use and accepted by most professionals as a design standard. Appendix A shows a partial listing of these tables for spans ranging from 6'–0" through 16'–0". Although shorter beams may be required in a residence, generally, only the F_v value will need to be determined to find the beam size. Beams longer than sixteen feet are typically holding enough weight that a glu-lam beam should be used.

To use the information in Appendix A, "W" must be known. The type of wood must also be known so that the maximum values for F_b, F_v, and E can be used. In the beam solved in the last example, this value would be W = 4800#. If SPF is to be used, F_b = 900, F_v = 65, and E = 1.3. Because the beam is 12 feet long, look in the 12' span section of the table. Because the F_b is 900, your answer will come from this column. Proceed down this column until you find a W value that is equal to or larger than the W to be supported (4800 lb). 4 × 14 (5,315) and 6 × 12 (6,061) will work. Check the F_v values for each. This number must be less than 65. In our example, both seem to fail but this IS NOT THE CASE. Consider what the 6 × 12 column has told you. If you were to have a 12'-long beam, and supported 6,061 pounds, the beam would be under 71 units of stress in F_v. The problem is you only want the beam to hold 4,800 lbs, not 6,061. In this case, you still have to figure F_v by using the formula $\frac{3}{65}$ = 2bd. We worked this in the last example and know that a 6 × 12 will work. To determine if E is suitable, examine the E value for the 6 × 12. You will see the number 845. This represents .845 unit of stress.

The maximum E value for SPF is 1.3. Since .845 is less than 1.3, the beam works.

Try solving the same beam for a beam of Douglas fir. It would seem to be the same process with different numbers. It is, with a twist. The values to be used include: W = 4,800, F_b = 1,300, F_v = 85, and E = 1.6. Enter the 1,300 F_b column until a weight is found equal to or greater than 4,800 lb. You could use a 4 × 12. Notice the F_v is 101. Because 101 is greater than 85, the beam appears to fail. Instead of working the F_v formula, there is a short-cut. Because we are only asking the beam to support 4,800 lb, go to the left of the W values until the W value is closer to 4,800. As you move to the left in the W column, you'll find that at 4,921 lb, the beam has F_v = 93. Since your beam only holds 4,800 lb, you can continue to the left. At 4,511 lbs, the beam has an F_v of 85. 85 is the maximum F_v value, but at this point the 12' beam cannot support the desired W of 4,800.

Try a 4 × 14. Enter the F_b 1,300 column. The maximum supported weight is 7,678 lb. Using the W values for a 4 × 14, move to the left until you find a number close to 4,800. The F_b 900 column is as close as you can get with a W value of 5,315. A beam holding 5,315 lb will have 84 units of F_v stress. A 4 × 14 beam is safe. Its E value is .720. .720 is less than 1.6, so E is safe also. Compare the values for a 6 × 10 and you will find that it, too, is safe. Enter the table in the 1,300 F_b column and you will find the beam could support 5,974 lb. Move to the left and you will see the weight to be supported falls between 4,596 and 5,055 lb. Each has an F_v value less than the maximum of 85. Staying in the 5,055 column (which is more than our beam will have to support), the E value is 1.250, which is less than the maximum of 1.7 for Douglas fir.

Laminated Beams

Two beam problems have now been solved using the tables that are found in this chapter. Both beams were chosen from standard dimensioned lumber. Often glued laminated beams, or glu-lams, are used because of their superior strength. Using a glu-lam can greatly reduce the depth of a beam as compared to conventional lumber. Glu-lam beams are determined in the same manner as standard lumber, but different values are used. See Figure 47–15. Figure 47–16 gives values for glu-lams made of Douglas fir. You will also need to consult the building code for safe values for glu-lam beams. For beams constructed of Douglas fir the values are F_b = 2200, F_v = 165, and E = 1.7.

SPECIES AND COMMERCIAL GRADE	EXTREME FIBER BENDING F_b	HORIZONTAL SHEAR F_v	COMPRESSION PERPENDICULAR TO GRAIN $F_c\perp$	MODULUS OF ELASTICITY E
DFL #1	1350	85	385	1,600,000
22FV4				
DF/DF	2200	165	385	1,700,000
Hem-Fir #1	1050	70	245	1,300,000
22F E2				
HF/HF	2200	155	245	1,400,000
SPF	900	65	265	1,300,000
22F-E-1				
SP/SP	2200	200	385	1,400,000

Figure 47–15 Comparative values of common framing lumber with laminated beams of equal materials. Values based on the *Uniform Building Code.*

PROPERTIES OF GLU-LAM BEAMS					
SIZE (b)(d)	S	A	(2)(b)(d)	I	(384)(E)(I) *
3 1/8 × 9.0	42.2	28.1	56.3	189.8	123,901
3 1/8 × 10.5	57.4	32.8	65.6	301.5	196,819
3 1/8 × 12.0	75.0	37.5	75.0	450.0	293,760
3 1/8 × 13.5	94.9	42.2	84.4	640.7	418,249
3 1/8 × 15.0	117.2	46.9	93.8	878.9	573,746
5 1/8 × 9.0	69.2	46.1	92.0	311.3	203,217
5 1/8 × 10.5	94.2	53.8	107.6	494.4	322,744
5 1/8 × 12.0	123.0	61.5	123.0	738.0	481,766
5 1/8 × 13.5	155.7	69.2	138.4	1,050.8	685,962
5 1/8 × 15.0	192.2	76.9	153.8	1,441.4	940,946
5 1/8 × 16.5	232.5	84.6	169.0	1,918.5	1,252,397
6 3/4 × 10.5	124.0	70.9	141.8	651.2	425,103
6 3/4 × 12.0	162.0	81.0	162.0	972.0	634,522
6 3/4 × 13.5	205.0	91.1	182.6	1,384.0	903,475
6 3/4 × 15.0	253.1	101.3	202.0	1,898.4	1,239,276
6 3/4 × 16.5	306.3	111.4	222.8	2,526.8	1,649,495

*All values for 384 × E × I are written in units per million. All E values are figured for Doug fir @ E = 1.7. Verify local conditions.

Figure 47–16 Structural properties of glu-lam beams. The (2)(b)(d) and the (384)(E)(I) columns are set up for Douglas fir. If a different type of wood is to be used, you must use different values for these columns.

DETERMINING SIMPLE BEAMS WITH UNIFORM LOADS TEST

DIRECTIONS

Answer the questions with short complete statements or drawings as needed on an 8½ × 11 drawing sheet as follows:

1. Use ⅛ in. guidelines for all lettering.
2. Letter your name, Determining Simple Beams with Uniform Loads Test, and the date at the top of the sheet.
3. Letter the question number and provide the answer. You do not need to write out the question.

4. Use the tables and formulas found in this chapter to answer questions 6 through 10. Answer questions 6 through 10 each on a separate sheet of paper. Show all work.
5. Your grade will be based on correct answers.

QUESTIONS

1. What is a simple beam?
2. Explain the difference between a uniform and a concentrated load.

3. List three common categories of stress that must be known before a beam size can be determined.

4. Define the following notations: W, w, R, L, l, E, I, S, F_v, and F_b.

5. List two methods of determining beams other than using formulas.

6. List the values for W, w, and R for a floor beam that has an L of 10 ft and is centered in a room 20 ft wide.

7. A 4 × 6 DFL beam, with an L of 6 ft, and a W of 2800 lb will be used to span an opening for a window. Will it fail in F_v?

8. A 4 × 14 DFL is being used as a ridge beam. L = 12′, W = 4650 lb. Will this beam have a safe E value? Assume $D_{max} = l/360$.

9. If the soil bearing pressure is 1500 psf and the concrete has a strength of 2500 psi what size footing is needed to support a load of 4600 pounds?

10. What size DFL #2 girder will be required if w = 600 and L = 6 ft? Determine all necessary values to find the needed S, F_v and E stresses.

Chapter 48
Determining Simple Beams with Nonuniform Loads

YOU HAVE been introduced to sizing beams by the use of span tables and mathematical formulas. The procedures worked because loading patterns and support methods remained constant. In this chapter you will be introduced to formulas that are needed when loading patterns vary. Don't skip over that word "introduced." This chapter is not intended to make you an engineer, but to acquaint you with some basic formulas needed for determining light framing member sizes.

SIMPLE BEAM WITH A LOAD CONCENTRATED AT THE CENTER

Often in light construction, load-bearing walls of an upper floor may not line up with the bearing walls of the floor below as shown in Figure 48–1. This type of loading occurs when the function of the lower room dictates that no post be placed in the center. Since no post can be used on the lower floor, a beam will be required to span from wall to wall, and be centered below the upper level post. This beam will

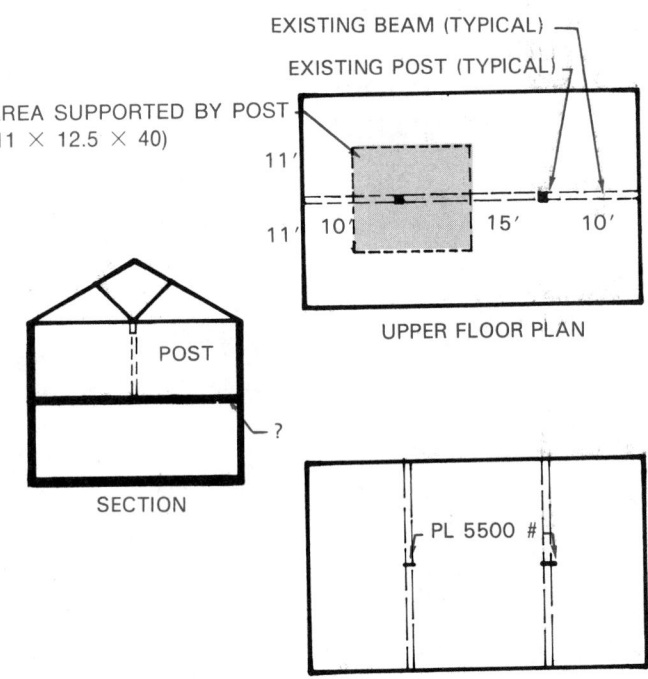

Figure 48–1 An engineer's sketch to help determine loads on a beam showing a load concentrated at the center.

773

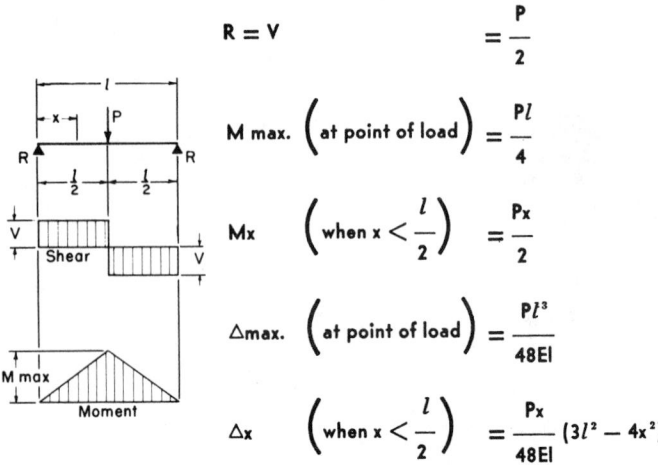

$$R = V = \frac{P}{2}$$

$$M \text{ max.} \left(\text{at point of load} \right) = \frac{Pl}{4}$$

$$M_x \left(\text{when } x < \frac{l}{2} \right) = \frac{Px}{2}$$

$$\Delta\text{max.} \left(\text{at point of load} \right) = \frac{Pl^3}{48EI}$$

$$\Delta_x \left(\text{when } x < \frac{l}{2} \right) = \frac{Px}{48EI}(3l^2 - 4x^2)$$

Figure 48–2 Shear and moment diagrams for a simple beam with a load concentrated at the center. *Data reproduced courtesy Western Wood Products Association.*

have no loads to support other than the weight from the post.

In order to size the beam needed to support the upper area, use the formulas presented in Figure 48–2. Notice that a new symbol, P, has been added to represent a point, or concentrated load. The point load is the sum of the reactions from each end of the beam.

Figure 48–3 shows a sample worksheet for this beam. Notice that the procedure used to solve for this beam is similar to the one used to determine a simple beam with uniform loads; only the formulas are different. With this procedure you must determine the amount of point loads for the upper beams. The sketch shows the upper floor plan with each point load. It is always a good idea to sketch the loading diagram and formulas in case you need to refer to the information about the beam in the future.

22' BEAM @ LIVING RM.

$P = W = 5500^\#$ $V = 2750$ $L = 22'$ $l = 264$ $l^3 = 18,399,744$

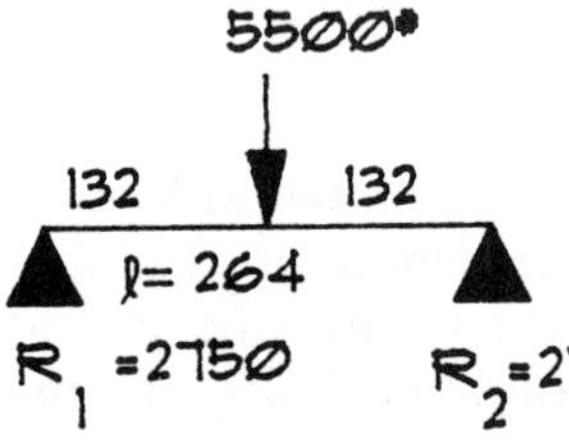

5500#

132   132

$l = 264$

$R_1 = 2750$ $R_2 = 2750$

$$M = \frac{(P)(l)}{4} = M = \frac{(5500)(264)}{4} =$$

$$\frac{1,452,000}{4} = 363,000 = M$$

$$S = \frac{M}{fb} = \frac{363,000}{2200} = S = 165 \quad \text{USE } 5\frac{1}{8} \times 15 \ (S=192$$
$$\text{or } 6\frac{3}{4} \times 13.5 \ (S=205$$

$$fv = \frac{(3)(V)}{2bd} = \frac{(3)(2750)}{165} = \frac{8250}{165} = 50 \quad \text{BOTH BM. O.K}$$

$$E_{max} = \frac{l}{360} = \frac{264}{360} = .73 \qquad E = \frac{(P)(l^3)}{(48)(E)(I)} =$$

$$E = \frac{(5500)(18.4)}{(48 \times 1.7)(1384)} = \frac{101,200}{112,934} = .89 > .73 = \text{FAIL}$$

$$? \ 5\frac{1}{8} \times 15 = I = 1441.4 = \frac{101,200}{117,618} = .86 > .73 = \text{FAIL}$$

$$? \ 6\frac{3}{4} \times 15 = I = 1898.4 = \frac{101,200}{154,909} = 65 < .73 = \boxed{\text{USE } 6\frac{3}{4} \times 15 \ f \ 2200 \\ \text{GLU-LAM BEAM}}$$

Figure 48–3 Worksheet for a beam with a load concentrated at the center. It is a good idea to include the location of the beam, a sketch of the loading, needed formulas, and the selected beam.

Occasionally you will be asked to explain how a beam size was determined weeks or months after it was done. Sketches will help you decode your calculations.

Once the point loads are known, determine M. Once M is known, divide it by the F_b value of the lumber to be used. This will provide the S value for the beam. Try to use a beam that has a depth equal to the depth of the floor joist but still has an S value greater than the S value just computed. Experience in structural work allows the designer to estimate fairly accurately when determining beams. In this case, with a length of 22 ft, the modulus of elasticity is going to govern the selection of this beam. The depth of the beam is going to greatly influence the size of beam needed for modulus of elasticity. In order to reduce the depth of this beam, a glu-lam beam will be used.

In Figure 48–3 three different beams have been selected that have the minimum required section modulus. Once the section modulus is known, the beam can be checked for modulus of elasticity. Because of the length of the beam, horizontal shear will not be a factor. Determine the F_v required for this beam, though, for the experience.

To determine the modulus of elasticity, first determine the maximum allowable limit. Divide l by 360. This beam is allowed to sag .73 of an in. Now use the formula in Figure 48–2 to determine how much the beam will actually deflect. Notice that the 6¾ × 13½ and the 5⅛ × 15 beams were each safe in S but failed in E. The 6¾ × 15 glu-lam is the smallest beam that can be used safely.

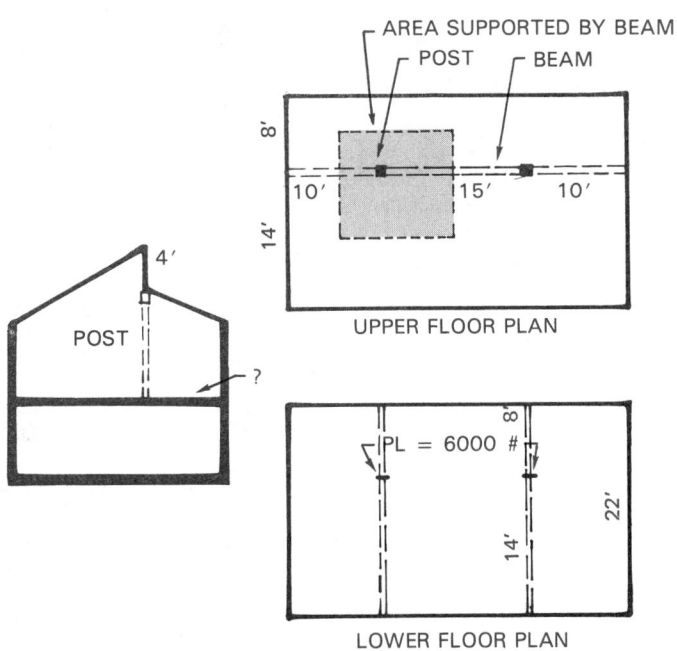

Figure 48–4 An engineer's sketch for a beam with a load concentrated at any point on the beam.

SIMPLE BEAM WITH A LOAD CONCENTRATED AT ANY POINT

A simple beam with a load concentrated at any point is similar to a beam with a concentrated load at the center. Figure 48–4 shows a sample floor plan which will result in concentrated off-center loads at the lower floor level. Figure 48–5 shows the diagrams and formulas that would be used to determine the

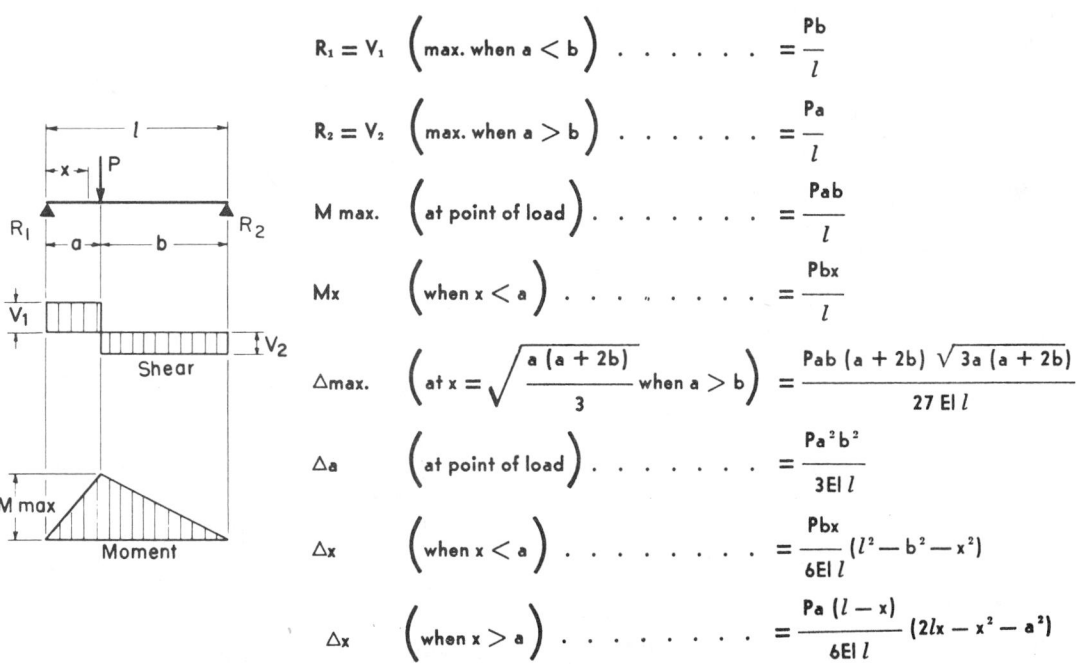

$$R_1 = V_1 \left(\text{max. when } a < b\right) \quad \ldots \ldots \quad = \frac{Pb}{l}$$

$$R_2 = V_2 \left(\text{max. when } a > b\right) \quad \ldots \ldots \quad = \frac{Pa}{l}$$

$$M \text{ max.} \left(\text{at point of load}\right) \quad \ldots \ldots \quad = \frac{Pab}{l}$$

$$Mx \left(\text{when } x < a\right) \quad \ldots \ldots \quad = \frac{Pbx}{l}$$

$$\Delta \text{max.} \left(\text{at } x = \sqrt{\frac{a(a+2b)}{3}} \text{ when } a > b\right) = \frac{Pab(a+2b)\sqrt{3a(a+2b)}}{27 \, EI \, l}$$

$$\Delta a \left(\text{at point of load}\right) \quad \ldots \ldots \quad = \frac{Pa^2b^2}{3EI \, l}$$

$$\Delta x \left(\text{when } x < a\right) \quad \ldots \ldots \quad = \frac{Pbx}{6EI \, l}(l^2 - b^2 - x^2)$$

$$\Delta x \left(\text{when } x > a\right) \quad \ldots \ldots \quad = \frac{Pa(l-x)}{6EI \, l}(2lx - x^2 - a^2)$$

Figure 48–5 Shear and moment diagrams for a simple beam with a load concentrated at any point on the beam. *Courtesy Western Wood Products Association.*

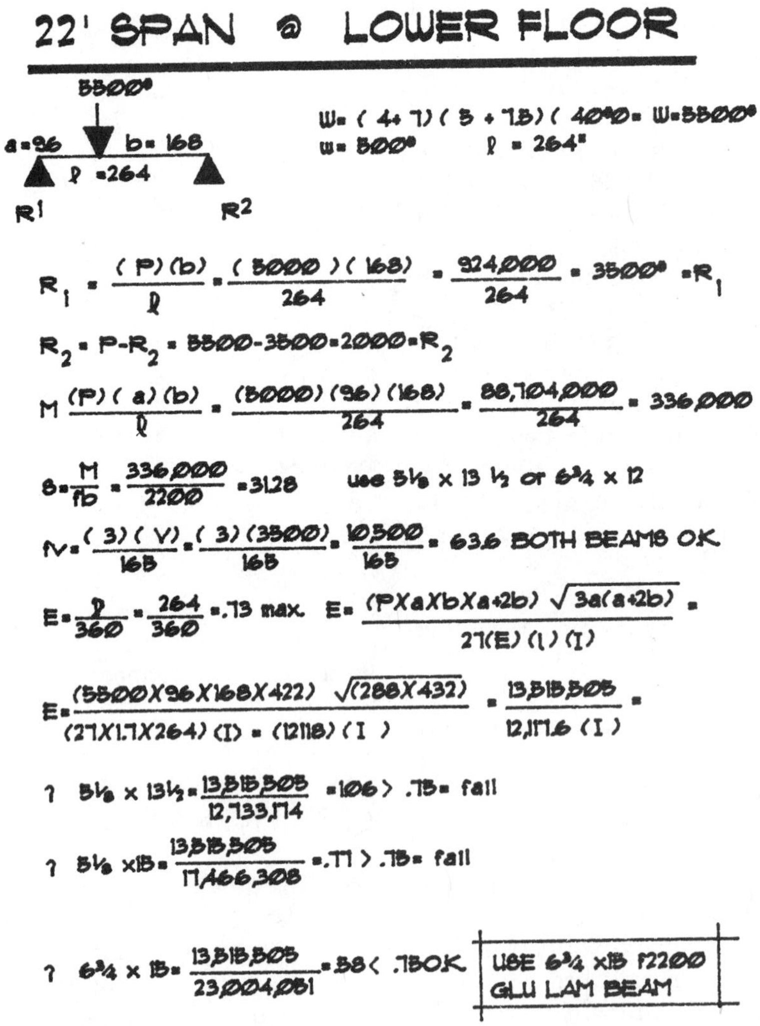

22' SPAN @ LOWER FLOOR

$$W = (4+7)(5+7.5)(40\#) = W = 5500\#$$
$$w = 500\# \qquad \ell = 264"$$

$$R_1 = \frac{(P)(b)}{\ell} = \frac{(5000)(168)}{264} = \frac{924,000}{264} = 3500\# = R_1$$

$$R_2 = P - R_2 = 5500 - 3500 = 2000 = R_2$$

$$M \frac{(P)(a)(b)}{\ell} = \frac{(5000)(96)(168)}{264} = \frac{88,704,000}{264} = 336,000 = M$$

$$S = \frac{M}{fb} = \frac{336,000}{2200} = 312.8 \qquad \text{use } 5\tfrac{1}{8} \times 13\tfrac{1}{2} \text{ or } 6\tfrac{3}{4} \times 12$$

$$fv = \frac{(3)(V)}{168} = \frac{(3)(3500)}{168} = \frac{10500}{168} = 63.6 \text{ BOTH BEAMS O.K.}$$

$$E = \frac{\ell}{360} = \frac{264}{360} = .73 \text{ max.} \qquad E = \frac{(P \times a \times b \times a + 2b)\sqrt{3a(a+2b)}}{27(E)(\ell)(I)}$$

$$E = \frac{(5500 \times 96 \times 168 \times 422)\sqrt{(288 \times 432)}}{(27 \times 1.7 \times 264)(I) = (12118)(I)} = \frac{13,518,505}{12,117.6(I)} =$$

$$? \quad 5\tfrac{1}{8} \times 13\tfrac{1}{2} = \frac{13,518,505}{12,733,174} = 1.06 > .73 = \text{fail}$$

$$? \quad 5\tfrac{1}{8} \times 15 = \frac{13,518,505}{17,466,308} = .77 > .73 = \text{fail}$$

$$? \quad 6\tfrac{3}{4} \times 15 = \frac{13,518,505}{23,004,081} = .58 < .73 \text{ O.K.} \qquad \boxed{\text{USE } 6\tfrac{3}{4} \times 15 \text{ f2200 GLU LAM BEAM}}$$

Figure 48–6 Workshop for a beam with a load concentrated off center.

beams of the lower floor plan. Figure 48–6 shows the worksheet for this beam.

CANTILEVERED BEAM WITH A UNIFORM LOAD

This loading pattern typically occurs where floor joists of a deck cantilever past the supporting wall. One major difference of this type of loading is that the live loads of decks are almost double the normal floor live loads. Figure 48–7 shows the diagrams and formulas for a cantilevered beam or joist. Figure 48–8 shows the worksheet to determine the spacing of floor joist at a three ft deck cantilever.

CANTILEVERED BEAM WITH A POINT LOAD AT THE FREE END

This type of beam results when a beam or joist is cantilevered and is supporting a point load. Floor joists that are cantilevered and support a wall and

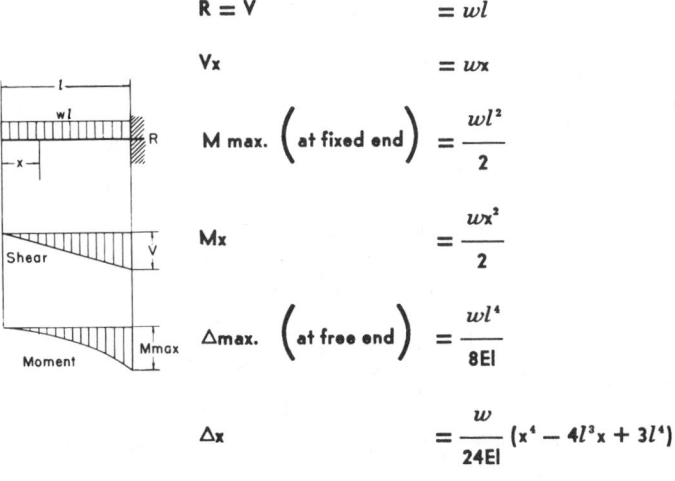

$$R = V = wl$$

$$V_x = wx$$

$$M \text{ max.} \left(\text{at fixed end}\right) = \frac{wl^2}{2}$$

$$M_x = \frac{wx^2}{2}$$

$$\Delta \text{max.} \left(\text{at free end}\right) = \frac{wl^4}{8EI}$$

$$\Delta_x = \frac{w}{24EI}(x^4 - 4l^3x + 3l^4)$$

Figure 48–7 Shear and moment diagrams for a cantilevered beam with a uniform load. *Data reproduced courtesy Western Wood Products Association.*

roof can be sized by using the formulas in Figure 48–9. Figure 48–10 shows the worksheet for determining the size and spacing of floor joists to cantilever two ft and support a bearing wall.

You have now been exposed to four standard formulas used by designers to size beams. Each of these, as well as other formulas, can be found in the product manuals of the wood associations.

FLOOR JOIST, 36" CANTILEVER

W = 210#

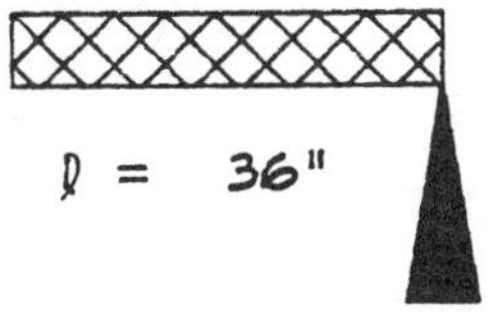

$W = 210^{\#}$ $w = 70^{\#}$ $V = 210$

$L = 3'$ $\ell = 36"$ $\ell = 36"$

$\ell^2 = 1296$ $\ell^4 = 1,679,616 \,(\, 1.68\,)$

$$M = \frac{(w)(\ell^2)}{2} = \frac{(70)(1296)}{2} = \frac{90{,}720}{2} = 45{,}360$$

$$S = \frac{M}{fb} = \frac{45{,}360}{1450} = 31.28$$ use 2x 12 @ 12" o.c.

$$fV = \frac{(3)(V)}{fb} = \frac{(3)(210)}{95} = \frac{630}{95} = 6.6 \quad 2 \times 12 \text{ OK}$$

$$E_{max} = \frac{\ell}{360} = \frac{36}{360} = .1 \text{ MAX}$$

$$E = \frac{(w)(\ell^4)}{(8)(E)(I)} = \frac{(70)(168)}{(8)(1.6)(178)} = \frac{118}{2278} = .05 < .1 \text{ ok}$$

USE 2 × 12 F.J. @ 12" o.c.

Figure 48–8 Worksheet for a cantilevered beam with a uniform load.

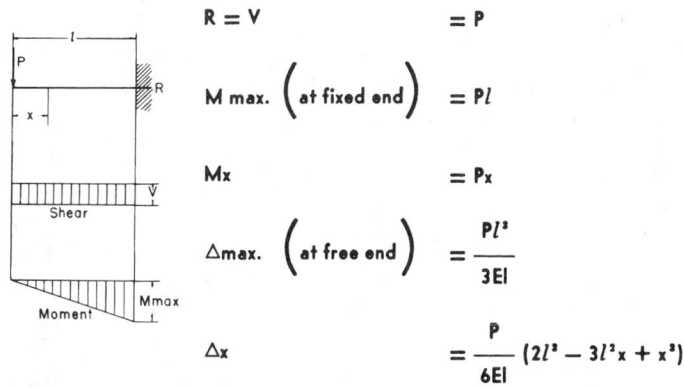

$R = V \qquad = P$

$M \max. \left(\text{at fixed end}\right) = P\ell$

$Mx \qquad = Px$

$\Delta max. \left(\text{at free end}\right) = \dfrac{P\ell^3}{3EI}$

$\Delta x \qquad = \dfrac{P}{6EI}(2\ell^3 - 3\ell^2 x + x^3)$

Figure 48–9 Shear and moment diagrams for a cantilevered beam with a concentrated load at the free end. *Data reproduced courtesy Western Wood Products Association.*

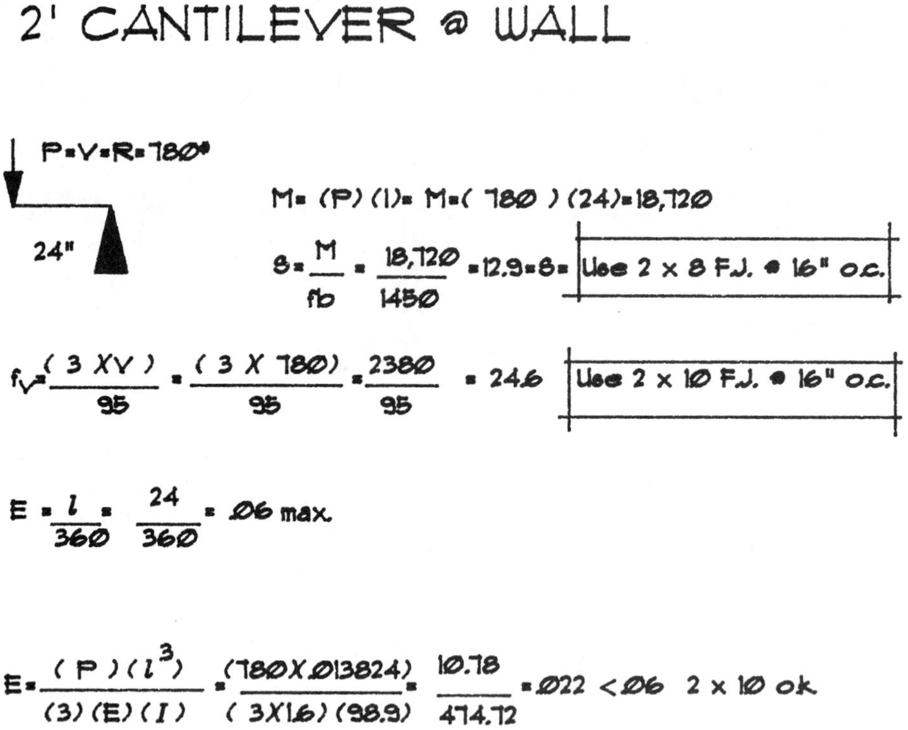

2' CANTILEVER @ WALL

$P = V = R = 780^\#$

24"

$M = (P)(l) = M = (780)(24) = 18,720$

$S = \dfrac{M}{fb} = \dfrac{18,720}{1450} = 12.9 = S =$ | Use 2 x 8 F.J. @ 16" o.c. |

$f_v = \dfrac{(3 \times V)}{95} = \dfrac{(3 \times 780)}{95} = \dfrac{2380}{95} = 24.6$ | Use 2 x 10 F.J. @ 16" o.c. |

$E = \dfrac{l}{360} = \dfrac{24}{360} = .06$ max.

$E = \dfrac{(P)(l^3)}{(3)(E)(I)} = \dfrac{(780 \times .013824)}{(3 \times 1.6)(98.9)} = \dfrac{10.78}{474.72} = .022 < .06 \quad 2 \times 10 \text{ ok}$

Figure 48–10 Worksheet for a cantilevered beam with a concentrated load at the free end.

DETERMINING SIMPLE BEAMS WITH NONUNIFORM LOADS TEST

DIRECTIONS

Answer the questions with short complete statements or drawings as needed on an 8½ × 11 drawing sheet as follows:

1. Use ⅛ in. guidelines for all lettering.
2. Letter your name, Determining Simple Beams with Nonuniform Loads Test, and the date at the top of the sheet.
3. Letter the question number and provide the answer. You do not need to write out the question.
4. Use the formulas in this chapter and tables in this section to answer the questions. Draw loading sketches as required and show all work.
5. Your grade will be based on correct answers.

QUESTIONS

1. Determine the minimum size beam needed to span 14 ft with a concentrated load of 3200 lb at the center. Assume the beam to be DFL. What size piers will be needed to resist the reactions if soil loads are 2000 psf?
2. Using Southern pine, determine the size of beam needed to cantilever 3.5 ft and support a concentrated load of 4000 lb at the free end.
3. Your family would like to add a deck to their existing house. 2 × 8 DFL #2 floor joists will be used. How far can the floor joists span? Can these floor joists extend 2 ft past a supporting girder using standard spacing?
4. Using SPF, determine what size beam will be needed to span 12 ft with a concentrated load of 2500 lb placed 3 ft from one end. What size piers will be required to support the loads if the soil pressure is 1500 psf?
5. Use DFL and determine the size of beam required to support the loads of problem 4.

CM-1430

Section Thirteen
Commercial Designs

Chapter 49

Commercial Construction Projects

OFFICE PRACTICE
TYPES OF DRAWINGS
TEST

OFFICE PRACTICE

THE DIRECTION that you choose to follow in your architectural education will affect the type of office practice that you can expect to find after you complete your formal education. In Chapter 14 you were introduced to the residential design sequence that you can expect to find in an architect's or designer's office. Although the design process is similar for commercial projects, the actual office practice for them is different.

Some offices that are staffed by designers and drafters work on commercial projects although in most cases these offices are the exception and not the rule. In most states, laws regulate who may or may not design and draw commercial structures. Designers and drafters are typically limited to drawing residential structures and commercial projects with limited square footage without the direct su-

pervision of a licensed architect or engineer. A drafter or designer should verify with the local building department exactly what can or cannot be drawn legally.

Some of you will get your first drafting experience during your upper-level architecture classes as you pursue your degree in architecture. Most offices staffed by architects hire drafters who are junior or senior architectural candidates or graduate students doing their post-graduate work toward their license.

For drafters with junior college degrees, a common place to seek a job drawing commercial projects would be at an engineering firm. Many structural engineers hire drafters and designers to complement their design teams. The design and drawing procedure will be quite similar to that of a residential office described in Chapter 8. As a new employee, you will be given jobs that are typically not the office favorites. These might include making corrections or lettering drawings that were drawn by others on the staff. As your linework and lettering speed and quality improve, so will the variety of drafting projects that you work on.

No matter what your drawing level, you will be required to research your drawing project. The two major tools that you will be using will be Sweets catalogs and the building code covering your area. Chapter 50 will introduce you to building codes as they apply to commercial projects.

Sweets catalogs are a collection of vendors' brochures that are used in nearly every architectural and engineering office. In residential construction, a drafter may be required to conduct a limited amount of research, but because of the simplicity of most houses, that research is typically not a time-consuming part of the project. In commercial projects, because of the various materials that are available, the drafter usually spends several hours a week researching product information during the first year of practice. As you become more familiar with products that are commonly used in your area, your research time will decrease, but will still be required.

Figure 49–1 shows an example from the Simpson Strong-Tie catalog of Sweets. This column cap (CC) is a common connector used to fasten beams to wood post. A common method of specifying this connection in the calculations might include only the use of a CC cap. The drafter would be required to determine the size of the post and the size of the beam to be supported, and then select the proper cap. The post size is determined by looking at the floor plan. The beam is determined by looking at the framing plan.

To determine the size cap needed at the intersection of two 6 × 14 beams (end-to-end) resting on a 6 × 6 post, a drafter would use the information in Figure 49–1. The width of a 6-in-wide member is really 5½ inches wide. You will need to find a cap that has a W2 size of 5½", and a W1 dimension of 5½ inches. A CC66 is the one that is needed.

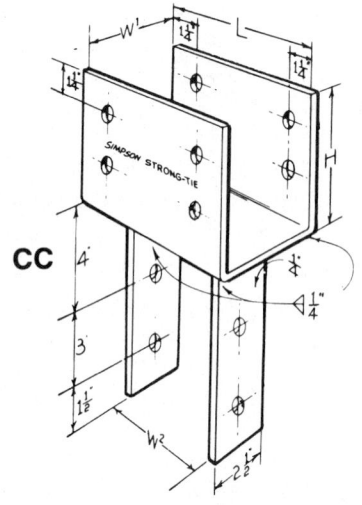

CC* (Strap may be rotated 90° as shown)

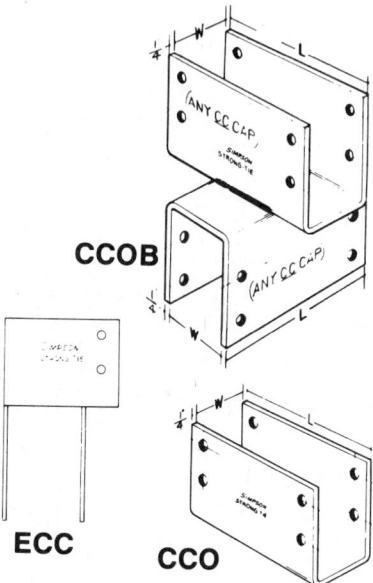

CCOB

ECC   **CCO**

COLUMN CAP

FACTORY VALUES! Precision factory gang-punched holes speed installation and insure full bolt values.

SPECIFICATIONS

1. Special corrosion protection Linear Polymer Formula (Simpson Gray).
2. Straps are fillet-welded both sides to bottom of cap.
3. Straps are centered upon the cap unless otherwise specified
4. For complete CC values consult Approval No. 1211.
5. For CCOB beam column cap values, utilize Table or consult Approval No. 1211, applying values no greater than the lesser element employed.
6. **MATERIAL:** ¼" hot-rolled steel.

For special, custom or rough lumber sizes, provide dimensions.

*Note: Any W2 dimension may be specified in combination with any column cap size given. For example, specify as "CC65" for a 5" column and 6" (nominal) beam width requirement. **COLUMN CAP ONLY** may be specified for field-welding to pipe or other column condition by specifying as "CCO—". **SPECIAL COLUMN CAPS** with W1, "L", "H", and hole schedules different from above may be special ordered. CCOB—Any two CCO's may be specified for back-to-back welding to create the CCOB cross beam connector. For end conditions specify ECC column caps and provide dimensions in accordance with Table.

*Column straps may be rotated 90° on special orders where W1 is greater than W2.

Model No.	W1	W2*	L*	H	Holes for Cap Bolt	Holes for Strap Bolt	Bolt Values	Seat Load Vertical**
CC44	3⅝"	3⅝"	7"	4"	(2) ⅝ MB	(2) ⅝ MB	3024	9430
CC3¼-4	3¼"	3⅝"	11"	6½"	(4) ⅝ MB	(2) ⅝ MB	6050	15470
CC3¼-6	3¼"	5½"	11"	6½"	(4) ⅝ MB	(2) ⅝ MB	6050	15470
CC5¼-6	5¼"	5½"	13"	8"	(4) ¾ MB	(2) ¾ MB	9310	29980
CC5¼-8	5¼"	7½"	13"	8"	(4) ¾ MB	(2) ¾ MB	9310	29980
CC64	5½"	3⅝"	11"	6½"	(4) ⅝ MB	(2) ⅝ MB	6050	23290
CC46	3⅝"	5½"	11"	6½"	(4) ⅝ MB	(2) ⅝ MB	6050	14820
CC66	5½"	5½"	11"	6½"	(4) ⅝ MB	(2) ⅝ MB	6050	23290
CC68	5½"	7½"	11"	6½"	(4) ⅝ MB	(2) ⅝ MB	6050	23290
CC76	6⅞"	5½"	13"	8"	(4) ¾ MB	(2) ¾ MB	9625	40220
CC7-7	6⅞"	6⅞"	13"	8"	(4) ¾ MB	(2) ¾ MB	9625	40220
CC7-8	6⅞"	7½"	13"	8"	(4) ¾ MB	(2) ¾ MB	9625	40220
CC86	7½"	5½"	13"	8"	(4) ¾ MB	(2) ¾ MB	9625	40220
CC88	7½"	7½"	13"	8"	(4) ¾ MB	(2) ¾ MB	9400	37540
CC96	8⅞"	5½"	13"	8"	(4) ¾ MB	(2) ¾ MB	9400	43790
CC98	8⅞"	7½"	13"	8"	(4) ¾ MB	(2) ¾ MB	9400	37540
CC106	9½"	5½"	13"	8"	(4) ¾ MB	(2) ¾ MB	9400	47550

**Subject to:
   As limited by nominal beam sizes @ 385 psi or normal Glulam sizes @ 450 psi of seat area.
   End bearing value of post, L/R of post, or other values to be deducted.
   *ECC Models are approximately 4" shorter than the "L" dimension given in Table, that provides for half the number of cap bolts with consequent decrease in bolt and seat load values.

ACCEPTED—see Research Recommendation No. 1211 of the International Conference of Building Officials (Uniform Building Code).

Figure 49–1 Vendors' catalogs are needed to determine many components shown on details. This page, from the Simpson Strong-Tie Company, can be used to determine the cap dimensions at post-to-beam details.

TYPES OF DRAWINGS

Most of the information to which you have been introduced while learning about residential architecture can be applied to commercial projects as well. There will be differences, of course, but the basic principles and procedures of drafting will be the same. Many of the differences will be discussed in this chapter.

Calculations

One of the prime differences of a commercial project from residential drafting is your need to work with engineer's calculations. No matter if you work for a designer, architect, or engineer, you will need to use a set of calculations as you draw the plans for a commercial project. In residential drafting, engineer's calcs are used to determine sizes of retaining walls, and occasionally for a connection. In commercial drafting a set of calculations is provided for the entire structure detailing everything from beam sizes to the size and number of nails to use in a wall.

Although called "engineer's calcs," these calculations may be prepared by an engineer, an architect or a drafter. Experienced drafters and designers occasionally prepare calculations for residential projects. By state law, commercial calculations are required to be signed by a licensed architect or engineer. Because of the complexity of many concrete and steel structures, architects typically design and coordinate the drafting of the project, but hire a consulting engineer to design the structural members. The architect typically designs the structure and decides where structural columns and beams will be located, and an engineer determines the stress and required size to resist this stress.

Figure 49–2 shows a page from the engineer's calcs. Most calcs are divided into three areas. The calc for a specific area usually begins with a statement of the problem. In Figure 49–2 the engineer is determining the size of the roof sheathing to be used for a warehouse. The second area of the calcs is the

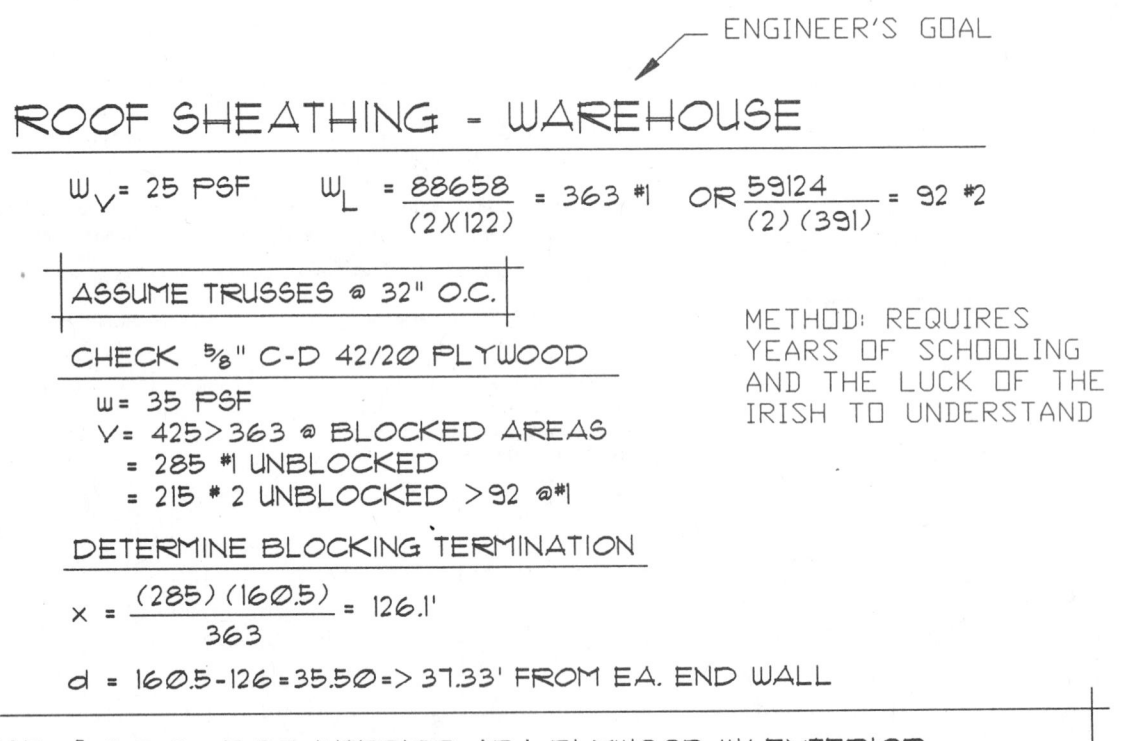

Figure 49–2 Engineer's calculations typically contain a problem to be solved, mathematical solutions, and specifications to be placed on the drawing.

mathematical formula used to determine the stress and needed reaction to that stress. This area of the calculations is of little meaning to the inexperienced drafter. But, since the part of the calcs that you will need is the solution area, you will note that the engineer placed the solution to the math problem in a box for easy reference. This is the information that the drafter needs to place on the plans.

Most calculations start at the highest level of the structure, and work down to the foundation level. This allows loads to be accumulated as formulas are worked out so that loads from a past solution can be used on a lower level. Figure 49–3 shows the calculations that were used to determine the loads on a column.

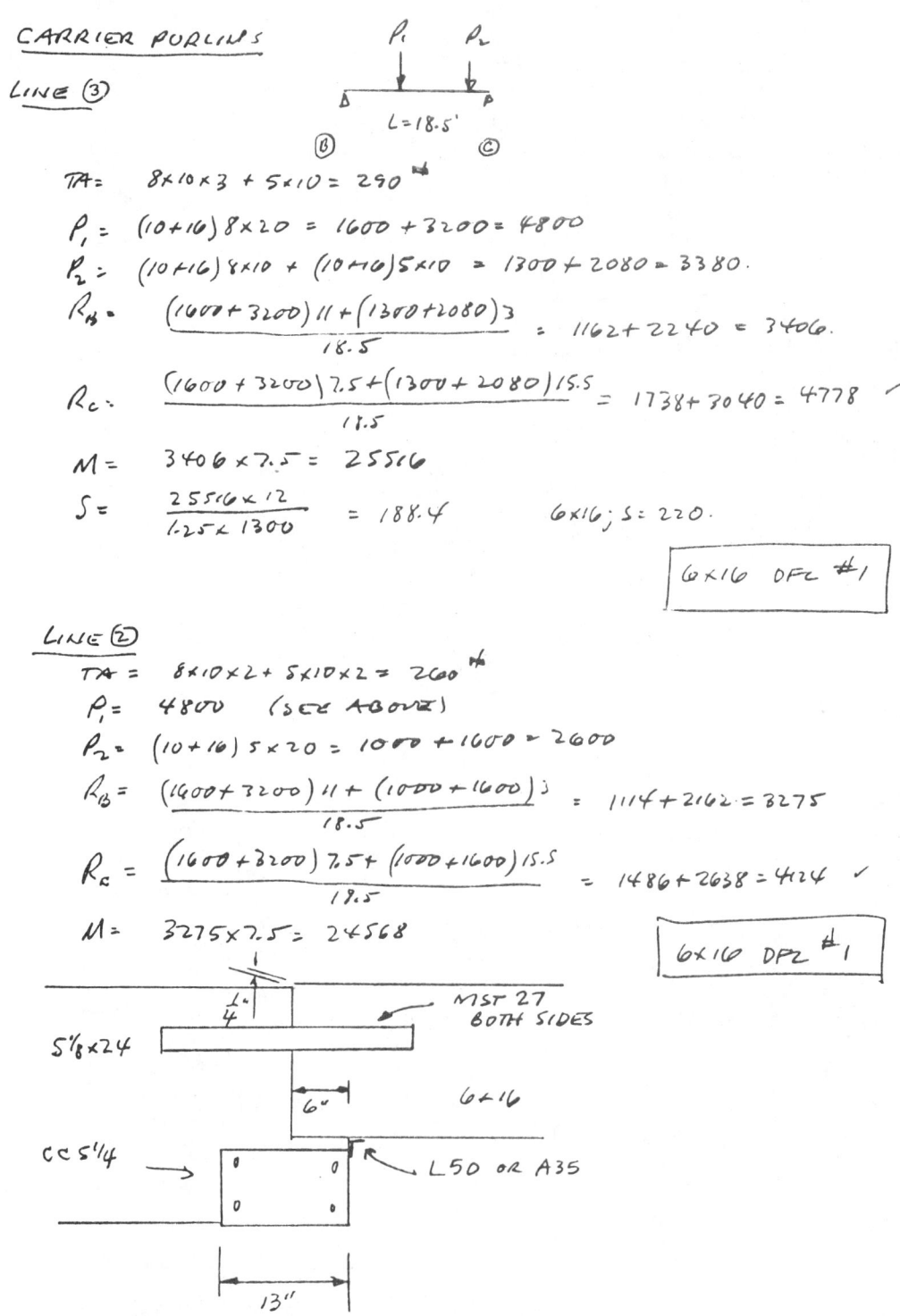

Figure 49–3 A sample of engineer's calculations to determine the loading criteria at a beam connection over a column. The drafter would be required to draw the detail using proper line quality. *Courtesy Structureform Masters, Inc.*

Figure 49–4 shows the drawing that the drafter produced from the calcs. Notice that there are items on the drawing that were not on the specifications. This is where the experience of the construction process is used. Based on past experience and a knowledge of the construction process, the drafter is able to draw such items as the shim without having it specified. Depending on the engineer and the experience level of the drafting team, the calcs may or may not contain sketches. If the engineer is specifying a common construction technique to a skilled drafting team, usually a sketch would not be required. The information to draw this detail was compiled from the foundation, grading, roof, and floor plans as well as the sections and other areas of the calcs.

Floor Plans

Commercial projects are similar to residential projects in their components. Each will use similar types of drawings to display basic information. The floor plan of a commercial project is used to show the locations of materials in the same way that a residential floor plan does. The difference in the floor plan comes in the type of material being specified. Figure 49–5 shows an example of a floor plan for an

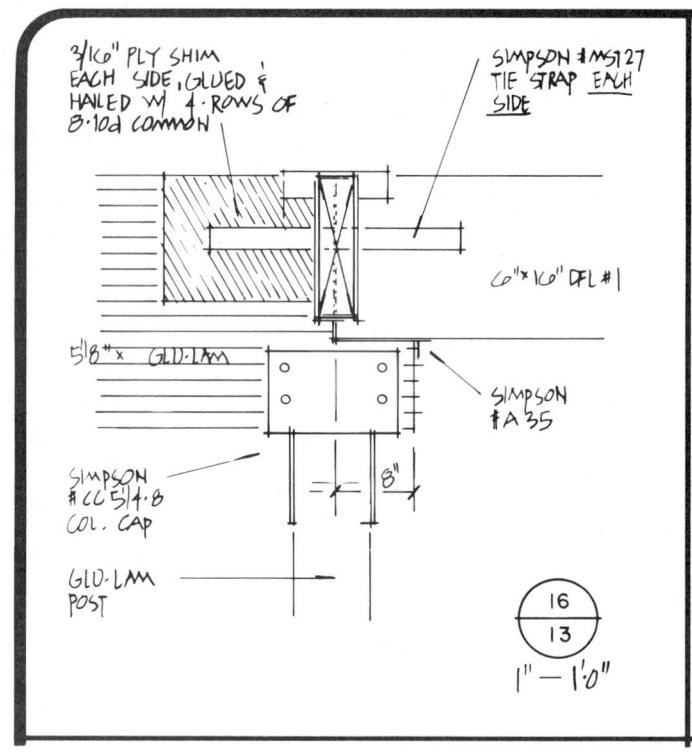

Figure 49–4 A detail drawn to convey the information in the engineer's calculations shown in Figure 49–3.

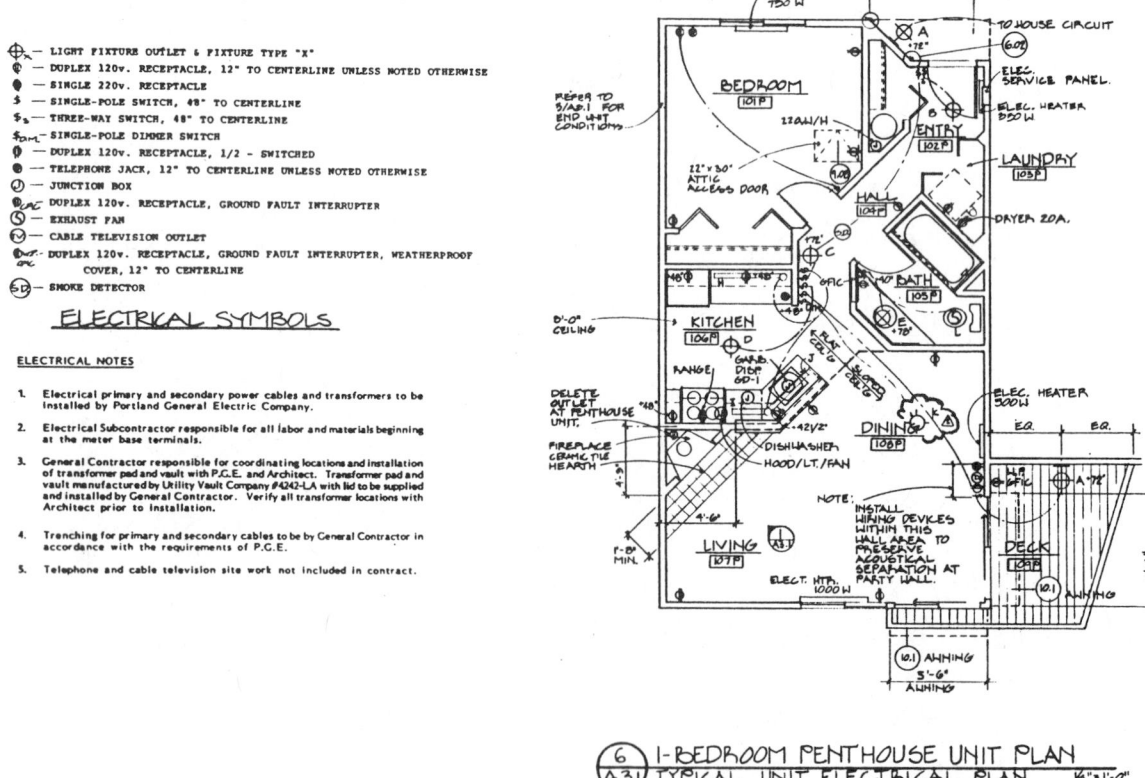

Figure 49–5 A typical unit floor plan for an apartment project. *Courtesy Guthrie, Slusarenko, and Leeb, Architects.*

apartment project. This plan is very similar to a residential plan. Information common to all units of this type is placed on the typical floor plan. To show how units fit together within the project, a building floor plan is also drawn as seen in Figure 49–6. This plan is usually drawn at a scale of ⅛″ = 1′–0″ or smaller. Multiunit apartment buildings may be one of the major types of drawing projects that you will work on as a drafter.

Another common type of floor plan that you can expect to work on would be the plan for an office complex. Figure 49–7 shows the floor plan for this type of development. Using methods similar to those of an apartment project, the overall floor plan is drawn at a scale of ⅛″ = 1′–0″ or smaller. Areas of the floor plan which are complex are then drawn at ¼″ = 1′–0″ as seen in Figure 49–8. Figure 49–9 shows the floor plan for a 7-ELEVEN convenience store. Many of the drawings of this chapter are based on this plan.

Electrical Plans

On a set of residential plans, an electrical plan was drawn to provide information for the locations of outlets, switches, light fixtures and other related information for the electrician. A similar electrical plan is also provided for a set of commercial drawings. Information for the electrical plans is usually specified by the owner or by major tenants. This information is then given to an electrical engineer who will specify how the actual circuitry is to be installed. The engineer will typically mark the needed information on a print of the floor plan. This print is then given to a drafter who transfers the information to a Mylar® copy of the floor plan. Because of the complexity of the electrical needs for commercial projects, a separate plan is often drawn to show the power outlet needs as seen in Figure 49–10, along with a plan for the lighting needs as seen in Figure 49–11. In addition, a plan was provided for electrical needs at the roof level in this sample set and is shown in Figure 49–12. Schematic drawings have also been provided by the electrical engineer and must be drawn by the drafter as shown in Figures 49–13 and 49–14.

Reflected Ceiling Plan

Acoustical ceilings are typically used on commercial projects and supported by wires in what is called a t-bar system. A reflected ceiling plan shows how the ceiling tiles are to be placed. The plan also typically shows the location of light panels or ceiling-mounted heat registers. Figure 49–15 shows an example of a reflected ceiling plan. The drafter must

work with information provided by both the electrical and the mechanical contractor to draw this plan properly.

Mechanical Plans

The mechanical plans for commercial projects are used in the same manner as in residential projects. These plans show the location of heating and cooling equipment as well as the duct runs. As with other plans, the mechanical contractor will mark all equipment sizes and duct runs on a print and a drafter will then redraw the information on a Mylar® copy of the floor plan. Figure 49–16 shows an example of a mechanical plan. Figures 49–17, 49–18, and 49–19 show examples of details that supplement the plan view.

Plumbing Plan

As with other plans that are generated from the floor plan, the information for the plumbing plan is supplied by the contractor and redrawn by a drafter. Depending on the complexity of the project, the plumbing plan may be divided into sewer and fresh water plans. Figure 49–20 shows an example of a plumbing plan which combines both systems on one plan. Notice that this plan shows far more detail and dimensions than the plans used for residential projects. Because of the simplicity of most residential projects, the skill of the plumber is relied upon to place the water and sewer lines. Because of the complexity of commercial projects, more details are usually placed on the plumbing plan. Figures 49–21 and 49–22 show examples of the details that the drafter was required to place on the plan view.

Foundation Plans

Foundations in commercial work are typically concrete slabs because of their durability and low labor cost. As seen in Figure 49–23, the foundation for a commercial project is similar to that of a residential project. The size of the footings will vary, but the same type of stresses affect a commercial project that affect a residence. They differ only in their magnitude. In commercial projects it is common to have both a slab and a foundation plan. The slab, or slab-on-grade plan as it is sometimes called, is a plan view of the construction of the floor system and specifies the size and location of concrete pours. A slab-on-grade plan can be seen in Figure 49–24. The foundation plan is used to show below-grade concrete work. An example of a foundation plan can be seen in Figure 49–25.

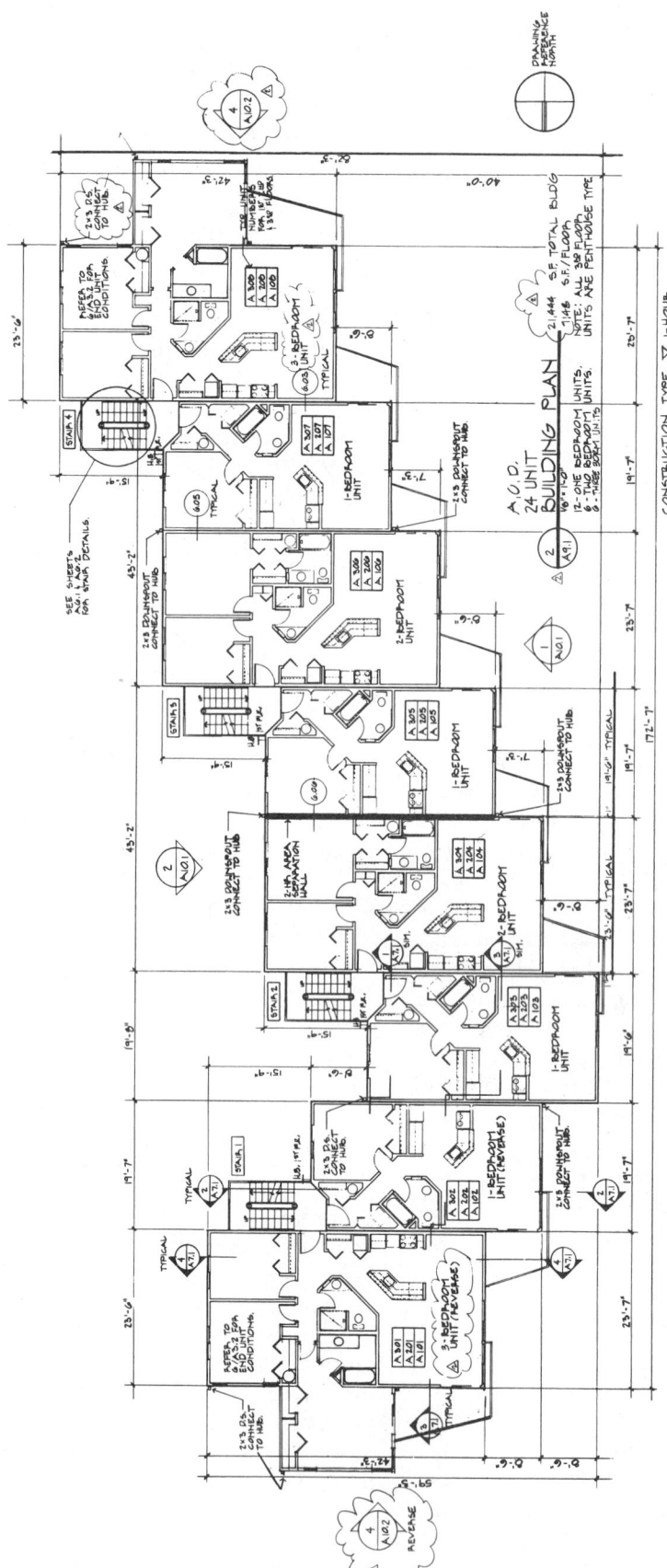

Figure 49-6 A plan showing the configuration of each building floor is usually shown at a smaller scale than the typical unit plan. *Courtesy Guthrie, Slusarenko, and Leeb, Architects.*

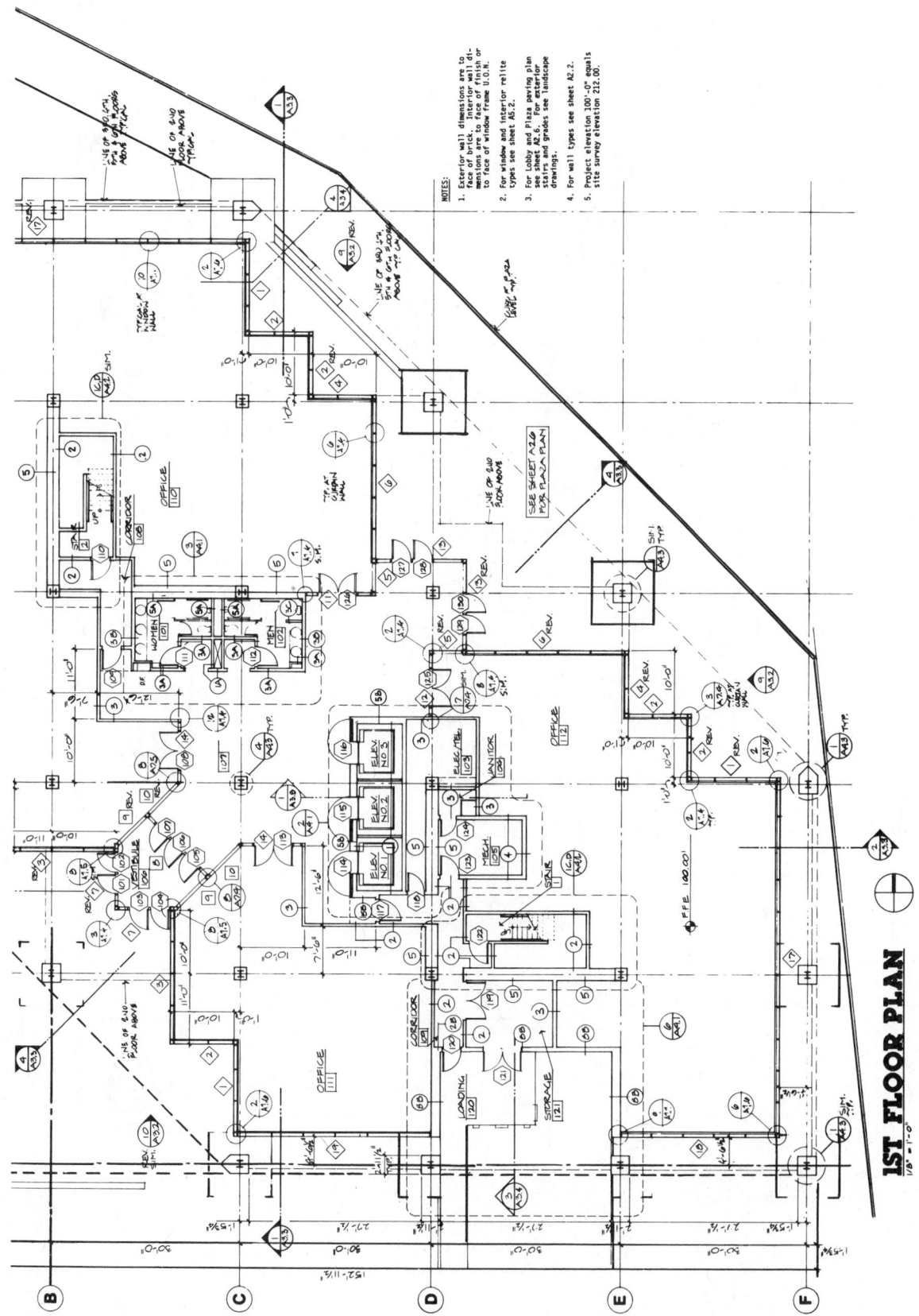

1ST FLOOR PLAN
1/8" = 1'-0"

Figure 49-7 The design and drafting of an office complex is a common project in the field of architecture. *Courtesy Guthrie, Slusarenko, and Leeb, Architects.*

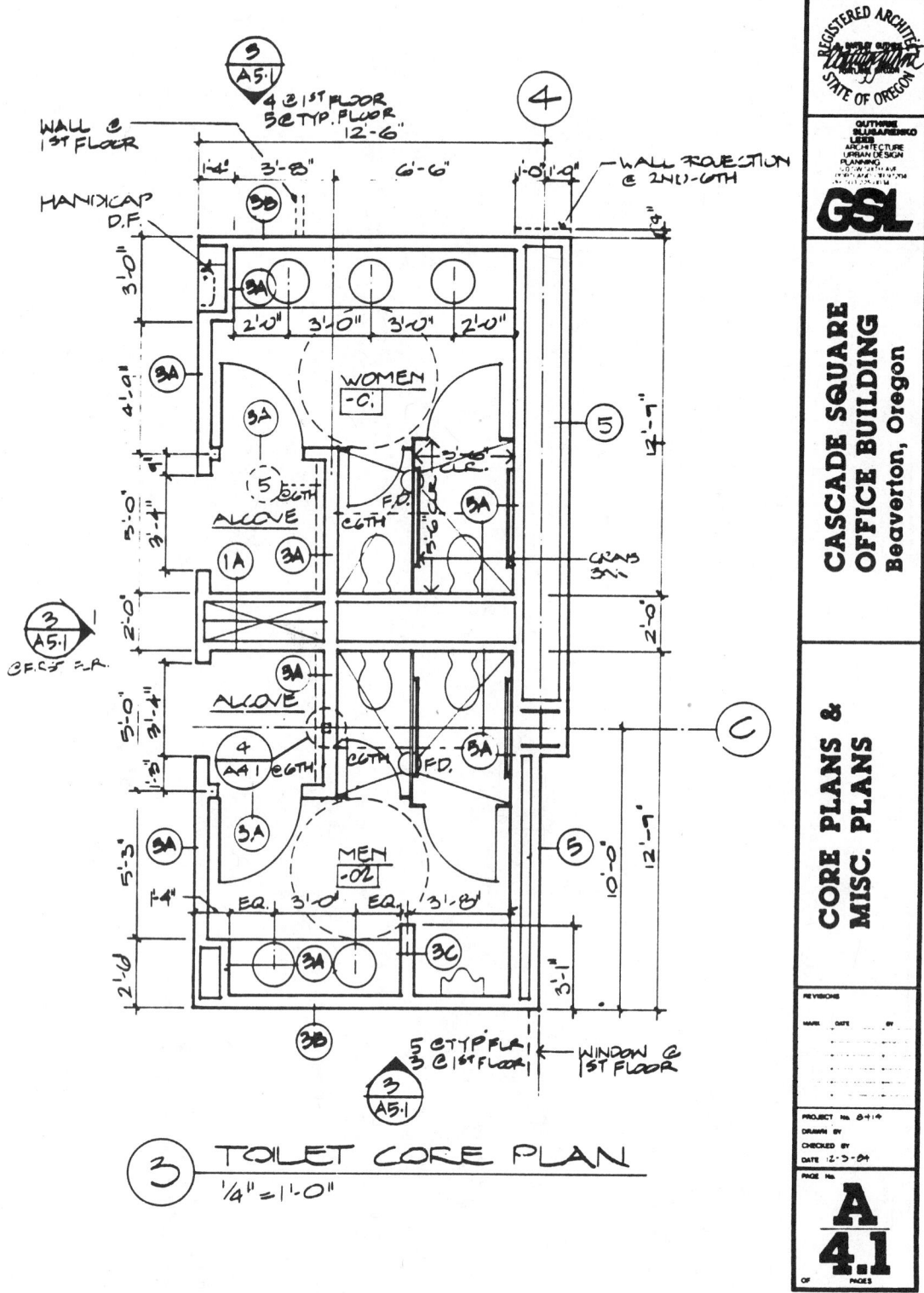

Figure 49–8 Areas of the office project floor plan are often enlarged to provide clarity. *Courtesy Guthrie, Slusarenko, and Leeb, Architects.*

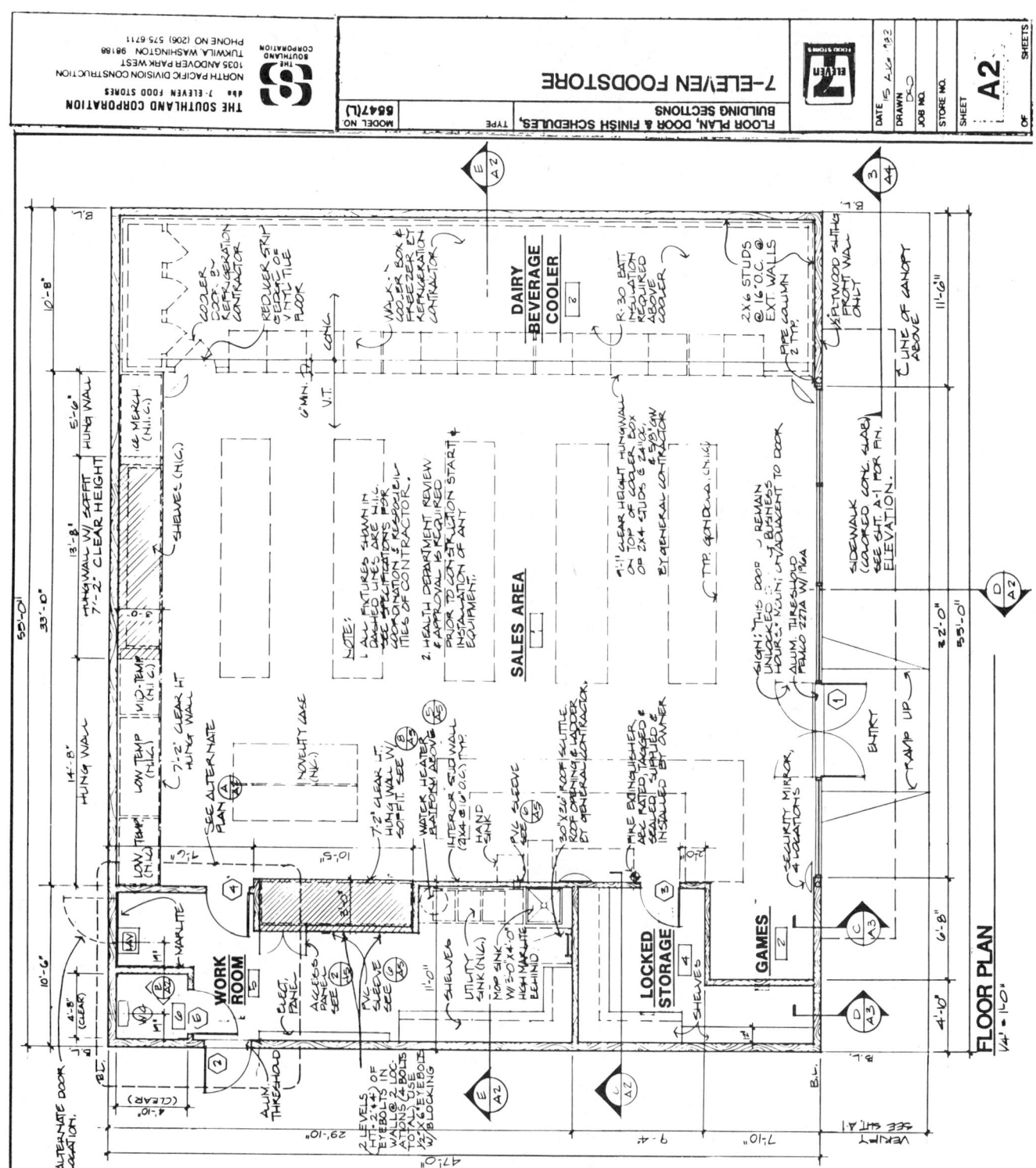

Figure 49-9 A floor plan for a convenience store. Courtesy the Southland Corporation.

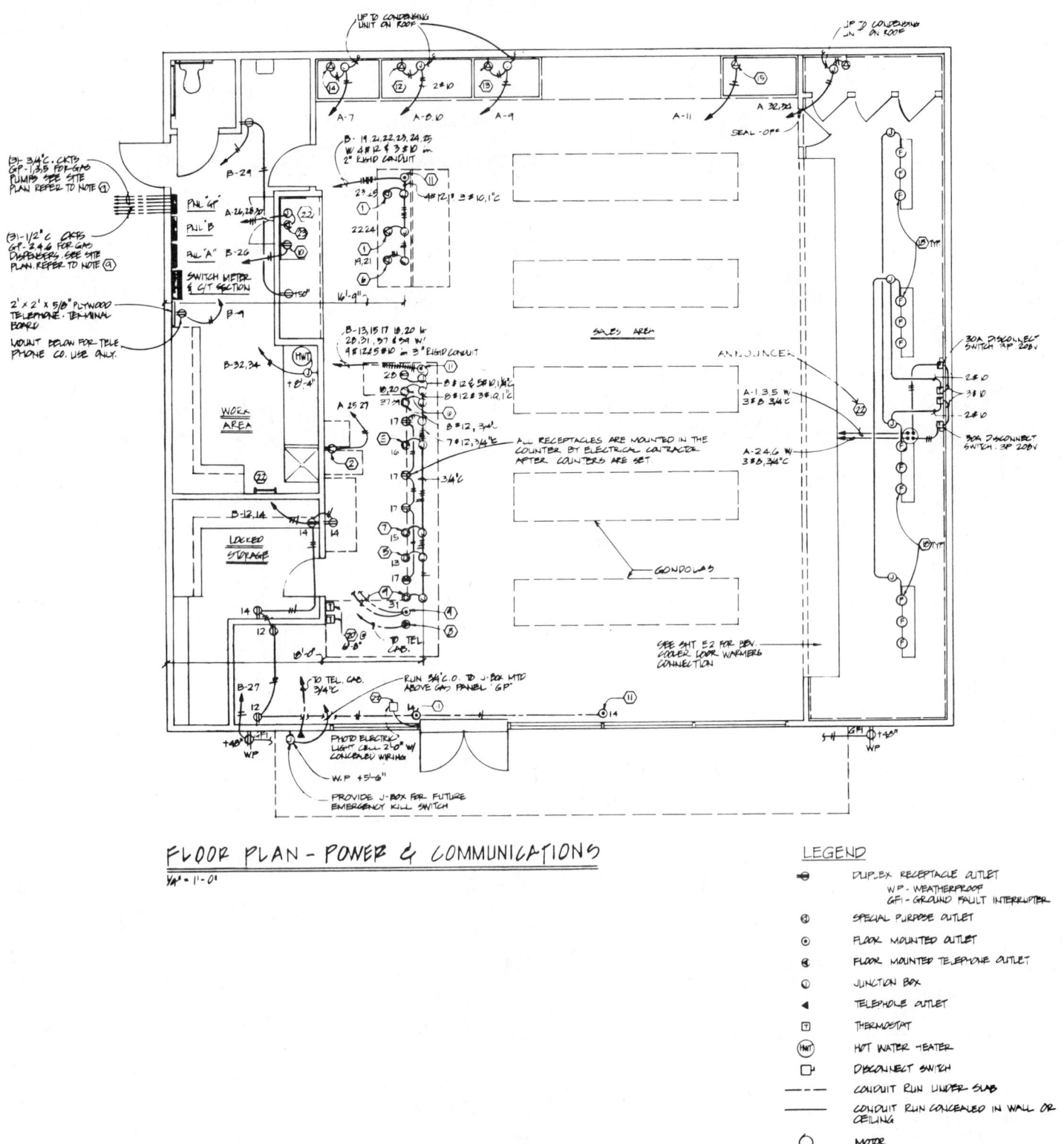

Figure 49–10 A plan is drawn to show power supplies. *Courtesy the Southland Corporation.*

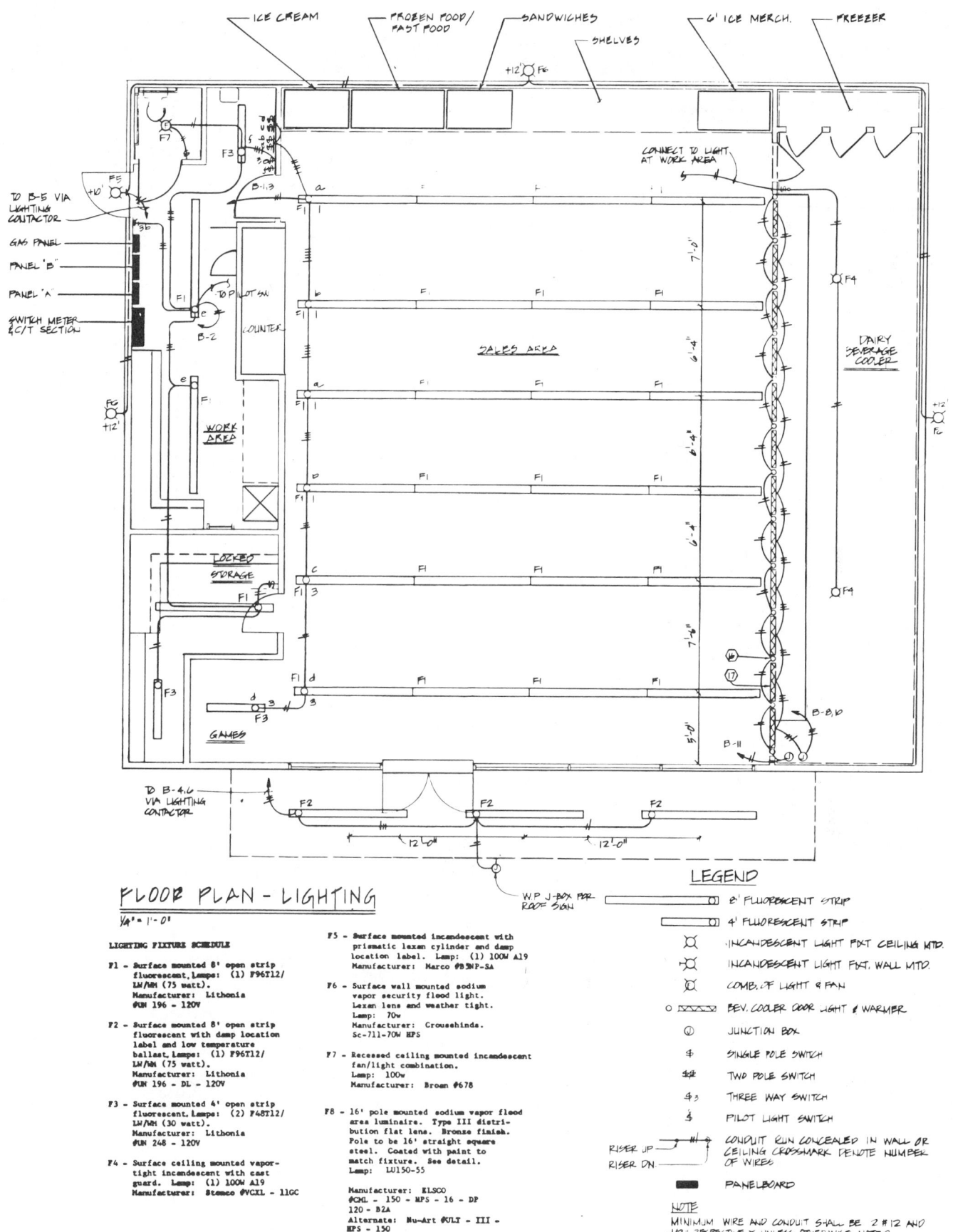

ICE CREAM — FROZEN FOOD/ FAST FOOD — SANDWICHES — SHELVES — 6' ICE MERCH. — FREEZER

CONNECT TO LIGHT AT WORK AREA

TO B-5 VIA LIGHTING CONTACTOR

GAS PANEL
PANEL 'B'
PANEL 'A'
SWITCH METER & C/T SECTION

TO PILOT SW.

COUNTER

SALES AREA

WORK AREA

LOCKED STORAGE

GAMES

DAIRY BEVERAGE COOLER

B-8,10

B-11

TO B-4,6 VIA LIGHTING CONTACTOR

12'-0"   12'-0"

W.P. J-BOX FOR ROOF SIGN

FLOOR PLAN - LIGHTING
1/4" = 1'-0"

LIGHTING FIXTURE SCHEDULE

F1 – Surface mounted 8' open strip fluorescent, Lamps: (1) F96T12/ LW/WM (75 watt).
Manufacturer: Lithonia
#UN 196 - 120V

F2 – Surface mounted 8' open strip fluorescent with damp location label and low temperature ballast, Lamps: (1) F96T12/ LW/WM (75 watt).
Manufacturer: Lithonia
#UN 196 - DL - 120V

F3 – Surface mounted 4' open strip fluorescent, Lamps: (2) F48T12/ LW/WM (30 watt).
Manufacturer: Lithonia
#UN 248 - 120V

F4 – Surface ceiling mounted vapor-tight incandescent with cast guard. Lamp: (1) 100W A19
Manufacturer: Stemco #VCXL - 11GC

F5 – Surface mounted incandescent with prismatic lexan cylinder and damp location label. Lamp: (1) 100W A19
Manufacturer: Marco #B3NP-SA

F6 – Surface wall mounted sodium vapor security flood light. Lexan lens and weather tight. Lamp: 70w
Manufacturer: Crousehinds. Sc-711-70W HPS

F7 – Recessed ceiling mounted incandescent fan/light combination. Lamp: 100w
Manufacturer: Broan #678

F8 – 16' pole mounted sodium vapor flood area luminaire. Type III distribution flat lens. Bronze finish. Pole to be 16' straight square steel. Coated with paint to match fixture. See detail. Lamp: LU150-55
Manufacturer: ELSCO
#CML - 150 - MPS - 16 - DP 120 - B2A
Alternate: Nu-Art #ULT - III - MPS - 150

LEGEND

	8' FLUORESCENT STRIP
	4' FLUORESCENT STRIP
⊗	INCANDESCENT LIGHT FIXT. CEILING MTD.
⊗	INCANDESCENT LIGHT FIXT. WALL MTD.
⊗	COMB. OF LIGHT & FAN
O ⋙	BEV. COOLER DOOR LIGHT & WARMER
ⓙ	JUNCTION BOX
$	SINGLE POLE SWITCH
$$	TWO POLE SWITCH
$₃	THREE WAY SWITCH
$	PILOT LIGHT SWITCH
	CONDUIT RUN CONCEALED IN WALL OR CEILING CROSSMARK DENOTE NUMBER OF WIRES
RISER UP	
RISER DN	
▬	PANELBOARD

NOTE
MINIMUM WIRE AND CONDUIT SHALL BE 2 #12 AND 1/2" RESPECTIVELY UNLESS OTHERWISE NOTED.

Figure 49–11 Lighting needs are shown using an overlay of the floor plan. *Courtesy The Southland Corporation.*

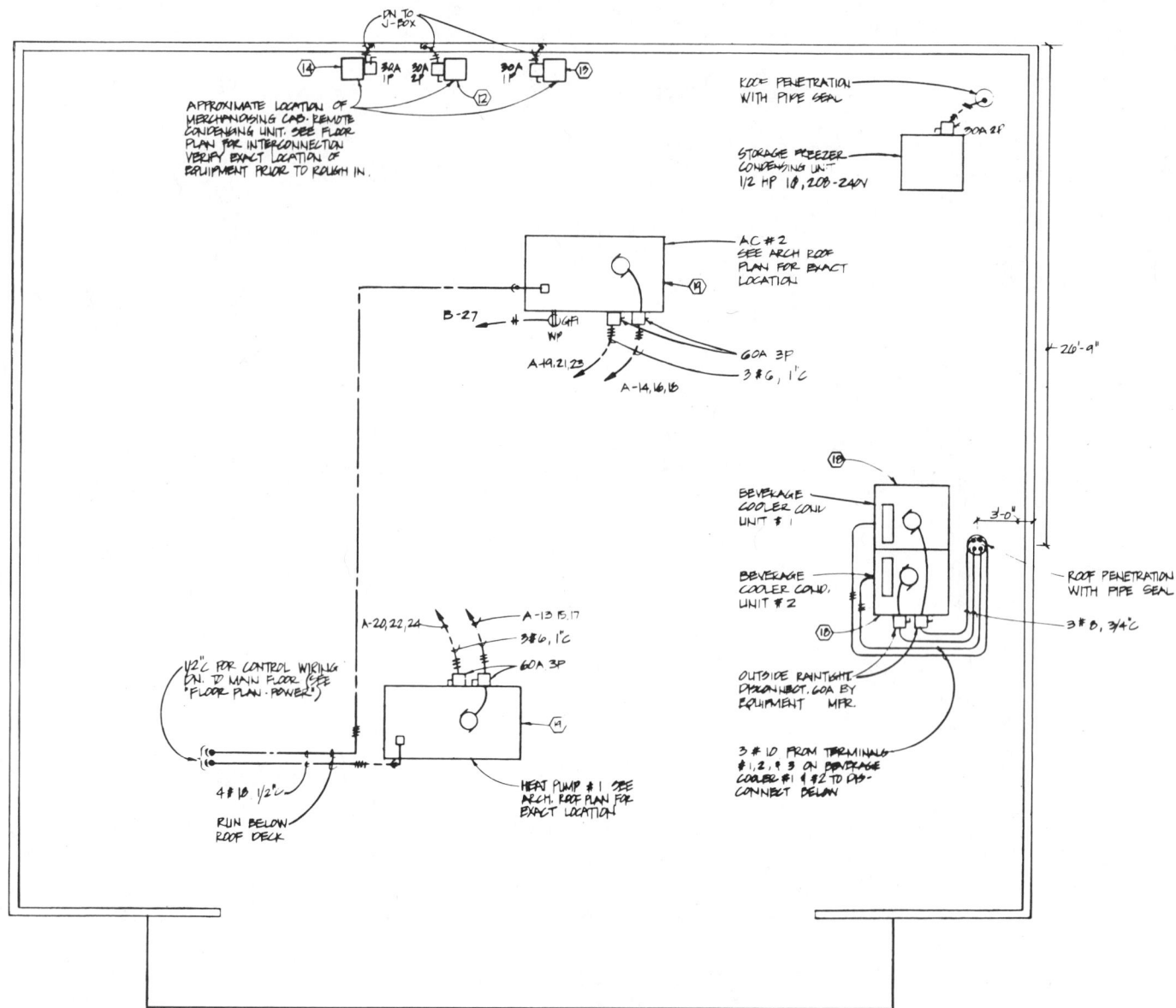

ROOF PLAN - ELECTRICAL

¼" = 1'-0"

Figure 49-12 To supplement the power supply and lighting plans, a plan showing the electrical needs of equipment on the roof is also drawn. *Courtesy The Southland Corporation.*

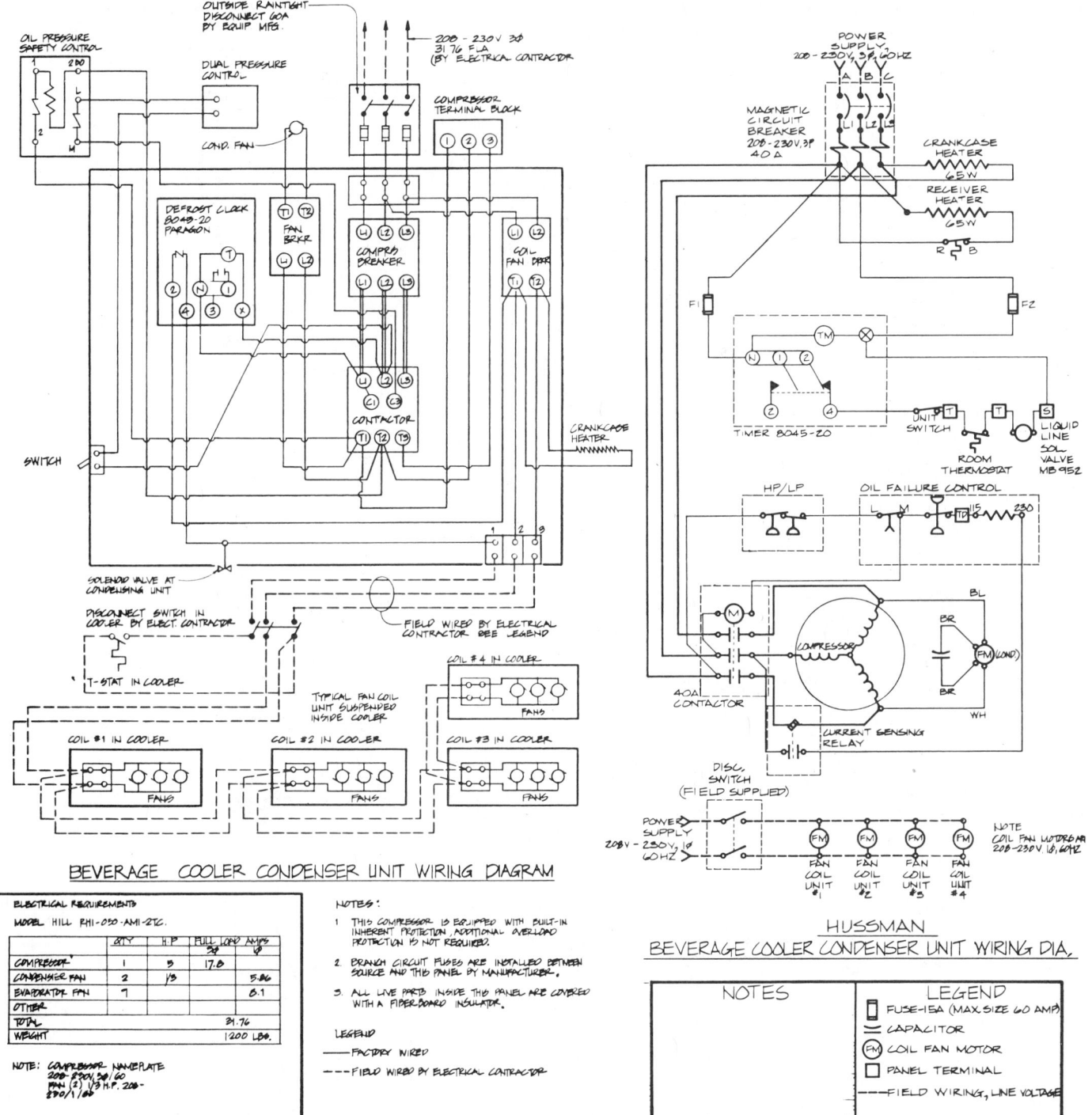

BEVERAGE COOLER CONDENSER UNIT WIRING DIAGRAM

HUSSMAN
BEVERAGE COOLER CONDENSER UNIT WIRING DIA.

ELECTRICAL REQUIREMENTS

MODEL HILL RHI-050-AMI-2TC.

	QTY	H.P	FULL LOAD AMPS 3∅	1∅
COMPRESSOR	1	5	17.8	
CONDENSER FAN	2	1/3		5.86
EVAPORATOR FAN	7			8.1
OTHER				
TOTAL			31.76	
WEIGHT			1200 LBS.	

NOTE: COMPRESSOR NAMEPLATE
200-230V 3∅/60
FAN (2) 1/3 H.P. 200-
230/1/60

NOTES:

1 THIS COMPRESSOR IS EQUIPPED WITH BUILT-IN INHERENT PROTECTION, ADDITIONAL OVERLOAD PROTECTION IS NOT REQUIRED.

2 BRANCH CIRCUIT FUSES ARE INSTALLED BETWEEN SOURCE AND THIS PANEL BY MANUFACTURER.

3 ALL LIVE PARTS INSIDE THIS PANEL ARE COVERED WITH A FIBERBOARD INSULATOR.

LEGEND

———— FACTORY WIRED

----- FIELD WIRED BY ELECTRICAL CONTRACTOR

NOTES

LEGEND

□ FUSE-15A (MAX SIZE 60 AMP)

= CAPACITOR

(FM) COIL FAN MOTOR

□ PANEL TERMINAL

----- FIELD WIRING, LINE VOLTAGE

Figure 49–13 A drafter is often required to draw schematic diagrams to help explain electrical needs. *Courtesy The Southland Corporation.*

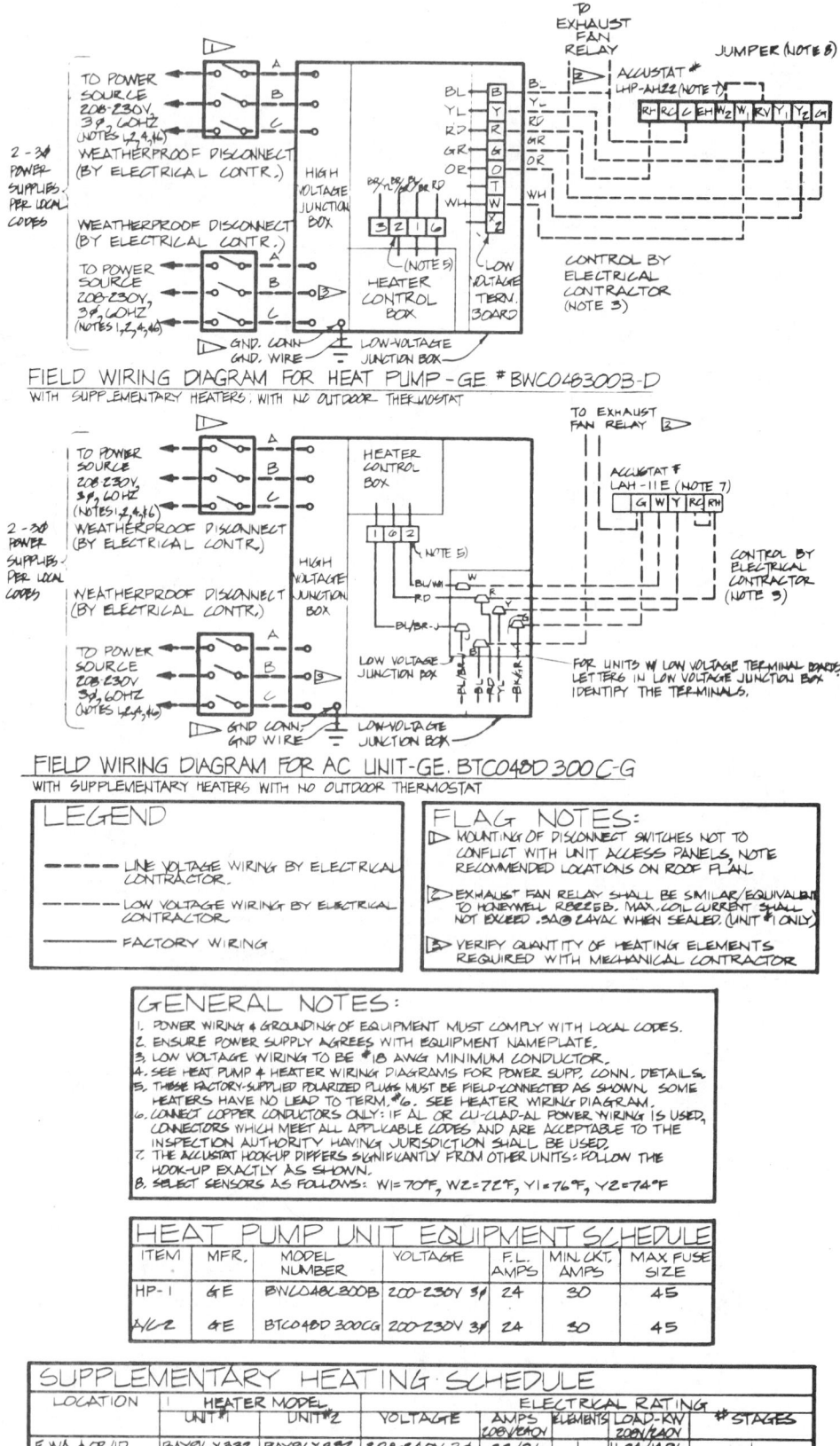

FIELD WIRING DIAGRAM FOR HEAT PUMP - GE # BWC0483003-D
WITH SUPPLEMENTARY HEATERS, WITH NO OUTDOOR THERMOSTAT

FIELD WIRING DIAGRAM FOR AC UNIT-GE. BTC048D 300C-G
WITH SUPPLEMENTARY HEATERS WITH NO OUTDOOR THERMOSTAT

LEGEND

---------- LINE VOLTAGE WIRING BY ELECTRICAL CONTRACTOR.

———————— LOW VOLTAGE WIRING BY ELECTRICAL CONTRACTOR.

———— FACTORY WIRING

FLAG NOTES:

1. MOUNTING OF DISCONNECT SWITCHES NOT TO CONFLICT WITH UNIT ACCESS PANELS, NOTE RECOMMENDED LOCATIONS ON ROOF PLAN.

2. EXHAUST FAN RELAY SHALL BE SIMILAR/EQUIVALENT TO HONEYWELL R8222B. MAX. COIL CURRENT SHALL NOT EXCEED .5A @ 24VAC WHEN SEALED. (UNIT #1 ONLY)

3. VERIFY QUANTITY OF HEATING ELEMENTS REQUIRED WITH MECHANICAL CONTRACTOR

GENERAL NOTES:

1. POWER WIRING & GROUNDING OF EQUIPMENT MUST COMPLY WITH LOCAL CODES.
2. ENSURE POWER SUPPLY AGREES WITH EQUIPMENT NAMEPLATE.
3. LOW VOLTAGE WIRING TO BE #18 AWG MINIMUM CONDUCTOR.
4. SEE HEAT PUMP & HEATER WIRING DIAGRAMS FOR POWER SUPP. CONN. DETAILS.
5. THESE FACTORY-SUPPLIED POLARIZED PLUGS MUST BE FIELD-CONNECTED AS SHOWN. SOME HEATERS HAVE NO LEAD TO TERM. #6. SEE HEATER WIRING DIAGRAM.
6. CONNECT COPPER CONDUCTORS ONLY: IF AL OR CU-CLAD-AL POWER WIRING IS USED, CONNECTORS WHICH MEET ALL APPLICABLE CODES AND ARE ACCEPTABLE TO THE INSPECTION AUTHORITY HAVING JURISDICTION SHALL BE USED.
7. THE ACCUSTAT HOOK-UP DIFFERS SIGNIFICANTLY FROM OTHER UNITS: FOLLOW THE HOOK-UP EXACTLY AS SHOWN.
8. SELECT SENSORS AS FOLLOWS: W1=70°F, W2=72°F, Y1=76°F, Y2=74°F

HEAT PUMP UNIT EQUIPMENT SCHEDULE

ITEM	MFR.	MODEL NUMBER	VOLTAGE	F.L. AMPS	MIN. CKT. AMPS	MAX FUSE SIZE
HP-1	GE	BWC048C300B	200-230V 3∅	24	30	45
AC-2	GE	BTC048D 300CG	200-230V 3∅	24	30	45

SUPPLEMENTARY HEATING SCHEDULE

LOCATION	HEATER MODEL		ELECTRICAL RATING				
	UNIT #1	UNIT #2	VOLTAGE	AMPS 208V/240V	ELEMENTS	LOAD-KW 208V/240V	# STAGES
E. WA & OR/ID.	BAY96X332	BAY96X332	208-240V, 3∅	32/36	1	11.24/14.96	1
W. WA & OR	BAY96X331	BAY96X331	208-240V, 3∅	28/24	1	8.08/9.96	1

Figure 49–14 Schedules and wiring diagrams are used to supplement the electrical plans. *Courtesy The Southland Corporation.*

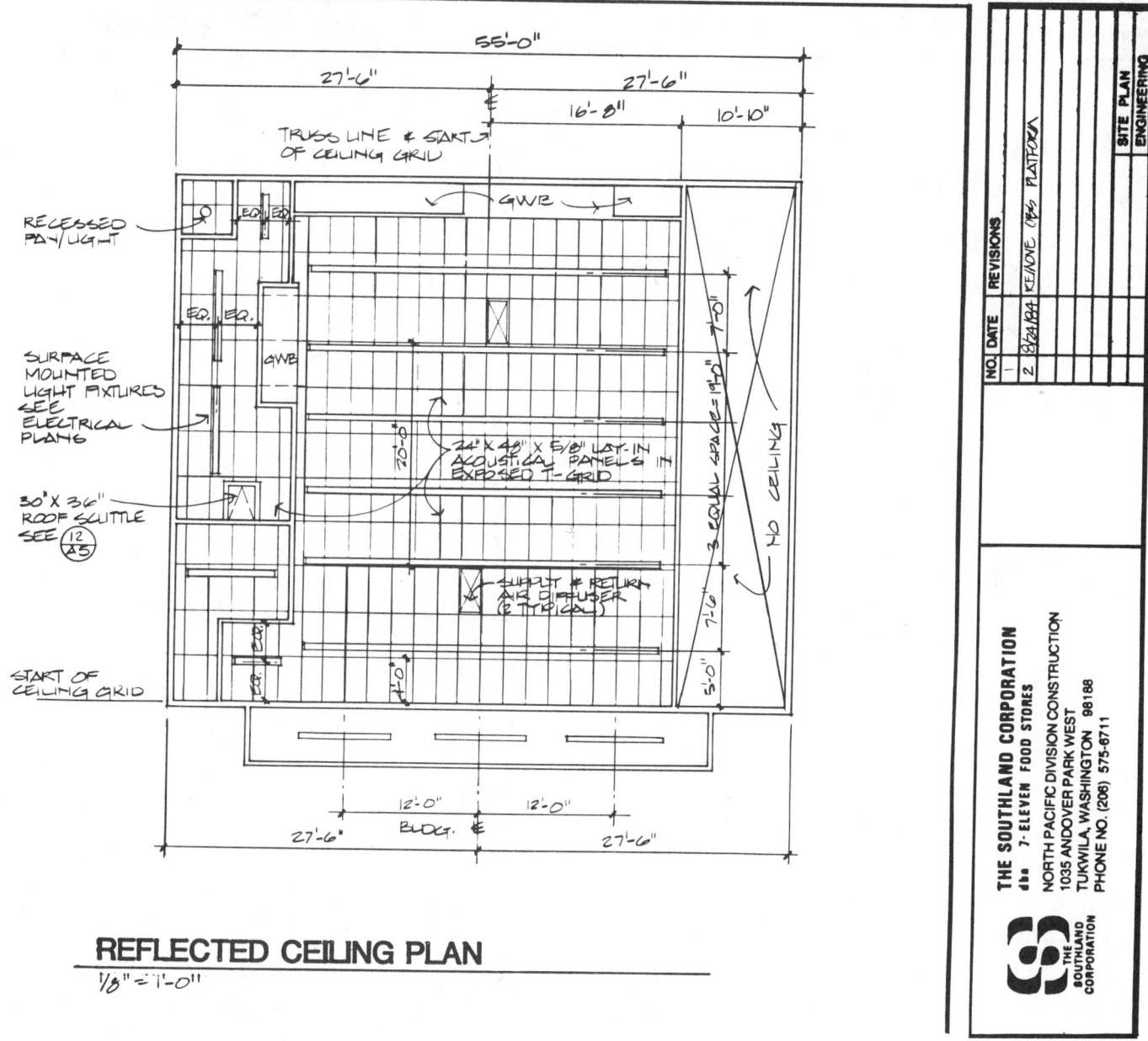

REFLECTED CEILING PLAN
1/8" = 1'-0"

Figure 49–15 A reflected ceiling plan is used to show the layout for the suspended ceiling system. *Courtesy The Southland Corporation.*

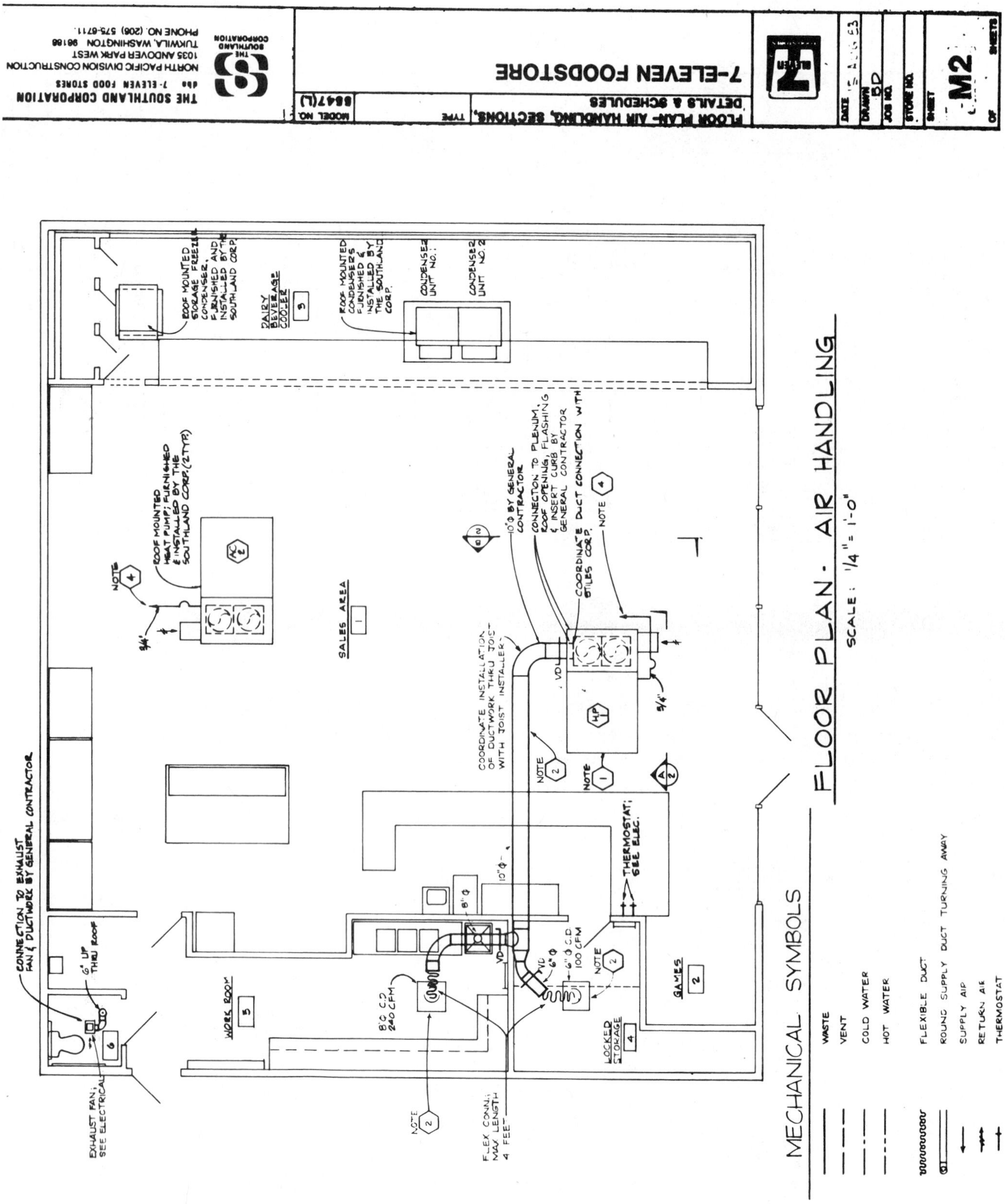

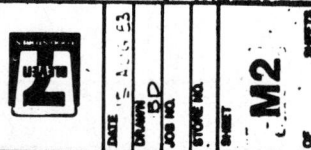

Figure 49–16 A mechanical plan is drawn to show the heating and air-conditioning requirements. *Courtesy The Southland Corporation.*

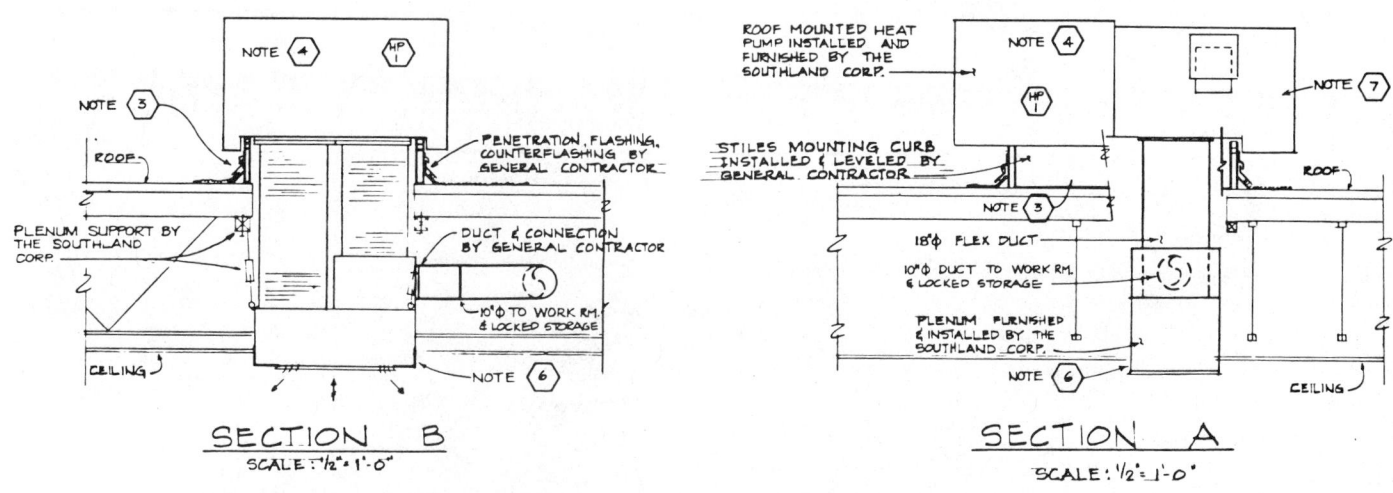

Figure 49–17 Details are required to show how HVAC equipment is to be installed. *Courtesy The Southland Corporation.*

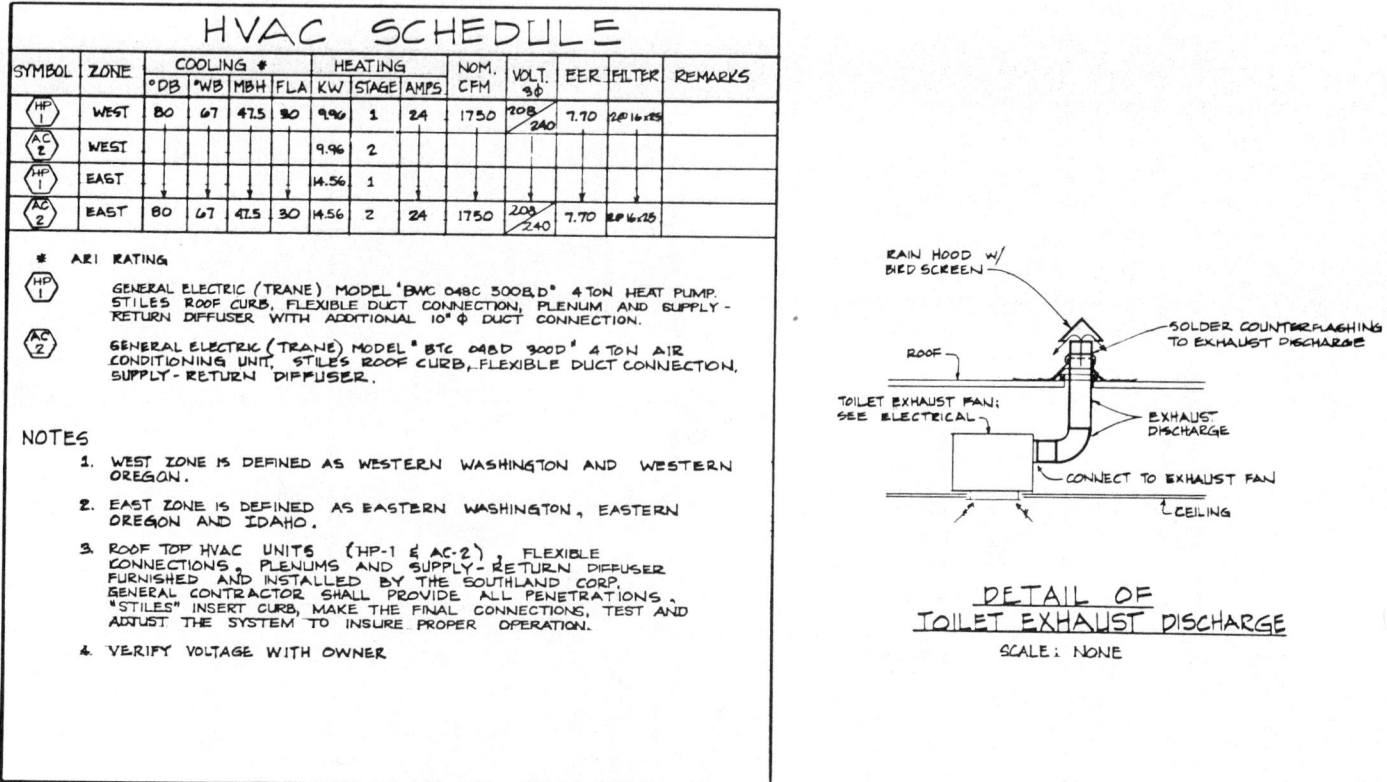

HVAC SCHEDULE

SYMBOL	ZONE	COOLING *				HEATING			NOM. CFM	VOLT. 3∅	EER	FILTER	REMARKS
		°DB	°WB	MBH	FLA	KW	STAGE	AMPS					
HP 1	WEST	80	67	47.5	30	9.96	1	24	1750	208/240	7.70	2∅ 16x25	
AC 2	WEST					9.96	2						
HP 1	EAST					14.56	1						
AC 2	EAST	80	67	47.5	30	14.56	2	24	1750	208/240	7.70	2∅ 16x25	

*   ARI RATING

HP 1   GENERAL ELECTRIC (TRANE) MODEL "BWC 048C 500B,D" 4 TON HEAT PUMP. STILES ROOF CURB, FLEXIBLE DUCT CONNECTION, PLENUM AND SUPPLY-RETURN DIFFUSER WITH ADDITIONAL 10"∅ DUCT CONNECTION.

AC 2   GENERAL ELECTRIC (TRANE) MODEL "BTC 048D 300D" 4 TON AIR CONDITIONING UNIT. STILES ROOF CURB, FLEXIBLE DUCT CONNECTION, SUPPLY-RETURN DIFFUSER.

NOTES

1. WEST ZONE IS DEFINED AS WESTERN WASHINGTON AND WESTERN OREGON.

2. EAST ZONE IS DEFINED AS EASTERN WASHINGTON, EASTERN OREGON AND IDAHO.

3. ROOF TOP HVAC UNITS (HP-1 & AC-2), FLEXIBLE CONNECTIONS, PLENUMS AND SUPPLY-RETURN DIFFUSER FURNISHED AND INSTALLED BY THE SOUTHLAND CORP. GENERAL CONTRACTOR SHALL PROVIDE ALL PENETRATIONS, "STILES" INSERT CURB, MAKE THE FINAL CONNECTIONS, TEST AND ADJUST THE SYSTEM TO INSURE PROPER OPERATION.

4. VERIFY VOLTAGE WITH OWNER

DETAIL OF TOILET EXHAUST DISCHARGE
SCALE: NONE

Figure 49–18 The drafter typically will have to letter schedules required to supplement the HVAC plan. *Courtesy The Southland Corporation.*

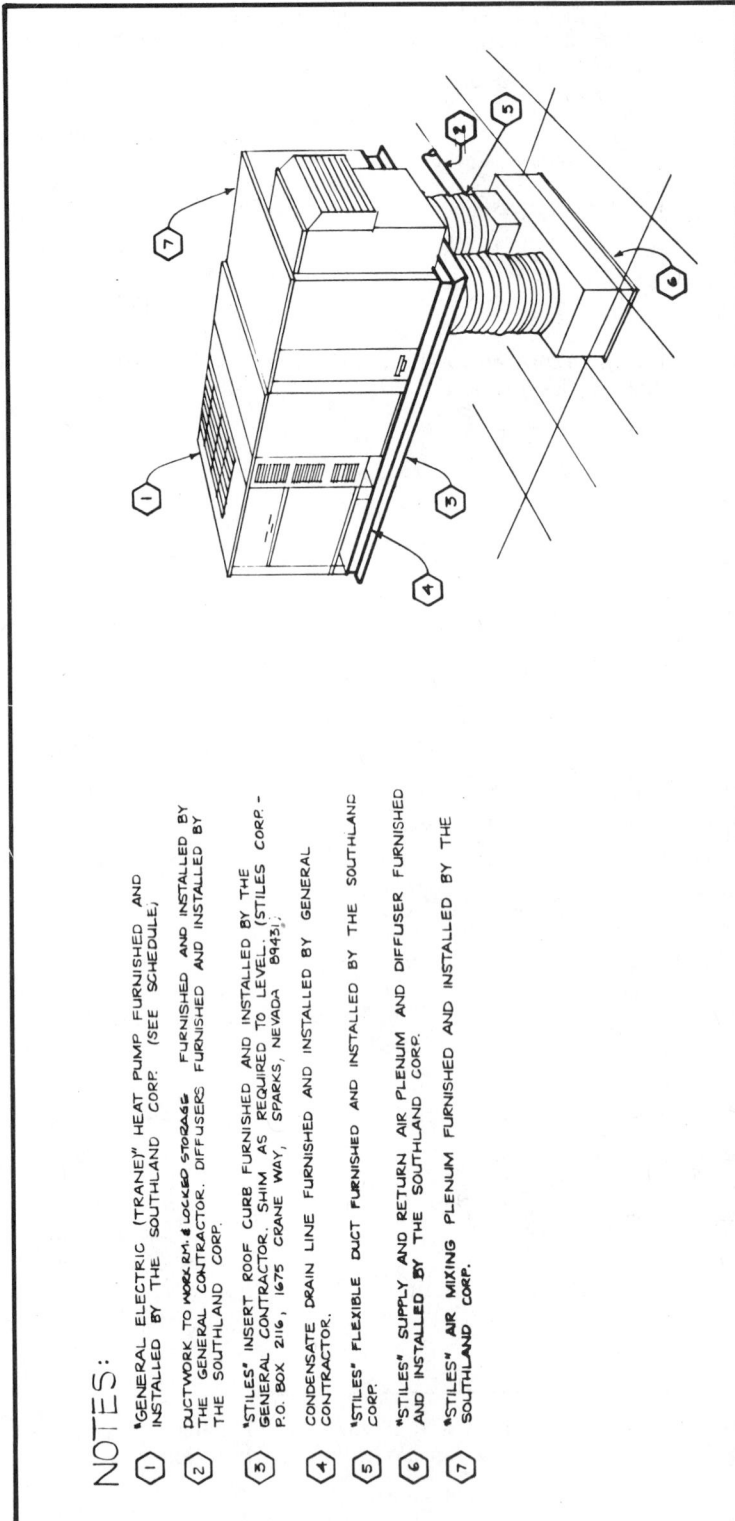

NOTES:

1. "GENERAL ELECTRIC ("TRANE") HEAT PUMP FURNISHED AND INSTALLED BY THE SOUTHLAND CORP. (SEE SCHEDULE,

2. DUCTWORK TO MODEL RM. & LOCKED STORAGE FURNISHED AND INSTALLED BY THE GENERAL CONTRACTOR. DIFFUSERS FURNISHED AND INSTALLED BY THE SOUTHLAND CORP.

3. "STILES" INSERT ROOF CURB FURNISHED AND INSTALLED BY THE GENERAL CONTRACTOR. SHIM AS REQUIRED TO LEVEL. (STILES CORP. - P.O. BOX 2116, 1675 CRANE WAY, SPARKS, NEVADA 89431).

4. CONDENSATE DRAIN LINE FURNISHED AND INSTALLED BY GENERAL CONTRACTOR.

5. "STILES" FLEXIBLE DUCT FURNISHED AND INSTALLED BY THE SOUTHLAND CORP.

6. "STILES" SUPPLY AND RETURN AIR PLENUM AND DIFFUSER FURNISHED AND INSTALLED BY THE SOUTHLAND CORP.

7. "STILES" AIR MIXING PLENUM FURNISHED AND INSTALLED BY THE SOUTHLAND CORP.

Figure 49-19 HVAC details and notes. Courtesy The Southland Corporation.

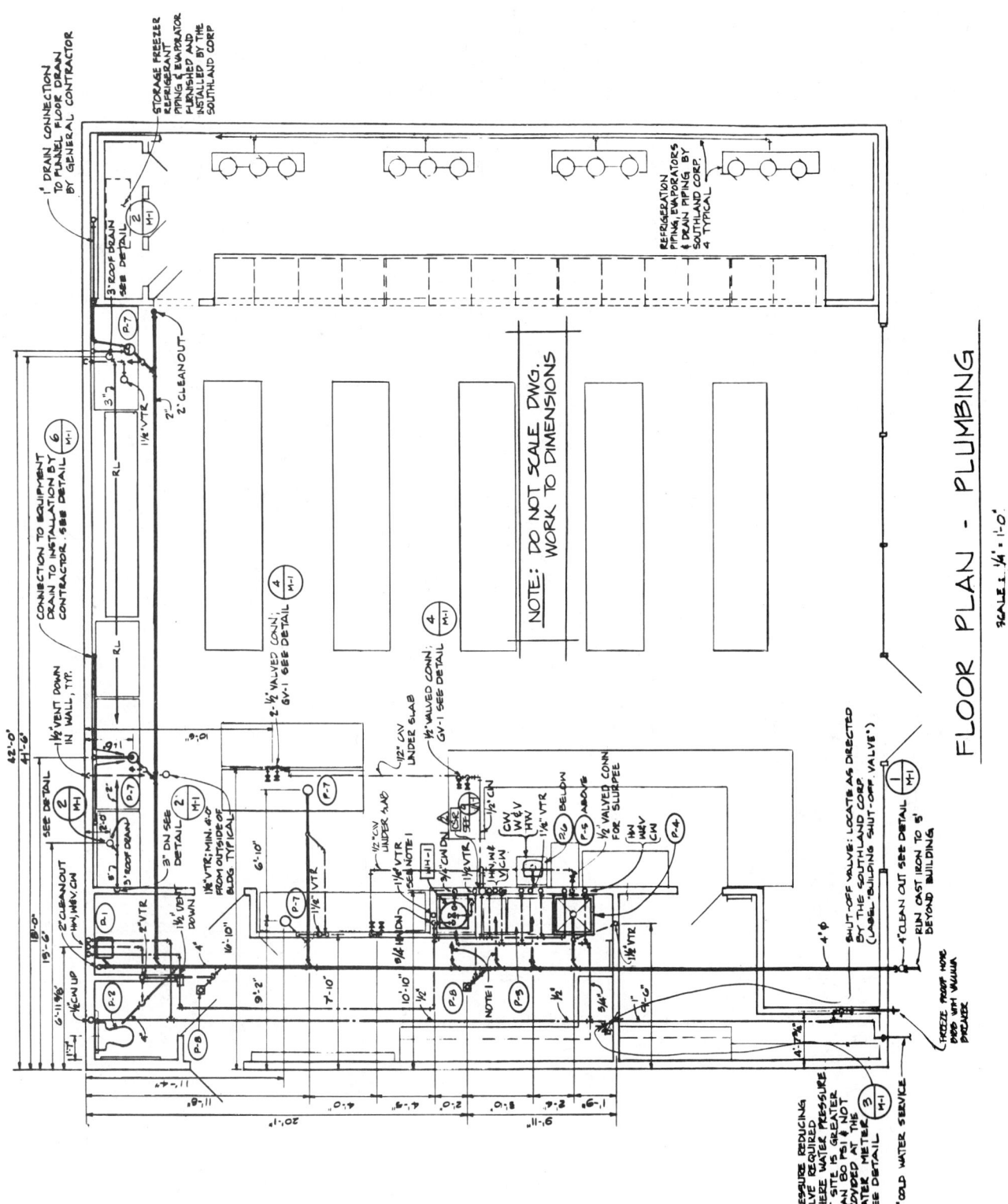

FLOOR PLAN - PLUMBING

SCALE: 1/4" = 1'-0"

NOTE: DO NOT SCALE DWG.
WORK TO DIMENSIONS

Figure 49-20 Required plumbing information is usually shown on an overlay of the floor plan. Courtesy The Southland Corporation.

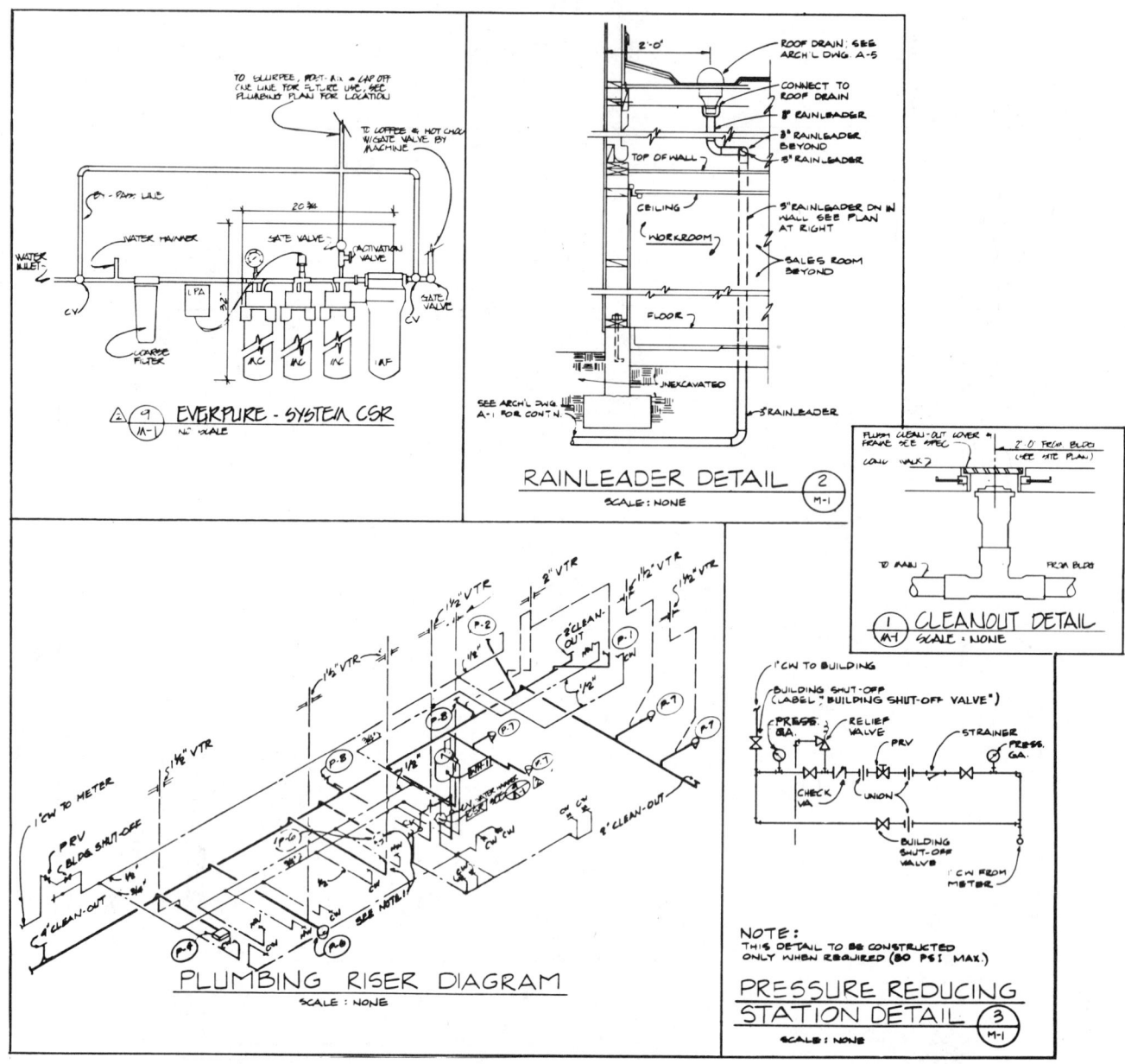

Figure 49–21 Details and schematic plumbing drawings. *Courtesy The Southland Corporation.*

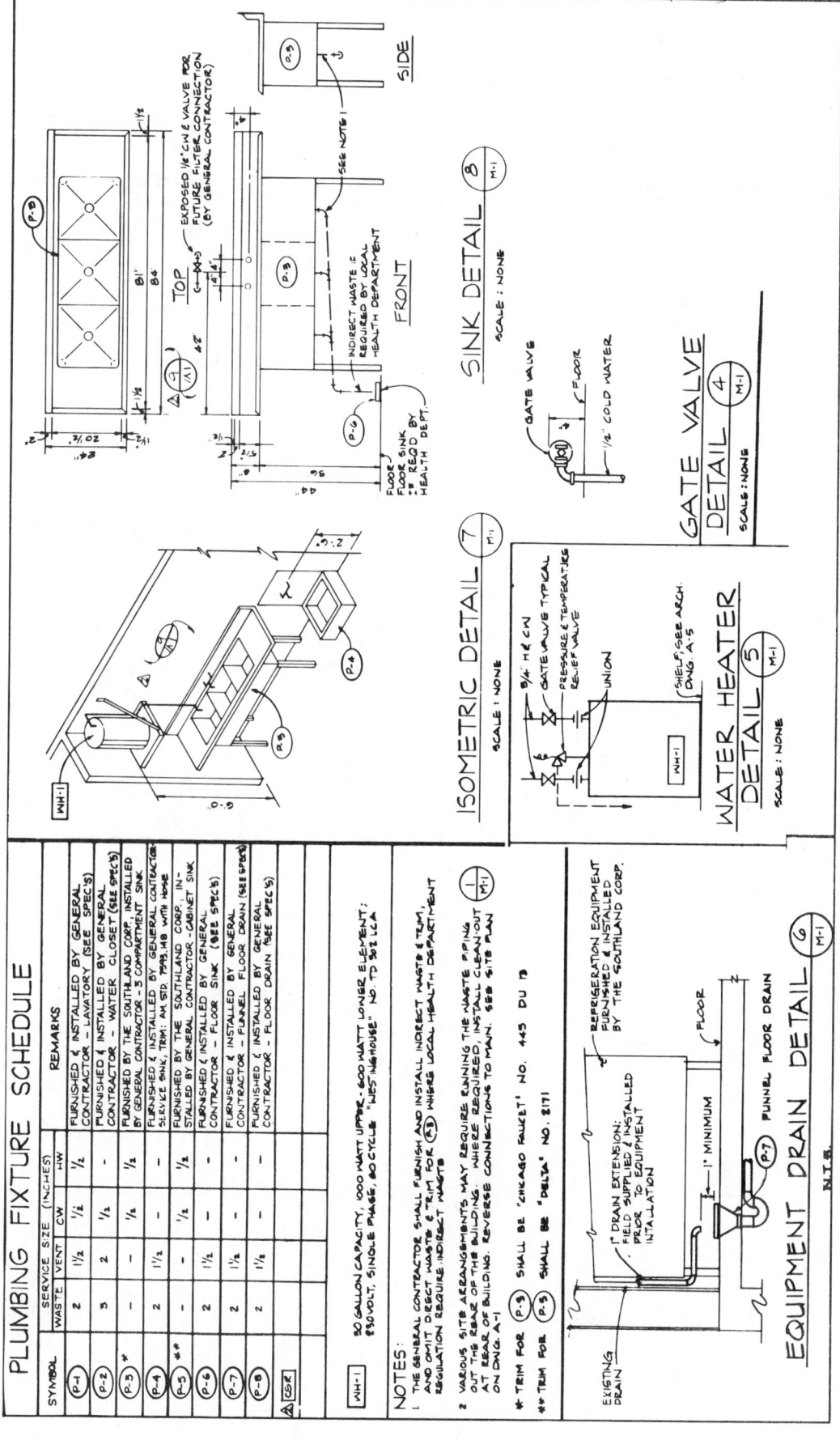

Figure 49-22 Notes, details, and schematic plumbing drawing. *Courtesy The Southland Corporation.*

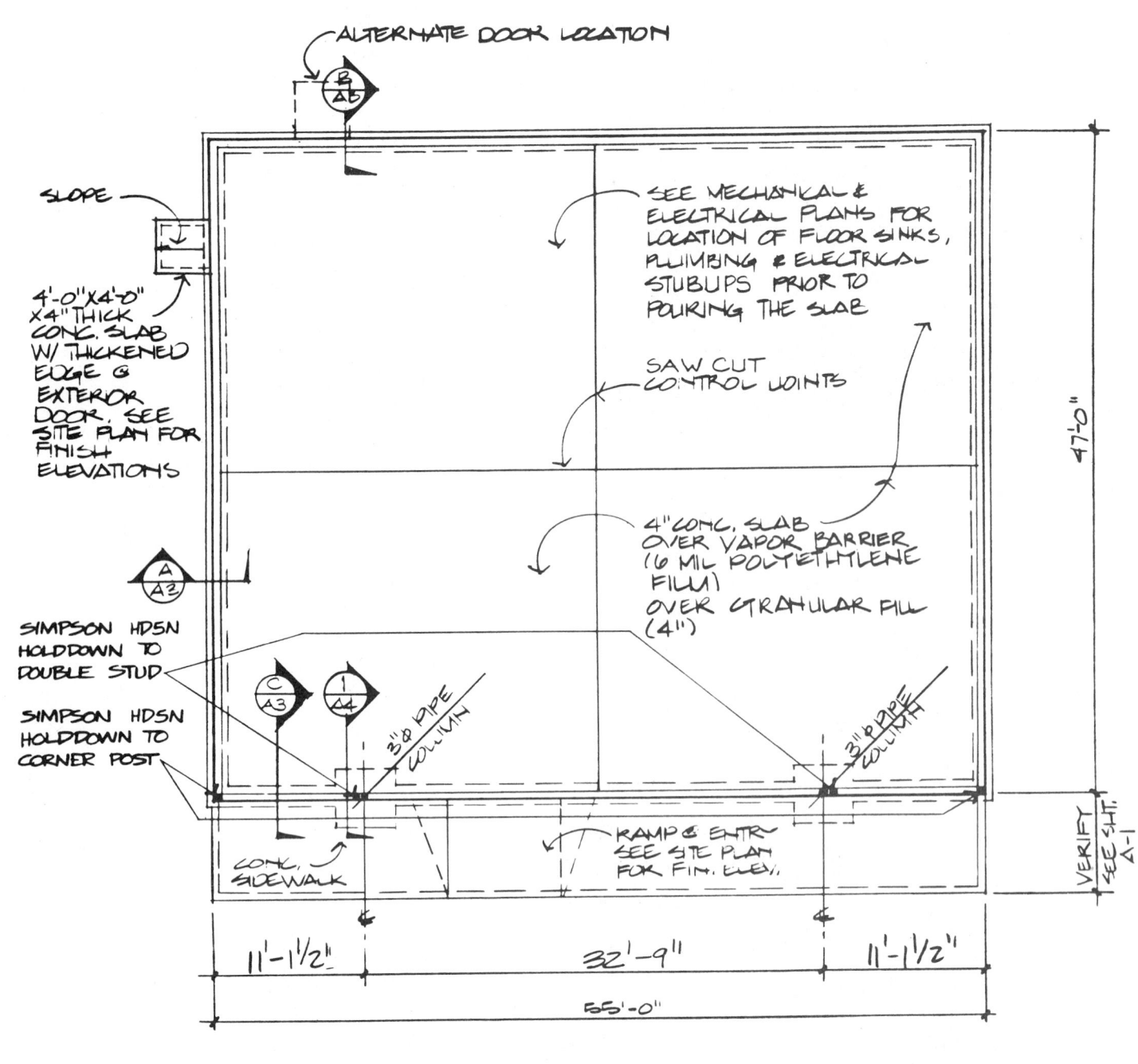

ALTERNATE DOOR LOCATION

SLOPE

4'-0"X4'-0" X4" THICK CONC. SLAB W/ THICKENED EDGE @ EXTERIOR DOOR, SEE SITE PLAN FOR FINISH ELEVATIONS

SEE MECHANICAL & ELECTRICAL PLANS FOR LOCATION OF FLOOR SINKS, PLUMBING & ELECTRICAL STUBUPS PRIOR TO POURING THE SLAB

SAW CUT CONTROL JOINTS

4" CONC. SLAB OVER VAPOR BARRIER (6 MIL POLYETHYLENE FILM) OVER GRANULAR FILL (4")

SIMPSON HD5N HOLDDOWN TO DOUBLE STUD

SIMPSON HD5N HOLDDOWN TO CORNER POST

3"Ø PIPE COLUMN

3"Ø PIPE COLUMN

CONC. SIDEWALK

RAMP & ENTRY SEE SITE PLAN FOR FIN. ELEV.

47'-0"

VERIFY SEE SHT. A-1

11'-1 1/2"   32'-9"   11'-1 1/2"

55'-0"

FOUNDATION PLAN

Figure 49-23 A concrete slab foundation is typically used for commercial structures. *Courtesy The Southland Corporation.*

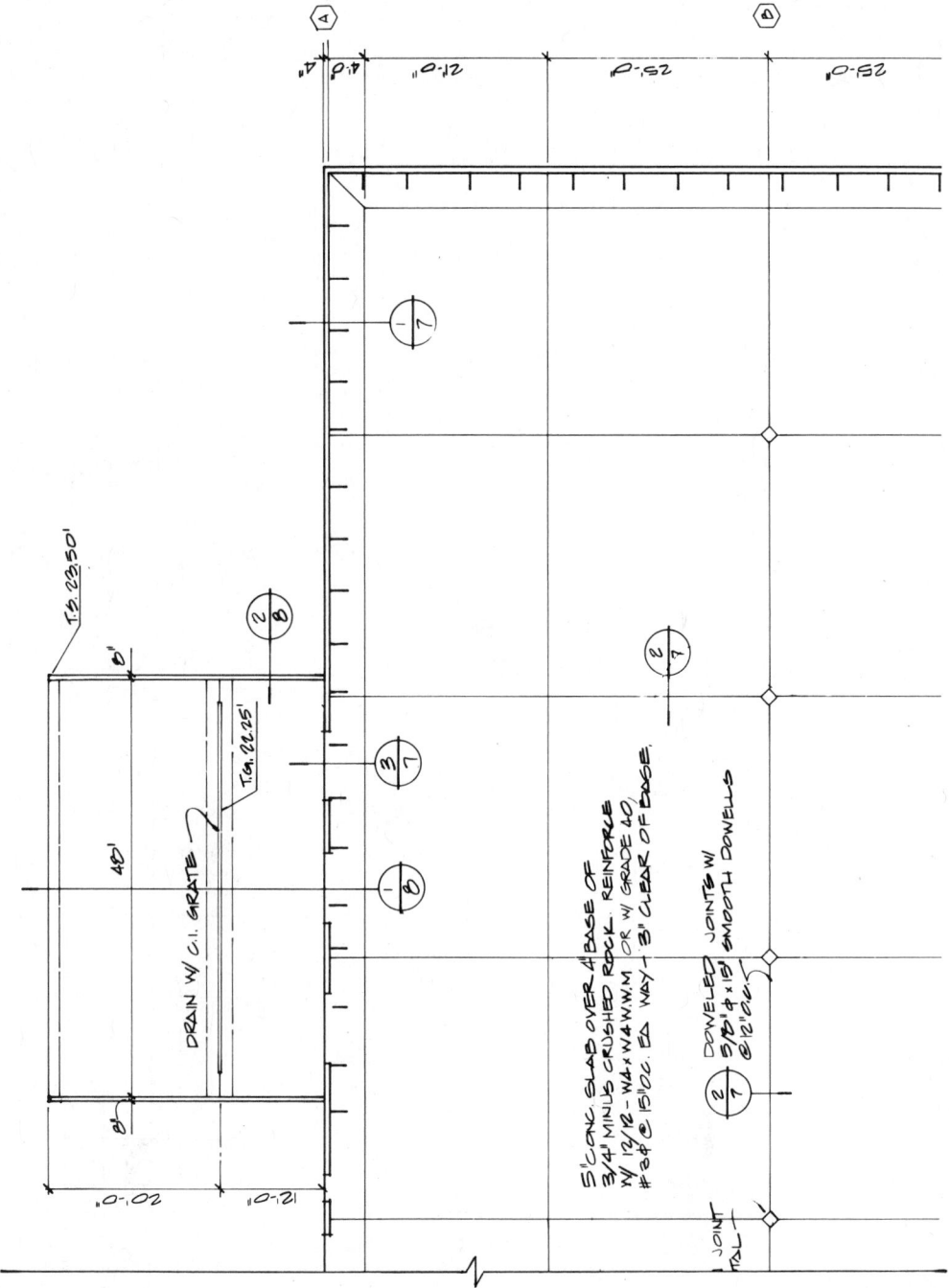

Figure 49-24 A slab-on-grade plan shows the size and location of all concrete pours. *Courtesy Structureform Masters, Inc.*

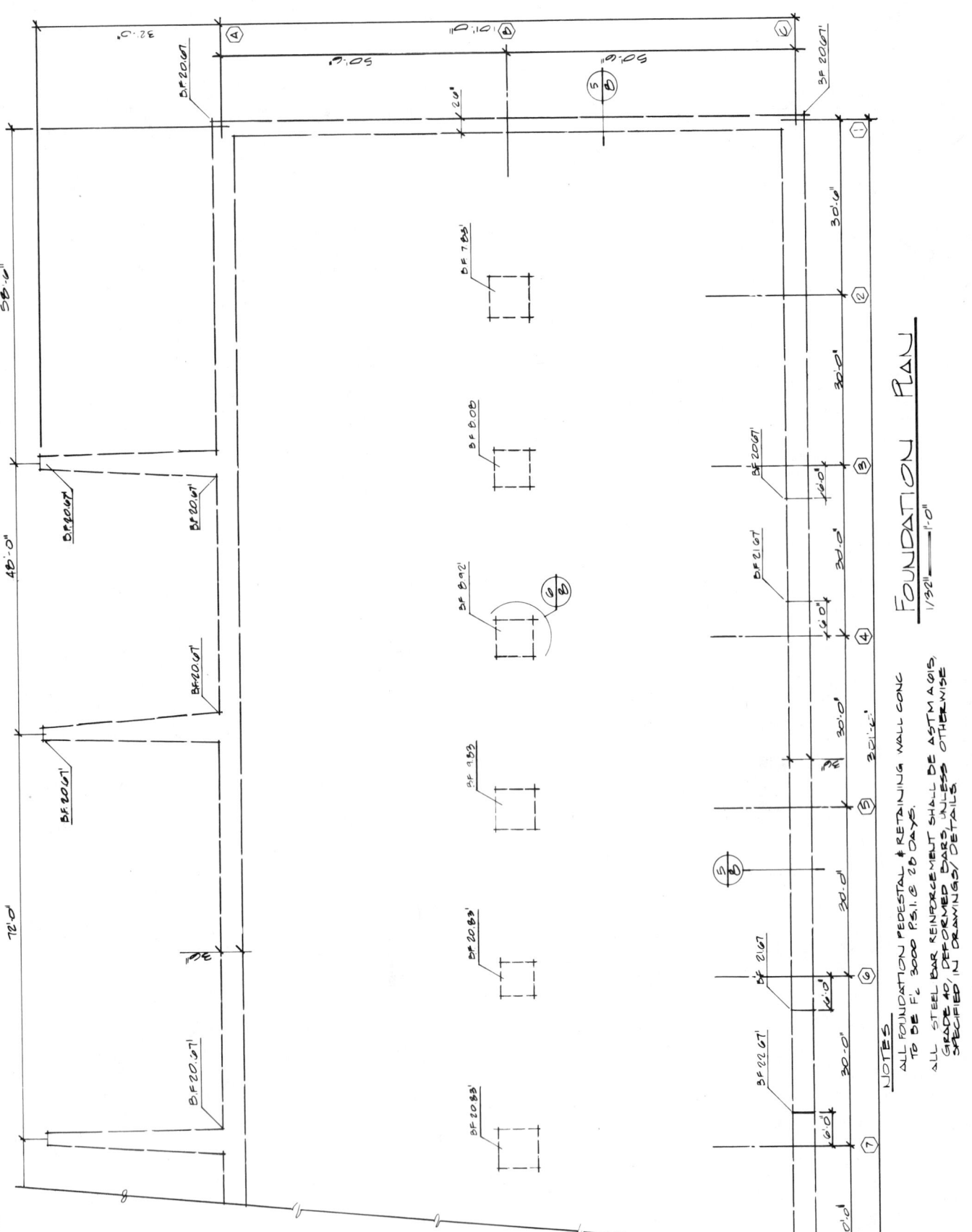

Figure 49–25 A foundation plan is used to show below-grade concrete work. Courtesy Structureform Masters, Inc.

Elevations

Elevations for commercial projects are very similar to the elevations required for a residential project. Figure 49–26 shows an example of an elevation for a restaurant. Notice that the elevation is used to show the same types of information as a residential elevation, but uses much more detail. Because the size of many commercial structures is so large, commercial projects are sometimes drawn at a scale of ⅛″ = 1′–0″ or smaller and have very little detail added as in Figure 49–27.

Sections

The drawing of sections for commercial projects is similar to residential projects, but the sections often have a different use in commercial projects. In residential projects, sections are used to show major types of construction. This use is also made of sections on commercial plans, but the sections are used primarily as a reference map of the structure. Sections are usually drawn at a scale of ¼″ = 1′–0″ or smaller and details of specific intersections are referenced to the sections. Figure 49–28 shows an example of this

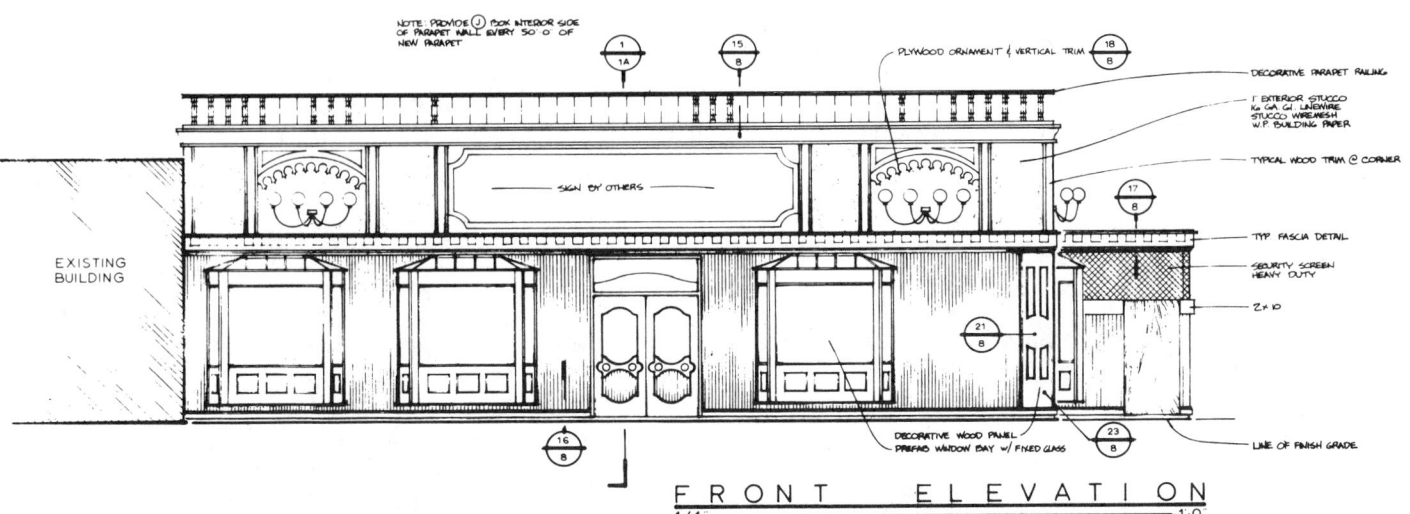

Figure 49–26 Elevations for commercial projects are similar to the elevations for residential projects. Exterior materials must be shown, as seen in this drawing for Farrell's. *Courtesy Structureform Masters, Inc.*

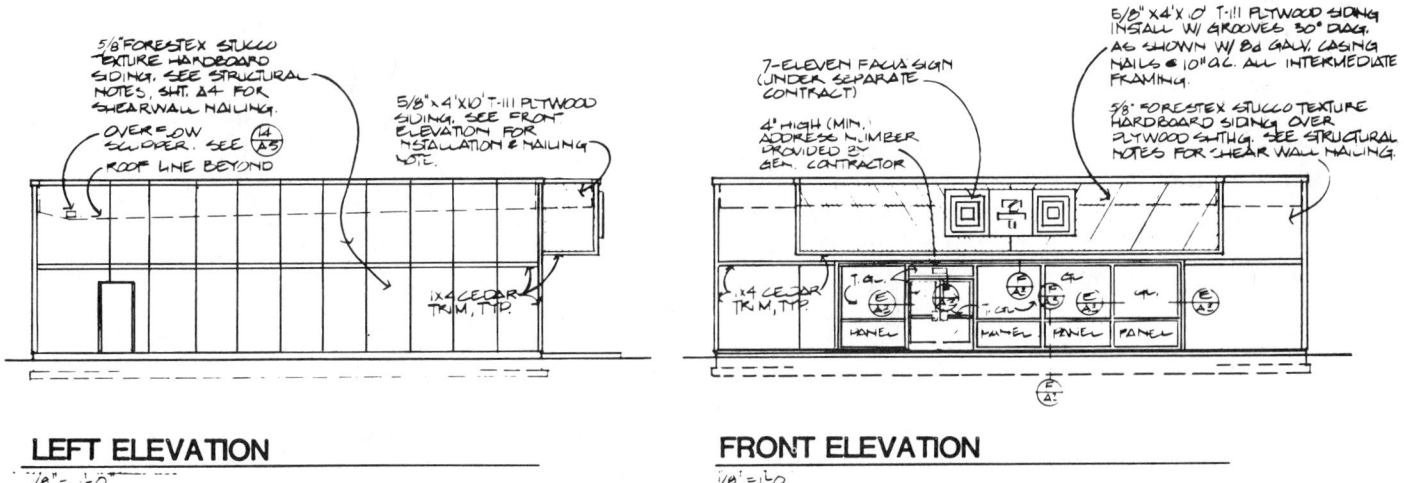

Figure 49–27 Elevations for commercial projects often require very little detail to be shown and can be drawn at a small scale. *Courtesy The Southland Corporation.*

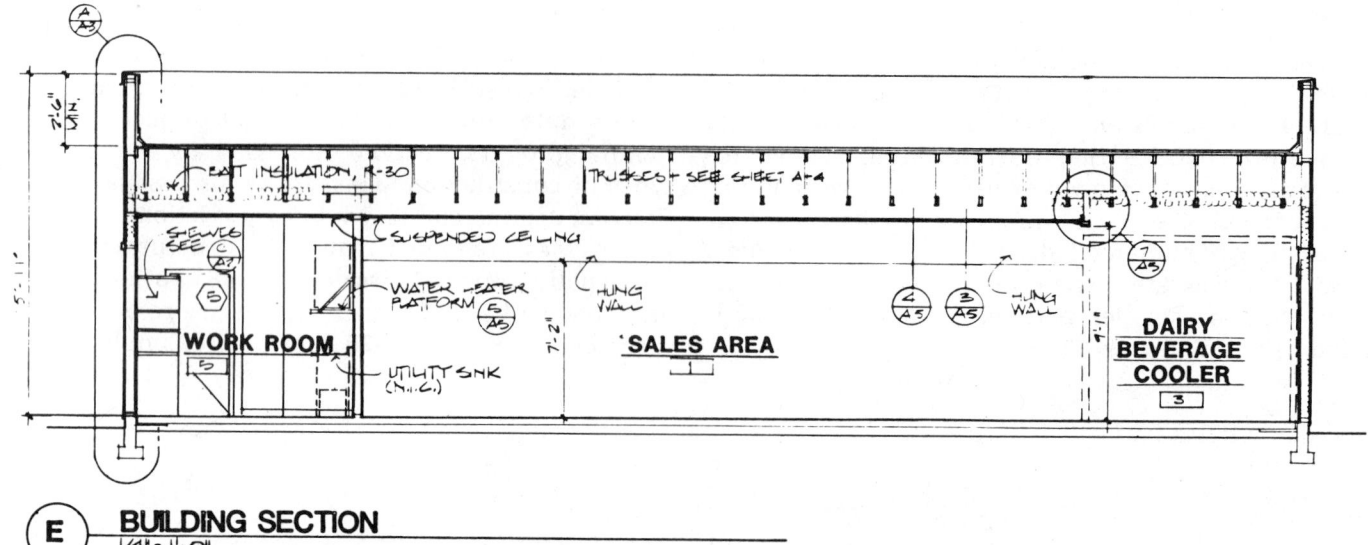

WORK ROOM

SALES AREA

DAIRY BEVERAGE COOLER

E   BUILDING SECTION
1/4" = 1'-0"

Figure 49-28 Sections for commercial projects are often drawn at a small scale to show major types of construction. Specific information is usually shown in details. *Courtesy The Southland Corporation.*

type of section. Another common method of drawing sections is to draw several partial sections as seen in Figure 49-29.

Details

On a residential plan you may draw details of a few special connections or of stock items such as fireplaces or footings. In commercial projects, drawing details is one of the primary jobs of the drafter. Because there are so many variables in construction techniques and materials, details are used to explain a specific area of construction. Figures 49-30 and 49-31 show some of the details that were required for the 7-ELEVEN store.

Roof Plans

Roof plans and roof drainage plans are typically used more in commercial projects than in residential work. Because the roof system is usually flat and contains concentrated loads from mechanical equipment, a detailed placement of beams and interior supports is usually required. Two of the most com-

mon types of roof systems used on commercial projects are the truss and the panelized systems. The use of trusses was discussed in Chapter 27. A panelized roof consists of large beams supporting smaller beams which in turn support 4×8 roofing panels. The system will be further discussed in Chapter 51. The roof plan can be seen in Figure 49-32 and the roof framing plan can be seen in Figure 49-33.

Interior Elevations

The kind of interior elevations drawn for a commercial project will depend on the type of project to be drawn. In an office or warehouse building, cabinets will be minimal and usually not drawn. For the office setting, an interior decorator may be used to coordinate and design interior spaces. On projects such as a restaurant, the drafter probably will be required to work closely with the supplier of the kitchen equipment to design an area that will suit both the users and the equipment. This requires coordinating the floor plan with the interior elevations. Figure 49-34 shows an example of an interior elevation detail for a restaurant.

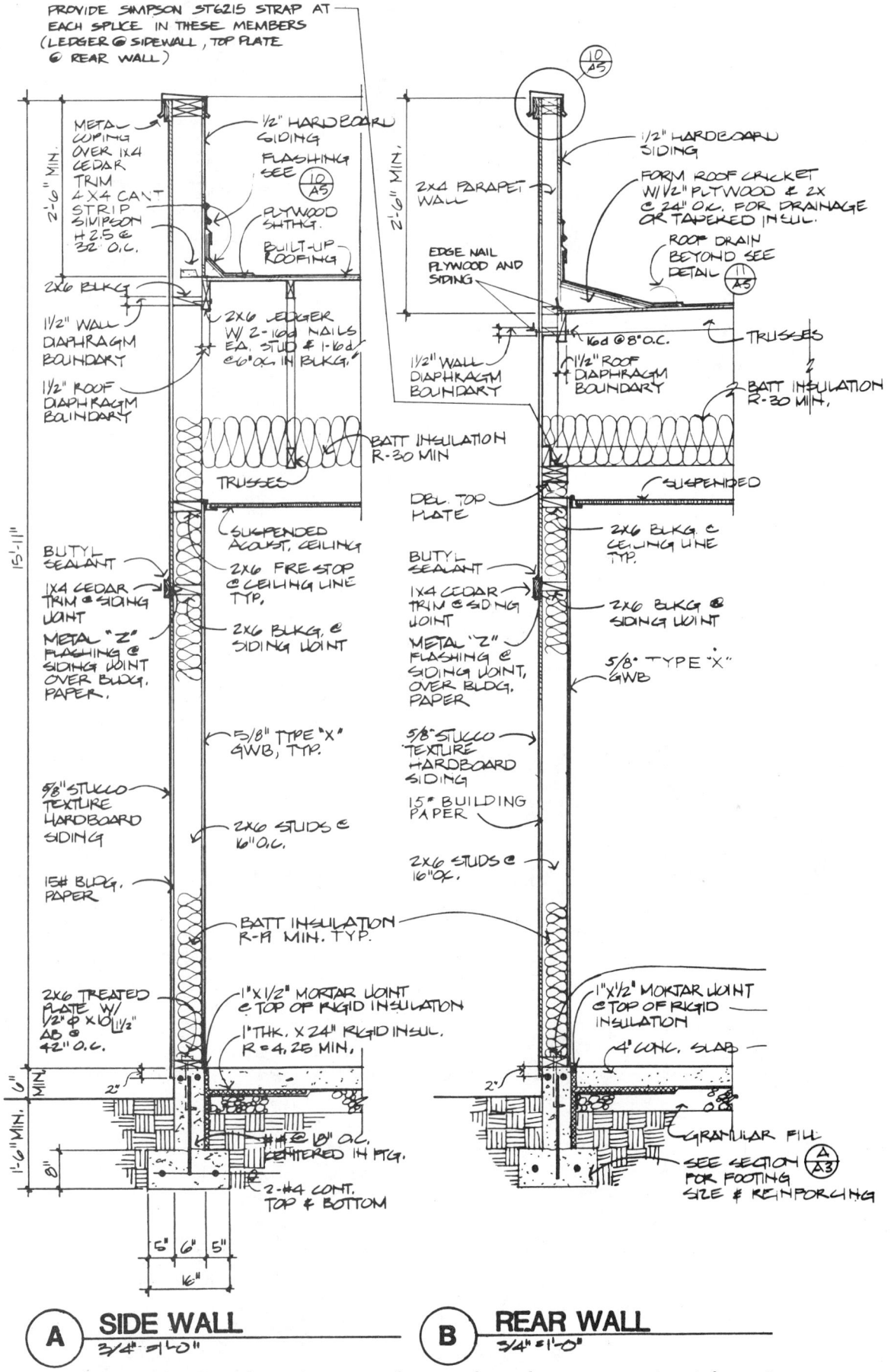

PROVIDE SIMPSON ST6215 STRAP AT
EACH SPLICE IN THESE MEMBERS
(LEDGER @ SIDEWALL, TOP PLATE
@ REAR WALL)

METAL COPING OVER 1x4 CEDAR TRIM
4 X 4 CANT STRIP SIMPSON +25 @ 32" O.C.

1/2" HARDBOARD SIDING

FLASHING SEE 10/A5

PLYWOOD SHTHG.

BUILT-UP ROOFING

2X6 BLKG.

1½" WALL DIAPHRAGM BOUNDARY

1½" ROOF DIAPHRAGM BOUNDARY

2X6 LEDGER W/ 2-16d NAILS EA. STUD & 1-16d @ 6" O.C. IN BLKG.

BATT INSULATION R-30 MIN

TRUSSES

BUTYL SEALANT

1X4 CEDAR TRIM @ SIDING JOINT

METAL "Z" FLASHING @ SIDING JOINT OVER BLDG. PAPER.

SUSPENDED ACOUST. CEILING

2X6 FIRE STOP @ CEILING LINE TYP.

2X6 BLKG. @ SIDING JOINT

5/8" TYPE "X" GWB, TYP.

5/8" STUCCO TEXTURE HARDBOARD SIDING

2X6 STUDS @ 16" O.C.

15# BLDG. PAPER

BATT INSULATION R-A MIN. TYP.

2X6 TREATED PLATE W/ ½" Ø X 10½" AB @ 42" O.C.

1" X ½" MORTAR JOINT @ TOP OF RIGID INSULATION

1" THK. X 24" RIGID INSUL. R=4.25 MIN.

6" MIN.

1'-6" MIN.

2"

8"

#4 @ 18" O.C. CENTERED IN FTG.

2 - #4 CONT. TOP & BOTTOM

5" 6" 5"
16"

15'-11"
2'-0" MIN.

2'-0" MIN.

10/A5

2X4 PARAPET WALL

1/2" HARDBOARD SIDING

FORM ROOF CRICKET W/ ½" PLYWOOD & 2X @ 24" O.C. FOR DRAINAGE OR TAPERED INSUL.

ROOF DRAIN BEYOND SEE DETAIL 11/A5

EDGE NAIL PLYWOOD AND SIDING

1½" WALL DIAPHRAGM BOUNDARY

16d @ 8" O.C.

1½" ROOF DIAPHRAGM BOUNDARY

TRUSSES

BATT INSULATION R-30 MIN.

DBL. TOP PLATE

SUSPENDED

2X6 BLKG. @ CEILING LINE TYP.

BUTYL SEALANT

1X4 CEDAR TRIM @ SIDING JOINT

METAL "Z" FLASHING @ SIDING JOINT, OVER BLDG. PAPER

2X6 BLKG @ SIDING JOINT

5/8" TYPE "X" GWB

5/8" STUCCO TEXTURE HARDBOARD SIDING

15# BUILDING PAPER

2X6 STUDS @ 16" O.C.

1" X ½" MORTAR JOINT @ TOP OF RIGID INSULATION

4" CONC. SLAB

2"

GRANULAR FILL

SEE SECTION A/A3 FOR FOOTING SIZE & REINFORCING

A **SIDE WALL**
3/4" = 1'-0"

B **REAR WALL**
3/4" = 1'-0"

Figure 49–29 Partial sections are often used to show construction information. *Courtesy The Southland Corporation.*

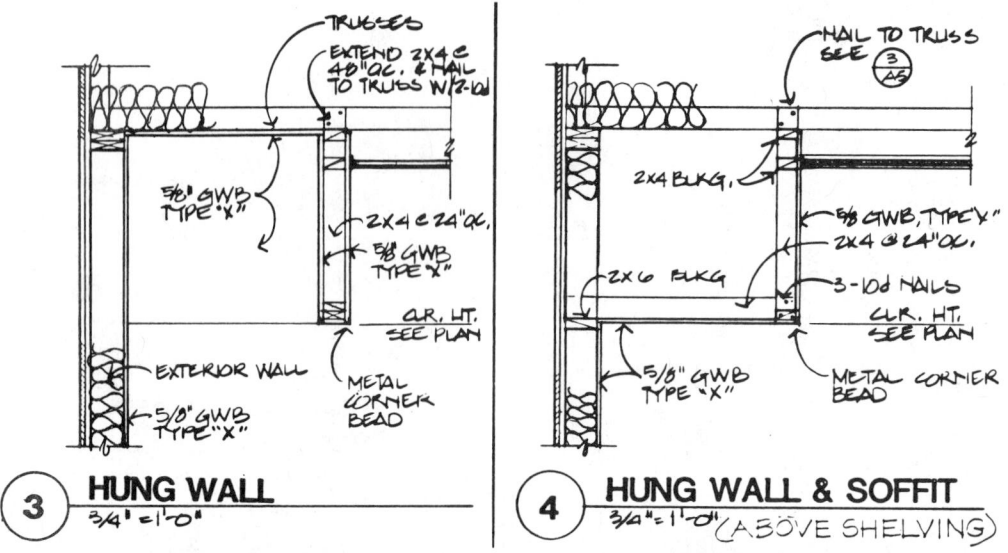

Figure 49–30 Drawing details is one of the most common jobs performed by drafters. *Courtesy The Southland Corporation.*

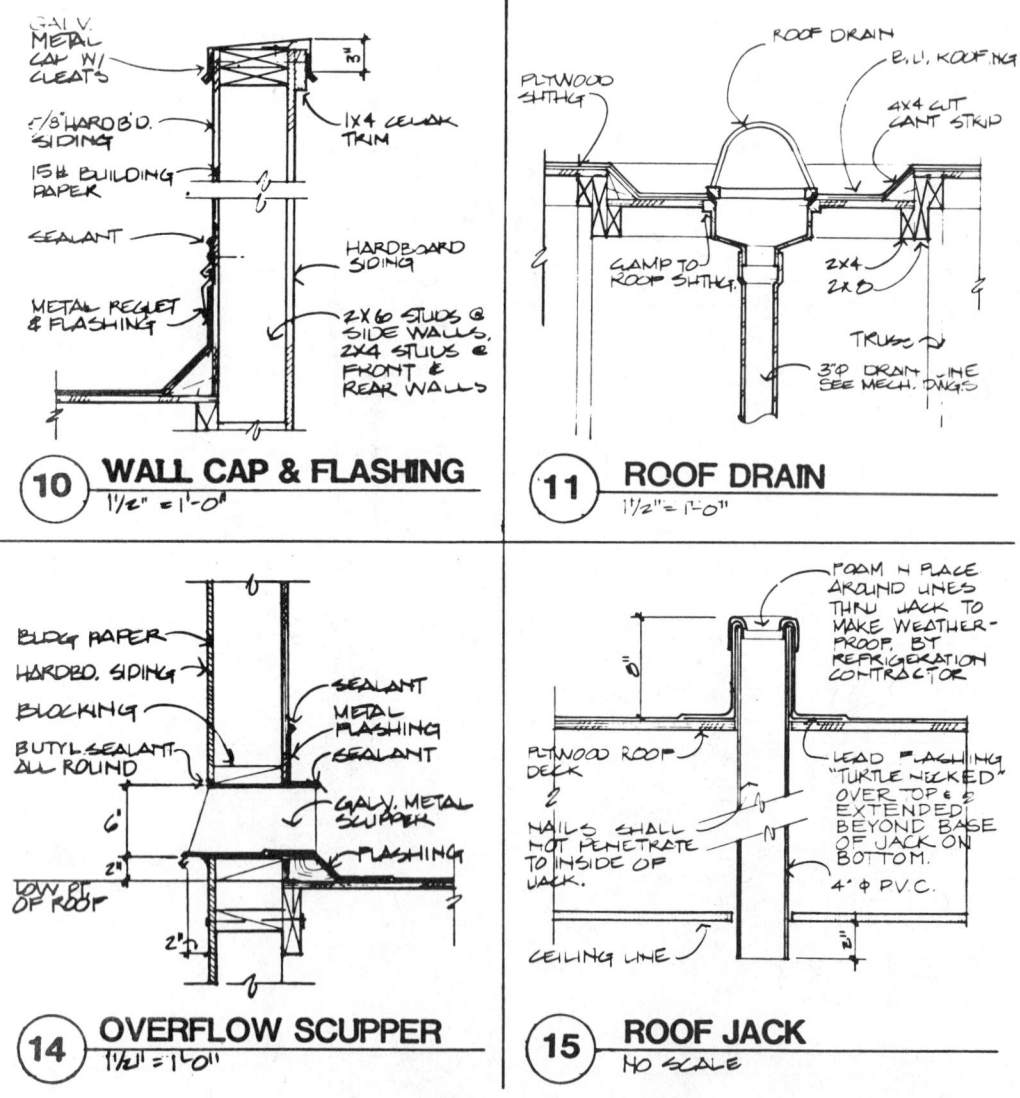

Figure 49–31 Details of roof construction. *Courtesy The Southland Corporation.*

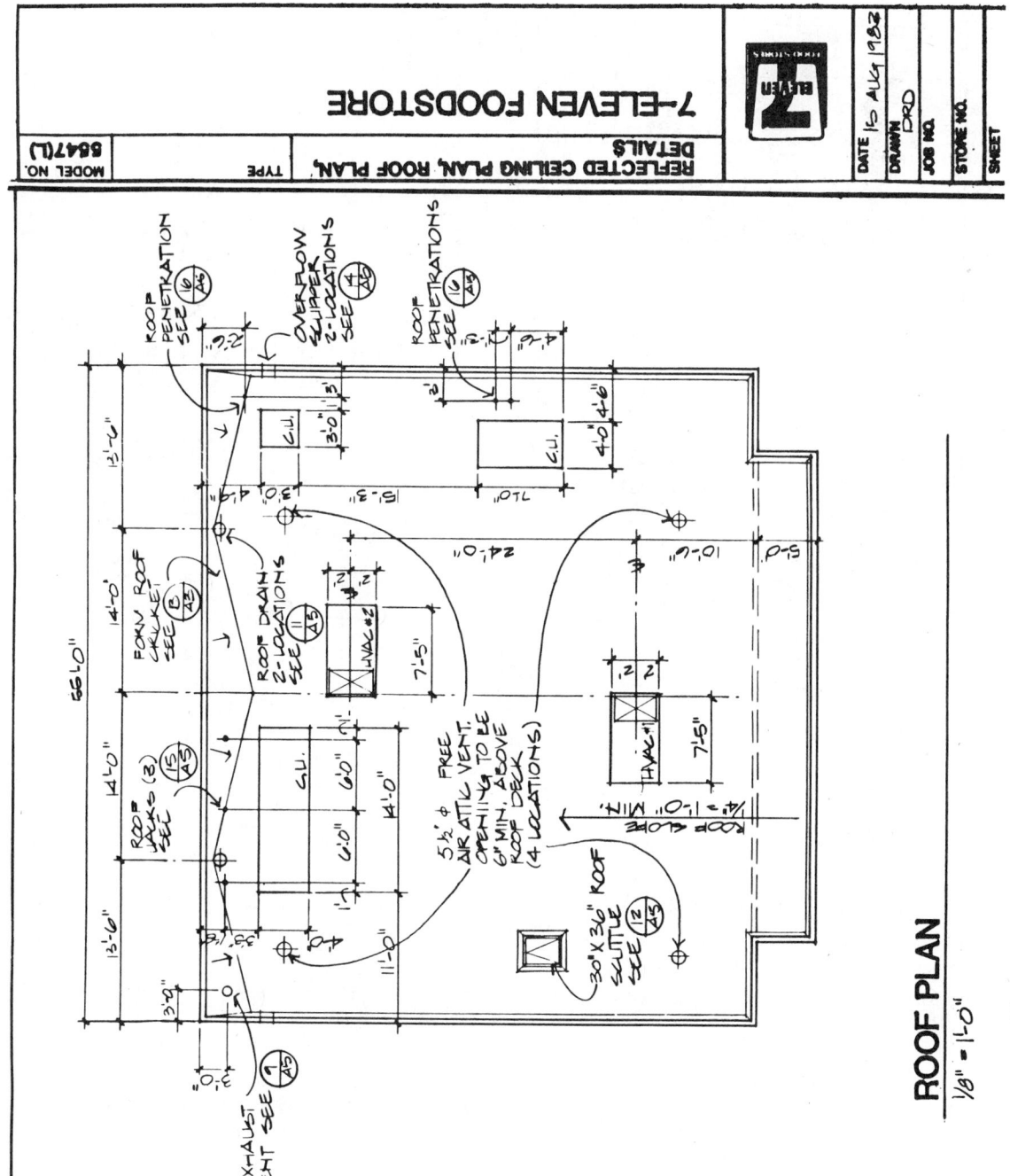

Figure 49-32 A roof plan is used to show construction components at the roof level. *Courtesy The Southland Corporation.*

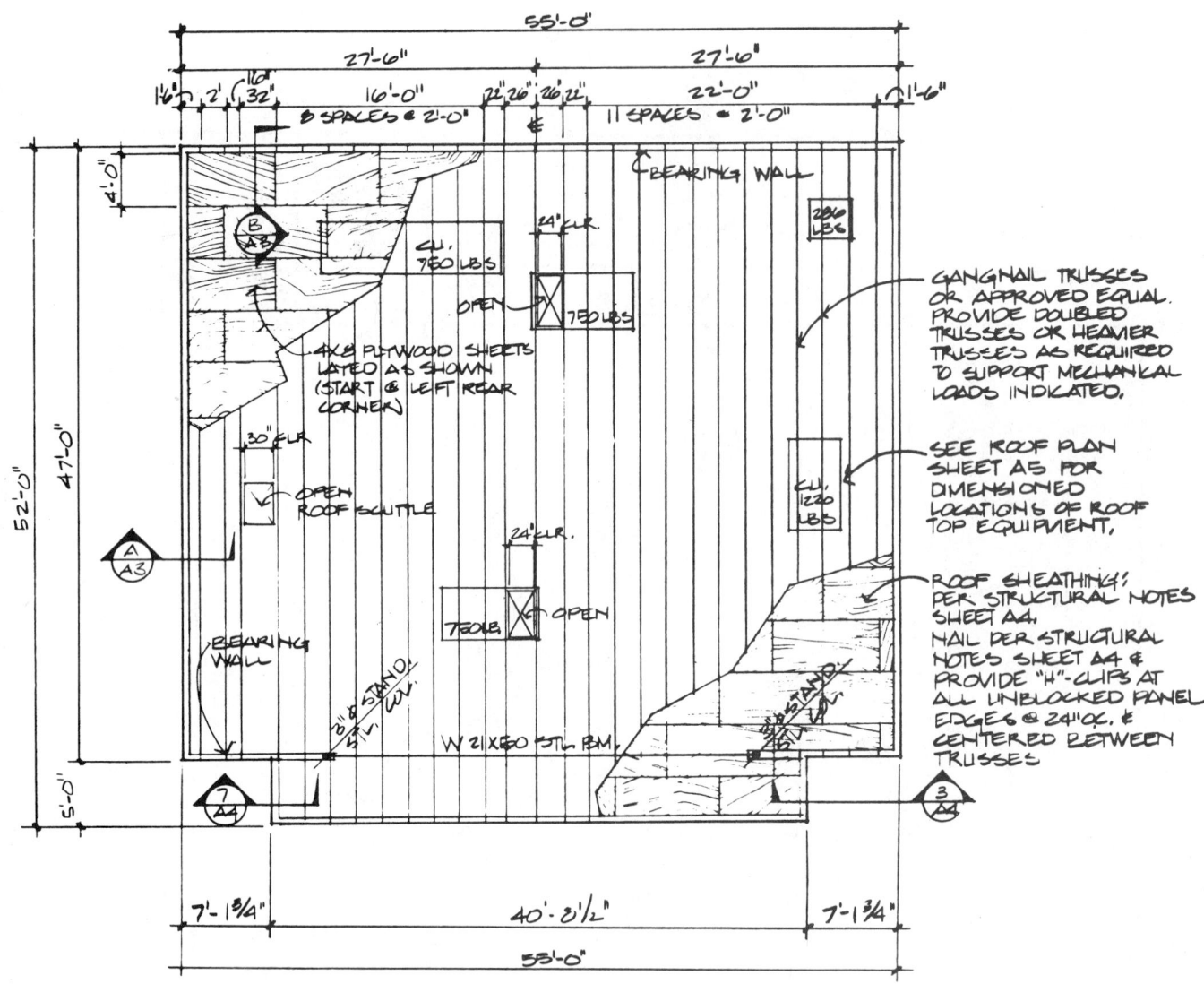

ROOF FRAMING PLAN
1/8" = 1'-0"

Figure 49–33 A roof framing plan is used to show structural components at the roof level. *Courtesy The Southland Corporation.*

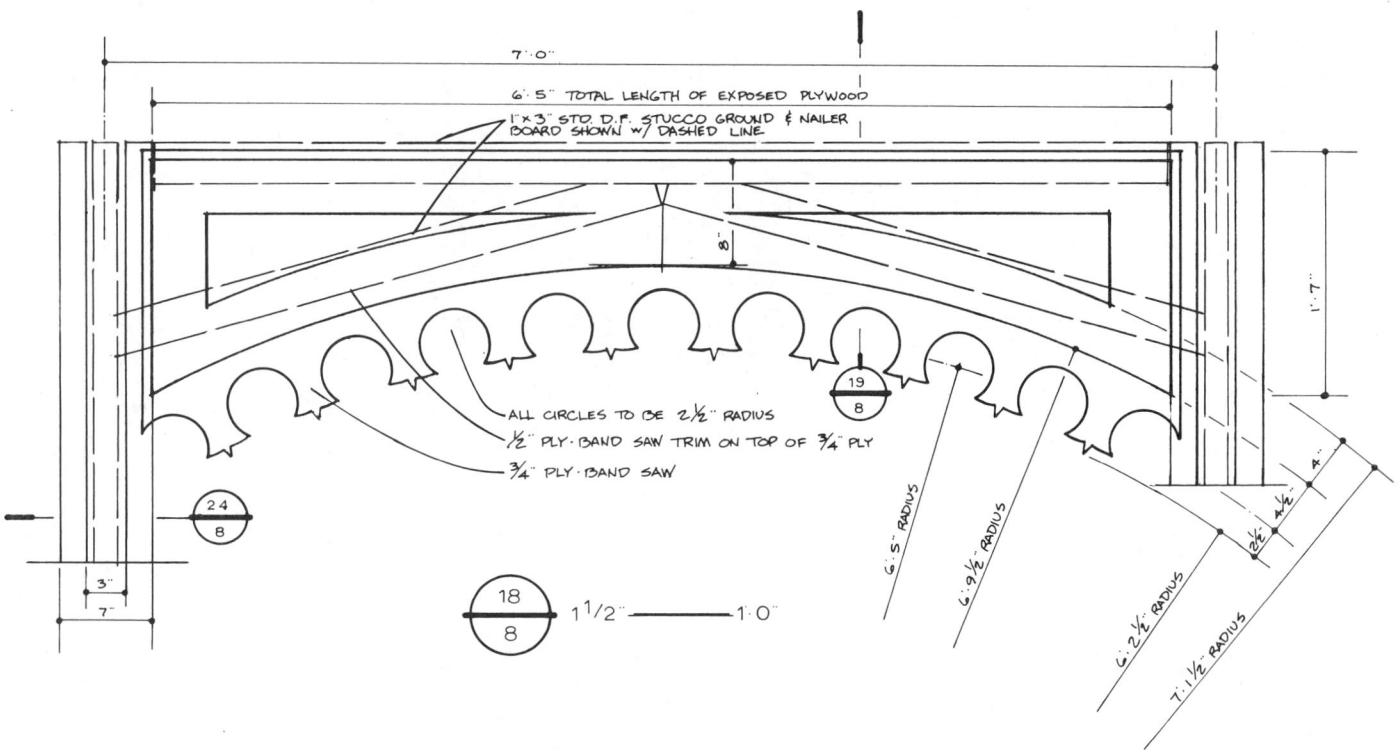

Figure 49–34 In addition to structural details, the drafter may be required to draw interior elevations and details, such as this trim detail for Farrell's. *Courtesy Structureform Masters, Inc.*

Plot Plans

The plot or site plan for a commercial project will resemble the plot plan for a residential project except for its size. One major difference is the need to plan and draw parking spaces, driveways, curbs, and walkways. In commercial projects, the plot plan is often drawn as part of the preliminary design study. Parking spaces are determined by the square footage of the building and the type of usage the building will receive. Parking requirements often dictate the layout of the floor plan. Figure 49–35 shows an example of a plot plan for an office building.

Grading Plan

Once basic information is placed on the plot plan to describe the structure a Mylar® print of the plan is usually given to a civil engineer or licensed surveyor so that a grading plan can be prepared. A drafter working for a civil engineer will then translate field notes into a grading plan as seen in Figure 49–36. Although titled a grading plan, the plan typically contains much more than just grading elevations. Drainage information is often placed on this plan as it relates to the structure, as well as walks and paving areas.

Landscape Plan

The size of the project will determine how the landscape plan is drawn. On a small project, a drafter may be given the job of drawing the landscape plan. When this is the case, the drafter must determine suitable plants for the area and the job site, and then specify the plants by their proper Latin name on the plan. On typical commercial projects, a Mylar® copy of the plot plan is given to a landscape architect who will specify the size, type, and location of plantings. A method of maintaining the plantings is also typically shown on the plan as seen in Figure 49–37.

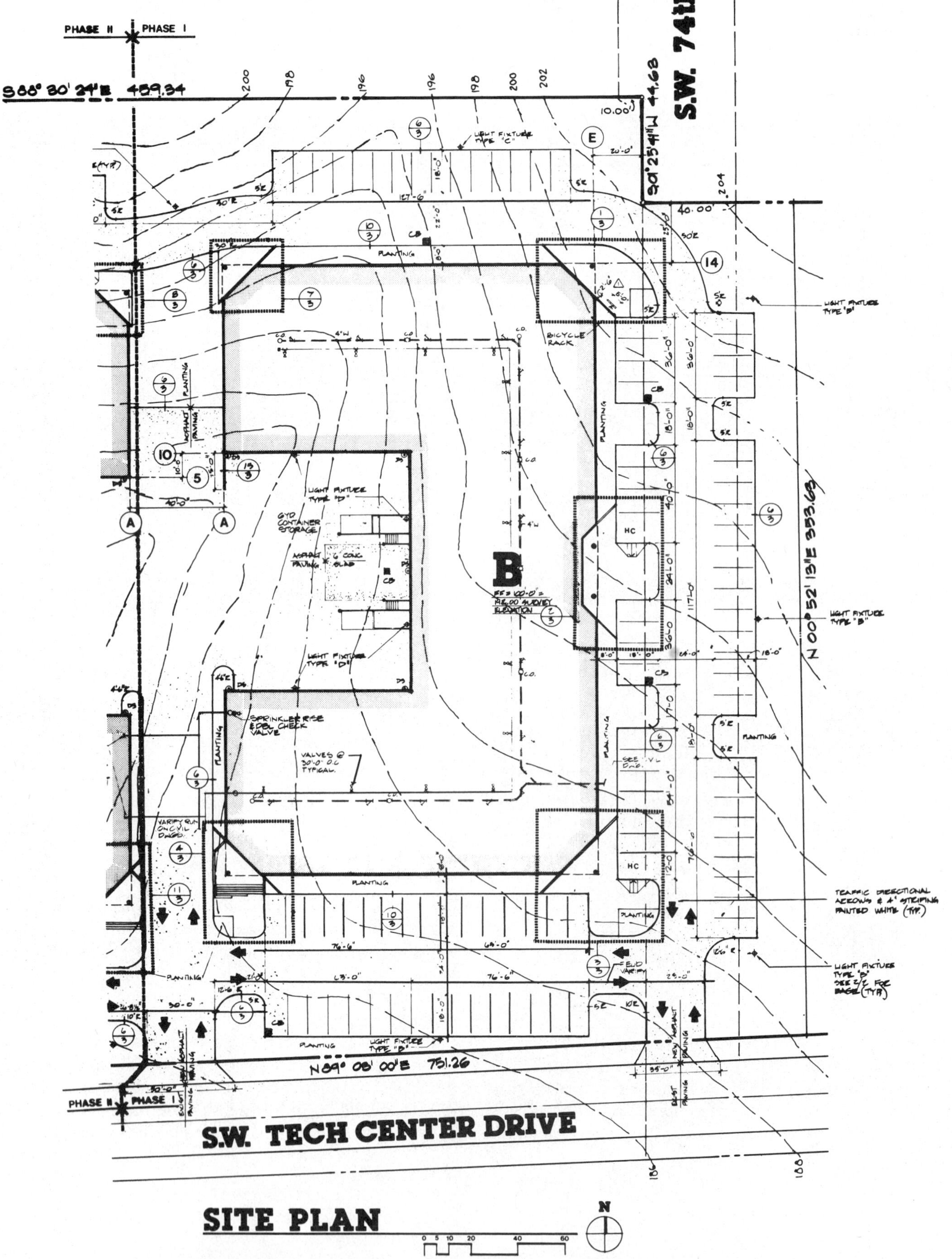

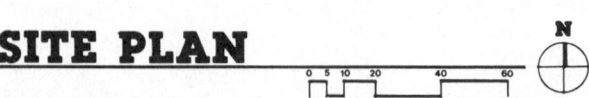

SITE PLAN

Figure 49–35 A plot, or site, plan for a commercial project is similar to a residential plan. Parking information is a major addition to a commercial plan. *Courtesy Guthrie, Slusarenko, and Leeb, Architects.*

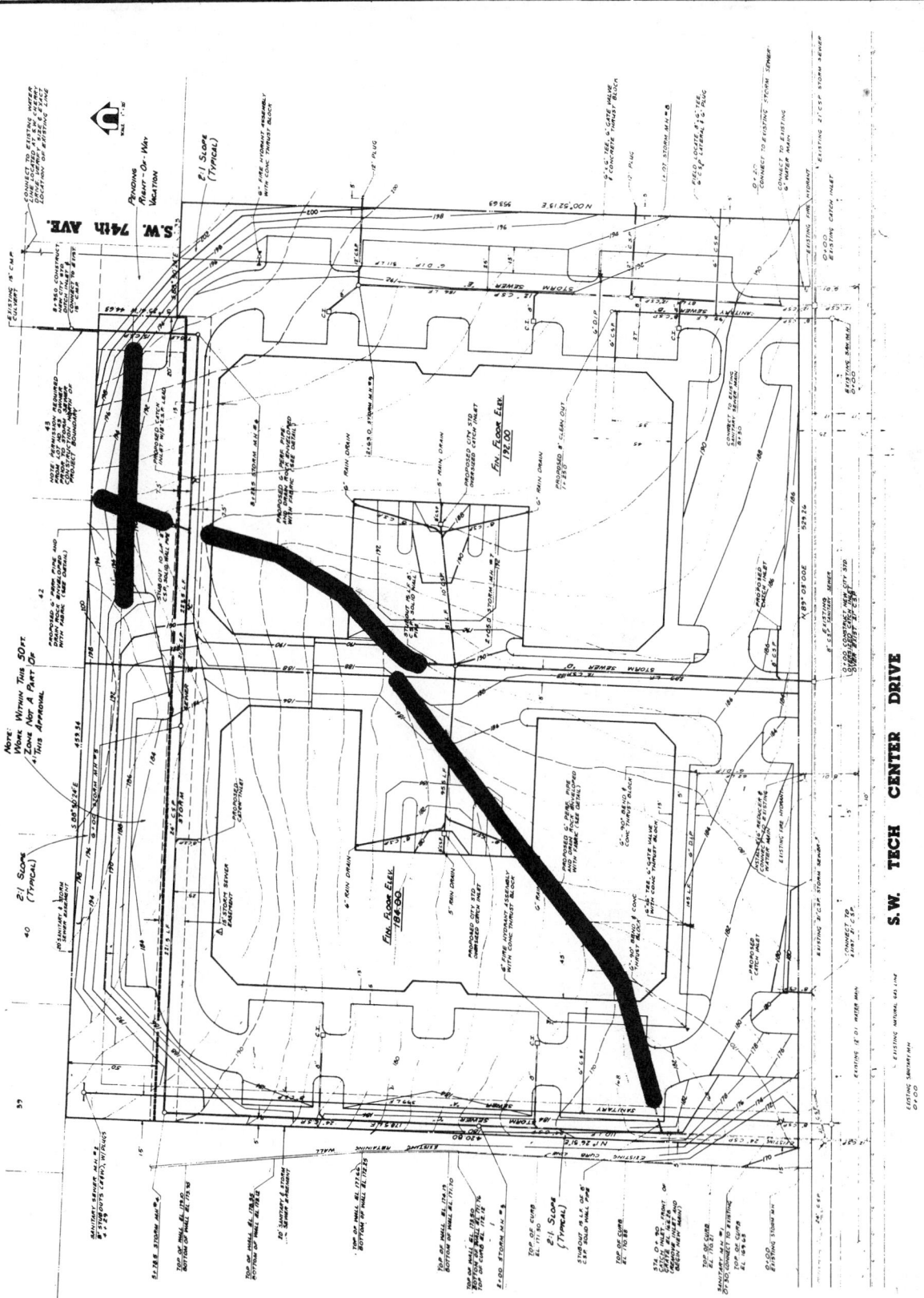

Figure 49-36 Grading information is often placed on an overlay of the plot plan to show cut and fill requirements of a job site. *Courtesy Guthrie, Slusarenko, and Leeb, Architects.*

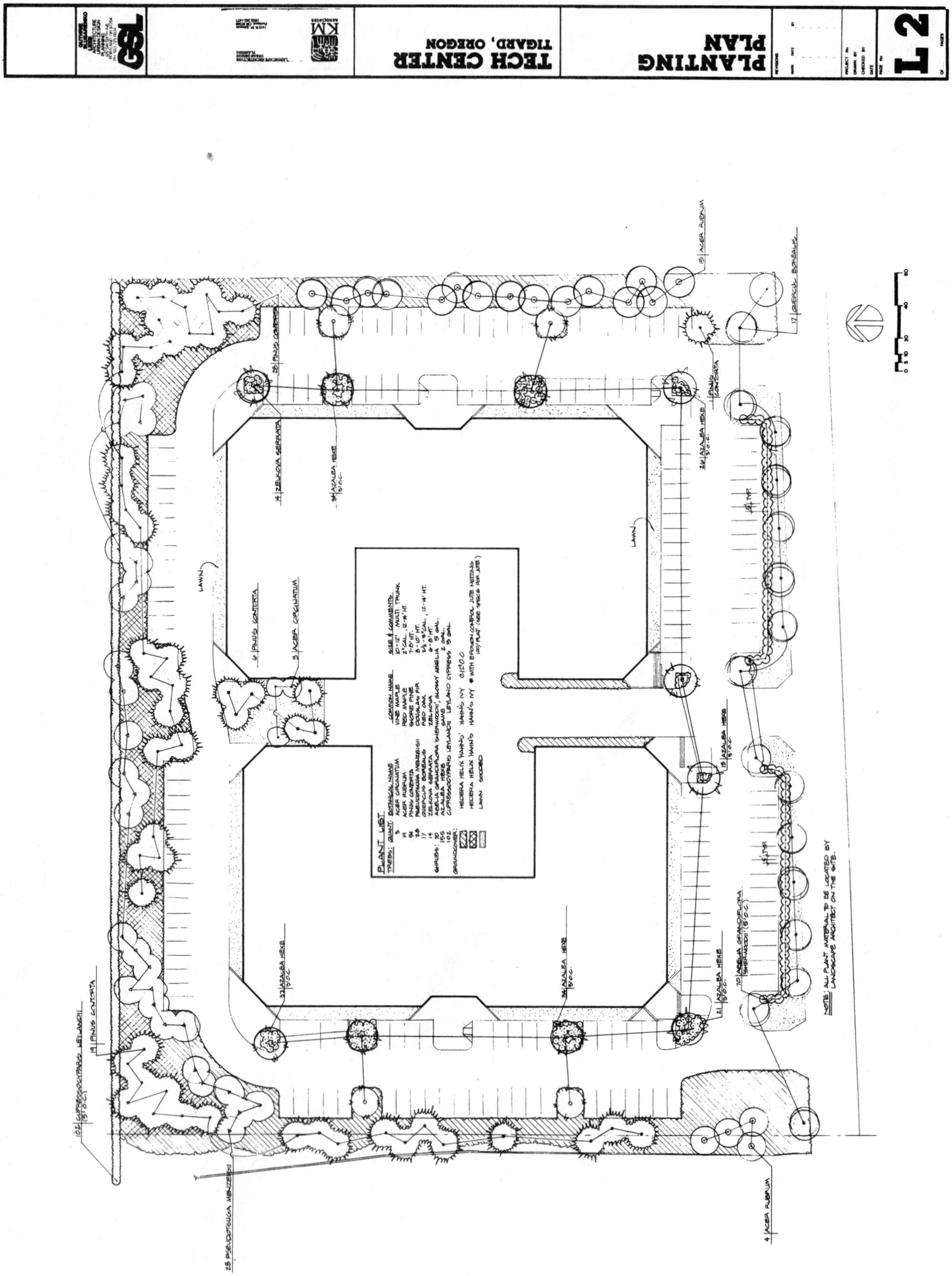

Figure 49-37 The planting or landscape plan is drawn as an overlay to the plot plan to show how the site will be planted and maintained. *Courtesy Guthrie, Slusarenko, and Leeb, Architects.*

CADD
applications

USING CADD FOR COMMERCIAL AND MULTIFAMILY PROJECTS

In most commercial architectural projects the architect works with consultants in the fields of mechanical, electrical, and structural engineering; plumbing systems; and interior design and space planning. These professionals use background drawings supplied by the architect to create their individual designs and plans. Background drawings are a subset of the information contained in the architect's floor plans.

Background drawings sent to individual consultants may contain different information. For example, the mechanical, electrical, and plumbing engineers need background drawings with sinks, toilets, showers, and utilities shown; these items may be omitted, to avoid confusion, on the structural background drawing. In multistory architectural projects, the background drawings may be used to coordinate floor-to-floor stacking relationships.

Multifamily housing projects provide a perfect application for CADD. Most of these projects have three or more unit plans which may be copied, mirrored, and rotated to create a complete multifamily plan. These projects normally begin with a unit plan such as the example shown in Figure 1. The most time-consuming part of the process is designing and drawing the unit plan. After the unit plan is drawn,

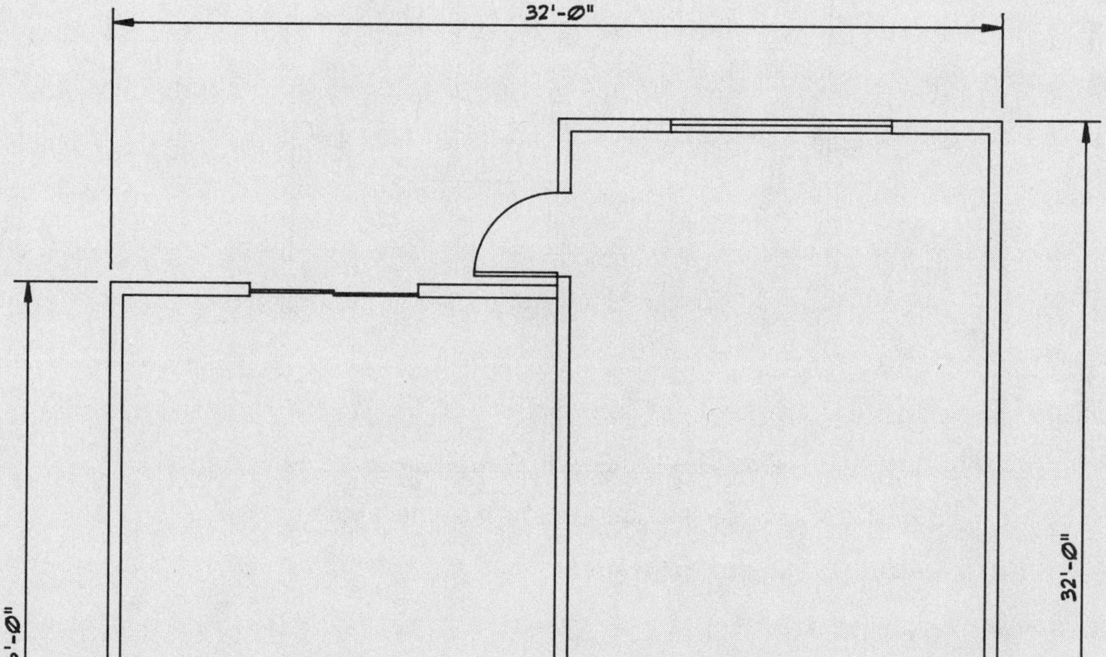

Figure 1 CADD-drawn unit plan for a multifamily housing project.

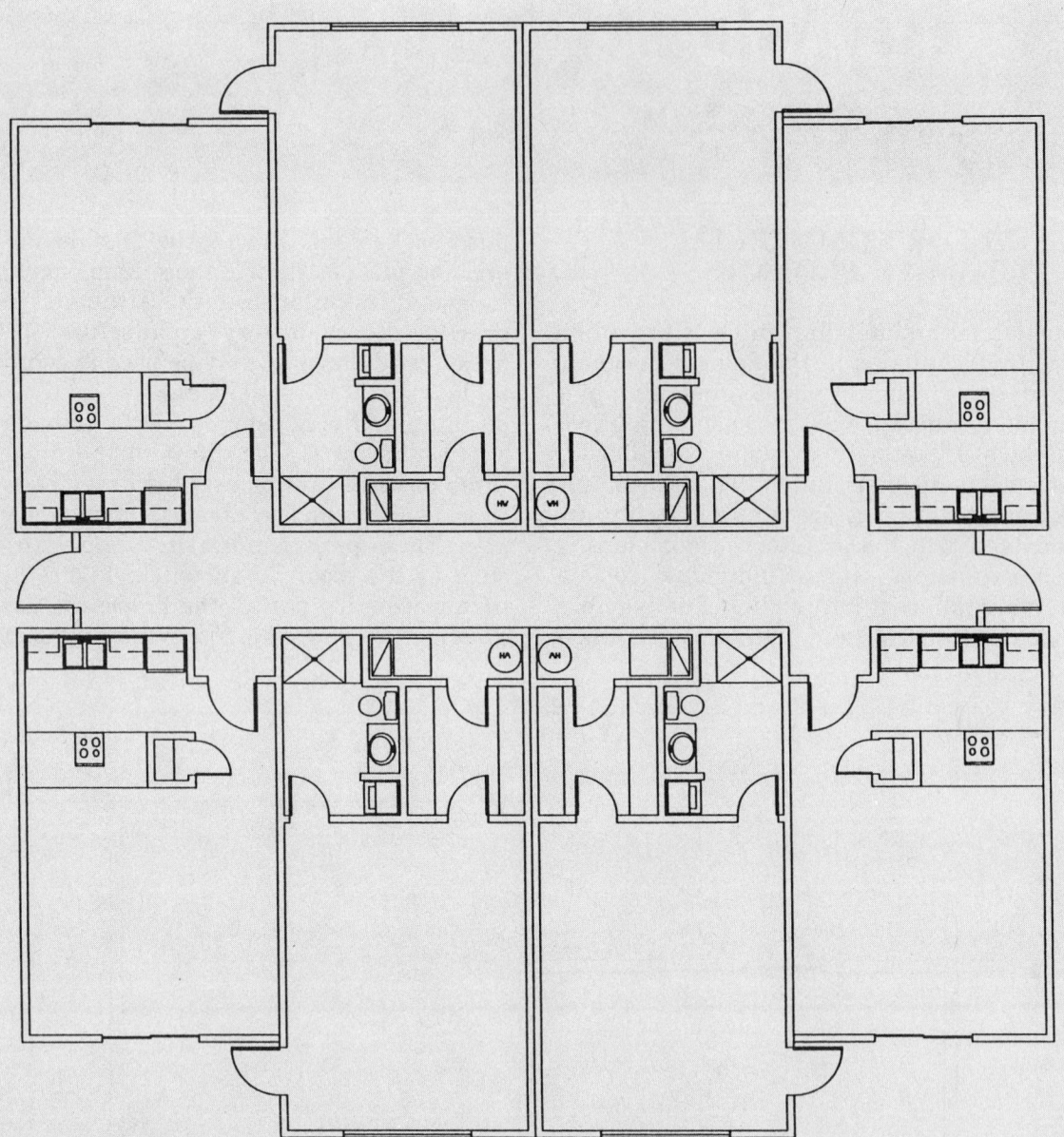

Figure 2 CADD copies the unit plan to show the entire arrangement.

all you have to do is mirror, copy, or rotate the unit plan as you create the arrangement for the multi-family building as shown in Figure 2.

When using CADD for architectural projects, it is important to relate one drawing to the next for accurate overlay purposes. The datum point method relates all plan drawings in the set through a common point. The datum point may be any convenient point on the drawing. Many drafters select the lower left corner of the drawing, represented by X and Y coordinates 0,0, as the datum point. Then, the lower right corner of each additional drawing is coordinated the same way. The relationship of the floor plans is established in relationship to the datum point, so each plan is aligned, one-over-the-other. Most projects begin with a schematic site plan at a reduced scale. If 0,0 is the lower left corner of the site plan, then the lower left corner of the floor plan drawing might have an X and Y coordinate of 57', 71' as shown in Figure 3. With this process, you can keep the orientation of each drawing related to every other drawing.

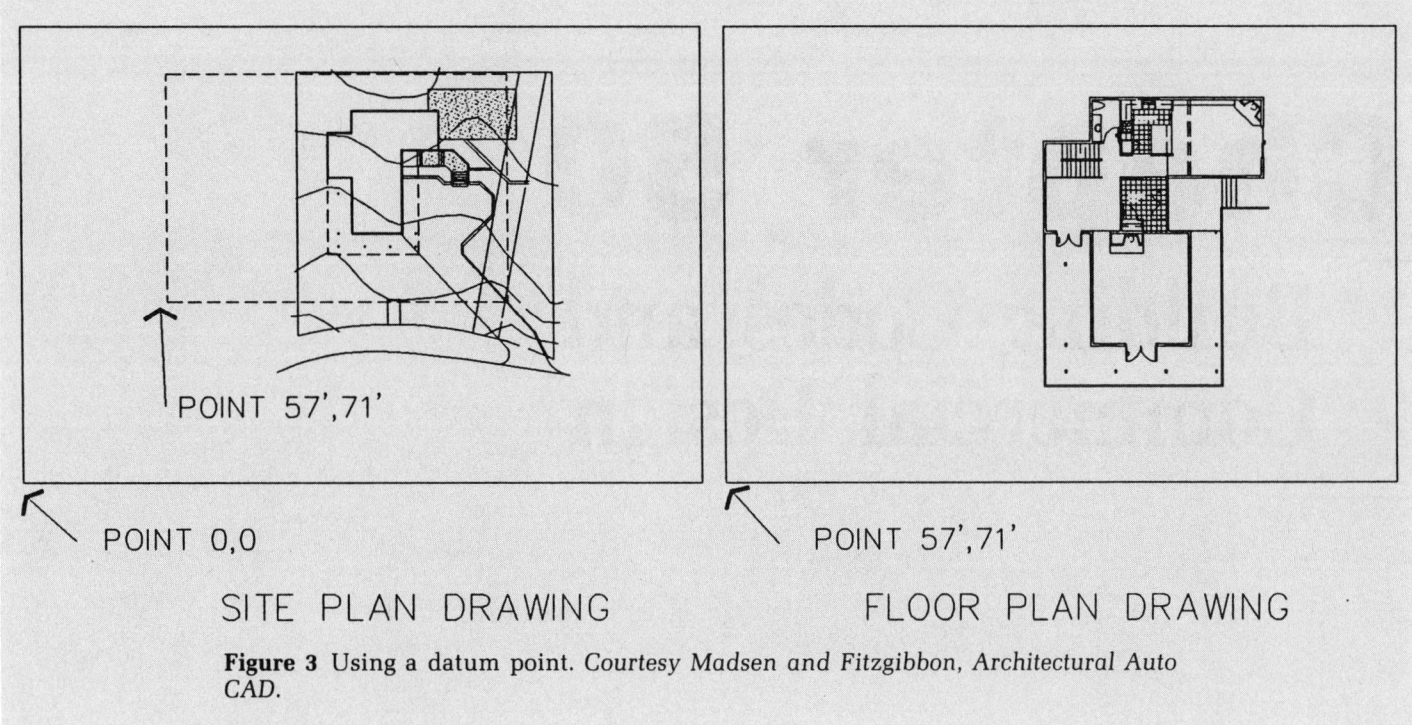

POINT 57',71'

POINT 0,0

POINT 57',71'

SITE PLAN DRAWING

FLOOR PLAN DRAWING

Figure 3 Using a datum point. *Courtesy Madsen and Fitzgibbon, Architectural Auto CAD.*

COMMERCIAL CONSTRUCTION PROJECTS TEST

DIRECTIONS

Answer the questions with short complete statements or drawings as needed on an 8½ × 11 drawing sheet as follows:

1. Use ⅛ in. guidelines for all lettering.
2. Letter your name, Commercial Construction Projects Test, and the date at the top of the sheet.
3. Letter the question number and provide the answer. You do not need to write out the question.
4. Do all lettering with vertical uppercase architectural letters. Answers may be prepared on a word processor if appropriate with course guidelines.
5. Your grade will be based on correct answers.

QUESTIONS

1. List three types of offices in which you might be able to work as a drafter.
2. List two major research tools that you will be using as a commercial drafter.
3. What is a reflected ceiling plan?
4. What are engineer's calculations?
5. What two types of plumbing plans may be drawn for a commercial project?
6. Describe two methods of drawing sections in commercial drawings.
7. List and describe two types of plans that are usually based on the plot plan.
8. What are the three parts of a set of calcs, and how do they affect a drafter?
9. Describe three plans that can be used to describe site-related material.
10. Describe the difference between two types of plans that are used to describe work done at or below the finished grade.

Chapter 50
Building Codes and Commercial Design

ONE OF the biggest differences you will notice between residential and commercial drafting is the increased dependency you will have on the building codes. You were introduced to residential building codes in Chapter 8 and have seen their effect on construction throughout the entire book. In residential drafting you may have been able to use a shortened version of the code such as *Dwelling Construction Under the Uniform Building Code.* If so, commercial construction drafting will be your first introduction to the full building code. As you draw commercial projects, the building codes will become much more influential. To be an effective drafter you must be able to use properly the code that governs your area. Although there are many different codes in use throughout the country, most will be similar to the Uniform Building Code (UBC), Basic National Building Code (BOCA), or the Standard Building Code (SBC).

If you haven't done so already, check with the building department in your area and determine the code that will cover your drafting. Typically you will spend approximately $50.00 to purchase a code book.

This may seem like a large expenditure to you now, but it will be one of your most useful drafting tools. Your code book should be considered a drafting tool just as pencils and vellum are. If possible, purchase the loose-leaf version of the code rather than the hardcover edition. The hardcover edition may look nicer sitting on your shelf, but this will be one book that will not just sit. The loose-leaf edition will allow you to update your codes with yearly amendments as well as state and local additions.

Purchase a code book as soon as possible in your drafting career, and don't hesitate to mark or place tabs on certain pages to identify key passages. You won't need to memorize the book, but you will need to refer to certain areas again and again. Page tabs will help you quickly find needed tables or formulas.

DETERMINE THE CATEGORIES

To effectively use a building code you must determine six classifications used to define a structure. These classifications will be used throughout the codes and include determining the occupancy group, location on the property, type of construction, floor area, height, and occupant load.

Occupancy Groups

The occupancy group specifies by whom or how the structure will be used. To protect the public adequately, buildings used for different purposes are designed to meet the hazards of that usage. Think of the occupancy group with which you are most familiar, the R occupancy. The R grouping not only covers the single-family residence, but also includes duplexes, apartments, lodging areas, and hotels. This one group covers single-family residences and multi-story apartments with hundreds of occupants. Obviously, the safety requirements for the multileveled apartment with hundreds of occupants should be different than a single-family residence.

The code that you are using will affect how the occupancy is listed. The letter of the occupancy listing generally is the first letter of the word that it represents. Figure 50–1 shows a detailed listing of occupancy categories from the UBC.

Structures often have more than one occupancy group within the structure. Separation must be provided at the wall or floor dividing these different occupancies. Figure 50–2 shows a listing of required separations based on UBC requirements. If you are working on a structure that has a 10,000 sq ft office area and a parking garage, the two areas must be separated. By using the table in Figure 50–1 you can see that the office area is a B-2 occupancy and the garage area is a B-3 occupancy. By using the table in Figure 50–2 you can determine that a wall with a one-hour rating must be provided between these two areas. The hourly rating is given to construction materials specifying the length of time that the item must resist structural damage that would be caused by a fire. Various ratings are assigned by the codes for materials ranging from nonrated to a four-hour rating. Whole chapters are assigned by each code to cover specific construction requirements for various materials. Chapter 43 of the UBC, section 1412 of BOCA, and chapter X of the SBC are the chapters that serve as an introduction to the fire resistance of materials.

Once the occupancy grouping is determined, you will need to turn to the section of the building code that introduces specifics on that occupancy grouping. Students often become frustrated with the amount of page turning that is required to find particular information in the codes. Often you will look in one section of the code only to be referred to another section of the code and then on to another. It may be frustrating, but the design of a structure is often complicated and requires patience.

Building Location and Size

When the occupancy of the structure was determined in Figure 50–1, information on the location of the structure to the property lines was also given. The type of occupancy will affect the location of a building on the property. The location to the property lines will also affect the size and amount of openings that are allowed in a wall. Notice that in the title to the table, the reader is referred to specific chapters within the code for information about openings based on size, location, and type of construction.

Type of Construction

Once the occupancy of the structure has been determined, the type of construction used to protect the occupants can be determined. The type of construction will determine the kind of building materials that can or cannot be used in the construction of the building. The kind of material used in construction will determine the ability of the structure to resist fire. Five general types of construction are typically specified by building codes and are represented by the numbers 1 through 5.

Construction in building types 1 and 2 requires the structural elements such as walls, floors, roofs, and exits to be constructed or protected by approved noncombustible materials such as steel, iron, concrete, or masonry. Construction in types 3, 4, and 5 can be of either steel, iron, concrete, masonry, or wood. In addition to specifying the structural framework, the type of construction will also dictate the material used for interior partitions, exit specifications, and a wide variety of other requirements for the building. Figure 50–3 shows the construction requirements for various areas of a structure based on the type of construction. Specific areas of the code must now be researched to determine how these requirements can be met.

Building Area

Once the type of construction has been determined, the size of the structure can be determined. Figure 50–4 shows a listing of allowable floor area based on the type of construction to be used. These are basic sq ft sizes which may be altered depending on the different construction techniques that can be used. If you are working on the plans for an office building with 20,000 sq ft, this table can be used to determine the type of construction that would be required. First determine the occupancy. By using Figure 50–1 you can find that the structure is a B-2 occupancy. In Figure 50–4 you can see that a B-2 structure of 20,000 sq ft could be constructed of either type 1 or type 2 F.R. (fire-resistant) construction materials. You will now need to turn to the areas of the code that cover these types of construction to determine types of materials that could be used.

Determine the Height

The occupancy and type of construction will determine the maximum height of the structure. Figure

TABLE NO. 5-A—WALL AND OPENING PROTECTION OF OCCUPANCIES BASED ON LOCATION ON PROPERTY
TYPES II ONE-HOUR, II-N AND V CONSTRUCTION: For exterior wall and opening protection of Types II One-hour, II-N and V buildings, see table below and Sections 504, 709, 1903 and 2203.
This table does not apply to Types I, II-F.R., III and IV construction, see Sections 1803, 1903, 2003 and 2103.

	GROUP	DESCRIPTION OF OCCUPANCY	FIRE RESISTANCE OF EXTERIOR WALLS	OPENINGS IN EXTERIOR WALLS
ASSEMBLY	A See also Section 602	1—Any assembly building with a stage and an occupant load of 1000 or more in the building	Not applicable (See Sections 602 and 603)	
		2—Any building or portion of a building having an assembly room with an occupant load of less than 1000 and a stage 2.1—Any building or portion of a building having an assembly room with an occupant load of 300 or more without a stage, including such buildings used for educational purposes and not classed as a Group E or Group B, Division 2 Occupancy	2 hours less than 10 feet, 1 hour less than 40 feet	Not permitted less than 5 feet Protected less than 10 feet
		3—Any building or portion of a building having an assembly room with an occupant load of less than 300 without a stage, including such buildings used for educational purposes and not classed as a Group E or Group B, Division 2 Occupancy	2 hours less than 5 feet, 1 hour less than 40 feet	Not permitted less than 5 feet Protected less than 10 feet
		4—Stadiums, reviewing stands and amusement park structures not included within other Group A Occupancies	1 hour less than 10 feet	Protected less than 10 feet
BUSINESS	B See also Section 702	1—Gasoline service stations, garages where no repair work is done except exchange of parts and maintenance requiring no open flame, welding, or use of Class I, II or III-A liquids 2—Drinking and dining establishments having an occupant load of less than 50, wholesale and retail stores, office buildings, printing plants, municipal police and fire stations, factories and workshops using material not highly flammable or combustible, storage and sales rooms for combustible goods, paint stores without bulk handling Buildings or portions of buildings having rooms used for educational purposes beyond the 12th grade, with less than 50 occupants in any room	1 hour less than 20 feet	Not permitted less than 5 feet Protected less than 10 feet
		3—Aircraft hangars where no repair work is done except exchange of parts and maintenance requiring no open flame, welding, or the use of Class I or II liquids Open parking garages (For requirements, See Section 709.) Heliports	1 hour less than 20 feet	Not permitted less than 5 feet Protected less than 20 feet
		4—Ice plants, power plants, pumping plants, cold storage and creameries Factories and workshops using noncombustible and nonexplosive materials Storage and sales rooms of noncombustible and nonexplosive materials	1 hour less than 5 feet	Not permitted less than 5 feet
EDUCATION	E See also Section 802	1—Any building used for educational purposes through the 12th grade by 50 or more persons for more than 12 hours per week or four hours in any one day 2—Any building used for educational purposes through the 12th grade by less than 50 persons for more than 12 hours per week or four hours in any one day 3—Any building used for day-care purposes for more than six children	2 hours less than 5 feet, 1 hour less than 10 feet[1]	Not permitted less than 5 feet Protected less than 10 feet[1]
HAZARDOUS	H See also Sections 902 and 903	1—Storage, handling, use or sale of hazardous and highly flammable or explosive materials other than Class I, II, or III-A liquids [See also Section 901 (a), Division 1.]	See Chapter 9 and the Fire Code	
		2—Storage, handling, use or sale of Classes I, II and III-A liquids; dry cleaning plants using Class I, II or III-A liquids; paint stores with bulk handling; paint shops and spray-painting rooms and shops [See also Section 901 (a), Division 2.] 3—Woodworking establishments, planing mills, box factories, buffing rooms for tire-rebuilding plants and picking rooms; shops, factories or warehouses where loose combustible fibers or dust are manufactured, processed, generated or stored; and pin-refinishing rooms	4 hours less than 5 feet, 2 hours less than 10 feet, 1 hour less than 20 feet	Not permitted less than 5 feet Protected less than 20 feet
		4—Repair garages not classified as a Group B, Division 1 Occupancy 5—Aircraft repair hangars	1 hour less than 60 feet	Protected less than 60 feet
		6—Semiconductor fabrication facilities and comparable research and development areas when the facilities in which hazardous production materials are used are designed and constructed in accordance with Section 911 and storage, handling and use of hazardous materials is in accordance with the Fire Code. [See also Section 901 (a), Division 6.]	4 hours less than 5 feet, 2 hours less than 10 feet, 1 hour less than 20 feet	Not permitted less than 5 feet, protected less than 20 feet
INSTITUTIONS	I See also Section 1002	1—Nurseries for the full-time care of children under the age of six (each accommodating more than five persons) Hospitals, sanitariums, nursing homes with nonambulatory patients and similar buildings (each accommodating more than five persons)	2 hours less than 5 feet, 1 hour elsewhere	Not permitted less than 5 feet Protected less than 10 feet
		2—Nursing homes for ambulatory patients, homes for children six years of age or over (each accommodating more than five persons)	1 hour	
		3—Mental hospitals, mental sanitariums, jails, prisons, reformatories and buildings where personal liberties of inmates are similarly restrained	2 hours less than 5 feet, 1 hour elsewhere	Not permitted less than 5 feet, protected less than 10 feet
	M[2]	1—Private garages, carports, sheds and agricultural buildings (See also Section 1101, Division 1.)	1 hour less than 3 feet (or may be protected on the exterior with materials approved for 1-hour fire-resistive construction)	Not permitted less than 3 feet
		2—Fences over 6 feet high, tanks and towers	Not regulated for fire resistance	
RESIDENTIAL	R See also Section 1202	1—Hotels and apartment houses Convents and monasteries (each accommodating more than 10 persons)	1 hour less than 5 feet	Not permitted less than 5 feet
		3—Dwellings and lodging houses	1 hour less than 3 feet	Not permitted less than 3 feet

[1]Group E, Divisions 2 and 3 Occupancies having an occupant load of not more than 20 may have exterior wall and opening protection as required for Group R, Division 3 Occupancies

[2]For agricultural buildings, see Appendix Chapter 11.

NOTES: (1) See Section 504 for types of walls affected and requirements covering percentage of openings permitted in exterior walls.
(2) For additional restrictions, see chapters under Occupancy and Types of Construction.
(3) For walls facing yards and public ways, see Part IV.
(4) Openings shall be protected by a fire assembly having a three-fourths-hour fire-protection rating.

Figure 50-1 Common occupancy listings. *Reproduced from the Uniform Building Code, 1985 edition. Courtesy The International Conference of Building Officials.*

TABLE NO. 5-B—REQUIRED SEPARATION IN BUILDINGS OF MIXED OCCUPANCY
(In Hours)

	A-1	A-2	A-2.1	A-3	A-4	B-1	B-2	B-3	B-4	E	H-1	H-2	H-3	H-4-5	H-6	I	M²	R-1	R-3
A-1		N	N	N	N	4	3	3	3	N	4	4	4	4	4	3	1	1	1
A-2	N		N	N	N	3	1	1	1	N	4	4	4	4	4	3	1	1	1
A-2.1	N	N		N	N	3	1	1	1	N	4	4	4	4	4	3	1	1	1
A-3	N	N	N		N	3	N	1	N	N	4	4	4	4	3	3	1	1	1
A-4	N	N	N	N		3	1	1	1	N	4	4	4	4	4	3	1	1	1
B-1	4	3	3	3	3		1	1	1	3	2	1	1	1	1	4	1	3¹	1
B-2	3	1	1	N	1	1		1	1	1	2	1	1	1	1	2	1	1	N
B-3	3	1	1	1	1	1	1		1	1	2	1	1	1	1	4	1	1	N
B-4	3	1	1	N	1	1	1	1		1	2	1	1	1	1	4	N	1	N
E	N	N	N	N	N	3	1	1	1		4	4	4	4	3	1	1	1	1
H-1	4	4	4	4	4	2	2	2	2	4		1	1	1	2	4	1	4	4
H-2	4	4	4	4	4	1	1	1	1	4	1		1	1	1	4	1	3	3
H-3	4	4	4	4	4	1	1	1	1	4	1	1		1	1	4	1	3	3
H-4-5	4	4	4	4	4	1	1	1	1	4	1	1	1		1	4	1	3	3
H-6	4	4	4	3	4	1	1	1	1	3	2	1	1	1		4	3	4	4
I	3	3	3	3	3	4	2	4	4	1	4	4	4	4	4		1	1	1
M²	1	1	1	1	1	1	1	1	N	1	1	1	1	1	3	1		1	1
R-1	1	1	1	1	1	3¹	1	1	1	1	4	3	3	3	4	1	1		N
R-3	1	1	1	1	1	1	N	N	N	1	4	3	3	3	4	1	1	N	

Note: For detailed requirements and exceptions, see Section 503.

¹The three-hour separation may be reduced to two hours where the Group B, Division 1 Occupancy is limited to the storage of passenger motor vehicles having a capacity of not more than nine persons. This shall not apply where provisions of Section 702 (a) apply.

²For Agricultural buildings, see also Appendix Chapter 11.

Figure 50–2 If a structure contains more than one occupancy grouping, the areas will need to be separated by protective construction methods to reduce the spread of fire. The fire rating of the separating construction can be determined by comparing the occupancy rating of each type of construction. An office (B-2) and a public parking garage (B-3) would require a 1-hour separation. *Reproduced from the* Uniform Building Code, *1985 edition. Courtesy The International Conference of Building Officials.*

50–5 shows an example of a table from the UBC used to determine the allowable height of a structure. The theoretical 20,000 sq ft office building could be 12 stories (or 160 ft) high if constructed of type 2 construction materials, or of unlimited height if built with type 1 materials. Remember that this height is based on building requirements governing fire and public safety. Zoning regulations for a specific area may further limit the height of the structure.

Determine the Occupant Load

You have already determined how the structure will be used. Now you must determine how many people may use the structure. Figure 50–6 is an example of the table used to compute the occupant load. In each occupancy, the intended size of the structure is divided by the occupant load factor to determine the occupant load. In a 20,000 sq ft office structure, the occupant load would be 200. This is found by dividing the size of 20,000 sq ft by the occupant factor of 100. The occupant load will be needed to determine the number of exits, the size and locations of doors, and many other construction requirements.

USING THE CODES

The need to determine the six classifications of a building may seem senseless to you as a beginning drafter. Although these are procedures that the designer, architect, or engineer will perform in the initial design stage, the drafter must be aware of these classifications as basic drafting functions are performed on the project. Many of the problems that the drafter will need the code to solve will require knowledge of the six basic code limitations. Practice using the tables presented in this text as well as similar tables of the code that govern your area.

Once you feel comfortable determining the basic categories of a structure, study the chapter of your building code that presents basic building requirements for a structure. If you're working with the UBC this would be Chapter 17. Article 5 contains general construction requirements if you're using BOCA. The SBC is structured somewhat differently than the other two national codes. Sections 5 and 6 contain general information that would be a good starting point for you to become familiar with in this code.

Table 401
FIRERESISTANCE RATINGS OF STRUCTURE ELEMENTS (IN HOURS)

Structure element Note a		Type of construction Section 401.0									
		Noncombustible					Noncombustible/Combustible			Combustible	
		Type 1 Section 402.0		Type 2 Section 403.0			Type 3 Section 404.0		Type 4 Section 405.0	Type 5 Section 406.0	
		Protected		Protected		Unprotected	Protected	Unprotected	Heavy timber	Protected	Unprotected
		1A	1B	2A	2B	2C	3A	3B	4	5A	5B
Exterior walls (Section 1406.0 and Note b)											
1 Fire separation of 30' or more	Bearing	4	3	2	1	0	2	2	2	1	0
	Nonbearing	0	0	0	0	0	0	0	0	0	0
Fire separation of less than 6'	Bearing	4	3	2	1½	1	2	2	2	1	1
	Nonbearing	2	2	1½	1	1	2	2	2	1	1
Fire separation of 6' or more but less than 11'	Bearing	4	3	2	1	0	2	2	2	1	1 Note i
	Nonbearing	2	2	1½	1	0	2	2	2	1	1 Note i
Fire separation of 11' or more but less than 30'	Bearing	4	3	2	1	0	2	2	2	1	1 Note i
	Nonbearing	1½	1½	1	1	0	1½	1½	see Sec. 405.0	1	1 Note i
2 Fire walls and party walls (Section 1407.0)		4	3	2	2	2	2	2	2	2	2
		◄——— Not less than fire grading of use group—(see Table 1402) ———►									
3 Fire separation assemblies (Sections 313.0, 1409.0 and 1412.0)		◄——— Fireresistance rating corresponding to fire grading of use group—(see Table 1402) ———►									
4 Fire enclosures of exits, exit hallways and stairways (Section 816.9.2, 1409.0 and Note c).		2	2	2	2	2	2	2	2	2	2
5 Shafts (other than exits) and elevator hoistways (Section 1410.0 and Note c)		2	2	2	2	2	2	2	2	1	1
		◄——————————— Noncombustible ———————————►									
6 Exit access corridors (Note g)		1	1	1	1	1	1	1	1	1	1
		◄——— Note e ———►									
Separation of tenant spaces		1	1	1	1	0	1	0	1	1	0
		◄——— Note e ———►									
7 Dwelling unit separations		1	1	1	1	1	1	1	1	1	1
		◄——— Note e ———►									
Other nonbearing partitions		0	0	0	0	0	0	0	0	0	0
		◄——— Note e ———►									
8 Interior bearing walls, bearing partitions, columns, girders, trusses (other than roof trusses) and framing (Section 1411.0)	Supporting more than one floor	4	3	2	1	0	1	0	see Sec. 405.0	1	0
	Supporting one floor only	3	2	1½	1	0	1	0	see Sec. 405.0	1	0
	Supporting a roof only	3	2	1½	1	0	1	0	see Sec. 405.0	1	0
9 Structural members supporting wall (Section 1411.0 and Note h)		3	2	1½	1	0	1	0	1	1	0
		◄——— Not less than fireresistance rating of wall supported ———►									
10 Floor construction including beams (Section 1412.0)		3	2	1½	1	0	1	0	see Sec. 405.0 Note d	1	0
11 Roof construction, including beams, trusses and framing, arches and roof deck (Section 1412.0 and Note f)	15' or less in height to lowest member	2	1½	1	1 (Note e)	0	1	0	see Sec. 405.0 Note d	1	0
	More than 15 but less than 20' in height to lowest lowest member	1	1	1	0 (Note e)	0	0	0	see Sec. 405.0 Note d	1	0
	20' or more in height to lowest member	0	0	0	0 (Note e)	0	0	0	see Sec. 405.0 Note d	0	0

Note a. For special high hazard uses involving a higher degree of fire severity and higher concentration of combustible contents, the fireresistance rating requirements for structural elements shall be increased accordingly (see Section 600.2).

Note b. The fire separation or fire exposure in feet as herein limited applies to the distance measured from the building face to the closest interior lot line, the center line of a street or public space or an imaginary line between two buildings on the same property (see definition of fire separation, exterior fire exposure in Section 201.0).

Note c. Exit and shaft enclosures connecting three floor levels or less shall have a fireresistance rating of not less than 1 hour (see Sections 1409.1.3 and 1410.3).

Note d. In Type 4 construction, members which are of material other than heavy timber shall have a fireresistance rating of not less than 1 hour (see Section 1224.2).

Note e. Fire-retardant treated wood, complying with Section 1403.5.1 may be used as provided in Section 1403.5.2 (see Section 1405.7).

Note f. Where the omission of fire protection from roof trusses, roof framing and decking is permitted, roofs in buildings of Type 1 and Type 2 construction shall be constructed of noncombustible materials without a specified fireresistance rating, or of Type 4 construction in buildings not over five stories or 65 feet in height (see Section 1413.4).

Note g. In all occupancies except Use Groups R-1 and R-2, exit access corridors serving 30 or fewer occupants may have a zero fireresistance rating. Exit access corridors contained within a dwelling unit shall not be required to have a fireresistance rating (see Section 810.4).

Note h. Structural members supporting fireresistance rated exit access corridor walls in buildings of Types 2C, 3B or 5B construction shall not be required to be fireresistance rated unless required by other provisions of this code (see Section 1409.4).

Note i. The exterior walls of buildings or structures of Type 5B construction with a fire separation of less than 15 feet shall have a fireresistance rating of not less than 1 hour except buildings of Use Group R-2, R-3 or U (see Section 1406.2).

Note j. 1 foot = 304.8 mm.

Figure 50–3 Construction requirements for various parts of a structure can be determined by using tables from the building code that governs your area. *Reproduced from BOAC Basic/National Building Code/1984, copyright 1983, Building Officials and Code Administrators International, Inc., 4051 West Flossmore Road, Country Club Hill, IL 60477. Published by arrangements with the author. All rights reserved.*

MOST PROTECTIVE   LEAST RESTRICTIVE

TABLE NO. 5-C—BASIC ALLOWABLE FLOOR AREA FOR BUILDINGS ONE STORY IN HEIGHT[1]
(In Square Feet)

OCCUPANCY	I F.R.	II F.R.	II ONE-HOUR	II N	III ONE-HOUR	III N	IV H.T.	V ONE-HOUR	V N
A-1	Unlimited	29,900	Not Permitted						
A) 2-2.1	Unlimited	29,900	13,500	Not Permitted	13,500	Not Permitted	13,500	10,500	Not Permitted
A) 3-4[2]	Unlimited	29,900	13,500	9,100	13,500	9,100	13,500	10,500	6,000
B) 1-2-3[3]	Unlimited	39,900	18,000	12,000	18,000	12,000	18,000	14,000	8,000
B-4	Unlimited	59,900	27,000	18,000	27,000	18,000	27,000	21,000	12,000
E	Unlimited	45,200	20,200	13,500	20,200	13,500	20,200	15,700	9,100
H) 1-2[4]	15,000	12,400	5,600	3,700	5,600	3,700	5,600	4,400	2,500
H) 3-4-5	Unlimited	24,800	11,200	7,500	11,200	7,500	11,200	8,800	5,100
H-6	Unlimited	39,900	18,000	12,000	18,000	12,000	18,000	14,000	8,000
I) 1-2	Unlimited	15,100	6,800	Not Permitted	6,800	Not Permitted	6,800	5,200	Not Permitted
I-3	Unlimited	15,100	Not Permitted[5]						
M[6]			See Chapter 11						
R-1	Unlimited	29,900	13,500	9,100[7]	13,500	9,100[7]	13,500	10,500	6,000[7]
R-3			Unlimited						

[1]For multistory buildings, see Section 505 (b).
[2]For limitations and exceptions, see Section 602 (a).
[3]For open parking garages, see Section 709.
[4]See Section 903.
[5]See Section 1002 (b).
[6]For agricultural buildings, see also Appendix Chapter 11.
[7]For limitations and exceptions, see Section 1202 (b).

N—No requirements for fire resistance
F.R.—Fire Resistive
H.T.—Heavy Timber

Figure 50-4 Building codes restrict the size of a structure based on the type of construction to help ensure public safety. *Reproduced from the* Uniform Building Code, *1985 edition. Courtesy The International Conference of Building Officials.*

TABLE NO. 5-D—MAXIMUM HEIGHT OF BUILDINGS

OCCUPANCY	I F.R.	II F.R.	II ONE-HOUR	II N	III ONE-HOUR	III N	IV H.T.	V ONE-HOUR	V N
MAXIMUM HEIGHT IN FEET	Unlimited	160	65	55	65	55	65	50	40
MAXIMUM HEIGHT IN STORIES									
A-1	Unlimited	4	Not Permitted						
A) 2-2.1	Unlimited	4	2	Not Permitted	2	Not Permitted	2	2	Not Permitted
A) 3-4[1]	Unlimited	12	2	1	2	1	2	2	1
B) 1-2-3[2]	Unlimited	12	4	2	4	2	4	3	2
B-4	Unlimited	12	4	2	4	2	4	3	2
E[3]	Unlimited	4	2	1	2	1	2	2	1
H-1	Unlimited	2	1	1	1	1	1	1	1
H) 2-3-4-5	Unlimited	5	2	1	2	1	2	2	1
H-6	3	3	3	2	3	2	3	3	1
I-1	Unlimited	3	1	Not Permitted	1	Not Permitted	1	1	Not Permitted
I-2	Unlimited	3	2	Not Permitted	2	Not Permitted	2	2	Not Permitted
I-3	Unlimited	2	Not Permitted[4]						
M[5]			See Chapter 11						
R-1	Unlimited	12	4	2[6]	4	2[6]	4	3	2[6]
R-3	Unlimited	3	3	3	3	3	3	3	3

[1]For limitations and exceptions, see Section 602 (a).
[2]For open parking garages, see Section 709.
[3]See Section 802 (c).
[4]See Section 1002 (b).
[5]For agricultural buildings, see also Appendix Chapter 11.
[6]For limitations and exceptions, see Section 1202 (b).

N—No requirements for fire resistance
F.R.—Fire Resistive
H.T.—Heavy Timber

Figure 50-5 The height of a structure is limited by codes based on the occupancy and the type of construction used in the structure. *Reproduced from the* Uniform Building Code, *1985 edition. Courtesy The International Conference of Building Officials.*

Once you feel at ease reading through the chapters dealing with general construction, work on the chapters of the code that deal with uses of different types of material. Start with the chapter that deals with the most common building material in your area. For most of you this will be the section governing the use of wood. The use of wood is covered in chapter 25 in the UBC, sections 1223 through 1227 of BOCA, and chapter 17 of the SBC. Although you will be familiar with the use of wood in residential structures, the building codes will open many new areas that were not required in residential construction.

TABLE NO. 33-A—MINIMUM EGRESS AND ACCESS REQUIREMENTS

USE[1]	MINIMUM OF TWO EXITS OTHER THAN ELEVATORS ARE REQUIRED WHERE NUMBER OF OCCUPANTS IS AT LEAST	OCCUPANT LOAD FACTOR[2] (Sq. Ft.)	ACCESS BY MEANS OF A RAMP OR AN ELEVATOR MUST BE PROVIDED FOR THE PHYSICALLY HANDICAPPED AS INDICATED[3]
1. Aircraft Hangars (no repair)	10	500	Yes
2. Auction Rooms	30	7	Yes
3. Assembly Areas, Concentrated Use (without fixed seats) Auditoriums Bowling Alleys (Assembly areas) Churches and Chapels Dance Floors Lobby Accessory to Assembly Occupancy Lodge Rooms Reviewing Stands Stadiums	50	7	Yes[4] [5]
4. Assembly Areas, Less-concentrated Use Conference Rooms Dining Rooms Drinking Establishments Exhibit Rooms Gymnasiums Lounges Stages	50	15	Yes[4] [6]
5. Children's Homes and Homes for the Aged	6	80	Yes[7]
6. Classrooms	50	20	Yes[8]
7. Dormitories	10	50	Yes[7]
8. Dwellings	10	300	No
9. Garage, Parking	30	200	Yes[9]
10. Hospitals and Sanitariums— Nursing Homes	6	80	Yes
11. Hotels and Apartments	10	200	Yes[10]
12. Kitchen—Commercial	30	200	No
13. Library Reading Room	50	50	Yes[4]
14. Locker Rooms	30	50	Yes
15. Malls (see Appendix Chapter 7)	—	—	—
16. Manufacturing Areas	30	200	Yes[7]
17. Mechanical Equipment Room	30	300	No
18. Nurseries for Children (Day-care)	7	35	Yes
19. Offices	30	100	Yes[7]
20. School Shops and Vocational Rooms	50	50	Yes
21. Skating Rinks	50	50 on the skating area; 15 on the deck	Yes[4]
22. Storage and Stock Rooms	30	300	No
23. Stores—Retail Sales Rooms Basement Ground Floor Upper Floors	11 50 10	20* 30 50	Yes Yes Yes
24. Swimming Pools	50	50 for the pool area; 15 on the deck	Yes[4]
25. Warehouses	30	500	No
26. All others	50	100	

[1]For additional provisions on number of exits from Group H and I Occupancies and from rooms containing fuel-fired equipment or cellulose nitrate, see Sections 3320, 3321 and 3322, respectively.

[2]This table shall not be used to determine working space requirements per person.

[3]Elevators shall not be construed as providing a required exit.

[4]Access to secondary areas on balconies or mezzanines may be by stairs only, except when such secondary areas contain the only available toilet facilities.

[5]Reviewing stands, grandstands and bleachers need not comply.

[6]Access requirements for conference rooms, dining rooms, lounges and exhibit rooms that are part of an office use shall be the same as required for the office use.

[7]Access to floors other than that closest to grade may be by stairs only, except when the only available toilet facilities are on other levels.

[8]When the floor closest to the grade offers the same programs and activities available on other floors, access to the other floors may be by stairs only, except when the only available toilet facilities are on other levels.

[9]Access to floors other than that closest to grade and to garages used in connection with apartment houses may be by stairs only.

[10]See Section 1213 for access to buildings and facilities in hotels and apartments.

[11]See Section 3303 for basement exit requirements.

*i.e., for every 20 ☐, one person is allowed in the building.

Figure 50–6 The occupant load of a structure is determined by dividing the intended size of the structure by the occupant load factor. *Reproduced from the Uniform Building Code, 1985 edition. Courtesy The International Conference of Building Officials.*

BUILDING CODES AND COMMERCIAL DESIGN TEST ████████████

DIRECTIONS

Answer the questions with short complete statements or drawings as needed on an 8½ × 11 drawing sheet as follows:

1. Use ⅛ in. guidelines for all lettering.
2. Letter your name, Building Codes and Commercial Design Test, and the date at the top of the sheet.
3. Letter the question number and provide the answer. You do not need to write out the question.
4. Use the tables in this chapter to answer the questions.
5. Do all lettering with vertical uppercase architectural letters. Answers may be prepared on a word processor if appropriate with course guidelines.
6. Your grade will be based on correct answers.

QUESTIONS

1. What is the occupancy rating of a room used to train 50 or more junior college drafters?
2. What fire rating would be required for a wall separating a single-family residence from a garage?
3. What is the height limitation on an office building of type 2-N construction?
4. What is the maximum allowable floor area of a public parking facility using type 4 construction methods?
5. What fire resistance would be required for the exterior walls of a structure used for full-time care of children that is within 5 ft of a property line?
6. What fire rating is required between a wall separating an A-1 occupancy from a B-1 occupancy?
7. What is the maximum height of a residence of type 2 through 5 construction?
8. You are drafting a 12,000 sq ft retail sales store. Determine the occupancy, the least restrictive type of construction to be used, maximum height and square footage, and the occupant load for each possible level.

Chapter 51
Common Commercial Construction Materials

AS YOU work on commercial projects you will be exposed to new types of structures and codes different from the ones you were using with residential drawing. You will also be using different types of materials than are typically used in residential construction. Most of the materials used in commercial construction can be used in residential construction, but they are not because of their cost and the associated cost of labor with each material. Wood is the exception. Common materials used in commercial construction include wood, concrete block, poured concrete, and steel.

WOOD

Wood is used in many types of commercial buildings in a manner similar to its use in residential construction. The western platform system, which was covered in Chapter 26, is a common framing method for multifamily and office buildings as well as others. Heavy wood timbers are also used for some commercial construction. As a drafter, you will need to be familiar with both types of construction.

Platform Construction

Platform construction methods in commercial projects are similar to residential methods. Wood is rarely used at the foundation level but is a common material for walls and intermediate and upper level floor systems. Trusses or truss joists are also common floor joist materials for commercial projects. Although each is used in residential construction, their primary usage is in commercial construction.

Walls. Wood is used to frame walls on many projects. The biggest difference in wood wall construction is not in the framing method but in the covering materials. Depending on the type of occupancy and the type of construction required, wood framed walls may require a special finish to achieve a required fire protection. Figure 51–1 shows several different methods of finishing a wood wall to achieve various fire ratings.

Roofs. Wood is also used to frame the roof system of many commercial projects. Joists, trusses and panelized systems are the most typically used framing

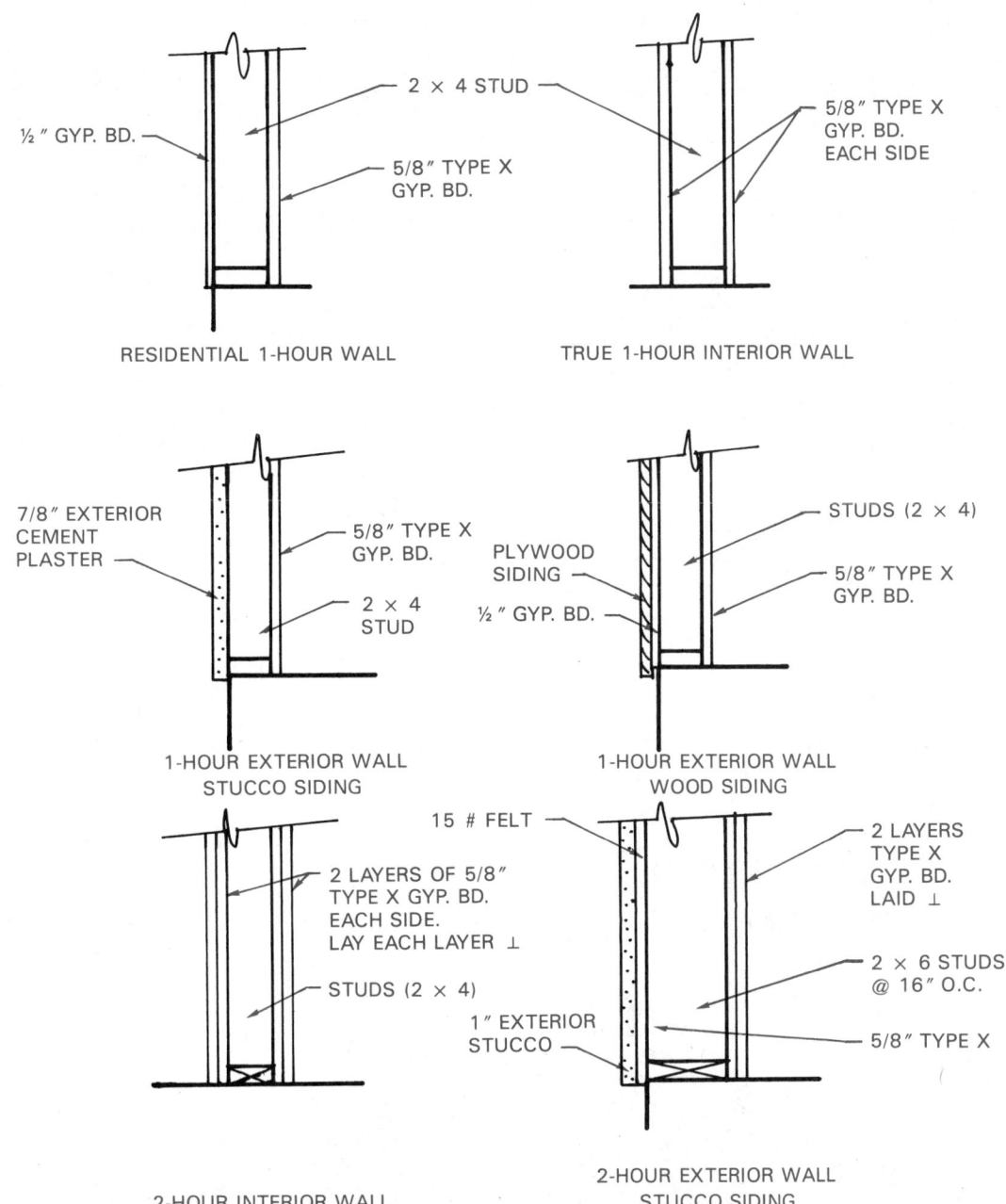

Figure 51–1 Walls often require special treatment to achieve the needed fire rating for certain types of construction (See Figure 50–2). Consult your local building code for complete descriptions of coverings.

systems. Both joist and truss systems have been discussed in Sections 6 and 7. These systems usually allow the joists or trusses to be placed at 24 or 32 in. O.C. for commercial uses. An example of a truss system can be seen in Figure 51–2. The panelized roof system typically uses beams placed approximately 20 to 30 ft apart. Smaller beams called purlins are then placed between the main beams typically using an 8 ft spacing. Joists that are 2 or 3 in. wide are then placed between these purlins at 24 in. O.C. The roof is then covered with plywood sheathing. Figure 51–3 shows an example of how a panelized roof is constructed. Figure 51–4 shows an example

of a roof framing plan for a panelized roof system. The availability of materials, labor practices, and use of the building will determine which type of roof will be used.

Heavy Timber Construction

In addition to standard uses of wood in the western platform system, large wood members are sometimes used for the structural framework of a building. This method of construction is typically used for both appearance and structural reasons. Heavy timbers have excellent structural and fire retardant qual-

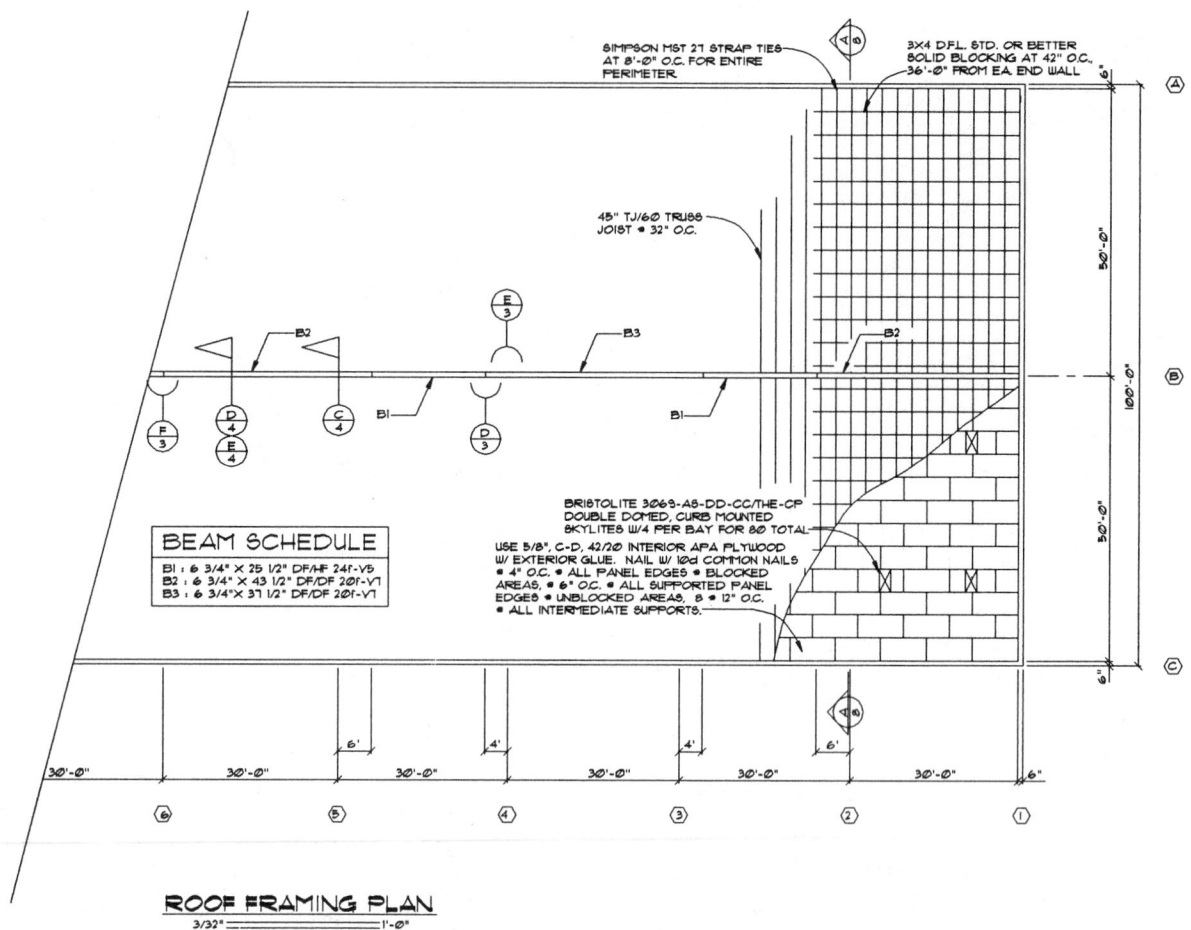

Figure 51–2 A roof plan using truss framing to span between supports.

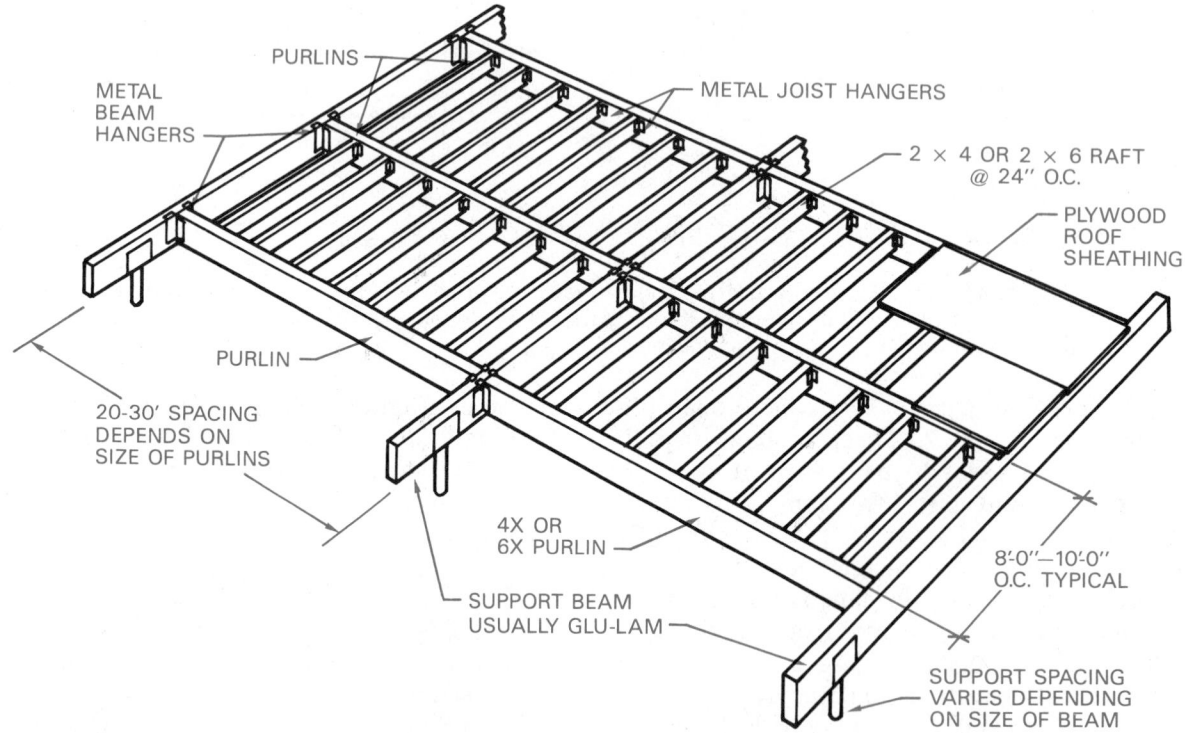

Figure 51–3 A panelized roof system is often used to provide roofing for large areas with limited supports.

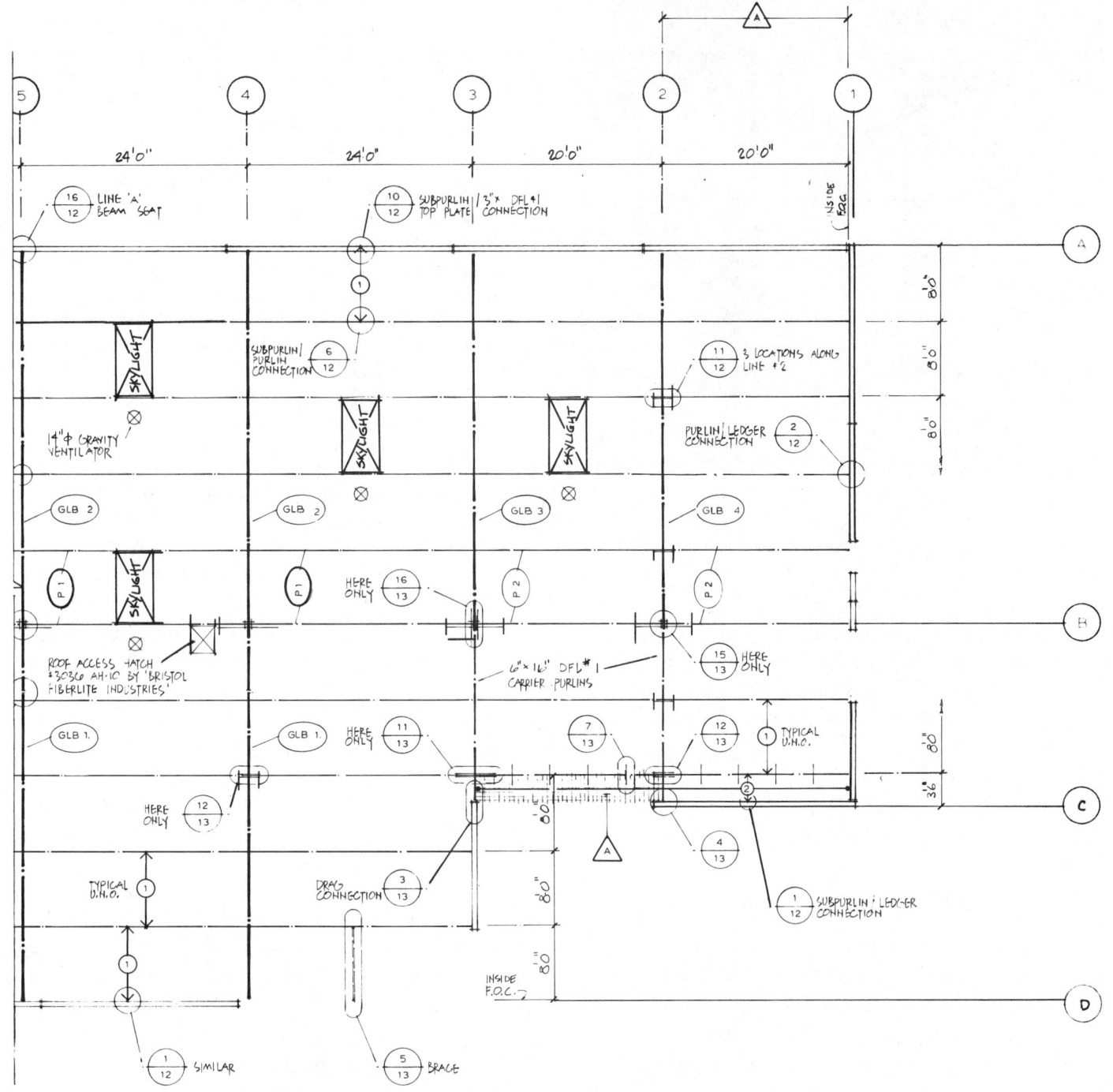

Figure 51–4 A panelized roof framing plan. *Courtesy Structureform Masters, Inc.*

ities. In a fire, heavy wood members will char on their exterior surfaces but will maintain their structural integrity long after an equal-sized steel beam will have failed. Figure 51–5 shows an examples of heavy timbers used to form the supports for a structure. A roof framed with heavy timbers will resemble the plan in Figure 51–4.

Laminated Beams

Because of the difficulty of producing large beams in long lengths from solid wood, large beams are typically constructed from smaller members laminated together to form the larger beam. Laminated beams are a common material for buildings such as gymnasiums and churches that require large amounts of open spaces. Three of the most common types of laminated beams are the single span, Tudor arch and the three-hinged arch beams. Examples of each can be seen in Figure 51–6.

The single span beam is often used in standard platform framing methods. These beams are typically referred to as glu-lams. Because of their increased

Figure 51–5 Timbers are often used in commercial construction because of their beauty and structural qualities. The structural system of St. Philip's Episcopal Church is formed by glue-laminated Southern pine arches and beams under a sweeping canopy of Southern pine roof decking. *Courtesy Southern Forest Products Association.*

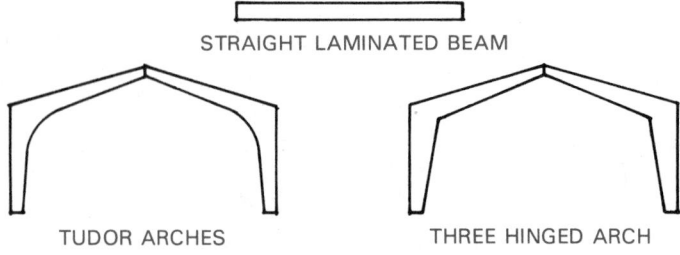

Figure 51–6 Common laminated beam shapes.

structural qualities, a laminated beam can be used to replace a much larger sawed beam. Laminated beams will often have a curve, or camber, built into the beam. The camber is designed into the beam to help resist the loads to be carried.

The Tudor and three-hinged arch members are a post-and-beam system combined into one member. These beams are specified on plans in a method similar to other beams. The drafter's major responsibility when working with either heavy timber construction or laminated beams will be in the drawing of connection details. Beam to beam, beam to column, and column to support are among the most common details drawn by drafters. Figure 51–7 shows common types of manufactured connectors used to connect

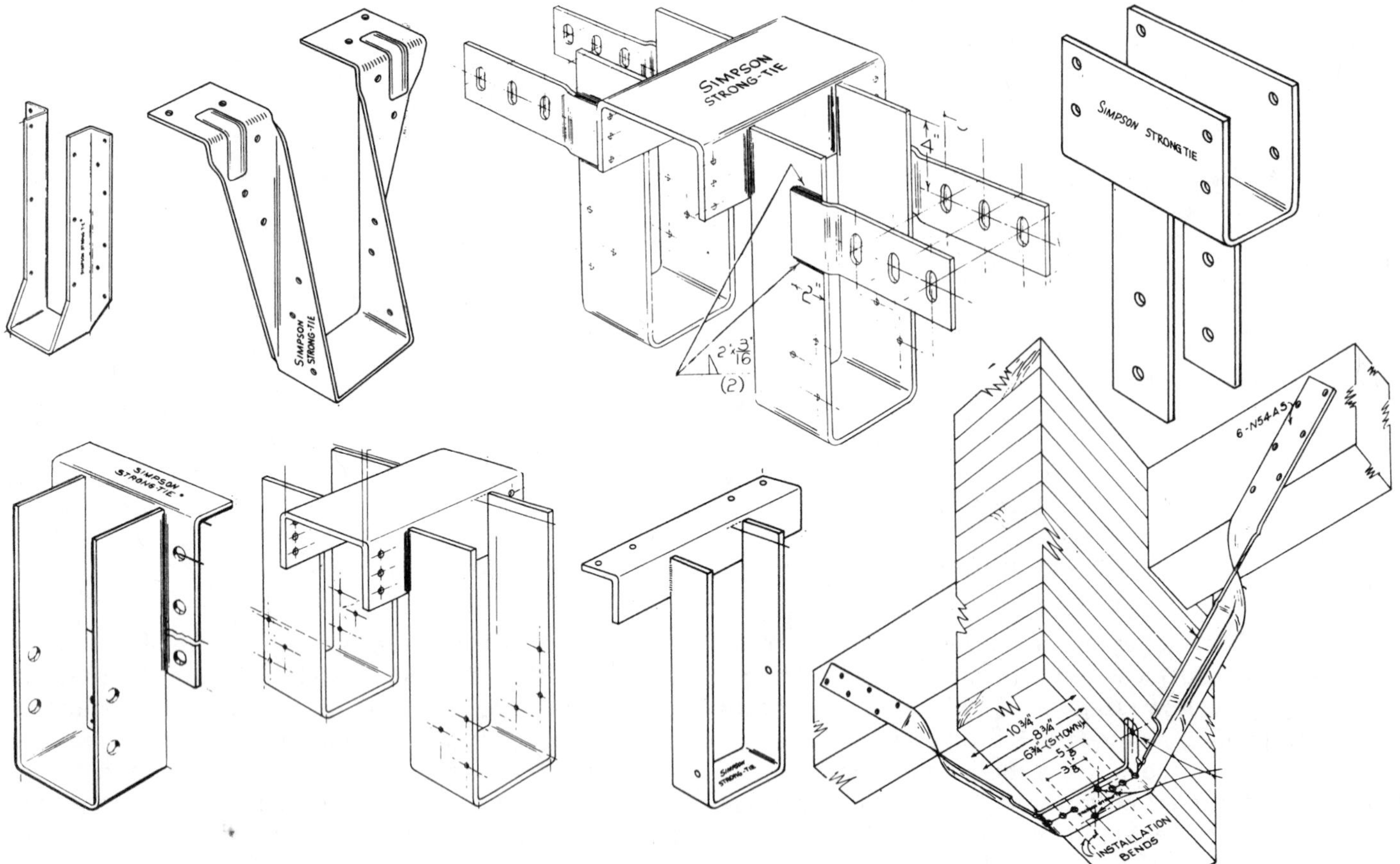

Figure 51–7 Common manufactured metal beam connectors. *Courtesy Simpson Strong-Tie Company, Inc.*

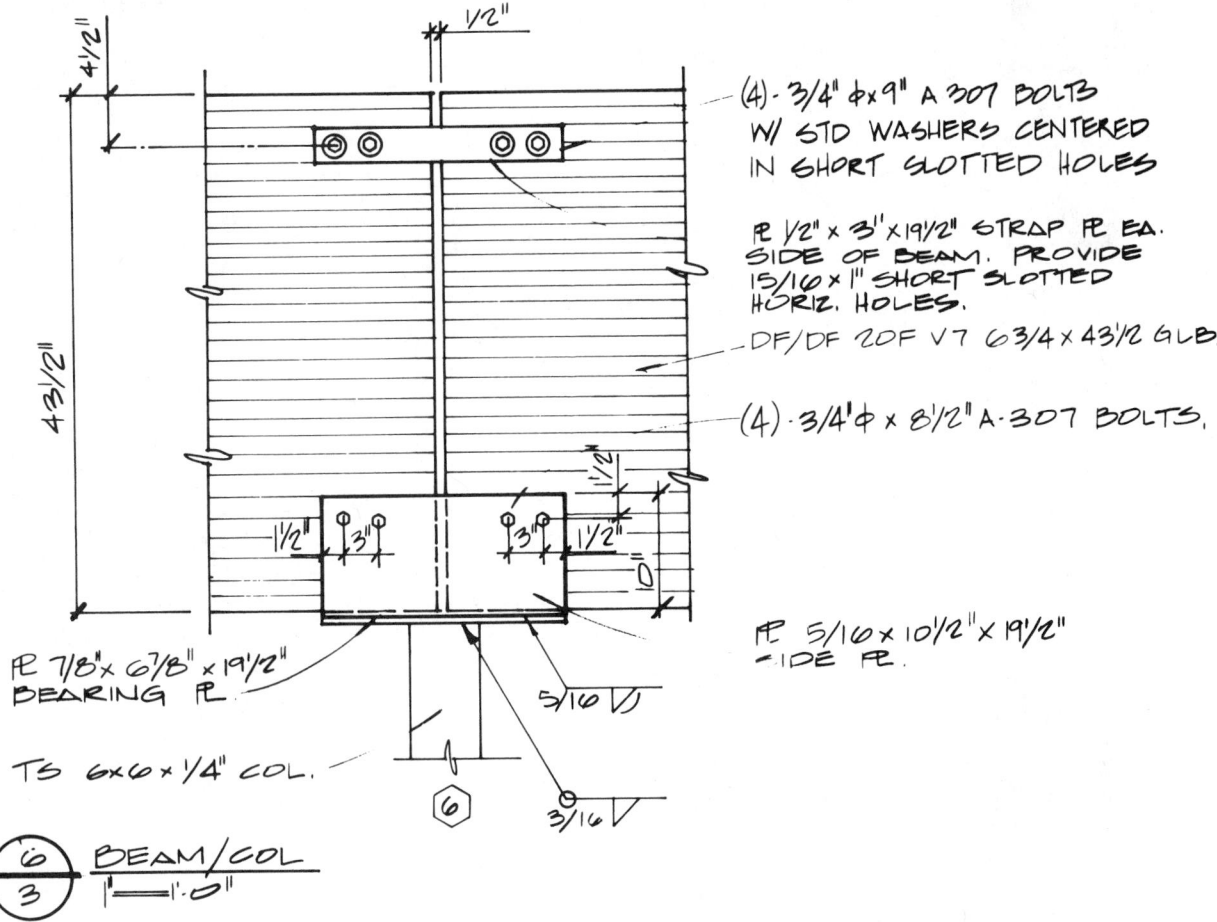

(4)·3/4" φ×9" A 307 BOLTS
W/ STD WASHERS CENTERED
IN SHORT SLOTTED HOLES

℄ 1/2" × 3" ×19½" STRAP ℄ EA.
SIDE OF BEAM. PROVIDE
15/16 × 1" SHORT SLOTTED
HORIZ. HOLES.

DF/DF 20F V7 63/4 × 43½ GLB.

(4)·3/4' φ × 8½" A·307 BOLTS.

℄ 5/16 × 10½" × 19½"
SIDE ℄.

℄ 7/8"× 67/8" × 19½"
BEARING ℄.

TS 6×6 × 1/4" COL.

6
3 BEAM/COL
1"═══1'·0"

Figure 51–8 When a prefabricated connector is not available in the proper size, a drafter will need to provide drawings for fabrication.

timbers. When the size of the beam does not match existing connectors, the drafter will be required to draw the fabrication details for a connector. Figure 51–8 shows an example of such a detail.

CONCRETE BLOCK

Concrete block is used in some areas for above-ground construction, but it is primarily used as a foundation material in residential construction. In commercial construction, concrete blocks are used to form the wall system for many types of buildings. Concrete blocks provide a durable and relatively inexpensive material to install and maintain. Blocks are typically manufactured in 8 × 8 × 16 modules. The sizes listed are width, height, then length. Other common sizes include 4 × 8 × 16, 6 × 8 × 16, and 12 × 8 × 16. The actual size of the block is smaller than the nominal size so that mortar joints can be included. Although the person responsible for the design will determine the size of the structure, it is important that the drafter be aware of the modular principles of concrete block construction. Lengths of

walls, locations of openings in a wall, and the heights of walls and openings must be based on the modular size of the block being used. Failure to maintain the modular layout can result in a tremendous increase in the cost of labor to cut and lay the blocks.

The drafter's major responsibility when working with concrete blocks will be to detail steel reinforcing patterns. Concrete blocks are often reinforced with a wire mesh at every other course of blocks. Where the risk of seismic danger is great, concrete blocks are often required to have reinforcing steel placed within the wall. These bars are placed in a grid pattern throughout the wall to help tie the blocks together. The steel is placed in a block that has a channel running through it. This cell is then filled with grout to form a header or bond beam within the wall. Figure 51–9 shows an example of a detail that a drafter would be required to draw to specify the bond beam.

When the concrete blocks are required to support a load from a beam, a pilaster is often placed in the wall to help transfer beam loads down into the footing. Pilasters are also used to provide vertical support to the wall when the wall is required to span long

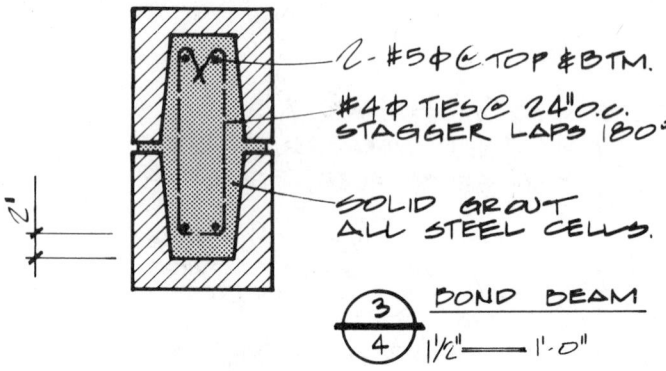

2 - #5∮ @ TOP & BTM.

#4∮ TIES @ 24" O.C.
STAGGER LAPS 180°

SOLID GROUT
ALL STEEL CELLS.

BOND BEAM
3/4   1½" ——— 1'-0"

Figure 51-9 When working with concrete block, the drafter is typically required to detail reinforcing.

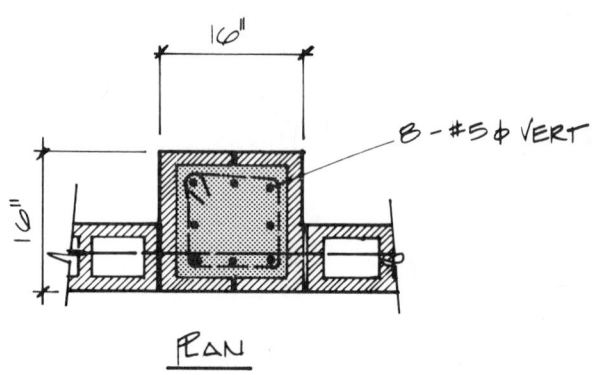

16"

8 - #5∮ VERT

PLAN

Figure 51-10 Pilasters are a common feature that require steel reinforcing.

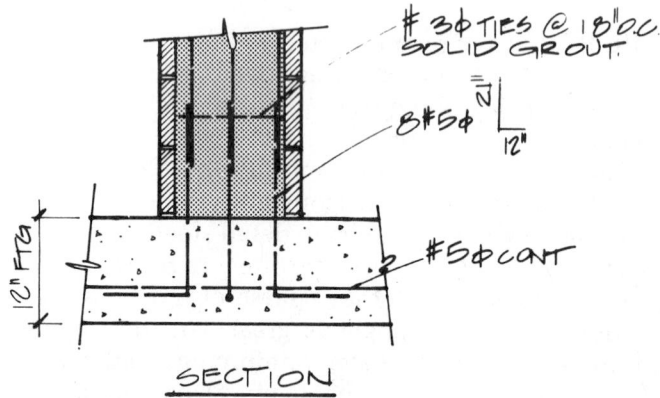

3∮ TIES @ 18" O.C.
SOLID GROUT

8 #5∮   2'/12"

#5∮ CONT

SECTION

distances. Examples of pilasters can be seen in Chapter 21. An example of a detail that the drafter might be required to draw can be seen in Figure 51-10. Wood can be attached to concrete in several ways. Two of the most common methods are by the use of a seat as seen in Figure 51-11, or a metal connector as seen in Figure 51-12.

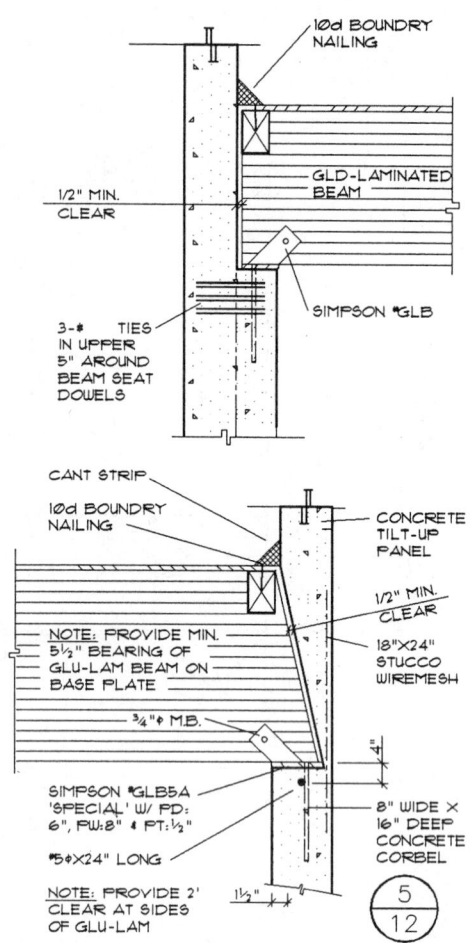

10d BOUNDRY NAILING

½" MIN.
CLEAR

GLD-LAMINATED BEAM

3-# TIES
IN UPPER
5" AROUND
BEAM SEAT
DOWELS

SIMPSON #GLB

CANT STRIP

10d BOUNDRY NAILING

CONCRETE TILT-UP PANEL

½" MIN.
CLEAR

NOTE: PROVIDE MIN.
5½" BEARING OF
GLU-LAM BEAM ON
BASE PLATE

18"X24"
STUCCO
WIREMESH

¾"∮ M.B.

SIMPSON #GLB5A
'SPECIAL' W/ PD:
6", PW:8" & PT:½"

8" WIDE X
16" DEEP
CONCRETE
CORBEL

#5∮X24" LONG

NOTE: PROVIDE 2'
CLEAR AT SIDES
OF GLU-LAM

1½"

5/12

Figure 51-11 Wood beams are often allowed to rest on a ledge. *Courtesy Structureform Masters, Inc.*

POURED CONCRETE

Concrete is a common building material composed of sand and gravel bonded together with cement and water. One of the most common types of cement is portland cement. Portland cement contains pulverized particles of limestone, cement rock, oyster shells, silica sand, shale, iron ore, and gypsum. The gypsum controls the time required for the cement to set.

Concrete can either be poured in place at the job site, formed off site and delivered ready to be erected into place, or formed at the job site and lifted into place. Your area of the country, the office that you work in, and the type of structure to be built will dictate which of these concrete construction methods you will be using.

Types of Drawings

As you work on concrete drawings, you will find that two types will typically be needed. Structural or engineering drawings are one type that is similar to other drawings that you have been exposed to.

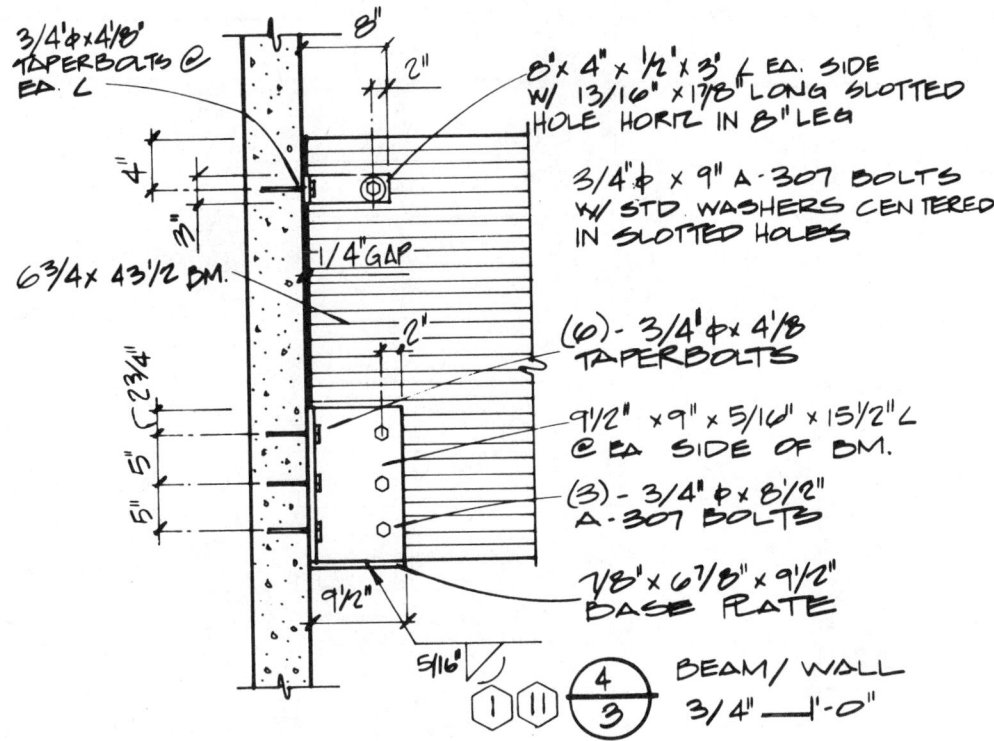

Figure 51–12 A metal hanger can be used to support beams when they intersect a wall.

These drawings will show general information that is required for sales, marketing, engineering, or erection purposes. Shop drawings are the other type, and they are needed to specify the fabrications process of the part. Depending on the complexity of the component and the structure, these two types of drawings may be combined. Figure 51–13 shows an example of an engineering drawing. An example of shop drawings can be seen in Figure 51–14. As a drafter in an architectural or engineering firm you typically will be drawing engineering drawings. The fabrication drawings are drawn by engineers and drafters at the fabricating company.

Cast in Place

You have been exposed to the methods of cast-in-place concrete for residential foundations and retaining walls. Commercial applications are similar, but the size of the casting and amount of reinforcing will vary greatly. In addition to foundation and floor systems, concrete is often used for walls, columns and floors above ground. Walls and columns are usually constructed by setting steel reinforcing in place and then surrounding it by wooden forms to contain the concrete. Once the concrete has been poured and allowed to set, the forms can be removed. As a drafter, you will be required to draw details showing not only sizes of the part to be constructed, but also steel placement within the wall or column. This will typically consist of drawing the vertical steel and the horizontal ties. Ties are wrapped around

the vertical steel to keep the column from separating when placed under a load. Figure 51–15 shows two examples of column reinforcing methods. Figure 51–16 shows the drawings required to detail the construction of a rectangular concrete column. Depending on the complexity of the object to be formed, the drafter may be required to draw the details for the column and for the forming system.

Concrete is also used on commercial projects to form an above-grade floor. The floor slab either can be supported by a steel deck or entirely self supporting. The steel deck system is typically used on structures constructed with a steel frame. Two of the most common poured-in-place concrete floor systems are the ribbed and waffle floor methods. Each can be seen in Figure 51–17.

The ribbed system is used in many office buildings. The ribs serve as floor joists to support the slab but are actually part of the slab. Spacing of the ribs will vary depending on the span and the reinforcing material. The waffle system is used to provide added support for the floor slab and is typically used in the floor system of parking garages.

Precast Concrete

Precast concrete construction consists of forming walls or other components off site and transporting the part to the job site. Figure 51–18 shows an example of a precast beam being lifted into place. In addition to detailing how precast members will be constructed, drawings must also include methods of

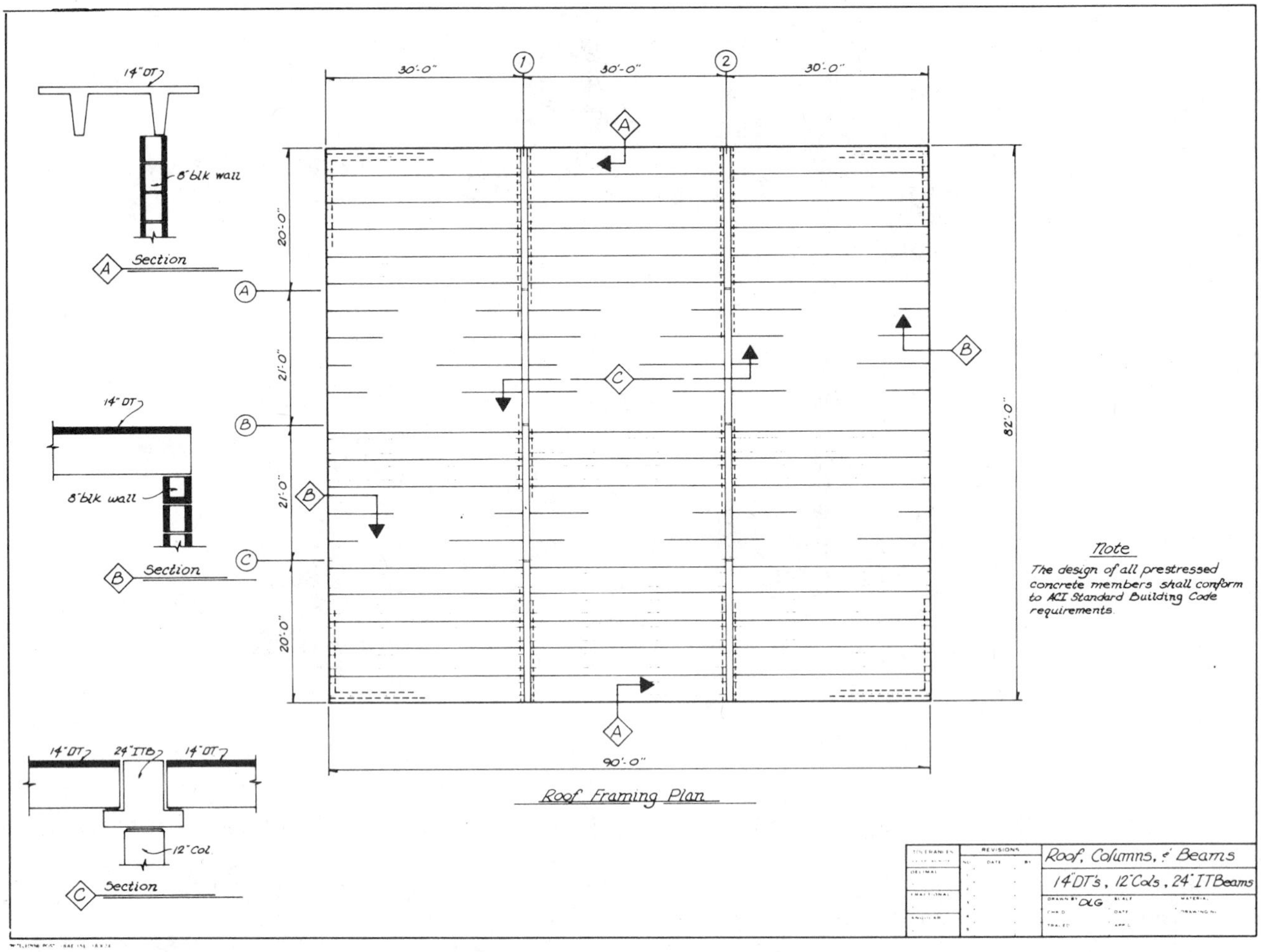

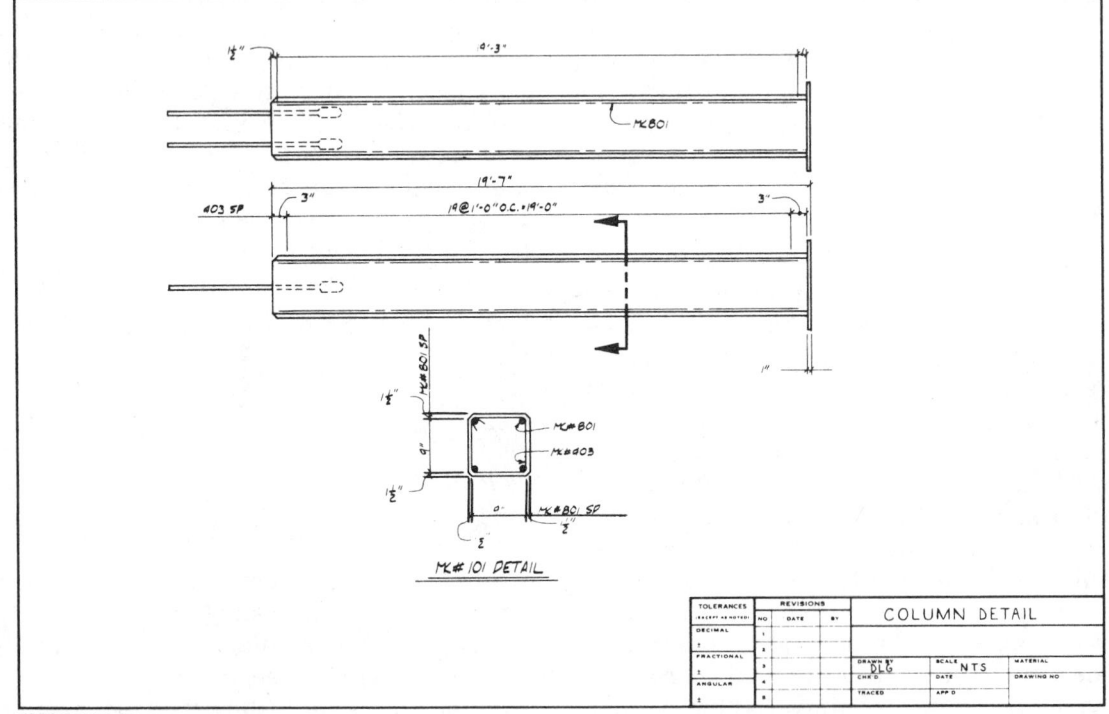

Figure 51–13 Precast concrete engineering drawing.

Figure 51–14 Precast concrete fabrication detail.

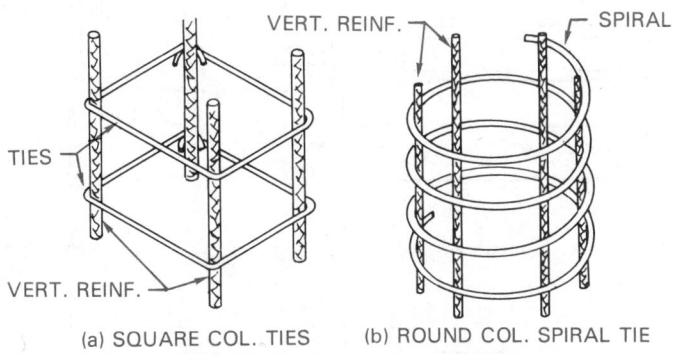

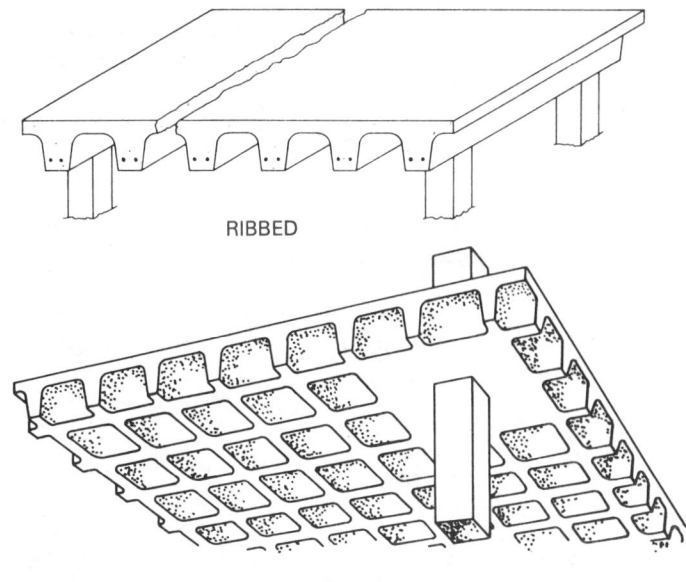

(a) SQUARE COL. TIES   (b) ROUND COL. SPIRAL TIE

Figure 51–15 Common methods of reinforcing poured concrete columns.

RIBBED

WAFFLE-SLAB

Figure 51–17 Two common concrete floor systems are the ribbed and waffle systems.

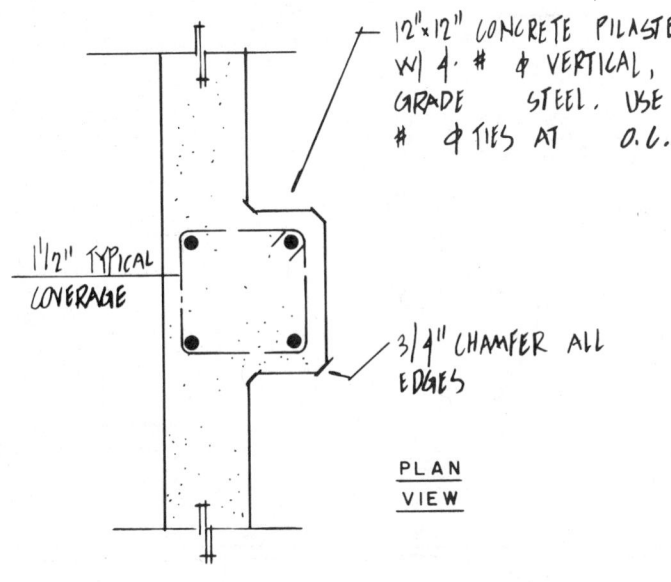

12"x12" CONCRETE PILASTER W/ 4 - # φ VERTICAL, GRADE STEEL. USE # φ TIES AT   O.C.

1½" TYPICAL COVERAGE

3/4" CHAMFER ALL EDGES

PLAN VIEW

1" — 1'· 0"

Figure 51–16 Typical reinforcing for a rectangular concrete column. *Courtesy Structureform Masters, Inc.*

Figure 51–18 Precast concrete beams and panels are often formed offsite, delivered to the job site, and then set into place by a crane.

Figure 51–19 Precast concrete panels are often welded to adjoining members.

transporting and lifting the part into place. Precast parts typically have an exposed metal flange so that the part can be connected to other parts. Figure 51–19 shows a precast wall section connected to a poured column. Figure 51–20 shows common details used for wall connections.

In addition to being precast, many concrete products are also prestressed. Concrete is prestressed by placing steel cables held in tension between the concrete forms while the concrete is poured around them. Once the concrete has hardened, the tension on the cables is released. As the cables attempt to regain their original shape, compression pressure is created within the concrete. The compression in the concrete helps prevent cracking and deflection and

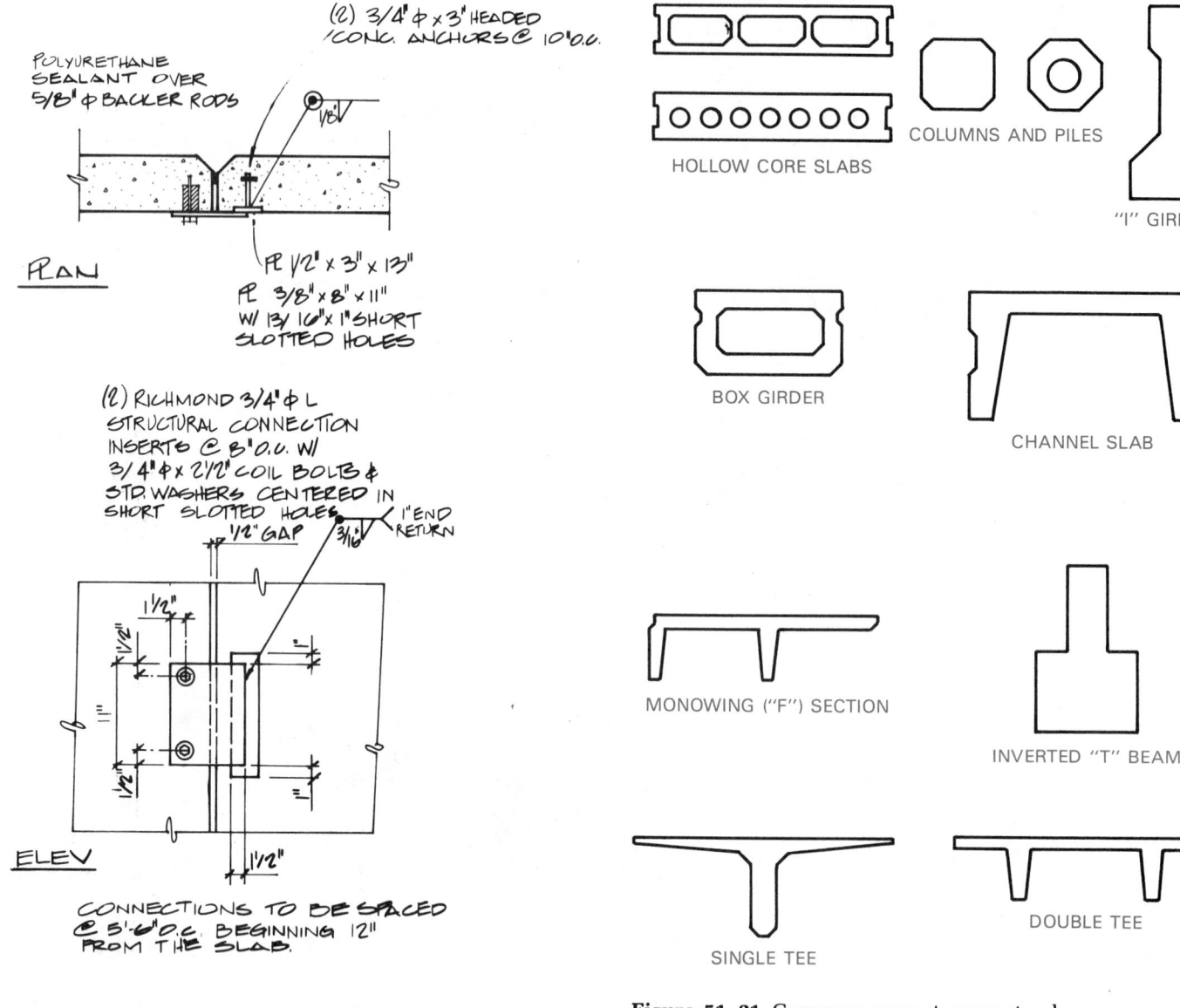

(2) 3/4" ⌀ × 3" HEADED
/CONC. ANCHORS @ 10" O.C.

POLYURETHANE
SEALANT OVER
5/8" ⌀ BACKER RODS

PLAN

PL 1/2" × 3" × 13"
PL 3/8" × 8" × 11"
W/ 13/16" × 1" SHORT
SLOTTED HOLES

(2) RICHMOND 3/4" ⌀ L
STRUCTURAL CONNECTION
INSERTS @ 8" O.C. W/
3/4" ⌀ × 2 1/2" COIL BOLTS &
STD. WASHERS CENTERED IN
SHORT SLOTTED HOLES

1/2" GAP   1" END RETURN

1 1/2"
1 1/2"
1"
1 1/2"

ELEV

1 1/2"

CONNECTIONS TO BE SPACED
@ 5'-6" O.C. BEGINNING 12"
FROM THE SLAB.

1/3   PANEL CONNECTOR
      1" = 1'-0"

Figure 51–20 A typical wall connection detail drawn by a drafter to explain how wall panels are connected.

often allows the size of the member to be reduced. Figure 51–21 shows common shapes that are typically used in prestressed construction.

Tilt-up

Tilt-up construction is a method using preformed wall panels which are lifted into place. Panels may either be formed at the job or off site. Forms for a wall are constructed in a horizontal position and the required steel is placed in the form. Concrete is then poured around the steel and allowed to harden. Once the panel has reached its design strength, it can then be lifted into place. When using this type of construction, the drafter will usually be drawing a plan

HOLLOW CORE SLABS

COLUMNS AND PILES

"I" GIRDER

BOX GIRDER

CHANNEL SLAB

MONOWING ("F") SECTION

INVERTED "T" BEAM

SINGLE TEE

DOUBLE TEE

Figure 51–21 Common precast concrete shapes.

view to specify the panel locations as seen in Figure 51–22. Figure 51–23 shows an example of a typical steel placement drawing.

STEEL CONSTRUCTION

Steel construction can be divided into the three categories of steel studs, prefabricated steel structures, and steel-framed structures.

Steel Studs

Prefabricated steel studs are used in many types of commercial structures to help meet the requirements of types 1, 2, and 3 construction methods. Steel studs offer lightweight, noncombustible, corrosion-resistant framing for interior walls, and load-bearing exterior walls up to four stories high. Steel members

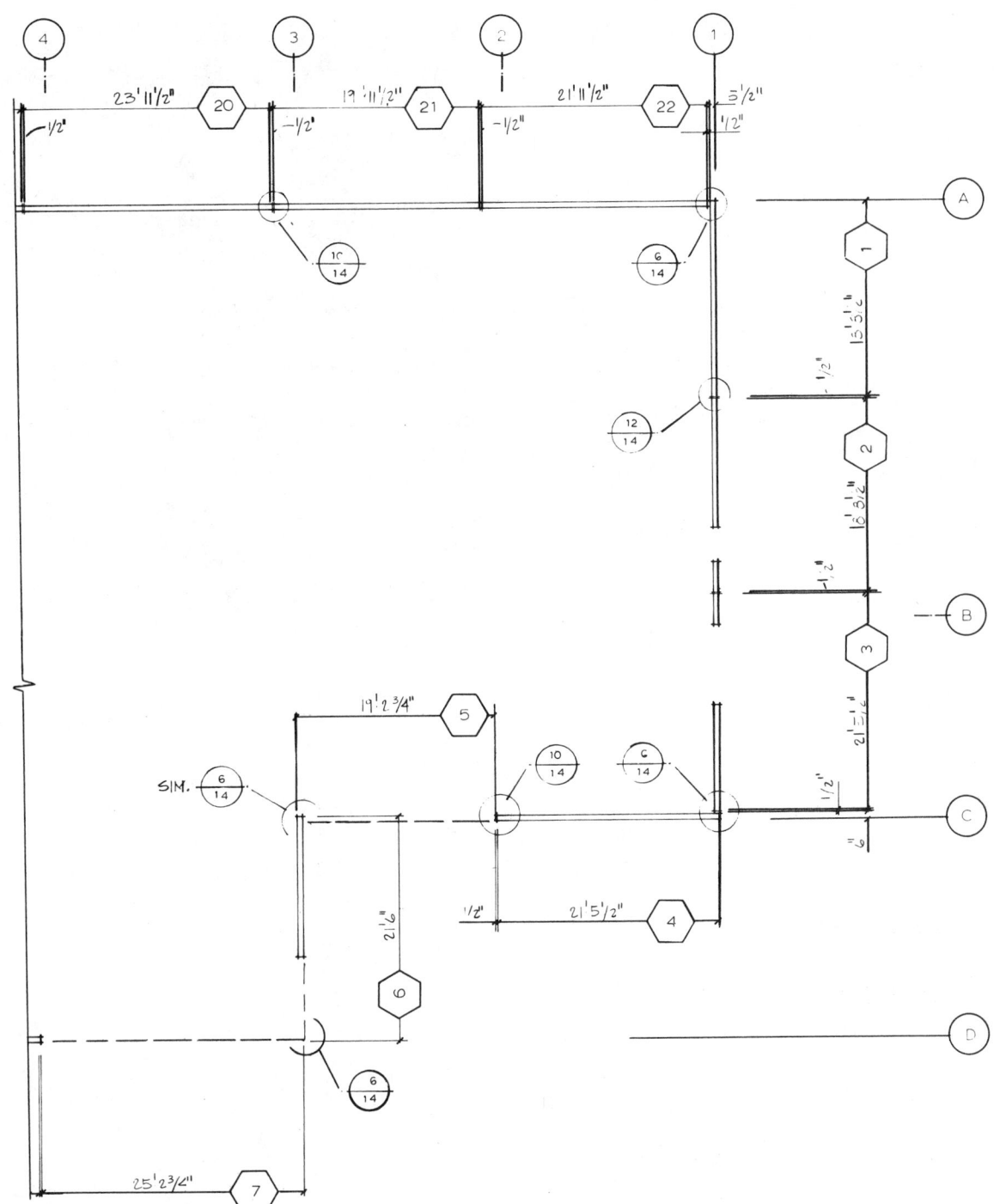

Figure 51–22 A plan view is often used to show panel locations. *Courtesy Structureform Masters, Inc.*

are available for use as studs or joists. Members are designed for rapid assembly and are predrilled for electrical and plumbing conduits. The standard 24 in. spacing reduces the number of studs required by about one-third when compared with common studs spacing of 16 in. O.C. Widths of studs can range from 3⅝ to 10 in. but can be manufactured in any width. The material used to produce studs ranges from 12 to 20 gage steel, depending on the loads to be sup-

ported. Figure 51–24 shows steel studs as they are typically used. Steel studs are mounted in a channel track at the top and bottom of the wall. This channel is similar to the top and bottom plates of a standard stud wall. Horizontal bridging is placed through the predrilled holes in the studs and then welded to the stud serving a function similar to solid blocking in a stud wall. Figure 51–25 shows components of steel stud framing.

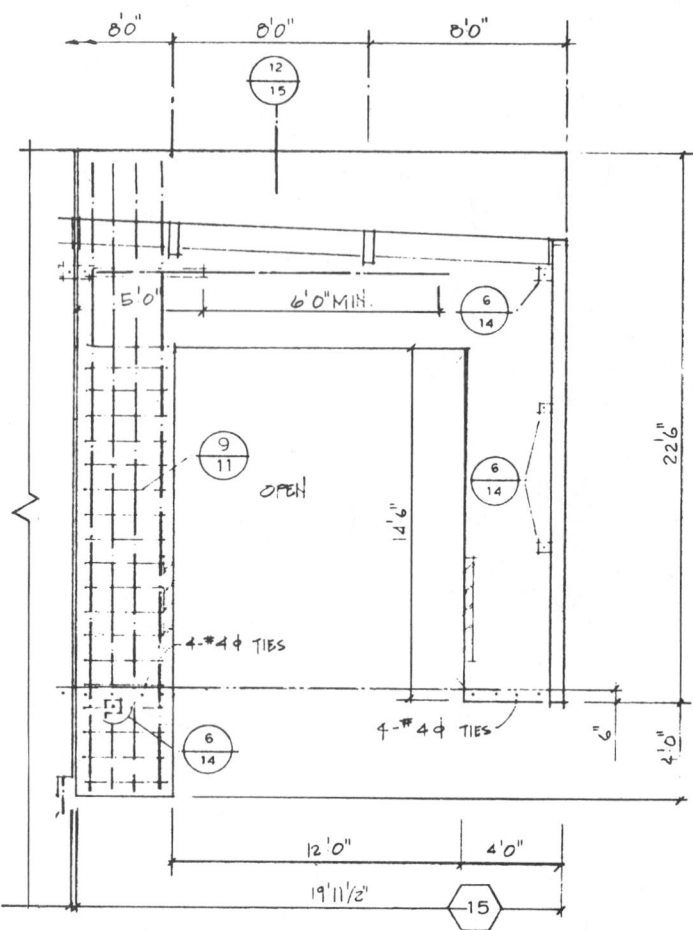

Figure 51-23 Steel locations in precast panels must be specified in details. *Courtesy Structureform Masters, Inc.*

Figure 51-24 Steel joists and studs are often used where noncombustible construction is required. *Courtesy United States Gypsum Company.*

Prefabricated Steel Structures

Prefabricated or metal buildings have become a common type of structure for commercial structures in many parts of the country. Because these structures are premanufactured, a drafter probably will not be drawing these in an architectural or engineering office. Although a drafter usually completes the plans for a metal building, the drafter is usually employed by the building manufacturer.

Steel-Framed Buildings

Steel-framed buildings will require engineering and shop drawings similar to those used for concrete structures. As a drafter in an engineering or architectural firm, you will most likely be drawing engineering drawings similar to the one in Figure 51-26. An engineer or drafter working for the steel fabricator will typically develop the shop drawings similar to the one in Figure 51-27.

As a drafter working on steel-framed structures, you will need to become familiar with the *Manual of Steel Construction* published by the American Institute of Steel Construction (AISC). In addition to

your building code, this manual will be one of your prime references since it will be helpful in determining dimensions and properties of common steel shapes.

Common Steel Products

Structural steel is typically identified as a plate, a bar or by its shape. Plates are flat pieces of steel of various thickness used at the intersection of different members. Figure 51-28 shows an example of a steel connector that uses top, side, and bottom plates. Plates are typically specified on a drawing by giving the thickness, width, and length in that order. The symbol ₤ is often used to specify plate material.

Bars are the smallest of structural steel products. Bars are either round, square, rectangular or hexagonal when seen in cross section. Bars are often used as supports or braces for other steel parts.

Structural steel is typically produced in the shapes that are seen in Figure 51-29. M, S, and W are the names given to steel shapes that have a cross-sectional area in the shape of the letter I. The three differ in the width of their flanges. The flange is the horizontal leg of the I shape and the vertical leg is the web. In addition to varied flange widths, the S shape flanges vary in depth.

Angles are structural steel components that have

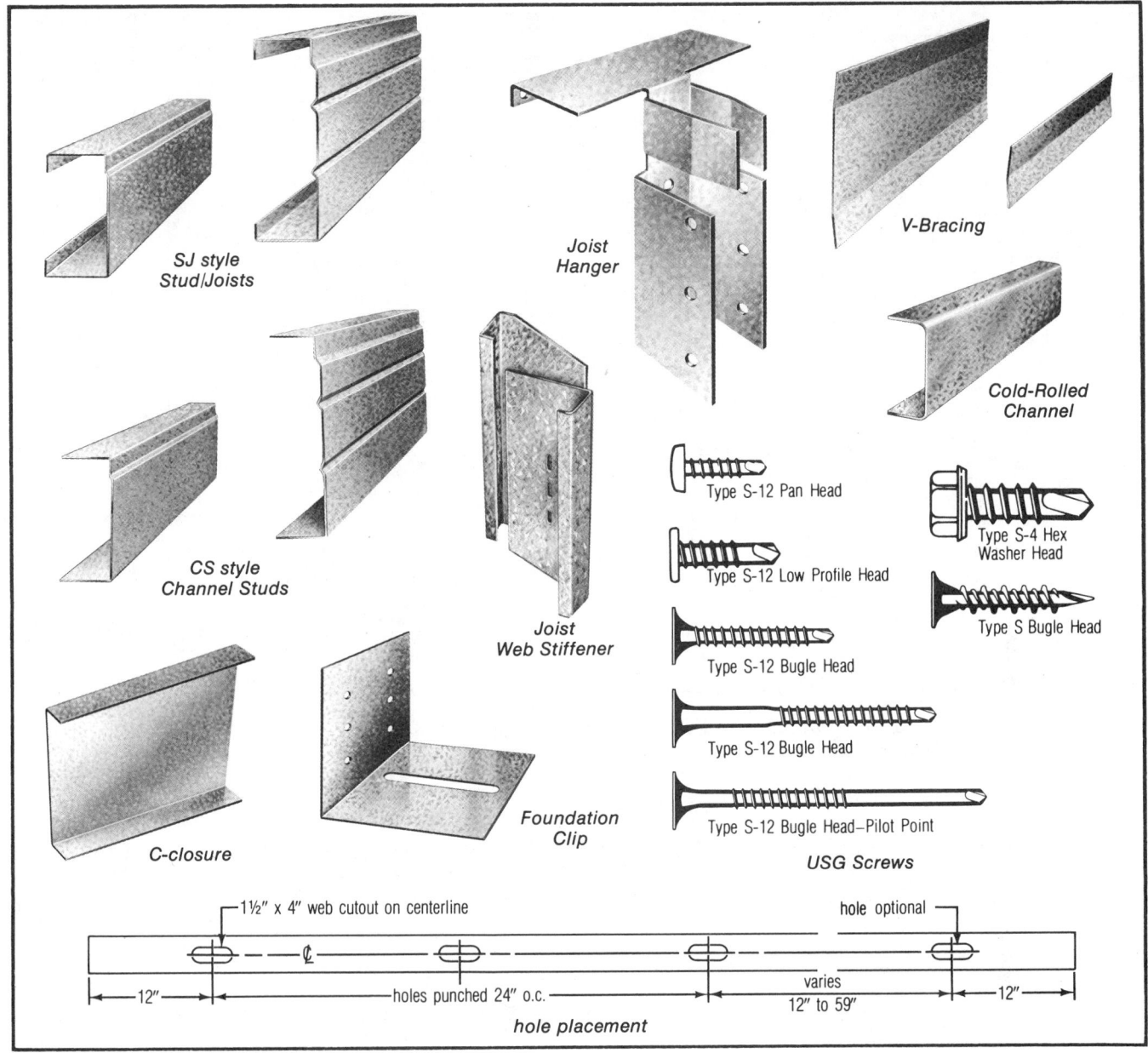

SJ style
Stud/Joists

CS style
Channel Studs

C-closure

Joist
Web Stiffener

Foundation
Clip

Joist
Hanger

V-Bracing

Cold-Rolled
Channel

Type S-12 Pan Head

Type S-12 Low Profile Head

Type S-12 Bugle Head

Type S-12 Bugle Head

Type S-12 Bugle Head–Pilot Point

Type S-4 Hex
Washer Head

Type S Bugle Head

USG Screws

1½" x 4" web cutout on centerline

hole optional

12"   C̶   holes punched 24" o.c.   varies
12" to 59"   12"

hole placement

Figure 51–25 Common components of steel stud construction. *Courtesy United States Gypsum Company.*

an L shape. The legs of the angle may be either equal or unequal in length but are usually equal in thickness. Channels have a squared C cross-sectional area and are represented by the letter C when specified in note form. Structural tees are cut from W, S, and M steel shapes by cutting the webs. Common designations include WT, ST, and MT.

Structural tubing is manufactured in square, rectangular, and round cross-sectional configurations. These members are used as columns to support loads from other members. Tubes are specified by the size of the outer wall followed by the thickness of the wall.

COMMON CONNECTION METHODS

Bolts

Bolts are used for many connections in lumber and steel construction. When specified on plans, the diameter and length of the bolt should be specified. Washers or plates are also specified so that the bolt head and nut will not be pulled through the hole made for the bolt. The strength of the bolt also needs to be specified. Bolts are classified as to their strength by the American Society for Testing and Materials (ASTM).

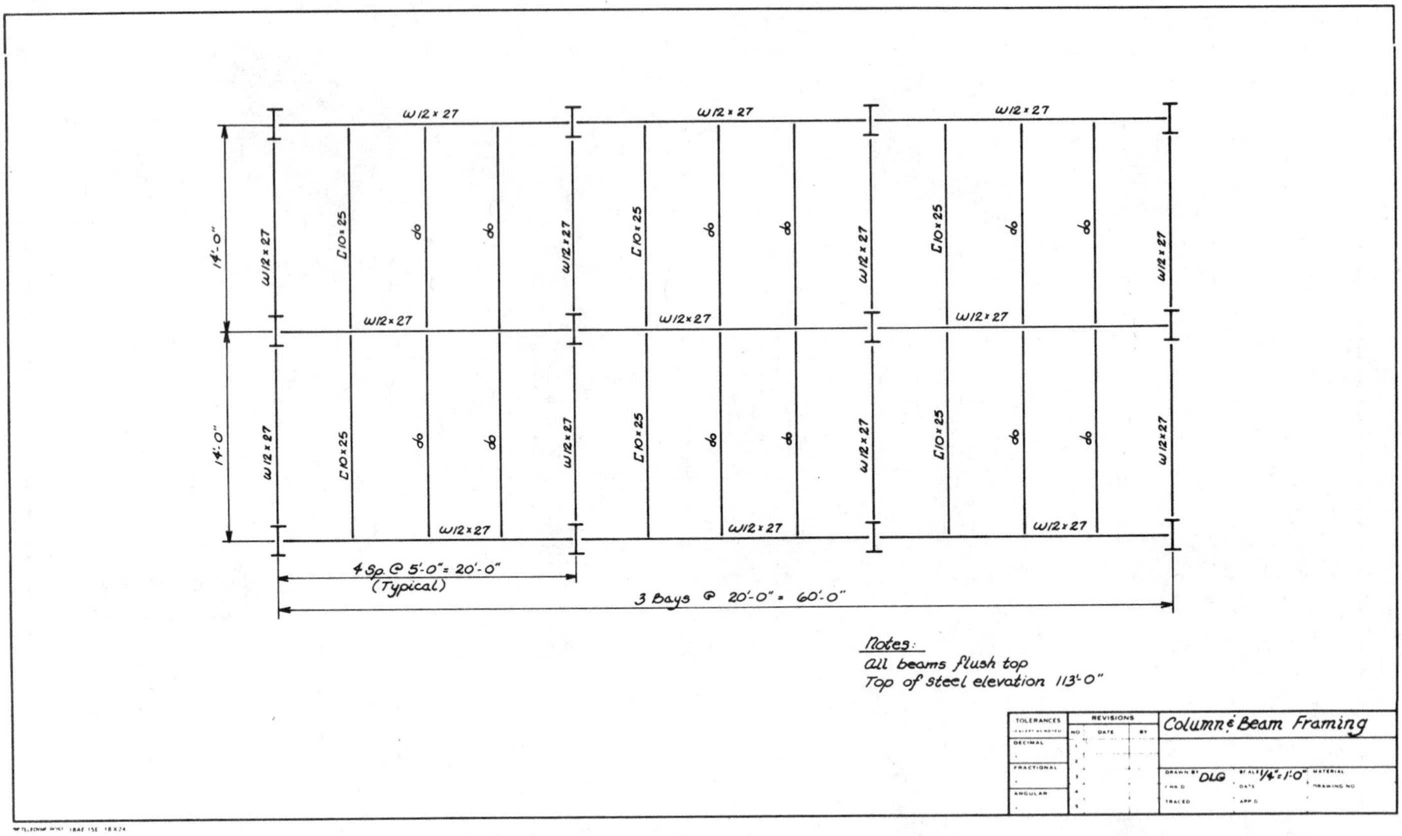

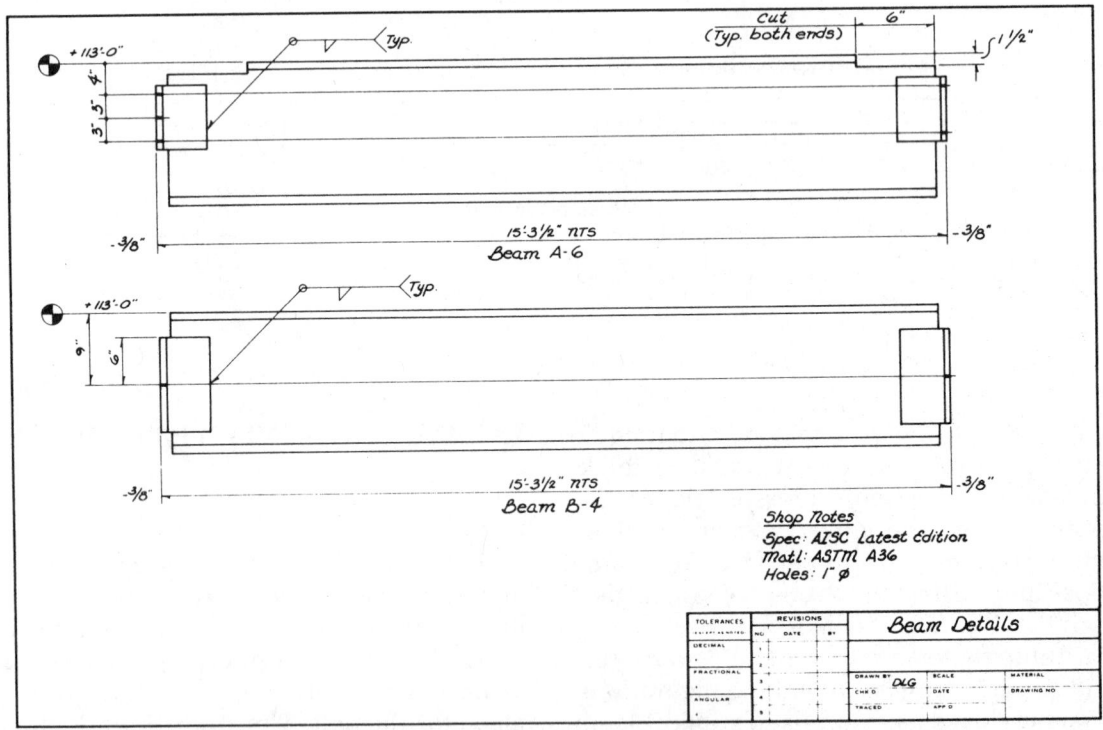

Figure 51–26 Structural steel engineering drawing. *From Goetsch, Structural Drafting, Delmar Publishers Inc.*

Figure 51–27 Structural steel fabrication drawings, such as this one, are used to show how individual components are to be made. *From Goetsch, Structural Drafting, Delmar Publishers Inc.*

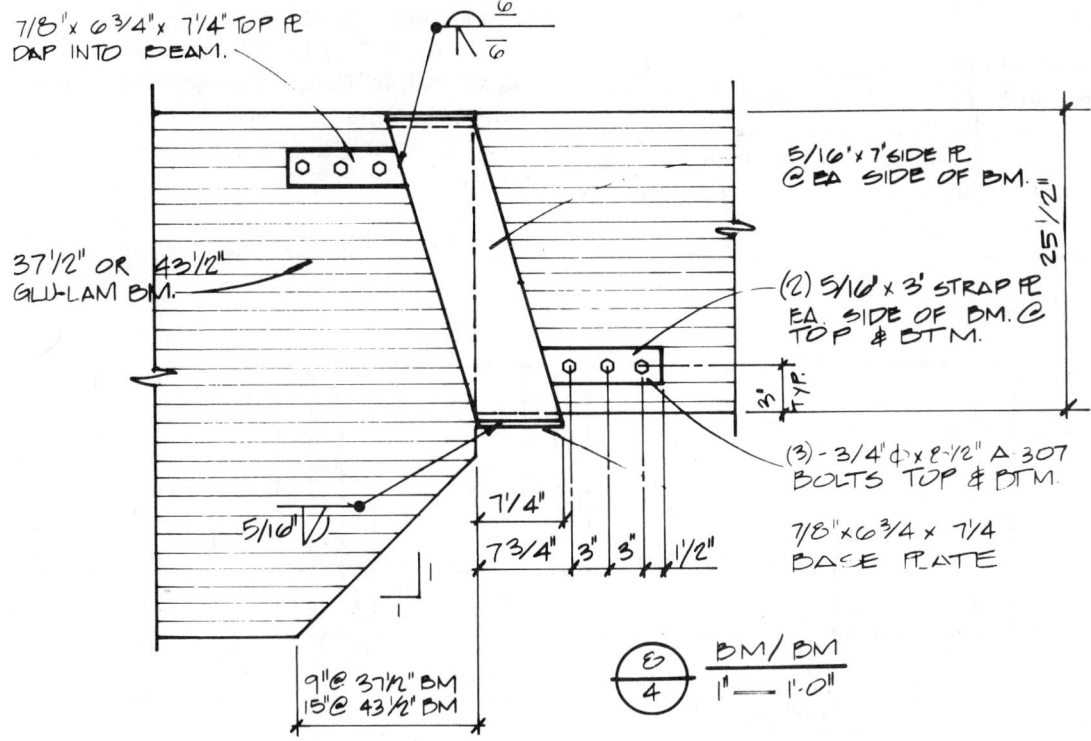

Figure 51–28 Steel plates are used to fabricate a beam connector.

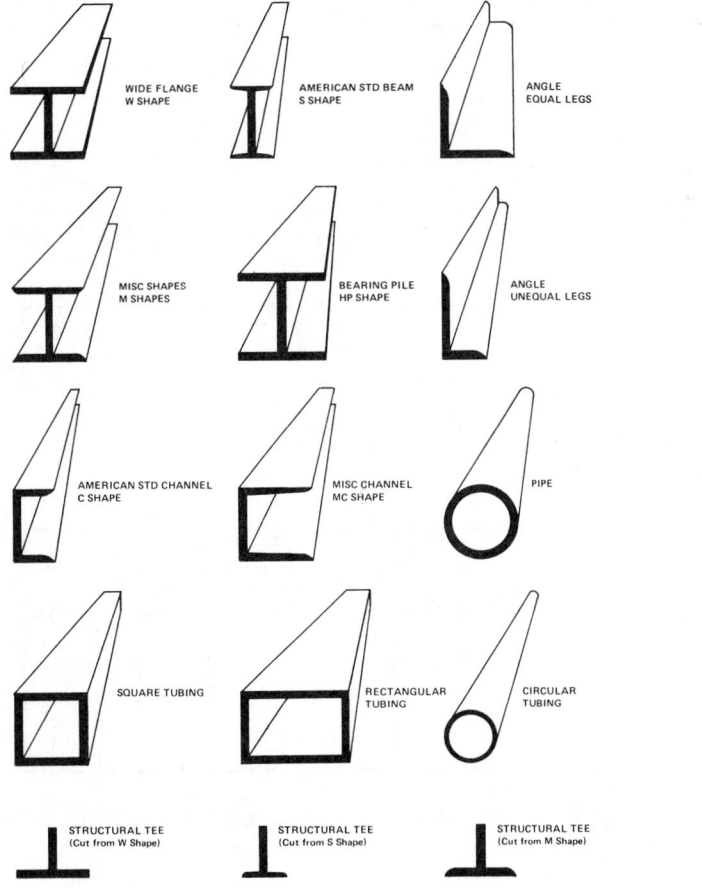

Figure 51–29 Standard structural steel shapes. *From Goetsch, Structural Drafting, Delmar Publishers Inc.*

Welds

Welds are classified according to the type of joint on which they are used. Four common welds used in construction are the fillet, back, plug or slot, and groove weld. Each type of weld can be seen in Figure 51–30. A symbol is used to designate the type of weld. Figure 51–31 shows common welding symbols used in construction. Welds are represented in details as shown in Figure 51–32. The horizontal line is a reference line connected to an angled leader line. Each line should be drawn using tools and not drawn freehand.

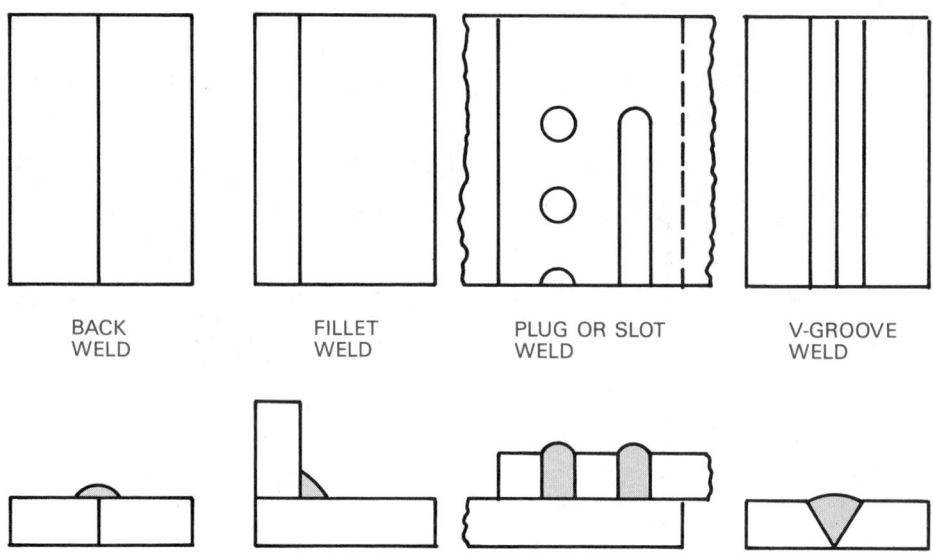

BACK WELD   FILLET WELD   PLUG OR SLOT WELD   V-GROOVE WELD

Figure 51–30 Common structural weld symbols.

BASIC WELD SYMBOLS FOR DRAFTING									
BACK	FILLET	PLUG OR SLOT	GROOVE						
			J	V	U	SQUARE	BEVEL	FLARE V	FLARE BEVEL
⌒	◺	▭	⊔	⋁	⋃	‖	⌵	⋎	⋔

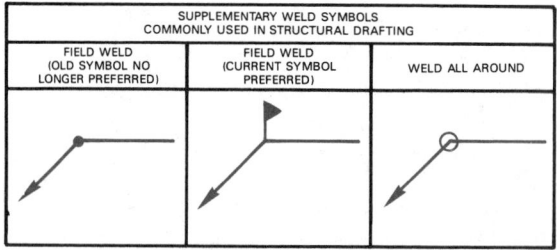

SUPPLEMENTARY WELD SYMBOLS COMMONLY USED IN STRUCTURAL DRAFTING		
FIELD WELD (OLD SYMBOL NO LONGER PREFERRED)	FIELD WELD (CURRENT SYMBOL PREFERRED)	WELD ALL AROUND

Figure 51–31 Basic welding symbols for structural drafting.

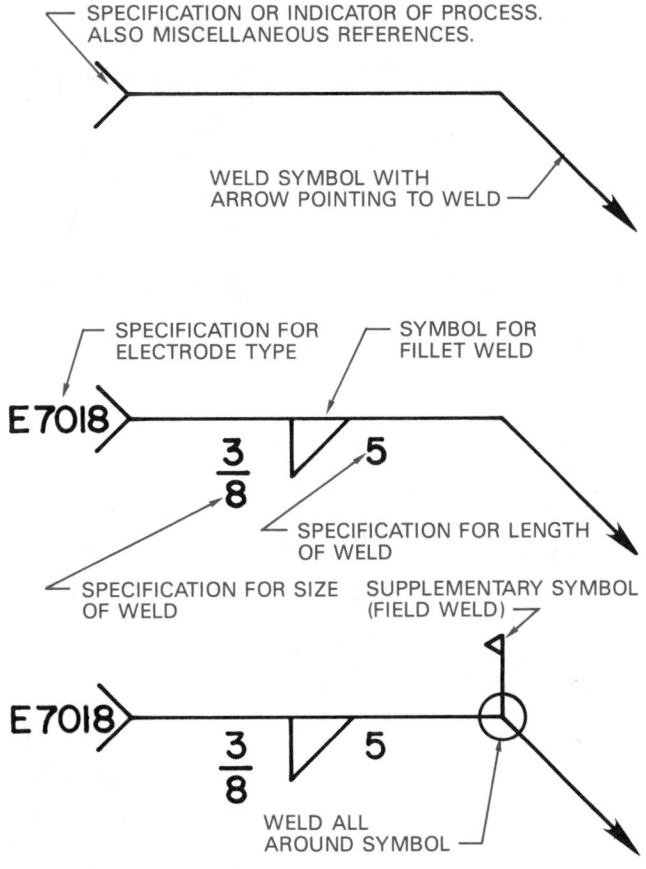

SPECIFICATION OR INDICATOR OF PROCESS. ALSO MISCELLANEOUS REFERENCES.

WELD SYMBOL WITH ARROW POINTING TO WELD

SPECIFICATION FOR ELECTRODE TYPE

SYMBOL FOR FILLET WELD

E 7018

$\frac{3}{8}$ 5

SPECIFICATION FOR LENGTH OF WELD

SPECIFICATION FOR SIZE OF WELD

SUPPLEMENTARY SYMBOL (FIELD WELD)

E 7018

$\frac{3}{8}$ 5

WELD ALL AROUND SYMBOL

EXPLANATION OF TYPICAL WELD SYMBOLS

Figure 51–32 Common elements of a weld symbol for structural drafting.

CADD
applications

USING CADD TO DRAW STRUCTURAL DETAILS

CADD has increased productivity in drawing structural details. One advantage is the use of standard details. Once a detail has been drawn, it may be automatically inserted into any drawing at any time. The detail may be inserted and used as is, or it may be inserted and modified to provide specific information that changes from one drawing to the next. Every time a CADD drafter draws a detail, it is saved in a drawing file for later use. With this process it is not necessary to draw the same drawing more than once. CADD structural packages are available that provide a variety of standard structural details. Most of these packages are based on parametric design, which means that the standard structural detail may be altered by supplying the computer with data. For example, a set of structural stairs may be drawn automatically by providing the computer with total rise, number of risers, tread dimension, reinforcing size and spacing, and railing information. A CADD structural tablet menu with a variety of structural details is shown in Figure 1.

Even when creating nonstandard original drawings, CADD is easier than manual drafting. Many CADD software packages have custom structural tablet menu overlays that provide standard structural shapes that may be inserted on the drawing at any time. This reduces the time for a drafter to individually draw these symbols with a pencil and manual template. Figure 2 shows a variety of CADD tablet menu overlays used to draw structural steel shapes. Drawing reinforcing bars in structural concrete drawings is aided by CADD tablet menu symbol libraries such as the one shown in Figure 3. Welding symbols similar to the one shown in Figure 4 are available on CADD tablet menu symbol libraries.

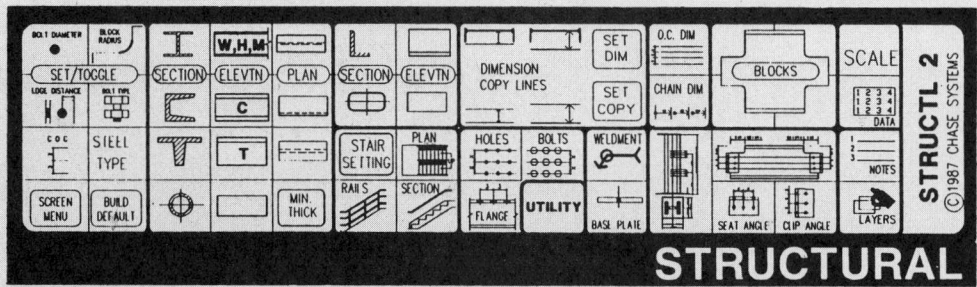

Figure 1 CADD structural tablet menu. *Courtesy Chase Systems.*

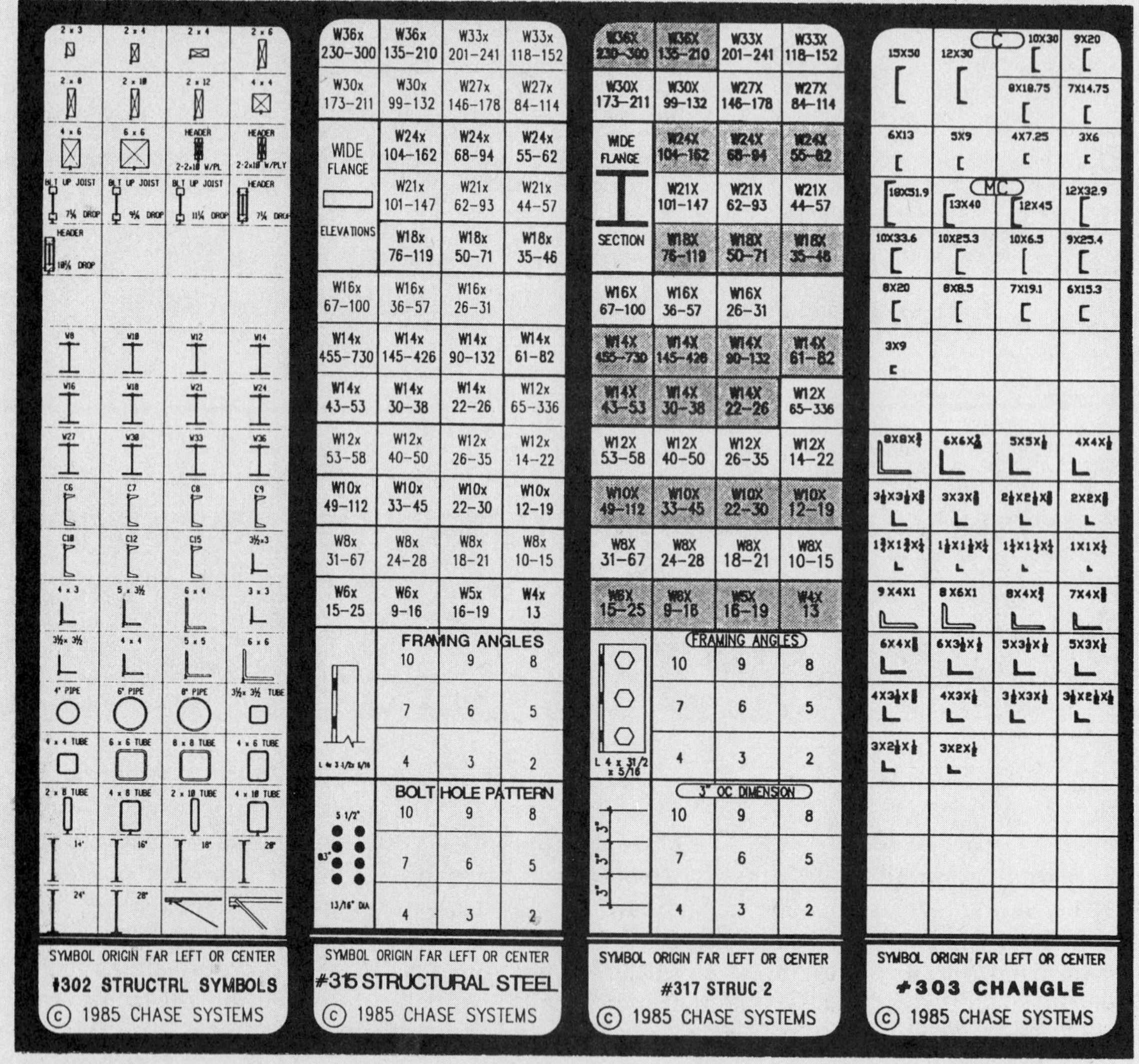

Figure 2 CADD tablet menu overlays for drawing structural steel shapes. *Courtesy Chase Systems.*

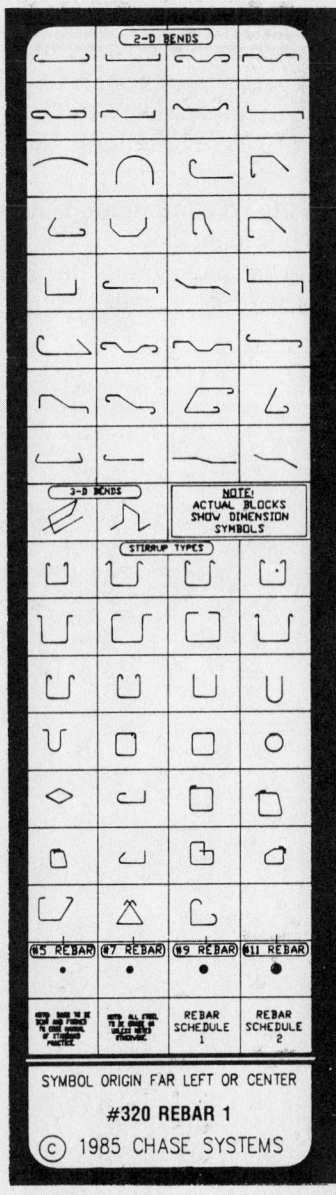

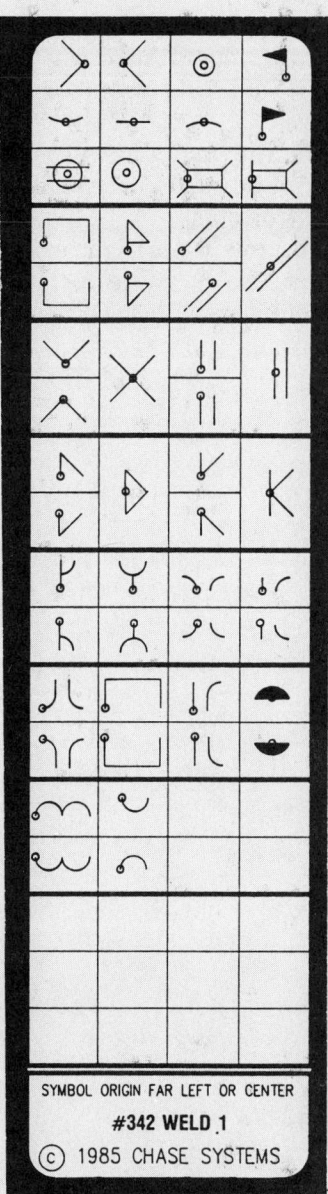

Figure 3 CADD tablet menu symbol library for drawing reinforcing bars. *Courtesy Chase Systems.*

Figure 4 CADD tablet menu welding symbol library. *Courtesy Chase Systems.*

COMMON COMMERCIAL CONSTRUCTION MATERIALS TEST

DIRECTIONS

Answer the questions with short complete statements or drawings as needed on an 8½ × 11 drawing sheet as follows:

1. Use ⅛ in. guidelines for all lettering.
2. Letter your name, Common Commercial Construction Materials Test, and the date at the top of the sheet.
3. Letter the question number and provide the answer. You do not need to write out the question.
4. Do all lettering with vertical uppercase architectural letters. If the answer requires line work, use proper drafting tools and technique. Answers may be prepared on a word processor if appropriate with course guidelines.
5. Your grade will be based on correct answers and quality of line technique.

QUESTIONS

1. Under what conditions can wood be used to frame a wall that requires a two-hour fire rating?
2. Why are the materials used to frame commercial buildings not typically used on residential projects?
3. Describe how a panelized roof is framed.
4. How does the F_b value for a DF/DF glu-lam beam compare with a DFL #1 beam?
5. Why is heavy timber a better construction material than steel in areas of high fire risk?
6. Describe two types of drawings typically required for steel and concrete projects.
7. How is concrete prestressed?
8. How are precast concrete panels usually connected to each other?
9. What is the recommended height limit for load-bearing steel studs.
10. Sketch the proper symbol for a 3/16 in. fillet weld, opposite side, field weld.

Chapter 52
Structural Drafting

THIS CHAPTER introduces basic concepts and drawing methods expected of an entry level drafter in an architect's or engineer's office. The project example at the end of this chapter will be working drawings for a concrete tilt-up warehouse.

There are two main drawing objectives: to coordinate various plans and to draw coordinated details that correspond to different areas of the building.

PLAN THE DRAWING

Before you begin drawing, search all plan views for similarities. Start at the upper level and work to the lowest. This should show you the loads that must be supported as your work progresses. As you work from top to bottom, you should see beams in the roof supported by columns on the floor plan, pedestals on the slab plan, and footings at the foundation. Had you begun at the foundation level, it might not have been clear why a given pier was in a particular location.

As you work on the various plans, you should also be studying details that relate to the plan. Details will give you a better understanding which, in turn, should result in faster drawing speeds.

As you draw, you may not be able to get your questions answered as quickly as they arise. This is typical of work situations—it is often difficult to find an engineer to answer your questions. Using a non-reproducible blue pencil, keep a list of your questions right on your drawing.

PROCEDURE—FROM CALCULATIONS TO WORKING DRAWING

As you work on projects for an architect or engineer, you will be given a set of calculations, sketches, and similar drawings that have been done by the office. The calculations are the mathematical solutions to particular problems. Calculations are printed in color following the related problem. As a drafter, you will be given a set of specifications and be expected to determine the goal of the engineer. You will then translate the results into working drawings. Typically, this will mean skipping over the math work. An example of a calculation can be seen in Figure 49–2. For the project you will be working on, the math has been omitted and only the material to be placed on the drawings has been shown.

Sketches an engineer provides are usually tools to help in the solution of the calculations. A drafter is expected to use the sketch as a guide to help determine size and material to be used.

NOTE: The sketches contained in this chapter are to be used as a guide only. As you progress through the project, you will find that some parts of a drawing do not match things that have already been drawn. It is your responsibility to coordinate the material that you draw with other drawings for this project. If you are unsure of what to draw, consult your instructor.

In addition to the calculations and sketches for this specific job, a drafter is expected to study similar jobs and details for common elements that can be used in the new drawing. This includes many common notes as well as common connection methods. A drafter would also be expected to consult vendor catalogs for specific details of prefabricated material. An example of a typical sketch and the working drawing which corresponds to it can be seen in Figure 1–1 and 1–2.

Drawing Layout

There is no one totally correct layout for this project. Usually, a project will be drawn so details and plans that relate to a given construction crew will be grouped together. Therefore, the roofer will never see the foundation plan. Often this technique of grouping details and plans requires material to be specified on plans more than once. As you lay out this project, two common methods might be used.

1. Group all plan views together, then all roof details, all concrete details, etc., in the same order that the plan views are presented.
2. Group a plan view with all related details: for instance, show the roof plan and then the roof details; the slab plan and then the slab details.

The layout format will not really be important until you have the plan views complete and you start to lay out details. By that time you should have a much better understanding of the project.

One frustration associated with this project and this type of drawing is that it cannot be completed without interruptions. You will be required to draw the basic drawing, stop, then solve a related problem at another level. You will be working on several drawings at the same time. The good news is that all drawings belong to the same project. It is common in an office to switch from one job to another several times a day depending on an engineer's or a client's appointments. On this project, you will be expected to shift from one drawing to another, keep them all coordinated, and still keep your sanity.

Material

Drafters in structural firms often work with several different drawing materials. These include ink on vellum or mylar, graphite on vellum, polyester on vellum, any combination of these, or CADD. The plan views, elevations, and panel elevations are well suited to CADD drafting because there are so many layering possibilities. Verify the drawing medium with your instructor whenever you start a drawing.

The material is not as important as the end result. Excellent line quality reflecting consistent width and density are a must for a structural detailer. Many of the details in this text are similar to what you will be drawing. The details feature several different line weights as should your drawings.

DETAIL COORDINATION

As you draw each detail, provide room for a title, scale, and detail marker under the detail. The title will typically tell the function of the drawing, such as BEAM/WALL CONNECTION, and should be neatly printed using ¼″ high lettering. The scale should be placed under the title in ⅛″ high lettering. A line should separate the two and should have a detail reference circle on the right end of the line. The reference circle should be about ¾″ in diameter with the line passing through the center of the circle. There will eventually be a detail number on the top of the line. On the bottom of the line, place the page number where the detail was drawn. Do not fill in the circles until all the drawing is complete.

Throughout the plans, you will be referring to a specific detail location for more information. Typically, circles ⅜″—½″ in diameter are used so the reference circle does not totally dominate the plan.

LETTERING

Lettering is an important skill to be mastered, even in this age of computers. You will probably get your initial job interview based solely on your lettering. Other than this minor detail, excellent lettering is essential for easy-to-use drawings. The best structural lettering has simple shapes, is easy to read, and quick to produce. Lettering must be uniform in size, angle, and spacing if you are to advance in the field. Practice lettering that has uniform angles of vertical strokes, uniform spacing, and proper placement of notes. Place notes so they require the shortest leader line without getting in the way of the drawing. Notes are often placed in the drawing or detail. Just be careful to keep the vertical strokes of letters away from lines in the drawing.

ORDER OF PRECEDENCE

This project may be unlike others you have done. Not only does it have sketches and engineer's calculations (calcs), it also has some very large errors. Most are so obvious (at the beginning) that you have no trouble finding them. They get tougher as you gain more knowledge. The errors are here to help you learn to think as a drafter. Because engineers are not perfect, you sometimes need to sort through conflicting information to solve a problem. Usually though, the engineer is correct, and you will find that you have misinterpreted the information. If you think you have found an error, do not make changes in the drawings until you have discussed them with the engineer. (In this case, discuss them with your

instructor.) To help you sort through conflicting information, use the following order of precedence.

1. Written changes by the engineer (your instructor) as change orders.
2. Verbal changes given by the engineer (your instructor).
3. Engineer's calcs (in color).
4. Sketches by engineer.
5. Lecturenotes and sketches.
6. Your own decision (should it come to this, please check with your instructor.)

OCCUPANCY

The space between grid 1—7.5 will be used for manufacturing wood cabinets including storage of stains, varnish, and glue. The space between grid 7.5—11 will be used for sales and office space. Before you start drawing, review chapter 50 and determine occupancy of each area, the least restrictive types of construction to be used, maximum height, square footage, and occupant load of each portion.

STRUCTURAL DRAFTING PROBLEMS

Students do not usually have adequate time to draw the entire set of plans required to construct this building. Your instructor may wish to add or delete drawings, or have you work individually or in teams. Verify with your instructor what problems will be drawn.

Problem 52–1. ROOF DRAINAGE PLAN.

Goal

The purpose of this drawing is to show the elevations of the roof supports. By changing the elevation of supports, you can control the flow of water and direct it to down-spouts.

Problem

The building on which you will work will be nearly as large as a football field. Therefore, you have

a large area that collects water. If the water is not quickly drained from the roof, it must be treated as a live load, and the beam sizes must be increased. This plan will show the slope of structural members and the roof, and it will show overflow drain locations. Use the sketch as a guide.

Method

At a scale of 1/16″ = 1′-0″ draw:

1. The outline of the entire structure with 6″ wide walls. Determine size of building from other sketches.
2. The center of the glu-lams at grid "B."
3. Four roof drains, overflow drains, and scuppers equally spaced on grids "A & C"; assume drains to be 8″ in diameter.
4. Dimension as per sketch.
5. Letter all elevations at drain.

6. Specify drains, overflows, and scuppers.
7. General notes: (1) Roof and overflow drains to be general purpose type with nonferrous domes and 4″ diameter outlets. (2) Overflow drains to be set with inlet 2″ above drain inlet and shall be independently connected to drain lines. (3) Scuppers to be 4″ high × 7″ wide with 4″ rectangular corrugated down-spouts. Provide a 6 × 9 conductor head at the top of down spouts.

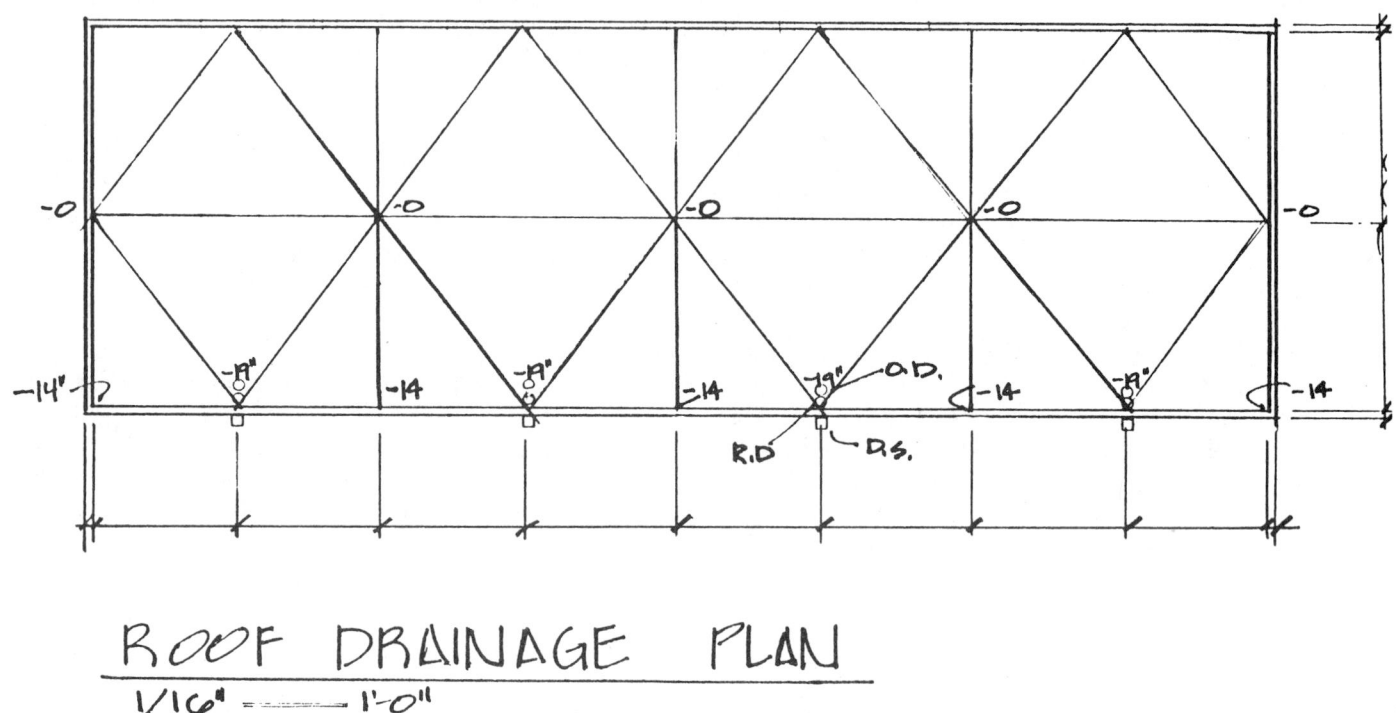

ROOF DRAINAGE PLAN
1/16″ = 1′-0″

Problem 52–2. ROOF FRAMING PLAN.

Goal

The purpose of this drawing is to show roof framing used to support the finished roofing. This structure will have a series of laminated beams which extend through the center of the structure at grid "B" from grid 1 through 11. It will also have a wood ledger bolted to each wall at grid "A & C." Trusses will span between the ledger and the glu-lams. Blocking will be shown at each end of the roof between the trusses. Above the trusses will be sheets of plywood. Four skylights will be equally placed in each bay. This plan will also show how the separation wall intersects the beams.

Problem

The building on which you are working is approximately 300′ × 100′ × 27′ high. The walls will act like a sail. To keep the structure rigid, the roof framing will be connected to the walls to form a rigid connection. In addition, a diaphragm will be built into each end of the structure. As the walls bend from wind or seismic pressure, the roof will shift in the direction of the pressure. As the pressure is decreased, the walls will return to their original shape. The rigid connections assure that, when the walls spring back to their original position, the roof will also return to its original position. If the connections at this level fail, the roof will fall from its supports. The roof framing plan is used to show how and where these items are located. Both ends of this structure are to be symmetrical. Use the sketches of the roof as a guide.

Method

Use a scale of 3/32″ = 1′-0″.
If you're unsure of what you are drawing, look through the roof framing and truss details.

1. Lay out and draw the walls.
2. Lay out and draw the locations of beams.
3. Dimension and label all grids.
4. Lay out truss, blocking, skylights, strap ties, and 4 × 8 plywood as per sketch and roof details.
5. Draw plywood over blocking and trusses and strap ties and skylights.
6. Draw 2-hour wall and roof area.
7. Letter general notes. (1) Beam sizes. Either specify beam size and type by beam, or provide a beam schedule. See engineer's calcs for size of beams 1–3. (2) Bay referencing. Use ¼″ hex

and print letter or number centered in hex. (3) Do not place detail markers on your plan at this time. These markers should be added to each plan as the details are drawn.

8. Local notes (verify notes with calculations).

1. Bristolite 3069–A.S.-DD-CC/WTH-C.P. double domed curb-mounted skylights with 4 per bay (80 total).

2. 45″ TJ/60 Truss joist at 32″ O.C.

3. 3 × 4 dfl std. and better solid blocking at 48″ O.C. 36′ out from each end wall.

4. Simpson MST 27 strap ties at 8′–0″ O.C. for entire perimeter. See Detail ***. (Place detail marker in note for future reference).

5. ⅝″ C-D 42/20 . . . . (See engineer's calcs for complete specifications and provide required information on drawing.)

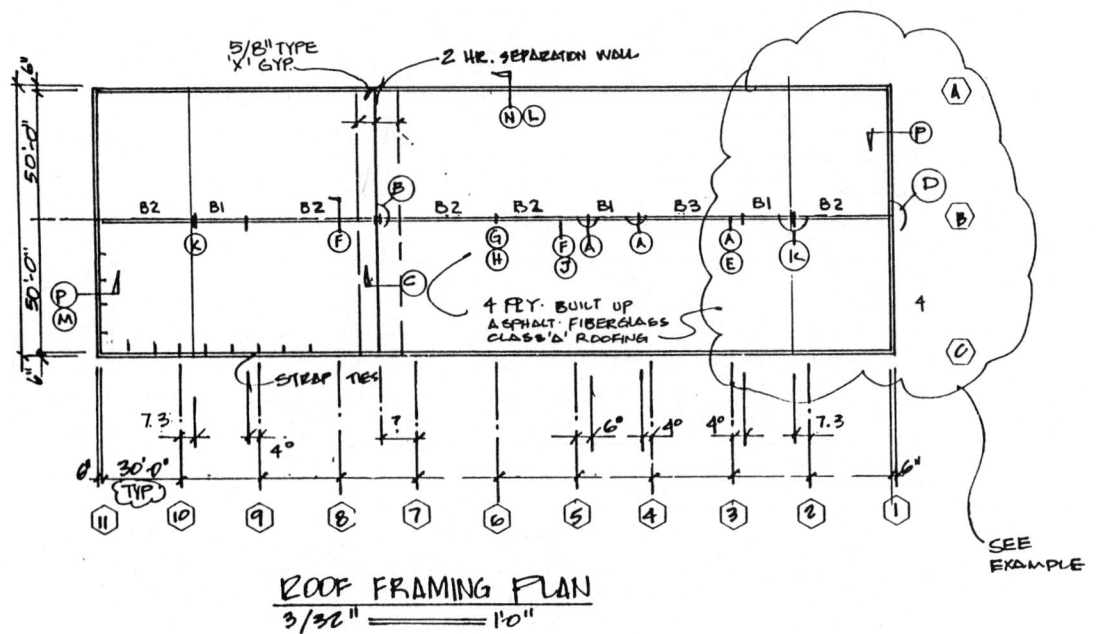

ROOF FRAMING PLAN
3/32″ = 1′0″

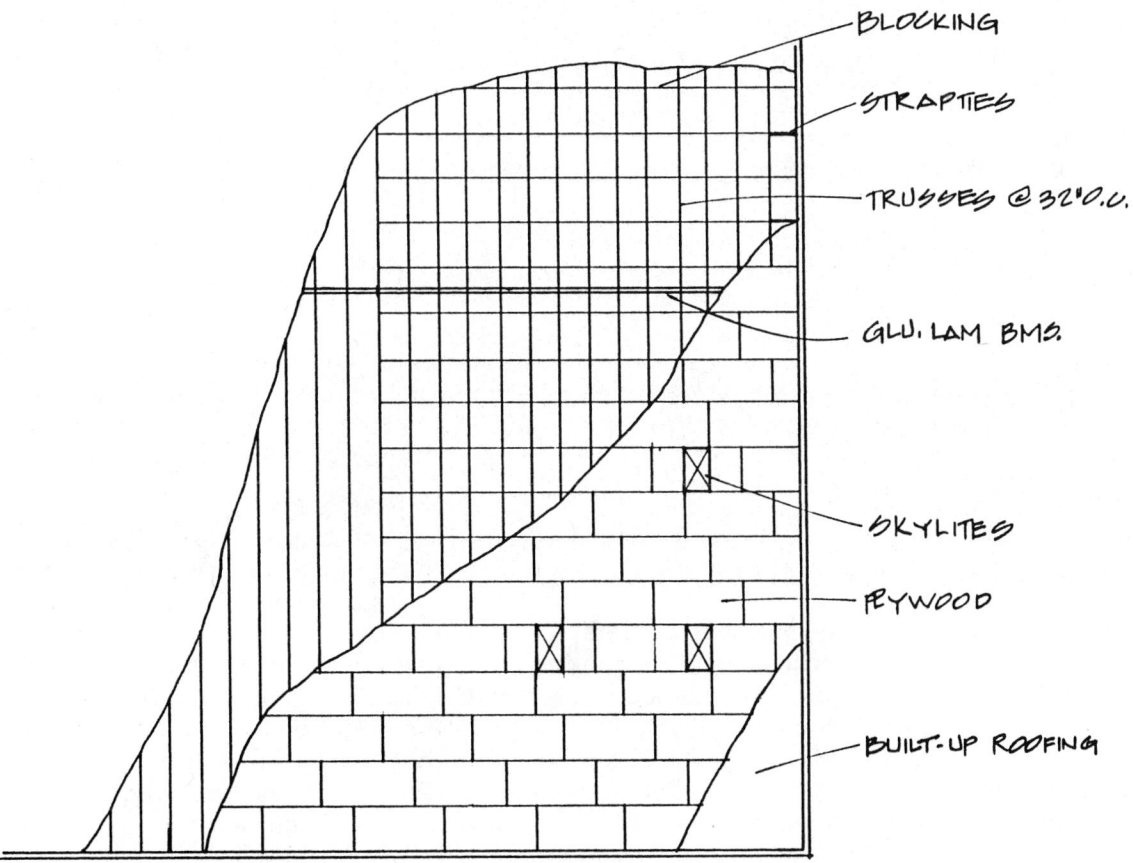

BLOCKING

STRAPTIES

TRUSSES @ 32″ O.C.

GLU. LAM BMS.

SKYLITES

PLYWOOD

BUILT-UP ROOFING

ROOF SHEATHING

w_V = 25 PSI

w_L = $\dfrac{88658}{(2)(122)}$ = .363 #/1

= $\dfrac{59124}{(2)(321)}$ = 92 #/1

ASSUME TRUSSES @ 32" O.C.

CHECK ⅝", C-D 42/20 PLYWOOD

w= 35 PSF 25 PSF

V= 425 #/1 BLOCKED > 363 #/1

= 285 #/1 UNBLOCKED

= 215 #/1 UNBLOCKED> 92 #/1

DETERMINE BLOCKING TERMINATION

x= $\dfrac{(285 \times 160.5)}{363}$ = 126.01'   d= 160.5-126 = 35.50 ⇒ 37.33 from end of wall

USE ⅝" C-D, 42/20, INTERIOR APA PLY W/ EXT. GLUE. LAY PERP. TO TRUSSES, STAGGER SEAMS AT EACH TRUSS. NAIL W/ 10d COMMON NAILS @ 4" O.C. @ ALL PANEL EDGES AND BLOCKED AREAS, @ 6" O.C. @ ALL SUPPORTED PANEL EDGES @ UNBLOCKED AREAS & @12" O.C. @ ALL INTERMEDIATE SUPPORTS.

ROOF BEAMS

BEAM 1= DF/HF 24f-V5 6¾ x25½ GLU- LAM
BEAM 2= DF/DF 20f- V7 6¾ x43½ GLU-LAM
BEAM 3= DF/DF 20f- V7 6¾ x 37½ GLU-LAM

ROOF TRUSSES

w_L =25 PSF w_Δ = 15 PSF   ASSUME TRUSSES @ 32"O.C.

ℓ = $\dfrac{122-1}{2}$ = 60.50'   w= (2.67)(25 + 15) =107 #/1

R= $\dfrac{(107)(60.5)}{2}$ =3237 Δ = $\dfrac{(60.50)(12)}{240}$ 3.03"

CHECK 45" TJ/60 TRUSS JOIST

w=109 #1 >107 #1   R= 4800# > 3237

Δ $\dfrac{(107 \times 60.50)^4}{(308000 \times 45 \cdot 2.3)^2}$ =2.55" < 3.03"

USE 45" TJ/60 TRUSS JOISTS AT 32" O.C.

Problem 52–3. SLAB ON GRADE.

Goal

This drawing will provide directions for pouring the concrete floor. Major items shown on this plan will include the floor slab and control joints, pedestal footings to support steel columns, loading docks, and doors.

Problem

The concrete slab is so large that the concrete crew will pour it in stages. This will account for the 30 × 25 grids. These control joints will also serve to minimize cracking. The 4' wide strip at the perimeter is to allow for movement of the concrete walls. The small squares at grid "B" are to allow for movement of the slab from the steel columns which support the roof.

Method

Your goals on this drawing are to determine door locations in the walls, slab control joints, and "L" connectors which will support the slab where it is over fill. Use a scale of 3/32 = 1'-0". Use the sketch as a guide for your drawing.

1. Lay out grids "A & C" and 1–11.
2. Lay out the exterior walls. Keep the drawing in the upper right corner of the page to allow for possible detail placement around the plan.
3. Lay out door openings using sketches of the panel elevations for locations.
4. Locate the loading docks. See slab details for the wall thickness. Locate the dock so that there is an equal amount of space at each side of the door and the dock walls. This is not the same as centering the dock on the center of the doors.

5. Lay out control joints at grid B, grids 2–10, 4′ perimeter, and pedestals. See wall details for the pedestal size. Draw at an appropriate scale.
6. Draw walls and control joints. Use varied line weight to distinguish between the two.
7. Draw the structural connectors using bold lines.
8. Dimension as per sketch.
9. Label the grids, elevations, and notes.
10. General notes: (1) All slab on grade concrete shall be 5″ thick F′c = 3500 p.s.i. @ 28 days. (2) All target strengths shall be in accordance with Chapter 4 of ACI 318 Building Code Requirements for reinforced concrete. (3) Reinforce with 12 × 12- w4 × w4 or grd 40, #3 @ 15″ O.C. each way centered in slab.

11. Local notes:

ON SKETCH	NOTE SHOULD READ
Doweled joints. . .	Doweled joints w/#5x 15″ smooth dowels @ 12″ O.C.
¼″ joint. . .	¼″ fiber isolation joints around entire pedestal.
5″ slab. . .	5″ slab over 4″ base minimum of ¾″ minus crushed rock. Reinforce w/ 12/12- 4/4 w.w.m. or grade 40, # 3 @ 15″ O.C. each way, 3″ clear of base.
L connectors. . .	¾″ dia. 'L' structural connection inserts w/ ¾″ diameter × 25″ coil rods @ 5′–7′ O.C. Provide 2″ min. rod penetration into inserts 2¾″ from top of slab.

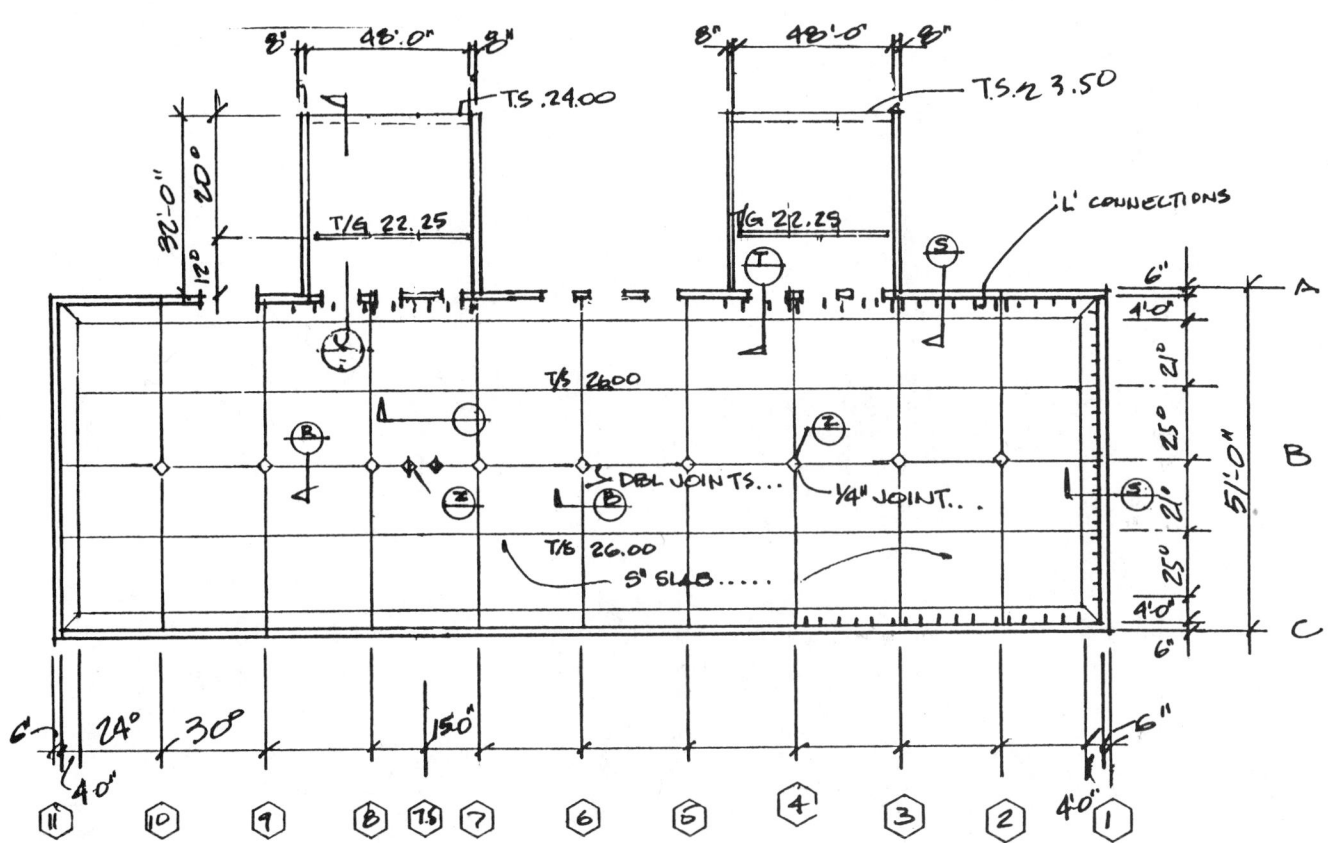

SLAB ON GRADE PLAN

3/32″ ═══ 1′0″

ADD PERSONAL DOORS SEE PANEL ELEVATIONS FOR LOCATIONS.

See PANEL ELEV. TO LOCATE ALL openings. Don't Dimen. openings on this PLAN

Problem 52–4. FOUNDATION PLAN.

Goal

The purpose of this drawing is to show concrete supports for the walls and columns. Supports will consist of a continuous footing at the perimeter of the structure and individual piers placed under the pedestals that support the columns.

Problem

This drawing will show the size and location of the footings as well as any change in their elevation. All elevations should be given using the proper symbol.

Method

Use a scale of 3/32″ = 1′–0″ for this drawing. Place the drawing in the upper right-hand corner of the page. Use the sketch of the foundation as a guide.

1. Lay out grids "A & C" and 1–11.

2. Lightly lay out the exterior face of the concrete walls and loading docks. This is for your reference only since only the retaining walls will be darkened on this plan.
3. Determine the size of the exterior footing and lay it out in the proper location. Refer to the foundation details for size information.
4. Draw the location of all elevation changes in the footing.
5. Determine the size of the pedestal footings. Since all footings are close in size, given the scale of the drawing, lay out all footings at the *average* size.
6. Draw all footings.
7. Dimension drawing as per sketch.
8. Label all grids, elevations, and notes.
9. General Notes. (1) All foundation, pedestal and retaining wall concrete shall be F'c 3000 PSI at 28 days. (2) All steel bar reinforcement shall be ASTM A615, Grade 40, deformed bars unless otherwise specified in drawings or details.
10. Local notes. None required.

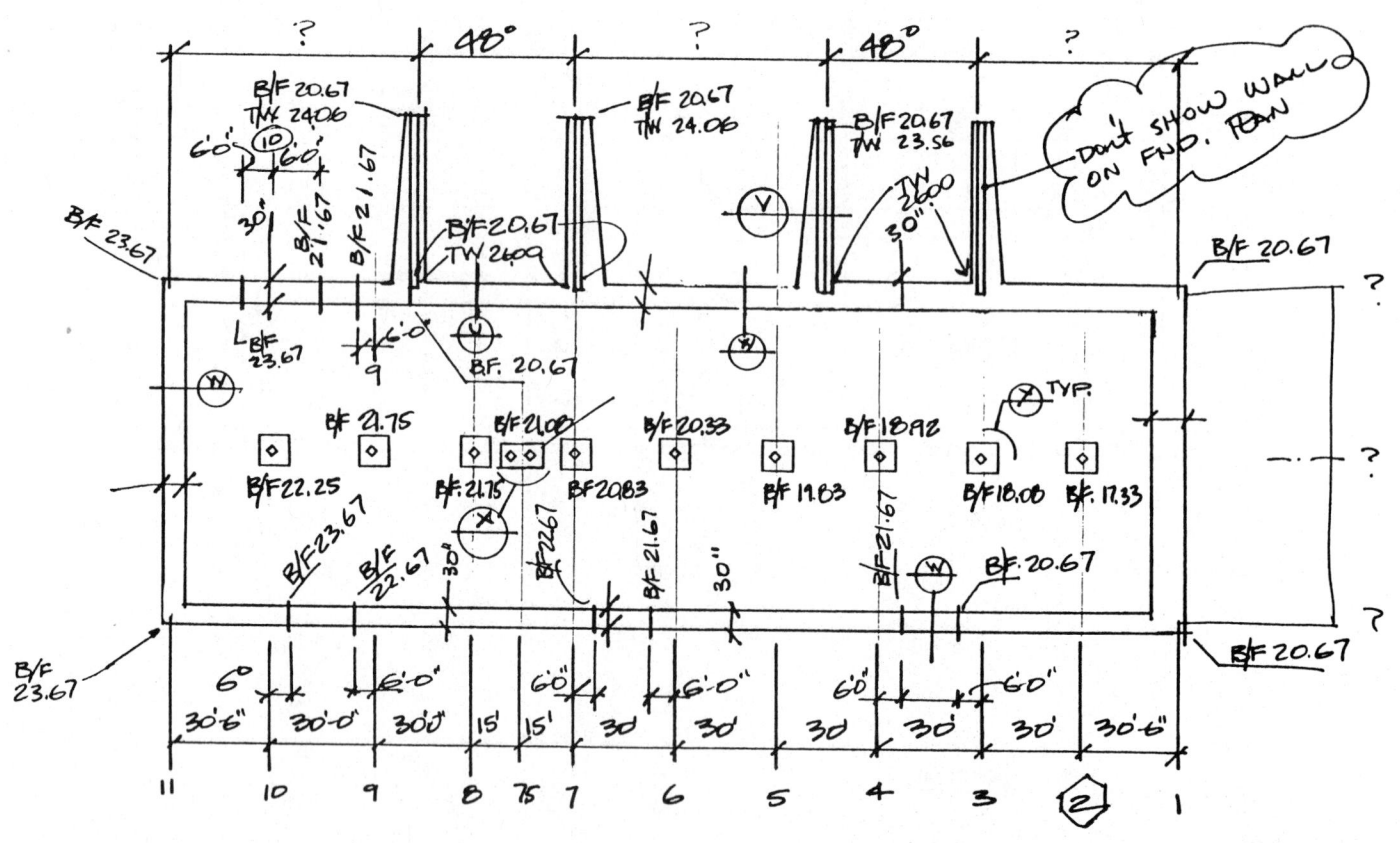

Problem 52–5. ROOF BEAM DETAILS.

Goal

The purpose of these details is to show how the glu-lam beams are attached in end-to-end connections, to columns, and to the wall at grid 1 and 11. Use the sketches and calcs as a guide for your drawings.

DETAIL A: BEAM TO BEAM. Use of a saddle to hang 25.5″ beam from large beams.

DETAIL B: BEAM TO WALL. Beams supported on columns with 2-hour wall between. Gyp. bd. to remain unbroken.

DETAIL C: WALL TO ROOF. Similar to "B" but shows roof between beam and concrete walls.

DETAIL D: BEAM TO WALL. Top and side views to show plates for beam support.

DETAIL E & F: BEAM TO COLUMN. Both show bearing-plate connections to steel column.

DETAIL G: BEAM TO COLUMN. Intersection of two beams over a steel column. All other beam intersections are in midspan and are not over a column.

Method

These drawings should be done in two stages. Lay out and final drawing with lettering and dimensions. Use the calcs, sketches, and the vendor's material of Figure 49–1.

1. Determine the location of details. Details should be either drawn with the roof drainage and framing plans or on a separate sheet. In addition, determine what order the details will be presented. Place the details in an order that reflects their relationship to the building, not the order that the engineer thought of them.

2. Lightly block out each detail allowing approximately 15 minutes per detail. Given this brief amount of time, only draw major features such as beam sizes, metal brackets, and bolt centerlines.

3. Draw beams with finish line quality. Use several line types or colors. Draw steel plates and brackets as boldest lines, beam outlines slightly thinner, followed by bolts or other connectors, followed by glu-lam lines. Use layouts similar to Figures 51–9 and 51–29. Lam-lines should be lighter than other lines: almost a cross between a construction and an object line. Represent steel plates in side view with pairs of parallel thin lines at 45 degrees.

4. Dimension all information from the sketch or calcs. Remember, some information can be placed within the drawing. Keep extension lines approximately 1–1½″ long. Interrupt lam lines as required for easy reading.

5. Place weld information on details as required. Be sure you understand what you are connecting before you order a weld. Also, be mindful of symbols for "this side, or opposite side".

6. Notes. Place notes in or near the drawing as required. Similar information in two details can be covered in one note carefully placed between the two details.

7. Place detail markers, title, and scale below each detail. Do not yet place any information in the circle, however.

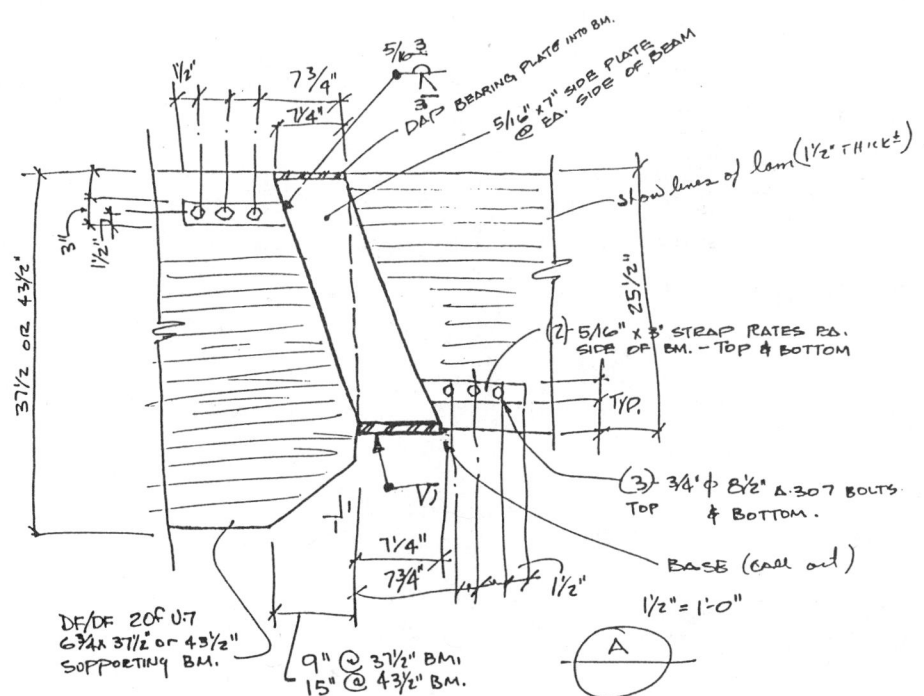

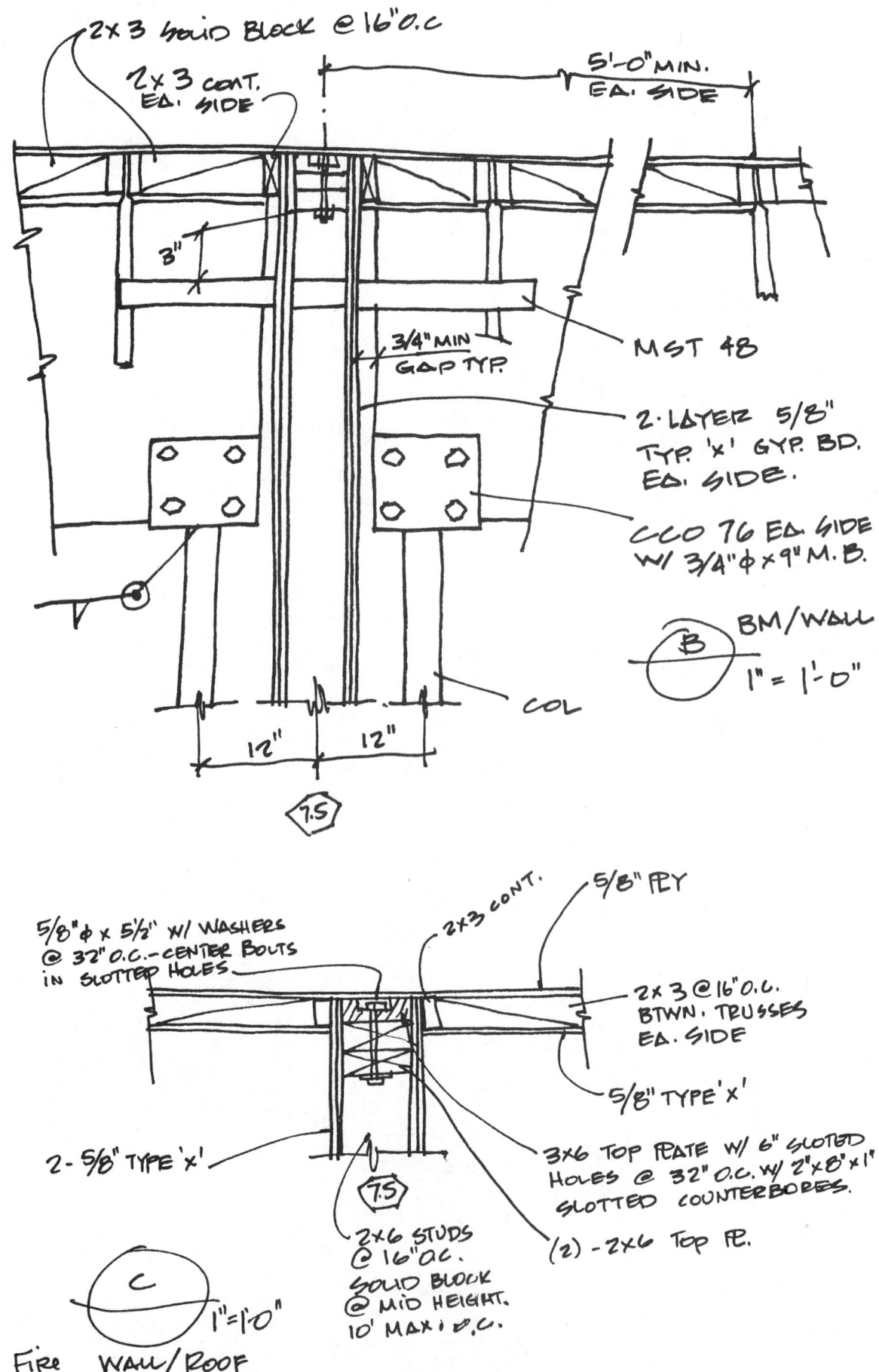

2×3 SOLID BLOCK @ 16" O.C.

2×3 CONT. EA. SIDE

5'-0" MIN. EA. SIDE

3"

3/4" MIN GAP TYP.

MST 48

2-LAYER 5/8" TYP. 'X' GYP. BD. EA. SIDE.

CCO 76 EA. SIDE W/ 3/4" ⌀ × 9" M.B.

BM/WALL

B

1" = 1'-0"

12"   12"

COL

7.5

5/8" ⌀ × 5 1/2" W/ WASHERS @ 32" O.C.—CENTER BOLTS IN SLOTTED HOLES.

2×3 CONT.

5/8" PLY

2×3 @ 16" O.C. BTWN. TRUSSES EA. SIDE

5/8" TYPE 'X'

3×6 TOP PLATE W/ 6" SLOTTED HOLES @ 32" O.C. W/ 2"×8"×1" SLOTTED COUNTERBORES.

(2) -2×6 TOP PL.

2-5/8" TYPE 'X'

7.5

2×6 STUDS @ 16" O.C. SOLID BLOCK @ MID HEIGHT. 10' MAX. O.C.

C

1" = 1'-0"

FIRE WALL/ROOF

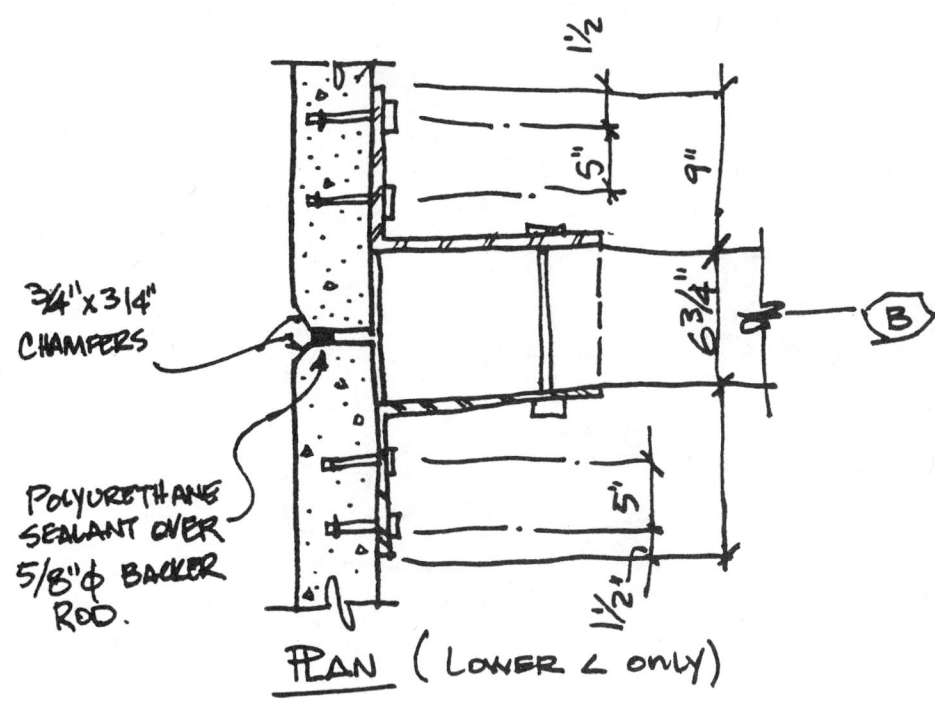

1½
5"
9"
6¾"
B
3/4"x3/4"
CHAMFERS
POLYURETHANE
SEALANT OVER
5/8"φ BACKER
ROD.
5"
1½"
PLAN (LOWER ∠ ONLY)

8"
1/4" GAP
(1) 3/4"φ x 4⅛" TAPER BOLT EA '∠'
8"x 4"x½" x 3" '∠' EA. SIDE, OF BM.
W/ 13/16" x 1⅞" LONG SLOTED
HOLE HORIZ. IN 8" LEG.
?
?
6¾x 43½
GLU-LAM BM
43½"
(1) -3/4"φ x 9" A-307 BOLT
W/ STD. WASHERS CENTERED
IN SLOTTED HOLES
2"
(6).
9½"x 9"x 5/16"x 1'-3½" '∠'
EA. SIDE OF BM
(3)-3/4"φ x 8½" A-307
BOLTS
?
BM/WALL
D
6"
9½"
1"=1'-0"
11
1
SECTION

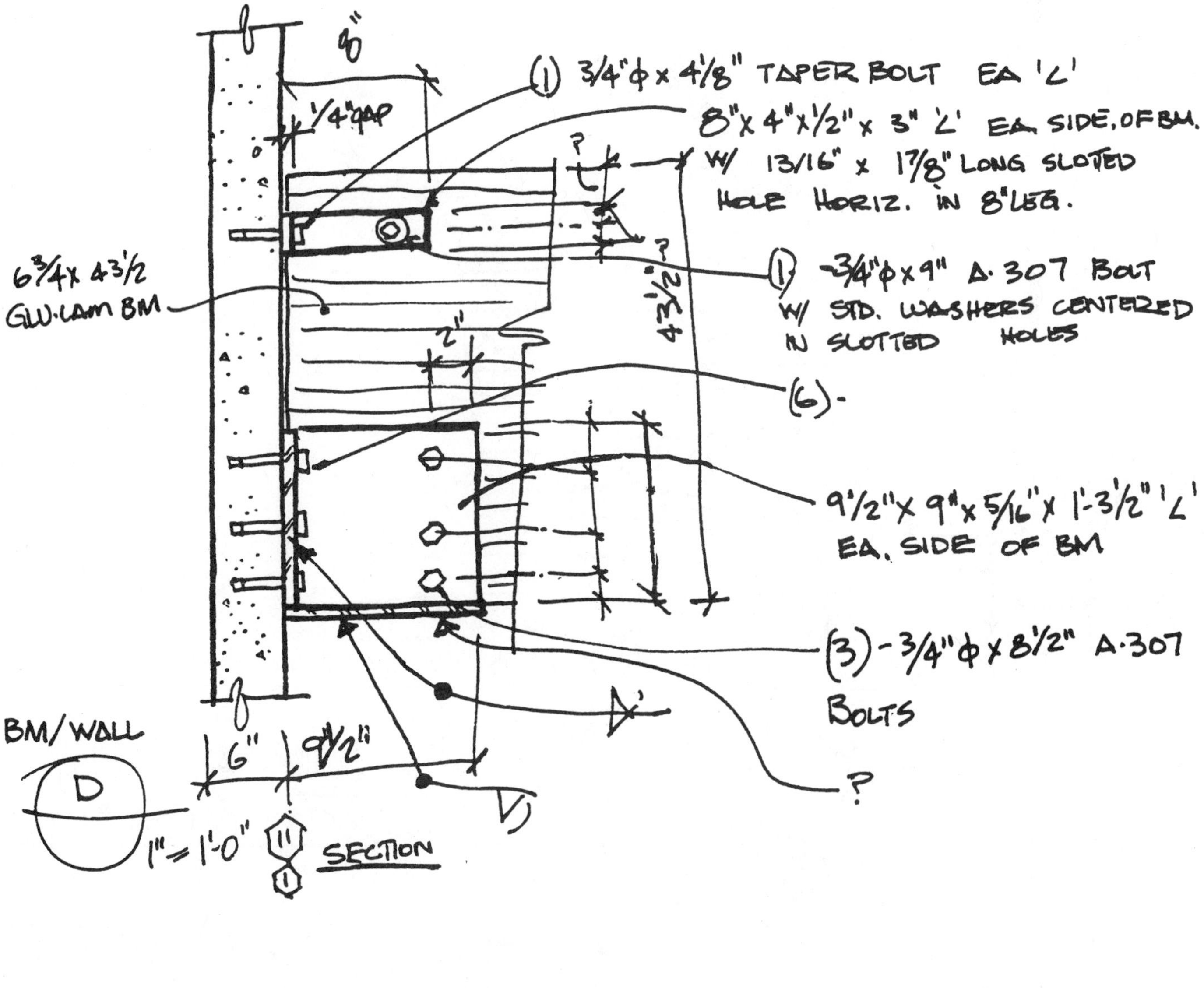

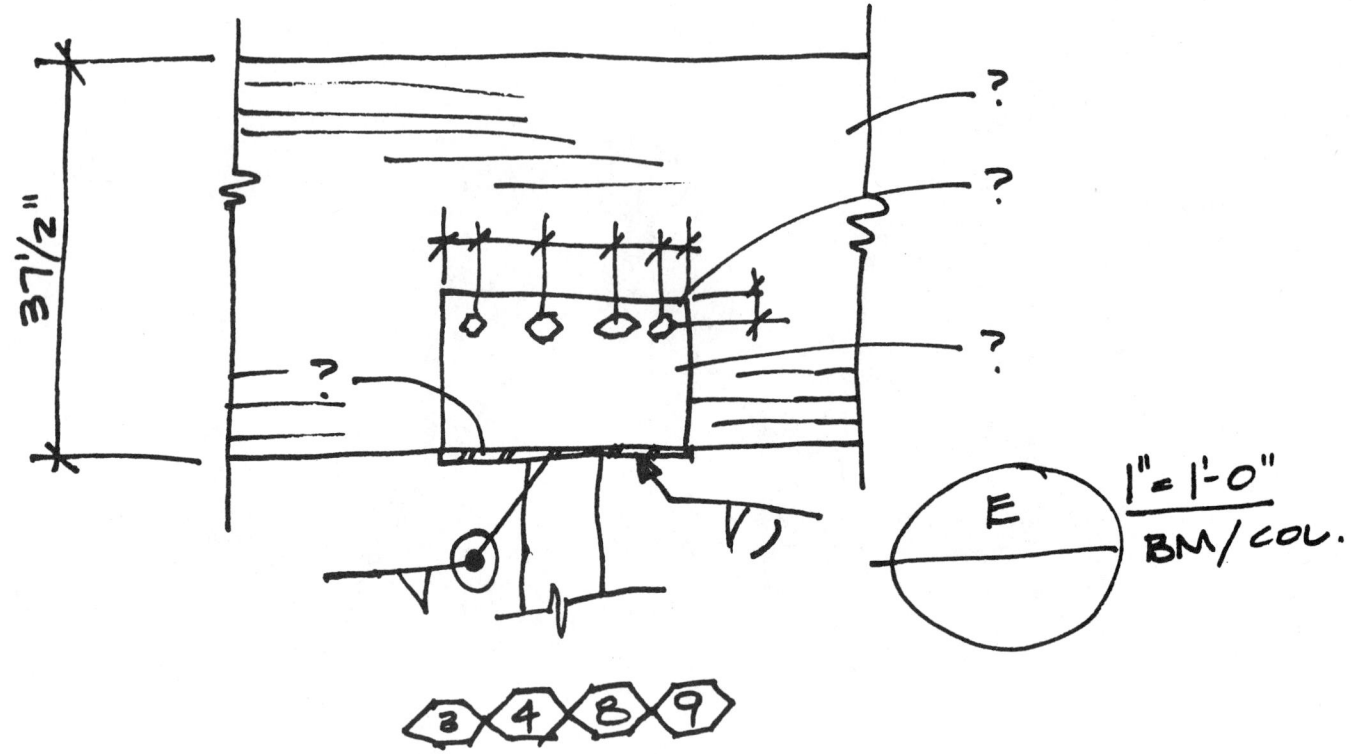

37½"

?
?
?
?

E   1"=1'-0"
BM/COL.

3 4 8 9

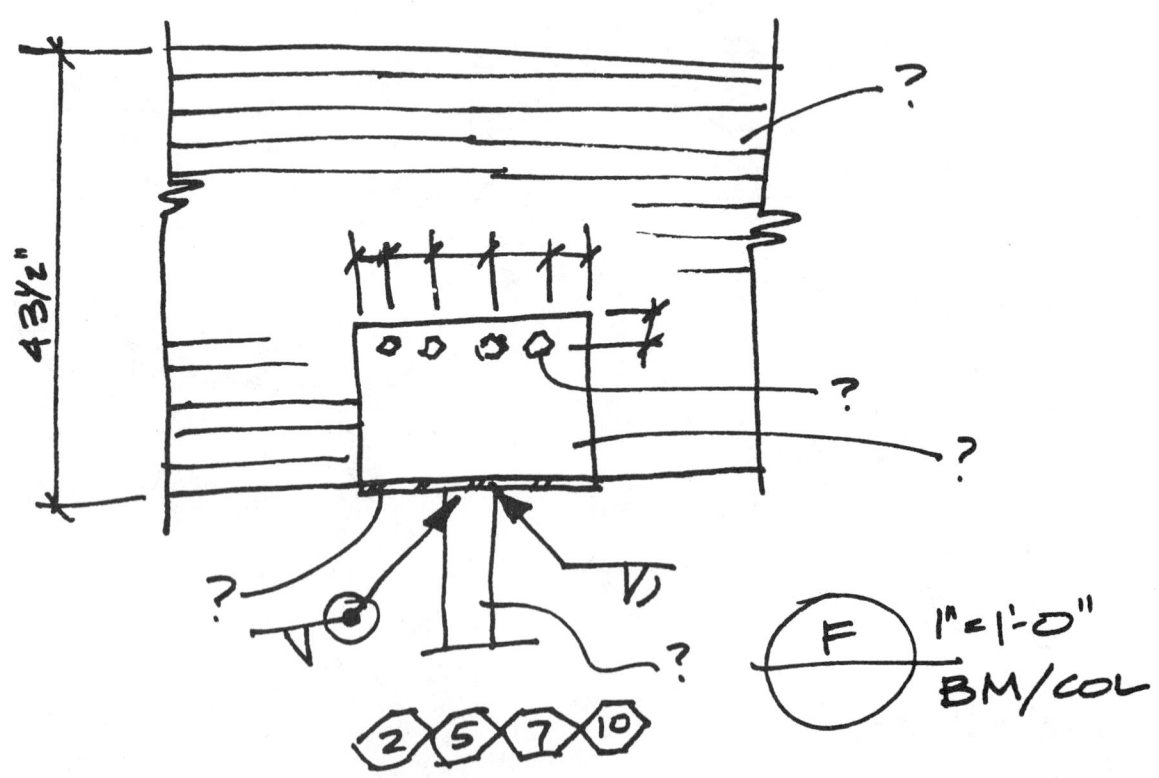

43½"

?
?
?
?
?

F   1"=1'-0"
BM/COL

2 5 7 10

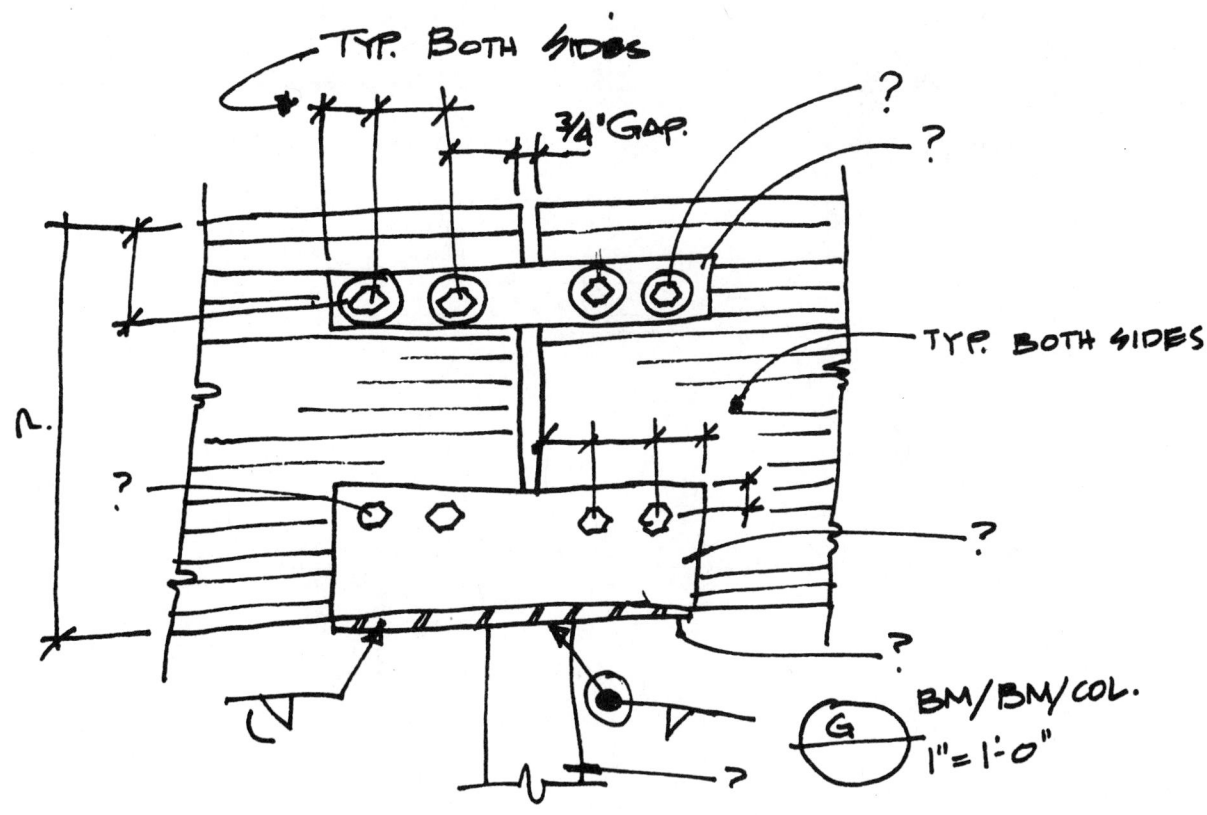

TYP. BOTH SIDES

3/4" GAP

?

?

TYP. BOTH SIDES

?

?

?

?

BM/BM/COL.
1" = 1'-0"

ROOF / BEAM-BEAM

ASSUME : ALL BOLTS TO BE ¾" DIA. 3" O.C. UNLESS NOTED
PROVIDE 1½" MIN. PLATE EDGE TO BOLT CENTER TYP UNLESS
NOTED
ALL BOLTS TO BE 3½" FROM TOP AND BOTTOM OF BEAMS.
ALL WELDS AT BM CINNECTIONS TO BE 5/16" UNLESS NOTED.
PROVIDE ⅜ FILLET WELD ● COL / P. UNLESS NOTED

HINGE CONNECTORS

USE: 5/16" SIDE P's w/ ⅞" x 6 ⅞ x 7 ¼" BEARING P's ●TOP AND BOTTOM
5/16" SIDE STRAPS W/ (3) ¾" ● BOLTS.

BEAM / TILT UP WALL

USE 9½ x 1'-3½" x 5/16 FABRICATED SIDE ANGLES W/ ⅞ x 6⅞ x 9½
BEARING P. USE (6) ¾● x 4⅛ TAPERBOLTS ● 5"O.C. EACH SIDE OF
ANGLE & (4) ¾" ● BOLTS ● 5" O.C. THRU

BEAM / FIREWALL

USE: ⅝" TYPE 'X' GYP. BD. MIN 5' EACH SIDE OF WALL. VERIFY TRUSS
LOCATION AND DIMEN. DETAIL ACCORDINGLY.
PLACE MST 48 3" MAX. FROM BOTTOM OF P.

BEAM / COLUMN. (3,4,8,9)

USE: 5/16 x 10 x 22 SIDE P W/ ⅞ x 6⅞ x 22 BEARING P
(4) ¾● BOLTS ● 6¼" O.C.
USE A TS 6 x 6 x ¼ COLUMN W/ ¼ FILLET TO P

BEAM / COLUMN (2,5,7,10)

5/16" x 10 x 24½ SIDE P W/ ⅞" x 6⅞ x 24½" BEARING P W/
(4) ¾● BOLTS ● 7" O.C.
USE A TS 6 x 6 x 5/16 COLUMN W/ ¼ FILLET TO P

BEAM / COLUMN (6)

5/16 x 10 x 19 SIDE P W/ ⅞ X 6⅞ 19½ BEARING P
(4) ¾ ● BOLTS

TOP P TO BE ½ x 19½ x 3 STRAP P W/ 13/16 x 1" SHORT SLOTTED HORIZ.
HOLES (EA. SIDE OF BEAM) W/ (4) ¾● W/ STD WASHERS CENTERED EA.
SIDE   USE A TS 6 x 6 x 5/16 COLUMN W/ ¼ FILLET TO P

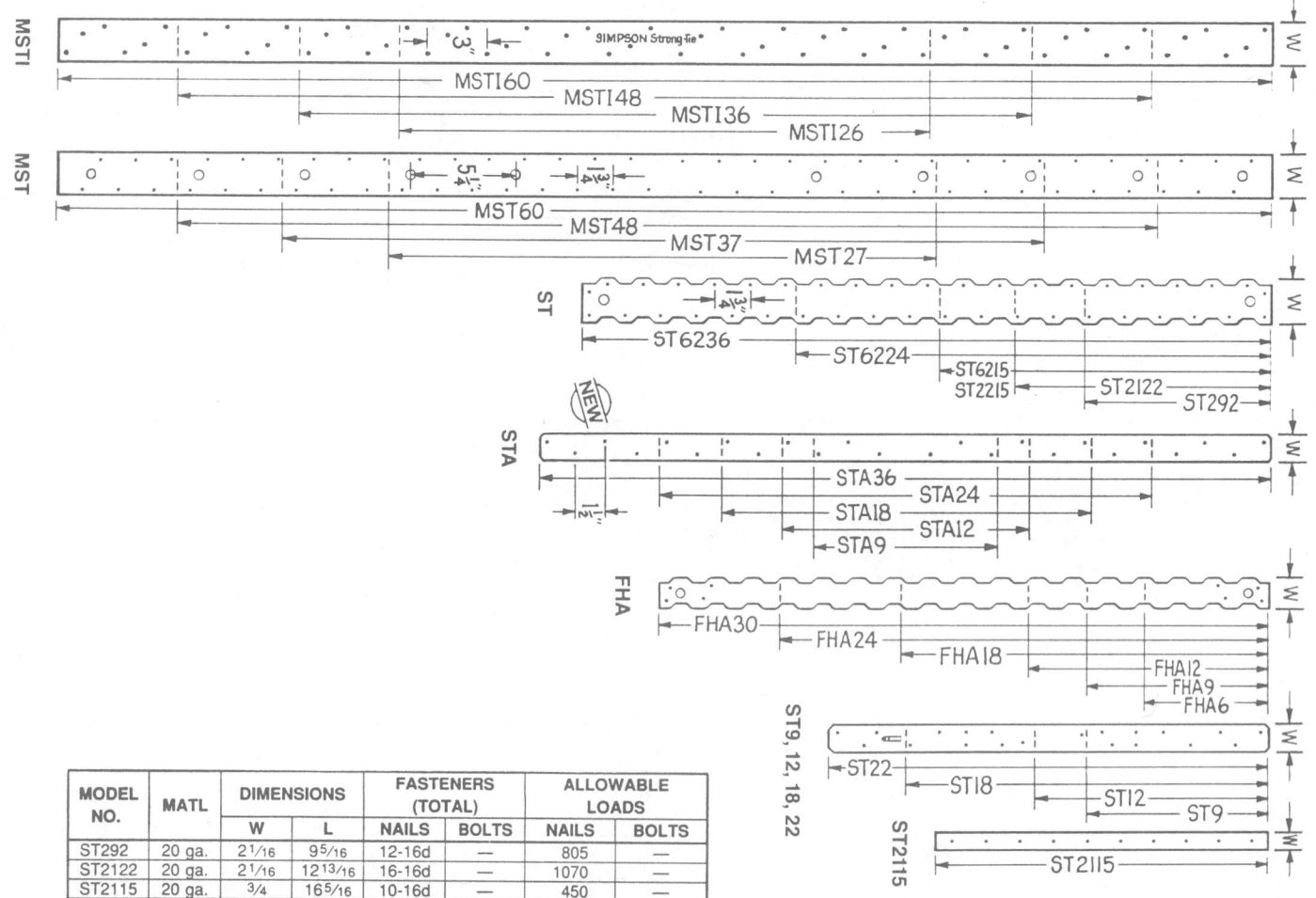

MODEL NO.	MATL	DIMENSIONS		FASTENERS (TOTAL)		ALLOWABLE LOADS	
		W	L	NAILS	BOLTS	NAILS	BOLTS
ST292	20 ga.	2 1/16	9 5/16	12-16d	—	805	—
ST2122	20 ga.	2 1/16	12 13/16	16-16d	—	1070	—
ST2115	20 ga.	3/4	16 5/16	10-16d	—	450	—
ST2215	20 ga.	2 1/16	16 5/16	20-16d	—	1210	—
ST6215	16 ga.	2 1/16	16 5/16	20-16d	—	1340	—
ST6224	16 ga.	2 1/16	23 5/16	28-16d	—	1875	—
ST6236	14 ga.	2 1/16	33 13/16	40-16d	—	2475	—
LST9*	18 ga.	1 1/4	9	8-16d	—	540	—
LST12*	18 ga.	1 1/4	11 5/8	10-16d	—	675	—
LST18*	18 ga.	1 1/4	17 3/4	14-16d	—	860	—
LST22*	18 ga.	1 1/4	21 5/8	14-16d	—	860	—
ST9*	16 ga.	1 1/4	9	8-16d	—	540	—
ST12*	16 ga.	1 1/4	11 5/8	10-16d	—	675	—
ST18*	16 ga.	1 1/4	17 3/4	14-16d	—	945	—
ST22*	16 ga.	1 1/4	21 5/8	18-16d	—	1215	—
STA9*	20 ga.	1 1/4	9	6-10d	—	350	—
STA12*	18 ga.	1 1/4	12	8-10d	—	470	—
STA18*	16 ga.	1 1/4	18	12-10d	—	705	—
STA24*	14 ga.	1 1/4	24	16-10d	—	940	—
STA36*	12 ga.	1 1/4	36	24-10d	—	1410	—
FHA6*	12 ga.	1 7/16	6	8-16d	—	535	—
FHA9	12 ga.	1 7/16	9	8-16d	—	535	—
FHA12	12 ga.	1 7/16	11 5/8	8-16d	—	535	—
FHA18	12 ga.	1 7/16	17 3/4	8-16d	—	535	—
FHA24	12 ga.	1 7/16	23 7/8	8-16d	—	535	—
FHA30	12 ga.	1 7/16	30	8-16d	—	535	—
MSTI26	12 ga.	2 1/16	26	26-10d	—	1525	—
MSTI36	12 ga.	2 1/16	36	36-10d	—	2115	—
MSTI48	12 ga.	2 1/16	48	48-10d	—	2820	—
MSTI60	12 ga.	2 1/16	60	60-10d	—	3525	—
MST27	12 ga.	2 1/16	27	30-16d	4-1/2	2005	2205
MST37	12 ga.	2 1/16	37 1/2	42-16d	6-1/2	2810	2860
MST48	12 ga.	2 1/16	48	50-16d	8-1/2	3345	3345
MST60	10 ga.	2 1/16	60	66-16d	8-1/2	4350	4060
HST2	7 ga.	2 1/2	21 1/4	—	6-5/8	—	4785
HST5	7 ga.	5	21 1/4	—	12-5/8	—	9670
HST3	3 ga.	3	25 1/2	—	6-3/4	—	6830
HST6	3 ga.	6	25 1/2	—	12-3/4	—	13665

Problem 52–6. TRUSS DETAILS.

Goal

The purpose of these details is to show how the trusses are connected in end-to-end connections, to beams, to ledgers, and to the wall at grid 1 and 11 and 'A & C'

DETAIL H: Basic truss-to-beam connection. Information in this detail should be reflected in all roof details.

DETAIL I: Remember that I, O, and Q are never used in the final detail callouts.

DETAIL J: Truss-to-beam at a column. Braces are added from the truss to the glu-lam so that the beam will not roll off the column as a result of wind pressure against the walls at grid A & C.

DETAIL K: Truss-to-truss connection at the inner edge of the roof diaphragm. This bolting will, in effect, make two trusses function as one. Make use of vendor specs for sizes.

DETAIL L: Ledger splice at grid "A & C."

DETAIL M: Ledger splice at grid 1 & 11.

DETAIL N: Truss-to-ledger connection at A & C, perpendicular.

DETAIL P: Truss-to-ledger connection at 1 and 11, parallel.

Method

These drawings should be done in two stages. Lay out and final drawing with lettering and dimensions. Use the calcs and the vendor's material to supply needed information.

1. Determine the location of details. Details should be either drawn with the beam details or on a separate sheet. In addition, determine what order the details will be presented. Place the details in an order that reflects their re-lationship to the building, not the order that the engineer thought of them.

2. Lay out each detail allowing approximately 15 minutes per detail. Given this brief amount of time, only draw major features such as beam or truss sizes, metal brackets and bolt centerlines. As you lay out the trusses, assume the web is 1" diameter aluminum placed at a 45 degree angle starting 6" from the end of the truss. The bottom chord of the truss *never* touches the beam. Also, carefully study the truss diagram provided by the vendor. The top chord, which supports the entire load on the truss, never touches the beam. The truss is supported by a metal connector.

3. Draw beams with finish line quality. Use several line types or colors. Draw steel plates and brackets as boldest lines, beam outlines slightly thinner, followed by bolts or other connectors, followed by glu-lam lines. Use Figures 51–9 and 51–29 as examples. Represent steel plates in side view with pairs of two parallel thin lines at 45 degrees.

4. Dimension all information from the sketch or calcs. Remember, some information can be placed within the drawing. Interrupt lam lines as required for easy reading.

5. Place weld information on details as required. Be sure you understand what you are connecting before you order a weld. Also, be mindful of symbols for "this side, or opposite side".

6. Notes. Place notes in or near the drawing as required. Similar information in two details can be covered in one note carefully placed between the two details.

7. Place detail markers and title and scale below each detail. Do not yet place any information in the circle, however.

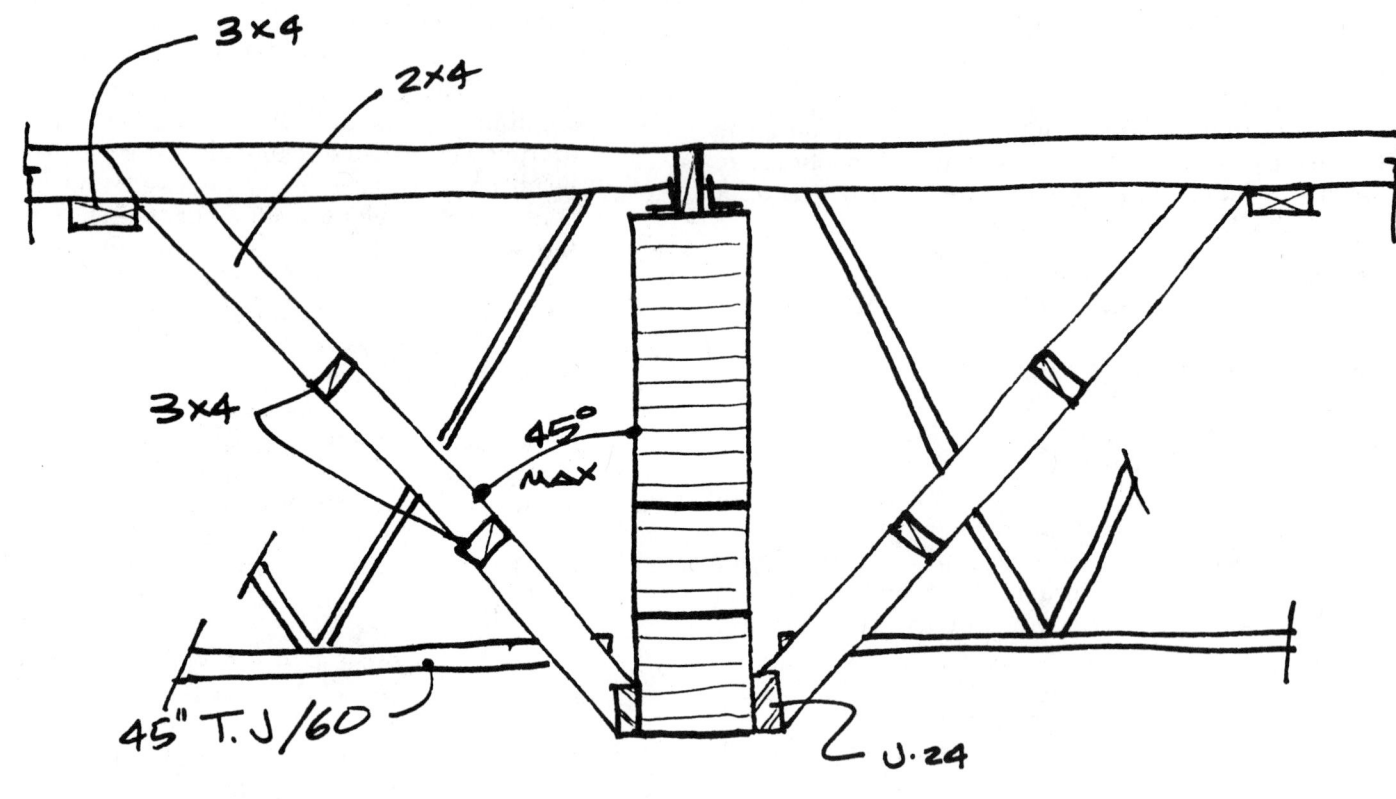

3×4

2×4

3×4

45° MAX

45" T.J /60

U.24

TRUSS/BEAM @ COL.

H

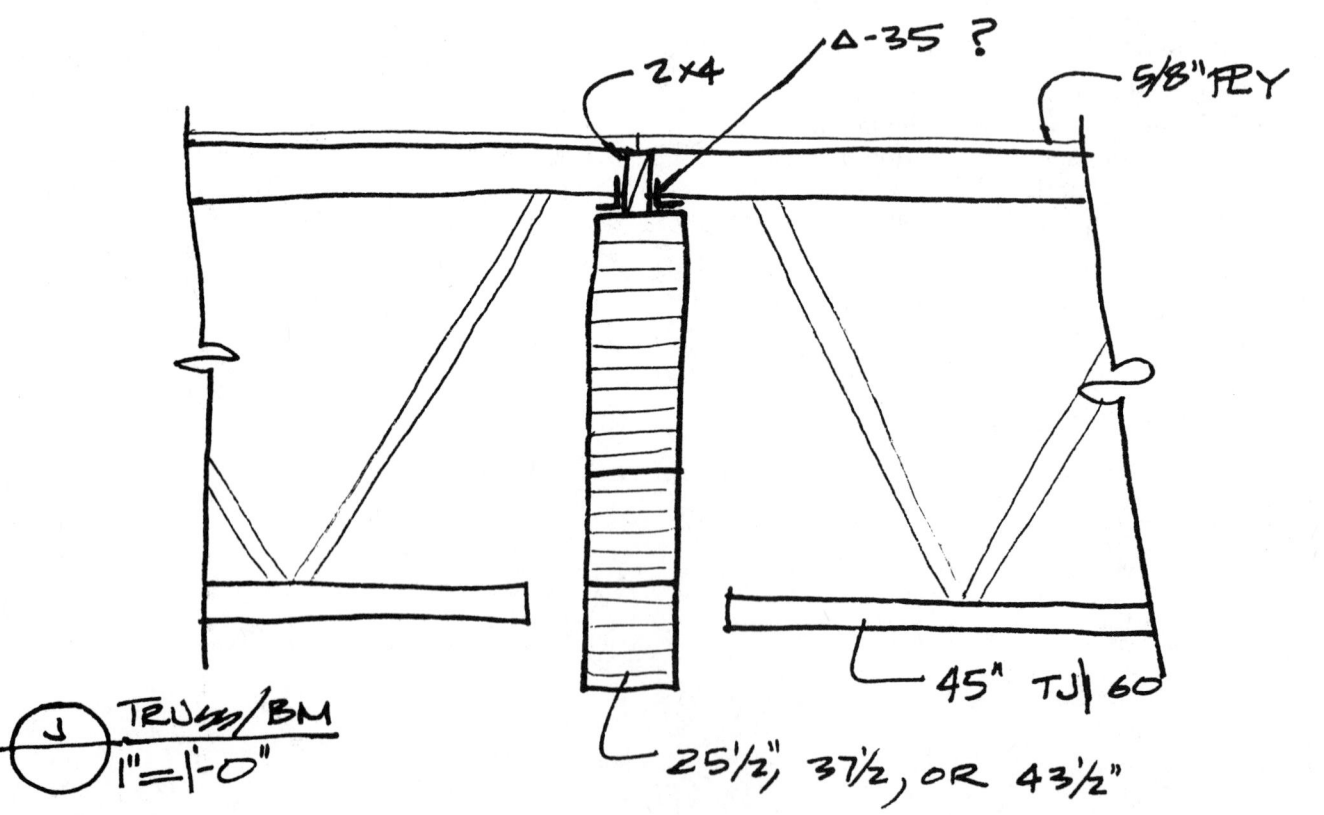

2×4

Δ-35 ?

5/8" PLY

45" TJ/60

J TRUSS/BM
1"=1'-0"

25½", 37½", OR 43½"

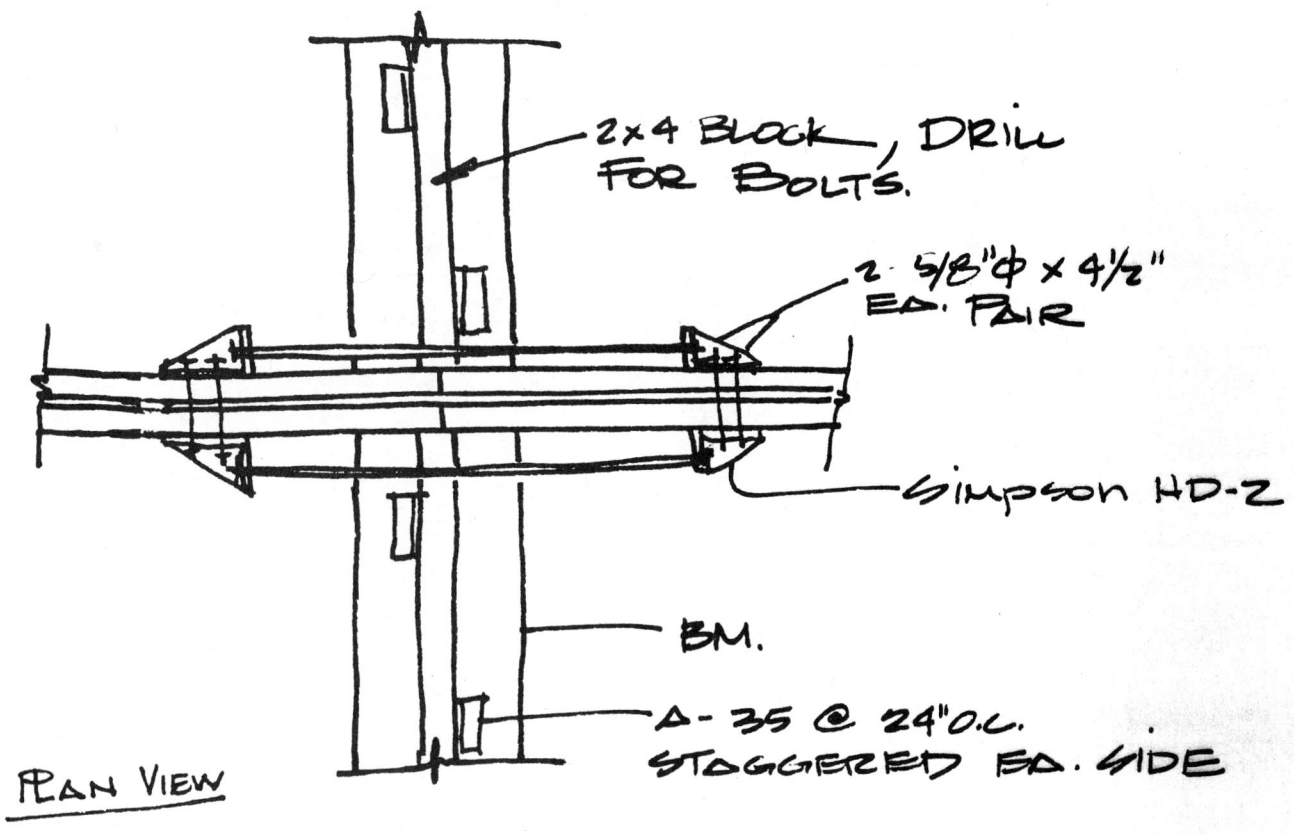

2×4 BLOCK, DRILL FOR BOLTS.

2· 5/8"⌀ × 4½" EA. PAIR

Simpson HD-2

BM.

A-35 @ 24" O.C. STAGGERED EA. SIDE

<u>PLAN VIEW</u>

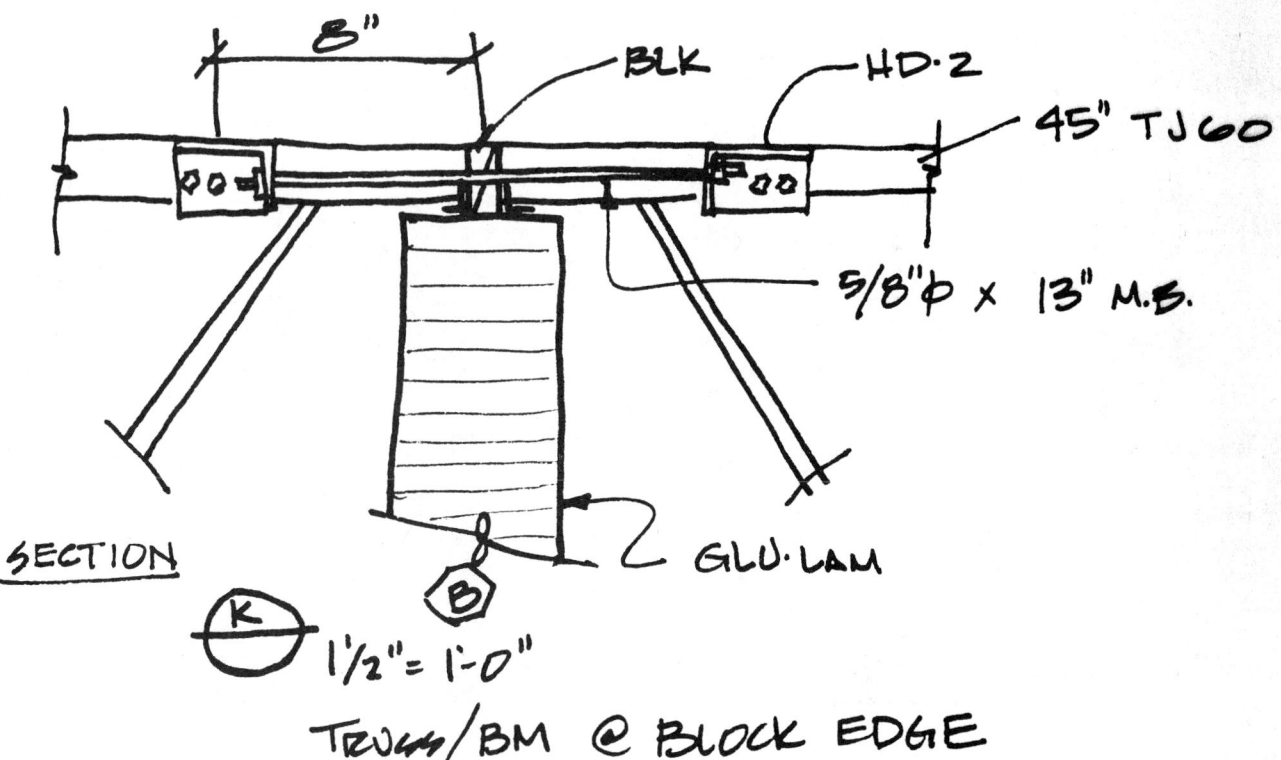

8"

BLK   HD·2

45" TJ 60

5/8"⌀ × 13" M.B.

GLU·LAM

<u>SECTION</u>

1½" = 1'-0"

K   B

TRUSS/BM @ BLOCK EDGE

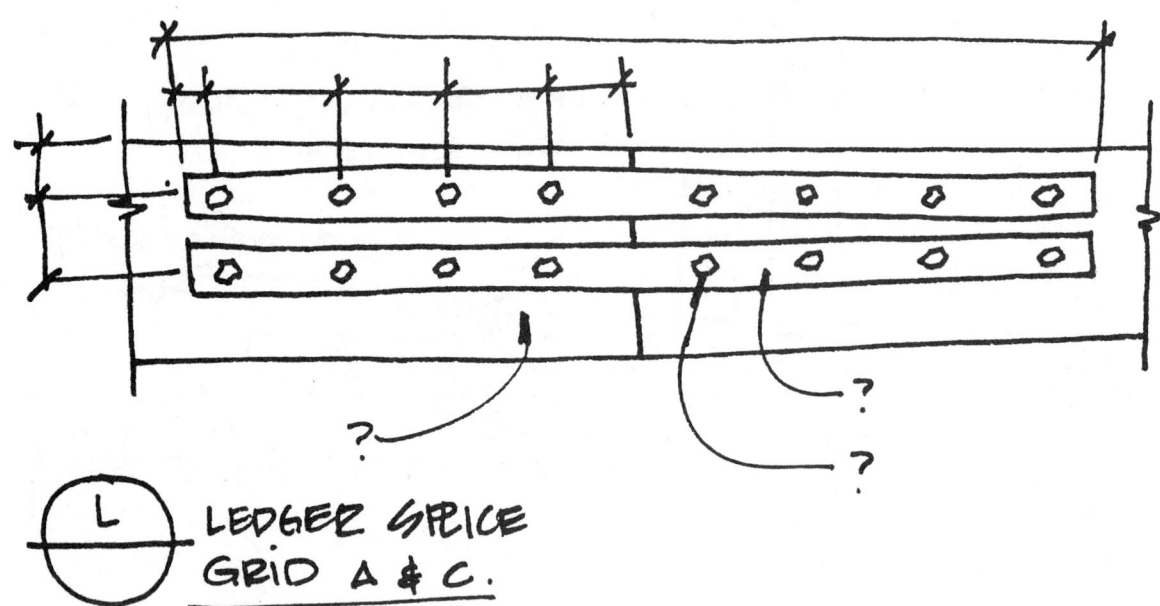

$\underbrace{L}$ LEDGER SPLICE
GRID A & C.
$\overline{3/4" = 1'-0"}$

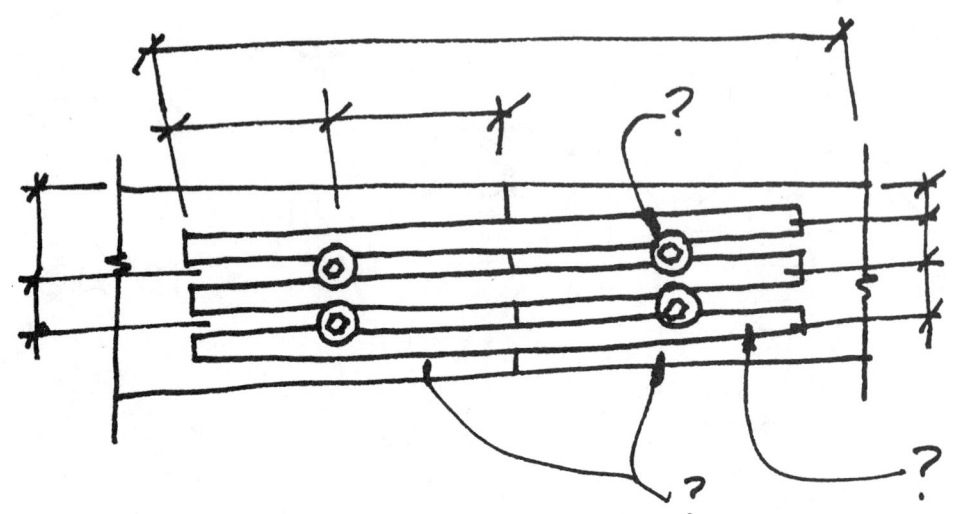

$\underbrace{M}$ LEDGER SPLICE
GRID 1 & 11
$\overline{3/4" = 1'-0"}$

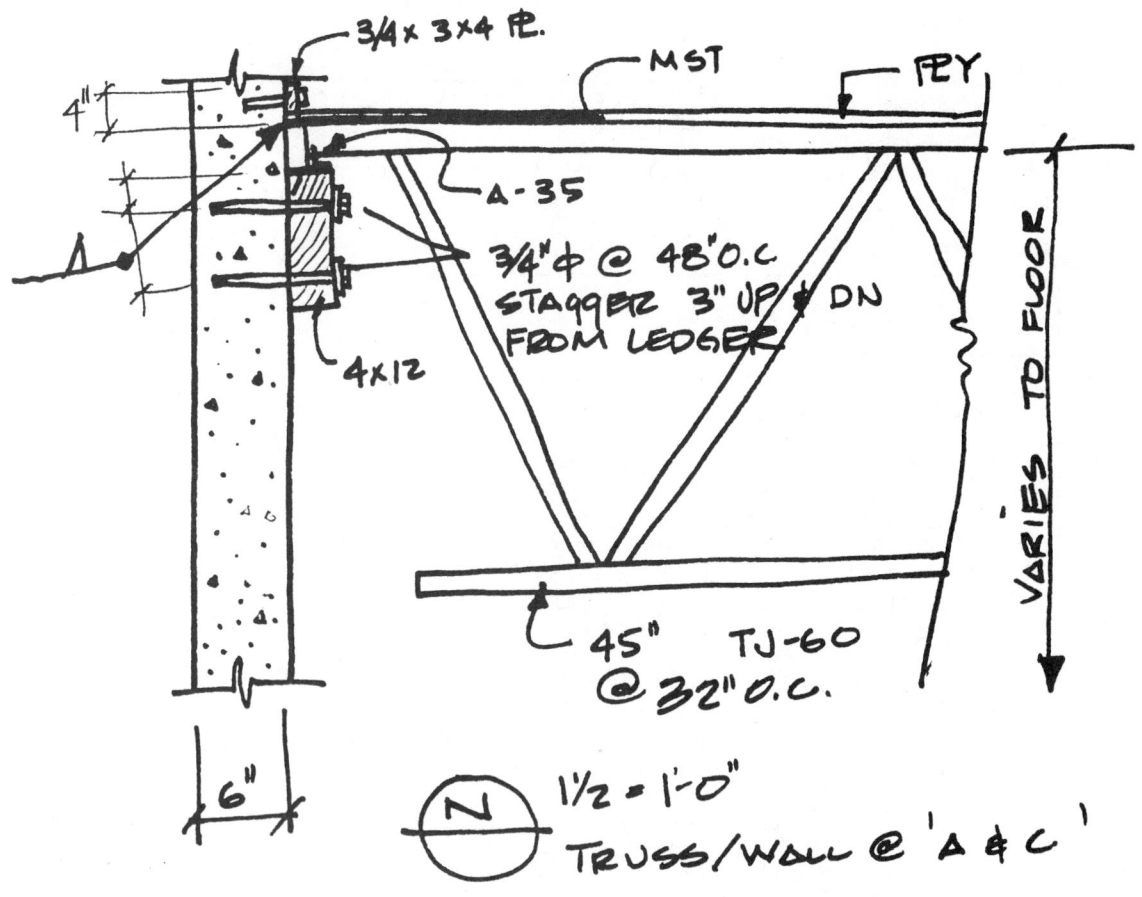

3/4 x 3x4 PL.
MST
PLY
4"
A-35
3/4"φ @ 48"O.C.
STAGGER 3" UP & DN
FROM LEDGER
4x12
45"   TJ-60
@ 32" O.C.
VARIES TO FLOOR
6"

Ⓝ 1½ = 1'-0"
TRUSS/WALL @ 'A & C'

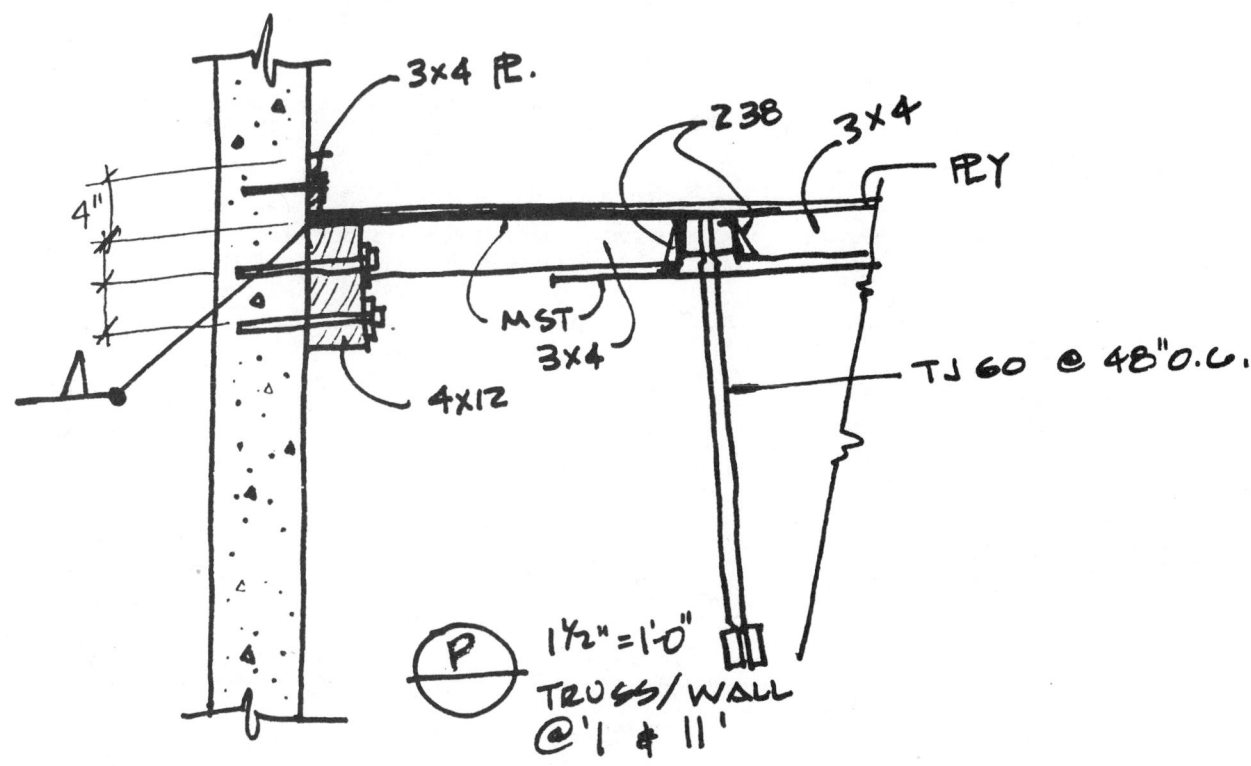

3x4 PL.
238   3x4
PLY
4"
MST
3x4
TJ 60 @ 48"O.C.
4x12

Ⓟ 1½" = 1'-0"
TRUSS/WALL
@ 'I & II'

TRUSS / BEAM DETAILS

ROOF LEDGERS: USE 4x12 D.F.L. #2

LEDGER SPLICES: USE (2) $\frac{1}{2}$ x 3 STRAP $\mathbb{P}$ EXTENDING 4 BOLTS ON
EACH SIDE OF SPLICE. USE $\frac{3}{4}\phi$ X 8" BOLTS @
20" O.C. W/ 2 ROWS @ 3$\frac{1}{2}$ O.C.

LEDGER SPLICE/ NON BEARING WALLS (1 & 11):
USE (3) SIMPSON MST48 STRAP TIES CENTERED OVER SPLICE @
3$\frac{1}{2}$"O.C.- 1$\frac{3}{4}$ DOWN FROM LEDGER TOP. PROVIDE (4) $\frac{3}{4}\phi$ x 8" BOLTS
THRU $\frac{1}{4}$ x 3"ϕ WASHERS CENTERED BETWEEN $\mathbb{P}$'s.

TRUSSES: USE 45" DEEP TJ/60 TRUSSJOIST @ 32" O.C.

ASSUME: 2.3" DEEP TOP AND BOTTOM CHORD.
1" ϕ ALUM. WEBS @ 45° ± 6" IN FROM END OF TOP CHORD.
BTM. CHORD TO BE 2" MIN. CLEAR OF BM.

TRUSS/BM CONNECTION:

PROVIDE 2x4 SOLID BLOCKING BTWN. TRUSSES OVER BEAM.
ATTACH TO GLU-LAM W/ SIMPSON CO. A-35 @ 32" O.C. @ EA. BLOCK
ALTERNATE SIDES & PROVIDE (2) EA. BLK. nAIL W/ n8 ALL HOLES.

TRUSS-BM/COLUMN PROVIDE 2x4 BRACE ALONG BEAM FOR

(2) TRUSS SPACES EA. SIDE OF COLUMN. USE 3x4 SOLID BLOCK BTWN.
BRACES. NAIL BLOCK TO BRACE W/ (5) 16d NAILS. PROVIDE 3x4x10'
NAILER @ TRUSSES. NAIL W/ (2) 16d'S EA. TRUSS. USE SIMPSON U-24 HGR.
2" UP FOM BTM. OF BEAM TO BRACE.   SET BRACE AT 45° MAX. FROM
BEAM.

TRUSS-BM @ BLOCKING EDGE: USE (2) SIMPSON HD-2

HOLDOWNS EITHER SIDE OF SPLICE W/ (2) $\frac{5}{8}$"ϕ x 4$\frac{1}{2}$" BOLTS THRU
TRUSS, AND $\frac{5}{8}$" ϕ x 15" BOLTS ACROSS SPLICE.

TRUSS/WALL (A & C): USE 4x12 DFL #2 TREATED LEDGER W/

$\frac{3}{4}$"ϕ x8" BOLTS @48" O.C. THRU $\frac{1}{4}$"x3ϕWASHERS. SOLID BLOCK BTWN.
TRUSSES @ LEDGER W/ 2x4 BLOCKS W/ (2) SIMPSON A-35 EA. BLK.
PROVIDE $\frac{3}{4}$" x 3"x4"$\mathbb{P}$ ABOVE PLYWOOD SHEATH. BOLT TO WALL W/
(1) $\frac{3}{4}$" 1 X 4$\frac{1}{8}$ BOLTS AT EA. 3rd TRUSS. WELD SIMPSON MST 27 STRAP
TO $\mathbb{P}$ W/ $\frac{1}{8}$" FILLET WELD AND NAIL TO TRUSSES W/ n8 EA. HOLE.

TRUSS/WALL (1, 11):

USE 4x12 DFL TREATED LEDGER W/ $\frac{3}{4}$"ϕ x 8" BOLTS @ 6'-0" O.C. THRU
$\frac{1}{8}$"ϕ x3" WASHERS. uSE 3x4$\mathbb{P}$ (SEE ABOVE) @ EA. 3rd TRUSS W/ MST27
STRAP.   PROVIDE 3x4 SOLID BLOCK @ 48" O.C. FOR 37.3' OUT FROM
WALL (SEE PLYWOOD DIAPHRAM SPECS.) cONNECT BLOCK TO TRUSS
W/ SIMPSON Z-38 HGR.

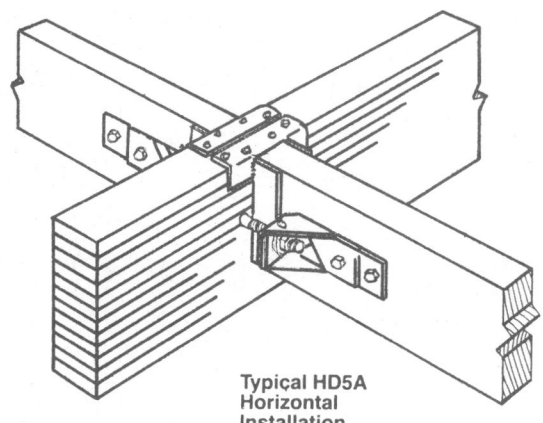

Typical HD5A
Horizontal
Installation

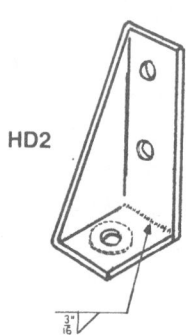

HD2

HDA/HD *HOLDOWNS*

MODEL NO.	MATERIAL		DIMENSIONS							FASTENERS				AVG ULT	MAXIMUM ALLOWABLE LOADS²					
	BASE	BODY	HB⁷	SB	W	H	B	SO	CL	CONC. ANCHOR			STUD BOLTS		LENGTH OF BOLT IN WOOD MEMBER					
										DIA	EMBEDMENT									
											2000³	3000⁴			1½	2	2½	3	3½	5½
HDA HOLDOWNS																				
HD2A	7 ga.	12 ga.	4½	2½	2½	8	2⅝	¼	1½	⅝	12	9	2-⅝	12150	1970	2585	3035	3270	3300	3315
HD5A	3 ga.	10 ga.	5¼	3	3³/₁₆	9⅜	3½	½	2¹/₁₆	¾	14	11	2-¾	20767	2370	3135	3850	4385	4670	4770
HD7A	3 ga.	3 ga.	6⅛	3½	3½	14¾	3¾	¾	2³/₁₆	1⅛	19	15	3-⅞	32663	3240	4310	6440	7570	8950	9555
HD20A	⅜	3 ga.	7	4	4¼	20¾	4⅛	⅞	2⅜	1¼	26	20	4-1	51000	—	—	—	—	13380	15040
HD HOLDOWNS																				
HD2	7 ga.	7 ga.	4⅜	2¾	2½	5¾	2½	2¾	1⅜	⅝	12	9	2-⅝	10916	1965	2585	3035	3265	3300	3315
HD5	3 ga.	7 ga.	5¼	3	2⅞	6⅜	3½	3⅝	2⅛	¾	14	11	2-¾	19000	2365	3135	3850	4385	4665	4765
HD6	3 ga.	3 ga.	5¼	3	2⅞	12½	3¼	3	1⅞	1	15	15	3-¾	18600	2770	3665	5430	6080	6080	6080
HD7	5/16	3 ga.	6⅛	3½	3½	11⅝	3⅜	3⅜	2⅛	1⅛	18	15	3-⅞	28600	3235	5195	6430	8050	8770	9260
HD9	⅜	3 ga.	7	4	3½	16½	4¼	3⅝	2⅛	1⅛	25	15	3-1	—	—	—	—	—	10675	12170
HD12	⅜	3 ga.	7	4	3½	20½	4¼	3⅝	2⅛	1⅛	30	15	4-1	43750	—	—	—	—	13665	15550
HD15	⅜	3 ga.	7	4	3½	24½	4¼	3⅝	2⅛	1¼	30	20	5-1	43750	—	—	—	—	—	17500

Z2 clips secure 2 x 4 flat blocking between joists or trusses to support sheathing.
Z4 and Z6 clips support fit-in joists when they are skewed.

MATERIAL: Z clips — see table; Angles — 12 gauge steel
FINISH: Galvanized
CODE ACCEPTANCE: Z4 and Z6 clips are ICBO accepted; see Evaluation Service No. 1258.

A311
Installed

A24
Installed

MODEL NO.	DIMENSIONS			FASTENERS			
	W₁	W₂	L	BASE		POST	
				BOLTS	NAILS	BOLTS	NAILS
A33	3	3	1½	—	4-10d	—	4-10d
A44	4½	4½	1½	—	4-10d	—	4-10d
A66	6	6	1½	2-⅜	—	2-⅜	—
A88	8	8	2	3-⅜	—	3-⅜	—
A24	4	2	2½	1-½	—	1-½	2-10d
A311	11	3⅝	2	1-½	—	1-½	2-10d

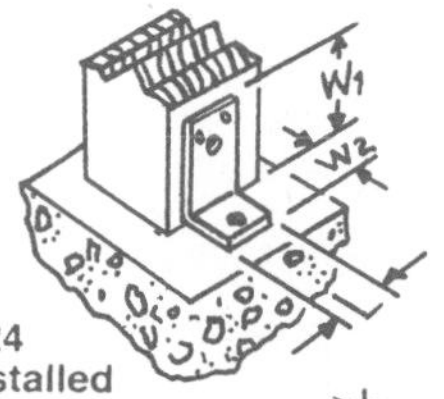

MODEL NO.	MATL	DIMENSIONS			
		W	H	B	TF
Z2	20 ga.	2⁵/₁₆	1½	1³/₈	1³/₈
Z4	12 ga.	1½	3½	2	1³/₈
Z6	12 ga.	1½	5⅜	2	1³/₈
Z28	28 ga.	2⁵/₁₆	2½	1³/₈	1³/₈
Z38	28 ga.	2⁵/₁₆	2½	1³/₈	1³/₈
Z44	12 ga.	2½	3½	2	1³/₈

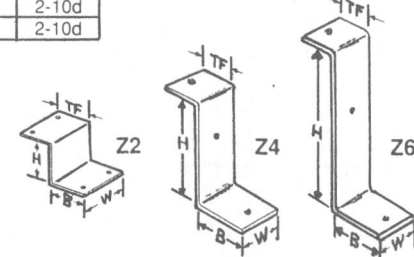

Z2   Z4   Z6

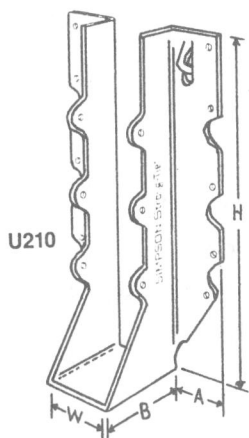

U210

MODEL NO.	JOIST SIZE	DIMENSIONS				FASTENERS		AVG ULT	ALLOWABLE LOADS[1,2]				
		W	H	B	A	HEADER	JOIST		UPLIFT	NORMAL 10d	NORMAL 16d	MAXIMUM 10d	MAXIMUM 16d
U24	2×4	1 9/16	3 1/8	1 1/2	7/8	4-16d	2-10d×1 1/2	2575	200	435	535	540	670
U26	2×6,8	1 9/16	4 3/4	2	1 1/4	6-16d	4-10d×1 1/2	3680	420	650	805	815	1005
U210	2×10,12,14	1 9/16	7 13/16	2	1 1/4	10-16d	6-10d×1 1/2	6200	630	1085	1340	1355	1675
U214	2×14,16	1 9/16	10	2	1 1/4	12-16d	8-10d×1 1/2	7200	840	1300	1610	1630	2010
U24R	ROUGH 2×4	2	3 5/8	2	1 1/4	4-16d	2-10d×1 1/2	2575	200	470	535	590	670
U26R	ROUGH 2×6,8	2	5 5/8	2	1 1/4	8-16d	4-10d×1 1/2	5000	420	945	1070	1180	1345
U210R	ROUGH 2×10,12,14	2	9 1/8	2	1 1/4	14-16d	6-10d×1 1/2	9800	630	1650	1875	2065	2350
U34	3×4	2 9/16	3 3/8	2	1 1/4	4-16d	2-10d×1 1/2	2600	200	470	535	590	670
U36	3×6,8	2 9/16	5 3/8	2	1 1/4	8-16d	4-10d×1 1/2	5000	420	945	1070	1180	1345
U310	3×10,12	2 9/16	8 7/8	2	1 1/4	14-16d	6-10d×1 1/2	9800	630	1650	1875	2065	2350
U314	3×14,16	2 9/16	10 1/2	2	1 1/4	16-16d	6-10d×1 1/2	11000	630	1890	2145	2360	2690
U24-2	(2) 2×4	3 1/8	3	2	1 1/4	4-16d	2-10d	2600	200	470	535	590	670
U26-2	(2) 2×6,8	3 1/8	5	2	1 1/4	8-16d	4-10d	5000	420	945	1070	1180	1345
U210-2	(2) 2×10,12,14	3 1/8	8 1/2	2	1 1/4	14-16d	6-10d	9800	630	1650	1875	2065	2350
U44	4×4	3 9/16	2 7/8	2	1 1/4	4-16d	2-10d	2600	200	470	535	590	670
U46	4×6,8	3 9/16	4 7/8	2	1 1/4	8-16d	4-10d	5000	420	945	1070	1180	1345
U410	4×10,12	3 9/16	8 3/8	2	1 1/4	14-16d	6-10d	9800	630	1650	1875	2065	2350
U414	4×14,16	3 9/16	10	2	1 1/4	16-16d	6-10d	11000	630	1890	2145	2360	2690
U44R	ROUGH 4×4	4	2 5/8	2	1 1/4	4-16d	2-16d	2600	200	470	535	590	670
U46R	ROUGH 4×6,8	4	4 5/8	2	1 1/4	8-16d	4-16d	5000	420	945	1070	1180	1345
U410R	ROUGH 4×10,12,14	4	8 1/8	2	1 1/4	14-16d	6-16d	9800	630	1650	1875	2065	2350
U26-3	(3) 2×6,8	4 5/8	4 1/4	2	1 1/4	8-16d	2-10d	5000	200	945	1070	1180	1345
U210-3	(3) 2×10,12,14	4 5/8	7 3/4	2	1 1/4	14-16d	6-10d	9800	630	1650	1875	2065	2350
U66	6×6,8	5 1/2	5	2	1 1/4	8-16d	4-10d	5000	420	945	1070	1180	1345
U610	6×10	5 1/2	8 1/2	2	1 1/4	8-16d	6-10d	9800	630	1650	1875	2065	2350
U66R	ROUGH 6×6,8	6	5	2	1 1/4	8-16d	4-16d	5000	420	945	1070	1180	1345
U610R	ROUGH 6×10,12,14	6	8 1/2	2	1 1/4	14-16d	6-16d	9800	630	1650	1875	2065	2350

1. The allowable loads under the "10d" column heading are the loads allowed when 10d common nails are used instead of the 16d header nails.

2. Uplift loads have been increased by 33% for wind or earthquake loading with no further increase allowed. Reduce allowable uplift by 33% for normal loading criteria such as in cantilever construction.

MODEL NO.	DIMENSIONS				FASTENERS		ALLOWABLE LOADS		
	W₁	W₂	L	H	BEAM	POST	UPLIFT[2]	DOWN[1] CC	DOWN[1] ECC
CC3 1/4-4	3 1/4	3 5/8	11	6 1/2	4-5/8 MB	2-5/8 MB	2795	15470	4920
CC3 1/4-6	3 1/4	5 1/2	11	6 1/2	4-5/8 MB	2-5/8 MB	2795	15470	7735
CC44	3 5/8	3 5/8	7	4	2-5/8 MB	2-5/8 MB	2430	9430	4715
CC46	3 5/8	5 1/2	11	6 1/2	4-5/8 MB	2-5/8 MB	3005	14820	7410
CC5 1/4-6	5 1/4	5 1/2	13	8	4-3/4 MB	2-3/4 MB	9440	29980	12615
CC5 1/4-8	5 1/4	7 1/2	13	8	4-3/4 MB	2-3/4 MB	9440	29980	17295
CC64	5 1/2	3 5/8	11	6 1/2	4-5/8 MB	2-5/8 MB	3750	23290	7410
CC66	5 1/2	5 1/2	11	6 1/2	4-5/8 MB	2-5/8 MB	3750	23290	11645
CC68	5 1/2	7 1/2	11	6 1/2	4-5/8 MB	2-5/8 MB	3750	23290	15880
CC76	6 7/8	5 1/2	13	8	4-3/4 MB	2-3/4 MB	9440	40220	16705
CC77	6 7/8	6 7/8	13	8	4-3/4 MB	2-3/4 MB	9440	40220	20500
CC78	6 7/8	7 1/2	13	8	4-3/4 MB	2-3/4 MB	9440	40220	22780
CC86	7 1/2	5 1/2	13	8	4-3/4 MB	2-3/4 MP	9440	37540	15880
CC88	7 1/2	7 1/2	13	8	4-3/4 MB	2-3/4 MB	9440	37540	21655
CC96	8 7/8	5 1/2	13	8	4-3/4 MB	2-3/4 MB	9025	51190	21655
CC98	8 7/8	7 1/2	13	8	4-3/4 MB	2-3/4 MB	9025	51190	29530
CC106	9 1/2	5 1/2	13	8	4-3/4 MB	2-3/4 MB	8745	47550	20115

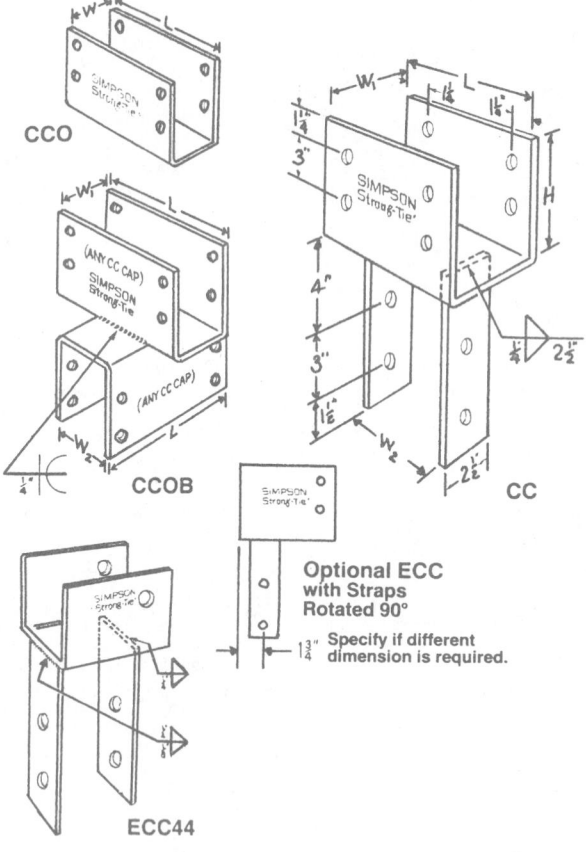

CCO

CCOB

CC

ECC44

Optional ECC with Straps Rotated 90°

Specify if different dimension is required.

Problem 52–7. SLAB DETAILS.

Goal

These drawings will provide information required to complete the floor slab, showing intersections in the concrete slab and door joints, and elevations.

Method

Use a scale as indicated on each detail. Place details on the same sheet as the slab, on grade plan, or on a separate sheet with all other concrete details.

1. Determine in what order the details will be presented. Place the details in an order that reflects their relationship to the building, not the order that the engineer thought of them.

2. Lay out each detail allowing approximately 15 minutes per detail. Given this brief amount of time, draw only major features such as slab outlines, and mesh and steel centerlines.

3. Draw all lines. Be careful that all rebar is drawn with the same type of line quality. Draw mesh as a thin line with the "X" spaced at 4″ O.C.

4. Dimension as per sketches.

5. Place detail markers on the slab plan and section.

6. Label as required.

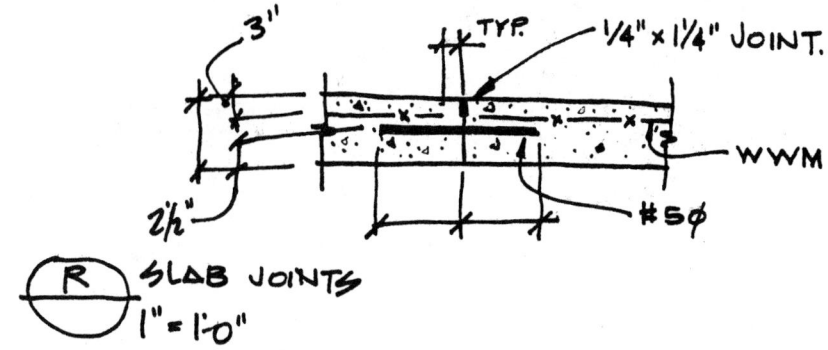

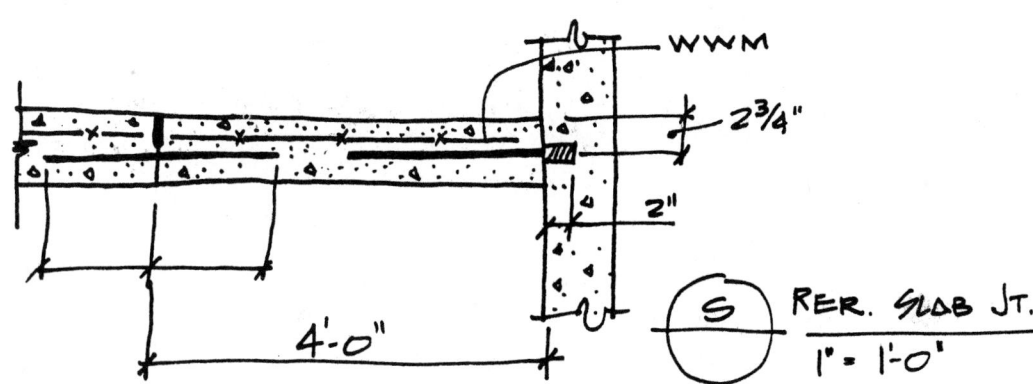

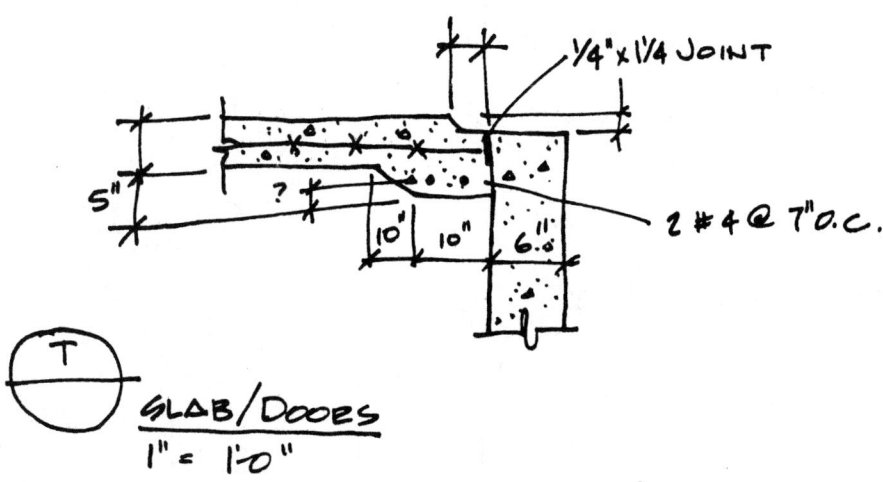

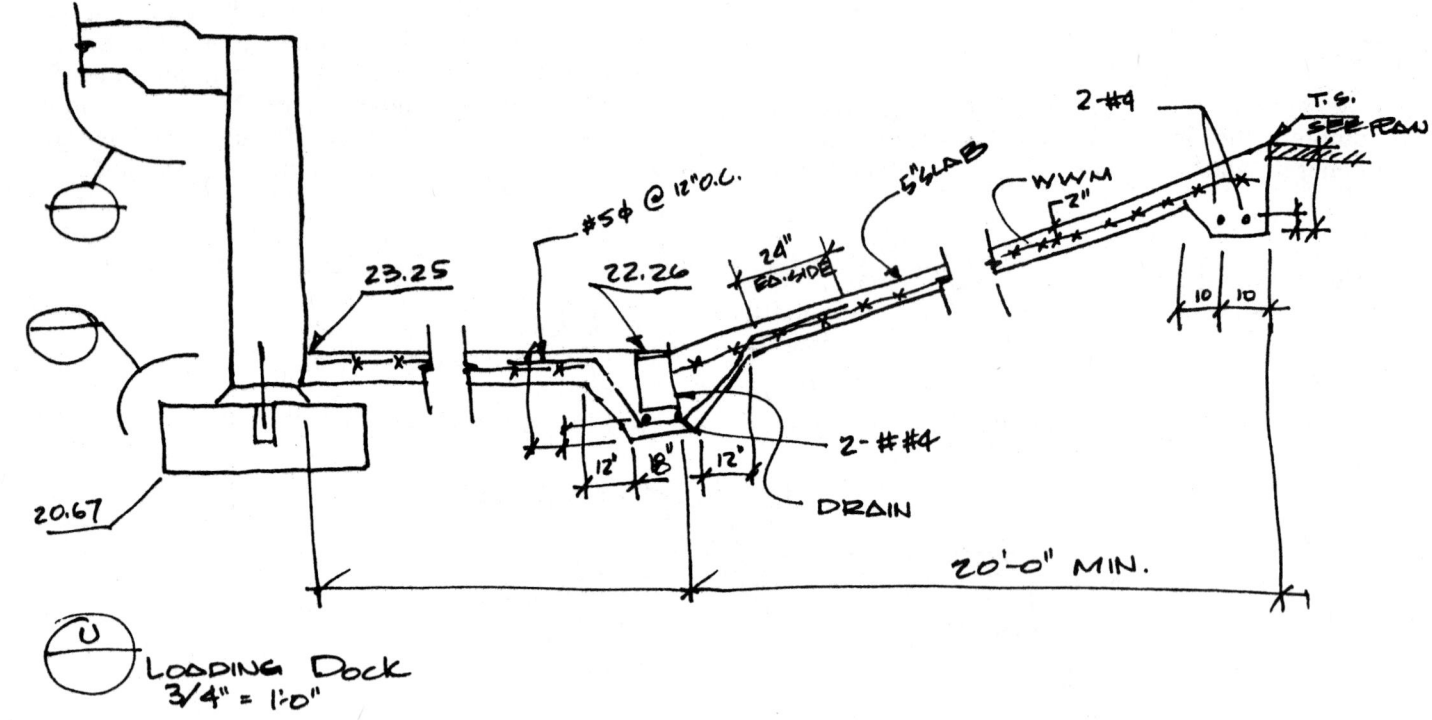

23.25 22.26 #5∮ @ 12"O.C. 24" EA. SIDE 5" SLAB WWM 2" 2-#4 T.S. SEE PLAN.

20.67

12" 8" 12" 2-#4 DRAIN 10 10 20'-0" MIN.

U LOADING DOCK
3/4" = 1'-0"

SLAB/ DOCK

SLAB: ALL SLAB ON GRADE CONC. TO BE F'c = 3500 PSI @ 28 DAYS. ALL TARGET STRENGTHS SHALL BE IN ACCORDANCE W/ CHAPTER 4 OF ACI 318 BUILDING CODE REQUIREMENTS FOR REINFORCED CONCRETE.   SLABS TO BE 5" THICK UNLESS NOTED W/ WWF 12x12 -W4xW4 OR GRD 40 #3 @ 15" O.C. EA. WAY CENTERED IN SLAB.

JOINTS: PROVIDE ¼" FIBER INSOLATION JOINTS W/ NEOPRENE JOINT SEALANT OVER ⅜"∮ BACKER BEAD AT ALL CONTROL JOINTS AND AROUND ALL FOUNDATION PEDESTALS.
PROVIDE #5 x 15" LONG SMOOTH DOWELLS @ 12"O.C. AT ALL CONTROL JOINTS UNLESS NOTED (SEE PER JTS.) COVER W/ PAPER SLEEVES ON EA SIDE OF JOINT.

KEEP WWM 2" MIN. CLEAR OF JOINT. KEEP #5's 2½" CLR OF BOTTOM OF SLAB.

PERP. JOINTS. SAME AS ABOVE EXCEPT: ALL SMOOTH DOWELLS TO BE #5x 30" LONG.

PROVIDE ¾"∮ 'L' STRUCTURAL CONNECTION INSERTS W/ ¾"∮ X 25"LONG COIL RODS @ 5'-7" O.C. PROVIDE 2" MIN ROD PENETRATION INTO INSERTS.

DOORS: PROVIDE 3" WIDE x ¾ x¾ CHAMFER IN SLAB AT ALL DOORS.

THICKEN SLAB AT ALL DOORS TO 10" AND PROVIDE (2) #4 2" CLR OF BTM. OF SLAB.

LOADING DOCK: PROVIDE 12' WIDE BASE PLATFORM W/ ¼"/12" SLOPE TO DRAIN. DRAIN TO BE 8" x 12" DEEP POLYESTER CONC DRAIN W/ C.I. GRATE. THICKEN SLAB @ GRATE TO 18" DP. W/ (2) #4 @ 15" O.C. 3" CLR OF BTM OF FTG.

PROVIDE 20' MIN SLOPE IN DOCK THICKEN SLAB TO 10" @ ENTRY W/ 2 #4 @ 6" O.C. 3" CLR OF BTM OF FTG.

Problem 52–8. FOUNDATION DETAILS.

Goal

These details will provide information on the concrete at the foundation level, showing either the exterior foundation or the pedestals.

Method

Use a scale as indicated on each detail. Place details on the same sheet as the foundation plan or on a separate sheet with all other concrete details. Use the sketches and the calcs as a guide for your drawing.

1. Determine in what order the details will be presented. Place the details in an order that reflects their relationship to the building, not the order that the engineer thought of them.
2. Determine the missing dimensions from the calculations prior to layout work.
3. Lay out each detail allowing approximately 15 minutes per detail. Given this brief amount of time, draw only major features such as concrete outlines and mesh and steel centerlines. Be sure to allow room for schedules by each detail where they are required. Be careful that all rebar is drawn with the same type of line quality as used in the slab details.
4. Dimension as per sketches.
5. Place detail markers on the foundation plan and section.
6. Label as required.

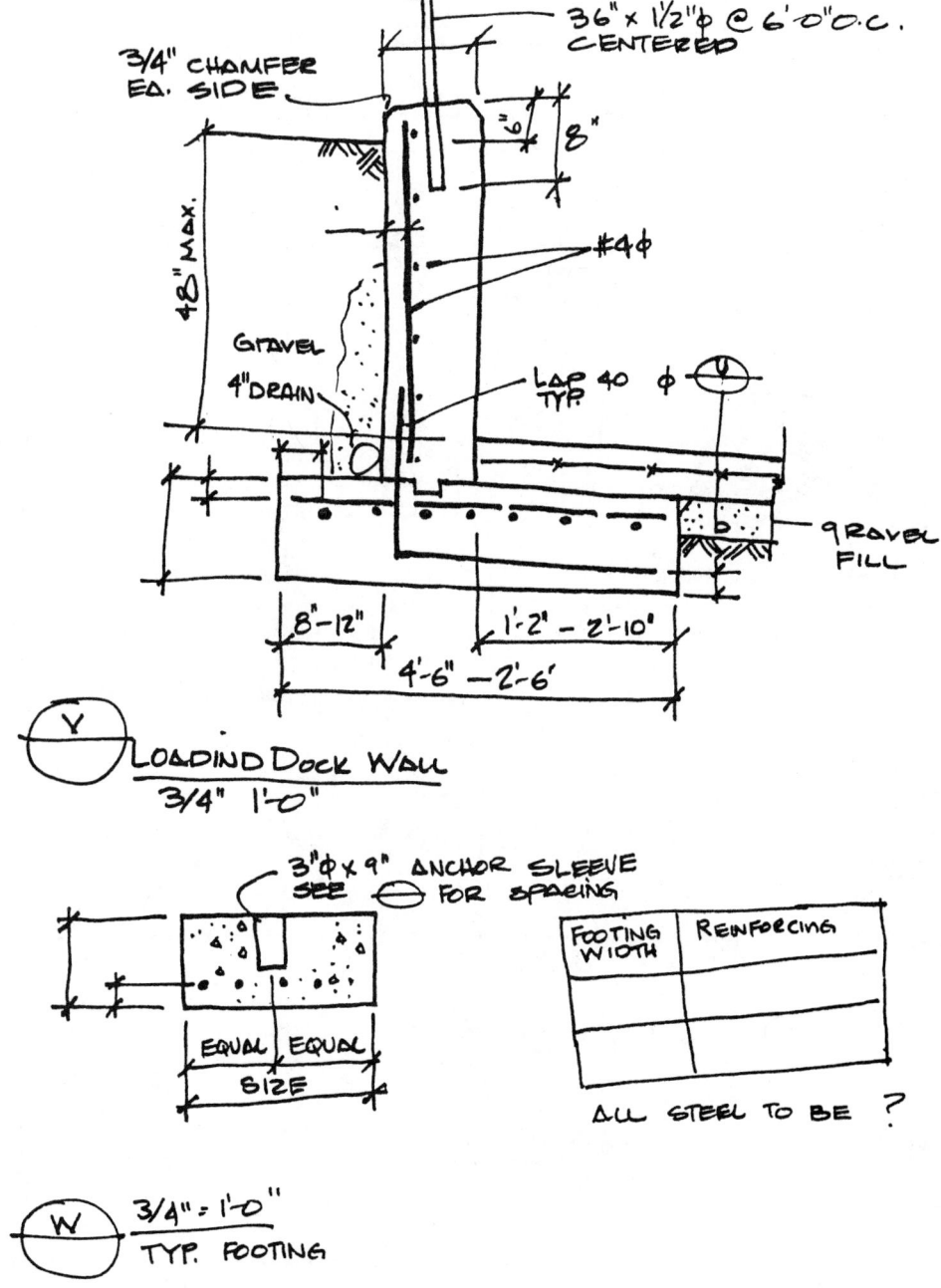

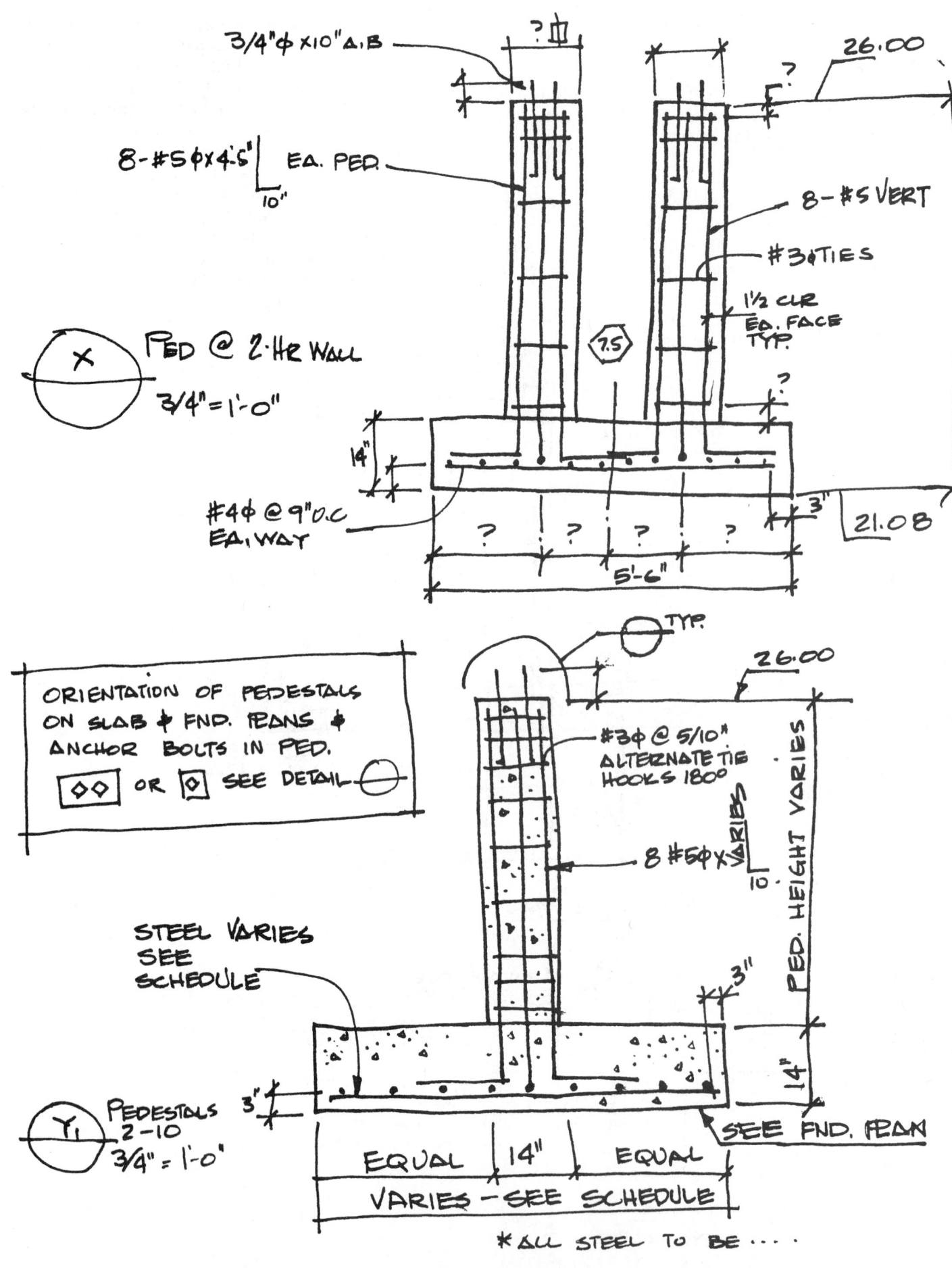

3/4"⌀ X10" A.B

8-#5⌀X4'5" EA. PED.
10"

26.00

8-#5 VERT

#3⌀TIES

1½ CLR
EA. FACE
TYP.

PED @ 2-HR WALL
3/4"=1'-0"

7.5

14"

#4⌀ @ 9"O.C
EA. WAY

3"

21.08

5'-6"

TYP.

26.00

ORIENTATION OF PEDESTALS
ON SLAB & FND. PLANS &
ANCHOR BOLTS IN PED.
◇◇ OR ◇ SEE DETAIL

#3⌀ @ 5/10"
ALTERNATE TIE
HOOKS 180°

8 #5⌀X VARIES
10

PED. HEIGHT VARIES

STEEL VARIES
SEE
SCHEDULE

3"

3"

14"

Y1 PEDESTALS
2-10
3/4" = 1'-0"

SEE FND. PLAN

EQUAL | 14" | EQUAL
VARIES - SEE SCHEDULE

* ALL STEEL TO BE . . . .

FOOTING	PEDESTAL HEIGHT	SIZE	REINFORCING STEEL				BTM OF FTG.
B-2	7.50	7'-0" φ	#	φ	@	O.C.	17.33
B-3							
B-4							
B-5							
B-6							
B-7							
B-7.5							
B-8							
B-9							
B-10							

ALL STEEL TO BE GRADE . . . . .   UNLESS NOTED

FOUNDATION

ASSUME: ALL FOUNDATION, PEDESTAL, AND RETAINING WALL CONC.
TO BE F'c =3000 PSI @ 28 DAYS.

ALL STEEL BAR REINFORCEMENT SHALL BE ASTM A615, GRADE 40,
DEFORMED BARS UNLESS OTHERWISE SPECIFIED IN DRAWINGS OR
DETAILS.

PEDESTALS USE 14"□ W/ (8)- GRADE 40 #5 VERT. RE-BAR 1½" CLR
OF PEDESTAL FACE (HEIGHT VARIES, SEE FOUNDATION PLAN AND
COMPLETE SCHEDULE). USE #3 HORIZ. TIES W/ TOP AND BOTTOM
(3) TIES @ 5" O.C. & INTERMEDIATES @ 10" O.C. HORIZ TIES TO BE
WITHIN 1½" OF TOP AND BOTTOM. PROVODE (4) ¾"φ x 10" A.B. IN
6½" GRID W/ 2½" BOLT PROJECTION.

PEDESTALS @ 7.5 SIMILAR TO TYPICAL PEDESTALS (ABOVE)
UNLESS NOTED. PROVIDE #3 HORIZ TIES (2) @ 5"O.C. WITHIN 1½" OF
TOP OF PEDESTAL, AND BALANCE @ 10"O.C. W/ LAST TIE WITHIN 1½"
OF BTM OF PED. USE 5'-6" x 3'-6" x 18" DEEP FOOTING.

PEDESTAL FOUNDATIONS (@B-6) USE A 6'□ x14" DP.
W/GRD. 40, #5 @10"O.C. EA.WAY 3" CLEAR OF BASE

PEDESTAL FOUND. (@ 2,5,7,10) USE 7'□ x 14" DP. W/
GRD. 40, #6 @ 10"O.C. EA.WAY 3" CLR OF BASE.

PEDESTAL FOUND. (@ 3,4,8,9,) USE 6.5□ x 14" DP. W/
GRADE 40, #6 @ 12"O.C. EACH WAY 3" CLEAR OF BASE.

FOUND.- LOAD BEAR.: 36" x 14" DP. W/ (3) GRD. 40,#5@ 9"O.C.
3" CLR OF FTG. BTM.

FOUND.- NON-BEAR(1&11) USE 26" x 14" DP. FOOTING W/
(2) GRD. 40, #5 @ 12"O.C. 3" CLR OF FTG. BTM.

RETAINING WALL: USE 8" THICK WALL W/GRD. 40, #4 @ 10" O.C.
EA. WAY, 2" CLR OF SOIL SIDE OF WALL. USE 14" THICK FOOTING x 4.5'
WIDE W/ GRADE 40, #4 @ 10" O.C. EA. WAY, 2" CLR OF TOP OF FOOTING.
PROVIDE #5 @ 10" O.C. EA. WAY 3" CLR OF BTM OF FTG. W/ #5 @ 10 O.C.
'L' SHAPED BAR W/ 24" MIN. PROJECTION INTO FOOTING. USE #4φ CONT.
@ "L". FOOTING TO TAPER FROM 8"-12" PROJECTION FROM WALL ON SOIL
SIDE AND BTWN. 1'-2"- 2'-10" ON DOCK SIDE. PROVIDE 4" φ DRAIN IN
12" x 24" MIN. ¾" MINUS GRAVEL BED.

Problem 52–9. TYPICAL CROSS-SECTION.

Goal

The purpose of this drawing is to show the vertical relationship of structural members. It functions as a reference map and is not intended to provide a detailed explanation of the connections. Most of the details that will be drawn will be referenced on this drawing.

Method

Using a scale of $3/16'' = 1'-0''$, draw the section. Do not draw the entire section.

1. Place a section marker in the same location on the roof drainage, roof framing, slab, and foundation plans before starting the drawing.
2. Establish base lines to represent the top of the slab floor and the wall at "C" and the beams at "B."
3. Determine the elevations of the footings at the wall and pedestal from the foundation plan. Your detail must match your reference marker, not your neighbor's or the engineer's sketch. The location of the reference marker will affect your wall size.
4. Establish vertical heights at "B & C", based on panel elevation.
5. Lay out the ledger, trusses, and beams.
6. Draw all items. Be careful to distinguish between concrete and wood members.
7. Dimension as per the sketch.
8. Label grids and local notes.

ON PROBLEM	NOTE SHOULD READ
⅝″ ply. . .	See note on roof calcs.
T.J.I. . . .	45″ TJ/60 joist at 24″ O.C.
6″ walls. . .	6″ tilt up conc. walls/
Roofing. . .	4 ply built-up asphaltic fiberglass class 'A' roofing.
Beam. . .	6¾″ × 25.5, 37.5 or 43.5 glu-lam beam

TYPICAL SECTION
$3/16'' = 1'-0''$

Problem 52–10. EXTERIOR ELEVATIONS.

Goal

These drawings will provide an external view of the building to be constructed.

Method

Typically, an elevation of each side of a structure would be drawn. Verify with your instructor which elevations will be drawn with your project. Use a scale of 3/32″ = 1′-0″ and follow the procedures outlined in chapters 24 and 25. For best use of a page, place the elevations in the upper portion of a sheet to allow room for other drawings. If you are using CADD, compare the elevations and the panel elevations so both drawings can be done in layers.

Layout

1. Draw a reference line to represent the slab. This line will never be on the finished drawing but will help locate the bottom of all doors.

2. Establish each end of the structure and each grid.
3. Establish the top of the walls using information on the typical cross-sections and details.
4. Establish finish grade elevations.
5. Lay out all door locations using the locations shown on the panel elevation sketches.
6. Locate loading docks based on the foundation plan.
7. Determine the locations of three strips, and sign as per sketch.
8. Draw the grade and loading dock using bold lines.
9. Draw the outline of the structure.
10. Draw grid lines as two, thin parallel lines.
11. Draw doors.
12. Draw stripes and sign.
13. Draw concrete symbols on some of the walls.
14. Label as per sketch.

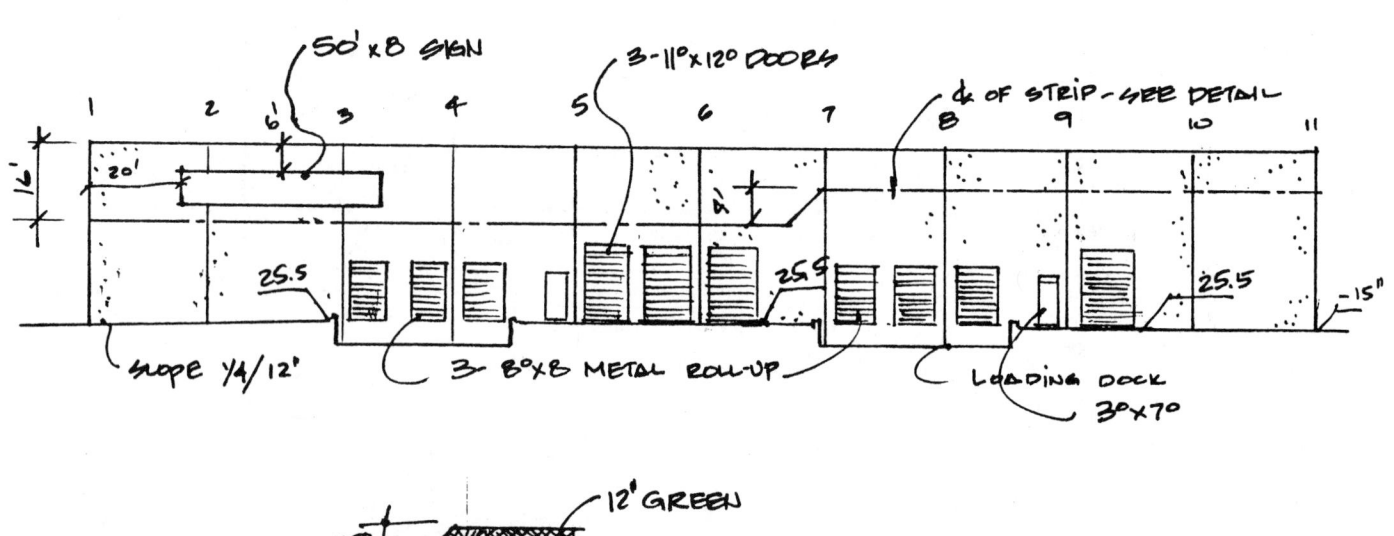

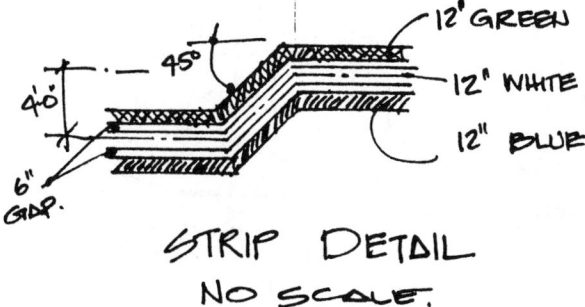

STRIP DETAIL
NO SCALE.

Problem 52–11. PANEL ELEVATIONS.

Goal

These drawings will provide an internal view of the walls to be constructed, showing wall shape and openings.

Method

Typically, an elevation of each panel of a structure would be drawn. Verify with your instructor if more than the north face will be drawn for your project. Use a scale of 3/32″ = 1′–0″. Due to the length of the structure, the sketch of the north panel elevations is shown on two separate drawings. Your drawings should reflect the true layout of the structure and include all information specified in the calcs. Place this drawing on the same sheet as the elevations. Use a print of the elevations to speed the layout, or set this up as a layer to be used on the exterior elevations if using CADD.

Layout

1. Draw a reference line to represent the slab. This line will never be on the finished drawing but will help locate the bottom of each panel.
2. Establish each end of the structure and each grid.
3. Establish the top of the walls using information on the sections and elevations.
4. Determine the foundation elevations and lay out the top of the footing.
5. Lay out all door locations.
6. Draw the outline of the panels.
7. Draw the grid lines.
8. Draw door openings.
9. Provide dimensions to describe all wall shapes and all door openings. Keep size location separate from location dimension.
10. Print all notes.

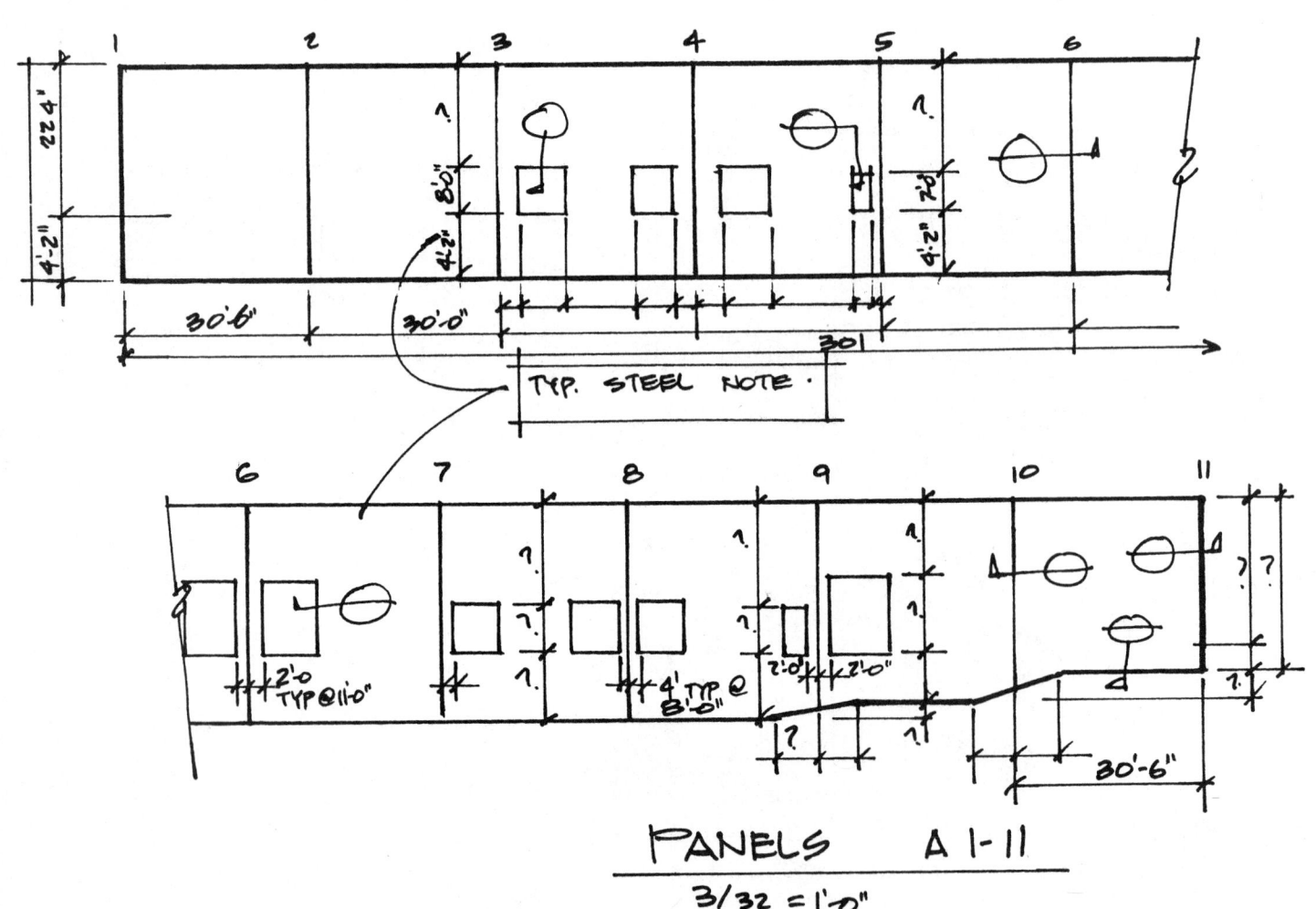

PANELS   A 1-11

3/32 = 1′-0″

Problem 52–12. PANEL DETAILS.

Goal

The purpose of these drawings is to show steel placement around any openings in the tilt-up walls. Steel could be shown on the panel elevations, but more clarity is gained by providing details.

Method

A detail will be provided for each size opening, to show typical steel placement. Be aware that all steel specified by the doors is in addition to any steel specified in the general note for the walls. Typical wall steel is usually only specified in a note and not shown. This allows special steel patterns to be shown and easily specified. Use a scale of ¼″ = 1′–0″ minimum. Place these details on the same sheet as the panel elevations. Reference these details to the section, and slab on grade plan.

1. Draw the door opening allowing approximately 7′–0″ on all four sides.
2. Lay out steel placements based on dimensions specified on the panel elevation sketches and calcs.
3. Draw the steel much bolder than the opening outline.
4. Dimension each opening as per the sketch.
5. Label all steel.

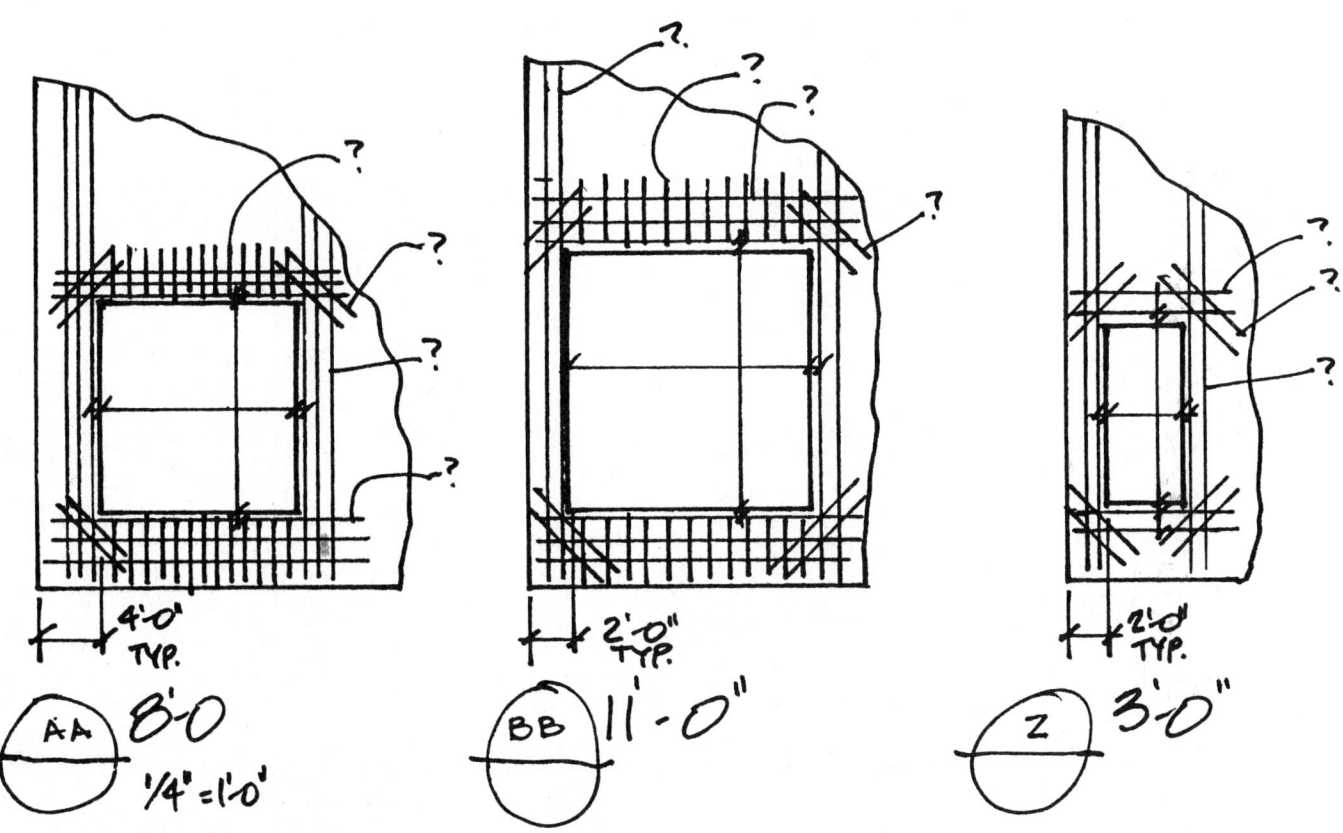

WALL PANELS

PANELS: ALL WALLS TO BE 6" THICK, 4000 PSI CONCRETE W/ GRADE 60-#5 @ 10"O.C. VERTICALLY & GRADE 40-#4 @ 12" O.C. HORIZONTALLY CENTERED IN WALL. EXTEND ALL WALL STEEL TO WITHIN 2" OF TOP AND BOTTOM.

ALL PANELS TO HAVE EXPOSED AGGREGATE FINISHED UNLESS NOTED

PROVIDE (2) GRADE 40, #5 x 4'-0" 45° DIAG. STEEL TYPICAL TOP AND BOTTOM OF ALL DOORS. TIE FIRST DIAG. TO INTERSECTION OF HORIZ. AND VERT. STEEL W/ SECOND BAR AT 8" O.C.

PANEL/PANEL: USE (2) 3/4"φ x 2 1/2" COIL INSERTS THRU 1"φ HOLES IN 11"h x 10"w x 3/8" ℞. INSERTS TO BE 1 1/2" MIN. FROM ℞ EDGES, 8"O.C. AND 3" MIN. FROM EDGE OF CONCRETE PANEL.

PROVIDE 3x 13 x 3/8" ℞ INSET FLUSH INTO CONC. 3" MIN. FROM PANEL EDGE W/ (2) 3/4"φ x3" HEADED CONCRETE ANCHORS @ 10" O.C. 1 1/2" MIN. FROM ℞ EDGES. WELD TO ℞ W/ 1/8" FILLET ALL AROUND @ FIELD. PROVIDE 1 1/2" MIN. LAP OF 11x10 ℞ OVER 3x13℞ & WELD W/ 1/4" FILLET WELD.

ALL CONNECTOR ℞ TO BE @ 5'-0" O.C. MAX. 12" MIN. FROM TOP AND BTM OF PANELS.

PANEL CORNERS: SIMILAR TO PANEL/PANEL JOINT UNLESS NOTED. USE 3/8"x 5"x3" x11" ℞.

ALL CORNER ℞ TO BE @ 6'-0" O.C. MAX. 12" MIN. FROM TOP AND BTM. OF PANEL EDGES.

PANEL/ FND.: 7/8" φ x14" STRUCTURAL CONNECTOR BY RICHMOND OR EQUAL, 8" MIN. INTO FND. WITH 5" MIN WALL PENETRATION. SET IN NON-SHRINK GROUT IN 3x9 ANCHOR SLEEVE IN FOUNDATION. USE:

6 PER PANEL @ GRID 11		
9 " " @ " 1
8 " " @ " C
8 " " @ " 1-4
7 " " @ " 4-7
6 " " @ " 7-11

11'-0" DOOR: IN ADDITION TO WALL STEEL PROVIDE:
(2) GRADE 60, #6 @ 8"O.C. 1" CLEAR OF EACH FACE VERTICALLY FOR FULL HEIGHT OF WALL.
(3) GRADE 60, #4 @ 12" O.C. HORIZONTALLY ABOVE AND BELOW DOORS, EXTEND 24" MIN EA. SIDE OF DOOR.

ABOVE AND BELOW DOOR PROVIDE GRD. 40, #4 @ 12"O.C VERT. EXTEND VERT. 36" ABOVE AND BELOW DOOR.

•••• ALL STEEL PATTERNS TO START WITHIN 1 1/2" OF WALL OPENINGS.

8'-0" DOOR: IN ADDITION TO WALL STEEL PROVIDE:
(3) GRADE 40, #5φ @ 8" O.C. @ 1" CLR OF EACH FACE VERTICALLY FOR FULL HEIGHT OF WALL.
(3) GRADE 60, #4 @ 12" O.C. HORIZONTALLY ABOVE AND BELOW DOORS, EXTEND 24" MIN EA. SIDE OF DOOR.

ABOVE AND BELOW DOOR PROVIDE GRD. 40, #4 @ 12"O.C VERT. EXTEND VERT. 36" ABOVE AND BELOW DOOR.

•••• ALL STEEL PATTERNS TO START WITHIN 1 1/2" OF WALL OPENINGS.

3'-0" DOOR: IN ADDITION TO WALL STEEL PROVIDE:
(2) GRADE 60, #6 @ 6" O.C. 1" CLR. OF EA. FACE VERTICALLY FOR FULL HEIGHT OF WALL.

(2) GRD 40, #5 x 7'-0" TOP AND BTM. @ 8" O.C.

Problem 52-13. WALL DETAILS.

Goal

The purpose of the wall details is to aid in the erection and connection of the concrete wall panels and to show connections between the steel columns and pedestals.

Method

Use the scale as indicated on each sketch. Place the details with the panel elevations, section, or with other concrete details.

1. Determine in what order the details will be presented. Place the details in an order that reflects their relationship to the building.

2. Lightly block out each detail allowing approximately 15 minutes per detail. Given this brief amount of time, draw only major items such as concrete, steel connector, and column outlines.

3. Draw details with finish line quality. Use several line types or colors to clearly distinguish between concrete, steel plates, and bolts.

4. Dimension all information based on sketches and calcs. Do not share dimension locations of bolts.

5. Place all weld symbols as required.

6. Place notes as required. Notes can be shared between details.

7. Place detail markers, title, and scale below each detail. Do not yet place information in the circle.

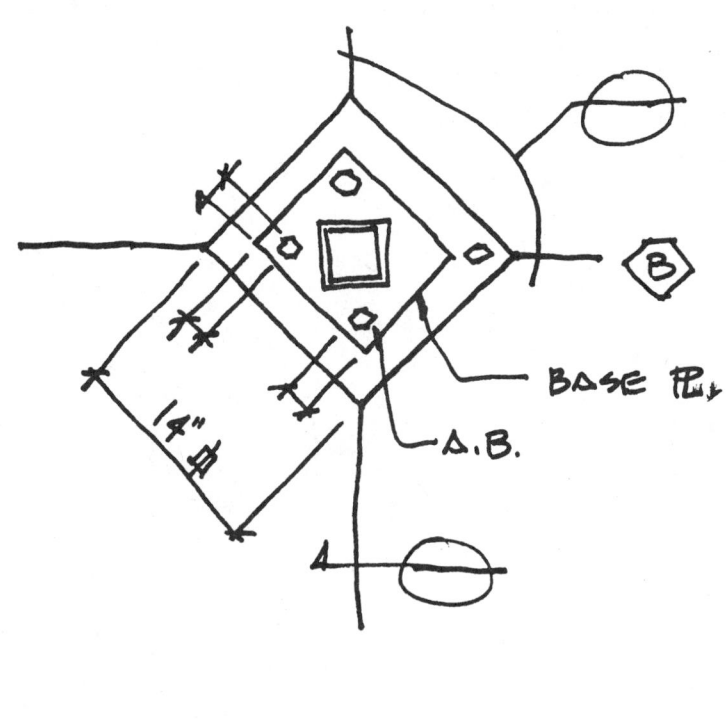

BASE PL.

A.B.

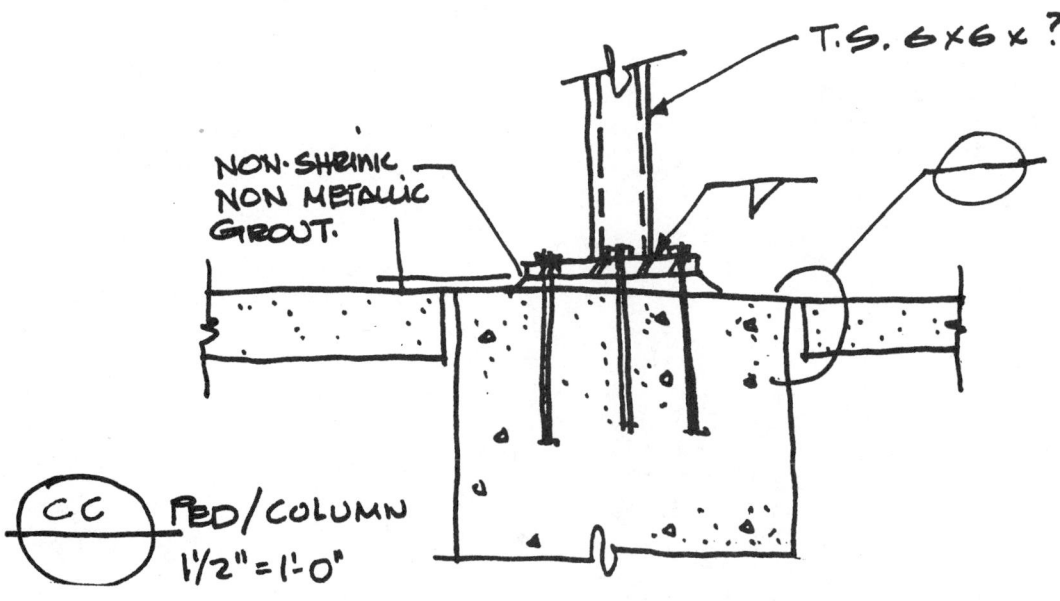

T.S. 6×6× ?

NON-SHRINK NON METALLIC GROUT.

CC PED/COLUMN
1½"=1'-0"

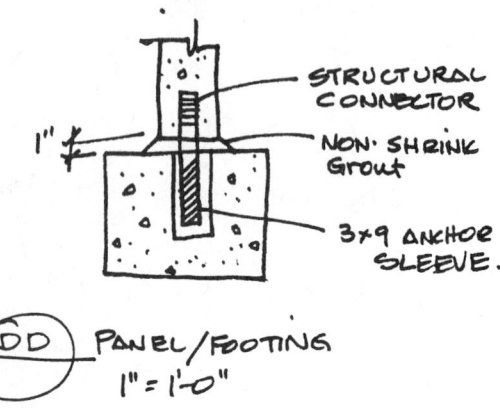

STRUCTURAL
CONNECTOR

NON· SHRINK
Grout

3×9 ANCHOR
SLEEVE.

DD PANEL/FOOTING
1" = 1'-0"

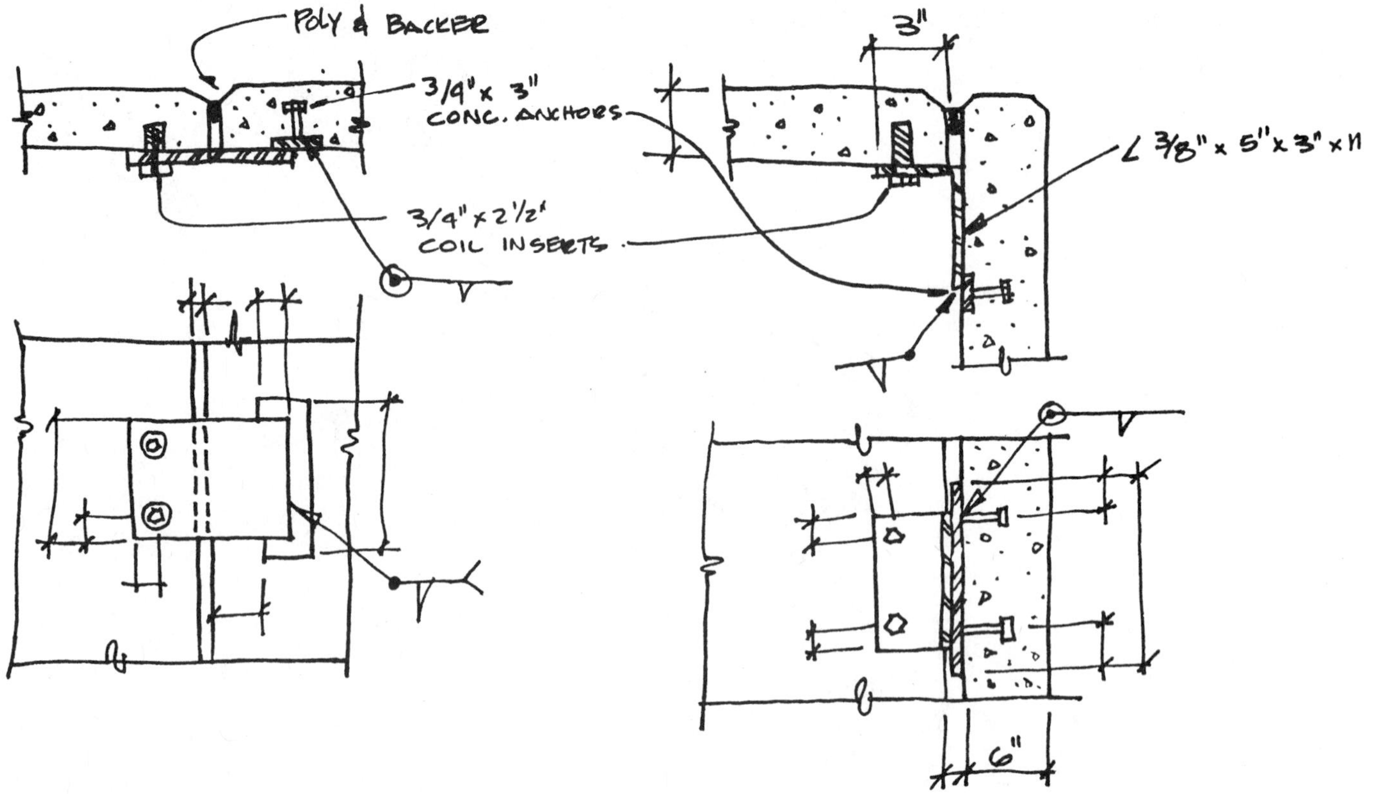

POLY & BACKER

3/4" x 3"
CONC. ANCHORS

3/4" x 2 1/2"
COIL INSERTS.

3"

L 3/8" x 5" x 3" x 11

6"

EE PANEL CONNECTIONS
1" = 1'-0"

FF PANEL CORNERS
1" = 1'-0"

Problem 52–14. PROJECT COORDINATION.

Goal

Up to this point, you have drawn plan views, elevations, sections, and details. These drawings must now be placed in a logical presentation order and be referenced to each other.

Method

1. Place all drawings in order. Suggested order: roof plan, roof details, slab plan, slab details, etc. through to the foundation level, sections, and elevations. Or, you can place all plan views from drainage to foundation in descending order, sections, elevations, panels and details.

2. Once the page order has been determined, place a page number in the title block. Structural drawings will always reflect the total number of pages in the title block as well as the actual page being viewed. In the title block, the numbers 2 of 7 would be placed on the second of seven pages.

3. Assign a page number to all details. All details drawn on page one would have a 1 placed in the lower half of the detail reference circle. All details drawn on page two would have a 2 placed in the lower half of the reference circle. This pattern should be repeated until all details have a page number.

4. Assign a reference letter to all details. Two methods may be used. Step "A" is the same for each method.

   A. Starting on page one, label each detail A, B, C. etc., until all details on page one have been assigned a letter. Start in one corner and work across or up and down the page. Do not skip all over the page as you assign reference letters.

   B. On page two, assign each detail a letter starting with the letter "A" and work through the alphabet. Use the same pattern that was used on page one. Repeat this process for all pages with details.

   OR

   B. On page two, instead of starting over at "A", use the letter that would follow the last letter used on the preceding detail. Never uses the letters I, O, or Q. After detail "Z" use AA, BB, etc.

   C. After all details have been referenced, make sure that each detail referenced on the plan views and sections, etc., has the correct reference symbol. Some details will be referenced on more than one plan. Most will be on the section.

Appendix A
Wood Beam Safe Load Table

This appendix shows a partial listing of span tables from *Wood Structural Design Data*, 1978 edition, courtesy of National Forest Products Association. Once the W, F_b, E, and F_v are known, spans can be determined for a simple beam of spans that are normally found in a residence. Refer to *Wood Structural Design Data* for a complete listing of all lumber sizes.

WOOD BEAM SAFE LOAD TABLE

SIZE OF BEAM		900	1,000	F_b 1,100	1,200	1,300	SIZE OF BEAM		900	1,000	F_b 1,100	1,200	1,300
				6'-0"							7'-0"		
4 x 4	W	714	793	873	952	1,032	4 x 6	W	1,512	1,680	1,848	2,016	2,184
	w	119	132	145	158	172		w	216	240	264	288	312
	F_v	43	48	53	58	63		F_v	58	65	72	78	85
	E	1,388	1,542	1,697	1,851	2,005		E	1,030	1,145	1,259	1,374	1,489
4 x 6	W	1,764	1,960	2,156	2,352	2,548	4 x 8	W	2,628	2,920	3,212	3,504	3,796
	w	294	326	359	392	424		w	375	417	458	500	542
	F_v	68	76	84	91	99		F_v	77	86	94	103	112
	E	883	981	1,079	1,175	1,276		E	782	868	955	1,042	1,129
4 x 8	W	3,066	3,406	3,747	4,088	4,428	4 x 10	W	5,278	4,753	5,228	5,704	6,179
	w	511	567	624	616	738		w	611	679	746	814	882
	F_v	90	100	110	120	130		F_v	99	110	121	132	143
	E	670	744	819	893	968		E	612	681	749	817	885
6 x 6	W	2,772	3,081	3,389	3,389	4,005	6 x 6	W	2,376	2,640	2,904	3,169	3,433
	w	462	513	564	616	667		w	339	377	414	452	490
	F_v	68	76	84	91	99		F_v	58	65	72	78	85
	E	883	981	1,079	1,178	1,276		E	1,030	1,145	1,259	1,374	1,489
6 x 8	W	5,156	5,729	6,302	6,875	7,447	6 x 8	W	4,419	4,910	5,401	5,892	6,383
	w	859	954	1,050	1,145	1,241		w	631	701	771	841	911
	F_v	93	104	114	125	135		F_v	80	89	98	107	116
	E	648	719	792	864	935		E	755	839	924	1,007	1,091

WOOD BEAM SAFE LOAD TABLE

SIZE OF BEAM		900	1,000	F_b 1,100	1,200	1,300	SIZE OF BEAM		900	1,000	F_b 1,100	1,200	1,300
				8'–0''							9'–0''		
4 x 6	W	1,323	1,470	1,617	1,764	1,911	4 x 8	W	2,044	2,271	2,498	2,725	2,952
	w	165	183	202	220	238		w	227	252	277	302	328
	F_v	51	57	63	68	74		F_v	60	67	73	80	87
	E	1,178	1,309	1,439	1,570	1,701		E	1,005	1,117	1,228	1,340	1,452
4 x 8	W	2,299	2,555	2,810	3,066	3,321	4 x 10	W	3,327	3,697	4,066	4,436	4,806
	w	287	319	351	383	415		w	369	410	451	492	534
	F_v	67	75	83	90	98		F_v	77	85	94	102	111
	E	893	993	1,092	1,191	1,291		E	788	875	963	1,050	1,138
4 x 10	W	3,743	4,159	4,575	4,991	5,407	4 x 12	W	3,921	5,468	6,015	6,562	7,109
	w	467	519	571	623	675		w	546	607	668	729	789
	F_v	86	96	105	115	125		F_v	93	104	114	125	135
	E	700	778	856	934	1,011		E	648	720	792	863	936
4 x 12	W	5,537	6,152	6,767	7,382	7,998	4 x 14	W	7,087	7,875	8,662	9,450	10,237
	w	692	769	845	922	999		w	787	875	962	1,050	1,137
	F_v	105	117	128	140	152		F_v	112	125	137	150	162
	E	576	640	703	768	832		E	540	600	660	720	780
4 x 14	W	7,973	8,859	9,745	10,361	11,517	6 x 8	W	3,437	3,819	4,201	4,583	4,965
	w	996	1,107	1,218	1,328	1,439		w	381	424	466	509	551
	F_v	126	140	154	168	182		F_v	62	69	76	83	90
	E	480	533	586	640	693		E	972	1,079	1,187	1,295	1,403
6 x 6	W	2,079	2,310	2,541	2,772	3,003	6 x 10	W	5,515	6,128	6,740	7,353	7,966
	w	259	288	317	346	375		w	612	680	748	817	885
	F_v	51	57	63	68	74		F_v	79	87	96	105	114
	E	1,178	1,309	1,439	1,570	1,701		E	767	852	937	1,023	1,108
6 x 8	W	3,867	4,296	4,726	5,156	5,585	6 x 12	W	8,081	8,979	9,877	10,775	11,673
	w	483	537	590	644	698		w	897	997	1,097	1,197	1,297
	F_v	70	78	86	93	101		F_v	95	106	117	127	138
	E	864	960	1,055	1,152	1,247		E	633	704	774	845	915
6 x 10	W	6,204	6,894	7,583	8,272	8,962	6 x 14	W	11,137	12,375	13,612	14,850	16,087
	w	775	861	947	1,034	1,120		w	1,237	1,375	1,512	1,650	1,787
	F_v	89	98	108	118	128		F_v	112	125	137	150	162
	E	682	757	833	909	985		E	540	600	659	720	779
6 x 12	W	9,092	10,102	11,112	12,122	13,133							
	w	1,136	1,262	1,389	1,515	1,641							
	F_v	107	119	131	143	155							
	E	563	626	688	751	813							
6 x 14	W	12,529	13,921	15,314	16,706	18,098							
	w	1,566	1,740	1,914	2,088	2,262							
	F_v	126	140	154	168	182							
	E	480	533	586	640	693							

WOOD BEAM SAFE LOAD TABLE

10'-0"

SIZE OF BEAM		F_b 900	1,000	1,100	1,200	1,300
4 x 10	W	2,994	3,327	3,660	3,992	4,325
	w	299	332	366	399	432
	F_v	69	77	84	92	100
	E	875	972	1,070	1,167	1,264
4 x 12	W	4,429	4,921	5,414	5,906	6,398
	w	442	492	541	590	639
	F_v	84	93	103	112	121
	E	720	800	880	960	1,040
4 x 14	W	6,378	7,087	7,796	8,505	9,213
	w	637	708	779	850	921
	F_v	101	112	123	135	146
	E	600	666	733	800	866
6 x 8	W	3,093	3,437	3,781	4,125	4,468
	w	309	343	378	412	446
	F_v	56	62	68	75	81
	E	1,079	1,199	1,319	1,439	1,559
6 x 10	W	4,963	5,515	6,066	6,618	7,169
	w	496	551	606	661	716
	F_v	71	79	87	95	102
	E	852	947	1,042	1,136	1,231
6 x 12	W	7,273	8,081	8,890	9,698	10,506
	w	727	808	889	969	1,050
	W	86	95	105	115	124
	E	704	782	860	939	1,017
6 x 14	W	10,023	11,137	12,251	13,365	14,478
	w	1,002	1,113	1,225	1,336	1,447
	F_v	101	112	123	135	146
	E	600	666	733	800	866

11'-0"

SIZE OF BEAM		F_b 900	1,000	1,100	1,200	1,300
4 x 8	W	1,672	1,858	2,044	2,229	2,415
	w	152	168	185	202	219
	F_v	49	54	60	65	71
	E	1,228	1,365	1,502	1,638	1,775
4 x 10	W	2,722	3,024	3,327	3,629	3,932
	w	247	274	302	329	357
	F_v	63	70	77	84	91
	E	963	1,070	1,177	1,284	1,391
4 x 12	W	4,026	4,474	4,921	5,369	5,816
	w	366	406	447	488	528
	F_v	76	85	93	102	110
	E	792	879	968	1,055	1,143
4 x 14	W	5,798	6,443	7,087	7,731	8,376
	w	527	585	644	702	761
	F_v	92	102	112	122	132
	E	660	733	806	880	953
6 x 8	W	2,812	3,125	3,437	3,750	4,062
	w	255	284	312	340	369
	F_v	51	56	62	68	73
	E	1,187	1,319	1,451	1,585	1,715
6 x 10	W	4,512	5,013	5,515	6,016	6,518
	w	410	455	501	546	592
	F_v	64	71	79	86	93
	E	937	1,042	1,146	1,250	1,350
6 x 12	W	6,612	7,347	8,081	8,816	9,551
	w	601	667	734	801	868
	F_v	78	87	95	104	113
	E	774	860	946	1,033	1,119
6 x 14	W	9,112	10,125	11,137	12,150	13,162
	w	828	920	1,012	1,104	1,196
	F_v	92	102	112	122	132
	E	659	733	806	880	953

WOOD BEAM SAFE LOAD TABLE

SIZE OF BEAM		900	1,000	F_b 1,100	1,200	1,300	SIZE OF BEAM		900	1,000	F_b 1,100	1,200	1,300
				12'-0"							13'-0"		
4 x 8	W	1,533	1,703	1,873	2,044	2,214	4 x 8	W	1,415	1,572	1,729	1,886	2,044
	w	127	141	156	170	184		w	108	120	133	145	157
	F_v	45	50	55	60	65		F_v	41	46	51	55	60
	E	1,340	1,489	1,638	1,787	1,936		E	1,452	1,613	1,775	1,936	2,097
4 x 10	W	2,495	3,772	3,050	3,327	3,604	4 x 10	W	2,303	2,559	2,815	3,071	3,327
	w	207	231	254	277	300		w	177	196	216	236	255
	F_v	57	64	70	77	83		F_v	53	59	65	71	77
	E	1,050	1,167	1,284	1,401	1,517		E	1,138	1,264	1,391	1,517	1,644
4 x 12	W	3,691	4,101	4,511	4,921	5,332	4 x 12	W	3,407	3,786	4,164	4,543	4,921
	w	307	341	375	410	444		w	262	291	320	349	378
	F_v	70	78	85	93	101		F_v	64	72	79	86	93
	E	863	960	1,055	1,151	1,247		E	936	1,039	1,143	1,247	1,351
4 x 14	W	5,315	5,906	6,496	7,087	7,678	4 x 14	W	4,906	5,451	5,997	6,542	7,087
	w	442	492	541	590	639		w	377	419	461	503	545
	F_v	84	93	103	112	121		F_v	77	86	95	103	112
	E	720	800	880	960	1,040		E	780	866	953	1,039	1,126
6 x 8	W	2,578	2,864	3,151	3,437	3,723	6 x 8	W	2,379	2,644	2,908	3,173	3,437
	w	214	238	262	286	310		w	183	203	223	244	264
	F_v	46	52	57	62	67		F_v	43	48	52	57	62
	E	1,295	1,439	1,583	1,727	1,871		E	1,403	1,559	1,715	1,871	2,027
6 x 10	W	4,136	4,596	5,055	5,515	5,974	6 x 10	W	3,818	4,242	4,666	5,091	5,515
	w	344	383	421	459	497		w	293	326	358	391	424
	F_v	59	65	72	79	85		F_v	54	60	66	73	79
	E	1,023	1,136	1,250	1,364	1,477		E	1,108	1,231	1,354	1,477	1,601
6 x 12	W	6,061	6,734	7,408	8,081	8,755	6 x 12	W	5,595	6,216	6,838	7,460	8,081
	w	505	561	617	673	729		w	430	478	526	573	621
	F_v	71	79	87	95	103		F_v	66	73	81	88	95
	E	845	939	1,033	1,126	1,220		E	915	1,017	1,119	1,220	1,322
6 x 14	W	8,353	9,281	10,209	11,137	12,065	6 x 14	W	7,710	8,567	9,424	10,280	11,137
	w	696	773	850	928	1,005		w	593	659	724	790	856
	F_v	84	93	103	112	121		F_v	77	86	95	103	112
	E	720	800	880	960	1,040		E	779	866	953	1,039	1,126

WOOD BEAM SAFE LOAD TABLE

SIZE OF BEAM		900	1,000	F_b 1,100	1,200	1,300	SIZE OF BEAM		900	1,000	F_b 1,100	1,200	1,300
				14'-0"							15'-0"		
4 x 8	W	1,314	1,460	1,606	1,752	1,898	4 x 8	W	1,226	1,362	1,499	1,635	1,771
	w	93	104	114	125	135		w	81	90	99	109	118
	F_v	38	43	47	51	56		F_v	36	40	44	48	52
	E	1,564	1,737	1,911	2,085	2,259		E	1,675	1,862	2,048	2,234	2,420
4 x 10	W	2,139	2,376	2,614	2,852	3,089	4 x 10	W	1,996	2,218	2,440	2,661	2,883
	w	152	169	186	203	220		w	133	147	162	177	192
	F_v	49	55	60	66	71		F_v	46	51	56	61	66
	E	1,225	1,362	1,498	1,634	1,770		E	1,313	1,459	1,605	1,751	1,897
4 x 12	W	3,164	3,515	3,867	4,218	4,570	4 x 12	W	2,953	3,281	3,609	3,937	4,265
	w	226	251	276	301	326		w	196	218	240	262	284
	F_v	60	66	73	80	87		F_v	56	62	68	75	81
	E	1,008	1,119	1,231	1,343	1,455		E	1,079	1,199	1,319	1,439	1,559
4 x 14	W	4,556	5,062	5,568	6,075	6,581	4 x 14	W	4,252	4,725	5,197	5,670	6,142
	w	325	361	397	433	470		w	283	315	346	378	409
	F_v	72	80	88	96	104		F_v	67	75	82	90	97
	E	840	933	1,026	1,119	1,213		E	900	1,000	1,099	1,199	1,299
6 x 8	W	2,209	2,455	2,700	2,946	3,191	6 x 8	W	2,062	2,291	2,520	2,750	2,979
	w	157	175	192	210	227		w	137	152	168	183	198
	F_v	40	44	49	53	58		F_v	37	41	45	50	54
	E	1,511	1,679	1,847	2,015	2,183		E	1,619	1,799	1,979	2,159	2,339
6 x 10	W	3,545	3,939	4,333	4,727	5,121	6 x 10	W	3,309	3,676	4,044	4,412	4,779
	w	253	281	309	337	365		w	220	245	269	294	318
	F_v	50	56	62	67	73		F_v	47	52	58	63	68
	E	1,193	1,326	1,458	1,591	1,724		E	1,278	1,421	1,563	1,705	1,847
6 x 12	W	5,195	5,772	6,350	6,927	7,504	6 x 12	W	4,849	5,387	5,926	6,465	7,004
	w	371	412	453	494	536		w	323	359	395	431	466
	F_v	61	68	75	82	88		F_v	57	63	70	76	83
	E	986	1,095	1,205	1,314	1,424		E	1,056	1,173	1,291	1,408	1,526
6 x 14	W	7,159	7,955	8,750	9,546	10,341	6 x 14	W	6,682	7,425	8,167	8,910	9,652
	w	511	568	625	681	738		w	445	495	544	594	643
	F_v	72	80	88	96	104		F_v	67	75	82	90	97
	E	839	933	1,026	1,119	1,213		E	900	1,000	1,099	1,199	1,299

WOOD BEAM SAFE LOAD TABLE

SIZE OF BEAM		900	1,000	F_b 1,100	1,200	1,300	SIZE OF BEAM		900	1,000	F_b 1,100	1,200	1,300
				16'–0"									
4 x 8	W	1,149	1,277	1,405	1,533	1,660							
	w	71	79	87	95	103							
	F_v	33	37	41	45	49							
	E	1,787	1,986	2,184	2,383	2,582							
4 x 10	W	1,871	2,079	2,287	2,495	2,703							
	w	116	129	142	155	168							
	F_v	43	48	52	57	62							
	E	1,401	1,556	1,712	1,868	2,023							
4 x 12	W	2,768	3,076	3,383	3,691	3,999							
	w	173	192	211	230	249							
	F_v	52	58	64	70	76							
	E	1,151	1,279	1,407	1,535	1,663							
4 x 14	W	3,986	4,429	4,872	5,315	5,758							
	w	249	276	304	332	359							
	F_v	63	70	77	84	91							
	E	960	1,066	1,173	1,279	1,386							
6 x 8	W	1,933	2,148	2,363	2,578	2,792							
	w	120	134	147	161	174							
	F_v	35	39	42	46	50							
	E	1,727	1,919	2,111	2,303	2,495							
6 x 10	W	3,102	3,447	3,791	4,196	4,481							
	w	193	215	236	258	280							
	F_v	44	49	54	59	64							
	E	1,364	1,515	1,667	1,818	1,970							
6 x 12	W	4,546	5,051	5,556	6,061	6,566							
	w	284	315	347	378	410							
	F_v	53	59	65	71	77							
	E	1,126	1,252	1,377	1,502	1,627							
6 x 14	W	6,264	6,960	7,657	8,353	9,049							
	w	391	435	478	522	565							
	F_v	63	70	77	84	91							
	E	960	1,066	1,173	1,279	1,386							

Appendix B
CABO Tables

Courtesy of the Council of American Building Officials, *CABO One-
and Two-Family Dwelling Code*, 1989 edition.

Table No. R-402.6a
HEADER DESIGN CHART
(Douglas Fir-Larch, Southern Pine No. 2,
Roof Load = 20 LL + 10 DL; Floor Load = 40 LL + 10 DL)
$F_b = 1,200 \quad E = 1,600,000 \quad F_v = 90$

HEADER SUPPORTING:	HEADER SIZE:	MAXIMUM ALLOWABLE HEADER SPAN (Ft.-In.)								
		DESIGN PROCEDURE								
		Nonstruct. Sheath.			1/2" Insul. Board Sheath.*			1/2" Plywood Sheath.**		
		House Depth (Ft.)			House Depth (Ft.)			House Depth (Ft.)		
		24'	28'	32'	24'	28'	32'	24'	28'	32'
Roof	2-2 × 4	4-7	4-6	4-3	4-11	4-8	4-6	5-7	5-4	5-1
	2-2 × 6	6-8	6-4	5-11	6-11	6-7	6-4	7-7	7-3	7-0
	2-2 × 8	8-3	8-0	7-7	8-6	8-2	7-11	8-11	8-7	8-4
	2-2 × 10	9-10	9-6	9-3	10-0	9-8	9-4	10-4	10-0	9-9
	2-2 × 12	11-4	10-11	10-7	11-5	11-1	10-9	11-10	11-5	11-1
Roof plus one story (Bearing)	2-2 × 4	5-2	4-11	4-9	5-4	5-1	4-10	5-8	5-5	5-2
	2-2 × 6	6-9	6-5	6-0	6-11	6-7	6-3	7-4	7-0	6-8
	2-2 × 8	8-0	7-5	7-0	8-1	7-8	7-3	8-5	8-2	7-9
	2-2 × 10	9-3	8-9	8-3	9-4	9-0	8-5	9-7	9-3	8-11
	2-2 × 12	10-5	10-1	9-7	10-6	10-2	9-9	10-10	10-5	10-1
Roof plus one story (No bearing)	2-2 × 4	4-8	4-5	4-3	4-9	4-6	4-3	5-1	4-10	4-8
	2-2 × 6	5-10	5-5	5-1	6-0	5-7	5-3	6-7	6-2	5-9
	2-2 × 8	6-9	6-3	5-11	7-0	6-6	6-1	7-6	7-0	6-7
	2-2 × 10	8-0	7-5	6-11	8-2	7-7	7-1	8-8	8-1	7-7
	2-2 × 12	9-3	8-7	8-1	9-5	8-9	8-3	9-11	9-3	8-8
Roof plus two stories (Bearing)	2-2 × 4	4-8	4-5	4-3	4-9	4-6	4-3	5-1	4-10	4-8
	2-2 × 6	5-10	5-5	5-1	6-0	5-7	5-3	6-7	6-2	5-9
	2-2 × 8	6-9	6-3	5-11	7-0	6-6	6-1	7-6	7-0	6-7
	2-2 × 10	8-0	7-5	6-11	8-2	7-7	7-1	8-8	8-1	7-7
	2-2 × 12	9-3	8-7	8-1	9-5	8-9	8-3	9-11	9-3	8-8
Roof plus two stories (No bearing)	2-2 × 4	3-11	3-8	3-5	4-1	3-9	3-7	4-5	4-2	4-0
	2-2 × 6	4-8	4-4	4-0	4-10	4-5	4-2	5-3	4-11	4-7
	2-2 × 8	5-5	5-0	4-8	5-7	5-2	4-10	6-0	5-7	5-3
	2-2 × 10	6-4	5-11	5-6	6-6	6-0	5-8	6-11	6-5	6-0
	2-2 × 12	7-5	6-10	6-5	7-6	7-0	6-6	7-11	7-4	6-11

* Sheathing or combined sheathing/siding having a minimum density of 18 pcf.

** Minimum 1/2-inch plywood sheathing or combined sheathing/siding applied between the bottom of the header, the top of the top plate and between the center lines of the broken vertical studs at the ends of the header and nailed to the header, top plates, cripples and studs—6 inches o.c. at the edges and 12 inches o.c. at intermediate framing.

Note: Linear interpolation for house widths not in table are permitted. For example, assume a 26-foot-wide house with 1/2-inch plywood sheathing—roof load, 2 × 6 header: allowable header span = 7 feet 5 inches.

Tables based on maximum 1 1/2-foot overhangs and band joists used at floors.

■ symbol represents supporting beam or structural bearing wall below floor.

● symbol represents location of header.

Header spans identified as having "no bearing" construction apply to both interior and exterior load-bearing walls which have tributary areas equal to one-half the house depth. Header spans identified with "bearing" construction apply only to exterior bearing walls with tributary areas equal to one fourth of the house depth.

Nominal 4-inch size single headers may be substituted for nominal 2-inch double headers.

Table No. R-402.6b
HEADER DESIGN CHART
(Douglas Fir-Larch, Southern Pine No. 2)
Roof Load = 30 LL + 10 DL; Floor Load = 40 LL + 10 DL)
F_b = 1,200   E = 1,600,000 F_v = 90

HEADER SUPPORTING:	HEADER SIZE:	MAXIMUM ALLOWABLE HEADER SPAN (Ft.-In.)								
		DESIGN PROCEDURE								
		Nonstruct. Sheath.			1/2" Insul. Board Sheath.*			1/2" Plywood Sheath.*		
		House Depth (Ft.)			House Depth (Ft.)			House Depth (Ft.)		
		24'	28'	32'	24'	28'	32'	24'	28'	32'
Roof	2-2 × 4	4-2	3-11	3-8	4-5	4-3	4-1	5-1	4-10	4-8
	2-2 × 6	5-10	5-6	5-2	6-3	5-10	5-6	6-11	6-7	6-4
	2-2 × 8	7-6	7-0	6-7	7-10	7-3	6-10	8-4	8-0	7-7
	2-2 × 10	9-2	8-8	8-2	9-3	8-11	8-5	9-8	9-4	9-1
	2-2 × 12	10-6	10-2	9-10	10-8	10-4	10-0	11-0	10-8	10-4
Roof plus one story (Bearing)	2-2 × 4	4-11	4-8	4-6	5-0	4-9	4-7	5-4	5-1	4-11
	2-2 × 6	6-3	5-10	5-6	6-6	6-1	5-8	6-11	6-7	6-3
	2-2 × 8	7-4	6-10	6-5	7-7	7-0	6-7	8-1	7-7	7-1
	2-2 × 10	8-7	8-1	7-6	8-10	8-2	7-8	9-2	8-8	8-2
	2-2 × 12	10-0	9-4	8-9	10-1	9-6	8-11	10-4	9-11	9-5
Roof plus one story (No bearing)	2-2 × 4	4-5	4-3	4-0	4-9	4-4	4-2	4-10	4-8	4-5
	2-2 × 6	5-5	5-1	4-9	5-8	5-3	4-11	6-2	5-9	5-5
	2-2 × 8	6-4	5-11	5-6	6-6	6-1	5-8	7-0	6-6	6-2
	2-2 × 10	7-6	6-11	6-6	7-7	7-1	6-8	8-1	7-6	7-0
	2-2 × 12	8-8	8-1	7-7	8-10	8-2	7-8	9-3	8-8	8-1
Roof plus two stories (Bearing)	2-2 × 4	4-5	4-3	4-0	4-9	4-4	4-2	4-10	4-8	4-5
	2-2 × 6	5-5	5-1	4-9	5-8	5-3	4-11	6-2	5-9	5-5
	2-2 × 8	6-4	5-11	5-6	6-6	6-1	5-8	7-0	6-6	6-2
	2-2 × 10	7-6	6-11	6-6	7-7	7-1	6-8	8-1	7-6	7-1
	2-2 × 12	8-8	8-1	7-7	8-10	8-2	7-8	9-3	8-8	8-1
Roof plus two stories (No bearing)	2-2 × 4	3-9	3-6	3-3	3-11	3-8	3-5	4-3	4-0	3-9
	2-2 × 6	4-5	4-1	3-10	4-7	4-3	4-0	5-1	4-8	4-5
	2-2 × 8	5-2	4-10	4-6	5-4	4-11	4-8	5-9	5-4	5-0
	2-2 × 10	6-1	5-8	5-4	6-3	5-9	5-5	6-7	6-2	5-9
	2-2 × 12	7-1	6-7	6-2	7-2	6-8	6-3	7-7	7-1	6-7

*See notes to Table No. R-402.6a.

Table No. R-402.6c
HEADER DESIGN CHART
(Hem Fir No. 2, Roof Load = 20 LL + 10 DL; Floor Load = 40 LL + 10 DL)
F_b = 1,000   E = 1,400,000 F_v = 75

HEADER SUPPORTING:	HEADER SIZE:	MAXIMUM ALLOWABLE HEADER SPAN (Ft.-In.)								
		DESIGN PROCEDURE								
		Nonstruct. Sheath.			1/2" Insul. Board Sheath.*			1/2" Plywood Sheath.*		
		House Depth (Ft.)			House Depth (Ft.)			House Depth (Ft.)		
		24'	28'	32'	24'	28'	32'	24'	28'	32'
Roof	2-2 × 4	4-5	4-2	3-11	4-8	4-5	4-3	5-1	4-10	5-3
	2-2 × 6	6-2	5-9	5-5	6-7	6-1	5-9	7-7	7-1	6-8
	2-2 × 8	7-10	7-4	6-11	8-3	7-8	7-3	9-1	8-6	8-0
	2-2 × 10	9-6	9-2	8-8	9-8	9-4	9-1	10-0	9-8	9-5
	2-2 × 12	10-11	10-7	10-3	11-1	10-8	10-5	11-5	11-1	10-9
Roof plus one story (Bearing)	2-2 × 4	4-12	4-9	4-6	5-1	4-10	4-8	5-5	5-2	5-0
	2-2 × 6	6-3	5-10	5-5	6-6	6-1	5-8	7-0	6-8	6-3
	2-2 × 8	7-4	6-10	6-4	7-6	7-0	6-7	8-1	7-7	7-1
	2-2 × 10	8-7	8-0	7-6	8-10	8-2	7-8	9-4	8-8	8-2
	2-2 × 12	10-0	9-4	8-9	10-2	9-6	8-11	10-5	10-0	9-4
Roof plus one story (No bearing)	2-2 × 4	4-5	4-2	3-11	4-7	4-4	4-1	4-10	4-8	4-5
	2-2 × 6	5-4	4-11	4-7	5-6	5-1	4-9	6-1	5-7	5-3
	2-2 × 8	6-2	5-9	5-5	6-4	5-11	5-6	6-10	6-5	6-0
	2-2 × 10	7-3	6-9	6-4	7-5	6-11	6-6	7-11	7-4	6-11
	2-2 × 12	8-5	7-10	7-4	8-7	8-0	7-6	9-1	8-5	7-11
Roof plus two stories (Bearing)	2-2 × 4	4-5	4-2	3-11	4-7	4-4	4-1	4-10	4-8	4-5
	2-2 × 6	5-4	4-11	4-7	5-6	5-1	4-9	6-1	5-7	5-3
	2-2 × 8	6-2	5-9	5-5	6-4	5-11	5-6	6-10	6-5	6-0
	2-2 × 10	7-3	6-9	6-4	7-5	6-11	6-6	7-11	7-4	6-11
	2-2 × 12	8-5	7-10	7-4	8-7	8-0	7-6	9-1	8-5	7-11
Roof plus two stories (No bearing)	2-2 × 4	3-7	3-4	3-1	3-9	3-6	3-3	4-2	3-10	3-7
	2-2 × 6	4-3	3-11	3-8	4-5	4-1	3-10	4-10	4-6	4-2
	2-2 × 8	4-11	4-7	4-3	5-1	4-9	4-5	5-6	5-1	4-9
	2-2 × 10	5-10	5-5	5-1	5-11	5-6	5-2	6-4	5-10	5-6
	2-2 × 12	6-9	6-3	5-10	6-10	6-4	6-0	7-3	6-8	6-3

*See notes to Table No. R-402.6a.

Table No. R-402.6d
HEADER DESIGN CHART
(Hem Fir No. 2, Roof Load = 30 LL + 10 DL; Floor Load = 40 LL + 10 DL)
F_b = 1,000   E = 1,400,000 F_v = 75

HEADER SUPPORTING:	HEADER SIZE:	MAXIMUM ALLOWABLE HEADER SPAN (Ft.-In.)								
		DESIGN PROCEDURE								
		Nonstruct. Sheath.			1/2" Insul. Board Sheath.*			1/2" Plywood Sheath.*		
		House Depth (Ft.)			House Depth (Ft.)			House Depth (Ft.)		
		24'	28'	32'	24'	28'	32'	24'	28'	32'
Roof	2-2 × 4	3-10	3-7	3-5	4-2	3-11	3-8	4-10	4-7	4-5
	2-2 × 6	5-4	5-0	4-9	5-8	5-4	5-0	6-7	6-2	5-9
	2-2 × 8	6-10	6-4	6-0	7-1	6-8	6-3	7-10	7-4	6-11
	2-2 × 10	8-6	7-11	7-6	8-9	8-2	7-8	9-4	8-9	8-3
	2-2 × 12	10-2	9-6	8-11	10-4	9-9	9-2	10-8	10-3	9-9
Roof plus one story (Bearing)	2-2 × 4	4-8	4-5	4-3	4-9	4-7	4-5	5-2	4-11	4-8
	2-2 × 6	5-9	5-3	5-0	5-11	5-6	5-2	6-6	6-1	5-8
	2-2 × 8	6-8	6-3	5-10	6-11	6-5	6-0	7-5	6-11	6-6
	2-2 × 10	7-10	7-4	6-11	8-0	7-6	7-0	8-6	7-11	7-6
	2-2 × 12	9-2	8-6	8-0	9-4	8-8	8-2	9-9	9-1	8-7
Roof plus one story (No bearing)	2-2 × 4	4-2	3-11	3-8	4-4	4-1	3-10	4-8	4-5	4-3
	2-2 × 6	5-0	4-7	4-4	5-2	4-9	4-6	5-8	5-3	4-11
	2-2 × 8	5-9	5-5	5-1	6-0	5-7	5-2	6-5	6-0	5-7
	2-2 × 10	6-10	6-4	5-11	6-11	6-6	6-1	7-5	6-10	6-5
	2-2 × 12	7-11	7-4	6-11	8-1	7-6	7-0	8-6	7-11	7-5
Roof plus two stories (Bearing)	2-2 × 4	4-2	3-11	3-8	4-4	4-1	3-10	4-8	4-5	4-3
	2-2 × 6	5-0	4-7	4-4	5-2	4-9	4-6	5-8	5-3	5-7
	2-2 × 8	5-9	5-5	5-1	6-0	5-7	5-2	6-5	6-0	6-5
	2-2 × 10	6-10	6-4	5-11	6-11	6-6	6-1	7-5	6-10	6-5
	2-2 × 12	7-11	7-4	6-11	8-1	7-6	7-0	8-6	7-11	7-5
Roof plus two stories (No bearing)	2-2 × 4	3-5	3-2	3-0	3-7	3-4	3-1	3-11	3-8	3-5
	2-2 × 6	4-1	3-9	3-6	4-2	3-11	3-8	4-7	4-3	4-0
	2-2 × 8	4-9	4-5	4-1	4-10	4-6	4-3	5-3	4-10	4-7
	2-2 × 10	5-7	5-2	4-10	5-8	5-3	4-11	6-0	5-7	5-3
	2-2 × 12	6-5	6-0	5-7	6-7	6-1	5-9	6-11	6-5	6-0

*See notes to Table No. R-402.6a

Table No. R-402.6e
HEADER DESIGN CHART
(Spruce-Pine-Fir No. 2, Roof Load = 20 LL + 10 DL;
Floor Load = 40 LL + 10 DL)
F_b = 875   E = 1,300,000 F_v = 70

HEADER SUPPORTING:	HEADER SIZE:	MAXIMUM ALLOWABLE HEADER SPAN (Ft.-In.)								
		DESIGN PROCEDURE								
		Nonstruct. Sheath.			1/2" Insul. Board Sheath.*			1/2" Plywood Sheath.*		
		House Depth (Ft.)			House Depth (Ft.)			House Depth (Ft.)		
		24'	28'	32'	24'	28'	32'	24'	28'	32'
Roof	2-2 × 4	4-2	3-11	3-8	4-5	4-3	4-0	5-2	5-0	4-9
	2-2 × 6	5-10	5-5	5-1	6-2	5-9	5-5	7-1	6-7	6-3
	2-2 × 8	7-4	6-10	6-6	7-8	7-2	6-9	8-6	7-11	7-6
	2-2 × 10	9-2	8-7	8-1	9-5	8-9	8-3	9-10	9-6	8-11
	2-2 × 12	10-9	10-3	9-8	10-10	10-6	9-11	11-3	10-10	10-6
Roof plus one story (Bearing)	2-2 × 4	4-10	4-7	4-4	5-0	4-9	4-6	5-4	5-1	4-10
	2-2 × 6	5-10	5-6	5-2	6-1	5-8	5-4	6-8	6-3	5-10
	2-2 × 8	6-10	6-4	6-0	7-1	6-7	6-2	7-7	7-1	6-8
	2-2 × 10	8-1	7-6	7-1	8-3	7-8	7-2	8-9	8-2	7-8
	2-2 × 12	9-4	8-8	8-2	9-6	8-10	8-4	10-0	9-4	8-9
Roof plus one story (No bearing)	2-2 × 4	4-3	3-11	3-8	4-5	4-1	3-10	4-9	4-6	4-3
	2-2 × 6	5-0	4-7	4-4	5-2	4-9	4-5	5-8	5-3	4-11
	2-2 × 8	5-9	5-4	5-0	6-0	5-6	5-2	6-5	6-0	5-7
	2-2 × 10	6-10	6-4	5-11	6-11	6-5	6-1	7-5	6-10	6-5
	2-2 × 12	7-11	7-4	6-11	8-1	7-6	7-0	8-6	7-11	7-5
Roof plus two stories (Bearing)	2-2 × 4	4-3	3-11	3-8	4-5	4-1	3-10	4-9	4-6	4-3
	2-2 × 6	5-0	4-7	4-4	5-2	4-9	4-5	5-8	5-3	4-11
	2-2 × 8	5-9	5-4	5-0	6-0	5-6	5-2	6-5	6-0	5-7
	2-2 × 10	6-10	6-4	5-11	6-11	6-5	6-1	7-5	6-10	6-5
	2-2 × 12	7-11	7-4	6-11	8-1	7-6	7-0	8-6	7-11	7-5
Roof plus two stories (No bearing)	2-2 × 4	3-4	3-1	2-11	3-6	3-3	3-0	3-10	3-7	3-4
	2-2 × 6	4-0	3-8	3-5	4-1	3-10	3-7	4-6	4-2	3-11
	2-2 × 8	4-7	4-3	4-0	4-9	4-5	4-2	5-1	4-9	4-5
	2-2 × 10	5-5	5-1	4-9	5-7	5-2	4-10	5-11	5-6	5-2
	2-2 × 12	6-4	5-10	5-6	6-5	6-0	5-7	6-9	6-3	5-11

*See notes to Table No. R-402.6a

Table No. R-402.6f
HEADER DESIGN CHART
(Spruce-Pine-Fir No. 2, Roof Load = 30 LL + 10 DL;
Floor Load = 40 LL + 10 DL)
F_b = 875　　E = 1,300,000　　F_v = 70

HEADER SUPPORTING:	HEADER SIZE:	MAXIMUM ALLOWABLE HEADER SPAN (Ft.-In.)								
		DESIGN PROCEDURE								
		Nonstruct. Sheath.			1/2" Insul. Board Sheath.*			1/2" Plywood Sheath.*		
		House Depth (Ft.)			House Depth (Ft.)			House Depth (Ft.)		
		24'	28'	32'	24'	28'	32'	24'	28'	32'
Roof	2-2 × 4	3-7	3-4	3-2	3-11	3-8	3-5	4-10	4-6	4-3
	2-2 × 6	5-0	4-8	4-5	5-4	5-0	4-8	6-2	5-9	5-5
	2-2 × 8	6-5	5-11	5-7	6-8	6-3	5-11	7-4	6-11	6-6
	2-2 × 10	8-0	7-5	7-0	8-2	7-7	7-2	8-10	8-3	7-9
	2-2 × 12	9-6	8-11	8-5	9-9	9-1	8-7	10-5	9-8	9-2
Roof plus one story (Bearing)	2-2 × 4	4-7	4-3	4-0	4-8	4-5	4-2	5-0	4-9	4-7
	2-2 × 6	5-4	5-0	4-8	5-6	5-2	4-10	6-1	5-8	5-4
	2-2 × 8	6-3	5-10	5-6	6-5	6-0	5-8	6-11	6-5	6-1
	2-2 × 10	7-4	6-10	6-5	7-6	7-0	6-7	8-0	7-5	7-0
	2-2 × 12	8-6	7-11	7-6	8-8	8-1	7-7	9-2	8-6	8-0
Roof plus one story (No bearing)	2-2 × 4	3-11	3-8	3-5	4-1	3-10	3-7	4-6	4-3	3-11
	2-2 × 6	4-8	4-4	4-1	4-10	4-6	4-2	5-3	4-11	4-7
	2-2 × 8	5-5	5-0	4-9	5-7	5-2	4-10	6-0	5-7	5-3
	2-2 × 10	6-5	5-11	5-7	6-6	6-1	5-8	6-11	6-5	6-0
	2-2 × 12	7-5	6-10	6-5	7-6	7-0	6-7	7-11	7-4	6-11
Roof plus two stories (Bearing)	2-2 × 4	3-11	3-8	3-5	4-1	3-10	3-7	4-6	4-3	3-11
	2-2 × 6	4-8	4-4	4-1	4-10	4-6	4-2	5-3	4-11	4-7
	2-2 × 8	5-5	5-0	4-9	5-7	5-2	4-10	6-0	5-7	5-3
	2-2 × 10	6-5	5-11	5-7	6-6	6-1	5-8	6-11	6-5	6-0
	2-2 × 12	7-5	6-10	6-5	7-6	7-0	6-7	7-11	7-4	6-11
Roof plus two stories (No bearing)	2-2 × 4	3-3	3-0	2-10	3-4	3-1	2-11	3-8	3-5	3-3
	2-2 × 6	3-10	3-6	3-4	3-11	3-8	3-5	4-4	4-0	3-9
	2-2 × 8	4-5	4-1	3-10	4-6	4-3	4-0	4-11	4-6	4-3
	2-2 × 10	5-2	4-10	4-6	5-4	4-11	4-7	5-8	5-3	4-11
	2-2 × 12	6-0	5-7	5-3	6-2	5-9	5-4	6-6	6-0	5-8

*See notes to Table No. R-402.6a

Table No. 6-A

ALLOWABLE SPANS FOR FLOOR JOISTS

40 Lbs. Per Sq. Ft. Live Load

(All rooms except those used for sleeping areas and attic floors.)
Strength — Live Load of 40 lbs. per sq. ft. plus dead load of
10 lbs. per sq. ft. determines the fiber stress value shown.

DESIGN CRITERIA:
Deflection — For 40 lbs. per sq. ft. live load
Limited to span in inches divided by 360.

HOW TO USE TABLES: Enter Table with span of joists (upper figure in each square). Determine size and spacing (first column) based on stress grade (lower figure in each square) and modulus of elasticity (top row) of lumber to be used.

Modulus of Elasticity, "E", in 1,000,000 psi

Each cell shows the allowable span (upper figure, ft-in) over the extreme fiber stress "Fb" in pounds per square inch (lower figure).

JOIST SIZE	SPACING (IN)	0.4	0.5	0.6	0.7	0.8	0.9	1.0	1.1	1.2	1.3	1.4	1.5	1.6	1.7	1.8	1.9	2.0	2.2	2.4
2x6	12.0	6-9 / 450	7-3 / 520	7-9 / 590	8-2 / 660	8-6 / 720	8-10 / 780	9-2 / 830	9-6 / 890	9-9 / 940	10-0 / 990	10-3 / 1040	10-6 / 1090	10-9 / 1140	10-11 / 1190	11-2 / 1230	11-4 / 1280	11-7 / 1320	11-11 / 1410	12-3 / 1490
	13.7	6-6 / 470	7-0 / 550	7-5 / 620	7-9 / 690	8-2 / 750	8-6 / 810	8-9 / 870	9-1 / 930	9-4 / 980	9-7 / 1040	9-10 / 1090	10-0 / 1140	10-3 / 1190	10-6 / 1240	10-8 / 1290	10-10 / 1340	11-1 / 1380	11-5 / 1470	11-9 / 1560
	16.0	6-2 / 500	6-7 / 580	7-0 / 650	7-5 / 720	7-9 / 790	8-0 / 860	8-4 / 920	8-7 / 980	8-10 / 1040	9-1 / 1090	9-4 / 1150	9-6 / 1200	9-9 / 1250	9-11 / 1310	10-2 / 1360	10-4 / 1410	10-6 / 1460	10-10 / 1550	11-2 / 1640
	19.2	5-9 / 530	6-3 / 610	6-7 / 690	7-0 / 770	7-3 / 840	7-7 / 910	7-10 / 970	8-1 / 1040	8-4 / 1100	8-7 / 1160	8-9 / 1220	9-0 / 1280	9-2 / 1330	9-4 / 1390	9-6 / 1440	9-8 / 1500	9-10 / 1550	10-2 / 1650	10-6 / 1750
	24.0	5-4 / 570	5-9 / 660	6-2 / 750	6-6 / 830	6-9 / 900	7-0 / 980	7-3 / 1050	7-6 / 1120	7-9 / 1190	7-11 / 1250	8-2 / 1310	8-4 / 1380	8-6 / 1440	8-8 / 1500	8-10 / 1550	9-0 / 1610	9-2 / 1670	9-6 / 1780	9-9 / 1880
	32.0					6-2 / 1010	6-5 / 1090	6-7 / 1150	6-10 / 1230	7-0 / 1300	7-3 / 1390	7-5 / 1450	7-7 / 1520	7-9 / 1590	7-11 / 1660	8-0 / 1690	8-2 / 1760	8-4 / 1840	8-7 / 1950	8-10 / 2060
2x8	12.0	8-11 / 450	9-7 / 520	10-2 / 590	10-9 / 660	11-3 / 720	11-8 / 780	12-1 / 830	12-6 / 890	12-10 / 940	13-2 / 990	13-6 / 1040	13-10 / 1090	14-2 / 1140	14-5 / 1190	14-8 / 1230	15-0 / 1280	15-3 / 1320	15-9 / 1410	16-2 / 1490
	13.7	8-6 / 470	9-2 / 550	9-9 / 620	10-3 / 690	10-9 / 750	11-2 / 810	11-7 / 870	11-11 / 930	12-3 / 980	12-7 / 1040	12-11 / 1090	13-3 / 1140	13-6 / 1190	13-10 / 1240	14-1 / 1290	14-4 / 1340	14-7 / 1380	15-0 / 1470	15-6 / 1560
	16.0	8-1 / 500	8-9 / 580	9-3 / 650	9-9 / 720	10-2 / 790	10-7 / 850	11-0 / 920	11-4 / 980	11-8 / 1040	12-0 / 1090	12-3 / 1150	12-7 / 1200	12-10 / 1250	13-1 / 1310	13-4 / 1360	13-7 / 1410	13-10 / 1460	14-3 / 1550	14-8 / 1640
	19.2	7-7 / 530	8-2 / 610	8-9 / 690	9-2 / 770	9-7 / 840	10-0 / 910	10-4 / 970	10-8 / 1040	11-0 / 1100	11-3 / 1160	11-7 / 1220	11-10 / 1280	12-1 / 1330	12-4 / 1390	12-7 / 1440	12-10 / 1500	13-0 / 1550	13-5 / 1650	13-10 / 1750
	24.0	7-1 / 570	7-7 / 660	8-1 / 750	8-6 / 830	8-11 / 900	9-3 / 980	9-7 / 1050	9-11 / 1120	10-2 / 1190	10-6 / 1250	10-9 / 1310	11-0 / 1380	11-3 / 1440	11-5 / 1500	11-8 / 1550	11-11 / 1610	12-1 / 1670	12-6 / 1780	12-10 / 1880
	32.0					8-1 / 990	8-5 / 1080	8-9 / 1170	9-0 / 1230	9-3 / 1300	9-6 / 1370	9-9 / 1450	10-0 / 1520	10-2 / 1570	10-5 / 1650	10-7 / 1700	10-10 / 1790	11-0 / 1840	11-4 / 1950	11-8 / 2070
2x10	12.0	11-4 / 450	12-3 / 520	13-0 / 590	13-8 / 660	14-4 / 720	14-11 / 780	15-5 / 830	15-11 / 890	16-5 / 940	16-10 / 990	17-3 / 1040	17-8 / 1090	18-0 / 1140	18-5 / 1190	18-9 / 1230	19-1 / 1280	19-5 / 1320	20-1 / 1410	20-8 / 1490
	13.7	10-10 / 470	11-8 / 550	12-5 / 620	13-1 / 690	13-8 / 750	14-3 / 810	14-9 / 870	15-3 / 930	15-8 / 980	16-1 / 1040	16-6 / 1090	16-11 / 1140	17-3 / 1190	17-7 / 1240	17-11 / 1290	18-3 / 1340	18-7 / 1380	19-2 / 1470	19-9 / 1560
	16.0	10-4 / 500	11-1 / 580	11-10 / 650	12-5 / 720	13-0 / 790	13-6 / 860	14-0 / 920	14-6 / 980	14-11 / 1040	15-3 / 1090	15-8 / 1150	16-0 / 1200	16-5 / 1250	16-9 / 1310	17-0 / 1360	17-4 / 1410	17-8 / 1460	18-3 / 1550	18-9 / 1640
	19.2	9-9 / 530	10-6 / 610	11-1 / 690	11-8 / 770	12-3 / 840	12-9 / 910	13-2 / 970	13-7 / 1040	14-0 / 1100	14-5 / 1160	14-9 / 1220	15-1 / 1280	15-5 / 1330	15-9 / 1390	16-0 / 1440	16-4 / 1500	16-7 / 1550	17-2 / 1650	17-8 / 1750
	24.0	9-0 / 570	9-9 / 660	10-4 / 750	10-10 / 830	11-4 / 900	11-10 / 980	12-3 / 1050	12-8 / 1120	13-0 / 1190	13-4 / 1250	13-8 / 1310	14-0 / 1380	14-4 / 1440	14-7 / 1500	14-11 / 1550	15-2 / 1610	15-5 / 1670	15-11 / 1780	16-5 / 1880
	32.0					10-4 / 1000	10-9 / 1080	11-1 / 1150	11-6 / 1240	11-10 / 1310	12-2 / 1380	12-5 / 1440	12-9 / 1520	13-0 / 1580	13-3 / 1640	13-6 / 1700	13-9 / 1770	14-0 / 1830	14-6 / 1970	14-11 / 2080
2x12	12.0	13-10 / 450	14-11 / 520	15-10 / 590	16-8 / 660	17-5 / 720	18-1 / 780	18-9 / 830	19-4 / 890	19-11 / 940	20-6 / 990	21-0 / 1040	21-6 / 1090	21-11 / 1140	22-5 / 1190	22-10 / 1230	23-3 / 1280	23-7 / 1320	24-5 / 1410	25-1 / 1490
	13.7	13-3 / 470	14-3 / 550	15-2 / 620	15-11 / 690	16-8 / 750	17-4 / 810	17-11 / 870	18-6 / 930	19-1 / 980	19-7 / 1040	20-1 / 1090	20-6 / 1140	21-0 / 1190	21-5 / 1240	21-10 / 1290	22-3 / 1340	22-7 / 1380	23-4 / 1470	24-0 / 1560
	16.0	12-7 / 500	13-6 / 580	14-4 / 650	15-2 / 720	15-10 / 790	16-5 / 860	17-0 / 920	17-7 / 980	18-1 / 1040	18-7 / 1090	19-1 / 1150	19-6 / 1200	19-11 / 1250	20-4 / 1310	20-9 / 1360	21-1 / 1410	21-6 / 1460	22-2 / 1550	22-10 / 1640
	19.2	11-10 / 530	12-9 / 610	13-6 / 690	14-3 / 770	14-11 / 840	15-6 / 910	16-0 / 970	16-7 / 1040	17-0 / 1100	17-6 / 1160	17-11 / 1220	18-4 / 1280	18-9 / 1330	19-2 / 1390	19-6 / 1440	19-10 / 1500	20-2 / 1550	20-10 / 1650	21-6 / 1750
	24.0	11-0 / 570	11-10 / 660	12-7 / 750	13-3 / 830	13-10 / 900	14-4 / 980	14-11 / 1050	15-4 / 1120	15-10 / 1190	16-3 / 1250	16-8 / 1310	17-0 / 1380	17-5 / 1440	17-9 / 1500	18-1 / 1550	18-5 / 1610	18-9 / 1670	19-4 / 1780	19-11 / 1880
	32.0					12-7 / 1000	13-1 / 1080	13-6 / 1150	13-11 / 1220	14-4 / 1300	14-9 / 1380	15-2 / 1450	15-6 / 1520	15-10 / 1580	16-2 / 1650	16-5 / 1700	16-9 / 1770	17-0 / 1830	17-7 / 1950	18-1 / 2070

NOTE: The extreme fiber stress in bending, "Fb", in pounds per square inch is shown below each span.

Table No. 7-B
ALLOWABLE SPAN FOR CEILING JOISTS

20 Lbs. Per Sq. Ft. Live Load
(Limited attic storage where development of future rooms is not possible)
(Gypsum Ceiling)

DESIGN CRITERIA:
Deflection — For 20 lbs. per sq. ft. live load. Limited to span in inches divided by 240.
Strength — Live load of 20 lbs. per sq. ft. plus dead load of 10 lbs. per sq. ft. determines fiber stress value.

HOW TO USE TABLES: Enter Table with span of joists (upper figure in each square). Determine size and spacing (first column) based on stress grade (lower figure in each square) and modulus of elasticity (top row) of lumber to be used.

Each cell shows the allowable span (feet-inches) over the extreme fiber stress "Fb" (psi).

Modulus of Elasticity, "E", in 1,000,000 psi

JOIST SIZE	SPACING (IN)	0.4	0.5	0.6	0.7	0.8	0.9	1.0	1.1	1.2	1.3	1.4	1.5	1.6	1.7	1.8	1.9	2.0	2.2	2.4
2x4	12.0	6-2 / 560	6-8 / 660	7-1 / 740	7-6 / 820	7-10 / 900	8-1 / 970	8-5 / 1040	8-8 / 1110	8-11 / 1170	9-2 / 1240	9-5 / 1300	9-8 / 1360	9-10 / 1420	10-0 / 1480	10-3 / 1540	10-5 / 1600	10-7 / 1650	10-11 / 1760	11-3 / 1860
2x4	13.7	5-11 / 590	6-5 / 690	6-9 / 770	7-2 / 860	7-6 / 940	7-9 / 1010	8-1 / 1090	8-4 / 1160	8-7 / 1230	8-9 / 1300	9-0 / 1360	9-3 / 1420	9-5 / 1490	9-7 / 1550	9-9 / 1610	10-0 / 1670	10-2 / 1730	10-6 / 1840	10-9 / 1950
2x4	16.0	5-8 / 620	6-1 / 720	6-5 / 810	6-9 / 900	7-1 / 990	7-5 / 1070	7-8 / 1140	7-11 / 1220	8-1 / 1290	8-4 / 1360	8-7 / 1430	8-9 / 1500	8-11 / 1570	9-1 / 1630	9-4 / 1690	9-6 / 1760	9-8 / 1820	9-11 / 1940	10-3 / 2050
2x4	19.2	5-4 / 660	5-9 / 770	6-1 / 870	6-5 / 960	6-8 / 1050	6-11 / 1130	7-2 / 1220	7-5 / 1300	7-8 / 1370	7-10 / 1450	8-1 / 1520	8-3 / 1590	8-5 / 1660	8-7 / 1730	8-9 / 1800	8-11 / 1870	9-1 / 1930	9-4 / 2060	9-8 / 2180
2x4	24.0	4-11 / 710	5-4 / 830	5-8 / 930	5-11 / 1030	6-2 / 1130	6-5 / 1220	6-8 / 1310	6-11 / 1400	7-1 / 1480	7-3 / 1560	7-6 / 1640	7-8 / 1720	7-10 / 1790	8-0 / 1870	8-1 / 1940	8-3 / 2010	8-5 / 2080	8-8 / 2220	8-11 / 2350
2x6	12.0	9-9 / 560	10-6 / 660	11-2 / 740	11-9 / 820	12-3 / 900	12-9 / 970	13-3 / 1040	13-8 / 1110	14-1 / 1170	14-5 / 1240	14-9 / 1300	15-2 / 1360	15-6 / 1420	15-9 / 1480	16-1 / 1540	16-4 / 1600	16-8 / 1650	17-2 / 1760	17-8 / 1860
2x6	13.7	9-4 / 590	10-0 / 690	10-8 / 770	11-3 / 860	11-9 / 940	12-3 / 1010	12-8 / 1090	13-1 / 1160	13-5 / 1230	13-10 / 1300	14-2 / 1360	14-6 / 1420	14-9 / 1490	15-1 / 1550	15-5 / 1610	15-8 / 1670	15-11 / 1730	16-5 / 1840	16-11 / 1950
2x6	16.0	8-10 / 620	9-6 / 720	10-2 / 810	10-8 / 900	11-2 / 990	11-7 / 1070	12-0 / 1140	12-5 / 1220	12-9 / 1290	13-1 / 1360	13-5 / 1430	13-9 / 1500	14-1 / 1570	14-4 / 1630	14-7 / 1690	14-11 / 1760	15-2 / 1820	15-7 / 1940	16-1 / 2050
2x6	19.2	8-4 / 660	9-0 / 770	9-6 / 870	10-0 / 960	10-6 / 1050	10-11 / 1130	11-4 / 1220	11-8 / 1300	12-0 / 1370	12-4 / 1450	12-8 / 1520	12-11 / 1590	13-3 / 1660	13-6 / 1730	13-9 / 1800	14-0 / 1870	14-3 / 1930	14-8 / 2060	15-2 / 2180
2x6	24.0	7-9 / 710	8-4 / 830	8-10 / 930	9-4 / 1030	9-9 / 1130	10-2 / 1220	10-6 / 1310	10-10 / 1400	11-2 / 1480	11-5 / 1560	11-9 / 1640	12-0 / 1720	12-3 / 1790	12-6 / 1870	12-9 / 1940	13-0 / 2010	13-3 / 2080	13-8 / 2220	14-1 / 2350
2x8	12.0	12-10 / 560	13-10 / 660	14-8 / 740	15-6 / 820	16-2 / 900	16-10 / 970	17-5 / 1040	18-0 / 1110	18-6 / 1170	19-0 / 1240	19-6 / 1300	19-11 / 1360	20-5 / 1420	20-10 / 1480	21-2 / 1540	21-7 / 1600	21-11 / 1650	22-8 / 1760	23-4 / 1860
2x8	13.7	12-3 / 590	13-3 / 690	14-1 / 770	14-10 / 860	15-6 / 940	16-1 / 1010	16-8 / 1090	17-2 / 1160	17-9 / 1230	18-2 / 1300	18-8 / 1360	19-1 / 1420	19-6 / 1490	19-11 / 1550	20-3 / 1610	20-8 / 1670	21-0 / 1730	21-8 / 1840	22-4 / 1950
2x8	16.0	11-8 / 620	12-7 / 720	13-4 / 810	14-1 / 900	14-8 / 990	15-3 / 1070	15-10 / 1140	16-4 / 1220	16-10 / 1290	17-3 / 1360	17-9 / 1430	18-2 / 1500	18-6 / 1570	18-11 / 1630	19-3 / 1690	19-7 / 1760	19-11 / 1820	20-7 / 1940	21-2 / 2050
2x8	19.2	11-0 / 660	11-10 / 770	12-7 / 870	13-3 / 960	13-10 / 1050	14-5 / 1130	14-11 / 1220	15-5 / 1300	15-10 / 1370	16-3 / 1450	16-8 / 1520	17-1 / 1590	17-5 / 1660	17-9 / 1730	18-2 / 1800	18-5 / 1870	18-9 / 1930	19-5 / 2060	19-11 / 2180
2x8	24.0	10-2 / 710	11-0 / 830	11-8 / 930	12-3 / 1030	12-10 / 1130	13-4 / 1220	13-10 / 1310	14-3 / 1400	14-8 / 1480	15-1 / 1560	15-6 / 1640	15-10 / 1720	16-2 / 1790	16-6 / 1870	16-10 / 1940	17-2 / 2010	17-5 / 2080	18-0 / 2220	18-6 / 2350
2x10	12.0	16-5 / 560	17-8 / 660	18-9 / 740	19-9 / 820	20-8 / 900	21-6 / 970	22-3 / 1040	22-11 / 1110	23-8 / 1170	24-3 / 1240	24-10 / 1300	25-5 / 1360	26-0 / 1420	26-6 / 1480	27-1 / 1540	27-6 / 1600	28-0 / 1650	28-11 / 1760	29-9 / 1860
2x10	13.7	15-8 / 590	16-11 / 690	17-11 / 770	18-11 / 860	19-9 / 940	20-6 / 1010	21-3 / 1090	21-11 / 1160	22-7 / 1230	23-3 / 1300	23-9 / 1360	24-4 / 1420	24-10 / 1490	25-5 / 1550	25-10 / 1610	26-4 / 1670	26-10 / 1730	27-8 / 1840	28-6 / 1950
2x10	16.0	14-11 / 620	16-0 / 720	17-0 / 810	17-11 / 900	18-9 / 990	19-6 / 1070	20-2 / 1140	20-10 / 1220	21-6 / 1290	22-1 / 1360	22-7 / 1430	23-2 / 1500	23-8 / 1570	24-1 / 1630	24-7 / 1690	25-0 / 1760	25-5 / 1820	26-3 / 1940	27-1 / 2050
2x10	19.2	14-0 / 660	15-1 / 770	16-0 / 870	16-11 / 960	17-8 / 1060	18-4 / 1130	19-0 / 1220	19-7 / 1300	20-2 / 1370	20-9 / 1450	21-3 / 1520	21-9 / 1590	22-3 / 1660	22-8 / 1730	23-2 / 1800	23-7 / 1870	23-11 / 1930	24-9 / 2060	25-5 / 2180
2x10	24.0	13-0 / 710	14-0 / 830	14-11 / 930	15-8 / 1030	16-5 / 1130	17-0 / 1220	17-8 / 1310	18-3 / 1400	18-9 / 1480	19-3 / 1560	19-9 / 1640	20-2 / 1720	20-8 / 1790	21-1 / 1870	21-6 / 1940	21-10 / 2010	22-3 / 2060	22-11 / 2220	23-8 / 2350

NOTE: The extreme fiber stress in bending, "Fb", in pounds per square inch is shown below each span.

Table No. 7-C
ALLOWABLE SPAN FOR CEILING JOISTS

10 Lbs. Per Sq. Ft. Live Load
(No attic storage and roof slope not steeper than 3 in 12)

(Plaster Ceiling)

DESIGN CRITERIA:
Deflection – For 10 lbs. per sq. ft. live load. Limited to span in inches divided by 360.
Strength – Live load of 10 lbs. per sq. ft. plus dead load of 5 lbs. per sq. ft. determines fiber stress value.

HOW TO USE TABLES: Enter Table with span of joists (upper figure in each square). Determine size and spacing (first column) based on stress grade (lower figure in each square) and modulus of elasticity (top row) of lumber to be used.

Each cell shows: span (upper figure) / extreme fiber stress in bending "Fb" in psi (lower figure).

Modulus of Elasticity, "E", in 1,000,000 psi

JOIST SIZE	SPACING (IN)	0.4	0.5	0.6	0.7	0.8	0.9	1.0	1.1	1.2	1.3	1.4	1.5	1.6	1.7	1.8	1.9	2.0	2.2	2.4
2x4	12.0	6-10/340	7-4/400	7-10/450	8-3/500	8-7/540	8-11/590	9-3/630	9-7/670	9-10/710	10-1/750	10-4/790	10-7/830	10-10/860	11-1/900	11-3/930	11-6/970	11-8/1000	12-1/1070	12-5/1130
	13.7	6-6/360	7-0/410	7-6/470	7-10/520	8-3/570	8-7/610	8-10/660	9-2/700	9-5/740	9-8/780	9-11/820	10-2/860	10-4/900	10-7/940	10-9/970	11-0/1010	11-2/1050	11-6/1110	11-10/1180
	16.0	6-2/380	6-8/440	7-1/490	7-6/550	7-10/600	8-1/650	8-5/690	8-8/740	8-11/780	9-2/830	9-5/870	9-8/910	9-10/950	10-0/990	10-3/1030	10-5/1060	10-7/1100	10-11/1170	11-3/1240
	19.2	5-10/400	6-3/460	6-8/520	7-0/580	7-4/630	7-8/690	7-11/740	8-2/790	8-5/830	8-8/880	8-10/920	9-1/970	9-3/1010	9-5/1050	9-8/1090	9-10/1130	10-0/1170	10-4/1250	10-7/1320
	24.0	5-5/430	5-10/500	6-2/560	6-6/630	6-10/680	7-1/740	7-4/790	7-7/850	7-10/900	8-0/950	8-3/990	8-5/1040	8-7/1090	8-9/1130	8-11/1170	9-1/1220	9-3/1260	9-7/1340	9-10/1420
2x6	12.0	10-9/340	11-7/400	12-3/450	12-11/500	13-6/540	14-1/590	14-7/630	15-0/670	15-6/710	15-11/750	16-3/790	16-8/830	17-0/860	17-4/900	17-8/930	18-0/970	18-4/1000	18-11/1070	19-6/1130
	13.7	10-3/360	11-1/410	11-9/470	12-4/520	12-11/570	13-5/610	13-11/660	14-4/700	14-9/740	15-2/780	15-7/820	15-11/860	16-3/900	16-7/940	16-11/970	17-3/1010	17-6/1050	18-1/1110	18-8/1180
	16.0	9-9/380	10-6/440	11-2/490	11-9/550	12-3/600	12-9/650	13-3/690	13-8/740	14-1/780	14-5/830	14-9/870	15-2/910	15-6/950	15-9/990	16-1/1030	16-4/1060	16-8/1100	17-2/1170	17-8/1240
	19.2	9-2/400	9-10/460	10-6/520	11-1/580	11-7/630	12-0/690	12-5/740	12-10/790	13-3/830	13-7/880	13-11/920	14-3/970	14-7/1010	14-10/1050	15-2/1090	15-5/1130	15-8/1170	16-2/1250	16-8/1320
	24.0	8-6/430	9-2/500	9-9/560	10-3/630	10-9/680	11-2/740	11-7/790	11-11/850	12-3/900	12-7/950	12-11/990	13-3/1040	13-6/1090	13-9/1130	14-1/1170	14-4/1220	14-7/1260	15-0/1340	15-6/1420
2x8	12.0	14-2/340	15-3/400	16-2/450	17-0/500	17-10/540	18-6/590	19-2/630	19-10/670	20-5/710	20-11/750	21-5/790	21-11/830	22-5/860	22-11/900	23-4/930	23-9/970	24-2/1000	24-11/1070	25-8/1130
	13.7	13-6/360	14-7/410	15-6/470	16-3/520	17-0/570	17-9/610	18-4/660	18-11/700	19-6/740	20-0/780	20-6/820	21-0/860	21-5/900	21-11/940	22-4/970	22-9/1010	23-1/1050	23-10/1110	24-7/1180
	16.0	12-10/380	13-10/440	14-8/490	15-6/550	16-2/600	16-10/650	17-5/690	18-0/740	18-6/780	19-0/830	19-6/870	19-11/910	20-5/950	20-10/990	21-2/1030	21-7/1060	21-11/1100	22-8/1170	23-4/1240
	19.2	12-1/400	13-0/460	13-10/520	14-7/580	15-3/630	15-10/690	16-5/740	16-11/790	17-5/830	17-11/880	18-4/920	18-9/970	19-2/1010	19-7/1050	19-11/1090	20-4/1130	20-8/1170	21-4/1250	21-11/1320
	24.0	11-3/430	12-1/500	12-10/560	13-6/630	14-2/680	14-8/740	15-3/790	15-9/850	16-2/900	16-7/950	17-0/990	17-5/1040	17-10/1090	18-2/1130	18-6/1170	18-10/1220	19-2/1260	19-10/1340	20-5/1420
2x10	12.0	18-0/340	19-5/400	20-8/450	21-9/500	22-9/540	23-8/590	24-6/630	25-3/670	26-0/710	26-9/750	27-5/790	28-0/830	28-7/860	29-2/900	29-9/930	30-4/970	30-10/1000	31-10/1070	32-9/1130
	13.7	17-3/360	18-7/410	19-9/470	20-9/520	21-9/570	22-7/610	23-5/660	24-2/700	24-10/740	25-7/780	26-2/820	26-10/860	27-5/900	27-11/940	28-6/970	29-0/1010	29-6/1050	30-5/1110	31-4/1180
	16.0	16-5/380	17-8/440	18-9/490	19-9/550	20-8/600	21-6/650	22-3/690	22-11/740	23-8/780	24-3/830	24-10/870	25-5/910	26-0/950	26-6/990	27-1/1030	27-6/1060	28-0/1100	28-11/1170	29-9/1240
	19.2	15-5/400	16-7/460	17-8/520	18-7/580	19-5/630	20-2/690	20-11/740	21-7/790	22-3/830	22-10/880	23-5/920	23-11/970	24-6/1010	25-0/1050	25-5/1090	25-11/1130	26-4/1170	27-3/1250	28-0/1320
	24.0	14-4/430	15-5/500	16-5/560	17-3/630	18-0/680	18-9/740	19-5/790	20-1/850	20-8/900	21-2/950	21-9/990	22-3/1040	22-9/1090	23-2/1130	23-8/1170	24-1/1220	24-6/1260	25-3/1340	26-0/1420

NOTE: The extreme fiber stress in bending, "Fb", in pounds per square inch is shown below each span.

Table No. 7-D
ALLOWABLE SPAN FOR CEILING JOISTS

10 Lbs. Per Sq. Ft. Live Load
(No attic storage and roof slope not steeper than 3 in 12)

(Gypsum Ceiling)

DESIGN CRITERIA:
Deflection – For 10 lbs. per sq. ft. live load.
 Limited to span in inches divided by 240.
Strength – Live load of 10 lbs. per sq. ft. plus
dead load of 5 lbs. per sq. ft. determines
fiber stress value.

HOW TO USE TABLES: Enter Table with span of joists (upper figure in each square). Determine size and spacing (first column) based on stress grade (lower figure in each square) and modulus of elasticity (top row) of lumber to be used.

Each cell shows allowable span (feet-inches) over extreme fiber stress "Fb" (psi).

Joist Size	Spacing (IN)	E=0.4	E=0.5	E=0.6	E=0.7	E=0.8	E=0.9	E=1.0	E=1.1	E=1.2	E=1.3	E=1.4	E=1.5	E=1.6	E=1.7	E=1.8	E=1.9	E=2.0	E=2.2	E=2.4
2×4	12.0	7-10/450	8-5/520	8-11/590	9-5/650	9-10/710	10-3/770	10-7/830	10-11/880	11-3/930	11-7/980	11-10/1030	12-2/1080	12-5/1130	12-8/1180	12-11/1220	13-2/1270	13-4/1310	13-9/1400	14-2/1480
2×4	13.7	7-6/470	8-1/540	8-7/610	9-0/680	9-5/740	9-9/800	10-2/860	10-6/920	10-9/970	11-1/1030	11-4/1080	11-7/1130	11-10/1180	12-1/1230	12-4/1280	12-7/1320	12-9/1370	13-2/1460	13-7/1550
2×4	16.0	7-1/490	7-8/570	8-1/650	8-7/720	8-11/780	9-4/850	9-8/910	9-11/970	10-3/1030	10-6/1080	10-9/1140	11-0/1190	11-3/1240	11-6/1290	11-9/1340	11-11/1390	12-2/1440	12-6/1540	12-11/1630
2×4	19.2	6-8/520	7-2/610	7-8/690	8-1/760	8-5/830	8-9/900	9-1/970	9-4/1030	9-8/1090	9-11/1150	10-2/1210	10-4/1270	10-7/1320	10-10/1380	11-0/1430	11-3/1480	11-5/1530	11-9/1630	12-2/1730
2×4	24.0	6-2/560	6-8/660	7-1/740	7-6/820	7-10/900	8-1/970	8-5/1040	8-8/1110	8-11/1170	9-2/1240	9-5/1300	9-8/1360	9-10/1420	10-0/1480	10-3/1540	10-5/1600	10-7/1650	10-11/1760	11-3/1860
2×6	12.0	12-3/450	13-3/520	14-1/590	14-9/650	15-6/710	16-1/770	16-8/830	17-2/880	17-8/930	18-2/980	18-8/1030	19-1/1080	19-6/1130	19-11/1180	20-3/1220	20-8/1270	21-0/1310	21-8/1400	22-4/1480
2×6	13.7	11-9/470	12-8/540	13-5/610	14-2/680	14-9/740	15-5/800	15-11/860	16-5/920	16-11/970	17-5/1030	17-10/1080	18-3/1130	18-8/1180	19-0/1230	19-5/1280	19-9/1320	20-1/1370	20-9/1460	21-4/1550
2×6	16.0	11-2/490	12-0/570	12-9/650	13-5/720	14-1/780	14-7/850	15-2/910	15-7/970	16-1/1030	16-6/1080	16-11/1140	17-4/1190	17-8/1240	18-1/1290	18-5/1340	18-9/1390	19-1/1440	19-8/1540	20-3/1630
2×6	19.2	10-6/520	11-4/610	12-0/690	12-8/760	13-3/830	13-9/900	14-3/970	14-8/1030	15-2/1090	15-7/1150	15-11/1210	16-4/1270	16-8/1320	17-0/1380	17-4/1430	17-8/1480	17-11/1530	18-6/1630	19-1/1730
2×6	24.0	9-9/560	10-6/660	11-2/740	11-9/820	12-3/900	12-9/970	13-3/1040	13-8/1110	14-1/1170	14-5/1240	14-9/1300	15-2/1360	15-6/1420	15-9/1480	16-1/1540	16-4/1600	16-8/1650	17-2/1760	17-8/1860
2×8	12.0	16-2/450	17-5/520	18-6/590	19-6/650	20-5/710	21-2/770	21-11/830	22-8/880	23-4/930	24-0/980	24-7/1030	25-2/1080	25-8/1130	26-2/1180	26-9/1220	27-2/1270	27-8/1310	28-7/1400	29-5/1480
2×8	13.7	15-6/470	16-8/540	17-9/610	18-8/680	19-6/740	20-3/800	21-0/860	21-8/920	22-4/970	22-11/1030	23-6/1080	24-0/1130	24-7/1180	25-1/1230	25-7/1280	26-0/1320	26-6/1370	27-4/1460	28-1/1550
2×8	16.0	14-8/490	15-10/570	16-10/650	17-9/720	18-6/780	19-3/850	19-11/910	20-7/970	21-2/1030	21-9/1080	22-4/1140	22-10/1190	23-4/1240	23-10/1290	24-3/1340	24-8/1390	25-2/1440	25-11/1540	26-9/1630
2×8	19.2	13-10/520	14-11/610	15-10/690	16-8/760	17-5/830	18-2/900	18-9/970	19-5/1030	19-11/1090	20-6/1150	21-0/1210	21-6/1270	21-11/1320	22-5/1380	22-10/1430	23-3/1480	23-8/1530	24-5/1630	25-2/1730
2×8	24.0	12-10/560	13-10/660	14-8/740	15-6/820	16-2/900	16-10/970	17-5/1040	18-0/1110	18-6/1170	19-0/1240	19-6/1300	19-11/1360	20-5/1420	20-10/1480	21-2/1540	21-7/1600	21-11/1650	22-8/1760	23-4/1860
2×10	12.0	20-8/450	22-3/520	23-8/590	24-10/650	26-0/710	27-1/770	28-0/830	28-11/880	29-9/930	30-7/980	31-4/1030	32-1/1080	32-9/1130	33-5/1180	34-1/1220	34-8/1270	35-4/1310	36-5/1400	37-6/1480
2×10	13.7	19-9/470	21-3/540	22-7/610	23-9/680	24-10/740	25-10/800	26-10/860	27-8/920	28-6/970	29-3/1030	30-0/1080	30-8/1130	31-4/1180	32-0/1230	32-7/1280	33-2/1320	33-9/1370	34-10/1460	35-10/1550
2×10	16.0	18-9/490	20-2/570	21-6/650	22-7/720	23-8/780	24-7/850	25-5/910	26-3/970	27-1/1030	27-9/1080	28-6/1140	29-2/1190	29-9/1240	30-5/1290	31-0/1340	31-6/1390	32-1/1440	33-1/1540	34-1/1630
2×10	19.2	17-8/520	19-0/610	20-2/690	21-3/760	22-3/830	23-2/900	23-11/970	24-9/1030	25-5/1090	26-2/1150	26-10/1210	27-5/1270	28-0/1320	28-7/1380	29-2/1430	29-8/1480	30-2/1530	31-2/1630	32-1/1730
2×10	24.0	16-5/560	17-8/660	18-9/740	19-9/820	20-8/900	21-6/970	22-3/1040	22-11/1110	23-8/1170	24-3/1240	24-10/1300	25-5/1360	26-0/1420	26-6/1480	27-1/1540	27-6/1600	28-0/1650	28-11/1760	29-9/1860

Modulus of Elasticity, "E", in 1,000,000 psi

NOTE: The extreme fiber stress in bending, "Fb", in pounds per square inch is shown below each span.

Table No. 7-E
ALLOWABLE SPAN FOR LOW OR HIGH SLOPE RAFTERS

20 Lbs. Per Sq. Ft. Live Load
(Supporting Gypsum Ceiling)

DESIGN CRITERIA:
Strength – 15 lbs. per sq. ft. dead load plus 20 lbs. per sq. ft. live load determines fiber stress.
Deflection – For 20 lbs. per sq. ft. live load. Limited to span in inches divided by 240.

RAFTERS: Spans are measured along the horizontal projection and loads are considered as applied on the horizontal projection.

HOW TO USE TABLES: Enter table with span of rafters (upper figure in each square). Determine size and spacing (last column) based on stress grade (top row) and modulus of elasticity (lower figure in each square) of lumber to be used.

Each cell shows allowable span (feet-inches) over modulus of elasticity "E".

Allowable Extreme Fiber Stress in Bending, "Fb" (psi) — 300 to 1300

SIZE	SPACING (IN)	300	400	500	600	700	800	900	1000	1100	1200	1300
2x6	12.0	6-7 / 0.12	7-7 / 0.19	8-6 / 0.26	9-4 / 0.35	10-0 / 0.44	10-9 / 0.54	11-5 / 0.64	12-0 / 0.75	12-7 / 0.86	13-2 / 0.98	13-8 / 1.11
	13.7	6-2 / 0.12	7-1 / 0.18	7-11 / 0.25	8-8 / 0.33	9-5 / 0.41	10-0 / 0.50	10-8 / 0.60	11-3 / 0.70	11-9 / 0.81	12-4 / 0.92	12-10 / 1.04
	16.0	5-8 / 0.11	6-7 / 0.16	7-4 / 0.23	8-1 / 0.30	8-8 / 0.38	9-4 / 0.46	9-10 / 0.55	10-5 / 0.65	10-11 / 0.75	11-5 / 0.85	11-10 / 0.96
	19.2	5-2 / 0.10	6-0 / 0.15	6-9 / 0.21	7-4 / 0.27	7-11 / 0.35	8-6 / 0.42	9-0 / 0.51	9-6 / 0.59	9-11 / 0.68	10-5 / 0.78	10-10 / 0.88
	24.0	4-8 / 0.09	5-4 / 0.13	6-0 / 0.19	6-7 / 0.25	7-1 / 0.31	7-7 / 0.38	8-1 / 0.45	8-6 / 0.53	8-11 / 0.61	9-4 / 0.70	9-8 / 0.78
2x8	12.0	8-8 / 0.12	10-0 / 0.19	11-2 / 0.26	12-3 / 0.35	13-3 / 0.44	14-2 / 0.54	15-0 / 0.64	15-10 / 0.75	16-7 / 0.86	17-4 / 0.98	18-0 / 1.11
	13.7	8-1 / 0.12	9-4 / 0.18	10-6 / 0.25	11-6 / 0.33	12-5 / 0.41	13-3 / 0.50	14-0 / 0.60	14-10 / 0.70	15-6 / 0.81	16-3 / 0.92	16-10 / 1.04
	16.0	7-6 / 0.11	8-8 / 0.16	9-8 / 0.23	10-7 / 0.30	11-6 / 0.38	12-3 / 0.46	13-0 / 0.55	13-8 / 0.65	14-4 / 0.75	15-0 / 0.85	15-7 / 0.96
	19.2	6-10 / 0.10	7-11 / 0.15	8-10 / 0.21	9-8 / 0.27	10-6 / 0.35	11-2 / 0.42	11-10 / 0.51	12-6 / 0.59	13-1 / 0.68	13-8 / 0.78	14-3 / 0.88
	24.0	6-2 / 0.09	7-1 / 0.13	7-11 / 0.19	8-8 / 0.25	9-4 / 0.31	10-0 / 0.38	10-7 / 0.45	11-2 / 0.53	11-9 / 0.61	12-3 / 0.70	12-9 / 0.78
2x10	12.0	11-1 / 0.12	12-9 / 0.19	14-3 / 0.26	15-8 / 0.35	16-11 / 0.44	18-1 / 0.54	19-2 / 0.64	20-2 / 0.75	21-2 / 0.86	22-1 / 0.98	23-0 / 1.11
	13.7	10-4 / 0.12	11-11 / 0.18	13-4 / 0.25	14-8 / 0.33	15-10 / 0.41	16-11 / 0.50	17-11 / 0.60	18-11 / 0.70	19-10 / 0.81	20-8 / 0.92	21-6 / 1.04
	16.0	9-7 / 0.11	11-1 / 0.16	12-4 / 0.23	13-6 / 0.30	14-8 / 0.38	15-8 / 0.46	16-7 / 0.55	17-6 / 0.65	18-4 / 0.75	19-2 / 0.85	19-11 / 0.96
	19.2	8-9 / 0.10	10-1 / 0.15	11-3 / 0.21	12-4 / 0.27	13-4 / 0.35	14-3 / 0.42	15-2 / 0.51	15-11 / 0.59	16-9 / 0.68	17-6 / 0.78	18-2 / 0.88
	24.0	7-10 / 0.09	9-0 / 0.13	10-1 / 0.19	11-1 / 0.25	11-11 / 0.31	12-9 / 0.38	13-6 / 0.45	14-3 / 0.53	15-0 / 0.61	15-8 / 0.70	16-3 / 0.78
2x12	12.0	13-5 / 0.12	15-6 / 0.19	17-4 / 0.26	19-0 / 0.35	20-6 / 0.44	21-11 / 0.54	23-3 / 0.64	24-7 / 0.75	25-9 / 0.86	26-11 / 0.98	28-0 / 1.11
	13.7	12-7 / 0.12	14-6 / 0.18	16-3 / 0.25	17-9 / 0.33	19-3 / 0.41	20-6 / 0.50	21-9 / 0.60	23-0 / 0.70	24-1 / 0.81	25-2 / 0.92	26-2 / 1.04
	16.0	11-8 / 0.11	13-5 / 0.16	15-0 / 0.23	16-6 / 0.30	17-9 / 0.38	19-0 / 0.46	20-2 / 0.55	21-3 / 0.65	22-4 / 0.75	23-3 / 0.85	24-3 / 0.96
	19.2	10-8 / 0.10	12-3 / 0.15	13-9 / 0.21	15-0 / 0.27	16-3 / 0.35	17-4 / 0.42	18-5 / 0.51	19-5 / 0.59	20-4 / 0.68	21-3 / 0.78	22-2 / 0.88
	24.0	9-6 / 0.09	11-0 / 0.13	12-3 / 0.19	13-5 / 0.25	14-6 / 0.31	15-6 / 0.38	16-6 / 0.45	17-4 / 0.53	18-2 / 0.61	19-0 / 0.70	19-10 / 0.78

Allowable Extreme Fiber Stress in Bending, "Fb" (psi) — 1400 to 2700

1400	1500	1600	1700	1800	1900	2000	2100	2200	2400	2700	RAFTER SPACING (IN)	SIZE (IN)
14-2 / 1.24	14-8 / 1.37	15-2 / 1.51	15-8 / 1.66	16-1 / 1.81	16-7 / 1.96	17-0 / 2.12	17-5 / 2.28	17-10 / 2.44			12.0	2x6
13-3 / 1.16	13-9 / 1.29	14-2 / 1.42	14-8 / 1.55	15-1 / 1.69	15-6 / 1.83	15-11 / 1.98	16-3 / 2.13	16-8 / 2.28	17-5 / 2.60		13.7	
12-4 / 1.07	12-9 / 1.19	13-2 / 1.31	13-7 / 1.44	13-11 / 1.56	14-4 / 1.70	14-8 / 1.83	15-1 / 1.97	15-5 / 2.11	16-1 / 2.41		16.0	
11-3 / 0.98	11-7 / 1.09	12-0 / 1.20	12-4 / 1.31	12-9 / 1.43	13-1 / 1.55	13-5 / 1.67	13-9 / 1.80	14-1 / 1.93	14-8 / 2.20		19.2	
10-0 / 0.88	10-5 / 0.97	10-9 / 1.07	11-1 / 1.17	11-5 / 1.28	11-8 / 1.39	12-0 / 1.50	12-4 / 1.61	12-7 / 1.73	13-2 / 1.97	13-11 / 2.35	24.0	
18-9 / 1.24	19-5 / 1.37	20-0 / 1.51	20-8 / 1.66	21-3 / 1.81	21-10 / 1.96	22-4 / 2.12	22-11 / 2.28	23-6 / 2.44			12.0	2x8
17-6 / 1.16	18-2 / 1.29	18-9 / 1.42	19-4 / 1.55	19-10 / 1.69	20-5 / 1.83	20-11 / 1.98	21-5 / 2.13	21-11 / 2.28	22-11 / 2.60		13.7	
16-3 / 1.07	16-9 / 1.19	17-4 / 1.31	17-10 / 1.44	18-5 / 1.56	18-11 / 1.70	19-5 / 1.83	19-10 / 1.97	20-4 / 2.11	21-3 / 2.41		16.0	
14-10 / 0.98	15-4 / 1.09	15-10 / 1.20	16-4 / 1.31	16-9 / 1.43	17-3 / 1.55	17-8 / 1.67	18-2 / 1.80	18-7 / 1.93	19-5 / 2.20		19.2	
13-3 / 0.88	13-8 / 0.97	14-2 / 1.07	14-7 / 1.17	15-0 / 1.28	15-5 / 1.39	15-10 / 1.50	16-3 / 1.61	16-7 / 1.73	17-4 / 1.97	18-5 / 2.35	24.0	
23-11 / 1.24	24-9 / 1.37	25-6 / 1.51	26-4 / 1.66	27-1 / 1.81	27-10 / 1.96	28-7 / 2.12	29-3 / 2.28	29-11 / 2.44			12.0	2x10
22-4 / 1.16	23-2 / 1.29	23-11 / 1.42	24-7 / 1.55	25-4 / 1.69	26-0 / 1.83	26-8 / 1.98	27-4 / 2.13	28-0 / 2.28	29-3 / 2.60		13.7	
20-8 / 1.07	21-5 / 1.19	22-1 / 1.31	22-10 / 1.44	23-5 / 1.56	24-1 / 1.70	24-9 / 1.83	25-4 / 1.97	25-11 / 2.11	27-1 / 2.41		16.0	
18-11 / 0.98	19-7 / 1.09	20-2 / 1.20	20-10 / 1.31	21-5 / 1.43	22-0 / 1.55	22-7 / 1.67	23-2 / 1.80	23-8 / 1.93	24-9 / 2.20		19.2	
16-11 / 0.88	17-6 / 0.97	18-1 / 1.07	18-7 / 1.17	19-2 / 1.28	19-8 / 1.39	20-2 / 1.50	20-8 / 1.61	21-2 / 1.73	22-1 / 1.97	23-5 / 2.35	24.0	
29-1 / 1.24	30-1 / 1.37	31-1 / 1.51	32-0 / 1.66	32-11 / 1.81	33-10 / 1.96	34-9 / 2.12	35-7 / 2.28	36-5 / 2.44			12.0	2x12
27-2 / 1.16	28-2 / 1.29	29-1 / 1.42	29-11 / 1.55	30-10 / 1.69	31-8 / 1.83	32-6 / 1.98	33-3 / 2.13	34-1 / 2.28	35-7 / 2.60		13.7	
25-2 / 1.07	26-0 / 1.19	26-11 / 1.31	27-9 / 1.44	28-6 / 1.56	29-4 / 1.70	30-1 / 1.83	30-10 / 1.97	31-6 / 2.11	32-11 / 2.41		16.0	
23-0 / 0.98	23-9 / 1.09	24-7 / 1.20	25-4 / 1.31	26-0 / 1.43	26-9 / 1.55	27-5 / 1.67	28-2 / 1.80	28-9 / 1.93	30-1 / 2.20		19.2	
20-6 / 0.88	21-3 / 0.97	21-11 / 1.07	22-8 / 1.17	23-3 / 1.28	23-11 / 1.39	24-7 / 1.50	25-2 / 1.61	25-9 / 1.73	26-11 / 1.97	28-6 / 2.35	24.0	

NOTE: The modulus of elasticity, "E", in 1,000,000 pounds per square inch is shown below each span.

Table No. 7-F
ALLOWABLE SPAN FOR LOW OR HIGH SLOPE RAFTERS

30 Lbs. Per Sq. Ft. Live Load
(Supporting Gypsum Ceiling)

DESIGN CRITERIA:
Strength – 15 lbs. per sq. ft. dead load plus 30 lbs. per sq. ft. live load determines fiber stress.
Deflection – For 30 lbs. per sq. ft. live load. Limited to span in inches divided by 240.

RAFTERS: Spans are measured along the horizontal projection and loads are considered as applied on the horizontal projection.

HOW TO USE TABLES: Enter table with span of rafters (upper figure in each square). Determine size and spacing (last column) based on stress grade (top row) and modulus of elasticity (lower figure in each square) of lumber to be used.

Each cell shows allowable span (upper figure) / modulus of elasticity "E" (lower figure).

Allowable Extreme Fiber Stress in Bending, "F_b" (psi)

RAFTER SIZE	SPACING (IN)	300	400	500	600	700	800	900	1000	1100	1200	1300	1400	1500	1600	1700	1800	1900	2000	2100	2200	2400	2700
2×6	12.0	5-10 / 0.13	6-8 / 0.19	7-6 / 0.27	8-2 / 0.36	8-10 / 0.45	9-6 / 0.55	10-0 / 0.66	10-7 / 0.77	11-1 / 0.89	11-7 / 1.01	12-1 / 1.14	12-6 / 1.28	13-0 / 1.41	13-5 / 1.56	13-10 / 1.71	14-2 / 1.86	14-7 / 2.02	15-0 / 2.18	15-4 / 2.34	15-8 / 2.51		
	13.7	5-5 / 0.12	6-3 / 0.18	7-0 / 0.25	7-8 / 0.33	8-3 / 0.42	8-10 / 0.52	9-5 / 0.61	9-11 / 0.72	10-5 / 0.83	10-10 / 0.95	11-3 / 1.07	11-9 / 1.19	12-2 / 1.32	12-6 / 1.46	12-11 / 1.60	13-3 / 1.74	13-8 / 1.89	14-0 / 2.04	14-4 / 2.19	14-8 / 2.35		
	16.0	5-0 / 0.11	5-10 / 0.17	6-6 / 0.24	7-1 / 0.31	7-8 / 0.39	8-2 / 0.48	8-8 / 0.57	9-2 / 0.67	9-7 / 0.77	10-0 / 0.88	10-5 / 0.99	10-10 / 1.10	11-3 / 1.22	11-7 / 1.35	11-11 / 1.48	12-4 / 1.61	12-8 / 1.75	13-0 / 1.89	13-3 / 2.03	13-7 / 2.18	14-2 / 2.48	
	19.2	4-7 / 0.10	5-4 / 0.15	5-11 / 0.22	6-6 / 0.28	7-0 / 0.36	7-6 / 0.44	7-11 / 0.52	8-4 / 0.61	8-9 / 0.70	9-2 / 0.80	9-6 / 0.90	9-11 / 1.01	10-3 / 1.12	10-7 / 1.23	10-11 / 1.35	11-3 / 1.47	11-6 / 1.59	11-10 / 1.72	12-2 / 1.85	12-5 / 1.99	13-0 / 2.26	
	24.0	4-1 / 0.09	4-9 / 0.14	5-4 / 0.19	5-10 / 0.25	6-3 / 0.32	6-8 / 0.39	7-1 / 0.46	7-6 / 0.54	7-10 / 0.63	8-2 / 0.72	8-6 / 0.81	8-10 / 0.90	9-2 / 1.00	9-6 / 1.10	9-9 / 1.21	10-0 / 1.31	10-4 / 1.43	10-7 / 1.54	10-10 / 1.66	11-1 / 1.78	11-7 / 2.02	12-4 / 2.41
2×8	12.0	7-8 / 0.13	8-10 / 0.19	9-10 / 0.27	10-10 / 0.36	11-8 / 0.45	12-6 / 0.55	13-3 / 0.66	13-11 / 0.77	14-8 / 0.89	15-3 / 1.01	15-11 / 1.14	16-6 / 1.28	17-1 / 1.41	17-8 / 1.56	18-2 / 1.71	18-9 / 1.86	19-3 / 2.02	19-9 / 2.18	20-3 / 2.34	20-8 / 2.51		
	13.7	7-2 / 0.12	8-3 / 0.18	9-3 / 0.25	10-1 / 0.33	10-11 / 0.42	11-8 / 0.52	12-5 / 0.61	13-1 / 0.72	13-8 / 0.83	14-4 / 0.95	14-11 / 1.07	15-5 / 1.19	16-0 / 1.32	16-6 / 1.46	17-0 / 1.60	17-6 / 1.74	18-0 / 1.89	18-5 / 2.04	18-11 / 2.19	19-4 / 2.35		
	16.0	6-7 / 0.11	7-8 / 0.17	8-7 / 0.24	9-4 / 0.31	10-1 / 0.39	10-10 / 0.48	11-6 / 0.57	12-1 / 0.67	12-8 / 0.77	13-3 / 0.88	13-9 / 0.99	14-4 / 1.10	14-10 / 1.22	15-3 / 1.35	15-9 / 1.48	16-3 / 1.61	16-8 / 1.75	17-1 / 1.89	17-6 / 2.03	17-11 / 2.18	18-9 / 2.48	
	19.2	6-1 / 0.10	7-0 / 0.15	7-10 / 0.22	8-7 / 0.28	9-3 / 0.36	9-10 / 0.44	10-6 / 0.52	11-0 / 0.61	11-7 / 0.70	12-1 / 0.80	12-7 / 0.90	13-1 / 1.01	13-6 / 1.12	13-11 / 1.23	14-5 / 1.35	14-10 / 1.47	15-2 / 1.59	15-7 / 1.72	16-0 / 1.85	16-4 / 1.99	17-1 / 2.26	
	24.0	5-5 / 0.09	6-3 / 0.14	7-0 / 0.19	7-8 / 0.25	8-3 / 0.32	8-10 / 0.39	9-4 / 0.46	9-10 / 0.54	10-4 / 0.63	10-10 / 0.72	11-3 / 0.81	11-8 / 0.90	12-1 / 1.00	12-6 / 1.10	12-10 / 1.21	13-3 / 1.31	13-7 / 1.43	13-11 / 1.54	14-4 / 1.66	14-8 / 1.78	15-3 / 2.02	16-3 / 2.41
2×10	12.0	9-9 / 0.13	11-3 / 0.19	12-7 / 0.27	13-9 / 0.36	14-11 / 0.45	15-11 / 0.55	16-11 / 0.66	17-10 / 0.77	18-8 / 0.89	19-6 / 1.01	20-4 / 1.14	21-1 / 1.28	21-10 / 1.41	22-6 / 1.56	23-3 / 1.71	23-11 / 1.86	24-6 / 2.02	25-2 / 2.18	25-10 / 2.34	26-5 / 2.51		
	13.7	9-1 / 0.12	10-6 / 0.18	11-9 / 0.25	12-11 / 0.33	13-11 / 0.42	14-11 / 0.52	15-10 / 0.61	16-8 / 0.72	17-6 / 0.83	18-3 / 0.95	19-0 / 1.07	19-8 / 1.19	20-5 / 1.32	21-1 / 1.46	21-9 / 1.60	22-4 / 1.74	22-11 / 1.89	23-7 / 2.04	24-2 / 2.19	24-8 / 2.35		
	16.0	8-5 / 0.11	9-9 / 0.17	10-11 / 0.24	11-11 / 0.31	12-11 / 0.39	13-9 / 0.48	14-8 / 0.57	15-5 / 0.67	16-2 / 0.77	16-11 / 0.88	17-7 / 0.99	18-3 / 1.10	18-11 / 1.22	19-6 / 1.35	20-1 / 1.48	20-8 / 1.61	21-3 / 1.75	21-10 / 1.89	22-4 / 2.03	22-10 / 2.18	23-11 / 2.48	
	19.2	7-8 / 0.10	8-11 / 0.15	9-11 / 0.22	10-11 / 0.28	11-9 / 0.36	12-7 / 0.44	13-4 / 0.52	14-1 / 0.61	14-9 / 0.70	15-5 / 0.80	16-1 / 0.90	16-8 / 1.01	17-3 / 1.12	17-10 / 1.23	18-4 / 1.35	18-11 / 1.47	19-5 / 1.59	19-11 / 1.72	20-5 / 1.85	20-10 / 1.99	21-10 / 2.26	
	24.0	6-11 / 0.09	8-0 / 0.14	8-11 / 0.19	9-9 / 0.25	10-6 / 0.32	11-3 / 0.39	11-11 / 0.46	12-7 / 0.54	13-2 / 0.63	13-9 / 0.72	14-4 / 0.81	14-11 / 0.90	15-5 / 1.00	15-11 / 1.10	16-5 / 1.21	16-11 / 1.31	17-4 / 1.43	17-10 / 1.54	18-3 / 1.66	18-8 / 1.78	19-6 / 2.02	20-8 / 2.41
2×12	12.0	11-10 / 0.13	13-8 / 0.19	15-4 / 0.27	16-9 / 0.36	18-1 / 0.45	19-4 / 0.55	20-6 / 0.66	21-8 / 0.77	22-8 / 0.89	23-9 / 1.01	24-8 / 1.14	25-7 / 1.28	26-6 / 1.41	27-5 / 1.56	28-3 / 1.71	29-1 / 1.86	29-10 / 2.02	30-7 / 2.18	31-4 / 2.34	32-1 / 2.51		
	13.7	11-1 / 0.12	12-10 / 0.18	14-4 / 0.25	15-8 / 0.33	16-11 / 0.42	18-1 / 0.52	19-3 / 0.61	20-3 / 0.72	21-3 / 0.83	22-2 / 0.95	23-1 / 1.07	24-0 / 1.19	24-10 / 1.32	25-7 / 1.46	26-5 / 1.60	27-2 / 1.74	27-11 / 1.89	28-8 / 2.04	29-4 / 2.19	30-0 / 2.35		
	16.0	10-3 / 0.11	11-10 / 0.17	13-3 / 0.24	14-6 / 0.31	15-8 / 0.39	16-9 / 0.48	17-9 / 0.57	18-9 / 0.67	19-8 / 0.77	20-6 / 0.88	21-5 / 0.99	22-2 / 1.10	23-0 / 1.22	23-9 / 1.35	24-5 / 1.48	25-2 / 1.61	25-10 / 1.75	26-6 / 1.89	27-2 / 2.03	27-10 / 2.18	29-1 / 2.48	
	19.2	9-5 / 0.10	10-10 / 0.15	12-1 / 0.22	13-3 / 0.28	14-4 / 0.36	15-4 / 0.44	16-3 / 0.52	17-1 / 0.61	17-11 / 0.70	18-9 / 0.80	19-6 / 0.90	20-3 / 1.01	21-0 / 1.12	21-8 / 1.23	22-4 / 1.35	23-0 / 1.47	23-7 / 1.59	24-2 / 1.72	24-10 / 1.85	25-5 / 1.99	26-6 / 2.26	
	24.0	8-5 / 0.09	9-8 / 0.14	10-10 / 0.19	11-10 / 0.25	12-10 / 0.32	13-8 / 0.39	14-6 / 0.46	15-4 / 0.54	16-1 / 0.63	16-9 / 0.72	17-5 / 0.81	18-1 / 0.90	18-9 / 1.00	19-4 / 1.10	20-0 / 1.21	20-6 / 1.31	21-1 / 1.43	21-8 / 1.54	22-2 / 1.66	22-8 / 1.78	23-9 / 2.02	25-2 / 2.41

NOTE: The modulus of elasticity, "E", in 1,000,000 pounds per square inch is shown below each span.

Table No. 7-G
ALLOWABLE SPAN FOR LOW OR HIGH SLOPE RAFTERS

40 Lbs. Per Sq. Ft. Live Load
(Supporting Gypsum Ceiling)

DESIGN CRITERIA:
Strength – 15 lbs. per sq. ft. dead load plus 40 lbs. per sq. ft. live load determines fiber stress.
Deflection – For 40 lbs. per sq. ft. live load. Limited to span in inches divided by 240.

RAFTERS: Spans are measured along the horizontal projection and loads are considered as applied on the horizontal projection.

HOW TO USE TABLES: Enter table with span of rafters (upper figure in each square). Determine size and spacing (last column) based on stress grade (top row) and modulus of elasticity (lower figure in each square) of lumber to be used.

The span/E value pairs below are given as "span (ft-in) / E". Modulus of elasticity "E" in 1,000,000 pounds per square inch is shown below each span.

Rafter Size	Spacing (IN)	Fb 300	Fb 400	Fb 500	Fb 600	Fb 700	Fb 800	Fb 900	Fb 1000	Fb 1100	Fb 1200	Fb 1300	Fb 1400	Fb 1500	Fb 1600	Fb 1700	Fb 1800	Fb 1900	Fb 2000	Fb 2100	Fb 2200	Fb 2400	Fb 2700
2x6	12.0	5-3 / 0.12	6-1 / 0.19	6-9 / 0.27	7-5 / 0.35	8-0 / 0.44	8-7 / 0.54	9-1 / 0.65	9-7 / 0.76	10-0 / 0.88	10-6 / 1.00	10-11 / 1.13	11-4 / 1.26	11-9 / 1.40	12-1 / 1.54	12-6 / 1.68	12-10 / 1.83	13-2 / 1.99	13-6 / 2.15	13-10 / 2.31	14-2 / 2.48		
2x6	13.7	4-11 / 0.12	5-8 / 0.18	6-4 / 0.25	6-11 / 0.33	7-6 / 0.42	8-0 / 0.51	8-6 / 0.61	8-11 / 0.71	9-5 / 0.82	9-10 / 0.93	10-3 / 1.05	10-7 / 1.18	11-0 / 1.31	11-4 / 1.44	11-8 / 1.57	12-0 / 1.72	12-4 / 1.86	12-8 / 2.01	13-0 / 2.16	13-3 / 2.32		
2x6	16.0	4-6 / 0.11	5-3 / 0.17	5-10 / 0.23	6-5 / 0.31	6-11 / 0.39	7-5 / 0.47	7-10 / 0.56	8-3 / 0.66	8-8 / 0.76	9-1 / 0.86	9-5 / 0.98	9-10 / 1.09	10-2 / 1.21	10-6 / 1.33	10-10 / 1.46	11-1 / 1.59	11-5 / 1.72	11-9 / 1.86	12-0 / 2.00	12-4 / 2.15	12-10 / 2.45	
2x6	19.2	4-2 / 0.11	4-9 / 0.15	5-4 / 0.21	5-10 / 0.28	6-4 / 0.35	6-9 / 0.43	7-2 / 0.51	7-7 / 0.60	7-11 / 0.69	8-3 / 0.79	8-8 / 0.89	8-11 / 0.99	9-3 / 1.10	9-7 / 1.22	9-10 / 1.33	10-2 / 1.45	10-5 / 1.57	10-8 / 1.70	11-0 / 1.83	11-3 / 1.96	11-9 / 2.23	
2x6	24.0	3-8 / 0.09	4-3 / 0.14	4-9 / 0.19	5-3 / 0.25	5-8 / 0.31	6-1 / 0.38	6-5 / 0.46	6-9 / 0.54	7-1 / 0.62	7-5 / 0.71	7-9 / 0.80	8-0 / 0.89	8-3 / 0.99	8-7 / 1.09	8-10 / 1.19	9-1 / 1.30	9-4 / 1.41	9-7 / 1.52	9-10 / 1.63	10-0 / 1.75	10-6 / 2.00	11-1 / 2.38
2x8	12.0	6-11 / 0.12	8-0 / 0.19	8-11 / 0.27	9-9 / 0.35	10-7 / 0.44	11-3 / 0.54	12-0 / 0.65	12-7 / 0.76	13-3 / 0.88	13-10 / 1.00	14-5 / 1.13	14-11 / 1.26	15-5 / 1.40	16-0 / 1.54	16-5 / 1.68	16-11 / 1.83	17-5 / 1.99	17-10 / 2.15	18-3 / 2.31	18-9 / 2.48		
2x8	13.7	6-6 / 0.12	7-6 / 0.18	8-4 / 0.25	9-2 / 0.33	9-11 / 0.42	10-7 / 0.51	11-2 / 0.61	11-10 / 0.71	12-5 / 0.82	12-11 / 0.93	13-6 / 1.05	14-0 / 1.18	14-6 / 1.31	14-11 / 1.44	15-5 / 1.57	15-10 / 1.72	16-3 / 1.86	16-8 / 2.01	17-1 / 2.16	17-6 / 2.32		
2x8	16.0	6-0 / 0.11	6-11 / 0.17	7-9 / 0.23	8-6 / 0.31	9-2 / 0.39	9-9 / 0.47	10-4 / 0.56	10-11 / 0.66	11-6 / 0.76	12-0 / 0.86	12-6 / 0.98	12-11 / 1.09	13-5 / 1.21	13-10 / 1.33	14-3 / 1.46	14-8 / 1.59	15-1 / 1.72	15-5 / 1.86	15-10 / 2.00	16-3 / 2.15	16-11 / 2.45	
2x8	19.2	5-6 / 0.10	6-4 / 0.15	7-1 / 0.21	7-9 / 0.28	8-4 / 0.35	8-11 / 0.43	9-6 / 0.51	10-0 / 0.60	10-6 / 0.69	10-11 / 0.79	11-5 / 0.89	11-10 / 0.99	12-3 / 1.10	12-7 / 1.22	13-0 / 1.33	13-5 / 1.45	13-9 / 1.57	14-1 / 1.70	14-6 / 1.83	14-10 / 1.96	15-5 / 2.23	
2x8	24.0	4-11 / 0.09	5-8 / 0.14	6-4 / 0.19	6-11 / 0.25	7-6 / 0.31	8-0 / 0.38	8-6 / 0.46	8-11 / 0.54	9-4 / 0.62	9-9 / 0.71	10-2 / 0.80	10-7 / 0.89	10-11 / 0.99	11-3 / 1.09	11-8 / 1.19	12-0 / 1.30	12-4 / 1.41	12-7 / 1.52	12-11 / 1.63	13-3 / 1.75	13-10 / 2.00	14-8 / 2.38
2x10	12.0	8-10 / 0.12	10-2 / 0.19	11-5 / 0.27	12-6 / 0.35	13-6 / 0.44	14-5 / 0.54	15-3 / 0.65	16-1 / 0.76	16-11 / 0.88	17-8 / 1.00	18-4 / 1.13	19-1 / 1.26	19-9 / 1.40	20-4 / 1.54	21-0 / 1.68	21-7 / 1.83	22-2 / 1.99	22-9 / 2.15	23-4 / 2.31	23-11 / 2.48		
2x10	13.7	8-3 / 0.12	9-6 / 0.18	10-8 / 0.25	11-8 / 0.33	12-7 / 0.42	13-6 / 0.51	14-3 / 0.61	15-1 / 0.71	15-10 / 0.82	16-6 / 0.93	17-2 / 1.05	17-10 / 1.18	18-5 / 1.31	19-1 / 1.44	19-8 / 1.57	20-2 / 1.72	20-9 / 1.86	21-4 / 2.01	21-10 / 2.16	22-4 / 2.32		
2x10	16.0	7-8 / 0.11	8-10 / 0.17	9-10 / 0.23	10-10 / 0.31	11-8 / 0.39	12-6 / 0.47	13-3 / 0.56	13-11 / 0.66	14-8 / 0.76	15-3 / 0.86	15-11 / 0.98	16-6 / 1.09	17-1 / 1.21	17-8 / 1.33	18-2 / 1.46	18-9 / 1.59	19-3 / 1.72	19-9 / 1.86	20-2 / 2.00	20-8 / 2.15	21-7 / 2.45	
2x10	19.2	7-0 / 0.10	8-1 / 0.15	9-0 / 0.21	9-10 / 0.28	10-8 / 0.35	11-5 / 0.43	12-1 / 0.51	12-9 / 0.60	13-4 / 0.69	13-11 / 0.79	14-6 / 0.89	15-1 / 0.99	15-7 / 1.10	16-1 / 1.22	16-7 / 1.33	17-1 / 1.45	17-7 / 1.57	18-0 / 1.70	18-5 / 1.83	18-11 / 1.96	19-9 / 2.23	
2x10	24.0	6-3 / 0.09	7-2 / 0.14	8-1 / 0.19	8-10 / 0.25	9-6 / 0.31	10-2 / 0.38	10-10 / 0.46	11-5 / 0.54	11-11 / 0.62	12-6 / 0.71	13-0 / 0.80	13-6 / 0.89	13-11 / 0.99	14-5 / 1.09	14-10 / 1.19	15-3 / 1.30	15-8 / 1.41	16-1 / 1.52	16-6 / 1.63	16-11 / 1.75	17-8 / 2.00	18-9 / 2.38
2x12	12.0	10-9 / 0.12	12-5 / 0.19	13-10 / 0.27	15-2 / 0.35	16-5 / 0.44	17-6 / 0.54	18-7 / 0.65	19-7 / 0.76	20-6 / 0.88	21-5 / 1.00	22-4 / 1.13	23-2 / 1.26	24-0 / 1.40	24-9 / 1.54	25-6 / 1.68	26-3 / 1.83	27-0 / 1.99	27-8 / 2.15	28-5 / 2.31	29-1 / 2.48		
2x12	13.7	10-0 / 0.12	11-7 / 0.18	12-11 / 0.25	14-2 / 0.33	15-4 / 0.42	16-5 / 0.51	17-5 / 0.61	18-4 / 0.71	19-3 / 0.82	20-1 / 0.93	20-11 / 1.05	21-8 / 1.18	22-5 / 1.31	23-2 / 1.44	23-11 / 1.57	24-7 / 1.72	25-3 / 1.86	25-11 / 2.01	26-7 / 2.16	27-2 / 2.32		
2x12	16.0	9-3 / 0.11	10-9 / 0.17	12-0 / 0.23	13-2 / 0.31	14-2 / 0.39	15-2 / 0.47	16-1 / 0.56	17-0 / 0.66	17-9 / 0.76	18-7 / 0.86	19-4 / 0.98	20-1 / 1.09	20-9 / 1.21	21-5 / 1.33	22-1 / 1.46	22-9 / 1.59	23-5 / 1.72	24-0 / 1.86	24-7 / 2.00	25-2 / 2.15	26-3 / 2.45	
2x12	19.2	8-6 / 0.10	9-10 / 0.15	11-0 / 0.21	12-0 / 0.28	12-11 / 0.35	13-10 / 0.43	14-8 / 0.51	15-6 / 0.60	16-3 / 0.69	17-0 / 0.79	17-8 / 0.89	18-4 / 0.99	19-0 / 1.10	19-7 / 1.22	20-2 / 1.33	20-9 / 1.45	21-4 / 1.57	21-11 / 1.70	22-5 / 1.83	23-0 / 1.96	24-0 / 2.23	
2x12	24.0	7-7 / 0.09	8-9 / 0.14	9-10 / 0.19	10-9 / 0.25	11-7 / 0.31	12-5 / 0.38	13-2 / 0.46	13-10 / 0.54	14-6 / 0.62	15-2 / 0.71	15-9 / 0.80	16-5 / 0.89	17-0 / 0.99	17-6 / 1.09	18-1 / 1.19	18-7 / 1.30	19-1 / 1.41	19-7 / 1.52	20-1 / 1.63	20-6 / 1.75	21-5 / 2.00	22-9 / 2.38

NOTE: The modulus of elasticity, "E", in 1,000,000 pounds per square inch is shown below each span.

Table No. 7-I
ALLOWABLE SPAN FOR LOW OR HIGH SLOPE RAFTERS

30 Lbs. Per Sq. Ft. Live Load
(Supporting Plaster Ceiling)

DESIGN CRITERIA:
Strength – 15 lbs. per sq. ft. dead load plus 30 lbs. per sq. ft. live load determines fiber stress.
Deflection – For 30 lbs. per sq. ft. live load. Limited to span in inches divided by 360.

RAFTERS: Spans are measured along the horizontal projection and loads are considered as applied on the horizontal projection.

HOW TO USE TABLES: Enter table with span of rafters (upper figure in each square). Determine size and spacing (last column) based on stress grade (top row) and modulus of elasticity (lower figure in each square) of lumber to be used.

Each cell shows span (upper figure) and modulus of elasticity "E" (lower figure).

Allowable Extreme Fiber Stress in Bending, "F_b" (psi)

RAFTER SIZE	SPACING (IN)	300	400	500	600	700	800	900	1000	1100	1200	1300
2x6	12.0	5-10 0.19	6-8 0.29	7-6 0.41	8-2 0.54	8-10 0.68	9-6 0.83	10-0 0.99	10-7 1.15	11-1 1.33	11-7 1.52	12-1 1.71
	13.7	5-5 0.18	6-3 0.27	7-0 0.38	7-8 0.50	8-3 0.63	8-10 0.77	9-5 0.92	9-11 1.08	10-5 1.25	10-10 1.42	11-3 1.60
	16.0	5-0 0.16	5-10 0.25	6-6 0.35	7-1 0.46	7-8 0.59	8-2 0.72	8-8 0.85	9-2 1.00	9-7 1.15	10-0 1.31	10-5 1.48
	19.2	4-7 0.15	5-4 0.23	5-11 0.32	6-6 0.42	7-0 0.53	7-6 0.65	7-11 0.78	8-4 0.91	8-9 1.05	9-2 1.20	9-6 1.35
	24.0	4-1 0.13	4-9 0.21	5-4 0.29	5-10 0.38	6-3 0.48	6-8 0.58	7-1 0.70	7-6 0.82	7-10 0.94	8-2 1.07	8-6 1.21
2x8	12.0	7-8 0.19	8-10 0.29	9-10 0.41	10-10 0.54	11-8 0.68	12-6 0.83	13-3 0.99	13-11 1.15	14-8 1.33	15-3 1.52	15-11 1.71
	13.7	7-2 0.18	8-3 0.27	9-3 0.38	10-1 0.50	10-11 0.63	11-8 0.77	12-5 0.92	13-1 1.08	13-8 1.25	14-4 1.42	14-11 1.60
	16.0	6-7 0.16	7-8 0.25	8-7 0.35	9-4 0.46	10-1 0.59	10-10 0.72	11-6 0.85	12-1 1.00	12-8 1.15	13-3 1.31	13-9 1.48
	19.2	6-1 0.15	7-0 0.23	7-10 0.32	8-7 0.42	9-3 0.53	9-10 0.65	10-6 0.78	11-0 0.91	11-7 1.06	12-1 1.20	12-7 1.35
	24.0	5-5 0.13	6-3 0.21	7-0 0.29	7-8 0.38	8-3 0.48	8-10 0.58	9-4 0.70	9-10 0.82	10-4 0.94	10-10 1.07	11-3 1.21
2x10	12.0	9-9 0.19	11-3 0.29	12-7 0.41	13-9 0.54	14-11 0.68	15-11 0.83	16-11 0.99	17-10 1.15	18-8 1.33	19-6 1.52	20-4 1.71
	13.7	9-1 0.18	10-6 0.27	11-9 0.38	12-11 0.50	13-11 0.63	14-11 0.77	15-10 0.92	16-8 1.08	17-6 1.25	18-3 1.42	19-0 1.60
	16.0	8-5 0.16	9-9 0.25	10-11 0.35	11-11 0.46	12-11 0.59	13-9 0.72	14-8 0.85	15-5 1.00	16-2 1.15	16-11 1.31	17-7 1.48
	19.2	7-8 0.15	8-11 0.23	9-11 0.32	10-11 0.42	11-9 0.53	12-7 0.65	13-4 0.78	14-1 0.91	14-9 1.06	15-5 1.20	16-1 1.35
	24.0	6-11 0.13	8-0 0.21	8-11 0.29	9-9 0.38	10-6 0.48	11-3 0.58	11-11 0.70	12-7 0.82	13-2 0.94	13-9 1.07	14-4 1.21
2x12	12.0	11-10 0.19	13-8 0.29	15-4 0.41	16-9 0.54	18-1 0.68	19-4 0.83	20-6 0.99	21-8 1.15	22-8 1.33	23-9 1.52	24-8 1.71
	13.7	11-1 0.18	12-10 0.27	14-4 0.38	15-8 0.50	16-11 0.63	18-1 0.77	19-3 0.92	20-3 1.08	21-3 1.25	22-2 1.42	23-1 1.60
	16.0	10-3 0.16	11-10 0.25	13-3 0.35	14-6 0.46	15-8 0.59	16-9 0.72	17-9 0.85	18-9 1.00	19-8 1.15	20-6 1.31	21-5 1.48
	19.2	9-5 0.15	10-10 0.23	12-1 0.32	13-3 0.42	14-4 0.53	15-4 0.65	16-3 0.78	17-1 0.91	17-11 1.06	18-9 1.20	19-6 1.35
	24.0	8-5 0.13	9-8 0.21	10-10 0.29	11-10 0.38	12-10 0.48	13-8 0.58	14-6 0.70	15-4 0.82	16-1 0.94	16-9 1.07	17-5 1.21

Allowable Extreme Fiber Stress in Bending, "F_b" (psi)

1300	1400	1500	1600	1700	1800	1900	2000	2100	RAFTER SPACING (IN)	RAFTER SIZE (IN)
12-1 1.71	12-6 1.91	13-0 2.12	13-5 2.34	13-10 2.56					12.0	
11-3 1.60	11-9 1.79	12-2 1.98	12-6 2.19	12-11 2.39					13.7	
10-5 1.48	10-10 1.66	11-3 1.84	11-7 2.02	11-11 2.22	12-4 2.41				16.0	2x6
9-6 1.35	9-11 1.51	10-3 1.68	10-7 1.85	10-11 2.02	11-3 2.20	11-6 2.39	11-10 2.58		19.2	
8-6 1.21	8-10 1.35	9-2 1.50	9-6 1.65	9-9 1.81	10-0 1.97	10-4 2.14	10-7 2.31	10-10 2.48	24.0	
15-11 1.71	16-6 1.91	17-1 2.12	17-8 2.34	18-2 2.56					12.0	
14-11 1.60	15-5 1.79	16-0 1.98	16-6 2.19	17-0 2.39					13.7	
13-9 1.48	14-4 1.66	14-10 1.84	15-3 2.02	15-9 2.22	16-3 2.41				16.0	2x8
12-7 1.35	13-1 1.51	13-6 1.68	13-11 1.85	14-5 2.02	14-10 2.20	15-2 2.39	15-7 2.58		19.2	
11-3 1.21	11-8 1.35	12-1 1.50	12-6 1.65	12-10 1.81	13-3 1.97	13-7 2.14	13-11 2.31	14-4 2.48	24.0	
20-4 1.71	21-1 1.91	21-10 2.12	22-6 2.34	23-3 2.56					12.0	
19-0 1.60	19-8 1.79	20-5 1.98	21-1 2.19	21-9 2.39					13.7	
17-7 1.48	18-3 1.66	18-11 1.84	19-6 2.02	20-1 2.22	20-8 2.41				16.0	2x10
16-1 1.35	16-8 1.51	17-3 1.68	17-10 1.85	18-4 2.02	18-11 2.20	19-5 2.39	19-11 2.58		19.2	
14-4 1.21	14-11 1.35	15-5 1.50	15-11 1.65	16-5 1.81	16-11 1.97	17-4 2.14	17-10 2.31	18-3 2.48	24.0	
24-8 1.71	25-7 1.91	26-6 2.12	27-5 2.34	28-3 2.56					12.0	
23-1 1.60	24-0 1.79	24-10 1.98	25-7 2.19	26-5 2.39					13.7	
21-5 1.48	22-2 1.66	23-0 1.84	23-9 2.02	24-5 2.22	25-2 2.41				16.0	2x12
19-6 1.35	20-3 1.51	21-0 1.68	21-8 1.85	22-4 2.02	23-0 2.20	23-7 2.39	24-2 2.58		19.2	
17-5 1.21	18-1 1.35	18-9 1.50	19-4 1.65	20-0 1.81	20-6 1.97	21-1 2.14	21-8 2.31	22-2 2.48	24.0	

NOTE: The modulus of elasticity, "E", in 1,000,000 pounds per square inch is shown below each span.

Table No. 7-L
ALLOWABLE SPAN FOR LOW SLOPE RAFTERS
Slope 3 in 12 or less — 30 Lbs. Per Sq. Ft. Live Load
(No Finished Ceiling)

DESIGN CRITERIA:
Strength – 10 lbs. per sq. ft. dead load plus 30 lbs. per sq. ft. live load determines fiber stress.
Deflection — For 30 lbs. per sq. ft. live load. Limited to span in inches divided by 240.

RAFTERS: Spans are measured along the horizontal projection and loads are considered as applied on the horizontal projection.

HOW TO USE TABLES: Enter table with span of rafters (upper figure in each square). Determine size and spacing (last column) based on stress grade (top row) and modulus of elasticity (lower figure in each square) of lumber to be used.

Values shown as span (feet-inches) / modulus of elasticity "E".

RAFTER SIZE (IN)	SPACING (IN)	300	400	500	600	700	800	900	1000	1100	1200	1300	1400	1500	1600	1700	1800	1900	2000	2100	2200	2400
2x6	12.0	6-2/0.15	7-1/0.23	7-11/.32	8-8/0.43	9-5/0.54	10-0/0.66	10-8/0.78	11-3/0.92	11-9/1.06	12-4/1.21	12-10/1.36	13-3/1.52	13-9/1.69	14-2/1.86	14-8/2.04	15-1/2.22	15-6/2.41	15-11/2.60			
	13.7	5-9/0.14	6-8/0.22	7-5/0.30	8-2/0.40	8-9/0.50	9-5/0.61	10-0/0.73	10-6/0.86	11-0/0.99	11-6/1.13	12-0/1.27	12-5/1.42	12-10/1.58	13-3/1.74	13-8/1.90	14-1/2.08	14-6/2.25	14-10/2.43			
	16.0	5-4/0.13	6-2/0.20	6-11/0.28	7-6/0.37	8-2/0.47	8-8/0.57	9-3/0.68	9-9/0.80	10-2/0.92	10-8/1.05	11-1/1.18	11-6/1.32	11-11/1.46	12-4/1.61	12-8/1.76	13-1/1.92	13-5/2.08	13-9/2.25	14-1/2.42	14-5/2.60	
	19.2	4-10/0.12	5-7/0.18	6-3/0.26	6-11/0.34	7-5/0.43	7-11/0.52	8-5/0.62	8-11/0.73	9-4/0.84	9-9/0.95	10-1/1.08	10-6/1.20	10-10/1.33	11-3/1.47	11-7/1.61	11-11/1.75	12-3/1.90	12-7/2.05	12-10/2.21	13-2/2.37	
	24.0	4-4/0.11	5-0/0.16	5-7/0.23	6-2/0.30	6-8/0.38	7-1/0.46	7-6/0.55	7-11/0.65	8-4/0.75	8-8/0.85	9-1/0.96	9-5/1.08	9-9/1.19	10-0/1.31	10-4/1.44	10-8/1.57	10-11/1.70	11-3/1.84	11-6/1.98	11-9/2.12	12-4/2.41
2x8	12.0	8-1/0.15	9-4/0.23	10-6/0.32	11-6/0.43	12-5/0.54	13-3/0.66	14-0/0.78	14-10/0.92	15-6/1.06	16-3/1.21	16-10/1.36	17-6/1.52	18-2/1.69	18-9/1.86	19-4/2.04	19-10/2.22	20-5/2.41	20-11/2.60			
	13.7	7-7/0.14	8-9/0.22	9-9/0.30	10-9/0.40	11-7/0.50	12-5/0.61	13-2/0.73	13-10/0.86	14-6/0.99	15-2/1.13	15-9/1.27	16-5/1.42	16-11/1.58	17-6/1.74	18-1/1.90	18-7/2.08	19-1/2.25	19-7/2.43			
	16.0	7-0/0.13	8-1/0.20	9-1/0.28	9-11/0.37	10-9/0.47	11-6/0.57	12-2/0.68	12-10/0.80	13-5/0.92	14-0/1.05	14-7/1.18	15-2/1.32	15-8/1.46	16-3/1.61	16-9/1.76	17-2/1.92	17-8/2.08	18-2/2.25	18-7/2.42	19-0/2.60	
	19.2	6-5/0.12	7-5/0.18	8-3/0.26	9-1/0.34	9-9/0.43	10-6/0.52	11-1/0.62	11-8/0.73	12-3/0.84	12-10/0.95	13-4/1.08	13-10/1.20	14-4/1.33	14-10/1.47	15-3/1.61	15-8/1.75	16-2/1.90	16-7/2.06	16-11/2.21	17-4/2.37	
	24.0	5-9/0.11	6-7/0.16	7-5/0.23	8-1/0.30	8-9/0.38	9-4/0.46	9-11/0.55	10-6/0.65	11-0/0.75	11-6/0.85	11-11/0.96	12-5/1.08	12-10/1.19	13-3/1.31	13-8/1.44	14-0/1.57	14-5/1.70	14-10/1.84	15-2/1.98	15-6/2.12	16-3/2.41
2x10	12.0	10-4/0.15	11-11/0.23	13-4/0.32	14-8/0.43	15-10/0.54	16-11/0.66	17-11/0.78	18-11/0.92	19-10/1.06	20-8/1.21	21-6/1.36	22-4/1.52	23-2/1.69	23-11/1.86	24-7/2.04	25-4/2.22	26-0/2.41	26-8/2.60			
	13.7	9-8/0.14	11-2/0.22	12-6/0.30	13-8/0.40	14-9/0.50	15-10/0.61	16-9/0.73	17-8/0.86	18-6/0.99	19-4/1.13	20-2/1.27	20-11/1.42	21-8/1.58	22-4/1.74	23-0/1.90	23-8/2.08	24-4/2.25	25-0/2.43			
	16.0	8-11/0.13	10-4/0.20	11-7/0.28	12-8/0.37	13-8/0.47	14-8/0.57	15-6/0.68	16-4/0.80	17-2/0.92	17-11/1.05	18-8/1.18	19-4/1.32	20-0/1.46	20-8/1.61	21-4/1.76	21-11/1.92	22-6/2.08	23-2/2.25	23-8/2.42	24-3/2.60	
	19.2	8-2/0.12	9-5/0.18	10-7/0.26	11-7/0.34	12-6/0.43	13-4/0.52	14-2/0.62	14-11/0.73	15-8/0.84	16-4/0.95	17-0/1.08	17-8/1.20	18-3/1.33	18-11/1.47	19-6/1.61	20-0/1.75	20-7/1.90	21-1/2.06	21-8/2.21	22-2/2.37	
	24.0	7-4/0.11	8-5/0.16	9-5/0.23	10-4/0.30	11-2/0.38	11-11/0.46	12-8/0.55	13-4/0.65	14-0/0.75	14-8/0.85	15-3/0.96	15-10/1.08	16-4/1.19	16-11/1.31	17-5/1.44	17-11/1.57	18-5/1.70	18-11/1.84	19-4/1.98	19-10/2.12	20-8/2.41
2x12	12.0	12-7/0.15	14-6/0.23	16-3/0.32	17-9/0.43	19-3/0.54	20-6/0.66	21-9/0.78	23-0/0.92	24-1/1.06	25-2/1.21	26-2/1.36	27-2/1.52	28-2/1.69	29-1/1.86	29-11/2.04	30-10/2.22	31-8/2.41	32-6/2.60			
	13.7	11-9/0.14	13-7/0.22	15-2/0.30	16-8/0.40	18-0/0.50	19-3/0.61	20-5/0.73	21-6/0.86	22-6/0.99	23-6/1.13	24-6/1.27	25-5/1.42	26-4/1.58	27-2/1.74	28-0/1.90	28-10/2.08	29-7/2.25	30-5/2.43			
	16.0	10-11/0.13	12-7/0.20	14-1/0.28	15-5/0.37	16-8/0.47	17-9/0.57	18-10/0.68	19-11/0.80	20-10/0.92	21-9/1.05	22-8/1.18	23-6/1.32	24-4/1.46	25-2/1.61	25-11/1.76	26-8/1.92	27-5/2.08	28-2/2.25	28-10/2.42	29-6/2.60	
	19.2	9-11/0.12	11-6/0.18	12-10/0.26	14-1/0.34	15-2/0.43	16-3/0.52	17-3/0.62	18-2/0.73	19-0/0.84	19-11/0.95	20-8/1.08	21-6/1.20	22-3/1.33	23-0/1.47	23-8/1.61	24-4/1.75	25-0/1.90	25-8/2.05	26-4/2.21	26-11/2.37	
	24.0	8-11/0.11	10-3/0.16	11-6/0.23	12-7/0.30	13-7/0.38	14-6/0.46	15-5/0.55	16-3/0.65	17-0/0.75	17-9/0.85	18-6/0.96	19-3/1.08	19-11/1.19	20-6/1.31	21-2/1.44	21-9/1.57	22-5/1.70	23-0/1.84	23-6/1.98	24-1/2.12	25-2/2.41

Column header: Allowable Extreme Fiber Stress In Bending, "Fb" (psi). Last column (right side): RAFTER SIZE (IN) / SPACING (IN).

NOTE: The modulus of elasticity, "E", in 1,000,000 pounds per square inch is shown below each span.

Table No. 7-0
ALLOWABLE SPAN FOR HIGH SLOPE RAFTERS
Slope over 3 in 12 – 30 Lbs. Per Sq. Ft. Live Load
(Heavy Roof Covering)

DESIGN CRITERIA:
Strength – 15 lbs. per sq. ft. dead load plus 30 lbs. per sq. ft. live load determines fiber stress.
Deflection – For 30 lbs. per sq. ft. live load. Limited to span in inches divided by 180.

RAFTERS: Spans are measured along the horizontal projection and loads are considered as applied on the horizontal projection.

HOW TO USE TABLES: Enter table with span of rafters (upper figure in each square). Determine size and spacing (last column) based on stress grade (top row) and modulus of elasticity (lower figure in each square) of lumber to be used.

Each cell shows the allowable span (feet-inches, upper figure) / modulus of elasticity "E" (lower figure).

Allowable Extreme Fiber Stress in Bending, F_b (psi) — 200 through 1400

Rafter Size (in)	Spacing (in)	200	300	400	500	600	700	800	900	1000	1100	1200	1300	1400
2x4	12.0	3-0 / 0.05	3-8 / 0.09	4-3 / 0.15	4-9 / 0.20	5-3 / 0.27	5-8 / 0.34	6-0 / 0.41	6-5 / 0.49	6-9 / 0.58	7-1 / 0.67	7-5 / 0.76	7-8 / 0.86	8-0 / 0.96
2x4	13.7	2-10 / 0.05	3-5 / 0.09	4-0 / 0.14	4-5 / 0.19	4-11 / 0.25	5-3 / 0.32	5-8 / 0.39	6-0 / 0.46	6-4 / 0.54	6-7 / 0.62	6-11 / 0.71	7-2 / 0.80	7-5 / 0.89
2x4	16.0	2-7 / 0.04	3-2 / 0.08	3-8 / 0.13	4-1 / 0.18	4-6 / 0.23	4-11 / 0.29	5-3 / 0.36	5-6 / 0.43	5-10 / 0.50	6-1 / 0.58	6-5 / 0.66	6-8 / 0.74	6-11 / 0.83
2x4	19.2	2-5 / 0.04	2-11 / 0.08	3-4 / 0.12	3-9 / 0.16	4-1 / 0.21	4-5 / 0.27	4-9 / 0.33	5-1 / 0.39	5-4 / 0.46	5-7 / 0.53	5-10 / 0.60	6-1 / 0.68	6-4 / 0.76
2x4	24.0	2-2 / 0.04	2-7 / 0.07	3-0 / 0.10	3-4 / 0.14	3-8 / 0.19	4-0 / 0.24	4-3 / 0.29	4-6 / 0.35	4-9 / 0.41	5-0 / 0.47	5-3 / 0.54	5-5 / 0.61	5-8 / 0.68
2x6	12.0	4-9 / 0.05	5-10 / 0.09	6-8 / 0.15	7-6 / 0.20	8-2 / 0.27	8-10 / 0.34	9-6 / 0.41	10-0 / 0.49	10-7 / 0.58	11-1 / 0.67	11-7 / 0.76	12-1 / 0.86	12-6 / 0.96
2x6	13.7	4-5 / 0.05	5-5 / 0.09	6-3 / 0.14	7-0 / 0.19	7-8 / 0.25	8-3 / 0.32	8-10 / 0.39	9-5 / 0.46	9-11 / 0.54	10-5 / 0.62	10-10 / 0.71	11-3 / 0.80	11-9 / 0.89
2x6	16.0	4-1 / 0.04	5-0 / 0.08	5-10 / 0.13	6-6 / 0.18	7-1 / 0.23	7-8 / 0.29	8-2 / 0.36	8-8 / 0.43	9-2 / 0.50	9-7 / 0.58	10-0 / 0.66	10-5 / 0.74	10-10 / 0.83
2x6	19.2	3-9 / 0.04	4-7 / 0.08	5-4 / 0.12	5-11 / 0.16	6-6 / 0.21	7-0 / 0.27	7-6 / 0.33	7-11 / 0.39	8-4 / 0.46	8-9 / 0.53	9-2 / 0.60	9-6 / 0.68	9-11 / 0.76
2x6	24.0	3-4 / 0.04	4-1 / 0.07	4-9 / 0.10	5-4 / 0.14	5-10 / 0.19	6-3 / 0.24	6-8 / 0.29	7-1 / 0.35	7-6 / 0.41	7-10 / 0.47	8-2 / 0.54	8-6 / 0.61	8-10 / 0.68
2x8	12.0	6-3 / 0.05	7-8 / 0.09	8-10 / 0.15	9-10 / 0.20	10-10 / 0.27	11-8 / 0.34	12-6 / 0.41	13-3 / 0.49	13-11 / 0.58	14-8 / 0.67	15-3 / 0.76	15-11 / 0.86	16-6 / 0.96
2x8	13.7	5-10 / 0.05	7-2 / 0.09	8-3 / 0.14	9-3 / 0.19	10-1 / 0.25	10-11 / 0.32	11-8 / 0.39	12-5 / 0.46	13-1 / 0.54	13-8 / 0.62	14-4 / 0.71	14-11 / 0.80	15-5 / 0.89
2x8	16.0	5-5 / 0.04	6-7 / 0.08	7-8 / 0.13	8-7 / 0.18	9-4 / 0.23	10-1 / 0.29	10-10 / 0.36	11-6 / 0.43	12-1 / 0.50	12-8 / 0.58	13-3 / 0.66	13-9 / 0.74	14-4 / 0.83
2x8	19.2	4-11 / 0.04	6-1 / 0.08	7-0 / 0.12	7-10 / 0.16	8-7 / 0.21	9-3 / 0.27	9-10 / 0.33	10-6 / 0.39	11-0 / 0.46	11-7 / 0.53	12-1 / 0.60	12-7 / 0.68	13-1 / 0.76
2x8	24.0	4-5 / 0.04	5-5 / 0.07	6-3 / 0.10	7-0 / 0.14	7-8 / 0.19	8-3 / 0.24	8-10 / 0.29	9-4 / 0.35	9-10 / 0.41	10-4 / 0.47	10-10 / 0.54	11-3 / 0.61	11-8 / 0.68
2x10	12.0	8-0 / 0.05	9-9 / 0.09	11-3 / 0.15	12-7 / 0.20	13-9 / 0.27	14-11 / 0.34	15-11 / 0.41	16-11 / 0.49	17-10 / 0.58	18-8 / 0.67	19-6 / 0.76	20-4 / 0.86	21-0 / 0.96
2x10	13.7	7-5 / 0.05	9-1 / 0.09	10-6 / 0.14	11-9 / 0.19	12-11 / 0.25	13-11 / 0.32	14-11 / 0.39	15-10 / 0.46	16-8 / 0.54	17-6 / 0.62	18-3 / 0.71	19-0 / 0.80	19-8 / 0.89
2x10	16.0	6-11 / 0.04	8-5 / 0.08	9-9 / 0.13	10-11 / 0.18	11-11 / 0.23	12-11 / 0.29	13-9 / 0.36	14-8 / 0.43	15-5 / 0.50	16-2 / 0.58	16-11 / 0.66	17-6 / 0.74	18-3 / 0.83
2x10	19.2	6-4 / 0.04	7-8 / 0.08	8-11 / 0.12	9-11 / 0.16	10-11 / 0.21	11-9 / 0.27	12-7 / 0.33	13-4 / 0.39	14-1 / 0.46	14-9 / 0.53	15-5 / 0.60	16-1 / 0.68	16-8 / 0.76
2x10	24.0	5-8 / 0.04	6-11 / 0.07	8-0 / 0.10	8-11 / 0.14	9-9 / 0.19	10-6 / 0.24	11-3 / 0.29	11-11 / 0.35	12-7 / 0.41	13-2 / 0.47	13-9 / 0.54	14-4 / 0.61	14-11 / 0.68

Allowable Extreme Fiber Stress in Bending, F_b (psi) — 1500 through 3000

Rafter Size (in)	Spacing (in)	1500	1600	1700	1800	1900	2000	2100	2200	2400	2700	3000
2x4	12.0	8-3 / 1.06	8-6 / 1.17	8-9 / 1.28	9-0 / 1.39	9-3 / 1.51	9-6 / 1.63	9-9 / 1.76	10-0 / 1.88	10-5 / 2.15	11-1 / 2.56	
2x4	13.7	7-9 / 0.99	8-0 / 1.09	8-3 / 1.20	8-5 / 1.30	8-8 / 1.41	8-11 / 1.53	9-2 / 1.64	9-4 / 1.76	9-9 / 2.01	10-4 / 2.40	
2x4	16.0	7-2 / 0.92	7-5 / 1.01	7-7 / 1.11	7-10 / 1.21	8-0 / 1.31	8-3 / 1.41	8-5 / 1.52	8-8 / 1.63	9-0 / 1.86	9-7 / 2.22	10-1 / 2.60
2x4	19.2	6-6 / 0.84	6-9 / 0.92	6-11 / 1.01	7-2 / 1.10	7-4 / 1.20	7-6 / 1.29	7-9 / 1.39	7-11 / 1.49	8-3 / 1.70	8-9 / 2.03	9-3 / 2.37
2x4	24.0	5-10 / 0.75	6-0 / 0.83	6-3 / 0.90	6-5 / 0.99	6-7 / 1.07	6-9 / 1.15	6-11 / 1.24	7-1 / 1.33	7-5 / 1.52	7-10 / 1.81	8-3 / 2.12
2x6	12.0	13-0 / 1.06	13-5 / 1.17	13-10 / 1.28	14-2 / 1.39	14-7 / 1.51	15-0 / 1.63	15-4 / 1.76	15-8 / 1.88	16-5 / 2.15	17-5 / 2.56	
2x6	13.7	12-2 / 0.99	12-6 / 1.09	12-11 / 1.20	13-3 / 1.30	13-8 / 1.41	14-0 / 1.53	14-4 / 1.64	14-8 / 1.76	15-4 / 2.01	16-3 / 2.40	
2x6	16.0	11-3 / 0.92	11-7 / 1.01	11-11 / 1.11	12-4 / 1.21	12-8 / 1.31	13-0 / 1.41	13-3 / 1.52	13-7 / 1.63	14-2 / 1.86	15-1 / 2.22	15-11 / 2.60
2x6	19.2	10-3 / 0.84	10-7 / 0.92	10-11 / 1.01	11-3 / 1.10	11-6 / 1.20	11-10 / 1.29	12-2 / 1.39	12-5 / 1.49	13-0 / 1.70	13-9 / 2.03	14-6 / 2.37
2x6	24.0	9-2 / 0.75	9-6 / 0.83	9-9 / 0.90	10-0 / 0.99	10-4 / 1.07	10-7 / 1.15	10-10 / 1.24	11-1 / 1.33	11-7 / 1.52	12-4 / 1.81	13-0 / 2.12
2x8	12.0	17-1 / 1.06	17-8 / 1.17	18-2 / 1.28	18-9 / 1.39	19-3 / 1.51	19-9 / 1.63	20-3 / 1.76	20-8 / 1.88	21-7 / 2.15	22-11 / 2.56	
2x8	13.7	16-0 / 0.99	16-6 / 1.09	17-0 / 1.20	17-6 / 1.30	18-0 / 1.41	18-5 / 1.53	18-11 / 1.64	19-4 / 1.76	20-3 / 2.01	21-5 / 2.40	
2x8	16.0	14-10 / 0.92	15-3 / 1.01	15-9 / 1.11	16-3 / 1.21	16-8 / 1.31	17-1 / 1.41	17-6 / 1.52	17-11 / 1.63	18-9 / 1.86	19-10 / 2.22	20-11 / 2.60
2x8	19.2	13-6 / 0.84	13-11 / 0.92	14-5 / 1.01	14-10 / 1.10	15-2 / 1.20	15-7 / 1.29	16-0 / 1.39	16-4 / 1.49	17-1 / 1.70	18-2 / 2.03	19-1 / 2.37
2x8	24.0	12-1 / 0.75	12-6 / 0.83	12-10 / 0.90	13-3 / 0.99	13-7 / 1.07	13-11 / 1.15	14-4 / 1.24	14-8 / 1.33	15-3 / 1.52	16-3 / 1.81	17-1 / 2.12
2x10	12.0	21-10 / 1.06	22-6 / 1.17	23-3 / 1.28	23-11 / 1.39	24-6 / 1.51	25-2 / 1.63	25-10 / 1.76	26-5 / 1.88	27-7 / 2.15	29-3 / 2.56	
2x10	13.7	20-5 / 0.99	21-1 / 1.09	21-9 / 1.20	22-4 / 1.30	22-11 / 1.41	23-7 / 1.53	24-2 / 1.64	24-8 / 1.76	25-10 / 2.01	27-4 / 2.40	
2x10	16.0	18-11 / 0.92	19-6 / 1.01	20-1 / 1.11	20-8 / 1.21	21-3 / 1.31	21-10 / 1.41	22-4 / 1.52	22-10 / 1.63	23-11 / 1.86	25-4 / 2.22	26-8 / 2.60
2x10	19.2	17-3 / 0.84	17-10 / 0.92	18-4 / 1.01	18-11 / 1.10	19-5 / 1.20	19-11 / 1.29	20-5 / 1.39	20-10 / 1.49	21-10 / 1.70	23-2 / 2.03	24-5 / 2.37
2x10	24.0	15-5 / 0.75	15-11 / 0.83	16-5 / 0.90	16-11 / 0.99	17-4 / 1.07	17-10 / 1.15	18-3 / 1.24	18-8 / 1.33	19-6 / 1.52	20-8 / 1.81	21-10 / 2.12

NOTE: The modulus of elasticity, "E", in 1,000,000 pounds per square inch is shown below each span.

Table No. 7-R

ALLOWABLE SPAN FOR HIGH SLOPE RAFTERS

Slope over 3 in 12 — 30 Lbs. Per Sq. Ft. Live Load

(Light Roof Covering)

DESIGN CRITERIA:
Strength — 7 lbs. per sq. ft. dead load plus 30 lbs. per sq. ft. live load determines fiber stress.
Deflection — For 30 lbs. per sq. ft. live load. Limited to span in inches divided by 180.

RAFTERS: Spans are measured along the horizontal projection and loads are considered as applied on the horizontal projection.

HOW TO USE TABLES: Enter table with span of rafters (upper figure in each square). Determine size and spacing (last column) based on stress grade (top row) and modulus of elasticity (lower figure in each square) of lumber to be used.

NOTE: The modulus of elasticity, "E", in 1,000,000 pounds per square inch is shown below each span.

Each cell shows allowable span (ft‑in) over required modulus of elasticity "E" (in 1,000,000 psi).

Allowable Extreme Fiber Stress in Bending, "Fb" (psi.) — 200 to 1300

Rafter Size	Spacing (in)	200	300	400	500	600	700	800	900	1000	1100	1200	1300
2x4	12.0	3-4 / 0.07	4-1 / 0.13	4-8 / 0.20	5-3 / 0.27	5-9 / 0.36	6-3 / 0.45	6-8 / 0.55	7-1 / 0.66	7-5 / 0.77	7-9 / 0.89	8-2 / 1.02	8-6 / 1.15
2x4	13.7	3-1 / 0.06	3-10 / 0.12	4-5 / 0.18	4-11 / 0.26	5-5 / 0.34	5-10 / 0.42	6-3 / 0.52	6-7 / 0.62	6-11 / 0.72	7-3 / 0.84	7-7 / 0.95	7-11 / 1.07
2x4	16.0	2-11 / 0.06	3-6 / 0.11	4-1 / 0.17	4-7 / 0.24	5-0 / 0.31	5-5 / 0.39	5-9 / 0.48	6-1 / 0.57	6-5 / 0.67	6-9 / 0.77	7-1 / 0.88	7-4 / 0.99
2x4	19.2	2-8 / 0.05	3-3 / 0.10	3-9 / 0.15	4-2 / 0.22	4-7 / 0.28	4-11 / 0.36	5-3 / 0.44	5-7 / 0.52	5-10 / 0.61	6-2 / 0.71	6-5 / 0.80	6-8 / 0.91
2x4	24.0	2-4 / 0.05	2-11 / 0.09	3-4 / 0.14	3-9 / 0.19	4-1 / 0.25	4-5 / 0.32	4-8 / 0.39	5-0 / 0.47	5-3 / 0.55	5-6 / 0.63	5-9 / 0.72	6-0 / 0.81
2x6	12.0	5-3 / 0.07	6-5 / 0.13	7-5 / 0.20	8-3 / 0.27	9-1 / 0.36	9-9 / 0.45	10-5 / 0.55	11-1 / 0.66	11-8 / 0.77	12-3 / 0.89	12-9 / 1.02	13-4 / 1.15
2x6	13.7	4-11 / 0.06	6-0 / 0.12	6-11 / 0.18	7-9 / 0.26	8-5 / 0.34	9-2 / 0.42	9-9 / 0.52	10-4 / 0.62	10-11 / 0.72	11-5 / 0.84	12-0 / 0.95	12-5 / 1.07
2x6	16.0	4-6 / 0.06	5-6 / 0.11	6-5 / 0.17	7-2 / 0.24	7-10 / 0.31	8-5 / 0.39	9-1 / 0.48	9-7 / 0.57	10-1 / 0.67	10-7 / 0.77	11-1 / 0.88	11-6 / 0.99
2x6	19.2	4-2 / 0.05	5-1 / 0.10	5-10 / 0.15	6-6 / 0.22	7-2 / 0.28	7-9 / 0.36	8-3 / 0.44	8-9 / 0.52	9-3 / 0.61	9-8 / 0.71	10-1 / 0.80	10-6 / 0.91
2x6	24.0	3-8 / 0.05	4-6 / 0.09	5-3 / 0.14	5-10 / 0.19	6-5 / 0.25	6-11 / 0.32	7-5 / 0.39	7-10 / 0.47	8-3 / 0.55	8-8 / 0.63	9-1 / 0.72	9-5 / 0.81
2x8	12.0	6-11 / 0.07	8-5 / 0.13	9-9 / 0.20	10-11 / 0.27	11-11 / 0.36	12-10 / 0.45	13-9 / 0.55	14-7 / 0.66	15-5 / 0.77	16-2 / 0.89	16-10 / 1.02	17-7 / 1.15
2x8	13.7	6-5 / 0.06	7-11 / 0.12	9-1 / 0.18	10-2 / 0.26	11-2 / 0.34	12-1 / 0.42	12-10 / 0.52	13-8 / 0.62	14-5 / 0.72	15-1 / 0.84	15-9 / 0.95	16-5 / 1.07
2x8	16.0	6-0 / 0.06	7-4 / 0.11	8-5 / 0.17	9-5 / 0.24	10-4 / 0.31	11-2 / 0.39	11-11 / 0.48	12-8 / 0.57	13-4 / 0.67	14-0 / 0.77	14-7 / 0.88	15-2 / 0.99
2x8	19.2	5-5 / 0.05	6-8 / 0.10	7-8 / 0.15	8-7 / 0.22	9-5 / 0.28	10-2 / 0.36	10-11 / 0.44	11-6 / 0.52	12-2 / 0.61	12-9 / 0.71	13-4 / 0.80	13-10 / 0.91
2x8	24.0	4-10 / 0.05	6-0 / 0.09	6-11 / 0.14	7-8 / 0.19	8-5 / 0.25	9-1 / 0.32	9-9 / 0.39	10-4 / 0.47	10-11 / 0.55	11-5 / 0.63	11-11 / 0.72	12-5 / 0.81
2x10	12.0	8-9 / 0.07	10-9 / 0.13	12-5 / 0.20	13-11 / 0.27	15-2 / 0.36	16-5 / 0.45	17-7 / 0.55	18-7 / 0.66	19-8 / 0.77	20-7 / 0.89	21-6 / 1.02	22-5 / 1.15
2x10	13.7	8-3 / 0.06	10-1 / 0.12	11-7 / 0.18	13-0 / 0.26	14-3 / 0.34	15-4 / 0.42	16-5 / 0.52	17-5 / 0.62	18-4 / 0.72	19-3 / 0.84	20-1 / 0.95	20-11 / 1.07
2x10	16.0	7-7 / 0.06	9-4 / 0.11	10-9 / 0.17	12-0 / 0.24	13-2 / 0.31	14-3 / 0.39	15-2 / 0.48	16-2 / 0.57	17-0 / 0.67	17-10 / 0.77	18-7 / 0.88	19-5 / 0.99
2x10	19.2	6-11 / 0.05	8-6 / 0.10	9-10 / 0.15	11-0 / 0.22	12-0 / 0.28	13-0 / 0.36	13-11 / 0.44	14-9 / 0.52	15-6 / 0.61	16-3 / 0.71	17-0 / 0.80	17-8 / 0.91
2x10	24.0	6-2 / 0.05	7-7 / 0.09	8-9 / 0.14	9-10 / 0.19	10-9 / 0.25	11-7 / 0.32	12-5 / 0.39	13-2 / 0.47	13-11 / 0.55	14-7 / 0.63	15-2 / 0.72	15-10 / 0.81

Allowable Extreme Fiber Stress in Bending, "Fb" (psi.) — 1400 to 2700

Rafter Size	Spacing (in)	1400	1500	1600	1700	1800	1900	2000	2100	2200	2400	2700
2x4	12.0	8-9 / 1.28	9-1 / 1.42	9-5 / 1.57	9-8 / 1.72	10-0 / 1.87	10-3 / 2.03	10-6 / 2.19	10-9 / 2.36	11-0 / 2.53		
2x4	13.7	8-3 / 1.20	8-6 / 1.33	8-9 / 1.47	9-1 / 1.61	9-4 / 1.75	9-7 / 1.90	9-9 / 2.05	10-1 / 2.20	10-4 / 2.36		
2x4	16.0	7-7 / 1.11	7-11 / 1.23	8-2 / 1.36	8-5 / 1.49	8-8 / 1.62	8-10 / 1.76	9-1 / 1.90	9-4 / 2.04	9-7 / 2.19	10-0 / 2.49	
2x4	19.2	6-11 / 1.01	7-2 / 1.12	7-5 / 1.24	7-8 / 1.36	7-11 / 1.48	8-1 / 1.60	8-4 / 1.73	8-6 / 1.86	8-9 / 2.00	9-1 / 2.28	
2x4	24.0	6-3 / 0.91	6-5 / 1.01	6-8 / 1.11	6-10 / 1.21	7-1 / 1.32	7-3 / 1.43	7-5 / 1.55	7-7 / 1.67	7-9 / 1.79	8-2 / 2.04	8-8 / 2.43
2x6	12.0	13-10 / 1.28	14-4 / 1.42	14-9 / 1.57	15-3 / 1.72	15-8 / 1.87	16-1 / 2.03	16-6 / 2.19	16-11 / 2.36	17-4 / 2.53		
2x6	13.7	12-11 / 1.20	13-4 / 1.33	13-10 / 1.47	14-3 / 1.61	14-8 / 1.75	15-1 / 1.90	15-5 / 2.05	15-10 / 2.20	16-2 / 2.36		
2x6	16.0	12-0 / 1.11	12-5 / 1.23	12-9 / 1.36	13-2 / 1.49	13-7 / 1.62	13-11 / 1.76	14-4 / 1.90	14-8 / 2.04	15-0 / 2.19	15-8 / 2.49	
2x6	19.2	10-11 / 1.01	11-4 / 1.12	11-8 / 1.24	12-0 / 1.36	12-5 / 1.48	12-9 / 1.60	13-1 / 1.73	13-4 / 1.86	13-8 / 2.00	14-4 / 2.28	
2x6	24.0	9-9 / 0.91	10-1 / 1.01	10-5 / 1.11	10-9 / 1.21	11-1 / 1.32	11-5 / 1.43	11-8 / 1.55	12-0 / 1.67	12-3 / 1.79	12-9 / 2.04	13-7 / 2.43
2x8	12.0	18-2 / 1.28	18-10 / 1.42	19-6 / 1.57	20-1 / 1.72	20-8 / 1.87	21-3 / 2.03	21-9 / 2.19	22-4 / 2.36	22-10 / 2.53		
2x8	13.7	17-0 / 1.20	17-8 / 1.33	18-2 / 1.47	18-9 / 1.61	19-4 / 1.75	19-10 / 1.90	20-4 / 2.05	20-10 / 2.20	21-4 / 2.36		
2x8	16.0	15-9 / 1.11	16-4 / 1.23	16-10 / 1.36	17-4 / 1.49	17-11 / 1.62	18-4 / 1.76	18-10 / 1.90	19-4 / 2.04	19-9 / 2.19	20-8 / 2.49	
2x8	19.2	14-5 / 1.01	14-11 / 1.12	15-5 / 1.24	15-10 / 1.36	16-4 / 1.48	16-9 / 1.60	17-2 / 1.73	17-8 / 1.86	18-1 / 2.00	18-10 / 2.28	
2x8	24.0	12-10 / 0.91	13-4 / 1.01	13-9 / 1.11	14-2 / 1.21	14-7 / 1.32	15-0 / 1.43	15-5 / 1.55	15-9 / 1.67	16-2 / 1.79	16-10 / 2.04	17-11 / 2.43
2x10	12.0	23-3 / 1.28	24-1 / 1.42	24-10 / 1.57	25-7 / 1.72	26-4 / 1.87	27-1 / 2.03	27-9 / 2.19	28-5 / 2.36	29-1 / 2.53		
2x10	13.7	21-9 / 1.20	22-6 / 1.33	23-3 / 1.47	23-11 / 1.61	24-8 / 1.75	25-4 / 1.90	26-0 / 2.05	26-7 / 2.20	27-3 / 2.36		
2x10	16.0	20-1 / 1.11	20-10 / 1.23	21-6 / 1.36	22-2 / 1.49	22-10 / 1.62	23-5 / 1.76	24-1 / 1.90	24-8 / 2.04	25-3 / 2.19		
2x10	19.2	18-4 / 1.01	19-0 / 1.12	19-8 / 1.24	20-3 / 1.36	20-10 / 1.48	21-5 / 1.60	21-11 / 1.73	22-6 / 1.86	23-0 / 2.00	24-1 / 2.28	
2x10	24.0	16-5 / 0.91	17-0 / 1.01	17-7 / 1.11	18-1 / 1.21	18-7 / 1.32	19-2 / 1.43	19-8 / 1.55	20-1 / 1.67	20-7 / 1.79	21-6 / 2.04	22-10 / 2.43

Table No. R-602.2.1b
ALLOWABLE SPAN FOR GIRDERS AND REQUIRED SIZE OF COLUMNS AND FOOTINGS TO SUPPORT ROOFS, INTERIOR BEARING PARTITIONS AND FLOORS

SIZE OF GIRDER REQUIRED		SPACING OF GIRDER2 "S"	TYPE OF LOADING3			SIZE OF COLUMNS REQUIRED4		SIZE OF PLAIN CONCRETE FOOTING REQUIRED4
Wood1			A	B	C	Steel	Wood	
4" × 12"	6" × 10"	10' 15' 20'	5'-6" 4'-0" —	— — —	— — —	3" Steel pipe5	4" × 4"	2' × 2' × 8"
(7)	6" × 12"	10' 15' 20'	8'-6" 6'-0" 4'-6"	5'-0" 4'-0" —	— — —			
(7)	(7)	10' 15' 20'	12'-0" 10'-0" 8'-0"	9'-0" 8'-0" 7'-0"	8'-0" 7'-0" 6'-0"		6" × 6"	4' × 4' × 16"6
(7)	(7)	10' 15' 20'	16'-0" 13'-6" 12'-0"	12'-6" 10'-6" 9'-6"	11'-0" 10'-0" 8'-0"		8" × 8"	4'-3" × 4'-3" × 17"6
(7)	(7)	10' 15' 20'	20'-0" 17'-0" 15'-0"	16'-0" 13'-6" 12'-0"	13'-6" 11'-6" 10'-0"			

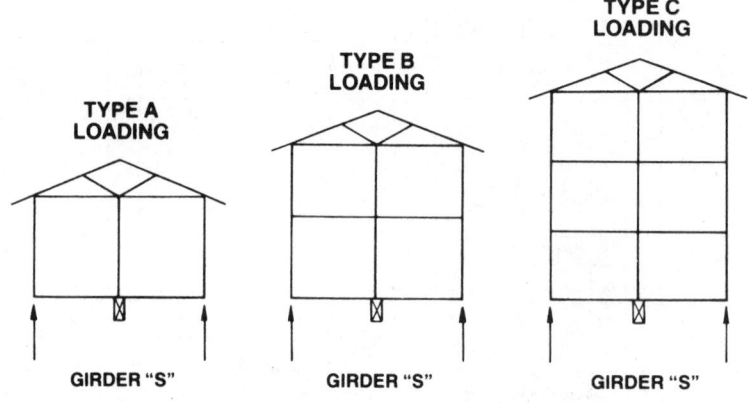

TYPE A LOADING — GIRDER "S"

TYPE B LOADING — GIRDER "S"

TYPE C LOADING — GIRDER "S"

[1]Spans for wood girders are based on No. 2 grade lumber. No. 3 grade may be used with appropriate design.

[2]The spacing "S" is the tributary load in the girder. It is found by adding the unsupported spans of the floor joists on each side which are supported by the girder and dividing by 2.

[3]Figures under "type of loading" columns are the allowable girder spans.

[4]Required size of columns is based on girder support from two sides. Size of footing is based on allowable soil pressure of 2,000 pounds per square foot.

[5]Standard weight.

[6]Footing thickness is based on the use of plain concrete with a specified compressive strength of not less than 2,500 pounds per square inch at 28 days. If approved, the footing thickness may be reduced based on an engineering design utilizing higher-strength concrete and/or reinforcement.

[7]Girder will require an approved design.

Table No. R-602.2.1a
ALLOWABLE SPAN FOR GIRDERS SUPPORTING ONE FLOOR ONLY[3]

SIZE OF WOOD GIRDER[4]		FLOOR LIVE LOAD (psf)	SPACING OF GIRDERS[2] "S"				
			4'	6'	8'	10'	16'
4" × 4"	—	30	5'-6"	4'-6"	3'-6"	3'-0"	2'-6"
		40	5'-0"	4'-0"	3'-6"	3'-0"	2'-6"
4" × 6"	—	30	8'-0"	6'-6"	5'-6"	5'-0"	4'-6"
		40	7'-6"	6'-0"	5'-6"	4'-6"	4'-0"
4" × 8"	6" × 6"	30	11'-0"	9'-0"	8'-0"	7'-0"	5'-6"
		40	10'-0"	8'-6"	7'-6"	6'-6"	5'-0"
4" × 10"	6" × 8"	30	14'-0"	11'-6"	10'-0"	8'-6"	6'-0"
		40	13'-0"	10'-6"	9'-6"	8'-6"	5'-6"
4" × 12"	6" × 10"	30	16'-6"	14'-0"	12'-0"	11'-0"	9'-0"
		40	16'-0"	12'-6"	11'-0"	10'-0"	8'-0"

[1]Spans are based on No. 2 grade lumber.

[2]The spacing "S" is the tributary load to the girder. It is found by adding the unsupported spans of the floor joists on each side which are supported by the girder and dividing by 2.

[3]Spans and girder sizes may be computed independently of the above table when designed in accordance with accepted engineering practice and substantiating data are provided and submitted as required.

Table No. R-201.4
MINIMUM UNIFORMLY DISTRIBUTED LIVE LOADS

USE	LIVE LOAD
Balconies (exterior)	60
Decks	40
Fire escapes	40
Garages (passenger cars only)	50
Attics (no storage with roof slope not steeper than 3 in 12)	10
Attics (limited attic storage)	20
Dwelling units (except sleeping rooms)	40
Sleeping rooms	30
Stairs	40

Table No. R-402.3d
MAXIMUM STUD SPACING (INCHES)

STUD SIZE	SUPPORTING ROOF AND CEILING ONLY	SUPPORTING ONE FLOOR ROOF AND CEILING	SUPPORTING TWO FLOORS ROOF AND CEILING	SUPPORTING ONE FLOOR ONLY
2 × 4	24[1]	16	—	24[1]
3 × 4	24[1]	24	16	24
2 × 5	24	24	—	24
2 × 6	24	24	16	24

[1]Shall be reduced to 16 inches if Utility grade studs are used.

Table No. R-503.4.1
ALLOWABLE SPANS FOR LINTELS
SUPPORTING MASONRY VENEER

SIZE OF STEEL ANGLE[1] [3]	NO STORY ABOVE	ONE STORY ABOVE	TWO STORIES ABOVE	NO. OF 1/2" OR EQUIVALENT REINFORCING BARS[2]
3 × 3 × 1/4	6'-0"	3'-6"	3'-0"	1
4 × 3 × 1/4	8'-0"	5'-0"	3'-0"	1
6 × 3 1/2 × 1/4	14'-0"	8'-0"	3'-6"	2
2-6 × 3 1/2 × 1/4	20'-0"	11'-0"	5'-0"	4

[1]Long leg of the angle shall be placed in a vertical position.

[2]Depth of reinforced lintels shall be not less than 8 inches and all cells of hollow masonry lintels shall be grouted solid. Reinforcing bars shall extend not less than 8 inches into the support.

[3]Steel members indicated are adequate typical examples; other steel members meeting structural design requirements may be used.

Table No. R-402.3a
FASTENER SCHEDULE FOR STRUCTURAL MEMBERS

DESCRIPTION OF BUILDING MATERIALS	NUMBER & TYPE OF FASTENER 1 2 3 5	SPACING OF FASTENERS
Joist to sill or girder, toe nail	3-8d	—
1" × 6" subfloor or less to each joist, face nail	2-8d 2 staples, 1¾"	— —
Wider than 1" × 6" subfloor to each joist, face nail	3-8d 4 staples, 1¾"	— —
2" subfloor to joist or girder, blind and face nail	2-16d	—
Sole plate to joist or blocking, face nail	16d	16" o.c.
Top or sole plate to stud, end nail	2-16d	—
Stud to sole plate, toe nail	3-8d or 2-16d	—
Double studs, face nail	16d	24" o.c.
Double top plates, face nail	16d	24" o.c.
Top plates, laps and intersections, face nail	2-16d	—
Continued header, two pieces	16d	16" o.c. along each edge
Ceiling joists to plate, toe nail	3-8d	—
Continuous header to stud, toe nail	4-8d	—
Ceiling joist, taps over partitions, face nail	3-16d	—
Ceiling joist to parallel rafters, face nail	3-16d	—
Rafter to plate, toe nail	2-16d	—
1" brace to each stud and plate, face nail	2-8d 2 staples, 1¾"	— —
1" × 6" sheathing to each bearing, face nail	2-8d 2 staples, 1¾"	— —
1" × 8" sheathing to each bearing, face nail	2-8d 3 staples, 1¾"	— —
Wider than 1" × 8" sheathing to each bearing, face nail	3-8d 4 staples, 1¾"	— —
Built-up corner studs	16d	24" o.c.
Built-up girder and beams	16d	32" o.c. at top and bottom and staggered two 20d at ends and at each splice
2" planks	2-16d	At each bearing
Roof rafters to ridge, valley or hip rafters: toe nail / face nail	4-16d 3-16d	— —
Rafter ties to rafters, face nail	3-8d	—

DESCRIPTION OF BUILDING MATERIALS	DESCRIPTION OF FASTENER 2 3 5	SPACING OF FASTENERS — Edges	SPACING OF FASTENERS — Intermediate Supports 4
Plywood and particleboard, roof and wall sheathing to frame			
5/16"-1/2"	6d Staple 16 ga.	6"	12"
19/32"-3/4"	8d smooth or 6d deformed	6"	12"
7/8"-1"	8d	6"	12"
1 1/8"-1 1/4"	10d smooth or 8d deformed	6"	12"
Other wall sheathing 7			
1/2" fiberboard sheathing 6	1 1/2" galvanized roofing nail 6d common nail Staple 16 ga., 1 1/8" long	3"	6"
25/32" fiberboard sheathing 6	1 3/4" galvanized roofing nail 8d common nail Staple 16 ga., 1 1/2" long	3"	6"
1/2" gypsum sheathing	1 1/2" galvanized roofing nail 6d common nail Staple 16 ga., 1 1/2" long	4"	8"
Particleboard roof and wall sheathing 5/16"-1/2"	6d common nail	6"	12"
5/8"-3/4"	8d common nail Staple 16 ga., 1 1/2" long	6"	12"
Plywood and particleboard, combination subfloor-underlayment to framing			
3/4" and less	6d deformed	6"	12"
7/8"-1"	8d deformed	6"	12"
1 1/8"-1 1/4"	10d smooth or 8d deformed	6"	6"

1 All nails are smooth-common, box or deformed shanks except where otherwise stated.

2 Nail is a general description and may be T-head, modified round head or round head.

3 Staples are No. 16 gauge wire and have a minimum 7/16-inch O.D. crown width.

4 Nails shall be spaced at not more than 6 inches o.c. at all supports where spans are 48 inches or greater.

5 The number of fasteners required for connections not included in this table shall be based on values set forth in Table No. R-402.3a(1).

6 Four-foot by 8-foot or 4-foot by 9-foot panels shall be applied vertically.

7 Gypsum sheathing shall conform to ASTM C79 listed in Section S-26.402. Fiberboard sheathing shall conform to AHA 194.1, ASTM D277, and ASTM C208 listed in Section S-26.402. Other sheathing materials shall be approved by the building official.

Table No. R-402.3a(1)
ALTERNATE ATTACHMENTS

NOMINAL MATERIAL THICKNESS	DESCRIPTION[1] [2] OF FASTENER & LENGTH	SPACING[3] OF FASTENERS	
		Edges	Intermediate Supports
Plywood or Particleboard Subfloor, Roof and Wall Sheathing to Framing			
5/16"	.097 - .099 Nail 1 1/2" Staple 15 ga. 1 3/8"	6"	12"
3/8"	Staple 15 ga. 1 3/8"	6"	12"
	.097 - .099 Nail 1 1/2"	4"	10"
15/32" and 1/2"	Staple 15 ga. 1 1/2"	6"	12"
	.097 - .099 Nail 1 5/8"	3"	6"
19/32" and 5/8"	.113 Nail 1 7/8" Staple 15 and 16 ga. 1 5/8"	6"	12"
	.097 - .099 Nail 1 3/4"	3"	6"
23/32" and 3/4"	Staple 14 ga. 1 3/4"	6"	12"
	Staple 15 ga. 1 3/4"	5"	10"
	.097 - .099 Nail 1 7/8"	3"	6"
1"	Staple 14 ga. 2"	5"	10"
	.113 Nail 2 1/4" Staple 15 ga. 2"	4"	8"
	.097 - .099 Nail 2 1/8"	3"	6"
Floor Underlayment; Plywood—Hardboard—Particleboard			
1/4" and 5/16"	.097 - .099 Nail 1 1/2" Staple 15 and 16 ga. 1 1/4"	6"	12"
	.080 Nail 1 1/4"	5"	10"
	Staple 18 ga. 3/16 crown 7/8"	3"	6"
3/8"	.097 - .099 Nail 1 1/2" Staple 15 and 16 ga. 1 3/8"	6"	12"
	.080 Nail 1 3/8"	5"	10"
1/2"	.113 Nail 1 7/8" Staple 15 and 16 ga. 1 1/2"	6"	12"
	.097 - .099 Nail 1 3/4"	5"	10"

[1]Nail is a general description and may be T-head, modified round head, or round head.

[2]Staples shall have a minimum crown width of 7/16-inch o.d. except as noted.

[3]Nails or staples shall be spaced at not more than 6 inches o.c. at all supports where spans are 48 inches or greater. Nails or staples shall be spaced at not more than 10 inches o.c. at intermediate supports for floors.

Appendix C
Joist Connectors

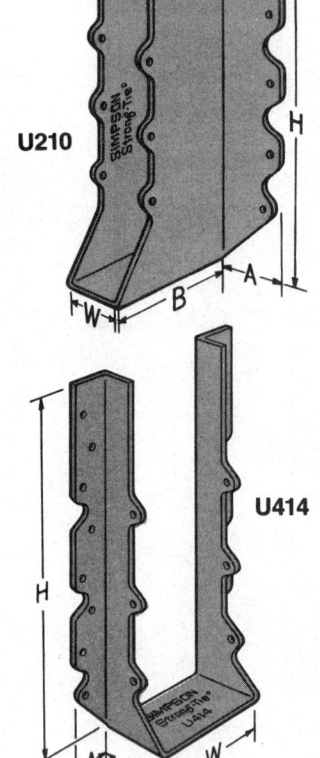

MATERIAL: 16 gauge steel
FINISH: Galvanized
OPTIONS AVAILABLE: Sloped and/or skewed models, see SLOPED AND/OR SKEWED U AND HU HANGERS on page 29.
CODE ACCEPTANCE: ICBO accepted; see Evaluation Report No. 1258.

MODEL NO.	JOIST SIZE	DIMENSIONS				FASTENERS		AVG. ULT.	ALLOWABLE LOADS [1]			
		W	H	B	A	HEADER	JOIST		NORMAL		MAXIMUM	
									10d	16d	10d	16d
U24	2x4	1⁹/₁₆	3 ¹/₈	1¹/₂	⁷/₈	4 – 16d	2 – 10dx1 ¹/₂	2575	435	535	540	670
U26	2x6,8	1⁹/₁₆	4 ³/₄	2	1¹/₄	6 – 16d	4 – 10dx1 ¹/₂	3680	650	805	815	1005
U210	2x10,12,14	1⁹/₁₆	7¹³/₁₆	2	1¹/₄	10 – 16d	6 – 10dx1 ¹/₂	6200	1085	1270	1355	1420
U214	2x14,16	1⁹/₁₆	10	2	1¹/₄	12 – 16d	8 – 10dx1 ¹/₂	7200	1300	1525	1630	1750
U24R	ROUGH 2x4	2	3⁵/₈	2	1¹/₄	4 – 16d	2 – 10dx1 ¹/₂	2575	435	755	540	755
U26R	ROUGH 2x6,8	2	5⁵/₈	2	1¹/₄	8 – 16d	4 – 10dx1 ¹/₂	3680	650	1160	815	1160
U210R	ROUGH 2x10,12,14	2	9¹/₈	2	1¹/₄	14 – 16d	6 – 10dx1 ¹/₂	6200	1085	1270	1355	1420
U34	3x4	2⁹/₁₆	3³/₈	2	1¹/₄	4 – 16d	2 – 10d	2600	470	535	590	670
U36	3x6,8	2⁹/₁₆	5³/₈	2	1¹/₄	8 – 16d	4 – 10d	5000	945	1070	1180	1345
U310	3x10,12	2⁹/₁₆	8⁷/₈	2	1¹/₄	14 – 16d	6 – 10d	9800	1650	1875	2065	2350
U314	3x14,16	2⁹/₁₆	10¹/₂	2	1¹/₄	16 – 16d	6 – 10d	11000	1890	2145	2360	2690
U24–2	(2) 2x4	3¹/₈	3	2	1¹/₄	4 – 16d	2 – 10d	2600	470	535	590	670
U26–2	(2) 2x6,8	3¹/₈	5	2	1¹/₄	8 – 16d	4 – 10d	5000	945	1070	1180	1345
U210–2	(2) 2x10,12,14	3¹/₈	8¹/₂	2	1¹/₄	14 – 16d	6 – 10d	9800	1650	1875	2065	2350
U44	4x4	3⁹/₁₆	2⁷/₈	2	1¹/₄	4 – 16d	2 – 10d	2600	470	535	590	670
U46	4x6,8	3⁹/₁₆	4⁷/₈	2	1¹/₄	8 – 16d	4 – 10d	5000	945	1070	1180	1345
U410	4x10,12	3⁹/₁₆	8³/₈	2	1¹/₄	14 – 16d	6 – 10d	9800	1650	1875	2065	2350
U414	4x14,16	3⁹/₁₆	10	2	1¹/₄	16 – 16d	6 – 10d	11000	1890	2145	2360	2690
U44R	ROUGH 4x4	4	2⁵/₈	2	1¹/₄	4 – 16d	2 – 16d	2600	470	535	590	670
U46R	ROUGH 4x6,8	4	4⁵/₈	2	1¹/₄	8 – 16d	4 – 16d	5000	945	1070	1180	1345
U410R	ROUGH 4x10,12,14	4	8¹/₈	2	1¹/₄	14 – 16d	6 – 16d	9800	1650	1875	2065	2350
U26–3	(3) 2x6,8	4⁵/₈	4¹/₄	2	⁷/₈	8 – 16d	2 – 10d	5000	945	1070	1180	1345
U210–3	(3) 2x10,12,14	4⁵/₈	7³/₄	2	⁷/₈	14 – 16d	6 – 10d	9800	1650	1875	2065	2350
U66	6x6,8	5¹/₂	5	2	1¹/₄	8 – 16d	4 – 10d	5000	945	1070	1180	1345
U610	6x10	5¹/₂	8¹/₂	2	1¹/₄	14 – 16d	6 – 10d	9800	1650	1875	2065	2350
U66R	ROUGH 6x6,8	6	5	2	1¹/₄	8 – 16d	4 – 16d	5000	945	1070	1180	1345
U610R	ROUGH 6x10,12,14	6	8¹/₂	2	1¹/₄	14 – 16d	6 – 16d	9800	1650	1875	2065	2350

1. The allowable loads under the "10d" column heading are the loads allowed when 10d common nails are used instead of the 16d header nails.

Courtesy Simpson Strong-Tie.

HU/HHU HEAVY DUTY JOIST HANGERS

MODEL NO.	JOIST SIZE	DIMENSIONS				FASTENERS[1]		AVG. ULT.	ALLOWABLE LOADS		
		W	H	B	A	HEADER	JOIST		UPLIFT	NORM.	MAX.
HU26	2x4,6	1⁹/₁₆	3¹/₁₆	2	1¹/₈	4 – 16d	2 – 10dx1¹/₂	2600	210	535	670
HU28	2x8	1⁹/₁₆	5¹/₄	2	1¹/₈	6 – 16d	4 – 10dx1¹/₂	3700	420	805	1010
HU210	2x10	1⁹/₁₆	7¹/₈	2	1¹/₈	8 – 16d	4 – 10dx1¹/₂	4900	420	1070	1345
HU212	2x12	1⁹/₁₆	9	2	1¹/₈	10 – 16d	6 – 10dx1¹/₂	6200	630	1340	1680
HU214	2x14	1⁹/₁₆	10¹/₈	2¹/₂	1¹/₈	12 – 16d	6 – 10dx1¹/₂	8500	630	1610	2015
HU34	3x4	2⁹/₁₆	3³/₈	2	1¹/₈	4 – 16d	2 – 10d	2600	210	535	670
HU36	3x6	2⁹/₁₆	5³/₈	2	1¹/₈	8 – 16d	4 – 10d	9474	420	1070	1345
HU38	3x8	2⁹/₁₆	7¹/₈	2	1¹/₈	10 – 16d	4 – 10d	11383	420	1340	1680
HU310	3x10	2⁹/₁₆	8⁷/₈	2	1¹/₈	14 – 16d	6 – 10d	14566	630	1875	2350
HU312	3x12	2⁹/₁₆	10⁵/₈	2¹/₂	1¹/₄	16 – 16d	6 – 10d	14316	630	2145	2690
HU314	3x14	2⁹/₁₆	12³/₈	2¹/₂	1¹/₄	18 – 16d	8 – 10d	14900	840	2410	3010
HU316	3x16	2⁹/₁₆	14¹/₈	2¹/₂	1¹/₄	20 – 16d	8 – 10d	14900	840	2680	3360
HU24 – 2	(2) 2x4	3¹/₈	3¹/₁₆	2	1¹/₈	4 – 16d	2 – 10d	2600	210	535	670
HU26 – 2	(2) 2x6	3¹/₈	5¹/₁₆	2	1¹/₈	8 – 16d	4 – 10d	9474	420	1070	1345
HHU26 – 2	(2) 2x6	3¹/₈	5¹/₁₆	2¹/₂	1¹/₄	8 – N20AN	4 – N20AN	9474	695	1390	1740
HU28 – 2	(2) 2x8	3¹/₈	6¹³/₁₆	2	1¹/₈	10 – 16d	4 – 10d	11383	420	1340	1680
HHU28 – 2	(2) 2x8	3¹/₈	6¹³/₁₆	2¹/₂	1¹/₄	10 – N20AN	4 – N20AN	11383	695	1740	2170
HU210 – 2	(2) 2x10	3¹/₈	8⁹/₁₆	2	1¹/₈	14 – 16d	6 – 10d	14566	630	1875	2350
HHU210 – 2	(2) 2x10	3¹/₈	8⁹/₁₆	2¹/₂	1¹/₄	14 – N20AN	6 – N20AN	14566	1045	2435	3040
HU212 – 2	(2) 2x12	3¹/₈	10⁵/₁₆	2¹/₂	1¹/₄	16 – 16d	6 – 10d	14316	630	2145	2690
HHU212 – 2	(2) 2x12	3¹/₈	10⁵/₁₆	2¹/₂	1¹/₄	16 – N20AN	6 – N20AN	14316	1045	2780	3475
HU214 – 2	(2) 2x14	3¹/₈	12¹/₁₆	2¹/₂	1¹/₄	18 – 16d	8 – 10d	14900	840	2410	3010
HHU214 – 2	(2) 2x14	3¹/₈	12¹/₁₆	2¹/₂	1¹/₄	18 – N20AN	8 – N20AN	14900	1390	3130	3910
HHU216 – 2	3¹/₈ LAM.	3¹/₈	13⁷/₈	2¹/₂	1¹/₄	20 – N20A	8 – N20A	14900	1390	3475	4345
HU44	4x4	3⁹/₁₆	2⁷/₈	2	1¹/₈	4 – 16d	2 – 10d	2600	210	535	670
HU46	4x6	3⁹/₁₆	4⁷/₈	2	1¹/₈	8 – 16d	4 – 10d	9474	420	1070	1345
HHU46	4x6	3⁹/₁₆	4⁷/₈	2¹/₂	1¹/₄	8 – N20AN	4 – N20AN	9474	695	1390	1740
HU48	4x8	3⁹/₁₆	6⁵/₈	2	1¹/₈	10 – 16d	4 – 10d	11383	420	1340	1680
HHU48	4x8	3⁹/₁₆	6⁵/₈	2¹/₂	1¹/₄	10 – N20AN	4 – N20AN	11383	695	1740	2170
HU410	4x10	3⁹/₁₆	8³/₈	2	1¹/₈	14 – 16d	6 – 10d	14566	630	1875	2350
HHU410	4x10	3⁹/₁₆	8³/₈	2¹/₂	1¹/₄	14 – N20AN	6 – N20AN	14566	1045	2435	3040
HU412	4x12	3⁹/₁₆	10¹/₈	2¹/₂	1¹/₄	16 – 16d	6 – 10d	14316	630	2145	2690
HHU412	4x12	3⁹/₁₆	10¹/₈	2¹/₂	1¹/₄	16 – N20AN	6 – N20AN	14316	1045	2780	3475
HU414	4x14	3⁹/₁₆	11⁷/₈	2¹/₂	1¹/₄	18 – 16d	8 – 10d	14900	840	2410	3010
HHU414	4x14	3⁹/₁₆	11⁷/₈	2¹/₂	1¹/₄	18 – N20AN	8 – N20AN	14900	1390	3130	3910
HU416	4x16	3⁹/₁₆	13⁵/₈	2¹/₂	1¹/₄	20 – 16d	8 – 10d	14900	840	2680	3360
HHU416	4x16	3⁹/₁₆	13⁵/₈	2¹/₂	1¹/₄	20 – N20AN	8 – N20AN	14900	1390	3475	4345
HHU5.125/12	5¹/₈ LAM.	5¹/₄	10¹/₈	2¹/₂	1¹/₄	16 – N20A	6 – N20A	14316	1045	2780	3475
HHU5.125/16	5¹/₈ LAM.	5¹/₄	13⁵/₈	2¹/₂	1¹/₄	20 – N20A	8 – N20A	14900	1390	3475	4345
HU66	6x6	5¹/₂	5	2	1¹/₄	8 – 16d	4 – 16d	9474	420	1070	1345
HHU66	6x6	5¹/₂	5	2	1¹/₄	8 – N20AN	4 – N20AN	9474	695	1390	1740
HU68	6x8	5¹/₂	6⁵/₈	2	1¹/₄	10 – 16d	4 – 16d	11383	420	1340	1680
HHU68	6x8	5¹/₂	6⁵/₈	2	1¹/₄	10 – N20AN	4 – N20AN	11383	695	1740	2170
HU610	6x10	5¹/₂	8³/₈	2	1¹/₄	14 – 16d	6 – 16d	14566	630	1875	2350
HHU610	6x10	5¹/₂	8³/₈	2	1¹/₄	14 – N20AN	6 – N20AN	14566	1045	2435	3040
HU612	6x12	5¹/₂	10¹/₈	2¹/₂	1¹/₄	16 – 16d	6 – 16d	14316	630	2145	2690
HHU612	6x12	5¹/₂	10¹/₈	2¹/₂	1¹/₄	16 – N20AN	6 – N20AN	14316	1045	2780	3475
HU614	6x14	5¹/₂	11⁷/₈	2¹/₂	1¹/₄	18 – 16d	8 – 16d	14900	840	2410	3010
HHU614	6x14	5¹/₂	11⁷/₈	2¹/₂	1¹/₄	18 – N20AN	8 – N20AN	14900	1390	3130	3910
HU616	6x16	5¹/₂	13⁵/₈	2¹/₂	1¹/₄	20 – 16d	8 – 16d	14900	840	2680	3360
HHU616	6x16	5¹/₂	13⁵/₈	2¹/₂	1¹/₄	20 – N20AN	8 – N20AN	14900	1390	3475	4345

SIMPSON Strong-Tie CONNECTORS

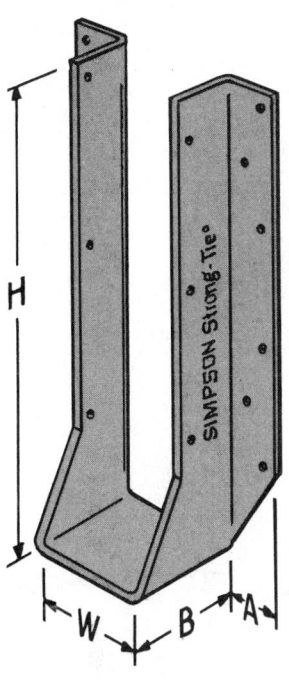

HU HHU

Projection seat on most models for maximum bearing and section economy.

1. N20AN and N20A fasteners are included with HHU models.

Courtesy Simpson Strong-Tie.

Glossary

ACOUSTICS The science of sound and sound control.

ADOBE A heavy clay soil used in many southwestern states to make sun-dried bricks.

AGGREGATE Stone, gravel, cinder, or slag used as one of the components of concrete.

AIR-DRIED LUMBER Lumber that has been stored in yards or sheds for a period of time after cutting. Building codes typically assume a 19 percent moisture content when determining joist and beams of air-dried lumber.

AIR DUCT A pipe, typically made of sheet metal, that carries air from a source such as a furnace or air conditioner to a room within a structure.

AIR TRAP A "U"-shaped piped placed in wastewater lines to prevent backflow of sewer gas.

ALCOVE A small room adjoining a larger room, often separated by an archway.

AMPERE (AMPS) A measure of electrical current.

ANCHOR A metal tie or strap used to tie building members to each other.

ANCHOR BOLT A threaded bolt used to fasten wooden structural members to masonry.

ANGLE IRON A structural piece of steel shaped to form a 90 degree angle.

APPRAISAL The estimated value of a piece of property.

APRON The inside trim board placed below a window sill. The term is also used to apply to a curb around a driveway or parking area.

AREAWAY A subsurface enclosure to admit light and air to a basement. Sometimes called a window well.

ASBESTOS A mineral that does not burn or conduct heat; it is usually used for roofing material.

ASHLAR MASONRY Squared masonry units laid with a horizontal bed joint.

ASH PIT An area in the bottom of the firebox of a fireplace to collect ash.

ASPHALT An insoluble material used for making floor tile and for waterproofing walls and roofs.

ASPHALTIC CONCRETE A mixture of asphalt and aggregate which is used for driveways.

ASPHALT SHINGLE Roof shingles made of asphalt-saturated felt and covered with mineral granules.

ASSESSED VALUE The value assigned by governmental agencies to determine the taxes to be assessed on structures and land.

ATTIC The area formed between the ceiling joists and rafters.

ATRIUM An inside courtyard of a structure which may be either open at the top or covered with a roof.

AWNING WINDOW A window that is hinged along the top edge.

BACKFILL Earth, gravel, or sand placed in the trench around the footing and stem wall after the foundation has cured.

BAFFLE A shield, usually made of scrap material, to keep insulation from plugging eave vents. Also used to describe wind- or sound-deadening devices.

BALCONY A deck or patio that is above ground level.

BALLOON FRAMING A building construction method that has vertical wall members that extend uninterrupted from the foundation to the roof.

BAND JOIST A joist set at the edge of the structure that runs parallel to the other joist. Also called a rim joist.

BANISTER A handrail beside a stairway.

BASEBOARD The finish trim where the wall and floor intersect, or an electric wall heater that extends along the floor.

BASE COURSE The lowest course in brick or concrete masonary unit construction.

BASE LINE A reference line.

BASEMENT A level of a structure that is built either entirely below grade level (full basement) or partially below grade (daylite basement).

BATT A blanket insulation usually made of fiberglass to be used between framing members.

BATTEN A board used to hide the seams when other boards are joined together.

BATTER BOARD A horizontal board used to form footings.

BAY A division of space within a building, usually divided by beams or columns.

BEAM A horizontal structural member that is used to support roof or wall loads. Often called a header.

BEAMED CEILING A ceiling that has support beams that are exposed to view.

BEARING PLATE A support member, often a steel plate used to spread weight over a larger area.

BEARING WALL A wall that supports vertical loads in addition to its own weight.

BENCH MARK A reference point used by surveyors to establish grades and construction heights.

BENDING One of three major forces acting on a beam. It is the tendency of a beam to bend or sag between its supports.

BENDING MOMENT A measure of the forces that cause a beam to break by bending. Represented by (M).

BEVELED SIDING Siding that has a tapered thickness.

BIBB An outdoor faucet which is threaded so that a hose may be attached.

BILL OF MATERIAL A part of a set of plans that lists all of the material needed to construct a structure.

BIRD BLOCK A block placed between rafters to maintain a uniform spacing and to keep animals out of the attic.

BIRD'S MOUTH A notch cut into a rafter to provide a bearing surface where the rafter intersects the top plate.

BLIND NAILING Driving nails in such a way that the heads are concealed from view.

BLOCKING Framing members, typically wood, placed between joist, rafters or studs to provide rigidity. Also called bridging.

BOARD AND BATTEN A type of siding using vertical boards with small wood strips (battens) used to cover the joints of the boards.

BOARD FOOT The amount of wood contained in a piece of lumber 1 in. thick by 12 in. wide by 12 in. long.

BOND The morter joint between two masonry units, or a pattern in which masonry units are arranged.

BOND BEAM A reinforced concrete beam used to strengthen masonry walls.

BOTTOM CHORD The lower, usually horizontal, member of a truss.

BOX BEAM A hollow built-up structural unit.

BRIDGING Cross blocking between horizontal members used to add stiffness. Also called blocking.

BREEZEWAY A covered walkway with open sides between two different parts of a structure.

BROKER A representative of the seller in property sales.

Btu British thermal unit. A unit used to measure heat.

BUILDING CODE Legal requirements designed to protect the public by providing guidelines for structural, electrical, plumbing, and mechanical areas of a structure.

BUILDING LINE An imaginary line determined by zoning departments to specify on which area of a lot a structure may be built (also known as a setback).

BUILDING PAPER A waterproofed paper used to prevent the passage of air and water into a structure.

BUILDING PERMIT A permit to build a structure issued by a governmental agency after the plans for the structure have been examined and the structure is found to comply with all building code requirements.

BUILT-UP BEAM A beam built of smaller members that are bolted or nailed together.

BUILT-UP ROOF A roof composed of three or more layers of felt, asphalt, pitch, or coal tar.

BULLNOSE Rounded edges of cabinet trim.

BUTT JOINT The junction where two members meet in a square-cut joint; end to end, or edge to edge.

BUTTRESS A projection from a wall often located below roof beams to provide support to the roof loads and to keep long walls in the vertical position.

CABINET WORK The interior finish woodwork of a structure, especially cabinetry.

CANTILEVER Projected construction that is fastened at only one end.

CANT STRIP A small built-up area between two intersecting roof shapes to divert water.

CARPORT A covered automobile parking structure that is typically not fully enclosed.

CARRIAGE The horizontal part of a stair stringer that supports the tread.

CASEMENT WINDOW A hinged window that swings outward.

CASING The metal, plastic, or wood trim around a door or a window.

CATCH BASIN An underground reservoir for water drained from a roof before it flows to a storm drain.

CATHEDRAL WINDOW A window with an upper edge which is parallel to the roof pitch.

CAULKING A soft, waterproof material used to seal seams and cracks in construction.

CAVITY WALL A masonry wall formed with an air space between each exterior face.

CEILING JOIST The horizontal member of the roof which is used to resist the outward spread of the rafters and to provide a surface on which to mount the finished ceiling.

CEMENT A powder of alumina, silica, lime, iron oxide, and magnesia pulverized and used as an ingredient in mortar and concrete.

CENTRAL HEATING A heating system in which heat is distributed throughout a structure from a single source.

CESSPOOL An underground catch basin for the collection and dispersal of sewage.

CHAMFER A beveled edge formed by removing the sharp corner of a piece of material.

CHANNEL A standard form of structural steel with three sides at right angles to each other forming the letter C.

CHASE A recessed area of column formed between structural members for electrical, mechanical, or plumbing materials.

CHECK Lengthwise cracks in a board caused by natural drying.

CHECK VALVE A valve in a pipe that permits flow in only one direction.

CHIMNEY An upright structure connected to a fireplace or furnace that passes smoke and gases to outside air.

CHORD The upper and lower members of a truss which are supported by the web.

CINDER BLOCK A block made of cinder and cement used in construction.

CIRCUIT BREAKER A safety device which opens and closes an electrical circuit.

CLAPBOARD A tapered board used for siding that overlaps the board below it.

CLEARANCE A clear space between building materials to allow for air flow or access.

CLERESTORY A window or group of windows which are placed above the normal window height, often between two roof levels.

COLLAR TIES A horizontal tie between rafters near the ridge to help resist the tendency of the rafters to separate.

COLONIAL A style of architecture and furniture adapted from the American colonial period.

COLUMN A vertical structural support, usually round and made of steel.

COMMON WALL The partition that divides two different dwelling units.

COMPRESSION A force that crushes or compacts.

COMPUTER AIDED DRAFTING Using a computer as a drafting aid.

COMPUTER INPUT Information placed into a computer.

COMPUTER MAINFRAME The main computer that controls many smaller desk terminals.

COMPUTER OUTPUT Information which is displayed or printed by a computer.

COMPUTER SOFTWARE Programs used to control a computer.

CONCENTRATED LOAD A load centralized in a small area. Usually the weight supported by a post results in a concentrated load.

CONCRETE A building material made from cement, sand, gravel, and water.

CONCRETE BLOCKS Blocks of concrete that are precast. The standard size is $8 \times 8 \times 16$.

CONDENSATION The formation of water on a surface when warm air comes in contact with a cold surface.

CONDUCTOR Any material that permits the flow of electricity. A drain pipe that diverts water from the roof (a downspout).

CONDUIT A bendable pipe or tubing used to encase electrical wiring.

CONSTRUCTION LOAN A mortgage loan to provide cash to the builder for material and labor that is typically repaid when the structure is completed.

CONTINUOUS BEAM A single beam that is supported by more than two supports.

CONTOURS A line that represents land formations.

CONTRACTOR The manager of a construction project, or one specific phase of it.

CONTROL JOINT An expansion joint in a masonry wall formed by raking mortar from the vertical joint.

CONVENIENCE OUTLET An electrical receptacle through which current is drawn for the electrical system of an appliance.

COPING A masonry cap placed on top of a block wall to protect it from water penetration.

CORBEL A ledge formed in a wall by building out successive courses of masonry.

CORNICE The part of the roof that extends out from the wall. Sometimes referred to as the eave.

COUNTERFLASH A metal flashing used under normal flashing to provide a waterproof seam.

COURSE A continuous row of building material such as shingles, stone or brick.

COURT An unroofed space surrounded by walls.

CRAWL SPACE The area between the floor joists and the ground.

CRICKET A diverter built to direct water away from an area of a roof where it would otherwise collect such as behind a chimney.

CRIPPLE A wall stud that is cut at less than full length.

CROSS BRACING Boards fastened diagonally between structural members such as floor joists to provide rigidity.

CROSSHATCH Thin lines drawn about 1/16″ apart, typically at 45 degrees, to show masonry in plan view or wood that has been sectioned.

CUL-DE-SAC A dead end street with no outlet which provides a circular turn-around.

CULVERT An underground passageway for water, usually part of a drainage system.

CUPOLA A small structure built above the main roof level to provide light or ventilation.

CURE The process of concrete drying to its maximum design strength, usually taking 28 days.

CURTAIN WALL An exterior wall which provides no structural support.

DAMPER A movable plate that controls the amount of draft for a woodstove, fireplace, or furnace.

DATUM A reference point for starting a survey.

DEADENING Material used to control the transmission of sound.

DEAD LOAD The weight of building materials or other unmoveable objects in a structure.

DECKING A wood material used to form the floor or roof, typically used in 1 and 2 in. thicknesses.

DENSITY The number of people allowed to live in a specific area of land or to work in a specific area of a structure.

DEPRECIATION Loss of monetary value.

DESIGNER A person who designs buildings, but is not licensed as is an architect.

DIGITIZER An input tool for computer aided drafting used to draw on a flat bed plotter. The device translates images to numbers for transmission to the computer.

DISK Computer storage units that store information or programs used to run the computer.

DIVERTER A metal strip used to divert water.

DORMER A structure which projects from a sloping roof to form another roofed area. This new area is typically used to provide a surface to install a window.

DOUBLE HUNG A type of window in which the upper and lower halves slide past each other to provide an opening at the top and bottom of the window.

DOWNSPOUT A pipe which carries rain water from the gutters of the roof to the ground.

DRAIN A collector for a pipe that carries water.

DRESSED LUMBER Lumber that has been surfaced by a planing machine to give the wood a smooth finish.

DRY ROT A type of wood decay caused by fungi that leaves the wood a soft powder.

DRYWALL An interior wall covering installed in large sheets made from gypsum board.

DRY WELL A shallow well used to disperse water from the gutter system.

DUCTS Pipes, typically made of sheet metal, used to conduct hot or cold air of the HVAC system.

DUPLEX OUTLET A standard electrical convenience outlet with two receptacles.

DUTCH DOOR A type of door that is divided horizontally in the center so that each half of the door may be opened separately.

DUTCH HIP A type of roof shape that combines features of a gable and a hip roof.

EASEMENT An area of land that cannot be built upon because it provides access to a structure or to utilities such as power or sewer lines.

EAVE The lower part of the roof that projects from the wall. See cornice.

EGRESS A term used in building codes to describe access.

ELASTIC LIMIT The extent a material can be bent and still return to its original shape.

ELBOW An L-shaped plumbing pipe.

ELEVATION The height of a specific point in relation to another point. The exterior views of a structure.

ELL An extension of the structure at a right angle to the main structure.

EMINENT DOMAIN The right of a government to condemn private property so that it may be obtained for public use.

ENAMEL A paint that produces a hard, glossy, smooth finish.

EQUITY The value of real estate in excess of the balance owed on the mortgage.

ERGONOMICS The study of human space and movement needs as they relate to a given work area, such as a kitchen.

EXCAVATION The removal of soil for construction purposes.

EXPANSION JOINT A joint installed in concrete construction to reduce cracking and to provide workable areas.

FABRICATION Work done on a structure away from the job site.

FACADE The exterior covering of a structure.

FACE BRICK Brick that is used on the visible surface to cover other masonry products.

FACE GRAIN The pattern in the visible veneer of plywood.

FASCIA A horizontal board nailed to the end of rafters or trusses to conceal their ends.

FEDERAL HOUSING ADMINISTRATION (FHA) A governmental agency that insures home loans made by private lending institutions.

FELT A tar-impregnated paper used for water protection under roofing and siding materials. Sometimes used under concrete slabs for moisture resistance.

FIBER BENDING STRESS The measurement of structural members used to determine their stiffness.

FIBERBOARD Fibrous wood products that have been pressed into a sheet. Typically used for the interior construction of cabinets and for a covering for the subfloor.

FILL Material used to raise an area for construction. Typically gravel or sand is used to provide a raised, level building area.

FILLED INSULATION Insulation material that is blown or poured into place in attics and walls.

FILLET WELD A weld between two surfaces that butt at 90° to each other with the weld filling the inside corner.

FINISHED LUMBER Wood that has been milled with a smooth finish suitable for use as trim and other finish work.

FINISHED SIZE Sometimes called the dressed size, the finished size represents the actual size of lumber after all milling operations and is typically about ½ in. smaller than the nominal size, which is the size of lumber before planing.

NOMINAL SIZE (IN.)	FINISHED SIZE (IN.)
1	3/4
2	1 1/2
4	3 1/2
6	5 1/2
8	7 1/4
10	9 1/4
12	11 1/4
14	13 1/4

FIREBRICK A refractory brick capable of withstanding high temperatures and used for lining fireplaces and furnaces.

FIREBOX The combustion chamber of the fireplace where the fire occurs.

FIREBRICK A brick made of a refractory material that can withstand great amounts of heat and is used to line the visible face of the firebox.

FIRE CUT An angular cut on the end of a joist or rafter that is supported by masonry. The cut allows the wood member to fall away from the wall without damaging a masonry wall when the wood is damaged by fire.

FIRE DOOR A door used between different types of construction which has been rated as being able to withstand fire for a certain amount of time.

FIREPROOFING Any material that is used to cover structural materials to increase their fire rating.

FIRE RATED A rating given to building materials to specify the amount of time the material can resist damage caused by fire.

FIRE-STOP Blocking placed between studs or other structural members to resist the spread of fire.

FIRE WALL A wall constructed of materials resulting in a specified time that the wall can resist fire before structural damage will occur.

FLAGSTONE Flat stones used typically for floor and wall coverings.

FLASHING Metal used to prevent water leaking through surface intersections.

FLAT ROOF A roof with a minimal roof pitch, usually about ⅛" per 12".

FLOOR PLUG A 110 convenience outlet located in the floor.

FLUE A passage inside of the chimney to conduct smoke and gases away from a firebox to outside air.

FLUE LINER A terra-cotta pipe used to provide a smooth flue surface so that unburned materials will not cling to the flue.

FOOTING The lowest member of a foundation system used to spread the loads of a structure across supporting soil.

FOOTING FORM The wooden mold used to give concrete its shape as it cures.

FOUNDATION The system used to support a building's loads and made up of stem walls, footings, and piers. The term is used in many areas to refer to the footing.

FRAME The structural skeleton of a building.

FROST LINE The depth to which soil will freeze.

FURRING Wood strips attached to structural members that are used to provide a level surface for finishing materials when different-sized structural members are used.

GABLE A type of roof with two sloping surfaces that intersect at the ridge of the structure.

GABLE END WALL The triangular wall that is formed at each end of a gable roof between the top plate of the wall and the rafters.

GALVANIZED Steel products that have had zinc applied to the exterior surface to provide protection from rusting.

GAMBREL A type of roof formed with two planes on each side. The lower pitch is steeper than the upper portion of the roof.

GIRDER A horizontal support member at the foundation level.

GLUED-LAMINATED TIMBER (GLU-LAM) A structural member made up of layers of lumber that are glued together.

GRADE The designation of the quality of a manufactured piece of wood.

GRADING The moving of soil to effect the elevation of land at a construction site.

GRAVEL STOP A metal strip used to retain gravel at the edge of built-up roofs.

GREEN LUMBER Lumber that has not been kiln-dried and still contains moisture.

GROUND FAULT CIRCUIT INTERRUPTER (GFCI OR GFI) A 110 convenience outlet with a built-in circuit breaker. GFCI outlets are to be used within 5'-0" of any water source.

GROUT A mixture of cement, sand, and water used to fill joints in masonry and tile construction.

GUARDRAIL A horizontal protective railing used around stairwells, balconies, and changes of floor elevation greater than 30 in.

GUSSET A plate added to the side of intersecting structural members to help form a secure connection and to reduce stress.

GUTTER A metal or plastic drainage system for collecting and disposing of water from roofs.

GYPSUM BOARD An interior finishing material made of gypsum and fiberglass and covered with paper which is installed in large sheets.

HALF-TIMBER A frame construction method where spaces between wood members are filled with masonry.

HANGER A metal support bracket used to attach two structural members.

HARDBOARD Sheet material formed of compressed wood fibers used as an underlayment for flooring.

HEAD The upper portion of a door or window frame.

HEADER A horizontal structural member used to support other structural members over openings such as doors and windows.

HEADER COURSE A horizontal masonry course with the end of each masonry unit exposed.

HEADROOM The vertical clearance in a room over a stairway.

HEARTH The fire-resistant floor within and extending a minimum of 18 in. in front of the firebox.

HEARTWOOD The inner core of a tree trunk.

HIP The exterior edge formed by two sloping roof surfaces.

HIP ROOF A roof shape with four sloping sides.

HORIZONTAL SHEAR One of three major forces acting on a beam, it is the tendency of the fibers of a beam to slide past each other in a horizontal direction.

HOSE BIBB A water outlet that is threaded to receive a hose.

HUMIDIFIER A mechanical device that controls the amount of moisture inside of a structure.

I BEAM The generic term for a wide flange or American standard steel beam with a cross section in the shape of the letter I.

INDIRECT LIGHTING Mechanical lighting that is reflected off a surface.

INSULATION Material used to restrict the flow of heat, cold, or sound from one surface to another.

ISOMETRIC A drawing method which enables three surfaces of an object to be seen in one view, with the base of each surface drawn at 30° to the horizontal plane.

JACK RAFTER A rafter which is cut shorter than the other rafters to allow for an opening in the roof.

JACK STUD A wall member which is cut shorter than other studs to allow for an opening such as a window. Also called a cripple stud.

JALOUSIE A type of window made of thin horizontal panels that can be rotated between the open and closed position.

JAMB The vertical members of a door or window frame.

JOIST A horizontal structural member used in repetitive patterns to support floor and ceiling loads.

KILN A heating unit for the removal of moisture from wood.

KILN DRIED A method of drying lumber in a kiln or oven. Kiln dried lumber has a reduced moisture content when compared to lumber that has been air dried.

KING STUD A full-length stud placed at the end of a header.

KIP Used in some engineering formulas to represent 1,000 pounds.

KNEE WALL A wall of less than full height.

KNOT A branch or limb of a tree that is cut through in the process of manufacturing lumber.

LALLY COLUMN A vertical steel column that is used to support floor or foundation loads.

LAMINATED Several layers of material that have been glued together under pressure.

LANDING A platform between two flights of stairs.

LATERAL Sideways action in a structure caused by wind or seismic forces.

LATH Wood or sheet metal strips which are attached to the structural frame to support plaster.

LATTICE A grille made by criss-crossing strips of material.

LAVATORY A bathroom sink, or the room which is equipped with a washbasin.

LEDGER A horizontal member which is attached to the side of wall members to provide support for rafters or joists.

LIEN A monetary claim on property.

LINTEL A horizontal steel member used to provide support for masonry over an opening.

LIVE LOAD The loads from all movable objects within a structure including loads from furniture and people. External loads from snow and wind are also considered live loads.

LOAD-BEARING WALL A support wall which holds floor or roof loads in addition to its own weight.

LOOKOUT A beam used to support eave loads.

LOUVER An opening with horizontal slats to allow for ventilation.

MANSARD A four-sided, steep-sloped roof.

MANTEL A decorative shelf above the opening of a fireplace.

MARKET VALUE The amount that property can be sold for.

MESH A metal reinforcing material placed in concrete slabs and masonry walls to help resist cracking.

METAL TIES A manufactured piece of metal for joining two structural members together.

METAL WALL TIES Corrugated metal strips used to bond brick veneer to its support wall.

MILLWORK Finished woodwork that has been manufactured in a milling plant. Examples are window and door frames, mantels, moldings, and stairway components.

MINERAL WOOL An insulating material made of fibrous foam.

MODULE A standardized unit of measurement.

MODULAS OF ELASTICITY (E) The degree of stiffness of beam.

MOISTURE BARRIER Typically a plastic material used to restrict moisture vapor from penetrating into a structure.

MOLDING Decorative strips, usually made of wood, used to conceal the seam in other finishing materials.

MOMENT The tendency of a force to rotate around a certain point.

MONOLITHIC Concrete construction created in one pouring.

MONUMENT A boundary marker set to mark property corners.

MORTAR A combination of cement, sand, and water used to bond masonry units together.

MORTGAGE A contract pledging the sale of property upon full payment of purchase price.

MORTGAGEE The lender of the money to the mortgagor for the purchase of property.

MORTGAGOR The buyer of property who is paying off the mortgage to the mortgagee.

MUD ROOM A room or utility entrance where soiled clothing can be removed before entering the main portion of the residence.

MUDSILL The horizontal wood member that rests on concrete to support other wood members.

MULLION A horizontal or vertical divider between sections of a window.

MUNTIN A horizontal or vertical divider within a section of a window.

NAILER A wood member bolted to concrete or steel members to provide a nailing surface for attaching other wood members.

NEWEL The end post of a stair railing.

NOMINAL SIZE An approximate size achieved by rounding the actual material size to the nearest larger whole number.

NONBEARING WALL A wall which supports no loads other than its own weight. Some building codes consider walls which support only ceiling loads as nonbearing.

NONFERROUS METAL Metal, such as copper or brass, that contains no iron.

NOSING The rounded front edge of a tread which extends past the riser.

OBSCURE GLASS Glass that is not transparent.

ON CENTER A measurement taken from the center of one member to the center of another member.

ORIENTATION The locating of a structure on property based on the location of the sun, prevailing winds, view, and noise.

OUTLET An electrical receptacle which allows for current to be drawn from the system.

OUTRIGGER A support for roof sheathing and the fascia which extends past the wall line perpendicular to the rafters.

OVERHANG The horizontal measurement of the distance the roof projects from a wall.

OVERLAY DRAFTING The practice of drawing a structure in several layers which must be combined to produce the finished drawing.

PAD An isolated concrete pier.

PARAPET A portion of wall that extends above the edge of the roof.

PARGING A thin coat of plaster used to smooth a masonry surface.

PARQUET FLOORING Wood flooring laid to form patterns.

PARTITION An interior wall.

PARTY WALL A wall dividing two adjoining spaces such as apartments or offices.

PENNY The length of a nail represented by the letter "d". "16d" is read as "sixteen penny".

PERSPECTIVE A drawing method which provides the illusion of depth by the use of vanishing points.

PHOTODRAFTING The use of photography to produce a base drawing on which additional drawings can be added.

PIER A concrete or masonry foundation support.

PILASTER A reinforcing column built into or against a masonry wall.

PILING A vertical foundation support driven into the ground to provide support on stable soil or rock.

PITCH A description of roof angle comparing the vertical rise to the horizontal run.

PLANK Lumber which is 1½ to 3½ in. in thickness.

PLASTER A mix of sand, cement, and water, used to cover walls and ceilings.

PLAT A map of an area of land which shows the boundaries of individual lots.

PLATE A horizontal member at the top (top plate) or bottom (sole plate or sill) of walls used to connect the vertical wall members.

PLENUM An air space for transporting air from the HVAC system.

PLOT A parcel of land.

PLOTTER An output device used in computer aided drafting to draw lines and symbols.

PLUMB True vertical.

PLYWOOD Wood composed of three or more layers, with the grain of each layer placed at 90° to each other and bonded with glue.

POCHÉ A shading method using graphite applied with a soft tissue in a rubbing motion.

PORCH A covered entrance to a structure.

PORTICO A roof supported by columns instead of walls.

PORTLAND CEMENT A hydraulic cement made of silica, lime, and aluminum that has become the most common cement used in the construction industry because of its strength.

POST A vertical wood structural member usually 4 × 4 or larger.

PRECAST A concrete component which has been cast in a location other than the one in which it will be used.

PREFABRICATED Buildings or components that are built away from the job site and transported ready to be used.

PRESTRESSED A concrete component that is placed in compression as it is cast to help resist deflection.

PRINCIPAL The original amount of money loaned before interest is applied.

PROGRAM A set of instructions which controls the functions of a computer.

PURLIN A horizontal roof member which is laid perpendicular to rafters to help limit deflection.

PURLIN BRACE A support member which extends from the purlin down to a load-bearing wall or header.

QUAD A courtyard surrounded by the walls of buildings.

QUARRY TILE An unglazed, machine-made tile.

QUARTER ROUND Wood molding that has the profile of one-quarter of a circle.

RABBET A rectangular groove cut on the edge of a board.

RAFTER The inclined structural member of a roof system designed to support roof loads.

RAFTER/CEILING JOIST An inclined structural member which supports both the ceiling and the roof materials.

RAKE JOINT A recessed mortar joint.

REACTION The upward forces acting at the supports of a beam.

REBAR Reinforcing steel used to strengthen concrete.

REFERENCE BUBBLE A symbol used to designate the origin of details and sections.

REGISTER An opening in a duct for the supply of heated or cooled air.

REINFORCED CONCRETE Concrete that has steel rebar placed in it to resist tension.

RHEOSTAT An electrical control device used to regulate the current reaching a light fixture. A dimmer switch.

RELATIVE HUMIDITY The amount of water vapor in the atmosphere compared to the maximum possible amount at the same temperature.

RENDERING An artistic process applied to drawings to add realism.

RESTRAINING WALL A masonry wall supported only at the bottom by a footing that is designed to resist soil loads.

RETAINING WALL A masonry wall supported at the top and bottom, designed to resist soil loads.

R-FACTOR A unit of thermal resistance applied to the insulating value of a specific building material.

RIBBON A structural wood member framed into studs to support joists or rafters.

RIDGE The uppermost area of two intersecting roof planes.

RIDGE BOARD A horizontal member that rafters are aligned against to resist their downward force.

RIDGE BRACE A support member used to transfer the weight from the ridge board to a bearing wall or beam. The brace is typically spaced at 48 in. O.C., and may not exceed a 45° angle from vertical.

RIM JOIST A joist at the perimeter of a structure that runs parallel to the other floor joist.

RISE The amount of vertical distance between one tread and another.

RISER The vertical member of stairs between the treads.

ROLL ROOFING Roofing material of fiber or asphalt that is shipped in rolls.

ROOF DRAIN A receptacle for removal of roof water.

ROUGH FLOOR The subfloor, usually hardboard, which serves as a base for the finished floor.

ROUGH HARDWARE Hardware used in construction, such as nails, bolts, and metal connectors, that will not be seen when the project is complete.

ROUGH IN To prepare a room for plumbing or electrical additions by running wires or piping for a future fixture.

ROUGH LUMBER Lumber that has not been surfaced but has been trimmed on all four sides.

ROUGH OPENING The unfinished opening between framing members allowed for doors, windows, or other assemblies.

ROWLOCK A pattern for laying masonry units so that the end of the unit is exposed.

RUN The horizontal distance of a set of steps or the measurement describing the depth of one step.

SADDLE A small gable-shaped roof used to divert water from behind a chimney.

SASH An individual frame around a window.

SCAB A short member that overlaps the butt joint of two other members used to fasten those members.

SCALE A measuring instrument used to draw materials at reduced size.

SCHEDULE A written list of similar components such as windows or doors.

SCRATCH COAT The first coat of stucco which is scratched to provide a good bonding surface for the second coat.

SEASONING The process of removing moisture from green lumber by either air- (natural) or kiln-drying.

SECTION A type of drawing showing an object as if it had been cut through to show interior construction.

SEISMIC Earthquake-related forces.

SEPTIC TANK A tank in which sewage is decomposed by bacteria and dispersed by drain tiles.

SERVICE CONNECTION The wires that run to a structure from a power pole or transformer.

SETBACK The minimum distance required between the structure and the property line.

SHAKE A hand-split wooden roof shingle.

SHEAR The stress that occurs when two forces from opposite directions are acting on the same member. Shearing stress tends to cut a member just as scissors cut paper.

SHEAR PANEL A plywood panel applied to walls to resist wind and seismic forces by keeping the studs in a vertical position.

SHEATHING A covering material placed over walls, floors and roofs which serves as a backing for finishing materials.

SHIM A piece of material used to fill a space between two surfaces.

SHIPLAP A siding pattern of overlapping rabbeted edges.

SILL A horizontal wood member placed at the bottom of walls and openings in walls.

SKYLIGHT An opening in the roof to allow light and ventilation that is usually covered with glass or plastic.

SLAB A concrete floor system typically poured at ground level.

SLEEPERS Strips of wood placed over a concrete slab in order to attach other wood members.

SMOKE CHAMBER The portion of the chimney located directly over the firebox which acts as a funnel between the firebox and the chimney.

SMOKE SHELF A shelf located at the bottom of the smoke chamber to prevent down-drafts from the chimney from entering the firebox.

SOFFIT A lowered ceiling, typically found in kitchens, halls, and bathrooms to allow for recessed lighting or HVAC ducts.

SOIL STACK The main vertical waste-water pipe.

SOLDIER A masonry unit laid on end with its narrow surface exposed.

SOLE PLATE The plate placed at the bottom of a wall.

SPACKLE The covering of sheetrock joints with joint compound.

SPAN The horizontal distance between two supporting members.

SPECIFICATIONS Written descriptions or requirements to specify how a structure is to be constructed.

SPLICE Two similar members that are joined together in a straight line usually by nailing or bolting.

SPLIT-LEVEL A house that has two levels, one about a half a level above or below the other.

SQUARE An area of roofing covering 100 square feet.

STACK A vertical plumbing pipe.

STAIR WELL The opening in the floor where a stair will be framed.

STILE A vertical member of a cabinet, door, or decorative panel.

STIRRUP A U-shaped metal bracket used to support wood beams.

STOCK Common sizes of building materials as they are sold.

STOP A wooden strip used to hold windows in place.

STRESS A live or dead load acting on a structural member. Stress results as the fibers of a beam resist an external force.

STRESSED-SKIN PANEL A hollow, built-up member typically used as a beam.

STRETCHER A course of masonry laid horizontally with the end of the unit exposed.

STRINGER The inclined support member of a stair that supports the risers and treads.

STUCCO A type of plaster made from Portland cement, sand, water, and a coloring agent that is applied to exterior walls.

STUD The vertical framing member of a wall which is usually 2 × 4 or 2 × 6 in size.

SUBFLOOR The flooring surface which is laid on the floor joist and serves as a base layer for the finished floor.

SUMP A recessed area in a basement floor to collect water so that it can be removed by a pump.

SURFACED LUMBER Lumber that has been smoothed on at least one side.

SWALE A recessed area formed in the ground to help divert ground water away from a structure.

TAMP To compact soil or concrete.

TENSILE STRENGTH The resistance of a material or beam to the tendency to stretch.

TENSION Forces that cause a material to stretch or pull apart.

TERMITE SHIELD A strip of sheet metal used at the intersection of concrete and wood surfaces near ground level to prevent termites from entering the wood.

TERRA-COTTA Hard-baked clay typically used as a liner for chimneys.

THERMAL CONDUCTOR A material suitable for transmitting heat.

THERMAL RESISTANCE Represented by the letter R, resistance measures the ability of a material to resist the flow of heat.

THERMOSTAT A mechanical device for controlling the output of HVAC units.

THRESHOLD The beveled member directly under a door.

THROAT The narrow opening to the chimney that is just above the firebox. The throat of a chimney is where the damper is placed.

TILT UP A method of construction in which concrete walls are cast in a horizontal position and then lifted into place.

TIMBER Lumber with a cross-sectional size of 4 × 6 inches or larger.

TOENAIL Nails driven into a member at an angle.

TONGUE AND GROOVE A joint where the edge of one member fits into a groove in the next member.

TRANSOM A window located over a door.

TRAP A U-shaped pipe below plumbing fixtures which holds water to prevent odor and sewer gas from entering the fixture.

TREAD The horizontal member of a stair on which the foot is placed.

TRIMMER Joist or rafters that are used to frame an opening in a floor, ceiling, or roof.

TRUSS A prefabricated or job-built construction member formed of triangular shapes used to support roof or floor loads over long spans.

TRUSS A framework made in triangular-shaped segments used for spanning distances greater than is possible using standard components and methods.

ULTIMATE STRENGTH The unit stress within a member just before it breaks.

UNIT STRESS The maximum permissible stress a structural member can resist without failing. Represented by (f).

VALLEY The internal corner formed between two intersecting roof surfaces.

VAPOR BARRIER Material that is used to block the flow of water vapor into a structure. Typically 6 mil (.006 in.) black plastic.

VAULT An inclined ceiling area.

VENEER A thin outer covering or nonload bearing masonry face material.

VENTILATION The process of supplying and removing air from a structure.

VENT PIPE Pipes that provide air into the waste lines to allow drainage by connecting each plumbing fixture to the vent stack.

VENT STACK A vertical pipe of a plumbing system used to equalize pressure within the system and to vent sewer gases.

VERTICAL SHEAR One of three major stresses acting on a beam, it is the tendency of a beam to drop between its supports.

VESTIBULE A small entrance or lobby.

WAINSCOT A paneling applied to the lower portion of a wall.

WALLBOARD Large flat sheets of gypsum, typically ½ or ⅝ in. thick, used to finish interior walls.

WARP Variation from true shape.

WATERPROOF Material or a type of construction that prevents the absorption of water.

WEATHER STRIP A fabric or plastic material placed along the edges of doors, windows, and skylites to reduce air infiltration.

WEEP HOLE An opening normally in the bottom course of a masonry to allow for drainage.

WORK TRIANGLE The triangular area created in the kitchen by drawing a line from the sink, to the refrigerator, and to the cooking area.

WYTHE A single unit thickness of a masonry wall.

Abbreviations

Drafters and designers print many abbreviations to conserve space. Using standard abbreviations ensures that drawings are interpreted accurately.

Here are three guidelines for proper use:

1. Abbreviations are in capital letters.
2. A period is used only when the abbreviation may be confused with a word.
3. Several words use the same abbreviation; use is defined by the location.

access panel	**ap**
acoustic	**ac.**
acoustic plaster	**ac. pl.**
actual	**act.**
addition	**add.**
adhesive	**adh.**
adjustable	**adj.**
aggregate	**aggr.**
air conditioning	**A.C.**
alternate	**alt.**
alternating current	**ac**
aluminum	**alum.**
American Institute of Architects	**A.I.A.**
American Institute of Building Designers	**A.I.B.D.**
American Institute of Steel Construction	**A.I.S.C.**
American Institute of Timber Construction	**A.I.T.C.**

American National Standards Institute	**A.N.S.I.**
American Plywood Association	**A.P.A.**
American Society of Civil Engineers	**A.S.C.E.**
American Society of Heating, Refrigerating, and Air Conditioning Engineers	**A.S.H.R.A.E.**
American Society of Landscape Architects	**A.S.L.A.**
American Society for Testing and Materials	**A.S.T.M.**
amount	**amt.**
ampere	**amp.**
anchor bolt	**A.B.**
angle	$\angle$
approximate	**approx.**
approved	**appd.**
architectural	**arch.**
area	**a**
asbestos	**asb.**
asphalt	**asph.**
asphaltic concrete	**asph. conc.**
at	**@**
automatic	**auto.**
avenue	**ave.**
average	**avg.**
balcony	**balc.**
base	**b**

basement	**basm.**	circuit breaker	**cir bkr**
Basic National Building Code	**BOCA**	class	**cl.**
batten	**batt.**	cleanout	**C.O.**
bathroom	**b**	clear	**clr**
bathtub	**bt.**	coated	**ctd.**
beam	**bm.**	cold water	**C.W.**
bearing	**br.**	column	**col.**
bedroom	**br**	combination	**comb.**
bench mark	**B.M.**	common	**com.**
bending moment	**bm**	composition	**comp**
better	**btr.**	computer-aided drafting	**CAD**
between	**btwn.**	concrete	**conc.**
beveled	**bev.**	concrete masonry unit	**C.M.U.**
bidet	**bdt.**	conduit	**cnd.**
block	**blk.**	construction	**const.**
blocking	**blkg.**	Construction Standards Institute	**CSI**
blower	**blo.**	continuous	**cont.**
board	**bd.**	contractor	**contr.**
board feet	**bd ft**	control joint	**C.J.**
both sides	**B.S.**	copper	**cop.**
both ways	**B.W.**	corridor	**corr.**
bottom	**btm.**	corrugate	**corr.**
bottom of footing	**B.F.**	countersink	**csk.**
boulevard	**blvd.**	courses	**c.**
brass	**br.**	cubic	**cu.**
brick	**brk.**	cubic feet	**cu ft**
British thermal unit	**Btu**	cubic feet per minute	**cfm**
bronze	**brz.**	cubic inch	**cu. in.**
broom closet	**bc**	cubic yard	**cu yd**
building	**bldg.**		
building line	**bL**	damper	**dpr.**
built-in	**blt-in**	dampproofing	**dp.**
buzzer	**buz.**	dead load	**DL**
by	**×**	decibel	**db.**
		decking	**dk.**
cabinet	**cab.**	deflection	**d.**
cast concrete	**c conc.**	degree	**° or deg.**
cast iron	**C.I.**	design	**dsgn**
catalog	**cat.**	detail	**det.**
catch basin	**C.B.**	diagonal	**diag.**
caulking	**calk.**	diameter	**φ or dia.**
ceiling	**clg.**	diffuser	**dif.**
ceiling diffuser	**C.D.**	dimension	**dimen.**
ceiling joist	**C.J. or ceil.**	dining room	**dr.**
	jst.	dishwasher	**D/W**
cement	**cem.**	disposal	**disp.**
center	**ctr.**	ditto	**″ or do**
center to center	**C-C**	division	**div.**
centerline	**₵**	door	**dr.**
centimeter	**cm.**	double	**dbl.**
ceramic	**cer**	double hung	**D.H.**
chamfer	**cham.**	Douglas fir	**DF**
channel	**C**	down	**dn.**
check	**chk.**	downspout	**D.S.**
cinder block	**cin. blk.**	drain	**D**
circle	**cir.**	drawing	**dwg.**
circuit	**cir.**	drinking fountain	**D.F.**

dryer	**d.**	front	**fnt.**
drywall	**D.W.**	full size	**fs**
		furnace	**furn.**
each	**ea.**	furred ceiling	**fc**
each face	**E.F.**	future	**fut.**
each way	**E.W.**		
east	**e.**	gallon	**gal**
elbow	**el.**	galvanized	**galv.**
electrical	**elect.**	galvanized iron	**g.i.**
elevation	**elev.**	gage	**ga.**
enamel	**enam.**	garage	**gar.**
engineer	**engr.**	gas	**g.**
entrance	**ent.**	girder	**gird.**
Environmental Protection		glass	**gl.**
Agency	**EPA**	glue laminated	**glu-lam**
Equal	**eq**	grade	**gr.**
Equipment	**equip.**	grade beam	**gr. bm.**
estimate	**est.**	grating	**grtg.**
excavate	**exc.**	gravel	**gvl.**
exhaust	**exh.**	grille	**gr.**
existing	**exist.**	ground	**gnd.**
expansion joint	**exp. jt.**	ground fault circuit interrupter	**gfci**
exposed	**expo.**	grout	**gt.**
extension	**extn.**	gypsum	**gyp.**
exterior	**ext.**	gypsum board	**gyp. bd.**
fabricate	**fab.**	hardboard	**hdb.**
face brick	**F.B.**	hardware	**hdw.**
face of studs	**f.o.s.**	hardwood	**hdwd.**
Fahrenheit	**F**	head	**hd.**
Federal Housing Administration	**F.H.A.**	header	**hdr.**
feet / foot	**' or ft**	heater	**htr.**
feet per minute	**fpm**	heating	**htg.**
finished	**fin.**	heating/ventilating/air	
finished floor	**fin. fl.**	conditioning	**HVAC**
finished grade	**fin. gr.**	height	**ht.**
finished opening	**F.O.**	hemlock	**hem**
firebrick	**fbrk.**	hemlock-fir	**hem-fir**
fire hydrant	**F.H.**	hollow core	**h.c.**
fireproof	**f.p.**	horizontal	**horiz.**
fixture	**fix.**	horsepower	**H.P.**
flammable	**flam.**	hose bibb	**H.B.**
flange	**flg.**	hot water	**H.W.**
flashing	**fl.**	hot water heater	**H.W.H.**
flexible	**flex.**	hundred	**c**
floor	**flr.**		
floor drain	**F.D.**	illuminate	**illum.**
floor joist	**fl. jst.**	incandescent	**incan.**
floor sink	**F.S.**	inch	**" or in.**
fluorescent	**fluor.**	inch pounds	**in. lb.**
folding	**fldg.**	incinerator	**incin.**
foot	**(') ft**	inflammable	**infl.**
foot candle	**fc.**	inside diameter	**I.D.**
footing	**ftg.**	inside face	**I.F.**
foot pounds	**ft. lb.**	inspection	**insp.**
forced air unit	**F.A.U.**	install	**inst.**
foundation	**fnd.**	insulate	**ins.**

insulation	**insul.**	molding	**mldg.**
interior	**int.**	motor	**mot.**
International Conference of		mullion	**mull.**
Building Officials	**ICBO**		
iron	**i**	National Association of Home	
		Builders	**N.A.H.B.**
jamb	**jmb.**	National Bureau of Standards	**N.B.S.**
joint	**jt.**	natural	**nat.**
joist	**jst.**	natural grade	**nat. gr.**
junction	**jct.**	noise reduction coefficient	**N.R.C.**
junction box	**J-box**	nominal	**nom.**
		not applicable	**n.a.**
kiln dried	**K.D.**	not in contract	**N.I.C.**
kilowatt	**kW**	not to scale	**N.T.S.**
kilowatt hour	**kWh**	number	**# or no.**
Kip (1,000 lb.)	**K**		
kitchen	**kit.**	obscure	**obs.**
knockout	**K.O.**	on center	**O.C.**
		opening	**opg.**
laboratory	**lab.**	opposite	**opp.**
laminated	**lam.**	ounce	**oz**
landing	**ldg.**	outside diameter	**O.D.**
laundry	**lau.**	outside face	**O.F.**
lavatory	**lav.**	overhead	**ovhd.**
length	**lgth.**		
level	**lev.**	painted	**ptd.**
light	**lt.**	pair	**pr.**
linear feet	**lin. ft**	panel	**pnl.**
linen closet	**L. cL.**	parallel	**// or par.**
linoleum	**lino.**	part	**pt.**
live load	**LL**	partition	**part.**
living room	**liv.**	pavement	**pvmt.**
long	**lg.**	penny	**d**
louver	**lv.**	per	**/**
lumber	**lum.**	perforate	**perf.**
		perimeter	**per.**
machine bolt	**M.B.**	permanent	**perm.**
manhole	**M.H.**	perpendicular	**⊥ or perp.**
manufacturer	**manuf.**	pi (3.1416)	**π**
marble	**mrb.**	plaster	**pls.**
masonry	**mas.**	plasterboard	**pls. bd.**
material	**mat.**	plastic	**plas.**
maximum	**max.**	plate	**℔ or pl.**
mechanical	**mech.**	platform	**plat.**
medicine cabinet	**M.C.**	plumbing	**plmb.**
medium	**med.**	plywood	**ply.**
membrane	**memb.**	polished	**pol.**
metal	**mtl.**	polyethelyne	**poly.**
meter	**m**	polyvinyl chloride	**PVC**
mile	**mi**	position	**pos.**
minimum	**min.**	pound	**# or lb**
minute	**(') min.**	pounds per square foot	**psf**
mirror	**mirr.**	pounds per square inch	**psi**
miscellaneous	**misc.**	precast	**prcst.**
mixture	**mix.**	prefabricated	**prefab.**
model	**mod.**	preferred	**pfd.**
modular	**mod.**	preliminary	**prelim.**

pressure treated	**p.t.**	socket	**soc.**
property	**prop.**	soil pipe	**S.P.**
pull chain	**P.C.**	solid block	**sol. blk.**
pushbutton	**P.B.**	solid core	**S.C.**
		Southern Building Code	**S.B.C.**
quality	**qty.**	Southern pine	**SP**
quantity	**qty.**	Southern Pine Inspection	
		Bureau	**S.P.I.B.**
radiator	**rad.**	specifications	**specs.**
radius	**r or rad.**	spruce-pine-fir	**SPF**
random length & width	**R L & W**	square	**□ or sq**
range	**r.**	square feet	**# or sq ft**
receptacle	**recp.**	square inch	**# or sq in**
recessed	**rec.**	stainless steel	**sst.**
redwood	**rdwd.**	stand pipe	**st. p.**
reference	**ref.**	standard	**std.**
refrigerator	**refr.**	steel	**stl.**
register	**reg.**	stirrup	**stir.**
reinforcing	**reinf.**	stock	**stk.**
reinforcing bar	**rebar**	storage	**sto.**
reproduce	**repro.**	storm drain	**S.D.**
required	**reqd.**	street	**st.**
resistance moment	**rm**	structural	**str.**
return	**ret.**	structural clay tile	**S.C.T.**
revision	**rev.**	substitute	**sub.**
ridge	**rdg.**	supply	**sup.**
riser	**ris.**	surface	**sur.**
roof	**rf.**	surface four sides	**S4S**
roof drain	**R.D.**	surface two sides	**S2S**
roofing	**rfg.**	suspended ceiling	**susp. clg.**
room	**rm.**	switch	**sw.**
rough	**rgh.**	symbol	**sym.**
rough opening	**R.O.**	symmetrical	**sym.**
round	**φ or rd**	synthetic	**syn.**
		system	**sys.**
safety	**saf.**	tangent	**tan.**
sanitary	**san.**	tar and gravel	**t & g**
scale	**sc.**	tee	**t**
schedule	**sch.**	telephone	**tel.**
screen	**scrn.**	television	**tv.**
screw	**scr.**	temperature	**temp.**
second	**sec.**	terra-cotta	**T.C.**
section	**sect.**	terrazzo	**tz.**
select	**sel.**	thermostat	**thrm.**
select structural	**sel. st.**	thickness	**thk.**
self-closing	**s.c.**	thousand	**m**
service	**serv.**	thousand board feet	**MBF**
sewer	**sew.**	threshold	**thr.**
sheathing	**shtg.**	through	**thru**
sheet	**sht.**	toilet	**tol.**
shower	**sh.**	tongue and groove	**T & G**
side	**s.**	top of wall	**T.W.**
siding	**sdg.**	total	**tot.**
sill cock	**S.C.**	tread	**tr.**
similar	**sim.**	tubing	**tub.**
single hung	**S.H.**	typical	**typ.**

Underwriters' Laboratories, Inc.	**UL**	wainscot	**wsct.**
unfinished	**unfin.**	wall vent	**W.V.**
Uniform Building Code	**UBC**	washing machine	**wm**
United States Department of Housing and Urban Development	**H.U.D.**	waste stack	**W.S.**
		water closet	**W.C.**
urinal	**ur.**	water heater	**W.H.**
utility	**util.**	waterproof	**W.P.**
		watt	**W**
V-joint	**V-jt.**	weather stripping	**ws**
valve	**v**	weatherproof	**wp.**
vanity	**van.**	weep hole	**wh**
vapor barrier	**v.b.**	weight	**wt.**
vapor proof	**vap. prf.**	welded wire fabric	**W.W.F.**
ventilation	**vent.**	west	**w**
vent pipe	**vp**	white pine	**WP**
vent stack	**V.S.**	wide flange	**W or WF**
vent through roof	**V.T.R.**	width	**w**
vertical	**vert.**	window	**wdw.**
vertical grain	**vert. gr.**	with	**w**
vinyl	**vin.**	without	**w/o**
vinyl asbestos tile	**V.A.T.**	wood	**wd**
vinyl base	**V.B.**	wrought iron	**W.I.**
vinyl tile	**V.T.**		
vitreous	**vit.**	yard	**yd**
vitreous clay tile	**V.C.T.**	yellow pine	**YP**
volt	**v**		
volume	**vol.**	zinc	**zn.**

Index